INDEX OF TIDE TABLE COVERAGE

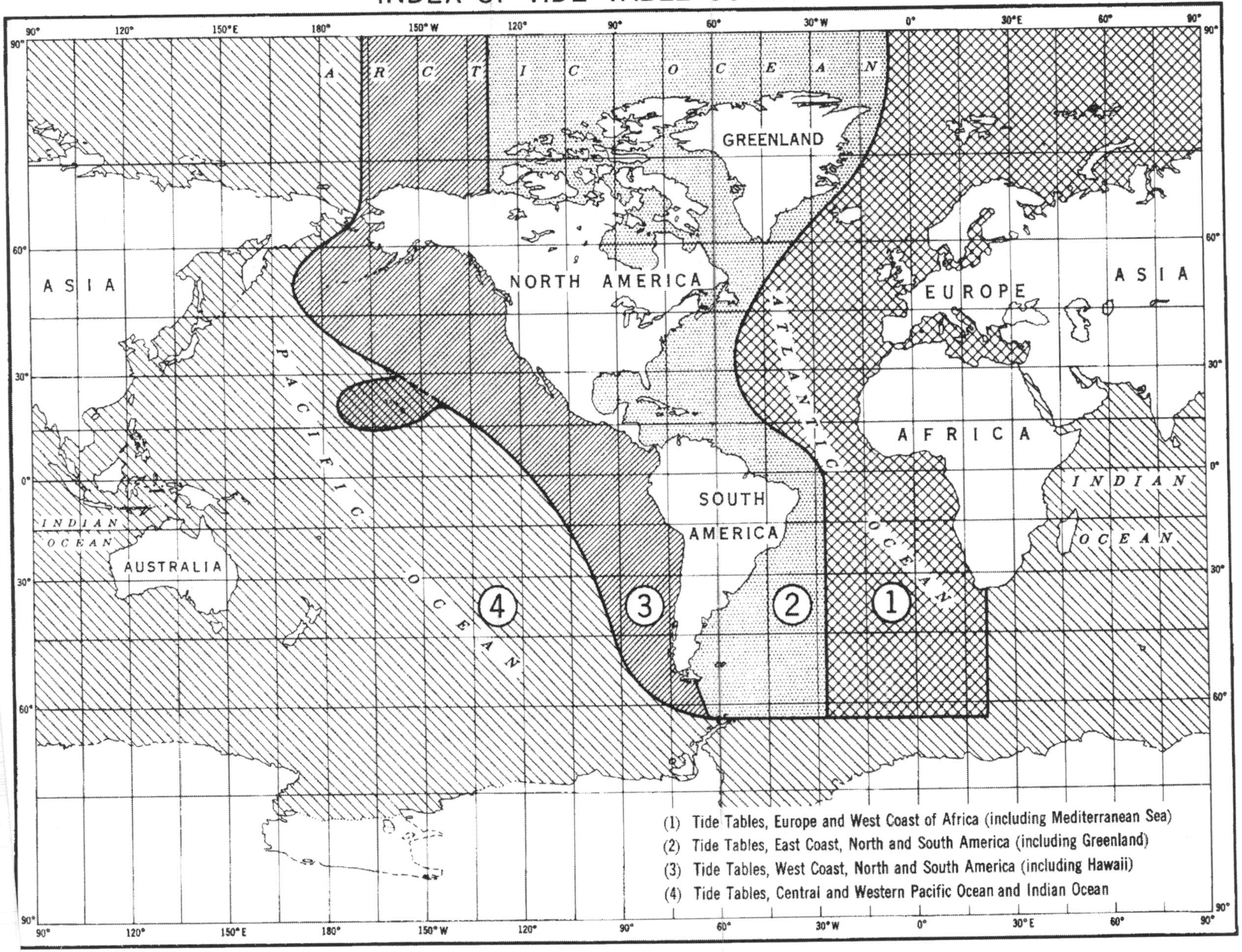
ARCTIC OCEAN
GREENLAND
NORTH AMERICA
EUROPE
ASIA
ASIA
ATLANTIC OCEAN
AFRICA
INDIAN OCEAN
INDIAN OCEAN
SOUTH AMERICA
AUSTRALIA
PACIFIC OCEAN
1
2
3
4
(1) Tide Tables, Europe and West Coast of Africa (including Mediterranean Sea)
(2) Tide Tables, East Coast, North and South America (including Greenland)
(3) Tide Tables, West Coast, North and South America (including Hawaii)
(4) Tide Tables, Central and Western Pacific Ocean and Indian Ocean

This publication contains tide and/or tidal current predictions and associated information produced by and obtained from the Department of Commerce, National Oceanic and Atmospheric Administration, National Ocean Service. This is not a National Ocean Service publication. The National Ocean Service is not responsible for any reproduction errors. These predictions satisfy all U.S. Coast Guard requirements including: 33 CFR Ch. I (7-1-91 Edition), 164.33 Charts and Publications.

Tide Tables 2017

East Coast of North and South America, Including Greenland

HIGH AND LOW WATER PREDICTIONS

North Wind Publishing

Brewer, Maine, USA

North Wind Publishing
P.O. Box 3655
Brewer, ME 04915
northwindpublishing.com
info@northwindpublishing.com

Printed in the United States of America.

ISBN-13: 978-0-9983192-0-9

ISBN-10: 090-9983192-0-1

East Coast of North and South America

Including Greenland

Issued 2016

SOURCES OF ADDITIONAL INFORMATION

THE NATIONAL OCEAN SERVICE IS NO LONGER PRINTING AND DISTRIBUTING THE TIDE AND TIDAL CURRENT TABLES

Tide and Tidal current data continue to be updated, generated and published by the NOAA/ National Ocean Service; however, the printing and distribution in book-form is now done by several private companies working from information provided by NOS.

NOS now offers two vehicles for obtaining predictions. First, the complete set of Tables as camera-ready page-images will be available on CD-ROM. The CD-ROM vehicle is primarily intended for use by federal or private printers who wish to print in book-form the full set of Tables for distribution to resellers and the general public. Second, for domestic tide stations, predictions are available on the NOS, Center for Operational Oceanographic Products and Services (CO-OPS), website, (http://tidesandcurrents.noaa.gov/).

In addition to predictions, the website provides updated information on the status of the Tables as they are finalized each year. Notices concerning the most recent Table updates and publication cut-off dates are included.

For the names of companies printing and distributing the Tables, please call or write to:

National Ocean Service
Oceanographic Division, N/OPS3
1305 East-West Highway
Silver Spring, MD 20910
(301) 713-2815, fax (301) 713-4500

A list of authorized sales agents is published in the Nautical Chart Catalogs or may be obtained on request from the National Ocean Service.

TECHNICAL ASSISTANCE:

Technical questions relating to ***tide and current predictions,*** as well as requests for ***special predictions***, should be addressed to:

National Ocean Service
Oceanographic Division, N/OPS3
1305 East-West Highway
Silver Spring, MD 20910
(301) 713-2815

Technical questions relating to ***actual tide observations, tidal datums, and other information necessary*** for ***engineering projects*** should be addressed to:

National Ocean Service
Oceanographic Division, N/OPS3
1305 East-West Highway
Silver Spring, MD 20910
(301) 713-2815

Technical questions relating to *other publications and nautical charts* should be addressed to:

National Ocean Service
Navigation Services Division
1315 East-West Highway
Silver Spring, MD 20910
(888) 990-NOAA (6622)

SOURCES OF ADDITIONAL INFORMATION

WEBSITES

Center for Operational Oceanographic Products and Services
(PORTS® * Predictions * Observations * Bench Marks * Tides Online * Great Lakes Online)
http://tidesandcurrents.noaa.gov

Marine Chart Division - http://www.nauticalcharts.noaa.gov

Office for Coastal Management - http://www.coast.noaa.gov

Ocean Predictions Center - http://www.opc.ncep.noaa.gov

National Center for Environmental Information - https://www.ncei.noaa.gov

National Centers for Environmental Predictions - http://www.ncep.noaa.gov

National Climatic Data Center - http://www.ncdc.noaa.gov

National Data Buoy Center - http://www.ndbc.noaa.gov

National Geodetic Survey - http://www.ngs.noaa.gov

National Geophysical Data Center - http://www.ngdc.noaa.gov

National Ocean Service - http://www.oceanservice.noaa.gov

National Oceanic and Atmospheric Administration - http://www.noaa.gov

National Oceanographic Data Center - http://www.nodc.noaa.gov

National Weather Service - http://www.weather.gov

U.S. Coast Guard - http://www.uscg.mil

U.S. Geological Survey - http://www.usgs.gov

U.S. Naval Observatory - http://www.usno.navy.mil

U.S. Naval Oceanographic Office - http://www.usno.navy.mil/NAVO

CORRECTIONS:

Corrections to this publication, after the date of printing, may appear in the Notice to Mariners. They may also appear in the Local Notice to Mariners, published weekly, by the various United States Coast Guard Districts.

CONTENTS

IMPORTANT NOTICES

For the most part, tide predictions for U.S. reference stations are based upon analyses of tide observations for periods of at least one year. Since the extremes of meteorological conditions have been excluded from the analyses and predictions, the predicted tidal heights should be considered as those expected under average weather conditions. During times when weather conditions differ from what is considered average for the area, the mariner must take note of the corresponding differences between predicted levels and those actually observed. Generally, prolonged onshore winds or a low barometric pressure can produce higher levels than predicted, while the opposite can result in lower levels than those predicted.

Exclusive of weather conditions, the astronomical tide is subject to range variations which should be noted. Decreased ranges may be expected near the times when the Moon is in apogee (apogean tides) or in quadrature (neap tides), and increased ranges may be expected when the Moon is in perigee (perigean tides) or in a new or full position (spring tides). A larger diurnal range may also result when the Moon is in its maximum declination (tropic tides). The actual range will depend upon the extent to which combinations of these positions reinforce or detract one from the other. The effect of these astronomical lineups is included in the predictions and may be apparent upon inspection.

The mariner may be kept aware of the times of these astronomical events by referring to the astronomical data listed in this book. He should realize, however, that there is generally a time lag from a few hours to several days from the time of the astronomical event to the time of the resultant tide. During times of storm surges or when extreme weather conditions are imminent, the mariner should closely follow local weather forecasts as they relate to the effects upon the tide levels.

Effective January 1, 1989, the chart datum and tidal datum chart, for all nautical charts, bathymetric maps, and tide tables covering the east coast of the United States and areas of the Caribbean Islands were changed from mean low water (MLW) to mean lower low water (MLLW). Notice of changes in tidal datums established through the "National Tidal Datum Convention of 1980" Federal Register, vol. 45, No. 207, Thursday, October 23, 1980, p. 70296-70297.

DAYLIGHT-SAVING TIME IS NOT USED IN THIS PUBLICATION. All daily tide predictions and predictions compiled by the use of Table 2 data are based on the standard time meridian indicated for each location. Predicted times may be converted to daylight saving times, where necessary, by adding 1 hour to these data. In converting times from the Astronomical Data page on the inside back cover, it should be remembered that daylight saving time is based on a meridian 15o east of the normal standard meridian for a particular place.

NOS, in partnership with other agencies and institutions, has established a series of Physical Oceanographic Real Time Systems (PORTS®) in selected areas. These PORTS® sites provide constantly updated information on tide and tidal current conditions, water temperature, and weather conditions. This information is updated every six minutes. PORTS® sites are currently in operation at several major harbors with future sites to be added. The information is accessible through a computer data connection or by a voice response system at the following sites:

PORTS® SITES	VOICE ACCESS	INTERNET ACCESS
CAPE COD	Not Available	www.tidesandcurrents.noaa.gov
CHARLESTON HARBOR	855-216-2137	"
CHERRY POINT	888-817-7794	"
CHESAPEAKE BAY	866-CH-PORTS (866-247-6787)	"
DELAWARE RIVER & BAY	866-30-PORTS (866-307-6787)	"
HOUSTON/GALVESTON	866-HG-PORTS (866-447-6787)	"
HUMBOLDT BAY	855-876-5015	"
JACKSONVILLE	855-901-1549	"
LAKE CHARLES	888-817-7692	"
LOS ANGELES/LONG BEACH	Not Available	"
LOWER COLUMBIA RIVER	888-53-PORTS (888-537-6787)	"
LOWER MISSISSIPPI RIVER	888-817-7767	"

IMPORTANT NOTICES

PORTS® SITES	VOICE ACCESS	INTERNET ACCESS
MOBILE BAY	877-84-PORTS (877-847-6787)	www.tidesandcurrents.noaa.gov
MORGAN CITY	888-312-4113	"
NARRAGANSETT BAY	866-75-PORTS (866-757-6787)	"
NEW HAVEN	888-80-PORTS (888-807-6787)	"
NEW LONDON	855-626-0509	"
NEW YORK/NEW JERSEY	866-21-PORTS (866-217-6787)	"
PASCAGOULA	888-257-1857	"
PORT OF ANCHORAGE	866-AK-PORTS (866-257-6787)	"
PORT FOURCHON	855-687-2084	"
SABINE NECHES	888-257-1859	"
SAN FRANCISCO BAY	866-SB-PORTS (866-727-6787)	"
SAVANNAH	855-907-3136	"
SOO LOCKS	301-713-9596	"
TACOMA	888-60-PORTS (888-607-6787)	"
TAMPA BAY	866-TB-PORTS (866-827-6787)	"

PUBLISHED CAUTIONARY NOTICES

Published in Local Notice to Mariners and United States Coast Pilot Notices

DAILY TIDE PREDICTIONS UPDATED FOR CUBA

In 2016, the NOAA/National Ocean Services', Center for Operational Oceanographic Products and Services (CO-OPS) started an exchange of daily tide predictions with Servicio Hidrografico y Geodesico de La Republica de Cuba. As a result of this exchange of information, the Tide Tables – East Coast of North and South America will now include daily tide predictions for four reference stations in Cuba, beginning with the 2017 Tide Tables.

Havana; Moa, Holguin; Santiago de Cuba; Bahia de Cienfuegos

Tide predictions at these stations will be updated annually. As the exchange of tide prediction information between NOAA and authorities in Cuba matures, it is expected that subordinate stations along the coast of Cuba will be updated and there may be some changes in the stations at which daily predictions are provided. Mariners should expect changes to the tide predictions provided in Cuba for several years. It is anticipated that most of these changes will be to the subordinate stations provided.

For additional information, please contact CO-OPS via e-mail at Tide.Predictions@noaa.gov or (301) 713-2815.

(Issued: October1, 2016)

IMPORTANT NOTICES

OBSERVED TIDAL CONDITIONS DIFFER FROM TIDAL PREDICTIONS IN THE HUDSON RIVER

The observed tides along the Hudson River have been reported to differ significantly from the published tide predictions; particularly in the northern section of the river from Newburgh to Albany, New York. Based on limited reports and comparisons to USGS stream gauges, it appears that high tides are occurring approximately 1 hour earlier than predicted.

NOAA has no information on what may be causing the difference between predictions and observations. This could be the result of natural changes (shoaling, erosion, etc) or artificial changes (dredging, construction, etc) in the Hudson River. Based on preliminary evidence, this does not appear to be a temporary condition and may indicate a long term change in the tidal conditions of the Hudson River.

NOAA does not have any water level stations operating along the length of the Hudson River, with the nearest operating station being located at The Battery, New York. Without observational data in the area, the extent of the difference between predictions and observations cannot be confirmed; neither can the areas affected by this change. Resources are not available for the installation and operation of water level stations along the Hudson River.

Mariners operating in this area are urged to use caution.

(Issued: May 24, 2010)

TIDAL CURRENT PREDICTIONS INSIDE U.S. ESTUARIES

At present there are several U.S. estuaries with operational Physical Oceanographic Real Time Systems (PORTS) installed. PORTS systems are presently being installed in several additional estuaries. Over the next ten years there are projected to be twenty or more additional systems installed. In the past, the tidal current reference station has always been located at the entrance to each estuary. All tidal current secondary stations both inside and outside (along the coast) have been referred to the reference station at the entrance to the estuary. This will no longer be the case in estuaries with an operational PORTS system.

Estuaries with an operational PORTS system will have at least two reference stations. One will be the historic station at the entrance to the estuary. All secondary stations along the coast will continue to be referred to this station. The second tidal current reference station will be the primary PORTS station within the estuary. All secondary locations within the estuary itself will be referred to this location. Depending on the circulation dynamics of the estuary, daily tidal current predictions may be provided for one or more additional stations within the estuary.

(Issued October 1, 1999)

ARANSAS PASS – CORPUS CHRISTI BAY, TX

The Aransas-Corpus Christi Pilots have reported that published tidal current predictions for Aransas Pass deviate from observations by as much as two (2) hours. The published predictions must be used with extreme caution. The Pilots should be consulted for critical transits. Tidal Current predictions of the National Ocean Service (NOS) are derived from analysis of observed data at tidal harmonic frequencies which in turn are based on predictable astronomic positions of the moon and sun. The problem in many areas of the Gulf of Mexico, including the south Texas coast, is that localized meteorological conditions can significantly effect and alter the times of maximum flood and ebb currents. Real-time observation and reporting systems, such as the Physical Oceanographic Real Time System (PORTS) installed in the Galveston-Houston area, are the only means of providing accurate tidal current data for areas such as this.

(Issued July 17, 1997)

IMPORTANT NOTICES

BISCAYNE BAY/PORT OF MIAMI, FL

The Biscayne Bay Pilots report that recent dredging and construction by the US Corps of Engineers (COE) supporting Miami port expansion has significantly effected the currents in Miami Harbor. Both flood and ebb currents should be expected to be stronger than indicated in official published predictions. The actual times for maximum and slack currents should be expected to deviate from the published predictions. Funding to support a survey to obtain new data for more accurate tidal current predictions is not available at this time. Installation of a Physical Oceanographic Real Time System (PORTS), like the one in operation in Tampa Bay, would be the best solution for long term marine safety.

(Issued July 17, 1997)

CHARLESTON HARBOR, SC

The US Army Corps of Engineers (CEO) is planning dredging and construction projects for Charleston Harbor in 1996-1997. Such projects in the past in other areas have resulted in dramatic changes in the observed tidal currents of those areas. Once dredging and/or construction operations commence, the Tidal Current predictions for this region should be considered questionable and potentially dangerous to rely upon. Tide predictions will also be affected but to a lesser degree. Funding for a real time system to monitor the Tidal Currents and a resurvey of the area after COE operations are complete is presently not available. Therefore, once COE operations begin and until such time as a real-time system is installed or a resurvey of the area conducted, the National Oceanic and Atmospheric Administration, National Ocean Service will be unable to provide accurate Tidal Current predictions necessary for marine safety and navigation in this area.

(Issued June 5, 1996)

CHESAPEAKE & DELAWARE CANAL AND BALTIMORE HARBOR CONNECTING CHANNELS

The US Army Corps of Engineers (COE) is planning a project involving the Chesapeake & Delaware Canal (C&D) and the channels in the upper Chesapeake Bay connecting the canal to Baltimore, MD in 1996-1997. Such projects in the past in other areas have resulted in dramatic changes in the observed tidal currents of those areas. Once the project begins, the Tidal Current predictions for the C&D Canal and the channels connecting the canal to Baltimore should be considered questionable and potentially dangerous to rely upon. Tide predictions will be affected but to a lesser degree. Funding for a real-time system to monitor the Tidal Currents and a resurvey of these areas after COE operations are complete is presently not available. Therefore, once COE operations begin and until such time as a real-time system is installed or a resurvey of the area conducted, the National Oceanic and Atmospheric Administration, National Ocean Service will be unable to provide accurate Tidal Current predictions necessary for marine safety and navigation in this area.

(Issued June 5, 1996)

ST. AUGUSTINE, FL – ATLANTIC INTRACOASTAL WATERWAY

The US Coast Guard (USCG) has reported a problem involving the Tidal Currents in the Atlantic Intracoastal Waterway (AICW) in the St. Augustine, FL area. The specific location is the Bridge of Lions over the waterway. Numerous accidents have occurred at this site which are related to the currents in the waterway. There is no National Ocean Service (NOS) Tidal Current Station at or near the Bridge of Lions. Thus the NOS cannot, at this time, make Tidal Current predictions for this location. The USCG states that the cause of the accidents is loss of maneuverability (control) as a vessel passes under the bridge. The loss of maneuverability results in the vessel striking the bridge supports. The USCG states in part:

> "The affect of a 'fair' tide on a navigating vessel is to reduce the vessel's ability to maneuver. When a vessel is proceeding with a current (fair tide), less water flows across the vessel's rudders. This condition has the affect of reducing the vessel's maneuverability for a given speed over ground (all other things being equal).

IMPORTANT NOTICES

The Bridge of Lions is a difficult bridge to navigate, even under ideal conditions. This circa 1926 Bascule bridge has a horizontal clearance of only 76' verses the 90' horizontal clearance of most of the other bridges on this section of the AICW."

In addition, according to the US Coast Pilot, Vol 4, Chapter 12, Tidal Currents in excess of 2 knots often run at right angles to the bridge opening. The Coast Pilot advises mariners to transit the bridge at minimal Tidal Current conditions. Funding for real-time monitoring of the Tidal Currents or a survey to obtain Tidal Current observations upon which to base Tidal Current predictions for this location is not presently available. A consortium of local, state, and federal officials in conjunction with the private sector and commercial shipping interests are presently studying various options to provide accurate Tidal Current predictions necessary for marine safety and navigation at this location.

(Issued June 5, 1996)

WILMINGTON AND CAPE FEAR RIVER, NC

The US Army Corps of Engineers (COE) is due to begin dredging operations in the Wilmington and Cape Fear River area in 1997. The plans call for the deepening of the channel approaching Wilmington and extending up the Cape Fear River. Such actions in the past in other areas have resulted in dramatic changes in the observed tidal currents of those areas. Once dredging operations commence, the Tidal Current predictions for this region should be considered questionable at best and potentially dangerous to rely upon. Tide predictions will also be affected but to a lesser degree. Funding for a real-time system to monitor the Tidal Currents during the project and a resurvey of the area after COE operations are complete is presently not available. Therefore, once COE operations begin and until such time as a real-time system is installed or a resurvey of the area conducted, the National Oceanic and Atmospheric Administration, National Ocean Service will be unable to provide accurate Tidal Current predictions necessary for marine safety and navigation in this area.

(Issued June 5, 1996)

HAMPTON ROADS, VA

Tidal currents in Hampton Roads and Elizabeth River have been significantly altered by dredging and construction of a new bridge/tunnel. Recent dredging by the U.S. Army Corps of Engineers has deepened the channels by 10 feet to a depth of 50 feet. Pilots and officials at the Norfolk Naval Base report hazardous conditions including significantly higher than predicted maximum current velocities, and significant deviation in the predicted times of maximum current. Mariners should exercise EXTREME CAUTION and DISCRETION in the use of published NOS tidal current predictions for this area. Funding for a Quality Assurance study and a full scale resurvey of the area is presently not available.

(Issued March 24, 1992)

CHINCOTEAGUE CHANNEL, VA

United States Coast Guard (USCG) Personnel at the Chincoteague Coast Guard Station, VA report that the times of high and low water computed from differences in Table 2 of the East Coast Tide Tables are frequently off by as much as an hour. The channel is subject to shoaling and is frequently dredged. Exercise caution in using Table 2 Tide differences for this area.

(Issued May 17, 1991)

INTRODUCTION

Tide tables for the use of mariners have been published by the National Ocean Service (formerly the Coast and Geodetic Survey) since 1853. For a number of years these tables appeared as appendixes to the annual reports of the Superintendent of the Survey, and consisted of detailed instructions enabling the mariner to make his own prediction of tides as the occasion arose.

The first tables to give predictions for each day were those for the year 1867. They gave the times and heights of high waters only and were published in two separate parts, one for the Atlantic coast and the other for the Pacific coast of the United States. Together they contained daily predictions for 19 stations and tidal differences for 124 stations. A few years later predictions for the low waters were also included, and for the year 1896 the tables were extended to include the entire maritime world, with full predictions for 70 ports and tidal differences for about 3,000 stations.

The tidal tables are now issued in four volumes, as follows: *Europe and West Coast of Africa (including the Mediterranean Sea); East Coast of North and South America (including Greenland); West Coast of North and South America (including the Hawaiian Islands); Central and Western Pacific Ocean and Indian Ocean.* Together, they contain daily predictions for more than 250 reference ports and differences and other constants for more than 6,500 stations.

This edition of the Tide Tables, *East Coast of North and South America*, contains full daily predictions for more than 70 reference ports and differences and other constants for more than 2,500 stations in North America, South America, and Greenland. It also contains a table for obtaining the approximate height of the tide at any time, a table of local mean time of sunrise and sunset for every 5th day of the year for different latitudes, a table for the reduction of local mean time to standard time, a table of moonrise and moonset for 8 places, a table of the Greenwich mean time of the Moons' phases, apogee, perigee, greatest north and south and zero declination, and the time of the solar equinoxes and solstices, and a glossary of terms.

Up to and including the tide tables for the year 1884, all the tide predictions were computed by means of auxiliary tables and curves constructed from the results of tide observations at the different ports. From 1885 to 1911, inclusively, the predictions were generally made by means of the Ferrel Tide-predicting machine. From 1912 to 1965, inclusively, they were made by means of the Coast and Geodetic Survey tide-predicting machine No. 2. Since 1966, predictions have been made by electronic computer.

In the preparation of these tables all available observations were used. In some cases, however, the observations were insufficient for obtaining final results. As further information becomes available it will be included in subsequent editions. All persons using these tables are invited to send information or suggestions for increasing their usefulness to the National Ocean Service, Oceanographic Division, 1305 East-West Highway, N/OPS3, Silver Spring, Maryland 20910, U.S.A.

The information presented in *Table 4 - Local mean time of sunrise and sunset* and in *Table 6 - Moonrise and Moonset* is computed by the National Ocean Service using the Interactive Computer Ephemeris Program provided by the United States Naval Observatory.

In accordance with cooperative arrangements between the National Ocean Service and the authorities listed below, predictions for the following stations appear in this issue:

Canadian Hydrographic Service.—Harrington Harbour, Quebec, Halifax, St. John, Pictou, and Argentia.

Directoria de Hidrografia e Navegacao, Brazil.—Recife, Rio de Janeiro, and Santos.

Servicio Hidrografico, Argentina.—Buenos Aires, Puerto Ingeniero White, Comodoro Rivadiva, and Punta Loyola.

LIST OF REFERENCE STATIONS

Station Name	Page	Datum below mean sea-level	Updated	Data Series
Albany, New York	80	2.49	1966	3 years (1984-1987)
Amuay, Venezuela	264	0.65		
Apalachicola, Florida	192	0.92	1999	3 years (1995-1997)
Argentia, Newfoundland	4	4.30		
Atlantic City, New Jersey	88	2.23	2006	5 years (1999-2003)
Baltimore, Maryland	108	0.82	2001	5 years (1994-1998)
Bar Harbor, Maine	32	5.71	2003	5 years (1992-1996)
Bayonne Bridge, Staten Island, New York	76	2.78	1999	4 years (1990-1991,1994-1995)
Boston, Massachusetts	40	5.22	2001	5 years (1994-1998)
Breakwater Harbor, Delaware	92	2.27	2001	5 years (1994-1998)
Bridgeport, Connecticut	64	3.61	2001	5 years (1994-1998)
Buenos Aires, Argentina	288	2.60		
Cape Hatteras, North Carolina	132	1.65	1998	4 years (1988-1991)
Cedar Key, Florida	184	2.03	2003	5 years (1992-1997)
Charleston, South Carolina	144	2.95	2003	5 years (1996-2000)
Charlotte Amalie, St. Thomas Island	252	0.38	2002	8 years (1984-1991)
Chesapeake Bay Bridge Tunnel, Virginia	116	1.45	2006	5 years (1999-2003)
Cienfuegos, Cuba	304			
Comodoro Rivadavia, Argentina	296	10.30		
Cristobal (Colon), Panama	232	0.38		
Dauphin Island, Alabama	200	0.57	1998	4 years (1993-1996)
Duck Pier, North Carolina	124	1.81	2003	5 years (1996-2000)
Eastport, Maine	28	9.71	2001	5 years (1994-1998)
Fernandina Beach, Amelia River, Florida	152	3.35	2003	3 years (1998-2000)
Galveston (Galveston Channel), Texas	216	0.82	2006	5 years (1999-2003)
Grand Isle (East Point), Louisiana	212	0.56	2006	5 years (1999-2003)
Halifax, Nova Scotia	20	4.30		
Hampton Roads (Sewells Pt.), Virginia	120	1.38	2002	5 years (1995-1999)
Harrington Harbour, Quebec	12	3.50		
Havana, Cuba	308			
Isla Zapara (Malecon), Venezuela	260	2.70		
Key West, Florida	172	0.92	2003	5 years (1996-2000)
Kings Point, Long Island, New York	68	3.87	2006	5 years (1999-2003)
Lime Tree Bay, St. Croix Island	256	0.38	2002	3 years (1995-1997)
Magueyes Island, Puerto Rico	244	0.34	2002	3 years (1995-1997)
Mayport, Florida	156	2.46	2005	3 years (2001-2003)
Miami, Government Cut, Florida	164	1.43	2005	2 years (1985-1986)
Moa, Holguin, Cuba	316			
Mobile, Alabama	204	0.83	2016	6 years (2008-2013)
Montauk, Fort Pond Bay, New York	56	1.09	2003	5 years (1996-2000)
Myrtle Beach (Springmaid Pier), South Carolina	140	2.75	2006	5 years (1999-2003)
Nantucket, Massachusetts	44	1.79	2005	5 years (1999-2003)
Naples, Florida	176	1.69	2003	4 years (1992-1996)
New London, Connecticut	60	1.55	2001	5 years (1994-1998)
New York (The Battery), New York	72	2.58	2006	5 years (1999-2003)
Newport, Rhode Island	52	1.77	2001	5 years (1994-1998)
Ocean City, Maryland	104	1.87	1999	5 years (1985-1989)
Oregon Inlet, North Carolina	128	0.66	1999	4 years (1995-1998)
Padre Island (south end), Texas	224	0.86	1998	1 year (1963)
Pensacola, Florida	196	0.62	2003	5 years (1996-2000)
Philadelphia, Pennsylvania	100	3.47	2006	5 years (1999-2003)
Pictou, Nova Scotia	8	3.90		

LIST OF REFERENCE STATIONS

Station Name	Page	Datum below mean sea-level	Updated	Data Series
Port Canaveral (Trident Pier), Florida	160	1.92	2003	5 years (1997-2001)
Port O'Connor, Texas....................................	220	0.42	1999	29 days beginning 2/1/1989
Portland, Maine	36	4.93	2001	5 years (1993-1997)
Puerto Ingeniero White, Argentina	292	8.50		
Punta Gorda, Venezuela	268	3.30		
Punta Loyola, Argentina	300	20.30		
Quebec, Quebec	16	8.50		
Recife, Brazil	276	3.70		
Reedy Point, Delaware.................................	96	2.99	2006	5 years (1999-2003)
Rio de Janeiro, Brazil	280	2.30		
Saint John, New Brunswick...........................	24	14.50		
San Juan, Puerto Rico	248	0.78	1999	4 years (1983-1996)
Sandy Hook, New Jersey	84	2.56	2006	5 years (1999-2003)
Santiago de Cuba..	312			
Santos, Brazil	284	2.50		
Savannah River Entrance, Georgia..............	148	3.80	2003	5 years (1996-2000)
Settlement Point, Grand Bahama Island	240	1.45	2002	4 years (1986-1988,1990)
South Pass, Louisiana.................................	208	0.68	1999	3 years (1989-1991)
St. Georges Island, Bermuda	236	1.35	2002	4 years (1990-1993)
St. Marks River Entrance, Florida	188	1.93	1996	358 days beginning 9/1/1970
St. Petersburg, Florida	180	1.19	2006	5 years (1999-2003)
Suriname River Entrance, Surinam...............	272	4.28		
Tampico Harbor (Madero), Mexico...............	228	0.84		
*Vaca Key, Florida Bay, Florida	168	0.52	2017	6 year (2009-2014)
Washington, D.C.	112	1.56	2001	5 years (1994-1998)
Wilmington, North Carolina	136	2.33	2006	5 years (1999-2003)
Woods Hole, Massachusetts........................	48	1.04	2005	5 years (1999-2003)

* New or updated station

Each datum figure above represents the difference in elevation between the local mean sea (or river) level and the reference level from which the predicted heights in table 1 were calculated.

Local mean sea level datum should not be confused with the National Geodetic Vertical Datum which is the datum of the geodetic level net of the United States. Relationships between geodetic and local tidal datums are published in connection with the tidal benchmark data of the National Ocean Service.

TABLE 1.— DAILY TIDE PREDICTIONS

EXPLANATION OF TABLE

This table contains the predicted times and heights of the high and low waters for each day of the year at a number of places which are designated as *reference stations*. By using tidal differences from Table 2, one can calculate the approximate times and heights of the tide at many other places which are called *subordinate stations*. Instructions on the use of the tidal differences are found in the explanation of Table 2.

High water is the maximum height reached by each rising tide, and low water is the minimum height reached by each falling tide. High and low waters can be selected from the predictions by the comparison of consecutive heights. Because of diurnal inequality at certain places, however, there may be a difference of only a few tenths of a foot between one high water and low water of a day, but a marked difference in height between the other high water and low water. Therefore, in using the Tide Tables it is essential to note carefully the heights as well as the times of the tides.

Time.— The kind of time used for the predictions at each reference station is indicated by the time meridian at the bottom of each page. Daylight-saving time is not used in this publication. If daylight-saving time is required, add one (1) hour to the predicted time.

Datum.— The datum from which the predicted heights are recorded is the same as that used for the nautical charts of the locality. The datum for the Atlantic coast of the United States is mean lower low water (MLLW). For foreign coasts a datum approximating to mean low water springs, Indian spring low water, or the lowest possible low water is generally used. The depression of the datum below mean sea level (MSL) for each of the reference stations of this volume is given on the preceding page.

Depth of water.— The nautical charts published by the United States and other maritime nations show the depth of the water as referred to a low water datum corresponding to that from which the predicted tidal heights are recorded. To find the actual depth of water at any time, the height of the tide should be added to the charted depth. If the height of the tide is negative—that is, if there is a minus sign (—) before the tabular height—the height should be subtracted from the charted depth. For any time between high and low water, the height of the tide may be estimated from the heights of the preceding and the following tides, or Table 3 may be used. The reference stations in Table 1 contain the heights in centimeters as well as in feet.

Variation in sea level.— Changes in winds and barometric conditions cause variations in sea level from day to day. In general, with onshore winds or a low barometer the heights of both the high and low waters will be higher than predicted, while with offshore winds or a high barometer they will be lower. There are also seasonal variations in sea level, but these variations have been included in the predictions for each station. At ocean stations the seasonal variation in sea level is usually less than half a foot.

At stations on tidal rivers the average seasonal variation in river level due to freshets and droughts may be considerably more than a foot. The predictions for these stations include an allowance for this seasonal variation representing average freshet and drought conditions. Unusual freshets or droughts, however, will cause the tides to be higher or lower, respectively, than predicted.

Number of tides.— There are usually two high and two low waters in a day. Tides follow the Moon more closely than they do the Sun, and the lunar or tidal day is about 50 minutes longer than the solar day. This causes the tide to occur later each day, and a tide that has occurred near the end of one calendar day will be followed by a corresponding tide that may skip the next day and occur in the early morning of the third day. Thus, on certain days of each month only a single high or a single low water occurs. At some stations, during portions of each month, the tide becomes diurnal—that is, only one high and one low water will occur during the period of a lunar day.

Relation of tide to current.— In using these tables of tide predictions bear in mind that they give the times and heights of high and low waters and not the times of turning of the current or slack water. For stations on the outer coast there is usually a small difference between the time of high or low water and the beginning of ebb or flood current, but for places in narrow channels, landlocked harbors, or on

1

TABLE 1.—DAILY TIDE PREDICTIONS

tidal rivers, the time of slack water may differ by several hours from the time of high or low water stand. The relation of the times of high and low water to the turning of the current depends upon a number of factors, so no simple or general rule can be given. For the predicted time of slack water, and other current data, reference should be made to the Tidal Current Tables prepared by the National Ocean Service, for the Atlantic and the Pacific coast of North America and Asia.

Typical tide curves.— The variations in the tide from day to day and from place to place are illustrated on the opposite page by the tide curves for representative ports along the Atlantic and Gulf coasts of the United States. Note that the range of tide for stations along the Atlantic coast varies from place to place but that the type is uniformly semidiurnal with the principal variations following the changes in the Moon's distance and phase. In the Gulf of Mexico, however, the type of tide differs considerably and the range of tide is uniformly small. At certain ports such as Pensacola there is usually only one high and one low water a day while at other ports such as Galveston the inequality is such that the tide is semidiurnal around the times the Moon is on the Equator but becomes diurnal around the times of maximum north or south declination of the Moon. In the Gulf of Mexico, consequently, the principal variations in the tide are due to the changing declination of the Moon. Key West, at the entrance to the Gulf of Mexico, has a type of tide which is a mixture of semidiurnal and diurnal types. Here the tide is semidiurnal but there is considerable inequality in the heights of high and low waters. By reference to the curves it will be seen that where the inequality is large there are times when there is only a few tenths of a foot difference between high water and low water.

TYPICAL TIDE CURVES FOR UNITED STATES PORTS

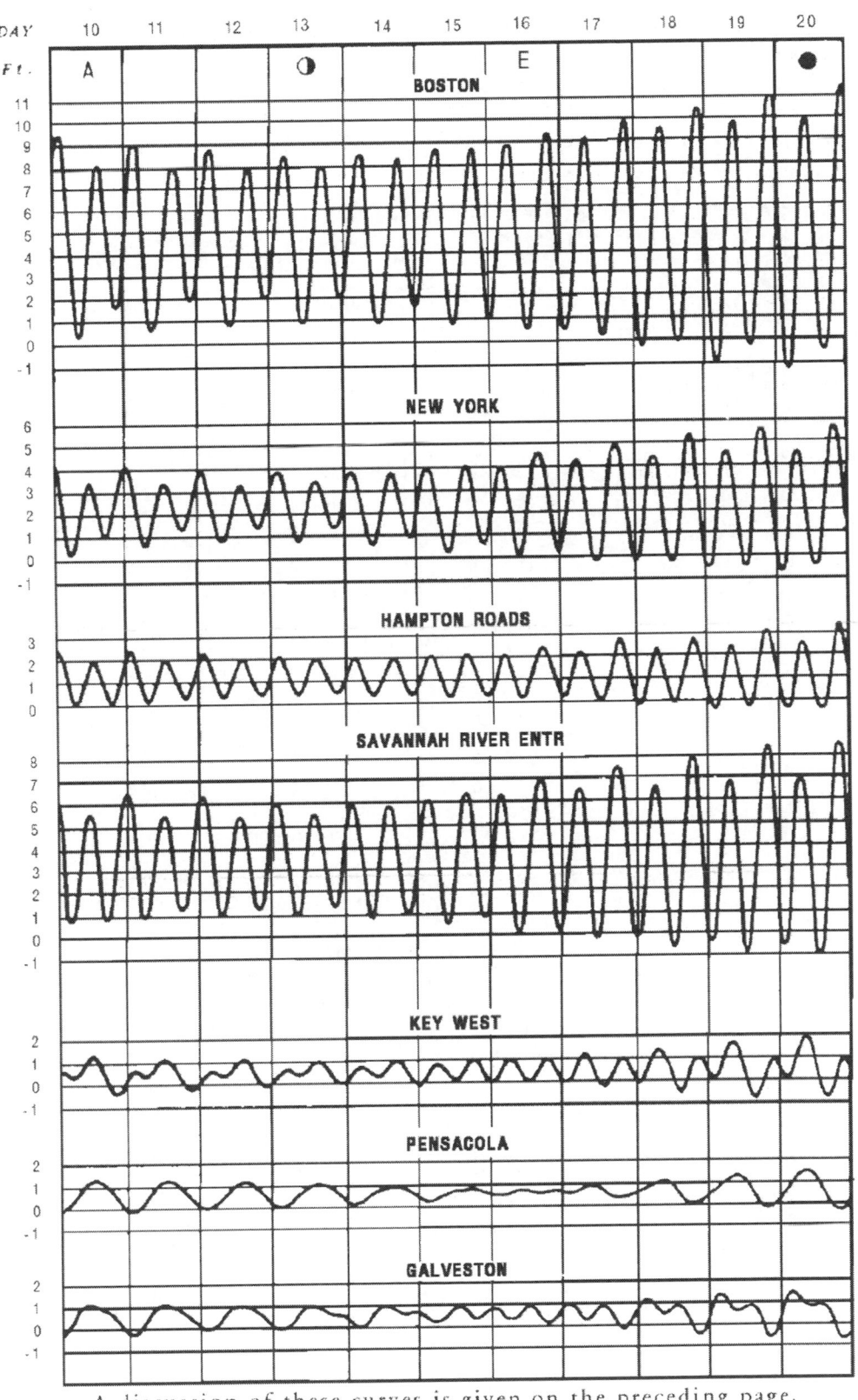

A discussion of these curves is given on the preceding page.

Lunar data: A – Moon in apogee
☽ – last quarter
E – Moon on Equater
● – new Moon

Argentia, Newfoundland, 2017
Times and Heights of High and Low Waters

January

Day	Time	ft	cm	Day	Time	ft	cm
1 Su	0330	2.0	60	**16** M	0402	1.6	50
	1009	7.9	240		1114	7.9	240
	1557	2.0	60		1631	2.0	60
	2227	6.9	210		2325	6.9	210
2 M	0406	2.0	60	**17** Tu	0442	2.0	60
	1050	7.5	230		1158	7.2	220
	1631	2.0	60		1710	2.3	70
	2312	6.9	210				
3 Tu	0444	2.0	60	**18** W	0013	6.9	210
	1133	7.5	230		0524	2.3	70
	1708	2.0	60		1245	6.9	210
					1752	2.6	80
4 W	0001	6.6	200	**19** Th	0104	6.6	200
	0527	2.3	70		0611	2.6	80
	1219	7.2	220		1337	6.6	200
	1750	2.0	60		1841	3.0	90
5 Th	0055	6.6	200	**20** F	0157	6.2	190
	0615	2.3	70		0709	3.0	90
	1312	6.9	210		1435	5.9	180
	1839	2.3	70		1950	3.0	90
6 F	0154	6.6	200	**21** Sa	0254	6.2	190
	0715	2.6	80		0852	3.3	100
	1413	6.6	200		1533	5.9	180
	1941	2.3	70		2122	3.0	90
7 Sa	0259	6.9	210	**22** Su	0353	6.2	190
	0838	2.6	80		1017	3.3	100
	1521	6.6	200		1632	5.6	170
	2101	2.3	70		2223	3.0	90
8 Su	0409	6.9	210	**23** M	0451	6.6	200
	1017	2.3	70		1114	3.0	90
	1632	6.6	200		1726	5.9	180
	2218	2.0	60		2312	2.6	80
9 M	0516	7.2	220	**24** Tu	0545	6.6	200
	1125	2.0	60		1202	3.0	90
	1738	6.6	200		1813	5.9	180
	2318	2.0	60		2359	2.3	70
10 Tu	0617	7.9	240	**25** W	0634	6.9	210
	1222	1.6	50		1246	2.6	80
	1839	6.9	210		1854	6.2	190
11 W	0013	1.6	50	**26** Th	0043	2.3	70
	0714	8.2	250		0716	7.2	220
	1313	1.6	50		1325	2.3	70
	1932	7.2	220		1932	6.6	200
12 Th	0105	1.6	50	**27** F	0125	2.0	60
	0806	8.5	260		0756	7.5	230
	1358	1.3	40		1401	2.0	60
	2021	7.2	220		2009	6.9	210
13 F	0153	1.3	40	**28** Sa	0204	1.6	50
	0856	8.5	260		0833	7.9	240
	1439	1.3	40		1434	2.0	60
	2108	7.2	220		2047	6.9	210
14 Sa	0239	1.3	40	**29** Su	0240	1.6	50
	0944	8.5	260		0911	7.9	240
	1517	1.6	50		1505	1.6	50
	2153	7.2	220		2126	7.2	220
15 Su	0321	1.6	50	**30** M	0315	1.6	50
	1029	8.2	250		0949	7.9	240
	1554	1.6	50		1536	1.6	50
	2238	7.2	220		2206	7.2	220
				31 Tu	0351	1.6	50
					1028	7.9	240
					1609	1.6	50
					2250	7.2	220

February

Day	Time	ft	cm	Day	Time	ft	cm
1 W	0428	1.6	50	**16** Th	0456	2.0	60
	1110	7.5	230		1154	6.6	200
	1645	1.6	50		1716	2.3	70
	2338	7.2	220				
2 Th	0508	1.6	50	**17** F	0012	6.6	200
	1156	7.2	220		0535	2.6	80
	1725	1.6	50		1240	6.2	190
					1756	2.6	80
3 F	0030	7.2	220	**18** Sa	0102	6.6	200
	0553	2.0	60		0620	3.0	90
	1249	6.9	210		1336	5.9	180
	1810	2.0	60		1844	3.0	90
4 Sa	0130	6.9	210	**19** Su	0159	6.2	190
	0647	2.3	70		0723	3.3	100
	1351	6.6	200		1438	5.6	170
	1906	2.3	70		2001	3.3	100
5 Su	0238	6.9	210	**20** M	0301	6.2	190
	0803	2.6	80		0936	3.6	110
	1502	6.2	190		1541	5.6	170
	2021	2.6	80		2146	3.3	100
6 M	0350	6.9	210	**21** Tu	0405	6.2	190
	1015	2.6	80		1046	3.3	100
	1616	6.2	190		1642	5.6	170
	2159	2.6	80		2245	3.0	90
7 Tu	0501	7.2	220	**22** W	0507	6.6	200
	1127	2.3	70		1139	3.0	90
	1728	6.6	200		1738	5.9	180
	2312	2.3	70		2337	2.6	80
8 W	0607	7.5	230	**23** Th	0603	6.9	210
	1222	2.0	60		1224	2.6	80
	1831	6.9	210		1826	6.2	190
9 Th	0010	2.0	60	**24** F	0024	2.3	70
	0705	7.9	240		0650	7.2	220
	1308	2.0	60		1302	2.3	70
	1924	7.2	220		1908	6.6	200
10 F	0102	2.0	60	**25** Sa	0107	2.0	60
	0756	8.2	250		0731	7.5	230
	1346	1.6	50		1337	2.0	60
	2009	7.2	220		1947	6.9	210
11 Sa	0147	1.6	50	**26** Su	0146	1.6	50
	0842	8.5	260		0810	7.9	240
	1421	1.6	50		1409	1.6	50
	2050	7.5	230		2025	7.2	220
12 Su	0227	1.6	50	**27** M	0222	1.3	40
	0923	8.2	250		0848	8.2	250
	1454	1.6	50		1440	1.3	40
	2129	7.5	230		2104	7.5	230
13 M	0305	1.3	40	**28** Tu	0257	1.0	30
	1001	7.9	240		0926	7.9	240
	1528	1.6	50		1511	1.3	40
	2207	7.2	220		2144	7.5	230
14 Tu	0342	1.6	50				
	1038	7.5	230				
	1603	1.6	50				
	2246	7.2	220				
15 W	0418	2.0	60				
	1114	7.2	220				
	1638	2.0	60				
	2327	6.9	210				

March

Day	Time	ft	cm	Day	Time	ft	cm
1 W	0332	1.0	30	**16** Th	0354	1.6	50
	1006	7.9	240		1034	6.9	210
	1545	1.3	40		1608	1.6	50
	2228	7.5	230		2249	6.9	210
2 Th	0409	1.0	30	**17** F	0428	2.0	60
	1049	7.5	230		1110	6.6	200
	1622	1.3	40		1643	2.0	60
	2316	7.5	230		2329	6.9	210
3 F	0448	1.3	40	**18** Sa	0504	2.3	70
	1136	7.2	220		1152	6.2	190
	1701	1.6	50		1719	2.6	80
4 Sa	0011	7.2	220	**19** Su	0015	6.6	200
	0532	1.6	50		0544	2.6	80
	1231	6.9	210		1242	5.9	180
	1745	2.0	60		1759	3.0	90
5 Su	0114	7.2	220	**20** M	0109	6.6	200
	0625	2.3	70		0632	3.3	100
	1338	6.6	200		1345	5.6	170
	1838	2.6	80		1850	3.3	100
6 M	0224	6.9	210	**21** Tu	0212	6.2	190
	0743	3.0	90		0834	3.6	110
	1453	6.2	190		1451	5.6	170
	1953	3.0	90		2052	3.3	100
7 Tu	0336	6.9	210	**22** W	0318	6.2	190
	1026	2.6	80		1015	3.3	100
	1608	6.2	190		1557	5.6	170
	2219	3.0	90		2215	3.3	100
8 W	0448	7.2	220	**23** Th	0425	6.6	200
	1127	2.6	80		1110	3.0	90
	1721	6.2	190		1700	5.9	180
	2325	2.6	80		2311	2.6	80
9 Th	0557	7.5	230	**24** F	0527	6.9	210
	1215	2.3	70		1153	2.6	80
	1823	6.6	200		1754	6.2	190
					2359	2.3	70
10 F	0016	2.3	70	**25** Sa	0619	7.2	220
	0655	7.5	230		1231	2.3	70
	1253	2.0	60		1840	6.6	200
	1912	6.9	210				
11 Sa	0059	2.0	60	**26** Su	0042	2.0	60
	0743	7.9	240		0703	7.5	230
	1325	1.6	50		1305	1.6	50
	1953	7.2	220		1921	7.2	220
12 Su	0137	1.6	50	**27** M	0122	1.3	40
	0823	7.9	240		0743	7.9	240
	1355	1.6	50		1337	1.3	40
	2029	7.5	230		2000	7.5	230
13 M	0212	1.6	50	**28** Tu	0159	1.0	30
	0859	7.9	240		0823	7.9	240
	1427	1.3	40		1410	1.0	30
	2103	7.5	230		2041	7.9	240
14 Tu	0246	1.3	40	**29** W	0235	0.7	20
	0931	7.5	230		0903	7.9	240
	1459	1.3	40		1445	1.0	30
	2137	7.5	230		2123	7.9	240
15 W	0320	1.6	50	**30** Th	0312	0.7	20
	1002	7.2	220		0945	7.9	240
	1534	1.6	50		1521	1.0	30
	2212	7.2	220		2209	7.9	240
				31 F	0350	1.0	30
					1029	7.5	230
					1559	1.0	30
					2259	7.9	240

Time meridian 52° 30' W. 0000 is midnight. 1200 is noon. Times are not adjusted for Daylight Saving Time.
Heights are referred to the Canadian chart datum of soundings. Subtract 1.9 feet (62 centimeters) to refer these levels to the datum of N.O.S. charts.

Argentia, Newfoundland, 2017

Times and Heights of High and Low Waters

April

Day	Time	ft	cm	Day	Time	ft	cm
1 Sa	0431	1.3	40	16 Su	0439	2.3	70
	1120	7.2	220		1116	6.2	190
	1640	1.6	50		1648	2.3	70
	2358	7.5	230		2340	6.9	210
2 Su	0516	1.6	50	17 M	0516	2.6	80
	1221	6.6	200		1203	5.9	180
	1724	2.0	60		1726	2.6	80
3 M	0104	7.2	220	18 Tu	0031	6.6	200
	0609	2.3	70		0559	3.0	90
	1334	6.2	190		1302	5.6	170
	1817	2.6	80		1810	3.0	90
4 Tu	0212	6.9	210	19 W	0128	6.6	200
	0822	3.0	90		0701	3.3	100
	1447	6.2	190		1407	5.6	170
	1938	3.3	100		1918	3.3	100
5 W	0322	6.9	210	20 Th	0232	6.6	200
	1020	2.6	80		0932	3.3	100
	1559	6.2	190		1513	5.6	170
	2232	3.0	90		2135	3.3	100
6 Th	0434	6.9	210	21 F	0338	6.6	200
	1114	2.6	80		1031	3.0	90
	1708	6.6	200		1618	5.9	180
	2327	2.6	80		2238	3.0	90
7 F	0543	6.9	210	22 Sa	0444	6.6	200
	1155	2.3	70		1114	2.6	80
	1807	6.6	200		1717	6.2	190
					2328	2.3	70
8 Sa	0011	2.3	70	23 Su	0542	6.9	210
	0639	7.2	220		1151	2.0	60
	1227	2.0	60		1808	6.9	210
	1853	6.9	210				
9 Su	0048	2.0	60	24 M	0013	2.0	60
	0724	7.2	220		0631	7.2	220
	1255	1.6	50		1227	1.6	50
	1931	7.2	220		1853	7.2	220
10 M	0120	1.6	50	25 Tu	0054	1.3	40
	0800	7.2	220		0715	7.5	230
	1326	1.6	50		1303	1.3	40
	2005	7.5	230		1936	7.9	240
11 Tu	0152	1.6	50	26 W	0134	1.0	30
	0832	7.2	220		0758	7.9	240
	1358	1.3	40		1341	1.0	30
	2037	7.5	230		2019	8.2	250
12 W	0225	1.6	50	27 Th	0214	0.7	20
	0900	6.9	210		0841	7.9	240
	1432	1.3	40		1420	0.7	20
	2110	7.5	230		2105	8.2	250
13 Th	0257	1.6	50	28 F	0254	0.7	20
	0929	6.9	210		0925	7.5	230
	1506	1.3	40		1459	1.0	30
	2143	7.2	220		2154	8.2	250
14 F	0330	1.6	50	29 Sa	0335	1.0	30
	1001	6.6	200		1013	7.5	230
	1540	1.6	50		1540	1.0	30
	2218	7.2	220		2248	8.2	250
15 Sa	0404	2.0	60	30 Su	0418	1.3	40
	1036	6.6	200		1109	7.2	220
	1614	2.0	60		1623	1.6	50
	2257	6.9	210		2349	7.9	240

May

Day	Time	ft	cm	Day	Time	ft	cm
1 M	0504	1.6	50	16 Tu	0456	2.6	80
	1215	6.6	200		1136	5.9	180
	1709	2.3	70		1702	2.6	80
2 Tu	0053	7.5	230	17 W	0001	6.9	210
	0558	2.3	70		0536	2.6	80
	1327	6.6	200		1230	5.9	180
	1804	2.6	80		1745	3.0	90
3 W	0158	7.2	220	18 Th	0053	6.9	210
	0845	3.0	90		0625	3.0	90
	1433	6.2	190		1329	5.9	180
	2022	3.3	100		1841	3.0	90
4 Th	0304	6.9	210	19 F	0150	6.6	200
	0958	2.6	80		0736	3.0	90
	1539	6.2	190		1431	5.9	180
	2218	3.0	90		2008	3.0	90
5 F	0414	6.6	200	20 Sa	0252	6.6	200
	1047	2.6	80		0924	3.0	90
	1643	6.6	200		1535	6.2	190
	2310	2.6	80		2152	3.0	90
6 Sa	0520	6.6	200	21 Su	0358	6.6	200
	1123	2.3	70		1021	2.6	80
	1740	6.6	200		1637	6.6	200
	2352	2.3	70		2251	2.3	70
7 Su	0615	6.6	200	22 M	0501	6.6	200
	1153	2.0	60		1106	2.0	60
	1827	6.9	210		1734	6.9	210
					2340	2.0	60
8 M	0027	2.0	60	23 Tu	0557	6.9	210
	0659	6.9	210		1148	1.6	50
	1223	2.0	60		1826	7.5	230
	1906	7.2	220				
9 Tu	0059	2.0	60	24 W	0027	1.3	40
	0734	6.9	210		0647	7.2	220
	1256	1.6	50		1231	1.3	40
	1941	7.2	220		1914	7.9	240
10 W	0131	1.6	50	25 Th	0111	1.0	30
	0804	6.6	200		0735	7.5	230
	1331	1.3	40		1314	1.0	30
	2013	7.5	230		2002	8.2	250
11 Th	0204	1.6	50	26 F	0156	0.7	20
	0832	6.6	200		0821	7.5	230
	1406	1.3	40		1357	1.0	30
	2045	7.5	230		2051	8.5	260
12 F	0237	1.6	50	27 Sa	0240	0.7	20
	0902	6.6	200		0909	7.5	230
	1441	1.6	50		1441	1.0	30
	2119	7.5	230		2143	8.5	260
13 Sa	0311	1.6	50	28 Su	0323	1.0	30
	0934	6.6	200		1000	7.2	220
	1516	1.6	50		1525	1.3	40
	2154	7.2	220		2239	8.2	250
14 Su	0344	2.0	60	29 M	0408	1.3	40
	1010	6.2	190		1058	7.2	220
	1550	2.0	60		1610	1.6	50
	2233	7.2	220		2337	7.9	240
15 M	0419	2.3	70	30 Tu	0454	2.0	60
	1050	6.2	190		1202	6.9	210
	1625	2.3	70		1658	2.3	70
	2315	7.2	220				
				31 W	0037	7.5	230
					0544	2.3	70
					1307	6.6	200
					1751	2.6	80

June

Day	Time	ft	cm	Day	Time	ft	cm
1 Th	0138	7.2	220	16 F	0022	6.9	210
	0648	3.0	90		0556	2.6	80
	1408	6.6	200		1256	6.2	190
	1903	3.0	90		1815	2.6	80
2 F	0240	6.9	210	17 Sa	0113	6.6	200
	0916	3.0	90		0646	2.6	80
	1508	6.2	190		1352	6.2	190
	2142	3.0	90		1916	3.0	90
3 Sa	0344	6.6	200	18 Su	0211	6.6	200
	1006	3.0	90		0749	2.6	80
	1608	6.6	200		1454	6.6	200
	2237	2.6	80		2039	2.6	80
4 Su	0447	6.2	190	19 M	0315	6.2	190
	1042	2.6	80		0909	2.6	80
	1705	6.6	200		1559	6.6	200
	2322	2.6	80		2207	2.6	80
5 M	0543	6.2	190	20 Tu	0423	6.6	200
	1116	2.3	70		1017	2.3	70
	1755	6.9	210		1704	7.2	220
					2310	2.0	60
6 Tu	0000	2.3	70	21 W	0526	6.6	200
	0629	6.2	190		1112	1.6	50
	1151	2.0	60		1802	7.5	230
	1838	6.9	210				
7 W	0036	2.3	70	22 Th	0005	1.6	50
	0706	6.2	190		0623	6.9	210
	1229	2.0	60		1203	1.3	40
	1916	7.2	220		1857	8.2	250
8 Th	0111	2.0	60	23 F	0056	1.3	40
	0738	6.2	190		0716	7.2	220
	1307	1.6	50		1252	1.3	40
	1950	7.2	220		1950	8.5	260
9 F	0146	2.0	60	24 Sa	0144	1.3	40
	0808	6.6	200		0807	7.5	230
	1345	1.6	50		1341	1.0	30
	2025	7.5	230		2041	8.9	270
10 Sa	0220	2.0	60	25 Su	0230	1.0	30
	0839	6.6	200		0857	7.5	230
	1422	1.6	50		1429	1.3	40
	2059	7.5	230		2134	8.9	270
11 Su	0255	2.0	60	26 M	0314	1.3	40
	0913	6.6	200		0948	7.5	230
	1458	2.0	60		1515	1.3	40
	2135	7.5	230		2226	8.5	260
12 M	0329	2.0	60	27 Tu	0356	1.6	50
	0949	6.6	200		1041	7.2	220
	1533	2.0	60		1559	1.6	50
	2213	7.5	230		2319	8.2	250
13 Tu	0403	2.0	60	28 W	0438	2.0	60
	1029	6.6	200		1138	6.9	210
	1608	2.3	70		1645	2.0	60
	2254	7.5	230				
14 W	0438	2.3	70	29 Th	0013	7.5	230
	1114	6.2	190		0521	2.3	70
	1645	2.3	70		1235	6.9	210
	2336	7.2	220		1732	2.3	70
15 Th	0515	2.3	70	30 F	0109	7.2	220
	1203	6.2	190		0608	2.6	80
	1727	2.6	80		1332	6.6	200
					1826	2.6	80

Time meridian 52° 30' W. 0000 is midnight. 1200 is noon. Times are not adjusted for Daylight Saving Time.
Heights are referred to the Canadian chart datum of soundings. Subtract 1.9 feet (62 centimeters) to refer these levels to the datum of N.O.S. charts.

Argentia, Newfoundland, 2017

Times and Heights of High and Low Waters

July

Day	Time (h m)	Height ft	Height cm
1 Sa	0206	6.9	210
	0707	3.0	90
	1428	6.6	200
	1941	3.0	90
2 Su	0305	6.2	190
	0842	3.0	90
	1525	6.6	200
	2144	3.0	90
3 M	0405	6.2	190
	0953	3.0	90
	1622	6.6	200
	2242	3.0	90
4 Tu	0502	5.9	180
	1039	2.6	80
	1717	6.6	200
	2330	2.6	80
5 W	0553	5.9	180
	1123	2.3	70
	1807	6.9	210
6 Th	0013	2.6	80
	0636	6.2	190
	1205	2.3	70
	1850	7.2	220
7 F	0052	2.3	70
	0712	6.2	190
	1247	2.0	60
	1929	7.2	220
8 Sa	0130	2.3	70
	0745	6.6	200
	1329	2.0	60
	2005	7.5	230
9 Su ○	0206	2.0	60
	0819	6.6	200
	1408	2.0	60
	2041	7.5	230
10 M	0241	2.0	60
	0854	6.6	200
	1444	2.0	60
	2117	7.9	240
11 Tu	0314	2.0	60
	0930	6.9	210
	1519	2.0	60
	2154	7.9	240
12 W	0346	2.0	60
	1010	6.9	210
	1554	2.0	60
	2232	7.5	230
13 Th	0418	2.0	60
	1052	6.9	210
	1629	2.0	60
	2312	7.5	230
14 F	0451	2.0	60
	1137	6.6	200
	1708	2.0	60
	2355	7.2	220
15 Sa	0529	2.0	60
	1225	6.6	200
	1751	2.3	70
16 Su ☽	0042	6.9	210
	0612	2.3	70
	1320	6.6	200
	1842	2.6	80
17 M	0137	6.6	200
	0705	2.3	70
	1421	6.6	200
	1948	2.6	80
18 Tu	0242	6.2	190
	0812	2.3	70
	1530	6.9	210
	2125	2.6	80
19 W	0352	6.2	190
	0934	2.3	70
	1639	7.2	220
	2252	2.3	70
20 Th	0502	6.6	200
	1044	2.0	60
	1745	7.5	230
	2354	2.0	60
21 F	0606	6.9	210
	1144	2.0	60
	1845	8.2	250
22 Sa	0049	1.6	50
	0704	7.2	220
	1240	1.6	50
	1940	8.5	260
23 Su ●	0138	1.3	40
	0756	7.2	220
	1332	1.3	40
	2032	8.9	270
24 M	0221	1.3	40
	0845	7.5	230
	1420	1.3	40
	2121	8.9	270
25 Tu	0300	1.3	40
	0931	7.5	230
	1504	1.3	40
	2208	8.5	260
26 W	0338	1.6	50
	1018	7.2	220
	1546	1.6	50
	2254	8.2	250
27 Th	0414	1.6	50
	1105	7.2	220
	1626	1.6	50
	2340	7.5	230
28 F	0452	2.0	60
	1154	6.9	210
	1707	2.0	60
29 Sa	0029	7.2	220
	0532	2.3	70
	1245	6.6	200
	1750	2.6	80
30 Su ◑	0121	6.6	200
	0617	2.6	80
	1339	6.6	200
	1842	3.0	90
31 M	0218	6.2	190
	0714	3.0	90
	1436	6.2	190
	2003	3.3	100

August

Day	Time (h m)	Height ft	Height cm
1 Tu	0317	5.9	180
	0847	3.3	100
	1534	6.2	190
	2159	3.3	100
2 W	0416	5.9	180
	1003	3.0	90
	1634	6.6	200
	2259	3.3	100
3 Th	0513	5.9	180
	1056	3.0	90
	1731	6.6	200
	2349	3.0	90
4 F	0603	5.9	180
	1144	2.6	80
	1822	6.9	210
5 Sa	0033	2.6	80
	0645	6.2	190
	1230	2.3	70
	1905	7.2	220
6 Su	0113	2.3	70
	0723	6.6	200
	1313	2.0	60
	1944	7.5	230
7 M ○	0149	2.3	70
	0758	6.6	200
	1353	2.0	60
	2020	7.9	240
8 Tu	0222	2.0	60
	0833	6.9	210
	1429	1.6	50
	2056	7.9	240
9 W	0253	1.6	50
	0910	7.2	220
	1504	1.6	50
	2132	7.9	240
10 Th	0323	1.6	50
	0948	7.2	220
	1537	1.6	50
	2209	7.9	240
11 F	0353	1.6	50
	1028	7.2	220
	1611	1.6	50
	2247	7.5	230
12 Sa	0426	1.6	50
	1111	7.2	220
	1648	1.6	50
	2329	7.2	220
13 Su	0502	1.6	50
	1159	7.2	220
	1728	2.0	60
14 M ◑	0017	6.9	210
	0543	2.0	60
	1254	6.9	210
	1815	2.3	70
15 Tu	0113	6.6	200
	0632	2.3	70
	1357	6.9	210
	1916	2.6	80
16 W	0219	6.2	190
	0734	2.6	80
	1508	6.9	210
	2101	3.0	90
17 Th	0333	6.2	190
	0901	2.6	80
	1621	7.2	220
	2252	2.6	80
18 F	0448	6.2	190
	1034	2.6	80
	1732	7.5	230
	2354	2.3	70
19 Sa	0558	6.6	200
	1142	2.3	70
	1836	7.9	240
20 Su	0045	2.0	60
	0657	6.9	210
	1239	2.0	60
	1931	8.2	250
21 M ●	0127	1.6	50
	0746	7.2	220
	1328	1.6	50
	2019	8.5	260
22 Tu	0204	1.6	50
	0830	7.5	230
	1411	1.3	40
	2103	8.5	260
23 W	0238	1.3	40
	0911	7.5	230
	1450	1.3	40
	2144	8.2	250
24 Th	0312	1.3	40
	0950	7.5	230
	1526	1.3	40
	2223	7.9	240
25 F	0346	1.6	50
	1031	7.2	220
	1603	1.6	50
	2301	7.2	220
26 Sa	0421	2.0	60
	1112	7.2	220
	1640	2.0	60
	2341	6.9	210
27 Su	0458	2.0	60
	1157	6.9	210
	1718	2.3	70
28 M	0027	6.6	200
	0537	2.6	80
	1247	6.6	200
	1801	2.6	80
29 Tu ◑	0123	5.9	180
	0622	3.0	90
	1343	6.6	200
	1857	3.3	100
30 W	0225	5.6	170
	0726	3.3	100
	1444	6.2	190
	2108	3.6	110
31 Th	0327	5.6	170
	0923	3.3	100
	1547	6.2	190
	2229	3.3	100

September

Day	Time (h m)	Height ft	Height cm
1 F	0429	5.6	170
	1030	3.0	90
	1651	6.6	200
	2324	3.3	100
2 Sa	0527	5.9	180
	1122	3.0	90
	1749	6.9	210
3 Su	0009	3.0	90
	0616	6.2	190
	1210	2.3	70
	1837	7.2	220
4 M	0048	2.3	70
	0656	6.6	200
	1254	2.0	60
	1918	7.5	230
5 Tu	0123	2.0	60
	0734	6.9	210
	1334	1.6	50
	1955	7.5	230
6 W ○	0155	1.6	50
	0810	7.2	220
	1409	1.3	40
	2031	7.9	240
7 Th	0225	1.3	40
	0846	7.5	230
	1443	1.3	40
	2107	7.9	240
8 F	0255	1.3	40
	0924	7.5	230
	1516	1.0	30
	2145	7.9	240
9 Sa	0327	1.3	40
	1005	7.5	230
	1551	1.0	30
	2224	7.5	230
10 Su	0401	1.3	40
	1049	7.5	230
	1627	1.3	40
	2308	7.2	220
11 M	0438	1.3	40
	1139	7.5	230
	1708	1.6	50
	2357	6.9	210
12 Tu	0519	1.6	50
	1236	7.2	220
	1754	2.0	60
13 W ◑	0058	6.6	200
	0606	2.3	70
	1343	6.9	210
	1855	2.6	80
14 Th	0210	6.2	190
	0707	2.6	80
	1454	6.9	210
	2139	3.0	90
15 F	0326	6.2	190
	0851	2.6	80
	1608	6.9	210
	2255	2.6	80
16 Sa	0443	6.2	190
	1052	2.6	80
	1721	7.2	220
	2348	2.3	70
17 Su	0551	6.6	200
	1151	2.3	70
	1825	7.5	230
18 M	0031	2.0	60
	0646	6.9	210
	1239	2.0	60
	1918	7.9	240
19 Tu	0107	1.6	50
	0731	7.2	220
	1320	1.6	50
	2003	7.9	240
20 W ●	0139	1.6	50
	0811	7.5	230
	1356	1.3	40
	2042	7.9	240
21 Th	0210	1.3	40
	0847	7.5	230
	1431	1.3	40
	2117	7.5	230
22 F	0243	1.3	40
	0923	7.5	230
	1505	1.3	40
	2150	7.2	220
23 Sa	0317	1.3	40
	0959	7.5	230
	1539	1.6	50
	2223	6.9	210
24 Su	0351	1.6	50
	1037	7.2	220
	1614	1.6	50
	2259	6.6	200
25 M	0427	2.0	60
	1117	6.9	210
	1650	2.3	70
	2340	6.2	190
26 Tu	0503	2.3	70
	1202	6.6	200
	1729	2.6	80
27 W ◑	0031	5.9	180
	0543	3.0	90
	1255	6.6	200
	1816	3.0	90
28 Th	0134	5.6	170
	0632	3.3	100
	1355	6.2	190
	1937	3.6	110
29 F	0238	5.6	170
	0815	3.6	110
	1459	6.2	190
	2154	3.3	100
30 Sa	0342	5.6	170
	0958	3.3	100
	1605	6.2	190
	2252	3.3	100

Time meridian 52° 30' W. 0000 is midnight. 1200 is noon. Times are not adjusted for Daylight Saving Time.
Heights are referred to the Canadian chart datum of soundings. Subtract 1.9 feet (62 centimeters) to refer these levels to the datum of N.O.S. charts.

Argentia, Newfoundland, 2017

Times and Heights of High and Low Waters

October

Day	Time (h m)	Height (ft)	Height (cm)
1 Su	0445	5.9	180
	1055	3.0	90
	1709	6.6	200
	2337	2.6	80
2 M	0540	6.2	190
	1145	2.6	80
	1802	6.9	210
3 Tu	0016	2.3	70
	0625	6.6	200
	1229	2.0	60
	1847	7.2	220
4 W	0050	2.0	60
	0705	6.9	210
	1308	1.6	50
	1926	7.5	230
5 Th ○	0122	1.6	50
	0743	7.5	230
	1344	1.0	40
	2004	7.5	230
6 F	0154	1.3	40
	0821	7.5	230
	1419	1.0	30
	2042	7.9	240
7 Sa	0226	1.0	30
	0901	7.9	240
	1454	0.7	20
	2121	7.5	230
8 Su	0301	1.0	30
	0944	7.9	240
	1531	1.0	30
	2203	7.5	230
9 M	0338	1.0	30
	1032	7.9	240
	1609	1.0	30
	2250	7.2	220
10 Tu	0417	1.3	40
	1125	7.5	230
	1652	1.6	50
	2345	6.9	210
11 W	0459	1.6	50
	1226	7.5	230
	1740	2.0	60
12 Th ◑	0053	6.6	200
	0548	2.3	70
	1334	7.2	220
	1843	2.6	80
13 F	0208	6.2	190
	0651	3.0	90
	1443	6.9	210
	2142	2.6	80
14 Sa	0320	6.2	190
	0955	3.0	90
	1555	6.9	210
	2244	2.6	80
15 Su	0432	6.2	190
	1059	2.6	80
	1708	6.9	210
	2331	2.3	70
16 M	0536	6.6	200
	1149	2.3	70
	1810	7.2	220
17 Tu	0008	2.0	60
	0629	6.9	210
	1230	2.0	60
	1901	7.2	220
18 W	0038	1.6	50
	0711	7.2	220
	1305	1.6	50
	1942	7.2	220
19 Th ●	0109	1.6	50
	0749	7.5	230
	1337	1.6	50
	2018	7.2	220
20 F	0141	1.3	40
	0823	7.5	230
	1410	1.3	40
	2049	7.2	220
21 Sa	0215	1.3	40
	0857	7.5	230
	1443	1.3	40
	2119	6.9	210
22 Su	0250	1.3	40
	0932	7.5	230
	1517	1.6	50
	2150	6.6	200
23 M	0325	1.6	50
	1007	7.2	220
	1551	2.0	60
	2225	6.6	200
24 Tu	0359	2.0	60
	1046	7.2	220
	1626	2.3	70
	2305	6.2	190
25 W	0435	2.3	70
	1128	6.9	210
	1704	2.6	80
	2352	5.9	180
26 Th	0513	2.6	80
	1217	6.6	200
	1747	3.0	90
27 F ◐	0049	5.6	170
	0557	3.0	90
	1312	6.6	200
	1844	3.3	100
28 Sa	0152	5.6	170
	0659	3.3	100
	1412	6.2	190
	2102	3.3	100
29 Su	0254	5.6	170
	0911	3.3	100
	1516	6.2	190
	2210	3.3	100
30 M	0358	5.9	180
	1020	3.0	90
	1621	6.2	190
	2257	2.6	80
31 Tu	0457	6.2	190
	1112	2.6	80
	1721	6.6	200
	2335	2.3	70

November

Day	Time (h m)	Height (ft)	Height (cm)
1 W	0549	6.6	200
	1157	2.0	60
	1811	6.9	210
2 Th	0010	2.0	60
	0634	7.2	220
	1238	1.6	50
	1855	7.2	220
3 F	0045	1.3	40
	0716	7.5	230
	1317	1.3	40
	1937	7.5	230
4 Sa ○	0121	1.0	30
	0758	7.9	240
	1355	1.0	30
	2018	7.5	230
5 Su	0159	1.0	30
	0842	8.2	250
	1434	0.7	20
	2100	7.5	230
6 M	0238	1.0	30
	0929	8.2	250
	1514	1.0	30
	2146	7.5	230
7 Tu	0318	1.0	30
	1020	8.2	250
	1556	1.0	30
	2238	7.2	220
8 W	0400	1.3	40
	1116	7.9	240
	1641	1.6	50
	2338	6.9	210
9 Th	0446	2.0	60
	1218	7.5	230
	1731	2.0	60
10 F ○	0049	6.6	200
	0536	2.3	70
	1323	7.2	220
	1836	2.6	80
11 Sa	0158	6.6	200
	0643	3.0	90
	1429	6.9	210
	2122	2.6	80
12 Su	0304	6.2	190
	0945	3.0	90
	1538	6.9	210
	2221	2.6	80
13 M	0410	6.6	200
	1045	2.6	80
	1647	6.6	200
	2303	2.3	70
14 Tu	0511	6.6	200
	1133	2.3	70
	1748	6.6	200
	2336	2.3	70
15 W	0603	6.9	210
	1212	2.0	60
	1838	6.9	210
16 Th	0006	2.0	60
	0647	7.2	220
	1245	2.0	60
	1919	6.9	210
17 F	0038	1.6	50
	0726	7.5	230
	1317	1.6	50
	1952	6.6	200
18 Sa ●	0113	1.6	50
	0801	7.5	230
	1350	1.6	50
	2023	6.6	200
19 Su	0150	1.3	40
	0835	7.5	230
	1424	1.6	50
	2052	6.6	200
20 M	0226	1.6	50
	0909	7.5	230
	1458	2.0	60
	2124	6.6	200
21 Tu	0302	1.6	50
	0944	7.5	230
	1532	2.0	60
	2159	6.2	190
22 W	0338	2.0	60
	1022	7.2	220
	1608	2.3	70
	2238	6.2	190
23 Th	0414	2.3	70
	1102	7.2	220
	1645	2.3	70
	2323	5.9	180
24 F	0451	2.6	80
	1146	6.9	210
	1725	2.6	80
25 Sa	0014	5.9	180
	0533	3.0	90
	1235	6.9	210
	1811	3.0	90
26 Su ◐	0109	5.9	180
	0624	3.0	90
	1328	6.6	200
	1911	3.3	100
27 M	0208	5.9	180
	0737	3.3	100
	1427	6.2	190
	2051	3.0	90
28 Tu	0309	5.9	180
	0925	3.0	90
	1531	6.2	190
	2159	2.6	80
29 W	0411	6.2	190
	1030	2.6	80
	1634	6.2	190
	2245	2.3	70
30 Th	0510	6.6	200
	1121	2.3	70
	1732	6.6	200
	2327	2.0	60

December

Day	Time (h m)	Height (ft)	Height (cm)
1 F	0602	7.2	220
	1207	1.6	50
	1823	6.9	210
2 Sa	0008	1.6	50
	0651	7.5	230
	1251	1.3	40
	1910	7.2	220
3 Su ○	0051	1.3	40
	0739	8.2	250
	1335	1.0	30
	1956	7.5	230
4 M	0135	1.0	30
	0827	8.5	260
	1419	1.0	30
	2044	7.5	230
5 Tu	0219	1.0	30
	0918	8.5	260
	1503	1.0	30
	2133	7.5	230
6 W	0304	1.0	30
	1011	8.5	260
	1547	1.3	40
	2228	7.2	220
7 Th	0349	1.3	40
	1107	8.2	250
	1633	1.6	50
	2328	6.9	210
8 F	0436	2.0	60
	1206	7.9	240
	1721	2.0	60
9 Sa	0034	6.9	210
	0527	2.3	70
	1307	7.5	230
	1816	2.6	80
10 Su ○	0137	6.6	200
	0628	2.6	80
	1409	6.9	210
	1942	3.0	90
11 M	0237	6.6	200
	0905	3.0	90
	1513	6.6	200
	2143	3.0	90
12 Tu	0338	6.6	200
	1015	2.6	80
	1618	6.6	200
	2225	2.6	80
13 W	0438	6.6	200
	1105	2.6	80
	1718	6.2	190
	2259	2.3	70
14 Th	0532	6.9	210
	1147	2.3	70
	1809	6.2	190
	2334	2.3	70
15 F	0620	6.9	210
	1224	2.3	70
	1852	6.2	190
16 Sa	0011	2.0	60
	0702	7.2	220
	1259	2.3	70
	1928	6.2	190
17 Su	0050	2.0	60
	0740	7.5	230
	1333	2.0	60
	1959	6.6	200
18 M ●	0130	1.6	50
	0815	7.5	230
	1408	2.0	60
	2030	6.6	200
19 Tu	0208	1.6	50
	0850	7.5	230
	1443	2.0	60
	2103	6.6	200
20 W	0246	2.0	60
	0925	7.5	230
	1518	2.0	60
	2138	6.6	200
21 Th	0323	2.0	60
	1001	7.5	230
	1553	2.0	60
	2216	6.6	200
22 F	0358	2.3	70
	1039	7.5	230
	1627	2.3	70
	2258	6.2	190
23 Sa	0434	2.3	70
	1119	7.2	220
	1703	2.3	70
	2344	6.2	190
24 Su	0513	2.6	80
	1202	6.9	210
	1741	2.6	80
25 M	0033	6.2	190
	0557	2.6	80
	1250	6.6	200
	1824	2.6	80
26 Tu ◐	0125	6.2	190
	0649	3.0	90
	1343	6.6	200
	1918	2.6	80
27 W	0223	6.2	190
	0758	3.0	90
	1443	6.2	190
	2027	2.6	80
28 Th	0327	6.6	200
	0931	2.6	80
	1549	6.2	190
	2143	2.3	70
29 F	0433	6.9	210
	1044	2.3	70
	1654	6.6	200
	2243	2.0	60
30 Sa	0534	7.2	220
	1141	2.0	60
	1754	6.9	210
	2336	1.6	50
31 Su	0630	7.9	240
	1233	1.6	50
	1849	7.2	220

Time meridian 52° 30' W. 0000 is midnight. 1200 is noon. Times are not adjusted for Daylight Saving Time.
Heights are referred to the Canadian chart datum of soundings. Subtract 1.9 feet (62 centimeters) to refer these levels to the datum of N.O.S. charts.

Pictou, Nova Scotia, 2017

Times and Heights of High and Low Waters

January

Day	Time	ft	cm		Day	Time	ft	cm
1 Su	0542	1.6	50		16 M	0628	1.3	40
	1240	5.6	170			1316	5.6	170
	1746	3.6	110			1837	3.0	90
	2340	5.9	180					
2 M	0619	1.6	50		17 Tu	0047	5.9	180
	1317	5.6	170			0710	2.0	60
	1829	3.3	100			1355	5.6	170
						1924	3.0	90
3 Tu	0022	5.9	180		18 W	0136	5.6	170
	0658	1.6	50			0751	2.3	70
	1353	5.6	170			1433	5.6	170
	1914	3.3	100			2014	3.0	90
4 W	0108	5.6	170		19 Th	0229	5.2	160
	0739	2.0	60			0831	2.6	80
	1431	5.6	170			1511	5.2	160
	2004	3.3	100			2110	3.0	90
5 Th ☽	0203	5.2	160		20 F	0334	4.9	150
	0823	2.3	70			0913	3.0	90
	1510	5.6	170			1548	5.2	160
	2101	3.0	90			2217	3.0	90
6 F	0312	4.9	150		21 Sa	0449	4.6	140
	0912	2.6	80			0959	3.6	110
	1554	5.6	170			1628	5.2	160
	2206	2.6	80			2331	2.6	80
7 Sa	0436	4.9	150		22 Su	0605	4.6	140
	1009	3.0	90			1052	3.6	110
	1643	5.9	180			1714	5.2	160
	2317	2.3	70					
8 Su	0601	4.9	150		23 M	0038	2.6	80
	1114	3.3	100			0714	4.6	140
	1738	5.9	180			1152	3.9	120
						1805	5.2	160
9 M	0026	2.0	60		24 Tu	0135	2.3	70
	0718	4.9	150			0816	4.6	140
	1222	3.3	100			1252	3.9	120
	1837	6.2	190			1859	5.6	170
10 Tu	0131	1.6	50		25 W	0221	2.0	60
	0826	5.2	160			0907	4.9	150
	1328	3.6	110			1347	3.9	120
	1938	6.2	190			1952	5.6	170
11 W	0230	1.3	40		26 Th	0301	2.0	60
	0926	5.6	170			0949	4.9	150
	1429	3.6	110			1436	3.9	120
	2037	6.6	200			2040	5.9	180
12 Th ○	0324	1.0	30		27 F ●	0337	1.6	50
	1020	5.6	170			1027	5.2	160
	1525	3.3	100			1522	3.6	110
	2131	6.6	200			2126	5.9	180
13 F	0413	0.7	20		28 Sa	0412	1.6	50
	1108	5.9	180			1102	5.2	160
	1616	3.3	100			1605	3.3	100
	2223	6.6	200			2209	5.9	180
14 Sa	0500	1.0	30		29 Su	0447	1.3	40
	1153	5.9	180			1136	5.6	170
	1705	3.0	90			1646	3.3	100
	2312	6.6	200			2252	5.9	180
15 Su	0545	1.0	30		30 M	0522	1.3	40
	1236	5.9	180			1210	5.6	170
	1751	3.0	90			1728	3.0	90
	2359	6.2	190			2336	5.9	180
					31 Tu	0558	1.3	40
						1243	5.6	170
						1811	2.6	80

February

Day	Time	ft	cm		Day	Time	ft	cm
1 W	0021	5.9	180		16 Th	0116	5.2	160
	0636	1.6	50			0713	2.3	70
	1317	5.6	170			1337	5.2	160
	1856	2.6	80			1938	2.3	70
2 Th	0109	5.6	170		17 F	0202	4.9	150
	0716	2.0	60			0746	3.0	90
	1352	5.6	170			1405	5.2	160
	1944	2.3	70			2024	2.3	70
3 F	0203	5.2	160		18 Sa ○	0255	4.6	140
	0758	2.3	70			0820	3.3	100
	1430	5.9	180			1433	5.2	160
	2038	2.3	70			2118	2.6	80
4 Sa ☽	0309	4.9	150		19 Su	0401	4.6	140
	0846	2.6	80			0856	3.6	110
	1513	5.9	180			1506	5.2	160
	2142	2.3	70			2225	2.6	80
5 Su	0428	4.9	150		20 M	0516	4.3	130
	0941	3.0	90			0942	3.6	110
	1604	5.9	180			1550	5.2	160
	2253	2.0	60			2339	2.6	80
6 M	0551	4.9	150		21 Tu	0629	4.3	130
	1048	3.3	100			1047	3.9	120
	1706	5.9	180			1648	5.2	160
7 Tu	0008	1.6	50		22 W	0047	2.3	70
	0710	4.9	150			0736	4.6	140
	1202	3.6	110			1202	3.9	120
	1816	5.9	180			1802	5.2	160
8 W	0119	1.6	50		23 Th	0143	2.3	70
	0820	4.9	150			0832	4.6	140
	1313	3.6	110			1311	3.9	120
	1925	5.9	180			1916	5.2	160
9 Th	0221	1.3	40		24 F	0228	2.0	60
	0919	5.2	160			0915	4.9	150
	1417	3.3	100			1409	3.6	110
	2028	6.2	190			2017	5.6	170
10 F ○	0315	1.0	30		25 Sa	0307	1.6	50
	1007	5.6	170			0953	4.9	150
	1513	3.3	100			1459	3.3	100
	2124	6.2	190			2109	5.6	170
11 Sa	0402	1.0	30		26 Su ●	0344	1.6	50
	1049	5.6	170			1027	5.2	160
	1603	3.0	90			1544	3.0	90
	2215	6.2	190			2158	5.9	180
12 Su	0445	1.0	30		27 M	0420	1.3	40
	1127	5.6	170			1100	5.6	170
	1648	2.6	80			1627	2.6	80
	2302	6.2	190			2244	5.9	180
13 M	0525	1.3	40		28 Tu	0457	1.3	40
	1203	5.6	170			1133	5.6	170
	1731	2.6	80			1710	2.0	60
	2347	5.9	180			2330	5.9	180
14 Tu	0603	1.6	50					
	1236	5.6	170					
	1813	2.3	70					
15 W	0031	5.6	170					
	0639	2.0	60					
	1308	5.6	170					
	1855	2.3	70					

March

Day	Time	ft	cm		Day	Time	ft	cm
1 W	0534	1.6	50		16 Th	0018	5.6	170
	1206	5.9	180			0607	2.3	70
	1753	2.0	60			1221	5.6	170
						1827	1.6	50
2 Th	0018	5.9	180		17 F	0059	5.2	160
	0613	1.6	50			0638	2.6	80
	1240	5.9	180			1247	5.2	160
	1837	1.6	50			1905	2.0	60
3 F	0108	5.6	170		18 Sa ○	0142	4.9	150
	0654	2.0	60			0709	3.0	90
	1316	5.9	180			1312	5.2	160
	1925	1.6	50			1945	2.0	60
4 Sa	0203	5.2	160		19 Su	0229	4.6	140
	0738	2.6	80			0741	3.3	100
	1355	5.9	180			1339	5.2	160
	2019	1.6	50			2031	2.3	70
5 Su ☽	0309	4.9	150		20 M ☾	0326	4.6	140
	0816	3.0	90			0816	3.6	110
	1439	5.9	180			1413	5.2	160
	2122	1.6	50			2125	2.3	70
6 M	0426	4.9	150		21 Tu	0433	4.3	130
	0925	3.3	100			0902	3.6	110
	1534	5.6	170			1456	5.2	160
	2235	1.6	50			2232	2.3	70
7 Tu	0546	4.9	150		22 W	0542	4.3	130
	1036	3.6	110			1008	3.6	110
	1647	5.6	170			1555	4.9	150
	2354	1.6	50			2343	2.3	70
8 W	0702	4.9	150		23 Th	0647	4.6	140
	1153	3.6	110			1129	3.6	110
	1807	5.6	170			1715	4.9	150
9 Th	0107	1.6	50		24 F	0047	2.3	70
	0808	4.9	150			0743	4.6	140
	1306	3.3	100			1242	3.6	110
	1921	5.6	170			1846	4.9	150
10 F	0209	1.6	50		25 Sa	0141	2.0	60
	0901	5.2	160			0829	4.9	150
	1409	3.3	100			1343	3.3	100
	2024	5.6	170			1956	5.2	160
11 Sa	0259	1.3	40		26 Su	0227	2.0	60
	0943	5.2	160			0907	4.9	150
	1502	2.6	80			1435	2.6	80
	2119	5.6	170			2053	5.6	170
12 Su ○	0343	1.3	40		27 M ●	0309	1.6	50
	1019	5.2	160			0943	5.2	160
	1549	2.3	70			1522	2.3	70
	2208	5.9	180			2145	5.6	170
13 M	0423	1.6	50		28 Tu	0349	1.6	50
	1053	5.6	170			1018	5.6	170
	1631	2.0	60			1606	1.6	50
	2253	5.9	180			2234	5.9	180
14 Tu	0459	2.0	60		29 W	0429	1.6	50
	1124	5.6	170			1053	5.9	180
	1711	2.0	60			1650	1.3	40
	2336	5.6	170			2323	5.9	180
15 W	0534	2.0	60		30 Th	0510	2.0	60
	1154	5.6	170			1129	5.9	180
	1749	1.6	50			1734	1.0	30
					31 F	0013	5.9	180
						0552	2.0	60
						1206	5.9	180
						1820	1.0	30

Time meridian 60° W. 0000 is midnight. 1200 is noon. Times are not adjusted for Daylight Saving Time.
Heights are referred to the Canadian chart datum of soundings.

Pictou, Nova Scotia, 2017

Times and Heights of High and Low Waters

April

Day	Time	ft	cm	Day	Time	ft	cm
1 Sa	0105	5.6	170	**16** Su	0128	4.9	150
	0635	2.3	70		0640	3.3	100
	1245	5.9	180		1231	5.2	160
	1909	1.0	30		1914	1.6	50
2 Su	0203	5.2	160	**17** M	0212	4.9	150
	0722	2.6	80		0714	3.3	100
	1327	5.9	180		1301	5.2	160
	2003	1.0	30		1956	2.0	60
3 M ◐	0310	5.2	160	**18** Tu	0303	4.6	140
	0815	3.3	100		0754	3.6	110
	1416	5.6	170		1337	5.2	160
	2106	1.3	40		2044	2.0	60
4 Tu	0423	4.9	150	**19** W ◑	0400	4.6	140
	0918	3.3	100		0844	3.6	110
	1518	5.6	170		1422	4.9	150
	2220	1.6	50		2142	2.0	60
5 W	0535	4.9	150	**20** Th	0459	4.6	140
	1033	3.6	110		0950	3.6	110
	1641	5.2	160		1522	4.9	150
	2336	1.6	50		2246	2.3	70
6 Th	0643	4.9	150	**21** F	0556	4.6	140
	1151	3.3	100		1105	3.6	110
	1804	5.2	160		1648	4.6	140
					2349	2.3	70
7 F	0046	1.6	50	**22** Sa	0647	4.6	140
	0741	4.9	150		1215	3.3	100
	1301	3.0	90		1823	4.9	150
	1917	5.2	160				
8 Sa	0146	2.0	60	**23** Su	0048	2.3	70
	0828	5.2	160		0733	4.9	150
	1359	2.6	80		1316	2.6	80
	2018	5.2	160		1936	4.9	150
9 Su	0235	2.0	60	**24** M	0142	2.0	60
	0906	5.2	160		0815	5.2	160
	1449	2.3	70		1410	2.3	70
	2111	5.2	160		2037	5.2	160
10 M	0317	2.0	60	**25** Tu	0230	2.0	60
	0941	5.2	160		0855	5.6	170
	1533	2.0	60		1458	1.6	50
	2159	5.6	170		2132	5.6	170
11 Tu ○	0355	2.3	70	**26** W ●	0316	2.0	60
	1013	5.2	160		0934	5.9	180
	1612	1.6	50		1545	1.0	30
	2243	5.6	170		2224	5.6	170
12 W	0431	2.3	70	**27** Th	0401	2.3	70
	1044	5.6	170		1014	5.9	180
	1650	1.3	40		1630	0.7	20
	2325	5.2	160		2315	5.9	180
13 Th	0504	2.6	80	**28** F	0446	2.3	70
	1113	5.6	170		1055	6.2	190
	1726	1.3	40		1717	0.3	10
14 F	0006	5.2	160	**29** Sa	0007	5.9	180
	0536	3.0	90		0532	2.6	80
	1139	5.6	170		1137	6.2	190
	1801	1.3	40		1804	0.3	10
15 Sa	0046	5.2	160	**30** Su	0102	5.6	170
	0608	3.0	90		0620	2.6	80
	1204	5.2	160		1221	6.2	190
	1837	1.6	50		1855	0.3	10

May

Day	Time	ft	cm	Day	Time	ft	cm
1 M	0201	5.6	170	**16** Tu	0157	4.9	150
	0711	3.0	90		0656	3.6	110
	1309	5.9	180		1237	5.2	160
	1951	0.7	20		1931	1.6	50
2 Tu ◐	0305	5.2	160	**17** W	0243	4.9	150
	0808	3.3	100		0739	3.6	110
	1405	5.6	170		1316	5.2	160
	2053	1.3	40		2017	1.6	50
3 W	0411	5.2	160	**18** Th ◑	0331	4.9	150
	0913	3.3	100		0831	3.6	110
	1515	5.2	160		1405	4.9	150
	2203	1.6	50		2107	2.0	60
4 Th	0513	5.2	160	**19** F	0420	4.9	150
	1027	3.3	100		0932	3.3	100
	1638	4.9	150		1509	4.9	150
	2312	2.0	60		2203	2.0	60
5 F	0610	4.9	150	**20** Sa	0507	4.9	150
	1142	3.0	90		1039	3.3	100
	1756	4.9	150		1635	4.6	140
					2301	2.3	70
6 Sa	0017	2.0	60	**21** Su	0553	4.9	150
	0701	5.2	160		1145	3.0	90
	1248	2.6	80		1803	4.6	140
	1907	4.9	150				
7 Su	0113	2.3	70	**22** M	0001	2.3	70
	0745	5.2	160		0638	5.2	160
	1344	2.3	70		1247	2.3	70
	2008	4.9	150		1917	4.9	150
8 M	0203	2.3	70	**23** Tu	0059	2.3	70
	0824	5.2	160		0723	5.6	170
	1432	2.0	60		1343	1.6	50
	2101	5.2	160		2020	5.2	160
9 Tu	0246	2.6	80	**24** W	0154	2.6	80
	0859	5.2	160		0809	5.9	180
	1514	1.6	50		1435	1.0	30
	2149	5.2	160		2118	5.2	160
10 W ○	0325	2.6	80	**25** Th ●	0246	2.6	80
	0933	5.2	160		0855	5.9	180
	1553	1.3	40		1524	0.7	20
	2232	5.2	160		2213	5.6	170
11 Th	0401	3.0	90	**26** F	0336	2.6	80
	1005	5.6	170		0942	6.2	190
	1630	1.3	40		1613	0.3	10
	2314	5.2	160		2306	5.9	180
12 F	0435	3.0	90	**27** Sa	0426	2.6	80
	1036	5.6	170		1029	6.2	190
	1705	1.3	40		1702	0.0	0
	2354	5.2	160				
13 Sa	0509	3.3	100	**28** Su	0000	5.9	180
	1104	5.6	170		0515	2.6	80
	1739	1.3	40		1117	6.2	190
					1752	0.3	10
14 Su	0034	5.2	160	**29** M	0055	5.9	180
	0543	3.3	100		0606	3.0	90
	1133	5.6	170		1207	6.2	190
	1814	1.3	40		1844	0.3	10
15 M	0115	4.9	150	**30** Tu	0151	5.6	170
	0618	3.3	100		0659	3.0	90
	1203	5.2	160		1300	5.9	180
	1851	1.6	50		1939	0.7	20
				31 W	0249	5.6	170
					0756	3.0	90
					1359	5.6	170
					2038	1.3	40

June

Day	Time	ft	cm	Day	Time	ft	cm
1 Th ◐	0346	5.2	160	**16** F	0259	4.9	150
	0859	3.0	90		0812	3.3	100
	1509	5.2	160		1402	4.9	150
	2140	1.6	50		2040	2.0	60
2 F	0440	5.2	160	**17** Sa ○	0340	4.9	150
	1009	3.0	90		0908	3.0	90
	1625	4.9	150		1505	4.9	150
	2241	2.0	60		2129	2.0	60
3 Sa	0529	5.2	160	**18** Su	0421	5.2	160
	1119	2.6	80		1010	3.0	90
	1739	4.9	150		1624	4.6	140
	2340	2.3	70		2223	2.3	70
4 Su	0616	5.2	160	**19** M	0504	5.2	160
	1224	2.3	70		1115	2.3	70
	1849	4.9	150		1745	4.6	140
					2321	2.6	80
5 M	0035	2.6	80	**20** Tu	0550	5.6	170
	0659	5.2	160		1218	2.0	60
	1321	2.0	60		1858	4.9	150
	1951	4.9	150				
6 Tu	0125	3.0	90	**21** W	0022	2.6	80
	0740	5.2	160		0640	5.6	170
	1411	1.6	50		1318	1.3	40
	2045	4.9	150		2004	4.9	150
7 W	0211	3.0	90	**22** Th	0122	3.0	90
	0819	5.2	160		0733	5.9	180
	1455	1.6	50		1415	1.0	30
	2134	4.9	150		2105	5.2	160
8 Th	0252	3.3	100	**23** F ●	0220	3.0	90
	0857	5.6	170		0827	6.2	190
	1535	1.3	40		1509	0.7	20
	2219	4.9	150		2202	5.6	170
9 F ○	0331	3.3	100	**24** Sa	0316	3.0	90
	0932	5.6	170		0921	6.2	190
	1612	1.3	40		1601	0.3	10
	2300	4.9	150		2257	5.6	170
10 Sa	0408	3.3	100	**25** Su	0409	3.0	90
	1006	5.6	170		1014	6.6	200
	1647	1.3	40		1652	0.3	10
	2340	5.2	160		2349	5.6	170
11 Su	0444	3.3	100	**26** M	0501	3.0	90
	1040	5.6	170		1106	6.6	200
	1722	1.3	40		1742	0.3	10
12 M	0019	5.2	160	**27** Tu	0041	5.6	170
	0521	3.3	100		0552	3.0	90
	1113	5.6	170		1159	6.2	190
	1757	1.3	40		1833	0.7	20
13 Tu	0058	5.2	160	**28** W	0131	5.6	170
	0559	3.3	100		0643	2.6	80
	1149	5.6	170		1252	5.9	180
	1834	1.3	40		1924	1.0	30
14 W	0138	4.9	150	**29** Th	0222	5.6	170
	0639	3.3	100		0736	2.6	80
	1227	5.2	160		1350	5.6	170
	1913	1.6	50		2016	1.3	40
15 Th	0218	4.9	150	**30** F ◐	0311	5.2	160
	0723	3.3	100		0834	2.6	80
	1310	5.2	160		1452	5.2	160
	1954	1.6	50		2109	2.0	60

Time meridian 60° W. 0000 is midnight. 1200 is noon. Times are not adjusted for Daylight Saving Time.
Heights are referred to the Canadian chart datum of soundings.

Pictou, Nova Scotia, 2017
Times and Heights of High and Low Waters

July

Day	Time (h m)	ft	cm	Day	Time (h m)	ft	cm
1 Sa	0358	5.2	160	16 Su ◯	0258	5.2	160
	0937	2.6	80		0842	2.6	80
	1602	4.9	150		1459	4.9	150
	2204	2.3	70		2059	2.3	70
2 Su	0444	5.2	160	17 M	0338	5.2	160
	1046	2.6	80		0941	2.3	70
	1714	4.6	140		1612	4.6	140
	2259	2.6	80		2151	2.6	80
3 M	0528	5.2	160	18 Tu	0422	5.6	170
	1153	2.3	70		1046	2.0	60
	1822	4.6	140		1729	4.6	140
	2353	3.0	90		2250	3.0	90
4 Tu	0613	5.2	160	19 W	0512	5.6	170
	1254	2.0	60		1153	1.6	50
	1926	4.6	140		1843	4.9	150
					2354	3.0	90
5 W	0045	3.3	100	20 Th	0609	5.9	180
	0657	5.2	160		1259	1.3	40
	1347	2.0	60		1952	4.9	150
	2024	4.6	140				
6 Th	0134	3.3	100	21 F	0059	3.0	90
	0742	5.2	160		0710	5.9	180
	1435	1.6	50		1401	1.0	30
	2115	4.9	150		2055	5.2	160
7 F	0219	3.3	100	22 Sa	0202	3.0	90
	0825	5.6	170		0811	6.2	190
	1517	1.6	50		1459	0.7	20
	2200	4.9	150		2152	5.2	160
8 Sa	0302	3.3	100	23 Su ●	0300	3.0	90
	0906	5.6	170		0910	6.2	190
	1555	1.3	40		1552	0.7	20
	2241	4.9	150		2244	5.6	170
9 Su ◯	0342	3.3	100	24 M	0355	3.0	90
	0945	5.6	170		1005	6.6	200
	1631	1.3	40		1642	0.3	10
	2320	4.9	150		2332	5.6	170
10 M	0421	3.3	100	25 Tu	0446	2.6	80
	1023	5.6	170		1058	6.2	190
	1705	1.3	40		1729	0.7	20
	2357	5.2	160				
11 Tu	0459	3.3	100	26 W	0017	5.6	170
	1102	5.6	170		0535	2.6	80
	1740	1.3	40		1149	6.2	190
					1815	1.0	30
12 W	0033	5.2	160	27 Th	0101	5.6	170
	0539	3.3	100		0622	2.3	70
	1142	5.6	170		1240	5.9	180
	1815	1.3	40		1901	1.3	40
13 Th	0110	5.2	160	28 F	0143	5.6	170
	0620	3.0	90		0711	2.3	70
	1223	5.6	170		1333	5.6	170
	1852	1.3	40		1946	1.6	50
14 F	0145	5.2	160	29 Sa	0225	5.2	160
	0703	3.0	90		0802	2.3	70
	1309	5.2	160		1429	5.2	160
	1931	1.6	50		2032	2.3	70
15 Sa	0222	5.2	160	30 Su ◑	0307	5.2	160
	0749	2.6	80		0858	2.3	70
	1359	5.2	160		1533	4.9	150
	2013	2.0	60		2120	2.6	80
				31 M	0349	5.2	160
					1004	2.3	70
					1641	4.6	140
					2211	3.0	90

August

Day	Time (h m)	ft	cm	Day	Time (h m)	ft	cm
1 Tu	0434	5.2	160	16 W	0344	5.6	170
	1115	2.3	70		1022	2.0	60
	1750	4.6	140		1720	4.9	150
	2305	3.3	100		2227	3.3	100
2 W	0522	5.2	160	17 Th	0443	5.6	170
	1221	2.3	70		1135	1.6	50
	1855	4.6	140		1834	4.9	150
					2336	3.3	100
3 Th	0001	3.6	110	18 F	0550	5.6	170
	0613	5.2	160		1246	1.3	40
	1320	2.0	60		1943	4.9	150
	1955	4.6	140				
4 F	0056	3.6	110	19 Sa	0046	3.3	100
	0706	5.2	160		0700	5.9	180
	1412	2.0	60		1352	1.3	40
	2049	4.6	140		2045	5.2	160
5 Sa	0146	3.6	110	20 Su	0151	3.0	90
	0756	5.2	160		0806	5.9	180
	1456	1.6	50		1450	1.0	30
	2134	4.9	150		2138	5.2	160
6 Su	0233	3.3	100	21 M ●	0249	3.0	90
	0842	5.6	170		0905	6.2	190
	1535	1.6	50		1541	1.0	30
	2214	4.9	150		2224	5.6	170
7 M ◯	0316	3.3	100	22 Tu	0342	2.6	80
	0926	5.6	170		0959	6.2	190
	1610	1.3	40		1627	1.0	30
	2251	4.9	150		2306	5.6	170
8 Tu	0357	3.0	90	23 W	0430	2.3	70
	1009	5.6	170		1049	6.2	190
	1643	1.3	40		1710	1.0	30
	2326	5.2	160		2345	5.6	170
9 W	0437	3.0	90	24 Th	0515	2.0	60
	1051	5.9	180		1138	6.2	190
	1717	1.3	40		1751	1.3	40
	2359	5.2	160				
10 Th	0517	2.6	80	25 F	0022	5.6	170
	1133	5.6	170		0559	2.0	60
	1751	1.3	40		1225	5.9	180
					1831	2.0	60
11 F	0033	5.2	160	26 Sa	0058	5.2	160
	0558	2.6	80		0642	2.0	60
	1216	5.6	170		1314	5.6	170
	1828	1.6	50		1911	2.3	70
12 Sa	0106	5.2	160	27 Su	0133	5.2	160
	0640	2.3	70		0728	2.0	60
	1303	5.6	170		1405	5.2	160
	1906	2.0	60		1950	2.6	80
13 Su	0140	5.2	160	28 M	0207	5.2	160
	0726	2.3	70		0817	2.0	60
	1354	5.2	160		1502	4.9	150
	1947	2.3	70		2032	3.0	90
14 M ◑	0216	5.6	170	29 Tu ◑	0243	5.2	160
	0816	2.0	60		0915	2.3	70
	1453	4.9	150		1606	4.6	140
	2032	2.6	80		2118	3.3	100
15 Tu	0256	5.6	170	30 W	0323	4.9	150
	0915	2.0	60		1026	2.3	70
	1603	4.9	150		1714	4.6	140
	2125	3.0	90		2212	3.6	110
				31 Th	0415	4.9	150
					1139	2.3	70
					1819	4.6	140
					2315	3.6	110

September

Day	Time (h m)	ft	cm	Day	Time (h m)	ft	cm
1 F	0520	4.9	150	16 Sa	0543	5.6	170
	1244	2.3	70		1235	1.6	50
	1921	4.6	140		1932	5.2	160
2 Sa	0018	3.6	110	17 Su	0041	3.3	100
	0626	5.2	160		0657	5.6	170
	1339	2.0	60		1340	1.6	50
	2015	4.6	140		2028	5.2	160
3 Su	0116	3.6	110	18 M	0145	3.0	90
	0726	5.2	160		0803	5.9	180
	1425	2.0	60		1435	1.3	40
	2059	4.9	150		2115	5.2	160
4 M	0206	3.3	100	19 Tu	0240	2.6	80
	0819	5.6	170		0859	5.9	180
	1503	1.6	50		1523	1.6	50
	2138	4.9	150		2155	5.6	170
5 Tu	0252	3.0	90	20 W ●	0328	2.3	70
	0907	5.6	170		0951	5.9	180
	1538	1.6	50		1605	1.6	50
	2213	5.2	160		2232	5.6	170
6 W	0334	2.6	80	21 Th ◯	0412	2.0	60
	0952	5.9	180		1039	5.9	180
	1612	1.6	50		1645	2.0	60
	2246	5.2	160		2306	5.6	170
7 Th	0414	2.3	70	22 F	0454	1.6	50
	1037	5.9	180		1125	5.9	180
	1647	1.6	50		1722	2.0	60
	2318	5.2	160		2339	5.6	170
8 F	0454	2.0	60	23 Sa	0534	1.6	50
	1121	5.9	180		1210	5.9	180
	1723	1.6	50		1758	2.6	80
	2351	5.6	170				
9 Sa	0535	2.0	60	24 Su	0010	5.6	170
	1206	5.9	180		0614	1.6	50
	1759	2.0	60		1255	5.6	170
					1834	3.0	90
10 Su	0024	5.6	170	25 M	0040	5.6	170
	0618	1.6	50		0654	1.6	50
	1254	5.6	170		1341	5.2	160
	1839	2.3	70		1910	3.3	100
11 M	0058	5.6	170	26 Tu	0108	5.2	160
	0703	1.6	50		0737	2.0	60
	1346	5.6	170		1432	4.9	150
	1922	2.6	80		1946	3.3	100
12 Tu	0136	5.6	170	27 W ◑	0138	5.2	160
	0754	1.6	50		0826	2.3	70
	1447	5.2	160		1531	4.9	150
	2009	3.0	90		2027	3.6	110
13 W ◯	0219	5.6	170	28 Th	0212	5.2	160
	0853	1.6	50		0925	2.3	70
	1559	4.9	150		1635	4.6	140
	2105	3.3	100		2119	3.9	120
14 Th	0312	5.6	170	29 F	0259	4.9	150
	1003	1.6	50		1037	2.6	80
	1714	4.9	150		1738	4.6	140
	2213	3.3	100		2228	3.9	120
15 F	0423	5.6	170	30 Sa	0407	4.9	150
	1120	1.6	50		1148	2.6	80
	1826	4.9	150		1838	4.6	140
	2328	3.6	110		2340	3.9	120

Time meridian 60° W. 0000 is midnight. 1200 is noon. Times are not adjusted for Daylight Saving Time.
Heights are referred to the Canadian chart datum of soundings.

Pictou, Nova Scotia, 2017
Times and Heights of High and Low Waters

October

Day	Time (h m)	Height (ft)	Height (cm)
1 Su	0538 / 1248 / 1930	4.9 / 2.3 / 4.9	150 / 70 / 150
2 M	0044 / 0653 / 1338 / 2014	3.6 / 5.2 / 2.3 / 4.9	110 / 160 / 70 / 150
3 Tu	0138 / 0753 / 1420 / 2052	3.3 / 5.2 / 2.3 / 5.2	100 / 160 / 70 / 160
4 W	0225 / 0846 / 1458 / 2127	3.0 / 5.6 / 2.0 / 5.2	90 / 170 / 60 / 160
5 Th ○	0308 / 0934 / 1536 / 2200	2.3 / 5.6 / 2.0 / 5.6	70 / 170 / 60 / 170
6 F	0349 / 1021 / 1613 / 2234	2.0 / 5.9 / 2.0 / 5.9	60 / 180 / 60 / 180
7 Sa	0431 / 1108 / 1652 / 2308	1.6 / 5.9 / 2.3 / 5.9	50 / 180 / 70 / 180
8 Su	0513 / 1155 / 1732 / 2343	1.3 / 5.9 / 2.3 / 5.9	40 / 180 / 70 / 180
9 M	0556 / 1245 / 1815	1.0 / 5.9 / 2.6	30 / 180 / 80
10 Tu	0021 / 0643 / 1340 / 1900	6.2 / 1.0 / 5.6 / 3.0	190 / 30 / 170 / 90
11 W	0102 / 0735 / 1443 / 1951	5.9 / 1.3 / 5.6 / 3.3	180 / 40 / 170 / 100
12 Th ◗	0149 / 0835 / 1553 / 2052	5.9 / 1.3 / 5.2 / 3.6	180 / 40 / 160 / 110
13 F	0250 / 0946 / 1704 / 2205	5.6 / 1.6 / 5.2 / 3.6	170 / 50 / 160 / 110
14 Sa	0412 / 1103 / 1811 / 2324	5.6 / 2.0 / 5.2 / 3.6	170 / 60 / 160 / 110
15 Su	0538 / 1216 / 1910	5.2 / 2.0 / 5.2	160 / 60 / 160
16 M	0036 / 0653 / 1319 / 1959	3.3 / 5.6 / 2.0 / 5.2	100 / 170 / 60 / 160
17 Tu	0137 / 0757 / 1412 / 2042	3.0 / 5.6 / 2.0 / 5.6	90 / 170 / 60 / 170
18 W	0228 / 0853 / 1457 / 2119	2.3 / 5.6 / 2.3 / 5.6	70 / 170 / 70 / 170
19 Th ●	0313 / 0943 / 1538 / 2153	2.0 / 5.9 / 2.3 / 5.6	60 / 180 / 70 / 170
20 F	0354 / 1029 / 1615 / 2226	1.6 / 5.9 / 2.6 / 5.6	50 / 180 / 80 / 170
21 Sa	0433 / 1113 / 1651 / 2257	1.3 / 5.9 / 3.0 / 5.9	40 / 180 / 90 / 180
22 Su	0511 / 1155 / 1725 / 2326	1.3 / 5.6 / 3.3 / 5.6	40 / 170 / 100 / 170
23 M	0548 / 1237 / 1759 / 2353	1.6 / 5.6 / 3.3 / 5.6	50 / 170 / 100 / 170
24 Tu	0625 / 1320 / 1833	1.6 / 5.2 / 3.6	50 / 160 / 110
25 W	0019 / 0703 / 1406 / 1908	5.6 / 2.0 / 5.2 / 3.6	170 / 60 / 160 / 110
26 Th	0048 / 0745 / 1457 / 1948	5.6 / 2.0 / 4.9 / 3.9	170 / 60 / 150 / 120
27 F ◖	0123 / 0833 / 1554 / 2038	5.2 / 2.3 / 4.9 / 3.9	160 / 70 / 150 / 120
28 Sa	0207 / 0931 / 1651 / 2143	5.2 / 2.6 / 4.9 / 3.9	160 / 80 / 150 / 120
29 Su	0309 / 1035 / 1745 / 2258	4.9 / 2.6 / 4.9 / 3.9	150 / 80 / 150 / 120
30 M	0444 / 1138 / 1834	4.9 / 2.6 / 4.9	150 / 80 / 150
31 Tu	0006 / 0616 / 1236 / 1917	3.6 / 4.9 / 2.6 / 5.2	110 / 150 / 80 / 160

November

Day	Time (h m)	Height (ft)	Height (cm)
1 W	0104 / 0726 / 1327 / 1957	3.0 / 5.2 / 2.6 / 5.2	90 / 160 / 80 / 160
2 Th	0154 / 0823 / 1413 / 2034	2.6 / 5.2 / 2.6 / 5.6	80 / 160 / 80 / 170
3 F	0240 / 0916 / 1457 / 2112	2.0 / 5.6 / 2.6 / 5.9	60 / 170 / 80 / 180
4 Sa ○	0324 / 1005 / 1540 / 2150	1.6 / 5.9 / 2.6 / 6.2	50 / 180 / 80 / 190
5 Su	0408 / 1054 / 1623 / 2229	1.0 / 5.9 / 3.0 / 6.2	30 / 180 / 90 / 190
6 M	0452 / 1144 / 1707 / 2309	0.7 / 6.2 / 3.0 / 6.6	20 / 190 / 90 / 200
7 Tu	0539 / 1236 / 1753 / 2352	0.7 / 5.9 / 3.3 / 6.6	20 / 180 / 100 / 200
8 W	0627 / 1332 / 1843	0.7 / 5.9 / 3.3	20 / 180 / 100
9 Th	0038 / 0720 / 1434 / 1937	6.2 / 1.0 / 5.9 / 3.6	190 / 30 / 180 / 110
10 F ○	0131 / 0819 / 1539 / 2040	5.9 / 1.3 / 5.6 / 3.6	180 / 40 / 170 / 110
11 Sa	0238 / 0927 / 1643 / 2153	5.6 / 1.6 / 5.6 / 3.6	170 / 50 / 170 / 110
12 Su	0402 / 1038 / 1742 / 2311	5.2 / 2.0 / 5.6 / 3.3	160 / 60 / 170 / 100
13 M	0527 / 1147 / 1835	5.2 / 2.3 / 5.6	160 / 70 / 170
14 Tu	0022 / 0643 / 1248 / 1921	3.0 / 5.2 / 2.6 / 5.6	90 / 160 / 80 / 170
15 W	0122 / 0748 / 1340 / 2002	2.6 / 5.2 / 3.0 / 5.6	80 / 160 / 90 / 170
16 Th	0212 / 0844 / 1426 / 2039	2.3 / 5.6 / 3.0 / 5.6	70 / 170 / 90 / 170
17 F	0256 / 0934 / 1507 / 2114	2.0 / 5.6 / 3.3 / 5.9	60 / 170 / 100 / 180
18 Sa ●	0337 / 1019 / 1545 / 2148	1.6 / 5.6 / 3.3 / 5.9	50 / 170 / 100 / 180
19 Su	0415 / 1101 / 1620 / 2219	1.6 / 5.6 / 3.6 / 5.9	50 / 170 / 110 / 180
20 M	0451 / 1142 / 1655 / 2248	1.3 / 5.6 / 3.6 / 5.9	40 / 170 / 110 / 180
21 Tu	0526 / 1221 / 1729 / 2316	1.6 / 5.6 / 3.6 / 5.9	50 / 170 / 110 / 180
22 W	0601 / 1301 / 1803 / 2344	1.6 / 5.2 / 3.9 / 5.9	50 / 160 / 120 / 180
23 Th	0636 / 1342 / 1839	2.0 / 5.2 / 3.9	60 / 160 / 120
24 F	0016 / 0714 / 1425 / 1920	5.6 / 2.0 / 5.2 / 3.9	170 / 60 / 160 / 120
25 Sa	0052 / 0756 / 1511 / 2008	5.6 / 2.3 / 5.2 / 3.9	170 / 70 / 160 / 120
26 Su ◖	0137 / 0842 / 1558 / 2106	5.2 / 2.3 / 5.2 / 3.9	160 / 70 / 160 / 120
27 M	0235 / 0935 / 1645 / 2213	4.9 / 2.6 / 5.2 / 3.6	150 / 80 / 160 / 110
28 Tu	0400 / 1033 / 1730 / 2322	4.9 / 2.6 / 5.2 / 3.3	150 / 80 / 160 / 100
29 W	0537 / 1132 / 1813	4.9 / 3.0 / 5.6	150 / 90 / 170
30 Th	0025 / 0655 / 1231 / 1856	3.0 / 4.9 / 3.0 / 5.6	90 / 150 / 90 / 170

December

Day	Time (h m)	Height (ft)	Height (cm)
1 F	0121 / 0759 / 1326 / 1940	2.3 / 5.2 / 3.3 / 5.9	70 / 160 / 100 / 180
2 Sa	0212 / 0857 / 1419 / 2026	1.6 / 5.6 / 3.3 / 6.2	50 / 170 / 100 / 190
3 Su ○	0301 / 0950 / 1509 / 2112	1.3 / 5.9 / 3.3 / 6.6	40 / 180 / 100 / 200
4 M	0349 / 1042 / 1558 / 2158	0.7 / 5.9 / 3.3 / 6.6	20 / 180 / 100 / 200
5 Tu	0436 / 1134 / 1647 / 2246	0.7 / 6.2 / 3.3 / 6.9	20 / 190 / 100 / 210
6 W	0525 / 1226 / 1736 / 2334	0.7 / 6.2 / 3.3 / 6.6	20 / 190 / 100 / 200
7 Th	0615 / 1320 / 1828	0.7 / 5.9 / 3.3	20 / 180 / 100
8 F	0025 / 0707 / 1416 / 1922	6.6 / 1.0 / 5.9 / 3.6	200 / 30 / 180 / 110
9 Sa	0122 / 0802 / 1513 / 2022	6.2 / 1.3 / 5.6 / 3.6	190 / 40 / 170 / 110
10 Su ○	0227 / 0901 / 1609 / 2129	5.6 / 2.0 / 5.6 / 3.3	170 / 60 / 170 / 100
11 M	0345 / 1004 / 1701 / 2244	5.2 / 2.3 / 5.6 / 3.3	160 / 70 / 170 / 100
12 Tu	0508 / 1106 / 1750 / 2357	5.2 / 3.0 / 5.6 / 3.0	160 / 90 / 170 / 90
13 W	0625 / 1206 / 1835	4.9 / 3.3 / 5.6	150 / 100 / 170
14 Th	0100 / 0733 / 1301 / 1918	2.6 / 4.9 / 3.3 / 5.6	80 / 150 / 100 / 170
15 F	0153 / 0833 / 1350 / 1959	2.3 / 5.2 / 3.6 / 5.9	70 / 160 / 110 / 180
16 Sa	0240 / 0924 / 1434 / 2038	2.0 / 5.2 / 3.6 / 5.9	60 / 160 / 110 / 180
17 Su	0321 / 1009 / 1514 / 2114	1.6 / 5.2 / 3.9 / 5.9	50 / 160 / 120 / 180
18 M ●	0359 / 1050 / 1551 / 2148	1.6 / 5.2 / 3.9 / 5.9	50 / 160 / 120 / 180
19 Tu	0435 / 1127 / 1627 / 2221	1.6 / 5.6 / 3.9 / 5.9	50 / 170 / 120 / 180
20 W	0509 / 1204 / 1703 / 2252	1.6 / 5.6 / 3.9 / 5.9	50 / 170 / 120 / 180
21 Th	0542 / 1240 / 1739 / 2325	1.6 / 5.2 / 3.9 / 5.9	50 / 160 / 120 / 180
22 F	0615 / 1315 / 1817 / 2359	1.6 / 5.2 / 3.9 / 5.9	50 / 160 / 120 / 180
23 Sa	0650 / 1352 / 1857	2.0 / 5.2 / 3.6	60 / 160 / 110
24 Su	0039 / 0727 / 1429 / 1942	5.6 / 2.0 / 5.2 / 3.6	170 / 60 / 160 / 110
25 M	0124 / 0807 / 1506 / 2034	5.2 / 2.3 / 5.2 / 3.6	160 / 70 / 160 / 110
26 Tu ◖	0219 / 0851 / 1545 / 2133	5.2 / 2.6 / 5.2 / 3.3	160 / 80 / 160 / 100
27 W	0333 / 0940 / 1626 / 2238	4.9 / 3.0 / 5.6 / 3.0	150 / 90 / 170 / 90
28 Th	0503 / 1037 / 1710 / 2345	4.9 / 3.0 / 5.6 / 2.6	150 / 90 / 170 / 80
29 F	0626 / 1140 / 1759	4.9 / 3.3 / 5.9	150 / 100 / 180
30 Sa	0048 / 0737 / 1244 / 1853	2.0 / 4.9 / 3.6 / 6.2	60 / 150 / 110 / 190
31 Su	0147 / 0840 / 1345 / 1949	1.6 / 5.2 / 3.6 / 6.6	50 / 160 / 110 / 200

Time meridian 60° W. 0000 is midnight. 1200 is noon. Times are not adjusted for Daylight Saving Time.
Heights are referred to the Canadian chart datum of soundings.

Harrington Harbour, Quebec, 2017
Times and Heights of High and Low Waters

January

Day	Time (h m)	Height (ft)	Height (cm)		Day	Time (h m)	Height (ft)	Height (cm)
1 Su	0010	5.2	160		16 M	0057	5.6	170
	0613	1.0	30			0706	1.0	30
	1257	6.2	190			1340	6.2	190
	1917	2.0	60			2000	1.6	50
2 M	0049	5.2	160		17 Tu	0142	5.2	160
	0653	1.3	40			0753	1.6	50
	1335	6.2	190			1420	5.9	180
	1958	2.0	60			2044	2.0	60
3 Tu	0132	4.9	150		18 W	0232	5.2	160
	0738	1.6	50			0844	2.0	60
	1417	5.9	180			1502	5.2	160
	2043	2.0	60			2130	2.0	60
4 W	0223	4.9	150		19 Th ☽	0330	4.9	150
	0831	2.0	60			0942	2.3	70
	1504	5.6	170			1547	4.9	150
	2132	2.0	60			2221	2.3	70
5 Th ☾	0325	4.9	150		20 F	0441	4.9	150
	0935	2.3	70			1052	3.0	90
	1558	5.6	170			1642	4.6	140
	2227	2.0	60			2319	2.3	70
6 F	0440	4.9	150		21 Sa	0602	4.9	150
	1050	2.3	70			1210	3.0	90
	1659	5.2	160			1746	4.3	130
	2326	1.6	50					
7 Sa	0600	5.2	160		22 Su	0021	2.3	70
	1209	2.3	70			0717	4.9	150
	1807	4.9	150			1326	3.0	90
						1854	4.3	130
8 Su	0028	1.6	50		23 M	0120	2.0	60
	0714	5.6	170			0816	5.2	160
	1325	2.3	70			1429	2.6	80
	1912	4.9	150			1953	4.3	130
9 M	0128	1.3	40		24 Tu	0211	1.6	50
	0817	6.2	190			0902	5.6	170
	1432	2.0	60			1517	2.6	80
	2013	5.2	160			2042	4.6	140
10 Tu	0224	1.0	30		25 W	0255	1.6	50
	0912	6.6	200			0941	5.9	180
	1530	2.0	60			1557	2.3	70
	2107	5.2	160			2124	4.6	140
11 W	0316	0.7	20		26 Th	0333	1.3	40
	1003	6.9	210			1017	6.2	190
	1621	1.6	50			1633	2.0	60
	2158	5.2	160			2203	4.9	150
12 Th ○	0405	0.3	10		27 F ●	0409	1.0	30
	1051	7.2	220			1051	6.2	190
	1708	1.6	50			1707	2.0	60
	2245	5.6	170			2240	5.2	160
13 F	0452	0.3	10		28 Sa	0445	1.0	30
	1136	7.2	220			1125	6.6	200
	1753	1.6	50			1740	1.6	50
	2329	5.6	170			2316	5.2	160
14 Sa	0537	0.3	10		29 Su	0521	0.7	20
	1219	6.9	210			1158	6.6	200
	1836	1.6	50			1814	1.6	50
						2354	5.6	170
15 Su	0013	5.6	170		30 M	0558	0.7	20
	0622	0.7	20			1233	6.6	200
	1300	6.6	200			1849	1.6	50
	1918	1.6	50					
					31 Tu	0033	5.6	170
						0639	1.0	30
						1309	6.2	190
						1927	1.3	40

February

Day	Time (h m)	Height (ft)	Height (cm)		Day	Time (h m)	Height (ft)	Height (cm)
1 W	0116	5.6	170		16 Th	0157	5.2	160
	0723	1.3	40			0809	2.0	60
	1348	5.9	180			1410	5.2	160
	2008	1.6	50			2035	1.6	50
2 Th	0204	5.2	160		17 F	0245	5.2	160
	0814	1.6	50			0858	2.3	70
	1430	5.6	170			1445	4.6	140
	2054	1.6	50			2118	2.0	60
3 F	0302	5.2	160		18 Sa ◯	0344	4.9	150
	0915	2.0	60			0958	2.6	80
	1520	5.2	160			1529	4.3	130
	2148	1.6	50			2211	2.0	60
4 Sa ☾	0413	5.2	160		19 Su	0459	4.6	140
	1028	2.3	70			1114	3.0	90
	1620	4.9	150			1630	4.3	130
	2250	1.6	50			2317	2.3	70
5 Su	0536	5.2	160		20 M	0625	4.9	150
	1150	2.6	80			1238	3.0	90
	1733	4.6	140			1752	3.9	120
	2359	1.6	50					
6 M	0659	5.6	170		21 Tu	0028	2.0	60
	1313	2.3	70			0736	4.9	150
	1851	4.6	140			1353	3.0	90
						1912	3.9	120
7 Tu	0108	1.3	40		22 W	0132	2.0	60
	0809	5.9	180			0830	5.2	160
	1425	2.3	70			1447	2.6	80
	2001	4.6	140			2013	4.3	130
8 W	0211	1.0	30		23 Th	0224	1.6	50
	0906	6.2	190			0912	5.6	170
	1522	2.0	60			1528	2.3	70
	2059	4.9	150			2101	4.6	140
9 Th	0306	0.7	20		24 F	0308	1.3	40
	0955	6.6	200			0949	5.9	180
	1610	1.6	50			1604	2.0	60
	2149	5.2	160			2142	4.9	150
10 F ○	0355	0.7	20		25 Sa	0347	1.0	30
	1039	6.6	200			1023	6.2	190
	1652	1.3	40			1637	1.6	50
	2233	5.6	170			2220	5.2	160
11 Sa	0440	0.3	10		26 Su ●	0425	0.7	20
	1118	6.6	200			1057	6.2	190
	1732	1.3	40			1710	1.3	40
	2315	5.6	170			2258	5.6	170
12 Su	0523	0.3	10		27 M	0504	0.7	20
	1156	6.6	200			1130	6.2	190
	1809	1.3	40			1743	1.0	30
	2355	5.6	170			2337	5.9	180
13 M	0604	0.7	20		28 Tu	0543	0.7	20
	1230	6.2	190			1205	6.2	190
	1845	1.3	40			1818	1.0	30
14 Tu	0034	5.6	170					
	0644	1.0	30					
	1304	5.9	180					
	1921	1.3	40					
15 W	0114	5.6	170					
	0725	1.3	40					
	1336	5.6	170					
	1957	1.6	50					

March

Day	Time (h m)	Height (ft)	Height (cm)		Day	Time (h m)	Height (ft)	Height (cm)
1 W	0017	5.9	180		16 Th	0049	5.6	170
	0626	0.7	20			0702	1.3	40
	1241	6.2	190			1257	5.2	160
	1855	1.0	30			1912	1.3	40
2 Th	0100	5.9	180		17 F	0127	5.6	170
	0711	1.0	30			0742	2.0	60
	1320	5.9	180			1327	4.9	150
	1936	1.0	30			1945	1.3	40
3 F	0148	5.9	180		18 Sa ◯	0210	5.2	160
	0803	1.3	40			0826	2.3	70
	1402	5.2	160			1359	4.6	140
	2022	1.0	30			2022	1.6	50
4 Sa	0245	5.6	170		19 Su	0259	4.9	150
	0904	2.0	60			0920	2.6	80
	1451	4.9	150			1439	4.3	130
	2115	1.3	40			2109	2.0	60
5 Su ☾	0354	5.6	170		20 M ◯	0404	4.9	150
	1016	2.3	70			1027	2.6	80
	1552	4.6	140			1533	3.9	120
	2220	1.3	40			2212	2.0	60
6 M	0519	5.2	160		21 Tu	0524	4.6	140
	1140	2.3	70			1147	3.0	90
	1713	4.3	130			1655	3.9	120
	2336	1.6	50			2330	2.0	60
7 Tu	0646	5.6	170		22 W	0643	4.9	150
	1305	2.3	70			1305	2.6	80
	1842	4.3	130			1830	3.9	120
8 W	0053	1.3	40		23 Th	0046	2.0	60
	0758	5.6	170			0745	4.9	150
	1415	2.0	60			1405	2.3	70
	1956	4.6	140			1942	4.3	130
9 Th	0201	1.3	40		24 F	0148	1.6	50
	0854	5.9	180			0831	5.2	160
	1509	2.0	60			1449	2.0	60
	2053	4.9	150			2034	4.6	140
10 F	0257	1.0	30		25 Sa	0239	1.3	40
	0939	6.2	190			0911	5.6	170
	1552	1.6	50			1526	1.6	50
	2140	5.2	160			2118	4.9	150
11 Sa	0345	0.7	20		26 Su	0323	1.0	30
	1019	6.2	190			0948	5.9	180
	1630	1.3	40			1600	1.3	40
	2221	5.6	170			2158	5.6	170
12 Su ○	0428	0.7	20		27 M ●	0404	0.7	20
	1054	6.2	190			1023	5.9	180
	1704	1.0	30			1634	1.0	30
	2259	5.6	170			2238	5.9	180
13 M	0508	0.7	20		28 Tu	0446	0.7	20
	1127	5.9	180			1059	5.9	180
	1738	1.0	30			1709	0.7	20
	2336	5.9	180			2318	6.2	190
14 Tu	0546	1.0	30		29 W	0529	0.7	20
	1158	5.6	170			1136	5.9	180
	1810	1.0	30			1746	0.3	10
15 W	0012	5.9	180		30 Th	0001	6.2	190
	0624	1.0	30			0614	0.7	20
	1227	5.6	170			1215	5.9	180
	1841	1.0	30			1825	0.3	10
					31 F	0046	6.2	190
						0703	1.0	30
						1256	5.6	170
						1908	0.7	20

Time meridian 60° W. 0000 is midnight. 1200 is noon. Times are not adjusted for Daylight Saving Time.
Heights are referred to the Canadian chart datum of soundings.

Harrington Harbour, Quebec, 2017

Times and Heights of High and Low Waters

April

Day	Time	ft	cm	Day	Time	ft	cm
1 Sa	0136	6.2	190	**16 Su**	0143	5.6	170
	0756	1.3	40		0805	2.0	60
	1341	4.9	150		1328	4.3	130
	1955	0.7	20		1940	1.6	50
2 Su	0233	5.9	180	**17 M**	0228	5.2	160
	0858	2.0	60		0854	2.3	70
	1432	4.6	140		1408	4.3	130
	2051	1.0	30		2024	1.6	50
3 M ☽	0341	5.6	170	**18 Tu**	0323	4.9	150
	1010	2.3	70		0953	2.6	80
	1537	4.3	130		1501	3.9	120
	2159	1.3	40		2123	2.0	60
4 Tu	0504	5.2	160	**19 W ☽**	0431	4.9	150
	1130	2.3	70		1102	2.6	80
	1704	3.9	120		1617	3.9	120
	2319	1.6	50		2238	2.0	60
5 W	0628	5.2	160	**20 Th**	0545	4.9	150
	1249	2.3	70		1211	2.3	70
	1837	4.3	130		1750	3.9	120
					2358	2.0	60
6 Th	0040	1.6	50	**21 F**	0650	4.9	150
	0738	5.2	160		1312	2.3	70
	1354	2.0	60		1906	4.3	130
	1949	4.6	140				
7 F	0150	1.3	40	**22 Sa**	0108	2.0	60
	0831	5.6	170		0743	5.2	160
	1444	1.6	50		1400	2.0	60
	2043	4.9	150		2003	4.6	140
8 Sa	0246	1.3	40	**23 Su**	0206	1.6	50
	0914	5.6	170		0827	5.2	160
	1524	1.3	40		1442	1.3	40
	2127	5.2	160		2050	5.2	160
9 Su	0332	1.0	30	**24 M**	0257	1.3	40
	0951	5.6	170		0908	5.6	170
	1600	1.3	40		1520	1.0	30
	2205	5.6	170		2134	5.9	180
10 M	0414	1.0	30	**25 Tu**	0344	1.0	30
	1024	5.6	170		0948	5.6	170
	1633	1.0	30		1558	0.7	20
	2242	5.9	180		2217	6.2	190
11 Tu ○	0453	1.0	30	**26 W ●**	0429	0.7	20
	1055	5.2	160		1029	5.6	170
	1705	1.0	30		1637	0.3	10
	2317	5.9	180		2300	6.6	200
12 W	0530	1.3	40	**27 Th**	0516	0.7	20
	1125	5.2	160		1110	5.6	170
	1735	1.0	30		1717	0.0	0
	2352	5.9	180		2346	6.9	210
13 Th	0607	1.3	40	**28 F**	0604	1.0	30
	1154	4.9	150		1153	5.6	170
	1804	1.0	30		1759	0.0	0
14 F	0027	5.9	180	**29 Sa**	0034	6.6	200
	0644	1.6	50		0656	1.0	30
	1224	4.9	150		1237	5.2	160
	1834	1.0	30		1846	0.3	10
15 Sa	0103	5.6	170	**30 Su**	0126	6.6	200
	0722	2.0	60		0752	1.3	40
	1254	4.6	140		1326	4.9	150
	1905	1.3	40		1936	0.7	20

May

Day	Time	ft	cm	Day	Time	ft	cm
1 M	0223	6.2	190	**16 Tu**	0205	5.6	170
	0853	1.6	50		0834	2.3	70
	1421	4.6	140		1350	4.3	130
	2035	1.0	30		1957	1.6	50
2 Tu ☽	0330	5.6	170	**17 W**	0254	5.2	160
	1000	2.0	60		0926	2.3	70
	1529	4.3	130		1442	3.9	120
	2144	1.3	40		2052	2.0	60
3 W	0444	5.2	160	**18 Th ☽**	0351	4.9	150
	1111	2.0	60		1023	2.3	70
	1653	4.3	130		1550	3.9	120
	2302	1.6	50		2159	2.0	60
4 Th	0559	5.2	160	**19 F**	0453	4.9	150
	1219	2.0	60		1122	2.3	70
	1821	4.3	130		1711	4.3	130
					2316	2.0	60
5 F	0022	2.0	60	**20 Sa**	0556	4.9	150
	0705	5.2	160		1219	2.0	60
	1319	2.0	60		1827	4.6	140
	1932	4.6	140				
6 Sa	0131	1.6	50	**21 Su**	0029	2.0	60
	0757	5.2	160		0652	4.9	150
	1409	1.6	50		1311	1.6	50
	2025	4.9	150		1929	4.9	150
7 Su	0229	1.6	50	**22 M**	0134	1.6	50
	0841	4.9	150		0743	5.2	160
	1450	1.3	40		1358	1.3	40
	2109	5.2	160		2022	5.6	170
8 M	0317	1.6	50	**23 Tu**	0231	1.6	50
	0918	4.9	150		0830	5.2	160
	1527	1.3	40		1442	1.0	30
	2148	5.6	170		2110	6.2	190
9 Tu	0359	1.6	50	**24 W**	0324	1.3	40
	0953	4.9	150		0916	5.2	160
	1601	1.0	30		1526	0.3	10
	2224	5.9	180		2158	6.6	200
10 W ○	0438	1.6	50	**25 Th ●**	0414	1.0	30
	1025	4.9	150		1002	5.2	160
	1633	1.0	30		1610	0.3	10
	2259	5.9	180		2245	6.9	210
11 Th	0516	1.6	50	**26 F**	0505	1.0	30
	1056	4.9	150		1048	5.2	160
	1703	1.0	30		1655	0.0	0
	2334	5.9	180		2334	6.9	210
12 F	0552	1.6	50	**27 Sa**	0556	1.0	30
	1127	4.6	140		1135	5.2	160
	1733	1.0	30		1741	0.0	0
13 Sa	0008	5.9	180	**28 Su**	0024	6.9	210
	0629	1.6	50		0648	1.3	40
	1158	4.6	140		1223	4.9	150
	1804	1.0	30		1830	0.3	10
14 Su	0044	5.9	180	**29 M**	0117	6.6	200
	0707	2.0	60		0743	1.3	40
	1231	4.6	140		1314	4.9	150
	1836	1.3	40		1922	0.7	20
15 M	0123	5.6	170	**30 Tu**	0212	6.2	190
	0748	2.0	60		0840	1.6	50
	1308	4.3	130		1410	4.6	140
	1913	1.3	40		2021	1.0	30
				31 W	0312	5.9	180
					0939	2.0	60
					1514	4.6	140
					2126	1.6	50

June

Day	Time	ft	cm	Day	Time	ft	cm
1 Th ☽	0415	5.6	170	**16 F**	0316	5.2	160
	1039	2.0	60		0945	2.0	60
	1630	4.3	130		1524	4.3	130
	2238	2.0	60		2131	2.0	60
2 F	0520	5.2	160	**17 Sa ○**	0409	5.2	160
	1139	2.0	60		1037	2.0	60
	1750	4.6	140		1635	4.6	140
	2353	2.0	60		2241	2.0	60
3 Sa	0621	4.9	150	**18 Su**	0507	4.9	150
	1236	2.0	60		1132	2.0	60
	1902	4.9	150		1750	4.9	150
					2355	2.0	60
4 Su	0104	2.0	60	**19 M**	0606	4.9	150
	0715	4.9	150		1226	1.6	50
	1328	1.6	50		1857	5.2	160
	1959	5.2	160				
5 M	0205	2.0	60	**20 Tu**	0105	2.0	60
	0802	4.6	140		0703	4.9	150
	1414	1.6	50		1320	1.3	40
	2047	5.2	160		1957	5.6	170
6 Tu	0257	2.0	60	**21 W**	0210	2.0	60
	0843	4.6	140		0758	4.9	150
	1454	1.3	40		1411	1.0	30
	2128	5.6	170		2051	6.2	190
7 W	0342	2.0	60	**22 Th**	0308	1.6	50
	0921	4.6	140		0851	5.2	160
	1531	1.3	40		1501	0.7	20
	2206	5.9	180		2143	6.6	200
8 Th	0423	2.0	60	**23 F ●**	0402	1.3	40
	0957	4.6	140		0942	5.2	160
	1606	1.0	30		1550	0.3	10
	2242	5.9	180		2234	6.9	210
9 F ○	0501	2.0	60	**24 Sa**	0454	1.3	40
	1031	4.6	140		1032	5.2	160
	1638	1.0	30		1639	0.0	0
	2318	5.9	180		2324	6.9	210
10 Sa	0537	2.0	60	**25 Su**	0545	1.3	40
	1104	4.6	140		1121	5.2	160
	1710	1.0	30		1728	0.0	0
	2353	5.9	180				
11 Su	0614	2.0	60	**26 M**	0014	6.9	210
	1138	4.6	140		0636	1.3	40
	1742	1.0	30		1210	5.2	160
					1817	0.3	10
12 M	0028	5.9	180	**27 Tu**	0104	6.6	200
	0651	2.0	60		0726	1.6	50
	1214	4.6	140		1259	5.2	160
	1817	1.3	40		1909	0.7	20
13 Tu	0105	5.9	180	**28 W**	0154	6.2	190
	0729	2.0	60		0816	1.6	50
	1252	4.6	140		1352	4.9	150
	1855	1.3	40		2003	1.0	30
14 W	0145	5.6	170	**29 Th**	0245	5.9	180
	0811	2.0	60		0907	1.6	50
	1334	4.6	140		1449	4.9	150
	1938	1.6	50		2102	1.6	50
15 Th	0228	5.6	170	**30 F ☽**	0337	5.6	170
	0856	2.0	60		0959	2.0	60
	1424	4.3	130		1555	4.6	140
	2030	1.6	50		2207	2.0	60

Time meridian 60° W. 0000 is midnight. 1200 is noon. Times are not adjusted for Daylight Saving Time.
Heights are referred to the Canadian chart datum of soundings.

Harrington Harbour, Quebec, 2017
Times and Heights of High and Low Waters

July

Day	Time (h m)	Height (ft)	Height (cm)		Day	Time (h m)	Height (ft)	Height (cm)
1 Sa	0431	4.9	150		16 Su	0330	5.2	160
	1054	2.0	60			0956	2.0	60
	1709	4.6	140			1604	4.9	150
	2317	2.3	70		◐	2215	2.3	70
2 Su	0528	4.6	140		17 M	0425	4.9	150
	1150	2.0	60			1051	1.6	50
	1823	4.9	150			1718	4.9	150
						2329	2.3	70
3 M	0029	2.6	80		18 Tu	0527	4.9	150
	0625	4.6	140			1150	1.6	50
	1245	2.0	60			1833	5.2	160
	1928	5.2	160					
4 Tu	0136	2.6	80		19 W	0045	2.3	70
	0719	4.6	140			0632	4.9	150
	1337	1.6	50			1251	1.3	40
	2022	5.2	160			1940	5.9	180
5 W	0234	2.3	70		20 Th	0155	2.0	60
	0809	4.6	140			0736	4.9	150
	1424	1.6	50			1350	1.0	30
	2108	5.6	170			2040	6.2	190
6 Th	0323	2.3	70		21 F	0258	2.0	60
	0853	4.6	140			0835	4.9	150
	1505	1.3	40			1446	0.7	20
	2149	5.9	180			2134	6.6	200
7 F	0405	2.3	70		22 Sa	0353	1.6	50
	0932	4.6	140			0929	5.2	160
	1543	1.3	40			1538	0.3	10
	2226	5.9	180			2225	6.9	210
8 Sa	0443	2.0	60		23 Su	0443	1.6	50
	1009	4.6	140			1020	5.2	160
	1617	1.0	30			1628	0.3	10
	2301	5.9	180		●	2313	6.9	210
9 Su	0519	2.0	60		24 M	0530	1.3	40
	1045	4.6	140			1108	5.6	170
	1651	1.0	30			1716	0.3	10
○	2335	6.2	190			2359	6.9	210
10 M	0553	2.0	60		25 Tu	0616	1.3	40
	1121	4.9	150			1155	5.6	170
	1725	1.0	30			1804	0.3	10
11 Tu	0010	6.2	190		26 W	0044	6.6	200
	0628	2.0	60			0659	1.3	40
	1157	4.9	150			1241	5.6	170
	1801	1.0	30			1851	0.7	20
12 W	0045	5.9	180		27 Th	0126	6.2	190
	0704	2.0	60			0743	1.6	50
	1236	4.9	150			1328	5.2	160
	1839	1.3	40			1940	1.3	40
13 Th	0121	5.9	180		28 F	0208	5.6	170
	0742	2.0	60			0827	1.6	50
	1317	4.9	150			1418	5.2	160
	1922	1.3	40			2033	1.6	50
14 F	0200	5.9	180		29 Sa	0251	5.2	160
	0823	2.0	60			0914	2.0	60
	1403	4.9	150			1515	4.9	150
	2010	1.6	50			2131	2.3	70
15 Sa	0242	5.6	170		30 Su	0337	4.9	150
	0907	2.0	60			1004	2.0	60
	1458	4.9	150			1622	4.9	150
	2107	2.0	60		◐	2237	2.6	80
					31 M	0429	4.6	140
						1059	2.0	60
						1738	4.9	150
						2350	2.6	80

August

Day	Time (h m)	Height (ft)	Height (cm)		Day	Time (h m)	Height (ft)	Height (cm)
1 Tu	0530	4.3	130		16 W	0458	4.6	140
	1159	2.0	60			1122	1.6	50
	1853	4.9	150			1818	5.6	170
2 W	0104	2.6	80		17 Th	0034	2.3	70
	0636	4.3	130			0614	4.6	140
	1300	2.0	60			1232	1.3	40
	1956	5.2	160			1931	5.9	180
3 Th	0208	2.6	80		18 F	0148	2.3	70
	0736	4.3	130			0727	4.6	140
	1354	1.6	50			1338	1.0	30
	2046	5.6	170			2033	6.2	190
4 F	0300	2.6	80		19 Sa	0250	2.0	60
	0827	4.3	130			0829	4.9	150
	1441	1.6	50			1437	1.0	30
	2127	5.6	170			2126	6.6	200
5 Sa	0343	2.3	70		20 Su	0342	1.6	50
	0911	4.6	140			0923	5.2	160
	1521	1.3	40			1530	0.7	20
	2204	5.9	180			2214	6.6	200
6 Su	0420	2.3	70		21 M	0427	1.6	50
	0950	4.9	150			1010	5.6	170
	1558	1.3	40			1619	0.3	10
	2239	5.9	180		●	2257	6.6	200
7 M	0454	2.0	60		22 Tu	0509	1.3	40
	1026	4.9	150			1055	5.6	170
	1633	1.0	30			1704	0.3	10
○	2312	6.2	190			2337	6.6	200
8 Tu	0526	2.0	60		23 W	0549	1.3	40
	1102	5.2	160			1137	5.9	180
	1708	1.0	30			1748	0.7	20
	2345	6.2	190					
9 W	0559	1.6	50		24 Th	0015	6.2	190
	1139	5.2	160			0627	1.3	40
	1745	1.0	30			1219	5.9	180
						1832	1.0	30
10 Th	0018	6.2	190		25 F	0052	5.9	180
	0633	1.6	50			0704	1.3	40
	1217	5.2	160			1302	5.6	170
	1823	1.0	30			1916	1.3	40
11 F	0053	5.9	180		26 Sa	0127	5.6	170
	0708	1.6	50			0743	1.6	50
	1258	5.2	160			1346	5.6	170
	1906	1.3	40			2003	2.0	60
12 Sa	0130	5.9	180		27 Su	0203	5.2	160
	0747	1.6	50			0823	1.6	50
	1343	5.2	160			1436	5.2	160
	1954	1.6	50			2055	2.3	70
13 Su	0210	5.6	170		28 M	0243	4.6	140
	0829	1.6	50			0909	2.0	60
	1436	5.2	160			1536	5.2	160
	2050	2.0	60			2157	2.6	80
14 M	0255	5.2	160		29 Tu	0330	4.3	130
	0919	1.6	50			1004	2.3	70
	1539	5.2	160			1649	4.9	150
◐	2157	2.3	70		◐	2310	3.0	90
15 Tu	0351	4.9	150		30 W	0432	4.3	130
	1017	1.6	50			1109	2.3	70
	1656	5.2	160			1811	4.9	150
	2314	2.3	70					
					31 Th	0028	3.0	90
						0550	3.9	120
						1219	2.3	70
						1922	4.9	150

September

Day	Time (h m)	Height (ft)	Height (cm)		Day	Time (h m)	Height (ft)	Height (cm)
1 F	0138	3.0	90		16 Sa	0142	2.3	70
	0706	4.3	130			0727	4.6	140
	1323	2.0	60			1332	1.3	40
	2016	5.2	160			2024	5.9	180
2 Sa	0232	2.6	80		17 Su	0239	2.0	60
	0804	4.3	130			0827	4.9	150
	1415	1.6	50			1431	1.0	30
	2058	5.6	170			2113	6.2	190
3 Su	0314	2.3	70		18 M	0325	1.6	50
	0849	4.6	140			0916	5.2	160
	1458	1.6	50			1522	1.0	30
	2135	5.9	180			2155	6.2	190
4 M	0349	2.0	60		19 Tu	0405	1.3	40
	0929	4.9	150			0959	5.9	180
	1536	1.3	40			1608	0.7	20
	2209	5.9	180			2234	6.2	190
5 Tu	0421	2.0	60		20 W	0442	1.3	40
	1006	5.2	160			1040	5.9	180
	1613	1.0	30			1651	0.7	20
	2242	6.2	190		●	2309	5.9	180
6 W	0453	1.6	50		21 Th	0517	1.3	40
	1042	5.6	170			1119	6.2	190
	1650	1.0	30			1732	1.0	30
○	2314	6.2	190			2343	5.9	180
7 Th	0525	1.3	40		22 F	0551	1.3	40
	1119	5.9	180			1157	6.2	190
	1727	1.0	30			1812	1.3	40
	2347	6.2	190					
8 F	0558	1.3	40		23 Sa	0015	5.6	170
	1158	5.9	180			0625	1.3	40
	1808	1.0	30			1236	5.9	180
						1853	1.6	50
9 Sa	0022	5.9	180		24 Su	0047	5.2	160
	0633	1.3	40			0659	1.3	40
	1239	5.9	180			1317	5.9	180
	1852	1.3	40			1937	2.0	60
10 Su	0059	5.6	170		25 M	0120	4.9	150
	0711	1.3	40			0734	1.6	50
	1325	5.9	180			1401	5.6	170
	1941	1.6	50			2025	2.3	70
11 M	0140	5.2	160		26 Tu	0155	4.6	140
	0755	1.3	40			0815	2.0	60
	1418	5.9	180			1454	5.2	160
	2039	2.0	60			2122	2.6	80
12 Tu	0227	4.9	150		27 W	0238	4.3	130
	0846	1.6	50			0905	2.3	70
	1522	5.6	170			1600	4.9	150
	2148	2.3	70		◐	2230	3.0	90
13 W	0326	4.6	140		28 Th	0337	3.9	120
	0949	1.6	50			1012	2.3	70
	1642	5.6	170			1721	4.9	150
◐	2308	2.6	80			2346	3.0	90
14 Th	0442	4.3	130		29 F	0503	3.9	120
	1103	1.6	50			1130	2.3	70
	1809	5.6	170			1837	4.9	150
15 F	0030	2.3	70		30 Sa	0057	3.0	90
	0610	4.3	130			0631	4.3	130
	1221	1.6	50			1243	2.3	70
	1924	5.9	180			1935	5.2	160

Time meridian 60° W. 0000 is midnight. 1200 is noon. Times are not adjusted for Daylight Saving Time.
Heights are referred to the Canadian chart datum of soundings.

Harrington Harbour, Quebec, 2017

Times and Heights of High and Low Waters

October

Day	Time	ft	cm
1 Su	0153	2.6	80
	0737	4.6	140
	1343	2.0	60
	2020	5.6	170
2 M	0236	2.3	70
	0825	4.9	150
	1430	1.6	50
	2058	5.6	170
3 Tu	0311	2.0	60
	0905	5.2	160
	1512	1.3	40
	2133	5.9	180
4 W	0344	1.6	50
	0943	5.6	170
	1551	1.3	40
	2207	5.9	180
5 Th ○	0416	1.3	40
	1021	5.9	180
	1630	1.0	30
	2241	5.9	180
6 F	0449	1.0	30
	1059	6.2	190
	1711	1.0	30
	2316	5.9	180
7 Sa	0523	1.0	30
	1139	6.6	200
	1754	1.0	30
	2353	5.9	180
8 Su	0600	0.7	20
	1222	6.6	200
	1840	1.3	40
9 M	0033	5.6	170
	0641	1.0	30
	1310	6.6	200
	1932	1.6	50
10 Tu	0116	5.2	160
	0727	1.0	30
	1405	6.2	190
	2033	2.0	60
11 W	0207	4.9	150
	0822	1.3	40
	1511	5.9	180
	2143	2.3	70
12 Th ◐	0311	4.6	140
	0929	1.6	50
	1631	5.6	170
	2301	2.3	70
13 F	0435	4.3	130
	1049	2.0	60
	1757	5.6	170
14 Sa	0019	2.3	70
	0608	4.6	140
	1211	2.0	60
	1909	5.6	170
15 Su	0125	2.3	70
	0724	4.9	150
	1324	1.6	50
	2005	5.9	180
16 M	0218	2.0	60
	0820	5.2	160
	1423	1.3	40
	2051	5.9	180
17 Tu	0301	1.6	50
	0906	5.6	170
	1512	1.3	40
	2131	5.9	180
18 W	0338	1.3	40
	0947	5.9	180
	1556	1.3	40
	2206	5.9	180
19 Th ●	0413	1.3	40
	1025	6.2	190
	1637	1.3	40
	2239	5.6	170
20 F	0446	1.3	40
	1101	6.2	190
	1716	1.3	40
	2311	5.6	170
21 Sa	0518	1.3	40
	1138	6.2	190
	1755	1.6	50
	2342	5.2	160
22 Su	0549	1.3	40
	1214	6.2	190
	1834	2.0	60
23 M	0013	4.9	150
	0621	1.3	40
	1252	5.9	180
	1915	2.3	70
24 Tu	0045	4.9	150
	0654	1.6	50
	1333	5.9	180
	2000	2.3	70
25 W	0120	4.6	140
	0730	2.0	60
	1420	5.6	170
	2051	2.6	80
26 Th	0201	4.3	130
	0816	2.0	60
	1517	5.2	160
	2151	3.0	90
27 F ◐	0255	4.3	130
	0916	2.3	70
	1626	4.9	150
	2258	3.0	90
28 Sa	0414	3.9	120
	1033	2.6	80
	1739	4.9	150
29 Su	0005	2.6	80
	0547	4.3	130
	1153	2.6	80
	1842	5.2	160
30 M	0103	2.6	80
	0700	4.6	140
	1302	2.3	70
	1932	5.2	160
31 Tu	0149	2.3	70
	0754	4.9	150
	1357	2.0	60
	2014	5.6	170

November

Day	Time	ft	cm
1 W	0228	2.0	60
	0838	5.6	170
	1444	1.6	50
	2053	5.6	170
2 Th	0304	1.3	40
	0918	5.9	180
	1528	1.3	40
	2131	5.9	180
3 F	0339	1.0	30
	0959	6.6	200
	1611	1.3	40
	2209	5.9	180
4 Sa ○	0416	0.7	20
	1040	6.9	210
	1656	1.3	40
	2248	5.9	180
5 Su	0454	0.7	20
	1123	6.9	210
	1742	1.3	40
	2329	5.6	170
6 M	0535	0.7	20
	1209	6.9	210
	1831	1.3	40
7 Tu	0013	5.6	170
	0619	0.7	20
	1259	6.9	210
	1925	1.6	50
8 W	0059	5.2	160
	0708	1.0	30
	1356	6.6	200
	2026	2.0	60
9 Th	0154	4.9	150
	0805	1.3	40
	1500	6.2	190
	2132	2.3	70
10 F ○	0259	4.6	140
	0913	1.6	50
	1614	5.9	180
	2243	2.3	70
11 Sa	0422	4.6	140
	1032	2.0	60
	1731	5.6	170
	2352	2.3	70
12 Su	0553	4.6	140
	1154	2.0	60
	1840	5.6	170
13 M	0055	2.0	60
	0708	4.9	150
	1307	2.0	60
	1936	5.6	170
14 Tu	0147	2.0	60
	0805	5.2	160
	1408	2.0	60
	2022	5.6	170
15 W	0231	1.6	50
	0851	5.9	180
	1459	1.6	50
	2102	5.2	160
16 Th	0309	1.3	40
	0932	6.2	190
	1543	1.6	50
	2138	5.2	160
17 F	0345	1.3	40
	1010	6.2	190
	1624	1.6	50
	2211	5.2	160
18 Sa ●	0418	1.3	40
	1046	6.6	200
	1703	1.6	50
	2244	5.2	160
19 Su	0450	1.3	40
	1122	6.6	200
	1741	2.0	60
	2315	4.9	150
20 M	0522	1.3	40
	1157	6.2	190
	1818	2.0	60
	2347	4.9	150
21 Tu	0553	1.3	40
	1234	6.2	190
	1857	2.3	70
22 W	0020	4.9	150
	0625	1.6	50
	1312	5.9	180
	1938	2.3	70
23 Th	0055	4.6	140
	0701	1.6	50
	1353	5.9	180
	2023	2.6	80
24 F	0136	4.6	140
	0743	2.0	60
	1441	5.6	170
	2113	2.6	80
25 Sa	0225	4.3	130
	0835	2.3	70
	1536	5.2	160
	2209	2.6	80
26 Su ◐	0331	4.3	130
	0941	2.3	70
	1637	5.2	160
	2307	2.6	80
27 M	0453	4.3	130
	1058	2.6	80
	1740	5.2	160
28 Tu	0004	2.3	70
	0613	4.6	140
	1213	2.6	80
	1837	5.2	160
29 W	0056	2.0	60
	0716	5.2	160
	1319	2.3	70
	1927	5.2	160
30 Th	0142	1.6	50
	0807	5.6	170
	1415	2.0	60
	2013	5.6	170

December

Day	Time	ft	cm
1 F	0224	1.3	40
	0854	6.2	190
	1506	1.6	50
	2057	5.6	170
2 Sa	0306	1.0	30
	0939	6.6	200
	1555	1.6	50
	2141	5.6	170
3 Su ○	0348	0.7	20
	1024	7.2	220
	1643	1.3	40
	2225	5.6	170
4 M	0432	0.3	10
	1111	7.2	220
	1732	1.3	40
	2311	5.6	170
5 Tu	0517	0.3	10
	1159	7.2	220
	1822	1.6	50
	2358	5.6	170
6 W	0604	0.3	10
	1251	7.2	220
	1915	1.6	50
7 Th	0047	5.2	160
	0655	0.7	20
	1345	6.9	210
	2011	2.0	60
8 F	0141	4.9	150
	0751	1.0	30
	1442	6.2	190
	2110	2.0	60
9 Sa	0243	4.9	150
	0854	1.6	50
	1545	5.9	180
	2210	2.3	70
10 Su ○	0356	4.9	150
	1006	2.0	60
	1651	5.6	170
	2312	2.3	70
11 M	0519	4.9	150
	1124	2.3	70
	1755	5.2	160
12 Tu	0012	2.0	60
	0638	4.9	150
	1239	2.3	70
	1854	5.2	160
13 W	0108	2.0	60
	0742	5.2	160
	1346	2.3	70
	1946	4.9	150
14 Th	0157	1.6	50
	0833	5.6	170
	1442	2.3	70
	2030	4.9	150
15 F	0240	1.6	50
	0917	5.9	180
	1529	2.3	70
	2110	4.9	150
16 Sa	0319	1.3	40
	0956	6.2	190
	1611	2.0	60
	2147	4.9	150
17 Su	0355	1.3	40
	1033	6.2	190
	1650	2.0	60
	2221	4.9	150
18 M ●	0429	1.3	40
	1108	6.6	200
	1727	2.0	60
	2254	4.9	150
19 Tu	0501	1.3	40
	1143	6.6	200
	1803	2.3	70
	2327	4.9	150
20 W	0533	1.3	40
	1217	6.2	190
	1838	2.3	70
21 Th	0001	4.9	150
	0606	1.3	40
	1252	6.2	190
	1915	2.3	70
22 F	0037	4.9	150
	0641	1.3	40
	1329	5.9	180
	1953	2.3	70
23 Sa	0116	4.9	150
	0720	1.6	50
	1408	5.9	180
	2035	2.3	70
24 Su	0200	4.6	140
	0806	2.0	60
	1452	5.6	170
	2121	2.3	70
25 M	0255	4.6	140
	0901	2.3	70
	1541	5.2	160
	2211	2.3	70
26 Tu ◐	0403	4.6	140
	1009	2.6	80
	1637	5.2	160
	2306	2.3	70
27 W	0521	4.9	150
	1125	2.6	80
	1738	5.2	160
28 Th	0002	2.0	60
	0634	5.2	160
	1240	2.6	80
	1838	4.9	150
29 F	0057	1.6	50
	0737	5.6	170
	1348	2.3	70
	1935	5.2	160
30 Sa	0149	1.3	40
	0832	6.2	190
	1448	2.0	60
	2029	5.2	160
31 Su	0240	1.0	30
	0924	6.9	210
	1542	1.6	50
	2120	5.2	160

Time meridian 60° W. 0000 is midnight. 1200 is noon. Times are not adjusted for Daylight Saving Time.
Heights are referred to the Canadian chart datum of soundings.

Quebec, Quebec, 2017

Times and Heights of High and Low Waters

January

Day	Time	ft	cm	Day	Time	ft	cm
1 Su	0345	0.7	20	16 M	0427	0.7	20
	0809	14.4	440		0854	15.7	480
	1536	1.0	30		1630	1.0	30
	2015	17.1	520		2106	17.1	520
2 M	0421	0.7	20	17 Tu	0509	0.7	20
	0848	14.4	440		0936	15.1	460
	1615	1.0	30		1712	1.0	30
	2054	16.7	510		2151	16.1	490
3 Tu	0500	0.7	20	18 W	0545	1.0	30
	0930	14.4	440		1024	14.4	440
	1700	0.7	20		1757	1.3	40
	2139	16.1	490		2242	14.4	440
4 W	0542	0.7	20	19 Th	0624	1.0	30
	1012	14.4	440		1118	14.1	430
	1751	1.0	30		1845	1.6	50
	2230	15.1	460		2339	13.5	410
5 Th	0627	0.7	20	20 F	0706	1.6	50
	1109	14.4	440		1215	13.8	420
	1848	1.0	30		1945	2.0	60
	2330	14.4	440				
6 F	0718	0.7	20	21 Sa	0042	12.5	380
	1209	14.4	440		0751	2.0	60
	1954	1.0	30		1321	13.8	420
					2051	2.0	60
7 Sa	0039	14.1	430	22 Su	0154	11.8	360
	0821	0.7	20		0851	2.3	70
	1318	14.8	450		1427	13.8	420
	2109	0.7	20		2203	2.0	60
8 Su	0151	13.8	420	23 M	0306	12.1	370
	0924	0.7	20		0957	2.3	70
	1421	15.7	480		1524	13.8	420
	2224	0.3	10		2306	1.6	50
9 M	0303	13.8	420	24 Tu	0409	12.5	380
	1030	0.7	20		1100	2.0	60
	1527	16.4	500		1618	14.8	450
	2333	0.3	10				
10 Tu	0406	14.1	430	25 W	0006	1.0	30
	1130	0.7	20		0500	13.1	400
	1624	17.4	530		1154	1.6	50
					1703	15.4	470
11 W	0036	0.3	10	26 Th	0054	1.0	30
	0506	14.4	440		0539	13.8	420
	1230	0.3	10		1242	1.3	40
	1718	18.0	550		1739	16.4	500
12 Th	0130	0.3	10	27 F	0136	1.0	30
	0557	14.8	450		0612	14.1	430
	1324	0.7	20		1324	1.0	30
	1806	18.4	560		1815	17.1	520
13 F	0221	0.3	10	28 Sa	0215	0.7	20
	0642	15.4	470		0645	14.4	440
	1415	0.7	20		1406	1.0	30
	1854	18.4	560		1848	17.4	530
14 Sa	0306	0.7	20	29 Su	0248	1.0	30
	0727	15.7	480		0715	15.1	460
	1503	0.7	20		1445	0.7	20
	1936	18.4	560		1921	17.4	530
15 Su	0348	0.7	20	30 M	0324	0.7	20
	0809	15.7	480		0748	15.4	470
	1548	1.0	30		1527	0.7	20
	2021	17.7	540		1957	17.4	530
				31 Tu	0400	0.7	20
					0824	15.7	480
					1609	0.7	20
					2036	17.4	530

February

Day	Time	ft	cm	Day	Time	ft	cm
1 W	0439	0.7	20	16 Th	0506	0.7	20
	0903	16.1	490		0942	15.1	460
	1651	0.7	20		1727	0.7	20
	2118	16.7	510		2203	14.4	440
2 Th	0521	0.7	20	17 F	0539	1.0	30
	0948	15.7	480		1024	14.4	440
	1739	1.0	30		1806	1.3	40
	2209	15.4	470		2251	13.5	410
3 F	0603	0.7	20	18 Sa	0609	1.3	40
	1039	15.4	470		1115	13.8	420
	1833	0.7	20		1851	1.6	50
	2306	14.4	440		2345	12.1	370
4 Sa	0651	0.7	20	19 Su	0645	2.0	60
	1139	15.1	460		1212	13.5	410
	1936	0.7	20		1948	2.3	70
5 Su	0012	13.8	420	20 M	0054	11.5	350
	0748	1.0	30		0736	2.6	80
	1245	15.1	460		1321	13.1	400
	2048	0.7	20		2100	2.3	70
6 M	0130	13.1	400	21 Tu	0215	11.2	340
	0854	1.0	30		0851	2.6	80
	1400	15.1	460		1433	13.5	410
	2203	0.7	20		2218	1.6	50
7 Tu	0248	13.1	400	22 W	0327	11.8	360
	1006	1.0	30		1012	2.3	70
	1512	16.1	490		1536	13.8	420
	2318	0.7	20		2324	1.3	40
8 W	0400	13.8	420	23 Th	0424	12.8	390
	1118	0.7	20		1118	1.6	50
	1615	16.7	510		1627	14.8	450
9 Th	0021	0.3	10	24 F	0021	0.7	20
	0500	14.1	430		0509	13.5	410
	1218	0.7	20		1215	1.3	40
	1712	17.4	530		1712	16.1	490
10 F	0115	0.3	10	25 Sa	0106	0.7	20
	0548	14.8	450		0545	14.1	430
	1315	0.3	10		1303	0.7	20
	1800	17.7	540		1751	16.7	510
11 Sa	0203	0.3	10	26 Su	0145	0.7	20
	0633	15.4	470		0621	15.1	460
	1403	0.7	20		1348	0.7	20
	1842	17.7	540		1824	17.4	530
12 Su	0248	0.3	10	27 M	0224	0.7	20
	0712	16.1	490		0648	16.1	490
	1448	0.7	20		1430	0.7	20
	1921	17.7	540		1900	17.7	540
13 M	0324	0.3	10	28 Tu	0300	0.3	10
	0748	16.1	490		0721	16.4	500
	1530	0.7	20		1512	0.3	10
	2000	17.1	520		1936	17.7	540
14 Tu	0400	0.7	20				
	0824	16.1	490				
	1609	0.7	20				
	2039	16.7	510				
15 W	0436	0.7	20				
	0903	15.7	480				
	1648	0.7	20				
	2121	15.7	480				

March

Day	Time	ft	cm	Day	Time	ft	cm
1 W	0339	0.3	10	16 Th	0400	1.0	30
	0757	17.1	520		0827	16.7	510
	1554	0.3	10		1621	0.7	20
	2015	17.4	530		2048	15.4	470
2 Th	0415	0.3	10	17 F	0427	1.0	30
	0836	17.1	520		0903	16.4	500
	1639	0.3	10		1654	1.0	30
	2100	16.7	510		2127	14.4	440
3 F	0454	0.7	20	18 Sa	0454	1.3	40
	0924	17.1	520		0942	15.4	470
	1724	0.7	20		1730	1.3	40
	2151	15.7	480		2209	13.8	420
4 Sa	0536	0.7	20	19 Su	0524	1.6	50
	1012	16.4	500		1024	14.8	450
	1815	0.7	20		1803	1.6	50
	2245	14.4	440		2300	12.8	390
5 Su	0624	0.7	20	20 M	0554	2.3	70
	1112	15.7	480		1118	14.1	430
	1918	0.7	20		1857	2.3	70
	2357	13.8	420				
6 M	0718	1.3	40	21 Tu	0003	11.8	360
	1224	15.1	460		0639	3.0	90
	2027	1.0	30		1221	13.5	410
					1957	2.6	80
7 Tu	0118	13.1	400	22 W	0115	11.5	350
	0830	1.6	50		0739	3.3	100
	1342	15.1	460		1336	13.5	410
	2145	1.0	30		2118	2.3	70
8 W	0239	13.1	400	23 Th	0242	12.1	370
	0948	1.6	50		0918	3.0	90
	1500	15.4	470		1448	14.1	430
	2300	0.7	20		2233	1.6	50
9 Th	0351	14.1	430	24 F	0345	13.1	400
	1106	1.3	40		1039	2.3	70
	1609	16.4	500		1548	14.8	450
					2336	1.0	30
10 F	0003	1.0	30	25 Sa	0433	14.1	430
	0448	14.4	440		1142	1.3	40
	1209	1.0	30		1639	16.1	490
	1706	16.7	510				
11 Sa	0057	0.7	20	26 Su	0027	0.7	20
	0536	15.4	470		0509	15.1	460
	1303	1.0	30		1236	1.0	30
	1751	17.1	520		1718	16.7	510
12 Su	0139	1.0	30	27 M	0112	0.7	20
	0618	16.1	490		0545	16.4	500
	1351	0.7	20		1327	0.7	20
	1830	17.4	530		1757	17.7	540
13 M	0218	1.0	30	28 Tu	0151	1.0	30
	0651	16.7	510		0618	17.4	530
	1433	0.7	20		1412	0.7	20
	1906	17.4	530		1833	18.0	550
14 Tu	0254	1.0	30	29 W	0233	1.0	30
	0724	16.7	510		0651	18.0	550
	1512	0.7	20		1457	1.0	30
	1939	17.1	520		1912	18.0	550
15 W	0327	1.0	30	30 Th	0312	1.0	30
	0754	16.7	510		0727	18.7	570
	1548	1.0	30		1542	1.0	30
	2015	16.4	500		1954	17.7	540
				31 F	0351	1.3	40
					0809	18.7	570
					1627	1.0	30
					2039	17.1	520

Time meridian 75° W. 0000 is midnight. 1200 is noon. Times are not adjusted for Daylight Saving Time.
Heights are referred to the Canadian chart datum of soundings.

Quebec, Quebec, 2017
Times and Heights of High and Low Waters

April

Day	Time	ft	cm	Day	Time	ft	cm
1 Sa	0433	1.3	40	16 Su	0421	2.0	60
	0857	18.4	560		0903	16.7	510
	1715	1.3	40		1706	1.6	50
	2130	16.1	490		2136	14.4	440
2 Su	0515	1.3	40	17 M	0451	2.3	70
	0948	17.7	540		0942	15.7	480
	1806	1.3	40		1739	2.0	60
	2227	14.8	450		2224	13.8	420
3 M	0603	1.6	50	18 Tu	0524	3.0	90
	1051	16.7	510		1033	14.8	450
	1906	1.6	50		1821	2.3	70
	2342	14.1	430		2318	13.1	400
4 Tu	0700	2.3	70	19 W	0606	3.3	100
	1203	15.7	480		1133	14.4	440
	2012	1.6	50		1918	2.6	80
5 W	0103	13.8	420	20 Th	0027	12.8	390
	0815	2.6	80		0715	3.6	110
	1327	15.4	470		1239	14.1	430
	2127	1.6	50		2033	2.6	80
6 Th	0224	14.1	430	21 F	0142	13.1	400
	0939	2.3	70		0839	3.6	110
	1445	15.4	470		1351	14.4	440
	2236	1.3	40		2145	2.3	70
7 F	0336	14.8	450	22 Sa	0248	14.1	430
	1054	2.0	60		1003	2.6	80
	1554	15.7	480		1457	15.1	460
	2339	1.3	40		2251	1.6	50
8 Sa	0430	15.4	470	23 Su	0339	14.8	450
	1157	1.6	50		1112	2.0	60
	1648	16.4	500		1554	15.7	480
					2345	1.6	50
9 Su	0030	1.3	40	24 M	0424	16.4	500
	0515	16.4	500		1212	1.6	50
	1251	1.3	40		1642	17.1	520
	1733	16.7	510				
10 M	0112	1.3	40	25 Tu	0036	1.3	40
	0554	17.1	520		0506	17.7	540
	1336	1.3	40		1306	1.3	40
	1812	16.7	510		1727	17.4	530
11 Tu	0151	1.3	40	26 W	0121	1.3	40
	0627	17.4	530		0542	18.7	570
	1415	1.3	40		1354	1.0	30
	1845	16.7	510		1809	17.7	540
12 W	0224	1.3	40	27 Th	0203	1.3	40
	0657	17.4	530		0621	19.4	590
	1451	1.0	30		1442	1.0	30
	1918	16.4	500		1854	17.7	540
13 Th	0254	1.3	40	28 F	0245	1.3	40
	0727	17.7	540		0703	19.7	600
	1527	1.0	30		1530	1.0	30
	1948	16.1	490		1936	17.4	530
14 F	0324	1.3	40	29 Sa	0327	1.3	40
	0754	17.4	530		0748	19.7	600
	1557	1.3	40		1615	1.3	40
	2018	15.7	480		2024	16.7	510
15 Sa	0354	1.6	50	30 Su	0412	1.3	40
	0827	17.1	520		0839	19.0	580
	1630	1.6	50		1703	1.3	40
	2054	15.1	460		2118	16.1	490

May

Day	Time	ft	cm	Day	Time	ft	cm
1 M	0454	1.6	50	16 Tu	0427	2.3	70
	0936	18.0	550		0921	16.4	500
	1751	1.3	40		1718	1.6	50
	2218	15.1	460		2200	14.1	430
2 Tu	0545	2.0	60	17 W	0506	2.6	80
	1039	17.1	520		1006	15.4	470
	1851	1.6	50		1800	2.0	60
	2333	14.8	450		2251	13.8	420
3 W	0645	2.6	80	18 Th	0551	3.0	90
	1151	16.1	490		1100	14.8	450
	1954	1.6	50		1851	2.0	60
					2354	13.5	410
4 Th	0048	14.4	440	19 F	0651	3.0	90
	0800	2.6	80		1200	14.4	440
	1309	15.4	470		1951	2.0	60
	2100	1.6	50				
5 F	0206	14.8	450	20 Sa	0100	13.8	420
	0921	2.6	80		0809	3.0	90
	1424	15.1	460		1309	14.4	440
	2206	1.6	50		2057	2.0	60
6 Sa	0306	15.1	460	21 Su	0200	14.4	440
	1033	2.3	70		0927	2.3	70
	1530	15.4	470		1415	14.8	450
	2306	1.6	50		2203	1.6	50
7 Su	0403	15.7	480	22 M	0257	15.4	470
	1139	2.0	60		1039	1.3	40
	1627	15.4	470		1518	15.4	470
	2357	1.6	50		2303	1.3	40
8 M	0451	16.7	510	23 Tu	0348	16.7	510
	1233	1.6	50		1145	1.0	30
	1712	15.7	480		1615	15.7	480
					2354	1.3	40
9 Tu	0039	1.6	50	24 W	0433	18.0	550
	0530	17.4	530		1242	0.7	20
	1315	1.6	50		1706	16.4	500
	1751	15.7	480				
10 W	0118	1.6	50	25 Th	0045	1.0	30
	0603	17.4	530		0518	19.0	580
	1357	1.3	40		1336	1.0	30
	1824	15.7	480		1751	16.7	510
11 Th	0151	1.6	50	26 F	0133	1.0	30
	0633	17.7	540		0603	19.7	600
	1430	1.3	40		1427	1.0	30
	1857	15.7	480		1839	17.1	520
12 F	0224	1.6	50	27 Sa	0221	1.3	40
	0703	17.7	540		0648	20.0	610
	1503	1.3	40		1515	1.0	30
	1927	15.4	470		1927	16.7	510
13 Sa	0254	1.6	50	28 Su	0306	1.3	40
	0733	17.7	540		0736	20.0	610
	1536	1.6	40		1603	1.0	30
	2000	15.4	470		2015	16.4	500
14 Su	0324	1.6	50	29 M	0354	1.3	40
	0803	17.4	530		0827	19.4	590
	1609	1.6	50		1648	1.3	40
	2033	14.8	450		2109	16.1	490
15 M	0354	2.0	60	30 Tu	0442	1.6	50
	0839	17.1	520		0924	18.4	560
	1642	1.6	50		1739	1.3	40
	2115	14.8	450		2206	15.4	470
				31 W	0533	1.6	50
					1024	17.4	530
					1830	1.3	40
					2315	14.8	450

June

Day	Time	ft	cm	Day	Time	ft	cm
1 Th	0630	2.3	70	16 F	0539	2.0	60
	1133	16.1	490		1033	15.4	470
	1927	1.3	40		1827	1.3	40
					2321	14.4	440
2 F	0021	14.4	440	17 Sa	0636	2.3	70
	0736	2.3	70		1130	14.8	450
	1242	15.1	460		1921	1.3	40
	2024	1.6	50				
3 Sa	0130	14.8	450	18 Su	0018	14.1	430
	0851	2.3	70		0742	2.0	60
	1351	14.4	440		1233	14.4	440
	2127	1.6	50		2018	1.3	40
4 Su	0236	15.1	460	19 M	0115	14.8	450
	1003	2.0	60		0857	1.6	50
	1500	14.4	440		1339	14.1	430
	2224	1.6	50		2121	1.0	30
5 M	0330	15.4	470	20 Tu	0215	15.4	470
	1109	1.6	50		1012	1.0	30
	1600	14.4	440		1448	14.4	440
	2318	1.6	50		2221	1.0	30
6 Tu	0421	16.1	490	21 W	0315	16.7	510
	1206	1.3	40		1118	0.7	20
	1651	14.4	440		1548	14.8	450
					2321	1.0	30
7 W	0003	1.6	50	22 Th	0406	17.7	540
	0503	16.7	510		1221	0.7	20
	1254	1.3	40		1645	15.1	460
	1733	14.4	440				
8 Th	0045	1.6	50	23 F	0018	0.7	20
	0539	17.1	520		0457	18.7	570
	1333	1.3	40		1318	0.7	20
	1809	14.8	450		1739	15.7	480
9 F	0121	1.6	50	24 Sa	0112	0.7	20
	0612	17.4	530		0548	19.4	590
	1409	1.3	40		1412	0.7	20
	1842	14.8	450		1827	16.1	490
10 Sa	0157	1.6	50	25 Su	0203	1.0	30
	0645	17.4	530		0636	19.7	600
	1442	1.3	40		1500	0.7	20
	1915	14.8	450		1918	16.1	490
11 Su	0230	1.6	50	26 M	0251	1.0	30
	0715	17.4	530		0727	19.4	590
	1515	1.3	40		1548	0.7	20
	1945	14.8	450		2006	16.1	490
12 M	0303	1.6	50	27 Tu	0342	1.0	30
	0748	17.4	530		0818	19.0	580
	1548	1.3	40		1633	0.7	20
	2018	14.8	450		2057	16.1	490
13 Tu	0336	1.6	50	28 W	0430	1.0	30
	0821	17.1	520		0909	18.0	550
	1624	1.3	40		1718	1.0	30
	2057	14.4	440		2151	15.4	470
14 W	0412	1.6	50	29 Th	0518	1.3	40
	0900	16.7	510		1006	17.1	520
	1700	1.0	30		1806	1.0	30
	2139	14.4	440		2248	15.1	460
15 Th	0451	2.0	60	30 F	0612	1.6	50
	0945	16.1	490		1103	15.4	470
	1742	1.3	40		1851	1.0	30
	2224	14.4	440		2348	14.8	450

Time meridian 75° W. 0000 is midnight. 1200 is noon. Times are not adjusted for Daylight Saving Time.
Heights are referred to the Canadian chart datum of soundings.

Quebec, Quebec, 2017

Times and Heights of High and Low Waters

July

Day	Time	Height (ft)	Height (cm)
1 Sa	0709	2.0	60
	1206	14.4	440
	1942	1.3	40
2 Su	0051	14.4	440
	0815	2.0	60
	1315	13.8	420
	2036	1.6	50
3 M	0151	14.4	440
	0924	1.6	50
	1424	13.1	400
	2136	1.6	50
4 Tu	0251	14.8	450
	1030	1.6	50
	1530	13.1	400
	2230	2.0	60
5 W	0345	15.1	460
	1130	1.3	40
	1624	13.5	410
	2324	1.6	50
6 Th	0433	15.4	470
	1224	1.0	30
	1712	13.8	420
7 F	0012	1.6	50
	0515	16.1	490
	1309	1.0	30
	1754	14.1	430
8 Sa ○	0054	1.3	40
	0554	16.7	510
	1348	0.7	20
	1827	14.4	440
9 Su	0133	1.3	40
	0624	17.1	520
	1424	1.0	30
	1900	14.4	440
10 M	0209	1.3	40
	0657	17.1	520
	1457	1.0	30
	1930	14.4	440
11 Tu	0245	1.3	40
	0730	17.4	530
	1533	1.0	30
	2003	14.8	450
12 W	0324	1.0	30
	0803	17.1	520
	1609	0.7	20
	2036	14.8	450
13 Th	0400	1.0	30
	0842	16.7	510
	1642	0.7	20
	2115	14.8	450
14 F	0442	1.0	30
	0921	16.4	500
	1721	0.7	20
	2157	14.8	450
15 Sa	0527	1.3	40
	1009	15.4	470
	1803	0.7	20
	2245	14.8	450
16 Su ☽	0618	1.3	40
	1100	14.8	450
	1851	0.7	20
	2339	14.8	450
17 M	0721	1.3	40
	1203	14.1	430
	1942	1.0	30
18 Tu	0039	15.1	460
	0830	1.3	40
	1312	14.1	430
	2045	1.0	30
19 W	0145	15.7	480
	0945	1.0	30
	1424	13.8	420
	2151	1.0	30
20 Th	0248	16.4	500
	1057	0.7	20
	1533	14.1	430
	2257	1.0	30
21 F	0348	17.4	530
	1206	0.7	20
	1633	14.1	430
	2357	0.7	20
22 Sa	0448	18.0	550
	1303	0.7	20
	1727	14.8	450
23 Su ●	0057	0.7	20
	0539	18.7	570
	1357	0.7	20
	1821	15.4	470
24 M	0151	0.7	20
	0630	19.0	580
	1445	0.7	20
	1906	16.1	490
25 Tu	0242	0.7	20
	0715	18.7	570
	1530	0.7	20
	1951	16.4	500
26 W	0327	1.0	30
	0803	18.4	560
	1612	0.7	20
	2039	16.1	490
27 Th	0415	0.7	20
	0848	17.7	540
	1651	0.7	20
	2124	16.1	490
28 F	0500	1.0	30
	0936	16.7	510
	1733	0.7	20
	2212	15.4	470
29 Sa	0545	1.0	30
	1027	15.1	460
	1812	1.0	30
	2303	14.8	450
30 Su ☾	0633	1.3	40
	1124	14.1	430
	1851	1.3	40
31 M	0000	14.4	440
	0730	1.6	50
	1227	13.1	400
	1936	1.6	50

August

Day	Time	Height (ft)	Height (cm)
1 Tu	0100	14.4	440
	0836	2.0	60
	1333	12.1	370
	2036	2.3	70
2 W	0206	14.1	430
	0948	2.0	60
	1448	12.1	370
	2139	2.3	70
3 Th	0306	14.1	430
	1054	1.3	40
	1551	12.5	380
	2242	2.0	60
4 F	0400	14.8	450
	1151	1.0	30
	1645	12.8	390
	2339	1.6	50
5 Sa	0448	15.4	470
	1242	1.0	30
	1730	13.5	410
6 Su	0027	1.3	40
	0530	16.1	490
	1327	0.7	20
	1806	14.1	430
7 M ○	0112	1.3	40
	0606	16.7	510
	1400	0.7	20
	1839	14.4	440
8 Tu	0151	1.0	30
	0639	17.1	520
	1436	0.7	20
	1909	14.8	450
9 W	0227	1.0	30
	0709	17.4	530
	1512	0.7	20
	1939	15.1	460
10 Th	0309	0.7	20
	0745	17.4	530
	1545	0.3	10
	2012	15.4	470
11 F	0348	0.7	20
	0818	17.1	520
	1621	0.3	10
	2048	15.7	480
12 Sa	0430	0.7	20
	0900	16.4	500
	1657	0.3	10
	2127	15.7	480
13 Su	0515	0.7	20
	0942	15.7	480
	1736	0.7	20
	2212	15.7	480
14 M ☽	0606	1.0	30
	1036	14.8	450
	1821	0.7	20
	2306	15.4	470
15 Tu	0703	1.0	30
	1136	14.1	430
	1915	1.0	30
16 W	0012	15.4	470
	0809	1.0	30
	1251	13.5	410
	2015	1.3	40
17 Th	0121	15.4	470
	0927	1.0	30
	1409	13.1	400
	2127	1.3	40
18 F	0233	16.1	490
	1042	0.7	20
	1521	13.5	410
	2239	1.0	30
19 Sa	0342	16.7	510
	1148	0.7	20
	1627	13.8	420
	2345	0.7	20
20 Su	0442	17.4	530
	1248	0.3	10
	1724	14.8	450
21 M ●	0048	0.7	20
	0533	17.7	540
	1339	0.3	10
	1809	15.4	470
22 Tu	0139	0.7	20
	0621	18.0	550
	1424	0.3	10
	1854	16.1	490
23 W	0227	0.7	20
	0703	18.0	550
	1506	0.3	10
	1933	16.4	500
24 Th	0312	0.7	20
	0745	17.7	540
	1545	0.7	20
	2012	16.4	500
25 F	0354	0.7	20
	0824	17.1	520
	1621	0.7	20
	2051	16.4	500
26 Sa	0436	0.7	20
	0906	16.1	490
	1654	0.7	20
	2133	16.1	490
27 Su	0515	1.0	30
	0951	14.8	450
	1727	1.0	30
	2215	15.1	460
28 M	0554	1.3	40
	1039	13.8	420
	1800	1.3	40
	2306	14.4	440
29 Tu ☾	0639	1.6	50
	1136	12.8	390
	1836	2.0	60
30 W	0003	14.1	430
	0739	2.3	70
	1239	11.8	360
	1927	2.6	80
31 Th	0109	13.8	420
	0851	2.3	70
	1400	11.5	350
	2033	3.0	90

September

Day	Time	Height (ft)	Height (cm)
1 F	0218	13.8	420
	1006	2.0	60
	1512	11.8	360
	2157	2.6	80
2 Sa	0321	14.1	430
	1112	1.3	40
	1612	12.5	380
	2303	2.0	60
3 Su	0415	14.8	450
	1206	1.0	30
	1657	13.5	410
4 M	0000	1.6	50
	0500	15.7	480
	1254	0.7	20
	1736	14.1	430
5 Tu	0048	1.0	30
	0539	16.4	500
	1333	0.7	20
	1809	14.8	450
6 W	0130	1.0	30
	0612	17.1	520
	1409	0.7	20
	1839	15.7	480
7 Th	0212	0.7	20
	0645	17.4	530
	1442	0.7	20
	1909	16.1	490
8 F	0251	0.7	20
	0721	17.4	530
	1518	0.7	20
	1942	16.7	510
9 Sa	0333	0.7	20
	0754	17.1	520
	1554	0.7	20
	2015	17.1	520
10 Su	0415	0.7	20
	0836	16.7	510
	1630	0.7	20
	2057	17.1	520
11 M	0500	1.0	30
	0918	16.1	490
	1712	1.0	30
	2142	16.7	510
12 Tu	0548	1.0	30
	1012	14.8	450
	1754	1.0	30
	2239	16.4	500
13 W ☽	0645	1.3	40
	1118	14.1	430
	1845	1.6	50
	2348	15.7	480
14 Th	0751	1.3	40
	1236	13.5	410
	1951	2.0	60
15 F	0103	15.4	470
	0909	1.0	30
	1400	13.1	400
	2109	1.6	50
16 Sa	0221	15.7	480
	1027	1.0	30
	1515	13.8	420
	2230	1.3	40
17 Su	0333	16.4	500
	1133	1.0	30
	1615	14.4	440
	2339	1.0	30
18 M	0436	16.7	510
	1230	0.7	20
	1709	15.4	470
19 Tu	0039	1.0	30
	0524	17.4	530
	1318	0.7	20
	1754	16.4	500
20 W ●	0130	1.0	30
	0609	17.4	530
	1400	0.7	20
	1833	16.7	510
21 Th	0215	0.7	20
	0645	17.4	530
	1439	0.7	20
	1909	17.1	520
22 F	0254	0.7	20
	0724	17.1	520
	1512	1.0	30
	1942	17.1	520
23 Sa	0333	0.7	20
	0757	16.4	500
	1545	0.7	20
	2015	16.7	510
24 Su	0409	1.0	30
	0836	15.4	470
	1612	1.0	30
	2051	16.4	500
25 M	0445	1.0	30
	0915	14.4	440
	1642	1.0	30
	2133	15.7	480
26 Tu	0521	1.3	40
	1000	13.8	420
	1712	1.6	50
	2215	14.8	450
27 W ☾	0557	1.6	50
	1051	12.8	390
	1745	2.3	70
	2309	14.4	440
28 Th	0645	2.3	70
	1151	11.8	360
	1827	3.0	90
29 F	0012	13.8	420
	0748	2.6	80
	1309	11.5	350
	1921	3.3	100
30 Sa	0127	13.5	410
	0909	2.3	70
	1427	11.8	360
	2057	3.0	90

Time meridian 75° W. 0000 is midnight. 1200 is noon. Times are not adjusted for Daylight Saving Time. Heights are referred to the Canadian chart datum of soundings.

Quebec, Quebec, 2017

Times and Heights of High and Low Waters

October

Day	Time (h m)	Height (ft)	Height (cm)
1 Su	0236	13.8	420
	1024	1.6	50
	1530	12.8	390
	2224	2.3	70
2 M	0336	14.4	440
	1121	1.3	40
	1621	13.8	420
	2327	1.6	50
3 Tu	0424	15.1	460
	1212	1.0	30
	1700	14.4	440
4 W	0021	1.0	30
	0506	16.1	490
	1254	1.0	30
	1733	15.7	480
5 Th ○	0106	1.0	30
	0542	16.7	510
	1333	0.7	20
	1803	16.7	510
6 F	0151	0.7	20
	0618	17.1	520
	1409	0.7	20
	1836	17.4	530
7 Sa	0233	0.7	20
	0657	17.4	530
	1445	0.7	20
	1909	17.7	540
8 Su	0315	0.7	20
	0733	17.1	520
	1524	0.7	20
	1948	18.0	550
9 M	0400	0.7	20
	0815	16.4	500
	1606	0.7	20
	2033	17.7	540
10 Tu	0445	0.7	20
	0906	15.4	470
	1645	1.0	30
	2124	17.4	530
11 W	0536	1.0	30
	1000	14.4	440
	1730	1.0	30
	2224	16.7	510
12 Th ◐	0633	1.0	30
	1109	13.8	420
	1827	1.6	50
	2333	15.7	480
13 F	0736	1.0	30
	1230	13.5	410
	1936	2.0	60
14 Sa	0054	15.1	460
	0851	1.0	30
	1354	13.5	410
	2100	2.0	60
15 Su	0212	15.1	460
	1006	1.0	30
	1506	14.4	440
	2218	1.6	50
16 M	0327	15.4	470
	1109	1.0	30
	1606	14.8	450
	2327	1.0	30
17 Tu	0424	16.1	490
	1203	1.0	30
	1654	16.1	490
18 W	0024	1.0	30
	0512	16.4	500
	1251	1.0	30
	1736	16.7	510
19 Th ●	0115	1.0	30
	0554	16.4	500
	1330	1.0	30
	1812	17.1	520
20 F	0157	1.0	30
	0630	16.4	500
	1406	1.0	30
	1845	17.4	530
21 Sa	0233	1.0	30
	0703	16.1	490
	1439	1.0	30
	1915	17.4	530
22 Su	0312	0.7	20
	0736	15.7	480
	1509	1.0	30
	1945	17.1	520
23 M	0345	1.0	30
	0809	15.1	460
	1539	1.0	30
	2021	16.7	510
24 Tu	0418	1.0	30
	0845	14.4	440
	1606	1.3	40
	2057	16.1	490
25 W	0451	1.0	30
	0927	13.8	420
	1636	1.6	50
	2136	15.1	460
26 Th	0524	1.6	50
	1015	13.1	400
	1709	2.3	70
	2224	14.4	440
27 F ◑	0606	2.0	60
	1112	12.5	380
	1751	3.0	90
	2324	14.1	430
28 Sa	0703	2.3	70
	1221	11.8	360
	1848	3.3	100
29 Su	0030	13.5	410
	0812	2.3	70
	1333	12.1	370
	2012	3.0	90
30 M	0145	13.8	420
	0924	2.3	70
	1442	12.8	390
	2139	2.3	70
31 Tu	0245	13.8	420
	1027	1.3	40
	1536	14.1	430
	2248	1.6	50

November

Day	Time (h m)	Height (ft)	Height (cm)
1 W	0345	14.8	450
	1124	1.0	30
	1618	14.8	450
	2348	0.7	20
2 Th	0433	15.7	480
	1209	0.7	20
	1654	16.1	490
3 F	0042	0.7	20
	0515	16.1	490
	1254	0.7	20
	1730	17.4	530
4 Sa ○	0130	0.3	10
	0554	16.4	500
	1336	0.7	20
	1806	18.0	550
5 Su	0215	0.3	10
	0633	16.7	510
	1418	0.7	20
	1845	18.7	570
6 M	0300	0.3	10
	0718	16.4	500
	1500	0.7	20
	1927	18.7	570
7 Tu	0348	0.7	20
	0803	16.1	490
	1545	0.7	20
	2015	18.4	560
8 W	0433	0.7	20
	0854	15.1	460
	1627	1.0	30
	2109	17.7	540
9 Th	0524	0.7	20
	0951	14.4	440
	1715	1.0	30
	2212	16.7	510
10 F ○	0618	1.0	30
	1100	14.1	430
	1815	1.6	50
	2321	16.1	490
11 Sa	0721	1.0	30
	1218	13.8	420
	1924	2.0	60
12 Su	0036	15.1	460
	0830	1.0	30
	1333	14.1	430
	2045	2.0	60
13 M	0154	14.8	450
	0936	1.0	30
	1442	14.4	440
	2200	1.3	40
14 Tu	0306	14.8	450
	1039	1.0	30
	1545	15.1	460
	2312	1.0	30
15 W	0406	14.8	450
	1133	1.0	30
	1633	16.1	490
16 Th	0006	1.0	30
	0457	15.1	460
	1218	0.7	20
	1715	16.7	510
17 F	0054	0.7	20
	0539	15.1	460
	1257	1.0	30
	1751	16.7	510
18 Sa ●	0139	0.7	20
	0615	15.1	460
	1333	1.0	30
	1824	17.1	520
19 Su	0215	0.7	20
	0648	14.8	450
	1409	1.0	30
	1854	17.1	520
20 M	0251	0.7	20
	0721	14.8	450
	1442	1.0	30
	1924	17.1	520
21 Tu	0321	0.7	20
	0751	14.4	440
	1512	1.0	30
	1957	16.7	510
22 W	0354	1.0	30
	0827	14.1	430
	1542	1.3	40
	2030	16.4	500
23 Th	0430	1.0	30
	0903	13.8	420
	1612	1.6	50
	2109	15.7	480
24 F	0503	1.0	30
	0948	13.5	410
	1648	2.0	60
	2154	14.8	450
25 Sa	0542	1.3	40
	1039	12.8	390
	1730	2.3	70
	2245	14.1	430
26 Su ◑	0627	1.6	50
	1136	12.8	390
	1824	2.6	80
	2342	14.1	430
27 M	0727	1.6	50
	1239	12.8	390
	1936	2.6	80
28 Tu	0051	13.8	420
	0830	1.6	50
	1342	13.5	410
	2057	2.0	60
29 W	0200	13.8	420
	0936	1.3	40
	1439	14.1	430
	2209	1.3	40
30 Th	0300	14.1	430
	1036	1.0	30
	1530	15.1	460
	2318	0.7	20

December

Day	Time (h m)	Height (ft)	Height (cm)
1 F	0357	14.8	450
	1130	0.7	20
	1615	16.4	500
2 Sa	0015	0.3	10
	0445	15.1	460
	1221	0.7	20
	1700	17.7	540
3 Su ○	0109	0.3	10
	0530	15.7	480
	1309	0.7	20
	1742	18.7	570
4 M	0200	0.3	10
	0615	15.7	480
	1357	0.7	20
	1824	19.0	580
5 Tu	0248	0.3	10
	0703	15.7	480
	1442	0.7	20
	1912	19.0	580
6 W	0336	0.3	10
	0751	15.7	480
	1530	0.7	20
	2003	18.7	570
7 Th	0424	0.7	20
	0842	15.1	460
	1615	0.7	20
	2057	18.0	550
8 F	0512	0.7	20
	0942	14.8	450
	1706	1.0	30
	2157	17.1	520
9 Sa	0606	0.7	20
	1045	14.4	440
	1803	1.3	40
	2303	16.1	490
10 Su ○	0700	0.7	20
	1154	14.1	430
	1906	1.6	50
11 M	0012	14.8	450
	0757	1.0	30
	1303	14.1	430
	2018	1.6	50
12 Tu	0127	14.1	430
	0900	1.0	30
	1412	14.4	440
	2133	1.3	40
13 W	0239	14.1	430
	1000	1.0	30
	1512	14.8	450
	2245	1.0	30
14 Th	0342	13.8	420
	1057	1.0	30
	1603	15.4	470
	2345	0.7	20
15 F	0436	14.1	430
	1145	1.0	30
	1648	16.1	490
16 Sa	0033	0.7	20
	0521	14.1	430
	1230	1.0	30
	1727	16.4	500
17 Su	0118	0.7	20
	0557	14.1	430
	1309	1.0	30
	1803	16.4	500
18 M ●	0157	0.7	20
	0633	14.1	430
	1345	1.0	30
	1836	16.7	510
19 Tu	0233	0.7	20
	0706	14.1	430
	1421	1.0	30
	1906	16.7	510
20 W	0306	0.7	20
	0736	14.1	430
	1451	1.0	30
	1936	16.7	510
21 Th	0339	0.7	20
	0809	14.1	430
	1527	1.0	30
	2012	16.4	500
22 F	0412	0.7	20
	0842	13.8	420
	1600	1.0	30
	2048	16.1	490
23 Sa	0445	1.0	30
	0918	13.8	420
	1636	1.3	40
	2127	15.7	480
24 Su	0524	0.7	20
	1006	13.8	420
	1718	1.6	50
	2212	14.8	450
25 M	0603	1.0	30
	1051	13.5	410
	1809	1.6	50
	2303	14.1	430
26 Tu ◑	0651	1.0	30
	1148	13.5	410
	1909	1.6	50
27 W	0003	14.1	430
	0748	1.3	40
	1248	13.8	420
	2021	1.6	50
28 Th	0112	13.8	420
	0848	1.0	30
	1348	14.1	430
	2136	1.0	30
29 F	0218	13.8	420
	0951	1.0	30
	1448	15.1	460
	2248	0.7	20
30 Sa	0324	14.1	430
	1054	0.7	20
	1542	16.4	500
	2354	0.3	10
31 Su	0421	14.1	430
	1151	0.7	20
	1636	17.4	530

Time meridian 75° W. 0000 is midnight. 1200 is noon. Times are not adjusted for Daylight Saving Time.
Heights are referred to the Canadian chart datum of soundings.

Halifax, Nova Scotia, 2017
Times and Heights of High and Low Waters

January

Day	Time	ft	cm	Day	Time	ft	cm
1 Su	0353	2.0	60	**16** M	0518	1.6	50
	0944	5.9	180		1040	5.9	180
	1623	1.0	30		1732	1.0	30
	2224	5.6	170		2314	5.9	180
2 M	0440	2.0	60	**17** Tu	0611	1.6	50
	1024	5.9	180		1125	5.6	170
	1707	1.0	30		1819	1.3	40
	2303	5.6	170		2357	5.9	180
3 Tu	0533	2.0	60	**18** W	0704	1.6	50
	1106	5.6	170		1212	5.2	160
	1755	1.0	30		1906	1.6	50
	2344	5.6	170				
4 W	0630	2.0	60	**19** Th ◐	0043	5.6	170
	1151	5.6	170		0756	2.0	60
	1846	1.3	40		1301	4.9	150
					1955	1.6	50
5 Th ◑	0030	5.6	170	**20** F	0132	5.6	170
	0728	1.6	50		0847	2.0	60
	1243	5.2	160		1358	4.6	140
	1939	1.3	40		2045	2.0	60
6 F	0120	5.6	170	**21** Sa	0228	5.2	160
	0827	1.6	50		0937	2.0	60
	1343	5.2	160		1503	4.6	140
	2036	1.3	40		2138	2.0	60
7 Sa	0218	5.6	170	**22** Su	0328	5.2	160
	0927	1.3	40		1026	1.6	50
	1453	5.2	160		1612	4.6	140
	2135	1.3	40		2231	2.3	70
8 Su	0322	5.9	180	**23** M	0426	5.2	160
	1027	1.0	30		1113	1.6	50
	1607	5.2	160		1713	4.9	150
	2237	1.3	40		2321	2.0	60
9 M	0427	6.2	190	**24** Tu	0516	5.2	160
	1127	0.7	20		1157	1.3	40
	1716	5.2	160		1803	4.9	150
	2340	1.3	40				
10 Tu	0529	6.2	190	**25** W	0007	2.0	60
	1227	0.3	10		0602	5.6	170
	1817	5.6	170		1239	1.0	30
					1847	5.2	160
11 W	0042	1.0	30	**26** Th	0048	2.0	60
	0628	6.6	200		0644	5.6	170
	1323	0.0	0		1320	1.0	30
	1914	5.9	180		1927	5.2	160
12 Th ○	0141	1.0	30	**27** F ●	0128	1.6	50
	0723	6.6	200		0724	5.9	180
	1416	0.0	0		1400	0.7	20
	2008	6.2	190		2006	5.6	170
13 F	0237	1.0	30	**28** Sa	0208	1.6	50
	0816	6.6	200		0804	5.9	180
	1507	0.0	0		1440	0.7	20
	2058	6.2	190		2044	5.6	170
14 Sa	0331	1.0	30	**29** Su	0249	1.3	40
	0906	6.6	200		0844	6.2	190
	1556	0.3	10		1519	0.3	10
	2146	6.2	190		2122	5.6	170
15 Su	0425	1.3	40	**30** M	0333	1.3	40
	0954	6.2	190		0925	5.9	180
	1644	0.7	20		1600	0.7	20
	2231	6.2	190		2200	5.9	180
				31 Tu	0420	1.3	40
					1006	5.9	180
					1644	0.7	20
					2240	5.9	180

February

Day	Time	ft	cm	Day	Time	ft	cm
1 W	0513	1.3	40	**16** Th	0616	1.6	50
	1049	5.9	180		1139	5.2	160
	1731	0.7	20		1813	1.6	50
	2321	5.9	180				
2 Th	0609	1.3	40	**17** F	0002	5.6	170
	1135	5.6	170		0704	2.0	60
	1824	1.0	30		1224	4.9	150
					1859	2.0	60
3 F	0005	5.9	180	**18** Sa ○	0047	5.2	160
	0709	1.3	40		0753	2.0	60
	1226	5.2	160		1313	4.9	150
	1922	1.3	40		1952	2.3	70
4 Sa ◐	0055	5.6	170	**19** Su	0137	5.2	160
	0809	1.3	40		0843	2.0	60
	1323	5.2	160		1412	4.6	140
	2023	1.3	40		2049	2.3	70
5 Su	0152	5.6	170	**20** M	0235	4.9	150
	0911	1.0	30		0934	2.0	60
	1432	4.9	150		1524	4.6	140
	2126	1.3	40		2145	2.3	70
6 M	0258	5.6	170	**21** Tu	0339	4.9	150
	1013	1.0	30		1024	1.6	50
	1550	4.9	150		1634	4.6	140
	2230	1.3	40		2239	2.3	70
7 Tu	0410	5.9	180	**22** W	0440	5.2	160
	1114	0.7	20		1114	1.6	50
	1704	5.2	160		1730	4.9	150
	2333	1.3	40		2329	2.0	60
8 W	0518	5.9	180	**23** Th	0531	5.6	170
	1213	0.7	20		1202	1.3	40
	1807	5.6	170		1816	5.2	160
9 Th	0034	1.3	40	**24** F	0015	2.0	60
	0617	6.2	190		0616	5.6	170
	1309	0.3	10		1247	1.0	30
	1902	5.9	180		1857	5.2	160
10 F ○	0130	1.0	30	**25** Sa	0059	1.6	50
	0711	6.2	190		0658	5.9	180
	1400	0.3	10		1330	0.7	20
	1951	6.2	190		1935	5.6	170
11 Sa	0222	1.0	30	**26** Su ●	0142	1.3	40
	0801	6.2	190		0740	6.2	190
	1447	0.3	10		1411	0.3	10
	2037	6.2	190		2014	5.9	180
12 Su	0311	1.0	30	**27** M	0227	1.0	30
	0847	6.2	190		0822	6.2	190
	1532	0.3	10		1452	0.3	10
	2120	6.2	190		2053	5.9	180
13 M	0358	1.3	40	**28** Tu	0313	1.0	30
	0932	6.2	190		0904	6.2	190
	1613	0.7	20		1534	0.3	10
	2201	6.2	190		2133	6.2	190
14 Tu	0443	1.3	40				
	1015	5.9	180				
	1653	1.0	30				
	2241	5.9	180				
15 W	0529	1.6	50				
	1057	5.6	170				
	1732	1.3	40				
	2321	5.9	180				

March

Day	Time	ft	cm	Day	Time	ft	cm
1 W	0402	0.7	20	**16** Th	0445	1.3	40
	0948	5.9	180		1029	5.6	170
	1619	0.3	10		1645	1.6	50
	2215	6.2	190		2244	5.9	180
2 Th	0455	0.7	20	**17** F	0524	1.6	50
	1033	5.9	180		1109	5.2	160
	1710	0.7	20		1720	2.0	60
	2258	5.9	180		2323	5.6	170
3 F	0552	0.7	20	**18** Sa	0608	1.6	50
	1120	5.6	170		1150	5.2	160
	1808	1.0	30		1807	2.3	70
	2344	5.9	180				
4 Sa	0653	1.0	30	**19** Su	0003	5.6	170
	1212	5.6	170		0656	2.0	60
	1912	1.3	40		1234	4.9	150
					1904	2.3	70
5 Su ◑	0034	5.9	180	**20** M ◐	0048	5.2	160
	0755	1.0	30		0748	2.0	60
	1309	5.2	160		1327	4.9	150
	2017	1.3	40		2005	2.6	80
6 M	0132	5.6	170	**21** Tu	0141	4.9	150
	0858	1.0	30		0841	2.0	60
	1418	4.9	150		1433	4.6	140
	2121	1.6	50		2104	2.6	80
7 Tu	0241	5.6	170	**22** W	0246	4.9	150
	1000	1.0	30		0935	2.0	60
	1540	4.9	150		1549	4.9	150
	2225	1.6	50		2159	2.3	70
8 W	0359	5.6	170	**23** Th	0355	5.2	160
	1101	1.0	30		1029	1.6	50
	1658	5.2	160		1651	4.9	150
	2327	1.3	40		2252	2.3	70
9 Th	0510	5.6	170	**24** F	0454	5.2	160
	1159	0.7	20		1120	1.3	40
	1757	5.6	170		1739	5.2	160
					2342	1.6	50
10 F	0024	1.3	40	**25** Sa	0544	5.6	170
	0608	5.9	180		1209	1.0	30
	1252	0.7	20		1821	5.6	170
	1846	5.9	180				
11 Sa	0117	1.0	30	**26** Su	0030	1.3	40
	0658	5.9	180		0629	5.9	180
	1341	0.7	20		1254	0.7	20
	1930	5.9	180		1900	5.9	180
12 Su ○	0205	1.0	30	**27** M ●	0118	1.0	30
	0743	6.2	190		0714	5.9	180
	1425	0.7	20		1338	0.3	10
	2012	6.2	190		1940	6.2	190
13 M	0248	1.0	30	**28** Tu	0205	0.7	20
	0827	6.2	190		0758	5.9	180
	1504	0.7	20		1422	0.3	10
	2051	6.2	190		2022	6.2	190
14 Tu	0329	1.0	30	**29** W	0254	0.3	10
	0908	5.9	180		0844	6.2	190
	1540	1.0	30		1507	0.3	10
	2129	5.9	180		2105	6.6	200
15 W	0407	1.3	40	**30** Th	0344	0.3	10
	0949	5.9	180		0931	5.9	180
	1613	1.3	40		1557	0.3	10
	2207	5.9	180		2150	6.6	200
				31 F	0439	0.3	10
					1019	5.9	180
					1654	0.7	20
					2236	6.2	190

Time meridian 60° W. 0000 is midnight. 1200 is noon. Times are not adjusted for Daylight Saving Time.
Heights are referred to the Canadian chart datum of soundings.

Halifax, Nova Scotia, 2017
Times and Heights of High and Low Waters

April

Day	Time	ft	cm	Day	Time	ft	cm
1 Sa	0537	0.3	10	16 Su	0521	1.6	50
	1108	5.6	170		1121	5.2	160
	1758	1.0	30		1728	2.3	70
	2325	5.9	180		2325	5.6	170
2 Su	0639	0.7	20	17 M	0608	2.0	60
	1201	5.6	170		1202	5.2	160
	1905	1.3	40		1827	2.6	80
3 M	0017	5.9	180	18 Tu	0006	5.2	160
	0742	0.7	20		0700	2.0	60
	1259	5.2	160		1249	4.9	150
	2012	1.6	50		1929	2.6	80
4 Tu	0117	5.6	170	19 W	0054	5.2	160
	0844	1.0	30		0755	2.0	60
	1409	4.9	150		1347	4.9	150
	2116	1.6	50		2028	2.6	80
5 W	0228	5.2	160	20 Th	0153	4.9	150
	0945	1.0	30		0850	2.0	60
	1533	5.2	160		1456	4.9	150
	2218	1.6	50		2124	2.3	70
6 Th	0350	5.2	160	21 F	0303	4.9	150
	1044	1.0	30		0944	1.6	50
	1646	5.2	160		1603	5.2	160
	2317	1.3	40		2218	2.0	60
7 F	0500	5.6	170	22 Sa	0411	5.2	160
	1140	1.0	30		1037	1.3	40
	1739	5.6	170		1655	5.6	170
					2311	1.6	50
8 Sa	0011	1.3	40	23 Su	0508	5.6	170
	0554	5.6	170		1128	1.0	30
	1232	1.0	30		1740	5.9	180
	1823	5.9	180				
9 Su	0101	1.0	30	24 M	0003	1.0	30
	0641	5.6	170		0559	5.6	170
	1318	1.0	30		1217	0.7	20
	1904	5.9	180		1823	6.2	190
10 M	0145	1.0	30	25 Tu	0053	0.7	20
	0724	5.9	180		0648	5.9	180
	1359	1.0	30		1305	0.7	20
	1942	5.9	180		1907	6.6	200
11 Tu	0224	1.0	30	26 W	0144	0.0	0
	0805	5.9	180		0736	5.9	180
	1437	1.0	30		1354	0.3	10
	2020	5.9	180		1952	6.6	200
12 W	0259	1.0	30	27 Th	0235	0.0	0
	0846	5.9	180		0825	5.9	180
	1509	1.3	40		1445	0.3	10
	2056	5.9	180		2040	6.6	200
13 Th	0333	1.0	30	28 F	0328	-0.3	-10
	0925	5.6	170		0915	5.9	180
	1538	1.6	50		1541	0.7	20
	2132	5.9	180		2129	6.6	200
14 F	0406	1.3	40	29 Sa	0423	0.0	0
	1004	5.6	170		1006	5.9	180
	1606	2.0	60		1643	1.0	30
	2209	5.9	180		2218	6.2	190
15 Sa	0441	1.3	40	30 Su	0522	0.3	10
	1042	5.2	160		1058	5.9	180
	1641	2.3	70		1749	1.3	40
	2246	5.6	170		2309	6.2	190

May

Day	Time	ft	cm	Day	Time	ft	cm
1 M	0623	0.3	10	16 Tu	0533	1.6	50
	1152	5.6	170		1135	5.2	160
	1857	1.3	40		1758	2.6	80
					2334	5.2	160
2 Tu	0003	5.6	170	17 W	0624	1.6	50
	0725	0.7	20		1218	5.2	160
	1250	5.6	170		1858	2.6	80
	2002	1.6	50				
3 W	0103	5.2	160	18 Th	0019	5.2	160
	0825	1.0	30		0717	1.6	50
	1357	5.2	160		1308	5.2	160
	2104	1.6	50		1955	2.6	80
4 Th	0213	5.2	160	19 F	0111	5.2	160
	0924	1.0	30		0811	1.6	50
	1513	5.2	160		1406	5.2	160
	2204	1.6	50		2051	2.3	70
5 F	0332	4.9	150	20 Sa	0215	4.9	150
	1021	1.3	40		0904	1.6	50
	1620	5.6	170		1509	5.2	160
	2300	1.3	40		2146	2.0	60
6 Sa	0440	5.2	160	21 Su	0325	5.2	160
	1115	1.3	40		0956	1.3	40
	1711	5.6	170		1606	5.6	170
	2352	1.3	40		2241	1.3	40
7 Su	0534	5.2	160	22 M	0431	5.2	160
	1206	1.3	40		1050	1.3	40
	1755	5.6	170		1658	5.9	180
					2336	1.0	30
8 M	0039	1.0	30	23 Tu	0529	5.6	170
	0620	5.2	160		1143	1.0	30
	1253	1.3	40		1747	6.2	190
	1834	5.9	180				
9 Tu	0121	1.0	30	24 W	0031	0.3	10
	0703	5.6	170		0623	5.6	170
	1334	1.3	40		1238	0.7	20
	1912	5.9	180		1837	6.6	200
10 W	0159	1.0	30	25 Th	0124	0.0	0
	0744	5.6	170		0716	5.9	180
	1410	1.6	50		1333	0.7	20
	1949	5.9	180		1927	6.9	210
11 Th	0233	1.0	30	26 F	0218	-0.3	-10
	0825	5.6	170		0809	6.2	190
	1442	1.6	50		1430	0.7	20
	2026	5.9	180		2019	6.9	210
12 F	0304	1.0	30	27 Sa	0312	-0.3	-10
	0904	5.6	170		0902	6.2	190
	1510	2.0	60		1529	0.7	20
	2102	5.9	180		2111	6.6	200
13 Sa	0336	1.0	30	28 Su	0408	-0.3	-10
	0941	5.6	170		0955	6.2	190
	1540	2.0	60		1632	1.0	30
	2138	5.9	180		2203	6.6	200
14 Su	0410	1.3	40	29 M	0506	0.0	0
	1018	5.6	170		1047	5.9	180
	1616	2.3	70		1737	1.3	40
	2215	5.6	170		2256	6.2	190
15 M	0449	1.3	40	30 Tu	0604	0.3	10
	1056	5.6	170		1140	5.9	180
	1702	2.3	70		1842	1.6	50
	2254	5.6	170		2349	5.9	180
				31 W	0703	0.7	20
					1235	5.6	170
					1945	1.6	50

June

Day	Time	ft	cm	Day	Time	ft	cm
1 Th	0045	5.2	160	16 F	0645	1.6	50
	0801	1.0	30		1235	5.6	170
	1333	5.6	170		1924	2.3	70
	2044	1.6	50				
2 F	0148	4.9	150	17 Sa	0040	5.2	160
	0857	1.3	40		0736	1.6	50
	1437	5.2	160		1325	5.6	170
	2141	1.6	50		2020	2.0	60
3 Sa	0259	4.9	150	18 Su	0138	5.2	160
	0951	1.3	40		0829	1.6	50
	1540	5.6	170		1421	5.6	170
	2235	1.3	40		2117	1.6	50
4 Su	0408	4.9	150	19 M	0245	5.2	160
	1045	1.6	50		0923	1.3	40
	1635	5.6	170		1521	5.9	180
	2326	1.3	40		2214	1.3	40
5 M	0506	4.9	150	20 Tu	0356	5.2	160
	1137	1.6	50		1019	1.3	40
	1722	5.6	170		1620	5.9	180
					2313	0.7	20
6 Tu	0013	1.0	30	21 W	0502	5.2	160
	0556	5.2	160		1118	1.3	40
	1224	1.6	50		1718	6.2	190
	1804	5.6	170				
7 W	0055	1.0	30	22 Th	0010	0.3	10
	0641	5.2	160		0602	5.6	170
	1307	1.6	50		1219	1.0	30
	1844	5.6	170		1813	6.6	200
8 Th	0132	1.0	30	23 F	0107	0.0	0
	0723	5.2	160		0659	5.9	180
	1344	1.6	50		1319	1.0	30
	1922	5.6	170		1908	6.9	210
9 F	0206	1.0	30	24 Sa	0203	-0.3	-10
	0804	5.6	170		0754	6.2	190
	1416	2.0	60		1418	1.0	30
	1959	5.6	170		2003	6.9	210
10 Sa	0239	1.0	30	25 Su	0257	-0.3	-10
	0843	5.6	170		0849	6.2	190
	1447	2.0	60		1518	1.0	30
	2037	5.9	180		2057	6.6	200
11 Su	0312	1.0	30	26 M	0351	0.0	0
	0920	5.6	170		0941	6.2	190
	1519	2.0	60		1618	1.0	30
	2114	5.9	180		2149	6.6	200
12 M	0347	1.0	30	27 Tu	0446	0.0	0
	0957	5.6	170		1032	6.2	190
	1556	2.3	70		1719	1.3	40
	2152	5.9	180		2240	6.2	190
13 Tu	0425	1.3	40	28 W	0540	0.3	10
	1033	5.6	170		1121	5.9	180
	1640	2.3	70		1819	1.3	40
	2230	5.6	170		2330	5.9	180
14 W	0508	1.3	40	29 Th	0635	0.7	20
	1111	5.6	170		1210	5.9	180
	1731	2.3	70		1918	1.6	50
	2309	5.6	170				
15 Th	0555	1.3	40	30 F	0021	5.2	160
	1151	5.6	170		0729	1.0	30
	1827	2.3	70		1259	5.6	170
	2352	5.6	170		2015	1.6	50

Time meridian 60° W. 0000 is midnight. 1200 is noon. Times are not adjusted for Daylight Saving Time.
Heights are referred to the Canadian chart datum of soundings.

Halifax, Nova Scotia, 2017

Times and Heights of High and Low Waters

July

Day	Time	ft	cm	Day	Time	ft	cm
1 Sa	0116	4.9	150	**16 Su** ○	0016	5.2	160
	0822	1.3	40		0707	1.3	40
	1354	5.6	170		1252	5.6	170
	2110	1.6	50		1954	1.6	50
2 Su	0218	4.9	150	**17 M**	0110	5.2	160
	0915	1.6	50		0802	1.3	40
	1453	5.2	160		1344	5.6	170
	2203	1.6	50		2052	1.3	40
3 M	0325	4.6	140	**18 Tu**	0214	5.2	160
	1009	1.6	50		0859	1.6	50
	1552	5.2	160		1444	5.9	180
	2253	1.3	40		2153	1.0	30
4 Tu	0431	4.6	140	**19 W**	0326	5.2	160
	1101	2.0	60		1001	1.3	40
	1646	5.2	160		1550	5.9	180
	2341	1.3	40		2254	0.7	20
5 W	0527	4.9	150	**20 Th**	0440	5.2	160
	1151	2.0	60		1104	1.3	40
	1734	5.6	170		1655	6.2	190
					2354	0.3	10
6 Th	0024	1.3	40	**21 F**	0546	5.6	170
	0617	4.9	150		1207	1.3	40
	1236	2.0	60		1757	6.6	200
	1817	5.6	170				
7 F	0103	1.0	30	**22 Sa**	0053	0.3	10
	0701	5.2	160		0645	5.9	180
	1315	2.0	60		1308	1.0	30
	1857	5.6	170		1855	6.6	200
8 Sa	0139	1.0	30	**23 Su** ●	0148	0.0	0
	0742	5.2	160		0741	6.2	190
	1349	2.0	60		1407	1.0	30
	1937	5.6	170		1950	6.6	200
9 Su ○	0215	1.0	30	**24 M**	0241	0.0	0
	0820	5.6	170		0834	6.2	190
	1422	2.0	60		1504	1.0	30
	2015	5.9	180		2043	6.6	200
10 M	0250	1.0	30	**25 Tu**	0332	0.0	0
	0857	5.6	170		0923	6.2	190
	1457	2.0	60		1559	1.0	30
	2053	5.9	180		2132	6.6	200
11 Tu	0326	1.0	30	**26 W**	0422	0.3	10
	0933	5.6	170		1010	6.2	190
	1535	2.0	60		1654	1.3	40
	2131	5.9	180		2220	6.2	190
12 W	0404	1.0	30	**27 Th**	0511	0.7	20
	1010	5.6	170		1055	6.2	190
	1618	2.0	60		1749	1.3	40
	2209	5.9	180		2306	5.9	180
13 Th	0444	1.0	30	**28 F**	0600	1.0	30
	1046	5.6	170		1138	5.9	180
	1706	2.0	60		1843	1.6	50
	2248	5.6	170		2353	5.6	170
14 F	0528	1.0	30	**29 Sa**	0650	1.3	40
	1125	5.6	170		1223	5.6	170
	1759	2.0	60		1937	1.6	50
	2330	5.6	170				
15 Sa	0615	1.3	40	**30 Su** ☽	0041	4.9	150
	1206	5.6	170		0741	1.6	50
	1856	2.0	60		1311	5.6	170
					2030	1.6	50
				31 M	0135	4.9	150
					0833	2.0	60
					1405	5.2	160
					2122	1.6	50

August

Day	Time	ft	cm	Day	Time	ft	cm
1 Tu	0238	4.6	140	**16 W**	0152	4.9	150
	0926	2.0	60		0848	1.6	50
	1505	5.2	160		1418	5.6	170
	2212	1.6	50		2137	1.0	30
2 W	0349	4.6	140	**17 Th**	0305	4.9	150
	1021	2.0	60		0952	1.6	50
	1607	5.2	160		1529	5.9	180
	2301	1.6	50		2239	1.0	30
3 Th	0455	4.6	140	**18 F**	0425	5.2	160
	1113	2.0	60		1057	1.3	40
	1702	5.2	160		1641	5.9	180
	2347	1.3	40		2340	0.7	20
4 F	0550	4.9	150	**19 Sa**	0535	5.6	170
	1200	2.0	60		1200	1.3	40
	1750	5.2	160		1747	6.2	190
5 Sa	0029	1.3	40	**20 Su**	0038	0.3	10
	0635	5.2	160		0634	5.9	180
	1241	2.0	60		1259	1.0	30
	1833	5.6	170		1845	6.2	190
6 Su	0109	1.0	30	**21 M** ●	0132	0.3	10
	0716	5.2	160		0726	6.2	190
	1318	2.0	60		1355	1.0	30
	1914	5.9	180		1937	6.6	200
7 M ○	0147	1.0	30	**22 Tu**	0223	0.3	10
	0754	5.6	170		0814	6.2	190
	1355	1.6	50		1447	1.0	30
	1953	5.9	180		2026	6.2	190
8 Tu	0225	0.7	20	**23 W**	0309	0.3	10
	0830	5.6	170		0859	6.2	190
	1433	1.6	50		1537	1.0	30
	2031	5.9	180		2112	6.2	190
9 W	0302	0.7	20	**24 Th**	0354	0.3	10
	0907	5.6	170		0942	6.2	190
	1513	1.3	40		1625	1.0	30
	2109	5.9	180		2157	5.9	180
10 Th	0339	0.7	20	**25 F**	0437	0.7	20
	0943	5.6	170		1023	6.2	190
	1556	1.3	40		1713	1.3	40
	2148	5.9	180		2240	5.9	180
11 F	0419	0.7	20	**26 Sa**	0520	1.3	40
	1020	5.9	180		1103	5.9	180
	1644	1.3	40		1801	1.3	40
	2228	5.9	180		2323	5.6	170
12 Sa	0502	1.0	30	**27 Su**	0604	1.6	50
	1058	5.9	180		1145	5.9	180
	1736	1.3	40		1850	1.6	50
	2311	5.6	170				
13 Su	0550	1.0	30	**28 M**	0007	5.2	160
	1139	5.9	180		0652	2.0	60
	1833	1.3	40		1228	5.6	170
	2357	5.6	170		1941	1.6	50
14 M ☽	0645	1.3	40	**29 Tu** ☽	0056	4.9	150
	1224	5.6	170		0745	2.3	70
	1933	1.3	40		1318	5.2	160
					2031	2.0	60
15 Tu	0050	5.2	160	**30 W**	0153	4.6	140
	0745	1.3	40		0841	2.3	70
	1316	5.6	170		1415	4.9	150
	2034	1.3	40		2122	2.0	60
				31 Th	0303	4.6	140
					0938	2.3	70
					1521	4.9	150
					2212	2.0	60

September

Day	Time	ft	cm	Day	Time	ft	cm
1 F	0418	4.6	140	**16 Sa**	0418	5.2	160
	1031	2.3	70		1053	1.6	50
	1626	4.9	150		1634	5.6	170
	2302	1.6	50		2326	0.7	20
2 Sa	0518	4.9	150	**17 Su**	0526	5.6	170
	1121	2.3	70		1153	1.3	40
	1720	5.2	160		1739	5.9	180
	2349	1.3	40				
3 Su	0604	5.2	160	**18 M**	0022	0.7	20
	1205	2.0	60		0620	5.9	180
	1805	5.6	170		1250	1.0	30
					1833	5.9	180
4 M	0033	1.0	30	**19 Tu**	0114	0.7	20
	0645	5.2	160		0706	6.2	190
	1247	1.6	50		1341	1.0	30
	1847	5.9	180		1922	6.2	190
5 Tu	0114	0.7	20	**20 W** ●	0202	0.7	20
	0722	5.6	170		0750	6.2	190
	1327	1.3	40		1428	1.0	30
	1927	5.9	180		2007	6.2	190
6 W ○	0154	0.7	20	**21 Th**	0245	0.7	20
	0758	5.6	170		0831	6.2	190
	1409	1.0	30		1512	1.0	30
	2006	5.9	180		2051	5.9	180
7 Th	0232	0.3	10	**22 F**	0325	1.0	30
	0835	5.9	180		0911	6.2	190
	1451	1.0	30		1553	1.0	30
	2046	5.9	180		2133	5.9	180
8 F	0311	0.3	10	**23 Sa**	0402	1.3	40
	0912	5.9	180		0949	6.2	190
	1536	0.7	20		1634	1.0	30
	2127	5.9	180		2214	5.6	170
9 Sa	0352	0.7	20	**24 Su**	0438	1.6	50
	0951	5.9	180		1028	5.9	180
	1624	0.7	20		1715	1.3	40
	2210	5.9	180		2255	5.6	170
10 Su	0438	0.7	20	**25 M**	0516	2.0	60
	1032	5.9	180		1107	5.6	170
	1718	1.0	30		1759	1.6	50
	2254	5.6	170		2337	5.2	160
11 M	0531	1.0	30	**26 Tu**	0601	2.3	70
	1115	5.9	180		1149	5.6	170
	1816	1.0	30		1846	2.0	60
	2342	5.6	170				
12 Tu	0633	1.3	40	**27 W** ☽	0021	4.9	150
	1202	5.9	180		0657	2.3	70
	1918	1.0	30		1234	5.2	160
					1936	2.0	60
13 W ☽	0036	5.2	160	**28 Th**	0112	4.9	150
	0739	1.6	50		0757	2.6	80
	1256	5.6	170		1326	4.9	150
	2021	1.0	30		2027	2.0	60
14 Th	0138	5.2	160	**29 F**	0216	4.9	150
	0844	1.6	50		0855	2.6	80
	1359	5.6	170		1429	4.9	150
	2124	1.0	30		2120	2.0	60
15 F	0254	4.9	150	**30 Sa**	0331	4.9	150
	0949	1.6	50		0949	2.6	80
	1515	5.6	170		1540	4.9	150
	2226	1.0	30		2212	1.6	50

Time meridian 60° W. 0000 is midnight. 1200 is noon. Times are not adjusted for Daylight Saving Time.
Heights are referred to the Canadian chart datum of soundings.

Halifax, Nova Scotia, 2017

Times and Heights of High and Low Waters

October

Day	Time (h m)	Height (ft)	Height (cm)		Day	Time (h m)	Height (ft)	Height (cm)
1 Su	0437	4.9	150		16 M	0510	5.6	170
	1041	2.3	70			1143	1.3	40
	1641	5.2	160			1727	5.6	170
	2303	1.6	50					
2 M	0526	5.2	160		17 Tu	0003	1.0	30
	1129	2.0	60			0559	5.9	180
	1731	5.2	160			1236	1.0	30
	2351	1.3	40			1818	5.6	170
3 Tu	0607	5.6	170		18 W	0054	1.0	30
	1215	1.6	50			0642	5.9	180
	1816	5.6	170			1324	1.0	30
						1904	5.9	180
4 W	0035	1.0	30		19 Th ●	0139	1.0	30
	0645	5.6	170			0722	6.2	190
	1259	1.0	30			1407	0.7	20
	1858	5.9	180			1947	5.9	180
5 Th ○	0118	0.7	20		20 F	0220	1.0	30
	0722	5.9	180			0801	6.2	190
	1345	0.7	20			1446	0.7	20
	1940	5.9	180			2029	5.9	180
6 F	0159	0.3	10		21 Sa	0257	1.3	40
	0801	6.2	190			0839	5.9	180
	1430	0.3	10			1523	1.0	30
	2024	5.9	180			2110	5.6	170
7 Sa	0242	0.3	10		22 Su	0331	1.6	50
	0841	6.2	190			0917	5.9	180
	1517	0.3	10			1558	1.0	30
	2108	5.9	180			2151	5.6	170
8 Su	0328	0.7	20		23 M	0402	2.0	60
	0924	6.2	190			0955	5.9	180
	1608	0.3	10			1633	1.3	40
	2154	5.9	180			2230	5.6	170
9 M	0420	0.7	20		24 Tu	0437	2.3	70
	1009	6.2	190			1033	5.6	170
	1703	0.3	10			1712	1.6	50
	2242	5.9	180			2310	5.2	160
10 Tu	0520	1.0	30		25 W	0521	2.3	70
	1056	6.2	190			1113	5.6	170
	1803	0.7	20			1756	1.6	50
	2332	5.6	170			2351	5.2	160
11 W	0628	1.3	40		26 Th	0616	2.6	80
	1146	5.9	180			1155	5.2	160
	1906	0.7	20			1845	2.0	60
12 Th ◑	0027	5.2	160		27 F ◐	0037	5.2	160
	0735	1.6	50			0717	2.6	80
	1242	5.6	170			1242	5.2	160
	2008	1.0	30			1937	2.0	60
13 F	0131	5.2	160		28 Sa	0132	4.9	150
	0841	1.6	50			0815	2.6	80
	1347	5.2	160			1338	4.9	150
	2110	1.0	30			2030	2.0	60
14 Sa	0249	5.2	160		29 Su	0239	4.9	150
	0944	1.6	50			0909	2.6	80
	1506	5.2	160			1445	4.9	150
	2210	1.0	30			2123	1.6	50
15 Su	0409	5.2	160		30 M	0346	5.2	160
	1045	1.6	50			1002	2.3	70
	1625	5.2	160			1554	4.9	150
	2309	1.0	30			2215	1.6	50
					31 Tu	0439	5.2	160
						1053	2.0	60
						1652	5.2	160
						2306	1.3	40

November

Day	Time (h m)	Height (ft)	Height (cm)		Day	Time (h m)	Height (ft)	Height (cm)
1 W	0523	5.6	170		16 Th	0031	1.3	40
	1143	1.3	40			0613	5.9	180
	1742	5.6	170			1302	1.0	30
	2354	1.0	30			1844	5.6	170
2 Th	0604	5.9	180		17 F	0116	1.3	40
	1232	0.7	20			0653	5.9	180
	1829	5.6	170			1344	0.7	20
						1927	5.6	170
3 F	0042	1.0	30		18 Sa ●	0157	1.3	40
	0645	6.2	190			0732	5.9	180
	1321	0.3	10			1421	0.7	20
	1915	5.9	180			2009	5.6	170
4 Sa ○	0129	0.7	20		19 Su	0233	1.6	50
	0728	6.6	200			0810	5.9	180
	1410	0.0	0			1455	0.7	20
	2002	5.9	180			2050	5.6	170
5 Su	0218	0.7	20		20 M	0305	2.0	60
	0814	6.6	200			0848	5.9	180
	1500	0.0	0			1528	1.0	30
	2051	5.9	180			2129	5.6	170
6 M	0310	0.7	20		21 Tu	0336	2.0	60
	0901	6.6	200			0926	5.9	180
	1553	0.0	0			1601	1.3	40
	2141	5.9	180			2208	5.6	170
7 Tu	0408	1.0	30		22 W	0409	2.3	70
	0951	6.6	200			1005	5.6	170
	1650	0.0	0			1638	1.3	40
	2232	5.9	180			2246	5.6	170
8 W	0513	1.3	40		23 Th	0451	2.6	80
	1041	6.2	190			1043	5.6	170
	1750	0.3	10			1718	1.6	50
	2324	5.9	180			2325	5.6	170
9 Th	0621	1.3	40		24 F	0542	2.6	80
	1134	5.9	180			1123	5.6	170
	1851	0.7	20			1805	1.6	50
10 F ○	0020	5.6	170		25 Sa	0006	5.2	160
	0728	1.6	50			0639	2.6	80
	1231	5.6	170			1206	5.2	160
	1953	0.7	20			1855	2.0	60
11 Sa	0123	5.2	160		26 Su ◑	0053	5.2	160
	0832	1.6	50			0736	2.6	80
	1336	5.2	160			1255	5.2	160
	2052	1.0	30			1947	1.6	50
12 Su	0234	5.2	160		27 M	0148	5.2	160
	0933	1.6	50			0831	2.3	70
	1451	5.2	160			1353	4.9	150
	2150	1.0	30			2040	1.6	50
13 M	0346	5.6	170		28 Tu	0247	5.2	160
	1031	1.3	40			0925	2.0	60
	1607	5.2	160			1500	4.9	150
	2247	1.3	40			2132	1.6	50
14 Tu	0444	5.6	170		29 W	0344	5.6	170
	1126	1.3	40			1018	1.6	50
	1708	5.2	160			1607	4.9	150
	2340	1.3	40			2224	1.3	40
15 W	0531	5.6	170		30 Th	0435	5.9	180
	1217	1.0	30			1112	1.0	30
	1759	5.2	160			1706	5.2	160
						2316	1.3	40

December

Day	Time (h m)	Height (ft)	Height (cm)		Day	Time (h m)	Height (ft)	Height (cm)
1 F	0523	6.2	190		16 Sa	0052	1.6	50
	1205	0.7	20			0626	5.6	170
	1759	5.6	170			1319	1.0	30
						1907	5.2	160
2 Sa	0010	1.0	30		17 Su	0134	1.6	50
	0611	6.6	200			0707	5.6	170
	1258	0.3	10			1356	1.0	30
	1852	5.6	170			1950	5.6	170
3 Su ○	0104	1.0	30		18 M ●	0210	2.0	60
	0701	6.6	200			0746	5.9	180
	1351	0.0	0			1431	1.0	30
	1943	5.9	180			2030	5.6	170
4 M	0159	0.7	20		19 Tu	0241	2.0	60
	0752	6.9	210			0825	5.9	180
	1444	-0.3	-10			1504	1.0	30
	2036	5.9	180			2109	5.6	170
5 Tu	0257	1.0	30		20 W	0312	2.0	60
	0844	6.9	210			0903	5.9	180
	1539	-0.3	-10			1537	1.0	30
	2129	6.2	190			2146	5.6	170
6 W	0359	1.0	30		21 Th	0345	2.3	70
	0937	6.6	200			0941	5.9	180
	1635	0.0	0			1612	1.3	40
	2222	6.2	190			2222	5.6	170
7 Th	0503	1.3	40		22 F	0425	2.3	70
	1029	6.2	190			1019	5.6	170
	1734	0.3	10			1650	1.3	40
	2315	5.9	180			2259	5.6	170
8 F	0609	1.3	40		23 Sa	0511	2.3	70
	1122	5.9	180			1057	5.6	170
	1833	0.3	10			1733	1.3	40
						2337	5.6	170
9 Sa	0008	5.9	180		24 Su	0604	2.3	70
	0713	1.6	50			1137	5.2	160
	1218	5.6	170			1820	1.6	50
	1931	0.7	20					
10 Su ○	0104	5.6	170		25 M	0019	5.6	170
	0814	1.6	50			0659	2.3	70
	1317	5.2	160			1221	5.2	160
	2029	1.0	30			1910	1.6	50
11 M	0205	5.6	170		26 Tu ◑	0104	5.6	170
	0913	1.3	40			0755	2.3	70
	1424	4.9	150			1313	5.2	160
	2125	1.3	40			2001	1.6	50
12 Tu	0309	5.6	170		27 W	0155	5.6	170
	1009	1.3	40			0850	2.0	60
	1536	4.9	150			1414	4.9	150
	2220	1.3	40			2054	1.6	50
13 W	0408	5.6	170		28 Th	0251	5.6	170
	1102	1.3	40			0946	1.3	40
	1640	4.9	150			1524	4.9	150
	2314	1.3	40			2149	1.6	50
14 Th	0459	5.6	170		29 F	0350	5.9	180
	1152	1.0	30			1044	1.0	30
	1734	4.9	150			1632	5.2	160
						2247	1.3	40
15 F	0005	1.6	50		30 Sa	0448	6.2	190
	0544	5.6	170			1141	0.7	20
	1238	1.0	30			1734	5.2	160
	1823	5.2	160			2347	1.3	40
					31 Su	0544	6.6	200
						1238	0.3	10
						1831	5.6	170

Time meridian 60° W. 0000 is midnight. 1200 is noon. Times are not adjusted for Daylight Saving Time.
Heights are referred to the Canadian chart datum of soundings.

Saint John, New Brunswick, 2017
Times and Heights of High and Low Waters

January

Day	Time	ft	cm	Day	Time	ft	cm
1 Su	0128	24.6	750	16 M	0215	25.9	790
	0737	4.3	130		0827	3.3	100
	1342	25.6	780		1434	26.2	800
	2000	3.3	100		2054	2.6	80
2 M	0207	24.6	750	17 Tu	0304	25.3	770
	0817	4.3	130		0918	3.9	120
	1423	25.6	780		1525	25.3	770
	2042	3.3	100		2143	3.6	110
3 Tu	0249	24.9	760	18 W	0355	24.6	750
	0902	4.3	130		1010	4.6	140
	1507	25.3	770		1618	24.3	740
	2127	3.3	100		2235	4.6	140
4 W	0335	24.9	760	19 Th ◐	0448	24.0	730
	0950	4.3	130		1104	5.2	160
	1556	24.9	760		1713	23.3	710
	2216	3.3	100		2329	5.2	160
5 Th ◑	0425	24.9	760	20 F	0543	23.6	720
	1043	3.9	120		1201	5.9	180
	1650	24.9	760		1811	22.6	690
	2310	3.6	110				
6 F	0520	25.3	770	21 Sa	0025	5.9	180
	1140	3.9	120		0640	23.3	710
	1749	24.6	750		1259	5.9	180
					1910	22.3	680
7 Sa	0008	3.6	110	22 Su	0122	6.2	190
	0619	25.6	780		0736	23.3	710
	1242	3.3	100		1356	5.9	180
	1851	24.9	760		2007	22.3	680
8 Su	0108	3.3	100	23 M	0217	6.6	200
	0720	26.2	800		0829	23.3	710
	1344	2.6	80		1449	5.6	170
	1954	24.9	760		2059	22.3	680
9 M	0210	3.0	90	24 Tu	0308	6.2	190
	0822	26.9	820		0918	23.6	720
	1446	2.0	60		1537	5.2	160
	2056	25.6	780		2147	22.6	690
10 Tu	0310	2.6	80	25 W	0354	5.9	180
	0921	27.6	840		1003	24.3	740
	1545	1.3	40		1621	4.6	140
	2155	25.9	790		2230	23.3	710
11 W	0408	2.3	70	26 Th	0436	5.2	160
	1018	27.9	850		1044	24.9	760
	1641	1.0	30		1701	3.9	120
	2252	26.2	800		2309	24.0	730
12 Th ○	0504	2.0	60	27 F ●	0516	4.9	150
	1113	28.2	860		1123	25.3	770
	1735	0.7	20		1740	3.3	100
	2345	26.6	810		2347	24.6	750
13 F	0557	2.0	60	28 Sa	0554	4.3	130
	1205	27.9	850		1201	25.9	790
	1827	1.0	30		1817	2.6	80
14 Sa	0036	26.6	810	29 Su	0023	24.9	760
	0648	2.3	70		0632	3.6	110
	1255	27.6	840		1239	26.2	800
	1916	1.3	40		1855	2.3	70
15 Su	0126	26.2	800	30 M	0101	25.6	780
	0738	2.6	80		0712	3.3	100
	1345	26.9	820		1318	26.6	810
	2005	2.0	60		1935	2.0	60
				31 Tu	0141	25.9	790
					0753	3.0	90
					1359	26.2	800
					2017	2.0	60

February

Day	Time	ft	cm	Day	Time	ft	cm
1 W	0223	25.9	790	16 Th	0318	24.6	750
	0838	2.6	80		0933	4.6	140
	1444	26.2	800		1541	24.0	730
	2103	2.3	70		2156	4.9	150
2 Th	0309	25.9	790	17 F	0407	24.0	730
	0926	3.0	90		1023	5.2	160
	1533	25.6	780		1632	23.0	700
	2152	2.6	80		2245	5.6	170
3 F	0400	25.9	790	18 Sa ○	0458	23.3	710
	1020	3.0	90		1116	5.9	180
	1628	25.3	770		1726	22.3	680
	2246	3.3	100		2339	6.6	200
4 Sa ◐	0457	25.6	780	19 Su	0553	23.0	700
	1118	3.3	100		1212	6.6	200
	1728	24.6	750		1824	21.7	660
	2346	3.6	110				
5 Su	0558	25.6	780	20 M	0035	6.9	210
	1222	3.3	100		0650	22.6	690
	1833	24.3	740		1310	6.6	200
					1922	21.7	660
6 M	0050	3.9	120	21 Tu	0133	7.2	220
	0702	25.6	780		0746	22.6	690
	1327	3.3	100		1406	6.2	190
	1939	24.3	740		2018	21.7	660
7 Tu	0155	3.9	120	22 W	0227	6.9	210
	0807	25.9	790		0839	23.3	710
	1432	3.0	90		1458	5.6	170
	2044	24.6	750		2109	22.3	680
8 W	0258	3.6	110	23 Th	0317	6.2	190
	0910	26.6	810		0927	24.0	730
	1533	2.3	70		1544	4.9	150
	2144	25.3	770		2154	23.3	710
9 Th	0357	3.0	90	24 F	0402	5.2	160
	1008	26.9	820		1011	24.6	750
	1630	2.0	60		1627	3.9	120
	2240	25.6	780		2235	24.0	730
10 F ○	0452	2.6	80	25 Sa	0444	4.3	130
	1101	27.2	830		1052	25.6	780
	1722	1.6	50		1708	3.0	90
	2331	25.9	790		2314	24.9	760
11 Sa	0542	2.6	80	26 Su ●	0524	3.3	100
	1150	27.2	830		1132	26.2	800
	1810	1.6	50		1748	2.0	60
					2353	25.9	790
12 Su	0018	26.2	800	27 M	0605	2.3	70
	0630	2.6	80		1212	26.9	820
	1237	26.9	820		1828	1.3	40
	1856	2.0	60				
13 M	0104	25.9	790	28 Tu	0033	26.6	810
	0716	2.6	80		0646	1.6	50
	1323	26.6	810		1253	27.2	830
	1940	2.3	70		1909	1.0	30
14 Tu	0148	25.6	780				
	0801	3.3	100				
	1408	25.6	780				
	2024	3.0	90				
15 W	0232	25.3	770				
	0846	3.6	110				
	1454	24.9	760				
	2109	3.9	120				

March

Day	Time	ft	cm	Day	Time	ft	cm
1 W	0114	26.9	820	16 Th	0201	25.3	770
	0729	1.3	40		0816	3.6	110
	1336	26.9	820		1424	24.6	750
	1953	1.3	40		2036	4.3	130
2 Th	0159	27.2	830	17 F	0243	24.6	750
	0816	1.3	40		0859	4.3	130
	1423	26.6	810		1507	23.6	720
	2040	1.6	50		2118	5.2	160
3 F ○	0247	26.9	820	18 Sa ○	0327	24.0	730
	0906	1.6	50		0943	5.2	160
	1514	25.9	790		1553	23.0	700
	2131	2.3	70		2204	6.2	190
4 Sa	0340	26.6	810	19 Su	0414	23.3	710
	1001	2.3	70		1032	5.9	180
	1611	25.3	770		1643	22.0	670
	2228	3.3	100		2253	6.9	210
5 Su ◑	0438	25.9	790	20 M ○	0505	22.6	690
	1101	3.0	90		1124	6.6	200
	1713	24.6	750		1737	21.7	660
	2330	3.9	120		2348	7.5	230
6 M	0542	25.3	770	21 Tu	0601	22.3	680
	1207	3.6	110		1221	6.6	200
	1820	24.0	730		1835	21.3	650
7 Tu	0037	4.3	130	22 W	0046	7.5	230
	0650	24.9	760		0659	22.3	680
	1316	3.6	110		1319	6.6	200
	1929	24.0	730		1933	21.7	660
8 W	0144	4.6	140	23 Th	0143	7.2	220
	0758	25.3	770		0756	22.6	690
	1422	3.6	110		1414	5.9	180
	2035	24.3	740		2026	22.3	680
9 Th	0248	3.9	120	24 F	0236	6.2	190
	0901	25.6	780		0847	23.6	720
	1522	3.0	90		1504	4.9	150
	2134	24.6	750		2114	23.3	710
10 F	0347	3.6	110	25 Sa	0325	4.9	150
	0957	25.9	790		0934	24.6	750
	1617	2.6	80		1550	3.6	110
	2227	25.3	770		2158	24.6	750
11 Sa	0439	3.0	90	26 Su	0410	3.6	110
	1048	26.2	800		1018	25.6	780
	1706	2.3	70		1633	2.6	80
	2315	25.6	780		2240	25.9	790
12 Su ○	0527	3.0	90	27 M ●	0453	2.3	70
	1135	26.2	800		1101	26.6	810
	1751	2.3	70		1716	1.6	50
	2358	25.9	790		2322	26.9	820
13 M	0611	2.6	80	28 Tu	0537	1.3	40
	1218	26.2	800		1144	27.2	830
	1833	2.6	80		1759	0.7	20
14 Tu	0040	25.9	790	29 W	0005	27.6	840
	0654	2.6	80		0621	0.3	10
	1300	25.9	790		1228	27.6	840
	1914	3.0	90		1843	0.7	20
15 W	0121	25.6	780	30 Th	0049	28.2	860
	0735	3.0	90		0707	0.3	10
	1342	25.3	770		1315	27.6	840
	1955	3.6	110		1930	0.7	20
				31 F	0137	27.9	850
					0756	0.3	10
					1405	26.9	820
					2020	1.3	40

Time meridian 60° W. 0000 is midnight. 1200 is noon. Times are not adjusted for Daylight Saving Time.
Heights are referred to the Canadian chart datum of soundings.

Saint John, New Brunswick, 2017

Times and Heights of High and Low Waters

April

Day	Time	ft	cm	Day	Time	ft	cm
1 Sa	0227	27.6	840	16 Su	0251	24.0	730
	0849	1.0	30		0908	4.9	150
	1459	26.2	800		1518	23.0	700
	2114	2.3	70		2126	6.2	190
2 Su	0323	26.6	810	17 M	0334	23.6	720
	0946	2.0	60		0953	5.6	170
	1557	25.3	770		1603	22.3	680
	2213	3.3	100		2213	6.9	210
3 M	0423	25.9	790	18 Tu	0422	23.0	700
	1048	3.0	90		1041	6.2	190
	1702	24.3	740		1654	22.0	670
	2318	4.3	130		2304	7.2	220
4 Tu	0530	24.9	760	19 W	0515	22.6	690
	1155	3.6	110		1135	6.2	190
	1811	23.6	720		1749	22.0	670
5 W	0026	4.9	150	20 Th	0001	7.2	220
	0639	24.6	750		0612	22.3	680
	1304	3.9	120		1232	6.2	190
	1920	23.6	720		1846	22.3	680
6 Th	0134	4.9	150	21 F	0059	6.9	210
	0747	24.6	750		0710	23.0	700
	1409	3.9	120		1328	5.6	170
	2024	24.0	730		1941	23.0	700
7 F	0237	4.3	130	22 Sa	0154	5.9	180
	0849	24.9	760		0805	23.6	720
	1508	3.6	110		1421	4.6	140
	2121	24.6	750		2032	24.0	730
8 Sa	0334	3.9	120	23 Su	0246	4.6	140
	0944	25.3	770		0856	24.6	750
	1600	3.3	100		1511	3.3	100
	2211	25.3	770		2120	25.3	770
9 Su	0424	3.3	100	24 M	0335	3.0	90
	1033	25.3	770		0944	25.6	780
	1647	3.0	90		1558	2.3	70
	2256	25.6	780		2206	26.6	810
10 M	0510	3.0	90	25 Tu	0423	1.6	50
	1118	25.6	780		1031	26.6	810
	1730	3.0	90		1645	1.3	40
	2337	25.6	780		2252	27.9	850
11 Tu	0552	3.0	90	26 W	0510	0.3	10
	1159	25.3	770		1118	27.2	830
	1811	3.3	100		1732	0.7	20
					2339	28.5	870
12 W	0016	25.6	780	27 Th	0558	-0.3	-10
	0631	3.0	90		1206	27.6	840
	1239	24.9	760		1820	0.3	10
	1849	3.6	110				
13 Th	0054	25.6	780	28 F	0027	28.9	880
	0710	3.3	100		0648	-0.3	-10
	1318	24.6	750		1257	27.6	840
	1927	4.3	130		1910	0.7	20
14 F	0132	25.3	770	29 Sa	0118	28.5	870
	0748	3.6	110		0739	0.0	0
	1356	24.0	730		1349	26.9	820
	2005	4.9	150		2003	1.6	50
15 Sa	0211	24.6	750	30 Su	0211	27.9	850
	0827	4.3	130		0834	0.7	20
	1436	23.6	720		1445	26.2	800
	2044	5.6	170		2059	2.6	80

May

Day	Time	ft	cm	Day	Time	ft	cm
1 M	0308	26.9	820	16 Tu	0301	24.0	730
	0932	2.0	60		0920	4.9	150
	1545	25.3	770		1530	23.0	700
	2159	3.6	110		2139	6.6	200
2 Tu	0410	25.9	790	17 W	0346	23.6	720
	1035	3.0	90		1006	5.2	160
	1650	24.3	740		1617	22.6	690
	2304	4.6	140		2228	6.9	210
3 W	0515	24.9	760	18 Th	0435	23.3	710
	1140	3.6	110		1056	5.6	170
	1757	24.0	730		1708	22.6	690
					2321	6.6	200
4 Th	0012	4.9	150	19 F	0529	23.0	700
	0624	24.3	740		1150	5.6	170
	1246	4.3	130		1802	23.0	700
	1903	24.0	730				
5 F	0118	4.9	150	20 Sa	0017	6.2	190
	0730	24.3	740		0626	23.3	710
	1349	4.3	130		1245	4.9	150
	2004	24.3	740		1857	23.6	720
6 Sa	0219	4.6	140	21 Su	0114	5.2	160
	0831	24.3	740		0723	24.0	730
	1446	3.9	120		1340	4.3	130
	2059	24.6	750		1951	24.9	760
7 Su	0315	3.9	120	22 M	0209	3.9	120
	0925	24.6	750		0818	24.9	760
	1538	3.9	120		1434	3.3	100
	2149	24.9	760		2044	25.9	790
8 M	0404	3.6	110	23 Tu	0303	2.6	80
	1014	24.6	750		0911	25.6	780
	1625	3.9	120		1526	2.3	70
	2233	25.3	770		2135	27.2	830
9 Tu	0449	3.3	100	24 W	0355	1.0	30
	1058	24.9	760		1004	26.6	810
	1707	3.9	120		1617	1.3	40
	2314	25.3	770		2225	28.2	860
10 W	0530	3.0	90	25 Th	0447	0.0	0
	1139	24.6	750		1055	27.2	830
	1747	3.9	120		1708	0.7	20
	2353	25.3	770		2316	28.9	880
11 Th	0609	3.3	100	26 F	0538	-0.7	-20
	1218	24.6	750		1147	27.6	840
	1825	4.3	130		1759	0.7	20
12 F	0030	25.3	770	27 Sa	0008	29.2	890
	0646	3.3	100		0631	-0.7	-20
	1255	24.3	740		1240	27.6	840
	1901	4.9	150		1853	1.0	30
13 Sa	0106	24.9	760	28 Su	0101	28.9	880
	0723	3.6	110		0724	0.0	0
	1331	24.0	730		1335	26.9	820
	1938	5.2	160		1948	1.6	50
14 Su	0143	24.6	750	29 M	0156	28.2	860
	0759	4.3	130		0819	0.7	20
	1409	23.6	720		1431	26.2	800
	2015	5.6	170		2044	2.6	80
15 M	0221	24.3	740	30 Tu	0253	26.9	820
	0838	4.6	140		0917	1.6	50
	1447	23.3	710		1530	25.6	780
	2055	6.2	190		2143	3.6	110
				31 W	0352	25.9	790
					1016	3.0	90
					1631	24.6	750
					2245	4.3	130

June

Day	Time	ft	cm	Day	Time	ft	cm
1 Th	0455	24.9	760	16 F	0402	24.0	730
	1117	3.6	110		1022	4.6	140
	1733	24.3	740		1631	23.6	720
	2349	4.9	150		2246	5.6	170
2 F	0559	24.3	740	17 Sa	0453	24.0	730
	1219	4.3	130		1113	4.6	140
	1836	24.3	740		1723	24.0	730
					2340	5.2	160
3 Sa	0052	4.9	150	18 Su	0548	24.0	730
	0703	24.0	730		1207	4.3	130
	1320	4.6	140		1819	24.6	750
	1936	24.3	740				
4 Su	0153	4.6	140	19 M	0038	4.6	140
	0803	23.6	720		0646	24.3	740
	1417	4.6	140		1304	3.9	120
	2031	24.6	750		1915	25.6	780
5 M	0249	4.3	130	20 Tu	0136	3.6	110
	0859	24.0	730		0745	24.9	760
	1510	4.6	140		1401	3.3	100
	2121	24.6	750		2012	26.6	810
6 Tu	0339	3.9	120	21 W	0234	2.3	70
	0949	24.0	730		0844	25.6	780
	1558	4.6	140		1458	2.3	70
	2207	24.9	760		2108	27.6	840
7 W	0425	3.6	110	22 Th	0331	1.3	40
	1035	24.0	730		0941	26.2	800
	1642	4.6	140		1554	1.6	50
	2250	24.9	760		2204	28.2	860
8 Th	0507	3.6	110	23 F	0427	0.3	10
	1117	24.0	730		1036	26.9	820
	1723	4.9	150		1649	1.3	40
	2329	25.3	770		2258	28.9	880
9 F	0546	3.6	110	24 Sa	0521	0.0	0
	1155	24.0	730		1131	27.2	830
	1801	4.9	150		1744	1.3	40
					2352	28.9	880
10 Sa	0006	25.3	770	25 Su	0615	-0.3	-10
	0623	3.6	110		1225	27.2	830
	1232	24.0	730		1838	1.3	40
	1837	5.2	160				
11 Su	0042	25.3	770	26 M	0046	28.5	870
	0659	3.6	110		0709	0.3	10
	1307	24.0	730		1319	26.9	820
	1913	5.2	160		1932	2.0	60
12 M	0118	24.9	760	27 Tu	0140	27.9	850
	0735	3.9	120		0802	1.0	30
	1343	24.0	730		1413	26.2	800
	1949	5.6	170		2026	2.6	80
13 Tu	0154	24.9	760	28 W	0234	26.9	820
	0812	4.3	130		0856	1.6	50
	1420	23.6	720		1508	25.6	780
	2028	5.6	170		2122	3.3	100
14 W	0233	24.6	750	29 Th	0330	25.9	790
	0852	4.3	130		0951	2.6	80
	1459	23.6	720		1604	24.9	760
	2110	5.6	170		2219	4.3	130
15 Th	0315	24.3	740	30 F	0428	24.9	760
	0935	4.6	140		1047	3.6	110
	1543	23.6	720		1702	24.6	750
	2156	5.6	170		2318	4.6	140

Time meridian 60° W. 0000 is midnight. 1200 is noon. Times are not adjusted for Daylight Saving Time.
Heights are referred to the Canadian chart datum of soundings.

Saint John, New Brunswick, 2017

Times and Heights of High and Low Waters

July

Day	Time	ft	cm	Day	Time	ft	cm
1 Sa	0527	24.0	730	16 Su	0422	24.6	750
	1145	4.6	140		1041	3.9	120
	1801	24.3	740		1651	24.9	760
				◗	2309	4.3	130
2 Su	0018	5.2	160	17 M	0517	24.3	740
	0629	23.3	710		1136	3.9	120
	1244	4.9	150		1746	25.3	770
	1859	24.0	730				
3 M	0118	5.2	160	18 Tu	0008	3.9	120
	0729	23.3	710		0617	24.3	740
	1342	5.2	160		1234	3.9	120
	1956	24.0	730		1846	25.6	780
4 Tu	0216	4.9	150	19 W	0109	3.3	100
	0826	23.0	700		0719	24.6	750
	1438	5.6	170		1335	3.6	110
	2049	24.3	740		1947	26.2	800
5 W	0309	4.6	140	20 Th	0212	2.6	80
	0919	23.3	710		0822	24.9	760
	1528	5.6	170		1437	3.0	90
	2138	24.3	740		2048	26.9	820
6 Th	0357	4.3	130	21 F	0313	1.6	50
	1007	23.3	710		0923	25.6	780
	1614	5.2	160		1537	2.6	80
	2223	24.6	750		2148	27.6	840
7 F	0441	4.3	130	22 Sa	0411	1.0	30
	1051	23.6	720		1022	26.2	800
	1656	5.2	160		1634	2.0	60
	2303	24.9	760		2244	28.2	860
8 Sa	0521	3.9	120	23 Su	0507	0.7	20
	1130	23.6	720		1117	26.6	810
	1735	5.2	160		1730	1.6	50
	2341	25.3	770	●	2339	28.2	860
9 Su	0558	3.6	110	24 M	0601	0.3	10
	1206	24.0	730		1210	26.9	820
○	1811	4.9	150		1823	1.6	50
10 M	0017	25.3	770	25 Tu	0031	28.2	860
	0634	3.6	110		0652	0.7	20
	1241	24.3	740		1301	26.6	810
	1847	4.9	150		1914	2.0	60
11 Tu	0053	25.3	770	26 W	0122	27.6	840
	0709	3.3	100		0742	1.3	40
	1316	24.3	740		1352	26.2	800
	1924	4.6	140		2005	2.6	80
12 W	0129	25.3	770	27 Th	0212	26.9	820
	0746	3.3	100		0831	2.0	60
	1352	24.6	750		1441	25.9	790
	2002	4.6	140		2055	3.3	100
13 Th	0207	25.3	770	28 F	0303	25.9	790
	0825	3.3	100		0921	3.0	90
	1431	24.6	750		1532	25.3	770
	2042	4.6	140		2147	3.9	120
14 F	0248	25.3	770	29 Sa	0356	24.9	760
	0906	3.6	110		1013	3.9	120
	1513	24.6	750		1625	24.6	750
	2127	4.3	130		2242	4.6	140
15 Sa	0332	24.9	760	30 Su	0451	24.0	730
	0951	3.6	110		1107	4.9	150
	1559	24.6	750		1721	24.0	730
	2215	4.3	130	◐	2339	5.2	160
				31 M	0549	23.0	700
					1204	5.6	170
					1818	23.6	720

August

Day	Time	ft	cm	Day	Time	ft	cm
1 Tu	0038	5.6	170	16 W	0555	24.3	740
	0650	22.3	680		1213	3.9	120
	1303	6.2	190		1824	25.6	780
	1917	23.3	710				
2 W	0137	5.6	180	17 Th	0050	3.6	110
	0749	22.3	680		0701	24.3	740
	1400	6.2	190		1318	3.9	120
	2013	23.3	710		1930	25.6	780
3 Th	0233	5.6	170	18 F	0156	3.0	90
	0845	22.3	680		0808	24.6	750
	1454	6.2	190		1423	3.6	110
	2105	23.6	720		2035	26.2	800
4 F	0324	5.2	160	19 Sa	0259	2.6	80
	0935	22.6	690		0911	24.9	760
	1543	5.9	180		1525	3.3	100
	2152	24.0	730		2136	26.9	820
5 Sa	0410	4.6	140	20 Su	0359	2.0	60
	1020	23.0	700		1010	25.6	780
	1626	5.6	170		1623	2.6	80
	2235	24.6	750		2233	27.2	830
6 Su	0451	4.3	130	21 M	0454	1.3	40
	1059	23.6	720		1104	26.2	800
	1706	4.9	150		1716	2.3	70
	2314	24.9	760	●	2325	27.6	840
7 M	0529	3.6	110	22 Tu	0545	1.3	40
	1137	24.3	740		1154	26.6	810
	1743	4.6	140		1807	2.0	60
○	2351	25.6	780				
8 Tu	0606	3.3	100	23 W	0014	27.2	830
	1212	24.6	750		0633	1.3	40
	1820	3.9	120		1241	26.6	810
					1854	2.0	60
9 W	0026	25.9	790	24 Th	0101	26.9	820
	0642	3.0	90		0719	1.6	50
	1247	24.9	760		1327	26.2	800
	1857	3.6	110		1941	2.6	80
10 Th	0103	25.9	790	25 F	0148	26.2	800
	0719	2.6	80		0804	2.3	70
	1324	25.3	770		1412	25.9	790
	1935	3.3	100		2027	3.0	90
11 F	0141	25.9	790	26 Sa	0235	25.3	770
	0757	2.3	70		0850	3.3	100
	1402	25.6	780		1459	25.3	770
	2016	3.0	90		2115	3.9	120
12 Sa	0222	25.9	790	27 Su	0323	24.6	750
	0839	2.6	80		0937	4.3	130
	1445	25.6	780		1548	24.6	750
	2101	3.0	90		2205	4.6	140
13 Su	0307	25.6	780	28 M	0414	23.6	720
	0925	3.0	90		1028	5.2	160
	1532	25.6	780		1639	23.6	720
	2150	3.3	100		2258	5.6	170
14 M	0357	24.9	760	29 Tu	0509	22.6	690
	1015	3.3	100		1122	6.2	190
	1624	25.6	780		1735	23.0	700
◐	2244	3.3	100	◐	2355	6.2	190
15 Tu	0453	24.6	750	30 W	0607	22.0	670
	1111	3.6	110		1220	6.9	210
	1721	25.6	780		1833	22.6	690
	2345	3.6	110				
				31 Th	0054	6.6	200
					0707	21.7	660
					1319	7.2	220
					1932	22.6	690

September

Day	Time	ft	cm	Day	Time	ft	cm
1 F	0152	6.2	190	16 Sa	0145	3.6	110
	0805	21.7	660		0759	24.0	730
	1415	6.9	210		1414	4.3	130
	2027	23.0	700		2026	25.6	780
2 Sa	0246	5.9	180	17 Su	0249	3.3	100
	0857	22.3	680		0902	24.6	750
	1506	6.6	200		1516	3.6	110
	2117	23.6	720		2127	25.9	790
3 Su	0334	5.2	160	18 M	0347	2.6	80
	0944	23.0	700		0958	25.3	770
	1552	5.6	170		1612	3.0	90
	2201	24.3	740		2222	26.2	800
4 M	0417	4.3	130	19 Tu	0440	2.3	70
	1025	23.6	720		1049	25.9	790
	1633	4.6	140		1703	2.6	80
	2242	24.9	760		2311	26.6	810
5 Tu	0456	3.6	110	20 W	0527	2.0	60
	1103	24.6	750		1136	26.2	800
	1712	3.9	120		1750	2.3	70
	2320	25.6	780	●	2357	26.6	810
6 W	0534	2.6	80	21 Th	0612	2.0	60
	1140	25.3	770		1219	26.2	800
	1750	3.0	90		1834	2.3	70
○	2357	26.2	800				
7 Th	0612	2.3	70	22 F	0041	26.2	800
	1216	25.9	790		0655	2.6	80
	1829	2.3	70		1302	26.2	800
					1917	2.6	80
8 F	0035	26.6	810	23 Sa	0124	25.6	780
	0650	1.6	50		0737	3.0	90
	1255	26.6	810		1344	25.6	780
	1909	2.0	60		1959	3.0	90
9 Sa	0115	26.6	810	24 Su	0207	24.9	760
	0731	1.6	50		0819	3.9	120
	1336	26.6	810		1427	25.3	770
	1952	1.6	50		2043	3.6	110
10 Su	0158	26.2	800	25 M	0252	24.0	730
	0814	2.0	60		0903	4.9	150
	1420	26.6	810		1511	24.3	740
	2038	2.0	60		2129	4.6	140
11 M	0246	25.9	790	26 Tu	0339	23.3	710
	0902	2.6	80		0950	5.9	180
	1509	26.2	800		1559	23.6	720
	2129	2.3	70		2218	5.6	170
12 Tu	0338	25.3	770	27 W	0429	22.3	680
	0955	3.3	100		1040	6.6	200
	1603	25.9	790		1651	23.0	700
	2226	3.0	90	◑	2311	6.2	190
13 W	0437	24.6	750	28 Th	0524	21.7	660
	1054	3.9	120		1135	7.2	220
	1704	25.3	770		1747	22.3	680
○	2329	3.6	110				
14 Th	0541	24.0	730	29 F	0008	6.6	200
	1159	4.6	140		0622	21.3	650
	1810	24.9	760		1233	7.5	230
					1846	22.3	680
15 F	0037	3.6	110	30 Sa	0106	6.6	200
	0650	24.0	730		0720	21.7	660
	1307	4.6	140		1331	7.2	220
	1920	24.9	760		1943	22.6	690

Time meridian 60° W. 0000 is midnight. 1200 is noon. Times are not adjusted for Daylight Saving Time.
Heights are referred to the Canadian chart datum of soundings.

Saint John, New Brunswick, 2017

Times and Heights of High and Low Waters

October

Day	Time	Height (ft)	Height (cm)
1 Su	0201 / 0814 / 1425 / 2036	6.2 / 22.3 / 6.6 / 23.3	190 / 680 / 200 / 710
2 M	0252 / 0902 / 1513 / 2123	5.2 / 23.0 / 5.6 / 24.0	160 / 700 / 170 / 730
3 Tu	0337 / 0945 / 1557 / 2206	4.3 / 24.0 / 4.3 / 24.9	130 / 730 / 130 / 760
4 W	0419 / 1026 / 1638 / 2246	3.3 / 24.9 / 3.0 / 25.6	100 / 760 / 90 / 780
5 Th ○	0459 / 1105 / 1720 / 2327	2.3 / 26.2 / 2.0 / 26.2	70 / 800 / 60 / 800
6 F	0540 / 1145 / 1801	1.6 / 26.9 / 1.3	50 / 820 / 40
7 Sa	0008 / 0622 / 1227 / 1845	26.9 / 1.3 / 27.6 / 0.7	820 / 40 / 840 / 20
8 Su	0052 / 0706 / 1311 / 1931	26.9 / 1.3 / 27.6 / 0.7	820 / 40 / 840 / 20
9 M	0138 / 0753 / 1359 / 2020	26.6 / 1.6 / 27.6 / 1.0	810 / 50 / 840 / 30
10 Tu	0229 / 0844 / 1451 / 2114	26.2 / 2.3 / 26.9 / 1.6	800 / 70 / 820 / 50
11 W	0324 / 0940 / 1548 / 2213	25.3 / 3.3 / 26.2 / 2.6	770 / 100 / 800 / 80
12 Th ◑	0426 / 1042 / 1652 / 2318	24.6 / 4.3 / 25.3 / 3.3	750 / 130 / 770 / 100
13 F	0532 / 1149 / 1800	24.0 / 4.6 / 24.9	730 / 140 / 760
14 Sa	0026 / 0642 / 1258 / 1910	3.9 / 24.0 / 4.9 / 24.6	120 / 730 / 150 / 750
15 Su	0134 / 0749 / 1404 / 2016	3.9 / 24.3 / 4.3 / 24.9	120 / 740 / 130 / 760
16 M	0236 / 0850 / 1504 / 2115	3.6 / 24.6 / 3.9 / 25.3	110 / 750 / 120 / 770
17 Tu	0332 / 0944 / 1558 / 2208	3.3 / 25.3 / 3.3 / 25.6	100 / 770 / 100 / 780
18 W	0422 / 1032 / 1647 / 2255	3.0 / 25.6 / 2.6 / 25.6	90 / 780 / 80 / 780
19 Th ●	0508 / 1116 / 1731 / 2339	3.0 / 25.9 / 2.6 / 25.6	90 / 790 / 80 / 780
20 F	0551 / 1157 / 1813	3.0 / 25.9 / 2.6	90 / 790 / 80
21 Sa	0021 / 0632 / 1237 / 1854	25.3 / 3.3 / 25.9 / 2.6	770 / 100 / 790 / 80
22 Su	0102 / 0711 / 1317 / 1934	24.9 / 3.9 / 25.6 / 3.3	760 / 120 / 780 / 100
23 M	0143 / 0751 / 1357 / 2015	24.3 / 4.6 / 24.9 / 3.9	740 / 140 / 760 / 120
24 Tu	0224 / 0832 / 1439 / 2057	24.0 / 5.2 / 24.3 / 4.6	730 / 160 / 740 / 140
25 W	0307 / 0915 / 1522 / 2141	23.3 / 6.2 / 23.6 / 5.2	710 / 190 / 720 / 160
26 Th	0352 / 1001 / 1610 / 2229	22.6 / 6.9 / 23.0 / 5.9	690 / 210 / 700 / 180
27 F ◐	0442 / 1052 / 1702 / 2322	22.0 / 7.2 / 22.6 / 6.2	670 / 220 / 690 / 190
28 Sa	0536 / 1147 / 1758	22.0 / 7.5 / 22.3	670 / 230 / 680
29 Su	0017 / 0632 / 1244 / 1855	6.6 / 22.0 / 7.2 / 22.6	200 / 670 / 220 / 690
30 M	0113 / 0726 / 1339 / 1949	5.9 / 22.6 / 6.6 / 23.0	180 / 690 / 200 / 700
31 Tu	0205 / 0817 / 1430 / 2040	5.2 / 23.3 / 5.2 / 24.0	160 / 710 / 160 / 730

November

Day	Time	Height (ft)	Height (cm)
1 W	0254 / 0903 / 1518 / 2127	4.3 / 24.6 / 3.9 / 24.9	130 / 750 / 120 / 760
2 Th	0340 / 0948 / 1604 / 2212	3.3 / 25.9 / 2.6 / 25.6	100 / 790 / 80 / 780
3 F	0425 / 1032 / 1649 / 2257	2.3 / 26.9 / 1.3 / 26.6	70 / 820 / 40 / 810
4 Sa ○	0509 / 1116 / 1735 / 2343	1.3 / 27.9 / 0.3 / 26.9	40 / 850 / 10 / 820
5 Su	0556 / 1202 / 1823	1.0 / 28.5 / 0.0	30 / 870 / 0
6 M	0031 / 0644 / 1251 / 1912	27.2 / 1.0 / 28.5 / 0.0	830 / 30 / 870 / 0
7 Tu	0122 / 0735 / 1342 / 2005	26.9 / 1.6 / 28.2 / 0.7	820 / 50 / 860 / 20
8 W	0215 / 0829 / 1437 / 2101	26.2 / 2.3 / 27.2 / 1.3	800 / 70 / 830 / 40
9 Th	0313 / 0927 / 1536 / 2201	25.6 / 3.3 / 26.2 / 2.3	780 / 100 / 800 / 70
10 F ○	0415 / 1030 / 1640 / 2305	24.9 / 3.9 / 25.3 / 3.3	760 / 120 / 770 / 100
11 Sa	0521 / 1136 / 1748	24.3 / 4.6 / 24.6	740 / 140 / 750
12 Su	0011 / 0628 / 1244 / 1856	3.9 / 24.3 / 4.6 / 24.3	120 / 740 / 140 / 740
13 M	0116 / 0732 / 1348 / 1959	3.9 / 24.3 / 4.6 / 24.3	120 / 740 / 140 / 740
14 Tu	0216 / 0831 / 1447 / 2058	3.9 / 24.6 / 3.9 / 24.6	120 / 750 / 120 / 750
15 W	0311 / 0923 / 1540 / 2150	3.9 / 25.3 / 3.6 / 24.6	120 / 770 / 110 / 750
16 Th	0401 / 1011 / 1628 / 2237	3.6 / 25.6 / 3.0 / 24.9	110 / 780 / 90 / 760
17 F	0447 / 1055 / 1712 / 2321	3.6 / 25.6 / 3.0 / 24.9	110 / 780 / 90 / 760
18 Sa ●	0529 / 1136 / 1753	3.9 / 25.6 / 3.0	120 / 780 / 90
19 Su	0002 / 0609 / 1215 / 1832	24.6 / 4.3 / 25.6 / 3.0	750 / 130 / 780 / 90
20 M	0041 / 0648 / 1253 / 1911	24.3 / 4.6 / 25.3 / 3.6	740 / 140 / 770 / 110
21 Tu	0120 / 0726 / 1331 / 1949	24.0 / 5.2 / 24.9 / 3.9	730 / 160 / 760 / 120
22 W	0158 / 0804 / 1410 / 2028	23.6 / 5.6 / 24.6 / 4.6	720 / 170 / 750 / 140
23 Th	0237 / 0844 / 1450 / 2108	23.3 / 6.2 / 24.0 / 4.9	710 / 190 / 730 / 150
24 F	0319 / 0927 / 1534 / 2152	23.0 / 6.6 / 23.6 / 5.2	700 / 200 / 720 / 160
25 Sa	0404 / 1013 / 1621 / 2240	22.6 / 6.9 / 23.0 / 5.6	690 / 210 / 700 / 170
26 Su ◐	0452 / 1104 / 1712 / 2331	22.6 / 6.9 / 23.0 / 5.6	690 / 210 / 700 / 170
27 M	0544 / 1158 / 1807	22.6 / 6.6 / 23.0	690 / 200 / 700
28 Tu	0025 / 0638 / 1253 / 1902	5.6 / 23.3 / 5.9 / 23.3	170 / 710 / 180 / 710
29 W	0118 / 0730 / 1348 / 1956	4.9 / 24.0 / 4.9 / 24.0	150 / 730 / 150 / 730
30 Th	0211 / 0822 / 1440 / 2049	4.3 / 25.3 / 3.6 / 24.9	130 / 770 / 110 / 760

December

Day	Time	Height (ft)	Height (cm)
1 F	0302 / 0911 / 1531 / 2140	3.3 / 26.2 / 2.3 / 25.6	100 / 800 / 70 / 780
2 Sa	0352 / 1001 / 1622 / 2230	2.3 / 27.6 / 1.0 / 26.6	70 / 840 / 30 / 810
3 Su ○	0443 / 1051 / 1713 / 2321	1.6 / 28.5 / 0.0 / 26.9	50 / 870 / 0 / 820
4 M	0534 / 1142 / 1804	1.3 / 28.9 / -0.3	40 / 880 / -10
5 Tu	0013 / 0626 / 1234 / 1857	27.2 / 1.0 / 28.9 / -0.3	830 / 30 / 880 / -10
6 W	0107 / 0720 / 1327 / 1951	27.2 / 1.6 / 28.5 / 0.3	830 / 50 / 870 / 10
7 Th	0202 / 0815 / 1423 / 2047	26.6 / 2.3 / 27.6 / 1.0	810 / 70 / 840 / 30
8 F	0259 / 0913 / 1522 / 2146	25.9 / 3.0 / 26.6 / 2.0	790 / 90 / 810 / 60
9 Sa	0359 / 1014 / 1623 / 2246	25.3 / 3.6 / 25.6 / 3.0	770 / 110 / 780 / 90
10 Su ○	0502 / 1117 / 1727 / 2348	24.6 / 4.3 / 24.6 / 3.6	750 / 130 / 750 / 110
11 M	0605 / 1221 / 1832	24.6 / 4.6 / 24.3	750 / 140 / 740
12 Tu	0050 / 0706 / 1324 / 1935	4.3 / 24.3 / 4.6 / 24.0	130 / 740 / 140 / 730
13 W	0150 / 0804 / 1423 / 2033	4.6 / 24.6 / 4.3 / 24.0	140 / 750 / 130 / 730
14 Th	0245 / 0858 / 1516 / 2127	4.6 / 24.9 / 3.9 / 24.0	140 / 760 / 120 / 730
15 F	0337 / 0947 / 1605 / 2216	4.6 / 24.9 / 3.6 / 24.3	140 / 760 / 110 / 740
16 Sa	0424 / 1032 / 1650 / 2300	4.6 / 25.3 / 3.3 / 24.3	140 / 770 / 100 / 740
17 Su	0507 / 1114 / 1732 / 2341	4.6 / 25.3 / 3.3 / 24.3	140 / 770 / 100 / 740
18 M ●	0547 / 1153 / 1811	4.9 / 25.3 / 3.6	150 / 770 / 110
19 Tu	0020 / 0625 / 1230 / 1848	24.0 / 4.9 / 25.3 / 3.6	730 / 150 / 770 / 110
20 W	0056 / 0702 / 1307 / 1924	24.0 / 5.2 / 25.3 / 3.9	730 / 160 / 770 / 120
21 Th	0132 / 0738 / 1344 / 2001	24.0 / 5.6 / 24.9 / 4.3	730 / 170 / 760 / 130
22 F	0209 / 0816 / 1421 / 2039	23.6 / 5.6 / 24.6 / 4.3	720 / 170 / 750 / 130
23 Sa	0247 / 0856 / 1501 / 2119	23.6 / 5.6 / 24.3 / 4.6	720 / 170 / 740 / 140
24 Su	0328 / 0939 / 1545 / 2203	23.6 / 5.9 / 24.0 / 4.9	720 / 180 / 730 / 150
25 M	0413 / 1025 / 1632 / 2251	23.6 / 5.9 / 23.6 / 4.9	720 / 180 / 720 / 150
26 Tu ◐	0501 / 1117 / 1724 / 2342	23.6 / 5.6 / 23.6 / 4.9	720 / 170 / 720 / 150
27 W	0554 / 1211 / 1820	24.0 / 5.2 / 23.6	730 / 160 / 720
28 Th	0037 / 0648 / 1309 / 1917	4.6 / 24.6 / 4.3 / 24.0	140 / 750 / 130 / 730
29 F	0133 / 0744 / 1406 / 2015	3.9 / 25.3 / 3.3 / 24.6	120 / 780 / 100 / 750
30 Sa	0229 / 0840 / 1503 / 2112	3.3 / 26.6 / 2.0 / 25.6	100 / 810 / 60 / 780
31 Su	0325 / 0936 / 1559 / 2208	2.6 / 27.6 / 1.0 / 26.2	80 / 840 / 30 / 800

Time meridian 60° W. 0000 is midnight. 1200 is noon. Times are not adjusted for Daylight Saving Time.
Heights are referred to the Canadian chart datum of soundings.

Eastport, Maine, 2017

Times and Heights of High and Low Waters

January

Day	Time	Height ft	Height cm	Day	Time	Height ft	Height cm
1 Su	0030	18.5	564	16 M	0115	19.7	600
	0645	0.8	24		0734	-0.3	-9
	1244	19.6	597		1334	20.1	613
	1911	-0.4	-12		2000	-0.9	-27
2 M	0111	18.6	567	17 Tu	0203	19.2	585
	0728	0.8	24		0822	0.4	12
	1326	19.5	594		1423	19.2	585
	1954	-0.3	-9		2048	0.0	0
3 Tu	0154	18.7	570	18 W	0252	18.6	567
	0813	0.8	24		0912	1.1	34
	1412	19.3	588		1514	18.2	555
	2040	-0.2	-6		2136	0.9	27
4 W	0242	18.8	573	19 Th	0343	18.0	549
	0903	0.9	27		1003	1.8	55
	1502	19.0	579		1607	17.3	527
	2130	0.0	0		2227	1.7	52
5 Th	0333	18.9	576	20 F	0435	17.5	533
	0956	0.8	24		1057	2.2	67
	1557	18.7	570		1702	16.7	509
	2223	0.3	9		2320	2.3	70
6 F	0429	19.0	579	21 Sa	0530	17.3	527
	1055	0.7	21		1153	2.4	73
	1656	18.5	564		1759	16.3	497
	2321	0.4	12				
7 Sa	0528	19.3	588	22 Su	0015	2.6	79
	1156	0.4	12		0625	17.3	527
	1758	18.5	564		1249	2.3	70
					1855	16.3	497
8 Su	0022	0.4	12	23 M	0109	2.6	79
	0628	19.8	604		0718	17.6	536
	1259	-0.2	-6		1343	1.9	58
	1901	18.7	570		1949	16.6	506
9 M	0123	0.1	3	24 Tu	0201	2.4	73
	0728	20.4	622		0809	18.0	549
	1400	-0.9	-27		1434	1.4	43
	2002	19.2	585		2038	17.0	518
10 Tu	0223	-0.4	-12	25 W	0250	1.9	58
	0827	21.1	643		0856	18.5	564
	1459	-1.7	-52		1520	0.7	21
	2100	19.7	600		2124	17.5	533
11 W	0320	-0.9	-27	26 Th	0336	1.4	43
	0922	21.6	658		0940	19.1	582
	1554	-2.3	-70		1604	0.1	3
	2155	20.1	613		2206	18.0	549
12 Th	0414	-1.3	-40	27 F	0419	0.9	27
	1016	21.9	668		1021	19.6	597
	1647	-2.7	-82		1645	-0.5	-15
	2247	20.4	622		2247	18.5	564
13 F	0506	-1.4	-43	28 Sa	0500	0.4	12
	1107	21.9	668		1101	20.0	610
	1737	-2.7	-82		1726	-0.9	-27
	2338	20.4	622		2326	19.0	579
14 Sa	0556	-1.3	-40	29 Su	0541	0.0	0
	1157	21.6	658		1141	20.3	619
	1825	-2.3	-70		1807	-1.2	-37
15 Su	0026	20.2	616	30 M	0006	19.3	588
	0645	-0.9	-27		0623	-0.3	-9
	1246	21.0	640		1222	20.4	622
	1913	-1.7	-52		1848	-1.3	-40
				31 Tu	0047	19.6	597
					0706	-0.4	-12
					1305	20.3	619
					1931	-1.2	-37

February

Day	Time	Height ft	Height cm	Day	Time	Height ft	Height cm
1 W	0131	19.8	604	16 Th	0215	18.7	570
	0752	-0.4	-12		0836	0.8	24
	1351	20.0	610		1438	18.2	555
	2017	-0.9	-27		2057	1.1	34
2 Th	0217	19.8	604	17 F	0301	18.1	552
	0841	-0.3	-9		0923	1.5	46
	1440	19.6	597		1526	17.3	527
	2106	-0.5	-15		2144	1.9	58
3 F	0308	19.7	600	18 Sa	0350	17.5	533
	0934	-0.1	-3		1013	2.1	64
	1535	19.0	579		1618	16.5	503
	2200	0.0	0		2235	2.6	79
4 Sa	0404	19.5	594	19 Su	0443	17.1	521
	1033	0.2	6		1106	2.5	76
	1635	18.5	564		1713	16.0	488
	2259	0.5	15		2329	3.0	91
5 Su	0505	19.4	591	20 M	0539	16.9	515
	1135	0.3	9		1203	2.6	79
	1738	18.1	552		1811	15.9	485
6 M	0001	0.8	24	21 Tu	0026	3.1	94
	0608	19.4	591		0635	17.0	518
	1240	0.1	3		1300	2.4	73
	1843	18.1	552		1908	16.1	491
7 Tu	0105	0.7	21	22 W	0122	2.8	85
	0711	19.7	600		0730	17.4	530
	1344	-0.4	-12		1355	1.8	55
	1947	18.5	564		2001	16.6	506
8 W	0208	0.2	6	23 Th	0215	2.2	67
	0812	20.2	616		0821	18.1	552
	1444	-1.0	-30		1445	1.0	30
	2047	19.0	579		2050	17.4	530
9 Th	0306	-0.3	-9	24 F	0304	1.4	43
	0910	20.7	631		0909	18.9	576
	1540	-1.6	-49		1532	0.2	6
	2142	19.6	597		2135	18.2	555
10 F	0401	-0.9	-27	25 Sa	0350	0.5	15
	1003	21.1	643		0953	19.7	600
	1631	-2.0	-61		1616	-0.6	-18
	2232	20.0	610		2217	19.0	579
11 Sa	0451	-1.2	-37	26 Su	0433	-0.3	-9
	1052	21.2	646		1035	20.3	619
	1719	-2.1	-64		1659	-1.3	-40
	2319	20.2	616		2259	19.8	604
12 Su	0538	-1.2	-37	27 M	0517	-0.9	-27
	1139	21.1	643		1117	20.8	634
	1804	-1.9	-58		1741	-1.7	-52
					2340	20.4	622
13 M	0004	20.1	613	28 Tu	0600	-1.4	-43
	0623	-1.0	-30		1200	21.0	640
	1223	20.6	628		1824	-1.9	-58
	1848	-1.4	-43				
14 Tu	0048	19.8	604				
	0707	-0.5	-15				
	1308	19.9	607				
	1930	-0.6	-18				
15 W	0131	19.3	588				
	0751	0.1	3				
	1352	19.1	582				
	2013	0.2	6				

March

Day	Time	Height ft	Height cm	Day	Time	Height ft	Height cm
1 W	0023	20.8	634	16 Th	0059	19.4	591
	0645	-1.7	-52		0721	-0.1	-3
	1244	21.0	640		1322	18.8	573
	1908	-1.8	-55		1940	0.6	18
2 Th	0107	20.9	637	17 F	0140	18.9	576
	0732	-1.6	-49		0802	0.5	15
	1331	20.6	628		1404	18.1	552
	1955	-1.4	-43		2021	1.3	40
3 F	0155	20.7	631	18 Sa	0223	18.3	558
	0822	-1.3	-40		0845	1.2	37
	1422	20.0	610		1449	17.3	527
	2046	-0.7	-21		2105	2.1	64
4 Sa	0247	20.3	619	19 Su	0309	17.7	539
	0916	-0.8	-24		0932	1.8	55
	1517	19.2	585		1538	16.6	506
	2141	0.0	0		2153	2.7	82
5 Su	0344	19.8	604	20 M	0400	17.1	521
	1015	-0.2	-6		1023	2.3	70
	1617	18.4	561		1631	16.1	491
	2241	0.7	21		2246	3.1	94
6 M	0446	19.2	585	21 Tu	0454	16.8	512
	1118	0.2	6		1119	2.6	79
	1722	17.9	546		1727	15.9	485
	2345	1.1	34		2343	3.2	98
7 Tu	0551	19.0	579	22 W	0552	16.8	512
	1224	0.3	9		1217	2.4	73
	1829	17.8	543		1825	16.2	494
8 W	0051	1.1	34	23 Th	0041	2.9	88
	0657	19.1	582		0649	17.2	524
	1329	0.1	3		1313	1.9	58
	1934	18.1	552		1920	16.8	512
9 Th	0155	0.7	21	24 F	0137	2.2	67
	0800	19.5	594		0743	17.9	546
	1430	-0.4	-12		1407	1.1	34
	2034	18.7	570		2012	17.6	536
10 F	0253	0.0	0	25 Sa	0229	1.3	40
	0857	19.9	607		0834	18.8	573
	1524	-0.9	-27		1457	0.2	6
	2127	19.3	588		2100	18.7	570
11 Sa	0346	-0.5	-15	26 Su	0318	0.2	6
	0949	20.3	619		0921	19.7	600
	1614	-1.3	-40		1544	-0.7	-21
	2215	19.8	604		2145	19.7	600
12 Su	0434	-1.2	-37	27 M	0405	-0.9	-27
	1035	20.5	625		1007	20.6	628
	1658	-1.4	-43		1629	-1.5	-46
	2258	20.0	610		2229	20.7	631
13 M	0518	-1.1	-34	28 Tu	0451	-1.8	-55
	1119	20.4	622		1052	21.2	646
	1740	-1.2	-37		1714	-2.0	-61
	2340	20.0	610		2313	21.4	652
14 Tu	0600	-0.9	-27	29 W	0537	-2.4	-73
	1200	20.0	610		1137	21.4	652
	1820	-0.8	-24		1759	-2.2	-67
					2358	21.8	664
15 W	0020	19.8	604	30 Th	0624	-2.7	-82
	0640	-0.6	-18		1224	21.3	649
	1241	19.5	594		1846	-2.0	-61
	1900	-0.1	-3				
				31 F	0045	21.8	664
					0713	-2.5	-76
					1313	20.9	637
					1935	-1.5	-46

Time meridian 75° W. 0000 is midnight. 1200 is noon. Times are not adjusted for Daylight Saving Time.
Heights are referred to mean lower low water which is the chart datum of soundings.

Eastport, Maine, 2017

Times and Heights of High and Low Waters

April

Day	Time (h m)	Height (ft)	Height (cm)
1 Sa	0135	21.4	652
	0804	-2.0	-61
	1406	20.2	616
	2028	-0.7	-21
2 Su	0229	20.7	631
	0859	-1.3	-40
	1502	19.3	588
	2124	0.1	3
3 M	0327	19.9	607
	0959	-0.5	-15
	1603	18.5	564
	2225	0.8	24
4 Tu	0430	19.2	585
	1102	0.1	3
	1708	18.0	549
	2330	1.3	40
5 W	0536	18.7	570
	1207	0.4	12
	1815	17.9	546
6 Th	0036	1.3	40
	0643	18.7	570
	1311	0.4	12
	1919	18.1	552
7 F	0140	0.9	27
	0745	18.9	576
	1411	0.1	3
	2016	18.7	570
8 Sa	0237	0.3	9
	0841	19.2	585
	1504	-0.3	-9
	2107	19.2	585
9 Su	0328	-0.2	-6
	0931	19.5	594
	1551	-0.5	-15
	2153	19.6	597
10 M	0414	-0.6	-18
	1015	19.7	600
	1634	-0.5	-15
	2234	19.8	604
11 Tu	0456	-0.7	-21
	1056	19.6	597
	1714	-0.3	-9
	2313	19.9	607
12 W	0535	-0.7	-21
	1136	19.4	591
	1753	0.0	0
	2351	19.7	600
13 Th	0614	-0.4	-12
	1214	19.0	579
	1831	0.5	15
14 F	0029	19.4	591
	0652	0.0	0
	1254	18.5	564
	1909	1.0	30
15 Sa	0108	18.9	576
	0732	0.4	12
	1334	18.0	549
	1949	1.6	49
16 Su	0150	18.4	561
	0813	1.0	30
	1417	17.4	530
	2032	2.2	67
17 M	0234	17.9	546
	0858	1.5	46
	1503	16.9	515
	2118	2.7	82
18 Tu	0321	17.4	530
	0947	1.9	58
	1553	16.5	503
	2209	3.0	91
19 W	0414	17.1	521
	1039	2.1	64
	1647	16.4	500
	2304	3.0	91
20 Th	0510	17.1	521
	1135	2.1	64
	1743	16.7	509
21 F	0001	2.7	82
	0607	17.4	530
	1232	1.7	52
	1839	17.3	527
22 Sa	0058	2.0	61
	0703	18.0	549
	1327	1.0	30
	1932	18.2	555
23 Su	0153	1.0	30
	0757	18.9	576
	1419	0.1	3
	2023	19.4	591
24 M	0245	-0.2	-6
	0848	19.8	604
	1510	-0.7	-21
	2112	20.5	625
25 Tu	0336	-1.4	-43
	0937	20.6	628
	1559	-1.5	-46
	2159	21.4	652
26 W	0425	-2.4	-73
	1026	21.2	646
	1647	-2.0	-61
	2247	22.1	674
27 Th	0514	-3.0	-91
	1115	21.5	655
	1736	-2.1	-64
	2335	22.4	683
28 F	0604	-3.2	-98
	1205	21.4	652
	1826	-1.9	-58
29 Sa	0025	22.3	680
	0655	-3.0	-91
	1256	20.9	637
	1917	-1.4	-43
30 Su	0117	21.8	664
	0748	-2.4	-73
	1350	20.3	619
	2011	-0.7	-21

May

Day	Time (h m)	Height (ft)	Height (cm)
1 M	0212	21.0	640
	0844	-1.6	-49
	1448	19.5	594
	2109	0.1	3
2 Tu	0311	20.0	610
	0942	-0.8	-24
	1548	18.8	573
	2210	0.8	24
3 W	0414	19.2	585
	1044	0.0	0
	1652	18.3	558
	2313	1.2	37
4 Th	0518	18.6	567
	1146	0.5	15
	1756	18.2	555
5 F	0017	1.3	40
	0623	18.4	561
	1248	0.6	18
	1857	18.3	558
6 Sa	0118	1.0	30
	0723	18.4	561
	1345	0.6	18
	1952	18.7	570
7 Su	0215	0.6	18
	0818	18.6	567
	1437	0.5	15
	2042	19.1	582
8 M	0305	0.2	6
	0907	18.7	570
	1524	0.4	12
	2126	19.4	591
9 Tu	0350	-0.1	-3
	0951	18.8	573
	1607	0.4	12
	2207	19.6	597
10 W	0431	-0.3	-9
	1032	18.8	573
	1647	0.6	18
	2246	19.6	597
11 Th	0510	-0.3	-9
	1111	18.7	570
	1725	0.8	24
	2324	19.5	594
12 F	0548	-0.2	-6
	1150	18.5	564
	1803	1.1	34
13 Sa	0002	19.3	588
	0626	0.1	3
	1228	18.2	555
	1842	1.4	43
14 Su	0041	18.9	576
	0705	0.4	12
	1308	17.9	546
	1921	1.8	55
15 M	0121	18.6	567
	0746	0.7	21
	1349	17.5	533
	2003	2.1	64
16 Tu	0203	18.2	555
	0829	1.1	34
	1433	17.3	527
	2048	2.4	73
17 W	0249	17.9	546
	0915	1.3	40
	1520	17.1	521
	2136	2.5	76
18 Th	0338	17.7	539
	1005	1.5	46
	1611	17.2	524
	2229	2.5	76
19 F	0432	17.6	536
	1057	1.4	43
	1705	17.5	533
	2324	2.1	64
20 Sa	0528	17.8	543
	1152	1.2	37
	1800	18.1	552
21 Su	0022	1.5	46
	0625	18.3	558
	1248	0.7	21
	1854	19.0	579
22 M	0119	0.5	15
	0721	18.9	576
	1344	0.1	3
	1948	20.0	610
23 Tu	0214	-0.6	-18
	0816	19.7	600
	1437	-0.6	-18
	2040	21.0	640
24 W	0308	-1.7	-52
	0910	20.4	622
	1530	-1.3	-40
	2132	21.9	668
25 Th	0401	-2.6	-79
	1002	20.9	637
	1622	-1.7	-52
	2223	22.4	683
26 F	0453	-3.1	-94
	1054	21.2	646
	1714	-1.8	-55
	2314	22.6	689
27 Sa	0545	-3.3	-101
	1146	21.1	643
	1806	-1.7	-52
28 Su	0006	22.4	683
	0638	-3.1	-94
	1240	20.8	634
	1900	-1.3	-40
29 M	0100	21.8	664
	0731	-2.6	-79
	1335	20.3	619
	1955	-0.7	-21
30 Tu	0156	21.0	640
	0826	-1.8	-55
	1431	19.7	600
	2051	0.0	0
31 W	0253	20.1	613
	0923	-1.0	-30
	1530	19.1	582
	2150	0.6	18

June

Day	Time (h m)	Height (ft)	Height (cm)
1 Th	0353	19.2	585
	1021	-0.1	-3
	1629	18.6	567
	2250	1.1	34
2 F	0455	18.5	564
	1119	0.5	15
	1729	18.4	561
	2351	1.3	40
3 Sa	0556	18.1	552
	1217	0.9	27
	1827	18.4	561
4 Su	0050	1.2	37
	0654	17.8	543
	1313	1.2	37
	1921	18.5	564
5 M	0145	1.0	30
	0749	17.8	543
	1405	1.2	37
	2010	18.8	573
6 Tu	0236	0.7	21
	0838	17.9	546
	1453	1.2	37
	2056	19.0	579
7 W	0322	0.4	12
	0924	18.0	549
	1537	1.2	37
	2139	19.2	585
8 Th	0404	0.2	6
	1006	18.1	552
	1619	1.2	37
	2219	19.2	585
9 F	0444	0.1	3
	1046	18.1	552
	1658	1.3	40
	2258	19.2	585
10 Sa	0523	0.1	3
	1125	18.1	552
	1738	1.4	43
	2337	19.1	582
11 Su	0602	0.1	3
	1204	18.0	549
	1817	1.5	46
12 M	0016	19.0	579
	0641	0.2	6
	1243	17.9	546
	1857	1.7	52
13 Tu	0056	18.8	573
	0721	0.4	12
	1323	17.8	543
	1938	1.8	55
14 W	0137	18.6	567
	0803	0.5	15
	1405	17.8	543
	2021	1.9	58
15 Th	0221	18.4	561
	0847	0.7	21
	1450	17.9	546
	2108	1.8	55
16 F	0308	18.3	558
	0934	0.7	21
	1539	18.1	552
	2158	1.7	52
17 Sa	0359	18.2	555
	1024	0.8	24
	1631	18.4	561
	2253	1.4	43
18 Su	0454	18.3	558
	1118	0.7	21
	1725	18.9	576
	2350	0.8	24
19 M	0552	18.5	564
	1215	0.5	15
	1821	19.5	594
20 Tu	0048	0.1	3
	0651	18.9	576
	1312	0.1	3
	1917	20.3	619
21 W	0147	-0.7	-21
	0749	19.4	591
	1409	-0.4	-12
	2013	21.1	643
22 Th	0244	-1.6	-49
	0846	19.9	607
	1506	-0.9	-27
	2108	21.8	664
23 F	0340	-2.4	-73
	0941	20.4	622
	1601	-1.3	-40
	2202	22.2	677
24 Sa	0434	-2.9	-88
	1035	20.7	631
	1655	-1.6	-49
	2256	22.4	683
25 Su	0528	-3.1	-94
	1129	20.8	634
	1749	-1.5	-46
	2349	22.2	677
26 M	0620	-3.0	-91
	1222	20.6	628
	1842	-1.3	-40
27 Tu	0042	21.7	661
	0713	-2.5	-76
	1316	20.3	619
	1936	-0.8	-24
28 W	0137	20.9	637
	0805	-1.8	-55
	1410	19.8	604
	2030	-0.2	-6
29 Th	0231	20.0	610
	0858	-1.0	-30
	1505	19.3	588
	2125	0.4	12
30 F	0327	19.1	582
	0952	-0.1	-3
	1600	18.8	573
	2221	1.0	30

Time meridian 75° W. 0000 is midnight. 1200 is noon. Times are not adjusted for Daylight Saving Time.
Heights are referred to mean lower low water which is the chart datum of soundings.

Eastport, Maine, 2017
Times and Heights of High and Low Waters

July

Day	Time	ft	cm		Day	Time	ft	cm
1 Sa	0424	18.3	558		16 Su	0332	18.7	570
	1046	0.7	21			0956	0.2	6
	1655	18.4	561			1601	19.1	582
	2317	1.4	43		☽	2225	0.6	18
2 Su	0522	17.6	536		17 M	0426	18.5	564
	1141	1.3	40			1050	0.4	12
	1750	18.2	555			1656	19.4	591
						2323	0.3	9
3 M	0014	1.5	46		18 Tu	0525	18.5	564
	0619	17.2	524			1147	0.4	12
	1235	1.7	52			1754	19.7	600
	1844	18.1	552					
4 Tu	0109	1.5	46		19 W	0023	-0.1	-3
	0714	17.1	521			0626	18.6	567
	1328	1.9	58			1247	0.3	9
	1935	18.3	558			1853	20.2	616
5 W	0201	1.3	40		20 Th	0124	-0.7	-21
	0805	17.2	524			0727	18.9	576
	1418	1.9	58			1347	-0.1	-3
	2024	18.5	564			1952	20.8	634
6 Th	0250	1.0	30		21 F	0224	-1.4	-43
	0853	17.3	527			0826	19.4	591
	1505	1.8	55			1447	-0.5	-15
	2109	18.7	570			2050	21.3	649
7 F	0335	0.6	18		22 Sa	0322	-2.0	-61
	0938	17.5	533			0924	19.9	607
	1549	1.6	49			1544	-1.0	-30
	2152	18.9	576			2145	21.7	661
8 Sa	0417	0.3	9		23 Su	0417	-2.5	-76
	1020	17.7	539			1018	20.3	619
	1631	1.5	46			1638	-1.4	-43
○	2233	19.1	582		●	2239	21.9	668
9 Su	0458	0.1	3		24 M	0510	-2.7	-82
	1100	17.9	546			1111	20.5	625
	1712	1.3	40			1731	-1.5	-46
	2313	19.2	585			2332	21.8	664
10 M	0537	0.0	0		25 Tu	0602	-2.6	-79
	1139	18.0	549			1203	20.5	625
	1752	1.2	37			1823	-1.3	-40
	2352	19.2	585					
11 Tu	0617	-0.1	-3		26 W	0023	21.3	649
	1218	18.2	555			0651	-2.2	-67
	1832	1.2	37			1253	20.3	619
						1914	-1.0	-30
12 W	0031	19.2	585		27 Th	0114	20.6	628
	0657	-0.1	-3			0740	-1.5	-46
	1257	18.3	558			1343	19.8	604
	1913	1.1	34			2004	-0.4	-12
13 Th	0112	19.1	582		28 F	0205	19.8	604
	0738	-0.1	-3			0829	-0.7	-21
	1339	18.5	564			1434	19.3	588
	1956	1.0	30			2055	0.3	9
14 F	0155	19.0	579		29 Sa	0257	18.8	573
	0821	0.0	0			0919	0.2	6
	1422	18.7	570			1524	18.7	570
	2042	0.9	27			2146	0.9	27
15 Sa	0241	18.9	576		30 Su	0349	17.9	546
	0906	0.1	3			1009	1.1	34
	1510	18.9	576			1616	18.2	555
	2132	0.8	24		☾	2239	1.5	46
					31 M	0444	17.2	524
						1101	1.8	55
						1710	17.8	543
						2334	1.8	55

August

Day	Time	ft	cm		Day	Time	ft	cm
1 Tu	0540	16.7	509		16 W	0504	18.3	558
	1155	2.3	70			1126	0.6	18
	1804	17.6	536			1732	19.6	597
2 W	0029	1.9	58		17 Th	0004	-0.1	-3
	0635	16.5	503			0607	18.2	555
	1249	2.5	76			1229	0.6	18
	1858	17.7	539			1835	19.8	604
3 Th	0123	1.8	55		18 F	0107	-0.4	-12
	0730	16.6	506			0710	18.5	564
	1342	2.4	73			1331	0.3	9
	1949	17.9	546			1936	20.2	616
4 F	0215	1.4	43		19 Sa	0209	-1.0	-30
	0820	16.9	515			0811	19.0	579
	1432	2.2	67			1432	-0.2	-6
	2038	18.3	558			2035	20.7	631
5 Sa	0303	1.0	30		20 Su	0307	-1.6	-49
	0907	17.2	524			0909	19.6	597
	1519	1.8	55			1529	-0.8	-24
	2123	18.7	570			2131	21.1	643
6 Su	0347	0.5	15		21 M	0401	-2.0	-61
	0951	17.7	539			1002	20.1	613
	1603	1.3	40			1623	-1.2	-37
	2206	19.0	579		●	2224	21.3	649
7 M	0429	0.0	0		22 Tu	0452	-2.2	-67
	1032	18.1	552			1053	20.4	622
	1645	0.9	27			1713	-1.4	-43
○	2246	19.3	588			2314	21.2	646
8 Tu	0510	-0.3	-9		23 W	0540	-2.1	-64
	1111	18.5	564			1141	20.4	622
	1726	0.6	18			1802	-1.4	-43
	2326	19.6	597					
9 W	0550	-0.6	-18		24 Th	0002	20.8	634
	1150	18.8	573			0627	-1.7	-52
	1807	0.3	9			1227	20.2	616
						1849	-1.0	-30
10 Th	0006	19.7	600		25 F	0049	20.2	616
	0630	-0.7	-21			0712	-1.0	-30
	1230	19.1	582			1313	19.8	604
	1848	0.1	3			1935	-0.4	-12
11 F	0047	19.7	600		26 Sa	0136	19.4	591
	0712	-0.7	-21			0757	-0.2	-6
	1311	19.4	591			1359	19.2	585
	1932	-0.1	-3			2021	0.3	9
12 Sa	0130	19.6	597		27 Su	0223	18.5	564
	0755	-0.6	-18			0843	0.7	21
	1355	19.6	597			1446	18.6	567
	2018	-0.1	-3			2109	1.0	30
13 Su	0217	19.3	588		28 M	0312	17.6	536
	0841	-0.3	-9			0930	1.6	49
	1443	19.6	597			1536	17.9	546
	2108	-0.1	-3			2159	1.6	49
14 M	0308	19.0	579		29 Tu	0404	16.8	512
	0932	0.0	0			1020	2.3	70
	1535	19.6	597			1628	17.4	530
☾	2203	0.0	0		☾	2252	2.1	64
15 Tu	0404	18.6	567		30 W	0459	16.3	497
	1027	0.4	12			1114	2.8	85
	1632	19.5	594			1722	17.2	524
	2302	0.0	0			2347	2.3	70
					31 Th	0555	16.1	491
						1209	3.0	91
						1818	17.2	524

September

Day	Time	ft	cm		Day	Time	ft	cm
1 F	0043	2.2	67		16 Sa	0053	-0.2	-6
	0651	16.2	494			0658	18.3	558
	1304	2.8	85			1319	0.6	18
	1913	17.4	530			1924	19.6	597
2 Sa	0137	1.8	55		17 Su	0154	-0.6	-18
	0744	16.7	509			0759	18.9	576
	1357	2.3	70			1420	0.0	0
	2004	17.9	546			2023	20.1	613
3 Su	0227	1.2	37		18 M	0252	-1.1	-34
	0833	17.3	527			0855	19.5	594
	1446	1.7	52			1516	-0.6	-18
	2051	18.5	564			2118	20.5	625
4 M	0314	0.5	15		19 Tu	0344	-1.5	-46
	0918	17.9	546			0946	20.1	613
	1532	1.0	30			1607	-1.1	-34
	2135	19.1	582			2208	20.6	628
5 Tu	0358	-0.1	-3		20 W	0432	-1.6	-49
	1000	18.6	567			1033	20.4	622
	1616	0.3	9			1654	-1.3	-40
	2217	19.6	597		●	2255	20.6	628
6 W	0440	-0.6	-18		21 Th	0517	-1.4	-43
	1041	19.3	588			1117	20.4	622
	1658	-0.3	-9			1739	-1.2	-37
○	2258	20.0	610			2339	20.2	616
7 Th	0521	-1.0	-30		22 F	0600	-1.0	-30
	1121	19.8	604			1159	20.2	616
	1740	-0.8	-24			1822	-0.9	-27
	2340	20.2	616					
8 F	0602	-1.2	-37		23 Sa	0022	19.6	597
	1202	20.2	616			0642	-0.3	-9
	1824	-1.1	-34			1241	19.7	600
						1905	-0.3	-9
9 Sa	0022	20.3	619		24 Su	0105	18.9	576
	0645	-1.2	-37			0724	0.5	15
	1244	20.4	622			1324	19.1	582
	1909	-1.2	-37			1948	0.3	9
10 Su	0107	20.1	613		25 M	0150	18.1	552
	0730	-0.9	-27			0807	1.3	40
	1330	20.4	622			1408	18.5	564
	1957	-1.1	-34			2033	1.0	30
11 M	0156	19.7	600		26 Tu	0236	17.4	530
	0819	-0.5	-15			0852	2.1	64
	1419	20.2	616			1455	17.8	543
	2048	-0.8	-24			2120	1.6	49
12 Tu	0249	19.1	582		27 W	0325	16.7	509
	0911	0.1	3			0941	2.7	82
	1514	19.9	607			1546	17.3	527
	2144	-0.4	-12		☾	2211	2.1	64
13 W	0346	18.6	567		28 Th	0419	16.2	494
	1009	0.6	18			1033	3.1	94
	1613	19.5	594			1641	16.9	515
☾	2245	-0.1	-3			2305	2.4	73
14 Th	0449	18.1	552		29 F	0514	16.0	488
	1111	0.9	27			1129	3.3	101
	1716	19.3	588			1737	16.9	515
	2349	0.0	0					
15 F	0554	18.0	549		30 Sa	0001	2.3	70
	1215	0.9	27			0611	16.2	494
	1821	19.3	588			1225	3.0	91
						1833	17.2	524

Time meridian 75° W   0000 is midnight. 1200 is noon. Times are not adjusted for Daylight Saving Time.
Heights are referred to mean lower low water which is the chart datum of soundings.

Eastport, Maine, 2017

Times and Heights of High and Low Waters

October

Day	Time (h m)	Height (ft)	Height (cm)
1 Su	0056	2.0	61
	0705	16.7	509
	1320	2.4	73
	1926	17.7	539
2 M	0149	1.3	40
	0755	17.5	533
	1411	1.6	49
	2016	18.4	561
3 Tu	0237	0.5	15
	0842	18.4	561
	1459	0.6	18
	2102	19.2	585
4 W	0323	-0.2	-6
	0926	19.4	591
	1545	-0.3	-9
	2146	19.9	607
5 Th ○	0407	-0.9	-27
	1008	20.2	616
	1629	-1.1	-34
	2230	20.4	622
6 F	0451	-1.4	-43
	1051	20.9	637
	1714	-1.7	-52
	2314	20.7	631
7 Sa	0535	-1.6	-49
	1134	21.3	649
	1800	-2.1	-64
	2359	20.7	631
8 Su	0620	-1.5	-46
	1219	21.4	652
	1847	-2.1	-64
9 M	0047	20.5	625
	0708	-1.1	-34
	1307	21.3	649
	1937	-1.8	-55
10 Tu	0137	20.0	610
	0759	-0.6	-18
	1359	20.8	634
	2031	-1.3	-40
11 W	0232	19.3	588
	0854	0.1	3
	1456	20.1	613
	2128	-0.7	-21
12 Th ◑	0332	18.7	570
	0953	0.7	21
	1557	19.5	594
	2230	-0.2	-6
13 F	0435	18.2	555
	1057	1.1	34
	1702	19.1	582
	2334	0.1	3
14 Sa	0541	18.1	552
	1202	1.1	34
	1808	19.0	579
15 Su	0037	0.1	3
	0645	18.4	561
	1306	0.7	21
	1911	19.2	585
16 M	0138	-0.2	-6
	0745	19.0	579
	1406	0.2	6
	2010	19.5	594
17 Tu	0234	-0.5	-15
	0838	19.6	597
	1500	-0.4	-12
	2102	19.8	604
18 W	0324	-0.8	-24
	0926	20.0	610
	1549	-0.8	-24
	2150	19.9	607
19 Th ●	0410	-0.8	-24
	1011	20.3	619
	1634	-1.0	-30
	2234	19.8	604
20 F	0453	-0.6	-18
	1052	20.3	619
	1716	-0.9	-27
	2316	19.5	594
21 Sa	0533	-0.2	-6
	1132	20.0	610
	1757	-0.6	-18
	2356	19.1	582
22 Su	0613	0.4	12
	1212	19.6	597
	1837	-0.2	-6
23 M	0037	18.5	564
	0653	1.0	30
	1252	19.1	582
	1917	0.4	12
24 Tu	0119	17.9	546
	0734	1.7	52
	1334	18.5	564
	2000	0.9	27
25 W	0203	17.3	527
	0817	2.3	70
	1419	17.9	546
	2045	1.5	46
26 Th	0249	16.8	512
	0904	2.8	85
	1507	17.4	530
	2133	1.9	58
27 F ◐	0340	16.4	500
	0954	3.2	98
	1600	17.0	518
	2225	2.2	67
28 Sa	0434	16.3	497
	1049	3.2	98
	1655	16.9	515
	2319	2.2	67
29 Su	0529	16.5	503
	1145	3.0	91
	1751	17.1	521
30 M	0014	1.9	58
	0623	17.1	521
	1240	2.4	73
	1846	17.6	536
31 Tu	0108	1.3	40
	0715	17.9	546
	1334	1.4	43
	1938	18.4	561

November

Day	Time (h m)	Height (ft)	Height (cm)
1 W	0159	0.6	18
	0804	19.0	579
	1425	0.3	9
	2028	19.2	585
2 Th	0248	-0.2	-6
	0851	20.0	610
	1514	-0.8	-24
	2115	20.0	610
3 F	0335	-1.0	-30
	0937	21.0	640
	1602	-1.7	-52
	2202	20.6	628
4 Sa ○	0422	-1.5	-46
	1022	21.8	664
	1649	-2.5	-76
	2249	21.0	640
5 Su	0509	-1.7	-52
	1109	22.2	677
	1738	-2.8	-85
	2338	21.0	640
6 M	0558	-1.7	-52
	1157	22.2	677
	1827	-2.8	-85
7 Tu	0028	20.8	634
	0648	-1.3	-40
	1248	21.9	668
	1919	-2.4	-73
8 W	0120	20.2	616
	0741	-0.7	-21
	1342	21.2	646
	2014	-1.8	-55
9 Th	0217	19.6	597
	0838	-0.1	-3
	1439	20.4	622
	2112	-1.1	-34
10 F ◑	0316	19.0	579
	0938	0.6	18
	1541	19.6	597
	2212	-0.4	-12
11 Sa	0419	18.5	564
	1041	1.0	30
	1645	19.0	579
	2315	0.1	3
12 Su	0524	18.4	561
	1145	1.1	34
	1751	18.7	570
13 M	0017	0.3	9
	0627	18.6	567
	1248	0.9	27
	1853	18.6	567
14 Tu	0117	0.3	9
	0725	19.0	579
	1347	0.4	12
	1951	18.8	573
15 W	0211	0.2	6
	0817	19.4	591
	1441	0.0	0
	2043	18.9	576
16 Th	0301	0.1	3
	0904	19.7	600
	1529	-0.4	-12
	2130	19.0	579
17 F	0346	0.1	3
	0948	19.9	607
	1612	-0.6	-18
	2213	19.0	579
18 Sa ●	0428	0.2	6
	1028	20.0	610
	1653	-0.5	-15
	2253	18.9	576
19 Su	0508	0.5	15
	1107	19.8	604
	1732	-0.4	-12
	2333	18.6	567
20 M	0547	0.9	27
	1146	19.5	594
	1811	-0.1	-3
21 Tu	0012	18.2	555
	0625	1.3	40
	1225	19.2	585
	1850	0.3	9
22 W	0052	17.9	546
	0705	1.8	55
	1305	18.7	570
	1931	0.7	21
23 Th	0133	17.5	533
	0747	2.2	67
	1347	18.2	555
	2013	1.1	34
24 F	0217	17.1	521
	0831	2.5	76
	1432	17.8	543
	2058	1.5	46
25 Sa	0304	16.9	515
	0919	2.8	85
	1521	17.5	533
	2147	1.7	52
26 Su ◐	0354	16.9	515
	1010	2.8	85
	1613	17.3	527
	2238	1.8	55
27 M	0446	17.1	521
	1104	2.6	79
	1708	17.3	527
	2332	1.6	49
28 Tu	0540	17.6	536
	1201	2.1	64
	1804	17.7	539
29 W	0027	1.2	37
	0634	18.4	561
	1257	1.2	37
	1900	18.3	558
30 Th	0121	0.6	18
	0730	19.4	591
	1351	0.1	3
	1954	19.0	579

December

Day	Time (h m)	Height (ft)	Height (cm)
1 F	0214	-0.1	-3
	0818	20.4	622
	1445	-1.0	-30
	2046	19.8	604
2 Sa	0305	-0.8	-24
	0908	21.4	652
	1536	-2.0	-61
	2137	20.5	625
3 Su ○	0356	-1.4	-43
	0958	22.2	677
	1627	-2.8	-85
	2228	20.9	637
4 M	0447	-1.8	-55
	1048	22.6	689
	1718	-3.2	-98
	2319	21.1	643
5 Tu	0538	-1.8	-55
	1138	22.7	692
	1810	-3.2	-98
6 W	0011	20.9	637
	0630	-1.6	-49
	1231	22.3	680
	1902	-2.9	-88
7 Th	0104	20.6	628
	0724	-1.1	-34
	1325	21.6	658
	1957	-2.2	-67
8 F	0200	20.0	610
	0820	-0.5	-15
	1422	20.7	631
	2052	-1.4	-43
9 Sa	0258	19.4	591
	0919	0.2	6
	1521	19.7	600
	2150	-0.6	-18
10 Su ◑	0358	18.9	576
	1019	0.8	24
	1623	18.9	576
	2250	0.1	3
11 M	0459	18.6	567
	1121	1.1	34
	1726	18.3	558
	2350	0.6	18
12 Tu	0600	18.5	564
	1223	1.1	34
	1828	18.0	549
13 W	0049	0.9	27
	0658	18.7	570
	1322	0.9	27
	1926	17.9	546
14 Th	0144	1.0	30
	0751	18.9	576
	1416	0.6	18
	2019	18.0	549
15 F	0235	1.0	30
	0839	19.2	585
	1505	0.3	9
	2107	18.1	552
16 Sa	0321	1.0	30
	0923	19.4	591
	1549	0.0	0
	2151	18.2	555
17 Su	0404	0.9	27
	1005	19.5	594
	1630	-0.1	-3
	2232	18.3	558
18 M ●	0444	1.0	30
	1044	19.5	594
	1709	-0.2	-6
	2311	18.2	555
19 Tu	0523	1.1	34
	1123	19.4	591
	1748	-0.1	-3
	2349	18.1	552
20 W	0601	1.3	40
	1201	19.3	588
	1826	0.1	3
21 Th	0027	18.0	549
	0640	1.5	46
	1240	19.0	579
	1905	0.3	9
22 F	0106	17.8	543
	0720	1.7	52
	1320	18.7	570
	1945	0.5	15
23 Sa	0147	17.7	539
	0802	1.9	58
	1402	18.4	561
	2027	0.8	24
24 Su	0230	17.6	536
	0846	2.0	61
	1447	18.1	552
	2112	1.0	30
25 M	0316	17.7	539
	0935	2.0	61
	1536	17.8	543
	2201	1.2	37
26 Tu ◐	0406	17.8	543
	1027	1.9	58
	1629	17.7	539
	2253	1.2	37
27 W	0500	18.2	555
	1123	1.6	49
	1726	17.8	543
	2348	1.1	34
28 Th	0556	18.8	573
	1222	0.9	27
	1824	18.1	552
29 F	0046	0.7	21
	0652	19.5	594
	1321	0.1	3
	1923	18.7	570
30 Sa	0143	0.1	3
	0748	20.5	625
	1418	-1.0	-30
	2020	19.4	591
31 Su	0240	-0.5	-15
	0843	21.4	652
	1514	-2.0	-61
	2115	20.1	613

Time meridian 75° W. 0000 is midnight. 1200 is noon. Times are not adjusted for Daylight Saving Time.
Heights are referred to mean lower low water which is the chart datum of soundings.

Bar Harbor, Maine, 2017

Times and Heights of High and Low Waters

January

Day	Time	ft	cm	Day	Time	ft	cm
1 Su	0023	10.5	320	**16** M	0115	11.5	351
	0622	0.9	27		0723	0.0	0
	1230	11.5	351		1332	11.9	363
	1852	-0.2	-6		1952	-0.5	-15
2 M	0102	10.6	323	**17** Tu	0205	11.1	338
	0703	0.9	27		0814	0.5	15
	1311	11.4	347		1422	11.2	341
	1933	-0.1	-3		2041	0.1	3
3 Tu	0144	10.7	326	**18** W	0254	10.8	329
	0749	0.8	24		0907	0.9	27
	1357	11.3	344		1515	10.5	320
	2018	-0.1	-3		2131	0.7	21
4 W	0231	10.8	329	**19** Th	0345	10.4	317
	0839	0.8	24		1002	1.2	37
	1448	11.1	338		1609	10.0	305
	2107	0.1	3	◑	2223	1.2	37
5 Th	0322	11.0	335	**20** F	0438	10.2	311
	0935	0.7	21		1059	1.4	43
	1544	10.9	332		1706	9.5	290
◐	2201	0.2	6		2317	1.6	49
6 F	0418	11.2	341	**21** Sa	0533	10.1	308
	1037	0.5	15		1157	1.5	46
	1646	10.7	326		1805	9.3	283
	2300	0.3	9				
7 Sa	0518	11.4	347	**22** Su	0012	1.8	55
	1141	0.2	6		0627	10.1	308
	1751	10.7	326		1253	1.4	43
					1901	9.3	283
8 Su	0002	0.3	9	**23** M	0106	1.8	55
	0620	11.8	360		0719	10.3	314
	1247	-0.2	-6		1346	1.1	34
	1857	10.8	329		1954	9.4	287
9 M	0105	0.1	3	**24** Tu	0156	1.7	52
	0721	12.2	372		0808	10.6	323
	1349	-0.7	-21		1434	0.8	24
	2000	11.1	338		2042	9.7	296
10 Tu	0206	-0.1	-3	**25** W	0243	1.4	43
	0821	12.7	387		0852	10.9	332
	1448	-1.2	-37		1517	0.4	12
	2059	11.4	347		2125	10.0	305
11 W	0303	-0.4	-12	**26** Th	0325	1.2	37
	0917	13.0	396		0934	11.2	341
	1544	-1.6	-49		1558	0.1	3
	2154	11.7	357		2205	10.3	314
12 Th	0358	-0.6	-18	**27** F	0405	0.9	27
	1010	13.2	402		1013	11.5	351
	1636	-1.8	-55		1635	-0.2	-6
○	2247	11.9	363	●	2242	10.6	323
13 F	0451	-0.7	-21	**28** Sa	0443	0.6	18
	1102	13.2	402		1050	11.8	360
	1726	-1.7	-52		1712	-0.4	-12
	2337	11.9	363		2319	10.9	332
14 Sa	0542	-0.6	-18	**29** Su	0521	0.4	12
	1152	12.9	393		1129	11.9	363
	1815	-1.5	-46		1749	-0.6	-18
					2357	11.1	338
15 Su	0027	11.7	357	**30** M	0600	0.2	6
	0632	-0.3	-9		1208	12.0	366
	1242	12.5	381		1827	-0.6	-18
	1904	-1.0	-30				
				31 Tu	0036	11.3	344
					0642	0.1	3
					1251	11.9	363
					1909	-0.6	-18

February

Day	Time	ft	cm	Day	Time	ft	cm
1 W	0119	11.5	351	**16** Th	0213	10.8	329
	0728	0.0	0		0829	0.7	21
	1337	11.7	357		1436	10.4	317
	1954	-0.4	-12		2048	0.9	27
2 Th	0206	11.5	351	**17** F	0259	10.5	320
	0819	0.0	0		0918	1.1	34
	1428	11.4	347		1525	9.9	302
	2043	-0.2	-6		2136	1.4	43
3 F	0257	11.6	354	**18** Sa	0347	10.2	311
	0915	0.1	3		1011	1.4	43
	1525	11.0	335		1619	9.4	287
◐	2138	0.1	3	○	2227	1.9	58
4 Sa	0354	11.5	351	**19** Su	0440	9.9	302
	1017	0.2	6		1107	1.6	49
	1627	10.7	326		1716	9.1	277
	2239	0.4	12		2323	2.1	64
5 Su	0456	11.5	351	**20** M	0536	9.9	302
	1124	0.1	3		1206	1.6	49
	1735	10.5	320		1815	9.0	274
	2344	0.6	18				
6 M	0602	11.6	354	**21** Tu	0021	2.1	64
	1232	0.0	0		0633	10.0	305
	1844	10.5	320		1302	1.5	46
					1912	9.2	280
7 Tu	0051	0.5	15	**22** W	0116	2.0	61
	0708	11.9	363		0727	10.2	311
	1337	-0.4	-12		1354	1.1	34
	1949	10.7	326		2003	9.5	290
8 W	0155	0.3	9	**23** Th	0207	1.6	49
	0810	12.2	372		0816	10.6	323
	1438	-0.8	-24		1441	0.7	21
	2049	11.1	338		2049	9.9	302
9 Th	0254	-0.1	-3	**24** F	0253	1.2	37
	0907	12.5	381		0901	11.1	338
	1532	-1.1	-34		1524	0.2	6
	2143	11.5	351		2131	10.5	320
10 F	0349	-0.4	-12	**25** Sa	0335	0.7	21
	1000	12.7	387		0943	11.6	354
	1623	-1.3	-40		1603	-0.2	-6
○	2233	11.7	357		2211	11.0	335
11 Sa	0439	-0.6	-18	**26** Su	0416	0.2	6
	1049	12.8	390		1024	12.0	366
	1710	-1.3	-40		1642	-0.6	-18
	2320	11.8	360	●	2249	11.4	347
12 Su	0526	-0.6	-18	**27** M	0456	-0.3	-9
	1136	12.6	384		1105	12.3	375
	1755	-1.1	-34		1721	-0.9	-27
					2329	11.8	360
13 M	0004	11.7	357	**28** Tu	0538	-0.6	-18
	0612	-0.4	-12		1147	12.4	378
	1221	12.2	372		1802	-1.0	-30
	1838	-0.7	-21				
14 Tu	0047	11.5	351				
	0657	-0.1	-3				
	1305	11.6	354				
	1920	-0.2	-6				
15 W	0130	11.2	341				
	0742	0.3	9				
	1350	11.0	335				
	2003	0.4	12				

March

Day	Time	ft	cm	Day	Time	ft	cm
1 W	0011	12.1	369	**16** Th	0055	11.3	344
	0622	-0.8	-24		0711	0.1	3
	1232	12.3	375		1319	10.8	329
	1845	-0.9	-27		1927	0.7	21
2 Th	0055	12.2	372	**17** F	0134	10.9	332
	0710	-0.8	-24		0753	0.5	15
	1320	12.0	366		1401	10.3	314
	1932	-0.6	-18		2008	1.2	37
3 F	0144	12.2	372	**18** Sa	0216	10.6	323
	0802	-0.7	-21		0837	0.9	27
	1413	11.6	354		1446	9.8	299
	2023	-0.2	-6		2052	1.6	49
4 Sa	0236	12.0	366	**19** Su	0300	10.2	311
	0859	-0.4	-12		0925	1.2	37
	1510	11.1	338		1535	9.4	287
	2120	0.2	6		2140	2.0	61
5 Su	0335	11.7	357	**20** M	0350	9.9	302
	1002	-0.1	-3		1018	1.5	46
	1614	10.6	323		1629	9.1	277
◐	2224	0.6	18	○	2235	2.2	67
6 M	0440	11.5	351	**21** Tu	0445	9.8	299
	1110	0.1	3		1115	1.6	49
	1724	10.4	317		1727	9.0	274
	2333	0.8	24		2333	2.3	70
7 Tu	0549	11.4	347	**22** W	0544	9.8	299
	1219	0.1	3		1213	1.5	46
	1834	10.4	317		1825	9.2	280
8 W	0042	0.8	24	**23** Th	0031	2.1	64
	0657	11.5	351		0642	10.0	305
	1325	-0.1	-3		1308	1.2	37
	1939	10.6	323		1919	9.6	293
9 Th	0147	0.5	15	**24** F	0126	1.6	49
	0800	11.7	357		0735	10.5	320
	1425	-0.4	-12		1358	0.8	24
	2038	11.0	335		2008	10.1	308
10 F	0245	0.1	3	**25** Sa	0216	1.0	30
	0857	12.0	366		0825	11.0	335
	1518	-0.7	-21		1444	0.2	6
	2129	11.4	347		2053	10.8	329
11 Sa	0338	-0.3	-9	**26** Su	0302	0.3	9
	0948	12.2	372		0911	11.6	354
	1606	-0.8	-24		1528	-0.3	-9
	2216	11.7	357		2136	11.5	351
12 Su	0425	-0.5	-15	**27** M	0347	-0.3	-9
	1035	12.2	372		0956	12.1	369
	1650	-0.8	-24		1610	-0.8	-24
○	2259	11.8	360	●	2218	12.1	369
13 M	0509	-0.5	-15	**28** Tu	0431	-0.9	-27
	1118	12.0	366		1040	12.4	378
	1731	-0.6	-18		1652	-1.0	-30
	2339	11.7	357		2301	12.6	384
14 Tu	0550	-0.4	-12	**29** W	0516	-1.3	-40
	1159	11.7	357		1126	12.5	381
	1810	-0.3	-9		1736	-1.1	-34
					2346	12.9	393
15 W	0017	11.5	351	**30** Th	0603	-1.5	-46
	0631	-0.2	-6		1214	12.4	378
	1239	11.3	344		1823	-1.0	-30
	1848	0.2	6				
				31 F	0033	12.9	393
					0653	-1.5	-46
					1305	12.1	369
					1913	-0.7	-21

Time meridian 75° W. 0000 is midnight. 1200 is noon. Times are not adjusted for Daylight Saving Time.
Heights are referred to mean lower low water which is the chart datum of soundings.

Bar Harbor, Maine, 2017

Times and Heights of High and Low Waters

April

Day	Time	Height ft	Height cm		Day	Time	Height ft	Height cm
1 Sa	0124	12.7	387		16 Su	0139	10.7	326
	0747	-1.2	-37			0802	0.7	21
	1400	11.7	357			1413	9.8	299
	2007	-0.2	-6			2015	1.7	52
2 Su	0219	12.3	375		17 M	0221	10.4	317
	0845	-0.8	-24			0847	1.0	30
	1459	11.1	338			1458	9.5	290
	2107	0.3	9			2101	2.0	61
3 M	0320	11.9	363		18 Tu	0308	10.1	308
	0949	-0.4	-12			0935	1.2	37
	1604	10.7	326			1548	9.3	283
	2213	0.7	21			2152	2.2	67
4 Tu	0427	11.4	347		19 W	0400	9.9	302
	1057	0.0	0			1028	1.3	40
	1713	10.5	320			1642	9.3	283
	2323	0.9	27			2248	2.1	64
5 W	0536	11.2	341		20 Th	0457	9.9	302
	1205	0.1	3			1123	1.3	40
	1821	10.5	320			1738	9.5	290
						2346	1.9	58
6 Th	0032	0.8	24		21 F	0555	10.1	308
	0644	11.2	341			1219	1.1	34
	1309	0.1	3			1832	9.9	302
	1924	10.7	326					
7 F	0135	0.5	15		22 Sa	0043	1.4	43
	0747	11.3	344			0652	10.5	320
	1407	-0.1	-3			1312	0.7	21
	2021	11.1	338			1924	10.5	320
8 Sa	0232	0.2	6		23 Su	0137	0.8	24
	0842	11.5	351			0746	11.0	335
	1458	-0.2	-6			1402	0.2	6
	2110	11.4	347			2014	11.2	341
9 Su	0322	-0.1	-3		24 M	0229	0.0	0
	0932	11.6	354			0838	11.5	351
	1545	-0.3	-9			1450	-0.3	-9
	2154	11.6	354			2101	12.0	366
10 M	0407	-0.4	-12		25 Tu	0318	-0.8	-24
	1016	11.6	354			0927	12.0	366
	1626	-0.2	-6			1537	-0.8	-24
	2235	11.7	357			2148	12.7	387
11 Tu	0449	-0.4	-12		26 W	0406	-1.4	-43
	1057	11.4	347			1017	12.3	375
	1705	0.0	0			1624	-1.0	-30
	2312	11.6	354			2235	13.1	399
12 W	0528	-0.4	-12		27 Th	0455	-1.9	-58
	1136	11.2	341			1106	12.5	381
	1742	0.3	9			1712	-1.1	-34
	2348	11.5	351			2323	13.4	408
13 Th	0605	-0.2	-6		28 F	0545	-2.0	-61
	1214	10.9	332			1157	12.4	378
	1818	0.6	18			1803	-0.9	-27
14 F	0023	11.3	344		29 Sa	0014	13.3	405
	0643	0.1	3			0638	-1.9	-58
	1252	10.5	320			1251	12.1	369
	1855	1.0	30			1856	-0.6	-18
15 Sa	0100	11.0	335		30 Su	0107	13.0	396
	0722	0.4	12			0733	-1.6	-49
	1331	10.2	311			1347	11.7	357
	1933	1.4	43			1953	-0.2	-6

May

Day	Time	Height ft	Height cm		Day	Time	Height ft	Height cm
1 M	0205	12.5	381		16 Tu	0150	10.6	323
	0832	-1.1	-34			0815	0.7	21
	1448	11.3	344			1427	9.8	299
	2055	0.3	9			2028	1.8	55
2 Tu	0306	11.9	363		17 W	0234	10.4	317
	0935	-0.6	-18			0900	0.8	24
	1552	10.9	332			1513	9.7	296
	2201	0.7	21			2116	1.9	58
3 W	0412	11.4	347		18 Th	0323	10.3	314
	1040	-0.2	-6			0948	0.9	27
	1657	10.7	326			1603	9.8	299
	2309	0.8	24			2209	1.8	55
4 Th	0520	11.0	335		19 F	0416	10.2	311
	1144	0.1	3			1040	0.9	27
	1802	10.7	326			1655	10.0	305
						2306	1.5	46
5 F	0015	0.8	24		20 Sa	0513	10.3	314
	0625	10.9	332			1134	0.7	21
	1246	0.2	6			1749	10.5	320
	1902	10.9	332					
6 Sa	0117	0.6	18		21 Su	0004	1.1	34
	0726	10.9	332			0612	10.5	320
	1342	0.3	9			1228	0.4	12
	1956	11.1	338			1844	11.0	335
7 Su	0212	0.3	9		22 M	0102	0.4	12
	0821	10.9	332			0710	10.9	332
	1432	0.3	9			1323	0.1	3
	2045	11.3	344			1937	11.7	357
8 M	0301	0.1	3		23 Tu	0157	-0.3	-9
	0910	10.9	332			0806	11.3	344
	1518	0.3	9			1416	-0.3	-9
	2128	11.4	347			2029	12.4	378
9 Tu	0346	-0.1	-3		24 W	0251	-1.0	-30
	0954	10.9	332			0901	11.8	360
	1559	0.4	12			1508	-0.7	-21
	2208	11.5	351			2120	13.0	396
10 W	0427	-0.2	-6		25 Th	0344	-1.7	-52
	1035	10.8	329			0955	12.1	369
	1638	0.6	18			1559	-0.9	-27
	2245	11.5	351			2211	13.4	408
11 Th	0505	-0.2	-6		26 F	0436	-2.1	-64
	1113	10.7	326			1048	12.2	372
	1714	0.8	24			1652	-0.9	-27
	2320	11.4	347			2303	13.6	415
12 F	0542	-0.1	-3		27 Sa	0529	-2.2	-67
	1150	10.5	320			1142	12.2	372
	1750	1.0	30			1745	-0.8	-24
	2355	11.2	341			2357	13.5	411
13 Sa	0618	0.1	3		28 Su	0623	-2.1	-64
	1227	10.3	314			1237	12.0	366
	1827	1.2	37			1841	-0.6	-18
14 Su	0031	11.0	335		29 M	0052	13.1	399
	0655	0.3	9			0719	-1.7	-52
	1305	10.1	308			1333	11.7	357
	1904	1.5	46			1939	-0.2	-6
15 M	0109	10.8	329		30 Tu	0150	12.6	384
	0734	0.5	15			0817	-1.2	-37
	1345	9.9	302			1432	11.4	347
	1944	1.7	52			2040	0.2	6
					31 W	0250	11.9	363
						0916	-0.7	-21
						1533	11.1	338
						2143	0.5	15

June

Day	Time	Height ft	Height cm		Day	Time	Height ft	Height cm
1 Th	0353	11.4	347		16 F	0252	10.6	323
	1017	-0.2	-6			0914	0.4	12
	1634	10.9	332			1529	10.4	317
	2247	0.7	21			2137	1.3	40
2 F	0456	10.9	332		17 Sa	0344	10.6	323
	1117	0.2	6			1003	0.4	12
	1735	10.9	332			1619	10.6	323
	2350	0.8	24			2232	1.1	34
3 Sa	0559	10.6	323		18 Su	0439	10.6	323
	1215	0.5	15			1056	0.4	12
	1832	10.9	332			1713	11.0	335
						2331	0.7	21
4 Su	0050	0.7	21		19 M	0539	10.6	323
	0658	10.4	317			1152	0.3	9
	1310	0.7	21			1809	11.5	351
	1925	11.0	335					
5 M	0145	0.5	15		20 Tu	0031	0.1	3
	0753	10.3	314			0640	10.8	329
	1401	0.8	24			1249	0.1	3
	2014	11.1	338			1906	12.0	366
6 Tu	0235	0.3	9		21 W	0131	-0.5	-15
	0843	10.3	314			0740	11.1	338
	1447	0.9	27			1347	-0.2	-6
	2058	11.2	341			2003	12.6	384
7 W	0320	0.2	6		22 Th	0229	-1.1	-34
	0928	10.3	314			0839	11.4	347
	1530	0.9	27			1444	-0.4	-12
	2139	11.3	344			2058	13.1	399
8 Th	0402	0.0	0		23 F	0326	-1.6	-49
	1010	10.3	314			0936	11.8	360
	1610	1.0	30			1540	-0.7	-21
	2217	11.3	344			2153	13.4	408
9 F	0441	0.0	0		24 Sa	0420	-2.0	-61
	1049	10.3	314			1032	12.0	366
	1648	1.1	34			1635	-0.8	-24
	2254	11.3	344			2247	13.5	411
10 Sa	0518	0.0	0		25 Su	0514	-2.1	-64
	1127	10.2	311			1126	12.0	366
	1725	1.2	37			1730	-0.7	-21
	2330	11.2	341			2342	13.4	408
11 Su	0554	0.1	3		26 M	0608	-2.0	-61
	1203	10.2	311			1221	12.0	366
	1801	1.3	40			1825	-0.6	-18
12 M	0006	11.1	338		27 Tu	0036	13.0	396
	0631	0.2	6			0702	-1.6	-49
	1240	10.1	308			1316	11.8	360
	1839	1.4	43			1922	-0.3	-9
13 Tu	0043	11.0	335		28 W	0132	12.5	381
	0708	0.3	9			0756	-1.2	-37
	1318	10.1	308			1411	11.5	351
	1918	1.5	46			2020	0.1	3
14 W	0123	10.9	332		29 Th	0229	11.9	363
	0747	0.3	9			0852	-0.6	-18
	1359	10.1	308			1507	11.3	344
	2000	1.5	46			2119	0.4	12
15 Th	0206	10.7	326		30 F	0327	11.2	341
	0829	0.4	12			0947	-0.1	-3
	1442	10.2	311			1604	11.0	335
	2046	1.5	46			2219	0.7	21

Time meridian 75° W. 0000 is midnight. 1200 is noon. Times are not adjusted for Daylight Saving Time.
Heights are referred to mean lower low water which is the chart datum of soundings.

Bar Harbor, Maine, 2017

Times and Heights of High and Low Waters

July

Day	Time	Height (ft)	Height (cm)
1 Sa	0426	10.7	326
	1043	0.4	12
	1700	10.8	329
	2318	0.9	27
2 Su	0526	10.2	311
	1139	0.8	24
	1755	10.7	326
3 M	0016	0.9	27
	0624	9.9	302
	1233	1.1	34
	1848	10.7	326
4 Tu	0112	0.9	27
	0720	9.8	299
	1325	1.3	40
	1939	10.8	329
5 W	0203	0.7	21
	0812	9.8	299
	1414	1.3	40
	2026	10.9	332
6 Th	0251	0.5	15
	0859	9.9	302
	1459	1.3	40
	2109	11.0	335
7 F	0334	0.3	9
	0943	10.0	305
	1542	1.3	40
	2150	11.2	341
8 Sa ○	0415	0.2	6
	1023	10.1	308
	1621	1.2	37
	2228	11.2	341
9 Su	0453	0.1	3
	1101	10.2	311
	1659	1.2	37
	2305	11.3	344
10 M	0529	0.0	0
	1137	10.2	311
	1736	1.1	34
	2342	11.3	344
11 Tu	0605	0.0	0
	1214	10.3	314
	1813	1.1	34
12 W	0019	11.3	344
	0641	0.0	0
	1251	10.4	317
	1852	1.1	34
13 Th	0058	11.2	341
	0719	0.0	0
	1330	10.6	323
	1934	1.0	30
14 F	0140	11.1	338
	0800	0.0	0
	1412	10.7	326
	2019	0.9	27
15 Sa	0226	11.0	335
	0844	0.1	3
	1458	10.9	332
	2110	0.7	21
16 Su ☽	0317	10.8	329
	0933	0.2	6
	1549	11.2	341
	2205	0.6	18
17 M	0413	10.7	326
	1026	0.3	9
	1643	11.4	347
	2305	0.3	9
18 Tu	0514	10.6	323
	1124	0.3	9
	1742	11.7	357
19 W	0008	0.0	0
	0617	10.7	326
	1225	0.3	9
	1843	12.1	369
20 Th	0112	-0.5	-15
	0722	10.8	329
	1327	0.1	3
	1944	12.5	381
21 F	0213	-0.9	-27
	0823	11.2	341
	1428	-0.2	-6
	2043	12.9	393
22 Sa	0311	-1.4	-43
	0922	11.5	351
	1526	-0.5	-15
	2139	13.2	402
23 Su ●	0406	-1.7	-52
	1017	11.8	360
	1621	-0.7	-21
	2234	13.3	405
24 M	0459	-1.8	-55
	1111	12.0	366
	1715	-0.7	-21
	2327	13.1	399
25 Tu	0551	-1.7	-52
	1202	12.0	366
	1809	-0.6	-18
26 W	0019	12.8	390
	0641	-1.4	-43
	1253	11.8	360
	1901	-0.4	-12
27 Th	0111	12.3	375
	0731	-0.9	-27
	1344	11.6	354
	1955	0.0	0
28 F	0203	11.6	354
	0821	-0.4	-12
	1435	11.3	344
	2049	0.4	12
29 Sa	0256	11.0	335
	0912	0.2	6
	1527	10.9	332
	2144	0.7	21
30 Su ☾	0351	10.4	317
	1004	0.8	24
	1619	10.6	323
	2240	1.0	30
31 M	0447	9.9	302
	1058	1.3	40
	1713	10.4	317
	2337	1.2	37

August

Day	Time	Height (ft)	Height (cm)
1 Tu	0545	9.5	290
	1152	1.6	49
	1807	10.4	317
2 W	0034	1.2	37
	0642	9.4	287
	1246	1.7	52
	1900	10.4	317
3 Th	0127	1.1	34
	0736	9.4	287
	1338	1.7	52
	1950	10.6	323
4 F	0217	0.9	27
	0826	9.6	293
	1427	1.5	46
	2037	10.8	329
5 Sa	0303	0.6	18
	0911	9.8	299
	1511	1.3	40
	2120	11.0	335
6 Su	0344	0.3	9
	0952	10.1	308
	1553	1.1	34
	2200	11.2	341
7 M ○	0423	0.1	3
	1030	10.3	314
	1631	0.9	27
	2238	11.4	347
8 Tu	0500	-0.1	-3
	1107	10.6	323
	1709	0.7	21
	2316	11.5	351
9 W	0536	-0.2	-6
	1143	10.8	329
	1747	0.5	15
	2354	11.6	354
10 Th	0612	-0.3	-9
	1221	11.0	335
	1826	0.4	12
11 F	0034	11.6	354
	0650	-0.3	-9
	1300	11.2	341
	1909	0.3	9
12 Sa	0117	11.4	347
	0732	-0.2	-6
	1343	11.4	347
	1956	0.2	6
13 Su	0204	11.3	344
	0817	-0.1	-3
	1431	11.5	351
	2047	0.2	6
14 M ☾	0256	11.0	335
	0908	0.1	3
	1523	11.6	354
	2144	0.1	3
15 Tu	0354	10.7	326
	1004	0.4	12
	1621	11.6	354
	2247	0.1	3
16 W	0457	10.5	320
	1105	0.5	15
	1723	11.7	357
	2352	0.0	0
17 Th	0603	10.5	320
	1210	0.5	15
	1828	11.9	363
18 F	0058	-0.3	-9
	0709	10.7	326
	1316	0.3	9
	1931	12.2	372
19 Sa	0200	-0.7	-21
	0812	11.0	335
	1418	0.0	0
	2032	12.5	381
20 Su	0258	-1.1	-34
	0910	11.4	347
	1515	-0.4	-12
	2128	12.8	390
21 M ●	0352	-1.3	-40
	1003	11.8	360
	1609	-0.6	-18
	2221	12.9	393
22 Tu	0442	-1.4	-43
	1053	12.0	366
	1700	-0.7	-21
	2311	12.7	387
23 W	0530	-1.3	-40
	1140	12.0	366
	1750	-0.7	-21
	2359	12.4	378
24 Th	0616	-1.0	-30
	1227	11.8	360
	1838	-0.4	-12
25 F	0047	11.9	363
	0702	-0.5	-15
	1312	11.5	351
	1926	-0.1	-3
26 Sa	0134	11.3	344
	0747	0.1	3
	1358	11.2	341
	2014	0.4	12
27 Su	0223	10.7	326
	0834	0.7	21
	1445	10.8	329
	2105	0.8	24
28 M	0313	10.1	308
	0923	1.2	37
	1535	10.4	317
	2158	1.1	34
29 Tu ☽	0407	9.6	293
	1015	1.7	52
	1627	10.2	311
	2254	1.4	43
30 W	0503	9.3	283
	1110	1.9	58
	1722	10.0	305
	2351	1.4	43
31 Th	0601	9.2	280
	1206	2.0	61
	1818	10.1	308

September

Day	Time	Height (ft)	Height (cm)
1 F	0047	1.3	40
	0657	9.2	280
	1301	1.9	58
	1912	10.2	311
2 Sa	0139	1.1	34
	0748	9.5	290
	1352	1.7	52
	2002	10.5	320
3 Su	0226	0.8	24
	0835	9.8	299
	1438	1.3	40
	2047	10.9	332
4 M	0309	0.4	12
	0917	10.3	314
	1521	0.9	27
	2129	11.2	341
5 Tu	0348	0.1	3
	0955	10.7	326
	1601	0.5	15
	2208	11.5	351
6 W ○	0426	-0.2	-6
	1033	11.1	338
	1640	0.1	3
	2247	11.8	360
7 Th	0503	-0.4	-12
	1111	11.5	351
	1720	-0.2	-6
	2328	11.9	363
8 F	0541	-0.5	-15
	1150	11.7	357
	1801	-0.4	-12
9 Sa	0010	11.9	363
	0622	-0.5	-15
	1232	11.9	363
	1846	-0.5	-15
10 Su	0055	11.7	357
	0706	-0.4	-12
	1317	12.0	366
	1935	-0.5	-15
11 M	0145	11.4	347
	0754	-0.1	-3
	1407	12.0	366
	2029	-0.4	-12
12 Tu	0240	11.0	335
	0848	0.2	6
	1503	11.8	360
	2128	-0.2	-6
13 W ☾	0340	10.7	326
	0948	0.5	15
	1604	11.6	354
	2233	-0.1	-3
14 Th	0446	10.5	320
	1054	0.7	21
	1710	11.6	354
	2341	0.0	0
15 F	0554	10.5	320
	1203	0.7	21
	1818	11.6	354
16 Sa	0047	-0.2	-6
	0700	10.7	326
	1309	0.4	12
	1923	11.8	360
17 Su	0149	-0.5	-15
	0801	11.1	338
	1410	0.0	0
	2023	12.1	369
18 M	0245	-0.8	-24
	0857	11.5	351
	1506	-0.3	-9
	2117	12.3	375
19 Tu	0336	-0.9	-27
	0947	11.8	360
	1557	-0.6	-18
	2207	12.3	375
20 W ●	0423	-1.0	-30
	1033	12.0	366
	1644	-0.7	-21
	2254	12.2	372
21 Th	0507	-0.8	-24
	1116	12.0	366
	1729	-0.7	-21
	2338	11.9	363
22 F	0549	-0.4	-12
	1158	11.8	360
	1813	-0.4	-12
23 Sa	0021	11.4	347
	0631	0.0	0
	1239	11.5	351
	1856	-0.1	-3
24 Su	0105	10.9	332
	0712	0.6	18
	1320	11.1	338
	1940	0.3	9
25 M	0149	10.4	317
	0755	1.1	34
	1404	10.7	326
	2026	0.7	21
26 Tu	0236	9.9	302
	0841	1.6	49
	1450	10.3	314
	2116	1.1	34
27 W ☽	0326	9.5	290
	0931	1.9	58
	1541	10.0	305
	2209	1.4	43
28 Th	0420	9.2	280
	1026	2.2	67
	1636	9.9	302
	2305	1.5	46
29 F	0517	9.1	277
	1123	2.2	67
	1733	9.8	299
30 Sa	0001	1.5	46
	0613	9.2	280
	1220	2.0	61
	1829	10.0	305

Time meridian 75° W. 0000 is midnight. 1200 is noon. Times are not adjusted for Daylight Saving Time.
Heights are referred to mean lower low water which is the chart datum of soundings.

Bar Harbor, Maine, 2017

Times and Heights of High and Low Waters

October

Day	h m	ft	cm
1 Su	0055	1.2	37
	0706	9.6	293
	1313	1.7	52
	1921	10.3	314
2 M	0143	0.9	27
	0753	10.0	305
	1401	1.2	37
	2009	10.8	329
3 Tu	0228	0.5	15
	0837	10.6	323
	1446	0.6	18
	2054	11.2	341
4 W	0309	0.0	0
	0918	11.2	341
	1529	0.0	0
	2137	11.6	354
5 Th ○	0350	-0.3	-9
	0958	11.7	357
	1611	-0.5	-15
	2219	11.9	363
6 F	0430	-0.6	-18
	1038	12.2	372
	1653	-0.9	-27
	2302	12.1	369
7 Sa	0511	-0.7	-21
	1121	12.5	381
	1738	-1.2	-37
	2348	12.1	369
8 Su	0556	-0.7	-21
	1206	12.6	384
	1826	-1.2	-37
9 M	0037	11.9	363
	0643	-0.5	-15
	1254	12.6	384
	1917	-1.1	-34
10 Tu	0129	11.5	351
	0735	-0.1	-3
	1348	12.3	375
	2014	-0.8	-24
11 W	0227	11.1	338
	0833	0.3	9
	1447	12.0	366
	2115	-0.5	-15
12 Th ◐	0330	10.8	329
	0937	0.6	18
	1551	11.6	354
	2221	-0.2	-6
13 F	0437	10.6	323
	1046	0.8	24
	1700	11.4	347
	2328	-0.1	-3
14 Sa	0545	10.6	323
	1155	0.7	21
	1808	11.4	347
15 Su	0034	-0.1	-3
	0649	10.9	332
	1300	0.4	12
	1912	11.5	351
16 M	0134	-0.3	-9
	0748	11.2	341
	1400	0.1	3
	2011	11.6	354
17 Tu	0228	-0.4	-12
	0840	11.6	354
	1453	-0.3	-9
	2103	11.7	357
18 W	0317	-0.5	-15
	0928	11.8	360
	1542	-0.5	-15
	2151	11.7	357
19 Th ●	0401	-0.4	-12
	1011	11.9	363
	1626	-0.6	-18
	2235	11.6	354
20 F	0443	-0.2	-6
	1051	11.9	363
	1708	-0.6	-18
	2317	11.3	344
21 Sa	0522	0.1	3
	1130	11.7	357
	1748	-0.4	-12
	2357	11.0	335
22 Su	0601	0.5	15
	1207	11.4	347
	1828	-0.1	-3
23 M	0037	10.6	323
	0640	0.9	27
	1246	11.1	338
	1908	0.3	9
24 Tu	0118	10.2	311
	0720	1.4	43
	1326	10.7	326
	1951	0.7	21
25 W	0201	9.8	299
	0803	1.7	52
	1410	10.4	317
	2036	1.0	30
26 Th	0248	9.5	290
	0851	2.0	61
	1458	10.1	308
	2126	1.3	40
27 F ◑	0338	9.3	283
	0943	2.2	67
	1550	9.9	302
	2218	1.4	43
28 Sa	0432	9.2	280
	1038	2.2	67
	1646	9.8	299
	2312	1.4	43
29 Su	0526	9.4	287
	1135	2.0	61
	1742	9.9	302
30 M	0006	1.2	37
	0619	9.8	299
	1230	1.6	49
	1837	10.2	311
31 Tu	0056	0.9	27
	0709	10.3	314
	1322	1.0	30
	1929	10.6	323

November

Day	h m	ft	cm
1 W	0144	0.5	15
	0755	11.0	335
	1410	0.3	9
	2018	11.1	338
2 Th	0230	0.0	0
	0840	11.7	357
	1457	-0.4	-12
	2105	11.6	354
3 F	0314	-0.4	-12
	0924	12.3	375
	1543	-1.0	-30
	2152	11.9	363
4 Sa ○	0359	-0.7	-21
	1009	12.8	390
	1630	-1.5	-46
	2239	12.1	369
5 Su	0445	-0.9	-27
	1055	13.2	402
	1718	-1.8	-55
	2328	12.1	369
6 M	0533	-0.8	-24
	1144	13.2	402
	1808	-1.8	-55
7 Tu	0020	12.0	366
	0624	-0.6	-18
	1236	13.0	396
	1902	-1.6	-49
8 W	0115	11.7	357
	0720	-0.2	-6
	1332	12.6	384
	2000	-1.2	-37
9 Th	0214	11.3	344
	0820	0.2	6
	1432	12.1	369
	2101	-0.7	-21
10 F ◐	0317	11.0	335
	0925	0.5	15
	1537	11.7	357
	2206	-0.4	-12
11 Sa	0423	10.8	329
	1034	0.7	21
	1645	11.3	344
	2311	-0.1	-3
12 Su	0529	10.8	329
	1142	0.7	21
	1753	11.1	338
13 M	0014	0.0	0
	0631	11.0	335
	1246	0.5	15
	1856	11.0	335
14 Tu	0113	0.1	3
	0728	11.3	344
	1344	0.2	6
	1954	11.1	338
15 W	0206	0.0	0
	0820	11.5	351
	1437	-0.1	-3
	2046	11.1	338
16 Th	0254	0.1	3
	0906	11.7	357
	1524	-0.3	-9
	2133	11.1	338
17 F	0338	0.2	6
	0948	11.7	357
	1607	-0.4	-12
	2216	11.0	335
18 Sa ●	0419	0.3	9
	1027	11.7	357
	1647	-0.4	-12
	2256	10.8	329
19 Su	0457	0.6	18
	1104	11.6	354
	1726	-0.3	-9
	2334	10.6	323
20 M	0535	0.9	27
	1140	11.4	347
	1803	0.0	0
21 Tu	0012	10.3	314
	0612	1.1	34
	1217	11.1	338
	1841	0.2	6
22 W	0050	10.1	308
	0650	1.4	43
	1255	10.8	329
	1920	0.5	15
23 Th	0131	9.8	299
	0730	1.7	52
	1336	10.6	323
	2002	0.7	21
24 F	0213	9.7	296
	0814	1.9	58
	1420	10.3	314
	2046	1.0	30
25 Sa	0259	9.6	293
	0902	2.0	61
	1508	10.1	308
	2134	1.1	34
26 Su ◑	0348	9.6	293
	0954	2.0	61
	1600	10.0	305
	2224	1.1	34
27 M	0439	9.8	299
	1049	1.8	55
	1656	10.0	305
	2316	1.0	30
28 Tu	0532	10.1	308
	1146	1.4	43
	1752	10.2	311
29 W	0009	0.8	24
	0624	10.7	326
	1242	0.8	24
	1849	10.5	320
30 Th	0101	0.5	15
	0715	11.3	344
	1336	0.1	3
	1943	10.9	332

December

Day	h m	ft	cm
1 F	0152	0.0	0
	0806	12.0	366
	1428	-0.6	-18
	2036	11.4	347
2 Sa	0243	-0.4	-12
	0855	12.7	387
	1519	-1.3	-40
	2128	11.8	360
3 Su ○	0333	-0.7	-21
	0945	13.2	402
	1609	-1.8	-55
	2220	12.1	369
4 M	0423	-0.9	-27
	1035	13.5	411
	1701	-2.1	-64
	2312	12.2	372
5 Tu	0515	-0.9	-27
	1127	13.6	415
	1753	-2.1	-64
6 W	0005	12.1	369
	0608	-0.7	-21
	1220	13.3	405
	1847	-1.9	-58
7 Th	0100	11.9	363
	0705	-0.4	-12
	1317	12.9	393
	1944	-1.4	-43
8 F	0158	11.6	354
	0805	-0.1	-3
	1417	12.3	375
	2043	-0.9	-27
9 Sa	0259	11.3	344
	0909	0.3	9
	1519	11.7	357
	2144	-0.4	-12
10 Su ◑	0401	11.1	338
	1014	0.6	18
	1624	11.1	338
	2246	0.0	0
11 M	0504	11.0	335
	1120	0.7	21
	1730	10.8	329
	2347	0.3	9
12 Tu	0605	11.0	335
	1223	0.6	18
	1832	10.5	320
13 W	0046	0.5	15
	0702	11.1	338
	1322	0.4	12
	1931	10.5	320
14 Th	0140	0.6	18
	0754	11.2	341
	1415	0.2	6
	2024	10.4	317
15 F	0229	0.7	21
	0841	11.4	347
	1503	0.0	0
	2112	10.5	320
16 Sa	0314	0.7	21
	0924	11.4	347
	1547	-0.1	-3
	2155	10.5	320
17 Su	0356	0.8	24
	1004	11.5	351
	1627	-0.2	-6
	2235	10.4	317
18 M ●	0434	0.9	27
	1041	11.5	351
	1704	-0.1	-3
	2313	10.4	317
19 Tu	0511	1.0	30
	1117	11.4	347
	1741	0.0	0
	2349	10.3	314
20 W	0548	1.1	34
	1153	11.2	341
	1817	0.1	3
21 Th	0025	10.2	311
	0624	1.3	40
	1230	11.1	338
	1853	0.3	9
22 F	0102	10.1	308
	0702	1.4	43
	1308	10.9	332
	1931	0.4	12
23 Sa	0141	10.0	305
	0742	1.5	46
	1348	10.7	326
	2011	0.6	18
24 Su	0222	10.0	305
	0826	1.6	49
	1432	10.5	320
	2053	0.7	21
25 M ◑	0307	10.1	308
	0914	1.5	46
	1521	10.3	314
	2140	0.8	24
26 Tu	0355	10.3	314
	1008	1.4	43
	1614	10.2	311
	2231	0.8	24
27 W	0448	10.6	323
	1105	1.1	34
	1712	10.2	311
	2326	0.7	21
28 Th	0543	11.0	335
	1205	0.6	18
	1813	10.4	317
29 F	0023	0.5	15
	0640	11.5	351
	1305	0.0	0
	1914	10.7	326
30 Sa	0121	0.2	6
	0736	12.2	372
	1403	-0.7	-21
	2012	11.1	338
31 Su	0217	-0.2	-6
	0832	12.8	390
	1459	-1.3	-40
	2109	11.6	354

Time meridian 75° W. 0000 is midnight. 1200 is noon. Times are not adjusted for Daylight Saving Time.
Heights are referred to mean lower low water which is the chart datum of soundings.

Portland, Maine, 2017

Times and Heights of High and Low Waters

January

Day	Time	ft	cm		Day	Time	ft	cm
1 Su	0044	8.8	268		16 M	0138	9.7	296
	0636	0.7	21			0738	-0.1	-3
	1247	9.9	302			1350	10.1	308
	1908	-0.3	-9			2009	-0.6	-18
2 M	0123	8.9	271		17 Tu	0226	9.4	287
	0718	0.6	18			0830	0.3	9
	1329	9.8	299			1441	9.5	290
	1949	-0.3	-9			2058	0.0	0
3 Tu	0205	9.0	274		18 W	0316	9.1	277
	0804	0.6	18			0923	0.7	21
	1415	9.7	296			1534	8.9	271
	2034	-0.2	-6			2148	0.5	15
4 W	0251	9.2	280		19 Th	0407	8.9	271
	0855	0.6	18			1019	1.0	30
	1506	9.5	290			1629	8.4	256
	2124	-0.1	-3			2240	1.0	30
5 Th	0342	9.3	283		20 F	0459	8.7	265
	0952	0.5	15			1118	1.2	37
	1602	9.3	283			1727	8.0	244
	2218	0.0	0			2334	1.3	40
6 F	0438	9.5	290		21 Sa	0554	8.6	262
	1053	0.3	9			1218	1.2	37
	1704	9.1	277			1827	7.8	238
	2316	0.1	3					
7 Sa	0537	9.8	299		22 Su	0029	1.5	46
	1158	0.1	3			0648	8.6	262
	1810	9.0	274			1315	1.1	34
						1925	7.8	238
8 Su	0017	0.1	3		23 M	0122	1.5	46
	0638	10.1	308			0739	8.8	268
	1304	-0.3	-9			1408	0.9	27
	1917	9.1	277			2018	7.9	241
9 M	0119	0.0	0		24 Tu	0211	1.4	43
	0740	10.5	320			0827	9.0	274
	1407	-0.8	-24			1455	0.6	18
	2021	9.4	287			2105	8.1	247
10 Tu	0220	-0.2	-6		25 W	0257	1.2	37
	0839	10.9	332			0911	9.3	283
	1506	-1.2	-37			1537	0.3	9
	2121	9.7	296			2148	8.4	256
11 W	0318	-0.5	-15		26 Th	0338	1.0	30
	0935	11.2	341			0952	9.6	293
	1602	-1.6	-49			1615	0.0	0
	2216	9.9	302			2227	8.6	262
12 Th	0412	-0.7	-21		27 F	0417	0.7	21
	1029	11.4	347			1030	9.8	299
	1654	-1.7	-52			1652	-0.3	-9
	2309	10.0	305			2304	8.9	271
13 F	0505	-0.7	-21		28 Sa	0455	0.4	12
	1120	11.3	344			1108	10.1	308
	1744	-1.7	-52			1728	-0.5	-15
	2359	10.1	308			2340	9.1	277
14 Sa	0556	-0.6	-18		29 Su	0534	0.2	6
	1211	11.1	338			1146	10.2	311
	1833	-1.5	-46			1805	-0.7	-21
15 Su	0049	9.9	302		30 M	0017	9.3	283
	0647	-0.4	-12			0614	0.0	0
	1301	10.7	326			1226	10.2	311
	1921	-1.1	-34			1843	-0.7	-21
					31 Tu	0057	9.5	290
						0657	-0.1	-3
						1309	10.2	311
						1925	-0.7	-21

February

Day	Time	ft	cm		Day	Time	ft	cm
1 W	0139	9.7	296		16 Th	0233	9.2	280
	0744	-0.2	-6			0845	0.5	15
	1356	10.0	305			1455	8.8	268
	2010	-0.6	-18			2103	0.7	21
2 Th	0226	9.8	299		17 F	0318	8.9	271
	0835	-0.2	-6			0934	0.9	27
	1447	9.7	296			1545	8.3	253
	2100	-0.4	-12			2149	1.2	37
3 F	0317	9.8	299		18 Sa	0406	8.6	262
	0932	-0.1	-3			1027	1.2	37
	1544	9.3	283			1639	7.9	241
	2154	-0.1	-3			2240	1.6	49
4 Sa	0413	9.8	299		19 Su	0458	8.4	256
	1034	0.0	0			1125	1.3	40
	1647	9.0	274			1738	7.6	232
	2254	0.2	6			2336	1.8	55
5 Su	0514	9.9	302		20 M	0554	8.4	256
	1141	-0.1	-3			1225	1.3	40
	1755	8.8	268			1838	7.5	229
	2358	0.3	9					
6 M	0620	10.0	305		21 Tu	0034	1.8	55
	1250	-0.2	-6			0652	8.5	259
	1905	8.8	268			1323	1.2	37
						1935	7.7	235
7 Tu	0105	0.3	9		22 W	0129	1.7	52
	0726	10.2	311			0746	8.7	265
	1356	-0.5	-15			1414	0.9	27
	2012	9.0	274			2027	8.0	244
8 W	0209	0.1	3		23 Th	0220	1.3	40
	0829	10.5	320			0835	9.1	277
	1456	-0.9	-27			1500	0.5	15
	2112	9.4	287			2112	8.4	256
9 Th	0308	-0.2	-6		24 F	0305	0.9	27
	0926	10.7	326			0920	9.5	290
	1551	-1.2	-37			1541	0.1	3
	2206	9.7	296			2153	8.8	268
10 F	0403	-0.5	-15		25 Sa	0348	0.5	15
	1019	10.9	332			1002	9.9	302
	1641	-1.3	-40			1620	-0.3	-9
	2255	9.9	302			2232	9.2	280
11 Sa	0453	-0.6	-18		26 Su	0429	0.0	0
	1109	10.9	332			1042	10.2	311
	1728	-1.3	-40			1658	-0.7	-21
	2342	10.0	305			2310	9.7	296
12 Su	0541	-0.6	-18		27 M	0510	-0.4	-12
	1155	10.7	326			1123	10.5	320
	1812	-1.1	-34			1737	-0.9	-27
						2349	10.0	305
13 M	0026	9.9	302		28 Tu	0553	-0.7	-21
	0627	-0.5	-15			1206	10.5	320
	1240	10.3	314			1818	-1.0	-30
	1855	-0.8	-24					
14 Tu	0108	9.7	296					
	0713	-0.2	-6					
	1324	9.9	302					
	1937	-0.3	-9					
15 W	0150	9.5	290					
	0758	0.1	3					
	1409	9.3	283					
	2019	0.2	6					

March

Day	Time	ft	cm		Day	Time	ft	cm
1 W	0031	10.3	314		16 Th	0114	9.6	293
	0638	-0.9	-27			0727	0.1	3
	1251	10.4	317			1339	9.2	280
	1902	-1.0	-30			1942	0.6	18
2 Th	0115	10.4	317		17 F	0152	9.3	283
	0727	-0.9	-27			0809	0.4	12
	1340	10.2	311			1421	8.7	265
	1948	-0.7	-21			2021	1.0	30
3 F	0203	10.4	317		18 Sa	0233	9.1	277
	0819	-0.8	-24			0852	0.7	21
	1432	9.8	299			1506	8.3	253
	2039	-0.4	-12			2104	1.4	43
4 Sa	0255	10.3	314		19 Su	0317	8.8	268
	0916	-0.5	-15			0940	1.0	30
	1530	9.4	287			1555	7.9	241
	2135	0.0	0			2152	1.7	52
5 Su	0353	10.1	308		20 M	0407	8.5	259
	1019	-0.3	-9			1034	1.3	40
	1635	9.0	274			1650	7.7	235
	2238	0.4	12			2246	1.9	58
6 M	0458	9.9	302		21 Tu	0502	8.4	256
	1127	-0.1	-3			1131	1.4	43
	1746	8.7	265			1749	7.6	232
	2346	0.6	18			2344	2.0	61
7 Tu	0607	9.8	299		22 W	0601	8.4	256
	1238	-0.1	-3			1230	1.3	40
	1857	8.8	268			1848	7.8	238
8 W	0056	0.6	18		23 Th	0043	1.8	55
	0716	9.9	302			0659	8.6	262
	1344	-0.3	-9			1325	1.0	30
	2003	9.0	274			1942	8.1	247
9 Th	0201	0.4	12		24 F	0139	1.4	43
	0820	10.1	308			0753	9.0	274
	1444	-0.5	-15			1415	0.6	18
	2101	9.3	283			2030	8.6	262
10 F	0300	0.0	0		25 Sa	0229	0.9	27
	0918	10.3	314			0843	9.5	290
	1537	-0.7	-21			1500	0.1	3
	2152	9.7	296			2114	9.2	280
11 Sa	0353	-0.3	-9		26 Su	0316	0.3	9
	1009	10.4	317			0929	9.9	302
	1624	-0.8	-24			1543	-0.3	-9
	2238	9.9	302			2156	9.8	299
12 Su	0441	-0.5	-15		27 M	0401	-0.4	-12
	1055	10.4	317			1015	10.4	317
	1707	-0.7	-21			1625	-0.7	-21
	2320	10.0	305			2238	10.4	317
13 M	0525	-0.5	-15		28 Tu	0446	-0.9	-27
	1138	10.2	311			1100	10.6	323
	1748	-0.5	-15			1708	-1.0	-30
	2359	10.0	305			2321	10.8	329
14 Tu	0606	-0.4	-12		29 W	0532	-1.3	-40
	1219	10.0	305			1146	10.7	326
	1826	-0.2	-6			1753	-1.1	-34
15 W	0037	9.8	299		30 Th	0005	11.1	338
	0647	-0.2	-6			0620	-1.5	-46
	1258	9.6	293			1234	10.6	323
	1904	0.1	3			1839	-1.0	-30
					31 F	0052	11.1	338
						0711	-1.4	-43
						1326	10.3	314
						1929	-0.7	-21

Time meridian 75° W. 0000 is midnight. 1200 is noon. Times are not adjusted for Daylight Saving Time.
Heights are referred to mean lower low water which is the chart datum of soundings.

Portland, Maine, 2017

Times and Heights of High and Low Waters

April

Day	Time	ft	cm
1 Sa	0143	11.0	335
	0804	-1.2	-37
	1421	9.9	302
	2022	-0.2	-6
2 Su	0237	10.7	326
	0903	-0.8	-24
	1521	9.5	290
	2121	0.2	6
3 M	0338	10.3	314
	1006	-0.4	-12
	1627	9.1	277
	2226	0.6	18
4 Tu	0445	9.9	302
	1114	-0.1	-3
	1736	8.9	271
	2337	0.8	24
5 W	0555	9.7	296
	1223	0.0	0
	1845	9.0	274
6 Th	0047	0.8	24
	0705	9.6	293
	1328	0.0	0
	1948	9.2	280
7 F	0151	0.6	18
	0808	9.7	296
	1426	-0.1	-3
	2044	9.5	290
8 Sa	0249	0.2	6
	0904	9.9	302
	1517	-0.2	-6
	2133	9.8	299
9 Su	0339	0.0	0
	0953	9.9	302
	1602	-0.2	-6
	2216	10.0	305
10 M	0425	-0.2	-6
	1038	9.9	302
	1643	-0.1	-3
	2255	10.0	305
11 Tu	0506	-0.3	-9
	1118	9.8	299
	1721	0.1	3
	2332	10.0	305
12 W	0545	-0.2	-6
	1157	9.6	293
	1757	0.4	12
13 Th	0006	9.9	302
	0622	-0.1	-3
	1234	9.3	283
	1832	0.7	21
14 F	0041	9.7	296
	0659	0.1	3
	1312	9.0	274
	1908	1.0	30
15 Sa	0117	9.5	290
	0738	0.3	9
	1351	8.7	265
	1946	1.3	40
16 Su	0155	9.3	283
	0818	0.6	18
	1434	8.4	256
	2027	1.6	49
17 M	0238	9.0	274
	0902	0.9	27
	1519	8.1	247
	2113	1.8	55
18 Tu	0325	8.8	268
	0950	1.1	34
	1610	8.0	244
	2204	2.0	61
19 W	0417	8.7	265
	1043	1.2	37
	1704	8.0	244
	2300	2.0	61
20 Th	0513	8.6	262
	1139	1.2	37
	1800	8.2	250
	2359	1.7	52
21 F	0612	8.8	268
	1234	0.9	27
	1854	8.6	262
22 Sa	0057	1.3	40
	0709	9.1	277
	1327	0.6	18
	1945	9.1	277
23 Su	0152	0.7	21
	0804	9.5	290
	1418	0.1	3
	2034	9.8	299
24 M	0244	0.0	0
	0856	10.0	305
	1506	-0.3	-9
	2121	10.4	317
25 Tu	0334	-0.7	-21
	0947	10.4	317
	1553	-0.7	-21
	2207	11.0	335
26 W	0423	-1.2	-37
	1036	10.6	323
	1640	-0.9	-27
	2253	11.5	351
27 Th	0513	-1.6	-49
	1127	10.7	326
	1728	-0.9	-27
	2342	11.7	357
28 F	0603	-1.8	-55
	1218	10.6	323
	1818	-0.8	-24
29 Sa	0032	11.7	357
	0656	-1.7	-52
	1313	10.4	317
	1911	-0.5	-15
30 Su	0125	11.4	347
	0751	-1.4	-43
	1410	10.1	308
	2008	-0.1	-3

May

Day	Time	ft	cm
1 M	0223	11.0	335
	0850	-1.0	-30
	1511	9.7	296
	2109	0.4	12
2 Tu	0324	10.5	320
	0953	-0.5	-15
	1615	9.4	287
	2215	0.7	21
3 W	0431	10.0	305
	1058	-0.1	-3
	1722	9.3	283
	2324	0.9	27
4 Th	0539	9.6	293
	1203	0.1	3
	1826	9.3	283
5 F	0032	0.9	27
	0646	9.5	290
	1305	0.3	9
	1926	9.5	290
6 Sa	0134	0.7	21
	0748	9.4	287
	1401	0.3	9
	2020	9.6	293
7 Su	0231	0.5	15
	0843	9.4	287
	1451	0.4	12
	2107	9.8	299
8 M	0320	0.2	6
	0932	9.4	287
	1535	0.5	15
	2150	9.9	302
9 Tu	0405	0.1	3
	1016	9.4	287
	1616	0.6	18
	2228	10.0	305
10 W	0445	0.0	0
	1057	9.3	283
	1653	0.7	21
	2303	10.0	305
11 Th	0523	0.0	0
	1135	9.2	280
	1728	0.9	27
	2337	9.9	302
12 F	0559	0.1	3
	1211	9.0	274
	1803	1.1	34
13 Sa	0012	9.8	299
	0635	0.2	6
	1248	8.8	268
	1838	1.3	40
14 Su	0047	9.7	296
	0711	0.3	9
	1326	8.6	262
	1916	1.5	46
15 M	0125	9.5	290
	0750	0.5	15
	1406	8.5	259
	1956	1.6	49
16 Tu	0206	9.3	283
	0831	0.7	21
	1449	8.4	256
	2041	1.7	52
17 W	0251	9.1	277
	0915	0.8	24
	1535	8.4	256
	2130	1.8	55
18 Th	0340	9.0	274
	1003	0.9	27
	1625	8.5	259
	2223	1.7	52
19 F	0433	9.0	274
	1055	0.8	24
	1717	8.7	265
	2320	1.5	46
20 Sa	0530	9.0	274
	1149	0.7	21
	1810	9.1	277
21 Su	0019	1.1	34
	0629	9.2	280
	1244	0.4	12
	1904	9.7	296
22 M	0118	0.5	15
	0728	9.5	290
	1338	0.1	3
	1956	10.3	314
23 Tu	0214	-0.2	-6
	0825	9.8	299
	1431	-0.2	-6
	2048	10.9	332
24 W	0308	-0.8	-24
	0921	10.2	311
	1523	-0.5	-15
	2139	11.5	351
25 Th	0402	-1.4	-43
	1015	10.4	317
	1615	-0.7	-21
	2230	11.8	360
26 F	0454	-1.8	-55
	1109	10.6	323
	1707	-0.7	-21
	2322	12.0	366
27 Sa	0548	-1.9	-58
	1203	10.5	320
	1800	-0.6	-18
28 Su	0015	11.9	363
	0642	-1.8	-55
	1259	10.4	317
	1855	-0.4	-12
29 M	0110	11.6	354
	0737	-1.5	-46
	1357	10.2	311
	1953	0.0	0
30 Tu	0208	11.1	338
	0835	-1.1	-34
	1456	9.9	302
	2054	0.3	9
31 W	0309	10.5	320
	0934	-0.6	-18
	1557	9.7	296
	2158	0.7	21

June

Day	Time	ft	cm
1 Th	0412	10.0	305
	1035	-0.1	-3
	1658	9.5	290
	2304	0.9	27
2 F	0516	9.5	290
	1135	0.3	9
	1759	9.5	290
3 Sa	0008	0.9	27
	0620	9.2	280
	1234	0.5	15
	1856	9.5	290
4 Su	0109	0.8	24
	0720	9.0	274
	1328	0.7	21
	1948	9.6	293
5 M	0205	0.7	21
	0816	8.9	271
	1419	0.9	27
	2036	9.7	296
6 Tu	0255	0.5	15
	0906	8.9	271
	1504	1.0	30
	2119	9.8	299
7 W	0341	0.4	12
	0951	8.8	268
	1545	1.1	34
	2159	9.9	302
8 Th	0422	0.3	9
	1033	8.8	268
	1624	1.1	34
	2236	9.9	302
9 F	0500	0.2	6
	1111	8.8	268
	1700	1.2	37
	2311	9.9	302
10 Sa	0536	0.2	6
	1149	8.8	268
	1736	1.3	40
	2346	9.8	299
11 Su	0611	0.2	6
	1225	8.7	265
	1812	1.4	43
12 M	0022	9.8	299
	0647	0.3	9
	1302	8.7	265
	1850	1.4	43
13 Tu	0100	9.7	296
	0724	0.3	9
	1340	8.6	262
	1930	1.5	46
14 W	0140	9.6	293
	0803	0.4	12
	1421	8.7	265
	2013	1.5	46
15 Th	0223	9.5	290
	0845	0.4	12
	1504	8.8	268
	2100	1.4	43
16 F	0310	9.3	283
	0930	0.4	12
	1550	9.0	274
	2152	1.3	40
17 Sa	0401	9.3	283
	1019	0.4	12
	1640	9.3	283
	2248	1.1	34
18 Su	0457	9.2	280
	1112	0.4	12
	1733	9.6	293
	2347	0.7	21
19 M	0556	9.3	283
	1208	0.3	9
	1828	10.1	308
20 Tu	0048	0.2	6
	0658	9.4	287
	1305	0.1	3
	1925	10.6	323
21 W	0149	-0.3	-9
	0759	9.6	293
	1402	-0.1	-3
	2021	11.1	338
22 Th	0247	-0.9	-27
	0859	9.9	302
	1459	-0.3	-9
	2116	11.5	351
23 F	0344	-1.4	-43
	0957	10.1	308
	1554	-0.5	-15
	2211	11.8	360
24 Sa	0439	-1.7	-52
	1053	10.3	314
	1649	-0.6	-18
	2305	11.9	363
25 Su	0533	-1.8	-55
	1149	10.4	317
	1744	-0.6	-18
26 M	0000	11.8	360
	0627	-1.7	-52
	1244	10.3	314
	1840	-0.4	-12
27 Tu	0055	11.5	351
	0720	-1.4	-43
	1339	10.2	311
	1937	-0.1	-3
28 W	0151	11.0	335
	0815	-1.0	-30
	1435	10.0	305
	2035	0.2	6
29 Th	0248	10.4	317
	0910	-0.5	-15
	1531	9.8	299
	2134	0.5	15
30 F	0347	9.8	299
	1005	0.0	0
	1627	9.6	293
	2236	0.8	24

Time meridian 75° W. 0000 is midnight. 1200 is noon. Times are not adjusted for Daylight Saving Time.
Heights are referred to mean lower low water which is the chart datum of soundings.

Portland, Maine, 2017

Times and Heights of High and Low Waters

July

Day	Time	ft	cm
1 Sa	0446	9.3	283
	1101	0.4	12
	1723	9.5	290
	2337	1.0	30
2 Su	0546	8.9	271
	1156	0.8	24
	1818	9.4	287
3 M	0037	1.0	30
	0646	8.6	262
	1250	1.1	34
	1911	9.4	287
4 Tu	0133	0.9	27
	0742	8.4	256
	1342	1.3	40
	2000	9.4	287
5 W	0225	0.8	24
	0834	8.4	256
	1430	1.4	43
	2046	9.5	290
6 Th	0312	0.6	18
	0922	8.4	256
	1514	1.4	43
	2129	9.6	293
7 F	0355	0.5	15
	1005	8.5	259
	1555	1.3	40
	2208	9.7	296
8 Sa ○	0434	0.3	9
	1045	8.6	262
	1633	1.3	40
	2246	9.8	299
9 Su	0511	0.3	9
	1123	8.7	265
	1710	1.2	37
	2322	9.9	302
10 M	0546	0.2	6
	1159	8.7	265
	1747	1.2	37
	2359	9.9	302
11 Tu	0621	0.1	3
	1235	8.8	268
	1825	1.1	34
12 W	0036	9.9	302
	0657	0.1	3
	1312	8.9	271
	1905	1.0	30
13 Th	0116	9.8	299
	0735	0.1	3
	1351	9.1	277
	1948	0.9	27
14 F	0158	9.7	296
	0816	0.1	3
	1433	9.3	283
	2035	0.8	24
15 Sa	0244	9.6	293
	0901	0.1	3
	1519	9.5	290
	2126	0.7	21
16 Su ◑	0335	9.4	287
	0949	0.1	3
	1609	9.7	296
	2222	0.6	18
17 M	0431	9.3	283
	1043	0.2	6
	1703	10.0	305
	2322	0.4	12
18 Tu	0532	9.2	280
	1140	0.2	6
	1801	10.3	314
19 W	0025	0.1	3
	0636	9.2	280
	1240	0.2	6
	1901	10.6	323
20 Th	0129	-0.3	-9
	0741	9.3	283
	1341	0.1	3
	2001	11.0	335
21 F	0231	-0.8	-24
	0843	9.6	293
	1441	-0.2	-6
	2100	11.3	344
22 Sa	0329	-1.2	-37
	0943	9.9	302
	1539	-0.4	-12
	2157	11.5	351
23 Su ●	0424	-1.5	-46
	1039	10.1	308
	1635	-0.5	-15
	2252	11.6	354
24 M	0517	-1.6	-49
	1133	10.3	314
	1730	-0.6	-18
	2346	11.5	351
25 Tu	0609	-1.5	-46
	1225	10.3	314
	1823	-0.5	-15
26 W	0038	11.2	341
	0659	-1.2	-37
	1316	10.2	311
	1917	-0.2	-6
27 Th	0130	10.7	326
	0749	-0.8	-24
	1407	10.0	305
	2010	0.1	3
28 F	0223	10.2	311
	0839	-0.3	-9
	1457	9.8	299
	2105	0.4	12
29 Sa	0316	9.6	293
	0930	0.2	6
	1549	9.5	290
	2201	0.8	24
30 Su ◐	0411	9.0	274
	1021	0.7	21
	1641	9.3	283
	2259	1.0	30
31 M	0508	8.5	259
	1114	1.2	37
	1734	9.1	277
	2357	1.2	37

August

Day	Time	ft	cm
1 Tu	0606	8.2	250
	1208	1.5	46
	1828	9.0	274
2 W	0055	1.2	37
	0704	8.1	247
	1302	1.6	49
	1920	9.1	277
3 Th	0149	1.1	34
	0759	8.1	247
	1353	1.6	49
	2010	9.2	280
4 F	0239	0.9	27
	0849	8.2	250
	1441	1.5	46
	2056	9.4	287
5 Sa	0323	0.7	21
	0934	8.4	256
	1524	1.3	40
	2139	9.6	293
6 Su	0404	0.5	15
	1015	8.6	262
	1605	1.1	34
	2218	9.8	299
7 M ○	0441	0.2	6
	1052	8.8	268
	1643	0.9	27
	2256	9.9	302
8 Tu	0516	0.1	3
	1129	9.0	274
	1721	0.7	21
	2334	10.0	305
9 W	0552	-0.1	-3
	1204	9.2	280
	1800	0.6	18
10 Th	0012	10.1	308
	0628	-0.2	-6
	1242	9.4	287
	1840	0.4	12
11 F	0052	10.1	308
	0707	-0.2	-6
	1321	9.6	293
	1924	0.3	9
12 Sa	0136	9.9	302
	0749	-0.2	-6
	1404	9.8	299
	2012	0.2	6
13 Su	0223	9.8	299
	0834	-0.1	-3
	1451	10.0	305
	2104	0.2	6
14 M ◐	0315	9.5	290
	0925	0.1	3
	1542	10.1	308
	2201	0.2	6
15 Tu	0412	9.3	283
	1020	0.2	6
	1639	10.1	308
	2303	0.1	3
16 W	0515	9.1	277
	1120	0.4	12
	1741	10.2	311
17 Th	0009	0.0	0
	0622	9.0	274
	1224	0.4	12
	1845	10.4	317
18 F	0115	-0.2	-6
	0729	9.1	277
	1329	0.3	9
	1949	10.7	326
19 Sa	0218	-0.6	-18
	0833	9.4	287
	1431	0.0	0
	2050	10.9	332
20 Su	0316	-0.9	-27
	0931	9.8	299
	1529	-0.3	-9
	2147	11.1	338
21 M ●	0410	-1.1	-34
	1025	10.1	308
	1624	-0.5	-15
	2240	11.2	341
22 Tu	0500	-1.2	-37
	1115	10.2	311
	1715	-0.6	-18
	2331	11.1	338
23 W	0548	-1.1	-34
	1202	10.3	314
	1805	-0.5	-15
24 Th	0019	10.8	329
	0634	-0.8	-24
	1248	10.2	311
	1854	-0.3	-9
25 F	0107	10.3	314
	0719	-0.4	-12
	1334	10.0	305
	1942	0.0	0
26 Sa	0154	9.8	299
	0804	0.1	3
	1419	9.7	296
	2031	0.4	12
27 Su	0243	9.3	283
	0850	0.6	18
	1505	9.4	287
	2122	0.8	24
28 M	0333	8.7	265
	0938	1.1	34
	1554	9.1	277
	2216	1.1	34
29 Tu ◐	0427	8.3	253
	1029	1.5	46
	1646	8.8	268
	2312	1.3	40
30 W	0524	8.0	244
	1123	1.8	55
	1741	8.7	265
31 Th	0011	1.4	43
	0623	7.9	241
	1220	1.9	58
	1837	8.8	268

September

Day	Time	ft	cm
1 F	0107	1.3	40
	0719	7.9	241
	1314	1.8	55
	1931	8.9	271
2 Sa	0159	1.1	34
	0811	8.1	247
	1405	1.6	49
	2021	9.2	280
3 Su	0245	0.8	24
	0857	8.4	256
	1451	1.3	40
	2106	9.5	290
4 M	0327	0.5	15
	0938	8.8	268
	1533	0.9	27
	2147	9.8	299
5 Tu	0405	0.2	6
	1017	9.1	277
	1613	0.5	15
	2227	10.0	305
6 W ○	0442	-0.1	-3
	1054	9.5	290
	1653	0.2	6
	2306	10.2	311
7 Th	0519	-0.3	-9
	1131	9.8	299
	1734	-0.1	-3
	2347	10.3	314
8 F	0558	-0.4	-12
	1210	10.1	308
	1817	-0.3	-9
9 Sa	0029	10.3	314
	0639	-0.4	-12
	1252	10.3	314
	1903	-0.4	-12
10 Su	0115	10.1	308
	0723	-0.3	-9
	1337	10.4	317
	1952	-0.4	-12
11 M	0205	9.9	302
	0811	-0.1	-3
	1426	10.4	317
	2046	-0.3	-9
12 Tu	0300	9.5	290
	0904	0.2	6
	1521	10.3	314
	2145	-0.2	-6
13 W ◐	0400	9.2	280
	1003	0.4	12
	1622	10.2	311
	2249	0.0	0
14 Th	0506	9.0	274
	1108	0.6	18
	1728	10.1	308
	2357	0.0	0
15 F	0615	9.0	274
	1216	0.6	18
	1836	10.1	308
16 Sa	0105	-0.1	-3
	0722	9.2	280
	1322	0.4	12
	1942	10.3	314
17 Su	0207	-0.3	-9
	0823	9.5	290
	1424	0.1	3
	2042	10.5	320
18 M	0303	-0.6	-18
	0918	9.9	302
	1521	-0.2	-6
	2137	10.7	326
19 Tu	0354	-0.7	-21
	1008	10.1	308
	1612	-0.4	-12
	2227	10.7	326
20 W ●	0441	-0.7	-21
	1054	10.3	314
	1700	-0.5	-15
	2314	10.6	323
21 Th ○	0525	-0.5	-15
	1137	10.3	314
	1745	-0.5	-15
	2359	10.3	314
22 F	0606	-0.3	-9
	1218	10.2	311
	1829	-0.3	-9
23 Sa	0042	9.9	302
	0647	0.1	3
	1258	9.9	302
	1912	0.0	0
24 Su	0125	9.5	290
	0728	0.6	18
	1339	9.6	293
	1956	0.4	12
25 M	0210	9.0	274
	0810	1.0	30
	1422	9.3	283
	2042	0.7	21
26 Tu	0256	8.6	262
	0855	1.4	43
	1508	9.0	274
	2132	1.1	34
27 W ◐	0347	8.2	250
	0944	1.8	55
	1558	8.7	265
	2225	1.3	40
28 Th	0441	7.9	241
	1038	2.0	61
	1653	8.6	262
	2322	1.5	46
29 F	0539	7.9	241
	1135	2.1	64
	1750	8.6	262
30 Sa	0019	1.4	43
	0635	8.0	244
	1232	1.9	58
	1847	8.7	265

Time meridian 75° W. 0000 is midnight. 1200 is noon. Times are not adjusted for Daylight Saving Time.
Heights are referred to mean lower low water which is the chart datum of soundings.

Portland, Maine, 2017

Times and Heights of High and Low Waters

October

Day	Time (h m)	Height (ft)	Height (cm)
1 Su	0112	1.2	37
	0728	8.2	250
	1326	1.6	49
	1940	9.0	274
2 M	0201	0.9	27
	0815	8.6	262
	1415	1.2	37
	2028	9.4	287
3 Tu	0244	0.5	15
	0858	9.1	277
	1500	0.6	18
	2113	9.7	296
4 W	0325	0.2	6
	0938	9.6	293
	1543	0.1	3
	2156	10.1	308
5 Th ○	0405	-0.2	-6
	1017	10.1	308
	1626	-0.4	-12
	2239	10.3	314
6 F	0446	-0.5	-15
	1058	10.5	320
	1709	-0.8	-24
	2322	10.5	320
7 Sa	0528	-0.6	-18
	1140	10.8	329
	1755	-1.0	-30
8 Su	0008	10.4	317
	0612	-0.6	-18
	1225	11.0	335
	1843	-1.1	-34
9 M	0057	10.3	314
	0700	-0.4	-12
	1313	11.0	335
	1935	-1.0	-30
10 Tu	0150	10.0	305
	0752	-0.1	-3
	1406	10.8	329
	2031	-0.7	-21
11 W	0248	9.6	293
	0848	0.2	6
	1504	10.5	320
	2132	-0.4	-12
12 Th ☽	0351	9.3	283
	0951	0.6	18
	1609	10.2	311
	2238	-0.1	-3
13 F	0458	9.1	277
	1059	0.8	24
	1717	10.0	305
	2346	0.0	0
14 Sa	0607	9.2	280
	1209	0.7	21
	1827	9.9	302
15 Su	0052	0.0	0
	0712	9.4	287
	1316	0.5	15
	1933	10.0	305
16 M	0152	-0.1	-3
	0810	9.7	296
	1416	0.2	6
	2032	10.1	308
17 Tu	0246	-0.2	-6
	0902	10.0	305
	1510	-0.1	-3
	2125	10.1	308
18 W	0335	-0.2	-6
	0949	10.2	311
	1559	-0.4	-12
	2213	10.1	308
19 Th ●	0419	-0.2	-6
	1032	10.3	314
	1644	-0.4	-12
	2257	10.0	305
20 F	0500	0.0	0
	1111	10.3	314
	1725	-0.4	-12
	2338	9.8	299
21 Sa	0538	0.3	9
	1148	10.1	308
	1805	-0.2	-6
22 Su	0018	9.5	290
	0616	0.6	18
	1225	9.9	302
	1845	0.0	0
23 M	0058	9.1	277
	0654	1.0	30
	1303	9.6	293
	1925	0.3	9
24 Tu	0139	8.8	268
	0733	1.3	40
	1343	9.3	283
	2006	0.6	18
25 W	0222	8.5	259
	0816	1.6	49
	1426	9.1	277
	2051	0.9	27
26 Th	0309	8.2	250
	0902	1.9	58
	1514	8.8	268
	2140	1.2	37
27 F ☾	0359	8.0	244
	0954	2.0	61
	1606	8.6	262
	2233	1.3	40
28 Sa	0453	8.0	244
	1049	2.1	64
	1702	8.5	259
	2327	1.3	40
29 Su	0548	8.1	247
	1147	1.9	58
	1800	8.6	262
30 M	0021	1.2	37
	0640	8.5	259
	1243	1.5	46
	1855	8.9	271
31 Tu	0112	0.9	27
	0729	8.9	271
	1336	1.0	30
	1947	9.2	280

November

Day	Time (h m)	Height (ft)	Height (cm)
1 W	0159	0.5	15
	0815	9.5	290
	1425	0.4	12
	2037	9.6	293
2 Th	0245	0.1	3
	0900	10.1	308
	1513	-0.3	-9
	2125	10.0	305
3 F	0330	-0.3	-9
	0943	10.7	326
	1600	-0.9	-27
	2212	10.3	314
4 Sa ○	0415	-0.6	-18
	1028	11.2	341
	1647	-1.3	-40
	2300	10.5	320
5 Su	0501	-0.7	-21
	1114	11.5	351
	1735	-1.6	-49
	2350	10.5	320
6 M	0549	-0.7	-21
	1203	11.5	351
	1826	-1.6	-49
7 Tu	0042	10.3	314
	0640	-0.5	-15
	1254	11.4	347
	1920	-1.4	-43
8 W	0137	10.1	308
	0735	-0.2	-6
	1350	11.1	338
	2017	-1.1	-34
9 Th	0236	9.8	299
	0834	0.2	6
	1450	10.6	323
	2118	-0.7	-21
10 F ○	0339	9.5	290
	0939	0.5	15
	1555	10.2	311
	2223	-0.3	-9
11 Sa	0446	9.4	287
	1048	0.7	21
	1704	9.8	299
	2329	0.0	0
12 Su	0552	9.4	287
	1157	0.7	21
	1813	9.6	293
13 M	0032	0.1	3
	0654	9.5	290
	1303	0.5	15
	1918	9.5	290
14 Tu	0131	0.2	6
	0751	9.8	299
	1403	0.2	6
	2016	9.5	290
15 W	0224	0.2	6
	0842	10.0	305
	1456	0.0	0
	2109	9.5	290
16 Th	0312	0.2	6
	0927	10.1	308
	1543	-0.2	-6
	2156	9.5	290
17 F	0355	0.3	9
	1008	10.1	308
	1626	-0.3	-9
	2238	9.4	287
18 Sa ●	0435	0.5	15
	1046	10.1	308
	1706	-0.3	-9
	2318	9.2	280
19 Su	0512	0.7	21
	1122	10.0	305
	1743	-0.1	-3
	2356	9.1	277
20 M	0548	0.9	27
	1157	9.8	299
	1820	0.0	0
21 Tu	0033	8.8	268
	0624	1.1	34
	1233	9.7	296
	1857	0.2	6
22 W	0111	8.6	262
	0702	1.3	40
	1311	9.4	287
	1936	0.5	15
23 Th	0152	8.4	256
	0742	1.5	46
	1352	9.2	280
	2016	0.7	21
24 F	0234	8.3	253
	0826	1.7	52
	1436	9.0	274
	2100	0.9	27
25 Sa	0320	8.2	250
	0914	1.8	55
	1525	8.8	268
	2148	1.0	30
26 Su ☾	0409	8.2	250
	1007	1.8	55
	1617	8.6	262
	2238	1.0	30
27 M	0500	8.4	256
	1103	1.6	49
	1713	8.6	262
	2331	0.9	27
28 Tu	0552	8.7	265
	1200	1.3	40
	1810	8.8	268
29 W	0024	0.7	21
	0644	9.2	280
	1257	0.8	24
	1908	9.0	274
30 Th	0116	0.4	12
	0735	9.8	299
	1352	0.1	3
	2003	9.4	287

December

Day	Time (h m)	Height (ft)	Height (cm)
1 F	0208	0.0	0
	0824	10.4	317
	1445	-0.6	-18
	2057	9.8	299
2 Sa	0258	-0.3	-9
	0914	11.0	335
	1536	-1.2	-37
	2149	10.1	308
3 Su ○	0348	-0.6	-18
	1003	11.5	351
	1627	-1.7	-52
	2241	10.3	314
4 M	0439	-0.8	-24
	1053	11.8	360
	1718	-2.0	-61
	2333	10.4	317
5 Tu	0530	-0.8	-24
	1145	11.8	360
	1811	-2.0	-61
6 W	0027	10.3	314
	0624	-0.7	-21
	1239	11.6	354
	1905	-1.8	-55
7 Th	0123	10.2	311
	0720	-0.4	-12
	1335	11.2	341
	2001	-1.4	-43
8 F	0221	9.9	302
	0819	-0.1	-3
	1435	10.7	326
	2100	-0.9	-27
9 Sa	0322	9.7	296
	0923	0.3	9
	1538	10.1	308
	2201	-0.4	-12
10 Su ○	0424	9.5	290
	1030	0.5	15
	1644	9.6	293
	2304	0.0	0
11 M	0527	9.4	287
	1137	0.6	18
	1751	9.2	280
12 Tu	0005	0.3	9
	0628	9.5	290
	1242	0.6	18
	1855	9.0	274
13 W	0104	0.5	15
	0725	9.6	293
	1342	0.4	12
	1954	8.9	271
14 Th	0158	0.6	18
	0816	9.7	296
	1436	0.2	6
	2048	8.9	271
15 F	0247	0.7	21
	0903	9.8	299
	1524	0.0	0
	2135	8.9	271
16 Sa	0331	0.8	24
	0945	9.8	299
	1607	-0.1	-3
	2218	8.9	271
17 Su	0411	0.8	24
	1023	9.9	302
	1646	-0.1	-3
	2258	8.8	268
18 M ●	0448	0.9	27
	1059	9.8	299
	1723	-0.1	-3
	2335	8.8	268
19 Tu	0524	0.9	27
	1134	9.8	299
	1758	0.0	0
20 W	0011	8.7	265
	0600	1.0	30
	1209	9.7	296
	1833	0.1	3
21 Th	0046	8.6	262
	0636	1.1	34
	1246	9.5	290
	1908	0.2	6
22 F	0123	8.5	259
	0714	1.2	37
	1324	9.3	283
	1945	0.3	9
23 Sa	0202	8.5	259
	0755	1.3	40
	1405	9.2	280
	2025	0.4	12
24 Su	0243	8.5	259
	0840	1.3	40
	1449	9.0	274
	2108	0.5	15
25 M	0327	8.6	262
	0929	1.3	40
	1538	8.8	268
	2155	0.6	18
26 Tu ☾	0415	8.8	268
	1023	1.2	37
	1632	8.7	265
	2247	0.6	18
27 W	0507	9.1	277
	1121	0.9	27
	1731	8.7	265
	2342	0.5	15
28 Th	0602	9.5	290
	1222	0.5	15
	1832	8.8	268
29 F	0039	0.3	9
	0658	10.0	305
	1322	-0.1	-3
	1933	9.1	277
30 Sa	0136	0.0	0
	0754	10.5	320
	1421	-0.7	-21
	2033	9.4	287
31 Su	0232	-0.3	-9
	0850	11.1	338
	1516	-1.3	-40
	2130	9.8	299

Time meridian 75° W. 0000 is midnight. 1200 is noon. Times are not adjusted for Daylight Saving Time.
Heights are referred to mean lower low water which is the chart datum of soundings.

Boston, Massachusetts, 2017
Times and Heights of High and Low Waters

January

Day	Time	ft	cm	Day	Time	ft	cm
1 Su	0059	9.3	283	16 M	0144	10.1	308
	0657	0.6	18		0744	-0.2	-6
	1305	10.3	314		1358	10.6	323
	1927	-0.4	-12		2015	-0.6	-18
2 M	0140	9.3	283	17 Tu	0232	9.9	302
	0741	0.6	18		0835	0.3	9
	1348	10.2	311		1448	10.0	305
	2011	-0.4	-12		2102	-0.1	-3
3 Tu	0224	9.4	287	18 W	0321	9.5	290
	0828	0.7	21		0926	0.7	21
	1435	10.1	308		1539	9.4	287
	2057	-0.3	-9		2151	0.5	15
4 W	0310	9.6	293	19 Th	0411	9.3	283
	0919	0.5	15		1020	1.1	34
	1526	9.9	302		1633	8.8	268
	2146	-0.2	-6		2242	1.0	30
5 Th	0401	9.7	296	20 F	0502	9.1	277
	1014	0.4	12		1116	1.3	40
	1621	9.7	296		1729	8.4	256
	2239	0.0	0		2334	1.4	43
6 F	0455	10.0	305	21 Sa	0555	9.0	274
	1113	0.3	9		1214	1.4	43
	1721	9.5	290		1826	8.2	250
	2336	0.0	0				
7 Sa	0552	10.3	314	22 Su	0027	1.6	49
	1214	0.0	0		0649	9.0	274
	1823	9.5	290		1310	1.3	40
					1924	8.1	247
8 Su	0034	0.0	0	23 M	0120	1.6	49
	0650	10.6	323		0741	9.2	280
	1316	-0.4	-12		1404	1.0	30
	1926	9.6	293		2018	8.2	250
9 M	0133	-0.1	-3	24 Tu	0211	1.5	46
	0749	11.0	335		0830	9.4	287
	1416	-0.9	-27		1453	0.7	21
	2028	9.8	299		2107	8.4	256
10 Tu	0231	-0.3	-9	25 W	0258	1.2	37
	0847	11.4	347		0916	9.7	296
	1514	-1.3	-40		1537	0.4	12
	2127	10.0	305		2152	8.7	265
11 W	0327	-0.6	-18	26 Th	0343	1.0	30
	0943	11.7	357		1000	10.0	305
	1609	-1.6	-49		1620	0.0	0
	2223	10.2	311		2234	9.0	274
12 Th	0421	-0.7	-21	27 F	0427	0.7	21
	1037	11.8	360		1041	10.3	314
	1701	-1.8	-55		1700	-0.3	-9
	2316	10.4	317		2314	9.3	283
13 F	0514	-0.8	-24	28 Sa	0509	0.4	12
	1129	11.8	360		1121	10.5	320
	1751	-1.8	-55		1740	-0.6	-18
					2354	9.5	290
14 Sa	0007	10.4	317	29 Su	0551	0.1	3
	0605	-0.7	-21		1202	10.7	326
	1219	11.6	354		1821	-0.8	-24
	1840	-1.6	-49				
15 Su	0056	10.3	314	30 M	0033	9.8	299
	0655	-0.5	-15		0634	-0.1	-3
	1309	11.1	338		1244	10.7	326
	1927	-1.2	-37		1902	-0.9	-27
				31 Tu	0114	10.0	305
					0719	-0.2	-6
					1327	10.6	323
					1946	-0.8	-24

February

Day	Time	ft	cm	Day	Time	ft	cm
1 W	0157	10.1	308	16 Th	0241	9.7	296
	0806	-0.3	-9		0851	0.5	15
	1414	10.4	317		1503	9.3	283
	2032	-0.7	-21		2111	0.7	21
2 Th	0244	10.2	311	17 F	0326	9.4	287
	0857	-0.2	-6		0940	0.9	27
	1505	10.1	308		1552	8.7	265
	2121	-0.4	-12		2158	1.2	37
3 F	0334	10.3	314	18 Sa	0414	9.1	277
	0952	-0.2	-6		1032	1.2	37
	1601	9.7	296		1645	8.3	253
	2214	-0.1	-3		2249	1.6	49
4 Sa	0429	10.3	314	19 Su	0506	8.9	271
	1051	-0.1	-3		1128	1.4	43
	1701	9.4	287		1741	8.0	244
	2312	0.1	3		2343	1.8	55
5 Su	0528	10.3	314	20 M	0601	8.8	268
	1154	-0.1	-3		1225	1.5	46
	1805	9.2	280		1840	7.9	241
6 M	0013	0.3	9	21 Tu	0038	1.8	55
	0630	10.5	320		0657	8.9	271
	1258	-0.3	-9		1321	1.3	40
	1911	9.2	280		1937	8.1	247
7 Tu	0115	0.2	6	22 W	0132	1.7	52
	0733	10.7	326		0751	9.2	280
	1401	-0.5	-15		1414	1.0	30
	2015	9.4	287		2029	8.3	253
8 W	0216	0.0	0	23 Th	0224	1.3	40
	0834	10.9	332		0841	9.6	293
	1500	-0.9	-27		1502	0.5	15
	2116	9.7	296		2117	8.7	265
9 Th	0313	-0.2	-6	24 F	0312	0.9	27
	0932	11.2	341		0928	10.0	305
	1554	-1.2	-37		1547	0.1	3
	2211	10.0	305		2201	9.2	280
10 F	0408	-0.5	-15	25 Sa	0358	0.4	12
	1025	11.3	344		1013	10.4	317
	1645	-1.3	-40		1630	-0.4	-12
	2301	10.2	311		2243	9.7	296
11 Sa	0458	-0.6	-18	26 Su	0443	-0.1	-3
	1115	11.3	344		1056	10.7	326
	1732	-1.3	-40		1712	-0.8	-24
	2348	10.3	314		2324	10.1	308
12 Su	0547	-0.7	-21	27 M	0527	-0.5	-15
	1202	11.1	338		1138	11.0	335
	1817	-1.1	-34		1754	-1.0	-30
13 M	0032	10.3	314	28 Tu	0005	10.5	320
	0633	-0.5	-15		0612	-0.8	-24
	1247	10.8	329		1222	11.1	338
	1901	-0.8	-24		1837	-1.1	-34
14 Tu	0115	10.2	311				
	0719	-0.3	-9				
	1332	10.4	317				
	1943	-0.4	-12				
15 W	0158	9.9	302				
	0805	0.1	3				
	1417	9.8	299				
	2027	0.1	3				

March

Day	Time	ft	cm	Day	Time	ft	cm
1 W	0047	10.8	329	16 Th	0123	10.1	308
	0658	-1.0	-30		0735	0.0	0
	1308	11.0	335		1347	9.7	296
	1921	-1.1	-34		1952	0.5	15
2 Th	0132	10.9	332	17 F	0203	9.8	299
	0746	-1.0	-30		0818	0.4	12
	1356	10.7	326		1430	9.2	280
	2008	-0.8	-24		2035	0.9	27
3 F	0219	10.9	332	18 Sa	0246	9.5	290
	0838	-0.9	-27		0904	0.7	21
	1448	10.3	314		1516	8.8	268
	2059	-0.5	-15		2120	1.4	43
4 Sa	0311	10.8	329	19 Su	0332	9.2	280
	0933	-0.6	-18		0952	1.1	34
	1545	9.8	299		1606	8.4	256
	2154	0.0	0		2208	1.7	52
5 Su	0408	10.6	323	20 M	0422	9.0	274
	1033	-0.3	-9		1045	1.4	43
	1646	9.4	287		1700	8.2	250
	2253	0.3	9		2301	1.9	58
6 M	0509	10.4	317	21 Tu	0516	8.9	271
	1136	-0.1	-3		1141	1.5	46
	1752	9.1	277		1757	8.1	247
	2356	0.6	18		2357	2.0	61
7 Tu	0614	10.3	314	22 W	0613	8.9	271
	1242	-0.1	-3		1237	1.4	43
	1900	9.1	277		1854	8.2	250
8 W	0100	0.6	18	23 Th	0054	1.8	55
	0720	10.3	314		0709	9.1	277
	1346	-0.2	-6		1332	1.1	34
	2005	9.3	283		1948	8.6	262
9 Th	0203	0.4	12	24 F	0148	1.4	43
	0824	10.5	320		0803	9.5	290
	1445	-0.4	-12		1423	0.6	18
	2104	9.6	293		2038	9.1	277
10 F	0301	0.1	3	25 Sa	0239	0.8	24
	0921	10.7	326		0853	10.0	305
	1539	-0.6	-18		1510	0.1	3
	2156	9.9	302		2124	9.6	293
11 Sa	0354	-0.2	-6	26 Su	0328	0.2	6
	1013	10.8	329		0941	10.5	320
	1627	-0.7	-21		1556	-0.4	-12
	2243	10.2	311		2208	10.2	311
12 Su	0443	-0.4	-12	27 M	0415	-0.5	-15
	1100	10.8	329		1028	10.9	332
	1711	-0.7	-21		1641	-0.8	-24
	2326	10.3	314		2252	10.8	329
13 M	0528	-0.5	-15	28 Tu	0502	-1.0	-30
	1144	10.7	326		1114	11.2	341
	1752	-0.5	-15		1725	-1.1	-34
					2336	11.3	344
14 Tu	0006	10.3	314	29 W	0549	-1.4	-43
	0611	-0.4	-12		1201	11.3	344
	1225	10.4	317		1811	-1.2	-37
	1832	-0.3	-9				
15 W	0045	10.3	314	30 Th	0021	11.5	351
	0653	-0.3	-9		0638	-1.6	-49
	1306	10.1	308		1249	11.2	341
	1912	0.1	3		1858	-1.1	-34
				31 F	0108	11.6	354
					0728	-1.6	-49
					1340	10.9	332
					1947	-0.8	-24

Time meridian 75° W. 0000 is midnight. 1200 is noon. Times are not adjusted for Daylight Saving Time.
Heights are referred to mean lower low water which is the chart datum of soundings.

Boston, Massachusetts, 2017
Times and Heights of High and Low Waters

April

Day	Time	ft	cm
1 Sa	0158	11.5	351
	0820	-1.3	-40
	1434	10.4	317
	2039	-0.4	-12
2 Su	0252	11.2	341
	0916	-0.9	-27
	1532	10.0	305
	2136	0.1	3
3 M	0350	10.8	329
	1016	-0.4	-12
	1634	9.6	293
	2237	0.6	18
4 Tu	0453	10.4	317
	1119	-0.1	-3
	1740	9.3	283
	2341	0.8	24
5 W	0600	10.1	308
	1225	0.1	3
	1847	9.3	283
6 Th	0047	0.8	24
	0708	10.1	308
	1328	0.2	6
	1950	9.5	290
7 F	0150	0.6	18
	0811	10.1	308
	1427	0.1	3
	2047	9.8	299
8 Sa	0248	0.4	12
	0907	10.2	311
	1518	0.0	0
	2137	10.0	305
9 Su	0339	0.1	3
	0957	10.3	314
	1604	0.0	0
	2220	10.2	311
10 M	0425	-0.1	-3
	1042	10.2	311
	1645	0.0	0
	2300	10.3	314
11 Tu	0508	-0.2	-6
	1123	10.2	311
	1725	0.2	6
	2337	10.4	317
12 W	0548	-0.2	-6
	1202	10.0	305
	1803	0.3	9
13 Th	0014	10.3	314
	0628	-0.1	-3
	1241	9.8	299
	1841	0.6	18
14 F	0051	10.2	311
	0708	0.1	3
	1321	9.5	290
	1921	0.9	27
15 Sa	0130	10.0	305
	0749	0.3	9
	1402	9.2	280
	2002	1.2	37
16 Su	0211	9.7	296
	0832	0.6	18
	1446	8.9	271
	2046	1.5	46
17 M	0255	9.5	290
	0918	0.9	27
	1533	8.6	262
	2133	1.8	55
18 Tu	0343	9.2	280
	1007	1.2	37
	1624	8.4	256
	2225	1.9	58
19 W	0436	9.1	277
	1100	1.3	40
	1717	8.4	256
	2320	1.9	58
20 Th	0531	9.1	277
	1155	1.2	37
	1812	8.6	262
21 F	0016	1.7	52
	0628	9.3	283
	1249	1.0	30
	1905	9.0	274
22 Sa	0112	1.3	40
	0723	9.6	293
	1342	0.6	18
	1957	9.6	293
23 Su	0206	0.6	18
	0817	10.0	305
	1433	0.1	3
	2046	10.2	311
24 M	0258	-0.1	-3
	0909	10.5	320
	1521	-0.4	-12
	2133	10.9	332
25 Tu	0348	-0.8	-24
	1000	10.9	332
	1610	-0.8	-24
	2220	11.5	351
26 W	0438	-1.4	-43
	1050	11.1	338
	1657	-1.0	-30
	2308	11.9	363
27 Th	0528	-1.8	-55
	1140	11.2	341
	1746	-1.1	-34
	2356	12.1	369
28 F	0618	-2.0	-61
	1232	11.2	341
	1836	-1.0	-30
29 Sa	0046	12.1	369
	0710	-1.9	-58
	1325	10.9	332
	1927	-0.7	-21
30 Su	0139	11.9	363
	0804	-1.5	-46
	1420	10.5	320
	2022	-0.2	-6

May

Day	Time	ft	cm
1 M	0235	11.4	347
	0900	-1.1	-34
	1519	10.2	311
	2119	0.2	6
2 Tu	0334	10.9	332
	0959	-0.5	-15
	1621	9.8	299
	2220	0.6	18
3 W	0438	10.4	317
	1100	-0.1	-3
	1725	9.6	293
	2324	0.9	27
4 Th	0543	10.0	305
	1203	0.3	9
	1828	9.6	293
5 F	0030	0.9	27
	0649	9.8	299
	1304	0.5	15
	1928	9.7	296
6 Sa	0132	0.8	24
	0751	9.7	296
	1401	0.5	15
	2022	9.9	302
7 Su	0229	0.6	18
	0846	9.7	296
	1451	0.6	18
	2110	10.1	308
8 M	0319	0.4	12
	0935	9.7	296
	1536	0.6	18
	2153	10.2	311
9 Tu	0404	0.2	6
	1020	9.7	296
	1617	0.7	21
	2231	10.3	314
10 W	0445	0.1	3
	1100	9.6	293
	1656	0.8	24
	2309	10.3	314
11 Th	0525	0.0	0
	1139	9.6	293
	1734	0.9	27
	2345	10.3	314
12 F	0603	0.0	0
	1218	9.4	287
	1813	1.0	30
13 Sa	0022	10.2	311
	0642	0.2	6
	1257	9.3	283
	1852	1.2	37
14 Su	0101	10.1	308
	0722	0.3	9
	1337	9.1	277
	1933	1.4	43
15 M	0142	9.9	302
	0804	0.5	15
	1419	9.0	274
	2017	1.6	49
16 Tu	0225	9.7	296
	0848	0.7	21
	1504	8.8	268
	2103	1.7	52
17 W	0311	9.5	290
	0935	0.8	24
	1552	8.8	268
	2152	1.8	55
18 Th	0401	9.4	287
	1024	0.9	27
	1642	8.9	271
	2246	1.7	52
19 F	0454	9.4	287
	1116	0.9	27
	1733	9.1	277
	2341	1.4	43
20 Sa	0550	9.5	290
	1210	0.7	21
	1826	9.6	293
21 Su	0038	1.0	30
	0646	9.7	296
	1303	0.4	12
	1918	10.1	308
22 M	0134	0.4	12
	0743	10.0	305
	1356	0.1	3
	2009	10.7	326
23 Tu	0229	-0.3	-9
	0838	10.3	314
	1449	-0.3	-9
	2100	11.4	347
24 W	0323	-1.0	-30
	0933	10.7	326
	1540	-0.6	-18
	2151	11.9	363
25 Th	0415	-1.6	-49
	1029	10.9	332
	1632	-0.8	-24
	2243	12.3	375
26 F	0508	-2.0	-61
	1121	11.0	335
	1723	-0.9	-27
	2334	12.4	378
27 Sa	0600	-2.1	-64
	1214	11.0	335
	1815	-0.8	-24
28 Su	0027	12.3	375
	0653	-2.0	-61
	1309	10.9	332
	1909	-0.6	-18
29 M	0122	12.0	366
	0747	-1.6	-49
	1405	10.6	323
	2004	-0.2	-6
30 Tu	0218	11.5	351
	0842	-1.1	-34
	1503	10.3	314
	2101	0.2	6
31 W	0317	10.9	332
	0938	-0.6	-18
	1602	10.1	308
	2201	0.6	18

June

Day	Time	ft	cm
1 Th	0418	10.4	317
	1036	0.0	0
	1701	9.9	302
	2303	0.9	27
2 F	0520	9.9	302
	1135	0.4	12
	1801	9.8	299
3 Sa	0006	1.0	30
	0622	9.5	290
	1233	0.7	21
	1857	9.8	299
4 Su	0107	1.0	30
	0722	9.3	283
	1327	0.9	27
	1950	9.9	302
5 M	0203	0.8	24
	0818	9.2	280
	1417	1.1	34
	2037	10.0	305
6 Tu	0254	0.6	18
	0908	9.2	280
	1503	1.1	34
	2121	10.1	308
7 W	0339	0.5	15
	0953	9.2	280
	1546	1.2	37
	2201	10.2	311
8 Th	0420	0.3	9
	1035	9.2	280
	1626	1.2	37
	2240	10.2	311
9 F	0500	0.2	6
	1115	9.2	280
	1706	1.2	37
	2319	10.2	311
10 Sa	0539	0.2	6
	1155	9.2	280
	1746	1.2	37
	2357	10.2	311
11 Su	0618	0.2	6
	1234	9.2	280
	1826	1.3	40
12 M	0036	10.2	311
	0658	0.2	6
	1313	9.1	277
	1908	1.3	40
13 Tu	0116	10.1	308
	0738	0.3	9
	1354	9.1	277
	1950	1.4	43
14 W	0158	9.9	302
	0821	0.4	12
	1436	9.1	277
	2035	1.4	43
15 Th	0243	9.8	299
	0905	0.4	12
	1521	9.2	280
	2124	1.4	43
16 F	0331	9.7	296
	0952	0.5	15
	1608	9.4	287
	2216	1.2	37
17 Sa	0422	9.6	293
	1042	0.5	15
	1658	9.7	296
	2311	1.0	30
18 Su	0517	9.6	293
	1135	0.4	12
	1750	10.1	308
19 M	0008	0.6	18
	0615	9.7	296
	1230	0.3	9
	1844	10.5	320
20 Tu	0106	0.1	3
	0713	9.9	302
	1325	0.1	3
	1938	11.1	338
21 W	0203	-0.5	-15
	0812	10.1	308
	1420	-0.2	-6
	2033	11.6	354
22 Th	0300	-1.1	-34
	0910	10.4	317
	1515	-0.4	-12
	2127	12.0	366
23 F	0355	-1.5	-46
	1007	10.6	323
	1609	-0.6	-18
	2222	12.3	375
24 Sa	0449	-1.9	-58
	1103	10.8	329
	1703	-0.8	-24
	2316	12.3	375
25 Su	0542	-2.0	-61
	1158	10.8	329
	1757	-0.7	-21
26 M	0010	12.2	372
	0635	-1.8	-55
	1252	10.8	329
	1851	-0.6	-18
27 Tu	0105	11.9	363
	0727	-1.5	-46
	1346	10.6	323
	1945	-0.3	-9
28 W	0200	11.4	347
	0820	-1.1	-34
	1441	10.4	317
	2040	0.1	3
29 Th	0255	10.8	329
	0913	-0.5	-15
	1535	10.2	311
	2137	0.5	15
30 F	0352	10.2	311
	1007	0.1	3
	1630	10.0	305
	2235	0.8	24

Time meridian 75° W. 0000 is midnight. 1200 is noon. Times are not adjusted for Daylight Saving Time.
Heights are referred to mean lower low water which is the chart datum of soundings.

Boston, Massachusetts, 2017

Times and Heights of High and Low Waters

July

Day	Time	Height (ft)	Height (cm)
1 Sa	0450	9.6	293
	1101	0.6	18
	1725	9.8	299
	2335	1.0	30
2 Su	0549	9.2	280
	1155	1.0	30
	1819	9.7	296
3 M	0034	1.1	34
	0647	8.9	271
	1249	1.3	40
	1911	9.7	296
4 Tu	0130	1.1	34
	0743	8.8	268
	1340	1.4	43
	2000	9.7	296
5 W	0222	0.9	27
	0835	8.7	265
	1428	1.5	46
	2047	9.8	299
6 Th	0309	0.8	24
	0923	8.8	268
	1514	1.4	43
	2131	10.0	305
7 F	0353	0.6	18
	1007	8.9	271
	1557	1.4	43
	2213	10.1	308
8 Sa ○	0434	0.4	12
	1049	9.0	274
	1639	1.3	40
	2253	10.2	311
9 Su	0514	0.2	6
	1129	9.1	277
	1720	1.1	34
	2333	10.3	314
10 M	0553	0.1	3
	1208	9.2	280
	1801	1.1	34
11 Tu	0012	10.3	314
	0632	0.1	3
	1247	9.3	283
	1843	1.0	30
12 W	0052	10.3	314
	0712	0.0	0
	1327	9.4	287
	1925	0.9	27
13 Th	0134	10.2	311
	0753	0.0	0
	1408	9.5	290
	2010	0.9	27
14 F	0218	10.1	308
	0837	0.1	3
	1451	9.7	296
	2058	0.8	24
15 Sa	0305	10.0	305
	0923	0.1	3
	1537	9.9	302
	2149	0.7	21
16 Su ◐	0356	9.8	299
	1012	0.2	6
	1627	10.1	308
	2244	0.5	15
17 M	0451	9.7	296
	1105	0.3	9
	1720	10.4	317
	2342	0.3	9
18 Tu	0550	9.6	293
	1202	0.3	9
	1816	10.7	326
19 W	0042	-0.1	-3
	0650	9.7	296
	1259	0.2	6
	1913	11.1	338
20 Th	0142	-0.5	-15
	0752	9.8	299
	1358	0.0	0
	2012	11.5	351
21 F	0241	-0.9	-27
	0852	10.0	305
	1455	-0.2	-6
	2109	11.8	360
22 Sa	0337	-1.3	-40
	0950	10.3	314
	1551	-0.5	-15
	2206	12.0	366
23 Su ●	0432	-1.6	-49
	1046	10.5	320
	1646	-0.6	-18
	2301	12.0	366
24 M	0524	-1.7	-52
	1140	10.7	326
	1739	-0.7	-21
	2354	11.9	363
25 Tu	0615	-1.6	-49
	1232	10.7	326
	1832	-0.6	-18
26 W	0047	11.6	354
	0705	-1.3	-40
	1323	10.6	323
	1923	-0.3	-9
27 Th	0138	11.1	338
	0754	-0.8	-24
	1413	10.5	320
	2015	0.0	0
28 F	0230	10.6	323
	0843	-0.3	-9
	1502	10.2	311
	2108	0.4	12
29 Sa	0322	10.0	305
	0932	0.3	9
	1553	9.9	302
	2202	0.8	24
30 Su ◐	0416	9.4	287
	1023	0.9	27
	1644	9.7	296
	2258	1.1	34
31 M	0511	8.9	271
	1115	1.3	40
	1736	9.5	290
	2354	1.3	40

August

Day	Time	Height (ft)	Height (cm)
1 Tu	0608	8.6	262
	1208	1.6	49
	1829	9.4	287
2 W	0051	1.3	40
	0704	8.4	256
	1301	1.7	52
	1921	9.4	287
3 Th	0145	1.2	37
	0759	8.4	256
	1352	1.7	52
	2011	9.6	293
4 F	0235	1.0	30
	0849	8.6	262
	1441	1.6	49
	2059	9.8	299
5 Sa	0321	0.7	21
	0936	8.8	268
	1527	1.4	43
	2143	10.0	305
6 Su	0404	0.5	15
	1019	9.0	274
	1611	1.1	34
	2226	10.2	311
7 M ○	0445	0.2	6
	1100	9.2	280
	1653	0.9	27
	2307	10.4	317
8 Tu	0524	0.0	0
	1139	9.5	290
	1735	0.6	18
	2347	10.5	320
9 W	0604	-0.2	-6
	1217	9.7	296
	1817	0.4	12
10 Th	0028	10.5	320
	0644	-0.3	-9
	1257	9.9	302
	1901	0.3	9
11 F	0110	10.5	320
	0726	-0.3	-9
	1338	10.1	308
	1946	0.2	6
12 Sa	0154	10.4	317
	0809	-0.2	-6
	1421	10.3	314
	2034	0.1	3
13 Su	0242	10.2	311
	0856	-0.1	-3
	1508	10.4	317
	2126	0.1	3
14 M ◐	0334	9.9	302
	0947	0.1	3
	1600	10.5	320
	2222	0.1	3
15 Tu	0431	9.7	296
	1041	0.3	9
	1655	10.6	323
	2321	0.0	0
16 W	0531	9.5	290
	1140	0.4	12
	1754	10.7	326
17 Th	0023	-0.1	-3
	0634	9.5	290
	1240	0.4	12
	1856	10.9	332
18 F	0125	-0.4	-12
	0737	9.6	293
	1341	0.2	6
	1957	11.1	338
19 Sa	0225	-0.7	-21
	0839	9.9	302
	1440	0.0	0
	2056	11.4	347
20 Su	0321	-1.0	-30
	0936	10.2	311
	1537	-0.3	-9
	2153	11.6	354
21 M ●	0415	-1.2	-37
	1030	10.5	320
	1630	-0.6	-18
	2247	11.6	354
22 Tu	0505	-1.2	-37
	1121	10.7	326
	1722	-0.6	-18
	2337	11.5	351
23 W	0553	-1.1	-34
	1209	10.7	326
	1811	-0.6	-18
24 Th	0026	11.2	341
	0639	-0.8	-24
	1255	10.6	323
	1900	-0.4	-12
25 F	0114	10.8	329
	0724	-0.4	-12
	1340	10.4	317
	1948	-0.1	-3
26 Sa	0201	10.2	311
	0810	0.1	3
	1425	10.2	311
	2036	0.3	9
27 Su	0250	9.7	296
	0856	0.7	21
	1512	9.8	299
	2126	0.8	24
28 M	0340	9.1	277
	0944	1.2	37
	1600	9.5	290
	2218	1.1	34
29 Tu ◐	0432	8.7	265
	1034	1.6	49
	1651	9.3	283
	2313	1.4	43
30 W	0528	8.4	256
	1127	1.9	58
	1745	9.2	280
31 Th	0009	1.5	46
	0625	8.3	253
	1222	2.0	61
	1840	9.2	280

September

Day	Time	Height (ft)	Height (cm)
1 F	0104	1.4	43
	0720	8.3	253
	1316	1.9	58
	1934	9.3	283
2 Sa	0157	1.2	37
	0813	8.5	259
	1407	1.6	49
	2024	9.6	293
3 Su	0245	0.9	27
	0900	8.9	271
	1456	1.3	40
	2111	9.9	302
4 M	0329	0.5	15
	0944	9.2	280
	1541	0.9	27
	2156	10.2	311
5 Tu	0411	0.2	6
	1026	9.6	293
	1625	0.5	15
	2238	10.5	320
6 W	0453	-0.2	-6
	1105	10.0	305
	1708	0.1	3
	2320	10.7	326
7 Th	0533	-0.4	-12
	1145	10.3	314
	1752	-0.2	-6
8 F	0002	10.8	329
	0615	-0.5	-15
	1226	10.6	323
	1836	-0.5	-15
9 Sa	0046	10.7	326
	0658	-0.5	-15
	1308	10.8	329
	1923	-0.6	-18
10 Su	0133	10.6	323
	0744	-0.4	-12
	1354	10.9	332
	2012	-0.6	-18
11 M	0223	10.3	314
	0832	-0.1	-3
	1443	10.9	332
	2105	-0.4	-12
12 Tu	0317	10.0	305
	0925	0.2	6
	1537	10.8	329
	2203	-0.2	-6
13 W ◐	0415	9.7	296
	1022	0.4	12
	1636	10.7	326
	2303	-0.1	-3
14 Th	0518	9.4	287
	1123	0.6	18
	1738	10.6	323
15 F	0006	-0.1	-3
	0623	9.4	287
	1226	0.6	18
	1843	10.6	323
16 Sa	0110	-0.2	-6
	0727	9.6	293
	1328	0.4	12
	1946	10.8	329
17 Su	0210	-0.4	-12
	0827	9.9	302
	1428	0.1	3
	2046	10.9	332
18 M	0305	-0.6	-18
	0923	10.3	314
	1524	-0.2	-6
	2142	11.0	335
19 Tu	0357	-0.7	-21
	1013	10.5	320
	1616	-0.4	-12
	2232	11.0	335
20 W ●	0444	-0.7	-21
	1059	10.7	326
	1704	-0.6	-18
	2320	10.9	332
21 Th	0528	-0.5	-15
	1143	10.7	326
	1750	-0.5	-15
22 F	0005	10.7	326
	0611	-0.3	-9
	1225	10.6	323
	1835	-0.3	-9
23 Sa	0049	10.3	314
	0653	0.1	3
	1306	10.4	317
	1919	0.0	0
24 Su	0132	9.9	302
	0736	0.6	18
	1348	10.1	308
	2004	0.3	9
25 M	0217	9.4	287
	0820	1.0	30
	1431	9.8	299
	2050	0.7	21
26 Tu	0304	9.0	274
	0906	1.5	46
	1518	9.5	290
	2139	1.1	34
27 W ◑	0355	8.6	262
	0955	1.8	55
	1608	9.2	280
	2231	1.4	43
28 Th	0449	8.4	256
	1048	2.1	64
	1703	9.0	274
	2326	1.5	46
29 F	0545	8.3	253
	1143	2.1	64
	1759	9.0	274
30 Sa	0022	1.5	46
	0640	8.4	256
	1238	2.0	61
	1854	9.2	280

Time meridian 75° W. 0000 is midnight. 1200 is noon. Times are not adjusted for Daylight Saving Time.
Heights are referred to mean lower low water which is the chart datum of soundings.

Boston, Massachusetts, 2017
Times and Heights of High and Low Waters

October

Day	Time (h m)	Height (ft)	Height (cm)
1 Su	0115	1.2	37
	0733	8.7	265
	1332	1.6	49
	1947	9.5	290
2 M	0205	0.9	27
	0821	9.1	277
	1422	1.1	34
	2036	9.8	299
3 Tu	0251	0.5	15
	0906	9.6	293
	1510	0.6	18
	2123	10.2	311
4 W	0336	0.1	3
	0949	10.1	308
	1556	0.0	0
	2208	10.5	320
5 Th (O)	0419	-0.3	-9
	1030	10.6	323
	1641	-0.5	-15
	2252	10.8	329
6 F	0502	-0.6	-18
	1112	11.0	335
	1727	-0.9	-27
	2338	10.9	332
7 Sa	0546	-0.7	-21
	1156	11.4	347
	1813	-1.2	-37
8 Su	0024	10.9	332
	0632	-0.7	-21
	1241	11.5	351
	1902	-1.3	-40
9 M	0113	10.7	326
	0720	-0.5	-15
	1329	11.5	351
	1953	-1.1	-34
10 Tu	0206	10.4	317
	0811	-0.2	-6
	1422	11.3	344
	2047	-0.9	-27
11 W	0302	10.0	305
	0906	0.2	6
	1518	11.0	335
	2145	-0.5	-15
12 Th (◐)	0402	9.7	296
	1005	0.5	15
	1620	10.7	326
	2247	-0.2	-6
13 F	0506	9.5	290
	1108	0.7	21
	1725	10.4	317
	2350	0.0	0
14 Sa	0612	9.5	290
	1213	0.7	21
	1832	10.3	314
15 Su	0053	0.0	0
	0715	9.7	296
	1317	0.6	18
	1936	10.3	314
16 M	0153	0.0	0
	0814	10.0	305
	1417	0.3	9
	2035	10.4	317
17 Tu	0247	-0.1	-3
	0906	10.3	314
	1511	-0.1	-3
	2128	10.4	317
18 W	0336	-0.2	-6
	0953	10.6	323
	1601	-0.3	-9
	2217	10.4	317
19 Th (●)	0421	-0.1	-3
	1036	10.7	326
	1646	-0.4	-12
	2301	10.3	314
20 F	0503	0.0	0
	1116	10.7	326
	1729	-0.4	-12
	2343	10.1	308
21 Sa	0543	0.3	9
	1155	10.6	323
	1810	-0.2	-6
22 Su	0024	9.8	299
	0623	0.6	18
	1234	10.4	317
	1852	0.0	0
23 M	0105	9.5	290
	0704	0.9	27
	1313	10.1	308
	1934	0.3	9
24 Tu	0148	9.2	280
	0746	1.3	40
	1355	9.8	299
	2017	0.6	18
25 W	0232	8.9	271
	0831	1.6	49
	1440	9.5	290
	2104	0.9	27
26 Th	0320	8.6	262
	0918	1.9	58
	1529	9.2	280
	2153	1.2	37
27 F (◑)	0411	8.4	256
	1010	2.1	64
	1621	9.0	274
	2245	1.3	40
28 Sa	0504	8.4	256
	1104	2.1	64
	1716	9.0	274
	2339	1.3	40
29 Su	0558	8.6	262
	1200	1.9	58
	1812	9.1	277
30 M	0032	1.1	34
	0650	8.9	271
	1255	1.5	46
	1906	9.3	283
31 Tu	0123	0.8	24
	0740	9.4	287
	1348	0.9	27
	1959	9.7	296

November

Day	Time (h m)	Height (ft)	Height (cm)
1 W	0212	0.4	12
	0827	10.0	305
	1438	0.3	9
	2049	10.1	308
2 Th	0259	0.0	0
	0912	10.6	323
	1527	-0.4	-12
	2137	10.4	317
3 F	0346	-0.4	-12
	0957	11.2	341
	1615	-1.0	-30
	2226	10.7	326
4 Sa (O)	0433	-0.7	-21
	1042	11.7	357
	1703	-1.5	-46
	2314	10.9	332
5 Su	0520	-0.8	-24
	1129	12.0	366
	1752	-1.8	-55
6 M	0004	10.9	332
	0608	-0.8	-24
	1218	12.0	366
	1843	-1.8	-55
7 Tu	0056	10.8	329
	0659	-0.6	-18
	1309	11.9	363
	1935	-1.6	-49
8 W	0150	10.5	320
	0752	-0.3	-9
	1404	11.6	354
	2030	-1.2	-37
9 Th	0247	10.2	311
	0848	0.1	3
	1502	11.1	338
	2128	-0.8	-24
10 F (O)	0348	9.9	302
	0948	0.4	12
	1604	10.6	323
	2228	-0.4	-12
11 Sa	0451	9.7	296
	1052	0.7	21
	1710	10.2	311
	2331	0.0	0
12 Su	0555	9.7	296
	1157	0.7	21
	1816	10.0	305
13 M	0032	0.2	6
	0657	9.8	299
	1302	0.6	18
	1920	9.8	299
14 Tu	0131	0.3	9
	0754	10.1	308
	1402	0.4	12
	2019	9.8	299
15 W	0224	0.3	9
	0845	10.3	314
	1456	0.1	3
	2111	9.8	299
16 Th	0312	0.3	9
	0931	10.4	317
	1544	-0.1	-3
	2159	9.7	296
17 F	0356	0.4	12
	1012	10.5	320
	1627	-0.2	-6
	2242	9.7	296
18 Sa (●)	0437	0.5	15
	1051	10.5	320
	1708	-0.2	-6
	2322	9.6	293
19 Su	0516	0.7	21
	1128	10.4	317
	1747	-0.2	-6
20 M	0001	9.4	287
	0556	0.9	27
	1206	10.3	314
	1827	0.0	0
21 Tu	0041	9.2	280
	0636	1.0	30
	1245	10.1	308
	1907	0.2	6
22 W	0121	9.0	274
	0717	1.3	40
	1325	9.9	302
	1948	0.4	12
23 Th	0203	8.9	271
	0800	1.5	46
	1408	9.6	293
	2032	0.6	18
24 F	0248	8.7	265
	0845	1.7	52
	1454	9.4	287
	2118	0.8	24
25 Sa	0335	8.6	262
	0934	1.8	55
	1543	9.2	280
	2206	1.0	30
26 Su (◑)	0424	8.6	262
	1027	1.8	55
	1636	9.1	277
	2257	1.0	30
27 M	0515	8.8	268
	1122	1.6	49
	1731	9.1	277
	2349	0.9	27
28 Tu	0607	9.2	280
	1218	1.2	37
	1826	9.2	280
29 W	0042	0.6	18
	0658	9.7	296
	1313	0.7	21
	1922	9.5	290
30 Th	0134	0.3	9
	0748	10.3	314
	1407	0.0	0
	2016	9.8	299

December

Day	Time (h m)	Height (ft)	Height (cm)
1 F	0225	-0.1	-3
	0838	10.9	332
	1459	-0.7	-21
	2109	10.2	311
2 Sa	0316	-0.4	-12
	0927	11.5	351
	1551	-1.4	-43
	2201	10.5	320
3 Su (O)	0406	-0.8	-24
	1017	12.0	366
	1642	-1.9	-58
	2253	10.7	326
4 M	0456	-1.0	-30
	1107	12.3	375
	1733	-2.1	-64
	2346	10.8	329
5 Tu	0547	-1.0	-30
	1159	12.3	375
	1825	-2.2	-67
6 W	0039	10.8	329
	0640	-0.9	-27
	1252	12.1	369
	1918	-2.0	-61
7 Th	0134	10.6	323
	0734	-0.6	-18
	1347	11.7	357
	2012	-1.6	-49
8 F	0230	10.4	317
	0830	-0.2	-6
	1445	11.2	341
	2108	-1.0	-30
9 Sa	0329	10.1	308
	0930	0.2	6
	1545	10.5	320
	2205	-0.5	-15
10 Su (O)	0429	9.9	302
	1032	0.5	15
	1648	10.0	305
	2305	0.0	0
11 M	0530	9.8	299
	1136	0.7	21
	1753	9.5	290
12 Tu	0004	0.4	12
	0630	9.8	299
	1240	0.7	21
	1856	9.3	283
13 W	0102	0.6	18
	0727	9.8	299
	1341	0.6	18
	1956	9.1	277
14 Th	0156	0.8	24
	0818	9.9	302
	1435	0.4	12
	2050	9.1	277
15 F	0245	0.8	24
	0905	10.1	308
	1524	0.2	6
	2138	9.1	277
16 Sa	0330	0.9	27
	0947	10.1	308
	1607	0.1	3
	2221	9.1	277
17 Su	0411	0.9	27
	1027	10.2	311
	1647	0.0	0
	2301	9.1	277
18 M (●)	0452	0.9	27
	1105	10.2	311
	1725	-0.1	-3
	2340	9.1	277
19 Tu	0531	0.9	27
	1143	10.2	311
	1804	-0.1	-3
20 W	0018	9.1	277
	0611	1.0	30
	1221	10.1	308
	1842	0.0	0
21 Th	0057	9.0	274
	0651	1.0	30
	1300	10.0	305
	1922	0.1	3
22 F	0136	9.0	274
	0732	1.1	34
	1341	9.8	299
	2002	0.2	6
23 Sa	0217	8.9	271
	0816	1.2	37
	1424	9.6	293
	2045	0.4	12
24 Su	0300	8.9	271
	0902	1.3	40
	1510	9.4	287
	2130	0.5	15
25 M (O)	0346	9.0	274
	0952	1.3	40
	1559	9.2	280
	2218	0.6	18
26 Tu (◑)	0435	9.2	280
	1046	1.1	34
	1653	9.1	277
	2310	0.6	18
27 W	0526	9.5	290
	1142	0.8	24
	1749	9.1	277
28 Th	0004	0.5	15
	0619	9.9	302
	1240	0.4	12
	1848	9.3	283
29 F	0059	0.3	9
	0713	10.4	317
	1338	-0.2	-6
	1946	9.5	290
30 Sa	0154	0.0	0
	0808	11.0	335
	1435	-0.9	-27
	2044	9.9	302
31 Su	0249	-0.4	-12
	0902	11.5	351
	1529	-1.5	-46
	2140	10.2	311

Time meridian 75° W. 0000 is midnight. 1200 is noon. Times are not adjusted for Daylight Saving Time.
Heights are referred to mean lower low water which is the chart datum of soundings.

Nantucket, Massachusetts, 2017

Times and Heights of High and Low Waters

January

Day	Time	ft	cm	Day	Time	ft	cm
1 Su	0208	2.7	82	**16** M	0300	3.2	98
	0729	0.5	15		0829	0.1	3
	1407	3.5	107		1509	3.5	107
	2014	-0.1	-3		2106	-0.2	-6
2 M	0251	2.8	85	**17** Tu	0349	3.2	98
	0815	0.4	12		0924	0.2	6
	1452	3.4	104		1600	3.3	101
	2056	-0.1	-3		2155	0.0	0
3 Tu	0335	2.9	88	**18** W	0437	3.1	94
	0905	0.4	12		1021	0.3	9
	1541	3.4	104		1652	3.0	91
	2142	-0.1	-3		2244	0.2	6
4 W	0422	3.1	94	**19** Th ◐	0525	3.1	94
	1000	0.3	9		1119	0.4	12
	1633	3.2	98		1745	2.8	85
	2230	-0.1	-3		2334	0.3	9
5 Th ◑	0512	3.2	98	**20** F	0614	3.1	94
	1058	0.2	6		1218	0.4	12
	1728	3.1	94		1840	2.6	79
	2321	0.0	0				
6 F	0604	3.4	104	**21** Sa	0025	0.5	15
	1159	0.1	3		0703	3.1	94
	1827	3.0	91		1316	0.4	12
					1935	2.5	76
7 Sa	0015	0.0	0	**22** Su	0115	0.6	18
	0658	3.6	110		0751	3.2	98
	1302	0.0	0		1411	0.4	12
	1929	2.9	88		2029	2.4	73
8 Su	0111	0.0	0	**23** M	0203	0.6	18
	0754	3.8	116		0838	3.2	98
	1403	-0.2	-6		1501	0.3	9
	2031	2.9	88		2120	2.4	73
9 M	0207	0.0	0	**24** Tu	0249	0.6	18
	0851	3.9	119		0925	3.3	101
	1503	-0.4	-12		1546	0.2	6
	2133	2.9	88		2207	2.5	76
10 Tu	0303	-0.1	-3	**25** W	0334	0.6	18
	0948	4.1	125		1009	3.3	101
	1600	-0.5	-15		1628	0.2	6
	2234	2.9	88		2251	2.5	76
11 W	0359	-0.1	-3	**26** Th	0416	0.5	15
	1044	4.1	125		1053	3.4	104
	1654	-0.6	-18		1707	0.1	3
	2331	3.0	91		2333	2.6	79
12 Th ○	0453	-0.1	-3	**27** F ●	0457	0.4	12
	1140	4.1	125		1135	3.5	107
	1747	-0.6	-18		1746	0.0	0
13 F	0026	3.1	94	**28** Sa	0014	2.7	82
	0548	-0.1	-3		0539	0.3	9
	1233	4.1	125		1218	3.5	107
	1838	-0.6	-18		1824	-0.1	-3
14 Sa	0119	3.1	94	**29** Su	0055	2.8	85
	0641	-0.1	-3		0622	0.2	6
	1326	3.9	119		1301	3.5	107
	1928	-0.5	-15		1904	-0.1	-3
15 Su	0210	3.1	94	**30** M	0137	2.9	88
	0735	0.0	0		0707	0.2	6
	1418	3.7	113		1345	3.5	107
	2017	-0.3	-9		1945	-0.2	-6
				31 Tu	0221	3.0	91
					0755	0.1	3
					1432	3.4	104
					2028	-0.2	-6

February

Day	Time	ft	cm	Day	Time	ft	cm
1 W	0306	3.2	98	**16** Th	0353	3.1	94
	0846	0.0	0		0948	0.2	6
	1522	3.3	101		1617	2.9	88
	2114	-0.2	-6		2204	0.3	9
2 Th	0354	3.3	101	**17** F	0438	3.1	94
	0941	0.0	0		1041	0.3	9
	1615	3.2	98		1706	2.7	82
	2203	-0.1	-3		2252	0.4	12
3 F ◐	0445	3.4	104	**18** Sa ○	0525	3.1	94
	1040	-0.1	-3		1136	0.3	9
	1712	3.0	91		1757	2.5	76
	2256	-0.1	-3		2341	0.5	15
4 Sa	0539	3.6	110	**19** Su	0614	3.1	94
	1141	-0.1	-3		1232	0.4	12
	1812	2.9	88		1850	2.5	76
	2352	0.0	0				
5 Su	0637	3.7	113	**20** M	0032	0.6	18
	1244	-0.2	-6		0704	3.1	94
	1915	2.8	85		1327	0.4	12
					1944	2.4	73
6 M	0050	0.0	0	**21** Tu	0123	0.6	18
	0737	3.8	116		0755	3.1	94
	1347	-0.2	-6		1418	0.3	9
	2019	2.8	85		2036	2.4	73
7 Tu	0150	0.0	0	**22** W	0212	0.6	18
	0837	3.8	116		0846	3.2	98
	1447	-0.3	-9		1506	0.3	9
	2123	2.8	85		2126	2.5	76
8 W	0248	0.0	0	**23** Th	0259	0.5	15
	0937	3.9	119		0934	3.3	101
	1545	-0.4	-12		1549	0.2	6
	2222	2.9	88		2212	2.6	79
9 Th	0345	-0.1	-3	**24** F	0345	0.4	12
	1034	3.9	119		1021	3.3	101
	1638	-0.4	-12		1631	0.1	3
	2318	3.0	91		2256	2.7	82
10 F ○	0440	-0.1	-3	**25** Sa	0429	0.3	9
	1129	3.9	119		1107	3.4	104
	1729	-0.4	-12		1711	0.0	0
					2339	2.8	85
11 Sa	0010	3.0	91	**26** Su ●	0514	0.1	3
	0534	-0.1	-3		1152	3.5	107
	1221	3.8	116		1751	-0.1	-3
	1817	-0.4	-12				
12 Su	0058	3.1	94	**27** M	0022	3.0	91
	0625	-0.1	-3		0600	0.0	0
	1310	3.6	110		1238	3.5	107
	1903	-0.3	-9		1832	-0.2	-6
13 M	0143	3.1	94	**28** Tu	0105	3.2	98
	0716	-0.1	-3		0647	-0.2	-6
	1357	3.5	107		1325	3.5	107
	1948	-0.2	-6		1915	-0.2	-6
14 Tu	0227	3.2	98				
	0806	0.0	0				
	1444	3.3	101				
	2033	0.0	0				
15 W	0310	3.2	98				
	0856	0.1	3				
	1530	3.1	94				
	2118	0.1	3				

March

Day	Time	ft	cm	Day	Time	ft	cm
1 W	0151	3.3	101	**16** Th	0231	3.2	98
	0737	-0.3	-9		0829	0.0	0
	1415	3.4	104		1501	2.9	88
	2000	-0.2	-6		2041	0.3	9
2 Th	0238	3.5	107	**17** F	0311	3.2	98
	0829	-0.3	-9		0916	0.1	3
	1507	3.3	101		1545	2.8	85
	2048	-0.2	-6		2125	0.4	12
3 F	0328	3.6	110	**18** Sa	0354	3.2	98
	0925	-0.3	-9		1005	0.2	6
	1601	3.1	94		1631	2.6	79
	2139	-0.1	-3		2211	0.5	15
4 Sa	0422	3.7	113	**19** Su	0440	3.1	94
	1023	-0.3	-9		1055	0.3	9
	1700	3.0	91		1720	2.5	76
	2234	0.0	0		2259	0.6	18
5 Su ◑	0519	3.7	113	**20** M ◐	0529	3.1	94
	1125	-0.3	-9		1148	0.3	9
	1801	2.9	88		1811	2.5	76
	2333	0.0	0		2350	0.7	21
6 M	0620	3.7	113	**21** Tu	0621	3.1	94
	1228	-0.2	-6		1240	0.3	9
	1905	2.8	85		1903	2.5	76
7 Tu	0035	0.1	3	**22** W	0042	0.7	21
	0723	3.7	113		0713	3.1	94
	1331	-0.2	-6		1332	0.3	9
	2010	2.8	85		1954	2.5	76
8 W	0137	0.1	3	**23** Th	0133	0.6	18
	0826	3.7	113		0806	3.1	94
	1432	-0.2	-6		1420	0.3	9
	2112	2.9	88		2044	2.6	79
9 Th	0237	0.1	3	**24** F	0224	0.5	15
	0928	3.6	110		0857	3.2	98
	1528	-0.2	-6		1506	0.2	6
	2211	2.9	88		2132	2.7	82
10 F	0335	0.0	0	**25** Sa	0313	0.3	9
	1026	3.6	110		0948	3.3	101
	1620	-0.2	-6		1550	0.1	3
	2303	3.0	91		2218	2.9	88
11 Sa	0430	0.0	0	**26** Su	0401	0.1	3
	1119	3.5	107		1037	3.3	101
	1707	-0.2	-6		1633	0.0	0
	2350	3.1	94		2303	3.1	94
12 Su ○	0521	-0.1	-3	**27** M ●	0450	-0.1	-3
	1208	3.4	104		1126	3.4	104
	1752	-0.1	-3		1716	-0.1	-3
					2348	3.3	101
13 M	0033	3.2	98	**28** Tu	0538	-0.3	-9
	0609	-0.1	-3		1216	3.4	104
	1253	3.3	101		1800	-0.2	-6
	1835	0.0	0				
14 Tu	0113	3.2	98	**29** W	0034	3.5	107
	0656	-0.1	-3		0628	-0.5	-15
	1336	3.2	98		1306	3.4	104
	1917	0.1	3		1846	-0.2	-6
15 W	0152	3.2	98	**30** Th	0122	3.7	113
	0742	0.0	0		0720	-0.6	-18
	1419	3.0	91		1358	3.3	101
	1958	0.2	6		1934	-0.2	-6
				31 F	0213	3.8	116
					0814	-0.6	-18
					1453	3.2	98
					2025	-0.2	-6

Time meridian 75° W. 0000 is midnight. 1200 is noon. Times are not adjusted for Daylight Saving Time.
Heights are referred to mean lower low water which is the chart datum of soundings.

Nantucket, Massachusetts, 2017
Times and Heights of High and Low Waters

April

Day	Time	ft	cm	Day	Time	ft	cm
1 Sa	0306	3.9	119	16 Su	0316	3.2	98
	0910	-0.6	-18		0931	0.1	3
	1549	3.1	94		1601	2.6	79
	2119	-0.1	-3		2133	0.6	18
2 Su	0402	3.8	116	17 M	0402	3.2	98
	1008	-0.5	-15		1018	0.2	6
	1649	3.0	91		1647	2.6	79
	2217	0.0	0		2220	0.7	21
3 M	0502	3.8	116	18 Tu	0450	3.1	94
	1109	-0.3	-9		1106	0.2	6
	1750	2.9	88		1736	2.6	79
	2318	0.1	3		2310	0.7	21
4 Tu	0604	3.7	113	19 W	0541	3.1	94
	1211	-0.2	-6		1156	0.3	9
	1854	2.9	88		1825	2.6	79
5 W	0022	0.2	6	20 Th	0002	0.7	21
	0709	3.6	110		0633	3.1	94
	1313	-0.1	-3		1246	0.3	9
	1958	2.9	88		1915	2.7	82
6 Th	0126	0.2	6	21 F	0056	0.6	18
	0814	3.5	107		0726	3.1	94
	1413	-0.1	-3		1335	0.2	6
	2059	3.0	91		2004	2.8	85
7 F	0228	0.2	6	22 Sa	0150	0.4	12
	0916	3.4	104		0820	3.1	94
	1507	0.0	0		1422	0.2	6
	2154	3.1	94		2053	3.0	91
8 Sa	0326	0.1	3	23 Su	0243	0.2	6
	1014	3.3	101		0913	3.2	98
	1556	0.0	0		1509	0.1	3
	2243	3.2	98		2140	3.2	98
9 Su	0419	0.0	0	24 M	0335	0.0	0
	1106	3.2	98		1007	3.2	98
	1642	0.1	3		1555	0.0	0
	2326	3.2	98		2228	3.5	107
10 M	0507	0.0	0	25 Tu	0426	-0.3	-9
	1153	3.1	94		1100	3.3	101
	1724	0.2	6		1642	-0.1	-3
					2316	3.7	113
11 Tu	0005	3.3	101	26 W	0518	-0.5	-15
	0553	0.0	0		1153	3.3	101
	1236	3.0	91		1730	-0.2	-6
	1805	0.2	6				
12 W	0041	3.3	101	27 Th	0006	3.9	119
	0636	-0.1	-3		0610	-0.7	-21
	1315	2.9	88		1247	3.3	101
	1845	0.3	9		1819	-0.2	-6
13 Th	0117	3.3	101	28 F	0057	4.1	125
	0719	0.0	0		0704	-0.8	-24
	1355	2.8	85		1342	3.3	101
	1925	0.4	12		1911	-0.2	-6
14 F	0154	3.3	101	29 Sa	0151	4.1	125
	0802	0.0	0		0758	-0.7	-21
	1435	2.8	85		1438	3.2	98
	2006	0.5	15		2004	-0.1	-3
15 Sa	0234	3.3	101	30 Su	0247	4.1	125
	0846	0.0	0		0854	-0.7	-21
	1517	2.7	82		1536	3.1	94
	2048	0.6	18		2101	0.0	0

May

Day	Time	ft	cm	Day	Time	ft	cm
1 M	0345	4.0	122	16 Tu	0329	3.3	101
	0952	-0.5	-15		0944	0.1	3
	1636	3.1	94		1618	2.7	82
	2200	0.1	3		2144	0.7	21
2 Tu	0445	3.8	116	17 W	0416	3.2	98
	1051	-0.4	-12		1029	0.2	6
	1737	3.1	94		1704	2.7	82
	2303	0.2	6		2234	0.7	21
3 W	0548	3.6	110	18 Th	0505	3.2	98
	1152	-0.2	-6		1116	0.2	6
	1839	3.1	94		1751	2.8	85
					2327	0.6	18
4 Th	0009	0.3	9	19 F	0557	3.1	94
	0652	3.4	104		1203	0.2	6
	1251	-0.1	-3		1839	2.9	88
	1940	3.1	94				
5 F	0114	0.3	9	20 Sa	0022	0.5	15
	0757	3.3	101		0650	3.1	94
	1348	0.1	3		1252	0.2	6
	2038	3.2	98		1927	3.1	94
6 Sa	0216	0.3	9	21 Su	0119	0.3	9
	0859	3.1	94		0745	3.1	94
	1440	0.2	6		1342	0.1	3
	2130	3.3	101		2016	3.3	101
7 Su	0313	0.2	6	22 M	0215	0.1	3
	0957	3.0	91		0842	3.1	94
	1528	0.2	6		1431	0.1	3
	2216	3.3	101		2106	3.6	110
8 M	0405	0.1	3	23 Tu	0310	-0.1	-3
	1048	2.9	88		0939	3.1	94
	1612	0.3	9		1521	0.0	0
	2257	3.3	101		2157	3.8	116
9 Tu	0451	0.1	3	24 W	0405	-0.4	-12
	1134	2.9	88		1036	3.2	98
	1654	0.4	12		1612	-0.1	-3
	2334	3.4	104		2249	4.1	125
10 W	0534	0.0	0	25 Th	0459	-0.6	-18
	1215	2.8	85		1102	3.2	98
	1734	0.5	15		1703	-0.1	-3
					2342	4.2	128
11 Th	0009	3.4	104	26 F	0553	-0.7	-21
	0616	0.0	0		1229	3.2	98
	1253	2.7	82		1756	-0.2	-6
	1813	0.5	15				
12 F	0045	3.4	104	27 Sa	0036	4.3	131
	0656	0.0	0		0647	-0.8	-24
	1330	2.7	82		1326	3.2	98
	1853	0.6	18		1849	-0.1	-3
13 Sa	0122	3.4	104	28 Su	0132	4.3	131
	0737	0.0	0		0741	-0.7	-21
	1409	2.7	82		1423	3.2	98
	1933	0.6	18		1945	-0.1	-3
14 Su	0202	3.4	104	29 M	0229	4.2	128
	0818	0.1	3		0837	-0.6	-18
	1450	2.7	82		1520	3.2	98
	2014	0.7	21		2043	0.0	0
15 M	0245	3.3	101	30 Tu	0327	4.0	122
	0900	0.1	3		0933	-0.5	-15
	1533	2.7	82		1619	3.2	98
	2058	0.7	21		2143	0.2	6
				31 W	0427	3.8	116
					1030	-0.3	-9
					1717	3.3	101
					2246	0.3	9

June

Day	Time	ft	cm	Day	Time	ft	cm
1 Th	0528	3.6	110	16 F	0435	3.3	101
	1127	-0.1	-3		1039	0.2	6
	1816	3.3	101		1718	3.0	91
	2351	0.3	9		2257	0.5	15
2 F	0630	3.3	101	17 Sa	0526	3.2	98
	1223	0.1	3		1126	0.2	6
	1913	3.3	101		1805	3.2	98
					2354	0.4	12
3 Sa	0056	0.4	12	18 Su	0620	3.1	94
	0732	3.1	94		1215	0.1	3
	1318	0.2	6		1854	3.4	104
	2008	3.4	104				
4 Su	0158	0.3	9	19 M	0052	0.2	6
	0833	3.0	91		0717	3.1	94
	1409	0.3	9		1307	0.1	3
	2058	3.4	104		1945	3.6	110
5 M	0254	0.3	9	20 Tu	0151	0.0	0
	0931	2.8	85		0815	3.1	94
	1456	0.4	12		1359	0.1	3
	2143	3.4	104		2038	3.9	119
6 Tu	0345	0.3	9	21 W	0249	-0.2	-6
	1023	2.7	82		0915	3.0	91
	1540	0.5	15		1453	0.0	0
	2224	3.4	104		2132	4.1	125
7 W	0431	0.2	6	22 Th	0345	-0.4	-12
	1108	2.7	82		1014	3.1	94
	1623	0.6	18		1546	0.0	0
	2302	3.4	104		2227	4.3	131
8 Th	0513	0.2	6	23 F	0441	-0.5	-15
	1149	2.7	82		1113	3.1	94
	1703	0.6	18		1641	-0.1	-3
	2339	3.5	107		2323	4.4	134
9 F	0553	0.1	3	24 Sa	0535	-0.6	-18
	1227	2.6	79		1211	3.2	98
	1743	0.7	21		1735	-0.1	-3
10 Sa	0016	3.5	107	25 Su	0019	4.4	134
	0632	0.1	3		0629	-0.6	-18
	1304	2.7	82		1308	3.2	98
	1823	0.7	21		1831	-0.1	-3
11 Su	0055	3.5	107	26 M	0116	4.3	131
	0711	0.1	3		0723	-0.6	-18
	1343	2.7	82		1404	3.3	101
	1903	0.7	21		1927	0.0	0
12 M	0136	3.5	107	27 Tu	0212	4.2	128
	0750	0.1	3		0816	-0.5	-15
	1423	2.7	82		1500	3.3	101
	1944	0.7	21		2025	0.1	3
13 Tu	0218	3.4	104	28 W	0309	4.0	122
	0830	0.1	3		0910	-0.3	-9
	1505	2.8	85		1555	3.4	104
	2027	0.7	21		2124	0.2	6
14 W	0301	3.4	104	29 Th	0406	3.7	113
	0911	0.1	3		1003	-0.2	-6
	1548	2.8	85		1650	3.4	104
	2113	0.7	21		2225	0.3	9
15 Th	0347	3.3	101	30 F	0503	3.5	107
	0954	0.1	3		1057	0.0	0
	1632	2.9	88		1745	3.4	104
	2203	0.6	18		2328	0.4	12

Time meridian 75° W. 0000 is midnight. 1200 is noon. Times are not adjusted for Daylight Saving Time.
Heights are referred to mean lower low water which is the chart datum of soundings.

Nantucket, Massachusetts, 2017
Times and Heights of High and Low Waters

July

Day	Time	ft	cm		Day	Time	ft	cm
1 Sa	0602	3.2	98		16 Su	0502	3.2	98
	1150	0.2	6			1054	0.2	6
	1838	3.4	104			1735	3.5	107
					◐	2330	0.3	9
2 Su	0030	0.4	12		17 M	0557	3.1	94
	0701	3.0	91			1145	0.2	6
	1243	0.4	12			1826	3.7	113
	1930	3.4	104					
3 M	0131	0.4	12		18 Tu	0030	0.2	6
	0800	2.8	85			0655	3.1	94
	1333	0.5	15			1239	0.2	6
	2019	3.4	104			1920	3.9	119
4 Tu	0227	0.4	12		19 W	0130	0.0	0
	0856	2.7	82			0755	3.0	91
	1422	0.6	18			1334	0.1	3
	2105	3.4	104			2016	4.0	122
5 W	0318	0.4	12		20 Th	0230	-0.1	-3
	0948	2.7	82			0857	3.0	91
	1508	0.7	21			1431	0.1	3
	2148	3.5	107			2114	4.2	128
6 Th	0404	0.3	9		21 F	0327	-0.3	-9
	1034	2.6	79			0957	3.1	94
	1551	0.7	21			1527	0.1	3
	2229	3.5	107			2211	4.3	131
7 F	0446	0.3	9		22 Sa	0423	-0.4	-12
	1116	2.6	79			1057	3.1	94
	1633	0.7	21			1623	0.0	0
	2309	3.5	107			2309	4.3	131
8 Sa ○	0526	0.3	9		23 Su ●	0517	-0.4	-12
	1155	2.7	82			1154	3.2	98
	1714	0.7	21			1719	-0.1	-3
	2349	3.5	107					
9 Su	0605	0.2	6		24 M	0005	4.3	131
	1234	2.7	82			0610	-0.4	-12
	1754	0.7	21			1249	3.3	101
						1814	0.0	0
10 M	0030	3.5	107		25 Tu	0100	4.2	128
	0642	0.2	6			0701	-0.4	-12
	1313	2.8	85			1343	3.4	104
	1834	0.7	21			1910	0.0	0
11 Tu	0111	3.5	107		26 W	0155	4.0	122
	0720	0.2	6			0752	-0.3	-9
	1353	2.8	85			1435	3.4	104
	1916	0.6	18			2005	0.1	3
12 W	0153	3.5	107		27 Th	0248	3.8	116
	0759	0.2	6			0842	-0.1	-3
	1435	2.9	88			1526	3.5	107
	2000	0.6	18			2102	0.2	6
13 Th	0236	3.5	107		28 F	0342	3.6	110
	0839	0.1	3			0932	0.1	3
	1517	3.0	91			1616	3.5	107
	2047	0.5	15			2159	0.3	9
14 F	0322	3.4	104		29 Sa	0435	3.3	101
	0921	0.1	3			1023	0.3	9
	1601	3.2	98			1706	3.4	104
	2137	0.5	15			2258	0.4	12
15 Sa	0410	3.3	101		30 Su ◑	0530	3.1	94
	1006	0.2	6			1114	0.4	12
	1647	3.3	101			1756	3.4	104
	2232	0.4	12			2357	0.5	15
					31 M	0625	2.9	88
						1205	0.6	18
						1846	3.4	104

August

Day	Time	ft	cm		Day	Time	ft	cm
1 Tu	0056	0.5	15		16 W	0011	0.1	3
	0720	2.8	85			0641	3.0	91
	1256	0.7	21			1217	0.2	6
	1935	3.4	104			1901	3.9	119
2 W	0152	0.5	15		17 Th	0112	0.0	0
	0815	2.7	82			0742	3.0	91
	1346	0.8	24			1316	0.2	6
	2023	3.4	104			2001	4.0	122
3 Th	0244	0.5	15		18 F	0213	-0.1	-3
	0906	2.6	79			0844	3.0	91
	1434	0.8	24			1415	0.2	6
	2110	3.4	104			2101	4.1	125
4 F	0331	0.5	15		19 Sa	0311	-0.1	-3
	0953	2.6	79			0945	3.1	94
	1520	0.8	24			1514	0.1	3
	2155	3.5	107			2200	4.1	125
5 Sa	0414	0.4	12		20 Su	0406	-0.2	-6
	1037	2.7	82			1042	3.2	98
	1603	0.7	21			1610	0.0	0
	2239	3.5	107			2257	4.1	125
6 Su	0454	0.4	12		21 M ●	0458	-0.2	-6
	1119	2.7	82			1137	3.3	101
	1645	0.7	21			1706	0.0	0
	2321	3.6	110			2353	4.1	125
7 M ○	0532	0.3	9		22 Tu	0548	-0.2	-6
	1159	2.8	85			1228	3.4	104
	1726	0.6	18			1759	0.0	0
8 Tu	0003	3.6	110		23 W	0045	3.9	119
	0610	0.3	9			0637	-0.1	-3
	1239	2.9	88			1317	3.5	107
	1808	0.5	15			1852	0.0	0
9 W	0045	3.6	110		24 Th	0136	3.8	116
	0647	0.2	6			0724	0.0	0
	1320	3.0	91			1405	3.5	107
	1851	0.5	15			1945	0.1	3
10 Th	0129	3.6	110		25 F	0226	3.6	110
	0726	0.2	6			0811	0.1	3
	1401	3.2	98			1451	3.5	107
	1936	0.4	12			2037	0.2	6
11 F	0213	3.5	107		26 Sa	0316	3.4	104
	0807	0.2	6			0858	0.3	9
	1444	3.3	101			1537	3.5	107
	2024	0.3	9			2130	0.3	9
12 Sa	0300	3.4	104		27 Su	0405	3.2	98
	0850	0.2	6			0946	0.5	15
	1529	3.4	104			1623	3.4	104
	2116	0.2	6			2224	0.4	12
13 Su	0351	3.3	101		28 M	0455	3.0	91
	0936	0.2	6			1035	0.6	18
	1617	3.6	110			1711	3.4	104
	2211	0.2	6			2320	0.5	15
14 M ◐	0444	3.2	98		29 Tu ◑	0547	2.8	85
	1026	0.2	6			1126	0.8	24
	1709	3.7	113			1800	3.4	104
	2310	0.1	3					
15 Tu	0541	3.1	94		30 W	0016	0.5	15
	1120	0.2	6			0639	2.7	82
	1804	3.8	116			1218	0.8	24
						1850	3.3	101
					31 Th	0111	0.6	18
						0732	2.7	82
						1310	0.9	27
						1941	3.3	101

September

Day	Time	ft	cm		Day	Time	ft	cm
1 F	0203	0.6	18		16 Sa	0157	0.0	0
	0823	2.7	82			0834	3.1	94
	1400	0.8	24			1405	0.3	9
	2031	3.4	104			2051	3.9	119
2 Sa	0251	0.5	15		17 Su	0254	0.0	0
	0911	2.7	82			0933	3.2	98
	1448	0.8	24			1504	0.2	6
	2120	3.4	104			2151	3.9	119
3 Su	0335	0.5	15		18 M	0347	0.0	0
	0957	2.8	85			1028	3.4	104
	1533	0.7	21			1601	0.1	3
	2206	3.5	107			2248	3.8	116
4 M	0416	0.4	12		19 Tu	0437	0.0	0
	1040	2.9	88			1119	3.5	107
	1616	0.6	18			1654	0.0	0
	2251	3.5	107			2341	3.7	113
5 Tu	0454	0.4	12		20 W ●	0524	0.1	3
	1121	3.0	91			1206	3.5	107
	1659	0.5	15			1745	0.0	0
	2335	3.5	107					
6 W	0533	0.3	9		21 Th	0030	3.6	110
	1202	3.2	98			0610	0.1	3
	1743	0.3	9			1250	3.6	110
						1835	0.0	0
7 Th	0019	3.6	110		22 F	0118	3.5	107
	0612	0.2	6			0654	0.3	9
	1244	3.3	101			1332	3.6	110
	1828	0.2	6			1923	0.1	3
8 F	0105	3.5	107		23 Sa	0203	3.3	101
	0652	0.2	6			0738	0.4	12
	1327	3.5	107			1413	3.5	107
	1915	0.1	3			2011	0.1	3
9 Sa	0152	3.5	107		24 Su	0248	3.1	94
	0735	0.2	6			0822	0.5	15
	1412	3.6	110			1455	3.5	107
	2004	0.0	0			2100	0.2	6
10 Su	0242	3.4	104		25 M	0334	3.0	91
	0821	0.2	6			0908	0.7	21
	1500	3.7	113			1540	3.4	104
	2057	0.0	0			2150	0.3	9
11 M	0334	3.3	101		26 Tu	0421	2.9	88
	0910	0.2	6			0956	0.8	24
	1552	3.8	116			1626	3.4	104
	2153	0.0	0			2241	0.4	12
12 Tu	0430	3.2	98		27 W ◑	0510	2.8	85
	1004	0.3	9			1046	0.9	27
	1647	3.9	119			1716	3.3	101
	2253	0.0	0			2334	0.5	15
13 W ◐	0529	3.1	94		28 Th	0600	2.7	82
	1101	0.3	9			1138	0.9	27
	1746	3.9	119			1807	3.3	101
	2354	0.0	0					
14 Th	0630	3.1	94		29 F	0027	0.5	15
	1201	0.3	9			0651	2.7	82
	1847	3.9	119			1231	0.9	27
						1859	3.3	101
15 F	0056	0.0	0		30 Sa	0119	0.6	18
	0733	3.1	94			0742	2.8	85
	1303	0.3	9			1323	0.9	27
	1949	3.9	119			1951	3.3	101

Time meridian 75° W. 0000 is midnight. 1200 is noon. Times are not adjusted for Daylight Saving Time. Heights are referred to mean lower low water which is the chart datum of soundings.

Nantucket, Massachusetts, 2017

Times and Heights of High and Low Waters

October

Day	Time	ft	cm	Day	Time	ft	cm
1 Su	0207	0.5	15	16 M	0234	0.1	3
	0830	2.9	88		0920	3.4	104
	1413	0.7	21		1456	0.2	6
	2042	3.3	101		2141	3.6	110
2 M	0251	0.5	15	17 Tu	0326	0.1	3
	0916	3.0	91		1011	3.5	107
	1501	0.6	18		1552	0.1	3
	2131	3.4	104		2237	3.5	107
3 Tu	0333	0.4	12	18 W	0414	0.2	6
	1000	3.1	94		1058	3.6	110
	1547	0.4	12		1643	0.1	3
	2219	3.4	104		2328	3.4	104
4 W	0414	0.3	9	19 Th ●	0459	0.3	9
	1043	3.3	101		1141	3.6	110
	1632	0.2	6		1731	0.0	0
	2306	3.4	104				
5 Th ○	0455	0.2	6	20 F	0015	3.2	98
	1126	3.5	107		0541	0.4	12
	1718	0.0	0		1221	3.6	110
	2353	3.5	107		1817	0.0	0
6 F	0537	0.2	6	21 Sa	0058	3.1	94
	1209	3.7	113		0623	0.5	15
	1806	-0.1	-3		1259	3.6	110
					1901	0.0	0
7 Sa	0042	3.4	104	22 Su	0140	3.0	91
	0620	0.1	3		0705	0.6	18
	1255	3.8	116		1337	3.5	107
	1855	-0.3	-9		1945	0.1	3
8 Su	0132	3.4	104	23 M	0222	2.9	88
	0706	0.1	3		0748	0.7	21
	1343	4.0	122		1418	3.5	107
	1946	-0.3	-9		2030	0.2	6
9 M	0225	3.3	101	24 Tu	0304	2.8	85
	0755	0.1	3		0832	0.8	24
	1435	4.0	122		1500	3.4	104
	2040	-0.3	-9		2116	0.3	9
10 Tu	0320	3.3	101	25 W	0349	2.8	85
	0848	0.2	6		0918	0.8	24
	1530	4.0	122		1546	3.3	101
	2137	-0.3	-9		2204	0.3	9
11 W	0418	3.2	98	26 Th	0435	2.8	85
	0944	0.3	9		1007	0.9	27
	1629	4.0	122		1635	3.3	101
	2236	-0.2	-6		2253	0.4	12
12 Th ◐	0518	3.1	94	27 F ◐	0524	2.7	82
	1045	0.3	9		1058	0.9	27
	1730	3.9	119		1726	3.2	98
	2338	-0.1	-3		2343	0.5	15
13 F	0620	3.1	94	28 Sa	0613	2.8	85
	1148	0.4	12		1151	0.9	27
	1834	3.8	116		1818	3.2	98
14 Sa	0039	0.0	0	29 Su	0032	0.5	15
	0722	3.2	98		0702	2.9	88
	1253	0.3	9		1245	0.8	24
	1938	3.7	113		1911	3.2	98
15 Su	0139	0.0	0	30 M	0120	0.5	15
	0823	3.3	101		0749	3.0	91
	1356	0.3	9		1337	0.7	21
	2041	3.6	110		2003	3.2	98
				31 Tu	0205	0.4	12
					0836	3.1	94
					1428	0.5	15
					2055	3.2	98

November

Day	Time	ft	cm	Day	Time	ft	cm
1 W	0250	0.3	9	16 Th	0348	0.3	9
	0921	3.3	101		1035	3.6	110
	1518	0.2	6		1630	0.1	3
	2146	3.2	98		2314	3.0	91
2 Th	0334	0.2	6	17 F	0432	0.4	12
	1006	3.6	110		1115	3.6	110
	1607	0.0	0		1716	0.1	3
	2237	3.3	101		2358	2.9	88
3 F	0418	0.1	3	18 Sa ●	0514	0.5	15
	1052	3.8	116		1152	3.6	110
	1656	-0.2	-6		1758	0.0	0
	2328	3.3	101				
4 Sa ○	0504	0.1	3	19 Su	0038	2.8	85
	1139	4.0	122		0554	0.6	18
	1745	-0.4	-12		1229	3.5	107
					1839	0.0	0
5 Su	0020	3.3	101	20 M	0116	2.8	85
	0551	0.0	0		0635	0.6	18
	1228	4.1	125		1306	3.5	107
	1836	-0.5	-15		1921	0.1	3
6 M	0113	3.3	101	21 Tu	0155	2.7	82
	0641	0.0	0		0716	0.7	21
	1320	4.2	128		1346	3.5	107
	1929	-0.6	-18		2002	0.1	3
7 Tu	0208	3.3	101	22 W	0235	2.7	82
	0733	0.0	0		0758	0.7	21
	1414	4.2	128		1428	3.4	104
	2024	-0.5	-15		2045	0.2	6
8 W	0305	3.2	98	23 Th	0318	2.7	82
	0828	0.1	3		0843	0.8	24
	1512	4.1	125		1512	3.3	101
	2120	-0.4	-12		2129	0.2	6
9 Th	0403	3.2	98	24 F	0402	2.7	82
	0927	0.2	6		0930	0.8	24
	1612	4.0	122		1559	3.3	101
	2219	-0.3	-9		2214	0.3	9
10 F ◐	0504	3.2	98	25 Sa	0448	2.8	85
	1030	0.3	9		1019	0.8	24
	1715	3.8	116		1649	3.2	98
	2319	-0.2	-6		2300	0.3	9
11 Sa	0606	3.2	98	26 Su ◐	0535	2.8	85
	1135	0.3	9		1112	0.8	24
	1819	3.6	110		1740	3.1	94
					2347	0.3	9
12 Su	0019	0.0	0	27 M	0623	2.9	88
	0707	3.3	101		1207	0.7	21
	1242	0.3	9		1832	3.1	94
	1924	3.5	107				
13 M	0117	0.1	3	28 Tu	0034	0.3	9
	0806	3.4	104		0710	3.1	94
	1346	0.3	9		1302	0.5	15
	2028	3.3	101		1926	3.0	91
14 Tu	0211	0.2	6	29 W	0121	0.3	9
	0901	3.5	107		0757	3.3	101
	1447	0.2	6		1356	0.3	9
	2128	3.2	98		2020	3.0	91
15 W	0302	0.2	6	30 Th	0209	0.2	6
	0951	3.5	107		0845	3.5	107
	1541	0.1	3		1449	0.1	3
	2224	3.1	94		2115	3.0	91

December

Day	Time	ft	cm	Day	Time	ft	cm
1 F	0257	0.1	3	16 Sa	0405	0.5	15
	0933	3.8	116		1049	3.5	107
	1542	-0.2	-6		1657	0.1	3
	2210	3.1	94		2337	2.7	82
2 Sa	0346	0.0	0	17 Su	0447	0.6	18
	1023	4.0	122		1126	3.5	107
	1634	-0.4	-12		1738	0.1	3
	2304	3.1	94				
3 Su ○	0436	0.0	0	18 M ●	0015	2.6	79
	1114	4.2	128		0528	0.6	18
	1726	-0.6	-18		1203	3.5	107
	2359	3.2	98		1817	0.1	3
4 M	0527	-0.1	-3	19 Tu	0051	2.6	79
	1206	4.3	131		0608	0.6	18
	1819	-0.7	-21		1241	3.5	107
					1856	0.1	3
5 Tu	0054	3.2	98	20 W	0128	2.6	79
	0619	-0.1	-3		0648	0.6	18
	1301	4.3	131		1320	3.4	104
	1912	-0.7	-21		1935	0.1	3
6 W	0150	3.2	98	21 Th	0207	2.7	82
	0714	-0.1	-3		0729	0.6	18
	1357	4.3	131		1401	3.4	104
	2006	-0.7	-21		2014	0.1	3
7 Th	0247	3.2	98	22 F	0247	2.7	82
	0811	0.0	0		0812	0.7	21
	1455	4.1	125		1444	3.3	101
	2101	-0.5	-15		2055	0.1	3
8 F	0346	3.3	101	23 Sa	0329	2.7	82
	0911	0.1	3		0857	0.7	21
	1555	3.9	119		1528	3.2	98
	2158	-0.4	-12		2136	0.2	6
9 Sa	0445	3.3	101	24 Su	0413	2.8	85
	1014	0.2	6		0945	0.6	18
	1656	3.7	113		1615	3.1	94
	2255	-0.2	-6		2219	0.2	6
10 Su ◐	0544	3.3	101	25 M	0458	2.9	88
	1119	0.3	9		1037	0.6	18
	1759	3.4	104		1705	3.0	91
	2353	0.0	0		2304	0.2	6
11 M	0644	3.4	104	26 Tu ◐	0544	3.1	94
	1226	0.3	9		1132	0.5	15
	1904	3.2	98		1758	3.0	91
					2352	0.2	6
12 Tu	0049	0.1	3	27 W	0632	3.2	98
	0741	3.4	104		1229	0.3	9
	1331	0.3	9		1853	2.9	88
	2008	3.0	91				
13 W	0143	0.2	6	28 Th	0042	0.2	6
	0835	3.5	107		0721	3.4	104
	1431	0.2	6		1326	0.1	3
	2109	2.9	88		1950	2.9	88
14 Th	0234	0.4	12	29 F	0133	0.1	3
	0924	3.5	107		0813	3.7	113
	1525	0.2	6		1423	-0.1	-3
	2205	2.8	85		2048	2.9	88
15 F	0321	0.4	12	30 Sa	0226	0.0	0
	1009	3.5	107		0905	3.9	119
	1614	0.1	3		1519	-0.3	-9
	2254	2.7	82		2146	2.9	88
				31 Su	0319	-0.1	-3
					0959	4.1	125
					1614	-0.5	-15
					2243	3.0	91

Time meridian 75° W. 0000 is midnight. 1200 is noon. Times are not adjusted for Daylight Saving Time.
Heights are referred to mean lower low water which is the chart datum of soundings.

Woods Hole, Massachusetts, 2017

Times and Heights of High and Low Waters

January

Day	Time	ft	cm		Day	Time	ft	cm
1 Su	0412	0.1	3		16 M	0553	0.1	3
	1009	2.1	64			1056	2.1	64
	1720	0.0	0			1849	-0.1	-3
	2230	1.5	46			2319	1.8	55
2 M	0508	0.2	6		17 Tu	0709	0.2	6
	1054	2.1	64			1144	1.8	55
	1810	0.0	0			1946	0.1	3
	2319	1.6	49					
3 Tu	0610	0.2	6		18 W	0011	1.7	52
	1141	2.0	61			0825	0.3	9
	1901	0.0	0			1233	1.5	46
						2042	0.2	6
4 W	0011	1.7	52		19 Th	0104	1.6	49
	0718	0.2	6			0933	0.4	12
	1232	1.9	58			1323	1.3	40
	1952	0.0	0		◯	2134	0.3	9
5 Th ☾	0106	1.8	55		20 F	0159	1.5	46
	0828	0.2	6			1036	0.4	12
	1327	1.8	55			1415	1.2	37
	2043	0.0	0			2217	0.4	12
6 F	0205	1.9	58		21 Sa	0257	1.5	46
	0935	0.0	0			1134	0.4	12
	1426	1.7	52			1510	1.1	34
	2133	-0.1	-3			2131	0.4	12
7 Sa	0307	2.1	64		22 Su	0356	1.6	49
	1040	-0.1	-3			1223	0.4	12
	1527	1.7	52			1605	1.1	34
	2223	-0.2	-6			2206	0.4	12
8 Su	0408	2.3	70		23 M	0450	1.7	52
	1144	-0.3	-9			1302	0.3	9
	1626	1.7	52			1656	1.2	37
	2316	-0.3	-9			2250	0.3	9
9 M	0506	2.5	76		24 Tu	0537	1.8	55
	1245	-0.4	-12			1327	0.3	9
	1722	1.8	55			1743	1.3	40
						2340	0.2	6
10 Tu	0012	-0.3	-9		25 W	0620	1.9	58
	0600	2.7	82			1342	0.1	3
	1343	-0.5	-15			1826	1.4	43
	1815	1.9	58					
11 W	0111	-0.4	-12		26 Th	0032	0.1	3
	0651	2.8	85			0700	2.1	64
	1436	-0.6	-18			1407	0.0	0
	1906	2.0	61			1908	1.5	46
12 Th ◯	0210	-0.4	-12		27 F ●	0125	0.0	0
	0740	2.8	85			0739	2.2	67
	1526	-0.6	-18			1443	-0.1	-3
	1956	2.0	61			1950	1.6	49
13 F	0304	-0.4	-12		28 Sa	0217	-0.1	-3
	0829	2.7	82			0819	2.2	67
	1615	-0.6	-18			1523	-0.2	-6
	2046	2.0	61			2033	1.7	52
14 Sa	0357	-0.3	-9		29 Su	0308	-0.2	-6
	0918	2.6	79			0901	2.2	67
	1705	-0.5	-15			1605	-0.2	-6
	2136	1.9	58			2118	1.8	55
15 Su	0451	-0.1	-3		30 M	0401	-0.2	-6
	1007	2.3	70			0944	2.2	67
	1756	-0.3	-9			1649	-0.2	-6
	2228	1.9	58			2205	1.8	55
					31 Tu	0456	-0.1	-3
						1030	2.1	64
						1736	-0.2	-6
						2254	1.9	58

February

Day	Time	ft	cm		Day	Time	ft	cm
1 W	0558	-0.1	-3		16 Th	0729	0.3	9
	1119	2.0	61			1159	1.4	43
	1826	-0.1	-3			1835	0.4	12
	2347	1.9	58					
2 Th	0706	0.0	0		17 F	0029	1.6	49
	1210	1.9	58			0846	0.4	12
	1921	-0.1	-3			1247	1.3	40
						1912	0.5	15
3 F ◑	0042	2.0	61		18 Sa ◯	0122	1.5	46
	0818	0.0	0			0952	0.4	12
	1305	1.7	52			1338	1.1	34
	2017	-0.1	-3			1620	0.6	18
						1746*	0.7	21
4 Sa	0141	2.0	61		19 Su	0219	1.4	43
	0927	-0.1	-3			1049	0.4	12
	1403	1.6	49			1432	1.0	30
	2114	-0.1	-3			1705	0.6	18
						1829*	0.7	21
5 Su	0244	2.1	64		20 M	0319	1.4	43
	1033	-0.2	-6			1136	0.4	12
	1504	1.6	49			1529	1.0	30
	2212	-0.1	-3			2138	0.4	12
6 M	0348	2.2	67		21 Tu	0417	1.5	46
	1136	-0.3	-9			1207	0.4	12
	1605	1.6	49			1624	1.1	34
	2313	-0.2	-6			2229	0.3	9
7 Tu	0448	2.3	70		22 W	0508	1.6	49
	1235	-0.4	-12			1223	0.3	9
	1702	1.7	52			1713	1.3	40
						2321	0.2	6
8 W	0016	-0.3	-9		23 Th	0551	1.8	55
	0543	2.5	76			1251	0.1	3
	1330	-0.5	-15			1758	1.5	46
	1756	1.8	55					
9 Th	0118	-0.3	-9		24 F	0016	0.0	0
	0633	2.5	76			0632	2.0	61
	1421	-0.5	-15			1328	0.0	0
	1846	1.9	58			1841	1.6	49
10 F ◯	0213	-0.4	-12		25 Sa	0111	-0.1	-3
	0721	2.5	76			0712	2.2	64
	1507	-0.5	-15			1409	-0.1	-3
	1935	2.0	61			1924	1.8	55
11 Sa	0302	-0.3	-9		26 Su ●	0205	-0.3	-9
	0807	2.5	76			0753	2.2	67
	1551	-0.4	-12			1450	-0.2	-6
	2023	2.1	64			2007	2.0	61
12 Su	0348	-0.3	-9		27 M	0257	-0.4	-12
	0853	2.3	70			0835	2.3	70
	1634	-0.3	-9			1533	-0.3	-9
	2111	2.0	61			2053	2.1	64
13 M	0431	-0.1	-3		28 Tu	0351	-0.4	-12
	0939	2.1	64			0921	2.2	67
	1714	-0.1	-3			1617	-0.3	-9
	2159	2.0	61			2141	2.2	67
14 Tu	0516	0.0	0					
	1026	1.9	58					
	1750	0.1	3					
	2248	1.9	58					
15 W	0609	0.2	6					
	1112	1.7	52					
	1815	0.3	9					
	2338	1.7	52					

March

Day	Time	ft	cm		Day	Time	ft	cm
1 W	0447	-0.4	-12		16 Th	0514	0.1	3
	1008	2.1	64			1041	1.6	49
	1704	-0.2	-6			1651	0.3	9
	2232	2.2	67			2305	1.9	58
2 Th	0549	-0.3	-9		17 F	0558	0.3	9
	1058	2.0	61			1127	1.4	43
	1756	-0.1	-3			1728	0.4	12
	2325	2.2	67			2354	1.7	52
3 F	0657	-0.3	-9		18 Sa	0659	0.4	12
	1151	1.8	55			1215	1.3	40
	1854	-0.1	-3			1817	0.5	15
4 Sa	0022	2.2	67		19 Su	0044	1.5	46
	0809	-0.2	-6			0822	0.4	12
	1246	1.7	52			1303	1.1	34
	1959	0.0	0			1550	0.6	18
						1727*	0.7	21
5 Su	0121	2.1	64		20 M ◯	0138	1.4	43
	0917	-0.2	-6			0925	0.5	15
	1343	1.6	49			1356	1.1	34
	2107	0.0	0			1633	0.6	18
						1810*	0.8	24
6 M	0224	2.1	64		21 Tu	0235	1.4	43
	1022	-0.3	-9			1002	0.4	12
	1444	1.5	46			1452	1.1	34
	2215	0.0	0			1724	0.7	21
						1847*	0.8	24
7 Tu	0328	2.1	64		22 W	0334	1.4	43
	1123	-0.3	-9			1038	0.4	12
	1545	1.6	49			1549	1.2	37
	2323	-0.1	-3			2208	0.4	12
8 W	0429	2.1	64		23 Th	0428	1.6	49
	1220	-0.3	-9			1118	0.2	6
	1643	1.7	52			1641	1.4	43
						2303	0.2	6
9 Th	0026	-0.2	-6		24 F	0516	1.7	52
	0524	2.2	67			1201	0.1	3
	1313	-0.4	-12			1728	1.6	49
	1736	1.8	55			2359	0.0	0
10 F	0123	-0.2	-6		25 Sa	0559	1.9	58
	0613	2.2	67			1245	0.0	0
	1401	-0.4	-12			1813	1.9	58
	1826	2.0	61					
11 Sa	0214	-0.3	-9		26 Su	0056	-0.2	-6
	0659	2.2	67			0642	2.1	64
	1444	-0.3	-9			1330	-0.2	-6
	1913	2.1	64			1858	2.1	64
12 Su ◯	0259	-0.3	-9		27 M ●	0152	-0.4	-12
	0743	2.2	67			0725	2.2	67
	1523	-0.2	-6			1415	-0.3	-9
	1959	2.2	67			1943	2.4	73
13 M	0338	-0.2	-6		28 Tu	0247	-0.5	-15
	0827	2.1	64			0810	2.3	70
	1555	-0.1	-3			1500	-0.3	-9
	2045	2.2	67			2030	2.5	76
14 Tu	0413	-0.1	-3		29 W	0342	-0.6	-18
	0911	1.9	58			0858	2.2	67
	1612	0.1	3			1546	-0.3	-9
	2131	2.1	64			2120	2.6	79
15 W	0442	0.0	0		30 Th	0439	-0.6	-18
	0956	1.8	55			0947	2.1	64
	1624	0.2	6			1636	-0.2	-6
	2218	2.0	61			2212	2.6	79
					31 F	0541	-0.5	-15
						1039	2.0	61
						1730	-0.1	-3
						2306	2.5	76

Time meridian 75° W. 0000 is midnight. 1200 is noon. Times are not adjusted for Daylight Saving Time.
Heights are referred to mean lower low water which is the chart datum of soundings.
* See Page 320 for the remaining tides on this day.

Woods Hole, Massachusetts, 2017

Times and Heights of High and Low Waters

April

Day	Time (h m)	Height (ft)	Height (cm)
1 Sa	0648	-0.4	-12
	1133	1.8	55
	1834	0.0	0
2 Su	0003	2.4	73
	0757	-0.4	-12
	1228	1.7	52
	1948	0.1	3
3 M	0102	2.2	67
	0903	-0.3	-9
	1325	1.6	49
	2106	0.1	3
4 Tu	0203	2.1	64
	1005	-0.3	-9
	1425	1.6	49
	2218	0.0	0
5 W	0305	2.0	61
	1104	-0.3	-9
	1525	1.6	49
	2324	0.0	0
6 Th	0406	1.9	58
	1159	-0.2	-6
	1623	1.7	52
7 F	0025	-0.1	-3
	0501	1.9	58
	1250	-0.2	-6
	1716	1.9	58
8 Sa	0120	-0.1	-3
	0549	1.9	58
	1336	-0.1	-3
	1805	2.1	64
9 Su	0208	-0.1	-3
	0633	1.9	58
	1417	0.0	0
	1850	2.2	67
10 M	0251	-0.1	-3
	0716	1.9	58
	1448	0.1	3
	1935	2.3	70
11 Tu	0327	-0.1	-3
	0759	1.8	55
	1454	0.2	6
	2019	2.3	70
12 W	0356	0.0	0
	0842	1.8	55
	1501	0.2	6
	2103	2.2	67
13 Th	0416	0.0	0
	0926	1.7	52
	1530	0.3	9
	2148	2.1	64
14 F	0444	0.1	3
	1011	1.5	46
	1606	0.4	12
	2234	2.0	61
15 Sa	0527	0.2	6
	1058	1.4	43
	1650	0.5	15
	2321	1.8	55
16 Su	0620	0.3	9
	1144	1.3	40
	1447	0.6	18
	1607	0.7	21
	1742	0.6	18
17 M	0008	1.7	52
	0720	0.4	12
	1232	1.2	37
	1523	0.6	18
	1701*	0.8	24
18 Tu	0057	1.6	49
	0818	0.4	12
	1322	1.2	37
	1604	0.7	21
	1746*	0.8	24
19 W	0149	1.5	46
	0907	0.4	12
	1415	1.2	37
	1654	0.9	24
	1823*	0.9	27
20 Th	0245	1.5	46
	0951	0.3	9
	1511	1.3	40
	2148	0.4	12
21 F	0342	1.6	49
	1034	0.2	6
	1606	1.6	49
	2245	0.2	6
22 Sa	0435	1.7	52
	1118	0.1	3
	1657	1.8	55
	2342	0.0	0
23 Su	0524	1.9	58
	1203	0.0	0
	1746	2.2	67
24 M	0042	-0.2	-6
	0611	2.1	64
	1251	-0.1	-3
	1833	2.5	76
25 Tu	0141	-0.4	-12
	0658	2.2	67
	1340	-0.2	-6
	1921	2.7	82
26 W	0238	-0.6	-18
	0746	2.2	67
	1429	-0.3	-9
	2009	2.9	88
27 Th	0334	-0.6	-18
	0835	2.2	67
	1520	-0.3	-9
	2100	2.9	88
28 F	0431	-0.7	-21
	0927	2.1	64
	1613	-0.2	-6
	2153	2.9	88
29 Sa	0531	-0.6	-18
	1020	2.0	61
	1711	-0.1	-3
	2248	2.7	82
30 Su	0635	-0.5	-15
	1114	1.9	58
	1820	0.0	0
	2344	2.5	76

May

Day	Time (h m)	Height (ft)	Height (cm)
1 M	0741	-0.4	-12
	1210	1.8	55
	1941	0.1	3
2 Tu	0041	2.3	70
	0844	-0.3	-9
	1306	1.7	52
	2100	0.2	6
3 W	0140	2.1	64
	0944	-0.2	-6
	1405	1.7	52
	2210	0.1	3
4 Th	0239	1.9	58
	1040	-0.2	-6
	1504	1.7	52
	2315	0.1	3
5 F	0337	1.7	52
	1133	-0.1	-3
	1601	1.9	58
6 Sa	0016	0.1	3
	0431	1.7	52
	1223	0.0	0
	1654	2.0	61
7 Su	0110	0.1	3
	0520	1.7	52
	1308	0.2	6
	1742	2.2	67
8 M	0158	0.1	3
	0605	1.7	52
	1343	0.3	9
	1827	2.3	70
9 Tu	0239	0.1	3
	0648	1.7	52
	1335	0.3	9
	1911	2.4	73
10 W	0313	0.1	3
	0731	1.7	52
	1338	0.3	9
	1954	2.4	73
11 Th	0339	0.1	3
	0814	1.7	52
	1412	0.3	9
	2037	2.3	70
12 F	0356	0.1	3
	0858	1.6	49
	1453	0.4	12
	2121	2.2	67
13 Sa	0424	0.2	6
	0943	1.6	49
	1537	0.4	12
	2206	2.1	64
14 Su	0505	0.2	6
	1029	1.5	46
	1625	0.5	15
	2250	2.0	61
15 M	0554	0.3	9
	1115	1.4	43
	1719	0.6	18
	2335	1.9	58
16 Tu	0647	0.3	9
	1202	1.4	43
	1458	0.7	21
	1629	0.8	24
	1820	0.7	21
17 W	0020	1.8	55
	0739	0.3	9
	1249	1.4	43
	1541	0.8	24
	1716*	0.9	27
18 Th	0107	1.7	52
	0828	0.3	9
	1340	1.4	43
	1631	0.9	27
	1755*	1.0	30
19 F	0200	1.7	52
	0913	0.3	9
	1435	1.6	49
	2129	0.5	15
20 Sa	0257	1.7	52
	0956	0.2	6
	1531	1.8	55
	2227	0.3	9
21 Su	0355	1.8	55
	1040	0.1	3
	1627	2.1	64
	2327	0.1	3
22 M	0450	1.9	58
	1126	0.0	0
	1719	2.5	76
23 Tu	0029	-0.1	-3
	0542	2.0	61
	1216	-0.1	-3
	1810	2.8	85
24 W	0130	-0.4	-12
	0633	2.1	64
	1308	-0.2	-6
	1900	3.0	91
25 Th	0229	-0.5	-15
	0723	2.2	67
	1403	-0.2	-6
	1950	3.1	94
26 F	0325	-0.6	-18
	0814	2.2	67
	1458	-0.2	-6
	2042	3.1	94
27 Sa	0421	-0.6	-18
	0906	2.2	67
	1555	-0.2	-6
	2135	3.0	91
28 Su	0518	-0.6	-18
	0959	2.1	64
	1657	0.0	0
	2229	2.8	85
29 M	0618	-0.5	-15
	1054	2.0	61
	1808	0.1	3
	2324	2.6	79
30 Tu	0720	-0.4	-12
	1149	1.9	58
	1929	0.2	6
31 W	0019	2.3	70
	0820	-0.2	-6
	1245	1.9	58
	2046	0.3	9

June

Day	Time (h m)	Height (ft)	Height (cm)
1 Th	0113	2.1	64
	0918	-0.1	-3
	1341	1.9	58
	2155	0.3	9
2 F	0208	1.8	55
	1013	0.0	0
	1439	1.9	58
	2259	0.3	9
3 Sa	0303	1.6	49
	1104	0.2	6
	1535	1.9	58
4 Su	0000	0.3	9
	0357	1.5	46
	1153	0.3	9
	1629	2.1	64
5 M	0054	0.3	9
	0448	1.5	46
	1234	0.4	12
	1718	2.2	67
6 Tu	0142	0.3	9
	0535	1.5	46
	1151	0.5	15
	1804	2.3	70
7 W	0222	0.3	9
	0620	1.6	49
	1212	0.5	15
	1848	2.4	73
8 Th	0255	0.3	9
	0703	1.6	49
	1252	0.4	12
	1931	2.4	73
9 F	0318	0.2	6
	0746	1.6	49
	1339	0.4	12
	2013	2.4	73
10 Sa	0334	0.2	6
	0830	1.6	49
	1428	0.4	12
	2056	2.3	70
11 Su	0403	0.2	6
	0914	1.6	49
	1517	0.4	12
	2138	2.2	67
12 M	0442	0.2	6
	0959	1.6	49
	1607	0.5	15
	2221	2.2	67
13 Tu	0527	0.2	6
	1045	1.6	49
	1701	0.6	18
	2304	2.1	64
14 W	0615	0.3	9
	1131	1.6	49
	1439	0.8	24
	1550	0.9	27
	1801*	0.6	18
15 Th	0704	0.3	9
	1218	1.6	49
	1523	0.9	27
	1640	1.0	30
	1905	0.6	18
16 F	0034	1.9	58
	0752	0.3	9
	1308	1.7	52
	2010	0.6	18
17 Sa	0125	1.9	58
	0838	0.3	9
	1402	1.9	58
	2113	0.5	15
18 Su	0221	1.8	55
	0923	0.2	6
	1500	2.1	64
	2214	0.3	9
19 M	0321	1.8	55
	1008	0.1	3
	1559	2.4	73
	2316	0.1	3
20 Tu	0420	1.9	58
	1056	0.0	0
	1655	2.6	79
21 W	0019	-0.1	-3
	0516	2.0	61
	1148	0.0	0
	1749	2.9	88
22 Th	0121	-0.3	-9
	0609	2.1	64
	1245	-0.1	-3
	1841	3.1	94
23 F	0218	-0.4	-12
	0701	2.2	67
	1344	-0.2	-6
	1933	3.2	98
24 Sa	0313	-0.5	-15
	0752	2.2	67
	1444	-0.2	-6
	2024	3.2	98
25 Su	0406	-0.5	-15
	0845	2.3	70
	1543	-0.1	-3
	2116	3.1	94
26 M	0500	-0.5	-15
	0938	2.2	67
	1645	0.0	0
	2208	2.9	88
27 Tu	0556	-0.4	-12
	1032	2.2	67
	1754	0.1	3
	2301	2.6	79
28 W	0653	-0.2	-6
	1126	2.1	64
	1910	0.3	9
	2352	2.3	70
29 Th	0751	0.0	0
	1220	2.0	61
	2025	0.4	12
30 F	0044	2.0	61
	0848	0.1	3
	1314	2.0	61
	2133	0.4	12

Time meridian 75° W. 0000 is midnight. 1200 is noon. Times are not adjusted for Daylight Saving Time.
Heights are referred to mean lower low water which is the chart datum of soundings.
* See Page 320 for the remaining tides on this day.

Woods Hole, Massachusetts, 2017

Times and Heights of High and Low Waters

July

Day	Time	ft	cm		Day	Time	ft	cm
1 Sa	0135	1.8	55		16 Su ◖	0058	2.0	61
	0942	0.3	9			0806	0.3	9
	1410	2.0	61			1334	2.1	64
	2237	0.5	15			2101	0.4	12
2 Su	0228	1.6	49		17 M	0154	1.9	58
	1033	0.4	12			0855	0.3	9
	1506	2.0	61			1434	2.3	70
	2338	0.5	15			2205	0.3	9
3 M	0322	1.4	43		18 Tu	0254	1.9	58
	1119	0.6	18			0945	0.2	6
	1602	2.0	61			1535	2.5	76
						2307	0.1	3
4 Tu	0033	0.5	15		19 W	0354	1.9	58
	0415	1.4	43			1036	0.1	3
	1035	0.6	18			1635	2.7	82
	1654	2.1	64					
5 W	0121	0.5	15		20 Th	0010	-0.1	-3
	0505	1.4	43			0453	2.0	61
	1055	0.6	18			1132	0.0	0
	1741	2.2	67			1731	2.9	88
6 Th	0159	0.4	12		21 F	0110	-0.2	-6
	0552	1.5	46			0548	2.1	64
	1136	0.5	15			1232	0.0	0
	1826	2.3	70			1824	3.1	94
7 F	0229	0.4	12		22 Sa	0205	-0.3	-9
	0636	1.6	49			0640	2.2	67
	1224	0.5	15			1335	-0.1	-3
	1908	2.4	73			1914	3.1	94
8 Sa ○	0247	0.4	12		23 Su ●	0257	-0.4	-12
	0720	1.7	52			0732	2.3	70
	1317	0.4	12			1437	-0.1	-3
	1949	2.4	73			2004	3.1	94
9 Su	0304	0.3	9		24 M	0347	-0.4	-12
	0802	1.7	52			0823	2.4	73
	1410	0.4	12			1535	-0.1	-3
	2030	2.4	73			2054	3.0	91
10 M	0335	0.2	6		25 Tu	0437	-0.3	-9
	0846	1.8	55			0914	2.4	73
	1501	0.4	12			1633	0.0	0
	2111	2.4	73			2144	2.7	82
11 Tu	0414	0.2	6		26 W	0527	-0.2	-6
	0930	1.8	55			1006	2.3	70
	1553	0.4	12			1736	0.2	6
	2152	2.3	70			2234	2.5	76
12 W	0456	0.2	6		27 Th	0620	0.0	0
	1015	1.8	55			1059	2.3	70
	1647	0.5	15			1846	0.3	9
	2235	2.2	67			2323	2.2	67
13 Th	0541	0.3	9		28 F	0716	0.2	6
	1101	1.8	55			1151	2.2	67
	1745	0.5	15			1958	0.5	15
	2319	2.1	64					
14 F	0629	0.3	9		29 Sa	0012	1.9	58
	1149	1.9	58			0813	0.4	12
	1849	0.5	15			1244	2.1	64
						2107	0.5	15
15 Sa	0006	2.1	64		30 Su ◗	0102	1.7	52
	0717	0.3	9			0908	0.6	18
	1240	2.0	61			1338	2.0	61
	1956	0.5	15			2211	0.6	18
					31 M	0154	1.5	46
						0431	1.0	30
						0541	1.1	34
						1000	0.7	21
						1434*	1.9	58

August

Day	Time	ft	cm		Day	Time	ft	cm
1 Tu	0248	1.4	43		16 W	0232	1.8	55
	0933	0.8	24			0932	0.3	9
	1532	2.0	61			1514	2.5	76
						2259	0.1	3
2 W	0004	0.6	18		17 Th	0334	1.9	58
	0343	1.4	43			1029	0.2	6
	0948	0.7	21			1616	2.7	82
	1627	2.0	61			2359	-0.1	-3
3 Th	0051	0.6	18		18 F	0433	2.0	61
	0436	1.4	43			1130	0.1	3
	1027	0.7	21			1713	2.8	85
	1717	2.1	64					
4 F	0126	0.6	18		19 Sa	0055	-0.2	-6
	0525	1.5	46			0529	2.1	64
	1114	0.6	18			1235	0.0	0
	1802	2.2	67			1806	2.9	88
5 Sa	0148	0.5	15		20 Su	0148	-0.2	-6
	0610	1.7	52			0621	2.3	70
	1206	0.5	15			1338	0.0	0
	1843	2.3	70			1855	2.9	88
6 Su	0200	0.4	12		21 M ●	0237	-0.3	-9
	0653	1.8	55			0711	2.4	73
	1300	0.4	12			1435	-0.1	-3
	1923	2.4	73			1942	2.9	88
7 M ○	0225	0.3	9		22 Tu	0324	-0.2	-6
	0735	1.9	58			0800	2.5	76
	1354	0.3	9			1528	0.0	0
	2002	2.4	73			2029	2.7	82
8 Tu	0301	0.2	6		23 W	0408	-0.1	-3
	0817	2.0	61			0849	2.5	76
	1447	0.3	9			1620	0.1	3
	2042	2.4	73			2117	2.5	76
9 W	0340	0.2	6		24 Th	0452	0.1	3
	0900	2.0	61			0939	2.5	76
	1539	0.3	9			1714	0.2	6
	2123	2.4	73			2204	2.3	70
10 Th	0422	0.2	6		25 F	0535	0.3	9
	0945	2.1	64			1029	2.4	73
	1633	0.3	9			1816	0.4	12
	2207	2.3	70			2252	2.0	61
11 F	0506	0.2	6		26 Sa	0619	0.5	15
	1032	2.2	67			1119	2.2	67
	1732	0.3	9			1925	0.5	15
	2254	2.2	67			2341	1.8	55
12 Sa	0554	0.3	9		27 Su	0704	0.7	21
	1122	2.2	67			1211	2.1	64
	1837	0.3	9			2034	0.6	18
	2343	2.1	64					
13 Su	0645	0.3	9		28 M	0030	1.6	49
	1215	2.3	70			0718	0.8	24
	1946	0.3	9			1304	2.0	61
						2138	0.6	18
14 M	0036	2.0	61		29 Tu ◗	0121	1.5	46
	0740	0.3	9			0400	0.9	27
	1311	2.3	70			0527	1.0	30
	2053	0.3	9			1400*	1.9	58
15 Tu	0132	1.9	58		30 W	0214	1.4	43
	0835	0.3	9			0833	0.8	24
	1411	2.4	73			1458	1.8	55
	2158	0.2	6			2326	0.7	21
					31 Th	0311	1.3	40
						0920	0.8	24
						1557	1.9	58

September

Day	Time	ft	cm		Day	Time	ft	cm
1 F	0006	0.6	18		16 Sa	0415	2.0	61
	0406	1.4	43			1142	0.1	3
	1007	0.7	21			1654	2.5	76
	1649	2.0	61					
2 Sa	0030	0.6	18		17 Su	0037	-0.1	-3
	0457	1.6	49			0511	2.2	67
	1058	0.6	18			1244	0.0	0
	1734	2.1	64			1746	2.6	79
3 Su	0037	0.5	15		18 M	0128	-0.2	-6
	0543	1.7	52			0602	2.4	73
	1150	0.5	15			1341	0.0	0
	1814	2.2	67			1833	2.6	79
4 M	0104	0.4	12		19 Tu	0214	-0.1	-3
	0625	1.9	58			0650	2.5	76
	1245	0.3	9			1432	0.0	0
	1853	2.3	70			1918	2.5	76
5 Tu	0142	0.3	9		20 W ●	0256	0.0	0
	0707	2.1	64			0737	2.6	79
	1339	0.2	6			1520	0.0	0
	1932	2.4	73			2003	2.4	73
6 W ○	0222	0.2	6		21 Th	0334	0.1	3
	0749	2.2	67			0824	2.6	79
	1433	0.1	3			1605	0.1	3
	2013	2.4	73			2048	2.3	70
7 Th	0304	0.1	3		22 F	0403	0.3	9
	0832	2.4	73			0911	2.5	76
	1526	0.1	3			1650	0.2	6
	2056	2.4	73			2134	2.1	64
8 F	0347	0.1	3		23 Sa	0419	0.4	12
	0918	2.4	73			0958	2.4	73
	1621	0.0	0			1740	0.4	12
	2142	2.3	70			2221	1.9	58
9 Sa	0432	0.1	3		24 Su	0439	0.6	18
	1006	2.5	76			1047	2.3	70
	1721	0.1	3			1842	0.5	15
	2231	2.2	67			2309	1.7	52
10 Su	0521	0.2	6		25 M	0512	0.7	21
	1058	2.5	76			1138	2.1	64
	1826	0.1	3			1952	0.6	18
	2323	2.1	64			2358	1.5	46
11 M	0617	0.3	9		26 Tu	0255	0.8	24
	1153	2.5	76			0414	0.9	27
	1937	0.1	3			0557	0.8	24
						1229	1.9	58
						2056	0.6	18
12 Tu	0017	1.9	58		27 W ◖	0049	1.4	43
	0719	0.3	9			0331	0.9	27
	1251	2.5	76			0508	1.0	30
	2045	0.1	3			0655*	0.9	27
						1323*	1.8	55
13 W ◗	0114	1.9	58		28 Th	0142	1.3	40
	0825	0.3	9			0412	0.9	27
	1352	2.4	73			0551	1.0	30
	2148	0.0	0			0758	0.9	27
						1420*	1.7	52
14 Th	0214	1.8	55		29 F	0238	1.3	40
	0931	0.3	9			0500	1.0	30
	1455	2.4	73			0627	1.1	34
	2247	0.0	0			0856	0.8	24
						1518*	1.7	52
15 F	0316	1.9	58		30 Sa	0335	1.4	43
	1037	0.2	6			0950	0.7	21
	1557	2.5	76			1612	1.8	55
	2344	-0.1	-3			2306	0.5	15

Time meridian 75° W. 0000 is midnight. 1200 is noon. Times are not adjusted for Daylight Saving Time.
Heights are referred to mean lower low water which is the chart datum of soundings.
* See Page 320 for the remaining tides on this day.

Woods Hole, Massachusetts, 2017

Times and Heights of High and Low Waters

October

Day	Time	ft	cm
1 Su	0427	1.6	49
	1042	0.6	18
	1658	1.9	58
	2337	0.4	12
2 M	0514	1.8	55
	1135	0.4	12
	1740	2.1	64
3 Tu	0017	0.3	9
	0557	2.0	61
	1229	0.2	6
	1821	2.2	67
4 W	0059	0.2	6
	0639	2.3	70
	1325	0.1	3
	1902	2.3	70
5 Th O	0143	0.1	3
	0722	2.5	76
	1420	-0.1	-3
	1945	2.3	70
6 F	0228	0.0	0
	0807	2.7	82
	1515	-0.2	-6
	2031	2.3	70
7 Sa	0314	0.0	0
	0854	2.8	85
	1611	-0.2	-6
	2119	2.2	67
8 Su	0402	0.0	0
	0944	2.8	85
	1711	-0.2	-6
	2210	2.1	64
9 M	0454	0.1	3
	1038	2.7	82
	1816	-0.1	-3
	2304	2.0	61
10 Tu	0554	0.2	6
	1134	2.6	79
	1925	-0.1	-3
	2359	1.9	58
11 W	0705	0.3	9
	1232	2.5	76
	2031	-0.1	-3
12 Th ☽	0057	1.8	55
	0822	0.3	9
	1333	2.4	73
	2133	-0.1	-3
13 F	0157	1.8	55
	0936	0.2	6
	1434	2.3	70
	2231	-0.2	-6
14 Sa	0258	1.9	58
	1043	0.2	6
	1535	2.2	67
	2325	-0.2	-6
15 Su	0357	2.0	61
	1146	0.1	3
	1632	2.2	67
16 M	0016	-0.1	-3
	0452	2.2	67
	1245	0.0	0
	1722	2.2	67
17 Tu	0104	-0.1	-3
	0542	2.3	70
	1338	0.0	0
	1808	2.2	67
18 W	0148	0.0	0
	0629	2.5	76
	1426	0.0	0
	1852	2.1	64
19 Th ●	0224	0.1	3
	0714	2.6	79
	1510	0.0	0
	1936	2.1	64
20 F	0246	0.2	6
	0759	2.6	79
	1550	0.1	3
	2019	2.0	61
21 Sa	0250	0.3	9
	0844	2.5	76
	1626	0.2	6
	2104	1.8	55
22 Su	0311	0.4	12
	0930	2.4	73
	1700	0.3	9
	2150	1.7	52
23 M	0344	0.5	15
	1017	2.2	67
	1740	0.4	12
	2238	1.6	49
24 Tu	0425	0.6	18
	1105	2.1	64
	1837	0.5	15
	2327	1.4	43
25 W	0228	0.7	21
	0348	0.8	24
	0515	0.7	21
	1155	1.9	58
	1947	0.5	15
26 Th	0017	1.3	40
	0303	0.8	24
	0442	0.9	27
	0618	0.8	24
	1245*	1.7	52
27 F ☽	0109	1.3	40
	0343	0.8	24
	0526	1.0	30
	0727	0.8	24
	1337*	1.7	52
28 Sa	0203	1.3	40
	0428	0.9	27
	0604	1.1	34
	0831	0.8	24
	1431*	1.6	49
29 Su	0258	1.4	43
	0929	0.6	18
	1525	1.7	52
	2217	0.4	12
30 M	0352	1.6	49
	1023	0.5	15
	1616	1.8	55
	2255	0.3	9
31 Tu	0441	1.8	55
	1118	0.3	9
	1703	1.9	58
	2336	0.1	3

November

Day	Time	ft	cm
1 W	0527	2.1	64
	1214	0.1	3
	1748	2.0	61
2 Th	0020	0.0	0
	0612	2.4	73
	1311	-0.1	-3
	1834	2.1	64
3 F	0107	-0.1	-3
	0658	2.7	82
	1408	-0.3	-9
	1920	2.2	67
4 Sa O	0155	-0.2	-6
	0745	2.9	88
	1504	-0.4	-12
	2007	2.2	67
5 Su	0245	-0.2	-6
	0834	3.0	91
	1601	-0.4	-12
	2057	2.2	67
6 M	0337	-0.1	-3
	0925	3.0	91
	1700	-0.4	-12
	2150	2.1	64
7 Tu	0433	-0.1	-3
	1020	2.8	85
	1803	-0.4	-12
	2244	2.0	61
8 W	0538	0.1	3
	1116	2.7	82
	1908	-0.3	-9
	2341	1.9	58
9 Th	0654	0.2	6
	1213	2.5	76
	2013	-0.3	-9
10 F O	0038	1.8	55
	0817	0.2	6
	1311	2.3	70
	2113	-0.3	-9
11 Sa	0137	1.8	55
	0932	0.2	6
	1410	2.1	64
	2209	-0.2	-6
12 Su	0237	1.8	55
	1039	0.1	3
	1508	1.9	58
	2303	-0.2	-6
13 M	0337	1.9	58
	1141	0.1	3
	1604	1.8	55
	2353	-0.1	-3
14 Tu	0432	2.1	64
	1238	0.1	3
	1655	1.8	55
15 W	0040	0.0	0
	0522	2.2	67
	1331	0.0	0
	1742	1.8	55
16 Th	0121	0.1	3
	0608	2.4	73
	1417	0.0	0
	1826	1.8	55
17 F	0148	0.2	6
	0652	2.4	73
	1458	0.1	3
	1909	1.7	52
18 Sa ●	0130	0.3	9
	0736	2.5	76
	1533	0.1	3
	1952	1.7	52
19 Su	0154	0.3	9
	0819	2.4	73
	1602	0.2	6
	2036	1.7	52
20 M	0230	0.3	9
	0904	2.3	70
	1625	0.2	6
	2121	1.6	49
21 Tu	0312	0.4	12
	0949	2.2	67
	1656	0.3	9
	2208	1.5	46
22 W	0358	0.4	12
	1035	2.0	61
	1740	0.3	9
	2256	1.4	43
23 Th	0450	0.6	18
	1121	1.9	58
	1832	0.4	12
	2344	1.3	40
24 F	0240	0.7	21
	0408	0.8	24
	0551	0.7	21
	1207	1.7	52
	1925	0.4	12
25 Sa	0034	1.3	40
	0319	0.7	21
	0457	0.9	27
	0658	0.7	21
	1253*	1.6	49
26 Su ☽	0124	1.3	40
	0403	0.8	24
	0538	1.0	30
	0805	0.7	21
	1343*	1.6	49
27 M	0218	1.4	43
	0907	0.5	15
	1436	1.6	49
	2136	0.2	6
28 Tu	0313	1.6	49
	1004	0.4	12
	1532	1.6	49
	2217	0.1	3
29 W	0407	1.9	58
	1101	0.2	6
	1626	1.7	52
	2300	0.0	0
30 Th	0458	2.2	67
	1200	0.0	0
	1717	1.9	58
	2347	-0.1	-3

December

Day	Time	ft	cm
1 F	0548	2.5	76
	1259	-0.2	-6
	1807	2.0	61
2 Sa	0037	-0.2	-6
	0637	2.8	85
	1358	-0.4	-12
	1856	2.1	64
3 Su O	0129	-0.3	-9
	0726	3.0	91
	1454	-0.6	-18
	1946	2.1	64
4 M	0224	-0.4	-12
	0816	3.1	94
	1549	-0.6	-18
	2037	2.1	64
5 Tu	0320	-0.3	-9
	0908	3.0	91
	1646	-0.6	-18
	2130	2.0	61
6 W	0419	-0.3	-9
	1002	2.9	88
	1745	-0.6	-18
	2224	2.0	61
7 Th	0525	-0.1	-3
	1056	2.6	79
	1846	-0.5	-15
	2320	1.9	58
8 F	0642	0.0	0
	1151	2.4	73
	1948	-0.4	-12
9 Sa	0017	1.8	55
	0805	0.1	3
	1246	2.1	64
	2048	-0.3	-9
10 Su O	0114	1.8	55
	0918	0.1	3
	1341	1.8	55
	2145	-0.2	-6
11 M	0213	1.8	55
	1026	0.1	3
	1437	1.6	49
	2239	-0.1	-3
12 Tu	0312	1.8	55
	1128	0.1	3
	1533	1.5	46
	2330	0.0	0
13 W	0408	1.9	58
	1226	0.1	3
	1625	1.4	43
14 Th	0018	0.1	3
	0500	2.0	61
	1319	0.1	3
	1714	1.4	43
15 F	0058	0.2	6
	0547	2.2	67
	1404	0.1	3
	1800	1.5	46
16 Sa	0019	0.3	9
	0631	2.2	67
	1443	0.1	3
	1843	1.5	46
17 Su	0041	0.2	6
	0714	2.3	70
	1514	0.1	3
	1927	1.5	46
18 M ●	0121	0.2	6
	0757	2.3	70
	1537	0.1	3
	2010	1.5	46
19 Tu	0206	0.2	6
	0840	2.2	67
	1554	0.1	3
	2054	1.5	46
20 W	0253	0.2	6
	0923	2.1	64
	1624	0.1	3
	2139	1.5	46
21 Th	0342	0.3	9
	1006	2.0	61
	1704	0.1	3
	2225	1.4	43
22 F	0433	0.4	12
	1048	1.9	58
	1750	0.2	6
	2311	1.4	43
23 Sa	0530	0.4	12
	1131	1.8	55
	1838	0.2	6
	2358	1.4	43
24 Su	0634	0.5	15
	1214	1.7	52
	1927	0.2	6
25 M O	0046	1.4	43
	0345	0.7	21
	0507	0.8	24
	0740	0.6	15
	1302*	1.6	49
26 Tu ☽	0138	1.5	46
	0845	0.4	12
	1354	1.5	46
	2059	0.1	3
27 W	0234	1.7	52
	0947	0.2	6
	1453	1.5	46
	2144	0.0	0
28 Th	0334	1.9	58
	1047	0.1	3
	1552	1.6	49
	2231	-0.1	-3
29 F	0431	2.2	67
	1148	-0.1	-3
	1649	1.7	52
	2321	-0.2	-6
30 Sa	0526	2.5	76
	1249	-0.3	-9
	1743	1.8	55
31 Su	0015	-0.3	-9
	0618	2.8	85
	1347	-0.5	-15
	1835	2.0	61

Time meridian 75° W. 0000 is midnight. 1200 is noon. Times are not adjusted for Daylight Saving Time.
Heights are referred to mean lower low water which is the chart datum of soundings.
* See Page 320 for the remaining tides on this day.

Newport, Rhode Island, 2017

Times and Heights of High and Low Waters

January

Day	Time	ft	cm	Day	Time	ft	cm
1 Su	0236	0.1	3	**16** M	0329	0.0	0
	0930	3.8	116		1036	3.9	119
	1516	0.0	0		1606	0.1	3
	2157	3.4	104		2305	3.8	116
2 M	0316	0.1	3	**17** Tu	0414	0.2	6
	1015	3.7	113		1125	3.5	107
	1551	0.1	3		1643	0.3	9
	2245	3.4	104		2356	3.5	107
3 Tu	0359	0.2	6	**18** W	0502	0.5	15
	1105	3.6	110		1214	3.2	98
	1631	0.1	3		1725	0.4	12
	2336	3.5	107				
4 W	0448	0.3	9	**19** Th	0047	3.3	101
	1158	3.5	107		0600	0.7	21
	1719	0.1	3		1303	2.9	88
					1816	0.5	15
5 Th	0030	3.6	110	**20** F	0137	3.2	98
	0550	0.5	15		0714	0.8	24
	1254	3.5	107		1352	2.7	82
	1816	0.2	6		1914	0.6	18
6 F	0126	3.7	113	**21** Sa	0230	3.1	94
	0709	0.5	15		0835	0.8	24
	1352	3.4	104		1446	2.6	79
	1920	0.1	3		2016	0.6	18
7 Sa	0226	3.8	116	**22** Su	0328	3.0	91
	0843	0.4	12		0937	0.7	21
	1455	3.4	104		1545	2.6	79
	2027	0.1	3		2114	0.5	15
8 Su	0331	4.0	122	**23** M	0424	3.1	94
	1001	0.2	6		1026	0.5	15
	1601	3.5	107		1641	2.7	82
	2130	-0.1	-3		2205	0.3	9
9 M	0436	4.3	131	**24** Tu	0512	3.2	98
	1102	0.0	0		1109	0.3	9
	1704	3.7	113		1728	2.8	85
	2228	-0.2	-6		2252	0.2	6
10 Tu	0535	4.5	137	**25** W	0554	3.4	104
	1155	-0.1	-3		1150	0.2	6
	1801	4.0	122		1809	3.0	91
	2322	-0.4	-12		2335	0.0	0
11 W	0630	4.7	143	**26** Th	0631	3.6	110
	1247	-0.2	-6		1230	0.0	0
	1854	4.2	128		1848	3.2	98
12 Th	0015	-0.4	-12	**27** F	0018	-0.1	-3
	0721	4.8	146		0709	3.7	113
	1337	-0.3	-9		1309	-0.1	-3
	1945	4.3	131		1928	3.4	104
13 F	0107	-0.4	-12	**28** Sa	0100	-0.2	-6
	0811	4.7	143		0747	3.9	119
	1421	-0.3	-9		1345	-0.3	-9
	2035	4.3	131		2008	3.5	107
14 Sa	0157	-0.4	-12	**29** Su	0141	-0.3	-9
	0859	4.5	137		0827	3.9	119
	1458	-0.2	-6		1419	-0.3	-9
	2124	4.2	128		2050	3.6	110
15 Su	0244	-0.2	-6	**30** M	0222	-0.3	-9
	0948	4.2	128		0910	3.9	119
	1532	-0.1	-3		1452	-0.4	-12
	2214	4.0	122		2134	3.7	113
				31 Tu	0303	-0.3	-9
					0956	3.8	116
					1528	-0.4	-12
					2222	3.7	113

February

Day	Time	ft	cm	Day	Time	ft	cm
1 W	0346	-0.2	-6	**16** Th	0428	0.2	6
	1045	3.7	113		1135	3.0	91
	1607	-0.3	-9		1639	0.2	6
	2313	3.7	113				
2 Th	0434	0.0	0	**17** F	0003	3.1	94
	1139	3.5	107		0515	0.4	12
	1652	-0.2	-6		1220	2.7	82
					1723	0.3	9
3 F	0008	3.7	113	**18** Sa	0049	2.9	88
	0532	0.2	6		0613	0.6	18
	1235	3.4	104		1306	2.5	76
	1746	-0.1	-3		1816	0.5	15
4 Sa	0105	3.7	113	**19** Su	0137	2.8	85
	0649	0.3	9		0729	0.7	21
	1334	3.3	101		1355	2.4	73
	1850	0.0	0		1921	0.5	15
5 Su	0206	3.7	113	**20** M	0231	2.7	82
	0846	0.3	9		0850	0.6	18
	1437	3.2	98		1452	2.3	70
	2002	0.0	0		2031	0.5	15
6 M	0313	3.8	116	**21** Tu	0332	2.7	82
	1007	0.2	6		0952	0.5	15
	1545	3.3	101		1554	2.4	73
	2115	0.0	0		2134	0.3	9
7 Tu	0421	3.9	119	**22** W	0430	2.9	88
	1105	0.0	0		1040	0.3	9
	1649	3.5	107		1649	2.7	82
	2221	-0.2	-6		2227	0.1	3
8 W	0523	4.1	125	**23** Th	0518	3.1	94
	1155	-0.1	-3		1121	0.1	3
	1747	3.7	113		1736	3.0	91
	2317	-0.3	-9		2314	-0.1	-3
9 Th	0617	4.3	131	**24** F	0600	3.4	104
	1241	-0.2	-6		1159	-0.1	-3
	1839	4.0	122		1819	3.3	101
					2358	-0.3	-9
10 F	0008	-0.4	-12	**25** Sa	0641	3.6	110
	0707	4.4	134		1236	-0.3	-9
	1321	-0.3	-9		1901	3.5	107
	1928	4.1	125				
11 Sa	0057	-0.4	-12	**26** Su	0041	-0.5	-15
	0754	4.3	131		0722	3.9	119
	1356	-0.3	-9		1313	-0.5	-15
	2015	4.1	125		1943	3.8	116
12 Su	0143	-0.4	-12	**27** M	0125	-0.6	-18
	0838	4.2	128		0805	4.0	122
	1426	-0.3	-9		1349	-0.6	-18
	2101	4.0	122		2026	3.9	119
13 M	0226	-0.4	-12	**28** Tu	0208	-0.6	-18
	0922	3.9	119		0849	4.0	122
	1455	-0.2	-6		1426	-0.7	-21
	2146	3.9	119		2112	4.0	122
14 Tu	0306	-0.2	-6				
	1006	3.6	110				
	1526	-0.1	-3				
	2231	3.6	110				
15 W	0346	0.0	0				
	1050	3.3	101				
	1601	0.0	0				
	2317	3.4	104				

March

Day	Time	ft	cm	Day	Time	ft	cm
1 W	0251	-0.6	-18	**16** Th	0320	-0.1	-3
	0937	3.9	119		1016	3.2	98
	1504	-0.6	-18		1525	0.0	0
	2201	4.0	122		2237	3.4	104
2 Th	0335	-0.5	-15	**17** F	0359	0.1	3
	1027	3.7	113		1057	2.9	88
	1545	-0.5	-15		1602	0.1	3
	2253	3.9	119		2319	3.1	94
3 F	0423	-0.2	-6	**18** Sa	0441	0.3	9
	1122	3.5	107		1140	2.7	82
	1630	-0.4	-12		1643	0.3	9
	2349	3.8	116				
4 Sa	0520	0.0	0	**19** Su	0002	2.9	88
	1219	3.4	104		0529	0.5	15
	1723	-0.1	-3		1225	2.5	76
					1731	0.5	15
5 Su	0048	3.7	113	**20** M	0047	2.7	82
	0644	0.3	9		0632	0.6	18
	1319	3.2	98		1312	2.4	73
	1828	0.1	3		1832	0.6	18
6 M	0150	3.6	110	**21** Tu	0137	2.7	82
	0857	0.3	9		0752	0.7	21
	1422	3.2	98		1405	2.4	73
	1948	0.2	6		1945	0.6	18
7 Tu	0258	3.6	110	**22** W	0234	2.7	82
	1006	0.2	6		0906	0.6	18
	1530	3.3	101		1504	2.5	76
	2119	0.1	3		2059	0.5	15
8 W	0407	3.6	110	**23** Th	0336	2.8	85
	1059	0.1	3		0959	0.4	12
	1635	3.4	104		1605	2.8	85
	2228	0.0	0		2159	0.2	6
9 Th	0509	3.8	116	**24** F	0435	3.1	94
	1144	0.0	0		1041	0.1	3
	1732	3.7	113		1659	3.1	94
	2320	-0.1	-3		2249	0.0	0
10 F	0602	3.9	119	**25** Sa	0525	3.4	104
	1222	-0.1	-3		1120	-0.1	-3
	1822	3.9	119		1747	3.5	107
					2335	-0.3	-9
11 Sa	0005	-0.2	-6	**26** Su	0611	3.7	113
	0650	4.0	122		1157	-0.4	-12
	1252	-0.2	-6		1832	3.9	119
	1909	4.1	125				
12 Su	0046	-0.3	-9	**27** M	0021	-0.5	-15
	0733	4.0	122		0656	4.0	122
	1319	-0.2	-6		1237	-0.6	-18
	1953	4.1	125		1917	4.2	128
13 M	0126	-0.4	-12	**28** Tu	0107	-0.6	-18
	0815	3.9	119		0742	4.1	125
	1347	-0.3	-9		1317	-0.7	-21
	2035	4.0	122		2003	4.4	134
14 Tu	0204	-0.3	-9	**29** W	0154	-0.7	-21
	0856	3.7	113		0829	4.2	128
	1417	-0.2	-6		1359	-0.7	-21
	2116	3.9	119		2051	4.5	137
15 W	0242	-0.3	-9	**30** Th	0240	-0.6	-18
	0936	3.4	104		0919	4.1	125
	1450	-0.2	-6		1442	-0.7	-21
	2156	3.6	110		2141	4.5	137
				31 F	0327	-0.5	-15
					1011	3.9	119
					1526	-0.5	-15
					2235	4.3	131

Time meridian 75° W. 0000 is midnight. 1200 is noon. Times are not adjusted for Daylight Saving Time.
Heights are referred to mean lower low water which is the chart datum of soundings.

Newport, Rhode Island, 2017

Times and Heights of High and Low Waters

April

Day	Time	ft	cm	Day	Time	ft	cm
1 Sa	0416	-0.2	-6	**16** Su	0413	0.4	12
	1107	3.7	113		1106	2.9	88
	1613	-0.2	-6		1611	0.5	15
	2332	4.1	125		2320	3.1	94
2 Su	0515	0.1	3	**17** M	0456	0.5	15
	1205	3.6	110		1151	2.8	85
	1707	0.1	3		1656	0.6	18
3 M	0033	3.9	119	**18** Tu	0006	3.0	91
	0707	0.3	9		0547	0.7	21
	1306	3.5	107		1238	2.7	82
	1815	0.3	9		1751	0.8	24
4 Tu	0135	3.7	113	**19** W	0055	2.9	88
	0848	0.4	12		0653	0.8	24
	1408	3.4	104		1328	2.8	85
	1954	0.5	15		1900	0.8	24
5 W	0241	3.6	110	**20** Th	0148	2.9	88
	0951	0.3	9		0805	0.7	21
	1513	3.5	107		1423	2.9	88
	2140	0.4	12		2017	0.7	21
6 Th	0349	3.6	110	**21** F	0247	3.1	94
	1040	0.3	9		0904	0.5	15
	1617	3.6	110		1522	3.2	98
	2238	0.3	9		2125	0.5	15
7 F	0450	3.6	110	**22** Sa	0350	3.3	101
	1120	0.2	6		0952	0.3	9
	1713	3.8	116		1621	3.5	107
	2320	0.2	6		2221	0.2	6
8 Sa	0542	3.7	113	**23** Su	0448	3.5	107
	1149	0.1	3		1035	0.0	0
	1803	4.0	122		1715	3.9	119
	2356	0.1	3		2311	-0.1	-3
9 Su	0628	3.8	116	**24** M	0540	3.9	119
	1211	0.1	3		1118	-0.3	-9
	1847	4.1	125		1804	4.4	134
					2359	-0.3	-9
10 M	0030	0.0	0	**25** Tu	0630	4.1	125
	0710	3.8	116		1201	-0.4	-12
	1236	0.0	0		1853	4.7	143
	1929	4.2	128				
11 Tu	0105	-0.1	-3	**26** W	0049	-0.5	-15
	0750	3.7	113		0720	4.3	131
	1307	0.0	0		1246	-0.6	-18
	2008	4.1	125		1942	4.9	149
12 W	0142	-0.1	-3	**27** Th	0140	-0.5	-15
	0829	3.6	110		0810	4.4	134
	1341	0.0	0		1333	-0.6	-18
	2046	4.0	122		2032	5.0	152
13 Th	0220	-0.1	-3	**28** F	0231	-0.5	-15
	0907	3.4	104		0901	4.3	131
	1418	0.1	3		1421	-0.5	-15
	2123	3.8	116		2124	4.9	149
14 F	0257	0.0	0	**29** Sa	0321	-0.3	-9
	0945	3.2	98		0955	4.2	128
	1454	0.2	6		1509	-0.3	-9
	2200	3.5	107		2219	4.7	143
15 Sa	0334	0.2	6	**30** Su	0412	-0.1	-3
	1024	3.0	91		1052	4.1	125
	1532	0.3	9		1600	0.0	0
	2239	3.3	101		2317	4.4	134

May

Day	Time	ft	cm	Day	Time	ft	cm
1 M	0515	0.2	6	**16** Tu	0429	0.6	18
	1151	3.9	119		1121	3.1	94
	1656	0.3	9		1628	0.7	21
					2334	3.3	101
2 Tu	0017	4.1	125	**17** W	0512	0.7	21
	0702	0.4	12		1208	3.1	94
	1250	3.8	116		1717	0.9	27
	1808	0.6	18				
3 W	0118	3.9	119	**18** Th	0022	3.3	101
	0824	0.5	15		0605	0.7	21
	1351	3.8	116		1257	3.2	98
	2016	0.7	21		1820	0.9	27
4 Th	0219	3.7	113	**19** F	0114	3.3	101
	0923	0.5	15		0706	0.7	21
	1452	3.8	116		1349	3.3	101
	2137	0.7	21		1935	0.8	24
5 F	0323	3.6	110	**20** Sa	0210	3.3	101
	1008	0.5	15		0806	0.5	15
	1554	3.9	119		1446	3.6	110
	2228	0.6	18		2049	0.6	18
6 Sa	0424	3.5	107	**21** Su	0311	3.5	107
	1041	0.5	15		0902	0.3	9
	1650	4.0	122		1545	3.9	119
	2306	0.5	15		2152	0.4	12
7 Su	0517	3.6	110	**22** M	0413	3.7	113
	1104	0.5	15		0953	0.1	3
	1740	4.1	125		1644	4.3	131
	2337	0.4	12		2247	0.1	3
8 M	0603	3.6	110	**23** Tu	0512	3.9	119
	1126	0.4	12		1042	-0.1	-3
	1823	4.2	128		1739	4.7	143
					2340	-0.1	-3
9 Tu	0008	0.3	9	**24** W	0607	4.2	128
	0645	3.6	110		1130	-0.3	-9
	1156	0.3	9		1831	5.0	152
	1904	4.2	128				
10 W	0042	0.2	6	**25** Th	0033	-0.3	-9
	0724	3.6	110		0659	4.4	134
	1231	0.3	9		1219	-0.4	-12
	1941	4.2	128		1923	5.2	158
11 Th	0120	0.2	6	**26** F	0128	-0.3	-9
	0802	3.6	110		0752	4.5	137
	1309	0.3	9		1311	-0.4	-12
	2017	4.1	125		2015	5.2	158
12 F	0159	0.2	6	**27** Sa	0223	-0.3	-9
	0839	3.5	107		0845	4.5	137
	1348	0.3	9		1403	-0.3	-9
	2053	3.9	119		2108	5.1	155
13 Sa	0237	0.2	6	**28** Su	0315	-0.2	-6
	0916	3.3	101		0939	4.4	134
	1428	0.4	12		1456	-0.1	-3
	2129	3.7	113		2203	4.9	149
14 Su	0314	0.3	9	**29** M	0407	0.0	0
	0955	3.2	98		1035	4.3	131
	1506	0.5	15		1548	0.2	6
	2206	3.6	110		2300	4.5	137
15 M	0351	0.5	15	**30** Tu	0505	0.3	9
	1037	3.1	94		1133	4.2	128
	1545	0.6	18		1645	0.5	15
	2248	3.4	104		2358	4.2	128
				31 W	0625	0.5	15
					1231	4.1	125
					1756	0.8	24

June

Day	Time	ft	cm	Day	Time	ft	cm
1 Th	0055	3.9	119	**16** F	0527	0.5	15
	0742	0.6	18		1230	3.4	104
	1329	4.0	122		1748	0.8	24
	1955	0.9	27				
2 F	0152	3.7	113	**17** Sa	0047	3.5	107
	0838	0.7	21		0620	0.5	15
	1427	3.9	119		1320	3.6	110
	2111	0.9	27		1859	0.8	24
3 Sa	0251	3.5	107	**18** Su	0141	3.5	107
	0920	0.7	21		0719	0.4	12
	1525	3.9	119		1415	3.8	116
	2201	0.8	24		2016	0.6	18
4 Su	0350	3.4	104	**19** M	0240	3.5	107
	0949	0.7	21		0819	0.2	6
	1622	3.9	119		1515	4.1	125
	2239	0.8	24		2128	0.4	12
5 M	0445	3.3	101	**20** Tu	0344	3.6	110
	1014	0.6	18		0917	0.0	0
	1712	4.0	122		1617	4.4	134
	2310	0.7	21		2229	0.2	6
6 Tu	0534	3.4	104	**21** W	0447	3.8	116
	1046	0.6	18		1012	-0.1	-3
	1757	4.1	125		1717	4.7	143
	2343	0.5	15		2325	0.0	0
7 W	0617	3.4	104	**22** Th	0546	4.0	122
	1122	0.5	15		1105	-0.3	-9
	1837	4.1	125		1813	5.0	152
8 Th	0019	0.4	12	**23** F	0021	-0.2	-6
	0657	3.5	107		0641	4.3	131
	1201	0.4	12		1158	-0.4	-12
	1915	4.1	125		1907	5.1	155
9 F	0059	0.3	9	**24** Sa	0118	-0.2	-6
	0735	3.5	107		0735	4.4	134
	1242	0.4	12		1253	-0.4	-12
	1951	4.0	122		1959	5.1	155
10 Sa	0140	0.3	9	**25** Su	0213	-0.3	-9
	0812	3.4	104		0828	4.5	137
	1324	0.4	12		1349	-0.3	-9
	2026	3.9	119		2052	5.0	152
11 Su	0219	0.3	9	**26** M	0304	-0.2	-6
	0850	3.4	104		0921	4.5	137
	1405	0.4	12		1443	-0.1	-3
	2102	3.8	116		2145	4.8	146
12 M	0255	0.3	9	**27** Tu	0350	0.0	0
	0928	3.3	101		1016	4.4	134
	1445	0.5	15		1535	0.1	3
	2139	3.7	113		2239	4.4	134
13 Tu	0330	0.4	12	**28** W	0435	0.1	3
	1009	3.3	101		1111	4.2	128
	1524	0.6	18		1628	0.4	12
	2221	3.6	110		2334	4.1	125
14 W	0404	0.5	15	**29** Th	0524	0.3	9
	1054	3.3	101		1207	4.1	125
	1605	0.7	21		1729	0.7	21
	2306	3.5	107				
15 Th	0442	0.5	15	**30** F	0028	3.8	116
	1141	3.3	101		0618	0.5	15
	1651	0.7	21		1301	3.9	119
	2355	3.5	107		1853	0.8	24

Time meridian 75° W. 0000 is midnight. 1200 is noon. Times are not adjusted for Daylight Saving Time.
Heights are referred to mean lower low water which is the chart datum of soundings.

Newport, Rhode Island, 2017

Times and Heights of High and Low Waters

July

Day	Time	ft	cm	Day	Time	ft	cm
1 Sa	0121	3.5	107	16 Su ◗	0024	3.4	104
	0714	0.6	18		0544	0.1	3
	1356	3.8	116		1255	3.7	113
	2023	0.9	27		1830	0.5	15
2 Su	0214	3.2	98	17 M	0119	3.4	104
	0802	0.7	21		0642	0.1	3
	1451	3.7	113		1351	3.8	116
	2121	0.9	27		1951	0.5	15
3 M	0311	3.0	91	18 Tu	0218	3.3	101
	0846	0.7	21		0745	0.1	3
	1548	3.6	110		1451	4.0	122
	2203	0.8	24		2114	0.3	9
4 Tu	0408	3.0	91	19 W	0322	3.4	104
	0929	0.6	18		0849	0.0	0
	1641	3.6	110		1557	4.2	128
	2241	0.7	21		2222	0.1	3
5 W	0501	3.0	91	20 Th	0428	3.6	110
	1011	0.5	15		0950	-0.2	-6
	1728	3.7	113		1700	4.4	134
	2318	0.5	15		2319	-0.1	-3
6 Th	0547	3.1	94	21 F	0529	3.8	116
	1053	0.4	12		1048	-0.3	-9
	1810	3.7	113		1758	4.6	140
	2357	0.4	12				
7 F	0628	3.2	98	22 Sa	0013	-0.2	-6
	1136	0.3	9		0625	4.1	125
	1848	3.8	116		1144	-0.4	-12
					1852	4.8	146
8 Sa ○	0038	0.3	9	23 Su ●	0107	-0.3	-9
	0707	3.3	101		0718	4.3	131
	1219	0.3	9		1240	-0.4	-12
	1924	3.8	116		1944	4.8	146
9 Su	0119	0.2	6	24 M	0157	-0.3	-9
	0744	3.3	101		0810	4.3	131
	1303	0.2	6		1335	-0.4	-12
	1959	3.8	116		2035	4.7	143
10 M	0158	0.1	3	25 Tu	0241	-0.3	-9
	0822	3.4	104		0901	4.3	131
	1345	0.2	6		1428	-0.3	-9
	2036	3.8	116		2124	4.4	134
11 Tu	0233	0.1	3	26 W	0319	-0.2	-6
	0901	3.4	104		0953	4.2	128
	1425	0.2	6		1517	-0.1	-3
	2115	3.7	113		2214	4.1	125
12 W	0305	0.1	3	27 Th	0354	-0.1	-3
	0942	3.4	104		1045	4.1	125
	1504	0.3	9		1604	0.2	6
	2156	3.7	113		2305	3.8	116
13 Th	0338	0.1	3	28 F	0430	0.1	3
	1026	3.4	104		1137	3.8	116
	1545	0.3	9		1653	0.4	12
	2242	3.6	110		2356	3.4	104
14 F	0413	0.1	3	29 Sa	0511	0.3	9
	1114	3.5	107		1229	3.6	110
	1630	0.4	12		1751	0.6	18
	2332	3.5	107				
15 Sa	0455	0.1	3	30 Su ◐	0046	3.1	94
	1203	3.6	110		0557	0.4	12
	1723	0.5	15		1320	3.4	104
					1906	0.8	24
				31 M	0136	2.9	88
					0652	0.5	15
					1412	3.3	101
					2025	0.8	24

August

Day	Time	ft	cm	Day	Time	ft	cm
1 Tu	0229	2.7	82	16 W	0202	3.2	98
	0750	0.6	18		0720	0.0	0
	1507	3.2	98		1434	3.8	116
	2124	0.7	21		2120	0.2	6
2 W	0326	2.6	79	17 Th	0306	3.2	98
	0848	0.5	15		0832	-0.1	-3
	1605	3.2	98		1541	3.9	119
	2210	0.6	18		2225	0.1	3
3 Th	0424	2.6	79	18 F	0413	3.4	104
	0942	0.4	12		0940	-0.2	-6
	1656	3.2	98		1646	4.1	125
	2252	0.4	12		2317	-0.1	-3
4 F	0514	2.8	85	19 Sa	0514	3.6	110
	1030	0.3	9		1042	-0.3	-9
	1740	3.3	101		1745	4.3	131
	2332	0.2	6				
5 Sa	0557	2.9	88	20 Su	0005	-0.3	-9
	1116	0.1	3		0610	3.9	119
	1819	3.5	107		1137	-0.4	-12
					1837	4.4	134
6 Su	0012	0.1	3	21 M ●	0050	-0.4	-12
	0637	3.1	94		0701	4.1	125
	1200	0.0	0		1230	-0.5	-15
	1855	3.6	110		1927	4.4	134
7 M ○	0051	-0.1	-3	22 Tu	0130	-0.4	-12
	0715	3.3	101		0751	4.2	128
	1243	-0.1	-3		1321	-0.5	-15
	1932	3.7	113		2014	4.3	131
8 Tu	0128	-0.2	-6	23 W	0206	-0.4	-12
	0753	3.4	104		0839	4.2	128
	1325	-0.1	-3		1409	-0.4	-12
	2010	3.7	113		2101	4.1	125
9 W	0203	-0.2	-6	24 Th	0239	-0.3	-9
	0833	3.5	107		0926	4.1	125
	1406	-0.2	-6		1453	-0.2	-6
	2050	3.7	113		2147	3.8	116
10 Th	0236	-0.3	-9	25 F	0312	-0.2	-6
	0915	3.5	107		1014	3.9	119
	1446	-0.1	-3		1535	-0.1	-3
	2133	3.6	110		2234	3.4	104
11 F	0309	-0.3	-9	26 Sa	0346	-0.1	-3
	1000	3.6	110		1103	3.6	110
	1527	-0.1	-3		1618	0.2	6
	2220	3.5	107		2321	3.1	94
12 Sa	0345	-0.3	-9	27 Su	0424	0.1	3
	1048	3.6	110		1152	3.4	104
	1612	0.0	0		1705	0.4	12
	2311	3.4	104				
13 Su	0427	-0.2	-6	28 M	0010	2.8	85
	1140	3.6	110		0508	0.3	9
	1704	0.2	6		1240	3.1	94
					1804	0.6	18
14 M ◐	0005	3.3	101	29 Tu ◐	0058	2.6	79
	0515	-0.2	-6		0559	0.4	12
	1234	3.7	113		1329	2.9	88
	1810	0.3	9		1921	0.7	21
15 Tu	0102	3.2	98	30 W	0148	2.5	76
	0613	-0.1	-3		0702	0.5	15
	1332	3.7	113		1421	2.8	85
	1941	0.3	9		2040	0.6	18
				31 Th	0242	2.4	73
					0811	0.5	15
					1519	2.8	85
					2138	0.5	15

September

Day	Time	ft	cm	Day	Time	ft	cm
1 F	0341	2.5	76	16 Sa	0359	3.4	104
	0915	0.4	12		0947	0.0	0
	1615	2.9	88		1633	3.8	116
	2223	0.3	9		2310	-0.1	-3
2 Sa	0436	2.6	79	17 Su	0500	3.7	113
	1009	0.2	6		1046	-0.2	-6
	1703	3.0	91		1730	4.0	122
	2303	0.1	3		2349	-0.2	-6
3 Su	0522	2.9	88	18 M	0554	4.0	122
	1056	0.0	0		1136	-0.3	-9
	1744	3.2	98		1821	4.1	125
	2340	-0.1	-3				
4 M	0604	3.1	94	19 Tu	0023	-0.3	-9
	1140	-0.2	-6		0643	4.1	125
	1823	3.5	107		1221	-0.3	-9
					1907	4.1	125
5 Tu	0016	-0.3	-9	20 W ●	0054	-0.3	-9
	0643	3.4	104		0730	4.2	128
	1222	-0.3	-9		1305	-0.4	-12
	1902	3.6	110		1952	4.0	122
6 W	0052	-0.4	-12	21 Th	0125	-0.3	-9
	0724	3.6	110		0814	4.2	128
	1304	-0.4	-12		1347	-0.3	-9
	1943	3.7	113		2035	3.8	116
7 Th	0127	-0.5	-15	22 F	0158	-0.3	-9
	0805	3.8	116		0858	4.0	122
	1347	-0.4	-12		1427	-0.2	-6
	2025	3.8	116		2118	3.6	110
8 F	0203	-0.6	-18	23 Sa	0232	-0.2	-6
	0848	3.9	119		0941	3.8	116
	1429	-0.4	-12		1506	-0.1	-3
	2111	3.7	113		2201	3.3	101
9 Sa	0240	-0.6	-18	24 Su	0308	-0.1	-3
	0935	3.9	119		1025	3.5	107
	1512	-0.4	-12		1546	0.1	3
	2200	3.6	110		2246	3.0	91
10 Su	0320	-0.5	-15	25 M	0346	0.1	3
	1025	3.9	119		1111	3.3	101
	1557	-0.2	-6		1629	0.3	9
	2252	3.4	104		2332	2.7	82
11 M	0403	-0.4	-12	26 Tu	0428	0.3	9
	1119	3.8	116		1157	3.0	91
	1650	0.0	0		1719	0.5	15
	2349	3.3	101				
12 Tu	0452	-0.2	-6	27 W ◐	0020	2.6	79
	1217	3.7	113		0517	0.5	15
	1758	0.2	6		1245	2.8	85
					1824	0.7	21
13 W ○	0048	3.2	98	28 Th	0108	2.5	76
	0552	0.0	0		0617	0.6	18
	1317	3.7	113		1333	2.7	82
	2005	0.3	9		1949	0.7	21
14 Th	0149	3.2	98	29 F	0159	2.4	73
	0705	0.1	3		0731	0.6	18
	1420	3.7	113		1426	2.7	82
	2128	0.2	6		2058	0.6	18
15 F	0253	3.2	98	30 Sa	0254	2.5	76
	0829	0.1	3		0845	0.5	15
	1528	3.7	113		1523	2.8	85
	2224	0.0	0		2147	0.4	12

Time meridian 75° W. 0000 is midnight. 1200 is noon. Times are not adjusted for Daylight Saving Time.
Heights are referred to mean lower low water which is the chart datum of soundings.

Newport, Rhode Island, 2017

Times and Heights of High and Low Waters

October

Day	Time	Height (ft)	Height (cm)
1 Su	0351	2.7	82
	0945	0.3	9
	1617	3.0	91
	2226	0.2	6
2 M	0443	3.0	91
	1033	0.1	3
	1705	3.2	98
	2302	-0.1	-3
3 Tu	0529	3.4	104
	1117	-0.1	-3
	1749	3.5	107
	2337	-0.3	-9
4 W	0612	3.7	113
	1200	-0.3	-9
	1833	3.7	113
5 Th ○	0013	-0.5	-15
	0655	4.0	122
	1243	-0.5	-15
	1917	3.9	119
6 F	0051	-0.6	-18
	0739	4.2	128
	1328	-0.5	-15
	2002	4.0	122
7 Sa	0132	-0.7	-21
	0824	4.3	131
	1413	-0.5	-15
	2050	3.9	119
8 Su	0214	-0.6	-18
	0913	4.4	134
	1459	-0.4	-12
	2141	3.8	116
9 M	0258	-0.5	-15
	1005	4.3	131
	1547	-0.2	-6
	2236	3.7	113
10 Tu	0344	-0.3	-9
	1101	4.1	125
	1641	0.0	0
	2334	3.5	107
11 W	0436	-0.1	-3
	1201	3.9	119
	1759	0.3	9
12 Th ◑	0035	3.5	107
	0538	0.2	6
	1303	3.8	116
	2011	0.3	9
13 F	0136	3.4	104
	0701	0.4	12
	1406	3.7	113
	2119	0.3	9
14 Sa	0240	3.5	107
	0854	0.4	12
	1512	3.7	113
	2211	0.2	6
15 Su	0344	3.7	113
	1005	0.2	6
	1616	3.7	113
	2253	0.1	3
16 M	0444	3.9	119
	1054	0.1	3
	1712	3.8	116
	2325	0.0	0
17 Tu	0536	4.1	125
	1134	0.0	0
	1801	3.9	119
	2350	0.0	0
18 W	0624	4.2	128
	1210	0.0	0
	1846	3.9	119
19 Th ●	0016	-0.1	-3
	0708	4.3	131
	1246	-0.1	-3
	1928	3.8	116
20 F	0046	-0.1	-3
	0750	4.3	131
	1324	-0.1	-3
	2009	3.7	113
21 Sa	0121	-0.1	-3
	0830	4.1	125
	1402	0.0	0
	2050	3.5	107
22 Su	0158	0.0	0
	0910	3.9	119
	1440	0.1	3
	2130	3.3	101
23 M	0236	0.1	3
	0949	3.6	110
	1519	0.2	6
	2212	3.1	94
24 Tu	0315	0.3	9
	1031	3.4	104
	1559	0.4	12
	2256	2.9	88
25 W	0356	0.4	12
	1114	3.1	94
	1643	0.6	18
	2342	2.7	82
26 Th	0441	0.6	18
	1200	3.0	91
	1736	0.7	21
27 F ◐	0030	2.7	82
	0536	0.8	24
	1248	2.9	88
	1845	0.8	24
28 Sa	0118	2.7	82
	0645	0.8	24
	1337	2.9	88
	1959	0.7	21
29 Su	0209	2.8	85
	0805	0.8	24
	1431	3.0	91
	2055	0.5	15
30 M	0305	3.0	91
	0912	0.6	18
	1528	3.1	94
	2139	0.3	9
31 Tu	0401	3.3	101
	1005	0.3	9
	1624	3.3	101
	2218	0.0	0

November

Day	Time	Height (ft)	Height (cm)
1 W	0453	3.7	113
	1052	0.0	0
	1716	3.6	110
	2257	-0.2	-6
2 Th	0541	4.1	125
	1137	-0.2	-6
	1804	3.9	119
	2338	-0.4	-12
3 F	0628	4.5	137
	1223	-0.4	-12
	1853	4.1	125
4 Sa ○	0020	-0.6	-18
	0715	4.7	143
	1311	-0.4	-12
	1941	4.2	128
5 Su	0105	-0.6	-18
	0804	4.8	146
	1400	-0.4	-12
	2032	4.2	128
6 M	0152	-0.6	-18
	0854	4.8	146
	1450	-0.3	-9
	2124	4.1	125
7 Tu	0240	-0.4	-12
	0948	4.7	143
	1540	-0.1	-3
	2220	4.0	122
8 W	0330	-0.2	-6
	1045	4.4	134
	1636	0.1	3
	2319	3.9	119
9 Th	0424	0.1	3
	1145	4.2	128
	1801	0.4	12
10 F ○	0019	3.8	116
	0528	0.4	12
	1247	4.0	122
	1950	0.4	12
11 Sa	0120	3.8	116
	0709	0.6	18
	1348	3.8	116
	2056	0.4	12
12 Su	0222	3.8	116
	0905	0.6	18
	1450	3.7	113
	2147	0.4	12
13 M	0324	3.9	119
	1006	0.5	15
	1552	3.6	110
	2226	0.3	9
14 Tu	0423	4.0	122
	1050	0.4	12
	1649	3.6	110
	2253	0.3	9
15 W	0516	4.1	125
	1125	0.4	12
	1739	3.7	113
	2315	0.3	9
16 Th	0603	4.2	128
	1156	0.3	9
	1823	3.7	113
	2341	0.2	6
17 F	0646	4.3	131
	1228	0.2	6
	1905	3.7	113
18 Sa ●	0013	0.2	6
	0726	4.2	128
	1303	0.2	6
	1945	3.6	110
19 Su	0050	0.1	3
	0804	4.1	125
	1340	0.2	6
	2023	3.5	107
20 M	0130	0.2	6
	0841	4.0	122
	1419	0.2	6
	2102	3.4	104
21 Tu	0210	0.2	6
	0918	3.8	116
	1457	0.3	9
	2141	3.2	98
22 W	0250	0.4	12
	0956	3.5	107
	1535	0.4	12
	2222	3.0	91
23 Th	0330	0.5	15
	1036	3.4	104
	1614	0.6	18
	2306	2.9	88
24 F	0412	0.7	21
	1120	3.2	98
	1657	0.7	21
	2352	2.9	88
25 Sa	0459	0.8	24
	1207	3.1	94
	1748	0.7	21
26 Su ◐	0040	2.9	88
	0559	0.9	27
	1256	3.1	94
	1847	0.7	21
27 M	0129	3.1	94
	0712	0.9	27
	1348	3.1	94
	1948	0.6	18
28 Tu	0223	3.3	101
	0829	0.7	21
	1445	3.2	98
	2043	0.4	12
29 W	0320	3.6	110
	0933	0.5	15
	1546	3.4	104
	2133	0.1	3
30 Th	0418	3.9	119
	1027	0.2	6
	1645	3.6	110
	2220	-0.1	-3

December

Day	Time	Height (ft)	Height (cm)
1 F	0513	4.3	131
	1116	-0.1	-3
	1739	3.9	119
	2307	-0.4	-12
2 Sa	0605	4.7	143
	1206	-0.2	-6
	1831	4.2	128
	2354	-0.5	-15
3 Su ○	0656	5.0	152
	1258	-0.4	-12
	1923	4.3	131
4 M	0044	-0.6	-18
	0747	5.1	155
	1350	-0.4	-12
	2015	4.4	134
5 Tu	0135	-0.5	-15
	0839	5.0	152
	1442	-0.3	-9
	2108	4.4	134
6 W	0227	-0.4	-12
	0933	4.9	149
	1533	-0.2	-6
	2203	4.3	131
7 Th	0319	-0.2	-6
	1029	4.6	140
	1626	0.1	3
	2301	4.1	125
8 F	0413	0.1	3
	1127	4.3	131
	1731	0.3	9
9 Sa	0000	4.0	122
	0516	0.5	15
	1225	4.0	122
	1903	0.4	12
10 Su ◐	0059	3.9	119
	0655	0.7	21
	1323	3.7	113
	2015	0.5	15
11 M	0158	3.9	119
	0846	0.7	21
	1422	3.5	107
	2108	0.5	15
12 Tu	0258	3.9	119
	0948	0.7	21
	1523	3.4	104
	2147	0.5	15
13 W	0358	3.9	119
	1034	0.6	18
	1622	3.3	101
	2214	0.5	15
14 Th	0453	3.9	119
	1109	0.6	18
	1714	3.4	104
	2240	0.4	12
15 F	0541	4.0	122
	1138	0.5	15
	1800	3.4	104
	2311	0.4	12
16 Sa	0624	4.0	122
	1210	0.4	12
	1842	3.4	104
	2348	0.3	9
17 Su	0703	4.0	122
	1245	0.3	9
	1921	3.5	107
18 M ●	0027	0.2	6
	0740	4.0	122
	1323	0.2	6
	1959	3.4	104
19 Tu	0109	0.2	6
	0816	3.9	119
	1401	0.2	6
	2035	3.4	104
20 W	0150	0.2	6
	0851	3.8	116
	1438	0.2	6
	2113	3.3	101
21 Th	0230	0.3	9
	0927	3.6	110
	1513	0.3	9
	2151	3.2	98
22 F	0309	0.4	12
	1005	3.5	107
	1547	0.3	9
	2232	3.1	94
23 Sa	0348	0.5	15
	1047	3.4	104
	1623	0.4	12
	2317	3.1	94
24 Su	0430	0.6	18
	1132	3.3	101
	1703	0.4	12
25 M	0004	3.1	94
	0520	0.7	21
	1222	3.2	98
	1751	0.4	12
26 Tu ◐	0054	3.2	98
	0624	0.7	21
	1314	3.2	98
	1849	0.4	12
27 W	0147	3.4	104
	0741	0.7	21
	1411	3.2	98
	1950	0.3	9
28 Th	0245	3.6	110
	0859	0.5	15
	1513	3.3	101
	2050	0.1	3
29 F	0347	3.9	119
	1004	0.2	6
	1618	3.5	107
	2148	-0.2	-6
30 Sa	0449	4.3	131
	1101	0.0	0
	1718	3.8	116
	2242	-0.4	-12
31 Su	0546	4.6	140
	1154	-0.2	-6
	1813	4.0	122
	2335	-0.5	-15

Time meridian 75° W. 0000 is midnight. 1200 is noon. Times are not adjusted for Daylight Saving Time.
Heights are referred to mean lower low water which is the chart datum of soundings.

Montauk, Fort Pond Bay, New York, 2017

Times and Heights of High and Low Waters

January

Day	Time	ft	cm	Day	Time	ft	cm
1 Su	0454	0.0	0	**16** M	0553	-0.2	-6
	1056	2.2	67		1140	2.1	64
	1740	-0.3	-9		1827	-0.3	-9
	2328	1.7	52				
2 M	0547	0.1	3	**17** Tu	0009	2.0	61
	1136	2.1	64		0652	0.0	0
	1828	-0.2	-6		1229	1.9	58
					1919	-0.2	-6
3 Tu	0013	1.7	52	**18** W	0102	1.9	58
	0644	0.1	3		0753	0.1	3
	1220	2.0	61		1321	1.6	49
	1918	-0.2	-6		2011	0.0	0
4 W	0100	1.8	55	**19** Th	0157	1.9	58
	0745	0.1	3		0853	0.2	6
	1308	1.9	58		1416	1.4	43
	2008	-0.2	-6		2101	0.1	3
5 Th	0152	1.9	58	**20** F	0256	1.8	55
	0846	0.0	0		0950	0.2	6
	1404	1.8	55		1516	1.3	40
	2059	-0.2	-6		2150	0.2	6
6 F	0250	2.0	61	**21** Sa	0356	1.8	55
	0946	-0.1	-3		1044	0.2	6
	1506	1.7	52		1616	1.2	37
	2151	-0.2	-6		2237	0.2	6
7 Sa	0351	2.2	67	**22** Su	0453	1.9	58
	1044	-0.3	-9		1134	0.2	6
	1609	1.7	52		1711	1.3	40
	2244	-0.3	-9		2324	0.2	6
8 Su	0449	2.4	73	**23** M	0543	1.9	58
	1142	-0.4	-12		1220	0.1	3
	1708	1.7	52		1800	1.3	40
	2338	-0.4	-12				
9 M	0544	2.6	79	**24** Tu	0010	0.2	6
	1238	-0.6	-18		0628	2.0	61
	1803	1.8	55		1302	0.0	0
					1845	1.4	43
10 Tu	0033	-0.5	-15	**25** W	0055	0.1	3
	0637	2.8	85		0710	2.1	64
	1331	-0.7	-21		1342	-0.1	-3
	1856	1.9	58		1927	1.6	49
11 W	0127	-0.6	-18	**26** Th	0138	0.0	0
	0728	2.8	85		0751	2.2	67
	1422	-0.8	-24		1422	-0.3	-9
	1948	2.0	61		2009	1.7	52
12 Th	0220	-0.6	-18	**27** F	0221	-0.1	-3
	0819	2.8	85		0830	2.3	70
	1511	-0.8	-24		1502	-0.4	-12
	2040	2.1	64		2050	1.7	52
13 F	0312	-0.6	-18	**28** Sa	0304	-0.2	-6
	0910	2.7	82		0909	2.3	70
	1559	-0.8	-24		1542	-0.4	-12
	2132	2.1	64		2132	1.8	55
14 Sa	0404	-0.5	-15	**29** Su	0348	-0.2	-6
	1000	2.6	79		0949	2.3	70
	1648	-0.7	-21		1624	-0.5	-15
	2225	2.1	64		2214	1.9	58
15 Su	0457	-0.4	-12	**30** M	0435	-0.2	-6
	1050	2.4	73		1029	2.2	67
	1737	-0.5	-15		1707	-0.4	-12
	2317	2.1	64		2257	2.0	61
				31 Tu	0526	-0.2	-6
					1111	2.2	67
					1753	-0.4	-12
					2341	2.0	61

February

Day	Time	ft	cm	Day	Time	ft	cm
1 W	0622	-0.2	-6	**16** Th	0026	2.1	64
	1156	2.0	61		0713	0.1	3
	1843	-0.3	-9		1246	1.6	49
					1923	0.2	6
2 Th	0028	2.1	64	**17** F	0117	2.0	61
	0723	-0.2	-6		0810	0.2	6
	1244	1.9	58		1338	1.5	46
	1935	-0.2	-6		2014	0.3	9
3 F	0120	2.1	64	**18** Sa	0213	1.9	58
	0824	-0.2	-6		0906	0.3	9
	1339	1.7	52		1435	1.3	40
	2030	-0.2	-6		2106	0.4	12
4 Sa	0220	2.2	67	**19** Su	0314	1.8	55
	0926	-0.2	-6		1000	0.3	9
	1442	1.6	49		1538	1.3	40
	2127	-0.2	-6		2158	0.4	12
5 Su	0325	2.2	67	**20** M	0417	1.8	55
	1026	-0.3	-9		1052	0.3	9
	1548	1.6	49		1639	1.3	40
	2225	-0.2	-6		2250	0.4	12
6 M	0431	2.3	70	**21** Tu	0513	1.9	58
	1125	-0.4	-12		1141	0.2	6
	1651	1.7	52		1732	1.4	43
	2324	-0.3	-9		2340	0.3	9
7 Tu	0531	2.4	73	**22** W	0601	2.0	61
	1222	-0.5	-15		1226	0.1	3
	1749	1.8	55		1818	1.6	49
8 W	0022	-0.4	-12	**23** Th	0028	0.2	6
	0625	2.5	76		0643	2.1	64
	1315	-0.6	-18		1309	0.0	0
	1842	1.9	58		1900	1.7	52
9 Th	0118	-0.5	-15	**24** F	0114	0.0	0
	0716	2.6	79		0723	2.2	67
	1405	-0.6	-18		1350	-0.2	-6
	1933	2.1	64		1940	1.9	58
10 F	0210	-0.5	-15	**25** Sa	0159	-0.2	-6
	0804	2.6	79		0801	2.3	70
	1451	-0.7	-21		1431	-0.3	-9
	2023	2.2	67		2020	2.1	64
11 Sa	0300	-0.5	-15	**26** Su	0243	-0.3	-9
	0852	2.5	76		0840	2.4	73
	1536	-0.6	-18		1511	-0.4	-12
	2112	2.2	67		2101	2.2	67
12 Su	0348	-0.5	-15	**27** M	0329	-0.4	-12
	0939	2.4	73		0921	2.4	73
	1620	-0.5	-15		1552	-0.5	-15
	2201	2.3	70		2143	2.3	70
13 M	0437	-0.4	-12	**28** Tu	0416	-0.4	-12
	1026	2.2	67		1003	2.4	73
	1703	-0.4	-12		1635	-0.4	-12
	2249	2.2	67		2227	2.4	73
14 Tu	0526	-0.2	-6				
	1112	2.1	64				
	1748	-0.2	-6				
	2337	2.2	67				
15 W	0618	0.0	0				
	1158	1.9	58				
	1834	0.0	0				

March

Day	Time	ft	cm	Day	Time	ft	cm
1 W	0507	-0.4	-12	**16** Th	0545	0.0	0
	1048	2.3	70		1130	1.9	58
	1721	-0.3	-9		1750	0.3	9
	2313	2.5	76		2351	2.3	70
2 Th	0603	-0.4	-12	**17** F	0635	0.2	6
	1135	2.2	67		1216	1.8	55
	1811	-0.2	-6		1836	0.4	12
3 F	0002	2.5	76	**18** Sa	0039	2.1	64
	0702	-0.3	-9		0728	0.3	9
	1226	2.0	61		1306	1.6	49
	1907	-0.1	-3		1928	0.6	18
4 Sa	0056	2.4	73	**19** Su	0132	2.0	61
	0804	-0.2	-6		0823	0.4	12
	1321	1.8	55		1400	1.5	46
	2007	0.0	0		2025	0.6	18
5 Su	0157	2.4	73	**20** M	0231	1.9	58
	0907	-0.2	-6		0918	0.4	12
	1424	1.7	52		1502	1.5	46
	2110	0.0	0		2122	0.6	18
6 M	0305	2.3	70	**21** Tu	0335	1.9	58
	1008	-0.2	-6		1010	0.4	12
	1532	1.7	52		1605	1.5	46
	2213	0.0	0		2217	0.6	18
7 Tu	0415	2.3	70	**22** W	0435	1.9	58
	1107	-0.2	-6		1059	0.4	12
	1638	1.8	55		1701	1.6	49
	2315	0.0	0		2310	0.5	15
8 W	0518	2.3	70	**23** Th	0525	2.0	61
	1204	-0.2	-6		1146	0.2	6
	1737	1.9	58		1748	1.8	55
9 Th	0014	-0.1	-3	**24** F	0000	0.3	9
	0613	2.4	73		0609	2.1	64
	1256	-0.3	-9		1231	0.1	3
	1830	2.1	64		1829	2.0	61
10 F	0110	-0.2	-6	**25** Sa	0048	0.1	3
	0702	2.4	73		0649	2.3	70
	1344	-0.3	-9		1314	-0.1	-3
	1918	2.3	70		1908	2.3	70
11 Sa	0200	-0.3	-9	**26** Su	0135	-0.1	-3
	0747	2.4	73		0729	2.4	73
	1428	-0.3	-9		1356	-0.2	-6
	2004	2.4	73		1948	2.5	76
12 Su	0247	-0.3	-9	**27** M	0222	-0.3	-9
	0832	2.4	73		0810	2.5	76
	1509	-0.3	-9		1438	-0.3	-9
	2050	2.5	76		2029	2.7	82
13 M	0331	-0.3	-9	**28** Tu	0309	-0.4	-12
	0916	2.3	70		0853	2.5	76
	1549	-0.2	-6		1521	-0.3	-9
	2135	2.5	76		2113	2.8	85
14 Tu	0415	-0.2	-6	**29** W	0358	-0.5	-15
	1000	2.2	67		0939	2.5	76
	1628	-0.1	-3		1605	-0.3	-9
	2220	2.5	76		2159	2.9	88
15 W	0459	-0.1	-3	**30** Th	0449	-0.5	-15
	1045	2.1	64		1027	2.4	73
	1708	0.1	3		1653	-0.2	-6
	2305	2.4	73		2249	2.9	88
				31 F	0544	-0.4	-12
					1117	2.3	70
					1745	-0.1	-3
					2341	2.9	88

Time meridian 75° W. 0000 is midnight. 1200 is noon. Times are not adjusted for Daylight Saving Time.
Heights are referred to mean lower low water which is the chart datum of soundings.

Montauk, Fort Pond Bay, New York, 2017

Times and Heights of High and Low Waters

April

Day	Time	ft	cm		Day	Time	ft	cm
1 Sa	0643	-0.3	-9		16 Su	0007	2.3	70
	1210	2.2	67			0653	0.3	9
	1845	0.1	3			1239	1.8	55
						1850	0.7	21
2 Su	0037	2.7	82		17 M	0056	2.2	67
	0745	-0.2	-6			0746	0.4	12
	1307	2.0	61			1331	1.7	52
	1950	0.2	6			1949	0.8	24
3 M	0138	2.5	76		18 Tu	0149	2.1	64
	0847	-0.1	-3			0839	0.5	15
	1410	2.0	61			1429	1.7	52
	2056	0.2	6			2048	0.8	24
4 Tu	0247	2.4	73		19 W	0248	2.0	61
	0948	0.0	0			0930	0.5	15
	1518	1.9	58			1529	1.7	52
	2202	0.2	6			2145	0.7	21
5 W	0357	2.3	70		20 Th	0347	2.0	61
	1047	0.0	0			1019	0.4	12
	1625	2.0	61			1625	1.9	58
	2306	0.2	6			2239	0.6	18
6 Th	0502	2.3	70		21 F	0441	2.1	64
	1142	0.0	0			1105	0.3	9
	1725	2.2	67			1712	2.1	64
						2331	0.4	12
7 F	0006	0.1	3		22 Sa	0528	2.2	67
	0557	2.3	70			1151	0.2	6
	1233	0.0	0			1754	2.3	70
	1815	2.3	70					
8 Sa	0100	0.1	3		23 Su	0022	0.2	6
	0643	2.3	70			0611	2.3	70
	1319	0.0	0			1236	0.0	0
	1900	2.5	76			1834	2.6	79
9 Su	0148	0.0	0		24 M	0111	-0.1	-3
	0726	2.2	67			0655	2.4	73
	1401	0.0	0			1321	-0.1	-3
	1943	2.6	79			1916	2.9	88
10 M	0232	-0.1	-3		25 Tu	0201	-0.3	-9
	0808	2.2	67			0739	2.5	76
	1440	0.1	3			1405	-0.2	-6
	2025	2.7	82			2000	3.1	94
11 Tu	0312	-0.1	-3		26 W	0250	-0.5	-15
	0851	2.2	67			0826	2.5	76
	1517	0.1	3			1451	-0.2	-6
	2108	2.7	82			2046	3.2	98
12 W	0352	0.0	0		27 Th	0340	-0.6	-18
	0934	2.1	64			0915	2.5	76
	1553	0.2	6			1538	-0.2	-6
	2151	2.7	82			2136	3.3	101
13 Th	0433	0.0	0		28 F	0432	-0.5	-15
	1019	2.1	64			1006	2.5	76
	1630	0.4	12			1629	-0.1	-3
	2235	2.6	79			2229	3.2	98
14 F	0516	0.1	3		29 Sa	0527	-0.5	-15
	1104	2.0	61			1059	2.4	73
	1710	0.5	15			1725	0.0	0
	2320	2.5	76			2323	3.1	94
15 Sa	0602	0.2	6		30 Su	0625	-0.3	-9
	1151	1.9	58			1155	2.3	70
	1756	0.6	18			1827	0.1	3

May

Day	Time	ft	cm		Day	Time	ft	cm
1 M	0020	2.9	88		16 Tu	0024	2.3	70
	0725	-0.2	-6			0712	0.4	12
	1253	2.2	67			1304	1.8	55
	1934	0.3	9			1918	0.8	24
2 Tu	0121	2.6	79		17 W	0110	2.2	67
	0826	-0.1	-3			0803	0.4	12
	1356	2.2	67			1356	1.8	55
	2042	0.4	12			2017	0.8	24
3 W	0225	2.4	73		18 Th	0200	2.1	64
	0925	0.0	0			0852	0.4	12
	1502	2.2	67			1450	1.9	58
	2149	0.4	12			2114	0.7	21
4 Th	0333	2.2	67		19 F	0255	2.1	64
	1021	0.1	3			0939	0.3	9
	1608	2.2	67			1543	2.1	64
	2253	0.4	12			2209	0.6	18
5 F	0438	2.1	64		20 Sa	0351	2.1	64
	1115	0.2	6			1032	0.3	9
	1707	2.4	73			1632	2.3	70
	2352	0.3	9			2302	0.4	12
6 Sa	0533	2.1	64		21 Su	0444	2.1	64
	1204	0.2	6			1112	0.2	6
	1756	2.5	76			1717	2.6	79
						2356	0.1	3
7 Su	0045	0.3	9		22 M	0534	2.2	67
	0619	2.0	61			1159	0.1	3
	1249	0.2	6			1802	2.8	85
	1839	2.6	79					
8 M	0132	0.2	6		23 Tu	0048	-0.1	-3
	0702	2.0	61			0622	2.3	70
	1330	0.3	9			1247	0.0	0
	1920	2.7	82			1847	3.1	94
9 Tu	0213	0.1	3		24 W	0140	-0.3	-9
	0743	2.0	61			0711	2.4	73
	1408	0.3	9			1336	-0.1	-3
	2001	2.7	82			1934	3.3	101
10 W	0251	0.1	3		25 Th	0231	-0.5	-15
	0826	2.0	61			0801	2.5	76
	1445	0.4	12			1425	-0.2	-6
	2042	2.7	82			2024	3.4	104
11 Th	0329	0.1	3		26 F	0322	-0.6	-18
	0909	2.0	61			0852	2.5	76
	1521	0.4	12			1517	-0.2	-6
	2125	2.7	82			2117	3.4	104
12 F	0408	0.1	3		27 Sa	0414	-0.6	-18
	0954	2.0	61			0946	2.5	76
	1559	0.5	15			1610	-0.2	-6
	2209	2.6	79			2211	3.3	101
13 Sa	0449	0.2	6		28 Su	0508	-0.5	-15
	1041	2.0	61			1042	2.5	76
	1639	0.6	18			1708	0.0	0
	2254	2.5	76			2306	3.1	94
14 Su	0534	0.2	6		29 M	0604	-0.3	-9
	1127	1.9	58			1138	2.4	73
	1726	0.7	21			1810	0.1	3
	2338	2.4	73					
15 M	0622	0.3	9		30 Tu	0003	2.9	88
	1215	1.9	58			0702	-0.2	-6
	1819	0.8	24			1236	2.4	73
						1917	0.3	9
					31 W	0100	2.6	79
						0800	-0.1	-3
						1337	2.3	70
						2025	0.4	12

June

Day	Time	ft	cm		Day	Time	ft	cm
1 Th	0200	2.3	70		16 F	0119	2.2	67
	0857	0.1	3			0816	0.3	9
	1440	2.3	70			1409	2.1	64
	2130	0.4	12			2045	0.6	18
2 F	0302	2.1	64		17 Sa	0209	2.1	64
	0951	0.2	6			0903	0.3	9
	1543	2.4	73			1500	2.2	67
	2233	0.4	12			2142	0.5	15
3 Sa	0404	2.0	61		18 Su	0306	2.1	64
	1042	0.3	9			0949	0.2	6
	1641	2.4	73			1552	2.4	73
	2332	0.4	12			2237	0.3	9
4 Su	0501	1.9	58		19 M	0405	2.1	64
	1131	0.4	12			1037	0.2	6
	1731	2.5	76			1644	2.7	82
						2332	0.1	3
5 M	0024	0.4	12		20 Tu	0501	2.1	64
	0550	1.8	55			1127	0.1	3
	1216	0.4	12			1734	3.0	91
	1815	2.6	79					
6 Tu	0110	0.3	9		21 W	0027	-0.1	-3
	0635	1.8	55			0554	2.2	67
	1257	0.5	15			1219	0.0	0
	1856	2.6	79			1824	3.2	98
7 W	0150	0.3	9		22 Th	0121	-0.3	-9
	0717	1.9	58			0646	2.3	70
	1337	0.5	15			1312	-0.1	-3
	1937	2.7	82			1914	3.3	101
8 Th	0228	0.2	6		23 F	0213	-0.5	-15
	0800	1.9	58			0739	2.4	73
	1415	0.5	15			1406	-0.2	-6
	2019	2.7	82			2006	3.4	104
9 F	0305	0.2	6		24 Sa	0304	-0.5	-15
	0845	1.9	58			0832	2.5	76
	1453	0.5	15			1500	-0.2	-6
	2102	2.7	82			2100	3.4	104
10 Sa	0343	0.1	3		25 Su	0355	-0.5	-15
	0930	2.0	61			0927	2.5	76
	1533	0.5	15			1554	-0.2	-6
	2145	2.6	79			2154	3.2	98
11 Su	0424	0.1	3		26 M	0447	-0.5	-15
	1017	2.0	61			1023	2.5	76
	1616	0.6	18			1652	-0.1	-3
	2229	2.6	79			2248	3.1	94
12 M	0506	0.2	6		27 Tu	0540	-0.3	-9
	1104	2.0	61			1119	2.5	76
	1702	0.6	18			1752	0.1	3
	2312	2.5	76			2342	2.8	85
13 Tu	0552	0.2	6		28 W	0635	-0.2	-6
	1150	2.0	61			1215	2.5	76
	1753	0.7	21			1856	0.2	6
	2353	2.4	73					
14 W	0639	0.2	6		29 Th	0035	2.5	76
	1235	2.0	61			0730	0.0	0
	1850	0.7	21			1312	2.5	76
						2001	0.4	12
15 Th	0035	2.3	70		30 F	0130	2.2	67
	0728	0.3	9			0824	0.1	3
	1321	2.0	61			1410	2.4	73
	1948	0.7	21			2105	0.5	15

Time meridian 75° W. 0000 is midnight. 1200 is noon. Times are not adjusted for Daylight Saving Time.
Heights are referred to mean lower low water which is the chart datum of soundings.

Montauk, Fort Pond Bay, New York, 2017

Times and Heights of High and Low Waters

July

Day	Time (h m)	Height ft	Height cm
1 Sa	0227	2.0	61
	0917	0.3	9
	1510	2.4	73
	2205	0.5	15
2 Su	0327	1.8	55
	1007	0.4	12
	1608	2.4	73
	2303	0.5	15
3 M	0426	1.7	52
	1055	0.5	15
	1701	2.4	73
	2355	0.5	15
4 Tu	0520	1.7	52
	1141	0.6	18
	1749	2.5	76
5 W	0042	0.4	12
	0607	1.7	52
	1224	0.6	18
	1832	2.5	76
6 Th	0122	0.4	12
	0652	1.8	55
	1307	0.6	18
	1915	2.6	79
7 F	0201	0.3	9
	0736	1.9	58
	1348	0.5	15
	1957	2.6	79
8 Sa ○	0238	0.2	6
	0820	1.9	58
	1429	0.5	15
	2039	2.6	79
9 Su	0317	0.1	3
	0905	2.0	61
	1511	0.4	12
	2121	2.6	79
10 M	0356	0.1	3
	0951	2.0	61
	1554	0.5	15
	2203	2.6	79
11 Tu	0437	0.1	3
	1036	2.1	64
	1640	0.5	15
	2243	2.5	76
12 W	0520	0.1	3
	1119	2.1	64
	1729	0.5	15
	2323	2.4	73
13 Th	0605	0.1	3
	1202	2.1	64
	1824	0.5	15
14 F	0003	2.3	70
	0652	0.2	6
	1245	2.2	67
	1921	0.5	15
15 Sa	0046	2.2	67
	0740	0.2	6
	1330	2.3	70
	2020	0.5	15
16 Su ○	0135	2.1	64
	0829	0.3	9
	1421	2.4	73
	2118	0.4	12
17 M	0232	2.0	61
	0918	0.2	6
	1518	2.6	79
	2215	0.2	6
18 Tu	0334	2.0	61
	1010	0.2	6
	1616	2.8	85
	2312	0.1	3
19 W	0435	2.1	64
	1104	0.1	3
	1712	3.0	91
20 Th	0008	-0.1	-3
	0533	2.1	64
	1200	0.0	0
	1806	3.1	94
21 F	0103	-0.2	-6
	0627	2.3	70
	1256	-0.1	-3
	1859	3.3	101
22 Sa	0155	-0.4	-12
	0720	2.4	73
	1352	-0.2	-6
	1951	3.3	101
23 Su ●	0245	-0.4	-12
	0814	2.5	76
	1446	-0.2	-6
	2043	3.2	98
24 M	0334	-0.4	-12
	0908	2.6	79
	1540	-0.2	-6
	2135	3.1	94
25 Tu	0423	-0.4	-12
	1002	2.7	82
	1634	-0.1	-3
	2226	2.9	88
26 W	0512	-0.2	-6
	1055	2.7	82
	1731	0.1	3
	2317	2.7	82
27 Th	0603	-0.1	-3
	1148	2.6	79
	1830	0.3	9
28 F	0007	2.4	73
	0655	0.1	3
	1241	2.6	79
	1931	0.4	12
29 Sa	0058	2.2	67
	0747	0.3	9
	1335	2.5	76
	2032	0.5	15
30 Su ☽	0152	1.9	58
	0839	0.5	15
	1432	2.4	73
	2131	0.6	18
31 M	0250	1.8	55
	0930	0.6	18
	1531	2.4	73
	2227	0.6	18

August

Day	Time (h m)	Height ft	Height cm
1 Tu	0351	1.7	52
	1019	0.7	21
	1629	2.4	73
	2319	0.6	18
2 W	0449	1.7	52
	1107	0.7	21
	1722	2.4	73
3 Th	0006	0.6	18
	0541	1.7	52
	1154	0.7	21
	1809	2.5	76
4 F	0049	0.5	15
	0627	1.8	55
	1239	0.6	18
	1852	2.5	76
5 Sa	0129	0.4	12
	0711	2.0	61
	1323	0.5	15
	1934	2.6	79
6 Su	0207	0.3	9
	0754	2.1	64
	1406	0.4	12
	2014	2.6	79
7 M ○	0246	0.2	6
	0837	2.2	67
	1449	0.4	12
	2054	2.7	82
8 Tu	0325	0.1	3
	0920	2.3	70
	1532	0.3	9
	2133	2.6	79
9 W	0405	0.1	3
	1002	2.3	70
	1617	0.3	9
	2213	2.6	79
10 Th	0446	0.1	3
	1044	2.4	73
	1706	0.3	9
	2253	2.5	76
11 F	0530	0.1	3
	1126	2.5	76
	1800	0.4	12
	2335	2.4	73
12 Sa	0616	0.2	6
	1209	2.5	76
	1857	0.4	12
13 Su	0020	2.3	70
	0706	0.3	9
	1256	2.6	79
	1957	0.4	12
14 M ☽	0111	2.2	67
	0759	0.3	9
	1350	2.6	79
	2057	0.3	9
15 Tu	0209	2.1	64
	0854	0.3	9
	1451	2.7	82
	2156	0.2	6
16 W	0313	2.0	61
	0951	0.3	9
	1555	2.8	85
	2254	0.1	3
17 Th	0417	2.1	64
	1049	0.2	6
	1657	2.9	88
	2351	0.0	0
18 F	0517	2.2	67
	1148	0.1	3
	1753	3.0	91
19 Sa	0045	-0.1	-3
	0613	2.4	73
	1246	0.0	0
	1845	3.1	94
20 Su	0136	-0.2	-6
	0705	2.5	76
	1341	-0.1	-3
	1935	3.1	94
21 M ●	0224	-0.2	-6
	0756	2.7	82
	1434	-0.1	-3
	2024	3.1	94
22 Tu	0311	-0.2	-6
	0847	2.8	85
	1525	-0.1	-3
	2113	2.9	88
23 W	0356	-0.2	-6
	0938	2.8	85
	1615	0.0	0
	2201	2.8	85
24 Th	0441	0.0	0
	1028	2.8	85
	1707	0.1	3
	2249	2.6	79
25 F	0527	0.2	6
	1117	2.8	85
	1801	0.3	9
	2338	2.4	73
26 Sa	0615	0.4	12
	1207	2.7	82
	1857	0.5	15
27 Su	0027	2.2	67
	0705	0.6	18
	1259	2.5	76
	1955	0.6	18
28 M	0119	2.0	61
	0758	0.7	21
	1354	2.4	73
	2053	0.7	21
29 Tu ☽	0215	1.8	55
	0851	0.8	24
	1453	2.3	70
	2148	0.7	21
30 W	0317	1.8	55
	0944	0.9	27
	1555	2.3	70
	2239	0.7	21
31 Th	0419	1.8	55
	1035	0.8	24
	1653	2.3	70
	2327	0.7	21

September

Day	Time (h m)	Height ft	Height cm
1 F	0515	1.9	58
	1125	0.8	24
	1743	2.4	73
2 Sa	0011	0.6	18
	0602	2.0	61
	1212	0.7	21
	1826	2.5	76
3 Su	0052	0.5	15
	0645	2.1	64
	1258	0.6	18
	1906	2.6	79
4 M	0132	0.3	9
	0726	2.3	70
	1342	0.4	12
	1944	2.7	82
5 Tu	0211	0.2	6
	0806	2.4	73
	1425	0.3	9
	2022	2.7	82
6 W ○	0251	0.1	3
	0845	2.6	79
	1509	0.2	6
	2101	2.7	82
7 Th	0330	0.1	3
	0926	2.7	82
	1555	0.2	6
	2142	2.7	82
8 F	0411	0.1	3
	1007	2.8	85
	1644	0.1	3
	2225	2.6	79
9 Sa	0455	0.1	3
	1051	2.8	85
	1737	0.2	6
	2310	2.5	76
10 Su	0543	0.2	6
	1138	2.8	85
	1835	0.2	6
	2359	2.4	73
11 M	0636	0.3	9
	1229	2.8	85
	1936	0.2	6
12 Tu	0053	2.2	67
	0735	0.4	12
	1326	2.8	85
	2038	0.2	6
13 W ☽	0152	2.1	64
	0837	0.4	12
	1431	2.8	85
	2138	0.2	6
14 Th	0258	2.1	64
	0939	0.4	12
	1539	2.8	85
	2236	0.2	6
15 F	0405	2.2	67
	1041	0.4	12
	1644	2.8	85
	2332	0.1	3
16 Sa	0506	2.3	70
	1141	0.3	9
	1741	2.9	88
17 Su	0025	0.0	0
	0601	2.5	76
	1238	0.1	3
	1831	2.9	88
18 M	0115	0.0	0
	0651	2.7	82
	1331	0.1	3
	1918	2.9	88
19 Tu	0201	0.0	0
	0738	2.8	85
	1421	0.0	0
	2004	2.8	85
20 W ●	0244	0.0	0
	0825	2.9	88
	1509	0.0	0
	2049	2.7	82
21 Th	0326	0.1	3
	0912	3.0	91
	1555	0.1	3
	2135	2.6	79
22 F	0408	0.2	6
	0958	2.9	88
	1641	0.2	6
	2221	2.4	73
23 Sa	0449	0.4	12
	1045	2.8	85
	1730	0.3	9
	2309	2.3	70
24 Su	0533	0.6	18
	1133	2.7	82
	1821	0.5	15
	2357	2.1	64
25 M	0621	0.7	21
	1223	2.6	79
	1916	0.6	18
26 Tu	0048	2.0	61
	0715	0.9	27
	1316	2.4	73
	2013	0.7	21
27 W ☽	0144	1.9	58
	0813	1.0	30
	1415	2.3	70
	2107	0.7	21
28 Th	0246	1.8	55
	0910	1.0	30
	1518	2.2	67
	2159	0.7	21
29 F	0350	1.8	55
	1004	0.9	27
	1618	2.3	70
	2246	0.7	21
30 Sa	0447	2.0	61
	1055	0.8	24
	1710	2.3	70
	2331	0.6	18

Time meridian 75° W. 0000 is midnight. 1200 is noon. Times are not adjusted for Daylight Saving Time.
Heights are referred to mean lower low water which is the chart datum of soundings.

Montauk, Fort Pond Bay, New York, 2017

Times and Heights of High and Low Waters

October

Day	Time (h m)	Height (ft)	Height (cm)
1 Su	0535	2.1	64
	1144	0.7	21
	1753	2.4	73
2 M	0013	0.4	12
	0616	2.3	70
	1231	0.5	15
	1832	2.5	76
3 Tu	0054	0.3	9
	0655	2.5	76
	1316	0.3	9
	1910	2.6	79
4 W	0135	0.2	6
	0732	2.7	82
	1401	0.2	6
	1948	2.6	79
5 Th ○	0215	0.1	3
	0811	2.8	85
	1447	0.0	0
	2029	2.7	82
6 F	0256	0.0	0
	0851	3.0	91
	1534	-0.1	-3
	2112	2.6	79
7 Sa	0339	0.0	0
	0935	3.1	94
	1624	-0.1	-3
	2159	2.6	79
8 Su	0424	0.1	3
	1022	3.1	94
	1717	-0.1	-3
	2248	2.5	76
9 M	0514	0.2	6
	1113	3.1	94
	1815	0.0	0
	2341	2.4	73
10 Tu	0612	0.3	9
	1208	3.0	91
	1916	0.1	3
11 W	0037	2.2	67
	0716	0.4	12
	1308	2.8	85
	2018	0.1	3
12 Th ☽	0139	2.2	67
	0823	0.4	12
	1414	2.7	82
	2119	0.1	3
13 F	0246	2.2	67
	0929	0.4	12
	1523	2.6	79
	2217	0.1	3
14 Sa	0354	2.2	67
	1032	0.4	12
	1628	2.6	79
	2312	0.1	3
15 Su	0455	2.4	73
	1133	0.3	9
	1725	2.5	76
16 M	0003	0.1	3
	0548	2.6	79
	1229	0.2	6
	1814	2.5	76
17 Tu	0051	0.1	3
	0636	2.7	82
	1320	0.1	3
	1859	2.5	76
18 W	0136	0.1	3
	0720	2.9	88
	1408	0.1	3
	1942	2.5	76
19 Th ●	0217	0.1	3
	0803	2.9	88
	1451	0.1	3
	2025	2.4	73
20 F	0256	0.2	6
	0846	2.9	88
	1534	0.1	3
	2109	2.3	70
21 Sa	0335	0.3	9
	0930	2.9	88
	1616	0.1	3
	2154	2.2	67
22 Su	0413	0.4	12
	1015	2.8	85
	1700	0.3	9
	2241	2.1	64
23 M	0453	0.6	18
	1102	2.6	79
	1747	0.4	12
	2330	2.0	61
24 Tu	0539	0.7	21
	1150	2.5	76
	1839	0.5	15
25 W	0020	1.9	58
	0634	0.8	24
	1242	2.3	70
	1933	0.6	18
26 Th	0115	1.8	55
	0735	0.9	27
	1337	2.2	67
	2027	0.6	18
27 F ☾	0214	1.8	55
	0835	0.9	27
	1436	2.1	64
	2118	0.6	18
28 Sa	0316	1.8	55
	0931	0.8	24
	1535	2.1	64
	2205	0.5	15
29 Su	0414	1.9	58
	1024	0.7	21
	1628	2.1	64
	2249	0.4	12
30 M	0502	2.1	64
	1114	0.6	18
	1714	2.2	67
	2332	0.3	9
31 Tu	0543	2.3	70
	1203	0.4	12
	1755	2.3	70

November

Day	Time (h m)	Height (ft)	Height (cm)
1 W	0015	0.2	6
	0621	2.6	79
	1250	0.1	3
	1835	2.4	73
2 Th	0058	0.0	0
	0659	2.8	85
	1338	-0.1	-3
	1916	2.4	73
3 F	0141	-0.1	-3
	0739	3.0	91
	1426	-0.3	-9
	2000	2.5	76
4 Sa ○	0225	-0.2	-6
	0822	3.1	94
	1514	-0.4	-12
	2046	2.5	76
5 Su	0310	-0.2	-6
	0909	3.2	98
	1605	-0.4	-12
	2136	2.4	73
6 M	0359	-0.1	-3
	1000	3.2	98
	1658	-0.4	-12
	2228	2.4	73
7 Tu	0453	0.0	0
	1054	3.1	94
	1755	-0.3	-9
	2324	2.3	70
8 W	0553	0.1	3
	1151	2.9	88
	1855	-0.2	-6
9 Th	0022	2.2	67
	0700	0.2	6
	1250	2.7	82
	1956	-0.1	-3
10 F ○	0124	2.2	67
	0809	0.3	9
	1354	2.5	76
	2056	0.0	0
11 Sa	0230	2.2	67
	0916	0.3	9
	1501	2.3	70
	2153	0.0	0
12 Su	0338	2.2	67
	1021	0.3	9
	1606	2.2	67
	2247	0.0	0
13 M	0440	2.3	70
	1121	0.2	6
	1704	2.1	64
	2338	0.0	0
14 Tu	0532	2.5	76
	1217	0.1	3
	1754	2.1	64
15 W	0025	0.1	3
	0618	2.6	79
	1307	0.1	3
	1838	2.0	61
16 Th	0109	0.1	3
	0700	2.7	82
	1352	0.0	0
	1920	2.0	61
17 F	0150	0.1	3
	0741	2.7	82
	1433	0.0	0
	2002	2.0	61
18 Sa ●	0228	0.2	6
	0822	2.7	82
	1512	0.0	0
	2045	2.0	61
19 Su	0305	0.3	9
	0905	2.7	82
	1552	0.0	0
	2130	1.9	58
20 M	0342	0.3	9
	0949	2.6	79
	1633	0.1	3
	2217	1.9	58
21 Tu	0422	0.4	12
	1035	2.5	76
	1716	0.1	3
	2305	1.8	55
22 W	0507	0.5	15
	1122	2.3	70
	1804	0.2	6
	2354	1.7	52
23 Th	0559	0.6	18
	1210	2.2	67
	1855	0.3	9
24 F	0046	1.7	52
	0658	0.7	21
	1258	2.0	61
	1947	0.3	9
25 Sa	0140	1.7	52
	0759	0.7	21
	1350	1.9	58
	2036	0.3	9
26 Su ☾	0236	1.7	52
	0857	0.6	18
	1444	1.9	58
	2123	0.3	9
27 M	0331	1.8	55
	0951	0.5	15
	1538	1.8	55
	2208	0.2	6
28 Tu	0421	2.0	61
	1043	0.3	9
	1629	1.9	58
	2253	0.1	3
29 W	0505	2.2	67
	1135	0.1	3
	1716	2.0	61
	2338	0.0	0
30 Th	0546	2.5	76
	1225	-0.1	-3
	1801	2.1	64

December

Day	Time (h m)	Height (ft)	Height (cm)
1 F	0024	-0.2	-6
	0628	2.8	85
	1316	-0.4	-12
	1847	2.1	64
2 Sa	0111	-0.3	-9
	0713	3.0	91
	1405	-0.6	-18
	1934	2.2	67
3 Su ○	0159	-0.4	-12
	0800	3.1	94
	1455	-0.7	-21
	2023	2.2	67
4 M	0249	-0.5	-15
	0850	3.2	98
	1546	-0.7	-21
	2115	2.3	70
5 Tu	0341	-0.4	-12
	0943	3.1	94
	1639	-0.7	-21
	2210	2.2	67
6 W	0436	-0.4	-12
	1037	3.0	91
	1734	-0.6	-18
	2306	2.2	67
7 Th	0537	-0.2	-6
	1133	2.8	85
	1831	-0.5	-15
8 F	0004	2.2	67
	0642	-0.1	-3
	1230	2.5	76
	1930	-0.4	-12
9 Sa	0105	2.1	64
	0751	0.0	0
	1330	2.2	67
	2029	-0.3	-9
10 Su ○	0208	2.1	64
	0858	0.1	3
	1432	2.0	61
	2125	-0.2	-6
11 M	0313	2.1	64
	1003	0.1	3
	1536	1.8	55
	2219	-0.1	-3
12 Tu	0416	2.2	67
	1104	0.1	3
	1636	1.7	52
	2310	0.0	0
13 W	0510	2.2	67
	1200	0.1	3
	1729	1.6	49
	2358	0.0	0
14 Th	0557	2.3	70
	1250	0.0	0
	1815	1.6	49
15 F	0043	0.1	3
	0640	2.4	73
	1333	0.0	0
	1858	1.6	49
16 Sa	0124	0.1	3
	0721	2.4	73
	1413	-0.1	-3
	1940	1.7	52
17 Su	0203	0.1	3
	0802	2.4	73
	1450	-0.1	-3
	2023	1.7	52
18 M ●	0240	0.1	3
	0844	2.4	73
	1528	-0.1	-3
	2108	1.7	52
19 Tu	0319	0.1	3
	0928	2.3	70
	1606	-0.1	-3
	2154	1.7	52
20 W	0359	0.2	6
	1012	2.3	70
	1647	-0.1	-3
	2241	1.7	52
21 Th	0443	0.2	6
	1056	2.2	67
	1731	-0.1	-3
	2328	1.6	49
22 F	0531	0.3	9
	1139	2.0	61
	1818	0.0	0
23 Sa	0014	1.6	49
	0626	0.4	12
	1221	1.9	58
	1906	0.0	0
24 Su	0101	1.6	49
	0724	0.4	12
	1304	1.8	55
	1954	0.0	0
25 M ○	0150	1.7	52
	0823	0.3	9
	1351	1.7	52
	2042	0.0	0
26 Tu ☾	0241	1.7	52
	0919	0.2	6
	1445	1.6	49
	2128	0.0	0
27 W	0333	1.9	58
	1014	0.1	3
	1543	1.6	49
	2216	-0.1	-3
28 Th	0425	2.1	64
	1108	-0.1	-3
	1639	1.7	52
	2304	-0.2	-6
29 F	0514	2.4	73
	1202	-0.3	-9
	1731	1.8	55
	2355	-0.3	-9
30 Sa	0603	2.6	79
	1255	-0.5	-15
	1822	1.9	58
31 Su	0047	-0.5	-15
	0652	2.8	85
	1347	-0.7	-21
	1912	2.0	61

Time meridian 75° W. 0000 is midnight. 1200 is noon. Times are not adjusted for Daylight Saving Time.
Heights are referred to mean lower low water which is the chart datum of soundings.

New London, Connecticut, 2017
Times and Heights of High and Low Waters

January

Day	Time (h m)	Height (ft)	Height (cm)
1 Su	0517	0.2	6
	1116	2.8	85
	1756	-0.2	-6
	2351	2.3	70
2 M	0607	0.2	6
	1158	2.7	82
	1843	-0.1	-3
3 Tu	0035	2.4	73
	0702	0.2	6
	1243	2.6	79
	1933	-0.1	-3
4 W	0123	2.4	73
	0801	0.2	6
	1334	2.5	76
	2024	-0.1	-3
5 Th ☽	0217	2.5	76
	0902	0.1	3
	1433	2.4	73
	2117	-0.1	-3
6 F	0317	2.7	82
	1002	0.0	0
	1537	2.3	70
	2211	-0.1	-3
7 Sa	0419	2.8	85
	1102	-0.1	-3
	1641	2.3	70
	2307	-0.1	-3
8 Su	0517	3.0	91
	1201	-0.3	-9
	1740	2.3	70
9 M	0003	-0.2	-6
	0611	3.2	98
	1258	-0.5	-15
	1834	2.4	73
10 Tu	0100	-0.3	-9
	0703	3.3	101
	1352	-0.6	-18
	1926	2.5	76
11 W	0154	-0.4	-12
	0754	3.4	104
	1443	-0.7	-21
	2017	2.6	79
12 Th ○	0247	-0.4	-12
	0844	3.4	104
	1532	-0.7	-21
	2108	2.6	79
13 F	0338	-0.4	-12
	0935	3.3	101
	1619	-0.7	-21
	2200	2.7	82
14 Sa	0429	-0.4	-12
	1025	3.1	94
	1707	-0.6	-18
	2252	2.7	82
15 Su	0521	-0.2	-6
	1116	2.9	88
	1756	-0.4	-12
	2344	2.7	82
16 M	0615	-0.1	-3
	1206	2.7	82
	1846	-0.2	-6
17 Tu	0035	2.6	79
	0712	0.1	3
	1256	2.4	73
	1937	0.0	0
18 W	0129	2.5	76
	0810	0.2	6
	1350	2.2	67
	2028	0.1	3
19 Th ◔	0225	2.5	76
	0909	0.3	9
	1448	2.0	61
	2120	0.3	9
20 F	0324	2.4	73
	1006	0.3	9
	1550	1.9	58
	2211	0.4	12
21 Sa	0423	2.5	76
	1101	0.3	9
	1650	1.9	58
	2302	0.4	12
22 Su	0518	2.5	76
	1153	0.3	9
	1744	1.9	58
	2352	0.4	12
23 M	0607	2.6	79
	1241	0.2	6
	1832	2.0	61
24 Tu	0040	0.3	9
	0652	2.7	82
	1324	0.1	3
	1916	2.1	64
25 W	0125	0.3	9
	0734	2.7	82
	1405	-0.1	-3
	1958	2.2	67
26 Th	0207	0.2	6
	0814	2.8	85
	1445	-0.2	-6
	2038	2.3	70
27 F ●	0248	0.1	3
	0853	2.8	85
	1524	-0.3	-9
	2118	2.3	70
28 Sa	0329	0.0	0
	0932	2.9	88
	1603	-0.4	-12
	2158	2.4	73
29 Su	0411	-0.1	-3
	1011	2.9	88
	1644	-0.4	-12
	2239	2.5	76
30 M	0457	-0.1	-3
	1052	2.8	85
	1727	-0.3	-9
	2320	2.5	76
31 Tu	0546	-0.1	-3
	1134	2.7	82
	1812	-0.3	-9

February

Day	Time (h m)	Height (ft)	Height (cm)
1 W	0004	2.6	79
	0641	-0.1	-3
	1220	2.6	79
	1902	-0.2	-6
2 Th	0052	2.7	82
	0739	-0.1	-3
	1310	2.5	76
	1955	-0.1	-3
3 F ◑	0146	2.7	82
	0841	-0.1	-3
	1408	2.3	70
	2051	-0.1	-3
4 Sa	0248	2.8	85
	0942	-0.1	-3
	1514	2.2	67
	2149	0.0	0
5 Su	0356	2.8	85
	1044	-0.2	-6
	1622	2.2	67
	2249	-0.1	-3
6 M	0500	2.9	88
	1144	-0.3	-9
	1725	2.2	67
	2349	-0.1	-3
7 Tu	0559	3.0	91
	1241	-0.4	-12
	1821	2.3	70
8 W	0048	-0.2	-6
	0653	3.1	94
	1335	-0.5	-15
	1913	2.5	76
9 Th	0143	-0.3	-9
	0743	3.1	94
	1425	-0.5	-15
	2003	2.6	79
10 F ○	0235	-0.4	-12
	0831	3.1	94
	1512	-0.6	-18
	2051	2.7	82
11 Sa	0325	-0.4	-12
	0918	3.0	91
	1557	-0.5	-15
	2139	2.8	85
12 Su	0412	-0.4	-12
	1005	2.9	88
	1641	-0.4	-12
	2227	2.8	85
13 M	0500	-0.3	-9
	1051	2.8	85
	1724	-0.3	-9
	2314	2.8	85
14 Tu	0548	-0.1	-3
	1137	2.6	79
	1809	-0.1	-3
15 W	0001	2.7	82
	0639	0.0	0
	1224	2.4	73
	1855	0.1	3
16 Th	0050	2.6	79
	0732	0.2	6
	1313	2.2	67
	1944	0.3	9
17 F	0142	2.5	76
	0827	0.3	9
	1407	2.0	61
	2035	0.4	12
18 Sa ◔	0239	2.4	73
	0922	0.4	12
	1507	1.9	58
	2128	0.5	15
19 Su	0340	2.4	73
	1017	0.4	12
	1611	1.9	58
	2222	0.5	15
20 M	0440	2.4	73
	1110	0.3	9
	1710	1.9	58
	2315	0.5	15
21 Tu	0535	2.4	73
	1200	0.3	9
	1802	2.0	61
22 W	0007	0.4	12
	0623	2.5	76
	1247	0.1	3
	1847	2.1	64
23 Th	0055	0.3	9
	0706	2.7	82
	1331	0.0	0
	1929	2.3	70
24 F	0140	0.1	3
	0747	2.8	85
	1413	-0.1	-3
	2008	2.4	73
25 Sa	0224	0.0	0
	0826	2.9	88
	1453	-0.3	-9
	2047	2.6	79
26 Su ●	0307	-0.2	-6
	0905	2.9	88
	1534	-0.4	-12
	2126	2.7	82
27 M	0351	-0.3	-9
	0945	2.9	88
	1615	-0.4	-12
	2207	2.8	85
28 Tu	0437	-0.4	-12
	1028	2.9	88
	1658	-0.4	-12
	2250	2.9	88

March

Day	Time (h m)	Height (ft)	Height (cm)
1 W	0527	-0.4	-12
	1113	2.8	85
	1744	-0.3	-9
	2336	3.0	91
2 Th	0622	-0.3	-9
	1200	2.7	82
	1834	-0.2	-6
3 F	0026	3.0	91
	0720	-0.3	-9
	1253	2.5	76
	1930	-0.1	-3
4 Sa	0123	2.9	88
	0821	-0.2	-6
	1351	2.3	70
	2029	0.0	0
5 Su ◑	0227	2.9	88
	0923	-0.1	-3
	1457	2.2	67
	2132	0.1	3
6 M	0337	2.8	85
	1025	-0.1	-3
	1607	2.2	67
	2235	0.1	3
7 Tu	0446	2.8	85
	1125	-0.1	-3
	1713	2.3	70
	2338	0.0	0
8 W	0548	2.9	88
	1223	-0.2	-6
	1810	2.4	73
9 Th	0038	-0.1	-3
	0642	2.9	88
	1316	-0.3	-9
	1901	2.6	79
10 F	0133	-0.2	-6
	0731	2.9	88
	1405	-0.3	-9
	1948	2.7	82
11 Sa	0224	-0.2	-6
	0816	2.9	88
	1450	-0.3	-9
	2032	2.8	85
12 Su ○	0310	-0.3	-9
	0859	2.8	85
	1532	-0.3	-9
	2116	2.9	88
13 M	0354	-0.3	-9
	0942	2.8	85
	1612	-0.2	-6
	2200	3.0	91
14 Tu	0438	-0.2	-6
	1026	2.7	82
	1652	0.0	0
	2244	2.9	88
15 W	0521	-0.1	-3
	1110	2.5	76
	1732	0.1	3
	2328	2.9	88
16 Th	0607	0.0	0
	1155	2.4	73
	1814	0.3	9
17 F	0014	2.8	85
	0655	0.2	6
	1242	2.3	70
	1901	0.5	15
18 Sa	0103	2.6	79
	0746	0.3	9
	1333	2.1	64
	1952	0.6	18
19 Su	0156	2.5	76
	0839	0.4	12
	1430	2.0	61
	2047	0.7	21
20 M ◔	0255	2.4	73
	0932	0.4	12
	1532	2.0	61
	2143	0.7	21
21 Tu	0358	2.4	73
	1025	0.4	12
	1634	2.1	64
	2238	0.7	21
22 W	0457	2.4	73
	1117	0.4	12
	1728	2.2	67
	2332	0.5	15
23 Th	0548	2.5	76
	1206	0.3	9
	1814	2.3	70
24 F	0023	0.4	12
	0632	2.7	82
	1253	0.1	3
	1856	2.5	76
25 Sa	0111	0.2	6
	0714	2.8	85
	1337	0.0	0
	1935	2.7	82
26 Su	0158	-0.1	-3
	0754	2.9	88
	1420	-0.2	-6
	2013	2.9	88
27 M ●	0244	-0.3	-9
	0835	3.0	91
	1502	-0.3	-9
	2054	3.1	94
28 Tu	0331	-0.4	-12
	0918	3.0	91
	1545	-0.3	-9
	2137	3.3	101
29 W	0419	-0.5	-15
	1004	2.9	88
	1630	-0.3	-9
	2223	3.4	104
30 Th	0510	-0.5	-15
	1053	2.9	88
	1718	-0.2	-6
	2313	3.4	104
31 F	0604	-0.4	-12
	1144	2.7	82
	1811	-0.1	-3

Time meridian 75° W. 0000 is midnight. 1200 is noon. Times are not adjusted for Daylight Saving Time.
Heights are referred to mean lower low water which is the chart datum of soundings.

New London, Connecticut, 2017
Times and Heights of High and Low Waters

April

Day	Time	ft	cm	Day	Time	ft	cm
1 Sa	0006	3.3	101	16 Su	0029	2.8	85
	0702	-0.3	-9		0709	0.3	9
	1238	2.6	79		1304	2.3	70
	1909	0.1	3		1914	0.8	24
2 Su	0104	3.2	98	17 M	0118	2.6	79
	0802	-0.2	-6		0800	0.4	12
	1338	2.5	76		1357	2.2	67
	2013	0.2	6		2010	0.8	24
3 M ◑	0209	3.0	91	18 Tu	0212	2.5	76
	0904	-0.1	-3		0852	0.4	12
	1444	2.4	73		1456	2.2	67
	2118	0.2	6		2106	0.8	24
4 Tu	0320	2.9	88	19 W ◐	0312	2.5	76
	1005	0.0	0		0943	0.4	12
	1554	2.4	73		1555	2.3	70
	2223	0.2	6		2202	0.8	24
5 W	0431	2.8	85	20 Th	0411	2.5	76
	1104	0.0	0		1034	0.4	12
	1700	2.5	76		1649	2.4	73
	2326	0.2	6		2257	0.6	18
6 Th	0534	2.8	85	21 F	0505	2.6	79
	1201	0.0	0		1124	0.3	9
	1757	2.7	82		1736	2.6	79
					2350	0.4	12
7 F	0026	0.1	3	22 Sa	0553	2.7	82
	0627	2.8	85		1212	0.2	6
	1253	0.0	0		1819	2.8	85
	1846	2.8	85				
8 Sa	0120	0.0	0	23 Su	0042	0.2	6
	0714	2.7	82		0637	2.8	85
	1341	0.0	0		1259	0.1	3
	1929	2.9	88		1859	3.0	91
9 Su	0209	0.0	0	24 M	0133	-0.1	-3
	0757	2.7	82		0721	2.9	88
	1424	0.0	0		1345	-0.1	-3
	2011	3.0	91		1940	3.3	101
10 M	0254	-0.1	-3	25 Tu	0222	-0.3	-9
	0838	2.7	82		0805	3.0	91
	1505	0.1	3		1431	-0.2	-6
	2052	3.1	94		2024	3.5	107
11 Tu ○	0335	-0.1	-3	26 W ●	0311	-0.5	-15
	0919	2.6	79		0852	3.0	91
	1543	0.2	6		1517	-0.2	-6
	2133	3.1	94		2110	3.6	110
12 W	0415	-0.1	-3	27 Th	0401	-0.6	-18
	1001	2.6	79		0942	3.0	91
	1620	0.3	9		1605	-0.2	-6
	2215	3.1	94		2200	3.7	113
13 Th	0455	0.0	0	28 F	0452	-0.6	-18
	1045	2.5	76		1033	2.9	88
	1658	0.4	12		1656	-0.1	-3
	2258	3.0	91		2254	3.6	110
14 F	0537	0.1	3	29 Sa	0546	-0.5	-15
	1129	2.4	73		1128	2.8	85
	1739	0.5	15		1751	0.0	0
	2343	2.9	88		2349	3.5	107
15 Sa	0621	0.2	6	30 Su	0643	-0.3	-9
	1215	2.4	73		1224	2.8	85
	1823	0.6	18		1852	0.1	3

May

Day	Time	ft	cm	Day	Time	ft	cm
1 M	0048	3.3	101	16 Tu	0044	2.8	85
	0742	-0.2	-6		0726	0.3	9
	1325	2.7	82		1328	2.4	73
	1957	0.3	9		1937	0.8	24
2 Tu ◐	0151	3.1	94	17 W	0132	2.7	82
	0842	-0.1	-3		0815	0.4	12
	1429	2.6	79		1420	2.4	73
	2103	0.3	9		2033	0.8	24
3 W	0259	2.9	88	18 Th ◐	0224	2.6	79
	0941	0.0	0		0905	0.4	12
	1537	2.7	82		1514	2.5	76
	2208	0.4	12		2129	0.8	24
4 Th	0408	2.7	82	19 F	0321	2.6	79
	1039	0.1	3		0954	0.4	12
	1642	2.7	82		1607	2.6	79
	2310	0.3	9		2225	0.6	18
5 F	0511	2.6	79	20 Sa	0418	2.6	79
	1134	0.2	6		1034	0.3	9
	1737	2.9	88		1656	2.8	85
					2320	0.4	12
6 Sa	0010	0.3	9	21 Su	0512	2.6	79
	0605	2.6	79		1133	0.2	6
	1225	0.2	6		1742	3.1	94
	1825	3.0	91				
7 Su	0103	0.2	6	22 M	0015	0.2	6
	0651	2.6	79		0601	2.7	82
	1313	0.3	9		1222	0.1	3
	1907	3.1	94		1826	3.3	101
8 M	0151	0.1	3	23 Tu	0108	-0.1	-3
	0734	2.5	76		0650	2.8	85
	1356	0.3	9		1312	0.0	0
	1947	3.1	94		1911	3.6	110
9 Tu	0234	0.1	3	24 W	0201	-0.3	-9
	0814	2.5	76		0738	2.9	88
	1436	0.4	12		1403	-0.1	-3
	2027	3.2	98		1959	3.7	113
10 W ○	0314	0.1	3	25 Th ●	0252	-0.5	-15
	0856	2.5	76		0837	2.9	88
	1514	0.4	12		1453	-0.1	-3
	2107	3.2	98		2048	3.8	116
11 Th	0352	0.1	3	26 F	0343	-0.6	-18
	0938	2.5	76		0920	2.9	88
	1551	0.5	15		1544	-0.1	-3
	2149	3.2	98		2141	3.8	116
12 F	0431	0.1	3	27 Sa	0434	-0.6	-18
	1022	2.5	76		1015	2.9	88
	1629	0.6	18		1638	-0.1	-3
	2232	3.1	94		2236	3.7	113
13 Sa	0510	0.1	3	28 Su	0527	-0.5	-15
	1107	2.5	76		1111	2.9	88
	1709	0.6	18		1734	0.0	0
	2315	3.0	91		2333	3.6	110
14 Su	0552	0.2	6	29 M	0623	-0.3	-9
	1152	2.5	76		1208	2.9	88
	1753	0.7	21		1835	0.2	6
	2359	2.9	88				
15 M	0638	0.3	9	30 Tu	0030	3.3	101
	1239	2.4	73		0720	-0.2	-6
	1843	0.8	24		1307	2.8	85
					1939	0.3	9
				31 W	0130	3.1	94
					0817	0.0	0
					1409	2.8	85
					2043	0.4	12

June

Day	Time	ft	cm	Day	Time	ft	cm
1 Th ◐	0232	2.8	85	16 F	0143	2.7	82
	0914	0.1	3		0829	0.3	9
	1512	2.8	85		1432	2.7	82
	2147	0.4	12		2100	0.6	18
2 F	0337	2.6	79	17 Sa ○	0236	2.6	79
	1009	0.2	6		0918	0.3	9
	1614	2.9	88		1524	2.8	85
	2248	0.4	12		2157	0.5	15
3 Sa	0440	2.5	76	18 Su	0335	2.6	79
	1102	0.3	9		1007	0.3	9
	1710	3.0	91		1617	3.0	91
	2347	0.4	12		2253	0.3	9
4 Su	0536	2.4	73	19 M	0434	2.6	79
	1153	0.4	12		1058	0.2	6
	1758	3.0	91		1709	3.2	98
					2350	0.1	3
5 M	0040	0.4	12	20 Tu	0530	2.6	79
	0624	2.4	73		1151	0.2	6
	1241	0.5	15		1759	3.5	107
	1841	3.1	94				
6 Tu	0128	0.3	9	21 W	0047	-0.1	-3
	0708	2.4	73		0623	2.7	82
	1325	0.5	15		1245	0.1	3
	1922	3.2	98		1848	3.7	113
7 W	0211	0.2	6	22 Th	0141	-0.3	-9
	0750	2.4	73		0714	2.8	85
	1406	0.6	18		1340	0.0	0
	2003	3.2	98		1939	3.8	116
8 Th	0250	0.2	6	23 F ●	0234	-0.4	-12
	0832	2.4	73		0807	2.9	88
	1446	0.6	18		1434	-0.1	-3
	2044	3.2	98		2031	3.8	116
9 F ○	0328	0.1	3	24 Sa	0325	-0.5	-15
	0915	2.5	76		0900	2.9	88
	1524	0.6	18		1527	-0.1	-3
	2126	3.2	98		2124	3.8	116
10 Sa	0406	0.1	3	25 Su	0416	-0.5	-15
	0959	2.5	76		0956	3.0	91
	1603	0.6	18		1621	-0.1	-3
	2208	3.1	94		2219	3.7	113
11 Su	0444	0.1	3	26 M	0507	-0.4	-12
	1044	2.5	76		1052	3.0	91
	1644	0.6	18		1717	0.0	0
	2250	3.0	91		2314	3.5	107
12 M	0525	0.2	6	27 Tu	0559	-0.3	-9
	1129	2.5	76		1148	3.0	91
	1728	0.7	21		1816	0.2	6
	2332	3.0	91				
13 Tu	0608	0.2	6	28 W	0009	3.3	101
	1213	2.5	76		0653	-0.2	-6
	1816	0.7	21		1244	3.0	91
					1917	0.3	9
14 W	0014	2.9	88	29 Th	0104	3.0	91
	0654	0.2	6		0748	0.0	0
	1258	2.5	76		1341	3.0	91
	1908	0.8	24		2019	0.4	12
15 Th	0056	2.8	85	30 F ◐	0201	2.7	82
	0741	0.3	9		0842	0.2	6
	1344	2.6	79		1440	2.9	88
	2003	0.7	21		2120	0.5	15

Time meridian 75° W. 0000 is midnight. 1200 is noon. Times are not adjusted for Daylight Saving Time.
Heights are referred to mean lower low water which is the chart datum of soundings.

New London, Connecticut, 2017

Times and Heights of High and Low Waters

July

Day	Time	Height (ft)	Height (cm)	Day	Time	Height (ft)	Height (cm)
1 Sa	0301	2.5	76	16 Su	0202	2.6	79
	0935	0.3	9		0846	0.3	9
	1539	2.9	88		1446	3.0	91
	2220	0.5	15	☽	2133	0.4	12
2 Su	0403	2.4	73	17 M	0301	2.6	79
	1027	0.5	15		0938	0.3	9
	1636	3.0	91		1544	3.1	94
	2317	0.5	15		2231	0.3	9
3 M	0502	2.3	70	18 Tu	0405	2.5	76
	1118	0.6	18		1032	0.3	9
	1728	3.0	91		1643	3.3	101
					2330	0.1	3
4 Tu	0011	0.5	15	19 W	0506	2.6	79
	0554	2.3	70		1128	0.2	6
	1207	0.6	18		1739	3.5	107
	1814	3.1	94				
5 W	0100	0.4	12	20 Th	0027	-0.1	-3
	0641	2.3	70		0602	2.6	79
	1254	0.7	21		1226	0.1	3
	1858	3.1	94		1832	3.6	110
6 Th	0143	0.4	12	21 F	0123	-0.2	-6
	0725	2.3	70		0656	2.8	85
	1338	0.7	21		1323	0.0	0
	1940	3.1	94		1924	3.7	113
7 F	0223	0.3	9	22 Sa	0215	-0.3	-9
	0808	2.4	73		0749	2.9	88
	1419	0.6	18		1419	-0.1	-3
	2021	3.1	94		2016	3.7	113
8 Sa	0301	0.2	6	23 Su	0306	-0.4	-12
	0851	2.5	76		0842	3.0	91
	1500	0.6	18		1512	-0.1	-3
○	2103	3.1	94	●	2108	3.7	113
9 Su	0339	0.2	6	24 M	0355	-0.4	-12
	0934	2.5	76		0936	3.1	94
	1539	0.6	18		1605	-0.1	-3
	2144	3.1	94		2200	3.5	107
10 M	0417	0.1	3	25 Tu	0444	-0.3	-9
	1018	2.6	79		1029	3.1	94
	1620	0.6	18		1659	0.0	0
	2225	3.1	94		2252	3.4	104
11 Tu	0456	0.1	3	26 W	0533	-0.2	-6
	1101	2.6	79		1123	3.1	94
	1703	0.6	18		1754	0.1	3
	2305	3.0	91		2344	3.1	94
12 W	0538	0.1	3	27 Th	0623	0.0	0
	1143	2.7	82		1215	3.1	94
	1750	0.6	18		1851	0.3	9
	2344	3.0	91				
13 Th	0622	0.2	6	28 F	0035	2.9	88
	1224	2.7	82		0714	0.2	6
	1842	0.6	18		1308	3.0	91
					1949	0.4	12
14 F	0026	2.9	88	29 Sa	0128	2.7	82
	0708	0.2	6		0806	0.3	9
	1307	2.8	85		1403	3.0	91
	1937	0.5	15		2048	0.5	15
15 Sa	0110	2.8	85	30 Su	0224	2.4	73
	0756	0.3	9		0859	0.5	15
	1354	2.9	88		1500	2.9	88
	2035	0.5	15	☾	2146	0.6	18
				31 M	0325	2.3	70
					0951	0.6	18
					1559	2.9	88
					2242	0.6	18

August

Day	Time	Height (ft)	Height (cm)	Day	Time	Height (ft)	Height (cm)
1 Tu	0426	2.2	67	16 W	0345	2.5	76
	1042	0.7	21		1014	0.3	9
	1655	2.9	88		1624	3.3	101
	2335	0.6	18		2311	0.1	3
2 W	0523	2.2	67	17 Th	0450	2.5	76
	1133	0.8	24		1113	0.3	9
	1746	2.9	88		1725	3.4	104
3 Th	0025	0.5	15	18 F	0009	0.0	0
	0613	2.3	70		0549	2.7	82
	1223	0.7	21		1213	0.2	6
	1833	3.0	91		1820	3.5	107
4 F	0110	0.5	15	19 Sa	0104	-0.1	-3
	0659	2.4	73		0643	2.8	85
	1309	0.7	21		1311	0.1	3
	1916	3.0	91		1912	3.5	107
5 Sa	0151	0.4	12	20 Su	0156	-0.2	-6
	0742	2.5	76		0734	3.0	91
	1353	0.6	18		1406	0.0	0
	1957	3.1	94		2002	3.5	107
6 Su	0230	0.3	9	21 M	0245	-0.3	-9
	0824	2.6	79		0824	3.1	94
	1434	0.5	15		1459	-0.1	-3
	2038	3.1	94	●	2051	3.5	107
7 M	0308	0.2	6	22 Tu	0332	-0.2	-6
	0905	2.7	82		0914	3.2	98
	1515	0.5	15		1549	-0.1	-3
○	2117	3.1	94		2139	3.3	101
8 Tu	0347	0.1	3	23 W	0418	-0.2	-6
	0946	2.7	82		1004	3.2	98
	1556	0.4	12		1639	0.0	0
	2156	3.1	94		2227	3.2	98
9 W	0426	0.1	3	24 Th	0503	0.0	0
	1027	2.8	85		1053	3.2	98
	1640	0.4	12		1729	0.1	3
	2235	3.1	94		2316	3.0	91
10 Th	0506	0.1	3	25 F	0549	0.2	6
	1107	2.9	88		1143	3.2	98
	1727	0.3	9		1821	0.3	9
	2316	3.0	91				
11 F	0549	0.1	3	26 Sa	0004	2.8	85
	1148	2.9	88		0637	0.4	12
	1818	0.3	9		1233	3.1	94
	2358	2.9	88		1916	0.4	12
12 Sa	0635	0.2	6	27 Su	0055	2.6	79
	1232	3.0	91		0727	0.5	15
	1914	0.3	9		1324	3.0	91
					2012	0.6	18
13 Su	0045	2.8	85	28 M	0149	2.4	73
	0725	0.3	9		0819	0.7	21
	1321	3.1	94		1420	2.9	88
	2013	0.3	9		2108	0.6	18
14 M	0138	2.6	79	29 Tu	0248	2.3	70
	0819	0.3	9		0913	0.8	24
	1417	3.1	94		1520	2.8	85
○	2113	0.3	9	◑	2202	0.7	21
15 Tu	0239	2.5	76	30 W	0351	2.2	67
	0915	0.3	9		1007	0.9	27
	1520	3.2	98		1620	2.8	85
	2212	0.2	6		2255	0.7	21
				31 Th	0451	2.3	70
					1100	0.9	27
					1716	2.8	85
					2345	0.6	18

September

Day	Time	Height (ft)	Height (cm)	Day	Time	Height (ft)	Height (cm)
1 F	0544	2.4	73	16 Sa	0539	2.8	85
	1151	0.8	24		1204	0.2	6
	1805	2.9	88		1810	3.3	101
2 Sa	0031	0.5	15	17 Su	0045	0.0	0
	0631	2.5	76		0631	2.9	88
	1239	0.7	21		1301	0.1	3
	1849	3.0	91		1900	3.3	101
3 Su	0114	0.4	12	18 M	0136	-0.1	-3
	0714	2.6	79		0720	3.1	94
	1324	0.6	18		1355	0.0	0
	1929	3.0	91		1946	3.3	101
4 M	0155	0.3	9	19 Tu	0223	-0.1	-3
	0754	2.7	82		0806	3.2	98
	1407	0.4	12		1444	0.0	0
	2008	3.1	94		2031	3.2	98
5 Tu	0235	0.2	6	20 W	0307	-0.1	-3
	0832	2.9	88		0851	3.3	101
	1449	0.3	9		1532	0.0	0
	2046	3.1	94	●	2116	3.1	94
6 W	0314	0.1	3	21 Th	0350	0.0	0
	0911	3.0	91		0937	3.3	101
	1532	0.2	6		1618	0.0	0
○	2125	3.1	94		2201	3.0	91
7 Th	0353	0.0	0	22 F	0432	0.2	6
	0950	3.1	94		1023	3.3	101
	1617	0.1	3		1703	0.1	3
	2206	3.1	94		2247	2.8	85
8 F	0434	0.0	0	23 Sa	0514	0.3	9
	1030	3.2	98		1109	3.2	98
	1705	0.1	3		1751	0.3	9
	2249	3.0	91		2335	2.7	82
9 Sa	0518	0.1	3	24 Su	0558	0.5	15
	1114	3.2	98		1157	3.1	94
	1757	0.1	3		1841	0.4	12
	2335	2.9	88				
10 Su	0606	0.2	6	25 M	0024	2.5	76
	1202	3.3	101		0646	0.7	21
	1853	0.1	3		1247	3.0	91
					1933	0.5	15
11 M	0025	2.8	85	26 Tu	0116	2.4	73
	0659	0.3	9		0739	0.8	24
	1254	3.3	101		1341	2.8	85
	1953	0.2	6		2028	0.6	18
12 Tu	0121	2.6	79	27 W	0214	2.3	70
	0757	0.4	12		0835	0.9	27
	1355	3.2	98		1440	2.7	82
	2054	0.2	6	◑	2121	0.7	21
13 W	0224	2.5	76	28 Th	0316	2.3	70
	0859	0.4	12		0931	0.9	27
	1502	3.2	98		1542	2.7	82
○	2154	0.2	6		2213	0.7	21
14 Th	0333	2.5	76	29 F	0418	2.3	70
	1001	0.4	12		1026	0.9	27
	1611	3.2	98		1641	2.7	82
	2254	0.1	3		2303	0.6	18
15 F	0439	2.6	79	30 Sa	0513	2.4	73
	1103	0.3	9		1118	0.8	24
	1714	3.2	98		1732	2.8	85
	2351	0.1	3		2350	0.5	15

Time meridian 75° W. 0000 is midnight. 1200 is noon. Times are not adjusted for Daylight Saving Time.
Heights are referred to mean lower low water which is the chart datum of soundings.

New London, Connecticut, 2017
Times and Heights of High and Low Waters

October

Day	Time	ft	cm	Time	ft	cm	Time	ft	cm	Time	ft	cm
1 Su	0600	2.6	79	1207	0.7	21	1816	2.9	88			
2 M	0035	0.4	12	0642	2.7	82	1254	0.5	15	1857	2.9	88
3 Tu	0117	0.3	9	0720	2.9	88	1339	0.3	9	1935	3.0	91
4 W	0158	0.1	3	0757	3.1	94	1424	0.1	3	2014	3.1	94
5 Th ○	0239	0.0	0	0835	3.2	98	1509	0.0	0	2054	3.1	94
6 F	0321	0.0	0	0915	3.4	104	1555	-0.1	-3	2137	3.0	91
7 Sa	0404	0.0	0	0958	3.5	107	1644	-0.2	-6	2224	3.0	91
8 Su	0449	0.0	0	1046	3.5	107	1737	-0.1	-3	2314	2.9	88
9 M	0540	0.1	3	1137	3.5	107	1833	-0.1	-3			
10 Tu	0008	2.8	85	0637	0.3	9	1234	3.4	104	1933	0.0	0
11 W	0107	2.6	79	0740	0.3	9	1337	3.2	98	2035	0.1	3
12 Th ◐	0212	2.6	79	0845	0.4	12	1446	3.1	94	2135	0.1	3
13 F	0321	2.6	79	0950	0.4	12	1556	3.0	91	2234	0.1	3
14 Sa	0429	2.7	82	1053	0.3	9	1701	3.0	91	2330	0.1	3
15 Su	0528	2.8	85	1154	0.2	6	1757	3.0	91			
16 M	0024	0.1	3	0619	3.0	91	1250	0.1	3	1845	3.0	91
17 Tu	0113	0.0	0	0704	3.2	98	1342	0.0	0	1929	2.9	88
18 W	0159	0.1	3	0747	3.3	101	1429	0.0	0	2011	2.9	88
19 Th ●	0241	0.1	3	0829	3.3	101	1514	0.0	0	2053	2.8	85
20 F	0322	0.2	6	0911	3.3	101	1556	0.0	0	2136	2.7	82
21 Sa	0401	0.3	9	0954	3.3	101	1638	0.1	3	2221	2.6	79
22 Su	0441	0.4	12	1038	3.2	98	1721	0.2	6	2307	2.5	76
23 M	0522	0.6	18	1124	3.1	94	1807	0.3	9	2355	2.4	73
24 Tu	0608	0.7	21	1213	2.9	88	1856	0.4	12			
25 W	0046	2.4	73	0700	0.8	24	1304	2.8	85	1947	0.5	15
26 Th	0142	2.3	70	0757	0.9	27	1400	2.6	79	2040	0.6	18
27 F ◐	0241	2.3	70	0854	0.9	27	1459	2.6	79	2131	0.5	15
28 Sa	0342	2.3	70	0949	0.9	27	1558	2.6	79	2220	0.5	15
29 Su	0438	2.4	73	1042	0.7	21	1652	2.6	79	2307	0.4	12
30 M	0525	2.6	79	1133	0.6	18	1739	2.7	82	2353	0.3	9
31 Tu	0607	2.8	85	1223	0.4	12	1821	2.8	85			

November

Day	Time	ft	cm	Time	ft	cm	Time	ft	cm	Time	ft	cm
1 W	0038	0.2	6	0645	3.0	91	1311	0.1	3	1902	2.9	88
2 Th	0122	0.1	3	0723	3.2	98	1359	-0.1	-3	1943	2.9	88
3 F	0206	0.0	0	0803	3.4	104	1447	-0.3	-9	2026	2.9	88
4 Sa	0251	-0.1	-3	0845	3.6	110	1535	-0.4	-12	2112	2.9	88
5 Su ○	0337	-0.1	-3	0932	3.6	110	1625	-0.4	-12	2202	2.9	88
6 M	0426	-0.1	-3	1024	3.6	110	1718	-0.4	-12	2255	2.8	85
7 Tu	0520	0.0	0	1119	3.5	107	1814	-0.3	-9	2352	2.7	82
8 W	0619	0.1	3	1217	3.4	104	1913	-0.2	-6			
9 Th	0052	2.7	82	0723	0.2	6	1320	3.2	98	2013	-0.1	-3
10 F ○	0157	2.6	79	0830	0.3	9	1427	3.0	91	2113		
11 Sa	0305	2.6	79	0936	0.3	9	1536	2.8	85	2211	0.0	0
12 Su	0412	2.7	82	1039	0.3	9	1641	2.7	82	2306	0.1	3
13 M	0512	2.9	88	1140	0.2	6	1738	2.7	82	2359	0.1	3
14 Tu	0602	3.0	91	1236	0.1	3	1827	2.6	79			
15 W	0048	0.1	3	0646	3.1	94	1327	0.0	0	1910	2.6	79
16 Th	0134	0.2	6	0727	3.2	98	1413	0.0	0	1951	2.5	76
17 F	0216	0.2	6	0807	3.2	98	1455	0.0	0	2032	2.5	76
18 Sa ●	0256	0.3	9	0847	3.2	98	1535	0.0	0	2114	2.5	76
19 Su	0334	0.3	9	0929	3.1	94	1614	0.0	0	2157	2.4	73
20 M	0412	0.4	12	1012	3.1	94	1654	0.1	3	2243	2.4	73
21 Tu	0452	0.5	15	1057	2.9	88	1736	0.2	6	2330	2.4	73
22 W	0536	0.6	18	1143	2.8	85	1821	0.2	6			
23 Th	0019	2.3	70	0625	0.7	21	1230	2.7	82	1909	0.3	9
24 F	0110	2.3	70	0720	0.8	24	1320	2.6	79	1959	0.3	9
25 Sa	0204	2.3	70	0816	0.8	24	1413	2.5	76	2049	0.3	9
26 Su ☽	0300	2.3	70	0912	0.7	21	1509	2.4	73	2137	0.3	9
27 M	0355	2.4	73	1007	0.6	18	1605	2.4	73	2225	0.3	9
28 Tu	0444	2.6	79	1100	0.4	12	1656	2.4	73	2313	0.2	6
29 W	0529	2.8	85	1153	0.2	6	1744	2.5	76			
30 Th	0000	0.1	3	0611	3.0	91	1245	-0.1	-3	1829	2.6	79

December

Day	Time	ft	cm	Time	ft	cm	Time	ft	cm	Time	ft	cm
1 F	0049	-0.1	-3	0653	3.3	101	1336	-0.3	-9	1914	2.7	82
2 Sa	0137	-0.2	-6	0736	3.5	107	1426	-0.5	-15	2001	2.7	82
3 Su ○	0226	-0.3	-9	0823	3.6	110	1516	-0.6	-18	2050	2.8	85
4 M	0316	-0.3	-9	0913	3.7	113	1607	-0.7	-21	2142	2.8	85
5 Tu	0408	-0.3	-9	1007	3.6	110	1659	-0.6	-18	2237	2.7	82
6 W	0503	-0.2	-6	1102	3.5	107	1753	-0.5	-15	2335	2.7	82
7 Th	0602	-0.1	-3	1200	3.3	101	1849	-0.4	-12			
8 F	0034	2.7	82	0705	0.0	0	1259	3.0	91	1948	-0.3	-9
9 Sa	0136	2.6	79	0811	0.1	3	1402	2.7	82	2046	-0.1	-3
10 Su ○	0241	2.6	79	0916	0.2	6	1507	2.5	76	2143	0.0	0
11 M	0346	2.7	82	1019	0.2	6	1613	2.4	73	2238	0.0	0
12 Tu	0447	2.8	85	1120	0.1	3	1713	2.3	70	2331	0.1	3
13 W	0539	2.8	85	1217	0.1	3	1804	2.2	67			
14 Th	0022	0.2	6	0625	2.9	88	1308	0.0	0	1849	2.2	67
15 F	0108	0.2	6	0707	3.0	91	1353	0.0	0	1931	2.2	67
16 Sa	0152	0.2	6	0747	3.0	91	1434	-0.1	-3	2012	2.2	67
17 Su	0232	0.3	9	0827	3.0	91	1512	-0.1	-3	2053	2.3	70
18 M ●	0311	0.3	9	0909	2.9	88	1550	-0.1	-3	2136	2.3	70
19 Tu	0349	0.3	9	0951	2.9	88	1628	-0.1	-3	2221	2.3	70
20 W	0428	0.3	9	1034	2.8	85	1707	0.0	0	2306	2.3	70
21 Th	0510	0.4	12	1116	2.7	82	1748	0.0	0	2351	2.3	70
22 F	0556	0.4	12	1159	2.6	79	1833	0.1	3			
23 Sa	0037	2.3	70	0646	0.5	15	1242	2.5	76	1919	0.1	3
24 Su	0123	2.3	70	0741	0.5	15	1327	2.4	73	2008	0.1	3
25 M	0212	2.3	70	0837	0.5	15	1417	2.3	70	2056	0.1	3
26 Tu ☽	0305	2.4	73	0933	0.4	12	1514	2.2	67	2145	0.1	3
27 W	0358	2.5	76	1029	0.2	6	1613	2.2	67	2235	0.1	3
28 Th	0450	2.8	85	1126	0.0	0	1709	2.3	70	2327	0.0	0
29 F	0539	3.0	91	1221	-0.2	-6	1801	2.4	73			
30 Sa	0020	-0.1	-3	0628	3.2	98	1315	-0.4	-12	1851	2.5	76
31 Su	0114	-0.3	-9	0716	3.4	104	1407	-0.6	-18	1940	2.6	79

Time meridian 75° W. 0000 is midnight. 1200 is noon. Times are not adjusted for Daylight Saving Time.
Heights are referred to mean lower low water which is the chart datum of soundings.

Bridgeport, Connecticut, 2017

Times and Heights of High and Low Waters

January

Day	Time	ft	cm	Day	Time	ft	cm
1 Su	0054	6.6	201	16 M	0143	7.1	216
	0659	0.2	6		0756	-0.2	-6
	1304	7.1	216		1402	7.0	213
	1929	-0.3	-9		2023	-0.3	-9
2 M	0136	6.6	201	17 Tu	0231	6.9	210
	0744	0.2	6		0848	0.1	3
	1348	7.0	213		1452	6.6	201
	2013	-0.3	-9		2111	0.0	0
3 Tu	0220	6.6	201	18 W	0321	6.7	204
	0833	0.3	9		0941	0.3	9
	1437	6.8	207		1545	6.2	189
	2101	-0.2	-6		2201	0.4	12
4 W	0309	6.7	204	19 Th	0413	6.5	198
	0927	0.3	9		1036	0.5	15
	1531	6.6	201		1640	5.9	180
	2153	-0.1	-3	◐	2252	0.6	18
5 Th	0402	6.8	207	20 F	0506	6.4	195
	1027	0.2	6		1133	0.6	18
	1630	6.5	198		1736	5.7	174
◐	2249	0.0	0		2346	0.8	24
6 F	0500	6.9	210	21 Sa	0601	6.3	192
	1130	0.1	3		1229	0.6	18
	1732	6.4	195		1833	5.6	171
	2348	0.0	0				
7 Sa	0600	7.1	216	22 Su	0040	0.8	24
	1233	-0.1	-3		0655	6.4	195
	1836	6.4	195		1323	0.5	15
					1928	5.7	174
8 Su	0048	-0.1	-3	23 M	0132	0.8	24
	0700	7.4	226		0746	6.5	198
	1336	-0.4	-12		1413	0.4	12
	1938	6.6	201		2019	5.9	180
9 M	0147	-0.2	-6	24 Tu	0222	0.6	18
	0800	7.6	232		0835	6.6	201
	1435	-0.7	-21		1459	0.1	3
	2037	6.8	207		2106	6.1	186
10 Tu	0245	-0.4	-12	25 W	0308	0.4	12
	0857	7.9	241		0920	6.8	207
	1530	-0.9	-27		1543	-0.1	-3
	2132	7.0	213		2150	6.3	192
11 W	0340	-0.6	-18	26 Th	0352	0.3	9
	0951	8.0	244		1002	6.9	210
	1623	-1.1	-34		1624	-0.3	-9
	2226	7.2	219		2231	6.5	198
12 Th	0434	-0.7	-21	27 F	0434	0.1	3
	1044	8.0	244		1043	7.1	216
	1714	-1.2	-37		1704	-0.5	-15
○	2316	7.3	223	●	2310	6.7	204
13 F	0525	-0.7	-21	28 Sa	0515	-0.1	-3
	1134	7.9	241		1123	7.2	219
	1802	-1.1	-34		1744	-0.6	-18
					2350	6.8	207
14 Sa	0006	7.3	223	29 Su	0557	-0.2	-6
	0616	-0.6	-18		1203	7.3	223
	1224	7.7	235		1824	-0.7	-21
	1850	-0.9	-27				
15 Su	0054	7.2	219	30 M	0029	7.0	213
	0706	-0.4	-12		0639	-0.3	-9
	1313	7.4	226		1244	7.3	223
	1937	-0.6	-18		1905	-0.7	-21
				31 Tu	0111	7.1	216
					0724	-0.3	-9
					1329	7.2	219
					1948	-0.6	-18

February

Day	Time	ft	cm	Day	Time	ft	cm
1 W	0155	7.1	216	16 Th	0240	6.8	207
	0813	-0.3	-9		0901	0.2	6
	1417	7.0	213		1506	6.2	189
	2035	-0.4	-12		2115	0.5	15
2 Th	0243	7.1	216	17 F	0327	6.6	201
	0907	-0.2	-6		0951	0.5	15
	1510	6.7	204		1557	5.9	180
	2127	-0.2	-6		2204	0.8	24
3 F	0336	7.1	216	18 Sa	0418	6.3	192
	1006	-0.1	-3		1044	0.7	21
	1609	6.5	198		1651	5.7	174
◐	2224	0.0	0	◐	2258	1.0	30
4 Sa	0435	7.1	216	19 Su	0512	6.2	189
	1109	0.0	0		1141	0.8	24
	1712	6.3	192		1748	5.6	171
	2325	0.1	3		2354	1.1	34
5 Su	0538	7.1	216	20 M	0609	6.1	186
	1215	-0.1	-3		1238	0.8	24
	1818	6.3	192		1846	5.6	171
6 M	0029	0.1	3	21 Tu	0052	1.0	30
	0642	7.2	219		0706	6.2	189
	1320	-0.2	-6		1332	0.6	18
	1922	6.4	195		1941	5.8	177
7 Tu	0133	0.0	0	22 W	0146	0.8	24
	0746	7.3	223		0759	6.4	195
	1421	-0.5	-15		1423	0.4	12
	2023	6.6	201		2031	6.1	186
8 W	0233	-0.2	-6	23 Th	0237	0.6	18
	0845	7.5	229		0848	6.6	201
	1517	-0.7	-21		1509	0.1	3
	2119	6.9	210		2117	6.4	195
9 Th	0329	-0.4	-12	24 F	0324	0.3	9
	0940	7.6	232		0933	6.9	210
	1608	-0.8	-24		1553	-0.2	-6
	2211	7.1	216		2200	6.7	204
10 F	0422	-0.6	-18	25 Sa	0408	0.0	0
	1031	7.7	235		1017	7.2	219
	1656	-0.9	-27		1635	-0.5	-15
○	2259	7.3	223		2241	7.0	213
11 Sa	0511	-0.7	-21	26 Su	0452	-0.3	-9
	1119	7.7	235		1059	7.4	226
	1742	-0.9	-27		1716	-0.7	-21
	2345	7.4	226	●	2322	7.3	223
12 Su	0558	-0.6	-18	27 M	0535	-0.5	-15
	1205	7.5	229		1141	7.5	229
	1825	-0.7	-21		1757	-0.8	-24
13 M	0029	7.3	223	28 Tu	0003	7.5	229
	0643	-0.5	-15		0619	-0.7	-21
	1249	7.2	219		1225	7.5	229
	1906	-0.5	-15		1840	-0.8	-24
14 Tu	0112	7.2	219				
	0728	-0.3	-9				
	1333	6.9	210				
	1948	-0.2	-6				
15 W	0156	7.0	213				
	0814	0.0	0				
	1419	6.5	198				
	2030	0.2	6				

March

Day	Time	ft	cm	Day	Time	ft	cm
1 W	0046	7.6	232	16 Th	0121	7.2	219
	0706	-0.7	-21		0741	-0.1	-3
	1310	7.4	226		1347	6.6	201
	1925	-0.6	-18		1953	0.4	12
2 Th	0131	7.7	235	17 F	0202	7.0	213
	0755	-0.6	-18		0823	0.2	6
	1400	7.2	219		1431	6.3	192
	2013	-0.4	-12		2035	0.7	21
3 F	0220	7.6	232	18 Sa	0245	6.7	204
	0849	-0.5	-15		0909	0.5	15
	1453	6.9	210		1518	6.1	186
	2106	-0.2	-6		2121	1.0	30
4 Sa	0315	7.4	226	19 Su	0332	6.4	195
	0948	-0.2	-6		0959	0.7	21
	1552	6.6	201		1609	5.8	177
	2205	0.1	3		2213	1.2	37
5 Su	0415	7.2	219	20 M	0425	6.2	189
	1052	0.0	0		1053	0.9	27
	1656	6.4	195		1704	5.8	177
◐	2309	0.3	9	◐	2311	1.3	40
6 M	0521	7.0	213	21 Tu	0523	6.1	186
	1159	0.0	0		1151	0.9	27
	1803	6.3	192		1802	5.8	177
7 Tu	0016	0.3	9	22 W	0010	1.2	37
	0628	7.0	213		0622	6.2	189
	1304	0.0	0		1248	0.8	24
	1908	6.5	198		1859	6.0	183
8 W	0122	0.2	6	23 Th	0108	1.0	30
	0733	7.1	216		0719	6.3	192
	1405	-0.2	-6		1342	0.6	18
	2009	6.7	204		1952	6.3	192
9 Th	0223	0.0	0	24 F	0202	0.7	21
	0833	7.2	219		0812	6.6	201
	1501	-0.3	-9		1432	0.2	6
	2104	7.0	213		2040	6.7	204
10 F	0318	-0.2	-6	25 Sa	0253	0.3	9
	0927	7.4	226		0901	7.0	213
	1551	-0.5	-15		1518	-0.1	-3
	2154	7.2	219		2126	7.1	216
11 Sa	0409	-0.4	-12	26 Su	0340	-0.1	-3
	1016	7.4	226		0947	7.3	223
	1636	-0.5	-15		1603	-0.4	-12
	2239	7.4	226		2210	7.5	229
12 Su	0455	-0.5	-15	27 M	0427	-0.5	-15
	1101	7.4	226		1033	7.6	232
	1718	-0.5	-15		1646	-0.6	-18
○	2322	7.5	229	●	2253	7.8	238
13 M	0538	-0.5	-15	28 Tu	0513	-0.8	-24
	1144	7.3	223		1118	7.7	235
	1757	-0.3	-9		1730	-0.7	-21
					2336	8.1	247
14 Tu	0002	7.5	229	29 W	0559	-1.0	-30
	0620	-0.4	-12		1205	7.7	235
	1225	7.1	216		1815	-0.7	-21
	1835	-0.1	-3				
15 W	0041	7.4	226	30 Th	0022	8.2	250
	0700	-0.3	-9		0648	-1.0	-30
	1306	6.9	210		1253	7.6	232
	1913	0.1	3		1903	-0.6	-18
				31 F	0110	8.2	250
					0739	-0.8	-24
					1344	7.4	226
					1953	-0.3	-9

Time meridian 75° W. 0000 is midnight. 1200 is noon. Times are not adjusted for Daylight Saving Time.
Heights are referred to mean lower low water which is the chart datum of soundings.

Bridgeport, Connecticut, 2017
Times and Heights of High and Low Waters

April

Day	Time (h m)	Height (ft)	Height (cm)
1 Sa	0201	8.0	244
	0833	-0.6	-18
	1439	7.1	216
	2049	0.0	0
2 Su	0257	7.6	232
	0933	-0.3	-9
	1538	6.8	207
	2150	0.3	9
3 M	0359	7.3	223
	1036	0.0	0
	1642	6.6	201
	2256	0.5	15
4 Tu	0506	7.0	213
	1142	0.2	6
	1748	6.6	201
5 W	0004	0.5	15
	0614	6.9	210
	1246	0.2	6
	1852	6.7	204
6 Th	0109	0.4	12
	0719	6.9	210
	1346	0.1	3
	1952	6.9	210
7 F	0210	0.2	6
	0818	7.0	213
	1439	0.0	0
	2045	7.2	219
8 Sa	0304	0.0	0
	0910	7.1	216
	1527	-0.1	-3
	2133	7.4	226
9 Su	0352	-0.2	-6
	0957	7.2	219
	1611	-0.1	-3
	2216	7.6	232
10 M	0436	-0.3	-9
	1041	7.2	219
	1651	0.0	0
	2256	7.6	232
11 Tu	0517	-0.3	-9
	1121	7.1	216
	1729	0.1	3
	2334	7.6	232
12 W	0555	-0.3	-9
	1201	7.0	213
	1805	0.3	9
13 Th	0012	7.5	229
	0633	-0.2	-6
	1240	6.8	207
	1842	0.5	15
14 F	0049	7.3	223
	0711	0.0	0
	1319	6.7	204
	1920	0.7	21
15 Sa	0128	7.1	216
	0751	0.2	6
	1400	6.5	198
	2001	0.9	27
16 Su	0209	6.9	210
	0834	0.4	12
	1444	6.3	192
	2046	1.1	34
17 M	0254	6.6	201
	0920	0.7	21
	1532	6.1	186
	2136	1.2	37
18 Tu	0344	6.4	195
	1012	0.8	24
	1625	6.1	186
	2232	1.3	40
19 W	0439	6.3	192
	1107	0.9	27
	1720	6.1	186
	2331	1.3	40
20 Th	0538	6.3	192
	1203	0.8	24
	1816	6.3	192
21 F	0030	1.1	34
	0637	6.4	195
	1259	0.6	18
	1910	6.6	201
22 Sa	0127	0.7	21
	0733	6.7	204
	1351	0.3	9
	2001	7.0	213
23 Su	0220	0.3	9
	0826	7.0	213
	1441	0.0	0
	2050	7.5	229
24 M	0311	-0.2	-6
	0917	7.3	223
	1529	-0.2	-6
	2137	7.9	241
25 Tu	0401	-0.6	-18
	1006	7.6	232
	1616	-0.5	-15
	2224	8.3	253
26 W	0450	-0.9	-27
	1055	7.7	235
	1704	-0.6	-18
	2311	8.5	259
27 Th	0540	-1.1	-34
	1145	7.8	238
	1752	-0.6	-18
28 F	0000	8.6	262
	0631	-1.1	-34
	1236	7.7	235
	1843	-0.4	-12
29 Sa	0051	8.5	259
	0723	-0.9	-27
	1328	7.5	229
	1936	-0.2	-6
30 Su	0144	8.2	250
	0818	-0.6	-18
	1424	7.3	223
	2034	0.1	3

May

Day	Time (h m)	Height (ft)	Height (cm)
1 M	0242	7.8	238
	0916	-0.3	-9
	1523	7.1	216
	2136	0.3	9
2 Tu	0344	7.4	226
	1018	0.0	0
	1625	7.0	213
	2241	0.5	15
3 W	0448	7.1	216
	1120	0.2	6
	1729	6.9	210
	2347	0.6	18
4 Th	0554	6.8	207
	1221	0.3	9
	1831	7.0	213
5 F	0051	0.5	15
	0657	6.8	207
	1319	0.3	9
	1928	7.2	219
6 Sa	0150	0.4	12
	0755	6.8	207
	1411	0.3	9
	2020	7.3	223
7 Su	0243	0.2	6
	0847	6.8	207
	1459	0.3	9
	2106	7.5	229
8 M	0330	0.0	0
	0934	6.9	210
	1542	0.4	12
	2149	7.6	232
9 Tu	0413	-0.1	-3
	1017	6.9	210
	1622	0.4	12
	2229	7.6	232
10 W	0453	-0.1	-3
	1058	6.9	210
	1700	0.5	15
	2307	7.6	232
11 Th	0531	-0.1	-3
	1137	6.8	207
	1737	0.6	18
	2344	7.5	229
12 F	0608	0.0	0
	1215	6.8	207
	1814	0.7	21
13 Sa	0021	7.3	223
	0645	0.1	3
	1254	6.7	204
	1853	0.8	24
14 Su	0059	7.2	219
	0724	0.2	6
	1334	6.6	201
	1933	1.0	30
15 M	0139	7.0	213
	0805	0.4	12
	1416	6.5	198
	2017	1.1	34
16 Tu	0222	6.8	207
	0849	0.5	15
	1501	6.4	195
	2105	1.2	37
17 W	0310	6.7	204
	0937	0.6	18
	1550	6.4	195
	2158	1.2	37
18 Th	0402	6.6	201
	1028	0.6	18
	1641	6.5	198
	2255	1.1	34
19 F	0458	6.5	198
	1122	0.6	18
	1735	6.7	204
	2354	0.9	27
20 Sa	0557	6.6	201
	1217	0.5	15
	1829	7.0	213
21 Su	0052	0.6	18
	0656	6.8	207
	1312	0.3	9
	1923	7.4	226
22 M	0149	0.2	6
	0753	7.0	213
	1405	0.1	3
	2015	7.8	238
23 Tu	0244	-0.2	-6
	0848	7.2	219
	1457	-0.1	-3
	2107	8.2	250
24 W	0337	-0.6	-18
	0941	7.4	226
	1548	-0.3	-9
	2158	8.5	259
25 Th	0430	-0.9	-27
	1034	7.6	232
	1640	-0.4	-12
	2249	8.7	265
26 F	0522	-1.1	-34
	1126	7.7	235
	1732	-0.4	-12
	2341	8.7	265
27 Sa	0614	-1.1	-34
	1219	7.7	235
	1825	-0.4	-12
28 Su	0034	8.5	259
	0707	-0.9	-27
	1312	7.6	232
	1921	-0.2	-6
29 M	0129	8.2	250
	0801	-0.7	-21
	1408	7.5	229
	2018	0.1	3
30 Tu	0226	7.8	238
	0857	-0.4	-12
	1505	7.3	223
	2119	0.3	9
31 W	0325	7.4	226
	0955	-0.1	-3
	1604	7.2	219
	2221	0.5	15

June

Day	Time (h m)	Height (ft)	Height (cm)
1 Th	0426	7.0	213
	1053	0.2	6
	1703	7.2	219
	2324	0.6	18
2 F	0528	6.7	204
	1150	0.4	12
	1802	7.2	219
3 Sa	0026	0.6	18
	0628	6.6	201
	1245	0.5	15
	1857	7.2	219
4 Su	0123	0.5	15
	0725	6.5	198
	1337	0.6	18
	1949	7.3	223
5 M	0216	0.4	12
	0818	6.5	198
	1425	0.7	21
	2036	7.4	226
6 Tu	0303	0.3	9
	0906	6.5	198
	1510	0.7	21
	2120	7.4	226
7 W	0347	0.2	6
	0950	6.6	201
	1552	0.7	21
	2201	7.5	229
8 Th	0427	0.1	3
	1032	6.7	204
	1632	0.8	24
	2240	7.4	226
9 F	0506	0.1	3
	1112	6.7	204
	1711	0.8	24
	2319	7.4	226
10 Sa	0544	0.1	3
	1151	6.7	204
	1750	0.8	24
	2357	7.3	223
11 Su	0621	0.1	3
	1230	6.7	204
	1829	0.9	27
12 M	0035	7.2	219
	0700	0.2	6
	1309	6.7	204
	1910	0.9	27
13 Tu	0114	7.1	216
	0739	0.2	6
	1350	6.7	204
	1952	1.0	30
14 W	0156	7.0	213
	0821	0.3	9
	1432	6.7	204
	2039	1.0	30
15 Th	0241	6.9	210
	0906	0.3	9
	1518	6.8	207
	2129	1.0	30
16 F	0331	6.8	207
	0955	0.4	12
	1607	6.9	210
	2224	0.9	27
17 Sa	0425	6.7	204
	1046	0.4	12
	1659	7.1	216
	2322	0.7	21
18 Su	0524	6.7	204
	1141	0.4	12
	1754	7.3	223
19 M	0022	0.5	15
	0624	6.7	204
	1237	0.3	9
	1850	7.6	232
20 Tu	0122	0.1	3
	0724	6.9	210
	1333	0.2	6
	1946	8.0	244
21 W	0220	-0.2	-6
	0822	7.0	213
	1430	0.0	0
	2041	8.3	253
22 Th	0316	-0.6	-18
	0919	7.3	223
	1525	-0.2	-6
	2136	8.5	259
23 F	0411	-0.8	-24
	1014	7.5	229
	1620	-0.3	-9
	2231	8.6	262
24 Sa	0504	-0.9	-27
	1108	7.6	232
	1714	-0.4	-12
	2324	8.6	262
25 Su	0557	-1.0	-30
	1201	7.7	235
	1809	-0.3	-9
26 M	0018	8.4	256
	0649	-0.8	-24
	1254	7.7	235
	1904	-0.2	-6
27 Tu	0111	8.1	247
	0741	-0.6	-18
	1347	7.6	232
	2000	0.0	0
28 W	0206	7.8	238
	0833	-0.4	-12
	1441	7.5	229
	2057	0.2	6
29 Th	0301	7.3	223
	0926	0.0	0
	1536	7.4	226
	2155	0.5	15
30 F	0358	6.9	210
	1019	0.3	9
	1631	7.3	223
	2254	0.6	18

Time meridian 75° W. 0000 is midnight. 1200 is noon. Times are not adjusted for Daylight Saving Time.
Heights are referred to mean lower low water which is the chart datum of soundings.

Bridgeport, Connecticut, 2017

Times and Heights of High and Low Waters

July

Day	Time	ft	cm
1 Sa	0456	6.6	201
	1113	0.5	15
	1727	7.2	219
	2353	0.7	21
2 Su	0554	6.4	195
	1207	0.8	24
	1821	7.1	216
3 M	0049	0.7	21
	0650	6.3	192
	1259	0.9	27
	1913	7.1	216
4 Tu	0143	0.6	18
	0744	6.2	189
	1349	1.0	30
	2002	7.2	219
5 W	0232	0.5	15
	0835	6.3	192
	1437	1.0	30
	2049	7.2	219
6 Th	0317	0.4	12
	0921	6.4	195
	1522	0.9	27
	2133	7.3	223
7 F	0359	0.3	9
	1005	6.5	198
	1604	0.9	27
	2214	7.3	223
8 Sa ○	0439	0.2	6
	1046	6.6	201
	1646	0.8	24
	2254	7.3	223
9 Su	0518	0.1	3
	1126	6.7	204
	1726	0.8	24
	2333	7.3	223
10 M	0556	0.1	3
	1205	6.8	207
	1806	0.7	21
11 Tu	0012	7.3	223
	0635	0.0	0
	1243	6.9	210
	1847	0.7	21
12 W	0051	7.3	223
	0714	0.0	0
	1322	7.0	213
	1929	0.7	21
13 Th	0132	7.2	219
	0755	0.1	3
	1404	7.0	213
	2014	0.7	21
14 F	0217	7.1	216
	0838	0.1	3
	1448	7.1	216
	2104	0.6	18
15 Sa	0305	7.0	213
	0925	0.2	6
	1536	7.2	219
	2158	0.6	18
16 Su ◑	0359	6.9	210
	1016	0.3	9
	1628	7.4	226
	2256	0.5	15
17 M	0457	6.7	204
	1112	0.4	12
	1725	7.5	229
	2358	0.3	9
18 Tu	0559	6.7	204
	1210	0.4	12
	1824	7.7	235
19 W	0100	0.1	3
	0701	6.8	207
	1310	0.3	9
	1924	7.9	241
20 Th	0201	-0.1	-3
	0802	6.9	210
	1410	0.1	3
	2023	8.2	250
21 F	0259	-0.4	-12
	0901	7.2	219
	1508	-0.1	-3
	2120	8.3	253
22 Sa	0354	-0.6	-18
	0957	7.4	226
	1604	-0.2	-6
	2215	8.4	256
23 Su ●	0447	-0.8	-24
	1050	7.6	232
	1659	-0.3	-9
	2309	8.4	256
24 M	0538	-0.8	-24
	1142	7.7	235
	1752	-0.3	-9
25 Tu	0000	8.3	253
	0627	-0.7	-21
	1232	7.8	238
	1845	-0.2	-6
26 W	0051	8.0	244
	0716	-0.5	-15
	1322	7.7	235
	1937	0.0	0
27 Th	0142	7.6	232
	0804	-0.2	-6
	1412	7.6	232
	2030	0.2	6
28 F	0233	7.2	219
	0852	0.1	3
	1502	7.4	226
	2123	0.5	15
29 Sa	0326	6.8	207
	0942	0.5	15
	1554	7.2	219
	2218	0.7	21
30 Su ◐	0420	6.5	198
	1033	0.8	24
	1647	7.1	216
	2314	0.9	27
31 M	0516	6.2	189
	1126	1.0	30
	1740	6.9	210

August

Day	Time	ft	cm
1 Tu	0010	0.9	27
	0613	6.1	186
	1219	1.2	37
	1834	6.9	210
2 W	0104	0.9	27
	0708	6.1	186
	1312	1.2	37
	1927	6.9	210
3 Th	0156	0.8	24
	0800	6.2	189
	1403	1.1	34
	2017	7.0	213
4 F	0243	0.6	18
	0849	6.4	195
	1451	1.0	30
	2103	7.1	216
5 Sa	0328	0.5	15
	0934	6.6	201
	1536	0.8	24
	2147	7.2	219
6 Su	0409	0.3	9
	1017	6.8	207
	1619	0.7	21
	2228	7.3	223
7 M ○	0449	0.1	3
	1057	6.9	210
	1701	0.6	18
	2308	7.4	226
8 Tu	0528	0.0	0
	1136	7.1	216
	1741	0.5	15
	2347	7.5	229
9 W	0607	-0.1	-3
	1214	7.2	219
	1823	0.4	12
10 Th	0027	7.5	229
	0646	-0.1	-3
	1253	7.3	223
	1906	0.3	9
11 F	0109	7.4	226
	0727	-0.1	-3
	1335	7.4	226
	1951	0.3	9
12 Sa	0154	7.3	223
	0811	0.0	0
	1419	7.5	229
	2041	0.3	9
13 Su	0244	7.1	216
	0859	0.2	6
	1509	7.5	229
	2136	0.3	9
14 M ◐	0338	6.9	210
	0952	0.3	9
	1603	7.6	232
	2236	0.4	12
15 Tu	0438	6.7	204
	1050	0.5	15
	1702	7.6	232
	2339	0.3	9
16 W	0541	6.7	204
	1152	0.5	15
	1805	7.6	232
17 Th	0043	0.2	6
	0645	6.7	204
	1255	0.4	12
	1908	7.8	238
18 F	0145	0.0	0
	0747	6.9	210
	1357	0.3	9
	2010	7.9	241
19 Sa	0244	-0.2	-6
	0846	7.2	219
	1456	0.0	0
	2107	8.1	247
20 Su	0338	-0.4	-12
	0941	7.5	229
	1552	-0.2	-6
	2202	8.2	250
21 M ●	0429	-0.5	-15
	1032	7.7	235
	1644	-0.3	-9
	2252	8.2	250
22 Tu	0517	-0.6	-18
	1121	7.8	238
	1735	-0.3	-9
	2341	8.0	244
23 W	0603	-0.4	-12
	1208	7.9	241
	1823	-0.2	-6
24 Th	0028	7.8	238
	0647	-0.2	-6
	1253	7.8	238
	1911	0.0	0
25 F	0115	7.5	229
	0731	0.1	3
	1339	7.6	232
	1959	0.2	6
26 Sa	0202	7.1	216
	0815	0.4	12
	1425	7.4	226
	2048	0.5	15
27 Su	0251	6.7	204
	0902	0.7	21
	1513	7.1	216
	2138	0.8	24
28 M	0342	6.4	195
	0951	1.0	30
	1604	6.9	210
	2232	1.0	30
29 Tu ◐	0437	6.2	189
	1043	1.3	40
	1658	6.7	204
	2327	1.1	34
30 W	0533	6.0	183
	1139	1.4	43
	1754	6.6	201
31 Th	0023	1.1	34
	0630	6.1	186
	1235	1.4	43
	1849	6.7	204

September

Day	Time	ft	cm
1 F	0116	1.0	30
	0724	6.2	189
	1329	1.2	37
	1942	6.8	207
2 Sa	0206	0.8	24
	0814	6.4	195
	1420	1.0	30
	2031	7.0	213
3 Su	0252	0.6	18
	0900	6.7	204
	1507	0.8	24
	2116	7.2	219
4 M	0335	0.3	9
	0943	7.0	213
	1551	0.5	15
	2159	7.4	226
5 Tu	0416	0.1	3
	1024	7.2	219
	1633	0.3	9
	2240	7.5	229
6 W ○	0456	-0.1	-3
	1104	7.5	229
	1715	0.1	3
	2321	7.6	232
7 Th	0536	-0.2	-6
	1143	7.7	235
	1758	0.0	0
8 F	0003	7.7	235
	0617	-0.2	-6
	1224	7.8	238
	1843	-0.1	-3
9 Sa	0047	7.6	232
	0700	-0.1	-3
	1307	7.9	241
	1930	-0.1	-3
10 Su	0134	7.4	226
	0746	0.0	0
	1354	7.9	241
	2022	0.0	0
11 M	0225	7.2	219
	0836	0.2	6
	1446	7.8	238
	2118	0.1	3
12 Tu	0322	6.9	210
	0933	0.4	12
	1543	7.6	232
	2220	0.3	9
13 W ◐	0423	6.8	207
	1035	0.6	18
	1646	7.5	229
	2325	0.3	9
14 Th	0528	6.7	204
	1140	0.6	18
	1752	7.5	229
15 F	0029	0.3	9
	0633	6.8	207
	1246	0.5	15
	1857	7.5	229
16 Sa	0131	0.1	3
	0735	7.0	213
	1348	0.3	9
	1959	7.7	235
17 Su	0228	-0.1	-3
	0832	7.3	223
	1446	0.1	3
	2055	7.8	238
18 M	0320	-0.2	-6
	0924	7.6	232
	1539	-0.2	-6
	2147	7.9	241
19 Tu	0408	-0.3	-9
	1012	7.8	238
	1629	-0.3	-9
	2235	7.8	238
20 W ●	0453	-0.3	-9
	1058	7.9	241
	1715	-0.3	-9
	2320	7.7	235
21 Th	0535	-0.2	-6
	1141	7.9	241
	1800	-0.2	-6
22 F	0004	7.5	229
	0616	0.1	3
	1223	7.8	238
	1843	0.0	0
23 Sa	0048	7.2	219
	0657	0.3	9
	1305	7.6	232
	1927	0.2	6
24 Su	0131	6.9	210
	0738	0.7	21
	1347	7.3	223
	2011	0.5	15
25 M	0217	6.6	201
	0822	1.0	30
	1433	7.1	216
	2058	0.8	24
26 Tu	0305	6.3	192
	0910	1.2	37
	1522	6.8	207
	2149	1.0	30
27 W ◐	0357	6.1	186
	1002	1.4	43
	1615	6.6	201
	2243	1.1	34
28 Th	0453	6.1	186
	1059	1.5	46
	1712	6.4	195
	2339	1.2	37
29 F	0549	6.1	186
	1157	1.4	43
	1809	6.5	198
30 Sa	0034	1.0	30
	0645	6.3	192
	1253	1.3	40
	1904	6.6	201

Time meridian 75° W. 0000 is midnight. 1200 is noon. Times are not adjusted for Daylight Saving Time.
Heights are referred to mean lower low water which is the chart datum of soundings.

Bridgeport, Connecticut, 2017
Times and Heights of High and Low Waters

October

Day	Time	ft	cm	Day	Time	ft	cm
1 Su	0125	0.8	24	16 M	0209	0.0	0
	0736	6.5	198		0815	7.4	226
	1346	1.0	30		1434	0.0	0
	1955	6.8	207		2040	7.4	226
2 M	0213	0.6	18	17 Tu	0259	-0.1	-3
	0823	6.9	210		0905	7.7	235
	1434	0.7	21		1525	-0.2	-6
	2042	7.1	216		2130	7.5	229
3 Tu	0258	0.3	9	18 W	0345	-0.1	-3
	0907	7.2	219		0951	7.8	238
	1520	0.3	9		1611	-0.3	-9
	2127	7.4	226		2215	7.4	226
4 W	0341	0.0	0	19 Th	0427	0.0	0
	0949	7.6	232		1033	7.9	241
	1605	0.0	0		1655	-0.3	-9
	2211	7.6	232	●	2259	7.3	223
5 Th	0423	-0.2	-6	20 F	0508	0.1	3
	1031	7.9	241		1114	7.8	238
	1649	-0.3	-9		1736	-0.2	-6
○	2254	7.7	235		2340	7.2	219
6 F	0506	-0.3	-9	21 Sa	0546	0.3	9
	1112	8.1	247		1153	7.7	235
	1734	-0.5	-15		1816	0.0	0
	2339	7.7	235				
7 Sa	0549	-0.3	-9	22 Su	0021	7.0	213
	1156	8.2	250		0625	0.5	15
	1821	-0.5	-15		1232	7.5	229
					1856	0.2	6
8 Su	0026	7.6	232	23 M	0102	6.7	204
	0635	-0.2	-6		0705	0.8	24
	1242	8.2	250		1313	7.2	219
	1911	-0.5	-15		1938	0.4	12
9 M	0115	7.4	226	24 Tu	0145	6.5	198
	0724	0.0	0		0747	1.0	30
	1332	8.1	247		1356	6.9	210
	2004	-0.3	-9		2021	0.6	18
10 Tu	0209	7.2	219	25 W	0231	6.3	192
	0818	0.2	6		0833	1.2	37
	1427	7.9	241		1443	6.7	204
	2102	-0.1	-3		2109	0.8	24
11 W	0307	7.0	213	26 Th	0320	6.2	189
	0918	0.4	12		0924	1.4	43
	1528	7.6	232		1534	6.5	198
	2205	0.1	3		2200	1.0	30
12 Th	0410	6.8	207	27 F	0413	6.1	186
	1022	0.6	18		1019	1.4	43
	1633	7.4	226		1629	6.3	192
◐	2310	0.3	9	◐	2255	1.0	30
13 F	0515	6.8	207	28 Sa	0508	6.1	186
	1130	0.6	18		1118	1.4	43
	1740	7.3	223		1726	6.3	192
					2349	0.9	27
14 Sa	0014	0.2	6	29 Su	0602	6.3	192
	0620	6.9	210		1215	1.2	37
	1236	0.5	15		1822	6.4	195
	1845	7.3	223				
15 Su	0114	0.1	3	30 M	0042	0.7	21
	0720	7.2	219		0654	6.6	201
	1338	0.3	9		1309	0.9	27
	1946	7.3	223		1916	6.7	204
				31 Tu	0132	0.5	15
					0743	7.0	213
					1401	0.5	15
					2006	6.9	210

November

Day	Time	ft	cm	Day	Time	ft	cm
1 W	0220	0.2	6	16 Th	0320	0.1	3
	0830	7.4	226		0928	7.6	232
	1450	0.0	0		1552	-0.2	-6
	2055	7.2	219		2155	6.9	210
2 Th	0306	-0.1	-3	17 F	0402	0.2	6
	0915	7.8	238		1009	7.6	232
	1537	-0.4	-12		1634	-0.3	-9
	2142	7.4	226		2237	6.9	210
3 F	0351	-0.3	-9	18 Sa	0441	0.3	9
	0959	8.1	247		1048	7.6	232
	1625	-0.7	-21		1713	-0.3	-9
	2229	7.6	232	●	2317	6.8	207
4 Sa	0437	-0.4	-12	19 Su	0520	0.4	12
	1045	8.4	256		1127	7.4	226
	1713	-0.9	-27		1751	-0.1	-3
○	2317	7.6	232		2357	6.7	204
5 Su	0524	-0.5	-15	20 M	0558	0.5	15
	1132	8.5	259		1205	7.3	223
	1802	-0.9	-27		1829	0.0	0
6 M	0006	7.6	232	21 Tu	0036	6.6	201
	0613	-0.4	-12		0636	0.7	21
	1221	8.4	256		1244	7.1	216
	1853	-0.8	-24		1908	0.2	6
7 Tu	0058	7.4	226	22 W	0117	6.4	195
	0705	-0.2	-6		0717	0.8	24
	1314	8.2	250		1325	6.8	207
	1948	-0.6	-18		1950	0.3	9
8 W	0153	7.2	219	23 Th	0159	6.3	192
	0802	0.0	0		0801	1.0	30
	1411	7.9	241		1409	6.6	201
	2046	-0.3	-9		2034	0.5	15
9 Th	0252	7.0	213	24 F	0245	6.2	189
	0903	0.2	6		0849	1.1	34
	1512	7.5	229		1456	6.4	195
	2147	-0.1	-3		2121	0.6	18
10 F	0354	6.9	210	25 Sa	0334	6.2	189
	1009	0.4	12		0941	1.2	37
	1617	7.2	219		1547	6.3	192
○	2250	0.1	3		2212	0.7	21
11 Sa	0458	6.9	210	26 Su	0425	6.2	189
	1116	0.5	15		1038	1.1	34
	1723	7.0	213		1643	6.2	189
	2352	0.1	3	◐	2305	0.6	18
12 Su	0601	7.0	213	27 M	0518	6.4	195
	1221	0.4	12		1135	0.9	27
	1828	6.9	210		1739	6.3	192
					2358	0.5	15
13 M	0051	0.1	3	28 Tu	0611	6.6	201
	0700	7.2	219		1232	0.6	18
	1322	0.2	6		1836	6.4	195
	1927	6.9	210				
14 Tu	0145	0.1	3	29 W	0051	0.3	9
	0754	7.4	226		0703	7.0	213
	1417	0.0	0		1327	0.2	6
	2021	6.9	210		1931	6.7	204
15 W	0235	0.1	3	30 Th	0142	0.1	3
	0843	7.5	229		0753	7.4	226
	1507	-0.2	-6		1420	-0.2	-6
	2110	6.9	210		2024	6.9	210

December

Day	Time	ft	cm	Day	Time	ft	cm
1 F	0233	-0.2	-6	16 Sa	0336	0.3	9
	0843	7.8	238		0945	7.2	219
	1512	-0.6	-18		1611	-0.2	-6
	2115	7.1	216		2215	6.5	198
2 Sa	0322	-0.4	-12	17 Su	0417	0.3	9
	0932	8.2	250		1025	7.2	219
	1603	-1.0	-30		1650	-0.2	-6
	2206	7.3	223		2255	6.5	198
3 Su	0412	-0.6	-18	18 M	0456	0.3	9
	1022	8.4	256		1104	7.2	219
	1653	-1.2	-37		1728	-0.2	-6
○	2257	7.4	226	●	2334	6.5	198
4 M	0503	-0.7	-21	19 Tu	0535	0.4	12
	1112	8.5	259		1142	7.1	216
	1744	-1.2	-37		1805	-0.2	-6
	2348	7.5	229				
5 Tu	0555	-0.7	-21	20 W	0012	6.5	198
	1204	8.4	256		0613	0.5	15
	1837	-1.1	-34		1221	7.0	213
					1843	-0.1	-3
6 W	0041	7.4	226	21 Th	0051	6.4	195
	0649	-0.5	-15		0653	0.5	15
	1259	8.1	247		1259	6.8	207
	1931	-0.9	-27		1921	0.0	0
7 Th	0136	7.3	223	22 F	0131	6.4	195
	0747	-0.3	-9		0734	0.6	18
	1355	7.8	238		1340	6.7	204
	2027	-0.7	-21		2002	0.1	3
8 F	0233	7.1	216	23 Sa	0212	6.3	192
	0847	-0.1	-3		0818	0.7	21
	1454	7.4	226		1423	6.5	198
	2125	-0.4	-12		2045	0.2	6
9 Sa	0333	7.0	213	24 Su	0256	6.3	192
	0950	0.1	3		0907	0.7	21
	1556	7.0	213		1511	6.4	195
	2224	-0.1	-3		2132	0.3	9
10 Su	0434	6.9	210	25 M	0344	6.4	195
	1055	0.3	9		1000	0.7	21
	1700	6.7	204		1603	6.3	192
○	2324	0.0	0		2223	0.3	9
11 M	0535	6.9	210	26 Tu	0435	6.5	198
	1159	0.3	9		1057	0.6	18
	1802	6.5	198		1700	6.2	189
				◐	2317	0.3	9
12 Tu	0022	0.2	6	27 W	0529	6.7	204
	0633	7.0	213		1156	0.4	12
	1259	0.2	6		1759	6.2	189
	1902	6.4	195				
13 W	0116	0.2	6	28 Th	0012	0.2	6
	0727	7.1	216		0625	7.0	213
	1355	0.1	3		1256	0.0	0
	1957	6.4	195		1858	6.4	195
14 Th	0207	0.2	6	29 F	0108	0.0	0
	0817	7.2	219		0720	7.3	223
	1445	-0.1	-3		1353	-0.3	-9
	2047	6.4	195		1956	6.6	201
15 F	0253	0.3	9	30 Sa	0204	-0.2	-6
	0903	7.2	219		0816	7.7	235
	1530	-0.2	-6		1449	-0.7	-21
	2133	6.5	198		2052	6.8	207
				31 Su	0259	-0.5	-15
					0910	8.0	244
					1543	-1.0	-30
					2146	7.1	216

Time meridian 75° W. 0000 is midnight. 1200 is noon. Times are not adjusted for Daylight Saving Time.
Heights are referred to mean lower low water which is the chart datum of soundings.

Kings Point, Long Island, New York, 2017

Times and Heights of High and Low Waters

January

Date	Day	Time	ft	cm
1	Su	0030	7.2	219
		0645	0.0	0
		1241	7.8	238
		1914	-0.4	-12
2	M	0111	7.3	223
		0728	0.0	0
		1326	7.8	238
		1957	-0.4	-12
3	Tu	0156	7.4	226
		0816	0.1	3
		1414	7.7	235
		2043	-0.3	-9
4	W	0244	7.5	229
		0910	0.1	3
		1507	7.5	229
		2134	-0.2	-6
5	Th ☽	0337	7.6	232
		1009	0.2	6
		1604	7.2	219
		2230	-0.1	-3
6	F	0434	7.6	232
		1119	0.2	6
		1707	7.0	213
		2332	0.0	0
7	Sa	0538	7.7	235
		1254	0.0	0
		1820	7.0	213
8	Su	0041	0.0	0
		0649	7.9	241
		1415	-0.4	-12
		1941	7.1	216
9	M	0203	-0.2	-6
		0802	8.2	250
		1517	-0.8	-24
		2051	7.3	223
10	Tu	0317	-0.4	-12
		0907	8.5	259
		1614	-1.2	-37
		2150	7.6	232
11	W	0417	-0.6	-18
		1004	8.6	262
		1706	-1.4	-43
		2244	7.8	238
12	Th ○	0512	-0.8	-24
		1057	8.7	265
		1756	-1.5	-46
		2335	7.9	241
13	F	0604	-0.8	-24
		1149	8.6	262
		1845	-1.4	-43
14	Sa	0026	7.9	241
		0654	-0.7	-21
		1240	8.3	253
		1933	-1.1	-34
15	Su	0117	7.8	238
		0745	-0.5	-15
		1331	7.9	241
		2021	-0.8	-24
16	M	0208	7.6	232
		0838	-0.1	-3
		1423	7.5	229
		2110	-0.4	-12
17	Tu	0259	7.4	226
		0934	0.2	6
		1517	7.1	216
		2200	0.1	3
18	W	0351	7.2	219
		1032	0.4	12
		1614	6.6	201
		2253	0.4	12
19	Th ◐	0447	7.0	213
		1131	0.6	18
		1716	6.3	192
		2347	0.7	21
20	F	0545	6.8	207
		1228	0.6	18
		1819	6.2	189
21	Sa	0042	0.8	24
		0643	6.8	207
		1323	0.6	18
		1918	6.2	189
22	Su	0135	0.9	27
		0738	6.9	210
		1415	0.4	12
		2012	6.3	192
23	M	0225	0.8	24
		0828	7.0	213
		1504	0.2	6
		2100	6.5	198
24	Tu	0312	0.6	18
		0913	7.2	219
		1548	0.0	0
		2143	6.7	204
25	W	0353	0.4	12
		0951	7.3	223
		1629	-0.2	-6
		2221	6.8	207
26	Th	0428	0.3	9
		1021	7.5	229
		1704	-0.3	-9
		2251	7.0	213
27	F ●	0452	0.1	3
		1041	7.6	232
		1730	-0.4	-12
		2310	7.1	216
28	Sa	0516	-0.1	-3
		1107	7.8	238
		1749	-0.6	-18
		2333	7.3	223
29	Su	0550	-0.3	-9
		1142	8.0	244
		1818	-0.7	-21
30	M	0007	7.6	232
		0629	-0.4	-12
		1223	8.0	244
		1854	-0.8	-24
31	Tu	0048	7.8	238
		0712	-0.5	-15
		1308	8.0	244
		1935	-0.7	-21

February

Date	Day	Time	ft	cm
1	W	0133	7.9	241
		0800	-0.4	-12
		1356	7.8	238
		2020	-0.6	-18
2	Th	0221	7.9	241
		0852	-0.3	-9
		1448	7.5	229
		2111	-0.4	-12
3	F ☽	0313	7.9	241
		0952	-0.1	-3
		1545	7.2	219
		2207	-0.1	-3
4	Sa	0411	7.7	235
		1112	0.1	3
		1650	6.9	210
		2312	0.1	3
5	Su	0518	7.6	232
		1256	0.0	0
		1814	6.7	204
6	M	0045	0.2	6
		0643	7.6	232
		1407	-0.3	-9
		1944	6.9	210
7	Tu	0214	0.0	0
		0808	7.8	238
		1508	-0.7	-21
		2050	7.2	219
8	W	0319	-0.3	-9
		0912	8.1	247
		1603	-1.0	-30
		2146	7.6	232
9	Th	0415	-0.6	-18
		1006	8.3	253
		1653	-1.3	-40
		2237	7.8	238
10	F ○	0507	-0.8	-24
		1056	8.4	256
		1741	-1.3	-40
		2325	8.0	244
11	Sa	0555	-0.9	-27
		1143	8.3	253
		1826	-1.2	-37
12	Su	0010	8.0	244
		0641	-0.8	-24
		1228	8.1	247
		1909	-1.0	-30
13	M	0053	7.9	241
		0725	-0.6	-18
		1311	7.8	238
		1949	-0.6	-18
14	Tu	0135	7.7	235
		0808	-0.3	-9
		1353	7.4	226
		2026	-0.1	-3
15	W	0215	7.5	229
		0851	0.1	3
		1435	7.0	213
		2052	0.3	9
16	Th	0253	7.2	219
		0935	0.4	12
		1518	6.6	201
		2106	0.7	21
17	F	0332	6.9	210
		1029	0.7	21
		1609	6.3	192
		2145	0.9	27
18	Sa ◐	0418	6.7	204
		1133	0.9	27
		1717	6.0	183
		2236	1.2	37
19	Su	0525	6.5	198
		1235	1.0	30
		1829	6.0	183
		2351	1.3	40
20	M	0644	6.4	195
		1332	0.9	27
		1930	6.1	186
21	Tu	0138	1.2	37
		0746	6.6	201
		1424	0.7	21
		2023	6.3	192
22	W	0231	0.9	27
		0836	6.8	207
		1511	0.4	12
		2108	6.6	201
23	Th	0317	0.6	18
		0917	7.1	216
		1553	0.1	3
		2145	6.9	210
24	F	0355	0.3	9
		0948	7.4	226
		1629	-0.2	-6
		2213	7.2	219
25	Sa	0427	-0.1	-3
		1014	7.8	238
		1657	-0.4	-12
		2235	7.5	229
26	Su ●	0459	-0.4	-12
		1046	8.0	244
		1722	-0.7	-21
		2306	7.9	241
27	M	0535	-0.7	-21
		1123	8.2	250
		1754	-0.8	-24
		2343	8.2	250
28	Tu	0615	-0.9	-27
		1206	8.3	253
		1832	-0.9	-27

March

Date	Day	Time	ft	cm
1	W	0025	8.4	256
		0658	-0.9	-27
		1251	8.2	250
		1914	-0.8	-24
2	Th	0111	8.5	259
		0746	-0.8	-24
		1340	8.0	244
		2000	-0.6	-18
3	F	0200	8.4	256
		0840	-0.5	-15
		1433	7.6	232
		2051	-0.3	-9
4	Sa	0254	8.1	247
		0946	-0.2	-6
		1532	7.2	219
		2151	0.1	3
5	Su ☽	0354	7.8	238
		1127	0.1	3
		1645	6.9	210
		2315	0.4	12
6	M	0509	7.5	229
		1248	0.0	0
		1823	6.8	207
7	Tu	0101	0.4	12
		0654	7.4	226
		1354	-0.2	-6
		1942	7.0	213
8	W	0211	0.1	3
		0809	7.6	232
		1453	-0.5	-15
		2043	7.4	226
9	Th	0311	-0.3	-9
		0908	7.9	241
		1546	-0.8	-24
		2136	7.8	238
10	F	0405	-0.6	-18
		1000	8.1	247
		1636	-1.0	-30
		2224	8.1	247
11	Sa	0454	-0.8	-24
		1047	8.2	250
		1721	-1.0	-30
		2308	8.2	250
12	Su ○	0540	-0.9	-27
		1130	8.2	250
		1803	-0.8	-24
		2349	8.2	250
13	M	0623	-0.8	-24
		1211	8.0	244
		1842	-0.6	-18
14	Tu	0027	8.1	247
		0703	-0.5	-15
		1249	7.7	235
		1916	-0.2	-6
15	W	0100	7.9	241
		0738	-0.2	-6
		1324	7.4	226
		1933	0.2	6
16	Th	0128	7.7	235
		0800	0.1	3
		1355	7.1	216
		1942	0.5	15
17	F	0154	7.4	226
		0812	0.4	12
		1425	6.8	207
		2014	0.7	21
18	Sa	0227	7.2	219
		0846	0.6	18
		1502	6.5	198
		2056	1.0	30
19	Su	0308	6.9	210
		0931	0.8	24
		1546	6.3	192
		2145	1.2	37
20	M ◐	0355	6.7	204
		1025	1.0	30
		1641	6.1	186
		2242	1.3	40
21	Tu	0451	6.5	198
		1130	1.1	34
		1810	6.1	186
		2346	1.3	40
22	W	0600	6.5	198
		1324	1.0	30
		1929	6.3	192
23	Th	0106	1.2	37
		0729	6.7	204
		1419	0.7	21
		2018	6.7	204
24	F	0225	0.8	24
		0823	7.1	216
		1504	0.4	12
		2055	7.1	216
25	Sa	0315	0.3	9
		0904	7.5	229
		1541	0.0	0
		2125	7.6	232
26	Su	0357	-0.2	-6
		0942	7.9	241
		1614	-0.3	-9
		2158	8.1	247
27	M ●	0437	-0.6	-18
		1021	8.2	250
		1650	-0.6	-18
		2237	8.5	259
28	Tu	0519	-0.9	-27
		1104	8.4	256
		1728	-0.8	-24
		2318	8.8	268
29	W	0602	-1.1	-34
		1149	8.5	259
		1810	-0.8	-24
30	Th	0003	9.0	274
		0648	-1.1	-34
		1237	8.4	256
		1855	-0.7	-21
31	F	0051	8.9	271
		0738	-0.9	-27
		1328	8.1	247
		1944	-0.4	-12

Time meridian 75° W. 0000 is midnight. 1200 is noon. Times are not adjusted for Daylight Saving Time.
Heights are referred to mean lower low water which is the chart datum of soundings.

Kings Point, Long Island, New York, 2017

Times and Heights of High and Low Waters

April

Day	Time	ft	cm		Day	Time	ft	cm
1 Sa	0143	8.7	265		16 Su	0146	7.4	226
	0837	-0.6	-18			0810	0.5	15
	1424	7.8	238			1422	6.8	207
	2039	0.0	0			2023	1.0	30
2 Su	0239	8.3	253		17 M	0228	7.2	219
	0958	-0.2	-6			0854	0.7	21
	1530	7.4	226			1504	6.7	204
	2152	0.4	12			2111	1.2	37
3 M ◑	0346	7.8	238		18 Tu	0314	7.0	213
	1122	0.0	0			0944	0.8	24
	1655	7.1	216			1552	6.6	201
	2339	0.6	18			2205	1.3	40
4 Tu	0521	7.4	226		19 W ◐	0406	6.9	210
	1232	0.0	0			1039	0.9	27
	1820	7.1	216			1647	6.6	201
						2304	1.3	40
5 W	0055	0.4	12		20 Th	0504	6.8	207
	0651	7.4	226			1140	0.9	27
	1335	-0.1	-3			1748	6.7	204
	1929	7.4	226					
6 Th	0159	0.1	3		21 F	0009	1.1	34
	0758	7.6	232			0609	6.9	210
	1432	-0.3	-9			1244	0.8	24
	2028	7.7	235			1852	7.0	213
7 F	0256	-0.2	-6		22 Sa	0120	0.8	24
	0855	7.8	238			0716	7.2	219
	1525	-0.5	-15			1346	0.5	15
	2119	8.1	247			1949	7.5	229
8 Sa	0349	-0.5	-15		23 Su	0228	0.3	9
	0945	8.0	244			0816	7.6	232
	1613	-0.6	-18			1441	0.1	3
	2205	8.3	253			2038	8.1	247
9 Su	0437	-0.7	-21		24 M	0325	-0.2	-6
	1030	8.0	244			0908	8.0	244
	1657	-0.5	-15			1530	-0.2	-6
	2247	8.4	256			2123	8.6	262
10 M	0521	-0.7	-21		25 Tu	0415	-0.7	-21
	1112	8.0	244			0956	8.3	253
	1738	-0.3	-9			1617	-0.5	-15
	2325	8.3	253			2209	9.0	274
11 Tu ○	0602	-0.6	-18		26 W ●	0503	-1.1	-34
	1151	7.8	238			1044	8.5	259
	1815	-0.1	-3			1703	-0.7	-21
	2359	8.2	250			2255	9.3	283
12 W	0639	-0.4	-12		27 Th	0552	-1.2	-37
	1227	7.6	232			1133	8.5	259
	1843	0.3	9			1750	-0.7	-21
						2344	9.3	283
13 Th	0027	8.0	244		28 F	0642	-1.2	-37
	0710	-0.1	-3			1225	8.4	256
	1258	7.4	226			1840	-0.5	-15
	1847	0.5	15					
14 F	0046	7.8	238		29 Sa	0035	9.2	280
	0718	0.1	3			0738	-1.0	-30
	1322	7.2	219			1320	8.2	250
	1905	0.7	21			1934	-0.2	-6
15 Sa	0112	7.6	232		30 Su	0130	8.8	268
	0735	0.3	9			0843	-0.7	-21
	1347	7.0	213			1422	7.9	241
	1940	0.8	24			2040	0.1	3

May

Day	Time	ft	cm		Day	Time	ft	cm
1 M	0232	8.3	253		16 Tu	0157	7.5	229
	0956	-0.3	-9			0825	0.5	15
	1534	7.6	232			1432	7.0	213
	2210	0.4	12			2043	1.0	30
2 Tu ○	0349	7.8	238		17 W	0243	7.4	226
	1106	-0.1	-3			0913	0.6	18
	1652	7.5	229			1518	7.0	213
	2330	0.5	15			2135	1.1	34
3 W	0518	7.5	229		18 Th ◐	0333	7.3	223
	1211	0.0	0			1004	0.6	18
	1804	7.5	229			1609	7.1	216
						2231	1.1	34
4 Th	0038	0.4	12		19 F	0428	7.2	219
	0634	7.4	226			1059	0.6	18
	1311	0.0	0			1704	7.2	219
	1908	7.7	235			2333	0.9	27
5 F	0139	0.2	6		20 Sa	0528	7.2	219
	0738	7.5	229			1157	0.6	18
	1406	-0.1	-3			1803	7.5	229
	2005	8.0	244					
6 Sa	0235	-0.1	-3		21 Su	0039	0.6	18
	0833	7.6	232			0632	7.3	223
	1458	-0.1	-3			1256	0.4	12
	2055	8.2	250			1902	7.9	241
7 Su	0327	-0.3	-9		22 M	0149	0.2	6
	0923	7.7	235			0737	7.6	232
	1546	-0.1	-3			1355	0.1	3
	2141	8.4	256			1959	8.4	256
8 M	0415	-0.5	-15		23 Tu	0257	-0.3	-9
	1009	7.7	235			0838	7.9	241
	1631	0.0	0			1453	-0.1	-3
	2222	8.4	256			2053	8.9	271
9 Tu	0459	-0.5	-15		24 W	0357	-0.7	-21
	1050	7.7	235			0933	8.2	250
	1711	0.2	6			1549	-0.4	-12
	2300	8.3	253			2145	9.3	283
10 W ○	0540	-0.4	-12		25 Th ●	0452	-1.1	-34
	1130	7.6	232			1027	8.4	256
	1747	0.4	12			1643	-0.5	-15
	2333	8.2	250			2236	9.4	287
11 Th	0616	-0.2	-6		26 F	0545	-1.2	-37
	1205	7.5	229			1120	8.4	256
	1814	0.6	18			1737	-0.5	-15
	2357	8.0	244			2329	9.4	287
12 F	0646	0.0	0		27 Sa	0639	-1.2	-37
	1236	7.3	223			1216	8.4	256
	1816	0.8	24			1833	-0.4	-12
13 Sa	0013	7.8	238		28 Su	0024	9.2	280
	0653	0.2	6			0736	-1.0	-30
	1256	7.2	219			1315	8.2	250
	1838	0.8	24			1935	-0.2	-6
14 Su	0040	7.7	235		29 M	0123	8.8	268
	0709	0.3	9			0837	-0.8	-24
	1318	7.1	216			1419	8.1	247
	1914	0.9	27			2047	0.1	3
15 M	0115	7.6	232		30 Tu	0230	8.3	253
	0743	0.3	9			0940	-0.5	-15
	1351	7.0	213			1526	7.9	241
	1956	1.0	30			2201	0.3	9
					31 W	0344	7.9	241
						1043	-0.2	-6
						1634	7.8	238
						2311	0.4	12

June

Day	Time	ft	cm		Day	Time	ft	cm
1 Th ◐	0459	7.5	229		16 F ◐	0306	7.6	232
	1143	0.0	0			0934	0.3	9
	1739	7.8	238			1538	7.6	232
						2203	0.8	24
2 F	0014	0.4	12		17 Sa ○	0359	7.5	229
	0608	7.3	223			1026	0.3	9
	1241	0.1	3			1631	7.7	235
	1840	7.8	238			2303	0.7	21
3 Sa	0114	0.3	9		18 Su	0457	7.4	226
	0710	7.3	223			1122	0.3	9
	1336	0.2	6			1727	8.0	244
	1936	8.0	244					
4 Su	0209	0.1	3		19 M	0008	0.5	15
	0806	7.3	223			0600	7.4	226
	1428	0.3	9			1220	0.3	9
	2027	8.1	247			1828	8.2	250
5 M	0301	-0.1	-3		20 Tu	0122	0.2	6
	0857	7.3	223			0707	7.5	229
	1516	0.4	12			1321	0.2	6
	2113	8.2	250			1929	8.6	262
6 Tu	0349	-0.2	-6		21 W	0241	-0.2	-6
	0943	7.4	226			0815	7.7	235
	1602	0.4	12			1426	0.0	0
	2156	8.2	250			2030	8.9	271
7 W	0434	-0.2	-6		22 Th	0347	-0.6	-18
	1026	7.4	226			0917	8.0	244
	1643	0.5	15			1532	-0.2	-6
	2235	8.1	247			2128	9.2	280
8 Th	0515	-0.2	-6		23 F ●	0444	-1.0	-30
	1106	7.4	226			1015	8.2	250
	1721	0.7	21			1635	-0.3	-9
	2309	8.0	244			2224	9.3	283
9 F ○	0552	-0.1	-3		24 Sa	0539	-1.2	-37
	1143	7.3	223			1112	8.3	253
	1750	0.8	24			1736	-0.4	-12
	2334	7.9	241			2320	9.2	280
10 Sa	0623	0.1	3		25 Su	0632	-1.2	-37
	1214	7.3	223			1209	8.4	256
	1757	0.8	24			1834	-0.4	-12
	2348	7.8	238					
11 Su	0637	0.2	6		26 M	0018	9.0	274
	1233	7.2	219			0725	-1.0	-30
	1817	0.8	24			1307	8.3	253
						1934	-0.2	-6
12 M	0014	7.8	238		27 Tu	0118	8.7	265
	0649	0.2	6			0820	-0.8	-24
	1252	7.2	219			1406	8.2	250
	1853	0.8	24			2037	0.0	0
13 Tu	0050	7.7	235		28 W	0221	8.3	253
	0721	0.2	6			0916	-0.5	-15
	1324	7.3	223			1506	8.1	247
	1934	0.8	24			2141	0.2	6
14 W	0131	7.7	235		29 Th	0325	7.9	241
	0801	0.2	6			1013	-0.1	-3
	1404	7.3	223			1606	7.9	241
	2019	0.8	24			2244	0.4	12
15 Th	0217	7.7	235		30 F ◐	0430	7.5	229
	0846	0.3	9			1111	0.2	6
	1449	7.4	226			1705	7.8	238
	2109	0.8	24			2345	0.5	15

Time meridian 75° W. 0000 is midnight. 1200 is noon. Times are not adjusted for Daylight Saving Time.
Heights are referred to mean lower low water which is the chart datum of soundings.

Kings Point, Long Island, New York, 2017

Times and Heights of High and Low Waters

July

Day	Time	ft	cm	Day	Time	ft	cm
1 Sa	0534	7.2	219	16 Su ☽	0335	7.6	232
	1207	0.5	15		0958	0.2	6
	1804	7.8	238		1602	8.1	247
					2239	0.5	15
2 Su	0043	0.5	15	17 M	0432	7.5	229
	0636	7.0	213		1053	0.3	9
	1301	0.7	21		1659	8.2	250
	1901	7.8	238		2347	0.4	12
3 M	0139	0.4	12	18 Tu	0536	7.3	223
	0734	6.9	210		1154	0.4	12
	1354	0.8	24		1801	8.3	253
	1954	7.8	238				
4 Tu	0231	0.3	9	19 W	0115	0.2	6
	0826	7.0	213		0648	7.3	223
	1444	0.8	24		1300	0.4	12
	2043	7.8	238		1909	8.5	259
5 W	0320	0.2	6	20 Th	0236	-0.1	-3
	0915	7.1	216		0804	7.5	229
	1531	0.8	24		1418	0.2	6
	2128	7.9	241		2019	8.7	265
6 Th	0405	0.1	3	21 F	0339	-0.5	-15
	1000	7.2	219		0911	7.8	238
	1614	0.8	24		1536	0.0	0
	2209	7.9	241		2123	8.9	271
7 F	0447	0.0	0	22 Sa	0436	-0.9	-27
	1041	7.3	223		1010	8.1	247
	1653	0.8	24		1639	-0.3	-9
	2245	7.9	241		2222	9.0	274
8 Sa ○	0525	0.0	0	23 Su ●	0528	-1.1	-34
	1118	7.3	223		1105	8.3	253
	1725	0.8	24		1736	-0.4	-12
	2312	7.8	238		2318	9.0	274
9 Su	0557	0.1	3	24 M	0618	-1.1	-34
	1149	7.3	223		1159	8.4	256
	1741	0.7	21		1830	-0.4	-12
	2327	7.8	238				
10 M	0616	0.1	3	25 Tu	0013	8.8	268
	1206	7.3	223		0707	-0.9	-27
	1800	0.7	21		1251	8.4	256
	2352	7.9	241		1923	-0.3	-9
11 Tu	0629	0.1	3	26 W	0107	8.6	262
	1224	7.4	226		0757	-0.7	-21
	1834	0.6	18		1344	8.4	256
					2017	-0.1	-3
12 W	0027	7.9	241	27 Th	0202	8.2	250
	0659	0.0	0		0846	-0.3	-9
	1257	7.6	232		1436	8.2	250
	1913	0.5	15		2114	0.2	6
13 Th	0109	7.9	241	28 F	0257	7.7	235
	0737	0.0	0		0938	0.1	3
	1337	7.7	235		1529	8.0	244
	1958	0.5	15		2212	0.4	12
14 F	0154	7.9	241	29 Sa	0355	7.3	223
	0820	0.0	0		1031	0.6	18
	1422	7.9	241		1624	7.7	235
	2046	0.4	12		2310	0.6	18
15 Sa	0242	7.8	238	30 Su ☾	0456	7.0	213
	0907	0.1	3		1126	0.9	27
	1510	8.0	244		1721	7.5	229
	2139	0.5	15				
				31 M	0008	0.8	24
					0558	6.7	204
					1222	1.1	34
					1820	7.4	226

August

Day	Time	ft	cm	Day	Time	ft	cm
1 Tu	0104	0.8	24	16 W	0521	7.2	219
	0657	6.7	204		1138	0.6	18
	1317	1.2	37		1744	8.1	247
	1917	7.4	226				
2 W	0157	0.7	21	17 Th	0122	0.3	9
	0753	6.8	207		0645	7.3	223
	1409	1.2	37		1307	0.6	18
	2010	7.4	226		1906	8.2	250
3 Th	0247	0.6	18	18 F	0230	-0.1	-3
	0844	6.9	210		0807	7.5	229
	1458	1.1	34		1436	0.3	9
	2058	7.5	229		2025	8.4	256
4 F	0333	0.4	12	19 Sa	0329	-0.4	-12
	0930	7.1	216		0910	7.9	241
	1543	1.0	30		1540	0.0	0
	2141	7.7	235		2128	8.7	265
5 Sa	0416	0.3	9	20 Su	0423	-0.7	-21
	1011	7.3	223		1005	8.2	250
	1624	0.8	24		1636	-0.3	-9
	2217	7.8	238		2223	8.8	268
6 Su	0454	0.2	6	21 M ●	0513	-0.9	-27
	1048	7.4	226		1055	8.5	259
	1657	0.7	21		1728	-0.5	-15
	2245	7.8	238		2313	8.8	268
7 M ○	0526	0.1	3	22 Tu	0600	-0.9	-27
	1115	7.5	229		1143	8.6	262
	1720	0.5	15		1818	-0.5	-15
	2303	7.9	241				
8 Tu	0545	0.0	0	23 W	0002	8.6	262
	1130	7.6	232		0645	-0.7	-21
	1742	0.4	12		1230	8.6	262
	2329	8.1	247		1905	-0.4	-12
9 W	0603	-0.1	-3	24 Th	0049	8.4	256
	1154	7.8	238		0729	-0.4	-12
	1815	0.2	6		1315	8.5	259
					1953	-0.1	-3
10 Th	0005	8.2	250	25 F	0137	8.0	244
	0634	-0.2	-6		0811	0.1	3
	1229	8.1	247		1359	8.2	250
	1854	0.1	3		2042	0.2	6
11 F	0047	8.2	250	26 Sa	0225	7.6	232
	0712	-0.2	-6		0853	0.5	15
	1310	8.2	250		1444	7.9	241
	1938	0.1	3		2133	0.6	18
12 Sa	0132	8.1	247	27 Su	0315	7.2	219
	0755	-0.1	-3		0935	1.0	30
	1356	8.4	256		1530	7.6	232
	2026	0.1	3		2228	0.9	27
13 Su	0222	7.9	241	28 M	0411	6.8	207
	0842	0.0	0		1025	1.3	40
	1445	8.4	256		1623	7.3	223
	2120	0.2	6		2326	1.1	34
14 M	0315	7.7	235	29 Tu ☽	0513	6.6	201
	0934	0.2	6		1130	1.6	49
	1538	8.3	253		1727	7.1	216
	2222	0.4	12				
15 Tu	0413	7.4	226	30 W	0023	1.1	34
	1032	0.5	15		0617	6.5	198
	1637	8.2	250		1233	1.6	49
	2345	0.4	12		1833	7.0	213
				31 Th	0118	1.1	34
					0716	6.6	201
					1330	1.6	49
					1932	7.1	216

September

Day	Time	ft	cm	Day	Time	ft	cm
1 F	0209	1.0	30	16 Sa	0218	-0.1	-3
	0809	6.8	207		0806	7.7	235
	1422	1.4	43		1436	0.3	9
	2023	7.3	223		2030	8.2	250
2 Sa	0257	0.8	24	17 Su	0314	-0.4	-12
	0856	7.1	216		0904	8.1	247
	1508	1.1	34		1534	-0.1	-3
	2107	7.5	229		2126	8.4	256
3 Su	0339	0.5	15	18 M	0406	-0.6	-18
	0937	7.3	223		0954	8.5	259
	1550	0.8	24		1626	-0.4	-12
	2144	7.7	235		2216	8.6	262
4 M	0416	0.3	9	19 Tu	0453	-0.7	-21
	1010	7.5	229		1040	8.7	265
	1624	0.5	15		1715	-0.6	-18
	2210	7.9	241		2302	8.5	259
5 Tu	0445	0.1	3	20 W ●	0538	-0.6	-18
	1031	7.8	238		1124	8.7	265
	1651	0.3	9		1801	-0.6	-18
	2233	8.1	247		2346	8.4	256
6 W	0506	0.0	0	21 Th	0620	-0.4	-12
	1051	8.1	247		1205	8.7	265
	1720	0.0	0		1845	-0.4	-12
	2305	8.3	253				
7 Th	0532	-0.2	-6	22 F	0029	8.1	247
	1123	8.4	256		0658	0.0	0
	1755	-0.2	-6		1243	8.5	259
	2343	8.4	256		1927	-0.1	-3
8 F	0607	-0.3	-9	23 Sa	0110	7.8	238
	1201	8.6	262		0731	0.4	12
	1835	-0.3	-9		1318	8.2	250
					2006	0.3	9
9 Sa	0026	8.4	256	24 Su	0150	7.4	226
	0647	-0.3	-9		0744	0.8	24
	1244	8.8	268		1350	7.9	241
	1920	-0.3	-9		2043	0.6	18
10 Su	0113	8.2	250	25 M	0230	7.1	216
	0732	-0.1	-3		0806	1.1	34
	1332	8.8	268		1424	7.5	229
	2010	-0.1	-3		2106	0.9	27
11 M	0204	8.0	244	26 Tu	0314	6.8	207
	0820	0.1	3		0845	1.4	43
	1423	8.6	262		1504	7.2	219
	2106	0.1	3		2141	1.2	37
12 Tu	0259	7.7	235	27 W ◐	0410	6.6	201
	0915	0.4	12		0935	1.6	49
	1518	8.4	256		1552	6.9	210
	2220	0.4	12		2324	1.4	43
13 W ○	0402	7.4	226	28 Th	0523	6.4	195
	1020	0.7	21		1033	1.8	55
	1622	8.1	247		1656	6.8	207
14 Th	0003	0.4	12	29 F	0027	1.3	40
	0523	7.2	219		0630	6.5	198
	1157	0.8	24		1227	1.8	55
	1744	7.9	241		1835	6.8	207
15 F	0116	0.2	6	30 Sa	0122	1.2	37
	0657	7.3	223		0727	6.7	204
	1330	0.6	18		1335	1.5	46
	1922	8.0	244		1937	7.0	213

Time meridian 75° W. 0000 is midnight. 1200 is noon. Times are not adjusted for Daylight Saving Time.
Heights are referred to mean lower low water which is the chart datum of soundings.

Kings Point, Long Island, New York, 2017

Times and Heights of High and Low Waters

October

Day	Time (h m)	Height (ft)	Height (cm)
1 Su	0210	1.0	30
	0814	7.0	213
	1426	1.1	34
	2023	7.3	223
2 M	0252	0.7	21
	0852	7.4	226
	1509	0.7	21
	2059	7.6	232
3 Tu	0326	0.4	12
	0920	7.8	238
	1546	0.3	9
	2129	7.9	241
4 W	0353	0.1	3
	0944	8.2	250
	1620	-0.1	-3
	2202	8.2	250
5 Th ○	0424	-0.2	-6
	1015	8.6	262
	1656	-0.4	-12
	2239	8.4	256
6 F	0501	-0.4	-12
	1053	8.9	271
	1736	-0.6	-18
	2321	8.5	259
7 Sa	0541	-0.4	-12
	1135	9.1	277
	1819	-0.7	-21
8 Su	0007	8.4	256
	0624	-0.4	-12
	1221	9.1	277
	1906	-0.6	-18
9 M	0056	8.2	250
	0712	-0.2	-6
	1311	9.0	274
	2000	-0.4	-12
10 Tu	0150	7.9	241
	0804	0.1	3
	1405	8.6	262
	2106	0.0	0
11 W	0250	7.6	232
	0905	0.5	15
	1505	8.2	250
	2239	0.2	6
12 Th ☽	0404	7.4	226
	1036	0.8	24
	1620	7.8	238
	2356	0.2	6
13 F	0537	7.3	223
	1216	0.7	21
	1803	7.7	235
14 Sa	0102	0.0	0
	0654	7.6	232
	1325	0.4	12
	1921	7.8	238
15 Su	0200	-0.2	-6
	0756	7.9	241
	1425	0.0	0
	2022	8.0	244
16 M	0255	-0.4	-12
	0850	8.3	253
	1520	-0.3	-9
	2115	8.2	250
17 Tu	0345	-0.5	-15
	0938	8.6	262
	1611	-0.6	-18
	2202	8.2	250
18 W	0431	-0.5	-15
	1022	8.7	265
	1658	-0.7	-21
	2247	8.2	250
19 Th ●	0515	-0.3	-9
	1102	8.7	265
	1742	-0.6	-18
	2328	8.0	244
20 F	0554	-0.1	-3
	1139	8.6	262
	1823	-0.4	-12
21 Sa	0008	7.8	238
	0629	0.3	9
	1212	8.3	253
	1901	-0.1	-3
22 Su	0044	7.5	229
	0650	0.6	18
	1238	8.0	244
	1932	0.2	6
23 M	0118	7.2	219
	0655	0.9	27
	1304	7.7	235
	1939	0.5	15
24 Tu	0147	7.0	213
	0726	1.1	34
	1336	7.5	229
	2003	0.7	21
25 W	0220	6.8	207
	0808	1.3	40
	1417	7.2	219
	2043	0.9	27
26 Th	0301	6.6	201
	0856	1.4	43
	1503	7.0	213
	2132	1.1	34
27 F ☽	0349	6.5	198
	0950	1.6	49
	1555	6.8	207
	2228	1.1	34
28 Sa	0447	6.5	198
	1051	1.6	49
	1653	6.7	204
	2330	1.1	34
29 Su	0558	6.6	201
	1159	1.4	43
	1759	6.8	207
30 M	0034	0.9	27
	0701	7.0	213
	1315	1.0	30
	1907	7.1	216
31 Tu	0130	0.6	18
	0744	7.4	226
	1416	0.6	18
	2002	7.4	226

November

Day	Time (h m)	Height (ft)	Height (cm)
1 W	0218	0.3	9
	0823	7.9	241
	1505	0.1	3
	2047	7.8	238
2 Th	0303	0.0	0
	0902	8.5	259
	1550	-0.4	-12
	2131	8.1	247
3 F	0347	-0.3	-9
	0944	8.9	271
	1635	-0.8	-24
	2216	8.3	253
4 Sa ○	0432	-0.5	-15
	1027	9.2	280
	1720	-1.0	-30
	2302	8.4	256
5 Su	0518	-0.6	-18
	1113	9.3	283
	1808	-1.0	-30
	2351	8.3	253
6 M	0606	-0.5	-15
	1203	9.3	283
	1900	-0.9	-27
7 Tu	0043	8.1	247
	0657	-0.3	-9
	1255	9.0	274
	2000	-0.7	-21
8 W	0141	7.9	241
	0755	0.0	0
	1353	8.5	259
	2114	-0.4	-12
9 Th	0249	7.6	232
	0910	0.4	12
	1500	8.1	247
	2230	-0.2	-6
10 F ☽	0409	7.4	226
	1050	0.5	15
	1628	7.6	232
	2338	-0.1	-3
11 Sa	0529	7.5	229
	1205	0.4	12
	1756	7.5	229
12 Su	0040	-0.2	-6
	0637	7.7	235
	1309	0.2	6
	1905	7.5	229
13 M	0138	-0.2	-6
	0737	8.0	244
	1408	-0.1	-3
	2004	7.6	232
14 Tu	0231	-0.3	-9
	0830	8.3	253
	1502	-0.4	-12
	2057	7.7	235
15 W	0321	-0.4	-12
	0918	8.5	259
	1552	-0.6	-18
	2144	7.8	238
16 Th	0408	-0.3	-9
	1001	8.5	259
	1638	-0.7	-21
	2228	7.7	235
17 F	0451	-0.1	-3
	1041	8.5	259
	1721	-0.6	-18
	2309	7.6	232
18 Sa ●	0530	0.1	3
	1117	8.3	253
	1801	-0.4	-12
	2348	7.4	226
19 Su	0604	0.4	12
	1147	8.0	244
	1837	-0.2	-6
20 M	0023	7.2	219
	0620	0.6	18
	1209	7.8	238
	1904	0.1	3
21 Tu	0052	7.0	213
	0626	0.8	24
	1231	7.6	232
	1906	0.3	9
22 W	0113	6.9	210
	0658	0.9	27
	1303	7.4	226
	1931	0.4	12
23 Th	0142	6.8	207
	0739	1.0	30
	1343	7.3	223
	2010	0.5	15
24 F	0220	6.7	204
	0825	1.1	34
	1427	7.1	216
	2056	0.6	18
25 Sa	0304	6.7	204
	0916	1.1	34
	1516	7.0	213
	2146	0.6	18
26 Su ☽	0353	6.7	204
	1011	1.1	34
	1609	6.9	210
	2240	0.6	18
27 M	0446	6.9	210
	1112	1.0	30
	1707	6.8	207
	2336	0.5	15
28 Tu	0543	7.1	216
	1217	0.7	21
	1809	6.9	210
29 W	0032	0.3	9
	0641	7.5	229
	1324	0.3	9
	1912	7.2	219
30 Th	0128	0.1	3
	0736	8.0	244
	1429	-0.1	-3
	2011	7.5	229

December

Day	Time (h m)	Height (ft)	Height (cm)
1 F	0223	-0.2	-6
	0828	8.5	259
	1527	-0.6	-18
	2104	7.8	238
2 Sa	0317	-0.5	-15
	0917	8.9	271
	1620	-1.0	-30
	2155	8.0	244
3 Su ○	0409	-0.7	-21
	1007	9.2	280
	1712	-1.3	-40
	2246	8.2	250
4 M	0501	-0.8	-24
	1057	9.3	283
	1804	-1.3	-40
	2339	8.2	250
5 Tu	0555	-0.7	-21
	1150	9.1	277
	1859	-1.2	-37
6 W	0035	8.0	244
	0651	-0.5	-15
	1246	8.8	268
	1959	-1.0	-30
7 Th	0136	7.9	241
	0756	-0.3	-9
	1347	8.4	256
	2103	-0.7	-21
8 F	0244	7.7	235
	0917	0.0	0
	1459	7.9	241
	2209	-0.5	-15
9 Sa	0356	7.6	232
	1035	0.2	6
	1619	7.5	229
	2313	-0.3	-9
10 Su ☽	0506	7.5	229
	1144	0.1	3
	1734	7.2	219
11 M	0013	-0.2	-6
	0611	7.6	232
	1247	0.0	0
	1841	7.1	216
12 Tu	0110	-0.2	-6
	0711	7.8	238
	1345	-0.2	-6
	1941	7.1	216
13 W	0204	-0.1	-3
	0805	7.9	241
	1439	-0.4	-12
	2034	7.2	219
14 Th	0255	-0.1	-3
	0854	8.0	244
	1529	-0.5	-15
	2123	7.2	219
15 F	0343	0.0	0
	0939	8.1	247
	1616	-0.6	-18
	2208	7.3	223
16 Sa	0427	0.0	0
	1020	8.0	244
	1659	-0.6	-18
	2249	7.2	219
17 Su	0507	0.2	6
	1057	7.9	241
	1739	-0.5	-15
	2328	7.2	219
18 M ●	0542	0.3	9
	1129	7.7	235
	1814	-0.3	-9
19 Tu	0003	7.0	213
	0605	0.4	12
	1151	7.6	232
	1841	-0.1	-3
20 W	0030	6.9	210
	0609	0.5	15
	1208	7.5	229
	1845	0.0	0
21 Th	0046	6.9	210
	0637	0.5	15
	1238	7.4	226
	1907	0.0	0
22 F	0111	6.9	210
	0715	0.5	15
	1315	7.3	223
	1943	0.0	0
23 Sa	0147	6.9	210
	0758	0.6	18
	1358	7.3	223
	2025	0.1	3
24 Su	0229	6.9	210
	0846	0.6	18
	1445	7.1	216
	2111	0.1	3
25 M	0315	7.0	213
	0938	0.6	18
	1535	7.0	213
	2201	0.2	6
26 Tu ☽	0405	7.2	219
	1035	0.5	15
	1630	6.9	210
	2255	0.2	6
27 W	0500	7.3	223
	1137	0.4	12
	1730	6.9	210
	2352	0.1	3
28 Th	0558	7.6	232
	1245	0.1	3
	1835	7.0	213
29 F	0051	0.0	0
	0659	8.0	244
	1402	-0.2	-6
	1941	7.2	219
30 Sa	0153	-0.2	-6
	0800	8.3	253
	1513	-0.7	-21
	2044	7.5	229
31 Su	0256	-0.5	-15
	0858	8.7	265
	1613	-1.1	-34
	2142	7.8	238

Time meridian 75° W. 0000 is midnight. 1200 is noon. Times are not adjusted for Daylight Saving Time.
Heights are referred to mean lower low water which is the chart datum of soundings.

New York (The Battery), New York, 2017

Times and Heights of High and Low Waters

January

Day	Time (h m)	Height (ft)	Height (cm)
1 Su	0354	0.1	3
	0945	4.8	146
	1634	-0.3	-9
	2221	4.0	122
2 M	0431	0.1	3
	1028	4.7	143
	1713	-0.2	-6
	2308	4.0	122
3 Tu	0514	0.3	9
	1118	4.6	140
	1757	-0.1	-3
	2359	4.1	125
4 W	0611	0.4	12
	1212	4.5	137
	1852	0.0	0
5 Th ☽	0051	4.3	131
	0728	0.5	15
	1309	4.4	134
	1956	0.0	0
6 F	0148	4.4	134
	0843	0.4	12
	1410	4.3	131
	2100	-0.1	-3
7 Sa	0249	4.6	140
	0948	0.1	3
	1518	4.2	128
	2159	-0.3	-9
8 Su	0355	4.8	146
	1048	-0.2	-6
	1628	4.3	131
	2255	-0.5	-15
9 M	0501	5.1	155
	1145	-0.5	-15
	1734	4.4	134
	2350	-0.7	-21
10 Tu	0600	5.4	165
	1239	-0.8	-24
	1832	4.6	140
11 W	0044	-0.8	-24
	0654	5.6	171
	1333	-1.0	-30
	1926	4.8	146
12 Th ○	0138	-0.9	-27
	0745	5.7	174
	1423	-1.1	-34
	2017	4.8	146
13 F	0229	-0.9	-27
	0834	5.6	171
	1512	-1.1	-34
	2109	4.8	146
14 Sa	0318	-0.8	-24
	0925	5.4	165
	1559	-1.0	-30
	2202	4.7	143
15 Su	0406	-0.6	-18
	1016	5.1	155
	1644	-0.8	-24
	2255	4.6	140
16 M	0454	-0.3	-9
	1107	4.8	146
	1731	-0.4	-12
	2347	4.4	134
17 Tu	0543	0.1	3
	1157	4.5	137
	1819	-0.1	-3
18 W	0036	4.3	131
	0638	0.4	12
	1246	4.2	128
	1911	0.2	6
19 Th ◑	0125	4.2	128
	0738	0.7	21
	1335	3.9	119
	2005	0.4	12
20 F	0213	4.1	125
	0839	0.7	21
	1426	3.7	113
	2059	0.5	15
21 Sa	0305	4.1	125
	0936	0.7	21
	1522	3.5	107
	2149	0.5	15
22 Su	0359	4.1	125
	1028	0.6	18
	1622	3.5	107
	2237	0.4	12
23 M	0453	4.2	128
	1116	0.4	12
	1718	3.6	110
	2322	0.3	9
24 Tu	0542	4.4	134
	1203	0.2	6
	1807	3.7	113
25 W	0007	0.2	6
	0625	4.6	140
	1248	0.0	0
	1850	3.9	119
26 Th	0052	0.0	0
	0704	4.8	146
	1331	-0.2	-6
	1928	4.1	125
27 F ●	0135	-0.1	-3
	0740	4.9	149
	1413	-0.4	-12
	2004	4.2	128
28 Sa	0218	-0.2	-6
	0814	5.0	152
	1453	-0.5	-15
	2038	4.3	131
29 Su	0259	-0.3	-9
	0849	5.0	152
	1532	-0.6	-18
	2115	4.3	131
30 M	0339	-0.3	-9
	0928	5.0	152
	1610	-0.6	-18
	2156	4.4	134
31 Tu	0420	-0.3	-9
	1012	4.9	149
	1649	-0.5	-15
	2243	4.5	137

February

Day	Time (h m)	Height (ft)	Height (cm)
1 W	0506	-0.1	-3
	1102	4.7	143
	1731	-0.4	-12
	2334	4.5	137
2 Th	0600	0.1	3
	1157	4.5	137
	1823	-0.2	-6
3 F ◐	0028	4.6	140
	0709	0.2	6
	1254	4.3	131
	1926	-0.1	-3
4 Sa ○	0125	4.6	140
	0823	0.2	6
	1356	4.2	128
	2035	0.0	0
5 Su	0228	4.7	143
	0931	0.1	3
	1504	4.1	125
	2140	-0.1	-3
6 M	0337	4.8	146
	1032	-0.1	-3
	1617	4.1	125
	2239	-0.3	-9
7 Tu	0447	4.9	149
	1129	-0.4	-12
	1724	4.3	131
	2336	-0.5	-15
8 W	0550	5.1	155
	1223	-0.6	-18
	1822	4.6	140
9 Th	0030	-0.6	-18
	0644	5.3	162
	1315	-0.8	-24
	1914	4.8	146
10 F ○	0123	-0.7	-21
	0733	5.4	165
	1404	-0.9	-27
	2002	4.9	149
11 Sa	0213	-0.8	-24
	0819	5.4	165
	1450	-0.9	-27
	2049	4.9	149
12 Su	0300	-0.7	-21
	0905	5.2	158
	1533	-0.8	-24
	2136	4.9	149
13 M	0345	-0.5	-15
	0950	5.0	152
	1615	-0.6	-18
	2223	4.8	146
14 Tu	0428	-0.3	-9
	1036	4.7	143
	1655	-0.3	-9
	2310	4.6	140
15 W	0512	0.0	0
	1123	4.4	134
	1736	0.0	0
	2355	4.4	134
16 Th	0559	0.4	12
	1209	4.1	125
	1820	0.4	12
17 F	0040	4.3	131
	0653	0.7	21
	1256	3.8	116
	1910	0.7	21
18 Sa ○	0126	4.1	125
	0754	0.8	24
	1344	3.6	110
	2008	0.9	27
19 Su	0214	4.0	122
	0855	0.9	27
	1438	3.5	107
	2106	0.9	27
20 M	0308	4.0	122
	0951	0.8	24
	1539	3.4	104
	2200	0.8	24
21 Tu	0407	4.1	125
	1042	0.6	18
	1641	3.6	110
	2250	0.6	18
22 W	0503	4.3	131
	1130	0.4	12
	1734	3.8	116
	2338	0.4	12
23 Th	0552	4.5	137
	1216	0.1	3
	1819	4.0	122
24 F	0024	0.2	6
	0634	4.8	146
	1300	-0.1	-3
	1858	4.3	131
25 Sa	0110	-0.1	-3
	0713	5.0	152
	1343	-0.4	-12
	1935	4.6	140
26 Su ●	0155	-0.3	-9
	0750	5.2	158
	1424	-0.6	-18
	2011	4.8	146
27 M	0239	-0.5	-15
	0828	5.2	158
	1505	-0.7	-21
	2049	4.9	149
28 Tu	0323	-0.6	-18
	0910	5.2	158
	1545	-0.7	-21
	2131	5.0	152

March

Day	Time (h m)	Height (ft)	Height (cm)
1 W	0408	-0.6	-18
	0957	5.1	155
	1626	-0.7	-21
	2219	5.1	155
2 Th	0455	-0.4	-12
	1050	4.9	149
	1710	-0.5	-15
	2313	5.0	152
3 F ○	0550	-0.2	-6
	1147	4.7	143
	1801	-0.2	-6
4 Sa	0009	5.0	152
	0654	0.1	3
	1246	4.4	134
	1905	0.1	3
5 Su ◐	0109	4.9	149
	0806	0.2	6
	1349	4.3	131
	2017	0.2	6
6 M	0213	4.8	146
	0914	0.1	3
	1457	4.2	128
	2124	0.2	6
7 Tu	0323	4.7	143
	1015	0.0	0
	1607	4.3	131
	2225	0.0	0
8 W	0435	4.8	146
	1111	-0.2	-6
	1713	4.5	137
	2322	-0.1	-3
9 Th	0538	5.0	152
	1204	-0.4	-12
	1809	4.7	143
10 F	0016	-0.3	-9
	0631	5.1	155
	1254	-0.5	-15
	1858	5.0	152
11 Sa	0107	-0.4	-12
	0717	5.2	158
	1340	-0.6	-18
	1943	5.1	155
12 Su ○	0155	-0.5	-15
	0800	5.2	158
	1424	-0.6	-18
	2026	5.2	158
13 M	0240	-0.5	-15
	0842	5.1	155
	1505	-0.5	-15
	2107	5.1	155
14 Tu	0322	-0.4	-12
	0924	4.9	149
	1544	-0.3	-9
	2149	5.0	152
15 W	0403	-0.2	-6
	1006	4.7	143
	1621	0.0	0
	2230	4.8	146
16 Th	0443	0.1	3
	1050	4.4	134
	1656	0.3	9
	2312	4.6	140
17 F	0525	0.4	12
	1135	4.1	125
	1731	0.6	18
	2354	4.5	137
18 Sa ○	0610	0.7	21
	1221	3.9	119
	1810	0.9	27
19 Su	0037	4.3	131
	0706	0.9	27
	1308	3.7	113
	1905	1.2	37
20 M ◐	0121	4.1	125
	0810	1.0	30
	1358	3.6	110
	2018	1.2	37
21 Tu	0211	4.1	125
	0910	1.0	30
	1454	3.6	110
	2121	1.2	37
22 W	0310	4.1	125
	1004	0.8	24
	1555	3.7	113
	2216	0.9	27
23 Th	0413	4.2	128
	1053	0.6	18
	1652	4.0	122
	2307	0.6	18
24 F	0510	4.5	137
	1139	0.3	9
	1741	4.3	131
	2356	0.3	9
25 Sa	0558	4.8	146
	1225	0.0	0
	1824	4.7	143
26 Su	0044	0.0	0
	0642	5.1	155
	1309	-0.3	-9
	1903	5.1	155
27 M ●	0132	-0.4	-12
	0723	5.3	162
	1353	-0.5	-15
	1942	5.4	165
28 Tu	0219	-0.6	-18
	0806	5.4	165
	1437	-0.7	-21
	2024	5.6	171
29 W	0306	-0.7	-21
	0852	5.4	165
	1520	-0.7	-21
	2109	5.7	174
30 Th	0354	-0.7	-21
	0943	5.2	158
	1604	-0.6	-18
	2159	5.6	171
31 F	0443	-0.6	-18
	1039	5.0	152
	1651	-0.4	-12
	2255	5.5	168

Time meridian 75° W. 0000 is midnight. 1200 is noon. Times are not adjusted for Daylight Saving Time.
Heights are referred to mean lower low water which is the chart datum of soundings.

New York (The Battery), New York, 2017

Times and Heights of High and Low Waters

April

Day	Time	Height (ft)	Height (cm)
1 Sa	0538	-0.3	-9
	1139	4.8	146
	1745	-0.1	-3
	2355	5.3	162
2 Su	0640	0.0	0
	1241	4.6	140
	1849	0.3	9
3 M ◑	0057	5.1	155
	0748	0.2	6
	1343	4.5	137
	2000	0.5	15
4 Tu	0201	4.9	149
	0855	0.2	6
	1448	4.4	134
	2109	0.5	15
5 W	0309	4.8	146
	0955	0.1	3
	1554	4.5	137
	2210	0.3	9
6 Th	0417	4.8	146
	1050	0.0	0
	1656	4.7	143
	2306	0.2	6
7 F	0519	4.8	146
	1140	-0.1	-3
	1751	4.9	149
	2358	0.0	0
8 Sa	0611	4.9	149
	1228	-0.2	-6
	1838	5.2	158
9 Su	0047	-0.1	-3
	0656	5.0	152
	1312	-0.2	-6
	1920	5.3	162
10 M	0134	-0.2	-6
	0738	5.0	152
	1355	-0.2	-6
	2000	5.4	165
11 Tu ○	0218	-0.2	-6
	0818	4.9	149
	1434	-0.1	-3
	2037	5.3	162
12 W	0259	-0.2	-6
	0857	4.8	146
	1512	0.1	3
	2115	5.2	158
13 Th	0339	-0.1	-3
	0938	4.6	140
	1548	0.3	9
	2152	5.0	152
14 F	0418	0.1	3
	1021	4.4	134
	1621	0.5	15
	2230	4.9	149
15 Sa	0456	0.4	12
	1106	4.2	128
	1653	0.8	24
	2310	4.7	143
16 Su	0536	0.6	18
	1151	4.0	122
	1722	1.1	34
	2350	4.5	137
17 M	0623	0.8	24
	1236	3.9	119
	1759	1.3	40
18 Tu	0033	4.4	134
	0722	1.0	30
	1321	3.8	116
	1917	1.4	43
19 W ○	0120	4.3	131
	0825	1.0	30
	1410	3.8	116
	2039	1.4	43
20 Th	0214	4.3	131
	0922	0.9	27
	1505	4.0	122
	2141	1.1	34
21 F	0315	4.4	134
	1013	0.6	18
	1603	4.3	131
	2235	0.8	24
22 Sa	0419	4.5	137
	1101	0.3	9
	1657	4.6	140
	2327	0.4	12
23 Su	0517	4.8	146
	1147	0.0	0
	1746	5.1	155
24 M	0018	0.0	0
	0608	5.1	155
	1234	-0.3	-9
	1831	5.5	168
25 Tu	0109	-0.3	-9
	0656	5.3	162
	1322	-0.5	-15
	1915	5.8	177
26 W ●	0159	-0.6	-18
	0744	5.4	165
	1409	-0.6	-18
	2000	6.0	183
27 Th	0249	-0.8	-24
	0834	5.4	165
	1457	-0.6	-18
	2049	6.1	186
28 F	0339	-0.8	-24
	0929	5.3	162
	1545	-0.5	-15
	2142	6.0	183
29 Sa	0430	-0.7	-21
	1029	5.1	155
	1635	-0.3	-9
	2241	5.8	177
30 Su	0524	-0.5	-15
	1131	4.9	149
	1730	0.0	0
	2343	5.5	168

May

Day	Time	Height (ft)	Height (cm)
1 M	0624	-0.2	-6
	1232	4.8	146
	1833	0.4	12
2 Tu ◐	0045	5.2	158
	0728	0.1	3
	1332	4.7	143
	1942	0.6	18
3 W	0146	5.0	152
	0832	0.2	6
	1433	4.7	143
	2050	0.7	21
4 Th	0248	4.8	146
	0931	0.2	6
	1533	4.8	146
	2151	0.6	18
5 F	0352	4.7	143
	1024	0.1	3
	1632	4.9	149
	2246	0.5	15
6 Sa	0452	4.6	140
	1112	0.1	3
	1726	5.1	155
	2337	0.3	9
7 Su	0544	4.7	143
	1158	0.1	3
	1812	5.2	158
8 M	0025	0.2	6
	0631	4.7	143
	1241	0.1	3
	1854	5.4	165
9 Tu	0110	0.1	3
	0713	4.7	143
	1323	0.1	3
	1932	5.4	165
10 W ○	0154	0.0	0
	0753	4.7	143
	1403	0.2	6
	2008	5.4	165
11 Th	0236	0.0	0
	0833	4.6	140
	1442	0.3	9
	2044	5.3	162
12 F	0316	0.0	0
	0913	4.4	134
	1518	0.5	15
	2119	5.2	158
13 Sa	0354	0.1	3
	0955	4.3	131
	1553	0.7	21
	2154	5.0	152
14 Su	0432	0.3	9
	1039	4.1	125
	1625	0.9	27
	2231	4.8	146
15 M	0510	0.5	15
	1123	4.0	122
	1656	1.1	34
	2310	4.7	143
16 Tu	0550	0.7	21
	1206	4.0	122
	1731	1.2	37
	2353	4.6	140
17 W	0639	0.8	24
	1248	4.0	122
	1826	1.4	43
18 Th ◑	0040	4.5	137
	0738	0.8	24
	1332	4.1	125
	1954	1.3	40
19 F	0131	4.5	137
	0837	0.7	21
	1421	4.3	131
	2105	1.1	34
20 Sa	0228	4.5	137
	0931	0.5	15
	1515	4.6	140
	2205	0.8	24
21 Su	0332	4.6	140
	1022	0.3	9
	1613	4.9	149
	2259	0.4	12
22 M	0437	4.7	143
	1112	0.0	0
	1709	5.4	165
	2353	0.0	0
23 Tu	0537	4.9	149
	1202	-0.3	-9
	1801	5.8	177
24 W	0047	-0.3	-9
	0632	5.1	155
	1253	-0.4	-12
	1851	6.1	186
25 Th ●	0140	-0.6	-18
	0725	5.2	158
	1345	-0.5	-15
	1941	6.3	192
26 F	0232	-0.8	-24
	0819	5.3	162
	1437	-0.6	-18
	2032	6.3	192
27 Sa	0324	-0.9	-27
	0916	5.2	158
	1528	-0.5	-15
	2128	6.1	186
28 Su	0415	-0.8	-24
	1016	5.1	155
	1620	-0.3	-9
	2227	5.9	180
29 M	0508	-0.6	-18
	1118	5.0	152
	1715	0.0	0
	2329	5.6	171
30 Tu	0603	-0.3	-9
	1218	5.0	152
	1815	0.4	12
31 W	0028	5.3	162
	0703	0.0	0
	1315	4.9	149
	1920	0.6	18

June

Day	Time	Height (ft)	Height (cm)
1 Th ◐	0125	5.0	152
	0803	0.1	3
	1410	4.9	149
	2026	0.8	24
2 F	0222	4.7	143
	0900	0.2	6
	1506	4.9	149
	2126	0.7	21
3 Sa	0319	4.5	137
	0952	0.3	9
	1601	4.9	149
	2221	0.7	21
4 Su	0417	4.4	134
	1040	0.3	9
	1654	5.0	152
	2311	0.5	15
5 M	0512	4.3	131
	1125	0.3	9
	1742	5.2	158
	2359	0.4	12
6 Tu	0602	4.4	134
	1208	0.4	12
	1825	5.3	162
7 W	0044	0.3	9
	0647	4.4	134
	1250	0.4	12
	1904	5.3	162
8 Th	0129	0.2	6
	0728	4.4	134
	1332	0.5	15
	1941	5.4	165
9 F ○	0211	0.1	3
	0809	4.4	134
	1413	0.5	15
	2017	5.3	162
10 Sa	0252	0.1	3
	0849	4.3	131
	1452	0.6	18
	2051	5.2	158
11 Su	0331	0.1	3
	0930	4.3	131
	1529	0.7	21
	2125	5.1	155
12 M	0409	0.2	6
	1012	4.2	128
	1604	0.8	24
	2200	4.9	149
13 Tu	0446	0.3	9
	1053	4.1	125
	1638	0.9	27
	2239	4.8	146
14 W	0523	0.4	12
	1134	4.1	125
	1714	1.0	30
	2322	4.7	143
15 Th	0603	0.5	15
	1215	4.2	128
	1802	1.1	34
16 F	0009	4.7	143
	0653	0.6	18
	1258	4.4	134
	1917	1.2	37
17 Sa ○	0100	4.6	140
	0752	0.5	15
	1345	4.6	140
	2033	1.0	30
18 Su	0156	4.6	140
	0851	0.4	12
	1438	4.9	149
	2138	0.8	24
19 M	0257	4.6	140
	0947	0.2	6
	1537	5.2	158
	2236	0.4	12
20 Tu	0405	4.6	140
	1041	0.0	0
	1639	5.5	168
	2332	0.0	0
21 W	0512	4.8	146
	1135	-0.2	-6
	1738	5.8	177
22 Th	0027	-0.3	-9
	0613	5.0	152
	1230	-0.4	-12
	1833	6.1	186
23 F ●	0122	-0.6	-18
	0709	5.1	155
	1325	-0.5	-15
	1926	6.2	189
24 Sa	0215	-0.8	-24
	0805	5.2	158
	1419	-0.5	-15
	2019	6.2	189
25 Su	0307	-0.9	-27
	0901	5.2	158
	1512	-0.4	-12
	2114	6.1	186
26 M	0357	-0.8	-24
	1000	5.2	158
	1604	-0.3	-9
	2211	5.8	177
27 Tu	0448	-0.6	-18
	1059	5.1	155
	1657	0.0	0
	2310	5.5	168
28 W	0539	-0.4	-12
	1156	5.1	155
	1752	0.3	9
29 Th	0006	5.2	158
	0632	-0.1	-3
	1250	5.0	152
	1852	0.6	18
30 F ◑	0059	4.9	149
	0728	0.2	6
	1341	4.9	149
	1955	0.8	24

Time meridian 75° W. 0000 is midnight. 1200 is noon. Times are not adjusted for Daylight Saving Time.
Heights are referred to mean lower low water which is the chart datum of soundings.

New York (The Battery), New York, 2017

Times and Heights of High and Low Waters

July

Day	Time	Height (ft)	Height (cm)
1 Sa	0151	4.6	140
	0824	0.4	12
	1433	4.9	149
	2056	0.9	27
2 Su	0244	4.3	131
	0917	0.5	15
	1525	4.9	149
	2152	0.9	27
3 M	0340	4.2	128
	1005	0.6	18
	1618	4.9	149
	2243	0.8	24
4 Tu	0437	4.1	125
	1051	0.6	18
	1708	5.0	152
	2330	0.6	18
5 W	0531	4.1	125
	1135	0.6	18
	1754	5.1	155
6 Th	0016	0.5	15
	0620	4.2	128
	1219	0.6	18
	1836	5.2	158
7 F	0101	0.3	9
	0704	4.3	131
	1303	0.6	18
	1915	5.3	162
8 Sa ○	0145	0.2	6
	0745	4.3	131
	1346	0.6	18
	1952	5.3	162
9 Su	0226	0.1	3
	0824	4.4	134
	1427	0.6	18
	2026	5.3	162
10 M	0306	0.1	3
	0902	4.4	134
	1507	0.6	18
	2100	5.2	158
11 Tu	0344	0.1	3
	0940	4.3	131
	1544	0.6	18
	2134	5.1	155
12 W	0420	0.1	3
	1018	4.4	134
	1621	0.7	21
	2212	5.0	152
13 Th	0456	0.2	6
	1058	4.4	134
	1700	0.8	24
	2256	4.9	149
14 F	0533	0.3	9
	1141	4.6	140
	1747	0.9	27
	2345	4.8	146
15 Sa	0617	0.3	9
	1227	4.7	143
	1852	1.0	30
16 Su ◑	0037	4.7	143
	0712	0.4	12
	1316	4.9	149
	2007	0.9	27
17 M	0134	4.6	140
	0817	0.4	12
	1410	5.1	155
	2116	0.7	21
18 Tu	0236	4.5	137
	0920	0.3	9
	1511	5.3	162
	2217	0.4	12
19 W	0345	4.5	137
	1019	0.1	3
	1617	5.5	168
	2314	0.1	3
20 Th	0455	4.7	143
	1116	-0.1	-3
	1721	5.8	177
21 F	0010	-0.2	-6
	0559	4.9	149
	1213	-0.2	-6
	1820	6.0	183
22 Sa	0105	-0.5	-15
	0657	5.1	155
	1308	-0.4	-12
	1914	6.1	186
23 Su ●	0157	-0.7	-21
	0751	5.2	158
	1403	-0.4	-12
	2006	6.1	186
24 M	0248	-0.8	-24
	0844	5.3	162
	1455	-0.4	-12
	2058	6.0	183
25 Tu	0336	-0.7	-21
	0939	5.3	162
	1545	-0.2	-6
	2151	5.7	174
26 W	0423	-0.6	-18
	1033	5.3	162
	1635	0.0	0
	2245	5.4	165
27 Th	0510	-0.3	-9
	1127	5.2	158
	1726	0.3	9
	2337	5.1	155
28 F	0558	0.0	0
	1218	5.1	155
	1820	0.7	21
29 Sa	0028	4.8	146
	0648	0.4	12
	1307	4.9	149
	1920	0.9	27
30 Su ◑	0118	4.5	137
	0742	0.7	21
	1356	4.8	146
	2021	1.1	34
31 M	0209	4.2	128
	0837	0.8	24
	1445	4.8	146
	2119	1.1	34

August

Day	Time	Height (ft)	Height (cm)
1 Tu	0303	4.0	122
	0929	0.9	27
	1538	4.7	143
	2211	1.0	30
2 W	0402	3.9	119
	1017	0.9	27
	1631	4.8	146
	2300	0.8	24
3 Th	0500	4.0	122
	1104	0.9	27
	1722	4.9	149
	2346	0.6	18
4 F	0551	4.1	125
	1150	0.8	24
	1808	5.1	155
5 Sa	0031	0.5	15
	0637	4.3	131
	1235	0.7	21
	1849	5.2	158
6 Su	0115	0.3	9
	0717	4.4	134
	1319	0.6	18
	1926	5.3	162
7 M ○	0157	0.1	3
	0755	4.6	140
	1402	0.5	15
	2000	5.3	162
8 Tu	0237	0.0	0
	0830	4.6	140
	1443	0.4	12
	2034	5.3	162
9 W	0315	0.0	0
	0904	4.7	143
	1524	0.4	12
	2109	5.3	162
10 Th	0352	-0.1	-3
	0941	4.8	146
	1604	0.4	12
	2148	5.2	158
11 F	0428	0.0	0
	1022	4.9	149
	1646	0.5	15
	2234	5.0	152
12 Sa	0505	0.1	3
	1108	5.0	152
	1734	0.6	18
	2326	4.9	149
13 Su	0548	0.2	6
	1159	5.1	155
	1835	0.7	21
14 M ◑	0022	4.7	143
	0644	0.4	12
	1252	5.2	158
	1948	0.8	24
15 Tu	0121	4.6	140
	0753	0.5	15
	1350	5.2	158
	2058	0.7	21
16 W	0225	4.5	137
	0902	0.4	12
	1454	5.3	162
	2201	0.4	12
17 Th	0335	4.5	137
	1004	0.3	9
	1603	5.4	165
	2258	0.1	3
18 F	0446	4.7	143
	1103	0.1	3
	1710	5.6	171
	2353	-0.1	-3
19 Sa	0549	4.9	149
	1159	-0.1	-3
	1810	5.8	177
20 Su	0046	-0.4	-12
	0645	5.2	158
	1254	-0.2	-6
	1902	5.9	180
21 M ●	0137	-0.5	-15
	0736	5.4	165
	1347	-0.3	-9
	1951	5.9	180
22 Tu	0225	-0.6	-18
	0824	5.5	168
	1437	-0.3	-9
	2038	5.8	177
23 W	0311	-0.6	-18
	0913	5.5	168
	1525	-0.2	-6
	2126	5.6	171
24 Th	0355	-0.4	-12
	1002	5.4	165
	1611	0.1	3
	2215	5.3	162
25 F	0437	-0.1	-3
	1052	5.3	162
	1658	0.4	12
	2305	4.9	149
26 Sa	0520	0.3	9
	1141	5.1	155
	1747	0.7	21
	2355	4.6	140
27 Su	0605	0.6	18
	1228	4.9	149
	1841	1.0	30
28 M	0044	4.3	131
	0655	1.0	30
	1315	4.8	146
	1941	1.2	37
29 Tu ◑	0135	4.1	125
	0752	1.2	37
	1403	4.7	143
	2041	1.2	37
30 W	0228	4.0	122
	0850	1.3	40
	1455	4.6	140
	2137	1.1	34
31 Th	0326	3.9	119
	0944	1.2	37
	1551	4.6	140
	2227	1.0	30

September

Day	Time	Height (ft)	Height (cm)
1 F	0426	4.0	122
	1033	1.1	34
	1646	4.7	143
	2314	0.8	24
2 Sa	0520	4.2	128
	1121	0.9	27
	1735	4.9	149
	2359	0.6	18
3 Su	0606	4.4	134
	1206	0.7	21
	1818	5.1	155
4 M	0042	0.3	9
	0646	4.6	140
	1252	0.5	15
	1856	5.3	162
5 Tu	0124	0.1	3
	0722	4.9	149
	1336	0.3	9
	1931	5.4	165
6 W ○	0204	-0.1	-3
	0755	5.1	155
	1420	0.2	6
	2007	5.5	168
7 Th	0243	-0.2	-6
	0830	5.2	158
	1503	0.1	3
	2044	5.4	165
8 F	0322	-0.2	-6
	0907	5.3	162
	1546	0.1	3
	2127	5.3	162
9 Sa	0401	-0.2	-6
	0950	5.4	165
	1631	0.2	6
	2216	5.1	155
10 Su	0441	0.0	0
	1040	5.4	165
	1721	0.3	9
	2312	4.9	149
11 M	0527	0.2	6
	1136	5.4	165
	1822	0.5	15
12 Tu	0013	4.7	143
	0624	0.4	12
	1235	5.3	162
	1932	0.6	18
13 W ◑	0116	4.6	140
	0736	0.6	18
	1338	5.3	162
	2042	0.6	18
14 Th	0221	4.5	137
	0848	0.6	18
	1444	5.2	158
	2145	0.4	12
15 F	0331	4.6	140
	0953	0.4	12
	1554	5.3	162
	2242	0.1	3
16 Sa	0438	4.8	146
	1051	0.2	6
	1701	5.4	165
	2335	-0.1	-3
17 Su	0538	5.1	155
	1146	0.1	3
	1758	5.6	171
18 M	0026	-0.3	-9
	0631	5.3	162
	1239	-0.1	-3
	1848	5.7	174
19 Tu	0114	-0.4	-12
	0718	5.5	168
	1329	-0.2	-6
	1933	5.7	174
20 W ●	0200	-0.4	-12
	0802	5.6	171
	1417	-0.2	-6
	2016	5.5	168
21 Th	0243	-0.3	-9
	0845	5.6	171
	1503	-0.1	-3
	2100	5.3	162
22 F	0324	-0.2	-6
	0929	5.5	168
	1547	0.1	3
	2145	5.0	152
23 Sa	0403	0.1	3
	1013	5.3	162
	1630	0.3	9
	2232	4.7	143
24 Su	0442	0.5	15
	1059	5.1	155
	1714	0.6	18
	2321	4.4	134
25 M	0521	0.8	24
	1145	4.9	149
	1802	0.9	27
26 Tu	0012	4.2	128
	0603	1.2	37
	1232	4.7	143
	1857	1.2	37
27 W ◑	0102	4.0	122
	0659	1.4	43
	1319	4.5	137
	1959	1.3	40
28 Th	0155	3.9	119
	0806	1.5	46
	1410	4.5	137
	2059	1.2	37
29 F	0250	3.9	119
	0907	1.5	46
	1505	4.5	137
	2151	1.0	30
30 Sa	0347	4.0	122
	1001	1.3	40
	1602	4.6	140
	2238	0.8	24

Time meridian 75° W. 0000 is midnight. 1200 is noon. Times are not adjusted for Daylight Saving Time.
Heights are referred to mean lower low water which is the chart datum of soundings.

New York (The Battery), New York, 2017

Times and Heights of High and Low Waters

October

Day	Time	ft	cm	Day	Time	ft	cm
1 Su	0442	4.2	128	16 M	0523	5.1	155
	1050	1.0	30		1131	0.1	3
	1655	4.8	146		1741	5.2	158
	2323	0.5	15				
2 M	0529	4.5	137	17 Tu	0002	-0.2	-6
	1137	0.7	21		0613	5.4	165
	1741	5.0	152		1222	0.0	0
					1829	5.3	162
3 Tu	0005	0.3	9	18 W	0048	-0.3	-9
	0610	4.8	146		0657	5.5	168
	1224	0.4	12		1310	-0.1	-3
	1822	5.2	158		1913	5.2	158
4 W	0048	0.0	0	19 Th	0132	-0.3	-9
	0646	5.2	158		0738	5.6	171
	1310	0.1	3		1356	-0.1	-3
	1901	5.4	165		● 1954	5.1	155
5 Th	0130	-0.2	-6	20 F	0213	-0.2	-6
	0722	5.4	165		0818	5.6	171
	1356	-0.1	-3		1440	-0.1	-3
	○ 1940	5.4	165		2034	5.0	152
6 F	0211	-0.3	-9	21 Sa	0253	0.0	0
	0759	5.7	174		0856	5.5	168
	1442	-0.2	-6		1522	0.0	0
	2021	5.4	165		2116	4.7	143
7 Sa	0253	-0.4	-12	22 Su	0331	0.2	6
	0840	5.8	177		0936	5.3	162
	1529	-0.3	-9		1603	0.2	6
	2108	5.3	162		2201	4.5	137
8 Su	0336	-0.3	-9	23 M	0407	0.5	15
	0926	5.8	177		1017	5.0	152
	1617	-0.2	-6		1644	0.4	12
	2201	5.1	155		2249	4.2	128
9 M	0421	-0.2	-6	24 Tu	0442	0.8	24
	1019	5.7	174		1101	4.8	146
	1709	0.0	0		1727	0.7	21
	2303	4.9	149		2339	4.0	122
10 Tu	0511	0.1	3	25 W	0517	1.1	34
	1120	5.5	168		1147	4.6	140
	1808	0.2	6		1815	0.9	27
11 W	0007	4.7	143	26 Th	0030	3.9	119
	0611	0.4	12		0600	1.3	40
	1224	5.4	165		1234	4.4	134
	1916	0.4	12		1913	1.1	34
12 Th	0111	4.6	140	27 F	0119	3.8	116
	0723	0.6	18		0711	1.5	46
	1328	5.2	158		1322	4.3	131
	☽ 2024	0.4	12		☾ 2014	1.1	34
13 F	0216	4.6	140	28 Sa	0210	3.8	116
	0835	0.6	18		0825	1.5	46
	1435	5.1	155		1413	4.3	131
	2127	0.2	6		2110	0.9	27
14 Sa	0322	4.7	143	29 Su	0302	3.9	119
	0940	0.5	15		0925	1.3	40
	1542	5.1	155		1508	4.4	134
	2223	0.1	3		2159	0.7	21
15 Su	0425	4.9	149	30 M	0355	4.2	128
	1038	0.3	9		1018	1.0	30
	1645	5.1	155		1604	4.5	137
	2314	-0.1	-3		2244	0.4	12
				31 Tu	0444	4.5	137
					1107	0.6	18
					1657	4.7	143
					2327	0.1	3

November

Day	Time	ft	cm	Day	Time	ft	cm
1 W	0529	4.9	149	16 Th	0020	-0.2	-6
	1156	0.3	9		0634	5.3	162
	1746	4.9	149		1250	-0.1	-3
					1851	4.7	143
2 Th	0011	-0.2	-6	17 F	0103	-0.2	-6
	0611	5.3	162		0714	5.4	165
	1244	-0.1	-3		1335	-0.1	-3
	1831	5.1	155		1932	4.6	140
3 F	0056	-0.4	-12	18 Sa	0144	-0.1	-3
	0652	5.7	174		0752	5.4	165
	1334	-0.4	-12		1418	-0.1	-3
	1916	5.2	158		● 2012	4.5	137
4 Sa	0142	-0.6	-18	19 Su	0224	0.0	0
	0734	5.9	180		0828	5.3	162
	1423	-0.6	-18		1459	-0.1	-3
	○ 2002	5.3	162		2052	4.4	134
5 Su	0228	-0.6	-18	20 M	0302	0.2	6
	0818	6.0	183		0905	5.1	155
	1512	-0.7	-21		1539	0.0	0
	2053	5.1	155		2134	4.2	128
6 M	0316	-0.6	-18	21 Tu	0339	0.4	12
	0908	6.0	183		0943	4.9	149
	1602	-0.6	-18		1618	0.2	6
	2150	5.0	152		2220	4.0	122
7 Tu	0405	-0.4	-12	22 W	0413	0.6	18
	1004	5.8	177		1022	4.7	143
	1655	-0.4	-12		1657	0.4	12
	2253	4.8	146		2307	3.8	116
8 W	0457	-0.1	-3	23 Th	0446	0.8	24
	1107	5.5	168		1105	4.5	137
	1753	-0.2	-6		1739	0.5	15
	2358	4.7	143		2354	3.7	113
9 Th	0558	0.2	6	24 F	0520	1.0	30
	1212	5.3	162		1149	4.4	134
	1856	0.0	0		1826	0.7	21
10 F	0101	4.6	140	25 Sa	0039	3.7	113
	0707	0.4	12		0607	1.2	37
	1316	5.1	155		1234	4.3	131
	○ 2002	0.1	3		1922	0.8	24
11 Sa	0203	4.6	140	26 Su	0124	3.7	113
	0817	0.5	15		0731	1.3	40
	1419	4.9	149		1322	4.2	128
	2104	0.0	0		☾ 2021	0.7	21
12 Su	0305	4.7	143	27 M	0210	3.9	119
	0922	0.5	15		0844	1.1	34
	1522	4.7	143		1414	4.2	128
	2159	-0.1	-3		2114	0.5	15
13 M	0405	4.8	146	28 Tu	0300	4.1	125
	1020	0.3	9		0944	0.8	24
	1623	4.7	143		1512	4.3	131
	2249	-0.2	-6		2203	0.2	6
14 Tu	0501	5.0	152	29 W	0354	4.5	137
	1113	0.2	6		1038	0.5	15
	1718	4.7	143		1613	4.4	134
	2336	-0.2	-6		2250	-0.1	-3
15 W	0551	5.2	158	30 Th	0448	4.9	149
	1202	0.0	0		1130	0.1	3
	1807	4.7	143		1711	4.6	140
					2338	-0.4	-12

December

Day	Time	ft	cm	Day	Time	ft	cm
1 F	0538	5.3	162	16 Sa	0035	-0.1	-3
	1221	-0.3	-9		0651	5.0	152
	1805	4.8	146		1312	-0.1	-3
					1911	4.2	128
2 Sa	0027	-0.6	-18	17 Su	0117	0.0	0
	0626	5.7	174		0729	5.1	155
	1313	-0.6	-18		1355	-0.2	-6
	1856	4.9	149		1952	4.2	128
3 Su	0117	-0.8	-24	18 M	0158	0.0	0
	0714	5.9	180		0806	5.0	152
	1405	-0.9	-27		1436	-0.2	-6
	○ 1947	5.0	152		● 2031	4.1	125
4 M	0208	-0.9	-27	19 Tu	0238	0.1	3
	0803	6.0	183		0841	4.9	149
	1456	-1.0	-30		1516	-0.2	-6
	2040	5.0	152		2111	4.0	122
5 Tu	0259	-0.9	-27	20 W	0315	0.2	6
	0855	5.9	180		0917	4.8	146
	1547	-1.0	-30		1554	-0.1	-3
	2138	4.9	149		2152	3.9	119
6 W	0350	-0.7	-21	21 Th	0351	0.3	9
	0953	5.7	174		0953	4.6	140
	1639	-0.9	-27		1631	0.0	0
	2240	4.8	146		2233	3.8	116
7 Th	0444	-0.5	-15	22 F	0424	0.5	15
	1055	5.5	168		1029	4.5	137
	1733	-0.6	-18		1707	0.1	3
	2343	4.7	143		2314	3.7	113
8 F	0542	-0.1	-3	23 Sa	0457	0.6	18
	1157	5.2	158		1109	4.3	131
	1832	-0.4	-12		1744	0.3	9
					2354	3.7	113
9 Sa	0044	4.6	140	24 Su	0535	0.8	24
	0646	0.2	6		1152	4.2	128
	1257	4.9	149		1827	0.3	9
	1934	-0.2	-6				
10 Su	0142	4.6	140	25 M	0035	3.8	116
	0754	0.4	12		0634	0.9	27
	1355	4.6	140		1239	4.2	128
	○ 2034	-0.1	-3		1923	0.4	12
11 M	0239	4.6	140	26 Tu	0119	4.0	122
	0859	0.4	12		0759	0.8	24
	1454	4.4	134		1330	4.1	125
	2130	-0.1	-3		☾ 2024	0.3	9
12 Tu	0337	4.6	140	27 W	0210	4.2	128
	0958	0.3	9		0910	0.6	18
	1553	4.2	128		1429	4.1	125
	2220	-0.1	-3		2122	0.1	3
13 W	0433	4.7	143	28 Th	0307	4.5	137
	1051	0.2	6		1010	0.3	9
	1651	4.1	125		1534	4.1	125
	2307	-0.1	-3		2217	-0.2	-6
14 Th	0524	4.8	146	29 F	0409	4.8	146
	1140	0.1	3		1106	-0.1	-3
	1743	4.2	128		1642	4.3	131
	2352	-0.1	-3		2310	-0.4	-12
15 F	0610	5.0	152	30 Sa	0510	5.2	158
	1227	0.0	0		1201	-0.5	-15
	1829	4.2	128		1744	4.5	137
				31 Su	0004	-0.7	-21
					0607	5.5	168
					1255	-0.8	-24
					1840	4.7	143

Time meridian 75° W. 0000 is midnight. 1200 is noon. Times are not adjusted for Daylight Saving Time.
Heights are referred to mean lower low water which is the chart datum of soundings.

Bayonne Bridge, Staten Island, New York, 2017

Times and Heights of High and Low Waters

January

Day	Time	ft	cm	Day	Time	ft	cm
1 Su	0402	0.0	0	16 M	0500	-0.4	-12
	0935	5.3	162		1103	5.3	162
	1641	-0.4	-12		1736	-0.5	-15
	2207	4.5	137		2345	4.9	149
2 M	0439	0.1	3	17 Tu	0546	0.0	0
	1018	5.2	158		1154	4.9	149
	1718	-0.3	-9		1820	-0.1	-3
	2254	4.5	137				
3 Tu	0519	0.2	6	18 W	0035	4.7	143
	1108	5.1	155		0635	0.4	12
	1758	-0.2	-6		1243	4.5	137
	2348	4.6	140		1906	0.2	6
4 W	0608	0.4	12	19 Th	0123	4.6	140
	1205	5.0	152		0733	0.7	21
	1847	-0.1	-3		1331	4.3	131
				◗	1959	0.5	15
5 Th	0045	4.7	143	20 F	0211	4.5	137
	0717	0.5	15		0838	0.8	24
	1305	4.8	146		1421	4.0	122
◐	1950	-0.1	-3		2056	0.6	18
6 F	0143	4.9	149	21 Sa	0300	4.4	134
	0841	0.5	15		0940	0.8	24
	1407	4.7	143		1514	3.9	119
	2100	-0.1	-3		2150	0.6	18
7 Sa	0244	5.1	155	22 Su	0353	4.5	137
	0954	0.2	6		1034	0.6	18
	1514	4.7	143		1613	3.8	116
	2204	-0.3	-9		2239	0.5	15
8 Su	0350	5.3	162	23 M	0449	4.6	140
	1057	-0.2	-6		1124	0.4	12
	1625	4.7	143		1712	3.9	119
	2302	-0.5	-15		2326	0.4	12
9 M	0457	5.6	171	24 Tu	0541	4.8	146
	1155	-0.5	-15		1211	0.1	3
	1733	4.9	149		1804	4.1	125
	2359	-0.8	-24				
10 Tu	0559	5.9	180	25 W	0013	0.2	6
	1252	-0.9	-27		0626	5.1	155
	1833	5.1	155		1257	-0.1	-3
					1849	4.3	131
11 W	0055	-0.9	-27	26 Th	0058	0.0	0
	0655	6.2	189		0706	5.3	162
	1346	-1.1	-34		1341	-0.4	-12
	1927	5.3	162		1928	4.5	137
12 Th	0149	-1.0	-30	27 F	0144	-0.2	-6
	0745	6.3	192		0741	5.4	165
	1437	-1.3	-40		1424	-0.6	-18
○	2017	5.4	165	●	2003	4.7	143
13 F	0241	-1.0	-30	28 Sa	0227	-0.3	-9
	0834	6.2	189		0814	5.5	168
	1525	-1.3	-40		1504	-0.7	-21
	2108	5.4	165		2036	4.8	146
14 Sa	0330	-0.9	-27	29 Su	0309	-0.4	-12
	0922	6.0	183		0847	5.6	171
	1611	-1.2	-37		1543	-0.8	-24
	2159	5.2	158		2110	4.9	149
15 Su	0416	-0.7	-21	30 M	0349	-0.4	-12
	1012	5.6	171		0923	5.5	168
	1654	-0.9	-27		1620	-0.8	-24
	2252	5.1	155		2149	4.9	149
				31 Tu	0429	-0.3	-9
					1005	5.4	165
					1657	-0.7	-21
					2234	5.0	152

February

Day	Time	ft	cm	Day	Time	ft	cm
1 W	0512	-0.2	-6	16 Th	0554	0.3	9
	1055	5.2	158		1202	4.5	137
	1737	-0.5	-15		1809	0.3	9
	2326	5.0	152				
2 Th	0601	0.0	0	17 F	0036	4.6	140
	1151	5.0	152		0639	0.7	21
	1823	-0.3	-9		1248	4.2	128
					1847	0.7	21
3 F	0023	5.1	155	18 Sa	0121	4.5	137
	0704	0.2	6		0739	0.9	27
	1251	4.8	146		1336	4.0	122
◑	1922	-0.1	-3	◯	1942	0.9	27
4 Sa	0122	5.1	155	19 Su	0208	4.4	134
	0823	0.3	9		0850	1.0	30
	1353	4.6	140		1428	3.8	116
	2034	-0.1	-3		2054	1.0	30
5 Su	0224	5.1	155	20 M	0300	4.4	134
	0938	0.2	6		0953	0.9	27
	1500	4.5	137		1527	3.8	116
	2144	-0.1	-3		2157	0.9	27
6 M	0331	5.2	158	21 Tu	0359	4.4	134
	1042	-0.1	-3		1048	0.6	18
	1611	4.6	140		1631	3.9	119
	2247	-0.3	-9		2252	0.7	21
7 Tu	0442	5.4	165	22 W	0459	4.6	140
	1141	-0.4	-12		1138	0.3	9
	1720	4.7	143		1729	4.1	125
	2345	-0.5	-15		2343	0.4	12
8 W	0547	5.6	171	23 Th	0552	4.9	149
	1236	-0.7	-21		1225	0.0	0
	1821	5.0	152		1818	4.4	134
9 Th	0041	-0.7	-21	24 F	0032	0.1	3
	0643	5.8	177		0637	5.3	162
	1328	-0.9	-27		1310	-0.3	-9
	1914	5.3	162		1859	4.8	146
10 F	0134	-0.8	-24	25 Sa	0119	-0.2	-6
	0732	6.0	183		0716	5.5	168
	1417	-1.1	-34		1354	-0.6	-18
○	2002	5.4	165		1937	5.1	155
11 Sa	0224	-0.9	-27	26 Su	0206	-0.4	-12
	0818	5.9	180		0753	5.7	174
	1503	-1.1	-34		1436	-0.8	-24
	2048	5.5	168	●	2012	5.3	162
12 Su	0311	-0.8	-24	27 M	0251	-0.6	-18
	0902	5.8	177		0829	5.8	177
	1545	-1.0	-30		1517	-0.9	-27
	2133	5.4	165		2049	5.5	168
13 M	0354	-0.7	-21	28 Tu	0335	-0.7	-21
	0946	5.5	168		0909	5.7	174
	1624	-0.7	-21		1556	-0.9	-27
	2219	5.2	158		2129	5.6	171
14 Tu	0435	-0.4	-12				
	1030	5.2	158				
	1700	-0.4	-12				
	2305	5.0	152				
15 W	0514	-0.1	-3				
	1116	4.8	146				
	1735	0.0	0				
	2351	4.8	146				

March

Day	Time	ft	cm	Day	Time	ft	cm
1 W	0418	-0.7	-21	16 Th	0445	0.0	0
	0953	5.6	171		1038	4.8	146
	1636	-0.8	-24		1654	0.2	6
	2215	5.6	171		2302	5.0	152
2 Th	0503	-0.5	-15	17 F	0520	0.3	9
	1044	5.4	165		1121	4.5	137
	1717	-0.6	-18		1721	0.5	15
	2308	5.5	168		2342	4.8	146
3 F	0553	-0.2	-6	18 Sa	0557	0.6	18
	1142	5.1	155		1205	4.3	131
	1804	-0.3	-9		1750	0.8	24
4 Sa	0006	5.4	165	19 Su	0024	4.6	140
	0654	0.1	3		0643	0.9	27
	1243	4.9	149		1252	4.1	125
	1903	0.0	0		1829	1.1	34
5 Su	0106	5.3	162	20 M	0109	4.5	137
	0809	0.3	9		0750	1.1	34
	1346	4.7	143		1342	4.0	122
◑	2016	0.2	6	◗	1937	1.3	40
6 M	0210	5.2	158	21 Tu	0159	4.5	137
	0922	0.2	6		0906	1.1	34
	1452	4.6	140		1439	4.0	122
	2130	0.2	6		2109	1.2	37
7 Tu	0318	5.2	158	22 W	0259	4.5	137
	1027	0.0	0		1007	0.9	27
	1601	4.7	143		1541	4.1	125
	2234	0.0	0		2216	1.0	30
8 W	0428	5.3	162	23 Th	0405	4.7	143
	1124	-0.2	-6		1100	0.5	15
	1708	4.9	149		1645	4.3	131
	2332	-0.2	-6		2311	0.7	21
9 Th	0533	5.4	165	24 F	0507	4.9	149
	1217	-0.5	-15		1148	0.2	6
	1807	5.2	158		1739	4.7	143
10 F	0026	-0.4	-12	25 Sa	0003	0.3	9
	0628	5.6	171		0600	5.3	162
	1306	-0.6	-18		1235	-0.2	-6
	1857	5.5	168		1825	5.2	158
11 Sa	0118	-0.5	-15	26 Su	0053	-0.1	-3
	0716	5.7	174		0645	5.6	171
	1353	-0.7	-21		1320	-0.5	-15
	1942	5.6	171		1906	5.6	171
12 Su	0206	-0.6	-18	27 M	0143	-0.4	-12
	0759	5.7	174		0727	5.9	180
	1436	-0.7	-21		1405	-0.7	-21
○	2024	5.7	174	●	1946	6.0	183
13 M	0250	-0.6	-18	28 Tu	0231	-0.7	-21
	0839	5.6	171		0809	6.0	183
	1516	-0.6	-18		1449	-0.9	-27
	2105	5.6	171		2026	6.2	189
14 Tu	0331	-0.5	-15	29 W	0319	-0.8	-24
	0919	5.4	165		0853	5.9	180
	1552	-0.4	-12		1532	-0.9	-27
	2144	5.5	168		2109	6.3	192
15 W	0410	-0.3	-9	30 Th	0405	-0.8	-24
	0958	5.1	155		0941	5.8	177
	1625	-0.1	-3		1616	-0.8	-24
	2223	5.3	162		2157	6.2	189
				31 F	0453	-0.7	-21
					1035	5.5	168
					1701	-0.5	-15
					2252	6.0	183

Time meridian 75° W. 0000 is midnight. 1200 is noon. Times are not adjusted for Daylight Saving Time.
Heights are referred to mean lower low water which is the chart datum of soundings.

Bayonne Bridge, Staten Island, New York, 2017

Times and Heights of High and Low Waters

April

Day	Time (h m)	Height (ft)	Height (cm)
1 Sa	0545	-0.4	-12
	1136	5.3	162
	1750	-0.2	-6
	2353	5.8	177
2 Su	0644	0.0	0
	1239	5.1	155
	1850	0.2	6
3 M ◐	0056	5.6	171
	0754	0.2	6
	1342	4.9	149
	2002	0.4	12
4 Tu	0159	5.4	165
	0904	0.2	6
	1444	4.9	149
	2116	0.5	15
5 W	0304	5.2	158
	1007	0.1	3
	1548	5.0	152
	2220	0.4	12
6 Th	0411	5.2	158
	1102	0.0	0
	1651	5.1	155
	2317	0.2	6
7 F	0513	5.3	162
	1152	-0.2	-6
	1747	5.4	165
8 Sa	0009	0.0	0
	0607	5.4	165
	1239	-0.3	-9
	1836	5.7	174
9 Su	0058	-0.2	-6
	0654	5.5	168
	1324	-0.3	-9
	1919	5.8	177
10 M	0144	-0.2	-6
	0736	5.5	168
	1405	-0.2	-6
	1958	5.9	180
11 Tu ○	0227	-0.3	-9
	0815	5.4	165
	1444	-0.1	-3
	2035	5.8	177
12 W	0308	-0.2	-6
	0852	5.3	162
	1519	0.0	0
	2110	5.7	174
13 Th	0345	-0.1	-3
	0928	5.1	155
	1551	0.3	9
	2143	5.5	168
14 F	0421	0.1	3
	1005	4.8	146
	1620	0.5	15
	2214	5.3	162
15 Sa	0455	0.3	9
	1044	4.5	137
	1647	0.8	24
	2247	5.1	155
16 Su	0529	0.6	18
	1126	4.4	134
	1716	1.0	30
	2325	4.9	149
17 M	0607	0.8	24
	1213	4.2	128
	1752	1.2	37
18 Tu	0013	4.8	146
	0659	1.0	30
	1303	4.2	128
	1845	1.4	43
19 W ◑	0106	4.7	143
	0812	1.1	34
	1356	4.2	128
	2014	1.4	43
20 Th	0204	4.8	146
	0921	0.9	27
	1453	4.4	134
	2137	1.2	37
21 F	0307	4.8	146
	1017	0.6	18
	1554	4.7	143
	2239	0.8	24
22 Sa	0414	5.0	152
	1108	0.3	9
	1653	5.1	155
	2334	0.4	12
23 Su	0517	5.3	162
	1156	-0.1	-3
	1746	5.6	171
24 M	0027	0.0	0
	0611	5.6	171
	1244	-0.4	-12
	1834	6.1	186
25 Tu	0119	-0.4	-12
	0700	5.9	180
	1333	-0.6	-18
	1919	6.5	198
26 W ●	0211	-0.7	-21
	0748	6.0	183
	1421	-0.7	-21
	2004	6.7	204
27 Th	0302	-0.9	-27
	0836	6.0	183
	1509	-0.8	-24
	2051	6.7	204
28 F	0352	-0.9	-27
	0928	5.8	177
	1557	-0.7	-21
	2141	6.6	201
29 Sa	0442	-0.8	-24
	1026	5.6	171
	1646	-0.4	-12
	2239	6.3	192
30 Su	0534	-0.5	-15
	1129	5.4	165
	1737	-0.1	-3
	2342	6.0	183

May

Day	Time (h m)	Height (ft)	Height (cm)
1 M	0631	-0.2	-6
	1232	5.3	162
	1837	0.3	9
2 Tu ◐	0045	5.7	174
	0735	0.1	3
	1332	5.2	158
	1946	0.6	18
3 W	0146	5.5	168
	0841	0.2	6
	1431	5.2	158
	2057	0.7	21
4 Th	0246	5.3	162
	0942	0.2	6
	1529	5.2	158
	2201	0.6	18
5 F	0346	5.1	155
	1035	0.2	6
	1627	5.4	165
	2256	0.5	15
6 Sa	0445	5.1	155
	1123	0.1	3
	1721	5.6	171
	2347	0.3	9
7 Su	0539	5.1	155
	1208	0.1	3
	1809	5.7	174
8 M	0034	0.2	6
	0627	5.2	158
	1250	0.1	3
	1852	5.9	180
9 Tu	0120	0.1	3
	0710	5.2	158
	1331	0.2	6
	1931	6.0	183
10 W ○	0203	0.0	0
	0749	5.2	158
	1411	0.3	9
	2007	5.9	180
11 Th	0244	0.0	0
	0827	5.1	155
	1447	0.4	12
	2040	5.8	177
12 F	0323	0.1	3
	0903	4.9	149
	1522	0.5	15
	2110	5.6	171
13 Sa	0359	0.2	6
	0938	4.7	143
	1554	0.7	21
	2137	5.5	168
14 Su	0434	0.3	9
	1015	4.6	140
	1624	0.9	27
	2207	5.3	162
15 M	0508	0.5	15
	1054	4.4	134
	1655	1.0	30
	2245	5.2	158
16 Tu	0544	0.6	18
	1140	4.4	134
	1731	1.2	37
	2333	5.1	155
17 W	0627	0.8	24
	1229	4.4	134
	1818	1.3	40
18 Th ◑	0028	5.0	152
	0723	0.8	24
	1320	4.6	140
	1930	1.4	43
19 F	0125	5.0	152
	0830	0.8	24
	1412	4.8	146
	2058	1.2	37
20 Sa	0224	5.0	152
	0932	0.5	15
	1509	5.1	155
	2207	0.9	27
21 Su	0328	5.1	155
	1027	0.3	9
	1609	5.5	168
	2306	0.5	15
22 M	0435	5.3	162
	1119	0.0	0
	1708	5.9	180
23 Tu	0002	0.0	0
	0538	5.5	168
	1210	-0.3	-9
	1804	6.4	195
24 W	0057	-0.4	-12
	0635	5.7	174
	1303	-0.5	-15
	1855	6.7	204
25 Th ●	0152	-0.7	-21
	0728	5.9	180
	1356	-0.6	-18
	1944	6.9	210
26 F	0246	-0.9	-27
	0820	5.9	180
	1449	-0.7	-21
	2034	6.9	210
27 Sa	0337	-1.0	-30
	0915	5.8	177
	1540	-0.6	-18
	2127	6.7	204
28 Su	0428	-0.9	-27
	1014	5.7	174
	1631	-0.4	-12
	2226	6.4	195
29 M	0519	-0.7	-21
	1117	5.5	168
	1723	0.0	0
	2329	6.1	186
30 Tu	0612	-0.4	-12
	1219	5.5	168
	1820	0.3	9
31 W	0030	5.8	177
	0710	-0.1	-3
	1316	5.4	165
	1924	0.6	18

June

Day	Time (h m)	Height (ft)	Height (cm)
1 Th ◐	0126	5.5	168
	0811	0.2	6
	1410	5.4	165
	2032	0.8	24
2 F	0221	5.2	158
	0909	0.3	9
	1503	5.4	165
	2135	0.8	24
3 Sa	0315	5.0	152
	1002	0.3	9
	1557	5.4	165
	2231	0.7	21
4 Su	0411	4.9	149
	1049	0.4	12
	1649	5.5	168
	2320	0.6	18
5 M	0506	4.8	146
	1133	0.4	12
	1738	5.7	174
6 Tu	0007	0.4	12
	0557	4.8	146
	1215	0.4	12
	1823	5.8	177
7 W	0053	0.3	9
	0642	4.9	149
	1257	0.5	15
	1903	5.9	180
8 Th	0137	0.2	6
	0724	4.9	149
	1338	0.5	15
	1940	5.9	180
9 F ○	0220	0.1	3
	0803	4.9	149
	1418	0.6	18
	2014	5.8	177
10 Sa	0300	0.1	3
	0840	4.8	146
	1456	0.6	18
	2044	5.7	174
11 Su	0339	0.1	3
	0916	4.7	143
	1533	0.7	21
	2112	5.6	171
12 M	0415	0.2	6
	0950	4.6	140
	1607	0.8	24
	2142	5.5	168
13 Tu	0450	0.3	9
	1028	4.5	137
	1641	0.9	27
	2219	5.3	162
14 W	0524	0.4	12
	1111	4.6	140
	1717	1.0	30
	2306	5.3	162
15 Th	0602	0.5	15
	1159	4.7	143
	1801	1.1	34
16 F	0000	5.2	158
	0647	0.5	15
	1248	4.9	149
	1902	1.2	37
17 Sa ○	0056	5.2	158
	0745	0.5	15
	1340	5.1	155
	2024	1.1	34
18 Su	0154	5.1	155
	0849	0.4	12
	1434	5.4	165
	2138	0.9	27
19 M	0255	5.1	155
	0950	0.2	6
	1534	5.7	174
	2241	0.5	15
20 Tu	0402	5.2	158
	1046	0.0	0
	1636	6.1	186
	2340	0.1	3
21 W	0510	5.3	162
	1142	-0.2	-6
	1738	6.4	195
22 Th	0037	-0.3	-9
	0613	5.5	168
	1238	-0.4	-12
	1834	6.7	204
23 F ●	0134	-0.6	-18
	0711	5.7	174
	1335	-0.5	-15
	1928	6.9	210
24 Sa	0229	-0.8	-24
	0805	5.8	177
	1430	-0.6	-18
	2020	6.9	210
25 Su	0321	-1.0	-30
	0900	5.8	177
	1524	-0.5	-15
	2113	6.7	204
26 M	0411	-0.9	-27
	0958	5.7	174
	1615	-0.4	-12
	2210	6.4	195
27 Tu	0500	-0.8	-24
	1058	5.6	171
	1706	-0.1	-3
	2309	6.1	186
28 W	0549	-0.5	-15
	1157	5.6	171
	1759	0.3	9
29 Th	0007	5.7	174
	0640	-0.1	-3
	1252	5.5	168
	1856	0.6	18
30 F ◐	0100	5.4	165
	0734	0.2	6
	1342	5.4	165
	1959	0.9	27

Time meridian 75° W. 0000 is midnight. 1200 is noon. Times are not adjusted for Daylight Saving Time.
Heights are referred to mean lower low water which is the chart datum of soundings.

Bayonne Bridge, Staten Island, New York, 2017

Times and Heights of High and Low Waters

July

Day	Time	ft	cm	Day	Time	ft	cm
1 Sa	0151	5.1	155	**16 Su** ◗	0034	5.2	158
	0830	0.4	12		0709	0.3	9
	1432	5.4	165		1312	5.4	165
	2102	1.0	30		2000	1.0	30
2 Su	0241	4.8	146	**17 M**	0132	5.1	155
	0923	0.6	18		0813	0.3	9
	1522	5.4	165		1408	5.6	171
	2159	0.9	27		2116	0.8	24
3 M	0334	4.6	140	**18 Tu**	0233	5.1	155
	1011	0.6	18		0920	0.2	6
	1612	5.4	165		1507	5.9	180
	2250	0.8	24		2223	0.5	15
4 Tu	0429	4.5	137	**19 W**	0340	5.1	155
	1056	0.7	21		1023	0.1	3
	1703	5.4	165		1612	6.1	186
	2338	0.7	21		2323	0.1	3
5 W	0523	4.6	140	**20 Th**	0451	5.2	158
	1140	0.7	21		1122	-0.1	-3
	1751	5.6	171		1718	6.3	192
6 Th	0024	0.5	15	**21 F**	0020	-0.2	-6
	0614	4.6	140		0557	5.4	165
	1223	0.6	18		1220	-0.3	-9
	1835	5.7	174		1819	6.6	201
7 F	0109	0.4	12	**22 Sa**	0116	-0.5	-15
	0659	4.7	143		0656	5.6	171
	1307	0.6	18		1318	-0.4	-12
	1915	5.8	177		1914	6.7	204
8 Sa ○	0153	0.2	6	**23 Su** ●	0210	-0.8	-24
	0740	4.8	146		0751	5.8	177
	1351	0.6	18		1414	-0.5	-15
	1950	5.8	177		2006	6.7	204
9 Su	0235	0.1	3	**24 M**	0302	-0.9	-27
	0818	4.8	146		0844	5.8	177
	1433	0.6	18		1507	-0.5	-15
	2022	5.8	177		2057	6.6	201
10 M	0315	0.0	0	**25 Tu**	0350	-0.9	-27
	0853	4.8	146		0937	5.8	177
	1513	0.6	18		1557	-0.3	-9
	2052	5.7	174		2149	6.3	192
11 Tu	0353	0.0	0	**26 W**	0435	-0.7	-21
	0926	4.8	146		1032	5.7	174
	1551	0.6	18		1645	-0.1	-3
	2123	5.6	171		2243	5.9	180
12 W	0428	0.0	0	**27 Th**	0520	-0.4	-12
	1001	4.8	146		1127	5.6	171
	1628	0.7	21		1733	0.3	9
	2200	5.5	168		2337	5.6	171
13 Th	0503	0.1	3	**28 F**	0604	0.0	0
	1042	4.9	149		1220	5.5	168
	1706	0.8	24		1824	0.6	18
	2245	5.4	165				
14 F	0538	0.2	6	**29 Sa**	0029	5.2	158
	1129	5.0	152		0650	0.4	12
	1749	0.9	27		1309	5.4	165
	2338	5.3	162		1920	0.9	27
15 Sa	0619	0.2	6	**30 Su** ◖	0118	4.9	149
	1220	5.2	158		0741	0.7	21
	1845	1.0	30		1356	5.3	162
					2022	1.1	34
				31 M	0206	4.7	143
					0836	0.9	27
					1443	5.2	158
					2122	1.1	34

August

Day	Time	ft	cm	Day	Time	ft	cm
1 Tu	0256	4.5	137	**16 W**	0221	5.0	152
	0929	1.0	30		0901	0.4	12
	1532	5.2	158		1450	5.8	177
	2217	1.0	30		2208	0.5	15
2 W	0351	4.4	134	**17 Th**	0329	5.0	152
	1019	1.0	30		1008	0.3	9
	1625	5.2	158		1557	6.0	183
	2306	0.9	27		2308	0.2	6
3 Th	0449	4.4	134	**18 F**	0439	5.1	155
	1106	0.9	27		1109	0.1	3
	1718	5.3	162		1705	6.1	186
	2353	0.7	21				
4 F	0544	4.5	137	**19 Sa**	0004	-0.1	-3
	1152	0.8	24		0545	5.4	165
	1806	5.5	168		1207	-0.1	-3
					1807	6.3	192
5 Sa	0039	0.5	15	**20 Su**	0058	-0.4	-12
	0632	4.7	143		0643	5.7	174
	1238	0.7	21		1303	-0.3	-9
	1848	5.7	174		1901	6.5	198
6 Su	0123	0.3	9	**21 M** ●	0150	-0.6	-18
	0714	4.9	149		0735	5.9	180
	1324	0.6	18		1357	-0.4	-12
	1926	5.8	177		1951	6.5	198
7 M ○	0207	0.1	3	**22 Tu**	0239	-0.7	-21
	0752	5.0	152		0824	6.0	183
	1410	0.5	15		1449	-0.4	-12
	2000	5.8	177		2038	6.4	195
8 Tu	0248	-0.1	-3	**23 W**	0324	-0.7	-21
	0826	5.1	155		0912	6.0	183
	1453	0.4	12		1536	-0.3	-9
	2031	5.8	177		2124	6.1	186
9 W	0326	-0.1	-3	**24 Th**	0407	-0.5	-15
	0858	5.2	158		1001	5.9	180
	1534	0.4	12		1621	0.0	0
	2104	5.8	177		2212	5.8	177
10 Th	0403	-0.2	-6	**25 F**	0447	-0.2	-6
	0933	5.3	162		1050	5.7	174
	1613	0.4	12		1705	0.3	9
	2142	5.7	174		2302	5.4	165
11 F	0438	-0.1	-3	**26 Sa**	0525	0.2	6
	1013	5.4	165		1140	5.5	168
	1654	0.5	15		1749	0.6	18
	2228	5.6	171		2352	5.1	155
12 Sa	0515	0.0	0	**27 Su**	0603	0.6	18
	1101	5.5	168		1228	5.3	162
	1738	0.6	18		1837	1.0	30
	2320	5.4	165				
13 Su	0555	0.1	3	**28 M**	0042	4.8	146
	1154	5.6	171		0644	1.0	30
	1833	0.7	21		1315	5.2	158
					1934	1.2	37
14 M ◖	0018	5.2	158	**29 Tu** ◖	0130	4.5	137
	0644	0.3	9		0736	1.2	37
	1250	5.7	174		1401	5.1	155
	1944	0.8	24		2038	1.3	40
15 Tu	0118	5.1	155	**30 W**	0220	4.4	134
	0748	0.4	12		0839	1.3	40
	1348	5.8	177		1450	5.0	152
	2100	0.7	21		2139	1.3	40
				31 Th	0314	4.3	131
					0939	1.3	40
					1543	5.0	152
					2231	1.1	34

September

Day	Time	ft	cm	Day	Time	ft	cm
1 F	0413	4.4	134	**16 Sa**	0430	5.2	158
	1033	1.2	37		1059	0.2	6
	1639	5.2	158		1654	5.9	180
	2319	0.8	24		2346	-0.1	-3
2 Sa	0510	4.5	137	**17 Su**	0533	5.5	168
	1122	1.0	30		1155	0.0	0
	1732	5.4	165		1754	6.1	186
3 Su	0005	0.5	15	**18 M**	0037	-0.3	-9
	0601	4.8	146		0628	5.8	177
	1210	0.7	21		1249	-0.1	-3
	1818	5.6	171		1846	6.2	189
4 M	0050	0.3	9	**19 Tu**	0126	-0.4	-12
	0644	5.1	155		0717	6.0	183
	1258	0.5	15		1340	-0.2	-6
	1857	5.8	177		1932	6.2	189
5 Tu	0133	0.0	0	**20 W** ●	0212	-0.5	-15
	0721	5.3	162		0801	6.1	186
	1345	0.3	9		1428	-0.2	-6
	1934	5.9	180		2016	6.1	186
6 W ○	0215	-0.2	-6	**21 Th**	0255	-0.4	-12
	0756	5.6	171		0844	6.1	186
	1430	0.1	3		1514	-0.2	-6
	2008	6.0	183		2058	5.9	180
7 Th	0256	-0.3	-9	**22 F**	0335	-0.2	-6
	0830	5.7	174		0927	6.0	183
	1514	0.0	0		1556	0.0	0
	2045	6.0	183		2140	5.5	168
8 F	0335	-0.3	-9	**23 Sa**	0412	0.1	3
	0906	5.9	180		1010	5.7	174
	1558	0.0	0		1636	0.3	9
	2125	5.8	177		2225	5.2	158
9 Sa	0413	-0.3	-9	**24 Su**	0446	0.4	12
	0948	5.9	180		1054	5.5	168
	1641	0.1	3		1715	0.6	18
	2212	5.6	171		2313	4.9	149
10 Su	0453	-0.2	-6	**25 M**	0518	0.8	24
	1037	5.9	180		1140	5.3	162
	1728	0.3	9		1756	0.9	27
	2308	5.4	165				
11 M	0536	0.0	0	**26 Tu**	0003	4.6	140
	1133	5.9	180		0550	1.1	34
	1824	0.5	15		1227	5.1	155
					1844	1.2	37
12 Tu	0009	5.2	158	**27 W** ◑	0053	4.4	134
	0627	0.3	9		0629	1.4	43
	1234	5.8	177		1313	4.9	149
	1932	0.7	21		1946	1.3	40
13 W ◖	0113	5.1	155	**28 Th**	0143	4.3	131
	0733	0.5	15		0732	1.5	46
	1335	5.8	177		1402	4.9	149
	2047	0.6	18		2054	1.3	40
14 Th	0217	5.0	152	**29 F**	0236	4.3	131
	0849	0.6	18		0853	1.5	46
	1439	5.8	177		1454	4.9	149
	2154	0.4	12		2152	1.1	34
15 F	0323	5.1	155	**30 Sa**	0332	4.4	134
	0958	0.4	12		0958	1.3	40
	1547	5.8	177		1552	5.0	152
	2252	0.2	6		2242	0.9	27

Time meridian 75° W. 0000 is midnight. 1200 is noon   Times are not adjusted for Daylight Saving Time.
Heights are referred to mean lower low water which is the chart datum of soundings.

Bayonne Bridge, Staten Island, New York, 2017

Times and Heights of High and Low Waters

October

Day	Time (h m)	Height (ft)	Height (cm)		Day	Time (h m)	Height (ft)	Height (cm)
1 Su	0430	4.6	140		16 M	0517	5.6	171
	1052	1.1	34			1141	0.1	3
	1649	5.2	158			1736	5.7	174
	2328	0.5	15					
2 M	0522	4.9	149		17 Tu	0013	-0.2	-6
	1142	0.7	21			0610	5.8	177
	1740	5.4	165			1232	-0.1	-3
						1827	5.8	177
3 Tu	0013	0.2	6		18 W	0059	-0.3	-9
	0608	5.3	162			0656	6.0	183
	1231	0.4	12			1321	-0.3	-9
	1824	5.7	174			1911	5.8	177
4 W	0057	-0.1	-3		19 Th ●	0143	-0.3	-9
	0648	5.7	174			0738	6.1	186
	1319	0.1	3			1407	-0.2	-6
	1905	5.9	180			1953	5.7	174
5 Th ○	0141	-0.3	-9		20 F	0224	-0.2	-6
	0725	6.0	183			0817	6.1	186
	1407	-0.1	-3			1451	-0.1	-3
	1944	6.0	183			2032	5.5	168
6 F	0224	-0.4	-12		21 Sa	0303	0.0	0
	0803	6.2	189			0854	5.9	180
	1455	-0.3	-9			1531	0.0	0
	2025	6.0	183			2111	5.2	158
7 Sa	0307	-0.5	-15		22 Su	0338	0.3	9
	0842	6.4	195			0931	5.7	174
	1541	-0.3	-9			1610	0.2	6
	2109	5.9	180			2151	4.9	149
8 Su	0350	-0.5	-15		23 M	0411	0.5	15
	0927	6.4	195			1008	5.5	168
	1628	-0.3	-9			1646	0.4	12
	2200	5.6	171			2234	4.6	140
9 M	0433	-0.3	-9		24 Tu	0440	0.8	24
	1018	6.2	189			1046	5.2	158
	1718	-0.1	-3			1723	0.7	21
	2259	5.4	165			2321	4.4	134
10 Tu	0520	0.0	0		25 W	0510	1.0	30
	1117	6.0	183			1129	5.0	152
	1814	0.2	6			1803	0.9	27
11 W	0005	5.2	158		26 Th	0012	4.2	128
	0615	0.3	9			0544	1.3	40
	1222	5.9	180			1217	4.8	146
	1920	0.4	12			1853	1.1	34
12 Th ◐	0109	5.1	155		27 F ◑	0103	4.2	128
	0723	0.5	15			0633	1.5	46
	1327	5.7	174			1307	4.8	146
	2031	0.4	12			1959	1.2	37
13 F	0212	5.1	155		28 Sa	0153	4.2	128
	0838	0.6	18			0755	1.5	46
	1430	5.6	171			1400	4.8	146
	2136	0.3	9			2105	1.0	30
14 Sa	0315	5.1	155		29 Su	0245	4.3	131
	0947	0.5	15			0917	1.4	43
	1535	5.6	171			1456	4.8	146
	2233	0.1	3			2200	0.8	24
15 Su	0418	5.3	162		30 M	0340	4.6	140
	1047	0.3	9			1019	1.0	30
	1638	5.6	171			1556	5.0	152
	2325	-0.1	-3			2248	0.4	12
					31 Tu	0435	5.0	152
						1112	0.6	18
						1655	5.2	158
						2334	0.1	3

November

Day	Time (h m)	Height (ft)	Height (cm)		Day	Time (h m)	Height (ft)	Height (cm)
1 W	0526	5.4	165		16 Th	0031	-0.2	-6
	1203	0.2	6			0633	5.8	177
	1748	5.4	165			1300	-0.1	-3
						1849	5.2	158
2 Th	0020	-0.2	-6		17 F	0113	-0.1	-3
	0613	5.9	180			0714	5.9	180
	1254	-0.1	-3			1345	-0.2	-6
	1836	5.7	174			1931	5.2	158
3 F	0107	-0.5	-15		18 Sa ●	0154	-0.1	-3
	0656	6.3	192			0752	5.9	180
	1345	-0.4	-12			1428	-0.2	-6
	1921	5.8	177			2009	5.1	155
4 Sa ○	0154	-0.6	-18		19 Su	0233	0.1	3
	0739	6.5	198			0827	5.8	177
	1436	-0.6	-18			1508	-0.1	-3
	2007	5.8	177			2047	4.9	149
5 Su	0242	-0.7	-21		20 M	0309	0.2	6
	0823	6.6	201			0900	5.6	171
	1526	-0.7	-21			1546	0.0	0
	2055	5.7	174			2124	4.7	143
6 M	0329	-0.7	-21		21 Tu	0342	0.4	12
	0910	6.6	201			0932	5.4	165
	1615	-0.7	-21			1622	0.1	3
	2149	5.6	171			2201	4.4	134
7 Tu	0417	-0.5	-15		22 W	0413	0.6	18
	1004	6.4	195			1003	5.1	155
	1706	-0.5	-15			1657	0.3	9
	2251	5.3	162			2242	4.3	131
8 W	0507	-0.3	-9		23 Th	0443	0.8	24
	1106	6.1	186			1038	5.0	152
	1801	-0.3	-9			1732	0.5	15
	2357	5.2	158			2327	4.1	125
9 Th	0603	0.1	3		24 F	0516	1.0	30
	1212	5.8	177			1122	4.8	146
	1902	0.0	0			1811	0.7	21
10 F ○	0101	5.1	155		25 Sa	0015	4.1	125
	0709	0.4	12			0558	1.1	34
	1315	5.6	171			1213	4.7	143
	2009	0.1	3			1902	0.7	21
11 Sa	0201	5.1	155		26 Su ◐	0104	4.2	128
	0822	0.5	15			0658	1.2	37
	1416	5.4	165			1308	4.7	143
	2113	0.1	3			2006	0.7	21
12 Su	0300	5.1	155		27 M	0154	4.3	131
	0930	0.5	15			0828	1.2	37
	1516	5.2	158			1404	4.7	143
	2209	0.0	0			2110	0.5	15
13 M	0359	5.3	162		28 Tu	0248	4.6	140
	1030	0.3	9			0942	0.9	27
	1616	5.2	158			1505	4.7	143
	2300	-0.1	-3			2205	0.2	6
14 Tu	0456	5.5	168		29 W	0345	5.0	152
	1123	0.1	3			1042	0.5	15
	1713	5.2	158			1609	4.9	149
	2347	-0.2	-6			2256	-0.1	-3
15 W	0547	5.7	174		30 Th	0444	5.4	165
	1213	0.0	0			1137	0.1	3
	1804	5.2	158			1712	5.1	155
						2346	-0.4	-12

December

Day	Time (h m)	Height (ft)	Height (cm)		Day	Time (h m)	Height (ft)	Height (cm)
1 F	0539	5.8	177		16 Sa	0044	0.0	0
	1231	-0.3	-9			0650	5.5	168
	1809	5.3	162			1321	-0.2	-6
						1909	4.7	143
2 Sa	0037	-0.7	-21		17 Su	0125	0.0	0
	0630	6.3	192			0729	5.6	171
	1325	-0.7	-21			1404	-0.2	-6
	1901	5.5	168			1949	4.7	143
3 Su	0129	-0.9	-27		18 M ●	0206	0.0	0
	0719	6.5	198			0805	5.5	168
	1418	-1.0	-30			1445	-0.3	-9
	1951	5.6	171			2027	4.6	140
4 M	0221	-1.0	-30		19 Tu	0244	0.1	3
	0807	6.7	204			0838	5.4	165
	1510	-1.1	-34			1523	-0.3	-9
	2042	5.6	171			2102	4.5	137
5 Tu	0312	-1.0	-30		20 W	0320	0.2	6
	0857	6.6	201			0908	5.3	162
	1601	-1.1	-34			1559	-0.2	-6
	2138	5.5	168			2136	4.4	134
6 W	0403	-0.9	-27		21 Th	0353	0.3	9
	0952	6.3	192			0935	5.1	155
	1651	-1.0	-30			1633	-0.1	-3
	2239	5.3	162			2209	4.2	128
7 Th	0454	-0.6	-18		22 F	0425	0.4	12
	1053	6.0	183			1007	5.0	152
	1743	-0.8	-24			1706	0.0	0
	2342	5.2	158			2245	4.2	128
8 F	0548	-0.3	-9		23 Sa	0458	0.6	18
	1156	5.7	174			1046	4.8	146
	1839	-0.5	-15			1740	0.1	3
						2328	4.2	128
9 Sa	0044	5.1	155		24 Su	0535	0.7	21
	0650	0.1	3			1134	4.7	143
	1257	5.4	165			1818	0.2	6
	1940	-0.2	-6					
10 Su ○	0141	5.1	155		25 M	0017	4.3	131
	0758	0.3	9			0623	0.8	24
	1354	5.1	155			1227	4.6	140
	2042	-0.1	-3			1909	0.3	9
11 M	0237	5.0	152		26 Tu ◐	0108	4.5	137
	0907	0.4	12			0737	0.9	27
	1450	4.8	146			1324	4.6	140
	2139	0.0	0			2014	0.3	9
12 Tu	0332	5.1	155		27 W	0203	4.7	143
	1007	0.3	9			0905	0.7	21
	1547	4.7	143			1425	4.6	140
	2231	0.0	0			2121	0.1	3
13 W	0428	5.2	158		28 Th	0302	5.0	152
	1101	0.2	6			1014	0.4	12
	1645	4.6	140			1531	4.6	140
	2317	-0.1	-3			2221	-0.2	-6
14 Th	0520	5.3	162		29 F	0406	5.3	162
	1150	0.1	3			1114	0.0	0
	1738	4.6	140			1641	4.7	143
						2317	-0.5	-15
15 F	0001	-0.1	-3		30 Sa	0510	5.7	174
	0608	5.4	165			1211	-0.5	-15
	1237	-0.1	-3			1746	5.0	152
	1826	4.6	140					
					31 Su	0013	-0.8	-24
						0609	6.1	186
						1307	-0.9	-27
						1844	5.2	158

Time meridian 75° W. 0000 is midnight. 1200 is noon. Times are not adjusted for Daylight Saving Time.
Heights are referred to mean lower low water which is the chart datum of soundings.

Albany, New York, 2017

Times and Heights of High and Low Waters

January

Day	Time (h m)	Height (ft)	Height (cm)
1 Su	0105	0.0	0
	0605	4.5	137
	1256	0.2	6
	1745	5.5	168
2 M	0146	0.0	0
	0638	4.6	140
	1343	0.2	6
	1831	5.5	168
3 Tu	0229	0.0	0
	0720	4.7	143
	1435	0.3	9
	1923	5.4	165
4 W	0314	0.0	0
	0811	4.9	149
	1534	0.4	12
	2023	5.2	158
5 Th	0405	0.1	3
	0909	4.9	149
	1639	0.4	12
	2133	5.0	152
6 F	0500	0.1	3
	1014	5.0	152
	1746	0.4	12
	2248	4.9	149
7 Sa	0559	0.1	3
	1120	5.1	155
	1851	0.3	9
	2357	4.8	146
8 Su	0659	0.0	0
	1223	5.2	158
	1953	0.1	3
9 M	0100	4.8	146
	0758	-0.1	-3
	1322	5.4	165
	2052	-0.2	-6
10 Tu	0158	4.9	149
	0854	-0.2	-6
	1416	5.6	171
	2147	-0.4	-12
11 W	0252	5.0	152
	0948	-0.3	-9
	1508	5.6	171
	2240	-0.5	-15
12 Th	0344	5.0	152
	1040	-0.4	-12
	1558	5.6	171
	2330	-0.6	-18
13 F	0435	5.0	152
	1131	-0.3	-9
	1649	5.5	168
14 Sa	0019	-0.5	-15
	0527	5.0	152
	1220	-0.3	-9
	1741	5.4	165
15 Su	0106	-0.5	-15
	0621	4.9	149
	1309	-0.1	-3
	1835	5.2	158
16 M	0153	-0.3	-9
	0714	4.9	149
	1359	0.1	3
	1929	5.1	155
17 Tu	0239	-0.2	-6
	0808	4.9	149
	1450	0.3	9
	2023	5.0	152
18 W	0325	0.0	0
	0900	4.9	149
	1542	0.4	12
	2117	4.8	146
19 Th	0411	0.1	3
	0952	4.9	149
	1636	0.5	15
	2211	4.7	143
20 F	0458	0.2	6
	1043	4.9	149
	1732	0.6	18
	2306	4.6	140
21 Sa	0546	0.3	9
	1135	5.0	152
	1828	0.6	18
22 Su	0001	4.5	137
	0635	0.4	12
	1226	5.0	152
	1923	0.5	15
23 M	0054	4.5	137
	0724	0.4	12
	1315	5.1	155
	2015	0.3	9
24 Tu	0144	4.5	137
	0812	0.3	9
	1400	5.3	162
	2104	0.1	3
25 W	0231	4.6	140
	0859	0.2	6
	1441	5.3	162
	2151	0.0	0
26 Th	0314	4.6	140
	0945	0.2	6
	1519	5.4	165
	2235	-0.1	-3
27 F	0354	4.6	140
	1030	0.1	3
	1552	5.5	168
	2317	-0.1	-3
28 Sa	0430	4.7	143
	1114	0.0	0
	1623	5.5	168
	2358	-0.1	-3
29 Su	0504	4.8	146
	1159	0.0	0
	1655	5.5	168
30 M	0039	-0.1	-3
	0536	4.9	149
	1245	0.0	0
	1734	5.5	168
31 Tu	0120	-0.1	-3
	0611	5.0	152
	1333	0.1	3
	1821	5.5	168

February

Day	Time (h m)	Height (ft)	Height (cm)
1 W	0202	-0.1	-3
	0654	5.1	155
	1425	0.2	6
	1916	5.4	165
2 Th	0248	0.0	0
	0745	5.2	158
	1523	0.3	9
	2019	5.2	158
3 F	0338	0.1	3
	0843	5.3	162
	1625	0.3	9
	2127	5.1	155
4 Sa	0434	0.2	6
	0948	5.3	162
	1729	0.4	12
	2236	4.9	149
5 Su	0535	0.2	6
	1057	5.3	162
	1833	0.3	9
	2343	4.9	149
6 M	0637	0.2	6
	1204	5.3	162
	1935	0.1	3
7 Tu	0046	4.9	149
	0738	0.1	3
	1306	5.4	165
	2033	-0.1	-3
8 W	0143	5.1	155
	0836	-0.1	-3
	1403	5.6	171
	2127	-0.3	-9
9 Th	0237	5.2	158
	0931	-0.2	-6
	1455	5.7	174
	2219	-0.4	-12
10 F	0328	5.3	162
	1023	-0.3	-9
	1545	5.7	174
	2307	-0.4	-12
11 Sa	0417	5.4	165
	1112	-0.2	-6
	1633	5.6	171
	2353	-0.4	-12
12 Su	0505	5.4	165
	1200	-0.1	-3
	1721	5.5	168
13 M	0037	-0.2	-6
	0554	5.3	162
	1246	0.0	0
	1810	5.4	165
14 Tu	0120	0.0	0
	0642	5.2	158
	1333	0.3	9
	1859	5.2	158
15 W	0202	0.2	6
	0731	5.2	158
	1419	0.5	15
	1950	5.0	152
16 Th	0243	0.4	12
	0820	5.1	155
	1508	0.7	21
	2042	4.9	149
17 F	0324	0.6	18
	0908	5.1	155
	1600	0.8	24
	2135	4.7	143
18 Sa	0407	0.7	21
	0958	5.1	155
	1654	0.9	27
	2230	4.6	140
19 Su	0454	0.9	27
	1049	5.0	152
	1750	0.9	27
	2326	4.5	137
20 M	0547	0.9	27
	1142	5.1	155
	1847	0.8	24
21 Tu	0021	4.5	137
	0642	0.9	27
	1234	5.1	155
	1941	0.7	21
22 W	0113	4.6	140
	0736	0.8	24
	1324	5.3	162
	2031	0.5	15
23 Th	0201	4.8	146
	0829	0.7	21
	1409	5.4	165
	2119	0.4	12
24 F	0245	4.9	149
	0920	0.5	15
	1449	5.5	168
	2204	0.3	9
25 Sa	0324	5.1	155
	1008	0.3	9
	1527	5.6	171
	2248	0.2	6
26 Su	0400	5.2	158
	1056	0.2	6
	1603	5.7	174
	2329	0.1	3
27 M	0434	5.4	165
	1143	0.1	3
	1641	5.7	174
28 Tu	0011	0.1	3
	0507	5.5	168
	1231	0.1	3
	1724	5.7	174

March

Day	Time (h m)	Height (ft)	Height (cm)
1 W	0053	0.2	6
	0545	5.7	174
	1321	0.2	6
	1814	5.7	174
2 Th	0137	0.2	6
	0629	5.8	177
	1414	0.3	9
	1911	5.5	168
3 F	0224	0.3	9
	0722	5.8	177
	1511	0.4	12
	2015	5.4	165
4 Sa	0316	0.4	12
	0823	5.7	174
	1611	0.5	15
	2121	5.3	162
5 Su	0414	0.5	15
	0931	5.6	171
	1713	0.5	15
	2226	5.2	158
6 M	0516	0.6	18
	1041	5.6	171
	1815	0.5	15
	2330	5.3	162
7 Tu	0619	0.5	15
	1149	5.6	171
	1915	0.3	9
8 W	0031	5.4	165
	0721	0.4	12
	1252	5.7	174
	2012	0.2	6
9 Th	0128	5.6	171
	0819	0.3	9
	1349	5.8	177
	2105	0.0	0
10 F	0221	5.8	177
	0913	0.1	3
	1441	5.9	180
	2154	-0.1	-3
11 Sa	0310	5.9	180
	1004	0.0	0
	1529	5.9	180
	2240	-0.1	-3
12 Su	0356	6.0	183
	1052	0.1	3
	1614	5.9	180
	2324	0.0	0
13 M	0441	6.0	183
	1138	0.2	6
	1659	5.8	177
14 Tu	0005	0.2	6
	0525	5.9	180
	1223	0.4	12
	1744	5.6	171
15 W	0044	0.5	15
	0608	5.8	177
	1306	0.6	18
	1830	5.4	165
16 Th	0121	0.7	21
	0651	5.7	174
	1350	0.8	24
	1918	5.3	162
17 F	0157	0.9	27
	0733	5.6	171
	1435	1.0	30
	2008	5.1	155
18 Sa	0232	1.1	34
	0816	5.5	168
	1523	1.1	34
	2100	5.0	152
19 Su	0309	1.3	40
	0859	5.5	168
	1615	1.2	37
	2153	4.9	149
20 M	0356	1.4	43
	0948	5.4	165
	1710	1.3	40
	2249	4.8	146
21 Tu	0455	1.5	46
	1045	5.3	162
	1807	1.3	40
	2345	4.8	146
22 W	0559	1.5	46
	1145	5.4	165
	1902	1.2	37
23 Th	0038	5.0	152
	0702	1.4	43
	1242	5.5	168
	1955	1.0	30
24 F	0127	5.2	158
	0800	1.1	34
	1332	5.6	171
	2044	0.8	24
25 Sa	0212	5.4	165
	0855	0.9	27
	1418	5.8	177
	2131	0.7	21
26 Su	0251	5.7	174
	0947	0.7	21
	1500	5.9	180
	2216	0.6	18
27 M	0328	5.9	180
	1037	0.5	15
	1542	6.0	183
	2259	0.5	15
28 Tu	0403	6.1	186
	1126	0.4	12
	1625	6.0	183
	2342	0.5	15
29 W	0439	6.3	192
	1216	0.3	9
	1712	5.9	180
30 Th	0027	0.5	15
	0520	6.4	195
	1307	0.4	12
	1805	5.9	180
31 F	0113	0.6	18
	0607	6.4	195
	1400	0.4	12
	1904	5.7	174

Time meridian 75° W. 0000 is midnight. 1200 is noon. Times are not adjusted for Daylight Saving Time.
Heights are referred to mean low water during lowest river stages which is the chart datum of soundings.

Albany, New York, 2017

Times and Heights of High and Low Waters

April

Day	Time	ft	cm	Day	Time	ft	cm
1 Sa	0203	0.7	21	**16** Su	0143	1.5	46
	0703	6.3	192		0659	6.0	183
	1456	0.5	15		1449	1.3	40
	2007	5.7	174		2024	5.2	158
2 Su	0257	0.9	27	**17** M	0218	1.6	49
	0808	6.1	186		0727	6.0	183
	1555	0.6	18		1537	1.4	43
	2111	5.6	171		2116	5.1	155
3 M	0357	0.9	27	**18** Tu	0306	1.7	52
	0918	6.0	183		0811	5.9	180
	1655	0.7	21		1629	1.4	43
	2214	5.6	171		2209	5.1	155
4 Tu	0459	1.0	30	**19** W	0408	1.8	55
	1027	5.9	180		0906	5.7	174
	1754	0.6	18		1725	1.4	43
	2315	5.7	174		2304	5.1	155
5 W	0601	0.9	27	**20** Th	0520	1.8	55
	1134	5.8	177		1023	5.6	171
	1852	0.5	15		1820	1.4	43
					2358	5.3	162
6 Th	0015	5.9	180	**21** F	0629	1.7	52
	0702	0.8	24		1150	5.6	171
	1236	5.9	180		1914	1.3	40
	1947	0.4	12				
7 F	0111	6.1	186	**22** Sa	0048	5.5	168
	0800	0.6	18		0732	1.4	43
	1332	6.0	183		1252	5.7	174
	2038	0.3	9		2006	1.1	34
8 Sa	0202	6.3	192	**23** Su	0135	5.8	177
	0854	0.5	15		0831	1.1	34
	1422	6.1	186		1345	5.8	177
	2126	0.3	9		2055	0.9	27
9 Su	0250	6.5	198	**24** M	0216	6.1	186
	0944	0.4	12		0925	0.9	27
	1509	6.1	186		1433	5.9	180
	2211	0.3	9		2142	0.8	24
10 M	0334	6.5	198	**25** Tu	0256	6.4	195
	1031	0.4	12		1018	0.6	18
	1553	6.0	183		1519	6.0	183
	2253	0.5	15		2229	0.7	21
11 Tu	0416	6.5	198	**26** W	0334	6.6	201
	1116	0.5	15		1109	0.5	15
	1636	5.9	180		1607	6.0	183
	2332	0.7	21		2315	0.7	21
12 W	0456	6.4	195	**27** Th	0414	6.7	204
	1159	0.7	21		1200	0.4	12
	1719	5.8	177		1657	5.9	180
13 Th	0008	0.9	27	**28** F	0002	0.8	24
	0534	6.3	192		0459	6.7	204
	1241	0.8	24		1252	0.4	12
	1802	5.6	171		1753	5.8	177
14 F	0042	1.1	34	**29** Sa	0052	0.8	24
	0610	6.2	189		0549	6.6	201
	1323	1.0	30		1345	0.4	12
	1848	5.4	165		1852	5.8	177
15 Sa	0113	1.3	40	**30** Su	0144	0.9	27
	0640	6.1	186		0649	6.4	195
	1405	1.1	34		1440	0.5	15
	1935	5.3	162		1955	5.7	174

May

Day	Time	ft	cm	Day	Time	ft	cm
1 M	0240	1.0	30	**16** Tu	0149	1.5	46
	0756	6.2	189		0648	6.1	186
	1536	0.5	15		1503	1.1	34
	2057	5.7	174		2035	5.1	155
2 Tu	0339	1.1	34	**17** W	0237	1.6	49
	0905	6.1	186		0735	6.0	183
	1633	0.6	18		1550	1.1	34
	2158	5.8	177		2124	5.1	155
3 W	0440	1.1	34	**18** Th	0337	1.6	49
	1011	5.9	180		0828	5.9	180
	1730	0.6	18		1641	1.1	34
	2257	5.9	180		2216	5.2	158
4 Th	0541	1.0	30	**19** F	0449	1.7	52
	1114	5.9	180		0930	5.7	174
	1825	0.5	15		1736	1.1	34
	2355	6.1	186		2310	5.4	165
5 F	0641	0.9	27	**20** Sa	0600	1.6	49
	1214	5.9	180		1050	5.5	168
	1918	0.5	15		1831	1.1	34
6 Sa	0050	6.3	192	**21** Su	0004	5.6	171
	0738	0.8	24		0706	1.3	40
	1309	5.9	180		1211	5.5	168
	2008	0.4	12		1926	0.9	27
7 Su	0140	6.5	198	**22** M	0055	5.9	180
	0832	0.6	18		0807	1.0	30
	1400	5.9	180		1313	5.5	168
	2055	0.4	12		2019	0.8	24
8 M	0227	6.6	201	**23** Tu	0142	6.2	189
	0922	0.5	15		0905	0.7	21
	1446	5.9	180		1407	5.6	171
	2139	0.5	15		2110	0.7	21
9 Tu	0310	6.7	204	**24** W	0226	6.4	195
	1009	0.5	15		0959	0.4	12
	1530	5.9	180		1459	5.6	171
	2220	0.6	18		2201	0.6	18
10 W	0350	6.6	201	**25** Th	0310	6.6	201
	1054	0.5	15		1052	0.2	6
	1613	5.7	174		1550	5.6	171
	2258	0.8	24		2251	0.6	18
11 Th	0427	6.5	198	**26** F	0355	6.6	201
	1136	0.6	18		1144	0.1	3
	1655	5.6	171		1642	5.6	171
	2334	1.0	30		2341	0.6	18
12 F	0502	6.4	195	**27** Sa	0443	6.6	201
	1217	0.7	21		1236	0.1	3
	1737	5.4	165		1738	5.5	168
13 Sa	0007	1.2	37	**28** Su	0033	0.6	18
	0531	6.3	192		0537	6.4	195
	1258	0.8	24		1328	0.1	3
	1820	5.2	158		1837	5.5	168
14 Su	0038	1.3	40	**29** M	0126	0.7	21
	0549	6.2	189		0637	6.2	189
	1338	0.9	27		1420	0.1	3
	1904	5.1	155		1938	5.5	168
15 M	0111	1.4	43	**30** Tu	0221	0.8	24
	0610	6.2	189		0742	6.0	183
	1419	1.0	30		1514	0.2	6
	1949	5.1	155		2038	5.5	168
				31 W	0319	0.8	24
					0847	5.8	177
					1607	0.2	6
					2137	5.6	171

June

Day	Time	ft	cm	Day	Time	ft	cm
1 Th	0418	0.9	27	**16** F	0318	1.1	34
	0949	5.6	171		0803	5.6	171
	1701	0.2	6		1600	0.5	15
	2234	5.8	177		2119	5.1	155
2 F	0518	0.9	27	**17** Sa	0425	1.1	34
	1049	5.5	168		0902	5.4	165
	1754	0.3	9		1652	0.5	15
	2330	5.9	180		2216	5.2	158
3 Sa	0616	0.8	24	**18** Su	0535	1.1	34
	1147	5.4	165		1015	5.1	155
	1845	0.3	9		1750	0.5	15
					2317	5.4	165
4 Su	0023	6.0	183	**19** M	0642	0.9	27
	0713	0.7	21		1137	5.0	152
	1242	5.4	165		1848	0.5	15
	1934	0.3	9				
5 M	0114	6.2	189	**20** Tu	0016	5.6	171
	0807	0.5	15		0745	0.6	18
	1334	5.4	165		1246	5.0	152
	2021	0.3	9		1946	0.4	12
6 Tu	0201	6.3	192	**21** W	0111	5.8	177
	0858	0.4	12		0845	0.3	9
	1422	5.4	165		1346	5.0	152
	2105	0.4	12		2043	0.3	9
7 W	0244	6.3	192	**22** Th	0202	6.0	183
	0945	0.3	9		0941	0.0	0
	1507	5.3	162		1441	5.1	155
	2147	0.5	15		2137	0.2	6
8 Th	0323	6.3	192	**23** F	0252	6.1	186
	1030	0.2	6		1035	-0.2	-6
	1550	5.2	158		1534	5.1	155
	2226	0.6	18		2231	0.1	3
9 F	0400	6.2	189	**24** Sa	0341	6.2	189
	1113	0.2	6		1126	-0.4	-12
	1633	5.1	155		1627	5.1	155
	2303	0.7	21		2323	0.1	3
10 Sa	0433	6.1	186	**25** Su	0432	6.1	186
	1154	0.3	9		1217	-0.5	-15
	1714	4.9	149		1722	5.1	155
	2339	0.8	24				
11 Su	0500	6.0	183	**26** M	0015	0.1	3
	1233	0.3	9		0526	5.9	180
	1755	4.8	146		1307	-0.5	-15
					1819	5.1	155
12 M	0015	0.9	27	**27** Tu	0107	0.2	6
	0518	6.0	183		0624	5.7	174
	1312	0.4	12		1357	-0.4	-12
	1834	4.8	146		1916	5.1	155
13 Tu	0052	0.9	27	**28** W	0201	0.3	9
	0544	5.9	180		0724	5.5	168
	1352	0.4	12		1447	-0.3	-9
	1912	4.8	146		2014	5.2	158
14 W	0133	1.0	30	**29** Th	0256	0.4	12
	0624	5.9	180		0824	5.3	162
	1432	0.5	15		1537	-0.2	-6
	1950	4.9	149		2110	5.2	158
15 Th	0221	1.0	30	**30** F	0352	0.5	15
	0711	5.8	177		0922	5.1	155
	1514	0.5	15		1627	-0.1	-3
	2030	5.0	152		2205	5.3	162

Time meridian 75° W. 0000 is midnight. 1200 is noon. Times are not adjusted for Daylight Saving Time.
Heights are referred to mean low water during lowest river stages which is the chart datum of soundings.

Albany, New York, 2017

Times and Heights of High and Low Waters

July

Day	Time (h m)	Height (ft)	Height (cm)
1 Sa	0450	0.5	15
	1019	4.9	149
	1718	0.0	0
	2259	5.4	165
2 Su	0548	0.5	15
	1116	4.8	146
	1807	0.0	0
	2352	5.5	168
3 M	0645	0.4	12
	1212	4.7	143
	1857	0.1	3
4 Tu	0043	5.5	168
	0739	0.3	9
	1305	4.7	143
	1944	0.1	3
5 W	0131	5.6	171
	0831	0.1	3
	1356	4.7	143
	2030	0.2	6
6 Th	0215	5.7	174
	0919	-0.1	-3
	1443	4.7	143
	2114	0.2	6
7 F	0256	5.7	174
	1005	-0.2	-6
	1527	4.6	140
	2156	0.2	6
8 Sa ○	0334	5.7	174
	1048	-0.2	-6
	1609	4.6	140
	2237	0.3	9
9 Su	0408	5.6	171
	1129	-0.3	-9
	1650	4.5	137
	2317	0.3	9
10 M	0437	5.6	171
	1208	-0.2	-6
	1728	4.5	137
	2357	0.3	9
11 Tu	0459	5.5	168
	1246	-0.2	-6
	1803	4.5	137
12 W	0038	0.3	9
	0526	5.5	168
	1324	-0.2	-6
	1835	4.6	140
13 Th	0122	0.4	12
	0606	5.5	168
	1402	-0.2	-6
	1906	4.7	143
14 F	0210	0.4	12
	0652	5.4	165
	1442	-0.2	-6
	1946	4.9	149
15 Sa	0305	0.5	15
	0745	5.2	158
	1526	-0.1	-3
	2034	5.0	152
16 Su ◑	0408	0.6	18
	0844	4.9	149
	1616	0.0	0
	2132	5.1	155
17 M	0515	0.6	18
	0957	4.7	143
	1715	0.0	0
	2237	5.1	155
18 Tu	0622	0.4	12
	1116	4.5	137
	1818	0.1	3
	2344	5.2	158
19 W	0725	0.2	6
	1227	4.5	137
	1921	0.0	0
20 Th	0047	5.4	165
	0826	-0.1	-3
	1329	4.5	137
	2021	-0.1	-3
21 F	0145	5.5	168
	0922	-0.4	-12
	1425	4.6	140
	2119	-0.2	-6
22 Sa	0238	5.6	171
	1016	-0.7	-21
	1519	4.7	143
	2213	-0.3	-9
23 Su ●	0330	5.7	174
	1106	-0.8	-24
	1611	4.8	146
	2306	-0.4	-12
24 M	0421	5.6	171
	1155	-0.9	-27
	1703	4.8	146
	2357	-0.4	-12
25 Tu	0513	5.5	168
	1243	-0.9	-27
	1757	4.9	149
26 W	0047	-0.3	-9
	0606	5.3	162
	1330	-0.8	-24
	1850	4.9	149
27 Th	0138	-0.1	-3
	0701	5.1	155
	1416	-0.6	-18
	1945	4.9	149
28 F	0230	0.0	0
	0756	4.9	149
	1503	-0.5	-15
	2038	4.9	149
29 Sa	0324	0.2	6
	0852	4.7	143
	1549	-0.3	-9
	2130	4.9	149
30 Su ◐	0419	0.3	9
	0947	4.5	137
	1636	-0.1	-3
	2222	4.9	149
31 M	0515	0.4	12
	1043	4.3	131
	1725	0.0	0
	2315	4.9	149

August

Day	Time (h m)	Height (ft)	Height (cm)
1 Tu	0612	0.3	9
	1139	4.2	128
	1815	0.1	3
2 W	0007	5.0	152
	0708	0.2	6
	1235	4.1	125
	1905	0.2	6
3 Th	0058	5.1	155
	0800	0.0	0
	1328	4.2	128
	1954	0.2	6
4 F	0145	5.2	158
	0850	-0.2	-6
	1417	4.2	128
	2042	0.1	3
5 Sa	0228	5.2	158
	0936	-0.3	-9
	1502	4.3	131
	2128	0.0	0
6 Su	0307	5.3	162
	1019	-0.5	-15
	1544	4.3	131
	2213	0.0	0
7 M ○	0343	5.3	162
	1101	-0.5	-15
	1622	4.4	134
	2257	-0.1	-3
8 Tu	0415	5.3	162
	1140	-0.6	-18
	1658	4.4	134
	2340	-0.1	-3
9 W	0443	5.3	162
	1218	-0.6	-18
	1730	4.5	137
10 Th	0024	-0.1	-3
	0513	5.2	158
	1256	-0.6	-18
	1759	4.7	143
11 F	0110	0.0	0
	0552	5.2	158
	1335	-0.5	-15
	1831	4.8	146
12 Sa	0159	0.0	0
	0639	5.1	155
	1415	-0.5	-15
	1914	5.0	152
13 Su	0254	0.1	3
	0733	4.9	149
	1459	-0.4	-12
	2004	5.1	155
14 M ◑	0354	0.2	6
	0837	4.7	143
	1550	-0.3	-9
	2102	5.1	155
15 Tu	0458	0.2	6
	0950	4.4	134
	1651	-0.1	-3
	2211	5.0	152
16 W	0603	0.1	3
	1104	4.3	131
	1757	-0.1	-3
	2323	5.0	152
17 Th	0706	-0.1	-3
	1212	4.3	131
	1902	-0.1	-3
18 F	0031	5.1	155
	0806	-0.3	-9
	1314	4.4	134
	2004	-0.3	-9
19 Sa	0132	5.2	158
	0902	-0.6	-18
	1410	4.6	140
	2102	-0.4	-12
20 Su	0227	5.4	165
	0954	-0.8	-24
	1503	4.8	146
	2157	-0.5	-15
21 M ●	0318	5.4	165
	1044	-1.0	-30
	1553	4.9	149
	2248	-0.6	-18
22 Tu	0407	5.4	165
	1131	-1.0	-30
	1643	5.0	152
	2338	-0.5	-15
23 W	0456	5.3	162
	1216	-0.9	-27
	1732	5.0	152
24 Th	0027	-0.4	-12
	0545	5.1	155
	1259	-0.8	-24
	1821	4.9	149
25 F	0115	-0.2	-6
	0635	4.9	149
	1342	-0.5	-15
	1911	4.9	149
26 Sa	0204	0.0	0
	0727	4.7	143
	1424	-0.3	-9
	2001	4.9	149
27 Su	0254	0.2	6
	0820	4.5	137
	1506	-0.1	-3
	2051	4.8	146
28 M	0346	0.4	12
	0914	4.3	131
	1550	0.1	3
	2141	4.8	146
29 Tu ◐	0440	0.4	12
	1009	4.1	125
	1637	0.3	9
	2233	4.7	143
30 W	0536	0.5	15
	1106	4.0	122
	1728	0.4	12
	2326	4.7	143
31 Th	0632	0.4	12
	1203	4.0	122
	1823	0.5	15

September

Day	Time (h m)	Height (ft)	Height (cm)
1 F	0019	4.8	146
	0726	0.2	6
	1257	4.0	122
	1917	0.4	12
2 Sa	0110	4.9	149
	0816	0.0	0
	1347	4.2	128
	2010	0.3	9
3 Su	0156	5.0	152
	0903	-0.2	-6
	1433	4.3	131
	2101	0.1	3
4 M	0238	5.1	155
	0947	-0.3	-9
	1514	4.5	137
	2149	0.0	0
5 Tu	0316	5.2	158
	1029	-0.5	-15
	1551	4.6	140
	2236	-0.1	-3
6 W ○	0351	5.2	158
	1110	-0.5	-15
	1625	4.8	146
	2322	-0.2	-6
7 Th	0424	5.2	158
	1149	-0.5	-15
	1655	4.9	149
8 F	0009	-0.2	-6
	0500	5.2	158
	1228	-0.5	-15
	1726	5.1	155
9 Sa	0057	-0.2	-6
	0541	5.1	155
	1308	-0.5	-15
	1802	5.2	158
10 Su	0147	-0.1	-3
	0631	5.0	152
	1351	-0.4	-12
	1848	5.3	162
11 M	0242	0.0	0
	0729	4.8	146
	1439	-0.3	-9
	1941	5.3	162
12 Tu	0340	0.1	3
	0836	4.7	143
	1534	-0.1	-3
	2044	5.2	158
13 W ◑	0442	0.1	3
	0945	4.5	137
	1636	0.0	0
	2157	5.1	155
14 Th	0545	0.1	3
	1053	4.5	137
	1742	0.0	0
	2310	5.1	155
15 F	0646	-0.1	-3
	1158	4.5	137
	1846	0.0	0
16 Sa	0018	5.1	155
	0744	-0.3	-9
	1259	4.7	143
	1948	-0.2	-6
17 Su	0119	5.3	162
	0839	-0.5	-15
	1354	5.0	152
	2045	-0.4	-12
18 M	0213	5.4	165
	0930	-0.7	-21
	1446	5.2	158
	2139	-0.5	-15
19 Tu	0303	5.5	168
	1018	-0.8	-24
	1534	5.3	162
	2230	-0.5	-15
20 W ●	0350	5.4	165
	1103	-0.8	-24
	1620	5.4	165
	2318	-0.4	-12
21 Th	0436	5.3	162
	1146	-0.6	-18
	1705	5.3	162
22 F	0005	-0.3	-9
	0522	5.1	155
	1227	-0.4	-12
	1750	5.3	162
23 Sa	0051	-0.1	-3
	0608	4.9	149
	1306	-0.2	-6
	1835	5.2	158
24 Su	0136	0.2	6
	0657	4.7	143
	1344	0.1	3
	1920	5.1	155
25 M	0223	0.4	12
	0748	4.5	137
	1421	0.3	9
	2006	5.0	152
26 Tu	0312	0.5	15
	0841	4.3	131
	1459	0.5	15
	2053	4.9	149
27 W ◑	0403	0.6	18
	0935	4.2	128
	1543	0.7	21
	2143	4.8	146
28 Th	0457	0.7	21
	1031	4.1	125
	1637	0.8	24
	2237	4.8	146
29 F	0552	0.6	18
	1127	4.1	125
	1738	0.8	24
	2334	4.8	146
30 Sa	0646	0.5	15
	1222	4.2	128
	1840	0.7	21

Time meridian 75° W. 0000 is midnight. 1200 is noon. Times are not adjusted for Daylight Saving Time.
Heights are referred to mean low water during lowest river stages which is the chart datum of soundings.

Albany, New York, 2017

Times and Heights of High and Low Waters

October

Day	Time (h m)	Height (ft)	Height (cm)
1 Su	0029	4.9	149
	0737	0.3	9
	1313	4.4	134
	1938	0.6	18
2 M	0119	5.0	152
	0826	0.1	3
	1359	4.6	140
	2033	0.4	12
3 Tu	0205	5.1	155
	0911	0.0	0
	1440	4.8	146
	2125	0.2	6
4 W	0246	5.2	158
	0955	-0.2	-6
	1517	5.1	155
	2215	0.0	0
5 Th ○	0325	5.3	162
	1037	-0.3	-9
	1550	5.3	162
	2304	-0.1	-3
6 F	0403	5.3	162
	1119	-0.3	-9
	1622	5.5	168
	2353	-0.1	-3
7 Sa	0445	5.3	162
	1201	-0.3	-9
	1657	5.6	171
8 Su	0042	-0.1	-3
	0531	5.2	158
	1244	-0.2	-6
	1738	5.7	174
9 M	0134	-0.1	-3
	0625	5.0	152
	1331	-0.1	-3
	1828	5.7	174
10 Tu	0228	0.0	0
	0726	4.9	149
	1423	0.0	0
	1927	5.6	171
11 W	0326	0.1	3
	0832	4.8	146
	1520	0.1	3
	2037	5.4	165
12 Th ☽	0425	0.1	3
	0937	4.8	146
	1623	0.2	6
	2149	5.3	162
13 F	0525	0.1	3
	1041	4.8	146
	1727	0.2	6
	2258	5.3	162
14 Sa	0624	-0.1	-3
	1143	4.9	149
	1830	0.1	3
15 Su	0003	5.3	162
	0720	-0.2	-6
	1241	5.1	155
	1930	0.0	0
16 M	0103	5.4	165
	0813	-0.4	-12
	1336	5.4	165
	2027	-0.2	-6
17 Tu	0156	5.5	168
	0903	-0.5	-15
	1426	5.6	171
	2120	-0.3	-9
18 W	0245	5.5	168
	0950	-0.6	-18
	1513	5.7	174
	2210	-0.3	-9
19 Th ●	0330	5.5	168
	1034	-0.5	-15
	1556	5.7	174
	2258	-0.2	-6
20 F	0414	5.3	162
	1115	-0.3	-9
	1639	5.7	174
	2343	-0.1	-3
21 Sa	0458	5.2	158
	1154	-0.1	-3
	1719	5.6	171
22 Su	0027	0.1	3
	0543	4.9	149
	1230	0.2	6
	1759	5.5	168
23 M	0110	0.3	9
	0629	4.7	143
	1305	0.4	12
	1838	5.3	162
24 Tu	0154	0.5	15
	0717	4.5	137
	1338	0.6	18
	1915	5.2	158
25 W	0238	0.6	18
	0808	4.4	134
	1412	0.7	21
	1952	5.2	158
26 Th	0325	0.7	21
	0900	4.3	131
	1454	0.9	27
	2031	5.1	155
27 F ☾	0415	0.7	21
	0952	4.3	131
	1548	1.0	30
	2127	5.0	152
28 Sa	0508	0.7	21
	1046	4.3	131
	1655	1.0	30
	2235	4.9	149
29 Su	0601	0.7	21
	1140	4.4	134
	1803	1.0	30
	2339	4.9	149
30 M	0654	0.5	15
	1231	4.6	140
	1906	0.8	24
31 Tu	0036	5.0	152
	0744	0.4	12
	1319	4.9	149
	2005	0.6	18

November

Day	Time (h m)	Height (ft)	Height (cm)
1 W	0128	5.1	155
	0833	0.2	6
	1401	5.1	155
	2101	0.3	9
2 Th	0214	5.2	158
	0919	0.1	3
	1439	5.4	165
	2154	0.1	3
3 F	0258	5.2	158
	1005	0.0	0
	1516	5.6	171
	2245	0.0	0
4 Sa ○	0342	5.3	162
	1050	-0.1	-3
	1553	5.8	177
	2336	-0.1	-3
5 Su	0429	5.2	158
	1136	-0.1	-3
	1633	5.9	180
6 M	0027	-0.2	-6
	0519	5.1	155
	1224	-0.1	-3
	1720	5.9	180
7 Tu	0119	-0.1	-3
	0616	5.0	152
	1314	0.0	0
	1815	5.8	177
8 W	0213	-0.1	-3
	0718	4.9	149
	1408	0.1	3
	1920	5.6	171
9 Th	0308	-0.1	-3
	0821	4.9	149
	1506	0.2	6
	2030	5.5	168
10 F ○	0405	0.0	0
	0923	5.0	152
	1607	0.2	6
	2138	5.4	165
11 Sa	0502	-0.1	-3
	1024	5.1	155
	1709	0.2	6
	2243	5.3	162
12 Su	0558	-0.1	-3
	1123	5.2	158
	1811	0.2	6
	2344	5.3	162
13 M	0652	-0.2	-6
	1221	5.4	165
	1910	0.1	3
14 Tu	0042	5.3	162
	0744	-0.3	-9
	1314	5.6	171
	2006	-0.1	-3
15 W	0134	5.4	165
	0833	-0.4	-12
	1404	5.7	174
	2059	-0.2	-6
16 Th	0223	5.4	165
	0919	-0.4	-12
	1449	5.8	177
	2149	-0.2	-6
17 F	0309	5.3	162
	1003	-0.3	-9
	1532	5.9	180
	2236	-0.1	-3
18 Sa ●	0353	5.2	158
	1044	-0.1	-3
	1612	5.8	177
	2320	0.0	0
19 Su	0436	5.0	152
	1122	0.1	3
	1651	5.7	174
20 M	0003	0.1	3
	0520	4.8	146
	1158	0.3	9
	1727	5.5	168
21 Tu	0045	0.2	6
	0604	4.6	140
	1232	0.5	15
	1759	5.4	165
22 W	0126	0.3	9
	0649	4.5	137
	1305	0.6	18
	1824	5.4	165
23 Th	0207	0.4	12
	0734	4.4	134
	1340	0.7	21
	1849	5.3	162
24 F	0249	0.5	15
	0821	4.4	134
	1422	0.8	24
	1928	5.3	162
25 Sa	0334	0.5	15
	0908	4.4	134
	1514	0.8	24
	2018	5.2	158
26 Su ☽	0422	0.6	18
	0957	4.4	134
	1619	0.9	27
	2118	5.0	152
27 M	0513	0.5	15
	1048	4.5	137
	1728	0.9	27
	2234	4.9	149
28 Tu	0606	0.5	15
	1141	4.7	143
	1836	0.8	24
	2348	4.9	149
29 W	0700	0.4	12
	1232	5.0	152
	1939	0.6	18
30 Th	0050	4.9	149
	0753	0.2	6
	1319	5.2	158
	2037	0.3	9

December

Day	Time (h m)	Height (ft)	Height (cm)
1 F	0144	5.0	152
	0844	0.1	3
	1403	5.5	168
	2133	0.1	3
2 Sa	0234	5.0	152
	0935	0.0	0
	1446	5.7	174
	2227	-0.1	-3
3 Su ○	0323	5.1	155
	1025	-0.1	-3
	1530	5.8	177
	2319	-0.2	-6
4 M	0413	5.0	152
	1115	-0.1	-3
	1617	5.9	180
5 Tu	0010	-0.3	-9
	0506	5.0	152
	1206	-0.1	-3
	1708	5.8	177
6 W	0102	-0.3	-9
	0603	4.9	149
	1259	-0.1	-3
	1807	5.7	174
7 Th	0154	-0.3	-9
	0703	4.9	149
	1353	-0.1	-3
	1912	5.5	168
8 F	0247	-0.3	-9
	0804	4.9	149
	1450	0.0	0
	2018	5.4	165
9 Sa	0341	-0.3	-9
	0904	5.0	152
	1548	0.1	3
	2121	5.3	162
10 Su ○	0435	-0.3	-9
	1002	5.1	155
	1648	0.1	3
	2221	5.2	158
11 M	0528	-0.3	-9
	1100	5.2	158
	1748	0.1	3
	2320	5.1	155
12 Tu	0621	-0.3	-9
	1155	5.3	162
	1847	0.1	3
13 W	0016	5.1	155
	0712	-0.3	-9
	1249	5.5	168
	1943	0.0	0
14 Th	0110	5.0	152
	0801	-0.3	-9
	1339	5.6	171
	2036	-0.1	-3
15 F	0200	5.0	152
	0848	-0.3	-9
	1424	5.7	174
	2126	-0.2	-6
16 Sa	0247	5.0	152
	0932	-0.2	-6
	1507	5.7	174
	2213	-0.2	-6
17 Su	0331	4.9	149
	1013	-0.1	-3
	1547	5.6	171
	2257	-0.2	-6
18 M ●	0415	4.8	146
	1052	0.1	3
	1624	5.5	168
	2339	-0.1	-3
19 Tu	0457	4.7	143
	1130	0.2	6
	1659	5.5	168
20 W	0019	0.0	0
	0539	4.5	137
	1206	0.3	9
	1729	5.4	165
21 Th	0058	0.1	3
	0620	4.4	134
	1242	0.4	12
	1751	5.3	162
22 F	0136	0.1	3
	0659	4.4	134
	1320	0.4	12
	1819	5.3	162
23 Sa	0215	0.2	6
	0736	4.4	134
	1403	0.5	15
	1859	5.3	162
24 Su	0254	0.2	6
	0809	4.5	137
	1453	0.6	18
	1948	5.2	158
25 M	0337	0.2	6
	0847	4.6	140
	1552	0.7	21
	2043	5.0	152
26 Tu ☾	0424	0.3	9
	0937	4.7	143
	1700	0.7	21
	2148	4.8	146
27 W	0518	0.3	9
	1036	4.8	146
	1809	0.7	21
	2306	4.7	143
28 Th	0617	0.2	6
	1139	5.0	152
	1914	0.5	15
29 F	0017	4.7	143
	0716	0.2	6
	1239	5.2	158
	2015	0.3	9
30 Sa	0118	4.7	143
	0814	0.1	3
	1333	5.4	165
	2113	0.0	0
31 Su	0213	4.8	146
	0910	-0.1	-3
	1424	5.6	171
	2208	-0.2	-6

Time meridian 75° W. 0000 is midnight. 1200 is noon. Times are not adjusted for Daylight Saving Time.
Heights are referred to mean low water during lowest river stages which is the chart datum of soundings.

Sandy Hook, New Jersey, 2017
Times and Heights of High and Low Waters

January

Day	Time (h m)	Height (ft)	Height (cm)
1 Su	0325	0.0	0
	0926	5.0	152
	1604	-0.3	-9
	2157	4.1	125
2 M	0404	0.1	3
	1010	4.9	149
	1642	-0.2	-6
	2245	4.2	128
3 Tu	0447	0.2	6
	1100	4.8	146
	1725	-0.2	-6
	2337	4.3	131
4 W	0540	0.4	12
	1154	4.6	140
	1816	-0.1	-3
5 Th ☽	0031	4.4	134
	0648	0.5	15
	1250	4.5	137
	1917	-0.1	-3
6 F	0127	4.6	140
	0805	0.4	12
	1350	4.4	134
	2022	-0.2	-6
7 Sa	0226	4.8	146
	0915	0.2	6
	1454	4.4	134
	2124	-0.3	-9
8 Su	0329	5.1	155
	1017	-0.2	-6
	1600	4.4	134
	2222	-0.5	-15
9 M	0433	5.4	165
	1115	-0.5	-15
	1704	4.6	140
	2318	-0.7	-21
10 Tu	0532	5.6	171
	1211	-0.8	-24
	1803	4.8	146
11 W	0013	-0.9	-27
	0627	5.8	177
	1305	-1.0	-30
	1857	5.0	152
12 Th ○	0107	-0.9	-27
	0718	5.9	180
	1356	-1.1	-34
	1949	5.0	152
13 F	0159	-0.9	-27
	0807	5.9	180
	1445	-1.1	-34
	2039	5.0	152
14 Sa	0248	-0.8	-24
	0856	5.7	174
	1531	-1.0	-30
	2131	4.9	149
15 Su	0336	-0.6	-18
	0945	5.4	165
	1615	-0.7	-21
	2222	4.7	143
16 M	0422	-0.3	-9
	1034	5.0	152
	1658	-0.5	-15
	2313	4.6	140
17 Tu	0509	0.0	0
	1124	4.7	143
	1743	-0.1	-3
18 W	0003	4.4	134
	0600	0.4	12
	1212	4.3	131
	1830	0.2	6
19 Th ◐	0051	4.3	131
	0657	0.6	18
	1300	4.0	122
	1923	0.4	12
20 F	0139	4.2	128
	0800	0.8	24
	1350	3.8	116
	2018	0.5	15
21 Sa	0228	4.2	128
	0900	0.7	21
	1442	3.7	113
	2111	0.5	15
22 Su	0320	4.3	131
	0954	0.6	18
	1539	3.6	110
	2201	0.4	12
23 M	0413	4.4	134
	1043	0.4	12
	1636	3.7	113
	2248	0.3	9
24 Tu	0504	4.6	140
	1130	0.2	6
	1728	3.8	116
	2333	0.2	6
25 W	0551	4.8	146
	1216	0.0	0
	1814	4.0	122
26 Th	0019	0.0	0
	0633	5.0	152
	1300	-0.2	-6
	1855	4.2	128
27 F ●	0103	-0.1	-3
	0712	5.1	155
	1342	-0.4	-12
	1934	4.3	131
28 Sa	0147	-0.2	-6
	0749	5.2	158
	1423	-0.5	-15
	2012	4.5	137
29 Su	0229	-0.3	-9
	0828	5.2	158
	1502	-0.6	-18
	2052	4.5	137
30 M	0310	-0.3	-9
	0908	5.2	158
	1541	-0.6	-18
	2134	4.6	140
31 Tu	0352	-0.3	-9
	0953	5.1	155
	1619	-0.6	-18
	2222	4.7	143

February

Day	Time (h m)	Height (ft)	Height (cm)
1 W	0436	-0.1	-3
	1042	4.9	149
	1701	-0.4	-12
	2313	4.7	143
2 Th	0528	0.0	0
	1136	4.7	143
	1749	-0.3	-9
3 F ◐	0008	4.8	146
	0631	0.2	6
	1233	4.5	137
	1848	-0.1	-3
4 Sa	0105	4.8	146
	0746	0.3	9
	1333	4.4	134
	1957	-0.1	-3
5 Su	0205	4.9	149
	0858	0.2	6
	1438	4.3	131
	2105	-0.1	-3
6 M	0310	5.0	152
	1002	-0.1	-3
	1545	4.3	131
	2207	-0.3	-9
7 Tu	0416	5.1	155
	1101	-0.3	-9
	1651	4.5	137
	2305	-0.4	-12
8 W	0518	5.4	165
	1156	-0.6	-18
	1750	4.7	143
9 Th	0000	-0.6	-18
	0613	5.6	171
	1248	-0.8	-24
	1843	4.9	149
10 F ○	0053	-0.7	-21
	0703	5.7	174
	1336	-0.9	-27
	1932	5.1	155
11 Sa	0143	-0.8	-24
	0749	5.6	171
	1422	-0.9	-27
	2019	5.1	155
12 Su	0230	-0.7	-21
	0834	5.5	168
	1505	-0.8	-24
	2105	5.1	155
13 M	0314	-0.6	-18
	0919	5.2	158
	1544	-0.6	-18
	2151	4.9	149
14 Tu	0357	-0.3	-9
	1003	4.9	149
	1622	-0.3	-9
	2237	4.8	146
15 W	0438	0.0	0
	1049	4.6	140
	1700	0.0	0
	2322	4.6	140
16 Th	0521	0.3	9
	1135	4.3	131
	1739	0.3	9
17 F	0007	4.4	134
	0610	0.6	18
	1221	4.0	122
	1823	0.6	18
18 Sa ○	0053	4.3	131
	0708	0.8	24
	1309	3.8	116
	1919	0.8	24
19 Su	0140	4.2	128
	0813	0.9	27
	1401	3.6	110
	2022	0.9	27
20 M	0232	4.2	128
	0914	0.8	24
	1457	3.6	110
	2121	0.8	24
21 Tu	0328	4.2	128
	1008	0.6	18
	1557	3.7	113
	2215	0.6	18
22 W	0425	4.4	134
	1057	0.4	12
	1654	3.9	119
	2304	0.4	12
23 Th	0517	4.7	143
	1144	0.1	3
	1743	4.2	128
	2352	0.1	3
24 F	0603	5.0	152
	1229	-0.1	-3
	1827	4.5	137
25 Sa	0039	-0.1	-3
	0645	5.2	158
	1312	-0.4	-12
	1907	4.7	143
26 Su ●	0125	-0.3	-9
	0726	5.4	165
	1354	-0.6	-18
	1947	5.0	152
27 M	0210	-0.5	-15
	0806	5.5	168
	1435	-0.7	-21
	2028	5.2	158
28 Tu	0254	-0.6	-18
	0849	5.4	165
	1516	-0.7	-21
	2112	5.2	158

March

Day	Time (h m)	Height (ft)	Height (cm)
1 W	0339	-0.5	-15
	0936	5.3	162
	1557	-0.7	-21
	2159	5.3	162
2 Th	0425	-0.4	-12
	1027	5.1	155
	1640	-0.5	-15
	2252	5.2	158
3 F	0517	-0.2	-6
	1123	4.8	146
	1728	-0.3	-9
	2348	5.2	158
4 Sa	0618	0.1	3
	1221	4.6	140
	1827	0.0	0
5 Su ◐	0047	5.1	155
	0730	0.2	6
	1322	4.4	134
	1938	0.2	6
6 M	0148	5.0	152
	0842	0.2	6
	1426	4.3	131
	2050	0.2	6
7 Tu	0253	5.0	152
	0947	0.1	3
	1533	4.4	134
	2154	0.1	3
8 W	0400	5.0	152
	1045	-0.1	-3
	1638	4.6	140
	2252	-0.1	-3
9 Th	0502	5.2	158
	1137	-0.3	-9
	1736	4.9	149
	2346	-0.3	-9
10 F	0557	5.3	162
	1226	-0.5	-15
	1827	5.1	155
11 Sa	0037	-0.4	-12
	0645	5.4	165
	1312	-0.6	-18
	1912	5.3	162
12 Su ○	0125	-0.5	-15
	0729	5.4	165
	1355	-0.6	-18
	1955	5.4	165
13 M	0209	-0.5	-15
	0810	5.3	162
	1435	-0.5	-15
	2037	5.3	162
14 Tu	0251	-0.4	-12
	0851	5.1	155
	1512	-0.3	-9
	2118	5.2	158
15 W	0331	-0.2	-6
	0933	4.9	149
	1547	-0.1	-3
	2159	5.0	152
16 Th	0410	0.0	0
	1015	4.6	140
	1621	0.2	6
	2240	4.8	146
17 F	0449	0.3	9
	1059	4.3	131
	1654	0.5	15
	2323	4.6	140
18 Sa	0530	0.6	18
	1145	4.0	122
	1731	0.8	24
19 Su	0006	4.4	134
	0620	0.8	24
	1232	3.8	116
	1819	1.1	34
20 M ◐	0053	4.3	131
	0722	1.0	30
	1322	3.7	113
	1927	1.2	37
21 Tu	0143	4.2	128
	0829	1.0	30
	1416	3.7	113
	2039	1.1	34
22 W	0239	4.3	131
	0928	0.8	24
	1515	3.8	116
	2140	0.9	27
23 Th	0339	4.4	134
	1020	0.6	18
	1614	4.1	125
	2234	0.6	18
24 F	0436	4.7	143
	1107	0.3	9
	1707	4.4	134
	2324	0.3	9
25 Sa	0528	5.0	152
	1153	-0.1	-3
	1754	4.8	146
26 Su	0013	-0.1	-3
	0615	5.3	162
	1238	-0.3	-9
	1838	5.2	158
27 M ●	0101	-0.4	-12
	0700	5.5	168
	1323	-0.6	-18
	1921	5.6	171
28 Tu	0149	-0.6	-18
	0744	5.6	171
	1407	-0.7	-21
	2004	5.8	177
29 W	0237	-0.7	-21
	0830	5.6	171
	1451	-0.8	-24
	2050	5.9	180
30 Th	0325	-0.7	-21
	0919	5.4	165
	1535	-0.7	-21
	2139	5.8	177
31 F	0414	-0.6	-18
	1014	5.2	158
	1621	-0.4	-12
	2234	5.7	174

Time meridian 75° W. 0000 is midnight. 1200 is noon. Times are not adjusted for Daylight Saving Time.
Heights are referred to mean lower low water which is the chart datum of soundings.

Sandy Hook, New Jersey, 2017

Times and Heights of High and Low Waters

April

Day	Time (h m)	Height (ft)	Height (cm)
1 Sa	0506	-0.3	-9
	1112	5.0	152
	1712	-0.1	-3
	2332	5.5	168
2 Su	0606	0.0	0
	1212	4.8	146
	1812	0.2	6
3 M ☾	0032	5.3	162
	0714	0.2	6
	1313	4.6	140
	1923	0.4	12
4 Tu	0133	5.1	155
	0825	0.3	9
	1415	4.6	140
	2036	0.5	15
5 W	0236	5.0	152
	0928	0.2	6
	1518	4.6	140
	2140	0.4	12
6 Th	0340	4.9	149
	1024	0.0	0
	1620	4.8	146
	2237	0.2	6
7 F	0441	5.0	152
	1114	-0.1	-3
	1716	5.0	152
	2329	0.0	0
8 Sa	0535	5.1	155
	1200	-0.2	-6
	1805	5.3	162
9 Su	0018	-0.1	-3
	0622	5.2	158
	1243	-0.2	-6
	1849	5.5	168
10 M	0103	-0.2	-6
	0705	5.2	158
	1324	-0.2	-6
	1929	5.5	168
11 Tu ○	0147	-0.2	-6
	0745	5.1	155
	1402	-0.1	-3
	2007	5.5	168
12 W	0228	-0.2	-6
	0824	5.0	152
	1439	0.0	0
	2045	5.4	165
13 Th	0307	-0.1	-3
	0904	4.7	143
	1514	0.2	6
	2122	5.2	158
14 F	0344	0.1	3
	0945	4.5	137
	1547	0.5	15
	2201	5.0	152
15 Sa	0421	0.3	9
	1028	4.3	131
	1620	0.7	21
	2240	4.8	146
16 Su	0500	0.5	15
	1113	4.1	125
	1654	1.0	30
	2323	4.6	140
17 M	0543	0.8	24
	1159	3.9	119
	1735	1.2	37
18 Tu	0008	4.5	137
	0636	0.9	27
	1247	3.9	119
	1834	1.3	40
19 W ◐	0058	4.4	134
	0741	1.0	30
	1338	3.9	119
	1954	1.3	40
20 Th	0152	4.4	134
	0844	0.9	27
	1433	4.1	125
	2103	1.1	34
21 F	0251	4.5	137
	0938	0.6	18
	1531	4.4	134
	2201	0.8	24
22 Sa	0352	4.7	143
	1028	0.3	9
	1627	4.8	146
	2255	0.4	12
23 Su	0450	5.0	152
	1116	0.0	0
	1719	5.2	158
	2346	0.0	0
24 M	0543	5.3	162
	1203	-0.3	-9
	1808	5.7	174
25 Tu	0038	-0.4	-12
	0633	5.5	168
	1251	-0.6	-18
	1854	6.1	186
26 W ●	0129	-0.6	-18
	0722	5.6	171
	1339	-0.7	-21
	1941	6.3	192
27 Th	0220	-0.8	-24
	0811	5.6	171
	1427	-0.7	-21
	2029	6.3	192
28 F	0311	-0.8	-24
	0904	5.5	168
	1515	-0.6	-18
	2121	6.2	189
29 Sa	0401	-0.7	-21
	1000	5.3	162
	1605	-0.4	-12
	2217	6.0	183
30 Su	0454	-0.5	-15
	1100	5.1	155
	1658	0.0	0
	2317	5.7	174

May

Day	Time (h m)	Height (ft)	Height (cm)
1 M	0552	-0.2	-6
	1201	4.9	149
	1758	0.3	9
2 Tu ○	0016	5.4	165
	0656	0.1	3
	1300	4.8	146
	1907	0.6	18
3 W	0116	5.2	158
	0802	0.2	6
	1359	4.8	146
	2017	0.7	21
4 Th	0215	5.0	152
	0903	0.2	6
	1458	4.8	146
	2121	0.6	18
5 F	0314	4.8	146
	0957	0.2	6
	1556	5.0	152
	2217	0.5	15
6 Sa	0413	4.8	146
	1044	0.1	3
	1650	5.1	155
	2308	0.3	9
7 Su	0507	4.8	146
	1128	0.1	3
	1739	5.3	162
	2355	0.2	6
8 M	0555	4.8	146
	1210	0.1	3
	1822	5.5	168
9 Tu	0039	0.1	3
	0638	4.8	146
	1250	0.1	3
	1901	5.6	171
10 W ○	0122	0.0	0
	0719	4.8	146
	1329	0.2	6
	1939	5.6	171
11 Th	0204	0.0	0
	0759	4.7	143
	1407	0.3	9
	2015	5.5	168
12 F	0243	0.0	0
	0838	4.6	140
	1444	0.4	12
	2051	5.3	162
13 Sa	0321	0.1	3
	0918	4.4	134
	1519	0.6	18
	2127	5.2	158
14 Su	0359	0.3	9
	1000	4.2	128
	1554	0.8	24
	2205	5.0	152
15 M	0436	0.4	12
	1044	4.1	125
	1628	1.0	30
	2246	4.8	146
16 Tu	0515	0.6	18
	1129	4.1	125
	1707	1.1	34
	2331	4.7	143
17 W	0600	0.7	21
	1216	4.1	125
	1758	1.3	40
18 Th ◐	0021	4.6	140
	0655	0.8	24
	1304	4.2	128
	1910	1.3	40
19 F	0113	4.6	140
	0757	0.7	21
	1355	4.4	134
	2026	1.1	34
20 Sa	0210	4.7	143
	0855	0.5	15
	1451	4.7	143
	2130	0.8	24
21 Su	0311	4.8	146
	0949	0.2	6
	1549	5.1	155
	2227	0.4	12
22 M	0413	4.9	149
	1040	-0.1	-3
	1646	5.5	168
	2322	0.0	0
23 Tu	0513	5.1	155
	1130	-0.3	-9
	1740	6.0	183
24 W	0016	-0.3	-9
	0608	5.3	162
	1221	-0.5	-15
	1831	6.3	192
25 Th ●	0110	-0.6	-18
	0701	5.5	168
	1314	-0.6	-18
	1921	6.5	198
26 F	0204	-0.8	-24
	0754	5.5	168
	1406	-0.6	-18
	2012	6.5	198
27 Sa	0256	-0.9	-27
	0849	5.4	165
	1458	-0.5	-15
	2105	6.4	195
28 Su	0347	-0.8	-24
	0946	5.3	162
	1550	-0.3	-9
	2202	6.1	186
29 M	0439	-0.6	-18
	1046	5.2	158
	1644	0.0	0
	2300	5.8	177
30 Tu	0533	-0.3	-9
	1145	5.1	155
	1741	0.3	9
	2358	5.5	168
31 W	0631	0.0	0
	1242	5.0	152
	1845	0.6	18

June

Day	Time (h m)	Height (ft)	Height (cm)
1 Th ☾	0053	5.2	158
	0732	0.2	6
	1337	5.0	152
	1952	0.8	24
2 F	0148	4.9	149
	0830	0.3	9
	1431	5.0	152
	2055	0.8	24
3 Sa	0243	4.7	143
	0923	0.3	9
	1525	5.0	152
	2151	0.7	21
4 Su	0338	4.5	137
	1010	0.3	9
	1618	5.1	155
	2241	0.6	18
5 M	0433	4.5	137
	1053	0.3	9
	1707	5.3	162
	2328	0.4	12
6 Tu	0524	4.5	137
	1135	0.3	9
	1752	5.4	165
7 W	0013	0.3	9
	0610	4.5	137
	1216	0.4	12
	1832	5.5	168
8 Th	0057	0.2	6
	0653	4.5	137
	1258	0.4	12
	1911	5.5	168
9 F ○	0139	0.1	3
	0734	4.5	137
	1339	0.5	15
	1948	5.5	168
10 Sa	0220	0.1	3
	0814	4.5	137
	1418	0.5	15
	2024	5.4	165
11 Su	0259	0.1	3
	0854	4.4	134
	1457	0.6	18
	2100	5.2	158
12 M	0337	0.2	6
	0934	4.3	131
	1533	0.7	21
	2137	5.1	155
13 Tu	0413	0.3	9
	1016	4.2	128
	1609	0.9	27
	2217	5.0	152
14 W	0450	0.4	12
	1100	4.2	128
	1648	1.0	30
	2302	4.9	149
15 Th	0530	0.5	15
	1145	4.3	131
	1734	1.1	34
	2351	4.8	146
16 F	0617	0.5	15
	1233	4.5	137
	1837	1.1	34
17 Sa ○	0043	4.8	146
	0713	0.5	15
	1323	4.7	143
	1952	1.0	30
18 Su	0138	4.8	146
	0814	0.4	12
	1417	5.0	152
	2101	0.8	24
19 M	0238	4.8	146
	0913	0.2	6
	1516	5.3	162
	2203	0.4	12
20 Tu	0343	4.8	146
	1009	-0.1	-3
	1616	5.7	174
	2300	0.0	0
21 W	0447	5.0	152
	1103	-0.3	-9
	1715	6.0	183
	2357	-0.3	-9
22 Th	0547	5.1	155
	1158	-0.4	-12
	1811	6.3	192
23 F ●	0053	-0.6	-18
	0644	5.3	162
	1253	-0.5	-15
	1904	6.5	198
24 Sa	0147	-0.8	-24
	0738	5.4	165
	1348	-0.6	-18
	1956	6.5	198
25 Su	0239	-0.8	-24
	0833	5.4	165
	1442	-0.5	-15
	2049	6.4	195
26 M	0330	-0.8	-24
	0929	5.4	165
	1534	-0.3	-9
	2144	6.1	186
27 Tu	0419	-0.6	-18
	1026	5.3	162
	1626	-0.1	-3
	2239	5.8	177
28 W	0509	-0.4	-12
	1122	5.2	158
	1719	0.3	9
	2334	5.4	165
29 Th	0600	-0.1	-3
	1216	5.1	155
	1817	0.6	18
30 F ☾	0026	5.1	155
	0654	0.2	6
	1308	5.0	152
	1919	0.8	24

Time meridian 75° W. 0000 is midnight. 1200 is noon. Times are not adjusted for Daylight Saving Time.
Heights are referred to mean lower low water which is the chart datum of soundings.

Sandy Hook, New Jersey, 2017

Times and Heights of High and Low Waters

July

Day	Time (h m)	Height (ft)	Height (cm)	Day	Time (h m)	Height (ft)	Height (cm)
1 Sa	0117	4.8	146	16 Su ◗	0019	4.9	149
	0750	0.4	12		0637	0.3	9
	1359	5.0	152		1255	5.0	152
	2022	0.9	27		1926	0.9	27
2 Su	0208	4.5	137	17 M	0115	4.8	146
	0843	0.5	15		0739	0.3	9
	1449	5.0	152		1350	5.2	158
	2120	0.9	27		2039	0.7	21
3 M	0301	4.3	131	18 Tu	0216	4.7	143
	0932	0.6	18		0844	0.2	6
	1541	5.0	152		1450	5.4	165
	2211	0.8	24		2144	0.4	12
4 Tu	0357	4.2	128	19 W	0321	4.7	143
	1017	0.6	18		0946	0.1	3
	1631	5.1	155		1553	5.7	174
	2259	0.6	18		2243	0.1	3
5 W	0451	4.2	128	20 Th	0428	4.8	146
	1101	0.6	18		1044	-0.1	-3
	1719	5.2	158		1656	6.0	183
	2344	0.5	15		2340	-0.2	-6
6 Th	0541	4.3	131	21 F	0531	5.0	152
	1145	0.6	18		1141	-0.3	-9
	1803	5.3	162		1755	6.2	189
7 F	0029	0.3	9	22 Sa	0036	-0.5	-15
	0627	4.4	134		0629	5.3	162
	1229	0.5	15		1237	-0.4	-12
	1844	5.4	165		1849	6.4	195
8 Sa ○	0113	0.2	6	23 Su ●	0129	-0.6	-18
	0709	4.5	137		0723	5.4	165
	1312	0.5	15		1333	-0.5	-15
	1923	5.5	168		1940	6.4	195
9 Su	0155	0.1	3	24 M	0220	-0.7	-21
	0749	4.5	137		0815	5.5	168
	1355	0.5	15		1425	-0.4	-12
	2000	5.4	165		2031	6.2	189
10 M	0235	0.1	3	25 Tu	0309	-0.7	-21
	0828	4.5	137		0908	5.5	168
	1435	0.5	15		1516	-0.3	-9
	2036	5.4	165		2122	6.0	183
11 Tu	0313	0.1	3	26 W	0355	-0.6	-18
	0906	4.5	137		1000	5.4	165
	1514	0.6	18		1605	-0.1	-3
	2113	5.3	162		2213	5.7	174
12 W	0349	0.1	3	27 Th	0439	-0.3	-9
	0946	4.5	137		1053	5.3	162
	1552	0.6	18		1653	0.3	9
	2153	5.2	158		2304	5.3	162
13 Th	0425	0.2	6	28 F	0524	0.0	0
	1029	4.6	140		1144	5.2	158
	1632	0.7	21		1744	0.6	18
	2237	5.1	155		2355	4.9	149
14 F	0502	0.2	6	29 Sa	0611	0.4	12
	1115	4.7	143		1233	5.0	152
	1717	0.8	24		1841	0.9	27
	2326	5.0	152				
15 Sa	0545	0.3	9	30 Su ◐	0044	4.6	140
	1204	4.8	146		0702	0.6	18
	1814	0.9	27		1321	4.9	149
					1942	1.1	34
				31 M	0133	4.3	131
					0757	0.8	24
					1410	4.9	149
					2042	1.1	34

August

Day	Time (h m)	Height (ft)	Height (cm)	Day	Time (h m)	Height (ft)	Height (cm)
1 Tu	0225	4.2	128	16 W	0202	4.7	143
	0851	0.9	27		0825	0.4	12
	1500	4.8	146		1431	5.5	168
	2137	1.0	30		2129	0.5	15
2 W	0320	4.1	125	17 Th	0308	4.7	143
	0942	0.9	27		0931	0.3	9
	1553	4.9	149		1537	5.6	171
	2227	0.8	24		2229	0.2	6
3 Th	0417	4.1	125	18 F	0415	4.8	146
	1029	0.8	24		1031	0.1	3
	1645	5.0	152		1641	5.8	177
	2314	0.7	21		2325	-0.1	-3
4 F	0511	4.2	128	19 Sa	0518	5.1	155
	1116	0.7	21		1128	-0.1	-3
	1733	5.2	158		1741	6.0	183
	2359	0.5	15				
5 Sa	0559	4.4	134	20 Su	0018	-0.3	-9
	1201	0.6	18		0615	5.4	165
	1817	5.3	162		1224	-0.3	-9
					1834	6.2	189
6 Su	0043	0.3	9	21 M ●	0109	-0.5	-15
	0642	4.6	140		0706	5.6	171
	1246	0.5	15		1317	-0.3	-9
	1857	5.5	168		1923	6.2	189
7 M ○	0126	0.2	6	22 Tu ○	0157	-0.6	-18
	0722	4.7	143		0755	5.7	174
	1330	0.4	12		1407	-0.3	-9
	1934	5.5	168		2010	6.1	186
8 Tu	0206	0.0	0	23 W	0243	-0.5	-15
	0800	4.8	146		0843	5.7	174
	1413	0.3	9		1455	-0.2	-6
	2011	5.5	168		2057	5.8	177
9 W	0245	0.0	0	24 Th	0325	-0.4	-12
	0837	4.9	149		0930	5.6	171
	1454	0.3	9		1541	0.0	0
	2049	5.5	168		2144	5.5	168
10 Th	0322	-0.1	-3	25 F	0406	-0.1	-3
	0916	5.0	152		1019	5.4	165
	1534	0.4	12		1625	0.3	9
	2129	5.4	165		2232	5.1	155
11 F	0358	0.0	0	26 Sa	0445	0.2	6
	0959	5.0	152		1107	5.2	158
	1616	0.4	12		1710	0.6	18
	2215	5.2	158		2320	4.8	146
12 Sa	0436	0.0	0	27 Su	0526	0.6	18
	1046	5.1	155		1154	5.0	152
	1702	0.6	18		1800	0.9	27
	2306	5.1	155				
13 Su	0518	0.2	6	28 M	0009	4.5	137
	1138	5.2	158		0611	0.9	27
	1758	0.7	21		1241	4.9	149
					1857	1.1	34
14 M ◐	0002	4.9	149	29 Tu ◐	0058	4.2	128
	0610	0.3	9		0705	1.2	37
	1232	5.3	162		1328	4.8	146
	1907	0.8	24		2000	1.2	37
15 Tu	0100	4.8	146	30 W	0150	4.1	125
	0714	0.4	12		0806	1.3	40
	1330	5.4	165		1419	4.7	143
	2022	0.7	21		2100	1.2	37
				31 Th	0245	4.0	122
					0905	1.2	37
					1512	4.7	143
					2153	1.0	30

September

Day	Time (h m)	Height (ft)	Height (cm)	Day	Time (h m)	Height (ft)	Height (cm)
1 F	0342	4.1	125	16 Sa	0404	4.9	149
	0958	1.1	34		1021	0.2	6
	1607	4.8	146		1627	5.6	171
	2241	0.8	24		2308	0.0	0
2 Sa	0438	4.2	128	17 Su	0505	5.2	158
	1047	0.9	27		1117	0.0	0
	1659	5.0	152		1725	5.8	177
	2326	0.6	18		2358	-0.2	-6
3 Su	0528	4.5	137	18 M	0559	5.5	168
	1134	0.7	21		1209	-0.1	-3
	1745	5.3	162		1817	5.9	180
4 M	0010	0.3	9	19 Tu	0046	-0.4	-12
	0612	4.8	146		0647	5.7	174
	1220	0.5	15		1300	-0.2	-6
	1827	5.5	168		1903	5.9	180
5 Tu	0052	0.1	3	20 W ●	0131	-0.4	-12
	0651	5.0	152		0732	5.8	177
	1305	0.3	9		1347	-0.2	-6
	1906	5.6	171		1947	5.8	177
6 W ○	0133	-0.1	-3	21 Th	0213	-0.3	-9
	0729	5.2	158		0816	5.8	177
	1349	0.1	3		1433	-0.1	-3
	1945	5.7	174		2030	5.5	168
7 Th	0213	-0.2	-6	22 F	0253	-0.2	-6
	0807	5.4	165		0858	5.7	174
	1433	0.1	3		1515	0.0	0
	2025	5.6	171		2113	5.2	158
8 F	0252	-0.2	-6	23 Sa	0331	0.1	3
	0847	5.5	168		0942	5.5	168
	1516	0.0	0		1557	0.3	9
	2108	5.5	168		2158	4.9	149
9 Sa	0332	-0.2	-6	24 Su	0407	0.4	12
	0931	5.6	171		1026	5.2	158
	1601	0.1	3		1638	0.5	15
	2156	5.3	162		2245	4.6	140
10 Su	0412	-0.1	-3	25 M	0443	0.7	21
	1021	5.6	171		1111	5.0	152
	1649	0.3	9		1722	0.8	24
	2251	5.1	155		2334	4.3	131
11 M	0457	0.1	3	26 Tu	0523	1.0	30
	1116	5.5	168		1158	4.8	146
	1746	0.5	15		1812	1.1	34
	2349	4.9	149				
12 Tu	0550	0.3	9	27 W ◗	0025	4.1	125
	1214	5.5	168		0611	1.3	40
	1854	0.6	18		1246	4.7	143
					1913	1.2	37
13 W ◗	0050	4.7	143	28 Th	0116	4.0	122
	0657	0.5	15		0716	1.5	46
	1315	5.4	165		1336	4.6	140
	2008	0.6	18		2017	1.2	37
14 Th	0153	4.7	143	29 F	0209	4.0	122
	0812	0.6	18		0825	1.4	43
	1418	5.4	165		1429	4.6	140
	2115	0.5	15		2115	1.1	34
15 F	0258	4.7	143	30 Sa	0304	4.1	125
	0920	0.5	15		0925	1.3	40
	1523	5.5	168		1524	4.7	143
	2214	0.2	6		2204	0.8	24

Time meridian 75° W. 0000 is midnight. 1200 is noon. Times are not adjusted for Daylight Saving Time.
Heights are referred to mean lower low water which is the chart datum of soundings.

Sandy Hook, New Jersey, 2017

Times and Heights of High and Low Waters

October

Day	Time	ft	cm		Day	Time	ft	cm
1 Su	0400	4.3	131		**16** M	0448	5.2	158
	1017	1.0	30			1103	0.1	3
	1619	4.9	149			1706	5.3	162
	2250	0.5	15			2334	-0.2	-6
2 M	0451	4.6	140		**17** Tu	0540	5.5	168
	1105	0.7	21			1153	0.0	0
	1709	5.1	155			1756	5.4	165
	2333	0.2	6					
3 Tu	0537	5.0	152		**18** W	0019	-0.3	-9
	1152	0.4	12			0626	5.7	174
	1754	5.4	165			1241	-0.1	-3
						1841	5.4	165
4 W	0016	0.0	0		**19** Th ●	0101	-0.3	-9
	0619	5.3	162			0708	5.8	177
	1239	0.1	3			1326	-0.2	-6
	1837	5.6	171			1923	5.3	162
5 Th ○	0058	-0.2	-6		**20** F	0142	-0.2	-6
	0659	5.6	171			0748	5.8	177
	1326	-0.1	-3			1409	-0.1	-3
	1919	5.7	174			2004	5.1	155
6 F	0141	-0.4	-12		**21** Sa	0220	0.0	0
	0739	5.9	180			0827	5.6	171
	1412	-0.3	-9			1451	0.0	0
	2002	5.6	171			2045	4.9	149
7 Sa	0224	-0.4	-12		**22** Su	0257	0.2	6
	0822	6.0	183			0906	5.4	165
	1459	-0.3	-9			1530	0.2	6
	2048	5.5	168			2127	4.6	140
8 Su	0307	-0.4	-12		**23** M	0333	0.5	15
	0908	6.0	183			0947	5.2	158
	1547	-0.2	-6			1609	0.4	12
	2140	5.3	162			2212	4.3	131
9 M	0352	-0.2	-6		**24** Tu	0408	0.7	21
	1000	5.9	180			1029	4.9	149
	1638	-0.1	-3			1649	0.6	18
	2238	5.0	152			2301	4.1	125
10 Tu	0441	0.0	0		**25** W	0444	1.0	30
	1058	5.7	174			1115	4.7	143
	1734	0.2	6			1734	0.8	24
	2340	4.8	146			2350	3.9	119
11 W	0537	0.3	9		**26** Th	0526	1.2	37
	1200	5.5	168			1203	4.6	140
	1840	0.4	12			1826	1.0	30
12 Th ☽	0042	4.7	143		**27** F ☾	0041	3.9	119
	0645	0.6	18			0624	1.4	43
	1302	5.4	165			1252	4.5	137
	1952	0.4	12			1929	1.1	34
13 F	0144	4.7	143		**28** Sa	0131	3.9	119
	0800	0.6	18			0739	1.4	43
	1404	5.3	162			1344	4.5	137
	2058	0.3	9			2030	0.9	27
14 Sa	0247	4.8	146		**29** Su	0223	4.0	122
	0909	0.5	15			0847	1.3	40
	1507	5.2	158			1438	4.5	137
	2156	0.1	3			2123	0.7	21
15 Su	0350	5.0	152		**30** M	0317	4.3	131
	1009	0.3	9			0944	0.9	27
	1609	5.3	162			1533	4.7	143
	2247	-0.1	-3			2210	0.4	12
					31 Tu	0410	4.6	140
						1035	0.6	18
						1628	4.9	149
						2255	0.1	3

November

Day	Time	ft	cm		Day	Time	ft	cm
1 W	0459	5.1	155		**16** Th	0602	5.5	168
	1124	0.2	6			1219	-0.1	-3
	1719	5.1	155			1817	4.8	146
	2339	-0.2	-6					
2 Th	0546	5.5	168		**17** F	0031	-0.2	-6
	1214	-0.1	-3			0643	5.6	171
	1808	5.3	162			1304	-0.1	-3
						1900	4.8	146
3 F	0025	-0.5	-15		**18** Sa ●	0111	-0.1	-3
	0630	5.9	180			0722	5.5	168
	1303	-0.4	-12			1346	-0.2	-6
	1854	5.4	165			1940	4.7	143
4 Sa ○	0111	-0.6	-18		**19** Su	0150	0.0	0
	0715	6.1	186			0759	5.5	168
	1353	-0.6	-18			1427	-0.1	-3
	1942	5.5	168			2020	4.5	137
5 Su	0158	-0.7	-21		**20** M	0228	0.2	6
	0800	6.2	189			0836	5.3	162
	1443	-0.7	-21			1506	0.0	0
	2032	5.3	162			2101	4.3	131
6 M	0246	-0.6	-18		**21** Tu	0305	0.4	12
	0850	6.2	189			0914	5.1	155
	1533	-0.6	-18			1545	0.1	3
	2126	5.2	158			2143	4.1	125
7 Tu	0335	-0.5	-15		**22** W	0341	0.6	18
	0944	6.0	183			0954	4.9	149
	1625	-0.5	-15			1622	0.3	9
	2226	5.0	152			2228	3.9	119
8 W	0427	-0.2	-6		**23** Th	0416	0.8	24
	1044	5.7	174			1036	4.6	140
	1721	-0.2	-6			1702	0.5	15
	2328	4.8	146			2315	3.8	116
9 Th	0525	0.1	3		**24** F	0454	0.9	27
	1145	5.5	168			1121	4.5	137
	1823	0.0	0			1745	0.6	18
10 F ○	0030	4.7	143		**25** Sa	0003	3.8	116
	0631	0.4	12			0541	1.1	34
	1246	5.3	162			1209	4.4	134
	1930	0.1	3			1838	0.7	21
11 Sa	0130	4.7	143		**26** Su ☾	0051	3.9	119
	0744	0.5	15			0647	1.2	37
	1346	5.1	155			1259	4.3	131
	2035	0.1	3			1937	0.6	18
12 Su	0230	4.8	146		**27** M	0140	4.0	122
	0852	0.5	15			0803	1.1	34
	1446	4.9	149			1352	4.4	134
	2132	0.0	0			2035	0.5	15
13 M	0329	4.9	149		**28** Tu	0232	4.3	131
	0952	0.3	9			0908	0.8	24
	1545	4.8	146			1448	4.4	134
	2222	-0.1	-3			2128	0.2	6
14 Tu	0425	5.1	155		**29** W	0326	4.6	140
	1045	0.2	6			1005	0.4	12
	1641	4.8	146			1547	4.6	140
	2307	-0.2	-6			2217	-0.1	-3
15 W	0516	5.3	162		**30** Th	0421	5.0	152
	1133	0.0	0			1058	0.0	0
	1732	4.8	146			1646	4.8	146
	2350	-0.2	-6			2306	-0.4	-12

December

Day	Time	ft	cm		Day	Time	ft	cm
1 F	0514	5.5	168		**16** Sa	0002	-0.1	-3
	1150	-0.3	-9			0618	5.2	158
	1741	5.0	152			1240	-0.1	-3
	2355	-0.7	-21			1837	4.3	131
2 Sa	0605	5.9	180		**17** Su	0043	0.0	0
	1243	-0.7	-21			0657	5.2	158
	1833	5.1	155			1323	-0.2	-6
						1918	4.3	131
3 Su ○	0046	-0.8	-24		**18** M ●	0124	0.0	0
	0654	6.2	189			0735	5.2	158
	1336	-0.9	-27			1404	-0.2	-6
	1925	5.2	158			1958	4.3	131
4 M	0137	-0.9	-27		**19** Tu	0204	0.1	3
	0743	6.3	192			0812	5.1	155
	1428	-1.0	-30			1444	-0.2	-6
	2017	5.2	158			2037	4.2	128
5 Tu	0229	-0.9	-27		**20** W	0243	0.2	6
	0835	6.2	189			0849	5.0	152
	1519	-1.0	-30			1521	-0.1	-3
	2112	5.1	155			2117	4.0	122
6 W	0321	-0.8	-24		**21** Th	0319	0.3	9
	0930	6.0	183			0926	4.8	146
	1610	-0.9	-27			1558	0.0	0
	2211	4.9	149			2157	3.9	119
7 Th	0414	-0.5	-15		**22** F	0355	0.4	12
	1028	5.7	174			1004	4.6	140
	1704	-0.6	-18			1634	0.1	3
	2312	4.8	146			2239	3.9	119
8 F	0510	-0.2	-6		**23** Sa	0431	0.6	18
	1128	5.4	165			1045	4.5	137
	1800	-0.4	-12			1710	0.2	6
						2323	3.9	119
9 Sa	0012	4.7	143		**24** Su	0511	0.7	21
	0612	0.1	3			1130	4.4	134
	1226	5.1	155			1752	0.3	9
	1902	-0.2	-6					
10 Su	0109	4.7	143		**25** M	0009	4.0	122
	0720	0.4	12			0604	0.8	24
	1322	4.8	146			1219	4.3	131
	2003	-0.1	-3			1843	0.3	9
11 M	0205	4.7	143		**26** Tu ☾	0057	4.1	125
	0828	0.4	12			0716	0.8	24
	1418	4.5	137			1312	4.3	131
	2100	0.0	0			1944	0.2	6
12 Tu	0301	4.7	143		**27** W	0149	4.4	134
	0929	0.4	12			0831	0.6	18
	1515	4.3	131			1410	4.3	131
	2151	-0.1	-3			2045	0.0	0
13 W	0356	4.8	146		**28** Th	0246	4.6	140
	1022	0.2	6			0936	0.3	9
	1611	4.3	131			1512	4.3	131
	2237	-0.1	-3			2143	-0.2	-6
14 Th	0448	5.0	152		**29** F	0347	5.0	152
	1111	0.1	3			1034	-0.1	-3
	1705	4.3	131			1617	4.4	134
	2320	-0.1	-3			2237	-0.5	-15
15 F	0535	5.1	155		**30** Sa	0447	5.4	165
	1156	0.0	0			1130	-0.4	-12
	1753	4.3	131			1719	4.7	143
						2332	-0.7	-21
					31 Su	0544	5.8	177
						1225	-0.8	-24
						1816	4.9	149

Time meridian 75° W. 0000 is midnight. 1200 is noon. Times are not adjusted for Daylight Saving Time.
Heights are referred to mean lower low water which is the chart datum of soundings.

Atlantic City, New Jersey, 2017
Times and Heights of High and Low Waters

January

Day	Time	ft	cm	Day	Time	ft	cm
1 Su	0245	0.0	0	16 M	0355	-0.3	-9
	0907	4.5	137		1008	4.4	134
	1536	-0.2	-6		1639	-0.4	-12
	2131	3.4	104		2246	3.7	113
2 M	0328	0.1	3	17 Tu	0447	0.0	0
	0947	4.4	134		1054	4.0	122
	1617	-0.2	-6		1726	-0.2	-6
	2216	3.4	104		2337	3.6	110
3 Tu	0417	0.1	3	18 W	0540	0.3	9
	1031	4.2	128		1143	3.7	113
	1703	-0.2	-6		1814	0.1	3
	2306	3.5	107				
4 W	0513	0.2	6	19 Th	0030	3.5	107
	1122	4.0	122		0637	0.5	15
	1753	-0.2	-6		1235	3.3	101
				◗	1903	0.3	9
5 Th	0003	3.6	110	20 F	0125	3.4	104
	0616	0.3	9		0736	0.6	18
	1220	3.8	116		1331	3.1	94
◑	1847	-0.2	-6		1953	0.4	12
6 F	0107	3.8	116	21 Sa	0220	3.5	107
	0725	0.2	6		0836	0.6	18
	1325	3.7	113		1430	3.0	91
	1946	-0.3	-9		2043	0.4	12
7 Sa	0212	4.0	122	22 Su	0313	3.6	110
	0835	0.1	3		0933	0.6	18
	1433	3.6	110		1527	2.9	88
	2046	-0.4	-12		2132	0.3	9
8 Su	0317	4.4	134	23 M	0403	3.8	116
	0942	-0.1	-3		1025	0.4	12
	1540	3.7	113		1620	3.0	91
	2146	-0.6	-18		2219	0.2	6
9 M	0417	4.7	143	24 Tu	0450	4.0	122
	1044	-0.4	-12		1112	0.2	6
	1643	3.8	116		1708	3.1	94
	2243	-0.7	-21		2303	0.1	3
10 Tu	0514	5.0	152	25 W	0533	4.2	128
	1141	-0.7	-21		1155	0.1	3
	1741	3.9	119		1752	3.2	98
	2339	-0.9	-27		2345	0.0	0
11 W	0607	5.2	158	26 Th	0614	4.4	134
	1235	-0.9	-27		1236	-0.1	-3
	1835	4.0	122		1833	3.4	104
12 Th	0032	-0.9	-27	27 F	0026	-0.2	-6
	0658	5.3	162		0653	4.6	140
	1327	-0.9	-27		1314	-0.3	-9
○	1927	4.0	122	●	1912	3.5	107
13 F	0124	-0.9	-27	28 Sa	0106	-0.3	-9
	0747	5.2	158		0731	4.6	140
	1416	-0.9	-27		1352	-0.4	-12
	2018	4.0	122		1951	3.6	110
14 Sa	0215	-0.8	-24	29 Su	0147	-0.3	-9
	0835	5.0	152		0809	4.7	143
	1505	-0.8	-24		1430	-0.5	-15
	2107	4.0	122		2030	3.7	113
15 Su	0305	-0.6	-18	30 M	0229	-0.4	-12
	0921	4.8	146		0847	4.6	140
	1552	-0.6	-18		1509	-0.5	-15
	2156	3.8	116		2111	3.8	116
				31 Tu	0314	-0.3	-9
					0928	4.5	137
					1551	-0.5	-15
					2154	3.9	119

February

Day	Time	ft	cm	Day	Time	ft	cm
1 W	0404	-0.2	-6	16 Th	0502	0.2	6
	1012	4.3	131		1101	3.6	110
	1635	-0.5	-15		1723	0.2	6
	2243	3.9	119		2337	3.6	110
2 Th	0459	-0.1	-3	17 F	0553	0.5	15
	1102	4.0	122		1147	3.3	101
	1725	-0.4	-12		1807	0.4	12
	2339	4.0	122				
3 F	0601	0.1	3	18 Sa	0028	3.5	107
	1200	3.7	113		0648	0.7	21
	1820	-0.3	-9		1240	3.0	91
◗				◗	1856	0.6	18
4 Sa	0042	4.0	122	19 Su	0124	3.5	107
	0710	0.1	3		0749	0.8	24
	1306	3.5	107		1341	2.9	88
	1922	-0.2	-6		1950	0.6	18
5 Su	0151	4.1	125	20 M	0224	3.6	110
	0821	0.1	3		0850	0.7	21
	1419	3.4	104		1445	2.8	85
	2026	-0.3	-9		2046	0.6	18
6 M	0300	4.3	131	21 Tu	0321	3.7	113
	0929	-0.1	-3		0946	0.6	18
	1529	3.5	107		1544	2.9	88
	2130	-0.4	-12		2140	0.5	15
7 Tu	0404	4.5	137	22 W	0413	3.9	119
	1032	-0.3	-9		1036	0.4	12
	1634	3.6	110		1636	3.1	94
	2231	-0.5	-15		2230	0.3	9
8 W	0502	4.8	146	23 Th	0500	4.2	128
	1129	-0.5	-15		1121	0.2	6
	1732	3.8	116		1722	3.3	101
	2328	-0.6	-18		2317	0.0	0
9 Th	0556	4.9	149	24 F	0544	4.4	134
	1221	-0.7	-21		1203	-0.1	-3
	1824	4.0	122		1805	3.6	110
10 F	0021	-0.7	-21	25 Sa	0002	-0.2	-6
	0645	5.0	152		0625	4.6	140
	1310	-0.8	-24		1242	-0.3	-9
○	1913	4.1	125		1846	3.8	116
11 Sa	0111	-0.8	-24	26 Su	0045	-0.4	-12
	0731	5.0	152		0705	4.7	143
	1355	-0.8	-24		1321	-0.5	-15
	1958	4.1	125	●	1926	4.1	125
12 Su	0158	-0.7	-21	27 M	0129	-0.5	-15
	0814	4.8	146		0746	4.8	146
	1439	-0.7	-21		1401	-0.6	-18
	2042	4.1	125		2006	4.3	131
13 M	0244	-0.5	-15	28 Tu	0214	-0.6	-18
	0856	4.6	140		0827	4.7	143
	1520	-0.5	-15		1442	-0.7	-21
	2125	4.0	122		2049	4.4	134
14 Tu	0330	-0.3	-9				
	0937	4.3	131				
	1601	-0.3	-9				
	2208	3.9	119				
15 W	0415	0.0	0				
	1018	3.9	119				
	1641	0.0	0				
	2251	3.8	116				

March

Day	Time	ft	cm	Day	Time	ft	cm
1 W	0302	-0.5	-15	16 Th	0345	0.0	0
	0910	4.6	140		0945	3.9	119
	1525	-0.6	-18		1558	0.2	6
	2134	4.5	137		2209	4.1	125
2 Th	0352	-0.4	-12	17 F	0428	0.3	9
	0957	4.3	131		1024	3.6	110
	1611	-0.5	-15		1634	0.4	12
	2224	4.5	137		2250	3.9	119
3 F	0448	-0.2	-6	18 Sa	0513	0.5	15
	1049	4.0	122		1106	3.3	101
	1702	-0.4	-12		1714	0.6	18
	2319	4.4	134		2336	3.8	116
4 Sa	0550	-0.1	-3	19 Su	0604	0.7	21
	1148	3.7	113		1155	3.1	94
	1800	-0.2	-6		1800	0.8	24
5 Su	0023	4.3	131	20 M	0029	3.7	113
	0658	0.1	3		0701	0.8	24
	1257	3.5	107		1254	2.9	88
◗	1904	0.0	0	◗	1855	0.9	27
6 M	0134	4.3	131	21 Tu	0130	3.7	113
	0808	0.1	3		0802	0.8	24
	1411	3.4	104		1400	2.9	88
	2012	0.0	0		1958	0.9	27
7 Tu	0245	4.3	131	22 W	0232	3.7	113
	0917	0.0	0		0900	0.7	21
	1522	3.5	107		1504	3.0	91
	2120	0.0	0		2059	0.7	21
8 W	0352	4.4	134	23 Th	0330	3.9	119
	1019	-0.1	-3		0953	0.5	15
	1626	3.7	113		1559	3.3	101
	2222	-0.2	-6		2156	0.5	15
9 Th	0450	4.6	140	24 F	0422	4.2	128
	1114	-0.3	-9		1040	0.3	9
	1721	3.9	119		1648	3.6	110
	2318	-0.3	-9		2247	0.2	6
10 F	0542	4.7	143	25 Sa	0509	4.4	134
	1203	-0.4	-12		1124	0.0	0
	1810	4.1	125		1733	4.0	122
					2336	-0.1	-3
11 Sa	0009	-0.4	-12	26 Su	0554	4.6	140
	0628	4.7	143		1206	-0.3	-9
	1248	-0.5	-15		1816	4.3	131
	1854	4.3	131				
12 Su	0056	-0.5	-15	27 M	0023	-0.4	-12
	0711	4.7	143		0638	4.8	146
	1329	-0.5	-15		1248	-0.5	-15
○	1936	4.4	134	●	1859	4.6	140
13 M	0140	-0.5	-15	28 Tu	0111	-0.6	-18
	0751	4.6	140		0721	4.8	146
	1408	-0.4	-12		1331	-0.7	-21
	2015	4.4	134		1942	4.9	149
14 Tu	0223	-0.4	-12	29 W	0159	-0.7	-21
	0829	4.4	134		0806	4.8	146
	1446	-0.3	-9		1415	-0.7	-21
	2053	4.3	131		2027	5.0	152
15 W	0304	-0.2	-6	30 Th	0249	-0.7	-21
	0907	4.2	128		0853	4.6	140
	1522	-0.1	-3		1501	-0.7	-21
	2130	4.2	128		2115	5.1	155
				31 F	0341	-0.6	-18
					0944	4.4	134
					1550	-0.5	-15
					2207	5.0	152

Time meridian 75° W. 0000 is midnight. 1200 is noon. Times are not adjusted for Daylight Saving Time.
Heights are referred to mean lower low water which is the chart datum of soundings.

Atlantic City, New Jersey, 2017
Times and Heights of High and Low Waters

April

Day	Time	Height (ft)	Height (cm)
1 Sa	0438	-0.4	-12
	1039	4.1	125
	1644	-0.2	-6
	2303	4.8	146
2 Su	0539	-0.1	-3
	1141	3.8	116
	1744	0.0	0
3 M ☽	0008	4.6	140
	0646	0.1	3
	1251	3.6	110
	1851	0.2	6
4 Tu	0118	4.4	134
	0754	0.1	3
	1404	3.6	110
	2001	0.3	9
5 W	0229	4.3	131
	0900	0.1	3
	1512	3.7	113
	2108	0.3	9
6 Th	0335	4.3	131
	0959	0.0	0
	1613	3.9	119
	2210	0.1	3
7 F	0432	4.4	134
	1052	-0.1	-3
	1705	4.1	125
	2304	0.0	0
8 Sa	0522	4.4	134
	1138	-0.2	-6
	1750	4.3	131
	2354	-0.1	-3
9 Su	0606	4.4	134
	1220	-0.2	-6
	1832	4.5	137
10 M	0039	-0.2	-6
	0647	4.4	134
	1259	-0.2	-6
	1910	4.6	140
11 Tu ○	0121	-0.2	-6
	0726	4.3	131
	1336	-0.1	-3
	1946	4.6	140
12 W	0201	-0.2	-6
	0803	4.2	128
	1411	0.0	0
	2022	4.6	140
13 Th	0240	0.0	0
	0839	4.0	122
	1444	0.2	6
	2057	4.5	137
14 F	0319	0.1	3
	0916	3.8	116
	1518	0.4	12
	2134	4.4	134
15 Sa	0359	0.3	9
	0954	3.5	107
	1553	0.6	18
	2212	4.2	128
16 Su	0441	0.5	15
	1035	3.3	101
	1631	0.7	21
	2254	4.1	125
17 M	0527	0.7	21
	1121	3.2	98
	1715	0.9	27
	2342	3.9	119
18 Tu	0619	0.8	24
	1215	3.1	94
	1809	1.0	30
19 W ◐	0038	3.8	116
	0715	0.8	24
	1317	3.1	94
	1912	1.0	30
20 Th	0140	3.9	119
	0812	0.7	21
	1421	3.2	98
	2018	0.9	27
21 F	0241	4.0	122
	0905	0.5	15
	1519	3.5	107
	2120	0.6	18
22 Sa	0338	4.1	125
	0956	0.2	6
	1611	3.9	119
	2217	0.3	9
23 Su	0430	4.4	134
	1043	-0.1	-3
	1659	4.4	134
	2310	-0.1	-3
24 M	0520	4.5	137
	1129	-0.4	-12
	1746	4.8	146
25 Tu	0001	-0.4	-12
	0609	4.7	143
	1215	-0.6	-18
	1833	5.1	155
26 W ●	0052	-0.6	-18
	0658	4.7	143
	1302	-0.7	-21
	1920	5.4	165
27 Th	0144	-0.8	-24
	0747	4.7	143
	1350	-0.7	-21
	2008	5.5	168
28 F	0236	-0.8	-24
	0838	4.6	140
	1439	-0.6	-18
	2058	5.5	168
29 Sa	0330	-0.6	-18
	0932	4.3	131
	1532	-0.4	-12
	2152	5.3	162
30 Su	0427	-0.5	-15
	1030	4.1	125
	1628	-0.2	-6
	2249	5.0	152

May

Day	Time	Height (ft)	Height (cm)
1 M	0527	-0.2	-6
	1133	3.9	119
	1730	0.1	3
	2352	4.7	143
2 Tu ◐	0631	0.0	0
	1241	3.8	116
	1837	0.3	9
3 W	0059	4.5	137
	0734	0.1	3
	1350	3.8	116
	1945	0.5	15
4 Th	0207	4.3	131
	0836	0.1	3
	1454	3.9	119
	2051	0.5	15
5 F	0310	4.2	128
	0932	0.1	3
	1552	4.1	125
	2152	0.4	12
6 Sa	0406	4.1	125
	1023	0.1	3
	1641	4.3	131
	2246	0.3	9
7 Su	0455	4.1	125
	1108	0.1	3
	1725	4.4	134
	2334	0.2	6
8 M	0540	4.1	125
	1148	0.1	3
	1805	4.6	140
9 Tu	0018	0.1	3
	0620	4.1	125
	1226	0.1	3
	1842	4.7	143
10 W ○	0059	0.0	0
	0659	4.0	122
	1302	0.1	3
	1918	4.7	143
11 Th	0139	0.0	0
	0737	3.9	119
	1337	0.2	6
	1954	4.7	143
12 F	0218	0.1	3
	0814	3.8	116
	1411	0.3	9
	2029	4.7	143
13 Sa	0256	0.2	6
	0851	3.6	110
	1445	0.5	15
	2105	4.6	140
14 Su	0335	0.3	9
	0930	3.5	107
	1520	0.6	18
	2142	4.4	134
15 M	0415	0.4	12
	1009	3.4	104
	1558	0.8	24
	2222	4.3	131
16 Tu	0457	0.5	15
	1053	3.3	101
	1643	0.9	27
	2306	4.2	128
17 W	0543	0.6	18
	1142	3.2	98
	1735	0.9	27
	2356	4.1	125
18 Th ◐	0633	0.6	18
	1239	3.3	101
	1836	1.0	30
19 F	0053	4.0	122
	0726	0.5	15
	1339	3.5	107
	1941	0.8	24
20 Sa	0153	4.0	122
	0820	0.3	9
	1438	3.8	116
	2046	0.6	18
21 Su	0254	4.1	125
	0913	0.1	3
	1534	4.2	128
	2148	0.3	9
22 M	0353	4.2	128
	1004	-0.1	-3
	1627	4.7	143
	2246	0.0	0
23 Tu	0449	4.4	134
	1055	-0.4	-12
	1718	5.1	155
	2341	-0.4	-12
24 W	0543	4.5	137
	1146	-0.6	-18
	1809	5.4	165
25 Th ●	0035	-0.6	-18
	0636	4.5	137
	1237	-0.7	-21
	1900	5.7	174
26 F	0129	-0.8	-24
	0730	4.5	137
	1328	-0.7	-21
	1951	5.7	174
27 Sa	0223	-0.8	-24
	0824	4.4	134
	1421	-0.6	-18
	2043	5.7	174
28 Su	0317	-0.7	-21
	0920	4.3	131
	1516	-0.4	-12
	2137	5.4	165
29 M	0413	-0.5	-15
	1018	4.2	128
	1613	-0.1	-3
	2234	5.1	155
30 Tu	0510	-0.3	-9
	1119	4.0	122
	1714	0.1	3
	2333	4.8	146
31 W	0609	-0.1	-3
	1222	3.9	119
	1818	0.4	12

June

Day	Time	Height (ft)	Height (cm)
1 Th ◐	0034	4.4	134
	0708	0.0	0
	1326	3.9	119
	1923	0.6	18
2 F	0136	4.2	128
	0805	0.2	6
	1427	4.0	122
	2027	0.6	18
3 Sa	0237	4.0	122
	0858	0.2	6
	1522	4.1	125
	2127	0.6	18
4 Su	0332	3.8	116
	0947	0.3	9
	1611	4.3	131
	2221	0.5	15
5 M	0423	3.8	116
	1032	0.3	9
	1655	4.4	134
	2310	0.4	12
6 Tu	0509	3.7	113
	1114	0.3	9
	1736	4.6	140
	2355	0.3	9
7 W	0552	3.7	113
	1152	0.3	9
	1814	4.7	143
8 Th	0036	0.2	6
	0632	3.7	113
	1230	0.3	9
	1852	4.8	146
9 F ○	0116	0.2	6
	0712	3.7	113
	1306	0.3	9
	1928	4.8	146
10 Sa	0155	0.2	6
	0751	3.6	110
	1342	0.4	12
	2005	4.8	146
11 Su	0234	0.2	6
	0829	3.6	110
	1418	0.5	15
	2041	4.7	143
12 M	0311	0.2	6
	0907	3.5	107
	1455	0.6	18
	2118	4.6	140
13 Tu	0350	0.3	9
	0946	3.4	104
	1534	0.7	21
	2156	4.5	137
14 W	0429	0.4	12
	1027	3.4	104
	1618	0.7	21
	2237	4.3	131
15 Th	0511	0.4	12
	1113	3.5	107
	1709	0.8	24
	2323	4.2	128
16 F	0557	0.4	12
	1205	3.6	110
	1807	0.8	24
17 Sa ◐	0015	4.1	125
	0647	0.3	9
	1302	3.8	116
	1912	0.8	24
18 Su	0114	4.0	122
	0740	0.2	6
	1402	4.1	125
	2018	0.6	18
19 M	0218	4.0	122
	0836	0.0	0
	1502	4.5	137
	2123	0.3	9
20 Tu	0321	4.1	125
	0932	-0.2	-6
	1600	4.9	149
	2225	0.0	0
21 W	0423	4.1	125
	1027	-0.4	-12
	1655	5.2	158
	2324	-0.3	-9
22 Th	0522	4.3	131
	1122	-0.5	-15
	1750	5.5	168
23 F ●	0020	-0.5	-15
	0619	4.3	131
	1217	-0.6	-18
	1843	5.7	174
24 Sa	0115	-0.7	-21
	0715	4.4	134
	1311	-0.6	-18
	1936	5.8	177
25 Su	0208	-0.7	-21
	0809	4.4	134
	1405	-0.6	-18
	2028	5.7	174
26 M	0301	-0.7	-21
	0904	4.4	134
	1500	-0.4	-12
	2121	5.4	165
27 Tu	0354	-0.5	-15
	1000	4.3	131
	1556	-0.1	-3
	2214	5.1	155
28 W	0447	-0.3	-9
	1056	4.2	128
	1654	0.2	6
	2307	4.7	143
29 Th	0540	-0.1	-3
	1154	4.1	125
	1753	0.4	12
30 F ◐	0003	4.4	134
	0634	0.1	3
	1252	4.0	122
	1854	0.6	18

Time meridian 75° W. 0000 is midnight. 1200 is noon. Times are not adjusted for Daylight Saving Time.
Heights are referred to mean lower low water which is the chart datum of soundings.

Atlantic City, New Jersey, 2017

Times and Heights of High and Low Waters

July

Day	Time	ft	cm	Day	Time	ft	cm
1 Sa	0100	4.0	122	16 Su ◑	0614	0.2	6
	0727	0.3	9		1231	4.2	128
	1350	4.0	122		1850	0.7	21
	1956	0.8	24				
2 Su	0157	3.8	116	17 M	0046	4.0	122
	0818	0.4	12		0708	0.1	3
	1444	4.1	125		1332	4.4	134
	2055	0.8	24		1957	0.6	18
3 M	0254	3.6	110	18 Tu	0152	3.9	119
	0908	0.5	15		0807	0.1	3
	1535	4.2	128		1436	4.7	143
	2151	0.7	21		2105	0.4	12
4 Tu	0347	3.5	107	19 W	0300	3.9	119
	0954	0.5	15		0907	-0.1	-3
	1621	4.3	131		1539	5.0	152
	2242	0.6	18		2209	0.1	3
5 W	0436	3.5	107	20 Th	0406	4.0	122
	1038	0.5	15		1007	-0.2	-6
	1705	4.5	137		1639	5.3	162
	2328	0.5	15		2309	-0.1	-3
6 Th	0522	3.5	107	21 F	0508	4.2	128
	1120	0.5	15		1106	-0.4	-12
	1746	4.6	140		1735	5.5	168
7 F	0011	0.4	12	22 Sa	0006	-0.4	-12
	0606	3.6	110		0606	4.3	131
	1200	0.4	12		1202	-0.5	-15
	1826	4.8	146		1829	5.7	174
8 Sa O	0052	0.3	9	23 Su ●	0059	-0.5	-15
	0647	3.6	110		0700	4.4	134
	1239	0.4	12		1257	-0.5	-15
	1904	4.8	146		1921	5.7	174
9 Su	0130	0.2	6	24 M	0150	-0.6	-18
	0727	3.7	113		0753	4.5	137
	1317	0.4	12		1351	-0.5	-15
	1942	4.9	149		2011	5.6	171
10 M	0208	0.2	6	25 Tu	0240	-0.6	-18
	0805	3.7	113		0845	4.5	137
	1355	0.4	12		1443	-0.3	-9
	2018	4.8	146		2100	5.4	165
11 Tu	0245	0.2	6	26 W	0329	-0.4	-12
	0843	3.7	113		0936	4.5	137
	1433	0.4	12		1536	-0.1	-3
	2055	4.8	146		2149	5.0	152
12 W	0322	0.2	6	27 Th	0417	-0.2	-6
	0921	3.7	113		1027	4.4	134
	1514	0.5	15		1629	0.2	6
	2132	4.6	140		2237	4.6	140
13 Th	0359	0.2	6	28 F	0505	0.0	0
	1001	3.8	116		1118	4.3	131
	1559	0.6	18		1723	0.5	15
	2211	4.5	137		2327	4.3	131
14 F	0440	0.2	6	29 Sa	0554	0.3	9
	1045	3.9	119		1211	4.2	128
	1649	0.6	18		1820	0.8	24
	2256	4.4	134				
15 Sa	0524	0.2	6	30 Su ◑	0019	3.9	119
	1135	4.0	122		0643	0.5	15
	1746	0.7	21		1305	4.1	125
	2347	4.2	128		1919	0.9	27
				31 M	0114	3.6	110
					0733	0.7	21
					1400	4.1	125
					2019	1.0	30

August

Day	Time	ft	cm	Day	Time	ft	cm
1 Tu	0212	3.4	104	16 W	0138	3.9	119
	0824	0.8	24		0747	0.3	9
	1454	4.1	125		1418	4.8	146
	2116	1.0	30		2052	0.5	15
2 W	0310	3.4	104	17 Th	0249	3.9	119
	0914	0.8	24		0852	0.2	6
	1545	4.3	131		1525	5.0	152
	2209	0.9	27		2157	0.3	9
3 Th	0404	3.4	104	18 F	0357	4.0	122
	1003	0.8	24		0955	0.0	0
	1632	4.4	134		1626	5.2	158
	2258	0.7	21		2256	0.0	0
4 F	0453	3.5	107	19 Sa	0458	4.2	128
	1048	0.7	21		1055	-0.1	-3
	1716	4.6	140		1723	5.4	165
	2341	0.6	18		2350	-0.2	-6
5 Sa	0538	3.6	110	20 Su	0554	4.4	134
	1131	0.5	15		1151	-0.3	-9
	1758	4.8	146		1815	5.5	168
6 Su	0022	0.4	12	21 M ●	0041	-0.3	-9
	0620	3.7	113		0645	4.6	140
	1213	0.4	12		1244	-0.3	-9
	1838	4.9	149		1904	5.5	168
7 M O	0100	0.3	9	22 Tu	0129	-0.4	-12
	0700	3.9	119		0734	4.7	143
	1253	0.3	9		1335	-0.3	-9
	1916	5.0	152		1951	5.4	165
8 Tu	0137	0.2	6	23 W	0215	-0.3	-9
	0738	4.0	122		0821	4.8	146
	1333	0.3	9		1424	-0.2	-6
	1953	5.0	152		2036	5.2	158
9 W	0213	0.1	3	24 Th	0259	-0.2	-6
	0816	4.1	125		0906	4.7	143
	1413	0.3	9		1512	0.0	0
	2030	4.9	149		2120	4.9	149
10 Th	0250	0.1	3	25 F	0342	0.0	0
	0854	4.2	128		0952	4.6	140
	1456	0.3	9		1601	0.3	9
	2108	4.8	146		2204	4.5	137
11 F	0328	0.1	3	26 Sa	0425	0.3	9
	0934	4.3	131		1037	4.5	137
	1541	0.4	12		1650	0.6	18
	2149	4.6	140		2249	4.1	125
12 Sa	0409	0.1	3	27 Su	0509	0.6	18
	1018	4.4	134		1125	4.3	131
	1632	0.5	15		1743	0.8	24
	2234	4.4	134		2337	3.8	116
13 Su	0455	0.1	3	28 M	0555	0.8	24
	1108	4.4	134		1216	4.2	128
	1730	0.6	18		1839	1.0	30
	2327	4.2	128				
14 M ◑	0546	0.2	6	29 Tu ◑	0031	3.5	107
	1206	4.5	137		0644	1.0	30
	1834	0.6	18		1311	4.1	125
					1938	1.2	37
15 Tu	0028	4.0	122	30 W	0131	3.4	104
	0644	0.3	9		0738	1.1	34
	1310	4.6	140		1408	4.1	125
	1943	0.6	18		2037	1.1	34
				31 Th	0233	3.3	101
					0833	1.1	34
					1505	4.2	128
					2133	1.1	34

September

Day	Time	ft	cm	Day	Time	ft	cm
1 F	0331	3.4	104	16 Sa	0351	4.1	125
	0927	1.0	30		0947	0.3	9
	1556	4.4	134		1615	5.1	155
	2222	0.9	27		2241	0.1	3
2 Sa	0422	3.6	110	17 Su	0449	4.4	134
	1016	0.8	24		1046	0.1	3
	1643	4.6	140		1710	5.2	158
	2306	0.7	21		2332	-0.1	-3
3 Su	0508	3.8	116	18 M	0541	4.6	140
	1102	0.7	21		1140	-0.1	-3
	1727	4.8	146		1759	5.2	158
	2346	0.5	15				
4 M	0550	4.0	122	19 Tu	0019	-0.2	-6
	1146	0.5	15		0628	4.8	146
	1807	4.9	149		1231	-0.1	-3
					1845	5.2	158
5 Tu	0024	0.3	9	20 W ●	0103	-0.2	-6
	0630	4.2	128		0712	4.9	149
	1228	0.3	9		1318	-0.1	-3
	1847	5.0	152		1928	5.1	155
6 W O	0102	0.1	3	21 Th	0145	-0.1	-3
	0708	4.4	134		0754	5.0	152
	1310	0.2	6		1404	0.0	0
	1925	5.1	155		2010	4.9	149
7 Th	0139	0.0	0	22 F	0225	0.0	0
	0746	4.6	140		0835	4.9	149
	1353	0.1	3		1448	0.1	3
	2004	5.0	152		2050	4.6	140
8 F	0217	-0.1	-3	23 Sa	0304	0.2	6
	0826	4.8	146		0915	4.8	146
	1438	0.1	3		1532	0.4	12
	2045	4.9	149		2131	4.3	131
9 Sa	0258	-0.1	-3	24 Su	0343	0.5	15
	0908	4.9	149		0956	4.6	140
	1526	0.2	6		1617	0.6	18
	2129	4.7	143		2213	4.0	122
10 Su	0342	0.0	0	25 M	0422	0.8	24
	0955	4.9	149		1039	4.4	134
	1619	0.3	9		1705	0.8	24
	2218	4.4	134		2258	3.7	113
11 M	0430	0.1	3	26 Tu	0505	1.0	30
	1047	4.9	149		1126	4.3	131
	1718	0.4	12		1758	1.0	30
	2314	4.2	128		2350	3.4	104
12 Tu	0525	0.3	9	27 W ◑	0553	1.2	37
	1147	4.8	146		1220	4.1	125
	1823	0.5	15		1855	1.2	37
13 W ◑	0020	3.9	119	28 Th	0050	3.3	101
	0627	0.4	12		0649	1.3	40
	1254	4.8	146		1320	4.1	125
	1932	0.6	18		1954	1.2	37
14 Th	0133	3.9	119	29 F	0154	3.3	101
	0734	0.5	15		0749	1.3	40
	1406	4.8	146		1419	4.1	125
	2041	0.5	15		2050	1.1	34
15 F	0245	3.9	119	30 Sa	0255	3.4	104
	0843	0.4	12		0848	1.2	37
	1514	4.9	149		1515	4.3	131
	2144	0.3	9		2140	0.9	27

Time meridian 75° W. 0000 is midnight. 1200 is noon. Times are not adjusted for Daylight Saving Time. Heights are referred to mean lower low water which is the chart datum of soundings.

Atlantic City, New Jersey, 2017

Times and Heights of High and Low Waters

October

Day	Time (h m)	Height (ft)	Height (cm)
1 Su	0348	3.6	110
	0942	0.9	27
	1605	4.4	134
	2224	0.7	21
2 M	0434	3.9	119
	1031	0.7	21
	1650	4.6	140
	2306	0.4	12
3 Tu	0516	4.2	128
	1118	0.4	12
	1733	4.8	146
	2345	0.1	3
4 W	0557	4.6	140
	1203	0.2	6
	1815	4.9	149
5 Th ○	0025	-0.1	-3
	0637	4.9	149
	1248	0.0	0
	1857	5.0	152
6 F	0105	-0.2	-6
	0718	5.1	155
	1334	-0.2	-6
	1939	4.9	149
7 Sa	0146	-0.3	-9
	0801	5.3	162
	1422	-0.2	-6
	2024	4.8	146
8 Su	0231	-0.3	-9
	0846	5.3	162
	1513	-0.1	-3
	2113	4.6	140
9 M	0318	-0.1	-3
	0936	5.3	162
	1608	0.0	0
	2206	4.3	131
10 Tu	0410	0.1	3
	1030	5.1	155
	1708	0.2	6
	2306	4.1	125
11 W	0509	0.3	9
	1132	5.0	152
	1813	0.3	9
12 Th ◐	0015	3.9	119
	0614	0.5	15
	1241	4.8	146
	1921	0.4	12
13 F	0129	3.9	119
	0725	0.5	15
	1353	4.7	143
	2027	0.3	9
14 Sa	0239	4.0	122
	0834	0.5	15
	1500	4.7	143
	2127	0.2	6
15 Su	0342	4.2	128
	0938	0.4	12
	1600	4.8	146
	2221	0.1	3
16 M	0436	4.5	137
	1036	0.2	6
	1653	4.8	146
	2310	0.0	0
17 Tu	0525	4.7	143
	1128	0.1	3
	1740	4.8	146
	2354	-0.1	-3
18 W	0608	4.9	149
	1215	0.0	0
	1823	4.7	143
19 Th ●	0035	-0.1	-3
	0649	5.0	152
	1300	0.0	0
	1904	4.6	140
20 F	0114	0.0	0
	0727	5.0	152
	1343	0.0	0
	1943	4.4	134
21 Sa	0151	0.1	3
	0805	4.9	149
	1424	0.1	3
	2022	4.2	128
22 Su	0228	0.3	9
	0842	4.8	146
	1505	0.3	9
	2100	4.0	122
23 M	0303	0.5	15
	0920	4.7	143
	1548	0.5	15
	2141	3.7	113
24 Tu	0340	0.7	21
	1000	4.5	137
	1632	0.7	21
	2224	3.5	107
25 W	0420	0.9	27
	1043	4.3	131
	1720	0.9	27
	2313	3.3	101
26 Th	0506	1.1	34
	1133	4.1	125
	1812	1.0	30
27 F ◑	0009	3.2	98
	0600	1.2	37
	1229	4.0	122
	1907	1.0	30
28 Sa	0112	3.2	98
	0702	1.2	37
	1329	4.0	122
	2001	0.9	27
29 Su	0212	3.3	101
	0806	1.1	34
	1427	4.1	125
	2052	0.7	21
30 M	0307	3.6	110
	0904	0.9	27
	1520	4.2	128
	2138	0.5	15
31 Tu	0356	4.0	122
	0958	0.6	18
	1610	4.3	131
	2223	0.2	6

November

Day	Time (h m)	Height (ft)	Height (cm)
1 W	0441	4.4	134
	1049	0.3	9
	1657	4.5	137
	2306	-0.1	-3
2 Th	0525	4.8	146
	1138	0.0	0
	1744	4.6	140
	2350	-0.3	-9
3 F	0608	5.1	155
	1227	-0.3	-9
	1830	4.7	143
4 Sa ○	0034	-0.5	-15
	0653	5.4	165
	1316	-0.5	-15
	1917	4.7	143
5 Su	0120	-0.6	-18
	0739	5.5	168
	1407	-0.5	-15
	2007	4.5	137
6 M	0208	-0.5	-15
	0828	5.6	171
	1500	-0.5	-15
	2059	4.4	134
7 Tu	0259	-0.4	-12
	0920	5.4	165
	1556	-0.3	-9
	2155	4.2	128
8 W	0354	-0.2	-6
	1016	5.2	158
	1655	-0.2	-6
	2258	4.0	122
9 Th	0455	0.1	3
	1118	4.9	149
	1758	0.0	0
10 F ◐	0006	3.8	116
	0602	0.3	9
	1225	4.7	143
	1903	0.1	3
11 Sa	0117	3.8	116
	0712	0.4	12
	1334	4.5	137
	2006	0.1	3
12 Su	0224	4.0	122
	0820	0.4	12
	1439	4.3	131
	2104	0.1	3
13 M	0324	4.1	125
	0924	0.4	12
	1538	4.3	131
	2156	0.0	0
14 Tu	0417	4.4	134
	1021	0.2	6
	1631	4.2	128
	2244	-0.1	-3
15 W	0504	4.5	137
	1112	0.1	3
	1717	4.2	128
	2327	-0.1	-3
16 Th	0546	4.7	143
	1158	0.0	0
	1800	4.1	125
17 F	0007	-0.1	-3
	0625	4.8	146
	1241	0.0	0
	1840	4.0	122
18 Sa ●	0044	0.0	0
	0702	4.8	146
	1322	0.0	0
	1919	3.9	119
19 Su	0120	0.1	3
	0738	4.8	146
	1402	0.0	0
	1957	3.8	116
20 M	0155	0.2	6
	0814	4.7	143
	1442	0.1	3
	2035	3.6	110
21 Tu	0231	0.4	12
	0851	4.6	140
	1521	0.2	6
	2114	3.4	104
22 W	0306	0.5	15
	0929	4.4	134
	1602	0.4	12
	2155	3.3	101
23 Th	0345	0.7	21
	1009	4.2	128
	1645	0.5	15
	2239	3.2	98
24 F	0428	0.8	24
	1053	4.1	125
	1731	0.6	18
	2329	3.1	94
25 Sa	0518	0.9	27
	1142	3.9	119
	1819	0.6	18
26 Su ◑	0025	3.1	94
	0617	1.0	30
	1236	3.8	116
	1910	0.5	15
27 M	0124	3.3	101
	0722	0.9	27
	1334	3.8	116
	2001	0.4	12
28 Tu	0221	3.6	110
	0825	0.7	21
	1433	3.9	119
	2051	0.2	6
29 W	0315	3.9	119
	0925	0.4	12
	1529	4.0	122
	2141	-0.1	-3
30 Th	0405	4.4	134
	1022	0.1	3
	1623	4.1	125
	2230	-0.4	-12

December

Day	Time (h m)	Height (ft)	Height (cm)
1 F	0455	4.8	146
	1116	-0.2	-6
	1716	4.2	128
	2319	-0.6	-18
2 Sa	0543	5.2	158
	1208	-0.5	-15
	1807	4.3	131
3 Su ○	0008	-0.8	-24
	0632	5.5	168
	1301	-0.8	-24
	1859	4.3	131
4 M	0059	-0.9	-27
	0722	5.6	171
	1353	-0.9	-27
	1952	4.3	131
5 Tu	0150	-0.8	-24
	0814	5.6	171
	1447	-0.8	-24
	2046	4.2	128
6 W	0244	-0.7	-21
	0907	5.4	165
	1542	-0.7	-21
	2144	4.1	125
7 Th	0341	-0.5	-15
	1002	5.1	155
	1639	-0.6	-18
	2244	3.9	119
8 F	0441	-0.2	-6
	1101	4.8	146
	1738	-0.4	-12
	2348	3.8	116
9 Sa	0545	0.1	3
	1203	4.4	134
	1837	-0.2	-6
10 Su ◑	0054	3.8	116
	0652	0.3	9
	1307	4.1	125
	1937	-0.1	-3
11 M	0159	3.8	116
	0759	0.3	9
	1410	3.9	119
	2033	-0.1	-3
12 Tu	0258	4.0	122
	0902	0.3	9
	1510	3.7	113
	2126	0.0	0
13 W	0351	4.1	125
	1000	0.3	9
	1604	3.6	110
	2214	0.0	0
14 Th	0439	4.3	131
	1052	0.2	6
	1652	3.6	110
	2258	0.0	0
15 F	0521	4.4	134
	1138	0.1	3
	1736	3.5	107
	2338	0.0	0
16 Sa	0601	4.5	137
	1221	0.0	0
	1817	3.5	107
17 Su	0017	0.0	0
	0638	4.6	140
	1302	-0.1	-3
	1857	3.5	107
18 M ●	0054	0.0	0
	0715	4.6	140
	1341	-0.1	-3
	1935	3.4	104
19 Tu	0130	0.0	0
	0752	4.6	140
	1419	-0.1	-3
	2013	3.4	104
20 W	0205	0.1	3
	0828	4.5	137
	1457	0.0	0
	2051	3.3	101
21 Th	0241	0.2	6
	0904	4.4	134
	1534	0.1	3
	2129	3.2	98
22 F	0319	0.3	9
	0941	4.2	128
	1612	0.1	3
	2209	3.2	98
23 Sa	0400	0.5	15
	1020	4.0	122
	1652	0.2	6
	2252	3.1	94
24 Su	0446	0.6	18
	1102	3.9	119
	1735	0.2	6
	2340	3.2	98
25 M	0540	0.6	18
	1151	3.7	113
	1822	0.2	6
26 Tu ◑	0035	3.4	104
	0643	0.6	18
	1246	3.6	110
	1913	0.1	3
27 W	0134	3.6	110
	0749	0.5	15
	1348	3.6	110
	2008	-0.1	-3
28 Th	0235	3.9	119
	0855	0.3	9
	1452	3.6	110
	2104	-0.3	-9
29 F	0333	4.3	131
	0957	0.0	0
	1554	3.7	113
	2200	-0.5	-15
30 Sa	0429	4.7	143
	1056	-0.4	-12
	1653	3.8	116
	2255	-0.8	-24
31 Su	0523	5.1	155
	1152	-0.7	-21
	1750	4.0	122
	2349	-0.9	-27

Time meridian 75° W. 0000 is midnight. 1200 is noon. Times are not adjusted for Daylight Saving Time.
Heights are referred to mean lower low water which is the chart datum of soundings.

Breakwater Harbor, Delaware, 2017

Times and Heights of High and Low Waters

January

Day	Time	ft	cm		Day	Time	ft	cm
1 Su	0354	-0.2	-6		**16** M	0455	-0.4	-12
	1027	4.6	140			1121	4.6	140
	1641	-0.2	-6			1737	-0.3	-9
	2250	3.6	110			2352	3.8	116
2 M	0438	-0.1	-3		**17** Tu	0546	-0.1	-3
	1109	4.5	137			1206	4.2	128
	1724	-0.2	-6			1824	-0.1	-3
	2336	3.6	110					
3 Tu	0526	0.0	0		**18** W	0041	3.7	113
	1155	4.4	134			0639	0.2	6
	1810	-0.2	-6			1254	3.8	116
						1912	0.1	3
4 W	0026	3.7	113		**19** Th ◑	0133	3.6	110
	0621	0.1	3			0736	0.4	12
	1245	4.2	128			1344	3.5	107
	1900	-0.2	-6			2002	0.2	6
5 Th ◐	0122	3.8	116		**20** F	0228	3.6	110
	0721	0.1	3			0837	0.6	18
	1341	4.0	122			1439	3.3	101
	1954	-0.2	-6			2053	0.4	12
6 F	0222	4.0	122		**21** Sa	0325	3.7	113
	0827	0.1	3			0940	0.6	18
	1442	3.8	116			1537	3.1	94
	2052	-0.3	-9			2146	0.4	12
7 Sa	0325	4.2	128		**22** Su	0421	3.8	116
	0936	0.0	0			1040	0.6	18
	1547	3.7	113			1636	3.1	94
	2151	-0.4	-12			2237	0.3	9
8 Su	0429	4.5	137		**23** M	0514	3.9	119
	1043	-0.1	-3			1134	0.4	12
	1653	3.7	113			1730	3.1	94
	2251	-0.5	-15			2325	0.2	6
9 M	0530	4.8	146		**24** Tu	0602	4.1	125
	1146	-0.4	-12			1222	0.3	9
	1756	3.8	116			1819	3.2	98
	2348	-0.7	-21					
10 Tu	0628	5.1	155		**25** W	0010	0.1	3
	1244	-0.6	-18			0647	4.4	134
	1854	3.9	119			1304	0.1	3
						1903	3.4	104
11 W	0043	-0.8	-24		**26** Th	0052	-0.1	-3
	0722	5.3	162			0728	4.5	137
	1338	-0.7	-21			1343	-0.1	-3
	1948	4.0	122			1945	3.5	107
12 Th O	0136	-0.9	-27		**27** F ●	0133	-0.2	-6
	0813	5.3	162			0808	4.7	143
	1429	-0.8	-24			1420	-0.2	-6
	2040	4.1	125			2025	3.7	113
13 F	0227	-0.9	-27		**28** Sa	0213	-0.3	-9
	0902	5.3	162			0847	4.8	146
	1518	-0.8	-24			1457	-0.3	-9
	2129	4.1	125			2105	3.8	116
14 Sa	0317	-0.8	-24		**29** Su	0254	-0.4	-12
	0949	5.1	155			0927	4.8	146
	1605	-0.7	-21			1536	-0.4	-12
	2217	4.0	122			2146	3.9	119
15 Su	0406	-0.6	-18		**30** M	0337	-0.5	-15
	1035	4.9	149			1007	4.7	143
	1651	-0.5	-15			1615	-0.5	-15
	2304	4.0	122			2228	4.0	122
					31 Tu	0422	-0.4	-12
						1049	4.6	140
						1658	-0.5	-15
						2314	4.1	125

February

Day	Time	ft	cm		Day	Time	ft	cm
1 W	0511	-0.3	-9		**16** Th	0602	0.2	6
	1134	4.4	134			1212	3.8	116
	1743	-0.5	-15			1822	0.2	6
2 Th	0003	4.1	125		**17** F	0043	3.8	116
	0604	-0.2	-6			0652	0.4	12
	1224	4.2	128			1258	3.5	107
	1832	-0.4	-12			1907	0.4	12
3 F ◑	0058	4.2	128		**18** Sa ○	0133	3.8	116
	0704	0.0	0			0748	0.6	18
	1320	3.9	119			1349	3.2	98
	1927	-0.3	-9			1957	0.5	15
4 Sa	0158	4.2	128		**19** Su	0229	3.7	113
	0810	0.1	3			0849	0.7	21
	1422	3.7	113			1447	3.1	94
	2027	-0.2	-6			2053	0.6	18
5 Su	0304	4.3	131		**20** M	0329	3.7	113
	0920	0.1	3			0953	0.7	21
	1531	3.5	107			1549	3.0	91
	2130	-0.2	-6			2150	0.6	18
6 M	0412	4.5	137		**21** Tu	0429	3.9	119
	1030	0.0	0			1052	0.6	18
	1641	3.5	107			1650	3.1	94
	2234	-0.3	-9			2245	0.4	12
7 Tu	0517	4.7	143		**22** W	0524	4.1	125
	1135	-0.2	-6			1143	0.5	15
	1746	3.7	113			1744	3.3	101
	2335	-0.4	-12			2336	0.2	6
8 W	0617	4.9	149		**23** Th	0614	4.3	131
	1233	-0.4	-12			1228	0.2	6
	1845	3.8	116			1832	3.5	107
9 Th	0032	-0.6	-18		**24** F	0023	0.0	0
	0711	5.0	152			0659	4.5	137
	1325	-0.5	-15			1309	0.0	0
	1937	4.0	122			1916	3.8	116
10 F O	0125	-0.7	-21		**25** Sa	0108	-0.2	-6
	0801	5.1	155			0741	4.7	143
	1413	-0.6	-18			1348	-0.2	-6
	2025	4.2	128			1958	4.0	122
11 Sa	0214	-0.7	-21		**26** Su ●	0151	-0.4	-12
	0846	5.1	155			0822	4.9	149
	1457	-0.6	-18			1427	-0.4	-12
	2109	4.2	128			2040	4.3	131
12 Su	0301	-0.7	-21		**27** M	0235	-0.6	-18
	0929	4.9	149			0903	4.9	149
	1539	-0.6	-18			1507	-0.6	-18
	2152	4.2	128			2122	4.5	137
13 M	0346	-0.5	-15		**28** Tu	0320	-0.6	-18
	1010	4.7	143			0946	4.9	149
	1620	-0.4	-12			1548	-0.6	-18
	2233	4.2	128			2206	4.6	140
14 Tu	0430	-0.3	-9					
	1050	4.4	134					
	1700	-0.2	-6					
	2314	4.1	125					
15 W	0515	-0.1	-3					
	1130	4.1	125					
	1740	0.0	0					
	2357	4.0	122					

March

Day	Time	ft	cm		Day	Time	ft	cm
1 W	0407	-0.6	-18		**16** Th	0447	0.0	0
	1029	4.7	143			1057	4.0	122
	1632	-0.6	-18			1659	0.2	6
	2252	4.7	143			2318	4.3	131
2 Th	0457	-0.5	-15		**17** F	0529	0.2	6
	1116	4.5	137			1137	3.8	116
	1718	-0.5	-15			1737	0.4	12
	2342	4.7	143					
3 F ◑	0551	-0.3	-9		**18** Sa	0000	4.1	125
	1208	4.2	128			0615	0.4	12
	1809	-0.3	-9			1220	3.5	107
						1819	0.6	18
4 Sa	0037	4.6	140		**19** Su	0047	4.0	122
	0651	-0.1	-3			0705	0.6	18
	1305	3.9	119			1309	3.3	101
	1905	-0.2	-6			1907	0.7	21
5 Su ◑	0139	4.5	137		**20** M ◑	0140	3.9	119
	0757	0.1	3			0801	0.8	24
	1410	3.7	113			1404	3.2	98
	2007	0.0	0			2002	0.8	24
6 M	0247	4.5	137		**21** Tu	0239	3.9	119
	0908	0.2	6			0902	0.8	24
	1522	3.6	110			1505	3.2	98
	2115	0.1	3			2103	0.8	24
7 Tu	0358	4.5	137		**22** W	0340	3.9	119
	1018	0.1	3			1002	0.7	21
	1634	3.6	110			1607	3.3	101
	2223	0.0	0			2203	0.6	18
8 W	0506	4.6	140		**23** Th	0440	4.1	125
	1122	0.0	0			1057	0.6	18
	1738	3.8	116			1705	3.5	107
	2326	-0.1	-3			2300	0.4	12
9 Th	0606	4.7	143		**24** F	0534	4.3	131
	1218	-0.1	-3			1145	0.3	9
	1834	4.0	122			1757	3.8	116
						2352	0.1	3
10 F	0023	-0.3	-9		**25** Sa	0623	4.5	137
	0658	4.8	146			1230	0.0	0
	1307	-0.3	-9			1844	4.2	128
	1923	4.2	128					
11 Sa	0114	-0.4	-12		**26** Su	0041	-0.2	-6
	0745	4.8	146			0709	4.7	143
	1351	-0.4	-12			1313	-0.2	-6
	2007	4.4	134			1929	4.5	137
12 Su O	0200	-0.5	-15		**27** M ●	0129	-0.4	-12
	0827	4.8	146			0754	4.9	149
	1432	-0.4	-12			1355	-0.5	-15
	2047	4.5	137			2014	4.8	146
13 M	0244	-0.5	-15		**28** Tu	0216	-0.6	-18
	0906	4.7	143			0839	4.9	149
	1510	-0.3	-9			1437	-0.6	-18
	2125	4.5	137			2058	5.1	155
14 Tu	0325	-0.4	-12		**29** W	0304	-0.7	-21
	0943	4.5	137			0924	4.9	149
	1546	-0.2	-6			1521	-0.7	-21
	2202	4.5	137			2145	5.2	158
15 W	0406	-0.2	-6		**30** Th	0353	-0.7	-21
	1020	4.3	131			1011	4.7	143
	1622	0.0	0			1607	-0.6	-18
	2239	4.4	134			2233	5.2	158
					31 F	0445	-0.6	-18
						1101	4.5	137
						1656	-0.4	-12
						2324	5.1	155

Time meridian 75° W. 0000 is midnight. 1200 is noon. Times are not adjusted for Daylight Saving Time.
Heights are referred to mean lower low water which is the chart datum of soundings.

Breakwater Harbor, Delaware, 2017

Times and Heights of High and Low Waters

April

Day	Time	ft	cm	Day	Time	ft	cm
1 Sa	0540	-0.4	-12	**16** Su	0544	0.4	12
	1155	4.2	128		1150	3.5	107
	1749	-0.2	-6		1740	0.6	18
2 Su	0021	5.0	152	**17** M	0010	4.3	131
	0640	-0.1	-3		0630	0.6	18
	1255	3.9	119		1237	3.4	104
	1847	0.0	0		1827	0.8	24
3 M	0123	4.8	146	**18** Tu	0100	4.1	125
	0745	0.1	3		0721	0.7	21
	1402	3.8	116		1329	3.3	101
	1953	0.2	6		1921	0.9	27
4 Tu	0231	4.6	140	**19** W	0155	4.1	125
	0854	0.2	6		0817	0.7	21
	1513	3.7	113		1427	3.4	104
	2103	0.3	9		2020	0.8	24
5 W	0342	4.5	137	**20** Th	0254	4.1	125
	1002	0.2	6		0914	0.7	21
	1623	3.8	116		1527	3.5	107
	2212	0.3	9		2123	0.7	21
6 Th	0449	4.5	137	**21** F	0353	4.2	128
	1104	0.2	6		1009	0.5	15
	1725	4.0	122		1625	3.8	116
	2315	0.2	6		2223	0.5	15
7 F	0548	4.5	137	**22** Sa	0450	4.3	131
	1157	0.1	3		1100	0.2	6
	1818	4.2	128		1720	4.1	125
					2320	0.2	6
8 Sa	0011	0.0	0	**23** Su	0544	4.5	137
	0639	4.6	140		1149	0.0	0
	1243	0.0	0		1811	4.5	137
	1904	4.4	134				
9 Su	0100	-0.1	-3	**24** M	0014	-0.1	-3
	0724	4.5	137		0635	4.6	140
	1324	-0.1	-3		1236	-0.3	-9
	1945	4.6	140		1859	4.9	149
10 M	0144	-0.2	-6	**25** Tu	0106	-0.4	-12
	0804	4.5	137		0725	4.7	143
	1402	-0.1	-3		1322	-0.5	-15
	2022	4.7	143		1947	5.3	162
11 Tu	0226	-0.2	-6	**26** W	0157	-0.6	-18
	0841	4.4	134		0814	4.8	146
	1438	0.0	0		1408	-0.6	-18
	2057	4.7	143		2035	5.5	168
12 W	0305	-0.1	-3	**27** Th	0248	-0.7	-21
	0916	4.2	128		0904	4.7	143
	1512	0.1	3		1456	-0.7	-21
	2132	4.7	143		2125	5.6	171
13 Th	0343	0.0	0	**28** F	0340	-0.7	-21
	0952	4.1	125		0955	4.6	140
	1547	0.2	6		1545	-0.6	-18
	2208	4.6	140		2215	5.6	171
14 F	0422	0.1	3	**29** Sa	0433	-0.6	-18
	1029	3.9	119		1048	4.4	134
	1622	0.3	9		1637	-0.4	-12
	2245	4.5	137		2309	5.4	165
15 Sa	0502	0.3	9	**30** Su	0529	-0.4	-12
	1107	3.7	113		1144	4.2	128
	1659	0.5	15		1732	-0.2	-6
	2326	4.4	134				

May

Day	Time	ft	cm	Day	Time	ft	cm
1 M	0006	5.2	158	**16** Tu	0602	0.5	15
	0628	-0.2	-6		1210	3.5	107
	1245	4.0	122		1756	0.7	21
	1832	0.1	3				
2 Tu	0107	4.9	149	**17** W	0028	4.3	131
	0731	0.0	0		0648	0.5	15
	1350	3.9	119		1300	3.5	107
	1938	0.3	9		1847	0.8	24
3 W	0212	4.6	140	**18** Th	0118	4.2	128
	0835	0.2	6		0739	0.5	15
	1458	3.9	119		1354	3.6	110
	2048	0.4	12		1945	0.8	24
4 Th	0319	4.4	134	**19** F	0213	4.2	128
	0938	0.2	6		0832	0.4	12
	1604	4.0	122		1451	3.8	116
	2156	0.4	12		2047	0.7	21
5 F	0423	4.3	131	**20** Sa	0310	4.2	128
	1036	0.2	6		0925	0.3	9
	1703	4.2	128		1548	4.0	122
	2258	0.4	12		2150	0.5	15
6 Sa	0521	4.3	131	**21** Su	0409	4.2	128
	1127	0.2	6		1019	0.1	3
	1754	4.4	134		1644	4.4	134
	2353	0.3	9		2251	0.2	6
7 Su	0612	4.2	128	**22** M	0507	4.3	131
	1212	0.1	3		1111	-0.2	-6
	1839	4.5	137		1739	4.8	146
					2349	-0.1	-3
8 M	0042	0.2	6	**23** Tu	0603	4.4	134
	0657	4.2	128		1202	-0.4	-12
	1252	0.1	3		1832	5.2	158
	1918	4.7	143				
9 Tu	0125	0.1	3	**24** W	0045	-0.4	-12
	0737	4.1	125		0658	4.5	137
	1330	0.1	3		1252	-0.6	-18
	1955	4.8	146		1923	5.5	168
10 W	0206	0.0	0	**25** Th	0139	-0.6	-18
	0814	4.0	122		0725	4.5	137
	1405	0.2	6		1342	-0.7	-21
	2030	4.8	146		2015	5.7	174
11 Th	0244	0.0	0	**26** F	0232	-0.7	-21
	0850	3.9	119		0845	4.5	137
	1440	0.2	6		1434	-0.7	-21
	2106	4.8	146		2107	5.8	177
12 F	0322	0.1	3	**27** Sa	0326	-0.7	-21
	0927	3.8	116		0939	4.4	134
	1515	0.3	9		1526	-0.6	-18
	2142	4.8	146		2200	5.7	174
13 Sa	0400	0.2	6	**28** Su	0420	-0.7	-21
	1004	3.7	113		1034	4.3	131
	1551	0.4	12		1620	-0.4	-12
	2219	4.7	143		2254	5.5	168
14 Su	0438	0.3	9	**29** M	0515	-0.5	-15
	1043	3.6	110		1130	4.2	128
	1629	0.5	15		1716	-0.2	-6
	2259	4.6	140		2349	5.2	158
15 M	0518	0.4	12	**30** Tu	0611	-0.3	-9
	1125	3.5	107		1230	4.1	125
	1710	0.6	18		1816	0.1	3
	2341	4.5	137				
				31 W	0047	4.9	149
					0710	-0.1	-3
					1331	4.0	122
					1920	0.3	9

June

Day	Time	ft	cm	Day	Time	ft	cm
1 Th	0147	4.6	140	**16** F	0048	4.4	134
	0809	0.1	3		0705	0.2	6
	1434	4.0	122		1324	3.8	116
	2026	0.5	15		1917	0.6	18
2 F	0248	4.3	131	**17** Sa	0139	4.3	131
	0906	0.2	6		0755	0.2	6
	1535	4.1	125		1419	4.0	122
	2131	0.5	15		2018	0.5	15
3 Sa	0349	4.1	125	**18** Su	0235	4.2	128
	1001	0.2	6		0848	0.1	3
	1631	4.2	128		1516	4.3	131
	2233	0.5	15		2122	0.4	12
4 Su	0446	3.9	119	**19** M	0334	4.1	125
	1050	0.3	9		0943	-0.1	-3
	1722	4.4	134		1614	4.6	140
	2329	0.5	15		2225	0.2	6
5 M	0537	3.8	116	**20** Tu	0435	4.1	125
	1136	0.3	9		1038	-0.2	-6
	1808	4.5	137		1712	5.0	152
					2327	-0.1	-3
6 Tu	0018	0.4	12	**21** W	0536	4.1	125
	0624	3.8	116		1133	-0.4	-12
	1217	0.3	9		1808	5.3	162
	1849	4.6	140				
7 W	0103	0.3	9	**22** Th	0026	-0.3	-9
	0707	3.7	113		0635	4.2	128
	1256	0.3	9		1227	-0.5	-15
	1927	4.7	143		1904	5.6	171
8 Th	0144	0.2	6	**23** F	0122	-0.5	-15
	0746	3.7	113		0732	4.3	131
	1334	0.3	9		1321	-0.6	-18
	2005	4.8	146		1958	5.7	174
9 F	0223	0.2	6	**24** Sa	0217	-0.6	-18
	0825	3.7	113		0828	4.3	131
	1410	0.3	9		1415	-0.6	-18
	2042	4.8	146		2051	5.8	177
10 Sa	0301	0.2	6	**25** Su	0311	-0.7	-21
	0903	3.7	113		0923	4.4	134
	1447	0.3	9		1509	-0.6	-18
	2119	4.8	146		2144	5.7	174
11 Su	0338	0.2	6	**26** M	0403	-0.6	-18
	0942	3.6	110		1017	4.3	131
	1524	0.4	12		1603	-0.4	-12
	2157	4.8	146		2237	5.5	168
12 M	0415	0.2	6	**27** Tu	0456	-0.5	-15
	1021	3.6	110		1112	4.3	131
	1603	0.4	12		1659	-0.2	-6
	2236	4.7	143		2329	5.2	158
13 Tu	0454	0.2	6	**28** W	0548	-0.3	-9
	1102	3.6	110		1207	4.2	128
	1645	0.5	15		1756	0.0	0
	2317	4.6	140				
14 W	0535	0.3	9	**29** Th	0022	4.8	146
	1146	3.6	110		0641	-0.1	-3
	1730	0.5	15		1303	4.2	128
					1855	0.3	9
15 Th	0000	4.5	137	**30** F	0116	4.5	137
	0618	0.3	9		0734	0.1	3
	1233	3.7	113		1400	4.1	125
	1821	0.6	18		1956	0.5	15

Time meridian 75° W. 0000 is midnight. 1200 is noon. Times are not adjusted for Daylight Saving Time.
Heights are referred to mean lower low water which is the chart datum of soundings.

Breakwater Harbor, Delaware, 2017

Times and Heights of High and Low Waters

July

Day	Time	ft	cm	Day	Time	ft	cm
1 Sa	0211	4.1	125	**16** Su	0112	4.3	131
	0827	0.2	6		0723	0.0	0
	1456	4.1	125		1351	4.3	131
	2059	0.6	18	◗	1955	0.4	12
2 Su	0307	3.9	119	**17** M	0207	4.1	125
	0919	0.3	9		0817	0.0	0
	1552	4.2	128		1449	4.6	140
	2200	0.7	21		2100	0.4	12
3 M	0404	3.7	113	**18** Tu	0308	4.0	122
	1009	0.4	12		0914	-0.1	-3
	1644	4.3	131		1549	4.8	146
	2258	0.6	18		2205	0.2	6
4 Tu	0458	3.6	110	**19** W	0412	4.0	122
	1057	0.4	12		1012	-0.2	-6
	1732	4.4	134		1651	5.1	155
	2350	0.6	18		2309	0.1	3
5 W	0548	3.5	107	**20** Th	0516	4.0	122
	1141	0.4	12		1111	-0.3	-9
	1817	4.5	137		1751	5.3	162
6 Th	0037	0.5	15	**21** F	0010	-0.2	-6
	0635	3.5	107		0618	4.1	125
	1224	0.4	12		1209	-0.4	-12
	1859	4.7	143		1848	5.5	168
7 F	0119	0.4	12	**22** Sa	0107	-0.3	-9
	0718	3.6	110		0717	4.2	128
	1304	0.4	12		1305	-0.5	-15
	1939	4.8	146		1943	5.6	171
8 Sa	0159	0.3	9	**23** Su	0201	-0.5	-15
	0759	3.6	110		0813	4.3	131
	1343	0.3	9		1400	-0.5	-15
○	2018	4.8	146	●	2036	5.6	171
9 Su	0236	0.2	6	**24** M	0253	-0.5	-15
	0838	3.7	113		0906	4.4	134
	1422	0.3	9		1453	-0.5	-15
	2056	4.8	146		2127	5.5	168
10 M	0313	0.2	6	**25** Tu	0342	-0.5	-15
	0918	3.7	113		0957	4.5	137
	1501	0.3	9		1546	-0.4	-12
	2135	4.8	146		2216	5.3	162
11 Tu	0350	0.1	3	**26** W	0431	-0.4	-12
	0957	3.8	116		1047	4.5	137
	1541	0.3	9		1638	-0.2	-6
	2213	4.8	146		2304	5.0	152
12 W	0427	0.1	3	**27** Th	0518	-0.2	-6
	1038	3.8	116		1137	4.4	134
	1623	0.3	9		1731	0.1	3
	2253	4.7	143		2352	4.7	143
13 Th	0507	0.1	3	**28** F	0606	0.0	0
	1121	3.9	119		1227	4.3	131
	1709	0.3	9		1825	0.3	9
	2335	4.6	140				
14 F	0549	0.1	3	**29** Sa	0040	4.3	131
	1207	4.0	122		0654	0.2	6
	1759	0.4	12		1318	4.3	131
					1922	0.6	18
15 Sa	0021	4.4	134	**30** Su	0130	4.0	122
	0634	0.0	0		0743	0.4	12
	1256	4.2	128		1411	4.2	128
	1854	0.4	12	☾	2021	0.8	24
				31 M	0223	3.7	113
					0833	0.5	15
					1505	4.2	128
					2122	0.8	24

August

Day	Time	ft	cm	Day	Time	ft	cm
1 Tu	0319	3.5	107	**16** W	0252	3.9	119
	0925	0.6	18		0852	0.1	3
	1600	4.2	128		1531	4.9	149
	2221	0.8	24		2151	0.3	9
2 W	0416	3.4	104	**17** Th	0359	3.9	119
	1016	0.7	21		0955	0.0	0
	1653	4.3	131		1636	5.1	155
	2316	0.8	24		2256	0.2	6
3 Th	0511	3.4	104	**18** F	0506	4.0	122
	1105	0.6	18		1057	-0.1	-3
	1742	4.5	137		1738	5.2	158
					2357	0.0	0
4 F	0005	0.7	21	**19** Sa	0608	4.2	128
	0601	3.5	107		1157	-0.2	-6
	1152	0.5	15		1836	5.4	165
	1828	4.6	140				
5 Sa	0049	0.5	15	**20** Su	0052	-0.2	-6
	0647	3.6	110		0705	4.3	131
	1235	0.4	12		1253	-0.3	-9
	1911	4.8	146		1930	5.5	168
6 Su	0129	0.4	12	**21** M	0143	-0.3	-9
	0730	3.7	113		0757	4.5	137
	1317	0.3	9		1347	-0.4	-12
	1952	4.9	149	●	2020	5.4	165
7 M	0206	0.3	9	**22** Tu	0231	-0.3	-9
	0811	3.9	119		0846	4.6	140
	1358	0.2	6		1437	-0.3	-9
○	2031	4.9	149		2106	5.3	162
8 Tu	0243	0.2	6	**23** W	0316	-0.3	-9
	0851	4.0	122		0932	4.7	143
	1438	0.2	6		1527	-0.2	-6
	2110	4.9	149		2151	5.1	155
9 W	0319	0.1	3	**24** Th	0400	-0.2	-6
	0931	4.1	125		1018	4.7	143
	1520	0.1	3		1615	-0.1	-3
	2149	4.9	149		2235	4.8	146
10 Th	0357	0.0	0	**25** F	0443	0.0	0
	1012	4.3	131		1102	4.6	140
	1603	0.1	3		1703	0.2	6
	2229	4.8	146		2318	4.5	137
11 F	0437	0.0	0	**26** Sa	0526	0.2	6
	1055	4.4	134		1147	4.5	137
	1650	0.2	6		1752	0.4	12
	2312	4.7	143				
12 Sa	0519	0.0	0	**27** Su	0002	4.2	128
	1141	4.5	137		0609	0.4	12
	1741	0.2	6		1233	4.4	134
	2359	4.5	137		1844	0.7	21
13 Su	0605	0.0	0	**28** M	0049	3.9	119
	1231	4.6	140		0655	0.6	18
	1837	0.3	9		1323	4.3	131
					1940	0.9	27
14 M	0051	4.3	131	**29** Tu	0140	3.6	110
	0656	0.0	0		0745	0.8	24
	1327	4.7	143		1417	4.2	128
☾	1938	0.4	12	☽	2039	1.0	30
15 Tu	0148	4.1	125	**30** W	0236	3.5	107
	0752	0.1	3		0839	0.9	27
	1427	4.8	146		1513	4.2	128
	2044	0.4	12		2140	1.0	30
				31 Th	0335	3.4	104
					0934	0.9	27
					1610	4.3	131
					2236	0.9	27

September

Day	Time	ft	cm	Day	Time	ft	cm
1 F	0433	3.5	107	**16** Sa	0500	4.1	125
	1028	0.8	24		1049	0.2	6
	1704	4.4	134		1727	5.1	155
	2327	0.8	24		2343	0.1	3
2 Sa	0526	3.6	110	**17** Su	0559	4.3	131
	1119	0.7	21		1149	0.0	0
	1753	4.6	140		1823	5.2	158
3 Su	0011	0.6	18	**18** M	0035	0.0	0
	0614	3.8	116		0652	4.5	137
	1206	0.5	15		1243	-0.1	-3
	1838	4.7	143		1914	5.2	158
4 M	0052	0.4	12	**19** Tu	0122	-0.1	-3
	0658	4.0	122		0740	4.7	143
	1250	0.3	9		1334	-0.2	-6
	1921	4.9	149		2000	5.1	155
5 Tu	0130	0.3	9	**20** W	0206	-0.2	-6
	0740	4.2	128		0824	4.9	149
	1333	0.2	6		1421	-0.2	-6
	2002	5.0	152	●	2043	5.0	152
6 W	0208	0.1	3	**21** Th	0247	-0.1	-3
	0821	4.5	137		0906	4.9	149
	1415	0.0	0		1506	-0.1	-3
○	2042	5.0	152		2124	4.8	146
7 Th	0246	0.0	0	**22** F	0326	0.0	0
	0902	4.7	143		0946	4.9	149
	1459	0.0	0		1551	0.1	3
	2123	5.0	152		2204	4.6	140
8 F	0325	-0.1	-3	**23** Sa	0405	0.2	6
	0945	4.8	146		1026	4.8	146
	1545	-0.1	-3		1635	0.2	6
	2206	4.8	146		2244	4.3	131
9 Sa	0407	-0.1	-3	**24** Su	0445	0.4	12
	1030	4.9	149		1107	4.7	143
	1633	0.0	0		1720	0.5	15
	2251	4.7	143		2326	4.0	122
10 Su	0451	-0.1	-3	**25** M	0525	0.6	18
	1117	5.0	152		1151	4.5	137
	1725	0.1	3		1808	0.7	21
	2341	4.4	134				
11 M	0540	0.0	0	**26** Tu	0011	3.8	116
	1210	5.0	152		0609	0.8	24
	1822	0.2	6		1238	4.4	134
					1859	0.9	27
12 Tu	0035	4.2	128	**27** W	0100	3.6	110
	0633	0.1	3		0657	1.0	30
	1307	4.9	149		1330	4.3	131
	1925	0.4	12	☽	1955	1.0	30
13 W	0136	4.0	122	**28** Th	0155	3.4	104
	0733	0.2	6		0752	1.1	34
	1411	4.9	149		1427	4.2	128
☾	2032	0.4	12		2054	1.0	30
14 Th	0244	3.9	119	**29** F	0255	3.4	104
	0837	0.3	9		0850	1.1	34
	1518	4.9	149		1525	4.2	128
	2140	0.4	12		2151	1.0	30
15 F	0353	3.9	119	**30** Sa	0354	3.5	107
	0944	0.3	9		0949	1.0	30
	1625	5.0	152		1621	4.3	131
	2245	0.3	9		2242	0.8	24

Time meridian 75° W. 0000 is midnight. 1200 is noon. Times are not adjusted for Daylight Saving Time.
Heights are referred to mean lower low water which is the chart datum of soundings.

Breakwater Harbor, Delaware, 2017

Times and Heights of High and Low Waters

October

Day	Time (h m)	Height (ft)	Height (cm)
1 Su	0449	3.7	113
	1043	0.8	24
	1714	4.5	137
	2328	0.6	18
2 M	0539	4.0	122
	1134	0.5	15
	1801	4.7	143
3 Tu	0010	0.4	12
	0624	4.3	131
	1221	0.3	9
	1846	4.8	146
4 W	0051	0.1	3
	0708	4.6	140
	1307	0.1	3
	1930	4.9	149
5 Th ○	0131	-0.1	-3
	0751	4.9	149
	1353	-0.1	-3
	2013	4.9	149
6 F	0212	-0.2	-6
	0835	5.1	155
	1440	-0.3	-9
	2058	4.9	149
7 Sa	0255	-0.3	-9
	0920	5.3	162
	1528	-0.3	-9
	2144	4.7	143
8 Su	0339	-0.3	-9
	1007	5.4	165
	1618	-0.2	-6
	2233	4.5	137
9 M	0427	-0.2	-6
	1057	5.3	162
	1712	-0.1	-3
	2325	4.3	131
10 Tu	0518	-0.1	-3
	1152	5.2	158
	1810	0.1	3
11 W	0023	4.1	125
	0615	0.1	3
	1251	5.1	155
	1913	0.2	6
12 Th ◐	0128	4.0	122
	0718	0.3	9
	1356	4.9	149
	2020	0.3	9
13 F	0237	3.9	119
	0826	0.4	12
	1505	4.8	146
	2127	0.3	9
14 Sa	0347	4.0	122
	0935	0.4	12
	1612	4.8	146
	2229	0.2	6
15 Su	0451	4.2	128
	1041	0.3	9
	1713	4.8	146
	2325	0.1	3
16 M	0547	4.4	134
	1140	0.2	6
	1807	4.8	146
17 Tu	0013	0.0	0
	0637	4.7	143
	1232	0.0	0
	1855	4.8	146
18 W	0057	-0.1	-3
	0721	4.8	146
	1320	0.0	0
	1939	4.7	143
19 Th ●	0138	-0.1	-3
	0802	4.9	149
	1405	-0.1	-3
	2019	4.5	137
20 F	0216	0.0	0
	0840	5.0	152
	1447	0.0	0
	2058	4.4	134
21 Sa	0253	0.1	3
	0917	4.9	149
	1528	0.1	3
	2135	4.2	128
22 Su	0330	0.2	6
	0954	4.9	149
	1609	0.2	6
	2213	4.0	122
23 M	0407	0.4	12
	1033	4.7	143
	1650	0.4	12
	2254	3.8	116
24 Tu	0446	0.6	18
	1114	4.6	140
	1734	0.6	18
	2337	3.6	110
25 W	0528	0.8	24
	1159	4.4	134
	1822	0.7	21
26 Th	0025	3.5	107
	0614	0.9	27
	1248	4.3	131
	1913	0.8	24
27 F ◑	0117	3.4	104
	0707	1.0	30
	1342	4.2	128
	2007	0.9	27
28 Sa	0215	3.4	104
	0806	1.0	30
	1439	4.1	125
	2102	0.8	24
29 Su	0313	3.5	107
	0906	0.9	27
	1535	4.2	128
	2154	0.6	18
30 M	0409	3.8	116
	1005	0.7	21
	1630	4.3	131
	2242	0.4	12
31 Tu	0501	4.1	125
	1100	0.5	15
	1722	4.4	134
	2328	0.1	3

November

Day	Time (h m)	Height (ft)	Height (cm)
1 W	0550	4.5	137
	1152	0.2	6
	1811	4.5	137
2 Th	0013	-0.1	-3
	0637	4.8	146
	1242	-0.1	-3
	1859	4.6	140
3 F	0057	-0.4	-12
	0723	5.2	158
	1332	-0.4	-12
	1946	4.7	143
4 Sa ○	0142	-0.5	-15
	0810	5.4	165
	1421	-0.5	-15
	2035	4.6	140
5 Su	0228	-0.6	-18
	0858	5.6	171
	1512	-0.6	-18
	2124	4.5	137
6 M	0316	-0.6	-18
	0947	5.6	171
	1604	-0.5	-15
	2216	4.4	134
7 Tu	0406	-0.4	-12
	1040	5.5	168
	1659	-0.4	-12
	2312	4.2	128
8 W	0500	-0.2	-6
	1135	5.3	162
	1757	-0.2	-6
9 Th	0011	4.0	122
	0559	0.0	0
	1235	5.0	152
	1859	0.0	0
10 F ◐	0116	3.9	119
	0703	0.2	6
	1339	4.8	146
	2003	0.1	3
11 Sa	0225	3.9	119
	0812	0.3	9
	1446	4.6	140
	2107	0.1	3
12 Su	0332	4.0	122
	0922	0.4	12
	1551	4.4	134
	2207	0.1	3
13 M	0434	4.2	128
	1028	0.3	9
	1652	4.3	131
	2300	0.0	0
14 Tu	0529	4.4	134
	1127	0.2	6
	1746	4.3	131
	2348	0.0	0
15 W	0617	4.6	140
	1218	0.1	3
	1833	4.2	128
16 Th	0031	0.0	0
	0700	4.7	143
	1305	0.0	0
	1916	4.1	125
17 F	0110	0.0	0
	0739	4.8	146
	1348	0.0	0
	1956	4.0	122
18 Sa ●	0148	0.0	0
	0815	4.8	146
	1428	0.0	0
	2033	3.9	119
19 Su	0224	0.1	3
	0851	4.8	146
	1507	0.0	0
	2110	3.8	116
20 M	0259	0.1	3
	0928	4.8	146
	1546	0.1	3
	2147	3.7	113
21 Tu	0336	0.3	9
	1005	4.7	143
	1625	0.2	6
	2226	3.6	110
22 W	0414	0.4	12
	1044	4.5	137
	1705	0.3	9
	2308	3.4	104
23 Th	0454	0.5	15
	1126	4.4	134
	1748	0.4	12
	2352	3.4	104
24 F	0538	0.6	18
	1212	4.2	128
	1833	0.5	15
25 Sa	0042	3.3	101
	0628	0.7	21
	1301	4.1	125
	1922	0.5	15
26 Su ◑	0135	3.4	104
	0724	0.8	24
	1354	4.0	122
	2014	0.4	12
27 M	0231	3.5	107
	0825	0.7	21
	1449	4.0	122
	2106	0.3	9
28 Tu	0328	3.8	116
	0927	0.6	18
	1546	4.0	122
	2157	0.1	3
29 W	0424	4.1	125
	1027	0.3	9
	1642	4.1	125
	2248	-0.1	-3
30 Th	0517	4.5	137
	1125	0.0	0
	1737	4.2	128
	2338	-0.4	-12

December

Day	Time (h m)	Height (ft)	Height (cm)
1 F	0608	4.9	149
	1220	-0.3	-9
	1830	4.2	128
2 Sa	0027	-0.6	-18
	0659	5.3	162
	1313	-0.6	-18
	1923	4.3	131
3 Su ○	0116	-0.8	-24
	0749	5.5	168
	1405	-0.7	-21
	2015	4.3	131
4 M	0206	-0.9	-27
	0840	5.7	174
	1457	-0.8	-24
	2108	4.3	131
5 Tu	0257	-0.9	-27
	0931	5.6	171
	1550	-0.8	-24
	2201	4.2	128
6 W	0349	-0.7	-21
	1024	5.5	168
	1644	-0.7	-21
	2257	4.1	125
7 Th	0444	-0.5	-15
	1119	5.2	158
	1740	-0.5	-15
	2355	4.0	122
8 F	0543	-0.3	-9
	1216	4.9	149
	1838	-0.3	-9
9 Sa	0057	3.9	119
	0645	0.0	0
	1316	4.6	140
	1937	-0.2	-6
10 Su ◐	0201	3.9	119
	0752	0.2	6
	1419	4.3	131
	2038	-0.1	-3
11 M	0306	3.9	119
	0901	0.3	9
	1522	4.0	122
	2136	0.0	0
12 Tu	0408	4.1	125
	1007	0.3	9
	1623	3.8	116
	2230	0.0	0
13 W	0504	4.2	128
	1108	0.3	9
	1719	3.7	113
	2318	0.0	0
14 Th	0553	4.3	131
	1201	0.2	6
	1808	3.7	113
15 F	0003	0.0	0
	0636	4.5	137
	1248	0.1	3
	1853	3.6	110
16 Sa	0043	0.0	0
	0716	4.6	140
	1330	0.0	0
	1933	3.6	110
17 Su	0122	0.0	0
	0753	4.6	140
	1410	0.0	0
	2011	3.6	110
18 M ●	0159	0.0	0
	0830	4.7	143
	1447	-0.1	-3
	2048	3.5	107
19 Tu	0235	0.0	0
	0906	4.6	140
	1524	0.0	0
	2124	3.5	107
20 W	0311	0.0	0
	0943	4.6	140
	1600	0.0	0
	2202	3.4	104
21 Th	0348	0.1	3
	1020	4.5	137
	1637	0.0	0
	2241	3.4	104
22 F	0427	0.2	6
	1059	4.4	134
	1716	0.1	3
	2323	3.4	104
23 Sa	0509	0.3	9
	1140	4.2	128
	1757	0.1	3
24 Su	0008	3.4	104
	0556	0.4	12
	1225	4.1	125
	1841	0.1	3
25 M	0057	3.5	107
	0649	0.4	12
	1314	3.9	119
	1930	0.1	3
26 Tu ◑	0151	3.6	110
	0748	0.4	12
	1408	3.8	116
	2022	0.0	0
27 W	0249	3.8	116
	0852	0.4	12
	1506	3.7	113
	2116	-0.1	-3
28 Th	0348	4.1	125
	0957	0.2	6
	1607	3.7	113
	2212	-0.3	-9
29 F	0446	4.5	137
	1100	-0.1	-3
	1708	3.8	116
	2307	-0.5	-15
30 Sa	0544	4.9	149
	1159	-0.4	-12
	1807	3.9	119
31 Su	0002	-0.7	-21
	0639	5.2	158
	1256	-0.6	-18
	1904	4.0	122

Time meridian 75° W. 0000 is midnight. 1200 is noon. Times are not adjusted for Daylight Saving Time.
Heights are referred to mean lower low water which is the chart datum of soundings.

Reedy Point, Delaware, 2017

Times and Heights of High and Low Waters

January

Day	Time	ft	cm	Day	Time	ft	cm
1 Su	0041	4.7	143	**16** M	0141	5.1	155
	0715	-0.2	-6		0819	-0.4	-12
	1248	5.6	171		1400	5.5	168
	2003	-0.1	-3		2057	-0.4	-12
2 M	0117	4.8	146	**17** Tu	0231	5.0	152
	0757	-0.1	-3		0908	-0.2	-6
	1328	5.6	171		1450	5.3	162
	2045	-0.1	-3		2141	-0.3	-9
3 Tu	0159	4.9	149	**18** W	0321	5.0	152
	0844	-0.1	-3		0957	0.0	0
	1415	5.5	168		1542	5.1	155
	2130	-0.1	-3		2226	-0.1	-3
4 W	0249	4.9	149	**19** Th	0414	4.9	149
	0939	0.0	0		1048	0.1	3
	1509	5.4	165		1636	4.9	149
	2219	-0.1	-3		2312	-0.1	-3
5 Th	0345	5.0	152	**20** F	0507	5.0	152
	1042	0.0	0		1141	0.1	3
	1611	5.3	162		1731	4.8	146
	2314	-0.2	-6				
6 F	0448	5.1	155	**21** Sa	0000	0.0	0
	1149	0.1	3		0600	5.0	152
	1718	5.1	155		1236	0.2	6
					1826	4.8	146
7 Sa	0012	-0.2	-6	**22** Su	0050	0.0	0
	0553	5.3	162		0653	5.1	155
	1256	0.0	0		1331	0.1	3
	1825	5.0	152		1919	4.8	146
8 Su	0113	-0.3	-9	**23** M	0140	-0.1	-3
	0657	5.4	165		0744	5.2	158
	1401	-0.2	-6		1425	0.0	0
	1929	5.0	152		2010	4.8	146
9 M	0213	-0.4	-12	**24** Tu	0230	-0.1	-3
	0758	5.6	171		0832	5.3	162
	1503	-0.4	-12		1516	-0.1	-3
	2029	5.1	155		2058	4.8	146
10 Tu	0311	-0.6	-18	**25** W	0319	-0.2	-6
	0856	5.8	177		0917	5.4	165
	1602	-0.5	-15		1605	-0.2	-6
	2126	5.1	155		2143	4.8	146
11 W	0407	-0.7	-21	**26** Th	0406	-0.3	-9
	0951	5.9	180		1000	5.5	168
	1657	-0.7	-21		1651	-0.3	-9
	2220	5.2	158		2225	4.9	149
12 Th	0501	-0.7	-21	**27** F	0451	-0.3	-9
	1043	6.0	183		1039	5.6	171
	1749	-0.8	-24		1735	-0.3	-9
	2312	5.2	158		2304	4.9	149
13 F	0553	-0.7	-21	**28** Sa	0535	-0.4	-12
	1134	5.9	180		1116	5.6	171
	1838	-0.7	-21		1817	-0.3	-9
					2341	4.9	149
14 Sa	0003	5.2	158	**29** Su	0618	-0.4	-12
	0643	-0.7	-21		1153	5.7	174
	1223	5.8	177		1858	-0.3	-9
	1926	-0.7	-21				
15 Su	0052	5.1	155	**30** M	0018	5.0	152
	0731	-0.5	-15		0701	-0.4	-12
	1311	5.7	174		1232	5.7	174
	2012	-0.5	-15		1939	-0.3	-9
				31 Tu	0056	5.1	155
					0747	-0.3	-9
					1314	5.7	174
					2021	-0.3	-9

February

Day	Time	ft	cm	Day	Time	ft	cm
1 W	0139	5.2	158	**16** Th	0241	5.2	158
	0836	-0.2	-6		0922	0.0	0
	1401	5.6	171		1505	5.1	155
	2106	-0.3	-9		2141	0.1	3
2 Th	0227	5.3	162	**17** F	0328	5.1	155
	0931	-0.1	-3		1010	0.2	6
	1455	5.4	165		1555	4.9	149
	2155	-0.2	-6		2224	0.2	6
3 F	0323	5.3	162	**18** Sa	0418	5.1	155
	1031	0.0	0		1101	0.3	9
	1556	5.2	158		1649	4.8	146
	2250	-0.2	-6		2311	0.3	9
4 Sa	0425	5.3	162	**19** Su	0511	5.1	155
	1136	0.0	0		1155	0.4	12
	1702	5.0	152		1745	4.7	143
	2351	-0.1	-3				
5 Su	0532	5.3	162	**20** M	0002	0.3	9
	1241	0.0	0		0606	5.1	155
	1809	4.9	149		1251	0.3	9
					1840	4.7	143
6 M	0053	-0.2	-6	**21** Tu	0056	0.3	9
	0638	5.4	165		0701	5.2	158
	1346	-0.1	-3		1347	0.3	9
	1914	4.9	149		1934	4.8	146
7 Tu	0155	-0.3	-9	**22** W	0151	0.2	6
	0742	5.5	168		0753	5.3	162
	1447	-0.3	-9		1441	0.2	6
	2015	5.0	152		2024	4.9	149
8 W	0255	-0.4	-12	**23** Th	0245	0.0	0
	0841	5.7	174		0842	5.4	165
	1544	-0.4	-12		1531	0.0	0
	2112	5.2	158		2111	5.0	152
9 Th	0351	-0.5	-15	**24** F	0336	-0.1	-3
	0937	5.8	177		0928	5.6	171
	1638	-0.6	-18		1619	-0.1	-3
	2205	5.3	162		2154	5.1	155
10 F	0445	-0.6	-18	**25** Sa	0425	-0.2	-6
	1028	5.9	180		1010	5.7	174
	1728	-0.6	-18		1705	-0.2	-6
	2255	5.4	165		2235	5.3	162
11 Sa	0535	-0.6	-18	**26** Su	0513	-0.3	-9
	1117	5.8	177		1052	5.8	177
	1814	-0.6	-18		1749	-0.3	-9
	2342	5.4	165		2315	5.4	165
12 Su	0623	-0.6	-18	**27** M	0600	-0.4	-12
	1203	5.8	177		1133	5.9	180
	1858	-0.5	-15		1831	-0.3	-9
					2354	5.6	171
13 M	0028	5.4	165	**28** Tu	0647	-0.4	-12
	0708	-0.5	-15		1215	5.9	180
	1247	5.6	171		1914	-0.3	-9
	1940	-0.4	-12				
14 Tu	0112	5.3	162				
	0753	-0.3	-9				
	1332	5.5	168				
	2021	-0.2	-6				
15 W	0156	5.3	162				
	0837	-0.1	-3				
	1417	5.3	162				
	2101	0.0	0				

March

Day	Time	ft	cm	Day	Time	ft	cm
1 W	0035	5.7	174	**16** Th	0121	5.6	171
	0735	-0.4	-12		0808	0.1	3
	1300	5.8	177		1346	5.4	165
	1958	-0.2	-6		2019	0.3	9
2 Th	0119	5.7	174	**17** F	0201	5.5	168
	0827	-0.3	-9		0850	0.2	6
	1349	5.6	171		1430	5.2	158
	2044	-0.2	-6		2056	0.4	12
3 F	0209	5.7	174	**18** Sa	0242	5.5	168
	0922	-0.1	-3		0934	0.4	12
	1444	5.4	165		1516	5.0	152
	2136	-0.1	-3		2135	0.5	15
4 Sa	0305	5.7	174	**19** Su	0327	5.4	165
	1021	0.0	0		1021	0.5	15
	1544	5.2	158		1607	4.9	149
	2232	0.0	0		2220	0.6	18
5 Su	0408	5.6	171	**20** M	0418	5.3	162
	1123	0.1	3		1114	0.6	18
	1650	5.1	155		1702	4.9	149
	2333	0.1	3		2313	0.6	18
6 M	0515	5.5	168	**21** Tu	0514	5.3	162
	1226	0.1	3		1209	0.6	18
	1757	5.0	152		1758	4.9	149
7 Tu	0036	0.1	3	**22** W	0012	0.6	18
	0623	5.5	168		0612	5.3	162
	1329	0.0	0		1306	0.5	15
	1901	5.1	155		1853	4.9	149
8 W	0139	0.0	0	**23** Th	0112	0.5	15
	0727	5.6	171		0709	5.4	165
	1428	-0.1	-3		1401	0.4	12
	2001	5.3	162		1946	5.1	155
9 Th	0238	-0.1	-3	**24** F	0210	0.3	9
	0827	5.7	174		0802	5.6	171
	1524	-0.2	-6		1454	0.3	9
	2057	5.4	165		2035	5.3	162
10 F	0334	-0.3	-9	**25** Sa	0306	0.1	3
	0921	5.8	177		0852	5.7	174
	1615	-0.3	-9		1544	0.1	3
	2148	5.6	171		2120	5.5	168
11 Sa	0427	-0.4	-12	**26** Su	0359	0.0	0
	1011	5.9	180		0939	5.9	180
	1702	-0.4	-12		1632	0.0	0
	2235	5.7	174		2204	5.8	177
12 Su	0515	-0.4	-12	**27** M	0451	-0.2	-6
	1057	5.8	177		1025	6.0	183
	1746	-0.3	-9		1718	-0.1	-3
	2320	5.8	177		2247	6.0	183
13 M	0601	-0.3	-9	**28** Tu	0541	-0.3	-9
	1140	5.8	177		1111	6.0	183
	1828	-0.2	-6		1803	-0.2	-6
					2330	6.2	189
14 Tu	0002	5.7	174	**29** W	0631	-0.4	-12
	0645	-0.2	-6		1157	6.0	183
	1222	5.7	174		1848	-0.2	-6
	1906	0.0	0				
15 W	0042	5.7	174	**30** Th	0014	6.2	189
	0727	-0.1	-3		0723	-0.3	-9
	1304	5.5	168		1245	5.9	180
	1943	0.1	3		1935	-0.1	-3
				31 F	0101	6.3	192
					0815	-0.2	-6
					1337	5.7	174
					2025	0.0	0

Time meridian 75° W. 0000 is midnight. 1200 is noon. Times are not adjusted for Daylight Saving Time.
Heights are referred to mean lower low water which is the chart datum of soundings.

Reedy Point, Delaware, 2017

Times and Heights of High and Low Waters

April

Day	Time	ft	cm		Day	Time	ft	cm
1 Sa	0153	6.2	189		16 Su	0159	5.8	177
	0910	-0.1	-3			0902	0.5	15
	1433	5.5	168			1440	5.1	155
	2118	0.1	3			2052	0.7	21
2 Su	0250	6.0	183		17 M	0238	5.7	174
	1008	0.0	0			0947	0.6	18
	1534	5.3	162			1527	5.0	152
	2216	0.3	9			2136	0.8	24
3 M	0353	5.8	177		18 Tu	0324	5.6	171
	1108	0.1	3			1035	0.7	21
	1639	5.3	162			1619	5.0	152
	2317	0.3	9			2229	0.8	24
4 Tu	0500	5.7	174		19 W	0419	5.6	171
	1208	0.2	6			1128	0.7	21
	1744	5.3	162			1714	5.1	155
						2330	0.8	24
5 W	0019	0.3	9		20 Th	0520	5.5	168
	0607	5.7	174			1224	0.6	18
	1308	0.1	3			1810	5.2	158
	1846	5.4	165					
6 Th	0121	0.3	9		21 F	0034	0.7	21
	0710	5.7	174			0622	5.6	171
	1405	0.0	0			1320	0.5	15
	1944	5.6	171			1905	5.4	165
7 F	0220	0.1	3		22 Sa	0136	0.6	18
	0808	5.8	177			0720	5.7	174
	1458	-0.1	-3			1414	0.4	12
	2038	5.8	177			1956	5.7	174
8 Sa	0315	0.0	0		23 Su	0236	0.4	12
	0901	5.8	177			0815	5.8	177
	1547	-0.1	-3			1506	0.2	6
	2127	6.0	183			2046	6.0	183
9 Su	0406	-0.1	-3		24 M	0334	0.1	3
	0949	5.9	180			0908	5.9	180
	1633	-0.1	-3			1557	0.1	3
	2213	6.1	186			2133	6.2	189
10 M	0454	-0.1	-3		25 Tu	0429	-0.1	-3
	1034	5.8	177			0958	6.0	183
	1715	0.0	0			1646	0.0	0
	2255	6.1	186			2220	6.5	198
11 Tu	0539	-0.1	-3		26 W	0522	-0.2	-6
	1116	5.8	177			1048	6.0	183
	1755	0.1	3			1735	-0.1	-3
	2334	6.1	186			2307	6.6	201
12 W	0621	0.0	0		27 Th	0615	-0.3	-9
	1157	5.6	171			1138	5.9	180
	1832	0.3	9			1824	0.0	0
						2355	6.7	204
13 Th	0012	6.0	183		28 F	0708	-0.3	-9
	0702	0.1	3			1230	5.8	177
	1237	5.5	168			1914	0.0	0
	1907	0.5	15					
14 F	0048	5.9	180		29 Sa	0045	6.6	201
	0741	0.2	6			0802	-0.2	-6
	1317	5.4	165			1324	5.7	174
	1941	0.6	18			2007	0.1	3
15 Sa	0123	5.9	180		30 Su	0138	6.4	195
	0821	0.4	12			0857	-0.1	-3
	1357	5.2	158			1421	5.6	171
	2015	0.7	21			2102	0.3	9

May

Day	Time	ft	cm		Day	Time	ft	cm
1 M	0236	6.2	189		16 Tu	0200	5.9	180
	0952	0.0	0			0917	0.6	18
	1522	5.5	168			1450	5.1	155
	2159	0.4	12			2103	0.8	24
2 Tu	0338	6.0	183		17 W	0242	5.9	180
	1049	0.1	3			1002	0.6	18
	1624	5.4	165			1537	5.2	158
	2259	0.5	15			2154	0.9	27
3 W	0443	5.8	177		18 Th	0334	5.8	177
	1146	0.1	3			1050	0.6	18
	1727	5.5	168			1630	5.2	158
	2359	0.5	15			2254	0.9	27
4 Th	0547	5.8	177		19 F	0434	5.8	177
	1242	0.1	3			1143	0.5	15
	1827	5.7	174			1727	5.4	165
5 F	0059	0.4	12		20 Sa	0000	0.8	24
	0648	5.7	174			0538	5.7	174
	1336	0.1	3			1238	0.5	15
	1923	5.9	180			1824	5.6	171
6 Sa	0157	0.3	9		21 Su	0105	0.7	21
	0744	5.8	177			0641	5.7	174
	1427	0.1	3			1334	0.3	9
	2014	6.1	186			1919	5.9	180
7 Su	0251	0.2	6		22 M	0209	0.5	15
	0835	5.8	177			0741	5.8	177
	1515	0.1	3			1429	0.2	6
	2102	6.2	189			2012	6.2	189
8 M	0342	0.1	3		23 Tu	0310	0.3	9
	0923	5.8	177			0838	5.8	177
	1600	0.1	3			1523	0.1	3
	2147	6.3	192			2104	6.5	198
9 Tu	0429	0.1	3		24 W	0408	0.0	0
	1008	5.7	174			0933	5.9	180
	1642	0.2	6			1617	0.0	0
	2228	6.3	192			2155	6.7	204
10 W	0514	0.1	3		25 Th	0504	-0.1	-3
	1051	5.6	171			1027	5.9	180
	1722	0.3	9			1709	0.0	0
	2307	6.3	192			2246	6.8	207
11 Th	0557	0.2	6		26 F	0559	-0.3	-9
	1132	5.5	168			1120	5.8	177
	1759	0.5	15			1802	0.0	0
	2344	6.2	189			2337	6.8	207
12 F	0638	0.2	6		27 Sa	0653	-0.3	-9
	1212	5.4	165			1214	5.7	174
	1835	0.6	18			1855	0.1	3
13 Sa	0018	6.1	186		28 Su	0029	6.7	204
	0717	0.3	9			0746	-0.3	-9
	1250	5.3	162			1309	5.7	174
	1909	0.7	21			1949	0.2	6
14 Su	0051	6.0	183		29 M	0124	6.5	198
	0757	0.4	12			0839	-0.2	-6
	1328	5.2	158			1405	5.6	171
	1942	0.8	24			2044	0.3	9
15 M	0124	6.0	183		30 Tu	0220	6.3	192
	0836	0.5	15			0932	-0.1	-3
	1407	5.1	155			1504	5.6	171
	2019	0.8	24			2140	0.4	12
					31 W	0320	6.1	186
						1025	0.0	0
						1604	5.6	171
						2237	0.5	15

June

Day	Time	ft	cm		Day	Time	ft	cm
1 Th	0421	5.9	180		16 F	0302	6.0	183
	1118	0.1	3			1017	0.4	12
	1703	5.7	174			1551	5.5	168
	2335	0.5	15			2228	0.8	24
2 F	0521	5.8	177		17 Sa	0400	5.9	180
	1211	0.1	3			1106	0.4	12
	1801	5.8	177			1648	5.6	171
						2333	0.8	24
3 Sa	0033	0.5	15		18 Su	0504	5.8	177
	0619	5.7	174			1200	0.3	9
	1302	0.1	3			1747	5.8	177
	1855	6.0	183					
4 Su	0129	0.5	15		19 M	0040	0.7	21
	0714	5.6	171			0609	5.7	174
	1351	0.2	6			1258	0.3	9
	1946	6.1	186			1846	6.1	186
5 M	0223	0.4	12		20 Tu	0146	0.5	15
	0806	5.6	171			0713	5.6	171
	1439	0.2	6			1357	0.2	6
	2034	6.2	189			1944	6.3	192
6 Tu	0314	0.3	9		21 W	0249	0.3	9
	0855	5.6	171			0813	5.7	174
	1524	0.3	9			1455	0.1	3
	2119	6.3	192			2040	6.6	201
7 W	0403	0.2	6		22 Th	0350	0.1	3
	0941	5.5	168			0911	5.7	174
	1608	0.3	9			1552	0.0	0
	2201	6.3	192			2135	6.7	204
8 Th	0448	0.2	6		23 F	0447	-0.1	-3
	1025	5.5	168			1008	5.7	174
	1649	0.4	12			1648	0.0	0
	2240	6.3	192			2228	6.8	207
9 F	0532	0.2	6		24 Sa	0542	-0.2	-6
	1107	5.4	165			1102	5.7	174
	1728	0.5	15			1743	0.0	0
	2317	6.2	189			2321	6.8	207
10 Sa	0614	0.3	9		25 Su	0635	-0.3	-9
	1147	5.3	162			1157	5.7	174
	1806	0.6	18			1837	0.0	0
	2352	6.2	189					
11 Su	0654	0.3	9		26 M	0014	6.7	204
	1224	5.2	158			0727	-0.3	-9
	1843	0.7	21			1251	5.7	174
						1930	0.1	3
12 M	0024	6.1	186		27 Tu	0107	6.5	198
	0733	0.4	12			0817	-0.2	-6
	1301	5.1	155			1345	5.7	174
	1919	0.7	21			2023	0.2	6
13 Tu	0056	6.1	186		28 W	0201	6.3	192
	0812	0.5	15			0907	-0.1	-3
	1337	5.2	158			1441	5.6	171
	1957	0.8	24			2117	0.4	12
14 W	0131	6.1	186		29 Th	0256	6.1	186
	0851	0.5	15			0956	0.0	0
	1416	5.2	158			1537	5.7	174
	2040	0.8	24			2211	0.5	15
15 Th	0213	6.0	183		30 F	0353	5.8	177
	0932	0.5	15			1045	0.1	3
	1500	5.3	162			1633	5.7	174
	2130	0.8	24			2306	0.6	18

Time meridian 75° W. 0000 is midnight. 1200 is noon. Times are not adjusted for Daylight Saving Time.
Heights are referred to mean lower low water which is the chart datum of soundings.

Reedy Point, Delaware, 2017

Times and Heights of High and Low Waters

July

Day	Time (h m)	Height (ft)	Height (cm)	Day	Time (h m)	Height (ft)	Height (cm)
1 Sa	0450	5.7	174	16 Su	0335	5.9	180
	1134	0.2	6		1036	0.3	9
	1728	5.8	177		1615	5.8	177
				◐	2315	0.8	24
2 Su	0002	0.6	18	17 M	0439	5.7	174
	0546	5.6	171		1131	0.3	9
	1224	0.3	9		1717	6.0	183
	1821	5.9	180				
3 M	0057	0.6	18	18 Tu	0022	0.7	21
	0641	5.5	168		0546	5.6	171
	1312	0.3	9		1231	0.3	9
	1913	6.0	183		1820	6.2	189
4 Tu	0151	0.5	15	19 W	0128	0.6	18
	0734	5.5	168		0651	5.5	168
	1400	0.3	9		1333	0.2	6
	2002	6.1	186		1922	6.3	192
5 W	0243	0.4	12	20 Th	0232	0.4	12
	0824	5.4	165		0754	5.5	168
	1448	0.4	12		1434	0.2	6
	2048	6.2	189		2021	6.5	198
6 Th	0333	0.4	12	21 F	0332	0.2	6
	0912	5.4	165		0854	5.6	171
	1533	0.4	12		1534	0.1	3
	2132	6.3	192		2118	6.6	201
7 F	0420	0.3	9	22 Sa	0429	0.0	0
	0958	5.4	165		0951	5.7	174
	1617	0.4	12		1631	0.0	0
	2213	6.3	192		2213	6.7	204
8 Sa	0505	0.3	9	23 Su	0523	-0.2	-6
	1041	5.3	162		1046	5.7	174
	1700	0.5	15		1725	0.0	0
○	2252	6.2	189	●	2306	6.7	204
9 Su	0548	0.3	9	24 M	0615	-0.2	-6
	1121	5.3	162		1138	5.8	177
	1741	0.5	15		1818	0.0	0
	2327	6.2	189		2357	6.6	201
10 M	0628	0.3	9	25 Tu	0704	-0.2	-6
	1158	5.2	158		1230	5.8	177
	1821	0.6	18		1910	0.1	3
11 Tu	0001	6.2	189	26 W	0047	6.4	195
	0708	0.3	9		0751	-0.1	-3
	1233	5.2	158		1321	5.8	177
	1900	0.6	18		2000	0.3	9
12 W	0034	6.2	189	27 Th	0137	6.2	189
	0746	0.4	12		0837	0.0	0
	1308	5.3	162		1412	5.8	177
	1940	0.7	21		2051	0.4	12
13 Th	0110	6.2	189	28 F	0228	6.0	183
	0825	0.4	12		0923	0.1	3
	1346	5.4	165		1504	5.8	177
	2024	0.7	21		2142	0.6	18
14 F	0151	6.1	186	29 Sa	0320	5.8	177
	0904	0.3	9		1008	0.3	9
	1429	5.6	171		1556	5.7	174
	2114	0.7	21		2234	0.7	21
15 Sa	0239	6.0	183	30 Su	0415	5.6	171
	0947	0.3	9		1054	0.4	12
	1518	5.7	174		1649	5.8	177
	2211	0.8	24	◐	2327	0.8	24
				31 M	0510	5.4	165
					1142	0.5	15
					1743	5.8	177

August

Day	Time (h m)	Height (ft)	Height (cm)	Day	Time (h m)	Height (ft)	Height (cm)
1 Tu	0021	0.8	24	16 W	0009	0.8	24
	0606	5.4	165		0530	5.4	165
	1230	0.5	15		1213	0.4	12
	1835	5.9	180		1801	6.1	186
2 W	0116	0.7	21	17 Th	0113	0.6	18
	0700	5.3	162		0637	5.4	165
	1320	0.5	15		1317	0.4	12
	1926	6.0	183		1906	6.3	192
3 Th	0209	0.6	18	18 F	0216	0.4	12
	0752	5.3	162		0741	5.5	168
	1410	0.5	15		1419	0.3	9
	2015	6.1	186		2007	6.4	195
4 F	0300	0.5	15	19 Sa	0315	0.2	6
	0842	5.3	162		0840	5.6	171
	1459	0.5	15		1519	0.1	3
	2101	6.2	189		2105	6.5	198
5 Sa	0349	0.4	12	20 Su	0410	0.0	0
	0929	5.4	165		0936	5.8	177
	1546	0.4	12		1615	0.0	0
	2144	6.2	189		2158	6.6	201
6 Su	0435	0.3	9	21 M	0502	-0.1	-3
	1012	5.4	165		1029	5.9	180
	1632	0.4	12		1708	0.0	0
	2224	6.3	192	●	2249	6.6	201
7 M	0518	0.3	9	22 Tu	0551	-0.2	-6
	1052	5.4	165		1118	6.0	183
	1716	0.4	12		1759	0.0	0
○	2302	6.3	192		2337	6.5	198
8 Tu	0600	0.3	9	23 W	0637	-0.1	-3
	1129	5.4	165		1206	6.0	183
	1759	0.4	12		1848	0.1	3
	2337	6.3	192				
9 W	0640	0.3	9	24 Th	0024	6.3	192
	1205	5.5	168		0721	0.0	0
	1842	0.5	15		1253	6.0	183
					1936	0.3	9
10 Th	0013	6.3	192	25 F	0110	6.1	186
	0719	0.3	9		0803	0.2	6
	1240	5.6	171		1339	5.9	180
	1925	0.5	15		2023	0.5	15
11 F	0050	6.2	189	26 Sa	0157	5.9	180
	0758	0.3	9		0845	0.3	9
	1318	5.8	177		1426	5.9	180
	2012	0.6	18		2110	0.7	21
12 Sa	0133	6.1	186	27 Su	0246	5.7	174
	0838	0.3	9		0927	0.5	15
	1402	5.9	180		1515	5.8	177
	2103	0.7	21		2159	0.8	24
13 Su	0222	6.0	183	28 M	0338	5.5	168
	0922	0.3	9		1010	0.6	18
	1452	6.0	183		1606	5.8	177
	2200	0.7	21		2250	0.9	27
14 M	0318	5.8	177	29 Tu	0432	5.3	162
	1013	0.4	12		1057	0.7	21
	1550	6.0	183		1659	5.7	174
◐	2303	0.8	24	◐	2343	0.9	27
15 Tu	0422	5.6	171	30 W	0528	5.2	158
	1110	0.4	12		1146	0.8	24
	1654	6.1	186		1753	5.8	177
				31 Th	0038	0.9	27
					0624	5.2	158
					1239	0.7	21
					1847	5.9	180

September

Day	Time (h m)	Height (ft)	Height (cm)	Day	Time (h m)	Height (ft)	Height (cm)
1 F	0132	0.8	24	16 Sa	0158	0.4	12
	0718	5.3	162		0728	5.5	168
	1332	0.7	21		1405	0.3	9
	1939	6.0	183		1954	6.3	192
2 Sa	0224	0.7	21	17 Su	0255	0.2	6
	0809	5.3	162		0827	5.7	174
	1425	0.6	18		1504	0.2	6
	2027	6.1	186		2051	6.4	195
3 Su	0314	0.5	15	18 M	0348	0.0	0
	0856	5.4	165		0920	5.9	180
	1516	0.5	15		1559	0.1	3
	2112	6.2	189		2142	6.4	195
4 M	0401	0.4	12	19 Tu	0438	-0.1	-3
	0940	5.6	171		1010	6.1	186
	1604	0.4	12		1650	0.0	0
	2154	6.3	192		2230	6.4	195
5 Tu	0446	0.3	9	20 W	0524	-0.1	-3
	1021	5.7	174		1057	6.1	186
	1652	0.3	9		1739	0.1	3
	2234	6.3	192	●	2316	6.3	192
6 W	0528	0.2	6	21 Th	0607	0.0	0
	1059	5.8	177		1141	6.1	186
	1738	0.3	9		1826	0.2	6
○	2312	6.3	192				
7 Th	0609	0.2	6	22 F	0000	6.1	186
	1136	5.9	180		0649	0.2	6
	1823	0.3	9		1224	6.1	186
	2351	6.3	192		1911	0.3	9
8 F	0650	0.2	6	23 Sa	0043	5.9	180
	1214	6.0	183		0728	0.3	9
	1910	0.4	12		1306	6.0	183
					1955	0.5	15
9 Sa	0032	6.2	189	24 Su	0127	5.7	174
	0731	0.2	6		0806	0.5	15
	1254	6.1	186		1348	5.9	180
	2000	0.4	12		2039	0.7	21
10 Su	0117	6.1	186	25 M	0212	5.5	168
	0814	0.3	9		0845	0.7	21
	1340	6.2	189		1432	5.8	177
	2053	0.5	15		2124	0.8	24
11 M	0208	5.9	180	26 Tu	0301	5.3	162
	0902	0.3	9		0925	0.8	24
	1432	6.2	189		1519	5.7	174
	2151	0.6	18		2213	0.9	27
12 Tu	0306	5.6	171	27 W	0353	5.2	158
	0956	0.4	12		1010	0.8	24
	1532	6.1	186		1611	5.7	174
	2252	0.7	21	◐	2304	0.9	27
13 W	0411	5.4	165	28 Th	0448	5.1	155
	1056	0.5	15		1101	0.9	27
	1639	6.1	186		1706	5.7	174
◐	2355	0.7	21		2358	0.9	27
14 Th	0519	5.4	165	29 F	0545	5.1	155
	1200	0.5	15		1156	0.8	24
	1747	6.1	186		1803	5.7	174
15 F	0058	0.6	18	30 Sa	0052	0.8	24
	0626	5.4	165		0639	5.2	158
	1304	0.4	12		1253	0.7	21
	1853	6.2	189		1857	5.8	177

Time meridian 75° W. 0000 is midnight. 1200 is noon. Times are not adjusted for Daylight Saving Time. Heights are referred to mean lower low water which is the chart datum of soundings.

Reedy Point, Delaware, 2017
Times and Heights of High and Low Waters

October

Day	Time	Height (ft)	Height (cm)	Day	Time	Height (ft)	Height (cm)
1 Su	0145	0.7	21	**16** M	0232	0.0	0
	0731	5.3	162		0810	5.8	177
	1350	0.6	18		1447	0.1	3
	1948	5.9	180		2033	6.1	186
2 M	0236	0.5	15	**17** Tu	0323	-0.1	-3
	0820	5.5	168		0902	6.0	183
	1444	0.5	15		1540	0.0	0
	2036	6.1	186		2123	6.1	186
3 Tu	0324	0.3	9	**18** W	0410	-0.2	-6
	0905	5.7	174		0950	6.1	186
	1536	0.3	9		1631	-0.1	-3
	2121	6.2	189		2210	6.1	186
4 W	0410	0.2	6	**19** Th ●	0455	-0.1	-3
	0947	5.9	180		1034	6.2	189
	1627	0.2	6		1718	0.0	0
	2204	6.2	189		2254	6.0	183
5 Th ○	0454	0.1	3	**20** F	0536	0.0	0
	1027	6.1	186		1116	6.1	186
	1716	0.1	3		1803	0.1	3
	2246	6.2	189		2336	5.8	177
6 F	0538	0.0	0	**21** Sa	0616	0.2	6
	1108	6.2	189		1156	6.1	186
	1805	0.1	3		1846	0.2	6
	2330	6.1	186				
7 Sa	0621	0.0	0	**22** Su	0017	5.6	171
	1149	6.3	192		0653	0.3	9
	1855	0.1	3		1234	6.0	183
					1928	0.4	12
8 Su	0015	6.0	183	**23** M	0059	5.4	165
	0706	0.1	3		0729	0.5	15
	1233	6.4	195		1312	5.9	180
	1947	0.2	6		2009	0.5	15
9 M	0103	5.9	180	**24** Tu	0141	5.2	158
	0753	0.1	3		0804	0.6	18
	1322	6.3	192		1351	5.8	177
	2042	0.3	9		2052	0.6	18
10 Tu	0157	5.6	171	**25** W	0225	5.1	155
	0845	0.3	9		0842	0.7	21
	1417	6.2	189		1433	5.7	174
	2139	0.4	12		2137	0.7	21
11 W	0256	5.4	165	**26** Th	0313	4.9	149
	0942	0.4	12		0925	0.7	21
	1518	6.1	186		1521	5.6	171
	2239	0.4	12		2225	0.8	24
12 Th ◐	0401	5.3	162	**27** F ◑	0405	4.9	149
	1043	0.4	12		1016	0.7	21
	1626	6.0	183		1615	5.5	168
	2339	0.4	12		2316	0.7	21
13 F	0508	5.3	162	**28** Sa	0500	4.9	149
	1146	0.4	12		1113	0.7	21
	1734	5.9	180		1713	5.5	168
14 Sa	0039	0.3	9	**29** Su	0009	0.6	18
	0613	5.4	165		0556	5.0	152
	1249	0.4	12		1214	0.6	18
	1839	6.0	183		1810	5.6	171
15 Su	0137	0.2	6	**30** M	0102	0.5	15
	0714	5.6	171		0649	5.2	158
	1349	0.2	6		1314	0.5	15
	1939	6.0	183		1906	5.7	174
				31 Tu	0154	0.3	9
					0740	5.4	165
					1412	0.3	9
					1957	5.8	177

November

Day	Time	Height (ft)	Height (cm)	Day	Time	Height (ft)	Height (cm)
1 W	0245	0.1	3	**16** Th	0341	-0.3	-9
	0827	5.7	174		0927	6.0	183
	1508	0.2	6		1609	-0.2	-6
	2047	5.9	180		2147	5.6	171
2 Th	0333	0.0	0	**17** F	0424	-0.2	-6
	0913	5.9	180		1010	6.0	183
	1602	0.0	0		1655	-0.2	-6
	2135	5.9	180		2231	5.5	168
3 F	0421	-0.2	-6	**18** Sa ●	0506	-0.1	-3
	0957	6.2	189		1051	6.0	183
	1655	-0.1	-3		1740	-0.1	-3
	2222	5.9	180		2313	5.4	165
4 Sa	0508	-0.2	-6	**19** Su	0545	0.0	0
	1042	6.3	192		1130	5.9	180
	1748	-0.2	-6		1822	0.0	0
	2309	5.8	177		2353	5.2	158
5 Su ○	0555	-0.2	-6	**20** M	0622	0.1	3
	1128	6.4	195		1207	5.8	177
	1840	-0.2	-6		1902	0.1	3
	2358	5.7	174				
6 M	0644	-0.2	-6	**21** Tu	0033	5.1	155
	1216	6.4	195		0657	0.3	9
	1933	-0.2	-6		1242	5.7	174
					1942	0.2	6
7 Tu	0050	5.6	171	**22** W	0112	4.9	149
	0736	-0.1	-3		0731	0.3	9
	1308	6.3	192		1318	5.6	171
	2028	-0.1	-3		2022	0.3	9
8 W	0145	5.4	165	**23** Th	0152	4.8	146
	0830	0.0	0		0807	0.4	12
	1404	6.1	186		1354	5.5	168
	2124	0.0	0		2103	0.4	12
9 Th	0245	5.2	158	**24** F	0234	4.7	143
	0928	0.1	3		0848	0.4	12
	1506	5.9	180		1436	5.5	168
	2221	0.0	0		2147	0.4	12
10 F ○	0348	5.1	155	**25** Sa	0320	4.7	143
	1028	0.2	6		0937	0.5	15
	1611	5.8	177		1525	5.4	165
	2319	0.0	0		2234	0.4	12
11 Sa	0453	5.2	158	**26** Su ◑	0411	4.7	143
	1129	0.2	6		1033	0.5	15
	1717	5.7	174		1621	5.4	165
					2325	0.3	9
12 Su	0016	0.0	0	**27** M	0506	4.9	149
	0556	5.3	162		1135	0.4	12
	1230	0.2	6		1721	5.3	162
	1820	5.6	171				
13 M	0111	-0.1	-3	**28** Tu	0017	0.2	6
	0655	5.5	168		0602	5.0	152
	1330	0.1	3		1238	0.3	9
	1918	5.7	174		1821	5.4	165
14 Tu	0204	-0.2	-6	**29** W	0111	0.0	0
	0750	5.7	174		0657	5.3	162
	1426	-0.1	-3		1341	0.2	6
	2011	5.7	174		1919	5.4	165
15 W	0254	-0.3	-9	**30** Th	0205	-0.1	-3
	0840	5.9	180		0749	5.6	171
	1519	-0.1	-3		1442	0.0	0
	2100	5.7	174		2014	5.5	168

December

Day	Time	Height (ft)	Height (cm)	Day	Time	Height (ft)	Height (cm)
1 F	0258	-0.3	-9	**16** Sa	0353	-0.3	-9
	0840	5.9	180		0945	5.7	174
	1540	-0.2	-6		1631	-0.3	-9
	2107	5.5	168		2207	5.1	155
2 Sa	0350	-0.4	-12	**17** Su	0436	-0.3	-9
	0930	6.1	186		1027	5.7	174
	1636	-0.4	-12		1715	-0.3	-9
	2159	5.5	168		2250	5.0	152
3 Su ○	0442	-0.5	-15	**18** M ●	0516	-0.2	-6
	1020	6.3	192		1106	5.7	174
	1730	-0.5	-15		1757	-0.2	-6
	2250	5.5	168		2330	4.9	149
4 M	0534	-0.6	-18	**19** Tu	0554	-0.1	-3
	1110	6.3	192		1142	5.6	171
	1824	-0.5	-15		1838	-0.1	-3
	2342	5.4	165				
5 Tu	0626	-0.5	-15	**20** W	0009	4.8	146
	1201	6.3	192		0631	0.0	0
	1918	-0.5	-15		1217	5.5	168
					1917	0.0	0
6 W	0035	5.3	162	**21** Th	0045	4.7	143
	0719	-0.5	-15		0707	0.0	0
	1255	6.2	189		1251	5.5	168
	2011	-0.5	-15		1955	0.0	0
7 Th	0131	5.2	158	**22** F	0121	4.7	143
	0814	-0.4	-12		0743	0.1	3
	1351	6.0	183		1324	5.5	168
	2105	-0.4	-12		2033	0.1	3
8 F	0229	5.1	155	**23** Sa	0157	4.7	143
	0911	-0.3	-9		0822	0.1	3
	1450	5.7	174		1402	5.4	165
	2159	-0.4	-12		2112	0.1	3
9 Sa	0329	5.1	155	**24** Su	0237	4.7	143
	1009	-0.1	-3		0906	0.1	3
	1552	5.5	168		1446	5.4	165
	2253	-0.3	-9		2154	0.0	0
10 Su ○	0431	5.1	155	**25** M	0323	4.8	146
	1107	-0.1	-3		0959	0.2	6
	1654	5.4	165		1538	5.3	162
	2347	-0.3	-9		2240	0.0	0
11 M	0531	5.2	158	**26** Tu ◑	0416	4.9	149
	1207	0.0	0		1100	0.2	6
	1754	5.3	162		1638	5.2	158
					2333	-0.1	-3
12 Tu	0040	-0.3	-9	**27** W	0515	5.0	152
	0629	5.3	162		1207	0.2	6
	1305	-0.1	-3		1742	5.1	155
	1851	5.3	162				
13 W	0132	-0.3	-9	**28** Th	0030	-0.2	-6
	0723	5.5	168		0615	5.2	158
	1401	-0.1	-3		1314	0.1	3
	1945	5.2	158		1845	5.1	155
14 Th	0221	-0.4	-12	**29** F	0128	-0.3	-9
	0814	5.6	171		0715	5.5	168
	1454	-0.2	-6		1418	-0.1	-3
	2035	5.2	158		1946	5.1	155
15 F	0308	-0.4	-12	**30** Sa	0227	-0.4	-12
	0901	5.7	174		0812	5.7	174
	1544	-0.3	-9		1519	-0.3	-9
	2122	5.2	158		2044	5.2	158
				31 Su	0325	-0.5	-15
					0908	5.9	180
					1618	-0.5	-15
					2139	5.2	158

Time meridian 75° W. 0000 is midnight. 1200 is noon. Times are not adjusted for Daylight Saving Time.
Heights are referred to mean lower low water which is the chart datum of soundings.

Philadelphia, Pennsylvania, 2017
Times and Heights of High and Low Waters

January

Day	Time (h m)	Height (ft)	Height (cm)	Day	Time (h m)	Height (ft)	Height (cm)
1 Su	0325	5.1	155	**16** M	0412	5.5	168
	1003	-0.4	-12		1056	-0.7	-21
	1533	6.0	183		1633	5.9	180
	2244	-0.4	-12		2330	-0.7	-21
2 M	0406	5.1	155	**17** Tu	0503	5.4	165
	1048	-0.4	-12		1144	-0.6	-18
	1615	6.0	183		1723	5.7	174
	2328	-0.4	-12				
3 Tu	0449	5.2	158	**18** W	0016	-0.7	-21
	1136	-0.4	-12		0554	5.4	165
	1702	5.9	180		1234	-0.5	-15
					1816	5.5	168
4 W	0015	-0.5	-15	**19** Th ◗	0102	-0.6	-18
	0539	5.3	162		0645	5.4	165
	1230	-0.4	-12		1325	-0.4	-12
	1758	5.8	177		1909	5.3	162
5 Th ◖	0105	-0.5	-15	**20** F	0149	-0.6	-18
	0634	5.4	165		0738	5.4	165
	1329	-0.3	-9		1418	-0.4	-12
	1858	5.6	171		2003	5.2	158
6 F	0159	-0.5	-15	**21** Sa	0237	-0.5	-15
	0733	5.5	168		0830	5.5	168
	1432	-0.3	-9		1512	-0.4	-12
	2001	5.5	168		2056	5.1	155
7 Sa	0256	-0.5	-15	**22** Su	0327	-0.5	-15
	0833	5.7	174		0922	5.5	168
	1535	-0.3	-9		1606	-0.4	-12
	2102	5.5	168		2149	5.1	155
8 Su	0354	-0.5	-15	**23** M	0418	-0.5	-15
	0933	5.9	180		1013	5.6	171
	1638	-0.4	-12		1659	-0.4	-12
	2202	5.4	165		2240	5.1	155
9 M	0452	-0.6	-18	**24** Tu	0508	-0.6	-18
	1030	6.1	186		1102	5.8	177
	1737	-0.5	-15		1750	-0.5	-15
	2300	5.5	168		2329	5.1	155
10 Tu	0549	-0.7	-21	**25** W	0556	-0.6	-18
	1126	6.3	192		1148	5.9	180
	1835	-0.7	-21		1839	-0.5	-15
	2355	5.5	168				
11 W	0644	-0.8	-24	**26** Th	0015	5.2	158
	1220	6.4	195		0644	-0.6	-18
	1929	-0.8	-24		1232	5.9	180
					1925	-0.5	-15
12 Th ○	0049	5.6	171	**27** F ●	0058	5.2	158
	0737	-0.8	-24		0729	-0.6	-18
	1312	6.4	195		1313	6.0	183
	2021	-0.8	-24		2010	-0.5	-15
13 F	0141	5.6	171	**28** Sa	0140	5.2	158
	0828	-0.8	-24		0815	-0.6	-18
	1403	6.4	195		1353	6.0	183
	2110	-0.9	-27		2054	-0.5	-15
14 Sa	0232	5.5	168	**29** Su	0220	5.2	158
	0918	-0.8	-24		0900	-0.6	-18
	1453	6.2	189		1433	6.0	183
	2158	-0.8	-24		2137	-0.5	-15
15 Su	0322	5.5	168	**30** M	0300	5.3	162
	1007	-0.7	-21		0945	-0.6	-18
	1543	6.1	186		1514	6.0	183
	2245	-0.8	-24		2220	-0.6	-18
				31 Tu	0341	5.4	165
					1032	-0.6	-18
					1558	6.0	183
					2304	-0.6	-18

February

Day	Time (h m)	Height (ft)	Height (cm)	Day	Time (h m)	Height (ft)	Height (cm)
1 W	0425	5.5	168	**16** Th	0517	5.7	174
	1122	-0.6	-18		1202	-0.4	-12
	1646	5.9	180		1742	5.5	168
	2351	-0.6	-18				
2 Th	0514	5.6	171	**17** F	0021	-0.3	-9
	1216	-0.5	-15		0605	5.6	171
	1741	5.7	174		1250	-0.3	-9
					1833	5.4	165
3 F ◗	0041	-0.6	-18	**18** Sa ○	0106	-0.3	-9
	0609	5.6	171		0656	5.6	171
	1314	-0.4	-12		1340	-0.2	-6
	1840	5.5	168		1926	5.2	158
4 Sa	0135	-0.5	-15	**19** Su	0153	-0.2	-6
	0709	5.7	174		0748	5.6	171
	1415	-0.3	-9		1433	-0.1	-3
	1942	5.4	165		2020	5.2	158
5 Su	0232	-0.5	-15	**20** M	0244	-0.2	-6
	0811	5.8	177		0841	5.6	171
	1517	-0.3	-9		1528	-0.1	-3
	2044	5.3	162		2113	5.2	158
6 M	0332	-0.4	-12	**21** Tu	0337	-0.2	-6
	0912	5.9	180		0934	5.7	174
	1619	-0.3	-9		1623	-0.1	-3
	2145	5.3	162		2206	5.2	158
7 Tu	0432	-0.5	-15	**22** W	0430	-0.2	-6
	1012	6.0	183		1025	5.8	177
	1719	-0.5	-15		1715	-0.1	-3
	2244	5.4	165		2256	5.3	162
8 W	0530	-0.6	-18	**23** Th	0523	-0.3	-9
	1110	6.2	189		1114	6.0	183
	1815	-0.6	-18		1806	-0.2	-6
	2339	5.5	168		2343	5.4	165
9 Th	0626	-0.7	-21	**24** F	0614	-0.3	-9
	1204	6.3	192		1201	6.1	186
	1908	-0.7	-21		1854	-0.2	-6
10 F ○	0032	5.7	174	**25** Sa	0028	5.6	171
	0718	-0.7	-21		0703	-0.4	-12
	1255	6.3	192		1245	6.2	189
	1958	-0.7	-21		1941	-0.3	-9
11 Sa	0122	5.7	174	**26** Su	0111	5.7	174
	0809	-0.7	-21		0752	-0.5	-15
	1344	6.3	192		1328	6.3	192
	2046	-0.7	-21		2026 ●	-0.3	-9
12 Su	0210	5.8	177	**27** M	0152	5.9	180
	0857	-0.7	-21		0840	-0.5	-15
	1431	6.2	189		1410	6.3	192
	2131	-0.7	-21		2110	-0.3	-9
13 M	0257	5.8	177	**28** Tu	0234	6.0	183
	0944	-0.6	-18		0928	-0.5	-15
	1518	6.1	186		1454	6.3	192
	2214	-0.6	-18		2155	-0.3	-9
14 Tu	0343	5.8	177				
	1030	-0.5	-15				
	1605	5.9	180				
	2257	-0.5	-15				
15 W	0430	5.7	174				
	1115	-0.5	-15				
	1653	5.7	174				
	2339	-0.4	-12				

March

Day	Time (h m)	Height (ft)	Height (cm)	Day	Time (h m)	Height (ft)	Height (cm)
1 W	0316	6.1	186	**16** Th	0356	6.3	192
	1017	-0.5	-15		1047	0.0	0
	1541	6.2	189		1623	6.0	183
	2240	-0.3	-9		2301	0.2	6
2 Th	0402	6.2	189	**17** F	0440	6.2	189
	1109	-0.4	-12		1131	0.1	3
	1631	6.1	186		1709	5.8	177
	2328	-0.3	-9		2341	0.2	6
3 F	0453	6.2	189	**18** Sa	0525	6.2	189
	1202	-0.3	-9		1216	0.1	3
	1726	5.9	180		1758	5.7	174
4 Sa	0019	-0.2	-6	**19** Su	0023	0.3	9
	0549	6.2	189		0613	6.1	186
	1259	-0.2	-6		1304	0.2	6
	1825	5.7	174		1849	5.6	171
5 Su ◗	0114	-0.1	-3	**20** M ○	0109	0.3	9
	0649	6.2	189		0704	6.0	183
	1359	-0.1	-3		1355	0.3	9
	1927	5.6	171		1942	5.5	168
6 M	0213	-0.1	-3	**21** Tu	0200	0.4	12
	0752	6.1	186		0758	6.0	183
	1500	0.0	0		1449	0.4	12
	2029	5.6	171		2036	5.5	168
7 Tu	0313	0.0	0	**22** W	0256	0.4	12
	0855	6.2	189		0852	6.1	186
	1600	-0.1	-3		1544	0.4	12
	2130	5.7	174		2129	5.6	171
8 W	0413	-0.1	-3	**23** Th	0353	0.4	12
	0956	6.2	189		0946	6.2	189
	1658	-0.2	-6		1638	0.4	12
	2228	5.8	177		2220	5.8	177
9 Th	0511	-0.2	-6	**24** F	0450	0.3	9
	1053	6.3	192		1038	6.3	192
	1754	-0.3	-9		1731	0.3	9
	2323	6.0	183		2309	6.0	183
10 F	0607	-0.3	-9	**25** Sa	0545	0.2	6
	1147	6.4	195		1127	6.5	198
	1845	-0.3	-9		1821	0.2	6
					2355	6.3	192
11 Sa	0014	6.2	189	**26** Su	0637	0.1	3
	0659	-0.3	-9		1214	6.6	201
	1237	6.5	198		1909	0.2	6
	1933	-0.3	-9				
12 Su ○	0102	6.3	192	**27** M ●	0040	6.5	198
	0748	-0.3	-9		0729	0.0	0
	1324	6.5	198		1300	6.7	204
	2018	-0.3	-9		1956	0.1	3
13 M	0147	6.4	195	**28** Tu	0123	6.7	204
	0835	-0.3	-9		0820	-0.1	-3
	1409	6.4	195		1347	6.7	204
	2101	-0.2	-6		2042	0.1	3
14 Tu	0231	6.4	195	**29** W	0207	6.9	210
	0920	-0.2	-6		0910	-0.1	-3
	1453	6.3	192		1434	6.7	204
	2142	0.0	0		2129	0.1	3
15 W	0314	6.4	195	**30** Th	0253	7.0	213
	1004	-0.1	-3		1002	-0.1	-3
	1537	6.1	186		1523	6.6	201
	2222	0.1	3		2217	0.1	3
				31 F	0342	7.0	213
					1054	-0.1	-3
					1616	6.4	195
					2307	0.2	6

Time meridian 75° W. 0000 is midnight. 1200 is noon. Times are not adjusted for Daylight Saving Time.
Heights are referred to mean lower low water which is the chart datum of soundings.

Philadelphia, Pennsylvania, 2017

Times and Heights of High and Low Waters

April

Day	Time (h m)	ft	cm
1 Sa	0434	7.0	213
	1148	0.0	0
	1712	6.2	189
2 Su	0000	0.3	9
	0531	6.9	210
	1244	0.1	3
	1811	6.1	186
3 M	0055	0.4	12
	0632	6.7	204
	1341	0.2	6
	1912	6.1	186
4 Tu	0154	0.4	12
	0734	6.6	201
	1440	0.3	9
	2014	6.1	186
5 W	0254	0.4	12
	0837	6.5	198
	1538	0.2	6
	2114	6.2	189
6 Th	0353	0.4	12
	0937	6.6	201
	1634	0.2	6
	2211	6.4	195
7 F	0451	0.3	9
	1034	6.6	201
	1728	0.1	3
	2304	6.6	201
8 Sa	0546	0.2	6
	1126	6.7	204
	1818	0.1	3
	2353	6.8	207
9 Su	0638	0.1	3
	1215	6.7	204
	1905	0.1	3
10 M	0039	6.9	210
	0726	0.1	3
	1301	6.7	204
	1948	0.2	6
11 Tu	0122	7.0	213
	0812	0.2	6
	1345	6.6	201
	2030	0.4	12
12 W	0204	7.0	213
	0856	0.2	6
	1428	6.4	195
	2110	0.5	15
13 Th	0244	6.9	210
	0939	0.3	9
	1511	6.3	192
	2148	0.7	21
14 F	0324	6.9	210
	1021	0.4	12
	1554	6.2	189
	2226	0.7	21
15 Sa	0405	6.8	207
	1102	0.5	15
	1639	6.1	186
	2304	0.8	24
16 Su	0447	6.7	204
	1145	0.5	15
	1725	6.0	183
	2345	0.8	24
17 M	0532	6.6	201
	1230	0.6	18
	1814	5.9	180
18 Tu	0030	0.8	24
	0620	6.5	198
	1319	0.7	21
	1905	5.9	180
19 W	0121	0.8	24
	0714	6.5	198
	1411	0.7	21
	1958	5.9	180
20 Th	0218	0.8	24
	0810	6.5	198
	1505	0.7	21
	2051	6.1	186
21 F	0318	0.8	24
	0906	6.6	201
	1600	0.7	21
	2143	6.3	192
22 Sa	0418	0.7	21
	1000	6.7	204
	1654	0.6	18
	2233	6.6	201
23 Su	0516	0.6	18
	1052	6.8	207
	1746	0.5	15
	2322	6.9	210
24 M	0612	0.5	15
	1143	6.9	210
	1836	0.5	15
25 Tu	0009	7.2	219
	0707	0.3	9
	1233	6.9	210
	1926	0.4	12
26 W	0055	7.4	226
	0800	0.2	6
	1323	6.9	210
	2015	0.4	12
27 Th	0142	7.6	232
	0852	0.2	6
	1413	6.8	207
	2105	0.4	12
28 F	0231	7.6	232
	0945	0.1	3
	1505	6.7	204
	2155	0.5	15
29 Sa	0322	7.6	232
	1038	0.2	6
	1600	6.6	201
	2247	0.5	15
30 Su	0416	7.4	226
	1131	0.2	6
	1657	6.5	198
	2340	0.6	18

May

Day	Time (h m)	ft	cm
1 M	0514	7.2	219
	1226	0.3	9
	1756	6.4	195
2 Tu	0036	0.6	18
	0614	7.0	213
	1321	0.3	9
	1856	6.4	195
3 W	0134	0.7	21
	0715	6.9	210
	1417	0.3	9
	1956	6.5	198
4 Th	0232	0.7	21
	0816	6.8	207
	1512	0.3	9
	2054	6.6	201
5 F	0331	0.7	21
	0914	6.7	204
	1606	0.3	9
	2149	6.8	207
6 Sa	0428	0.6	18
	1009	6.7	204
	1658	0.3	9
	2240	7.0	213
7 Su	0522	0.5	15
	1101	6.7	204
	1747	0.3	9
	2329	7.2	219
8 M	0614	0.4	12
	1150	6.7	204
	1833	0.4	12
9 Tu	0014	7.3	223
	0702	0.4	12
	1236	6.6	201
	1917	0.5	15
10 W	0056	7.3	223
	0748	0.4	12
	1320	6.5	198
	1958	0.7	21
11 Th	0137	7.3	223
	0832	0.5	15
	1403	6.4	195
	2038	0.8	24
12 F	0216	7.2	219
	0914	0.5	15
	1445	6.3	192
	2117	0.9	27
13 Sa	0255	7.1	216
	0955	0.6	18
	1528	6.2	189
	2155	1.0	30
14 Su	0334	7.0	213
	1036	0.7	21
	1610	6.1	186
	2233	1.0	30
15 M	0413	7.0	213
	1118	0.7	21
	1654	6.0	183
	2314	1.0	30
16 Tu	0454	6.9	210
	1201	0.7	21
	1740	6.0	183
	2358	0.9	27
17 W	0539	6.8	207
	1246	0.7	21
	1829	6.1	186
18 Th	0049	0.9	27
	0631	6.8	207
	1335	0.7	21
	1920	6.2	189
19 F	0146	1.0	30
	0728	6.7	204
	1428	0.7	21
	2013	6.4	195
20 Sa	0247	1.0	30
	0826	6.7	204
	1522	0.7	21
	2106	6.6	201
21 Su	0349	0.9	27
	0924	6.7	204
	1617	0.6	18
	2158	6.9	210
22 M	0450	0.8	24
	1020	6.8	207
	1712	0.6	18
	2250	7.3	223
23 Tu	0548	0.6	18
	1114	6.8	207
	1805	0.5	15
	2340	7.5	229
24 W	0645	0.5	15
	1207	6.8	207
	1858	0.5	15
25 Th	0030	7.7	235
	0740	0.3	9
	1300	6.8	207
	1950	0.5	15
26 F	0120	7.8	238
	0834	0.2	6
	1353	6.7	204
	2042	0.5	15
27 Sa	0211	7.8	238
	0927	0.2	6
	1447	6.6	201
	2134	0.5	15
28 Su	0304	7.7	235
	1020	0.2	6
	1542	6.5	198
	2227	0.6	18
29 M	0359	7.5	229
	1112	0.2	6
	1639	6.5	198
	2321	0.6	18
30 Tu	0455	7.3	223
	1204	0.2	6
	1736	6.5	198
31 W	0015	0.6	18
	0553	7.1	216
	1257	0.2	6
	1834	6.5	198

June

Day	Time (h m)	ft	cm
1 Th	0111	0.7	21
	0652	6.9	210
	1349	0.2	6
	1932	6.6	201
2 F	0208	0.7	21
	0750	6.7	204
	1442	0.2	6
	2028	6.7	204
3 Sa	0304	0.7	21
	0846	6.6	201
	1533	0.2	6
	2121	6.9	210
4 Su	0401	0.6	18
	0941	6.5	198
	1624	0.3	9
	2212	7.1	216
5 M	0455	0.5	15
	1033	6.5	198
	1713	0.3	9
	2300	7.2	219
6 Tu	0546	0.5	15
	1122	6.5	198
	1759	0.4	12
	2346	7.3	223
7 W	0635	0.4	12
	1209	6.4	195
	1844	0.5	15
8 Th	0029	7.3	223
	0722	0.4	12
	1254	6.3	192
	1926	0.7	21
9 F	0110	7.2	219
	0806	0.5	15
	1338	6.2	189
	2008	0.8	24
10 Sa	0150	7.2	219
	0849	0.5	15
	1420	6.1	186
	2048	0.9	27
11 Su	0228	7.1	216
	0930	0.6	18
	1501	6.0	183
	2127	0.9	27
12 M	0306	7.0	213
	1011	0.6	18
	1542	5.9	180
	2207	0.9	27
13 Tu	0344	7.0	213
	1052	0.6	18
	1624	5.9	180
	2249	0.9	27
14 W	0422	6.9	210
	1133	0.5	15
	1707	6.0	183
	2334	0.8	24
15 Th	0505	6.8	207
	1217	0.5	15
	1753	6.1	186
16 F	0024	0.8	24
	0555	6.8	207
	1303	0.5	15
	1843	6.3	192
17 Sa	0120	0.9	27
	0652	6.7	204
	1354	0.4	12
	1936	6.5	198
18 Su	0221	0.9	27
	0752	6.6	201
	1448	0.5	15
	2032	6.7	204
19 M	0324	0.8	24
	0853	6.5	198
	1544	0.5	15
	2127	7.0	213
20 Tu	0426	0.7	21
	0952	6.5	198
	1641	0.4	12
	2221	7.3	223
21 W	0527	0.6	18
	1049	6.5	198
	1738	0.4	12
	2315	7.5	229
22 Th	0625	0.4	12
	1144	6.5	198
	1833	0.4	12
23 F	0007	7.7	235
	0721	0.3	9
	1239	6.5	198
	1928	0.4	12
24 Sa	0100	7.7	235
	0815	0.2	6
	1333	6.5	198
	2021	0.4	12
25 Su	0152	7.7	235
	0908	0.1	3
	1427	6.5	198
	2114	0.4	12
26 M	0245	7.6	232
	0959	0.0	0
	1522	6.4	195
	2207	0.4	12
27 Tu	0339	7.4	226
	1049	0.0	0
	1617	6.4	195
	2259	0.5	15
28 W	0434	7.1	216
	1139	0.0	0
	1712	6.4	195
	2352	0.5	15
29 Th	0529	6.9	210
	1228	0.0	0
	1807	6.5	198
30 F	0045	0.6	18
	0624	6.7	204
	1318	0.1	3
	1902	6.5	198

Time meridian 75° W. 0000 is midnight. 1200 is noon. Times are not adjusted for Daylight Saving Time.
Heights are referred to mean lower low water which is the chart datum of soundings.

Philadelphia, Pennsylvania, 2017

Times and Heights of High and Low Waters

July

Day	Time	Height (ft)	Height (cm)	Day	Time	Height (ft)	Height (cm)
1 Sa	0140	0.6	18	16 Su	0101	0.7	21
	0720	6.5	198		0625	6.5	198
	1407	0.1	3		1325	0.3	9
	1956	6.6	201	◗	1904	6.6	201
2 Su	0235	0.6	18	17 M	0201	0.8	24
	0815	6.3	192		0726	6.4	195
	1457	0.2	6		1420	0.3	9
	2048	6.8	207		2002	6.8	207
3 M	0330	0.6	18	18 Tu	0304	0.8	24
	0909	6.2	189		0828	6.3	192
	1547	0.2	6		1518	0.4	12
	2140	6.9	210		2100	7.0	213
4 Tu	0424	0.5	15	19 W	0407	0.7	21
	1002	6.2	189		0929	6.2	189
	1636	0.3	9		1617	0.4	12
	2229	7.0	213		2158	7.2	219
5 W	0516	0.4	12	20 Th	0508	0.5	15
	1052	6.2	189		1028	6.2	189
	1724	0.3	9		1716	0.3	9
	2316	7.1	216		2254	7.4	226
6 Th	0606	0.4	12	21 F	0606	0.4	12
	1141	6.1	186		1125	6.3	192
	1810	0.4	12		1813	0.3	9
					2349	7.5	229
7 F	0001	7.1	216	22 Sa	0702	0.2	6
	0653	0.4	12		1221	6.4	195
	1227	6.1	186		1908	0.3	9
	1855	0.5	15				
8 Sa	0043	7.1	216	23 Su	0043	7.6	232
	0738	0.4	12		0755	0.1	3
	1311	6.0	183		1315	6.4	195
O	1939	0.6	18	●	2002	0.2	6
9 Su	0124	7.0	213	24 M	0135	7.5	229
	0822	0.4	12		0846	0.0	0
	1354	5.9	180		1407	6.5	198
	2021	0.6	18		2054	0.3	9
10 M	0203	7.0	213	25 Tu	0226	7.4	226
	0904	0.4	12		0936	0.0	0
	1435	5.9	180		1500	6.5	198
	2103	0.7	21		2145	0.3	9
11 Tu	0241	6.9	210	26 W	0318	7.2	219
	0945	0.4	12		1023	0.0	0
	1514	5.9	180		1551	6.5	198
	2145	0.7	21		2236	0.4	12
12 W	0318	6.9	210	27 Th	0409	7.0	213
	1026	0.4	12		1110	0.0	0
	1554	5.9	180		1643	6.5	198
	2229	0.7	21		2326	0.5	15
13 Th	0357	6.8	207	28 F	0501	6.7	204
	1107	0.3	9		1156	0.1	3
	1635	6.1	186		1735	6.5	198
	2315	0.7	21				
14 F	0439	6.8	207	29 Sa	0017	0.5	15
	1150	0.3	9		0553	6.5	198
	1720	6.2	189		1243	0.1	3
					1827	6.5	198
15 Sa	0005	0.7	21	30 Su	0109	0.6	18
	0528	6.7	204		0647	6.3	192
	1235	0.3	9		1330	0.2	6
	1809	6.4	195	◖	1919	6.6	201
				31 M	0202	0.6	18
					0741	6.1	186
					1418	0.3	9
					2012	6.6	201

August

Day	Time	Height (ft)	Height (cm)	Day	Time	Height (ft)	Height (cm)
1 Tu	0256	0.6	18	16 W	0247	0.8	24
	0836	6.0	183		0810	6.2	189
	1508	0.3	9		1457	0.5	15
	2104	6.7	204		2039	7.0	213
2 W	0350	0.6	18	17 Th	0349	0.7	21
	0929	6.0	183		0912	6.1	186
	1558	0.4	12		1557	0.5	15
	2155	6.8	207		2140	7.1	216
3 Th	0443	0.5	15	18 F	0449	0.6	18
	1021	6.0	183		1012	6.2	189
	1648	0.4	12		1657	0.4	12
	2244	6.9	210		2238	7.3	223
4 F	0534	0.5	15	19 Sa	0547	0.4	12
	1111	6.0	183		1109	6.4	195
	1737	0.4	12		1755	0.3	9
	2331	7.0	213		2333	7.4	226
5 Sa	0622	0.4	12	20 Su	0642	0.2	6
	1158	6.0	183		1204	6.5	198
	1824	0.4	12		1850	0.3	9
6 Su	0015	7.0	213	21 M	0026	7.4	226
	0708	0.4	12		0733	0.1	3
	1243	6.1	186		1256	6.6	201
	1911	0.5	15	●	1943	0.3	9
7 M	0057	7.0	213	22 Tu	0117	7.4	226
	0753	0.4	12		0822	0.1	3
	1326	6.1	186		1346	6.7	204
O	1956	0.5	15		2034	0.3	9
8 Tu	0137	7.0	213	23 W	0206	7.3	223
	0835	0.4	12		0909	0.1	3
	1406	6.1	186		1435	6.7	204
	2040	0.5	15		2123	0.4	12
9 W	0216	7.0	213	24 Th	0254	7.1	216
	0917	0.4	12		0954	0.2	6
	1445	6.2	189		1523	6.7	204
	2125	0.6	18		2212	0.5	15
10 Th	0254	6.9	210	25 F	0342	6.9	210
	0959	0.3	9		1038	0.3	9
	1524	6.3	192		1611	6.7	204
	2210	0.6	18		2259	0.6	18
11 F	0335	6.9	210	26 Sa	0431	6.7	204
	1040	0.3	9		1122	0.3	9
	1605	6.4	195		1659	6.7	204
	2258	0.6	18		2347	0.7	21
12 Sa	0419	6.8	207	27 Su	0521	6.4	195
	1124	0.3	9		1205	0.4	12
	1650	6.5	198		1749	6.6	201
	2350	0.7	21				
13 Su	0509	6.6	201	28 M	0036	0.7	21
	1210	0.3	9		0613	6.2	189
	1740	6.7	204		1250	0.5	15
					1840	6.6	201
14 M	0045	0.7	21	29 Tu	0127	0.8	24
	0606	6.4	195		0707	6.1	186
	1301	0.3	9		1337	0.6	18
◖	1837	6.8	207	◖	1932	6.6	201
15 Tu	0145	0.8	24	30 W	0219	0.8	24
	0707	6.3	192		0801	6.0	183
	1357	0.4	12		1427	0.6	18
	1938	6.9	210		2025	6.7	204
				31 Th	0313	0.8	24
					0855	6.0	183
					1518	0.6	18
					2118	6.7	204

September

Day	Time	Height (ft)	Height (cm)	Day	Time	Height (ft)	Height (cm)
1 F	0406	0.7	21	16 Sa	0430	0.6	18
	0948	6.0	183		0957	6.4	195
	1611	0.6	18		1640	0.5	15
	2209	6.8	207		2223	7.2	219
2 Sa	0458	0.6	18	17 Su	0526	0.4	12
	1039	6.1	186		1054	6.6	201
	1703	0.6	18		1738	0.4	12
	2258	7.0	213		2318	7.3	223
3 Su	0548	0.6	18	18 M	0619	0.3	9
	1127	6.2	189		1147	6.8	207
	1754	0.5	15		1832	0.3	9
	2344	7.1	216				
4 M	0636	0.5	15	19 Tu	0009	7.3	223
	1212	6.3	192		0709	0.2	6
	1843	0.5	15		1237	6.9	210
					1924	0.3	9
5 Tu	0028	7.1	216	20 W	0058	7.3	223
	0721	0.5	15		0756	0.2	6
	1255	6.4	195		1324	7.0	213
	1930	0.5	15	●	2013	0.4	12
6 W	0109	7.1	216	21 Th	0144	7.2	219
	0805	0.4	12		0841	0.3	9
	1336	6.5	198		1410	7.0	213
O	2017	0.5	15		2101	0.5	15
7 Th	0150	7.1	216	22 F	0230	7.0	213
	0848	0.4	12		0923	0.4	12
	1415	6.6	201		1454	7.0	213
	2105	0.5	15		2147	0.6	18
8 F	0231	7.0	213	23 Sa	0315	6.8	207
	0931	0.4	12		1005	0.5	15
	1455	6.8	207		1539	6.9	210
	2153	0.6	18		2232	0.7	21
9 Sa	0314	6.9	210	24 Su	0402	6.6	201
	1014	0.4	12		1046	0.6	18
	1538	6.9	210		1624	6.8	207
	2243	0.6	18		2317	0.8	24
10 Su	0401	6.8	207	25 M	0450	6.3	192
	1100	0.4	12		1127	0.7	21
	1625	7.0	213		1710	6.8	207
	2335	0.7	21				
11 M	0453	6.6	201	26 Tu	0003	0.8	24
	1149	0.5	15		0540	6.2	189
	1718	7.0	213		1210	0.8	24
					1759	6.7	204
12 Tu	0031	0.8	24	27 W	0051	0.9	27
	0550	6.4	195		0632	6.0	183
	1242	0.5	15		1255	0.8	24
	1816	7.0	213	◗	1851	6.6	201
13 W	0129	0.8	24	28 Th	0142	0.9	27
	0652	6.2	189		0725	5.9	180
	1339	0.6	18		1345	0.8	24
◖	1919	7.0	213		1944	6.6	201
14 Th	0230	0.8	24	29 F	0234	0.9	27
	0755	6.2	189		0819	5.9	180
	1439	0.6	18		1439	0.8	24
	2022	7.0	213		2039	6.7	204
15 F	0331	0.7	21	30 Sa	0328	0.9	27
	0858	6.2	189		0913	6.0	183
	1540	0.6	18		1534	0.8	24
	2124	7.1	216		2132	6.8	207

Time meridian 75° W. 0000 is midnight. 1200 is noon. Times are not adjusted for Daylight Saving Time.
Heights are referred to mean lower low water which is the chart datum of soundings.

Philadelphia, Pennsylvania, 2017

Times and Heights of High and Low Waters

October

Day	Time (h m)	Height (ft)	Height (cm)
1 Su	0421	0.8	24
	1004	6.2	189
	1629	0.7	21
	2222	6.9	210
2 M	0512	0.6	18
	1053	6.4	195
	1723	0.6	18
	2310	7.0	213
3 Tu	0600	0.5	15
	1139	6.6	201
	1815	0.5	15
	2356	7.1	216
4 W	0647	0.5	15
	1222	6.8	207
	1905	0.5	15
5 Th ○	0040	7.1	216
	0733	0.4	12
	1304	7.0	213
	1955	0.4	12
6 F	0124	7.1	216
	0818	0.4	12
	1346	7.1	216
	2045	0.4	12
7 Sa	0208	7.0	213
	0903	0.4	12
	1429	7.2	219
	2135	0.5	15
8 Su	0254	6.9	210
	0950	0.4	12
	1514	7.3	223
	2227	0.5	15
9 M	0344	6.7	204
	1038	0.4	12
	1604	7.2	219
	2320	0.6	18
10 Tu	0438	6.5	198
	1129	0.5	15
	1659	7.2	219
11 W	0016	0.6	18
	0537	6.3	192
	1224	0.6	18
	1759	7.0	213
12 Th ☽	0113	0.6	18
	0638	6.2	189
	1322	0.6	18
	1903	6.9	210
13 F	0212	0.6	18
	0741	6.2	189
	1422	0.6	18
	2006	6.9	210
14 Sa	0310	0.5	15
	0843	6.3	192
	1523	0.6	18
	2108	6.9	210
15 Su	0407	0.4	12
	0942	6.5	198
	1622	0.5	15
	2206	7.0	213
16 M	0502	0.3	9
	1037	6.7	204
	1719	0.4	12
	2300	7.0	213
17 Tu	0554	0.1	3
	1129	6.9	210
	1813	0.3	9
	2350	7.0	213
18 W	0642	0.1	3
	1216	7.0	213
	1903	0.3	9
19 Th ●	0037	7.0	213
	0728	0.2	6
	1301	7.1	216
	1952	0.3	9
20 F	0122	6.8	207
	0811	0.3	9
	1344	7.1	216
	2037	0.4	12
21 Sa	0206	6.7	204
	0852	0.4	12
	1426	7.0	213
	2122	0.5	15
22 Su	0250	6.5	198
	0932	0.6	18
	1508	6.9	210
	2205	0.6	18
23 M	0334	6.3	192
	1012	0.7	21
	1550	6.8	207
	2248	0.7	21
24 Tu	0420	6.1	186
	1051	0.7	21
	1634	6.7	204
	2332	0.7	21
25 W	0507	5.9	180
	1132	0.7	21
	1720	6.6	201
26 Th	0017	0.7	21
	0556	5.8	177
	1216	0.7	21
	1809	6.5	198
27 F ◐	0105	0.7	21
	0648	5.7	174
	1305	0.7	21
	1902	6.5	198
28 Sa	0155	0.7	21
	0741	5.7	174
	1359	0.7	21
	1957	6.4	195
29 Su	0248	0.7	21
	0834	5.9	180
	1457	0.7	21
	2051	6.5	198
30 M	0341	0.6	18
	0926	6.0	183
	1555	0.6	18
	2144	6.6	201
31 Tu	0433	0.5	15
	1016	6.3	192
	1652	0.5	15
	2235	6.7	204

November

Day	Time (h m)	Height (ft)	Height (cm)
1 W	0524	0.3	9
	1104	6.6	201
	1747	0.4	12
	2323	6.8	207
2 Th	0613	0.2	6
	1149	6.8	207
	1841	0.3	9
3 F	0011	6.8	207
	0701	0.2	6
	1234	7.1	216
	1934	0.2	6
4 Sa ○	0058	6.7	204
	0749	0.1	3
	1319	7.2	219
	2026	0.1	3
5 Su	0145	6.7	204
	0838	0.1	3
	1405	7.3	223
	2118	0.1	3
6 M	0235	6.5	198
	0927	0.1	3
	1454	7.3	223
	2210	0.1	3
7 Tu	0327	6.3	192
	1018	0.2	6
	1547	7.2	219
	2304	0.2	6
8 W	0423	6.2	189
	1111	0.2	6
	1643	7.0	213
	2358	0.2	6
9 Th	0521	6.0	183
	1206	0.2	6
	1743	6.8	207
10 F ☽	0054	0.2	6
	0622	6.0	183
	1304	0.3	9
	1845	6.7	204
11 Sa	0150	0.2	6
	0724	6.0	183
	1403	0.3	9
	1947	6.5	198
12 Su	0246	0.1	3
	0824	6.1	186
	1503	0.3	9
	2047	6.5	198
13 M	0341	0.0	0
	0922	6.3	192
	1601	0.2	6
	2144	6.5	198
14 Tu	0435	-0.1	-3
	1016	6.5	198
	1658	0.1	3
	2238	6.5	198
15 W	0525	-0.2	-6
	1106	6.7	204
	1751	0.0	0
	2327	6.5	198
16 Th	0613	-0.2	-6
	1153	6.8	207
	1841	-0.1	-3
17 F	0014	6.4	195
	0658	-0.1	-3
	1237	6.8	207
	1929	0.0	0
18 Sa ●	0059	6.3	192
	0741	0.0	0
	1319	6.8	207
	2014	0.0	0
19 Su	0143	6.1	186
	0822	0.1	3
	1400	6.7	204
	2057	0.1	3
20 M	0226	5.9	180
	0902	0.3	9
	1440	6.6	201
	2139	0.2	6
21 Tu	0308	5.8	177
	0941	0.3	9
	1520	6.5	198
	2221	0.3	9
22 W	0351	5.6	171
	1019	0.3	9
	1601	6.4	195
	2302	0.3	9
23 Th	0435	5.5	168
	1059	0.3	9
	1644	6.3	192
	2345	0.3	9
24 F	0521	5.4	165
	1142	0.3	9
	1730	6.2	189
25 Sa	0029	0.3	9
	0609	5.4	165
	1229	0.3	9
	1820	6.1	186
26 Su ◑	0117	0.2	6
	0700	5.4	165
	1323	0.3	9
	1913	6.1	186
27 M	0207	0.2	6
	0752	5.5	168
	1422	0.3	9
	2009	6.0	183
28 Tu	0300	0.1	3
	0845	5.7	174
	1522	0.3	9
	2105	6.1	186
29 W	0354	0.0	0
	0937	6.0	183
	1623	0.2	6
	2159	6.1	186
30 Th	0447	-0.1	-3
	1028	6.3	192
	1721	0.0	0
	2252	6.2	189

December

Day	Time (h m)	Height (ft)	Height (cm)
1 F	0540	-0.2	-6
	1117	6.6	201
	1818	-0.1	-3
	2343	6.2	189
2 Sa	0632	-0.3	-9
	1206	6.9	210
	1913	-0.2	-6
3 Su ○	0034	6.2	189
	0724	-0.3	-9
	1255	7.0	213
	2007	-0.3	-9
4 M	0125	6.1	186
	0815	-0.4	-12
	1345	7.0	213
	2100	-0.4	-12
5 Tu	0217	6.0	183
	0907	-0.4	-12
	1437	7.0	213
	2152	-0.4	-12
6 W	0310	5.9	180
	0959	-0.4	-12
	1530	6.8	207
	2245	-0.4	-12
7 Th	0406	5.8	177
	1053	-0.3	-9
	1627	6.6	201
	2338	-0.4	-12
8 F	0503	5.7	174
	1147	-0.3	-9
	1725	6.4	195
9 Sa	0030	-0.4	-12
	0602	5.7	174
	1243	-0.2	-6
	1824	6.2	189
10 Su ☽	0124	-0.4	-12
	0701	5.7	174
	1341	-0.2	-6
	1924	6.0	183
11 M	0217	-0.5	-15
	0759	5.8	177
	1439	-0.2	-6
	2022	5.9	180
12 Tu	0311	-0.5	-15
	0856	5.9	180
	1536	-0.2	-6
	2118	5.8	177
13 W	0403	-0.5	-15
	0949	6.1	186
	1632	-0.3	-9
	2211	5.8	177
14 Th	0454	-0.6	-18
	1040	6.2	189
	1726	-0.4	-12
	2302	5.8	177
15 F	0542	-0.5	-15
	1127	6.3	192
	1816	-0.4	-12
	2350	5.7	174
16 Sa	0628	-0.5	-15
	1212	6.3	192
	1904	-0.4	-12
17 Su	0036	5.6	171
	0712	-0.4	-12
	1255	6.3	192
	1949	-0.4	-12
18 M ●	0120	5.5	168
	0753	-0.3	-9
	1336	6.3	192
	2032	-0.3	-9
19 Tu	0202	5.4	165
	0834	-0.2	-6
	1416	6.2	189
	2114	-0.3	-9
20 W	0244	5.3	162
	0914	-0.2	-6
	1455	6.1	186
	2154	-0.2	-6
21 Th	0324	5.2	158
	0953	-0.2	-6
	1534	6.0	183
	2234	-0.2	-6
22 F	0405	5.1	155
	1033	-0.2	-6
	1613	5.9	180
	2315	-0.2	-6
23 Sa	0447	5.1	155
	1115	-0.2	-6
	1654	5.9	180
	2356	-0.3	-9
24 Su	0530	5.1	155
	1201	-0.2	-6
	1740	5.8	177
25 M ○	0040	-0.3	-9
	0617	5.2	158
	1253	-0.2	-6
	1832	5.7	174
26 Tu ◑	0128	-0.3	-9
	0709	5.3	162
	1351	-0.1	-3
	1929	5.6	171
27 W	0221	-0.4	-12
	0804	5.5	168
	1453	-0.1	-3
	2028	5.5	168
28 Th	0317	-0.4	-12
	0859	5.7	174
	1556	-0.2	-6
	2126	5.5	168
29 F	0414	-0.4	-12
	0955	6.0	183
	1657	-0.3	-9
	2223	5.6	171
30 Sa	0511	-0.5	-15
	1049	6.3	192
	1757	-0.4	-12
	2318	5.6	171
31 Su	0607	-0.6	-18
	1142	6.5	198
	1853	-0.6	-18

Time meridian 75° W. 0000 is midnight. 1200 is noon. Times are not adjusted for Daylight Saving Time.
Heights are referred to mean lower low water which is the chart datum of soundings.

Ocean City, Maryland, 2017

Times and Heights of High and Low Waters

January

Day	Time	ft	cm
1 Su	0259	-0.1	-3
	0924	4.0	122
	1546	0.0	0
	2142	3.0	91
2 M	0344	-0.1	-3
	1006	3.9	119
	1631	0.0	0
	2228	3.1	94
3 Tu	0434	0.0	0
	1051	3.7	113
	1719	0.0	0
	2317	3.1	94
4 W	0529	0.1	3
	1139	3.6	110
	1809	0.0	0
5 Th	0012	3.2	98
	0629	0.1	3
	1233	3.4	104
	1901	-0.1	-3
6 F	0113	3.3	101
	0732	0.1	3
	1333	3.2	98
	1956	-0.2	-6
7 Sa	0216	3.5	107
	0837	0.1	3
	1436	3.1	94
	2053	-0.4	-12
8 Su	0319	3.8	116
	0942	-0.1	-3
	1537	3.1	94
	2151	-0.5	-15
9 M	0418	4.0	122
	1046	-0.3	-9
	1636	3.1	94
	2248	-0.7	-21
10 Tu	0515	4.3	131
	1145	-0.5	-15
	1732	3.1	94
	2344	-0.9	-27
11 W	0609	4.4	134
	1240	-0.6	-18
	1827	3.2	98
12 Th	0037	-1.0	-30
	0702	4.4	134
	1331	-0.7	-21
	1920	3.2	98
13 F	0128	-1.0	-30
	0753	4.4	134
	1419	-0.7	-21
	2011	3.2	98
14 Sa	0218	-0.9	-27
	0841	4.2	128
	1506	-0.6	-18
	2100	3.2	98
15 Su	0308	-0.8	-24
	0928	4.0	122
	1553	-0.5	-15
	2149	3.1	94
16 M	0358	-0.5	-15
	1014	3.7	113
	1640	-0.3	-9
	2237	3.0	91
17 Tu	0449	-0.2	-6
	1059	3.4	104
	1727	-0.2	-6
	2325	2.9	88
18 W	0542	0.0	0
	1145	3.1	94
	1813	0.0	0
19 Th	0017	2.9	88
	0636	0.3	9
	1235	2.8	85
	1900	0.1	3
20 F	0112	2.8	85
	0732	0.4	12
	1328	2.6	79
	1947	0.2	6
21 Sa	0210	2.9	88
	0830	0.5	15
	1424	2.5	76
	2036	0.3	9
22 Su	0306	3.0	91
	0927	0.5	15
	1518	2.5	76
	2126	0.2	6
23 M	0358	3.2	98
	1022	0.5	15
	1609	2.5	76
	2216	0.1	3
24 Tu	0446	3.4	104
	1112	0.4	12
	1657	2.6	79
	2303	0.0	0
25 W	0531	3.6	110
	1156	0.2	6
	1742	2.8	85
	2348	-0.2	-6
26 Th	0614	3.8	116
	1237	0.1	3
	1826	2.9	88
27 F	0032	-0.3	-9
	0656	3.9	119
	1317	-0.1	-3
	1909	3.1	94
28 Sa	0114	-0.4	-12
	0738	4.0	122
	1357	-0.2	-6
	1953	3.2	98
29 Su	0157	-0.5	-15
	0820	4.1	125
	1438	-0.3	-9
	2036	3.3	101
30 M	0241	-0.5	-15
	0902	4.0	122
	1520	-0.3	-9
	2120	3.4	104
31 Tu	0328	-0.4	-12
	0944	3.9	119
	1604	-0.3	-9
	2206	3.4	104

February

Day	Time	ft	cm
1 W	0418	-0.3	-9
	1029	3.7	113
	1651	-0.3	-9
	2255	3.5	107
2 Th	0513	-0.2	-6
	1117	3.5	107
	1741	-0.3	-9
	2349	3.5	107
3 F	0612	-0.1	-3
	1211	3.2	98
	1834	-0.2	-6
4 Sa	0049	3.5	107
	0715	0.0	0
	1310	3.0	91
	1931	-0.3	-9
5 Su	0154	3.6	110
	0821	0.0	0
	1415	2.8	85
	2031	-0.3	-9
6 M	0301	3.7	113
	0928	0.0	0
	1520	2.8	85
	2133	-0.4	-12
7 Tu	0404	3.8	116
	1033	-0.2	-6
	1622	2.9	88
	2234	-0.6	-18
8 W	0502	4.0	122
	1133	-0.3	-9
	1719	3.0	91
	2331	-0.7	-21
9 Th	0557	4.1	125
	1225	-0.5	-15
	1812	3.1	94
10 F	0025	-0.9	-27
	0647	4.1	125
	1313	-0.6	-18
	1903	3.2	98
11 Sa	0114	-0.9	-27
	0735	4.1	125
	1357	-0.6	-18
	1950	3.3	101
12 Su	0201	-0.9	-27
	0820	4.0	122
	1439	-0.6	-18
	2036	3.3	101
13 M	0247	-0.7	-21
	0902	3.8	116
	1520	-0.4	-12
	2120	3.3	101
14 Tu	0332	-0.5	-15
	0944	3.5	107
	1601	-0.3	-9
	2204	3.2	98
15 W	0418	-0.2	-6
	1025	3.3	101
	1643	-0.1	-3
	2248	3.2	98
16 Th	0506	0.0	0
	1108	3.0	91
	1726	0.1	3
	2334	3.1	94
17 F	0556	0.3	9
	1153	2.7	82
	1811	0.2	6
18 Sa	0024	3.0	91
	0649	0.5	15
	1243	2.6	79
	1859	0.4	12
19 Su	0120	2.9	88
	0744	0.6	18
	1338	2.4	73
	1950	0.4	12
20 M	0219	3.0	91
	0841	0.7	21
	1437	2.4	73
	2044	0.4	12
21 Tu	0317	3.1	94
	0938	0.6	18
	1533	2.5	76
	2138	0.3	9
22 W	0410	3.3	101
	1032	0.5	15
	1624	2.7	82
	2230	0.1	3
23 Th	0459	3.5	107
	1120	0.3	9
	1712	2.9	88
	2320	-0.1	-3
24 F	0544	3.8	116
	1205	0.1	3
	1758	3.2	98
25 Sa	0007	-0.3	-9
	0628	4.0	122
	1247	-0.1	-3
	1843	3.4	104
26 Su	0052	-0.5	-15
	0712	4.1	125
	1328	-0.3	-9
	1927	3.6	110
27 M	0138	-0.6	-18
	0755	4.1	125
	1409	-0.4	-12
	2012	3.8	116
28 Tu	0224	-0.6	-18
	0839	4.1	125
	1452	-0.5	-15
	2058	3.9	119

March

Day	Time	ft	cm
1 W	0312	-0.6	-18
	0923	3.9	119
	1537	-0.5	-15
	2146	3.9	119
2 Th	0403	-0.5	-15
	1010	3.7	113
	1624	-0.4	-12
	2236	3.9	119
3 F	0459	-0.3	-9
	1059	3.4	104
	1716	-0.3	-9
	2330	3.8	116
4 Sa	0558	-0.1	-3
	1153	3.2	98
	1812	-0.2	-6
5 Su	0029	3.7	113
	0701	0.0	0
	1254	2.9	88
	1911	-0.1	-3
6 M	0136	3.6	110
	0807	0.1	3
	1401	2.8	85
	2015	-0.1	-3
7 Tu	0245	3.6	110
	0915	0.1	3
	1509	2.8	85
	2119	-0.2	-6
8 W	0351	3.7	113
	1020	0.0	0
	1612	2.9	88
	2223	-0.3	-9
9 Th	0450	3.8	116
	1117	-0.1	-3
	1708	3.1	94
	2321	-0.5	-15
10 F	0542	3.8	116
	1207	-0.3	-9
	1758	3.2	98
11 Sa	0013	-0.6	-18
	0629	3.8	116
	1250	-0.4	-12
	1844	3.4	104
12 Su	0100	-0.6	-18
	0713	3.8	116
	1330	-0.4	-12
	1928	3.5	107
13 M	0143	-0.6	-18
	0754	3.7	113
	1408	-0.4	-12
	2010	3.6	110
14 Tu	0225	-0.5	-15
	0834	3.6	110
	1445	-0.3	-9
	2051	3.6	110
15 W	0307	-0.3	-9
	0914	3.4	104
	1522	-0.1	-3
	2131	3.6	110
16 Th	0349	-0.1	-3
	0953	3.2	98
	1601	0.1	3
	2212	3.5	107
17 F	0433	0.1	3
	1034	3.0	91
	1642	0.3	9
	2256	3.4	104
18 Sa	0520	0.4	12
	1117	2.8	85
	1727	0.4	12
	2342	3.2	98
19 Su	0610	0.6	18
	1204	2.7	82
	1815	0.6	18
20 M	0035	3.1	94
	0703	0.7	21
	1258	2.6	79
	1908	0.6	18
21 Tu	0133	3.1	94
	0758	0.8	24
	1356	2.6	79
	2003	0.6	18
22 W	0233	3.2	98
	0854	0.7	21
	1455	2.7	82
	2100	0.5	15
23 Th	0330	3.4	104
	0949	0.6	18
	1550	2.9	88
	2157	0.3	9
24 F	0422	3.6	110
	1040	0.4	12
	1640	3.2	98
	2250	0.1	3
25 Sa	0510	3.8	116
	1128	0.1	3
	1728	3.5	107
	2341	-0.2	-6
26 Su	0556	4.0	122
	1212	-0.1	-3
	1815	3.8	116
27 M	0030	-0.5	-15
	0642	4.1	125
	1256	-0.3	-9
	1901	4.1	125
28 Tu	0118	-0.6	-18
	0728	4.1	125
	1340	-0.5	-15
	1949	4.3	131
29 W	0207	-0.7	-21
	0815	4.1	125
	1424	-0.6	-18
	2037	4.5	137
30 Th	0257	-0.7	-21
	0903	3.9	119
	1511	-0.5	-15
	2126	4.5	137
31 F	0350	-0.5	-15
	0952	3.7	113
	1601	-0.4	-12
	2218	4.4	134

Time meridian 75° W. 0000 is midnight. 1200 is noon. Times are not adjusted for Daylight Saving Time.
Heights are referred to mean lower low water which is the chart datum of soundings.

Ocean City, Maryland, 2017

Times and Heights of High and Low Waters

April

Day	Time	ft	cm	Day	Time	ft	cm
1 Sa	0446	-0.4	-12	16 Su	0449	0.4	12
	1043	3.4	104		1046	2.9	88
	1655	-0.3	-9		1648	0.6	18
	2312	4.2	128		2308	3.5	107
2 Su	0546	-0.1	-3	17 M	0537	0.6	18
	1139	3.2	98		1131	2.8	85
	1753	-0.1	-3		1737	0.7	21
					2356	3.4	104
3 M	0012	3.9	119	18 Tu	0627	0.7	21
	0649	0.0	0		1222	2.7	82
	1241	3.0	91		1830	0.7	21
	1856	0.0	0				
4 Tu	0119	3.7	113	19 W	0051	3.3	101
	0754	0.1	3		0720	0.8	24
	1350	2.9	88		1319	2.8	85
	2001	0.1	3		1926	0.7	21
5 W	0229	3.6	110	20 Th	0149	3.4	104
	0859	0.2	6		0814	0.7	21
	1459	2.9	88		1419	2.9	88
	2107	0.1	3		2024	0.6	18
6 Th	0335	3.6	110	21 F	0247	3.5	107
	1000	0.1	3		0907	0.6	18
	1602	3.1	94		1515	3.2	98
	2211	0.0	0		2123	0.4	12
7 F	0433	3.6	110	22 Sa	0342	3.6	110
	1055	0.0	0		0959	0.3	9
	1654	3.3	101		1608	3.5	107
	2309	-0.1	-3		2220	0.2	6
8 Sa	0522	3.6	110	23 Su	0434	3.8	116
	1141	-0.1	-3		1049	0.1	3
	1740	3.4	104		1658	3.9	119
	2359	-0.2	-6		2315	-0.1	-3
9 Su	0606	3.6	110	24 M	0523	3.9	119
	1221	-0.1	-3		1137	-0.2	-6
	1822	3.6	110		1747	4.3	131
10 M	0043	-0.3	-9	25 Tu	0008	-0.4	-12
	0646	3.5	107		0612	4.0	122
	1258	-0.1	-3		1224	-0.4	-12
	1903	3.8	116		1836	4.6	140
11 Tu	0124	-0.3	-9	26 W	0100	-0.6	-18
	0726	3.5	107		0702	4.0	122
	1334	-0.1	-3		1311	-0.6	-18
	1942	3.8	116		1926	4.8	146
12 W	0203	-0.2	-6	27 Th	0151	-0.7	-21
	0805	3.4	104		0752	4.0	122
	1410	0.0	0		1359	-0.6	-18
	2021	3.9	119		2017	4.8	146
13 Th	0243	-0.1	-3	28 F	0242	-0.7	-21
	0844	3.3	101		0843	3.8	116
	1446	0.1	3		1448	-0.6	-18
	2101	3.8	116		2108	4.8	146
14 F	0323	0.0	0	29 Sa	0336	-0.6	-18
	0923	3.2	98		0935	3.6	110
	1524	0.2	6		1540	-0.5	-15
	2141	3.8	116		2201	4.6	140
15 Sa	0404	0.2	6	30 Su	0433	-0.4	-12
	1004	3.0	91		1028	3.4	104
	1604	0.4	12		1636	-0.3	-9
	2223	3.6	110		2256	4.4	134

May

Day	Time	ft	cm	Day	Time	ft	cm
1 M	0532	-0.2	-6	16 Tu	0508	0.6	18
	1125	3.2	98		1103	2.9	88
	1736	-0.1	-3		1704	0.7	21
	2355	4.0	122		2324	3.6	110
2 Tu	0634	0.0	0	17 W	0556	0.6	18
	1227	3.0	91		1152	2.9	88
	1840	0.1	3		1757	0.7	21
3 W	0059	3.8	116	18 Th	0014	3.5	107
	0735	0.1	3		0645	0.6	18
	1335	3.0	91		1245	2.9	88
	1946	0.2	6		1853	0.7	21
4 Th	0206	3.5	107	19 F	0108	3.5	107
	0836	0.2	6		0736	0.5	15
	1444	3.1	94		1343	3.1	94
	2052	0.3	9		1952	0.6	18
5 F	0310	3.4	104	20 Sa	0206	3.5	107
	0932	0.2	6		0828	0.4	12
	1544	3.2	98		1441	3.4	104
	2155	0.2	6		2052	0.4	12
6 Sa	0406	3.3	101	21 Su	0303	3.6	110
	1023	0.1	3		0920	0.2	6
	1634	3.4	104		1537	3.8	116
	2252	0.2	6		2152	0.2	6
7 Su	0454	3.3	101	22 M	0358	3.7	113
	1107	0.1	3		1012	0.0	0
	1717	3.6	110		1630	4.2	128
	2341	0.1	3		2251	-0.1	-3
8 M	0536	3.3	101	23 Tu	0452	3.7	113
	1147	0.1	3		1104	-0.3	-9
	1757	3.7	113		1721	4.5	137
					2347	-0.3	-9
9 Tu	0024	0.0	0	24 W	0544	3.8	116
	0616	3.2	98		1155	-0.5	-15
	1224	0.0	0		1813	4.8	146
	1836	3.9	119				
10 W	0103	0.0	0	25 Th	0042	-0.6	-18
	0656	3.2	98		0637	3.8	116
	1301	0.0	0		1245	-0.7	-21
	1915	4.0	122		1906	5.0	152
11 Th	0141	0.0	0	26 F	0135	-0.7	-21
	0736	3.2	98		0730	3.8	116
	1337	0.1	3		1336	-0.7	-21
	1954	4.0	122		1958	5.0	152
12 F	0219	0.1	3	27 Sa	0228	-0.7	-21
	0816	3.2	98		0824	3.7	113
	1414	0.2	6		1428	-0.7	-21
	2034	4.0	122		2052	4.9	149
13 Sa	0258	0.2	6	28 Su	0322	-0.6	-18
	0856	3.1	94		0918	3.5	107
	1452	0.3	9		1522	-0.5	-15
	2115	3.9	119		2145	4.7	143
14 Su	0339	0.3	9	29 M	0417	-0.4	-12
	0937	3.0	91		1012	3.4	104
	1533	0.4	12		1618	-0.3	-9
	2156	3.8	116		2239	4.4	134
15 M	0422	0.4	12	30 Tu	0514	-0.3	-9
	1019	2.9	88		1109	3.3	101
	1616	0.6	18		1718	-0.1	-3
	2238	3.7	113		2335	4.0	122
				31 W	0612	-0.1	-3
					1209	3.2	98
					1821	0.1	3

June

Day	Time	ft	cm	Day	Time	ft	cm
1 Th	0033	3.7	113	16 F	0612	0.4	12
	0709	0.0	0		1215	3.2	98
	1312	3.1	94		1825	0.6	18
	1925	0.3	9				
2 F	0135	3.4	104	17 Sa	0033	3.6	110
	0804	0.1	3		0702	0.3	9
	1417	3.2	98		1311	3.4	104
	2028	0.4	12		1924	0.5	15
3 Sa	0235	3.2	98	18 Su	0130	3.5	107
	0856	0.2	6		0753	0.2	6
	1516	3.3	101		1410	3.6	110
	2130	0.4	12		2025	0.4	12
4 Su	0331	3.1	94	19 M	0229	3.5	107
	0944	0.2	6		0846	0.1	3
	1606	3.4	104		1508	3.9	119
	2228	0.4	12		2128	0.2	6
5 M	0419	3.0	91	20 Tu	0327	3.5	107
	1029	0.2	6		0940	-0.1	-3
	1649	3.6	110		1605	4.3	131
	2318	0.3	9		2230	0.0	0
6 Tu	0503	3.0	91	21 W	0425	3.5	107
	1111	0.2	6		1036	-0.4	-12
	1730	3.8	116		1700	4.6	140
					2329	-0.2	-6
7 W	0001	0.3	9	22 Th	0520	3.5	107
	0544	3.0	91		1130	-0.6	-18
	1150	0.2	6		1754	4.8	146
	1809	3.9	119				
8 Th	0040	0.2	6	23 F	0025	-0.4	-12
	0626	3.0	91		0616	3.6	110
	1229	0.1	3		1224	-0.7	-21
	1849	4.0	122		1848	4.9	149
9 F	0118	0.2	6	24 Sa	0119	-0.6	-18
	0707	3.0	91		0710	3.6	110
	1308	0.1	3		1317	-0.8	-24
	1930	4.1	125		1942	5.0	152
10 Sa	0156	0.2	6	25 Su	0212	-0.6	-18
	0749	3.1	94		0805	3.6	110
	1346	0.2	6		1410	-0.7	-21
	2010	4.1	125		2035	4.8	146
11 Su	0235	0.2	6	26 M	0304	-0.6	-18
	0830	3.1	94		0859	3.5	107
	1426	0.2	6		1504	-0.6	-18
	2051	4.0	122		2127	4.6	140
12 M	0315	0.3	9	27 Tu	0356	-0.4	-12
	0912	3.0	91		0953	3.5	107
	1506	0.3	9		1559	-0.4	-12
	2131	4.0	122		2218	4.3	131
13 Tu	0356	0.4	12	28 W	0449	-0.3	-9
	0953	3.0	91		1047	3.4	104
	1550	0.4	12		1657	-0.1	-3
	2212	3.9	119		2310	3.9	119
14 W	0440	0.4	12	29 Th	0542	-0.1	-3
	1037	3.0	91		1142	3.3	101
	1637	0.5	15		1756	0.1	3
	2255	3.8	116				
15 Th	0525	0.4	12	30 F	0002	3.6	110
	1123	3.1	94		0634	0.0	0
	1729	0.6	18		1239	3.2	98
	2342	3.7	113		1856	0.4	12

Time meridian 75° W. 0000 is midnight. 1200 is noon. Times are not adjusted for Daylight Saving Time.
Heights are referred to mean lower low water which is the chart datum of soundings.

Ocean City, Maryland, 2017

Times and Heights of High and Low Waters

July

Day	Time (h m)	Height (ft)	Height (cm)
1 Sa	0057	3.2	98
	0725	0.2	6
	1339	3.2	98
	1957	0.5	15
2 Su	0153	3.0	91
	0813	0.3	9
	1437	3.3	101
	2057	0.6	18
3 M	0249	2.9	88
	0901	0.3	9
	1530	3.4	104
	2155	0.6	18
4 Tu	0341	2.8	85
	0948	0.4	12
	1617	3.6	110
	2247	0.6	18
5 W	0428	2.8	85
	1034	0.3	9
	1700	3.7	113
	2333	0.5	15
6 Th	0513	2.9	88
	1118	0.3	9
	1742	3.9	119
7 F	0014	0.4	12
	0556	3.0	91
	1200	0.2	6
	1824	4.0	122
8 Sa ○	0053	0.3	9
	0639	3.0	91
	1241	0.2	6
	1905	4.1	125
9 Su	0131	0.3	9
	0722	3.1	94
	1322	0.1	3
	1946	4.1	125
10 M	0209	0.2	6
	0804	3.2	98
	1402	0.2	6
	2027	4.2	128
11 Tu	0248	0.2	6
	0846	3.2	98
	1444	0.2	6
	2107	4.1	125
12 W	0328	0.3	9
	0928	3.3	101
	1527	0.3	9
	2147	4.0	122
13 Th	0410	0.3	9
	1011	3.3	101
	1614	0.4	12
	2229	3.9	119
14 F	0454	0.3	9
	1057	3.4	104
	1706	0.4	12
	2314	3.8	116
15 Sa	0541	0.3	9
	1147	3.5	107
	1802	0.5	15
16 Su ◐	0004	3.6	110
	0630	0.2	6
	1242	3.6	110
	1902	0.5	15
17 M	0100	3.4	104
	0722	0.1	3
	1342	3.8	116
	2004	0.4	12
18 Tu	0201	3.3	101
	0817	0.0	0
	1444	4.1	125
	2108	0.3	9
19 W	0303	3.3	101
	0915	-0.1	-3
	1544	4.3	131
	2212	0.1	3
20 Th	0403	3.3	101
	1014	-0.3	-9
	1642	4.6	140
	2313	-0.1	-3
21 F	0502	3.4	104
	1112	-0.5	-15
	1738	4.7	143
22 Sa	0010	-0.3	-9
	0558	3.5	107
	1208	-0.6	-18
	1832	4.8	146
23 Su ●	0103	-0.4	-12
	0653	3.6	110
	1302	-0.7	-21
	1925	4.8	146
24 M	0153	-0.5	-15
	0746	3.7	113
	1354	-0.7	-21
	2016	4.7	143
25 Tu	0242	-0.5	-15
	0838	3.7	113
	1446	-0.5	-15
	2106	4.5	137
26 W	0330	-0.4	-12
	0929	3.7	113
	1538	-0.3	-9
	2153	4.2	128
27 Th	0418	-0.2	-6
	1019	3.6	110
	1631	0.0	0
	2240	3.8	116
28 F	0505	0.0	0
	1109	3.5	107
	1726	0.2	6
	2327	3.5	107
29 Sa	0553	0.2	6
	1200	3.4	104
	1822	0.5	15
30 Su ◑	0016	3.2	98
	0641	0.3	9
	1254	3.3	101
	1919	0.7	21
31 M	0109	2.9	88
	0729	0.5	15
	1352	3.3	101
	2017	0.8	24

August

Day	Time (h m)	Height (ft)	Height (cm)
1 Tu	0206	2.8	85
	0818	0.6	18
	1448	3.4	104
	2115	0.8	24
2 W	0302	2.7	82
	0908	0.6	18
	1541	3.5	107
	2210	0.8	24
3 Th	0354	2.8	85
	0958	0.5	15
	1629	3.7	113
	2300	0.7	21
4 F	0442	2.9	88
	1046	0.4	12
	1714	3.9	119
	2343	0.6	18
5 Sa	0528	3.1	94
	1132	0.3	9
	1757	4.0	122
6 Su	0023	0.5	15
	0611	3.2	98
	1216	0.2	6
	1839	4.2	128
7 M ○	0102	0.4	12
	0654	3.4	104
	1258	0.1	3
	1920	4.3	131
8 Tu	0140	0.3	9
	0737	3.5	107
	1340	0.1	3
	2001	4.3	131
9 W	0219	0.2	6
	0819	3.6	110
	1422	0.1	3
	2041	4.3	131
10 Th	0258	0.2	6
	0902	3.7	113
	1507	0.1	3
	2122	4.2	128
11 F	0340	0.1	3
	0945	3.8	116
	1555	0.2	6
	2205	4.0	122
12 Sa	0424	0.2	6
	1032	3.9	119
	1647	0.3	9
	2250	3.8	116
13 Su	0511	0.2	6
	1122	3.9	119
	1744	0.4	12
	2340	3.6	110
14 M ◑	0602	0.2	6
	1217	4.0	122
	1844	0.5	15
15 Tu	0037	3.4	104
	0657	0.2	6
	1319	4.0	122
	1948	0.5	15
16 W	0140	3.2	98
	0755	0.1	3
	1424	4.1	125
	2053	0.4	12
17 Th	0245	3.2	98
	0857	0.1	3
	1528	4.3	131
	2158	0.3	9
18 F	0349	3.3	101
	0959	-0.1	-3
	1628	4.5	137
	2259	0.1	3
19 Sa	0448	3.4	104
	1059	-0.3	-9
	1724	4.6	140
	2355	-0.1	-3
20 Su	0544	3.6	110
	1155	-0.4	-12
	1817	4.6	140
21 M ●	0045	-0.2	-6
	0637	3.7	113
	1248	-0.5	-15
	1907	4.6	140
22 Tu	0131	-0.3	-9
	0727	3.8	116
	1338	-0.5	-15
	1955	4.5	137
23 W	0215	-0.3	-9
	0815	3.9	119
	1427	-0.4	-12
	2040	4.3	131
24 Th	0258	-0.2	-6
	0902	3.9	119
	1515	-0.2	-6
	2124	4.0	122
25 F	0341	0.0	0
	0947	3.9	119
	1603	0.1	3
	2207	3.7	113
26 Sa	0424	0.2	6
	1033	3.8	116
	1653	0.4	12
	2251	3.4	104
27 Su	0509	0.4	12
	1120	3.6	110
	1745	0.6	18
	2337	3.1	94
28 M	0555	0.6	18
	1210	3.5	107
	1839	0.8	24
29 Tu ◑	0028	2.9	88
	0644	0.7	21
	1305	3.5	107
	1935	1.0	30
30 W	0124	2.8	85
	0735	0.8	24
	1404	3.5	107
	2032	1.0	30
31 Th	0223	2.8	85
	0828	0.8	24
	1502	3.6	110
	2128	1.0	30

September

Day	Time (h m)	Height (ft)	Height (cm)
1 F	0320	2.9	88
	0922	0.8	24
	1555	3.7	113
	2220	0.9	27
2 Sa	0411	3.1	94
	1014	0.6	18
	1642	3.9	119
	2306	0.8	24
3 Su	0458	3.3	101
	1103	0.5	15
	1726	4.1	125
	2348	0.6	18
4 M	0542	3.5	107
	1150	0.3	9
	1809	4.2	128
5 Tu	0028	0.4	12
	0626	3.7	113
	1234	0.1	3
	1850	4.4	134
6 W	0107	0.2	6
	0709	4.0	122
	1318	0.0	0
	1932	4.4	134
7 Th	0147	0.1	3
	0752	4.1	125
	1402	0.0	0
	2015	4.4	134
8 F	0227	0.0	0
	0836	4.3	131
	1448	0.0	0
	2058	4.3	131
9 Sa	0310	0.0	0
	0921	4.4	134
	1538	0.1	3
	2142	4.1	125
10 Su	0355	0.1	3
	1009	4.4	134
	1631	0.2	6
	2230	3.8	116
11 M	0444	0.2	6
	1101	4.3	131
	1729	0.4	12
	2322	3.6	110
12 Tu	0538	0.2	6
	1157	4.3	131
	1830	0.5	15
13 W ◑	0020	3.3	101
	0637	0.3	9
	1301	4.2	128
	1935	0.5	15
14 Th	0126	3.2	98
	0739	0.3	9
	1408	4.2	128
	2041	0.5	15
15 F	0234	3.2	98
	0844	0.2	6
	1515	4.2	128
	2145	0.4	12
16 Sa	0340	3.3	101
	0948	0.1	3
	1616	4.3	131
	2244	0.2	6
17 Su	0439	3.5	107
	1049	0.0	0
	1710	4.3	131
	2337	0.1	3
18 M	0531	3.7	113
	1145	-0.2	-6
	1800	4.3	131
19 Tu	0023	-0.1	-3
	0620	3.9	119
	1235	-0.2	-6
	1846	4.3	131
20 W ●	0105	-0.1	-3
	0706	4.1	125
	1322	-0.2	-6
	1930	4.2	128
21 Th ○	0145	-0.1	-3
	0750	4.1	125
	1407	-0.2	-6
	2012	4.0	122
22 F	0224	0.0	0
	0833	4.1	125
	1451	0.0	0
	2054	3.8	116
23 Sa	0303	0.1	3
	0915	4.1	125
	1535	0.2	6
	2135	3.6	110
24 Su	0343	0.3	9
	0958	4.0	122
	1621	0.5	15
	2217	3.3	101
25 M	0425	0.5	15
	1042	3.8	116
	1709	0.7	21
	2301	3.1	94
26 Tu	0511	0.7	21
	1129	3.7	113
	1800	0.9	27
	2350	3.0	91
27 W ◑	0600	0.9	27
	1221	3.6	110
	1854	1.1	34
28 Th	0044	2.8	85
	0653	1.0	30
	1319	3.5	107
	1949	1.1	34
29 F	0144	2.8	85
	0748	1.0	30
	1418	3.6	110
	2044	1.1	34
30 Sa	0243	3.0	91
	0845	0.9	27
	1515	3.7	113
	2136	1.0	30

Time meridian 75° W. 0000 is midnight. 1200 is noon. Times are not adjusted for Daylight Saving Time.
Heights are referred to mean lower low water which is the chart datum of soundings.

Ocean City, Maryland, 2017

Times and Heights of High and Low Waters

October

Day	Time	ft	cm	Day	Time	ft	cm
1 Su	0337	3.2	98	16 M	0428	3.6	110
	0940	0.8	24		1039	0.2	6
	1605	3.9	119		1652	4.0	122
	2224	0.8	24		2314	0.1	3
2 M	0426	3.5	107	17 Tu	0517	3.8	116
	1032	0.6	18		1133	0.0	0
	1651	4.1	125		1739	3.9	119
	2309	0.5	15		2357	0.0	0
3 Tu	0512	3.8	116	18 W	0602	4.0	122
	1122	0.3	9		1221	0.0	0
	1735	4.2	128		1822	3.9	119
	2352	0.3	9				
4 W	0556	4.1	125	19 Th ●	0037	0.0	0
	1209	0.1	3		0644	4.1	125
	1819	4.3	131		1305	0.0	0
					1903	3.8	116
5 Th ○	0033	0.1	3	20 F	0114	0.0	0
	0640	4.4	134		0724	4.2	128
	1256	-0.1	-3		1346	0.0	0
	1903	4.4	134		1943	3.7	113
6 F	0115	-0.1	-3	21 Sa	0151	0.0	0
	0726	4.6	140		0805	4.2	128
	1343	-0.2	-6		1427	0.1	3
	1948	4.3	131		2024	3.5	107
7 Sa	0158	-0.2	-6	22 Su	0228	0.2	6
	0812	4.7	143		0845	4.2	128
	1431	-0.2	-6		1508	0.3	9
	2034	4.2	128		2104	3.4	104
8 Su	0242	-0.2	-6	23 M	0307	0.3	9
	0900	4.8	146		0927	4.1	125
	1522	-0.1	-3		1551	0.5	15
	2122	4.0	122		2146	3.2	98
9 M	0330	-0.1	-3	24 Tu	0347	0.5	15
	0950	4.7	143		1009	3.9	119
	1617	0.1	3		1636	0.7	21
	2212	3.7	113		2229	3.0	91
10 Tu	0422	0.0	0	25 W	0431	0.7	21
	1043	4.6	140		1054	3.8	116
	1715	0.2	6		1725	0.8	24
	2307	3.5	107		2315	2.9	88
11 W	0519	0.2	6	26 Th	0520	0.9	27
	1141	4.4	134		1142	3.6	110
	1818	0.4	12		1816	1.0	30
12 Th ◐	0007	3.3	101	27 F ◐	0007	2.8	85
	0621	0.3	9		0613	1.0	30
	1244	4.2	128		1236	3.5	107
	1922	0.4	12		1908	1.0	30
13 F	0114	3.2	98	28 Sa	0104	2.9	88
	0726	0.4	12		0709	1.0	30
	1353	4.1	125		1333	3.5	107
	2027	0.4	12		2000	0.9	27
14 Sa	0225	3.2	98	29 Su	0204	3.0	91
	0833	0.4	12		0806	0.9	27
	1500	4.0	122		1430	3.6	110
	2128	0.3	9		2051	0.8	24
15 Su	0332	3.4	104	30 M	0300	3.2	98
	0938	0.3	9		0904	0.8	24
	1600	4.0	122		1523	3.7	113
	2225	0.2	6		2141	0.6	18
				31 Tu	0352	3.6	110
					0959	0.6	18
					1613	3.9	119
					2228	0.4	12

November

Day	Time	ft	cm	Day	Time	ft	cm
1 W	0440	3.9	119	16 Th	0541	3.9	119
	1053	0.3	9		1206	0.1	3
	1700	4.0	122		1755	3.4	104
	2314	0.1	3				
2 Th	0527	4.3	131	17 F	0007	0.0	0
	1145	0.0	0		0621	4.0	122
	1747	4.1	125		1247	0.0	0
					1836	3.3	101
3 F	0000	-0.2	-6	18 Sa ●	0044	-0.1	-3
	0613	4.6	140		0700	4.1	125
	1235	-0.2	-6		1327	0.1	3
	1835	4.1	125		1916	3.2	98
4 Sa	0045	-0.4	-12	19 Su ○	0121	0.0	0
	0701	4.9	149		0740	4.1	125
	1325	-0.4	-12		1405	0.1	3
	1923	4.1	125		1956	3.2	98
5 Su	0131	-0.5	-15	20 M	0158	0.1	3
	0751	5.0	152		0820	4.1	125
	1415	-0.4	-12		1444	0.2	6
	2013	3.9	119		2037	3.1	94
6 M	0219	-0.5	-15	21 Tu	0236	0.2	6
	0841	5.0	152		0900	4.0	122
	1508	-0.3	-9		1524	0.3	9
	2104	3.8	116		2118	3.0	91
7 Tu	0309	-0.4	-12	22 W	0316	0.3	9
	0933	4.9	149		0941	3.9	119
	1603	-0.2	-6		1607	0.5	15
	2157	3.6	110		2201	2.9	88
8 W	0404	-0.2	-6	23 Th	0359	0.5	15
	1027	4.7	143		1024	3.8	116
	1701	0.0	0		1652	0.6	18
	2253	3.4	104		2245	2.8	85
9 Th	0503	0.0	0	24 F	0445	0.6	18
	1125	4.4	134		1108	3.6	110
	1803	0.1	3		1740	0.7	21
	2354	3.2	98		2333	2.8	85
10 F ○	0606	0.1	3	25 Sa	0537	0.7	21
	1226	4.1	125		1208	3.5	107
	1905	0.2	6		1828	0.7	21
11 Sa	0101	3.1	94	26 Su ◐	0026	2.8	85
	0712	0.3	9		0632	0.8	24
	1332	3.8	116		1248	3.4	104
	2006	0.2	6		1918	0.6	18
12 Su	0211	3.2	98	27 M	0123	3.0	91
	0819	0.3	9		0729	0.7	21
	1438	3.6	110		1344	3.4	104
	2104	0.2	6		2008	0.5	15
13 M	0317	3.3	101	28 Tu	0221	3.2	98
	0924	0.3	9		0828	0.6	18
	1538	3.5	107		1440	3.5	107
	2158	0.1	3		2058	0.3	9
14 Tu	0413	3.5	107	29 W	0316	3.5	107
	1025	0.2	6		0927	0.4	12
	1629	3.5	107		1534	3.5	107
	2245	0.0	0		2149	0.1	3
15 W	0459	3.7	113	30 Th	0408	3.9	119
	1119	0.2	6		1025	0.2	6
	1714	3.4	104		1626	3.6	110
	2328	0.0	0		2239	-0.2	-6

December

Day	Time	ft	cm	Day	Time	ft	cm
1 F	0459	4.3	131	16 Sa	0558	3.7	113
	1121	-0.1	-3		1228	0.1	3
	1718	3.7	113		1809	2.9	88
	2330	-0.5	-15				
2 Sa	0549	4.6	140	17 Su	0016	-0.1	-3
	1215	-0.4	-12		0637	3.8	116
	1809	3.7	113		1306	0.1	3
					1850	2.9	88
3 Su ○	0019	-0.7	-21	18 M ●	0055	-0.1	-3
	0640	4.9	149		0717	3.9	119
	1308	-0.6	-18		1343	0.0	0
	1901	3.7	113		1931	2.9	88
4 M	0109	-0.8	-24	19 Tu	0133	-0.1	-3
	0732	5.0	152		0757	3.9	119
	1400	-0.6	-18		1421	0.1	3
	1953	3.7	113		2012	2.9	88
5 Tu	0200	-0.8	-24	20 W	0211	-0.1	-3
	0825	4.9	149		0837	3.9	119
	1453	-0.6	-18		1459	0.1	3
	2047	3.6	110		2053	2.9	88
6 W	0252	-0.8	-24	21 Th	0251	0.0	0
	0918	4.8	146		0917	3.8	116
	1547	-0.5	-15		1539	0.2	6
	2141	3.4	104		2135	2.9	88
7 Th	0347	-0.6	-18	22 F	0332	0.2	6
	1011	4.5	137		0957	3.7	113
	1643	-0.4	-12		1621	0.3	9
	2237	3.3	101		2217	2.8	85
8 F	0446	-0.4	-12	23 Sa	0417	0.3	9
	1106	4.2	128		1038	3.6	110
	1741	-0.2	-6		1705	0.3	9
	2335	3.1	94		2301	2.8	85
9 Sa	0548	-0.1	-3	24 Su	0505	0.4	12
	1203	3.8	116		1121	3.5	107
	1840	-0.1	-3		1750	0.3	9
					2350	2.9	88
10 Su ○	0039	3.1	94	25 M	0559	0.5	15
	0652	0.1	3		1209	3.3	101
	1304	3.5	107		1838	0.3	9
	1937	0.0	0				
11 M	0146	3.1	94	26 Tu ◐	0044	3.0	91
	0758	0.2	6		0656	0.5	15
	1406	3.2	98		1302	3.2	98
	2031	0.0	0		1928	0.2	6
12 Tu	0251	3.2	98	27 W	0142	3.2	98
	0903	0.3	9		0756	0.4	12
	1506	3.0	91		1400	3.2	98
	2123	0.0	0		2019	0.0	0
13 W	0348	3.3	101	28 Th	0241	3.5	107
	1005	0.3	9		0858	0.2	6
	1559	2.9	88		1459	3.2	98
	2212	0.0	0		2114	-0.2	-6
14 Th	0436	3.5	107	29 F	0339	3.8	116
	1100	0.2	6		1000	0.0	0
	1645	2.9	88		1556	3.2	98
	2256	0.0	0		2209	-0.4	-12
15 F	0518	3.6	110	30 Sa	0434	4.2	128
	1147	0.1	3		1100	-0.2	-6
	1728	2.9	88		1652	3.3	101
	2337	-0.1	-3		2304	-0.7	-21
				31 Su	0529	4.5	137
					1158	-0.5	-15
					1747	3.4	104
					2358	-0.9	-27

Time meridian 75° W. 0000 is midnight. 1200 is noon. Times are not adjusted for Daylight Saving Time.
Heights are referred to mean lower low water which is the chart datum of soundings.

Baltimore, Maryland, 2017

Times and Heights of High and Low Waters

January

Day	Time	Height (ft)	Height (cm)
1 Su	0322	-0.1	-3
	0824	0.7	21
	1419	-0.3	-9
	2054	1.2	37
2 M	0400	-0.1	-3
	0910	0.7	21
	1507	-0.2	-6
	2136	1.2	37
3 Tu	0438	-0.1	-3
	1000	0.7	21
	1601	-0.2	-6
	2222	1.1	34
4 W	0519	-0.2	-6
	1054	0.8	24
	1704	-0.1	-3
	2311	1.1	34
5 Th ☽	0601	-0.2	-6
	1152	0.9	27
	1818	0.0	0
6 F	0003	1.0	30
	0646	-0.3	-9
	1254	1.0	30
	1938	0.0	0
7 Sa	0058	0.9	27
	0734	-0.4	-12
	1357	1.1	34
	2056	0.0	0
8 Su	0156	0.8	24
	0825	-0.4	-12
	1459	1.2	37
	2207	0.0	0
9 M	0255	0.7	21
	0918	-0.5	-15
	1600	1.3	40
	2311	-0.1	-3
10 Tu	0355	0.7	21
	1013	-0.5	-15
	1658	1.4	43
11 W	0008	-0.1	-3
	0452	0.7	21
	1108	-0.6	-18
	1753	1.4	43
12 Th ○	0101	-0.2	-6
	0548	0.7	21
	1202	-0.6	-18
	1845	1.4	43
13 F	0150	-0.2	-6
	0642	0.7	21
	1256	-0.5	-15
	1935	1.3	40
14 Sa	0237	-0.2	-6
	0735	0.8	24
	1350	-0.5	-15
	2023	1.3	40
15 Su	0321	-0.2	-6
	0827	0.8	24
	1443	-0.4	-12
	2109	1.2	37
16 M	0404	-0.2	-6
	0919	0.8	24
	1536	-0.3	-9
	2154	1.1	34
17 Tu	0445	-0.2	-6
	1013	0.8	24
	1632	-0.2	-6
	2238	1.0	30
18 W	0526	-0.2	-6
	1108	0.8	24
	1733	-0.1	-3
	2322	0.9	27
19 Th ☾	0605	-0.2	-6
	1207	0.8	24
	1839	0.0	0
20 F	0008	0.8	24
	0645	-0.2	-6
	1307	0.8	24
	1948	0.1	3
21 Sa	0055	0.7	21
	0727	-0.3	-9
	1407	0.9	27
	2056	0.1	3
22 Su	0145	0.6	18
	0810	-0.3	-9
	1504	0.9	27
	2157	0.1	3
23 M	0237	0.6	18
	0856	-0.3	-9
	1555	1.0	30
	2250	0.1	3
24 Tu	0329	0.6	18
	0942	-0.3	-9
	1641	1.0	30
	2337	0.0	0
25 W	0419	0.6	18
	1028	-0.3	-9
	1722	1.1	34
26 Th	0019	0.0	0
	0507	0.6	18
	1113	-0.4	-12
	1800	1.1	34
27 F ●	0057	-0.1	-3
	0551	0.6	18
	1157	-0.4	-12
	1837	1.1	34
28 Sa	0134	-0.1	-3
	0634	0.7	21
	1241	-0.4	-12
	1914	1.2	37
29 Su	0209	-0.1	-3
	0717	0.7	21
	1326	-0.4	-12
	1953	1.2	37
30 M	0245	-0.2	-6
	0801	0.8	24
	1412	-0.3	-9
	2033	1.2	37
31 Tu	0320	-0.2	-6
	0847	0.8	24
	1503	-0.3	-9
	2115	1.1	34

February

Day	Time	Height (ft)	Height (cm)
1 W	0358	-0.2	-6
	0937	0.9	27
	1600	-0.2	-6
	2200	1.0	30
2 Th	0438	-0.3	-9
	1031	1.0	30
	1704	-0.1	-3
	2249	1.0	30
3 F ◑	0521	-0.3	-9
	1129	1.0	30
	1817	-0.1	-3
	2341	0.9	27
4 Sa	0610	-0.3	-9
	1231	1.1	34
	1935	0.0	0
5 Su	0038	0.8	24
	0704	-0.4	-12
	1336	1.2	37
	2049	0.0	0
6 M	0139	0.7	21
	0803	-0.4	-12
	1442	1.2	37
	2157	0.0	0
7 Tu	0241	0.7	21
	0905	-0.4	-12
	1547	1.2	37
	2256	-0.1	-3
8 W	0342	0.7	21
	1006	-0.5	-15
	1647	1.3	40
	2349	-0.1	-3
9 Th	0440	0.8	24
	1104	-0.5	-15
	1742	1.3	40
10 F ○	0038	-0.1	-3
	0535	0.8	24
	1200	-0.5	-15
	1832	1.3	40
11 Sa	0122	-0.1	-3
	0626	0.9	27
	1252	-0.4	-12
	1918	1.2	37
12 Su	0203	-0.1	-3
	0715	0.9	27
	1342	-0.4	-12
	2001	1.2	37
13 M	0242	-0.1	-3
	0803	0.9	27
	1431	-0.3	-9
	2042	1.1	34
14 Tu	0317	-0.1	-3
	0851	0.9	27
	1519	-0.2	-6
	2122	1.0	30
15 W	0351	-0.1	-3
	0939	0.9	27
	1609	-0.1	-3
	2201	0.9	27
16 Th	0425	-0.1	-3
	1028	0.9	27
	1703	0.0	0
	2242	0.9	27
17 F	0501	-0.1	-3
	1120	0.9	27
	1802	0.1	3
	2326	0.8	24
18 Sa ☾	0541	-0.1	-3
	1214	0.9	27
	1907	0.2	6
19 Su	0014	0.7	21
	0628	-0.1	-3
	1311	1.0	30
	2013	0.2	6
20 M	0106	0.7	21
	0719	-0.1	-3
	1409	1.0	30
	2113	0.2	6
21 Tu	0201	0.7	21
	0814	-0.1	-3
	1505	1.0	30
	2206	0.2	6
22 W	0257	0.7	21
	0910	-0.2	-6
	1556	1.0	30
	2253	0.1	3
23 Th	0349	0.7	21
	1003	-0.2	-6
	1643	1.1	34
	2335	0.1	3
24 F	0438	0.8	24
	1054	-0.2	-6
	1726	1.1	34
25 Sa	0013	0.0	0
	0524	0.9	27
	1143	-0.2	-6
	1807	1.2	37
26 Su	0050	0.0	0
	0608	0.9	27
	1231	-0.2	-6
	1847 ●	1.2	37
27 M	0125	0.0	0
	0652	1.0	30
	1319	-0.2	-6
	1928	1.2	37
28 Tu	0201	-0.1	-3
	0737	1.1	34
	1410	-0.2	-6
	2010	1.2	37

March

Day	Time	Height (ft)	Height (cm)
1 W	0237	-0.1	-3
	0825	1.2	37
	1504	-0.2	-6
	2054	1.1	34
2 Th	0316	-0.2	-6
	0916	1.2	37
	1602	-0.1	-3
	2141	1.1	34
3 F ○	0359	-0.2	-6
	1010	1.3	40
	1707	0.0	0
	2232	1.0	30
4 Sa	0447	-0.2	-6
	1108	1.3	40
	1817	0.0	0
	2327	0.9	27
5 Su ◑	0542	-0.2	-6
	1210	1.3	40
	1928	0.1	3
6 M	0026	0.9	27
	0645	-0.2	-6
	1317	1.3	40
	2036	0.1	3
7 Tu	0130	0.9	27
	0753	-0.2	-6
	1426	1.3	40
	2138	0.1	3
8 W	0233	0.9	27
	0902	-0.2	-6
	1533	1.3	40
	2233	0.1	3
9 Th	0334	1.0	30
	1006	-0.2	-6
	1634	1.3	40
	2322	0.1	3
10 F	0430	1.0	30
	1105	-0.2	-6
	1727	1.3	40
11 Sa	0007	0.1	3
	0522	1.1	34
	1159	-0.2	-6
	1813	1.3	40
12 Su ○	0047	0.1	3
	0610	1.2	37
	1249	-0.2	-6
	1855	1.2	37
13 M	0123	0.1	3
	0656	1.2	37
	1335	-0.1	-3
	1934	1.2	37
14 Tu	0155	0.1	3
	0740	1.2	37
	1420	-0.1	-3
	2012	1.1	34
15 W	0225	0.1	3
	0822	1.3	40
	1505	0.0	0
	2049	1.1	34
16 Th	0254	0.1	3
	0905	1.3	40
	1550	0.1	3
	2127	1.0	30
17 F	0327	0.1	3
	0948	1.2	37
	1638	0.2	6
	2208	1.0	30
18 Sa ☾	0403	0.1	3
	1033	1.2	37
	1730	0.3	9
	2252	0.9	27
19 Su	0446	0.1	3
	1121	1.2	37
	1826	0.3	9
	2340	0.9	27
20 M ◑	0537	0.1	3
	1213	1.2	37
	1925	0.3	9
21 Tu	0034	0.9	27
	0635	0.1	3
	1309	1.2	37
	2021	0.3	9
22 W	0130	0.9	27
	0737	0.2	6
	1407	1.2	37
	2113	0.3	9
23 Th	0226	1.0	30
	0840	0.1	3
	1504	1.2	37
	2200	0.3	9
24 F	0319	1.0	30
	0940	0.1	3
	1556	1.2	37
	2243	0.2	6
25 Sa	0408	1.1	34
	1036	0.1	3
	1645	1.3	40
	2322	0.2	6
26 Su	0455	1.2	37
	1130	0.0	0
	1731	1.3	40
27 M ●	0000	0.2	6
	0542	1.3	40
	1222	0.0	0
	1816	1.3	40
28 Tu	0037	0.1	3
	0628	1.5	46
	1314	0.0	0
	1900	1.3	40
29 W	0115	0.1	3
	0715	1.6	49
	1408	0.0	0
	1946	1.2	37
30 Th	0155	0.0	0
	0804	1.6	49
	1505	0.0	0
	2033	1.2	37
31 F	0238	0.0	0
	0856	1.7	52
	1604	0.1	3
	2124	1.1	34

Time meridian 75° W. 0000 is midnight. 1200 is noon. Times are not adjusted for Daylight Saving Time.
Heights are referred to mean lower low water which is the chart datum of soundings.

Baltimore, Maryland, 2017

Times and Heights of High and Low Waters

April

Day	Time (h m)	ft	cm	Day	Time (h m)	ft	cm
1 Sa	0325	0.0	0	**16** Su	0317	0.3	9
	0950	1.7	52		0951	1.5	46
	1706	0.1	3		1703	0.4	12
	2218	1.1	34		2224	1.1	34
2 Su	0420	0.1	3	**17** M	0403	0.3	9
	1048	1.6	49		1034	1.5	46
	1810	0.2	6		1750	0.4	12
	2317	1.1	34		2313	1.1	34
3 M ◐	0523	0.1	3	**18** Tu	0455	0.4	12
	1151	1.5	46		1122	1.4	43
	1914	0.2	6		1840	0.4	12
4 Tu	0019	1.1	34	**19** W	0006	1.1	34
	0635	0.1	3		0556	0.4	12
	1258	1.5	46		1216	1.4	43
	2015	0.3	9	○	1930	0.4	12
5 W	0123	1.1	34	**20** Th	0100	1.2	37
	0750	0.1	3		0703	0.4	12
	1407	1.4	43		1313	1.4	43
	2111	0.3	9		2019	0.4	12
6 Th	0226	1.2	37	**21** F	0155	1.2	37
	0901	0.1	3		0812	0.4	12
	1513	1.4	43		1412	1.4	43
	2202	0.3	9		2104	0.4	12
7 F	0325	1.3	40	**22** Sa	0248	1.3	40
	1006	0.1	3		0918	0.4	12
	1611	1.4	43		1508	1.4	43
	2248	0.3	9		2148	0.3	9
8 Sa	0419	1.4	43	**23** Su	0339	1.5	46
	1104	0.1	3		1019	0.3	9
	1702	1.3	40		1601	1.4	43
	2329	0.3	9		2229	0.3	9
9 Su	0508	1.4	43	**24** M	0428	1.6	49
	1156	0.1	3		1118	0.3	9
	1746	1.3	40		1652	1.4	43
					2309	0.2	6
10 M	0005	0.3	9	**25** Tu	0517	1.7	52
	0554	1.5	46		1214	0.2	6
	1244	0.1	3		1742	1.3	40
	1826	1.3	40		2350	0.2	6
11 Tu ○	0036	0.3	9	**26** W ●	0606	1.9	58
	0636	1.5	46		1310	0.2	6
	1329	0.2	6		1832	1.3	40
	1903	1.2	37				
12 W	0105	0.2	6	**27** Th	0032	0.1	3
	0716	1.6	49		0655	1.9	58
	1412	0.2	6		1406	0.2	6
	1941	1.2	37		1922	1.3	40
13 Th	0133	0.2	6	**28** F	0117	0.1	3
	0755	1.6	49		0745	2.0	61
	1454	0.3	9		1502	0.2	6
	2018	1.1	34		2014	1.3	40
14 F	0203	0.3	9	**29** Sa	0206	0.1	3
	0832	1.6	49		0837	2.0	61
	1536	0.3	9		1558	0.2	6
	2057	1.1	34		2108	1.2	37
15 Sa	0238	0.3	9	**30** Su	0300	0.2	6
	0910	1.5	46		0932	1.9	58
	1618	0.4	12		1656	0.3	9
	2139	1.1	34		2206	1.2	37

May

Day	Time (h m)	ft	cm	Day	Time (h m)	ft	cm
1 M	0402	0.3	9	**16** Tu	0329	0.5	15
	1030	1.8	55		0958	1.7	52
	1754	0.3	9		1718	0.5	15
	2306	1.3	40		2248	1.2	37
2 Tu ◐	0512	0.3	9	**17** W	0423	0.6	18
	1131	1.7	52		1044	1.6	49
	1851	0.3	9		1800	0.5	15
					2338	1.3	40
3 W	0009	1.3	40	**18** Th ○	0525	0.6	18
	0628	0.4	12		1134	1.6	49
	1236	1.6	49		1844	0.5	15
	1946	0.4	12				
4 Th	0113	1.4	43	**19** F	0031	1.3	40
	0744	0.4	12		0634	0.6	18
	1341	1.5	46		1229	1.5	46
	2037	0.4	12		1928	0.4	12
5 F	0215	1.5	46	**20** Sa	0124	1.4	43
	0855	0.4	12		0747	0.6	18
	1442	1.4	43		1326	1.5	46
	2125	0.4	12		2012	0.4	12
6 Sa	0313	1.5	46	**21** Su	0218	1.6	49
	1000	0.4	12		0858	0.5	15
	1538	1.4	43		1423	1.4	43
	2207	0.4	12		2055	0.3	9
7 Su	0405	1.6	49	**22** M	0311	1.7	52
	1057	0.4	12		1005	0.5	15
	1626	1.3	40		1520	1.4	43
	2244	0.4	12		2139	0.3	9
8 M	0453	1.7	52	**23** Tu	0403	1.9	58
	1149	0.4	12		1108	0.4	12
	1711	1.3	40		1616	1.3	40
	2318	0.4	12		2223	0.2	6
9 Tu	0536	1.7	52	**24** W	0455	2.0	61
	1237	0.4	12		1208	0.4	12
	1752	1.2	37		1711	1.3	40
	2348	0.4	12		2309	0.2	6
10 W ○	0616	1.8	55	**25** Th ●	0546	2.1	64
	1321	0.4	12		1304	0.3	9
	1831	1.2	37		1805	1.3	40
					2358	0.2	6
11 Th	0017	0.4	12	**26** F	0637	2.2	67
	0653	1.8	55		1359	0.3	9
	1403	0.4	12		1900	1.3	40
	1911	1.2	37				
12 F	0048	0.4	12	**27** Sa	0049	0.2	6
	0728	1.8	55		0729	2.2	67
	1442	0.4	12		1452	0.3	9
	1951	1.2	37		1956	1.3	40
13 Sa	0123	0.4	12	**28** Su	0144	0.2	6
	0803	1.8	55		0821	2.1	64
	1520	0.4	12		1545	0.3	9
	2032	1.2	37		2052	1.3	40
14 Su	0200	0.4	12	**29** M	0244	0.3	9
	0839	1.7	52		0915	2.0	61
	1558	0.5	15		1637	0.3	9
	2115	1.2	37		2151	1.3	40
15 M	0242	0.5	15	**30** Tu	0349	0.4	12
	0916	1.7	52		1011	1.9	58
	1637	0.5	15		1729	0.3	9
	2200	1.2	37		2251	1.4	43
				31 W	0500	0.5	15
					1108	1.7	52
					1820	0.4	12
					2353	1.5	46

June

Day	Time (h m)	ft	cm	Day	Time (h m)	ft	cm
1 Th ◐	0615	0.5	15	**16** F	0501	0.7	21
	1207	1.6	49		1102	1.6	49
	1910	0.4	12		1801	0.4	12
2 F	0056	1.5	46	**17** Sa	0612	0.7	21
	0730	0.5	15		1153	1.6	49
	1305	1.5	46		1842	0.4	12
	1957	0.4	12				
3 Sa	0157	1.6	49	**18** Su	0055	1.6	49
	0841	0.6	18		0728	0.7	21
	1402	1.4	43		1248	1.5	46
	2040	0.4	12		1925	0.3	9
4 Su	0254	1.7	52	**19** M	0151	1.7	52
	0947	0.6	18		0844	0.6	18
	1455	1.3	40		1346	1.4	43
	2120	0.4	12		2010	0.3	9
5 M	0347	1.8	55	**20** Tu	0246	1.9	58
	1046	0.5	15		0955	0.6	18
	1545	1.2	37		1446	1.3	40
	2156	0.4	12		2058	0.2	6
6 Tu	0434	1.8	55	**21** W	0341	2.0	61
	1138	0.5	15		1100	0.5	15
	1632	1.2	37		1546	1.3	40
	2230	0.4	12		2148	0.2	6
7 W	0516	1.9	58	**22** Th	0435	2.1	64
	1226	0.5	15		1159	0.4	12
	1717	1.2	37		1645	1.2	37
	2304	0.4	12		2240	0.2	6
8 Th	0554	1.9	58	**23** F ●	0529	2.2	67
	1309	0.5	15		1254	0.4	12
	1800	1.2	37		1743	1.3	40
	2338	0.4	12		2335	0.2	6
9 F ○	0630	1.9	58	**24** Sa	0621	2.2	67
	1348	0.5	15		1345	0.3	9
	1843	1.2	37		1841	1.3	40
10 Sa	0015	0.4	12	**25** Su	0032	0.2	6
	0704	1.9	58		0714	2.2	67
	1424	0.5	15		1435	0.3	9
	1926	1.2	37		1938	1.3	40
11 Su	0053	0.4	12	**26** M	0131	0.3	9
	0737	1.9	58		0806	2.1	64
	1459	0.5	15		1523	0.3	9
	2008	1.2	37		2034	1.4	43
12 M	0135	0.5	15	**27** Tu	0233	0.3	9
	0812	1.8	55		0857	2.0	61
	1534	0.5	15		1610	0.3	9
	2051	1.2	37		2131	1.4	43
13 Tu	0218	0.5	15	**28** W	0337	0.4	12
	0849	1.8	55		0949	1.8	55
	1609	0.4	12		1656	0.3	9
	2135	1.3	40		2230	1.5	46
14 W	0306	0.6	18	**29** Th	0444	0.5	15
	0930	1.8	55		1041	1.7	52
	1645	0.4	12		1742	0.4	12
	2221	1.3	40		2329	1.5	46
15 Th	0400	0.6	18	**30** F ◐	0555	0.6	18
	1014	1.7	52		1132	1.6	49
	1722	0.4	12		1826	0.4	12
	2309	1.4	43				

Time meridian 75° W. 0000 is midnight. 1200 is noon. Times are not adjusted for Daylight Saving Time.
Heights are referred to mean lower low water which is the chart datum of soundings.

Baltimore, Maryland, 2017

Times and Heights of High and Low Waters

July

Day	Time	Height (ft)	Height (cm)
1 Sa	0030	1.6	49
	0709	0.7	21
	1224	1.4	43
	1908	0.4	12
2 Su	0130	1.7	52
	0820	0.7	21
	1316	1.3	40
	1949	0.4	12
3 M	0228	1.7	52
	0927	0.7	21
	1409	1.2	37
	2028	0.4	12
4 Tu	0321	1.8	55
	1027	0.7	21
	1502	1.2	37
	2107	0.4	12
5 W	0408	1.8	55
	1120	0.6	18
	1553	1.2	37
	2147	0.4	12
6 Th	0451	1.9	58
	1206	0.6	18
	1644	1.1	34
	2228	0.4	12
7 F	0530	1.9	58
	1246	0.6	18
	1732	1.2	37
	2310	0.4	12
8 Sa ○	0605	1.9	58
	1323	0.5	15
	1817	1.2	37
	2352	0.4	12
9 Su	0640	1.9	58
	1357	0.5	15
	1901	1.2	37
10 M	0034	0.5	15
	0714	1.9	58
	1430	0.5	15
	1943	1.3	40
11 Tu	0118	0.5	15
	0749	1.9	58
	1502	0.4	12
	2024	1.3	40
12 W	0203	0.5	15
	0826	1.8	55
	1535	0.4	12
	2107	1.4	43
13 Th	0252	0.6	18
	0905	1.8	55
	1608	0.4	12
	2152	1.4	43
14 F	0346	0.6	18
	0948	1.7	52
	1643	0.4	12
	2241	1.5	46
15 Sa ◗	0448	0.7	21
	1034	1.6	49
	1720	0.3	9
	2333	1.6	49
16 Su ◑	0601	0.7	21
	1124	1.5	46
	1801	0.3	9
17 M	0028	1.8	55
	0719	0.7	21
	1219	1.4	43
	1845	0.3	9
18 Tu	0126	1.9	58
	0836	0.7	21
	1319	1.3	40
	1935	0.2	6
19 W	0224	2.0	61
	0947	0.6	18
	1421	1.3	40
	2029	0.2	6
20 Th	0322	2.1	64
	1049	0.5	15
	1525	1.2	37
	2126	0.2	6
21 F	0419	2.1	64
	1145	0.5	15
	1627	1.3	40
	2226	0.2	6
22 Sa	0515	2.2	67
	1236	0.4	12
	1727	1.3	40
	2326	0.2	6
23 Su ●	0608	2.2	67
	1324	0.4	12
	1824	1.4	43
24 M	0025	0.3	9
	0659	2.1	64
	1409	0.4	12
	1919	1.4	43
25 Tu	0124	0.3	9
	0748	2.0	61
	1453	0.4	12
	2013	1.5	46
26 W	0223	0.4	12
	0836	1.9	58
	1535	0.4	12
	2108	1.6	49
27 Th	0323	0.5	15
	0922	1.8	55
	1615	0.4	12
	2202	1.6	49
28 F	0425	0.6	18
	1008	1.7	52
	1654	0.4	12
	2258	1.6	49
29 Sa	0531	0.7	21
	1054	1.5	46
	1733	0.4	12
	2355	1.7	52
30 Su ◖	0642	0.8	24
	1141	1.4	43
	1812	0.4	12
31 M	0053	1.7	52
	0753	0.8	24
	1231	1.3	40
	1852	0.4	12

August

Day	Time	Height (ft)	Height (cm)
1 Tu	0151	1.8	55
	0900	0.8	24
	1325	1.2	37
	1936	0.4	12
2 W	0245	1.8	55
	0959	0.8	24
	1422	1.2	37
	2023	0.4	12
3 Th	0334	1.8	55
	1050	0.7	21
	1519	1.2	37
	2111	0.4	12
4 F	0419	1.8	55
	1134	0.7	21
	1613	1.2	37
	2200	0.5	15
5 Sa	0500	1.9	58
	1212	0.6	18
	1704	1.2	37
	2248	0.5	15
6 Su	0537	1.9	58
	1247	0.6	18
	1750	1.3	40
	2335	0.5	15
7 M ○	0613	1.9	58
	1320	0.5	15
	1833	1.3	40
8 Tu	0021	0.5	15
	0648	1.9	58
	1352	0.5	15
	1915	1.4	43
9 W	0106	0.5	15
	0724	1.9	58
	1423	0.4	12
	1956	1.5	46
10 Th	0154	0.6	18
	0802	1.8	55
	1455	0.4	12
	2039	1.5	46
11 F	0244	0.6	18
	0841	1.8	55
	1527	0.4	12
	2124	1.6	49
12 Sa	0341	0.7	21
	0924	1.7	52
	1602	0.3	9
	2214	1.7	52
13 Su	0445	0.7	21
	1011	1.6	49
	1641	0.3	9
	2307	1.8	55
14 M ◗	0558	0.7	21
	1102	1.5	46
	1724	0.3	9
15 Tu	0003	1.9	58
	0715	0.7	21
	1159	1.4	43
	1814	0.3	9
16 W	0103	2.0	61
	0829	0.7	21
	1301	1.3	40
	1911	0.3	9
17 Th	0205	2.0	61
	0935	0.6	18
	1407	1.3	40
	2014	0.3	9
18 F	0307	2.1	64
	1033	0.6	18
	1512	1.3	40
	2120	0.3	9
19 Sa	0406	2.1	64
	1125	0.5	15
	1615	1.4	43
	2224	0.3	9
20 Su	0502	2.1	64
	1212	0.5	15
	1713	1.4	43
	2325	0.3	9
21 M ●	0554	2.0	61
	1256	0.4	12
	1808	1.5	46
22 Tu ○	0023	0.3	9
	0642	2.0	61
	1337	0.4	12
	1901	1.6	49
23 W	0119	0.4	12
	0727	1.9	58
	1416	0.4	12
	1952	1.7	52
24 Th	0214	0.5	15
	0810	1.8	55
	1452	0.4	12
	2042	1.7	52
25 F	0308	0.6	18
	0851	1.7	52
	1526	0.4	12
	2132	1.7	52
26 Sa	0405	0.7	21
	0933	1.6	49
	1600	0.4	12
	2222	1.7	52
27 Su	0506	0.8	24
	1015	1.5	46
	1635	0.4	12
	2314	1.8	55
28 M	0612	0.8	24
	1101	1.4	43
	1713	0.4	12
29 Tu ◗	0008	1.8	55
	0719	0.8	24
	1151	1.3	40
	1757	0.5	15
30 W	0103	1.8	55
	0823	0.8	24
	1247	1.2	37
	1847	0.5	15
31 Th	0158	1.8	55
	0920	0.8	24
	1347	1.2	37
	1943	0.5	15

September

Day	Time	Height (ft)	Height (cm)
1 F	0250	1.8	55
	1008	0.8	24
	1447	1.2	37
	2040	0.5	15
2 Sa	0338	1.8	55
	1050	0.7	21
	1543	1.3	40
	2136	0.5	15
3 Su	0421	1.8	55
	1127	0.6	18
	1634	1.3	40
	2230	0.5	15
4 M	0502	1.8	55
	1202	0.6	18
	1720	1.4	43
	2320	0.5	15
5 Tu	0540	1.8	55
	1235	0.5	15
	1803	1.5	46
6 W ○	0008	0.5	15
	0617	1.8	55
	1307	0.5	15
	1845	1.6	49
7 Th	0057	0.5	15
	0656	1.8	55
	1338	0.4	12
	1928	1.7	52
8 F	0148	0.6	18
	0736	1.8	55
	1411	0.4	12
	2012	1.8	55
9 Sa	0242	0.6	18
	0817	1.7	52
	1445	0.3	9
	2059	1.9	58
10 Su	0341	0.6	18
	0903	1.6	49
	1523	0.3	9
	2149	1.9	58
11 M	0447	0.7	21
	0952	1.5	46
	1606	0.3	9
	2243	2.0	61
12 Tu	0557	0.7	21
	1046	1.4	43
	1656	0.3	9
	2342	2.0	61
13 W ◗	0708	0.7	21
	1147	1.3	40
	1754	0.3	9
14 Th	0044	2.0	61
	0815	0.7	21
	1252	1.3	40
	1901	0.4	12
15 F	0149	2.0	61
	0916	0.6	18
	1400	1.3	40
	2012	0.4	12
16 Sa	0253	2.0	61
	1010	0.6	18
	1505	1.4	43
	2122	0.4	12
17 Su	0352	1.9	58
	1059	0.5	15
	1606	1.5	46
	2227	0.4	12
18 M	0446	1.9	58
	1143	0.5	15
	1702	1.6	49
	2326	0.4	12
19 Tu	0535	1.9	58
	1223	0.4	12
	1754	1.7	52
20 W ●	0022	0.4	12
	0619	1.8	55
	1300	0.4	12
	1843	1.7	52
21 Th	0114	0.5	15
	0700	1.7	52
	1334	0.4	12
	1930	1.8	55
22 F	0205	0.5	15
	0740	1.6	49
	1404	0.4	12
	2015	1.8	55
23 Sa	0256	0.6	18
	0818	1.5	46
	1434	0.4	12
	2100	1.8	55
24 Su	0348	0.7	21
	0858	1.4	43
	1505	0.4	12
	2145	1.8	55
25 M	0442	0.7	21
	0940	1.4	43
	1540	0.4	12
	2231	1.8	55
26 Tu	0540	0.8	24
	1025	1.3	40
	1620	0.4	12
	2319	1.7	52
27 W ◖	0639	0.8	24
	1117	1.2	37
	1708	0.5	15
28 Th ○	0010	1.7	52
	0737	0.8	24
	1214	1.2	37
	1804	0.5	15
29 F	0103	1.7	52
	0829	0.7	21
	1314	1.2	37
	1906	0.6	18
30 Sa	0156	1.7	52
	0916	0.7	21
	1415	1.2	37
	2010	0.6	18

Time meridian 75° W. 0000 is midnight. 1200 is noon. Times are not adjusted for Daylight Saving Time.
Heights are referred to mean lower low water which is the chart datum of soundings.

Baltimore, Maryland, 2017

Times and Heights of High and Low Waters

October

Day	Time (h m)	Height (ft)	Height (cm)
1 Su	0248	1.7	52
	0958	0.6	18
	1511	1.3	40
	2112	0.6	18
2 M	0335	1.7	52
	1036	0.6	18
	1602	1.4	43
	2209	0.5	15
3 Tu	0419	1.7	52
	1111	0.5	15
	1649	1.5	46
	2304	0.5	15
4 W	0501	1.7	52
	1145	0.4	12
	1733	1.6	49
	2357	0.5	15
5 Th ○	0543	1.7	52
	1218	0.3	9
	1817	1.7	52
6 F	0050	0.5	15
	0625	1.6	49
	1252	0.3	9
	1902	1.8	55
7 Sa	0144	0.5	15
	0709	1.6	49
	1328	0.2	6
	1948	1.9	58
8 Su	0241	0.5	15
	0754	1.5	46
	1407	0.2	6
	2036	2.0	61
9 M	0341	0.5	15
	0843	1.4	43
	1450	0.2	6
	2128	2.0	61
10 Tu	0444	0.5	15
	0937	1.3	40
	1539	0.2	6
	2224	2.0	61
11 W	0549	0.5	15
	1035	1.3	40
	1637	0.3	9
	2323	1.9	58
12 Th ☽	0654	0.5	15
	1139	1.2	37
	1744	0.3	9
13 F	0027	1.9	58
	0755	0.5	15
	1246	1.3	40
	1859	0.4	12
14 Sa	0132	1.8	55
	0851	0.5	15
	1354	1.3	40
	2014	0.4	12
15 Su	0235	1.8	55
	0942	0.5	15
	1458	1.4	43
	2124	0.4	12
16 M	0332	1.7	52
	1028	0.4	12
	1557	1.5	46
	2228	0.4	12
17 Tu	0423	1.6	49
	1109	0.3	9
	1651	1.6	49
	2326	0.4	12
18 W	0509	1.6	49
	1146	0.3	9
	1741	1.7	52
19 Th ●	0019	0.4	12
	0551	1.5	46
	1219	0.3	9
	1826	1.7	52
20 F	0109	0.4	12
	0630	1.4	43
	1249	0.3	9
	1909	1.7	52
21 Sa	0158	0.5	15
	0709	1.4	43
	1318	0.2	6
	1950	1.8	55
22 Su	0245	0.5	15
	0747	1.3	40
	1347	0.2	6
	2030	1.7	52
23 M	0332	0.6	18
	0827	1.2	37
	1420	0.3	9
	2110	1.7	52
24 Tu	0419	0.6	18
	0910	1.2	37
	1457	0.3	9
	2151	1.7	52
25 W	0507	0.6	18
	0956	1.1	34
	1539	0.3	9
	2234	1.6	49
26 Th	0557	0.6	18
	1046	1.1	34
	1628	0.4	12
	2321	1.6	49
27 F ☾	0646	0.6	18
	1142	1.1	34
	1725	0.4	12
28 Sa	0011	1.5	46
	0735	0.5	15
	1240	1.1	34
	1829	0.5	15
29 Su	0103	1.5	46
	0820	0.5	15
	1339	1.1	34
	1937	0.5	15
30 M	0155	1.5	46
	0902	0.4	12
	1435	1.2	37
	2044	0.5	15
31 Tu	0245	1.5	46
	0941	0.3	9
	1528	1.3	40
	2148	0.4	12

November

Day	Time (h m)	Height (ft)	Height (cm)
1 W	0334	1.4	43
	1018	0.2	6
	1617	1.5	46
	2248	0.4	12
2 Th	0421	1.4	43
	1054	0.1	3
	1704	1.6	49
	2346	0.4	12
3 F	0508	1.4	43
	1131	0.1	3
	1751	1.7	52
4 Sa ○	0043	0.3	9
	0555	1.3	40
	1210	0.0	0
	1839	1.8	55
5 Su	0140	0.3	9
	0643	1.2	37
	1251	0.0	0
	1927	1.9	58
6 M	0237	0.3	9
	0734	1.2	37
	1337	0.0	0
	2018	1.9	58
7 Tu	0334	0.3	9
	0827	1.1	34
	1426	0.0	0
	2111	1.9	58
8 W	0433	0.3	9
	0923	1.1	34
	1523	0.0	0
	2207	1.8	55
9 Th	0532	0.3	9
	1024	1.1	34
	1627	0.1	3
	2306	1.7	52
10 F ○	0630	0.3	9
	1128	1.1	34
	1739	0.2	6
11 Sa	0008	1.6	49
	0727	0.2	6
	1236	1.1	34
	1855	0.2	6
12 Su	0110	1.5	46
	0819	0.2	6
	1343	1.2	37
	2010	0.2	6
13 M	0209	1.4	43
	0908	0.2	6
	1447	1.3	40
	2120	0.3	9
14 Tu	0303	1.3	40
	0952	0.1	3
	1546	1.4	43
	2223	0.3	9
15 W	0353	1.3	40
	1032	0.1	3
	1639	1.4	43
	2321	0.3	9
16 Th	0438	1.2	37
	1107	0.0	0
	1727	1.5	46
17 F	0014	0.3	9
	0520	1.1	34
	1139	0.0	0
	1810	1.5	46
18 Sa ●	0103	0.3	9
	0600	1.1	34
	1209	0.0	0
	1849	1.6	49
19 Su	0149	0.3	9
	0640	1.0	30
	1239	0.0	0
	1927	1.6	49
20 M	0232	0.3	9
	0720	1.0	30
	1312	0.0	0
	2003	1.5	46
21 Tu	0313	0.3	9
	0801	0.9	27
	1347	0.0	0
	2040	1.5	46
22 W	0353	0.3	9
	0844	0.9	27
	1426	0.1	3
	2117	1.5	46
23 Th	0433	0.3	9
	0929	0.9	27
	1509	0.1	3
	2157	1.4	43
24 F	0515	0.3	9
	1017	0.9	27
	1558	0.2	6
	2240	1.4	43
25 Sa	0558	0.3	9
	1109	0.9	27
	1652	0.2	6
	2326	1.3	40
26 Su ☾	0641	0.2	6
	1204	0.9	27
	1755	0.3	9
27 M	0015	1.3	40
	0724	0.1	3
	1301	1.0	30
	1905	0.3	9
28 Tu	0106	1.2	37
	0805	0.1	3
	1358	1.1	34
	2018	0.3	9
29 W	0159	1.2	37
	0846	0.0	0
	1453	1.2	37
	2128	0.2	6
30 Th	0251	1.1	34
	0927	-0.1	-3
	1546	1.3	40
	2234	0.2	6

December

Day	Time (h m)	Height (ft)	Height (cm)
1 F	0343	1.0	30
	1009	-0.2	-6
	1637	1.5	46
	2336	0.1	3
2 Sa	0436	1.0	30
	1052	-0.3	-9
	1728	1.6	49
3 Su ○	0035	0.1	3
	0528	0.9	27
	1137	-0.3	-9
	1819	1.7	52
4 M	0131	0.0	0
	0621	0.9	27
	1226	-0.3	-9
	1910	1.7	52
5 Tu	0225	0.0	0
	0715	0.9	27
	1318	-0.3	-9
	2002	1.7	52
6 W	0319	0.0	0
	0811	0.9	27
	1413	-0.3	-9
	2056	1.6	49
7 Th	0413	0.0	0
	0908	0.9	27
	1513	-0.2	-6
	2151	1.5	46
8 F	0506	0.0	0
	1009	0.9	27
	1619	-0.1	-3
	2247	1.4	43
9 Sa	0559	0.0	0
	1112	0.9	27
	1730	-0.1	-3
	2344	1.3	40
10 Su ○	0652	-0.1	-3
	1218	1.0	30
	1844	0.0	0
11 M	0040	1.2	37
	0742	-0.1	-3
	1325	1.0	30
	1958	0.1	3
12 Tu	0135	1.1	34
	0828	-0.1	-3
	1430	1.1	34
	2109	0.1	3
13 W	0227	1.0	30
	0912	-0.2	-6
	1530	1.2	37
	2213	0.1	3
14 Th	0317	0.9	27
	0951	-0.2	-6
	1623	1.2	37
	2311	0.1	3
15 F	0404	0.8	24
	1028	-0.2	-6
	1710	1.3	40
16 Sa	0003	0.1	3
	0449	0.8	24
	1102	-0.2	-6
	1752	1.3	40
17 Su	0050	0.1	3
	0533	0.7	21
	1136	-0.2	-6
	1830	1.3	40
18 M ●	0132	0.1	3
	0615	0.7	21
	1212	-0.2	-6
	1906	1.3	40
19 Tu	0211	0.1	3
	0656	0.7	21
	1248	-0.2	-6
	1940	1.3	40
20 W	0247	0.1	3
	0738	0.7	21
	1326	-0.2	-6
	2015	1.3	40
21 Th	0322	0.0	0
	0819	0.7	21
	1406	-0.2	-6
	2050	1.2	37
22 F	0358	0.0	0
	0902	0.7	21
	1449	-0.1	-3
	2128	1.2	37
23 Sa	0434	0.0	0
	0948	0.7	21
	1535	-0.1	-3
	2207	1.2	37
24 Su	0511	0.0	0
	1036	0.7	21
	1627	0.0	0
	2250	1.1	34
25 M	0550	-0.1	-3
	1128	0.8	24
	1728	0.0	0
	2337	1.0	30
26 Tu ☾	0630	-0.2	-6
	1224	0.9	27
	1839	0.1	3
27 W	0027	1.0	30
	0712	-0.2	-6
	1322	1.0	30
	1957	0.1	3
28 Th	0120	0.9	27
	0757	-0.3	-9
	1420	1.1	34
	2112	0.1	3
29 F	0215	0.8	24
	0843	-0.4	-12
	1517	1.2	37
	2222	0.0	0
30 Sa	0312	0.8	24
	0932	-0.4	-12
	1614	1.3	40
	2324	0.0	0
31 Su	0410	0.7	21
	1024	-0.5	-15
	1709	1.4	43

Time meridian 75° W. 0000 is midnight. 1200 is noon. Times are not adjusted for Daylight Saving Time.
Heights are referred to mean lower low water which is the chart datum of soundings.

Washington, D.C., 2017

Times and Heights of High and Low Waters

January

Day	Time	ft	cm	Day	Time	ft	cm
1 Su	0448	-0.2	-6	16 M	0538	-0.4	-12
	0952	2.4	73		1054	2.7	82
	1644	-0.2	-6		1755	-0.3	-9
	2201	2.8	85		2316	2.7	82
2 M	0526	-0.2	-6	17 Tu	0622	-0.3	-9
	1031	2.5	76		1144	2.6	79
	1729	-0.1	-3		1845	-0.2	-6
	2245	2.8	85				
3 Tu	0605	-0.2	-6	18 W	0008	2.6	79
	1115	2.6	79		0706	-0.2	-6
	1817	-0.1	-3		1234	2.6	79
	2334	2.7	82		1935	-0.1	-3
4 W	0647	-0.2	-6	19 Th ◖	0101	2.4	73
	1204	2.6	79		0748	-0.1	-3
	1912	-0.1	-3		1326	2.5	76
					2027	0.0	0
5 Th ◑	0028	2.6	79	20 F	0156	2.3	70
	0734	-0.2	-6		0832	-0.1	-3
	1258	2.7	82		1419	2.5	76
	2014	-0.1	-3		2121	0.0	0
6 F	0128	2.6	79	21 Sa	0251	2.3	70
	0826	-0.2	-6		0918	0.0	0
	1357	2.7	82		1512	2.5	76
	2121	-0.1	-3		2216	0.1	3
7 Sa	0233	2.5	76	22 Su	0345	2.2	67
	0924	-0.3	-9		1008	0.0	0
	1459	2.8	85		1604	2.5	76
	2230	-0.2	-6		2310	0.1	3
8 Su	0339	2.5	76	23 M	0438	2.2	67
	1028	-0.3	-9		1100	0.0	0
	1602	2.9	88		1654	2.5	76
	2335	-0.2	-6				
9 M	0442	2.5	76	24 Tu	0002	0.0	0
	1133	-0.3	-9		0528	2.3	70
	1702	3.0	91		1153	0.0	0
					1742	2.5	76
10 Tu	0036	-0.3	-9	25 W	0052	0.0	0
	0542	2.5	76		0615	2.3	70
	1235	-0.4	-12		1244	-0.1	-3
	1801	3.0	91		1826	2.6	79
11 W	0133	-0.4	-12	26 Th	0138	-0.1	-3
	0638	2.6	79		0658	2.3	70
	1334	-0.4	-12		1333	-0.1	-3
	1857	3.0	91		1907	2.6	79
12 Th ○	0226	-0.5	-15	27 F ●	0222	-0.1	-3
	0732	2.7	82		0738	2.4	73
	1430	-0.5	-15		1420	-0.2	-6
	1950	3.0	91		1946	2.7	82
13 F	0317	-0.6	-18	28 Sa	0304	-0.2	-6
	0824	2.7	82		0816	2.5	76
	1524	-0.5	-15		1505	-0.2	-6
	2043	3.0	91		2025	2.7	82
14 Sa	0406	-0.5	-15	29 Su	0344	-0.2	-6
	0914	2.7	82		0852	2.5	76
	1615	-0.5	-15		1550	-0.2	-6
	2134	2.9	88		2104	2.8	85
15 Su	0453	-0.5	-15	30 M	0424	-0.3	-9
	1004	2.7	82		0929	2.6	79
	1705	-0.4	-12		1634	-0.2	-6
	2225	2.8	85		2145	2.8	85
				31 Tu	0502	-0.3	-9
					1009	2.7	82
					1721	-0.2	-6
					2230	2.8	85

February

Day	Time	ft	cm	Day	Time	ft	cm
1 W	0542	-0.3	-9	16 Th	0621	-0.1	-3
	1053	2.8	85		1153	2.8	85
	1810	-0.2	-6		1859	0.0	0
	2319	2.8	85				
2 Th	0625	-0.3	-9	17 F	0024	2.5	76
	1142	2.9	88		0657	0.0	0
	1904	-0.2	-6		1238	2.7	82
					1945	0.1	3
3 F ◐	0013	2.7	82	18 Sa ◐	0114	2.4	73
	0711	-0.2	-6		0734	0.1	3
	1235	2.9	88		1326	2.6	79
	2004	-0.1	-3		2035	0.2	6
4 Sa	0112	2.6	79	19 Su	0207	2.4	73
	0805	-0.2	-6		0818	0.2	6
	1334	2.9	88		1418	2.6	79
	2108	-0.1	-3		2128	0.3	9
5 Su	0216	2.5	76	20 M	0302	2.3	70
	0906	-0.2	-6		0910	0.2	6
	1437	2.9	88		1513	2.5	76
	2214	-0.1	-3		2224	0.3	9
6 M	0322	2.5	76	21 Tu	0357	2.3	70
	1012	-0.1	-3		1010	0.2	6
	1543	2.9	88		1608	2.6	79
	2317	-0.2	-6		2319	0.3	9
7 Tu	0426	2.5	76	22 W	0449	2.4	73
	1119	-0.2	-6		1112	0.2	6
	1647	2.9	88		1700	2.6	79
8 W	0017	-0.2	-6	23 Th	0012	0.2	6
	0526	2.6	79		0538	2.5	76
	1223	-0.2	-6		1211	0.1	3
	1747	2.9	88		1750	2.7	82
9 Th	0114	-0.3	-9	24 F	0102	0.1	3
	0623	2.7	82		0623	2.5	76
	1321	-0.3	-9		1306	0.1	3
	1844	3.0	91		1836	2.7	82
10 F ○	0206	-0.4	-12	25 Sa	0148	0.0	0
	0716	2.8	85		0705	2.6	79
	1416	-0.4	-12		1357	0.0	0
	1937	3.0	91		1919	2.8	85
11 Sa	0255	-0.4	-12	26 Su ●	0232	0.0	0
	0806	2.8	85		0745	2.8	85
	1508	-0.4	-12		1446	-0.1	-3
	2028	3.0	91		2002	2.9	88
12 Su	0341	-0.4	-12	27 M	0314	-0.1	-3
	0854	2.9	88		0824	2.9	88
	1557	-0.4	-12		1534	-0.1	-3
	2116	2.9	88		2045	3.0	91
13 M	0425	-0.3	-9	28 Tu	0356	-0.2	-6
	0940	2.9	88		0904	3.0	91
	1644	-0.3	-9		1621	-0.2	-6
	2203	2.9	88		2129	3.0	91
14 Tu	0506	-0.2	-6				
	1024	2.8	85				
	1729	-0.2	-6				
	2249	2.8	85				
15 W	0545	-0.1	-3				
	1108	2.8	85				
	1814	-0.1	-3				
	2336	2.7	82				

March

Day	Time	ft	cm	Day	Time	ft	cm
1 W	0437	-0.2	-6	16 Th	0505	0.1	3
	0946	3.1	94		1032	3.1	94
	1710	-0.2	-6		1744	0.1	3
	2215	3.0	91		2304	2.8	85
2 Th	0519	-0.2	-6	17 F	0536	0.2	6
	1032	3.2	98		1110	3.0	91
	1800	-0.1	-3		1823	0.2	6
	2305	2.9	88		2348	2.7	82
3 F	0605	-0.1	-3	18 Sa	0608	0.3	9
	1121	3.2	98		1149	2.9	88
	1855	-0.1	-3		1903	0.3	9
4 Sa	0000	2.8	85	19 Su	0033	2.6	79
	0655	-0.1	-3		0644	0.3	9
	1215	3.2	98		1231	2.9	88
	1953	0.0	0		1946	0.4	12
5 Su ◐	0100	2.8	85	20 M ◐	0122	2.6	79
	0752	0.0	0		0729	0.4	12
	1315	3.1	94		1319	2.8	85
	2054	0.0	0		2035	0.5	15
6 M	0204	2.7	82	21 Tu	0216	2.6	79
	0855	0.1	3		0823	0.4	12
	1421	3.0	91		1414	2.7	82
	2157	0.0	0		2131	0.5	15
7 Tu	0310	2.7	82	22 W	0311	2.6	79
	1002	0.1	3		0925	0.5	15
	1529	3.0	91		1515	2.7	82
	2258	0.0	0		2230	0.5	15
8 W	0413	2.7	82	23 Th	0405	2.6	79
	1108	0.0	0		1032	0.4	12
	1634	3.0	91		1615	2.8	85
	2357	0.0	0		2327	0.4	12
9 Th	0512	2.8	85	24 F	0456	2.7	82
	1210	0.0	0		1138	0.4	12
	1735	3.0	91		1710	2.8	85
10 F	0051	-0.1	-3	25 Sa	0020	0.3	9
	0607	2.9	88		0544	2.9	88
	1307	-0.1	-3		1237	0.3	9
	1830	3.0	91		1802	2.9	88
11 Sa	0142	-0.1	-3	26 Su	0109	0.2	6
	0658	3.0	91		0628	3.0	91
	1400	-0.2	-6		1333	0.2	6
	1922	3.1	94		1850	3.0	91
12 Su ○	0229	-0.1	-3	27 M ●	0156	0.1	3
	0745	3.1	94		0712	3.2	98
	1450	-0.2	-6		1425	0.1	3
	2010	3.1	94		1937	3.1	94
13 M	0313	-0.1	-3	28 Tu	0241	0.1	3
	0830	3.1	94		0754	3.3	101
	1537	-0.2	-6		1515	0.0	0
	2055	3.0	91		2023	3.1	94
14 Tu	0354	0.0	0	29 W	0326	0.0	0
	0913	3.1	94		0838	3.4	104
	1621	-0.1	-3		1605	-0.1	-3
	2139	3.0	91		2111	3.1	94
15 W	0431	0.0	0	30 Th	0411	0.0	0
	0953	3.1	94		0923	3.5	107
	1703	0.0	0		1656	-0.1	-3
	2222	2.9	88		2200	3.1	94
				31 F	0457	0.0	0
					1011	3.5	107
					1748	0.0	0
					2252	3.1	94

Time meridian 75° W. 0000 is midnight. 1200 is noon. Times are not adjusted for Daylight Saving Time.
Heights are referred to mean lower low water which is the chart datum of soundings.

Washington, D.C., 2017
Times and Heights of High and Low Waters

April

Day	Time (h m)	Height (ft)	Height (cm)
1 Sa	0548	0.1	3
	1102	3.5	107
	1842	0.0	0
	2348	3.0	91
2 Su	0642	0.2	6
	1159	3.4	104
	1939	0.1	3
3 M ☽	0048	2.9	88
	0742	0.2	6
	1301	3.2	98
	2038	0.1	3
4 Tu	0152	2.9	88
	0846	0.3	9
	1409	3.1	94
	2137	0.2	6
5 W	0257	2.9	88
	0951	0.3	9
	1517	3.1	94
	2236	0.2	6
6 Th	0358	3.0	91
	1054	0.2	6
	1621	3.1	94
	2332	0.2	6
7 F	0455	3.1	94
	1154	0.1	3
	1720	3.1	94
8 Sa	0025	0.1	3
	0548	3.2	98
	1249	0.1	3
	1813	3.1	94
9 Su	0114	0.1	3
	0637	3.3	101
	1341	0.0	0
	1903	3.1	94
10 M	0200	0.1	3
	0722	3.3	101
	1429	0.0	0
	1949	3.1	94
11 Tu ○	0241	0.2	6
	0805	3.3	101
	1515	0.0	0
	2032	3.1	94
12 W	0320	0.2	6
	0844	3.3	101
	1557	0.1	3
	2114	3.0	91
13 Th	0355	0.3	9
	0921	3.3	101
	1637	0.2	6
	2154	3.0	91
14 F	0427	0.4	12
	0956	3.3	101
	1715	0.3	9
	2234	2.9	88
15 Sa	0457	0.4	12
	1030	3.2	98
	1751	0.4	12
	2313	2.8	85
16 Su	0529	0.5	15
	1105	3.1	94
	1826	0.5	15
	2354	2.8	85
17 M	0609	0.5	15
	1145	3.1	94
	1904	0.5	15
18 Tu	0038	2.8	85
	0655	0.6	18
	1231	3.0	91
	1949	0.6	18
19 W ◐	0128	2.8	85
	0748	0.6	18
	1325	2.9	88
	2040	0.6	18
20 Th	0222	2.8	85
	0849	0.6	18
	1426	2.9	88
	2138	0.5	15
21 F	0318	2.9	88
	0957	0.6	18
	1530	2.9	88
	2236	0.5	15
22 Sa	0412	3.0	91
	1105	0.5	15
	1631	3.0	91
	2333	0.4	12
23 Su	0503	3.1	94
	1209	0.4	12
	1727	3.0	91
24 M	0026	0.3	9
	0552	3.3	101
	1308	0.3	9
	1820	3.1	94
25 Tu	0117	0.2	6
	0639	3.5	107
	1403	0.1	3
	1911	3.2	98
26 W ●	0207	0.2	6
	0726	3.6	110
	1456	0.0	0
	2001	3.2	98
27 Th	0256	0.1	3
	0813	3.7	113
	1548	0.0	0
	2051	3.2	98
28 F	0347	0.1	3
	0902	3.7	113
	1640	0.0	0
	2143	3.2	98
29 Sa	0438	0.2	6
	0952	3.7	113
	1732	0.0	0
	2237	3.2	98
30 Su	0533	0.2	6
	1046	3.6	110
	1826	0.0	0
	2334	3.1	94

May

Day	Time (h m)	Height (ft)	Height (cm)
1 M	0630	0.3	9
	1144	3.4	104
	1921	0.1	3
2 Tu ◐	0035	3.1	94
	0730	0.3	9
	1248	3.3	101
	2017	0.2	6
3 W	0137	3.1	94
	0832	0.3	9
	1355	3.2	98
	2114	0.2	6
4 Th	0240	3.1	94
	0934	0.3	9
	1501	3.1	94
	2210	0.2	6
5 F	0339	3.2	98
	1035	0.3	9
	1603	3.1	94
	2303	0.2	6
6 Sa	0435	3.2	98
	1134	0.3	9
	1659	3.1	94
	2354	0.2	6
7 Su	0526	3.3	101
	1228	0.2	6
	1751	3.1	94
8 M	0042	0.2	6
	0613	3.4	104
	1319	0.2	6
	1839	3.1	94
9 Tu	0127	0.3	9
	0657	3.4	104
	1406	0.2	6
	1925	3.0	91
10 W ○	0208	0.3	9
	0738	3.4	104
	1451	0.2	6
	2008	3.0	91
11 Th	0246	0.4	12
	0816	3.4	104
	1532	0.2	6
	2049	3.0	91
12 F	0322	0.4	12
	0851	3.3	101
	1611	0.3	9
	2128	2.9	88
13 Sa	0355	0.5	15
	0924	3.3	101
	1648	0.4	12
	2205	2.9	88
14 Su	0427	0.5	15
	0956	3.3	101
	1723	0.4	12
	2242	2.9	88
15 M	0502	0.5	15
	1031	3.2	98
	1757	0.4	12
	2319	2.9	88
16 Tu	0543	0.6	18
	1110	3.2	98
	1833	0.5	15
	2359	2.9	88
17 W	0629	0.6	18
	1156	3.1	94
	1914	0.5	15
18 Th ◐	0045	2.9	88
	0721	0.6	18
	1249	3.1	94
	2001	0.5	15
19 F	0138	2.9	88
	0821	0.6	18
	1348	3.0	91
	2053	0.4	12
20 Sa	0234	3.0	91
	0927	0.6	18
	1451	3.0	91
	2149	0.4	12
21 Su	0330	3.2	98
	1037	0.5	15
	1555	3.0	91
	2247	0.4	12
22 M	0425	3.3	101
	1143	0.4	12
	1655	3.0	91
	2344	0.3	9
23 Tu	0519	3.5	107
	1245	0.3	9
	1752	3.1	94
24 W	0041	0.2	6
	0610	3.6	110
	1342	0.1	3
	1847	3.1	94
25 Th ●	0137	0.2	6
	0701	3.7	113
	1437	0.0	0
	1940	3.2	98
26 F	0232	0.1	3
	0752	3.8	116
	1530	-0.1	-3
	2033	3.2	98
27 Sa	0327	0.1	3
	0843	3.8	116
	1622	-0.1	-3
	2126	3.2	98
28 Su	0422	0.1	3
	0936	3.7	113
	1714	-0.1	-3
	2221	3.2	98
29 M	0518	0.2	6
	1031	3.5	107
	1806	0.0	0
	2317	3.1	94
30 Tu	0615	0.2	6
	1129	3.4	104
	1859	0.0	0
31 W	0016	3.1	94
	0713	0.3	9
	1231	3.2	98
	1952	0.1	3

June

Day	Time (h m)	Height (ft)	Height (cm)
1 Th ◐	0116	3.1	94
	0813	0.3	9
	1335	3.1	94
	2045	0.2	6
2 F	0216	3.1	94
	0913	0.3	9
	1438	3.0	91
	2138	0.2	6
3 Sa	0314	3.2	98
	1012	0.3	9
	1538	2.9	88
	2229	0.3	9
4 Su	0408	3.2	98
	1109	0.3	9
	1633	2.9	88
	2319	0.3	9
5 M	0459	3.3	101
	1203	0.3	9
	1725	2.9	88
6 Tu	0007	0.3	9
	0546	3.3	101
	1253	0.2	6
	1814	2.9	88
7 W	0052	0.3	9
	0630	3.3	101
	1341	0.2	6
	1859	2.9	88
8 Th	0134	0.4	12
	0711	3.3	101
	1425	0.2	6
	1943	2.9	88
9 F ○	0214	0.4	12
	0749	3.3	101
	1506	0.2	6
	2023	2.9	88
10 Sa	0252	0.4	12
	0824	3.3	101
	1545	0.3	9
	2102	2.9	88
11 Su	0329	0.5	15
	0857	3.2	98
	1622	0.3	9
	2138	2.8	85
12 M	0405	0.5	15
	0929	3.2	98
	1657	0.3	9
	2212	2.9	88
13 Tu	0443	0.5	15
	1004	3.2	98
	1731	0.3	9
	2247	2.9	88
14 W	0524	0.5	15
	1044	3.2	98
	1806	0.3	9
	2325	2.9	88
15 Th	0609	0.5	15
	1129	3.1	94
	1845	0.3	9
16 F	0010	3.0	91
	0701	0.6	18
	1220	3.1	94
	1928	0.3	9
17 Sa ○	0101	3.1	94
	0759	0.6	18
	1318	3.0	91
	2016	0.3	9
18 Su	0156	3.2	98
	0905	0.5	15
	1420	3.0	91
	2110	0.3	9
19 M	0255	3.3	101
	1015	0.5	15
	1525	2.9	88
	2209	0.3	9
20 Tu	0353	3.4	104
	1122	0.3	9
	1629	2.9	88
	2311	0.2	6
21 W	0451	3.5	107
	1224	0.2	6
	1729	3.0	91
22 Th	0014	0.2	6
	0546	3.6	110
	1323	0.1	3
	1826	3.0	91
23 F ●	0115	0.1	3
	0641	3.7	113
	1418	0.0	0
	1921	3.1	94
24 Sa	0214	0.1	3
	0734	3.7	113
	1511	-0.1	-3
	2015	3.1	94
25 Su	0310	0.1	3
	0827	3.7	113
	1602	-0.1	-3
	2108	3.2	98
26 M	0406	0.1	3
	0921	3.6	110
	1653	-0.1	-3
	2201	3.2	98
27 Tu	0501	0.1	3
	1015	3.5	107
	1742	-0.1	-3
	2256	3.2	98
28 W	0556	0.2	6
	1111	3.3	101
	1832	0.0	0
	2351	3.1	94
29 Th	0652	0.2	6
	1209	3.2	98
	1921	0.1	3
30 F ◐	0048	3.1	94
	0748	0.3	9
	1308	3.0	91
	2010	0.2	6

Time meridian 75° W. 0000 is midnight. 1200 is noon. Times are not adjusted for Daylight Saving Time.
Heights are referred to mean lower low water which is the chart datum of soundings.

Washington, D.C., 2017

Times and Heights of High and Low Waters

July

Day	Time	Height (ft)	Height (cm)
1 Sa	0145	3.1	94
	0846	0.4	12
	1408	2.9	88
	2100	0.3	9
2 Su	0242	3.1	94
	0943	0.4	12
	1507	2.8	85
	2150	0.3	9
3 M	0336	3.1	94
	1039	0.4	12
	1603	2.8	85
	2239	0.4	12
4 Tu	0427	3.2	98
	1133	0.4	12
	1656	2.8	85
	2328	0.4	12
5 W	0516	3.2	98
	1224	0.3	9
	1746	2.8	85
6 Th	0016	0.4	12
	0601	3.2	98
	1312	0.3	9
	1832	2.8	85
7 F	0101	0.4	12
	0644	3.2	98
	1356	0.3	9
	1916	2.8	85
8 Sa ○	0145	0.4	12
	0723	3.2	98
	1438	0.2	6
	1957	2.8	85
9 Su	0227	0.4	12
	0759	3.2	98
	1517	0.2	6
	2035	2.8	85
10 M	0307	0.4	12
	0833	3.2	98
	1555	0.2	6
	2109	2.9	88
11 Tu	0347	0.4	12
	0907	3.2	98
	1630	0.2	6
	2142	2.9	88
12 W	0427	0.4	12
	0942	3.2	98
	1705	0.2	6
	2217	3.0	91
13 Th	0509	0.4	12
	1022	3.2	98
	1740	0.2	6
	2255	3.0	91
14 F	0554	0.5	15
	1107	3.2	98
	1817	0.2	6
	2340	3.1	94
15 Sa	0645	0.5	15
	1157	3.1	94
	1859	0.2	6
16 Su ◑	0030	3.2	98
	0743	0.5	15
	1253	3.0	91
	1947	0.2	6
17 M	0125	3.3	101
	0849	0.5	15
	1356	2.9	88
	2041	0.2	6
18 Tu	0225	3.3	101
	0958	0.4	12
	1503	2.9	88
	2143	0.3	9
19 W	0327	3.4	104
	1104	0.3	9
	1608	2.9	88
	2251	0.2	6
20 Th	0429	3.5	107
	1206	0.2	6
	1711	2.9	88
	2358	0.2	6
21 F	0529	3.6	110
	1304	0.1	3
	1809	3.0	91
22 Sa	0101	0.1	3
	0626	3.6	110
	1359	0.0	0
	1904	3.1	94
23 Su ●	0200	0.1	3
	0721	3.6	110
	1450	-0.1	-3
	1957	3.2	98
24 M	0256	0.0	0
	0814	3.6	110
	1540	-0.1	-3
	2049	3.2	98
25 Tu	0349	0.0	0
	0905	3.5	107
	1628	-0.1	-3
	2139	3.3	101
26 W	0442	0.1	3
	0957	3.4	104
	1714	0.0	0
	2230	3.2	98
27 Th	0534	0.2	6
	1049	3.3	101
	1800	0.0	0
	2321	3.2	98
28 F	0626	0.3	9
	1141	3.1	94
	1845	0.2	6
29 Sa	0013	3.2	98
	0719	0.4	12
	1236	3.0	91
	1930	0.3	9
30 Su ◑	0106	3.1	94
	0813	0.5	15
	1333	2.8	85
	2016	0.4	12
31 M	0201	3.1	94
	0909	0.5	15
	1431	2.7	82
	2104	0.4	12

August

Day	Time	Height (ft)	Height (cm)
1 Tu	0256	3.1	94
	1004	0.5	15
	1528	2.7	82
	2154	0.5	15
2 W	0350	3.1	94
	1059	0.5	15
	1623	2.7	82
	2247	0.5	15
3 Th	0442	3.1	94
	1150	0.5	15
	1715	2.7	82
	2339	0.5	15
4 F	0530	3.1	94
	1239	0.4	12
	1803	2.8	85
5 Sa	0029	0.5	15
	0615	3.1	94
	1324	0.4	12
	1847	2.8	85
6 Su	0117	0.4	12
	0656	3.2	98
	1406	0.3	9
	1928	2.9	88
7 M ○	0203	0.4	12
	0734	3.2	98
	1447	0.2	6
	2005	2.9	88
8 Tu	0246	0.4	12
	0810	3.2	98
	1525	0.2	6
	2040	3.0	91
9 W	0329	0.4	12
	0845	3.3	101
	1601	0.2	6
	2113	3.1	94
10 Th	0411	0.4	12
	0922	3.3	101
	1637	0.2	6
	2148	3.2	98
11 F	0455	0.4	12
	1002	3.3	101
	1713	0.2	6
	2228	3.3	101
12 Sa	0542	0.4	12
	1047	3.2	98
	1751	0.2	6
	2313	3.3	101
13 Su	0634	0.4	12
	1137	3.1	94
	1835	0.2	6
14 M ◑	0003	3.4	104
	0732	0.5	15
	1234	3.0	91
	1925	0.3	9
15 Tu	0059	3.4	104
	0837	0.5	15
	1337	2.9	88
	2024	0.3	9
16 W	0202	3.4	104
	0943	0.4	12
	1446	2.9	88
	2131	0.3	9
17 Th	0308	3.4	104
	1048	0.4	12
	1554	2.9	88
	2242	0.3	9
18 F	0414	3.4	104
	1149	0.2	6
	1656	3.0	91
	2349	0.2	6
19 Sa	0516	3.5	107
	1246	0.1	3
	1755	3.1	94
20 Su	0050	0.1	3
	0614	3.5	107
	1338	0.0	0
	1849	3.2	98
21 M ●	0147	0.1	3
	0708	3.6	110
	1428	-0.1	-3
	1940	3.3	101
22 Tu	0241	0.0	0
	0759	3.5	107
	1515	-0.1	-3
	2028	3.4	104
23 W	0332	0.0	0
	0848	3.5	107
	1600	0.0	0
	2115	3.4	104
24 Th	0421	0.1	3
	0936	3.4	104
	1643	0.0	0
	2201	3.4	104
25 F	0509	0.2	6
	1023	3.3	101
	1724	0.2	6
	2247	3.3	101
26 Sa	0558	0.3	9
	1111	3.1	94
	1804	0.3	9
	2334	3.2	98
27 Su	0646	0.5	15
	1201	2.9	88
	1843	0.4	12
28 M	0022	3.1	94
	0737	0.6	18
	1254	2.8	85
	1924	0.5	15
29 Tu ◑	0114	3.1	94
	0829	0.7	21
	1351	2.7	82
	2010	0.6	18
30 W	0209	3.0	91
	0923	0.7	21
	1449	2.7	82
	2104	0.6	18
31 Th	0307	3.0	91
	1018	0.7	21
	1546	2.7	82
	2203	0.6	18

September

Day	Time	Height (ft)	Height (cm)
1 F	0402	3.0	91
	1111	0.6	18
	1640	2.7	82
	2301	0.6	18
2 Sa	0455	3.0	91
	1201	0.5	15
	1729	2.8	85
	2357	0.5	15
3 Su	0542	3.1	94
	1247	0.4	12
	1814	2.9	88
4 M	0049	0.5	15
	0626	3.2	98
	1331	0.3	9
	1855	3.0	91
5 Tu	0137	0.4	12
	0706	3.2	98
	1412	0.3	9
	1932	3.1	94
6 W ○	0224	0.3	9
	0744	3.3	101
	1451	0.2	6
	2008	3.2	98
7 Th	0309	0.3	9
	0822	3.3	101
	1530	0.2	6
	2043	3.3	101
8 F	0355	0.3	9
	0902	3.3	101
	1607	0.1	3
	2121	3.4	104
9 Sa	0441	0.3	9
	0944	3.3	101
	1646	0.2	6
	2203	3.5	107
10 Su	0530	0.3	9
	1030	3.2	98
	1729	0.2	6
	2249	3.5	107
11 M	0623	0.4	12
	1121	3.1	94
	1816	0.3	9
	2341	3.5	107
12 Tu	0722	0.4	12
	1219	3.0	91
	1912	0.3	9
13 W ◑	0039	3.4	104
	0824	0.4	12
	1324	2.9	88
	2016	0.4	12
14 Th	0145	3.3	101
	0928	0.4	12
	1434	2.9	88
	2127	0.4	12
15 F	0255	3.3	101
	1031	0.3	9
	1541	2.9	88
	2235	0.3	9
16 Sa	0403	3.3	101
	1130	0.2	6
	1643	3.0	91
	2339	0.2	6
17 Su	0506	3.4	104
	1224	0.1	3
	1740	3.2	98
18 M	0038	0.1	3
	0602	3.4	104
	1316	0.0	0
	1832	3.3	101
19 Tu	0133	0.1	3
	0654	3.5	107
	1403	0.0	0
	1921	3.4	104
20 W ●	0224	0.0	0
	0743	3.4	104
	1448	0.0	0
	2007	3.4	104
21 Th	0313	0.0	0
	0829	3.4	104
	1530	0.0	0
	2050	3.5	107
22 F	0359	0.1	3
	0913	3.3	101
	1610	0.1	3
	2132	3.4	104
23 Sa	0445	0.2	6
	0957	3.2	98
	1647	0.2	6
	2213	3.3	101
24 Su	0529	0.4	12
	1041	3.0	91
	1721	0.4	12
	2254	3.3	101
25 M	0612	0.5	15
	1126	2.9	88
	1755	0.4	12
	2336	3.1	94
26 Tu	0657	0.6	18
	1214	2.8	85
	1832	0.5	15
27 W ◑	0022	3.0	91
	0744	0.7	21
	1307	2.7	82
	1918	0.6	18
28 Th	0114	2.9	88
	0836	0.7	21
	1404	2.6	79
	2013	0.6	18
29 F	0214	2.9	88
	0930	0.7	21
	1503	2.6	79
	2116	0.7	21
30 Sa	0315	2.9	88
	1024	0.7	21
	1558	2.7	82
	2221	0.6	18

Time meridian 75° W. 0000 is midnight. 1200 is noon. Times are not adjusted for Daylight Saving Time.
Heights are referred to mean lower low water which is the chart datum of soundings.

Washington, D.C., 2017

Times and Heights of High and Low Waters

October

Date	Time (h m)	ft	cm
1 Su	0412	2.9	88
	1116	0.5	15
	1649	2.8	85
	2322	0.5	15
2 M	0504	3.0	91
	1205	0.4	12
	1735	2.9	88
3 Tu	0018	0.4	12
	0551	3.1	94
	1251	0.3	9
	1817	3.1	94
4 W	0111	0.3	9
	0634	3.2	98
	1334	0.2	6
	1857	3.2	98
5 Th ○	0200	0.2	6
	0717	3.2	98
	1416	0.1	3
	1935	3.4	104
6 F	0249	0.2	6
	0759	3.2	98
	1458	0.1	3
	2015	3.5	107
7 Sa	0337	0.1	3
	0842	3.2	98
	1540	0.1	3
	2057	3.6	110
8 Su	0426	0.1	3
	0927	3.2	98
	1624	0.1	3
	2141	3.6	110
9 M	0517	0.2	6
	1015	3.1	94
	1711	0.1	3
	2230	3.5	107
10 Tu	0611	0.2	6
	1108	3.0	91
	1805	0.2	6
	2323	3.4	104
11 W	0709	0.3	9
	1208	2.9	88
	1905	0.3	9
12 Th ◐	0024	3.3	101
	0809	0.3	9
	1313	2.9	88
	2011	0.3	9
13 F	0133	3.2	98
	0910	0.3	9
	1422	2.9	88
	2118	0.3	9
14 Sa	0244	3.1	94
	1009	0.2	6
	1527	2.9	88
	2224	0.2	6
15 Su	0352	3.1	94
	1106	0.1	3
	1628	3.0	91
	2325	0.1	3
16 M	0452	3.2	98
	1200	0.0	0
	1723	3.2	98
17 Tu	0023	0.0	0
	0547	3.2	98
	1250	0.0	0
	1814	3.3	101
18 W	0116	0.0	0
	0637	3.2	98
	1336	0.0	0
	1900	3.3	101
19 Th ●	0206	-0.1	-3
	0724	3.2	98
	1420	0.0	0
	1944	3.4	104
20 F	0253	0.0	0
	0808	3.1	94
	1500	0.0	0
	2025	3.4	104
21 Sa	0337	0.0	0
	0851	3.1	94
	1538	0.1	3
	2104	3.3	101
22 Su	0420	0.1	3
	0932	3.0	91
	1612	0.2	6
	2141	3.2	98
23 M	0501	0.3	9
	1013	2.9	88
	1643	0.3	9
	2218	3.1	94
24 Tu	0540	0.4	12
	1054	2.7	82
	1715	0.4	12
	2255	3.0	91
25 W	0619	0.5	15
	1136	2.7	82
	1753	0.4	12
	2336	2.9	88
26 Th	0659	0.5	15
	1222	2.6	79
	1838	0.5	15
27 F ◑	0022	2.8	85
	0745	0.5	15
	1314	2.5	76
	1932	0.5	15
28 Sa	0117	2.8	85
	0836	0.5	15
	1410	2.6	79
	2033	0.5	15
29 Su	0219	2.7	82
	0930	0.5	15
	1507	2.6	79
	2139	0.5	15
30 M	0322	2.8	85
	1024	0.4	12
	1601	2.7	82
	2245	0.4	12
31 Tu	0419	2.8	85
	1117	0.3	9
	1650	2.9	88
	2346	0.3	9

November

Date	Time (h m)	ft	cm
1 W	0512	2.9	88
	1206	0.1	3
	1736	3.0	91
2 Th	0043	0.2	6
	0601	3.0	91
	1254	0.0	0
	1821	3.2	98
3 F	0137	0.0	0
	0648	3.0	91
	1341	0.0	0
	1904	3.4	104
4 Sa	0229	0.0	0
	0735	3.0	91
	1428	-0.1	-3
	1949	3.5	107
5 Su	0320	-0.1	-3
	0822	3.0	91
	1516	-0.1	-3
	2035	3.5	107
6 M	0411	-0.1	-3
	0910	3.0	91
	1606	-0.1	-3
	2123	3.5	107
7 Tu	0503	-0.1	-3
	1001	2.9	88
	1659	-0.1	-3
	2215	3.4	104
8 W	0557	-0.1	-3
	1056	2.9	88
	1756	0.0	0
	2311	3.3	101
9 Th	0652	0.0	0
	1156	2.8	85
	1857	0.0	0
10 F ○	0013	3.1	94
	0749	0.0	0
	1300	2.8	85
	2000	0.1	3
11 Sa	0121	3.0	91
	0847	0.0	0
	1405	2.8	85
	2104	0.1	3
12 Su	0230	2.9	88
	0944	0.0	0
	1509	2.8	85
	2207	0.0	0
13 M	0334	2.9	88
	1039	-0.1	-3
	1608	2.9	88
	2307	0.0	0
14 Tu	0433	2.9	88
	1131	-0.1	-3
	1702	3.0	91
15 W	0003	-0.1	-3
	0527	2.9	88
	1221	-0.1	-3
	1751	3.1	94
16 Th	0056	-0.2	-6
	0616	2.9	88
	1307	-0.1	-3
	1837	3.1	94
17 F	0145	-0.2	-6
	0703	2.8	85
	1350	-0.1	-3
	1920	3.1	94
18 Sa ●	0231	-0.2	-6
	0747	2.8	85
	1431	-0.1	-3
	2000	3.1	94
19 Su	0315	-0.1	-3
	0828	2.7	82
	1508	0.0	0
	2038	3.1	94
20 M	0356	0.0	0
	0909	2.7	82
	1543	0.1	3
	2114	3.0	91
21 Tu	0434	0.1	3
	0947	2.6	79
	1616	0.1	3
	2149	2.9	88
22 W	0511	0.1	3
	1025	2.5	76
	1649	0.1	3
	2223	2.8	85
23 Th	0546	0.2	6
	1102	2.5	76
	1727	0.2	6
	2301	2.8	85
24 F	0621	0.2	6
	1141	2.5	76
	1810	0.2	6
	2344	2.7	82
25 Sa	0700	0.2	6
	1226	2.5	76
	1900	0.2	6
26 Su ◐	0034	2.7	82
	0745	0.2	6
	1316	2.5	76
	1956	0.3	9
27 M	0131	2.6	79
	0835	0.1	3
	1411	2.5	76
	2100	0.2	6
28 Tu	0232	2.6	79
	0929	0.1	3
	1508	2.6	79
	2208	0.2	6
29 W	0334	2.6	79
	1024	0.0	0
	1603	2.8	85
	2314	0.1	3
30 Th	0433	2.6	79
	1120	-0.1	-3
	1656	2.9	88

December

Date	Time (h m)	ft	cm
1 F	0016	0.0	0
	0528	2.7	82
	1215	-0.2	-6
	1746	3.1	94
2 Sa	0114	-0.2	-6
	0621	2.7	82
	1310	-0.2	-6
	1836	3.2	98
3 Su ○	0209	-0.3	-9
	0712	2.8	85
	1404	-0.3	-9
	1926	3.3	101
4 M	0302	-0.4	-12
	0803	2.8	85
	1458	-0.3	-9
	2017	3.3	101
5 Tu	0354	-0.4	-12
	0854	2.8	85
	1552	-0.3	-9
	2109	3.3	101
6 W	0446	-0.4	-12
	0947	2.8	85
	1648	-0.3	-9
	2203	3.2	98
7 Th	0538	-0.4	-12
	1042	2.7	82
	1745	-0.3	-9
	2300	3.0	91
8 F	0631	-0.3	-9
	1140	2.7	82
	1843	-0.2	-6
9 Sa	0001	2.9	88
	0725	-0.3	-9
	1241	2.7	82
	1943	-0.2	-6
10 Su ◑	0104	2.7	82
	0819	-0.3	-9
	1343	2.7	82
	2044	-0.2	-6
11 M	0209	2.6	79
	0913	-0.2	-6
	1443	2.7	82
	2144	-0.2	-6
12 Tu	0310	2.6	79
	1006	-0.2	-6
	1541	2.7	82
	2243	-0.2	-6
13 W	0408	2.6	79
	1058	-0.2	-6
	1635	2.8	85
	2339	-0.2	-6
14 Th	0502	2.5	76
	1148	-0.2	-6
	1725	2.8	85
15 F	0032	-0.2	-6
	0552	2.5	76
	1236	-0.2	-6
	1812	2.8	85
16 Sa	0121	-0.2	-6
	0639	2.5	76
	1321	-0.2	-6
	1856	2.8	85
17 Su	0207	-0.2	-6
	0724	2.5	76
	1403	-0.2	-6
	1937	2.8	85
18 M ●	0250	-0.2	-6
	0806	2.5	76
	1443	-0.1	-3
	2015	2.8	85
19 Tu	0331	-0.2	-6
	0846	2.4	73
	1521	-0.1	-3
	2051	2.7	82
20 W	0409	-0.1	-3
	0923	2.4	73
	1556	-0.1	-3
	2126	2.7	82
21 Th	0444	-0.1	-3
	0958	2.4	73
	1632	-0.1	-3
	2159	2.7	82
22 F	0517	-0.1	-3
	1032	2.4	73
	1709	0.0	0
	2235	2.7	82
23 Sa	0550	-0.1	-3
	1107	2.4	73
	1750	0.0	0
	2316	2.6	79
24 Su	0626	-0.1	-3
	1147	2.5	76
	1836	0.0	0
25 M ◐	0003	2.6	79
	0706	-0.1	-3
	1234	2.5	76
	1928	0.0	0
26 Tu ◑	0055	2.5	76
	0751	-0.1	-3
	1326	2.6	79
	2027	0.0	0
27 W	0153	2.5	76
	0842	-0.2	-6
	1422	2.7	82
	2135	0.0	0
28 Th	0256	2.4	73
	0937	-0.2	-6
	1521	2.8	85
	2245	0.0	0
29 F	0358	2.4	73
	1039	-0.2	-6
	1620	2.9	88
	2351	-0.2	-6
30 Sa	0459	2.5	76
	1143	-0.3	-9
	1717	3.0	91
31 Su	0052	-0.3	-9
	0557	2.5	76
	1246	-0.3	-9
	1813	3.1	94

Time meridian 75° W. 0000 is midnight. 1200 is noon. Times are not adjusted for Daylight Saving Time.
Heights are referred to mean lower low water which is the chart datum of soundings.

Chesapeake Bay Bridge Tunnel, Virginia, 2017

Times and Heights of High and Low Waters

January

Day	Time	ft	cm	Day	Time	ft	cm
1 Su	0333	-0.1	-3	**16** M	0445	-0.3	-9
	0958	2.7	82		1102	2.7	82
	1615	-0.2	-6		1722	-0.3	-9
	2221	2.2	67		2330	2.4	73
2 M	0418	-0.1	-3	**17** Tu	0537	-0.1	-3
	1038	2.6	79		1146	2.4	73
	1658	-0.2	-6		1807	-0.1	-3
	2306	2.2	67				
3 Tu	0507	0.0	0	**18** W	0019	2.3	70
	1122	2.5	76		0630	0.1	3
	1744	-0.2	-6		1231	2.2	67
	2356	2.3	70		1853	0.0	0
4 W	0602	0.0	0	**19** Th	0110	2.2	67
	1211	2.4	73		0727	0.2	6
	1835	-0.2	-6		1319	2.0	61
				☽	1940	0.1	3
5 Th	0051	2.4	73	**20** F	0204	2.2	67
	0703	0.0	0		0826	0.3	9
	1306	2.3	70		1412	1.9	58
☾	1930	-0.2	-6		2030	0.1	3
6 F	0152	2.5	76	**21** Sa	0301	2.2	67
	0810	0.0	0		0926	0.4	12
	1407	2.2	67		1509	1.8	55
	2029	-0.3	-9		2121	0.1	3
7 Sa	0257	2.6	79	**22** Su	0358	2.2	67
	0919	0.0	0		1021	0.3	9
	1513	2.2	67		1608	1.8	55
	2130	-0.4	-12		2211	0.1	3
8 Su	0403	2.7	82	**23** M	0451	2.3	70
	1025	-0.1	-3		1111	0.2	6
	1621	2.2	67		1703	1.8	55
	2231	-0.5	-15		2259	0.0	0
9 M	0507	2.9	88	**24** Tu	0540	2.4	73
	1128	-0.3	-9		1156	0.2	6
	1727	2.3	70		1752	1.9	58
	2330	-0.6	-18		2345	-0.1	-3
10 Tu	0607	3.1	94	**25** W	0623	2.5	76
	1226	-0.4	-12		1237	0.0	0
	1828	2.4	73		1837	2.0	61
11 W	0026	-0.6	-18	**26** Th	0028	-0.2	-6
	0703	3.2	98		0704	2.6	79
	1321	-0.5	-15		1315	-0.1	-3
	1925	2.4	73		1918	2.1	64
12 Th	0121	-0.7	-21	**27** F	0110	-0.2	-6
	0755	3.2	98		0743	2.7	82
	1413	-0.6	-18		1353	-0.2	-6
○	2017	2.5	76	●	1958	2.2	67
13 F	0213	-0.7	-21	**28** Sa	0151	-0.3	-9
	0844	3.2	98		0821	2.8	85
	1502	-0.6	-18		1431	-0.3	-9
	2107	2.5	76		2038	2.3	70
14 Sa	0305	-0.6	-18	**29** Su	0233	-0.3	-9
	0931	3.0	91		0859	2.8	85
	1550	-0.5	-15		1510	-0.3	-9
	2155	2.5	76		2119	2.4	73
15 Su	0355	-0.4	-12	**30** M	0317	-0.3	-9
	1017	2.9	88		0938	2.8	85
	1636	-0.4	-12		1551	-0.4	-12
	2243	2.4	73		2201	2.5	76
				31 Tu	0403	-0.3	-9
					1019	2.7	82
					1633	-0.4	-12
					2246	2.5	76

February

Day	Time	ft	cm	Day	Time	ft	cm
1 W	0452	-0.2	-6	**16** Th	0549	0.1	3
	1103	2.6	79		1149	2.2	67
	1719	-0.4	-12		1801	0.1	3
	2335	2.6	79				
2 Th	0546	-0.1	-3	**17** F	0019	2.4	73
	1152	2.5	76		0637	0.3	9
	1810	-0.3	-9		1232	2.1	64
					1845	0.2	6
3 F	0030	2.6	79	**18** Sa	0107	2.3	70
	0646	0.0	0		0730	0.4	12
	1246	2.3	70		1320	1.9	58
☾	1906	-0.3	-9	○	1934	0.3	9
4 Sa	0130	2.6	79	**19** Su	0201	2.2	67
	0753	0.0	0		0828	0.5	15
	1347	2.2	67		1415	1.9	58
	2007	-0.2	-6		2029	0.3	9
5 Su	0237	2.6	79	**20** M	0301	2.2	67
	0903	0.0	0		0927	0.5	15
	1456	2.1	64		1516	1.8	55
	2112	-0.3	-9		2126	0.3	9
6 M	0348	2.7	82	**21** Tu	0402	2.3	70
	1012	0.0	0		1023	0.4	12
	1610	2.1	64		1618	1.9	58
	2217	-0.3	-9		2221	0.2	6
7 Tu	0457	2.8	85	**22** W	0459	2.4	73
	1117	-0.1	-3		1114	0.3	9
	1719	2.2	67		1714	2.0	61
	2320	-0.4	-12		2312	0.1	3
8 W	0559	2.9	88	**23** Th	0548	2.5	76
	1215	-0.3	-9		1159	0.2	6
	1821	2.4	73		1803	2.2	67
9 Th	0018	-0.5	-15	**24** F	0000	0.0	0
	0654	3.0	91		0633	2.7	82
	1308	-0.4	-12		1241	0.0	0
	1915	2.5	76		1848	2.4	73
10 F	0112	-0.5	-15	**25** Sa	0046	-0.2	-6
	0744	3.0	91		0715	2.8	85
	1356	-0.4	-12		1321	-0.1	-3
○	2004	2.6	79		1931	2.5	76
11 Sa	0202	-0.5	-15	**26** Su	0130	-0.3	-9
	0829	3.0	91		0755	2.9	88
	1441	-0.4	-12		1402	-0.3	-9
	2049	2.6	79	●	2013	2.7	82
12 Su	0249	-0.5	-15	**27** M	0215	-0.4	-12
	0912	2.9	88		0836	2.9	88
	1523	-0.4	-12		1443	-0.4	-12
	2132	2.6	79		2056	2.8	85
13 M	0335	-0.4	-12	**28** Tu	0301	-0.4	-12
	0952	2.8	85		0917	2.9	88
	1604	-0.3	-9		1525	-0.4	-12
	2213	2.6	79		2140	2.9	88
14 Tu	0419	-0.2	-6				
	1031	2.6	79				
	1642	-0.2	-6				
	2254	2.5	76				
15 W	0503	0.0	0				
	1109	2.4	73				
	1721	0.0	0				
	2335	2.4	73				

March

Day	Time	ft	cm	Day	Time	ft	cm
1 W	0348	-0.4	-12	**16** Th	0432	0.1	3
	1001	2.8	85		1036	2.5	76
	1609	-0.4	-12		1639	0.1	3
	2227	2.9	88		2256	2.7	82
2 Th	0439	-0.3	-9	**17** F	0512	0.2	6
	1047	2.7	82		1113	2.3	70
	1657	-0.3	-9		1717	0.2	6
	2317	2.9	88		2336	2.6	79
3 F	0533	-0.2	-6	**18** Sa	0554	0.4	12
	1136	2.6	79		1154	2.2	67
	1749	-0.3	-9		1759	0.4	12
4 Sa	0011	2.9	88	**19** Su	0020	2.5	76
	0633	0.0	0		0642	0.5	15
	1232	2.4	73		1239	2.1	64
	1847	-0.1	-3		1847	0.4	12
5 Su	0113	2.8	85	**20** M	0110	2.4	73
	0739	0.1	3		0735	0.6	18
	1335	2.3	70		1331	2.0	61
☾	1951	-0.1	-3	○	1942	0.5	15
6 M	0222	2.7	82	**21** Tu	0207	2.3	70
	0850	0.1	3		0833	0.6	18
	1448	2.2	67		1430	2.0	61
	2101	0.0	0		2041	0.5	15
7 Tu	0336	2.7	82	**22** W	0309	2.3	70
	1000	0.1	3		0931	0.5	15
	1605	2.3	70		1532	2.1	64
	2210	-0.1	-3		2141	0.4	12
8 W	0448	2.8	85	**23** Th	0410	2.4	73
	1104	0.0	0		1026	0.4	12
	1714	2.4	73		1632	2.2	67
	2314	-0.1	-3		2238	0.3	9
9 Th	0549	2.9	88	**24** F	0506	2.6	79
	1200	0.0	0		1116	0.3	9
	1812	2.5	76		1726	2.4	73
					2330	0.1	3
10 F	0011	-0.2	-6	**25** Sa	0556	2.7	82
	0642	2.9	88		1202	0.1	3
	1249	-0.1	-3		1815	2.7	82
	1902	2.7	82				
11 Sa	0102	-0.3	-9	**26** Su	0020	-0.1	-3
	0729	2.9	88		0642	2.9	88
	1334	-0.2	-6		1246	-0.1	-3
	1947	2.8	85		1902	2.9	88
12 Su	0149	-0.3	-9	**27** M	0108	-0.3	-9
	0810	2.9	88		0727	3.0	91
	1415	-0.2	-6		1330	-0.2	-6
○	2027	2.8	85	●	1947	3.1	94
13 M	0232	-0.3	-9	**28** Tu	0156	-0.4	-12
	0849	2.9	88		0812	3.0	91
	1452	-0.2	-6		1414	-0.3	-9
	2105	2.8	85		2033	3.2	98
14 Tu	0313	-0.2	-6	**29** W	0244	-0.4	-12
	0925	2.7	82		0857	3.0	91
	1528	-0.1	-3		1459	-0.4	-12
	2142	2.8	85		2120	3.3	101
15 W	0353	-0.1	-3	**30** Th	0334	-0.4	-12
	1001	2.6	79		0943	2.9	88
	1603	0.0	0		1547	-0.4	-12
	2218	2.8	85		2209	3.3	101
				31 F	0426	-0.3	-9
					1032	2.8	85
					1637	-0.3	-9
					2300	3.2	98

Time meridian 75° W. 0000 is midnight. 1200 is noon. Times are not adjusted for Daylight Saving Time.
Heights are referred to mean lower low water which is the chart datum of soundings.

Chesapeake Bay Bridge Tunnel, Virginia, 2017

Times and Heights of High and Low Waters

April

Day	Time	ft	cm	Day	Time	ft	cm
1 Sa	0522	-0.2	-6	16 Su	0520	0.4	12
	1125	2.7	82		1123	2.3	70
	1732	-0.1	-3		1721	0.5	15
	2356	3.1	94		2342	2.6	79
2 Su	0622	0.0	0	17 M	0603	0.5	15
	1223	2.5	76		1207	2.2	67
	1833	0.0	0		1808	0.5	15
3 M	0058	2.9	88	18 Tu	0029	2.5	76
	0727	0.1	3		0652	0.5	15
	1329	2.4	73		1256	2.2	67
	1941	0.1	3		1902	0.6	18
4 Tu	0208	2.8	85	19 W	0122	2.4	73
	0837	0.2	6		0747	0.6	18
	1443	2.4	73		1351	2.2	67
	2053	0.2	6		2001	0.6	18
5 W	0323	2.7	82	20 Th	0220	2.4	73
	0944	0.2	6		0843	0.5	15
	1558	2.4	73		1451	2.3	70
	2203	0.2	6		2103	0.5	15
6 Th	0434	2.7	82	21 F	0320	2.5	76
	1045	0.2	6		0939	0.4	12
	1703	2.6	79		1551	2.4	73
	2305	0.1	3		2203	0.3	9
7 F	0533	2.8	85	22 Sa	0420	2.6	79
	1138	0.1	3		1032	0.2	6
	1757	2.7	82		1648	2.7	82
					2300	0.1	3
8 Sa	0000	0.0	0	23 Su	0515	2.7	82
	0624	2.8	85		1122	0.1	3
	1224	0.1	3		1741	2.9	88
	1843	2.8	85		2354	-0.1	-3
9 Su	0049	0.0	0	24 M	0608	2.8	85
	0708	2.8	85		1210	-0.1	-3
	1306	0.0	0		1832	3.2	98
	1924	2.9	88				
10 M	0132	-0.1	-3	25 Tu	0046	-0.3	-9
	0747	2.8	85		0658	2.9	88
	1343	0.0	0		1258	-0.3	-9
	2002	3.0	91		1921	3.4	104
11 Tu	0212	-0.1	-3	26 W	0137	-0.4	-12
	0823	2.7	82		0747	3.0	91
	1419	0.0	0		1346	-0.4	-12
	2037	3.0	91		2011	3.5	107
12 W	0250	0.0	0	27 Th	0228	-0.4	-12
	0858	2.6	79		0837	3.0	91
	1452	0.1	3		1436	-0.4	-12
	2111	3.0	91		2101	3.6	110
13 Th	0327	0.1	3	28 F	0320	-0.4	-12
	0932	2.6	79		0927	2.9	88
	1527	0.2	6		1527	-0.4	-12
	2146	2.9	88		2152	3.5	107
14 F	0403	0.1	3	29 Sa	0414	-0.3	-9
	1007	2.5	76		1020	2.8	85
	1602	0.3	9		1620	-0.2	-6
	2222	2.8	85		2246	3.4	104
15 Sa	0440	0.3	9	30 Su	0510	-0.2	-6
	1044	2.4	73		1115	2.7	82
	1640	0.4	12		1718	-0.1	-3
	2300	2.7	82		2343	3.2	98

May

Day	Time	ft	cm	Day	Time	ft	cm
1 M	0610	0.0	0	16 Tu	0533	0.4	12
	1215	2.6	79		1140	2.3	70
	1821	0.1	3		1738	0.5	15
					2356	2.6	79
2 Tu	0044	3.0	91	17 W	0618	0.4	12
	0713	0.1	3		1227	2.3	70
	1321	2.5	76		1830	0.5	15
	1930	0.2	6				
3 W	0152	2.8	85	18 Th	0044	2.5	76
	0818	0.2	6		0709	0.4	12
	1432	2.5	76		1319	2.3	70
	2041	0.3	9		1927	0.5	15
4 Th	0302	2.7	82	19 F	0138	2.5	76
	0921	0.2	6		0802	0.3	9
	1541	2.6	79		1415	2.4	73
	2149	0.3	9		2029	0.4	12
5 F	0409	2.6	79	20 Sa	0237	2.5	76
	1018	0.2	6		0857	0.2	6
	1642	2.7	82		1514	2.6	79
	2250	0.2	6		2131	0.3	9
6 Sa	0507	2.6	79	21 Su	0337	2.5	76
	1108	0.2	6		0952	0.1	3
	1734	2.8	85		1613	2.8	85
	2343	0.2	6		2232	0.1	3
7 Su	0557	2.6	79	22 M	0437	2.6	79
	1152	0.2	6		1045	-0.1	-3
	1818	2.9	88		1710	3.1	94
					2330	-0.1	-3
8 M	0030	0.1	3	23 Tu	0535	2.7	82
	0641	2.5	76		1138	-0.2	-6
	1232	0.1	3		1805	3.3	101
	1857	2.9	88				
9 Tu	0112	0.1	3	24 W	0025	-0.3	-9
	0719	2.5	76		0631	2.7	82
	1309	0.1	3		1230	-0.4	-12
	1934	3.0	91		1858	3.5	107
10 W	0150	0.1	3	25 Th	0119	-0.4	-12
	0756	2.5	76		0725	2.8	85
	1344	0.1	3		1323	-0.4	-12
	2008	3.0	91		1951	3.6	110
11 Th	0226	0.1	3	26 F	0213	-0.5	-15
	0831	2.5	76		0819	2.8	85
	1419	0.2	6		1416	-0.4	-12
	2043	3.0	91		2044	3.6	110
12 F	0301	0.1	3	27 Sa	0306	-0.5	-15
	0906	2.4	73		0913	2.8	85
	1454	0.2	6		1510	-0.4	-12
	2118	2.9	88		2137	3.5	107
13 Sa	0336	0.1	3	28 Su	0400	-0.4	-12
	0942	2.4	73		1007	2.8	85
	1531	0.3	9		1606	-0.3	-9
	2154	2.8	85		2232	3.3	101
14 Su	0413	0.2	6	29 M	0456	-0.3	-9
	1019	2.3	70		1104	2.7	82
	1610	0.4	12		1705	-0.1	-3
	2232	2.7	82		2328	3.1	94
15 M	0451	0.3	9	30 Tu	0553	-0.1	-3
	1058	2.3	70		1203	2.7	82
	1651	0.4	12		1808	0.0	0
	2312	2.6	79				
				31 W	0026	2.9	88
					0652	0.0	0
					1305	2.6	79
					1914	0.2	6

June

Day	Time	ft	cm	Day	Time	ft	cm
1 Th	0128	2.7	82	16 F	0013	2.5	76
	0751	0.1	3		0635	0.2	6
	1410	2.6	79		1250	2.4	73
	2022	0.3	9		1859	0.4	12
2 F	0231	2.5	76	17 Sa	0105	2.5	76
	0848	0.2	6		0727	0.1	3
	1513	2.6	79		1345	2.6	79
	2127	0.3	9		2001	0.3	9
3 Sa	0334	2.4	73	18 Su	0201	2.4	73
	0942	0.2	6		0821	0.1	3
	1611	2.7	82		1443	2.7	82
	2226	0.3	9		2104	0.2	6
4 Su	0432	2.3	70	19 M	0302	2.4	73
	1031	0.2	6		0918	0.0	0
	1702	2.7	82		1543	2.9	88
	2319	0.2	6		2207	0.1	3
5 M	0523	2.3	70	20 Tu	0405	2.4	73
	1115	0.2	6		1015	-0.1	-3
	1747	2.8	85		1644	3.1	94
					2308	-0.1	-3
6 Tu	0005	0.2	6	21 W	0508	2.5	76
	0608	2.3	70		1112	-0.3	-9
	1156	0.2	6		1743	3.3	101
	1827	2.9	88				
7 W	0047	0.2	6	22 Th	0007	-0.2	-6
	0649	2.3	70		0609	2.6	79
	1234	0.2	6		1208	-0.4	-12
	1905	2.9	88		1840	3.5	107
8 Th	0125	0.1	3	23 F	0103	-0.4	-12
	0727	2.3	70		0708	2.7	82
	1312	0.2	6		1304	-0.4	-12
	1941	2.9	88		1935	3.5	107
9 F	0201	0.1	3	24 Sa	0157	-0.4	-12
	0804	2.3	70		0804	2.8	85
	1349	0.2	6		1359	-0.4	-12
	2017	2.9	88		2029	3.5	107
10 Sa	0236	0.1	3	25 Su	0251	-0.5	-15
	0841	2.3	70		0859	2.8	85
	1427	0.2	6		1455	-0.4	-12
	2053	2.9	88		2123	3.4	104
11 Su	0311	0.1	3	26 M	0344	-0.4	-12
	0918	2.3	70		0953	2.8	85
	1505	0.2	6		1551	-0.3	-9
	2130	2.8	85		2215	3.3	101
12 M	0347	0.1	3	27 Tu	0437	-0.3	-9
	0955	2.3	70		1047	2.8	85
	1544	0.3	9		1649	-0.1	-3
	2207	2.7	82		2308	3.1	94
13 Tu	0425	0.2	6	28 W	0530	-0.2	-6
	1034	2.3	70		1142	2.7	82
	1626	0.3	9		1748	0.0	0
	2246	2.7	82				
14 W	0505	0.2	6	29 Th	0001	2.8	85
	1115	2.3	70		0623	-0.1	-3
	1712	0.4	12		1239	2.7	82
	2328	2.6	79		1850	0.2	6
15 Th	0548	0.2	6	30 F	0055	2.6	79
	1200	2.4	73		0716	0.1	3
	1803	0.4	12		1336	2.6	79
					1953	0.3	9

Time meridian 75° W. 0000 is midnight. 1200 is noon. Times are not adjusted for Daylight Saving Time.
Heights are referred to mean lower low water which is the chart datum of soundings.

Chesapeake Bay Bridge Tunnel, Virginia, 2017

Times and Heights of High and Low Waters

July

Day	Time	ft	cm		Day	Time	ft	cm
1 Sa	0152	2.4	73		16 Su	0037	2.5	76
	0808	0.2	6			0656	0.1	3
	1434	2.6	79			1318	2.8	85
	2055	0.4	12		☽ 1938	0.3	9
2 Su	0250	2.2	67		17 M	0133	2.4	73
	0859	0.3	9			0751	0.0	0
	1531	2.6	79			1417	2.9	88
	2154	0.4	12			2043	0.3	9
3 M	0348	2.1	64		18 Tu	0236	2.4	73
	0948	0.3	9			0851	0.0	0
	1623	2.7	82			1520	3.0	91
	2247	0.4	12			2148	0.2	6
4 Tu	0442	2.1	64		19 W	0342	2.4	73
	1035	0.3	9			0952	-0.1	-3
	1711	2.7	82			1624	3.2	98
	2334	0.3	9			2252	0.0	0
5 W	0531	2.1	64		20 Th	0450	2.5	76
	1119	0.3	9			1053	-0.2	-6
	1755	2.8	85			1727	3.3	101
						2352	-0.1	-3
6 Th	0017	0.3	9		21 F	0554	2.6	79
	0616	2.2	67			1153	-0.2	-6
	1202	0.2	6			1826	3.4	104
	1836	2.8	85					
7 F	0056	0.2	6		22 Sa	0048	-0.2	-6
	0658	2.3	70			0654	2.7	82
	1243	0.2	6			1250	-0.3	-9
	1915	2.9	88			1923	3.5	107
8 Sa	0133	0.2	6		23 Su	0142	-0.3	-9
	0738	2.3	70			0750	2.8	85
	1323	0.2	6			1347	-0.3	-9
○ 1953	2.9	88		● 2016	3.5	107
9 Su	0209	0.1	3		24 M	0233	-0.3	-9
	0816	2.4	73			0844	2.9	88
	1402	0.2	6			1441	-0.3	-9
	2030	2.9	88			2106	3.4	104
10 M	0244	0.1	3		25 Tu	0323	-0.3	-9
	0853	2.4	73			0935	3.0	91
	1442	0.2	6			1535	-0.2	-6
	2106	2.9	88			2155	3.2	98
11 Tu	0320	0.1	3		26 W	0411	-0.2	-6
	0931	2.5	76			1024	2.9	88
	1522	0.2	6			1629	0.0	0
	2143	2.8	85			2243	3.0	91
12 W	0358	0.1	3		27 Th	0459	-0.1	-3
	1010	2.5	76			1114	2.9	88
	1604	0.2	6			1723	0.1	3
	2221	2.8	85			2330	2.8	85
13 Th	0437	0.1	3		28 F	0546	0.1	3
	1051	2.5	76			1203	2.8	85
	1650	0.3	9			1818	0.3	9
	2302	2.7	82					
14 F	0519	0.1	3		29 Sa	0018	2.6	79
	1135	2.6	79			0633	0.2	6
	1741	0.3	9			1254	2.7	82
	2347	2.6	79			1916	0.4	12
15 Sa	0605	0.1	3		30 Su	0107	2.4	73
	1224	2.7	82			0721	0.3	9
	1837	0.3	9			1347	2.7	82
					◑ 2015	0.5	15
					31 M	0201	2.2	67
						0811	0.4	12
						1441	2.7	82
						2113	0.6	18

August

Day	Time	ft	cm		Day	Time	ft	cm
1 Tu	0258	2.1	64		16 W	0219	2.5	76
	0902	0.5	15			0832	0.2	6
	1537	2.7	82			1503	3.1	94
	2208	0.6	18			2134	0.3	9
2 W	0357	2.1	64		17 Th	0330	2.5	76
	0954	0.5	15			0938	0.1	3
	1630	2.7	82			1612	3.2	98
	2258	0.5	15			2239	0.2	6
3 Th	0452	2.2	67		18 F	0441	2.6	79
	1044	0.5	15			1042	0.1	3
	1720	2.8	85			1717	3.3	101
	2342	0.5	15			2339	0.1	3
4 F	0542	2.3	70		19 Sa	0546	2.7	82
	1131	0.4	12			1144	0.0	0
	1805	2.8	85			1816	3.4	104
5 Sa	0023	0.4	12		20 Su	0034	0.0	0
	0627	2.4	73			0645	2.9	88
	1215	0.3	9			1241	-0.1	-3
	1847	2.9	88			1910	3.4	104
6 Su	0101	0.3	9		21 M	0124	-0.1	-3
	0708	2.5	76			0737	3.0	91
	1257	0.3	9			1335	-0.1	-3
	1926	3.0	91		● 2000	3.4	104
7 M	0137	0.2	6		22 Tu	0212	-0.1	-3
	0748	2.6	79			0826	3.1	94
	1338	0.2	6			1427	-0.1	-3
○ 2003	3.0	91			2047	3.3	101
8 Tu	0214	0.1	3		23 W	0257	-0.1	-3
	0826	2.7	82			0912	3.2	98
	1419	0.2	6			1516	0.0	0
	2040	3.0	91			2131	3.2	98
9 W	0250	0.1	3		24 Th	0340	0.0	0
	0904	2.8	85			0956	3.2	98
	1500	0.2	6			1605	0.1	3
	2118	3.0	91			2213	3.0	91
10 Th	0328	0.1	3		25 F	0422	0.1	3
	0944	2.8	85			1040	3.1	94
	1544	0.2	6			1653	0.3	9
	2157	2.9	88			2256	2.8	85
11 F	0408	0.1	3		26 Sa	0504	0.3	9
	1026	2.9	88			1123	3.0	91
	1631	0.3	9			1742	0.5	15
	2239	2.9	88			2338	2.6	79
12 Sa	0451	0.1	3		27 Su	0546	0.4	12
	1111	3.0	91			1208	2.9	88
	1722	0.3	9			1833	0.6	18
	2325	2.7	82					
13 Su	0538	0.1	3		28 M	0024	2.4	73
	1200	3.0	91			0631	0.6	18
	1818	0.3	9			1256	2.8	85
						1928	0.7	21
14 M	0016	2.6	79		29 Tu	0113	2.3	70
	0630	0.1	3			0721	0.7	21
	1255	3.0	91			1349	2.7	82
◑ 1920	0.4	12		◑ 2025	0.8	24
15 Tu	0114	2.5	76		30 W	0210	2.2	67
	0728	0.2	6			0815	0.7	21
	1357	3.1	94			1446	2.7	82
	2027	0.4	12			2122	0.8	24
					31 Th	0311	2.2	67
						0913	0.7	21
						1545	2.7	82
						2215	0.7	21

September

Day	Time	ft	cm		Day	Time	ft	cm
1 F	0412	2.3	70		16 Sa	0439	2.7	82
	1008	0.7	21			1037	0.3	9
	1640	2.8	85			1709	3.2	98
	2302	0.7	21			2325	0.2	6
2 Sa	0506	2.4	73		17 Su	0541	2.9	88
	1059	0.6	18			1138	0.2	6
	1729	2.9	88			1806	3.3	101
	2344	0.5	15					
3 Su	0553	2.6	79		18 M	0017	0.1	3
	1146	0.5	15			0634	3.1	94
	1813	3.0	91			1233	0.1	3
						1856	3.3	101
4 M	0024	0.4	12		19 Tu	0104	0.1	3
	0636	2.7	82			0722	3.2	98
	1230	0.4	12			1324	0.1	3
	1854	3.1	94			1942	3.3	101
5 Tu	0102	0.3	9		20 W	0147	0.0	0
	0717	2.9	88			0806	3.3	101
	1313	0.3	9			1411	0.1	3
	1933	3.1	94		● 2024	3.2	98
6 W	0140	0.2	6		21 Th	0227	0.1	3
	0757	3.0	91			0847	3.3	101
	1356	0.2	6			1456	0.1	3
○ 2013	3.1	94			2104	3.1	94
7 Th	0218	0.1	3		22 F	0306	0.2	6
	0837	3.2	98			0926	3.3	101
	1440	0.1	3			1539	0.3	9
	2052	3.1	94			2143	2.9	88
8 F	0258	0.0	0		23 Sa	0344	0.3	9
	0918	3.3	101			1004	3.2	98
	1525	0.1	3			1622	0.4	12
	2134	3.1	94			2221	2.8	85
9 Sa	0340	0.0	0		24 Su	0421	0.4	12
	1002	3.3	101			1044	3.1	94
	1614	0.2	6			1705	0.5	15
	2218	3.0	91			2301	2.6	79
10 Su	0425	0.1	3		25 M	0501	0.6	18
	1049	3.3	101			1125	3.0	91
	1706	0.3	9			1751	0.7	21
	2307	2.8	85			2344	2.5	76
11 M	0515	0.2	6		26 Tu	0544	0.7	21
	1140	3.3	101			1210	2.9	88
	1803	0.4	12			1840	0.8	24
12 Tu	0001	2.7	82		27 W	0031	2.3	70
	0610	0.3	9			0633	0.8	24
	1238	3.2	98			1300	2.8	85
	1907	0.4	12		◑ 1934	0.9	27
13 W	0102	2.6	79		28 Th	0126	2.3	70
	0712	0.3	9			0729	0.9	27
	1342	3.2	98			1356	2.7	82
◑ 2015	0.5	15			2031	0.9	27
14 Th	0211	2.6	79		29 F	0226	2.3	70
	0821	0.4	12			0830	0.9	27
	1452	3.2	98			1455	2.7	82
	2124	0.4	12			2126	0.8	24
15 F	0327	2.6	79		30 Sa	0329	2.4	73
	0931	0.4	12			0929	0.8	24
	1603	3.2	98			1554	2.7	82
	2228	0.3	9			2216	0.7	21

Time meridian 75° W. 0000 is midnight. 1200 is noon Times are not adjusted for Daylight Saving Time.
Heights are referred to mean lower low water which is the chart datum of soundings.

Chesapeake Bay Bridge Tunnel, Virginia, 2017

Times and Heights of High and Low Waters

October

Day	Time	ft	cm		Day	Time	ft	cm
1 Su	0426	2.5	76		16 M	0531	3.0	91
	1024	0.7	21			1131	0.3	9
	1647	2.8	85			1750	3.1	94
	2301	0.6	18			2356	0.1	3
2 M	0516	2.7	82		17 Tu	0620	3.1	94
	1115	0.5	15			1223	0.2	6
	1734	2.9	88			1838	3.0	91
	2343	0.4	12					
3 Tu	0601	2.9	88		18 W	0039	0.1	3
	1202	0.4	12			0704	3.2	98
	1818	3.0	91			1310	0.1	3
						1920	3.0	91
4 W	0024	0.2	6		19 Th ●	0119	0.1	3
	0644	3.1	94			0743	3.3	101
	1248	0.2	6			1353	0.1	3
	1901	3.1	94			2000	2.9	88
5 Th O	0105	0.1	3		20 F	0156	0.1	3
	0727	3.3	101			0820	3.3	101
	1333	0.1	3			1434	0.2	6
	1944	3.1	94			2037	2.8	85
6 F	0147	0.0	0		21 Sa	0232	0.2	6
	0810	3.5	107			0856	3.3	101
	1420	0.0	0			1513	0.3	9
	2028	3.1	94			2113	2.7	82
7 Sa	0230	-0.1	-3		22 Su	0308	0.3	9
	0854	3.6	110			0932	3.2	98
	1508	0.0	0			1552	0.3	9
	2113	3.1	94			2150	2.6	79
8 Su	0315	-0.1	-3		23 M	0344	0.4	12
	0940	3.6	110			1009	3.1	94
	1558	0.1	3			1631	0.5	15
	2201	3.0	91			2228	2.5	76
9 M	0403	0.0	0		24 Tu	0422	0.5	15
	1030	3.5	107			1048	3.0	91
	1652	0.2	6			1712	0.6	18
	2253	2.8	85			2310	2.4	73
10 Tu	0456	0.1	3		25 W	0504	0.6	18
	1124	3.4	104			1130	2.8	85
	1751	0.3	9			1757	0.7	21
	2350	2.7	82			2355	2.3	70
11 W	0555	0.3	9		26 Th	0552	0.7	21
	1223	3.3	101			1217	2.7	82
	1855	0.4	12			1847	0.7	21
12 Th ☽	0055	2.6	79		27 F ☾	0047	2.2	67
	0702	0.4	12			0646	0.8	24
	1330	3.2	98			1309	2.6	79
	2004	0.4	12			1940	0.7	21
13 F	0208	2.6	79		28 Sa	0144	2.3	70
	0814	0.4	12			0746	0.8	24
	1442	3.1	94			1405	2.6	79
	2111	0.4	12			2035	0.7	21
14 Sa	0324	2.7	82		29 Su	0244	2.3	70
	0926	0.4	12			0847	0.7	21
	1553	3.0	91			1502	2.6	79
	2213	0.3	9			2127	0.5	15
15 Su	0433	2.8	85		30 M	0342	2.5	76
	1032	0.4	12			0946	0.6	18
	1656	3.0	91			1559	2.6	79
	2308	0.2	6			2215	0.4	12
					31 Tu	0436	2.7	82
						1041	0.4	12
						1651	2.7	82
						2302	0.2	6

November

Day	Time	ft	cm		Day	Time	ft	cm
1 W	0525	3.0	91		16 Th	0012	0.0	0
	1133	0.2	6			0642	3.1	94
	1741	2.8	85			1254	0.1	3
	2347	0.0	0			1857	2.6	79
2 Th	0612	3.2	98		17 F	0050	0.0	0
	1223	0.0	0			0720	3.1	94
	1829	2.9	88			1335	0.1	3
						1935	2.5	76
3 F	0032	-0.2	-6		18 Sa ●	0127	0.0	0
	0658	3.4	104			0756	3.1	94
	1312	-0.1	-3			1413	0.1	3
	1917	3.0	91			2011	2.5	76
4 Sa O	0118	-0.3	-9		19 Su	0202	0.1	3
	0745	3.6	110			0830	3.1	94
	1401	-0.2	-6			1449	0.1	3
	2005	3.0	91			2047	2.4	73
5 Su	0205	-0.3	-9		20 M	0237	0.1	3
	0833	3.7	113			0905	3.0	91
	1452	-0.2	-6			1525	0.2	6
	2055	2.9	88			2124	2.4	73
6 M	0254	-0.3	-9		21 Tu	0314	0.2	6
	0923	3.6	110			0941	2.9	88
	1544	-0.2	-6			1602	0.2	6
	2146	2.8	85			2201	2.3	70
7 Tu	0346	-0.2	-6		22 W	0352	0.3	9
	1015	3.5	107			1018	2.8	85
	1639	-0.1	-3			1640	0.3	9
	2241	2.7	82			2241	2.2	67
8 W	0442	-0.1	-3		23 Th	0433	0.4	12
	1110	3.4	104			1058	2.7	82
	1738	0.0	0			1721	0.4	12
	2340	2.6	79			2324	2.2	67
9 Th	0543	0.1	3		24 F	0518	0.5	15
	1210	3.2	98			1141	2.6	79
	1841	0.1	3			1806	0.4	12
10 F ◐	0047	2.6	79		25 Sa	0011	2.1	64
	0651	0.2	6			0608	0.5	15
	1315	3.0	91			1227	2.5	76
	1947	0.2	6			1855	0.4	12
11 Sa	0159	2.5	76		26 Su ☾	0103	2.1	64
	0804	0.3	9			0705	0.6	18
	1425	2.8	85			1318	2.4	73
	2051	0.2	6			1946	0.3	9
12 Su	0312	2.6	79		27 M	0200	2.2	67
	0916	0.3	9			0806	0.5	15
	1533	2.7	82			1413	2.4	73
	2150	0.1	3			2039	0.2	6
13 M	0418	2.7	82		28 Tu	0258	2.4	73
	1021	0.3	9			0908	0.4	12
	1635	2.7	82			1511	2.4	73
	2243	0.1	3			2131	0.1	3
14 Tu	0513	2.9	88		29 W	0355	2.6	79
	1118	0.2	6			1008	0.2	6
	1729	2.6	79			1609	2.4	73
	2330	0.0	0			2222	-0.1	-3
15 W	0600	3.0	91		30 Th	0450	2.9	88
	1209	0.2	6			1105	0.0	0
	1815	2.6	79			1706	2.5	76
						2313	-0.3	-9

December

Day	Time	ft	cm		Day	Time	ft	cm
1 F	0543	3.1	94		16 Sa	0022	-0.1	-3
	1159	-0.2	-6			0657	2.8	85
	1800	2.6	79			1314	0.0	0
						1911	2.2	67
2 Sa	0003	-0.4	-12		17 Su	0100	-0.1	-3
	0634	3.3	101			0733	2.8	85
	1252	-0.3	-9			1351	0.0	0
	1854	2.7	82			1948	2.2	67
3 Su O	0054	-0.5	-15		18 M ●	0137	-0.1	-3
	0725	3.5	107			0808	2.8	85
	1345	-0.4	-12			1426	0.0	0
	1946	2.7	82			2025	2.2	67
4 M	0145	-0.6	-18		19 Tu	0213	-0.1	-3
	0817	3.5	107			0843	2.8	85
	1437	-0.5	-15			1501	0.0	0
	2039	2.7	82			2101	2.2	67
5 Tu	0238	-0.6	-18		20 W	0250	0.0	0
	0908	3.5	107			0918	2.7	82
	1530	-0.5	-15			1536	0.0	0
	2133	2.7	82			2138	2.1	64
6 W	0332	-0.5	-15		21 Th	0328	0.0	0
	1001	3.4	104			0954	2.6	79
	1625	-0.4	-12			1612	0.0	0
	2229	2.6	79			2216	2.1	64
7 Th	0429	-0.4	-12		22 F	0407	0.1	3
	1056	3.2	98			1031	2.5	76
	1722	-0.3	-9			1650	0.0	0
	2328	2.5	76			2256	2.1	64
8 F	0530	-0.2	-6		23 Sa	0450	0.2	6
	1153	3.0	91			1110	2.5	76
	1821	-0.2	-6			1730	0.1	3
						2339	2.1	64
9 Sa	0031	2.5	76		24 Su	0537	0.2	6
	0636	0.0	0			1152	2.4	73
	1254	2.7	82			1815	0.1	3
	1922	-0.1	-3					
10 Su ◐	0139	2.4	73		25 M O	0027	2.1	64
	0746	0.1	3			0630	0.3	9
	1358	2.5	76			1239	2.3	70
	2022	-0.1	-3			1903	0.0	0
11 M	0247	2.5	76		26 Tu ☾	0120	2.2	67
	0856	0.2	6			0730	0.3	9
	1503	2.4	73			1331	2.2	67
	2119	0.0	0			1956	0.0	0
12 Tu	0351	2.5	76		27 W	0217	2.3	70
	1001	0.2	6			0833	0.2	6
	1605	2.3	70			1430	2.2	67
	2212	0.0	0			2051	-0.1	-3
13 W	0447	2.6	79		28 Th	0317	2.5	76
	1058	0.1	3			0937	0.1	3
	1700	2.2	67			1532	2.2	67
	2259	-0.1	-3			2148	-0.3	-9
14 Th	0535	2.7	82		29 F	0418	2.7	82
	1149	0.1	3			1039	-0.1	-3
	1749	2.2	67			1635	2.2	67
	2342	-0.1	-3			2244	-0.4	-12
15 F	0618	2.8	85		30 Sa	0517	3.0	91
	1234	0.0	0			1138	-0.3	-9
	1832	2.2	67			1736	2.3	70
						2340	-0.6	-18
					31 Su	0615	3.2	98
						1235	-0.5	-15
						1835	2.4	73

Time meridian 75° W. 0000 is midnight. 1200 is noon. Times are not adjusted for Daylight Saving Time.
Heights are referred to mean lower low water which is the chart datum of soundings.

Hampton Roads (Sewells Pt.), Virginia, 2017

Times and Heights of High and Low Waters

January

Day	Time	ft	cm	Day	Time	ft	cm
1 Su	0438	-0.1	-3	16 M	0541	-0.3	-9
	1056	2.6	79		1156	2.5	76
	1720	-0.2	-6		1814	-0.3	-9
	2315	2.2	67				
2 M	0521	-0.1	-3	17 Tu	0023	2.3	70
	1138	2.5	76		0631	-0.1	-3
	1802	-0.2	-6		1242	2.3	70
					1859	-0.1	-3
3 Tu	0000	2.2	67	18 W	0112	2.2	67
	0610	0.0	0		0723	0.1	3
	1223	2.4	73		1328	2.1	64
	1846	-0.2	-6		1945	0.0	0
4 W	0050	2.3	70	19 Th ◓	0203	2.2	67
	0704	0.0	0		0817	0.2	6
	1314	2.3	70		1418	2.0	61
	1936	-0.2	-6		2034	0.1	3
5 Th ◑	0146	2.3	70	20 F	0258	2.1	64
	0806	0.0	0		0915	0.3	9
	1411	2.2	67		1511	1.8	55
	2030	-0.2	-6		2125	0.1	3
6 F	0247	2.4	73	21 Sa	0354	2.1	64
	0912	0.0	0		1013	0.3	9
	1513	2.2	67		1607	1.8	55
	2128	-0.2	-6		2218	0.1	3
7 Sa	0352	2.5	76	22 Su	0450	2.2	67
	1020	0.0	0		1111	0.3	9
	1618	2.1	64		1703	1.8	55
	2229	-0.3	-9		2311	0.1	3
8 Su	0457	2.7	82	23 M	0544	2.2	67
	1127	-0.1	-3		1204	0.2	6
	1723	2.2	67		1756	1.8	55
	2329	-0.4	-12				
9 M	0559	2.8	85	24 Tu	0001	0.0	0
	1229	-0.3	-9		0633	2.3	70
	1824	2.3	70		1252	0.1	3
					1844	1.9	58
10 Tu	0028	-0.5	-15	25 W	0049	0.0	0
	0659	2.9	88		0718	2.4	73
	1326	-0.4	-12		1337	0.0	0
	1922	2.3	70		1929	2.0	61
11 W	0125	-0.6	-18	26 Th	0134	-0.1	-3
	0754	3.0	91		0759	2.5	76
	1419	-0.5	-15		1418	-0.1	-3
	2017	2.4	73		2012	2.1	64
12 Th ○	0219	-0.6	-18	27 F ●	0216	-0.2	-6
	0846	3.0	91		0839	2.6	79
	1510	-0.5	-15		1458	-0.2	-6
	2108	2.5	76		2052	2.2	67
13 F	0311	-0.6	-18	28 Sa	0258	-0.2	-6
	0936	3.0	91		0918	2.7	82
	1558	-0.5	-15		1537	-0.3	-9
	2158	2.5	76		2132	2.3	70
14 Sa	0402	-0.5	-15	29 Su	0340	-0.3	-9
	1024	2.9	88		0957	2.7	82
	1644	-0.5	-15		1616	-0.3	-9
	2247	2.5	76		2213	2.4	73
15 Su	0452	-0.4	-12	30 M	0422	-0.3	-9
	1110	2.7	82		1037	2.7	82
	1730	-0.4	-12		1655	-0.3	-9
	2335	2.4	73		2255	2.4	73
				31 Tu	0507	-0.3	-9
					1119	2.6	79
					1736	-0.3	-9
					2341	2.5	76

February

Day	Time	ft	cm	Day	Time	ft	cm
1 W	0556	-0.2	-6	16 Th	0029	2.4	73
	1205	2.5	76		0644	0.1	3
	1821	-0.3	-9		1245	2.2	67
					1858	0.1	3
2 Th	0030	2.5	76	17 F	0115	2.3	70
	0650	-0.1	-3		0732	0.2	6
	1255	2.4	73		1328	2.0	61
	1910	-0.3	-9		1943	0.2	6
3 F ◑	0125	2.5	76	18 Sa ◓	0204	2.2	67
	0749	0.0	0		0825	0.4	12
	1351	2.2	67		1417	1.9	58
	2004	-0.2	-6		2033	0.2	6
4 Sa	0226	2.5	76	19 Su	0300	2.1	64
	0855	0.0	0		0923	0.4	12
	1453	2.1	64		1513	1.8	55
	2105	-0.2	-6		2128	0.3	9
5 Su	0333	2.6	79	20 M	0400	2.1	64
	1004	0.0	0		1024	0.4	12
	1600	2.1	64		1613	1.8	55
	2209	-0.2	-6		2226	0.3	9
6 M	0441	2.6	79	21 Tu	0459	2.2	67
	1112	0.0	0		1122	0.4	12
	1708	2.1	64		1713	1.9	58
	2314	-0.3	-9		2323	0.2	6
7 Tu	0547	2.7	82	22 W	0554	2.3	70
	1215	-0.1	-3		1214	0.3	9
	1812	2.2	67		1808	2.0	61
8 W	0016	-0.4	-12	23 Th	0017	0.1	3
	0648	2.8	85		0644	2.4	73
	1311	-0.2	-6		1302	0.1	3
	1910	2.3	70		1857	2.1	64
9 Th	0114	-0.4	-12	24 F	0106	0.0	0
	0743	2.9	88		0729	2.6	79
	1403	-0.3	-9		1345	0.0	0
	2003	2.5	76		1942	2.3	70
10 F ○	0208	-0.5	-15	25 Sa	0152	-0.1	-3
	0833	2.9	88		0812	2.7	82
	1451	-0.4	-12		1427	-0.2	-6
	2052	2.5	76		2026	2.5	76
11 Sa	0258	-0.5	-15	26 Su ●	0237	-0.2	-6
	0919	2.9	88		0853	2.8	85
	1535	-0.4	-12		1507	-0.3	-9
	2138	2.6	79		2108	2.6	79
12 Su	0345	-0.4	-12	27 M	0321	-0.3	-9
	1003	2.8	85		0935	2.8	85
	1617	-0.4	-12		1547	-0.3	-9
	2222	2.6	79		2151	2.7	82
13 M	0430	-0.4	-12	28 Tu	0407	-0.3	-9
	1044	2.7	82		1017	2.8	85
	1657	-0.3	-9		1629	-0.4	-12
	2305	2.5	76		2235	2.8	85
14 Tu	0515	-0.2	-6				
	1124	2.5	76				
	1737	-0.2	-6				
	2347	2.5	76				
15 W	0559	-0.1	-3				
	1204	2.3	70				
	1817	-0.1	-3				

March

Day	Time	ft	cm	Day	Time	ft	cm
1 W	0454	-0.3	-9	16 Th	0528	0.0	0
	1101	2.7	82		1129	2.4	73
	1712	-0.4	-12		1737	0.1	3
	2322	2.8	85		2351	2.6	79
2 Th	0543	-0.2	-6	17 F	0610	0.2	6
	1148	2.6	79		1207	2.3	70
	1758	-0.3	-9		1816	0.2	6
3 F	0013	2.8	85	18 Sa	0032	2.5	76
	0637	-0.1	-3		0653	0.3	9
	1239	2.5	76		1247	2.1	64
	1849	-0.2	-6		1858	0.3	9
4 Sa	0108	2.8	85	19 Su	0117	2.4	73
	0736	0.0	0		0742	0.4	12
	1336	2.3	70		1332	2.0	61
	1946	-0.1	-3		1946	0.4	12
5 Su ◑	0210	2.7	82	20 M ◓	0209	2.3	70
	0841	0.1	3		0836	0.5	15
	1439	2.2	67		1426	2.0	61
	2048	-0.1	-3		2041	0.5	15
6 M	0318	2.6	79	21 Tu	0307	2.2	67
	0950	0.1	3		0935	0.5	15
	1548	2.2	67		1526	2.0	61
	2156	0.0	0		2141	0.5	15
7 Tu	0429	2.6	79	22 W	0409	2.3	70
	1057	0.1	3		1034	0.5	15
	1657	2.2	67		1628	2.0	61
	2303	-0.1	-3		2243	0.4	12
8 W	0536	2.7	82	23 Th	0509	2.4	73
	1158	0.0	0		1130	0.4	12
	1800	2.4	73		1727	2.2	67
					2341	0.3	9
9 Th	0006	-0.1	-3	24 F	0604	2.5	76
	0635	2.7	82		1220	0.2	6
	1253	-0.1	-3		1820	2.4	73
	1857	2.5	76				
10 F	0103	-0.2	-6	25 Sa	0035	0.1	3
	0728	2.8	85		0653	2.6	79
	1342	-0.1	-3		1307	0.1	3
	1947	2.6	79		1909	2.6	79
11 Sa	0155	-0.3	-9	26 Su	0126	0.0	0
	0815	2.8	85		0740	2.8	85
	1427	-0.2	-6		1351	-0.1	-3
	2033	2.7	82		1956	2.8	85
12 Su ○	0242	-0.3	-9	27 M ●	0214	-0.2	-6
	0859	2.8	85		0826	2.8	85
	1508	-0.2	-6		1434	-0.2	-6
	2115	2.8	85		2042	3.0	91
13 M	0326	-0.3	-9	28 Tu	0302	-0.3	-9
	0939	2.7	82		0911	2.9	88
	1547	-0.2	-6		1518	-0.3	-9
	2155	2.8	85		2128	3.1	94
14 Tu	0408	-0.2	-6	29 W	0350	-0.3	-9
	1016	2.6	79		0957	2.9	88
	1624	-0.1	-3		1603	-0.4	-12
	2234	2.7	82		2216	3.2	98
15 W	0448	-0.1	-3	30 Th	0440	-0.3	-9
	1053	2.5	76		1044	2.8	85
	1700	0.0	0		1649	-0.3	-9
	2312	2.7	82		2305	3.2	98
				31 F	0531	-0.2	-6
					1133	2.7	82
					1739	-0.3	-9
					2357	3.1	94

Time meridian 75° W. 0000 is midnight. 1200 is noon. Times are not adjusted for Daylight Saving Time.
Heights are referred to mean lower low water which is the chart datum of soundings.

Hampton Roads (Sewells Pt.), Virginia, 2017

Times and Heights of High and Low Waters

April

Day	Time	ft	cm
1 Sa	0626	-0.1	-3
	1227	2.6	79
	1832	-0.1	-3
2 Su	0054	3.0	91
	0724	0.2	6
	1325	2.5	76
	1931	0.0	0
3 M	0157	2.8	85
	0828	0.1	3
	1429	2.4	73
	2036	0.1	3
4 Tu	0305	2.7	82
	0933	0.2	6
	1537	2.4	73
	2145	0.1	3
5 W	0414	2.7	82
	1037	0.2	6
	1644	2.4	73
	2252	0.1	3
6 Th	0519	2.6	79
	1136	0.2	6
	1745	2.5	76
	2354	0.1	3
7 F	0617	2.7	82
	1229	0.1	3
	1839	2.6	79
8 Sa	0049	0.0	0
	0708	2.7	82
	1316	0.0	0
	1927	2.8	85
9 Su	0139	0.0	0
	0753	2.7	82
	1358	0.0	0
	2010	2.8	85
10 M	0224	-0.1	-3
	0834	2.7	82
	1437	0.0	0
	2050	2.9	88
11 Tu	0305	-0.1	-3
	0912	2.6	79
	1515	0.0	0
	2128	2.9	88
12 W	0345	0.0	0
	0948	2.6	79
	1551	0.0	0
	2204	2.8	85
13 Th	0423	0.0	0
	1024	2.5	76
	1627	0.1	3
	2241	2.8	85
14 F	0502	0.1	3
	1059	2.4	73
	1703	0.2	6
	2318	2.7	82
15 Sa	0541	0.2	6
	1135	2.3	70
	1741	0.3	9
	2357	2.6	79
16 Su	0622	0.3	9
	1214	2.2	67
	1821	0.4	12
17 M	0039	2.5	76
	0707	0.4	12
	1258	2.1	64
	1907	0.5	15
18 Tu	0127	2.4	73
	0756	0.5	15
	1348	2.1	64
	2000	0.5	15
19 W	0221	2.4	73
	0850	0.5	15
	1445	2.1	64
	2100	0.5	15
20 Th	0321	2.4	73
	0947	0.5	15
	1546	2.2	67
	2203	0.5	15
21 F	0422	2.4	73
	1042	0.4	12
	1646	2.4	73
	2305	0.3	9
22 Sa	0520	2.5	76
	1135	0.2	6
	1743	2.6	79
23 Su	0004	0.2	6
	0615	2.6	79
	1225	0.1	3
	1836	2.8	85
24 M	0059	0.0	0
	0707	2.7	82
	1314	-0.1	-3
	1927	3.0	91
25 Tu	0151	-0.2	-6
	0757	2.8	85
	1402	-0.2	-6
	2017	3.2	98
26 W	0242	-0.3	-9
	0846	2.8	85
	1450	-0.3	-9
	2106	3.3	101
27 Th	0333	-0.4	-12
	0936	2.9	88
	1539	-0.4	-12
	2157	3.4	104
28 F	0425	-0.3	-9
	1027	2.8	85
	1629	-0.3	-9
	2249	3.3	101
29 Sa	0518	-0.3	-9
	1119	2.7	82
	1722	-0.2	-6
	2344	3.2	98
30 Su	0613	-0.2	-6
	1215	2.6	79
	1818	-0.1	-3

May

Day	Time	ft	cm
1 M	0041	3.0	91
	0710	0.0	0
	1314	2.5	76
	1919	0.0	0
2 Tu	0143	2.9	88
	0810	0.1	3
	1417	2.5	76
	2023	0.1	3
3 W	0247	2.7	82
	0912	0.2	6
	1522	2.5	76
	2130	0.2	6
4 Th	0353	2.6	79
	1011	0.2	6
	1625	2.5	76
	2236	0.2	6
5 F	0455	2.5	76
	1107	0.2	6
	1723	2.6	79
	2336	0.2	6
6 Sa	0551	2.5	76
	1157	0.2	6
	1815	2.7	82
7 Su	0030	0.1	3
	0640	2.5	76
	1243	0.1	3
	1902	2.8	85
8 M	0118	0.1	3
	0725	2.5	76
	1325	0.1	3
	1944	2.8	85
9 Tu	0201	0.1	3
	0806	2.5	76
	1405	0.1	3
	2023	2.9	88
10 W	0242	0.0	0
	0844	2.4	73
	1443	0.1	3
	2101	2.9	88
11 Th	0321	0.1	3
	0921	2.4	73
	1520	0.1	3
	2138	2.8	85
12 F	0400	0.1	3
	0957	2.4	73
	1557	0.2	6
	2214	2.8	85
13 Sa	0438	0.1	3
	1033	2.3	70
	1634	0.2	6
	2251	2.7	82
14 Su	0516	0.2	6
	1110	2.3	70
	1712	0.3	9
	2329	2.6	79
15 M	0556	0.3	9
	1149	2.2	67
	1752	0.4	12
16 Tu	0009	2.5	76
	0638	0.3	9
	1231	2.2	67
	1837	0.4	12
17 W	0053	2.5	76
	0723	0.4	12
	1319	2.2	67
	1928	0.5	15
18 Th	0143	2.4	73
	0812	0.3	9
	1412	2.2	67
	2026	0.5	15
19 F	0239	2.4	73
	0904	0.3	9
	1510	2.3	70
	2129	0.4	12
20 Sa	0339	2.4	73
	0958	0.2	6
	1609	2.5	76
	2233	0.3	9
21 Su	0439	2.4	73
	1053	0.1	3
	1708	2.7	82
	2334	0.1	3
22 M	0538	2.5	76
	1147	0.0	0
	1805	2.9	88
23 Tu	0033	0.0	0
	0635	2.6	79
	1240	-0.2	-6
	1900	3.1	94
24 W	0129	-0.2	-6
	0730	2.7	82
	1332	-0.3	-9
	1954	3.3	101
25 Th	0223	-0.3	-9
	0824	2.7	82
	1425	-0.4	-12
	2047	3.4	104
26 F	0317	-0.4	-12
	0917	2.8	85
	1518	-0.4	-12
	2140	3.4	104
27 Sa	0410	-0.4	-12
	1010	2.7	82
	1611	-0.4	-12
	2234	3.3	101
28 Su	0503	-0.3	-9
	1104	2.7	82
	1706	-0.3	-9
	2329	3.2	98
29 M	0557	-0.2	-6
	1200	2.7	82
	1804	-0.1	-3
30 Tu	0025	3.0	91
	0651	-0.1	-3
	1258	2.6	79
	1903	0.0	0
31 W	0123	2.8	85
	0747	0.0	0
	1358	2.5	76
	2005	0.1	3

June

Day	Time	ft	cm
1 Th	0223	2.6	79
	0843	0.1	3
	1458	2.5	76
	2109	0.2	6
2 F	0323	2.5	76
	0938	0.1	3
	1558	2.5	76
	2211	0.3	9
3 Sa	0422	2.3	70
	1031	0.2	6
	1654	2.6	79
	2310	0.3	9
4 Su	0516	2.3	70
	1120	0.2	6
	1745	2.6	79
5 M	0003	0.2	6
	0607	2.3	70
	1207	0.2	6
	1832	2.7	82
6 Tu	0052	0.2	6
	0653	2.3	70
	1251	0.1	3
	1915	2.7	82
7 W	0136	0.1	3
	0735	2.3	70
	1333	0.1	3
	1956	2.8	85
8 Th	0218	0.1	3
	0815	2.3	70
	1413	0.1	3
	2035	2.8	85
9 F	0258	0.1	3
	0854	2.3	70
	1452	0.1	3
	2113	2.8	85
10 Sa	0337	0.1	3
	0932	2.3	70
	1531	0.2	6
	2151	2.7	82
11 Su	0415	0.1	3
	1009	2.3	70
	1609	0.2	6
	2227	2.7	82
12 M	0453	0.1	3
	1047	2.3	70
	1648	0.2	6
	2305	2.6	79
13 Tu	0531	0.1	3
	1126	2.3	70
	1729	0.3	9
	2344	2.6	79
14 W	0611	0.2	6
	1207	2.3	70
	1813	0.3	9
15 Th	0026	2.5	76
	0652	0.2	6
	1253	2.3	70
	1903	0.3	9
16 F	0113	2.5	76
	0738	0.2	6
	1343	2.4	73
	1959	0.3	9
17 Sa	0206	2.4	73
	0828	0.1	3
	1439	2.5	76
	2101	0.3	9
18 Su	0304	2.4	73
	0921	0.1	3
	1538	2.6	79
	2205	0.2	6
19 M	0405	2.4	73
	1017	0.0	0
	1639	2.8	85
	2309	0.1	3
20 Tu	0507	2.4	73
	1114	-0.1	-3
	1739	3.0	91
21 W	0011	0.0	0
	0608	2.5	76
	1212	-0.2	-6
	1838	3.2	98
22 Th	0109	-0.2	-6
	0707	2.5	76
	1309	-0.3	-9
	1935	3.3	101
23 F	0206	-0.3	-9
	0804	2.6	79
	1405	-0.4	-12
	2031	3.3	101
24 Sa	0300	-0.4	-12
	0859	2.7	82
	1500	-0.4	-12
	2125	3.3	101
25 Su	0352	-0.4	-12
	0953	2.7	82
	1555	-0.4	-12
	2218	3.2	98
26 M	0444	-0.4	-12
	1047	2.7	82
	1650	-0.3	-9
	2311	3.1	94
27 Tu	0535	-0.3	-9
	1141	2.7	82
	1746	-0.2	-6
28 W	0004	2.9	88
	0626	-0.2	-6
	1236	2.7	82
	1842	0.0	0
29 Th	0057	2.7	82
	0717	-0.1	-3
	1331	2.6	79
	1940	0.1	3
30 F	0151	2.5	76
	0808	0.1	3
	1427	2.6	79
	2040	0.3	9

Time meridian 75° W. 0000 is midnight. 1200 is noon. Times are not adjusted for Daylight Saving Time.
Heights are referred to mean lower low water which is the chart datum of soundings.

Hampton Roads (Sewells Pt.), Virginia, 2017
Times and Heights of High and Low Waters

July

Day	Time	ft	cm		Day	Time	ft	cm
1 Sa	0246	2.3	70		16 Su	0140	2.4	73
	0859	0.1	3			0757	0.1	3
	1523	2.5	76			1413	2.7	82
	2139	0.3	9		◗	2039	0.3	9
2 Su	0342	2.2	67		17 M	0237	2.4	73
	0950	0.2	6			0851	0.0	0
	1618	2.5	76			1513	2.8	85
	2237	0.4	12			2144	0.2	6
3 M	0436	2.1	64		18 Tu	0340	2.4	73
	1040	0.2	6			0950	0.2	6
	1710	2.6	79			1617	2.9	88
	2331	0.4	12			2250	0.2	6
4 Tu	0528	2.1	64		19 W	0444	2.4	73
	1129	0.3	9			1051	-0.1	-3
	1759	2.6	79			1720	3.0	91
						2353	0.1	3
5 W	0021	0.3	9		20 Th	0548	2.4	73
	0617	2.1	64			1152	-0.2	-6
	1216	0.2	6			1822	3.1	94
	1846	2.7	82					
6 Th	0107	0.3	9		21 F	0053	-0.1	-3
	0703	2.2	67			0649	2.6	79
	1302	0.2	6			1252	-0.2	-6
	1929	2.7	82			1920	3.2	98
7 F	0151	0.2	6		22 Sa	0149	-0.2	-6
	0746	2.2	67			0747	2.7	82
	1345	0.2	6			1350	-0.3	-9
	2010	2.7	82			2016	3.3	101
8 Sa	0232	0.1	3		23 Su	0242	-0.3	-9
	0827	2.3	70			0842	2.8	85
	1427	0.2	6			1445	-0.3	-9
○	2049	2.8	85		●	2109	3.3	101
9 Su	0311	0.1	3		24 M	0332	-0.3	-9
	0906	2.3	70			0935	2.8	85
	1507	0.2	6			1539	-0.3	-9
	2127	2.8	85			2200	3.2	98
10 M	0349	0.1	3		25 Tu	0421	-0.3	-9
	0945	2.3	70			1026	2.9	88
	1547	0.2	6			1632	-0.2	-6
	2204	2.8	85			2249	3.1	94
11 Tu	0427	0.1	3		26 W	0508	-0.2	-6
	1023	2.4	73			1116	2.8	85
	1627	0.2	6			1724	-0.1	-3
	2242	2.7	82			2337	2.9	88
12 W	0504	0.1	3		27 Th	0554	-0.1	-3
	1102	2.4	73			1206	2.8	85
	1708	0.2	6			1816	0.1	3
	2320	2.7	82					
13 Th	0542	0.1	3		28 F	0025	2.7	82
	1143	2.5	76			0640	0.0	0
	1753	0.2	6			1256	2.7	82
						1909	0.2	6
14 F	0002	2.6	79		29 Sa	0114	2.5	76
	0623	0.1	3			0727	0.2	6
	1228	2.5	76			1348	2.6	79
	1843	0.3	9			2004	0.4	12
15 Sa	0048	2.5	76		30 Su	0204	2.3	70
	0707	0.1	3			0815	0.3	9
	1318	2.6	79			1441	2.6	79
	1938	0.3	9		◖	2100	0.5	15
					31 M	0257	2.2	67
						0906	0.4	12
						1536	2.5	76
						2157	0.5	15

August

Day	Time	ft	cm		Day	Time	ft	cm
1 Tu	0352	2.1	64		16 W	0323	2.4	73
	0958	0.4	12			0931	0.1	3
	1631	2.5	76			1601	3.0	91
	2254	0.5	15			2235	0.3	9
2 W	0447	2.1	64		17 Th	0430	2.4	73
	1051	0.4	12			1036	0.1	3
	1724	2.6	79			1707	3.1	94
	2346	0.5	15			2339	0.2	6
3 Th	0540	2.1	64		18 F	0536	2.5	76
	1142	0.4	12			1140	0.0	0
	1814	2.6	79			1810	3.2	98
4 F	0035	0.4	12		19 Sa	0037	0.1	3
	0630	2.2	67			0637	2.7	82
	1231	0.3	9			1241	-0.1	-3
	1900	2.7	82			1908	3.2	98
5 Sa	0120	0.3	9		20 Su	0131	0.0	0
	0715	2.3	70			0733	2.8	85
	1318	0.3	9			1338	-0.1	-3
	1942	2.8	85			2001	3.3	101
6 Su	0202	0.2	6		21 M	0221	-0.1	-3
	0758	2.4	73			0825	2.9	88
	1401	0.2	6			1431	-0.1	-3
	2022	2.8	85		●	2051	3.2	98
7 M	0241	0.2	6		22 Tu	0308	-0.1	-3
	0839	2.5	76			0915	3.0	91
	1443	0.2	6			1522	-0.1	-3
○	2101	2.9	88			2138	3.2	98
8 Tu	0319	0.1	3		23 W	0353	-0.1	-3
	0918	2.6	79			1002	3.0	91
	1524	0.2	6			1611	0.0	0
	2139	2.9	88			2223	3.0	91
9 W	0357	0.1	3		24 Th	0436	0.0	0
	0957	2.7	82			1047	3.0	91
	1606	0.2	6			1659	0.1	3
	2217	2.9	88			2307	2.9	88
10 Th	0434	0.0	0		25 F	0518	0.1	3
	1037	2.7	82			1132	2.9	88
	1649	0.2	6			1746	0.2	6
	2257	2.8	85			2350	2.7	82
11 F	0513	0.0	0		26 Sa	0601	0.2	6
	1119	2.8	85			1218	2.8	85
	1735	0.2	6			1834	0.4	12
	2340	2.7	82					
12 Sa	0555	0.1	3		27 Su	0034	2.5	76
	1205	2.8	85			0644	0.3	9
	1825	0.3	9			1305	2.7	82
						1925	0.5	15
13 Su	0027	2.6	79		28 M	0120	2.3	70
	0640	0.1	3			0730	0.5	15
	1256	2.9	88			1355	2.6	79
	1921	0.3	9			2018	0.7	21
14 M	0119	2.5	76		29 Tu	0210	2.2	67
	0731	0.1	3			0820	0.6	18
	1353	2.9	88			1449	2.6	79
◖	2023	0.4	12		◖	2115	0.7	21
15 Tu	0218	2.5	76		30 W	0305	2.2	67
	0828	0.1	3			0914	0.6	18
	1455	2.9	88			1547	2.6	79
	2129	0.4	12			2212	0.7	21
					31 Th	0404	2.2	67
						1012	0.6	18
						1644	2.6	79
						2307	0.7	21

September

Day	Time	ft	cm		Day	Time	ft	cm
1 F	0502	2.2	67		16 Sa	0527	2.7	82
	1108	0.6	18			1132	0.2	6
	1737	2.7	82			1759	3.1	94
	2358	0.6	18					
2 Sa	0554	2.3	70		17 Su	0021	0.2	6
	1200	0.5	15			0626	2.8	85
	1826	2.8	85			1232	0.1	3
						1854	3.2	98
3 Su	0044	0.5	15		18 M	0111	0.1	3
	0642	2.5	76			0719	3.0	91
	1249	0.4	12			1326	0.0	0
	1910	2.9	88			1945	3.2	98
4 M	0126	0.3	9		19 Tu	0158	0.0	0
	0727	2.6	79			0807	3.1	94
	1335	0.3	9			1417	0.0	0
	1951	2.9	88			2031	3.1	94
5 Tu	0206	0.2	6		20 W	0242	0.0	0
	0808	2.8	85			0853	3.2	98
	1418	0.2	6			1504	0.0	0
	2032	3.0	91		●	2114	3.1	94
6 W	0245	0.1	3		21 Th	0323	0.0	0
	0849	2.9	88			0935	3.2	98
	1501	0.2	6			1549	0.1	3
○	2112	3.0	91			2155	2.9	88
7 Th	0324	0.1	3		22 F	0403	0.1	3
	0930	3.0	91			1017	3.1	94
	1545	0.1	3			1632	0.2	6
	2152	3.0	91			2235	2.8	85
8 F	0403	0.0	0		23 Sa	0442	0.2	6
	1012	3.1	94			1058	3.0	91
	1630	0.1	3			1716	0.3	9
	2235	2.9	88			2314	2.7	82
9 Sa	0445	0.0	0		24 Su	0521	0.3	9
	1056	3.1	94			1139	2.9	88
	1718	0.2	6			1800	0.5	15
	2320	2.8	85			2355	2.5	76
10 Su	0529	0.1	3		25 M	0601	0.5	15
	1144	3.2	98			1222	2.8	85
	1810	0.3	9			1846	0.6	18
11 M	0009	2.7	82		26 Tu	0038	2.4	73
	0618	0.1	3			0645	0.6	18
	1237	3.1	94			1309	2.7	82
	1908	0.3	9			1936	0.7	21
12 Tu	0104	2.6	79		27 W	0126	2.3	70
	0712	0.2	6			0735	0.7	21
	1337	3.1	94			1401	2.6	79
	2010	0.4	12		◖	2030	0.8	24
13 W	0206	2.5	76		28 Th	0220	2.2	67
	0813	0.3	9			0830	0.8	24
	1442	3.0	91			1459	2.6	79
◖	2116	0.4	12			2128	0.8	24
14 Th	0313	2.5	76		29 F	0320	2.2	67
	0919	0.3	9			0930	0.8	24
	1551	3.0	91			1558	2.6	79
	2223	0.4	12			2224	0.7	21
15 F	0422	2.6	79		30 Sa	0420	2.3	70
	1027	0.3	9			1030	0.7	21
	1658	3.1	94			1654	2.6	79
	2325	0.3	9			2316	0.6	18

Time meridian 75° W. 0000 is midnight. 1200 is noon. Times are not adjusted for Daylight Saving Time.
Heights are referred to mean lower low water which is the chart datum of soundings.

Hampton Roads (Sewells Pt.), Virginia, 2017

Times and Heights of High and Low Waters

October

Day	Time (h m)	Height (ft)	Height (cm)
1 Su	0516 / 1126 / 1746	2.4 / 0.6 / 2.7	73 / 18 / 82
2 M	0003 / 0606 / 1218 / 1833	0.5 / 2.6 / 0.5 / 2.8	15 / 79 / 15 / 85
3 Tu	0047 / 0652 / 1306 / 1917	0.3 / 2.8 / 0.3 / 2.9	9 / 85 / 9 / 88
4 W	0129 / 0736 / 1353 / 2000	0.2 / 3.0 / 0.2 / 3.0	6 / 91 / 6 / 91
5 Th ○	0210 / 0819 / 1439 / 2044	0.1 / 3.1 / 0.1 / 3.0	3 / 94 / 3 / 91
6 F	0251 / 0903 / 1525 / 2128	0.0 / 3.3 / 0.0 / 3.0	0 / 101 / 0 / 91
7 Sa	0334 / 0948 / 1613 / 2214	-0.1 / 3.4 / 0.0 / 2.9	-3 / 104 / 0 / 88
8 Su	0419 / 1036 / 1703 / 2302	-0.1 / 3.4 / 0.1 / 2.8	-3 / 104 / 3 / 85
9 M	0507 / 1127 / 1757 / 2354	0.0 / 3.3 / 0.2 / 2.7	0 / 101 / 6 / 82
10 Tu	0559 / 1222 / 1855	0.1 / 3.2 / 0.3	3 / 98 / 9
11 W	0052 / 0657 / 1324 / 1957	2.6 / 0.2 / 3.1 / 0.3	79 / 6 / 94 / 9
12 Th ◑	0156 / 0802 / 1430 / 2103	2.6 / 0.3 / 3.0 / 0.4	79 / 9 / 91 / 12
13 F	0305 / 0910 / 1539 / 2207	2.6 / 0.3 / 2.9 / 0.3	79 / 9 / 88 / 9
14 Sa	0413 / 1019 / 1645 / 2306	2.6 / 0.3 / 2.9 / 0.3	79 / 9 / 88 / 9
15 Su	0516 / 1123 / 1744	2.7 / 0.3 / 2.9	82 / 9 / 88
16 M	0000 / 0612 / 1221 / 1837	0.2 / 2.9 / 0.2 / 2.9	6 / 88 / 6 / 88
17 Tu	0048 / 0702 / 1313 / 1925	0.1 / 3.0 / 0.1 / 2.9	3 / 91 / 3 / 88
18 W	0132 / 0747 / 1400 / 2008	0.1 / 3.1 / 0.1 / 2.9	3 / 94 / 3 / 88
19 Th ●	0213 / 0829 / 1445 / 2049	0.0 / 3.1 / 0.1 / 2.8	0 / 94 / 3 / 85
20 F	0252 / 0909 / 1526 / 2127	0.1 / 3.1 / 0.1 / 2.7	3 / 94 / 3 / 82
21 Sa	0330 / 0948 / 1607 / 2205	0.1 / 3.1 / 0.2 / 2.6	3 / 94 / 6 / 79
22 Su	0408 / 1026 / 1647 / 2242	0.2 / 3.0 / 0.3 / 2.5	6 / 91 / 9 / 76
23 M	0445 / 1105 / 1728 / 2320	0.3 / 2.9 / 0.4 / 2.4	9 / 88 / 12 / 73
24 Tu	0524 / 1145 / 1811	0.4 / 2.8 / 0.5	12 / 85 / 15
25 W	0001 / 0607 / 1228 / 1857	2.3 / 0.5 / 2.6 / 0.6	70 / 15 / 79 / 18
26 Th	0047 / 0654 / 1317 / 1948	2.2 / 0.6 / 2.5 / 0.6	67 / 18 / 76 / 18
27 F ◐	0138 / 0747 / 1410 / 2042	2.2 / 0.7 / 2.5 / 0.7	67 / 21 / 76 / 21
28 Sa	0236 / 0847 / 1508 / 2136	2.2 / 0.7 / 2.4 / 0.6	67 / 21 / 73 / 18
29 Su	0336 / 0949 / 1606 / 2228	2.3 / 0.7 / 2.5 / 0.5	70 / 21 / 76 / 15
30 M	0434 / 1049 / 1701 / 2318	2.4 / 0.5 / 2.5 / 0.3	73 / 15 / 76 / 9
31 Tu	0527 / 1145 / 1753	2.6 / 0.4 / 2.6	79 / 12 / 79

November

Day	Time (h m)	Height (ft)	Height (cm)
1 W	0005 / 0617 / 1237 / 1842	0.2 / 2.8 / 0.2 / 2.7	6 / 85 / 6 / 82
2 Th	0051 / 0705 / 1327 / 1930	0.0 / 3.0 / 0.0 / 2.8	0 / 91 / 0 / 85
3 F	0136 / 0752 / 1417 / 2017	-0.1 / 3.2 / -0.1 / 2.8	-3 / 98 / -3 / 85
4 Sa ○	0222 / 0840 / 1506 / 2105	-0.2 / 3.4 / -0.2 / 2.9	-6 / 104 / -6 / 88
5 Su	0309 / 0929 / 1556 / 2154	-0.3 / 3.4 / -0.2 / 2.8	-9 / 104 / -6 / 85
6 M	0358 / 1019 / 1649 / 2246	-0.3 / 3.4 / -0.2 / 2.7	-9 / 104 / -6 / 82
7 Tu	0449 / 1112 / 1743 / 2341	-0.2 / 3.3 / -0.1 / 2.7	-6 / 101 / -3 / 82
8 W	0544 / 1209 / 1840	-0.1 / 3.2 / 0.0	-3 / 98 / 0
9 Th	0040 / 0644 / 1310 / 1941	2.6 / 0.0 / 3.0 / 0.1	79 / 0 / 91 / 3
10 F ◐	0144 / 0750 / 1414 / 2043	2.5 / 0.2 / 2.8 / 0.1	76 / 6 / 85 / 3
11 Sa	0251 / 0858 / 1520 / 2144	2.5 / 0.2 / 2.7 / 0.1	76 / 6 / 82 / 3
12 Su	0357 / 1006 / 1624 / 2241	2.6 / 0.2 / 2.6 / 0.1	79 / 6 / 79 / 3
13 M	0458 / 1109 / 1722 / 2333	2.7 / 0.2 / 2.6 / 0.1	82 / 6 / 79 / 3
14 Tu	0553 / 1206 / 1815	2.8 / 0.1 / 2.6	85 / 3 / 79
15 W	0021 / 0642 / 1256 / 1901	0.0 / 2.9 / 0.1 / 2.5	0 / 88 / 3 / 76
16 Th	0104 / 0726 / 1342 / 1944	0.0 / 2.9 / 0.0 / 2.5	0 / 88 / 0 / 76
17 F	0145 / 0807 / 1424 / 2024	0.0 / 2.9 / 0.0 / 2.5	0 / 88 / 0 / 76
18 Sa ●	0224 / 0845 / 1505 / 2101	0.0 / 2.9 / 0.0 / 2.4	0 / 88 / 0 / 73
19 Su	0302 / 0923 / 1544 / 2138	0.0 / 2.9 / 0.1 / 2.4	0 / 88 / 3 / 73
20 M	0339 / 1000 / 1622 / 2215	0.1 / 2.8 / 0.1 / 2.3	3 / 85 / 3 / 70
21 Tu	0416 / 1037 / 1701 / 2252	0.2 / 2.7 / 0.2 / 2.2	6 / 82 / 6 / 67
22 W	0455 / 1115 / 1742 / 2331	0.2 / 2.6 / 0.3 / 2.2	6 / 79 / 9 / 67
23 Th	0535 / 1155 / 1824	0.3 / 2.5 / 0.3	9 / 76 / 9
24 F	0014 / 0619 / 1238 / 1909	2.1 / 0.4 / 2.4 / 0.4	64 / 12 / 73 / 12
25 Sa	0102 / 0709 / 1326 / 1957	2.1 / 0.5 / 2.3 / 0.4	64 / 15 / 70 / 12
26 Su ◐	0155 / 0806 / 1420 / 2048	2.1 / 0.5 / 2.3 / 0.3	64 / 15 / 70 / 9
27 M	0252 / 0908 / 1517 / 2140	2.2 / 0.5 / 2.3 / 0.2	67 / 15 / 70 / 6
28 Tu	0350 / 1011 / 1615 / 2232	2.3 / 0.4 / 2.3 / 0.1	70 / 12 / 70 / 3
29 W	0448 / 1111 / 1713 / 2324	2.5 / 0.2 / 2.4 / -0.1	76 / 6 / 73 / -3
30 Th	0543 / 1209 / 1808	2.7 / 0.0 / 2.4	82 / 0 / 73

December

Day	Time (h m)	Height (ft)	Height (cm)
1 F	0015 / 0636 / 1304 / 1901	-0.2 / 3.0 / -0.1 / 2.5	-6 / 91 / -3 / 76
2 Sa	0106 / 0729 / 1357 / 1954	-0.4 / 3.1 / -0.3 / 2.6	-12 / 94 / -9 / 79
3 Su ○	0157 / 0820 / 1449 / 2045	-0.5 / 3.3 / -0.4 / 2.6	-15 / 101 / -12 / 79
4 M	0248 / 0912 / 1541 / 2138	-0.5 / 3.3 / -0.4 / 2.6	-15 / 101 / -12 / 79
5 Tu	0340 / 1005 / 1633 / 2231	-0.5 / 3.3 / -0.4 / 2.6	-15 / 101 / -12 / 79
6 W	0434 / 1058 / 1727 / 2327	-0.5 / 3.2 / -0.4 / 2.6	-15 / 98 / -12 / 79
7 Th	0531 / 1154 / 1821	-0.3 / 3.0 / -0.3	-9 / 91 / -9
8 F	0025 / 0630 / 1252 / 1918	2.5 / -0.2 / 2.8 / -0.2	76 / -6 / 85 / -6
9 Sa	0126 / 0733 / 1352 / 2015	2.4 / 0.0 / 2.6 / -0.1	73 / 0 / 79 / -3
10 Su ○	0229 / 0838 / 1453 / 2113	2.4 / 0.1 / 2.4 / -0.1	73 / 3 / 73 / -3
11 M	0332 / 0944 / 1555 / 2208	2.4 / 0.1 / 2.3 / 0.0	73 / 3 / 70 / 0
12 Tu	0432 / 1046 / 1653 / 2301	2.5 / 0.1 / 2.2 / 0.0	76 / 3 / 67 / 0
13 W	0528 / 1143 / 1746 / 2350	2.5 / 0.1 / 2.2 / 0.0	76 / 3 / 67 / 0
14 Th	0617 / 1234 / 1834	2.6 / 0.1 / 2.2	79 / 3 / 67
15 F	0036 / 0703 / 1321 / 1918	-0.1 / 2.6 / 0.0 / 2.2	-3 / 79 / 0 / 67
16 Sa	0118 / 0745 / 1403 / 1959	-0.1 / 2.7 / 0.0 / 2.2	-3 / 82 / 0 / 67
17 Su	0159 / 0824 / 1443 / 2038	-0.1 / 2.7 / -0.1 / 2.2	-3 / 82 / -3 / 67
18 M ●	0238 / 0902 / 1522 / 2115	-0.1 / 2.7 / -0.1 / 2.1	-3 / 82 / -3 / 64
19 Tu	0316 / 0938 / 1600 / 2152	-0.1 / 2.6 / -0.1 / 2.1	-3 / 79 / -3 / 64
20 W	0354 / 1015 / 1637 / 2229	0.0 / 2.6 / 0.0 / 2.1	0 / 79 / 0 / 64
21 Th	0432 / 1051 / 1715 / 2306	0.0 / 2.5 / 0.0 / 2.1	0 / 76 / 0 / 64
22 F	0510 / 1127 / 1753 / 2346	0.1 / 2.4 / 0.0 / 2.1	3 / 73 / 0 / 64
23 Sa	0552 / 1207 / 1833	0.1 / 2.3 / 0.0	3 / 70 / 0
24 Su	0029 / 0638 / 1250 / 1916	2.1 / 0.2 / 2.3 / 0.0	64 / 6 / 70 / 0
25 M	0118 / 0731 / 1339 / 2003	2.1 / 0.2 / 2.2 / 0.0	64 / 6 / 67 / 0
26 Tu ◐	0212 / 0831 / 1434 / 2055	2.2 / 0.2 / 2.1 / 0.0	67 / 6 / 64 / 0
27 W	0310 / 0935 / 1535 / 2151	2.3 / 0.2 / 2.1 / -0.1	70 / 6 / 64 / -3
28 Th	0412 / 1040 / 1637 / 2248	2.5 / 0.1 / 2.1 / -0.2	76 / 3 / 64 / -6
29 F	0513 / 1143 / 1738 / 2345	2.6 / -0.1 / 2.2 / -0.4	79 / -3 / 67 / -12
30 Sa	0612 / 1242 / 1837	2.8 / -0.2 / 2.3	85 / -6 / 70
31 Su	0042 / 0709 / 1338 / 1934	-0.5 / 3.0 / -0.4 / 2.4	-15 / 91 / -12 / 73

Time meridian 75° W. 0000 is midnight. 1200 is noon. Times are not adjusted for Daylight Saving Time.
Heights are referred to mean lower low water which is the chart datum of soundings.

Duck Pier, North Carolina, 2017

Times and Heights of High and Low Waters

January

Day	Time	ft	cm	Day	Time	ft	cm
1 Su	0249	0.0	0	16 M	0354	-0.2	-6
	0908	3.6	110		1004	3.5	107
	1533	-0.2	-6		1633	-0.3	-9
	2132	2.9	88		2238	3.1	94
2 M	0334	0.0	0	17 Tu	0445	0.0	0
	0950	3.5	107		1049	3.2	98
	1615	-0.2	-6		1718	-0.1	-3
	2218	2.9	88		2329	3.0	91
3 Tu	0423	0.1	3	18 W	0538	0.3	9
	1036	3.4	104		1136	2.9	88
	1701	-0.2	-6		1803	0.0	0
	2309	3.0	91				
4 W	0518	0.1	3	19 Th	0022	2.9	88
	1126	3.2	98		0635	0.4	12
	1750	-0.2	-6		1225	2.6	79
					1850	0.2	6
5 Th	0004	3.1	94	20 F	0118	2.9	88
	0618	0.2	6		0737	0.6	18
	1221	3.1	94		1319	2.4	73
	1843	-0.2	-6		1941	0.3	9
6 F	0103	3.3	101	21 Sa	0216	2.9	88
	0724	0.1	3		0841	0.6	18
	1321	3.0	91		1417	2.3	70
	1941	-0.3	-9		2033	0.3	9
7 Sa	0206	3.5	107	22 Su	0312	3.0	91
	0833	0.1	3		0941	0.5	15
	1425	2.9	88		1517	2.3	70
	2040	-0.4	-12		2125	0.2	6
8 Su	0310	3.7	113	23 M	0403	3.1	94
	0941	-0.1	-3		1032	0.4	12
	1530	2.9	88		1612	2.4	73
	2140	-0.5	-15		2214	0.2	6
9 M	0411	3.9	119	24 Tu	0449	3.2	98
	1044	-0.3	-9		1117	0.3	9
	1633	2.9	91		1701	2.5	76
	2239	-0.6	-18		2300	0.1	3
10 Tu	0509	4.1	125	25 W	0532	3.4	104
	1143	-0.5	-15		1157	0.1	3
	1732	3.1	94		1745	2.6	79
	2336	-0.7	-21		2343	-0.1	-3
11 W	0604	4.2	128	26 Th	0612	3.5	107
	1236	-0.6	-18		1235	-0.1	-3
	1828	3.2	98		1827	2.8	85
12 Th	0031	-0.8	-24	27 F	0025	-0.2	-6
	0656	4.3	131		0650	3.6	110
	1327	-0.7	-21		1312	-0.2	-6
	1920	3.3	101		1907	2.9	88
13 F	0123	-0.8	-24	28 Sa	0107	-0.3	-9
	0745	4.2	128		0729	3.7	113
	1416	-0.7	-21		1349	-0.3	-9
	2011	3.3	101		1947	3.0	91
14 Sa	0214	-0.7	-21	29 Su	0149	-0.3	-9
	0833	4.0	122		0808	3.7	113
	1503	-0.6	-18		1428	-0.4	-12
	2100	3.3	101		2028	3.1	94
15 Su	0304	-0.5	-15	30 M	0233	-0.3	-9
	0919	3.8	116		0848	3.7	113
	1548	-0.5	-15		1508	-0.5	-15
	2149	3.2	98		2111	3.2	98
				31 Tu	0318	-0.3	-9
					0930	3.6	110
					1549	-0.5	-15
					2156	3.3	101

February

Day	Time	ft	cm	Day	Time	ft	cm
1 W	0408	-0.2	-6	16 Th	0458	0.2	6
	1015	3.4	104		1054	2.8	85
	1634	-0.4	-12		1711	0.1	3
	2246	3.3	101		2330	3.0	91
2 Th	0502	-0.1	-3	17 F	0546	0.4	12
	1105	3.2	98		1138	2.6	79
	1723	-0.4	-12		1754	0.3	9
	2340	3.4	104				
3 F	0601	0.0	0	18 Sa	0020	2.9	88
	1200	3.0	91		0640	0.6	18
	1817	-0.3	-9		1228	2.4	73
					1843	0.4	12
4 Sa	0040	3.4	104	19 Su	0116	2.9	88
	0707	0.1	3		0740	0.7	21
	1301	2.9	88		1325	2.3	70
	1917	-0.3	-9		1938	0.5	15
5 Su	0145	3.5	107	20 M	0216	2.9	88
	0818	0.1	3		0843	0.6	18
	1407	2.8	85		1428	2.3	70
	2021	-0.3	-9		2037	0.4	12
6 M	0253	3.6	110	21 Tu	0315	3.0	91
	0929	0.0	0		0943	0.5	15
	1517	2.8	85		1530	2.4	73
	2126	-0.3	-9		2135	0.3	9
7 Tu	0359	3.7	113	22 W	0409	3.1	94
	1034	-0.2	-6		1034	0.4	12
	1623	2.9	88		1625	2.5	76
	2229	-0.4	-12		2228	0.2	6
8 W	0500	3.8	116	23 Th	0457	3.3	101
	1132	-0.3	-9		1118	0.2	6
	1723	3.1	94		1714	2.8	85
	2328	-0.6	-18		2316	0.0	0
9 Th	0554	3.9	119	24 F	0541	3.5	107
	1223	-0.5	-15		1200	0.0	0
	1817	3.2	98		1758	3.0	91
10 F	0022	-0.6	-18	25 Sa	0002	-0.2	-6
	0644	4.0	122		0623	3.6	110
	1311	-0.6	-18		1239	-0.2	-6
	1907	3.3	101		1840	3.2	98
11 Sa	0112	-0.6	-18	26 Su	0047	-0.4	-12
	0730	3.9	119		0703	3.8	116
	1355	-0.6	-18		1319	-0.4	-12
	1953	3.4	104		1922	3.4	104
12 Su	0200	-0.6	-18	27 M	0131	-0.5	-15
	0813	3.8	116		0745	3.8	116
	1436	-0.5	-15		1359	-0.5	-15
	2037	3.4	104		2005	3.6	110
13 M	0245	-0.4	-12	28 Tu	0217	-0.5	-15
	0854	3.6	110		0827	3.8	116
	1515	-0.4	-12		1441	-0.6	-18
	2119	3.4	104		2049	3.7	113
14 Tu	0329	-0.2	-6				
	0933	3.4	104				
	1553	-0.2	-6				
	2201	3.3	101				
15 W	0413	0.0	0				
	1013	3.1	94				
	1631	-0.1	-3				
	2245	3.1	94				

March

Day	Time	ft	cm	Day	Time	ft	cm
1 W	0304	-0.5	-15	16 Th	0343	0.0	0
	0911	3.7	113		0940	3.1	94
	1524	-0.6	-18		1549	0.1	3
	2135	3.8	116		2205	3.4	104
2 Th	0354	-0.4	-12	17 F	0422	0.2	6
	0958	3.5	107		1019	2.9	88
	1610	-0.5	-15		1627	0.3	9
	2225	3.8	116		2247	3.2	98
3 F	0448	-0.3	-9	18 Sa	0505	0.4	12
	1048	3.3	101		1101	2.7	82
	1701	-0.4	-12		1708	0.4	12
	2320	3.7	113		2332	3.1	94
4 Sa	0548	-0.1	-3	19 Su	0553	0.6	18
	1144	3.1	94		1149	2.5	76
	1757	-0.2	-6		1756	0.5	15
5 Su	0020	3.6	110	20 M	0023	3.0	91
	0653	0.1	3		0647	0.7	21
	1247	2.9	88		1243	2.4	73
	1859	-0.1	-3		1851	0.6	18
6 M	0127	3.5	107	21 Tu	0121	2.9	88
	0805	0.1	3		0747	0.7	21
	1357	2.8	85		1344	2.4	73
	2008	0.0	0		1952	0.6	18
7 Tu	0239	3.5	107	22 W	0222	3.0	91
	0917	0.1	3		0847	0.6	18
	1510	2.9	88		1447	2.5	76
	2119	-0.1	-3		2055	0.5	15
8 W	0349	3.6	110	23 Th	0321	3.1	94
	1021	0.0	0		0943	0.4	12
	1618	3.0	91		1545	2.7	82
	2224	-0.2	-6		2153	0.3	9
9 Th	0450	3.6	110	24 F	0415	3.3	101
	1117	-0.1	-3		1033	0.2	6
	1715	3.2	98		1638	3.0	91
	2323	-0.3	-9		2247	0.1	3
10 F	0543	3.7	113	25 Sa	0504	3.5	107
	1206	-0.3	-9		1119	0.0	0
	1806	3.4	104		1725	3.3	101
					2337	-0.2	-6
11 Sa	0014	-0.4	-12	26 Su	0551	3.6	110
	0630	3.7	113		1203	-0.3	-9
	1249	-0.3	-9		1811	3.6	110
	1850	3.5	107				
12 Su	0101	-0.4	-12	27 M	0025	-0.4	-12
	0712	3.7	113		0636	3.8	116
	1328	-0.3	-9		1246	-0.4	-12
	1931	3.6	110		1856	3.9	119
13 M	0144	-0.4	-12	28 Tu	0113	-0.6	-18
	0751	3.6	110		0721	3.8	116
	1405	-0.3	-9		1329	-0.6	-18
	2010	3.6	110		1941	4.1	125
14 Tu	0225	-0.3	-9	29 W	0201	-0.6	-18
	0827	3.4	104		0806	3.8	116
	1440	-0.2	-6		1414	-0.6	-18
	2048	3.6	110		2027	4.2	128
15 W	0304	-0.1	-3	30 Th	0251	-0.6	-18
	0904	3.3	101		0853	3.7	113
	1514	-0.1	-3		1500	-0.6	-18
	2126	3.5	107		2116	4.2	128
				31 F	0342	-0.5	-15
					0942	3.5	107
					1549	-0.5	-15
					2207	4.1	125

Time meridian 75° W. 0000 is midnight. 1200 is noon. Times are not adjusted for Daylight Saving Time. Heights are referred to mean lower low water which is the chart datum of soundings.

Duck Pier, North Carolina, 2017
Times and Heights of High and Low Waters

April

Day	Time (h m)	Height (ft)	Height (cm)	Day	Time (h m)	Height (ft)	Height (cm)
1 Sa	0437	-0.4	-12	16 Su	0434	0.4	12
	1035	3.3	101		1032	2.7	82
	1643	-0.3	-9		1632	0.5	15
	2303	4.0	122		2254	3.2	98
2 Su	0536	-0.1	-3	17 M	0518	0.5	15
	1133	3.1	94		1118	2.6	79
	1742	-0.1	-3		1719	0.6	18
					2341	3.1	94
3 M	0004	3.7	113	18 Tu	0607	0.5	15
	0641	0.0	0		1209	2.6	79
	1238	3.0	91		1813	0.7	21
	1847	0.1	3				
4 Tu	0111	3.6	110	19 W	0035	3.0	91
	0751	0.1	3		0701	0.6	18
	1351	3.0	91		1306	2.6	79
	2000	0.2	6		1913	0.7	21
5 W	0224	3.4	104	20 Th	0133	3.0	91
	0900	0.2	6		0758	0.5	15
	1504	3.0	91		1406	2.8	85
	2113	0.2	6		2016	0.6	18
6 Th	0334	3.4	104	21 F	0232	3.1	94
	1002	0.1	3		0854	0.4	12
	1608	3.2	98		1505	3.0	91
	2218	0.1	3		2118	0.4	12
7 F	0435	3.4	104	22 Sa	0330	3.2	98
	1055	0.0	0		0947	0.2	6
	1702	3.4	104		1600	3.3	101
	2314	0.0	0		2216	0.1	3
8 Sa	0526	3.4	104	23 Su	0425	3.4	104
	1141	0.0	0		1037	-0.1	-3
	1749	3.5	107		1652	3.7	113
					2311	-0.2	-6
9 Su	0003	-0.1	-3	24 M	0517	3.5	107
	0610	3.4	104		1125	-0.3	-9
	1221	-0.1	-3		1741	4.0	122
	1830	3.7	113				
10 M	0047	-0.2	-6	25 Tu	0003	-0.4	-12
	0649	3.4	104		0607	3.7	113
	1258	-0.1	-3		1213	-0.5	-15
	1907	3.7	113		1829	4.3	131
11 Tu	0127	-0.2	-6	26 W	0054	-0.6	-18
	0726	3.3	101		0656	3.7	113
	1332	0.0	0		1300	-0.6	-18
	1943	3.8	116		1918	4.5	137
12 W	0204	-0.1	-3	27 Th	0145	-0.7	-21
	0801	3.2	98		0746	3.7	113
	1405	0.0	0		1349	-0.7	-21
	2018	3.7	113		2007	4.5	137
13 Th	0240	0.0	0	28 F	0237	-0.7	-21
	0836	3.1	94		0836	3.6	110
	1438	0.1	3		1439	-0.6	-18
	2054	3.6	110		2058	4.5	137
14 F	0316	0.1	3	29 Sa	0330	-0.6	-18
	0912	3.0	91		0929	3.5	107
	1513	0.2	6		1532	-0.5	-15
	2131	3.5	107		2151	4.3	131
15 Sa	0354	0.2	6	30 Su	0425	-0.5	-15
	0951	2.9	88		1024	3.4	104
	1551	0.4	12		1628	-0.2	-6
	2211	3.4	104		2247	4.1	125

May

Day	Time (h m)	Height (ft)	Height (cm)	Day	Time (h m)	Height (ft)	Height (cm)
1 M	0524	-0.3	-9	16 Tu	0450	0.3	9
	1124	3.2	98		1052	2.7	82
	1729	0.0	0		1650	0.6	18
	2347	3.8	116		2308	3.2	98
2 Tu	0626	-0.1	-3	17 W	0535	0.3	9
	1230	3.1	94		1141	2.7	82
	1836	0.2	6		1742	0.6	18
					2357	3.1	94
3 W	0053	3.5	107	18 Th	0624	0.3	9
	0731	0.1	3		1234	2.8	85
	1340	3.1	94		1840	0.6	18
	1949	0.3	9				
4 Th	0202	3.3	101	19 F	0051	3.1	94
	0834	0.1	3		0716	0.3	9
	1449	3.2	98		1330	3.0	91
	2100	0.3	9		1942	0.5	15
5 F	0310	3.2	98	20 Sa	0149	3.1	94
	0933	0.1	3		0810	0.1	3
	1549	3.3	101		1428	3.2	98
	2205	0.2	6		2046	0.3	9
6 Sa	0409	3.1	94	21 Su	0249	3.1	94
	1024	0.1	3		0904	0.0	0
	1641	3.5	107		1525	3.5	107
	2300	0.2	6		2147	0.1	3
7 Su	0500	3.1	94	22 M	0347	3.2	98
	1108	0.1	3		0958	-0.2	-6
	1725	3.6	110		1620	3.9	119
	2347	0.1	3		2246	-0.2	-6
8 M	0544	3.1	94	23 Tu	0444	3.3	101
	1148	0.1	3		1051	-0.4	-12
	1804	3.7	113		1713	4.2	128
					2343	-0.4	-12
9 Tu	0030	0.0	0	24 W	0539	3.4	104
	0623	3.0	91		1143	-0.6	-18
	1223	0.1	3		1806	4.5	137
	1841	3.8	116				
10 W	0108	0.0	0	25 Th	0037	-0.6	-18
	0700	3.0	91		0633	3.5	107
	1258	0.1	3		1235	-0.7	-21
	1916	3.8	116		1858	4.6	140
11 Th	0143	0.0	0	26 F	0130	-0.7	-21
	0735	3.0	91		0727	3.6	110
	1332	0.1	3		1328	-0.7	-21
	1951	3.8	116		1950	4.6	140
12 F	0218	0.0	0	27 Sa	0223	-0.8	-24
	0811	2.9	88		0820	3.6	110
	1407	0.2	6		1421	-0.6	-18
	2026	3.7	113		2042	4.5	137
13 Sa	0253	0.1	3	28 Su	0316	-0.7	-21
	0848	2.9	88		0915	3.5	107
	1443	0.3	9		1516	-0.5	-15
	2103	3.6	110		2135	4.3	131
14 Su	0329	0.2	6	29 M	0411	-0.6	-18
	0927	2.8	85		1012	3.4	104
	1522	0.4	12		1614	-0.3	-9
	2142	3.5	107		2230	4.0	122
15 M	0408	0.2	6	30 Tu	0507	-0.4	-12
	1008	2.7	82		1111	3.3	101
	1604	0.5	15		1715	0.0	0
	2223	3.3	101		2328	3.7	113
				31 W	0604	-0.2	-6
					1214	3.3	101
					1820	0.2	6

June

Day	Time (h m)	Height (ft)	Height (cm)	Day	Time (h m)	Height (ft)	Height (cm)
1 Th	0028	3.4	104	16 F	0552	0.1	3
	0702	0.0	0		1204	3.0	91
	1318	3.2	98		1813	0.5	15
	1929	0.3	9				
2 F	0131	3.1	94	17 Sa	0018	3.2	98
	0800	0.1	3		0641	0.0	0
	1422	3.3	101		1259	3.2	98
	2038	0.4	12		1914	0.4	12
3 Sa	0234	2.9	88	18 Su	0114	3.1	94
	0855	0.1	3		0733	0.0	0
	1520	3.3	101		1356	3.4	104
	2142	0.4	12		2018	0.3	9
4 Su	0333	2.8	85	19 M	0214	3.1	94
	0945	0.2	6		0829	-0.2	-6
	1611	3.4	104		1455	3.7	113
	2237	0.3	9		2122	0.1	3
5 M	0426	2.8	85	20 Tu	0315	3.1	94
	1029	0.2	6		0925	-0.3	-9
	1656	3.5	107		1553	4.0	122
	2325	0.3	9		2225	-0.1	-3
6 Tu	0512	2.7	82	21 W	0417	3.2	98
	1110	0.2	6		1022	-0.4	-12
	1736	3.6	110		1650	4.3	131
					2324	-0.4	-12
7 W	0007	0.2	6	22 Th	0516	3.3	101
	0553	2.8	85		1119	-0.6	-18
	1148	0.2	6		1746	4.5	137
	1813	3.7	113				
8 Th	0045	0.1	3	23 F	0021	-0.6	-18
	0633	2.8	85		0614	3.4	104
	1225	0.2	6		1215	-0.6	-18
	1850	3.7	113		1840	4.6	140
9 F	0121	0.1	3	24 Sa	0115	-0.7	-21
	0711	2.8	85		0710	3.5	107
	1302	0.2	6		1310	-0.6	-18
	1926	3.7	113		1933	4.6	140
10 Sa	0156	0.1	3	25 Su	0208	-0.7	-21
	0748	2.8	85		0805	3.5	107
	1340	0.2	6		1406	-0.6	-18
	2002	3.7	113		2026	4.5	137
11 Su	0231	0.0	0	26 M	0300	-0.7	-21
	0826	2.8	85		0859	3.5	107
	1418	0.3	9		1501	-0.4	-12
	2039	3.6	110		2118	4.2	128
12 M	0307	0.1	3	27 Tu	0352	-0.6	-18
	0905	2.8	85		0954	3.5	107
	1458	0.3	9		1558	-0.2	-6
	2117	3.5	107		2210	4.0	122
13 Tu	0344	0.1	3	28 W	0443	-0.4	-12
	0945	2.8	85		1050	3.4	104
	1541	0.4	12		1656	0.0	0
	2157	3.4	104		2303	3.6	110
14 W	0424	0.1	3	29 Th	0535	-0.2	-6
	1028	2.8	85		1148	3.4	104
	1626	0.5	15		1756	0.2	6
	2240	3.3	101		2356	3.3	101
15 Th	0506	0.1	3	30 F	0626	0.0	0
	1114	2.9	88		1246	3.3	101
	1717	0.5	15		1900	0.4	12
	2326	3.2	98				

Time meridian 75° W. 0000 is midnight. 1200 is noon. Times are not adjusted for Daylight Saving Time.
Heights are referred to mean lower low water which is the chart datum of soundings.

Duck Pier, North Carolina, 2017
Times and Heights of High and Low Waters

July

Day	Time	ft	cm	Time	ft	cm	Time	ft	cm	Time	ft	cm
1 Sa	0052	3.0	91	0718	0.1	3	1345	3.3	101	2006	0.5	15
2 Su	0150	2.8	85	0810	0.2	6	1441	3.3	101	2109	0.6	18
3 M	0248	2.6	79	0859	0.3	9	1534	3.4	104	2206	0.5	15
4 Tu	0344	2.6	79	0947	0.4	12	1621	3.4	104	2256	0.5	15
5 W	0435	2.6	79	1032	0.3	9	1704	3.5	107	2339	0.4	12
6 Th	0522	2.6	79	1115	0.3	9	1745	3.6	110			
7 F	0018	0.3	9	0604	2.7	82	1156	0.3	9	1824	3.7	113
8 Sa ○	0055	0.2	6	0645	2.8	85	1236	0.3	9	1901	3.7	113
9 Su	0130	0.1	3	0724	2.9	88	1316	0.2	6	1938	3.7	113
10 M	0205	0.0	0	0803	2.9	88	1356	0.2	6	2015	3.7	113
11 Tu	0241	0.0	0	0841	3.0	91	1437	0.3	9	2053	3.7	113
12 W	0318	0.0	0	0921	3.1	94	1520	0.3	9	2133	3.6	110
13 Th	0356	0.0	0	1003	3.1	94	1606	0.3	9	2215	3.5	107
14 F	0437	0.0	0	1048	3.2	98	1656	0.4	12	2300	3.4	104
15 Sa	0522	0.0	0	1137	3.4	104	1751	0.4	12	2351	3.2	98
16 Su ◑	0610	0.0	0	1231	3.5	107	1852	0.4	12			
17 M	0047	3.1	94	0703	-0.1	-3	1329	3.7	113	1956	0.3	9
18 Tu	0148	3.0	91	0801	-0.1	-3	1430	3.9	119	2103	0.2	6
19 W	0252	3.0	91	0901	-0.2	-6	1532	4.1	125	2208	0.0	0
20 Th	0356	3.1	94	1002	-0.3	-9	1632	4.3	131	2309	-0.2	-6
21 F	0459	3.3	101	1102	-0.4	-12	1730	4.4	134			
22 Sa	0005	-0.4	-12	0558	3.4	104	1200	-0.5	-15	1825	4.5	137
23 Su ●	0059	-0.5	-15	0655	3.6	110	1257	-0.5	-15	1918	4.5	137
24 M	0150	-0.5	-15	0748	3.7	113	1351	-0.4	-12	2009	4.4	134
25 Tu	0239	-0.5	-15	0840	3.7	113	1445	-0.3	-9	2057	4.1	125
26 W	0326	-0.4	-12	0931	3.7	113	1538	-0.1	-3	2145	3.9	119
27 Th	0412	-0.3	-9	1022	3.6	110	1631	0.1	3	2232	3.6	110
28 F	0458	-0.1	-3	1113	3.5	107	1726	0.4	12	2320	3.2	98
29 Sa	0544	0.1	3	1205	3.5	107	1823	0.6	18			
30 Su ◑	0010	3.0	91	0631	0.3	9	1259	3.4	104	1924	0.7	21
31 M	0103	2.7	82	0720	0.5	15	1354	3.3	101	2027	0.8	24

August

Day	Time	ft	cm	Time	ft	cm	Time	ft	cm	Time	ft	cm
1 Tu	0200	2.6	79	0811	0.6	18	1450	3.4	104	2126	0.8	24
2 W	0300	2.6	79	0904	0.6	18	1542	3.4	104	2219	0.7	21
3 Th	0357	2.6	79	0955	0.6	18	1630	3.5	107	2304	0.6	18
4 F	0448	2.7	82	1043	0.5	15	1714	3.6	110	2345	0.4	12
5 Sa	0534	2.8	85	1128	0.4	12	1755	3.7	113			
6 Su	0022	0.3	9	0616	3.0	91	1211	0.3	9	1834	3.8	116
7 M ○	0058	0.2	6	0656	3.1	94	1253	0.3	9	1912	3.9	119
8 Tu	0134	0.1	3	0735	3.3	101	1334	0.2	6	1950	3.9	119
9 W	0210	0.0	0	0814	3.4	104	1416	0.2	6	2029	3.8	116
10 Th	0248	-0.1	-3	0855	3.5	107	1501	0.2	6	2109	3.8	116
11 F	0327	-0.1	-3	0937	3.6	110	1547	0.2	6	2152	3.6	110
12 Sa	0409	-0.1	-3	1023	3.7	113	1638	0.3	9	2238	3.5	107
13 Su	0454	0.0	0	1113	3.8	116	1733	0.4	12	2330	3.3	101
14 M ◑	0544	0.0	0	1208	3.8	116	1835	0.4	12			
15 Tu	0027	3.2	98	0640	0.1	3	1308	3.9	119	1941	0.4	12
16 W	0130	3.1	94	0741	0.1	3	1412	4.0	122	2049	0.3	9
17 Th	0237	3.1	94	0845	0.1	3	1517	4.1	125	2155	0.2	6
18 F	0345	3.2	98	0950	0.0	0	1620	4.2	128	2255	0.0	0
19 Sa	0448	3.4	104	1052	-0.1	-3	1718	4.3	131	2350	-0.1	-3
20 Su	0547	3.6	110	1150	-0.2	-6	1812	4.4	134			
21 M ●	0040	-0.2	-6	0640	3.8	116	1245	-0.2	-6	1902	4.3	131
22 Tu	0127	-0.3	-9	0730	3.9	119	1337	-0.2	-6	1948	4.2	128
23 W	0212	-0.3	-9	0817	4.0	122	1426	-0.1	-3	2033	4.0	122
24 Th	0254	-0.2	-6	0903	3.9	119	1515	0.1	3	2116	3.8	116
25 F	0336	0.0	0	0948	3.9	119	1603	0.3	9	2159	3.5	107
26 Sa	0416	0.2	6	1033	3.7	113	1651	0.5	15	2242	3.2	98
27 Su	0458	0.4	12	1120	3.6	110	1742	0.7	21	2328	3.0	91
28 M	0542	0.6	18	1210	3.5	107	1837	0.9	27			
29 Tu ◑	0019	2.8	85	0630	0.7	21	1304	3.4	104	1936	1.0	30
30 W	0116	2.7	82	0724	0.8	24	1401	3.4	104	2037	1.0	30
31 Th	0218	2.7	82	0821	0.9	27	1458	3.4	104	2133	0.9	27

September

Day	Time	ft	cm	Time	ft	cm	Time	ft	cm	Time	ft	cm
1 F	0319	2.8	85	0918	0.8	24	1551	3.5	107	2221	0.8	24
2 Sa	0413	2.9	88	1011	0.7	21	1638	3.6	110	2303	0.6	18
3 Su	0501	3.1	94	1059	0.6	18	1721	3.8	116	2343	0.4	12
4 M	0544	3.3	101	1145	0.4	12	1802	3.9	119			
5 Tu	0020	0.2	6	0625	3.5	107	1228	0.3	9	1842	4.0	122
6 W ○	0058	0.1	3	0705	3.7	113	1312	0.2	6	1922	4.0	122
7 Th	0136	0.0	0	0746	3.9	119	1356	0.1	3	2003	4.0	122
8 F	0216	-0.1	-3	0828	4.1	125	1442	0.1	3	2046	3.9	119
9 Sa	0258	-0.1	-3	0912	4.1	125	1531	0.1	3	2131	3.8	116
10 Su	0342	0.0	0	1000	4.2	128	1623	0.2	6	2220	3.6	110
11 M	0430	0.1	3	1051	4.2	128	1719	0.3	9	2314	3.4	104
12 Tu	0524	0.2	6	1148	4.1	125	1822	0.4	12			
13 W ◑	0014	3.3	101	0623	0.3	9	1251	4.1	125	1929	0.5	15
14 Th	0121	3.2	98	0729	0.3	9	1358	4.0	122	2039	0.4	12
15 F	0232	3.3	101	0838	0.3	9	1506	4.1	125	2143	0.3	9
16 Sa	0340	3.4	104	0945	0.2	6	1610	4.1	125	2241	0.2	6
17 Su	0442	3.6	110	1047	0.1	3	1706	4.2	128	2332	0.1	3
18 M	0535	3.8	116	1143	0.0	0	1757	4.2	128			
19 Tu	0018	0.0	0	0624	4.0	122	1234	0.0	0	1843	4.1	125
20 W ●	0101	-0.1	-3	0709	4.1	125	1322	0.0	0	1925	4.0	122
21 Th	0141	0.0	0	0751	4.2	128	1407	0.1	3	2006	3.8	116
22 F	0220	0.1	3	0832	4.1	125	1450	0.3	9	2046	3.6	110
23 Sa	0257	0.2	6	0912	4.0	122	1533	0.4	12	2125	3.4	104
24 Su	0334	0.4	12	0954	3.9	119	1616	0.6	18	2206	3.2	98
25 M	0413	0.6	18	1037	3.7	113	1701	0.8	24	2251	3.0	91
26 Tu	0456	0.8	24	1123	3.6	110	1751	0.9	27	2340	2.9	88
27 W ◑	0544	0.9	27	1214	3.4	104	1845	1.0	30			
28 Th	0036	2.8	85	0639	1.0	30	1311	3.4	104	1944	1.0	30
29 F	0137	2.8	85	0739	1.1	34	1409	3.4	104	2041	1.0	30
30 Sa	0239	2.9	88	0840	1.0	30	1505	3.5	107	2132	0.8	24

Time meridian 75° W. 0000 is midnight. 1200 is noon. Times are not adjusted for Daylight Saving Time.
Heights are referred to mean lower low water which is the chart datum of soundings.

Duck Pier, North Carolina, 2017

Times and Heights of High and Low Waters

October

Day	Time	ft	cm		Day	Time	ft	cm
1 Su	0335	3.1	94		16 M	0432	3.7	113
	0937	0.8	24			1042	0.3	9
	1556	3.6	110			1651	3.8	116
	2217	0.6	18			2310	0.1	3
2 M	0424	3.3	101		17 Tu	0522	3.9	119
	1029	0.6	18			1135	0.2	6
	1643	3.7	113			1739	3.8	116
	2259	0.4	12			2353	0.1	3
3 Tu	0509	3.6	110		18 W	0606	4.1	125
	1117	0.4	12			1222	0.1	3
	1727	3.9	119			1821	3.7	113
	2340	0.2	6					
4 W	0552	3.9	119		19 Th ●	0033	0.1	3
	1203	0.2	6			0647	4.2	128
	1810	4.0	122			1306	0.1	3
						1901	3.6	110
5 Th ○	0021	0.0	0		20 F	0109	0.1	3
	0634	4.2	128			0725	4.2	128
	1249	0.0	0			1347	0.2	6
	1854	4.0	122			1939	3.5	107
6 F	0103	-0.1	-3		21 Sa	0145	0.2	6
	0718	4.4	134			0802	4.1	125
	1336	-0.1	-3			1426	0.3	9
	1938	4.0	122			2016	3.4	104
7 Sa	0146	-0.2	-6		22 Su	0220	0.3	9
	0802	4.5	137			0840	4.0	122
	1425	-0.1	-3			1505	0.4	12
	2024	3.9	119			2055	3.2	98
8 Su	0231	-0.2	-6		23 M	0256	0.5	15
	0849	4.5	137			0918	3.9	119
	1515	0.0	0			1544	0.5	15
	2112	3.8	116			2135	3.1	94
9 M	0319	-0.1	-3		24 Tu	0335	0.6	18
	0939	4.5	137			0959	3.7	113
	1609	0.1	3			1626	0.7	21
	2205	3.6	110			2218	2.9	88
10 Tu	0411	0.0	0		25 W	0417	0.8	24
	1033	4.4	134			1043	3.6	110
	1707	0.2	6			1711	0.8	24
	2302	3.4	104			2306	2.8	85
11 W	0508	0.2	6		26 Th	0505	0.9	27
	1132	4.2	128			1131	3.4	104
	1810	0.3	9			1801	0.9	27
						2359	2.8	85
12 Th ◐	0005	3.3	101		27 F ◐	0559	1.0	30
	0612	0.4	12			1223	3.3	101
	1237	4.0	122			1854	0.9	27
	1918	0.4	12					
13 F	0116	3.3	101		28 Sa	0057	2.8	85
	0722	0.5	15			0658	1.0	30
	1346	3.9	119			1319	3.3	101
	2026	0.4	12			1948	0.8	24
14 Sa	0229	3.4	104		29 Su	0157	2.9	88
	0834	0.5	15			0800	1.0	30
	1455	3.9	119			1416	3.3	101
	2128	0.3	9			2041	0.6	18
15 Su	0335	3.5	107		30 M	0254	3.1	94
	0942	0.4	12			0900	0.8	24
	1557	3.8	116			1510	3.4	104
	2222	0.2	6			2129	0.4	12
					31 Tu	0345	3.4	104
						0956	0.6	18
						1602	3.5	107
						2216	0.2	6

November

Day	Time	ft	cm		Day	Time	ft	cm
1 W	0433	3.8	116		16 Th	0546	3.9	119
	1048	0.3	9			1208	0.2	6
	1651	3.7	113			1759	3.2	98
	2301	0.0	0					
2 Th	0520	4.1	125		17 F	0004	0.1	3
	1139	0.0	0			0624	4.0	122
	1739	3.8	116			1249	0.1	3
	2346	-0.2	-6			1837	3.2	98
3 F	0606	4.4	134		18 Sa ●	0039	0.1	3
	1228	-0.2	-6			0700	4.0	122
	1827	3.8	116			1327	0.2	6
						1914	3.1	94
4 Sa ○	0032	-0.4	-12		19 Su	0114	0.2	6
	0652	4.6	140			0736	4.0	122
	1318	-0.3	-9			1404	0.2	6
	1915	3.8	116			1951	3.1	94
5 Su	0119	-0.4	-12		20 M	0149	0.2	6
	0740	4.7	143			0812	3.9	119
	1408	-0.4	-12			1440	0.3	9
	2004	3.8	116			2029	3.0	91
6 M	0208	-0.4	-12		21 Tu	0226	0.3	9
	0830	4.7	143			0849	3.8	116
	1501	-0.3	-9			1517	0.3	9
	2056	3.7	113			2108	2.9	88
7 Tu	0300	-0.3	-9		22 W	0305	0.5	15
	0922	4.6	140			0928	3.6	110
	1555	-0.2	-6			1556	0.4	12
	2151	3.5	107			2150	2.8	85
8 W	0355	-0.1	-3		23 Th	0346	0.6	18
	1017	4.4	134			1009	3.5	107
	1654	-0.1	-3			1637	0.5	15
	2251	3.4	104			2235	2.7	82
9 Th	0454	0.1	3		24 F	0432	0.7	21
	1116	4.1	125			1053	3.3	101
	1756	0.1	3			1722	0.5	15
	2356	3.3	101			2324	2.7	82
10 F ○	0600	0.3	9		25 Sa	0523	0.8	24
	1220	3.9	119			1141	3.2	98
	1900	0.2	6			1810	0.5	15
11 Sa	0107	3.3	101		26 Su ◑	0018	2.7	82
	0712	0.4	12			0619	0.8	24
	1328	3.6	110			1233	3.1	94
	2005	0.2	6			1901	0.4	12
12 Su	0218	3.4	104		27 M	0114	2.9	88
	0825	0.4	12			0720	0.7	21
	1436	3.5	107			1329	3.1	94
	2104	0.2	6			1952	0.3	9
13 M	0322	3.5	107		28 Tu	0211	3.1	94
	0933	0.4	12			0823	0.6	18
	1537	3.4	104			1426	3.1	94
	2157	0.1	3			2044	0.1	3
14 Tu	0417	3.7	113		29 W	0306	3.4	104
	1032	0.3	9			0923	0.4	12
	1631	3.4	104			1522	3.2	98
	2244	0.1	3			2135	-0.1	-3
15 W	0504	3.8	116		30 Th	0359	3.8	116
	1123	0.2	6			1021	0.1	3
	1717	3.3	101			1617	3.3	101
	2326	0.1	3			2226	-0.3	-9

December

Day	Time	ft	cm		Day	Time	ft	cm
1 F	0450	4.1	125		16 Sa	0602	3.7	113
	1116	-0.2	-6			1231	0.1	3
	1710	3.4	104			1815	2.8	85
	2316	-0.5	-15					
2 Sa	0541	4.4	134		17 Su	0013	0.0	0
	1209	-0.4	-12			0639	3.7	113
	1803	3.5	107			1308	0.1	3
						1853	2.8	85
3 Su ○	0007	-0.6	-18		18 M ●	0049	0.0	0
	0631	4.6	140			0714	3.7	113
	1301	-0.6	-18			1343	0.0	0
	1855	3.6	110			1930	2.8	85
4 M	0058	-0.7	-21		19 Tu	0126	0.1	3
	0722	4.7	143			0750	3.7	113
	1353	-0.6	-18			1417	0.0	0
	1947	3.6	110			2007	2.8	85
5 Tu	0150	-0.7	-21		20 W	0203	0.1	3
	0814	4.6	140			0826	3.6	110
	1446	-0.6	-18			1452	0.1	3
	2041	3.5	107			2045	2.7	82
6 W	0244	-0.6	-18		21 Th	0241	0.2	6
	0906	4.5	137			0903	3.5	107
	1540	-0.5	-15			1528	0.1	3
	2137	3.4	104			2125	2.7	82
7 Th	0340	-0.4	-12		22 F	0321	0.3	9
	1001	4.2	128			0941	3.4	104
	1636	-0.4	-12			1606	0.1	3
	2236	3.3	101			2207	2.7	82
8 F	0440	-0.2	-6		23 Sa	0404	0.4	12
	1058	3.9	119			1021	3.2	98
	1734	-0.3	-9			1647	0.1	3
	2339	3.3	101			2252	2.7	82
9 Sa	0545	0.1	3		24 Su	0452	0.4	12
	1158	3.6	110			1105	3.1	94
	1834	-0.1	-3			1731	0.1	3
						2341	2.8	85
10 Su ○	0046	3.2	98		25 M	0546	0.5	15
	0655	0.2	6			1154	3.0	91
	1301	3.3	101			1818	0.1	3
	1934	0.0	0					
11 M	0154	3.3	101		26 Tu ◑	0034	2.9	88
	0807	0.3	9			0645	0.5	15
	1406	3.1	94			1248	2.9	88
	2032	0.0	0			1910	0.0	0
12 Tu	0257	3.3	101		27 W	0131	3.1	94
	0915	0.3	9			0748	0.4	12
	1508	2.9	88			1346	2.9	88
	2126	0.0	0			2004	-0.1	-3
13 W	0353	3.4	104		28 Th	0230	3.4	104
	1014	0.3	9			0853	0.2	6
	1604	2.8	85			1447	2.9	88
	2214	0.0	0			2100	-0.3	-9
14 Th	0441	3.5	107		29 F	0328	3.7	113
	1106	0.2	6			0956	0.0	0
	1653	2.8	85			1547	3.0	91
	2257	0.0	0			2156	-0.5	-15
15 F	0524	3.6	110		30 Sa	0425	4.0	122
	1151	0.2	6			1055	-0.3	-9
	1736	2.8	85			1646	3.1	94
	2336	0.0	0			2252	-0.7	-21
					31 Su	0520	4.2	128
						1152	-0.5	-15
						1743	3.2	98
						2347	-0.8	-24

Time meridian 75° W. 0000 is midnight. 1200 is noon. Times are not adjusted for Daylight Saving Time.
Heights are referred to mean lower low water which is the chart datum of soundings.

Oregon Inlet, North Carolina, 2017

Times and Heights of High and Low Waters

January

Day	Time (h m)	Height (ft)	Height (cm)
1 Su	0325	0.0	0
	0928	1.0	30
	1643	-0.1	-3
	2201	0.8	24
2 M	0410	0.0	0
	1010	1.0	30
	1720	-0.1	-3
	2248	0.8	24
3 Tu	0502	0.0	0
	1057	1.0	30
	1758	0.0	0
	2339	0.9	27
4 W	0602	0.1	3
	1148	0.9	27
	1842	0.0	0
5 Th ☽	0035	0.9	27
	0710	0.1	3
	1246	0.9	27
	1932	0.0	0
6 F	0137	1.0	30
	0827	0.1	3
	1350	0.9	27
	2030	0.0	0
7 Sa	0241	1.1	34
	0943	0.1	3
	1500	0.8	24
	2134	0.0	0
8 Su	0345	1.1	34
	1053	0.1	3
	1609	0.9	27
	2240	0.0	0
9 M	0446	1.2	37
	1157	0.0	0
	1712	0.9	27
	2342	-0.1	-3
10 Tu	0543	1.3	40
	1255	-0.1	-3
	1809	0.9	27
11 W	0041	-0.1	-3
	0636	1.3	40
	1349	-0.1	-3
	1903	0.9	27
12 Th ○	0137	-0.1	-3
	0727	1.3	40
	1441	-0.1	-3
	1955	1.0	30
13 F	0231	-0.1	-3
	0815	1.2	37
	1530	-0.1	-3
	2046	1.0	30
14 Sa	0323	-0.1	-3
	0902	1.2	37
	1617	-0.1	-3
	2137	0.9	27
15 Su	0415	-0.1	-3
	0949	1.1	34
	1703	-0.1	-3
	2228	0.9	27
16 M	0507	0.0	0
	1035	1.0	30
	1748	-0.1	-3
	2321	0.9	27
17 Tu	0600	0.0	0
	1122	0.9	27
	1832	-0.1	-3
18 W	0015	0.8	24
	0655	0.0	0
	1214	0.7	21
	1918	-0.1	-3
19 Th ◗	0111	0.8	24
	0750	0.1	3
	1312	0.7	21
	2004	0.0	0
20 F	0208	0.8	24
	0847	0.1	3
	1419	0.6	18
	2052	0.0	0
21 Sa	0304	0.8	24
	0944	0.0	0
	1525	0.6	18
	2141	0.0	0
22 Su	0355	0.8	24
	1038	0.0	0
	1622	0.6	18
	2229	0.0	0
23 M	0442	0.8	24
	1129	0.0	0
	1711	0.6	18
	2315	0.0	0
24 Tu	0523	0.8	24
	1217	0.0	0
	1753	0.6	18
	2357	0.0	0
25 W	0601	0.9	27
	1301	-0.1	-3
	1831	0.7	21
26 Th	0036	-0.1	-3
	0636	0.9	27
	1344	-0.1	-3
	1906	0.7	21
27 F ●	0115	-0.1	-3
	0712	1.0	30
	1424	-0.1	-3
	1941	0.7	21
28 Sa	0154	-0.1	-3
	0748	1.0	30
	1502	-0.1	-3
	2018	0.8	24
29 Su	0234	-0.1	-3
	0827	1.1	34
	1538	-0.1	-3
	2058	0.9	27
30 M	0318	0.0	0
	0908	1.1	34
	1613	-0.1	-3
	2141	0.9	27
31 Tu	0407	0.0	0
	0952	1.0	30
	1648	-0.1	-3
	2227	1.0	30

February

Day	Time (h m)	Height (ft)	Height (cm)
1 W	0500	0.0	0
	1039	1.0	30
	1727	0.0	0
	2317	1.0	30
2 Th	0600	0.0	0
	1131	0.9	27
	1813	0.0	0
3 F ◐	0011	1.1	34
	0708	0.1	3
	1228	0.9	27
	1907	0.0	0
4 Sa	0112	1.1	34
	0822	0.1	3
	1333	0.8	24
	2012	0.1	3
5 Su	0218	1.1	34
	0935	0.1	3
	1446	0.8	24
	2124	0.1	3
6 M	0326	1.1	34
	1043	0.1	3
	1558	0.8	24
	2233	0.0	0
7 Tu	0430	1.2	37
	1145	0.0	0
	1702	0.9	27
	2337	0.0	0
8 W	0528	1.2	37
	1241	0.0	0
	1800	0.9	27
9 Th	0035	0.0	0
	0621	1.2	37
	1332	-0.1	-3
	1852	1.0	30
10 F ○	0129	-0.1	-3
	0710	1.2	37
	1420	-0.1	-3
	1941	1.0	30
11 Sa	0220	-0.1	-3
	0756	1.2	37
	1504	-0.1	-3
	2029	1.0	30
12 Su	0309	-0.1	-3
	0840	1.1	34
	1546	-0.1	-3
	2115	1.0	30
13 M	0357	0.0	0
	0923	1.0	30
	1626	-0.1	-3
	2159	1.0	30
14 Tu	0443	0.0	0
	1006	0.9	27
	1705	-0.1	-3
	2244	0.9	27
15 W	0529	0.0	0
	1049	0.8	24
	1743	0.0	0
	2328	0.9	27
16 Th	0615	0.0	0
	1134	0.7	21
	1821	0.0	0
17 F	0015	0.9	27
	0704	0.1	3
	1225	0.7	21
	1902	0.0	0
18 Sa ◗	0105	0.8	24
	0757	0.1	3
	1326	0.6	18
	1949	0.1	3
19 Su	0159	0.8	24
	0854	0.1	3
	1438	0.6	18
	2041	0.1	3
20 M	0256	0.8	24
	0953	0.1	3
	1543	0.6	18
	2136	0.1	3
21 Tu	0350	0.8	24
	1049	0.0	0
	1636	0.6	18
	2228	0.1	3
22 W	0437	0.9	27
	1140	0.0	0
	1721	0.7	21
	2318	0.0	0
23 Th	0520	0.9	27
	1226	0.0	0
	1800	0.8	24
24 F	0006	0.0	0
	0601	1.0	30
	1308	-0.1	-3
	1838	0.8	24
25 Sa	0052	0.0	0
	0641	1.1	34
	1348	-0.1	-3
	1916	0.9	27
26 Su ●	0139	0.0	0
	0723	1.1	34
	1425	-0.1	-3
	1955	1.0	30
27 M	0226	0.0	0
	0805	1.1	34
	1502	-0.1	-3
	2037	1.1	34
28 Tu	0315	0.0	0
	0849	1.1	34
	1538	0.0	0
	2120	1.2	37

March

Day	Time (h m)	Height (ft)	Height (cm)
1 W	0407	0.0	0
	0935	1.1	34
	1617	0.0	0
	2207	1.2	37
2 Th	0502	0.0	0
	1024	1.0	30
	1701	0.1	3
	2256	1.2	37
3 F ○	0602	0.1	3
	1116	1.0	30
	1752	0.1	3
	2351	1.2	37
4 Sa	0708	0.1	3
	1215	0.9	27
	1853	0.1	3
5 Su ◐	0052	1.2	37
	0817	0.1	3
	1323	0.9	27
	2004	0.2	6
6 M	0159	1.2	37
	0926	0.1	3
	1440	0.9	27
	2118	0.2	6
7 Tu	0309	1.2	37
	1031	0.1	3
	1553	0.9	27
	2227	0.1	3
8 W	0414	1.2	37
	1129	0.1	3
	1656	0.9	27
	2330	0.1	3
9 Th	0512	1.2	37
	1222	0.0	0
	1751	1.0	30
10 F	0027	0.1	3
	0604	1.1	34
	1309	0.0	0
	1840	1.1	34
11 Sa	0120	0.0	0
	0651	1.1	34
	1353	0.0	0
	1926	1.1	34
12 Su ○	0209	0.0	0
	0735	1.1	34
	1433	-0.1	-3
	2009	1.1	34
13 M	0254	0.0	0
	0817	1.0	30
	1511	0.0	0
	2050	1.1	34
14 Tu	0338	0.0	0
	0858	1.0	30
	1546	0.0	0
	2129	1.1	34
15 W	0419	0.0	0
	0937	0.9	27
	1618	0.0	0
	2207	1.0	30
16 Th	0459	0.0	0
	1017	0.8	24
	1647	0.0	0
	2244	1.0	30
17 F	0540	0.1	3
	1058	0.8	24
	1719	0.1	3
	2323	0.9	27
18 Sa	0623	0.1	3
	1142	0.7	21
	1757	0.1	3
19 Su	0005	0.9	27
	0712	0.1	3
	1234	0.7	21
	1843	0.2	6
20 M ◗	0052	0.9	27
	0808	0.1	3
	1337	0.6	18
	1936	0.2	6
21 Tu	0146	0.9	27
	0908	0.1	3
	1451	0.7	21
	2034	0.2	6
22 W	0244	0.9	27
	1005	0.1	3
	1554	0.7	21
	2136	0.2	6
23 Th	0340	0.9	27
	1056	0.1	3
	1643	0.8	24
	2237	0.2	6
24 F	0433	1.0	30
	1143	0.0	0
	1726	0.9	27
	2335	0.1	3
25 Sa	0522	1.0	30
	1225	0.0	0
	1807	1.0	30
26 Su	0031	0.1	3
	0610	1.1	34
	1305	0.0	0
	1849	1.1	34
27 M ●	0124	0.0	0
	0656	1.1	34
	1345	0.0	0
	1931	1.2	37
28 Tu	0217	0.0	0
	0743	1.1	34
	1424	0.0	0
	2015	1.3	40
29 W	0309	0.0	0
	0830	1.1	34
	1506	0.0	0
	2100	1.4	43
30 Th	0404	0.0	0
	0919	1.1	34
	1551	0.0	0
	2148	1.4	43
31 F	0500	0.0	0
	1010	1.0	30
	1641	0.1	3
	2239	1.4	43

Time meridian 75° W. 0000 is midnight. 1200 is noon. Times are not adjusted for Daylight Saving Time.
Heights are referred to mean lower low water which is the chart datum of soundings.

Oregon Inlet, North Carolina, 2017

Times and Heights of High and Low Waters

April

Day	Time	ft	cm
1 Sa	0600	0.1	3
	1105	1.0	30
	1738	0.1	3
	2334	1.3	40
2 Su	0703	0.1	3
	1206	0.9	27
	1844	0.2	6
3 M ●	0035	1.3	40
	0808	0.1	3
	1319	0.9	27
	1956	0.2	6
4 Tu	0141	1.2	37
	0912	0.1	3
	1437	0.9	27
	2108	0.2	6
5 W	0250	1.2	37
	1012	0.1	3
	1548	0.9	27
	2216	0.2	6
6 Th	0354	1.1	34
	1107	0.1	3
	1647	1.0	30
	2318	0.2	6
7 F	0451	1.1	34
	1156	0.0	0
	1738	1.1	34
8 Sa	0015	0.1	3
	0542	1.1	34
	1241	0.0	0
	1825	1.1	34
9 Su	0107	0.1	3
	0629	1.0	30
	1322	0.0	0
	1907	1.1	34
10 M	0154	0.1	3
	0712	1.0	30
	1359	0.0	0
	1946	1.2	37
11 Tu ○	0237	0.1	3
	0753	0.9	27
	1433	0.0	0
	2024	1.1	34
12 W	0318	0.1	3
	0832	0.9	27
	1504	0.0	0
	2059	1.1	34
13 Th	0357	0.0	0
	0909	0.8	24
	1530	0.0	0
	2132	1.1	34
14 F	0434	0.1	3
	0946	0.8	24
	1555	0.1	3
	2206	1.0	30
15 Sa	0513	0.1	3
	1024	0.7	21
	1627	0.1	3
	2241	1.0	30
16 Su	0554	0.1	3
	1105	0.7	21
	1706	0.1	3
	2320	1.0	30
17 M	0641	0.1	3
	1152	0.7	21
	1751	0.2	6
18 Tu	0004	1.0	30
	0733	0.1	3
	1249	0.7	21
	1843	0.2	6
19 W ○	0054	1.0	30
	0827	0.1	3
	1356	0.7	21
	1942	0.2	6
20 Th	0149	1.0	30
	0919	0.1	3
	1503	0.8	24
	2048	0.2	6
21 F	0248	1.0	30
	1008	0.1	3
	1600	0.9	27
	2158	0.2	6
22 Sa	0347	1.0	30
	1054	0.0	0
	1650	1.0	30
	2306	0.2	6
23 Su	0444	1.1	34
	1138	0.0	0
	1736	1.1	34
24 M	0009	0.1	3
	0538	1.1	34
	1221	0.0	0
	1822	1.3	40
25 Tu	0108	0.1	3
	0630	1.1	34
	1305	0.0	0
	1908	1.4	43
26 W ●	0204	0.0	0
	0721	1.1	34
	1351	0.0	0
	1954	1.4	43
27 Th	0300	0.0	0
	0811	1.1	34
	1439	0.0	0
	2042	1.5	46
28 F	0356	0.0	0
	0902	1.1	34
	1530	0.0	0
	2132	1.5	46
29 Sa	0453	0.0	0
	0956	1.0	30
	1626	0.1	3
	2224	1.4	43
30 Su	0552	0.0	0
	1053	1.0	30
	1726	0.1	3
	2319	1.4	43

May

Day	Time	ft	cm
1 M	0652	0.1	3
	1158	0.9	27
	1833	0.2	6
2 Tu ◑	0017	1.3	40
	0752	0.1	3
	1312	0.9	27
	1942	0.2	6
3 W	0121	1.2	37
	0851	0.1	3
	1427	0.9	27
	2052	0.2	6
4 Th	0226	1.1	34
	0946	0.0	0
	1534	1.0	30
	2159	0.2	6
5 F	0329	1.0	30
	1038	0.0	0
	1630	1.0	30
	2301	0.2	6
6 Sa	0426	1.0	30
	1125	0.0	0
	1720	1.1	34
	2357	0.2	6
7 Su	0518	0.9	27
	1209	0.0	0
	1804	1.1	34
8 M	0048	0.1	3
	0604	0.9	27
	1249	0.0	0
	1845	1.1	34
9 Tu	0134	0.1	3
	0648	0.9	27
	1325	0.0	0
	1923	1.1	34
10 W ○	0216	0.1	3
	0728	0.8	24
	1357	0.0	0
	1958	1.1	34
11 Th	0256	0.1	3
	0806	0.8	24
	1425	0.0	0
	2031	1.1	34
12 F	0335	0.0	0
	0841	0.8	24
	1449	0.0	0
	2103	1.1	34
13 Sa	0414	0.0	0
	0916	0.7	21
	1515	0.1	3
	2135	1.1	34
14 Su	0453	0.0	0
	0953	0.7	21
	1548	0.1	3
	2209	1.1	34
15 M	0535	0.1	3
	1033	0.7	21
	1626	0.1	3
	2246	1.1	34
16 Tu	0618	0.1	3
	1119	0.7	21
	1711	0.2	6
	2329	1.0	30
17 W	0702	0.1	3
	1212	0.7	21
	1803	0.2	6
18 Th ◐	0016	1.0	30
	0748	0.1	3
	1312	0.7	21
	1903	0.2	6
19 F	0109	1.0	30
	0834	0.1	3
	1417	0.8	24
	2011	0.2	6
20 Sa	0207	1.0	30
	0919	0.0	0
	1518	0.9	27
	2125	0.2	6
21 Su	0309	1.0	30
	1006	0.0	0
	1614	1.1	34
	2240	0.2	6
22 M	0410	1.0	30
	1054	0.0	0
	1706	1.2	37
	2349	0.1	3
23 Tu	0510	1.0	30
	1143	0.0	0
	1757	1.3	40
24 W	0052	0.1	3
	0606	1.1	34
	1234	0.0	0
	1846	1.4	43
25 Th ●	0151	0.0	0
	0700	1.1	34
	1326	-0.1	-3
	1936	1.5	46
26 F	0248	0.0	0
	0753	1.1	34
	1419	0.0	0
	2026	1.5	46
27 Sa	0345	0.0	0
	0846	1.0	30
	1514	0.0	0
	2117	1.5	46
28 Su	0441	0.0	0
	0941	1.0	30
	1612	0.0	0
	2209	1.4	43
29 M	0537	0.0	0
	1040	1.0	30
	1712	0.1	3
	2302	1.3	40
30 Tu	0633	0.0	0
	1145	0.9	27
	1816	0.1	3
	2357	1.2	37
31 W	0729	0.0	0
	1255	0.9	27
	1922	0.2	6

June

Day	Time	ft	cm
1 Th ◑	0056	1.1	34
	0823	0.0	0
	1406	0.9	27
	2029	0.2	6
2 F	0158	1.0	30
	0915	0.0	0
	1510	1.0	30
	2134	0.2	6
3 Sa	0300	0.9	27
	1005	0.0	0
	1606	1.0	30
	2236	0.2	6
4 Su	0358	0.9	27
	1051	0.0	0
	1655	1.0	30
	2332	0.2	6
5 M	0451	0.8	24
	1135	0.0	0
	1739	1.1	34
6 Tu	0023	0.2	6
	0539	0.8	24
	1215	0.0	0
	1820	1.1	34
7 W	0109	0.1	3
	0623	0.8	24
	1251	0.0	0
	1858	1.1	34
8 Th	0152	0.1	3
	0703	0.8	24
	1324	0.0	0
	1933	1.1	34
9 F ○	0233	0.1	3
	0739	0.8	24
	1352	0.0	0
	2005	1.1	34
10 Sa	0313	0.1	3
	0814	0.7	21
	1417	0.0	0
	2036	1.1	34
11 Su	0353	0.1	3
	0849	0.7	21
	1446	0.0	0
	2107	1.1	34
12 M	0433	0.0	0
	0925	0.7	21
	1519	0.1	3
	2141	1.1	34
13 Tu	0512	0.1	3
	1006	0.7	21
	1558	0.1	3
	2219	1.1	34
14 W	0551	0.1	3
	1051	0.7	21
	1643	0.2	6
	2300	1.1	34
15 Th	0630	0.1	3
	1141	0.8	24
	1736	0.2	6
	2347	1.1	34
16 F	0709	0.1	3
	1237	0.8	24
	1836	0.2	6
17 Sa ○	0039	1.1	34
	0751	0.1	3
	1338	0.9	27
	1944	0.2	6
18 Su	0136	1.0	30
	0837	0.1	3
	1440	1.0	30
	2059	0.2	6
19 M	0239	1.0	30
	0928	0.1	3
	1542	1.2	37
	2218	0.2	6
20 Tu	0343	1.0	30
	1021	0.0	0
	1640	1.3	40
	2331	0.2	6
21 W	0445	1.0	30
	1117	0.0	0
	1735	1.4	43
22 Th	0037	0.1	3
	0545	1.1	34
	1214	0.0	0
	1828	1.5	46
23 F ●	0137	0.1	3
	0641	1.1	34
	1310	0.0	0
	1920	1.5	46
24 Sa	0234	0.1	3
	0736	1.1	34
	1406	0.0	0
	2011	1.5	46
25 Su	0329	0.0	0
	0830	1.1	34
	1502	0.0	0
	2101	1.5	46
26 M	0423	0.0	0
	0925	1.1	34
	1558	0.0	0
	2151	1.4	43
27 Tu	0515	0.0	0
	1022	1.0	30
	1656	0.1	3
	2241	1.3	40
28 W	0607	0.0	0
	1123	1.0	30
	1756	0.2	6
	2333	1.2	37
29 Th	0658	0.0	0
	1227	1.0	30
	1857	0.2	6
30 F ◑	0028	1.1	34
	0749	0.0	0
	1333	1.0	30
	1959	0.3	9

Time meridian 75° W. 0000 is midnight. 1200 is noon. Times are not adjusted for Daylight Saving Time.
Heights are referred to mean lower low water which is the chart datum of soundings.

Oregon Inlet, North Carolina, 2017
Times and Heights of High and Low Waters

July

Day	Time	ft	cm	Day	Time	ft	cm
1 Sa	0126	1.0	30	16 Su ☽	0015	1.2	37
	0839	0.1	3		0715	0.2	6
	1436	1.0	30		1305	1.1	34
	2102	0.3	9		1926	0.3	9
2 Su	0228	0.9	27	17 M	0112	1.1	34
	0928	0.1	3		0806	0.2	6
	1533	1.0	30		1409	1.2	37
	2202	0.3	9		2044	0.3	9
3 M	0328	0.9	27	18 Tu	0216	1.1	34
	1015	0.1	3		0903	0.2	6
	1624	1.0	30		1515	1.3	40
	2259	0.3	9		2205	0.3	9
4 Tu	0423	0.8	24	19 W	0322	1.1	34
	1100	0.1	3		1003	0.1	3
	1711	1.0	30		1618	1.4	43
	2350	0.2	6		2318	0.3	9
5 W	0513	0.8	24	20 Th	0428	1.1	34
	1142	0.0	0		1105	0.1	3
	1753	1.1	34		1717	1.4	43
6 Th	0038	0.2	6	21 F	0023	0.3	9
	0557	0.8	24		0529	1.1	34
	1220	0.0	0		1204	0.1	3
	1832	1.1	34		1813	1.5	46
7 F	0123	0.2	6	22 Sa	0122	0.2	6
	0637	0.8	24		0626	1.2	37
	1254	0.0	0		1301	0.1	3
	1907	1.1	34		1905	1.5	46
8 Sa ○	0206	0.1	3	23 Su ●	0217	0.2	6
	0713	0.8	24		0721	1.2	37
	1324	0.0	0		1357	0.1	3
	1939	1.1	34		1955	1.5	46
9 Su	0247	0.1	3	24 M	0309	0.2	6
	0748	0.8	24		0814	1.2	37
	1354	0.1	3		1451	0.1	3
	2010	1.2	37		2043	1.5	46
10 M	0327	0.1	3	25 Tu	0358	0.1	3
	0823	0.8	24		0907	1.2	37
	1425	0.1	3		1544	0.1	3
	2041	1.2	37		2130	1.4	43
11 Tu	0405	0.1	3	26 W	0447	0.1	3
	0900	0.8	24		1000	1.2	37
	1500	0.1	3		1638	0.2	6
	2116	1.2	37		2218	1.3	40
12 W	0442	0.1	3	27 Th	0534	0.1	3
	0940	0.9	27		1054	1.1	34
	1540	0.2	6		1732	0.2	6
	2154	1.2	37		2306	1.2	37
13 Th	0518	0.1	3	28 F	0622	0.2	6
	1024	0.9	27		1150	1.1	34
	1626	0.2	6		1827	0.3	9
	2237	1.2	37		2357	1.1	34
14 F	0553	0.2	6	29 Sa	0710	0.2	6
	1112	1.0	30		1250	1.1	34
	1719	0.2	6		1923	0.3	9
	2323	1.2	37				
15 Sa	0631	0.2	6	30 Su ☾	0052	1.0	30
	1206	1.0	30		0759	0.2	6
	1818	0.3	9		1351	1.0	30
					2021	0.4	12
				31 M	0153	1.0	30
					0848	0.2	6
					1451	1.0	30
					2120	0.4	12

August

Day	Time	ft	cm	Day	Time	ft	cm
1 Tu	0256	0.9	27	16 W	0200	1.2	37
	0937	0.2	6		0851	0.3	9
	1547	1.0	30		1453	1.4	43
	2218	0.4	12		2159	0.4	12
2 W	0354	0.9	27	17 Th	0310	1.2	37
	1023	0.2	6		0958	0.3	9
	1637	1.1	34		1601	1.4	43
	2312	0.3	9		2308	0.4	12
3 Th	0445	0.9	27	18 F	0418	1.2	37
	1107	0.2	6		1101	0.3	9
	1722	1.1	34		1702	1.5	46
4 F	0003	0.3	9	19 Sa	0009	0.4	12
	0530	0.9	27		0519	1.3	40
	1147	0.2	6		1200	0.2	6
	1801	1.1	34		1757	1.5	46
5 Sa	0050	0.3	9	20 Su	0104	0.3	9
	0610	0.9	27		0615	1.3	40
	1224	0.2	6		1256	0.2	6
	1836	1.2	37		1848	1.6	49
6 Su	0133	0.3	9	21 M ●	0155	0.3	9
	0646	1.0	30		0707	1.3	40
	1300	0.2	6		1349	0.2	6
	1909	1.2	37		1936	1.5	46
7 M ○	0214	0.2	6	22 Tu	0242	0.3	9
	0721	1.0	30		0757	1.4	43
	1335	0.2	6		1440	0.2	6
	1941	1.3	40		2023	1.5	46
8 Tu	0252	0.2	6	23 W	0328	0.2	6
	0757	1.0	30		0845	1.3	40
	1411	0.2	6		1530	0.2	6
	2016	1.3	40		2108	1.4	43
9 W	0329	0.2	6	24 Th	0412	0.3	9
	0835	1.1	34		0933	1.3	40
	1450	0.2	6		1618	0.3	9
	2053	1.3	40		2152	1.3	40
10 Th	0404	0.2	6	25 F	0456	0.3	9
	0915	1.1	34		1020	1.3	40
	1532	0.2	6		1705	0.3	9
	2133	1.3	40		2237	1.2	37
11 F	0439	0.3	9	26 Sa	0540	0.3	9
	0959	1.2	37		1108	1.2	37
	1619	0.3	9		1753	0.3	9
	2217	1.3	40		2324	1.2	37
12 Sa	0515	0.3	9	27 Su	0626	0.3	9
	1047	1.2	37		1159	1.2	37
	1711	0.3	9		1842	0.4	12
	2304	1.3	40				
13 Su	0557	0.3	9	28 M	0015	1.1	34
	1139	1.3	40		0713	0.3	9
	1811	0.4	12		1254	1.1	34
	2357	1.2	37		1935	0.4	12
14 M ☽	0648	0.3	9	29 Tu ☾	0114	1.0	30
	1238	1.3	40		0802	0.4	12
	1921	0.4	12		1356	1.1	34
					2033	0.4	12
15 Tu	0055	1.2	37	30 W	0219	1.0	30
	0746	0.3	9		0852	0.4	12
	1343	1.3	40		1457	1.1	34
	2041	0.4	12		2133	0.4	12
				31 Th	0321	1.0	30
					0941	0.3	9
					1553	1.1	34
					2230	0.4	12

September

Day	Time	ft	cm	Day	Time	ft	cm
1 F	0415	1.0	30	16 Sa	0414	1.3	40
	1028	0.3	9		1057	0.4	12
	1641	1.1	34		1646	1.5	46
	2323	0.4	12		2350	0.4	12
2 Sa	0501	1.0	30	17 Su	0512	1.3	40
	1112	0.3	9		1156	0.3	9
	1722	1.2	37		1741	1.5	46
3 Su	0010	0.4	12	18 M	0041	0.4	12
	0541	1.1	34		0605	1.4	43
	1155	0.3	9		1250	0.3	9
	1759	1.3	40		1830	1.5	46
4 M	0053	0.3	9	19 Tu	0128	0.3	9
	0617	1.1	34		0653	1.4	43
	1236	0.3	9		1340	0.3	9
	1835	1.3	40		1917	1.4	43
5 Tu	0133	0.3	9	20 W ●	0212	0.3	9
	0653	1.2	37		0739	1.4	43
	1317	0.2	6		1428	0.2	6
	1912	1.4	43		2001	1.4	43
6 W ○	0210	0.3	9	21 Th	0254	0.3	9
	0730	1.3	40		0822	1.4	43
	1359	0.2	6		1513	0.3	9
	1950	1.4	43		2044	1.3	40
7 Th	0246	0.3	9	22 F	0335	0.3	9
	0809	1.3	40		0904	1.4	43
	1443	0.2	6		1556	0.3	9
	2031	1.4	43		2126	1.3	40
8 F	0322	0.3	9	23 Sa	0414	0.3	9
	0851	1.4	43		0945	1.3	40
	1529	0.3	9		1638	0.3	9
	2114	1.4	43		2208	1.2	37
9 Sa	0359	0.4	12	24 Su	0454	0.4	12
	0936	1.4	43		1026	1.3	40
	1618	0.3	9		1719	0.3	9
	2159	1.4	43		2251	1.1	34
10 Su	0442	0.4	12	25 M	0534	0.4	12
	1024	1.5	46		1109	1.2	37
	1713	0.4	12		1802	0.4	12
	2248	1.3	40		2337	1.1	34
11 M	0531	0.4	12	26 Tu	0618	0.4	12
	1117	1.5	46		1155	1.1	34
	1816	0.4	12		1851	0.4	12
	2342	1.3	40				
12 Tu	0630	0.4	12	27 W ☽	0029	1.0	30
	1217	1.4	43		0705	0.4	12
	1927	0.5	15		1247	1.1	34
					1947	0.4	12
13 W ☽	0043	1.3	40	28 Th	0132	1.0	30
	0737	0.4	12		0757	0.4	12
	1323	1.4	43		1346	1.1	34
	2041	0.5	15		2047	0.4	12
14 Th	0153	1.2	37	29 F	0240	1.0	30
	0847	0.4	12		0850	0.4	12
	1435	1.4	43		1447	1.1	34
	2151	0.5	15		2145	0.4	12
15 F	0306	1.2	37	30 Sa	0338	1.0	30
	0955	0.4	12		0943	0.4	12
	1545	1.4	43		1543	1.1	34
	2253	0.4	12		2237	0.4	12

Time meridian 75° W. 0000 is midnight. 1200 is noon. Times are not adjusted for Daylight Saving Time.
Heights are referred to mean lower low water which is the chart datum of soundings.

Oregon Inlet, North Carolina, 2017

Times and Heights of High and Low Waters

October

Day	Time	Height (ft)	Height (cm)
1 Su	0425	1.1	34
	1034	0.4	12
	1631	1.2	37
	2323	0.3	9
16 M	0503	1.3	40
	1147	0.3	9
	1722	1.3	40
2 M	0506	1.1	34
	1124	0.3	9
	1716	1.2	37
17 Tu	0014	0.3	9
	0551	1.4	43
	1240	0.3	9
	1811	1.3	40
3 Tu	0006	0.3	9
	0544	1.2	37
	1212	0.3	9
	1759	1.3	40
18 W	0059	0.3	9
	0636	1.4	43
	1329	0.2	6
	1857	1.2	37
4 W	0045	0.3	9
	0623	1.3	40
	1259	0.2	6
	1842	1.3	40
19 Th ●	0141	0.2	6
	0718	1.4	43
	1414	0.2	6
	1940	1.2	37
5 Th ○	0123	0.3	9
	0703	1.4	43
	1346	0.2	6
	1925	1.3	40
20 F	0220	0.2	6
	0758	1.4	43
	1455	0.2	6
	2021	1.1	34
6 F	0202	0.3	9
	0745	1.5	46
	1435	0.2	6
	2009	1.4	43
21 Sa	0257	0.3	9
	0836	1.3	40
	1535	0.2	6
	2101	1.1	34
7 Sa	0242	0.3	9
	0829	1.5	46
	1525	0.2	6
	2055	1.3	40
22 Su	0331	0.3	9
	0913	1.3	40
	1613	0.2	6
	2140	1.0	30
8 Su	0327	0.3	9
	0916	1.6	49
	1618	0.3	9
	2143	1.3	40
23 M	0404	0.3	9
	0949	1.2	37
	1651	0.2	6
	2219	1.0	30
9 M	0417	0.4	12
	1006	1.5	46
	1716	0.3	9
	2235	1.3	40
24 Tu	0438	0.3	9
	1027	1.1	34
	1731	0.3	9
	2300	0.9	27
10 Tu	0514	0.4	12
	1100	1.5	46
	1820	0.3	9
	2332	1.2	37
25 W	0516	0.3	9
	1107	1.1	34
	1817	0.3	9
	2347	0.9	27
11 W	0619	0.4	12
	1159	1.5	46
	1926	0.4	12
26 Th	0601	0.4	12
	1151	1.1	34
	1908	0.3	9
12 Th ☽	0037	1.2	37
	0729	0.4	12
	1305	1.4	43
	2032	0.4	12
27 F ☾	0041	0.9	27
	0654	0.4	12
	1241	1.0	30
	2002	0.3	9
13 F	0150	1.2	37
	0840	0.4	12
	1417	1.4	43
	2135	0.4	12
28 Sa	0144	0.9	27
	0752	0.4	12
	1337	1.0	30
	2055	0.3	9
14 Sa	0304	1.2	37
	0947	0.4	12
	1526	1.3	40
	2233	0.4	12
29 Su	0246	0.9	27
	0853	0.3	9
	1437	1.0	30
	2144	0.3	9
15 Su	0408	1.3	40
	1050	0.3	9
	1628	1.3	40
	2326	0.3	9
30 M	0339	1.0	30
	0954	0.3	9
	1536	1.1	34
	2230	0.2	6
31 Tu	0425	1.1	34
	1052	0.3	9
	1632	1.1	34
	2314	0.2	6

November

Day	Time	Height (ft)	Height (cm)
1 W	0509	1.2	37
	1147	0.2	6
	1723	1.1	34
	2356	0.2	6
16 Th	0029	0.1	3
	0617	1.2	37
	1312	0.1	3
	1836	1.0	30
2 Th	0553	1.3	40
	1240	0.1	3
	1813	1.2	37
17 F	0110	0.1	3
	0657	1.2	37
	1355	0.1	3
	1919	0.9	27
3 F	0040	0.2	6
	0638	1.4	43
	1332	0.1	3
	1901	1.2	37
18 Sa ●	0148	0.1	3
	0735	1.2	37
	1436	0.1	3
	1959	0.9	27
4 Sa ○	0125	0.2	6
	0723	1.5	46
	1425	0.1	3
	1949	1.2	37
19 Su	0222	0.1	3
	0810	1.1	34
	1514	0.1	3
	2037	0.9	27
5 Su	0212	0.2	6
	0811	1.5	46
	1518	0.1	3
	2038	1.2	37
20 M	0253	0.1	3
	0845	1.1	34
	1551	0.1	3
	2113	0.8	24
6 M	0304	0.2	6
	0900	1.5	46
	1614	0.1	3
	2129	1.2	37
21 Tu	0321	0.1	3
	0918	1.1	34
	1629	0.1	3
	2149	0.8	24
7 Tu	0359	0.2	6
	0951	1.5	46
	1712	0.1	3
	2223	1.1	34
22 W	0352	0.1	3
	0953	1.0	30
	1707	0.1	3
	2228	0.8	24
8 W	0501	0.2	6
	1045	1.4	43
	1813	0.2	6
	2322	1.1	34
23 Th	0429	0.2	6
	1030	1.0	30
	1748	0.1	3
	2310	0.7	21
9 Th	0608	0.3	9
	1143	1.3	40
	1914	0.2	6
24 F	0513	0.2	6
	1110	1.0	30
	1830	0.1	3
	2358	0.7	21
10 F ○	0030	1.1	34
	0717	0.3	9
	1246	1.3	40
	2014	0.2	6
25 Sa	0604	0.2	6
	1156	0.9	27
	1915	0.1	3
11 Sa	0143	1.1	34
	0827	0.3	9
	1355	1.2	37
	2112	0.2	6
26 Su ☾	0052	0.8	24
	0702	0.2	6
	1248	0.9	27
	2000	0.1	3
12 Su	0253	1.1	34
	0934	0.3	9
	1504	1.1	34
	2207	0.2	6
27 M	0150	0.8	24
	0807	0.2	6
	1347	0.9	27
	2047	0.1	3
13 M	0354	1.1	34
	1036	0.2	6
	1607	1.1	34
	2258	0.1	3
28 Tu	0248	0.9	27
	0914	0.2	6
	1449	0.9	27
	2134	0.1	3
14 Tu	0446	1.2	37
	1134	0.2	6
	1702	1.0	30
	2345	0.1	3
29 W	0343	1.0	30
	1020	0.1	3
	1552	0.9	27
	2223	0.1	3
15 W	0534	1.2	37
	1225	0.1	3
	1751	1.0	30
30 Th	0435	1.1	34
	1113	0.1	3
	1651	1.0	30
	2314	0.0	0

December

Day	Time	Height (ft)	Height (cm)
1 F	0525	1.3	40
	1221	0.0	0
	1746	1.0	30
16 Sa	0042	0.0	0
	0635	1.0	30
	1334	0.0	0
	1859	0.7	21
2 Sa	0005	0.0	0
	0615	1.4	43
	1318	0.0	0
	1839	1.0	30
17 Su	0120	0.0	0
	0712	1.0	30
	1414	-0.1	-3
	1938	0.7	21
3 Su	0058	0.0	0
	0704	1.4	43
	1413	0.0	0
	1930	1.1	34
18 M ●	0154	0.0	0
	0747	1.0	30
	1453	-0.1	-3
	2014	0.7	21
4 M	0152	0.0	0
	0754	1.4	43
	1509	-0.1	-3
	2022	1.1	34
19 Tu	0224	0.0	0
	0819	1.0	30
	1530	-0.1	-3
	2049	0.7	21
5 Tu	0249	0.0	0
	0845	1.4	43
	1604	0.0	0
	2115	1.0	30
20 W	0252	0.0	0
	0851	1.0	30
	1607	-0.1	-3
	2123	0.7	21
6 W	0347	0.0	0
	0936	1.4	43
	1700	0.0	0
	2210	1.0	30
21 Th	0322	0.0	0
	0924	0.9	27
	1642	-0.1	-3
	2158	0.7	21
7 Th	0449	0.0	0
	1029	1.3	40
	1755	0.0	0
	2310	1.0	30
22 F	0358	0.0	0
	0959	0.9	27
	1716	-0.1	-3
	2238	0.7	21
8 F	0554	0.1	3
	1124	1.2	37
	1851	0.0	0
23 Sa	0441	0.1	3
	1039	0.9	27
	1750	0.0	0
	2322	0.7	21
9 Sa	0015	1.0	30
	0700	0.1	3
	1224	1.1	34
	1947	0.0	0
24 Su	0530	0.1	3
	1123	0.9	27
	1826	0.0	0
10 Su ○	0124	1.0	30
	0807	0.1	3
	1330	1.0	30
	2042	0.0	0
25 M	0011	0.8	24
	0627	0.1	3
	1213	0.8	24
	1907	0.0	0
11 M	0231	1.0	30
	0913	0.1	3
	1438	0.9	27
	2135	0.0	0
26 Tu ☾	0105	0.8	24
	0730	0.1	3
	1310	0.8	24
	1954	0.0	0
12 Tu	0330	1.0	30
	1015	0.1	3
	1543	0.8	24
	2226	0.0	0
27 W	0204	0.9	27
	0840	0.1	3
	1413	0.8	24
	2046	0.0	0
13 W	0423	1.0	30
	1113	0.1	3
	1640	0.8	24
	2315	0.0	0
28 Th	0304	1.0	30
	0952	0.0	0
	1519	0.8	24
	2143	0.0	0
14 Th	0511	1.0	30
	1204	0.0	0
	1731	0.8	24
29 F	0403	1.1	34
	1101	0.0	0
	1624	0.8	24
	2242	0.0	0
15 F	0000	0.0	0
	0555	1.0	30
	1251	0.0	0
	1816	0.7	21
30 Sa	0500	1.2	37
	1205	0.0	0
	1724	0.9	27
	2342	-0.1	-3
31 Su	0555	1.3	40
	1304	-0.1	-3
	1820	0.9	27

Time meridian 75° W. 0000 is midnight. 1200 is noon. Times are not adjusted for Daylight Saving Time.
Heights are referred to mean lower low water which is the chart datum of soundings.

Cape Hatteras, North Carolina, 2017

Times and Heights of High and Low Waters

January

Day	Time	ft	cm	Day	Time	ft	cm
1 Su	0237	-0.1	-3	**16** M	0346	-0.3	-9
	0904	3.4	104		1005	3.3	101
	1532	-0.1	-3		1628	-0.3	-9
	2126	2.5	76		2236	2.8	85
2 M	0320	-0.1	-3	**17** Tu	0438	-0.1	-3
	0945	3.3	101		1053	3.0	91
	1612	-0.1	-3		1714	-0.2	-6
	2212	2.6	79		2329	2.7	82
3 Tu	0409	0.0	0	**18** W	0534	0.1	3
	1030	3.2	98		1142	2.6	79
	1655	-0.1	-3		1801	0.0	0
	2303	2.7	82				
4 W	0504	0.1	3	**19** Th	0024	2.6	79
	1119	3.0	91		0634	0.3	9
	1743	-0.1	-3		1233	2.4	73
	2359	2.8	85		1849	0.1	3
5 Th	0606	0.1	3	**20** F	0121	2.6	79
	1214	2.8	85		0738	0.4	12
	1835	-0.2	-6		1329	2.2	67
					1939	0.2	6
6 F	0101	3.0	91	**21** Sa	0218	2.6	79
	0714	0.1	3		0842	0.5	15
	1315	2.7	82		1426	2.1	64
	1931	-0.3	-9		2030	0.2	6
7 Sa	0204	3.2	98	**22** Su	0312	2.7	82
	0825	0.0	0		0940	0.4	12
	1419	2.6	79		1522	2.0	61
	2030	-0.4	-12		2120	0.1	3
8 Su	0308	3.4	104	**23** M	0402	2.8	85
	0934	-0.1	-3		1031	0.3	9
	1524	2.6	79		1613	2.1	64
	2130	-0.5	-15		2208	0.1	3
9 M	0408	3.7	113	**24** Tu	0447	3.0	91
	1037	-0.3	-9		1116	0.2	6
	1626	2.7	82		1659	2.2	67
	2228	-0.6	-18		2253	-0.1	-3
10 Tu	0505	3.9	119	**25** W	0529	3.1	94
	1135	-0.4	-12		1157	0.0	0
	1725	2.8	85		1742	2.3	70
	2324	-0.8	-24		2336	-0.2	-6
11 W	0600	4.0	122	**26** Th	0609	3.3	101
	1229	-0.6	-18		1236	-0.1	-3
	1820	2.9	88		1823	2.4	73
12 Th	0019	-0.8	-24	**27** F	0017	-0.3	-9
	0652	4.0	122		0647	3.4	104
	1319	-0.6	-18		1313	-0.2	-6
	1913	2.9	88		1902	2.5	76
13 F	0112	-0.8	-24	**28** Sa	0058	-0.4	-12
	0742	4.0	122		0725	3.4	104
	1408	-0.6	-18		1349	-0.3	-9
	2004	2.9	88		1942	2.6	79
14 Sa	0203	-0.7	-21	**29** Su	0139	-0.4	-12
	0831	3.8	116		0804	3.4	104
	1456	-0.6	-18		1426	-0.4	-12
	2055	2.9	88		2022	2.7	82
15 Su	0254	-0.5	-15	**30** M	0222	-0.4	-12
	0918	3.6	110		0843	3.4	104
	1542	-0.5	-15		1504	-0.4	-12
	2145	2.9	88		2105	2.8	85
				31 Tu	0307	-0.4	-12
					0925	3.3	101
					1543	-0.4	-12
					2151	2.9	88

February

Day	Time	ft	cm	Day	Time	ft	cm
1 W	0356	-0.3	-9	**16** Th	0457	0.1	3
	1009	3.1	94		1058	2.5	76
	1626	-0.4	-12		1707	0.0	0
	2241	3.0	91		2332	2.7	82
2 Th	0451	-0.2	-6	**17** F	0549	0.3	9
	1058	2.9	88		1144	2.3	70
	1714	-0.4	-12		1751	0.2	6
	2337	3.0	91				
3 F	0551	-0.1	-3	**18** Sa	0023	2.6	79
	1153	2.7	82		0647	0.4	12
	1806	-0.3	-9		1235	2.1	64
					1839	0.3	9
4 Sa	0038	3.1	94	**19** Su	0120	2.6	79
	0659	0.0	0		0750	0.5	15
	1254	2.5	76		1333	2.0	61
	1905	-0.3	-9		1934	0.3	9
5 Su	0144	3.2	98	**20** M	0219	2.6	79
	0811	0.0	0		0853	0.5	15
	1402	2.4	73		1435	2.0	61
	2009	-0.3	-9		2032	0.3	9
6 M	0251	3.3	101	**21** Tu	0316	2.7	82
	0922	-0.1	-3		0950	0.4	12
	1511	2.4	73		1533	2.0	61
	2114	-0.4	-12		2129	0.2	6
7 Tu	0355	3.5	107	**22** W	0408	2.9	88
	1026	-0.2	-6		1038	0.3	9
	1616	2.5	76		1625	2.2	67
	2217	-0.5	-15		2221	0.0	0
8 W	0454	3.6	110	**23** Th	0455	3.0	91
	1123	-0.4	-12		1121	0.1	3
	1715	2.7	82		1711	2.4	73
	2316	-0.6	-18		2308	-0.1	-3
9 Th	0548	3.7	113	**24** F	0538	3.2	98
	1214	-0.5	-15		1201	-0.1	-3
	1809	2.8	85		1754	2.6	79
					2354	-0.3	-9
10 F	0010	-0.7	-21	**25** Sa	0619	3.3	101
	0639	3.7	113		1239	-0.3	-9
	1302	-0.6	-18		1835	2.8	85
	1859	2.9	88				
11 Sa	0101	-0.7	-21	**26** Su	0038	-0.4	-12
	0726	3.7	113		0659	3.4	104
	1346	-0.6	-18		1316	-0.4	-12
	1946	3.0	91		1917	3.0	91
12 Su	0150	-0.6	-18	**27** M	0122	-0.5	-15
	0810	3.5	107		0740	3.5	107
	1428	-0.5	-15		1354	-0.5	-15
	2032	3.0	91		2000	3.2	98
13 M	0236	-0.5	-15	**28** Tu	0208	-0.6	-18
	0853	3.3	101		0822	3.4	104
	1509	-0.4	-12		1434	-0.6	-18
	2116	3.0	91		2044	3.3	101
14 Tu	0322	-0.3	-9				
	0935	3.1	94				
	1548	-0.3	-9				
	2200	2.9	88				
15 W	0409	-0.1	-3				
	1016	2.8	85				
	1627	-0.1	-3				
	2245	2.8	85				

March

Day	Time	ft	cm	Day	Time	ft	cm
1 W	0255	-0.6	-18	**16** Th	0341	0.0	0
	0905	3.3	101		0942	2.7	82
	1515	-0.6	-18		1543	0.0	0
	2131	3.4	104		2204	3.1	94
2 Th	0346	-0.5	-15	**17** F	0424	0.1	3
	0951	3.1	94		1020	2.5	76
	1600	-0.5	-15		1619	0.2	6
	2222	3.4	104		2245	3.0	91
3 F	0441	-0.3	-9	**18** Sa	0510	0.3	9
	1042	2.9	88		1102	2.3	70
	1649	-0.4	-12		1700	0.3	9
	2318	3.4	104		2331	2.8	85
4 Sa	0541	-0.1	-3	**19** Su	0601	0.5	15
	1138	2.7	82		1150	2.1	64
	1744	-0.3	-9		1746	0.4	12
5 Su	0019	3.3	101	**20** M	0023	2.8	85
	0648	0.0	0		0659	0.6	18
	1242	2.5	76		1246	2.1	64
	1847	-0.2	-6		1841	0.5	15
6 M	0127	3.3	101	**21** Tu	0122	2.7	82
	0800	0.0	0		0800	0.6	18
	1353	2.4	73		1348	2.1	64
	1956	-0.1	-3		1943	0.5	15
7 Tu	0237	3.3	101	**22** W	0223	2.8	85
	0910	0.0	0		0859	0.5	15
	1504	2.5	76		1450	2.2	67
	2106	-0.2	-6		2046	0.4	12
8 W	0342	3.4	104	**23** Th	0321	2.9	88
	1012	-0.1	-3		0951	0.4	12
	1610	2.6	79		1546	2.4	73
	2211	-0.2	-6		2145	0.2	6
9 Th	0442	3.4	104	**24** F	0413	3.0	91
	1107	-0.2	-6		1037	0.2	6
	1707	2.8	85		1636	2.7	82
	2310	-0.3	-9		2239	0.0	0
10 F	0535	3.5	107	**25** Sa	0500	3.2	98
	1155	-0.3	-9		1119	-0.1	-3
	1757	3.0	91		1722	3.0	91
					2328	-0.2	-6
11 Sa	0002	-0.4	-12	**26** Su	0546	3.4	104
	0622	3.5	107		1200	-0.3	-9
	1239	-0.4	-12		1807	3.3	101
	1844	3.1	94				
12 Su	0050	-0.4	-12	**27** M	0017	-0.4	-12
	0706	3.4	104		0630	3.4	104
	1319	-0.4	-12		1240	-0.4	-12
	1926	3.2	98		1851	3.5	107
13 M	0135	-0.4	-12	**28** Tu	0105	-0.6	-18
	0747	3.3	101		0714	3.5	107
	1357	-0.4	-12		1322	-0.6	-18
	2007	3.3	101		1937	3.8	116
14 Tu	0218	-0.3	-9	**29** W	0153	-0.6	-18
	0826	3.1	94		0759	3.4	104
	1433	-0.3	-9		1404	-0.6	-18
	2046	3.2	98		2024	3.9	119
15 W	0300	-0.2	-6	**30** Th	0244	-0.6	-18
	0904	2.8	85		0846	3.3	101
	1508	-0.1	-3		1449	-0.6	-18
	2124	3.2	98		2113	3.9	119
				31 F	0336	-0.5	-15
					0935	3.1	94
					1537	-0.5	-15
					2205	3.9	119

Time meridian 75° W. 0000 is midnight. 1200 is noon. Times are not adjusted for Daylight Saving Time.
Heights are referred to mean lower low water which is the chart datum of soundings.

Cape Hatteras, North Carolina, 2017

Times and Heights of High and Low Waters

April

Day	Time	ft	cm	Day	Time	ft	cm
1 Sa	0432	-0.3	-9	**16** Su	0439	0.3	9
	1029	2.9	88		1030	2.3	70
	1629	-0.3	-9		1619	0.4	12
	2302	3.7	113		2250	3.1	94
2 Su	0532	-0.2	-6	**17** M	0525	0.5	15
	1128	2.7	82		1115	2.2	67
	1728	-0.2	-6		1705	0.5	15
					2338	3.0	91
3 M ◐	0004	3.6	110	**18** Tu	0616	0.5	15
	0638	0.0	0		1208	2.2	67
	1235	2.6	79		1758	0.6	18
	1834	0.0	0				
4 Tu	0111	3.4	104	**19** W ◐	0032	2.9	88
	0747	0.1	3		0711	0.5	15
	1347	2.6	79		1307	2.2	67
	1947	0.1	3		1859	0.6	18
5 W	0221	3.3	101	**20** Th	0131	2.9	88
	0853	0.1	3		0807	0.5	15
	1458	2.7	82		1408	2.4	73
	2059	0.1	3		2005	0.5	15
6 Th	0326	3.3	101	**21** F	0230	2.9	88
	0953	0.0	0		0859	0.3	9
	1600	2.8	85		1506	2.6	79
	2205	0.0	0		2108	0.4	12
7 F	0424	3.2	98	**22** Sa	0327	3.0	91
	1044	-0.1	-3		0948	0.1	3
	1654	3.0	91		1600	3.0	91
	2302	0.0	0		2208	0.1	3
8 Sa	0515	3.2	98	**23** Su	0420	3.2	98
	1130	-0.1	-3		1034	-0.1	-3
	1742	3.2	98		1650	3.3	101
	2352	-0.1	-3		2303	-0.1	-3
9 Su	0601	3.2	98	**24** M	0510	3.3	101
	1210	-0.2	-6		1119	-0.3	-9
	1824	3.3	101		1738	3.7	113
					2356	-0.3	-9
10 M	0037	-0.1	-3	**25** Tu	0559	3.3	101
	0642	3.1	94		1204	-0.5	-15
	1248	-0.2	-6		1826	4.0	122
	1903	3.4	104				
11 Tu ○	0119	-0.2	-6	**26** W ●	0047	-0.5	-15
	0721	3.0	91		0648	3.4	104
	1322	-0.1	-3		1250	-0.6	-18
	1941	3.5	107		1915	4.2	128
12 W	0159	-0.1	-3	**27** Th	0139	-0.6	-18
	0758	2.9	88		0737	3.3	101
	1356	-0.1	-3		1337	-0.7	-21
	2016	3.5	107		2005	4.3	131
13 Th	0238	0.0	0	**28** F	0231	-0.6	-18
	0835	2.8	85		0828	3.2	98
	1429	0.0	0		1426	-0.6	-18
	2052	3.4	104		2056	4.3	131
14 F	0317	0.1	3	**29** Sa	0325	-0.5	-15
	0911	2.6	79		0921	3.1	94
	1503	0.2	6		1518	-0.5	-15
	2129	3.3	101		2150	4.2	128
15 Sa	0357	0.2	6	**30** Su	0422	-0.4	-12
	0949	2.5	76		1018	2.9	88
	1539	0.3	9		1614	-0.3	-9
	2208	3.2	98		2247	3.9	119

May

Day	Time	ft	cm	Day	Time	ft	cm
1 M	0521	-0.2	-6	**16** Tu	0456	0.4	12
	1119	2.8	85		1047	2.3	70
	1715	-0.1	-3		1633	0.5	15
	2348	3.7	113		2303	3.1	94
2 Tu ○	0624	-0.1	-3	**17** W	0541	0.4	12
	1227	2.7	82		1137	2.3	70
	1823	0.1	3		1725	0.6	18
					2353	3.0	91
3 W	0053	3.4	104	**18** Th ○	0629	0.4	12
	0728	0.0	0		1232	2.4	73
	1337	2.8	85		1824	0.6	18
	1936	0.3	9				
4 Th	0159	3.2	98	**19** F	0047	3.0	91
	0829	0.1	3		0720	0.3	9
	1443	2.9	88		1331	2.6	79
	2047	0.3	9		1929	0.5	15
5 F	0302	3.1	94	**20** Sa	0144	3.0	91
	0925	0.1	3		0811	0.2	6
	1543	3.0	91		1429	2.9	88
	2151	0.3	9		2035	0.4	12
6 Sa	0359	3.0	91	**21** Su	0243	3.0	91
	1014	0.0	0		0902	0.0	0
	1635	3.2	98		1525	3.2	98
	2247	0.2	6		2138	0.2	6
7 Su	0449	2.9	88	**22** M	0340	3.0	91
	1058	0.0	0		0952	-0.2	-6
	1720	3.3	101		1619	3.6	110
	2336	0.1	3		2238	-0.1	-3
8 M	0534	2.9	88	**23** Tu	0436	3.1	94
	1137	0.0	0		1042	-0.4	-12
	1801	3.4	104		1712	3.9	119
					2335	-0.3	-9
9 Tu	0021	0.1	3	**24** W	0530	3.2	98
	0615	2.8	85		1132	-0.6	-18
	1213	0.0	0		1804	4.2	128
	1839	3.5	107				
10 W ○	0101	0.1	3	**25** Th ●	0030	-0.5	-15
	0654	2.8	85		0623	3.2	98
	1248	0.0	0		1223	-0.7	-21
	1914	3.6	110		1855	4.4	134
11 Th	0140	0.1	3	**26** F	0124	-0.6	-18
	0731	2.7	82		0717	3.2	98
	1322	0.1	3		1314	-0.7	-21
	1950	3.6	110		1947	4.5	137
12 F	0218	0.1	3	**27** Sa	0218	-0.6	-18
	0808	2.6	79		0811	3.1	94
	1356	0.1	3		1407	-0.7	-21
	2025	3.5	107		2040	4.4	134
13 Sa	0256	0.1	3	**28** Su	0312	-0.5	-15
	0844	2.5	76		0906	3.1	94
	1431	0.2	6		1502	-0.5	-15
	2101	3.4	104		2134	4.2	128
14 Su	0334	0.2	6	**29** M	0408	-0.4	-12
	0923	2.4	73		1005	3.0	91
	1508	0.3	9		1559	-0.3	-9
	2139	3.3	101		2230	4.0	122
15 M	0414	0.3	9	**30** Tu	0504	-0.3	-9
	1003	2.4	73		1106	2.9	88
	1548	0.4	12		1701	-0.1	-3
	2219	3.2	98		2328	3.7	113
				31 W	0602	-0.2	-6
					1211	2.9	88
					1807	0.2	6

June

Day	Time	ft	cm	Day	Time	ft	cm
1 Th ◐	0029	3.4	104	**16** F	0552	0.2	6
	0701	-0.1	-3		1201	2.6	79
	1316	2.9	88		1756	0.5	15
	1917	0.3	9				
2 F	0130	3.1	94	**17** Sa ◐	0011	3.0	91
	0757	0.0	0		0640	0.1	3
	1420	2.9	88		1258	2.8	85
	2026	0.4	12		1900	0.4	12
3 Sa	0230	2.9	88	**18** Su	0107	2.9	88
	0850	0.1	3		0730	0.0	0
	1517	3.1	94		1357	3.1	94
	2130	0.4	12		2007	0.3	9
4 Su	0326	2.7	82	**19** M	0206	2.9	88
	0938	0.1	3		0823	-0.2	-6
	1608	3.2	98		1456	3.4	104
	2226	0.4	12		2114	0.2	6
5 M	0417	2.6	79	**20** Tu	0307	2.9	88
	1021	0.1	3		0917	-0.3	-9
	1654	3.3	101		1554	3.7	113
	2315	0.3	9		2217	0.0	0
6 Tu	0503	2.6	79	**21** W	0407	2.9	88
	1101	0.1	3		1012	-0.5	-15
	1735	3.4	104		1650	4.0	122
					2317	-0.2	-6
7 W	0000	0.3	9	**22** Th	0506	3.0	91
	0545	2.5	76		1107	-0.6	-18
	1139	0.1	3		1745	4.3	131
	1813	3.5	107				
8 Th	0041	0.2	6	**23** F ●	0014	-0.4	-12
	0625	2.5	76		0603	3.0	91
	1216	0.1	3		1202	-0.7	-21
	1849	3.5	107		1838	4.4	134
9 F ○	0120	0.1	3	**24** Sa	0109	-0.5	-15
	0704	2.5	76		0659	3.1	94
	1252	0.1	3		1256	-0.7	-21
	1925	3.6	110		1932	4.4	134
10 Sa	0157	0.1	3	**25** Su	0202	-0.6	-18
	0742	2.5	76		0754	3.1	94
	1328	0.1	3		1351	-0.7	-21
	2001	3.5	107		2024	4.3	131
11 Su	0234	0.1	3	**26** M	0255	-0.5	-15
	0820	2.5	76		0850	3.1	94
	1405	0.2	6		1447	-0.5	-15
	2037	3.5	107		2117	4.1	125
12 M	0312	0.2	6	**27** Tu	0348	-0.5	-15
	0858	2.4	73		0947	3.1	94
	1443	0.2	6		1544	-0.3	-9
	2114	3.4	104		2210	3.9	119
13 Tu	0349	0.2	6	**28** W	0440	-0.3	-9
	0939	2.4	73		1045	3.0	91
	1524	0.3	9		1643	-0.1	-3
	2153	3.3	101		2304	3.5	107
14 W	0428	0.2	6	**29** Th	0533	-0.2	-6
	1022	2.4	73		1145	3.0	91
	1609	0.4	12		1745	0.2	6
	2235	3.2	98		2359	3.2	98
15 Th	0509	0.2	6	**30** F ◐	0626	-0.1	-3
	1109	2.5	76		1246	2.9	88
	1659	0.4	12		1850	0.4	12
	2320	3.1	94				

Time meridian 75° W. 0000 is midnight. 1200 is noon. Times are not adjusted for Daylight Saving Time.
Heights are referred to mean lower low water which is the chart datum of soundings.

Cape Hatteras, North Carolina, 2017

Times and Heights of High and Low Waters

July

Day	Time	ft	cm	Day	Time	ft	cm
1 Sa	0055	2.9	88	16 Su ☽	0605	0.0	0
	0718	0.0	0		1230	3.1	94
	1346	3.0	91		1838	0.4	12
	1956	0.5	15				
2 Su	0151	2.7	82	17 M	0038	2.9	88
	0808	0.1	3		0657	-0.1	-3
	1443	3.0	91		1330	3.3	101
	2100	0.6	18		1946	0.3	9
3 M	0247	2.5	76	18 Tu	0139	2.8	85
	0857	0.2	6		0753	-0.2	-6
	1535	3.1	94		1432	3.5	107
	2157	0.5	15		2055	0.2	6
4 Tu	0340	2.4	73	19 W	0242	2.8	85
	0942	0.2	6		0851	-0.3	-9
	1622	3.2	98		1533	3.8	116
	2249	0.5	15		2201	0.1	3
5 W	0429	2.4	73	20 Th	0346	2.8	85
	1026	0.2	6		0951	-0.4	-12
	1706	3.3	101		1633	4.0	122
	2334	0.4	12		2302	-0.1	-3
6 Th	0514	2.4	73	21 F	0448	2.9	88
	1107	0.1	3		1050	-0.5	-15
	1746	3.4	104		1729	4.2	128
					2359	-0.2	-6
7 F	0016	0.3	9	22 Sa	0547	3.0	91
	0556	2.4	73		1147	-0.6	-18
	1147	0.1	3		1824	4.3	131
	1824	3.5	107				
8 Sa ○	0055	0.2	6	23 Su ●	0052	-0.4	-12
	0637	2.5	76		0643	3.1	94
	1226	0.1	3		1243	-0.6	-18
	1901	3.5	107		1916	4.3	131
9 Su	0132	0.2	6	24 M	0143	-0.4	-12
	0716	2.5	76		0738	3.2	98
	1305	0.1	3		1337	-0.6	-18
	1938	3.6	110		2007	4.2	128
10 M	0209	0.1	3	25 Tu	0233	-0.4	-12
	0755	2.6	79		0831	3.2	98
	1343	0.1	3		1431	-0.4	-12
	2014	3.6	110		2056	4.0	122
11 Tu	0245	0.1	3	26 W	0321	-0.4	-12
	0834	2.6	79		0924	3.2	98
	1423	0.1	3		1525	-0.2	-6
	2051	3.5	107		2145	3.7	113
12 W	0320	0.1	3	27 Th	0409	-0.2	-6
	0914	2.6	79		1017	3.2	98
	1504	0.2	6		1619	0.0	0
	2129	3.4	104		2234	3.4	104
13 Th	0357	0.1	3	28 F	0456	-0.1	-3
	0956	2.7	82		1111	3.1	94
	1549	0.2	6		1716	0.3	9
	2209	3.3	101		2324	3.1	94
14 F	0436	0.1	3	29 Sa	0543	0.1	3
	1043	2.8	85		1207	3.1	94
	1639	0.3	9		1816	0.5	15
	2254	3.2	98				
15 Sa	0518	0.0	0	30 Su ◖	0015	2.8	85
	1134	2.9	88		0632	0.2	6
	1736	0.4	12		1304	3.0	91
	2343	3.0	91		1919	0.7	21
				31 M	0109	2.6	79
					0721	0.3	9
					1401	3.0	91
					2022	0.7	21

August

Day	Time	ft	cm	Day	Time	ft	cm
1 Tu	0205	2.4	73	16 W	0122	2.8	85
	0812	0.4	12		0731	0.0	0
	1456	3.1	94		1414	3.7	113
	2122	0.7	21		2042	0.4	12
2 W	0301	2.4	73	17 Th	0229	2.8	85
	0902	0.4	12		0835	-0.1	-3
	1547	3.2	98		1519	3.8	116
	2216	0.7	21		2148	0.3	9
3 Th	0354	2.4	73	18 F	0336	2.9	88
	0951	0.4	12		0939	-0.2	-6
	1633	3.3	101		1620	4.0	122
	2303	0.6	18		2248	0.1	3
4 F	0442	2.4	73	19 Sa	0438	3.0	91
	1037	0.3	9		1041	-0.3	-9
	1716	3.4	104		1717	4.1	125
	2345	0.5	15		2343	-0.1	-3
5 Sa	0527	2.5	76	20 Su	0536	3.2	98
	1120	0.2	6		1138	-0.4	-12
	1756	3.5	107		1809	4.2	128
6 Su	0024	0.3	9	21 M ●	0033	-0.2	-6
	0608	2.6	79		0629	3.4	104
	1202	0.1	3		1232	-0.4	-12
	1834	3.6	110		1859	4.2	128
7 M ○	0100	0.2	6	22 Tu	0120	-0.2	-6
	0648	2.8	85		0720	3.5	107
	1242	0.1	3		1324	-0.3	-9
	1912	3.7	113		1947	4.0	122
8 Tu	0136	0.1	3	23 W	0205	-0.2	-6
	0727	2.9	88		0809	3.5	107
	1323	0.0	0		1414	-0.2	-6
	1948	3.7	113		2032	3.9	119
9 W	0211	0.1	3	24 Th	0249	-0.1	-3
	0807	3.0	91		0857	3.5	107
	1404	0.0	0		1504	0.0	0
	2026	3.6	110		2117	3.6	110
10 Th	0247	0.0	0	25 F	0331	0.0	0
	0847	3.1	94		0944	3.5	107
	1447	0.1	3		1553	0.2	6
	2105	3.5	107		2201	3.3	101
11 F	0324	0.0	0	26 Sa	0413	0.0	0
	0930	3.2	98		1032	3.4	104
	1533	0.1	3		1644	0.4	12
	2146	3.4	104		2246	3.0	91
12 Sa	0404	0.0	0	27 Su	0456	0.3	9
	1017	3.3	101		1121	3.2	98
	1624	0.2	6		1738	0.6	18
	2231	3.3	101		2333	2.8	85
13 Su	0447	0.0	0	28 M	0541	0.5	15
	1109	3.4	104		1214	3.2	98
	1720	0.3	9		1837	0.8	24
	2321	3.1	94				
14 M ○	0536	0.0	0	29 Tu ◖	0025	2.6	79
	1206	3.4	104		0631	0.6	18
	1823	0.4	12		1311	3.1	94
					1939	0.9	27
15 Tu	0018	2.9	88	30 W	0122	2.5	76
	0631	0.0	0		0725	0.7	21
	1308	3.6	110		1409	3.1	94
	1932	0.4	12		2041	0.9	27
				31 Th	0222	2.4	73
					0821	0.7	21
					1505	3.2	98
					2136	0.9	27

September

Day	Time	ft	cm	Day	Time	ft	cm
1 F	0319	2.5	76	16 Sa	0331	3.1	94
	0916	0.6	18		0935	0.1	3
	1556	3.3	101		1608	3.9	119
	2224	0.7	21		2233	0.2	6
2 Sa	0409	2.6	79	17 Su	0431	3.3	101
	1007	0.5	15		1036	0.0	0
	1642	3.4	104		1703	4.0	122
	2307	0.6	18		2324	0.1	3
3 Su	0455	2.8	85	18 M	0525	3.5	107
	1053	0.4	12		1131	-0.1	-3
	1723	3.6	110		1753	4.0	122
	2345	0.5	15				
4 M	0537	3.0	91	19 Tu	0010	0.0	0
	1137	0.2	6		0615	3.6	110
	1803	3.7	113		1223	-0.1	-3
					1840	3.9	119
5 Tu	0022	0.3	9	20 W ●	0053	0.0	0
	0618	3.2	98		0701	3.8	116
	1219	0.1	3		1311	-0.1	-3
	1841	3.8	116		1924	3.8	116
6 W ○	0058	0.2	6	21 Th	0134	0.0	0
	0658	3.4	104		0745	3.8	116
	1302	0.0	0		1357	0.0	0
	1920	3.8	116		2006	3.6	110
7 Th	0134	0.1	3	22 F	0213	0.1	3
	0739	3.5	107		0827	3.8	116
	1346	0.0	0		1442	0.2	6
	1959	3.7	113		2046	3.4	104
8 F	0212	0.0	0	23 Sa	0251	0.2	6
	0821	3.7	113		0909	3.7	113
	1431	0.0	0		1526	0.4	12
	2040	3.6	110		2127	3.2	98
9 Sa	0251	0.0	0	24 Su	0329	0.4	12
	0906	3.8	116		0951	3.6	110
	1519	0.1	3		1612	0.5	15
	2124	3.5	107		2209	3.0	91
10 Su	0334	0.0	0	25 M	0409	0.6	18
	0955	3.8	116		1036	3.4	104
	1611	0.2	6		1701	0.7	21
	2212	3.3	101		2253	2.8	85
11 M	0420	0.1	3	26 Tu	0451	0.7	21
	1048	3.8	116		1124	3.3	101
	1709	0.3	9		1754	0.9	27
	2306	3.1	94		2343	2.6	79
12 Tu	0513	0.1	3	27 W ◖	0540	0.9	27
	1147	3.8	116		1218	3.2	98
	1813	0.5	15		1853	1.0	30
13 W ○	0006	3.0	91	28 Th	0040	2.5	76
	0613	0.2	6		0636	0.9	27
	1252	3.8	116		1317	3.1	94
	1922	0.5	15		1953	1.0	30
14 Th	0114	2.9	88	29 F	0141	2.5	76
	0719	0.2	6		0737	0.9	27
	1400	3.8	116		1416	3.2	98
	2032	0.5	15		2050	1.0	30
15 F	0224	2.9	88	30 Sa	0240	2.6	79
	0828	0.2	6		0837	0.8	24
	1507	3.8	116		1511	3.3	101
	2136	0.4	12		2139	0.8	24

Time meridian 75° W. 0000 is midnight. 1200 is noon. Times are not adjusted for Daylight Saving Time.
Heights are referred to mean lower low water which is the chart datum of soundings.

Cape Hatteras, North Carolina, 2017

Times and Heights of High and Low Waters

October

Day	h m	ft	cm
1 Su	0333	2.8	85
	0933	0.7	21
	1600	3.4	104
	2222	0.7	21
2 M	0420	3.0	91
	1023	0.5	15
	1644	3.5	107
	2301	0.5	15
3 Tu	0504	3.3	101
	1110	0.3	9
	1726	3.6	110
	2340	0.3	9
4 W	0546	3.6	110
	1156	0.1	3
	1808	3.7	113
5 Th ○	0018	0.1	3
	0629	3.8	116
	1241	0.0	0
	1850	3.8	116
6 F	0057	0.0	0
	0712	4.0	122
	1328	-0.1	-3
	1933	3.7	113
7 Sa	0138	-0.1	-3
	0757	4.2	128
	1416	-0.1	-3
	2018	3.6	110
8 Su	0221	-0.1	-3
	0844	4.2	128
	1506	0.0	0
	2105	3.5	107
9 M	0308	-0.1	-3
	0935	4.2	128
	1600	0.1	3
	2157	3.3	101
10 Tu	0359	0.1	3
	1030	4.1	125
	1659	0.3	9
	2254	3.1	94
11 W	0456	0.2	6
	1131	4.0	122
	1804	0.4	12
	2359	3.0	91
12 Th ◑	0600	0.3	9
	1237	3.8	116
	1912	0.5	15
13 F	0110	3.0	91
	0711	0.4	12
	1346	3.8	116
	2019	0.4	12
14 Sa	0221	3.1	94
	0824	0.4	12
	1453	3.7	113
	2120	0.4	12
15 Su	0325	3.2	98
	0931	0.3	9
	1553	3.7	113
	2213	0.3	9
16 M	0422	3.4	104
	1031	0.2	6
	1646	3.7	113
	2301	0.2	6
17 Tu	0513	3.6	110
	1124	0.2	6
	1734	3.6	110
	2344	0.1	3
18 W	0558	3.8	116
	1212	0.1	3
	1818	3.6	110
19 Th ●	0024	0.1	3
	0640	3.9	119
	1257	0.1	3
	1859	3.5	107
20 F	0101	0.1	3
	0720	3.9	119
	1339	0.2	6
	1939	3.3	101
21 Sa	0138	0.2	6
	0758	3.9	119
	1420	0.3	9
	2017	3.2	98
22 Su	0213	0.3	9
	0836	3.8	116
	1501	0.4	12
	2055	3.0	91
23 M	0249	0.5	15
	0915	3.7	113
	1543	0.5	15
	2135	2.8	85
24 Tu	0327	0.6	18
	0956	3.5	107
	1627	0.7	21
	2217	2.7	82
25 W	0408	0.7	21
	1040	3.4	104
	1715	0.8	24
	2305	2.6	79
26 Th	0455	0.9	27
	1130	3.2	98
	1807	0.9	27
	2359	2.5	76
27 F ◐	0550	0.9	27
	1224	3.1	94
	1903	0.9	27
28 Sa	0058	2.5	76
	0651	1.0	30
	1322	3.1	94
	1957	0.8	24
29 Su	0158	2.7	82
	0754	0.9	27
	1419	3.1	94
	2047	0.7	21
30 M	0253	2.9	88
	0855	0.7	21
	1512	3.2	98
	2132	0.5	15
31 Tu	0343	3.2	98
	0950	0.5	15
	1601	3.3	101
	2215	0.3	9

November

Day	h m	ft	cm
1 W	0430	3.5	107
	1042	0.3	9
	1649	3.4	104
	2257	0.1	3
2 Th	0516	3.8	116
	1132	0.1	3
	1735	3.5	107
	2340	-0.1	-3
3 F	0601	4.1	125
	1221	-0.1	-3
	1821	3.6	110
4 Sa ○	0024	-0.3	-9
	0648	4.3	131
	1311	-0.2	-6
	1908	3.5	107
5 Su	0109	-0.3	-9
	0736	4.5	137
	1401	-0.3	-9
	1957	3.5	107
6 M	0157	-0.3	-9
	0826	4.5	137
	1454	-0.2	-6
	2049	3.4	104
7 Tu	0247	-0.3	-9
	0919	4.4	134
	1549	-0.1	-3
	2144	3.2	98
8 W	0342	-0.1	-3
	1015	4.2	128
	1647	0.0	0
	2244	3.1	94
9 Th	0442	0.1	3
	1116	4.0	122
	1750	0.2	6
	2350	3.0	91
10 F ◑	0549	0.3	9
	1220	3.7	113
	1854	0.2	6
11 Sa	0100	3.0	91
	0702	0.4	12
	1327	3.5	107
	1957	0.3	9
12 Su	0209	3.1	94
	0815	0.4	12
	1432	3.4	104
	2056	0.2	6
13 M	0312	3.3	101
	0922	0.4	12
	1532	3.3	101
	2148	0.2	6
14 Tu	0407	3.4	104
	1021	0.3	9
	1625	3.2	98
	2234	0.1	3
15 W	0456	3.6	110
	1113	0.2	6
	1712	3.2	98
	2316	0.1	3
16 Th	0539	3.7	113
	1159	0.2	6
	1755	3.1	94
	2355	0.1	3
17 F	0619	3.8	116
	1241	0.2	6
	1835	3.0	91
18 Sa ●	0031	0.1	3
	0657	3.8	116
	1322	0.2	6
	1913	2.9	88
19 Su	0106	0.2	6
	0733	3.8	116
	1400	0.2	6
	1951	2.8	85
20 M	0141	0.2	6
	0810	3.7	113
	1439	0.3	9
	2028	2.7	82
21 Tu	0217	0.3	9
	0846	3.6	110
	1518	0.4	12
	2107	2.6	79
22 W	0255	0.4	12
	0925	3.4	104
	1558	0.5	15
	2147	2.5	76
23 Th	0335	0.5	15
	1006	3.3	101
	1640	0.5	15
	2231	2.5	76
24 F	0420	0.6	18
	1050	3.2	98
	1725	0.6	18
	2321	2.4	73
25 Sa	0510	0.7	21
	1138	3.1	94
	1813	0.6	18
26 Su ◐	0015	2.5	76
	0608	0.7	21
	1231	3.0	91
	1903	0.5	15
27 M	0113	2.6	79
	0711	0.7	21
	1327	2.9	88
	1953	0.4	12
28 Tu	0210	2.8	85
	0816	0.6	18
	1423	3.0	91
	2042	0.2	6
29 W	0304	3.1	94
	0917	0.4	12
	1519	3.0	91
	2130	0.0	0
30 Th	0357	3.5	107
	1015	0.1	3
	1612	3.1	94
	2219	-0.2	-6

December

Day	h m	ft	cm
1 F	0447	3.8	116
	1110	-0.1	-3
	1704	3.2	98
	2307	-0.4	-12
2 Sa	0537	4.2	128
	1203	-0.3	-9
	1756	3.2	98
	2356	-0.6	-18
3 Su ○	0628	4.4	134
	1255	-0.5	-15
	1847	3.2	98
4 M	0046	-0.7	-21
	0719	4.5	137
	1347	-0.5	-15
	1940	3.2	98
5 Tu	0138	-0.7	-21
	0810	4.4	134
	1440	-0.5	-15
	2034	3.2	98
6 W	0232	-0.6	-18
	0904	4.3	131
	1534	-0.4	-12
	2130	3.1	94
7 Th	0328	-0.4	-12
	0959	4.1	125
	1630	-0.3	-9
	2230	3.0	91
8 F	0429	-0.2	-6
	1057	3.8	116
	1728	-0.2	-6
	2334	3.0	91
9 Sa	0535	0.0	0
	1158	3.5	107
	1828	-0.1	-3
10 Su ◑	0041	3.0	91
	0645	0.2	6
	1301	3.2	98
	1927	0.0	0
11 M	0148	3.0	91
	0757	0.3	9
	1404	3.0	91
	2024	0.0	0
12 Tu	0250	3.1	94
	0904	0.3	9
	1504	2.8	85
	2116	0.0	0
13 W	0345	3.2	98
	1004	0.3	9
	1559	2.7	82
	2204	0.0	0
14 Th	0434	3.3	101
	1056	0.2	6
	1647	2.6	79
	2247	0.0	0
15 F	0518	3.4	104
	1143	0.2	6
	1732	2.6	79
	2327	0.0	0
16 Sa	0558	3.5	107
	1224	0.1	3
	1812	2.6	79
17 Su	0004	0.0	0
	0635	3.5	107
	1303	0.1	3
	1851	2.6	79
18 M ●	0041	0.0	0
	0712	3.5	107
	1341	0.0	0
	1928	2.5	76
19 Tu	0117	0.0	0
	0747	3.5	107
	1417	0.1	3
	2005	2.5	76
20 W	0154	0.1	3
	0823	3.4	104
	1454	0.1	3
	2042	2.5	76
21 Th	0231	0.1	3
	0900	3.3	101
	1530	0.1	3
	2121	2.4	73
22 F	0310	0.2	6
	0937	3.2	98
	1607	0.2	6
	2202	2.4	73
23 Sa	0352	0.3	9
	1017	3.1	94
	1646	0.2	6
	2246	2.4	73
24 Su	0439	0.4	12
	1100	2.9	88
	1728	0.2	6
	2336	2.5	76
25 M	0533	0.4	12
	1148	2.8	85
	1814	0.2	6
26 Tu ◐	0030	2.6	79
	0634	0.4	12
	1242	2.7	82
	1903	0.1	3
27 W	0128	2.8	85
	0740	0.3	9
	1340	2.7	82
	1956	-0.1	-3
28 Th	0228	3.1	94
	0846	0.2	6
	1440	2.6	79
	2051	-0.2	-6
29 F	0326	3.4	104
	0950	0.0	0
	1541	2.7	82
	2146	-0.4	-12
30 Sa	0422	3.7	113
	1050	-0.2	-6
	1639	2.8	85
	2241	-0.6	-18
31 Su	0517	4.0	122
	1146	-0.5	-15
	1735	2.9	88
	2336	-0.8	-24

Time meridian 75° W. 0000 is midnight. 1200 is noon. Times are not adjusted for Daylight Saving Time.
Heights are referred to mean lower low water which is the chart datum of soundings.

Wilmington, North Carolina, 2017
Times and Heights of High and Low Waters

January

Day	Time (h m)	Height (ft)	Height (cm)	Day	Time (h m)	Height (ft)	Height (cm)
1 Su	0535	0.0	0	16 M	0015	4.3	131
	1055	4.5	137		0644	-0.2	-6
	1819	0.1	3		1238	4.6	140
	2305	4.0	122		1920	-0.1	-3
2 M	0616	0.0	0	17 Tu	0107	4.3	131
	1132	4.5	137		0732	0.0	0
	1900	0.1	3		1327	4.4	134
	2350	4.1	125		2005	0.0	0
3 Tu	0703	0.1	3	18 W	0158	4.2	128
	1222	4.5	137		0822	0.2	6
	1944	0.1	3		1415	4.2	128
					2051	0.1	3
4 W	0045	4.1	125	19 Th	0249	4.1	125
	0759	0.2	6		0915	0.3	9
	1321	4.4	134		1504	4.1	125
	2036	0.1	3		2139	0.2	6
5 Th ☾	0151	4.2	128	20 F	0339	4.1	125
	0907	0.3	9		1010	0.4	12
	1428	4.3	131		1554	3.9	119
	2135	0.0	0		2228	0.2	6
6 F	0304	4.3	131	21 Sa	0430	4.1	125
	1019	0.3	9		1104	0.4	12
	1538	4.2	128		1645	3.9	119
	2238	-0.1	-3		2318	0.2	6
7 Sa	0416	4.4	134	22 Su	0522	4.2	128
	1127	0.2	6		1158	0.3	9
	1646	4.2	128		1737	3.9	119
	2340	-0.2	-6				
8 Su	0525	4.6	140	23 M	0007	0.1	3
	1230	0.1	3		0614	4.2	128
	1751	4.3	131		1249	0.3	9
					1828	3.9	119
9 M	0040	-0.3	-9	24 Tu	0056	0.1	3
	0630	4.8	146		0704	4.4	134
	1330	-0.1	-3		1338	0.2	6
	1853	4.3	131		1917	4.0	122
10 Tu	0138	-0.4	-12	25 W	0143	0.0	0
	0730	5.0	152		0750	4.5	137
	1427	-0.2	-6		1425	0.2	6
	1951	4.4	134		2002	4.0	122
11 W	0234	-0.5	-15	26 Th	0229	0.0	0
	0826	5.1	155		0834	4.6	140
	1521	-0.3	-9		1511	0.1	3
	2045	4.5	137		2043	4.1	125
12 Th ○	0328	-0.6	-18	27 F ●	0314	-0.1	-3
	0919	5.1	155		0913	4.6	140
	1612	-0.4	-12		1554	0.1	3
	2138	4.5	137		2120	4.2	128
13 F	0419	-0.6	-18	28 Sa	0358	-0.1	-3
	1010	5.1	155		0947	4.7	143
	1702	-0.4	-12		1636	0.1	3
	2230	4.5	137		2152	4.2	128
14 Sa	0509	-0.5	-15	29 Su	0441	-0.1	-3
	1100	4.9	149		1018	4.7	143
	1749	-0.3	-9		1717	0.0	0
	2322	4.4	134		2220	4.3	131
15 Su	0557	-0.3	-9	30 M	0525	-0.1	-3
	1149	4.8	146		1048	4.7	143
	1834	-0.2	-6		1757	0.0	0
					2254	4.4	134
				31 Tu	0610	-0.1	-3
					1126	4.7	143
					1838	0.0	0
					2339	4.5	137

February

Day	Time (h m)	Height (ft)	Height (cm)	Day	Time (h m)	Height (ft)	Height (cm)
1 W	0659	0.0	0	16 Th	0119	4.4	134
	1215	4.6	140		0747	0.3	9
	1923	0.0	0		1337	4.2	128
					2002	0.4	12
2 Th	0034	4.5	137	17 F	0207	4.3	131
	0754	0.2	6		0834	0.5	15
	1314	4.5	137		1425	4.1	125
	2013	0.0	0		2044	0.5	15
3 F ☽	0139	4.5	137	18 Sa ☾	0256	4.2	128
	0857	0.3	9		0926	0.6	18
	1420	4.3	131		1514	3.9	119
	2112	0.1	3		2131	0.5	15
4 Sa	0251	4.5	137	19 Su	0346	4.2	128
	1005	0.3	9		1021	0.6	18
	1527	4.3	131		1605	3.9	119
	2216	0.1	3		2225	0.5	15
5 Su	0402	4.6	140	20 M	0439	4.2	128
	1111	0.3	9		1117	0.6	18
	1633	4.2	128		1658	3.9	119
	2321	0.0	0		2321	0.5	15
6 M	0510	4.6	140	21 Tu	0532	4.2	128
	1213	0.2	6		1210	0.5	15
	1737	4.3	131		1751	3.9	119
7 Tu	0022	-0.1	-3	22 W	0016	0.4	12
	0615	4.8	146		0625	4.3	131
	1312	0.0	0		1302	0.5	15
	1839	4.4	134		1842	4.1	125
8 W	0121	-0.3	-9	23 Th	0109	0.3	9
	0716	4.9	149		0715	4.5	137
	1407	-0.1	-3		1351	0.4	12
	1936	4.5	137		1930	4.2	128
9 Th	0217	-0.4	-12	24 F	0200	0.2	6
	0811	5.0	152		0801	4.6	140
	1500	-0.2	-6		1439	0.3	9
	2030	4.6	140		2014	4.4	134
10 F ○	0310	-0.4	-12	25 Sa	0250	0.1	3
	0902	5.0	152		0843	4.7	143
	1550	-0.3	-9		1524	0.2	6
	2121	4.7	143		2054	4.5	137
11 Sa	0401	-0.4	-12	26 Su ●	0338	0.0	0
	0949	5.0	152		0921	4.8	146
	1637	-0.2	-6		1608	0.1	3
	2210	4.7	143		2130	4.7	143
12 Su	0449	-0.3	-9	27 M	0426	-0.1	-3
	1035	4.9	149		0959	4.9	149
	1721	-0.2	-6		1651	0.0	0
	2258	4.7	143		2206	4.8	146
13 M	0534	-0.2	-6	28 Tu	0513	-0.1	-3
	1120	4.8	146		1037	4.9	149
	1803	0.0	0		1734	0.0	0
	2345	4.6	140		2246	4.9	149
14 Tu	0619	0.0	0				
	1205	4.6	140				
	1844	0.1	3				
15 W	0032	4.5	137				
	0702	0.1	3				
	1250	4.4	134				
	1923	0.2	6				

March

Day	Time (h m)	Height (ft)	Height (cm)	Day	Time (h m)	Height (ft)	Height (cm)
1 W	0601	-0.1	-3	16 Th	0634	0.3	9
	1121	4.8	146		1215	4.4	134
	1817	0.0	0		1840	0.4	12
	2333	4.9	149				
2 Th	0652	0.0	0	17 F	0039	4.6	140
	1212	4.7	143		0714	0.4	12
	1904	0.1	3		1259	4.2	128
					1912	0.6	18
3 F ☽	0029	4.9	149	18 Sa	0122	4.5	137
	0747	0.2	6		0756	0.6	18
	1312	4.5	137		1344	4.1	125
	1955	0.1	3		1944	0.6	18
4 Sa	0135	4.8	146	19 Su	0207	4.4	134
	0847	0.3	9		0842	0.7	21
	1415	4.4	134		1432	4.0	122
	2054	0.2	6		2025	0.7	21
5 Su ☾	0244	4.8	146	20 M ☾	0255	4.3	131
	0950	0.4	12		0935	0.7	21
	1519	4.4	134		1522	3.9	119
	2159	0.2	6		2121	0.7	21
6 M	0351	4.7	143	21 Tu	0347	4.2	128
	1054	0.3	9		1032	0.8	24
	1622	4.4	134		1615	3.9	119
	2304	0.2	6		2229	0.7	21
7 Tu	0456	4.7	143	22 W	0442	4.2	128
	1154	0.3	9		1128	0.7	21
	1725	4.4	134		1709	4.0	122
					2334	0.7	21
8 W	0006	0.1	3	23 Th	0538	4.3	131
	0559	4.8	146		1222	0.6	18
	1251	0.1	3		1802	4.2	128
	1825	4.6	140				
9 Th	0104	0.0	0	24 F	0034	0.5	15
	0658	4.9	149		0631	4.5	137
	1345	0.0	0		1314	0.5	15
	1921	4.7	143		1853	4.4	134
10 F	0159	-0.1	-3	25 Sa	0131	0.4	12
	0751	4.9	149		0721	4.6	140
	1436	-0.1	-3		1404	0.3	9
	2013	4.9	149		1941	4.6	140
11 Sa	0252	-0.2	-6	26 Su	0225	0.2	6
	0840	5.0	152		0808	4.8	146
	1524	-0.1	-3		1452	0.2	6
	2102	5.0	152		2025	4.9	149
12 Su ○	0341	-0.2	-6	27 M ●	0318	0.1	3
	0925	4.9	149		0852	4.9	149
	1609	-0.1	-3		1539	0.1	3
	2148	5.0	152		2108	5.1	155
13 M	0427	-0.1	-3	28 Tu	0409	-0.1	-3
	1008	4.9	149		0936	4.9	149
	1651	0.0	0		1625	0.0	0
	2231	5.0	152		2150	5.3	162
14 Tu	0511	0.0	0	29 W	0459	-0.1	-3
	1050	4.7	143		1021	4.9	149
	1730	0.2	6		1710	0.0	0
	2314	4.9	149		2236	5.3	162
15 W	0553	0.1	3	30 Th	0549	-0.1	-3
	1132	4.5	137		1110	4.8	146
	1807	0.3	9		1757	0.0	0
	2357	4.8	146		2327	5.3	162
				31 F	0641	0.0	0
					1206	4.7	143
					1846	0.1	3

Time meridian 75° W. 0000 is midnight. 1200 is noon. Times are not adjusted for Daylight Saving Time.
Heights are referred to mean lower low water which is the chart datum of soundings.

Wilmington, North Carolina, 2017

Times and Heights of High and Low Waters

April

Day	Time (h m)	Height (ft)	Height (cm)	Day	Time (h m)	Height (ft)	Height (cm)
1 Sa	0026	5.2	158	16 Su	0033	4.6	140
	0735	0.1	3		0723	0.5	15
	1306	4.6	140		1302	4.0	122
	1939	0.2	6		1858	0.6	18
2 Su	0130	5.1	155	17 M	0103	4.4	134
	0833	0.2	6		0803	0.6	18
	1409	4.5	137		1345	3.9	119
	2039	0.3	9		1937	0.7	21
3 M	0235	4.9	149	18 Tu	0139	4.4	134
	0934	0.3	9		0850	0.7	21
	1510	4.4	134		1432	3.9	119
	2142	0.3	9		2028	0.7	21
4 Tu	0338	4.8	146	19 W	0231	4.3	131
	1034	0.3	9		0945	0.7	21
	1611	4.5	137		1525	3.9	119
	2246	0.3	9		2137	0.7	21
5 W	0439	4.8	146	20 Th	0334	4.3	131
	1132	0.2	6		1043	0.6	18
	1710	4.6	140		1621	4.1	125
	2347	0.2	6		2253	0.7	21
6 Th	0539	4.7	143	21 F	0439	4.3	131
	1228	0.1	3		1140	0.5	15
	1808	4.7	143		1718	4.3	131
7 F	0045	0.1	3	22 Sa	0001	0.6	18
	0634	4.7	143		0541	4.4	134
	1319	0.0	0		1235	0.4	12
	1902	4.9	149		1814	4.5	137
8 Sa	0139	0.1	3	23 Su	0103	0.4	12
	0726	4.8	146		0638	4.6	140
	1409	-0.1	-3		1327	0.2	6
	1953	5.0	152		1907	4.8	146
9 Su	0230	0.0	0	24 M	0201	0.2	6
	0813	4.8	146		0731	4.7	143
	1455	-0.1	-3		1418	0.1	3
	2040	5.1	155		1957	5.1	155
10 M	0318	0.0	0	25 Tu	0257	0.0	0
	0858	4.7	143		0822	4.8	146
	1538	0.0	0		1509	-0.1	-3
	2123	5.1	155		2045	5.3	162
11 Tu	0404	0.0	0	26 W	0351	-0.1	-3
	0940	4.7	143		0912	4.8	146
	1619	0.1	3		1559	-0.1	-3
	2205	5.1	155		2134	5.5	168
12 W	0447	0.1	3	27 Th	0443	-0.2	-6
	1021	4.5	137		1003	4.8	146
	1656	0.3	9		1648	-0.2	-6
	2245	5.0	152		2224	5.5	168
13 Th	0528	0.2	6	28 F	0535	-0.2	-6
	1101	4.4	134		1057	4.7	143
	1731	0.4	12		1738	-0.1	-3
	2323	4.9	149		2319	5.4	165
14 F	0607	0.3	9	29 Sa	0628	-0.1	-3
	1141	4.2	128		1155	4.6	140
	1801	0.5	15		1830	-0.1	-3
15 Sa	0000	4.7	143	30 Su	0019	5.3	162
	0645	0.4	12		0721	-0.1	-3
	1222	4.1	125		1257	4.5	137
	1829	0.6	18		1924	0.1	3

May

Day	Time (h m)	Height (ft)	Height (cm)	Day	Time (h m)	Height (ft)	Height (cm)
1 M	0121	5.1	155	16 Tu	0004	4.5	137
	0816	0.0	0		0732	0.4	12
	1358	4.4	134		1248	3.8	116
	2022	0.2	6		1908	0.5	15
2 Tu	0222	4.9	149	17 W	0044	4.4	134
	0914	0.1	3		0814	0.4	12
	1457	4.4	134		1333	3.8	116
	2124	0.3	9		1957	0.5	15
3 W	0321	4.8	146	18 Th	0136	4.4	134
	1011	0.0	0		0903	0.4	12
	1555	4.5	137		1429	3.9	119
	2226	0.3	9		2101	0.6	18
4 Th	0417	4.6	140	19 F	0237	4.3	131
	1107	0.0	0		1000	0.3	9
	1652	4.6	140		1531	4.1	125
	2325	0.3	9		2219	0.6	18
5 F	0512	4.6	140	20 Sa	0343	4.3	131
	1200	-0.1	-3		1058	0.2	6
	1747	4.7	143		1634	4.3	131
					2332	0.5	15
6 Sa	0022	0.2	6	21 Su	0452	4.3	131
	0605	4.5	137		1156	0.1	3
	1250	-0.2	-6		1735	4.6	140
	1839	4.8	146				
7 Su	0115	0.1	3	22 M	0037	0.3	9
	0656	4.5	137		0557	4.4	134
	1337	-0.2	-6		1252	-0.1	-3
	1928	4.9	149		1835	4.9	149
8 M	0206	0.0	0	23 Tu	0138	0.1	3
	0743	4.5	137		0657	4.4	134
	1423	-0.1	-3		1347	-0.2	-6
	2015	5.0	152		1931	5.1	155
9 Tu	0253	0.0	0	24 W	0236	0.0	0
	0828	4.4	134		0754	4.5	137
	1505	-0.1	-3		1441	-0.3	-9
	2058	5.1	155		2025	5.3	162
10 W	0339	0.0	0	25 Th	0332	-0.2	-6
	0911	4.3	131		0849	4.5	137
	1546	0.1	3		1535	-0.3	-9
	2139	5.0	152		2118	5.4	165
11 Th	0422	0.1	3	26 F	0426	-0.3	-9
	0953	4.2	128		0944	4.5	137
	1623	0.2	6		1628	-0.4	-12
	2217	4.9	149		2212	5.4	165
12 F	0503	0.1	3	27 Sa	0519	-0.3	-9
	1033	4.1	125		1041	4.5	137
	1658	0.3	9		1720	-0.3	-9
	2253	4.8	146		2308	5.3	162
13 Sa	0541	0.2	6	28 Su	0611	-0.3	-9
	1111	4.0	122		1141	4.4	134
	1729	0.4	12		1813	-0.2	-6
	2324	4.6	140				
14 Su	0618	0.3	9	29 M	0007	5.2	158
	1146	3.9	119		0703	-0.3	-9
	1758	0.4	12		1242	4.3	131
	2344	4.5	137		1907	-0.1	-3
15 M	0655	0.4	12	30 Tu	0106	5.0	152
	1217	3.8	116		0756	-0.3	-9
	1829	0.5	15		1342	4.3	131
					2003	0.0	0
				31 W	0203	4.8	146
					0849	-0.2	-6
					1439	4.3	131
					2102	0.2	6

June

Day	Time (h m)	Height (ft)	Height (cm)	Day	Time (h m)	Height (ft)	Height (cm)
1 Th	0257	4.6	140	16 F	0106	4.4	134
	0943	-0.2	-6		0830	0.1	3
	1534	4.4	134		1349	4.0	122
	2201	0.2	6		2041	0.4	12
2 F	0350	4.4	134	17 Sa	0205	4.3	131
	1036	-0.2	-6		0923	0.0	0
	1628	4.4	134		1453	4.1	125
	2259	0.2	6		2155	0.4	12
3 Sa	0442	4.3	131	18 Su	0309	4.3	131
	1128	-0.3	-9		1022	-0.1	-3
	1720	4.5	137		1559	4.3	131
	2355	0.2	6		2309	0.4	12
4 Su	0533	4.2	128	19 M	0417	4.2	128
	1217	-0.3	-9		1122	-0.2	-6
	1812	4.6	140		1705	4.6	140
5 M	0048	0.1	3	20 Tu	0015	0.2	6
	0623	4.2	128		0526	4.2	128
	1303	-0.3	-9		1222	-0.3	-9
	1901	4.7	143		1809	4.8	146
6 Tu	0138	0.0	0	21 W	0118	0.1	3
	0712	4.1	125		0631	4.2	128
	1348	-0.2	-6		1321	-0.4	-12
	1947	4.8	146		1910	5.1	155
7 W	0226	0.0	0	22 Th	0217	-0.1	-3
	0759	4.1	125		0732	4.3	131
	1432	-0.1	-3		1419	-0.4	-12
	2031	4.8	146		2008	5.2	158
8 Th	0312	0.0	0	23 F	0314	-0.3	-9
	0843	4.0	122		0830	4.3	131
	1513	0.0	0		1515	-0.5	-15
	2113	4.8	146		2103	5.3	162
9 F	0355	0.0	0	24 Sa	0408	-0.4	-12
	0925	4.0	122		0927	4.4	134
	1552	0.1	3		1610	-0.5	-15
	2152	4.7	143		2158	5.3	162
10 Sa	0437	0.0	0	25 Su	0500	-0.4	-12
	1005	3.9	119		1024	4.4	134
	1629	0.1	3		1703	-0.5	-15
	2227	4.6	140		2253	5.2	158
11 Su	0516	0.1	3	26 M	0551	-0.5	-15
	1042	3.8	116		1123	4.3	131
	1703	0.2	6		1755	-0.4	-12
	2255	4.5	137		2349	5.0	152
12 M	0554	0.1	3	27 Tu	0641	-0.4	-12
	1112	3.7	113		1221	4.3	131
	1736	0.2	6		1847	-0.2	-6
	2311	4.5	137				
13 Tu	0630	0.2	6	28 W	0044	4.8	146
	1134	3.7	113		0730	-0.4	-12
	1811	0.3	9		1319	4.3	131
	2334	4.5	137		1941	0.0	0
14 W	0706	0.2	6	29 Th	0137	4.6	140
	1205	3.8	116		0820	-0.3	-9
	1851	0.3	9		1414	4.3	131
					2036	0.1	3
15 Th	0015	4.4	134	30 F	0228	4.4	134
	0745	0.1	3		0911	-0.3	-9
	1252	3.9	119		1507	4.3	131
	1939	0.3	9		2132	0.2	6

Time meridian 75° W. 0000 is midnight. 1200 is noon. Times are not adjusted for Daylight Saving Time.
Heights are referred to mean lower low water which is the chart datum of soundings.

Wilmington, North Carolina, 2017
Times and Heights of High and Low Waters

July

Day	Time	ft	cm	Day	Time	ft	cm
1 Sa	0318	4.3	131	16 Su ◑	0143	4.4	134
	1001	-0.2	-6		0854	-0.1	-3
	1558	4.3	131		1427	4.3	131
	2229	0.2	6		2141	0.4	12
2 Su	0408	4.1	125	17 M	0249	4.3	131
	1051	-0.2	-6		0954	-0.1	-3
	1649	4.4	134		1536	4.5	137
	2324	0.2	6		2251	0.4	12
3 M	0459	4.0	122	18 Tu	0358	4.2	128
	1140	-0.2	-6		1057	-0.2	-6
	1740	4.5	137		1644	4.6	140
					2357	0.3	9
4 Tu	0016	0.2	6	19 W	0507	4.1	125
	0550	3.9	119		1200	-0.3	-9
	1227	-0.2	-6		1751	4.8	146
	1830	4.5	137				
5 W	0107	0.1	3	20 Th	0059	0.1	3
	0640	3.9	119		0613	4.2	128
	1313	-0.2	-6		1301	-0.4	-12
	1918	4.6	140		1854	5.0	152
6 Th	0155	0.1	3	21 F	0158	-0.1	-3
	0728	3.9	119		0716	4.3	131
	1358	-0.1	-3		1400	-0.4	-12
	2003	4.7	143		1953	5.1	155
7 F	0242	0.0	0	22 Sa	0254	-0.2	-6
	0815	3.9	119		0814	4.4	134
	1441	-0.1	-3		1458	-0.5	-15
	2046	4.7	143		2049	5.2	158
8 Sa ○	0327	0.0	0	23 Su ●	0348	-0.3	-9
	0858	3.9	119		0911	4.4	134
	1523	0.0	0		1552	-0.5	-15
	2126	4.7	143		2142	5.2	158
9 Su	0409	0.0	0	24 M	0439	-0.4	-12
	0938	3.8	116		1006	4.5	137
	1603	0.0	0		1645	-0.4	-12
	2201	4.6	140		2234	5.1	155
10 M	0449	0.0	0	25 Tu	0527	-0.4	-12
	1013	3.8	116		1101	4.5	137
	1642	0.1	3		1736	-0.3	-9
	2230	4.6	140		2325	5.0	152
11 Tu	0527	0.1	3	26 W	0615	-0.4	-12
	1041	3.8	116		1156	4.4	134
	1720	0.1	3		1825	-0.2	-6
	2249	4.5	137				
12 W	0604	0.0	0	27 Th	0015	4.8	146
	1102	3.8	116		0701	-0.3	-9
	1759	0.2	6		1250	4.4	134
	2314	4.5	137		1915	0.0	0
13 Th	0641	0.0	0	28 F	0105	4.6	140
	1136	3.9	119		0747	-0.2	-6
	1841	0.2	6		1343	4.4	134
	2354	4.5	137		2006	0.2	6
14 F	0719	0.0	0	29 Sa	0155	4.4	134
	1224	4.1	125		0833	-0.1	-3
	1930	0.3	9		1434	4.3	131
					2100	0.3	9
15 Sa	0045	4.4	134	30 Su ◐	0244	4.2	128
	0803	-0.1	-3		0921	0.0	0
	1321	4.2	128		1524	4.3	131
	2031	0.4	12		2154	0.4	12
				31 M	0334	4.0	122
					1010	0.0	0
					1615	4.3	131
					2249	0.4	12

August

Day	Time	ft	cm	Day	Time	ft	cm
1 Tu	0424	3.9	119	16 W	0349	4.2	128
	1059	0.1	3		1040	0.0	0
	1705	4.4	134		1632	4.8	146
	2342	0.4	12		2341	0.4	12
2 W	0516	3.9	119	17 Th	0457	4.2	128
	1148	0.1	3		1145	-0.1	-3
	1756	4.4	134		1739	4.9	149
3 Th	0033	0.3	9	18 F	0041	0.2	6
	0607	3.9	119		0602	4.3	131
	1236	0.0	0		1246	-0.2	-6
	1846	4.5	137		1841	5.0	152
4 F	0122	0.3	9	19 Sa	0139	0.0	0
	0658	3.9	119		0703	4.4	134
	1324	0.0	0		1345	-0.3	-9
	1933	4.6	140		1939	5.1	155
5 Sa	0210	0.2	6	20 Su	0233	-0.1	-3
	0745	4.0	122		0800	4.6	140
	1410	0.0	0		1441	-0.3	-9
	2017	4.7	143		2032	5.2	158
6 Su	0255	0.2	6	21 M ●	0325	-0.2	-6
	0829	4.0	122		0854	4.7	143
	1455	0.0	0		1534	-0.3	-9
	2058	4.7	143		2122	5.2	158
7 M ○	0338	0.2	6	22 Tu	0414	-0.3	-9
	0910	4.1	125		0946	4.7	143
	1539	0.1	3		1625	-0.3	-9
	2134	4.7	143		2210	5.1	155
8 Tu	0420	0.1	3	23 W	0500	-0.3	-9
	0945	4.1	125		1037	4.7	143
	1622	0.1	3		1714	-0.1	-3
	2205	4.7	143		2256	4.9	149
9 W	0459	0.1	3	24 Th	0545	-0.2	-6
	1013	4.2	128		1127	4.7	143
	1704	0.1	3		1801	0.0	0
	2230	4.7	143		2343	4.7	143
10 Th	0537	0.0	0	25 F	0628	-0.1	-3
	1039	4.3	131		1217	4.6	140
	1747	0.2	6		1848	0.2	6
	2259	4.7	143				
11 F	0616	0.0	0	26 Sa	0030	4.5	137
	1115	4.4	134		0710	0.1	3
	1833	0.2	6		1307	4.5	137
	2339	4.6	140		1935	0.4	12
12 Sa	0656	0.0	0	27 Su	0119	4.3	131
	1203	4.5	137		0751	0.2	6
	1924	0.3	9		1357	4.4	134
					2024	0.6	18
13 Su	0030	4.5	137	28 M	0208	4.2	128
	0741	0.0	0		0835	0.3	9
	1302	4.5	137		1446	4.4	134
	2024	0.4	12		2116	0.7	21
14 M ◐	0132	4.4	134	29 Tu ◐	0258	4.0	122
	0833	0.0	0		0922	0.4	12
	1411	4.6	140		1536	4.3	131
	2130	0.5	15		2210	0.7	21
15 Tu	0240	4.3	131	30 W	0349	3.9	119
	0935	0.0	0		1013	0.4	12
	1523	4.7	143		1628	4.4	134
	2237	0.5	15		2304	0.7	21
				31 Th	0441	3.9	119
					1106	0.4	12
					1719	4.4	134
					2356	0.6	18

September

Day	Time	ft	cm	Day	Time	ft	cm
1 F	0534	4.0	122	16 Sa	0023	0.2	6
	1158	0.4	12		0551	4.5	137
	1810	4.5	137		1232	0.0	0
					1827	5.0	152
2 Sa	0046	0.5	15	17 Su	0118	0.1	3
	0625	4.0	122		0650	4.7	143
	1249	0.3	9		1329	-0.1	-3
	1859	4.6	140		1922	5.1	155
3 Su	0134	0.4	12	18 M	0210	-0.1	-3
	0714	4.2	128		0745	4.8	146
	1339	0.2	6		1424	-0.2	-6
	1944	4.7	143		2012	5.2	158
4 M	0221	0.3	9	19 Tu	0300	-0.1	-3
	0758	4.3	131		0836	5.0	152
	1428	0.2	6		1515	-0.1	-3
	2026	4.8	146		2059	5.1	155
5 Tu	0305	0.2	6	20 W ●	0347	-0.2	-6
	0839	4.4	134		0925	5.0	152
	1515	0.1	3		1605	-0.1	-3
	2103	4.9	149		2143	5.0	152
6 W	0348	0.2	6	21 Th	0431	-0.1	-3
	0915	4.5	137		1011	5.0	152
	1602	0.1	3		1651	0.0	0
	2137	4.9	149		2227	4.9	149
7 Th	0429	0.1	3	22 F	0513	0.0	0
	0947	4.7	143		1057	4.9	149
	1648	0.1	3		1736	0.2	6
	2209	4.9	149		2310	4.7	143
8 F	0510	0.1	3	23 Sa	0553	0.2	6
	1020	4.8	146		1142	4.8	146
	1735	0.2	6		1820	0.4	12
	2245	4.8	146		2355	4.5	137
9 Sa	0551	0.1	3	24 Su	0631	0.3	9
	1100	4.8	146		1228	4.7	143
	1824	0.3	9		1903	0.5	15
	2328	4.7	143				
10 Su	0635	0.1	3	25 M	0041	4.3	131
	1150	4.9	149		0707	0.5	15
	1917	0.4	12		1316	4.5	137
					1948	0.7	21
11 M	0023	4.6	140	26 Tu	0130	4.1	125
	0723	0.1	3		0744	0.6	18
	1253	4.8	146		1404	4.4	134
	2015	0.5	15		2036	0.8	24
12 Tu	0129	4.4	134	27 W ◐	0220	4.0	122
	0818	0.2	6		0826	0.6	18
	1406	4.8	146		1454	4.3	131
	2118	0.6	18		2127	0.8	24
13 W ○	0238	4.3	131	28 Th	0311	3.9	119
	0921	0.2	6		0918	0.7	21
	1517	4.8	146		1545	4.3	131
	2222	0.5	15		2222	0.8	24
14 Th	0345	4.3	131	29 F	0404	3.9	119
	1027	0.2	6		1018	0.7	21
	1623	4.8	146		1637	4.3	131
	2324	0.4	12		2315	0.7	21
15 F	0449	4.4	134	30 Sa	0456	4.0	122
	1131	0.1	3		1117	0.6	18
	1727	4.9	149		1729	4.4	134

Time meridian 75° W. 0000 is midnight. 1200 is noon. Times are not adjusted for Daylight Saving Time.
Heights are referred to mean lower low water which is the chart datum of soundings.

Wilmington, North Carolina, 2017
Times and Heights of High and Low Waters

October

Day	Time	ft	cm	Day	Time	ft	cm
1 Su	0007	0.6	18	16 M	0054	0.0	0
	0548	4.1	125		0635	4.8	146
	1214	0.5	15		1312	0.0	0
	1819	4.6	140		1900	4.9	149
2 M	0056	0.5	15	17 Tu	0145	-0.1	-3
	0638	4.3	131		0728	4.9	149
	1308	0.4	12		1404	-0.1	-3
	1906	4.7	143		1948	4.9	149
3 Tu	0143	0.3	9	18 W	0232	-0.2	-6
	0724	4.5	137		0816	5.1	155
	1400	0.3	9		1455	-0.1	-3
	1949	4.8	146		2034	4.9	149
4 W	0230	0.2	6	19 Th	0318	-0.2	-6
	0807	4.7	143		0902	5.1	155
	1452	0.2	6		1542	0.0	0
	2030	4.9	149	●	2117	4.8	146
5 Th O	0315	0.1	3	20 F	0401	-0.1	-3
	0846	4.9	149		0946	5.1	155
	1542	0.1	3		1628	0.1	3
	2109	4.9	149		2159	4.7	143
6 F	0359	0.0	0	21 Sa	0441	0.1	3
	0925	5.1	155		1028	5.0	152
	1631	0.1	3		1711	0.2	6
	2148	4.9	149		2240	4.5	137
7 Sa	0444	0.0	0	22 Su	0518	0.2	6
	1004	5.2	158		1109	4.8	146
	1721	0.1	3		1752	0.4	12
	2231	4.8	146		2322	4.3	131
8 Su	0529	0.0	0	23 M	0553	0.4	12
	1050	5.2	158		1150	4.7	143
	1812	0.2	6		1833	0.5	15
	2321	4.7	143				
9 M	0616	0.0	0	24 Tu	0004	4.1	125
	1145	5.1	155		0625	0.5	15
	1906	0.3	9		1233	4.5	137
					1913	0.6	18
10 Tu	0021	4.5	137	25 W	0049	4.0	122
	0708	0.1	3		0656	0.6	18
	1252	5.0	152		1317	4.4	134
	2003	0.4	12		1955	0.7	21
11 W	0128	4.4	134	26 Th	0137	3.8	116
	0805	0.2	6		0732	0.6	18
	1402	4.9	149		1404	4.3	131
	2103	0.5	15		2042	0.8	24
12 Th ☽	0234	4.4	134	27 F	0227	3.8	116
	0908	0.2	6		0821	0.6	18
	1509	4.9	149		1454	4.2	128
	2205	0.4	12	☾	2135	0.8	24
13 F	0338	4.4	134	28 Sa	0319	3.8	116
	1013	0.2	6		0924	0.7	21
	1611	4.8	146		1546	4.2	128
	2305	0.3	9		2229	0.7	21
14 Sa	0439	4.5	137	29 Su	0412	3.9	119
	1116	0.2	6		1034	0.6	18
	1711	4.9	149		1639	4.3	131
					2323	0.5	15
15 Su	0001	0.1	3	30 M	0505	4.1	125
	0539	4.6	140		1138	0.5	15
	1216	0.1	3		1732	4.4	134
	1807	4.9	149				
				31 Tu	0015	0.4	12
					0557	4.3	131
					1237	0.4	12
					1822	4.5	137

November

Day	Time	ft	cm	Day	Time	ft	cm
1 W	0105	0.2	6	16 Th	0203	-0.3	-9
	0647	4.6	140		0754	4.9	149
	1334	0.2	6		1432	-0.1	-3
	1911	4.7	143		2007	4.6	140
2 Th	0154	0.0	0	17 F	0248	-0.2	-6
	0734	4.9	149		0839	5.0	152
	1429	0.1	3		1519	-0.1	-3
	1957	4.8	146		2051	4.5	137
3 F	0243	-0.1	-3	18 Sa	0330	-0.1	-3
	0820	5.1	155		0921	5.0	152
	1522	0.0	0		1603	0.0	0
	2043	4.8	146	●	2133	4.4	134
4 Sa O	0331	-0.2	-6	19 Su	0410	0.0	0
	0905	5.3	162		1002	4.9	149
	1614	0.0	0		1646	0.1	3
	2129	4.8	146		2213	4.2	128
5 Su	0420	-0.2	-6	20 M	0447	0.1	3
	0952	5.3	162		1041	4.7	143
	1706	0.0	0		1726	0.2	6
	2218	4.7	143		2252	4.1	125
6 M	0509	-0.2	-6	21 Tu	0521	0.2	6
	1043	5.3	162		1118	4.6	140
	1758	0.0	0		1804	0.3	9
	2313	4.6	140		2330	3.9	119
7 Tu	0600	-0.2	-6	22 W	0552	0.3	9
	1142	5.2	158		1153	4.4	134
	1852	0.1	3		1841	0.4	12
8 W	0015	4.4	134	23 Th	0006	3.8	116
	0654	-0.1	-3		0622	0.4	12
	1247	5.0	152		1223	4.3	131
	1947	0.1	3		1919	0.5	15
9 Th	0120	4.3	131	24 F	0040	3.7	113
	0751	0.0	0		0656	0.4	12
	1352	4.9	149		1253	4.2	128
	2045	0.2	6		1959	0.5	15
10 F O	0224	4.3	131	25 Sa	0119	3.7	113
	0853	0.1	3		0741	0.4	12
	1454	4.8	146		1338	4.2	128
	2143	0.1	3		2045	0.5	15
11 Sa	0325	4.3	131	26 Su ☾	0211	3.7	113
	0956	0.2	6		0839	0.5	15
	1553	4.7	143		1435	4.2	128
	2241	0.0	0		2139	0.4	12
12 Su	0424	4.4	134	27 M	0311	3.9	119
	1058	0.1	3		0951	0.5	15
	1649	4.6	140		1537	4.2	128
	2336	-0.1	-3		2236	0.3	9
13 M	0521	4.6	140	28 Tu	0411	4.0	122
	1156	0.0	0		1103	0.4	12
	1742	4.6	140		1638	4.2	128
					2332	0.2	6
14 Tu	0028	-0.2	-6	29 W	0511	4.3	131
	0615	4.7	143		1208	0.3	9
	1251	0.0	0		1737	4.3	131
	1834	4.6	140				
15 W	0117	-0.3	-9	30 Th	0027	0.0	0
	0706	4.8	146		0609	4.6	140
	1343	-0.1	-3		1309	0.2	6
	1922	4.6	140		1834	4.4	134

December

Day	Time	ft	cm	Day	Time	ft	cm
1 F	0121	-0.2	-6	16 Sa	0218	-0.3	-9
	0704	4.8	146		0815	4.8	146
	1407	0.0	0		1453	-0.1	-3
	1928	4.5	137		2026	4.2	128
2 Sa	0214	-0.3	-9	17 Su	0300	-0.2	-6
	0757	5.1	155		0857	4.8	146
	1503	-0.1	-3		1538	-0.1	-3
	2020	4.6	140		2108	4.2	128
3 Su O	0307	-0.4	-12	18 M	0341	-0.1	-3
	0849	5.2	158		0938	4.7	143
	1557	-0.2	-6		1620	0.0	0
	2112	4.6	140	●	2149	4.1	125
4 M	0400	-0.5	-15	19 Tu	0419	-0.1	-3
	0941	5.3	162		1017	4.6	140
	1650	-0.3	-9		1659	0.1	3
	2205	4.6	140		2227	4.0	122
5 Tu	0452	-0.5	-15	20 W	0455	0.0	0
	1036	5.2	158		1052	4.5	137
	1742	-0.3	-9		1737	0.2	6
	2302	4.5	137		2301	3.9	119
6 W	0545	-0.4	-12	21 Th	0528	0.1	3
	1134	5.1	155		1121	4.4	134
	1834	-0.2	-6		1812	0.2	6
					2325	3.8	116
7 Th	0003	4.4	134	22 F	0600	0.1	3
	0639	-0.3	-9		1138	4.3	131
	1235	4.9	149		1847	0.3	9
	1927	-0.2	-6		2345	3.8	116
8 F	0105	4.3	131	23 Sa	0635	0.2	6
	0735	-0.2	-6		1204	4.3	131
	1335	4.8	146		1922	0.3	9
	2021	-0.1	-3				
9 Sa	0207	4.3	131	24 Su	0022	3.8	116
	0833	-0.1	-3		0716	0.2	6
	1433	4.6	140		1248	4.2	128
	2117	-0.1	-3		2002	0.2	6
10 Su O	0305	4.3	131	25 M	0112	3.9	119
	0934	0.0	0		0809	0.3	9
	1528	4.5	137		1342	4.2	128
	2212	-0.2	-6		2051	0.2	6
11 M	0402	4.3	131	26 Tu ☾	0210	4.0	122
	1034	0.1	3		0917	0.4	12
	1621	4.4	134		1443	4.2	128
	2306	-0.2	-6		2149	0.1	3
12 Tu	0457	4.4	134	27 W	0316	4.1	125
	1131	0.0	0		1033	0.4	12
	1713	4.3	131		1550	4.1	125
	2357	-0.3	-9		2251	0.0	0
13 W	0550	4.5	137	28 Th	0425	4.3	131
	1226	0.0	0		1143	0.3	9
	1804	4.3	131		1658	4.2	128
					2353	-0.1	-3
14 Th	0046	-0.3	-9	29 F	0534	4.5	137
	0641	4.6	140		1247	0.2	6
	1317	-0.1	-3		1803	4.2	128
	1854	4.2	128				
15 F	0133	-0.3	-9	30 Sa	0053	-0.3	-9
	0729	4.7	143		0639	4.8	146
	1406	-0.1	-3		1347	0.0	0
	1941	4.2	128		1904	4.3	131
				31 Su	0151	-0.4	-12
					0739	5.0	152
					1444	-0.2	-6
					2002	4.4	134

Time meridian 75° W. 0000 is midnight. 1200 is noon. Times are not adjusted for Daylight Saving Time.
Heights are referred to mean lower low water which is the chart datum of soundings.

Myrtle Beach (Springmaid Pier), South Carolina, 2017

Times and Heights of High and Low Waters

January

Day	Time	ft	cm
1 Su	0259	-0.1	-3
	0912	5.4	165
	1537	-0.1	-3
	2122	4.5	137
2 M	0341	0.0	0
	0956	5.2	158
	1618	-0.1	-3
	2212	4.5	137
3 Tu	0427	0.1	3
	1046	5.1	155
	1702	-0.1	-3
	2307	4.5	137
4 W	0518	0.2	6
	1141	5.0	152
	1751	-0.1	-3
5 Th ☾	0006	4.7	143
	0617	0.3	9
	1238	4.9	149
	1847	-0.2	-6
6 F	0106	4.9	149
	0725	0.3	9
	1336	4.8	146
	1948	-0.3	-9
7 Sa	0206	5.2	158
	0839	0.2	6
	1436	4.8	146
	2051	-0.5	-15
8 Su	0307	5.5	168
	0948	0.0	0
	1538	4.9	149
	2153	-0.7	-21
9 M	0409	5.8	177
	1050	-0.3	-9
	1639	5.0	152
	2251	-1.0	-30
10 Tu	0508	6.1	186
	1146	-0.6	-18
	1738	5.1	155
	2346	-1.2	-37
11 W	0604	6.3	192
	1240	-0.8	-24
	1832	5.3	162
12 Th ◯	0040	-1.3	-40
	0656	6.4	195
	1331	-0.9	-27
	1924	5.3	162
13 F	0132	-1.3	-40
	0746	6.3	192
	1420	-0.9	-27
	2015	5.3	162
14 Sa	0222	-1.1	-34
	0835	6.0	183
	1506	-0.7	-21
	2105	5.2	158
15 Su	0311	-0.9	-27
	0923	5.7	174
	1551	-0.5	-15
	2158	5.0	152
16 M	0359	-0.5	-15
	1013	5.3	162
	1635	-0.3	-9
	2252	4.7	143
17 Tu	0446	-0.1	-3
	1104	4.9	149
	1720	0.0	0
	2346	4.6	140
18 W	0536	0.2	6
	1154	4.5	137
	1806	0.2	6
19 Th ◐	0038	4.5	137
	0629	0.5	15
	1244	4.2	128
	1855	0.4	12
20 F	0129	4.4	134
	0727	0.7	21
	1333	4.0	122
	1950	0.5	15
21 Sa	0219	4.4	134
	0829	0.8	24
	1423	3.9	119
	2046	0.5	15
22 Su	0308	4.5	137
	0927	0.7	21
	1514	3.9	119
	2138	0.4	12
23 M	0358	4.6	140
	1018	0.5	15
	1605	3.9	119
	2226	0.2	6
24 Tu	0446	4.8	146
	1105	0.3	9
	1653	4.1	125
	2311	0.0	0
25 W	0531	5.0	152
	1149	0.1	3
	1738	4.2	128
	2354	-0.2	-6
26 Th	0613	5.3	162
	1231	-0.1	-3
	1820	4.4	134
27 F ●	0037	-0.4	-12
	0652	5.4	165
	1311	-0.3	-9
	1859	4.6	140
28 Sa	0118	-0.5	-15
	0730	5.5	168
	1351	-0.4	-12
	1938	4.7	143
29 Su	0200	-0.5	-15
	0809	5.6	171
	1431	-0.5	-15
	2018	4.8	146
30 M	0242	-0.5	-15
	0850	5.5	168
	1512	-0.6	-18
	2102	4.9	149
31 Tu	0326	-0.4	-12
	0934	5.3	162
	1554	-0.6	-18
	2151	4.9	149

February

Day	Time	ft	cm
1 W	0412	-0.3	-9
	1024	5.1	155
	1638	-0.5	-15
	2245	4.9	149
2 Th	0503	-0.1	-3
	1119	4.9	149
	1727	-0.5	-15
	2344	5.0	152
3 F ◯	0601	0.0	0
	1218	4.8	146
	1821	-0.4	-12
4 Sa	0045	5.1	155
	0708	0.2	6
	1318	4.6	140
	1924	-0.3	-9
5 Su	0147	5.2	158
	0824	0.2	6
	1421	4.6	140
	2032	-0.4	-12
6 M	0251	5.4	165
	0936	0.0	0
	1524	4.6	140
	2138	-0.5	-15
7 Tu	0354	5.5	168
	1039	-0.2	-6
	1627	4.8	146
	2239	-0.8	-24
8 W	0456	5.7	174
	1135	-0.4	-12
	1726	5.0	152
	2336	-1.0	-30
9 Th	0552	5.9	180
	1226	-0.6	-18
	1820	5.2	158
10 F ◯	0028	-1.1	-34
	0643	6.0	183
	1314	-0.7	-21
	1910	5.3	162
11 Sa	0118	-1.1	-34
	0730	5.9	180
	1358	-0.7	-21
	1956	5.4	165
12 Su	0205	-1.0	-30
	0814	5.7	174
	1440	-0.6	-18
	2042	5.3	162
13 M	0250	-0.8	-24
	0857	5.4	165
	1520	-0.5	-15
	2127	5.1	155
14 Tu	0333	-0.5	-15
	0940	5.1	155
	1558	-0.2	-6
	2214	4.9	149
15 W	0416	-0.2	-6
	1025	4.7	143
	1637	0.0	0
	2302	4.7	143
16 Th	0459	0.2	6
	1111	4.4	134
	1717	0.3	9
	2351	4.5	137
17 F	0545	0.5	15
	1200	4.1	125
	1800	0.5	15
18 Sa ◯	0041	4.4	134
	0636	0.7	21
	1249	3.9	119
	1851	0.7	21
19 Su	0131	4.3	131
	0735	0.9	27
	1339	3.8	116
	1950	0.7	21
20 M	0222	4.4	134
	0838	0.9	27
	1431	3.8	116
	2052	0.6	18
21 Tu	0314	4.5	137
	0937	0.7	21
	1524	3.9	119
	2149	0.5	15
22 W	0406	4.7	143
	1028	0.5	15
	1616	4.1	125
	2240	0.2	6
23 Th	0456	4.9	149
	1115	0.2	6
	1705	4.3	131
	2327	-0.1	-3
24 F	0541	5.2	158
	1158	-0.1	-3
	1751	4.7	143
25 Sa	0012	-0.4	-12
	0623	5.5	168
	1240	-0.3	-9
	1833	5.0	152
26 Su ●	0056	-0.6	-18
	0704	5.7	174
	1322	-0.6	-18
	1915	5.3	162
27 M	0140	-0.7	-21
	0745	5.7	174
	1403	-0.7	-21
	1957	5.5	168
28 Tu	0225	-0.7	-21
	0828	5.7	174
	1446	-0.8	-24
	2042	5.6	171

March

Day	Time	ft	cm
1 W	0311	-0.7	-21
	0914	5.5	168
	1530	-0.8	-24
	2132	5.6	171
2 Th	0359	-0.5	-15
	1006	5.3	162
	1616	-0.7	-21
	2226	5.5	168
3 F	0451	-0.3	-9
	1102	5.0	152
	1706	-0.5	-15
	2325	5.4	165
4 Sa	0549	-0.1	-3
	1203	4.8	146
	1802	-0.3	-9
5 Su ☾	0028	5.4	165
	0656	0.2	6
	1306	4.6	140
	1906	-0.1	-3
6 M	0132	5.3	162
	0811	0.3	9
	1410	4.6	140
	2018	-0.1	-3
7 Tu	0236	5.3	162
	0924	0.2	6
	1513	4.7	143
	2127	-0.2	-6
8 W	0341	5.4	165
	1026	0.0	0
	1616	4.8	146
	2230	-0.4	-12
9 Th	0442	5.5	168
	1120	-0.2	-6
	1714	5.1	155
	2325	-0.6	-18
10 F	0537	5.6	171
	1208	-0.3	-9
	1806	5.3	162
11 Sa	0016	-0.7	-21
	0626	5.6	171
	1252	-0.4	-12
	1852	5.5	168
12 Su ◯	0102	-0.7	-21
	0709	5.6	171
	1332	-0.5	-15
	1935	5.6	171
13 M	0146	-0.7	-21
	0750	5.5	168
	1410	-0.4	-12
	2016	5.5	168
14 Tu	0227	-0.5	-15
	0829	5.3	162
	1446	-0.2	-6
	2056	5.4	165
15 W	0307	-0.3	-9
	0907	5.0	152
	1522	0.0	0
	2136	5.2	158
16 Th	0346	0.0	0
	0948	4.7	143
	1558	0.2	6
	2219	4.9	149
17 F	0426	0.2	6
	1031	4.4	134
	1635	0.4	12
	2304	4.7	143
18 Sa	0508	0.5	15
	1117	4.1	125
	1716	0.7	21
	2353	4.6	140
19 Su	0555	0.7	21
	1207	4.0	122
	1803	0.8	24
20 M ◐	0044	4.5	137
	0648	0.9	27
	1258	3.9	119
	1859	0.9	27
21 Tu	0136	4.5	137
	0748	1.0	30
	1350	3.9	119
	2004	0.9	27
22 W	0229	4.6	140
	0850	0.9	27
	1444	4.1	125
	2108	0.7	21
23 Th	0322	4.7	143
	0946	0.6	18
	1537	4.3	131
	2205	0.5	15
24 F	0415	5.0	152
	1035	0.3	9
	1630	4.7	143
	2257	0.1	3
25 Sa	0504	5.3	162
	1122	0.0	0
	1719	5.1	155
	2345	-0.2	-6
26 Su	0551	5.6	171
	1206	-0.4	-12
	1806	5.5	168
27 M ●	0032	-0.5	-15
	0636	5.8	177
	1250	-0.7	-21
	1851	5.9	180
28 Tu	0120	-0.7	-21
	0721	5.9	180
	1335	-0.9	-27
	1936	6.2	189
29 W	0208	-0.8	-24
	0807	5.8	177
	1420	-0.9	-27
	2023	6.3	192
30 Th	0257	-0.8	-24
	0856	5.7	174
	1507	-0.9	-27
	2114	6.2	189
31 F	0347	-0.6	-18
	0950	5.4	165
	1556	-0.7	-21
	2209	6.1	186

Time meridian 75° W. 0000 is midnight. 1200 is noon. Times are not adjusted for Daylight Saving Time.
Heights are referred to mean lower low water which is the chart datum of soundings.

Myrtle Beach (Springmaid Pier), South Carolina, 2017

Times and Heights of High and Low Waters

April

Day	Time	ft	cm	Day	Time	ft	cm
1 Sa	0441	-0.4	-12	**16** Su	0439	0.5	15
	1049	5.1	155		1040	4.2	128
	1649	-0.4	-12		1641	0.8	24
	2310	5.9	180		2311	4.8	146
2 Su	0539	-0.1	-3	**17** M	0522	0.7	21
	1152	4.9	149		1129	4.0	122
	1747	-0.2	-6		1725	0.9	27
3 M ☽	0014	5.6	171	**18** Tu	0001	4.7	143
	0645	0.2	6		0610	0.8	24
	1256	4.8	146		1220	4.0	122
	1853	0.1	3		1817	1.0	30
4 Tu	0118	5.5	168	**19** W ◑	0053	4.7	143
	0758	0.3	9		0704	0.9	27
	1400	4.8	146		1313	4.1	125
	2005	0.2	6		1919	1.0	30
5 W	0221	5.3	162	**20** Th	0146	4.7	143
	0908	0.3	9		0803	0.8	24
	1502	4.9	149		1406	4.3	131
	2116	0.2	6		2025	0.9	27
6 Th	0323	5.3	162	**21** F	0239	4.9	149
	1007	0.2	6		0900	0.6	18
	1602	5.1	155		1500	4.6	140
	2218	0.0	0		2128	0.6	18
7 F	0422	5.3	162	**22** Sa	0332	5.0	152
	1058	0.0	0		0953	0.2	6
	1658	5.3	162		1554	5.1	155
	2312	-0.1	-3		2225	0.3	9
8 Sa	0516	5.3	162	**23** Su	0426	5.3	162
	1143	-0.1	-3		1043	-0.1	-3
	1747	5.5	168		1647	5.5	168
					2318	-0.1	-3
9 Su	0000	-0.2	-6	**24** M	0518	5.5	168
	0603	5.3	162		1131	-0.5	-15
	1224	-0.1	-3		1738	6.0	183
	1831	5.7	174				
10 M	0044	-0.3	-9	**25** Tu	0009	-0.5	-15
	0645	5.3	162		0608	5.7	174
	1301	-0.1	-3		1219	-0.8	-24
	1911	5.7	174		1827	6.4	195
11 Tu ○	0125	-0.3	-9	**26** W ●	0100	-0.7	-21
	0723	5.2	158		0657	5.8	177
	1338	-0.1	-3		1307	-1.0	-30
	1949	5.7	174		1915	6.7	204
12 W	0204	-0.2	-6	**27** Th	0151	-0.9	-27
	0800	5.0	152		0747	5.8	177
	1413	0.0	0		1356	-1.0	-30
	2025	5.6	171		2005	6.8	207
13 Th	0242	-0.1	-3	**28** F	0243	-0.9	-27
	0837	4.8	146		0839	5.7	174
	1448	0.2	6		1447	-0.9	-27
	2102	5.4	165		2057	6.7	204
14 F	0320	0.1	3	**29** Sa	0335	-0.7	-21
	0915	4.6	140		0935	5.4	165
	1524	0.4	12		1539	-0.7	-21
	2141	5.2	158		2154	6.4	195
15 Sa	0358	0.3	9	**30** Su	0430	-0.5	-15
	0955	4.4	134		1036	5.2	158
	1601	0.6	18		1634	-0.4	-12
	2224	5.0	152		2255	6.1	186

May

Day	Time	ft	cm	Day	Time	ft	cm
1 M	0527	-0.2	-6	**16** Tu	0455	0.5	15
	1140	5.0	152		1055	4.1	125
	1733	-0.1	-3		1656	0.9	27
	2359	5.8	177		2324	4.9	149
2 Tu ☾	0630	0.1	3	**17** W	0539	0.6	18
	1244	5.0	152		1147	4.2	128
	1838	0.2	6		1744	1.0	30
3 W	0101	5.5	168	**18** Th ◑	0015	4.9	149
	0737	0.2	6		0628	0.6	18
	1346	5.0	152		1229	4.3	131
	1949	0.4	12		1841	1.0	30
4 Th	0202	5.3	162	**19** F	0107	4.9	149
	0843	0.3	9		0721	0.5	15
	1445	5.1	155		1333	4.6	140
	2059	0.4	12		1946	0.9	27
5 F	0300	5.1	155	**20** Sa	0159	4.9	149
	0940	0.2	6		0817	0.3	9
	1542	5.2	158		1427	4.9	149
	2200	0.3	9		2053	0.7	21
6 Sa	0355	5.0	152	**21** Su	0254	5.0	152
	1029	0.2	6		0913	0.0	0
	1635	5.4	165		1522	5.4	165
	2252	0.2	6		2155	0.3	9
7 Su	0447	4.9	149	**22** M	0350	5.2	158
	1112	0.1	3		1007	-0.3	-9
	1723	5.5	168		1617	5.8	177
	2338	0.2	6		2252	-0.1	-3
8 M	0533	4.9	149	**23** Tu	0446	5.4	165
	1151	0.1	3		1059	-0.6	-18
	1806	5.6	171		1712	6.3	192
					2347	-0.4	-12
9 Tu	0021	0.1	3	**24** W	0541	5.5	168
	0616	4.9	149		1150	-0.9	-27
	1228	0.1	3		1805	6.7	204
	1844	5.7	174				
10 W ○	0101	0.0	0	**25** Th ●	0041	-0.7	-21
	0655	4.8	146		0635	5.6	171
	1304	0.1	3		1243	-1.0	-30
	1921	5.7	174		1856	6.9	210
11 Th	0139	0.0	0	**26** F	0135	-0.9	-27
	0732	4.8	146		0728	5.7	174
	1341	0.2	6		1335	-1.1	-34
	1956	5.7	174		1948	6.9	210
12 F	0218	0.1	3	**27** Sa	0228	-0.9	-27
	0808	4.6	140		0823	5.6	171
	1417	0.3	9		1429	-1.0	-30
	2032	5.5	168		2042	6.8	207
13 Sa	0256	0.2	6	**28** Su	0322	-0.8	-24
	0845	4.5	137		0839	5.4	165
	1454	0.4	12		1523	-0.8	-24
	2110	5.4	165		2139	6.5	198
14 Su	0334	0.3	9	**29** M	0416	-0.6	-18
	0924	4.3	131		1021	5.2	158
	1533	0.6	18		1619	-0.5	-15
	2151	5.2	158		2239	6.1	186
15 M	0414	0.4	12	**30** Tu	0511	-0.3	-9
	1007	4.2	128		1125	5.1	155
	1613	0.7	21		1717	-0.1	-3
	2236	5.0	152		2340	5.7	174
				31 W	0608	-0.1	-3
					1227	5.1	155
					1819	0.2	6

June

Day	Time	ft	cm	Day	Time	ft	cm
1 Th ☾	0039	5.4	165	**16** F	0556	0.3	9
	0709	0.1	3		1209	4.6	140
	1326	5.1	155		1812	0.8	24
	1926	0.5	15				
2 F	0136	5.1	155	**17** Sa	0034	5.0	152
	0809	0.2	6		0645	0.2	6
	1422	5.1	155		1303	4.9	149
	2033	0.6	18		1915	0.8	24
3 Sa	0229	4.8	146	**18** Su	0127	5.0	152
	0904	0.3	9		0740	0.0	0
	1515	5.2	158		1358	5.2	158
	2133	0.6	18		2022	0.6	18
4 Su	0321	4.7	143	**19** M	0223	5.0	152
	0952	0.3	9		0838	-0.2	-6
	1605	5.3	162		1454	5.6	171
	2225	0.5	15		2128	0.3	9
5 M	0411	4.5	137	**20** Tu	0321	5.1	155
	1035	0.2	6		0936	-0.5	-15
	1652	5.4	165		1551	6.0	183
	2311	0.4	12		2230	0.0	0
6 Tu	0459	4.5	137	**21** W	0420	5.2	158
	1116	0.2	6		1032	-0.7	-21
	1736	5.5	168		1649	6.4	195
	2354	0.3	9		2328	-0.3	-9
7 W	0544	4.5	137	**22** Th	0519	5.3	162
	1154	0.2	6		1127	-0.9	-27
	1816	5.6	171		1745	6.7	204
8 Th	0034	0.2	6	**23** F ●	0024	-0.6	-18
	0625	4.5	137		0616	5.4	165
	1233	0.2	6		1223	-1.1	-34
	1853	5.6	171		1840	6.9	210
9 F ○	0114	0.2	6	**24** Sa	0119	-0.8	-24
	0704	4.5	137		0712	5.5	168
	1311	0.2	6		1318	-1.1	-34
	1930	5.6	171		1933	6.9	210
10 Sa	0153	0.1	3	**25** Su	0213	-0.8	-24
	0741	4.4	134		0807	5.5	168
	1350	0.3	9		1413	-1.0	-30
	2006	5.6	171		2027	6.7	204
11 Su	0232	0.2	6	**26** M	0306	-0.8	-24
	0818	4.4	134		0903	5.4	165
	1429	0.4	12		1507	-0.8	-24
	2043	5.5	168		2121	6.4	195
12 M	0311	0.2	6	**27** Tu	0357	-0.6	-18
	0857	4.3	131		1002	5.3	162
	1509	0.5	15		1602	-0.5	-15
	2123	5.3	162		2218	6.0	183
13 Tu	0350	0.3	9	**28** W	0448	-0.4	-12
	0939	4.2	128		1103	5.2	158
	1549	0.6	18		1657	-0.1	-3
	2206	5.2	158		2315	5.6	171
14 W	0429	0.3	9	**29** Th	0539	-0.2	-6
	1025	4.2	128		1202	5.2	158
	1632	0.7	21		1754	0.3	9
	2252	5.0	152				
15 Th	0511	0.3	9	**30** F ☾	0011	5.2	158
	1116	4.3	131		0632	0.1	3
	1718	0.8	24		1259	5.1	155
	2342	5.0	152		1854	0.6	18

Time meridian 75° W. 0000 is midnight. 1200 is noon. Times are not adjusted for Daylight Saving Time.
Heights are referred to mean lower low water which is the chart datum of soundings.

Myrtle Beach (Springmaid Pier), South Carolina, 2017

Times and Heights of High and Low Waters

July

Day	h m	ft	cm	Day	h m	ft	cm
1 Sa	0104	4.9	149	**16** Su ◗	0007	5.0	152
	0726	0.3	9		0616	0.0	0
	1351	5.1	155		1237	5.2	158
	1957	0.8	24		1851	0.7	21
2 Su	0154	4.6	140	**17** M	0102	5.0	152
	0820	0.4	12		0710	-0.1	-3
	1441	5.1	155		1334	5.5	168
	2057	0.8	24		1959	0.6	18
3 M	0244	4.4	134	**18** Tu	0159	5.0	152
	0910	0.4	12		0810	-0.2	-6
	1530	5.2	158		1431	5.8	177
	2151	0.8	24		2109	0.4	12
4 Tu	0333	4.3	131	**19** W	0259	5.0	152
	0956	0.4	12		0912	-0.4	-12
	1617	5.2	158		1531	6.1	186
	2239	0.7	21		2213	0.1	3
5 W	0422	4.3	131	**20** Th	0401	5.1	155
	1040	0.4	12		1012	-0.6	-18
	1703	5.3	162		1631	6.4	195
	2323	0.6	18		2313	-0.1	-3
6 Th	0510	4.3	131	**21** F	0502	5.2	158
	1122	0.3	9		1111	-0.7	-21
	1745	5.5	168		1730	6.6	201
7 F	0005	0.4	12	**22** Sa	0010	-0.4	-12
	0554	4.3	131		0601	5.4	165
	1203	0.3	9		1208	-0.9	-27
	1826	5.6	171		1825	6.8	207
8 Sa ○	0047	0.3	9	**23** Su ●	0103	-0.6	-18
	0635	4.4	134		0656	5.6	171
	1244	0.2	6		1303	-0.9	-27
	1904	5.6	171		1918	6.8	207
9 Su	0127	0.2	6	**24** M	0155	-0.6	-18
	0714	4.5	137		0750	5.6	171
	1325	0.2	6		1357	-0.8	-24
	1941	5.7	174		2009	6.6	201
10 M	0206	0.2	6	**25** Tu	0245	-0.6	-18
	0752	4.5	137		0844	5.6	171
	1406	0.3	9		1450	-0.6	-18
	2018	5.6	171		2100	6.3	192
11 Tu	0245	0.1	3	**26** W	0332	-0.5	-15
	0830	4.5	137		0938	5.5	168
	1446	0.3	9		1541	-0.3	-9
	2057	5.5	168		2152	5.9	180
12 W	0324	0.1	3	**27** Th	0418	-0.3	-9
	0911	4.5	137		1034	5.4	165
	1528	0.4	12		1632	0.1	3
	2138	5.4	165		2244	5.5	168
13 Th	0403	0.1	3	**28** F	0504	0.0	0
	0957	4.6	140		1130	5.3	162
	1611	0.5	15		1723	0.4	12
	2224	5.2	158		2337	5.1	155
14 F	0443	0.1	3	**29** Sa	0550	0.3	9
	1048	4.7	143		1224	5.2	158
	1657	0.6	18		1817	0.8	24
	2314	5.1	155				
15 Sa	0527	0.0	0	**30** Su ◖	0028	4.8	146
	1142	4.9	149		0639	0.5	15
	1750	0.7	21		1315	5.1	155
					1914	1.0	30
				31 M	0117	4.5	137
					0730	0.7	21
					1403	5.1	155
					2014	1.1	34

August

Day	h m	ft	cm	Day	h m	ft	cm
1 Tu	0206	4.3	131	**16** W	0144	5.0	152
	0823	0.7	21		0751	0.0	0
	1451	5.1	155		1415	6.0	183
	2111	1.1	34		2055	0.6	18
2 W	0255	4.3	131	**17** Th	0245	5.1	155
	0916	0.7	21		0857	0.0	0
	1539	5.2	158		1516	6.2	189
	2203	1.0	30		2201	0.4	12
3 Th	0345	4.2	128	**18** F	0348	5.2	158
	1004	0.7	21		1000	-0.2	-6
	1627	5.3	162		1617	6.3	192
	2250	0.8	24		2300	0.1	3
4 F	0435	4.3	131	**19** Sa	0450	5.4	165
	1051	0.6	18		1100	-0.4	-12
	1713	5.5	168		1716	6.5	198
	2334	0.7	21		2355	-0.1	-3
5 Sa	0522	4.5	137	**20** Su	0548	5.6	171
	1135	0.4	12		1156	-0.5	-15
	1756	5.6	171		1811	6.6	201
6 Su	0016	0.5	15	**21** M ●	0045	-0.3	-9
	0605	4.6	140		0642	5.8	177
	1218	0.3	9		1249	-0.6	-18
	1836	5.8	177		1901	6.6	201
7 M ○	0056	0.3	9	**22** Tu	0133	-0.3	-9
	0646	4.8	146		0732	5.9	180
	1300	0.2	6		1341	-0.5	-15
	1914	5.8	177		1949	6.4	195
8 Tu	0136	0.2	6	**23** W	0219	-0.3	-9
	0724	4.9	149		0821	5.9	180
	1342	0.2	6		1430	-0.3	-9
	1952	5.9	180		2035	6.2	189
9 W	0215	0.1	3	**24** Th	0302	-0.2	-6
	0804	5.0	152		0910	5.8	177
	1424	0.2	6		1517	0.0	0
	2030	5.8	177		2121	5.8	177
10 Th	0254	0.0	0	**25** F	0344	0.0	0
	0845	5.1	155		1000	5.7	174
	1507	0.3	9		1603	0.3	9
	2112	5.7	174		2209	5.4	165
11 F	0334	0.0	0	**26** Sa	0425	0.3	9
	0931	5.2	158		1051	5.5	168
	1552	0.4	12		1649	0.7	21
	2158	5.5	168		2258	5.0	152
12 Sa	0416	0.0	0	**27** Su	0507	0.6	18
	1022	5.3	162		1143	5.3	162
	1640	0.5	15		1737	1.0	30
	2249	5.3	162		2348	4.7	143
13 Su	0501	0.0	0	**28** M	0551	0.8	24
	1117	5.5	168		1233	5.2	158
	1733	0.6	18		1829	1.2	37
	2345	5.2	158				
14 M ◖	0551	0.0	0	**29** Tu ◖	0038	4.5	137
	1215	5.6	171		0640	1.0	30
	1834	0.7	21		1322	5.1	155
					1926	1.4	43
15 Tu	0044	5.1	155	**30** W	0128	4.4	134
	0647	0.1	3		0735	1.1	34
	1315	5.8	177		1411	5.1	155
	1944	0.7	21		2026	1.4	43
				31 Th	0218	4.4	134
					0833	1.1	34
					1500	5.2	158
					2123	1.3	40

September

Day	h m	ft	cm	Day	h m	ft	cm
1 F	0309	4.4	134	**16** Sa	0339	5.4	165
	0929	1.0	30		0952	0.2	6
	1549	5.3	162		1605	6.3	192
	2213	1.1	34		2247	0.4	12
2 Sa	0359	4.5	137	**17** Su	0439	5.6	171
	1019	0.8	24		1051	0.0	0
	1637	5.5	168		1702	6.4	195
	2258	0.9	27		2338	0.2	6
3 Su	0448	4.8	146	**18** M	0535	5.9	180
	1106	0.6	18		1145	-0.1	-3
	1722	5.7	174		1754	6.4	195
	2341	0.6	18				
4 M	0533	5.0	152	**19** Tu	0024	0.0	0
	1151	0.5	15		0626	6.1	186
	1804	5.9	180		1235	-0.2	-6
					1842	6.4	195
5 Tu	0022	0.4	12	**20** W ●	0108	0.0	0
	0616	5.3	162		0712	6.2	189
	1235	0.3	9		1323	-0.1	-3
	1844	6.1	186		1926	6.2	189
6 W	0102	0.2	6	**21** Th ○	0149	0.0	0
	0656	5.6	171		0756	6.2	189
	1318	0.2	6		1408	0.1	3
	1923	6.1	186		2008	6.0	183
7 Th	0143	0.0	0	**22** F	0229	0.1	3
	0737	5.8	177		0840	6.1	186
	1403	0.2	6		1451	0.3	9
	2004	6.1	186		2049	5.6	171
8 F	0224	-0.1	-3	**23** Sa	0308	0.4	12
	0820	5.9	180		0923	5.9	180
	1448	0.2	6		1534	0.6	18
	2047	5.9	180		2132	5.3	162
9 Sa	0306	-0.1	-3	**24** Su	0346	0.6	18
	0907	6.0	183		1009	5.6	171
	1535	0.3	9		1616	0.9	27
	2135	5.7	174		2217	5.0	152
10 Su	0351	-0.1	-3	**25** M	0425	0.9	27
	0958	6.0	183		1057	5.4	165
	1625	0.5	15		1700	1.1	34
	2230	5.5	168		2306	4.7	143
11 M	0438	0.0	0	**26** Tu	0507	1.1	34
	1056	6.0	183		1148	5.3	162
	1720	0.6	18		1747	1.4	43
	2329	5.3	162		2358	4.5	137
12 Tu	0531	0.2	6	**27** W ◑	0554	1.3	40
	1157	6.0	183		1239	5.2	158
	1822	0.8	24		1841	1.5	46
13 W ◖	0032	5.2	158	**28** Th	0050	4.4	134
	0631	0.3	9		0648	1.4	43
	1300	6.0	183		1329	5.2	158
	1933	0.9	27		1939	1.5	46
14 Th	0134	5.2	158	**29** F	0141	4.4	134
	0738	0.4	12		0749	1.4	43
	1402	6.1	186		1419	5.2	158
	2045	0.8	24		2038	1.4	43
15 F	0237	5.2	158	**30** Sa	0232	4.5	137
	0847	0.3	9		0851	1.3	40
	1504	6.2	189		1509	5.4	165
	2150	0.6	18		2132	1.2	37

Time meridian 75° W. 0000 is midnight. 1200 is noon. Times are not adjusted for Daylight Saving Time.
Heights are referred to mean lower low water which is the chart datum of soundings.

Myrtle Beach (Springmaid Pier), South Carolina, 2017

Times and Heights of High and Low Waters

October

Day	Time (h m)	Height (ft)	Height (cm)	Day	Time (h m)	Height (ft)	Height (cm)
1 Su	0323	4.7	143	16 M	0427	5.8	177
	0946	1.1	34		1041	0.3	9
	1558	5.5	168		1645	6.0	183
	2219	0.9	27		2317	0.2	6
2 M	0412	5.0	152	17 Tu	0520	6.0	183
	1036	0.8	24		1132	0.2	6
	1645	5.8	177		1735	6.0	183
	2303	0.6	18				
3 Tu	0500	5.4	165	18 W	0000	0.1	3
	1123	0.5	15		0607	6.2	189
	1729	6.0	183		1219	0.1	3
	2345	0.3	9		1820	5.9	180
4 W	0545	5.8	177	19 Th ●	0040	0.1	3
	1209	0.3	9		0651	6.3	192
	1813	6.1	186		1303	0.2	6
					1901	5.8	177
5 Th ○	0028	0.0	0	20 F	0119	0.2	6
	0629	6.2	189		0731	6.3	192
	1255	0.1	3		1345	0.3	9
	1855	6.2	189		1940	5.6	171
6 F	0110	-0.2	-6	21 Sa	0156	0.3	9
	0712	6.5	198		0810	6.1	186
	1341	0.0	0		1425	0.4	12
	1939	6.2	189		2018	5.4	165
7 Sa	0154	-0.3	-9	22 Su	0233	0.5	15
	0757	6.6	201		0849	5.9	180
	1429	0.0	0		1505	0.6	18
	2025	6.1	186		2057	5.1	155
8 Su	0240	-0.3	-9	23 M	0310	0.7	21
	0846	6.6	201		0930	5.7	174
	1519	0.1	3		1545	0.8	24
	2116	5.8	177		2139	4.8	146
9 M	0328	-0.2	-6	24 Tu	0349	0.9	27
	0939	6.5	198		1014	5.5	168
	1612	0.3	9		1627	1.0	30
	2213	5.6	171		2225	4.6	140
10 Tu	0419	0.0	0	25 W	0429	1.1	34
	1038	6.4	195		1103	5.3	162
	1708	0.5	15		1711	1.2	37
	2316	5.4	165		2316	4.4	134
11 W	0515	0.2	6	26 Th	0514	1.3	40
	1142	6.2	189		1155	5.1	155
	1811	0.7	21		1800	1.3	40
12 Th ◗	0022	5.3	162	27 F ◖	0009	4.3	131
	0617	0.4	12		0604	1.4	43
	1247	6.1	186		1246	5.1	155
	1922	0.8	24		1854	1.4	43
13 F	0126	5.3	162	28 Sa	0102	4.4	134
	0727	0.5	15		0703	1.4	43
	1350	6.0	183		1336	5.1	155
	2033	0.7	21		1951	1.3	40
14 Sa	0229	5.4	165	29 Su	0153	4.5	137
	0838	0.5	15		0808	1.3	40
	1451	6.0	183		1426	5.2	158
	2136	0.6	18		2046	1.1	34
15 Su	0329	5.5	168	30 M	0244	4.8	146
	0944	0.4	12		0909	1.1	34
	1549	6.0	183		1516	5.4	165
	2229	0.4	12		2137	0.7	21
				31 Tu	0335	5.2	158
					1004	0.8	24
					1605	5.6	171
					2224	0.4	12

November

Day	Time (h m)	Height (ft)	Height (cm)	Day	Time (h m)	Height (ft)	Height (cm)
1 W	0426	5.6	171	16 Th	0546	5.9	180
	1054	0.5	15		1201	0.3	9
	1654	5.8	177		1755	5.3	162
	2309	0.0	0				
2 Th	0515	6.1	186	17 F	0012	0.1	3
	1144	0.2	6		0628	6.0	183
	1742	6.0	183		1242	0.2	6
	2355	-0.3	-9		1836	5.2	158
3 F	0602	6.5	198	18 Sa ●	0050	0.1	3
	1232	-0.1	-3		0706	6.0	183
	1829	6.1	186		1322	0.3	9
					1914	5.1	155
4 Sa ○	0041	-0.5	-15	19 Su	0126	0.2	6
	0649	6.8	207		0743	5.9	180
	1322	-0.3	-9		1401	0.3	9
	1917	6.1	186		1951	4.9	149
5 Su	0129	-0.7	-21	20 M	0203	0.3	9
	0737	7.0	213		0820	5.8	177
	1413	-0.3	-9		1439	0.4	12
	2006	6.0	183		2028	4.8	146
6 M	0218	-0.6	-18	21 Tu	0240	0.5	15
	0828	6.9	210		0858	5.6	171
	1505	-0.2	-6		1518	0.5	15
	2100	5.8	177		2106	4.5	137
7 Tu	0309	-0.5	-15	22 W	0319	0.6	18
	0922	6.7	204		0939	5.4	165
	1559	-0.1	-3		1558	0.7	21
	2158	5.5	168		2148	4.3	131
8 W	0403	-0.3	-9	23 Th	0358	0.8	24
	1022	6.5	198		1023	5.2	158
	1655	0.2	6		1639	0.8	24
	2303	5.3	162		2235	4.2	128
9 Th	0501	0.0	0	24 F	0440	1.0	30
	1126	6.2	189		1112	5.0	152
	1757	0.4	12		1723	0.9	27
					2327	4.2	128
10 F ○	0009	5.2	158	25 Sa	0527	1.1	34
	0604	0.3	9		1202	4.9	149
	1231	6.0	183		1811	0.9	27
	1904	0.5	15				
11 Sa	0114	5.2	158	26 Su ◖	0020	4.3	131
	0713	0.5	15		0621	1.1	34
	1333	5.8	177		1253	4.9	149
	2012	0.5	15		1903	0.9	27
12 Su	0215	5.3	162	27 M	0113	4.5	137
	0825	0.5	15		0723	1.1	34
	1432	5.6	171		1343	4.9	149
	2113	0.4	12		1958	0.7	21
13 M	0314	5.5	168	28 Tu	0206	4.8	146
	0930	0.5	15		0828	0.9	27
	1528	5.5	168		1434	5.0	152
	2206	0.3	9		2053	0.4	12
14 Tu	0409	5.6	171	29 W	0259	5.1	155
	1026	0.4	12		0930	0.7	21
	1622	5.4	165		1527	5.2	158
	2252	0.2	6		2146	0.0	0
15 W	0500	5.8	177	30 Th	0353	5.6	171
	1116	0.3	9		1027	0.3	9
	1711	5.3	162		1621	5.4	165
	2334	0.1	3		2236	-0.4	-12

December

Day	Time (h m)	Height (ft)	Height (cm)	Day	Time (h m)	Height (ft)	Height (cm)
1 F	0447	6.1	186	16 Sa	0604	5.5	168
	1120	-0.1	-3		1220	0.2	6
	1714	5.5	168		1811	4.6	140
	2326	-0.7	-21				
2 Sa	0539	6.5	198	17 Su	0023	0.0	0
	1213	-0.4	-12		0642	5.6	171
	1807	5.7	174		1259	0.1	3
					1850	4.6	140
3 Su ○	0017	-1.0	-30	18 M ●	0101	0.0	0
	0630	6.8	207		0719	5.6	171
	1305	-0.6	-18		1337	0.1	3
	1858	5.8	177		1927	4.6	140
4 M	0108	-1.1	-34	19 Tu	0138	0.0	0
	0721	6.9	210		0755	5.5	168
	1357	-0.7	-21		1415	0.1	3
	1950	5.7	174		2003	4.5	137
5 Tu	0200	-1.1	-34	20 W	0216	0.1	3
	0813	6.9	210		0832	5.4	165
	1450	-0.7	-21		1453	0.2	6
	2044	5.6	171		2039	4.3	131
6 W	0254	-1.0	-30	21 Th	0254	0.2	6
	0907	6.7	204		0910	5.2	158
	1544	-0.5	-15		1531	0.2	6
	2143	5.4	165		2117	4.2	128
7 Th	0348	-0.7	-21	22 F	0333	0.3	9
	1006	6.3	192		0950	5.0	152
	1639	-0.3	-9		1610	0.3	9
	2246	5.2	158		2200	4.1	125
8 F	0445	-0.4	-12	23 Sa	0413	0.5	15
	1108	5.9	180		1034	4.9	149
	1736	-0.1	-3		1650	0.4	12
	2351	5.1	155		2248	4.1	125
9 Sa	0546	0.0	0	24 Su	0456	0.6	18
	1210	5.6	171		1121	4.7	143
	1837	0.1	3		1733	0.4	12
					2340	4.2	128
10 Su ○	0054	5.1	155	25 M	0545	0.7	21
	0652	0.3	9		1211	4.7	143
	1310	5.3	162		1820	0.3	9
	1941	0.2	6				
11 M	0154	5.1	155	26 Tu ◖	0034	4.4	134
	0802	0.4	12		0643	0.7	21
	1406	5.0	152		1304	4.6	140
	2042	0.2	6		1914	0.2	6
12 Tu	0251	5.2	158	27 W	0130	4.7	143
	0908	0.5	15		0749	0.7	21
	1501	4.8	146		1358	4.7	143
	2136	0.2	6		2012	0.0	0
13 W	0345	5.3	162	28 Th	0226	5.1	155
	1005	0.4	12		0858	0.4	12
	1554	4.7	143		1454	4.8	146
	2223	0.1	3		2111	-0.3	-9
14 Th	0435	5.3	162	29 F	0324	5.4	165
	1055	0.4	12		1001	0.1	3
	1644	4.6	140		1553	4.9	149
	2305	0.1	3		2208	-0.6	-18
15 F	0522	5.4	165	30 Sa	0422	5.9	180
	1139	0.3	9		1100	-0.3	-9
	1730	4.6	140		1651	5.1	155
	2345	0.0	0		2303	-1.0	-30
				31 Su	0519	6.3	192
					1155	-0.6	-18
					1748	5.3	162
					2358	-1.3	-40

Time meridian 75° W. 0000 is midnight. 1200 is noon. Times are not adjusted for Daylight Saving Time.
Heights are referred to mean lower low water which is the chart datum of soundings.

Charleston, South Carolina, 2017

Times and Heights of High and Low Waters

January

Day	Time	Height (ft)	Height (cm)
1 Su	0321	-0.1	-3
	0942	5.6	171
	1606	-0.1	-3
	2150	4.8	146
2 M	0404	-0.1	-3
	1021	5.5	168
	1648	-0.1	-3
	2234	4.8	146
3 Tu	0452	0.0	0
	1105	5.4	165
	1735	-0.1	-3
	2325	4.9	149
4 W	0546	0.1	3
	1156	5.2	158
	1826	-0.1	-3
5 Th ◖	0022	5.0	152
	0647	0.2	6
	1253	5.1	155
	1922	-0.2	-6
6 F	0126	5.2	158
	0755	0.3	9
	1357	5.0	152
	2022	-0.3	-9
7 Sa	0233	5.4	165
	0905	0.2	6
	1503	5.0	152
	2123	-0.5	-15
8 Su	0340	5.7	174
	1012	-0.1	-3
	1609	5.0	152
	2224	-0.8	-24
9 M	0444	6.0	183
	1114	-0.3	-9
	1711	5.1	155
	2322	-1.0	-30
10 Tu	0545	6.3	192
	1212	-0.6	-18
	1810	5.3	162
11 W	0018	-1.2	-37
	0641	6.4	195
	1306	-0.8	-24
	1906	5.4	165
12 Th ○	0112	-1.3	-40
	0734	6.5	198
	1357	-0.8	-24
	1959	5.4	165
13 F	0203	-1.2	-37
	0825	6.4	195
	1446	-0.8	-24
	2050	5.4	165
14 Sa	0253	-1.1	-34
	0913	6.2	189
	1533	-0.7	-21
	2139	5.3	162
15 Su	0342	-0.8	-24
	0959	5.9	180
	1619	-0.5	-15
	2228	5.2	158
16 M	0431	-0.5	-15
	1044	5.6	171
	1705	-0.2	-6
	2317	5.0	152
17 Tu	0521	-0.1	-3
	1129	5.2	158
	1750	0.0	0
18 W	0007	4.9	149
	0612	0.3	9
	1214	4.9	149
	1836	0.2	6
19 Th ◐	0058	4.7	143
	0706	0.5	15
	1303	4.6	140
	1924	0.4	12
20 F	0151	4.7	143
	0802	0.7	21
	1354	4.4	134
	2014	0.5	15
21 Sa	0246	4.7	143
	0859	0.7	21
	1448	4.3	131
	2106	0.5	15
22 Su	0340	4.8	146
	0955	0.7	21
	1542	4.3	131
	2157	0.4	12
23 M	0432	5.0	152
	1047	0.5	15
	1634	4.4	134
	2247	0.2	6
24 Tu	0521	5.2	158
	1134	0.3	9
	1724	4.5	137
	2333	0.0	0
25 W	0607	5.4	165
	1219	0.1	3
	1810	4.6	140
26 Th	0017	-0.2	-6
	0651	5.5	168
	1301	-0.1	-3
	1854	4.8	146
27 F ●	0100	-0.3	-9
	0731	5.7	174
	1341	-0.3	-9
	1934	4.9	149
28 Sa	0141	-0.5	-15
	0810	5.7	174
	1421	-0.4	-12
	2013	5.0	152
29 Su	0223	-0.5	-15
	0847	5.7	174
	1501	-0.5	-15
	2053	5.1	155
30 M	0306	-0.5	-15
	0924	5.7	174
	1542	-0.5	-15
	2134	5.2	158
31 Tu	0351	-0.5	-15
	1004	5.6	171
	1625	-0.5	-15
	2218	5.2	158

February

Day	Time	Height (ft)	Height (cm)
1 W	0440	-0.3	-9
	1048	5.4	165
	1711	-0.5	-15
	2308	5.3	162
2 Th	0534	-0.2	-6
	1138	5.2	158
	1802	-0.5	-15
3 F ◐	0004	5.3	162
	0634	0.0	0
	1235	4.9	149
	1858	-0.4	-12
4 Sa	0107	5.3	162
	0740	0.1	3
	1339	4.8	146
	1959	-0.4	-12
5 Su	0215	5.4	165
	0849	0.1	3
	1447	4.7	143
	2103	-0.5	-15
6 M	0325	5.5	168
	0957	0.0	0
	1555	4.8	146
	2207	-0.6	-18
7 Tu	0432	5.7	174
	1059	-0.2	-6
	1659	4.9	149
	2308	-0.8	-24
8 W	0533	5.9	180
	1156	-0.4	-12
	1758	5.1	155
9 Th	0005	-1.0	-30
	0628	6.1	186
	1249	-0.6	-18
	1853	5.3	162
10 F ○	0057	-1.1	-34
	0719	6.1	186
	1337	-0.7	-21
	1943	5.4	165
11 Sa	0147	-1.1	-34
	0806	6.1	186
	1423	-0.7	-21
	2030	5.5	168
12 Su	0235	-1.0	-30
	0849	5.9	180
	1506	-0.6	-18
	2115	5.4	165
13 M	0321	-0.7	-21
	0931	5.7	174
	1548	-0.4	-12
	2158	5.3	162
14 Tu	0405	-0.4	-12
	1010	5.4	165
	1627	-0.2	-6
	2241	5.2	158
15 W	0450	-0.1	-3
	1050	5.1	155
	1706	0.1	3
	2324	5.0	152
16 Th	0535	0.2	6
	1132	4.8	146
	1746	0.3	9
17 F	0010	4.8	146
	0623	0.5	15
	1216	4.5	137
	1828	0.5	15
18 Sa ◐	0059	4.7	143
	0715	0.7	21
	1306	4.3	131
	1917	0.6	18
19 Su	0154	4.7	143
	0811	0.9	27
	1400	4.2	128
	2011	0.7	21
20 M	0251	4.7	143
	0909	0.8	24
	1458	4.2	128
	2109	0.6	18
21 Tu	0349	4.8	146
	1005	0.7	21
	1555	4.3	131
	2206	0.5	15
22 W	0443	5.0	152
	1056	0.5	15
	1649	4.5	137
	2259	0.2	6
23 Th	0533	5.3	162
	1144	0.2	6
	1739	4.7	143
	2349	-0.1	-3
24 F	0619	5.5	168
	1229	-0.1	-3
	1825	5.0	152
25 Sa	0035	-0.4	-12
	0702	5.7	174
	1311	-0.4	-12
	1908	5.2	158
26 Su ●	0121	-0.6	-18
	0744	5.8	177
	1353	-0.6	-18
	1951	5.5	168
27 M	0206	-0.7	-21
	0824	5.9	180
	1435	-0.7	-21
	2033	5.7	174
28 Tu	0252	-0.8	-24
	0905	5.8	177
	1518	-0.8	-24
	2117	5.8	177

March

Day	Time	Height (ft)	Height (cm)
1 W	0339	-0.7	-21
	0948	5.7	174
	1602	-0.8	-24
	2203	5.8	177
2 Th	0429	-0.5	-15
	1034	5.4	165
	1649	-0.7	-21
	2254	5.8	177
3 F	0523	-0.3	-9
	1126	5.2	158
	1741	-0.5	-15
	2351	5.7	174
4 Sa	0623	-0.1	-3
	1224	5.0	152
	1838	-0.4	-12
5 Su ◐	0054	5.6	171
	0727	0.1	3
	1329	4.8	146
	1941	-0.2	-6
6 M	0202	5.5	168
	0835	0.2	6
	1438	4.7	143
	2048	-0.2	-6
7 Tu	0312	5.5	168
	0941	0.1	3
	1546	4.8	146
	2153	-0.3	-9
8 W	0418	5.6	171
	1042	0.0	0
	1649	5.0	152
	2254	-0.4	-12
9 Th	0518	5.7	174
	1138	-0.2	-6
	1746	5.3	162
	2351	-0.6	-18
10 F	0611	5.8	177
	1228	-0.4	-12
	1837	5.5	168
11 Sa	0042	-0.7	-21
	0659	5.9	180
	1314	-0.5	-15
	1924	5.6	171
12 Su ○	0130	-0.7	-21
	0742	5.8	177
	1356	-0.5	-15
	2008	5.7	174
13 M	0215	-0.6	-18
	0822	5.7	174
	1436	-0.4	-12
	2048	5.7	174
14 Tu	0258	-0.5	-15
	0901	5.5	168
	1513	-0.2	-6
	2127	5.6	171
15 W	0339	-0.2	-6
	0938	5.3	162
	1549	0.0	0
	2205	5.5	168
16 Th	0420	0.0	0
	1015	5.0	152
	1624	0.2	6
	2244	5.3	162
17 F	0501	0.3	9
	1054	4.7	143
	1700	0.5	15
	2324	5.1	155
18 Sa	0544	0.6	18
	1135	4.5	137
	1739	0.7	21
19 Su	0009	4.9	149
	0631	0.8	24
	1222	4.4	134
	1824	0.8	24
20 M ◐	0101	4.8	146
	0724	0.9	27
	1315	4.3	131
	1918	0.9	27
21 Tu	0158	4.8	146
	0821	0.9	27
	1413	4.3	131
	2020	0.9	27
22 W	0259	4.9	149
	0919	0.8	24
	1513	4.4	134
	2123	0.7	21
23 Th	0357	5.0	152
	1014	0.6	18
	1610	4.7	143
	2223	0.4	12
24 F	0451	5.3	162
	1104	0.3	9
	1703	5.0	152
	2318	0.1	3
25 Sa	0541	5.5	168
	1152	-0.1	-3
	1753	5.4	165
26 Su	0009	-0.2	-6
	0628	5.7	174
	1238	-0.4	-12
	1840	5.7	174
27 M ●	0059	-0.5	-15
	0714	5.9	180
	1323	-0.7	-21
	1926	6.1	186
28 Tu	0148	-0.7	-21
	0759	5.9	180
	1408	-0.9	-27
	2013	6.3	192
29 W	0237	-0.8	-24
	0845	5.9	180
	1453	-0.9	-27
	2100	6.4	195
30 Th	0327	-0.8	-24
	0932	5.7	174
	1540	-0.9	-27
	2150	6.4	195
31 F	0419	-0.6	-18
	1022	5.5	168
	1630	-0.7	-21
	2242	6.3	192

Time meridian 75° W. 0000 is midnight. 1200 is noon. Times are not adjusted for Daylight Saving Time.
Heights are referred to mean lower low water which is the chart datum of soundings.

Charleston, South Carolina, 2017
Times and Heights of High and Low Waters

April

Day	Time (h m)	Height (ft)	Height (cm)	Day	Time (h m)	Height (ft)	Height (cm)
1 Sa	0513	-0.4	-12	16 Su	0512	0.6	18
	1117	5.3	162		1101	4.6	140
	1724	-0.5	-15		1659	0.7	21
	2340	6.1	186		2327	5.2	158
2 Su	0612	-0.1	-3	17 M	0555	0.7	21
	1217	5.1	155		1145	4.4	134
	1823	-0.2	-6		1744	0.9	27
3 M	0043	5.8	177	18 Tu	0014	5.1	155
	0715	0.1	3		0644	0.8	24
	1322	4.9	149		1235	4.4	134
	1926	0.0	0		1836	1.0	30
4 Tu	0149	5.6	171	19 W	0108	5.0	152
	0819	0.2	6		0737	0.8	24
	1429	4.9	149		1332	4.5	137
	2033	0.1	3		1937	0.9	27
5 W	0256	5.5	168	20 Th	0207	5.0	152
	0922	0.2	6		0833	0.7	21
	1534	5.1	155		1431	4.6	140
	2138	0.1	3		2042	0.8	24
6 Th	0359	5.5	168	21 F	0307	5.1	155
	1021	0.1	3		0929	0.5	15
	1634	5.3	162		1530	4.9	149
	2239	0.0	0		2147	0.6	18
7 F	0456	5.5	168	22 Sa	0405	5.3	162
	1114	0.0	0		1023	0.2	6
	1729	5.5	168		1626	5.3	162
	2334	-0.2	-6		2247	0.2	6
8 Sa	0546	5.6	171	23 Su	0459	5.5	168
	1202	-0.2	-6		1114	-0.2	-6
	1817	5.7	174		1720	5.8	177
					2343	-0.1	-3
9 Su	0024	-0.3	-9	24 M	0552	5.7	174
	0632	5.6	171		1204	-0.5	-15
	1245	-0.2	-6		1811	6.2	189
	1901	5.8	177				
10 M	0110	-0.3	-9	25 Tu	0037	-0.5	-15
	0714	5.5	168		0643	5.8	177
	1326	-0.2	-6		1252	-0.8	-24
	1942	5.9	180		1902	6.5	198
11 Tu	0154	-0.3	-9	26 W	0129	-0.7	-21
	0753	5.4	165		0733	5.8	177
	1403	-0.1	-3		1341	-1.0	-30
	2021	5.9	180		1953	6.8	207
12 W	0235	-0.2	-6	27 Th	0221	-0.8	-24
	0831	5.3	162		0824	5.8	177
	1439	0.0	0		1430	-1.0	-30
	2058	5.8	177		2044	6.8	207
13 Th	0314	0.0	0	28 F	0313	-0.8	-24
	0907	5.1	155		0916	5.7	174
	1513	0.2	6		1520	-0.9	-27
	2134	5.7	174		2136	6.8	207
14 F	0353	0.2	6	29 Sa	0407	-0.6	-18
	0944	4.9	149		1010	5.5	168
	1546	0.4	12		1613	-0.7	-21
	2210	5.5	168		2231	6.6	201
15 Sa	0432	0.4	12	30 Su	0502	-0.4	-12
	1021	4.7	143		1108	5.3	162
	1621	0.6	18		1709	-0.4	-12
	2247	5.3	162		2329	6.3	192

May

Day	Time (h m)	Height (ft)	Height (cm)	Day	Time (h m)	Height (ft)	Height (cm)
1 M	0559	-0.2	-6	16 Tu	0525	0.6	18
	1209	5.2	158		1115	4.5	137
	1808	-0.1	-3		1714	0.8	24
					2338	5.2	158
2 Tu	0030	6.0	183	17 W	0611	0.6	18
	0659	0.0	0		1202	4.5	137
	1312	5.1	155		1805	0.8	24
	1911	0.1	3				
3 W	0132	5.7	174	18 Th	0027	5.2	158
	0759	0.1	3		0700	0.5	15
	1416	5.1	155		1256	4.6	140
	2016	0.3	9		1903	0.8	24
4 Th	0233	5.5	168	19 F	0122	5.1	155
	0858	0.2	6		0754	0.4	12
	1517	5.2	158		1354	4.9	149
	2119	0.3	9		2008	0.7	21
5 F	0331	5.4	165	20 Sa	0221	5.2	158
	0954	0.1	3		0849	0.2	6
	1614	5.4	165		1453	5.2	158
	2218	0.3	9		2114	0.5	15
6 Sa	0425	5.3	162	21 Su	0321	5.3	162
	1044	0.0	0		0944	-0.1	-3
	1705	5.6	171		1552	5.6	171
	2312	0.2	6		2218	0.2	6
7 Su	0514	5.2	158	22 M	0419	5.4	165
	1130	0.0	0		1039	-0.4	-12
	1752	5.8	177		1649	6.0	183
					2318	-0.1	-3
8 M	0002	0.1	3	23 Tu	0517	5.5	168
	0559	5.2	158		1132	-0.7	-21
	1213	-0.1	-3		1745	6.5	198
	1835	5.9	180				
9 Tu	0047	0.0	0	24 W	0016	-0.4	-12
	0641	5.2	158		0613	5.6	171
	1253	0.0	0		1225	-1.0	-30
	1915	6.0	183		1840	6.8	207
10 W	0130	0.0	0	25 Th	0111	-0.7	-21
	0722	5.1	155		0709	5.6	171
	1330	0.0	0		1317	-1.1	-34
	1954	6.0	183		1934	6.9	210
11 Th	0211	0.0	0	26 F	0205	-0.8	-24
	0801	5.0	152		0804	5.6	171
	1406	0.1	3		1409	-1.1	-34
	2031	5.9	180		2028	7.0	213
12 F	0250	0.1	3	27 Sa	0259	-0.8	-24
	0839	4.9	149		0900	5.5	168
	1440	0.3	9		1502	-1.0	-30
	2107	5.8	177		2123	6.8	207
13 Sa	0328	0.2	6	28 Su	0352	-0.7	-21
	0916	4.7	143		0957	5.4	165
	1515	0.4	12		1557	-0.8	-24
	2142	5.6	171		2219	6.6	201
14 Su	0405	0.4	12	29 M	0446	-0.5	-15
	0954	4.6	140		1056	5.3	162
	1550	0.6	18		1653	-0.5	-15
	2217	5.5	168		2315	6.3	192
15 M	0444	0.5	15	30 Tu	0541	-0.3	-9
	1032	4.5	137		1155	5.2	158
	1629	0.7	21		1751	-0.2	-6
	2255	5.3	162				
				31 W	0012	5.9	180
					0637	-0.2	-6
					1255	5.2	158
					1852	0.1	3

June

Day	Time (h m)	Height (ft)	Height (cm)	Day	Time (h m)	Height (ft)	Height (cm)
1 Th	0108	5.6	171	16 F	0629	0.2	6
	0733	0.0	0		1226	4.8	146
	1355	5.2	158		1838	0.7	21
	1954	0.4	12				
2 F	0203	5.3	162	17 Sa	0047	5.2	158
	0828	0.1	3		0720	0.0	0
	1452	5.3	162		1323	5.1	155
	2054	0.5	15		1941	0.6	18
3 Sa	0257	5.1	155	18 Su	0144	5.2	158
	0920	0.1	3		0814	-0.1	-3
	1545	5.4	165		1422	5.4	165
	2152	0.5	15		2047	0.5	15
4 Su	0348	5.0	152	19 M	0245	5.2	158
	1009	0.1	3		0911	-0.4	-12
	1635	5.6	171		1523	5.8	177
	2246	0.4	12		2153	0.2	6
5 M	0436	4.9	149	20 Tu	0346	5.2	158
	1055	0.1	3		1008	-0.6	-18
	1722	5.7	174		1623	6.2	189
	2335	0.3	9		2257	-0.1	-3
6 Tu	0523	4.9	149	21 W	0448	5.3	162
	1138	0.1	3		1105	-0.8	-24
	1805	5.8	177		1723	6.5	198
					2356	-0.3	-9
7 W	0021	0.3	9	22 Th	0548	5.3	162
	0607	4.8	146		1201	-1.0	-30
	1219	0.1	3		1821	6.8	207
	1847	5.9	180				
8 Th	0104	0.2	6	23 F	0053	-0.6	-18
	0650	4.8	146		0648	5.4	165
	1258	0.1	3		1256	-1.1	-34
	1927	5.9	180		1918	6.9	210
9 F	0145	0.2	6	24 Sa	0148	-0.7	-21
	0732	4.7	143		0746	5.5	168
	1335	0.2	6		1351	-1.1	-34
	2006	5.9	180		2013	6.9	210
10 Sa	0224	0.2	6	25 Su	0242	-0.8	-24
	0812	4.7	143		0844	5.5	168
	1412	0.2	6		1445	-1.0	-30
	2043	5.8	177		2108	6.8	207
11 Su	0302	0.2	6	26 M	0334	-0.7	-21
	0851	4.6	140		0941	5.4	165
	1448	0.3	9		1540	-0.8	-24
	2119	5.7	174		2202	6.5	198
12 M	0340	0.3	9	27 Tu	0426	-0.6	-18
	0929	4.6	140		1038	5.4	165
	1526	0.4	12		1634	-0.5	-15
	2154	5.5	168		2254	6.2	189
13 Tu	0419	0.3	9	28 W	0518	-0.4	-12
	1007	4.5	137		1134	5.3	162
	1606	0.5	15		1730	-0.1	-3
	2230	5.4	165		2346	5.8	177
14 W	0459	0.3	9	29 Th	0610	-0.2	-6
	1048	4.6	140		1230	5.3	162
	1651	0.6	18		1827	0.2	6
	2310	5.4	165				
15 Th	0542	0.3	9	30 F	0037	5.5	168
	1134	4.7	143		0701	0.0	0
	1741	0.6	18		1325	5.2	158
	2355	5.3	162		1925	0.5	15

Time meridian 75° W. 0000 is midnight. 1200 is noon. Times are not adjusted for Daylight Saving Time.
Heights are referred to mean lower low water which is the chart datum of soundings.

Charleston, South Carolina, 2017

Times and Heights of High and Low Waters

July

Day	Time (h m)	Height (ft)	Height (cm)
1 Sa	0128	5.2	158
	0752	0.1	3
	1419	5.3	162
	2024	0.6	18
2 Su	0218	4.9	149
	0842	0.2	6
	1511	5.3	162
	2120	0.7	21
3 M	0308	4.8	146
	0930	0.2	6
	1601	5.4	165
	2214	0.7	21
4 Tu	0358	4.7	143
	1017	0.2	6
	1648	5.6	171
	2304	0.6	18
5 W	0446	4.6	140
	1102	0.2	6
	1734	5.7	174
	2351	0.5	15
6 Th	0534	4.7	143
	1145	0.2	6
	1818	5.8	177
7 F	0035	0.4	12
	0619	4.7	143
	1227	0.2	6
	1900	5.8	177
8 Sa ○	0116	0.3	9
	0703	4.7	143
	1307	0.2	6
	1941	5.8	177
9 Su	0157	0.2	6
	0746	4.7	143
	1347	0.2	6
	2019	5.8	177
10 M	0235	0.2	6
	0826	4.7	143
	1426	0.2	6
	2056	5.8	177
11 Tu	0314	0.2	6
	0904	4.7	143
	1505	0.3	9
	2131	5.7	174
12 W	0352	0.1	3
	0943	4.8	146
	1547	0.3	9
	2207	5.6	171
13 Th	0432	0.1	3
	1024	4.9	149
	1632	0.4	12
	2246	5.5	168
14 F	0515	0.0	0
	1110	5.0	152
	1723	0.5	15
	2330	5.4	165
15 Sa	0601	0.0	0
	1201	5.2	158
	1819	0.5	15
16 Su ◗	0021	5.3	162
	0651	-0.1	-3
	1258	5.4	165
	1921	0.5	15
17 M	0118	5.2	158
	0746	-0.2	-6
	1358	5.7	174
	2027	0.5	15
18 Tu	0220	5.1	155
	0845	-0.4	-12
	1501	6.0	183
	2134	0.3	9
19 W	0324	5.1	155
	0945	-0.5	-15
	1604	6.2	189
	2238	0.1	3
20 Th	0428	5.2	158
	1045	-0.7	-21
	1706	6.5	198
	2339	-0.1	-3
21 F	0530	5.3	162
	1143	-0.9	-27
	1806	6.7	204
22 Sa	0036	-0.4	-12
	0631	5.4	165
	1240	-1.0	-30
	1903	6.8	207
23 Su ●	0130	-0.5	-15
	0729	5.5	168
	1335	-1.0	-30
	1957	6.8	207
24 M	0222	-0.6	-18
	0826	5.6	171
	1428	-0.9	-27
	2049	6.6	201
25 Tu	0312	-0.6	-18
	0920	5.6	171
	1521	-0.6	-18
	2139	6.4	195
26 W	0401	-0.4	-12
	1013	5.6	171
	1613	-0.3	-9
	2227	6.1	186
27 Th	0448	-0.2	-6
	1106	5.5	168
	1705	0.0	0
	2314	5.7	174
28 F	0535	0.0	0
	1157	5.4	165
	1758	0.4	12
29 Sa	0001	5.4	165
	0622	0.2	6
	1249	5.3	162
	1852	0.7	21
30 Su ◖	0048	5.1	155
	0710	0.4	12
	1340	5.3	162
	1947	0.9	27
31 M	0137	4.9	149
	0758	0.5	15
	1431	5.3	162
	2043	1.0	30

August

Day	Time (h m)	Height (ft)	Height (cm)
1 Tu	0228	4.7	143
	0847	0.6	18
	1522	5.4	165
	2137	1.0	30
2 W	0319	4.6	140
	0937	0.6	18
	1612	5.5	168
	2229	0.9	27
3 Th	0410	4.7	143
	1025	0.5	15
	1701	5.6	171
	2317	0.8	24
4 F	0501	4.7	143
	1112	0.4	12
	1747	5.8	177
5 Sa	0002	0.6	18
	0549	4.8	146
	1157	0.3	9
	1831	5.9	180
6 Su	0045	0.4	12
	0634	4.9	149
	1240	0.2	6
	1913	6.0	183
7 M ○	0126	0.3	9
	0718	5.0	152
	1322	0.2	6
	1952	6.0	183
8 Tu	0205	0.2	6
	0759	5.1	155
	1404	0.2	6
	2030	6.0	183
9 W	0244	0.1	3
	0838	5.2	158
	1446	0.2	6
	2107	5.9	180
10 Th	0324	0.0	0
	0918	5.3	162
	1530	0.2	6
	2144	5.8	177
11 F	0405	0.0	0
	1001	5.4	165
	1617	0.3	9
	2225	5.7	174
12 Sa	0448	-0.1	-3
	1048	5.6	171
	1708	0.4	12
	2311	5.6	171
13 Su	0535	-0.1	-3
	1140	5.7	174
	1804	0.5	15
14 M ◖	0003	5.4	165
	0627	-0.1	-3
	1238	5.8	177
	1906	0.6	18
15 Tu	0101	5.3	162
	0724	-0.1	-3
	1341	5.9	180
	2012	0.6	18
16 W	0205	5.2	158
	0825	-0.1	-3
	1446	6.1	186
	2119	0.5	15
17 Th	0311	5.2	158
	0928	-0.2	-6
	1551	6.3	192
	2223	0.3	9
18 F	0416	5.3	162
	1030	-0.4	-12
	1654	6.5	198
	2322	0.1	3
19 Sa	0519	5.5	168
	1129	-0.5	-15
	1752	6.6	201
20 Su	0018	-0.1	-3
	0618	5.7	174
	1226	-0.6	-18
	1847	6.7	204
21 M ●	0109	-0.3	-9
	0713	5.8	177
	1319	-0.6	-18
	1938	6.7	204
22 Tu	0158	-0.3	-9
	0806	5.9	180
	1410	-0.5	-15
	2026	6.5	198
23 W	0245	-0.3	-9
	0856	5.9	180
	1500	-0.3	-9
	2111	6.3	192
24 Th	0330	-0.1	-3
	0944	5.9	180
	1549	0.0	0
	2155	6.0	183
25 F	0413	0.1	3
	1031	5.8	177
	1637	0.3	9
	2238	5.7	174
26 Sa	0456	0.3	9
	1118	5.6	171
	1725	0.7	21
	2322	5.4	165
27 Su	0539	0.6	18
	1206	5.5	168
	1815	1.0	30
28 M	0007	5.1	155
	0623	0.8	24
	1256	5.4	165
	1907	1.2	37
29 Tu ◖	0056	4.9	149
	0710	0.9	27
	1347	5.4	165
	2002	1.3	40
30 W	0147	4.8	146
	0801	1.0	30
	1441	5.4	165
	2056	1.3	40
31 Th	0241	4.7	143
	0854	1.0	30
	1533	5.5	168
	2149	1.2	37

September

Day	Time (h m)	Height (ft)	Height (cm)
1 F	0335	4.8	146
	0948	0.9	27
	1625	5.6	171
	2239	1.0	30
2 Sa	0428	5.0	152
	1039	0.8	24
	1713	5.8	177
	2326	0.8	24
3 Su	0517	5.1	155
	1127	0.6	18
	1758	6.0	183
4 M	0010	0.6	18
	0604	5.3	162
	1213	0.4	12
	1841	6.1	186
5 Tu	0052	0.4	12
	0648	5.5	168
	1258	0.2	6
	1922	6.2	189
6 W ○	0133	0.2	6
	0730	5.7	174
	1343	0.1	3
	2001	6.2	189
7 Th	0213	0.0	0
	0812	5.9	180
	1428	0.1	3
	2041	6.2	189
8 F	0255	-0.1	-3
	0855	6.1	186
	1514	0.2	6
	2122	6.1	186
9 Sa	0338	-0.1	-3
	0940	6.2	189
	1603	0.3	9
	2206	5.9	180
10 Su	0424	-0.1	-3
	1029	6.2	189
	1655	0.4	12
	2255	5.7	174
11 M	0513	0.0	0
	1123	6.2	189
	1752	0.6	18
	2350	5.5	168
12 Tu	0607	0.1	3
	1223	6.2	189
	1854	0.7	21
13 W ◗	0052	5.4	165
	0707	0.2	6
	1329	6.2	189
	2000	0.8	24
14 Th	0158	5.3	162
	0811	0.2	6
	1436	6.2	189
	2106	0.7	21
15 F	0306	5.4	165
	0916	0.1	3
	1541	6.3	192
	2208	0.5	15
16 Sa	0410	5.6	171
	1019	0.0	0
	1642	6.4	195
	2305	0.3	9
17 Su	0510	5.8	177
	1117	-0.1	-3
	1737	6.5	198
	2358	0.1	3
18 M	0605	6.0	183
	1212	-0.2	-6
	1828	6.6	201
19 Tu	0047	0.0	0
	0656	6.2	189
	1303	-0.2	-6
	1915	6.5	198
20 W ●	0132	0.0	0
	0744	6.3	192
	1352	-0.1	-3
	1959	6.4	195
21 Th	0216	0.0	0
	0829	6.3	192
	1438	0.0	0
	2041	6.1	186
22 F	0257	0.2	6
	0913	6.2	189
	1523	0.3	9
	2121	5.9	180
23 Sa	0336	0.4	12
	0955	6.0	183
	1607	0.6	18
	2201	5.6	171
24 Su	0415	0.6	18
	1037	5.9	180
	1651	0.9	27
	2242	5.3	162
25 M	0453	0.9	27
	1122	5.7	174
	1737	1.2	37
	2326	5.1	155
26 Tu	0534	1.1	34
	1209	5.5	168
	1825	1.4	43
27 W ◖	0014	4.9	149
	0620	1.3	40
	1300	5.4	165
	1917	1.5	46
28 Th	0106	4.8	146
	0712	1.3	40
	1355	5.4	165
	2012	1.5	46
29 F	0202	4.8	146
	0809	1.3	40
	1450	5.5	168
	2106	1.4	43
30 Sa	0258	4.9	149
	0907	1.2	37
	1543	5.6	171
	2158	1.2	37

Time meridian 75° W. 0000 is midnight. 1200 is noon. Times are not adjusted for Daylight Saving Time.
Heights are referred to mean lower low water which is the chart datum of soundings.

Charleston, South Carolina, 2017

Times and Heights of High and Low Waters

October

Day	Time	ft	cm		Day	Time	ft	cm
1 Su	0352	5.1	155		**16** M	0458	6.0	183
	1003	1.0	30			1104	0.2	6
	1634	5.8	177			1717	6.2	189
	2246	0.9	27			2335	0.2	6
2 M	0443	5.4	165		**17** Tu	0550	6.2	189
	1056	0.8	24			1157	0.1	3
	1721	6.0	183			1805	6.2	189
	2332	0.6	18					
3 Tu	0532	5.7	174		**18** W	0022	0.1	3
	1146	0.5	15			0637	6.3	192
	1805	6.2	189			1246	0.1	3
						1849	6.1	186
4 W	0016	0.3	9		**19** Th	0105	0.1	3
	0617	6.0	183			0721	6.4	195
	1234	0.2	6			1332	0.1	3
	1849	6.3	192		●	1931	6.0	183
5 Th	0059	0.0	0		**20** F	0145	0.2	6
	0702	6.3	192			0803	6.4	195
	1322	0.1	3			1415	0.2	6
O	1932	6.3	192			2010	5.8	177
6 F	0143	-0.2	-6		**21** Sa	0223	0.3	9
	0747	6.6	201			0842	6.3	192
	1410	0.0	0			1457	0.4	12
	2015	6.3	192			2049	5.6	171
7 Sa	0227	-0.3	-9		**22** Su	0300	0.5	15
	0833	6.7	204			0921	6.1	186
	1459	0.0	0			1538	0.6	18
	2101	6.1	186			2127	5.4	165
8 Su	0313	-0.3	-9		**23** M	0336	0.7	21
	0921	6.7	204			1000	5.9	180
	1549	0.1	3			1619	0.9	27
	2149	5.9	180			2207	5.2	158
9 M	0402	-0.2	-6		**24** Tu	0412	0.9	27
	1013	6.7	204			1041	5.7	174
	1643	0.3	9			1701	1.1	34
	2243	5.7	174			2248	5.0	152
10 Tu	0454	0.0	0		**25** W	0451	1.1	34
	1110	6.5	198			1124	5.6	171
	1741	0.5	15			1745	1.3	40
	2341	5.5	168			2333	4.8	146
11 W	0551	0.1	3		**26** Th	0534	1.3	40
	1212	6.4	195			1212	5.4	165
	1842	0.7	21			1833	1.4	43
12 Th	0046	5.4	165		**27** F	0024	4.8	146
	0653	0.3	9			0625	1.4	43
	1318	6.3	192			1305	5.3	162
◗	1947	0.7	21		☾	1925	1.4	43
13 F	0153	5.4	165		**28** Sa	0119	4.8	146
	0759	0.4	12			0723	1.4	43
	1424	6.2	189			1401	5.4	165
	2050	0.7	21			2019	1.2	37
14 Sa	0300	5.5	168		**29** Su	0217	4.9	149
	0905	0.4	12			0824	1.3	40
	1527	6.2	189			1456	5.5	168
	2150	0.5	15			2113	1.0	30
15 Su	0402	5.7	174		**30** M	0313	5.2	158
	1007	0.3	9			0926	1.1	34
	1625	6.2	189			1549	5.6	171
	2245	0.4	12			2204	0.7	21
					31 Tu	0407	5.5	168
						1024	0.8	24
						1640	5.8	177
						2253	0.3	9

November

Day	Time	ft	cm		Day	Time	ft	cm
1 W	0458	5.9	180		**16** Th	0616	6.2	189
	1118	0.4	12			1226	0.2	6
	1728	6.0	183			1822	5.6	171
	2341	0.0	0					
2 Th	0547	6.3	192		**17** F	0036	0.1	3
	1211	0.1	3			0658	6.2	189
	1816	6.1	186			1311	0.2	6
						1903	5.5	168
3 F	0028	-0.3	-9		**18** Sa	0116	0.1	3
	0636	6.7	204			0738	6.2	189
	1302	-0.1	-3			1353	0.2	6
	1904	6.1	186		●	1943	5.4	165
4 Sa	0115	-0.5	-15		**19** Su	0153	0.2	6
	0725	6.9	210			0816	6.1	186
	1352	-0.3	-9			1433	0.3	9
O	1952	6.1	186			2021	5.2	158
5 Su	0203	-0.6	-18		**20** M	0229	0.3	9
	0814	7.0	213			0853	6.0	183
	1443	-0.3	-9			1512	0.4	12
	2042	6.0	183			2059	5.1	155
6 M	0252	-0.6	-18		**21** Tu	0304	0.5	15
	0906	7.0	213			0930	5.8	177
	1536	-0.2	-6			1550	0.6	18
	2135	5.8	177			2136	4.9	149
7 Tu	0343	-0.5	-15		**22** W	0339	0.7	21
	1000	6.9	210			1007	5.6	171
	1630	0.0	0			1629	0.8	24
	2231	5.7	174			2215	4.8	146
8 W	0438	-0.3	-9		**23** Th	0417	0.8	24
	1058	6.6	201			1046	5.5	168
	1727	0.2	6			1709	0.9	27
	2332	5.5	168			2256	4.7	143
9 Th	0536	0.0	0		**24** F	0458	0.9	27
	1159	6.4	195			1128	5.3	162
	1827	0.4	12			1753	0.9	27
						2342	4.6	140
10 F	0037	5.4	165		**25** Sa	0546	1.0	30
	0639	0.2	6			1215	5.2	158
	1303	6.1	186			1841	0.9	27
O	1928	0.5	15					
11 Sa	0143	5.4	165		**26** Su	0035	4.7	143
	0744	0.4	12			0641	1.1	34
	1406	5.9	180			1308	5.2	158
	2029	0.5	15		◗	1933	0.8	24
12 Su	0247	5.5	168		**27** M	0132	4.8	146
	0849	0.4	12			0743	1.0	30
	1506	5.8	177			1404	5.2	158
	2127	0.4	12			2027	0.6	18
13 M	0346	5.7	174		**28** Tu	0231	5.1	155
	0950	0.4	12			0849	0.9	27
	1601	5.7	174			1502	5.3	162
	2221	0.2	6			2122	0.3	9
14 Tu	0441	5.9	180		**29** W	0329	5.4	165
	1047	0.3	9			0952	0.6	18
	1652	5.7	174			1558	5.4	165
	2309	0.1	3			2216	0.0	0
15 W	0531	6.0	183		**30** Th	0425	5.9	180
	1139	0.2	6			1052	0.2	6
	1739	5.6	171			1653	5.5	168
	2354	0.1	3			2308	-0.4	-12

December

Day	Time	ft	cm		Day	Time	ft	cm
1 F	0520	6.3	192		**16** Sa	0008	0.0	0
	1148	-0.1	-3			0634	5.9	180
	1747	5.7	174			1248	0.1	3
						1837	5.0	152
2 Sa	0000	-0.7	-21		**17** Su	0048	0.0	0
	0613	6.7	204			0715	5.9	180
	1243	-0.4	-12			1329	0.1	3
	1840	5.7	174			1918	4.9	149
3 Su	0051	-1.0	-30		**18** M	0126	0.0	0
	0706	6.9	210			0753	5.9	180
	1336	-0.6	-18			1408	0.1	3
O	1933	5.8	177		●	1957	4.9	149
4 M	0142	-1.1	-34		**19** Tu	0203	0.1	3
	0759	7.0	213			0831	5.8	177
	1428	-0.6	-18			1446	0.1	3
	2026	5.8	177			2035	4.8	146
5 Tu	0234	-1.1	-34		**20** W	0238	0.1	3
	0853	6.9	210			0907	5.6	171
	1521	-0.6	-18			1523	0.2	6
	2121	5.7	174			2111	4.7	143
6 W	0327	-0.9	-27		**21** Th	0314	0.2	6
	0948	6.8	207			0941	5.5	168
	1614	-0.5	-15			1600	0.3	9
	2218	5.5	168			2147	4.6	140
7 Th	0422	-0.7	-21		**22** F	0351	0.4	12
	1044	6.5	198			1016	5.3	162
	1709	-0.3	-9			1637	0.4	12
	2318	5.4	165			2225	4.6	140
8 F	0520	-0.4	-12		**23** Sa	0431	0.5	15
	1141	6.1	186			1052	5.2	158
	1805	-0.1	-3			1718	0.4	12
						2306	4.6	140
9 Sa	0020	5.3	162		**24** Su	0516	0.6	18
	0620	-0.1	-3			1133	5.1	155
	1240	5.8	177			1802	0.4	12
	1903	0.1	3			2354	4.6	140
10 Su	0122	5.3	162		**25** M	0608	0.6	18
	0723	0.2	6			1222	5.0	152
	1339	5.5	168			1851	0.3	9
◗	2001	0.1	3					
11 M	0224	5.3	162		**26** Tu	0049	4.8	146
	0827	0.4	12			0709	0.6	18
	1436	5.3	162			1317	4.9	149
	2057	0.2	6		◖	1945	0.1	3
12 Tu	0322	5.4	165		**27** W	0150	5.0	152
	0928	0.4	12			0815	0.6	18
	1531	5.1	155			1418	4.9	149
	2151	0.1	3			2043	-0.1	-3
13 W	0417	5.5	168		**28** Th	0252	5.3	162
	1025	0.4	12			0923	0.4	12
	1622	5.0	152			1521	5.0	152
	2240	0.1	3			2142	-0.4	-12
14 Th	0506	5.7	174		**29** F	0355	5.7	174
	1116	0.3	9			1028	0.1	3
	1710	5.0	152			1622	5.1	155
	2326	0.0	0			2240	-0.7	-21
15 F	0552	5.8	177		**30** Sa	0456	6.1	186
	1204	0.2	6			1128	-0.3	-9
	1755	5.0	152			1722	5.2	158
						2336	-1.0	-30
					31 Su	0554	6.4	195
						1225	-0.6	-18
						1820	5.4	165

Time meridian 75° W. 0000 is midnight. 1200 is noon. Times are not adjusted for Daylight Saving Time.
Heights are referred to mean lower low water which is the chart datum of soundings.

Savannah River Entrance, Georgia, 2017

Times and Heights of High and Low Waters

January

Day	Time	ft	cm		Day	Time	ft	cm
1 Su	0345	-0.1	-3		16 M	0448	-0.5	-15
	0950	7.3	223			1052	7.3	223
	1625	-0.2	-6			1715	-0.3	-9
	2206	6.5	198			2326	6.6	201
2 M	0427	-0.1	-3		17 Tu	0535	0.0	0
	1032	7.1	216			1140	6.9	210
	1707	-0.1	-3			1758	0.1	3
	2252	6.5	198					
3 Tu	0512	0.1	3		18 W	0016	6.4	195
	1119	7.0	213			0623	0.4	12
	1752	-0.1	-3			1228	6.5	198
	2345	6.6	201			1843	0.4	12
4 W	0603	0.2	6		19 Th	0107	6.3	192
	1213	6.8	207			0716	0.8	24
	1843	-0.1	-3			1317	6.2	189
					○	1931	0.6	18
5 Th	0042	6.7	204		20 F	0157	6.2	189
	0702	0.4	12			0814	1.0	30
	1310	6.7	204			1407	5.9	180
◐	1940	-0.1	-3			2024	0.8	24
6 F	0142	6.9	210		21 Sa	0248	6.2	189
	0810	0.4	12			0913	1.1	34
	1410	6.6	201			1458	5.8	177
	2042	-0.3	-9			2118	0.8	24
7 Sa	0243	7.2	219		22 Su	0341	6.3	192
	0920	0.3	9			1009	1.0	30
	1512	6.6	201			1551	5.8	177
	2145	-0.5	-15			2212	0.6	18
8 Su	0346	7.5	229		23 M	0434	6.5	198
	1027	0.0	0			1101	0.8	24
	1616	6.7	204			1644	5.9	180
	2246	-0.8	-24			2302	0.4	12
9 M	0449	7.8	238		24 Tu	0526	6.7	204
	1129	-0.3	-9			1149	0.5	15
	1719	6.8	207			1735	6.0	183
	2344	-1.1	-34			2350	0.2	6
10 Tu	0549	8.1	247		25 W	0613	6.9	210
	1227	-0.6	-18			1235	0.2	6
	1818	7.0	213			1822	6.2	189
11 W	0040	-1.3	-40		26 Th	0036	-0.1	-3
	0646	8.3	253			0657	7.1	216
	1322	-0.9	-27			1318	-0.1	-3
	1914	7.2	219			1906	6.4	195
12 Th	0134	-1.5	-46		27 F	0120	-0.3	-9
	0739	8.4	256			0737	7.3	223
	1414	-1.0	-30			1400	-0.3	-9
○	2006	7.2	219		●	1946	6.6	201
13 F	0225	-1.5	-46		28 Sa	0203	-0.5	-15
	0829	8.3	253			0815	7.4	226
	1502	-1.0	-30			1441	-0.5	-15
	2056	7.2	219			2025	6.8	207
14 Sa	0315	-1.3	-40		29 Su	0246	-0.6	-18
	0917	8.1	247			0853	7.5	229
	1548	-0.9	-27			1522	-0.7	-21
	2146	7.0	213			2104	6.9	210
15 Su	0402	-1.0	-30		30 M	0328	-0.7	-21
	1005	7.7	235			0931	7.4	226
	1632	-0.6	-18			1602	-0.7	-21
	2235	6.8	207			2146	6.9	210
					31 Tu	0412	-0.6	-18
						1013	7.3	223
						1645	-0.7	-21
						2232	7.0	213

February

Day	Time	ft	cm		Day	Time	ft	cm
1 W	0458	-0.4	-12		16 Th	0546	0.4	12
	1101	7.1	216			1148	6.3	192
	1730	-0.6	-18			1755	0.4	12
	2324	7.0	213					
2 Th	0549	-0.2	-6		17 F	0021	6.3	192
	1153	6.8	207			0632	0.8	24
	1820	-0.5	-15			1235	6.0	183
						1837	0.7	21
3 F	0021	7.0	213		18 Sa	0110	6.2	189
	0646	0.1	3			0723	1.1	34
	1251	6.6	201			1324	5.8	177
◐	1916	-0.4	-12		○	1927	0.9	27
4 Sa	0122	7.1	216		19 Su	0201	6.1	186
	0752	0.3	9			0822	1.2	37
	1352	6.4	195			1416	5.7	174
	2019	-0.3	-9			2024	1.0	30
5 Su	0224	7.2	219		20 M	0255	6.1	186
	0903	0.3	9			0922	1.2	37
	1456	6.4	195			1510	5.7	174
	2125	-0.4	-12			2125	0.9	27
6 M	0329	7.3	223		21 Tu	0351	6.2	189
	1012	0.1	3			1019	1.0	30
	1601	6.4	195			1605	5.8	177
	2229	-0.6	-18			2223	0.7	21
7 Tu	0433	7.5	229		22 W	0446	6.5	198
	1115	-0.2	-6			1112	0.7	21
	1705	6.6	201			1659	6.0	183
	2329	-0.9	-27			2317	0.4	12
8 W	0536	7.7	235		23 Th	0539	6.8	207
	1212	-0.4	-12			1200	0.3	9
	1805	6.8	207			1750	6.3	192
9 Th	0026	-1.1	-34		24 F	0007	0.0	0
	0633	7.9	241			0626	7.1	216
	1305	-0.7	-21			1246	-0.1	-3
	1900	7.0	213			1836	6.7	204
10 F	0119	-1.2	-37		25 Sa	0055	-0.3	-9
	0724	8.0	244			0709	7.4	226
	1354	-0.9	-27			1331	-0.4	-12
○	1950	7.2	219			1920	7.0	213
11 Sa	0209	-1.3	-40		26 Su	0141	-0.6	-18
	0811	8.0	244			0750	7.6	232
	1440	-0.9	-27			1414	-0.7	-21
	2036	7.2	219		●	2001	7.3	223
12 Su	0256	-1.1	-34		27 M	0227	-0.9	-27
	0855	7.8	238			0830	7.7	235
	1522	-0.8	-24			1456	-1.0	-30
	2121	7.2	219			2043	7.5	229
13 M	0340	-0.9	-27		28 Tu	0312	-0.9	-27
	0937	7.5	229			0912	7.6	232
	1602	-0.6	-18			1539	-1.1	-34
	2204	7.0	213			2127	7.7	235
14 Tu	0422	-0.5	-15					
	1020	7.1	216					
	1640	-0.3	-9					
	2248	6.8	207					
15 W	0504	-0.1	-3					
	1103	6.7	204					
	1717	0.1	3					
	2334	6.5	198					

March

Day	Time	ft	cm		Day	Time	ft	cm
1 W	0358	-0.9	-27		16 Th	0434	0.0	0
	0956	7.5	229			1028	6.7	204
	1623	-1.0	-30			1639	0.3	9
	2214	7.7	235			2253	6.9	210
2 Th	0445	-0.7	-21		17 F	0513	0.4	12
	1045	7.2	219			1110	6.3	192
	1709	-0.9	-27			1714	0.6	18
	2307	7.6	232			2336	6.6	201
3 F	0537	-0.4	-12		18 Sa	0554	0.8	24
	1139	6.9	210			1155	6.1	186
	1800	-0.6	-18			1753	0.8	24
◐					○			
4 Sa	0004	7.5	229		19 Su	0023	6.4	195
	0634	0.0	0			0640	1.1	34
	1238	6.6	201			1244	5.9	180
	1857	-0.3	-9			1839	1.1	34
5 Su	0106	7.3	223		20 M	0114	6.3	192
	0738	0.3	9			0734	1.3	40
	1340	6.5	198			1336	5.8	177
◐	2001	-0.1	-3		○	1934	1.2	37
6 M	0209	7.2	219		21 Tu	0208	6.2	189
	0848	0.4	12			0834	1.3	40
	1444	6.4	195			1430	5.8	177
	2109	-0.1	-3			2038	1.2	37
7 Tu	0314	7.2	219		22 W	0305	6.3	192
	0956	0.3	9			0934	1.1	34
	1549	6.5	198			1525	6.0	183
	2215	-0.2	-6			2142	1.0	30
8 W	0419	7.3	223		23 Th	0402	6.5	198
	1058	0.1	3			1030	0.8	24
	1653	6.7	204			1620	6.3	192
	2316	-0.4	-12			2241	0.7	21
9 Th	0520	7.4	226		24 F	0457	6.8	207
	1154	-0.2	-6			1122	0.4	12
	1752	6.9	210			1714	6.7	204
						2336	0.2	6
10 F	0011	-0.7	-21		25 Sa	0549	7.1	216
	0615	7.6	232			1211	-0.1	-3
	1244	-0.4	-12			1804	7.1	216
	1844	7.2	219					
11 Sa	0103	-0.8	-24		26 Su	0028	-0.2	-6
	0704	7.7	235			0636	7.4	226
	1331	-0.5	-15			1258	-0.5	-15
	1931	7.4	226			1851	7.6	232
12 Su	0151	-0.8	-24		27 M	0118	-0.6	-18
	0748	7.7	235			0722	7.7	235
	1414	-0.6	-18			1344	-0.9	-27
○	2014	7.5	229		●	1936	8.0	244
13 M	0235	-0.8	-24		28 Tu	0207	-0.9	-27
	0829	7.5	229			0806	7.8	238
	1453	-0.5	-15			1430	-1.1	-34
	2054	7.4	226			2021	8.3	253
14 Tu	0317	-0.6	-18		29 W	0255	-1.0	-30
	0908	7.3	223			0851	7.8	238
	1530	-0.3	-9			1516	-1.2	-37
	2133	7.3	223			2108	8.4	256
15 W	0356	-0.3	-9		30 Th	0344	-1.0	-30
	0947	7.0	213			0939	7.6	232
	1604	0.0	0			1602	-1.1	-34
	2212	7.1	216			2158	8.4	256
					31 F	0433	-0.8	-24
						1030	7.3	223
						1651	-0.9	-27
						2252	8.1	247

Time meridian 75° W. 0000 is midnight. 1200 is noon. Times are not adjusted for Daylight Saving Time.
Heights are referred to mean lower low water which is the chart datum of soundings.

Savannah River Entrance, Georgia, 2017

Times and Heights of High and Low Waters

April

Day	Time (h m)	Height (ft)	Height (cm)
1 Sa	0525	-0.5	-15
	1127	7.0	213
	1743	-0.5	-15
	2351	7.9	241
2 Su	0622	-0.1	-3
	1228	6.8	207
	1840	-0.2	-6
3 M ●	0053	7.6	232
	0724	0.3	9
	1331	6.6	201
	1945	0.1	3
4 Tu	0156	7.4	226
	0832	0.4	12
	1435	6.6	201
	2054	0.2	6
5 W	0258	7.2	219
	0938	0.4	12
	1538	6.7	204
	2200	0.2	6
6 Th	0400	7.2	219
	1038	0.2	6
	1638	6.9	210
	2300	0.0	0
7 F	0458	7.2	219
	1130	0.0	0
	1734	7.1	216
	2354	-0.2	-6
8 Sa	0551	7.3	223
	1218	-0.1	-3
	1824	7.4	226
9 Su	0043	-0.3	-9
	0638	7.3	223
	1302	-0.2	-6
	1908	7.6	232
10 M	0129	-0.4	-12
	0721	7.3	223
	1343	-0.2	-6
	1948	7.7	235
11 Tu ○	0212	-0.3	-9
	0801	7.2	219
	1421	-0.1	-3
	2026	7.7	235
12 W	0253	-0.2	-6
	0839	7.1	216
	1457	0.0	0
	2103	7.6	232
13 Th	0331	0.0	0
	0917	6.8	207
	1531	0.2	6
	2139	7.4	226
14 F	0408	0.2	6
	0956	6.6	201
	1605	0.5	15
	2217	7.1	216
15 Sa	0444	0.5	15
	1036	6.3	192
	1640	0.7	21
	2257	6.9	210
16 Su	0523	0.7	21
	1120	6.1	186
	1718	0.9	27
	2342	6.6	201
17 M	0606	1.0	30
	1208	6.0	183
	1802	1.1	34
18 Tu	0031	6.5	198
	0655	1.1	34
	1259	5.9	180
	1854	1.3	40
19 W ◐	0124	6.4	195
	0751	1.2	37
	1352	6.0	183
	1956	1.3	40
20 Th	0220	6.5	198
	0850	1.0	30
	1446	6.2	189
	2102	1.1	34
21 F	0316	6.6	201
	0948	0.7	21
	1542	6.6	201
	2206	0.8	24
22 Sa	0413	6.9	210
	1043	0.3	9
	1637	7.1	216
	2305	0.3	9
23 Su	0508	7.1	216
	1134	-0.2	-6
	1730	7.6	232
24 M	0000	-0.1	-3
	0601	7.4	226
	1225	-0.6	-18
	1822	8.1	247
25 Tu	0054	-0.5	-15
	0652	7.6	232
	1314	-1.0	-30
	1911	8.6	262
26 W ●	0147	-0.9	-27
	0741	7.7	235
	1404	-1.2	-37
	2000	8.8	268
27 Th	0238	-1.0	-30
	0830	7.7	235
	1453	-1.3	-40
	2050	8.9	271
28 F	0329	-1.0	-30
	0922	7.6	232
	1543	-1.2	-37
	2142	8.7	265
29 Sa	0420	-0.9	-27
	1017	7.3	223
	1634	-0.9	-27
	2238	8.4	256
30 Su	0513	-0.6	-18
	1116	7.1	216
	1727	-0.5	-15
	2338	8.1	247

May

Day	Time (h m)	Height (ft)	Height (cm)
1 M	0608	-0.2	-6
	1219	6.9	210
	1825	-0.1	-3
2 Tu ○	0039	7.7	235
	0708	0.1	3
	1321	6.8	207
	1928	0.3	9
3 W	0139	7.4	226
	0812	0.3	9
	1422	6.8	207
	2035	0.5	15
4 Th	0238	7.2	219
	0914	0.3	9
	1520	6.9	210
	2140	0.5	15
5 F	0335	7.1	216
	1010	0.3	9
	1617	7.0	213
	2239	0.4	12
6 Sa	0429	7.0	213
	1101	0.2	6
	1709	7.2	219
	2331	0.2	6
7 Su	0520	6.9	210
	1147	0.1	3
	1757	7.5	229
8 M	0020	0.1	3
	0607	6.9	210
	1229	0.0	0
	1841	7.6	232
9 Tu	0105	0.0	0
	0650	6.9	210
	1310	0.0	0
	1921	7.7	235
10 W ○	0147	0.0	0
	0731	6.9	210
	1348	0.1	3
	1958	7.7	235
11 Th	0227	0.0	0
	0811	6.8	207
	1425	0.2	6
	2035	7.6	232
12 F	0306	0.1	3
	0849	6.6	201
	1501	0.4	12
	2111	7.4	226
13 Sa	0343	0.3	9
	0927	6.4	195
	1536	0.5	15
	2147	7.2	219
14 Su	0420	0.4	12
	1007	6.2	189
	1613	0.7	21
	2226	7.0	213
15 M	0458	0.6	18
	1049	6.1	186
	1651	0.9	27
	2308	6.8	207
16 Tu	0539	0.7	21
	1135	6.0	183
	1734	1.0	30
	2355	6.7	204
17 W	0624	0.8	24
	1225	6.0	183
	1824	1.1	34
18 Th ◐	0046	6.6	201
	0715	0.8	24
	1318	6.2	189
	1922	1.2	37
19 F	0140	6.7	204
	0812	0.6	18
	1412	6.5	198
	2027	1.0	30
20 Sa	0235	6.8	207
	0909	0.4	12
	1507	6.9	210
	2133	0.7	21
21 Su	0332	6.9	210
	1006	0.0	0
	1603	7.4	226
	2235	0.3	9
22 M	0430	7.1	216
	1100	-0.4	-12
	1659	7.9	241
	2335	-0.1	-3
23 Tu	0527	7.2	219
	1154	-0.8	-24
	1754	8.4	256
24 W	0032	-0.5	-15
	0623	7.4	226
	1247	-1.1	-34
	1848	8.8	268
25 Th ●	0127	-0.8	-24
	0717	7.5	229
	1340	-1.3	-40
	1940	9.0	274
26 F	0221	-1.0	-30
	0810	7.5	229
	1432	-1.3	-40
	2033	9.0	274
27 Sa	0314	-1.0	-30
	0905	7.4	226
	1525	-1.2	-37
	2127	8.8	268
28 Su	0406	-0.9	-27
	1002	7.2	219
	1617	-0.9	-27
	2224	8.5	259
29 M	0458	-0.7	-21
	1103	7.0	213
	1711	-0.6	-18
	2322	8.1	247
30 Tu	0551	-0.4	-12
	1204	6.9	210
	1807	-0.1	-3
31 W	0021	7.7	235
	0647	-0.1	-3
	1304	6.8	207
	1908	0.3	9

June

Day	Time (h m)	Height (ft)	Height (cm)
1 Th ●	0117	7.3	223
	0745	0.2	6
	1401	6.9	210
	2011	0.6	18
2 F	0211	7.0	213
	0842	0.3	9
	1456	6.9	210
	2114	0.7	21
3 Sa	0303	6.8	207
	0936	0.3	9
	1548	7.0	213
	2211	0.6	18
4 Su	0354	6.7	204
	1026	0.3	9
	1638	7.2	219
	2304	0.5	15
5 M	0444	6.6	201
	1111	0.2	6
	1725	7.3	223
	2352	0.4	12
6 Tu	0532	6.5	198
	1154	0.2	6
	1810	7.5	229
7 W	0037	0.3	9
	0618	6.5	198
	1235	0.2	6
	1852	7.6	232
8 Th	0119	0.2	6
	0701	6.5	198
	1315	0.2	6
	1932	7.6	232
9 F ○	0201	0.2	6
	0743	6.5	198
	1355	0.3	9
	2010	7.5	229
10 Sa	0240	0.2	6
	0822	6.4	195
	1433	0.3	9
	2047	7.4	226
11 Su	0318	0.2	6
	0901	6.3	192
	1511	0.4	12
	2123	7.3	223
12 M	0356	0.3	9
	0940	6.2	189
	1550	0.5	15
	2200	7.1	216
13 Tu	0434	0.3	9
	1021	6.1	186
	1629	0.7	21
	2240	6.9	210
14 W	0514	0.4	12
	1106	6.1	186
	1712	0.8	24
	2325	6.8	207
15 Th	0557	0.4	12
	1155	6.2	189
	1800	0.9	27
16 F ●	0014	6.8	207
	0645	0.3	9
	1247	6.5	198
	1856	0.9	27
17 Sa ○	0107	6.8	207
	0738	0.2	6
	1341	6.8	207
	1959	0.8	24
18 Su	0202	6.8	207
	0835	0.0	0
	1437	7.2	219
	2105	0.6	18
19 M	0300	6.8	207
	0933	-0.3	-9
	1534	7.6	232
	2210	0.3	9
20 Tu	0359	6.9	210
	1030	-0.6	-18
	1632	8.1	247
	2312	0.0	0
21 W	0459	7.0	213
	1127	-0.9	-27
	1730	8.4	256
22 Th	0011	-0.4	-12
	0558	7.2	219
	1223	-1.1	-34
	1827	8.7	265
23 F ●	0108	-0.7	-21
	0656	7.3	223
	1319	-1.3	-40
	1923	8.9	271
24 Sa ○	0204	-0.9	-27
	0752	7.3	223
	1414	-1.3	-40
	2017	8.9	271
25 Su	0257	-1.0	-30
	0848	7.3	223
	1507	-1.2	-37
	2111	8.7	265
26 M	0348	-0.9	-27
	0945	7.2	219
	1600	-0.9	-27
	2206	8.4	256
27 Tu	0438	-0.7	-21
	1044	7.1	216
	1652	-0.6	-18
	2301	8.0	244
28 W	0528	-0.5	-15
	1143	7.0	213
	1746	-0.1	-3
	2356	7.5	229
29 Th	0619	-0.2	-6
	1239	6.9	210
	1842	0.3	9
30 F ○	0049	7.2	219
	0711	0.1	3
	1333	6.9	210
	1941	0.7	21

Time meridian 75° W. 0000 is midnight. 1200 is noon. Times are not adjusted for Daylight Saving Time.
Heights are referred to mean lower low water which is the chart datum of soundings.

Savannah River Entrance, Georgia, 2017

Times and Heights of High and Low Waters

July

Day	Time (h m)	Height (ft)	Height (cm)
1 Sa	0139	6.8	207
	0803	0.3	9
	1424	6.9	210
	2041	0.9	27
2 Su	0229	6.6	201
	0856	0.4	12
	1513	6.9	210
	2138	0.9	27
3 M	0317	6.4	195
	0945	0.5	15
	1602	7.0	213
	2231	0.9	27
4 Tu	0407	6.3	192
	1032	0.4	12
	1651	7.2	219
	2319	0.7	21
5 W	0456	6.3	192
	1117	0.4	12
	1738	7.3	223
6 Th	0005	0.6	18
	0545	6.3	192
	1201	0.3	9
	1823	7.4	226
7 F	0049	0.5	15
	0631	6.4	195
	1244	0.3	9
	1905	7.5	229
8 Sa ○	0132	0.3	9
	0715	6.4	195
	1327	0.3	9
	1945	7.5	229
9 Su	0213	0.2	6
	0756	6.4	195
	1408	0.3	9
	2023	7.5	229
10 M	0253	0.2	6
	0835	6.4	195
	1449	0.3	9
	2100	7.4	226
11 Tu	0331	0.1	3
	0914	6.4	195
	1529	0.4	12
	2136	7.3	223
12 W	0410	0.1	3
	0955	6.4	195
	1610	0.4	12
	2215	7.2	219
13 Th	0450	0.1	3
	1039	6.5	198
	1653	0.5	15
	2259	7.1	216
14 F	0532	0.0	0
	1127	6.6	201
	1741	0.6	18
	2348	7.0	213
15 Sa	0618	0.0	0
	1220	6.9	210
	1835	0.7	21
16 Su ◑	0041	6.9	210
	0710	0.0	0
	1315	7.2	219
	1937	0.7	21
17 M	0137	6.8	207
	0807	-0.1	-3
	1412	7.5	229
	2043	0.6	18
18 Tu	0235	6.8	207
	0907	-0.3	-9
	1511	7.8	238
	2150	0.4	12
19 W	0336	6.9	210
	1007	-0.5	-15
	1611	8.1	247
	2253	0.1	3
20 Th	0438	6.9	210
	1107	-0.8	-24
	1712	8.4	256
	2353	-0.2	-6
21 F	0539	7.1	216
	1205	-1.0	-30
	1811	8.6	262
22 Sa	0051	-0.5	-15
	0639	7.2	219
	1302	-1.1	-34
	1907	8.7	265
23 Su ●	0145	-0.7	-21
	0736	7.4	226
	1357	-1.1	-34
	2001	8.7	265
24 M	0237	-0.8	-24
	0830	7.4	226
	1450	-1.0	-30
	2053	8.5	259
25 Tu	0327	-0.7	-21
	0924	7.4	226
	1541	-0.8	-24
	2144	8.2	250
26 W	0414	-0.6	-18
	1019	7.3	223
	1631	-0.4	-12
	2234	7.8	238
27 Th	0500	-0.3	-9
	1113	7.1	216
	1720	0.1	3
	2325	7.4	226
28 F	0545	0.0	0
	1206	7.0	213
	1811	0.5	15
29 Sa	0014	7.0	213
	0631	0.3	9
	1257	6.9	210
	1904	0.9	27
30 Su ◐	0103	6.7	204
	0719	0.6	18
	1347	6.9	210
	2001	1.2	37
31 M	0152	6.5	198
	0809	0.8	24
	1435	6.9	210
	2058	1.3	40

August

Day	Time (h m)	Height (ft)	Height (cm)
1 Tu	0241	6.3	192
	0901	0.9	27
	1524	7.0	213
	2152	1.3	40
2 W	0330	6.3	192
	0952	0.8	24
	1614	7.0	213
	2243	1.1	34
3 Th	0421	6.3	192
	1041	0.8	24
	1704	7.2	219
	2331	0.9	27
4 F	0512	6.4	195
	1128	0.6	18
	1752	7.3	223
5 Sa	0016	0.7	21
	0601	6.5	198
	1214	0.5	15
	1837	7.5	229
6 Su	0100	0.5	15
	0646	6.6	201
	1259	0.4	12
	1918	7.6	232
7 M ○	0143	0.3	9
	0728	6.8	207
	1343	0.3	9
	1957	7.7	235
8 Tu	0224	0.1	3
	0809	6.9	210
	1426	0.2	6
	2035	7.7	235
9 W	0304	0.0	0
	0848	7.0	213
	1509	0.2	6
	2112	7.6	232
10 Th	0344	-0.1	-3
	0929	7.1	216
	1552	0.2	6
	2152	7.5	229
11 F	0425	-0.1	-3
	1013	7.2	219
	1637	0.3	9
	2236	7.3	223
12 Sa	0508	-0.1	-3
	1103	7.3	223
	1725	0.5	15
	2326	7.2	219
13 Su	0554	-0.1	-3
	1157	7.4	226
	1819	0.6	18
14 M ◑	0021	7.0	213
	0646	0.0	0
	1254	7.6	232
	1920	0.8	24
15 Tu	0119	6.9	210
	0744	0.0	0
	1353	7.8	238
	2026	0.8	24
16 W	0219	6.9	210
	0847	0.0	0
	1454	8.0	244
	2134	0.7	21
17 Th	0321	6.9	210
	0950	-0.2	-6
	1556	8.1	247
	2238	0.4	12
18 F	0424	7.0	213
	1052	-0.4	-12
	1657	8.3	253
	2337	0.1	3
19 Sa	0526	7.2	219
	1150	-0.6	-18
	1756	8.5	259
20 Su	0033	-0.1	-3
	0625	7.5	229
	1247	-0.7	-21
	1851	8.6	262
21 M ●	0126	-0.3	-9
	0720	7.6	232
	1340	-0.7	-21
	1942	8.6	262
22 Tu	0215	-0.4	-12
	0811	7.7	235
	1432	-0.6	-18
	2030	8.4	256
23 W	0301	-0.4	-12
	0900	7.7	235
	1520	-0.4	-12
	2117	8.1	247
24 Th	0345	-0.2	-6
	0949	7.6	232
	1607	0.0	0
	2203	7.8	238
25 F	0427	0.0	0
	1037	7.4	226
	1652	0.4	12
	2249	7.4	226
26 Sa	0507	0.4	12
	1126	7.3	223
	1738	0.8	24
	2336	7.0	213
27 Su	0548	0.7	21
	1215	7.1	216
	1825	1.2	37
28 M	0025	6.7	204
	0631	1.0	30
	1305	7.0	213
	1917	1.5	46
29 Tu ◐	0114	6.5	198
	0719	1.3	40
	1354	6.9	210
	2013	1.7	52
30 W	0204	6.4	195
	0812	1.4	43
	1445	6.9	210
	2109	1.7	52
31 Th	0255	6.3	192
	0909	1.4	43
	1536	7.0	213
	2203	1.5	46

September

Day	Time (h m)	Height (ft)	Height (cm)
1 F	0347	6.4	195
	1003	1.2	37
	1627	7.2	219
	2253	1.3	40
2 Sa	0438	6.6	201
	1055	1.0	30
	1717	7.4	226
	2340	1.0	30
3 Su	0528	6.8	207
	1144	0.8	24
	1804	7.6	232
4 M	0026	0.7	21
	0615	7.1	216
	1232	0.5	15
	1848	7.8	238
5 Tu	0109	0.4	12
	0659	7.3	223
	1318	0.3	9
	1928	7.9	241
6 W ○	0152	0.1	3
	0741	7.6	232
	1403	0.2	6
	2008	8.0	244
7 Th	0235	-0.1	-3
	0822	7.8	238
	1449	0.1	3
	2047	8.0	244
8 F	0317	-0.2	-6
	0904	7.9	241
	1534	0.1	3
	2129	7.8	238
9 Sa	0400	-0.2	-6
	0950	8.0	244
	1621	0.2	6
	2216	7.6	232
10 Su	0445	-0.2	-6
	1041	8.0	244
	1711	0.4	12
	2308	7.4	226
11 M	0533	0.0	0
	1137	8.0	244
	1805	0.7	21
12 Tu	0006	7.2	219
	0627	0.1	3
	1237	8.0	244
	1906	0.9	27
13 W ◑	0107	7.1	216
	0727	0.3	9
	1339	8.0	244
	2013	1.0	30
14 Th	0209	7.0	213
	0832	0.3	9
	1441	8.1	247
	2120	0.9	27
15 F	0312	7.1	216
	0938	0.2	6
	1543	8.1	247
	2223	0.6	18
16 Sa	0415	7.3	223
	1040	0.1	3
	1644	8.3	253
	2321	0.4	12
17 Su	0515	7.5	229
	1138	-0.1	-3
	1741	8.4	256
18 M	0014	0.1	3
	0611	7.8	238
	1232	-0.2	-6
	1833	8.4	256
19 Tu	0103	0.0	0
	0703	8.0	244
	1323	-0.3	-9
	1921	8.4	256
20 W ●	0149	-0.1	-3
	0750	8.1	247
	1412	-0.2	-6
	2005	8.2	250
21 Th	0233	0.0	0
	0834	8.1	247
	1458	0.0	0
	2048	8.0	244
22 F	0313	0.1	3
	0917	7.9	241
	1541	0.3	9
	2130	7.7	235
23 Sa	0352	0.4	12
	1000	7.7	235
	1623	0.7	21
	2212	7.3	223
24 Su	0429	0.7	21
	1044	7.5	229
	1704	1.0	30
	2257	7.0	213
25 M	0507	1.0	30
	1131	7.3	223
	1747	1.4	43
	2345	6.7	204
26 Tu	0546	1.3	40
	1220	7.1	216
	1834	1.7	52
27 W ◐	0035	6.5	198
	0632	1.6	49
	1311	7.0	213
	1926	1.9	58
28 Th	0126	6.4	195
	0724	1.7	52
	1403	6.9	210
	2023	1.9	58
29 F	0218	6.4	195
	0823	1.7	52
	1455	7.0	213
	2120	1.7	52
30 Sa	0310	6.6	201
	0924	1.6	49
	1547	7.2	219
	2213	1.4	43

Time meridian 75° W. 0000 is midnight. 1200 is noon. Times are not adjusted for Daylight Saving Time.
Heights are referred to mean lower low water which is the chart datum of soundings.

Savannah River Entrance, Georgia, 2017

Times and Heights of High and Low Waters

October

Day	Time	ft	cm		Day	Time	ft	cm
1 Su	0403	6.8	207		**16** M	0502	7.7	235
	1020	1.3	40			1124	0.2	6
	1638	7.4	226			1721	8.0	244
	2302	1.1	34			2352	0.2	6
2 M	0454	7.1	216		**17** Tu	0555	7.9	241
	1113	1.0	30			1216	0.1	3
	1727	7.6	232			1811	8.0	244
	2349	0.7	21					
3 Tu	0542	7.5	229		**18** W	0038	0.1	3
	1203	0.6	18			0643	8.1	247
	1813	7.9	241			1305	0.1	3
						1856	8.0	244
4 W	0035	0.3	9		**19** Th ●	0122	0.1	3
	0628	7.9	241			0727	8.2	250
	1252	0.3	9			1351	0.1	3
	1857	8.1	247			1939	7.9	241
5 Th ○	0120	0.0	0		**20** F	0203	0.2	6
	0713	8.3	253			0808	8.2	250
	1341	0.1	3			1434	0.2	6
	1940	8.2	250			2019	7.7	235
6 F	0205	-0.3	-9		**21** Sa	0241	0.3	9
	0757	8.5	259			0847	8.1	247
	1429	-0.1	-3			1515	0.5	15
	2023	8.1	247			2059	7.4	226
7 Sa	0250	-0.4	-12		**22** Su	0318	0.6	18
	0842	8.7	265			0926	7.9	241
	1517	-0.1	-3			1555	0.7	21
	2108	8.0	244			2139	7.1	216
8 Su	0336	-0.4	-12		**23** M	0354	0.8	24
	0930	8.7	265			1006	7.6	232
	1606	0.0	0			1633	1.0	30
	2158	7.8	238			2221	6.8	207
9 M	0424	-0.3	-9		**24** Tu	0430	1.1	34
	1023	8.6	262			1049	7.3	223
	1657	0.2	6			1713	1.3	40
	2253	7.5	229			2306	6.6	201
10 Tu	0514	-0.1	-3		**25** W	0508	1.3	40
	1121	8.4	256			1136	7.1	216
	1752	0.5	15			1755	1.5	46
	2354	7.3	223			2355	6.4	195
11 W	0610	0.2	6		**26** Th	0551	1.6	49
	1223	8.2	250			1226	6.9	210
	1853	0.8	24			1843	1.7	52
12 Th ☽	0058	7.1	216		**27** F ☾	0046	6.3	192
	0712	0.4	12			0640	1.7	52
	1326	8.1	247			1318	6.9	210
	1958	0.9	27			1937	1.7	52
13 F	0201	7.1	216		**28** Sa	0139	6.4	195
	0818	0.6	18			0738	1.8	55
	1428	8.0	244			1410	6.9	210
	2105	0.9	27			2034	1.6	49
14 Sa	0304	7.2	219		**29** Su	0231	6.5	198
	0925	0.5	15			0841	1.6	49
	1529	8.0	244			1503	7.0	213
	2206	0.7	21			2130	1.3	40
15 Su	0405	7.4	226		**30** M	0324	6.8	207
	1027	0.4	12			0943	1.4	43
	1627	8.0	244			1555	7.2	219
	2301	0.4	12			2222	0.9	27
					31 Tu	0417	7.2	219
						1041	1.0	30
						1647	7.4	226
						2312	0.4	12

November

Day	Time	ft	cm		Day	Time	ft	cm
1 W	0508	7.7	235		**16** Th	0011	0.1	3
	1135	0.6	18			0621	7.9	241
	1737	7.7	235			1244	0.2	6
						1831	7.3	223
2 Th	0001	0.0	0		**17** F	0053	0.1	3
	0558	8.2	250			0704	8.0	244
	1227	0.2	6			1329	0.2	6
	1826	7.9	241			1913	7.3	223
3 F	0049	-0.4	-12		**18** Sa ●	0133	0.2	6
	0646	8.6	262			0743	8.0	244
	1319	-0.2	-6			1411	0.3	9
	1913	8.0	244			1953	7.2	219
4 Sa ○	0137	-0.7	-21		**19** Su	0212	0.3	9
	0734	8.9	271			0821	7.9	241
	1410	-0.4	-12			1450	0.3	9
	2001	8.0	244			2032	7.0	213
5 Su	0226	-0.8	-24		**20** M	0249	0.4	12
	0822	9.1	277			0859	7.7	235
	1501	-0.4	-12			1528	0.5	15
	2050	7.9	241			2111	6.8	207
6 M	0315	-0.8	-24		**21** Tu	0324	0.6	18
	0913	9.0	274			0936	7.5	229
	1552	-0.4	-12			1606	0.7	21
	2142	7.7	235			2150	6.6	201
7 Tu	0406	-0.7	-21		**22** W	0400	0.8	24
	1007	8.8	268			1015	7.2	219
	1644	-0.2	-6			1643	0.9	27
	2240	7.4	226			2232	6.4	195
8 W	0458	-0.4	-12		**23** Th	0438	1.0	30
	1106	8.5	259			1057	7.0	213
	1738	0.1	3			1723	1.0	30
	2342	7.2	219			2317	6.2	189
9 Th	0554	0.0	0		**24** F	0518	1.2	37
	1208	8.2	250			1143	6.8	207
	1836	0.4	12			1806	1.1	34
10 F ○	0046	7.1	216		**25** Sa	0006	6.2	189
	0655	0.3	9			0604	1.3	40
	1311	7.9	241			1232	6.7	204
	1939	0.6	18			1855	1.2	37
11 Sa	0149	7.1	216		**26** Su ◐	0057	6.2	189
	0802	0.5	15			0658	1.4	43
	1411	7.7	235			1324	6.7	204
	2043	0.6	18			1949	1.1	34
12 Su	0250	7.2	219		**27** M	0150	6.4	195
	0908	0.6	18			0800	1.4	43
	1508	7.6	232			1417	6.7	204
	2143	0.5	15			2046	0.8	24
13 M	0349	7.3	223		**28** Tu	0244	6.8	207
	1010	0.5	15			0906	1.1	34
	1604	7.5	229			1511	6.9	210
	2237	0.4	12			2142	0.5	15
14 Tu	0444	7.5	229		**29** W	0339	7.2	219
	1106	0.4	12			1009	0.8	24
	1656	7.4	226			1607	7.0	213
	2326	0.2	6			2236	0.0	0
15 W	0535	7.7	235		**30** Th	0434	7.7	235
	1157	0.3	9			1108	0.4	12
	1745	7.4	226			1703	7.2	219
						2329	-0.4	-12

December

Day	Time	ft	cm		Day	Time	ft	cm
1 F	0529	8.2	250		**16** Sa	0025	0.1	3
	1204	-0.1	-3			0640	7.5	229
	1757	7.4	226			1305	0.2	6
						1847	6.7	204
2 Sa	0021	-0.8	-24		**17** Su	0106	0.1	3
	0622	8.6	262			0721	7.6	232
	1259	-0.5	-15			1346	0.1	3
	1850	7.6	232			1929	6.7	204
3 Su ○	0114	-1.1	-34		**18** M ●	0145	0.1	3
	0714	8.9	271			0759	7.5	229
	1352	-0.7	-21			1426	0.1	3
	1941	7.7	235			2008	6.6	201
4 M	0206	-1.3	-40		**19** Tu	0223	0.1	3
	0806	9.0	274			0836	7.4	226
	1445	-0.9	-27			1504	0.1	3
	2033	7.7	235			2046	6.5	198
5 Tu	0257	-1.3	-40		**20** W	0300	0.2	6
	0859	9.0	274			0913	7.3	223
	1536	-0.8	-24			1540	0.2	6
	2128	7.5	229			2124	6.4	195
6 W	0349	-1.2	-37		**21** Th	0336	0.3	9
	0953	8.7	265			0949	7.1	216
	1628	-0.7	-21			1617	0.3	9
	2225	7.3	223			2202	6.2	189
7 Th	0442	-0.9	-27		**22** F	0413	0.4	12
	1051	8.4	256			1026	6.9	210
	1720	-0.4	-12			1654	0.4	12
	2326	7.1	216			2243	6.1	186
8 F	0537	-0.4	-12		**23** Sa	0452	0.6	18
	1150	8.0	244			1106	6.7	204
	1815	-0.1	-3			1734	0.5	15
						2327	6.1	186
9 Sa	0029	7.0	213		**24** Su	0536	0.7	21
	0636	0.0	0			1151	6.6	201
	1249	7.6	232			1818	0.5	15
	1913	0.1	3					
10 Su ◐	0129	6.9	210		**25** M	0017	6.2	189
	0739	0.4	12			0626	0.8	24
	1346	7.3	223			1241	6.5	198
	2013	0.3	9			1908	0.5	15
11 M	0228	6.9	210		**26** Tu ◐	0110	6.4	195
	0844	0.5	15			0725	0.9	27
	1440	7.0	213			1335	6.5	198
	2112	0.3	9			2005	0.3	9
12 Tu	0324	7.0	213		**27** W	0206	6.7	204
	0947	0.6	18			0831	0.8	24
	1534	6.8	207			1432	6.5	198
	2207	0.3	9			2104	0.1	3
13 W	0418	7.1	216		**28** Th	0304	7.1	216
	1043	0.5	15			0939	0.6	18
	1626	6.7	204			1531	6.6	201
	2256	0.2	6			2204	-0.3	-9
14 Th	0509	7.3	223		**29** F	0404	7.5	229
	1134	0.4	12			1043	0.2	6
	1716	6.6	201			1632	6.7	204
	2342	0.1	3			2302	-0.7	-21
15 F	0556	7.4	226		**30** Sa	0504	7.9	241
	1221	0.3	9			1143	-0.3	-9
	1803	6.7	204			1732	7.0	213
						2358	-1.1	-34
					31 Su	0602	8.3	253
						1240	-0.7	-21
						1830	7.2	219

Time meridian 75° W. 0000 is midnight. 1200 is noon. Times are not adjusted for Daylight Saving Time.
Heights are referred to mean lower low water which is the chart datum of soundings.

Fernandina Beach, Amelia River, Florida, 2017

Times and Heights of High and Low Waters

January

Day	Time	ft	cm	Day	Time	ft	cm
1 Su	0400	-0.1	-3	16 M	0508	-0.4	-12
	1044	6.5	198		1142	6.5	198
	1641	-0.1	-3		1739	-0.3	-9
	2259	5.7	174				
2 M	0442	-0.1	-3	17 Tu	0009	5.9	180
	1124	6.4	195		0559	0.0	0
	1724	0.0	0		1225	6.1	186
	2342	5.7	174		1826	0.0	0
3 Tu	0530	0.1	3	18 W	0055	5.7	174
	1207	6.2	189		0653	0.4	12
	1811	0.0	0		1309	5.7	174
					1915	0.3	9
4 W	0030	5.8	177	19 Th ◐	0143	5.5	168
	0625	0.2	6		0750	0.7	21
	1255	6.1	186		1355	5.3	162
	1904	-0.1	-3		2006	0.4	12
5 Th ◗	0123	5.9	180	20 F	0234	5.4	165
	0728	0.3	9		0847	0.8	24
	1348	5.9	180		1444	5.1	155
	2001	-0.2	-6		2056	0.5	15
6 F	0222	6.0	183	21 Sa	0329	5.4	165
	0835	0.3	9		0942	0.8	24
	1449	5.8	177		1538	5.0	152
	2101	-0.3	-9		2146	0.5	15
7 Sa	0328	6.2	189	22 Su	0425	5.6	171
	0941	0.1	3		1034	0.8	24
	1556	5.7	174		1634	5.0	152
	2200	-0.5	-15		2236	0.4	12
8 Su	0437	6.5	198	23 M	0520	5.7	174
	1045	-0.1	-3		1125	0.6	18
	1703	5.8	177		1728	5.1	155
	2300	-0.8	-24		2325	0.2	6
9 M	0542	6.9	210	24 Tu	0610	6.0	183
	1146	-0.3	-9		1214	0.4	12
	1806	6.0	183		1819	5.3	162
	2358	-1.0	-30				
10 Tu	0642	7.2	219	25 W	0013	0.0	0
	1245	-0.6	-18		0657	6.2	189
	1904	6.2	189		1259	0.2	6
					1906	5.5	168
11 W	0055	-1.2	-37	26 Th	0058	-0.2	-6
	0738	7.4	226		0741	6.4	195
	1340	-0.8	-24		1341	-0.1	-3
	2000	6.3	192		1950	5.6	171
12 Th O	0149	-1.3	-40	27 F ●	0141	-0.4	-12
	0832	7.5	229		0823	6.5	198
	1431	-1.0	-30		1421	-0.3	-9
	2053	6.4	195		2033	5.8	177
13 F	0241	-1.3	-40	28 Sa	0222	-0.5	-15
	0922	7.4	226		0903	6.6	201
	1520	-0.9	-27		1500	-0.4	-12
	2144	6.4	195		2115	5.9	180
14 Sa	0330	-1.1	-34	29 Su	0303	-0.6	-18
	1011	7.2	219		0944	6.6	201
	1606	-0.8	-24		1538	-0.6	-18
	2234	6.3	192		2156	5.9	180
15 Su	0419	-0.8	-24	30 M	0344	-0.6	-18
	1057	6.9	210		1024	6.5	198
	1652	-0.6	-18		1617	-0.6	-18
	2322	6.1	186		2239	6.0	183
				31 Tu	0428	-0.5	-15
					1105	6.4	195
					1700	-0.6	-18
					2324	6.1	186

February

Day	Time	ft	cm	Day	Time	ft	cm
1 W	0516	-0.4	-12	16 Th	0016	5.8	177
	1149	6.2	189		0616	0.4	12
	1746	-0.5	-15		1229	5.5	168
					1828	0.3	9
2 Th	0012	6.1	186	17 F	0059	5.6	171
	0610	-0.2	-6		0707	0.7	21
	1237	6.0	183		1311	5.2	158
	1839	-0.5	-15		1915	0.5	15
3 F ◐	0104	6.1	186	18 Sa O	0145	5.5	168
	0712	0.0	0		0802	0.9	27
	1330	5.8	177		1358	5.0	152
	1936	-0.4	-12		2006	0.7	21
4 Sa	0203	6.2	189	19 Su	0237	5.4	165
	0817	0.1	3		0857	0.9	27
	1430	5.6	171		1451	4.9	149
	2038	-0.4	-12		2059	0.7	21
5 Su	0310	6.2	189	20 M	0335	5.4	165
	0923	0.1	3		0951	0.9	27
	1538	5.5	168		1549	4.9	149
	2140	-0.5	-15		2153	0.6	18
6 M	0421	6.4	195	21 Tu	0435	5.5	168
	1028	0.0	0		1044	0.7	21
	1647	5.6	171		1648	5.0	152
	2242	-0.7	-21		2246	0.4	12
7 Tu	0528	6.6	201	22 W	0532	5.8	177
	1130	-0.2	-6		1135	0.5	15
	1752	5.8	177		1744	5.3	162
	2343	-0.8	-24		2338	0.2	6
8 W	0629	6.8	207	23 Th	0623	6.1	186
	1229	-0.5	-15		1223	0.2	6
	1851	6.0	183		1834	5.5	168
9 Th	0041	-1.0	-30	24 F	0028	-0.1	-3
	0724	7.0	213		0710	6.3	192
	1323	-0.7	-21		1308	-0.1	-3
	1945	6.2	189		1922	5.8	177
10 F O	0135	-1.1	-34	25 Sa	0115	-0.4	-12
	0815	7.1	216		0754	6.6	201
	1413	-0.8	-24		1351	-0.4	-12
	2036	6.3	192		2007	6.1	186
11 Sa	0226	-1.1	-34	26 Su ●	0200	-0.6	-18
	0903	7.1	216		0837	6.7	204
	1458	-0.9	-27		1431	-0.6	-18
	2124	6.4	195		2051	6.4	195
12 Su	0313	-1.0	-30	27 M	0244	-0.8	-24
	0948	6.9	210		0920	6.7	204
	1541	-0.8	-24		1512	-0.8	-24
	2210	6.3	192		2135	6.5	198
13 M	0358	-0.7	-21	28 Tu	0329	-0.9	-27
	1030	6.6	201		1003	6.7	204
	1622	-0.5	-15		1553	-0.9	-27
	2253	6.2	189		2220	6.7	204
14 Tu	0443	-0.4	-12				
	1110	6.2	189				
	1703	-0.3	-9				
	2335	6.0	183				
15 W	0528	0.0	0				
	1150	5.9	180				
	1744	0.0	0				

March

Day	Time	ft	cm	Day	Time	ft	cm
1 W	0414	-0.8	-24	16 Th	0459	0.1	3
	1047	6.6	201		1116	5.8	177
	1637	-0.9	-27		1704	0.2	6
	2306	6.7	204		2339	6.1	186
2 Th	0503	-0.6	-18	17 F	0541	0.4	12
	1133	6.4	195		1154	5.5	168
	1724	-0.8	-24		1742	0.5	15
	2356	6.7	204				
3 F	0558	-0.4	-12	18 Sa	0018	5.9	180
	1223	6.1	186		0627	0.7	21
	1817	-0.6	-18		1234	5.3	162
					1826	0.7	21
4 Sa	0050	6.6	201	19 Su	0101	5.7	174
	0658	-0.1	-3		0718	0.9	27
	1317	5.9	180		1319	5.1	155
	1916	-0.4	-12		1915	0.9	27
5 Su ◐	0149	6.4	195	20 M ◐	0150	5.6	171
	0802	0.1	3		0812	1.0	30
	1417	5.7	174		1409	5.1	155
	2019	-0.3	-9		2011	0.9	27
6 M	0256	6.3	192	21 Tu	0245	5.5	168
	0908	0.2	6		0907	1.0	30
	1525	5.6	171		1506	5.1	155
	2124	-0.2	-6		2109	0.9	27
7 Tu	0406	6.4	195	22 W	0347	5.6	171
	1012	0.1	3		1001	0.9	27
	1634	5.6	171		1607	5.2	158
	2228	-0.3	-9		2207	0.7	21
8 W	0513	6.5	198	23 Th	0448	5.8	177
	1113	0.0	0		1053	0.6	18
	1739	5.9	180		1706	5.5	168
	2329	-0.4	-12		2303	0.4	12
9 Th	0613	6.6	201	24 F	0544	6.0	183
	1210	-0.2	-6		1143	0.3	9
	1837	6.1	186		1800	5.8	177
					2357	0.1	3
10 F	0027	-0.6	-18	25 Sa	0635	6.3	192
	0706	6.8	207		1231	-0.1	-3
	1302	-0.4	-12		1851	6.2	189
	1929	6.4	195				
11 Sa	0121	-0.7	-21	26 Su	0048	-0.3	-9
	0755	6.8	207		0722	6.6	201
	1350	-0.5	-15		1317	-0.4	-12
	2017	6.5	198		1939	6.6	201
12 Su O	0209	-0.7	-21	27 M ●	0138	-0.6	-18
	0840	6.7	204		0808	6.8	207
	1433	-0.6	-18		1401	-0.8	-24
	2102	6.6	201		2025	7.0	213
13 M	0254	-0.6	-18	28 Tu	0225	-0.8	-24
	0921	6.6	201		0854	6.8	207
	1513	-0.5	-15		1445	-1.0	-30
	2143	6.5	198		2112	7.2	219
14 Tu	0337	-0.5	-15	29 W	0312	-1.0	-30
	1001	6.3	192		0941	6.8	207
	1550	-0.3	-9		1529	-1.1	-34
	2223	6.4	195		2201	7.3	223
15 W	0418	-0.2	-6	30 Th	0400	-0.9	-27
	1039	6.1	186		1029	6.7	204
	1627	-0.1	-3		1615	-1.0	-30
	2301	6.3	192		2251	7.3	223
				31 F	0451	-0.7	-21
					1119	6.5	198
					1705	-0.8	-24
					2343	7.2	219

Time meridian 75° W. 0000 is midnight. 1200 is noon. Times are not adjusted for Daylight Saving Time.
Heights are referred to mean lower low water which is the chart datum of soundings.

Fernandina Beach, Amelia River, Florida, 2017

Times and Heights of High and Low Waters

April

Day	Time	ft	cm
1 Sa	0545	-0.4	-12
	1211	6.3	192
	1759	-0.5	-15
2 Su	0038	7.0	213
	0645	-0.1	-3
	1307	6.0	183
	1859	-0.2	-6
3 M ☽	0137	6.7	204
	0748	0.1	3
	1408	5.8	177
	2004	0.0	0
4 Tu	0241	6.5	198
	0853	0.2	6
	1514	5.8	177
	2110	0.1	3
5 W	0348	6.4	195
	0954	0.2	6
	1621	5.9	180
	2214	0.1	3
6 Th	0453	6.4	195
	1052	0.1	3
	1723	6.1	186
	2314	0.0	0
7 F	0551	6.4	195
	1147	0.0	0
	1819	6.3	192
8 Sa	0011	-0.1	-3
	0642	6.5	198
	1236	-0.2	-6
	1909	6.5	198
9 Su	0103	-0.2	-6
	0729	6.5	198
	1322	-0.2	-6
	1954	6.7	204
10 M	0150	-0.3	-9
	0812	6.4	195
	1403	-0.3	-9
	2036	6.7	204
11 Tu ○	0234	-0.3	-9
	0852	6.3	192
	1442	-0.2	-6
	2115	6.7	204
12 W	0314	-0.2	-6
	0930	6.1	186
	1518	-0.1	-3
	2153	6.6	201
13 Th	0353	0.0	0
	1007	5.9	180
	1552	0.1	3
	2229	6.5	198
14 F	0431	0.2	6
	1045	5.7	174
	1627	0.4	12
	2306	6.3	192
15 Sa	0510	0.5	15
	1123	5.5	168
	1704	0.6	18
	2344	6.1	186
16 Su	0552	0.7	21
	1203	5.4	165
	1744	0.8	24
17 M	0025	5.9	180
	0638	0.9	27
	1246	5.2	158
	1831	1.0	30
18 Tu	0110	5.8	177
	0730	1.0	30
	1334	5.3	158
	1927	1.0	30
19 W ○	0202	5.7	174
	0824	0.9	27
	1428	5.2	158
	2028	1.0	30
20 Th	0300	5.7	174
	0918	0.8	24
	1527	5.4	165
	2129	0.8	24
21 F	0401	5.8	177
	1011	0.5	15
	1627	5.7	174
	2228	0.5	15
22 Sa	0501	6.0	183
	1102	0.2	6
	1725	6.1	186
	2326	0.2	6
23 Su	0556	6.3	192
	1153	-0.2	-6
	1819	6.6	201
24 M	0021	-0.2	-6
	0648	6.5	198
	1243	-0.6	-18
	1910	7.1	216
25 Tu	0114	-0.6	-18
	0738	6.7	204
	1331	-0.9	-27
	2000	7.4	226
26 W ●	0206	-0.9	-27
	0828	6.7	204
	1419	-1.1	-34
	2051	7.7	235
27 Th	0256	-1.0	-30
	0919	6.7	204
	1507	-1.2	-37
	2143	7.7	235
28 F	0346	-1.0	-30
	1011	6.6	201
	1556	-1.1	-34
	2236	7.7	235
29 Sa	0437	-0.8	-24
	1104	6.5	198
	1647	-0.8	-24
	2330	7.5	229
30 Su	0532	-0.5	-15
	1159	6.3	192
	1743	-0.5	-15

May

Day	Time	ft	cm
1 M	0026	7.2	219
	0631	-0.2	-6
	1256	6.1	186
	1844	-0.1	-3
2 Tu ○	0123	6.9	210
	0732	0.0	0
	1356	6.0	183
	1949	0.1	3
3 W ○	0223	6.5	198
	0834	0.1	3
	1459	5.9	180
	2055	0.3	9
4 Th	0325	6.3	192
	0933	0.1	3
	1602	6.0	183
	2157	0.3	9
5 F	0425	6.2	189
	1027	0.1	3
	1702	6.2	189
	2256	0.3	9
6 Sa	0521	6.1	186
	1118	0.0	0
	1755	6.4	195
	2351	0.2	6
7 Su	0612	6.1	186
	1206	-0.1	-3
	1843	6.6	201
8 M	0041	0.1	3
	0657	6.0	183
	1250	-0.1	-3
	1927	6.7	204
9 Tu	0128	0.0	0
	0740	6.0	183
	1331	-0.1	-3
	2007	6.7	204
10 W ○	0210	0.0	0
	0820	5.9	180
	1410	0.0	0
	2046	6.7	204
11 Th	0250	0.0	0
	0859	5.8	177
	1446	0.1	3
	2124	6.6	201
12 F	0328	0.1	3
	0938	5.6	171
	1521	0.2	6
	2201	6.5	198
13 Sa	0405	0.2	6
	1016	5.5	168
	1556	0.4	12
	2238	6.4	195
14 Su	0442	0.4	12
	1056	5.4	165
	1632	0.5	15
	2316	6.2	189
15 M	0522	0.5	15
	1136	5.3	162
	1711	0.7	21
	2356	6.0	183
16 Tu	0605	0.6	18
	1219	5.2	158
	1757	0.8	24
17 W	0039	5.9	180
	0653	0.7	21
	1305	5.3	162
	1851	0.9	27
18 Th ○	0126	5.8	177
	0745	0.6	18
	1356	5.4	165
	1952	0.9	27
19 F	0219	5.8	177
	0838	0.4	12
	1451	5.6	171
	2055	0.7	21
20 Sa	0317	5.8	177
	0931	0.3	9
	1551	5.9	180
	2157	0.5	15
21 Su	0418	5.9	180
	1024	-0.2	-6
	1651	6.3	192
	2257	0.1	3
22 M	0518	6.1	186
	1118	-0.5	-15
	1748	6.8	207
	2355	-0.2	-6
23 Tu	0615	6.2	189
	1211	-0.8	-24
	1844	7.3	223
24 W	0051	-0.6	-18
	0710	6.4	195
	1303	-1.1	-34
	1938	7.6	232
25 Th ●	0146	-0.9	-27
	0804	6.5	198
	1355	-1.3	-40
	2032	7.8	238
26 F	0238	-1.0	-30
	0858	6.5	198
	1446	-1.3	-40
	2126	7.8	238
27 Sa	0330	-1.0	-30
	0954	6.5	198
	1538	-1.2	-37
	2221	7.7	235
28 Su	0422	-0.9	-27
	1049	6.4	195
	1631	-0.9	-27
	2316	7.5	229
29 M	0516	-0.7	-21
	1145	6.2	189
	1727	-0.6	-18
30 Tu	0010	7.2	219
	0613	-0.4	-12
	1242	6.1	186
	1827	-0.2	-6
31 W	0104	6.8	207
	0711	-0.2	-6
	1339	6.0	183
	1931	0.2	6

June

Day	Time	ft	cm
1 Th ☽	0159	6.4	195
	0810	-0.1	-3
	1437	6.0	183
	2035	0.3	9
2 F	0255	6.1	186
	0905	-0.1	-3
	1536	6.0	183
	2135	0.4	12
3 Sa	0351	5.8	177
	0956	0.0	0
	1633	6.1	186
	2232	0.4	12
4 Su	0445	5.7	174
	1045	0.0	0
	1725	6.2	189
	2324	0.4	12
5 M	0535	5.6	171
	1131	0.0	0
	1812	6.4	195
6 Tu	0014	0.3	9
	0621	5.6	171
	1215	0.0	0
	1856	6.5	198
7 W	0100	0.2	6
	0705	5.5	168
	1258	0.0	0
	1938	6.6	201
8 Th	0144	0.1	3
	0747	5.5	168
	1338	0.0	0
	2018	6.6	201
9 F ○	0224	0.1	3
	0829	5.5	168
	1416	0.0	0
	2057	6.5	198
10 Sa	0302	0.1	3
	0910	5.4	165
	1453	0.1	3
	2136	6.5	198
11 Su	0339	0.1	3
	0950	5.3	162
	1530	0.2	6
	2214	6.3	192
12 M	0416	0.2	6
	1031	5.3	162
	1607	0.3	9
	2253	6.2	189
13 Tu	0455	0.3	9
	1112	5.3	162
	1646	0.4	12
	2332	6.1	186
14 W	0536	0.3	9
	1154	5.3	162
	1731	0.5	15
15 Th	0013	6.0	183
	0621	0.3	9
	1239	5.4	165
	1824	0.6	18
16 F	0058	5.9	180
	0710	0.2	6
	1328	5.5	168
	1924	0.6	18
17 Sa ○	0147	5.8	177
	0803	0.0	0
	1421	5.8	177
	2027	0.5	15
18 Su	0242	5.8	177
	0857	-0.2	-6
	1520	6.1	186
	2130	0.3	9
19 M	0342	5.8	177
	0952	-0.5	-15
	1621	6.5	198
	2231	0.0	0
20 Tu	0444	5.9	180
	1047	-0.8	-24
	1722	6.9	210
	2331	-0.3	-9
21 W	0546	6.0	183
	1143	-1.0	-30
	1821	7.3	223
22 Th	0030	-0.6	-18
	0645	6.1	186
	1239	-1.2	-37
	1919	7.5	229
23 F ●	0126	-0.8	-24
	0742	6.2	189
	1334	-1.4	-43
	2015	7.7	235
24 Sa ○	0221	-1.0	-30
	0840	6.3	192
	1428	-1.4	-43
	2111	7.7	235
25 Su	0313	-1.0	-30
	0936	6.3	192
	1521	-1.3	-40
	2205	7.6	232
26 M	0405	-1.0	-30
	1033	6.3	192
	1614	-1.0	-30
	2258	7.3	223
27 Tu	0456	-0.8	-24
	1128	6.2	189
	1709	-0.6	-18
	2350	7.0	213
28 W	0550	-0.6	-18
	1222	6.1	186
	1807	-0.2	-6
29 Th	0041	6.6	201
	0644	-0.3	-9
	1315	6.0	183
	1908	0.2	6
30 F ☽	0130	6.2	189
	0739	-0.2	-6
	1409	5.9	180
	2009	0.4	12

Time meridian 75° W. 0000 is midnight. 1200 is noon. Times are not adjusted for Daylight Saving Time.
Heights are referred to mean lower low water which is the chart datum of soundings.

Fernandina Beach, Amelia River, Florida, 2017

Times and Heights of High and Low Waters

July

Day	Time	ft	cm	Day	Time	ft	cm
1 Sa	0221	5.8	177	16 Su ◗	0122	5.9	180
	0831	0.0	0		0732	-0.2	-6
	1503	5.9	180		1356	6.1	186
	2107	0.6	18		2004	0.4	12
2 Su	0312	5.6	171	17 M	0215	5.8	177
	0921	0.0	0		0828	-0.4	-12
	1557	6.0	183		1455	6.3	192
	2201	0.6	18		2108	0.3	9
3 M	0404	5.4	165	18 Tu	0315	5.8	177
	1008	0.1	3		0925	-0.6	-18
	1649	6.0	183		1558	6.6	201
	2253	0.6	18		2210	0.1	3
4 Tu	0455	5.3	162	19 W	0419	5.8	177
	1054	0.1	3		1023	-0.8	-24
	1738	6.2	189		1702	6.9	210
	2342	0.5	15		2311	-0.1	-3
5 W	0543	5.3	162	20 Th	0524	5.9	180
	1140	0.1	3		1121	-0.9	-27
	1823	6.3	192		1804	7.2	219
6 Th	0029	0.4	12	21 F	0011	-0.4	-12
	0630	5.3	162		0626	6.1	186
	1224	0.1	3		1220	-1.1	-34
	1907	6.4	195		1903	7.5	229
7 F	0114	0.2	6	22 Sa	0108	-0.6	-18
	0715	5.4	165		0725	6.2	189
	1307	0.0	0		1317	-1.2	-37
	1949	6.5	198		1959	7.6	232
8 Sa ○	0155	0.1	3	23 Su ●	0202	-0.8	-24
	0759	5.4	165		0823	6.4	195
	1348	0.0	0		1412	-1.2	-37
	2031	6.5	198		2054	7.6	232
9 Su	0235	0.1	3	24 M	0254	-0.9	-27
	0842	5.4	165		0919	6.4	195
	1428	0.0	0		1505	-1.1	-34
	2111	6.5	198		2146	7.5	229
10 M	0313	0.0	0	25 Tu	0344	-0.8	-24
	0925	5.4	165		1013	6.4	195
	1506	0.0	0		1556	-0.8	-24
	2151	6.4	195		2237	7.2	219
11 Tu	0350	0.0	0	26 W	0432	-0.7	-21
	1006	5.4	165		1106	6.4	195
	1545	0.1	3		1649	-0.4	-12
	2230	6.3	192		2325	6.9	210
12 W	0427	0.0	0	27 Th	0521	-0.4	-12
	1048	5.5	168		1156	6.3	192
	1626	0.2	6		1742	0.0	0
	2309	6.2	189				
13 Th	0507	0.0	0	28 F	0012	6.5	198
	1131	5.6	171		0610	-0.1	-3
	1711	0.3	9		1245	6.2	189
	2350	6.1	186		1838	0.4	12
14 F	0551	0.0	0	29 Sa	0057	6.1	186
	1215	5.7	174		0700	0.1	3
	1803	0.4	12		1334	6.0	183
					1936	0.7	21
15 Sa	0034	6.0	183	30 Su ◐	0143	5.7	174
	0639	-0.1	-3		0751	0.3	9
	1303	5.9	180		1424	6.0	183
	1902	0.4	12		2032	0.8	24
				31 M	0230	5.5	168
					0840	0.4	12
					1516	5.9	180
					2126	0.9	27

August

Day	Time	ft	cm	Day	Time	ft	cm
1 Tu	0321	5.3	162	16 W	0257	5.9	180
	0929	0.4	12		0905	-0.3	-9
	1608	6.0	183		1541	6.8	207
	2217	0.9	27		2153	0.3	9
2 W	0413	5.3	162	17 Th	0404	5.9	180
	1016	0.4	12		1005	-0.4	-12
	1659	6.1	186		1647	7.0	213
	2307	0.8	24		2254	0.2	6
3 Th	0505	5.3	162	18 F	0510	6.1	186
	1104	0.4	12		1105	-0.5	-15
	1748	6.3	192		1750	7.3	223
	2354	0.7	21		2353	0.0	0
4 F	0556	5.4	165	19 Sa	0613	6.3	192
	1151	0.3	9		1205	-0.6	-18
	1835	6.4	195		1849	7.5	229
5 Sa	0040	0.5	15	20 Su	0050	-0.2	-6
	0644	5.5	168		0711	6.5	198
	1237	0.2	6		1302	-0.7	-21
	1920	6.6	201		1943	7.6	232
6 Su	0124	0.3	9	21 M ●	0143	-0.4	-12
	0730	5.7	174		0807	6.7	204
	1322	0.1	3		1357	-0.7	-21
	2003	6.7	204		2035	7.5	229
7 M ○	0204	0.2	6	22 Tu	0232	-0.5	-15
	0814	5.8	177		0900	6.8	207
	1404	0.1	3		1448	-0.6	-18
	2044	6.7	204		2124	7.4	226
8 Tu	0243	0.0	0	23 W	0319	-0.5	-15
	0858	5.9	180		0950	6.8	207
	1445	0.0	0		1538	-0.4	-12
	2125	6.7	204		2211	7.1	216
9 W	0321	0.0	0	24 Th	0404	-0.3	-9
	0941	6.0	183		1039	6.7	204
	1526	0.0	0		1626	0.0	0
	2205	6.6	201		2256	6.8	207
10 Th	0400	-0.1	-3	25 F	0447	0.0	0
	1023	6.1	186		1125	6.6	201
	1608	0.1	3		1715	0.4	12
	2246	6.5	198		2339	6.4	195
11 F	0440	-0.1	-3	26 Sa	0532	0.3	9
	1107	6.2	189		1210	6.4	195
	1654	0.2	6		1805	0.7	21
	2328	6.4	195				
12 Sa	0523	-0.1	-3	27 Su	0021	6.1	186
	1153	6.3	192		0617	0.6	18
	1746	0.3	9		1255	6.3	192
					1858	1.0	30
13 Su	0013	6.3	192	28 M	0104	5.8	177
	0612	-0.1	-3		0705	0.8	24
	1242	6.4	195		1341	6.2	189
	1843	0.4	12		1952	1.2	37
14 M ○	0102	6.1	186	29 Tu ◐	0149	5.6	171
	0706	-0.1	-3		0755	0.9	27
	1336	6.6	201		1430	6.1	186
	1946	0.5	15		2046	1.3	40
15 Tu	0157	6.0	183	30 W	0238	5.5	168
	0804	-0.2	-6		0846	1.0	30
	1436	6.7	204		1523	6.1	186
	2050	0.5	15		2138	1.3	40
				31 Th	0332	5.5	168
					0938	1.0	30
					1618	6.2	189
					2228	1.2	37

September

Day	Time	ft	cm	Day	Time	ft	cm
1 F	0427	5.5	168	16 Sa	0500	6.4	195
	1028	0.9	27		1053	0.0	0
	1711	6.3	192		1736	7.3	223
	2317	1.0	30		2336	0.3	9
2 Sa	0521	5.7	174	17 Su	0601	6.7	204
	1118	0.7	21		1153	-0.1	-3
	1801	6.5	198		1833	7.4	226
3 Su	0004	0.8	24	18 M	0030	0.1	3
	0612	5.9	180		0658	6.9	210
	1207	0.6	18		1249	-0.2	-6
	1848	6.8	207		1925	7.5	229
4 M	0048	0.6	18	19 Tu	0121	0.0	0
	0700	6.2	189		0750	7.1	216
	1254	0.4	12		1342	-0.2	-6
	1932	6.9	210		2013	7.4	226
5 Tu	0131	0.3	9	20 W	0208	-0.1	-3
	0746	6.4	195		0839	7.2	219
	1339	0.2	6		1431	-0.1	-3
	2015	7.0	213	●	2059	7.3	223
6 W	0212	0.1	3	21 Th	0252	0.0	0
	0830	6.6	201		0925	7.2	219
○	1423	0.1	3		1517	0.1	3
	2057	7.0	213		2142	7.0	213
7 Th	0251	-0.1	-3	22 F	0333	0.1	3
	0914	6.8	207		1009	7.1	216
	1507	0.0	0		1602	0.3	9
	2140	7.0	213		2224	6.7	204
8 F	0332	-0.2	-6	23 Sa	0413	0.4	12
	0959	6.9	210		1052	6.9	210
	1551	0.1	3		1646	0.7	21
	2223	6.9	210		2304	6.4	195
9 Sa	0413	-0.2	-6	24 Su	0452	0.7	21
	1045	7.0	213		1133	6.7	204
	1638	0.2	6		1731	1.0	30
	2308	6.7	204		2344	6.2	189
10 Su	0458	-0.1	-3	25 M	0533	1.0	30
	1133	7.1	216		1214	6.6	201
	1730	0.4	12		1818	1.3	40
	2356	6.6	201				
11 M	0548	0.0	0	26 Tu	0025	5.9	180
	1225	7.1	216		0618	1.2	37
	1828	0.5	15		1258	6.4	195
					1909	1.5	46
12 Tu	0047	6.4	195	27 W	0109	5.8	177
	0645	0.1	3		0707	1.4	43
	1321	7.1	216		1345	6.3	192
	1930	0.7	21	◐	2003	1.6	49
13 W	0144	6.3	192	28 Th	0158	5.7	174
	0746	0.2	6		0801	1.5	46
	1422	7.1	216		1437	6.2	189
○	2035	0.7	21		2056	1.6	49
14 Th	0247	6.2	189	29 F	0251	5.7	174
	0849	0.2	6		0856	1.4	43
	1528	7.1	216		1533	6.3	192
	2138	0.6	18		2147	1.5	46
15 F	0354	6.2	189	30 Sa	0348	5.8	177
	0952	0.1	3		0951	1.3	40
	1634	7.2	219		1629	6.4	195
	2238	0.5	15		2236	1.3	40

Time meridian 75° W. 0000 is midnight. 1200 is noon. Times are not adjusted for Daylight Saving Time.
Heights are referred to mean lower low water which is the chart datum of soundings.

Fernandina Beach, Amelia River, Florida, 2017

Times and Heights of High and Low Waters

October

Day	Time	ft	cm
1 Su	0445	6.0	183
	1044	1.1	34
	1723	6.6	201
	2324	1.0	30
2 M	0539	6.3	192
	1136	0.9	27
	1812	6.8	207
3 Tu	0011	0.7	21
	0629	6.7	204
	1226	0.6	18
	1859	7.0	213
4 W	0056	0.4	12
	0716	7.0	213
	1315	0.3	9
	1944	7.2	219
5 Th ○	0139	0.1	3
	0802	7.3	223
	1402	0.1	3
	2029	7.2	219
6 F	0222	-0.2	-6
	0848	7.5	229
	1448	0.0	0
	2114	7.2	219
7 Sa	0305	-0.3	-9
	0935	7.7	235
	1535	0.0	0
	2201	7.1	216
8 Su	0349	-0.3	-9
	1025	7.7	235
	1623	0.1	3
	2249	7.0	213
9 M	0437	-0.2	-6
	1116	7.7	235
	1716	0.3	9
	2341	6.8	207
10 Tu	0529	0.0	0
	1210	7.6	232
	1813	0.5	15
11 W	0035	6.6	201
	0626	0.2	6
	1307	7.4	226
	1915	0.7	21
12 Th ☽	0134	6.5	198
	0730	0.4	12
	1409	7.3	223
	2019	0.8	24
13 F	0237	6.4	195
	0835	0.5	15
	1514	7.2	219
	2122	0.7	21
14 Sa	0344	6.5	198
	0940	0.5	15
	1618	7.1	216
	2221	0.6	18
15 Su	0449	6.6	201
	1041	0.5	15
	1719	7.2	219
	2316	0.4	12
16 M	0548	6.9	210
	1140	0.4	12
	1813	7.2	219
17 Tu	0009	0.3	9
	0642	7.1	216
	1235	0.3	9
	1903	7.2	219
18 W	0057	0.2	6
	0731	7.3	223
	1326	0.2	6
	1948	7.1	216
19 Th ●	0142	0.2	6
	0816	7.4	226
	1413	0.2	6
	2031	7.0	213
20 F	0223	0.2	6
	0859	7.4	226
	1456	0.3	9
	2112	6.8	207
21 Sa	0302	0.3	9
	0939	7.2	219
	1537	0.5	15
	2152	6.5	198
22 Su	0339	0.6	18
	1018	7.1	216
	1617	0.8	24
	2230	6.3	192
23 M	0416	0.8	24
	1057	6.9	210
	1658	1.0	30
	2309	6.1	186
24 Tu	0453	1.1	34
	1137	6.7	204
	1740	1.3	40
	2350	5.9	180
25 W	0534	1.3	40
	1218	6.5	198
	1827	1.5	46
26 Th	0033	5.8	177
	0620	1.5	46
	1302	6.3	192
	1917	1.6	49
27 F ☾	0120	5.7	174
	0714	1.6	49
	1351	6.3	192
	2010	1.6	49
28 Sa	0212	5.7	174
	0812	1.6	49
	1445	6.2	189
	2103	1.4	43
29 Su	0308	5.8	177
	0911	1.5	46
	1543	6.3	192
	2154	1.2	37
30 M	0407	6.1	186
	1008	1.2	37
	1640	6.4	195
	2243	0.9	27
31 Tu	0504	6.4	195
	1104	0.9	27
	1734	6.6	201
	2332	0.5	15

November

Day	Time	ft	cm
1 W	0557	6.9	210
	1158	0.6	18
	1824	6.9	210
2 Th	0020	0.1	3
	0647	7.3	223
	1250	0.2	6
	1913	7.0	213
3 F	0107	-0.2	-6
	0736	7.7	235
	1340	-0.1	-3
	2001	7.1	216
4 Sa ○	0154	-0.5	-15
	0825	7.9	241
	1430	-0.3	-9
	2050	7.1	216
5 Su	0241	-0.6	-18
	0916	8.1	247
	1518	-0.3	-9
	2140	7.1	216
6 M	0329	-0.7	-21
	1007	8.1	247
	1608	-0.2	-6
	2232	6.9	210
7 Tu	0418	-0.5	-15
	1101	7.9	241
	1701	0.0	0
	2326	6.8	207
8 W	0512	-0.2	-6
	1156	7.7	235
	1757	0.2	6
9 Th	0023	6.6	201
	0610	0.1	3
	1253	7.5	229
	1858	0.4	12
10 F ○	0122	6.5	198
	0714	0.4	12
	1352	7.2	219
	2001	0.5	15
11 Sa	0224	6.4	195
	0821	0.6	18
	1454	6.9	210
	2102	0.5	15
12 Su	0329	6.4	195
	0926	0.6	18
	1556	6.8	207
	2159	0.4	12
13 M	0432	6.6	201
	1027	0.6	18
	1655	6.7	204
	2253	0.4	12
14 Tu	0530	6.8	207
	1124	0.5	15
	1748	6.6	201
	2343	0.3	9
15 W	0622	7.0	213
	1218	0.4	12
	1837	6.6	201
16 Th	0030	0.2	6
	0709	7.1	216
	1307	0.4	12
	1922	6.5	198
17 F	0114	0.2	6
	0752	7.2	219
	1352	0.3	9
	2003	6.4	195
18 Sa ●	0155	0.2	6
	0833	7.2	219
	1434	0.3	9
	2043	6.3	192
19 Su	0233	0.3	9
	0912	7.1	216
	1513	0.4	12
	2122	6.2	189
20 M	0310	0.4	12
	0949	6.9	210
	1551	0.6	18
	2200	6.0	183
21 Tu	0345	0.6	18
	1027	6.8	207
	1628	0.7	21
	2239	5.8	177
22 W	0421	0.8	24
	1105	6.6	201
	1707	0.9	27
	2319	5.7	174
23 Th	0458	1.0	30
	1144	6.4	195
	1749	1.1	34
24 F	0000	5.6	171
	0541	1.1	34
	1225	6.2	189
	1834	1.1	34
25 Sa	0045	5.6	171
	0631	1.3	40
	1310	6.1	186
	1925	1.1	34
26 Su ☾	0134	5.6	171
	0730	1.3	40
	1400	6.0	183
	2017	1.0	30
27 M	0228	5.7	174
	0831	1.2	37
	1455	6.0	183
	2110	0.8	24
28 Tu	0326	6.0	183
	0933	1.0	30
	1555	6.1	186
	2202	0.5	15
29 W	0427	6.3	192
	1032	0.7	21
	1654	6.2	189
	2255	0.1	3
30 Th	0525	6.8	207
	1130	0.4	12
	1750	6.4	195
	2347	-0.3	-9

December

Day	Time	ft	cm
1 F	0620	7.2	219
	1226	0.0	0
	1844	6.6	201
2 Sa	0039	-0.6	-18
	0713	7.6	232
	1320	-0.4	-12
	1937	6.7	204
3 Su ○	0130	-0.9	-27
	0806	7.9	241
	1412	-0.6	-18
	2029	6.8	207
4 M	0220	-1.1	-34
	0859	8.0	244
	1502	-0.7	-21
	2122	6.8	207
5 Tu	0311	-1.1	-34
	0952	8.0	244
	1553	-0.7	-21
	2217	6.8	207
6 W	0402	-1.0	-30
	1046	7.9	241
	1645	-0.5	-15
	2312	6.6	201
7 Th	0456	-0.7	-21
	1140	7.6	232
	1739	-0.3	-9
8 F	0008	6.5	198
	0554	-0.3	-9
	1235	7.2	219
	1837	-0.1	-3
9 Sa	0105	6.3	192
	0656	0.1	3
	1330	6.8	207
	1937	0.1	3
10 Su ○	0205	6.2	189
	0802	0.4	12
	1427	6.5	198
	2036	0.2	6
11 M	0306	6.2	189
	0906	0.5	15
	1526	6.2	189
	2132	0.2	6
12 Tu	0408	6.3	192
	1006	0.6	18
	1624	6.0	183
	2224	0.2	6
13 W	0505	6.4	195
	1103	0.5	15
	1718	5.9	180
	2314	0.2	6
14 Th	0557	6.5	198
	1156	0.4	12
	1807	5.8	177
15 F	0001	0.1	3
	0644	6.7	204
	1244	0.3	9
	1853	5.8	177
16 Sa	0046	0.1	3
	0727	6.7	204
	1329	0.2	6
	1935	5.8	177
17 Su	0128	0.0	0
	0807	6.8	207
	1410	0.2	6
	2016	5.8	177
18 M ●	0207	0.0	0
	0846	6.8	207
	1449	0.1	3
	2055	5.8	177
19 Tu	0244	0.1	3
	0924	6.7	204
	1525	0.2	6
	2134	5.7	174
20 W	0320	0.2	6
	1002	6.5	198
	1601	0.3	9
	2213	5.6	171
21 Th	0355	0.3	9
	1038	6.4	195
	1637	0.4	12
	2252	5.5	168
22 F	0432	0.4	12
	1115	6.2	189
	1715	0.5	15
	2331	5.5	168
23 Sa	0512	0.6	18
	1154	6.1	186
	1756	0.5	15
24 Su	0013	5.5	168
	0558	0.7	21
	1235	5.9	180
	1843	0.5	15
25 M	0059	5.5	168
	0653	0.8	24
	1321	5.8	177
	1934	0.4	12
26 Tu ☾	0150	5.6	171
	0755	0.8	24
	1413	5.7	174
	2028	0.2	6
27 W	0247	5.8	177
	0859	0.6	18
	1513	5.7	174
	2124	0.0	0
28 Th	0350	6.1	186
	1002	0.4	12
	1616	5.7	174
	2221	-0.3	-9
29 F	0455	6.5	198
	1104	0.1	3
	1719	5.9	180
	2318	-0.6	-18
30 Sa	0556	7.0	213
	1203	-0.3	-9
	1819	6.1	186
31 Su	0014	-1.0	-30
	0654	7.3	223
	1300	-0.6	-18
	1916	6.3	192

Time meridian 75° W. 0000 is midnight. 1200 is noon. Times are not adjusted for Daylight Saving Time.
Heights are referred to mean lower low water which is the chart datum of soundings.

Mayport, Florida, 2017

Times and Heights of High and Low Waters

January

Day	Time (h m)	Height (ft)	Height (cm)
1 Su	0329	-0.2	-6
	1025	4.8	146
	1614	0.0	0
	2246	4.2	128
2 M	0413	-0.1	-3
	1106	4.8	146
	1657	0.0	0
	2331	4.3	131
3 Tu	0503	0.0	0
	1150	4.7	143
	1745	0.0	0
4 W	0019	4.3	131
	0600	0.2	6
	1238	4.6	140
	1840	0.0	0
5 Th ☾	0114	4.4	134
	0706	0.2	6
	1334	4.4	134
	1939	-0.1	-3
6 F	0216	4.5	137
	0815	0.2	6
	1437	4.3	131
	2039	-0.3	-9
7 Sa	0324	4.6	140
	0924	0.1	3
	1546	4.2	128
	2140	-0.5	-15
8 Su	0433	4.8	146
	1030	-0.1	-3
	1654	4.2	128
	2241	-0.7	-21
9 M	0536	5.0	152
	1133	-0.4	-12
	1757	4.3	131
	2341	-0.9	-27
10 Tu	0635	5.2	158
	1231	-0.7	-21
	1855	4.4	134
11 W	0037	-1.1	-34
	0729	5.3	162
	1325	-0.9	-27
	1951	4.4	134
12 Th ○	0131	-1.3	-40
	0822	5.3	162
	1416	-1.0	-30
	2043	4.5	137
13 F	0222	-1.3	-40
	0912	5.3	162
	1504	-1.0	-30
	2134	4.5	137
14 Sa	0312	-1.1	-34
	0959	5.1	155
	1552	-0.9	-27
	2223	4.4	134
15 Su	0402	-0.9	-27
	1045	4.9	149
	1640	-0.7	-21
	2311	4.3	131
16 M	0454	-0.5	-15
	1130	4.7	143
	1729	-0.4	-12
	2359	4.2	128
17 Tu	0549	-0.1	-3
	1215	4.5	137
	1820	-0.1	-3
18 W	0048	4.2	128
	0647	0.2	6
	1300	4.2	128
	1910	0.1	3
19 Th ◑	0138	4.1	125
	0745	0.4	12
	1348	4.0	122
	2000	0.2	6
20 F	0232	4.1	125
	0841	0.6	18
	1440	3.8	116
	2049	0.3	9
21 Sa	0329	4.1	125
	0935	0.6	18
	1536	3.8	116
	2138	0.3	9
22 Su	0424	4.2	128
	1028	0.6	18
	1631	3.7	113
	2226	0.3	9
23 M	0515	4.3	131
	1118	0.4	12
	1722	3.8	116
	2312	0.1	3
24 Tu	0602	4.4	134
	1205	0.3	9
	1809	3.8	116
	2357	-0.1	-3
25 W	0645	4.5	137
	1248	0.1	3
	1854	3.9	119
26 Th	0038	-0.3	-9
	0726	4.6	140
	1326	-0.1	-3
	1937	4.0	122
27 F ●	0117	-0.5	-15
	0806	4.7	143
	1402	-0.3	-9
	2019	4.1	125
28 Sa	0155	-0.6	-18
	0845	4.7	143
	1437	-0.5	-15
	2100	4.2	128
29 Su	0233	-0.7	-21
	0924	4.8	146
	1512	-0.5	-15
	2142	4.3	131
30 M	0314	-0.7	-21
	1005	4.7	143
	1550	-0.6	-18
	2226	4.3	131
31 Tu	0359	-0.6	-18
	1047	4.7	143
	1632	-0.6	-18
	2311	4.4	134

February

Day	Time (h m)	Height (ft)	Height (cm)
1 W	0449	-0.4	-12
	1132	4.6	140
	1720	-0.5	-15
2 Th	0000	4.5	137
	0547	-0.2	-6
	1221	4.4	134
	1815	-0.4	-12
3 F ◐	0055	4.5	137
	0652	0.0	0
	1317	4.2	128
	1915	-0.4	-12
4 Sa	0158	4.5	137
	0802	0.0	0
	1422	4.0	122
	2019	-0.4	-12
5 Su	0309	4.5	137
	0912	0.0	0
	1534	4.0	122
	2124	-0.5	-15
6 M	0421	4.6	140
	1018	-0.1	-3
	1645	4.0	122
	2228	-0.6	-18
7 Tu	0526	4.8	146
	1120	-0.4	-12
	1748	4.1	125
	2330	-0.8	-24
8 W	0624	4.9	149
	1218	-0.6	-18
	1846	4.3	131
9 Th	0027	-1.0	-30
	0718	5.0	152
	1310	-0.8	-24
	1939	4.4	134
10 F ○	0120	-1.2	-37
	0807	5.1	155
	1359	-1.0	-30
	2028	4.5	137
11 Sa	0210	-1.2	-37
	0853	5.0	152
	1443	-1.0	-30
	2115	4.5	137
12 Su	0256	-1.1	-34
	0937	4.9	149
	1526	-0.9	-27
	2159	4.4	134
13 M	0342	-0.9	-27
	1018	4.7	143
	1608	-0.7	-21
	2242	4.4	134
14 Tu	0428	-0.6	-18
	1058	4.5	137
	1649	-0.4	-12
	2323	4.3	131
15 W	0516	-0.2	-6
	1137	4.3	131
	1732	-0.1	-3
16 Th	0004	4.2	128
	0607	0.1	3
	1217	4.1	125
	1817	0.1	3
17 F	0047	4.1	125
	0701	0.4	12
	1300	3.9	119
	1905	0.4	12
18 Sa ◐	0135	4.0	122
	0757	0.6	18
	1349	3.8	116
	1955	0.5	15
19 Su	0229	4.0	122
	0852	0.7	21
	1444	3.7	113
	2047	0.5	15
20 M	0329	4.0	122
	0945	0.7	21
	1543	3.7	113
	2139	0.5	15
21 Tu	0428	4.1	125
	1037	0.6	18
	1641	3.7	113
	2231	0.3	9
22 W	0521	4.3	131
	1125	0.4	12
	1734	3.9	119
	2321	0.1	3
23 Th	0609	4.4	134
	1210	0.1	3
	1822	4.0	122
24 F	0008	-0.2	-6
	0654	4.6	140
	1251	-0.1	-3
	1908	4.2	128
25 Sa	0052	-0.5	-15
	0736	4.7	143
	1329	-0.4	-12
	1952	4.4	134
26 Su ●	0134	-0.7	-21
	0818	4.8	146
	1407	-0.7	-21
	2035	4.5	137
27 M	0217	-0.9	-27
	0900	4.9	149
	1445	-0.8	-24
	2120	4.7	143
28 Tu	0300	-0.9	-27
	0944	4.8	146
	1525	-0.9	-27
	2205	4.8	146

March

Day	Time (h m)	Height (ft)	Height (cm)
1 W	0347	-0.8	-24
	1029	4.7	143
	1609	-0.8	-24
	2253	4.8	146
2 Th	0438	-0.6	-18
	1116	4.6	140
	1658	-0.7	-21
	2344	4.8	146
3 F	0537	-0.4	-12
	1208	4.4	134
	1754	-0.5	-15
4 Sa	0040	4.8	146
	0642	-0.1	-3
	1306	4.2	128
	1858	-0.3	-9
5 Su ◐	0144	4.7	143
	0752	0.0	0
	1413	4.1	125
	2006	-0.2	-6
6 M	0256	4.6	140
	0901	0.1	3
	1526	4.0	122
	2113	-0.2	-6
7 Tu	0409	4.6	140
	1005	0.0	0
	1637	4.1	125
	2219	-0.3	-9
8 W	0514	4.8	146
	1106	-0.2	-6
	1739	4.3	131
	2320	-0.5	-15
9 Th	0611	4.9	149
	1201	-0.4	-12
	1834	4.5	137
10 F	0017	-0.7	-21
	0702	4.9	149
	1252	-0.6	-18
	1924	4.6	140
11 Sa	0108	-0.8	-24
	0748	4.9	149
	1337	-0.7	-21
	2010	4.7	143
12 Su ○	0155	-0.9	-27
	0831	4.9	149
	1419	-0.8	-24
	2053	4.7	143
13 M	0239	-0.8	-24
	0911	4.7	143
	1457	-0.7	-21
	2133	4.7	143
14 Tu	0321	-0.7	-21
	0949	4.6	140
	1534	-0.5	-15
	2211	4.6	140
15 W	0402	-0.4	-12
	1026	4.4	134
	1609	-0.2	-6
	2248	4.5	137
16 Th	0445	-0.1	-3
	1102	4.3	131
	1645	0.0	0
	2324	4.5	137
17 F	0529	0.2	6
	1140	4.1	125
	1723	0.3	9
18 Sa	0003	4.4	134
	0617	0.5	15
	1221	4.0	122
	1806	0.6	18
19 Su	0045	4.3	131
	0709	0.8	24
	1306	3.9	119
	1855	0.7	21
20 M ◐	0134	4.2	128
	0803	0.9	27
	1358	3.8	116
	1951	0.8	24
21 Tu	0231	4.2	128
	0857	0.9	27
	1457	3.8	116
	2049	0.8	24
22 W	0334	4.2	128
	0949	0.8	24
	1558	3.9	119
	2146	0.6	18
23 Th	0434	4.3	131
	1039	0.6	18
	1655	4.1	125
	2242	0.3	9
24 F	0528	4.5	137
	1126	0.3	9
	1748	4.3	131
	2335	0.0	0
25 Sa	0617	4.7	143
	1211	-0.1	-3
	1837	4.6	140
26 Su	0025	-0.4	-12
	0703	4.8	146
	1254	-0.5	-15
	1924	4.8	146
27 M ●	0113	-0.7	-21
	0749	4.9	149
	1336	-0.8	-24
	2010	5.1	155
28 Tu	0200	-0.9	-27
	0835	4.9	149
	1418	-1.0	-30
	2057	5.2	158
29 W	0247	-1.0	-30
	0923	4.9	149
	1502	-1.0	-30
	2146	5.3	162
30 Th	0336	-0.9	-27
	1012	4.8	146
	1548	-0.9	-27
	2237	5.3	162
31 F	0429	-0.7	-21
	1103	4.7	143
	1640	-0.7	-21
	2330	5.2	158

Time meridian 75° W   0000 is midnight. 1200 is noon. Times are not adjusted for Daylight Saving Time.
Heights are referred to mean lower low water which is the chart datum of soundings.

Mayport, Florida, 2017

Times and Heights of High and Low Waters

	April				April				May				May				June				June		
	Time	Height			Time	Height			Time	Height			Time	Height			Time	Height			Time	Height	
	h m	ft	cm		h m	ft	cm		h m	ft	cm		h m	ft	cm		h m	ft	cm		h m	ft	cm
1 Sa	0528 1158 1738	-0.4 4.5 -0.4	-12 137 -12	**16** Su	0536 1149 1718	0.6 4.1 0.7	18 125 21	**1** M	0015 0621 1248 1833	5.2 -0.2 4.5 -0.1	158 -6 137 -3	**16** Tu	0543 1205 1730	0.6 4.1 0.7	18 125 21	**1** Th	0155 0803 1436 2028	4.8 -0.1 4.5 0.2	146 -3 137 6	**16** F	0037 0643 1313 1857	4.6 0.3 4.3 0.5	140 9 131 15
2 Su	0028 0633 1258 1845	5.1 -0.1 4.4 -0.1	155 -3 134 -3	**17** M	0006 0622 1232 1805	4.5 0.8 4.0 0.8	137 24 122 24	**2** Tu	0116 0726 1353 1942	5.0 -0.1 4.4 0.1	152 -3 134 3	**17** W	0019 0630 1251 1824	4.6 0.7 4.1 0.8	140 21 125 24	**2** F	0254 0858 1538 2127	4.6 -0.1 4.6 0.3	140 -3 140 9	**17** Sa	0126 0735 1408 2001	4.5 0.1 4.5 0.5	137 3 137 15
3 M	0132 0741 1405 1955	4.9 0.1 4.3 0.0	149 3 131 0	**18** Tu	0051 0713 1321 1901	4.5 0.9 4.0 0.9	137 27 122 27	**3** W	0222 0829 1501 2049	4.9 0.0 4.5 0.2	149 0 137 6	**18** Th	0106 0720 1342 1925	4.5 0.6 4.2 0.8	137 18 128 24	**3** Sa	0353 0949 1634 2223	4.4 0.0 4.7 0.3	134 0 143 9	**18** Su	0223 0830 1508 2106	4.4 -0.1 4.6 0.3	134 -3 140 9
4 Tu	0242 0847 1517 2103	4.8 0.1 4.3 0.1	146 3 131 3	**19** W	0143 0806 1416 2002	4.4 0.9 4.1 0.9	134 27 125 27	**4** Th	0327 0926 1605 2151	4.7 0.0 4.6 0.2	143 0 140 6	**19** F	0159 0813 1439 2028	4.5 0.5 4.3 0.6	137 15 131 18	**4** Su	0446 1037 1725 2316	4.3 0.0 4.8 0.3	131 0 146 9	**19** M	0325 0925 1611 2210	4.4 -0.3 4.9 0.1	134 -9 149 3
5 W	0352 0949 1625 2208	4.7 0.1 4.4 0.0	143 3 134 0	**20** Th	0242 0858 1516 2104	4.4 0.8 4.2 0.7	134 24 128 21	**5** F	0428 1020 1703 2249	4.7 0.0 4.7 0.2	143 0 143 6	**20** Sa	0258 0906 1539 2132	4.5 0.2 4.5 0.4	137 6 137 12	**5** M	0535 1123 1811	4.2 0.0 4.8	128 0 146	**20** Tu	0430 1022 1712 2312	4.3 -0.6 5.1 -0.2	131 -18 155 -6
6 Th	0455 1046 1724 2307	4.8 0.0 4.6 -0.1	146 0 140 -3	**21** F	0343 0950 1616 2204	4.4 0.5 4.4 0.5	134 15 134 15	**6** Sa	0522 1111 1754 2342	4.6 0.0 4.9 0.1	140 0 149 3	**21** Su	0400 0959 1639 2234	4.5 -0.1 4.8 0.1	137 -3 146 3	**6** Tu	0006 0620 1206 1853	0.2 4.2 0.0 4.9	6 128 0 149	**21** W	0533 1120 1811	4.4 -0.8 5.3	134 -24 162
7 F	0550 1139 1817	4.8 -0.2 4.7	146 -6 143	**22** Sa	0443 1040 1712 2303	4.5 0.2 4.6 0.1	137 6 140 3	**7** Su	0610 1157 1840	4.6 -0.1 4.9	140 -3 149	**22** M	0500 1052 1736 2334	4.5 -0.4 5.1 -0.2	137 -12 155 -6	**7** W	0052 0703 1247 1932	0.1 4.1 -0.1 4.9	3 125 -3 149	**22** Th	0012 0633 1217 1908	-0.5 4.4 -1.1 5.5	-15 134 -34 168
8 Sa	0002 0639 1227 1905	-0.2 4.8 -0.3 4.9	-6 146 -9 149	**23** Su	0537 1130 1805 2358	4.7 -0.2 4.9 -0.3	143 -6 149 -9	**8** M	0032 0654 1240 1922	-0.1 4.5 -0.2 5.0	-3 137 -6 152	**23** Tu	0558 1146 1831	4.6 -0.7 5.4	140 -21 165	**8** Th	0134 0743 1324 2010	0.0 4.1 -0.1 4.8	0 125 -3 146	**23** F	0109 0732 1312 2004	-0.8 4.5 -1.2 5.6	-24 137 -37 171
9 Su	0052 0724 1311 1948	-0.4 4.8 -0.4 4.9	-12 146 -12 149	**24** M	0629 1218 1856	4.8 -0.6 5.2	146 -18 158	**9** Tu	0117 0735 1319 2001	-0.2 4.4 -0.2 5.0	-6 134 -6 152	**24** W	0031 0654 1238 1925	-0.6 4.6 -1.0 5.6	-18 140 -30 171	**9** F	0213 0822 1359 2046	-0.1 4.0 -0.1 4.8	-3 122 -3 146	**24** Sa	0203 0830 1406 2059	-1.0 4.5 -1.2 5.6	-30 137 -37 171
10 M	0138 0805 1350 2028	-0.5 4.7 -0.4 4.9	-15 143 -12 149	**25** Tu	0051 0720 1305 1946	-0.6 4.9 -0.9 5.5	-18 149 -27 168	**10** W	0158 0814 1355 2038	-0.2 4.3 -0.2 4.9	-6 131 -6 149	**25** Th	0125 0749 1330 2019	-0.9 4.7 -1.2 5.7	-27 143 -37 174	**10** Sa	0250 0901 1431 2122	0.0 4.0 0.0 4.8	0 122 0 146	**25** Su	0256 0926 1500 2153	-1.0 4.5 -1.1 5.5	-30 137 -34 168
11 Tu	0220 0843 1426 2106	-0.5 4.6 -0.4 4.9	-15 140 -12 149	**26** W	0142 0811 1352 2037	-0.9 4.9 -1.1 5.6	-27 149 -34 171	**11** Th	0237 0851 1428 2113	-0.2 4.2 -0.1 4.9	-6 128 -3 149	**26** F	0218 0845 1422 2113	-1.0 4.7 -1.2 5.7	-30 143 -37 174	**11** Su	0324 0940 1503 2158	0.1 4.0 0.1 4.7	3 122 3 143	**26** M	0349 1022 1556 2246	-1.0 4.6 -0.9 5.4	-30 140 -27 165
12 W	0300 0920 1500 2141	-0.4 4.5 -0.2 4.8	-12 137 -6 146	**27** Th	0232 0903 1440 2129	-1.0 4.9 -1.1 5.6	-30 149 -34 171	**12** F	0314 0928 1459 2147	-0.1 4.2 0.0 4.8	-3 128 0 146	**27** Sa	0311 0941 1514 2208	-1.0 4.6 -1.1 5.6	-30 140 -34 171	**12** M	0358 1019 1537 2235	0.2 4.0 0.2 4.7	6 122 6 143	**27** Tu	0443 1117 1654 2338	-0.8 4.5 -0.5 5.1	-24 137 -15 155
13 Th	0338 0956 1532 2215	-0.2 4.3 0.0 4.8	-6 131 0 146	**28** F	0324 0956 1530 2222	-0.9 4.8 -1.0 5.6	-27 146 -30 171	**13** Sa	0350 1005 1530 2222	0.1 4.1 0.2 4.7	3 125 6 143	**28** Su	0405 1037 1610 2303	-0.9 4.6 -0.8 5.4	-27 140 -24 165	**13** Tu	0432 1059 1617 2312	0.3 4.0 0.3 4.7	9 122 9 143	**28** W	0539 1212 1756	-0.6 4.5 -0.2	-18 137 -6
14 F	0416 1032 1604 2250	0.1 4.2 0.2 4.7	3 128 6 143	**29** Sa	0418 1051 1624 2317	-0.7 4.7 -0.7 5.4	-21 143 -21 165	**14** Su	0425 1043 1604 2258	0.3 4.1 0.4 4.7	9 125 12 143	**29** M	0503 1134 1711 2359	-0.7 4.5 -0.5 5.2	-21 137 -15 158	**14** W	0510 1140 1703 2353	0.3 4.1 0.4 4.6	9 125 12 140	**29** Th	0030 0636 1308 1900	4.9 -0.4 4.5 0.1	149 -12 137 3
15 Sa	0455 1109 1638 2327	0.3 4.2 0.4 4.6	9 128 12 140	**30** Su	0517 1148 1725	-0.5 4.6 -0.4	-15 140 -12	**15** M	0502 1123 1643 2337	0.5 4.1 0.6 4.6	15 125 18 140	**30** Tu	0604 1233 1817	-0.4 4.5 -0.1	-12 137 -3	**15** Th	0554 1225 1756	0.3 4.2 0.5	9 128 15	**30** F	0122 0731 1405 2001	4.6 -0.2 4.5 0.3	140 -6 137 9
												31 W	0056 0705 1334 1924	5.0 -0.3 4.5 0.1	152 -9 137 3								

Time meridian 75° W. 0000 is midnight. 1200 is noon. Times are not adjusted for Daylight Saving Time.
Heights are referred to mean lower low water which is the chart datum of soundings.

Mayport, Florida, 2017

Times and Heights of High and Low Waters

July

Day	Time	Height (ft)	Height (cm)		Day	Time	Height (ft)	Height (cm)
1 Sa	0216	4.4	134		16 Su ◯	0102	4.6	140
	0823	0.0	0			0705	-0.1	-3
	1502	4.5	137			1343	4.7	143
	2058	0.4	12			1940	0.4	12
2 Su	0311	4.2	128		17 M	0158	4.4	134
	0912	0.1	3			0801	-0.2	-6
	1558	4.6	140			1444	4.8	146
	2153	0.5	15			2047	0.3	9
3 M	0405	4.1	125		18 Tu	0301	4.3	131
	1000	0.1	3			0900	-0.3	-9
	1649	4.6	140			1550	5.0	152
	2245	0.5	15			2152	0.2	6
4 Tu	0455	4.0	122		19 W	0409	4.3	131
	1046	0.2	6			1000	-0.5	-15
	1737	4.7	143			1655	5.2	158
	2335	0.4	12			2256	-0.1	-3
5 W	0543	4.0	122		20 Th	0516	4.3	131
	1131	0.1	3			1101	-0.7	-21
	1821	4.8	146			1757	5.4	165
						2357	-0.3	-9
6 Th	0022	0.3	9		21 F	0619	4.4	134
	0628	4.0	122			1201	-0.9	-27
	1214	0.1	3			1855	5.5	168
	1902	4.8	146					
7 F	0106	0.2	6		22 Sa	0054	-0.6	-18
	0711	4.0	122			0718	4.5	137
	1254	0.0	0			1259	-1.0	-30
	1941	4.8	146			1951	5.6	171
8 Sa ◯	0146	0.1	3		23 Su ●	0148	-0.8	-24
	0753	4.0	122			0815	4.6	140
	1331	0.0	0			1354	-1.0	-30
	2019	4.8	146			2044	5.6	171
9 Su	0222	0.0	0		24 M	0239	-0.9	-27
	0833	4.0	122			0910	4.7	143
	1405	0.0	0			1447	-1.0	-30
	2057	4.8	146			2135	5.5	168
10 M	0256	0.0	0		25 Tu	0328	-0.8	-24
	0914	4.0	122			1003	4.7	143
	1440	0.0	0			1540	-0.7	-21
	2134	4.8	146			2224	5.3	162
11 Tu	0329	0.0	0		26 W	0418	-0.7	-21
	0954	4.1	125			1054	4.7	143
	1516	0.0	0			1634	-0.4	-12
	2211	4.8	146			2312	5.1	155
12 W	0402	0.1	3		27 Th	0508	-0.4	-12
	1035	4.2	128			1145	4.7	143
	1556	0.1	3			1731	0.0	0
	2249	4.8	146			2359	4.9	149
13 Th	0439	0.1	3		28 F	0600	-0.2	-6
	1117	4.3	131			1235	4.7	143
	1642	0.2	6			1830	0.3	9
	2330	4.7	143					
14 F	0522	0.1	3		29 Sa	0046	4.6	140
	1201	4.4	134			0652	0.1	3
	1735	0.4	12			1326	4.6	140
						1928	0.5	15
15 Sa	0013	4.7	143		30 Su ◑	0134	4.4	134
	0611	0.0	0			0742	0.3	9
	1249	4.6	140			1419	4.6	140
	1835	0.4	12			2025	0.7	21
					31 M	0225	4.2	128
						0832	0.4	12
						1514	4.6	140
						2119	0.8	24

August

Day	Time	Height (ft)	Height (cm)		Day	Time	Height (ft)	Height (cm)
1 Tu	0318	4.1	125		16 W	0249	4.5	137
	0920	0.5	15			0844	0.0	0
	1607	4.7	143			1537	5.2	158
	2211	0.8	24			2140	0.5	15
2 W	0412	4.1	125		17 Th	0400	4.5	137
	1007	0.6	18			0947	-0.1	-3
	1658	4.7	143			1644	5.4	165
	2301	0.8	24			2243	0.3	9
3 Th	0504	4.1	125		18 F	0507	4.6	140
	1054	0.5	15			1050	-0.2	-6
	1744	4.8	146			1746	5.5	168
	2349	0.7	21			2343	0.0	0
4 F	0552	4.1	125		19 Sa	0609	4.7	143
	1140	0.4	12			1151	-0.4	-12
	1828	4.9	149			1843	5.6	171
5 Sa	0033	0.5	15		20 Su	0038	-0.2	-6
	0638	4.2	128			0707	4.9	149
	1223	0.3	9			1248	-0.5	-15
	1910	5.0	152			1936	5.7	174
6 Su	0113	0.4	12		21 M ●	0130	-0.4	-12
	0722	4.3	131			0801	5.0	152
	1303	0.2	6			1342	-0.6	-18
	1949	5.0	152			2026	5.6	171
7 M ○	0150	0.2	6		22 Tu	0218	-0.5	-15
	0804	4.4	134			0852	5.1	155
	1341	0.1	3			1432	-0.5	-15
	2028	5.1	155			2114	5.5	168
8 Tu	0224	0.1	3		23 W	0304	-0.5	-15
	0846	4.5	137			0941	5.1	155
	1418	0.0	0			1521	-0.3	-9
	2107	5.1	155			2159	5.4	165
9 W	0257	0.0	0		24 Th	0348	-0.3	-9
	0927	4.6	140			1028	5.1	155
	1457	0.0	0			1611	-0.1	-3
	2146	5.1	155			2243	5.2	158
10 Th	0332	0.0	0		25 F	0433	0.0	0
	1009	4.7	143			1113	5.1	155
	1538	0.1	3			1702	0.3	9
	2226	5.0	152			2325	5.0	152
11 F	0410	0.0	0		26 Sa	0518	0.3	9
	1053	4.8	146			1158	5.0	152
	1625	0.2	6			1756	0.6	18
	2309	5.0	152					
12 Sa	0454	0.0	0		27 Su	0008	4.8	146
	1139	4.9	149			0606	0.6	18
	1719	0.4	12			1243	4.9	149
	2355	4.9	149			1852	0.9	27
13 Su	0544	0.1	3		28 M	0052	4.6	140
	1229	5.0	152			0656	0.8	24
	1820	0.5	15			1331	4.9	149
						1947	1.2	37
14 M ◑	0045	4.7	143		29 Tu ◑	0140	4.5	137
	0640	0.1	3			0746	1.0	30
	1324	5.1	155			1423	4.8	146
	1926	0.6	18			2041	1.3	40
15 Tu	0143	4.6	140		30 W	0232	4.4	134
	0741	0.1	3			0836	1.1	34
	1428	5.2	158			1518	4.9	149
	2034	0.6	18			2133	1.3	40
					31 Th	0328	4.4	134
						0926	1.1	34
						1613	4.9	149
						2222	1.3	40

September

Day	Time	Height (ft)	Height (cm)		Day	Time	Height (ft)	Height (cm)
1 F	0424	4.4	134		16 Sa	0501	5.0	152
	1016	1.0	30			1043	0.3	9
	1704	5.0	152			1734	5.7	174
	2310	1.1	34			2327	0.4	12
2 Sa	0516	4.5	137		17 Su	0600	5.2	158
	1104	0.9	27			1142	0.1	3
	1750	5.1	155			1828	5.8	177
	2354	0.9	27					
3 Su	0604	4.7	143		18 M	0020	0.2	6
	1150	0.7	21			0654	5.4	165
	1834	5.2	158			1237	0.0	0
						1918	5.8	177
4 M	0035	0.7	21		19 Tu	0109	0.0	0
	0649	4.8	146			0744	5.5	168
	1234	0.5	15			1328	-0.1	-3
	1916	5.3	162			2005	5.7	174
5 Tu	0113	0.5	15		20 W ●	0154	-0.1	-3
	0733	5.0	152			0831	5.5	168
	1316	0.3	9			1416	0.0	0
	1957	5.4	165			2049	5.6	171
6 W	0149	0.2	6		21 Th	0236	0.0	0
	0816	5.1	155			0916	5.5	168
	1357	0.2	6			1502	0.1	3
	2038	5.4	165			2131	5.4	165
7 Th	0225	0.1	3		22 F	0316	0.1	3
	0900	5.2	158			0958	5.5	168
	1438	0.1	3			1547	0.3	9
	2120	5.4	165			2212	5.2	158
8 F	0302	0.0	0		23 Sa	0355	0.4	12
	0944	5.4	165			1039	5.4	165
	1523	0.2	6			1632	0.6	18
	2204	5.3	162			2251	5.0	152
9 Sa	0343	0.0	0		24 Su	0435	0.7	21
	1030	5.5	168			1119	5.3	162
	1611	0.3	9			1720	1.0	30
	2250	5.2	158			2331	4.9	149
10 Su	0429	0.1	3		25 M	0517	1.0	30
	1119	5.5	168			1200	5.2	158
	1706	0.5	15			1812	1.3	40
	2339	5.1	155					
11 M	0521	0.2	6		26 Tu	0013	4.8	146
	1212	5.5	168			0602	1.2	37
	1808	0.7	21			1243	5.1	155
						1906	1.5	46
12 Tu	0034	5.0	152		27 W ◑	0059	4.7	143
	0621	0.4	12			0653	1.4	43
	1311	5.5	168			1331	5.1	155
	1917	0.8	24			1959	1.6	49
13 W ◑	0135	4.9	149		28 Th	0149	4.6	140
	0727	0.5	15			0747	1.5	46
	1417	5.5	168			1425	5.1	155
	2025	0.8	24			2051	1.6	49
14 Th	0244	4.8	146		29 F	0245	4.6	140
	0834	0.5	15			0842	1.5	46
	1527	5.5	168			1522	5.1	155
	2129	0.8	24			2139	1.6	49
15 F	0355	4.9	149		30 Sa	0342	4.7	143
	0940	0.4	12			0935	1.4	43
	1634	5.6	171			1617	5.2	158
	2230	0.6	18			2226	1.4	43

Time meridian 75° W. 0000 is midnight. 1200 is noon. Times are not adjusted for Daylight Saving Time.
Heights are referred to mean lower low water which is the chart datum of soundings.

Mayport, Florida, 2017

Times and Heights of High and Low Waters

October

Day	Time (h m)	ft	cm
1 Su	0437	4.9	149
	1026	1.2	37
	1708	5.3	162
	2310	1.2	37
2 M	0528	5.1	155
	1116	1.0	30
	1755	5.4	165
	2353	0.8	24
3 Tu	0616	5.3	162
	1204	0.7	21
	1839	5.5	168
4 W	0033	0.5	15
	0701	5.5	168
	1250	0.4	12
	1924	5.6	171
5 Th ○	0113	0.2	6
	0747	5.7	174
	1335	0.2	6
	2008	5.6	171
6 F	0153	0.0	0
	0833	5.8	177
	1421	0.1	3
	2054	5.6	171
7 Sa	0235	-0.1	-3
	0920	5.9	180
	1508	0.1	3
	2143	5.5	168
8 Su	0320	-0.1	-3
	1010	6.0	183
	1559	0.3	9
	2233	5.4	165
9 M	0408	0.1	3
	1102	6.0	183
	1655	0.5	15
	2327	5.2	158
10 Tu	0504	0.3	9
	1158	5.9	180
	1758	0.7	21
11 W	0025	5.1	155
	0607	0.5	15
	1259	5.8	177
	1907	0.8	24
12 Th ◑	0129	5.0	152
	0717	0.7	21
	1405	5.7	174
	2014	0.9	27
13 F	0238	5.0	152
	0827	0.8	24
	1514	5.6	171
	2116	0.8	24
14 Sa	0348	5.1	155
	0932	0.7	21
	1619	5.7	174
	2214	0.7	21
15 Su	0451	5.3	162
	1034	0.6	18
	1717	5.7	174
	2309	0.5	15
16 M	0548	5.5	168
	1131	0.5	15
	1809	5.7	174
	2359	0.4	12
17 Tu	0639	5.6	171
	1224	0.4	12
	1857	5.6	171
18 W	0045	0.2	6
	0725	5.7	174
	1313	0.3	9
	1941	5.5	168
19 Th ●	0128	0.2	6
	0809	5.7	174
	1359	0.3	9
	2023	5.4	165
20 F	0207	0.2	6
	0850	5.7	174
	1441	0.3	9
	2102	5.2	158
21 Sa	0244	0.3	9
	0929	5.6	171
	1523	0.5	15
	2141	5.1	155
22 Su	0320	0.5	15
	1006	5.5	168
	1604	0.8	24
	2219	4.9	149
23 M	0355	0.8	24
	1043	5.4	165
	1646	1.0	30
	2258	4.8	146
24 Tu	0431	1.1	34
	1121	5.3	162
	1731	1.3	40
	2339	4.7	143
25 W	0511	1.3	40
	1202	5.2	158
	1820	1.5	46
26 Th	0022	4.7	143
	0559	1.5	46
	1246	5.2	158
	1911	1.6	49
27 F ◑	0110	4.7	143
	0654	1.6	49
	1335	5.1	155
	2002	1.6	49
28 Sa	0203	4.7	143
	0752	1.6	49
	1430	5.1	155
	2050	1.5	46
29 Su	0300	4.8	146
	0850	1.5	46
	1526	5.1	155
	2137	1.3	40
30 M	0357	5.0	152
	0946	1.3	40
	1621	5.2	158
	2223	1.0	30
31 Tu	0451	5.2	158
	1041	1.0	30
	1714	5.3	162
	2309	0.7	21

November

Day	Time (h m)	ft	cm
1 W	0542	5.4	165
	1134	0.7	21
	1803	5.4	165
	2354	0.3	9
2 Th	0631	5.7	174
	1226	0.3	9
	1852	5.4	165
3 F	0040	-0.1	-3
	0720	5.9	180
	1315	0.0	0
	1941	5.4	165
4 Sa ○	0126	-0.3	-9
	0809	6.1	186
	1404	-0.1	-3
	2032	5.4	165
5 Su	0212	-0.4	-12
	0900	6.1	186
	1454	-0.2	-6
	2124	5.3	162
6 M	0300	-0.4	-12
	0953	6.1	186
	1546	0.0	0
	2218	5.2	158
7 Tu	0352	-0.2	-6
	1048	6.0	183
	1643	0.1	3
	2315	5.1	155
8 W	0450	0.1	3
	1145	5.9	180
	1746	0.4	12
9 Th	0014	5.0	152
	0555	0.3	9
	1245	5.7	174
	1852	0.5	15
10 F ○	0118	5.0	152
	0706	0.6	18
	1349	5.6	171
	1957	0.6	18
11 Sa	0226	5.0	152
	0815	0.7	21
	1454	5.4	165
	2057	0.6	18
12 Su	0333	5.1	155
	0919	0.7	21
	1557	5.4	165
	2153	0.5	15
13 M	0434	5.3	162
	1019	0.6	18
	1654	5.3	162
	2245	0.4	12
14 Tu	0530	5.4	165
	1115	0.5	15
	1746	5.2	158
	2334	0.3	9
15 W	0619	5.5	168
	1207	0.4	12
	1832	5.1	155
16 Th	0019	0.2	6
	0704	5.5	168
	1255	0.3	9
	1916	5.0	152
17 F	0101	0.2	6
	0746	5.5	168
	1339	0.3	9
	1956	4.9	149
18 Sa ●	0140	0.2	6
	0825	5.5	168
	1421	0.3	9
	2035	4.8	146
19 Su	0216	0.2	6
	0902	5.4	165
	1500	0.4	12
	2113	4.7	143
20 M	0249	0.4	12
	0937	5.3	162
	1537	0.5	15
	2150	4.6	140
21 Tu	0322	0.5	15
	1013	5.2	158
	1615	0.7	21
	2228	4.5	137
22 W	0355	0.7	21
	1049	5.1	155
	1653	0.9	27
	2308	4.5	137
23 Th	0432	0.9	27
	1127	5.0	152
	1734	1.1	34
	2349	4.4	134
24 F	0516	1.1	34
	1208	5.0	152
	1819	1.2	37
25 Sa	0034	4.4	134
	0607	1.2	37
	1253	4.9	149
	1907	1.2	37
26 Su ◐	0123	4.5	137
	0705	1.3	40
	1342	4.9	149
	1956	1.1	34
27 M	0217	4.6	140
	0807	1.2	37
	1437	4.8	146
	2046	0.8	24
28 Tu	0316	4.8	146
	0908	1.0	30
	1535	4.8	146
	2137	0.5	15
29 W	0414	5.0	152
	1008	0.7	21
	1634	4.9	149
	2228	0.2	6
30 Th	0510	5.3	162
	1106	0.4	12
	1730	4.9	149
	2320	-0.2	-6

December

Day	Time (h m)	ft	cm
1 F	0604	5.5	168
	1203	0.0	0
	1825	5.0	152
2 Sa	0012	-0.5	-15
	0657	5.7	174
	1257	-0.3	-9
	1919	5.0	152
3 Su	0103	-0.8	-24
	0750	5.9	180
	1349	-0.5	-15
	2013	5.0	152
4 M	0154	-0.9	-27
	0844	6.0	183
	1441	-0.6	-18
	2108	5.0	152
5 Tu	0245	-0.9	-27
	0939	5.9	180
	1533	-0.6	-18
	2204	4.9	149
6 W	0339	-0.7	-21
	1033	5.8	177
	1629	-0.4	-12
	2301	4.9	149
7 Th	0437	-0.5	-15
	1129	5.6	171
	1728	-0.2	-6
	2359	4.8	146
8 F	0541	-0.1	-3
	1226	5.4	165
	1831	0.0	0
9 Sa	0100	4.8	146
	0649	0.2	6
	1325	5.2	158
	1932	0.1	3
10 Su ○	0204	4.7	143
	0756	0.4	12
	1426	4.9	149
	2031	0.1	3
11 M	0309	4.8	146
	0900	0.4	12
	1527	4.8	146
	2125	0.2	6
12 Tu	0410	4.9	149
	0959	0.5	15
	1625	4.6	140
	2216	0.2	6
13 W	0505	5.0	152
	1054	0.4	12
	1717	4.6	140
	2305	0.1	3
14 Th	0555	5.0	152
	1146	0.3	9
	1805	4.5	137
	2351	0.1	3
15 F	0640	5.1	155
	1234	0.2	6
	1849	4.4	134
16 Sa	0034	0.0	0
	0721	5.1	155
	1318	0.1	3
	1930	4.3	131
17 Su	0114	0.0	0
	0800	5.0	152
	1359	0.1	3
	2009	4.3	131
18 M ●	0150	-0.1	-3
	0837	5.0	152
	1437	0.1	3
	2047	4.2	128
19 Tu	0224	0.0	0
	0912	4.9	149
	1512	0.1	3
	2124	4.2	128
20 W	0256	0.1	3
	0947	4.9	149
	1546	0.3	9
	2202	4.2	128
21 Th	0328	0.2	6
	1022	4.8	146
	1619	0.4	12
	2240	4.1	125
22 F	0404	0.3	9
	1058	4.7	143
	1653	0.5	15
	2320	4.2	128
23 Sa	0444	0.5	15
	1136	4.7	143
	1732	0.5	15
24 Su	0001	4.2	128
	0532	0.6	18
	1217	4.6	140
	1817	0.5	15
25 M	0047	4.3	131
	0627	0.7	21
	1302	4.5	137
	1908	0.4	12
26 Tu ◐	0138	4.4	134
	0729	0.7	21
	1355	4.4	134
	2001	0.2	6
27 W	0236	4.5	137
	0834	0.6	18
	1455	4.4	134
	2057	0.0	0
28 Th	0339	4.7	143
	0939	0.3	9
	1559	4.3	131
	2154	-0.3	-9
29 F	0442	4.9	149
	1042	0.0	0
	1703	4.4	134
	2252	-0.6	-18
30 Sa	0543	5.2	158
	1143	-0.3	-9
	1803	4.4	134
	2349	-0.9	-27
31 Su	0640	5.4	165
	1240	-0.6	-18
	1901	4.5	137

Time meridian 75° W. 0000 is midnight. 1200 is noon. Times are not adjusted for Daylight Saving Time.
Heights are referred to mean lower low water which is the chart datum of soundings.

Port Canaveral (Trident Pier), Florida, 2017

Times and Heights of High and Low Waters

January

Day	Time	ft	cm	Day	Time	ft	cm
1 Su	0307	-0.1	-3	16 M	0410	-0.3	-9
	0939	3.9	119		1031	3.8	116
	1556	0.1	3		1654	-0.2	-6
	2155	3.1	94		2259	3.2	98
2 M	0353	0.0	0	17 Tu	0504	0.0	0
	1020	3.8	116		1116	3.4	104
	1641	0.0	0		1742	-0.1	-3
	2241	3.1	94		2350	3.1	94
3 Tu	0444	0.1	3	18 W	0559	0.2	6
	1104	3.7	113		1202	3.1	94
	1728	0.0	0		1829	0.0	0
	2331	3.2	98				
4 W	0540	0.1	3	19 Th	0046	3.0	91
	1152	3.5	107		0655	0.4	12
	1817	-0.1	-3		1253	2.8	85
					1916	0.1	3
5 Th	0027	3.3	101	20 F	0145	3.0	91
	0641	0.2	6		0752	0.6	18
	1246	3.4	104		1348	2.6	79
	1909	-0.2	-6		2004	0.2	6
6 F	0129	3.5	107	21 Sa	0244	3.1	94
	0744	0.2	6		0849	0.6	18
	1346	3.3	101		1445	2.5	76
	2004	-0.3	-9		2052	0.2	6
7 Sa	0234	3.7	113	22 Su	0339	3.2	98
	0848	0.1	3		0946	0.6	18
	1449	3.2	98		1539	2.5	76
	2100	-0.5	-15		2142	0.1	3
8 Su	0337	4.0	122	23 M	0427	3.3	101
	0953	0.0	0		1039	0.5	15
	1551	3.2	98		1629	2.6	79
	2158	-0.7	-21		2231	0.0	0
9 M	0436	4.2	128	24 Tu	0512	3.4	104
	1056	-0.2	-6		1126	0.3	9
	1650	3.3	101		1716	2.6	79
	2256	-0.8	-24		2317	-0.1	-3
10 Tu	0533	4.4	134	25 W	0554	3.6	110
	1154	-0.3	-9		1209	0.2	6
	1747	3.4	104		1800	2.8	85
	2351	-0.9	-27				
11 W	0628	4.5	137	26 Th	0001	-0.3	-9
	1248	-0.4	-12		0635	3.7	113
	1843	3.4	104		1249	0.0	0
					1843	2.9	88
12 Th	0045	-1.0	-30	27 F	0043	-0.4	-12
	0721	4.6	140		0716	3.8	116
	1339	-0.5	-15		1328	-0.1	-3
	1937	3.5	107		1926	3.0	91
13 F	0136	-0.9	-27	28 Sa	0124	-0.5	-15
	0812	4.5	137		0756	3.9	119
	1428	-0.5	-15		1406	-0.2	-6
	2030	3.5	107		2008	3.1	94
14 Sa	0227	-0.8	-24	29 Su	0205	-0.5	-15
	0900	4.3	131		0836	3.9	119
	1516	-0.4	-12		1446	-0.3	-9
	2120	3.5	107		2051	3.2	98
15 Su	0318	-0.6	-18	30 M	0249	-0.5	-15
	0946	4.1	125		0916	3.9	119
	1605	-0.3	-9		1527	-0.3	-9
	2210	3.4	104		2135	3.3	101
				31 Tu	0336	-0.4	-12
					0958	3.8	116
					1611	-0.4	-12
					2221	3.4	104

February

Day	Time	ft	cm	Day	Time	ft	cm
1 W	0428	-0.3	-9	16 Th	0522	0.2	6
	1042	3.6	110		1122	3.0	91
	1658	-0.4	-12		1740	0.1	3
	2310	3.5	107		2358	3.1	94
2 Th	0524	0.1	3	17 F	0614	0.4	12
	1130	3.4	104		1207	2.7	82
	1749	-0.4	-12		1826	0.2	6
3 F	0006	3.5	107	18 Sa	0050	3.0	91
	0624	0.0	0		0708	0.5	15
	1224	3.2	98		1258	2.5	76
	1843	-0.4	-12		1915	0.2	6
4 Sa	0107	3.6	110	19 Su	0148	3.0	91
	0728	0.1	3		0803	0.6	18
	1325	3.0	91		1355	2.4	73
	1940	-0.5	-15		2006	0.3	9
5 Su	0214	3.7	113	20 M	0248	3.0	91
	0833	0.1	3		0859	0.6	18
	1430	2.9	88		1455	2.4	73
	2040	-0.5	-15		2100	0.2	6
6 M	0321	3.8	116	21 Tu	0343	3.2	98
	0939	0.0	0		0955	0.5	15
	1536	3.0	91		1551	2.5	76
	2141	-0.6	-18		2153	0.1	3
7 Tu	0423	4.0	122	22 W	0433	3.3	101
	1043	-0.1	-3		1046	0.4	12
	1638	3.1	94		1642	2.7	82
	2242	-0.7	-21		2245	0.0	0
8 W	0521	4.1	125	23 Th	0519	3.5	107
	1141	-0.3	-9		1133	0.2	6
	1736	3.2	98		1728	2.9	88
	2340	-0.8	-24		2333	-0.2	-6
9 Th	0616	4.2	128	24 F	0603	3.7	113
	1233	-0.4	-12		1215	0.0	0
	1831	3.4	104		1814	3.1	94
10 F	0033	-0.8	-24	25 Sa	0018	-0.4	-12
	0706	4.2	128		0645	3.8	116
	1321	-0.5	-15		1255	-0.2	-6
	1923	3.5	107		1858	3.3	101
11 Sa	0123	-0.8	-24	26 Su	0102	-0.5	-15
	0754	4.1	125		0728	3.9	119
	1405	-0.5	-15		1335	-0.4	-12
	2012	3.5	107		1943	3.5	107
12 Su	0210	-0.7	-21	27 M	0146	-0.6	-18
	0838	4.0	122		0810	4.0	122
	1448	-0.4	-12		1416	-0.5	-15
	2058	3.5	107		2028	3.7	113
13 M	0257	-0.5	-15	28 Tu	0232	-0.6	-18
	0920	3.8	116		0853	3.9	119
	1530	-0.4	-12		1458	-0.6	-18
	2143	3.5	107		2114	3.8	116
14 Tu	0344	-0.3	-9				
	1001	3.5	107				
	1613	-0.2	-6				
	2226	3.4	104				
15 W	0432	0.0	0				
	1041	3.2	98				
	1656	-0.1	-3				
	2311	3.2	98				

March

Day	Time	ft	cm	Day	Time	ft	cm
1 W	0321	-0.5	-15	16 Th	0403	0.1	3
	0937	3.8	116		1008	3.1	94
	1543	-0.6	-18		1612	0.1	3
	2202	3.9	119		2235	3.5	107
2 Th	0414	-0.4	-12	17 F	0449	0.3	9
	1023	3.6	110		1047	2.9	88
	1632	-0.5	-15		1655	0.2	6
	2252	3.9	119		2317	3.4	104
3 F	0511	-0.2	-6	18 Sa	0538	0.5	15
	1112	3.4	104		1129	2.7	82
	1725	-0.5	-15		1741	0.3	9
	2347	3.9	119				
4 Sa	0612	-0.1	-3	19 Su	0004	3.3	101
	1207	3.2	98		0629	0.6	18
	1821	-0.4	-12		1217	2.6	79
					1831	0.4	12
5 Su	0049	3.8	116	20 M	0056	3.2	98
	0715	0.1	3		0721	0.6	18
	1310	3.0	91		1312	2.5	76
	1922	-0.3	-9		1923	0.5	15
6 M	0157	3.8	116	21 Tu	0155	3.1	94
	0820	0.1	3		0815	0.7	21
	1419	3.0	91		1412	2.5	76
	2025	-0.3	-9		2018	0.4	12
7 Tu	0306	3.8	116	22 W	0254	3.2	98
	0926	0.1	3		0909	0.6	18
	1528	3.0	91		1512	2.7	82
	2130	-0.3	-9		2114	0.3	9
8 W	0411	3.8	116	23 Th	0348	3.3	101
	1029	0.0	0		1002	0.4	12
	1631	3.2	98		1606	2.9	88
	2233	-0.4	-12		2209	0.2	6
9 Th	0508	3.9	119	24 F	0438	3.5	107
	1126	-0.1	-3		1050	0.2	6
	1727	3.3	101		1655	3.1	94
	2331	-0.4	-12		2302	-0.1	-3
10 F	0600	3.9	119	25 Sa	0525	3.7	113
	1215	-0.2	-6		1136	0.0	0
	1819	3.5	107		1743	3.4	104
					2352	-0.3	-9
11 Sa	0023	-0.5	-15	26 Su	0610	3.8	116
	0648	3.9	119		1219	-0.3	-9
	1258	-0.3	-9		1830	3.8	116
	1907	3.6	110				
12 Su	0110	-0.5	-15	27 M	0040	-0.5	-15
	0732	3.8	116		0656	3.9	119
	1338	-0.3	-9		1302	-0.5	-15
	1952	3.7	113		1918	4.0	122
13 M	0154	-0.4	-12	28 Tu	0127	-0.6	-18
	0813	3.7	113		0742	4.0	122
	1416	-0.3	-9		1345	-0.6	-18
	2034	3.7	113		2005	4.3	131
14 Tu	0237	-0.3	-9	29 W	0216	-0.6	-18
	0852	3.5	107		0829	3.9	119
	1454	-0.2	-6		1429	-0.7	-21
	2115	3.7	113		2054	4.4	134
15 W	0319	-0.1	-3	30 Th	0307	-0.6	-18
	0930	3.4	104		0916	3.8	116
	1532	-0.1	-3		1517	-0.7	-21
	2154	3.6	110		2144	4.5	137
				31 F	0401	-0.4	-12
					1005	3.6	110
					1608	-0.6	-18
					2236	4.4	134

Time meridian 75° W. 0000 is midnight. 1200 is noon. Times are not adjusted for Daylight Saving Time.
Heights are referred to mean lower low water which is the chart datum of soundings.

Port Canaveral (Trident Pier), Florida, 2017

Times and Heights of High and Low Waters

April

Day	Time	ft	cm	Day	Time	ft	cm
1 Sa	0459	-0.2	-6	16 Su	0507	0.5	15
	1058	3.4	104		1059	2.8	85
	1704	-0.4	-12		1702	0.4	12
	2331	4.2	128		2327	3.5	107
2 Su	0601	-0.1	-3	17 M	0555	0.5	15
	1155	3.3	101		1144	2.7	82
	1804	-0.3	-9		1751	0.5	15
3 M ◐	0032	4.0	122	18 Tu	0015	3.4	104
	0704	0.1	3		0645	0.6	18
	1259	3.1	94		1236	2.6	79
	1908	-0.1	-3		1844	0.6	18
4 Tu	0140	3.9	119	19 W ◑	0108	3.3	101
	0807	0.1	3		0736	0.6	18
	1410	3.1	94		1334	2.7	82
	2013	0.0	0		1940	0.5	15
5 W	0250	3.8	116	20 Th	0205	3.3	101
	0910	0.1	3		0827	0.5	15
	1520	3.2	98		1433	2.8	85
	2119	0.0	0		2036	0.4	12
6 Th	0354	3.7	113	21 F	0302	3.4	104
	1010	0.1	3		0917	0.3	9
	1622	3.3	101		1529	3.1	94
	2222	0.0	0		2134	0.3	9
7 F	0450	3.7	113	22 Sa	0354	3.5	107
	1103	0.0	0		1007	0.1	3
	1716	3.5	107		1622	3.4	104
	2320	-0.1	-3		2230	0.0	0
8 Sa	0539	3.7	113	23 Su	0445	3.6	110
	1149	-0.1	-3		1056	-0.2	-6
	1804	3.7	113		1712	3.8	116
					2325	-0.2	-6
9 Su	0010	-0.1	-3	24 M	0534	3.7	113
	0624	3.6	110		1143	-0.4	-12
	1230	-0.1	-3		1802	4.2	128
	1848	3.8	116				
10 M	0055	-0.1	-3	25 Tu	0017	-0.4	-12
	0706	3.5	107		0624	3.8	116
	1307	-0.2	-6		1229	-0.7	-21
	1930	3.9	119		1853	4.5	137
11 Tu ○	0136	-0.1	-3	26 W ●	0109	-0.5	-15
	0745	3.4	104		0714	3.8	116
	1343	-0.1	-3		1316	-0.8	-24
	2009	3.9	119		1944	4.7	143
12 W	0216	0.0	0	27 Th	0200	-0.6	-18
	0823	3.3	101		0805	3.8	116
	1418	-0.1	-3		1404	-0.8	-24
	2047	3.9	119		2035	4.8	146
13 Th	0256	0.1	3	28 F	0253	-0.6	-18
	0901	3.2	98		0857	3.7	113
	1455	0.0	0		1454	-0.8	-24
	2125	3.8	116		2127	4.8	146
14 F	0337	0.2	6	29 Sa	0349	-0.5	-15
	0939	3.0	91		0950	3.6	110
	1534	0.2	6		1548	-0.6	-18
	2203	3.7	113		2220	4.6	140
15 Sa	0421	0.3	9	30 Su	0447	-0.3	-9
	1018	2.9	88		1044	3.4	104
	1616	0.3	9		1647	-0.4	-12
	2243	3.6	110		2316	4.4	134

May

Day	Time	ft	cm	Day	Time	ft	cm
1 M	0548	-0.2	-6	16 Tu	0526	0.4	12
	1143	3.3	101		1117	2.7	82
	1749	-0.2	-6		1718	0.5	15
					2341	3.5	107
2 Tu ◐	0016	4.1	125	17 W	0613	0.4	12
	0650	-0.1	-3		1205	2.7	82
	1248	3.2	98		1811	0.5	15
	1854	0.0	0				
3 W	0120	3.8	116	18 Th ◑	0029	3.4	104
	0750	0.0	0		0700	0.3	9
	1359	3.2	98		1300	2.8	85
	1959	0.1	3		1906	0.5	15
4 Th	0227	3.6	110	19 F	0122	3.4	104
	0848	0.0	0		0748	0.2	6
	1507	3.3	101		1358	3.0	91
	2104	0.2	6		2003	0.4	12
5 F	0329	3.5	107	20 Sa	0218	3.4	104
	0943	0.0	0		0837	0.0	0
	1607	3.4	104		1455	3.3	101
	2206	0.2	6		2102	0.2	6
6 Sa	0423	3.4	104	21 Su	0313	3.4	104
	1033	0.0	0		0927	-0.2	-6
	1658	3.6	110		1551	3.6	110
	2303	0.2	6		2201	0.0	0
7 Su	0511	3.3	101	22 M	0407	3.5	107
	1117	-0.1	-3		1018	-0.4	-12
	1744	3.7	113		1644	4.0	122
	2353	0.2	6		2259	-0.2	-6
8 M	0554	3.2	98	23 Tu	0501	3.5	107
	1157	-0.1	-3		1109	-0.7	-21
	1825	3.8	116		1737	4.4	134
					2356	-0.4	-12
9 Tu	0037	0.1	3	24 W	0554	3.6	110
	0635	3.2	98		1159	-0.9	-27
	1233	-0.1	-3		1830	4.6	140
	1905	3.9	119				
10 W ○	0116	0.1	3	25 Th ●	0050	-0.5	-15
	0715	3.1	94		0649	3.6	110
	1309	-0.1	-3		1250	-1.0	-30
	1943	3.9	119		1924	4.8	146
11 Th	0155	0.1	3	26 F	0144	-0.6	-18
	0754	3.0	91		0743	3.6	110
	1345	0.0	0		1341	-1.0	-30
	2021	3.9	119		2018	4.9	149
12 F	0234	0.2	6	27 Sa	0238	-0.6	-18
	0833	2.9	88		0839	3.6	110
	1423	0.0	0		1434	-0.9	-27
	2058	3.9	119		2111	4.8	146
13 Sa	0314	0.2	6	28 Su	0334	-0.5	-15
	0912	2.9	88		0934	3.5	107
	1502	0.1	3		1530	-0.7	-21
	2137	3.8	116		2205	4.6	140
14 Su	0356	0.3	9	29 M	0432	-0.4	-12
	0952	2.8	85		1030	3.4	104
	1543	0.3	9		1630	-0.5	-15
	2216	3.7	113		2259	4.3	131
15 M	0440	0.4	12	30 Tu	0531	-0.3	-9
	1033	2.7	82		1129	3.3	101
	1629	0.4	12		1733	-0.2	-6
	2257	3.6	110		2355	4.0	122
				31 W	0629	-0.2	-6
					1232	3.2	98
					1836	0.0	0

June

Day	Time	ft	cm	Day	Time	ft	cm
1 Th ◐	0054	3.7	113	16 F	0627	0.1	3
	0725	-0.2	-6		1230	2.9	88
	1339	3.2	98		1837	0.3	9
	1939	0.2	6				
2 F	0156	3.4	104	17 Sa	0047	3.4	104
	0818	-0.1	-3		0713	-0.1	-3
	1445	3.3	101		1326	3.2	98
	2042	0.3	9		1935	0.3	9
3 Sa	0255	3.2	98	18 Su	0141	3.3	101
	0908	-0.1	-3		0802	-0.2	-6
	1543	3.4	104		1425	3.4	104
	2142	0.4	12		2035	0.2	6
4 Su	0348	3.1	94	19 M	0238	3.3	101
	0955	-0.1	-3		0853	-0.4	-12
	1633	3.5	107		1523	3.8	116
	2239	0.4	12		2136	0.0	0
5 M	0436	2.9	88	20 Tu	0336	3.3	101
	1039	-0.1	-3		0946	-0.6	-18
	1717	3.6	110		1620	4.1	125
	2329	0.3	9		2237	-0.1	-3
6 Tu	0520	2.9	88	21 W	0432	3.3	101
	1120	-0.1	-3		1040	-0.8	-24
	1758	3.7	113		1715	4.4	134
					2336	-0.3	-9
7 W	0013	0.3	9	22 Th	0529	3.4	104
	0602	2.8	85		1135	-1.0	-30
	1200	-0.1	-3		1811	4.6	140
	1837	3.8	116				
8 Th	0053	0.2	6	23 F ●	0033	-0.5	-15
	0644	2.8	85		0627	3.4	104
	1238	-0.1	-3		1229	-1.1	-34
	1916	3.8	116		1906	4.8	146
9 F ○	0132	0.2	6	24 Sa	0127	-0.6	-18
	0725	2.8	85		0724	3.5	107
	1316	-0.1	-3		1323	-1.0	-30
	1955	3.9	119		2001	4.8	146
10 Sa	0210	0.2	6	25 Su	0221	-0.6	-18
	0806	2.8	85		0821	3.5	107
	1355	0.0	0		1417	-0.9	-27
	2034	3.8	116		2055	4.7	143
11 Su	0250	0.2	6	26 M	0316	-0.5	-15
	0847	2.7	82		0917	3.5	107
	1435	0.0	0		1513	-0.7	-21
	2113	3.8	116		2147	4.5	137
12 M	0331	0.2	6	27 Tu	0411	-0.5	-15
	0928	2.7	82		1013	3.4	104
	1517	0.1	3		1612	-0.5	-15
	2151	3.7	113		2239	4.2	128
13 Tu	0413	0.2	6	28 W	0507	-0.4	-12
	1009	2.7	82		1109	3.4	104
	1601	0.2	6		1712	-0.2	-6
	2231	3.6	110		2330	3.9	119
14 W	0457	0.2	6	29 Th	0601	-0.3	-9
	1052	2.7	82		1207	3.3	101
	1650	0.3	9		1813	0.1	3
	2312	3.5	107				
15 Th	0541	0.1	3	30 F ◐	0023	3.5	107
	1138	2.8	85		0653	-0.2	-6
	1742	0.3	9		1309	3.3	101
	2357	3.4	104		1913	0.3	9

Time meridian 75° W. 0000 is midnight. 1200 is noon. Times are not adjusted for Daylight Saving Time.
Heights are referred to mean lower low water which is the chart datum of soundings.

Port Canaveral (Trident Pier), Florida, 2017

Times and Heights of High and Low Waters

July

Day	Time	ft	cm	Day	Time	ft	cm
1 Sa	0118	3.2	98	16 Su	0018	3.4	104
	0742	-0.1	-3		0642	-0.2	-6
	1411	3.3	101		1259	3.5	107
	2012	0.4	12		1913 ◐	0.3	9
2 Su	0214	3.0	91	17 M	0112	3.3	101
	0829	0.0	0		0732	-0.3	-9
	1509	3.4	104		1359	3.7	113
	2110	0.5	15		2014	0.2	6
3 M	0308	2.8	85	18 Tu	0211	3.3	101
	0915	0.0	0		0825	-0.4	-12
	1600	3.4	104		1500	4.0	122
	2206	0.5	15		2116	0.2	6
4 Tu	0358	2.7	82	19 W	0312	3.2	98
	1000	0.0	0		0921	-0.6	-18
	1645	3.5	107		1600	4.2	128
	2258	0.5	15		2218	0.0	0
5 W	0444	2.7	82	20 Th	0412	3.3	101
	1044	0.0	0		1019	-0.7	-21
	1728	3.6	110		1658	4.5	137
	2344	0.4	12		2319	-0.1	-3
6 Th	0529	2.7	82	21 F	0511	3.4	104
	1128	0.0	0		1117	-0.8	-24
	1808	3.7	113		1755	4.6	140
7 F	0026	0.3	9	22 Sa	0016	-0.2	-6
	0612	2.7	82		0610	3.5	107
	1210	-0.1	-3		1213	-0.9	-27
	1849	3.8	116		1850	4.7	143
8 Sa	0105	0.3	9	23 Su	0110	-0.3	-9
	0656	2.8	85		0707	3.6	110
	1250	-0.1	-3		1308	-0.8	-24
	1929 O	3.8	116		1945 ●	4.7	143
9 Su	0144	0.2	6	24 M	0202	-0.4	-12
	0739	2.8	85		0804	3.7	113
	1331	-0.1	-3		1402	-0.7	-21
	2009	3.9	119		2036	4.6	140
10 M	0223	0.2	6	25 Tu	0253	-0.4	-12
	0821	2.8	85		0858	3.7	113
	1411	0.0	0		1456	-0.5	-15
	2048	3.9	119		2126	4.4	134
11 Tu	0302	0.1	3	26 W	0344	-0.3	-9
	0903	2.9	88		0951	3.7	113
	1453	0.0	0		1551	-0.3	-9
	2126	3.8	116		2214	4.1	125
12 W	0343	0.1	3	27 Th	0435	-0.2	-6
	0944	3.0	91		1043	3.6	110
	1538	0.1	3		1647	0.0	0
	2205	3.8	116		2300	3.8	116
13 Th	0425	0.1	3	28 F	0524	-0.1	-3
	1027	3.0	91		1136	3.5	107
	1626	0.2	6		1744	0.3	9
	2246	3.7	113		2348	3.5	107
14 F	0509	0.0	0	29 Sa	0613	0.0	0
	1113	3.2	98		1231	3.5	107
	1719	0.2	6		1841	0.5	15
	2329	3.6	110				
15 Sa	0554	-0.1	-3	30 Su	0037	3.2	98
	1204	3.3	101		0700	0.1	3
	1815	0.3	9		1328	3.4	104
					1937 ◐	0.7	21
				31 M	0130	3.0	91
					0746	0.2	6
					1426	3.4	104
					2032	0.8	24

August

Day	Time	ft	cm	Day	Time	ft	cm
1 Tu	0225	2.8	85	16 W	0152	3.4	104
	0833	0.3	9		0805	-0.1	-3
	1520	3.5	107		1442	4.2	128
	2127	0.8	24		2101	0.4	12
2 W	0319	2.8	85	17 Th	0257	3.4	104
	0921	0.3	9		0904	-0.2	-6
	1609	3.6	110		1545	4.4	134
	2220	0.8	24		2204	0.4	12
3 Th	0409	2.8	85	18 F	0359	3.5	107
	1010	0.3	9		1005	-0.3	-9
	1654	3.7	113		1645	4.5	137
	2308	0.7	21		2304	0.2	6
4 F	0456	2.9	88	19 Sa	0459	3.6	110
	1057	0.2	6		1105	-0.4	-12
	1737	3.8	116		1741	4.7	143
	2353	0.6	18				
5 Sa	0542	3.0	91	20 Su	0000	0.1	3
	1142	0.1	3		0557	3.8	116
	1819	3.9	119		1201	-0.4	-12
					1835	4.7	143
6 Su	0034	0.5	15	21 M	0051	0.0	0
	0626	3.1	94		0653	3.9	119
	1225	0.1	3		1255	-0.4	-12
	1900	4.0	122		1926 ●	4.7	143
7 M	0113	0.3	9	22 Tu	0139	-0.1	-3
	0710	3.2	98		0746	4.0	122
	1307	0.0	0		1347	-0.3	-9
	1940 O	4.1	125		2015	4.5	137
8 Tu	0151	0.2	6	23 W	0225	-0.1	-3
	0753	3.3	101		0837	4.1	125
	1349	0.0	0		1437	-0.1	-3
	2020	4.1	125		2101	4.4	134
9 W	0230	0.2	6	24 Th	0311	0.0	0
	0836	3.4	104		0926	4.1	125
	1432	0.1	3		1527	0.1	3
	2059	4.1	125		2145	4.1	125
10 Th	0310	0.1	3	25 F	0356	0.1	3
	0919	3.5	107		1013	4.0	122
	1517	0.1	3		1619	0.4	12
	2139	4.0	122		2228	3.8	116
11 F	0351	0.1	3	26 Sa	0442	0.3	9
	1003	3.7	113		1100	3.9	119
	1606	0.2	6		1712	0.6	18
	2221	3.9	119		2311	3.6	110
12 Sa	0436	0.0	0	27 Su	0528	0.4	12
	1049	3.8	116		1148	3.8	116
	1700	0.3	9		1805	0.8	24
	2306	3.8	116		2356	3.3	101
13 Su	0523	0.0	0	28 M	0615	0.6	18
	1140	3.9	119		1240	3.7	113
	1757	0.4	12		1858	1.0	30
	2355	3.6	110				
14 M	0614	0.0	0	29 Tu	0046	3.1	94
	1236	4.0	122		0703	0.7	21
	1857 ◐	0.5	15		1336	3.6	110
					1952 ◐	1.1	34
15 Tu	0051	3.5	107	30 W	0142	3.0	91
	0708	-0.1	-3		0752	0.7	21
	1338	4.1	125		1433	3.7	113
	1958	0.5	15		2045	1.1	34
				31 Th	0240	3.0	91
					0844	0.7	21
					1528	3.7	113
					2138	1.1	34

September

Day	Time	ft	cm	Day	Time	ft	cm
1 F	0335	3.1	94	16 Sa	0353	3.8	116
	0935	0.7	21		0956	0.2	6
	1616	3.9	119		1632	4.6	140
	2229	1.0	30		2249	0.5	15
2 Sa	0424	3.2	98	17 Su	0452	4.0	122
	1026	0.6	18		1056	0.1	3
	1701	4.0	122		1727	4.6	140
	2315	0.8	24		2342	0.4	12
3 Su	0511	3.4	104	18 M	0547	4.2	128
	1114	0.5	15		1152	0.1	3
	1744	4.1	125		1817	4.6	140
	2357	0.7	21				
4 M	0556	3.5	107	19 Tu	0029	0.3	9
	1159	0.4	12		0639	4.3	131
	1826	4.2	128		1243	0.1	3
					1905	4.5	137
5 Tu	0037	0.5	15	20 W	0113	0.2	6
	0640	3.7	113		0728	4.4	134
	1243	0.3	9		1331	0.2	6
	1907	4.3	131		1950 ●	4.4	134
6 W	0116	0.4	12	21 Th	0154	0.2	6
	0724	3.9	119		0814	4.5	137
	1327	0.2	6		1417	0.3	9
	1949 O	4.4	134		2033	4.3	131
7 Th	0155	0.2	6	22 F	0235	0.3	9
	0808	4.1	125		0858	4.5	137
	1411	0.2	6		1503	0.5	15
	2031	4.3	131		2114	4.0	122
8 F	0235	0.2	6	23 Sa	0315	0.5	15
	0853	4.3	131		0941	4.4	134
	1458	0.2	6		1550	0.7	21
	2114	4.3	131		2154	3.8	116
9 Sa	0318	0.1	3	24 Su	0357	0.6	18
	0939	4.4	134		1023	4.3	131
	1549	0.3	9		1638	0.9	27
	2158	4.1	125		2235	3.6	110
10 Su	0405	0.1	3	25 M	0442	0.8	24
	1027	4.5	137		1107	4.1	125
	1644	0.5	15		1728	1.1	34
	2245	4.0	122		2319	3.4	104
11 M	0456	0.2	6	26 Tu	0529	0.9	27
	1120	4.5	137		1154	4.0	122
	1742	0.6	18		1820	1.2	37
	2337	3.8	116				
12 Tu	0551	0.2	6	27 W	0006	3.3	101
	1217	4.5	137		0620	1.1	34
	1843	0.7	21		1246	3.9	119
					1912 ◑	1.3	40
13 W	0036	3.7	113	28 Th	0101	3.2	98
	0649	0.2	6		0712	1.1	34
	1321	4.4	134		1343	3.8	116
	1946 ◐	0.7	21		2004	1.3	40
14 Th	0141	3.6	110	29 F	0200	3.2	98
	0750	0.3	9		0805	1.1	34
	1428	4.5	137		1441	3.9	119
	2049	0.7	21		2056	1.2	37
15 F	0249	3.7	113	30 Sa	0259	3.3	101
	0853	0.2	6		0859	1.0	30
	1533	4.5	137		1534	4.0	122
	2151	0.6	18		2146	1.1	34

Time meridian 75° W. 0000 is midnight. 1200 is noon. Times are not adjusted for Daylight Saving Time.
Heights are referred to mean lower low water which is the chart datum of soundings.

Port Canaveral (Trident Pier), Florida, 2017

Times and Heights of High and Low Waters

October

Day	Time (h m)	Height (ft)	Height (cm)
1 Su	0351 / 0952 / 1621 / 2233	3.5 / 0.9 / 4.1 / 0.9	107 / 27 / 125 / 27
2 M	0439 / 1043 / 1706 / 2317	3.7 / 0.7 / 4.2 / 0.7	113 / 21 / 128 / 21
3 Tu	0525 / 1132 / 1749 / 2359	4.0 / 0.6 / 4.3 / 0.5	122 / 18 / 131 / 15
4 W	0610 / 1219 / 1833	4.3 / 0.4 / 4.4	131 / 12 / 134
5 Th ○	0040 / 0655 / 1305 / 1917	0.3 / 4.5 / 0.3 / 4.5	9 / 137 / 9 / 137
6 F	0121 / 0742 / 1352 / 2003	0.1 / 4.8 / 0.2 / 4.4	3 / 146 / 6 / 134
7 Sa	0204 / 0829 / 1441 / 2049	0.1 / 4.9 / 0.2 / 4.3	3 / 149 / 6 / 131
8 Su	0249 / 0918 / 1533 / 2137	0.0 / 5.0 / 0.3 / 4.2	0 / 152 / 9 / 128
9 M	0338 / 1008 / 1629 / 2228	0.1 / 5.0 / 0.5 / 4.1	3 / 152 / 15 / 125
10 Tu	0433 / 1102 / 1729 / 2323	0.2 / 4.9 / 0.6 / 3.9	6 / 149 / 18 / 119
11 W	0532 / 1200 / 1831	0.3 / 4.7 / 0.7	9 / 143 / 21
12 Th ◑	0024 / 0634 / 1305 / 1934	3.8 / 0.4 / 4.6 / 0.7	116 / 12 / 140 / 21
13 F	0132 / 0739 / 1413 / 2036	3.8 / 0.5 / 4.5 / 0.7	116 / 15 / 137 / 21
14 Sa	0243 / 0844 / 1518 / 2136	3.8 / 0.6 / 4.5 / 0.7	116 / 18 / 137 / 21
15 Su	0348 / 0948 / 1617 / 2231	4.0 / 0.5 / 4.4 / 0.6	122 / 15 / 134 / 18
16 M	0445 / 1048 / 1709 / 2321	4.2 / 0.5 / 4.4 / 0.5	128 / 15 / 134 / 15
17 Tu	0536 / 1143 / 1757	4.4 / 0.5 / 4.3	134 / 15 / 131
18 W	0005 / 0624 / 1231 / 1841	0.4 / 4.5 / 0.5 / 4.2	12 / 137 / 15 / 128
19 Th ●	0045 / 0708 / 1316 / 1923	0.3 / 4.6 / 0.5 / 4.1	9 / 140 / 15 / 125
20 F	0123 / 0750 / 1358 / 2004	0.4 / 4.6 / 0.6 / 4.0	12 / 140 / 18 / 122
21 Sa	0200 / 0831 / 1439 / 2044	0.4 / 4.6 / 0.7 / 3.8	12 / 140 / 21 / 116
22 Su	0238 / 0910 / 1522 / 2123	0.6 / 4.5 / 0.8 / 3.7	18 / 137 / 24 / 113
23 M	0318 / 0950 / 1606 / 2203	0.7 / 4.4 / 1.0 / 3.5	21 / 134 / 30 / 107
24 Tu	0400 / 1031 / 1653 / 2245	0.9 / 4.2 / 1.1 / 3.4	27 / 128 / 34 / 104
25 W	0447 / 1115 / 1743 / 2331	1.0 / 4.1 / 1.2 / 3.3	30 / 125 / 37 / 101
26 Th	0538 / 1202 / 1833	1.1 / 3.9 / 1.2	34 / 119 / 37
27 F ☽	0022 / 0631 / 1255 / 1924	3.2 / 1.2 / 3.8 / 1.2	98 / 37 / 116 / 37
28 Sa	0120 / 0726 / 1351 / 2013	3.2 / 1.2 / 3.8 / 1.1	98 / 37 / 116 / 34
29 Su	0219 / 0821 / 1446 / 2102	3.3 / 1.1 / 3.9 / 1.0	101 / 34 / 119 / 30
30 M	0315 / 0917 / 1537 / 2150	3.6 / 1.0 / 4.0 / 0.8	110 / 30 / 122 / 24
31 Tu	0405 / 1011 / 1625 / 2236	3.9 / 0.8 / 4.1 / 0.5	119 / 24 / 125 / 15

November

Day	Time (h m)	Height (ft)	Height (cm)
1 W	0453 / 1104 / 1712 / 2321	4.2 / 0.6 / 4.2 / 0.2	128 / 18 / 128 / 6
2 Th	0541 / 1155 / 1759	4.6 / 0.3 / 4.2	140 / 9 / 128
3 F	0005 / 0629 / 1244 / 1847	0.0 / 4.9 / 0.2 / 4.3	0 / 149 / 6 / 131
4 Sa ○	0050 / 0718 / 1333 / 1937	-0.2 / 5.1 / 0.1 / 4.3	-6 / 155 / 3 / 131
5 Su	0137 / 0808 / 1424 / 2027	-0.3 / 5.2 / 0.1 / 4.2	-9 / 158 / 3 / 128
6 M	0225 / 0859 / 1517 / 2119	-0.3 / 5.3 / 0.1 / 4.1	-9 / 162 / 3 / 125
7 Tu	0317 / 0951 / 1614 / 2212	-0.2 / 5.2 / 0.2 / 4.0	-6 / 158 / 6 / 122
8 W	0414 / 1045 / 1714 / 2309	0.0 / 5.0 / 0.4 / 3.9	0 / 152 / 12 / 119
9 Th	0515 / 1143 / 1816	0.2 / 4.7 / 0.4	6 / 143 / 12
10 F ○	0012 / 0620 / 1246 / 1918	3.7 / 0.4 / 4.5 / 0.5	113 / 12 / 137 / 15
11 Sa	0121 / 0726 / 1353 / 2017	3.7 / 0.5 / 4.2 / 0.5	113 / 15 / 128 / 15
12 Su	0233 / 0832 / 1458 / 2114	3.8 / 0.6 / 4.1 / 0.4	116 / 18 / 125 / 12
13 M	0338 / 0937 / 1556 / 2207	3.9 / 0.6 / 4.0 / 0.4	119 / 18 / 122 / 12
14 Tu	0433 / 1038 / 1647 / 2255	4.1 / 0.6 / 3.9 / 0.3	125 / 18 / 119 / 9
15 W	0522 / 1131 / 1733 / 2337	4.3 / 0.6 / 3.8 / 0.3	131 / 18 / 116 / 9
16 Th	0606 / 1218 / 1816	4.4 / 0.5 / 3.7	134 / 15 / 113
17 F	0016 / 0647 / 1259 / 1857	0.2 / 4.4 / 0.5 / 3.6	6 / 134 / 15 / 110
18 Sa ●	0054 / 0727 / 1339 / 1936	0.3 / 4.5 / 0.5 / 3.5	9 / 137 / 15 / 107
19 Su	0130 / 0805 / 1417 / 2016	0.3 / 4.4 / 0.6 / 3.4	9 / 134 / 18 / 104
20 M	0207 / 0843 / 1456 / 2055	0.4 / 4.4 / 0.6 / 3.3	12 / 134 / 18 / 101
21 Tu	0246 / 0922 / 1538 / 2135	0.5 / 4.2 / 0.7 / 3.2	15 / 128 / 21 / 98
22 W	0327 / 1001 / 1622 / 2216	0.6 / 4.1 / 0.8 / 3.1	18 / 125 / 24 / 94
23 Th	0411 / 1041 / 1708 / 2259	0.7 / 4.0 / 0.9 / 3.1	21 / 122 / 27 / 94
24 F	0500 / 1125 / 1755 / 2347	0.9 / 3.8 / 0.9 / 3.0	27 / 116 / 27 / 91
25 Sa	0552 / 1211 / 1843	0.9 / 3.7 / 0.8	27 / 113 / 24
26 Su ☾	0040 / 0647 / 1303 / 1931	3.1 / 0.9 / 3.6 / 0.7	94 / 27 / 110 / 21
27 M	0138 / 0744 / 1358 / 2019	3.2 / 0.9 / 3.6 / 0.6	98 / 27 / 110 / 18
28 Tu	0236 / 0841 / 1453 / 2107	3.4 / 0.8 / 3.6 / 0.3	104 / 24 / 110 / 9
29 W	0331 / 0939 / 1546 / 2156	3.8 / 0.6 / 3.7 / 0.1	116 / 18 / 113 / 3
30 Th	0423 / 1036 / 1638 / 2246	4.2 / 0.4 / 3.8 / -0.2	128 / 12 / 116 / -6

December

Day	Time (h m)	Height (ft)	Height (cm)
1 F	0514 / 1131 / 1729 / 2335	4.5 / 0.1 / 3.8 / -0.4	137 / 3 / 116 / -12
2 Sa	0605 / 1224 / 1821	4.8 / -0.1 / 3.9	146 / -3 / 119
3 Su	0025 / 0657 / 1316 / 1914	-0.6 / 5.0 / -0.2 / 3.9	-18 / 152 / -6 / 119
4 M	0115 / 0749 / 1408 / 2008	-0.7 / 5.1 / -0.3 / 3.9	-21 / 155 / -9 / 119
5 Tu	0206 / 0842 / 1501 / 2102	-0.7 / 5.1 / -0.3 / 3.9	-21 / 155 / -9 / 119
6 W	0300 / 0935 / 1557 / 2157	-0.6 / 5.0 / -0.2 / 3.8	-18 / 152 / -6 / 116
7 Th	0357 / 1028 / 1655 / 2254	-0.4 / 4.7 / -0.1 / 3.7	-12 / 143 / -3 / 113
8 F	0458 / 1124 / 1755 / 2355	-0.1 / 4.4 / 0.0 / 3.6	-3 / 134 / 0 / 110
9 Sa	0603 / 1222 / 1854	0.1 / 4.1 / 0.1	3 / 125 / 3
10 Su ○	0102 / 0708 / 1324 / 1950	3.5 / 0.3 / 3.8 / 0.1	107 / 9 / 116 / 3
11 M	0212 / 0814 / 1428 / 2045	3.6 / 0.5 / 3.5 / 0.1	110 / 15 / 107 / 3
12 Tu	0318 / 0919 / 1528 / 2136	3.7 / 0.5 / 3.4 / 0.1	113 / 15 / 104 / 3
13 W	0414 / 1020 / 1620 / 2224	3.8 / 0.5 / 3.2 / 0.1	116 / 15 / 98 / 3
14 Th	0502 / 1114 / 1707 / 2308	3.9 / 0.5 / 3.2 / 0.1	119 / 15 / 98 / 3
15 F	0545 / 1201 / 1750 / 2349	4.0 / 0.4 / 3.1 / 0.0	122 / 12 / 94 / 0
16 Sa	0625 / 1241 / 1831	4.0 / 0.4 / 3.1	122 / 12 / 94
17 Su	0027 / 0704 / 1318 / 1911	0.0 / 4.1 / 0.3 / 3.1	0 / 125 / 9 / 94
18 M ●	0105 / 0742 / 1355 / 1951	0.0 / 4.1 / 0.3 / 3.0	0 / 125 / 9 / 91
19 Tu	0142 / 0820 / 1432 / 2030	0.0 / 4.0 / 0.3 / 3.0	0 / 122 / 9 / 91
20 W	0221 / 0857 / 1511 / 2110	0.1 / 4.0 / 0.3 / 3.0	3 / 122 / 9 / 91
21 Th	0300 / 0935 / 1552 / 2149	0.2 / 3.9 / 0.4 / 2.9	6 / 119 / 12 / 88
22 F	0343 / 1013 / 1634 / 2230	0.3 / 3.8 / 0.4 / 2.9	9 / 116 / 12 / 88
23 Sa	0428 / 1052 / 1718 / 2314	0.4 / 3.6 / 0.4 / 2.9	12 / 110 / 12 / 88
24 Su	0518 / 1134 / 1803	0.5 / 3.5 / 0.3	15 / 107 / 9
25 M	0004 / 0612 / 1222 / 1849	3.0 / 0.5 / 3.3 / 0.2	91 / 15 / 101 / 6
26 Tu ☾	0059 / 0709 / 1314 / 1937	3.1 / 0.5 / 3.2 / 0.1	94 / 15 / 98 / 3
27 W	0158 / 0809 / 1412 / 2028	3.3 / 0.5 / 3.2 / -0.1	101 / 15 / 98 / -3
28 Th	0258 / 0910 / 1510 / 2121	3.6 / 0.3 / 3.2 / -0.3	110 / 9 / 98 / -9
29 F	0355 / 1011 / 1608 / 2216	4.0 / 0.1 / 3.3 / -0.6	122 / 3 / 101 / -18
30 Sa	0451 / 1110 / 1704 / 2310	4.3 / -0.1 / 3.4 / -0.8	131 / -3 / 104 / -24
31 Su	0545 / 1206 / 1800	4.6 / -0.3 / 3.5	140 / -9 / 107

Time meridian 75° W. 0000 is midnight. 1200 is noon. Times are not adjusted for Daylight Saving Time.
Heights are referred to mean lower low water which is the chart datum of soundings.

Miami, Government Cut, Florida, 2017

Times and Heights of High and Low Waters

January

Day	Time	ft	cm		Day	Time	ft	cm
1 Su	0344	-0.2	-6		**16** M	0451	-0.3	-9
	1037	2.4	73			1126	2.4	73
	1614	0.1	3			1721	-0.2	-6
	2249	2.2	67			2348	2.2	67
2 M	0427	-0.1	-3		**17** Tu	0540	-0.1	-3
	1119	2.4	73			1210	2.3	70
	1658	0.1	3			1811	-0.1	-3
	2335	2.2	67					
3 Tu	0514	-0.1	-3		**18** W	0037	2.1	64
	1202	2.3	70			0632	0.1	3
	1747	0.0	0			1254	2.1	64
						1903	0.0	0
4 W	0027	2.2	67		**19** Th	0128	2.0	61
	0607	0.0	0			0725	0.2	6
	1250	2.3	70			1341	1.9	58
	1843	0.0	0		☽	1956	0.0	0
5 Th	0125	2.2	67		**20** F	0222	1.9	58
	0708	0.1	3			0822	0.3	9
	1344	2.2	67			1431	1.8	55
☾	1944	-0.1	-3			2050	0.1	3
6 F	0228	2.2	67		**21** Sa	0319	1.8	55
	0813	0.1	3			0918	0.4	12
	1443	2.2	67			1525	1.8	55
	2047	-0.2	-6			2144	0.1	3
7 Sa	0334	2.3	70		**22** Su	0417	1.8	55
	0920	0.1	3			1013	0.4	12
	1546	2.2	67			1621	1.8	55
	2150	-0.3	-9			2234	0.0	0
8 Su	0440	2.4	73		**23** M	0512	1.9	58
	1023	0.0	0			1103	0.3	9
	1650	2.3	70			1716	1.8	55
	2250	-0.5	-15			2322	-0.1	-3
9 M	0542	2.5	76		**24** Tu	0603	2.0	61
	1123	-0.1	-3			1150	0.2	6
	1752	2.4	73			1806	1.9	58
	2347	-0.6	-18					
10 Tu	0640	2.6	79		**25** W	0006	-0.2	-6
	1219	-0.2	-6			0649	2.1	64
	1849	2.5	76			1234	0.1	3
						1854	2.0	61
11 W	0041	-0.7	-21		**26** Th	0047	-0.3	-9
	0733	2.7	82			0732	2.2	67
	1312	-0.3	-9			1314	0.0	0
	1943	2.6	79			1938	2.1	64
12 Th	0133	-0.8	-24		**27** F	0127	-0.3	-9
	0823	2.8	85			0814	2.3	70
	1404	-0.3	-9			1354	-0.1	-3
○	2035	2.6	79		●	2022	2.2	67
13 F	0224	-0.7	-21		**28** Sa	0206	-0.4	-12
	0911	2.8	85			0854	2.4	73
	1454	-0.4	-12			1432	-0.1	-3
	2125	2.6	79			2104	2.2	67
14 Sa	0314	-0.6	-18		**29** Su	0246	-0.4	-12
	0957	2.7	82			0934	2.4	73
	1543	-0.3	-9			1512	-0.2	-6
	2213	2.5	76			2147	2.3	70
15 Su	0402	-0.5	-15		**30** M	0327	-0.4	-12
	1042	2.6	79			1014	2.4	73
	1632	-0.3	-9			1553	-0.3	-9
	2301	2.4	73			2232	2.3	70
					31 Tu	0410	-0.4	-12
						1056	2.4	73
						1637	-0.3	-9
						2319	2.3	70

February

Day	Time	ft	cm		Day	Time	ft	cm
1 W	0457	-0.3	-9		**16** Th	0550	0.0	0
	1139	2.3	70			1210	2.0	61
	1726	-0.3	-9			1815	-0.1	-3
2 Th	0009	2.2	67		**17** F	0043	2.0	61
	0549	-0.2	-6			0637	0.2	6
	1226	2.2	67			1252	1.9	58
	1820	-0.3	-9			1903	0.0	0
3 F	0106	2.2	67		**18** Sa	0132	1.9	58
	0648	-0.1	-3			0729	0.3	9
	1320	2.1	64			1339	1.8	55
◐	1920	-0.3	-9		○	1957	0.1	3
4 Sa	0208	2.1	64		**19** Su	0226	1.8	55
	0752	0.0	0			0827	0.4	12
	1420	2.1	64			1433	1.7	52
	2025	-0.4	-12			2054	0.1	3
5 Su	0315	2.1	64		**20** M	0327	1.8	55
	0900	0.1	3			0926	0.4	12
	1527	2.1	64			1534	1.7	52
	2131	-0.4	-12			2151	0.1	3
6 M	0423	2.2	67		**21** Tu	0428	1.8	55
	1007	0.0	0			1023	0.4	12
	1635	2.1	64			1636	1.8	55
	2235	-0.5	-15			2244	0.0	0
7 Tu	0528	2.3	70		**22** W	0525	1.9	58
	1109	-0.1	-3			1115	0.3	9
	1739	2.2	67			1733	1.9	58
	2334	-0.6	-18			2333	-0.1	-3
8 W	0626	2.4	73		**23** Th	0616	2.1	64
	1206	-0.2	-6			1201	0.2	6
	1838	2.3	70			1825	2.0	61
9 Th	0029	-0.6	-18		**24** F	0018	-0.2	-6
	0718	2.5	76			0702	2.2	67
	1259	-0.3	-9			1244	0.0	0
	1932	2.4	73			1913	2.2	67
10 F	0120	-0.7	-21		**25** Sa	0101	-0.3	-9
	0806	2.6	79			0745	2.3	70
	1348	-0.4	-12			1326	-0.2	-6
○	2021	2.5	76			1959	2.3	70
11 Sa	0209	-0.7	-21		**26** Su	0143	-0.4	-12
	0851	2.6	79			0827	2.4	73
	1435	-0.4	-12			1407	-0.3	-9
	2107	2.5	76		●	2044	2.4	73
12 Su	0255	-0.6	-18		**27** M	0225	-0.5	-15
	0933	2.5	76			0908	2.5	76
	1520	-0.4	-12			1448	-0.4	-12
	2151	2.4	73			2128	2.5	76
13 M	0339	-0.5	-15		**28** Tu	0308	-0.5	-15
	1014	2.5	76			0950	2.5	76
	1603	-0.4	-12			1531	-0.5	-15
	2234	2.4	73			2214	2.5	76
14 Tu	0423	-0.3	-9					
	1053	2.3	70					
	1646	-0.3	-9					
	2316	2.2	67					
15 W	0506	-0.1	-3					
	1131	2.2	67					
	1729	-0.2	-6					
	2358	2.1	64					

March

Day	Time	ft	cm		Day	Time	ft	cm
1 W	0354	-0.4	-12		**16** Th	0433	0.0	0
	1033	2.5	76			1055	2.2	67
	1617	-0.5	-15			1650	-0.1	-3
	2302	2.5	76			2323	2.2	67
2 Th	0441	-0.3	-9		**17** F	0512	0.2	6
	1118	2.4	73			1132	2.1	64
	1706	-0.5	-15			1730	0.0	0
	2353	2.5	76					
3 F	0534	-0.2	-6		**18** Sa	0004	2.1	64
	1207	2.3	70			0553	0.3	9
	1801	-0.4	-12			1211	2.0	61
						1813	0.1	3
4 Sa	0049	2.4	73		**19** Su	0049	2.0	61
	0632	0.0	0			0640	0.4	12
	1302	2.2	67			1256	1.9	58
	1902	-0.3	-9			1903	0.2	6
5 Su	0151	2.3	70		**20** M	0140	1.9	58
	0737	0.1	3			0735	0.5	15
	1404	2.1	64			1348	1.8	55
◐	2008	-0.3	-9		◐	2000	0.3	9
6 M	0258	2.2	67		**21** Tu	0239	1.9	58
	0846	0.1	3			0837	0.5	15
	1513	2.1	64			1450	1.8	55
	2116	-0.3	-9			2102	0.3	9
7 Tu	0407	2.2	67		**22** W	0342	1.9	58
	0953	0.1	3			0938	0.5	15
	1623	2.2	67			1555	1.9	58
	2222	-0.3	-9			2201	0.2	6
8 W	0512	2.3	70		**23** Th	0442	2.0	61
	1056	0.0	0			1034	0.4	12
	1729	2.2	67			1658	2.0	61
	2322	-0.3	-9			2255	0.1	3
9 Th	0609	2.4	73		**24** F	0537	2.1	64
	1152	-0.1	-3			1124	0.2	6
	1827	2.4	73			1755	2.2	67
						2345	0.0	0
10 F	0016	-0.4	-12		**25** Sa	0627	2.3	70
	0700	2.5	76			1210	0.0	0
	1243	-0.2	-6			1846	2.4	73
	1918	2.5	76					
11 Sa	0105	-0.4	-12		**26** Su	0032	-0.2	-6
	0746	2.5	76			0713	2.5	76
	1329	-0.3	-9			1255	-0.2	-6
	2004	2.5	76			1934	2.6	79
12 Su	0151	-0.4	-12		**27** M	0118	-0.3	-9
	0827	2.6	79			0757	2.6	79
	1412	-0.3	-9			1339	-0.4	-12
○	2047	2.6	79		●	2022	2.7	82
13 M	0233	-0.3	-9		**28** Tu	0203	-0.4	-12
	0906	2.5	76			0841	2.7	82
	1453	-0.4	-12			1423	-0.5	-15
	2127	2.5	76			2109	2.8	85
14 Tu	0314	-0.3	-9		**29** W	0249	-0.4	-12
	0943	2.5	76			0925	2.7	82
	1533	-0.3	-9			1509	-0.6	-18
	2206	2.5	76			2156	2.8	85
15 W	0354	-0.1	-3		**30** Th	0336	-0.3	-9
	1019	2.4	73			1011	2.7	82
	1611	-0.2	-6			1557	-0.6	-18
	2244	2.4	73			2246	2.8	85
					31 F	0426	-0.2	-6
						1059	2.6	79
						1649	-0.5	-15
						2338	2.7	82

Time meridian 75° W. 0000 is midnight. 1200 is noon. Times are not adjusted for Daylight Saving Time.
Heights are referred to mean lower low water which is the chart datum of soundings.

Miami, Government Cut, Florida, 2017

Times and Heights of High and Low Waters

April

Day	Time h m	Height ft	Height cm	Day	Time h m	Height ft	Height cm
1 Sa	0520	-0.1	-3	16 Su	0518	0.4	12
	1151	2.5	76		1139	2.1	64
	1745	-0.4	-12		1732	0.2	6
2 Su	0034	2.6	79	17 M	0016	2.2	67
	0619	0.0	0		0601	0.5	15
	1248	2.4	73		1223	2.0	61
	1846	-0.2	-6		1817	0.3	9
3 M	0135	2.5	76	18 Tu	0104	2.1	64
	0724	0.2	6		0652	0.6	18
	1352	2.3	70		1314	1.9	58
	1953	-0.1	-3		1912	0.3	9
4 Tu	0240	2.4	73	19 W	0158	2.0	61
	0832	0.2	6		0751	0.6	18
	1501	2.2	67		1413	1.9	58
	2102	0.0	0		2014	0.4	12
5 W	0347	2.3	70	20 Th	0257	2.1	64
	0939	0.2	6		0853	0.5	15
	1610	2.3	70		1518	2.0	61
	2207	0.0	0		2117	0.3	9
6 Th	0450	2.4	73	21 F	0357	2.1	64
	1040	0.1	3		0952	0.4	12
	1714	2.3	70		1622	2.1	64
	2306	0.0	0		2216	0.2	6
7 F	0547	2.4	73	22 Sa	0454	2.2	67
	1134	0.0	0		1045	0.2	6
	1811	2.4	73		1722	2.3	70
	2358	-0.1	-3		2310	0.1	3
8 Sa	0636	2.5	76	23 Su	0547	2.4	73
	1222	-0.1	-3		1135	-0.1	-3
	1900	2.5	76		1817	2.5	76
9 Su	0046	-0.1	-3	24 M	0002	0.0	0
	0720	2.5	76		0637	2.5	76
	1306	-0.2	-6		1224	-0.3	-9
	1944	2.6	79		1909	2.7	82
10 M	0129	-0.1	-3	25 Tu	0051	-0.2	-6
	0800	2.5	76		0725	2.7	82
	1346	-0.2	-6		1311	-0.5	-15
	2024	2.6	79		1959	2.9	88
11 Tu	0209	-0.1	-3	26 W	0140	-0.2	-6
	0837	2.5	76		0813	2.7	82
	1425	-0.2	-6		1359	-0.6	-18
	2102	2.6	79		2049	3.0	91
12 W	0248	0.0	0	27 Th	0229	-0.3	-9
	0913	2.4	73		0902	2.8	85
	1502	-0.2	-6		1448	-0.7	-21
	2139	2.5	76		2139	3.0	91
13 Th	0325	0.1	3	28 F	0319	-0.2	-6
	0948	2.4	73		0951	2.8	85
	1538	-0.1	-3		1539	-0.6	-18
	2216	2.5	76		2230	3.0	91
14 F	0402	0.2	6	29 Sa	0411	-0.2	-6
	1023	2.3	70		1043	2.7	82
	1614	0.0	0		1633	-0.5	-15
	2253	2.4	73		2323	2.9	88
15 Sa	0439	0.3	9	30 Su	0507	-0.1	-3
	1100	2.2	67		1137	2.6	79
	1652	0.1	3		1730	-0.4	-12
	2333	2.3	70				

May

Day	Time h m	Height ft	Height cm	Day	Time h m	Height ft	Height cm
1 M	0018	2.7	82	16 Tu	0532	0.4	12
	0606	0.0	0		1158	2.0	61
	1235	2.5	76		1744	0.2	6
	1832	-0.2	-6				
2 Tu	0117	2.6	79	17 W	0035	2.2	67
	0710	0.1	3		0619	0.5	15
	1338	2.4	73		1247	2.0	61
	1937	0.0	0		1835	0.3	9
3 W	0218	2.5	76	18 Th	0123	2.2	67
	0816	0.2	6		0714	0.4	12
	1444	2.3	70		1343	2.0	61
	2043	0.1	3		1934	0.3	9
4 Th	0321	2.4	73	19 F	0217	2.1	64
	0920	0.2	6		0813	0.3	9
	1551	2.3	70		1444	2.1	64
	2146	0.1	3		2036	0.3	9
5 F	0421	2.3	70	20 Sa	0313	2.2	67
	1018	0.1	3		0912	0.2	6
	1653	2.3	70		1548	2.2	67
	2244	0.1	3		2138	0.2	6
6 Sa	0516	2.4	73	21 Su	0411	2.2	67
	1109	0.0	0		1009	0.0	0
	1748	2.4	73		1650	2.3	70
	2335	0.1	3		2237	0.1	3
7 Su	0605	2.4	73	22 M	0508	2.4	73
	1156	0.0	0		1103	-0.2	-6
	1836	2.5	76		1749	2.5	76
					2332	0.0	0
8 M	0021	0.1	3	23 Tu	0603	2.5	76
	0649	2.4	73		1155	-0.4	-12
	1238	-0.1	-3		1845	2.7	82
	1919	2.5	76				
9 Tu	0103	0.1	3	24 W	0026	-0.1	-3
	0728	2.4	73		0656	2.6	79
	1318	-0.1	-3		1246	-0.6	-18
	1959	2.5	76		1938	2.9	88
10 W	0143	0.1	3	25 Th	0118	-0.2	-6
	0806	2.4	73		0749	2.7	82
	1356	-0.1	-3		1338	-0.7	-21
	2037	2.5	76		2030	3.0	91
11 Th	0221	0.2	6	26 F	0210	-0.3	-9
	0843	2.4	73		0841	2.8	85
	1433	-0.1	-3		1430	-0.7	-21
	2114	2.5	76		2122	3.0	91
12 F	0258	0.2	6	27 Sa	0302	-0.3	-9
	0919	2.3	70		0934	2.8	85
	1509	-0.1	-3		1523	-0.7	-21
	2151	2.5	76		2214	3.0	91
13 Sa	0335	0.2	6	28 Su	0356	-0.2	-6
	0956	2.3	70		1027	2.7	82
	1544	0.0	0		1617	-0.6	-18
	2229	2.4	73		2306	2.9	88
14 Su	0412	0.3	9	29 M	0452	-0.1	-3
	1034	2.2	67		1122	2.6	79
	1621	0.1	3		1714	-0.4	-12
	2308	2.3	70		2359	2.7	82
15 M	0450	0.4	12	30 Tu	0551	-0.1	-3
	1115	2.1	64		1219	2.5	76
	1700	0.1	3		1814	-0.2	-6
	2350	2.3	70				
				31 W	0054	2.6	79
					0652	0.0	0
					1319	2.4	73
					1916	0.0	0

June

Day	Time h m	Height ft	Height cm	Day	Time h m	Height ft	Height cm
1 Th	0151	2.4	73	16 F	0053	2.2	67
	0753	0.0	0		0643	0.2	6
	1421	2.3	70		1318	2.1	64
	2018	0.1	3		1902	0.2	6
2 F	0248	2.3	70	17 Sa	0142	2.2	67
	0853	0.1	3		0739	0.1	3
	1523	2.2	67		1417	2.1	64
	2118	0.2	6		2003	0.2	6
3 Sa	0344	2.2	67	18 Su	0236	2.2	67
	0948	0.0	0		0838	0.0	0
	1623	2.2	67		1519	2.2	67
	2214	0.2	6		2106	0.2	6
4 Su	0438	2.2	67	19 M	0334	2.2	67
	1039	0.0	0		0937	-0.2	-6
	1718	2.3	70		1623	2.3	70
	2305	0.3	9		2208	0.1	3
5 M	0528	2.2	67	20 Tu	0434	2.3	70
	1125	0.0	0		1035	-0.3	-9
	1807	2.3	70		1725	2.5	76
	2352	0.3	9		2307	0.0	0
6 Tu	0613	2.2	67	21 W	0534	2.4	73
	1208	-0.1	-3		1131	-0.5	-15
	1851	2.3	70		1824	2.7	82
7 W	0035	0.2	6	22 Th	0003	-0.1	-3
	0655	2.2	67		0632	2.5	76
	1249	-0.1	-3		1226	-0.7	-21
	1932	2.4	73		1919	2.8	85
8 Th	0116	0.2	6	23 F	0058	-0.2	-6
	0735	2.2	67		0729	2.6	79
	1328	-0.1	-3		1320	-0.7	-21
	2011	2.4	73		2013	2.9	88
9 F	0155	0.2	6	24 Sa	0152	-0.3	-9
	0815	2.2	67		0824	2.7	82
	1405	-0.1	-3		1413	-0.8	-24
	2049	2.4	73		2105	2.9	88
10 Sa	0233	0.2	6	25 Su	0246	-0.3	-9
	0854	2.2	67		0917	2.7	82
	1442	-0.1	-3		1506	-0.7	-21
	2128	2.4	73		2156	2.9	88
11 Su	0310	0.2	6	26 M	0339	-0.3	-9
	0933	2.2	67		1011	2.7	82
	1518	-0.1	-3		1600	-0.6	-18
	2207	2.4	73		2246	2.8	85
12 M	0347	0.2	6	27 Tu	0434	-0.2	-6
	1013	2.1	64		1104	2.6	79
	1555	0.0	0		1655	-0.4	-12
	2246	2.3	70		2336	2.7	82
13 Tu	0425	0.3	9	28 W	0529	-0.2	-6
	1054	2.1	64		1158	2.5	76
	1634	0.0	0		1751	-0.2	-6
	2327	2.3	70				
14 W	0506	0.3	9	29 Th	0027	2.5	76
	1138	2.1	64		0626	-0.1	-3
	1717	0.1	3		1253	2.4	73
					1848	0.0	0
15 Th	0009	2.2	67	30 F	0117	2.4	73
	0552	0.3	9		0722	0.0	0
	1225	2.1	64		1350	2.2	67
	1806	0.1	3		1946	0.1	3

Time meridian 75° W. 0000 is midnight. 1200 is noon. Times are not adjusted for Daylight Saving Time.
Heights are referred to mean lower low water which is the chart datum of soundings.

Miami, Government Cut, Florida, 2017

Times and Heights of High and Low Waters

July

Day	Time	ft	cm	Day	Time	ft	cm
1 Sa	0209	2.2	67	16 Su	0113	2.3	70
	0819	0.0	0		0710	0.0	0
	1448	2.2	67		1354	2.2	67
	2044	0.3	9		1937	0.2	6
2 Su	0302	2.1	64	17 M	0207	2.3	70
	0913	0.0	0		0810	-0.1	-3
	1545	2.1	64		1456	2.3	70
	2139	0.3	9		2041	0.2	6
3 M	0354	2.1	64	18 Tu	0306	2.3	70
	1004	0.0	0		0912	-0.2	-6
	1641	2.1	64		1601	2.4	73
	2231	0.4	12		2145	0.2	6
4 Tu	0446	2.0	61	19 W	0410	2.3	70
	1052	0.0	0		1013	-0.3	-9
	1732	2.2	67		1705	2.5	76
	2319	0.4	12		2247	0.1	3
5 W	0535	2.1	64	20 Th	0514	2.4	73
	1137	0.0	0		1113	-0.4	-12
	1819	2.2	67		1806	2.7	82
					2346	0.0	0
6 Th	0004	0.3	9	21 F	0616	2.5	76
	0621	2.1	64		1210	-0.5	-15
	1220	-0.1	-3		1903	2.8	85
	1902	2.3	70				
7 F	0047	0.3	9	22 Sa	0042	-0.1	-3
	0705	2.1	64		0714	2.7	82
	1300	-0.1	-3		1304	-0.6	-18
	1944	2.3	70		1956	2.9	88
8 Sa ○	0128	0.3	9	23 Su ●	0136	-0.2	-6
	0748	2.2	67		0809	2.7	82
	1339	-0.1	-3		1358	-0.6	-18
	2024	2.4	73		2047	2.9	88
9 Su	0207	0.2	6	24 M	0228	-0.2	-6
	0830	2.2	67		0901	2.8	85
	1417	-0.1	-3		1450	-0.5	-15
	2104	2.4	73		2135	2.9	88
10 M	0245	0.2	6	25 Tu	0319	-0.2	-6
	0911	2.2	67		0952	2.8	85
	1454	-0.1	-3		1541	-0.4	-12
	2143	2.4	73		2222	2.8	85
11 Tu	0322	0.2	6	26 W	0410	-0.2	-6
	0952	2.2	67		1042	2.7	82
	1532	-0.1	-3		1631	-0.2	-6
	2223	2.4	73		2308	2.7	82
12 W	0400	0.1	3	27 Th	0501	-0.1	-3
	1034	2.2	67		1132	2.6	79
	1612	0.0	0		1723	-0.1	-3
	2302	2.4	73		2354	2.6	79
13 Th	0441	0.1	3	28 F	0552	0.0	0
	1118	2.2	67		1222	2.4	73
	1655	0.0	0		1815	0.1	3
	2343	2.4	73				
14 F	0525	0.1	3	29 Sa	0040	2.4	73
	1205	2.2	67		0644	0.1	3
	1743	0.1	3		1313	2.3	70
					1909	0.3	9
15 Sa	0026	2.3	70	30 Su ◑	0127	2.3	70
	0615	0.0	0		0738	0.2	6
	1256	2.2	67		1406	2.2	67
	1837	0.2	6		2004	0.5	15
				31 M	0216	2.2	67
					0832	0.2	6
					1501	2.1	64
					2100	0.6	18

August

Day	Time	ft	cm	Day	Time	ft	cm
1 Tu	0308	2.1	64	16 W	0249	2.4	73
	0925	0.3	9		0854	0.0	0
	1558	2.1	64		1545	2.6	79
	2154	0.6	18		2129	0.4	12
2 W	0403	2.1	64	17 Th	0356	2.5	76
	1016	0.2	6		0958	-0.1	-3
	1653	2.2	67		1650	2.7	82
	2245	0.6	18		2233	0.3	9
3 Th	0457	2.1	64	18 F	0502	2.6	79
	1105	0.2	6		1100	-0.1	-3
	1744	2.2	67		1751	2.8	85
	2333	0.5	15		2332	0.2	6
4 F	0548	2.2	67	19 Sa	0604	2.7	82
	1150	0.2	6		1157	-0.2	-6
	1831	2.3	70		1847	2.9	88
5 Sa	0017	0.5	15	20 Su	0027	0.1	3
	0636	2.2	67		0701	2.9	88
	1233	0.1	3		1251	-0.3	-9
	1915	2.4	73		1938	3.0	91
6 Su	0059	0.4	12	21 M ●	0119	0.0	0
	0722	2.3	70		0754	2.9	88
	1313	0.0	0		1342	-0.3	-9
	1957	2.5	76		2026	3.0	91
7 M ○	0139	0.3	9	22 Tu	0208	-0.1	-3
	0805	2.4	73		0844	3.0	91
	1352	0.0	0		1431	-0.2	-6
	2037	2.6	79		2111	3.0	91
8 Tu	0217	0.2	6	23 W	0256	-0.1	-3
	0848	2.5	76		0931	3.0	91
	1430	0.0	0		1518	-0.1	-3
	2116	2.6	79		2154	3.0	91
9 W	0255	0.2	6	24 Th	0342	0.0	0
	0930	2.5	76		1017	2.9	88
	1509	0.0	0		1604	0.1	3
	2156	2.7	82		2237	2.8	85
10 Th	0334	0.1	3	25 F	0428	0.1	3
	1013	2.6	79		1102	2.8	85
	1550	0.0	0		1651	0.2	6
	2235	2.6	79		2318	2.7	82
11 F	0415	0.1	3	26 Sa	0514	0.2	6
	1057	2.6	79		1147	2.7	82
	1634	0.1	3		1738	0.4	12
	2317	2.6	79				
12 Sa	0500	0.0	0	27 Su	0000	2.6	79
	1145	2.6	79		0602	0.3	9
	1722	0.2	6		1233	2.5	76
					1827	0.6	18
13 Su	0001	2.5	76	28 M	0043	2.4	73
	0550	0.0	0		0652	0.4	12
	1237	2.5	76		1322	2.4	73
	1816	0.3	9		1920	0.8	24
14 M ◑	0050	2.5	76	29 Tu ◑	0130	2.3	70
	0647	0.0	0		0746	0.5	15
	1335	2.5	76		1415	2.3	70
	1917	0.4	12		2017	0.9	27
15 Tu	0146	2.5	76	30 W	0223	2.2	67
	0749	0.0	0		0842	0.6	18
	1438	2.5	76		1512	2.3	70
	2023	0.4	12		2114	0.9	27
				31 Th	0321	2.2	67
					0938	0.6	18
					1611	2.3	70
					2209	0.9	27

September

Day	Time	ft	cm	Day	Time	ft	cm
1 F	0420	2.3	70	16 Sa	0454	2.8	85
	1030	0.5	15		1049	0.2	6
	1706	2.4	73		1735	3.0	91
	2300	0.8	24		2320	0.4	12
2 Sa	0516	2.4	73	17 Su	0555	3.0	91
	1118	0.5	15		1145	0.2	6
	1756	2.5	76		1829	3.1	94
	2345	0.7	21				
3 Su	0607	2.5	76	18 M	0013	0.3	9
	1202	0.4	12		0649	3.1	94
	1842	2.7	82		1237	0.1	3
					1917	3.1	94
4 M	0027	0.6	18	19 Tu	0101	0.2	6
	0654	2.6	79		0739	3.2	98
	1244	0.3	9		1324	0.1	3
	1925	2.8	85		2002	3.2	98
5 Tu	0107	0.4	12	20 W ●	0147	0.1	3
	0739	2.8	85		0824	3.2	98
	1324	0.2	6		1410	0.2	6
	2006	2.9	88		2044	3.1	94
6 W ○	0146	0.3	9	21 Th	0230	0.1	3
	0823	2.9	88		0908	3.2	98
	1405	0.2	6		1453	0.3	9
	2046	2.9	88		2124	3.1	94
7 Th	0226	0.2	6	22 F	0312	0.2	6
	0907	3.0	91		0950	3.1	94
	1446	0.2	6		1536	0.4	12
	2127	3.0	91		2203	3.0	91
8 F	0307	0.1	3	23 Sa	0353	0.3	9
	0951	3.0	91		1030	3.0	91
	1528	0.2	6		1617	0.6	18
	2208	2.9	88		2241	2.8	85
9 Sa	0350	0.1	3	24 Su	0435	0.4	12
	1037	3.0	91		1111	2.9	88
	1614	0.3	9		1700	0.7	21
	2252	2.9	88		2320	2.7	82
10 Su	0437	0.1	3	25 M	0518	0.5	15
	1126	3.0	91		1154	2.7	82
	1704	0.4	12		1745	0.9	27
	2339	2.8	85				
11 M	0529	0.1	3	26 Tu	0002	2.6	79
	1220	2.9	88		0604	0.7	21
	1800	0.5	15		1240	2.6	79
					1835	1.0	30
12 Tu	0032	2.8	85	27 W ◑	0048	2.5	76
	0627	0.2	6		0656	0.8	24
	1319	2.8	85		1331	2.5	76
	1902	0.6	18		1931	1.1	34
13 W ◑	0132	2.7	82	28 Th	0141	2.4	73
	0733	0.3	9		0754	0.9	27
	1423	2.8	85		1427	2.5	76
	2010	0.7	21		2031	1.1	34
14 Th	0238	2.7	82	29 F	0240	2.4	73
	0841	0.3	9		0854	0.9	27
	1531	2.8	85		1527	2.5	76
	2118	0.7	21		2130	1.1	34
15 F	0347	2.7	82	30 Sa	0343	2.4	73
	0947	0.3	9		0951	0.8	24
	1636	2.9	88		1624	2.6	79
	2222	0.6	18		2223	1.0	30

Time meridian 75° W. 0000 is midnight. 1200 is noon. Times are not adjusted for Daylight Saving Time.
Heights are referred to mean lower low water which is the chart datum of soundings.

Miami, Government Cut, Florida, 2017

Times and Heights of High and Low Waters

October

Day	Time	ft	cm		Day	Time	ft	cm
1 Su	0442	2.5	76		16 M	0542	3.0	91
	1042	0.7	21			1131	0.4	12
	1717	2.7	82			1807	3.1	94
	2309	0.8	24			2355	0.4	12
2 M	0536	2.7	82		17 Tu	0634	3.1	94
	1129	0.6	18			1220	0.4	12
	1804	2.8	85			1854	3.1	94
	2353	0.6	18					
3 Tu	0625	2.9	88		18 W	0041	0.3	9
	1213	0.5	15			0720	3.2	98
	1849	3.0	91			1305	0.4	12
						1936	3.1	94
4 W	0034	0.4	12		19 Th ●	0123	0.2	6
	0712	3.0	91			0803	3.2	98
	1256	0.4	12			1347	0.4	12
	1932	3.1	94			2016	3.1	94
5 Th ○	0115	0.3	9		20 F	0203	0.2	6
	0758	3.2	98			0844	3.2	98
	1339	0.3	9			1428	0.5	15
	2015	3.1	94			2054	3.0	91
6 F	0157	0.1	3		21 Sa	0242	0.3	9
	0843	3.3	101			0922	3.1	94
	1423	0.3	9			1507	0.6	18
	2058	3.2	98			2131	2.9	88
7 Sa	0241	0.1	3		22 Su	0321	0.4	12
	0930	3.3	101			1001	3.0	91
	1508	0.3	9			1546	0.7	21
	2143	3.2	98			2207	2.8	85
8 Su	0327	0.0	0		23 M	0359	0.5	15
	1018	3.3	101			1039	2.9	88
	1556	0.4	12			1626	0.8	24
	2230	3.1	94			2246	2.7	82
9 M	0417	0.1	3		24 Tu	0438	0.6	18
	1109	3.2	98			1120	2.8	85
	1648	0.5	15			1707	0.9	27
	2321	3.0	91			2326	2.6	79
10 Tu	0511	0.2	6		25 W	0520	0.7	21
	1204	3.1	94			1203	2.7	82
	1746	0.6	18			1753	1.0	30
11 W	0018	2.9	88		26 Th	0012	2.5	76
	0612	0.3	9			0608	0.8	24
	1304	3.0	91			1252	2.6	79
	1850	0.7	21			1845	1.1	34
12 Th ☽	0121	2.9	88		27 F ◐	0104	2.4	73
	0719	0.4	12			0703	0.9	27
	1408	3.0	91			1345	2.5	76
	1959	0.8	24			1945	1.1	34
13 F	0229	2.8	85		28 Sa	0202	2.4	73
	0829	0.5	15			0804	0.9	27
	1514	2.9	88			1442	2.5	76
	2107	0.7	21			2045	1.0	30
14 Sa	0338	2.8	85		29 Su	0304	2.4	73
	0936	0.5	15			0905	0.9	27
	1617	3.0	91			1539	2.6	79
	2210	0.6	18			2140	0.9	27
15 Su	0443	2.9	88		30 M	0405	2.6	79
	1036	0.5	15			1001	0.8	24
	1715	3.0	91			1633	2.7	82
	2305	0.5	15			2230	0.7	21
					31 Tu	0502	2.7	82
						1053	0.7	21
						1724	2.8	85
						2316	0.5	15

November

Day	Time	ft	cm		Day	Time	ft	cm
1 W	0555	2.9	88		16 Th	0018	0.2	6
	1141	0.5	15			0700	3.0	91
	1812	2.9	88			1243	0.4	12
						1909	2.8	85
2 Th	0001	0.3	9		17 F	0059	0.1	3
	0645	3.1	94			0741	3.0	91
	1227	0.4	12			1324	0.4	12
	1859	3.0	91			1948	2.8	85
3 F	0046	0.1	3		18 Sa ●	0138	0.1	3
	0733	3.3	101			0820	3.0	91
	1314	0.3	9			1404	0.5	15
	1945	3.1	94			2025	2.7	82
4 Sa ○	0132	-0.1	-3		19 Su	0216	0.2	6
	0822	3.4	104			0857	2.9	88
	1401	0.3	9			1442	0.5	15
	2032	3.2	98			2102	2.7	82
5 Su	0219	-0.2	-6		20 M	0253	0.2	6
	0910	3.4	104			0935	2.8	85
	1449	0.2	6			1519	0.6	18
	2121	3.2	98			2139	2.6	79
6 M	0308	-0.2	-6		21 Tu	0329	0.3	9
	1001	3.4	104			1013	2.8	85
	1540	0.3	9			1557	0.6	18
	2212	3.1	94			2218	2.5	76
7 Tu	0400	-0.1	-3		22 W	0406	0.4	12
	1053	3.3	101			1052	2.7	82
	1634	0.4	12			1636	0.7	21
	2306	3.0	91			2258	2.4	73
8 W	0456	0.0	0		23 Th	0445	0.5	15
	1148	3.2	98			1133	2.6	79
	1733	0.5	15			1718	0.8	24
						2342	2.3	70
9 Th	0004	2.9	88		24 F	0528	0.6	18
	0557	0.2	6			1217	2.5	76
	1246	3.0	91			1805	0.8	24
	1837	0.5	15					
10 F ○	0107	2.8	85		25 Sa	0031	2.3	70
	0704	0.3	9			0617	0.6	18
	1348	2.9	88			1305	2.4	73
	1945	0.6	18			1858	0.8	24
11 Sa	0214	2.8	85		26 Su ◐	0126	2.2	67
	0812	0.4	12			0715	0.7	21
	1451	2.8	85			1357	2.4	73
	2051	0.5	15			1956	0.7	21
12 Su	0322	2.7	82		27 M	0226	2.3	70
	0918	0.5	15			0817	0.7	21
	1552	2.8	85			1452	2.4	73
	2151	0.4	12			2054	0.6	18
13 M	0426	2.8	85		28 Tu	0327	2.4	73
	1018	0.5	15			0918	0.6	18
	1649	2.8	85			1548	2.4	73
	2245	0.3	9			2148	0.4	12
14 Tu	0524	2.9	88		29 W	0428	2.5	76
	1111	0.5	15			1015	0.5	15
	1741	2.8	85			1643	2.5	76
	2333	0.2	6			2240	0.2	6
15 W	0614	2.9	88		30 Th	0525	2.7	82
	1159	0.5	15			1109	0.4	12
	1827	2.8	85			1736	2.7	82
						2331	-0.1	-3

December

Day	Time	ft	cm		Day	Time	ft	cm
1 F	0619	2.9	88		16 Sa	0034	0.0	0
	1201	0.2	6			0718	2.6	79
	1829	2.8	85			1301	0.3	9
						1921	2.4	73
2 Sa	0021	-0.3	-9		17 Su	0114	-0.1	-3
	0711	3.0	91			0757	2.6	79
	1251	0.1	3			1341	0.3	9
	1920	2.9	88			2000	2.4	73
3 Su	0110	-0.4	-12		18 M ●	0152	-0.1	-3
	0803	3.2	98			0834	2.6	79
	1341	0.0	0			1419	0.3	9
O	2012	2.9	88			2038	2.4	73
4 M	0201	-0.5	-15		19 Tu	0229	-0.1	-3
	0853	3.2	98			0912	2.5	76
	1432	0.0	0			1456	0.3	9
	2104	3.0	91			2117	2.3	70
5 Tu	0252	-0.5	-15		20 W	0305	0.0	0
	0945	3.2	98			0950	2.5	76
	1525	0.0	0			1533	0.3	9
	2157	2.9	88			2156	2.3	70
6 W	0346	-0.4	-12		21 Th	0341	0.0	0
	1036	3.1	94			1028	2.4	73
	1620	0.0	0			1609	0.3	9
	2252	2.9	88			2236	2.2	67
7 Th	0441	-0.3	-9		22 F	0418	0.1	3
	1130	3.0	91			1106	2.4	73
	1717	0.1	3			1648	0.3	9
	2349	2.7	82			2318	2.1	64
8 F	0541	-0.1	-3		23 Sa	0457	0.2	6
	1225	2.8	85			1147	2.3	70
	1819	0.1	3			1730	0.3	9
9 Sa	0049	2.6	79		24 Su	0003	2.1	64
	0643	0.1	3			0542	0.3	9
	1322	2.7	82			1229	2.2	67
	1922	0.2	6			1817	0.3	9
10 Su ○	0152	2.5	76		25 M	0053	2.1	64
	0748	0.2	6			0634	0.3	9
	1420	2.6	79			1316	2.2	67
	2025	0.2	6			1911	0.3	9
11 M	0257	2.5	76		26 Tu ◐	0150	2.1	64
	0852	0.3	9			0733	0.3	9
	1519	2.5	76			1407	2.2	67
	2124	0.2	6			2010	0.1	3
12 Tu	0400	2.4	73		27 W	0251	2.1	64
	0952	0.4	12			0837	0.3	9
	1616	2.4	73			1504	2.2	67
	2218	0.1	3			2109	0.0	0
13 W	0458	2.5	76		28 Th	0355	2.2	67
	1046	0.4	12			0940	0.3	9
	1709	2.4	73			1605	2.2	67
	2307	0.0	0			2208	-0.2	-6
14 Th	0550	2.5	76		29 F	0458	2.4	73
	1135	0.4	12			1040	0.2	6
	1757	2.4	73			1705	2.3	70
	2352	0.0	0			2305	-0.4	-12
15 F	0636	2.5	76		30 Sa	0557	2.6	79
	1219	0.3	9			1137	0.0	0
	1841	2.4	73			1804	2.5	76
						2359	-0.6	-18
					31 Su	0653	2.7	82
						1231	-0.1	-3
						1901	2.6	79

Time meridian 75° W. 0000 is midnight. 1200 is noon. Times are not adjusted for Daylight Saving Time.
Heights are referred to mean lower low water which is the chart datum of soundings.

Vaca Key, Florida Bay, Florida, 2017

Times and Heights of High and Low Waters

January

Day	Time	ft	cm	Day	Time	ft	cm
1 Su	0239	0.9	27	16 M	0312	0.7	21
	0830	-0.2	-6		0859	-0.2	-6
	1723	0.6	18		1730	0.5	15
	2018	0.4	12		2113	0.1	3
2 M	0327	0.8	24	17 Tu	0400	0.6	18
	0915	-0.2	-6		0944	-0.1	-3
	1713	0.6	18		1716	0.5	15
	2111	0.3	9		2214	0.0	0
3 Tu	0416	0.8	24	18 W	0447	0.5	15
	1001	-0.1	-3		1030	-0.1	-3
	1733	0.6	18		1736	0.5	15
	2209	0.3	9		2318	0.0	0
4 W	0506	0.7	21	19 Th	0536	0.3	9
	1048	0.0	0		1116	0.0	0
	1804	0.6	18		1811	0.6	18
	2311	0.2	6		◗		
5 Th	0601	0.6	18	20 F	0025	-0.1	-3
	1137	0.1	3		0629	0.2	6
	1839	0.7	21		1203	0.0	0
◖					1852	0.6	18
6 F	0017	0.1	3	21 Sa	0133	-0.2	-6
	0706	0.4	12		1045	0.2	6
	1226	0.2	6		1253	0.1	3
	1917	0.7	21		1936	0.6	18
7 Sa	0125	0.0	0	22 Su	0237	-0.2	-6
	1102	0.4	12		2023	0.6	18
	1317	0.3	9				
	1956	0.8	24				
8 Su	0231	-0.1	-3	23 M	0329	-0.3	-9
	2036	0.8	24		2111	0.6	18
9 M	0332	-0.2	-6	24 Tu	0410	-0.3	-9
	1315	0.5	15		2201	0.6	18
	1500	0.4	12				
	2120	0.9	27				
10 Tu	0426	-0.2	-6	25 W	0447	-0.3	-9
	1406	0.5	15		1425	0.4	12
	1551	0.4	12		1609	0.3	9
	2210	0.9	27		2254	0.6	18
11 W	0515	-0.3	-9	26 Th	0524	-0.3	-9
	1451	0.5	15		1503	0.4	12
	1642	0.4	12		1653	0.3	9
	2311	0.9	27		2349	0.6	18
12 Th	0602	-0.3	-9	27 F	0602	-0.3	-9
	1532	0.5	15		1537	0.4	12
	1733	0.4	12		1737	0.3	9
○				●			
13 F	0019	0.9	27	28 Sa	0046	0.7	21
	0646	-0.2	-6		0642	-0.3	-9
	1610	0.5	15		1606	0.4	12
	1825	0.3	9		1823	0.3	9
14 Sa	0124	0.9	27	29 Su	0141	0.7	21
	0731	-0.2	-6		0723	-0.3	-9
	1644	0.5	15		1625	0.4	12
	1919	0.3	9		1912	0.2	6
15 Su	0221	0.8	24	30 M	0233	0.7	21
	0815	-0.2	-6		0806	-0.3	-9
	1714	0.5	15		1623	0.4	12
	2015	0.2	6		2003	0.1	3
				31 Tu	0322	0.6	18
					0849	-0.2	-6
					1627	0.4	12
					2056	0.0	0

February

Day	Time	ft	cm	Day	Time	ft	cm
1 W	0412	0.6	18	16 Th	0435	0.3	9
	0933	-0.2	-6		0954	-0.1	-3
	1651	0.5	15		1652	0.5	15
	2152	-0.1	-3		2243	-0.3	-9
2 Th	0502	0.4	12	17 F	0519	0.2	6
	1017	-0.1	-3		1036	-0.1	-3
	1723	0.5	15		1730	0.5	15
	2252	-0.2	-6		2339	-0.4	-12
3 F	0557	0.3	9	18 Sa	0849	0.0	0
	1101	0.0	0		1119	-0.1	-3
	1758	0.6	18		1812	0.5	15
◖	2355	-0.3	-9	◗			
4 Sa	0923	0.2	6	19 Su	0037	-0.4	-12
	1147	0.1	3		1027	0.0	0
	1837	0.6	18		1206	0.0	0
					1857	0.5	15
5 Su	0100	-0.3	-9	20 M	0136	-0.4	-12
	1919	0.6	18		1946	0.5	15
6 M	0207	-0.4	-12	21 Tu	0233	-0.4	-12
	2006	0.7	21		2038	0.5	15
7 Tu	0310	-0.4	-12	22 W	0326	-0.4	-12
	1259	0.3	9		2133	0.5	15
	1432	0.2	6				
	2059	0.7	21				
8 W	0407	-0.4	-12	23 Th	0412	-0.4	-12
	1343	0.3	9		1354	0.3	9
	1532	0.2	6		1546	0.2	6
	2159	0.7	21		2232	0.5	15
9 Th	0456	-0.3	-9	24 F	0454	-0.3	-9
	1423	0.3	9		1427	0.3	9
	1629	0.2	6		1634	0.2	6
	2309	0.7	21		2338	0.5	15
10 F	0541	-0.3	-9	25 Sa	0535	-0.3	-9
	1500	0.3	9		1457	0.3	9
	1723	0.2	6		1722	0.2	6
○							
11 Sa	0026	0.6	18	26 Su	0045	0.6	18
	0624	-0.3	-9		0616	-0.2	-6
	1533	0.4	12		1519	0.4	12
	1816	0.1	3	●	1809	0.1	3
12 Su	0134	0.6	18	27 M	0147	0.6	18
	0705	-0.2	-6		0657	-0.2	-6
	1601	0.4	12		1526	0.4	12
	1908	0.0	0		1858	0.0	0
13 M	0226	0.6	18	28 Tu	0241	0.6	18
	0747	-0.2	-6		0738	-0.1	-3
	1619	0.4	12		1521	0.4	12
	2001	0.0	0		1948	-0.1	-3
14 Tu	0311	0.5	15				
	0829	-0.2	-6				
	1607	0.4	12				
	2054	-0.1	-3				
15 W	0353	0.4	12				
	0911	-0.2	-6				
	1621	0.5	15				
	2148	-0.2	-6				

March

Day	Time	ft	cm	Day	Time	ft	cm
1 W	0332	0.5	15	16 Th	0402	0.4	12
	0820	-0.1	-3		0836	0.0	0
	1540	0.5	15		1537	0.6	18
	2041	-0.2	-6		2119	-0.3	-9
2 Th	0421	0.4	12	17 F	0431	0.3	9
	0902	0.0	0		0916	0.0	0
	1609	0.5	15		1613	0.6	18
	2135	-0.3	-9		2207	-0.4	-12
3 F	0513	0.3	9	18 Sa	0508	0.2	6
	0944	0.0	0		0956	0.0	0
	1643	0.6	18		1653	0.6	18
	2232	-0.4	-12		2257	-0.4	-12
4 Sa	0623	0.2	6	19 Su	0553	0.1	3
	1027	0.0	0		1037	0.0	0
	1721	0.6	18		1736	0.5	15
	2332	-0.4	-12		2350	-0.4	-12
5 Su	1804	0.6	18	20 M	1001	0.1	3
◖					1122	0.1	3
					1822	0.5	15
				◗			
6 M	0035	-0.4	-12	21 Tu	0045	-0.4	-12
	1851	0.6	18		1911	0.5	15
7 Tu	0140	-0.4	-12	22 W	0143	-0.4	-12
	1945	0.6	18		2006	0.5	15
8 W	0244	-0.4	-12	23 Th	0240	-0.3	-9
	1228	0.2	6		1237	0.3	9
	1419	0.2	6		1430	0.2	6
	2045	0.6	18		2106	0.5	15
9 Th	0342	-0.3	-9	24 F	0333	-0.2	-6
	1309	0.3	9		1311	0.4	12
	1525	0.1	3		1528	0.2	6
	2157	0.5	15		2215	0.5	15
10 F	0432	-0.2	-6	25 Sa	0420	-0.1	-3
	1346	0.3	9		1341	0.4	12
	1625	0.1	3		1619	0.2	6
					2346	0.5	15
11 Sa	0038	0.5	15	26 Su	0504	0.0	0
	0516	-0.1	-3		1405	0.4	12
	1420	0.4	12		1708	0.1	3
	1719	0.1	3				
12 Su	0142	0.5	15	27 M	0125	0.6	18
	0557	-0.1	-3		0545	0.0	0
	1450	0.4	12		1416	0.5	15
○	1809	0.0	0	●	1755	0.0	0
13 M	0232	0.5	15	28 Tu	0226	0.6	18
	0636	0.0	0		0626	0.1	3
	1511	0.4	12		1406	0.5	15
	1857	-0.1	-3		1844	-0.1	-3
14 Tu	0314	0.5	15	29 W	0320	0.6	18
	0716	0.0	0		0706	0.2	6
	1504	0.5	15		1423	0.6	18
	1944	-0.2	-6		1934	-0.2	-6
15 W	0344	0.4	12	30 Th	0413	0.6	18
	0756	0.0	0		0747	0.2	6
	1508	0.5	15		1453	0.7	21
	2031	-0.3	-9		2025	-0.3	-9
				31 F	0510	0.5	15
					0828	0.2	6
					1529	0.7	21
					2118	-0.4	-12

Time meridian 75° W. 0000 is midnight. 1200 is noon. Times are not adjusted for Daylight Saving Time.
Heights are referred to mean lower low water which is the chart datum of soundings.

Vaca Key, Florida Bay, Florida, 2017
Times and Heights of High and Low Waters

April

Day	Time	ft	cm	Day	Time	ft	cm
1 Sa	0620	0.4	12	**16** Su	0514	0.3	9
	0910	0.2	6		0918	0.2	6
	1608	0.8	24		1619	0.7	21
	2212	-0.4	-12		2221	-0.4	-12
2 Su	0744	0.3	9	**17** M	0800	0.3	9
	0955	0.2	6		1000	0.2	6
	1651	0.8	24		1703	0.7	21
	2309	-0.4	-12		2311	-0.4	-12
3 M ◖	1737	0.7	21	**18** Tu	1749	0.6	18
4 Tu	0009	-0.3	-9	**19** W ◗	0003	-0.3	-9
	1829	0.7	21		1840	0.6	18
5 W	0111	-0.3	-9	**20** Th	0059	-0.2	-6
	1104	0.3	9		1936	0.6	18
	1300	0.2	6				
	1927	0.6	18				
6 Th	0213	-0.2	-6	**21** F	0157	-0.1	-3
	1147	0.4	12		1146	0.4	12
	1417	0.2	6		1408	0.3	9
	2035	0.5	15		2041	0.5	15
7 F	0312	-0.1	-3	**22** Sa	0252	0.0	0
	1226	0.4	12		1218	0.5	15
	1527	0.2	6		1509	0.3	9
	2358	0.5	15		2205	0.5	15
8 Sa	0402	0.0	0	**23** Su	0343	0.1	3
	1302	0.5	15		1242	0.5	15
	1626	0.1	3		1603	0.2	6
9 Su	0103	0.6	18	**24** M	0051	0.6	18
	0446	0.1	3		0428	0.2	6
	1335	0.5	15		1247	0.6	18
	1715	0.1	3		1653	0.1	3
10 M	0157	0.6	18	**25** Tu	0154	0.7	21
	0525	0.2	6		0511	0.3	9
	1359	0.6	18		1225	0.7	21
	1800	0.0	0		1741	0.0	0
11 Tu ○	0247	0.6	18	**26** W ●	0250	0.7	21
	0604	0.2	6		0551	0.4	12
	1358	0.6	18		1251	0.8	24
	1842	-0.1	-3		1829	-0.1	-3
12 W	0333	0.5	15	**27** Th	0343	0.7	21
	0642	0.2	6		0631	0.4	12
	1350	0.7	21		1328	0.8	24
	1924	-0.2	-6		1918	-0.2	-6
13 Th	0416	0.5	15	**28** F	0436	0.6	18
	0720	0.2	6		0712	0.4	12
	1420	0.7	21		1409	0.9	27
	2006	-0.3	-9		2008	-0.3	-9
14 F	0456	0.4	12	**29** Sa	0530	0.6	18
	0759	0.2	6		0754	0.4	12
	1457	0.7	21		1453	0.9	27
	2049	-0.3	-9		2059	-0.3	-9
15 Sa	0532	0.4	12	**30** Su	0628	0.5	15
	0838	0.2	6		0839	0.4	12
	1537	0.7	21		1539	0.9	27
	2134	-0.4	-12		2152	-0.3	-9

May

Day	Time	ft	cm	Day	Time	ft	cm
1 M	0730	0.4	12	**16** Tu	0716	0.4	12
	0930	0.3	9		0930	0.3	9
	1627	0.9	27		1634	0.8	24
	2246	-0.3	-9		2238	-0.3	-9
2 Tu ◗	0831	0.4	12	**17** W	0818	0.4	12
	1028	0.3	9		1023	0.3	9
	1717	0.8	24		1721	0.7	21
	2342	-0.2	-6		2328	-0.2	-6
3 W	0927	0.4	12	**18** Th ◖	0915	0.5	15
	1138	0.3	9		1126	0.4	12
	1810	0.7	21		1812	0.7	21
4 Th	0040	-0.1	-3	**19** F	0022	-0.1	-3
	1016	0.5	15		1000	0.5	15
	1257	0.3	9		1235	0.4	12
	1911	0.6	18		1910	0.6	18
5 F	0139	0.0	0	**20** Sa	0117	0.0	0
	1059	0.5	15		0857	0.5	15
	1419	0.2	6		1345	0.3	9
	2243	0.5	15		2019	0.6	18
6 Sa	0236	0.1	3	**21** Su	0212	0.2	6
	1139	0.6	18		0923	0.6	18
	1532	0.2	6		1448	0.3	9
					2347	0.6	18
7 Su	0002	0.5	15	**22** M	0303	0.3	9
	0327	0.2	6		0958	0.7	21
	1214	0.7	21		1545	0.1	3
	1627	0.1	3				
8 M	0103	0.6	18	**23** Tu	0059	0.6	18
	0412	0.3	9		0350	0.4	12
	1242	0.7	21		1032	0.8	24
	1709	0.0	0		1636	0.0	0
9 Tu	0156	0.6	18	**24** W	0159	0.7	21
	0452	0.3	9		0433	0.5	15
	1238	0.7	21		1108	0.9	27
	1747	0.0	0		1725	-0.1	-3
10 W ○	0246	0.6	18	**25** Th ●	0253	0.7	21
	0530	0.4	12		0515	0.5	15
	1224	0.8	24		1149	1.0	30
	1823	-0.1	-3		1814	-0.2	-6
11 Th	0333	0.6	18	**26** F	0345	0.7	21
	0606	0.4	12		0556	0.5	15
	1258	0.8	24		1239	1.0	30
	1901	-0.2	-6		1902	-0.2	-6
12 F	0418	0.6	18	**27** Sa	0435	0.6	18
	0644	0.4	12		0639	0.5	15
	1339	0.8	24		1333	1.1	34
	1940	-0.2	-6		1951	-0.3	-9
13 Sa	0501	0.5	15	**28** Su	0523	0.6	18
	0722	0.4	12		0725	0.5	15
	1422	0.8	24		1426	1.1	34
	2021	-0.3	-9		2040	-0.3	-9
14 Su	0543	0.5	15	**29** M	0610	0.5	15
	0802	0.4	12		0816	0.4	12
	1505	0.8	24		1518	1.0	30
	2105	-0.3	-9		2130	-0.2	-6
15 M	0626	0.4	12	**30** Tu	0657	0.5	15
	0844	0.3	9		0913	0.4	12
	1549	0.8	24		1609	0.9	27
	2150	-0.3	-9		2221	-0.2	-6
				31 W	0744	0.5	15
					1017	0.4	12
					1700	0.8	24
					2313	-0.1	-3

June

Day	Time	ft	cm	Day	Time	ft	cm
1 Th ◖	0832	0.5	15	**16** F	0623	0.6	18
	1129	0.3	9		1105	0.4	12
	1754	0.7	21		1752	0.7	21
					2347	0.0	0
2 F	0006	0.0	0	**17** Sa	0702	0.6	18
	0918	0.6	18		1211	0.3	9
	1250	0.3	9		1850	0.6	18
	1853	0.5	15				
3 Sa	0102	0.1	3	**18** Su	0039	0.1	3
	1001	0.6	18		0742	0.7	21
	1417	0.2	6		1319	0.3	9
	2243	0.5	15		2004	0.5	15
4 Su	0157	0.2	6	**19** M	0131	0.3	9
	1040	0.7	21		0822	0.8	24
	1533	0.1	3		1425	0.2	6
	2355	0.5	15		2352	0.6	18
5 M	0249	0.3	9	**20** Tu	0222	0.4	12
	1108	0.7	21		0901	0.8	24
	1622	0.1	3		1525	0.1	3
6 Tu	0056	0.6	18	**21** W	0058	0.6	18
	0336	0.4	12		0310	0.5	15
	1020	0.8	24		0939	0.9	27
	1657	0.0	0		1619	0.0	0
7 W	0149	0.6	18	**22** Th	0155	0.7	21
	0417	0.4	12		0356	0.6	18
	1056	0.8	24		1019	1.0	30
	1729	-0.1	-3		1709	-0.1	-3
8 Th	0239	0.6	18	**23** F ●	0247	0.7	21
	0455	0.5	15		0441	0.6	18
	1136	0.9	27		1108	1.1	34
	1802	-0.1	-3		1757	-0.2	-6
9 F ○	0325	0.6	18	**24** Sa	0334	0.7	21
	0532	0.5	15		0527	0.6	18
	1220	0.9	27		1208	1.1	34
	1837	-0.2	-6		1844	-0.2	-6
10 Sa	0409	0.6	18	**25** Su	0418	0.6	18
	0610	0.5	15		0614	0.5	15
	1306	0.9	27		1311	1.1	34
	1915	-0.2	-6		1931	-0.1	-3
11 Su	0450	0.6	18	**26** M	0459	0.6	18
	0649	0.5	15		0705	0.5	15
	1353	0.9	27		1410	1.1	34
	1955	-0.2	-6		2018	-0.1	-3
12 M	0526	0.6	18	**27** Tu	0537	0.6	18
	0731	0.5	15		0800	0.4	12
	1439	0.9	27		1504	1.0	30
	2037	-0.2	-6		2105	-0.1	-3
13 Tu	0556	0.5	15	**28** W	0611	0.6	18
	0817	0.4	12		0859	0.4	12
	1525	0.9	27		1555	0.9	27
	2122	-0.2	-6		2153	0.0	0
14 W	0545	0.5	15	**29** Th	0641	0.6	18
	0907	0.4	12		1003	0.3	9
	1612	0.8	24		1646	0.8	24
	2208	-0.2	-6		2242	0.1	3
15 Th	0550	0.6	18	**30** F ◖	0641	0.6	18
	1003	0.4	12		1113	0.3	9
	1700	0.8	24		1737	0.6	18
	2256	-0.1	-3		2331	0.1	3

Time meridian 75° W. 0000 is midnight. 1200 is noon. Times are not adjusted for Daylight Saving Time.
Heights are referred to mean lower low water which is the chart datum of soundings.

Vaca Key, Florida Bay, Florida, 2017

Times and Heights of High and Low Waters

July

Day	Time	ft	cm	Day	Time	ft	cm
1 Sa	0643	0.7	21	16 Su ☽	0619	0.8	24
	1230	0.2	6		1147	0.2	6
	1833	0.5	15		1838	0.6	18
2 Su	0023	0.2	6	17 M	0001	0.3	9
	0719	0.7	21		0657	0.8	24
	1352	0.2	6		1253	0.2	6
	2232	0.4	12		2227	0.5	15
3 M	0117	0.3	9	18 Tu	0051	0.4	12
	0801	0.8	24		0738	0.9	27
	1508	0.1	3		1400	0.1	3
	2344	0.5	15		2348	0.6	18
4 Tu	0211	0.4	12	19 W	0142	0.5	15
	0846	0.8	24		0820	1.0	30
	1559	0.0	0		1503	0.0	0
5 W	0044	0.5	15	20 Th	0905	1.0	30
	0301	0.4	12		1600	0.0	0
	0932	0.9	27				
	1635	0.0	0				
6 Th	0136	0.6	18	21 F	0143	0.7	21
	0345	0.5	15		0326	0.6	18
	1018	0.9	27		0954	1.1	34
	1706	-0.1	-3		1651	0.0	0
7 F	0224	0.6	18	22 Sa	0229	0.7	21
	0425	0.5	15		0417	0.6	18
	1104	0.9	27		1052	1.1	34
	1738	-0.1	-3		1739	0.0	0
8 Sa ○	0308	0.6	18	23 Su ●	0310	0.7	21
	0503	0.5	15		0508	0.6	18
	1153	0.9	27		1158	1.2	37
	1813	-0.1	-3		1824	0.0	0
9 Su	1243	0.9	27	24 M	0348	0.7	21
	1850	-0.1	-3		0600	0.6	18
					1305	1.1	34
					1909	0.1	3
10 M	0423	0.6	18	25 Tu	0422	0.7	21
	0624	0.5	15		0653	0.5	15
	1333	1.0	30		1405	1.1	34
	1929	-0.1	-3		1953	0.1	3
11 Tu	0452	0.6	18	26 W	0452	0.7	21
	0709	0.5	15		0748	0.4	12
	1422	1.0	30		1458	1.0	30
	2011	-0.1	-3		2037	0.2	6
12 W	0505	0.6	18	27 Th	0510	0.7	21
	0757	0.5	15		0845	0.4	12
	1510	0.9	27		1547	0.9	27
	2055	0.0	0		2122	0.2	6
13 Th	0451	0.7	21	28 F	0501	0.8	24
	0849	0.4	12		0945	0.3	9
	1558	0.9	27		1634	0.8	24
	2139	0.0	0		2208	0.2	6
14 F	0511	0.7	21	29 Sa	0517	0.8	24
	0944	0.4	12		1048	0.3	9
	1647	0.8	24		1722	0.7	21
	2225	0.1	3		2255	0.3	9
15 Sa	0542	0.7	21	30 Su ☾	0551	0.9	27
	1043	0.3	9		1154	0.2	6
	1739	0.7	21		1813	0.5	15
	2313	0.2	6		2344	0.4	12
				31 M	0632	0.9	27
					1304	0.1	3
					2217	0.5	15

August

Day	Time	ft	cm	Day	Time	ft	cm
1 Tu	0036	0.4	12	16 W	0012	0.6	18
	0718	0.9	27		0701	1.1	34
	1412	0.1	3		1333	0.2	6
	2328	0.5	15				
2 W	0132	0.4	12	17 Th	0749	1.1	34
	0806	0.9	27		1439	0.2	6
	1512	0.1	3				
3 Th	0027	0.6	18	18 F	0843	1.2	37
	0226	0.5	15		1539	0.2	6
	0856	0.9	27				
	1558	0.1	3				
4 F	0116	0.7	21	19 Sa	0118	0.8	24
	0316	0.6	18		0307	0.7	21
	0948	1.0	30		0942	1.2	37
	1636	0.1	3		1631	0.2	6
5 Sa	0200	0.7	21	20 Su	0158	0.8	24
	0400	0.6	18		0405	0.7	21
	1041	1.0	30		1051	1.2	37
	1711	0.1	3		1718	0.3	9
6 Su	0240	0.7	21	21 M ●	0234	0.9	27
	0442	0.6	18		0459	0.7	21
	1135	1.0	30		1209	1.2	37
	1746	0.1	3		1801	0.3	9
7 M ○	0314	0.8	24	22 Tu	0308	0.9	27
	0523	0.7	21		0552	0.6	18
	1230	1.0	30		1325	1.2	37
	1824	0.2	6		1843	0.4	12
8 Tu	0344	0.8	24	23 W	0337	0.9	27
	0607	0.6	18		0644	0.6	18
	1324	1.1	34		1422	1.2	37
	1903	0.2	6		1924	0.4	12
9 W	0403	0.8	24	24 Th	0355	0.9	27
	0653	0.6	18		0736	0.5	15
	1415	1.1	34		1507	1.1	34
	1944	0.2	6		2006	0.5	15
10 Th	0356	0.8	24	25 F	0346	1.0	30
	0741	0.5	15		0828	0.4	12
	1504	1.1	34		1547	1.0	30
	2026	0.3	9		2049	0.5	15
11 F	0401	0.9	27	26 Sa	0359	1.0	30
	0832	0.4	12		0922	0.3	9
	1553	1.0	30		1627	0.9	27
	2110	0.3	9		2132	0.5	15
12 Sa	0428	0.9	27	27 Su	0431	1.1	34
	0925	0.3	9		1017	0.3	9
	1642	0.9	27		1709	0.8	24
	2153	0.4	12		2217	0.5	15
13 Su	0501	1.0	30	28 M	0509	1.1	34
	1022	0.3	9		1114	0.2	6
	1735	0.8	24		2026	0.7	21
	2237	0.5	15		2303	0.6	18
14 M ☾	0537	1.0	30	29 Tu ☾	0552	1.1	34
	1123	0.2	6		1213	0.2	6
	1839	0.7	21		2157	0.7	21
	2323	0.5	15		2354	0.6	18
15 Tu	0617	1.1	34	30 W	0639	1.1	34
	1227	0.2	6		1314	0.2	6
	2226	0.7	21				
				31 Th	0730	1.0	30
					1416	0.2	6

September

Day	Time	ft	cm	Day	Time	ft	cm
1 F	0824	1.0	30	16 Sa	0001	0.9	27
	1511	0.3	9		0154	0.9	27
					0827	1.3	40
					1513	0.4	12
2 Sa	0047	0.8	24	17 Su	0041	1.0	30
	0252	0.7	21		0301	0.8	24
	0921	1.1	34		0940	1.2	37
	1558	0.3	9		1606	0.5	15
3 Su	0126	0.9	27	18 M	0118	1.0	30
	0341	0.8	24		0402	0.8	24
	1022	1.1	34		1219	1.3	40
	1639	0.4	12		1652	0.6	18
4 M	0201	0.9	27	19 Tu	0152	1.1	34
	0426	0.8	24		0456	0.7	21
	1126	1.1	34		1327	1.3	40
	1717	0.4	12		1733	0.7	21
5 Tu	0230	1.0	30	20 W ●	0222	1.1	34
	0509	0.8	24		0546	0.7	21
	1232	1.2	37		1421	1.3	40
	1756	0.5	15		1813	0.7	21
6 W ○	0252	1.0	30	21 Th	0242	1.1	34
	0552	0.7	21		0634	0.6	18
	1332	1.2	37		1510	1.2	37
	1835	0.5	15		1853	0.8	24
7 Th	0253	1.0	30	22 F	0232	1.2	37
	0638	0.6	18		0721	0.5	15
	1425	1.2	37		1554	1.2	37
	1915	0.6	18		1933	0.8	24
8 F	0249	1.1	34	23 Sa	0239	1.2	37
	0725	0.5	15		0808	0.4	12
	1515	1.2	37		1632	1.1	34
	1956	0.6	18		2014	0.8	24
9 Sa	0312	1.1	34	24 Su	0311	1.3	40
	0815	0.4	12		0856	0.4	12
	1604	1.1	34		1652	1.0	30
	2037	0.7	21		2055	0.8	24
10 Su	0344	1.2	37	25 M	0349	1.3	40
	0907	0.3	9		0944	0.3	9
	1655	1.0	30		1708	0.9	27
	2119	0.7	21		2138	0.8	24
11 M	0419	1.2	37	26 Tu	0431	1.3	40
	1002	0.3	9		1035	0.3	9
	1757	0.9	27		2007	0.9	27
	2201	0.7	21		2222	0.8	24
12 Tu ☾	0458	1.3	40	27 W	0516	1.2	37
	1100	0.3	9		1128	0.3	9
13 W ○	0542	1.3	40	28 Th	0603	1.2	37
	1202	0.3	9		1224	0.3	9
14 Th	0630	1.3	40	29 F	0655	1.2	37
	1306	0.3	9		1323	0.4	12
					2326	1.0	30
15 F	0725	1.3	40	30 Sa	0123	0.9	27
	1412	0.4	12		0752	1.1	34
					1421	0.5	15

Time meridian 75° W. 0000 is midnight. 1200 is noon. Times are not adjusted for Daylight Saving Time.
Heights are referred to mean lower low water which is the chart datum of soundings.

Vaca Key, Florida Bay, Florida, 2017

Times and Heights of High and Low Waters

October

Day	Time	ft	cm
1 Su	0007	1.0	30
	0229	0.9	27
	0854	1.2	37
	1515	0.5	15
2 M	0042	1.1	34
	0324	0.9	27
	1004	1.2	37
	1602	0.6	18
3 Tu	0112	1.1	34
	0410	0.9	27
	1148	1.2	37
	1644	0.7	21
4 W	0135	1.1	34
	0454	0.8	24
	1320	1.3	40
	1724	0.8	24
5 Th ○	0135	1.2	37
	0538	0.7	21
	1416	1.3	40
	1803	0.9	27
6 F	0124	1.2	37
	0623	0.6	18
	1508	1.3	40
	1842	0.9	27
7 Sa	0149	1.3	40
	0710	0.5	15
	1559	1.3	40
	1922	0.9	27
8 Su	0223	1.4	43
	0759	0.4	12
	1654	1.2	37
	2003	0.9	27
9 M	0301	1.4	43
	0850	0.3	9
	1758	1.1	34
	2044	0.9	27
10 Tu	0342	1.5	46
	0943	0.3	9
	1916	1.0	30
	2128	0.9	27
11 W	0426	1.4	43
	1038	0.3	9
12 Th ☽	0513	1.4	43
	1136	0.4	12
13 F	0606	1.4	43
	1238	0.4	12
	2234	1.0	30
14 Sa	0032	0.9	27
	0706	1.3	40
	1341	0.5	15
	2318	1.1	34
15 Su	0150	0.9	27
	0816	1.2	37
	1441	0.6	18
	2357	1.1	34
16 M	0302	0.8	24
	1134	1.2	37
	1535	0.7	21
17 Tu	0033	1.2	37
	0403	0.8	24
	1243	1.2	37
	1621	0.8	24
18 W	0105	1.2	37
	0454	0.7	21
	1340	1.3	40
	1702	0.9	27
19 Th ●	0129	1.3	40
	0539	0.6	18
	1431	1.3	40
	1741	0.9	27
20 F	0112	1.3	40
	0621	0.5	15
	1520	1.2	37
	1820	0.9	27
21 Sa	0115	1.3	40
	0703	0.4	12
	1607	1.2	37
	1859	0.9	27
22 Su	0150	1.4	43
	0746	0.4	12
	1652	1.1	34
	1938	0.9	27
23 M	0230	1.4	43
	0829	0.3	9
	1739	1.1	34
	2019	0.9	27
24 Tu	0313	1.4	43
	0914	0.2	6
	1832	1.0	30
	2101	0.9	27
25 W	0357	1.3	40
	1000	0.2	6
	1938	1.0	30
	2146	0.9	27
26 Th	0442	1.3	40
	1049	0.3	9
27 F ☾	0531	1.2	37
	1141	0.3	9
28 Sa	0623	1.2	37
	1236	0.4	12
	2236	1.0	30
29 Su	0052	0.9	27
	0720	1.1	34
	1334	0.5	15
	2314	1.0	30
30 M	0201	0.9	27
	0826	1.1	34
	1429	0.6	18
	2345	1.1	34
31 Tu	0301	0.8	24
	0950	1.1	34
	1521	0.7	21

November

Day	Time	ft	cm
1 W	0006	1.1	34
	0351	0.8	24
	1239	1.2	37
	1606	0.8	24
	2317	1.2	37
2 Th	0437	0.7	21
	1339	1.2	37
	1648	0.9	27
	2341	1.3	40
3 F	0522	0.5	15
	1434	1.2	37
	1728	1.0	30
4 Sa ○	0014	1.3	40
	0607	0.4	12
	1526	1.2	37
	1807	1.0	30
5 Su	0053	1.4	43
	0654	0.3	9
	1618	1.2	37
	1847	1.0	30
6 M	0137	1.4	43
	0743	0.2	6
	1711	1.1	34
	1929	1.0	30
7 Tu	0224	1.5	46
	0832	0.2	6
	1805	1.1	34
	2014	1.0	30
8 W	0312	1.5	46
	0924	0.2	6
	1903	1.0	30
	2103	0.9	27
9 Th	0402	1.4	43
	1016	0.2	6
	2000	1.0	30
	2201	0.9	27
10 F ☽	0453	1.3	40
	1111	0.3	9
	2055	0.9	27
	2309	0.8	24
11 Sa	0548	1.2	37
	1208	0.4	12
	2143	1.0	30
12 Su	0026	0.8	24
	0649	1.1	34
	1306	0.5	15
	2227	1.0	30
13 M	0149	0.7	21
	1012	1.0	30
	1404	0.6	18
	2307	1.1	34
14 Tu	0305	0.6	18
	1140	1.0	30
	1458	0.7	21
	2342	1.1	34
15 W	0404	0.6	18
	1243	1.1	34
	1546	0.8	24
16 Th	0009	1.2	37
	0450	0.5	15
	1339	1.1	34
	1629	0.8	24
	2323	1.2	37
17 F	0529	0.4	12
	1430	1.1	34
	1709	0.9	27
	2348	1.2	37
18 Sa ●	0606	0.3	9
	1518	1.0	30
	1747	0.9	27
19 Su	0027	1.3	40
	0644	0.2	6
	1605	1.0	30
	1825	0.9	27
20 M	0111	1.3	40
	0722	0.2	6
	1649	1.0	30
	1905	0.8	24
21 Tu	0156	1.3	40
	0803	0.1	3
	1731	0.9	27
	1946	0.8	24
22 W	0242	1.2	37
	0845	0.1	3
	1812	0.9	27
	2029	0.8	24
23 Th	0328	1.2	37
	0930	0.1	3
	1852	0.9	27
	2117	0.8	24
24 F	0415	1.1	34
	1016	0.1	3
	1800	0.8	24
	2211	0.7	21
25 Sa	0503	1.1	34
	1105	0.2	6
	1834	0.9	27
	2313	0.7	21
26 Su ☾	0555	1.0	30
	1156	0.3	9
	1917	0.9	27
27 M	0020	0.7	21
	0652	0.9	27
	1250	0.4	12
	2001	0.9	27
28 Tu	0129	0.6	18
	0758	0.9	27
	1345	0.5	15
	2044	1.0	30
29 W	0232	0.6	18
	1131	0.8	24
	1437	0.6	18
	2124	1.0	30
30 Th	0327	0.4	12
	1243	0.9	27
	1525	0.7	21
	2201	1.1	34

December

Day	Time	ft	cm
1 F	0417	0.3	9
	1342	1.0	30
	1609	0.8	24
	2237	1.2	37
2 Sa	0504	0.2	6
	1436	1.0	30
	1651	0.8	24
	2316	1.2	37
3 Su ○	0551	0.1	3
	1527	1.0	30
	1733	0.9	27
4 M	0003	1.3	40
	0638	0.0	0
	1616	0.9	27
	1816	0.8	24
5 Tu	0101	1.3	40
	0726	0.0	0
	1702	0.9	27
	1902	0.8	24
6 W	0158	1.3	40
	0815	0.0	0
	1747	0.8	24
	1952	0.7	21
7 Th	0254	1.3	40
	0904	0.0	0
	1829	0.8	24
	2048	0.7	21
8 F	0347	1.2	37
	0953	0.1	3
	1911	0.8	24
	2150	0.6	18
9 Sa	0439	1.1	34
	1044	0.2	6
	1953	0.8	24
	2300	0.5	15
10 Su ☽	0533	0.9	27
	1136	0.3	9
	2035	0.8	24
11 M	0017	0.5	15
	0632	0.8	24
	1229	0.3	9
	2115	0.8	24
12 Tu	0140	0.4	12
	1017	0.7	21
	1324	0.4	12
	2030	0.9	27
13 W	0300	0.3	9
	1135	0.7	21
	1418	0.5	15
	2105	0.9	27
14 Th	0358	0.2	6
	1237	0.7	21
	1509	0.6	18
	2144	1.0	30
15 F	0439	0.1	3
	1332	0.7	21
	1555	0.6	18
	2225	1.0	30
16 Sa	0514	0.0	0
	1423	0.7	21
	1637	0.6	18
	2308	1.0	30
17 Su	0547	0.0	0
	1509	0.7	21
	1716	0.6	18
	2354	1.0	30
18 M ●	0622	-0.1	-3
	1553	0.7	21
	1756	0.6	18
19 Tu	0042	1.0	30
	0659	-0.1	-3
	1633	0.7	21
	1836	0.6	18
20 W	0131	1.0	30
	0738	-0.1	-3
	1709	0.7	21
	1919	0.6	18
21 Th	0220	1.0	30
	0819	-0.1	-3
	1737	0.7	21
	2005	0.5	15
22 F	0307	0.9	27
	0902	-0.1	-3
	1726	0.6	18
	2055	0.5	15
23 Sa	0354	0.9	27
	0946	-0.1	-3
	1725	0.7	21
	2149	0.4	12
24 Su	0442	0.8	24
	1032	0.0	0
	1756	0.7	21
	2247	0.4	12
25 M	0533	0.7	21
	1120	0.0	0
	1833	0.7	21
	2350	0.3	9
26 Tu ☾	0629	0.6	18
	1210	0.2	6
	1912	0.7	21
27 W	0055	0.2	6
	0735	0.5	15
	1301	0.3	9
	1953	0.8	24
28 Th	0159	0.1	3
	1132	0.5	15
	1352	0.4	12
	2032	0.8	24
29 F	0300	0.0	0
	1241	0.6	18
	1442	0.5	15
	2111	0.9	27
30 Sa	0355	-0.1	-3
	1339	0.6	18
	1529	0.5	15
	2150	1.0	30
31 Su	0446	-0.2	-6
	2234	1.0	30

Time meridian 75° W. 0000 is midnight. 1200 is noon. Times are not adjusted for Daylight Saving Time.
Heights are referred to mean lower low water which is the chart datum of soundings.

Key West, Florida, 2017

Times and Heights of High and Low Waters

January

Date	Time	Height (ft)	Height (cm)	Date	Time	Height (ft)	Height (cm)
1 Su	0536	-0.3	-9	16 M	0623	-0.2	-6
	1219	1.1	34		1255	1.2	37
	1703	0.3	9		1818	0.1	3
	2339	1.7	52				
2 M	0615	-0.2	-6	17 Tu	0045	1.5	46
	1259	1.2	37		0705	-0.1	-3
	1753	0.3	9		1336	1.2	37
					1919	0.2	6
3 Tu	0026	1.6	49	18 W	0134	1.3	40
	0657	-0.1	-3		0748	0.1	3
	1342	1.2	37		1419	1.2	37
	1853	0.3	9		2027	0.2	6
4 W	0120	1.5	46	19 Th ☽	0232	1.1	34
	0742	0.0	0		0834	0.2	6
	1427	1.3	40		1506	1.3	40
	2003	0.3	9		2141	0.2	6
5 Th ☾	0226	1.3	40	20 F	0344	0.9	27
	0831	0.1	3		0923	0.3	9
	1517	1.4	43		1558	1.3	40
	2121	0.2	6		2253	0.1	3
6 F	0347	1.1	34	21 Sa	0511	0.8	24
	0925	0.2	6		1016	0.4	12
	1611	1.5	46		1653	1.3	40
	2239	0.0	0		2358	0.0	0
7 Sa	0518	1.0	30	22 Su	0632	0.8	24
	1021	0.3	9		1109	0.4	12
	1709	1.6	49		1748	1.4	43
	2350	-0.2	-6				
8 Su	0641	1.0	30	23 M	0053	-0.1	-3
	1117	0.3	9		0731	0.8	24
	1807	1.8	55		1158	0.4	12
					1839	1.4	43
9 M	0053	-0.4	-12	24 Tu	0139	-0.2	-6
	0748	1.0	30		0816	0.8	24
	1213	0.3	9		1244	0.3	9
	1904	1.9	58		1926	1.5	46
10 Tu	0150	-0.5	-15	25 W	0219	-0.3	-9
	0843	1.0	30		0853	0.9	27
	1306	0.2	6		1325	0.3	9
	1958	2.0	61		2009	1.6	49
11 W	0242	-0.6	-18	26 Th	0255	-0.3	-9
	0931	1.0	30		0928	0.9	27
	1358	0.1	3		1405	0.2	6
	2050	2.0	61		2049	1.7	52
12 Th ○	0330	-0.6	-18	27 F ●	0329	-0.4	-12
	1014	1.1	34		1002	1.0	30
	1449	0.1	3		1445	0.2	6
	2139	2.0	61		2129	1.7	52
13 F	0416	-0.6	-18	28 Sa	0401	-0.4	-12
	1056	1.1	34		1036	1.1	34
	1539	0.1	3		1526	0.1	3
	2227	2.0	61		2209	1.7	52
14 Sa	0459	-0.5	-15	29 Su	0435	-0.4	-12
	1136	1.1	34		1110	1.1	34
	1630	0.1	3		1609	0.0	0
	2313	1.8	55		2250	1.7	52
15 Su	0542	-0.4	-12	30 M	0509	-0.4	-12
	1215	1.2	37		1145	1.2	37
	1723	0.1	3		1655	0.0	0
	2358	1.7	52		2333	1.6	49
				31 Tu	0545	-0.3	-9
					1221	1.2	37
					1746	0.0	0

February

Date	Time	Height (ft)	Height (cm)	Date	Time	Height (ft)	Height (cm)
1 W	0020	1.5	46	16 Th	0105	1.2	37
	0623	-0.2	-6		0656	0.1	3
	1258	1.3	40		1316	1.3	40
	1843	-0.1	-3		1945	0.0	0
2 Th	0114	1.3	40	17 F	0154	1.0	30
	0705	0.0	0		0734	0.2	6
	1340	1.4	43		1357	1.3	40
	1949	-0.1	-3		2049	0.1	3
3 F ◑	0218	1.1	34	18 Sa ○	0255	0.8	24
	0751	0.1	3		0818	0.3	9
	1429	1.4	43		1446	1.2	37
	2103	-0.1	-3		2201	0.1	3
4 Sa	0338	0.9	27	19 Su	0417	0.7	21
	0844	0.2	6		0912	0.4	12
	1528	1.5	46		1546	1.2	37
	2222	-0.2	-6		2313	0.0	0
5 Su	0513	0.8	24	20 M	0551	0.7	21
	0945	0.3	9		1016	0.4	12
	1637	1.5	46		1655	1.3	40
	2338	-0.3	-9				
6 M	0637	0.8	24	21 Tu	0016	-0.1	-3
	1050	0.3	9		0700	0.7	21
	1750	1.6	49		1119	0.4	12
					1802	1.3	40
7 Tu	0045	-0.4	-12	22 W	0107	-0.1	-3
	0742	0.8	24		0747	0.8	24
	1155	0.2	6		1215	0.4	12
	1856	1.7	52		1859	1.4	43
8 W	0142	-0.5	-15	23 Th	0149	-0.2	-6
	0832	0.9	27		0824	0.9	27
	1255	0.1	3		1303	0.3	9
	1955	1.8	55		1948	1.5	46
9 Th	0231	-0.5	-15	24 F	0225	-0.3	-9
	0915	1.0	30		0858	1.0	30
	1351	0.0	0		1348	0.2	6
	2047	1.8	55		2033	1.6	49
10 F ○	0315	-0.5	-15	25 Sa	0258	-0.3	-9
	0953	1.1	34		0930	1.1	34
	1443	0.0	0		1431	0.0	0
	2135	1.8	55		2116	1.7	52
11 Sa	0355	-0.4	-12	26 Su ●	0330	-0.3	-9
	1029	1.1	34		1002	1.2	37
	1532	-0.1	-3		1514	-0.1	-3
	2219	1.8	55		2159	1.7	52
12 Su	0432	-0.4	-12	27 M	0403	-0.3	-9
	1103	1.2	37		1034	1.3	40
	1621	-0.1	-3		1559	-0.2	-6
	2300	1.7	52		2242	1.7	52
13 M	0509	-0.3	-9	28 Tu	0437	-0.2	-6
	1135	1.3	40		1107	1.4	43
	1708	-0.1	-3		1647	-0.3	-9
	2340	1.5	46		2328	1.6	49
14 Tu	0544	-0.2	-6				
	1208	1.3	40				
	1757	-0.1	-3				
15 W	0021	1.3	40				
	0620	0.0	0				
	1241	1.3	40				
	1848	0.0	0				

March

Date	Time	Height (ft)	Height (cm)	Date	Time	Height (ft)	Height (cm)
1 W	0513	-0.2	-6	16 Th	0001	1.3	40
	1142	1.5	46		0535	0.1	3
	1738	-0.3	-9		1152	1.5	46
					1819	-0.1	-3
2 Th	0017	1.4	43	17 F	0042	1.2	37
	0550	0.0	0		0608	0.3	9
	1219	1.6	49		1225	1.5	46
	1833	-0.3	-9		1907	-0.1	-3
3 F	0112	1.2	37	18 Sa	0128	1.0	30
	0631	0.1	3		0641	0.4	12
	1302	1.6	49		1304	1.4	43
	1936	-0.3	-9		2002	0.0	0
4 Sa	0216	1.0	30	19 Su	0223	0.9	27
	0717	0.2	6		0720	0.4	12
	1353	1.6	49		1350	1.3	40
	2048	-0.3	-9		2108	0.1	3
5 Su ☾	0336	0.8	24	20 M ☽	0336	0.8	24
	0812	0.3	9		0811	0.5	15
	1457	1.6	49		1449	1.3	40
	2206	-0.2	-6		2220	0.1	3
6 M	0508	0.8	24	21 Tu	0504	0.8	24
	0920	0.4	12		0923	0.6	18
	1617	1.5	46		1601	1.3	40
	2324	-0.2	-6		2327	0.1	3
7 Tu	0628	0.8	24	22 W	0617	0.8	24
	1037	0.3	9		1041	0.5	15
	1741	1.6	49		1719	1.3	40
8 W	0031	-0.3	-9	23 Th	0022	0.0	0
	0727	0.9	27		0706	0.9	27
	1149	0.3	9		1147	0.5	15
	1853	1.6	49		1827	1.4	43
9 Th	0125	-0.3	-9	24 F	0105	0.0	0
	0813	1.0	30		0744	1.1	34
	1253	0.2	6		1241	0.3	9
	1953	1.7	52		1923	1.5	46
10 F	0210	-0.3	-9	25 Sa	0143	-0.1	-3
	0851	1.1	34		0818	1.2	37
	1349	0.0	0		1330	0.2	6
	2043	1.7	52		2014	1.6	49
11 Sa	0249	-0.2	-6	26 Su	0217	-0.1	-3
	0925	1.3	40		0850	1.4	43
	1439	-0.1	-3		1416	0.0	0
	2128	1.7	52		2101	1.7	52
12 Su ○	0325	-0.2	-6	27 M ●	0252	-0.1	-3
	0957	1.4	43		0922	1.5	46
	1526	-0.1	-3		1502	-0.2	-6
	2208	1.6	49		2148	1.7	52
13 M	0359	-0.1	-3	28 Tu	0326	-0.1	-3
	1026	1.4	43		0955	1.6	49
	1609	-0.2	-6		1549	-0.4	-12
	2246	1.5	46		2235	1.6	49
14 Tu	0431	0.0	0	29 W	0402	0.0	0
	1054	1.5	46		1030	1.8	55
	1652	-0.2	-6		1638	-0.5	-15
	2323	1.4	43		2324	1.5	46
15 W	0504	0.1	3	30 Th	0440	0.1	3
	1122	1.5	46		1107	1.8	55
	1735	-0.2	-6		1729	-0.5	-15
				31 F	0015	1.4	43
					0520	0.2	6
					1148	1.9	58
					1824	-0.5	-15

Time meridian 75° W. 0000 is midnight. 1200 is noon. Times are not adjusted for Daylight Saving Time.
Heights are referred to mean lower low water which is the chart datum of soundings.

Key West, Florida, 2017

Times and Heights of High and Low Waters

April

Day	Time	ft	cm	Day	Time	ft	cm
1 Sa	0111	1.2	37	16 Su	0110	1.1	34
	0603	0.2	6		0558	0.5	15
	1235	1.8	55		1224	1.5	46
	1926	-0.4	-12		1925	0.0	0
2 Su	0215	1.0	30	17 M	0203	1.0	30
	0652	0.3	9		0637	0.6	18
	1330	1.7	52		1309	1.5	46
	2034	-0.3	-9		2022	0.0	0
3 M	0331	0.9	27	18 Tu	0306	0.9	27
	0753	0.4	12		0729	0.6	18
	1439	1.6	49		1404	1.4	43
	2149	-0.2	-6		2126	0.1	3
4 Tu	0454	0.9	27	19 W	0419	0.9	27
	0910	0.5	15		0842	0.7	21
	1604	1.6	49		1513	1.4	43
	2302	-0.1	-3		2229	0.1	3
5 W	0606	1.0	30	20 Th	0525	1.0	30
	1034	0.4	12		1006	0.6	18
	1732	1.5	46		1633	1.4	43
					2324	0.1	3
6 Th	0005	0.0	0	21 F	0615	1.1	34
	0700	1.1	34		1119	0.5	15
	1150	0.3	9		1749	1.4	43
	1846	1.6	49				
7 F	0056	0.0	0	22 Sa	0011	0.1	3
	0743	1.3	40		0655	1.3	40
	1253	0.2	6		1219	0.3	9
	1945	1.6	49		1855	1.5	46
8 Sa	0138	0.0	0	23 Su	0052	0.1	3
	0820	1.4	43		0732	1.4	43
	1347	0.1	3		1311	0.1	3
	2034	1.6	49		1953	1.5	46
9 Su	0215	0.1	3	24 M	0131	0.1	3
	0852	1.5	46		0806	1.6	49
	1434	0.0	0		1401	-0.1	-3
	2117	1.5	46		2046	1.6	49
10 M	0248	0.1	3	25 Tu	0210	0.1	3
	0920	1.6	49		0842	1.8	55
	1516	-0.1	-3		1449	-0.4	-12
	2156	1.5	46		2137	1.6	49
11 Tu	0321	0.2	6	26 W	0248	0.1	3
	0947	1.7	52		0919	1.9	58
	1556	-0.2	-6		1538	-0.5	-15
	2232	1.4	43		2228	1.5	46
12 W	0352	0.2	6	27 Th	0328	0.2	6
	1013	1.7	52		0958	2.0	61
	1635	-0.2	-6		1628	-0.6	-18
	2308	1.3	40		2319	1.4	43
13 Th	0423	0.3	9	28 F	0409	0.2	6
	1042	1.7	52		1040	2.1	64
	1713	-0.2	-6		1720	-0.6	-18
	2345	1.2	37				
14 F	0454	0.3	9	29 Sa	0011	1.3	40
	1112	1.7	52		0453	0.3	9
	1754	-0.2	-6		1126	2.1	64
					1815	-0.5	-15
15 Sa	0025	1.2	37	30 Su	0107	1.2	37
	0525	0.4	12		0540	0.3	9
	1146	1.6	49		1218	2.0	61
	1837	-0.1	-3		1915	-0.4	-12

May

Day	Time	ft	cm	Day	Time	ft	cm
1 M	0208	1.1	34	16 Tu	0144	1.0	30
	0636	0.4	12		0609	0.6	18
	1316	1.8	55		1241	1.6	49
	2019	-0.2	-6		1945	0.0	0
2 Tu	0316	1.0	30	17 W	0238	1.0	30
	0744	0.5	15		0703	0.6	18
	1426	1.7	52		1332	1.5	46
	2125	-0.1	-3		2038	0.0	0
3 W	0427	1.1	34	18 Th	0335	1.1	34
	0906	0.5	15		0815	0.7	21
	1548	1.5	46		1435	1.4	43
	2230	0.0	0		2133	0.1	3
4 Th	0531	1.2	37	19 F	0430	1.2	37
	1031	0.5	15		0936	0.6	18
	1714	1.4	43		1551	1.3	40
	2326	0.1	3		2226	0.1	3
5 F	0623	1.3	40	20 Sa	0519	1.3	40
	1146	0.3	9		1051	0.4	12
	1829	1.4	43		1713	1.3	40
					2315	0.2	6
6 Sa	0015	0.2	6	21 Su	0603	1.4	43
	0706	1.5	46		1156	0.2	6
	1248	0.2	6		1828	1.3	40
	1930	1.4	43				
7 Su	0056	0.2	6	22 M	0001	0.2	6
	0742	1.6	49		0644	1.6	49
	1339	0.1	3		1253	0.0	0
	2020	1.3	40		1935	1.3	40
8 M	0133	0.3	9	23 Tu	0046	0.2	6
	0814	1.7	52		0724	1.8	55
	1423	-0.1	-3		1346	-0.3	-9
	2104	1.3	40		2033	1.3	40
9 Tu	0208	0.3	9	24 W	0129	0.2	6
	0842	1.7	52		0806	2.0	61
	1503	-0.1	-3		1437	-0.5	-15
	2142	1.3	40		2128	1.3	40
10 W	0241	0.3	9	25 Th	0213	0.2	6
	0910	1.8	55		0849	2.1	64
	1541	-0.2	-6		1528	-0.6	-18
	2218	1.2	37		2220	1.3	40
11 Th	0314	0.3	9	26 F	0257	0.2	6
	0939	1.8	55		0935	2.2	67
	1618	-0.3	-9		1619	-0.7	-21
	2254	1.2	37		2311	1.2	37
12 F	0346	0.4	12	27 Sa	0343	0.2	6
	1009	1.8	55		1022	2.2	67
	1655	-0.3	-9		1711	-0.7	-21
	2332	1.2	37				
13 Sa	0417	0.4	12	28 Su	0002	1.2	37
	1042	1.7	52		0432	0.3	9
	1733	-0.2	-6		1113	2.1	64
					1804	-0.5	-15
14 Su	0012	1.1	34	29 M	0054	1.1	34
	0450	0.5	15		0525	0.3	9
	1118	1.7	52		1207	2.0	61
	1813	-0.2	-6		1859	-0.4	-12
15 M	0055	1.1	34	30 Tu	0149	1.1	34
	0526	0.5	15		0625	0.4	12
	1157	1.6	49		1305	1.8	55
	1857	-0.1	-3		1956	-0.2	-6
				31 W	0247	1.1	34
					0736	0.4	12
					1410	1.6	49
					2053	-0.1	-3

June

Day	Time	ft	cm	Day	Time	ft	cm
1 Th	0347	1.2	37	16 F	0250	1.2	37
	0857	0.4	12		0754	0.5	15
	1524	1.4	43		1410	1.4	43
	2148	0.1	3		2043	0.1	3
2 F	0445	1.3	40	17 Sa	0337	1.3	40
	1019	0.4	12		0910	0.5	15
	1645	1.3	40		1522	1.3	40
	2240	0.2	6		2133	0.2	6
3 Sa	0537	1.4	43	18 Su	0425	1.4	43
	1133	0.3	9		1025	0.3	9
	1803	1.2	37		1645	1.2	37
	2327	0.3	9		2224	0.2	6
4 Su	0622	1.5	46	19 M	0512	1.6	49
	1234	0.2	6		1134	0.1	3
	1909	1.1	34		1808	1.1	34
					2315	0.3	9
5 M	0011	0.3	9	20 Tu	0601	1.7	52
	0700	1.6	49		1235	-0.2	-6
	1325	0.0	0		1921	1.1	34
	2002	1.1	34				
6 Tu	0051	0.4	12	21 W	0005	0.3	9
	0735	1.7	52		0650	1.9	58
	1408	-0.1	-3		1332	-0.4	-12
	2047	1.1	34		2023	1.1	34
7 W	0128	0.4	12	22 Th	0055	0.3	9
	0807	1.7	52		0740	2.1	64
	1448	-0.2	-6		1426	-0.5	-15
	2127	1.1	34		2118	1.1	34
8 Th	0204	0.4	12	23 F	0144	0.3	9
	0839	1.8	55		0830	2.2	67
	1525	-0.2	-6		1518	-0.6	-18
	2203	1.1	34		2209	1.1	34
9 F	0239	0.4	12	24 Sa	0234	0.2	6
	0912	1.8	55		0921	2.2	67
	1601	-0.3	-9		1608	-0.6	-18
	2239	1.1	34		2257	1.1	34
10 Sa	0313	0.4	12	25 Su	0325	0.2	6
	0946	1.8	55		1012	2.2	67
	1637	-0.3	-9		1658	-0.6	-18
	2316	1.1	34		2344	1.2	37
11 Su	0348	0.4	12	26 M	0417	0.2	6
	1022	1.8	55		1104	2.1	64
	1714	-0.3	-9		1747	-0.5	-15
	2355	1.1	34				
12 M	0424	0.5	15	27 Tu	0031	1.2	37
	1059	1.8	55		0513	0.3	9
	1751	-0.2	-6		1156	2.0	61
					1836	-0.3	-9
13 Tu	0036	1.1	34	28 W	0119	1.2	37
	0504	0.5	15		0615	0.3	9
	1139	1.7	52		1250	1.8	55
	1830	-0.2	-6		1924	-0.1	-3
14 W	0119	1.1	34	29 Th	0208	1.3	40
	0551	0.5	15		0723	0.4	12
	1222	1.6	49		1348	1.5	46
	1912	-0.1	-3		2013	0.0	0
15 Th	0204	1.1	34	30 F	0259	1.4	43
	0646	0.6	18		0837	0.4	12
	1311	1.5	46		1452	1.3	40
	1956	0.0	0		2101	0.2	6

Time meridian 75° W. 0000 is midnight. 1200 is noon. Times are not adjusted for Daylight Saving Time.
Heights are referred to mean lower low water which is the chart datum of soundings.

Key West, Florida, 2017

Times and Heights of High and Low Waters

July

Day	Time	ft	cm		Day	Time	ft	cm
1 Sa	0350	1.4	43		16 Su ◐	0247	1.5	46
	0955	0.3	9			0848	0.3	9
	1606	1.1	34			1504	1.2	37
	2150	0.3	9			2048	0.3	9
2 Su	0442	1.5	46		17 M	0335	1.6	49
	1107	0.3	9			1003	0.2	6
	1727	1.0	30			1629	1.1	34
	2239	0.4	12			2141	0.4	12
3 M	0530	1.6	49		18 Tu	0429	1.7	52
	1210	0.2	6			1115	0.0	0
	1841	1.0	30			1757	1.0	30
	2326	0.4	12			2237	0.4	12
4 Tu	0615	1.6	49		19 W	0528	1.9	58
	1303	0.1	3			1221	-0.2	-6
	1940	1.0	30			1913	1.0	30
						2334	0.4	12
5 W	0011	0.5	15		20 Th	0628	2.0	61
	0657	1.7	52			1321	-0.3	-9
	1349	0.0	0			2014	1.1	34
	2027	1.0	30					
6 Th	0053	0.5	15		21 F	0031	0.4	12
	0736	1.7	52			0726	2.1	64
	1430	-0.1	-3			1415	-0.4	-12
	2107	1.0	30			2106	1.1	34
7 F	0133	0.4	12		22 Sa	0126	0.3	9
	0815	1.8	55			0822	2.2	67
	1508	-0.2	-6			1506	-0.4	-12
	2143	1.0	30			2152	1.2	37
8 Sa ○	0211	0.4	12		23 Su ●	0220	0.3	9
	0852	1.8	55			0915	2.2	67
	1543	-0.2	-6			1553	-0.4	-12
	2218	1.1	34			2235	1.2	37
9 Su	0248	0.4	12		24 M	0314	0.2	6
	0930	1.9	58			1005	2.2	67
	1617	-0.2	-6			1638	-0.3	-9
	2253	1.1	34			2317	1.3	40
10 M	0326	0.4	12		25 Tu	0407	0.2	6
	1007	1.9	58			1055	2.1	64
	1651	-0.2	-6			1721	-0.2	-6
	2329	1.2	37			2357	1.4	43
11 Tu	0406	0.4	12		26 W	0502	0.2	6
	1046	1.8	55			1143	2.0	61
	1725	-0.2	-6			1803	-0.1	-3
12 W	0006	1.2	37		27 Th	0038	1.5	46
	0449	0.4	12			0600	0.3	9
	1126	1.8	55			1231	1.8	55
	1800	-0.1	-3			1845	0.1	3
13 Th	0044	1.3	40		28 F	0120	1.5	46
	0537	0.4	12			0701	0.3	9
	1209	1.7	52			1322	1.5	46
	1837	0.0	0			1927	0.2	6
14 F	0123	1.3	40		29 Sa	0203	1.6	49
	0632	0.4	12			0807	0.4	12
	1257	1.6	49			1417	1.3	40
	1917	0.1	3			2011	0.4	12
15 Sa	0203	1.4	43		30 Su ◐	0249	1.6	49
	0736	0.4	12			0919	0.4	12
	1354	1.4	43			1524	1.2	37
	2000	0.2	6			2058	0.5	15
					31 M	0339	1.6	49
						1031	0.3	9
						1645	1.0	30
						2150	0.6	18

August

Day	Time	ft	cm		Day	Time	ft	cm
1 Tu	0433	1.6	49		16 W	0358	1.9	58
	1137	0.3	9			1101	0.1	3
	1809	1.0	30			1753	1.1	34
	2243	0.6	18			2211	0.6	18
2 W	0529	1.7	52		17 Th	0509	2.0	61
	1235	0.2	6			1210	0.0	0
	1914	1.0	30			1905	1.2	37
	2335	0.6	18			2317	0.6	18
3 Th	0622	1.7	52		18 F	0619	2.1	64
	1325	0.1	3			1310	0.0	0
	2002	1.1	34			2001	1.2	37
4 F	0024	0.6	18		19 Sa	0020	0.5	15
	0710	1.8	55			0722	2.2	67
	1407	0.1	3			1402	-0.1	-3
	2041	1.1	34			2047	1.3	40
5 Sa	0108	0.6	18		20 Su	0119	0.5	15
	0754	1.9	58			0819	2.3	70
	1444	0.0	0			1448	-0.1	-3
	2115	1.2	37			2128	1.4	43
6 Su	0150	0.5	15		21 M ●	0214	0.4	12
	0835	1.9	58			0910	2.3	70
	1518	0.0	0			1530	0.0	0
	2148	1.3	40			2206	1.6	49
7 M ○	0230	0.5	15		22 Tu	0307	0.3	9
	0915	2.0	61			0958	2.2	67
	1549	0.0	0			1610	0.0	0
	2221	1.3	40			2242	1.7	52
8 Tu	0311	0.5	15		23 W	0358	0.3	9
	0954	2.0	61			1043	2.1	64
	1620	0.0	0			1647	0.2	6
	2254	1.4	43			2317	1.7	52
9 W	0352	0.4	12		24 Th	0449	0.3	9
	1034	2.0	61			1126	2.0	61
	1652	0.0	0			1724	0.3	9
	2328	1.5	46			2352	1.8	55
10 Th	0437	0.4	12		25 F	0540	0.3	9
	1115	1.9	58			1210	1.8	55
	1725	0.1	3			1801	0.4	12
11 F	0002	1.6	49		26 Sa	0027	1.8	55
	0525	0.3	9			0633	0.4	12
	1200	1.8	55			1255	1.6	49
	1800	0.2	6			1839	0.5	15
12 Sa	0038	1.7	52		27 Su	0105	1.8	55
	0619	0.3	9			0731	0.4	12
	1249	1.7	52			1345	1.4	43
	1839	0.3	9			1919	0.7	21
13 Su	0116	1.7	52		28 M	0146	1.8	55
	0719	0.3	9			0836	0.5	15
	1347	1.5	46			1445	1.3	40
	1921	0.4	12			2004	0.8	24
14 M ◐	0201	1.8	55		29 Tu ◐	0236	1.8	55
	0829	0.3	9			0947	0.5	15
	1458	1.3	40			1602	1.2	37
	2010	0.5	15			2059	0.8	24
15 Tu	0254	1.9	58		30 W	0335	1.7	52
	0945	0.2	6			1058	0.5	15
	1624	1.2	37			1731	1.2	37
	2107	0.6	18			2202	0.9	27
					31 Th	0442	1.8	55
						1201	0.4	12
						1841	1.2	37
						2305	0.9	27

September

Day	Time	ft	cm		Day	Time	ft	cm
1 F	0547	1.8	55		16 Sa	0617	2.2	67
	1253	0.4	12			1253	0.3	9
	1929	1.3	40			1941	1.5	46
2 Sa	0001	0.8	24		17 Su	0020	0.7	21
	0644	1.9	58			0721	2.3	70
	1335	0.3	9			1341	0.3	9
	2006	1.4	43			2022	1.7	52
3 Su	0049	0.8	24		18 M	0119	0.6	18
	0732	2.0	61			0815	2.3	70
	1411	0.3	9			1422	0.3	9
	2039	1.5	46			2059	1.8	55
4 M	0133	0.7	21		19 Tu	0212	0.5	15
	0816	2.1	64			0904	2.3	70
	1442	0.3	9			1459	0.4	12
	2110	1.6	49			2132	1.9	58
5 Tu	0215	0.6	18		20 W ●	0301	0.4	12
	0858	2.1	64			0948	2.2	67
	1512	0.3	9			1535	0.4	12
	2142	1.7	52			2204	2.0	61
6 W	0256	0.5	15		21 Th	0348	0.3	9
	0939	2.2	67			1029	2.1	64
	1543	0.3	9			1609	0.5	15
	2213	1.8	55			2234	2.1	64
7 Th	0339	0.4	12		22 F	0433	0.3	9
	1022	2.1	64			1109	2.0	61
	1614	0.3	9			1643	0.6	18
	2245	1.9	58			2305	2.1	64
8 F	0424	0.3	9		23 Sa	0518	0.3	9
	1106	2.0	61			1148	1.8	55
	1648	0.4	12			1717	0.7	21
	2318	2.0	61			2337	2.1	64
9 Sa	0513	0.2	6		24 Su	0605	0.4	12
	1153	1.9	58			1230	1.7	52
	1724	0.5	15			1751	0.8	24
	2355	2.1	64					
10 Su	0606	0.2	6		25 M	0012	2.0	61
	1245	1.7	52			0655	0.5	15
	1803	0.6	18			1317	1.5	46
						1828	0.9	27
11 M	0036	2.1	64		26 Tu	0052	2.0	61
	0705	0.2	6			0752	0.5	15
	1345	1.5	46			1413	1.4	43
	1847	0.7	21			1910	1.0	30
12 Tu	0124	2.1	64		27 W ◐	0140	1.9	58
	0814	0.3	9			0859	0.6	18
	1458	1.4	43			1525	1.4	43
	1939	0.8	24			2005	1.1	34
13 W ○	0224	2.1	64		28 Th	0240	1.9	58
	0930	0.3	9			1011	0.6	18
	1625	1.3	40			1649	1.3	40
	2044	0.9	27			2119	1.1	34
14 Th	0339	2.1	64		29 F	0353	1.8	55
	1048	0.3	9			1117	0.6	18
	1747	1.3	40			1759	1.4	43
	2159	0.9	27			2235	1.1	34
15 F	0501	2.1	64		30 Sa	0507	1.9	58
	1156	0.3	9			1210	0.6	18
	1851	1.4	43			1847	1.5	46
	2314	0.8	24			2338	1.0	30

Time meridian 75° W. 0000 is midnight. 1200 is noon. Times are not adjusted for Daylight Saving Time.
Heights are referred to mean lower low water which is the chart datum of soundings.

Key West, Florida, 2017

Times and Heights of High and Low Waters

October

Day	Time	ft	cm	Day	Time	ft	cm
1 Su	0612 / 1251 / 1924	2.0 / 0.6 / 1.6	61 / 18 / 49	16 M	0023 / 0716 / 1310 / 1952	0.7 / 2.1 / 0.5 / 1.9	21 / 64 / 15 / 58
2 M	0030 / 0706 / 1326 / 1956	0.9 / 2.1 / 0.5 / 1.8	27 / 64 / 15 / 55	17 Tu	0120 / 0809 / 1348 / 2026	0.6 / 2.1 / 0.6 / 2.0	18 / 64 / 18 / 61
3 Tu	0115 / 0755 / 1358 / 2028	0.7 / 2.1 / 0.5 / 1.9	21 / 64 / 15 / 58	18 W	0209 / 0855 / 1424 / 2058	0.4 / 2.1 / 0.6 / 2.1	12 / 64 / 18 / 64
4 W	0159 / 0840 / 1430 / 2059	0.6 / 2.2 / 0.5 / 2.0	18 / 67 / 15 / 61	19 Th ●	0254 / 0937 / 1458 / 2127	0.3 / 2.0 / 0.6 / 2.2	9 / 61 / 18 / 67
5 Th O	0242 / 0925 / 1502 / 2131	0.4 / 2.2 / 0.5 / 2.2	12 / 67 / 15 / 67	20 F	0336 / 1015 / 1531 / 2155	0.3 / 1.9 / 0.7 / 2.2	9 / 58 / 21 / 67
6 F	0326 / 1011 / 1536 / 2204	0.2 / 2.1 / 0.6 / 2.3	6 / 64 / 18 / 70	21 Sa	0417 / 1052 / 1603 / 2224	0.3 / 1.8 / 0.7 / 2.2	9 / 55 / 21 / 67
7 Sa	0412 / 1058 / 1612 / 2240	0.1 / 2.0 / 0.6 / 2.3	3 / 61 / 18 / 70	22 Su	0457 / 1130 / 1636 / 2256	0.3 / 1.7 / 0.8 / 2.2	9 / 52 / 24 / 67
8 Su	0501 / 1148 / 1651 / 2320	0.1 / 1.9 / 0.7 / 2.4	3 / 58 / 21 / 73	23 M	0539 / 1210 / 1709 / 2331	0.3 / 1.6 / 0.9 / 2.1	9 / 49 / 27 / 64
9 M	0555 / 1242 / 1733	0.1 / 1.7 / 0.8	3 / 52 / 24	24 Tu	0623 / 1255 / 1744	0.4 / 1.5 / 1.0	12 / 46 / 30
10 Tu	0006 / 0654 / 1344 / 1820	2.4 / 0.2 / 1.6 / 0.9	73 / 6 / 49 / 27	25 W	0010 / 0714 / 1347 / 1824	2.0 / 0.5 / 1.4 / 1.0	61 / 15 / 43 / 30
11 W	0100 / 0801 / 1456 / 1919	2.3 / 0.3 / 1.5 / 0.9	70 / 9 / 46 / 27	26 Th	0057 / 0812 / 1451 / 1918	2.0 / 0.5 / 1.4 / 1.1	61 / 15 / 43 / 34
12 Th ◗	0206 / 0915 / 1616 / 2033	2.2 / 0.4 / 1.4 / 1.0	67 / 12 / 43 / 30	27 F ◖	0154 / 0917 / 1602 / 2034	1.9 / 0.6 / 1.4 / 1.1	58 / 18 / 43 / 34
13 F	0328 / 1029 / 1729 / 2158	2.1 / 0.4 / 1.5 / 1.0	64 / 12 / 46 / 30	28 Sa	0304 / 1020 / 1707 / 2159	1.8 / 0.6 / 1.5 / 1.1	55 / 18 / 46 / 34
14 Sa	0455 / 1134 / 1827 / 2317	2.1 / 0.5 / 1.6 / 0.9	64 / 15 / 49 / 27	29 Su	0421 / 1113 / 1756 / 2310	1.8 / 0.6 / 1.6 / 1.0	55 / 18 / 49 / 30
15 Su	0612 / 1226 / 1913	2.1 / 0.5 / 1.8	64 / 15 / 55	30 M	0534 / 1157 / 1835	1.8 / 0.6 / 1.7	55 / 18 / 52
				31 Tu	0006 / 0637 / 1235 / 1910	0.8 / 1.9 / 0.6 / 1.9	24 / 58 / 18 / 58

November

Day	Time	ft	cm	Day	Time	ft	cm
1 W	0055 / 0732 / 1311 / 1944	0.6 / 1.9 / 0.6 / 2.0	18 / 58 / 18 / 61	16 Th	0203 / 0845 / 1348 / 2025	0.3 / 1.7 / 0.6 / 2.1	9 / 52 / 18 / 64
2 Th	0142 / 0823 / 1347 / 2018	0.4 / 2.0 / 0.6 / 2.2	12 / 61 / 18 / 67	17 F	0244 / 0925 / 1422 / 2054	0.2 / 1.6 / 0.6 / 2.1	6 / 49 / 18 / 64
3 F	0227 / 0912 / 1423 / 2053	0.1 / 1.9 / 0.6 / 2.3	3 / 58 / 18 / 70	18 Sa ●	0323 / 1002 / 1456 / 2124	0.1 / 1.6 / 0.6 / 2.1	3 / 49 / 18 / 64
4 Sa O	0313 / 1001 / 1501 / 2131	0.0 / 1.9 / 0.6 / 2.4	0 / 58 / 18 / 73	19 Su	0401 / 1038 / 1529 / 2154	0.1 / 1.5 / 0.7 / 2.1	3 / 46 / 21 / 64
5 Su	0401 / 1050 / 1541 / 2212	-0.1 / 1.8 / 0.6 / 2.5	-3 / 55 / 18 / 76	20 M	0439 / 1114 / 1602 / 2227	0.1 / 1.5 / 0.7 / 2.1	3 / 46 / 21 / 64
6 M	0452 / 1141 / 1623 / 2258	-0.2 / 1.7 / 0.7 / 2.5	-6 / 52 / 21 / 76	21 Tu	0517 / 1152 / 1636 / 2303	0.1 / 1.4 / 0.7 / 2.0	3 / 43 / 21 / 61
7 Tu	0545 / 1235 / 1710 / 2349	-0.1 / 1.6 / 0.7 / 2.4	-3 / 49 / 21 / 73	22 W	0558 / 1234 / 1712 / 2343	0.2 / 1.4 / 0.8 / 1.9	6 / 43 / 24 / 58
8 W	0643 / 1335 / 1803	0.0 / 1.5 / 0.8	0 / 46 / 24	23 Th	0642 / 1321 / 1753	0.2 / 1.3 / 0.9	6 / 40 / 27
9 Th	0046 / 0746 / 1440 / 1908	2.3 / 0.1 / 1.4 / 0.8	70 / 3 / 43 / 24	24 F	0027 / 0730 / 1414 / 1846	1.9 / 0.3 / 1.3 / 0.9	58 / 9 / 40 / 27
10 F ◖	0155 / 0853 / 1550 / 2028	2.1 / 0.3 / 1.4 / 0.9	64 / 9 / 43 / 27	25 Sa	0118 / 0822 / 1511 / 1955	1.8 / 0.4 / 1.3 / 0.9	55 / 12 / 40 / 27
11 Sa	0315 / 0959 / 1656 / 2156	2.0 / 0.4 / 1.5 / 0.8	61 / 12 / 46 / 24	26 Su	0220 / 0916 / 1607 / 2118	1.7 / 0.4 / 1.4 / 0.9	52 / 12 / 43 / 27
12 Su	0441 / 1058 / 1752 / 2316	1.9 / 0.5 / 1.7 / 0.7	58 / 15 / 52 / 21	27 M	0333 / 1008 / 1657 / 2235	1.6 / 0.5 / 1.5 / 0.7	49 / 15 / 46 / 21
13 M	0600 / 1149 / 1839	1.8 / 0.5 / 1.8	55 / 15 / 55	28 Tu	0453 / 1056 / 1741 / 2338	1.5 / 0.5 / 1.6 / 0.5	46 / 15 / 49 / 15
14 Tu	0022 / 0705 / 1232 / 1918	0.5 / 1.8 / 0.6 / 2.0	15 / 55 / 18 / 61	29 W	0607 / 1141 / 1821	1.5 / 0.5 / 1.8	46 / 15 / 55
15 W	0116 / 0759 / 1311 / 1953	0.4 / 1.7 / 0.6 / 2.0	12 / 52 / 18 / 61	30 Th	0033 / 0711 / 1224 / 1901	0.3 / 1.5 / 0.5 / 2.0	9 / 46 / 15 / 61

December

Day	Time	ft	cm	Day	Time	ft	cm
1 F	0124 / 0809 / 1306 / 1942	0.0 / 1.5 / 0.5 / 2.1	0 / 46 / 15 / 64	16 Sa	0232 / 0913 / 1352 / 2029	-0.1 / 1.2 / 0.5 / 1.9	-3 / 37 / 15 / 58
2 Sa	0213 / 0902 / 1349 / 2024	-0.2 / 1.5 / 0.5 / 2.3	-6 / 46 / 15 / 70	17 Su	0310 / 0949 / 1428 / 2102	-0.1 / 1.2 / 0.5 / 1.9	-3 / 37 / 15 / 58
3 Su O	0302 / 0952 / 1432 / 2109	-0.4 / 1.5 / 0.4 / 2.4	-12 / 46 / 12 / 73	18 M ●	0347 / 1023 / 1503 / 2135	-0.2 / 1.2 / 0.5 / 1.9	-6 / 37 / 15 / 58
4 M	0352 / 1041 / 1517 / 2156	-0.5 / 1.4 / 0.4 / 2.4	-15 / 43 / 12 / 73	19 Tu	0423 / 1057 / 1538 / 2210	-0.2 / 1.2 / 0.5 / 1.9	-6 / 37 / 15 / 58
5 Tu	0442 / 1131 / 1604 / 2246	-0.5 / 1.4 / 0.4 / 2.4	-15 / 43 / 12 / 73	20 W	0458 / 1133 / 1613 / 2247	-0.2 / 1.2 / 0.5 / 1.8	-6 / 37 / 15 / 55
6 W	0534 / 1221 / 1655 / 2340	-0.4 / 1.3 / 0.4 / 2.2	-12 / 40 / 12 / 67	21 Th	0534 / 1210 / 1651 / 2325	-0.1 / 1.2 / 0.5 / 1.8	-3 / 37 / 15 / 55
7 Th	0628 / 1314 / 1753	-0.2 / 1.3 / 0.5	-6 / 40 / 15	22 F	0612 / 1251 / 1734	-0.1 / 1.2 / 0.5	-3 / 37 / 15
8 F	0037 / 0724 / 1411 / 1900	2.1 / -0.1 / 1.3 / 0.5	64 / -3 / 40 / 15	23 Sa	0007 / 0650 / 1333 / 1825	1.7 / 0.0 / 1.2 / 0.6	52 / 0 / 37 / 18
9 Sa	0141 / 0821 / 1510 / 2019	1.9 / 0.1 / 1.4 / 0.6	58 / 3 / 43 / 18	24 Su	0053 / 0732 / 1418 / 1926	1.6 / 0.1 / 1.2 / 0.6	49 / 3 / 37 / 18
10 Su ◖	0255 / 0918 / 1611 / 2145	1.6 / 0.3 / 1.5 / 0.5	49 / 9 / 46 / 15	25 M	0148 / 0817 / 1505 / 2040	1.4 / 0.2 / 1.3 / 0.5	43 / 6 / 40 / 15
11 M	0417 / 1013 / 1708 / 2304	1.5 / 0.4 / 1.6 / 0.4	46 / 12 / 49 / 12	26 Tu ◖	0255 / 0905 / 1553 / 2157	1.3 / 0.3 / 1.4 / 0.4	40 / 9 / 43 / 12
12 Tu	0539 / 1104 / 1758	1.4 / 0.4 / 1.7	43 / 12 / 52	27 W	0416 / 0957 / 1643 / 2308	1.2 / 0.3 / 1.5 / 0.2	37 / 9 / 46 / 6
13 W	0010 / 0650 / 1151 / 1842	0.3 / 1.3 / 0.5 / 1.8	9 / 40 / 15 / 55	28 Th	0541 / 1049 / 1733	1.1 / 0.4 / 1.6	34 / 12 / 49
14 Th	0105 / 0747 / 1234 / 1920	0.1 / 1.3 / 0.5 / 1.8	3 / 40 / 15 / 55	29 F	0011 / 0656 / 1141 / 1824	-0.1 / 1.1 / 0.4 / 1.8	-3 / 34 / 12 / 55
15 F	0152 / 0833 / 1314 / 1955	0.0 / 1.2 / 0.5 / 1.9	0 / 37 / 15 / 58	30 Sa	0108 / 0758 / 1232 / 1915	-0.3 / 1.1 / 0.3 / 2.0	-9 / 34 / 9 / 61
				31 Su	0201 / 0852 / 1321 / 2007	-0.5 / 1.1 / 0.3 / 2.1	-15 / 34 / 9 / 64

Time meridian 75° W. 0000 is midnight. 1200 is noon. Times are not adjusted for Daylight Saving Time.
Heights are referred to mean lower low water which is the chart datum of soundings.

Naples, Florida, 2017

Times and Heights of High and Low Waters

January

Day	Time	ft	cm		Day	Time	ft	cm
1 Su	0041	2.8	85		**16** M	0210	2.6	79
	0815	-0.5	-15			0859	-0.3	-9
	1501	2.4	73			1527	2.3	70
	2014	1.1	34			2121	0.7	21
2 M	0121	2.7	82		**17** Tu	0307	2.3	70
	0855	-0.3	-9			0942	0.1	3
	1543	2.4	73			1609	2.3	70
	2105	1.1	34			2220	0.7	21
3 Tu	0213	2.5	76		**18** W	0411	2.0	61
	0937	-0.1	-3			1029	0.5	15
	1626	2.4	73			1653	2.3	70
	2208	0.9	27			2328	0.6	18
4 W	0324	2.2	67		**19** Th ☽	0520	1.8	55
	1026	0.2	6			1123	0.8	24
	1710	2.4	73			1741	2.3	70
	2322	0.8	24					
5 Th ☽	0459	2.0	61		**20** F	0038	0.5	15
	1124	0.5	15			0639	1.6	49
	1756	2.5	76			1226	1.1	34
						1834	2.3	70
6 F	0035	0.5	15		**21** Sa	0142	0.3	9
	0640	1.9	58			0810	1.6	49
	1230	0.8	24			1330	1.2	37
	1846	2.6	79			1930	2.4	73
7 Sa	0142	0.1	3		**22** Su	0238	0.1	3
	0812	1.9	58			0938	1.7	52
	1335	1.0	30			1429	1.3	40
	1940	2.7	82			2024	2.4	73
8 Su	0241	-0.3	-9		**23** M	0326	-0.1	-3
	0931	2.1	64			1028	1.8	55
	1437	1.1	34			1521	1.3	40
	2033	2.9	88			2112	2.5	76
9 M	0337	-0.7	-21		**24** Tu	0410	-0.3	-9
	1034	2.2	67			1100	2.0	61
	1535	1.2	37			1606	1.3	40
	2124	3.0	91			2154	2.6	79
10 Tu	0429	-1.0	-30		**25** W	0450	-0.5	-15
	1124	2.3	70			1131	2.1	64
	1629	1.1	34			1647	1.2	37
	2212	3.2	98			2232	2.7	82
11 W	0519	-1.1	-34		**26** Th	0528	-0.6	-18
	1208	2.3	70			1203	2.2	67
	1720	1.0	30			1724	1.1	34
	2258	3.2	98			2306	2.8	85
12 Th ○	0606	-1.2	-37		**27** F ●	0605	-0.7	-21
	1248	2.4	73			1236	2.2	67
	1808	0.9	27			1801	1.0	30
	2343	3.2	98			2338	2.8	85
13 F	0651	-1.1	-34		**28** Sa	0640	-0.8	-24
	1328	2.4	73			1310	2.3	70
	1855	0.8	24			1839	0.8	24
14 Sa	0029	3.1	94		**29** Su	0010	2.8	85
	0735	-0.9	-27			0716	-0.7	-21
	1407	2.4	73			1344	2.4	73
	1941	0.8	24			1918	0.7	21
15 Su	0117	2.9	88		**30** M	0046	2.8	85
	0817	-0.6	-18			0752	-0.6	-18
	1446	2.4	73			1419	2.4	73
	2029	0.7	21			2001	0.6	18
					31 Tu	0128	2.6	79
						0829	-0.4	-12
						1455	2.4	73
						2049	0.4	12

February

Day	Time	ft	cm		Day	Time	ft	cm
1 W	0221	2.4	73		**16** Th	0336	2.0	61
	0908	-0.1	-3			0935	0.6	18
	1531	2.4	73			1550	2.3	70
	2146	0.4	12			2235	0.4	12
2 Th	0329	2.1	64		**17** F	0439	1.8	55
	0951	0.3	9			1012	1.0	30
	1611	2.5	76			1637	2.3	70
	2253	0.2	6			2343	0.4	12
3 F ◐	0454	1.9	58		**18** Sa ○	0554	1.6	49
	1044	0.7	21			1107	1.2	37
	1658	2.5	76			1733	2.2	67
4 Sa	0007	0.1	3		**19** Su	0053	0.3	9
	0631	1.7	52			0723	1.6	49
	1154	1.0	30			1240	1.4	43
	1757	2.5	76			1841	2.2	67
5 Su	0119	-0.2	-6		**20** M	0157	0.1	3
	0813	1.7	52			0903	1.7	52
	1311	1.2	37			1356	1.4	43
	1907	2.6	79			1948	2.3	70
6 M	0224	-0.5	-15		**21** Tu	0252	0.0	0
	0943	1.9	58			1001	1.8	55
	1422	1.2	37			1454	1.4	43
	2017	2.7	82			2047	2.4	73
7 Tu	0323	-0.7	-21		**22** W	0339	-0.2	-6
	1041	2.0	61			1033	2.0	61
	1524	1.2	37			1542	1.2	37
	2118	2.8	85			2135	2.5	76
8 W	0416	-0.9	-27		**23** Th	0422	-0.4	-12
	1121	2.1	64			1103	2.1	64
	1619	1.0	30			1624	1.1	34
	2211	3.0	91			2217	2.7	82
9 Th	0505	-1.0	-30		**24** F	0501	-0.5	-15
	1153	2.2	67			1133	2.2	67
	1709	0.8	24			1703	0.9	27
	2258	3.0	91			2255	2.8	85
10 F ○	0550	-0.9	-27		**25** Sa	0538	-0.6	-18
	1223	2.3	70			1202	2.4	73
	1755	0.6	18			1742	0.6	18
	2342	3.0	91			2331	2.9	88
11 Sa	0632	-0.8	-24		**26** Su ●	0614	-0.6	-18
	1253	2.3	70			1232	2.5	76
	1839	0.5	15			1821	0.4	12
12 Su	0024	2.9	88		**27** M	0008	2.9	88
	0711	-0.6	-18			0650	-0.5	-15
	1324	2.4	73			1302	2.6	79
	1922	0.4	12			1902	0.2	6
13 M	0107	2.7	82		**28** Tu	0048	2.8	85
	0749	-0.4	-12			0726	-0.3	-9
	1357	2.4	73			1332	2.6	79
	2004	0.3	9			1945	0.0	0
14 Tu	0151	2.5	76					
	0825	0.0	0					
	1431	2.4	73					
	2049	0.3	9					
15 W	0240	2.2	67					
	0900	0.3	9					
	1509	2.4	73					
	2138	0.3	9					

March

Day	Time	ft	cm		Day	Time	ft	cm
1 W	0134	2.6	79		**16** Th	0219	2.3	70
	0803	-0.1	-3			0820	0.7	21
	1402	2.6	79			1408	2.5	76
	2033	-0.1	-3			2101	0.1	3
2 Th	0230	2.4	73		**17** F	0310	2.1	64
	0841	0.3	9			0846	0.9	27
	1436	2.7	82			1442	2.5	76
	2127	-0.2	-6			2150	0.2	6
3 F	0338	2.2	67		**18** Sa	0410	1.9	58
	0923	0.7	21			0903	1.2	37
	1516	2.6	79			1521	2.4	73
	2230	-0.2	-6			2250	0.3	9
4 Sa	0458	1.9	58		**19** Su	0521	1.8	55
	1015	1.0	30			0909	1.4	43
	1608	2.6	79			1616	2.3	70
	2343	-0.2	-6					
5 Su ◐	0631	1.8	55		**20** M ☽	0001	0.3	9
	1132	1.3	40			0642	1.7	52
	1721	2.5	76			0932	1.6	49
						1742	2.2	67
6 M	0057	-0.3	-9		**21** Tu	0110	0.2	6
	0821	1.8	55			0808	1.8	55
	1300	1.4	43			1320	1.6	49
	1850	2.5	76			1907	2.2	67
7 Tu	0205	-0.4	-12		**22** W	0209	0.1	3
	0951	2.0	61			0912	2.0	61
	1415	1.3	40			1425	1.4	43
	2012	2.6	79			2016	2.3	70
8 W	0306	-0.5	-15		**23** Th	0300	0.0	0
	1032	2.1	64			0951	2.1	64
	1517	1.1	34			1515	1.2	37
	2118	2.7	82			2111	2.5	76
9 Th	0359	-0.5	-15		**24** F	0345	-0.1	-3
	1100	2.2	67			1023	2.3	70
	1610	0.9	27			1558	1.0	30
	2211	2.8	85			2157	2.7	82
10 F	0446	-0.5	-15		**25** Sa	0427	-0.2	-6
	1124	2.3	70			1053	2.5	76
	1658	0.6	18			1639	0.6	18
	2256	2.8	85			2239	2.8	85
11 Sa	0529	-0.4	-12		**26** Su	0506	-0.2	-6
	1148	2.4	73			1122	2.6	79
	1741	0.4	12			1720	0.3	9
	2337	2.8	85			2320	2.9	88
12 Su ○	0608	-0.3	-9		**27** M ●	0544	-0.2	-6
	1213	2.5	76			1150	2.8	85
	1822	0.2	6			1802	0.0	0
13 M	0015	2.7	82		**28** Tu	0002	2.9	88
	0644	-0.1	-3			0622	-0.1	-3
	1239	2.6	79			1217	2.9	88
	1901	0.1	3			1845	-0.3	-9
14 Tu	0054	2.6	79		**29** W	0047	2.8	85
	0718	0.1	3			0700	0.2	6
	1307	2.6	79			1245	3.0	91
	1939	0.0	0			1930	-0.5	-15
15 W	0134	2.5	76		**30** Th	0139	2.7	82
	0751	0.3	9			0739	0.4	12
	1337	2.6	79			1316	3.0	91
	2019	0.0	0			2018	-0.5	-15
					31 F	0238	2.5	76
						0819	0.7	21
						1352	3.0	91
						2111	-0.5	-15

Time meridian 75° W. 0000 is midnight. 1200 is noon. Times are not adjusted for Daylight Saving Time.
Heights are referred to mean lower low water which is the chart datum of soundings.

Naples, Florida, 2017

Times and Heights of High and Low Waters

April

Day	Time (h m)	Height (ft)	Height (cm)
1 Sa	0346	2.3	70
	0903	1.1	34
	1436	2.9	88
	2212	-0.4	-12
2 Su	0502	2.1	64
	1000	1.3	40
	1537	2.7	82
	2322	-0.3	-9
3 M ☽	0628	2.0	61
	1124	1.5	46
	1706	2.6	79
4 Tu	0035	-0.2	-6
	0807	2.0	61
	1253	1.5	46
	1842	2.5	76
5 W	0143	-0.1	-3
	0920	2.2	67
	1408	1.3	40
	2006	2.5	76
6 Th	0243	-0.1	-3
	0956	2.3	70
	1508	1.0	30
	2114	2.6	79
7 F	0335	0.0	0
	1022	2.4	73
	1559	0.7	21
	2207	2.6	79
8 Sa	0421	0.0	0
	1044	2.5	76
	1644	0.4	12
	2251	2.7	82
9 Su	0502	0.2	6
	1108	2.6	79
	1724	0.2	6
	2329	2.7	82
10 M	0540	0.3	9
	1132	2.7	82
	1803	0.0	0
11 Tu ○	0005	2.6	79
	0615	0.5	15
	1157	2.8	85
	1840	-0.1	-3
12 W	0041	2.5	76
	0647	0.7	21
	1223	2.8	85
	1916	-0.2	-6
13 Th	0120	2.4	73
	0718	0.9	27
	1249	2.8	85
	1953	-0.1	-3
14 F	0204	2.3	70
	0745	1.0	30
	1315	2.8	85
	2032	-0.1	-3
15 Sa	0254	2.2	67
	0809	1.2	37
	1341	2.7	82
	2116	0.0	0
16 Su	0353	2.1	64
	0828	1.4	43
	1413	2.5	76
	2208	0.1	3
17 M	0458	2.0	61
	0853	1.6	49
	1455	2.4	73
	2311	0.2	6
18 Tu	0608	2.0	61
	1003	1.7	52
	1611	2.3	70
19 W ◑	0019	0.3	9
	0717	2.1	64
	1240	1.7	52
	1814	2.2	67
20 Th	0120	0.3	9
	0817	2.2	67
	1350	1.5	46
	1935	2.3	70
21 F	0214	0.2	6
	0901	2.4	73
	1443	1.2	37
	2040	2.4	73
22 Sa	0303	0.2	6
	0937	2.5	76
	1530	0.8	24
	2134	2.6	79
23 Su	0347	0.2	6
	1009	2.7	82
	1614	0.4	12
	2222	2.7	82
24 M	0430	0.2	6
	1038	2.9	88
	1658	0.0	0
	2309	2.8	85
25 Tu	0512	0.3	9
	1107	3.1	94
	1743	-0.4	-12
	2356	2.9	88
26 W ●	0553	0.5	15
	1136	3.2	98
	1828	-0.7	-21
27 Th	0046	2.8	85
	0635	0.7	21
	1207	3.3	101
	1915	-0.8	-24
28 F	0141	2.7	82
	0717	0.9	27
	1242	3.3	101
	2004	-0.8	-24
29 Sa	0242	2.5	76
	0801	1.1	34
	1324	3.2	98
	2057	-0.7	-21
30 Su	0348	2.4	73
	0850	1.3	40
	1415	3.0	91
	2155	-0.5	-15

May

Day	Time (h m)	Height (ft)	Height (cm)
1 M	0457	2.3	70
	0953	1.5	46
	1528	2.8	85
	2259	-0.3	-9
2 Tu ○	0608	2.2	67
	1115	1.6	49
	1659	2.6	79
3 W	0007	0.0	0
	0720	2.3	70
	1240	1.4	43
	1828	2.4	73
4 Th	0113	0.2	6
	0821	2.4	73
	1353	1.2	37
	1951	2.4	73
5 F	0212	0.3	9
	0903	2.5	76
	1452	0.9	27
	2102	2.4	73
6 Sa	0303	0.4	12
	0934	2.6	79
	1542	0.6	18
	2158	2.4	73
7 Su	0349	0.6	18
	1002	2.7	82
	1626	0.3	9
	2242	2.5	76
8 M	0431	0.7	21
	1029	2.8	85
	1706	0.1	3
	2320	2.5	76
9 Tu	0509	0.9	27
	1055	2.9	88
	1743	-0.1	-3
	2355	2.4	73
10 W ○	0545	1.0	30
	1122	3.0	91
	1820	-0.2	-6
11 Th	0031	2.4	73
	0618	1.1	34
	1147	3.0	91
	1856	-0.3	-9
12 F	0110	2.4	73
	0648	1.2	37
	1213	3.0	91
	1932	-0.3	-9
13 Sa	0154	2.3	70
	0717	1.3	40
	1237	2.9	88
	2010	-0.2	-6
14 Su	0243	2.3	70
	0744	1.4	43
	1304	2.8	85
	2051	-0.1	-3
15 M	0338	2.2	67
	0814	1.5	46
	1336	2.7	82
	2136	0.0	0
16 Tu	0435	2.2	67
	0857	1.6	49
	1419	2.6	79
	2229	0.1	3
17 W	0533	2.2	67
	1014	1.7	52
	1522	2.4	73
	2328	0.3	9
18 Th ◑	0630	2.3	70
	1156	1.6	49
	1709	2.3	70
19 F	0028	0.4	12
	0722	2.4	73
	1311	1.4	43
	1849	2.3	70
20 Sa	0125	0.4	12
	0808	2.5	76
	1409	1.0	30
	2006	2.3	70
21 Su	0217	0.5	15
	0847	2.7	82
	1501	0.6	18
	2111	2.4	73
22 M	0306	0.6	18
	0923	2.9	88
	1550	0.1	3
	2208	2.6	79
23 Tu	0354	0.7	21
	0956	3.1	94
	1638	-0.3	-9
	2300	2.7	82
24 W	0440	0.8	24
	1030	3.3	101
	1725	-0.7	-21
	2351	2.7	82
25 Th ●	0526	0.9	27
	1104	3.5	107
	1813	-0.9	-27
26 F	0044	2.7	82
	0612	1.1	34
	1142	3.5	107
	1902	-1.0	-30
27 Sa	0139	2.6	79
	0658	1.2	37
	1223	3.5	107
	1951	-1.0	-30
28 Su	0238	2.5	76
	0746	1.3	40
	1311	3.3	101
	2041	-0.8	-24
29 M	0337	2.5	76
	0839	1.4	43
	1410	3.1	94
	2135	-0.5	-15
30 Tu	0435	2.4	73
	0941	1.4	43
	1524	2.8	85
	2233	-0.2	-6
31 W	0532	2.4	73
	1056	1.4	43
	1644	2.6	79
	2335	0.1	3

June

Day	Time (h m)	Height (ft)	Height (cm)
1 Th ☽	0627	2.4	73
	1216	1.3	40
	1804	2.4	73
2 F	0036	0.4	12
	0719	2.5	76
	1328	1.0	30
	1925	2.2	67
3 Sa	0134	0.7	21
	0805	2.6	79
	1428	0.7	21
	2042	2.2	67
4 Su	0227	0.9	27
	0846	2.7	82
	1519	0.5	15
	2145	2.2	67
5 M	0315	1.0	30
	0921	2.8	85
	1604	0.2	6
	2233	2.2	67
6 Tu	0359	1.1	34
	0954	2.9	88
	1645	0.0	0
	2311	2.3	70
7 W	0439	1.2	37
	1025	3.0	91
	1723	-0.1	-3
	2346	2.3	70
8 Th	0516	1.3	40
	1055	3.0	91
	1800	-0.2	-6
9 F ○	0022	2.3	70
	0551	1.4	43
	1124	3.1	94
	1837	-0.3	-9
10 Sa	0100	2.3	70
	0624	1.4	43
	1152	3.1	94
	1913	-0.3	-9
11 Su	0142	2.3	70
	0656	1.4	43
	1218	3.0	91
	1950	-0.3	-9
12 M	0228	2.3	70
	0729	1.5	46
	1246	3.0	91
	2028	-0.2	-6
13 Tu	0317	2.3	70
	0806	1.5	46
	1320	2.8	85
	2108	-0.1	-3
14 W	0405	2.4	73
	0853	1.5	46
	1404	2.7	82
	2152	0.0	0
15 Th	0453	2.4	73
	0956	1.5	46
	1504	2.5	76
	2242	0.2	6
16 F	0541	2.5	76
	1115	1.4	43
	1628	2.3	70
	2338	0.4	12
17 Sa ○	0627	2.5	76
	1231	1.1	34
	1808	2.2	67
18 Su	0036	0.6	18
	0713	2.7	82
	1336	0.8	24
	1937	2.2	67
19 M	0133	0.8	24
	0757	2.8	85
	1434	0.3	9
	2053	2.3	70
20 Tu	0228	1.0	30
	0840	3.0	91
	1528	-0.1	-3
	2158	2.4	73
21 W	0322	1.1	34
	0922	3.2	98
	1620	-0.5	-15
	2255	2.5	76
22 Th	0414	1.2	37
	1003	3.4	104
	1710	-0.8	-24
	2347	2.6	79
23 F ●	0504	1.2	37
	1045	3.6	110
	1800	-1.0	-30
24 Sa	0038	2.6	79
	0554	1.2	37
	1129	3.6	110
	1848	-1.0	-30
25 Su	0129	2.6	79
	0643	1.2	37
	1216	3.6	110
	1935	-0.9	-27
26 M	0219	2.5	76
	0732	1.2	37
	1308	3.4	104
	2023	-0.7	-21
27 Tu	0309	2.5	76
	0824	1.2	37
	1406	3.1	94
	2111	-0.4	-12
28 W	0357	2.5	76
	0921	1.2	37
	1511	2.8	85
	2202	0.0	0
29 Th	0444	2.5	76
	1027	1.2	37
	1620	2.5	76
	2256	0.4	12
30 F ☽	0532	2.5	76
	1140	1.1	34
	1731	2.3	70
	2354	0.7	21

Time meridian 75° W. 0000 is midnight. 1200 is noon. Times are not adjusted for Daylight Saving Time.
Heights are referred to mean lower low water which is the chart datum of soundings.

Naples, Florida, 2017

Times and Heights of High and Low Waters

July

Day	Time	ft	cm		Day	Time	ft	cm
1 Sa	0621	2.6	79		16 Su ☽	0530	2.7	82
	1252	0.9	27			1156	0.9	27
	1848	2.1	64			1745	2.2	67
						2351	0.9	27
2 Su	0052	1.0	30		17 M	0617	2.8	85
	0710	2.6	79			1307	0.5	15
	1356	0.7	21			1919	2.1	64
	2011	2.0	61					
3 M	0149	1.2	37		18 Tu	0056	1.2	37
	0759	2.7	82			0710	2.9	88
	1451	0.5	15			1410	0.2	6
	2128	2.0	61			2045	2.2	67
4 Tu	0241	1.3	40		19 W	0200	1.3	40
	0844	2.8	85			0806	3.1	94
	1539	0.3	9			1509	-0.2	-6
	2223	2.1	64			2156	2.3	70
5 W	0329	1.4	43		20 Th	0300	1.4	43
	0926	2.9	88			0900	3.3	101
	1622	0.1	3			1604	-0.5	-15
	2301	2.2	67			2252	2.4	73
6 Th	0412	1.5	46		21 F	0356	1.4	43
	1003	3.0	91			0951	3.5	107
	1703	-0.1	-3			1656	-0.7	-21
	2334	2.2	67			2340	2.5	76
7 F	0452	1.5	46		22 Sa	0449	1.3	40
	1038	3.1	94			1039	3.6	110
	1741	-0.2	-6			1745	-0.8	-24
					○			
8 Sa ○	0008	2.3	70		23 Su ●	0023	2.6	79
	0529	1.4	43			0540	1.2	37
	1111	3.1	94			1126	3.6	110
	1817	-0.3	-9			1832	-0.8	-24
9 Su	0044	2.4	73		24 M	0104	2.6	79
	0604	1.4	43			0629	1.0	30
	1142	3.1	94			1213	3.6	110
	1853	-0.3	-9			1917	-0.6	-18
10 M	0122	2.4	73		25 Tu	0144	2.6	79
	0639	1.4	43			0716	1.0	30
	1211	3.1	94			1303	3.4	104
	1928	-0.3	-9			2000	-0.4	-12
11 Tu	0201	2.4	73		26 W	0225	2.6	79
	0715	1.3	40			0805	0.9	27
	1241	3.1	94			1355	3.2	98
	2004	-0.2	-6			2043	-0.1	-3
12 W	0243	2.5	76		27 Th	0307	2.6	79
	0754	1.3	40			0856	0.9	27
	1316	3.0	91			1451	2.9	88
	2040	-0.1	-3			2127	0.3	9
13 Th	0324	2.5	76		28 F	0350	2.6	79
	0839	1.2	37			0952	0.9	27
	1400	2.8	85			1551	2.6	79
	2119	0.1	3			2213	0.7	21
14 F	0405	2.6	79		29 Sa	0435	2.6	79
	0934	1.2	37			1057	0.9	27
	1457	2.6	79			1655	2.3	70
	2202	0.4	12			2306	1.1	34
15 Sa	0446	2.6	79		30 Su ☾	0524	2.6	79
	1042	1.1	34			1207	0.9	27
	1613	2.4	73			1807	2.1	64
	2252	0.7	21					
					31 M	0006	1.3	40
						0617	2.7	82
						1316	0.7	21
						1930	2.0	61

August

Day	Time	ft	cm		Day	Time	ft	cm
1 Tu	0110	1.5	46		16 W	0032	1.5	46
	0715	2.7	82			0635	3.0	91
	1417	0.6	18			1350	0.2	6
	2102	2.0	61			2046	2.3	70
2 W	0211	1.6	49		17 Th	0145	1.6	49
	0811	2.8	85			0748	3.1	94
	1509	0.4	12			1452	-0.1	-3
	2207	2.1	64			2155	2.4	73
3 Th	0303	1.6	49		18 F	0250	1.6	49
	0902	2.9	88			0853	3.3	101
	1556	0.2	6			1548	-0.3	-9
	2242	2.2	67			2243	2.5	76
4 F	0350	1.6	49		19 Sa	0347	1.4	43
	0946	3.0	91			0949	3.5	107
	1638	0.1	3			1640	-0.4	-12
	2312	2.3	70			2321	2.6	79
5 Sa	0431	1.5	46		20 Su	0439	1.2	37
	1025	3.1	94			1038	3.6	110
	1717	0.0	0			1727	-0.4	-12
	2343	2.4	73			2355	2.7	82
6 Su	0508	1.4	43		21 M ●	0528	1.0	30
	1101	3.2	98			1124	3.6	110
	1753	-0.1	-3			1812	-0.3	-9
7 M ○	0015	2.5	76		22 Tu	0027	2.7	82
	0544	1.3	40			0614	0.8	24
	1134	3.3	101			1209	3.5	107
	1829	-0.2	-6			1853	-0.1	-3
8 Tu	0048	2.6	79		23 W	0059	2.8	85
	0621	1.2	37			0658	0.7	21
	1206	3.3	101			1253	3.4	104
	1903	-0.1	-3			1933	0.1	3
9 W	0122	2.7	82		24 Th	0133	2.8	85
	0658	1.0	30			0742	0.6	18
	1238	3.2	98			1339	3.2	98
	1937	0.0	0			2012	0.4	12
10 Th	0156	2.7	82		25 F	0209	2.8	85
	0738	0.9	27			0827	0.6	18
	1315	3.1	94			1428	2.9	88
	2012	0.1	3			2050	0.8	24
11 F	0231	2.7	82		26 Sa	0248	2.8	85
	0822	0.8	24			0916	0.7	21
	1401	2.9	88			1521	2.6	79
	2048	0.4	12			2129	1.1	34
12 Sa	0305	2.8	85		27 Su	0332	2.8	85
	0913	0.8	24			1011	0.8	24
	1458	2.7	82			1622	2.4	73
	2128	0.7	21			2213	1.4	43
13 Su	0343	2.8	85		28 M	0422	2.7	82
	1014	0.7	21			1117	0.8	24
	1612	2.5	76			1731	2.2	67
	2214	1.0	30			2314	1.7	52
14 M ☾	0428	2.8	85		29 Tu ☾	0522	2.7	82
	1127	0.6	18			1229	0.8	24
	1740	2.3	70			1850	2.1	64
	2316	1.3	40					
15 Tu	0524	2.9	88		30 W	0033	1.8	55
	1241	0.4	12			0631	2.6	79
	1915	2.2	67			1336	0.7	21
						2020	2.2	67
					31 Th	0144	1.8	55
						0739	2.7	82
						1434	0.6	18
						2128	2.3	70

September

Day	Time	ft	cm		Day	Time	ft	cm
1 F	0241	1.7	52		16 Sa	0245	1.5	46
	0839	2.9	88			0852	3.2	98
	1524	0.5	15			1530	0.1	3
	2206	2.4	73			2220	2.7	82
2 Sa	0328	1.6	49		17 Su	0340	1.3	40
	0928	3.0	91			0949	3.4	104
	1607	0.3	9			1620	0.1	3
	2238	2.5	76			2251	2.8	85
3 Su	0408	1.5	46		18 M	0429	1.0	30
	1009	3.2	98			1038	3.4	104
	1647	0.2	6			1705	0.2	6
	2308	2.7	82			2318	2.9	88
4 M	0446	1.3	40		19 Tu	0514	0.7	21
	1047	3.3	101			1121	3.5	107
	1724	0.2	6			1747	0.3	9
	2338	2.8	85			2346	3.0	91
5 Tu	0523	1.1	34		20 W ●	0557	0.5	15
	1122	3.4	104			1201	3.4	104
	1759	0.1	3			1826	0.5	15
6 W	0007	2.9	88		21 Th	0013	3.0	91
	0600	0.9	27			0639	0.4	12
	1157	3.4	104			1241	3.3	101
	1834	0.2	6			1903	0.7	21
	○							
7 Th	0036	2.9	88		22 F	0042	3.1	94
	0639	0.7	21			0719	0.4	12
	1234	3.3	101			1322	3.1	94
	1908	0.3	9			1939	1.0	30
8 F	0104	3.0	91		23 Sa	0112	3.0	91
	0720	0.5	15			0759	0.4	12
	1315	3.2	98			1406	2.9	88
	1943	0.6	18			2013	1.2	37
9 Sa	0131	3.0	91		24 Su	0144	3.0	91
	0805	0.4	12			0842	0.5	15
	1405	3.0	91			1457	2.7	82
	2020	0.8	24			2046	1.5	46
10 Su	0202	3.1	94		25 M	0220	2.9	88
	0855	0.4	12			0930	0.6	18
	1506	2.8	85			1555	2.5	76
	2100	1.1	34			2120	1.7	52
11 M	0239	3.1	94		26 Tu	0306	2.8	85
	0953	0.4	12			1028	0.8	24
	1620	2.6	79			1701	2.4	73
	2148	1.5	46			2210	1.9	58
12 Tu	0329	3.0	91		27 W	0416	2.7	82
	1103	0.4	12			1138	0.8	24
	1744	2.4	73			1815	2.3	70
	2256	1.7	52			2351 ☾	2.0	61
13 W	0443	3.0	91		28 Th	0542	2.6	79
	1219	0.4	12			1249	0.8	24
	1915	2.4	73			1932	2.3	70
	☾							
14 Th	0024	1.8	55		29 F	0116	2.0	61
	0617	3.0	91			0702	2.6	79
	1330	0.3	9			1351	0.8	24
	2043	2.4	73			2037	2.5	76
15 F	0141	1.8	55		30 Sa	0216	1.8	55
	0743	3.1	94			0809	2.8	85
	1434	0.2	6			1443	0.7	21
	2142	2.6	79			2121	2.6	79

Time meridian 75° W. 0000 is midnight. 1200 is noon. Times are not adjusted for Daylight Saving Time.
Heights are referred to mean lower low water which is the chart datum of soundings.

Naples, Florida, 2017

Times and Heights of High and Low Waters

October

Day	Time	ft	cm	Day	Time	ft	cm
1 Su	0302	1.6	49	**16** M	0330	1.0	30
	0903	2.9	88		0948	3.1	94
	1529	0.6	18		1555	0.6	18
	2156	2.7	82		2214	2.9	88
2 M	0343	1.3	40	**17** Tu	0417	0.7	21
	0949	3.1	94		1035	3.2	98
	1610	0.5	15		1639	0.7	21
	2227	2.9	88		2240	3.0	91
3 Tu	0421	1.0	30	**18** W	0500	0.4	12
	1029	3.2	98		1116	3.2	98
	1648	0.5	15		1720	0.8	24
	2256	3.0	91		2306	3.1	94
4 W	0500	0.7	21	**19** Th	0540	0.2	6
	1108	3.3	101		1153	3.1	94
	1725	0.5	15		1758	1.0	30
	2324	3.1	94	●	2332	3.2	98
5 Th	0539	0.4	12	**20** F	0619	0.1	3
	1147	3.3	101		1230	3.0	91
	1802	0.6	18		1833	1.2	37
○	2349	3.2	98		2358	3.2	98
6 F	0620	0.2	6	**21** Sa	0657	0.1	3
	1229	3.3	101		1308	2.9	88
	1839	0.8	24		1907	1.3	40
7 Sa	0015	3.3	101	**22** Su	0024	3.2	98
	0703	0.0	0		0735	0.1	3
	1315	3.2	98		1350	2.8	85
	1917	1.0	30		1939	1.5	46
8 Su	0042	3.4	104	**23** M	0051	3.1	94
	0749	-0.1	-3		0814	0.2	6
	1410	3.0	91		1438	2.7	82
	1956	1.2	37		2009	1.7	52
9 M	0115	3.3	101	**24** Tu	0120	3.0	91
	0839	-0.1	-3		0857	0.4	12
	1514	2.8	85		1534	2.6	79
	2039	1.5	46		2040	1.8	55
10 Tu	0156	3.3	101	**25** W	0154	2.8	85
	0937	0.0	0		0947	0.5	15
	1626	2.7	82		1636	2.5	76
	2133	1.7	52		2122	1.9	58
11 W	0253	3.1	94	**26** Th	0244	2.7	82
	1043	0.2	6		1047	0.7	21
	1743	2.5	76		1741	2.4	73
	2250	1.9	58		2300	2.0	61
12 Th	0425	3.0	91	**27** F	0436	2.5	76
	1156	0.3	9		1155	0.8	24
	1905	2.5	76	◑	1846	2.5	76
◐							
13 F	0019	1.9	58	**28** Sa	0035	1.9	58
	0610	2.9	88		0613	2.5	76
	1307	0.4	12		1300	0.8	24
	2018	2.6	79		1945	2.6	79
14 Sa	0135	1.6	49	**29** Su	0141	1.7	52
	0738	2.9	88		0729	2.5	76
	1411	0.4	12		1355	0.8	24
	2109	2.7	82		2032	2.7	82
15 Su	0237	1.3	40	**30** M	0230	1.4	43
	0850	3.0	91		0832	2.7	82
	1506	0.5	15		1443	0.7	21
	2144	2.8	85		2110	2.8	85
				31 Tu	0314	1.0	30
					0924	2.8	85
					1528	0.8	24
					2143	3.0	91

November

Day	Time	ft	cm	Day	Time	ft	cm
1 W	0355	0.7	21	**16** Th	0444	0.1	3
	1011	3.0	91		1113	2.7	82
	1609	0.8	24		1652	1.2	37
	2213	3.2	98		2233	3.1	94
2 Th	0437	0.3	9	**17** F	0523	0.0	0
	1055	3.1	94		1147	2.7	82
	1650	0.9	27		1730	1.3	40
	2241	3.3	101		2300	3.1	94
3 F	0519	-0.1	-3	**18** Sa	0601	-0.2	-6
	1139	3.1	94		1222	2.7	82
	1731	1.0	30		1806	1.4	43
	2309	3.4	104	●	2327	3.1	94
4 Sa	0603	-0.4	-12	**19** Su	0638	-0.2	-6
	1225	3.1	94		1258	2.6	79
	1812	1.1	34		1840	1.5	46
○	2337	3.5	107		2353	3.1	94
5 Su	0648	-0.6	-18	**20** M	0714	-0.2	-6
	1316	3.0	91		1338	2.6	79
	1854	1.3	40		1912	1.5	46
6 M	0010	3.5	107	**21** Tu	0019	3.0	91
	0736	-0.6	-18		0752	-0.1	-3
	1412	2.9	88		1424	2.5	76
	1937	1.4	43		1944	1.6	49
7 Tu	0049	3.5	107	**22** W	0048	2.9	88
	0826	-0.5	-15		0831	0.0	0
	1515	2.8	85		1515	2.5	76
	2026	1.6	49		2018	1.7	52
8 W	0136	3.3	101	**23** Th	0121	2.8	85
	0921	-0.3	-9		0914	0.2	6
	1621	2.6	79		1609	2.4	73
	2125	1.7	52		2102	1.7	52
9 Th	0243	3.1	94	**24** F	0204	2.6	79
	1023	0.0	0		1003	0.3	9
	1727	2.6	79		1704	2.4	73
	2241	1.7	52		2213	1.8	55
10 F	0422	2.8	85	**25** Sa	0311	2.4	73
	1130	0.2	6		1059	0.5	15
	1833	2.6	79		1759	2.5	76
○					2343	1.6	49
11 Sa	0006	1.6	49	**26** Su	0509	2.3	70
	0558	2.7	82		1201	0.6	18
	1238	0.4	12		1851	2.5	76
	1933	2.6	79	◑			
12 Su	0121	1.3	40	**27** M	0056	1.4	43
	0725	2.6	79		0640	2.2	67
	1341	0.6	18		1300	0.7	21
	2023	2.7	82		1938	2.6	79
13 M	0223	1.0	30	**28** Tu	0153	1.0	30
	0842	2.6	79		0755	2.3	70
	1436	0.8	24		1354	0.8	24
	2102	2.8	85		2020	2.8	85
14 Tu	0316	0.6	18	**29** W	0242	0.6	18
	0944	2.7	82		0859	2.4	73
	1526	0.9	27		1443	0.9	27
	2135	2.9	88		2057	2.9	88
15 W	0402	0.3	9	**30** Th	0329	0.2	6
	1033	2.7	82		0955	2.6	79
	1611	1.0	30		1531	1.0	30
	2204	3.0	91		2131	3.1	94

December

Day	Time	ft	cm	Day	Time	ft	cm
1 F	0415	-0.2	-6	**16** Sa	0506	-0.3	-9
	1045	2.7	82		1144	2.3	70
	1617	1.1	34		1707	1.3	40
	2204	3.3	101		2238	2.9	88
2 Sa	0501	-0.6	-18	**17** Su	0544	-0.4	-12
	1133	2.8	85		1215	2.3	70
	1703	1.1	34		1744	1.4	43
	2238	3.4	104		2309	3.0	91
3 Su	0548	-0.9	-27	**18** M	0620	-0.5	-15
	1222	2.8	85		1248	2.3	70
	1749	1.2	37		1819	1.4	43
○	2314	3.5	107	●	2338	2.9	88
4 M	0635	-1.0	-30	**19** Tu	0656	-0.5	-15
	1313	2.8	85		1325	2.4	73
	1836	1.2	37		1852	1.4	43
	2354	3.5	107				
5 Tu	0723	-1.0	-30	**20** W	0007	2.9	88
	1407	2.7	82		0732	-0.4	-12
	1923	1.3	40		1406	2.4	73
					1926	1.3	40
6 W	0040	3.4	104	**21** Th	0036	2.8	85
	0812	-0.9	-27		0808	-0.3	-9
	1503	2.6	79		1450	2.4	73
	2015	1.3	40		2002	1.3	40
7 Th	0135	3.2	98	**22** F	0109	2.7	82
	0904	-0.6	-18		0845	-0.2	-6
	1559	2.5	76		1535	2.4	73
	2113	1.3	40		2045	1.3	40
8 F	0246	2.9	88	**23** Sa	0150	2.5	76
	0959	-0.2	-6		0925	0.0	0
	1654	2.5	76		1621	2.4	73
	2223	1.3	40		2140	1.3	40
9 Sa	0411	2.6	79	**24** Su	0245	2.3	70
	1059	0.1	3		1009	0.2	6
	1747	2.5	76		1707	2.4	73
	2341	1.1	34		2251	1.2	37
10 Su	0536	2.4	73	**25** M	0407	2.1	64
	1202	0.5	15		1100	0.5	15
	1840	2.5	76		1752	2.4	73
○							
11 M	0057	0.9	27	**26** Tu	0006	1.0	30
	0702	2.2	67		0548	2.0	61
	1304	0.7	21		1159	0.7	21
	1930	2.6	79	◑	1838	2.5	76
12 Tu	0201	0.6	18	**27** W	0113	0.6	18
	0828	2.2	67		0718	1.9	58
	1402	0.9	27		1301	0.9	27
	2016	2.7	82		1924	2.6	79
13 W	0256	0.3	9	**28** Th	0211	0.2	6
	0943	2.2	67		0838	2.0	61
	1455	1.1	34		1401	1.0	30
	2057	2.8	85		2010	2.8	85
14 Th	0343	0.0	0	**29** F	0304	-0.2	-6
	1036	2.2	67		0944	2.2	67
	1542	1.2	37		1457	1.1	34
	2133	2.8	85		2054	3.0	91
15 F	0426	-0.1	-3	**30** Sa	0355	-0.6	-18
	1114	2.3	70		1040	2.3	70
	1626	1.3	40		1550	1.2	37
	2207	2.9	88		2137	3.1	94
				31 Su	0445	-1.0	-30
					1129	2.4	73
					1642	1.1	34
					2221	3.3	101

Time meridian 75° W. 0000 is midnight. 1200 is noon. Times are not adjusted for Daylight Saving Time.
Heights are referred to mean lower low water which is the chart datum of soundings.

St. Petersburg, Florida, 2017

Times and Heights of High and Low Waters

January

Day	Time	ft	cm	Day	Time	ft	cm
1 Su	0231	2.1	64	**16** M	0336	1.8	55
	1016	-0.5	-15		1052	-0.3	-9
	1703	1.2	37		1730	1.3	40
	2117	0.9	27		2245	0.6	18
2 M	0318	2.0	61	**17** Tu	0428	1.6	49
	1055	-0.4	-12		1127	-0.1	-3
	1737	1.3	40		1802	1.4	43
	2221	0.8	24		2356	0.5	15
3 Tu	0411	1.8	55	**18** W	0531	1.3	40
	1136	-0.3	-9		1202	0.1	3
	1815	1.4	43		1838	1.5	46
	2336	0.7	21				
4 W	0515	1.6	49	**19** Th	0115	0.4	12
	1221	-0.1	-3		0653	1.1	34
	1856	1.5	46		1241	0.4	12
					1918	1.6	49
5 Th	0101	0.5	15	**20** F	0236	0.2	6
	0637	1.3	40		0843	0.9	27
	1307	0.2	6		1324	0.6	18
	1940	1.6	49		2003	1.7	52
6 F	0229	0.3	9	**21** Sa	0349	0.0	0
	0821	1.1	34		1039	0.9	27
	1356	0.4	12		1413	0.7	21
	2025	1.8	55		2050	1.7	52
7 Sa	0349	0.0	0	**22** Su	0450	-0.2	-6
	1016	1.1	34		1209	1.0	30
	1447	0.6	18		1510	0.9	27
	2113	1.9	58		2138	1.8	55
8 Su	0458	-0.3	-9	**23** M	0542	-0.3	-9
	1156	1.1	34		1310	1.1	34
	1538	0.8	24		1607	1.0	30
	2201	2.1	64		2225	1.9	58
9 M	0558	-0.6	-18	**24** Tu	0626	-0.5	-15
	1313	1.1	34		1353	1.1	34
	1629	0.9	27		1658	1.0	30
	2251	2.2	67		2309	1.9	58
10 Tu	0651	-0.8	-24	**25** W	0705	-0.6	-18
	1412	1.2	37		1425	1.1	34
	1719	1.0	30		1742	0.9	27
	2340	2.3	70		2350	2.0	61
11 W	0739	-0.9	-27	**26** Th	0741	-0.6	-18
	1458	1.2	37		1449	1.1	34
	1808	1.0	30		1823	0.9	27
12 Th	0028	2.3	70	**27** F	0030	2.1	64
	0823	-0.9	-27		0813	-0.7	-21
	1535	1.2	37		1509	1.2	37
	1857	0.9	27		1903	0.8	24
13 F	0115	2.3	70	**28** Sa	0109	2.1	64
	0904	-0.8	-24		0845	-0.6	-18
	1606	1.2	37		1527	1.2	37
	1948	0.8	24		1944	0.7	21
14 Sa	0201	2.2	67	**29** Su	0150	2.1	64
	0942	-0.7	-21		0917	-0.6	-18
	1634	1.2	37		1547	1.2	37
	2042	0.8	24		2030	0.6	18
15 Su	0248	2.0	61	**30** M	0234	2.0	61
	1018	-0.5	-15		0949	-0.5	-15
	1701	1.2	37		1611	1.3	40
	2140	0.7	21		2121	0.5	15
				31 Tu	0321	1.9	58
					1022	-0.3	-9
					1639	1.4	43
					2218	0.4	12

February

Day	Time	ft	cm	Day	Time	ft	cm
1 W	0415	1.7	52	**16** Th	0513	1.2	37
	1057	-0.1	-3		1059	0.4	12
	1712	1.5	46		1715	1.7	52
	2324	0.3	9				
2 Th	0518	1.4	43	**17** F	0021	0.2	6
	1134	0.2	6		0623	1.1	34
	1751	1.7	52		1129	0.6	18
					1752	1.7	52
3 F	0041	0.1	3	**18** Sa	0133	0.1	3
	0640	1.1	34		0808	0.9	27
	1212	0.4	12		1202	0.8	24
	1835	1.8	55		1836	1.7	52
4 Sa	0208	0.0	0	**19** Su	0251	0.0	0
	0837	0.9	27		1035	0.9	27
	1253	0.7	21		1245	0.8	24
	1928	1.9	58		1932	1.7	52
5 Su	0334	-0.2	-6	**20** M	0404	-0.1	-3
	1059	0.9	27		2040	1.7	52
	1345	0.8	24				
	2030	1.9	58				
6 M	0450	-0.5	-15	**21** Tu	0505	-0.2	-6
	1238	1.0	30		1257	1.1	34
	1456	0.9	27		1536	1.0	30
	2137	2.0	61		2149	1.8	55
7 Tu	0552	-0.6	-18	**22** W	0555	-0.4	-12
	1331	1.1	34		1324	1.2	37
	1614	1.0	30		1646	1.0	30
	2242	2.1	64		2249	1.9	58
8 W	0644	-0.7	-21	**23** Th	0636	-0.4	-12
	1407	1.2	37		1346	1.2	37
	1723	1.0	30		1739	0.9	27
	2341	2.2	67		2340	2.0	61
9 Th	0728	-0.7	-21	**24** F	0712	-0.5	-15
	1434	1.2	37		1403	1.3	40
	1820	0.9	27		1824	0.8	24
10 F	0034	2.2	67	**25** Sa	0026	2.0	61
	0807	-0.7	-21		0745	-0.5	-15
	1456	1.2	37		1419	1.3	40
	1911	0.7	21		1905	0.6	18
11 Sa	0121	2.1	64	**26** Su	0109	2.1	64
	0840	-0.6	-18		0815	-0.4	-12
	1516	1.3	40		1436	1.4	43
	1959	0.6	18		1947	0.5	15
12 Su	0205	2.0	61	**27** M	0153	2.0	61
	0910	-0.4	-12		0845	-0.3	-9
	1535	1.3	40		1455	1.5	46
	2046	0.5	15		2031	0.3	9
13 M	0248	1.8	55	**28** Tu	0239	1.9	58
	0938	-0.2	-6		0915	-0.1	-3
	1555	1.4	43		1518	1.6	49
	2133	0.4	12		2120	0.1	3
14 Tu	0331	1.7	52				
	1004	0.0	0				
	1617	1.5	46				
	2224	0.3	9				
15 W	0418	1.5	46				
	1031	0.2	6				
	1644	1.6	49				
	2318	0.2	6				

March

Day	Time	ft	cm	Day	Time	ft	cm
1 W	0328	1.8	55	**16** Th	0412	1.4	43
	0945	0.1	3		0938	0.5	15
	1545	1.8	55		1540	2.0	61
	2213	0.0	0		2247	0.0	0
2 Th	0424	1.6	49	**17** F	0503	1.3	40
	1015	0.3	9		1002	0.7	21
	1617	1.9	58		1610	2.0	61
	2315	-0.1	-3		2339	0.0	0
3 F	0531	1.3	40	**18** Sa	0608	1.2	37
	1045	0.6	18		1027	0.9	27
	1655	2.0	61		1645	2.0	61
4 Sa	0027	-0.1	-3	**19** Su	0041	0.0	0
	0704	1.1	34		0746	1.1	34
	1114	0.8	24		1051	1.0	30
	1741	2.0	61		1728	1.9	58
5 Su	0152	-0.2	-6	**20** M	0154	0.0	0
	0938	1.0	30		1824	1.9	58
	1140	0.9	27				
	1840	2.0	61				
6 M	0320	-0.3	-9	**21** Tu	0309	0.0	0
	1958	2.0	61		1942	1.8	55
7 Tu	0436	-0.4	-12	**22** W	0416	-0.1	-3
	1246	1.2	37		1211	1.3	40
	1459	1.1	34		1519	1.2	37
	2128	2.0	61		2110	1.8	55
8 W	0537	-0.4	-12	**23** Th	0509	-0.1	-3
	1309	1.3	40		1231	1.4	43
	1637	1.1	34		1637	1.1	34
	2247	2.0	61		2225	1.9	58
9 Th	0625	-0.4	-12	**24** F	0554	-0.2	-6
	1330	1.4	43		1249	1.5	46
	1745	0.9	27		1732	0.9	27
	2350	2.0	61		2326	1.9	58
10 F	0705	-0.4	-12	**25** Sa	0631	-0.2	-6
	1349	1.4	43		1306	1.6	49
	1837	0.7	21		1818	0.7	21
11 Sa	0042	2.0	61	**26** Su	0018	2.0	61
	0737	-0.3	-9		0705	-0.1	-3
	1406	1.5	46		1323	1.7	52
	1922	0.5	15		1901	0.5	15
12 Su	0127	1.9	58	**27** M	0107	2.0	61
	0805	-0.1	-3		0736	0.0	0
	1422	1.6	49		1341	1.8	55
	2002	0.4	12		1943	0.2	6
13 M	0208	1.8	55	**28** Tu	0155	2.0	61
	0829	0.1	3		0806	0.2	6
	1437	1.7	52		1403	1.9	58
	2041	0.2	6		2028	0.0	0
14 Tu	0248	1.7	52	**29** W	0245	1.9	58
	0852	0.2	6		0835	0.4	12
	1455	1.8	55		1428	2.1	64
	2121	0.1	3		2116	-0.2	-6
15 W	0328	1.6	49	**30** Th	0339	1.7	52
	0914	0.4	12		0903	0.6	18
	1515	1.9	58		1458	2.2	67
	2202	0.0	0		2209	-0.3	-9
				31 F	0441	1.5	46
					0929	0.8	24
					1532	2.3	70
					2309	-0.3	-9

Time meridian 75° W. 0000 is midnight. 1200 is noon. Times are not adjusted for Daylight Saving Time.
Heights are referred to mean lower low water which is the chart datum of soundings.

St. Petersburg, Florida, 2017
Times and Heights of High and Low Waters

April

Day	Time (h m)	Height (ft)	Height (cm)
1 Sa	0558	1.3	40
	0955	1.0	30
	1613	2.3	70
2 Su	0018	-0.3	-9
	0755	1.2	37
	1013	1.1	34
	1702	2.2	67
3 M ☽	0137	-0.2	-6
	1807	2.1	64
4 Tu	0259	-0.2	-6
	1940	2.0	61
5 W	0410	-0.2	-6
	1200	1.5	46
	1534	1.3	40
	2127	1.9	58
6 Th	0506	-0.1	-3
	1220	1.6	49
	1659	1.1	34
	2250	1.9	58
7 F	0550	0.0	0
	1239	1.7	52
	1757	0.8	24
	2354	1.9	58
8 Sa	0626	0.1	3
	1258	1.8	55
	1843	0.6	18
9 Su	0046	1.8	55
	0656	0.2	6
	1314	1.9	58
	1922	0.4	12
10 M	0131	1.8	55
	0721	0.4	12
	1329	2.0	61
	1958	0.2	6
11 Tu ○	0212	1.7	52
	0743	0.6	18
	1345	2.1	64
	2032	0.1	3
12 W	0250	1.6	49
	0804	0.7	21
	1402	2.2	67
	2106	0.0	0
13 Th	0330	1.5	46
	0824	0.8	24
	1424	2.2	67
	2143	-0.1	-3
14 F	0412	1.4	43
	0846	0.9	27
	1450	2.3	70
	2224	-0.1	-3
15 Sa	0501	1.4	43
	0910	1.0	30
	1521	2.3	70
	2310	-0.1	-3
16 Su	0603	1.3	40
	0935	1.1	34
	1558	2.2	67
17 M	0004	0.0	0
	0731	1.3	40
	1004	1.2	37
	1642	2.1	64
18 Tu	0107	0.0	0
	1738	2.0	61
19 W ◑	0214	0.0	0
	1030	1.4	43
	1304	1.3	40
	1855	1.9	58
20 Th	0318	0.1	3
	1059	1.5	46
	1501	1.3	40
	2029	1.8	55
21 F	0413	0.1	3
	1123	1.6	49
	1620	1.1	34
	2156	1.8	55
22 Sa	0500	0.1	3
	1144	1.7	52
	1718	0.8	24
	2307	1.9	58
23 Su	0541	0.2	6
	1205	1.9	58
	1806	0.5	15
24 M	0008	1.9	58
	0617	0.3	9
	1226	2.0	61
	1851	0.2	6
25 Tu	0105	1.9	58
	0650	0.5	15
	1250	2.2	67
	1937	0.0	0
26 W ●	0201	1.8	55
	0721	0.7	21
	1317	2.4	73
	2023	-0.3	-9
27 Th	0257	1.7	52
	0750	0.9	27
	1347	2.5	76
	2113	-0.4	-12
28 F	0357	1.6	49
	0817	1.0	30
	1422	2.6	79
	2206	-0.5	-15
29 Sa	0507	1.4	43
	0843	1.2	37
	1501	2.6	79
	2304	-0.4	-12
30 Su	0635	1.4	43
	0908	1.3	40
	1546	2.5	76

May

Day	Time (h m)	Height (ft)	Height (cm)
1 M	0009	-0.3	-9
	1640	2.4	73
2 Tu ○	0117	-0.2	-6
	1750	2.1	64
3 W	0226	-0.1	-3
	1033	1.6	49
	1351	1.4	43
	1930	1.9	58
4 Th	0327	0.1	3
	1057	1.7	52
	1546	1.2	37
	2118	1.8	55
5 F	0419	0.2	6
	1121	1.8	55
	1700	0.9	27
	2244	1.7	52
6 Sa	0501	0.3	9
	1144	1.9	58
	1753	0.6	18
	2351	1.7	52
7 Su	0536	0.5	15
	1204	2.0	61
	1837	0.4	12
8 M	0046	1.6	49
	0606	0.7	21
	1223	2.2	67
	1914	0.2	6
9 Tu	0135	1.6	49
	0632	0.8	24
	1241	2.3	70
	1949	0.0	0
10 W ○	0218	1.6	49
	0654	0.9	27
	1259	2.3	70
	2021	-0.1	-3
11 Th	0259	1.5	46
	0715	1.0	30
	1320	2.4	73
	2054	-0.2	-6
12 F	0338	1.5	46
	0736	1.1	34
	1345	2.5	76
	2129	-0.2	-6
13 Sa	0419	1.4	43
	0759	1.2	37
	1415	2.5	76
	2207	-0.2	-6
14 Su	0505	1.4	43
	0827	1.2	37
	1449	2.5	76
	2250	-0.2	-6
15 M	0559	1.4	43
	0901	1.3	40
	1529	2.4	73
	2338	-0.1	-3
16 Tu	0703	1.4	43
	0949	1.3	40
	1615	2.3	70
17 W	0030	0.0	0
	0808	1.5	46
	1107	1.4	43
	1711	2.1	64
18 Th ◑	0126	0.0	0
	0859	1.6	49
	1253	1.4	43
	1824	1.9	58
19 F	0221	0.1	3
	0937	1.7	52
	1435	1.2	37
	1954	1.8	55
20 Sa	0314	0.2	6
	1009	1.8	55
	1555	1.0	30
	2127	1.7	52
21 Su	0402	0.4	12
	1038	2.0	61
	1658	0.6	18
	2250	1.7	52
22 M	0446	0.5	15
	1106	2.1	64
	1751	0.3	9
23 Tu	0003	1.7	52
	0525	0.7	21
	1135	2.3	70
	1841	0.0	0
24 W	0109	1.7	52
	0600	0.9	27
	1207	2.5	76
	1931	-0.3	-9
25 Th ●	0212	1.6	49
	0633	1.1	34
	1241	2.7	82
	2020	-0.5	-15
26 F	0315	1.6	49
	0704	1.2	37
	1318	2.8	85
	2111	-0.5	-15
27 Sa	0419	1.5	46
	0735	1.3	40
	1359	2.8	85
	2203	-0.5	-15
28 Su	0527	1.4	43
	0808	1.3	40
	1444	2.7	82
	2257	-0.4	-12
29 M	0640	1.4	43
	0852	1.3	40
	1534	2.6	79
	2352	-0.3	-9
30 Tu	0746	1.5	46
	1003	1.4	43
	1631	2.4	73
31 W	0047	-0.1	-3
	0835	1.5	46
	1151	1.4	43
	1742	2.1	64

June

Day	Time (h m)	Height (ft)	Height (cm)
1 Th ☽	0142	0.1	3
	0913	1.7	52
	1350	1.3	40
	1914	1.8	55
2 F	0233	0.3	9
	0946	1.8	55
	1529	1.1	34
	2057	1.6	49
3 Sa	0320	0.5	15
	1016	2.0	61
	1642	0.8	24
	2228	1.5	46
4 Su	0402	0.7	21
	1045	2.1	64
	1736	0.5	15
	2343	1.5	46
5 M	0440	0.8	24
	1111	2.2	67
	1821	0.3	9
6 Tu	0046	1.5	46
	0513	1.0	30
	1136	2.3	70
	1901	0.1	3
7 W	0141	1.5	46
	0542	1.1	34
	1200	2.4	73
	1937	-0.1	-3
8 Th	0229	1.5	46
	0608	1.2	37
	1224	2.5	76
	2011	-0.1	-3
9 F ○	0311	1.4	43
	0632	1.2	37
	1251	2.5	76
	2044	-0.2	-6
10 Sa	0349	1.4	43
	0658	1.3	40
	1321	2.6	79
	2118	-0.2	-6
11 Su	0423	1.4	43
	0728	1.3	40
	1354	2.6	79
	2154	-0.2	-6
12 M	0458	1.4	43
	0805	1.3	40
	1432	2.5	76
	2232	-0.2	-6
13 Tu	0534	1.5	46
	0852	1.3	40
	1514	2.5	76
	2312	-0.1	-3
14 W	0614	1.5	46
	0953	1.3	40
	1602	2.3	70
	2356	0.0	0
15 Th	0656	1.6	49
	1108	1.3	40
	1658	2.2	67
16 F	0041	0.1	3
	0738	1.7	52
	1235	1.2	37
	1806	2.0	61
17 Sa ○	0129	0.2	6
	0819	1.8	55
	1406	1.0	30
	1931	1.8	55
18 Su	0217	0.4	12
	0858	2.0	61
	1527	0.8	24
	2107	1.6	49
19 M	0304	0.6	18
	0936	2.2	67
	1637	0.5	15
	2242	1.5	46
20 Tu	0350	0.8	24
	1015	2.4	73
	1738	0.1	3
21 W	0008	1.5	46
	0433	1.0	30
	1054	2.5	76
	1834	-0.2	-6
22 Th	0123	1.5	46
	0513	1.2	37
	1135	2.7	82
	1926	-0.4	-12
23 F ●	0229	1.5	46
	0551	1.3	40
	1219	2.8	85
	2017	-0.5	-15
24 Sa	0328	1.5	46
	0630	1.3	40
	1304	2.9	88
	2106	-0.5	-15
25 Su	0421	1.5	46
	0714	1.3	40
	1351	2.9	88
	2153	-0.4	-12
26 M	0508	1.5	46
	0805	1.3	40
	1440	2.8	85
	2239	-0.3	-9
27 Tu	0550	1.5	46
	0907	1.3	40
	1531	2.6	79
	2324	-0.1	-3
28 W	0629	1.6	49
	1021	1.3	40
	1628	2.3	70
29 Th	0007	0.1	3
	0708	1.7	52
	1148	1.2	37
	1732	2.0	61
30 F ☽	0050	0.3	9
	0747	1.8	55
	1321	1.1	34
	1852	1.7	52

Time meridian 75° W. 0000 is midnight. 1200 is noon. Times are not adjusted for Daylight Saving Time.
Heights are referred to mean lower low water which is the chart datum of soundings.

St. Petersburg, Florida, 2017

Times and Heights of High and Low Waters

July

Day	Time	Height (ft)	Height (cm)	Day	Time	Height (ft)	Height (cm)
1 Sa	0132	0.5	15	16 Su ◐	0040	0.5	15
	0826	1.9	58		0708	2.0	61
	1451	0.9	27		1338	0.8	24
	2029	1.5	46		1922	1.7	52
2 Su	0215	0.7	21	17 M	0124	0.8	24
	0905	2.1	64		0754	2.2	67
	1607	0.7	21		1503	0.6	18
	2208	1.4	43		2105	1.5	46
3 M	0259	0.9	27	18 Tu	0210	1.0	30
	0943	2.2	67		0842	2.4	73
	1708	0.4	12		1620	0.3	9
	2335	1.4	43		2254	1.5	46
4 Tu	0342	1.1	34	19 W	0259	1.2	37
	1020	2.3	70		0934	2.5	76
	1758	0.2	6		1728	0.1	3
5 W	0046	1.5	46	20 Th	0027	1.5	46
	0423	1.2	37		0350	1.3	40
	1055	2.4	73		1027	2.7	82
	1842	0.1	3		1827	-0.1	-3
6 Th	0144	1.5	46	21 F	0138	1.5	46
	0501	1.3	40		0442	1.4	43
	1129	2.4	73		1120	2.8	85
	1921	0.0	0		1920	-0.3	-9
7 F	0230	1.5	46	22 Sa	0231	1.5	46
	0536	1.3	40		0534	1.4	43
	1202	2.5	76		1212	2.9	88
	1957	-0.1	-3		2008	-0.3	-9
8 Sa O	0307	1.5	46	23 Su ●	0312	1.5	46
	0609	1.3	40		0627	1.3	40
	1235	2.6	79		1303	2.9	88
	2031	-0.1	-3		2052	-0.3	-9
9 Su	0335	1.5	46	24 M	0345	1.6	49
	0643	1.3	40		0721	1.3	40
	1310	2.6	79		1352	2.8	85
	2103	-0.1	-3		2132	-0.1	-3
10 M	0358	1.5	46	25 Tu	0413	1.6	49
	0722	1.3	40		0816	1.2	37
	1347	2.6	79		1441	2.7	82
	2135	-0.1	-3		2209	0.0	0
11 Tu	0421	1.5	46	26 W	0441	1.7	52
	0806	1.2	37		0915	1.1	34
	1426	2.6	79		1530	2.5	76
	2208	-0.1	-3		2244	0.2	6
12 W	0446	1.6	49	27 Th	0510	1.8	55
	0856	1.2	37		1017	1.1	34
	1509	2.5	76		1621	2.2	67
	2243	0.0	0		2318	0.4	12
13 Th	0515	1.7	52	28 F	0542	1.9	58
	0954	1.2	37		1125	1.0	30
	1557	2.4	73		1719	2.0	61
	2320	0.1	3		2353	0.7	21
14 F	0549	1.8	55	29 Sa	0618	2.0	61
	1100	1.1	34		1239	0.9	27
	1652	2.2	67		1829	1.7	52
	2359	0.3	9				
15 Sa	0627	1.9	58	30 Su ◐	0029	0.9	27
	1215	1.0	30		0658	2.1	64
	1758	1.9	58		1359	0.8	24
					2001	1.6	49
				31 M	0110	1.1	34
					0745	2.2	67
					1518	0.7	21
					2150	1.5	46

August

Day	Time	Height (ft)	Height (cm)	Day	Time	Height (ft)	Height (cm)
1 Tu	0157	1.2	37	16 W	0122	1.4	43
	0836	2.2	67		0758	2.5	76
	1628	0.5	15		1607	0.3	9
	2328	1.5	46		2327	1.6	49
2 W	0251	1.4	43	17 Th	0224	1.5	46
	0929	2.3	70		0908	2.6	79
	1726	0.4	12		1718	0.2	6
3 Th	0039	1.6	49	18 F	0041	1.6	49
	0348	1.4	43		0337	1.5	46
	1020	2.4	73		1018	2.7	82
	1815	0.2	6		1817	0.0	0
4 F	0128	1.6	49	19 Sa	0127	1.7	52
	0441	1.4	43		0447	1.5	46
	1108	2.5	76		1121	2.8	85
	1857	0.1	3		1906	0.0	0
5 Sa	0204	1.6	49	20 Su	0200	1.7	52
	0527	1.4	43		0548	1.4	43
	1150	2.5	76		1218	2.8	85
	1934	0.1	3		1949	0.0	0
6 Su	0230	1.6	49	21 M ●	0226	1.7	52
	0608	1.4	43		0643	1.2	37
	1229	2.6	79		1309	2.8	85
	2007	0.1	3		2026	0.1	3
7 M O	0250	1.6	49	22 Tu	0248	1.8	55
	0647	1.3	40		0733	1.1	34
	1307	2.6	79		1356	2.7	82
	2037	0.1	3		2058	0.3	9
8 Tu	0307	1.7	52	23 W	0309	1.9	58
	0727	1.2	37		0822	1.0	30
	1345	2.7	82		1441	2.6	79
	2107	0.2	6		2128	0.5	15
9 W	0325	1.7	52	24 Th	0331	2.0	61
	0810	1.1	34		0911	0.9	27
	1425	2.6	79		1526	2.4	73
	2136	0.2	6		2156	0.7	21
10 Th	0346	1.8	55	25 F	0355	2.1	64
	0857	1.0	30		1001	0.8	24
	1509	2.5	76		1613	2.2	67
	2207	0.4	12		2224	0.9	27
11 F	0413	1.9	58	26 Sa	0422	2.2	67
	0949	0.9	27		1055	0.8	24
	1557	2.4	73		1706	2.0	61
	2240	0.5	15		2253	1.0	30
12 Sa	0445	2.1	64	27 Su	0455	2.2	67
	1048	0.8	24		1155	0.8	24
	1653	2.2	67		1811	1.8	55
	2315	0.7	21		2326	1.2	37
13 Su	0522	2.2	67	28 M	0534	2.3	70
	1157	0.7	21		1304	0.7	21
	1801	1.9	58		1941	1.7	52
	2352	1.0	30				
14 M O	0605	2.3	70	29 Tu ◐	0005	1.4	43
	1317	0.6	18		0622	2.3	70
	1931	1.7	52		1422	0.7	21
					2137	1.6	49
15 Tu	0033	1.2	37	30 W	0058	1.5	46
	0657	2.4	73		0723	2.3	70
	1444	0.5	15		1539	0.6	18
	2131	1.6	49		2314	1.7	52
				31 Th	0214	1.6	49
					0836	2.3	70
					1645	0.5	15

September

Day	Time	Height (ft)	Height (cm)	Day	Time	Height (ft)	Height (cm)
1 F	0011	1.7	52	16 Sa	0019	1.8	55
	0333	1.6	49		0402	1.6	49
	0949	2.4	73		1022	2.6	79
	1738	0.4	12		1756	0.3	9
2 Sa	0047	1.8	55	17 Su	0048	1.9	58
	0437	1.5	46		0511	1.4	43
	1049	2.4	73		1130	2.6	79
	1822	0.4	12		1840	0.3	9
3 Su	0114	1.8	55	18 M	0111	1.9	58
	0527	1.4	43		0607	1.2	37
	1139	2.5	76		1226	2.6	79
	1858	0.3	9		1916	0.4	12
4 M	0134	1.8	55	19 Tu	0132	2.0	61
	0609	1.3	40		0655	1.0	30
	1223	2.6	79		1315	2.6	79
	1931	0.4	12		1947	0.6	18
5 Tu	0151	1.9	58	20 W ●	0150	2.1	64
	0648	1.1	34		0738	0.8	24
	1303	2.6	79		1359	2.5	76
	2000	0.4	12		2014	0.8	24
6 W O	0207	2.0	61	21 Th	0208	2.2	67
	0727	1.0	30		0819	0.7	21
	1344	2.6	79		1441	2.4	73
	2029	0.5	15		2039	0.9	27
7 Th	0225	2.1	64	22 F	0227	2.3	70
	0808	0.8	24		0859	0.6	18
	1426	2.6	79		1523	2.2	67
	2057	0.6	18		2103	1.1	34
8 F	0247	2.2	67	23 Sa	0250	2.4	73
	0853	0.7	21		0941	0.5	15
	1511	2.4	73		1607	2.1	64
	2126	0.8	24		2127	1.2	37
9 Sa	0314	2.3	70	24 Su	0316	2.4	73
	0942	0.6	18		1026	0.5	15
	1603	2.3	70		1658	1.9	58
	2156	1.0	30		2154	1.3	40
10 Su	0347	2.4	73	25 M	0347	2.5	76
	1038	0.5	15		1117	0.5	15
	1703	2.1	64		1801	1.8	55
	2228	1.2	37		2225	1.5	46
11 M	0425	2.5	76	26 Tu	0424	2.4	73
	1145	0.5	15		1217	0.6	18
	1820	1.8	55		1929	1.7	52
	2302	1.4	43		2304	1.6	49
12 Tu	0511	2.5	76	27 W ◐	0510	2.3	70
	1303	0.5	15		1329	0.6	18
	2009	1.7	52		2121	1.7	52
	2343	1.5	46				
13 W O	0610	2.5	76	28 Th	0008	1.6	49
	1431	0.4	12		0614	2.3	70
	2223	1.7	52		1444	0.6	18
					2240	1.8	55
14 Th	0047	1.6	49	29 F	0150	1.7	52
	0727	2.5	76		0741	2.2	67
	1554	0.3	9		1553	0.6	18
	2340	1.8	55		2322	1.9	58
15 F	0229	1.7	52	30 Sa	0324	1.6	49
	0859	2.5	76		0912	2.2	67
	1702	0.3	9		1648	0.5	15
					2350	1.9	58

Time meridian 75° W. 0000 is midnight. 1200 is noon. Times are not adjusted for Daylight Saving Time.
Heights are referred to mean lower low water which is the chart datum of soundings.

St. Petersburg, Florida, 2017
Times and Heights of High and Low Waters

183

October

Day	Time (h m)	Height (ft)	Height (cm)
1 Su	0430	1.5	46
	1025	2.3	70
	1733	0.5	15
2 M	0013	2.0	61
	0520	1.3	40
	1122	2.4	73
	1811	0.5	15
3 Tu	0032	2.0	61
	0602	1.1	34
	1211	2.4	73
	1845	0.6	18
4 W	0050	2.1	64
	0641	0.8	24
	1257	2.4	73
	1915	0.7	21
5 Th ○	0109	2.2	67
	0721	0.6	18
	1342	2.4	73
	1944	0.8	24
6 F	0130	2.4	73
	0802	0.4	12
	1429	2.3	70
	2012	1.0	30
7 Sa	0156	2.5	76
	0847	0.2	6
	1519	2.2	67
	2041	1.2	37
8 Su	0225	2.6	79
	0936	0.1	3
	1616	2.0	61
	2109	1.3	40
9 M	0300	2.7	82
	1032	0.1	3
	1725	1.9	58
	2139	1.5	46
10 Tu	0341	2.7	82
	1138	0.2	6
	1858	1.7	52
	2212	1.6	49
11 W	0431	2.6	79
	1253	0.2	6
12 Th ◗	0537	2.5	76
	1415	0.3	9
	2230	1.8	55
13 F	0058	1.7	52
	0710	2.4	73
	1530	0.3	9
	2307	1.8	55
14 Sa	0302	1.6	49
	0900	2.3	70
	1632	0.4	12
	2334	1.9	58
15 Su	0426	1.3	40
	1028	2.3	70
	1721	0.5	15
	2359	2.0	61
16 M	0527	1.1	34
	1136	2.3	70
	1801	0.6	18
17 Tu	0020	2.1	64
	0615	0.8	24
	1232	2.3	70
	1834	0.7	21
18 W	0040	2.2	67
	0657	0.6	18
	1320	2.2	67
	1901	0.9	27
19 Th ●	0058	2.3	70
	0735	0.4	12
	1404	2.1	64
	1925	1.0	30
20 F	0115	2.4	73
	0811	0.3	9
	1445	2.0	61
	1948	1.2	37
21 Sa	0135	2.5	76
	0846	0.2	6
	1525	1.9	58
	2010	1.3	40
22 Su	0158	2.5	76
	0923	0.2	6
	1608	1.8	55
	2033	1.4	43
23 M	0225	2.5	76
	1003	0.2	6
	1656	1.7	52
	2100	1.4	43
24 Tu	0257	2.5	76
	1048	0.2	6
	1756	1.7	52
	2132	1.5	46
25 W	0335	2.4	73
	1141	0.3	9
	1913	1.7	52
	2216	1.6	49
26 Th	0421	2.3	70
	1243	0.3	9
	2039	1.7	52
	2334	1.6	49
27 F ◐	0522	2.2	67
	1349	0.4	12
	2139	1.7	52
28 Sa	0127	1.6	49
	0647	2.0	61
	1453	0.4	12
	2216	1.8	55
29 Su	0303	1.4	43
	0827	2.0	61
	1548	0.5	15
	2245	1.9	58
30 M	0411	1.2	37
	0953	2.0	61
	1636	0.5	15
	2309	2.0	61
31 Tu	0503	0.9	27
	1101	2.0	61
	1717	0.6	18
	2331	2.1	64

November

Day	Time (h m)	Height (ft)	Height (cm)
1 W	0548	0.6	18
	1159	2.0	61
	1753	0.7	21
	2354	2.2	67
2 Th	0630	0.4	12
	1252	2.1	64
	1826	0.9	27
3 F	0018	2.4	73
	0712	0.1	3
	1344	2.0	61
	1857	1.0	30
4 Sa ○	0044	2.5	76
	0756	-0.1	-3
	1438	1.9	58
	1926	1.2	37
5 Su	0115	2.6	79
	0843	-0.3	-9
	1534	1.8	55
	1955	1.3	40
6 M	0150	2.7	82
	0933	-0.3	-9
	1637	1.7	52
	2024	1.4	43
7 Tu	0229	2.7	82
	1029	-0.3	-9
	1753	1.6	49
	2056	1.5	46
8 W	0315	2.7	82
	1131	-0.2	-6
	1927	1.6	49
	2139	1.5	46
9 Th	0409	2.5	76
	1238	0.0	0
	2052	1.6	49
	2310	1.5	46
10 F ○	0521	2.2	67
	1347	0.1	3
	2139	1.7	52
11 Sa	0124	1.5	46
	0702	2.0	61
	1452	0.2	6
	2212	1.8	55
12 Su	0315	1.2	37
	0856	1.9	58
	1547	0.4	12
	2240	1.9	58
13 M	0431	0.9	27
	1027	1.8	55
	1634	0.5	15
	2306	2.0	61
14 Tu	0527	0.6	18
	1138	1.8	55
	1712	0.7	21
	2330	2.1	64
15 W	0613	0.3	9
	1236	1.8	55
	1745	0.9	27
	2352	2.2	67
16 Th	0653	0.1	3
	1327	1.7	52
	1813	1.0	30
17 F	0013	2.3	70
	0729	0.0	0
	1413	1.7	52
	1838	1.1	34
18 Sa ●	0033	2.4	73
	0802	-0.1	-3
	1454	1.6	49
	1901	1.2	37
19 Su	0056	2.4	73
	0835	-0.2	-6
	1534	1.6	49
	1924	1.2	37
20 M	0122	2.4	73
	0909	-0.2	-6
	1613	1.5	46
	1950	1.3	40
21 Tu	0152	2.4	73
	0946	-0.2	-6
	1655	1.5	46
	2021	1.3	40
22 W	0227	2.4	73
	1027	-0.2	-6
	1742	1.5	46
	2101	1.3	40
23 Th	0307	2.3	70
	1112	-0.1	-3
	1835	1.5	46
	2156	1.3	40
24 F	0354	2.1	64
	1202	0.0	0
	1929	1.5	46
	2316	1.3	40
25 Sa	0452	2.0	61
	1256	0.1	3
	2018	1.6	49
26 Su ◐	0055	1.3	40
	0608	1.8	55
	1351	0.2	6
	2058	1.7	52
27 M	0228	1.1	34
	0742	1.6	49
	1444	0.3	9
	2132	1.8	55
28 Tu	0341	0.8	24
	0918	1.6	49
	1533	0.5	15
	2203	1.9	58
29 W	0440	0.5	15
	1040	1.6	49
	1618	0.6	18
	2233	2.1	64
30 Th	0530	0.2	6
	1151	1.6	49
	1659	0.8	24
	2304	2.2	67

December

Day	Time (h m)	Height (ft)	Height (cm)
1 F	0617	-0.2	-6
	1254	1.6	49
	1736	0.9	27
	2336	2.4	73
2 Sa	0704	-0.4	-12
	1354	1.6	49
	1811	1.0	30
3 Su ○	0010	2.5	76
	0751	-0.6	-18
	1452	1.5	46
	1844	1.1	34
4 M	0048	2.6	79
	0840	-0.7	-21
	1551	1.4	43
	1918	1.2	37
5 Tu	0130	2.7	82
	0930	-0.7	-21
	1650	1.4	43
	1955	1.2	37
6 W	0216	2.6	79
	1023	-0.6	-18
	1751	1.3	40
	2043	1.2	37
7 Th	0306	2.4	73
	1116	-0.5	-15
	1850	1.3	40
	2152	1.2	37
8 F	0404	2.2	67
	1211	-0.3	-9
	1941	1.4	43
	2329	1.2	37
9 Sa	0516	1.9	58
	1306	0.0	0
	2024	1.5	46
10 Su ○	0121	1.0	30
	0651	1.6	49
	1359	0.2	6
	2103	1.6	49
11 M	0302	0.8	24
	0842	1.4	43
	1449	0.4	12
	2138	1.8	55
12 Tu	0417	0.5	15
	1020	1.3	40
	1536	0.6	18
	2211	1.9	58
13 W	0515	0.2	6
	1139	1.3	40
	1618	0.8	24
	2241	2.0	61
14 Th	0602	-0.1	-3
	1244	1.3	40
	1655	0.9	27
	2310	2.1	64
15 F	0642	-0.3	-9
	1339	1.3	40
	1729	1.0	30
	2337	2.2	67
16 Sa	0719	-0.4	-12
	1425	1.3	40
	1800	1.1	34
17 Su	0004	2.2	67
	0753	-0.5	-15
	1505	1.3	40
	1828	1.1	34
18 M ●	0032	2.2	67
	0825	-0.5	-15
	1539	1.3	40
	1857	1.1	34
19 Tu	0103	2.2	67
	0858	-0.5	-15
	1609	1.3	40
	1929	1.1	34
20 W	0136	2.2	67
	0931	-0.5	-15
	1637	1.3	40
	2008	1.0	30
21 Th	0214	2.2	67
	1007	-0.4	-12
	1706	1.3	40
	2055	1.0	30
22 F	0255	2.1	64
	1044	-0.4	-12
	1739	1.3	40
	2152	1.0	30
23 Sa	0342	1.9	58
	1124	-0.3	-9
	1816	1.4	43
	2300	0.9	27
24 Su	0436	1.7	52
	1206	-0.1	-3
	1855	1.5	46
25 M	0021	0.8	24
	0543	1.5	46
	1251	0.0	0
	1936	1.6	49
26 Tu ◐	0146	0.7	21
	0708	1.3	40
	1339	0.2	6
	2017	1.7	52
27 W	0305	0.4	12
	0849	1.2	37
	1429	0.4	12
	2058	1.8	55
28 Th	0413	0.1	3
	1030	1.1	34
	1518	0.6	18
	2139	2.0	61
29 F	0513	-0.2	-6
	1156	1.2	37
	1606	0.8	24
	2221	2.1	64
30 Sa	0607	-0.5	-15
	1308	1.2	37
	1651	0.9	27
	2305	2.3	70
31 Su	0658	-0.8	-24
	1410	1.2	37
	1735	1.0	30
	2350	2.4	73

Time meridian 75° W. 0000 is midnight. 1200 is noon. Times are not adjusted for Daylight Saving Time.
Heights are referred to mean lower low water which is the chart datum of soundings.

Cedar Key, Florida, 2017

Times and Heights of High and Low Waters

January

Day	Time	ft	cm	Day	Time	ft	cm
1 Su	0246	3.7	113	16 M	0345	3.5	107
	0948	-0.6	-18		1031	-0.3	-9
	1618	3.1	94		1648	3.1	94
	2158	1.0	30		2245	0.7	21
2 M	0328	3.5	107	17 Tu	0431	3.2	98
	1024	-0.4	-12		1105	0.1	3
	1653	3.1	94		1721	3.1	94
	2244	0.9	27		2332	0.6	18
3 Tu	0416	3.4	104	18 W	0522	2.8	85
	1105	-0.2	-6		1140	0.4	12
	1732	3.1	94		1757	3.1	94
	2336	0.8	24				
4 W	0513	3.1	94	19 Th	0025	0.6	18
	1149	0.1	3		0623	2.5	76
	1815	3.2	98		1219	0.8	24
					1838	3.1	94
5 Th	0038	0.7	21	20 F	0128	0.6	18
	0624	2.8	85		0738	2.3	70
	1241	0.5	15		1307	1.1	34
	1905	3.2	98		1928	3.1	94
6 F	0150	0.5	15	21 Sa	0242	0.5	15
	0751	2.6	79		0906	2.2	67
	1344	0.8	24		1409	1.3	40
	2002	3.3	101		2025	3.1	94
7 Sa	0308	0.3	6	22 Su	0358	0.3	9
	0925	2.5	76		1032	2.2	67
	1456	1.1	34		1522	1.5	46
	2103	3.4	104		2125	3.2	98
8 Su	0422	-0.2	-6	23 M	0502	0.0	0
	1051	2.6	79		1140	2.4	73
	1609	1.3	40		1632	1.5	46
	2202	3.6	110		2221	3.3	101
9 M	0527	-0.6	-18	24 Tu	0553	-0.3	-9
	1202	2.8	85		1231	2.6	79
	1714	1.3	40		1730	1.4	43
	2259	3.7	113		2313	3.4	104
10 Tu	0622	-0.9	-27	25 W	0635	-0.5	-15
	1300	3.0	91		1312	2.8	85
	1812	1.2	37		1820	1.2	37
	2351	3.9	119		2358	3.5	107
11 W	0712	-1.1	-34	26 Th	0713	-0.6	-18
	1348	3.1	94		1347	2.9	88
	1903	1.1	34		1903	1.1	34
12 Th	0041	4.0	122	27 F	0041	3.6	110
	0758	-1.2	-37		0748	-0.7	-21
	1430	3.1	94		1419	3.0	91
	1950	1.0	30		1944	1.0	30
13 F	0129	4.0	122	28 Sa	0121	3.7	113
	0840	-1.1	-34		0822	-0.7	-21
	1508	3.2	98		1449	3.1	94
	2035	0.9	27		2023	0.8	24
14 Sa	0215	3.9	119	29 Su	0201	3.7	113
	0920	-0.9	-27		0855	-0.7	-21
	1543	3.1	94		1518	3.2	98
	2118	0.8	24		2103	0.7	21
15 Su	0300	3.7	113	30 M	0242	3.7	113
	0956	-0.6	-18		0929	-0.6	-18
	1616	3.1	94		1547	3.3	101
	2201	0.7	21		2143	0.5	15

February

Day	Time	ft	cm	Day	Time	ft	cm
1 W	0412	3.3	101	16 Th	0455	2.9	88
	1040	-0.1	-3		1055	0.5	15
	1651	3.4	104		1659	3.3	101
	2316	0.3	9		2339	0.3	9
2 Th	0506	3.0	91	17 F	0546	2.6	79
	1120	0.3	9		1128	0.8	24
	1729	3.4	104		1735	3.3	101
3 F	0013	0.2	6	18 Sa	0031	0.4	12
	0612	2.7	82		0650	2.3	70
	1206	0.7	21		1209	1.1	34
	1816	3.4	104		1820	3.2	98
4 Sa	0122	0.2	6	19 Su	0138	0.4	12
	0737	2.4	73		0815	2.1	64
	1303	1.1	34		1306	1.4	43
	1914	3.3	101		1919	3.1	94
5 Su	0244	0.0	0	20 M	0300	0.4	12
	0917	2.3	70		0952	2.1	64
	1419	1.4	43		1428	1.6	49
	2024	3.3	101		2032	3.0	91
6 M	0408	-0.2	-6	21 Tu	0420	0.2	6
	1054	2.4	73		1112	2.3	70
	1545	1.5	46		1555	1.6	49
	2138	3.4	104		2145	3.1	94
7 Tu	0518	-0.5	-15	22 W	0521	-0.1	-3
	1204	2.7	82		1205	2.6	79
	1702	1.4	43		1705	1.4	43
	2247	3.5	107		2248	3.3	101
8 W	0615	-0.8	-24	23 Th	0608	-0.3	-9
	1254	2.9	88		1244	2.8	85
	1803	1.2	37		1800	1.2	37
	2346	3.7	113		2341	3.4	104
9 Th	0702	-0.9	-27	24 F	0648	-0.5	-15
	1334	3.0	91		1317	3.0	91
	1854	0.9	27		1845	0.9	27
10 F	0038	3.8	116	25 Sa	0028	3.6	110
	0744	-0.9	-27		0724	-0.6	-18
	1408	3.1	94		1347	3.1	94
	1939	0.7	21		1927	0.6	18
11 Sa	0125	3.8	116	26 Su	0112	3.7	113
	0821	-0.8	-24		0758	-0.6	-18
	1438	3.2	98		1415	3.3	101
	2021	0.5	15		2006	0.4	12
12 Su	0209	3.8	116	27 M	0154	3.8	116
	0855	-0.6	-18		0832	-0.5	-15
	1507	3.3	101		1442	3.4	104
	2100	0.4	12		2046	0.1	3
13 M	0250	3.6	110	28 Tu	0237	3.7	113
	0927	-0.4	-12		0906	-0.3	-9
	1534	3.3	101		1510	3.5	107
	2138	0.3	9		2127	0.0	0
14 Tu	0330	3.4	104				
	0956	-0.1	-3				
	1601	3.3	101				
	2216	0.2	6				
15 W	0411	3.2	98				
	1025	0.2	6				
	1629	3.3	101				
	2255	0.2	6				

March

Day	Time	ft	cm	Day	Time	ft	cm
1 W	0322	3.6	110	16 Th	0352	3.2	98
	0941	-0.1	-3		0949	0.5	15
	1540	3.6	110		1541	3.6	110
	2210	-0.2	-6		2222	0.0	0
2 Th	0409	3.3	101	17 F	0432	2.9	88
	1016	0.2	6		1018	0.7	21
	1612	3.6	110		1610	3.5	107
	2258	-0.2	-6		2300	0.0	0
3 F	0502	3.0	91	18 Sa	0518	2.7	82
	1054	0.6	18		1050	1.0	30
	1650	3.6	110		1643	3.5	107
	2353	-0.1	-3		2345	0.2	6
4 Sa	0607	2.6	79	19 Su	0614	2.4	73
	1138	1.0	30		1129	1.3	40
	1736	3.5	107		1725	3.3	101
5 Su	0100	0.0	0	20 M	0043	0.3	9
	0730	2.3	70		0731	2.3	70
	1235	1.4	43		1224	1.5	46
	1837	3.3	101		1821	3.1	94
6 M	0224	0.0	0	21 Tu	0159	0.4	12
	0915	2.3	70		0905	2.3	70
	1358	1.6	49		1347	1.7	52
	1957	3.2	98		1941	3.0	91
7 Tu	0353	-0.1	-3	22 W	0324	0.4	12
	1051	2.4	73		1026	2.4	73
	1535	1.6	49		1522	1.6	49
	2126	3.2	98		2108	3.0	91
8 W	0505	-0.3	-9	23 Th	0436	0.2	6
	1151	2.7	82		1121	2.7	82
	1656	1.4	43		1639	1.4	43
	2243	3.4	104		2222	3.2	98
9 Th	0600	-0.4	-12	24 F	0529	0.0	0
	1232	2.9	88		1201	3.0	91
	1756	1.0	30		1736	1.0	30
	2345	3.5	107		2322	3.4	104
10 F	0644	-0.5	-15	25 Sa	0613	-0.2	-6
	1305	3.1	94		1234	3.2	98
	1844	0.7	21		1823	0.6	18
11 Sa	0035	3.6	110	26 Su	0013	3.6	110
	0722	-0.5	-15		0652	-0.2	-6
	1334	3.3	101		1304	3.4	104
	1926	0.4	12		1906	0.3	9
12 Su	0120	3.7	113	27 M	0101	3.7	113
	0755	-0.4	-12		0729	-0.2	-6
	1400	3.4	104		1333	3.6	110
	2004	0.2	6		1947	-0.1	-3
13 M	0200	3.6	110	28 Tu	0146	3.8	116
	0826	-0.2	-6		0805	0.0	0
	1425	3.5	107		1402	3.7	113
	2039	0.0	0		2028	-0.3	-9
14 Tu	0238	3.5	107	29 W	0232	3.7	113
	0854	0.0	0		0841	0.2	6
	1450	3.5	107		1432	3.8	116
	2114	-0.1	-3		2110	-0.5	-15
15 W	0315	3.4	104	30 Th	0319	3.6	110
	0922	0.3	9		0917	0.4	12
	1515	3.6	110		1504	3.9	119
	2147	-0.1	-3		2155	-0.6	-18
				31 F	0408	3.3	101
					0954	0.7	21
					1539	3.9	119
					2243	-0.5	-15

Time meridian 75° W. 0000 is midnight. 1200 is noon. Times are not adjusted for Daylight Saving Time.
Heights are referred to mean lower low water which is the chart datum of soundings.

Cedar Key, Florida, 2017

Times and Heights of High and Low Waters

April

Day	Time	ft	cm	Day	Time	ft	cm
1 Sa	0502	3.0	91	16 Su	0458	2.9	88
	1034	1.1	34		1023	1.3	40
	1619	3.8	116		1604	3.7	113
	2338	-0.3	-9		2312	0.1	3
2 Su	0606	2.7	82	17 M	0549	2.7	82
	1120	1.4	43		1104	1.5	46
	1708	3.6	110		1646	3.5	107
3 M	0043	-0.1	-3	18 Tu	0003	0.3	9
	0727	2.5	76		0656	2.6	79
	1222	1.6	49		1200	1.6	49
	1813	3.4	104		1740	3.3	101
4 Tu	0203	0.1	3	19 W	0108	0.4	12
	0903	2.5	76		0815	2.6	79
	1350	1.7	52		1319	1.7	52
	1942	3.1	94		1858	3.1	94
5 W	0329	0.2	6	20 Th	0225	0.5	15
	1024	2.6	79		0929	2.7	82
	1529	1.6	49		1450	1.6	49
	2119	3.1	94		2032	3.0	91
6 Th	0440	0.1	3	21 F	0339	0.4	12
	1116	2.9	88		1025	2.9	88
	1648	1.2	37		1608	1.3	40
	2239	3.2	98		2153	3.2	98
7 F	0533	0.1	3	22 Sa	0440	0.4	12
	1153	3.1	94		1108	3.2	98
	1745	0.8	24		1708	0.9	27
	2340	3.4	104		2300	3.4	104
8 Sa	0615	0.1	3	23 Su	0531	0.3	9
	1224	3.3	101		1144	3.5	107
	1830	0.4	12		1758	0.4	12
					2357	3.6	110
9 Su	0028	3.5	107	24 M	0615	0.3	9
	0651	0.1	3		1218	3.7	113
	1252	3.5	107		1844	0.0	0
	1909	0.1	3				
10 M	0110	3.5	107	25 Tu	0049	3.7	113
	0723	0.3	9		0657	0.4	12
	1318	3.6	110		1250	3.9	119
	1944	-0.1	-3		1927	-0.4	-12
11 Tu O	0149	3.5	107	26 W ●	0138	3.8	116
	0753	0.4	12		0736	0.6	18
	1343	3.7	113		1323	4.1	125
	2018	-0.2	-6		2011	-0.7	-21
12 W	0225	3.4	104	27 Th	0227	3.7	113
	0821	0.6	18		0815	0.8	24
	1408	3.8	116		1358	4.2	128
	2050	-0.2	-6		2056	-0.8	-24
13 Th	0301	3.3	101	28 F	0317	3.5	107
	0849	0.7	21		0855	1.0	30
	1434	3.8	116		1434	4.2	128
	2122	-0.2	-6		2142	-0.8	-24
14 F	0337	3.2	98	29 Sa	0407	3.3	101
	0918	0.9	27		0936	1.2	37
	1501	3.8	116		1514	4.2	128
	2155	-0.2	-6		2231	-0.6	-18
15 Sa	0415	3.0	91	30 Su	0502	3.1	94
	0948	1.1	34		1020	1.4	43
	1531	3.8	116		1559	4.0	122
	2230	-0.1	-3		2325	-0.3	-9

May

Day	Time	ft	cm	Day	Time	ft	cm
1 M	0603	2.9	88	16 Tu	0529	3.0	91
	1111	1.6	49		1048	1.6	49
	1652	3.7	113		1620	3.7	113
					2334	0.2	6
2 Tu	0025	0.0	0	17 W	0624	2.9	88
	0713	2.7	82		1144	1.7	52
	1217	1.7	52		1714	3.5	107
	1800	3.4	104				
3 W	0135	0.3	9	18 Th	0028	0.4	12
	0828	2.8	85		0726	3.0	91
	1342	1.7	52		1256	1.7	52
	1929	3.1	94		1827	3.2	98
4 Th	0250	0.5	15	19 F	0133	0.6	18
	0935	2.9	88		0828	3.1	94
	1514	1.5	46		1417	1.6	49
	2105	3.0	91		1957	3.1	94
5 F	0358	0.6	18	20 Sa	0242	0.7	21
	1025	3.1	94		0929	3.3	101
	1630	1.1	34		1534	1.2	37
	2225	3.1	94		2124	3.2	98
6 Sa	0452	0.7	21	21 Su	0348	0.8	24
	1104	3.4	104		1012	3.5	107
	1726	0.7	21		1639	0.7	21
	2327	3.2	98		2238	3.3	101
7 Su	0536	0.7	21	22 M	0446	0.8	24
	1137	3.6	110		1054	3.8	116
	1810	0.3	9		1733	0.2	6
					2342	3.5	107
8 M	0016	3.4	104	23 Tu	0537	0.9	27
	0613	0.8	24		1133	4.0	122
	1207	3.8	116		1823	-0.2	-6
	1849	0.0	0				
9 Tu	0058	3.4	104	24 W	0039	3.6	110
	0647	0.9	27		0624	1.0	30
	1236	3.9	119		1212	4.2	128
	1924	-0.1	-3		1911	-0.6	-18
10 W O	0137	3.4	104	25 Th ●	0132	3.7	113
	0719	1.0	30		0709	1.2	37
	1304	4.0	122		1251	4.4	134
	1957	-0.2	-6		1958	-0.8	-24
11 Th	0214	3.4	104	26 F	0223	3.7	113
	0750	1.1	34		0753	1.3	40
	1332	4.0	122		1331	4.5	137
	2030	-0.3	-9		2045	-0.9	-27
12 F	0249	3.3	101	27 Sa	0314	3.5	107
	0821	1.2	37		0836	1.4	43
	1400	4.0	122		1414	4.5	137
	2101	-0.2	-6		2132	-0.8	-24
13 Sa	0325	3.2	98	28 Su	0404	3.4	104
	0853	1.3	40		0921	1.5	46
	1430	4.0	122		1459	4.4	134
	2134	-0.2	-6		2220	-0.5	-15
14 Su	0403	3.2	98	29 M	0454	3.3	101
	0926	1.4	43		1009	1.6	49
	1502	3.9	119		1547	4.1	125
	2209	-0.1	-3		2309	-0.2	-6
15 M	0443	3.1	94	30 Tu	0546	3.1	94
	1004	1.5	46		1103	1.7	52
	1538	3.8	116		1642	3.8	116
	2248	0.0	0				
				31 W	0001	0.2	6
					0641	3.1	94
					1206	1.7	52
					1748	3.5	107

June

Day	Time	ft	cm	Day	Time	ft	cm
1 Th	0057	0.5	15	16 F	0637	3.4	104
	0738	3.1	94		1230	1.6	49
	1321	1.6	49		1805	3.4	104
	1908	3.2	98				
2 F	0158	0.8	24	17 Sa	0049	0.7	21
	0833	3.2	98		0730	3.4	104
	1444	1.4	43		1343	1.4	43
	2037	3.0	91		1929	3.2	98
3 Sa	0300	1.1	34	18 Su	0152	0.9	27
	0924	3.4	104		0825	3.6	110
	1600	1.1	34		1500	1.1	34
	2159	3.0	91		2058	3.1	94
4 Su	0358	1.2	37	19 M	0258	1.2	37
	1009	3.6	110		0918	3.8	116
	1659	0.7	21		1610	0.6	18
	2306	3.1	94		2220	3.2	98
5 M	0448	1.3	40	20 Tu	0404	1.3	40
	1048	3.8	116		1008	4.0	122
	1747	0.4	12		1712	0.2	6
					2331	3.4	104
6 Tu	0000	3.2	98	21 W	0503	1.4	43
	0532	1.4	43		1056	4.3	131
	1124	3.9	119		1807	-0.3	-9
	1828	0.1	3				
7 W	0045	3.3	101	22 Th	0032	3.5	107
	0611	1.4	43		0557	1.5	46
	1158	4.1	125		1143	4.5	137
	1905	-0.1	-3		1858	-0.6	-18
8 Th	0125	3.3	101	23 F ●	0127	3.6	110
	0648	1.5	46		0647	1.6	49
	1231	4.1	125		1229	4.6	140
	1939	-0.1	-3		1947	-0.7	-21
9 F O	0203	3.4	104	24 Sa	0218	3.6	110
	0723	1.5	46		0735	1.6	49
	1303	4.2	128		1315	4.7	143
	2012	-0.2	-6		2034	-0.7	-21
10 Sa	0239	3.3	101	25 Su	0305	3.6	110
	0758	1.6	49		0821	1.6	49
	1335	4.2	128		1402	4.6	140
	2045	-0.2	-6		2120	-0.6	-18
11 Su	0315	3.3	101	26 M	0350	3.5	107
	0833	1.6	49		0908	1.6	49
	1408	4.2	128		1449	4.5	137
	2118	-0.1	-3		2204	-0.4	-12
12 M	0350	3.3	101	27 Tu	0432	3.5	107
	0910	1.6	49		0956	1.5	46
	1443	4.1	125		1539	4.2	128
	2152	0.0	0		2247	0.0	0
13 Tu	0426	3.3	101	28 W	0514	3.4	104
	0950	1.6	49		1048	1.5	46
	1521	4.0	122		1631	3.9	119
	2228	0.1	3		2330	0.4	12
14 W	0505	3.3	101	29 Th	0556	3.4	104
	1035	1.7	52		1144	1.5	46
	1605	3.9	119		1730	3.5	107
	2309	0.2	6				
15 Th	0548	3.3	101	30 F	0014	0.8	24
	1128	1.7	52		0640	3.4	104
	1657	3.6	110		1248	1.4	43
	2355	0.4	12		1839	3.2	98

Time meridian 75° W. 0000 is midnight. 1200 is noon. Times are not adjusted for Daylight Saving Time.
Heights are referred to mean lower low water which is the chart datum of soundings.

Cedar Key, Florida, 2017
Times and Heights of High and Low Waters

July

Day	Time	ft	cm		Day	Time	ft	cm
1 Sa	0102	1.1	34		16 Su ☽	0013	0.9	27
	0728	3.5	107			0635	3.7	113
	1401	1.3	40			1312	1.2	37
	1959	3.0	91			1908	3.2	98
2 Su	0156	1.4	43		17 M	0109	1.3	40
	0819	3.6	110			0730	3.8	116
	1517	1.1	34			1429	0.9	27
	2124	2.9	88			2039	3.1	94
3 M	0255	1.6	49		18 Tu	0216	1.6	49
	0910	3.7	113			0830	3.9	119
	1625	0.8	24			1547	0.6	18
	2239	2.9	88			2209	3.1	94
4 Tu	0355	1.7	52		19 W	0329	1.8	55
	0959	3.9	119			0932	4.1	125
	1720	0.5	15			1656	0.2	6
	2340	3.1	94			2325	3.3	101
5 W	0450	1.8	55		20 Th	0438	1.8	55
	1045	4.0	122			1031	4.3	131
	1805	0.3	9			1755	-0.2	-6
6 Th	0029	3.2	98		21 F	0027	3.4	104
	0538	1.8	55			0538	1.8	55
	1127	4.1	125			1126	4.5	137
	1845	0.1	3			1848	-0.4	-12
7 F	0111	3.3	101		22 Sa	0119	3.5	110
	0621	1.7	52			0632	1.7	52
	1206	4.2	128			1218	4.7	143
	1922	0.0	0			1936	-0.5	-15
8 Sa ○	0149	3.4	104		23 Su ●	0204	3.6	110
	0701	1.7	52			0721	1.5	46
	1243	4.3	131			1307	4.7	143
	1956	-0.1	-3			2020	-0.5	-15
9 Su	0224	3.4	104		24 M	0244	3.6	110
	0740	1.7	52			0808	1.4	43
	1319	4.3	131			1355	4.7	143
	2028	-0.1	-3			2102	-0.3	-9
10 M	0257	3.5	107		25 Tu	0321	3.7	113
	0818	1.6	49			0854	1.3	40
	1355	4.3	131			1442	4.5	137
	2100	0.0	0			2141	-0.1	-3
11 Tu	0328	3.5	107		26 W	0356	3.7	113
	0856	1.6	49			0939	1.2	37
	1432	4.2	128			1528	4.2	128
	2133	0.0	0			2217	0.3	9
12 W	0400	3.5	107		27 Th	0429	3.7	113
	0936	1.5	46			1025	1.2	37
	1511	4.1	125			1616	3.9	119
	2207	0.1	3			2253	0.6	18
13 Th	0432	3.6	110		28 F	0503	3.7	113
	1019	1.5	46			1113	1.2	37
	1555	4.0	122			1707	3.6	110
	2244	0.3	9			2329	1.0	30
14 F	0508	3.6	110		29 Sa	0540	3.7	113
	1108	1.4	43			1206	1.2	37
	1646	3.7	113			1806	3.2	98
	2325	0.6	18					
15 Sa	0548	3.7	113		30 Su ☾	0008	1.3	40
	1204	1.3	40			0622	3.7	113
	1749	3.5	107			1309	1.2	37
						1917	3.0	91
					31 M	0055	1.6	49
						0712	3.7	113
						1422	1.1	34
						2041	2.8	85

August

Day	Time	ft	cm		Day	Time	ft	cm
1 Tu	0154	1.9	58		16 W	0145	1.9	58
	0810	3.7	113			0752	3.9	119
	1541	1.0	30			1528	0.6	18
	2207	2.8	85			2205	3.0	91
2 W	0304	2.0	61		17 Th	0307	2.0	61
	0912	3.8	116			0908	4.0	122
	1648	0.7	21			1644	0.3	9
	2316	3.0	91			2321	3.2	98
3 Th	0412	2.0	61		18 F	0424	1.9	58
	1009	3.9	119			1018	4.2	128
	1740	0.5	15			1745	0.0	0
4 F	0008	3.2	98		19 Sa	0017	3.4	104
	0510	1.9	58			0529	1.7	52
	1101	4.0	122			1120	4.4	134
	1823	0.3	9			1836	-0.2	-6
5 Sa	0050	3.3	101		20 Su	0100	3.6	110
	0559	1.8	55			0623	1.5	46
	1147	4.2	128			1214	4.5	137
	1900	0.1	3			1920	-0.3	-9
6 Su	0125	3.4	104		21 M ●	0138	3.7	113
	0643	1.6	49			0710	1.2	37
	1228	4.3	131			1303	4.6	140
	1934	0.1	3			2000	-0.2	-6
7 M ○	0157	3.5	107		22 Tu	0211	3.7	113
	0723	1.5	46			0755	1.0	30
	1307	4.3	131			1349	4.5	137
	2007	0.0	0			2037	0.0	0
8 Tu	0227	3.6	110		23 W	0242	3.8	116
	0802	1.4	43			0837	0.9	27
	1346	4.3	131			1432	4.4	134
	2038	0.1	3			2111	0.3	9
9 W	0256	3.7	113		24 Th	0312	3.8	116
	0840	1.2	37			0917	0.8	24
	1424	4.3	131			1515	4.1	125
	2110	0.2	6			2143	0.6	18
10 Th	0324	3.8	116		25 F	0341	3.8	116
	0919	1.1	34			0957	0.8	24
	1505	4.2	128			1558	3.9	119
	2144	0.3	9			2214	0.9	27
11 F	0353	3.8	116		26 Sa	0411	3.8	116
	1001	1.0	30			1038	0.8	24
	1549	4.0	122			1643	3.6	110
	2219	0.5	15			2246	1.2	37
12 Sa	0425	3.9	119		27 Su	0443	3.8	116
	1047	0.9	27			1123	0.9	27
	1639	3.8	116			1734	3.2	98
	2257	0.8	24			2321	1.4	43
13 Su	0502	3.9	119		28 M	0521	3.8	116
	1140	0.9	27			1216	1.0	30
	1739	3.4	104			1837	3.0	91
	2341	1.2	37					
14 M ☾	0547	3.9	119		29 Tu ☾	0004	1.7	52
	1245	0.8	24			0608	3.7	113
	1856	3.1	94			1322	1.1	34
						1958	2.8	85
15 Tu	0035	1.6	49		30 W	0102	1.9	58
	0643	3.9	119			0710	3.6	110
	1403	0.8	24			1444	1.0	30
	2030	3.0	91			2127	2.8	85
					31 Th	0218	2.1	64
						0824	3.6	110
						1604	0.9	27
						2242	2.9	88

September

Day	Time	ft	cm		Day	Time	ft	cm
1 F	0339	2.0	61		16 Sa	0419	1.8	55
	0936	3.7	113			1014	3.9	119
	1705	0.7	21			1728	0.2	6
	2335	3.1	94			2353	3.4	104
2 Sa	0446	1.8	55		17 Su	0523	1.4	43
	1037	3.8	116			1118	4.1	125
	1751	0.4	12			1816	0.1	3
3 Su	0016	3.3	101		18 M	0030	3.6	110
	0538	1.6	49			0614	1.1	34
	1129	4.0	122			1212	4.2	128
	1830	0.3	9			1857	0.1	3
4 M	0049	3.5	107		19 Tu	0102	3.7	113
	0623	1.3	40			0658	0.7	21
	1214	4.2	128			1258	4.3	131
	1905	0.2	6			1934	0.2	6
5 Tu	0120	3.6	110		20 W ●	0132	3.8	116
	0704	1.1	34			0739	0.5	15
	1255	4.3	131			1341	4.2	128
	1938	0.2	6			2007	0.4	12
6 W ○	0148	3.7	113		21 Th	0200	3.9	119
	0743	0.9	27			0817	0.4	12
	1336	4.3	131			1421	4.1	125
	2011	0.3	9			2038	0.6	18
7 Th	0215	3.8	116		22 F	0227	3.9	119
	0821	0.7	21			0854	0.3	9
	1417	4.2	128			1501	3.9	119
	2044	0.4	12			2108	0.9	27
8 F	0243	3.9	119		23 Sa	0254	3.9	119
	0900	0.5	15			0930	0.3	9
	1459	4.1	125			1540	3.7	113
	2118	0.6	18			2138	1.1	34
9 Sa	0312	4.0	122		24 Su	0322	3.9	119
	0942	0.4	12			1006	0.4	12
	1544	3.9	119			1621	3.4	104
	2154	0.9	27			2209	1.3	40
10 Su	0344	4.1	125		25 M	0353	3.9	119
	1028	0.4	12			1045	0.5	15
	1635	3.6	110			1708	3.2	98
	2232	1.2	37			2243	1.5	46
11 M	0422	4.1	125		26 Tu	0428	3.8	116
	1121	0.4	12			1131	0.7	21
	1735	3.3	101			1804	3.0	91
	2316	1.5	46			2326	1.7	52
12 Tu	0507	4.0	122		27 W ☾	0513	3.6	110
	1225	0.5	15			1228	0.8	24
	1852	3.0	91			1917	2.8	85
13 W ☽	0012	1.8	55		28 Th	0023	1.9	58
	0607	3.8	116			0614	3.4	104
	1344	0.6	18			1342	0.9	27
	2027	2.9	88			2041	2.8	85
14 Th	0128	2.0	61		29 F	0142	2.0	61
	0726	3.7	113			0735	3.3	101
	1511	0.5	15			1504	0.9	27
	2200	3.0	91			2156	2.9	88
15 F	0258	2.0	61		30 Sa	0307	1.9	58
	0855	3.8	116			0900	3.4	104
	1629	0.4	12			1615	0.8	24
	2306	3.2	98			2250	3.1	94

Time meridian 75° W. 0000 is midnight. 1200 is noon. Times are not adjusted for Daylight Saving Time.
Heights are referred to mean lower low water which is the chart datum of soundings.

Cedar Key, Florida, 2017
Times and Heights of High and Low Waters

October

Day	Time	ft	cm	Day	Time	ft	cm
1 Su	0419	1.6	49	16 M	0513	1.0	30
	1010	3.5	107		1115	3.7	113
	1708	0.6	18		1748	0.4	12
	2330	3.3	101		2351	3.6	110
2 M	0514	1.3	40	17 Tu	0602	0.6	18
	1107	3.8	116		1207	3.8	116
	1751	0.4	12		1827	0.5	15
3 Tu	0004	3.5	107	18 W	0022	3.7	113
	0600	0.9	27		0644	0.3	9
	1157	3.9	119		1252	3.9	119
	1829	0.4	12		1902	0.6	18
4 W	0035	3.7	113	19 Th ●	0051	3.9	119
	0642	0.6	18		0722	0.0	0
	1242	4.1	125		1332	3.8	116
	1906	0.4	12		1935	0.8	24
5 Th O	0104	3.8	116	20 F	0119	3.9	119
	0722	0.3	9		0758	-0.1	-3
	1326	4.1	125		1411	3.7	113
	1941	0.5	15		2006	0.9	27
6 F	0133	4.0	122	21 Sa	0146	3.9	119
	0802	0.0	0		0832	-0.1	-3
	1410	4.1	125		1448	3.6	110
	2017	0.7	21		2036	1.1	34
7 Sa	0203	4.1	125	22 Su	0214	3.9	119
	0843	-0.1	-3		0905	-0.1	-3
	1455	3.9	119		1526	3.5	107
	2054	0.9	27		2107	1.2	37
8 Su	0235	4.1	125	23 M	0243	3.9	119
	0927	-0.2	-6		0939	0.0	0
	1543	3.7	113		1605	3.3	101
	2132	1.2	37		2139	1.4	43
9 M	0311	4.1	125	24 Tu	0314	3.8	116
	1014	-0.1	-3		1016	0.1	3
	1635	3.4	104		1648	3.1	94
	2213	1.4	43		2216	1.5	46
10 Tu	0351	4.1	125	25 W	0350	3.7	113
	1107	0.0	0		1057	0.1	3
	1736	3.1	94		1738	2.9	88
	2300	1.6	49		2259	1.6	49
11 W	0440	3.9	119	26 Th	0433	3.5	107
	1209	0.2	6		1146	0.5	15
	1850	2.9	88		1839	2.8	85
					2356	1.8	55
12 Th ◑	0001	1.8	55	27 F ◐	0530	3.3	101
	0545	3.7	113		1247	0.6	18
	1324	0.4	12		1949	2.8	85
	2017	2.8	85				
13 F	0121	1.9	58	28 Sa	0109	1.8	55
	0712	3.5	107		0648	3.1	94
	1448	0.5	15		1359	0.7	21
	2136	3.0	91		2057	2.9	88
14 Sa	0253	1.8	55	29 Su	0232	1.6	49
	0848	3.4	104		0818	3.1	94
	1603	0.5	15		1511	0.7	21
	2234	3.2	98		2152	3.1	94
15 Su	0413	1.4	43	30 M	0345	1.3	40
	1011	3.5	107		0937	3.2	98
	1701	0.4	12		1613	0.7	21
	2316	3.4	104		2237	3.3	101
				31 Tu	0444	0.9	27
					1042	3.4	104
					1704	0.6	18
					2314	3.5	107

November

Day	Time	ft	cm	Day	Time	ft	cm
1 W	0534	0.5	15	16 Th	0628	-0.1	-3
	1138	3.6	110		1244	3.4	104
	1750	0.6	18		1829	1.0	30
	2348	3.7	113				
2 Th	0619	0.0	0	17 F	0013	3.8	116
	1229	3.7	113		0706	-0.3	-9
	1831	0.7	21		1325	3.4	104
					1904	1.1	34
3 F	0021	3.9	119	18 Sa ●	0043	3.8	116
	0702	-0.3	-9		0741	-0.4	-12
	1317	3.8	116		1403	3.4	104
	1912	0.8	24		1937	1.1	34
4 Sa O	0055	4.1	125	19 Su	0113	3.9	119
	0745	-0.6	-18		0814	-0.4	-12
	1405	3.8	116		1439	3.3	101
	1952	1.0	30		2010	1.2	37
5 Su	0129	4.2	128	20 M	0143	3.8	116
	0830	-0.7	-21		0847	-0.4	-12
	1453	3.6	110		1515	3.2	98
	2032	1.1	34		2043	1.3	40
6 M	0207	4.2	128	21 Tu	0215	3.8	116
	0915	-0.7	-21		0920	-0.3	-9
	1543	3.5	107		1552	3.1	94
	2114	1.3	40		2118	1.4	43
7 Tu	0248	4.2	128	22 W	0248	3.7	113
	1004	-0.6	-18		0955	-0.2	-6
	1636	3.2	98		1631	3.0	91
	2200	1.5	46		2157	1.4	43
8 W	0333	4.0	122	23 Th	0325	3.6	110
	1056	-0.4	-12		1032	-0.1	-3
	1734	3.0	91		1713	3.0	91
	2251	1.6	49		2241	1.5	46
9 Th	0427	3.8	116	24 F	0408	3.4	104
	1154	-0.1	-3		1114	0.1	3
	1838	2.9	88		1801	2.9	88
	2354	1.6	49		2333	1.5	46
10 F O	0533	3.4	104	25 Sa	0500	3.2	98
	1259	0.3	9		1204	0.3	9
	1946	2.9	88		1855	2.9	88
11 Sa	0112	1.6	49	26 Su ◐	0037	1.4	43
	0659	3.2	98		0609	3.0	91
	1411	0.5	15		1302	0.5	15
	2051	3.0	91		1952	3.0	91
12 Su	0239	1.4	43	27 M	0151	1.3	40
	0834	3.0	91		0734	2.8	85
	1521	0.7	21		1407	0.6	18
	2145	3.1	94		2047	3.1	94
13 M	0357	1.0	30	28 Tu	0305	1.0	30
	0959	3.1	94		0900	2.8	85
	1621	0.7	21		1513	0.8	24
	2230	3.3	101		2137	3.3	101
14 Tu	0457	0.6	18	29 W	0411	0.6	18
	1106	3.2	98		1015	3.0	91
	1710	0.8	24		1614	0.8	24
	2307	3.5	107		2222	3.5	107
15 W	0546	0.2	6	30 Th	0507	0.1	3
	1159	3.3	101		1120	3.2	98
	1752	0.9	27		1709	0.9	27
	2341	3.7	113		2303	3.7	113

December

Day	Time	ft	cm	Day	Time	ft	cm
1 F	0558	-0.4	-12	16 Sa	0651	-0.5	-15
	1218	3.3	101		1318	3.0	91
	1759	1.0	30		1837	1.2	37
	2343	3.9	119				
2 Sa	0646	-0.8	-24	17 Su	0014	3.7	113
	1311	3.4	104		0727	-0.6	-18
	1846	1.1	34		1356	3.1	94
					1915	1.2	37
3 Su O	0024	4.1	125	18 M ●	0049	3.7	113
	0733	-1.0	-30		0800	-0.6	-18
	1402	3.4	104		1431	3.1	94
	1931	1.2	37		1951	1.2	37
4 M	0106	4.2	128	19 Tu	0124	3.7	113
	0820	-1.1	-34		0833	-0.6	-18
	1452	3.4	104		1505	3.0	91
	2016	1.2	37		2027	1.2	37
5 Tu	0149	4.2	128	20 W	0158	3.7	113
	0907	-1.1	-34		0905	-0.5	-15
	1541	3.3	101		1538	3.0	91
	2102	1.3	40		2104	1.2	37
6 W	0236	4.1	125	21 Th	0234	3.6	110
	0955	-0.9	-27		0937	-0.4	-12
	1629	3.1	94		1611	3.0	91
	2150	1.3	40		2142	1.2	37
7 Th	0325	3.9	119	22 F	0311	3.5	107
	1043	-0.6	-18		1011	-0.3	-9
	1717	3.0	91		1645	3.0	91
	2243	1.3	40		2224	1.1	34
8 F	0420	3.6	110	23 Sa	0353	3.4	104
	1133	-0.2	-6		1047	-0.2	-6
	1807	3.0	91		1722	3.1	94
	2343	1.2	37		2311	1.1	34
9 Sa	0524	3.3	101	24 Su	0441	3.2	98
	1225	0.2	6		1127	0.0	0
	1859	2.9	88		1803	3.1	94
10 Su ◑	0052	1.1	34	25 M	0005	1.0	30
	0640	2.9	88		0540	2.9	88
	1322	0.5	15		1214	0.3	9
	1953	3.0	91		1849	3.1	94
11 M	0209	1.0	30	26 Tu ◐	0110	0.9	27
	0808	2.7	82		0656	2.7	82
	1424	0.8	24		1310	0.6	18
	2045	3.1	94		1941	3.2	98
12 Tu	0327	0.7	21	27 W	0222	0.6	18
	0935	2.6	79		0824	2.6	79
	1526	1.0	30		1415	0.9	27
	2135	3.2	98		2036	3.3	101
13 W	0433	0.3	9	28 Th	0336	0.3	9
	1050	2.7	82		0950	2.6	79
	1623	1.1	34		1525	1.1	34
	2220	3.4	104		2131	3.4	104
14 Th	0527	0.0	0	29 F	0442	-0.2	-6
	1149	2.8	85		1107	2.8	85
	1713	1.2	37		1632	1.2	37
	2301	3.5	107		2224	3.6	110
15 F	0611	-0.3	-9	30 Sa	0540	-0.6	-18
	1237	2.9	88		1212	3.0	91
	1757	1.2	37		1732	1.2	37
	2338	3.6	110		2314	3.8	116
				31 Su	0634	-1.0	-30
					1308	3.1	94
					1826	1.2	37

Time meridian 75° W. 0000 is midnight. 1200 is noon. Times are not adjusted for Daylight Saving Time.
Heights are referred to mean lower low water which is the chart datum of soundings.

St. Marks River Entrance, Florida, 2017

Times and Heights of High and Low Waters

January

Day	Time	Height (ft)	Height (cm)		Day	Time	Height (ft)	Height (cm)
1 Su	0300	3.3	101		16 M	0355	3.0	91
	0956	-0.7	-21			1036	-0.2	-6
	1624	3.1	94			1700	2.8	85
	2156	0.8	24			2253	0.6	18
2 M	0341	3.2	98		17 Tu	0439	2.6	79
	1031	-0.5	-15			1106	0.2	6
	1701	3.1	94			1731	2.7	82
	2243	0.7	21			2345	0.6	18
3 Tu	0429	3.0	91		18 W	0531	2.3	70
	1112	-0.3	-9			1136	0.6	18
	1740	3.0	91			1804	2.6	79
	2339	0.6	18					
4 W	0529	2.7	82		19 Th	0049	0.6	18
	1159	0.0	0			0640	2.0	61
	1824	2.9	88			1212	1.0	30
						1846	2.5	76
5 Th	0047	0.5	15		20 F	0209	0.5	15
	0648	2.5	76			0824	1.8	55
	1255	0.4	12			1305	1.3	40
	1916	2.9	88			1945	2.4	73
6 F	0207	0.3	9		21 Sa	0334	0.4	12
	0828	2.3	70			1014	1.9	58
	1401	0.8	24			1426	1.5	46
	2016	2.9	88			2106	2.4	73
7 Sa	0329	-0.1	-3		22 Su	0443	0.1	3
	1005	2.4	73			1126	2.1	64
	1513	1.0	30			1557	1.5	46
	2120	3.0	91			2219	2.5	76
8 Su	0441	-0.5	-15		23 M	0537	-0.2	-6
	1122	2.7	82			1212	2.3	70
	1624	1.2	37			1707	1.4	43
	2223	3.2	98			2313	2.6	79
9 M	0543	-0.9	-27		24 Tu	0620	-0.4	-12
	1223	2.9	88			1250	2.5	76
	1727	1.2	37			1758	1.3	40
	2320	3.3	101			2356	2.8	85
10 Tu	0637	-1.2	-37		25 W	0658	-0.6	-18
	1314	3.1	94			1324	2.7	82
	1823	1.1	34			1839	1.1	34
11 W	0013	3.5	107		26 Th	0033	3.0	91
	0726	-1.3	-40			0732	-0.8	-24
	1400	3.1	94			1356	2.9	88
	1912	1.0	30			1916	0.9	27
12 Th	0101	3.5	107		27 F	0108	3.1	94
	0811	-1.3	-40			0803	-0.9	-27
	1441	3.2	98			1426	3.0	91
	1958	0.9	27			1951	0.8	24
13 F	0147	3.5	107		28 Sa	0143	3.2	98
	0853	-1.2	-37			0833	-0.9	-27
	1520	3.1	94			1456	3.1	94
	2041	0.7	21			2027	0.6	18
14 Sa	0231	3.4	104		29 Su	0219	3.3	101
	0931	-0.9	-27			0903	-0.9	-27
	1555	3.0	91			1524	3.2	98
	2124	0.6	18			2104	0.4	12
15 Su	0313	3.2	98		30 M	0257	3.3	101
	1005	-0.6	-18			0934	-0.8	-24
	1628	2.9	88			1553	3.2	98
	2207	0.6	18			2144	0.3	9
					31 Tu	0339	3.2	98
						1006	-0.5	-15
						1624	3.2	98
						2227	0.1	3

February

Day	Time	Height (ft)	Height (cm)		Day	Time	Height (ft)	Height (cm)
1 W	0427	3.0	91		16 Th	0506	2.4	73
	1042	-0.2	-6			1046	0.7	21
	1656	3.2	98			1659	2.8	85
	2318	0.1	3			2359	0.3	9
2 Th	0524	2.7	82		17 F	0600	2.1	64
	1122	0.2	6			1115	1.0	30
	1733	3.1	94			1725	2.7	82
3 F	0020	0.0	0		18 Sa	0104	0.4	12
	0636	2.4	73			0718	1.9	58
	1210	0.7	21			1153	1.3	40
	1817	3.0	91			1800	2.5	76
4 Sa	0137	-0.1	-3		19 Su	0231	0.4	12
	0813	2.2	67			0915	1.9	58
	1312	1.1	34			1300	1.6	49
	1915	2.9	88			1903	2.4	73
5 Su	0306	-0.2	-6		20 M	0358	0.3	9
	0958	2.2	67			1054	2.1	64
	1432	1.4	43			1455	1.7	52
	2032	2.9	88			2112	2.3	70
6 M	0428	-0.5	-15		21 Tu	0504	0.1	3
	1119	2.5	76			1149	2.3	70
	1600	1.4	43			1640	1.6	49
	2158	3.0	91			2242	2.5	76
7 Tu	0535	-0.8	-24		22 W	0553	-0.2	-6
	1217	2.7	82			1228	2.6	79
	1716	1.3	40			1742	1.4	43
	2311	3.1	94			2336	2.7	82
8 W	0629	-1.0	-30		23 Th	0632	-0.4	-12
	1303	2.9	88			1301	2.8	85
	1816	1.1	34			1826	1.1	34
9 Th	0011	3.3	101		24 F	0019	3.0	91
	0716	-1.1	-34			0707	-0.6	-18
	1343	3.1	94			1331	3.0	91
	1906	0.8	24			1903	0.8	24
10 F	0101	3.4	104		25 Sa	0058	3.2	98
	0757	-1.0	-30			0739	-0.7	-21
	1419	3.2	98			1359	3.2	98
	1950	0.6	18			1939	0.6	18
11 Sa	0146	3.4	104		26 Su	0136	3.4	104
	0833	-0.9	-27			0809	-0.7	-21
	1451	3.2	98			1426	3.3	101
	2031	0.4	12			2014	0.3	9
12 Su	0227	3.4	104		27 M	0215	3.5	107
	0905	-0.6	-18			0839	-0.6	-18
	1521	3.2	98			1452	3.4	104
	2110	0.2	6			2051	0.0	0
13 M	0306	3.2	98		28 Tu	0255	3.5	107
	0933	-0.3	-9			0910	-0.4	-12
	1548	3.1	94			1519	3.5	107
	2148	0.1	3			2130	-0.2	-6
14 Tu	0344	3.0	91					
	0958	0.0	0					
	1612	3.1	94					
	2227	0.1	3					
15 W	0423	2.7	82					
	1021	0.3	9					
	1635	3.0	91					
	2309	0.2	6					

March

Day	Time	Height (ft)	Height (cm)		Day	Time	Height (ft)	Height (cm)
1 W	0339	3.4	104		16 Th	0407	3.0	91
	0941	-0.1	-3			0945	0.6	18
	1546	3.5	107			1550	3.3	101
	2213	-0.3	-9			2238	0.0	0
2 Th	0426	3.1	94		17 F	0446	2.7	82
	1015	0.2	6			1010	0.9	27
	1616	3.5	107			1611	3.2	98
	2301	-0.4	-12			2319	0.2	6
3 F	0521	2.8	85		18 Sa	0532	2.5	76
	1051	0.6	18			1040	1.1	34
	1650	3.4	104			1636	3.0	91
	2359	-0.3	-9					
4 Sa	0630	2.5	76		19 Su	0010	0.3	9
	1135	1.1	34			0635	2.2	67
	1730	3.3	101			1117	1.4	43
						1706	2.8	85
5 Su	0114	-0.2	-6		20 M	0122	0.5	15
	0804	2.2	67			0810	2.1	64
	1233	1.4	43			1215	1.7	52
	1825	3.1	94			1751	2.6	79
6 M	0246	-0.1	-3		21 Tu	0253	0.5	15
	0952	2.3	70			1000	2.2	67
	1401	1.7	52			1402	1.9	58
	1953	2.8	85			1930	2.4	73
7 Tu	0415	-0.2	-6		22 W	0413	0.4	12
	1111	2.5	76			1108	2.5	76
	1549	1.7	52			1606	1.8	55
	2148	2.8	85			2156	2.5	76
8 W	0523	-0.4	-12		23 Th	0510	0.1	3
	1203	2.8	85			1151	2.8	85
	1714	1.4	43			1718	1.5	46
	2312	3.0	91			2308	2.8	85
9 Th	0615	-0.5	-15		24 F	0555	-0.1	-3
	1243	3.0	91			1225	3.0	91
	1813	1.0	30			1805	1.1	34
						2359	3.1	94
10 F	0012	3.2	98		25 Sa	0632	-0.2	-6
	0658	-0.5	-15			1255	3.3	101
	1318	3.2	98			1844	0.7	21
	1859	0.6	18					
11 Sa	0100	3.3	101		26 Su	0044	3.3	101
	0735	-0.4	-12			0707	-0.2	-6
	1349	3.3	101			1323	3.5	107
	1940	0.3	9			1922	0.3	9
12 Su	0141	3.4	104		27 M	0127	3.5	107
	0806	-0.3	-9			0740	-0.2	-6
	1418	3.4	104			1350	3.6	110
	2018	0.1	3			1959	-0.1	-3
13 M	0219	3.4	104		28 Tu	0210	3.7	113
	0834	-0.1	-3			0813	0.0	0
	1444	3.4	104			1417	3.7	113
	2053	-0.1	-3			2038	-0.4	-12
14 Tu	0255	3.3	101		29 W	0253	3.7	113
	0858	0.1	3			0845	0.2	6
	1507	3.4	104			1444	3.8	116
	2128	-0.1	-3			2118	-0.6	-18
15 W	0330	3.1	94		30 Th	0338	3.5	107
	0921	0.4	12			0917	0.5	15
	1529	3.4	104			1512	3.9	119
	2202	-0.1	-3			2201	-0.7	-21
					31 F	0427	3.3	101
						0951	0.8	24
						1543	3.9	119
						2249	-0.6	-18

Time meridian 75° W. 0000 is midnight. 1200 is noon. Times are not adjusted for Daylight Saving Time.
Heights are referred to mean lower low water which is the chart datum of soundings.

St. Marks River Entrance, Florida, 2017

Times and Heights of High and Low Waters

April

Day	Time	ft	cm		Day	Time	ft	cm
1 Sa	0521	3.0	91		16 Su	0513	2.8	85
	1027	1.1	34			1018	1.3	40
	1618	3.7	113			1605	3.3	101
	2345	-0.4	-12			2334	0.2	6
2 Su	0627	2.6	79		17 M	0607	2.7	82
	1110	1.5	46			1059	1.6	49
	1658	3.5	107			1638	3.1	94
3 M	0056	-0.1	-3		18 Tu	0030	0.4	12
	0754	2.4	73			0720	2.5	76
	1210	1.8	55			1156	1.8	55
	1753	3.2	98			1723	2.9	88
4 Tu	0224	0.1	3		19 W	0144	0.5	15
	0934	2.5	76			0851	2.6	79
	1347	1.9	58			1327	2.0	61
	1928	2.8	85			1842	2.7	82
5 W	0352	0.2	6		20 Th	0303	0.5	15
	1047	2.7	82			1007	2.7	82
	1547	1.7	52			1521	1.8	55
	2145	2.8	85			2057	2.6	79
6 Th	0500	0.2	6		21 F	0410	0.4	12
	1136	2.9	88			1059	3.0	91
	1710	1.3	40			1642	1.5	46
	2311	2.9	88			2232	2.8	85
7 F	0552	0.2	6		22 Sa	0504	0.3	9
	1213	3.2	98			1137	3.2	98
	1805	0.9	27			1736	1.0	30
						2336	3.1	94
8 Sa	0009	3.1	94		23 Su	0550	0.3	9
	0632	0.2	6			1211	3.5	107
	1246	3.4	104			1821	0.5	15
	1848	0.5	15					
9 Su	0054	3.3	101		24 M	0028	3.4	104
	0705	0.3	9			0630	0.3	9
	1315	3.5	107			1241	3.7	113
	1927	0.2	6			1903	0.0	0
10 M	0133	3.3	101		25 Tu	0117	3.6	110
	0734	0.4	12			0708	0.4	12
	1342	3.6	110			1311	3.9	119
	2002	-0.1	-3			1944	-0.4	-12
11 Tu	0209	3.4	104		26 W	0204	3.7	113
	0800	0.6	18			0745	0.6	18
	1407	3.7	113			1342	4.0	122
	2036	-0.2	-6			2026	-0.7	-21
12 W	0243	3.3	101		27 Th	0251	3.7	113
	0824	0.7	21			0821	0.8	24
	1430	3.7	113			1413	4.1	125
	2108	-0.2	-6			2109	-0.8	-24
13 Th	0317	3.3	101		28 F	0338	3.6	110
	0849	0.8	24			0856	1.1	34
	1452	3.7	113			1446	4.2	128
	2141	-0.2	-6			2154	-0.8	-24
14 F	0352	3.2	98		29 Sa	0427	3.4	104
	0916	1.0	30			0933	1.3	40
	1514	3.6	110			1520	4.1	125
	2214	-0.1	-3			2242	-0.6	-18
15 Sa	0430	3.0	91		30 Su	0519	3.1	94
	0945	1.1	34			1013	1.5	46
	1538	3.5	107			1558	3.9	119
	2251	0.0	0			2335	-0.3	-9

May

Day	Time	ft	cm		Day	Time	ft	cm
1 M	0620	2.8	85		16 Tu	0545	3.0	91
	1100	1.7	52			1047	1.6	49
	1642	3.6	110			1624	3.4	104
						2355	0.2	6
2 Tu	0038	0.1	3		17 W	0641	2.9	88
	0734	2.7	82			1143	1.8	55
	1204	1.9	58			1712	3.2	98
	1739	3.2	98					
3 W	0153	0.4	12		18 Th	0050	0.4	12
	0856	2.7	82			0746	2.9	88
	1342	1.9	58			1300	1.9	58
	1917	2.8	85			1824	2.9	88
4 Th	0312	0.6	18		19 F	0156	0.5	15
	1005	2.8	85			0854	3.0	91
	1536	1.7	52			1434	1.7	52
	2133	2.7	82			2011	2.8	85
5 F	0421	0.8	24		20 Sa	0304	0.6	18
	1055	3.1	94			0952	3.2	98
	1656	1.2	37			1558	1.3	40
	2301	2.8	85			2155	2.9	88
6 Sa	0514	0.8	24		21 Su	0406	0.7	21
	1135	3.3	101			1039	3.4	104
	1750	0.8	24			1702	0.8	24
	2359	3.0	91			2312	3.1	94
7 Su	0555	0.9	27		22 M	0501	0.8	24
	1208	3.5	107			1120	3.6	110
	1833	0.4	12			1755	0.3	9
8 M	0044	3.1	94		23 Tu	0013	3.4	104
	0629	1.0	30			0551	0.9	27
	1239	3.6	110			1158	3.8	116
	1911	0.1	3			1844	-0.2	-6
9 Tu	0122	3.2	98		24 W	0108	3.6	110
	0659	1.1	34			0636	1.0	30
	1307	3.7	113			1235	4.0	122
	1946	-0.1	-3			1930	-0.6	-18
10 W	0158	3.3	101		25 Th	0159	3.7	113
	0726	1.1	34			0719	1.2	37
	1333	3.8	116			1312	4.2	128
	2020	-0.2	-6			2016	-0.9	-27
11 Th	0232	3.3	101		26 F	0248	3.7	113
	0754	1.1	34			0800	1.3	40
	1358	3.8	116			1350	4.3	131
	2052	-0.3	-9			2102	-1.0	-30
12 F	0305	3.3	101		27 Sa	0335	3.6	110
	0823	1.2	37			0840	1.4	43
	1423	3.8	116			1428	4.3	131
	2124	-0.2	-6			2148	-0.9	-27
13 Sa	0340	3.3	101		28 Su	0423	3.4	104
	0856	1.3	40			0922	1.5	46
	1448	3.8	116			1509	4.2	128
	2156	-0.2	-6			2235	-0.6	-18
14 Su	0417	3.2	98		29 M	0511	3.2	98
	0927	1.4	43			1006	1.6	49
	1516	3.7	113			1551	3.9	119
	2230	-0.1	-3			2323	-0.2	-6
15 M	0458	3.1	94		30 Tu	0602	3.0	91
	1004	1.5	46			1057	1.7	52
	1547	3.6	110			1638	3.6	110
	2309	0.1	3					
					31 W	0014	0.2	6
						0658	2.9	88
						1201	1.8	55
						1736	3.2	98

June

Day	Time	ft	cm		Day	Time	ft	cm
1 Th	0110	0.6	18		16 F	0010	0.3	9
	0802	2.9	88			0651	3.2	98
	1327	1.7	52			1234	1.5	46
	1902	2.7	82			1813	3.1	94
2 F	0213	1.0	30		17 Sa	0104	0.5	15
	0906	2.9	88			0744	3.3	101
	1506	1.5	46			1353	1.4	43
	2103	2.5	76			1943	2.9	88
3 Sa	0318	1.2	37		18 Su	0205	0.8	24
	1002	3.1	94			0841	3.3	101
	1629	1.1	34			1516	1.1	34
	2239	2.6	79			2124	2.9	88
4 Su	0417	1.4	43		19 M	0310	1.1	34
	1048	3.3	101			0937	3.5	107
	1727	0.7	21			1630	0.6	18
	2343	2.7	82			2251	3.0	91
5 M	0506	1.5	46		20 Tu	0414	1.3	40
	1128	3.4	104			1029	3.7	113
	1814	0.4	12			1733	0.1	3
6 Tu	0030	2.9	88		21 W	0000	3.3	101
	0546	1.5	46			0513	1.4	43
	1203	3.6	110			1119	3.9	119
	1854	0.1	3			1828	-0.4	-12
7 W	0110	3.0	91		22 Th	0059	3.5	107
	0622	1.5	46			0607	1.5	46
	1235	3.7	113			1206	4.1	125
	1931	0.0	0			1919	-0.7	-21
8 Th	0146	3.1	94		23 F	0152	3.6	110
	0656	1.5	46			0657	1.5	46
	1305	3.8	116			1252	4.3	131
	2005	-0.2	-6			2008	-0.9	-27
9 F	0220	3.2	98		24 Sa	0240	3.6	110
	0730	1.5	46			0744	1.5	46
	1334	3.8	116			1337	4.3	131
	2038	-0.2	-6			2054	-0.9	-27
10 Sa	0254	3.3	101		25 Su	0326	3.6	110
	0803	1.4	43			0829	1.5	46
	1402	3.8	116			1421	4.3	131
	2109	-0.2	-6			2139	-0.7	-21
11 Su	0328	3.3	101		26 M	0409	3.5	107
	0838	1.4	43			0914	1.5	46
	1431	3.8	116			1505	4.2	128
	2140	-0.2	-6			2221	-0.5	-15
12 M	0403	3.4	104		27 Tu	0450	3.4	104
	0914	1.4	43			1000	1.5	46
	1502	3.8	116			1550	3.9	119
	2212	-0.2	-6			2301	-0.1	-3
13 Tu	0440	3.3	101		28 W	0531	3.2	98
	0953	1.5	46			1050	1.5	46
	1537	3.7	113			1636	3.6	110
	2246	-0.1	-3			2341	0.4	12
14 W	0519	3.3	101		29 Th	0612	3.1	94
	1036	1.5	46			1148	1.5	46
	1617	3.6	110			1730	3.2	98
	2325	0.1	3					
15 Th	0602	3.3	101		30 F	0020	0.8	24
	1129	1.6	49			0658	3.1	94
	1707	3.4	104			1258	1.4	43
						1839	2.8	85

Time meridian 75° W. 0000 is midnight. 1200 is noon. Times are not adjusted for Daylight Saving Time.
Heights are referred to mean lower low water which is the chart datum of soundings.

St. Marks River Entrance, Florida, 2017

Times and Heights of High and Low Waters

July

Day	Time (h m)	Height (ft)	Height (cm)	Day	Time (h m)	Height (ft)	Height (cm)
1 Sa	0104	1.2	37	16 Su	0023	0.7	21
	0751	3.0	91		0644	3.5	107
	1423	1.3	40		1319	1.0	30
	2016	2.5	76		1925 ☽	3.0	91
2 Su	0156	1.5	46	17 M	0118	1.1	34
	0852	3.1	94		0737	3.5	107
	1549	1.1	34		1441	0.8	24
	2203	2.4	73		2104	2.9	88
3 M	0259	1.8	55	18 Tu	0223	1.4	43
	0952	3.2	98		0839	3.6	110
	1658	0.8	24		1603	0.4	12
	2320	2.6	79		2236	3.0	91
4 Tu	0404	1.9	58	19 W	0334	1.6	49
	1046	3.3	101		0946	3.7	113
	1752	0.5	15		1715	0.0	0
					2350	3.2	98
5 W	0013	2.7	82	20 Th	0444	1.7	52
	0502	1.9	58		1050	3.9	119
	1131	3.4	104		1815	-0.3	-9
	1836	0.3	9				
6 Th	0055	2.9	88	21 F	0049	3.4	104
	0551	1.8	55		0546	1.7	52
	1210	3.6	110		1149	4.1	125
	1915	0.1	3		1909	-0.6	-18
7 F	0131	3.1	94	22 Sa	0139	3.5	107
	0633	1.7	52		0642	1.6	49
	1245	3.7	113		1242	4.2	128
	1950	0.0	0		1957	-0.7	-21
8 Sa	0206	3.2	98	23 Su	0224	3.6	110
	0712	1.6	49		0733	1.5	46
	1318	3.8	116		1332	4.3	131
	2022 ○	-0.1	-3		2041 ●	-0.6	-18
9 Su	0238	3.3	101	24 M	0305	3.6	110
	0749	1.5	46		0819	1.3	40
	1349	3.9	119		1418	4.3	131
	2052	-0.2	-6		2121	-0.4	-12
10 M	0311	3.4	104	25 Tu	0342	3.6	110
	0825	1.4	43		0904	1.2	37
	1421	3.9	119		1502	4.2	128
	2121	-0.2	-6		2158	-0.1	-3
11 Tu	0342	3.5	107	26 W	0417	3.5	107
	0902	1.4	43		0949	1.1	34
	1454	3.9	119		1545	3.9	119
	2151	-0.2	-6		2231	0.2	6
12 W	0414	3.5	107	27 Th	0449	3.4	104
	0940	1.3	40		1034	1.1	34
	1531	3.9	119		1628	3.6	110
	2222	-0.1	-3		2301	0.6	18
13 Th	0446	3.6	110	28 F	0521	3.3	101
	1022	1.2	37		1123	1.1	34
	1613	3.7	113		1715	3.2	98
	2257	0.1	3		2331	1.0	30
14 F	0521	3.5	107	29 Sa	0553	3.2	98
	1110	1.2	37		1221	1.2	37
	1702	3.5	107		1811	2.9	88
	2336	0.3	9				
15 Sa	0600	3.5	107	30 Su	0002	1.4	43
	1208	1.1	34		0630	3.2	98
	1804	3.3	101		1333	1.2	37
					1928 ☽	2.5	76
				31 M	0042	1.7	52
					0721	3.1	94
					1459	1.2	37
					2113	2.4	73

August

Day	Time (h m)	Height (ft)	Height (cm)	Day	Time (h m)	Height (ft)	Height (cm)
1 Tu	0140	1.9	58	16 W	0148	1.7	52
	0838	3.1	94		0753	3.6	110
	1621	1.0	30		1544	0.4	12
	2248	2.5	76		2226	3.0	91
2 W	0302	2.1	64	17 Th	0308	1.9	58
	1001	3.1	94		0918	3.7	113
	1725	0.7	21		1701	0.2	6
	2349	2.7	82		2338	3.2	98
3 Th	0425	2.0	61	18 F	0428	1.9	58
	1104	3.3	101		1038	3.8	116
	1813	0.5	15		1803	-0.1	-3
4 F	0033	2.9	88	19 Sa	0032	3.4	104
	0528	1.9	58		0536	1.7	52
	1151	3.5	107		1144	4.0	122
	1853	0.3	9		1855	-0.3	-9
5 Sa	0110	3.1	94	20 Su	0118	3.5	107
	0616	1.8	55		0633	1.5	46
	1230	3.7	113		1239	4.2	128
	1928	0.1	3		1940	-0.3	-9
6 Su	0143	3.3	101	21 M	0158	3.6	110
	0657	1.6	49		0723	1.2	37
	1305	3.8	116		1328	4.3	131
	2000	0.0	0		2020 ●	-0.2	-6
7 M	0214	3.4	104	22 Tu	0233	3.7	113
	0735	1.4	43		0808	1.0	30
	1338	3.9	119		1413	4.2	128
	2029 ○	-0.1	-3		2055	0.0	0
8 Tu	0244	3.5	107	23 W	0306	3.7	113
	0811	1.3	40		0850	0.8	24
	1412	4.0	122		1454	4.1	125
	2057	-0.1	-3		2127	0.3	9
9 W	0312	3.6	110	24 Th	0335	3.7	113
	0847	1.1	34		0930	0.7	21
	1447	4.1	125		1534	3.9	119
	2125	0.0	0		2154	0.6	18
10 Th	0340	3.7	113	25 F	0402	3.6	110
	0925	1.0	30		1011	0.7	21
	1526	4.0	122		1614	3.6	110
	2155	0.1	3		2220	1.0	30
11 F	0408	3.8	116	26 Sa	0428	3.5	107
	1005	0.8	24		1053	0.8	24
	1608	3.9	119		1656	3.3	101
	2228	0.3	9		2246	1.3	40
12 Sa	0439	3.8	116	27 Su	0453	3.4	104
	1051	0.7	21		1141	1.0	30
	1658	3.7	113		1744	3.0	91
	2305	0.7	21		2314	1.5	46
13 Su	0513	3.8	116	28 M	0521	3.3	101
	1145	0.7	21		1242	1.1	34
	1757	3.3	101		1848	2.7	82
	2349	1.0	30		2351	1.8	55
14 M	0554	3.7	113	29 Tu	0559	3.2	98
	1252	0.7	21		1402	1.2	37
	1915 ☽	3.0	91		2021 ☽	2.5	76
15 Tu	0041	1.4	43	30 W	0047	2.0	61
	0645	3.7	113		0704	3.0	91
	1415	0.6	18		1534	1.1	34
	2052	2.9	88		2205	2.6	79
				31 Th	0218	2.2	67
					0906	3.0	91
					1647	0.9	27
					2315	2.8	85

September

Day	Time (h m)	Height (ft)	Height (cm)	Day	Time (h m)	Height (ft)	Height (cm)
1 F	0359	2.1	64	16 Sa	0424	1.8	55
	1036	3.2	98		1038	3.7	113
	1740	0.7	21		1745	0.2	6
2 Sa	0002	3.0	91	17 Su	0008	3.4	104
	0511	1.9	58		0531	1.5	46
	1130	3.4	104		1144	3.9	119
	1822	0.5	15		1834	0.2	6
3 Su	0038	3.2	98	18 M	0048	3.6	110
	0600	1.7	52		0625	1.1	34
	1211	3.6	110		1237	4.0	122
	1857	0.3	9		1915	0.2	6
4 M	0111	3.4	104	19 Tu	0123	3.7	113
	0640	1.4	43		0711	0.8	24
	1249	3.8	116		1322	4.1	125
	1928	0.2	6		1951	0.4	12
5 Tu	0140	3.6	110	20 W	0156	3.8	116
	0717	1.2	37		0752	0.6	18
	1325	4.0	122		1404	4.1	125
	1958	0.2	6		2022 ●	0.6	18
6 W	0207	3.7	113	21 Th	0225	3.8	116
	0753	0.9	27		0832	0.4	12
	1401	4.1	125		1443	4.0	122
	2027 ○	0.2	6		2050	0.8	24
7 Th	0234	3.8	116	22 F	0251	3.8	116
	0829	0.7	21		0909	0.4	12
	1440	4.2	128		1520	3.8	116
	2056	0.3	9		2116	1.0	30
8 F	0300	3.9	119	23 Sa	0315	3.7	113
	0907	0.5	15		0946	0.4	12
	1521	4.1	125		1557	3.6	110
	2127	0.5	15		2141	1.2	37
9 Sa	0327	4.0	122	24 Su	0339	3.7	113
	0948	0.3	9		1023	0.5	15
	1605	3.9	119		1636	3.4	104
	2200	0.8	24		2208	1.4	43
10 Su	0357	4.0	122	25 M	0403	3.5	107
	1033	0.3	9		1105	0.7	21
	1655	3.7	113		1721	3.1	94
	2237	1.1	34		2239	1.6	49
11 M	0431	4.0	122	26 Tu	0430	3.4	104
	1126	0.4	12		1156	0.9	27
	1754	3.3	101		1817	2.9	88
	2320	1.4	43		2319	1.8	55
12 Tu	0512	3.9	119	27 W	0505	3.2	98
	1233	0.5	15		1305	1.1	34
	1911	3.0	91		1935 ☽	2.7	82
13 W	0014	1.8	55	28 Th	0017	2.0	61
	0606	3.7	113		0559	3.0	91
	1357	0.6	18		1433	1.1	34
	2045 ☽	2.9	88		2113	2.7	82
14 Th	0127	2.0	61	29 F	0150	2.2	67
	0723	3.5	107		0754	2.8	85
	1528	0.5	15		1553	1.0	30
	2214	3.0	91		2229	2.9	88
15 F	0258	2.0	61	30 Sa	0336	2.0	61
	0907	3.5	107		0956	3.0	91
	1645	0.4	12		1653	0.9	27
	2319	3.2	98		2319	3.1	94

Time meridian 75° W. 0000 is midnight. 1200 is noon. Times are not adjusted for Daylight Saving Time.
Heights are referred to mean lower low water which is the chart datum of soundings.

St. Marks River Entrance, Florida, 2017

Times and Heights of High and Low Waters

October

Day	Time	ft	cm	Day	Time	ft	cm
1 Su	0448	1.8	55	16 M	0525	1.1	34
	1100	3.2	98		1142	3.5	107
	1738	0.7	21		1805	0.7	21
	2356	3.3	101				
2 M	0538	1.5	46	17 Tu	0013	3.5	107
	1148	3.5	107		0614	0.7	21
	1816	0.6	18		1231	3.7	113
					1844	0.7	21
3 Tu	0029	3.5	107	18 W	0046	3.7	113
	0618	1.1	34		0657	0.3	9
	1230	3.7	113		1314	3.8	116
	1850	0.5	15		1916	0.9	27
4 W	0058	3.6	110	19 Th ●	0116	3.8	116
	0656	0.7	21		0736	0.1	3
	1310	3.9	119		1353	3.8	116
	1923	0.5	15		1946	1.0	30
5 Th ○	0125	3.8	116	20 F	0144	3.8	116
	0734	0.4	12		0813	0.0	0
	1351	4.1	125		1429	3.7	113
	1954	0.6	18		2013	1.1	34
6 F	0152	3.9	119	21 Sa	0210	3.8	116
	0811	0.1	3		0848	0.0	0
	1433	4.1	125		1505	3.6	110
	2027	0.7	21		2040	1.2	37
7 Sa	0220	4.0	122	22 Su	0234	3.7	113
	0851	-0.1	-3		0922	0.1	3
	1517	4.0	122		1540	3.5	107
	2100	0.9	27		2108	1.3	40
8 Su	0249	4.1	125	23 M	0259	3.6	110
	0933	-0.2	-6		0958	0.2	6
	1603	3.8	116		1618	3.3	101
	2135	1.2	37		2139	1.4	43
9 M	0322	4.1	125	24 Tu	0325	3.5	107
	1020	-0.1	-3		1035	0.4	12
	1654	3.6	110		1700	3.1	94
	2214	1.4	43		2214	1.6	49
10 Tu	0358	4.0	122	25 W	0355	3.3	101
	1113	0.0	0		1119	0.6	18
	1753	3.2	98		1750	3.0	91
	2259	1.7	52		2258	1.7	52
11 W	0442	3.8	116	26 Th	0432	3.1	94
	1219	0.3	9		1215	0.8	24
	1906	3.0	91		1855	2.8	85
	2357	1.9	58		2358	1.9	58
12 Th ◗	0540	3.5	107	27 F ◖	0524	2.9	88
	1340	0.5	15		1326	0.9	27
	2033	2.9	88		2014	2.8	85
13 F	0120	2.0	61	28 Sa	0124	1.9	58
	0708	3.3	101		0655	2.7	82
	1507	0.6	18		1443	0.9	27
	2152	3.0	91		2129	2.9	88
14 Sa	0259	1.8	55	29 Su	0302	1.8	55
	0908	3.2	98		0901	2.7	82
	1622	0.6	18		1550	0.9	27
	2250	3.2	98		2224	3.0	91
15 Su	0423	1.5	46	30 M	0416	1.5	46
	1039	3.4	104		1023	3.0	91
	1720	0.6	18		1643	0.8	24
	2335	3.4	104		2305	3.2	98
				31 Tu	0509	1.0	30
					1121	3.2	98
					1728	0.7	21
					2340	3.4	104

November

Day	Time	ft	cm	Day	Time	ft	cm
1 W	0553	0.6	18	16 Th	0009	3.5	107
	1210	3.5	107		0643	-0.1	-3
	1808	0.7	21		1304	3.3	101
					1841	1.1	34
2 Th	0011	3.6	110	17 F	0040	3.5	107
	0634	0.2	6		0721	-0.3	-9
	1257	3.7	113		1341	3.3	101
	1846	0.8	24		1912	1.2	37
3 F	0042	3.7	113	18 Sa ●	0109	3.6	110
	0715	-0.2	-6		0756	-0.4	-12
	1342	3.9	119		1416	3.3	101
	1923	0.9	27		1942	1.2	37
4 Sa ○	0113	3.9	119	19 Su	0137	3.6	110
	0756	-0.5	-15		0831	-0.4	-12
	1427	3.9	119		1451	3.3	101
	2000	1.0	30		2012	1.2	37
5 Su	0145	4.0	122	20 M	0204	3.5	107
	0839	-0.7	-21		0904	-0.3	-9
	1513	3.8	116		1525	3.3	101
	2037	1.2	37		2044	1.2	37
6 M	0219	4.0	122	21 Tu	0232	3.4	104
	0924	-0.7	-21		0937	-0.2	-6
	1601	3.6	110		1601	3.2	98
	2115	1.3	40		2119	1.3	40
7 Tu	0257	4.0	122	22 W	0302	3.3	101
	1012	-0.6	-18		1012	-0.1	-3
	1651	3.3	101		1640	3.1	94
	2158	1.5	46		2157	1.3	40
8 W	0338	3.8	116	23 Th	0335	3.2	98
	1104	-0.3	-9		1050	0.1	3
	1747	3.1	94		1724	3.0	91
	2247	1.6	49		2242	1.4	43
9 Th	0426	3.6	110	24 F	0414	3.0	91
	1204	0.1	3		1134	0.3	9
	1851	2.9	88		1815	2.9	88
	2351	1.7	52		2338	1.5	46
10 F ○	0528	3.2	98	25 Sa	0505	2.8	85
	1315	0.4	12		1228	0.5	15
	2005	2.8	85		1914	2.8	85
11 Sa	0117	1.7	52	26 Su ◖	0051	1.5	46
	0702	2.9	88		0620	2.6	79
	1433	0.7	21		1331	0.6	18
	2115	2.9	88		2018	2.8	85
12 Su	0254	1.4	43	27 M	0217	1.4	43
	0905	2.8	85		0806	2.5	76
	1545	0.8	24		1439	0.7	21
	2212	3.0	91		2116	2.9	88
13 M	0415	1.0	30	28 Tu	0334	1.0	30
	1035	2.9	88		0943	2.6	79
	1644	0.9	27		1542	0.8	24
	2257	3.2	98		2205	3.1	94
14 Tu	0514	0.6	18	29 W	0435	0.5	15
	1136	3.1	94		1055	2.9	88
	1730	1.0	30		1638	0.8	24
	2335	3.3	101		2247	3.2	98
15 W	0601	0.2	6	30 Th	0527	0.0	0
	1224	3.2	98		1153	3.2	98
	1808	1.1	34		1728	0.9	27
					2326	3.4	104

December

Day	Time	ft	cm	Day	Time	ft	cm
1 F	0614	-0.4	-12	16 Sa	0012	3.2	98
	1246	3.4	104		0707	-0.5	-15
	1813	1.0	30		1331	2.9	88
					1847	1.2	37
2 Sa	0004	3.6	110	17 Su	0045	3.3	101
	0700	-0.8	-24		0743	-0.6	-18
	1335	3.5	107		1404	3.0	91
	1856	1.0	30		1921	1.1	34
3 Su ○	0042	3.8	116	18 M ●	0117	3.3	101
	0745	-1.1	-34		0817	-0.6	-18
	1422	3.6	110		1437	3.0	91
	1938	1.1	34		1955	1.1	34
4 M	0121	3.9	119	19 Tu	0147	3.3	101
	0831	-1.2	-37		0849	-0.6	-18
	1509	3.5	107		1510	3.1	94
	2020	1.2	37		2029	1.0	30
5 Tu	0202	3.9	119	20 W	0218	3.2	98
	0917	-1.1	-34		0919	-0.5	-15
	1554	3.3	101		1543	3.1	94
	2103	1.2	37		2105	1.0	30
6 W	0245	3.8	116	21 Th	0250	3.2	98
	1003	-0.9	-27		0950	-0.5	-15
	1641	3.1	94		1618	3.0	91
	2149	1.2	37		2143	1.0	30
7 Th	0331	3.6	110	22 F	0324	3.1	94
	1051	-0.5	-15		1023	-0.3	-9
	1729	2.9	88		1653	3.0	91
	2241	1.2	37		2226	1.0	30
8 F	0422	3.3	101	23 Sa	0404	2.9	88
	1141	-0.1	-3		1059	-0.2	-6
	1820	2.8	85		1732	2.9	88
	2343	1.2	37		2315	1.0	30
9 Sa	0523	2.9	88	24 Su	0452	2.7	82
	1237	0.3	9		1141	0.1	3
	1917	2.7	82		1815	2.8	85
10 Su ◖	0102	1.2	37	25 M	0015	1.0	30
	0650	2.5	76		0556	2.5	76
	1339	0.7	21		1232	0.3	9
	2019	2.7	82		1904	2.8	85
11 M	0233	0.9	27	26 Tu ◖	0129	0.8	24
	0846	2.3	70		0725	2.3	70
	1448	1.0	30		1333	0.6	18
	2119	2.7	82		1959	2.8	85
12 Tu	0354	0.6	18	27 W	0248	0.5	15
	1023	2.4	73		0907	2.3	70
	1553	1.2	37		1441	0.8	24
	2212	2.9	88		2057	2.9	88
13 W	0457	0.2	6	28 Th	0401	0.1	3
	1128	2.5	76		1033	2.5	76
	1648	1.3	40		1549	1.0	30
	2257	3.0	91		2153	3.0	91
14 Th	0546	-0.1	-3	29 F	0503	-0.4	-12
	1216	2.7	82		1140	2.8	85
	1733	1.3	40		1651	1.1	34
	2336	3.1	94		2245	3.2	98
15 F	0629	-0.4	-12	30 Sa	0558	-0.8	-24
	1256	2.8	85		1237	3.1	94
	1811	1.3	40		1747	1.1	34
					2335	3.4	104
				31 Su	0648	-1.2	-37
					1327	3.2	98
					1837	1.1	34

Time meridian 75° W. 0000 is midnight. 1200 is noon. Times are not adjusted for Daylight Saving Time.
Heights are referred to mean lower low water which is the chart datum of soundings.

Apalachicola, Florida, 2017

Times and Heights of High and Low Waters

January

Day	Time	ft	cm	Day	Time	ft	cm
1 Su	0415	1.3	40	**16** M	0013	0.6	18
	1159	-0.4	-12		0523	1.2	37
	1915	1.1	34		1248	-0.2	-6
					1923	1.1	34
2 M	0001	0.7	21	**17** Tu	0109	0.5	15
	0504	1.2	37		0620	1.0	30
	1231	-0.4	-12		1316	0.0	0
	1942	1.1	34		1947	1.1	34
3 Tu	0054	0.7	21	**18** W	0212	0.3	9
	0600	1.1	34		0726	0.9	27
	1307	-0.2	-6		1345	0.2	6
	2011	1.1	34		2013	1.1	34
4 W	0158	0.5	15	**19** Th	0323	0.2	6
	0707	1.0	30		0847	0.7	21
	1347	0.0	0		1416	0.3	9
	2042	1.2	37		2042	1.2	37
5 Th	0317	0.4	12	**20** F	0439	0.1	3
	0833	0.8	24		1032	0.7	21
	1431	0.2	6		1454	0.5	15
	2115	1.2	37		2117	1.2	37
6 F	0443	0.2	6	**21** Sa	0549	-0.1	-3
	1024	0.7	21		1242	0.7	21
	1522	0.4	12		1550	0.6	18
	2151	1.2	37		2157	1.2	37
7 Sa	0601	-0.1	-3	**22** Su	0650	-0.2	-6
	1236	0.8	24		1422	0.8	24
	1627	0.6	18		1715	0.7	21
	2231	1.3	40		2242	1.2	37
8 Su	0707	-0.3	-9	**23** M	0742	-0.3	-9
	1431	0.9	27		1515	0.9	27
	1747	0.8	24		1836	0.8	24
	2316	1.3	40		2332	1.2	37
9 M	0804	-0.5	-15	**24** Tu	0828	-0.4	-12
	1543	1.0	30		1553	1.0	30
	1905	0.9	27		1940	0.9	27
10 Tu	0007	1.4	43	**25** W	0024	1.2	37
	0856	-0.6	-18		0908	-0.5	-15
	1632	1.1	34		1625	1.1	34
	2009	0.9	27		2030	0.8	24
11 W	0100	1.4	43	**26** Th	0114	1.3	40
	0944	-0.7	-21		0944	-0.5	-15
	1712	1.1	34		1653	1.1	34
	2103	0.9	27		2112	0.8	24
12 Th	0154	1.4	43	**27** F	0201	1.3	40
	1028	-0.7	-21		1016	-0.5	-15
	1745	1.1	34		1717	1.1	34
	2151	0.9	27		2149	0.8	24
13 F	0247	1.4	43	**28** Sa	0248	1.3	40
	1108	-0.7	-21		1045	-0.5	-15
	1814	1.1	34		1740	1.1	34
	2237	0.8	24		2224	0.7	21
14 Sa	0339	1.4	43	**29** Su	0334	1.3	40
	1145	-0.5	-15		1112	-0.4	-12
	1838	1.1	34		1800	1.1	34
	2324	0.7	21		2301	0.6	18
15 Su	0430	1.3	40	**30** M	0422	1.3	40
	1218	-0.4	-12		1140	-0.4	-12
	1901	1.1	34		1821	1.1	34
					2342	0.5	15
				31 Tu	0514	1.2	37
					1209	-0.2	-6
					1844	1.1	34

February

Day	Time	ft	cm	Day	Time	ft	cm
1 W	0030	0.4	12	**16** Th	0123	0.2	6
	0612	1.1	34		0720	1.0	30
	1241	0.0	0		1254	0.4	12
	1909	1.2	37		1900	1.2	37
2 Th	0128	0.2	6	**17** F	0222	0.1	3
	0721	1.0	30		0833	0.9	27
	1314	0.2	6		1323	0.5	15
	1937	1.2	37		1931	1.3	40
3 F	0242	0.1	3	**18** Sa	0333	0.1	3
	0849	0.8	24		1006	0.8	24
	1349	0.4	12		1359	0.7	21
	2010	1.2	37		2008	1.3	40
4 Sa	0413	0.0	0	**19** Su	0452	0.0	0
	1050	0.8	24		1202	0.9	27
	1428	0.6	18		1458	0.8	24
	2051	1.3	40		2055	1.2	37
5 Su	0542	-0.2	-6	**20** M	0604	-0.1	-3
	2141	1.3	40		1339	1.0	30
					1642	0.9	27
					2152	1.2	37
6 M	0656	-0.3	-9	**21** Tu	0704	-0.2	-6
	1503	1.0	30		1431	1.0	30
	1729	0.9	27		1818	0.9	27
	2243	1.3	40		2258	1.2	37
7 Tu	0757	-0.5	-15	**22** W	0754	-0.2	-6
	1542	1.1	34		1507	1.1	34
	1904	0.9	27		1925	0.9	27
	2353	1.3	40				
8 W	0849	-0.5	-15	**23** Th	0005	1.3	40
	1614	1.1	34		0837	-0.3	-9
	2010	0.9	27		1537	1.2	37
					2015	0.8	24
9 Th	0101	1.3	40	**24** F	0106	1.3	40
	0934	-0.6	-18		0915	-0.3	-9
	1641	1.1	34		1603	1.2	37
	2101	0.8	24		2056	0.7	21
10 F	0204	1.4	43	**25** Sa	0201	1.4	43
	1015	-0.5	-15		0948	-0.3	-9
	1704	1.1	34		1624	1.2	37
	2146	0.7	21		2132	0.6	18
11 Sa	0259	1.4	43	**26** Su	0253	1.4	43
	1050	-0.4	-12		1018	-0.2	-6
	1723	1.1	34		1643	1.2	37
	2228	0.6	18		2208	0.5	15
12 Su	0350	1.3	40	**27** M	0343	1.4	43
	1120	-0.3	-9		1047	-0.1	-3
	1740	1.1	34		1701	1.2	37
	2308	0.4	12		2244	0.4	12
13 M	0438	1.3	40	**28** Tu	0435	1.4	43
	1145	-0.1	-3		1116	0.0	0
	1756	1.1	34		1720	1.2	37
	2350	0.3	9		2325	0.2	6
14 Tu	0528	1.2	37				
	1208	0.1	3				
	1814	1.2	37				
15 W	0034	0.3	9				
	0620	1.1	34				
	1230	0.2	6				
	1835	1.2	37				

March

Day	Time	ft	cm	Day	Time	ft	cm
1 W	0531	1.3	40	**16** Th	0002	0.1	3
	1145	0.2	6		0625	1.2	37
	1742	1.3	40		1150	0.6	18
					1729	1.4	43
2 Th	0011	0.1	3	**17** F	0041	0.1	3
	0632	1.2	37		0721	1.1	34
	1215	0.4	12		1217	0.7	21
	1808	1.3	40		1757	1.4	43
3 F	0107	0.0	0	**18** Sa	0126	0.1	3
	0745	1.1	34		0825	1.1	34
	1247	0.6	18		1251	0.8	24
	1839	1.4	43		1830	1.4	43
4 Sa	0218	0.0	0	**19** Su	0224	0.1	3
	0917	1.0	30		0943	1.1	34
	1321	0.8	24		1337	0.9	27
	1916	1.4	43		1911	1.4	43
5 Su	0348	-0.1	-3	**20** M	0340	0.1	3
	1123	1.0	30		1112	1.1	34
	1403	0.9	27		1451	1.0	30
	2004	1.4	43		2003	1.3	40
6 M	0520	-0.1	-3	**21** Tu	0501	0.1	3
	1337	1.1	34		1231	1.2	37
	1547	1.0	30		1636	1.0	30
	2107	1.3	40		2109	1.3	40
7 Tu	0637	-0.2	-6	**22** W	0610	0.1	3
	1427	1.1	34		1325	1.2	37
	1754	1.0	30		1806	1.0	30
	2231	1.3	40		2230	1.3	40
8 W	0739	-0.2	-6	**23** Th	0706	0.0	0
	1458	1.2	37		1403	1.3	40
	1914	0.9	27		1908	0.9	27
					2350	1.3	40
9 Th	0002	1.3	40	**24** F	0753	0.0	0
	0830	-0.2	-6		1433	1.3	40
	1525	1.2	37		1956	0.8	24
	2011	0.8	24				
10 F	0120	1.3	40	**25** Sa	0101	1.3	40
	0914	-0.2	-6		0834	0.0	0
	1547	1.2	37		1458	1.3	40
	2058	0.6	18		2036	0.6	18
11 Sa	0223	1.4	43	**26** Su	0203	1.4	43
	0950	-0.1	-3		0910	0.1	3
	1606	1.2	37		1519	1.3	40
	2139	0.5	15		2114	0.5	15
12 Su	0316	1.4	43	**27** M	0301	1.5	46
	1021	0.1	3		0944	0.2	6
	1621	1.2	37		1538	1.3	40
	2216	0.4	12		2151	0.3	9
13 M	0404	1.3	40	**28** Tu	0356	1.5	46
	1047	0.2	6		1017	0.3	9
	1634	1.2	37		1557	1.4	43
	2252	0.3	9		2230	0.1	3
14 Tu	0449	1.3	40	**29** W	0453	1.5	46
	1108	0.3	9		1048	0.5	15
	1649	1.3	40		1619	1.4	43
	2327	0.2	6		2312	0.0	0
15 W	0536	1.3	40	**30** Th	0553	1.4	43
	1128	0.5	15		1120	0.7	21
	1706	1.3	40		1645	1.5	46
					2359	-0.1	-3
				31 F	0658	1.4	43
					1153	0.9	27
					1715	1.6	49

Time meridian 75° W. 0000 is midnight. 1200 is noon. Times are not adjusted for Daylight Saving Time.
Heights are referred to mean lower low water which is the chart datum of soundings.

Apalachicola, Florida, 2017

Times and Heights of High and Low Waters

April

Day	Time	ft	cm
1 Sa	0055	-0.1	-3
	0812	1.3	40
	1229	1.0	30
	1751	1.6	49
2 Su	0203	-0.1	-3
	0940	1.2	37
	1315	1.1	34
	1836	1.5	46
3 M ◖	0326	0.0	0
	1120	1.2	37
	1434	1.1	34
	1933	1.5	46
4 Tu	0452	0.0	0
	1236	1.2	37
	1633	1.1	34
	2053	1.3	40
5 W	0606	0.0	0
	1322	1.3	40
	1808	1.0	30
	2238	1.3	40
6 Th	0707	0.1	3
	1354	1.3	40
	1914	0.8	24
7 F	0022	1.3	40
	0757	0.2	6
	1420	1.3	40
	2005	0.6	18
8 Sa	0142	1.3	40
	0839	0.3	9
	1441	1.3	40
	2049	0.5	15
9 Su	0243	1.3	40
	0915	0.4	12
	1458	1.3	40
	2128	0.3	9
10 M	0335	1.4	43
	0944	0.5	15
	1512	1.4	43
	2204	0.2	6
11 Tu ○	0421	1.4	43
	1008	0.7	21
	1527	1.4	43
	2237	0.1	3
12 W	0505	1.4	43
	1030	0.8	24
	1544	1.5	46
	2308	0.0	0
13 Th	0549	1.4	43
	1052	0.9	27
	1606	1.5	46
	2338	0.0	0
14 F	0635	1.3	40
	1118	0.9	27
	1633	1.5	46
15 Sa	0010	0.0	0
	0724	1.3	40
	1151	1.0	30
	1704	1.5	46
16 Su	0047	0.0	0
	0820	1.3	40
	1233	1.1	34
	1742	1.5	46
17 M	0133	0.1	3
	0921	1.3	40
	1331	1.1	34
	1826	1.4	43
18 Tu	0232	0.1	3
	1025	1.3	40
	1452	1.1	34
	1922	1.4	43
19 W ○	0344	0.2	6
	1124	1.3	40
	1627	1.1	34
	2035	1.3	40
20 Th	0456	0.2	6
	1212	1.4	43
	1748	1.0	30
	2204	1.2	37
21 F	0600	0.2	6
	1250	1.4	43
	1847	0.8	24
	2335	1.2	37
22 Sa	0654	0.3	9
	1321	1.4	43
	1934	0.6	18
23 Su	0057	1.3	40
	0742	0.4	12
	1346	1.4	43
	2016	0.4	12
24 M	0208	1.4	43
	0825	0.5	15
	1409	1.5	46
	2057	0.2	6
25 Tu	0313	1.5	46
	0905	0.6	18
	1432	1.5	46
	2137	0.0	0
26 W ●	0415	1.5	46
	0943	0.8	24
	1457	1.6	49
	2220	-0.1	-3
27 Th	0516	1.5	46
	1019	1.0	30
	1525	1.6	49
	2305	-0.2	-6
28 F	0617	1.5	46
	1055	1.1	34
	1557	1.7	52
	2354	-0.3	-9
29 Sa	0721	1.5	46
	1135	1.2	37
	1635	1.7	52
30 Su	0050	-0.2	-6
	0828	1.4	43
	1223	1.2	37
	1719	1.7	52

May

Day	Time	ft	cm
1 M	0152	-0.2	-6
	0937	1.4	43
	1329	1.2	37
	1813	1.6	49
2 Tu ○	0301	0.0	0
	1040	1.4	43
	1503	1.2	37
	1920	1.4	43
3 W	0412	0.1	3
	1130	1.4	43
	1642	1.0	30
	2052	1.3	40
4 Th	0519	0.2	6
	1209	1.4	43
	1801	0.8	24
	2246	1.2	37
5 F	0617	0.4	12
	1241	1.4	43
	1901	0.6	18
6 Sa	0035	1.2	37
	0707	0.5	15
	1307	1.4	43
	1951	0.4	12
7 Su	0159	1.2	37
	0750	0.6	18
	1329	1.4	43
	2035	0.2	6
8 M	0302	1.3	40
	0827	0.8	24
	1348	1.5	46
	2115	0.1	3
9 Tu	0355	1.3	40
	0859	0.9	27
	1406	1.5	46
	2151	0.0	0
10 W ○	0441	1.4	43
	0928	1.0	30
	1426	1.6	49
	2223	-0.1	-3
11 Th	0523	1.4	43
	0954	1.1	34
	1450	1.6	49
	2254	-0.1	-3
12 F	0603	1.4	43
	1023	1.1	34
	1518	1.6	49
	2323	-0.1	-3
13 Sa	0643	1.4	43
	1055	1.2	37
	1550	1.6	49
	2352	-0.1	-3
14 Su	0724	1.4	43
	1135	1.2	37
	1627	1.6	49
15 M	0024	-0.1	-3
	0808	1.4	43
	1223	1.2	37
	1708	1.5	46
16 Tu	0101	0.0	0
	0853	1.4	43
	1324	1.2	37
	1756	1.5	46
17 W	0147	0.0	0
	0939	1.4	43
	1440	1.1	34
	1855	1.4	43
18 Th ◑	0240	0.1	3
	1022	1.5	46
	1604	1.0	30
	2010	1.3	40
19 F	0340	0.2	6
	1101	1.5	46
	1720	0.9	27
	2143	1.2	37
20 Sa	0443	0.4	12
	1136	1.5	46
	1821	0.7	21
	2324	1.2	37
21 Su	0544	0.5	15
	1207	1.5	46
	1912	0.4	12
22 M	0058	1.2	37
	0641	0.7	21
	1235	1.5	46
	1959	0.2	6
23 Tu	0221	1.3	40
	0734	0.8	24
	1304	1.6	49
	2044	0.0	0
24 W	0333	1.4	43
	0822	1.0	30
	1334	1.7	52
	2129	-0.2	-6
25 Th ●	0438	1.5	46
	0907	1.1	34
	1408	1.7	52
	2215	-0.4	-12
26 F	0539	1.5	46
	0950	1.2	37
	1445	1.8	55
	2303	-0.4	-12
27 Sa	0635	1.5	46
	1034	1.3	40
	1527	1.8	55
	2352	-0.4	-12
28 Su	0729	1.5	46
	1123	1.3	40
	1613	1.8	55
29 M	0043	-0.3	-9
	0818	1.5	46
	1220	1.3	40
	1706	1.7	52
30 Tu	0135	-0.2	-6
	0904	1.4	43
	1332	1.2	37
	1806	1.5	46
31 W	0229	0.0	0
	0944	1.4	43
	1457	1.1	34
	1918	1.3	40

June

Day	Time	ft	cm
1 Th ◖	0323	0.2	6
	1021	1.4	43
	1623	0.9	27
	2049	1.2	37
2 F	0417	0.4	12
	1054	1.4	43
	1738	0.7	21
	2242	1.1	34
3 Sa	0510	0.6	18
	1124	1.5	46
	1840	0.4	12
4 Su	0039	1.1	34
	0600	0.8	24
	1152	1.5	46
	1932	0.2	6
5 M	0211	1.2	37
	0648	0.9	27
	1218	1.5	46
	2017	0.1	3
6 Tu	0319	1.2	37
	0732	1.0	30
	1245	1.6	49
	2059	-0.1	-3
7 W	0412	1.3	40
	0813	1.1	34
	1312	1.6	49
	2137	-0.1	-3
8 Th	0456	1.4	43
	0851	1.2	37
	1341	1.6	49
	2211	-0.2	-6
9 F ○	0534	1.4	43
	0927	1.2	37
	1412	1.7	52
	2243	-0.2	-6
10 Sa	0607	1.4	43
	1003	1.2	37
	1447	1.7	52
	2311	-0.2	-6
11 Su	0639	1.5	46
	1040	1.2	37
	1525	1.6	49
	2339	-0.2	-6
12 M	0710	1.5	46
	1122	1.2	37
	1606	1.6	49
13 Tu	0007	-0.1	-3
	0741	1.5	46
	1209	1.2	37
	1651	1.6	49
14 W	0038	-0.1	-3
	0813	1.5	46
	1305	1.1	34
	1742	1.5	46
15 Th	0114	0.0	0
	0846	1.5	46
	1411	1.1	34
	1842	1.3	40
16 F	0156	0.1	3
	0920	1.5	46
	1527	0.9	27
	1958	1.2	37
17 Sa ○	0242	0.3	9
	0953	1.5	46
	1644	0.7	21
	2133	1.1	34
18 Su	0335	0.5	15
	1025	1.6	49
	1752	0.5	15
	2323	1.1	34
19 M	0434	0.7	21
	1059	1.6	49
	1852	0.3	9
20 Tu	0114	1.2	37
	0538	0.9	27
	1134	1.7	52
	1945	0.0	0
21 W	0247	1.3	40
	0643	1.1	34
	1211	1.7	52
	2036	-0.2	-6
22 Th	0400	1.4	43
	0743	1.2	37
	1252	1.8	55
	2125	-0.4	-12
23 F ●	0459	1.5	46
	0838	1.3	40
	1337	1.8	55
	2213	-0.4	-12
24 Sa	0548	1.5	46
	0929	1.3	40
	1425	1.9	58
	2300	-0.4	-12
25 Su	0630	1.5	46
	1019	1.3	40
	1516	1.8	55
	2345	-0.4	-12
26 M	0708	1.5	46
	1112	1.2	37
	1609	1.8	55
27 Tu	0028	-0.2	-6
	0741	1.5	46
	1210	1.1	34
	1705	1.7	52
28 W	0109	-0.1	-3
	0811	1.5	46
	1315	1.0	30
	1806	1.5	46
29 Th	0149	0.1	3
	0839	1.5	46
	1429	0.9	27
	1915	1.3	40
30 F ◖	0227	0.4	12
	0908	1.5	46
	1548	0.7	21
	2040	1.2	37

Time meridian 75° W. 0000 is midnight. 1200 is noon. Times are not adjusted for Daylight Saving Time.
Heights are referred to mean lower low water which is the chart datum of soundings.

Apalachicola, Florida, 2017

Times and Heights of High and Low Waters

July

Day	Time	ft	cm
1 Sa	0307	0.6	18
	0937	1.5	46
	1703	0.6	18
	2228	1.1	34
2 Su	0349	0.8	24
	1008	1.6	49
	1809	0.4	12
3 M	0033	1.1	34
	0439	0.9	27
	1041	1.6	49
	1905	0.2	6
4 Tu	0218	1.2	37
	0538	1.1	34
	1116	1.6	49
	1955	0.0	0
5 W	0325	1.3	40
	0640	1.2	37
	1154	1.7	52
	2039	-0.1	-3
6 Th	0411	1.4	43
	0737	1.3	40
	1233	1.7	52
	2119	-0.1	-3
7 F	0447	1.4	43
	0826	1.3	40
	1313	1.7	52
	2156	-0.2	-6
8 Sa ○	0518	1.5	46
	0910	1.3	40
	1355	1.7	52
	2228	-0.2	-6
9 Su	0546	1.5	46
	0949	1.3	40
	1436	1.7	52
	2256	-0.1	-3
10 M	0610	1.5	46
	1027	1.2	37
	1518	1.7	52
	2322	-0.1	-3
11 Tu	0634	1.5	46
	1105	1.2	37
	1602	1.7	52
	2347	0.0	0
12 W	0657	1.5	46
	1148	1.1	34
	1649	1.6	49
13 Th	0015	0.0	0
	0721	1.5	46
	1236	1.0	30
	1742	1.5	46
14 F	0045	0.2	6
	0747	1.6	49
	1333	0.9	27
	1843	1.4	43
15 Sa	0120	0.3	9
	0815	1.6	49
	1443	0.8	24
	2000	1.3	40
16 Su ◗	0158	0.5	15
	0846	1.6	49
	1603	0.6	18
	2138	1.1	34
17 M	0241	0.8	24
	0920	1.7	52
	1724	0.4	12
	2341	1.1	34
18 Tu	0333	1.0	30
	0959	1.7	52
	1835	0.2	6
19 W	0149	1.2	37
	0443	1.1	34
	1045	1.8	55
	1936	0.0	0
20 Th	0318	1.4	43
	0609	1.3	40
	1136	1.8	55
	2031	-0.2	-6
21 F	0412	1.5	46
	0725	1.4	43
	1232	1.9	58
	2121	-0.3	-9
22 Sa	0453	1.5	46
	0827	1.4	43
	1329	1.9	58
	2207	-0.3	-9
23 Su ●	0527	1.5	46
	0920	1.3	40
	1426	1.9	58
	2249	-0.2	-6
24 M	0556	1.5	46
	1010	1.2	37
	1521	1.9	58
	2328	-0.1	-3
25 Tu	0621	1.5	46
	1059	1.1	34
	1615	1.8	55
26 W	0003	0.0	0
	0643	1.5	46
	1151	1.0	30
	1710	1.7	52
27 Th	0035	0.2	6
	0705	1.5	46
	1247	0.9	27
	1807	1.5	46
28 F	0104	0.4	12
	0727	1.6	49
	1349	0.8	24
	1912	1.4	43
29 Sa	0132	0.6	18
	0752	1.6	49
	1459	0.7	21
	2030	1.2	37
30 Su ◖	0202	0.8	24
	0821	1.6	49
	1615	0.6	18
	2210	1.2	37
31 M	0237	1.0	30
	0855	1.7	52
	1728	0.4	12

August

Day	Time	ft	cm
1 Tu	0015	1.2	37
	0327	1.1	34
	0935	1.7	52
	1831	0.3	9
2 W	0202	1.3	40
	0447	1.2	37
	1023	1.7	52
	1926	0.2	6
3 Th	0259	1.4	43
	0611	1.3	40
	1116	1.7	52
	2014	0.1	3
4 F	0337	1.5	46
	0719	1.3	40
	1210	1.7	52
	2056	0.0	0
5 Sa	0409	1.5	46
	0812	1.3	40
	1302	1.8	55
	2132	0.0	0
6 Su	0436	1.6	49
	0856	1.3	40
	1351	1.8	55
	2204	0.0	0
7 M ○	0500	1.6	49
	0934	1.2	37
	1437	1.8	55
	2232	0.1	3
8 Tu	0520	1.6	49
	1010	1.2	37
	1522	1.8	55
	2258	0.1	3
9 W	0539	1.6	49
	1045	1.1	34
	1608	1.8	55
	2322	0.2	6
10 Th	0558	1.6	49
	1123	1.0	30
	1657	1.7	52
	2348	0.3	9
11 F	0619	1.6	49
	1207	0.9	27
	1751	1.6	49
12 Sa	0017	0.5	15
	0642	1.7	52
	1258	0.8	24
	1855	1.5	46
13 Su	0048	0.7	21
	0710	1.7	52
	1404	0.6	18
	2015	1.4	43
14 M ◖	0123	0.9	27
	0743	1.8	55
	1527	0.5	15
	2159	1.3	40
15 Tu	0201	1.1	34
	0822	1.8	55
	1700	0.4	12
16 W	0017	1.3	40
	0250	1.2	37
	0911	1.8	55
	1820	0.2	6
17 Th	0219	1.4	43
	0429	1.3	40
	1012	1.9	58
	1925	0.1	3
18 F	0310	1.5	46
	0616	1.4	43
	1123	1.9	58
	2021	0.0	0
19 Sa	0345	1.6	49
	0731	1.4	43
	1234	1.9	58
	2109	0.0	0
20 Su	0415	1.6	49
	0828	1.3	40
	1340	1.9	58
	2152	0.0	0
21 M ●	0439	1.6	49
	0917	1.2	37
	1439	1.9	58
	2230	0.1	3
22 Tu	0500	1.6	49
	1002	1.1	34
	1533	1.9	58
	2303	0.3	9
23 W	0518	1.6	49
	1045	0.9	27
	1625	1.8	55
	2331	0.4	12
24 Th	0534	1.6	49
	1129	0.8	24
	1716	1.7	52
	2356	0.6	18
25 F	0552	1.6	49
	1215	0.7	21
	1810	1.6	49
26 Sa	0019	0.8	24
	0613	1.7	52
	1305	0.7	21
	1910	1.5	46
27 Su	0044	0.9	27
	0638	1.7	52
	1403	0.6	18
	2021	1.4	43
28 M	0113	1.1	34
	0709	1.8	55
	1515	0.6	18
	2151	1.4	43
29 Tu ◖	0152	1.2	37
	0748	1.8	55
	1633	0.5	15
	2339	1.4	43
30 W	0255	1.3	40
	0837	1.7	52
	1746	0.4	12
31 Th	0110	1.5	46
	0433	1.4	43
	0937	1.7	52
	1847	0.4	12

September

Day	Time	ft	cm
1 F	0203	1.5	46
	0603	1.4	43
	1047	1.7	52
	1938	0.3	9
2 Sa	0241	1.6	49
	0708	1.3	40
	1156	1.7	52
	2021	0.3	9
3 Su	0312	1.6	49
	0759	1.3	40
	1257	1.8	55
	2059	0.3	9
4 M	0337	1.7	52
	0840	1.2	37
	1351	1.8	55
	2131	0.3	9
5 Tu	0359	1.7	52
	0916	1.1	34
	1441	1.9	58
	2200	0.4	12
6 W ○	0417	1.7	52
	0951	1.0	30
	1529	1.9	58
	2227	0.4	12
7 Th	0435	1.7	52
	1025	0.8	24
	1618	1.8	55
	2253	0.6	18
8 F	0453	1.7	52
	1102	0.7	21
	1711	1.8	55
	2321	0.7	21
9 Sa	0514	1.8	55
	1144	0.6	18
	1809	1.7	52
	2350	0.9	27
10 Su	0539	1.8	55
	1234	0.5	15
	1917	1.6	49
11 M	0021	1.1	34
	0610	1.9	58
	1338	0.5	15
	2040	1.5	46
12 Tu	0056	1.2	37
	0647	1.9	58
	1502	0.4	12
	2229	1.5	46
13 W ◖	0140	1.4	43
	0735	1.9	58
	1638	0.4	12
14 Th	0035	1.5	46
	0304	1.4	43
	0837	1.8	55
	1800	0.3	9
15 F	0145	1.6	49
	0510	1.5	46
	0959	1.8	55
	1907	0.3	9
16 Sa	0223	1.6	49
	0637	1.4	43
	1131	1.8	55
	2001	0.3	9
17 Su	0253	1.6	49
	0739	1.2	37
	1254	1.8	55
	2048	0.3	9
18 M	0317	1.6	49
	0829	1.1	34
	1401	1.8	55
	2127	0.4	12
19 Tu	0337	1.6	49
	0913	0.9	27
	1458	1.8	55
	2201	0.5	15
20 W ●	0354	1.6	49
	0954	0.8	24
	1549	1.8	55
	2229	0.7	21
21 Th	0409	1.7	52
	1032	0.7	21
	1637	1.8	55
	2253	0.8	24
22 F	0424	1.7	52
	1109	0.6	18
	1725	1.7	52
	2315	1.0	30
23 Sa	0442	1.7	52
	1146	0.5	15
	1816	1.7	52
	2338	1.1	34
24 Su	0505	1.8	55
	1225	0.5	15
	1911	1.6	49
25 M	0005	1.2	37
	0533	1.8	55
	1311	0.5	15
	2015	1.5	46
26 Tu	0040	1.3	40
	0608	1.8	55
	1409	0.5	15
	2130	1.5	46
27 W ◗	0131	1.3	40
	0651	1.7	52
	1525	0.5	15
	2252	1.5	46
28 Th	0250	1.4	43
	0745	1.7	52
	1644	0.5	15
29 F	0004	1.6	49
	0431	1.4	43
	0856	1.6	49
	1751	0.5	15
30 Sa	0056	1.6	49
	0554	1.3	40
	1020	1.6	49
	1847	0.5	15

Time meridian 75° W. 0000 is midnight. 1200 is noon. Times are not adjusted for Daylight Saving Time.
Heights are referred to mean lower low water which is the chart datum of soundings.

Apalachicola, Florida, 2017

Times and Heights of High and Low Waters

October

Day	Time	ft	cm	Day	Time	ft	cm
1 Su	0135	1.6	49	16 M	0149	1.6	49
	0654	1.2	37		0738	0.9	27
	1141	1.6	49		1318	1.6	49
	1933	0.4	12		2014	0.6	18
2 M	0205	1.7	52	17 Tu	0212	1.6	49
	0741	1.1	34		0825	0.7	21
	1251	1.7	52		1425	1.6	49
	2013	0.5	15		2052	0.7	21
3 Tu	0230	1.7	52	18 W	0230	1.6	49
	0821	0.9	27		0907	0.5	15
	1351	1.7	52		1520	1.6	49
	2049	0.5	15		2124	0.8	24
4 W	0251	1.7	52	19 Th	0247	1.6	49
	0857	0.8	24		0945	0.4	12
	1446	1.8	55		1609	1.6	49
	2121	0.6	18	●	2151	0.9	27
5 Th O	0310	1.7	52	20 F	0303	1.7	52
	0932	0.6	18		1020	0.3	9
	1540	1.8	55		1655	1.6	49
	2152	0.8	24		2215	1.1	34
6 F	0329	1.7	52	21 Sa	0321	1.7	52
	1008	0.5	15		1052	0.2	6
	1634	1.8	55		1739	1.6	49
	2222	0.9	27		2238	1.1	34
7 Sa	0350	1.8	55	22 Su	0343	1.7	52
	1047	0.3	9		1124	0.2	6
	1731	1.8	55		1825	1.6	49
	2253	1.1	34		2305	1.2	37
8 Su	0416	1.8	55	23 M	0410	1.7	52
	1131	0.2	6		1157	0.2	6
	1832	1.7	52		1913	1.5	46
	2325	1.2	37		2338	1.2	37
9 M	0446	1.9	58	24 Tu	0443	1.7	52
	1222	0.2	6		1234	0.2	6
	1942	1.6	49		2006	1.5	46
10 Tu	0001	1.3	40	25 W	0021	1.3	40
	0522	1.9	58		0521	1.7	52
	1325	0.2	6		1319	0.3	9
	2104	1.6	49		2104	1.5	46
11 W	0045	1.4	43	26 Th	0120	1.3	40
	0606	1.9	58		0607	1.6	49
	1445	0.2	6		1416	0.3	9
	2237	1.5	46		2203	1.5	46
12 Th ◐	0157	1.4	43	27 F	0243	1.3	40
	0703	1.8	55		0704	1.5	46
	1612	0.3	9		1525	0.4	12
	2356	1.5	46	◐	2258	1.5	46
13 F	0352	1.4	43	28 Sa	0417	1.2	37
	0821	1.7	52		0819	1.4	43
	1730	0.3	9		1635	0.4	12
					2345	1.5	46
14 Sa	0046	1.5	46	29 Su	0534	1.1	34
	0533	1.3	40		0950	1.3	40
	1004	1.6	49		1736	0.4	12
	1835	0.4	12				
15 Su	0122	1.6	49	30 M	0022	1.6	49
	0644	1.1	34		0633	0.9	27
	1151	1.6	49		1122	1.3	40
	1929	0.5	15		1830	0.5	15
				31 Tu	0053	1.6	49
					0719	0.7	21
					1243	1.4	43
					1917	0.6	18

November

Day	Time	ft	cm	Day	Time	ft	cm
1 W	0119	1.6	49	16 Th	0124	1.5	46
	0801	0.5	15		0857	0.0	0
	1353	1.5	46		1544	1.3	40
	1959	0.7	21		2043	0.9	27
2 Th	0142	1.6	49	17 F	0145	1.5	46
	0839	0.3	9		0935	-0.1	-3
	1456	1.5	46		1631	1.4	43
	2039	0.8	24		2114	1.0	30
3 F	0205	1.6	49	18 Sa	0207	1.5	46
	0918	0.1	3		1010	-0.1	-3
	1556	1.6	49		1713	1.4	43
	2116	0.9	27	●	2143	1.1	34
4 Sa	0230	1.7	52	19 Su	0231	1.6	49
	0957	0.0	0		1042	-0.2	-6
	1654	1.6	49		1753	1.4	43
O	2152	1.1	34		2212	1.1	34
5 Su	0258	1.8	55	20 M	0300	1.6	49
	1040	-0.2	-6		1112	-0.2	-6
	1753	1.6	49		1830	1.4	43
	2228	1.2	37		2244	1.1	34
6 M	0331	1.8	55	21 Tu	0333	1.6	49
	1127	-0.2	-6		1141	-0.1	-3
	1854	1.6	49		1908	1.4	43
	2306	1.3	40		2322	1.1	34
7 Tu	0409	1.8	55	22 W	0410	1.5	46
	1219	-0.2	-6		1212	-0.1	-3
	1957	1.5	46		1948	1.4	43
	2351	1.3	40				
8 W	0453	1.8	55	23 Th	0009	1.1	34
	1318	-0.1	-3		0452	1.5	46
	2102	1.5	46		1246	-0.1	-3
					2029	1.4	43
9 Th	0051	1.3	40	24 F	0107	1.1	34
	0545	1.7	52		0540	1.4	43
	1425	0.0	0		1327	0.0	0
	2204	1.4	43		2111	1.4	43
10 F O	0219	1.2	37	25 Sa	0219	1.0	30
	0651	1.5	46		0637	1.3	40
	1537	0.1	3		1416	0.1	3
	2257	1.4	43		2152	1.4	43
11 Sa	0402	1.1	34	26 Su	0342	0.9	27
	0819	1.3	40		0750	1.1	34
	1645	0.3	9		1511	0.2	6
	2338	1.4	43	◐	2231	1.4	43
12 Su	0529	0.9	27	27 M	0500	0.8	24
	1011	1.2	37		0921	1.0	30
	1747	0.4	12		1611	0.3	9
					2306	1.4	43
13 M	0011	1.4	43	28 Tu	0602	0.6	18
	0635	0.7	21		1103	1.0	30
	1208	1.2	37		1713	0.4	12
	1841	0.5	15		2338	1.4	43
14 Tu	0039	1.4	43	29 W	0654	0.3	9
	0729	0.4	12		1239	1.1	34
	1340	1.3	40		1811	0.6	18
	1927	0.7	21				
15 W	0103	1.5	46	30 Th	0008	1.4	43
	0815	0.2	6		0740	0.1	3
	1448	1.3	40		1403	1.1	34
	2008	0.8	24		1906	0.7	21

December

Day	Time	ft	cm	Day	Time	ft	cm
1 F	0038	1.5	46	16 Sa	0054	1.4	43
	0824	-0.1	-3		0923	-0.4	-12
	1514	1.3	40		1644	1.2	37
	1956	0.9	27		2045	0.9	27
2 Sa	0109	1.5	46	17 Su	0126	1.4	43
	0908	-0.4	-12		0959	-0.4	-12
	1616	1.3	40		1720	1.2	37
	2043	1.0	30		2122	1.0	30
3 Su	0144	1.6	49	18 M	0201	1.4	43
	0953	-0.5	-15		1032	-0.5	-15
	1714	1.4	43		1751	1.2	37
O	2126	1.1	34	●	2158	1.0	30
4 M	0222	1.6	49	19 Tu	0237	1.4	43
	1039	-0.6	-18		1102	-0.4	-12
	1808	1.4	43		1819	1.2	37
	2209	1.1	34		2234	0.9	27
5 Tu	0305	1.7	52	20 W	0316	1.4	43
	1126	-0.6	-18		1128	-0.4	-12
	1858	1.3	40		1847	1.2	37
	2255	1.1	34		2312	0.9	27
6 W	0353	1.6	49	21 Th	0357	1.3	40
	1216	-0.5	-15		1154	-0.4	-12
	1946	1.3	40		1915	1.2	37
	2347	1.1	34		2354	0.8	24
7 Th	0445	1.5	46	22 F	0441	1.3	40
	1306	-0.4	-12		1221	-0.3	-9
	2030	1.2	37		1944	1.2	37
8 F	0052	1.0	30	23 Sa	0044	0.8	24
	0543	1.4	43		0530	1.2	37
	1358	-0.2	-6		1252	-0.2	-6
	2110	1.2	37		2014	1.2	37
9 Sa	0213	0.9	27	24 Su	0142	0.7	21
	0652	1.2	37		0626	1.1	34
	1452	0.0	0		1328	-0.1	-3
	2147	1.2	37		2045	1.2	37
10 Su O	0342	0.7	21	25 M	0252	0.6	18
	0819	1.0	30		0735	0.9	27
	1546	0.2	6		1409	0.0	0
	2221	1.2	37		2118	1.2	37
11 M	0506	0.5	15	26 Tu	0409	0.4	12
	1010	0.9	27		0904	0.8	24
	1641	0.4	12		1457	0.2	6
	2254	1.2	37	◐	2151	1.2	37
12 Tu	0614	0.2	6	27 W	0522	0.2	6
	1217	0.9	27		1052	0.8	24
	1736	0.6	18		1554	0.4	12
	2324	1.3	40		2226	1.3	40
13 W	0711	0.0	0	28 Th	0626	0.0	0
	1400	0.9	27		1247	0.8	24
	1829	0.7	21		1702	0.6	18
	2354	1.3	40		2303	1.3	40
14 Th	0800	-0.2	-6	29 F	0722	-0.3	-9
	1510	1.0	30		1424	0.9	27
	1918	0.8	24		1814	0.8	24
					2344	1.4	43
15 F	0024	1.3	40	30 Sa	0813	-0.5	-15
	0844	-0.3	-9		1537	1.1	34
	1603	1.1	34		1920	0.9	27
	2004	0.9	27				
				31 Su	0028	1.4	43
					0903	-0.6	-18
					1633	1.2	37
					2018	1.0	30

Time meridian 75° W. 0000 is midnight. 1200 is noon. Times are not adjusted for Daylight Saving Time.
Heights are referred to mean lower low water which is the chart datum of soundings.

Pensacola, Florida, 2017

Times and Heights of High and Low Waters

January

Day	Time (h m)	Height (ft)	Height (cm)	Day	Time (h m)	Height (ft)	Height (cm)
1 Su	1032	-0.6	-18	16 M	0034	0.8	24
					1036	-0.3	-9
2 M	0018	1.1	34	17 Tu	0057	0.6	18
	1056	-0.5	-15		1021	-0.1	-3
3 Tu	0055	0.9	27	18 W	0010	0.4	12
	1113	-0.3	-9		0939	0.0	0
					1759	0.4	12
4 W	0130	0.7	21	19 Th ☽	0810	0.0	0
	1116	-0.1	-3		1742	0.6	18
	2035	0.4	12				
5 Th ◖	1051	0.0	0	20 F	0512	-0.1	-3
	1846	0.5	15		1752	0.7	21
6 F	0356	0.0	0	21 Sa	0459	-0.3	-9
	1829	0.7	21		1817	0.8	24
7 Sa	0418	-0.2	-6	22 Su	0525	-0.4	-12
	1844	0.9	27		1852	0.9	27
8 Su	0507	-0.4	-12	23 M	0601	-0.5	-15
	1918	1.1	34		1933	1.0	30
9 M	0601	-0.6	-18	24 Tu	0640	-0.5	-15
	2002	1.2	37		2017	1.1	34
10 Tu	0658	-0.8	-24	25 W	0719	-0.6	-18
	2052	1.3	40		2101	1.1	34
11 W	0753	-0.8	-24	26 Th	0756	-0.6	-18
	2143	1.3	40		2144	1.1	34
12 Th ○	0845	-0.8	-24	27 F ●	0830	-0.6	-18
	2233	1.3	40		2225	1.1	34
13 F	0931	-0.8	-24	28 Sa	0900	-0.6	-18
	2319	1.2	37		2305	1.1	34
14 Sa	1007	-0.6	-18	29 Su	0925	-0.5	-15
					2348	0.9	27
15 Su	0000	1.0	30	30 M	0945	-0.4	-12
	1030	-0.5	-15				
				31 Tu	0033	0.8	24
					0954	-0.2	-6

February

Day	Time (h m)	Height (ft)	Height (cm)	Day	Time (h m)	Height (ft)	Height (cm)
1 W	0126	0.5	15	16 Th	0300	0.2	6
	0946	0.0	0		0602	0.1	3
	1656	0.3	9		1510	0.6	18
	2144	0.2	6				
2 Th	0243	0.3	9	17 F	0141	0.0	0
	0859	0.1	3		1535	0.7	21
	1620	0.5	15				
3 F ◐	0110	0.0	0	18 Sa ○	0253	-0.1	-3
	1631	0.7	21		1612	0.8	24
4 Sa	0254	-0.2	-6	19 Su	0347	-0.2	-6
	1706	0.9	27		1701	0.9	27
5 Su	0403	-0.4	-12	20 M	0436	-0.3	-9
	1756	1.0	30		1758	1.0	30
6 M	0505	-0.6	-18	21 Tu	0522	-0.4	-12
	1854	1.1	34		1857	1.0	30
7 Tu	0603	-0.7	-21	22 W	0604	-0.4	-12
	1955	1.2	37		1953	1.1	34
8 W	0657	-0.7	-21	23 Th	0642	-0.4	-12
	2054	1.2	37		2046	1.1	34
9 Th	0744	-0.7	-21	24 F	0715	-0.4	-12
	2148	1.2	37		2137	1.1	34
10 F ○	0824	-0.6	-18	25 Sa	0743	-0.4	-12
	2238	1.1	34		2227	1.0	30
11 Sa	0852	-0.4	-12	26 Su ●	0807	-0.2	-6
	2323	0.9	27		2321	0.9	27
12 Su	0907	-0.3	-9	27 M	0822	-0.1	-3
13 M	0006	0.7	21	28 Tu	0024	0.7	21
	0904	-0.1	-3		0823	0.1	3
					1359	0.3	9
					1837	0.2	6
14 Tu	0049	0.5	15				
	0839	0.1	3				
	1522	0.3	9				
	2019	0.2	6				
15 W	0136	0.3	9				
	0750	0.1	3				
	1501	0.5	15				
	2314	0.1	3				

March

Day	Time (h m)	Height (ft)	Height (cm)	Day	Time (h m)	Height (ft)	Height (cm)
1 W	0143	0.6	18	16 Th	1254	0.9	27
	0755	0.3	9		2236	0.0	0
	1333	0.5	15				
	2049	0.1	3				
2 Th	1343	0.7	21	17 F	1321	1.0	30
	2251	0.0	0		2358	0.0	0
3 F	1416	0.9	27	18 Sa	1358	1.0	30
4 Sa	0048	-0.2	-6	19 Su	0121	-0.1	-3
	1505	1.0	30		1445	1.1	34
5 Su ◐	0225	-0.3	-9	20 M ☽	0233	-0.1	-3
	1608	1.1	34		1544	1.1	34
6 M	0343	-0.4	-12	21 Tu	0332	-0.2	-6
	1720	1.2	37		1652	1.1	34
7 Tu	0448	-0.5	-15	22 W	0421	-0.2	-6
	1836	1.2	37		1805	1.1	34
8 W	0542	-0.4	-12	23 Th	0501	-0.2	-6
	1948	1.2	37		1916	1.1	34
9 Th	0626	-0.4	-12	24 F	0535	-0.1	-3
	2053	1.1	34		2025	1.1	34
10 F	0700	-0.2	-6	25 Sa	0602	0.0	0
	2152	1.0	30		2135	1.0	30
11 Sa	0719	-0.1	-3	26 Su	0623	0.1	3
	2249	0.9	27		2251	0.9	27
12 Su ○	0721	0.1	3	27 M ●	0630	0.3	9
	1357	0.3	9		1154	0.5	15
	1600	0.2	6		1712	0.3	9
	2347	0.7	21				
13 M	0703	0.3	9	28 Tu	0021	0.8	24
	1243	0.5	15		0613	0.5	15
	1825	0.3	9		1125	0.7	21
					1847	0.2	6
14 Tu	0055	0.6	18	29 W	0247	0.6	18
	0621	0.4	12		0447	0.5	15
	1229	0.6	18		1127	0.9	27
	1958	0.2	6		2011	0.0	0
15 W	0247	0.4	12	30 Th	1151	1.1	34
	0449	0.3	9		2137	-0.1	-3
	1236	0.8	24				
	2118	0.1	3				
				31 F	1229	1.3	40
					2308	-0.2	-6

Time meridian 90° W. 0000 is midnight. 1200 is noon. Times are not adjusted for Daylight Saving Time.
Heights are referred to mean lower low water which is the chart datum of soundings.

Pensacola, Florida, 2017

Times and Heights of High and Low Waters

April

Day	Time (h m)	Height (ft)	Height (cm)
1 Sa	1319	1.4	43
2 Su	0040	-0.2	-6
	1418	1.4	43
3 M ◐	0203	-0.3	-9
	1527	1.4	43
4 Tu	0312	-0.3	-9
	1644	1.3	40
5 W	0406	-0.2	-6
	1807	1.2	37
6 Th	0446	-0.1	-3
	1930	1.1	34
7 F	0511	0.1	3
	2050	0.9	27
8 Sa	0516	0.3	9
	1208	0.6	18
	1543	0.5	15
	2212	0.8	24
9 Su	0458	0.4	12
	1103	0.7	21
	1733	0.4	12
	2348	0.6	18
10 M	0410	0.5	15
	1046	0.9	27
	1844	0.3	9
11 Tu ○	1048	1.0	30
	1940	0.2	6
12 W	1101	1.1	34
	2031	0.1	3
13 Th	1121	1.2	37
	2122	0.0	0
14 F	1147	1.3	40
	2219	0.0	0
15 Sa	1220	1.3	40
	2323	0.0	0
16 Su	1259	1.3	40
17 M	0030	0.0	0
	1345	1.3	40
18 Tu	0130	-0.1	-3
	1437	1.3	40
19 W ◐	0221	-0.1	-3
	1538	1.2	37
20 Th	0302	0.0	0
	1651	1.2	37
21 F	0335	0.0	0
	1823	1.1	34
22 Sa	0359	0.2	6
	2009	0.9	27
23 Su	0412	0.4	12
	1052	0.7	21
	1600	0.5	15
	2207	0.8	24
24 M	0404	0.5	15
	1007	0.8	24
	1723	0.3	9
25 Tu	0051	0.7	21
	0253	0.6	18
	0955	1.0	30
	1831	0.1	3
26 W ●	1006	1.2	37
	1938	-0.1	-3
27 Th	1034	1.4	43
	2047	-0.2	-6
28 F	1114	1.6	49
	2201	-0.3	-9
29 Sa	1201	1.6	49
	2318	-0.3	-9
30 Su	1254	1.6	49

May

Day	Time (h m)	Height (ft)	Height (cm)
1 M	0031	-0.3	-9
	1351	1.6	49
2 Tu ◐	0134	-0.2	-6
	1450	1.4	43
3 W	0222	-0.1	-3
	1553	1.2	37
4 Th	0254	0.1	3
	1704	1.0	30
5 F	0306	0.2	6
	1208	0.8	24
	1452	0.7	21
	1849	0.8	24
6 Sa	0252	0.4	12
	1009	0.8	24
	1704	0.5	15
	2121	0.6	18
7 Su	0158	0.5	15
	0935	1.0	30
	1801	0.4	12
8 M	0929	1.1	34
	1845	0.2	6
9 Tu	0937	1.3	40
	1924	0.1	3
10 W ○	0953	1.4	43
	2002	0.0	0
11 Th	1016	1.4	43
	2042	-0.1	-3
12 F	1043	1.5	46
	2127	-0.1	-3
13 Sa	1114	1.5	46
	2216	-0.1	-3
14 Su	1149	1.5	46
	2307	-0.1	-3
15 M	1227	1.5	46
	2354	-0.1	-3
16 Tu	1306	1.4	43
17 W	0036	-0.1	-3
	1347	1.4	43
18 Th	0110	0.0	0
	1429	1.2	37
19 F	0137	0.1	3
	1517	1.1	34
20 Sa	0155	0.2	6
	1110	0.8	24
	1503	0.7	21
	1711	0.8	24
21 Su	0156	0.4	12
	0925	0.9	27
	1622	0.5	15
	2052	0.6	18
22 M	0119	0.5	15
	0851	1.0	30
	1714	0.3	9
23 Tu	0847	1.2	37
	1808	0.0	0
24 W	0903	1.4	43
	1905	-0.2	-6
25 Th ●	0935	1.6	49
	2007	-0.3	-9
26 F	1016	1.7	52
	2112	-0.4	-12
27 Sa	1103	1.8	55
	2217	-0.4	-12
28 Su	1153	1.8	55
	2318	-0.4	-12
29 M	1243	1.7	52
30 Tu	0010	-0.3	-9
	1330	1.5	46
31 W	0049	-0.1	-3
	1410	1.3	40

June

Day	Time (h m)	Height (ft)	Height (cm)
1 Th ◐	0110	0.0	0
	1425	1.0	30
2 F	0109	0.2	6
	1024	0.9	27
3 Sa	0037	0.4	12
	0849	0.9	27
	2250	0.5	15
4 Su	0823	1.1	34
	1811	0.3	9
5 M	0822	1.2	37
	1831	0.1	3
6 Tu	0835	1.4	43
	1901	0.0	0
7 W	0855	1.5	46
	1934	-0.1	-3
8 Th	0922	1.5	46
	2011	-0.1	-3
9 F ○	0952	1.6	49
	2051	-0.2	-6
10 Sa	1025	1.6	49
	2131	-0.2	-6
11 Su	1059	1.6	49
	2210	-0.2	-6
12 M	1134	1.6	49
	2246	-0.2	-6
13 Tu	1209	1.5	46
	2317	-0.2	-6
14 W	1242	1.4	43
	2343	-0.1	-3
15 Th	1314	1.3	40
16 F ◐	0002	0.0	0
	1336	1.1	34
17 Sa ◐	0011	0.2	6
	0957	0.9	27
18 Su	0000	0.4	12
	0806	0.9	27
	2252	0.5	15
19 M	0737	1.1	34
	1654	0.3	9
20 Tu	0740	1.3	40
	1737	0.0	0
21 W	0803	1.5	46
	1830	-0.2	-6
22 Th	0840	1.7	52
	1927	-0.4	-12
23 F ●	0925	1.8	55
	2026	-0.5	-15
24 Sa	1014	1.8	55
	2124	-0.5	-15
25 Su	1105	1.8	55
	2216	-0.4	-12
26 M	1153	1.7	52
	2300	-0.3	-9
27 Tu	1237	1.5	46
	2331	-0.1	-3
28 W	1313	1.3	40
	2344	0.1	3
29 Th	1330	1.1	34
	2335	0.3	9
30 F ◐	0924	0.9	27
	2253	0.4	12

Time meridian 90° W. 0000 is midnight. 1200 is noon. Times are not adjusted for Daylight Saving Time.
Heights are referred to mean lower low water which is the chart datum of soundings.

Pensacola, Florida, 2017
Times and Heights of High and Low Waters

July

Day	Time (h m)	Height (ft)	Height (cm)
1 Sa	0724 / 2105	0.9 / 0.4	27 / 12
2 Su	0701 / 1753	1.1 / 0.3	34 / 9
3 M	0707 / 1755	1.3 / 0.1	40 / 3
4 Tu	0727 / 1822	1.4 / 0.0	43 / 0
5 W	0755 / 1856	1.5 / -0.1	46 / -3
6 Th	0828 / 1933	1.5 / -0.1	46 / -3
7 F	0904 / 2011	1.6 / -0.2	49 / -6
8 Sa ○	0942 / 2047	1.6 / -0.2	49 / -6
9 Su	1018 / 2119	1.6 / -0.2	49 / -6
10 M	1054 / 2148	1.6 / -0.2	49 / -6
11 Tu	1128 / 2212	1.5 / -0.1	46 / -3
12 W	1202 / 2231	1.4 / 0.0	43 / 0
13 Th	1237 / 2244	1.3 / 0.1	40 / 3
14 F	1311 / 2245	1.1 / 0.3	34 / 9
15 Sa	0823 / 1049 / 1325 / 2223	0.8 / 0.7 / 0.8 / 0.4	24 / 21 / 24 / 12
16 Su ◐	0621 / 2051	0.9 / 0.5	27 / 15
17 M	0605 / 1603	1.1 / 0.3	34 / 9
18 Tu	0621 / 1650	1.3 / 0.1	40 / 3
19 W	0655 / 1744	1.5 / -0.1	46 / -3
20 Th	0741 / 1841	1.7 / -0.3	52 / -9
21 F	0833 / 1937	1.8 / -0.3	55 / -9
22 Sa	0927 / 2029	1.9 / -0.3	58 / -9
23 Su ●	1020 / 2116	1.8 / -0.3	55 / -9
24 M	1109 / 2153	1.7 / -0.1	52 / -3
25 Tu	1155 / 2218	1.6 / 0.0	49 / 0
26 W	1236 / 2225	1.3 / 0.2	40 / 6
27 Th	1312 / 2208	1.1 / 0.4	34 / 12
28 F	0656 / 0856 / 1328 / 2118	0.8 / 0.7 / 0.9 / 0.6	24 / 21 / 27 / 18
29 Sa	0511 / 1928	1.0 / 0.6	30 / 18
30 Su ◑	0505 / 1622	1.1 / 0.4	34 / 12
31 M	0524 / 1638	1.3 / 0.3	40 / 9

August

Day	Time (h m)	Height (ft)	Height (cm)
1 Tu	0556 / 1714	1.4 / 0.2	43 / 6
2 W	0636 / 1754	1.5 / 0.1	46 / 3
3 Th	0721 / 1835	1.5 / 0.0	46 / 0
4 F	0808 / 1913	1.6 / 0.0	49 / 0
5 Sa	0852 / 1948	1.6 / 0.0	49 / 0
6 Su	0934 / 2018	1.6 / 0.0	49 / 0
7 M ○	1014 / 2044	1.6 / 0.0	49 / 0
8 Tu	1053 / 2104	1.6 / 0.1	49 / 3
9 W	1134 / 2119	1.5 / 0.3	46 / 9
10 Th	1219 / 2126	1.3 / 0.4	40 / 12
11 F	1313 / 2116	1.1 / 0.6	34 / 18
12 Sa	0407 / 0903 / 1428 / 2035	0.9 / 0.8 / 0.9 / 0.7	27 / 24 / 27 / 21
13 Su	0343 / 1205	1.1 / 0.6	34 / 18
14 M ◐	0357 / 1409	1.2 / 0.4	37 / 12
15 Tu	0434 / 1530	1.4 / 0.2	43 / 6
16 W	0526 / 1637	1.6 / 0.1	49 / 3
17 Th	0627 / 1738	1.7 / 0.0	52 / 0
18 F	0731 / 1834	1.8 / -0.1	55 / -3
19 Sa	0833 / 1923	1.8 / -0.1	55 / -3
20 Su	0932 / 2006	1.8 / 0.0	55 / 0
21 M ●	1026 / 2038	1.7 / 0.2	52 / 6
22 Tu	1118 / 2056	1.5 / 0.4	46 / 12
23 W	1209 / 2052	1.3 / 0.6	40 / 18
24 Th	1304 / 2020	1.1 / 0.7	34 / 21
25 F	0216 / 0816 / 1416 / 1912	1.0 / 0.8 / 0.9 / 0.8	30 / 24 / 27 / 24
26 Sa	0211 / 1038	1.1 / 0.7	34 / 21
27 Su	0229 / 1244	1.3 / 0.6	40 / 18
28 M	0301 / 1415	1.4 / 0.5	43 / 15
29 Tu ◑	0345 / 1522	1.5 / 0.4	46 / 12
30 W	0439 / 1617	1.5 / 0.3	46 / 9
31 Th	0540 / 1706	1.6 / 0.3	49 / 9

September

Day	Time (h m)	Height (ft)	Height (cm)
1 F	0642 / 1748	1.6 / 0.2	49 / 6
2 Sa	0741 / 1824	1.6 / 0.2	49 / 6
3 Su	0834 / 1855	1.6 / 0.3	49 / 9
4 M	0924 / 1919	1.6 / 0.3	49 / 9
5 Tu	1014 / 1938	1.5 / 0.5	46 / 15
6 W ○	1108 / 1948	1.4 / 0.6	43 / 18
7 Th	1211 / 1944	1.3 / 0.8	40 / 24
8 F	0106 / 0633 / 1332 / 1914	0.9 / 0.8 / 1.1 / 0.9	27 / 24 / 34 / 27
9 Sa	0052 / 0824	1.1 / 0.7	34 / 21
10 Su	0106 / 1011	1.3 / 0.5	40 / 15
11 M	0139 / 1201	1.5 / 0.4	46 / 12
12 Tu	0229 / 1343	1.6 / 0.3	49 / 9
13 W ◐	0332 / 1506	1.7 / 0.2	52 / 6
14 Th	0446 / 1614	1.8 / 0.1	55 / 3
15 F	0604 / 1711	1.8 / 0.1	55 / 3
16 Sa	0721 / 1758	1.8 / 0.2	55 / 6
17 Su	0831 / 1834	1.7 / 0.3	52 / 9
18 M	0937 / 1857	1.6 / 0.5	49 / 15
19 Tu ●	1042 / 1859	1.4 / 0.7	43 / 21
20 W	0035 / 0426 / 1152 / 1834 / 2348	0.9 / 0.8 / 1.2 / 0.9 / 1.1	27 / 24 / 37 / 27 / 34
21 Th	0623 / 1320 / 1734 / 2343	0.7 / 1.1 / 1.0 / 1.2	21 / 34 / 30 / 37
22 F	0750 / 2357	0.7 / 1.4	21 / 43
23 Sa	0906	0.6	18
24 Su	0020 / 1020	1.5 / 0.5	46 / 15
25 M	0052 / 1139	1.5 / 0.5	46 / 15
26 Tu	0131 / 1259	1.6 / 0.4	49 / 12
27 W ◑	0219 / 1410	1.6 / 0.4	49 / 12
28 Th	0318 / 1509	1.6 / 0.4	49 / 12
29 F	0427 / 1556	1.6 / 0.3	49 / 9
30 Sa	0542 / 1634	1.6 / 0.4	49 / 12

Time meridian 90° W. 0000 is midnight. 1200 is noon. Times are not adjusted for Daylight Saving Time.
Heights are referred to mean lower low water which is the chart datum of soundings.

Pensacola, Florida, 2017

Times and Heights of High and Low Waters

October

Day	Time (h m)	Height (ft)	Height (cm)	Day	Time (h m)	Height (ft)	Height (cm)
1 Su	0655 / 1704	1.5 / 0.4	46 / 12	16 M	0831 / 1646 / 2317	1.3 / 0.6 / 0.9	40 / 18 / 27
2 M	0806 / 1727	1.5 / 0.5	46 / 15	17 Tu	0345 / 1006 / 1624 / 2223	0.8 / 1.1 / 0.8 / 1.1	24 / 34 / 24 / 34
3 Tu	0919 / 1741	1.4 / 0.7	43 / 21	18 W	0525 / 1207 / 1516 / 2210	0.7 / 1.0 / 0.9 / 1.2	21 / 30 / 27 / 37
4 W	0010 / 0328 / 1037 / 1742 / 2309	0.9 / 0.8 / 1.3 / 0.8 / 1.0	27 / 24 / 40 / 24 / 30	19 Th ●	0633 / 2217	0.5 / 1.4	15 / 43
5 Th ○	0515 / 1212 / 1717 / 2251	0.7 / 1.1 / 1.0 / 1.2	21 / 34 / 30 / 37	20 F	0729 / 2233	0.4 / 1.5	12 / 46
6 F	0636 / 2257	0.6 / 1.4	18 / 43	21 Sa	0821 / 2257	0.3 / 1.6	9 / 49
7 Sa	0751 / 2321	0.4 / 1.6	12 / 49	22 Su	0912 / 2325	0.3 / 1.6	9 / 49
8 Su	0909 / 2358	0.3 / 1.7	9 / 52	23 M	1009 / 2359	0.2 / 1.6	6 / 49
9 M	1034	0.2	6	24 Tu	1110	0.2	6
10 Tu	0047 / 1204	1.8 / 0.1	55 / 3	25 W	0037 / 1213	1.6 / 0.2	49 / 6
11 W	0145 / 1327	1.8 / 0.1	55 / 3	26 Th	0120 / 1309	1.6 / 0.2	49 / 6
12 Th ◗	0252 / 1437	1.8 / 0.1	55 / 3	27 F ◖	0209 / 1356	1.5 / 0.2	46 / 6
13 F	0409 / 1532	1.7 / 0.2	52 / 6	28 Sa	0303 / 1432	1.4 / 0.2	43 / 6
14 Sa	0534 / 1614	1.6 / 0.3	49 / 9	29 Su	0410 / 1500	1.3 / 0.3	40 / 9
15 Su	0702 / 1640	1.4 / 0.5	43 / 15	30 M	0544 / 1519 / 2351	1.2 / 0.4 / 0.9	37 / 12 / 27
				31 Tu	0223 / 0743 / 1525 / 2212	0.8 / 1.0 / 0.6 / 1.0	24 / 30 / 18 / 30

November

Day	Time (h m)	Height (ft)	Height (cm)	Day	Time (h m)	Height (ft)	Height (cm)
1 W	0414 / 0952 / 1509 / 2138	0.7 / 0.9 / 0.7 / 1.1	21 / 27 / 21 / 34	16 Th	0629 / 2113	0.2 / 1.4	6 / 43
2 Th	0519 / 2131	0.5 / 1.3	15 / 40	17 F	0710 / 2133	0.0 / 1.4	0 / 43
3 F ○	0618 / 2143	0.3 / 1.4	9 / 43	18 Sa ●	0750 / 2157	-0.1 / 1.5	-3 / 46
4 Sa	0719 / 2211	0.1 / 1.6	3 / 49	19 Su	0832 / 2226	-0.1 / 1.5	-3 / 46
5 Su	0824 / 2249	-0.1 / 1.7	-3 / 52	20 M	0917 / 2258	-0.1 / 1.5	-3 / 46
6 M	0936 / 2336	-0.2 / 1.8	-6 / 55	21 Tu	1005 / 2333	-0.2 / 1.5	-6 / 46
7 Tu	1051	-0.2	-6	22 W	1053	-0.2	-6
8 W	0028 / 1203	1.8 / -0.2	55 / -6	23 Th	0008 / 1136	1.4 / -0.2	43 / -6
9 Th	0124 / 1305	1.7 / -0.2	52 / -6	24 F	0044 / 1213	1.4 / -0.1	43 / -3
10 F ◖	0222 / 1354	1.6 / 0.0	49 / 0	25 Sa	0119 / 1243	1.3 / -0.1	40 / -3
11 Sa	0324 / 1427	1.4 / 0.1	43 / 3	26 Su ◗	0150 / 1305	1.1 / 0.0	34 / 0
12 Su	0435 / 1440 / 2329	1.1 / 0.3 / 0.9	34 / 9 / 27	27 M	0204 / 1317 / 2219	0.9 / 0.1 / 0.8	27 / 3 / 24
13 M	0246 / 0630 / 1424 / 2137	0.8 / 0.9 / 0.5 / 0.9	24 / 27 / 15 / 27	28 Tu	1313 / 2056	0.3 / 0.8	9 / 24
14 Tu	0447 / 0927 / 1318 / 2105	0.6 / 0.7 / 0.6 / 1.1	18 / 21 / 18 / 34	29 W	0433 / 0829 / 1225 / 2026	0.4 / 0.5 / 0.4 / 0.9	12 / 15 / 12 / 27
15 W	0544 / 2101	0.3 / 1.2	9 / 37	30 Th	0506 / 2025	0.2 / 1.1	6 / 34

December

Day	Time (h m)	Height (ft)	Height (cm)	Day	Time (h m)	Height (ft)	Height (cm)
1 F	0552 / 2042	-0.1 / 1.3	-3 / 40	16 Sa	0720 / 2107	-0.4 / 1.3	-12 / 40
2 Sa	0645 / 2114	-0.3 / 1.5	-9 / 46	17 Su	0759 / 2139	-0.4 / 1.3	-12 / 40
3 Su ○	0744 / 2155	-0.5 / 1.6	-15 / 49	18 M ●	0838 / 2213	-0.5 / 1.3	-15 / 40
4 M	0848 / 2243	-0.6 / 1.6	-18 / 49	19 Tu	0917 / 2247	-0.5 / 1.3	-15 / 40
5 Tu	0952 / 2333	-0.6 / 1.6	-18 / 49	20 W	0954 / 2321	-0.5 / 1.2	-15 / 37
6 W	1053	-0.6	-18	21 Th	1026 / 2353	-0.5 / 1.2	-15 / 37
7 Th	0024 / 1146	1.5 / -0.5	46 / -15	22 F	1053	-0.4	-12
8 F	0112 / 1226	1.4 / -0.4	43 / -12	23 Sa	0023 / 1115	1.1 / -0.4	34 / -12
9 Sa	0155 / 1250	1.1 / -0.2	34 / -6	24 Su	0049 / 1130	0.9 / -0.2	27 / -6
10 Su ◖	0221 / 1250 / 2159	0.8 / 0.0 / 0.6	24 / 0 / 18	25 M	0102 / 1135 / 2117	0.7 / -0.1 / 0.5	21 / -3 / 15
11 M	1213 / 2017	0.2 / 0.7	6 / 21	26 Tu ◗	1120 / 1934	0.0 / 0.6	0 / 18
12 Tu	0559 / 1952	0.2 / 0.9	6 / 27	27 W	1001 / 1909	0.1 / 0.7	3 / 21
13 W	0541 / 1955	0.0 / 1.0	0 / 30	28 Th	0440 / 1914	-0.1 / 0.9	-3 / 27
14 Th	0610 / 2012	-0.2 / 1.1	-6 / 34	29 F	0517 / 1939	-0.3 / 1.1	-9 / 34
15 F	0644 / 2037	-0.3 / 1.2	-9 / 37	30 Sa	0607 / 2018	-0.5 / 1.3	-15 / 40
				31 Su	0703 / 2105	-0.7 / 1.4	-21 / 43

Time meridian 90° W. 0000 is midnight. 1200 is noon. Times are not adjusted for Daylight Saving Time.
Heights are referred to mean lower low water which is the chart datum of soundings.

Dauphin Island, Alabama, 2017

Times and Heights of High and Low Waters

January

Day	Time (h m)	Height (ft)	Height (cm)
1 Su	1051	-0.5	-15
	2334	1.0	30
2 M	1117	-0.4	-12
3 Tu	0001	0.9	27
	1131	-0.3	-9
4 W	0012	0.7	21
	1121	-0.1	-3
	2227	0.5	15
5 Th ☽	1025	0.0	0
	1916	0.5	15
6 F	0747	0.0	0
	1829	0.6	18
7 Sa	0529	-0.2	-6
	1834	0.9	27
8 Su	0547	-0.4	-12
	1902	1.0	30
9 M	0631	-0.6	-18
	1941	1.2	37
10 Tu	0725	-0.7	-21
	2025	1.3	40
11 W	0822	-0.7	-21
	2111	1.3	40
12 Th ○	0919	-0.7	-21
	2157	1.2	37
13 F	1011	-0.6	-18
	2240	1.1	34
14 Sa	1053	-0.5	-15
	2319	1.0	30
15 Su	1120	-0.4	-12
	2352	0.8	24
16 M	1121	-0.2	-6
17 Tu	0010	0.6	18
	1040	-0.1	-3
	2337	0.4	12
18 W	0924	0.0	0
	1834	0.3	9
19 Th ☾	0746	0.0	0
	1739	0.5	15
20 F	0558	-0.1	-3
	1745	0.6	18
21 Sa	0525	-0.2	-6
	1809	0.8	24
22 Su	0541	-0.3	-9
	1840	0.9	27
23 M	0612	-0.4	-12
	1915	0.9	27
24 Tu	0650	-0.5	-15
	1953	1.0	30
25 W	0730	-0.5	-15
	2031	1.0	30
26 Th	0811	-0.6	-18
	2108	1.0	30
27 F ●	0850	-0.6	-18
	2145	1.0	30
28 Sa	0926	-0.5	-15
	2222	1.0	30
29 Su	0958	-0.5	-15
	2259	0.9	27
30 M	1022	-0.4	-12
	2333	0.7	21
31 Tu	1028	-0.2	-6

February

Day	Time (h m)	Height (ft)	Height (cm)
1 W	0000	0.5	15
	0954	0.0	0
	2244	0.3	9
2 Th	0813	0.1	3
	1642	0.4	12
3 F ☽	0444	0.0	0
	1633	0.6	18
4 Sa	0403	-0.2	-6
	1702	0.8	24
5 Su	0441	-0.4	-12
	1745	1.0	30
6 M	0532	-0.5	-15
	1835	1.1	34
7 Tu	0630	-0.6	-18
	1928	1.1	34
8 W	0729	-0.6	-18
	2020	1.1	34
9 Th	0826	-0.6	-18
	2110	1.1	34
10 F ○	0918	-0.5	-15
	2157	1.0	30
11 Sa	1003	-0.4	-12
	2240	0.8	24
12 Su	1032	-0.2	-6
	2319	0.7	21
13 M	1020	-0.1	-3
	2353	0.5	15
14 Tu	0857	0.1	3
15 W	0014	0.3	9
	0718	0.1	3
	1438	0.3	9
16 Th	0514	0.1	3
	1458	0.5	15
17 F	0312	0.0	0
	1533	0.6	18
18 Sa ☾	0323	-0.1	-3
	1614	0.7	21
19 Su	0358	-0.2	-6
	1700	0.8	24
20 M	0440	-0.3	-9
	1748	0.9	27
21 Tu	0525	-0.3	-9
	1836	0.9	27
22 W	0610	-0.4	-12
	1924	1.0	30
23 Th	0655	-0.4	-12
	2010	1.0	30
24 F	0737	-0.4	-12
	2056	1.0	30
25 Sa	0817	-0.3	-9
	2142	0.9	27
26 Su ●	0852	-0.2	-6
	2230	0.8	24
27 M	0918	-0.1	-3
	2323	0.6	18
28 Tu	0902	0.1	3

March

Day	Time (h m)	Height (ft)	Height (cm)
1 W	0030	0.4	12
	0723	0.3	9
	1247	0.4	12
	2028	0.2	6
2 Th	1313	0.6	18
3 F	0007	0.0	0
	1400	0.8	24
4 Sa	0148	-0.2	-6
	1456	0.9	27
5 Su ☽	0300	-0.3	-9
	1559	1.0	30
6 M	0406	-0.4	-12
	1705	1.1	34
7 Tu	0510	-0.4	-12
	1811	1.1	34
8 W	0612	-0.4	-12
	1915	1.1	34
9 Th	0711	-0.3	-9
	2015	1.0	30
10 F	0805	-0.2	-6
	2111	0.9	27
11 Sa	0854	0.0	0
	2204	0.8	24
12 Su ○	0933	0.1	3
	2259	0.6	18
13 M	0725	0.2	6
	1025	0.3	9
	1613	0.2	6
14 Tu	0003	0.5	15
	0535	0.4	12
	1103	0.5	15
	1853	0.2	6
15 W	1142	0.6	18
	2112	0.1	3
16 Th	1222	0.8	24
	2307	0.1	3
17 F	1304	0.9	27
18 Sa	0029	0.0	0
	1350	0.9	27
19 Su	0135	-0.1	-3
	1442	1.0	30
20 M ☾	0233	-0.1	-3
	1539	1.0	30
21 Tu	0327	-0.1	-3
	1640	1.0	30
22 W	0417	-0.1	-3
	1742	1.0	30
23 Th	0504	-0.1	-3
	1844	1.0	30
24 F	0546	-0.1	-3
	1945	1.0	30
25 Sa	0624	0.0	0
	2048	0.9	27
26 Su	0653	0.2	6
	2159	0.8	24
27 M ●	0651	0.3	9
	1047	0.4	12
	1516	0.3	9
	2333	0.6	18
28 Tu	0533	0.5	15
	1004	0.6	18
	1801	0.2	6
29 W	1028	0.8	24
	2009	0.1	3
30 Th	1110	1.0	30
	2202	0.0	0
31 F	1201	1.1	34
	2341	-0.1	-3

Time meridian 90° W. 0000 is midnight. 1200 is noon. Times are not adjusted for Daylight Saving Time.
Heights are referred to mean lower low water which is the chart datum of soundings.

Dauphin Island, Alabama, 2017

Times and Heights of High and Low Waters

April

Day	Time (h m)	Height (ft)	Height (cm)	Day	Time (h m)	Height (ft)	Height (cm)
1 Sa	1258	1.2	37	16 Su	1241	1.2	37
2 Su	0107	-0.2	-6	17 M	0029	0.0	0
	1401	1.3	40		1327	1.2	37
3 M ◖	0223	-0.2	-6	18 Tu	0124	0.0	0
	1510	1.3	40		1418	1.2	37
4 Tu	0330	-0.2	-6	19 W ◐	0214	0.0	0
	1623	1.2	37		1517	1.1	34
5 W	0429	-0.1	-3	20 Th	0258	0.0	0
	1738	1.1	34		1623	1.0	30
6 Th	0519	0.0	0	21 F	0334	0.1	3
	1853	1.0	30		1741	1.0	30
7 F	0553	0.2	6	22 Sa	0400	0.2	6
	2006	0.9	27		1916	0.8	24
8 Sa	0547	0.3	9	23 Su	0404	0.4	12
	2124	0.7	21		1047	0.6	18
					1436	0.5	15
					2118	0.7	21
9 Su	0439	0.5	15	24 M	0319	0.5	15
	0912	0.6	18		0913	0.7	21
	1548	0.4	12		1655	0.4	12
	2304	0.6	18				
10 M	0256	0.5	15	25 Tu	0901	0.9	27
	0921	0.7	21		1825	0.2	6
	1746	0.3	9				
11 Tu ○	0947	0.9	27	26 W ●	0922	1.1	34
	1914	0.2	6		1944	0.0	0
12 W	1017	1.0	30	27 Th	0958	1.3	40
	2025	0.1	3		2102	-0.1	-3
13 Th	1048	1.1	34	28 F	1043	1.4	43
	2129	0.1	3		2220	-0.2	-6
14 F	1122	1.2	37	29 Sa	1133	1.5	46
	2230	0.0	0		2336	-0.2	-6
15 Sa	1200	1.2	37	30 Su	1227	1.5	46
	2330	0.0	0				

May

Day	Time (h m)	Height (ft)	Height (cm)	Day	Time (h m)	Height (ft)	Height (cm)
1 M	0047	-0.2	-6	16 Tu	1235	1.3	40
	1325	1.4	43				
2 Tu ◐	0150	-0.1	-3	17 W	0032	0.0	0
	1425	1.3	40		1313	1.2	37
3 W	0239	0.0	0	18 Th ◐	0108	0.0	0
	1528	1.1	34		1352	1.1	34
4 Th	0311	0.2	6	19 F	0135	0.1	3
	1636	1.0	30		1425	0.9	27
5 F	0311	0.3	9	20 Sa	0147	0.2	6
	1759	0.8	24		1244	0.8	24
6 Sa	0224	0.5	15	21 Su	0129	0.4	12
	0912	0.7	21		0918	0.7	21
	1528	0.5	15		1710	0.4	12
	2013	0.6	18		1941	0.5	15
					2353	0.4	12
7 Su	0046	0.5	15	22 M	0818	0.9	27
	0827	0.8	24		1733	0.3	9
	1720	0.4	12				
8 M	0833	1.0	30	23 Tu	0810	1.1	34
	1823	0.2	6		1822	0.1	3
9 Tu	0853	1.1	34	24 W	0829	1.3	40
	1912	0.1	3		1918	-0.1	-3
10 W ○	0918	1.3	40	25 Th ●	0902	1.5	46
	1957	0.0	0		2020	-0.3	-9
11 Th	0946	1.3	40	26 F	0944	1.6	49
	2041	0.0	0		2125	-0.3	-9
12 F	1016	1.4	43	27 Sa	1030	1.7	52
	2127	-0.1	-3		2232	-0.3	-9
13 Sa	1048	1.4	43	28 Su	1119	1.6	49
	2215	-0.1	-3		2335	-0.3	-9
14 Su	1122	1.4	43	29 M	1209	1.5	46
	2304	-0.1	-3				
15 M	1158	1.3	40	30 Tu	0029	-0.2	-6
	2350	-0.1	-3		1256	1.4	43
				31 W	0108	0.0	0
					1339	1.2	37

June

Day	Time (h m)	Height (ft)	Height (cm)	Day	Time (h m)	Height (ft)	Height (cm)
1 Th ◐	0125	0.1	3	16 F	0004	0.1	3
	1407	0.9	27		1228	1.0	30
2 F	0103	0.3	9	17 Sa ○	0004	0.2	6
	1250	0.7	21		1036	0.8	24
	2355	0.4	12		2328	0.3	9
3 Sa	0816	0.8	24	18 Su	0810	0.8	24
	2146	0.4	12		2110	0.4	12
4 Su	0736	0.9	27	19 M	0719	1.0	30
	1821	0.3	9		1739	0.2	6
5 M	0740	1.1	34	20 Tu	0714	1.2	37
	1828	0.1	3		1800	0.0	0
6 Tu	0759	1.2	37	21 W	0735	1.4	43
	1856	0.0	0		1845	-0.2	-6
7 W	0824	1.3	40	22 Th	0810	1.5	46
	1930	-0.1	-3		1941	-0.3	-9
8 Th	0853	1.4	43	23 F ●	0852	1.6	49
	2007	-0.1	-3		2041	-0.4	-12
9 F ○	0923	1.4	43	24 Sa	0938	1.7	52
	2047	-0.2	-6		2142	-0.4	-12
10 Sa	0955	1.4	43	25 Su	1025	1.6	49
	2128	-0.2	-6		2239	-0.3	-9
11 Su	1027	1.4	43	26 M	1112	1.5	46
	2208	-0.2	-6		2327	-0.2	-6
12 M	1059	1.4	43	27 Tu	1155	1.4	43
	2245	-0.1	-3				
13 Tu	1130	1.3	40	28 W	0000	-0.1	-3
	2318	-0.1	-3		1230	1.2	37
14 W	1200	1.2	37	29 Th	0007	0.1	3
	2346	0.0	0		1248	0.9	27
					2332	0.3	9
15 Th	1224	1.1	34	30 F ◐	1135	0.7	21
					2212	0.4	12

Time meridian 90° W. 0000 is midnight. 1200 is noon. Times are not adjusted for Daylight Saving Time.
Heights are referred to mean lower low water which is the chart datum of soundings.

Dauphin Island, Alabama, 2017

Times and Heights of High and Low Waters

July

Day	Time	Height (ft)	Height (cm)	Day	Time	Height (ft)	Height (cm)
1 Sa	0710	0.8	24	16 Su ◯	0635	0.8	24
	2012	0.4	12		1859	0.4	12
2 Su	0628	0.9	27	17 M	0554	1.0	30
	1810	0.2	6		1654	0.2	6
3 M	0635	1.1	34	18 Tu	0602	1.2	37
	1757	0.1	3		1714	0.0	0
4 Tu	0657	1.2	37	19 W	0631	1.4	43
	1819	0.0	0		1759	-0.2	-6
5 W	0726	1.3	40	20 Th	0712	1.5	46
	1851	-0.1	-3		1854	-0.3	-9
6 Th	0758	1.4	43	21 F	0758	1.6	49
	1928	-0.1	-3		1953	-0.3	-9
7 F	0832	1.4	43	22 Sa	0848	1.7	52
	2007	-0.2	-6		2052	-0.3	-9
8 Sa ◯	0907	1.4	43	23 Su ●	0937	1.6	49
	2046	-0.2	-6		2148	-0.2	-6
9 Su	0940	1.4	43	24 M	1024	1.5	46
	2121	-0.1	-3		2234	-0.1	-3
10 M	1013	1.4	43	25 Tu	1108	1.4	43
	2153	-0.1	-3		2307	0.1	3
11 Tu	1044	1.3	40	26 W	1145	1.2	37
	2220	-0.1	-3		2308	0.3	9
12 W	1113	1.3	40	27 Th	1212	1.0	30
	2241	0.0	0		2210	0.4	12
13 Th	1138	1.1	34	28 F	1151	0.8	24
	2251	0.1	3		2029	0.5	15
14 F	1144	0.9	27	29 Sa	0454	0.8	24
	2238	0.3	9		1821	0.5	15
15 Sa	0938	0.8	24	30 Su ◖	0438	1.0	30
	2141	0.4	12		1639	0.3	9
				31 M	0459	1.1	34
					1640	0.2	6

August

Day	Time	Height (ft)	Height (cm)	Day	Time	Height (ft)	Height (cm)
1 Tu	0532	1.3	40	16 W	0505	1.5	46
	1708	0.1	3		1650	0.0	0
2 W	0610	1.3	40	17 Th	0558	1.6	49
	1746	0.1	3		1750	-0.1	-3
3 Th	0651	1.4	43	18 F	0654	1.7	52
	1828	0.0	0		1851	-0.1	-3
4 F	0732	1.4	43	19 Sa	0751	1.7	52
	1910	0.0	0		1951	0.0	0
5 Sa	0813	1.5	46	20 Su	0846	1.6	49
	1950	0.0	0		2048	0.1	3
6 Su	0851	1.5	46	21 M ●	0938	1.5	46
	2026	0.0	0		2139	0.2	6
7 M ◯	0929	1.4	43	22 Tu	1027	1.4	43
	2057	0.1	3		2218	0.4	12
8 Tu	1004	1.4	43	23 W	1113	1.2	37
	2122	0.1	3		2202	0.6	18
9 W	1039	1.3	40	24 Th	1200	1.0	30
	2138	0.3	9		1953	0.7	21
10 Th	1113	1.1	34	25 F	0052	0.8	24
	2136	0.4	12		0637	0.7	21
					1253	0.8	24
					1740	0.7	21
11 F	1142	0.9	27	26 Sa	0119	1.0	30
	2057	0.5	15		1144	0.6	18
12 Sa	0545	0.8	24	27 Su	0158	1.1	34
	1912	0.6	18		1335	0.5	15
13 Su	0340	0.9	27	28 M	0242	1.3	40
	1509	0.5	15		1427	0.4	12
14 M ◖	0344	1.1	34	29 Tu ◖	0330	1.3	40
	1508	0.3	9		1516	0.3	9
15 Tu	0418	1.3	40	30 W	0421	1.4	43
	1554	0.1	3		1605	0.3	9
				31 Th	0514	1.5	46
					1653	0.3	9

September

Day	Time	Height (ft)	Height (cm)	Day	Time	Height (ft)	Height (cm)
1 F	0607	1.5	46	16 Sa	0636	1.6	49
	1739	0.3	9		1823	0.3	9
2 Sa	0659	1.5	46	17 Su	0741	1.6	49
	1821	0.3	9		1915	0.4	12
3 Su	0747	1.5	46	18 M	0843	1.4	43
	1859	0.3	9		1958	0.6	18
4 M	0833	1.4	43	19 Tu ●	0945	1.3	40
	1931	0.4	12		1949	0.7	21
					2207	0.8	24
5 Tu	0919	1.4	43	20 W	0141	0.7	21
	1954	0.5	15		1052	1.1	34
					1754	0.8	24
					2159	0.9	27
6 W ◯	1008	1.3	40	21 Th	0504	0.7	21
	2000	0.6	18		1233	1.0	30
					1539	0.9	27
					2233	1.1	34
7 Th	1105	1.1	34	22 F	0725	0.7	21
	1926	0.7	21		2311	1.3	40
8 F	0034	0.8	24	23 Sa	0920	0.6	18
	0516	0.7	21		2350	1.4	43
	1229	0.9	27				
	1747	0.8	24				
9 Sa	0009	1.0	30	24 Su	1050	0.5	15
	0850	0.7	21				
10 Su	0034	1.2	37	25 M	0031	1.5	46
	1122	0.5	15		1201	0.4	12
11 M	0117	1.4	43	26 Tu	0116	1.5	46
	1256	0.4	12		1304	0.4	12
12 Tu	0211	1.5	46	27 W ◖	0206	1.5	46
	1410	0.2	6		1401	0.4	12
13 W ◯	0312	1.6	49	28 Th	0302	1.5	46
	1518	0.2	6		1453	0.4	12
14 Th	0419	1.7	52	29 F	0401	1.5	46
	1623	0.2	6		1539	0.4	12
15 F	0528	1.7	52	30 Sa	0503	1.5	46
	1725	0.2	6		1619	0.4	12

Time meridian 90° W. 0000 is midnight. 1200 is noon. Times are not adjusted for Daylight Saving Time.
Heights are referred to mean lower low water which is the chart datum of soundings.

Dauphin Island, Alabama, 2017

Times and Heights of High and Low Waters

October

Day	Time (h m)	Height (ft)	Height (cm)
1 Su	0606	1.4	43
	1653	0.5	15
2 M	0708	1.4	43
	1717	0.6	18
3 Tu	0813	1.3	40
	1726	0.7	21
4 W	0930	1.1	34
	1704	0.8	24
	2228	0.9	27
5 Th ○	0429	0.8	24
	1123	1.0	30
	1540	0.9	27
	2203	1.1	34
6 F	0634	0.7	21
	2217	1.3	40
7 Sa	0816	0.5	15
	2250	1.5	46
8 Su	0947	0.4	12
	2334	1.6	49
9 M	1112	0.2	6
10 Tu	0025	1.7	52
	1230	0.2	6
11 W	0123	1.8	55
	1341	0.1	3
12 Th ◐	0227	1.7	52
	1446	0.2	6
13 F	0336	1.6	49
	1542	0.3	9
14 Sa	0449	1.5	46
	1627	0.4	12
15 Su	0604	1.4	43
	1653	0.5	15
16 M	0722	1.2	37
	1637	0.7	21
17 Tu	0850	1.0	30
	1527	0.9	27
	2107	1.0	30
18 W	0423	0.7	21
	2110	1.2	37
19 Th ●	0612	0.6	18
	2132	1.3	40
20 F	0730	0.5	15
	2200	1.4	43
21 Sa	0834	0.4	12
	2231	1.5	46
22 Su	0930	0.3	9
	2304	1.6	49
23 M	1025	0.3	9
	2340	1.6	49
24 Tu	1120	0.2	6
25 W	0019	1.6	49
	1213	0.2	6
26 Th	0101	1.5	46
	1301	0.3	9
27 F ◑	0146	1.5	46
	1343	0.3	9
28 Sa	0234	1.4	43
	1417	0.3	9
29 Su	0326	1.3	40
	1443	0.4	12
30 M	0427	1.2	37
	1457	0.5	15
31 Tu	0556	1.0	30
	1448	0.6	18
	2211	0.9	27

November

Day	Time (h m)	Height (ft)	Height (cm)
1 W	0412	0.7	21
	0822	0.8	24
	1356	0.7	21
	2111	1.0	30
2 Th	0536	0.6	18
	2059	1.2	37
3 F ○	0641	0.4	12
	2113	1.4	43
4 Sa	0746	0.2	6
	2144	1.6	49
5 Su	0853	0.0	0
	2224	1.7	52
6 M	1003	-0.1	-3
	2310	1.8	55
7 Tu	1114	-0.1	-3
8 W	0001	1.7	52
	1221	-0.1	-3
9 Th	0055	1.7	52
	1319	0.0	0
10 F ◐	0150	1.5	46
	1406	0.1	3
11 Sa	0246	1.3	40
	1435	0.2	6
12 Su	0341	1.1	34
	1433	0.4	12
13 M	0435	0.9	27
	1345	0.6	18
	2113	0.8	24
14 Tu	1203	0.6	18
	2020	1.0	30
15 W	0557	0.5	15
	2022	1.2	37
16 Th	0642	0.3	9
	2041	1.3	40
17 F	0723	0.1	3
	2106	1.4	43
18 Sa ●	0804	0.0	0
	2134	1.5	46
19 Su	0846	0.0	0
	2205	1.5	46
20 M	0930	0.0	0
	2236	1.5	46
21 Tu	1015	-0.1	-3
	2309	1.4	43
22 W	1058	-0.1	-3
	2343	1.4	43
23 Th	1138	0.0	0
24 F	0015	1.3	40
	1212	0.0	0
25 Sa	0045	1.2	37
	1239	0.0	0
26 Su ◑	0109	1.1	34
	1257	0.1	3
27 M	0109	0.9	27
	1302	0.2	6
	2309	0.8	24
28 Tu	1240	0.3	9
	2105	0.8	24
29 W	1112	0.4	12
	2015	0.9	27
30 Th	0604	0.2	6
	2005	1.1	34

December

Day	Time (h m)	Height (ft)	Height (cm)
1 F	0628	0.0	0
	2020	1.3	40
2 Sa	0715	-0.2	-6
	2049	1.5	46
3 Su ○	0811	-0.3	-9
	2128	1.6	49
4 M	0913	-0.4	-12
	2213	1.6	49
5 Tu	1017	-0.5	-15
	2301	1.6	49
6 W	1118	-0.5	-15
	2349	1.5	46
7 Th	1211	-0.4	-12
8 F	0035	1.3	40
	1250	-0.2	-6
9 Sa	0116	1.1	34
	1308	0.0	0
10 Su ◐	0141	0.9	27
	1248	0.1	3
11 M	0034	0.6	18
	1138	0.3	9
	2014	0.6	18
12 Tu	0936	0.2	6
	1925	0.8	24
13 W	0646	0.1	3
	1928	1.0	30
14 Th	0637	-0.1	-3
	1948	1.1	34
15 F	0702	-0.2	-6
	2014	1.2	37
16 Sa	0735	-0.3	-9
	2044	1.3	40
17 Su	0812	-0.3	-9
	2115	1.3	40
18 M ●	0851	-0.4	-12
	2148	1.3	40
19 Tu	0930	-0.4	-12
	2220	1.2	37
20 W	1007	-0.4	-12
	2250	1.2	37
21 Th	1038	-0.4	-12
	2318	1.1	34
22 F	1104	-0.3	-9
	2343	1.0	30
23 Sa	1124	-0.3	-9
24 Su	0000	0.9	27
	1136	-0.2	-6
	2353	0.7	21
25 M	1132	-0.1	-3
	2210	0.6	18
26 Tu ◑	1058	0.0	0
	2002	0.6	18
27 W	0911	0.1	3
	1911	0.7	21
28 Th	0556	-0.1	-3
	1905	0.9	27
29 F	0557	-0.3	-9
	1923	1.1	34
30 Sa	0636	-0.5	-15
	1956	1.2	37
31 Su	0728	-0.6	-18
	2037	1.4	43

Time meridian 90° W. 0000 is midnight. 1200 is noon. Times are not adjusted for Daylight Saving Time.
Heights are referred to mean lower low water which is the chart datum of soundings.

Mobile, Alabama, 2017

Times and Heights of High and Low Waters

January

Day	Time	ft	cm	Day	Time	ft	cm
1 Su	0102	1.2	37	16 M	0132	0.9	27
	1128	-0.6	-18		1120	-0.3	-9
2 M	0141	1.1	34	17 Tu	0201	0.7	21
	1143	-0.5	-15		1109	-0.1	-3
					1938	0.5	15
					2319	0.4	12
3 Tu	0218	0.9	27	18 W	0201	0.5	15
	1152	-0.3	-9		1048	0.0	0
					1854	0.6	18
4 W	0245	0.7	21	19 Th	0924	0.0	0
	1156	-0.1	-3		1830	0.8	24
	2036	0.6	18	☽			
5 Th	1147	0.0	0	20 F	0742	-0.1	-3
	1956	0.7	21		1837	0.9	27
☾							
6 F	0749	0.1	3	21 Sa	0726	-0.2	-6
	1933	0.8	24		1903	1.0	30
7 Sa	0707	-0.2	-6	22 Su	0739	-0.4	-12
	1940	1.0	30		1941	1.1	34
8 Su	0735	-0.5	-15	23 M	0803	-0.5	-15
	2012	1.2	37		2027	1.2	37
9 M	0815	-0.7	-21	24 Tu	0832	-0.6	-18
	2058	1.4	43		2117	1.2	37
10 Tu	0857	-0.8	-24	25 W	0900	-0.6	-18
	2148	1.4	43		2207	1.3	40
11 W	0941	-0.9	-27	26 Th	0928	-0.6	-18
	2239	1.5	46		2254	1.3	40
12 Th	1022	-0.8	-24	27 F	0953	-0.6	-18
	2327	1.4	43		2339	1.3	40
○				●			
13 F	1059	-0.7	-21	28 Sa	1014	-0.6	-18
14 Sa	0012	1.3	40	29 Su	0023	1.2	37
	1124	-0.6	-18		1029	-0.5	-15
15 Su	0054	1.1	34	30 M	0109	1.1	34
	1130	-0.4	-12		1036	-0.4	-12
				31 Tu	0156	0.9	27
					1037	-0.2	-6
					1851	0.5	15
					2101	0.4	12

February

Day	Time	ft	cm	Day	Time	ft	cm
1 W	0246	0.7	21	16 Th	0230	0.4	12
	1035	0.0	0		0849	0.3	9
	1815	0.6	18		1643	0.9	27
	2308	0.3	9				
2 Th	0326	0.4	12	17 F	0541	0.2	6
	1020	0.1	3		1659	1.0	30
	1752	0.7	21				
3 F	0516	0.1	3	18 Sa	0549	0.0	0
	1747	0.9	27		1727	1.1	34
◐				○			
4 Sa	0551	-0.1	-3	19 Su	0622	-0.1	-3
	1807	1.1	34		1804	1.2	37
5 Su	0638	-0.4	-12	20 M	0657	-0.2	-6
	1845	1.3	40		1850	1.3	40
6 M	0724	-0.5	-15	21 Tu	0730	-0.3	-9
	1936	1.4	43		1945	1.3	40
7 Tu	0808	-0.7	-21	22 W	0800	-0.4	-12
	2037	1.4	43		2049	1.3	40
8 W	0848	-0.7	-21	23 Th	0828	-0.4	-12
	2140	1.4	43		2154	1.3	40
9 Th	0925	-0.6	-18	24 F	0853	-0.3	-9
	2238	1.4	43		2252	1.3	40
10 F	0955	-0.5	-15	25 Sa	0913	-0.3	-9
	2329	1.2	37		2348	1.2	37
○							
11 Sa	1012	-0.4	-12	26 Su	0926	-0.2	-6
				●			
12 Su	0015	1.1	34	27 M	0046	1.1	34
	1010	-0.2	-6		0930	0.0	0
					1717	0.6	18
					1921	0.5	15
13 M	0059	0.9	27	28 Tu	0157	1.0	30
	0959	0.0	0		0926	0.2	6
	1757	0.5	15		1636	0.6	18
	2028	0.4	12		2048	0.5	15
14 Tu	0142	0.7	21				
	0951	0.1	3				
	1724	0.6	18				
	2155	0.4	12				
15 W	0221	0.5	15				
	0938	0.2	6				
	1650	0.7	21				
	2347	0.3	9				

March

Day	Time	ft	cm	Day	Time	ft	cm
1 W	0334	0.8	24	16 Th	1451	1.2	37
	0919	0.4	12		2335	0.3	9
	1608	0.8	24				
	2207	0.3	9				
2 Th	0524	0.6	18	17 F	1518	1.3	40
	0901	0.5	15				
	1552	1.0	30				
3 F	0017	0.2	6	18 Sa	0212	0.3	9
	1603	1.2	37		1552	1.4	43
4 Sa	0331	0.1	3	19 Su	0349	0.2	6
	1634	1.4	43		1630	1.5	46
5 Su	0500	-0.1	-3	20 M	0501	0.1	3
	1716	1.5	46		1713	1.5	46
◐				☽			
6 M	0608	-0.3	-9	21 Tu	0556	0.0	0
	1805	1.5	46		1801	1.5	46
7 Tu	0702	-0.3	-9	22 W	0637	0.0	0
	1903	1.5	46		1857	1.5	46
8 W	0746	-0.3	-9	23 Th	0710	0.0	0
	2013	1.4	43		2011	1.4	43
9 Th	0822	-0.3	-9	24 F	0738	0.0	0
	2132	1.4	43		2141	1.3	40
10 F	0848	-0.1	-3	25 Sa	0800	0.1	3
	2244	1.2	37		2305	1.3	40
11 Sa	0858	0.1	3	26 Su	0813	0.3	9
	2346	1.1	34				
12 Su	0847	0.2	6	27 M	0027	1.2	37
	1610	0.7	21		0813	0.4	12
	1852	0.6	18		1447	0.8	24
○				●	1920	0.6	18
13 M	0049	1.0	30	28 Tu	0208	1.0	30
	0835	0.4	12		0805	0.6	18
	1539	0.8	24		1411	0.9	27
	2012	0.5	15		2029	0.5	15
14 Tu	0223	0.8	24	29 W	0405	0.9	27
	0829	0.5	15		0753	0.8	24
	1458	0.9	27		1344	1.1	34
	2114	0.4	12		2135	0.3	9
15 W	0427	0.7	21	30 Th	1350	1.4	43
	0820	0.6	18		2257	0.2	6
	1438	1.0	30				
	2215	0.4	12				
				31 F	1420	1.5	46

Time meridian 90° W. 0000 is midnight. 1200 is noon. Times are not adjusted for Daylight Saving Time.
Heights are referred to mean lower low water which is the chart datum of soundings.

Mobile, Alabama, 2017

Times and Heights of High and Low Waters

April

Day	Time (h m)	Height (ft)	Height (cm)	Day	Time (h m)	Height (ft)	Height (cm)
1 Sa	0121	0.1	3	16 Su	0114	0.3	9
	1501	1.7	52		1501	1.7	52
2 Su	0302	0.0	0	17 M	0232	0.2	6
	1549	1.7	52		1543	1.7	52
3 M ☾	0421	0.0	0	18 Tu	0334	0.2	6
	1638	1.7	52		1627	1.7	52
4 Tu	0529	0.0	0	19 W ○	0427	0.2	6
	1730	1.7	52		1712	1.6	49
5 W	0624	0.0	0	20 Th	0512	0.2	6
	1824	1.5	46		1802	1.5	46
6 Th	0705	0.1	3	21 F	0548	0.3	9
	1928	1.4	43		1911	1.4	43
7 F	0730	0.3	9	22 Sa	0613	0.4	12
	2114	1.2	37		2145	1.2	37
8 Sa	0729	0.5	15	23 Su	0624	0.6	18
	1418	0.9	27		1318	1.0	30
	1702	0.8	24		1751	0.9	27
	2336	1.1	34				
9 Su	0703	0.6	18	24 M	0004	1.1	34
	1345	1.0	30		0618	0.8	24
	1855	0.7	21		1239	1.1	34
					1918	0.7	21
10 M	0134	1.0	30	25 Tu	0217	1.0	30
	0648	0.7	21		0603	0.9	27
	1308	1.1	34		1209	1.2	37
	2001	0.6	18		2019	0.4	12
11 Tu ○	0342	0.9	27	26 W ●	1201	1.5	46
	0640	0.8	24		2118	0.2	6
	1243	1.2	37				
	2052	0.5	15				
12 W	1250	1.4	43	27 Th	1220	1.7	52
	2139	0.4	12		2227	0.1	3
13 Th	1313	1.5	46	28 F	1256	1.8	55
	2229	0.3	9		2356	0.0	0
14 F	1345	1.6	49	29 Sa	1340	1.9	58
	2336	0.3	9				
15 Sa	1421	1.7	52	30 Su	0124	0.0	0
					1429	1.9	58

May

Day	Time (h m)	Height (ft)	Height (cm)	Day	Time (h m)	Height (ft)	Height (cm)
1 M	0235	0.0	0	16 Tu	0130	0.2	6
	1520	1.9	58		1510	1.8	55
2 Tu ○	0336	0.1	3	17 W	0211	0.2	6
	1608	1.8	55		1551	1.7	52
3 W	0429	0.2	6	18 Th ○	0243	0.3	9
	1652	1.6	49		1630	1.6	49
4 Th	0510	0.4	12	19 F	0308	0.4	12
	1731	1.4	43		1706	1.4	43
5 F	0520	0.5	15	20 Sa	0324	0.5	15
	1803	1.2	37		1733	1.2	37
6 Sa	0440	0.7	21	21 Su	0330	0.7	21
	1228	1.1	34		1139	1.1	34
	2118	0.8	24		1921	0.8	24
	2351	0.9	27		2330	0.9	27
7 Su	0414	0.8	24	22 M	0322	0.8	24
	1158	1.2	37		1101	1.2	37
	2006	0.7	21		1935	0.6	18
8 M	1125	1.3	40	23 Tu	1038	1.4	43
	2022	0.5	15		2017	0.3	9
9 Tu	1116	1.5	46	24 W	1043	1.6	49
	2053	0.4	12		2106	0.1	3
10 W ○	1132	1.6	49	25 Th ●	1110	1.8	55
	2128	0.3	9		2201	0.0	0
11 Th	1158	1.7	52	26 F	1149	2.0	61
	2207	0.2	6		2305	-0.1	-3
12 F	1231	1.8	55	27 Sa	1235	2.0	61
	2252	0.2	6				
13 Sa	1307	1.8	55	28 Su	0010	-0.1	-3
	2345	0.2	6		1323	2.0	61
14 Su	1347	1.8	55	29 M	0110	-0.1	-3
					1413	2.0	61
15 M	0041	0.2	6	30 Tu	0159	0.0	0
	1428	1.8	55		1500	1.8	55
				31 W	0235	0.2	6
					1541	1.6	49

June

Day	Time (h m)	Height (ft)	Height (cm)	Day	Time (h m)	Height (ft)	Height (cm)
1 Th ☾	0247	0.4	12	16 F	0106	0.4	12
	1613	1.4	43		1603	1.4	43
2 F	0227	0.6	18	17 Sa	0117	0.5	15
	1624	1.2	37		1620	1.2	37
3 Sa	0203	0.7	21	18 Su	0120	0.7	21
	1058	1.1	34		0942	1.1	34
	2136	0.8	24				
4 Su	1017	1.3	40	19 M	0047	0.8	24
	2043	0.6	18		0858	1.3	40
					1934	0.6	18
5 M	0943	1.4	43	20 Tu	0851	1.5	46
	2038	0.4	12		2000	0.3	9
6 Tu	0951	1.5	46	21 W	0917	1.7	52
	2053	0.3	9		2041	0.1	3
7 W	1018	1.7	52	22 Th	1000	1.9	58
	2118	0.2	6		2128	-0.1	-3
8 Th	1051	1.8	55	23 F ●	1048	2.0	61
	2150	0.1	3		2218	-0.2	-6
9 F ○	1128	1.8	55	24 Sa	1138	2.0	61
	2225	0.1	3		2310	-0.2	-6
10 Sa	1207	1.8	55	25 Su	1229	2.0	61
	2301	0.1	3		2359	-0.1	-3
11 Su	1247	1.9	58	26 M	1319	2.0	61
	2335	0.1	3				
12 M	1329	1.8	55	27 Tu	0040	0.0	0
					1407	1.8	55
13 Tu	0006	0.1	3	28 W	0104	0.2	6
	1410	1.8	55		1449	1.6	49
14 W	0031	0.2	6	29 Th	0058	0.4	12
	1451	1.7	52		1523	1.4	43
15 Th	0051	0.2	6	30 F ☾	0034	0.6	18
	1529	1.6	49		1540	1.2	37

Time meridian 90° W. 0000 is midnight. 1200 is noon. Times are not adjusted for Daylight Saving Time.
Heights are referred to mean lower low water which is the chart datum of soundings.

Mobile, Alabama, 2017

Times and Heights of High and Low Waters

July

Day	Time	ft	cm	Day	Time	ft	cm
1 Sa	0008	0.7	21	16 Su	0646	1.2	37
	0816	1.1	34		2232	0.8	24
	2145	0.8	24	☽			
2 Su	0721	1.3	40	17 M	0636	1.4	43
	2014	0.6	18		1845	0.6	18
3 M	0730	1.4	43	18 Tu	0654	1.6	49
	2008	0.4	12		1916	0.4	12
4 Tu	0804	1.6	49	19 W	0735	1.7	52
	2023	0.3	9		1958	0.2	6
5 W	0848	1.7	52	20 Th	0833	1.9	58
	2048	0.2	6		2043	0.0	0
6 Th	0937	1.7	52	21 F	0939	2.0	61
	2117	0.1	3		2128	-0.1	-3
7 F	1025	1.8	55	22 Sa	1042	2.0	61
	2148	0.1	3		2213	-0.1	-3
8 Sa	1111	1.8	55	23 Su	1140	2.0	61
	2218	0.1	3		2254	0.0	0
○				●			
9 Su	1156	1.9	58	24 M	1234	1.9	58
	2244	0.1	3		2328	0.2	6
10 M	1240	1.8	55	25 Tu	1326	1.8	55
	2305	0.1	3		2342	0.4	12
11 Tu	1323	1.8	55	26 W	1416	1.6	49
	2320	0.2	6		2325	0.6	18
12 W	1407	1.7	52	27 Th	1502	1.4	43
	2329	0.3	9		2303	0.7	21
13 Th	1452	1.6	49	28 F	0615	1.1	34
	2335	0.4	12		1003	1.0	30
					1539	1.2	37
					2243	0.8	24
14 F	1536	1.4	43	29 Sa	0531	1.2	37
	2340	0.6	18		1159	0.9	27
					1552	1.0	30
					2135	0.9	27
15 Sa	0720	1.1	34	30 Su	0523	1.4	43
	1037	1.0	30		1902	0.8	24
	1614	1.2	37	☾			
	2337	0.7	21	31 M	0543	1.5	46
					1900	0.6	18

August

Day	Time	ft	cm	Day	Time	ft	cm
1 Tu	0616	1.6	49	16 W	0557	1.9	58
	1924	0.5	15		1851	0.3	9
2 W	0700	1.7	52	17 Th	0652	1.9	58
	1954	0.4	12		1943	0.2	6
3 Th	0756	1.8	55	18 F	0804	2.0	61
	2026	0.3	9		2029	0.2	6
4 F	0902	1.8	55	19 Sa	0929	2.0	61
	2056	0.3	9		2111	0.2	6
5 Sa	1006	1.8	55	20 Su	1047	1.9	58
	2124	0.3	9		2148	0.3	9
6 Su	1103	1.8	55	21 M	1153	1.9	58
	2148	0.3	9		2215	0.5	15
7 M	1153	1.8	55	●			
	2207	0.3	9	22 Tu	1257	1.7	52
○					2218	0.7	21
8 Tu	1243	1.8	55	23 W	1407	1.6	49
	2217	0.4	12		2155	0.8	24
9 W	1336	1.7	52	24 Th	0437	1.1	34
	2220	0.5	15		0822	1.0	30
					1529	1.4	43
					2139	1.0	30
10 Th	1435	1.6	49	25 F	0351	1.2	37
	2220	0.7	21		0929	0.9	27
					1654	1.3	40
					2126	1.1	34
11 F	0529	1.1	34	26 Sa	0321	1.4	43
	0851	1.0	30		1036	0.8	24
	1542	1.4	43				
	2220	0.8	24				
12 Sa	0501	1.2	37	27 Su	0334	1.6	49
	1005	0.9	27		1203	0.8	24
	1659	1.2	37				
	2212	1.0	30				
13 Su	0444	1.4	43	28 M	0403	1.7	52
	1141	0.8	24		1447	0.8	24
14 M	0449	1.6	49	29 Tu	0438	1.8	55
	1529	0.7	21		1713	0.7	21
☾				☾			
15 Tu	0516	1.7	52	30 W	0519	1.8	55
	1746	0.5	15		1821	0.6	18
				31 Th	0607	1.8	55
					1908	0.5	15

September

Day	Time	ft	cm	Day	Time	ft	cm
1 F	0706	1.8	55	16 Sa	0732	1.9	58
	1944	0.5	15		1958	0.4	12
2 Sa	0823	1.8	55	17 Su	0920	1.7	52
	2014	0.5	15		2032	0.6	18
3 Su	0948	1.8	55	18 M	1111	1.6	49
	2039	0.5	15		2050	0.7	21
4 M	1059	1.7	52	19 Tu	1243	1.5	46
	2057	0.6	18		2034	0.9	27
5 Tu	1203	1.7	52	●			
	2106	0.7	21	20 W	0236	1.2	37
6 W	1312	1.6	49		0657	1.0	30
	2106	0.8	24		1426	1.4	43
					2009	1.1	34
7 Th	0339	1.2	37	21 Th	0141	1.3	40
	0736	1.0	30		0804	0.8	24
	1435	1.5	46		1609	1.3	40
	2102	1.0	30		1959	1.2	37
8 F	0304	1.2	37	22 F	0102	1.4	43
	0837	0.9	27		0859	0.7	21
	1607	1.4	43				
	2058	1.1	34				
9 Sa	0236	1.4	43	23 Sa	0115	1.6	49
	0935	0.8	24		0950	0.6	18
	1744	1.3	40				
	2045	1.2	37				
10 Su	0236	1.6	49	24 Su	0144	1.7	52
	1043	0.7	21		1044	0.6	18
11 M	0301	1.8	55	25 M	0219	1.8	55
	1234	0.6	18		1156	0.6	18
12 Tu	0340	1.9	58	26 Tu	0258	1.8	55
	1519	0.5	15		1347	0.6	18
13 W	0426	2.0	61	27 W	0340	1.8	55
	1702	0.4	12		1526	0.6	18
○				☾			
14 Th	0518	2.0	61	28 Th	0426	1.8	55
	1817	0.4	12		1645	0.6	18
15 F	0618	1.9	58	29 F	0515	1.8	55
	1913	0.4	12		1745	0.6	18
				30 Sa	0611	1.7	52
					1828	0.6	18

Time meridian 90° W. 0000 is midnight. 1200 is noon. Times are not adjusted for Daylight Saving Time.
Heights are referred to mean lower low water which is the chart datum of soundings.

Mobile, Alabama, 2017

Times and Heights of High and Low Waters

October

Day	Time	Height (ft)	Height (cm)
1 Su	0726	1.6	49
	1858	0.6	18
2 M	0925	1.5	46
	1917	0.7	21
3 Tu	1113	1.4	43
	1923	0.8	24
4 W	0141	1.2	37
	0624	1.0	30
	1250	1.4	43
	1919	1.0	30
5 Th O	0103	1.2	37
	0727	0.8	24
	1446	1.3	40
	1913	1.1	34
6 F	0033	1.4	43
	0820	0.6	18
	1648	1.3	40
	1859	1.2	37
7 Sa	0028	1.6	49
	0913	0.5	15
8 Su	0047	1.7	52
	1013	0.4	12
9 M	0121	1.9	58
	1137	0.3	9
10 Tu	0205	2.0	61
	1332	0.3	9
11 W	0255	2.0	61
	1501	0.3	9
12 Th ◑	0349	1.9	58
	1616	0.3	9
13 F	0443	1.8	55
	1720	0.3	9
14 Sa	0538	1.7	52
	1812	0.5	15
15 Su	0639	1.5	46
	1841	0.6	18
16 M	0853	1.2	37
	1822	0.8	24
17 Tu	0051	1.1	34
	0531	1.0	30
	1241	1.1	34
	1740	1.0	30
18 W	0016	1.2	37
	0700	0.7	21
	1505	1.1	34
	1712	1.0	30
	2334	1.4	43
19 Th ●	0757	0.6	18
	2331	1.5	46
20 F	0842	0.4	12
	2351	1.7	52
21 Sa	0924	0.3	9
22 Su	0019	1.7	52
	1008	0.3	9
23 M	0052	1.8	55
	1058	0.2	6
24 Tu	0128	1.8	55
	1201	0.2	6
25 W	0208	1.8	55
	1313	0.3	9
26 Th	0250	1.7	52
	1413	0.3	9
27 F ◐	0334	1.6	49
	1459	0.3	9
28 Sa	0418	1.5	46
	1534	0.4	12
29 Su	0502	1.4	43
	1558	0.5	15
30 M	0551	1.2	37
	1610	0.6	18
31 Tu	0029	1.1	34
	0532	0.9	27
	0915	1.0	30
	1615	0.7	21
	2349	1.1	34

November

Day	Time	Height (ft)	Height (cm)
1 W	0640	0.7	21
	1226	0.9	27
	1609	0.8	24
	2319	1.2	37
2 Th	0725	0.5	15
	2302	1.4	43
3 F O	0811	0.3	9
	2308	1.5	46
4 Sa	0900	0.1	3
	2332	1.7	52
5 Su	0957	-0.1	-3
6 M	0007	1.8	55
	1107	-0.2	-6
7 Tu	0049	1.9	58
	1226	-0.2	-6
8 W	0137	1.9	58
	1335	-0.2	-6
9 Th	0228	1.8	55
	1431	-0.1	-3
10 F ◑	0318	1.6	49
	1514	0.1	3
11 Sa	0404	1.4	43
	1535	0.2	6
12 Su	0441	1.2	37
	1521	0.4	12
	2351	1.0	30
13 M	1456	0.6	18
	2317	1.0	30
14 Tu	0849	0.6	18
	2242	1.1	34
15 W	0812	0.4	12
	2215	1.3	40
16 Th	0820	0.2	6
	2222	1.4	43
17 F	0844	0.0	0
	2244	1.5	46
18 Sa ●	0916	-0.1	-3
	2314	1.6	49
19 Su	0951	-0.2	-6
	2346	1.6	49
20 M	1031	-0.2	-6
21 Tu	0021	1.6	49
	1114	-0.2	-6
22 W	0057	1.6	49
	1157	-0.2	-6
23 Th	0135	1.5	46
	1236	-0.1	-3
24 F	0213	1.4	43
	1305	-0.1	-3
25 Sa	0248	1.3	40
	1326	0.0	0
26 Su ◐	0316	1.1	34
	1341	0.1	3
27 M	0059	0.9	27
	1352	0.2	6
	2306	0.9	27
28 Tu	1355	0.3	9
	2222	0.9	27
29 W	0748	0.3	9
	2155	1.0	30
30 Th	0733	0.1	3
	2147	1.2	37

December

Day	Time	Height (ft)	Height (cm)
1 F	0803	-0.1	-3
	2200	1.4	43
2 Sa	0846	-0.4	-12
	2229	1.6	49
3 Su O	0936	-0.5	-15
	2307	1.7	52
4 M	1033	-0.6	-18
	2350	1.7	52
5 Tu	1132	-0.7	-21
6 W	0036	1.7	52
	1227	-0.6	-18
7 Th	0123	1.6	49
	1312	-0.5	-15
8 F	0209	1.4	43
	1341	-0.3	-9
9 Sa	0249	1.2	37
	1342	-0.1	-3
10 Su ◑	0315	0.9	27
	1320	0.1	3
	2228	0.7	21
11 M	1251	0.2	6
	2146	0.8	24
12 Tu	0856	0.2	6
	2106	0.9	27
13 W	0819	0.0	0
	2052	1.1	34
14 Th	0822	-0.2	-6
	2110	1.2	37
15 F	0839	-0.3	-9
	2139	1.3	40
16 Sa	0904	-0.4	-12
	2213	1.4	43
17 Su	0934	-0.5	-15
	2249	1.4	43
18 M ●	1006	-0.5	-15
	2327	1.4	43
19 Tu	1038	-0.5	-15
20 W	0004	1.4	43
	1107	-0.5	-15
21 Th	0041	1.3	40
	1129	-0.5	-15
22 F	0117	1.2	37
	1145	-0.4	-12
23 Sa	0150	1.1	34
	1156	-0.4	-12
24 Su	0219	0.9	27
	1205	-0.2	-6
25 M	0223	0.7	21
	1212	-0.1	-3
	2123	0.6	18
26 Tu ◐	1210	0.0	0
	2036	0.7	21
27 W	0915	0.1	3
	2017	0.9	27
28 Th	0720	-0.1	-3
	2022	1.0	30
29 F	0740	-0.4	-12
	2047	1.2	37
30 Sa	0817	-0.6	-18
	2125	1.4	43
31 Su	0902	-0.8	-24
	2210	1.5	46

Time meridian 90° W. 0000 is midnight. 1200 is noon. Times are not adjusted for Daylight Saving Time.
Heights are referred to mean lower low water which is the chart datum of soundings.

South Pass, Louisiana, 2017

Times and Heights of High and Low Waters

January

Day	Time	Height (ft)	Height (cm)	Day	Time	Height (ft)	Height (cm)
1 Su	0806 / 2156	-0.5 / 0.9	-15 / 27	16 M	0833 / 2227	-0.3 / 0.4	-9 / 12
2 M	0836 / 2228	-0.4 / 0.8	-12 / 24	17 Tu	0817 / 2122	-0.1 / 0.2	-3 / 6
3 Tu	0901 / 2249	-0.3 / 0.6	-9 / 18	18 W	0709 / 1622	0.0 / 0.2	0 / 6
4 W	0910 / 2037	-0.1 / 0.3	-3 / 9	19 Th	0445 / 1538	-0.1 / 0.4	-3 / 12
5 Th ◑	0836 / 1710	0.0 / 0.4	0 / 12	20 F	0310 / 1544	-0.2 / 0.5	-6 / 15
6 F	0318 / 1634	0.0 / 0.5	0 / 15	21 Sa	0307 / 1609	-0.3 / 0.6	-9 / 18
7 Sa	0241 / 1641	-0.2 / 0.7	-6 / 21	22 Su	0327 / 1644	-0.5 / 0.7	-15 / 21
8 Su	0314 / 1711	-0.5 / 0.9	-15 / 27	23 M	0355 / 1724	-0.6 / 0.8	-18 / 24
9 M	0358 / 1753	-0.7 / 1.0	-21 / 30	24 Tu	0426 / 1806	-0.6 / 0.8	-18 / 24
10 Tu	0445 / 1840	-0.8 / 1.1	-24 / 34	25 W	0459 / 1849	-0.7 / 0.9	-21 / 27
11 W	0534 / 1929	-0.9 / 1.1	-27 / 34	26 Th	0532 / 1930	-0.7 / 0.9	-21 / 27
12 Th ○	0622 / 2016	-0.8 / 1.1	-24 / 34	27 F ●	0604 / 2010	-0.6 / 0.9	-18 / 27
13 F	0708 / 2101	-0.8 / 1.0	-24 / 30	28 Sa	0634 / 2050	-0.6 / 0.8	-18 / 24
14 Sa	0748 / 2141	-0.6 / 0.8	-18 / 24	29 Su	0703 / 2129	-0.5 / 0.7	-15 / 21
15 Su	0819 / 2213	-0.5 / 0.6	-15 / 18	30 M	0727 / 2210	-0.4 / 0.6	-12 / 18
				31 Tu	0742 / 2250	-0.3 / 0.4	-9 / 12

February

Day	Time	Height (ft)	Height (cm)	Day	Time	Height (ft)	Height (cm)
1 W	0734 / 1537 / 1846 / 2320	-0.1 / 0.1 / 0.0 / 0.1	-3 / 3 / 0 / 3	16 Th	0249 / 1243	0.0 / 0.4	0 / 12
2 Th	0626 / 1419	0.0 / 0.3	0 / 9	17 F	0053 / 1310	-0.1 / 0.5	-3 / 15
3 F ◑	0054 / 1421	-0.1 / 0.5	-3 / 15	18 Sa ○	0119 / 1350	-0.2 / 0.6	-6 / 18
4 Sa	0125 / 1454	-0.3 / 0.6	-9 / 18	19 Su	0155 / 1441	-0.3 / 0.7	-9 / 21
5 Su	0211 / 1542	-0.6 / 0.8	-18 / 24	20 M	0232 / 1539	-0.4 / 0.8	-12 / 24
6 M	0259 / 1638	-0.7 / 0.9	-21 / 27	21 Tu	0310 / 1639	-0.5 / 0.8	-15 / 24
7 Tu	0348 / 1738	-0.8 / 1.0	-24 / 30	22 W	0347 / 1738	-0.5 / 0.9	-15 / 27
8 W	0436 / 1836	-0.8 / 1.0	-24 / 30	23 Th	0422 / 1833	-0.5 / 0.9	-15 / 27
9 Th	0521 / 1932	-0.8 / 0.9	-24 / 27	24 F	0455 / 1925	-0.4 / 0.9	-12 / 27
10 F ○	0603 / 2023	-0.6 / 0.8	-18 / 24	25 Sa	0526 / 2016	-0.4 / 0.8	-12 / 24
11 Sa	0638 / 2110	-0.5 / 0.7	-15 / 21	26 Su ●	0553 / 2109	-0.3 / 0.7	-9 / 21
12 Su	0701 / 2152	-0.3 / 0.5	-9 / 15	27 M	0613 / 2207	-0.1 / 0.6	-3 / 18
13 M	0704 / 2230	-0.1 / 0.4	-3 / 12	28 Tu	0617 / 1159 / 1605 / 2322	0.0 / 0.2 / 0.1 / 0.4	0 / 6 / 3 / 12
14 Tu	0637 / 1314 / 1707 / 2301	0.0 / 0.1 / 0.0 / 0.2	0 / 3 / 0 / 6				
15 W	0525 / 1235	0.1 / 0.3	3 / 9				

March

Day	Time	Height (ft)	Height (cm)	Day	Time	Height (ft)	Height (cm)
1 W	0545 / 1124 / 1843	0.2 / 0.4 / 0.1	6 / 12 / 3	16 Th	1031 / 2046	0.8 / 0.1	24 / 3
2 Th	1129 / 2120	0.6 / -0.1	18 / -3	17 F	1059 / 2216	0.9 / 0.0	27 / 0
3 F	1159 / 2317	0.7 / -0.2	21 / -6	18 Sa	1135 / 2330	0.9 / -0.1	27 / -3
4 Sa	1246	0.9	27	19 Su	1220	1.0	30
5 Su ◑	0035 / 1344	-0.4 / 1.0	-12 / 30	20 M	0030 / 1315	-0.1 / 1.0	-3 / 30
6 M	0138 / 1454	-0.5 / 1.0	-15 / 30	21 Tu	0121 / 1421	-0.1 / 1.0	-3 / 30
7 Tu	0234 / 1610	-0.5 / 1.0	-15 / 30	22 W	0207 / 1538	-0.1 / 1.0	-3 / 30
8 W	0325 / 1726	-0.5 / 1.0	-15 / 30	23 Th	0247 / 1659	-0.1 / 1.0	-3 / 30
9 Th	0410 / 1838	-0.4 / 0.9	-12 / 27	24 F	0324 / 1816	-0.1 / 1.0	-3 / 30
10 F	0448 / 1944	-0.2 / 0.8	-6 / 24	25 Sa	0356 / 1930	0.0 / 0.9	0 / 27
11 Sa	0516 / 2045	-0.1 / 0.7	-3 / 21	26 Su	0422 / 2048	0.2 / 0.8	6 / 24
12 Su ○	0527 / 2145	0.1 / 0.6	3 / 18	27 M ●	0435 / 0957 / 1502 / 2219	0.3 / 0.5 / 0.3 / 0.7	9 / 15 / 9 / 21
13 M	0513 / 1035 / 1602 / 2254	0.2 / 0.4 / 0.3 / 0.5	6 / 12 / 9 / 15	28 Tu	0420 / 0921 / 1643	0.5 / 0.6 / 0.2	15 / 18 / 6
14 Tu	0423 / 1010 / 1739	0.4 / 0.5 / 0.2	12 / 15 / 6	29 W	0919 / 1816	0.8 / 0.1	24 / 3
15 W	1013 / 1911	0.6 / 0.1	18 / 3	30 Th	0940 / 1948	1.0 / 0.0	30 / 0
				31 F	1016 / 2119	1.2 / -0.1	37 / -3

Time meridian 90° W. 0000 is midnight. 1200 is noon. Times are not adjusted for Daylight Saving Time.
Heights are referred to mean lower low water which is the chart datum of soundings.

South Pass, Louisiana, 2017

Times and Heights of High and Low Waters

April

Day	Time (h m)	Height (ft)	Height (cm)
1 Sa	1101	1.3	40
	2243	-0.2	-6
2 Su	1154	1.3	40
	2357	-0.2	-6
3 M ◐	1254	1.3	40
4 Tu	0100	-0.2	-6
	1404	1.2	37
5 W	0155	-0.1	-3
	1529	1.1	34
6 Th	0239	0.0	0
	1710	1.0	30
7 F	0312	0.2	6
	1852	0.9	27
8 Sa	0327	0.4	12
	1029	0.6	18
	1401	0.5	15
	2030	0.8	24
9 Su	0314	0.5	15
	0907	0.7	21
	1539	0.5	15
	2221	0.7	21
10 M	0217	0.6	18
	0838	0.8	24
	1644	0.4	12
11 Tu ○	0836	0.9	27
	1740	0.3	9
12 W	0847	1.1	34
	1831	0.2	6
13 Th	0906	1.1	34
	1922	0.1	3
14 F	0931	1.2	37
	2016	0.1	3
15 Sa	1002	1.3	40
	2114	0.1	3
16 Su	1038	1.3	40
	2214	0.0	0
17 M	1119	1.3	40
	2311	0.1	3
18 Tu	1205	1.3	40
19 W ◐	0003	0.1	3
	1300	1.2	37
20 Th	0049	0.1	3
	1412	1.1	34
21 F	0128	0.2	6
	1557	1.0	30
22 Sa	0200	0.3	9
	1808	0.9	27
23 Su	0220	0.4	12
	0904	0.7	21
	1407	0.6	18
	2021	0.8	24
24 M	0218	0.6	18
	0810	0.8	24
	1529	0.4	12
25 Tu	0752	1.0	30
	1638	0.2	6
26 W ●	0800	1.2	37
	1744	0.0	0
27 Th	0826	1.4	43
	1852	-0.1	-3
28 F	0902	1.5	46
	2001	-0.2	-6
29 Sa	0945	1.6	49
	2110	-0.2	-6
30 Su	1032	1.6	49
	2217	-0.2	-6

May

Day	Time (h m)	Height (ft)	Height (cm)
1 M	1121	1.5	46
	2319	-0.1	-3
2 Tu	1209	1.4	43
3 W	0012	0.0	0
	1255	1.2	37
4 Th	0052	0.2	6
	1323	1.0	30
5 F	0112	0.4	12
	1012	0.8	24
6 Sa	0101	0.5	15
	0823	0.8	24
	1547	0.6	18
	2111	0.7	21
	2329	0.6	18
7 Su	0738	1.0	30
	1621	0.4	12
8 M	0725	1.1	34
	1656	0.3	9
9 Tu	0730	1.2	37
	1730	0.2	6
10 W ○	0744	1.3	40
	1804	0.1	3
11 Th	0805	1.4	43
	1839	0.0	0
12 F	0829	1.4	43
	1917	0.0	0
13 Sa	0858	1.4	43
	1958	0.0	0
14 Su	0929	1.5	46
	2041	0.0	0
15 M	1003	1.4	43
	2125	0.0	0
16 Tu ◐	1039	1.4	43
	2209	0.0	0
17 W	1115	1.3	40
	2250	0.1	3
18 Th ◐	1150	1.2	37
	2325	0.2	6
19 F	1211	1.0	30
	2351	0.3	9
20 Sa	0936	0.9	27
	2358	0.5	15
21 Su	0740	0.9	27
	1459	0.5	15
	1948	0.6	18
	2307	0.5	15
22 M	0656	1.0	30
	1532	0.3	9
23 Tu	0646	1.1	34
	1618	0.1	3
24 W	0659	1.3	40
	1710	-0.1	-3
25 Th	0727	1.5	46
	1805	-0.3	-9
26 F ●	0805	1.7	52
	1902	-0.4	-12
27 Sa	0847	1.7	52
	2000	-0.4	-12
28 Su	0932	1.7	52
	2057	-0.3	-9
29 M	1016	1.6	49
	2151	-0.2	-6
30 Tu	1056	1.4	43
	2235	0.0	0
31 W	1123	1.2	37
	2304	0.2	6

June

Day	Time (h m)	Height (ft)	Height (cm)
1 Th ◐	1103	1.0	30
	2307	0.3	9
2 F	0842	0.8	24
	2212	0.5	15
3 Sa	0706	0.9	27
	1655	0.4	12
4 Su	0628	1.0	30
	1626	0.3	9
5 M	0622	1.1	34
	1642	0.1	3
6 Tu	0632	1.2	37
	1706	0.0	0
7 W	0650	1.3	40
	1734	-0.1	-3
8 Th	0713	1.4	43
	1803	-0.1	-3
9 F ○	0740	1.4	43
	1834	-0.2	-6
10 Sa	0809	1.4	43
	1907	-0.2	-6
11 Su	0840	1.4	43
	1941	-0.2	-6
12 M	0912	1.4	43
	2014	-0.1	-3
13 Tu	0944	1.4	43
	2047	-0.1	-3
14 W	1015	1.3	40
	2118	0.0	0
15 Th	1041	1.1	34
	2143	0.1	3
16 F	1048	1.0	30
	2157	0.2	6
17 Sa	0841	0.8	24
	2145	0.4	12
18 Su	0628	0.8	24
	1804	0.4	12
19 M	0546	0.9	27
	1520	0.2	6
20 Tu	0541	1.1	34
	1548	-0.1	-3
21 W	0559	1.3	40
	1630	-0.3	-9
22 Th	0632	1.5	46
	1718	-0.4	-12
23 F ●	0712	1.6	49
	1809	-0.5	-15
24 Sa	0758	1.7	52
	1901	-0.5	-15
25 Su	0844	1.6	49
	1952	-0.4	-12
26 M	0928	1.5	46
	2038	-0.3	-9
27 Tu	1008	1.3	40
	2115	-0.1	-3
28 W	1037	1.1	34
	2136	0.1	3
29 Th	1031	0.9	27
	2125	0.3	9
30 F ◐	0801	0.7	21
	2011	0.4	12

Time meridian 90° W. 0000 is midnight. 1200 is noon. Times are not adjusted for Daylight Saving Time.
Heights are referred to mean lower low water which is the chart datum of soundings.

South Pass, Louisiana, 2017

Times and Heights of High and Low Waters

July

Day	Time (h m)	Height (ft)	Height (cm)	Day	Time (h m)	Height (ft)	Height (cm)
1 Sa	0549	0.8	24	16 Su ☽	0448	0.8	24
	1702	0.3	9		1708	0.4	12
2 Su	0511	0.9	27	17 M	0414	0.9	27
	1558	0.2	6		1439	0.2	6
3 M	0510	1.0	30	18 Tu	0421	1.1	34
	1604	0.0	0		1501	-0.1	-3
4 Tu	0526	1.2	37	19 W	0449	1.3	40
	1625	-0.1	-3		1541	-0.3	-9
5 W	0551	1.2	37	20 Th	0531	1.5	46
	1651	-0.2	-6		1627	-0.4	-12
6 Th	0621	1.3	40	21 F	0618	1.6	49
	1720	-0.2	-6		1715	-0.5	-15
7 F	0653	1.4	43	22 Sa	0709	1.6	49
	1750	-0.2	-6		1804	-0.4	-12
8 Sa ○	0726	1.4	43	23 Su ●	0759	1.6	49
	1821	-0.2	-6		1851	-0.3	-9
9 Su	0800	1.4	43	24 M	0848	1.5	46
	1850	-0.2	-6		1933	-0.2	-6
10 M	0833	1.4	43	25 Tu	0932	1.3	40
	1918	-0.2	-6		2005	0.0	0
11 Tu	0906	1.3	40	26 W	1009	1.1	34
	1944	-0.1	-3		2019	0.2	6
12 W	0937	1.2	37	27 Th	1029	0.9	27
	2007	0.0	0		1959	0.4	12
13 Th	1006	1.1	34	28 F	0917	0.7	21
	2024	0.1	3		1842	0.5	15
14 F	1023	0.9	27	29 Sa	0333	0.8	24
	2027	0.2	6		1604	0.4	12
15 Sa	0844	0.7	21	30 Su ☾	0310	0.9	27
	1957	0.4	12		1449	0.3	9
				31 M	0324	1.1	34
					1456	0.2	6

August

Day	Time (h m)	Height (ft)	Height (cm)	Day	Time (h m)	Height (ft)	Height (cm)
1 Tu	0354	1.2	37	16 W	0315	1.4	43
	1520	0.1	3		1434	0.0	0
2 W	0431	1.3	40	17 Th	0411	1.6	49
	1549	0.0	0		1523	-0.1	-3
3 Th	0512	1.3	40	18 F	0512	1.6	49
	1621	-0.1	-3		1613	-0.2	-6
4 F	0555	1.4	43	19 Sa	0613	1.7	52
	1654	-0.1	-3		1701	-0.1	-3
5 Sa	0637	1.4	43	20 Su	0713	1.6	49
	1725	-0.1	-3		1745	0.0	0
6 Su	0718	1.4	43	21 M ●	0809	1.5	46
	1755	0.0	0		1823	0.2	6
7 M ○	0757	1.4	43	22 Tu	0901	1.4	43
	1821	0.0	0		1850	0.4	12
8 Tu	0834	1.4	43	23 W	0950	1.2	37
	1844	0.1	3		1854	0.6	18
9 W	0912	1.3	40	24 Th	1038	1.0	30
	1901	0.2	6		1819	0.7	21
10 Th	0949	1.1	34	25 F	0020	0.8	24
	1910	0.3	9		0540	0.7	21
					1129	0.9	27
					1645	0.8	24
11 F	1027	1.0	30	26 Sa	0002	1.0	30
	1859	0.5	15		0950	0.7	21
12 Sa	0252	0.8	24	27 Su	0018	1.1	34
	0611	0.7	21		1210	0.6	18
	1058	0.8	24				
	1805	0.6	18				
13 Su	0153	0.9	27	28 M	0051	1.3	40
	1303	0.6	18		1257	0.4	12
14 M ☾	0157	1.1	34	29 Tu ☾	0133	1.3	40
	1301	0.3	9		1339	0.4	12
15 Tu	0228	1.3	40	30 W	0225	1.4	43
	1346	0.1	3		1420	0.3	9
				31 Th	0325	1.5	46
					1459	0.3	9

September

Day	Time (h m)	Height (ft)	Height (cm)	Day	Time (h m)	Height (ft)	Height (cm)
1 F	0426	1.5	46	16 Sa	0458	1.7	52
	1536	0.3	9		1545	0.3	9
2 Sa	0526	1.5	46	17 Su	0615	1.6	49
	1611	0.3	9		1627	0.4	12
3 Su	0621	1.5	46	18 M	0727	1.5	46
	1642	0.3	9		1658	0.6	18
4 M	0712	1.5	46	19 Tu ●	0835	1.4	43
	1709	0.4	12		1712	0.8	24
					2317	0.9	27
5 Tu	0801	1.4	43	20 W	0148	0.8	24
	1730	0.5	15		0946	1.3	40
					1653	1.0	30
					2153	1.1	34
6 W ○	0852	1.4	43	21 Th	0406	0.9	27
	1742	0.6	18		1113	1.1	34
					1544	1.0	30
					2136	1.2	37
7 Th	0948	1.2	37	22 F	0542	0.8	24
	1740	0.8	24		2147	1.4	43
	2316	0.9	27				
8 F	0400	0.8	24	23 Sa	0713	0.7	21
	1059	1.1	34		2210	1.5	46
	1706	0.9	27				
	2255	1.1	34				
9 Sa	0619	0.8	24	24 Su	0842	0.7	21
	2304	1.3	40		2240	1.5	46
10 Su	0840	0.6	18	25 M	1006	0.6	18
	2334	1.4	43		2317	1.6	49
11 M	1038	0.5	15	26 Tu	1116	0.6	18
12 Tu	0018	1.6	49	27 W ☽	0002	1.6	49
	1200	0.3	9		1216	0.5	15
13 W ☽	0114	1.7	52	28 Th	0056	1.6	49
	1306	0.2	6		1307	0.5	15
14 Th	0222	1.7	52	29 F	0202	1.6	49
	1404	0.2	6		1352	0.5	15
15 F	0339	1.7	52	30 Sa	0320	1.6	49
	1457	0.2	6		1432	0.5	15

Time meridian 90° W. 0000 is midnight. 1200 is noon. Times are not adjusted for Daylight Saving Time.
Heights are referred to mean lower low water which is the chart datum of soundings.

South Pass, Louisiana, 2017

Times and Heights of High and Low Waters

October

Day	Time	Height (ft)	Height (cm)	Day	Time	Height (ft)	Height (cm)
1 Su	0442	1.5	46	16 M	0633	1.4	43
	1505	0.6	18		1507	0.8	24
					2155	1.1	34
2 M	0600	1.5	46	17 Tu	0151	1.0	30
	1532	0.7	21		0822	1.2	37
					1453	1.0	30
					2036	1.2	37
3 Tu	0715	1.4	43	18 W	0329	0.9	27
	1550	0.8	24		1037	1.1	34
	2237	1.0	30		1338	1.0	30
					2010	1.3	40
4 W	0052	0.9	27	19 Th ●	0437	0.8	24
	0832	1.3	40		2012	1.4	43
	1554	1.0	30				
	2117	1.1	34				
5 Th ○	0301	0.9	27	20 F	0534	0.7	21
	1003	1.2	37		2027	1.5	46
	1531	1.1	34				
	2054	1.2	37				
6 F	0431	0.8	24	21 Sa	0626	0.6	18
	2057	1.4	43		2049	1.6	49
7 Sa	0555	0.7	21	22 Su	0717	0.5	15
	2119	1.6	49		2116	1.7	52
8 Su	0720	0.5	15	23 M	0810	0.5	15
	2153	1.7	52		2147	1.7	52
9 M	0847	0.4	12	24 Tu	0906	0.5	15
	2236	1.8	55		2222	1.7	52
10 Tu	1010	0.3	9	25 W	1004	0.4	12
	2327	1.9	58		2301	1.7	52
11 W	1124	0.3	9	26 Th	1059	0.4	12
					2346	1.6	49
12 Th ☽	0026	1.9	58	27 F ◑	1149	0.5	15
	1229	0.3	9				
13 F	0134	1.8	55	28 Sa	0037	1.5	46
	1326	0.4	12		1232	0.5	15
14 Sa	0258	1.7	52	29 Su	0141	1.4	43
	1414	0.5	15		1306	0.6	18
15 Su	0442	1.5	46	30 M	0323	1.3	40
	1450	0.7	21		1332	0.7	21
				31 Tu	0545	1.2	37
					1344	0.8	24
					2027	1.1	34

November

Day	Time	Height (ft)	Height (cm)	Day	Time	Height (ft)	Height (cm)
1 W	0213	0.9	27	16 Th	0440	0.4	12
	0806	1.1	34		1911	1.4	43
	1331	0.9	27				
	1944	1.2	37				
2 Th	0321	0.7	21	17 F	0518	0.3	9
	1932	1.3	40		1929	1.4	43
3 F ○	0423	0.5	15	18 Sa ●	0554	0.2	6
	1943	1.5	46		1952	1.5	46
4 Sa	0524	0.3	9	19 Su	0630	0.1	3
	2008	1.7	52		2018	1.5	46
5 Su	0628	0.2	6	20 M	0707	0.1	3
	2043	1.8	55		2046	1.5	46
6 M	0734	0.1	3	21 Tu	0748	0.1	3
	2125	1.9	58		2118	1.5	46
7 Tu	0842	0.0	0	22 W	0830	0.1	3
	2211	1.9	58		2151	1.5	46
8 W	0950	0.0	0	23 Th	0914	0.1	3
	2300	1.8	55		2225	1.4	43
9 Th	1053	0.1	3	24 F	0955	0.1	3
	2350	1.6	49		2259	1.3	40
10 F ☽	1149	0.2	6	25 Sa	1033	0.2	6
					2329	1.2	37
11 Sa	0039	1.4	43	26 Su ◑	1103	0.3	9
	1232	0.4	12		2338	1.0	30
12 Su	0121	1.2	37	27 M	1122	0.4	12
	1257	0.6	18		2105	0.8	24
	2202	1.0	30				
13 M	0315	0.9	27	28 Tu	1121	0.5	15
	0356	1.0	30		1913	0.8	24
	1249	0.7	21				
	2000	1.0	30				
14 Tu	0321	0.7	21	29 W	0304	0.5	15
	1913	1.1	34		0743	0.6	18
					1008	0.5	15
					1833	0.9	27
15 W	0401	0.5	15	30 Th	0320	0.3	9
	1902	1.2	37		1826	1.1	34

December

Day	Time	Height (ft)	Height (cm)	Day	Time	Height (ft)	Height (cm)
1 F	0400	0.1	3	16 Sa	0519	-0.3	-9
	1841	1.3	40		1901	1.2	37
2 Sa	0448	-0.1	-3	17 Su	0549	-0.3	-9
	1909	1.4	43		1930	1.2	37
3 Su ○	0541	-0.3	-9	18 M ●	0621	-0.4	-12
	1947	1.6	49		2000	1.2	37
4 M	0637	-0.4	-12	19 Tu	0654	-0.4	-12
	2030	1.6	49		2032	1.2	37
5 Tu	0735	-0.5	-15	20 W	0727	-0.4	-12
	2116	1.6	49		2104	1.1	34
6 W	0833	-0.4	-12	21 Th	0759	-0.3	-9
	2202	1.5	46		2135	1.1	34
7 Th	0929	-0.3	-9	22 F	0830	-0.3	-9
	2246	1.3	40		2205	1.0	30
8 F	1018	-0.2	-6	23 Sa	0857	-0.2	-6
	2321	1.1	34		2231	0.8	24
9 Sa	1053	0.0	0	24 Su	0918	-0.1	-3
	2320	0.8	24		2240	0.7	21
10 Su ☽	1101	0.2	6	25 M	0926	0.0	0
	2036	0.7	21		2039	0.5	15
11 M	1005	0.4	12	26 Tu ◑	0906	0.1	3
	1838	0.7	21		1756	0.5	15
12 Tu	0401	0.3	9	27 W	0539	0.1	3
	1759	0.8	24		1715	0.6	18
13 W	0356	0.1	3	28 Th	0302	-0.1	-3
	1757	0.9	27		1714	0.8	24
14 Th	0420	-0.1	-3	29 F	0325	-0.3	-9
	1812	1.0	30		1735	0.9	27
15 F	0449	-0.2	-6	30 Sa	0405	-0.6	-18
	1835	1.1	34		1810	1.1	34
				31 Su	0452	-0.7	-21
					1853	1.2	37

Time meridian 90° W. 0000 is midnight. 1200 is noon. Times are not adjusted for Daylight Saving Time.
Heights are referred to mean lower low water which is the chart datum of soundings.

Grand Isle (East Point), Louisiana, 2017

Times and Heights of High and Low Waters

January

Day	Time (h m)	Height (ft)	Height (cm)	Day	Time (h m)	Height (ft)	Height (cm)
1 Su	0938	-0.4	-12	16 M	1017	-0.3	-9
	2316	0.7	21		2351	0.4	12
2 M	1006	-0.3	-9	17 Tu	1006	-0.1	-3
	2347	0.6	18		2222	0.2	6
3 Tu	1026	-0.2	-6	18 W	0900	0.0	0
					1808	0.2	6
4 W	0004	0.4	12	19 Th	0605	0.0	0
	1028	-0.1	-3		1714	0.3	9
	2056	0.3	9	☽			
5 Th	0943	0.0	0	20 F	0427	-0.1	-3
	1818	0.3	9		1713	0.4	12
◐							
6 F	0425	0.0	0	21 Sa	0430	-0.3	-9
	1747	0.4	12		1734	0.5	15
7 Sa	0404	-0.2	-6	22 Su	0454	-0.4	-12
	1757	0.6	18		1807	0.6	18
8 Su	0440	-0.4	-12	23 M	0525	-0.4	-12
	1828	0.8	24		1846	0.7	21
9 M	0526	-0.6	-18	24 Tu	0559	-0.5	-15
	1912	0.9	27		1927	0.7	21
10 Tu	0615	-0.7	-21	25 W	0634	-0.5	-15
	2000	0.9	27		2008	0.7	21
11 W	0706	-0.7	-21	26 Th	0709	-0.5	-15
	2051	0.9	27		2049	0.7	21
12 Th	0756	-0.7	-21	27 F	0742	-0.5	-15
	2140	0.9	27		2129	0.7	21
○				●			
13 F	0843	-0.6	-18	28 Sa	0814	-0.5	-15
	2226	0.8	24		2209	0.7	21
14 Sa	0925	-0.5	-15	29 Su	0842	-0.4	-12
	2306	0.7	21		2250	0.6	18
15 Su	0959	-0.4	-12	30 M	0906	-0.3	-9
	2338	0.5	15		2333	0.5	15
				31 Tu	0919	-0.2	-6

February

Day	Time (h m)	Height (ft)	Height (cm)	Day	Time (h m)	Height (ft)	Height (cm)
1 W	0017	0.3	9	16 Th	1418	0.4	12
	0906	-0.1	-3				
	1655	0.1	3				
	2129	0.0	0				
2 Th	0108	0.1	3	17 F	0145	0.0	0
	0744	0.0	0		1442	0.5	15
	1541	0.3	9				
3 F	0146	-0.1	-3	18 Sa	0231	-0.1	-3
	1544	0.4	12		1522	0.5	15
☽				○			
4 Sa	0239	-0.3	-9	19 Su	0315	-0.2	-6
	1616	0.6	18		1611	0.6	18
5 Su	0332	-0.4	-12	20 M	0358	-0.3	-9
	1705	0.7	21		1706	0.7	21
6 M	0425	-0.6	-18	21 Tu	0440	-0.3	-9
	1802	0.8	24		1804	0.7	21
7 Tu	0517	-0.6	-18	22 W	0520	-0.3	-9
	1902	0.8	24		1859	0.7	21
8 W	0609	-0.6	-18	23 Th	0559	-0.3	-9
	2001	0.8	24		1953	0.8	24
9 Th	0658	-0.6	-18	24 F	0635	-0.3	-9
	2057	0.8	24		2045	0.8	24
10 F	0744	-0.5	-15	25 Sa	0708	-0.3	-9
	2149	0.7	21		2138	0.7	21
○							
11 Sa	0823	-0.4	-12	26 Su	0738	-0.2	-6
	2237	0.6	18		2235	0.6	18
				●			
12 Su	0852	-0.2	-6	27 M	0800	0.0	0
	2322	0.5	15		2342	0.5	15
13 M	0905	-0.1	-3	28 Tu	0805	0.1	3
					1328	0.2	6
					1736	0.1	3
14 Tu	0006	0.3	9				
	0843	0.0	0				
	1555	0.1	3				
	1809	0.0	0				
15 W	0052	0.2	6				
	0721	0.1	3				
	1420	0.2	6				
	2344	0.1	3				

March

Day	Time (h m)	Height (ft)	Height (cm)	Day	Time (h m)	Height (ft)	Height (cm)
1 W	0116	0.4	12	16 Th	1144	0.6	18
	0725	0.2	6		2209	0.1	3
	1239	0.3	9				
	2025	0.1	3				
2 Th	1245	0.5	15	17 F	1217	0.7	21
	2243	0.0	0		2331	0.0	0
3 F	1319	0.6	18	18 Sa	1257	0.8	24
4 Sa	0029	-0.2	-6	19 Su	0043	0.0	0
	1409	0.8	24		1346	0.8	24
5 Su	0150	-0.3	-9	20 M	0147	0.0	0
	1511	0.9	27		1444	0.9	27
☽				○			
6 M	0259	-0.3	-9	21 Tu	0244	-0.1	-3
	1622	0.9	27		1550	0.9	27
7 Tu	0401	-0.4	-12	22 W	0334	-0.1	-3
	1738	0.9	27		1703	0.9	27
8 W	0457	-0.3	-9	23 Th	0418	0.0	0
	1854	0.9	27		1819	0.9	27
9 Th	0548	-0.3	-9	24 F	0458	0.0	0
	2006	0.8	24		1936	0.8	24
10 F	0632	-0.1	-3	25 Sa	0534	0.1	3
	2113	0.7	21		2056	0.8	24
11 Sa	0709	0.0	0	26 Su	0604	0.2	6
	2218	0.6	18		2225	0.7	21
12 Su	0731	0.1	3	27 M	0621	0.3	9
	2327	0.5	15		1104	0.4	12
○					1629	0.3	9
13 M	0727	0.2	6	●			
	1207	0.3	9	28 Tu	0017	0.6	18
	1716	0.2	6		0601	0.5	15
14 Tu	0055	0.5	15		1018	0.6	18
	0627	0.3	9		1815	0.2	6
	1121	0.4	12	29 W	1018	0.7	21
	1909	0.2	6		1946	0.1	3
15 W	1123	0.5	15	30 Th	1045	0.9	27
	2043	0.1	3		2112	0.0	0
				31 F	1127	1.0	30
					2237	-0.1	-3

Time meridian 90° W. 0000 is midnight. 1200 is noon. Times are not adjusted for Daylight Saving Time.
Heights are referred to mean lower low water which is the chart datum of soundings.

Grand Isle (East Point), Louisiana, 2017

Times and Heights of High and Low Waters

April

Day	Time (h m)	Height (ft)	Height (cm)		Day	Time (h m)	Height (ft)	Height (cm)
1 Sa	1218	1.1	34		16 Su	1156	1.1	34
	2358	-0.1	-3			2331	0.1	3
2 Su	1316	1.1	34		17 M	1240	1.1	34
3 M ◖	0114	-0.1	-3		18 Tu	0028	0.1	3
	1420	1.1	34			1330	1.1	34
4 Tu	0222	-0.1	-3		19 W ○	0121	0.1	3
	1534	1.0	30			1426	1.0	30
5 W	0322	0.0	0		20 Th	0209	0.1	3
	1701	0.9	27			1535	0.9	27
6 Th	0413	0.1	3		21 F	0250	0.2	6
	1841	0.8	24			1715	0.9	27
7 F	0453	0.2	6		22 Sa	0323	0.3	9
	2028	0.7	21			1937	0.8	24
8 Sa	0518	0.4	12		23 Su	0344	0.5	15
	1220	0.5	15			1006	0.6	18
	1503	0.4	12			1537	0.5	15
	2220	0.7	21			2220	0.7	21
9 Su	0512	0.5	15		24 M	0332	0.6	18
	1023	0.6	18			0906	0.7	21
	1703	0.4	12			1659	0.3	9
10 M	0048	0.6	18		25 Tu	0847	0.9	27
	0353	0.5	15			1806	0.2	6
	0939	0.7	21					
	1812	0.3	9					
11 Tu ○	0934	0.8	24		26 W ●	0859	1.0	30
	1908	0.2	6			1910	0.0	0
12 W	0948	0.9	27		27 Th	0930	1.2	37
	1958	0.2	6			2015	-0.1	-3
13 Th	1011	1.0	30		28 F	1012	1.3	40
	2047	0.1	3			2121	-0.1	-3
14 F	1041	1.0	30		29 Sa	1059	1.3	40
	2139	0.1	3			2229	-0.2	-6
15 Sa	1116	1.1	34		30 Su	1150	1.3	40
	2234	0.1	3			2335	-0.1	-3

May

Day	Time (h m)	Height (ft)	Height (cm)		Day	Time (h m)	Height (ft)	Height (cm)
1 M	1242	1.3	40		16 Tu	1157	1.2	37
						2328	0.1	3
2 Tu ○	0038	0.0	0		17 W	1234	1.1	34
	1333	1.2	37					
3 W	0133	0.1	3		18 Th ○	0006	0.1	3
	1421	1.0	30			1308	1.0	30
4 Th	0217	0.2	6		19 F	0038	0.2	6
	1450	0.8	24			1321	0.9	27
5 F	0242	0.4	12		20 Sa	0059	0.3	9
	1136	0.7	21			1029	0.7	21
6 Sa	0232	0.5	15		21 Su	0054	0.5	15
	0942	0.7	21			0836	0.8	24
	1711	0.5	15			1629	0.5	15
7 Su	0846	0.8	24		22 M	0753	0.9	27
	1746	0.4	12			1658	0.3	9
8 M	0827	0.9	27		23 Tu	0746	1.0	30
	1821	0.3	9			1743	0.1	3
9 Tu	0832	1.0	30		24 W	0802	1.2	37
	1855	0.2	6			1833	-0.1	-3
10 W ○	0848	1.1	34		25 Th ●	0834	1.3	40
	1929	0.1	3			1927	-0.2	-6
11 Th	0911	1.2	37		26 F	0916	1.4	43
	2004	0.1	3			2024	-0.3	-9
12 F	0939	1.2	37		27 Sa	1002	1.4	43
	2041	0.0	0			2122	-0.3	-9
13 Sa	1010	1.2	37		28 Su	1049	1.4	43
	2121	0.0	0			2219	-0.2	-6
14 Su	1044	1.2	37		29 M	1135	1.3	40
	2203	0.0	0			2312	-0.1	-3
15 M	1120	1.2	37		30 Tu	1215	1.2	37
	2246	0.0	0			2357	0.0	0
					31 W	1240	1.0	30

June

Day	Time (h m)	Height (ft)	Height (cm)		Day	Time (h m)	Height (ft)	Height (cm)
1 Th ◖	0027	0.2	6		16 F ◖	1151	0.9	27
	1210	0.8	24			2305	0.3	9
2 F	0030	0.3	9		17 Sa ○	0918	0.7	21
	0953	0.7	21			2235	0.4	12
	2321	0.5	15					
3 Sa	0821	0.8	24		18 Su	0723	0.8	24
	1755	0.4	12			1728	0.4	12
4 Su	0739	0.9	27		19 M	0646	0.9	27
	1744	0.3	9			1640	0.2	6
5 M	0730	1.0	30		20 Tu	0645	1.0	30
	1803	0.1	3			1709	0.0	0
6 Tu	0739	1.1	34		21 W	0707	1.2	37
	1829	0.0	0			1752	-0.2	-6
7 W	0758	1.1	34		22 Th	0743	1.3	40
	1858	0.0	0			1841	-0.3	-9
8 Th	0823	1.2	37		23 F ●	0826	1.4	43
	1928	-0.1	-3			1933	-0.4	-12
9 F ○	0851	1.2	37		24 Sa	0914	1.4	43
	2000	-0.1	-3			2026	-0.4	-12
10 Sa	0922	1.2	37		25 Su	1002	1.4	43
	2033	-0.1	-3			2116	-0.3	-9
11 Su	0954	1.2	37		26 M	1047	1.3	40
	2106	-0.1	-3			2203	-0.2	-6
12 M	1027	1.2	37		27 Tu	1127	1.2	37
	2139	-0.1	-3			2240	0.0	0
13 Tu	1059	1.2	37		28 W	1153	1.0	30
	2210	0.0	0			2302	0.1	3
14 W	1130	1.1	34		29 Th	1136	0.8	24
	2237	0.0	0			2252	0.3	9
15 Th	1154	1.0	30		30 F ◖	0858	0.7	21
	2258	0.1	3			2130	0.4	12

Time meridian 90° W. 0000 is midnight. 1200 is noon. Times are not adjusted for Daylight Saving Time.
Heights are referred to mean lower low water which is the chart datum of soundings.

Grand Isle (East Point), Louisiana, 2017
Times and Heights of High and Low Waters

July

Day	Time (h m)	Height (ft)	Height (cm)	Day	Time (h m)	Height (ft)	Height (cm)
1 Sa	0706	0.7	21	16 Su	0545	0.8	24
	1751	0.4	12		1706	0.4	12
2 Su	0627	0.8	24	17 M	0519	0.9	27
	1709	0.2	6		1551	0.2	6
3 M	0624	1.0	30	18 Tu	0530	1.1	34
	1722	0.1	3		1620	0.0	0
4 Tu	0639	1.1	34	19 W	0601	1.2	37
	1746	0.0	0		1702	-0.1	-3
5 W	0703	1.1	34	20 Th	0645	1.3	40
	1815	-0.1	-3		1751	-0.2	-6
6 Th	0734	1.2	37	21 F	0734	1.4	43
	1847	-0.1	-3		1841	-0.3	-9
7 F	0807	1.2	37	22 Sa	0827	1.4	43
	1918	-0.1	-3		1931	-0.3	-9
8 Sa ○	0840	1.2	37	23 Su ●	0918	1.4	43
	1950	-0.1	-3		2019	-0.2	-6
9 Su	0914	1.2	37	24 M	1007	1.3	40
	2019	-0.1	-3		2102	-0.1	-3
10 M	0947	1.2	37	25 Tu	1052	1.2	37
	2047	-0.1	-3		2136	0.1	3
11 Tu	1020	1.2	37	26 W	1129	1.0	30
	2112	0.0	0		2153	0.3	9
12 W	1050	1.1	34	27 Th	1147	0.9	27
	2132	0.1	3		2137	0.4	12
13 Th	1117	1.0	30	28 F	0831	0.7	21
	2144	0.2	6		2013	0.5	15
14 F	1128	0.8	24	29 Sa	0505	0.8	24
	2140	0.3	9		1643	0.5	15
15 Sa	0810	0.7	21	30 Su ◖	0435	0.9	27
	2055	0.4	12		1553	0.3	9
				31 M	0445	1.0	30
					1610	0.2	6

August

Day	Time (h m)	Height (ft)	Height (cm)	Day	Time (h m)	Height (ft)	Height (cm)
1 Tu	0512	1.1	34	16 W	0432	1.3	40
	1640	0.2	6		1555	0.1	3
2 W	0548	1.2	37	17 Th	0529	1.4	43
	1714	0.1	3		1648	0.0	0
3 Th	0629	1.2	37	18 F	0630	1.5	46
	1749	0.1	3		1740	0.0	0
4 F	0711	1.3	40	19 Sa	0732	1.5	46
	1824	0.0	0		1831	0.0	0
5 Sa	0752	1.3	40	20 Su	0832	1.4	43
	1857	0.0	0		1918	0.1	3
6 Su	0832	1.3	40	21 M ●	0929	1.4	43
	1927	0.1	3		1959	0.2	6
7 M ○	0911	1.3	40	22 Tu	1024	1.2	37
	1954	0.1	3		2030	0.4	12
8 Tu	0948	1.2	37	23 W	1117	1.1	34
	2016	0.2	6		2041	0.6	18
9 W	1026	1.1	34	24 Th	1213	0.9	27
	2033	0.3	9		2010	0.7	21
10 Th	1106	1.0	30	25 F	0216	0.8	24
	2038	0.4	12		0743	0.7	21
					1340	0.8	24
					1811	0.7	21
11 F	1148	0.9	27	26 Sa	0137	0.9	27
	2020	0.5	15		1125	0.6	18
12 Sa	0357	0.8	24	27 Su	0147	1.0	30
	0917	0.6	18		1310	0.5	15
	1231	0.7	21				
	1904	0.6	18				
13 Su	0306	0.9	27	28 M	0217	1.1	34
	1321	0.5	15		1407	0.5	15
14 M ◐	0312	1.0	30	29 Tu ◗	0300	1.2	37
	1410	0.4	12		1456	0.4	12
15 Tu	0344	1.2	37	30 W	0350	1.3	40
	1502	0.2	6		1542	0.3	9
				31 Th	0446	1.3	40
					1625	0.3	9

September

Day	Time (h m)	Height (ft)	Height (cm)	Day	Time (h m)	Height (ft)	Height (cm)
1 F	0544	1.3	40	16 Sa	0617	1.5	46
	1705	0.3	9		1715	0.3	9
2 Sa	0641	1.3	40	17 Su	0733	1.4	43
	1742	0.3	9		1801	0.4	12
3 Su	0734	1.3	40	18 M	0848	1.3	40
	1816	0.3	9		1839	0.6	18
4 M	0825	1.3	40	19 Tu ●	1002	1.2	37
	1844	0.4	12		1901	0.7	21
5 Tu	0916	1.3	40	20 W	1125	1.1	34
	1907	0.5	15		1849	0.8	24
					2325	0.9	27
6 W ○	1012	1.2	37	21 Th	0544	0.8	24
	1920	0.6	18		1326	1.0	30
					1721	0.9	27
					2254	1.0	30
7 Th	1118	1.1	34	22 F	0727	0.7	21
	1913	0.7	21		2302	1.2	37
8 F	0041	0.9	27	23 Sa	0854	0.6	18
	0548	0.8	24		2327	1.2	37
	1253	1.0	30				
	1823	0.9	27				
9 Sa	0011	1.0	30	24 Su	1014	0.6	18
	0812	0.7	21				
10 Su	0020	1.1	34	25 M	0001	1.3	40
	1015	0.6	18		1127	0.5	15
11 M	0052	1.3	40	26 Tu	0042	1.4	43
	1155	0.4	12		1234	0.5	15
12 Tu	0139	1.4	43	27 W ◗	0129	1.4	43
	1315	0.3	9		1335	0.5	15
13 W ○	0237	1.5	46	28 Th	0224	1.4	43
	1424	0.3	9		1429	0.5	15
14 Th	0345	1.5	46	29 F	0326	1.4	43
	1526	0.2	6		1516	0.5	15
15 F	0459	1.5	46	30 Sa	0436	1.4	43
	1623	0.2	6		1558	0.5	15

Time meridian 90° W. 0000 is midnight. 1200 is noon. Times are not adjusted for Daylight Saving Time.
Heights are referred to mean lower low water which is the chart datum of soundings.

Grand Isle (East Point), Louisiana, 2017

Times and Heights of High and Low Waters

October

Day	Time	Height (ft)	Height (cm)	Day	Time	Height (ft)	Height (cm)
1 Su	0550	1.3	40	16 M	0752	1.1	34
	1633	0.5	15		1644	0.7	21
					2344	0.9	27
2 M	0708	1.3	40	17 Tu	0321	0.8	24
	1703	0.6	18		1001	1.0	30
					1634	0.8	24
					2202	1.0	30
3 Tu	0829	1.2	37	18 W	0509	0.7	21
	1722	0.7	21		2123	1.1	34
4 W	1001	1.1	34	19 Th ●	0616	0.6	18
	1724	0.8	24		2121	1.2	37
	2233	0.9	27				
5 Th O	0439	0.8	24	20 F	0712	0.5	15
	1202	1.0	30		2138	1.3	40
	1645	0.9	27				
	2201	1.1	34				
6 F	0612	0.7	21	21 Sa	0802	0.4	12
	2205	1.2	37		2203	1.3	40
7 Sa	0734	0.5	15	22 Su	0851	0.4	12
	2230	1.3	40		2233	1.4	43
8 Su	0853	0.4	12	23 M	0941	0.4	12
	2308	1.5	46		2307	1.4	43
9 M	1011	0.3	9	24 Tu	1034	0.3	9
	2355	1.5	46		2345	1.4	43
10 Tu	1128	0.3	9	25 W	1128	0.3	9
11 W	0049	1.6	49	26 Th	0027	1.4	43
	1242	0.2	6		1220	0.3	9
12 Th ☽	0150	1.5	46	27 F ◑	0112	1.3	40
	1349	0.3	9		1309	0.4	12
13 F	0258	1.5	46	28 Sa	0200	1.3	40
	1449	0.3	9		1350	0.4	12
14 Sa	0418	1.4	43	29 Su	0256	1.2	37
	1540	0.4	12		1425	0.5	15
15 Su	0556	1.2	37	30 M	0415	1.0	30
	1620	0.6	18		1449	0.6	18
				31 Tu	0647	0.9	27
					1457	0.7	21
					2143	0.9	27

November

Day	Time	Height (ft)	Height (cm)	Day	Time	Height (ft)	Height (cm)
1 W	0354	0.7	21	16 Th	0615	0.3	9
	0956	0.8	24		2023	1.1	34
	1426	0.7	21				
	2051	1.0	30				
2 Th	0500	0.5	15	17 F	0651	0.2	6
	2038	1.1	34		2041	1.1	34
3 F O	0559	0.4	12	18 Sa ●	0727	0.1	3
	2050	1.2	37		2106	1.2	37
4 Sa	0657	0.2	6	19 Su	0804	0.0	0
	2119	1.4	43		2135	1.2	37
5 Su	0758	0.1	3	20 M	0841	0.0	0
	2158	1.5	46		2206	1.2	37
6 M	0901	0.0	0	21 Tu	0921	0.0	0
	2243	1.5	46		2239	1.2	37
7 Tu	1006	0.0	0	22 W	1002	0.0	0
	2333	1.5	46		2314	1.2	37
8 W	1112	0.0	0	23 Th	1042	0.0	0
					2348	1.1	34
9 Th	0023	1.4	43	24 F	1120	0.0	0
	1214	0.0	0				
10 F O	0114	1.3	40	25 Sa	0021	1.0	30
	1309	0.1	3		1153	0.1	3
11 Sa	0202	1.1	34	26 Su ◑	0048	0.9	27
	1354	0.3	9		1219	0.2	6
12 Su	0233	1.0	30	27 M	0052	0.8	24
	1421	0.4	12		1232	0.3	9
	2333	0.8	24		2219	0.7	21
13 M	1413	0.6	18	28 Tu	1217	0.4	12
	2129	0.8	24		2022	0.7	21
14 Tu	0505	0.6	18	29 W	0452	0.4	12
	2033	0.9	27		1940	0.8	24
15 W	0538	0.4	12	30 Th	0454	0.2	6
	2016	1.0	30		1934	0.9	27

December

Day	Time	Height (ft)	Height (cm)	Day	Time	Height (ft)	Height (cm)
1 F	0531	0.0	0	16 Sa	0651	-0.3	-9
	1951	1.0	30		2018	0.9	27
2 Sa	0618	-0.2	-6	17 Su	0724	-0.3	-9
	2022	1.2	37		2049	0.9	27
3 Su O	0710	-0.3	-9	18 M ●	0757	-0.4	-12
	2103	1.3	40		2121	0.9	27
4 M	0805	-0.4	-12	19 Tu	0831	-0.4	-12
	2149	1.3	40		2153	0.9	27
5 Tu	0903	-0.4	-12	20 W	0903	-0.4	-12
	2238	1.3	40		2225	0.9	27
6 W	1000	-0.4	-12	21 Th	0934	-0.3	-9
	2325	1.2	37		2256	0.8	24
7 Th	1054	-0.3	-9	22 F	1002	-0.3	-9
					2325	0.8	24
8 F	0009	1.0	30	23 Sa	1026	-0.2	-6
	1142	-0.2	-6		2348	0.7	21
9 Sa	0043	0.9	27	24 Su	1042	-0.1	-3
	1217	0.0	0		2353	0.5	15
10 Su O	0035	0.7	21	25 M	1043	0.0	0
	1226	0.1	3		2132	0.4	12
	2157	0.5	15				
11 M	1129	0.3	9	26 Tu ◑	1011	0.1	3
	2006	0.5	15		1903	0.4	12
12 Tu	0530	0.2	6	27 W	0616	0.1	3
	1922	0.6	18		1824	0.5	15
13 W	0525	0.0	0	28 Th	0428	-0.1	-3
	1915	0.7	21		1825	0.6	18
14 Th	0550	-0.1	-3	29 F	0451	-0.3	-9
	1928	0.8	24		1849	0.8	24
15 F	0620	-0.2	-6	30 Sa	0533	-0.5	-15
	1951	0.9	27		1926	0.9	27
				31 Su	0621	-0.6	-18
					2012	1.0	30

Time meridian 90° W. 0000 is midnight. 1200 is noon. Times are not adjusted for Daylight Saving Time.
Heights are referred to mean lower low water which is the chart datum of soundings.

Galveston (Galveston Channel), Texas, 2017

Times and Heights of High and Low Waters

January

Day	Time (h m)	Height (ft)	Height (cm)	Day	Time (h m)	Height (ft)	Height (cm)
1 Su	0243	0.9	27	**16** M	0126	0.5	15
	1132	-0.5	-15		0540	0.7	21
	1958	1.0	30		1249	-0.3	-9
					2026	0.8	24
2 M	0024	0.7	21	**17** Tu	0246	0.4	12
	0318	0.8	24		0709	0.5	15
	1211	-0.4	-12		1334	0.0	0
	2033	0.9	27		2057	0.8	24
3 Tu	0136	0.6	18	**18** W	0358	0.2	6
	0416	0.7	21		0858	0.5	15
	1254	-0.2	-6		1422	0.2	6
	2104	0.9	27		2125	0.7	21
4 W	0259	0.5	15	**19** Th	0454	0.1	3
	0656	0.6	18		1101	0.5	15
	1343	0.0	0		1524	0.4	12
	2130	0.8	24	☽	2150	0.7	21
5 Th	0404	0.3	9	**20** F	0537	-0.1	-3
	0944	0.5	15		1301	0.6	18
	1443	0.2	6		1728	0.5	15
☾	2154	0.8	24		2213	0.7	21
6 F	0455	0.0	0	**21** Sa	0615	-0.3	-9
	1147	0.6	18		1422	0.7	21
	1602	0.4	12		1915	0.6	18
	2219	0.8	24		2236	0.7	21
7 Sa	0543	-0.3	-9	**22** Su	0649	-0.4	-12
	1319	0.8	24		1507	0.8	24
	1742	0.6	18		2018	0.6	18
	2247	0.9	27		2302	0.7	21
8 Su	0631	-0.5	-15	**23** M	0721	-0.5	-15
	1428	1.0	30		1540	0.9	27
	1915	0.8	24		2052	0.7	21
	2322	0.9	27		2333	0.8	24
9 M	0719	-0.8	-24	**24** Tu	0753	-0.6	-18
	1525	1.1	34		1608	0.9	27
	2022	0.8	24		2101	0.7	21
10 Tu	0004	0.9	27	**25** W	0010	0.8	24
	0807	-0.9	-27		0825	-0.6	-18
	1615	1.2	37		1636	0.9	27
	2112	0.9	27		2103	0.7	21
11 W	0052	1.0	30	**26** Th	0048	0.8	24
	0856	-1.0	-30		0857	-0.7	-21
	1702	1.2	37		1705	0.9	27
	2154	0.9	27		2117	0.7	21
12 Th	0143	1.0	30	**27** F	0127	0.9	27
	0944	-1.0	-30		0931	-0.7	-21
	1748	1.1	34		1735	0.9	27
○	2236	0.8	24	●	2144	0.7	21
13 F	0236	1.0	30	**28** Sa	0209	0.9	27
	1032	-0.9	-27		1005	-0.6	-18
	1831	1.1	34		1804	0.9	27
	2322	0.7	21		2219	0.7	21
14 Sa	0331	0.9	27	**29** Su	0255	0.8	24
	1119	-0.7	-21		1041	-0.6	-18
	1912	1.0	30		1833	0.9	27
					2302	0.6	18
15 Su	0017	0.7	21	**30** M	0350	0.8	24
	0430	0.8	24		1118	-0.5	-15
	1205	-0.5	-15		1901	0.8	24
	1951	0.9	27		2352	0.5	15
				31 Tu	0459	0.7	21
					1158	-0.3	-9
					1926	0.8	24

February

Day	Time (h m)	Height (ft)	Height (cm)	Day	Time (h m)	Height (ft)	Height (cm)
1 W	0049	0.3	9	**16** Th	0205	0.1	3
	0629	0.6	18		0850	0.7	21
	1241	-0.1	-3		1338	0.4	12
	1949	0.8	24		1955	0.7	21
2 Th	0152	0.1	3	**17** F	0303	0.0	0
	0819	0.6	18		1032	0.7	21
	1330	0.2	6		1423	0.6	18
	2012	0.7	21		2013	0.7	21
3 F	0259	-0.1	-3	**18** Sa	0402	-0.1	-3
	1016	0.6	18		1220	0.8	24
	1430	0.4	12		1741	0.7	21
◑	2035	0.8	24	☾	2028	0.8	24
4 Sa	0406	-0.3	-9	**19** Su	0458	-0.1	-3
	1205	0.8	24		1344	0.9	27
	1559	0.7	21				
	2105	0.8	24				
5 Su	0510	-0.5	-15	**20** M	0549	-0.2	-6
	1330	0.9	27		1431	0.9	27
	1812	0.7	21				
	2147	0.8	24				
6 M	0610	-0.6	-18	**21** Tu	0635	-0.3	-9
	1433	1.0	30		1504	1.0	30
	1941	0.8	24		2051	0.8	24
	2246	0.9	27		2251	0.9	27
7 Tu	0707	-0.8	-24	**22** W	0718	-0.3	-9
	1522	1.1	34		1531	1.0	30
	2026	0.8	24		2035	0.8	24
	2352	0.9	27		2353	0.9	27
8 W	0801	-0.8	-24	**23** Th	0757	-0.4	-12
	1604	1.1	34		1557	1.0	30
	2101	0.8	24		2031	0.8	24
9 Th	0057	1.0	30	**24** F	0049	1.0	30
	0851	-0.8	-24		0835	-0.4	-12
	1642	1.0	30		1622	1.0	30
	2134	0.7	21		2049	0.8	24
10 F	0158	1.0	30	**25** Sa	0143	1.0	30
	0939	-0.7	-21		0912	-0.4	-12
	1717	1.0	30		1646	1.0	30
○	2209	0.7	21		2118	0.7	21
11 Sa	0257	1.0	30	**26** Su	0239	1.0	30
	1024	-0.6	-18		0950	-0.3	-9
	1749	0.9	27		1709	1.0	30
	2249	0.6	18	●	2155	0.6	18
12 Su	0355	0.9	27	**27** M	0338	1.0	30
	1106	-0.4	-12		1029	-0.2	-6
	1818	0.9	27		1731	0.9	27
	2332	0.5	15		2237	0.4	12
13 M	0457	0.8	24	**28** Tu	0443	1.0	30
	1146	-0.2	-6		1110	0.0	0
	1846	0.8	24		1752	0.9	27
					2324	0.3	9
14 Tu	0019	0.3	9				
	0604	0.8	24				
	1224	0.0	0				
	1911	0.8	24				
15 W	0110	0.2	6				
	0720	0.7	21				
	1300	0.2	6				
	1934	0.8	24				

March

Day	Time (h m)	Height (ft)	Height (cm)	Day	Time (h m)	Height (ft)	Height (cm)
1 W	0556	1.0	30	**16** Th	0007	0.2	6
	1154	0.2	6		0722	1.1	34
	1812	0.9	27		1239	0.7	21
					1802	1.0	30
2 Th	0016	0.1	3	**17** F	0047	0.2	6
	0717	1.0	30		0832	1.1	34
	1241	0.5	15		1318	0.9	27
	1832	0.9	27		1808	1.0	30
3 F	0113	-0.1	-3	**18** Sa	0133	0.2	6
	0849	1.0	30		0950	1.1	34
	1336	0.7	21		1411	0.9	27
	1852	0.9	27		1727	1.0	30
4 Sa	0217	-0.2	-6	**19** Su	0227	0.1	3
	1027	1.1	34		1114	1.1	34
	1451	0.9	27				
	1913	1.0	30				
5 Su	0327	-0.3	-9	**20** M	0327	0.1	3
	1202	1.1	34		1231	1.2	37
	1741	0.9	27				
◑	1943	1.0	30	☾			
6 M	0441	-0.3	-9	**21** Tu	0433	0.1	3
	1319	1.2	37		1327	1.2	37
7 Tu	0553	-0.3	-9	**22** W	0536	0.1	3
	1416	1.2	37		1405	1.2	37
	1959	0.9	27				
	2249	1.0	30				
8 W	0659	-0.3	-9	**23** Th	0633	0.1	3
	1458	1.2	37		1434	1.2	37
	2024	0.9	27		2008	1.0	30
					2351	1.1	34
9 Th	0011	1.1	34	**24** F	0722	0.1	3
	0757	-0.3	-9		1458	1.2	37
	1533	1.2	37		2004	0.9	27
	2051	0.9	27				
10 F	0122	1.1	34	**25** Sa	0101	1.2	37
	0848	-0.2	-6		0808	0.1	3
	1602	1.1	34		1520	1.2	37
	2119	0.7	21		2024	0.8	24
11 Sa	0225	1.2	37	**26** Su	0205	1.3	40
	0934	-0.1	-3		0852	0.2	6
	1627	1.1	34		1540	1.2	37
	2149	0.6	18		2055	0.7	21
12 Su	0324	1.2	37	**27** M	0308	1.3	40
	1016	0.1	3		0936	0.3	9
	1650	1.1	34		1559	1.2	37
○	2221	0.5	15	●	2132	0.5	15
13 M	0421	1.2	37	**28** Tu	0411	1.4	43
	1054	0.2	6		1021	0.5	15
	1711	1.0	30		1619	1.2	37
	2254	0.4	12		2214	0.3	9
14 Tu	0519	1.1	34	**29** W	0516	1.5	46
	1129	0.4	12		1108	0.7	21
	1730	1.0	30		1638	1.2	37
	2329	0.3	9		2300	0.1	3
15 W	0618	1.1	34	**30** Th	0625	1.5	46
	1203	0.6	18		1158	0.9	27
	1748	1.0	30		1657	1.2	37
					2350	0.0	0
				31 F	0738	1.5	46
					1255	1.0	30
					1715	1.2	37

Time meridian 90° W. 0000 is midnight. 1200 is noon. Times are not adjusted for Daylight Saving Time.
Heights are referred to mean lower low water which is the chart datum of soundings.
On days when the tide is diurnal, high water has an approximate stand of about 7 hours. Predictions are for beginning of stand.

Galveston (Galveston Channel), Texas, 2017

Times and Heights of High and Low Waters

April

Day	Time	ft	cm	Day	Time	ft	cm
1 Sa	0045	-0.1	-3	16 Su	0037	0.2	6
	0857	1.5	46		0912	1.5	46
	1409	1.1	34				
	1730	1.2	37				
2 Su	0147	-0.1	-3	17 M	0122	0.2	6
	1020	1.5	46		1019	1.4	43
3 M ◐	0258	-0.1	-3	18 Tu	0215	0.3	9
	1141	1.5	46		1124	1.4	43
4 Tu	0417	0.0	0	19 W ◑	0317	0.3	9
	1247	1.5	46		1217	1.4	43
5 W	0537	0.1	3	20 Th	0426	0.4	12
	1336	1.4	43		1256	1.4	43
	1948	1.1	34				
	2318	1.2	37				
6 Th	0650	0.2	6	21 F	0535	0.4	12
	1413	1.4	43		1324	1.4	43
	2012	1.0	30		1932	1.0	30
7 F	0044	1.2	37	22 Sa	0002	1.2	37
	0752	0.3	9		0638	0.5	15
	1441	1.3	40		1347	1.4	43
	2038	0.8	24		1934	0.9	27
8 Sa	0155	1.3	40	23 Su	0120	1.3	40
	0844	0.4	12		0736	0.6	18
	1503	1.3	40		1407	1.3	40
	2103	0.7	21		1958	0.6	18
9 Su	0257	1.4	43	24 M	0228	1.4	43
	0929	0.5	15		0830	0.7	21
	1523	1.2	37		1425	1.3	40
	2129	0.5	15		2031	0.4	12
10 M	0352	1.4	43	25 Tu	0331	1.6	49
	1009	0.7	21		0923	0.8	24
	1539	1.2	37		1444	1.3	40
	2154	0.4	12		2110	0.2	6
11 Tu ○	0444	1.4	43	26 W ●	0433	1.7	52
	1045	0.8	24		1016	1.0	30
	1555	1.2	37		1503	1.3	40
	2221	0.3	9		2153	0.0	0
12 W	0534	1.5	46	27 Th	0535	1.8	55
	1118	1.0	30		1110	1.1	34
	1608	1.2	37		1524	1.4	43
	2250	0.2	6		2240	-0.2	-6
13 Th	0624	1.5	46	28 F	0638	1.8	55
	1152	1.1	34		1208	1.3	40
	1618	1.2	37		1546	1.4	43
	2321	0.2	6		2330	-0.2	-6
14 F	0716	1.5	46	29 Sa	0743	1.8	55
	1230	1.1	34		1318	1.3	40
	1619	1.2	37		1607	1.4	43
	2357	0.2	6				
15 Sa	0811	1.5	46	30 Su	0025	-0.2	-6
	1317	1.1	34		0851	1.8	55
	1548	1.2	37				

May

Day	Time	ft	cm	Day	Time	ft	cm
1 M	0125	-0.1	-3	16 Tu	0039	0.1	3
	1001	1.7	52		0936	1.5	46
2 Tu ○	0233	0.1	3	17 W	0125	0.2	6
	1106	1.6	49		1027	1.5	46
3 W	0352	0.2	6	18 Th ◐	0218	0.3	9
	1200	1.5	46		1110	1.4	43
	1858	1.0	30				
	2202	1.1	34				
4 Th	0517	0.4	12	19 F	0320	0.4	12
	1242	1.5	46		1143	1.4	43
	1924	0.9	27		1911	0.9	27
	2352	1.2	37		2233	1.0	30
5 F	0635	0.5	15	20 Sa	0432	0.6	18
	1312	1.4	43		1208	1.3	40
	1951	0.7	21		1844	0.7	21
6 Sa	0120	1.3	40	21 Su	0021	1.1	34
	0742	0.7	21		0549	0.7	21
	1336	1.3	40		1229	1.3	40
	2018	0.6	18		1900	0.5	15
7 Su	0230	1.3	40	22 M	0141	1.3	40
	0838	0.8	24		0703	0.8	24
	1354	1.3	40		1248	1.3	40
	2042	0.4	12		1931	0.2	6
8 M	0327	1.4	43	23 Tu	0247	1.5	46
	0926	1.0	30		0811	1.0	30
	1410	1.3	40		1308	1.3	40
	2104	0.3	9		2008	-0.1	-3
9 Tu	0416	1.5	46	24 W	0347	1.6	49
	1007	1.1	34		0913	1.1	34
	1423	1.3	40		1330	1.3	40
	2126	0.2	6		2050	-0.3	-9
10 W ○	0500	1.5	46	25 Th ●	0445	1.7	52
	1043	1.2	37		1011	1.2	37
	1434	1.3	40		1355	1.4	43
	2151	0.1	3		2136	-0.4	-12
11 Th	0541	1.6	49	26 F	0541	1.8	55
	1116	1.2	37		1108	1.3	40
	1442	1.3	40		1425	1.4	43
	2218	0.0	0		2224	-0.5	-15
12 F	0622	1.6	49	27 Sa	0638	1.8	55
	1148	1.2	37		1209	1.3	40
	1443	1.3	40		1458	1.4	43
	2248	0.0	0		2315	-0.5	-15
13 Sa	0704	1.6	49	28 Su	0736	1.8	55
	2321	0.0	0		1324	1.3	40
					1532	1.4	43
14 Su	0751	1.6	49	29 M	0009	-0.4	-12
	2358	0.1	3		0835	1.7	52
15 M	0842	1.5	46	30 Tu	0107	-0.2	-6
					0931	1.6	49
				31 W	0210	0.1	3
					1022	1.5	46
					1743	0.9	27
					2017	1.0	30

June

Day	Time	ft	cm	Day	Time	ft	cm
1 Th	0322	0.3	9	16 F	0135	0.2	6
	1105	1.4	43		1004	1.3	40
	1817	0.8	24				
◑	2231	1.0	30				
2 F	0446	0.5	15	17 Sa	0230	0.4	12
	1139	1.3	40		1029	1.2	37
	1851	0.5	15		1735	0.6	18
				◑	2301	0.8	24
3 Sa	0025	1.0	30	18 Su	0338	0.6	18
	0612	0.7	21		1051	1.2	37
	1205	1.2	37		1753	0.3	9
	1922	0.4	12				
4 Su	0154	1.1	34	19 M	0043	1.0	30
	0728	0.9	27		0504	0.8	24
	1226	1.2	37		1110	1.2	37
	1949	0.2	6		1826	0.0	0
5 M	0300	1.3	40	20 Tu	0159	1.2	37
	0833	1.0	30		0635	1.0	30
	1242	1.2	37		1131	1.2	37
	2014	0.0	0		1905	-0.2	-6
6 Tu	0351	1.3	40	21 W	0301	1.4	43
	0927	1.1	34		0756	1.1	34
	1254	1.2	37		1157	1.2	37
	2036	-0.1	-3		1949	-0.5	-15
7 W	0431	1.4	43	22 Th	0356	1.5	46
	1012	1.1	34		0902	1.2	37
	1305	1.2	37		1230	1.3	40
	2100	-0.1	-3		2035	-0.7	-21
8 Th	0505	1.4	43	23 F ●	0448	1.6	49
	1047	1.1	34		0958	1.2	37
	1315	1.2	37		1311	1.3	40
	2125	-0.2	-6		2123	-0.7	-21
9 F	0538	1.5	46	24 Sa	0538	1.6	49
	1111	1.1	34		1048	1.2	37
	1323	1.2	37		1358	1.3	40
○	2153	-0.2	-6		2213	-0.7	-21
10 Sa	0612	1.5	46	25 Su	0628	1.6	49
	2223	-0.2	-6		1142	1.2	37
					1450	1.3	40
					2304	-0.6	-18
11 Su	0649	1.5	46	26 M	0717	1.5	46
	2256	-0.2	-6		1245	1.1	34
					1549	1.2	37
					2355	-0.4	-12
12 M	0729	1.4	43	27 Tu	0805	1.4	43
	2331	-0.1	-3		1406	1.0	30
					1702	1.1	34
13 Tu	0812	1.4	43	28 W	0048	-0.2	-6
					0849	1.3	40
					1531	0.8	24
					1841	0.9	27
14 W	0008	-0.1	-3	29 Th	0144	0.1	3
	0854	1.4	43		0928	1.2	37
					1636	0.6	18
					2042	0.8	24
15 Th	0049	0.0	0	30 F	0245	0.4	12
	0932	1.3	40		1002	1.2	37
					1726	0.4	12
				◑	2250	0.8	24

Time meridian 90° W. 0000 is midnight. 1200 is noon. Times are not adjusted for Daylight Saving Time.
Heights are referred to mean lower low water which is the chart datum of soundings.
On days when the tide is diurnal, high water has an approximate stand of about 7 hours. Predictions are for beginning of stand.

Galveston (Galveston Channel), Texas, 2017

Times and Heights of High and Low Waters

July

Day	Time	ft	cm	Day	Time	ft	cm
1 Sa	0403	0.6	18	16 Su ☽	0156	0.5	15
	1031	1.1	34		0912	1.1	34
	1807	0.2	6		1621	0.3	9
					2325	0.9	27
2 Su	0051	0.9	27	17 M	0302	0.8	24
	0545	0.8	24		0931	1.1	34
	1054	1.1	34		1707	0.0	0
	1842	0.1	3				
3 M	0221	1.1	34	18 Tu	0101	1.1	34
	0719	0.9	27		0435	1.0	30
	1113	1.1	34		0953	1.2	37
	1912	-0.1	-3		1755	-0.2	-6
4 Tu	0319	1.2	37	19 W	0210	1.3	40
	0834	1.0	30		0626	1.1	34
	1129	1.1	34		1024	1.2	37
	1940	-0.2	-6		1844	-0.5	-15
5 W	0359	1.3	40	20 Th	0305	1.4	43
	0932	1.0	30		0752	1.2	37
	1144	1.1	34		1108	1.3	40
	2007	-0.3	-9		1934	-0.6	-18
6 Th	0429	1.3	40	21 F	0354	1.5	46
	2034	-0.3	-9		0848	1.2	37
					1204	1.3	40
					2024	-0.7	-21
7 F	0456	1.3	40	22 Sa	0439	1.5	46
	2103	-0.3	-9		0932	1.2	37
					1305	1.3	40
					2114	-0.7	-21
8 Sa ○	0523	1.3	40	23 Su ●	0522	1.5	46
	1029	1.1	34		1015	1.2	37
	1254	1.2	37		1407	1.3	40
	2132	-0.4	-12		2204	-0.6	-18
9 Su	0553	1.3	40	24 M	0603	1.4	43
	1040	1.0	30		1103	1.1	34
	1323	1.1	34		1511	1.3	40
	2204	-0.3	-9		2253	-0.4	-12
10 M	0625	1.3	40	25 Tu	0642	1.4	43
	1109	1.0	30		1158	1.0	30
	1351	1.1	34		1619	1.2	37
	2236	-0.3	-9		2341	-0.2	-6
11 Tu	0658	1.3	40	26 W	0718	1.3	40
	1151	1.0	30		1302	0.8	24
	1419	1.1	34		1735	1.1	34
	2310	-0.2	-6				
12 W	0731	1.3	40	27 Th	0028	0.1	3
	1245	0.9	27		0752	1.2	37
	1456	1.0	30		1411	0.7	21
	2345	-0.1	-3		1906	0.9	27
13 Th	0802	1.2	37	28 F	0115	0.3	9
	1348	0.8	24		0823	1.2	37
	1606	0.9	27		1518	0.5	15
					2053	0.9	27
14 F	0024	0.1	3	29 Sa	0206	0.6	18
	0829	1.2	37		0850	1.1	34
	1446	0.7	21		1616	0.3	9
	1847	0.8	24		2254	0.9	27
15 Sa	0106	0.3	9	30 Su ☾	0314	0.8	24
	0852	1.1	34		0915	1.1	34
	1535	0.5	15		1706	0.2	6
	2122	0.8	24				
				31 M	0100	1.1	34
					0532	1.0	30
					0936	1.1	34
					1749	0.1	3

August

Day	Time	ft	cm	Day	Time	ft	cm
1 Tu	0226	1.2	37	16 W	0105	1.4	43
	0730	1.0	30		0453	1.2	37
	0955	1.1	34		0836	1.3	40
	1828	0.0	0		1729	-0.2	-6
2 W	0312	1.3	40	17 Th	0208	1.5	46
	1903	-0.1	-3		0708	1.3	40
					0938	1.4	43
					1828	-0.3	-9
3 Th	0342	1.3	40	18 F	0256	1.6	49
	1937	-0.2	-6		0800	1.3	40
					1059	1.4	43
					1924	-0.3	-9
4 F	0406	1.3	40	19 Sa	0337	1.6	49
	2009	-0.2	-6		0835	1.3	40
					1216	1.5	46
					2018	-0.3	-9
5 Sa	0428	1.4	43	20 Su	0414	1.6	49
	0933	1.1	34		0910	1.3	40
	1222	1.2	37		1326	1.5	46
	2041	-0.2	-6		2108	-0.2	-6
6 Su	0452	1.4	43	21 M ●	0448	1.5	46
	0933	1.1	34		0949	1.1	34
	1308	1.2	37		1433	1.5	46
	2113	-0.2	-6		2156	-0.1	-3
7 M ○	0517	1.4	43	22 Tu	0520	1.5	46
	0952	1.1	34		1032	1.0	30
	1354	1.2	37		1539	1.4	43
	2145	-0.1	-3		2242	0.1	3
8 Tu	0543	1.3	40	23 W	0549	1.4	43
	1023	1.1	34		1118	0.9	27
	1443	1.2	37		1646	1.4	43
	2218	-0.1	-3		2325	0.3	9
9 W	0609	1.3	40	24 Th	0616	1.4	43
	1102	1.0	30		1206	0.8	24
	1539	1.2	37		1759	1.3	40
	2253	0.1	3				
10 Th	0633	1.3	40	25 F	0007	0.6	18
	1146	0.9	27		0641	1.3	40
	1648	1.1	34		1258	0.6	18
	2329	0.2	6		1919	1.2	37
11 F	0655	1.3	40	26 Sa	0048	0.8	24
	1235	0.7	21		0704	1.3	40
	1815	1.0	30		1351	0.5	15
					2050	1.2	37
12 Sa	0008	0.4	12	27 Su	0132	1.0	30
	0715	1.2	37		0724	1.3	40
	1329	0.5	15		1447	0.4	12
	1958	1.0	30		2234	1.3	40
13 Su	0051	0.7	21	28 M	0235	1.2	37
	0733	1.2	37		0738	1.3	40
	1426	0.4	12		1543	0.4	12
	2150	1.1	34				
14 M	0142	0.9	27	29 Tu ☾	0027	1.4	43
	0749	1.3	40		1639	0.3	9
	1527	0.2	6				
	2338 ☾	1.2	37				
15 Tu	0253	1.1	34	30 W	0148	1.4	43
	0807	1.3	40		1731	0.3	9
	1628	0.0	0				
				31 Th	0229	1.5	46
					1819	0.2	6

September

Day	Time	ft	cm	Day	Time	ft	cm
1 F	0256	1.5	46	16 Sa	0228	1.8	55
	1902	0.2	6		0803	1.5	46
					1127	1.6	49
					1918	0.2	6
2 Sa	0319	1.5	46	17 Su	0302	1.7	52
	0902	1.3	40		0828	1.4	43
	1133	1.4	43		1248	1.6	49
	1941	0.2	6		2013	0.3	9
3 Su	0341	1.5	46	18 M	0331	1.7	52
	0850	1.3	40		0858	1.2	37
	1235	1.4	43		1359	1.6	49
	2017	0.2	6		2103	0.4	12
4 M	0402	1.5	46	19 Tu ●	0357	1.6	49
	0857	1.3	40		0932	1.1	34
	1331	1.4	43		1505	1.6	49
	2052	0.2	6		2148	0.6	18
5 Tu	0423	1.5	46	20 W	0421	1.6	49
	0919	1.2	37		1007	0.9	27
	1427	1.5	46		1607	1.6	49
	2127	0.3	9		2229	0.7	21
6 W ○	0444	1.5	46	21 Th	0443	1.6	49
	0950	1.1	34		1043	0.8	24
	1525	1.5	46		1710	1.6	49
	2202	0.4	12		2309	0.9	27
7 Th	0503	1.5	46	22 F	0503	1.5	46
	1027	0.9	27		1120	0.7	21
	1629	1.5	46		1813	1.6	49
	2240	0.6	18		2347	1.1	34
8 F	0522	1.5	46	23 Sa	0520	1.5	46
	1108	0.7	21		1158	0.6	18
	1739	1.5	46		1920	1.6	49
	2320	0.8	24				
9 Sa	0539	1.5	46	24 Su	0025	1.3	40
	1154	0.6	18		0532	1.5	46
	1857	1.5	46		1239	0.6	18
					2034	1.6	49
10 Su	0003	1.0	30	25 M	0109	1.4	43
	0554	1.5	46		0531	1.5	46
	1245	0.4	12		1325	0.5	15
	2025	1.5	46		2155	1.6	49
11 M	0052	1.2	37	26 Tu	1417	0.5	15
	0606	1.5	46		2322	1.6	49
	1343	0.3	9				
	2200	1.6	49				
12 Tu	0153	1.4	43	27 W ☽	1517	0.5	15
	0615	1.5	46				
	1448	0.2	6				
	2334	1.7	52				
13 W ○	0350	1.5	46	28 Th	0036	1.7	52
	0559	1.6	49		1621	0.5	15
	1558	0.2	6				
14 Th	0051	1.7	52	29 F	0122	1.7	52
	1710	0.1	3		1722	0.5	15
15 F	0147	1.8	55	30 Sa	0154	1.7	52
	1817	0.1	3		1816	0.5	15

Time meridian 90° W. 0000 is midnight. 1200 is noon. Times are not adjusted for Daylight Saving Time.
Heights are referred to mean lower low water which is the chart datum of soundings.
On days when the tide is diurnal, high water has an approximate stand of about 7 hours. Predictions are for beginning of stand.

Galveston (Galveston Channel), Texas, 2017
Times and Heights of High and Low Waters

October

Day	Time	ft	cm
1 Su	0218	1.7	52
	0831	1.4	43
	1138	1.5	46
	1904	0.6	18
2 M	0239	1.7	52
	0819	1.3	40
	1250	1.5	46
	1946	0.6	18
3 Tu	0258	1.7	52
	0828	1.2	37
	1353	1.6	49
	2027	0.7	21
4 W	0316	1.6	49
	0850	1.0	30
	1454	1.7	52
	2107	0.8	24
5 Th ○	0333	1.6	49
	0921	0.8	24
	1555	1.7	52
	2148	0.9	27
6 F	0349	1.6	49
	0958	0.6	18
	1658	1.8	55
	2231	1.1	34
7 Sa	0405	1.6	49
	1039	0.5	15
	1804	1.8	55
	2317	1.3	40
8 Su	0420	1.6	49
	1125	0.3	9
	1915	1.9	58
9 M	0007	1.5	46
	0433	1.7	52
	1216	0.2	6
	2032	1.9	58
10 Tu	0106	1.6	49
	0442	1.7	52
	1314	0.2	6
	2155	1.9	58
11 W	1420	0.2	6
	2315	1.9	58
12 Th ☽	1534	0.3	9
13 F	0020	1.9	58
	1653	0.4	12
14 Sa	0108	1.8	55
	0733	1.4	43
	1027	1.5	46
	1808	0.5	15
15 Su	0143	1.8	55
	0752	1.3	40
	1207	1.6	49
	1913	0.6	18
16 M	0212	1.7	52
	0818	1.1	34
	1327	1.6	49
	2009	0.7	21
17 Tu	0235	1.7	52
	0846	1.0	30
	1435	1.7	52
	2058	0.9	27
18 W	0256	1.6	49
	0915	0.8	24
	1536	1.7	52
	2141	1.0	30
19 Th ●	0314	1.6	49
	0943	0.6	18
	1632	1.7	52
	2220	1.2	37
20 F	0330	1.6	49
	1012	0.5	15
	1726	1.7	52
	2256	1.3	40
21 Sa	0344	1.6	49
	1042	0.4	12
	1818	1.8	55
	2330	1.4	43
22 Su	0353	1.6	49
	1114	0.4	12
	1912	1.7	52
23 M	0005	1.5	46
	0350	1.6	49
	1149	0.4	12
	2010	1.7	52
24 Tu	0048	1.5	46
	0310	1.6	49
	1228	0.4	12
	2114	1.7	52
25 W	1313	0.4	12
	2222	1.7	52
26 Th	1405	0.5	15
	2325	1.7	52
27 F ☾	1505	0.5	15
28 Sa	0012	1.7	52
	1610	0.6	18
29 Su	0045	1.7	52
	1716	0.7	21
30 M	0110	1.6	49
	0754	1.2	37
	1149	1.3	40
	1815	0.7	21
31 Tu	0130	1.6	49
	0743	1.0	30
	1307	1.4	43
	1909	0.8	24

November

Day	Time	ft	cm
1 W	0147	1.6	49
	0756	0.8	24
	1414	1.5	46
	2000	0.9	27
2 Th	0203	1.5	46
	0821	0.6	18
	1515	1.7	52
	2049	1.0	30
3 F ○	0219	1.5	46
	0855	0.3	9
	1614	1.8	55
	2137	1.2	37
4 Sa	0235	1.6	49
	0934	0.1	3
	1714	1.9	58
	2225	1.3	40
5 Su	0253	1.6	49
	1017	0.0	0
	1815	1.9	58
	2315	1.5	46
6 M	0313	1.6	49
	1105	-0.1	-3
	1919	1.9	58
7 Tu	0010	1.5	46
	0333	1.6	49
	1157	-0.1	-3
	2027	1.8	55
8 W	0125	1.5	46
	0347	1.6	49
	1255	-0.1	-3
	2137	1.8	55
9 Th	1359	0.1	3
	2242	1.7	52
10 F ○	1513	0.2	6
	2336	1.7	52
11 Sa	0644	1.2	37
	0858	1.3	40
	1634	0.4	12
12 Su	0017	1.6	49
	0703	1.0	30
	1109	1.2	37
	1754	0.6	18
13 M	0048	1.5	46
	0731	0.8	24
	1247	1.3	40
	1905	0.7	21
14 Tu	0113	1.5	46
	0801	0.6	18
	1406	1.4	43
	2005	0.9	27
15 W	0134	1.4	43
	0828	0.4	12
	1509	1.5	46
	2056	1.0	30
16 Th	0151	1.4	43
	0855	0.3	9
	1603	1.5	46
	2139	1.1	34
17 F	0206	1.4	43
	0920	0.2	6
	1650	1.6	49
	2215	1.2	37
18 Sa ●	0219	1.4	43
	0945	0.1	3
	1733	1.6	49
	2245	1.3	40
19 Su	0229	1.4	43
	1012	0.0	0
	1815	1.6	49
	2310	1.3	40
20 M	0234	1.4	43
	1041	0.0	0
	1858	1.5	46
	2336	1.3	40
21 Tu	0230	1.4	43
	1114	0.0	0
	1945	1.5	46
22 W	0012	1.3	40
	0214	1.4	43
	1150	0.0	0
	2036	1.5	46
23 Th	1230	0.1	3
	2130	1.4	43
24 F	1313	0.2	6
	2221	1.4	43
25 Sa	1403	0.3	9
	2302	1.4	43
26 Su ☽	1500	0.4	12
	2333	1.3	40
27 M	0741	0.8	24
	1003	0.9	27
	1606	0.5	15
	2356	1.3	40
28 Tu	0656	0.7	21
	1203	1.0	30
	1719	0.6	18
29 W	0015	1.3	40
	0658	0.5	15
	1324	1.1	34
	1830	0.8	24
30 Th	0031	1.2	37
	0721	0.2	6
	1430	1.3	40
	1935	0.9	27

December

Day	Time	ft	cm
1 F	0048	1.2	37
	0754	-0.1	-3
	1528	1.4	43
	2032	1.0	30
2 Sa	0108	1.3	40
	0832	-0.3	-9
	1623	1.6	49
	2124	1.1	34
3 Su ○	0133	1.3	40
	0915	-0.5	-15
	1718	1.6	49
	2213	1.2	37
4 M	0203	1.4	43
	1002	-0.6	-18
	1814	1.6	49
	2301	1.3	40
5 Tu	0238	1.4	43
	1052	-0.6	-18
	1911	1.6	49
	2355	1.2	37
6 W	0318	1.3	40
	1145	-0.6	-18
	2009	1.5	46
7 Th	0109	1.2	37
	0403	1.3	40
	1241	-0.4	-12
	2106	1.4	43
8 F	1342	-0.2	-6
	2157	1.3	40
9 Sa	0456	0.8	24
	0717	0.9	27
	1450	0.0	0
	2241	1.2	37
10 Su ○	0545	0.7	21
	0939	0.8	24
	1610	0.3	9
	2317	1.2	37
11 M	0625	0.4	12
	1143	0.9	27
	1737	0.5	15
	2346	1.1	34
12 Tu	0701	0.2	6
	1324	1.0	30
	1857	0.7	21
13 W	0010	1.1	34
	0734	0.0	0
	1439	1.1	34
	2005	0.8	24
14 Th	0031	1.0	30
	0804	-0.2	-6
	1536	1.1	34
	2100	0.9	27
15 F	0048	1.0	30
	0831	-0.3	-9
	1620	1.2	37
	2143	0.9	27
16 Sa	0104	1.0	30
	0856	-0.4	-12
	1656	1.2	37
	2212	1.0	30
17 Su	0120	1.1	34
	0922	-0.4	-12
	1730	1.2	37
	2224	1.0	30
18 M ●	0137	1.1	34
	0949	-0.4	-12
	1803	1.2	37
	2234	1.0	30
19 Tu	0155	1.1	34
	1019	-0.4	-12
	1838	1.2	37
	2256	0.9	27
20 W	0210	1.0	30
	1050	-0.4	-12
	1916	1.1	34
	2331	0.9	27
21 Th	0220	1.0	30
	1124	-0.4	-12
	1957	1.1	34
22 F	1159	-0.3	-9
	2039	1.1	34
23 Sa	1237	-0.2	-6
	2117	1.0	30
24 Su	1318	0.0	0
	2149	1.0	30
25 M	1407	0.1	3
	2215	0.9	27
26 Tu ☽	0533	0.4	12
	1024	0.5	15
	1507	0.3	9
	2236	0.9	27
27 W	0541	0.1	3
	1217	0.7	21
	1626	0.5	15
	2254	0.9	27
28 Th	0610	-0.1	-3
	1337	0.9	27
	1755	0.7	21
	2314	0.9	27
29 F	0647	-0.4	-12
	1439	1.0	30
	1914	0.8	24
	2339	0.9	27
30 Sa	0729	-0.7	-21
	1533	1.2	37
	2016	0.9	27
31 Su	0013	1.0	30
	0815	-0.9	-27
	1623	1.3	40
	2105	0.9	27

Time meridian 90° W. 0000 is midnight. 1200 is noon. Times are not adjusted for Daylight Saving Time.
Heights are referred to mean lower low water which is the chart datum of soundings.
On days when the tide is diurnal, high water has an approximate stand of about 7 hours. Predictions are for beginning of stand.

Port O'Connor, Texas, 2017

Times and Heights of High and Low Waters

January

Day	Time (h m)	Height (ft)	Height (cm)
1 Su	0021	0.4	12
	1337	-0.5	-15
2 M	0038	0.3	9
	1413	-0.4	-12
3 Tu	0048	0.2	6
	1446	-0.3	-9
4 W	0041	0.2	6
	1512	-0.2	-6
	2333	0.1	3
5 Th ☾	1435	-0.1	-3
	2226	0.1	3
6 F	0645	-0.2	-6
	2143	0.1	3
7 Sa	0715	-0.3	-9
	2118	0.2	6
8 Su	0757	-0.5	-15
	2116	0.3	9
9 M	0847	-0.6	-18
	2139	0.3	9
10 Tu	0940	-0.7	-21
	2226	0.4	12
11 W	1035	-0.7	-21
	2326	0.4	12
12 Th ○	1129	-0.8	-24
13 F	0031	0.3	9
	1220	-0.7	-21
14 Sa	0132	0.3	9
	1306	-0.7	-21
15 Su	0223	0.2	6
	1346	-0.6	-18
16 M	0013	0.1	3
	1417	-0.5	-15
	2351	0.0	0
17 Tu	1438	-0.4	-12
	2323	0.0	0
18 W	1440	-0.3	-9
	2217	0.0	0
19 Th ◑	0703	-0.3	-9
	2137	0.0	0
20 F	0657	-0.4	-12
	2113	0.0	0
21 Sa	0722	-0.4	-12
	2103	0.0	0
22 Su	0755	-0.5	-15
	2105	0.1	3
23 M	0834	-0.6	-18
	2117	0.1	3
24 Tu	0917	-0.6	-18
	2141	0.1	3
25 W	1001	-0.7	-21
	2222	0.1	3
26 Th	1046	-0.7	-21
	2317	0.1	3
27 F ●	1128	-0.7	-21
28 Sa	0022	0.1	3
	1208	-0.7	-21
29 Su	0132	0.1	3
	1244	-0.6	-18
30 M	0249	0.0	0
	1318	-0.6	-18
	2335	0.0	0
31 Tu	0144	-0.1	-3
	0417	0.0	0
	1350	-0.5	-15
	2248	-0.1	-3

February

Day	Time (h m)	Height (ft)	Height (cm)
1 W	0240	-0.2	-6
	0603	-0.1	-3
	1419	-0.4	-12
	2105	-0.1	-3
2 Th	0333	-0.3	-9
	0832	-0.2	-6
	1431	-0.3	-9
	2022	-0.1	-3
3 F ◑	0428	-0.4	-12
	1955	0.0	0
4 Sa	0526	-0.5	-15
	1945	0.1	3
5 Su	0628	-0.6	-18
	1954	0.1	3
6 M	0733	-0.7	-21
	2026	0.2	6
7 Tu	0839	-0.7	-21
	2119	0.2	6
8 W	0941	-0.7	-21
	2229	0.2	6
9 Th	1039	-0.7	-21
	2351	0.2	6
10 F ○	1130	-0.7	-21
11 Sa	0119	0.2	6
	1214	-0.6	-18
12 Su	0245	0.1	3
	1250	-0.5	-15
13 M	0408	0.0	0
	1318	-0.4	-12
	2205	-0.1	-3
14 Tu	0128	-0.2	-6
	0533	0.0	0
	1339	-0.3	-9
	2100	-0.1	-3
15 W	0226	-0.2	-6
	0710	-0.1	-3
	1353	-0.2	-6
	2000	0.0	0
16 Th	0317	-0.2	-6
	1933	0.0	0
17 F	0405	-0.3	-9
	1917	0.0	0
18 Sa ◑	0454	-0.3	-9
	1913	0.1	3
19 Su	0549	-0.4	-12
	1915	0.1	3
20 M	0650	-0.4	-12
	1922	0.2	6
21 Tu	0752	-0.4	-12
	1947	0.2	6
22 W	0851	-0.5	-15
	2035	0.2	6
23 Th	0944	-0.5	-15
	2202	0.2	6
24 F	1032	-0.5	-15
25 Sa	0008	0.2	6
	1114	-0.4	-12
26 Su ●	0157	0.2	6
	1152	-0.4	-12
27 M	0334	0.2	6
	1229	-0.3	-9
	2122	0.1	3
	2339	0.0	0
28 Tu	0508	0.2	6
	1304	-0.2	-6
	1918	0.0	0

March

Day	Time (h m)	Height (ft)	Height (cm)
1 W	0033	0.0	0
	0645	0.1	3
	1339	0.0	0
	1828	0.1	3
2 Th	0127	-0.1	-3
	0850	0.1	3
	1411	0.0	0
	1800	0.1	3
3 F	0224	-0.2	-6
	1747	0.2	6
4 Sa	0327	-0.3	-9
	1748	0.3	9
5 Su ◑	0438	-0.3	-9
	1807	0.4	12
6 M	0556	-0.4	-12
	1848	0.4	12
7 Tu	0716	-0.4	-12
	1943	0.5	15
8 W	0831	-0.4	-12
	2054	0.4	12
9 Th	0938	-0.3	-9
	2253	0.4	12
10 F	1035	-0.2	-6
11 Sa	0136	0.4	12
	1121	-0.2	-6
	2016	0.3	9
	2228	0.2	6
12 Su ○	0331	0.3	9
	1158	-0.1	-3
	2003	0.2	6
	2320	0.1	3
13 M	0503	0.3	9
	1227	0.1	3
	1914	0.2	6
14 Tu	0004	0.1	3
	0630	0.3	9
	1250	0.1	3
	1800	0.2	6
15 W	0043	0.1	3
	0809	0.3	9
	1314	0.2	6
	1724	0.3	9
16 Th	0119	0.0	0
	1036	0.3	9
	1341	0.2	6
	1704	0.3	9
17 F	0156	0.0	0
	1656	0.4	12
18 Sa	0238	0.0	0
	1457	0.4	12
19 Su	0331	0.0	0
	1537	0.5	15
20 M ◑	0436	0.0	0
	1625	0.5	15
21 Tu	0551	0.0	0
	1713	0.6	18
22 W	0706	0.0	0
	1800	0.6	18
23 Th	0815	0.0	0
	1841	0.6	18
24 F	0915	0.0	0
	1913	0.5	15
25 Sa	1007	0.1	3
	1930	0.5	15
	2139	0.4	12
26 Su	0206	0.5	15
	1054	0.2	6
	1917	0.4	12
	2204	0.3	9
27 M ●	0359	0.5	15
	1138	0.2	6
	1726	0.4	12
	2238	0.3	9
28 Tu	0536	0.6	18
	1224	0.3	9
	1614	0.4	12
	2319	0.2	6
29 W	0719	0.6	18
	1315	0.4	12
	1527	0.5	15
30 Th	0004	0.1	3
	0926	0.6	18
31 F	0055	0.0	0
	1137	0.7	21

Time meridian 90° W. 0000 is midnight. 1200 is noon. Times are not adjusted for Daylight Saving Time.
Heights are referred to mean lower low water which is the chart datum of soundings.

Port O'Connor, Texas, 2017

Times and Heights of High and Low Waters

April

Day	Time	ft	cm		Day	Time	ft	cm
1 Sa	0152	0.0	0		16 Su	0150	0.2	6
	1337	0.8	24			1311	0.9	27
2 Su	0257	0.0	0		17 M	0243	0.2	6
	1521	0.8	24			1411	0.9	27
3 M ☾	0411	0.0	0		18 Tu	0347	0.2	6
	1630	0.8	24			1506	0.9	27
4 Tu	0531	0.0	0		19 W	0458	0.3	9
	1717	0.8	24			1553	0.9	27
5 W	0654	0.1	3		20 Th	0611	0.3	9
	1739	0.8	24			1632	0.8	24
6 Th	0811	0.2	6		21 F	0720	0.4	12
	1747	0.7	21			1658	0.8	24
7 F	0919	0.2	6		22 Sa	0825	0.4	12
	1751	0.6	18			1703	0.7	21
	2142	0.5	15			2122	0.6	18
8 Sa	0223	0.6	18		23 Su	0211	0.7	21
	1015	0.3	9			0928	0.5	15
	1746	0.6	18			1545	0.6	18
	2208	0.5	15			2124	0.5	15
9 Su	0445	0.6	18		24 M	0452	0.7	21
	1101	0.4	12			1036	0.5	15
	1708	0.6	18			1358	0.6	18
	2240	0.4	12			2147	0.4	12
10 M	0625	0.7	21		25 Tu	0638	0.8	24
	1139	0.5	15			2220	0.3	9
	1544	0.6	18					
	2310	0.4	12					
11 Tu ○	0747	0.7	21		26 W ●	0804	0.9	27
	1214	0.5	15			2301	0.2	6
	1438	0.6	18					
	2337	0.3	9					
12 W	0900	0.7	21		27 Th	0924	1.0	30
	1304	0.6	18			2348	0.1	3
	1356	0.7	21					
13 Th	0004	0.3	9		28 F	1044	1.0	30
	1006	0.8	24					
14 F	0033	0.2	6		29 Sa	0040	0.1	3
	1108	0.8	24			1204	1.0	30
15 Sa	0107	0.2	6		30 Su	0139	0.1	3
	1209	0.8	24			1321	1.0	30

May

Day	Time	ft	cm		Day	Time	ft	cm
1 M	0243	0.1	3		16 Tu	0220	0.2	6
	1424	1.0	30			1323	0.9	27
2 Tu ☽	0352	0.2	6		17 W	0313	0.2	6
	1505	1.0	30			1404	0.9	27
3 W	0503	0.2	6		18 Th ☽	0408	0.3	9
	1526	0.9	27			1436	0.8	24
4 Th	0614	0.3	9		19 F	0503	0.3	9
	1536	0.8	24			1451	0.7	21
5 F	0720	0.5	15		20 Sa	0559	0.4	12
	1535	0.7	21			1417	0.7	21
	2128	0.6	18			2109	0.4	12
6 Sa	0321	0.7	21		21 Su	0413	0.5	15
	0821	0.6	18			0701	0.4	12
	1504	0.7	21			1239	0.6	18
	2134	0.5	15			2038	0.4	12
7 Su	0526	0.7	21		22 M	0602	0.6	18
	0918	0.6	18			0824	0.5	15
	1338	0.7	21			1108	0.6	18
	2157	0.4	12			2055	0.3	9
8 M	0656	0.8	24		23 Tu	0712	0.8	24
	2221	0.3	9			2125	0.1	3
9 Tu	0809	0.8	24		24 W	0812	0.8	24
	2244	0.3	9			2204	0.0	0
10 W ○	0902	0.9	27		25 Th ●	0910	0.9	27
	2308	0.2	6			2250	-0.1	-3
11 Th	0943	0.9	27		26 F	1010	1.0	30
	2334	0.2	6			2342	-0.1	-3
12 F	1020	0.9	27		27 Sa	1111	1.0	30
13 Sa	0006	0.2	6		28 Su	0037	-0.2	-6
	1102	0.9	27			1211	1.0	30
14 Su	0045	0.1	3		29 M	0135	-0.1	-3
	1148	0.9	27			1259	0.9	27
15 M	0130	0.1	3		30 Tu	0234	-0.1	-3
	1236	0.9	27			1328	0.8	24
					31 W	0330	0.0	0
						1341	0.7	21

June

Day	Time	ft	cm		Day	Time	ft	cm
1 Th ☾	0422	0.2	6		16 F ☾	0317	0.0	0
	1342	0.6	18			1252	0.5	15
2 F	0506	0.3	9		17 Sa ☽	0333	0.1	3
	1322	0.6	18			1150	0.4	12
	2050	0.3	9			2025	0.2	6
3 Sa	0318	0.4	12		18 Su	1047	0.4	12
	0532	0.3	9			1934	0.1	3
	1220	0.5	15					
	2044	0.2	6					
4 Su	1114	0.6	18		19 M	0950	0.5	15
	2105	0.1	3			1952	0.0	0
5 M	1019	0.6	18		20 Tu	0908	0.5	15
	2128	0.1	3			2025	-0.2	-6
6 Tu	0959	0.7	21		21 W	0832	0.6	18
	2151	0.0	0			2107	-0.3	-9
7 W	0935	0.7	21		22 Th	0857	0.7	21
	2215	-0.1	-3			2155	-0.4	-12
8 Th	0928	0.7	21		23 F ●	0943	0.7	21
	2243	-0.1	-3			2248	-0.4	-12
9 F ○	0947	0.7	21		24 Sa	1035	0.7	21
	2316	-0.1	-3			2342	-0.4	-12
10 Sa	1017	0.7	21		25 Su	1126	0.7	21
	2355	-0.1	-3					
11 Su	1052	0.7	21		26 M	0037	-0.4	-12
						1203	0.6	18
12 M	0036	-0.1	-3		27 Tu	0130	-0.3	-9
	1130	0.7	21			1215	0.5	15
13 Tu	0120	-0.1	-3		28 W	0217	-0.2	-6
	1205	0.7	21			1215	0.5	15
14 W	0202	-0.1	-3		29 Th	0257	-0.1	-3
	1236	0.6	18			1204	0.4	12
15 Th	0242	0.0	0		30 F ☾	0325	0.0	0
	1256	0.6	18			1127	0.3	9
						1924	0.1	3

Time meridian 90° W. 0000 is midnight. 1200 is noon. Times are not adjusted for Daylight Saving Time.
Heights are referred to mean lower low water which is the chart datum of soundings.

Port O'Connor, Texas, 2017
Times and Heights of High and Low Waters

July

Day	Time	ft	cm		Day	Time	ft	cm
1 Sa	1032	0.3	9		16 Su ☾	0915	0.3	9
	1924	0.0	0			1758	-0.1	-3
2 Su	0951	0.4	12		17 M	0838	0.3	9
	1950	-0.1	-3			1830	-0.2	-6
3 M	0923	0.4	12		18 Tu	0818	0.4	12
	2017	-0.2	-6			1912	-0.3	-9
4 Tu	0915	0.5	15		19 W	0812	0.5	15
	2045	-0.2	-6			2001	-0.4	-12
5 W	0915	0.5	15		20 Th	0830	0.6	18
	2115	-0.3	-9			2055	-0.4	-12
6 Th	0913	0.5	15		21 F	0909	0.6	18
	2149	-0.3	-9			2152	-0.5	-15
7 F	0919	0.5	15		22 Sa	0959	0.6	18
	2226	-0.3	-9			2249	-0.5	-15
8 Sa ○	0939	0.5	15		23 Su ●	1051	0.6	18
	2306	-0.3	-9			2343	-0.4	-12
9 Su	1007	0.5	15		24 M	1124	0.6	18
	2348	-0.3	-9					
10 M	1036	0.5	15		25 Tu	0032	-0.4	-12
						1108	0.5	15
11 Tu	0028	-0.3	-9		26 W	0116	-0.2	-6
	1103	0.5	15			1054	0.4	12
12 W	0107	-0.3	-9		27 Th	0150	-0.1	-3
	1122	0.4	12			1033	0.3	9
13 Th	0142	-0.2	-6		28 F	0213	0.0	0
	1129	0.4	12			0941	0.3	9
						1637	0.1	3
						2349	0.2	6
14 F	0211	-0.1	-3		29 Sa	0201	0.1	3
	1102	0.3	9			0854	0.3	9
						1720	0.0	0
15 Sa	0224	0.0	0		30 Su ☽	0826	0.4	12
	1001	0.3	9			1800	-0.1	-3
	1743	0.1	3		31 M	0810	0.4	12
						1838	-0.1	-3

August

Day	Time	ft	cm		Day	Time	ft	cm
1 Tu	0808	0.5	15		16 W	0703	0.7	21
	1916	-0.1	-3			1842	-0.1	-3
2 W	0814	0.5	15		17 Th	0728	0.8	24
	1957	-0.2	-6			1945	-0.2	-6
3 Th	0822	0.6	18		18 F	0810	0.8	24
	2040	-0.2	-6			2049	-0.2	-6
4 F	0833	0.6	18		19 Sa	0902	0.8	24
	2125	-0.2	-6			2150	-0.1	-3
5 Sa	0852	0.6	18		20 Su	0956	0.8	24
	2211	-0.2	-6			2245	-0.1	-3
6 Su	0917	0.6	18		21 M ●	1017	0.8	24
	2255	-0.2	-6			2335	0.0	0
7 M ○	0940	0.6	18		22 Tu	0932	0.7	21
	2336	-0.2	-6			1158	0.6	18
						1348	0.7	21
8 Tu	0958	0.6	18		23 W	0017	0.1	3
						0916	0.6	18
						1250	0.5	15
						1623	0.6	18
9 W	0013	-0.1	-3		24 Th	0050	0.3	9
	1008	0.5	15			0841	0.6	18
						1341	0.4	12
						1843	0.5	15
10 Th	0048	0.0	0		25 F	0113	0.4	12
	0958	0.5	15			0734	0.6	18
						1429	0.4	12
						2241	0.5	15
11 F	0118	0.1	3		26 Sa	0117	0.4	12
	0857	0.4	12			0655	0.6	18
	1452	0.2	6			1513	0.3	9
	1852	0.3	9					
12 Sa	0141	0.2	6		27 Su	0633	0.7	21
	0804	0.4	12			1555	0.3	9
	1524	0.2	6					
13 Su	0729	0.5	15		28 M	0627	0.8	24
	1603	0.1	3			1638	0.2	6
14 M ☽	0705	0.6	18		29 Tu ☽	0630	0.8	24
	1649	0.0	0			1724	0.2	6
15 Tu	0657	0.6	18		30 W	0636	0.9	27
	1743	-0.1	-3			1814	0.2	6
					31 Th	0641	0.9	27
						1909	0.2	6

September

Day	Time	ft	cm		Day	Time	ft	cm
1 F	0656	0.9	27		16 Sa	0713	1.2	37
	2005	0.2	6			2037	0.4	12
2 Sa	0722	0.9	27		17 Su	0729	1.2	37
	2059	0.2	6			2137	0.5	15
3 Su	0750	0.9	27		18 M	0727	1.1	34
	2149	0.3	9			2229	0.6	18
4 M	0813	0.9	27		19 Tu ●	0722	1.0	30
	2234	0.3	9			1101	0.9	27
						1453	1.0	30
						2312	0.7	21
5 Tu	0827	0.9	27		20 W	0701	1.0	30
	2314	0.4	12			1138	0.9	27
						1726	1.0	30
						2346	0.8	24
6 W ○	0827	0.8	24		21 Th	0555	1.0	30
	1153	0.7	21			1218	0.8	24
	1513	0.8	24			2008	1.0	30
	2352	0.5	15					
7 Th	0739	0.8	24		22 F	0010	0.9	27
	1219	0.7	21			0457	1.0	30
	1723	0.8	24			1256	0.7	21
8 F	0026	0.6	18		23 Sa	0422	1.1	34
	0620	0.8	24			1332	0.7	21
	1254	0.6	18					
	1935	0.8	24					
9 Sa	0058	0.7	21		24 Su	0411	1.1	34
	0538	0.8	24			1408	0.6	18
	1333	0.5	15					
10 Su	0511	0.9	27		25 M	0411	1.2	37
	1417	0.4	12			1446	0.6	18
11 M	0500	1.0	30		26 Tu	0402	1.2	37
	1508	0.4	12			1531	0.6	18
12 Tu	0458	1.1	34		27 W ☽	0343	1.3	40
	1607	0.3	9			1622	0.6	18
13 W ☽	0513	1.2	37		28 Th	0407	1.3	40
	1712	0.3	9			1721	0.6	18
14 Th	0549	1.2	37		29 F	0442	1.3	40
	1821	0.3	9			1824	0.6	18
15 F	0633	1.2	37		30 Sa	0518	1.3	40
	1931	0.3	9			1925	0.7	21

Time meridian 90° W. 0000 is midnight. 1200 is noon. Times are not adjusted for Daylight Saving Time.
Heights are referred to mean lower low water which is the chart datum of soundings.

Port O'Connor, Texas, 2017
Times and Heights of High and Low Waters

October

Day	Time	ft	cm		Day	Time	ft	cm
1 Su	0550	1.3	40		16 M	0510	1.3	40
	2021	0.7	21			2104	0.9	27
2 M	0614	1.2	37		17 Tu	0459	1.2	37
	2113	0.8	24			1023	1.1	34
						1619	1.2	37
						2149	1.0	30
3 Tu	0624	1.2	37		18 W	0409	1.2	37
	1045	1.0	30			1048	1.0	30
	1248	1.1	34			1848	1.2	37
	2200	0.9	27			2222	1.1	34
4 W	0559	1.1	34		19 Th ●	0302	1.2	37
	1036	1.0	30			1118	0.9	27
	1552	1.1	34					
	2244	1.0	30					
5 Th ○	0427	1.1	34		20 F	0207	1.3	40
	1059	0.9	27			1148	0.8	24
	1822	1.2	37					
	2327	1.0	30					
6 F	0328	1.1	34		21 Sa	0147	1.3	40
	1130	0.8	24			1217	0.8	24
	2054	1.2	37					
7 Sa	0012	1.1	34		22 Su	0145	1.3	40
	0248	1.2	37			1247	0.7	21
	1208	0.7	21					
	2254	1.3	40					
8 Su	0106	1.2	37		23 M	0120	1.4	43
	0223	1.3	40			1320	0.7	21
	1251	0.7	21					
9 M	0046	1.4	43		24 Tu	0112	1.4	43
	1342	0.6	18			1359	0.7	21
10 Tu	0207	1.5	46		25 W	0140	1.4	43
	1439	0.6	18			1446	0.7	21
11 W	0304	1.5	46		26 Th	0215	1.4	43
	1543	0.6	18			1540	0.7	21
12 Th ☽	0352	1.5	46		27 F ◑	0253	1.4	43
	1652	0.6	18			1638	0.7	21
13 F	0431	1.5	46		28 Sa	0328	1.4	43
	1801	0.6	18			1737	0.7	21
14 Sa	0455	1.4	43		29 Su	0357	1.3	40
	1909	0.7	21			1834	0.8	24
15 Su	0506	1.3	40		30 M	0416	1.3	40
	2010	0.8	24			1927	0.9	27
					31 Tu	0413	1.2	37
						2018	1.0	30

November

Day	Time	ft	cm		Day	Time	ft	cm
1 W	0305	1.1	34		16 Th	0044	1.0	30
	0945	1.0	30			1028	0.5	15
	1728	1.1	34					
	2108	1.0	30					
2 Th	0149	1.1	34		17 F	0007	1.1	34
	0959	0.8	24			1054	0.5	15
	1932	1.2	37					
	2201	1.1	34					
3 F ○	0049	1.2	37		18 Sa ●	0005	1.1	34
	1026	0.7	21			1120	0.4	12
	2110	1.3	40					
	2311	1.2	37					
4 Sa	0004	1.3	40		19 Su	0012	1.1	34
	1101	0.6	18			1147	0.4	12
	2239	1.3	40					
5 Su	1143	0.5	15		20 M	0010	1.1	34
	2352	1.4	43			1217	0.3	9
6 M	1232	0.4	12		21 Tu	0010	1.1	34
						1253	0.3	9
7 Tu	0053	1.4	43		22 W	0030	1.1	34
	1327	0.4	12			1335	0.3	9
8 W	0147	1.4	43		23 Th	0100	1.1	34
	1426	0.4	12			1421	0.3	9
9 Th	0231	1.4	43		24 F	0132	1.1	34
	1529	0.4	12			1509	0.3	9
10 F ☽	0258	1.3	40		25 Sa	0201	1.0	30
	1632	0.5	15			1558	0.3	9
11 Sa	0310	1.3	40		26 Su ◑	0224	1.0	30
	1732	0.6	18			1645	0.4	12
12 Su	0314	1.2	37		27 M	0235	0.9	27
	1828	0.7	21			1728	0.5	15
13 M	0309	1.1	34		28 Tu	0215	0.8	24
	1915	0.8	24			1803	0.6	18
14 Tu	0240	1.0	30		29 W	0059	0.8	24
	0941	0.8	24			0857	0.5	15
	1704	0.9	27			2351	0.8	24
	1948	0.8	24					
15 W	0141	1.0	30		30 Th	0903	0.4	12
	1001	0.6	18			2303	0.8	24

December

Day	Time	ft	cm		Day	Time	ft	cm
1 F	0927	0.2	6		16 Sa	1029	-0.1	-3
	2239	0.9	27			2312	0.6	18
2 Sa	1002	0.1	3		17 Su	1056	-0.2	-6
	2241	1.0	30			2328	0.6	18
3 Su ○	1044	0.0	0		18 M ●	1127	-0.2	-6
	2321	1.0	30			2340	0.6	18
4 M	1133	-0.1	-3		19 Tu	1201	-0.3	-9
						2351	0.6	18
5 Tu	0015	1.0	30		20 W	1240	-0.3	-9
	1226	-0.2	-6					
6 W	0111	1.0	30		21 Th	0009	0.6	18
	1322	-0.2	-6			1320	-0.3	-9
7 Th	0157	0.9	27		22 F	0031	0.5	15
	1418	-0.1	-3			1401	-0.3	-9
8 F	0209	0.9	27		23 Sa	0051	0.5	15
	1513	-0.1	-3			1441	-0.2	-6
9 Sa	0153	0.8	24		24 Su	0107	0.4	12
	1604	0.1	3			1518	-0.2	-6
10 Su ☽	0143	0.6	18		25 M	0110	0.3	9
	1647	0.2	6			1546	-0.1	-3
11 M	0126	0.6	18		26 Tu ◑	0029	0.3	9
	1716	0.3	9			1330	0.0	0
						2314	0.2	6
12 Tu	0041	0.5	15		27 W	0746	0.0	0
	0844	0.2	6			2216	0.2	6
	2350	0.5	15					
13 W	0906	0.1	3		28 Th	0755	-0.2	-6
	2308	0.6	18			2141	0.3	9
14 Th	0935	0.0	0		29 F	0824	-0.3	-9
	2250	0.6	18			2133	0.4	12
15 F	1002	-0.1	-3		30 Sa	0903	-0.4	-12
	2256	0.6	18			2152	0.4	12
					31 Su	0948	-0.5	-15
						2236	0.5	15

Time meridian 90° W. 0000 is midnight. 1200 is noon. Times are not adjusted for Daylight Saving Time.
Heights are referred to mean lower low water which is the chart datum of soundings.

Padre Island (south end), Texas, 2017

Times and Heights of High and Low Waters

January

Day	Time (h m)	Height ft	cm	Day	Time (h m)	Height ft	cm
1 Su	1013	-0.3	-9	16 M	0034	0.8	24
	1928	1.5	46		0321	0.9	27
					1125	-0.1	-3
					1919	1.1	34
2 M	1054	-0.2	-6	17 Tu	0118	0.7	21
	1948	1.4	43		0506	0.8	24
					1207	0.2	6
					1930	1.0	30
3 Tu	1139	0.0	0	18 W	0207	0.5	15
	2002	1.3	40		0716	0.7	21
					1248	0.5	15
					1935	1.0	30
4 W	1228	0.2	6	19 Th ◖	0255	0.3	9
	2010	1.2	37		0959	0.8	24
					1329	0.7	21
					1934	1.0	30
5 Th ◑	0312	0.5	15	20 F	0342	0.1	3
	0812	0.7	21		1920	1.0	30
	1328	0.5	15				
	2013	1.1	34				
6 F	0341	0.2	6	21 Sa	0426	0.0	0
	1104	0.9	27		1426	1.0	30
	1450	0.8	24				
	2009	1.0	30				
7 Sa	0420	-0.1	-3	22 Su	0509	-0.2	-6
	1303	1.1	34		1505	1.1	34
	1659	0.9	27				
	1952	1.0	30				
8 Su	0504	-0.5	-15	23 M	0549	-0.3	-9
	1420	1.3	40		1539	1.2	37
9 M	0552	-0.8	-24	24 Tu	0627	-0.4	-12
	1519	1.4	43		1610	1.2	37
10 Tu	0642	-0.9	-27	25 W	0703	-0.5	-15
	1611	1.5	46		1637	1.3	40
11 W	0732	-1.0	-30	26 Th	0738	-0.5	-15
	1658	1.5	46		1703	1.3	40
12 Th ○	0822	-1.0	-30	27 F ●	0813	-0.5	-15
	1740	1.5	46		1726	1.3	40
13 F	0910	-0.9	-27	28 Sa	0850	-0.5	-15
	1815	1.4	43		1747	1.3	40
14 Sa	0957	-0.7	-21	29 Su	0928	-0.4	-12
	1843	1.3	40		1805	1.2	37
15 Su	1042	-0.4	-12	30 M	1008	-0.3	-9
	1904	1.2	37		1819	1.1	34
					2347	0.8	24
				31 Tu	0301	0.9	27
					1051	-0.1	-3
					1829	1.0	30

February

Day	Time (h m)	Height ft	cm	Day	Time (h m)	Height ft	cm
1 W	0019	0.6	18	16 Th	0036	0.3	9
	0449	0.8	24		0740	0.8	24
	1138	0.1	3		1235	0.7	21
	1833	0.9	27		1744	0.9	27
2 Th	0100	0.3	9	17 F	0127	0.2	6
	0656	0.7	21		0959	0.9	27
	1231	0.4	12		1324	0.8	24
	1833	0.9	27		1724	0.9	27
3 F ◖	0148	0.0	0	18 Sa ◗	0221	0.1	3
	0924	0.8	24		1236	1.0	30
	1338	0.7	21				
	1826	0.9	27				
4 Sa	0242	-0.3	-9	19 Su	0317	0.0	0
	1149	1.0	30		1345	1.1	34
	1540	0.8	24				
	1756	0.9	27				
5 Su	0340	-0.5	-15	20 M	0411	-0.1	-3
	1323	1.1	34		1422	1.2	37
6 M	0438	-0.7	-21	21 Tu	0502	-0.2	-6
	1425	1.3	40		1451	1.2	37
7 Tu	0536	-0.8	-24	22 W	0549	-0.2	-6
	1514	1.3	40		1516	1.3	40
8 W	0632	-0.9	-27	23 Th	0633	-0.3	-9
	1555	1.3	40		1538	1.3	40
9 Th	0726	-0.8	-24	24 F	0714	-0.3	-9
	1629	1.3	40		1557	1.3	40
					2102	1.0	30
					2303	1.1	34
10 F ○	0816	-0.7	-21	25 Sa	0756	-0.3	-9
	1656	1.2	37		1614	1.2	37
	2127	1.0	30		2104	1.0	30
11 Sa	0031	1.1	34	26 Su ●	0031	1.1	34
	0904	-0.5	-15		0839	-0.2	-6
	1716	1.1	34		1628	1.1	34
	2151	0.9	27		2122	0.8	24
12 Su	0153	1.0	30	27 M	0150	1.1	34
	0949	-0.3	-9		0923	-0.1	-3
	1732	1.0	30		1639	1.0	30
	2226	0.7	21		2150	0.6	18
13 M	0310	1.0	30	28 Tu	0309	1.1	34
	1032	0.0	0		1010	0.1	3
	1743	0.9	27		1645	0.9	27
	2305	0.6	18		2225	0.4	12
14 Tu	0428	0.9	27				
	1113	0.2	6				
	1749	0.9	27				
	2349	0.4	12				
15 W	0555	0.9	27				
	1154	0.5	15				
	1750	0.9	27				

March

Day	Time (h m)	Height ft	cm	Day	Time (h m)	Height ft	cm
1 W	0433	1.0	30	16 Th	0625	1.2	37
	1101	0.3	9		1210	0.8	24
	1647	0.8	24		1537	0.9	27
	2307	0.2	6		2323	0.2	6
2 Th	0608	1.0	30	17 F	0751	1.2	37
	1159	0.6	18				
	1644	0.8	24				
	2357	-0.1	-3				
3 F	0757	1.1	34	18 Sa	0006	0.1	3
	1314	0.8	24		0933	1.2	37
	1629	0.9	27				
4 Sa	0054	-0.3	-9	19 Su	0056	0.1	3
	0958	1.2	37		1115	1.3	40
5 Su ◑	0158	-0.4	-12	20 M ◖	0154	0.1	3
	1145	1.3	40		1221	1.3	40
6 M	0306	-0.5	-15	21 Tu	0258	0.1	3
	1300	1.4	43		1302	1.4	43
7 Tu	0415	-0.5	-15	22 W	0401	0.1	3
	1352	1.4	43		1331	1.4	43
8 W	0521	-0.5	-15	23 Th	0500	0.1	3
	1431	1.4	43		1354	1.4	43
9 Th	0622	-0.4	-12	24 F	0554	0.1	3
	1500	1.3	40		1413	1.4	43
	1955	1.0	30		1942	1.1	34
	2252	1.1	34		2249	1.2	37
10 F	0719	-0.3	-9	25 Sa	0647	0.2	6
	1522	1.2	37		1428	1.3	40
	2007	1.0	30		1944	1.0	30
11 Sa	0027	1.2	37	26 Su	0021	1.2	37
	0810	-0.1	-3		0739	0.2	6
	1538	1.1	34		1441	1.2	37
	2031	0.8	24		2002	0.8	24
12 Su ○	0145	1.2	37	27 M ●	0139	1.3	40
	0859	0.1	3		0831	0.3	9
	1549	1.0	30		1449	1.1	34
	2101	0.6	18		2029	0.5	15
13 M	0255	1.2	37	28 Tu	0253	1.3	40
	0945	0.3	9		0927	0.5	15
	1556	1.0	30		1453	1.0	30
	2134	0.5	15		2103	0.2	6
14 Tu	0403	1.2	37	29 W	0409	1.4	43
	1031	0.5	15		1027	0.7	21
	1558	0.9	27		1452	0.9	27
	2208	0.4	12		2142	0.0	0
15 W	0511	1.2	37	30 Th	0528	1.4	43
	1117	0.7	21		1138	0.8	24
	1553	0.9	27		1441	0.9	27
	2244	0.3	9		2228	-0.2	-6
				31 F	0654	1.4	43
					2320	-0.4	-12

Time meridian 90° W. 0000 is midnight. 1200 is noon. Times are not adjusted for Daylight Saving Time.
Heights are referred to mean lower low water which is the chart datum of soundings.

Padre Island (south end), Texas, 2017

Times and Heights of High and Low Waters

April

Day	Time (h m)	Height (ft)	Height (cm)	Day	Time (h m)	Height (ft)	Height (cm)
1 Sa	0826	1.5	46	16 Su	0904	1.5	46
					2351	0.1	3
2 Su	0018	-0.4	-12	17 M	1008	1.5	46
	0957	1.5	46				
3 M ☽	0124	-0.4	-12	18 Tu	0043	0.2	6
	1114	1.6	49		1058	1.5	46
4 Tu	0236	-0.3	-9	19 W ☽	0144	0.3	9
	1210	1.6	49		1134	1.6	49
5 W	0349	-0.1	-3	20 Th	0251	0.3	9
	1250	1.5	46		1201	1.5	46
6 Th	0501	0.0	0	21 F	0402	0.4	12
	1318	1.4	43		1222	1.5	46
	1857	1.1	34		1857	1.0	30
	2230	1.2	37		2150	1.1	34
7 F	0607	0.2	6	22 Sa	0511	0.5	15
	1338	1.3	40		1238	1.4	43
	1908	0.9	27		1843	0.9	27
					2347	1.2	37
8 Sa	0013	1.2	37	23 Su	0618	0.5	15
	0708	0.4	12		1249	1.3	40
	1351	1.2	37		1857	0.6	18
	1931	0.7	21				
9 Su	0133	1.3	40	24 M	0113	1.3	40
	0805	0.6	18		0725	0.7	21
	1400	1.1	34		1256	1.1	34
	1959	0.5	15		1923	0.3	9
10 M	0243	1.4	43	25 Tu	0228	1.4	43
	0900	0.7	21		0835	0.8	24
	1403	1.1	34		1257	1.0	30
	2028	0.4	12		1956	0.0	0
11 Tu ○	0345	1.4	43	26 W ●	0340	1.5	46
	0956	0.9	27		0951	0.9	27
	1358	1.0	30		1249	1.0	30
	2057	0.2	6		2034	-0.3	-9
12 W	0445	1.4	43	27 Th	0451	1.6	49
	1059	0.9	27		2118	-0.5	-15
	1341	1.0	30				
	2127	0.1	3				
13 Th	0545	1.4	43	28 F	0603	1.7	52
	2158	0.1	3		2206	-0.6	-18
14 F	0647	1.4	43	29 Sa	0717	1.7	52
	2231	0.1	3		2258	-0.6	-18
15 Sa	0753	1.4	43	30 Su	0830	1.7	52
	2308	0.1	3		2355	-0.5	-15

May

Day	Time (h m)	Height (ft)	Height (cm)	Day	Time (h m)	Height (ft)	Height (cm)
1 M	0936	1.7	52	16 Tu	0916	1.6	49
					2356	0.0	0
2 Tu ☽	0058	-0.3	-9	17 W	0949	1.6	49
	1028	1.6	49				
3 W	0205	-0.1	-3	18 Th ☽	0049	0.2	6
	1107	1.5	46		1016	1.5	46
4 Th	0318	0.2	6	19 F	0151	0.3	9
	1133	1.4	43		1036	1.5	46
	1803	0.9	27				
	2137	1.0	30				
5 F	0432	0.4	12	20 Sa	0305	0.5	15
	1151	1.3	40		1051	1.3	40
	1812	0.8	24		1747	0.7	21
	2345	1.1	34		2250	0.9	27
6 Sa	0545	0.7	21	21 Su	0428	0.6	18
	1203	1.3	40		1100	1.2	37
	1836	0.5	15		1755	0.4	12
7 Su	0116	1.3	40	22 M	0037	1.1	34
	0656	0.8	24		0556	0.8	24
	1209	1.2	37		1104	1.1	34
	1904	0.3	9		1820	0.1	3
8 M	0229	1.4	43	23 Tu	0158	1.3	40
	0808	1.0	30		0727	0.9	27
	1207	1.1	34		1100	1.0	30
	1933	0.1	3		1853	-0.3	-9
9 Tu	0331	1.4	43	24 W	0309	1.4	43
	0926	1.0	30		1933	-0.6	-18
	1150	1.1	34				
	2002	0.0	0				
10 W ○	0426	1.5	46	25 Th ●	0415	1.6	49
	2030	-0.1	-3		2016	-0.8	-24
11 Th	0518	1.5	46	26 F	0519	1.6	49
	2058	-0.2	-6		2103	-1.0	-30
12 F	0609	1.5	46	27 Sa	0621	1.7	52
	2127	-0.2	-6		2153	-1.0	-30
13 Sa	0658	1.5	46	28 Su	0721	1.7	52
	2158	-0.2	-6		2244	-0.8	-24
14 Su	0748	1.5	46	29 M	0814	1.6	49
	2232	-0.1	-3		2338	-0.6	-18
15 M	0835	1.5	46	30 Tu	0858	1.5	46
	2311	-0.1	-3				
				31 W	0034	-0.3	-9
					0930	1.4	43

June

Day	Time (h m)	Height (ft)	Height (cm)	Day	Time (h m)	Height (ft)	Height (cm)
1 Th ☽	0133	0.0	0	16 F	0015	0.0	0
	0954	1.3	40		0901	1.3	40
	1656	0.7	21				
	1953	0.8	24				
2 F	0238	0.3	9	17 Sa ☽	0110	0.2	6
	1010	1.2	37		0912	1.2	37
	1707	0.5	15		1634	0.5	15
	2246	0.9	27		2114	0.7	21
3 Sa	0351	0.6	18	18 Su	0221	0.5	15
	1020	1.2	37		0918	1.1	34
	1734	0.3	9		1644	0.2	6
					2348	0.8	24
4 Su	0045	1.0	30	19 M	0356	0.7	21
	0516	0.8	24		0919	1.0	30
	1023	1.1	34		1712	-0.1	-3
	1806	0.1	3				
5 M	0209	1.2	37	20 Tu	0125	1.0	30
	0652	1.0	30		0555	0.9	27
	1016	1.1	34		0909	1.0	30
	1838	-0.1	-3		1749	-0.5	-15
6 Tu	0312	1.3	40	21 W	0237	1.2	37
	1909	-0.3	-9		1831	-0.8	-24
7 W	0405	1.3	40	22 Th	0339	1.4	43
	1940	-0.4	-12		1917	-1.0	-30
8 Th	0452	1.4	43	23 F ●	0437	1.5	46
	2009	-0.4	-12		2005	-1.2	-37
9 F ○	0535	1.4	43	24 Sa	0530	1.5	46
	2039	-0.5	-15		2055	-1.2	-37
10 Sa	0616	1.4	43	25 Su	0620	1.5	46
	2108	-0.4	-12		2145	-1.0	-30
11 Su	0654	1.4	43	26 M	0702	1.4	43
	2139	-0.4	-12		2234	-0.8	-24
12 M	0728	1.4	43	27 Tu	0737	1.3	40
	2211	-0.4	-12		2323	-0.5	-15
13 Tu	0759	1.4	43	28 W	0802	1.2	37
	2248	-0.3	-9				
14 W	0824	1.4	43	29 Th	0012	-0.2	-6
	2328	-0.1	-3		0821	1.2	37
					1454	0.6	18
					1804	0.7	21
15 Th	0845	1.4	43	30 F ☽	0102	0.2	6
					0834	1.1	34
					1531	0.4	12
					2054	0.7	21

Time meridian 90° W. 0000 is midnight. 1200 is noon. Times are not adjusted for Daylight Saving Time.
Heights are referred to mean lower low water which is the chart datum of soundings.

Padre Island (south end), Texas, 2017

Times and Heights of High and Low Waters

July

Day	Time (h m)	Height (ft)	Height (cm)	Day	Time (h m)	Height (ft)	Height (cm)
1 Sa	0156	0.5	15	16 Su	0052	0.4	12
	0842	1.0	30		0741	1.0	30
	1611	0.2	6		1506	0.2	6
	2337	0.8	24	◐	2221	0.8	24
2 Su	0305	0.7	21	17 M	0202	0.7	21
	0845	1.0	30		0738	0.9	27
	1652	0.0	0		1547	-0.1	-3
3 M	0134	1.0	30	18 Tu	0037	1.0	30
	0453	0.9	27		0404	0.9	27
	0835	1.0	30		0721	1.0	30
	1731	-0.2	-6		1634	-0.5	-15
4 Tu	0244	1.1	34	19 W	0158	1.2	37
	1809	-0.3	-9		1724	-0.7	-21
5 W	0334	1.2	37	20 Th	0258	1.4	43
	1845	-0.4	-12		1815	-0.9	-27
6 Th	0416	1.3	40	21 F	0349	1.5	46
	1919	-0.5	-15		1907	-1.0	-30
7 F	0455	1.3	40	22 Sa	0436	1.5	46
	1952	-0.5	-15		1959	-1.0	-30
8 Sa ○	0529	1.3	40	23 Su	0516	1.5	46
	2023	-0.5	-15	●	2049	-0.9	-27
9 Su	0559	1.3	40	24 M	0550	1.4	43
	2053	-0.5	-15		2138	-0.7	-21
10 M	0625	1.3	40	25 Tu	0615	1.3	40
	2125	-0.4	-12		1102	1.0	30
					1354	1.1	34
					2225	-0.4	-12
11 Tu	0647	1.3	40	26 W	0634	1.2	37
	2158	-0.4	-12		1139	0.9	27
					1526	1.0	30
					2311	-0.1	-3
12 W	0705	1.3	40	27 Th	0648	1.1	34
	2235	-0.2	-6		1226	0.7	21
					1704	0.9	27
					2355	0.2	6
13 Th	0720	1.3	40	28 F	0658	1.0	30
	2315	-0.1	-3		1318	0.5	15
					1900	0.9	27
14 F	0731	1.2	37	29 Sa	0040	0.5	15
	1424	0.6	18		0704	1.0	30
	1625	0.7	21		1412	0.3	9
	2359	0.2	6		2123	0.9	27
15 Sa	0738	1.1	34	30 Su ◐	0129	0.8	24
	1434	0.5	15		0704	1.0	30
	1926	0.7	21		1506	0.2	6
				31 M	0005	1.0	30
					0242	0.9	27
					0652	1.1	34
					1558	0.0	0

August

Day	Time (h m)	Height (ft)	Height (cm)	Day	Time (h m)	Height (ft)	Height (cm)
1 Tu	0149	1.1	34	16 W	0048	1.4	43
	1648	-0.1	-3		1601	-0.4	-12
2 W	0242	1.3	40	17 Th	0155	1.5	46
	1734	-0.2	-6		1703	-0.5	-15
3 Th	0322	1.3	40	18 F	0245	1.6	49
	1817	-0.2	-6		1803	-0.5	-15
4 F	0356	1.4	43	19 Sa	0327	1.6	49
	1856	-0.2	-6		1900	-0.5	-15
5 Sa	0425	1.4	43	20 Su	0400	1.6	49
	1931	-0.2	-6		1953	-0.4	-12
6 Su	0449	1.4	43	21 M	0426	1.5	46
	2005	-0.2	-6		0851	1.3	40
					1224	1.4	43
				●	2044	-0.2	-6
7 M ○	0509	1.4	43	22 Tu	0445	1.4	43
	2039	-0.2	-6		0916	1.1	34
					1348	1.4	43
					2132	0.0	0
8 Tu	0525	1.4	43	23 W	0458	1.3	40
	2114	-0.1	-3		0951	1.0	30
					1507	1.4	43
					2219	0.3	9
9 W	0538	1.3	40	24 Th	0508	1.2	37
	1045	1.1	34		1031	0.8	24
	1334	1.2	37		1626	1.3	40
	2151	0.0	0		2304	0.6	18
10 Th	0548	1.3	40	25 F	0514	1.2	37
	1107	1.0	30		1115	0.6	18
	1459	1.1	34		1750	1.3	40
	2231	0.2	6		2351	0.8	24
11 F	0556	1.2	37	26 Sa	0516	1.2	37
	1138	0.8	24		1202	0.5	15
	1633	1.0	30		1927	1.3	40
	2315	0.4	12				
12 Sa	0600	1.1	34	27 Su	0042	1.1	34
	1218	0.6	18		0511	1.2	37
	1823	1.0	30		1254	0.4	12
					2126	1.3	40
13 Su	0006	0.6	18	28 M	0155	1.2	37
	0559	1.1	34		0447	1.3	40
	1305	0.3	9		1350	0.4	12
	2037	1.1	34		2337	1.4	43
14 M ◐	0109	0.9	27	29 Tu ◐	1450	0.3	9
	0551	1.1	34				
	1400	0.0	0				
	2301	1.2	37				
15 Tu	0302	1.1	34	30 W	0103	1.5	46
	0520	1.2	37		1550	0.3	9
	1500	-0.2	-6	31 Th	0153	1.6	49
					1647	0.3	9

September

Day	Time (h m)	Height (ft)	Height (cm)	Day	Time (h m)	Height (ft)	Height (cm)
1 F	0229	1.6	49	16 Sa	0157	1.9	58
	1737	0.3	9		1750	0.2	6
2 Sa	0256	1.7	52	17 Su	0227	1.8	55
	1823	0.3	9		0733	1.5	46
					1029	1.6	49
					1850	0.3	9
3 Su	0316	1.7	52	18 M	0248	1.7	52
	1904	0.3	9		0741	1.4	43
					1213	1.7	52
					1947	0.5	15
4 M	0332	1.7	52	19 Tu	0303	1.6	49
	0835	1.4	43		0805	1.3	40
	1122	1.5	46		1335	1.7	52
	1944	0.4	12	●	2040	0.7	21
5 Tu	0345	1.6	49	20 W	0313	1.5	46
	0841	1.4	43		0836	1.1	34
	1239	1.5	46		1449	1.8	55
	2024	0.4	12		2131	0.9	27
6 W ○	0356	1.5	46	21 Th	0319	1.5	46
	0859	1.2	37		0910	0.9	27
	1351	1.5	46		1559	1.8	55
	2107	0.5	15		2222	1.1	34
7 Th	0404	1.5	46	22 F	0321	1.4	43
	0924	1.1	34		0946	0.7	21
	1503	1.5	46		1708	1.8	55
	2152	0.7	21		2316	1.3	40
8 F	0410	1.4	43	23 Sa	0316	1.4	43
	0956	0.8	24		1023	0.6	18
	1619	1.5	46		1821	1.8	55
	2242	0.9	27				
9 Sa	0411	1.3	40	24 Su	0023	1.4	43
	1034	0.6	18		0256	1.5	46
	1745	1.5	46		1103	0.6	18
	2340	1.1	34		1941	1.8	55
10 Su	0406	1.3	40	25 M	1146	0.6	18
	1120	0.4	12		2111	1.8	55
	1922	1.6	49				
11 M	0057	1.2	37	26 Tu	1235	0.6	18
	0348	1.3	40		2241	1.8	55
	1213	0.2	6				
	2113	1.7	52				
12 Tu	1314	0.1	3	27 W ◑	1331	0.7	21
	2300	1.8	55		2350	1.9	58
13 W ◐	1422	0.0	0	28 Th	1435	0.7	21
14 Th	0020	1.9	58	29 F	0035	1.9	58
	1534	0.0	0		1540	0.8	24
15 F	0116	1.9	58	30 Sa	0105	2.0	61
	1644	0.1	3		1641	0.8	24

Time meridian 90° W. 0000 is midnight. 1200 is noon. Times are not adjusted for Daylight Saving Time.
Heights are referred to mean lower low water which is the chart datum of soundings.

Padre Island (south end), Texas, 2017

Times and Heights of High and Low Waters

October

Day	Time	ft	cm	Day	Time	ft	cm
1 Su	0126	2.0	61	16 M	0102	1.9	58
	1736	0.8	24		0646	1.4	43
					1153	1.8	55
					1838	1.0	30
2 M	0142	1.9	58	17 Tu	0115	1.8	55
	0728	1.6	49		0708	1.2	37
	1058	1.7	52		1321	1.9	58
	1829	0.9	27		1941	1.2	37
3 Tu	0155	1.8	55	18 W	0122	1.7	52
	0730	1.5	46		0737	1.0	30
	1224	1.7	52		1434	1.9	58
	1920	0.9	27		2042	1.3	40
4 W	0205	1.8	55	19 Th ●	0125	1.6	49
	0746	1.3	40		0808	0.8	24
	1338	1.8	55		1540	2.0	61
	2013	1.0	30		2146	1.5	46
5 Th O	0212	1.6	49	20 F	0120	1.6	49
	0810	1.0	30		0840	0.6	18
	1447	1.9	58		1641	2.0	61
	2108	1.2	37				
6 F	0216	1.6	49	21 Sa	0913	0.5	15
	0841	0.8	24		1741	2.0	61
	1557	1.9	58				
	2209	1.3	40				
7 Sa	0213	1.5	46	22 Su	0945	0.5	15
	0917	0.5	15		1842	2.0	61
	1711	2.0	61				
	2324	1.4	43				
8 Su	0159	1.5	46	23 M	1019	0.5	15
	0959	0.3	9		1945	2.0	61
	1829	2.0	61				
9 M	1048	0.2	6	24 Tu	1056	0.5	15
	1954	2.1	64		2049	2.0	61
10 Tu	1142	0.1	3	25 W	1137	0.6	18
	2120	2.1	64		2149	2.1	64
11 W	1244	0.1	3	26 Th	1224	0.7	21
	2236	2.2	67		2235	2.1	64
12 Th ☾	1353	0.2	6	27 F ◐	1319	0.8	24
	2334	2.2	67		2309	2.1	64
13 F	1506	0.4	12	28 Sa	1421	0.9	27
					2332	2.0	61
14 Sa	0015	2.1	64	29 Su	1530	1.0	30
	1621	0.6	18		2350	2.0	61
15 Su	0043	2.0	61	30 M	0650	1.5	46
	0640	1.6	49		0948	1.6	49
	0955	1.7	52		1640	1.1	34
	1732	0.8	24				
				31 Tu	0003	1.9	58
					0632	1.3	40
					1147	1.6	49
					1750	1.2	37

November

Day	Time	ft	cm	Day	Time	ft	cm
1 W	0013	1.8	55	16 Th	0715	0.5	15
	0644	1.1	34		1523	1.9	58
	1310	1.8	55				
	1900	1.3	40				
2 Th	0018	1.7	52	17 F	0746	0.3	9
	0706	0.8	24		1620	1.9	58
	1422	1.9	58				
	2013	1.4	43				
3 F O	0019	1.6	49	18 Sa ●	0818	0.2	6
	0737	0.5	15		1713	1.9	58
	1529	2.0	61				
	2134	1.4	43				
4 Sa	0009	1.5	46	19 Su	0849	0.1	3
	0813	0.2	6		1803	1.9	58
	1636	2.1	64				
5 Su	0854	0.0	0	20 M	0920	0.1	3
	1744	2.2	67		1852	1.9	58
6 M	0940	-0.2	-6	21 Tu	0951	0.2	6
	1853	2.2	67		1939	1.9	58
7 Tu	1030	-0.2	-6	22 W	1024	0.2	6
	2002	2.2	67		2023	1.9	58
8 W	1124	-0.1	-3	23 Th	1059	0.3	9
	2105	2.2	67		2059	1.9	58
9 Th	1223	0.1	3	24 F	1138	0.4	12
	2156	2.1	64		2127	1.9	58
10 F ☽	1327	0.3	9	25 Sa	1223	0.6	18
	2234	2.0	61		2148	1.9	58
11 Sa	1436	0.6	18	26 Su ◐	1316	0.7	21
	2300	1.9	58		2205	1.8	55
12 Su	0546	1.3	40	27 M	1422	0.9	27
	0848	1.4	43		2217	1.7	52
	1550	0.9	27				
	2317	1.8	55				
13 M	0549	1.2	37	28 Tu	0535	1.0	30
	1118	1.5	46		1040	1.2	37
	1707	1.1	34		1543	1.0	30
	2328	1.7	52		2225	1.6	49
14 Tu	0613	0.9	27	29 W	0540	0.7	21
	1300	1.7	52		1231	1.4	43
	1825	1.3	40		1716	1.2	37
	2333	1.6	49		2228	1.5	46
15 W	0643	0.7	21	30 Th	0603	0.4	12
	1418	1.8	55		1351	1.6	49
	1945	1.4	43		1856	1.3	40
	2331	1.6	49		2224	1.4	43

December

Day	Time	ft	cm	Day	Time	ft	cm
1 F	0634	0.1	3	16 Sa	0728	-0.2	-6
	1458	1.7	52		1643	1.6	49
2 Sa	0712	-0.3	-9	17 Su	0801	-0.3	-9
	1601	1.9	58		1727	1.6	49
3 Su O	0754	-0.5	-15	18 M ●	0832	-0.3	-9
	1701	2.0	61		1808	1.6	49
4 M	0840	-0.7	-21	19 Tu	0903	-0.2	-6
	1801	2.0	61		1846	1.6	49
5 Tu	0929	-0.7	-21	20 W	0933	-0.2	-6
	1857	2.0	61		1918	1.6	49
6 W	1020	-0.6	-18	21 Th	1003	-0.1	-3
	1948	1.9	58		1944	1.6	49
7 Th	1112	-0.4	-12	22 F	1035	0.0	0
	2030	1.8	55		2004	1.6	49
8 F	1206	-0.1	-3	23 Sa	1110	0.1	3
	2101	1.7	52		2019	1.5	46
9 Sa	1303	0.2	6	24 Su	1150	0.3	9
	2123	1.6	49		2031	1.4	43
10 Su ☽	0421	1.0	30	25 M	1236	0.4	12
	0702	1.1	34		2040	1.3	40
	1403	0.6	18				
	2138	1.5	46				
11 M	0435	0.8	24	26 Tu ◐	0413	0.7	21
	1006	1.1	34		0837	0.8	24
	1513	0.9	27		1335	0.7	21
	2147	1.4	43		2045	1.2	37
12 Tu	0506	0.5	15	27 W	0421	0.4	12
	1221	1.2	37		1129	0.9	27
	1638	1.1	34		1502	0.8	24
	2150	1.4	43		2045	1.2	37
13 W	0542	0.3	9	28 Th	0449	0.1	3
	1354	1.4	43		1314	1.1	34
	1822	1.2	37		1707	1.0	30
	2144	1.3	40		2036	1.1	34
14 Th	0618	0.1	3	29 F	0526	-0.3	-9
	1501	1.5	46		1424	1.3	40
15 F	0653	-0.1	-3	30 Sa	0608	-0.6	-18
	1555	1.6	49		1523	1.5	46
				31 Su	0654	-0.9	-27
					1618	1.6	49

Time meridian 90° W. 0000 is midnight. 1200 is noon. Times are not adjusted for Daylight Saving Time.
Heights are referred to mean lower low water which is the chart datum of soundings.

Tampico Harbor (Madero), Mexico, 2017

Times and Heights of High and Low Waters

January

Day	Time (h m)	Height (ft)	Height (cm)
1 Su	0949	-0.2	-6
	1828	1.3	40
2 M	1029	-0.1	-3
	1848	1.3	40
3 Tu	1117	0.1	3
	1907	1.2	37
4 W	0154	0.7	21
	0458	0.8	24
	1211	0.3	9
	1924	1.2	37
5 Th ☽	0220	0.6	18
	0712	0.8	24
	1305	0.6	18
	1940	1.1	34
6 F	0300	0.3	9
	1036	0.9	27
	1416	0.8	24
	1953	1.0	30
7 Sa	0349	0.1	3
	1232	1.1	34
	1707	0.9	27
	1958	1.0	30
8 Su	0440	-0.2	-6
	1408	1.2	37
9 M	0532	-0.5	-15
	1459	1.3	40
10 Tu	0626	-0.7	-21
	1542	1.4	43
11 W	0719	-0.8	-24
	1623	1.3	40
12 Th ○	0807	-0.8	-24
	1700	1.3	40
13 F	0852	-0.7	-21
	1733	1.2	37
	2313	0.8	24
14 Sa	0129	0.9	27
	0934	-0.6	-18
	1758	1.1	34
	2350	0.7	21
15 Su	0245	0.8	24
	1018	-0.3	-9
	1817	1.0	30
16 M	0024	0.7	21
	0353	0.8	24
	1104	-0.1	-3
	1832	0.9	27
17 Tu	0056	0.5	15
	0515	0.7	21
	1152	0.2	6
	1844	0.9	27
18 W	0130	0.4	12
	0647	0.7	21
	1233	0.4	12
	1853	0.9	27
19 Th ☾	0207	0.3	9
	0930	0.7	21
	1308	0.6	18
	1857	0.9	27
20 F	0252	0.2	6
	1847	0.9	27
21 Sa	0341	0.0	0
	1433	1.0	30
22 Su	0428	-0.1	-3
	1448	1.1	34
23 M	0513	-0.2	-6
	1511	1.2	37
24 Tu	0557	-0.3	-9
	1534	1.2	37
25 W	0640	-0.4	-12
	1556	1.2	37
26 Th	0720	-0.4	-12
	1617	1.2	37
27 F ●	0756	-0.4	-12
	1636	1.3	40
28 Sa	0830	-0.3	-9
	1654	1.3	40
	2213	0.9	27
29 Su	0022	1.0	30
	0904	-0.2	-6
	1710	1.2	37
	2236	0.9	27
30 M	0157	1.0	30
	0939	-0.1	-3
	1726	1.2	37
	2312	0.8	24
31 Tu	0309	1.0	30
	1019	0.1	3
	1742	1.2	37
	2352	0.7	21

February

Day	Time (h m)	Height (ft)	Height (cm)
1 W	0429	0.9	27
	1110	0.3	9
	1757	1.1	34
2 Th	0033	0.5	15
	0609	0.9	27
	1209	0.6	18
	1810	1.1	34
3 F ☽	0116	0.3	9
	0823	0.9	27
	1307	0.8	24
	1819	1.0	30
4 Sa	0207	0.0	0
	1132	1.1	34
	1509	0.9	27
	1813	1.0	30
5 Su	0309	-0.2	-6
	1326	1.2	37
6 M	0415	-0.4	-12
	1424	1.3	40
7 Tu	0517	-0.5	-15
	1503	1.3	40
8 W	0618	-0.6	-18
	1535	1.3	40
9 Th	0715	-0.6	-18
	1603	1.2	37
	2112	0.9	27
	2340	1.0	30
10 F ○	0804	-0.5	-15
	1623	1.1	34
	2124	0.8	24
11 Sa	0101	0.9	27
	0846	-0.4	-12
	1638	1.0	30
	2142	0.7	21
12 Su	0215	0.9	27
	0924	-0.2	-6
	1651	1.0	30
	2206	0.6	18
13 M	0316	0.9	27
	1002	0.0	0
	1702	0.9	27
	2241	0.5	15
14 Tu	0419	0.9	27
	1042	0.2	6
	1714	0.9	27
	2326	0.4	12
15 W	0530	0.9	27
	1127	0.5	15
	1725	0.9	27
16 Th	0011	0.3	9
	0649	0.8	24
	1214	0.7	21
	1732	0.9	27
17 F	0053	0.2	6
	0919	0.9	27
	1255	0.8	24
	1729	0.9	27
18 Sa ☾	0137	0.1	3
	1623	1.0	30
19 Su	0230	0.0	0
	1341	1.1	34
20 M	0331	0.0	0
	1416	1.2	37
21 Tu	0430	-0.1	-3
	1439	1.3	40
22 W	0523	-0.1	-3
	1459	1.3	40
23 Th	0613	-0.1	-3
	1514	1.3	40
24 F	0659	-0.1	-3
	1527	1.3	40
	2051	1.0	30
	2321	1.1	34
25 Sa	0741	-0.1	-3
	1537	1.3	40
	2052	1.0	30
26 Su ●	0030	1.1	34
	0819	0.0	0
	1547	1.3	40
	2104	0.9	27
27 M	0147	1.1	34
	0857	0.1	3
	1559	1.2	37
	2126	0.7	21
28 Tu	0254	1.2	37
	0936	0.3	9
	1612	1.2	37
	2158	0.6	18

March

Day	Time (h m)	Height (ft)	Height (cm)
1 W	0402	1.2	37
	1023	0.5	15
	1626	1.1	34
	2243	0.4	12
2 Th	0523	1.2	37
	1126	0.7	21
	1639	1.1	34
	2338	0.2	6
3 F	0656	1.2	37
	1240	0.9	27
	1648	1.1	34
4 Sa	0035	0.0	0
	0956	1.2	37
	1410	1.0	30
	1637	1.1	34
5 Su ☽	0132	-0.1	-3
	1141	1.3	40
6 M	0238	-0.2	-6
	1302	1.4	43
7 Tu	0354	-0.2	-6
	1401	1.4	43
8 W	0505	-0.2	-6
	1437	1.3	40
9 Th	0611	-0.2	-6
	1459	1.2	37
	2017	0.9	27
	2313	1.0	30
10 F	0711	-0.1	-3
	1512	1.2	37
	2025	0.8	24
11 Sa	0030	1.1	34
	0800	0.0	0
	1519	1.1	34
	2038	0.7	21
12 Su ○	0145	1.1	34
	0840	0.1	3
	1524	1.0	30
	2055	0.6	18
13 M	0246	1.1	34
	0915	0.3	9
	1532	1.0	30
	2115	0.4	12
14 Tu	0341	1.1	34
	0950	0.5	15
	1541	1.0	30
	2141	0.3	9
15 W	0438	1.1	34
	1028	0.6	18
	1550	1.0	30
	2215	0.3	9
16 Th	0541	1.1	34
	1122	0.8	24
	1556	1.0	30
	2300	0.2	6
17 F	0649	1.1	34
	1228	0.9	27
	1553	1.0	30
	2351	0.1	3
18 Sa	0836	1.1	34
19 Su	0041	0.1	3
	1055	1.2	37
20 M ☾	0131	0.1	3
	1151	1.3	40
21 Tu	0229	0.2	6
	1244	1.3	40
22 W	0337	0.2	6
	1326	1.4	43
23 Th	0441	0.2	6
	1350	1.4	43
24 F	0538	0.2	6
	1404	1.4	43
	2002	1.0	30
	2252	1.1	34
25 Sa	0634	0.3	9
	1413	1.4	43
	1952	1.0	30
26 Su	0002	1.2	37
	0725	0.3	9
	1421	1.3	40
	2001	0.8	24
27 M ●	0119	1.3	40
	0812	0.4	12
	1432	1.2	37
	2021	0.6	18
28 Tu	0229	1.3	40
	0856	0.5	15
	1444	1.2	37
	2048	0.4	12
29 W	0333	1.4	43
	0943	0.7	21
	1457	1.2	37
	2123	0.2	6
30 Th	0443	1.4	43
	1045	0.9	27
	1509	1.1	34
	2207	0.0	0
31 F	0603	1.4	43
	1217	1.1	34
	1518	1.2	37
	2303	-0.1	-3

Time meridian 90° W. 0000 is midnight. 1200 is noon. Times are not adjusted for Daylight Saving Time.
Heights are referred to the chart datum of soundings.

Tampico Harbor (Madero), Mexico, 2017

Times and Heights of High and Low Waters

April

Day	Time	ft	cm	Day	Time	ft	cm
1 Sa	0732	1.4	43	16 Su	0801 / 2351	1.3 / 0.1	40 / 3
2 Su	0005 / 1002	-0.2 / 1.4	-6 / 43	17 M	1000	1.3	40
3 M ◐	0107 / 1116	-0.2 / 1.4	-6 / 43	18 Tu	0042 / 1049	0.2 / 1.4	6 / 43
4 Tu	0213 / 1211	-0.1 / 1.4	-3 / 43	19 W ◐	0134 / 1121	0.3 / 1.4	9 / 43
5 W	0333 / 1258	0.0 / 1.3	0 / 40	20 Th	0234 / 1145	0.4 / 1.4	12 / 43
6 Th	0451 / 1329 / 1917 / 2239	0.1 / 1.3 / 0.9 / 1.1	3 / 40 / 27 / 34	21 F	0348 / 1203 / 1926 / 2151	0.4 / 1.4 / 1.0 / 1.1	12 / 43 / 30 / 34
7 F	0602 / 1342 / 1927 / 2359	0.2 / 1.2 / 0.8 / 1.1	6 / 37 / 24 / 34	22 Sa	0459 / 1218 / 1845 / 2322	0.5 / 1.4 / 0.9 / 1.2	15 / 43 / 27 / 37
8 Sa	0707 / 1347 / 1943	0.4 / 1.1 / 0.6	12 / 34 / 18	23 Su	0607 / 1232 / 1854	0.6 / 1.3 / 0.7	18 / 40 / 21
9 Su	0117 / 0757 / 1352 / 2000	1.1 / 0.5 / 1.0 / 0.5	34 / 15 / 30 / 15	24 M	0041 / 0714 / 1246 / 1917	1.3 / 0.7 / 1.2 / 0.5	40 / 21 / 37 / 15
10 M	0223 / 0837 / 1359 / 2019	1.2 / 0.6 / 1.0 / 0.3	37 / 18 / 30 / 9	25 Tu	0159 / 0813 / 1302 / 1947	1.4 / 0.8 / 1.2 / 0.2	43 / 24 / 37 / 6
11 Tu ○	0315 / 0912 / 1408 / 2040	1.2 / 0.7 / 1.0 / 0.2	37 / 21 / 30 / 6	26 W ●	0304 / 0905 / 1318 / 2022	1.5 / 0.9 / 1.1 / -0.1	46 / 27 / 34 / -3
12 W	0403 / 0947 / 1417 / 2105	1.3 / 0.8 / 1.0 / 0.1	40 / 24 / 30 / 3	27 Th	0407 / 1004 / 1334 / 2102	1.5 / 1.0 / 1.1 / -0.3	46 / 30 / 34 / -9
13 Th	0455 / 1034 / 1423 / 2136	1.3 / 0.9 / 1.0 / 0.1	40 / 27 / 30 / 3	28 F	0517 / 1145 / 1345 / 2147	1.6 / 1.0 / 1.1 / -0.4	49 / 30 / 34 / -12
14 F	0550 / 1212 / 1420 / 2213	1.3 / 0.9 / 1.0 / 0.0	40 / 27 / 30 / 0	29 Sa	0629 / 2241	1.5 / -0.4	46 / -12
15 Sa	0648 / 2259	1.3 / 0.1	40 / 3	30 Su	0747 / 2344	1.5 / -0.3	46 / -9

May

Day	Time	ft	cm	Day	Time	ft	cm
1 M	0934	1.4	43	16 Tu	0835 / 2359	1.4 / 0.1	43 / 3
2 Tu ○	0047 / 1036	-0.2 / 1.4	-6 / 43	17 W	0936	1.4	43
3 W	0150 / 1110	0.0 / 1.3	0 / 40	18 Th ◐	0048 / 1007	0.2 / 1.4	6 / 43
4 Th	0305 / 1132 / 1757 / 2142	0.2 / 1.2 / 0.8 / 0.9	6 / 37 / 24 / 27	19 F	0139 / 1025	0.4 / 1.4	12 / 43
5 F	0429 / 1144 / 1816 / 2322	0.4 / 1.1 / 0.7 / 1.0	12 / 34 / 21 / 30	20 Sa	0248 / 1039 / 1729 / 2227	0.5 / 1.3 / 0.8 / 1.0	15 / 40 / 24 / 30
6 Sa	0546 / 1151 / 1839	0.6 / 1.0 / 0.5	18 / 30 / 15	21 Su	0419 / 1052 / 1739 / 2356	0.7 / 1.2 / 0.6 / 1.1	21 / 37 / 18 / 34
7 Su	0047 / 0702 / 1157 / 1902	1.1 / 0.7 / 1.0 / 0.4	34 / 21 / 30 / 12	22 M	0548 / 1106 / 1805	0.8 / 1.2 / 0.3	24 / 37 / 9
8 M	0204 / 0800 / 1204 / 1925	1.2 / 0.8 / 1.0 / 0.2	37 / 24 / 30 / 6	23 Tu	0125 / 0718 / 1120 / 1841	1.3 / 0.9 / 1.1 / 0.0	40 / 27 / 34 / 0
9 Tu	0258 / 0843 / 1212 / 1948	1.2 / 0.8 / 1.0 / 0.0	37 / 24 / 30 / 0	24 W	0236 / 0827 / 1135 / 1922	1.4 / 1.0 / 1.1 / -0.3	43 / 30 / 34 / -9
10 W ○	0342 / 0921 / 1217 / 2012	1.3 / 0.9 / 1.0 / -0.1	40 / 27 / 30 / -3	25 Th ●	0335 / 0926 / 1147 / 2004	1.5 / 1.0 / 1.1 / -0.5	46 / 30 / 34 / -15
11 Th	0424 / 1004 / 1208 / 2039	1.3 / 0.9 / 1.0 / -0.2	40 / 27 / 30 / -6	26 F	0434 / 2048	1.5 / -0.7	46 / -21
12 F	0510 / 2109	1.3 / -0.2	40 / -6	27 Sa	0536 / 2135	1.5 / -0.7	46 / -21
13 Sa	0556 / 2143	1.3 / -0.2	40 / -6	28 Su	0635 / 2228	1.5 / -0.6	46 / -18
14 Su	0642 / 2222	1.3 / -0.1	40 / -3	29 M	0732 / 2328	1.4 / -0.4	43 / -12
15 M	0731 / 2309	1.3 / 0.0	40 / 0	30 Tu	0834	1.3	40
				31 W	0029 / 0927	-0.2 / 1.2	-6 / 37

June

Day	Time	ft	cm	Day	Time	ft	cm
1 Th ○	0126 / 0954 / 1626 / 1936	0.1 / 1.1 / 0.7 / 0.8	3 / 34 / 21 / 24	16 F	0011 / 0824	0.2 / 1.3	6 / 40
2 F	0228 / 1007 / 1653 / 2227	0.4 / 1.0 / 0.6 / 0.8	12 / 30 / 18 / 24	17 Sa ◐	0101 / 0847 / 1555 / 2007	0.4 / 1.2 / 0.7 / 0.8	12 / 37 / 21 / 24
3 Sa	0354 / 1016 / 1722	0.6 / 1.0 / 0.4	18 / 30 / 12	18 Su	0159 / 0907 / 1615 / 2306	0.6 / 1.2 / 0.5 / 1.0	18 / 37 / 15 / 30
4 Su	0004 / 0526 / 1024 / 1752	0.9 / 0.7 / 0.9 / 0.2	27 / 21 / 27 / 6	19 M	0351 / 0927 / 1648	0.8 / 1.1 / 0.2	24 / 34 / 6
5 M	0144 / 0711 / 1032 / 1821	1.0 / 0.8 / 0.9 / 0.1	30 / 24 / 27 / 3	20 Tu	0046 / 0555 / 0946 / 1729	1.1 / 1.0 / 1.1 / -0.1	34 / 30 / 34 / -3
6 Tu	0245 / 0823 / 1039 / 1850	1.1 / 0.8 / 0.9 / -0.1	34 / 24 / 27 / -3	21 W	0211 / 0753 / 1005 / 1815	1.3 / 1.0 / 1.1 / -0.4	40 / 30 / 34 / -12
7 W	0325 / 1920	1.2 / -0.2	37 / -6	22 Th	0306 / 1904	1.4 / -0.6	43 / -18
8 Th	0401 / 1950	1.2 / -0.3	37 / -9	23 F ●	0356 / 1953	1.5 / -0.8	46 / -24
9 F ○	0437 / 2020	1.2 / -0.4	37 / -12	24 Sa	0446 / 2040	1.5 / -0.8	46 / -24
10 Sa	0513 / 2051	1.3 / -0.4	40 / -12	25 Su	0535 / 2127	1.4 / -0.7	43 / -21
11 Su	0549 / 2123	1.3 / -0.3	40 / -9	26 M	0618 / 2217	1.3 / -0.5	40 / -15
12 M	0624 / 2157	1.3 / -0.2	40 / -6	27 Tu	0653 / 1255 / 1505 / 2313	1.2 / 0.9 / 1.0 / -0.3	37 / 27 / 30 / -9
13 Tu	0656 / 2236	1.3 / -0.1	40 / -3	28 W	0722 / 1328 / 1626	1.1 / 0.8 / 0.9	34 / 24 / 27
14 W	0727 / 2322	1.3 / 0.1	40 / 3	29 Th	0009 / 0745 / 1408 / 1809	0.0 / 1.0 / 0.7 / 0.8	0 / 30 / 21 / 24
15 Th	0757	1.3	40	30 F ◐	0100 / 0802 / 1457 / 2016	0.3 / 1.0 / 0.5 / 0.7	9 / 30 / 15 / 21

Time meridian 90° W. 0000 is midnight. 1200 is noon. Times are not adjusted for Daylight Saving Time.
Heights are referred to the chart datum of soundings.

Tampico Harbor (Madero), Mexico, 2017
Times and Heights of High and Low Waters

July

Day	Time	ft	cm		Day	Time	ft	cm
1 Sa	0150	0.5	15		16 Su ☾	0041	0.6	18
	0816	0.9	27			0713	1.2	37
	1545	0.4	12			1423	0.5	15
	2259	0.8	24			2151	0.9	27
2 Su	0306	0.7	21		17 M	0140	0.8	24
	0826	0.9	27			0725	1.1	34
	1626	0.2	6			1514	0.2	6
						2354	1.1	34
3 M	0049	0.9	27		18 Tu	0419	1.0	30
	0521	0.8	24			0730	1.1	34
	0828	0.9	27			1608	0.0	0
	1703	0.0	0					
4 Tu	0222	1.1	34		19 W	0138	1.3	40
	1740	-0.1	-3			1702	-0.3	-9
5 W	0302	1.2	37		20 Th	0235	1.4	43
	1817	-0.2	-6			1758	-0.5	-15
6 Th	0333	1.2	37		21 F	0317	1.5	46
	1855	-0.3	-9			1854	-0.6	-18
7 F	0402	1.2	37		22 Sa	0357	1.5	46
	1931	-0.4	-12			1946	-0.7	-21
8 Sa ○	0429	1.2	37		23 Su ●	0434	1.4	43
	2004	-0.4	-12			0933	1.0	30
						1200	1.1	34
						2034	-0.6	-18
9 Su	0456	1.2	37		24 M	0507	1.3	40
	2036	-0.3	-9			0953	1.0	30
						1322	1.1	34
						2120	-0.4	-12
10 M	0522	1.3	40		25 Tu	0533	1.2	37
	2107	-0.2	-6			1024	0.9	27
						1436	1.1	34
						2206	-0.2	-6
11 Tu	0546	1.3	40		26 W	0553	1.1	34
	2139	-0.1	-3			1113	0.8	24
						1543	1.0	30
						2256	0.0	0
12 W	0607	1.3	40		27 Th	0610	1.0	30
	2214	0.0	0			1206	0.7	21
						1701	1.0	30
						2350	0.3	9
13 Th	0626	1.3	40		28 F	0624	1.0	30
	1257	0.9	27			1251	0.5	15
	1500	1.0	30			1830	0.9	27
	2257	0.2	6					
14 F	0644	1.3	40		29 Sa	0041	0.6	18
	1315	0.8	24			0635	1.0	30
	1631	0.9	27			1334	0.4	12
	2348	0.4	12			2036	0.9	27
15 Sa	0659	1.2	37		30 Su ☾	0127	0.8	24
	1343	0.7	21			0642	1.0	30
	1831	0.9	27			1421	0.3	9
						2312	1.0	30
					31 M	0246	0.9	27
						0635	1.0	30
						1516	0.2	6

August

Day	Time	ft	cm		Day	Time	ft	cm
1 Tu	0056	1.1	34		16 W	0017	1.4	43
	1610	0.1	3			1537	0.0	0
2 W	0213	1.2	37		17 Th	0138	1.5	46
	1658	0.0	0			1643	-0.2	-6
3 Th	0247	1.3	40		18 F	0227	1.6	49
	1744	-0.1	-3			1746	-0.3	-9
4 F	0313	1.3	40		19 Sa	0302	1.5	46
	1829	-0.1	-3			1848	-0.3	-9
5 Sa	0335	1.3	40		20 Su	0330	1.5	46
	1911	-0.1	-3			0831	1.2	37
						1132	1.3	40
						1943	-0.2	-6
6 Su	0354	1.3	40		21 M ●	0351	1.3	40
	0905	1.0	30			0843	1.1	34
	1107	1.1	34			1248	1.3	40
	1948	-0.1	-3			2030	-0.1	-3
7 M ○	0411	1.3	40		22 Tu	0407	1.2	37
	0909	1.1	34			0901	0.9	27
	1155	1.2	37			1402	1.3	40
	2021	0.0	0			2113	0.1	3
8 Tu	0427	1.3	40		23 W	0420	1.2	37
	0921	1.1	34			0924	0.8	24
	1255	1.2	37			1506	1.3	40
	2053	0.1	3			2155	0.3	9
9 W	0442	1.3	40		24 Th	0432	1.1	34
	0942	1.0	30			0955	0.7	21
	1401	1.2	37			1610	1.2	37
	2126	0.2	6			2242	0.5	15
10 Th	0458	1.3	40		25 F	0445	1.1	34
	1014	1.0	30			1038	0.6	18
	1502	1.2	37			1721	1.2	37
	2202	0.4	12			2340	0.7	21
11 F	0513	1.3	40		26 Sa	0457	1.1	34
	1059	0.9	27			1132	0.5	15
	1610	1.2	37			1839	1.2	37
	2247	0.6	18					
12 Sa	0528	1.3	40		27 Su	0040	0.9	27
	1150	0.7	21			0505	1.1	34
	1739	1.2	37			1224	0.4	12
	2349	0.8	24			2032	1.2	37
13 Su	0541	1.2	37		28 M	0143	1.0	30
	1239	0.5	15			0456	1.1	34
	1926	1.2	37			1312	0.4	12
						2255	1.3	40
14 M ☾	0056	1.0	30		29 Tu ☾	1405	0.3	9
	0551	1.2	37					
	1329	0.3	9					
	2248	1.3	40					
15 Tu	0242	1.1	34		30 W	0001	1.3	40
	0548	1.2	37			1507	0.3	9
	1428	0.1	3					
					31 Th	0107	1.4	43
						1612	0.3	9

September

Day	Time	ft	cm		Day	Time	ft	cm
1 F	0155	1.4	43		16 Sa	0146	1.6	49
	1708	0.3	9			1737	0.1	3
2 Sa	0222	1.5	46		17 Su	0215	1.5	46
	1759	0.3	9			0735	1.2	37
						1100	1.4	43
						1843	0.2	6
3 Su	0241	1.5	46		18 M	0231	1.4	43
	0818	1.2	37			0746	1.1	34
	1049	1.3	40			1215	1.4	43
	1847	0.3	9			1940	0.3	9
4 M	0254	1.5	46		19 Tu ●	0240	1.3	40
	0813	1.2	37			0804	0.9	27
	1142	1.3	40			1330	1.4	43
	1929	0.3	9			2027	0.5	15
5 Tu	0304	1.5	46		20 W	0248	1.2	37
	0820	1.1	34			0824	0.8	24
	1242	1.4	43			1436	1.5	46
	2007	0.4	12			2108	0.6	18
6 W ○	0314	1.5	46		21 Th	0257	1.2	37
	0835	1.1	34			0847	0.6	18
	1346	1.4	43			1533	1.5	46
	2043	0.5	15			2149	0.8	24
7 Th	0325	1.4	43		22 F	0307	1.2	37
	0856	0.9	27			0914	0.5	15
	1445	1.5	46			1631	1.5	46
	2120	0.7	21			2239	1.0	30
8 F	0338	1.4	43		23 Sa	0316	1.2	37
	0924	0.8	24			0946	0.4	12
	1546	1.5	46			1735	1.4	43
	2203	0.9	27					
9 Sa	0350	1.4	43		24 Su	0001	1.1	34
	1002	0.6	18			0319	1.2	37
	1659	1.5	46			1027	0.4	12
	2307	1.1	34			1842	1.4	43
10 Su	0401	1.3	40		25 M	1119	0.4	12
	1053	0.5	15			2008	1.4	43
	1826	1.5	46					
11 M	0036	1.2	37		26 Tu	1214	0.4	12
	0407	1.3	40			2215	1.5	46
	1153	0.3	9					
	2027	1.5	46					
12 Tu	1254	0.2	6		27 W ☾	1308	0.4	12
	2253	1.6	49			2307	1.5	46
13 W ☾	1357	0.1	3		28 Th	1406	0.5	15
	2357	1.7	52			2346	1.6	49
14 Th	1511	0.1	3		29 F	1515	0.5	15
15 F	0058	1.7	52		30 Sa	0021	1.6	49
	1628	0.1	3			1622	0.6	18

Time meridian 90° W. 0000 is midnight. 1200 is noon. Times are not adjusted for Daylight Saving Time.
Heights are referred to the chart datum of soundings.

Tampico Harbor (Madero), Mexico, 2017

Times and Heights of High and Low Waters

October

Day	Time	ft	cm	Day	Time	ft	cm
1 Su	0050	1.6	49	**16** M	0041	1.4	43
	0749	1.2	37		0645	1.0	30
	1004	1.3	40		1143	1.4	43
	1721	0.6	18		1838	0.6	18
2 M	0110	1.6	49	**17** Tu	0053	1.3	40
	0719	1.2	37		0707	0.8	24
	1111	1.4	43		1302	1.4	43
	1816	0.7	21		1940	0.8	24
3 Tu	0125	1.5	46	**18** W	0102	1.2	37
	0721	1.1	34		0731	0.6	18
	1212	1.4	43		1413	1.5	46
	1909	0.7	21		2029	0.9	27
4 W	0138	1.5	46	**19** Th	0112	1.2	37
	0734	1.0	30		0754	0.5	15
	1319	1.5	46		1508	1.5	46
	1956	0.8	24		2112 ●	1.0	30
5 Th ○	0150	1.5	46	**20** F	0122	1.2	37
	0755	0.8	24		0818	0.3	9
	1423	1.6	49		1559	1.5	46
	2040	0.9	27		2157	1.1	34
6 F	0203	1.4	43	**21** Sa	0128	1.2	37
	0822	0.6	18		0844	0.2	6
	1521	1.7	52		1651	1.5	46
	2126	1.1	34				
7 Sa	0215	1.4	43	**22** Su	0913	0.2	6
	0854	0.4	12		1745	1.5	46
	1625	1.7	52				
	2227	1.2	37				
8 Su	0226	1.4	43	**23** M	0948	0.2	6
	0933	0.2	6		1840	1.5	46
	1740	1.7	52				
9 M	0022	1.3	40	**24** Tu	1031	0.2	6
	0228	1.4	43		1940	1.5	46
	1022	0.1	3				
	1900	1.7	52				
10 Tu	1123	0.1	3	**25** W	1124	0.3	9
	2056	1.7	52		2108	1.5	46
11 W	1229	0.1	3	**26** Th	1220	0.4	12
	2231	1.7	52		2209	1.6	49
12 Th ☽	1335	0.1	3	**27** F ●	1313	0.5	15
	2319	1.7	52		2241	1.6	49
13 F	1449	0.3	9	**28** Sa	1410	0.6	18
	2356	1.6	49		2304	1.6	49
14 Sa	1612	0.4	12	**29** Su	1521	0.7	21
					2321	1.6	49
15 Su	0024	1.5	46	**30** M	0625	1.1	34
	0629	1.2	37		1021	1.2	37
	1021	1.3	40		1634	0.8	24
	1727	0.5	15		2335	1.5	46
				31 Tu	0616	1.0	30
					1133	1.3	40
					1741	0.9	27
					2348	1.5	46

November

Day	Time	ft	cm	Day	Time	ft	cm
1 W	0629	0.8	24	**16** Th	0700	0.2	6
	1244	1.4	43		1455	1.4	43
	1852	1.0	30		2047	1.0	30
					2328	1.1	34
2 Th	0001	1.4	43	**17** F	0727	0.1	3
	0652	0.6	18		1541	1.4	43
	1356	1.5	46				
	1956	1.1	34				
3 F ○	0014	1.3	40	**18** Sa ●	0754	-0.1	-3
	0722	0.3	9		1623	1.4	43
	1456	1.6	49				
	2051	1.1	34				
4 Sa	0026	1.3	40	**19** Su	0822	-0.1	-3
	0756	0.1	3		1706	1.4	43
	1554	1.7	52				
	2151	1.2	37				
5 Su	0033	1.3	40	**20** M	0851	-0.2	-6
	0834	-0.1	-3		1748	1.4	43
	1658	1.8	55				
6 M	0916	-0.2	-6	**21** Tu	0924	-0.1	-3
	1806	1.8	55		1830	1.4	43
7 Tu	1006	-0.3	-9	**22** W	1001	-0.1	-3
	1913	1.7	52		1911	1.4	43
8 W	1106	-0.2	-6	**23** Th	1045	0.1	3
	2033	1.7	52		1955	1.4	43
9 Th	1212	-0.1	-3	**24** F	1136	0.2	6
	2148	1.6	49		2042	1.5	46
10 F ☽	1316	0.1	3	**25** Sa	1226	0.4	12
	2227	1.5	46		2120	1.4	43
11 Sa	1424	0.3	9	**26** Su ◐	1313	0.5	15
	2248	1.4	43		2144	1.4	43
12 Su	0516	1.0	30	**27** M	1408	0.7	21
	0911	1.1	34		2201	1.4	43
	1549	0.6	18				
	2301	1.3	40				
13 M	0537	0.8	24	**28** Tu	0507	0.8	24
	1106	1.1	34		1042	1.0	30
	1712	0.7	21		1535	0.8	24
	2310	1.2	37		2215	1.3	40
14 Tu	0604	0.6	18	**29** W	0517	0.6	18
	1233	1.2	37		1203	1.2	37
	1836	0.9	27		1712	1.0	30
	2318	1.1	34		2228	1.3	40
15 W	0632	0.4	12	**30** Th	0542	0.3	9
	1357	1.3	40		1329	1.3	40
	1952	1.0	30		1854	1.1	34
	2324	1.1	34		2241	1.2	37

December

Day	Time	ft	cm	Day	Time	ft	cm
1 F	0615	0.1	3	**16** Sa	0703	-0.3	-9
	1434	1.5	46		1603	1.3	40
	2018	1.1	34				
	2252	1.2	37				
2 Sa	0655	-0.2	-6	**17** Su	0734	-0.4	-12
	1526	1.6	49		1635	1.3	40
3 Su ○	0738	-0.5	-15	**18** M ●	0805	-0.4	-12
	1619	1.6	49		1706	1.3	40
4 M	0821	-0.6	-18	**19** Tu	0836	-0.4	-12
	1716	1.6	49		1737	1.3	40
5 Tu	0907	-0.7	-21	**20** W	0908	-0.3	-9
	1810	1.6	49		1806	1.3	40
6 W	0957	-0.6	-18	**21** Th	0941	-0.2	-6
	1900	1.5	46		1833	1.3	40
7 Th	1055	-0.4	-12	**22** F	1017	-0.1	-3
	1946	1.4	43		1859	1.3	40
8 F	1158	-0.2	-6	**23** Sa	1058	0.1	3
	2028	1.3	40		1922	1.3	40
9 Sa	1257	0.1	3	**24** Su	1144	0.3	9
	2100	1.2	37		1942	1.3	40
10 Su ☽	0340	0.7	21	**25** M	1228	0.5	15
	0712	0.8	24		2001	1.2	37
	1356	0.4	12				
	2119	1.1	34				
11 M	0415	0.5	15	**26** Tu ◐	0327	0.6	18
	1005	0.9	27		0756	0.8	24
	1513	0.6	18		1313	0.6	18
	2133	1.0	30		2018	1.2	37
12 Tu	0450	0.3	9	**27** W	0350	0.4	12
	1151	1.0	30		1116	0.9	27
	1656	0.8	24		1418	0.8	24
	2143	1.0	30		2033	1.1	34
13 W	0524	0.2	6	**28** Th	0423	0.2	6
	1341	1.1	34		1303	1.1	34
	1903	0.9	27		1711	1.0	30
	2151	1.0	30		2045	1.1	34
14 Th	0558	0.0	0	**29** F	0502	-0.1	-3
	1447	1.2	37		1417	1.2	37
15 F	0630	-0.2	-6	**30** Sa	0547	-0.4	-12
	1528	1.2	37		1502	1.4	43
				31 Su	0636	-0.6	-18
					1544	1.5	46

Time meridian 90° W. 0000 is midnight. 1200 is noon. Times are not adjusted for Daylight Saving Time.
Heights are referred to the chart datum of soundings.

Cristobal (Colon), Panama, 2017

Times and Heights of High and Low Waters

January

Day	Time (h m)	Height (ft)	Height (cm)		Day	Time (h m)	Height (ft)	Height (cm)
1 Su	1422	1.0	30		**16** M	0514	0.6	18
	2243	-0.2	-6			0950	0.3	9
						1548	0.9	27
						2301	-0.3	-9
2 M	1507	1.0	30		**17** Tu	0555	0.7	21
	2302	-0.2	-6			1113	0.3	9
						1641	0.7	21
						2334	-0.2	-6
3 Tu	0609	0.6	18		**18** W	0632	0.8	24
	0958	0.4	12			1227	0.2	6
	1555	0.9	27			1733	0.6	18
	2321	-0.2	-6					
4 W	0623	0.7	21		**19** Th ☽	0003	-0.2	-6
	1129	0.4	12			0707	0.9	27
	1646	0.7	21			1333	0.2	6
	2344	-0.2	-6			1823	0.5	15
5 Th ◑	0649	0.9	27		**20** F	0028	-0.1	-3
	1248	0.3	9			0741	1.0	30
	1740	0.6	18			1434	0.1	3
						1913	0.4	12
6 F	0010	-0.2	-6		**21** Sa	0050	-0.1	-3
	0723	1.0	30			0813	1.0	30
	1401	0.2	6			1532	0.1	3
	1838	0.5	15			2003	0.3	9
7 Sa	0040	-0.2	-6		**22** Su	0110	0.0	0
	0802	1.2	37			0845	1.1	34
	1509	0.1	3			1628	0.0	0
	1940	0.3	9			2055	0.2	6
8 Su	0113	-0.2	-6		**23** M	0126	0.0	0
	0845	1.3	40			0918	1.1	34
	1615	-0.1	-3			1724	0.0	0
	2048	0.2	6			2154	0.1	3
9 M	0150	-0.2	-6		**24** Tu	0138	0.0	0
	0931	1.4	43			0952	1.1	34
	1718	-0.1	-3			1819	-0.1	-3
	2203	0.2	6			2308	0.1	3
10 Tu	0231	-0.1	-3		**25** W	0142	0.0	0
	1021	1.4	43			1027	1.1	34
	1819	-0.2	-6			1912	-0.1	-3
	2326	0.1	3					
11 W	0318	0.0	0		**26** Th	1105	1.1	34
	1112	1.4	43			1958	-0.1	-3
	1917	-0.3	-9					
12 Th ○	0055	0.2	6		**27** F ●	1145	1.1	34
	0412	0.1	3			2035	-0.2	-6
	1206	1.4	43					
	2011	-0.3	-9					
13 F	0220	0.2	6		**28** Sa	1228	1.0	30
	0521	0.1	3			2105	-0.2	-6
	1301	1.3	40					
	2100	-0.3	-9					
14 Sa	0331	0.3	9		**29** Su	1315	0.9	27
	0646	0.2	6			2129	-0.2	-6
	1357	1.2	37					
	2145	-0.3	-9					
15 Su	0427	0.5	15		**30** M	0431	0.3	9
	0820	0.3	9			0650	0.2	6
	1453	1.0	30			1406	0.9	27
	2225	-0.3	-9			2151	-0.2	-6
					31 Tu	0439	0.5	15
						0854	0.3	9
						1500	0.7	21
						2214	-0.2	-6

February

Day	Time (h m)	Height (ft)	Height (cm)		Day	Time (h m)	Height (ft)	Height (cm)
1 W	0503	0.6	18		**16** Th	0544	0.8	24
	1028	0.2	6			1216	0.1	3
	1556	0.6	18			1734	0.4	12
	2239	-0.2	-6			2321	-0.1	-3
2 Th	0535	0.8	24		**17** F	0618	0.8	24
	1146	0.1	3			1309	0.0	0
	1654	0.5	15			1822	0.4	12
	2308	-0.2	-6			2347	0.0	0
3 F ◐	0612	1.0	30		**18** Sa ○	0650	0.9	27
	1254	0.0	0			1357	0.0	0
	1753	0.4	12			1907	0.3	9
	2341	-0.2	-6					
4 Sa	0653	1.1	34		**19** Su	0011	0.0	0
	1356	-0.1	-3			0723	0.9	27
	1852	0.3	9			1443	-0.1	-3
						1949	0.2	6
5 Su	0017	-0.2	-6		**20** M	0035	0.0	0
	0736	1.2	37			0756	1.0	30
	1455	-0.1	-3			1529	-0.1	-3
	1951	0.3	9			2031	0.2	6
6 M	0057	-0.2	-6		**21** Tu	0059	0.0	0
	0822	1.3	40			0831	1.0	30
	1552	-0.2	-6			1615	-0.1	-3
	2052	0.2	6			2114	0.2	6
7 Tu	0140	-0.2	-6		**22** W	0124	0.0	0
	0911	1.3	40			0907	1.0	30
	1650	-0.2	-6			1701	-0.1	-3
	2157	0.2	6			2202	0.1	3
8 W	0227	-0.1	-3		**23** Th	0152	0.0	0
	1001	1.3	40			0945	1.0	30
	1747	-0.3	-9			1747	-0.1	-3
	2308	0.2	6			2255	0.1	3
9 Th	0319	0.0	0		**24** F	0228	0.0	0
	1054	1.2	37			1026	0.9	27
	1842	-0.3	-9			1830	-0.1	-3
						2355	0.2	6
10 F ○	0023	0.2	6		**25** Sa	0319	0.1	3
	0420	0.0	0			1112	0.9	27
	1149	1.1	34			1908	-0.1	-3
	1935	-0.2	-6					
11 Sa	0138	0.3	9		**26** Su ●	0055	0.2	6
	0535	0.1	3			0435	0.1	3
	1246	1.0	30			1203	0.8	24
	2025	-0.2	-6			1942	-0.1	-3
12 Su	0245	0.4	12		**27** M	0149	0.3	9
	0704	0.2	6			0615	0.2	6
	1345	0.9	27			1301	0.7	21
	2109	-0.2	-6			2013	-0.1	-3
13 M	0341	0.5	15		**28** Tu	0236	0.5	15
	0837	0.2	6			0758	0.1	3
	1446	0.7	21			1405	0.6	18
	2148	-0.2	-6			2045	-0.1	-3
14 Tu	0428	0.6	18					
	1002	0.2	6					
	1545	0.6	18					
	2223	-0.1	-3					
15 W	0508	0.7	21					
	1115	0.1	3					
	1641	0.5	15					
	2254	-0.1	-3					

March

Day	Time (h m)	Height (ft)	Height (cm)		Day	Time (h m)	Height (ft)	Height (cm)
1 W	0320	0.6	18		**16** Th	0408	0.7	21
	0928	0.1	3			1110	-0.1	-3
	1511	0.5	15			1702	0.4	12
	2119	-0.1	-3			2201	0.1	3
2 Th	0404	0.8	24		**17** F	0444	0.8	24
	1042	0.0	0			1156	-0.1	-3
	1615	0.4	12			1750	0.3	9
	2156	-0.1	-3			2231	0.1	3
3 F	0449	0.9	27		**18** Sa	0518	0.8	24
	1146	-0.1	-3			1237	-0.1	-3
	1716	0.4	12			1831	0.3	9
	2236	-0.1	-3			2300	0.1	3
4 Sa	0534	1.1	34		**19** Su	0552	0.9	27
	1243	-0.2	-6			1316	-0.2	-6
	1813	0.3	9			1907	0.3	9
	2319	-0.1	-3			2330	0.1	3
5 Su ◐	0621	1.2	37		**20** M	0627	0.9	27
	1336	-0.3	-9			1353	-0.2	-6
	1908	0.3	9			1941	0.3	9
6 M	0004	-0.1	-3		**21** Tu	0000	0.1	3
	0709	1.2	37			0702	0.9	27
	1428	-0.3	-9			1429	-0.2	-6
	2001	0.3	9			2014	0.3	9
7 Tu	0052	-0.1	-3		**22** W	0034	0.1	3
	0758	1.2	37			0739	0.9	27
	1520	-0.3	-9			1506	-0.2	-6
	2055	0.3	9			2048	0.3	9
8 W	0142	-0.1	-3		**23** Th	0113	0.1	3
	0849	1.1	34			0817	0.9	27
	1611	-0.3	-9			1542	-0.1	-3
	2151	0.3	9			2125	0.3	9
9 Th	0237	0.0	0		**24** F	0159	0.1	3
	0941	1.1	34			0859	0.8	24
	1703	-0.2	-6			1618	-0.1	-3
	2250	0.3	9			2206	0.3	9
10 F	0338	0.0	0		**25** Sa	0256	0.1	3
	1036	0.9	27			0945	0.8	24
	1754	-0.2	-6			1653	-0.1	-3
	2352	0.4	12			2252	0.4	12
11 Sa	0449	0.1	3		**26** Su	0407	0.1	3
	1134	0.8	24			1038	0.7	21
	1844	-0.1	-3			1728	0.0	0
						2343	0.5	15
12 Su ○	0054	0.4	12		**27** M ●	0533	0.1	3
	0612	0.1	3			1142	0.6	18
	1239	0.7	21			1805	0.0	0
	1931	-0.1	-3					
13 M	0152	0.5	15		**28** Tu	0036	0.6	18
	0741	0.1	3			0704	0.0	0
	1348	0.6	18			1256	0.5	15
	2015	0.0	0			1846	0.0	0
14 Tu	0244	0.6	18		**29** W	0130	0.7	21
	0904	0.1	3			0828	-0.1	-3
	1459	0.5	15			1415	0.4	12
	2054	0.0	0			1931	0.0	0
15 W	0328	0.6	18		**30** Th	0224	0.9	27
	1013	0.0	0			0938	-0.2	-6
	1605	0.4	12			1529	0.3	9
	2129	0.1	3			2020	0.0	0
					31 F	0316	1.0	30
						1039	-0.3	-9
						1635	0.3	9
						2113	0.0	0

Time meridian 75° W. 0000 is midnight. 1200 is noon. Times are not adjusted for Daylight Saving Time.
Heights are referred to the chart datum of soundings.

Cristobal (Colon), Panama, 2017

Times and Heights of High and Low Waters

April

Day	Time	ft	cm
1 Sa	0408	1.1	34
	1133	-0.4	-12
	1733	0.3	9
	2207	0.0	0
2 Su	0459	1.1	34
	1223	-0.4	-12
	1826	0.4	12
	2302	0.0	0
3 M	0550	1.2	37
	1311	-0.4	-12
	1916	0.4	12
	2357	0.0	0
4 Tu	0641	1.1	34
	1358	-0.4	-12
	2004	0.4	12
5 W	0055	0.0	0
	0732	1.1	34
	1443	-0.4	-12
	2053	0.5	15
6 Th	0155	0.0	0
	0825	0.9	27
	1528	-0.3	-9
	2142	0.5	15
7 F	0259	0.0	0
	0919	0.8	24
	1611	-0.2	-6
	2233	0.5	15
8 Sa	0411	0.1	3
	1017	0.6	18
	1653	-0.1	-3
	2323	0.6	18
9 Su	0532	0.1	3
	1124	0.5	15
	1733	0.0	0
10 M	0012	0.6	18
	0657	0.0	0
	1244	0.4	12
	1811	0.1	3
11 Tu	0100	0.7	21
	0817	0.0	0
	1416	0.3	9
	1847	0.2	6
12 W	0144	0.7	21
	0923	-0.1	-3
	1545	0.3	9
	1922	0.2	6
13 Th	0225	0.8	24
	1015	-0.2	-6
	1658	0.3	9
	1958	0.2	6
14 F	0303	0.8	24
	1057	-0.2	-6
	1749	0.3	9
	2036	0.2	6
15 Sa	0340	0.8	24
	1133	-0.2	-6
	1825	0.3	9
	2116	0.2	6
16 Su	0416	0.9	27
	1206	-0.3	-9
	1851	0.3	9
	2157	0.2	6
17 M	0452	0.9	27
	1238	-0.3	-9
	1914	0.3	9
	2239	0.2	6
18 Tu	0529	0.9	27
	1307	-0.3	-9
	1936	0.3	9
	2324	0.2	6
19 W	0606	0.9	27
	1337	-0.2	-6
	2000	0.4	12
20 Th	0013	0.2	6
	0645	0.8	24
	1405	-0.2	-6
	2027	0.4	12
21 F	0108	0.2	6
	0727	0.8	24
	1433	-0.2	-6
	2058	0.5	15
22 Sa	0210	0.1	3
	0812	0.7	21
	1501	-0.1	-3
	2135	0.6	18
23 Su	0322	0.1	3
	0904	0.6	18
	1530	-0.1	-3
	2217	0.7	21
24 M	0443	0.1	3
	1007	0.4	12
	1603	-0.1	-3
	2304	0.8	24
25 Tu	0606	0.0	0
	1124	0.3	9
	1640	0.0	0
	2355	0.9	27
26 W	0725	-0.1	-3
	1255	0.2	6
	1725	0.0	0
27 Th	0048	1.1	34
	0833	-0.3	-9
	1425	0.2	6
	1820	0.1	3
28 F	0143	1.1	34
	0932	-0.4	-12
	1542	0.2	6
	1924	0.1	3
29 Sa	0239	1.2	37
	1025	-0.5	-15
	1645	0.3	9
	2032	0.1	3
30 Su	0334	1.2	37
	1114	-0.5	-15
	1739	0.4	12
	2141	0.1	3

May

Day	Time	ft	cm
1 M	0428	1.2	37
	1200	-0.5	-15
	1827	0.4	12
	2249	0.1	3
2 Tu	0521	1.1	34
	1244	-0.5	-15
	1914	0.5	15
	2356	0.1	3
3 W	0613	1.0	30
	1326	-0.5	-15
	1959	0.6	18
4 Th	0103	0.1	3
	0706	0.9	27
	1406	-0.4	-12
	2044	0.7	21
5 F	0213	0.1	3
	0759	0.7	21
	1443	-0.3	-9
	2128	0.7	21
6 Sa	0327	0.1	3
	0855	0.6	18
	1517	-0.2	-6
	2212	0.8	24
7 Su	0446	0.1	3
	0959	0.4	12
	1546	0.0	0
	2254	0.8	24
8 M	0609	0.0	0
	1119	0.3	9
	1609	0.1	3
	2334	0.9	27
9 Tu	0726	-0.1	-3
	1307	0.2	6
	1620	0.1	3
10 W	0013	0.9	27
	0832	-0.1	-3
11 Th	0051	0.9	27
	0923	-0.2	-6
12 F	0128	0.9	27
	1005	-0.3	-9
13 Sa	0205	0.9	27
	1040	-0.3	-9
14 Su	0242	0.9	27
	1111	-0.3	-9
15 M	0319	0.9	27
	1138	-0.3	-9
16 Tu	0357	0.9	27
	1204	-0.3	-9
	1925	0.4	12
	2141	0.3	9
17 W	0436	0.9	27
	1227	-0.3	-9
	1928	0.4	12
	2254	0.3	9
18 Th	0515	0.8	24
	1250	-0.3	-9
	1942	0.5	15
19 F	0004	0.3	9
	0557	0.8	24
	1312	-0.3	-9
	2004	0.6	18
20 Sa	0115	0.2	6
	0642	0.7	21
	1335	-0.2	-6
	2033	0.7	21
21 Su	0229	0.2	6
	0732	0.5	15
	1400	-0.2	-6
	2109	0.9	27
22 M	0346	0.1	3
	0831	0.4	12
	1429	-0.2	-6
	2150	1.0	30
23 Tu	0504	0.0	0
	0942	0.3	9
	1501	-0.1	-3
	2236	1.1	34
24 W	0618	-0.1	-3
	1109	0.2	6
	1539	-0.1	-3
	2326	1.2	37
25 Th	0725	-0.3	-9
	1248	0.1	3
	1625	0.0	0
26 F	0019	1.3	40
	0824	-0.4	-12
	1422	0.1	3
	1724	0.0	0
27 Sa	0114	1.3	40
	0917	-0.5	-15
	1540	0.2	6
	1838	0.1	3
28 Su	0210	1.3	40
	1006	-0.5	-15
	1640	0.3	9
	2000	0.2	6
29 M	0306	1.3	40
	1052	-0.6	-18
	1731	0.4	12
	2123	0.2	6
30 Tu	0401	1.2	37
	1135	-0.5	-15
	1818	0.5	15
	2242	0.2	6
31 W	0455	1.1	34
	1215	-0.5	-15
	1902	0.6	18
	2358	0.2	6

June

Day	Time	ft	cm
1 Th	0548	0.9	27
	1253	-0.4	-12
	1945	0.8	24
2 F	0114	0.2	6
	0641	0.7	21
	1328	-0.3	-9
	2026	0.8	24
3 Sa	0229	0.2	6
	0735	0.6	18
	1359	-0.2	-6
	2106	0.9	27
4 Su	0346	0.1	3
	0833	0.4	12
	1425	-0.1	-3
	2145	1.0	30
5 M	0503	0.0	0
	0939	0.2	6
	1444	0.0	0
	2222	1.0	30
6 Tu	0618	0.0	0
	1106	0.1	3
	1451	0.0	0
	2258	1.0	30
7 W	0725	-0.1	-3
	2333	1.0	30
8 Th	0822	-0.2	-6
9 F	0007	1.0	30
	0908	-0.2	-6
10 Sa	0043	1.0	30
	0946	-0.3	-9
11 Su	0119	1.0	30
	1019	-0.3	-9
12 M	0156	1.0	30
	1046	-0.3	-9
13 Tu	0235	1.0	30
	1109	-0.3	-9
14 W	0314	0.9	27
	1129	-0.3	-9
15 Th	0355	0.9	27
	1148	-0.3	-9
	1900	0.5	15
	2250	0.4	12
16 F	0438	0.8	24
	1206	-0.3	-9
	1912	0.6	18
17 Sa	0013	0.3	9
	0524	0.7	21
	1226	-0.3	-9
	1935	0.8	24
18 Su	0129	0.3	9
	0614	0.5	15
	1249	-0.2	-6
	2006	0.9	27
19 M	0243	0.1	3
	0710	0.4	12
	1316	-0.2	-6
	2043	1.1	34
20 Tu	0355	0.0	0
	0814	0.3	9
	1347	-0.2	-6
	2125	1.2	37
21 W	0504	-0.1	-3
	0928	0.2	6
	1423	-0.2	-6
	2212	1.3	40
22 Th	0608	-0.2	-6
	1053	0.1	3
	1504	-0.1	-3
	2302	1.4	43
23 F	0708	-0.3	-9
	1227	0.1	3
	1553	0.0	0
	2355	1.4	43
24 Sa	0804	-0.4	-12
	1359	0.1	3
	1655	0.0	0
25 Su	0050	1.4	43
	0855	-0.5	-15
	1517	0.2	6
	1814	0.1	3
26 M	0147	1.3	40
	0942	-0.5	-15
	1618	0.3	9
	1945	0.2	6
27 Tu	0243	1.2	37
	1026	-0.5	-15
	1710	0.5	15
	2116	0.3	9
28 W	0340	1.1	34
	1107	-0.5	-15
	1756	0.6	18
	2242	0.3	9
29 Th	0435	0.9	27
	1145	-0.4	-12
	1839	0.8	24
30 F	0003	0.2	6
	0529	0.8	24
	1220	-0.3	-9
	1920	0.9	27

Time meridian 75° W. 0000 is midnight. 1200 is noon. Times are not adjusted for Daylight Saving Time.
Heights are referred to the chart datum of soundings.

Cristobal (Colon), Panama, 2017

Times and Heights of High and Low Waters

July

Day	Time	ft	cm	Day	Time	ft	cm
1 Sa	0119	0.2	6	16 Su	0028	0.3	9
	0623	0.6	18		0516	0.5	15
	1251	-0.3	-9		1146	-0.2	-6
	1958	1.0	30	◐	1900	1.0	30
2 Su	0231	0.1	3	17 M	0137	0.2	6
	0718	0.4	12		0611	0.4	12
	1318	-0.2	-6		1214	-0.2	-6
	2036	1.0	30		1936	1.1	34
3 M	0341	0.1	3	18 Tu	0241	0.0	0
	0814	0.3	9		0710	0.3	9
	1341	-0.1	-3		1246	-0.2	-6
	2111	1.1	34		2017	1.3	40
4 Tu	0448	0.0	0	19 W	0343	-0.1	-3
	0917	0.2	6		0813	0.2	6
	1357	0.0	0		1322	-0.2	-6
	2146	1.1	34		2102	1.4	43
5 W	0552	-0.1	-3	20 Th	0443	-0.1	-3
	1031	0.1	3		0922	0.2	6
	1403	0.0	0		1404	-0.2	-6
	2220	1.1	34		2150	1.4	43
6 Th	0653	-0.1	-3	21 F	0542	-0.2	-6
	2255	1.1	34		1037	0.1	3
					1451	-0.1	-3
					2241	1.4	43
7 F	0748	-0.2	-6	22 Sa	0640	-0.3	-9
	2330	1.1	34		1159	0.1	3
					1546	0.0	0
					2335	1.4	43
8 Sa	0836	-0.2	-6	23 Su	0734	-0.3	-9
O					1322	0.2	6
				●	1653	0.1	3
9 Su	0006	1.1	34	24 M	0031	1.3	40
	0915	-0.2	-6		0825	-0.3	-9
					1438	0.3	9
					1816	0.2	6
10 M	0044	1.0	30	25 Tu	0129	1.2	37
	0946	-0.2	-6		0912	-0.3	-9
					1542	0.4	12
					1950	0.2	6
11 Tu	0123	1.0	30	26 W	0228	1.0	30
	1011	-0.2	-6		0955	-0.3	-9
					1635	0.6	18
					2123	0.3	9
12 W	0204	0.9	27	27 Th	0327	0.9	27
	1031	-0.2	-6		1035	-0.3	-9
					1721	0.7	21
					2248	0.2	6
13 Th	0248	0.9	27	28 F	0426	0.8	24
	1048	-0.2	-6		1111	-0.2	-6
	1803	0.5	15		1803	0.8	24
	2136	0.4	12				
14 F	0334	0.8	24	29 Sa	0004	0.2	6
	1105	-0.2	-6		0522	0.6	18
	1809	0.6	18		1144	-0.2	-6
	2310	0.3	9		1843	0.9	27
15 Sa	0423	0.7	21	30 Su	0111	0.1	3
	1124	-0.2	-6		0617	0.5	15
	1830	0.8	24		1214	-0.1	-3
				◐	1920	1.0	30
				31 M	0212	0.1	3
					0709	0.4	12
					1241	-0.1	-3
					1955	1.1	34

August

Day	Time	ft	cm	Day	Time	ft	cm
1 Tu	0309	0.0	0	16 W	0223	-0.1	-3
	0800	0.3	9		0723	0.3	9
	1305	0.0	0		1228	-0.1	-3
	2030	1.1	34		1951	1.3	40
2 W	0404	0.0	0	17 Th	0317	-0.1	-3
	0852	0.2	6		0820	0.3	9
	1325	0.0	0		1312	-0.1	-3
	2104	1.1	34		2039	1.4	43
3 Th	0458	0.0	0	18 F	0411	-0.2	-6
	0947	0.2	6		0919	0.3	9
	1341	0.1	3		1401	-0.1	-3
	2139	1.1	34		2129	1.4	43
4 F	0552	0.0	0	19 Sa	0505	-0.2	-6
	1051	0.1	3		1023	0.3	9
	1351	0.0	0		1455	0.0	0
	2215	1.1	34		2222	1.3	40
5 Sa	0646	-0.1	-3	20 Su	0559	-0.2	-6
	2252	1.1	34		1132	0.3	9
					1558	0.1	3
					2318	1.2	37
6 Su	0735	-0.1	-3	21 M	0653	-0.1	-3
	2331	1.0	30		1244	0.4	12
					1713	0.2	6
				●			
7 M	0816	-0.1	-3	22 Tu	0017	1.1	34
O					0743	-0.1	-3
					1353	0.5	15
					1840	0.2	6
8 Tu	0013	1.0	30	23 W	0120	0.9	27
	0849	-0.1	-3		0831	-0.1	-3
					1455	0.6	18
					2013	0.2	6
9 W	0059	0.9	27	24 Th	0225	0.8	24
	0914	-0.1	-3		0915	0.0	0
	1618	0.4	12		1548	0.7	21
	1828	0.3	9		2139	0.2	6
10 Th	0148	0.8	24	25 F	0330	0.7	21
	0934	0.0	0		0955	0.0	0
	1621	0.5	15		1634	0.8	24
	2036	0.4	12		2253	0.1	3
11 F	0242	0.7	21	26 Sa	0432	0.6	18
	0954	0.0	0		1032	0.0	0
	1642	0.6	18		1716	0.9	27
	2210	0.3	9		2356	0.1	3
12 Sa	0338	0.6	18	27 Su	0529	0.5	15
	1016	0.0	0		1105	0.1	3
	1710	0.8	24		1754	1.0	30
	2326	0.2	6				
13 Su	0435	0.5	15	28 M	0050	0.0	0
	1042	-0.1	-3		0620	0.5	15
	1745	1.0	30		1136	0.1	3
					1831	1.0	30
14 M	0030	0.1	3	29 Tu	0138	0.0	0
	0531	0.5	15		0706	0.4	12
	1113	-0.1	-3		1204	0.1	3
◐	1823	1.1	34	◐	1906	1.1	34
15 Tu	0128	0.0	0	30 W	0223	0.0	0
	0627	0.4	12		0749	0.4	12
	1148	-0.1	-3		1232	0.1	3
	1906	1.2	37		1941	1.1	34
				31 Th	0307	0.0	0
					0830	0.4	12
					1258	0.1	3
					2016	1.1	34

September

Day	Time	ft	cm	Day	Time	ft	cm
1 F	0351	0.0	0	16 Sa	0332	-0.1	-3
	0911	0.3	9		0918	0.5	15
	1325	0.2	6		1412	0.1	3
	2052	1.1	34		2107	1.2	37
2 Sa	0435	0.0	0	17 Su	0421	-0.1	-3
	0955	0.3	9		1013	0.5	15
	1355	0.2	6		1515	0.1	3
	2130	1.0	30		2203	1.1	34
3 Su	0519	0.0	0	18 M	0510	0.0	0
	1043	0.3	9		1111	0.6	18
	1431	0.2	6		1628	0.2	6
	2210	1.0	30		2303	1.0	30
4 M	0602	0.1	3	19 Tu	0558	0.0	0
	1136	0.3	9		1211	0.7	21
	1519	0.2	6		1751	0.2	6
	2255	0.9	27				
5 Tu	0641	0.1	3	20 W	0010	0.8	24
	1231	0.4	12		0646	0.1	3
	1631	0.3	9		1309	0.7	21
	2345	0.8	24	●	1919	0.2	6
6 W	0715	0.1	3	21 Th	0124	0.7	21
	1322	0.5	15		0733	0.2	6
	1806	0.3	9		1404	0.8	24
O					2043	0.2	6
7 Th	0043	0.8	24	22 F	0241	0.6	18
	0745	0.1	3		0817	0.2	6
	1407	0.6	18		1454	0.9	27
	1946	0.3	9		2153	0.1	3
8 F	0148	0.7	21	23 Sa	0354	0.6	18
	0815	0.2	6		0859	0.3	9
	1450	0.7	21		1538	0.9	27
	2113	0.2	6		2251	0.0	0
9 Sa	0255	0.6	18	24 Su	0456	0.5	15
	0847	0.1	3		0938	0.3	9
	1533	0.9	27		1619	1.0	30
	2224	0.1	3		2339	0.0	0
10 Su	0400	0.5	15	25 M	0548	0.5	15
	0922	0.1	3		1015	0.3	9
	1617	1.0	30		1657	1.0	30
	2324	0.0	0				
11 M	0459	0.5	15	26 Tu	0021	0.0	0
	1002	0.1	3		0631	0.5	15
	1702	1.2	37		1049	0.3	9
					1734	1.0	30
12 Tu	0017	-0.1	-3	27 W	0059	0.0	0
	0553	0.5	15		0707	0.5	15
	1045	0.1	3		1123	0.3	9
	1748	1.3	40	◐	1810	1.1	34
13 W	0107	-0.1	-3	28 Th	0136	0.0	0
	0644	0.5	15		0741	0.5	15
	1132	0.1	3		1157	0.3	9
O	1836	1.3	40		1846	1.1	34
14 Th	0156	-0.2	-6	29 F	0211	0.0	0
	0734	0.5	15		0813	0.5	15
	1222	0.1	3		1232	0.3	9
	1924	1.3	40		1922	1.0	30
15 F	0244	-0.2	-6	30 Sa	0245	0.0	0
	0825	0.5	15		0846	0.5	15
	1314	0.1	3		1312	0.3	9
	2015	1.3	40		2000	1.0	30

Time meridian 75° W. 0000 is midnight. 1200 is noon. Times are not adjusted for Daylight Saving Time.
Heights are referred to the chart datum of soundings.

Cristobal (Colon), Panama, 2017

Times and Heights of High and Low Waters

October

Day	Time	ft	cm
1 Su	0319	0.0	0
	0920	0.5	15
	1358	0.3	9
	2040	0.9	27
2 M	0352	0.1	3
	0957	0.6	18
	1454	0.3	9
	2124	0.9	27
3 Tu	0424	0.1	3
	1038	0.6	18
	1603	0.3	9
	2216	0.8	24
4 W	0455	0.2	6
	1122	0.7	21
	1726	0.3	9
	2318	0.7	21
5 Th ○	0527	0.2	6
	1209	0.8	24
	1854	0.2	6
6 F	0034	0.6	18
	0603	0.2	6
	1259	0.9	27
	2015	0.1	3
7 Sa	0157	0.5	15
	0644	0.3	9
	1350	1.1	34
	2122	0.0	0
8 Su	0315	0.5	15
	0733	0.3	9
	1442	1.2	37
	2219	-0.1	-3
9 M	0421	0.5	15
	0828	0.3	9
	1533	1.3	40
	2310	-0.2	-6
10 Tu	0516	0.5	15
	0925	0.3	9
	1624	1.3	40
	2357	-0.2	-6
11 W	0606	0.5	15
	1024	0.2	6
	1715	1.4	43
12 Th ☽	0042	-0.3	-9
	0653	0.6	18
	1123	0.2	6
	1807	1.3	40
13 F	0127	-0.2	-6
	0739	0.6	18
	1224	0.2	6
	1858	1.3	40
14 Sa	0210	-0.2	-6
	0825	0.7	21
	1327	0.2	6
	1951	1.1	34
15 Su	0252	-0.1	-3
	0913	0.8	24
	1434	0.2	6
	2045	1.0	30
16 M	0334	0.0	0
	1002	0.8	24
	1548	0.2	6
	2145	0.8	24
17 Tu	0414	0.1	3
	1051	0.9	27
	1709	0.2	6
	2252	0.7	21
18 W	0453	0.2	6
	1140	0.9	27
	1834	0.2	6
19 Th ●	0014	0.6	18
	0530	0.3	9
	1229	1.0	30
	1954	0.1	3
20 F	0149	0.5	15
	0607	0.3	9
	1315	1.0	30
	2102	0.0	0
21 Sa	0327	0.5	15
	0643	0.4	12
	1359	1.0	30
	2157	0.0	0
22 Su	0450	0.5	15
	0723	0.4	12
	1440	1.1	34
	2241	-0.1	-3
23 M	0548	0.5	15
	0808	0.4	12
	1520	1.1	34
	2319	-0.1	-3
24 Tu	0625	0.5	15
	0856	0.4	12
	1558	1.1	34
	2353	-0.1	-3
25 W	0652	0.5	15
	0943	0.4	12
	1635	1.1	34
26 Th	0023	-0.1	-3
	0715	0.5	15
	1031	0.4	12
	1711	1.1	34
27 F ☾	0053	-0.1	-3
	0737	0.6	18
	1118	0.5	15
	1748	1.0	30
28 Sa	0120	-0.1	-3
	0759	0.6	18
	1209	0.4	12
	1826	1.0	30
29 Su	0147	0.0	0
	0824	0.7	21
	1304	0.4	12
	1906	0.9	27
30 M	0212	0.0	0
	0852	0.7	21
	1407	0.4	12
	1949	0.8	24
31 Tu	0237	0.1	3
	0924	0.8	24
	1517	0.4	12
	2038	0.7	21

November

Day	Time	ft	cm
1 W	0302	0.1	3
	1001	0.9	27
	1635	0.3	9
	2137	0.6	18
2 Th	0329	0.1	3
	1042	1.0	30
	1756	0.2	6
	2253	0.5	15
3 F	0359	0.2	6
	1128	1.2	37
	1911	0.1	3
4 Sa ○	0025	0.4	12
	0436	0.2	6
	1218	1.3	40
	2017	0.0	0
5 Su	0202	0.3	9
	0524	0.2	6
	1310	1.3	40
	2113	-0.2	-6
6 M	0324	0.4	12
	0627	0.3	9
	1405	1.4	43
	2203	-0.3	-9
7 Tu	0427	0.4	12
	0740	0.3	9
	1459	1.4	43
	2249	-0.3	-9
8 W	0519	0.5	15
	0856	0.3	9
	1553	1.4	43
	2334	-0.4	-12
9 Th	0605	0.6	18
	1009	0.3	9
	1647	1.3	40
10 F ○	0016	-0.3	-9
	0650	0.7	21
	1121	0.3	9
	1740	1.2	37
11 Sa	0057	-0.3	-9
	0734	0.8	24
	1233	0.3	9
	1834	1.1	34
12 Su	0136	-0.2	-6
	0818	0.9	27
	1346	0.3	9
	1928	0.9	27
13 M	0213	-0.1	-3
	0902	1.0	30
	1502	0.3	9
	2025	0.8	24
14 Tu	0247	0.0	0
	0946	1.0	30
	1622	0.2	6
	2129	0.6	18
15 W	0318	0.1	3
	1029	1.1	34
	1743	0.2	6
	2246	0.4	12
16 Th	0344	0.2	6
	1111	1.1	34
	1901	0.1	3
17 F	0028	0.4	12
	0400	0.3	9
	1152	1.1	34
	2009	0.0	0
18 Sa ●	1232	1.2	37
	2104	-0.1	-3
19 Su	1310	1.1	34
	2149	-0.1	-3
20 M	1348	1.1	34
	2226	-0.1	-3
21 Tu	1426	1.1	34
	2258	-0.2	-6
22 W	1503	1.1	34
	2326	-0.2	-6
23 Th	1541	1.1	34
	2351	-0.2	-6
24 F	1618	1.0	30
25 Sa	0014	-0.1	-3
	0729	0.6	18
	1046	0.5	15
	1657	1.0	30
26 Su ☽	0035	-0.1	-3
	0740	0.7	21
	1157	0.5	15
	1736	0.9	27
27 M	0056	-0.1	-3
	0758	0.8	24
	1307	0.5	15
	1819	0.8	24
28 Tu	0116	-0.1	-3
	0823	0.9	27
	1420	0.4	12
	1906	0.7	21
29 W	0138	0.0	0
	0853	1.0	30
	1534	0.3	9
	2001	0.5	15
30 Th	0202	0.0	0
	0930	1.2	37
	1649	0.2	6
	2107	0.4	12

December

Day	Time	ft	cm
1 F	0230	0.0	0
	1012	1.3	40
	1800	0.1	3
	2230	0.3	9
2 Sa	0302	0.1	3
	1058	1.4	43
	1904	-0.1	-3
3 Su ○	0006	0.2	6
	0342	0.1	3
	1148	1.4	43
	2001	-0.2	-6
4 M	0146	0.2	6
	0434	0.1	3
	1242	1.5	46
	2053	-0.3	-9
5 Tu	0310	0.3	9
	0544	0.2	6
	1337	1.5	46
	2141	-0.4	-12
6 W	0413	0.4	12
	0710	0.3	9
	1433	1.4	43
	2226	-0.4	-12
7 Th	0504	0.5	15
	0839	0.3	9
	1529	1.4	43
	2308	-0.4	-12
8 F	0551	0.6	18
	1004	0.4	12
	1624	1.2	37
	2349	-0.4	-12
9 Sa	0635	0.8	24
	1126	0.4	12
	1719	1.1	34
10 Su ○	0027	-0.3	-9
	0718	0.9	27
	1245	0.3	9
	1814	0.9	27
11 M	0103	-0.3	-9
	0801	1.0	30
	1402	0.3	9
	1911	0.7	21
12 Tu	0136	-0.2	-6
	0842	1.1	34
	1519	0.2	6
	2010	0.5	15
13 W	0205	-0.1	-3
	0922	1.2	37
	1635	0.1	3
	2116	0.4	12
14 Th	0229	0.0	0
	1002	1.2	37
	1749	0.1	3
	2237	0.3	9
15 F	0244	0.1	3
	1040	1.2	37
	1858	0.0	0
16 Sa	0031	0.2	6
	0236	0.1	3
	1117	1.2	37
	1958	-0.1	-3
17 Su	1154	1.2	37
	2049	-0.1	-3
18 M ●	1230	1.2	37
	2131	-0.2	-6
19 Tu	1306	1.1	34
	2205	-0.2	-6
20 W	1343	1.1	34
	2234	-0.2	-6
21 Th	1420	1.0	30
	2258	-0.2	-6
22 F	1459	1.0	30
	2318	-0.2	-6
23 Sa	1538	0.9	27
	2335	-0.2	-6
24 Su	0657	0.6	18
	1039	0.5	15
	1620	0.8	24
	2352	-0.1	-3
25 M	0704	0.7	21
	1202	0.4	12
	1703	0.7	21
26 Tu ☾	0009	-0.1	-3
	0722	0.9	27
	1317	0.4	12
	1751	0.6	18
27 W	0029	-0.1	-3
	0749	1.0	30
	1427	0.3	9
	1844	0.5	15
28 Th	0053	-0.1	-3
	0822	1.2	37
	1534	0.1	3
	1943	0.3	9
29 F	0121	-0.1	-3
	0901	1.3	40
	1639	0.0	0
	2051	0.2	6
30 Sa	0154	-0.1	-3
	0945	1.4	43
	1741	-0.1	-3
	2209	0.2	6
31 Su	0233	-0.1	-3
	1033	1.5	46
	1840	-0.2	-6
	2337	0.1	3

Time meridian 75° W. 0000 is midnight. 1200 is noon. Times are not adjusted for Daylight Saving Time.
Heights are referred to the chart datum of soundings.

St. Georges Island, Bermuda, 2017

Times and Heights of High and Low Waters

January

Day	Time	ft	cm	Day	Time	ft	cm
1 Su	0352	0.0	0	16 M	0457	-0.2	-6
	1015	2.9	88		1114	2.8	85
	1640	0.0	0		1734	-0.2	-6
	2238	2.3	70		2344	2.4	73
2 M	0434	0.1	3	17 Tu	0547	0.0	0
	1055	2.8	85		1159	2.5	76
	1720	0.0	0		1818	-0.1	-3
	2323	2.3	70				
3 Tu	0521	0.1	3	18 W	0034	2.3	70
	1138	2.7	82		0640	0.2	6
	1803	0.0	0		1246	2.3	70
					1904	0.1	3
4 W	0013	2.3	70	19 Th	0127	2.3	70
	0615	0.2	6		0737	0.4	12
	1228	2.5	76		1337	2.0	61
	1851	0.0	0	☽	1952	0.2	6
5 Th	0109	2.4	73	20 F	0223	2.2	67
	0717	0.3	9		0840	0.5	15
	1324	2.4	73		1433	1.9	58
☽	1945	0.0	0		2044	0.3	9
6 F	0212	2.5	76	21 Sa	0321	2.2	67
	0827	0.3	9		0945	0.5	15
	1427	2.3	70		1533	1.8	55
	2044	0.0	0		2139	0.3	9
7 Sa	0318	2.7	82	22 Su	0419	2.3	70
	0940	0.2	6		1046	0.5	15
	1535	2.2	67		1632	1.8	55
	2146	-0.1	-3		2233	0.3	9
8 Su	0423	2.9	88	23 M	0511	2.4	73
	1049	0.1	3		1140	0.4	12
	1642	2.2	67		1727	1.8	55
	2248	-0.2	-6		2324	0.2	6
9 M	0525	3.1	94	24 Tu	0559	2.5	76
	1153	-0.1	-3		1227	0.2	6
	1745	2.3	70		1815	1.9	58
	2348	-0.4	-12				
10 Tu	0622	3.2	98	25 W	0011	0.1	3
	1250	-0.3	-9		0643	2.6	79
	1844	2.4	73		1309	0.1	3
					1859	2.0	61
11 W	0045	-0.5	-15	26 Th	0054	-0.1	-3
	0716	3.4	104		0723	2.8	85
	1343	-0.4	-12		1347	0.0	0
	1938	2.5	76		1940	2.1	64
12 Th	0138	-0.6	-18	27 F	0136	-0.2	-6
	0807	3.4	104		0801	2.9	88
	1432	-0.5	-15		1425	-0.1	-3
○	2029	2.6	79	●	2019	2.2	67
13 F	0230	-0.6	-18	28 Sa	0216	-0.2	-6
	0856	3.4	104		0839	2.9	88
	1520	-0.5	-15		1501	-0.2	-6
	2119	2.6	79		2058	2.3	70
14 Sa	0320	-0.5	-15	29 Su	0256	-0.3	-9
	0943	3.2	98		0917	2.9	88
	1605	-0.4	-12		1537	-0.3	-9
	2207	2.6	79		2137	2.4	73
15 Su	0409	-0.4	-12	30 M	0337	-0.3	-9
	1029	3.0	91		0955	2.9	88
	1650	-0.3	-9		1614	-0.3	-9
	2255	2.5	76		2218	2.5	76
				31 Tu	0420	-0.2	-6
					1035	2.8	85
					1653	-0.3	-9
					2303	2.5	76

February

Day	Time	ft	cm	Day	Time	ft	cm
1 W	0507	-0.2	-6	16 Th	0602	0.1	3
	1118	2.6	79		1204	2.1	64
	1735	-0.3	-9		1814	0.0	0
	2351	2.5	76				
2 Th	0600	-0.1	-3	17 F	0037	2.3	70
	1206	2.4	73		0651	0.3	9
	1822	-0.2	-6		1248	1.9	58
					1856	0.1	3
3 F	0046	2.6	79	18 Sa	0127	2.2	67
	0700	0.1	3		0747	0.4	12
	1301	2.3	70		1338	1.8	55
	1916	-0.2	-6	○	1946	0.3	9
4 Sa	0148	2.6	79	19 Su	0224	2.1	64
	0809	0.1	3		0851	0.5	15
	1405	2.1	64		1438	1.6	49
☽	2017	-0.1	-3		2043	0.3	9
5 Su	0256	2.6	79	20 M	0326	2.1	64
	0923	0.1	3		0958	0.5	15
	1516	2.0	61		1544	1.6	49
	2125	-0.1	-3		2146	0.3	9
6 M	0406	2.7	82	21 Tu	0427	2.2	67
	1036	0.1	3		1059	0.4	12
	1628	2.0	61		1647	1.7	52
	2233	-0.2	-6		2246	0.2	6
7 Tu	0512	2.8	85	22 W	0522	2.3	70
	1142	-0.1	-3		1151	0.3	9
	1735	2.1	64		1741	1.8	55
	2337	-0.3	-9		2339	0.1	3
8 W	0611	3.0	91	23 Th	0610	2.5	76
	1239	-0.2	-6		1235	0.1	3
	1834	2.3	70		1829	2.0	61
9 Th	0036	-0.4	-12	24 F	0027	-0.1	-3
	0705	3.1	94		0654	2.6	79
	1330	-0.4	-12		1315	-0.1	-3
	1927	2.4	73		1912	2.2	67
10 F	0129	-0.5	-15	25 Sa	0112	-0.2	-6
	0754	3.1	94		0734	2.8	85
	1416	-0.5	-15		1353	-0.3	-9
○	2016	2.5	76		1953	2.4	73
11 Sa	0219	-0.6	-18	26 Su	0155	-0.4	-12
	0840	3.1	94		0814	2.9	88
	1459	-0.5	-15		1430	-0.4	-12
	2102	2.6	79	●	2033	2.5	76
12 Su	0305	-0.5	-15	27 M	0238	-0.5	-15
	0923	3.0	91		0853	2.9	88
	1540	-0.5	-15		1508	-0.5	-15
	2145	2.6	79		2115	2.7	82
13 M	0350	-0.4	-12	28 Tu	0321	-0.5	-15
	1004	2.8	85		0933	2.8	85
	1619	-0.4	-12		1546	-0.5	-15
	2227	2.6	79		2157	2.8	85
14 Tu	0433	-0.3	-9				
	1043	2.6	79				
	1657	-0.3	-9				
	2309	2.5	76				
15 W	0517	-0.1	-3				
	1123	2.4	73				
	1734	-0.1	-3				
	2352	2.4	73				

March

Day	Time	ft	cm	Day	Time	ft	cm
1 W	0407	-0.5	-15	16 Th	0448	-0.1	-3
	1015	2.7	82		1049	2.3	70
	1627	-0.5	-15		1654	-0.1	-3
	2243	2.8	85		2313	2.5	76
2 Th	0455	-0.4	-12	17 F	0529	0.0	0
	1100	2.6	79		1127	2.1	64
	1710	-0.5	-15		1730	0.0	0
	2332	2.8	85		2353	2.4	73
3 F	0548	-0.2	-6	18 Sa	0613	0.2	6
	1149	2.4	73		1207	1.9	58
	1759	-0.4	-12		1809	0.1	3
4 Sa	0027	2.7	82	19 Su	0039	2.3	70
	0648	-0.1	-3		0702	0.3	9
	1245	2.2	67		1254	1.8	55
	1854	-0.2	-6		1856	0.3	9
5 Su	0129	2.7	82	20 M	0131	2.2	67
	0755	0.0	0		0800	0.5	15
	1351	2.0	61		1350	1.6	49
☽	1959	-0.1	-3	☽	1952	0.4	12
6 M	0238	2.6	79	21 Tu	0232	2.1	64
	0910	0.1	3		0906	0.5	15
	1505	1.9	58		1457	1.6	49
	2111	-0.1	-3		2057	0.4	12
7 Tu	0351	2.6	79	22 W	0337	2.1	64
	1023	0.1	3		1010	0.4	12
	1620	2.0	61		1604	1.7	52
	2224	-0.1	-3		2204	0.3	9
8 W	0459	2.7	82	23 Th	0438	2.2	67
	1128	-0.1	-3		1106	0.3	9
	1727	2.1	64		1703	1.9	58
	2331	-0.2	-6		2304	0.2	6
9 Th	0559	2.7	82	24 F	0531	2.4	73
	1224	-0.2	-6		1153	0.1	3
	1825	2.3	70		1754	2.1	64
					2357	0.0	0
10 F	0029	-0.3	-9	25 Sa	0618	2.5	76
	0652	2.8	85		1236	-0.1	-3
	1312	-0.3	-9		1840	2.3	70
	1915	2.5	76				
11 Sa	0120	-0.4	-12	26 Su	0046	-0.2	-6
	0738	2.8	85		0702	2.7	82
	1354	-0.4	-12		1317	-0.3	-9
	1959	2.6	79		1924	2.6	79
12 Su	0206	-0.4	-12	27 M	0133	-0.4	-12
	0820	2.8	85		0745	2.8	85
	1433	-0.4	-12		1357	-0.5	-15
○	2041	2.7	82	●	2007	2.8	85
13 M	0249	-0.4	-12	28 Tu	0219	-0.5	-15
	0900	2.7	82		0828	2.8	85
	1510	-0.4	-12		1437	-0.6	-18
	2120	2.7	82		2051	3.0	91
14 Tu	0330	-0.4	-12	29 W	0305	-0.6	-18
	0937	2.6	79		0911	2.8	85
	1545	-0.4	-12		1519	-0.7	-21
	2157	2.7	82		2137	3.1	94
15 W	0409	-0.3	-9	30 Th	0353	-0.6	-18
	1013	2.5	76		0957	2.7	82
	1619	-0.3	-9		1602	-0.6	-18
	2235	2.6	79		2224	3.1	94
				31 F	0444	-0.5	-15
					1044	2.6	79
					1649	-0.5	-15
					2315	3.1	94

Time meridian 60° W. 0000 is midnight. 1200 is noon. Times are not adjusted for Daylight Saving Time.
Heights are referred to mean lower low water which is the chart datum of soundings.

St. Georges Island, Bermuda, 2017

Times and Heights of High and Low Waters

April

Day	Time	ft	cm	Day	Time	ft	cm
1 Sa	0538	-0.3	-9	**16** Su	0542	0.2	6
	1136	2.4	73		1135	1.9	58
	1741	-0.4	-12		1732	0.2	6
2 Su	0011	2.9	88	**17** M	0001	2.4	73
	0637	-0.2	-6		0627	0.3	9
	1235	2.2	67		1220	1.8	55
	1839	-0.2	-6		1816	0.3	9
3 M ☽	0113	2.8	85	**18** Tu	0049	2.3	70
	0744	0.0	0		0719	0.4	12
	1342	2.0	61		1313	1.7	52
	1946	-0.1	-3		1910	0.4	12
4 Tu	0223	2.6	79	**19** W ☽	0144	2.2	67
	0855	0.1	3		0818	0.4	12
	1456	2.0	61		1415	1.7	52
	2101	0.0	0		2013	0.4	12
5 W	0335	2.5	76	**20** Th	0246	2.2	67
	1006	0.1	3		0919	0.4	12
	1610	2.1	64		1521	1.8	55
	2215	0.0	0		2121	0.4	12
6 Th	0443	2.5	76	**21** F	0348	2.3	70
	1108	0.0	0		1015	0.3	9
	1715	2.2	67		1622	2.0	61
	2321	0.0	0		2226	0.2	6
7 F	0541	2.6	79	**22** Sa	0446	2.4	73
	1201	-0.1	-3		1106	0.1	3
	1810	2.4	73		1717	2.3	70
					2325	0.0	0
8 Sa	0018	-0.1	-3	**23** Su	0538	2.5	76
	0632	2.6	79		1153	-0.1	-3
	1246	-0.2	-6		1807	2.6	79
	1857	2.6	79				
9 Su	0106	-0.2	-6	**24** M	0019	-0.2	-6
	0716	2.6	79		0628	2.6	79
	1326	-0.3	-9		1238	-0.3	-9
	1939	2.7	82		1855	2.9	88
10 M	0150	-0.3	-9	**25** Tu	0110	-0.4	-12
	0756	2.6	79		0715	2.7	82
	1403	-0.3	-9		1323	-0.5	-15
	2017	2.8	85		1942	3.2	98
11 Tu ○	0230	-0.3	-9	**26** W ●	0200	-0.5	-15
	0834	2.5	76		0803	2.8	85
	1438	-0.3	-9		1407	-0.6	-18
	2053	2.8	85		2029	3.3	101
12 W	0308	-0.3	-9	**27** Th	0249	-0.6	-18
	0909	2.4	73		0850	2.8	85
	1511	-0.2	-6		1453	-0.7	-21
	2128	2.8	85		2118	3.4	104
13 Th	0346	-0.2	-6	**28** F	0340	-0.6	-18
	0945	2.3	70		0939	2.7	82
	1544	-0.2	-6		1541	-0.6	-18
	2204	2.7	82		2208	3.4	104
14 F	0423	-0.1	-3	**29** Sa	0432	-0.5	-15
	1020	2.2	67		1030	2.6	79
	1618	-0.1	-3		1632	-0.5	-15
	2240	2.6	79		2300	3.3	101
15 Sa	0501	0.0	0	**30** Su	0527	-0.3	-9
	1056	2.1	64		1125	2.4	73
	1653	0.1	3		1726	-0.3	-9
	2319	2.5	76		2357	3.1	94

May

Day	Time	ft	cm	Day	Time	ft	cm
1 M	0625	-0.2	-6	**16** Tu	0600	0.3	9
	1225	2.3	70		1153	1.9	58
	1827	-0.1	-3		1747	0.3	9
2 Tu ☽	0058	2.9	88	**17** W	0015	2.5	76
	0729	0.0	0		0646	0.3	9
	1332	2.2	67		1243	1.9	58
	1935	0.0	0		1837	0.4	12
3 W	0204	2.7	82	**18** Th ☽	0105	2.4	73
	0835	0.1	3		0737	0.4	12
	1443	2.2	67		1340	1.9	58
	2048	0.2	6		1937	0.4	12
4 Th	0312	2.5	76	**19** F	0201	2.3	70
	0940	0.1	3		0831	0.3	9
	1553	2.2	67		1441	2.0	61
	2200	0.2	6		2043	0.4	12
5 F	0417	2.4	73	**20** Sa	0301	2.3	70
	1039	0.0	0		0926	0.2	6
	1655	2.4	73		1543	2.3	70
	2305	0.1	3		2151	0.3	9
6 Sa	0515	2.4	73	**21** Su	0402	2.4	73
	1130	0.0	0		1020	0.0	0
	1748	2.5	76		1641	2.5	76
					2254	0.1	3
7 Su	0000	0.1	3	**22** M	0459	2.5	76
	0605	2.4	73		1112	-0.1	-3
	1214	-0.1	-3		1736	2.8	85
	1833	2.6	79		2353	-0.1	-3
8 M	0048	0.0	0	**23** Tu	0555	2.5	76
	0649	2.4	73		1202	-0.3	-9
	1254	-0.1	-3		1828	3.1	94
	1913	2.8	85				
9 Tu	0130	0.0	0	**24** W	0049	-0.3	-9
	0729	2.4	73		0648	2.6	79
	1330	-0.1	-3		1252	-0.5	-15
	1951	2.8	85		1919	3.4	104
10 W ○	0209	-0.1	-3	**25** Th ●	0142	-0.4	-12
	0806	2.4	73		0739	2.7	82
	1405	-0.1	-3		1342	-0.6	-18
	2026	2.9	88		2010	3.5	107
11 Th	0247	-0.1	-3	**26** F	0234	-0.5	-15
	0842	2.3	70		0831	2.7	82
	1439	-0.1	-3		1432	-0.6	-18
	2102	2.9	88		2101	3.6	110
12 F	0323	-0.1	-3	**27** Sa	0326	-0.5	-15
	0918	2.3	70		0923	2.7	82
	1514	-0.1	-3		1524	-0.6	-18
	2137	2.8	85		2153	3.5	107
13 Sa	0400	0.0	0	**28** Su	0419	-0.5	-15
	0954	2.2	67		1016	2.6	79
	1549	0.0	0		1617	-0.5	-15
	2213	2.8	85		2246	3.4	104
14 Su	0438	0.1	3	**29** M	0513	-0.3	-9
	1031	2.1	64		1112	2.5	76
	1625	0.1	3		1713	-0.3	-9
	2251	2.7	82		2341	3.2	98
15 M	0517	0.2	6	**30** Tu	0609	-0.2	-6
	1110	2.0	61		1212	2.4	73
	1703	0.2	6		1813	-0.1	-3
	2331	2.6	79				
				31 W	0039	2.9	88
					0707	-0.1	-3
					1315	2.4	73
					1918	0.1	3

June

Day	Time	ft	cm	Day	Time	ft	cm
1 Th ○	0140	2.7	82	**16** F	0033	2.5	76
	0807	0.1	3		0700	0.2	6
	1421	2.3	70		1309	2.2	67
	2026	0.3	9		1908	0.4	12
2 F	0242	2.5	76	**17** Sa ○	0124	2.5	76
	0906	0.1	3		0750	0.2	6
	1526	2.4	73		1407	2.3	70
	2135	0.3	9		2013	0.4	12
3 Sa	0343	2.3	70	**18** Su	0222	2.4	73
	1002	0.1	3		0844	0.1	3
	1625	2.4	73		1508	2.4	73
	2239	0.3	9		2121	0.3	9
4 Su	0441	2.3	70	**19** M	0324	2.4	73
	1052	0.1	3		0940	0.0	0
	1718	2.6	79		1610	2.7	82
	2335	0.3	9		2228	0.2	6
5 M	0532	2.2	67	**20** Tu	0426	2.4	73
	1137	0.1	3		1037	-0.1	-3
	1804	2.7	82		1709	3.0	91
					2331	0.0	0
6 Tu	0023	0.2	6	**21** W	0527	2.5	76
	0617	2.2	67		1133	-0.3	-9
	1219	0.1	3		1806	3.3	101
	1845	2.8	85				
7 W	0107	0.2	6	**22** Th	0030	-0.1	-3
	0659	2.2	67		0625	2.6	79
	1257	0.0	0		1228	-0.4	-12
	1924	2.9	88		1900	3.5	107
8 Th	0146	0.1	3	**23** F ●	0126	-0.3	-9
	0738	2.2	67		0720	2.6	79
	1335	0.0	0		1322	-0.5	-15
	2001	2.9	88		1954	3.6	110
9 F	0224	0.1	3	**24** Sa ○	0219	-0.4	-12
	0816	2.2	67		0814	2.7	82
	1411	0.0	0		1416	-0.6	-18
	2038	2.9	88		2046	3.6	110
10 Sa	0302	0.1	3	**25** Su	0311	-0.4	-12
	0854	2.2	67		0908	2.7	82
	1448	0.0	0		1509	-0.5	-15
	2114	2.9	88		2138	3.5	107
11 Su	0339	0.1	3	**26** M	0403	-0.4	-12
	0931	2.2	67		1001	2.7	82
	1525	0.1	3		1603	-0.4	-12
	2151	2.9	88		2229	3.4	104
12 M	0416	0.1	3	**27** Tu	0454	-0.3	-9
	1009	2.2	67		1056	2.7	82
	1602	0.1	3		1658	-0.2	-6
	2228	2.8	85		2321	3.2	98
13 Tu	0454	0.2	6	**28** W	0545	-0.2	-6
	1048	2.1	64		1151	2.6	79
	1641	0.2	6		1754	0.0	0
	2306	2.7	82				
14 W	0533	0.2	6	**29** Th	0014	2.9	88
	1129	2.1	64		0637	0.0	0
	1723	0.3	9		1249	2.5	76
	2347	2.6	79		1853	0.2	6
15 Th	0615	0.2	6	**30** F ☽	0108	2.7	82
	1216	2.1	64		0731	0.1	3
	1812	0.4	12		1348	2.5	76
					1956	0.4	12

Time meridian 60° W. 0000 is midnight. 1200 is noon. Times are not adjusted for Daylight Saving Time.
Heights are referred to mean lower low water which is the chart datum of soundings.

St. Georges Island, Bermuda, 2017

Times and Heights of High and Low Waters

July

Day	Time	ft	cm	Day	Time	ft	cm
1 Sa	0205	2.4	73	16 Su	0055	2.5	76
	0824	0.2	6		0714	0.2	6
	1448	2.5	76		1337	2.6	79
	2101	0.5	15	◗	1949	0.4	12
2 Su	0302	2.3	70	17 M	0152	2.4	73
	0917	0.3	9		0809	0.1	3
	1547	2.5	76		1439	2.7	82
	2204	0.5	15		2058	0.4	12
3 M	0400	2.1	64	18 Tu	0255	2.4	73
	1009	0.3	9		0908	0.1	3
	1641	2.5	76		1544	2.9	88
	2303	0.5	15		2208	0.3	9
4 Tu	0454	2.1	64	19 W	0402	2.4	73
	1058	0.3	9		1011	0.0	0
	1730	2.6	79		1648	3.1	94
	2354	0.4	12		2314	0.2	6
5 W	0543	2.1	64	20 Th	0507	2.4	73
	1143	0.3	9		1113	-0.2	-6
	1815	2.7	82		1749	3.3	101
6 Th	0039	0.4	12	21 F	0015	0.0	0
	0629	2.2	67		0608	2.5	76
	1226	0.2	6		1212	-0.3	-9
	1857	2.8	85		1846	3.4	104
7 F	0121	0.3	9	22 Sa	0111	-0.1	-3
	0711	2.2	67		0706	2.7	82
	1307	0.1	3		1309	-0.4	-12
	1936	2.9	88		1940	3.5	107
8 Sa	0200	0.2	6	23 Su	0204	-0.2	-6
	0751	2.3	70		0800	2.8	85
	1347	0.1	3		1404	-0.4	-12
	2014	3.0	91	●	2031	3.6	110
9 Su	0238	0.2	6	24 M	0254	-0.3	-9
	0829	2.3	70		0852	2.9	88
	1425	0.1	3		1456	-0.4	-12
○	2051	3.0	91		2121	3.5	107
10 M	0315	0.1	3	25 Tu	0342	-0.3	-9
	0907	2.3	70		0943	2.9	88
	1503	0.1	3		1548	-0.3	-9
	2128	3.0	91		2209	3.3	101
11 Tu	0351	0.1	3	26 W	0429	-0.2	-6
	0945	2.4	73		1033	2.9	88
	1541	0.1	3		1639	-0.2	-6
	2204	2.9	88		2256	3.1	94
12 W	0427	0.1	3	27 Th	0515	-0.1	-3
	1024	2.4	73		1123	2.8	85
	1621	0.2	6		1730	0.0	0
	2242	2.9	88		2344	2.9	88
13 Th	0504	0.1	3	28 F	0601	0.0	0
	1105	2.4	73		1214	2.7	82
	1704	0.2	6		1823	0.3	9
	2321	2.8	85				
14 F	0543	0.2	6	29 Sa	0032	2.6	79
	1150	2.4	73		0648	0.2	6
	1751	0.3	9		1307	2.6	79
					1919	0.5	15
15 Sa	0005	2.7	82	30 Su	0123	2.4	73
	0626	0.2	6		0736	0.3	9
	1240	2.5	76		1403	2.5	76
	1846	0.4	12	◖	2020	0.6	18
				31 M	0217	2.2	67
					0828	0.4	12
					1501	2.5	76
					2123	0.7	21

August

Day	Time	ft	cm	Day	Time	ft	cm
1 Tu	0315	2.1	64	16 W	0237	2.4	73
	0923	0.5	15		0847	0.2	6
	1559	2.5	76		1526	3.0	91
	2224	0.7	21		2154	0.4	12
2 W	0414	2.0	61	17 Th	0348	2.4	73
	1017	0.5	15		0955	0.1	3
	1654	2.6	79		1634	3.1	94
	2320	0.6	18		2301	0.3	9
3 Th	0509	2.1	64	18 F	0456	2.5	76
	1109	0.4	12		1102	0.0	0
	1743	2.7	82		1737	3.2	98
4 F	0008	0.5	15	19 Sa	0002	0.1	3
	0558	2.2	67		0559	2.6	79
	1157	0.3	9		1204	-0.1	-3
	1828	2.8	85		1834	3.4	104
5 Sa	0052	0.4	12	20 Su	0056	0.0	0
	0643	2.3	70		0655	2.8	85
	1242	0.2	6		1300	-0.2	-6
	1910	2.9	88		1926	3.4	104
6 Su	0131	0.3	9	21 M	0146	-0.1	-3
	0724	2.4	73		0747	2.9	88
	1323	0.2	6		1353	-0.3	-9
	1949	3.0	91	●	2015	3.4	104
7 M	0209	0.2	6	22 Tu	0232	-0.2	-6
	0803	2.5	76		0835	3.0	91
	1403	0.1	3		1442	-0.3	-9
○	2026	3.1	94		2101	3.4	104
8 Tu	0245	0.1	3	23 W	0316	-0.2	-6
	0842	2.6	79		0922	3.1	94
	1442	0.1	3		1530	-0.2	-6
	2103	3.1	94		2145	3.2	98
9 W	0320	0.1	3	24 Th	0358	-0.1	-3
	0920	2.6	79		1007	3.1	94
	1521	0.0	0		1616	-0.1	-3
	2139	3.0	91		2228	3.0	91
10 Th	0356	0.1	3	25 F	0439	0.0	0
	0959	2.7	82		1051	3.0	91
	1602	0.1	3		1703	0.1	3
	2217	3.0	91		2310	2.8	85
11 F	0432	0.1	3	26 Sa	0520	0.2	6
	1040	2.8	85		1136	2.9	88
	1646	0.1	3		1750	0.3	9
	2257	2.9	88		2354	2.6	79
12 Sa	0512	0.1	3	27 Su	0601	0.3	9
	1125	2.8	85		1222	2.7	82
	1734	0.2	6		1840	0.5	15
	2342	2.7	82				
13 Su	0555	0.1	3	28 M	0040	2.4	73
	1215	2.8	85		0646	0.5	15
	1829	0.3	9		1313	2.6	79
					1935	0.7	21
14 M	0032	2.6	79	29 Tu	0132	2.2	67
	0645	0.2	6		0737	0.6	18
	1313	2.9	88		1410	2.5	76
◖	1932	0.4	12	◖	2036	0.8	24
15 Tu	0130	2.4	73	30 W	0230	2.1	64
	0742	0.2	6		0835	0.7	21
	1417	2.9	88		1512	2.5	76
	2041	0.4	12		2141	0.8	24
				31 Th	0333	2.1	64
					0936	0.7	21
					1612	2.5	76
					2241	0.8	24

September

Day	Time	ft	cm	Day	Time	ft	cm
1 F	0433	2.1	64	16 Sa	0450	2.6	79
	1035	0.6	18		1057	0.2	6
	1707	2.6	79		1725	3.1	94
	2332	0.7	21		2348	0.2	6
2 Sa	0526	2.3	67	17 Su	0551	2.8	85
	1128	0.5	15		1158	0.1	3
	1755	2.8	85		1821	3.2	98
3 Su	0017	0.5	15	18 M	0039	0.1	3
	0613	2.4	73		0644	2.9	88
	1215	0.4	12		1252	-0.1	-3
	1838	2.9	88		1910	3.3	101
4 M	0057	0.4	12	19 Tu	0124	0.0	0
	0655	2.6	79		0731	3.1	94
	1258	0.2	6		1341	-0.1	-3
	1918	3.0	91		1956	3.2	98
5 Tu	0134	0.2	6	20 W	0207	-0.1	-3
	0735	2.7	82		0816	3.2	98
	1339	0.1	3		1427	-0.1	-3
	1956	3.1	94	●	2038	3.2	98
6 W	0210	0.1	3	21 Th	0246	0.0	0
	0813	2.9	88		0857	3.2	98
	1420	0.0	0		1511	-0.1	-3
○	2034	3.1	94		2118	3.0	91
7 Th	0246	0.0	0	22 F	0324	0.0	0
	0853	3.0	91		0938	3.2	98
	1501	0.0	0		1553	0.0	0
	2113	3.1	94		2158	2.9	88
8 F	0323	0.0	0	23 Sa	0401	0.1	3
	0933	3.1	94		1017	3.1	94
	1544	0.0	0		1634	0.2	6
	2153	3.0	91		2237	2.7	82
9 Sa	0401	0.0	0	24 Su	0438	0.3	9
	1016	3.2	98		1057	3.0	91
	1630	0.0	0		1717	0.4	12
	2235	2.9	88		2317	2.5	76
10 Su	0443	0.0	0	25 M	0517	0.4	12
	1102	3.2	98		1139	2.8	85
	1720	0.1	3		1802	0.5	15
	2322	2.8	85				
11 M	0529	0.1	3	26 Tu	0000	2.3	70
	1154	3.1	94		0559	0.6	18
	1816	0.3	9		1226	2.7	82
					1852	0.7	21
12 Tu	0015	2.6	79	27 W	0049	2.2	67
	0622	0.2	6		0648	0.7	21
	1253	3.1	94		1320	2.6	79
	1919	0.4	12	◖	1950	0.8	24
13 W	0117	2.4	73	28 Th	0147	2.1	64
	0724	0.3	9		0746	0.8	24
	1400	3.0	91		1421	2.5	76
◖	2030	0.5	15		2053	0.9	27
14 Th	0228	2.4	73	29 F	0252	2.1	64
	0834	0.3	9		0852	0.8	24
	1512	3.0	91		1525	2.5	76
	2142	0.5	15		2155	0.8	24
15 F	0341	2.4	73	30 Sa	0355	2.2	67
	0948	0.3	9		0957	0.8	24
	1622	3.0	91		1624	2.6	79
	2249	0.4	12		2249	0.7	21

Time meridian 60° W. 0000 is midnight. 1200 is noon. Times are not adjusted for Daylight Saving Time.
Heights are referred to mean lower low water which is the chart datum of soundings.

St. Georges Island, Bermuda, 2017

Times and Heights of High and Low Waters

October

Day	Time	ft	cm		Day	Time	ft	cm
1 Su	0451	2.3	70		**16** M	0540	2.9	88
	1054	0.6	18			1150	0.2	6
	1716	2.7	82			1803	3.0	91
	2335	0.5	15					
2 M	0539	2.5	76		**17** Tu	0016	0.1	3
	1144	0.4	12			0629	3.0	91
	1801	2.8	85			1242	0.1	3
						1851	3.0	91
3 Tu	0016	0.4	12		**18** W	0059	0.1	3
	0622	2.7	82			0713	3.2	98
	1230	0.3	9			1328	0.0	0
	1843	3.0	91			1934	3.0	91
4 W	0055	0.2	6		**19** Th ●	0139	0.0	0
	0704	3.0	91			0754	3.3	101
	1314	0.1	3			1411	0.0	0
	1924	3.0	91			2014	2.9	88
5 Th ○	0133	0.0	0		**20** F	0215	0.0	0
	0745	3.2	98			0832	3.3	101
	1358	0.0	0			1451	0.0	0
	2005	3.1	94			2052	2.8	85
6 F	0211	-0.1	-3		**21** Sa	0251	0.1	3
	0826	3.4	104			0909	3.3	101
	1442	-0.1	-3			1530	0.1	3
	2047	3.1	94			2129	2.7	82
7 Sa	0251	-0.1	-3		**22** Su	0326	0.2	6
	0909	3.5	107			0946	3.2	98
	1527	-0.1	-3			1608	0.2	6
	2130	3.0	91			2206	2.6	79
8 Su	0333	-0.1	-3		**23** M	0402	0.3	9
	0955	3.5	107			1023	3.1	94
	1616	-0.1	-3			1648	0.4	12
	2216	2.9	88			2244	2.4	73
9 M	0419	-0.1	-3		**24** Tu	0439	0.5	15
	1043	3.5	107			1103	2.9	88
	1707	0.1	3			1729	0.5	15
	2307	2.8	85			2326	2.3	70
10 Tu	0509	0.1	3		**25** W	0519	0.6	18
	1137	3.3	101			1146	2.7	82
	1804	0.2	6			1815	0.6	18
11 W	0003	2.6	79		**26** Th	0012	2.2	67
	0606	0.2	6			0606	0.7	21
	1238	3.2	98			1235	2.6	79
	1908	0.3	9			1907	0.7	21
12 Th ◐	0108	2.5	76		**27** F ☽	0106	2.1	64
	0712	0.3	9			0701	0.8	24
	1346	3.0	91			1331	2.5	76
	2018	0.4	12			2005	0.8	24
13 F	0221	2.4	73		**28** Sa	0208	2.1	64
	0826	0.4	12			0806	0.8	24
	1458	2.9	88			1432	2.5	76
	2128	0.4	12			2104	0.7	21
14 Sa	0335	2.5	76		**29** Su	0312	2.2	67
	0942	0.4	12			0913	0.8	24
	1607	2.9	88			1533	2.5	76
	2233	0.3	9			2159	0.6	18
15 Su	0442	2.7	82		**30** M	0410	2.4	73
	1051	0.3	9			1015	0.7	21
	1710	3.0	91			1629	2.6	79
	2328	0.2	6			2247	0.5	15
					31 Tu	0501	2.6	79
						1111	0.5	15
						1719	2.7	82
						2332	0.3	9

November

Day	Time	ft	cm		Day	Time	ft	cm
1 W	0548	2.9	88		**16** Th	0031	0.1	3
	1201	0.3	9			0653	3.1	94
	1807	2.8	85			1312	0.1	3
						1910	2.6	79
2 Th	0014	0.1	3		**17** F	0110	0.1	3
	0633	3.2	98			0732	3.2	98
	1249	0.1	3			1353	0.1	3
	1852	2.9	88			1950	2.6	79
3 F	0057	-0.1	-3		**18** Sa ●	0146	0.1	3
	0717	3.4	104			0809	3.2	98
	1336	-0.1	-3			1431	0.1	3
	1937	3.0	91			2027	2.5	76
4 Sa ○	0140	-0.2	-6		**19** Su	0222	0.1	3
	0802	3.6	110			0844	3.2	98
	1424	-0.2	-6			1508	0.1	3
	2023	3.0	91			2103	2.5	76
5 Su	0224	-0.3	-9		**20** M	0257	0.2	6
	0849	3.7	113			0920	3.1	94
	1512	-0.3	-9			1545	0.2	6
	2111	2.9	88			2140	2.4	73
6 M	0311	-0.3	-9		**21** Tu	0333	0.2	6
	0937	3.7	113			0957	3.0	91
	1602	-0.2	-6			1623	0.3	9
	2200	2.8	85			2218	2.3	70
7 Tu	0400	-0.2	-6		**22** W	0410	0.3	9
	1028	3.6	110			1034	2.9	88
	1655	-0.1	-3			1702	0.4	12
	2254	2.7	82			2257	2.2	67
8 W	0454	-0.1	-3		**23** Th	0449	0.5	15
	1123	3.4	104			1114	2.8	85
	1752	0.0	0			1744	0.4	12
	2353	2.6	79			2341	2.2	67
9 Th	0553	0.1	3		**24** F	0532	0.6	18
	1223	3.2	98			1157	2.6	79
	1854	0.2	6			1829	0.5	15
10 F ○	0058	2.5	76		**25** Sa	0030	2.1	64
	0701	0.3	9			0622	0.7	21
	1329	3.0	91			1246	2.5	76
	2000	0.3	9			1918	0.6	18
11 Sa	0210	2.5	76		**26** Su ☾	0125	2.1	64
	0815	0.4	12			0721	0.7	21
	1438	2.8	85			1340	2.4	73
	2106	0.3	9			2011	0.5	15
12 Su	0321	2.6	79		**27** M	0225	2.2	67
	0930	0.4	12			0827	0.7	21
	1546	2.7	82			1439	2.4	73
	2207	0.3	9			2104	0.5	15
13 M	0426	2.7	82		**28** Tu	0325	2.4	73
	1038	0.4	12			0933	0.6	18
	1647	2.7	82			1539	2.4	73
	2302	0.2	6			2157	0.3	9
14 Tu	0522	2.9	88		**29** W	0421	2.6	79
	1137	0.3	9			1036	0.4	12
	1741	2.7	82			1636	2.5	76
	2349	0.1	3			2247	0.1	3
15 W	0610	3.0	91		**30** Th	0514	2.9	88
	1228	0.2	6			1133	0.2	6
	1828	2.6	79			1730	2.6	79
						2336	-0.1	-3

December

Day	Time	ft	cm		Day	Time	ft	cm
1 F	0604	3.2	98		**16** Sa	0042	0.1	3
	1226	0.0	0			0709	3.0	91
	1822	2.7	82			1334	0.1	3
						1926	2.3	70
2 Sa	0025	-0.2	-6		**17** Su	0120	0.1	3
	0653	3.5	107			0747	3.0	91
	1317	-0.2	-6			1412	0.1	3
	1913	2.7	82			2004	2.3	70
3 Su ○	0114	-0.4	-12		**18** M ●	0158	0.0	0
	0742	3.6	110			0823	3.0	91
	1408	-0.3	-9			1449	0.0	0
	2003	2.8	85			2041	2.3	70
4 M	0203	-0.5	-15		**19** Tu	0234	0.1	3
	0832	3.7	113			0859	3.0	91
	1458	-0.4	-12			1525	0.1	3
	2054	2.8	85			2118	2.3	70
5 Tu	0254	-0.5	-15		**20** W	0311	0.1	3
	0922	3.7	113			0935	2.9	88
	1549	-0.4	-12			1601	0.1	3
	2147	2.8	85			2155	2.2	67
6 W	0346	-0.4	-12		**21** Th	0348	0.2	6
	1014	3.6	110			1011	2.8	85
	1642	-0.3	-9			1637	0.1	3
	2241	2.7	82			2233	2.2	67
7 Th	0441	-0.2	-6		**22** F	0426	0.2	6
	1108	3.4	104			1048	2.7	82
	1736	-0.2	-6			1714	0.2	6
	2339	2.6	79			2313	2.2	67
8 F	0541	0.0	0		**23** Sa	0506	0.3	9
	1205	3.1	94			1126	2.6	79
	1833	-0.1	-3			1753	0.2	6
						2357	2.1	64
9 Sa	0042	2.5	76		**24** Su	0552	0.4	12
	0645	0.2	6			1208	2.5	76
	1306	2.8	85			1835	0.3	9
	1933	0.1	3					
10 Su ○	0149	2.5	76		**25** M	0046	2.2	67
	0755	0.3	9			0644	0.5	15
	1410	2.6	79			1256	2.4	73
	2034	0.1	3			1921	0.3	9
11 M	0256	2.5	76		**26** Tu ☾	0141	2.2	67
	0908	0.4	12			0746	0.5	15
	1515	2.4	73			1351	2.3	70
	2133	0.2	6			2013	0.2	6
12 Tu	0400	2.6	79		**27** W	0241	2.4	73
	1016	0.4	12			0854	0.5	15
	1617	2.3	70			1453	2.2	67
	2228	0.2	6			2109	0.1	3
13 W	0457	2.7	82		**28** Th	0342	2.6	79
	1117	0.3	9			1002	0.3	9
	1713	2.3	70			1557	2.2	67
	2317	0.2	6			2207	0.0	0
14 Th	0546	2.8	85		**29** F	0442	2.8	85
	1209	0.3	9			1106	0.1	3
	1802	2.3	70			1659	2.3	70
						2304	-0.2	-6
15 F	0001	0.1	3		**30** Sa	0539	3.1	94
	0630	2.9	88			1205	-0.1	-3
	1254	0.2	6			1758	2.4	73
	1846	2.3	70					
					31 Su	0000	-0.4	-12
						0633	3.3	101
						1300	-0.3	-9
						1854	2.5	76

Time meridian 60° W. 0000 is midnight. 1200 is noon. Times are not adjusted for Daylight Saving Time.
Heights are referred to mean lower low water which is the chart datum of soundings.

Settlement Point, Grand Bahama Island, 2017

Times and Heights of High and Low Waters

January

Day	Time (h m)	ft	cm		Day	Time (h m)	ft	cm
1 Su	0320	-0.1	-3		16 M	0425	-0.3	-9
	0944	2.9	88			1042	2.9	88
	1607	-0.1	-3			1704	-0.3	-9
	2207	2.3	70			2313	2.5	76
2 M	0404	-0.1	-3		17 Tu	0516	-0.1	-3
	1025	2.9	88			1129	2.7	82
	1649	-0.1	-3			1750	-0.2	-6
	2253	2.4	73					
3 Tu	0452	0.0	0		18 W	0004	2.4	73
	1110	2.8	85			0609	0.1	3
	1733	-0.1	-3			1217	2.4	73
	2343	2.4	73			1837	-0.1	-3
4 W	0546	0.1	3		19 Th ○	0057	2.3	70
	1159	2.7	82			0705	0.2	6
	1822	-0.2	-6			1307	2.2	67
						1925	0.0	0
5 Th ☽	0039	2.5	76		20 F	0151	2.3	70
	0646	0.1	3			0803	0.3	9
	1254	2.6	79			1400	2.0	61
	1915	-0.2	-6			2015	0.1	3
6 F	0140	2.6	79		21 Sa	0246	2.3	70
	0751	0.1	3			0902	0.3	9
	1354	2.5	76			1455	1.9	58
	2013	-0.3	-9			2106	0.1	3
7 Sa	0243	2.8	85		22 Su	0340	2.4	73
	0859	0.0	0			1000	0.3	9
	1458	2.4	73			1549	1.9	58
	2112	-0.4	-12			2156	0.0	0
8 Su	0345	3.0	91		23 M	0430	2.4	73
	1006	-0.1	-3			1052	0.2	6
	1602	2.4	73			1641	1.9	58
	2212	-0.5	-15			2245	0.0	0
9 M	0446	3.1	94		24 Tu	0517	2.6	79
	1108	-0.2	-6			1140	0.1	3
	1703	2.5	76			1730	2.0	61
	2310	-0.6	-18			2331	-0.1	-3
10 Tu	0543	3.3	101		25 W	0601	2.7	82
	1207	-0.4	-12			1224	0.0	0
	1802	2.6	79			1815	2.1	64
11 W	0007	-0.7	-21		26 Th	0014	-0.2	-6
	0637	3.4	104			0643	2.8	85
	1301	-0.5	-15			1305	-0.1	-3
	1857	2.6	79			1857	2.2	67
12 Th ○	0101	-0.7	-21		27 F ●	0057	-0.3	-9
	0730	3.5	107			0723	2.9	88
	1353	-0.6	-18			1344	-0.2	-6
	1951	2.7	82			1939	2.3	70
13 F	0154	-0.7	-21		28 Sa	0138	-0.3	-9
	0820	3.4	104			0802	3.0	91
	1442	-0.6	-18			1423	-0.3	-9
	2042	2.7	82			2020	2.4	73
14 Sa	0245	-0.6	-18		29 Su	0220	-0.3	-9
	0908	3.3	101			0842	3.0	91
	1530	-0.5	-15			1501	-0.3	-9
	2133	2.7	82			2102	2.5	76
15 Su	0335	-0.5	-15		30 M	0303	-0.3	-9
	0956	3.1	94			0922	3.0	91
	1617	-0.4	-12			1541	-0.3	-9
	2223	2.6	79			2146	2.6	79
					31 Tu	0348	-0.3	-9
						1004	2.9	88
						1622	-0.4	-12
						2232	2.7	82

February

Day	Time (h m)	ft	cm		Day	Time (h m)	ft	cm
1 W	0437	-0.2	-6		16 Th	0532	0.1	3
	1049	2.8	85			1136	2.3	70
	1707	-0.3	-9			1749	0.0	0
	2322	2.7	82					
2 Th	0531	-0.1	-3		17 F	0010	2.4	73
	1138	2.7	82			0622	0.2	6
	1755	-0.3	-9			1222	2.1	64
						1834	0.1	3
3 F ○	0017	2.7	82		18 Sa ○	0100	2.3	70
	0630	0.0	0			0716	0.3	9
	1233	2.5	76			1312	2.0	61
	1849	-0.3	-9			1923	0.1	3
4 Sa	0118	2.8	85		19 Su	0154	2.3	70
	0735	0.0	0			0814	0.4	12
	1334	2.4	73			1407	1.9	58
	1949	-0.3	-9			2016	0.2	6
5 Su	0223	2.8	85		20 M	0251	2.3	70
	0844	0.0	0			0914	0.4	12
	1440	2.3	70			1505	1.9	58
	2052	-0.3	-9			2111	0.2	6
6 M	0328	2.9	88		21 Tu	0347	2.4	73
	0952	0.0	0			1011	0.3	9
	1547	2.3	70			1602	1.9	58
	2156	-0.4	-12			2206	0.1	3
7 Tu	0431	3.0	91		22 W	0439	2.5	76
	1056	-0.1	-3			1102	0.2	6
	1652	2.4	73			1655	2.1	64
	2258	-0.4	-12			2257	0.0	0
8 W	0530	3.1	94		23 Th	0527	2.7	82
	1154	-0.3	-9			1148	0.1	3
	1751	2.5	76			1743	2.2	67
	2356	-0.5	-15			2346	-0.1	-3
9 Th	0624	3.2	98		24 F	0611	2.8	85
	1247	-0.4	-12			1231	-0.1	-3
	1846	2.6	79			1829	2.4	73
10 F ○	0050	-0.6	-18		25 Sa	0031	-0.2	-6
	0715	3.2	98			0654	3.0	91
	1335	-0.5	-15			1311	-0.2	-6
	1936	2.7	82			1912	2.6	79
11 Sa	0140	-0.6	-18		26 Su ●	0116	-0.3	-9
	0802	3.2	98			0735	3.1	94
	1421	-0.5	-15			1351	-0.3	-9
	2024	2.7	82			1955	2.8	85
12 Su	0229	-0.5	-15		27 M	0201	-0.4	-12
	0847	3.1	94			0817	3.1	94
	1504	-0.5	-15			1431	-0.4	-12
	2110	2.7	82			2039	2.9	88
13 M	0315	-0.4	-12		28 Tu	0246	-0.4	-12
	0930	3.0	91			0859	3.1	94
	1546	-0.4	-12			1513	-0.5	-15
	2154	2.7	82			2124	3.0	91
14 Tu	0400	-0.3	-9					
	1012	2.8	85					
	1627	-0.3	-9					
	2238	2.6	79					
15 W	0445	-0.1	-3					
	1053	2.6	79					
	1708	-0.2	-6					
	2323	2.5	76					

March

Day	Time (h m)	ft	cm		Day	Time (h m)	ft	cm
1 W	0334	-0.4	-12		16 Th	0416	-0.1	-3
	0944	3.0	91			1019	2.5	76
	1556	-0.5	-15			1626	-0.1	-3
	2212	3.0	91			2244	2.6	79
2 Th	0424	-0.3	-9		17 F	0459	0.1	3
	1031	2.8	85			1059	2.3	70
	1642	-0.4	-12			1705	0.0	0
	2303	3.0	91			2327	2.5	76
3 F ○	0518	-0.2	-6		18 Sa ○	0544	0.2	6
	1122	2.7	82			1142	2.1	64
	1733	-0.4	-12			1747	0.1	3
	2359	3.0	91					
4 Sa	0617	-0.1	-3		19 Su	0013	2.4	73
	1218	2.5	76			0634	0.3	9
	1829	-0.3	-9			1230	2.0	61
						1834	0.2	6
5 Su ◐	0100	2.9	88		20 M ○	0105	2.4	73
	0722	0.0	0			0728	0.4	12
	1321	2.4	73			1324	1.9	58
	1932	-0.2	-6			1928	0.3	9
6 M	0206	2.9	88		21 Tu	0201	2.4	73
	0831	0.1	3			0827	0.4	12
	1430	2.3	70			1423	1.9	58
	2039	-0.2	-6			2027	0.3	9
7 Tu	0313	2.9	88		22 W	0259	2.4	73
	0940	0.0	0			0925	0.4	12
	1539	2.3	70			1523	2.0	61
	2146	-0.2	-6			2126	0.3	9
8 W	0418	2.9	88		23 Th	0355	2.5	76
	1043	-0.1	-3			1018	0.3	9
	1643	2.4	73			1618	2.2	67
	2249	-0.2	-6			2222	0.1	3
9 Th	0516	3.0	91		24 F	0447	2.7	82
	1138	-0.2	-6			1107	0.1	3
	1741	2.6	79			1710	2.4	73
	2347	-0.3	-9			2315	0.0	0
10 F	0609	3.0	91		25 Sa	0535	2.8	85
	1228	-0.3	-9			1152	-0.1	-3
	1832	2.7	82			1757	2.7	82
11 Sa	0039	-0.3	-9		26 Su	0005	-0.2	-6
	0657	3.0	91			0621	3.0	91
	1313	-0.3	-9			1235	-0.3	-9
	1919	2.8	85			1843	2.9	88
12 Su ○	0126	-0.4	-12		27 M ●	0053	-0.3	-9
	0741	3.0	91			0706	3.1	94
	1355	-0.4	-12			1317	-0.4	-12
	2003	2.8	85			1929	3.1	94
13 M	0211	-0.3	-9		28 Tu	0141	-0.5	-15
	0822	2.9	88			0751	3.1	94
	1434	-0.3	-9			1401	-0.5	-15
	2044	2.9	88			2015	3.3	101
14 Tu	0253	-0.3	-9		29 W	0229	-0.5	-15
	0902	2.8	85			0836	3.1	94
	1512	-0.3	-9			1445	-0.6	-18
	2124	2.8	85			2103	3.4	104
15 W	0335	-0.2	-6		30 Th	0319	-0.5	-15
	0941	2.6	79			0924	3.0	91
	1549	-0.2	-6			1532	-0.6	-18
	2204	2.7	82			2153	3.4	104
					31 F	0411	-0.4	-12
						1014	2.8	85
						1621	-0.5	-15
						2245	3.3	101

Time meridian 75° W. 0000 is midnight. 1200 is noon. Times are not adjusted for Daylight Saving Time.
Heights are referred to mean lower low water which is the chart datum of soundings.

Settlement Point, Grand Bahama Island, 2017

Times and Heights of High and Low Waters

April

Day	Time (h m)	Height (ft)	Height (cm)
1 Sa	0507	-0.3	-9
	1108	2.7	82
	1714	-0.4	-12
	2342	3.2	98
2 Su	0606	-0.2	-6
	1207	2.5	76
	1813	-0.2	-6
3 M ☽	0044	3.0	91
	0710	0.0	0
	1312	2.4	73
	1919	-0.1	-3
4 Tu	0150	2.9	88
	0818	0.0	0
	1421	2.4	73
	2028	0.0	0
5 W	0257	2.8	85
	0924	0.0	0
	1530	2.4	73
	2136	0.0	0
6 Th	0400	2.8	85
	1024	0.0	0
	1632	2.5	76
	2239	0.0	0
7 F	0458	2.8	85
	1117	-0.1	-3
	1727	2.6	79
	2335	-0.1	-3
8 Sa	0549	2.8	85
	1204	-0.2	-6
	1815	2.8	85
9 Su	0024	-0.1	-3
	0634	2.8	85
	1246	-0.2	-6
	1859	2.9	88
10 M	0109	-0.2	-6
	0716	2.8	85
	1325	-0.2	-6
	1939	2.9	88
11 Tu ○	0151	-0.2	-6
	0755	2.7	82
	1401	-0.2	-6
	2017	2.9	88
12 W	0231	-0.2	-6
	0833	2.6	79
	1437	-0.2	-6
	2054	2.9	88
13 Th	0310	-0.1	-3
	0911	2.5	76
	1513	-0.1	-3
	2132	2.8	85
14 F	0350	0.0	0
	0948	2.4	73
	1549	0.0	0
	2210	2.7	82
15 Sa	0430	0.1	3
	1027	2.2	67
	1626	0.1	3
	2250	2.7	82
16 Su	0513	0.2	6
	1109	2.1	64
	1707	0.2	6
	2334	2.6	79
17 M	0559	0.3	9
	1155	2.0	61
	1753	0.3	9
18 Tu	0022	2.5	76
	0649	0.4	12
	1247	2.0	61
	1846	0.4	12
19 W ○	0115	2.5	76
	0743	0.4	12
	1345	2.0	61
	1945	0.4	12
20 Th	0212	2.5	76
	0839	0.3	9
	1444	2.1	64
	2046	0.3	9
21 F	0309	2.5	76
	0932	0.2	6
	1541	2.3	70
	2147	0.2	6
22 Sa	0404	2.7	82
	1023	0.0	0
	1635	2.6	79
	2244	0.0	0
23 Su	0456	2.8	85
	1111	-0.2	-6
	1726	2.9	88
	2338	-0.2	-6
24 M	0546	2.9	88
	1158	-0.4	-12
	1815	3.2	98
25 Tu	0030	-0.4	-12
	0636	3.0	91
	1244	-0.5	-15
	1904	3.4	104
26 W ●	0121	-0.5	-15
	0725	3.0	91
	1331	-0.6	-18
	1953	3.5	107
27 Th	0212	-0.6	-18
	0814	3.0	91
	1420	-0.7	-21
	2043	3.6	110
28 F	0305	-0.6	-18
	0905	2.9	88
	1510	-0.7	-21
	2135	3.6	110
29 Sa	0358	-0.5	-15
	0959	2.8	85
	1602	-0.5	-15
	2229	3.5	107
30 Su	0454	-0.4	-12
	1055	2.7	82
	1658	-0.4	-12
	2326	3.3	101

May

Day	Time (h m)	Height (ft)	Height (cm)
1 M	0553	-0.2	-6
	1156	2.6	79
	1759	-0.2	-6
2 Tu ○	0027	3.1	94
	0655	-0.1	-3
	1301	2.5	76
	1905	0.0	0
3 W	0131	2.9	88
	0759	0.0	0
	1409	2.4	73
	2014	0.1	3
4 Th	0235	2.8	85
	0901	0.0	0
	1514	2.5	76
	2121	0.1	3
5 F	0336	2.7	82
	0958	0.0	0
	1614	2.6	79
	2222	0.1	3
6 Sa	0432	2.6	79
	1048	-0.1	-3
	1706	2.7	82
	2317	0.1	3
7 Su	0522	2.6	79
	1133	-0.1	-3
	1752	2.8	85
8 M	0005	0.0	0
	0607	2.5	76
	1214	-0.1	-3
	1834	2.9	88
9 Tu	0049	0.0	0
	0648	2.5	76
	1252	-0.2	-6
	1913	2.9	88
10 W ○	0130	-0.1	-3
	0727	2.5	76
	1329	-0.2	-6
	1950	2.9	88
11 Th	0209	-0.1	-3
	0805	2.4	73
	1404	-0.1	-3
	2027	2.9	88
12 F	0247	-0.1	-3
	0843	2.3	70
	1440	-0.1	-3
	2103	2.9	88
13 Sa	0326	0.0	0
	0921	2.3	70
	1517	0.0	0
	2141	2.8	85
14 Su	0405	0.1	3
	1000	2.2	67
	1555	0.1	3
	2220	2.8	85
15 M	0446	0.1	3
	1041	2.1	64
	1635	0.2	6
	2302	2.7	82
16 Tu	0529	0.2	6
	1126	2.1	64
	1720	0.3	9
	2346	2.6	79
17 W	0615	0.3	9
	1216	2.1	64
	1811	0.4	12
18 Th ○	0036	2.6	79
	0704	0.3	9
	1310	2.2	67
	1909	0.4	12
19 F	0129	2.6	79
	0756	0.2	6
	1408	2.3	70
	2011	0.3	9
20 Sa	0226	2.6	79
	0849	0.1	3
	1506	2.5	76
	2113	0.2	6
21 Su	0323	2.6	79
	0941	-0.1	-3
	1602	2.8	85
	2214	0.1	3
22 M	0419	2.7	82
	1033	-0.3	-9
	1656	3.1	94
	2312	-0.1	-3
23 Tu	0514	2.8	85
	1124	-0.4	-12
	1749	3.3	101
24 W	0008	-0.3	-9
	0608	2.9	88
	1215	-0.6	-18
	1841	3.6	110
25 Th ●	0102	-0.5	-15
	0701	2.9	88
	1306	-0.7	-21
	1933	3.7	113
26 F	0156	-0.5	-15
	0754	2.9	88
	1358	-0.7	-21
	2026	3.7	113
27 Sa	0250	-0.6	-18
	0848	2.9	88
	1451	-0.7	-21
	2119	3.7	113
28 Su	0344	-0.5	-15
	0943	2.8	85
	1546	-0.5	-15
	2213	3.5	107
29 M	0439	-0.4	-12
	1041	2.7	82
	1643	-0.3	-9
	2309	3.3	101
30 Tu	0536	-0.3	-9
	1141	2.6	79
	1743	-0.1	-3
31 W	0007	3.1	94
	0634	-0.2	-6
	1244	2.6	79
	1847	0.0	0

June

Day	Time (h m)	Height (ft)	Height (cm)
1 Th ◐	0106	2.9	88
	0733	-0.1	-3
	1347	2.6	79
	1952	0.2	6
2 F	0206	2.7	82
	0830	0.0	0
	1449	2.6	79
	2057	0.3	9
3 Sa	0304	2.6	79
	0924	0.0	0
	1547	2.6	79
	2157	0.3	9
4 Su	0359	2.5	76
	1013	0.0	0
	1638	2.7	82
	2252	0.2	6
5 M	0449	2.4	73
	1058	0.0	0
	1724	2.8	85
	2341	0.2	6
6 Tu	0535	2.3	70
	1140	0.0	0
	1806	2.9	88
7 W	0025	0.1	3
	0618	2.3	70
	1219	-0.1	-3
	1845	2.9	88
8 Th	0106	0.1	3
	0658	2.3	70
	1257	-0.1	-3
	1924	3.0	91
9 F ○	0145	0.0	0
	0738	2.3	70
	1335	-0.1	-3
	2001	3.0	91
10 Sa	0224	0.0	0
	0817	2.3	70
	1412	0.0	0
	2039	3.0	91
11 Su	0303	0.1	3
	0856	2.3	70
	1450	0.0	0
	2116	2.9	88
12 M	0341	0.1	3
	0935	2.3	70
	1529	0.1	3
	2154	2.9	88
13 Tu	0420	0.1	3
	1016	2.3	70
	1610	0.2	6
	2234	2.9	88
14 W	0500	0.2	6
	1100	2.3	70
	1654	0.3	9
	2316	2.8	85
15 Th	0543	0.2	6
	1147	2.3	70
	1744	0.3	9
16 F	0002	2.7	82
	0629	0.2	6
	1239	2.4	73
	1840	0.4	12
17 Sa ○	0053	2.7	82
	0718	0.1	3
	1336	2.6	79
	1941	0.3	9
18 Su	0149	2.6	79
	0810	0.0	0
	1434	2.8	85
	2045	0.3	9
19 M	0248	2.6	79
	0905	-0.1	-3
	1533	3.0	91
	2149	0.1	3
20 Tu	0348	2.7	82
	1000	-0.2	-6
	1631	3.2	98
	2250	0.0	0
21 W	0447	2.7	82
	1056	-0.4	-12
	1727	3.5	107
	2349	-0.2	-6
22 Th	0545	2.8	85
	1151	-0.5	-15
	1822	3.7	113
23 F ●	0045	-0.3	-9
	0641	2.9	88
	1246	-0.6	-18
	1916	3.8	116
24 Sa	0140	-0.4	-12
	0737	2.9	88
	1340	-0.6	-18
	2009	3.8	116
25 Su	0234	-0.4	-12
	0832	2.9	88
	1435	-0.6	-18
	2102	3.7	113
26 M	0326	-0.4	-12
	0927	2.9	88
	1529	-0.4	-12
	2155	3.6	110
27 Tu	0419	-0.3	-9
	1023	2.9	88
	1625	-0.2	-6
	2247	3.4	104
28 W	0512	-0.2	-6
	1120	2.8	85
	1722	0.0	0
	2341	3.1	94
29 Th	0605	-0.1	-3
	1218	2.7	82
	1822	0.2	6
30 F ◐	0035	2.9	88
	0659	0.0	0
	1317	2.7	82
	1923	0.3	9

Time meridian 75° W. 0000 is midnight. 1200 is noon. Times are not adjusted for Daylight Saving Time.
Heights are referred to mean lower low water which is the chart datum of soundings.

Settlement Point, Grand Bahama Island, 2017

Times and Heights of High and Low Waters

July

Day	Time	ft	cm	Day	Time	ft	cm
1 Sa	0131	2.7	82	16 Su	0025	2.8	85
	0752	0.1	3		0645	0.1	3
	1415	2.7	82		1307	2.9	88
	2025	0.4	12	◗	1918	0.4	12
2 Su	0226	2.5	76	17 M	0120	2.8	85
	0844	0.2	6		0738	0.1	3
	1511	2.7	82		1407	3.0	91
	2125	0.5	15		2023	0.4	12
3 M	0321	2.4	73	18 Tu	0221	2.7	82
	0933	0.2	6		0836	0.0	0
	1603	2.7	82		1509	3.2	98
	2220	0.5	15		2129	0.3	9
4 Tu	0413	2.3	70	19 W	0324	2.7	82
	1020	0.2	6		0936	-0.1	-3
	1651	2.8	85		1610	3.4	104
	2311	0.4	12		2233	0.2	6
5 W	0501	2.3	70	20 Th	0427	2.8	85
	1105	0.2	6		1036	-0.2	-6
	1736	2.9	88		1710	3.6	110
	2357	0.3	9		2333	0.0	0
6 Th	0547	2.3	70	21 F	0528	2.9	88
	1147	0.1	3		1134	-0.3	-9
	1817	3.0	91		1806	3.7	113
7 F	0039	0.3	9	22 Sa	0030	-0.1	-3
	0630	2.4	73		0626	3.0	91
	1228	0.1	3		1231	-0.4	-12
	1857	3.0	91		1901	3.8	116
8 Sa ○	0120	0.2	6	23 Su ●	0124	-0.2	-6
	0711	2.4	73		0722	3.1	94
	1308	0.1	3		1326	-0.4	-12
	1936	3.1	94		1953	3.8	116
9 Su	0159	0.2	6	24 M	0215	-0.2	-6
	0751	2.4	73		0816	3.1	94
	1348	0.1	3		1420	-0.3	-9
	2014	3.1	94		2044	3.8	116
10 M	0237	0.2	6	25 Tu	0305	-0.2	-6
	0831	2.5	76		0908	3.2	98
	1427	0.1	3		1512	-0.2	-6
	2052	3.1	94		2133	3.6	110
11 Tu	0314	0.2	6	26 W	0354	-0.2	-6
	0911	2.5	76		1000	3.1	94
	1507	0.2	6		1605	0.0	0
	2129	3.1	94		2222	3.4	104
12 W	0352	0.2	6	27 Th	0442	-0.1	-3
	0951	2.6	79		1052	3.1	94
	1548	0.2	6		1658	0.2	6
	2208	3.1	94		2311	3.2	98
13 Th	0431	0.2	6	28 F	0530	0.1	3
	1034	2.6	79		1145	3.0	91
	1633	0.3	9		1752	0.3	9
	2249	3.0	91				
14 F	0511	0.2	6	29 Sa	0000	2.9	88
	1121	2.7	82		0618	0.2	6
	1722	0.4	12		1238	2.9	88
	2335	2.9	88		1848	0.5	15
15 Sa	0556	0.2	6	30 Su ◑	0051	2.7	82
	1211	2.8	85		0708	0.3	9
	1817	0.4	12		1333	2.8	85
					1946	0.6	18
				31 M	0144	2.5	76
					0758	0.4	12
					1428	2.8	85
					2045	0.7	21

August

Day	Time	ft	cm	Day	Time	ft	cm
1 Tu	0239	2.4	73	16 W	0204	2.8	85
	0850	0.5	15		0816	0.2	6
	1523	2.8	85		1451	3.4	104
	2143	0.7	21		2114	0.5	15
2 W	0334	2.4	73	17 Th	0310	2.8	85
	0941	0.5	15		0920	0.2	6
	1614	2.9	88		1555	3.5	107
	2236	0.7	21		2219	0.4	12
3 Th	0427	2.4	73	18 F	0416	2.9	88
	1030	0.4	12		1023	0.1	3
	1702	3.0	91		1656	3.6	110
	2325	0.6	18		2320	0.3	9
4 F	0515	2.4	73	19 Sa	0517	3.0	91
	1117	0.4	12		1124	0.0	0
	1747	3.1	94		1753	3.7	113
5 Sa	0009	0.5	15	20 Su	0015	0.1	3
	0601	2.5	76		0614	3.2	98
	1201	0.3	9		1220	-0.1	-3
	1829	3.2	98		1846	3.8	116
6 Su	0050	0.4	12	21 M ●	0106	0.0	0
	0643	2.6	79		0708	3.3	101
	1243	0.3	9		1314	-0.1	-3
	1908	3.3	101		1935	3.8	116
7 M ○	0129	0.3	9	22 Tu	0154	0.0	0
	0724	2.8	85		0758	3.4	104
	1324	0.2	6		1405	-0.1	-3
	1947	3.3	101		2023	3.7	113
8 Tu	0206	0.3	9	23 W	0239	0.0	0
	0804	2.9	88		0847	3.4	104
	1405	0.2	6		1454	0.0	0
	2025	3.4	104		2108	3.6	110
9 W	0243	0.2	6	24 Th	0324	0.0	0
	0844	3.0	91		0934	3.4	104
	1446	0.2	6		1542	0.2	6
	2103	3.4	104		2153	3.4	104
10 Th	0321	0.2	6	25 F	0407	0.2	6
	0926	3.0	91		1020	3.3	101
	1529	0.3	9		1630	0.3	9
	2143	3.3	101		2238	3.2	98
11 F	0400	0.2	6	26 Sa	0450	0.3	9
	1009	3.1	94		1107	3.2	98
	1614	0.3	9		1718	0.5	15
	2225	3.2	98		2323	2.9	88
12 Sa	0441	0.2	6	27 Su	0534	0.4	12
	1056	3.1	94		1155	3.0	91
	1704	0.4	12		1809	0.7	21
	2311	3.1	94				
13 Su	0526	0.2	6	28 M	0010	2.7	82
	1147	3.2	98		0621	0.6	18
	1759	0.5	15		1246	2.9	88
					1904	0.8	24
14 M ◑	0002	3.0	91	29 Tu ◑	0101	2.6	79
	0617	0.2	6		0710	0.7	21
	1244	3.2	98		1341	2.9	88
	1900	0.5	15		2002	0.9	27
15 Tu	0100	2.9	88	30 W	0157	2.5	76
	0714	0.2	6		0804	0.7	21
	1346	3.3	101		1437	2.9	88
	2007	0.5	15		2101	0.9	27
				31 Th	0255	2.4	73
					0900	0.7	21
					1533	2.9	88
					2157	0.9	27

September

Day	Time	ft	cm	Day	Time	ft	cm
1 F	0351	2.5	76	16 Sa	0409	3.0	91
	0954	0.7	21		1016	0.3	9
	1625	3.0	91		1643	3.6	110
	2247	0.8	24		2305	0.4	12
2 Sa	0443	2.6	79	17 Su	0509	3.2	98
	1045	0.6	18		1116	0.2	6
	1712	3.1	94		1738	3.6	110
	2333	0.7	21		2357	0.2	6
3 Su	0530	2.8	85	18 M	0603	3.3	101
	1132	0.5	15		1211	0.2	6
	1756	3.3	101		1829	3.6	110
4 M	0014	0.5	15	19 Tu	0045	0.2	6
	0613	2.9	88		0653	3.4	104
	1216	0.4	12		1301	0.1	3
	1837	3.4	104		1915	3.6	110
5 Tu	0053	0.4	12	20 W ●	0129	0.1	3
	0655	3.1	94		0739	3.5	107
	1300	0.3	9		1349	0.1	3
	1917	3.5	107		1959	3.5	107
6 W ○	0131	0.3	9	21 Th	0211	0.1	3
	0736	3.3	101		0823	3.5	107
	1342	0.2	6		1434	0.2	6
	1956	3.5	107		2042	3.4	104
7 Th	0210	0.2	6	22 F	0251	0.2	6
	0817	3.4	104		0905	3.5	107
	1425	0.2	6		1518	0.3	9
	2037	3.5	107		2123	3.2	98
8 F	0249	0.2	6	23 Sa	0330	0.3	9
	0900	3.5	107		0947	3.4	104
	1510	0.2	6		1601	0.4	12
	2119	3.4	104		2204	3.0	91
9 Sa	0330	0.1	3	24 Su	0410	0.4	12
	0945	3.5	107		1029	3.3	101
	1558	0.3	9		1646	0.5	15
	2203	3.3	101		2246	2.8	85
10 Su	0413	0.2	6	25 M	0450	0.5	15
	1033	3.5	107		1113	3.1	94
	1649	0.4	12		1733	0.7	21
	2252	3.2	98		2331	2.7	82
11 M	0501	0.2	6	26 Tu	0534	0.7	21
	1126	3.5	107		1200	3.0	91
	1745	0.5	15		1823	0.8	24
	2346	3.0	91				
12 Tu	0555	0.3	9	27 W ◑	0020	2.5	76
	1225	3.5	107		0623	0.8	24
	1848	0.6	18		1253	2.9	88
					1919	0.9	27
13 W ◑	0047	2.9	88	28 Th	0116	2.4	73
	0656	0.4	12		0718	0.8	24
	1329	3.4	104		1349	2.9	88
	1955	0.6	18		2017	0.9	27
14 Th	0154	2.9	88	29 F	0215	2.4	73
	0802	0.4	12		0817	0.9	27
	1436	3.4	104		1447	2.9	88
	2103	0.6	18		2113	0.9	27
15 F	0303	2.9	88	30 Sa	0313	2.5	76
	0910	0.4	12		0915	0.8	24
	1542	3.5	107		1541	3.0	91
	2207	0.5	15		2205	0.8	24

Time meridian 75° W. 0000 is midnight. 1200 is noon. Times are not adjusted for Daylight Saving Time.
Heights are referred to mean lower low water which is the chart datum of soundings.

Settlement Point, Grand Bahama Island, 2017

Times and Heights of High and Low Waters

October

Day	Time	ft	cm
1 Su	0407	2.7	82
	1010	0.7	21
	1631	3.1	94
	2251	0.6	18
2 M	0456	2.9	88
	1101	0.6	18
	1718	3.2	98
	2334	0.5	15
3 Tu	0541	3.1	94
	1148	0.4	12
	1801	3.3	101
4 W	0014	0.3	9
	0624	3.3	101
	1234	0.3	9
	1844	3.4	104
5 Th ○	0055	0.2	6
	0707	3.5	107
	1319	0.1	3
	1927	3.4	104
6 F	0136	0.0	0
	0751	3.7	113
	1405	0.1	3
	2011	3.4	104
7 Sa	0218	0.0	0
	0836	3.8	116
	1453	0.0	0
	2056	3.4	104
8 Su	0302	0.0	0
	0924	3.8	116
	1543	0.1	3
	2144	3.3	101
9 M	0350	0.0	0
	1014	3.8	116
	1636	0.2	6
	2236	3.1	94
10 Tu	0441	0.1	3
	1109	3.7	113
	1734	0.3	9
	2334	3.0	91
11 W	0539	0.2	6
	1209	3.5	107
	1836	0.4	12
12 Th ◑	0037	2.9	88
	0643	0.4	12
	1314	3.4	104
	1943	0.5	15
13 F	0146	2.8	85
	0752	0.4	12
	1421	3.3	101
	2049	0.4	12
14 Sa	0256	2.9	88
	0902	0.4	12
	1526	3.3	101
	2151	0.4	12
15 Su	0400	3.0	91
	1008	0.4	12
	1626	3.3	101
	2246	0.3	9
16 M	0458	3.2	98
	1107	0.3	9
	1720	3.3	101
	2336	0.2	6
17 Tu	0549	3.3	101
	1200	0.2	6
	1809	3.3	101
18 W	0020	0.1	3
	0635	3.4	104
	1247	0.2	6
	1853	3.2	98
19 Th ●	0102	0.1	3
	0718	3.4	104
	1332	0.2	6
	1935	3.1	94
20 F	0140	0.1	3
	0758	3.4	104
	1414	0.2	6
	2015	3.0	91
21 Sa	0218	0.1	3
	0837	3.4	104
	1454	0.2	6
	2054	2.9	88
22 Su	0255	0.2	6
	0915	3.3	101
	1535	0.3	9
	2133	2.7	82
23 M	0333	0.3	9
	0955	3.2	98
	1616	0.4	12
	2213	2.6	79
24 Tu	0412	0.4	12
	1036	3.1	94
	1700	0.5	15
	2256	2.5	76
25 W	0453	0.6	18
	1120	2.9	88
	1747	0.6	18
	2344	2.4	73
26 Th	0540	0.7	21
	1208	2.8	85
	1837	0.7	21
27 F ◐	0036	2.3	70
	0633	0.8	24
	1301	2.8	85
	1931	0.7	21
28 Sa	0134	2.3	70
	0732	0.8	24
	1357	2.8	85
	2025	0.7	21
29 Su	0232	2.4	73
	0833	0.7	21
	1453	2.8	85
	2117	0.6	18
30 M	0328	2.6	79
	0932	0.6	18
	1546	2.9	88
	2205	0.4	12
31 Tu	0419	2.9	88
	1027	0.5	15
	1636	3.0	91
	2251	0.2	6

November

Day	Time	ft	cm
1 W	0507	3.1	94
	1118	0.3	9
	1724	3.1	94
	2335	0.0	0
2 Th	0554	3.4	104
	1208	0.1	3
	1812	3.2	98
3 F	0020	-0.1	-3
	0640	3.6	110
	1257	-0.1	-3
	1859	3.2	98
4 Sa ○	0105	-0.3	-9
	0727	3.8	116
	1347	-0.2	-6
	1947	3.2	98
5 Su	0151	-0.3	-9
	0815	3.9	119
	1437	-0.2	-6
	2036	3.2	98
6 M	0239	-0.3	-9
	0905	3.9	119
	1529	-0.2	-6
	2128	3.1	94
7 Tu	0331	-0.3	-9
	0958	3.8	116
	1623	-0.1	-3
	2223	3.0	91
8 W	0425	-0.1	-3
	1054	3.6	110
	1721	0.0	0
	2322	2.8	85
9 Th	0525	0.0	0
	1153	3.4	104
	1822	0.1	3
10 F ◑	0027	2.8	85
	0630	0.2	6
	1256	3.2	98
	1925	0.2	6
11 Sa	0135	2.7	82
	0740	0.3	9
	1401	3.1	94
	2028	0.2	6
12 Su	0242	2.8	85
	0849	0.3	9
	1505	3.0	91
	2128	0.1	3
13 M	0345	2.9	88
	0954	0.3	9
	1604	2.9	88
	2221	0.1	3
14 Tu	0441	3.0	91
	1053	0.3	9
	1657	2.8	85
	2309	0.0	0
15 W	0530	3.1	94
	1144	0.2	6
	1745	2.8	85
	2353	0.0	0
16 Th	0614	3.2	98
	1231	0.1	3
	1829	2.7	82
17 F	0033	0.0	0
	0655	3.2	98
	1313	0.1	3
	1910	2.7	82
18 Sa ●	0111	0.0	0
	0734	3.2	98
	1353	0.1	3
	1949	2.6	79
19 Su	0148	0.0	0
	0811	3.2	98
	1432	0.1	3
	2027	2.5	76
20 M	0225	0.1	3
	0849	3.1	94
	1511	0.1	3
	2106	2.4	73
21 Tu	0302	0.1	3
	0926	3.0	91
	1551	0.2	6
	2145	2.4	73
22 W	0340	0.2	6
	1005	2.9	88
	1632	0.3	9
	2227	2.3	70
23 Th	0421	0.3	9
	1046	2.8	85
	1714	0.3	9
	2311	2.2	67
24 F	0505	0.4	12
	1130	2.7	82
	1759	0.4	12
25 Sa	0000	2.2	67
	0555	0.5	15
	1218	2.6	79
	1847	0.4	12
26 Su ◐	0054	2.2	67
	0650	0.6	18
	1309	2.6	79
	1937	0.4	12
27 M	0150	2.3	70
	0751	0.5	15
	1404	2.6	79
	2028	0.3	9
28 Tu	0246	2.5	76
	0853	0.4	12
	1500	2.6	79
	2119	0.1	3
29 W	0341	2.8	85
	0952	0.3	9
	1555	2.7	82
	2209	-0.1	-3
30 Th	0434	3.0	91
	1049	0.1	3
	1649	2.7	82
	2259	-0.3	-9

December

Day	Time	ft	cm
1 F	0525	3.3	101
	1144	-0.1	-3
	1742	2.8	85
	2348	-0.4	-12
2 Sa	0616	3.5	107
	1237	-0.3	-9
	1834	2.9	88
3 Su ○	0039	-0.6	-18
	0706	3.7	113
	1329	-0.4	-12
	1926	2.9	88
4 M	0129	-0.6	-18
	0758	3.8	116
	1421	-0.5	-15
	2019	2.9	88
5 Tu	0221	-0.6	-18
	0849	3.8	116
	1514	-0.5	-15
	2113	2.9	88
6 W	0315	-0.6	-18
	0943	3.7	113
	1608	-0.4	-12
	2209	2.8	85
7 Th	0411	-0.4	-12
	1038	3.5	107
	1704	-0.3	-9
	2308	2.7	82
8 F	0511	-0.2	-6
	1134	3.3	101
	1802	-0.2	-6
9 Sa	0010	2.7	82
	0614	0.0	0
	1234	3.0	91
	1901	-0.1	-3
10 Su ◑	0115	2.6	79
	0720	0.1	3
	1335	2.8	85
	2000	-0.1	-3
11 M	0220	2.6	79
	0828	0.2	6
	1436	2.6	79
	2057	-0.1	-3
12 Tu	0321	2.7	82
	0933	0.2	6
	1535	2.5	76
	2150	-0.1	-3
13 W	0417	2.7	82
	1032	0.2	6
	1629	2.4	73
	2239	-0.1	-3
14 Th	0506	2.8	85
	1124	0.1	3
	1718	2.3	70
	2323	-0.1	-3
15 F	0551	2.9	88
	1210	0.1	3
	1803	2.3	70
16 Sa	0005	-0.1	-3
	0632	2.9	88
	1253	0.0	0
	1845	2.3	70
17 Su	0044	-0.1	-3
	0711	2.9	88
	1333	0.0	0
	1925	2.3	70
18 M ●	0122	-0.1	-3
	0748	2.9	88
	1411	0.0	0
	2003	2.3	70
19 Tu	0159	-0.1	-3
	0825	2.9	88
	1449	0.0	0
	2042	2.2	67
20 W	0237	-0.1	-3
	0902	2.9	88
	1527	0.0	0
	2121	2.2	67
21 Th	0315	0.0	0
	0940	2.8	85
	1605	0.0	0
	2201	2.2	67
22 F	0355	0.1	3
	1018	2.7	82
	1643	0.1	3
	2242	2.2	67
23 Sa	0437	0.2	6
	1058	2.7	82
	1723	0.1	3
	2327	2.2	67
24 Su	0523	0.3	9
	1140	2.6	79
	1806	0.1	3
25 M	0016	2.2	67
	0615	0.3	9
	1228	2.5	76
	1852	0.1	3
26 Tu ◐	0110	2.3	70
	0714	0.3	9
	1321	2.4	73
	1943	0.0	0
27 W	0207	2.5	76
	0817	0.3	9
	1418	2.4	73
	2036	-0.1	-3
28 Th	0305	2.7	82
	0921	0.1	3
	1518	2.4	73
	2132	-0.3	-9
29 F	0403	2.9	88
	1023	0.0	0
	1618	2.5	76
	2228	-0.4	-12
30 Sa	0500	3.2	98
	1122	-0.2	-6
	1716	2.5	76
	2323	-0.6	-18
31 Su	0555	3.4	104
	1218	-0.4	-12
	1813	2.7	82

Time meridian 75° W. 0000 is midnight. 1200 is noon. Times are not adjusted for Daylight Saving Time.
Heights are referred to mean lower low water which is the chart datum of soundings.

Magueyes Island, Puerto Rico, 2017

Times and Heights of High and Low Waters

January

Day	Time	ft	cm	Day	Time	ft	cm
1 Su	0137	-0.1	-3	16 M	0211	-0.1	-3
	1218	0.6	18		1151	0.4	12
2 M	0153	-0.1	-3	17 Tu	0211	0.0	0
	1240	0.6	18		1130	0.4	12
3 Tu	0158	0.0	0	18 W	0117	0.1	3
	1250	0.6	18		1040	0.3	9
					2150	0.1	3
4 W	0138	0.1	3	19 Th O	0926	0.3	9
	1230	0.5	15		2040	0.0	0
5 Th ◑	0032	0.1	3	20 F	0828	0.4	12
	1105	0.4	12		2042	0.0	0
	2304	0.1	3				
6 F	0913	0.5	15	21 Sa	0812	0.4	12
	2211	0.1	3		2110	-0.1	-3
7 Sa	0833	0.5	15	22 Su	0820	0.5	15
	2159	0.0	0		2148	-0.1	-3
8 Su	0837	0.6	18	23 M	0839	0.5	15
	2217	-0.1	-3		2230	-0.2	-6
9 M	0900	0.7	21	24 Tu	0904	0.5	15
	2250	-0.2	-6		2310	-0.2	-6
10 Tu	0931	0.7	21	25 W	0930	0.5	15
	2329	-0.2	-6		2346	-0.2	-6
11 W	1004	0.7	21	26 Th	0957	0.6	18
12 Th O	0010	-0.3	-9	27 F ●	0019	-0.2	-6
	1038	0.7	21		1023	0.6	18
13 F	0049	-0.3	-9	28 Sa	0049	-0.2	-6
	1109	0.6	18		1047	0.6	18
14 Sa	0123	-0.2	-6	29 Su	0116	-0.2	-6
	1134	0.6	18		1107	0.5	15
15 Su	0152	-0.1	-3	30 M	0140	-0.1	-3
	1150	0.5	15		1120	0.5	15
				31 Tu	0156	0.0	0
					1119	0.4	12

February

Day	Time	ft	cm	Day	Time	ft	cm
1 W	0152	0.1	3	16 Th	0819	0.3	9
	1051	0.4	12		1701	0.0	0
2 Th	0003	0.1	3	17 F	0714	0.3	9
	0939	0.3	9		1719	-0.1	-3
	1912	0.1	3				
3 F	0812	0.4	12	18 Sa O	0657	0.3	9
	1857	0.0	0		1750	-0.1	-3
4 Sa ◑	0737	0.4	12	19 Su	0710	0.4	12
	1923	-0.1	-3		1838	-0.1	-3
5 Su	0744	0.5	15	20 M	0733	0.4	12
	2015	-0.2	-6		1954	-0.2	-6
6 M	0808	0.6	18	21 Tu	0800	0.4	12
	2120	-0.2	-6		2128	-0.2	-6
7 Tu	0838	0.6	18	22 W	0827	0.5	15
	2225	-0.2	-6		2239	-0.2	-6
8 W	0909	0.6	18	23 Th	0854	0.5	15
	2323	-0.2	-6		2331	-0.2	-6
9 Th	0939	0.6	18	24 F	0918	0.5	15
10 F O	0013	-0.2	-6	25 Sa	0015	-0.1	-3
	1005	0.5	15		0939	0.5	15
11 Sa	0057	-0.2	-6	26 Su ●	0054	-0.1	-3
	1024	0.5	15		0956	0.5	15
12 Su	0134	-0.1	-3	27 M	0132	0.0	0
	1034	0.4	12		1003	0.4	12
13 M	0206	0.0	0	28 Tu	0209	0.1	3
	1031	0.3	9		0953	0.3	9
					1643	0.1	3
					2121	0.2	6
14 Tu	0230	0.0	0				
	1010	0.3	9				
	1713	0.1	3				
	2145	0.2	6				
15 W	0236	0.1	3				
	0926	0.3	9				
	1657	0.1	3				

March

Day	Time	ft	cm	Day	Time	ft	cm
1 W	0241	0.1	3	16 Th	1508	-0.1	-3
	0913	0.3	9				
	1611	0.1	3				
	2325	0.2	6				
2 Th	0254	0.1	3	17 F	0047	0.3	9
	0745	0.3	9		1522	-0.1	-3
	1605	0.0	0				
3 F	0553	0.3	9	18 Sa	0336	0.3	9
	1619	-0.1	-3		1543	-0.2	-6
4 Sa	0545	0.4	12	19 Su	0459	0.4	12
	1648	-0.1	-3		1608	-0.2	-6
5 Su ◑	0615	0.5	15	20 M O	0548	0.4	12
	1730	-0.2	-6		1638	-0.2	-6
6 M	0651	0.5	15	21 Tu	0627	0.4	12
	1828	-0.2	-6		1712	-0.1	-3
7 Tu	0727	0.5	15	22 W	0701	0.4	12
	2000	-0.2	-6		1754	-0.1	-3
8 W	0801	0.5	15	23 Th	0730	0.5	15
	2159	-0.1	-3		2103	0.0	0
9 Th	0829	0.5	15	24 F	0756	0.5	15
	2325	-0.1	-3		2311	0.0	0
10 F	0852	0.4	12	25 Sa	0817	0.4	12
					1645	0.0	0
					1912	0.1	3
11 Sa	0027	-0.1	-3	26 Su	0024	0.0	0
	0906	0.4	12		0830	0.4	12
					1545	0.1	3
					2006	0.2	6
12 Su O	0120	0.0	0	27 M ●	0128	0.1	3
	0909	0.3	9		0831	0.3	9
	1549	0.1	3		1502	0.1	3
	2005	0.2	6		2059	0.3	9
13 M	0209	0.1	3	28 Tu	0239	0.2	6
	0900	0.3	9		0805	0.3	9
	1516	0.1	3		1433	0.1	3
	2109	0.2	6		2156	0.4	12
14 Tu	0258	0.1	3	29 W	0426	0.1	3
	0833	0.2	6		0636	0.2	6
	1502	0.1	3		1422	0.0	0
	2209	0.3	9		2301	0.4	12
15 W	0356	0.1	3	30 Th	1428	-0.1	-3
	0737	0.2	6				
	1500	0.0	0				
	2315	0.3	9				
				31 F	0022	0.4	12
					1446	-0.2	-6

Time meridian 60° W. 0000 is midnight. 1200 is noon. Times are not adjusted for Daylight Saving Time.
Heights are referred to mean lower low water which is the chart datum of soundings.

Magueyes Island, Puerto Rico, 2017

Times and Heights of High and Low Waters

April

Day	Time	ft	cm	Day	Time	ft	cm
1 Sa	0208	0.5	15	16 Su	0143	0.4	12
	1513	-0.2	-6		1444	-0.2	-6
2 Su	0348	0.5	15	17 M	0304	0.4	12
	1546	-0.2	-6		1504	-0.2	-6
3 M ☽	0457	0.5	15	18 Tu	0410	0.5	15
	1620	-0.2	-6		1523	-0.1	-3
4 Tu	0548	0.5	15	19 W ☽	0500	0.5	15
	1652	-0.1	-3		1535	-0.1	-3
5 W	0628	0.5	15	20 Th	0538	0.5	15
	1714	-0.1	-3		1536	0.0	0
6 Th	0658	0.4	12	21 F	0608	0.5	15
	1647	0.0	0		1517	0.0	0
7 F	0717	0.4	12	22 Sa	0630	0.4	12
	1529	0.0	0		1442	0.1	3
	2001	0.1	3				
	2342	0.0	0				
8 Sa	0725	0.3	9	23 Su	0638	0.4	12
	1433	0.1	3		1403	0.1	3
	2021	0.2	6		2104	0.3	9
9 Su	0115	0.1	3	24 M	0144	0.2	6
	0718	0.3	9		0620	0.3	9
	1359	0.1	3		1330	0.1	3
	2052	0.3	9		2121	0.4	12
10 M	0238	0.1	3	25 Tu	1310	0.0	0
	0652	0.2	6		2153	0.5	15
	1343	0.0	0				
	2127	0.4	12				
11 Tu ○	1338	0.0	0	26 W ●	1305	-0.1	-3
	2204	0.4	12		2236	0.6	18
12 W	1341	-0.1	-3	27 Th	1316	-0.2	-6
	2245	0.4	12		2327	0.6	18
13 Th	1351	-0.1	-3	28 F	1338	-0.2	-6
	2332	0.4	12				
14 F	1406	-0.2	-6	29 Sa	0026	0.6	18
					1406	-0.3	-9
15 Sa	0029	0.4	12	30 Su	0132	0.6	18
	1424	-0.2	-6		1435	-0.3	-9

May

Day	Time	ft	cm	Day	Time	ft	cm
1 M	0239	0.6	18	16 Tu	0154	0.5	15
	1503	-0.2	-6		1421	-0.2	-6
2 Tu ☽	0339	0.5	15	17 W	0241	0.5	15
	1523	-0.1	-3		1430	-0.1	-3
3 W	0425	0.5	15	18 Th ○	0321	0.5	15
	1525	-0.1	-3		1427	0.0	0
4 Th	0455	0.5	15	19 F	0351	0.5	15
	1452	0.0	0		1407	0.0	0
5 F	0507	0.4	12	20 Sa	0405	0.5	15
	1355	0.1	3		1332	0.1	3
6 Sa	0456	0.3	9	21 Su	0343	0.4	12
	1309	0.1	3		1253	0.1	3
	2124	0.3	9		2149	0.4	12
7 Su	0235	0.2	6	22 M	1220	0.0	0
	0336	0.3	9		2125	0.5	15
	1242	0.0	0				
	2115	0.4	12				
8 M	1231	0.0	0	23 Tu	1203	0.0	0
	2130	0.5	15		2140	0.6	18
9 Tu	1232	-0.1	-3	24 W	1203	-0.1	-3
	2153	0.5	15		2209	0.7	21
10 W ○	1239	-0.1	-3	25 Th ●	1218	-0.2	-6
	2222	0.5	15		2247	0.7	21
11 Th	1253	-0.2	-6	26 F	1243	-0.3	-9
	2255	0.5	15		2331	0.7	21
12 F	1309	-0.2	-6	27 Sa	1313	-0.3	-9
	2334	0.5	15				
13 Sa	1328	-0.2	-6	28 Su	0017	0.7	21
					1344	-0.3	-9
14 Su	0017	0.5	15	29 M	0104	0.7	21
	1347	-0.2	-6		1411	-0.2	-6
15 M	0105	0.5	15	30 Tu	0146	0.6	18
	1406	-0.2	-6		1431	-0.2	-6
				31 W	0218	0.6	18
					1432	-0.1	-3

June

Day	Time	ft	cm	Day	Time	ft	cm
1 Th ☽	0234	0.5	15	16 F	0143	0.6	18
	1400	0.0	0		1324	0.0	0
2 F	0221	0.4	12	17 Sa	0135	0.5	15
	1258	0.1	3		1240	0.1	3
3 Sa	0103	0.4	12	18 Su	0020	0.5	15
	1204	0.1	3		1151	0.1	3
	2214	0.4	12		2201	0.5	15
4 Su	1136	0.0	0	19 M	1114	0.1	3
	2124	0.5	15		2114	0.6	18
5 M	1127	0.0	0	20 Tu	1059	0.0	0
	2122	0.5	15		2115	0.7	21
6 Tu	1132	-0.1	-3	21 W	1104	-0.1	-3
	2135	0.6	18		2136	0.7	21
7 W	1145	-0.2	-6	22 Th	1125	-0.2	-6
	2157	0.6	18		2208	0.8	24
8 Th	1203	-0.2	-6	23 F ●	1155	-0.2	-6
	2224	0.6	18		2244	0.8	24
9 F ○	1224	-0.2	-6	24 Sa	1229	-0.3	-9
	2254	0.6	18		2322	0.8	24
10 Sa	1246	-0.2	-6	25 Su	1303	-0.2	-6
	2326	0.6	18		2358	0.8	24
11 Su	1308	-0.2	-6	26 M	1334	-0.2	-6
12 M	0000	0.6	18	27 Tu	0028	0.7	21
	1327	-0.2	-6		1357	-0.1	-3
13 Tu	0033	0.6	18	28 W	0048	0.7	21
	1342	-0.2	-6		1405	0.0	0
14 W	0103	0.6	18	29 Th	0052	0.6	18
	1351	-0.1	-3		1342	0.1	3
15 Th	0128	0.6	18	30 F ☽	0029	0.5	15
	1347	0.0	0		1226	0.1	3
					2331	0.5	15

Time meridian 60° W. 0000 is midnight. 1200 is noon. Times are not adjusted for Daylight Saving Time.
Heights are referred to mean lower low water which is the chart datum of soundings.

Magueyes Island, Puerto Rico, 2017

Times and Heights of High and Low Waters

July

Day	Time (h m)	Height (ft)	Height (cm)
1 Sa	1101	0.1	3
	2205	0.5	15
2 Su	1023	0.1	3
	2110	0.5	15
3 M	1016	0.0	0
	2057	0.6	18
4 Tu	1027	0.0	0
	2105	0.6	18
5 W	1048	-0.1	-3
	2123	0.7	21
6 Th	1114	-0.1	-3
	2147	0.7	21
7 F	1142	-0.2	-6
	2213	0.7	21
8 Sa	1210	-0.2	-6
	2240	0.7	21
9 Su ○	1236	-0.1	-3
	2306	0.7	21
10 M	1258	-0.1	-3
	2331	0.7	21
11 Tu	1317	-0.1	-3
	2353	0.7	21
12 W	1329	0.0	0
13 Th	0008	0.7	21
	1330	0.1	3
14 F	0013	0.7	21
	1305	0.2	6
	2356	0.6	18
15 Sa	1157	0.2	6
	2256	0.6	18
16 Su ◐	1035	0.2	6
	2126	0.6	18
17 M	0947	0.2	6
	2038	0.7	21
18 Tu	0936	0.1	3
	2035	0.7	21
19 W	0952	0.0	0
	2053	0.8	24
20 Th	1025	-0.1	-3
	2122	0.9	27
21 F	1104	-0.1	-3
	2154	0.9	27
22 Sa	1146	-0.1	-3
	2227	0.9	27
23 Su ●	1227	-0.1	-3
	2257	0.8	24
24 M	1303	-0.1	-3
	2322	0.8	24
25 Tu	1333	0.0	0
	2335	0.7	21
26 W	1353	0.1	3
	2334	0.7	21
27 Th	1352	0.2	6
	2311	0.6	18
28 F	1246	0.3	9
	2224	0.6	18
29 Sa	0843	0.3	9
	2119	0.6	18
30 Su ◑	0805	0.2	6
	2026	0.6	18
31 M	0815	0.2	6
	2009	0.7	21

August

Day	Time (h m)	Height (ft)	Height (cm)
1 Tu	0845	0.1	3
	2016	0.7	21
2 W	0926	0.1	3
	2034	0.7	21
3 Th	1010	0.0	0
	2057	0.8	24
4 F	1052	0.0	0
	2122	0.8	24
5 Sa	1130	0.0	0
	2147	0.8	24
6 Su	1203	0.0	0
	2210	0.8	24
7 M ○	1232	0.1	3
	2230	0.8	24
8 Tu	1258	0.1	3
	2247	0.8	24
9 W	1318	0.2	6
	2257	0.8	24
10 Th	1331	0.3	9
	2255	0.7	21
11 F	1322	0.3	9
	2231	0.7	21
12 Sa	1003	0.4	12
	2133	0.6	18
13 Su	0704	0.4	12
	2014	0.7	21
14 M ◐	0648	0.3	9
	1932	0.7	21
15 Tu	0708	0.2	6
	1933	0.8	24
16 W	0752	0.1	3
	1954	0.9	27
17 Th	0853	0.1	3
	2024	0.9	27
18 F	0957	0.1	3
	2055	0.9	27
19 Sa	1056	0.1	3
	2126	0.9	27
20 Su	1149	0.1	3
	2152	0.9	27
21 M ●	1234	0.1	3
	2212	0.8	24
22 Tu	1314	0.2	6
	2220	0.8	24
23 W	1348	0.3	9
	2214	0.7	21
24 Th	1412	0.4	12
	2150	0.6	18
25 F	0457	0.4	12
	0951	0.5	15
	1417	0.4	12
	2104	0.6	18
26 Sa	0443	0.4	12
	1958	0.6	18
27 Su	0450	0.3	9
	1900	0.7	21
28 M	0510	0.3	9
	1846	0.7	21
29 Tu ◑	0543	0.2	6
	1859	0.7	21
30 W	0632	0.2	6
	1923	0.8	24
31 Th	0747	0.2	6
	1949	0.8	24

September

Day	Time (h m)	Height (ft)	Height (cm)
1 F	0915	0.2	6
	2015	0.8	24
2 Sa	1025	0.2	6
	2040	0.9	27
3 Su	1117	0.2	6
	2102	0.9	27
4 M	1159	0.3	9
	2120	0.9	27
5 Tu	1237	0.3	9
	2133	0.8	24
6 W ○	1312	0.4	12
	2138	0.8	24
7 Th	1345	0.5	15
	2128	0.7	21
8 F	0428	0.5	15
	0921	0.6	18
	1415	0.5	15
	2052	0.7	21
9 Sa	0401	0.5	15
	1124	0.6	18
	1419	0.5	15
	1935	0.7	21
10 Su	0355	0.4	12
	1750	0.7	21
11 M	0407	0.3	9
	1731	0.8	24
12 Tu	0434	0.3	9
	1758	0.9	27
13 W ◐	0514	0.2	6
	1833	0.9	27
14 Th	0610	0.2	6
	1909	0.9	27
15 F	0735	0.2	6
	1943	0.9	27
16 Sa	0926	0.3	9
	2012	0.9	27
17 Su	1055	0.3	9
	2035	0.9	27
18 M	1202	0.4	12
	2050	0.8	24
19 Tu	1258	0.4	12
	2052	0.8	24
20 W ●	0334	0.5	15
	0746	0.6	18
	1350	0.5	15
	2039	0.7	21
21 Th	0257	0.5	15
	0856	0.7	21
	1443	0.5	15
	2007	0.6	18
22 F	0243	0.5	15
	1000	0.7	21
	1545	0.5	15
	1904	0.6	18
23 Sa	0244	0.4	12
	1110	0.7	21
24 Su	0254	0.3	9
	1249	0.7	21
25 M	0311	0.3	9
	1533	0.7	21
26 Tu	0333	0.2	6
	1649	0.8	24
27 W ◑	0400	0.2	6
	1737	0.8	24
28 Th	0432	0.3	9
	1815	0.8	24
29 F	0508	0.3	9
	1847	0.8	24
30 Sa	0552	0.3	9
	1915	0.9	27

Time meridian 60° W. 0000 is midnight. 1200 is noon. Times are not adjusted for Daylight Saving Time.
Heights are referred to mean lower low water which is the chart datum of soundings.

Magueyes Island, Puerto Rico, 2017

Times and Heights of High and Low Waters

October

Day	Time	Height (ft)	Height (cm)		Day	Time	Height (ft)	Height (cm)
1 Su	0906 / 1937	0.4 / 0.9	12 / 27		16 M	0332 / 0734 / 1111 / 1909	0.4 / 0.5 / 0.4 / 0.7	12 / 15 / 12 / 21
2 M	1058 / 1955	0.4 / 0.8	12 / 24		17 Tu	0223 / 0759 / 1251 / 1901	0.5 / 0.6 / 0.5 / 0.7	15 / 18 / 15 / 21
3 Tu	0408 / 0714 / 1207 / 2005	0.4 / 0.5 / 0.4 / 0.8	12 / 15 / 12 / 24		18 W	0144 / 0835 / 1421 / 1830	0.5 / 0.7 / 0.5 / 0.6	15 / 21 / 15 / 18
4 W	0318 / 0803 / 1309 / 2003	0.5 / 0.6 / 0.5 / 0.7	15 / 18 / 15 / 21		19 Th ●	0125 / 0912	0.4 / 0.7	12 / 21
5 Th ○	0243 / 0852 / 1417 / 1938	0.5 / 0.7 / 0.6 / 0.7	15 / 21 / 18 / 21		20 F	0121 / 0951	0.4 / 0.8	12 / 24
6 F	0219 / 0945 / 1557 / 1818	0.5 / 0.7 / 0.6 / 0.7	15 / 21 / 18 / 21		21 Sa	0127 / 1033	0.3 / 0.8	9 / 24
7 Sa	0210 / 1048	0.4 / 0.8	12 / 24		22 Su	0139 / 1121	0.2 / 0.8	6 / 24
8 Su	0215 / 1208	0.3 / 0.8	9 / 24		23 M	0155 / 1220	0.2 / 0.8	6 / 24
9 M	0232 / 1353	0.3 / 0.9	9 / 27		24 Tu	0215 / 1336	0.2 / 0.8	6 / 24
10 Tu	0258 / 1531	0.2 / 0.9	6 / 27		25 W	0237 / 1458	0.2 / 0.8	6 / 24
11 W	0331 / 1639	0.2 / 0.9	6 / 27		26 Th	0258 / 1602	0.2 / 0.8	6 / 24
12 Th ◐	0407 / 1731	0.2 / 0.9	6 / 27		27 F ◑	0317 / 1650	0.2 / 0.8	6 / 24
13 F	0443 / 1811	0.3 / 0.9	9 / 27		28 Sa	0327 / 1725	0.3 / 0.8	9 / 24
14 Sa	0515 / 1842	0.3 / 0.9	9 / 27		29 Su	0322 / 1752	0.3 / 0.8	9 / 24
15 Su	0507 / 1902	0.4 / 0.8	12 / 24		30 M	0257 / 1810	0.4 / 0.8	12 / 24
					31 Tu	0221 / 1816	0.4 / 0.7	12 / 21

November

Day	Time	Height (ft)	Height (cm)		Day	Time	Height (ft)	Height (cm)
1 W	0145 / 0853 / 1329 / 1757	0.4 / 0.6 / 0.5 / 0.6	12 / 18 / 15 / 18		16 Th	0017 / 0912	0.3 / 0.7	9 / 21
2 Th	0116 / 0908	0.4 / 0.7	12 / 21		17 F	0018 / 0937	0.2 / 0.8	6 / 24
3 F	0059 / 0939	0.3 / 0.8	9 / 24		18 Sa ●	0028 / 1006	0.1 / 0.8	3 / 24
4 Sa ○	0055 / 1020	0.3 / 0.9	9 / 27		19 Su	0044 / 1040	0.1 / 0.8	3 / 24
5 Su	0106 / 1109	0.2 / 0.9	6 / 27		20 M	0103 / 1119	0.0 / 0.8	0 / 24
6 M	0126 / 1208	0.1 / 0.9	3 / 27		21 Tu	0124 / 1203	0.0 / 0.8	0 / 24
7 Tu	0154 / 1315	0.0 / 0.9	0 / 27		22 W	0145 / 1251	0.0 / 0.7	0 / 21
8 W	0225 / 1425	0.0 / 0.9	0 / 27		23 Th	0205 / 1342	0.0 / 0.7	0 / 21
9 Th	0255 / 1528	0.1 / 0.9	3 / 27		24 F	0220 / 1429	0.1 / 0.7	3 / 21
10 F ◑	0319 / 1616	0.1 / 0.8	3 / 24		25 Sa	0228 / 1508	0.1 / 0.7	3 / 21
11 Sa	0328 / 1649	0.2 / 0.8	6 / 24		26 Su ◑	0222 / 1537	0.2 / 0.7	6 / 21
12 Su	0302 / 1703	0.3 / 0.7	9 / 21		27 M	0158 / 1550	0.2 / 0.6	6 / 18
13 M	0158 / 1653	0.4 / 0.6	12 / 18		28 Tu	0120 / 1525	0.3 / 0.6	9 / 18
14 Tu	0101 / 0904 / 1405 / 1543	0.4 / 0.6 / 0.5 / 0.6	12 / 18 / 15 / 18		29 W	0041 / 0930	0.3 / 0.6	9 / 18
15 W	0029 / 0856	0.3 / 0.7	9 / 21		30 Th	0010 / 0908 / 2353	0.2 / 0.7 / 0.2	6 / 21 / 6

December

Day	Time	Height (ft)	Height (cm)		Day	Time	Height (ft)	Height (cm)
1 F	0921 / 2354	0.7 / 0.1	21 / 3		16 Sa	0938 / 2356	0.7 / -0.1	21 / -3
2 Sa	0950	0.8	24		17 Su	1005	0.7	21
3 Su ○	0009 / 1028	0.0 / 0.8	0 / 24		18 M ●	0020 / 1036	-0.1 / 0.7	-3 / 21
4 M	0034 / 1111	-0.1 / 0.9	-3 / 27		19 Tu	0045 / 1108	-0.1 / 0.7	-3 / 21
5 Tu	0105 / 1159	-0.1 / 0.9	-3 / 27		20 W	0109 / 1141	-0.1 / 0.7	-3 / 21
6 W	0137 / 1247	-0.1 / 0.8	-3 / 24		21 Th	0131 / 1213	-0.1 / 0.6	-3 / 18
7 Th	0208 / 1333	-0.1 / 0.8	-3 / 24		22 F	0148 / 1242	-0.1 / 0.6	-3 / 18
8 F	0233 / 1410	0.0 / 0.7	0 / 21		23 Sa	0157 / 1305	0.0 / 0.6	0 / 18
9 Sa	0242 / 1429	0.1 / 0.6	3 / 18		24 Su	0154 / 1317	0.0 / 0.6	0 / 18
10 Su ◑	0219 / 1417	0.2 / 0.6	6 / 18		25 M	0128 / 1303	0.1 / 0.5	3 / 15
11 M	0109 / 1241 / 2357	0.2 / 0.5 / 0.2	6 / 15 / 6		26 Tu ◑	0037 / 1138 / 2341	0.1 / 0.5 / 0.1	3 / 15 / 3
12 Tu	0944 / 2320	0.5 / 0.2	15 / 6		27 W	0933 / 2300	0.5 / 0.1	15 / 3
13 W	0859 / 2311	0.6 / 0.1	18 / 3		28 Th	0851 / 2243	0.6 / 0.0	18 / 0
14 Th	0900 / 2318	0.6 / 0.0	18 / 0		29 F	0853 / 2249	0.6 / -0.1	18 / -3
15 F	0915 / 2334	0.7 / -0.1	21 / -3		30 Sa	0914 / 2311	0.7 / -0.2	21 / -6
					31 Su	0945 / 2344	0.7 / -0.2	21 / -6

Time meridian 60° W. 0000 is midnight. 1200 is noon. Times are not adjusted for Daylight Saving Time.
Heights are referred to mean lower low water which is the chart datum of soundings.

San Juan, Puerto Rico, 2017

Times and Heights of High and Low Waters

January

Day	Time (h m)	Height (ft)	Height (cm)
1 Su	0412	-0.1	-3
	1127	1.6	49
	1806	0.4	12
	2259	0.9	27
2 M	0457	0.0	0
	1204	1.6	49
	1843	0.3	9
	2356	0.9	27
3 Tu	0548	0.1	3
	1242	1.5	46
	1921	0.3	9
4 W	0059	1.0	30
	0646	0.2	6
	1323	1.4	43
	2001	0.2	6
5 Th ☾	0206	1.1	34
	0754	0.3	9
	1407	1.3	40
	2045	0.0	0
6 F	0316	1.3	40
	0909	0.4	12
	1455	1.2	37
	2132	-0.1	-3
7 Sa	0424	1.4	43
	1027	0.4	12
	1548	1.1	34
	2223	-0.2	-6
8 Su	0529	1.5	46
	1143	0.4	12
	1644	1.0	30
	2316	-0.3	-9
9 M	0630	1.7	52
	1253	0.4	12
	1743	1.0	30
10 Tu	0011	-0.4	-12
	0728	1.8	55
	1356	0.3	9
	1842	0.9	27
11 W	0106	-0.5	-15
	0823	1.8	55
	1453	0.3	9
	1941	0.9	27
12 Th ○	0201	-0.5	-15
	0915	1.8	55
	1545	0.2	6
	2039	0.9	27
13 F	0255	-0.5	-15
	1004	1.8	55
	1633	0.2	6
	2136	0.9	27
14 Sa	0347	-0.4	-12
	1051	1.7	52
	1720	0.2	6
	2233	1.0	30
15 Su	0440	-0.2	-6
	1136	1.6	49
	1804	0.2	6
	2331	1.0	30
16 M	0532	-0.1	-3
	1218	1.5	46
	1846	0.1	3
17 Tu	0029	1.0	30
	0626	0.1	3
	1258	1.3	40
	1926	0.1	3
18 W	0128	1.1	34
	0722	0.2	6
	1336	1.2	37
	2006	0.1	3
19 Th ◖	0228	1.1	34
	0822	0.3	9
	1414	1.1	34
	2046	0.0	0
20 F	0328	1.1	34
	0925	0.4	12
	1452	1.0	30
	2127	0.0	0
21 Sa	0426	1.2	37
	1031	0.4	12
	1533	0.9	27
	2209	-0.1	-3
22 Su	0522	1.2	37
	1135	0.5	15
	1618	0.8	24
	2254	-0.1	-3
23 M	0613	1.3	40
	1233	0.4	12
	1705	0.8	24
	2339	-0.2	-6
24 Tu	0701	1.3	40
	1325	0.4	12
	1754	0.8	24
25 W	0023	-0.2	-6
	0746	1.4	43
	1412	0.4	12
	1843	0.8	24
26 Th	0107	-0.3	-9
	0827	1.5	46
	1454	0.4	12
	1931	0.8	24
27 F ●	0151	-0.3	-9
	0907	1.5	46
	1534	0.4	12
	2019	0.8	24
28 Sa	0234	-0.2	-6
	0945	1.5	46
	1611	0.3	9
	2108	0.9	27
29 Su	0318	-0.2	-6
	1022	1.5	46
	1648	0.3	9
	2159	0.9	27
30 M	0404	-0.1	-3
	1058	1.5	46
	1724	0.2	6
	2252	1.0	30
31 Tu	0454	0.0	0
	1135	1.5	46
	1800	0.1	3
	2349	1.1	34

February

Day	Time (h m)	Height (ft)	Height (cm)
1 W	0548	0.1	3
	1214	1.4	43
	1840	0.1	3
2 Th	0050	1.2	37
	0649	0.2	6
	1255	1.3	40
	1923	0.0	0
3 F	0154	1.3	40
	0756	0.3	9
	1340	1.1	34
	2010	-0.1	-3
4 Sa ☾	0301	1.3	40
	0909	0.3	9
	1430	1.0	30
	2103	-0.2	-6
5 Su	0409	1.4	43
	1024	0.4	12
	1526	0.9	27
	2159	-0.3	-9
6 M	0515	1.5	46
	1137	0.4	12
	1627	0.9	27
	2259	-0.4	-12
7 Tu	0617	1.6	49
	1242	0.3	9
	1731	0.9	27
	2358	-0.4	-12
8 W	0714	1.6	49
	1339	0.3	9
	1833	0.9	27
9 Th	0056	-0.4	-12
	0807	1.6	49
	1430	0.2	6
	1933	0.9	27
10 F ○	0152	-0.4	-12
	0856	1.6	49
	1517	0.2	6
	2030	1.0	30
11 Sa	0246	-0.3	-9
	0942	1.6	49
	1600	0.2	6
	2125	1.0	30
12 Su	0337	-0.3	-9
	1024	1.5	46
	1640	0.1	3
	2217	1.1	34
13 M	0428	-0.1	-3
	1103	1.4	43
	1718	0.1	3
	2309	1.1	34
14 Tu	0517	0.0	0
	1140	1.3	40
	1755	0.1	3
15 W	0000	1.1	34
	0607	0.1	3
	1216	1.1	34
	1831	0.1	3
16 Th	0052	1.1	34
	0659	0.2	6
	1251	1.0	30
	1908	0.0	0
17 F	0145	1.1	34
	0753	0.3	9
	1326	0.9	27
	1947	0.0	0
18 Sa ◖	0240	1.2	37
	0851	0.4	12
	1404	0.8	24
	2031	0.0	0
19 Su ◖	0337	1.2	37
	0952	0.4	12
	1446	0.8	24
	2118	-0.1	-3
20 M	0434	1.2	37
	1053	0.4	12
	1535	0.8	24
	2208	-0.1	-3
21 Tu	0529	1.2	37
	1150	0.4	12
	1628	0.8	24
	2300	-0.1	-3
22 W	0620	1.3	40
	1241	0.4	12
	1724	0.8	24
	2351	-0.2	-6
23 Th	0706	1.4	43
	1327	0.4	12
	1819	0.8	24
24 F	0041	-0.2	-6
	0749	1.4	43
	1408	0.3	9
	1913	0.9	27
25 Sa	0130	-0.2	-6
	0830	1.5	46
	1447	0.3	9
	2005	1.0	30
26 Su ●	0219	-0.2	-6
	0909	1.5	46
	1524	0.2	6
	2058	1.1	34
27 M	0309	-0.1	-3
	0948	1.5	46
	1601	0.2	6
	2150	1.2	37
28 Tu	0401	-0.1	-3
	1027	1.4	43
	1639	0.1	3
	2244	1.3	40

March

Day	Time (h m)	Height (ft)	Height (cm)
1 W	0455	0.0	0
	1106	1.3	40
	1719	0.0	0
	2340	1.4	43
2 Th	0553	0.1	3
	1148	1.2	37
	1802	-0.1	-3
3 F ○	0038	1.4	43
	0655	0.2	6
	1232	1.1	34
	1849	-0.2	-6
4 Sa	0140	1.5	46
	0800	0.3	9
	1321	1.0	30
	1942	-0.2	-6
5 Su ◖	0245	1.5	46
	0910	0.3	9
	1416	0.9	27
	2040	-0.2	-6
6 M	0352	1.5	46
	1020	0.3	9
	1518	0.9	27
	2142	-0.3	-9
7 Tu	0457	1.5	46
	1125	0.3	9
	1624	0.9	27
	2247	-0.3	-9
8 W	0559	1.5	46
	1224	0.3	9
	1730	0.9	27
	2350	-0.2	-6
9 Th	0654	1.5	46
	1314	0.3	9
	1833	1.0	30
10 F	0050	-0.2	-6
	0744	1.5	46
	1400	0.2	6
	1930	1.1	34
11 Sa	0147	-0.2	-6
	0830	1.4	43
	1441	0.2	6
	2024	1.2	37
12 Su ○	0240	-0.1	-3
	0911	1.4	43
	1518	0.1	3
	2113	1.2	37
13 M	0330	-0.1	-3
	0950	1.3	40
	1554	0.1	3
	2201	1.3	40
14 Tu	0418	0.0	0
	1026	1.2	37
	1628	0.1	3
	2246	1.3	40
15 W	0505	0.1	3
	1100	1.1	34
	1702	0.0	0
	2331	1.3	40
16 Th	0552	0.2	6
	1133	1.0	30
	1736	0.0	0
17 F	0016	1.3	40
	0640	0.2	6
	1207	0.9	27
	1812	0.0	0
18 Sa	0104	1.3	40
	0729	0.3	9
	1242	0.8	24
	1851	0.0	0
19 Su	0154	1.2	37
	0821	0.4	12
	1321	0.8	24
	1936	0.0	0
20 M ◖	0247	1.2	37
	0915	0.4	12
	1407	0.8	24
	2026	0.0	0
21 Tu	0342	1.2	37
	1010	0.4	12
	1501	0.8	24
	2121	0.0	0
22 W	0437	1.3	40
	1103	0.4	12
	1600	0.8	24
	2219	0.0	0
23 Th	0529	1.3	40
	1152	0.4	12
	1701	0.9	27
	2317	0.0	0
24 F	0617	1.3	40
	1236	0.3	9
	1801	1.0	30
25 Sa	0015	0.0	0
	0702	1.4	43
	1317	0.3	9
	1858	1.1	34
26 Su	0111	0.0	0
	0745	1.4	43
	1356	0.2	6
	1952	1.3	40
27 M ●	0207	0.0	0
	0828	1.4	43
	1435	0.1	3
	2046	1.4	43
28 Tu	0303	0.0	0
	0910	1.3	40
	1516	0.1	3
	2139	1.5	46
29 W	0400	0.0	0
	0953	1.2	37
	1557	-0.1	-3
	2233	1.6	49
30 Th	0457	0.1	3
	1037	1.1	34
	1642	-0.2	-6
	2328	1.7	52
31 F	0557	0.1	3
	1123	1.0	30
	1729	-0.2	-6

Time meridian 60° W. 0000 is midnight. 1200 is noon. Times are not adjusted for Daylight Saving Time.
Heights are referred to mean lower low water which is the chart datum of soundings.

San Juan, Puerto Rico, 2017

Times and Heights of High and Low Waters

April

Day	Time	ft	cm	Day	Time	ft	cm
1 Sa	0026	1.7	52	**16** Su	0029	1.4	43
	0658	0.2	6		0709	0.3	9
	1214	1.0	30		1203	0.7	21
	1822	-0.2	-6		1802	0.0	0
2 Su	0126	1.6	49	**17** M	0114	1.3	40
	0801	0.2	6		0756	0.4	12
	1309	0.9	27		1245	0.7	21
	1919	-0.2	-6		1847	0.0	0
3 M	0228	1.6	49	**18** Tu	0202	1.3	40
	0905	0.3	9		0843	0.4	12
	1411	0.9	27		1335	0.7	21
	2022	-0.2	-6		1938	0.1	3
4 Tu	0332	1.5	46	**19** W	0252	1.3	40
	1008	0.3	9		0931	0.4	12
	1519	0.9	27		1434	0.8	24
	2129	-0.1	-3		2035	0.1	3
5 W	0434	1.5	46	**20** Th	0342	1.3	40
	1105	0.3	9		1018	0.4	12
	1628	0.9	27		1538	0.9	27
	2237	-0.1	-3		2139	0.1	3
6 Th	0532	1.4	43	**21** F	0433	1.3	40
	1156	0.2	6		1102	0.3	9
	1733	1.0	30		1643	1.0	30
	2343	0.0	0		2245	0.2	6
7 F	0624	1.4	43	**22** Sa	0522	1.3	40
	1242	0.2	6		1145	0.2	6
	1833	1.1	34		1745	1.2	37
					2351	0.2	6
8 Sa	0045	0.0	0	**23** Su	0610	1.3	40
	0711	1.3	40		1227	0.1	3
	1322	0.1	3		1843	1.3	40
	1926	1.2	37				
9 Su	0141	0.1	3	**24** M	0055	0.2	6
	0754	1.2	37		0657	1.3	40
	1359	0.1	3		1309	0.0	0
	2015	1.3	40		1938	1.5	46
10 M	0234	0.1	3	**25** Tu	0157	0.1	3
	0833	1.1	34		0744	1.2	37
	1434	0.1	3		1352	-0.1	-3
	2100	1.4	43		2033	1.7	52
11 Tu	0323	0.1	3	**26** W	0257	0.1	3
	0909	1.1	34		0831	1.1	34
	1507	0.0	0		1436	-0.2	-6
	2143	1.4	43		2126	1.8	55
12 W	0410	0.2	6	**27** Th	0357	0.1	3
	0944	1.0	30		0919	1.1	34
	1540	0.0	0		1523	-0.3	-9
	2224	1.5	46		2221	1.8	55
13 Th	0455	0.2	6	**28** F	0456	0.1	3
	1018	0.9	27		1009	1.0	30
	1612	0.0	0		1612	-0.3	-9
	2305	1.4	43		2316	1.9	58
14 F	0540	0.2	6	**29** Sa	0554	0.1	3
	1052	0.8	24		1102	0.9	27
	1646	0.0	0		1704	-0.3	-9
	2346	1.4	43				
15 Sa	0624	0.3	9	**30** Su	0012	1.8	55
	1126	0.8	24		0654	0.2	6
	1723	0.0	0		1158	0.9	27
					1800	-0.3	-9

May

Day	Time	ft	cm	Day	Time	ft	cm
1 M	0110	1.7	52	**16** Tu	0042	1.4	43
	0753	0.2	6		0732	0.3	9
	1300	0.9	27		1217	0.7	21
	1901	-0.2	-6		1807	0.1	3
2 Tu	0208	1.6	49	**17** W	0123	1.4	43
	0851	0.2	6		0813	0.3	9
	1408	0.9	27		1311	0.8	24
	2006	-0.1	-3		1858	0.1	3
3 W	0306	1.5	46	**18** Th	0207	1.4	43
	0946	0.2	6		0854	0.3	9
	1518	0.9	27		1414	0.8	24
	2115	0.0	0		1958	0.2	6
4 Th	0403	1.4	43	**19** F	0252	1.4	43
	1036	0.2	6		0935	0.3	9
	1627	1.0	30		1520	1.0	30
	2225	0.1	3		2106	0.3	9
5 F	0455	1.3	40	**20** Sa	0340	1.3	40
	1122	0.1	3		1016	0.2	6
	1730	1.1	34		1626	1.1	34
	2333	0.2	6		2218	0.3	9
6 Sa	0544	1.2	37	**21** Su	0429	1.3	40
	1203	0.1	3		1059	0.1	3
	1826	1.3	40		1728	1.3	40
					2331	0.3	9
7 Su	0036	0.2	6	**22** M	0519	1.2	37
	0628	1.1	34		1143	-0.1	-3
	1241	0.0	0		1827	1.5	46
	1916	1.4	43				
8 M	0134	0.2	6	**23** Tu	0041	0.3	9
	0709	1.0	30		0610	1.1	34
	1316	0.0	0		1228	-0.2	-6
	2001	1.4	43		1924	1.7	52
9 Tu	0226	0.2	6	**24** W	0147	0.2	6
	0748	0.9	27		0702	1.1	34
	1350	-0.1	-3		1316	-0.3	-9
	2044	1.5	46		2019	1.8	55
10 W	0315	0.2	6	**25** Th	0250	0.2	6
	0825	0.9	27		0755	1.0	30
	1424	-0.1	-3		1405	-0.4	-12
	2124	1.5	46		2113	1.9	58
11 Th	0401	0.3	9	**26** F	0350	0.2	6
	0901	0.8	24		0849	0.9	27
	1457	-0.1	-3		1456	-0.4	-12
	2203	1.5	46		2208	2.0	61
12 F	0444	0.3	9	**27** Sa	0448	0.2	6
	0937	0.7	21		0945	0.9	27
	1532	-0.1	-3		1550	-0.4	-12
	2242	1.5	46		2302	1.9	58
13 Sa	0527	0.3	9	**28** Su	0544	0.2	6
	1013	0.7	21		1043	0.9	27
	1607	-0.1	-3		1645	-0.4	-12
	2321	1.5	46		2356	1.9	58
14 Su	0609	0.3	9	**29** M	0639	0.2	6
	1050	0.7	21		1144	0.9	27
	1644	0.0	0		1743	-0.3	-9
15 M	0001	1.5	46	**30** Tu	0050	1.8	55
	0650	0.3	9		0733	0.2	6
	1130	0.7	21		1249	0.9	27
	1723	0.0	0		1844	-0.1	-3
				31 W	0143	1.6	49
					0825	0.1	3
					1358	1.0	30
					1949	0.0	0

June

Day	Time	ft	cm	Day	Time	ft	cm
1 Th	0235	1.5	46	**16** F	0128	1.5	46
	0914	0.1	3		0813	0.3	9
	1508	1.0	30		1357	1.0	30
	2057	0.2	6		1935	0.3	9
2 F	0324	1.4	43	**17** Sa	0209	1.4	43
	0959	0.1	3		0852	0.2	6
	1614	1.1	34		1503	1.1	34
	2207	0.3	9		2045	0.4	12
3 Sa	0412	1.2	37	**18** Su	0254	1.3	40
	1041	0.0	0		0934	0.1	3
	1715	1.2	37		1608	1.3	40
	2316	0.3	9		2201	0.4	12
4 Su	0456	1.1	34	**19** M	0343	1.2	37
	1121	0.0	0		1018	-0.1	-3
	1809	1.3	40		1711	1.5	46
					2318	0.4	12
5 M	0021	0.4	12	**20** Tu	0436	1.1	34
	0539	1.0	30		1106	-0.2	-6
	1158	-0.1	-3		1812	1.6	49
	1858	1.4	43				
6 Tu	0120	0.4	12	**21** W	0030	0.4	12
	0620	0.9	27		0532	1.0	30
	1234	-0.1	-3		1157	-0.3	-9
	1942	1.5	46		1909	1.8	55
7 W	0213	0.4	12	**22** Th	0137	0.4	12
	0701	0.8	24		0629	1.0	30
	1311	-0.1	-3		1249	-0.4	-12
	2023	1.5	46		2005	1.9	58
8 Th	0301	0.3	9	**23** F	0239	0.3	9
	0741	0.8	24		0727	0.9	27
	1347	-0.2	-6		1343	-0.5	-15
	2104	1.6	49		2100	2.0	61
9 F	0345	0.3	9	**24** Sa	0337	0.3	9
	0820	0.7	21		0826	0.9	27
	1424	-0.2	-6		1438	-0.5	-15
	2143	1.6	49		2153	2.0	61
10 Sa	0427	0.3	9	**25** Su	0431	0.2	6
	0900	0.7	21		0926	0.9	27
	1501	-0.1	-3		1534	-0.4	-12
	2221	1.6	49		2246	1.9	58
11 Su	0508	0.3	9	**26** M	0523	0.2	6
	0940	0.7	21		1026	1.0	30
	1538	-0.1	-3		1630	-0.3	-9
	2258	1.6	49		2336	1.8	55
12 M	0547	0.3	9	**27** Tu	0613	0.2	6
	1021	0.7	21		1129	1.0	30
	1615	-0.1	-3		1728	-0.2	-6
	2335	1.5	46				
13 Tu	0625	0.3	9	**28** W	0025	1.7	52
	1106	0.7	21		0702	0.2	6
	1656	0.0	0		1234	1.0	30
					1827	0.0	0
14 W	0012	1.5	46	**29** Th	0112	1.6	49
	0701	0.3	9		0748	0.1	3
	1156	0.8	24		1340	1.1	34
	1741	0.1	3		1930	0.2	6
15 Th	0049	1.5	46	**30** F	0158	1.4	43
	0737	0.3	9		0832	0.1	3
	1254	0.8	24		1445	1.2	37
	1833	0.2	6		2036	0.3	9

Time meridian 60° W. 0000 is midnight. 1200 is noon. Times are not adjusted for Daylight Saving Time.
Heights are referred to mean lower low water which is the chart datum of soundings.

San Juan, Puerto Rico, 2017

Times and Heights of High and Low Waters

July

Day	Time	ft	cm	Day	Time	ft	cm
1 Sa	0241	1.3	40	**16** Su ○	0133	1.4	43
	0915	0.1	3		0811	0.1	3
	1549	1.2	37		1445	1.3	40
	2144	0.4	12		2037	0.5	15
2 Su	0324	1.1	34	**17** M	0218	1.3	40
	0956	0.0	0		0856	0.0	0
	1648	1.3	40		1551	1.5	46
	2253	0.5	15		2153	0.5	15
3 M	0406	1.0	30	**18** Tu	0309	1.2	37
	1036	0.0	0		0945	-0.1	-3
	1742	1.4	43		1655	1.6	49
	2358	0.5	15		2309	0.5	15
4 Tu	0449	0.9	27	**19** W	0405	1.1	34
	1116	-0.1	-3		1039	-0.2	-6
	1831	1.5	46		1756	1.8	55
5 W	0057	0.5	15	**20** Th	0020	0.5	15
	0533	0.9	27		0505	1.0	30
	1156	-0.1	-3		1135	-0.3	-9
	1916	1.5	46		1855	1.9	58
6 Th	0149	0.5	15	**21** F	0125	0.5	15
	0618	0.8	24		0608	1.0	30
	1237	-0.1	-3		1232	-0.4	-12
	1959	1.5	46		1951	1.9	58
7 F	0236	0.4	12	**22** Sa	0223	0.4	12
	0702	0.8	24		0710	1.0	30
	1318	-0.1	-3		1330	-0.4	-12
	2040	1.6	49		2045	2.0	61
8 Sa	0319	0.4	12	**23** Su ●	0316	0.4	12
	0747	0.8	24		0812	1.1	34
	1358	-0.1	-3		1427	-0.3	-9
	2119	1.6	49		2136	1.9	58
9 Su ○	0359	0.4	12	**24** M	0405	0.3	9
	0831	0.8	24		0912	1.1	34
	1437	-0.1	-3		1523	-0.2	-6
	2157	1.6	49		2224	1.9	58
10 M	0437	0.4	12	**25** Tu	0452	0.3	9
	0915	0.8	24		1012	1.2	37
	1517	0.0	0		1618	-0.1	-3
	2232	1.6	49		2310	1.8	55
11 Tu	0513	0.4	12	**26** W	0537	0.3	9
	1001	0.9	27		1112	1.2	37
	1557	0.0	0		1714	0.0	0
	2307	1.6	49		2354	1.7	52
12 W	0547	0.4	12	**27** Th	0620	0.2	6
	1049	0.9	27		1212	1.3	40
	1640	0.1	3		1811	0.2	6
	2341	1.6	49				
13 Th	0621	0.4	12	**28** F	0036	1.5	46
	1142	1.0	30		0702	0.2	6
	1728	0.2	6		1312	1.3	40
					1910	0.3	9
14 F	0016	1.5	46	**29** Sa	0117	1.4	43
	0654	0.3	9		0743	0.2	6
	1239	1.1	34		1412	1.3	40
	1822	0.3	9		2012	0.5	15
15 Sa	0053	1.5	46	**30** Su ◐	0156	1.2	37
	0731	0.2	6		0824	0.1	3
	1341	1.2	37		1512	1.4	43
	1925	0.4	12		2117	0.6	18
				31 M	0236	1.1	34
					0906	0.1	3
					1609	1.4	43
					2223	0.6	18

August

Day	Time	ft	cm	Day	Time	ft	cm
1 Tu	0319	1.0	30	**16** W	0248	1.2	37
	0949	0.1	3		0920	0.0	0
	1704	1.5	46		1639	1.8	55
	2326	0.6	18		2303	0.6	18
2 W	0404	1.0	30	**17** Th	0349	1.1	34
	1034	0.0	0		1020	-0.1	-3
	1756	1.5	46		1741	1.9	58
3 Th	0024	0.6	18	**18** F	0009	0.6	18
	0453	0.9	27		0455	1.1	34
	1120	0.0	0		1122	-0.1	-3
	1844	1.6	49		1840	1.9	58
4 F	0114	0.6	18	**19** Sa	0108	0.6	18
	0543	0.9	27		0601	1.2	37
	1206	0.0	0		1223	-0.1	-3
	1928	1.6	49		1934	1.9	58
5 Sa	0159	0.6	18	**20** Su	0200	0.5	15
	0633	0.9	27		0705	1.2	37
	1251	0.0	0		1322	-0.1	-3
	2010	1.6	49		2025	1.9	58
6 Su	0240	0.6	18	**21** M ●	0247	0.5	15
	0722	1.0	30		0805	1.3	40
	1335	0.0	0		1419	0.0	0
	2048	1.7	52		2112	1.9	58
7 M ○	0318	0.5	15	**22** Tu	0331	0.4	12
	0810	1.0	30		0903	1.4	43
	1418	0.1	3		1515	0.0	0
	2125	1.7	52		2156	1.8	55
8 Tu	0353	0.5	15	**23** W	0413	0.4	12
	0858	1.1	34		0959	1.5	46
	1502	0.1	3		1609	0.2	6
	2200	1.7	52		2238	1.7	52
9 W	0427	0.5	15	**24** Th	0453	0.3	9
	0947	1.2	37		1053	1.5	46
	1546	0.2	6		1702	0.3	9
	2234	1.7	52		2318	1.6	49
10 Th	0500	0.4	12	**25** F	0532	0.3	9
	1037	1.2	37		1146	1.5	46
	1634	0.3	9		1756	0.4	12
	2309	1.6	49		2356	1.4	43
11 F	0534	0.4	12	**26** Sa	0610	0.3	9
	1129	1.3	40		1239	1.5	46
	1725	0.4	12		1851	0.5	15
	2345	1.6	49				
12 Sa	0610	0.3	9	**27** Su	0033	1.3	40
	1225	1.4	43		0648	0.3	9
	1823	0.5	15		1333	1.5	46
					1948	0.6	18
13 Su	0023	1.5	46	**28** M	0111	1.2	37
	0650	0.2	6		0729	0.3	9
	1325	1.5	46		1428	1.5	46
	1927	0.6	18		2048	0.7	21
14 M ◑	0105	1.3	40	**29** Tu ◑	0151	1.1	34
	0734	0.1	3		0813	0.2	6
	1428	1.6	49		1524	1.5	46
	2037	0.6	18		2149	0.7	21
15 Tu	0153	1.3	40	**30** W	0235	1.1	34
	0825	0.0	0		0900	0.2	6
	1534	1.7	52		1619	1.5	46
	2151	0.7	21		2248	0.7	21
				31 Th	0326	1.0	30
					0951	0.2	6
					1713	1.6	49
					2342	0.7	21

September

Day	Time	ft	cm	Day	Time	ft	cm
1 F	0421	1.0	30	**16** Sa	0458	1.3	40
	1043	0.2	6		1114	0.1	3
	1802	1.6	49		1819	1.9	58
2 Sa	0030	0.7	21	**17** Su	0044	0.6	18
	0517	1.1	34		0604	1.3	40
	1135	0.2	6		1218	0.2	6
	1848	1.7	52		1911	1.9	58
3 Su	0113	0.7	21	**18** M	0131	0.5	15
	0611	1.1	34		0706	1.5	46
	1225	0.2	6		1318	0.2	6
	1929	1.7	52		1958	1.8	55
4 M	0152	0.6	18	**19** Tu	0213	0.5	15
	0704	1.2	37		0802	1.6	49
	1313	0.2	6		1415	0.3	9
	2008	1.7	52		2042	1.8	55
5 Tu	0228	0.6	18	**20** W ●	0252	0.4	12
	0754	1.3	40		0855	1.7	52
	1402	0.3	9		1509	0.3	9
	2045	1.7	52		2122	1.7	52
6 W ○	0303	0.5	15	**21** Th	0330	0.4	12
	0844	1.4	43		0945	1.7	52
	1450	0.3	9		1601	0.4	12
	2122	1.7	52		2201	1.5	46
7 Th	0337	0.5	15	**22** F	0406	0.3	9
	0933	1.5	46		1032	1.7	52
	1540	0.4	12		1652	0.5	15
	2158	1.7	52		2237	1.4	43
8 F	0412	0.4	12	**23** Sa	0441	0.3	9
	1024	1.6	49		1119	1.8	55
	1632	0.4	12		1742	0.5	15
	2235	1.6	49		2313	1.3	40
9 Sa	0449	0.3	9	**24** Su	0517	0.3	9
	1116	1.7	52		1206	1.7	52
	1728	0.5	15		1833	0.6	18
	2314	1.5	46		2349	1.2	37
10 Su	0529	0.2	6	**25** M	0554	0.3	9
	1211	1.8	55		1254	1.7	52
	1828	0.6	18		1925	0.7	21
	2357	1.4	43				
11 M	0614	0.2	6	**26** Tu	0027	1.1	34
	1310	1.8	55		0634	0.3	9
	1932	0.6	18		1344	1.7	52
					2019	0.7	21
12 Tu	0044	1.3	40	**27** W ◐	0108	1.1	34
	0704	0.1	3		0719	0.3	9
	1413	1.9	58		1436	1.6	49
	2040	0.7	21		2114	0.7	21
13 W ○	0138	1.2	37	**28** Th	0156	1.1	34
	0800	0.1	3		0809	0.4	12
	1517	1.9	58		1530	1.6	49
	2149	0.7	21		2208	0.8	24
14 Th ◑	0240	1.2	37	**29** F	0252	1.1	34
	0903	0.1	3		0904	0.4	12
	1622	1.9	58		1622	1.6	49
	2255	0.7	21		2257	0.8	24
15 F	0349	1.2	37	**30** Sa	0353	1.1	34
	1008	0.1	3		1002	0.4	12
	1723	1.9	58		1711	1.7	52
	2353	0.6	18		2342	0.7	21

Time meridian 60° W. 0000 is midnight. 1200 is noon. Times are not adjusted for Daylight Saving Time.
Heights are referred to mean lower low water which is the chart datum of soundings.

San Juan, Puerto Rico, 2017

Times and Heights of High and Low Waters

October

Day	Time	ft	cm	Day	Time	ft	cm
1 Su	0454	1.2	37	**16** M	0015	0.5	15
	1100	0.4	12		0608	1.5	46
	1757	1.7	52		1214	0.4	12
					1840	1.7	52
2 M	0022	0.7	21	**17** Tu	0057	0.4	12
	0552	1.3	40		0705	1.6	49
	1156	0.4	12		1315	0.4	12
	1839	1.7	52		1924	1.6	49
3 Tu	0100	0.6	18	**18** W	0136	0.4	12
	0647	1.4	43		0757	1.7	52
	1252	0.4	12		1411	0.5	15
	1920	1.7	52		2005	1.5	46
4 W	0136	0.5	15	**19** Th ●	0212	0.3	9
	0738	1.6	49		0844	1.8	55
	1346	0.5	15		1504	0.5	15
	2000	1.7	52		2043	1.4	43
5 Th ○	0212	0.4	12	**20** F	0247	0.3	9
	0829	1.7	52		0929	1.8	55
	1440	0.5	15		1554	0.5	15
	2039	1.6	49		2120	1.3	40
6 F	0250	0.3	9	**21** Sa	0321	0.2	6
	0919	1.9	58		1012	1.8	55
	1535	0.5	15		1642	0.5	15
	2120	1.5	46		2155	1.2	37
7 Sa	0329	0.2	6	**22** Su	0355	0.2	6
	1010	2.0	61		1054	1.8	55
	1632	0.5	15		1729	0.6	18
	2202	1.5	46		2231	1.1	34
8 Su	0411	0.2	6	**23** M	0430	0.2	6
	1103	2.0	61		1136	1.8	55
	1730	0.6	18		1816	0.6	18
	2247	1.4	43		2307	1.1	34
9 M	0456	0.1	3	**24** Tu	0507	0.3	9
	1158	2.0	61		1220	1.7	52
	1830	0.6	18		1903	0.7	21
	2335	1.3	40		2346	1.0	30
10 Tu	0546	0.1	3	**25** W	0547	0.3	9
	1256	2.0	61		1305	1.7	52
	1933	0.6	18		1951	0.7	21
11 W	0030	1.2	37	**26** Th	0030	1.0	30
	0641	0.1	3		0631	0.3	9
	1357	2.0	61		1351	1.7	52
	2037	0.6	18		2039	0.7	21
12 Th ◐	0132	1.2	37	**27** F ☾	0122	1.0	30
	0743	0.2	6		0720	0.4	12
	1459	1.9	58		1439	1.6	49
	2140	0.6	18		2126	0.7	21
13 F	0242	1.2	37	**28** Sa	0222	1.1	34
	0850	0.2	6		0817	0.4	12
	1600	1.9	58		1527	1.6	49
	2238	0.6	18		2210	0.7	21
14 Sa	0355	1.3	40	**29** Su	0328	1.1	34
	1000	0.3	9		0918	0.5	15
	1658	1.8	55		1614	1.6	49
	2329	0.6	18		2251	0.6	18
15 Su	0504	1.4	43	**30** M	0432	1.2	37
	1109	0.3	9		1023	0.5	15
	1751	1.8	55		1659	1.6	49
					2330	0.5	15
				31 Tu	0532	1.4	43
					1128	0.5	15
					1744	1.6	49

November

Day	Time	ft	cm	Day	Time	ft	cm
1 W	0008	0.4	12	**16** Th	0058	0.2	6
	0628	1.6	49		0746	1.7	52
	1231	0.5	15		1406	0.5	15
	1828	1.5	46		1924	1.2	37
2 Th	0047	0.3	9	**17** F	0134	0.1	3
	0721	1.7	52		0830	1.8	55
	1332	0.5	15		1457	0.5	15
	1913	1.5	46		2002	1.1	34
3 F	0128	0.2	6	**18** Sa ●	0208	0.1	3
	0812	1.9	58		0912	1.8	55
	1431	0.5	15		1545	0.5	15
	1958	1.4	43		2039	1.0	30
4 Sa ○	0210	0.0	0	**19** Su	0243	0.0	0
	0904	2.0	61		0952	1.8	55
	1530	0.5	15		1630	0.5	15
	2044	1.3	40		2116	1.0	30
5 Su	0254	0.0	0	**20** M	0318	0.0	0
	0956	2.1	64		1032	1.8	55
	1628	0.5	15		1714	0.5	15
	2132	1.3	40		2152	0.9	27
6 M	0341	-0.1	-3	**21** Tu	0354	0.1	3
	1050	2.1	64		1111	1.7	52
	1726	0.5	15		1757	0.5	15
	2223	1.2	37		2230	0.9	27
7 Tu	0432	-0.1	-3	**22** W	0431	0.1	3
	1145	2.1	64		1151	1.7	52
	1825	0.5	15		1839	0.6	18
	2319	1.1	34		2311	0.9	27
8 W	0526	-0.1	-3	**23** Th	0510	0.2	6
	1241	2.1	64		1231	1.6	49
	1924	0.5	15		1921	0.6	18
					2358	0.9	27
9 Th	0021	1.1	34	**24** F	0552	0.2	6
	0625	0.0	0		1311	1.6	49
	1339	2.0	61		2002	0.6	18
	2023	0.5	15				
10 F ○	0129	1.1	34	**25** Sa	0052	0.9	27
	0729	0.1	3		0640	0.3	9
	1436	1.9	58		1352	1.6	49
	2119	0.5	15		2042	0.5	15
11 Sa	0243	1.2	37	**26** Su ☽	0155	1.0	30
	0838	0.3	9		0735	0.4	12
	1532	1.8	55		1434	1.5	46
	2211	0.4	12		2121	0.5	15
12 Su	0356	1.3	40	**27** M	0302	1.1	34
	0950	0.4	12		0840	0.5	15
	1626	1.7	52		1517	1.5	46
	2258	0.4	12		2200	0.4	12
13 M	0504	1.4	43	**28** Tu	0407	1.2	37
	1101	0.4	12		0950	0.5	15
	1715	1.5	46		1603	1.4	43
	2341	0.3	9		2240	0.3	9
14 Tu	0604	1.5	46	**29** W	0509	1.4	43
	1208	0.5	15		1102	0.5	15
	1801	1.4	43		1650	1.4	43
					2321	0.1	3
15 W	0021	0.2	6	**30** Th	0607	1.6	49
	0658	1.6	49		1212	0.5	15
	1310	0.5	15		1739	1.3	40
	1844	1.3	40				

December

Day	Time	ft	cm	Day	Time	ft	cm
1 F	0005	0.0	0	**16** Sa	0059	-0.1	-3
	0702	1.8	55		0812	1.6	49
	1318	0.5	15		1444	0.4	12
	1829	1.2	37		1923	0.9	27
2 Sa	0051	-0.2	-6	**17** Su	0137	-0.1	-3
	0756	1.9	58		0853	1.6	49
	1421	0.4	12		1529	0.4	12
	1921	1.2	37		2003	0.8	24
3 Su ○	0139	-0.3	-9	**18** M ●	0214	-0.1	-3
	0849	2.0	61		0933	1.6	49
	1520	0.4	12		1611	0.4	12
	2013	1.1	34		2042	0.8	24
4 M	0229	-0.3	-9	**19** Tu	0251	-0.1	-3
	0943	2.1	64		1011	1.6	49
	1618	0.4	12		1652	0.4	12
	2108	1.1	34		2122	0.8	24
5 Tu	0321	-0.3	-9	**20** W	0328	-0.1	-3
	1036	2.1	64		1048	1.6	49
	1714	0.4	12		1731	0.4	12
	2205	1.0	30		2203	0.8	24
6 W	0415	-0.3	-9	**21** Th	0406	0.0	0
	1130	2.0	61		1125	1.6	49
	1809	0.3	9		1808	0.4	12
	2306	1.0	30		2247	0.8	24
7 Th	0512	-0.2	-6	**22** F	0444	0.0	0
	1223	1.9	58		1200	1.6	49
	1904	0.3	9		1844	0.4	12
					2335	0.8	24
8 F	0011	1.0	30	**23** Sa	0526	0.1	3
	0612	-0.1	-3		1234	1.5	46
	1316	1.8	55		1919	0.4	12
	1957	0.3	9				
9 Sa	0121	1.1	34	**24** Su	0030	0.9	27
	0716	0.1	3		0613	0.2	6
	1408	1.7	52		1309	1.5	46
	2047	0.2	6		1954	0.3	9
10 Su ○	0234	1.1	34	**25** M	0130	1.0	30
	0824	0.2	6		0708	0.3	9
	1458	1.5	46		1347	1.4	43
	2135	0.2	6		2031	0.2	6
11 M	0345	1.2	37	**26** Tu ☽	0235	1.1	34
	0936	0.4	12		0813	0.4	12
	1547	1.4	43		1428	1.3	40
	2220	0.1	3		2110	0.1	3
12 Tu	0451	1.3	40	**27** W	0340	1.2	37
	1048	0.4	12		0926	0.5	15
	1633	1.3	40		1514	1.2	37
	2303	0.1	3		2154	0.0	0
13 W	0549	1.4	43	**28** Th	0444	1.4	43
	1156	0.5	15		1042	0.5	15
	1718	1.1	34		1604	1.2	37
	2343	0.0	0		2241	-0.2	-6
14 Th	0642	1.5	46	**29** F	0545	1.5	46
	1259	0.5	15		1156	0.5	15
	1801	1.0	30		1658	1.1	34
					2331	-0.3	-9
15 F	0021	-0.1	-3	**30** Sa	0644	1.7	52
	0729	1.6	49		1304	0.4	12
	1354	0.5	15		1755	1.0	30
	1842	0.9	27				
				31 Su	0024	-0.4	-12
					0740	1.8	55
					1407	0.4	12
					1853	1.0	30

Time meridian 60° W. 0000 is midnight. 1200 is noon. Times are not adjusted for Daylight Saving Time.
Heights are referred to mean lower low water which is the chart datum of soundings.

Charlotte Amalie, St. Thomas Island, 2017

Times and Heights of High and Low Waters

January

Day	Time	ft	cm	Day	Time	ft	cm
1 Su	0240	-0.1	-3	16 M	0420	-0.1	-3
	1138	0.8	24		1216	0.6	18
					2000	0.1	3
					2333	0.2	6
2 M	0314	-0.1	-3	17 Tu	0519	0.1	3
	1212	0.8	24		1237	0.5	15
					2023	0.1	3
3 Tu	0356	0.0	0	18 W	0153	0.2	6
	1245	0.7	21		0635	0.1	3
	2056	0.1	3		1253	0.4	12
					2047	0.0	0
4 W	0032	0.2	6	19 Th ◗	0405	0.3	9
	0456	0.1	3		0812	0.2	6
	1317	0.7	21		1305	0.4	12
	2110	0.1	3		2114	-0.1	-3
5 Th ◐	0330	0.3	9	20 F	0510	0.4	12
	0719	0.2	6		1011	0.2	6
	1347	0.6	18		1307	0.3	9
	2129	0.0	0		2143	-0.1	-3
6 F	0506	0.4	12	21 Sa	0557	0.5	15
	0950	0.3	9		2214	-0.2	-6
	1414	0.5	15				
	2154	-0.1	-3				
7 Sa	0600	0.6	18	22 Su	0638	0.5	15
	1218	0.3	9		2247	-0.2	-6
	1431	0.4	12				
	2224	-0.2	-6				
8 Su	0648	0.7	21	23 M	0717	0.6	18
	2300	-0.2	-6		2322	-0.3	-9
9 M	0736	0.8	24	24 Tu	0753	0.6	18
	2340	-0.3	-9		2356	-0.3	-9
10 Tu	0823	0.8	24	25 W	0827	0.6	18
11 W	0023	-0.3	-9	26 Th	0031	-0.3	-9
	0910	0.8	24		0900	0.7	21
12 Th O	0109	-0.3	-9	27 F ●	0104	-0.3	-9
	0954	0.8	24		0932	0.7	21
13 F	0156	-0.3	-9	28 Sa	0139	-0.2	-6
	1037	0.8	24		1002	0.7	21
14 Sa	0242	-0.2	-6	29 Su	0216	-0.2	-6
	1115	0.8	24		1032	0.7	21
15 Su	0330	-0.2	-6	30 M	0257	-0.1	-3
	1149	0.7	21		1101	0.7	21
	1941	0.0	0		1847	0.1	3
	2153	0.1	3		2142	0.2	6
				31 Tu	0349	0.0	0
					1130	0.6	18
					1904	0.1	3
					2309	0.2	6

February

Day	Time	ft	cm	Day	Time	ft	cm
1 W	0500	0.1	3	16 Th	0058	0.3	9
	1158	0.5	15		0703	0.1	3
	1926	0.1	3		1140	0.3	9
					1925	0.0	0
2 Th	0056	0.3	9	17 F	0236	0.3	9
	0642	0.2	6		0836	0.1	3
	1225	0.4	12		1148	0.2	6
	1952	0.0	0		1957	-0.1	-3
3 F	0304	0.4	12	18 Sa O	0357	0.4	12
	0842	0.2	6		2034	-0.1	-3
	1247	0.3	9				
	2023	-0.1	-3				
4 Sa ◖	0434	0.5	15	19 Su	0459	0.4	12
	2101	-0.2	-6		2116	-0.2	-6
5 Su	0538	0.6	18	20 M	0549	0.5	15
	2146	-0.3	-9		2201	-0.2	-6
6 M	0632	0.7	21	21 Tu	0632	0.5	15
	2235	-0.3	-9		2246	-0.2	-6
7 Tu	0722	0.7	21	22 W	0711	0.6	18
	2327	-0.3	-9		2330	-0.2	-6
8 W	0809	0.7	21	23 Th	0746	0.6	18
9 Th	0019	-0.3	-9	24 F	0013	-0.2	-6
	0852	0.7	21		0819	0.6	18
10 F O	0111	-0.3	-9	25 Sa	0058	-0.2	-6
	0931	0.7	21		0849	0.6	18
					1614	0.1	3
					1856	0.2	6
11 Sa	0202	-0.2	-6	26 Su ●	0145	-0.1	-3
	1005	0.6	18		0919	0.6	18
	1723	0.1	3		1630	0.2	6
	2003	0.2	6		2001	0.3	9
12 Su	0252	-0.2	-6	27 M	0238	-0.1	-3
	1033	0.6	18		0947	0.6	18
	1744	0.1	3		1648	0.1	3
	2109	0.2	6		2106	0.3	9
13 M	0344	-0.1	-3	28 Tu	0340	0.0	0
	1056	0.5	15		1015	0.5	15
	1807	0.1	3		1708	0.1	3
	2217	0.2	6		2215	0.4	12
14 Tu	0441	0.0	0				
	1113	0.4	12				
	1831	0.0	0				
	2331	0.3	9				
15 W	0546	0.1	3				
	1128	0.3	9				
	1857	0.0	0				

March

Day	Time	ft	cm	Day	Time	ft	cm
1 W	0453	0.1	3	16 Th	0623	0.1	3
	1042	0.4	12		1015	0.2	6
	1731	0.0	0		1720	0.0	0
	2331	0.4	12				
2 Th	0619	0.1	3	17 F	0020	0.4	12
	1107	0.3	9		0741	0.1	3
	1800	0.0	0		1026	0.2	6
					1747	-0.1	-3
3 F O	0059	0.5	15	18 Sa	0128	0.4	12
	0758	0.2	6		1822	-0.1	-3
	1128	0.3	9				
	1836	-0.1	-3				
4 Sa	0235	0.5	15	19 Su	0240	0.5	15
	1921	-0.2	-6		1908	-0.1	-3
5 Su ◖	0359	0.6	18	20 M O	0347	0.5	15
	2015	-0.2	-6		2003	-0.1	-3
6 M	0507	0.6	18	21 Tu	0443	0.5	15
	2115	-0.2	-6		2102	-0.1	-3
7 Tu	0604	0.7	21	22 W	0531	0.6	18
	2218	-0.2	-6		2200	-0.1	-3
8 W	0655	0.7	21	23 Th	0612	0.6	18
	2321	-0.2	-6		1404	0.1	3
					1605	0.2	6
					2258	-0.1	-3
9 Th	0739	0.6	18	24 F	0649	0.6	18
	1459	0.1	3		1410	0.1	3
	1733	0.2	6		1726	0.2	6
					2357	-0.1	-3
10 F	0022	-0.2	-6	25 Sa	0722	0.6	18
	0817	0.6	18		1424	0.2	6
	1516	0.1	3		1831	0.3	9
	1841	0.2	6				
11 Sa	0120	-0.1	-3	26 Su	0059	0.0	0
	0848	0.5	15		0754	0.6	18
	1535	0.1	3		1440	0.2	6
	1941	0.3	9		1931	0.4	12
12 Su O	0217	-0.1	-3	27 M ●	0204	0.0	0
	0913	0.5	15		0823	0.5	15
	1556	0.1	3		1457	0.1	3
	2036	0.3	9		2030	0.5	15
13 M	0314	0.0	0	28 Tu	0315	0.1	3
	0932	0.4	12		0852	0.5	15
	1617	0.1	3		1517	0.1	3
	2130	0.4	12		2129	0.5	15
14 Tu	0413	0.0	0	29 W	0431	0.1	3
	0947	0.3	9		0919	0.4	12
	1637	0.0	0		1539	0.0	0
	2223	0.4	12		2231	0.6	18
15 W	0515	0.1	3	30 Th	0553	0.2	6
	1001	0.3	9		0944	0.3	9
	1658	0.0	0		1608	-0.1	-3
	2319	0.4	12		2338	0.6	18
				31 F	0723	0.1	3
					1004	0.2	6
					1644	-0.1	-3

Time meridian 60° W. 0000 is midnight. 1200 is noon. Times are not adjusted for Daylight Saving Time.
Heights are referred to mean lower low water which is the chart datum of soundings.

Charlotte Amalie, St. Thomas Island, 2017
Times and Heights of High and Low Waters

April

Day	Time	ft	cm		Day	Time	ft	cm
1 Sa	0051	0.7	21		16 Su	0046	0.6	18
	1729	-0.1	-3			1630	-0.1	-3
2 Su	0209	0.7	21		17 M	0143	0.6	18
	1826	-0.2	-6			1718	-0.1	-3
3 M ●	0324	0.7	21		18 Tu	0240	0.6	18
	1934	-0.1	-3			1824	0.0	0
4 Tu	0429	0.7	21		19 W ◐	0333	0.6	18
	2048	-0.1	-3			1943	0.0	0
5 W	0524	0.7	21		20 Th	0420	0.6	18
	1310	0.0	0			1230	0.1	3
	1553	0.1	3			1516	0.2	6
	2204	-0.1	-3			2105	0.1	3
6 Th	0610	0.6	18		21 F	0502	0.6	18
	1322	0.1	3			1236	0.1	3
	1723	0.2	6			1654	0.2	6
	2319	0.0	0			2227	0.1	3
7 F	0649	0.6	18		22 Sa	0540	0.6	18
	1340	0.1	3			1248	0.1	3
	1828	0.3	9			1801	0.4	12
						2351	0.1	3
8 Sa	0030	0.0	0		23 Su	0615	0.6	18
	0719	0.5	15			1303	0.1	3
	1359	0.1	3			1858	0.5	15
	1922	0.4	12					
9 Su	0138	0.1	3		24 M	0115	0.2	6
	0741	0.4	12			0647	0.5	15
	1419	0.1	3			1320	0.1	3
	2011	0.4	12			1952	0.6	18
10 M	0244	0.1	3		25 Tu	0239	0.2	6
	0758	0.4	12			0717	0.4	12
	1437	0.0	0			1340	0.0	0
	2055	0.5	15			2045	0.7	21
11 Tu ○	0348	0.1	3		26 W ●	0402	0.2	6
	0812	0.3	9			0745	0.3	9
	1453	0.0	0			1403	-0.1	-3
	2138	0.5	15			2140	0.8	24
12 W	0453	0.1	3		27 Th	0526	0.1	3
	0825	0.2	6			0809	0.2	6
	1508	0.0	0			1432	-0.1	-3
	2221	0.6	18			2237	0.8	24
13 Th	0601	0.1	3		28 F	1507	-0.2	-6
	0838	0.2	6			2337	0.8	24
	1520	-0.1	-3					
	2306	0.6	18					
14 F	1535	-0.1	-3		29 Sa	1549	-0.2	-6
	2354	0.6	18					
15 Sa	1557	-0.1	-3		30 Su	0041	0.8	24
						1640	-0.2	-6

May

Day	Time	ft	cm		Day	Time	ft	cm
1 M	0145	0.8	24		16 Tu	0102	0.7	21
	1743	-0.1	-3			1604	0.0	0
2 Tu ○	0247	0.8	24		17 W	0147	0.7	21
	1858	0.0	0			1652	0.0	0
3 W	0343	0.7	21		18 Th ◐	0230	0.7	21
	1143	0.0	0			1113	0.0	0
	1514	0.1	3			1335	0.1	3
	2023	0.0	0			1810	0.0	0
4 Th	0429	0.6	18		19 F	0312	0.7	21
	1155	0.1	3			1113	0.1	3
	1705	0.2	6			1611	0.2	6
	2151	0.1	3			2013	0.1	3
5 F	0507	0.6	18		20 Sa	0351	0.6	18
	1214	0.1	3			1124	0.1	3
	1810	0.3	9			1729	0.4	12
	2321	0.2	6			2213	0.3	9
6 Sa	0536	0.5	15		21 Su	0427	0.6	18
	1233	0.1	3			1139	0.1	3
	1901	0.4	12			1823	0.5	15
7 Su	0048	0.2	6		22 M	0007	0.3	9
	0556	0.4	12			0501	0.5	15
	1253	0.0	0			1157	0.0	0
	1945	0.5	15			1912	0.6	18
8 M	0211	0.2	6		23 Tu	0152	0.3	9
	0610	0.3	9			0531	0.4	12
	1311	0.0	0			1218	-0.1	-3
	2025	0.6	18			2001	0.7	21
9 Tu	0328	0.2	6		24 W	0329	0.2	6
	0621	0.3	9			0557	0.3	9
	1328	-0.1	-3			1245	-0.1	-3
	2102	0.6	18			2051	0.8	24
10 W ○	1343	-0.1	-3		25 Th ●	1316	-0.2	-6
	2138	0.7	21			2143	0.9	27
11 Th	1356	-0.1	-3		26 F	1353	-0.2	-6
	2215	0.7	21			2236	0.9	27
12 F	1411	-0.1	-3		27 Sa	1435	-0.3	-9
	2253	0.7	21			2331	0.9	27
13 Sa	1430	-0.1	-3		28 Su	1521	-0.2	-6
	2334	0.7	21					
14 Su	1455	-0.1	-3		29 M	0025	0.9	27
						1614	-0.1	-3
15 M	0017	0.7	21		30 Tu	0118	0.8	24
	1526	-0.1	-3			1716	0.0	0
					31 W	0206	0.8	24
						1021	0.0	0
						1315	0.1	3
						1832	0.0	0

June

Day	Time	ft	cm		Day	Time	ft	cm
1 Th ◐	0248	0.7	21		16 F	0136	0.8	24
	1033	0.1	3			0952	0.1	3
	1617	0.2	6			1421	0.2	6
	2003	0.1	3			1716	0.1	3
2 F	0321	0.6	18		17 Sa ◐	0210	0.7	21
	1052	0.1	3			1003	0.1	3
	1735	0.4	12			1647	0.4	12
	2143	0.3	9			2013	0.3	9
3 Sa	0346	0.5	15		18 Su	0243	0.6	18
	1113	0.0	0			1019	0.1	3
	1826	0.5	15			1741	0.5	15
	2332	0.3	9			2238	0.4	12
4 Su	0401	0.4	12		19 M	0314	0.5	15
	1134	0.0	0			1039	0.0	0
	1909	0.6	18			1828	0.6	18
5 M	0125	0.3	9		20 Tu	0053	0.3	9
	0408	0.4	12			0339	0.4	12
	1156	-0.1	-3			1104	-0.1	-3
	1947	0.6	18			1914	0.8	24
6 Tu	1217	-0.1	-3		21 W	1135	-0.2	-6
	2022	0.7	21			2002	0.9	27
7 W	1237	-0.1	-3		22 Th	1210	-0.2	-6
	2056	0.7	21			2050	0.9	27
8 Th	1258	-0.2	-6		23 F ●	1251	-0.3	-9
	2130	0.7	21			2140	1.0	30
9 F ○	1319	-0.2	-6		24 Sa	1336	-0.3	-9
	2204	0.8	24			2229	1.0	30
10 Sa	1340	-0.2	-6		25 Su	1423	-0.2	-6
	2239	0.8	24			2317	1.0	30
11 Su	1404	-0.1	-3		26 M	1513	-0.1	-3
	2315	0.8	24					
12 M	1431	-0.1	-3		27 Tu	0002	0.9	27
	2350	0.8	24			1607	0.0	0
13 Tu	1500	-0.1	-3		28 W	0042	0.8	24
						0849	0.1	3
						1108	0.2	6
						1709	0.1	3
14 W	0026	0.8	24		29 Th	0117	0.7	21
	1533	0.0	0			0905	0.2	6
						1352	0.3	9
						1826	0.2	6
15 Th	0101	0.8	24		30 F ◐	0144	0.7	21
	1611	0.1	3			0926	0.1	3
						1616	0.4	12
						2000	0.3	9

Time meridian 60° W. 0000 is midnight. 1200 is noon. Times are not adjusted for Daylight Saving Time.
Heights are referred to mean lower low water which is the chart datum of soundings.

Charlotte Amalie, St. Thomas Island, 2017

Times and Heights of High and Low Waters

July

Day	Time	Height (ft)	Height (cm)	Day	Time	Height (ft)	Height (cm)
1 Sa	0203	0.6	18	16 Su	0114	0.7	21
	0950	0.1	3		0854	0.2	6
	1723	0.5	15		1625	0.6	18
	2150	0.4	12	◐	2113	0.5	15
2 Su	0212	0.5	15	17 M	0139	0.6	18
	1014	0.0	0		0918	0.1	3
	1811	0.6	18		1725	0.7	21
					2341	0.4	12
3 M	1040	0.0	0	18 Tu	0153	0.5	15
	1852	0.7	21		0949	0.0	0
					1816	0.8	24
4 Tu	1107	-0.1	-3	19 W	1025	-0.1	-3
	1929	0.7	21		1905	0.9	27
5 W	1136	-0.1	-3	20 Th	1107	-0.1	-3
	2005	0.8	24		1953	1.0	30
6 Th	1204	-0.1	-3	21 F	1153	-0.2	-6
	2040	0.8	24		2041	1.0	30
7 F	1233	-0.1	-3	22 Sa	1242	-0.2	-6
	2113	0.8	24		2127	1.0	30
8 Sa	1302	-0.1	-3	23 Su	1333	-0.1	-3
	2146	0.8	24	●	2210	1.0	30
9 Su	1330	-0.1	-3	24 M	1425	-0.1	-3
○	2217	0.8	24		2250	0.9	27
10 M	1357	-0.1	-3	25 Tu	1519	0.0	0
	2247	0.9	27		2325	0.9	27
11 Tu	1426	0.0	0	26 W	0701	0.3	9
	2317	0.9	27		0954	0.4	12
					1617	0.2	6
					2354	0.8	24
12 W	1459	0.1	3	27 Th	0723	0.3	9
	2347	0.8	24		1129	0.4	12
					1724	0.3	9
13 Th	0809	0.2	6	28 F	0016	0.7	21
	1021	0.3	9		0748	0.3	9
	1539	0.2	6		1330	0.5	15
					1843	0.4	12
14 F	0016	0.8	24	29 Sa	0032	0.6	18
	0819	0.2	6		0814	0.2	6
	1211	0.3	9		1526	0.5	15
	1638	0.2	6		2017	0.4	12
15 Sa	0045	0.8	24	30 Su	0041	0.6	18
	0834	0.2	6		0843	0.2	6
	1434	0.4	12	◑	1637	0.6	18
	1848	0.3	9		2214	0.4	12
				31 M	0038	0.5	15
					0914	0.1	3
					1730	0.7	21

August

Day	Time	Height (ft)	Height (cm)	Day	Time	Height (ft)	Height (cm)
1 Tu	0948	0.1	3	16 W	0906	0.1	3
	1815	0.8	24		1754	1.0	30
2 W	1024	0.0	0	17 Th	0957	0.0	0
	1856	0.8	24		1846	1.0	30
3 Th	1102	0.0	0	18 F	1051	0.0	0
	1934	0.8	24		1934	1.1	34
4 F	1140	0.0	0	19 Sa	1147	0.0	0
	2010	0.9	27		2019	1.1	34
5 Sa	1217	0.0	0	20 Su	1244	0.1	3
	2042	0.9	27		2100	1.0	30
6 Su	1252	0.0	0	21 M	0428	0.4	12
	2112	0.9	27		0647	0.5	15
					1341	0.1	3
				●	2136	1.0	30
7 M	1327	0.1	3	22 Tu	0447	0.4	12
	2141	0.9	27		0758	0.5	15
○					1438	0.2	6
					2206	0.9	27
8 Tu	1404	0.1	3	23 W	0509	0.4	12
	2208	0.9	27		0905	0.6	18
					1538	0.3	9
					2230	0.8	24
9 W	0556	0.4	12	24 Th	0533	0.4	12
	0823	0.5	15		1014	0.6	18
	1444	0.2	6		1642	0.4	12
	2235	0.9	27		2249	0.7	21
10 Th	0611	0.4	12	25 F	0557	0.4	12
	0935	0.5	15		1128	0.7	21
	1536	0.3	9		1753	0.5	15
	2301	0.9	27		2303	0.7	21
11 F	0629	0.4	12	26 Sa	0624	0.3	9
	1054	0.5	15		1249	0.7	21
	1647	0.4	12		1914	0.5	15
	2328	0.8	24		2314	0.6	18
12 Sa	0649	0.3	9	27 Su	0653	0.3	9
	1225	0.6	18		1416	0.7	21
	1825	0.5	15		2051	0.5	15
	2353	0.7	21		2317	0.6	18
13 Su	0714	0.3	9	28 M	0726	0.3	9
	1414	0.7	21		1531	0.8	24
	2018	0.5	15				
14 M	0015	0.6	18	29 Tu	0805	0.2	6
	0744	0.2	6		1632	0.8	24
◐	1548	0.8	24	◐			
15 Tu	0822	0.1	3	30 W	0850	0.2	6
	1656	0.9	27		1723	0.9	27
				31 Th	0938	0.2	6
					1808	0.9	27

September

Day	Time	Height (ft)	Height (cm)	Day	Time	Height (ft)	Height (cm)
1 F	1026	0.2	6	16 Sa	1044	0.2	6
	1848	0.9	27		1901	1.1	34
2 Sa	1113	0.2	6	17 Su	0226	0.5	15
	1923	1.0	30		0520	0.6	18
					1150	0.3	9
					1941	1.0	30
3 Su	1159	0.2	6	18 M	0243	0.5	15
	1954	1.0	30		0632	0.6	18
					1255	0.3	9
					2013	1.0	30
4 M	0324	0.5	15	19 Tu	0303	0.5	15
	0554	0.6	18		0733	0.7	21
	1244	0.2	6		1359	0.4	12
	2023	1.0	30		2040	0.9	27
5 Tu	0339	0.5	15	20 W	0324	0.5	15
	0657	0.6	18		0831	0.8	24
	1332	0.3	9		1503	0.4	12
	2050	1.0	30	●	2100	0.8	24
6 W	0355	0.5	15	21 Th	0345	0.5	15
	0757	0.7	21		0925	0.8	24
	1425	0.4	12		1609	0.5	15
○	2116	0.9	27		2116	0.7	21
7 Th	0413	0.5	15	22 F	0405	0.4	12
	0857	0.7	21		1020	0.9	27
	1527	0.4	12		1719	0.5	15
	2143	0.9	27		2129	0.7	21
8 F	0431	0.5	15	23 Sa	0425	0.4	12
	1000	0.8	24		1115	0.9	27
	1640	0.5	15		1834	0.5	15
	2208	0.8	24		2140	0.6	18
9 Sa	0453	0.4	12	24 Su	0446	0.4	12
	1109	0.8	24		1213	0.9	27
	1805	0.6	18				
	2232	0.7	21				
10 Su	0519	0.4	12	25 M	0512	0.3	9
	1226	0.9	27		1317	0.9	27
	1942	0.5	15				
	2252	0.6	18				
11 M	0553	0.3	9	26 Tu	0546	0.3	9
	1352	0.9	27		1423	0.9	27
12 Tu	0636	0.2	6	27 W	0634	0.3	9
	1515	1.0	30	◐	1526	0.9	27
13 W	0730	0.2	6	28 Th	0734	0.3	9
◐	1625	1.0	30		1620	0.9	27
14 Th	0831	0.2	6	29 F	0837	0.3	9
	1724	1.1	34		1706	1.0	30
15 F	0937	0.2	6	30 Sa	0939	0.3	9
	1816	1.1	34		1746	1.0	30

Time meridian 60° W. 0000 is midnight. 1200 is noon. Times are not adjusted for Daylight Saving Time.
Heights are referred to mean lower low water which is the chart datum of soundings.

Charlotte Amalie, St. Thomas Island, 2017
Times and Heights of High and Low Waters

October

Day	Time (h m)	ft	cm		Day	Time (h m)	ft	cm
1 Su	0131	0.5	15		16 M	0113	0.5	15
	0419	0.6	18			0618	0.7	21
	1040	0.4	12			1201	0.4	12
	1820	1.0	30			1842	0.9	27
2 M	0141	0.5	15		17 Tu	0132	0.4	12
	0533	0.6	18			0715	0.8	24
	1140	0.4	12			1317	0.5	15
	1852	1.0	30			1906	0.8	24
3 Tu	0155	0.5	15		18 W	0152	0.4	12
	0632	0.7	21			0805	0.8	24
	1242	0.4	12			1431	0.5	15
	1921	0.9	27			1923	0.7	21
4 W	0210	0.5	15		19 Th ●	0210	0.4	12
	0727	0.8	24			0850	0.9	27
	1348	0.5	15			1543	0.5	15
	1949	0.9	27			1936	0.6	18
5 Th ○	0226	0.5	15		20 F	0227	0.3	9
	0821	0.9	27			0934	0.9	27
	1500	0.5	15			1656	0.5	15
	2015	0.8	24			1946	0.6	18
6 F	0243	0.4	12		21 Sa	0242	0.3	9
	0915	0.9	27			1016	1.0	30
	1617	0.6	18					
	2041	0.7	21					
7 Sa	0304	0.4	12		22 Su	0255	0.3	9
	1012	1.0	30			1100	1.0	30
	1740	0.6	18					
	2103	0.7	21					
8 Su	0329	0.3	9		23 M	0308	0.2	6
	1113	1.1	34			1146	1.0	30
	1913	0.5	15					
	2119	0.6	18					
9 M	0402	0.3	9		24 Tu	0328	0.2	6
	1221	1.1	34			1236	1.0	30
10 Tu	0444	0.2	6		25 W	0356	0.2	6
	1333	1.1	34			1330	1.0	30
11 W	0538	0.2	6		26 Th	0437	0.3	9
	1445	1.1	34			1423	1.0	30
12 Th ☽	0645	0.2	6		27 F ◐	0536	0.3	9
	1550	1.1	34			1512	1.0	30
13 F	0801	0.3	9		28 Sa	0702	0.4	12
	1645	1.1	34			1556	1.0	30
14 Sa	0049	0.4	12		29 Su	0012	0.4	12
	0325	0.5	15			0330	0.5	15
	0921	0.3	9			0834	0.4	12
	1732	1.0	30			1635	0.9	27
15 Su	0056	0.5	15		30 M	0016	0.4	12
	0508	0.6	18			0506	0.6	18
	1042	0.4	12			1002	0.5	15
	1811	1.0	30			1709	0.9	27
					31 Tu	0027	0.4	12
						0605	0.7	21
						1128	0.5	15
						1741	0.9	27

November

Day	Time (h m)	ft	cm		Day	Time (h m)	ft	cm
1 W	0041	0.4	12		16 Th	0052	0.2	6
	0655	0.8	24			0819	0.9	27
	1255	0.5	15			1523	0.4	12
	1811	0.8	24			1744	0.5	15
2 Th	0057	0.3	9		17 F	0111	0.1	3
	0744	0.9	27			0856	0.9	27
	1421	0.6	18					
	1840	0.7	21					
3 F	0115	0.3	9		18 Sa ●	0128	0.1	3
	0832	1.0	30			0932	0.9	27
	1546	0.5	15					
	1905	0.6	18					
4 Sa ○	0136	0.2	6		19 Su	0144	0.1	3
	0922	1.1	34			1009	0.9	27
	1713	0.4	12					
	1925	0.5	15					
5 Su	0204	0.1	3		20 M	0200	0.0	0
	1016	1.1	34			1046	0.9	27
6 M	0237	0.1	3		21 Tu	0219	0.0	0
	1112	1.1	34			1125	0.9	27
7 Tu	0316	0.1	3		22 W	0242	0.1	3
	1212	1.1	34			1206	0.9	27
8 W	0403	0.1	3		23 Th	0308	0.1	3
	1314	1.1	34			1248	0.9	27
9 Th	0459	0.1	3		24 F	0338	0.1	3
	1415	1.1	34			1329	0.9	27
10 F ○	0610	0.2	6		25 Sa	0411	0.2	6
	1509	1.0	30			1409	0.9	27
	2333	0.3	9					
11 Sa	0217	0.4	12		26 Su ◐	0451	0.3	9
	0736	0.3	9			1446	0.9	27
	1556	1.0	30			2300	0.3	9
	2337	0.3	9					
12 Su	0447	0.5	15		27 M	0445	0.4	12
	0910	0.4	12			0706	0.3	9
	1634	0.9	27			1522	0.8	24
	2353	0.3	9			2309	0.3	9
13 M	0600	0.6	18		28 Tu	0541	0.5	15
	1047	0.5	15			0938	0.4	12
	1703	0.8	24			1555	0.7	21
						2322	0.2	6
14 Tu	0013	0.3	9		29 W	0623	0.6	18
	0653	0.7	21			1139	0.5	15
	1224	0.5	15			1627	0.7	21
	1724	0.7	21			2339	0.1	3
15 W	0033	0.2	6		30 Th	0704	0.8	24
	0738	0.8	24			1329	0.5	15
	1355	0.5	15			1656	0.6	18
	1738	0.6	18			2359	0.1	3

December

Day	Time (h m)	ft	cm		Day	Time (h m)	ft	cm
1 F	0748	0.9	27		16 Sa	0029	-0.1	-3
	1511	0.4	12			0850	0.8	24
	1718	0.5	15					
2 Sa	0024	0.0	0		17 Su	0053	-0.1	-3
	0834	1.0	30			0924	0.8	24
3 Su ○	0055	-0.1	-3		18 M ●	0116	-0.2	-6
	0923	1.0	30			0957	0.8	24
4 M	0131	-0.1	-3		19 Tu	0140	-0.2	-6
	1014	1.1	34			1030	0.8	24
5 Tu	0212	-0.2	-6		20 W	0203	-0.1	-3
	1106	1.1	34			1104	0.8	24
6 W	0257	-0.1	-3		21 Th	0227	-0.1	-3
	1159	1.0	30			1136	0.8	24
7 Th	0347	-0.1	-3		22 F	0252	0.0	0
	1251	1.0	30			1209	0.8	24
8 F	0444	0.0	0		23 Sa	0318	0.0	0
	1339	0.9	27			1240	0.8	24
9 Sa	0554	0.1	3		24 Su	0347	0.1	3
	1421	0.8	24			1312	0.7	21
	2215	0.2	6			2136	0.1	3
10 Su ○	0335	0.3	9		25 M	0127	0.2	6
	0724	0.2	6			0413	0.1	3
	1455	0.7	21			1343	0.7	21
	2233	0.2	6			2146	0.1	3
11 M	0517	0.4	12		26 Tu ○	1413	0.6	18
	0910	0.3	9			2201	0.1	3
	1520	0.6	18					
	2255	0.1	3					
12 Tu	0614	0.6	18		27 W	0538	0.5	15
	1106	0.4	12			0958	0.4	12
	1536	0.5	15			1442	0.5	15
	2318	0.0	0			2221	0.0	0
13 W	0659	0.7	21		28 Th	0617	0.6	18
	1310	0.3	9			1221	0.3	9
	1539	0.4	12			1506	0.4	12
	2342	0.0	0			2246	-0.1	-3
14 Th	0739	0.7	21		29 F	0659	0.7	21
						2316	-0.2	-6
15 F	0005	-0.1	-3		30 Sa	0744	0.8	24
	0815	0.8	24			2352	-0.3	-9
					31 Su	0830	0.9	27

Time meridian 60° W. 0000 is midnight. 1200 is noon. Times are not adjusted for Daylight Saving Time.
Heights are referred to mean lower low water which is the chart datum of soundings.

Lime Tree Bay, St. Croix Island, 2017

Times and Heights of High and Low Waters

January

Day	Time (h m)	Height (ft)	Height (cm)	Day	Time (h m)	Height (ft)	Height (cm)
1 Su	0150	-0.1	-3	16 M	0226	-0.1	-3
	1210	0.7	21		1149	0.5	15
2 M	0218	-0.1	-3	17 Tu	0249	0.0	0
	1228	0.7	21		1131	0.4	12
3 Tu	0241	0.0	0	18 W	0253	0.1	3
	1237	0.6	18		1103	0.4	12
					1928	0.2	6
4 W	0252	0.1	3	19 Th	1028	0.4	12
	1230	0.6	18		1931	0.1	3
				◐			
5 Th	0156	0.2	6	20 F	0944	0.4	12
	1159	0.5	15		1958	0.0	0
	2132	0.2	6				
◑							
6 F	1051	0.5	15	21 Sa	0904	0.4	12
	2103	0.1	3		2035	-0.1	-3
7 Sa	0920	0.5	15	22 Su	0849	0.5	15
	2116	0.0	0		2117	-0.2	-6
8 Su	0852	0.6	18	23 M	0858	0.5	15
	2147	-0.1	-3		2200	-0.2	-6
9 M	0909	0.7	21	24 Tu	0918	0.5	15
	2227	-0.2	-6		2242	-0.3	-9
10 Tu	0941	0.7	21	25 W	0942	0.6	18
	2310	-0.3	-9		2322	-0.3	-9
11 W	1017	0.7	21	26 Th	1006	0.6	18
	2355	-0.3	-9		2359	-0.3	-9
12 Th	1053	0.7	21	27 F	1028	0.6	18
○				●			
13 F	0038	-0.3	-9	28 Sa	0035	-0.2	-6
	1124	0.7	21		1049	0.6	18
14 Sa	0118	-0.2	-6	29 Su	0109	-0.2	-6
	1146	0.6	18		1106	0.6	18
15 Su	0155	-0.2	-6	30 M	0142	-0.1	-3
	1155	0.6	18		1117	0.5	15
				31 Tu	0213	0.0	0
					1118	0.5	15

February

Day	Time (h m)	Height (ft)	Height (cm)	Day	Time (h m)	Height (ft)	Height (cm)
1 W	0238	0.1	3	16 Th	0314	0.1	3
	1103	0.4	12		0904	0.3	9
	1920	0.1	3		1706	0.0	0
	2151	0.2	6				
2 Th	0235	0.1	3	17 F	0820	0.3	9
	1026	0.4	12		1743	-0.1	-3
	1839	0.1	3				
3 F	0925	0.4	12	18 Sa	0736	0.3	9
	1853	0.0	0		1828	-0.1	-3
				○			
4 Sa	0815	0.4	12	19 Su	0726	0.4	12
	1927	-0.1	-3		1919	-0.2	-6
◐							
5 Su	0757	0.5	15	20 M	0743	0.4	12
	2013	-0.2	-6		2014	-0.2	-6
6 M	0818	0.6	18	21 Tu	0808	0.5	15
	2106	-0.3	-9		2110	-0.2	-6
7 Tu	0850	0.6	18	22 W	0834	0.5	15
	2201	-0.3	-9		2203	-0.2	-6
8 W	0925	0.6	18	23 Th	0859	0.5	15
	2255	-0.3	-9		2253	-0.2	-6
9 Th	0958	0.6	18	24 F	0921	0.5	15
	2345	-0.3	-9		2340	-0.2	-6
10 F	1025	0.6	18	25 Sa	0939	0.5	15
○							
11 Sa	0032	-0.2	-6	26 Su	0025	-0.1	-3
	1040	0.5	15		0952	0.5	15
				●			
12 Su	0115	-0.1	-3	27 M	0110	0.0	0
	1041	0.4	12		0956	0.4	12
13 M	0155	-0.1	-3	28 Tu	0156	0.0	0
	1029	0.4	12		0946	0.4	12
					1604	0.2	6
					2026	0.3	9
14 Tu	0231	0.0	0				
	1007	0.3	9				
	1628	0.1	3				
	2102	0.2	6				
15 W	0301	0.1	3				
	0939	0.3	9				
	1639	0.1	3				
	2319	0.2	6				

March

Day	Time (h m)	Height (ft)	Height (cm)	Day	Time (h m)	Height (ft)	Height (cm)
1 W	0243	0.1	3	16 Th	1511	-0.1	-3
	0918	0.3	9				
	1554	0.1	3				
	2235	0.3	9				
2 Th	0330	0.2	6	17 F	0007	0.3	9
	0826	0.3	9		1545	-0.1	-3
	1609	0.0	0				
3 F	0112	0.3	9	18 Sa	0149	0.4	12
	0414	0.2	6		1624	-0.2	-6
	0649	0.3	9				
	1641	-0.1	-3				
○							
4 Sa	0517	0.4	12	19 Su	0349	0.4	12
	1723	-0.2	-6		1707	-0.2	-6
5 Su	0602	0.5	15	20 M	0511	0.4	12
	1815	-0.2	-6		1756	-0.2	-6
◐				○			
6 M	0648	0.5	15	21 Tu	0603	0.4	12
	1914	-0.2	-6		1851	-0.2	-6
7 Tu	0732	0.5	15	22 W	0643	0.5	15
	2020	-0.2	-6		1953	-0.1	-3
8 W	0811	0.5	15	23 Th	0714	0.5	15
	2128	-0.2	-6		2100	-0.1	-3
9 Th	0843	0.5	15	24 F	0740	0.5	15
	2234	-0.1	-3		2210	0.0	0
10 F	0903	0.5	15	25 Sa	0758	0.5	15
	2337	-0.1	-3		2321	0.0	0
11 Sa	0909	0.4	12	26 Su	0807	0.4	12
12 Su	0035	0.0	0	27 M	0034	0.1	3
	0859	0.3	9		0801	0.4	12
	1444	0.2	6		1407	0.2	6
	1758	0.3	9		1940	0.3	9
○				●			
13 M	0130	0.1	3	28 Tu	0151	0.2	6
	0838	0.3	9		0735	0.3	9
	1414	0.2	6		1351	0.1	3
	1957	0.3	9		2109	0.4	12
14 Tu	0226	0.1	3	29 W	0331	0.2	6
	0810	0.2	6		0631	0.3	9
	1421	0.1	3		1400	0.0	0
	2124	0.3	9		2230	0.4	12
15 W	0327	0.1	3	30 Th	1425	-0.1	-3
	0733	0.2	6		2353	0.5	15
	1442	0.0	0				
	2243	0.3	9				
				31 F	1459	-0.2	-6

Time meridian 60° W. 0000 is midnight. 1200 is noon. Times are not adjusted for Daylight Saving Time.
Heights are referred to mean lower low water which is the chart datum of soundings.

Lime Tree Bay, St. Croix Island, 2017

Times and Heights of High and Low Waters

April

Day	Time	ft	cm	Day	Time	ft	cm
1 Sa	0125	0.5	15	16 Su	0113	0.5	15
	1540	-0.2	-6		1526	-0.2	-6
2 Su	0301	0.5	15	17 M	0217	0.5	15
	1625	-0.2	-6		1602	-0.2	-6 ◗
3 M ◗	0424	0.5	15	18 Tu	0318	0.5	15
	1716	-0.2	-6		1640	-0.1	-3
4 Tu	0528	0.5	15	19 W ◑	0409	0.5	15
	1811	-0.2	-6		1719	-0.1	-3
5 W	0615	0.5	15	20 Th	0450	0.5	15
	1912	-0.1	-3		1801	0.0	0
6 Th	0645	0.5	15	21 F	0519	0.5	15
	2025	0.0	0		1849	0.1	3
7 F	0655	0.4	12	22 Sa	0537	0.5	15
	2155	0.1	3		2021	0.2	6
8 Sa	0646	0.4	12	23 Su	0538	0.4	12
	1348	0.1	3		1312	0.2	6
	1721	0.2	6		1937	0.3	9
	2335	0.1	3		2326	0.2	6
9 Su	0622	0.3	9	24 M	0512	0.4	12
	1245	0.2	6		1233	0.2	6
	1927	0.3	9		2033	0.4	12
10 M	0118	0.2	6	25 Tu	1227	0.1	3
	0544	0.3	9		2124	0.5	15
	1242	0.1	3				
	2037	0.4	12				
11 Tu O	1257	0.0	0	26 W ●	1242	-0.1	-3
	2133	0.4	12		2218	0.6	18
12 W	1320	-0.1	-3	27 Th	1308	-0.2	-6
	2225	0.5	15		2315	0.6	18
13 Th	1347	-0.1	-3	28 F	1343	-0.2	-6
	2317	0.5	15				
14 F	1417	-0.2	-6	29 Sa	0014	0.7	21
					1421	-0.3	-9
15 Sa	0012	0.5	15	30 Su	0116	0.7	21
	1451	-0.2	-6		1502	-0.3	-9

May

Day	Time	ft	cm	Day	Time	ft	cm
1 M	0217	0.7	21	16 Tu	0130	0.6	18
	1544	-0.2	-6		1513	-0.2	-6
2 Tu ◑	0310	0.6	18	17 W	0207	0.6	18
	1624	-0.2	-6		1539	-0.1	-3
3 W	0349	0.6	18	18 Th O	0238	0.6	18
	1700	0.0	0		1557	0.0	0
4 Th	0407	0.5	15	19 F	0300	0.6	18
	1725	0.1	3		1550	0.1	3
5 F	0402	0.4	12	20 Sa	0309	0.5	15
	1635	0.2	6		1349	0.2	6
6 Sa	0335	0.4	12	21 Su	0254	0.5	15
	1209	0.2	6		1200	0.2	6
7 Su	0239	0.4	12	22 M	0140	0.5	15
	1132	0.1	3		1125	0.1	3
	2113	0.4	12		2132	0.5	15
8 M	1136	0.0	0	23 Tu	1122	0.0	0
	2116	0.5	15		2131	0.6	18
9 Tu	1153	-0.1	-3	24 W	1139	-0.1	-3
	2142	0.5	15		2203	0.7	21
10 W O	1216	-0.1	-3	25 Th ●	1207	-0.2	-6
	2213	0.6	18		2244	0.8	24
11 Th	1243	-0.2	-6	26 F	1242	-0.3	-9
	2249	0.6	18		2330	0.8	24
12 F	1313	-0.2	-6	27 Sa	1320	-0.3	-9
	2327	0.6	18				
13 Sa	1343	-0.2	-6	28 Su	0017	0.8	24
					1359	-0.3	-9
14 Su	0008	0.6	18	29 M	0101	0.8	24
	1414	-0.2	-6		1437	-0.3	-9
15 M	0049	0.6	18	30 Tu	0138	0.7	21
	1445	-0.2	-6		1511	-0.2	-6
				31 W	0200	0.6	18
					1538	0.0	0

June

Day	Time	ft	cm	Day	Time	ft	cm
1 Th ◗	0204	0.6	18	16 F	0123	0.7	21
	1545	0.1	3		1448	0.1	3
2 F	0149	0.5	15	17 Sa	0123	0.6	18
	1436	0.2	6		1310	0.2	6
3 Sa	0115	0.5	15	18 Su	0101	0.6	18
	1105	0.2	6		1055	0.2	6
					2358	0.5	15
4 Su	0022	0.5	15	19 M	1018	0.1	3
	1029	0.1	3		2205	0.6	18
	2256	0.5	15				
5 M	1035	0.0	0	20 Tu	1018	0.0	0
	2152	0.6	18		2126	0.7	21
6 Tu	1054	-0.1	-3	21 W	1038	-0.1	-3
	2147	0.6	18		2141	0.8	24
7 W	1120	-0.2	-6	22 Th	1109	-0.2	-6
	2203	0.6	18		2213	0.8	24
8 Th	1149	-0.2	-6	23 F ●	1147	-0.3	-9
	2227	0.7	21		2251	0.9	27
9 F O	1220	-0.2	-6	24 Sa	1227	-0.3	-9
	2256	0.7	21		2330	0.9	27
10 Sa	1251	-0.3	-9	25 Su	1307	-0.3	-9
	2326	0.7	21				
11 Su	1321	-0.2	-6	26 M	0006	0.8	24
	2356	0.7	21		1345	-0.2	-6
12 M	1349	-0.2	-6	27 Tu	0034	0.8	24
					1419	-0.1	-3
13 Tu	0024	0.7	21	28 W	0048	0.7	21
	1416	-0.2	-6		1446	0.0	0
14 W	0049	0.7	21	29 Th	0045	0.6	18
	1438	-0.1	-3		1458	0.1	3
15 Th	0110	0.7	21	30 F ◗	0025	0.6	18
	1454	0.0	0		1427	0.2	6
					2355	0.6	18

Time meridian 60° W. 0000 is midnight. 1200 is noon. Times are not adjusted for Daylight Saving Time.
Heights are referred to mean lower low water which is the chart datum of soundings.

Lime Tree Bay, St. Croix Island, 2017

Times and Heights of High and Low Waters

July

Day	Time	ft	cm
1 Sa	0947	0.2	6
	2316	0.6	18
2 Su	0911	0.1	3
	2229	0.6	18
3 M	0922	0.0	0
	2148	0.6	18
4 Tu	0948	0.0	0
	2134	0.7	21
5 W	1019	-0.1	-3
	2143	0.7	21
6 Th	1053	-0.2	-6
	2201	0.7	21
7 F	1128	-0.2	-6
	2224	0.7	21
8 Sa	1202	-0.2	-6
	2247	0.8	24
9 Su ○	1234	-0.2	-6
	2310	0.8	24
10 M	1304	-0.1	-3
	2331	0.8	24
11 Tu	1332	-0.1	-3
	2348	0.8	24
12 W	1357	0.0	0
13 Th	0002	0.8	24
	1417	0.1	3
14 F	0008	0.7	21
	1423	0.2	6
15 Sa	0003	0.7	21
	1320	0.3	9
	2338	0.6	18
16 Su ☽	0916	0.3	9
	2248	0.6	18
17 M	0848	0.2	6
	2134	0.7	21
18 Tu	0859	0.1	3
	2056	0.7	21
19 W	0927	0.0	0
	2105	0.8	24
20 Th	1006	-0.1	-3
	2133	0.9	27
21 F	1049	-0.2	-6
	2208	0.9	27
22 Sa	1134	-0.2	-6
	2244	0.9	27
23 Su ●	1218	-0.2	-6
	2315	0.9	27
24 M	1300	-0.1	-3
	2338	0.8	24
25 Tu	1338	0.0	0
	2345	0.8	24
26 W	1410	0.1	3
	2336	0.7	21
27 Th	1433	0.2	6
	2313	0.6	18
28 F	1436	0.3	9
	2243	0.6	18
29 Sa	0701	0.3	9
	2209	0.6	18
30 Su ☾	0708	0.2	6
	2132	0.6	18
31 M	0737	0.2	6
	2101	0.7	21

August

Day	Time	ft	cm
1 Tu	0815	0.1	3
	2051	0.7	21
2 W	0858	0.0	0
	2100	0.7	21
3 Th	0942	0.0	0
	2118	0.8	24
4 F	1026	0.0	0
	2139	0.8	24
5 Sa	1107	0.0	0
	2200	0.8	24
6 Su	1145	0.0	0
	2218	0.8	24
7 M ○	1220	0.0	0
	2234	0.8	24
8 Tu	1253	0.1	3
	2246	0.8	24
9 W	1324	0.1	3
	2253	0.8	24
10 Th	1352	0.2	6
	2253	0.7	21
11 F	1415	0.3	9
	2240	0.7	21
12 Sa	0654	0.4	12
	0953	0.5	15
	1412	0.4	12
	2210	0.7	21
13 Su	0622	0.4	12
	2119	0.7	21
14 M ☾	0634	0.3	9
	2014	0.7	21
15 Tu	0706	0.2	6
	1948	0.8	24
16 W	0750	0.1	3
	2004	0.9	27
17 Th	0842	0.0	0
	2036	0.9	27
18 F	0936	0.0	0
	2112	0.9	27
19 Sa	1031	0.0	0
	2146	0.9	27
20 Su	1124	0.0	0
	2215	0.9	27
21 M ●	1213	0.1	3
	2232	0.8	24
22 Tu	1259	0.2	6
	2231	0.8	24
23 W	1341	0.3	9
	2213	0.7	21
24 Th	1418	0.4	12
	2146	0.6	18
25 F	0359	0.5	15
	0858	0.6	18
	1449	0.5	15
	2113	0.6	18
26 Sa	0414	0.4	12
	1113	0.6	18
	1503	0.5	15
	2036	0.6	18
27 Su	0443	0.3	9
	1955	0.7	21
28 M	0522	0.3	9
	1920	0.7	21
29 Tu ☾	0607	0.2	6
	1917	0.7	21
30 W	0659	0.2	6
	1936	0.8	24
31 Th	0755	0.1	3
	2001	0.8	24

September

Day	Time	ft	cm
1 F	0853	0.1	3
	2026	0.8	24
2 Sa	0947	0.1	3
	2048	0.8	24
3 Su	1038	0.2	6
	2105	0.8	24
4 M	1124	0.2	6
	2118	0.8	24
5 Tu	1209	0.3	9
	2126	0.8	24
6 W ○	1252	0.4	12
	2126	0.8	24
7 Th	1337	0.4	12
	2116	0.7	21
8 F	0340	0.5	15
	0826	0.6	18
	1422	0.5	15
	2052	0.7	21
9 Sa	0335	0.5	15
	1025	0.7	21
	1510	0.6	18
	2006	0.7	21
10 Su	0350	0.4	12
	1247	0.7	21
	1600	0.6	18
	1837	0.7	21
11 M	0420	0.3	9
	1645	0.8	24
12 Tu	0500	0.2	6
	1735	0.9	27
13 W ☽	0549	0.2	6
	1823	0.9	27
14 Th	0647	0.2	6
	1909	0.9	27
15 F	0752	0.2	6
	1950	0.9	27
16 Sa	0900	0.2	6
	2024	0.9	27
17 Su	1009	0.3	9
	2048	0.9	27
18 M	1115	0.3	9
	2054	0.8	24
19 Tu	1217	0.4	12
	2040	0.7	21
20 W ●	0213	0.6	18
	0548	0.7	21
	1317	0.5	15
	2013	0.7	21
21 Th	0145	0.6	18
	0749	0.7	21
	1418	0.5	15
	1938	0.6	18
22 F	0156	0.5	15
	0916	0.7	21
	1525	0.5	15
	1852	0.6	18
23 Sa	0219	0.4	12
	1034	0.7	21
24 Su	0250	0.3	9
	1156	0.8	24
25 M	0325	0.3	9
	1335	0.8	24
26 Tu	0405	0.2	6
	1532	0.8	24
27 W ☽	0449	0.2	6
	1656	0.8	24
28 Th	0538	0.2	6
	1749	0.8	24
29 F	0633	0.2	6
	1827	0.8	24
30 Sa	0734	0.3	9
	1855	0.8	24

Time meridian 60° W. 0000 is midnight. 1200 is noon. Times are not adjusted for Daylight Saving Time.
Heights are referred to mean lower low water which is the chart datum of soundings.

Lime Tree Bay, St. Croix Island, 2017
Times and Heights of High and Low Waters

October

Day	Time	ft	cm	Day	Time	ft	cm
1 Su	0840	0.3	9	16 M	0927	0.5	15
	1916	0.8	24		1826	0.7	21
2 M	0951	0.4	12	17 Tu	0136	0.5	15
	1928	0.8	24		0457	0.6	18
					1114	0.5	15
					1755	0.7	21
3 Tu	1102	0.5	15	18 W	0022	0.6	18
	1932	0.8	24		0715	0.7	21
					1310	0.5	15
					1707	0.6	18
4 W	0232	0.5	15	19 Th	0020	0.5	15
	0548	0.6	18		0827	0.8	24 ●
	1215	0.5	15				
	1923	0.7	21				
5 Th	0142	0.6	18	20 F	0036	0.4	12
	0741	0.7	21		0923	0.8	24
	1333	0.6	18				
○	1858	0.7	21				
6 F	0133	0.5	15	21 Sa	0101	0.3	9
	0903	0.8	24		1014	0.8	24
	1516	0.6	18				
	1756	0.7	21				
7 Sa	0144	0.4	12	22 Su	0129	0.2	6
	1018	0.8	24		1105	0.9	27
8 Su	0207	0.3	9	23 M	0201	0.2	6
	1136	0.9	27		1200	0.9	27
9 M	0239	0.2	6	24 Tu	0235	0.1	3
	1302	0.9	27		1259	0.8	24
10 Tu	0318	0.2	6	25 W	0311	0.1	3
	1434	0.9	27		1402	0.8	24
11 W	0403	0.2	6	26 Th	0348	0.2	6
	1558	1.0	30		1501	0.8	24
12 Th	0452	0.2	6	27 F	0426	0.2	6
☽	1704	0.9	27	☾	1550	0.8	24
13 F	0546	0.2	6	28 Sa	0503	0.3	9
	1753	0.9	27		1626	0.8	24
14 Sa	0646	0.3	9	29 Su	0539	0.3	9
	1825	0.9	27		1650	0.8	24
15 Su	0757	0.4	12	30 M	0613	0.4	12
	1837	0.8	24		1702	0.8	24
				31 Tu	0246	0.5	15
					1659	0.7	21

November

Day	Time	ft	cm	Day	Time	ft	cm
1 W	0045	0.5	15	16 Th	0903	0.7	21
	0753	0.6	18		2334	0.2	6
	1057	0.5	15				
	1631	0.7	21				
2 Th	0015	0.5	15	17 F	0928	0.8	24
	0831	0.7	21				
3 F	0013	0.4	12	18 Sa	0000	0.1	3
	0915	0.8	24		1000	0.8	24
				●			
4 Sa	0027	0.3	9	19 Su	0029	0.0	0
	1004	0.9	27		1036	0.8	24
○							
5 Su	0053	0.2	6	20 M	0100	0.0	0
	1058	0.9	27		1114	0.8	24
6 M	0126	0.1	3	21 Tu	0132	0.0	0
	1156	1.0	30		1154	0.8	24
7 Tu	0204	0.0	0	22 W	0204	0.0	0
	1257	1.0	30		1234	0.8	24
8 W	0245	0.0	0	23 Th	0235	0.0	0
	1359	1.0	30		1313	0.8	24
9 Th	0327	0.1	3	24 F	0304	0.1	3
	1454	0.9	27		1347	0.8	24
10 F	0408	0.1	3	25 Sa	0329	0.1	3
	1536	0.9	27		1414	0.8	24
☽							
11 Sa	0445	0.2	6	26 Su	0346	0.2	6
	1556	0.8	24		1432	0.8	24
				☾			
12 Su	0514	0.3	9	27 M	0336	0.3	9
	1549	0.7	21		1437	0.7	21
13 M	0455	0.5	15	28 Tu	0127	0.4	12
	1516	0.7	21		1419	0.7	21
	2356	0.5	15		2338	0.4	12
14 Tu	1410	0.6	18	29 W	1306	0.6	18
	2312	0.4	12		2307	0.3	9
15 W	0901	0.7	21	30 Th	0926	0.7	21
	2316	0.3	9		2307	0.2	6

December

Day	Time	ft	cm	Day	Time	ft	cm
1 F	0918	0.8	24	16 Sa	0946	0.7	21
	2323	0.1	3		2334	-0.1	-3
2 Sa	0946	0.8	24	17 Su	1011	0.7	21
	2351	0.0	0				
3 Su	1026	0.9	27	18 M	0007	-0.2	-6
○					1040	0.7	21
				●			
4 M	0026	-0.1	-3	19 Tu	0041	-0.2	-6
	1111	0.9	27		1110	0.7	21
5 Tu	0105	-0.2	-6	20 W	0113	-0.2	-6
	1159	0.9	27		1139	0.7	21
6 W	0145	-0.2	-6	21 Th	0143	-0.1	-3
	1245	0.9	27		1205	0.7	21
7 Th	0225	-0.1	-3	22 F	0210	-0.1	-3
	1324	0.9	27		1228	0.7	21
8 F	0301	0.0	0	23 Sa	0234	0.0	0
	1350	0.8	24		1245	0.7	21
9 Sa	0331	0.1	3	24 Su	0250	0.1	3
	1354	0.7	21		1255	0.6	18
10 Su	0347	0.2	6	25 M	0248	0.2	6
☽	1334	0.6	18		1253	0.6	18
11 M	0308	0.3	9	26 Tu	0112	0.2	6
	1254	0.6	18		1231	0.6	18
	2240	0.3	9		2224	0.2	6
				☾			
12 Tu	1153	0.6	18	27 W	1131	0.5	15
	2200	0.2	6		2151	0.1	3
13 W	1025	0.6	18	28 Th	0944	0.6	18
	2209	0.1	3		2155	0.0	0
14 Th	0930	0.6	18	29 F	0904	0.6	18
	2233	0.0	0		2217	-0.1	-3
15 F	0928	0.7	21	30 Sa	0918	0.7	21
	2302	-0.1	-3		2250	-0.2	-6
				31 Su	0950	0.8	24
					2329	-0.3	-9

Time meridian 60° W. 0000 is midnight. 1200 is noon. Times are not adjusted for Daylight Saving Time.
Heights are referred to mean lower low water which is the chart datum of soundings.

Isla Zapara (Malecon), Venezuela, 2017
Times and Heights of High and Low Waters

January

Day	Time	ft	cm	Day	Time	ft	cm
1 Su	0035	1.1	34	**16** M	0205	0.8	24
	0723	3.8	116		0839	4.2	128
	1249	2.2	67		1445	1.6	49
	1858	4.1	125		2032	4.2	128
2 M	0119	1.1	34	**17** Tu	0305	1.0	30
	0809	3.9	119		0936	4.2	128
	1343	2.2	67		1547	1.5	46
	1947	4.1	125		2134	4.1	125
3 Tu	0205	1.1	34	**18** W	0402	1.2	37
	0853	4.0	122		1027	4.2	128
	1439	2.0	61		1643	1.4	43
	2040	4.1	125		2232	4.0	122
4 W	0253	1.1	34	**19** Th	0455	1.4	43
	0937	4.1	125		1112	4.2	128
	1535	1.7	52		1735	1.3	40
	2136	4.1	125		2325	3.9	119
5 Th	0342	1.2	37	**20** F	0543	1.5	46
	1020	4.3	131		1152	4.2	128
	1631	1.4	43		1820	1.2	37
	2233	4.1	125				
6 F	0434	1.2	37	**21** Sa	0012	3.8	116
	1106	4.5	137		0626	1.6	49
	1726	1.1	34		1229	4.2	128
	2332	4.2	128		1901	1.1	34
7 Sa	0528	1.2	37	**22** Su	0056	3.8	116
	1153	4.6	140		0703	1.7	52
	1821	0.7	21		1304	4.2	128
					1938	1.0	30
8 Su	0030	4.2	128	**23** M	0136	3.7	113
	0623	1.2	37		0736	1.8	55
	1243	4.8	146		1339	4.2	128
	1916	0.5	15		2011	1.0	30
9 M	0129	4.2	128	**24** Tu	0216	3.7	113
	0719	1.3	40		0806	1.8	55
	1335	4.9	149		1416	4.2	128
	2012	0.3	9		2044	0.9	27
10 Tu	0228	4.2	128	**25** W	0257	3.7	113
	0817	1.3	40		0837	1.8	55
	1429	4.9	149		1453	4.2	128
	2108	0.1	3		2117	0.9	27
11 W	0327	4.2	128	**26** Th	0338	3.7	113
	0918	1.4	43		0912	1.8	55
	1525	4.9	149		1531	4.3	131
	2205	0.1	3		2153	0.9	27
12 Th	0429	4.2	128	**27** F	0420	3.7	113
	1020	1.5	46		0951	1.8	55
	1623	4.8	146		1611	4.3	131
	2304	0.2	6		2231	0.9	27
13 F	0531	4.2	128	**28** Sa	0503	3.8	116
	1125	1.6	49		1035	1.8	55
	1723	4.7	143		1654	4.2	128
					2313	0.9	27
14 Sa	0003	0.4	12	**29** Su	0548	3.8	116
	0635	4.2	128		1124	1.8	55
	1232	1.6	49		1740	4.2	128
	1825	4.6	140		2357	0.9	27
15 Su	0104	0.6	18	**30** M	0634	3.8	116
	0738	4.2	128		1217	1.7	52
	1339	1.6	49		1830	4.1	125
	1929	4.4	134				
				31 Tu	0045	1.0	30
					0722	3.8	116
					1315	1.6	49
					1925	4.1	125

February

Day	Time	ft	cm	Day	Time	ft	cm
1 W	0136	1.1	34	**16** Th	0339	1.5	46
	0811	3.9	119		0945	3.7	113
	1415	1.4	43		1609	1.2	37
	2024	4.0	122		2205	3.7	113
2 Th	0230	1.2	37	**17** F	0432	1.6	49
	0902	4.0	122		1029	3.7	113
	1515	1.2	37		1656	1.2	37
	2125	4.0	122		2255	3.6	110
3 F	0326	1.2	37	**18** Sa	0517	1.6	49
	0955	4.2	128		1110	3.8	116
	1615	0.9	27		1738	1.1	34
	2227	4.0	122		2339	3.6	110
4 Sa	0424	1.2	37	**19** Su	0556	1.6	49
	1048	4.3	131		1148	3.8	116
	1713	0.6	18		1815	1.0	30
	2328	4.0	122				
5 Su	0523	1.2	37	**20** M	0020	3.6	110
	1141	4.4	134		0629	1.6	49
	1810	0.4	12		1225	3.9	119
					1849	0.9	27
6 M	0027	4.1	125	**21** Tu	0059	3.7	113
	0621	1.2	37		0658	1.6	49
	1235	4.6	140		1302	4.0	122
	1906	0.2	6		1921	0.9	27
7 Tu	0125	4.1	125	**22** W	0137	3.7	113
	0719	1.2	37		0728	1.6	49
	1329	4.7	143		1339	4.1	125
	2001	0.1	3		1954	0.8	24
8 W	0222	4.1	125	**23** Th	0215	3.8	116
	0817	1.2	37		0801	1.5	46
	1423	4.7	143		1418	4.2	128
	2056	0.1	3		2030	0.7	21
9 Th	0318	4.1	125	**24** F	0254	3.8	116
	0915	1.2	37		0838	1.4	43
	1518	4.7	143		1457	4.2	128
	2152	0.2	6		2108	0.7	21
10 F	0414	4.1	125	**25** Sa	0334	3.8	116
	1014	1.3	40		0920	1.4	43
	1614	4.6	140		1540	4.2	128
	2248	0.4	12		2150	0.7	21
11 Sa	0511	4.0	122	**26** Su	0415	3.8	116
	1114	1.3	40		1006	1.3	40
	1711	4.4	134		1625	4.2	128
	2345	0.7	21		2234	0.8	24
12 Su	0608	3.9	119	**27** M	0458	3.9	119
	1215	1.4	43		1057	1.2	37
	1810	4.2	128		1715	4.2	128
					2323	0.9	27
13 M	0044	0.9	27	**28** Tu	0545	3.9	119
	0706	3.9	119		1152	1.1	34
	1317	1.4	43		1810	4.1	125
	1910	4.1	125				
14 Tu	0143	1.1	34				
	0803	3.8	116				
	1418	1.4	43				
	2011	3.9	119				
15 W	0242	1.3	40				
	0856	3.8	116				
	1516	1.3	40				
	2110	3.8	116				

March

Day	Time	ft	cm	Day	Time	ft	cm
1 W	0015	1.0	30	**16** Th	0220	1.7	52
	0637	3.9	119		0807	3.4	104
	1252	0.9	27		1438	1.1	34
	1910	4.0	122		2047	3.6	110
2 Th	0113	1.1	34	**17** F	0317	1.7	52
	0733	3.9	119		0855	3.4	104
	1354	0.8	24		1526	1.1	34
	2014	4.0	122		2138	3.5	107
3 F	0214	1.2	37	**18** Sa	0408	1.8	55
	0832	4.0	122		0941	3.4	104
	1457	0.6	18		1609	1.1	34
	2120	4.0	122		2223	3.6	110
4 Sa	0318	1.2	37	**19** Su	0450	1.8	55
	0933	4.0	122		1024	3.4	104
	1559	0.4	12		1647	1.0	30
	2224	4.0	122		2305	3.6	110
5 Su	0423	1.2	37	**20** M	0524	1.7	52
	1034	4.1	125		1105	3.5	107
	1659	0.2	6		1721	1.0	30
	2326	4.1	125		2344	3.7	113
6 M	0525	1.2	37	**21** Tu	0554	1.7	52
	1133	4.3	131		1145	3.6	110
	1757	0.1	3		1755	0.9	27
7 Tu	0025	4.1	125	**22** W	0021	3.7	113
	0624	1.1	34		0622	1.5	46
	1229	4.4	134		1223	3.8	116
	1854	0.1	3		1829	0.8	24
8 W	0120	4.1	125	**23** Th	0057	3.8	116
	0722	1.0	30		0653	1.4	43
	1325	4.4	134		1302	3.9	119
	1948	0.2	6		1905	0.7	21
9 Th	0213	4.1	125	**24** F	0133	3.9	119
	0817	1.0	30		0729	1.3	40
	1419	4.4	134		1343	4.0	122
	2042	0.3	9		1944	0.7	21
10 F	0304	4.1	125	**25** Sa	0210	4.0	122
	0912	1.0	30		0809	1.1	34
	1513	4.4	134		1425	4.1	125
	2136	0.5	15		2025	0.7	21
11 Sa	0355	4.0	122	**26** Su	0248	4.0	122
	1007	1.0	30		0853	0.9	27
	1607	4.2	128		1511	4.2	128
	2230	0.8	24		2110	0.8	24
12 Su	0445	3.9	119	**27** M	0329	4.1	125
	1101	1.0	30		0942	0.7	21
	1701	4.1	125		1601	4.2	128
	2325	1.1	34		2159	0.9	27
13 M	0535	3.8	116	**28** Tu	0414	4.1	125
	1157	1.1	34		1035	0.6	18
	1757	3.9	119		1656	4.2	128
					2252	1.0	30
14 Tu	0022	1.3	40	**29** W	0503	4.1	125
	0626	3.6	110		1131	0.4	12
	1252	1.1	34		1756	4.1	125
	1855	3.8	116		2350	1.1	34
15 W	0121	1.5	46	**30** Th	0559	4.0	122
	0717	3.5	107		1232	0.3	9
	1346	1.1	34		1900	4.1	125
	1952	3.6	110				
				31 F	0055	1.3	40
					0701	4.0	122
					1335	0.2	6
					2007	4.1	125

Time meridian 67° 30' W. 0000 is midnight. 1200 is noon. Times are not adjusted for Daylight Saving Time. Heights are referred to the chart datum of soundings.

Isla Zapara (Malecon), Venezuela, 2017

Times and Heights of High and Low Waters

April

Day	Time	ft	cm	Day	Time	ft	cm
1 Sa	0203	1.3	40	16 Su	0338	2.0	61
	0807	4.0	122		0850	3.2	98
	1438	0.1	3		1514	1.0	30
	2115	4.1	125		2152	3.6	110
2 Su	0314	1.3	40	17 M	0417	2.0	61
	0914	4.0	122		0936	3.3	101
	1542	0.1	3		1550	1.0	30
	2220	4.2	128		2232	3.7	113
3 M ☽	0422	1.2	37	18 Tu	0448	1.9	58
	1020	4.1	125		1020	3.4	104
	1643	0.0	0		1625	0.9	27
	2320	4.3	131		2309	3.8	116
4 Tu	0525	1.1	34	19 W ☽	0516	1.8	55
	1123	4.2	128		1102	3.5	107
	1742	0.1	3		1701	0.9	27
					2344	3.9	119
5 W	0017	4.3	131	20 Th	0547	1.6	49
	0625	1.0	30		1143	3.7	113
	1222	4.2	128		1738	0.9	27
	1838	0.2	6				
6 Th	0109	4.3	131	21 F	0018	4.0	122
	0720	0.9	27		0622	1.4	43
	1319	4.2	128		1226	3.8	116
	1933	0.4	12		1818	0.8	24
7 F	0158	4.3	131	22 Sa	0052	4.2	128
	0814	0.8	24		0701	1.1	34
	1413	4.2	128		1310	4.0	122
	2026	0.7	21		1901	0.8	24
8 Sa	0245	4.2	128	23 Su	0128	4.3	131
	0906	0.8	24		0744	0.8	24
	1507	4.1	125		1357	4.1	125
	2118	0.9	27		1946	0.9	27
9 Su	0330	4.1	125	24 M	0207	4.4	134
	0956	0.8	24		0831	0.5	15
	1559	4.0	122		1447	4.2	128
	2210	1.2	37		2035	1.0	30
10 M	0413	3.9	119	25 Tu	0250	4.4	134
	1046	0.8	24		0922	0.3	9
	1652	3.8	116		1542	4.2	128
	2303	1.5	46		2128	1.1	34
11 Tu ○	0456	3.7	113	26 W ●	0337	4.4	134
	1135	0.8	24		1016	0.1	3
	1745	3.7	113		1640	4.2	128
	2358	1.7	52		2226	1.2	37
12 W	0540	3.5	107	27 Th	0430	4.4	134
	1223	0.9	27		1113	0.0	0
	1839	3.6	110		1743	4.2	128
					2330	1.4	43
13 Th	0056	1.9	58	28 F	0530	4.3	131
	0626	3.4	104		1214	-0.1	-3
	1310	0.9	27		1850	4.2	128
	1931	3.5	107				
14 F	0154	2.0	61	29 Sa	0039	1.5	46
	0714	3.3	101		0635	4.2	128
	1354	1.0	30		1316	-0.1	-3
	2022	3.5	107		1958	4.3	131
15 Sa	0250	2.0	61	30 Su	0153	1.5	46
	0802	3.2	98		0745	4.1	125
	1436	1.0	30		1420	-0.1	-3
	2109	3.6	110		2106	4.4	134

May

Day	Time	ft	cm	Day	Time	ft	cm
1 M	0306	1.4	43	16 Tu	0331	2.3	70
	0855	4.1	125		0846	3.3	101
	1523	0.0	0		1456	1.0	30
	2210	4.5	137		2158	3.9	119
2 Tu ○	0416	1.3	40	17 W	0404	2.1	64
	1004	4.1	125		0933	3.4	104
	1625	0.1	3		1533	1.0	30
	2308	4.5	137		2233	4.0	122
3 W	0519	1.1	34	18 Th ☽	0438	1.9	58
	1109	4.1	125		1019	3.5	107
	1724	0.3	9		1613	1.0	30
					2307	4.2	128
4 Th	0003	4.6	140	19 F	0514	1.7	52
	0618	0.9	27		1105	3.6	110
	1211	4.1	125		1654	1.0	30
	1820	0.5	15		2340	4.3	131
5 F	0052	4.6	140	20 Sa	0553	1.4	43
	0713	0.8	24		1152	3.8	116
	1309	4.1	125		1738	1.0	30
	1914	0.8	24				
6 Sa	0138	4.5	137	21 Su	0014	4.5	137
	0805	0.7	21		0637	1.0	30
	1405	4.0	122		1241	3.9	119
	2006	1.1	34		1824	1.0	30
7 Su	0221	4.4	134	22 M	0052	4.6	140
	0854	0.6	18		0723	0.6	18
	1458	3.9	119		1333	4.0	122
	2057	1.4	43		1914	1.1	34
8 M	0301	4.2	128	23 Tu	0133	4.7	143
	0941	0.6	18		0812	0.3	9
	1549	3.8	116		1428	4.1	125
	2146	1.7	52		2007	1.2	37
9 Tu	0339	4.0	122	24 W	0219	4.8	146
	1026	0.7	21		0904	0.0	0
	1640	3.7	113		1526	4.2	128
	2236	1.9	58		2104	1.3	40
10 W ○	0417	3.8	116	25 Th ●	0310	4.8	146
	1108	0.7	21		0959	-0.2	-6
	1729	3.6	110		1627	4.3	131
	2327	2.1	64		2205	1.5	46
11 Th	0456	3.7	113	26 F	0406	4.7	143
	1150	0.8	24		1056	-0.3	-9
	1818	3.6	110		1731	4.3	131
					2313	1.6	49
12 F	0020	2.3	70	27 Sa	0508	4.6	140
	0538	3.5	107		1156	-0.3	-9
	1229	0.9	27		1838	4.4	134
	1906	3.6	110				
13 Sa	0115	2.3	70	28 Su	0026	1.7	52
	0623	3.4	104		0614	4.5	137
	1307	0.9	27		1258	-0.2	-6
	1953	3.6	110		1946	4.5	137
14 Su	0207	2.4	73	29 M	0141	1.7	52
	0710	3.3	101		0724	4.3	131
	1343	1.0	30		1401	-0.1	-3
	2037	3.7	113		2052	4.6	140
15 M	0252	2.3	70	30 Tu	0254	1.5	46
	0758	3.3	101		0836	4.2	128
	1419	1.0	30		1503	0.1	3
	2119	3.8	116		2153	4.7	143
				31 W	0403	1.4	43
					0946	4.2	128
					1604	0.4	12
					2251	4.8	146

June

Day	Time	ft	cm	Day	Time	ft	cm
1 Th ☽	0507	1.1	34	16 F	0400	2.0	61
	1053	4.1	125		0940	3.6	110
	1703	0.6	18		1533	1.1	34
	2343	4.8	146		2230	4.3	131
2 F	0605	0.9	27	17 Sa ☽	0444	1.7	52
	1156	4.1	125		1032	3.7	113
	1759	0.9	27		1618	1.2	37
					2305	4.5	137
3 Sa	0030	4.8	146	18 Su	0529	1.3	40
	0659	0.8	24		1126	3.8	116
	1255	4.0	122		1706	1.2	37
	1853	1.2	37		2343	4.7	143
4 Su	0113	4.7	143	19 M	0616	0.9	27
	0749	0.7	21		1220	3.9	119
	1351	3.9	119		1757	1.3	40
	1943	1.5	46				
5 M	0152	4.5	137	20 Tu	0024	4.8	146
	0835	0.6	18		0705	0.5	15
	1443	3.8	116		1316	4.0	122
	2031	1.8	55		1850	1.4	43
6 Tu	0229	4.4	134	21 W	0109	5.0	152
	0918	0.6	18		0756	0.1	3
	1531	3.7	113		1414	4.1	125
	2117	2.0	61		1947	1.5	46
7 W	0304	4.2	128	22 Th	0159	5.0	152
	0959	0.6	18		0849	-0.1	-3
	1617	3.7	113		1513	4.2	128
	2202	2.2	67		2047	1.6	49
8 Th	0340	4.1	125	23 F ●	0252	5.0	152
	1036	0.7	21		0944	-0.3	-9
	1702	3.7	113		1614	4.3	131
	2246	2.4	73		2151	1.7	52
9 F ○	0418	3.9	119	24 Sa	0350	4.9	149
	1112	0.8	24		1041	-0.3	-9
	1747	3.7	113		1718	4.4	134
	2330	2.5	76		2300	1.8	55
10 Sa	0457	3.8	116	25 Su	0451	4.8	146
	1146	0.8	24		1139	-0.2	-6
	1832	3.7	113		1823	4.5	137
11 Su	0017	2.5	76	26 M	0012	1.8	55
	0540	3.7	113		0556	4.6	140
	1220	0.9	27		1240	-0.1	-3
	1917	3.8	116		1928	4.6	140
12 M	0104	2.6	79	27 Tu	0126	1.7	52
	0624	3.6	110		0705	4.4	134
	1255	0.9	27		1341	0.2	6
	2001	3.9	119		2032	4.7	143
13 Tu	0150	2.5	76	28 W	0238	1.6	49
	0711	3.6	110		0816	4.3	131
	1331	1.0	30		1443	0.4	12
	2042	4.0	122		2132	4.8	146
14 W	0235	2.4	73	29 Th	0346	1.4	43
	0759	3.5	107		0926	4.1	125
	1409	1.0	30		1543	0.7	21
	2121	4.1	125		2227	4.8	146
15 Th	0318	2.3	70	30 F ☽	0449	1.2	37
	0849	3.5	107		1034	4.0	122
	1450	1.1	34		1642	1.0	30
	2156	4.2	128		2317	4.8	146

Time meridian 67° 30' W. 0000 is midnight. 1200 is noon. Times are not adjusted for Daylight Saving Time.
Heights are referred to the chart datum of soundings.

Isla Zapara (Malecon), Venezuela, 2017
Times and Heights of High and Low Waters

July

Day	Time (h m)	Height (ft)	Height (cm)	Day	Time (h m)	Height (ft)	Height (cm)
1 Sa	0546	1.0	30	16 Su ◗	0417	1.5	46
	1138	3.9	119		1010	3.7	113
	1738	1.3	40		1553	1.4	43
					2236	4.6	140
2 Su	0002	4.8	146	17 M	0508	1.1	34
	0639	0.8	24		1109	3.8	116
	1237	3.9	119		1645	1.4	43
	1830	1.6	49		2319	4.8	146
3 M	0043	4.7	143	18 Tu	0559	0.7	21
	0726	0.7	21		1208	3.9	119
	1330	3.8	116		1740	1.5	46
	1918	1.8	55				
4 Tu	0120	4.6	140	19 W	0005	4.9	149
	0809	0.7	21		0650	0.3	9
	1418	3.8	116		1306	4.0	122
	2002	2.0	61		1838	1.5	46
5 W	0156	4.5	137	20 Th	0054	5.0	152
	0848	0.7	21		0742	0.1	3
	1502	3.7	113		1404	4.1	125
	2042	2.2	67		1937	1.6	49
6 Th	0230	4.4	134	21 F	0146	5.1	155
	0924	0.7	21		0835	-0.1	-3
	1544	3.7	113		1502	4.2	128
	2120	2.3	70		2038	1.7	52
7 F	0306	4.3	131	22 Sa	0241	5.1	155
	0957	0.7	21		0930	-0.2	-6
	1625	3.7	113		1602	4.3	131
	2157	2.4	73		2142	1.7	52
8 Sa ○	0343	4.2	128	23 Su ●	0338	5.0	152
	1029	0.8	24		1025	-0.1	-3
	1707	3.8	116		1702	4.4	134
	2235	2.5	76		2249	1.8	55
9 Su	0422	4.1	125	24 M	0438	4.8	146
	1102	0.8	24		1122	0.0	0
	1750	3.8	116		1804	4.5	137
	2317	2.5	76		2358	1.8	55
10 M	0502	4.0	122	25 Tu	0542	4.6	140
	1135	0.9	27		1221	0.3	9
	1834	3.9	119		1906	4.5	137
11 Tu	0002	2.5	76	26 W	0109	1.7	52
	0545	3.9	119		0648	4.4	134
	1211	0.9	27		1321	0.6	18
	1917	4.0	122		2007	4.6	140
12 W	0052	2.5	76	27 Th	0219	1.6	49
	0631	3.8	116		0757	4.2	128
	1250	1.0	30		1422	0.9	27
	1959	4.1	125		2105	4.6	140
13 Th	0143	2.4	73	28 F	0325	1.4	43
	0721	3.7	113		0907	4.0	122
	1331	1.1	34		1522	1.2	37
	2039	4.2	128		2158	4.6	140
14 F	0235	2.2	67	29 Sa	0426	1.2	37
	0815	3.7	113		1014	3.9	119
	1415	1.2	37		1621	1.4	43
	2117	4.3	131		2247	4.6	140
15 Sa	0326	1.9	58	30 Su ◗	0521	1.1	34
	0912	3.7	113		1117	3.8	116
	1502	1.3	40		1715	1.6	49
	2155	4.4	134		2330	4.6	140
				31 M	0611	0.9	27
					1212	3.8	116
					1805	1.8	55

August

Day	Time (h m)	Height (ft)	Height (cm)	Day	Time (h m)	Height (ft)	Height (cm)
1 Tu	0009	4.5	137	16 W	0543	0.5	15
	0655	0.8	24		1201	4.0	122
	1301	3.7	113		1736	1.6	49
	1849	2.0	61		2354	4.9	149
2 W	0046	4.5	137	17 Th	0636	0.2	6
	0735	0.8	24		1259	4.1	125
	1344	3.7	113		1835	1.6	49
	1928	2.1	64				
3 Th	0121	4.4	134	18 F	0046	5.0	152
	0810	0.8	24		0729	0.1	3
	1423	3.7	113		1356	4.2	128
	2003	2.2	67		1935	1.6	49
4 F	0156	4.4	134	19 Sa	0140	5.0	152
	0842	0.8	24		0822	0.0	0
	1502	3.8	116		1452	4.3	131
	2036	2.2	67		2035	1.6	49
5 Sa	0232	4.4	134	20 Su	0234	5.0	152
	0913	0.8	24		0916	0.1	3
	1541	3.8	116		1547	4.4	134
	2110	2.3	70		2137	1.6	49
6 Su	0310	4.4	134	21 M ●	0330	4.9	149
	0944	0.8	24		1010	0.2	6
	1621	3.9	119		1644	4.4	134
	2147	2.3	70		2240	1.6	49
7 M ○	0348	4.3	131	22 Tu	0429	4.7	143
	1017	0.8	24		1105	0.5	15
	1703	4.0	122		1741	4.4	134
	2230	2.3	70		2345	1.6	49
8 Tu	0429	4.2	128	23 W	0530	4.5	137
	1053	0.9	27		1202	0.8	24
	1745	4.0	122		1839	4.4	134
	2317	2.2	67				
9 W	0513	4.1	125	24 Th	0051	1.6	49
	1131	1.0	30		0634	4.2	128
	1827	4.1	125		1301	1.1	34
					1936	4.4	134
10 Th	0008	2.2	67	25 F	0156	1.5	46
	0601	4.0	122		0741	4.0	122
	1213	1.1	34		1402	1.4	43
	1910	4.1	125		2031	4.4	134
11 F	0103	2.0	61	26 Sa	0259	1.4	43
	0655	3.9	119		0848	3.8	116
	1259	1.2	37		1502	1.6	49
	1953	4.2	128		2123	4.3	131
12 Sa	0200	1.8	55	27 Su	0357	1.3	40
	0753	3.8	116		0953	3.7	113
	1349	1.3	40		1600	1.8	55
	2038	4.3	131		2210	4.3	131
13 Su	0257	1.5	46	28 M	0450	1.1	34
	0855	3.8	116		1051	3.7	113
	1442	1.5	46		1652	1.9	58
	2124	4.5	137		2253	4.3	131
14 M ◗	0354	1.2	37	29 Tu ◗	0536	1.0	30
	0959	3.8	116		1141	3.7	113
	1538	1.5	46		1738	2.0	61
	2213	4.6	140		2332	4.3	131
15 Tu	0449	0.8	24	30 W	0616	1.0	30
	1101	3.8	116		1225	3.7	113
	1637	1.6	49		1818	2.0	61
	2302	4.8	146				
				31 Th	0009	4.3	131
					0652	0.9	27
					1304	3.8	116
					1852	2.1	64

September

Day	Time (h m)	Height (ft)	Height (cm)	Day	Time (h m)	Height (ft)	Height (cm)
1 F	0045	4.4	134	16 Sa	0041	4.9	149
	0724	0.9	27		0716	0.2	6
	1341	3.8	116		1347	4.4	134
	1923	2.1	64		1937	1.5	46
2 Sa	0121	4.4	134	17 Su	0136	4.9	149
	0754	0.9	27		0809	0.3	9
	1418	3.9	119		1439	4.4	134
	1955	2.1	64		2035	1.5	46
3 Su	0158	4.4	134	18 M	0230	4.8	146
	0825	0.9	27		0901	0.5	15
	1455	4.0	122		1531	4.5	137
	2030	2.0	61		2133	1.5	46
4 M	0237	4.5	137	19 Tu	0325	4.7	143
	0857	0.9	27		0954	0.7	21
	1534	4.1	125		1623	4.4	134
	2109	2.0	61		2232	1.5	46
5 Tu	0317	4.4	134	20 W ●	0422	4.5	137
	0933	0.9	27		1048	1.0	30
	1613	4.1	125		1715	4.4	134
	2154	1.9	58		2331	1.5	46
6 W ○	0400	4.4	134	21 Th	0521	4.2	128
	1012	1.0	30		1144	1.3	40
	1653	4.2	128		1807	4.3	131
	2242	1.8	55				
7 Th	0447	4.3	131	22 F	0031	1.4	43
	1055	1.1	34		0622	4.0	122
	1736	4.2	128		1242	1.6	49
	2335	1.7	52		1900	4.2	128
8 F	0539	4.1	125	23 Sa	0131	1.4	43
	1141	1.2	37		0726	3.8	116
	1821	4.3	131		1342	1.8	55
					1951	4.1	125
9 Sa	0032	1.5	46	24 Su	0229	1.3	40
	0637	4.0	122		0829	3.7	113
	1233	1.4	43		1441	2.0	61
	1910	4.3	131		2041	4.1	125
10 Su	0132	1.3	40	25 M	0322	1.3	40
	0740	3.9	119		0928	3.7	113
	1329	1.5	46		1537	2.1	64
	2003	4.4	134		2127	4.1	125
11 M	0233	1.1	34	26 Tu	0410	1.2	37
	0846	3.9	119		1020	3.7	113
	1430	1.6	49		1626	2.1	64
	2058	4.5	137		2210	4.1	125
12 Tu	0333	0.8	24	27 W ◗	0452	1.2	37
	0952	3.9	119		1105	3.7	113
	1533	1.7	52		1707	2.2	67
	2155	4.6	140		2250	4.1	125
13 W ◗	0431	0.6	18	28 Th	0529	1.1	34
	1056	4.0	122		1145	3.8	116
	1636	1.7	52		1742	2.2	67
	2251	4.7	143		2329	4.2	128
14 Th	0528	0.4	12	29 F	0601	1.1	34
	1156	4.2	128		1223	3.9	119
	1738	1.6	49		1813	2.1	64
	2347	4.8	146				
15 F	0622	0.3	9	30 Sa	0007	4.3	131
	1253	4.3	131		0632	1.1	34
	1838	1.6	49		1258	4.0	122
					1843	2.0	61

Time meridian 67° 30' W. 0000 is midnight. 1200 is noon. Times are not adjusted for Daylight Saving Time.
Heights are referred to the chart datum of soundings.

Isla Zapara (Malecon), Venezuela, 2017

Times and Heights of High and Low Waters

October

Day	Time	ft	cm	Day	Time	ft	cm
1 Su	0044	4.4	134	16 M	0132	4.7	143
	0703	1.0	30		0755	0.7	21
	1334	4.1	125		1424	4.6	140
	1917	1.9	58		2032	1.3	40
2 M	0123	4.4	134	17 Tu	0227	4.6	140
	0736	1.0	30		0847	0.9	27
	1410	4.2	128		1512	4.6	140
	1955	1.8	55		2127	1.3	40
3 Tu	0204	4.5	137	18 W	0321	4.4	134
	0812	1.0	30		0939	1.2	37
	1446	4.3	131		1559	4.5	137
	2038	1.6	49		2221	1.3	40
4 W	0247	4.5	137	19 Th ●	0417	4.2	128
	0851	1.0	30		1031	1.5	46
	1524	4.4	134		1645	4.4	134
	2124	1.5	46		2315	1.3	40
5 Th ○	0333	4.4	134	20 F	0513	4.0	122
	0935	1.1	34		1125	1.8	55
	1605	4.4	134		1732	4.2	128
	2215	1.3	40				
6 F	0425	4.3	131	21 Sa	0009	1.3	40
	1022	1.2	37		0611	3.9	119
	1649	4.5	137		1221	2.0	61
	2309	1.1	34		1819	4.1	125
7 Sa	0521	4.2	128	22 Su	0102	1.3	40
	1114	1.4	43		0709	3.8	116
	1739	4.5	137		1319	2.2	67
					1906	4.0	122
8 Su	0008	1.0	30	23 M	0153	1.3	40
	0623	4.2	128		0806	3.7	113
	1211	1.5	46		1415	2.3	70
	1834	4.5	137		1953	3.9	119
9 M	0109	0.8	24	24 Tu	0240	1.3	40
	0729	4.1	125		0858	3.7	113
	1314	1.7	52		1506	2.4	73
	1934	4.6	140		2039	3.9	119
10 Tu	0211	0.6	18	25 W	0323	1.3	40
	0837	4.1	125		0946	3.7	113
	1422	1.7	52		1551	2.4	73
	2036	4.6	140		2123	4.0	122
11 W	0313	0.5	15	26 Th	0401	1.3	40
	0945	4.2	128		1028	3.8	116
	1530	1.7	52		1629	2.4	73
	2139	4.7	143		2206	4.0	122
12 Th ◑	0413	0.4	12	27 F ◐	0435	1.3	40
	1049	4.3	131		1106	3.9	119
	1637	1.7	52		1701	2.3	70
	2240	4.8	146		2246	4.1	125
13 F	0512	0.4	12	28 Sa	0506	1.2	37
	1148	4.4	134		1142	4.0	122
	1739	1.6	49		1732	2.2	67
	2339	4.8	146		2327	4.2	128
14 Sa	0608	0.4	12	29 Su	0539	1.2	37
	1243	4.5	137		1217	4.2	128
	1839	1.5	46		1806	2.0	61
15 Su	0036	4.8	146	30 M	0007	4.3	131
	0702	0.5	15		0613	1.2	37
	1335	4.6	140		1251	4.3	131
	1936	1.4	43		1843	1.8	55
				31 Tu	0049	4.4	134
					0650	1.1	34
					1325	4.4	134
					1925	1.6	49

November

Day	Time	ft	cm	Day	Time	ft	cm
1 W	0133	4.4	134	16 Th	0315	4.2	128
	0730	1.1	34		0923	1.6	49
	1401	4.6	140		1533	4.5	137
	2010	1.3	40		2206	1.1	34
2 Th	0219	4.4	134	17 F	0408	4.1	125
	0814	1.2	37		1013	1.9	58
	1441	4.7	143		1614	4.4	134
	2059	1.0	30		2255	1.1	34
3 F	0310	4.4	134	18 Sa ●	0501	3.9	119
	0902	1.3	40		1103	2.1	64
	1524	4.7	143		1656	4.2	128
	2151	0.8	24		2342	1.2	37
4 Sa ○	0405	4.4	134	19 Su	0552	3.8	116
	0953	1.4	43		1154	2.3	70
	1613	4.8	146		1738	4.1	125
	2247	0.6	18				
5 Su	0505	4.3	131	20 M	0027	1.3	40
	1050	1.5	46		0644	3.7	113
	1707	4.8	146		1245	2.4	73
	2346	0.5	15		1822	4.0	122
6 M	0609	4.3	131	21 Tu	0111	1.3	40
	1153	1.7	52		0734	3.7	113
	1806	4.8	146		1335	2.5	76
					1907	3.9	119
7 Tu	0047	0.4	12	22 W	0152	1.3	40
	0716	4.3	131		0822	3.7	113
	1302	1.8	55		1422	2.5	76
	1911	4.8	146		1952	3.9	119
8 W	0150	0.4	12	23 Th	0230	1.4	43
	0825	4.3	131		0907	3.8	116
	1413	1.8	55		1504	2.5	76
	2017	4.8	146		2037	3.9	119
9 Th	0253	0.3	9	24 F	0305	1.4	43
	0933	4.5	137		0948	3.9	119
	1524	1.7	52		1541	2.5	76
	2123	4.8	146		2121	4.0	122
10 F ◯	0355	0.4	12	25 Sa	0339	1.4	43
	1036	4.6	140		1027	4.0	122
	1631	1.6	49		1616	2.4	73
	2228	4.8	146		2204	4.0	122
11 Sa	0455	0.5	15	26 Su ◐	0414	1.3	40
	1134	4.7	143		1102	4.1	125
	1735	1.5	46		1652	2.2	67
	2330	4.7	143		2248	4.1	125
12 Su	0552	0.6	18	27 M	0450	1.3	40
	1228	4.8	146		1136	4.2	128
	1834	1.3	40		1731	1.9	58
					2332	4.2	128
13 M	0029	4.7	143	28 Tu	0529	1.3	40
	0647	0.8	24		1209	4.4	134
	1318	4.8	146		1813	1.6	49
	1930	1.2	37				
14 Tu	0126	4.6	140	29 W	0017	4.3	131
	0740	1.1	34		0611	1.3	40
	1405	4.7	143		1245	4.6	140
	2024	1.1	34		1858	1.3	40
15 W	0222	4.4	134	30 Th	0105	4.3	131
	0832	1.3	40		0655	1.3	40
	1450	4.6	140		1323	4.7	143
	2116	1.1	34		1946	1.0	30

December

Day	Time	ft	cm	Day	Time	ft	cm
1 F	0156	4.4	134	16 Sa	0350	3.9	119
	0744	1.3	40		0950	2.0	61
	1406	4.9	149		1543	4.3	131
	2037	0.7	21		2227	1.0	30
2 Sa	0250	4.4	134	17 Su	0436	3.8	116
	0835	1.4	43		1034	2.2	67
	1454	5.0	152		1621	4.2	128
	2131	0.4	12		2308	1.1	34
3 Su	0347	4.4	134	18 M ●	0522	3.7	113
	0931	1.5	46		1116	2.3	70
	1546	5.0	152		1700	4.1	125
○	2227	0.3	9		2347	1.2	37
4 M	0448	4.4	134	19 Tu	0607	3.7	113
	1032	1.6	49		1158	2.4	73
	1643	5.0	152		1741	4.0	122
	2326	0.2	6				
5 Tu	0553	4.4	134	20 W	0025	1.3	40
	1138	1.7	52		0653	3.7	113
	1745	5.0	152		1240	2.5	76
					1824	4.0	122
6 W	0028	0.2	6	21 Th	0101	1.3	40
	0700	4.4	134		0739	3.7	113
	1248	1.7	52		1323	2.5	76
	1851	4.9	149		1908	3.9	119
7 Th	0130	0.2	6	22 F	0137	1.4	43
	0808	4.5	137		0824	3.8	116
	1401	1.7	52		1405	2.5	76
	1959	4.8	146		1953	3.9	119
8 F	0234	0.3	9	23 Sa	0213	1.4	43
	0915	4.6	140		0906	3.8	116
	1512	1.6	49		1447	2.4	73
	2107	4.7	143		2039	3.9	119
9 Sa	0336	0.5	15	24 Su	0250	1.4	43
	1018	4.7	143		0944	3.9	119
	1620	1.5	46		1530	2.2	67
	2214	4.7	143		2126	3.9	119
10 Su ◯	0437	0.7	21	25 M	0329	1.4	43
	1115	4.8	146		1020	4.1	125
	1723	1.3	40		1614	2.0	61
	2318	4.6	140		2213	4.0	122
11 M	0536	0.9	27	26 Tu ◐	0410	1.4	43
	1209	4.8	146		1055	4.2	128
	1822	1.2	37		1659	1.7	52
					2302	4.0	122
12 Tu	0019	4.5	137	27 W	0454	1.4	43
	0632	1.1	34		1131	4.4	134
	1257	4.8	146		1746	1.3	40
	1917	1.0	30		2352	4.1	125
13 W	0117	4.3	131	28 Th	0540	1.3	40
	0725	1.3	40		1211	4.6	140
	1343	4.7	143		1834	1.0	30
	2009	1.0	30				
14 Th	0211	4.2	128	29 F	0043	4.2	128
	0816	1.6	49		0630	1.3	40
	1425	4.6	140		1254	4.8	146
	2058	0.9	27		1925	0.6	18
15 F	0302	4.0	122	30 Sa	0137	4.2	128
	0904	1.8	55		0722	1.3	40
	1504	4.5	137		1341	4.9	149
	2144	1.0	30		2017	0.3	9
				31 Su	0232	4.3	131
					0817	1.3	40
					1432	5.0	152
					2112	0.1	3

Time meridian 67° 30' W. 0000 is midnight. 1200 is noon. Times are not adjusted for Daylight Saving Time.
Heights are referred to the chart datum of soundings.

Amuay, Venezuela, 2017

Times and Heights of High and Low Waters

January

Day	Time (h m)	Height (ft)	Height (cm)	Day	Time (h m)	Height (ft)	Height (cm)
1 Su	0005	-0.4	-12	16 M	0055	-0.4	-12
	1549	1.0	30		0844	0.8	24
					1315	0.4	12
					1915	0.7	21
2 M	0045	-0.3	-9	17 Tu	0139	-0.3	-9
	0931	0.8	24		0928	0.9	27
	1233	0.7	21		1438	0.3	9
	1644	0.9	27		2045	0.6	18
3 Tu	0125	-0.3	-9	18 W	0222	-0.2	-6
	0946	0.8	24		1008	0.9	27
	1353	0.5	15		1559	0.2	6
	1754	0.8	24		2210	0.5	15
4 W	0207	-0.2	-6	19 Th ◖	0303	0.0	0
	1002	0.9	27		1045	0.9	27
	1508	0.4	12		1707	0.0	0
	1937	0.6	18		2325	0.4	12
5 Th ◑	0250	-0.1	-3	20 F	0342	0.1	3
	1020	1.0	30		1119	0.9	27
	1615	0.1	3		1758	-0.1	-3
	2209	0.5	15				
6 F	0335	0.0	0	21 Sa	0033	0.4	12
	1045	1.1	34		0421	0.2	6
	1717	-0.1	-3		1149	1.0	30
	2350	0.5	15		1839	-0.2	-6
7 Sa	0422	0.1	3	22 Su	0135	0.4	12
	1117	1.2	37		0500	0.2	6
	1813	-0.3	-9		1216	1.0	30
					1915	-0.3	-9
8 Su	0108	0.5	15	23 M	0232	0.4	12
	0511	0.2	6		0538	0.3	9
	1154	1.3	40		1238	1.0	30
	1907	-0.5	-15		1950	-0.4	-12
9 M	0216	0.6	18	24 Tu	0326	0.5	15
	0601	0.2	6		0615	0.3	9
	1236	1.4	43		1253	1.0	30
	1959	-0.7	-21		2025	-0.4	-12
10 Tu	0319	0.6	18	25 W	0418	0.5	15
	0653	0.3	9		0653	0.4	12
	1321	1.4	43		1305	1.0	30
	2051	-0.7	-21		2101	-0.5	-15
11 W	0419	0.6	18	26 Th	0509	0.5	15
	0746	0.4	12		0731	0.4	12
	1408	1.4	43		1324	1.0	30
	2142	-0.8	-24		2137	-0.5	-15
12 Th ○	0517	0.7	21	27 F ●	0556	0.5	15
	0842	0.4	12		0813	0.4	12
	1456	1.3	40		1352	1.0	30
	2232	-0.7	-21		2213	-0.5	-15
13 F	0613	0.7	21	28 Sa	0638	0.5	15
	0942	0.4	12		0902	0.4	12
	1548	1.2	37		1428	1.0	30
	2321	-0.7	-21		2251	-0.5	-15
14 Sa	0707	0.7	21	29 Su	0712	0.5	15
	1047	0.4	12		1000	0.4	12
	1644	1.0	30		1511	0.9	27
					2329	-0.4	-12
15 Su	0009	-0.6	-18	30 M	0739	0.5	15
	0757	0.8	24		1107	0.3	9
	1158	0.4	12		1602	0.8	24
	1751	0.9	27				
				31 Tu	0009	-0.4	-12
					0802	0.6	18
					1220	0.3	9
					1708	0.6	18

February

Day	Time (h m)	Height (ft)	Height (cm)	Day	Time (h m)	Height (ft)	Height (cm)
1 W	0051	-0.3	-9	16 Th	0138	0.0	0
	0825	0.7	21		0914	0.7	21
	1335	0.1	3		1506	0.0	0
	1850	0.5	15		2211	0.4	12
2 Th	0136	-0.2	-6	17 F	0221	0.1	3
	0852	0.8	24		0953	0.7	21
	1448	0.0	0		1608	-0.1	-3
	2114	0.4	12		2319	0.4	12
3 F ◖	0224	-0.1	-3	18 Sa ○	0306	0.2	6
	0926	0.9	27		1029	0.8	24
	1557	-0.2	-6		1700	-0.2	-6
	2251	0.4	12				
4 Sa	0315	0.0	0	19 Su	0018	0.4	12
	1007	1.0	30		0351	0.2	6
	1659	-0.4	-12		1102	0.8	24
					1743	-0.3	-9
5 Su	0005	0.5	15	20 M	0109	0.5	15
	0407	0.1	3		0436	0.3	9
	1052	1.1	34		1132	0.8	24
	1757	-0.6	-18		1823	-0.3	-9
6 M	0109	0.5	15	21 Tu	0156	0.5	15
	0501	0.1	3		0519	0.3	9
	1140	1.2	37		1158	0.9	27
	1851	-0.7	-21		1902	-0.4	-12
7 Tu	0207	0.5	15	22 W	0239	0.5	15
	0555	0.2	6		0601	0.3	9
	1229	1.2	37		1222	0.9	27
	1942	-0.7	-21		1939	-0.4	-12
8 W	0300	0.6	18	23 Th	0319	0.5	15
	0648	0.2	6		0643	0.3	9
	1319	1.2	37		1249	0.9	27
	2032	-0.8	-24		2016	-0.4	-12
9 Th	0352	0.6	18	24 F	0356	0.5	15
	0742	0.2	6		0726	0.3	9
	1409	1.2	37		1320	0.9	27
	2120	-0.7	-21		2053	-0.4	-12
10 F ○	0441	0.6	18	25 Sa	0428	0.5	15
	0836	0.2	6		0813	0.2	6
	1501	1.1	34		1359	0.9	27
	2206	-0.6	-18		2131	-0.4	-12
11 Sa	0530	0.6	18	26 Su ●	0456	0.5	15
	0933	0.2	6		0904	0.2	6
	1555	0.9	27		1444	0.9	27
	2251	-0.5	-15		2209	-0.3	-9
12 Su	0618	0.6	18	27 M	0520	0.5	15
	1032	0.2	6		1000	0.1	3
	1656	0.8	24		1540	0.8	24
	2334	-0.4	-12		2249	-0.2	-6
13 M	0705	0.6	18	28 Tu	0543	0.6	18
	1136	0.2	6		1102	0.0	0
	1807	0.6	18		1653	0.7	21
					2332	-0.1	-3
14 Tu	0015	-0.2	-6				
	0750	0.6	18				
	1244	0.1	3				
	1930	0.5	15				
15 W	0056	-0.1	-3				
	0833	0.7	21				
	1355	0.1	3				
	2054	0.5	15				

March

Day	Time (h m)	Height (ft)	Height (cm)	Day	Time (h m)	Height (ft)	Height (cm)
1 W	0611	0.7	21	16 Th	0008	0.3	9
	1209	-0.1	-3		0709	0.7	21
	1836	0.6	18		1311	0.0	0
					2109	0.6	18
2 Th	0019	0.0	0	17 F	0053	0.4	12
	0650	0.7	21		0746	0.7	21
	1318	-0.2	-6		1410	-0.1	-3
	2024	0.5	15		2215	0.6	18
3 F	0111	0.1	3	18 Sa	0143	0.4	12
	0740	0.8	24		0826	0.7	21
	1428	-0.3	-9		1505	-0.1	-3
	2150	0.6	18		2310	0.6	18
4 Sa	0207	0.2	6	19 Su	0236	0.4	12
	0837	0.9	27		0907	0.7	21
	1534	-0.4	-12		1557	-0.1	-3
	2301	0.6	18		2357	0.6	18
5 Su ◖	0306	0.2	6	20 M ◖	0328	0.5	15
	0936	1.0	30		0948	0.8	24
	1636	-0.5	-15		1643	-0.2	-6
6 M	0001	0.6	18	21 Tu	0038	0.7	21
	0405	0.2	6		0418	0.4	12
	1035	1.1	34		1028	0.8	24
	1734	-0.6	-18		1727	-0.2	-6
7 Tu	0055	0.7	21	22 W	0114	0.7	21
	0503	0.2	6		0505	0.4	12
	1133	1.1	34		1108	0.8	24
	1828	-0.6	-18		1807	-0.3	-9
8 W	0144	0.7	21	23 Th	0147	0.7	21
	0559	0.2	6		0549	0.4	12
	1229	1.1	34		1148	0.9	27
	1918	-0.6	-18		1847	-0.3	-9
9 Th	0230	0.7	21	24 F	0215	0.7	21
	0652	0.2	6		0634	0.3	9
	1324	1.1	34		1232	0.9	27
	2006	-0.5	-15		1925	-0.2	-6
10 F	0314	0.7	21	25 Sa	0238	0.7	21
	0745	0.1	3		0721	0.2	6
	1420	1.0	30		1320	0.9	27
	2050	-0.4	-12		2004	-0.2	-6
11 Sa	0357	0.7	21	26 Su	0256	0.7	21
	0836	0.1	3		0809	0.1	3
	1516	0.9	27		1414	0.9	27
	2132	-0.3	-9		2043	-0.1	-3
12 Su ○	0438	0.7	21	27 M ●	0313	0.8	24
	0928	0.1	3		0901	0.0	0
	1617	0.8	24		1517	0.8	24
	2212	-0.1	-3		2124	0.0	0
13 M	0517	0.7	21	28 Tu	0335	0.8	24
	1021	0.1	3		0956	-0.1	-3
	1723	0.7	21		1633	0.8	24
	2250	0.0	0		2208	0.1	3
14 Tu	0555	0.7	21	29 W	0405	0.9	27
	1116	0.0	0		1055	-0.2	-6
	1837	0.6	18		1800	0.7	21
	2328	0.2	6		2257	0.2	6
15 W	0632	0.6	18	30 Th	0445	1.0	30
	1213	0.0	0		1157	-0.3	-9
	1955	0.6	18		1928	0.7	21
					2351	0.4	12
				31 F	0536	1.0	30
					1301	-0.4	-12
					2047	0.8	24

Time meridian 67° 30' W. 0000 is midnight. 1200 is noon. Times are not adjusted for Daylight Saving Time. Heights are referred to the chart datum of soundings.

Amuay, Venezuela, 2017

Times and Heights of High and Low Waters

April

Day	Time (h m)	ft	cm	Day	Time (h m)	ft	cm
1 Sa	0052	0.4	12	**16** Su	0103	0.7	21
	0640	1.0	30		0440	0.9	27
	1406	-0.4	-12		1412	-0.1	-3
	2154	0.8	24		2258	0.9	27
2 Su	0158	0.5	15	**17** M	0206	0.7	21
	0755	1.0	30		0538	0.9	27
	1509	-0.5	-15		1501	-0.1	-3
	2252	0.9	27		2333	0.9	27
3 M ◐	0305	0.5	15	**18** Tu	0306	0.7	21
	0911	1.1	34		0654	0.9	27
	1610	-0.5	-15		1547	-0.1	-3
	2344	1.0	30				
4 Tu	0410	0.4	12	**19** W ◑	0004	0.9	27
	1023	1.1	34		0401	0.6	18
	1706	-0.4	-12		0827	0.8	24
					1630	-0.1	-3
5 W	0031	1.0	30	**20** Th	0030	0.9	27
	0511	0.4	12		0451	0.6	18
	1129	1.1	34		1000	0.9	27
	1758	-0.4	-12		1712	-0.1	-3
6 Th	0114	1.0	30	**21** F	0052	0.9	27
	0608	0.3	9		0538	0.4	12
	1232	1.1	34		1114	0.9	27
	1846	-0.3	-9		1753	0.0	0
7 F	0155	1.0	30	**22** Sa	0109	1.0	30
	0701	0.2	6		0626	0.3	9
	1333	1.0	30		1221	0.9	27
	1930	-0.1	-3		1833	0.0	0
8 Sa	0233	1.0	30	**23** Su	0123	1.0	30
	0751	0.1	3		0714	0.1	3
	1434	0.9	27		1327	0.9	27
	2011	0.0	0		1913	0.1	3
9 Su	0308	0.9	27	**24** M	0139	1.1	34
	0839	0.1	3		0804	0.0	0
	1537	0.9	27		1437	0.9	27
	2048	0.2	6		1955	0.2	6
10 M	0339	0.9	27	**25** Tu	0202	1.2	37
	0926	0.0	0		0855	-0.2	-6
	1643	0.8	24		1552	0.9	27
	2123	0.3	9		2040	0.3	9
11 Tu ○	0403	0.9	27	**26** W ●	0233	1.2	37
	1012	0.0	0		0949	-0.3	-9
	1753	0.8	24		1710	0.9	27
	2157	0.5	15		2129	0.5	15
12 W	0411	0.9	27	**27** Th	0311	1.3	40
	1059	0.0	0		1045	-0.4	-12
	1906	0.8	24		1827	0.9	27
	2233	0.6	18		2223	0.6	18
13 Th	0330	0.9	27	**28** F	0357	1.3	40
	1145	0.0	0		1143	-0.5	-15
	2017	0.8	24		1939	1.0	30
	2314	0.7	21		2325	0.7	21
14 F	0330	0.9	27	**29** Sa	0451	1.3	40
	1234	-0.1	-3		1243	-0.5	-15
	2122	0.8	24		2044	1.0	30
15 Sa	0004	0.7	21	**30** Su	0035	0.7	21
	0357	0.9	27		0558	1.2	37
	1323	-0.1	-3		1343	-0.5	-15
	2215	0.8	24		2142	1.1	34

May

Day	Time (h m)	ft	cm	Day	Time (h m)	ft	cm
1 M	0149	0.7	21	**16** Tu	0131	0.9	27
	0722	1.2	37		0437	1.0	30
	1443	-0.4	-12		1413	-0.1	-3
	2233	1.2	37		2304	1.1	34
2 Tu ◐	0304	0.7	21	**17** W	0240	0.9	27
	0850	1.1	34		0543	1.0	30
	1540	-0.4	-12		1456	-0.1	-3
	2319	1.2	37		2325	1.1	34
3 W	0415	0.6	18	**18** Th ○	0341	0.8	24
	1011	1.1	34		0708	0.9	27
	1633	-0.3	-9		1538	0.0	0
					2342	1.1	34
4 Th	0002	1.2	37	**19** F	0436	0.6	18
	0520	0.4	12		0857	0.8	24
	1125	1.0	30		1620	0.0	0
	1722	-0.1	-3		2355	1.1	34
5 F	0041	1.3	40	**20** Sa	0527	0.4	12
	0617	0.3	9		1055	0.8	24
	1235	1.0	30		1701	0.1	3
	1807	0.0	0				
6 Sa	0118	1.2	37	**21** Su	0007	1.2	37
	0709	0.2	6		0616	0.2	6
	1342	0.9	27		1227	0.8	24
	1847	0.2	6		1743	0.2	6
7 Su	0151	1.2	37	**22** M	0023	1.3	40
	0757	0.1	3		0705	0.0	0
	1448	0.9	27		1345	0.8	24
	1923	0.4	12		1827	0.3	9
8 M	0219	1.2	37	**23** Tu	0048	1.4	43
	0841	0.0	0		0755	-0.2	-6
	1555	0.9	27		1459	0.8	24
	1957	0.5	15		1912	0.4	12
9 Tu	0239	1.1	34	**24** W	0120	1.5	46
	0922	0.0	0		0846	-0.3	-9
	1704	0.9	27		1611	0.9	27
	2028	0.7	21		2001	0.6	18
10 W ○	0239	1.1	34	**25** Th ●	0158	1.5	46
	1002	-0.1	-3		0938	-0.5	-15
	1814	0.9	27		1721	0.9	27
	2059	0.8	24		2055	0.7	21
11 Th	0207	1.1	34	**26** F	0241	1.5	46
	1041	-0.1	-3		1032	-0.5	-15
	1926	0.9	27		1828	1.0	30
	2133	0.8	24		2155	0.8	24
12 F	0208	1.1	34	**27** Sa	0330	1.5	46
	1121	-0.1	-3		1127	-0.6	-18
					1930	1.1	34
					2302	0.8	24
13 Sa	0230	1.1	34	**28** Su	0425	1.4	43
	1202	-0.1	-3		1223	-0.5	-15
					2027	1.2	37
14 Su	0303	1.1	34	**29** M	0017	0.8	24
	1245	-0.1	-3		0533	1.3	40
	2207	1.0	30		1319	-0.5	-15
					2118	1.2	37
15 M	0018	0.9	27	**30** Tu	0137	0.8	24
	0345	1.1	34		0658	1.2	37
	1329	-0.1	-3		1414	-0.4	-12
	2238	1.0	30		2205	1.3	40
				31 W	0258	0.7	21
					0834	1.0	30
					1506	-0.2	-6
					2249	1.3	40

June

Day	Time (h m)	ft	cm	Day	Time (h m)	ft	cm
1 Th ◐	0416	0.6	18	**16** F	0318	0.7	21
	1002	1.0	30		0634	0.8	24
	1556	-0.1	-3		1452	0.1	3
	2329	1.4	43		2247	1.2	37
2 F	0524	0.4	12	**17** Sa ○	0418	0.5	15
	1122	0.9	27		0840	0.7	21
	1641	0.1	3		1534	0.2	6
					2258	1.3	40
3 Sa	0006	1.4	43	**18** Su	0512	0.3	9
	0622	0.2	6		1115	0.7	21
	1236	0.9	27		1617	0.3	9
	1723	0.3	9		2314	1.4	43
4 Su	0040	1.4	43	**19** M	0603	0.1	3
	0712	0.1	3		1246	0.7	21
	1347	0.8	24		1702	0.4	12
	1800	0.4	12		2340	1.5	46
5 M	0110	1.3	40	**20** Tu	0654	-0.2	-6
	0755	0.0	0		1400	0.8	24
	1455	0.8	24		1750	0.5	15
	1835	0.6	18				
6 Tu	0134	1.3	40	**21** W	0014	1.6	49
	0834	-0.1	-3		0744	-0.3	-9
	1602	0.9	27		1507	0.8	24
	1906	0.7	21		1840	0.6	18
7 W	0147	1.3	40	**22** Th	0053	1.7	52
	0910	-0.1	-3		0834	-0.5	-15
	1710	0.9	27		1611	0.9	27
	1937	0.8	24		1934	0.7	21
8 Th	0135	1.3	40	**23** F ●	0137	1.7	52
	0945	-0.2	-6		0925	-0.6	-18
					1712	1.0	30
					2031	0.7	21
9 F ○	0123	1.3	40	**24** Sa	0225	1.6	49
	1020	-0.2	-6		1016	-0.6	-18
					1810	1.0	30
					2134	0.8	24
10 Sa	0137	1.3	40	**25** Su	0316	1.6	49
	1056	-0.2	-6		1108	-0.6	-18
					1905	1.1	34
					2243	0.8	24
11 Su	0204	1.3	40	**26** M	0414	1.4	43
	1133	-0.2	-6		1200	-0.5	-15
					1957	1.2	37
					2358	0.8	24
12 M	0238	1.2	37	**27** Tu	0521	1.3	40
	1211	-0.1	-3		1252	-0.4	-12
					2045	1.2	37
13 Tu	0319	1.2	37	**28** W	0119	0.7	21
	1250	-0.1	-3		0648	1.1	34
	2204	1.1	34		1342	-0.2	-6
					2131	1.3	40
14 W	0054	1.0	30	**29** Th	0244	0.6	18
	0409	1.1	34		0826	0.9	27
	1330	-0.1	-3		1430	-0.1	-3
	2222	1.1	34		2213	1.3	40
15 Th	0209	0.9	27	**30** F ◐	0406	0.5	15
	0511	1.0	30		0958	0.8	24
	1411	0.0	0		1516	0.1	3
	2236	1.1	34		2252	1.4	43

Time meridian 67° 30' W. 0000 is midnight. 1200 is noon. Times are not adjusted for Daylight Saving Time.
Heights are referred to the chart datum of soundings.

Amuay, Venezuela, 2017

Times and Heights of High and Low Waters

July

Day	Time	Height ft	Height cm	Day	Time	Height ft	Height cm
1 Sa	0517	0.3	9	**16 Su**	0356	0.4	12
	1120	0.8	24		1003	0.7	21
	1559	0.3	9		1457	0.3	9
	2329	1.4	43	○	2202	1.4	43
2 Su	0613	0.2	6	**17 M**	0453	0.1	3
	1235	0.8	24		1145	0.7	21
	1640	0.4	12		1545	0.4	12
					2232	1.5	46
3 M	0002	1.4	43	**18 Tu**	0547	-0.1	-3
	0659	0.0	0		1259	0.8	24
	1345	0.8	24		1635	0.5	15
	1717	0.6	18		2310	1.6	49
4 Tu	0032	1.4	43	**19 W**	0638	-0.3	-9
	0738	-0.1	-3		1402	0.8	24
	1449	0.8	24		1728	0.6	18
	1753	0.7	21		2353	1.7	52
5 W	0055	1.4	43	**20 Th**	0728	-0.4	-12
	0813	-0.1	-3		1459	0.9	27
	1551	0.9	27		1823	0.7	21
	1829	0.8	24				
6 Th	0108	1.3	40	**21 F**	0040	1.7	52
	0846	-0.2	-6		0818	-0.5	-15
	1650	0.9	27		1553	1.0	30
	1903	0.8	24		1920	0.7	21
7 F	0105	1.3	40	**22 Sa**	0129	1.7	52
	0919	-0.2	-6		0907	-0.5	-15
					1646	1.0	30
					2020	0.7	21
8 Sa	0107	1.3	40	**23 Su**	0220	1.6	49
	0952	-0.2	-6		0956	-0.5	-15
○					1737	1.1	34
				●	2122	0.7	21
9 Su	0126	1.3	40	**24 M**	0314	1.5	46
	1026	-0.2	-6		1045	-0.4	-12
					1827	1.1	34
					2228	0.7	21
10 M	0155	1.3	40	**25 Tu**	0414	1.4	43
	1101	-0.2	-6		1132	-0.3	-9
					1916	1.2	37
					2340	0.7	21
11 Tu	0230	1.3	40	**26 W**	0526	1.2	37
	1137	-0.1	-3		1219	-0.1	-3
	2042	1.0	30		2003	1.2	37
	2310	0.9	27				
12 W	0313	1.2	37	**27 Th**	0057	0.6	18
	1213	-0.1	-3		0655	1.0	30
	2104	1.0	30		1306	0.1	3
					2048	1.3	40
13 Th	0025	0.9	27	**28 F**	0219	0.5	15
	0404	1.1	34		0831	0.9	27
	1251	0.0	0		1351	0.2	6
	2119	1.1	34		2130	1.3	40
14 F	0140	0.8	24	**29 Sa**	0340	0.4	12
	0509	0.9	27		1000	0.8	24
	1330	0.1	3		1435	0.4	12
	2131	1.1	34		2210	1.3	40
15 Sa	0251	0.6	18	**30 Su**	0449	0.3	9
	0645	0.8	24		1119	0.8	24
	1412	0.2	6		1519	0.5	15
	2143	1.2	37	◑	2248	1.4	43
				31 M	0542	0.2	6
					1229	0.9	27
					1602	0.6	18
					2322	1.4	43

August

Day	Time	Height ft	Height cm	Day	Time	Height ft	Height cm
1 Tu	0625	0.1	3	**16 W**	0526	-0.1	-3
	1331	0.9	27		1255	1.0	30
	1644	0.7	21		1625	0.7	21
	2353	1.4	43		2251	1.7	52
2 W	0701	0.0	0	**17 Th**	0618	-0.2	-6
	1426	0.9	27		1347	1.0	30
	1726	0.8	24		1723	0.7	21
					2344	1.7	52
3 Th	0019	1.4	43	**18 F**	0709	-0.3	-9
	0736	0.0	0		1436	1.1	34
	1517	0.9	27		1821	0.7	21
	1807	0.8	24				
4 F	0037	1.4	43	**19 Sa**	0037	1.7	52
	0809	-0.1	-3		0757	-0.3	-9
	1605	1.0	30		1523	1.1	34
	1848	0.9	27		1919	0.7	21
5 Sa	0048	1.4	43	**20 Su**	0131	1.7	52
	0842	-0.1	-3		0844	-0.3	-9
	1651	1.0	30		1609	1.2	37
	1929	0.9	27		2017	0.7	21
6 Su	0102	1.4	43	**21 M**	0226	1.6	49
	0915	-0.1	-3		0930	-0.2	-6
	1734	1.0	30		1654	1.2	37
	2013	0.9	27	●	2117	0.7	21
7 M	0125	1.3	40	**22 Tu**	0325	1.4	43
	0949	-0.1	-3		1015	0.0	0
	1814	1.0	30		1739	1.2	37
○	2101	0.9	27		2219	0.7	21
8 Tu	0158	1.3	40	**23 W**	0431	1.3	40
	1023	0.0	0		1058	0.1	3
	1847	1.0	30		1824	1.3	40
	2156	0.9	27		2324	0.6	18
9 W	0237	1.2	37	**24 Th**	0548	1.1	34
	1058	0.1	3		1141	0.3	9
	1913	1.0	30		1909	1.3	40
	2258	0.8	24				
10 Th	0325	1.1	34	**25 F**	0034	0.6	18
	1135	0.2	6		0716	1.0	30
	1931	1.1	34		1224	0.5	15
					1952	1.3	40
11 F	0006	0.7	21	**26 Sa**	0146	0.5	15
	0426	1.0	30		0845	1.0	30
	1213	0.3	9		1308	0.6	18
	1946	1.1	34		2035	1.3	40
12 Sa	0116	0.6	18	**27 Su**	0256	0.4	12
	0600	0.9	27		1005	1.0	30
	1255	0.4	12		1354	0.7	21
	2003	1.2	37		2117	1.3	40
13 Su	0226	0.4	12	**28 M**	0358	0.3	9
	0906	0.8	24		1115	1.0	30
	1341	0.5	15		1442	0.8	24
	2033	1.4	43		2157	1.3	40
14 M	0331	0.2	6	**29 Tu**	0449	0.1	3
	1044	0.8	24		1215	1.0	30
	1433	0.6	18		1532	0.9	27
◑	2113	1.5	46	◑	2235	1.4	43
15 Tu	0430	0.0	0	**30 W**	0532	0.2	6
	1156	0.9	27		1305	1.1	34
	1528	0.7	21		1621	0.9	27
	2200	1.6	49		2309	1.4	43
				31 Th	0610	0.1	3
					1350	1.1	34
					1709	0.9	27
					2338	1.4	43

September

Day	Time	Height ft	Height cm	Day	Time	Height ft	Height cm
1 F	0646	0.1	3	**16 Sa**	0643	-0.1	-3
	1431	1.1	34		1405	1.4	43
	1754	0.9	27		1827	0.8	24
2 Sa	0005	1.4	43	**17 Su**	0043	1.6	49
	0721	0.1	3		0730	0.0	0
	1509	1.1	34		1447	1.4	43
	1838	0.9	27		1924	0.8	24
3 Su	0029	1.4	43	**18 M**	0142	1.6	49
	0756	0.1	3		0815	0.1	3
	1544	1.1	34		1527	1.4	43
	1922	0.9	27		2020	0.7	21
4 M	0057	1.4	43	**19 Tu**	0243	1.5	46
	0830	0.1	3		0857	0.2	6
	1616	1.1	34		1606	1.4	43
	2008	0.9	27		2116	0.6	18
5 Tu	0132	1.4	43	**20 W**	0349	1.4	43
	0904	0.2	6		0937	0.4	12
	1642	1.1	34		1644	1.4	43
	2057	0.8	24	●	2213	0.6	18
6 W	0214	1.3	40	**21 Th**	0501	1.3	40
	0939	0.3	9		1017	0.6	18
	1701	1.2	37		1721	1.4	43
○	2151	0.7	21		2311	0.5	15
7 Th	0307	1.2	37	**22 F**	0620	1.2	37
	1016	0.4	12		1055	0.7	21
	1713	1.2	37		1757	1.4	43
	2249	0.6	18				
8 F	0418	1.1	34	**23 Sa**	0010	0.5	15
	1054	0.5	15		0742	1.1	34
	1727	1.3	40		1135	0.9	27
	2351	0.5	15		1832	1.4	43
9 Sa	0613	1.0	30	**24 Su**	0109	0.4	12
	1137	0.6	18		0901	1.1	34
	1754	1.4	43		1220	1.0	30
					1906	1.3	40
10 Su	0056	0.4	12	**25 M**	0207	0.4	12
	0814	1.0	30		1011	1.2	37
	1225	0.7	21		1311	1.0	30
	1837	1.5	46		1943	1.3	40
11 M	0202	0.3	9	**26 Tu**	0300	0.4	12
	0942	1.1	34		1108	1.2	37
	1320	0.8	24		1408	1.1	34
	1931	1.5	46		2025	1.3	40
12 Tu	0305	0.1	3	**27 W**	0349	0.3	9
	1051	1.1	34		1155	1.2	37
	1422	0.9	27		1507	1.1	34
	2033	1.6	49	◑	2112	1.3	40
13 W	0405	0.0	0	**28 Th**	0432	0.3	9
	1148	1.2	37		1235	1.3	40
	1525	0.9	27		1603	1.1	34
◑	2138	1.6	49		2157	1.4	43
14 Th	0501	-0.1	-3	**29 F**	0513	0.3	9
	1237	1.3	40		1310	1.3	40
	1628	0.9	27		1654	1.0	30
	2242	1.7	52		2240	1.4	43
15 F	0554	-0.1	-3	**30 Sa**	0551	0.3	9
	1322	1.3	40		1342	1.3	40
	1729	0.9	27		1742	1.0	30
	2343	1.7	52		2323	1.4	43

Time meridian 67° 30' W. 0000 is midnight. 1200 is noon. Times are not adjusted for Daylight Saving Time.
Heights are referred to the chart datum of soundings.

Amuay, Venezuela, 2017

Times and Heights of High and Low Waters

October

Day	Time	ft	cm	Day	Time	ft	cm
1 Su	0628	0.3	9	**16** M	0053	1.5	46
	1410	1.3	40		0657	0.2	6
	1828	0.9	27		1409	1.6	49
					1933	0.6	18
2 M	0006	1.4	43	**17** Tu	0159	1.4	43
	0704	0.3	9		0739	0.4	12
	1434	1.3	40		1445	1.6	49
	1914	0.8	24		2026	0.5	15
3 Tu	0054	1.3	40	**18** W	0306	1.3	40
	0739	0.4	12		0817	0.6	18
	1452	1.3	40		1517	1.5	46
	2002	0.7	21		2118	0.5	15
4 W	0147	1.3	40	**19** Th ●	0416	1.2	37
	0815	0.5	15		0853	0.7	21
	1504	1.4	43		1545	1.5	46
	2051	0.6	18		2208	0.4	12
5 Th ○	0251	1.2	37	**20** F	0531	1.2	37
	0852	0.6	18		0927	0.9	27
	1516	1.4	43		1606	1.5	46
	2143	0.5	15		2257	0.4	12
6 F	0410	1.2	37	**21** Sa	0648	1.2	37
	0931	0.7	21		1001	1.0	30
	1536	1.5	46		1607	1.4	43
	2239	0.4	12		2346	0.3	9
7 Sa	0543	1.2	37	**22** Su	0806	1.2	37
	1014	0.8	24		1038	1.1	34
	1607	1.6	49		1549	1.4	43
	2337	0.3	9				
8 Su	0715	1.2	37	**23** M	0034	0.3	9
	1103	0.9	27		0917	1.2	37
	1649	1.6	49		1123	1.1	34
					1600	1.4	43
9 M	0038	0.1	3	**24** Tu	0122	0.3	9
	0835	1.2	37		1014	1.3	40
	1201	1.0	30		1222	1.2	37
	1742	1.6	49		1631	1.4	43
10 Tu	0140	0.1	3	**25** W	0208	0.3	9
	0942	1.3	40		1057	1.3	40
	1307	1.1	34		1330	1.2	37
	1848	1.6	49		1716	1.4	43
11 W	0240	0.0	0	**26** Th	0253	0.3	9
	1038	1.4	43		1131	1.3	40
	1418	1.1	34		1439	1.2	37
	2004	1.6	49		1817	1.3	40
12 Th ◑	0339	0.0	0	**27** F ◐	0336	0.3	9
	1127	1.4	43		1202	1.3	40
	1529	1.0	30		1542	1.1	34
	2123	1.6	49		1933	1.3	40
13 F	0434	0.0	0	**28** Sa	0416	0.3	9
	1211	1.5	46		1228	1.4	43
	1636	1.0	30		1638	1.0	30
	2237	1.6	49		2104	1.2	37
14 Sa	0525	0.0	0	**29** Su	0455	0.3	9
	1253	1.5	46		1251	1.4	43
	1739	0.9	27		1728	0.9	27
	2347	1.5	46		2231	1.2	37
15 Su	0613	0.1	3	**30** M	0533	0.3	9
	1332	1.6	49		1310	1.4	43
	1837	0.8	24		1817	0.8	24
					2347	1.2	37
				31 Tu	0610	0.4	12
					1324	1.4	43
					1904	0.6	18

November

Day	Time	ft	cm	Day	Time	ft	cm
1 W	0058	1.1	34	**16** Th	0325	1.1	34
	0647	0.5	15		0733	0.7	21
	1335	1.5	46		1431	1.5	46
	1952	0.5	15		2117	0.2	6
2 Th	0211	1.1	34	**17** F	0437	1.0	30
	0725	0.6	18		0804	0.8	24
	1350	1.6	49		1450	1.5	46
	2042	0.3	9		2201	0.1	3
3 F	0328	1.1	34	**18** Sa ●	0551	1.0	30
	0806	0.7	21		0834	0.9	27
	1414	1.6	49		1449	1.4	43
	2133	0.1	3		2242	0.1	3
4 Sa ○	0448	1.1	34	**19** Su	1432	1.4	43
	0849	0.8	24		2322	0.1	3
	1446	1.7	52				
	2227	0.0	0				
5 Su	0608	1.1	34	**20** M	1440	1.4	43
	0938	0.9	27				
	1527	1.7	52				
	2322	-0.1	-3				
6 M	0722	1.2	37	**21** Tu	0003	0.1	3
	1035	1.0	30		1505	1.4	43
	1615	1.7	52				
7 Tu	0020	-0.2	-6	**22** W	0043	0.1	3
	0828	1.3	40		1539	1.3	40
	1142	1.1	34				
	1712	1.7	52				
8 W	0118	-0.2	-6	**23** Th	0124	0.1	3
	0924	1.3	40		1038	1.2	37
	1256	1.1	34		1246	1.1	34
	1821	1.6	49		1623	1.3	40
9 Th	0215	-0.2	-6	**24** F	0205	0.1	3
	1014	1.4	43		1103	1.2	37
	1414	1.0	30		1404	1.1	34
	1946	1.5	46		1716	1.2	37
10 F ○	0311	-0.2	-6	**25** Sa	0245	0.1	3
	1059	1.5	46		1125	1.2	37
	1531	0.9	27		1515	1.0	30
	2114	1.4	43		1824	1.1	34
11 Sa	0404	-0.1	-3	**26** Su ◐	0324	0.1	3
	1141	1.5	46		1143	1.2	37
	1643	0.8	24		1617	0.8	24
	2236	1.3	40		1953	1.0	30
12 Su	0453	0.0	0	**27** M	0403	0.2	6
	1221	1.6	49		1158	1.3	40
	1748	0.7	21		1711	0.7	21
	2352	1.2	37		2151	0.9	27
13 M	0538	0.2	6	**28** Tu	0442	0.2	6
	1258	1.6	49		1209	1.3	40
	1848	0.5	15		1802	0.5	15
					2347	0.8	24
14 Tu	0104	1.2	37	**29** W	0520	0.3	9
	0620	0.3	9		1220	1.4	43
	1333	1.6	49		1850	0.3	9
	1941	0.4	12				
15 W	0215	1.1	34	**30** Th	0113	0.8	24
	0658	0.5	15		0600	0.4	12
	1404	1.5	46		1237	1.5	46
	2031	0.3	9		1939	0.0	0

December

Day	Time	ft	cm	Day	Time	ft	cm
1 F	0230	0.8	24	**16** Sa	0439	0.8	24
	0642	0.5	15		0722	0.7	21
	1304	1.6	49		1408	1.3	40
	2029	-0.1	-3		2145	-0.2	-6
2 Sa	0343	0.9	27	**17** Su	0549	0.8	24
	0727	0.6	18		0750	0.7	21
	1339	1.7	52		1403	1.2	37
	2120	-0.3	-9		2221	-0.2	-6
3 Su ○	0454	0.9	27	**18** M ●	1357	1.2	37
	0816	0.7	21		2256	-0.2	-6
	1420	1.7	52				
	2212	-0.4	-12				
4 M	0602	1.0	30	**19** Tu	1413	1.2	37
	0911	0.8	24		2331	-0.2	-6
	1506	1.7	52				
	2305	-0.5	-15				
5 Tu	0705	1.0	30	**20** W	1441	1.2	37
	1014	0.8	24				
	1558	1.6	49				
6 W	0000	-0.5	-15	**21** Th	0007	-0.2	-6
	0802	1.1	34		1516	1.1	34
	1125	0.9	27				
	1658	1.5	46				
7 Th	0055	-0.5	-15	**22** F	0044	-0.2	-6
	0854	1.2	37		1001	0.9	27
	1243	0.8	24		1206	0.8	24
	1810	1.3	40		1558	1.0	30
8 F	0149	-0.4	-12	**23** Sa	0122	-0.2	-6
	0942	1.2	37		1021	0.9	27
	1405	0.8	24		1327	0.8	24
	1938	1.2	37		1649	0.9	27
9 Sa	0242	-0.3	-9	**24** Su	0159	-0.1	-3
	1026	1.3	40		1037	0.9	27
	1527	0.6	18		1443	0.7	21
	2112	1.0	30		1755	0.8	24
10 Su ○	0332	-0.2	-6	**25** M	0238	-0.1	-3
	1108	1.4	43		1049	1.0	30
	1644	0.5	15		1550	0.5	15
	2238	0.9	27		1928	0.6	18
11 M	0419	0.0	0	**26** Tu ◐	0317	0.0	0
	1147	1.4	43		1058	1.0	30
	1752	0.3	9		1649	0.3	9
	2357	0.9	27		2214	0.5	15
12 Tu	0502	0.1	3	**27** W	0357	0.1	3
	1224	1.4	43		1109	1.1	34
	1850	0.1	3		1742	0.1	3
13 W	0111	0.8	24	**28** Th	0008	0.5	15
	0542	0.3	9		0440	0.2	6
	1258	1.4	43		1129	1.3	40
	1941	0.0	0		1833	-0.2	-6
14 Th	0222	0.8	24	**29** F	0126	0.5	15
	0618	0.4	12		0524	0.2	6
	1329	1.4	43		1159	1.4	43
	2026	-0.1	-3		1922	-0.4	-12
15 F	0331	0.8	24	**30** Sa	0234	0.6	18
	0651	0.6	18		0611	0.3	9
	1354	1.3	40		1236	1.5	46
	2107	-0.2	-6		2012	-0.5	-15
				31 Su	0337	0.6	18
					0702	0.4	12
					1319	1.5	46
					2103	-0.7	-21

Time meridian 67° 30' W. 0000 is midnight. 1200 is noon. Times are not adjusted for Daylight Saving Time.
Heights are referred to the chart datum of soundings.

Punta Gorda, Venezuela, 2017

Times and Heights of High and Low Waters

January

Day	Time	ft	cm	Day	Time	ft	cm
1 Su	0052	-0.6	-18	16 M	0139	-1.0	-30
	0631	6.1	186		0731	6.1	186
	1300	0.6	18		1358	-0.1	-3
	1834	6.6	201		1933	6.3	192
2 M	0129	-0.4	-12	17 Tu	0223	-0.6	-18
	0709	6.2	189		0810	5.9	180
	1339	0.7	21		1445	0.1	3
	1916	6.5	198		2016	5.8	177
3 Tu	0209	-0.2	-6	18 W	0309	-0.1	-3
	0751	6.1	186		0852	5.6	171
	1426	0.7	21		1536	0.4	12
	2003	6.2	189		2103	5.4	165
4 W	0256	0.1	3	19 Th	0359	0.4	12
	0839	6.0	183		0938	5.3	162
	1524	0.8	24		1631	0.6	18
	2057	5.8	177		2156	5.0	152
5 Th	0353	0.4	12	20 F	0454	0.8	24
	0934	5.9	180		1031	5.1	155
	1633	0.8	24		1731	0.6	18
	2201	5.5	168		2258	4.6	140
6 F	0459	0.6	18	21 Sa	0554	1.0	30
	1037	5.9	180		1131	5.0	152
	1746	0.6	18		1833	0.6	18
	2317	5.2	158				
7 Sa	0609	0.7	21	22 Su	0008	4.5	137
	1147	5.9	180		0654	1.0	30
	1856	0.2	6		1235	5.0	152
					1931	0.3	9
8 Su	0038	5.2	158	23 M	0118	4.5	137
	0716	0.6	18		0752	1.0	30
	1258	6.1	186		1335	5.2	158
	2000	-0.3	-9		2025	0.0	0
9 M	0154	5.4	165	24 Tu	0219	4.7	143
	0818	0.3	9		0844	0.8	24
	1404	6.4	195		1428	5.5	168
	2058	-0.8	-24		2114	-0.3	-9
10 Tu	0259	5.8	177	25 W	0308	5.0	152
	0915	0.0	0		0931	0.5	15
	1503	6.7	204		1514	5.7	174
	2151	-1.3	-40		2159	-0.6	-18
11 W	0355	6.1	186	26 Th	0350	5.3	162
	1007	-0.2	-6		1013	0.3	9
	1555	7.0	213		1554	6.0	183
	2241	-1.6	-49		2240	-0.9	-27
12 Th	0444	6.3	192	27 F	0428	5.6	171
	1056	-0.4	-12		1053	0.1	3
	1644	7.1	216		1631	6.3	192
	2327	-1.7	-52		2318	-1.0	-30
13 F	0529	6.4	195	28 Sa	0502	5.8	177
	1143	-0.5	-15		1130	0.0	0
	1728	7.1	216		1707	6.5	198
					2355	-1.1	-34
14 Sa	0012	-1.6	-49	29 Su	0536	6.0	183
	0611	6.4	195		1207	-0.2	-6
	1228	-0.5	-15		1744	6.6	201
	1811	7.0	213				
15 Su	0056	-1.4	-43	30 M	0031	-1.0	-30
	0651	6.3	192		0611	6.2	189
	1313	-0.3	-9		1244	-0.2	-6
	1852	6.7	204		1822	6.6	201
				31 Tu	0108	-0.9	-27
					0649	6.3	192
					1323	-0.2	-6
					1903	6.4	195

February

Day	Time	ft	cm	Day	Time	ft	cm
1 W	0147	-0.7	-21	16 Th	0230	-0.1	-3
	0729	6.3	192		0807	5.7	174
	1408	-0.2	-6		1455	-0.1	-3
	1948	6.1	186		2024	5.4	165
2 Th	0232	-0.3	-9	17 F	0314	0.3	9
	0814	6.2	189		0846	5.4	165
	1502	-0.1	-3		1544	0.2	6
	2040	5.7	174		2110	5.0	152
3 F	0325	0.1	3	18 Sa	0404	0.8	24
	0905	6.0	183		0931	5.1	155
	1606	0.1	3		1642	0.5	15
	2141	5.3	162		2204	4.6	140
4 Sa	0430	0.4	12	19 Su	0505	1.1	34
	1005	5.7	174		1027	4.9	149
	1719	0.1	3		1746	0.6	18
	2255	4.9	149		2310	4.3	131
5 Su	0543	0.6	18	20 M	0611	1.2	37
	1117	5.6	171		1134	4.7	143
	1832	-0.1	-3		1850	0.5	15
6 M	0020	4.8	146	21 Tu	0026	4.3	131
	0656	0.6	18		0715	1.2	37
	1235	5.6	171		1246	4.8	146
	1941	-0.4	-12		1950	0.2	6
7 Tu	0142	5.0	152	22 W	0137	4.5	137
	0802	0.4	12		0813	0.9	27
	1349	5.8	177		1351	5.0	152
	2042	-0.9	-27		2043	-0.1	-3
8 W	0251	5.4	165	23 Th	0235	4.8	146
	0901	0.0	0		0904	0.5	15
	1453	6.1	186		1445	5.4	165
	2136	-1.3	-40		2131	-0.5	-15
9 Th	0346	5.7	174	24 F	0321	5.2	158
	0954	-0.4	-12		0948	0.2	6
	1547	6.4	195		1531	5.8	177
	2225	-1.6	-49		2213	-0.8	-24
10 F	0433	6.0	183	25 Sa	0401	5.6	171
	1042	-0.7	-21		1030	-0.2	-6
	1634	6.6	201		1612	6.2	189
	2310	-1.7	-52		2253	-1.1	-34
11 Sa	0514	6.2	189	26 Su	0437	6.0	183
	1126	-0.9	-27		1109	-0.5	-15
	1716	6.7	204		1651	6.4	195
	2353	-1.6	-49		2331	-1.2	-37
12 Su	0551	6.3	192	27 M	0513	6.3	192
	1208	-0.9	-27		1147	-0.8	-24
	1755	6.6	201		1729	6.6	201
13 M	0033	-1.4	-43	28 Tu	0008	-1.2	-37
	0625	6.2	189		0549	6.5	198
	1249	-0.8	-24		1226	-0.9	-27
	1832	6.4	195		1809	6.6	201
14 Tu	0112	-1.1	-34				
	0659	6.1	186				
	1329	-0.7	-21				
	1908	6.2	189				
15 W	0150	-0.6	-18				
	0732	5.9	180				
	1411	-0.4	-12				
	1945	5.8	177				

March

Day	Time	ft	cm	Day	Time	ft	cm
1 W	0046	-1.0	-30	16 Th	0118	-0.3	-9
	0627	6.7	204		0655	6.1	186
	1306	-1.0	-30		1338	-0.6	-18
	1850	6.5	198		1915	5.9	180
2 Th	0127	-0.8	-24	17 F	0154	0.1	3
	0707	6.6	201		0726	5.9	180
	1352	-0.8	-24		1417	-0.3	-9
	1936	6.2	189		1952	5.6	171
3 F	0212	-0.4	-12	18 Sa	0233	0.5	15
	0751	6.4	195		0802	5.7	174
	1443	-0.6	-18		1502	0.0	0
	2027	5.8	177		2033	5.3	162
4 Sa	0306	0.1	3	19 Su	0319	1.0	30
	0842	6.1	186		0844	5.4	165
	1545	-0.3	-9		1554	0.4	12
	2127	5.3	162		2121	4.9	149
5 Su	0411	0.5	15	20 M	0417	1.3	40
	0941	5.7	174		0934	5.0	152
	1657	-0.1	-3		1658	0.6	18
	2240	4.9	149		2221	4.6	140
6 M	0525	0.8	24	21 Tu	0527	1.5	46
	1054	5.4	165		1039	4.8	146
	1811	-0.1	-3		1806	0.7	21
	2334	4.5	137		2334	4.5	137
7 Tu	0007	4.7	143	22 W	0637	1.4	43
	0639	0.7	21		1155	4.7	143
	1218	5.3	162		1910	0.5	15
	1921	-0.3	-9				
8 W	0131	4.9	149	23 Th	0049	4.6	140
	0747	0.4	12		0739	1.1	34
	1338	5.5	168		1309	4.9	149
	2024	-0.6	-18		2007	0.2	6
9 Th	0239	5.3	162	24 F	0153	5.0	152
	0846	0.0	0		0833	0.6	18
	1444	5.8	177		1412	5.3	162
	2118	-1.0	-30		2057	-0.2	-6
10 F	0331	5.7	174	25 Sa	0244	5.4	165
	0938	-0.4	-12		0920	0.1	3
	1537	6.1	186		1503	5.8	177
	2206	-1.2	-37		2142	-0.5	-15
11 Sa	0414	6.1	186	26 Su	0328	5.9	180
	1024	-0.8	-24		1004	-0.4	-12
	1621	6.4	195		1549	6.2	189
	2249	-1.3	-40		2224	-0.8	-24
12 Su	0451	6.2	189	27 M	0408	6.4	195
	1106	-1.0	-30		1045	-0.8	-24
	1700	6.5	198		1631	6.5	198
	2329	-1.2	-37		2304	-0.9	-27
13 M	0524	6.3	192	28 Tu	0446	6.7	204
	1146	-1.1	-34		1125	-1.2	-37
	1736	6.5	198		1713	6.7	204
					2344	-0.9	-27
14 Tu	0007	-1.0	-30	29 W	0525	7.0	213
	0555	6.3	192		1207	-1.4	-43
	1224	-1.0	-30		1755	6.8	207
	1809	6.4	195				
15 W	0043	-0.7	-21	30 Th	0025	-0.8	-24
	0625	6.2	189		0604	7.1	216
	1301	-0.9	-27		1250	-1.4	-43
	1842	6.2	189		1839	6.7	204
				31 F	0109	-0.5	-15
					0646	7.0	213
					1336	-1.2	-37
					1925	6.4	195

Time meridian 67° 30' W. 0000 is midnight. 1200 is noon. Times are not adjusted for Daylight Saving Time.
Heights are referred to the chart datum of soundings.

Punta Gorda, Venezuela, 2017

Times and Heights of High and Low Waters

April

Day	Time (h m)	ft	cm	Day	Time (h m)	ft	cm
1 Sa	0157	-0.1	-3	16 Su	0200	0.9	27
	0732	6.7	204		0727	5.9	180
	1429	-0.9	-27		1427	0.0	0
	2017	5.9	180		2004	5.5	168
2 Su	0252	0.3	9	17 M	0242	1.2	37
	0823	6.3	192		0807	5.7	174
	1529	-0.5	-15		1515	0.3	9
	2117	5.5	168		2049	5.3	162
3 M	0357	0.7	21	18 Tu	0336	1.5	46
	0923	5.8	177		0855	5.4	165
	1638	-0.1	-3		1613	0.6	18
	2230	5.1	155		2144	5.0	152
4 Tu	0510	0.9	27	19 W	0445	1.6	49
	1037	5.4	165		0955	5.1	155
	1749	0.0	0		1720	0.8	24
	2353	5.0	152		2250	4.9	149
5 W	0622	0.9	27	20 Th	0556	1.6	49
	1202	5.2	158		1108	4.9	149
	1858	-0.1	-3		1826	0.7	21
6 Th	0113	5.2	158	21 F	0001	5.0	152
	0729	0.5	15		0701	1.2	37
	1323	5.3	162		1225	5.1	155
	2000	-0.3	-9		1926	0.5	15
7 F	0217	5.6	171	22 Sa	0106	5.3	162
	0827	0.1	3		0758	0.7	21
	1429	5.7	174		1334	5.4	165
	2053	-0.5	-15		2019	0.2	6
8 Sa	0307	5.9	180	23 Su	0202	5.8	177
	0917	-0.4	-12		0849	0.1	3
	1521	6.0	183		1432	5.8	177
	2141	-0.6	-18		2108	-0.1	-3
9 Su	0347	6.2	189	24 M	0251	6.3	192
	1002	-0.7	-21		0936	-0.5	-15
	1603	6.2	189		1524	6.2	189
	2223	-0.7	-21		2154	-0.4	-12
10 M	0422	6.4	195	25 Tu	0336	6.8	207
	1043	-1.0	-30		1020	-1.0	-30
	1641	6.3	192		1611	6.6	201
	2302	-0.6	-18		2238	-0.5	-15
11 Tu	0454	6.4	195	26 W	0419	7.1	216
	1121	-1.0	-30		1104	-1.4	-43
	1714	6.3	192		1657	6.8	207
	2339	-0.4	-12		2321	-0.5	-15
12 W	0523	6.5	198	27 Th	0501	7.4	226
	1158	-1.0	-30		1149	-1.6	-49
	1746	6.3	192		1742	6.9	210
13 Th	0014	-0.1	-3	28 F	0006	-0.4	-12
	0552	6.4	195		0544	7.4	226
	1234	-0.9	-27		1234	-1.6	-49
	1817	6.2	189		1828	6.7	204
14 F	0049	0.2	6	29 Sa	0053	-0.2	-6
	0621	6.3	192		0629	7.2	219
	1309	-0.6	-18		1323	-1.4	-43
	1849	6.0	183		1917	6.5	198
15 Sa	0124	0.5	15	30 Su	0144	0.2	6
	0652	6.2	189		0716	6.9	210
	1346	-0.3	-9		1415	-1.0	-30
	1924	5.8	177		2009	6.1	186

May

Day	Time (h m)	ft	cm	Day	Time (h m)	ft	cm
1 M	0240	0.5	15	16 Tu	0214	1.3	40
	0809	6.4	195		0739	5.9	180
	1514	-0.6	-18		1443	0.2	6
	2108	5.8	177		2023	5.6	171
2 Tu	0343	0.8	24	17 W	0304	1.5	46
	0909	5.9	180		0826	5.7	174
	1617	-0.2	-6		1534	0.5	15
	2216	5.5	168		2114	5.5	168
3 W	0451	1.0	30	18 Th	0406	1.6	49
	1020	5.4	165		0922	5.4	165
	1724	0.1	3		1635	0.7	21
	2330	5.4	165		2212	5.4	165
4 Th	0600	0.9	27	19 F	0516	1.5	46
	1140	5.2	158		1028	5.2	158
	1829	0.2	6		1740	0.8	24
					2316	5.5	168
5 F	0042	5.5	168	20 Sa	0622	1.2	37
	0704	0.6	18		1143	5.2	158
	1258	5.3	162		1842	0.7	21
	1929	0.2	6				
6 Sa	0143	5.7	174	21 Su	0021	5.8	177
	0801	0.2	6		0723	0.6	18
	1404	5.5	168		1256	5.4	165
	2023	0.1	3		1940	0.5	15
7 Su	0232	6.0	183	22 M	0121	6.2	189
	0851	-0.2	-6		0818	0.0	0
	1457	5.7	174		1402	5.7	174
	2111	0.0	0		2034	0.3	9
8 M	0313	6.2	189	23 Tu	0215	6.6	201
	0936	-0.6	-18		0909	-0.6	-18
	1540	5.9	180		1459	6.1	186
	2154	0.0	0		2125	0.0	0
9 Tu	0349	6.4	195	24 W	0306	7.0	213
	1018	-0.8	-24		0958	-1.1	-34
	1617	6.0	183		1552	6.5	198
	2234	0.1	3		2213	-0.1	-3
10 W	0422	6.5	198	25 Th	0354	7.3	223
	1056	-0.9	-27		1045	-1.5	-46
	1651	6.1	186		1642	6.7	204
	2312	0.2	6		2301	-0.2	-6
11 Th	0452	6.5	198	26 F	0441	7.5	229
	1133	-0.9	-27		1132	-1.7	-52
	1723	6.1	186		1730	6.8	207
	2348	0.4	12		2349	-0.1	-3
12 F	0522	6.5	198	27 Sa	0527	7.5	229
	1209	-0.8	-24		1220	-1.7	-52
	1755	6.1	186		1818	6.8	207
13 Sa	0023	0.6	18	28 Su	0039	0.0	0
	0552	6.4	195		0614	7.3	223
	1245	-0.6	-18		1309	-1.4	-43
	1827	6.0	183		1908	6.6	201
14 Su	0058	0.8	24	29 M	0130	0.2	6
	0624	6.3	192		0703	7.0	213
	1321	-0.3	-9		1400	-1.1	-34
	1902	5.9	180		1959	6.3	192
15 M	0134	1.1	34	30 Tu	0225	0.5	15
	0659	6.2	189		0756	6.5	198
	1400	-0.1	-3		1455	-0.6	-18
	1940	5.8	177		2054	6.1	186
				31 W	0324	0.7	21
					0852	6.0	183
					1553	-0.2	-6
					2153	5.8	177

June

Day	Time (h m)	ft	cm	Day	Time (h m)	ft	cm
1 Th	0427	0.8	24	16 F	0332	1.3	40
	0957	5.6	171		0855	5.7	174
	1653	0.2	6		1554	0.5	15
	2256	5.7	174		2138	5.9	180
2 F	0531	0.8	24	17 Sa	0437	1.2	37
	1108	5.2	158		0956	5.5	168
	1754	0.4	12		1656	0.7	21
	2359	5.7	174		2236	6.0	183
3 Sa	0632	0.6	18	18 Su	0544	1.0	30
	1221	5.1	155		1107	5.3	162
	1853	0.6	18		1801	0.8	24
					2339	6.1	186
4 Su	0059	5.8	177	19 M	0649	0.5	15
	0729	0.3	9		1222	5.4	165
	1328	5.2	158		1904	0.8	24
	1948	0.6	18				
5 M	0150	6.0	183	20 Tu	0043	6.4	195
	0821	0.0	0		0750	0.0	0
	1425	5.4	165		1334	5.6	171
	2038	0.6	18		2004	0.6	18
6 Tu	0235	6.1	186	21 W	0144	6.7	204
	0908	-0.3	-9		0846	-0.6	-18
	1512	5.6	171		1439	5.9	180
	2123	0.6	18		2101	0.4	12
7 W	0315	6.3	192	22 Th	0241	7.0	213
	0951	-0.5	-15		0938	-1.1	-34
	1552	5.7	174		1537	6.3	192
	2206	0.6	18		2154	0.2	6
8 Th	0351	6.4	195	23 F	0335	7.3	223
	1032	-0.7	-21		1029	-1.5	-46
	1628	5.8	177		1630	6.6	201
	2246	0.6	18		2245	0.0	0
9 F	0424	6.4	195	24 Sa	0425	7.4	226
	1110	-0.7	-21		1117	-1.6	-49
	1702	5.9	180		1719	6.7	204
	2324	0.7	21		2335	0.0	0
10 Sa	0456	6.5	198	25 Su	0514	7.4	226
	1147	-0.7	-21		1206	-1.6	-49
	1734	6.0	183		1807	6.8	207
11 Su	0001	0.8	24	26 M	0024	0.0	0
	0528	6.5	198		0602	7.3	223
	1224	-0.6	-18		1253	-1.5	-46
	1807	6.0	183		1854	6.7	204
12 M	0037	0.9	27	27 Tu	0114	0.1	3
	0602	6.4	195		0650	7.0	213
	1300	-0.4	-12		1342	-1.1	-34
	1841	6.0	183		1941	6.6	201
13 Tu	0113	1.1	34	28 W	0206	0.3	9
	0637	6.3	192		0739	6.6	201
	1337	-0.2	-6		1431	-0.6	-18
	1918	6.0	183		2029	6.3	192
14 W	0152	1.2	37	29 Th	0300	0.5	15
	0717	6.2	189		0830	6.1	186
	1416	0.0	0		1523	-0.2	-6
	1959	6.0	183		2119	6.1	186
15 Th	0237	1.3	40	30 F	0356	0.7	21
	0802	6.0	183		0926	5.7	174
	1501	0.3	9		1618	0.3	9
	2045	6.0	183		2212	5.9	180

Time meridian 67° 30' W. 0000 is midnight. 1200 is noon. Times are not adjusted for Daylight Saving Time.
Heights are referred to the chart datum of soundings.

Punta Gorda, Venezuela, 2017

Times and Heights of High and Low Waters

July

Day	Time	ft	cm
1 Sa	0455	0.7	21
	1027	5.3	162
	1715	0.7	21
	2309	5.8	177
2 Su	0555	0.7	21
	1135	5.0	152
	1813	1.0	30
3 M	0007	5.7	174
	0653	0.5	15
	1243	5.0	152
	1910	1.1	34
4 Tu	0103	5.8	177
	0747	0.3	9
	1346	5.1	155
	2003	1.1	34
5 W	0154	5.9	180
	0838	0.0	0
	1440	5.3	162
	2053	1.0	30
6 Th	0241	6.1	186
	0924	-0.2	-6
	1525	5.5	168
	2139	0.9	27
7 F	0322	6.2	189
	1007	-0.4	-12
	1605	5.7	174
	2221	0.9	27
8 Sa ○	0400	6.4	195
	1047	-0.5	-15
	1641	5.9	180
	2301	0.8	24
9 Su	0435	6.5	198
	1126	-0.6	-18
	1714	6.0	183
	2339	0.8	24
10 M	0509	6.6	201
	1202	-0.5	-15
	1747	6.2	189
11 Tu	0016	0.9	27
	0543	6.6	201
	1238	-0.4	-12
	1820	6.3	192
12 W	0052	0.9	27
	0619	6.6	201
	1313	-0.3	-9
	1855	6.4	195
13 Th	0130	0.9	27
	0658	6.5	198
	1350	-0.1	-3
	1934	6.4	195
14 F	0212	0.9	27
	0742	6.3	192
	1430	0.2	6
	2017	6.4	195
15 Sa	0302	0.9	27
	0831	6.0	183
	1519	0.5	15
	2105	6.4	195
16 Su ◗	0403	0.9	27
	0929	5.7	174
	1618	0.8	24
	2201	6.4	195
17 M	0511	0.8	24
	1038	5.4	165
	1726	1.1	34
	2304	6.3	192
18 Tu	0620	0.5	15
	1156	5.3	162
	1836	1.1	34
19 W	0012	6.4	195
	0726	0.1	3
	1314	5.5	168
	1942	1.0	30
20 Th	0120	6.6	201
	0826	-0.4	-12
	1425	5.8	177
	2043	0.7	21
21 F	0224	6.9	210
	0922	-0.9	-27
	1526	6.2	189
	2138	0.4	12
22 Sa	0322	7.2	219
	1014	-1.3	-40
	1619	6.6	201
	2230	0.2	6
23 Su ●	0414	7.4	226
	1102	-1.4	-43
	1707	6.8	207
	2320	0.0	0
24 M	0503	7.4	226
	1149	-1.4	-43
	1752	6.9	210
25 Tu	0007	-0.1	-3
	0549	7.3	223
	1234	-1.3	-40
	1834	6.9	210
26 W	0054	0.0	0
	0634	7.1	216
	1318	-0.9	-27
	1915	6.8	207
27 Th	0141	0.1	3
	0717	6.8	207
	1403	-0.4	-12
	1956	6.6	201
28 F	0230	0.3	9
	0802	6.3	192
	1449	0.1	3
	2038	6.4	195
29 Sa	0320	0.6	18
	0850	5.9	180
	1538	0.6	18
	2123	6.1	186
30 Su ◗	0415	0.8	24
	0942	5.4	165
	1631	1.1	34
	2213	5.9	180
31 M	0513	0.9	27
	1043	5.1	155
	1730	1.4	43
	2310	5.7	174

August

Day	Time	ft	cm
1 Tu	0613	0.9	27
	1152	4.9	149
	1830	1.6	49
2 W	0011	5.7	174
	0711	0.7	21
	1302	5.0	152
	1929	1.6	49
3 Th	0112	5.8	177
	0806	0.5	15
	1405	5.2	158
	2023	1.5	46
4 F	0207	6.0	183
	0856	0.2	6
	1456	5.5	168
	2113	1.3	40
5 Sa	0255	6.2	189
	0941	-0.1	-3
	1539	5.8	177
	2157	1.1	34
6 Su	0337	6.4	195
	1023	-0.3	-9
	1616	6.0	183
	2238	0.9	27
7 M ○	0415	6.7	204
	1102	-0.4	-12
	1650	6.3	192
	2316	0.7	21
8 Tu	0450	6.8	207
	1138	-0.4	-12
	1723	6.6	201
	2353	0.6	18
9 W	0526	6.9	210
	1213	-0.4	-12
	1756	6.8	207
10 Th	0029	0.6	18
	0602	6.9	210
	1248	-0.2	-6
	1830	6.9	210
11 F	0107	0.5	15
	0641	6.9	210
	1324	0.0	0
	1907	7.0	213
12 Sa	0148	0.6	18
	0723	6.7	204
	1403	0.3	9
	1949	7.0	213
13 Su	0236	0.6	18
	0812	6.3	192
	1450	0.7	21
	2036	6.9	210
14 M ◑	0335	0.7	21
	0908	6.0	183
	1549	1.1	34
	2131	6.7	204
15 Tu	0444	0.8	24
	1016	5.6	171
	1701	1.4	43
	2235	6.5	198
16 W	0557	0.6	18
	1137	5.4	165
	1816	1.5	46
	2349	6.4	195
17 Th	0706	0.3	9
	1302	5.6	171
	1926	1.4	43
18 F	0105	6.6	201
	0810	-0.1	-3
	1416	5.9	180
	2029	1.0	30
19 Sa	0214	6.8	207
	0906	-0.5	-15
	1516	6.4	195
	2125	0.6	18
20 Su	0313	7.1	216
	0958	-0.9	-27
	1607	6.8	207
	2216	0.2	6
21 M ●	0405	7.4	226
	1045	-1.0	-30
	1651	7.1	216
	2303	0.0	0
22 Tu	0451	7.5	229
	1129	-1.0	-30
	1731	7.2	219
	2348	-0.1	-3
23 W	0534	7.4	226
	1211	-0.8	-24
	1808	7.3	223
24 Th	0031	-0.1	-3
	0614	7.3	223
	1252	-0.5	-15
	1844	7.2	219
25 F	0114	0.0	0
	0652	7.0	213
	1332	0.0	0
	1919	7.0	213
26 Sa	0157	0.3	9
	0731	6.6	201
	1413	0.5	15
	1955	6.7	204
27 Su	0242	0.6	18
	0812	6.2	189
	1457	1.1	34
	2034	6.5	198
28 M	0332	0.9	27
	0858	5.7	174
	1547	1.6	49
	2119	6.2	189
29 Tu ◑	0429	1.1	34
	0952	5.4	165
	1645	1.9	58
	2212	5.9	180
30 W	0530	1.3	40
	1059	5.1	155
	1750	2.1	64
	2317	5.7	174
31 Th	0633	1.2	37
	1214	5.1	155
	1855	2.1	64

September

Day	Time	ft	cm
1 F	0027	5.8	177
	0732	1.0	30
	1325	5.3	162
	1953	1.9	58
2 Sa	0132	6.0	183
	0825	0.7	21
	1422	5.6	171
	2045	1.6	49
3 Su	0226	6.3	192
	0912	0.3	9
	1508	6.0	183
	2131	1.2	37
4 M	0312	6.6	201
	0955	0.1	3
	1546	6.4	195
	2213	0.9	27
5 Tu	0352	6.9	210
	1034	-0.1	-3
	1621	6.8	207
	2251	0.6	18
6 W ○	0430	7.1	216
	1111	-0.2	-6
	1655	7.1	216
	2329	0.4	12
7 Th	0507	7.3	223
	1147	-0.1	-3
	1729	7.4	226
8 F	0006	0.2	6
	0545	7.3	223
	1222	0.0	0
	1804	7.6	232
9 Sa	0045	0.2	6
	0624	7.2	219
	1259	0.3	9
	1842	7.6	232
10 Su	0127	0.2	6
	0708	7.0	213
	1341	0.6	18
	1924	7.5	229
11 M	0215	0.4	12
	0756	6.7	204
	1429	1.1	34
	2011	7.3	223
12 Tu	0314	0.6	18
	0852	6.2	189
	1530	1.5	46
	2106	6.9	210
13 W ◑	0423	0.8	24
	1002	5.8	177
	1645	1.8	55
	2213	6.6	201
14 Th	0537	0.8	24
	1126	5.6	171
	1802	1.9	58
	2333	6.4	195
15 F	0648	0.6	18
	1253	5.8	177
	1913	1.6	49
16 Sa	0055	6.5	198
	0753	0.3	9
	1406	6.2	189
	2016	1.2	37
17 Su	0206	6.8	207
	0849	-0.1	-3
	1503	6.7	204
	2110	0.7	21
18 M	0305	7.1	216
	0939	-0.4	-12
	1549	7.1	216
	2159	0.3	9
19 Tu	0354	7.4	226
	1024	-0.5	-15
	1629	7.4	226
	2244	0.0	0
20 W ●	0437	7.5	229
	1106	-0.4	-12
	1706	7.5	229
	2326	-0.1	-3
21 Th	0515	7.5	229
	1145	-0.2	-6
	1739	7.5	229
22 F	0006	-0.1	-3
	0551	7.3	223
	1223	0.1	3
	1811	7.5	229
23 Sa	0045	0.0	0
	0626	7.1	216
	1300	0.5	15
	1842	7.3	223
24 Su	0125	0.3	9
	0701	6.8	207
	1337	1.0	30
	1914	7.1	216
25 M	0206	0.6	18
	0738	6.4	195
	1417	1.5	46
	1950	6.8	207
26 Tu	0252	1.0	30
	0819	6.1	186
	1503	1.9	58
	2031	6.5	198
27 W ◑	0345	1.3	40
	0908	5.7	174
	1600	2.3	70
	2121	6.1	186
28 Th	0446	1.5	46
	1009	5.4	165
	1708	2.5	76
	2224	5.9	180
29 F	0551	1.6	49
	1123	5.3	162
	1818	2.5	76
	2338	5.8	177
30 Sa	0654	1.4	43
	1238	5.5	168
	1920	2.2	67

Time meridian 67° 30' W. 0000 is midnight. 1200 is noon. Times are not adjusted for Daylight Saving Time. Heights are referred to the chart datum of soundings.

Punta Gorda, Venezuela, 2017

Times and Heights of High and Low Waters

October

Day	Time	ft	cm	Day	Time	ft	cm
1 Su	0051	6.0	183	16 M	0154	6.6	201
	0750	1.1	34		0827	0.3	9
	1340	5.9	180		1442	6.9	210
	2014	1.8	55		2052	0.7	21
2 M	0152	6.3	192	17 Tu	0251	6.9	210
	0839	0.8	24		0916	0.1	3
	1430	6.3	192		1526	7.2	219
	2102	1.3	40		2140	0.3	9
3 Tu	0243	6.7	204	18 W	0339	7.2	219
	0923	0.5	15		1000	0.1	3
	1511	6.8	207		1604	7.5	229
	2145	0.8	24		2223	0.0	0
4 W	0327	7.0	213	19 Th ●	0419	7.3	223
	1003	0.2	6		1041	0.1	3
	1549	7.2	219		1638	7.6	232
	2225	0.4	12		2303	-0.2	-6
5 Th ○	0408	7.3	223	20 F	0455	7.2	219
	1042	0.1	3		1119	0.3	9
	1625	7.6	232		1709	7.6	232
	2305	0.1	3		2342	-0.1	-3
6 F	0448	7.5	229	21 Sa	0529	7.1	216
	1120	0.1	3		1156	0.6	18
	1702	7.9	241		1739	7.5	229
	2344	-0.1	-3				
7 Sa	0528	7.6	232	22 Su	0019	0.0	0
	1159	0.2	6		0601	7.0	213
	1739	8.1	247		1231	0.9	27
					1808	7.4	226
8 Su	0025	-0.2	-6	23 M	0056	0.2	6
	0610	7.5	229		0634	6.8	207
	1239	0.5	15		1307	1.3	40
	1819	8.1	247		1839	7.2	219
9 M	0110	-0.1	-3	24 Tu	0135	0.5	15
	0655	7.2	219		0709	6.5	198
	1323	0.9	27		1343	1.7	52
	1903	7.9	241		1914	6.9	210
10 Tu	0200	0.1	3	25 W	0216	0.9	27
	0745	6.8	207		0748	6.2	189
	1415	1.3	40		1425	2.0	61
	1951	7.5	229		1953	6.6	201
11 W	0258	0.5	15	26 Th	0304	1.2	37
	0842	6.4	195		0833	5.9	180
	1518	1.7	52		1518	2.3	70
	2048	7.0	213		2040	6.3	192
12 Th ◐	0405	0.8	24	27 F ◑	0402	1.5	46
	0952	6.0	183		0928	5.7	174
	1632	2.0	61		1624	2.5	76
	2157	6.6	201		2137	6.0	183
13 F	0518	0.9	27	28 Sa	0506	1.6	49
	1115	5.9	180		1033	5.6	171
	1747	2.0	61		1735	2.5	76
	2320	6.3	192		2247	5.8	177
14 Sa	0628	0.8	24	29 Su	0610	1.5	46
	1238	6.1	186		1144	5.7	174
	1857	1.6	49		1841	2.2	67
15 Su	0043	6.4	195	30 M	0003	5.9	180
	0731	0.6	18		0708	1.3	40
	1348	6.5	198		1250	6.0	183
	1958	1.2	37		1939	1.7	52
				31 Tu	0112	6.1	186
					0801	1.0	30
					1345	6.4	195
					2030	1.2	37

November

Day	Time	ft	cm	Day	Time	ft	cm
1 W	0209	6.5	198	16 Th	0319	6.6	201
	0848	0.7	21		0934	0.4	12
	1432	6.9	210		1536	7.1	216
	2116	0.6	18		2200	-0.1	-3
2 Th	0300	6.8	207	17 F	0400	6.7	204
	0932	0.5	15		1016	0.4	12
	1515	7.4	226		1610	7.2	219
	2159	0.1	3		2240	-0.3	-9
3 F	0346	7.2	219	18 Sa ●	0435	6.7	204
	1014	0.3	9		1054	0.5	15
	1556	7.8	238		1642	7.2	219
	2242	-0.3	-9		2319	-0.3	-9
4 Sa	0430	7.4	226	19 Su	0508	6.7	204
	1056	0.2	6		1131	0.7	21
	1637	8.1	247		1712	7.2	219
	2325	-0.6	-18		2356	-0.2	-6
5 Su	0514	7.5	229	20 M	0540	6.6	201
	1138	0.3	9		1207	0.9	27
	1719	8.2	250		1742	7.1	216
6 M	0009	-0.7	-21	21 Tu	0032	0.0	0
	0558	7.4	226		0612	6.5	198
	1223	0.5	15		1242	1.2	37
	1802	8.1	247		1813	7.0	213
7 Tu	0056	-0.6	-18	22 W	0109	0.2	6
	0645	7.2	219		0646	6.4	195
	1311	0.8	24		1317	1.4	43
	1848	7.9	241		1847	6.8	207
8 W	0147	-0.3	-9	23 Th	0148	0.5	15
	0736	6.8	207		0722	6.2	189
	1405	1.1	34		1356	1.7	52
	1938	7.5	229		1924	6.6	201
9 Th	0243	0.1	3	24 F	0230	0.7	21
	0833	6.5	198		0804	6.0	183
	1506	1.5	46		1441	1.9	58
	2035	6.9	210		2008	6.3	192
10 F ◐	0346	0.4	12	25 Sa	0320	1.0	30
	0939	6.1	186		0852	5.8	177
	1615	1.7	52		1539	2.1	64
	2142	6.4	195		2100	6.0	183
11 Sa	0454	0.7	21	26 Su ◑	0417	1.2	37
	1054	6.0	183		0948	5.7	174
	1726	1.7	52		1648	2.1	64
	2301	6.1	186		2202	5.8	177
12 Su	0601	0.8	24	27 M	0520	1.3	40
	1211	6.1	186		1051	5.7	174
	1834	1.4	43		1756	1.9	58
					2313	5.6	171
13 M	0022	6.0	183	28 Tu	0621	1.2	37
	0703	0.7	21		1156	5.9	180
	1318	6.3	192		1859	1.4	43
	1935	1.0	30				
14 Tu	0134	6.2	189	29 W	0027	5.7	174
	0759	0.6	18		0719	1.0	30
	1412	6.7	204		1258	6.3	192
	2029	0.5	15		1955	0.8	24
15 W	0232	6.4	195	30 Th	0134	6.0	183
	0849	0.5	15		0812	0.8	24
	1457	6.9	210		1353	6.7	204
	2117	0.1	3		2047	0.2	6

December

Day	Time	ft	cm	Day	Time	ft	cm
1 F	0233	6.3	192	16 Sa	0339	5.9	180
	0902	0.5	15		0951	0.5	15
	1444	7.2	219		1544	6.6	201
	2135	-0.4	-12		2218	-0.5	-15
2 Sa	0325	6.7	204	17 Su	0416	6.0	183
	0950	0.3	9		1032	0.5	15
	1531	7.6	232		1618	6.7	204
	2222	-0.8	-24		2257	-0.5	-15
3 Su ○	0414	6.9	210	18 M ●	0450	6.1	186
	1036	0.1	3		1110	0.6	18
	1617	7.8	238		1650	6.7	204
	2309	-1.1	-34		2335	-0.5	-15
4 M	0502	7.1	216	19 Tu	0522	6.1	186
	1123	0.1	3		1146	0.6	18
	1703	8.0	244		1722	6.7	204
	2355	-1.2	-37				
5 Tu	0549	7.1	216	20 W	0012	-0.5	-15
	1210	0.2	6		0553	6.1	186
	1749	7.9	241		1222	0.8	24
					1753	6.7	204
6 W	0043	-1.1	-34	21 Th	0048	-0.3	-9
	0637	6.9	210		0626	6.1	186
	1300	0.3	9		1256	0.9	27
	1837	7.6	232		1827	6.6	201
7 Th	0133	-0.9	-27	22 F	0124	-0.1	-3
	0727	6.7	204		0700	6.0	183
	1352	0.6	18		1332	1.0	30
	1927	7.2	219		1903	6.4	195
8 F	0227	-0.5	-15	23 Sa	0201	0.1	3
	0820	6.4	195		0738	6.0	183
	1450	0.8	24		1411	1.2	37
	2022	6.7	204		1943	6.2	189
9 Sa	0324	-0.1	-3	24 Su	0242	0.4	12
	0918	6.1	186		0820	5.9	180
	1552	1.0	30		1459	1.3	40
	2123	6.2	189		2030	5.9	180
10 Su ◐	0425	0.3	9	25 M	0330	0.6	18
	1022	5.9	180		0908	5.8	177
	1658	1.1	34		1559	1.3	40
	2233	5.7	174		2125	5.6	171
11 M	0527	0.6	18	26 Tu	0427	0.8	24
	1130	5.8	177		1003	5.7	174
	1803	1.0	30		1708	1.2	37
	2348	5.5	168		2230	5.4	165
12 Tu	0629	0.7	21	27 W	0532	1.0	30
	1236	5.9	180		1105	5.8	177
	1905	0.7	21		1817	0.9	27
					2344	5.2	158
13 W	0101	5.5	168	28 Th	0638	0.9	27
	0727	0.7	21		1212	5.9	180
	1334	6.1	186		1922	0.4	12
	2000	0.3	9				
14 Th	0204	5.6	171	29 F	0100	5.4	165
	0820	0.7	21		0739	0.7	21
	1423	6.3	192		1317	6.3	192
	2050	0.0	0		2020	-0.1	-3
15 F	0256	5.8	177	30 Sa	0208	5.6	171
	0907	0.6	18		0837	0.5	15
	1506	6.4	195		1417	6.6	201
	2136	-0.3	-9		2115	-0.7	-21
				31 Su	0308	6.0	183
					0930	0.1	3
					1512	7.0	213
					2205	-1.2	-37

Time meridian 67° 30' W. 0000 is midnight. 1200 is noon. Times are not adjusted for Daylight Saving Time.
Heights are referred to the chart datum of soundings.

Suriname River Entrance, Surinam, 2017

Times and Heights of High and Low Waters

January

Day	Time	ft	cm	Day	Time	ft	cm
1 Su	0008	0.7	21	16 M	0053	0.8	24
	0618	7.5	229		0703	7.5	229
	1222	1.1	34		1309	1.1	34
	1832	7.8	238		1920	7.6	232
2 M	0049	0.8	24	17 Tu	0134	1.1	34
	0701	7.4	226		0744	7.2	219
	1306	1.2	37		1352	1.4	43
	1917	7.7	235		2003	7.2	219
3 Tu	0134	0.9	27	18 W	0216	1.4	43
	0747	7.3	223		0828	7.0	213
	1354	1.3	40		1438	1.7	52
	2007	7.4	226		2050	6.8	207
4 W	0225	1.2	37	19 Th	0303	1.8	55
	0839	7.1	216		0916	6.7	204
	1450	1.5	46		1529	2.0	61
	2104	7.1	216		2142	6.5	198
5 Th	0321	1.4	43	20 F	0355	2.1	64
	0938	7.0	213		1010	6.4	195
	1553	1.6	49		1627	2.2	67
	2209	6.9	210		2242	6.2	189
6 F	0425	1.6	49	21 Sa	0455	2.4	73
	1044	6.9	210		1112	6.3	192
	1703	1.6	49		1733	2.3	70
	2320	6.8	207		2349	6.1	186
7 Sa	0534	1.7	52	22 Su	0600	2.5	76
	1152	7.0	213		1217	6.3	192
	1815	1.5	46		1839	2.2	67
8 Su	0031	6.9	210	23 M	0055	6.2	189
	0642	1.7	52		0703	2.4	73
	1259	7.3	223		1318	6.5	198
	1922	1.2	37		1940	2.0	61
9 M	0138	7.1	216	24 Tu	0154	6.4	195
	0745	1.5	46		0800	2.1	64
	1400	7.6	232		1412	6.8	207
	2022	0.9	27		2032	1.7	52
10 Tu	0236	7.3	223	25 W	0245	6.7	204
	0842	1.2	37		0849	1.9	58
	1455	7.9	241		1500	7.1	216
	2115	0.6	18		2117	1.3	40
11 W	0329	7.6	232	26 Th	0329	7.0	213
	0933	1.0	30		0932	1.5	46
	1545	8.1	247		1542	7.5	229
	2204	0.4	12		2159	1.0	30
12 Th	0416	7.7	235	27 F	0409	7.3	223
	1020	0.8	24		1013	1.2	37
	1631	8.2	250		1622	7.8	238
	2249	0.3	9		2238	0.7	21
13 F	0501	7.8	238	28 Sa	0448	7.6	232
	1104	0.8	24		1051	0.9	27
	1715	8.2	250		1701	8.0	244
	2332	0.3	9		2316	0.5	15
14 Sa	0542	7.8	238	29 Su	0525	7.8	238
	1146	0.8	24		1130	0.7	21
	1757	8.1	247		1740	8.2	250
					2354	0.4	12
15 Su	0013	0.5	15	30 M	0604	7.9	241
	0623	7.7	235		1209	0.6	18
	1228	0.9	27		1820	8.2	250
	1838	7.9	241				
				31 Tu	0034	0.4	12
					0644	7.9	241
					1251	0.6	18
					1903	8.1	247

February

Day	Time	ft	cm	Day	Time	ft	cm
1 W	0116	0.6	18	16 Th	0138	1.2	37
	0726	7.8	238		0746	7.4	226
	1336	0.7	21		1357	1.2	37
	1948	7.8	238		2008	7.1	216
2 Th	0201	0.9	27	17 F	0216	1.6	49
	0813	7.6	232		0826	7.0	213
	1426	1.0	30		1440	1.6	49
	2039	7.4	226		2052	6.7	204
3 F	0251	1.3	40	18 Sa	0301	2.0	61
	0905	7.3	223		0912	6.6	201
	1522	1.3	40		1530	2.0	61
	2138	7.0	213		2145	6.3	192
4 Sa	0350	1.7	52	19 Su	0354	2.4	73
	1006	7.0	213		1009	6.3	192
	1628	1.6	49		1632	2.3	70
	2247	6.7	204		2250	6.0	183
5 Su	0458	2.0	61	20 M	0501	2.7	82
	1117	6.8	207		1119	6.1	186
	1744	1.7	52		1746	2.4	73
6 M	0004	6.5	198	21 Tu	0007	5.9	180
	0615	2.1	64		0618	2.7	82
	1233	6.8	207		1235	6.1	186
	1900	1.6	49		1901	2.3	70
7 Tu	0120	6.6	201	22 W	0121	6.1	186
	0728	1.9	58		0730	2.5	76
	1343	7.1	216		1343	6.4	195
	2008	1.3	40		2005	1.9	58
8 W	0225	6.9	210	23 Th	0221	6.5	198
	0831	1.6	49		0827	2.0	61
	1444	7.4	226		1438	6.9	210
	2105	1.0	30		2056	1.5	46
9 Th	0319	7.3	223	24 F	0309	7.0	213
	0924	1.3	40		0915	1.6	49
	1536	7.7	235		1524	7.4	226
	2153	0.7	21		2140	1.0	30
10 F	0405	7.6	232	25 Sa	0351	7.4	226
	1010	1.0	30		0956	1.1	34
	1621	8.0	244		1606	7.9	241
	2236	0.5	15		2219	0.6	18
11 Sa	0446	7.8	238	26 Su	0429	7.8	238
	1052	0.7	21		1036	0.6	18
	1702	8.1	247		1645	8.2	250
	2315	0.4	12		2258	0.3	9
12 Su	0524	7.9	241	27 M	0507	8.2	250
	1130	0.6	18		1114	0.3	9
	1740	8.1	247		1724	8.5	259
	2351	0.5	15		2335	0.1	3
13 M	0559	7.9	241	28 Tu	0544	8.4	256
	1206	0.6	18		1153	0.1	3
	1816	8.0	244		1804	8.5	259
14 Tu	0026	0.6	18				
	0634	7.8	238				
	1242	0.7	21				
	1852	7.8	238				
15 W	0101	0.9	27				
	0709	7.6	232				
	1319	0.9	27				
	1929	7.5	229				

March

Day	Time	ft	cm	Day	Time	ft	cm
1 W	0014	0.2	6	16 Th	0028	0.8	24
	0623	8.4	256		0635	7.9	241
	1233	0.1	3		1246	0.6	18
	1845	8.4	256		1856	7.7	235
2 Th	0054	0.4	12	17 F	0101	1.1	34
	0703	8.3	253		0708	7.6	232
	1316	0.3	9		1321	0.9	27
	1929	8.0	244		1932	7.3	223
3 F	0137	0.7	21	18 Sa	0137	1.4	43
	0747	7.9	241		0745	7.3	223
	1403	0.6	18		1400	1.3	40
	2017	7.5	229		2012	6.9	210
4 Sa	0224	1.2	37	19 Su	0217	1.9	58
	0836	7.5	229		0826	6.8	207
	1456	1.1	34		1445	1.8	55
	2112	7.0	213		2100	6.4	195
5 Su	0320	1.8	55	20 M	0306	2.3	70
	0935	7.0	213		0918	6.4	195
	1600	1.6	49		1542	2.2	67
	2220	6.5	198		2202	6.0	183
6 M	0430	2.3	70	21 Tu	0411	2.7	82
	1047	6.6	201		1027	6.1	186
	1719	1.9	58		1657	2.4	73
	2343	6.2	189		2323	5.8	177
7 Tu	0554	2.5	76	22 W	0534	2.8	85
	1212	6.5	198		1152	6.0	183
	1843	1.9	58		1821	2.4	73
8 W	0107	6.3	192	23 Th	0046	6.0	183
	0717	2.3	70		0657	2.6	79
	1331	6.7	204		1310	6.3	192
	1956	1.7	52		1933	2.0	61
9 Th	0214	6.7	204	24 F	0151	6.5	198
	0822	1.9	58		0800	2.1	64
	1434	7.1	216		1411	6.8	207
	2052	1.3	40		2028	1.5	46
10 F	0306	7.1	216	25 Sa	0242	7.1	216
	0914	1.4	43		0850	1.4	43
	1524	7.5	229		1500	7.4	226
	2138	1.0	30		2114	1.0	30
11 Sa	0349	7.5	229	26 Su	0325	7.6	232
	0956	1.0	30		0934	0.8	24
	1606	7.8	238		1544	8.0	244
	2217	0.7	21		2155	0.5	15
12 Su	0426	7.8	238	27 M	0405	8.1	247
	1034	0.7	21		1014	0.3	9
	1643	8.0	244		1625	8.4	256
	2252	0.6	18		2234	0.2	6
13 M	0500	8.0	244	28 Tu	0443	8.5	259
	1108	0.5	15		1054	-0.1	-3
	1717	8.1	247		1705	8.6	262
	2325	0.5	15		2313	0.0	0
14 Tu	0532	8.1	247	29 W	0521	8.7	265
	1141	0.4	12		1134	-0.3	-9
	1750	8.1	247		1745	8.6	262
	2356	0.6	18		2352	0.1	3
15 W	0603	8.1	247	30 Th	0600	8.7	265
	1213	0.4	12		1214	-0.2	-6
	1823	7.9	241		1826	8.4	256
				31 F	0032	0.3	9
					0641	8.5	259
					1257	0.0	0
					1910	8.0	244

Time meridian 52° 30' W. 0000 is midnight. 1200 is noon. Times are not adjusted for Daylight Saving Time.
Heights are referred to the chart datum of soundings.
Seasonal variations in sea level have not been included in these predictions.

Suriname River Entrance, Surinam, 2017

Times and Heights of High and Low Waters

April

Day	Time	ft	cm	Day	Time	ft	cm
1 Sa	0115	0.8	24	16 Su	0104	1.4	43
	0725	8.1	247		0712	7.4	226
	1343	0.5	15		1329	1.2	37
	1958	7.5	229		1941	6.9	210
2 Su	0202	1.3	40	17 M	0144	1.8	55
	0813	7.5	229		0753	7.0	213
	1436	1.1	34		1413	1.6	49
	2053	6.9	210		2028	6.5	198
3 M	0258	2.0	61	18 Tu	0232	2.3	70
	0912	6.9	210		0844	6.6	201
	1540	1.7	52		1508	2.0	61
	2202	6.3	192		2128	6.1	186
4 Tu	0410	2.4	73	19 W	0335	2.6	79
	1027	6.4	195		0950	6.2	189
	1700	2.1	64		1620	2.3	70
	2327	6.1	186		2245	6.0	183
5 W	0539	2.6	79	20 Th	0456	2.7	82
	1155	6.3	192		1112	6.1	186
	1826	2.1	64		1741	2.2	67
6 Th	0051	6.3	192	21 F	0006	6.2	189
	0702	2.4	73		0619	2.5	76
	1315	6.5	198		1232	6.4	195
	1937	1.8	55		1854	1.9	58
7 F	0155	6.6	201	22 Sa	0114	6.6	201
	0806	1.9	58		0726	1.9	58
	1416	6.9	210		1337	6.9	210
	2031	1.5	46		1953	1.4	43
8 Sa	0244	7.1	216	23 Su	0208	7.2	219
	0854	1.4	43		0819	1.3	40
	1503	7.3	223		1430	7.4	226
	2114	1.2	37		2042	0.9	27
9 Su	0324	7.5	229	24 M	0254	7.8	238
	0934	1.0	30		0906	0.6	18
	1543	7.6	232		1517	8.0	244
	2151	0.9	27		2126	0.5	15
10 M	0359	7.8	238	25 Tu	0336	8.3	253
	1009	0.7	21		0949	0.1	3
	1618	7.8	238		1600	8.3	253
	2224	0.8	24		2208	0.2	6
11 Tu	0431	8.0	244	26 W	0417	8.7	265
	1042	0.5	15		1031	-0.2	-6
	1650	7.9	241		1643	8.5	259
	2255	0.7	21		2249	0.1	3
12 W	0502	8.1	247	27 Th	0458	8.8	268
	1113	0.4	12		1113	-0.4	-12
	1722	7.9	241		1725	8.5	259
	2326	0.7	21		2330	0.2	6
13 Th	0532	8.1	247	28 F	0539	8.8	268
	1145	0.4	12		1156	-0.3	-9
	1754	7.8	238		1808	8.3	253
	2357	0.9	27				
14 F	0603	8.0	244	29 Sa	0012	0.5	15
	1217	0.6	18		0622	8.5	259
	1826	7.6	232		1240	0.1	3
					1854	7.9	241
15 Sa	0029	1.1	34	30 Su	0057	0.9	27
	0636	7.7	235		0707	8.0	244
	1251	0.8	24		1328	0.6	18
	1902	7.3	223		1943	7.3	223

May

Day	Time	ft	cm	Day	Time	ft	cm
1 M	0146	1.5	46	16 Tu	0121	1.8	55
	0757	7.5	229		0731	7.1	216
	1421	1.1	34		1352	1.4	43
	2039	6.8	207		2007	6.6	201
2 Tu	0244	2.0	61	17 W	0210	2.1	64
	0857	6.9	210		0822	6.8	207
	1524	1.7	52		1445	1.7	52
	2147	6.4	195		2104	6.4	195
3 W	0354	2.4	73	18 Th	0311	2.3	70
	1009	6.4	195		0924	6.5	198
	1639	2.0	61		1550	1.9	58
	2305	6.2	189		2212	6.3	192
4 Th	0517	2.5	76	19 F	0423	2.4	73
	1132	6.3	192		1038	6.4	195
	1758	2.1	64		1702	2.0	61
					2325	6.5	198
5 F	0021	6.3	192	20 Sa	0539	2.2	67
	0634	2.3	70		1153	6.6	201
	1247	6.4	195		1812	1.8	55
	1905	2.0	61				
6 Sa	0123	6.6	201	21 Su	0032	6.8	207
	0736	2.0	61		0647	1.7	52
	1346	6.7	204		1259	7.0	213
	1958	1.7	52		1913	1.4	43
7 Su	0211	7.0	213	22 M	0129	7.3	223
	0824	1.5	46		0745	1.2	37
	1433	7.0	213		1357	7.4	226
	2041	1.4	43		2007	1.0	30
8 M	0252	7.3	223	23 Tu	0220	7.8	238
	0904	1.2	37		0836	0.6	18
	1513	7.3	223		1448	7.8	238
	2118	1.2	37		2056	0.7	21
9 Tu	0327	7.6	232	24 W	0308	8.3	253
	0940	0.9	27		0924	0.2	6
	1549	7.5	229		1536	8.1	247
	2152	1.0	30		2142	0.4	12
10 W	0400	7.8	238	25 Th	0353	8.6	262
	1013	0.7	21		1010	-0.1	-3
	1622	7.6	232		1622	8.3	253
	2225	1.0	30		2227	0.4	12
11 Th	0432	7.9	241	26 F	0437	8.7	265
	1046	0.6	18		1055	-0.2	-6
	1655	7.7	235		1707	8.2	250
	2257	1.0	30		2311	0.4	12
12 F	0504	8.0	244	27 Sa	0521	8.6	262
	1118	0.6	18		1140	-0.1	-3
	1728	7.6	232		1753	8.0	244
	2329	1.1	34		2356	0.7	21
13 Sa	0537	7.9	241	28 Su	0606	8.4	256
	1152	0.7	21		1227	0.2	6
	1802	7.4	226		1840	7.7	235
14 Su	0003	1.2	37	29 M	0043	1.0	30
	0611	7.7	235		0654	8.0	244
	1228	0.9	27		1315	0.6	18
	1838	7.2	219		1930	7.3	223
15 M	0040	1.5	46	30 Tu	0133	1.4	43
	0648	7.4	226		0745	7.5	229
	1307	1.1	34		1408	1.1	34
	1919	6.9	210		2024	6.9	210
				31 W	0229	1.9	58
					0842	7.0	213
					1505	1.6	49
					2125	6.6	201

June

Day	Time	ft	cm	Day	Time	ft	cm
1 Th	0333	2.2	67	16 F	0248	1.9	58
	0946	6.6	201		0901	6.9	210
	1610	1.9	58		1522	1.6	49
	2231	6.4	195		2140	6.7	204
2 F	0443	2.3	70	17 Sa	0351	1.9	58
	1057	6.4	195		1005	6.8	207
	1717	2.1	64		1625	1.7	52
	2338	6.4	195		2244	6.8	207
3 Sa	0552	2.2	67	18 Su	0500	1.8	55
	1205	6.4	195		1114	6.8	207
	1820	2.1	64		1731	1.6	49
					2349	7.0	213
4 Su	0038	6.6	201	19 M	0607	1.6	49
	0653	2.0	61		1222	7.0	213
	1305	6.5	198		1835	1.5	46
	1915	1.9	58				
5 M	0129	6.8	207	20 Tu	0052	7.3	223
	0745	1.7	52		0711	1.2	37
	1355	6.7	204		1325	7.2	219
	2002	1.7	52		1934	1.2	37
6 Tu	0214	7.1	216	21 W	0149	7.7	235
	0829	1.4	43		0809	0.8	24
	1439	6.9	210		1422	7.5	229
	2043	1.6	49		2029	1.0	30
7 W	0254	7.3	223	22 Th	0242	8.0	244
	0909	1.2	37		0902	0.4	12
	1518	7.1	216		1515	7.8	238
	2121	1.4	43		2120	0.8	24
8 Th	0331	7.5	229	23 F	0332	8.3	253
	0946	1.0	30		0952	0.2	6
	1555	7.3	223		1605	7.9	241
	2157	1.3	40		2209	0.7	21
9 F	0406	7.7	235	24 Sa	0421	8.4	256
	1022	0.9	27		1040	0.1	3
	1631	7.3	223		1653	8.0	244
	2232	1.2	37		2257	0.7	21
10 Sa	0441	7.7	235	25 Su	0508	8.4	256
	1057	0.8	24		1127	0.1	3
	1706	7.3	223		1740	7.9	241
	2308	1.2	37		2343	0.8	24
11 Su	0516	7.7	235	26 M	0554	8.3	253
	1133	0.8	24		1214	0.3	9
	1743	7.3	223		1826	7.7	235
	2344	1.3	40				
12 M	0553	7.7	235	27 Tu	0030	1.0	30
	1210	0.9	27		0641	8.0	244
	1821	7.2	219		1300	0.6	18
					1913	7.4	226
13 Tu	0023	1.4	43	28 W	0118	1.2	37
	0632	7.5	229		0729	7.6	232
	1251	1.0	30		1348	1.0	30
	1902	7.1	216		2001	7.1	216
14 W	0105	1.6	49	29 Th	0208	1.5	46
	0715	7.3	223		0820	7.2	219
	1335	1.2	37		1438	1.4	43
	1948	6.9	210		2052	6.9	210
15 Th	0153	1.7	52	30 F	0301	1.8	55
	0805	7.1	216		0914	6.8	207
	1425	1.4	43		1531	1.8	55
	2041	6.8	207		2147	6.6	201

Time meridian 52° 30' W. 0000 is midnight. 1200 is noon. Times are not adjusted for Daylight Saving Time.
Heights are referred to the chart datum of soundings.
Seasonal variations in sea level have not been included in these predictions.

Suriname River Entrance, Surinam, 2017

Times and Heights of High and Low Waters

July

Day	Time (h m)	Height (ft)	Height (cm)
1 Sa	0359	2.0	61
	1012	6.5	198
	1628	2.0	61
	2245	6.5	198
2 Su	0501	2.1	64
	1114	6.4	195
	1727	2.2	67
	2344	6.5	198
3 M	0602	2.1	64
	1216	6.3	192
	1826	2.2	67
4 Tu	0042	6.6	201
	0700	2.0	61
	1313	6.4	195
	1920	2.1	64
5 W	0134	6.7	204
	0753	1.8	55
	1404	6.6	201
	2009	1.9	58
6 Th	0221	7.0	213
	0839	1.5	46
	1450	6.8	207
	2054	1.8	55
7 F	0304	7.2	219
	0922	1.3	40
	1532	7.0	213
	2135	1.6	49
8 Sa	0345	7.4	226
	1001	1.1	34
	1611	7.1	216
	2214	1.4	43
9 Su ○	0423	7.6	232
	1039	1.0	30
	1649	7.3	223
	2251	1.3	40
10 M	0501	7.7	235
	1117	0.8	24
	1727	7.3	223
	2329	1.2	37
11 Tu	0539	7.7	235
	1155	0.8	24
	1805	7.4	226
12 W	0008	1.2	37
	0618	7.7	235
	1234	0.8	24
	1845	7.4	226
13 Th	0050	1.2	37
	0700	7.7	235
	1316	0.9	27
	1928	7.4	226
14 F	0135	1.2	37
	0746	7.5	229
	1402	1.1	34
	2015	7.3	223
15 Sa	0224	1.3	40
	0837	7.3	223
	1453	1.3	40
	2107	7.2	219
16 Su ○	0320	1.4	43
	0935	7.1	216
	1550	1.5	46
	2206	7.1	216
17 M	0424	1.5	46
	1039	6.9	210
	1653	1.7	52
	2311	7.1	216
18 Tu	0532	1.5	46
	1149	6.8	207
	1801	1.7	52
19 W	0018	7.2	219
	0641	1.3	40
	1258	6.9	210
	1907	1.6	49
20 Th	0123	7.4	226
	0747	1.1	34
	1403	7.2	219
	2009	1.4	43
21 F	0224	7.7	235
	0846	0.8	24
	1500	7.4	226
	2106	1.1	34
22 Sa	0318	8.0	244
	0939	0.5	15
	1552	7.6	232
	2157	0.9	27
23 Su ●	0409	8.2	250
	1028	0.3	9
	1640	7.8	238
	2245	0.7	21
24 M	0456	8.3	253
	1114	0.3	9
	1725	7.9	241
	2330	0.7	21
25 Tu	0541	8.2	250
	1157	0.4	12
	1807	7.8	238
26 W	0013	0.7	21
	0624	8.1	247
	1239	0.6	18
	1849	7.7	235
27 Th	0056	0.9	27
	0707	7.8	238
	1320	0.9	27
	1930	7.5	229
28 F	0139	1.1	34
	0750	7.4	226
	1402	1.2	37
	2013	7.2	219
29 Sa	0223	1.4	43
	0835	7.1	216
	1447	1.6	49
	2058	6.9	210
30 Su ◐	0312	1.7	52
	0924	6.7	204
	1536	2.0	61
	2149	6.6	201
31 M	0406	2.0	61
	1020	6.4	195
	1631	2.3	70
	2247	6.4	195

August

Day	Time (h m)	Height (ft)	Height (cm)
1 Tu	0507	2.2	67
	1123	6.1	186
	1734	2.4	73
	2350	6.3	192
2 W	0613	2.2	67
	1229	6.1	186
	1838	2.4	73
3 Th	0054	6.4	195
	0716	2.1	64
	1332	6.3	192
	1938	2.3	70
4 F	0152	6.6	201
	0812	1.9	58
	1426	6.5	198
	2031	2.0	61
5 Sa	0242	6.9	210
	0900	1.5	46
	1512	6.8	207
	2117	1.7	52
6 Su	0327	7.2	219
	0943	1.2	37
	1554	7.1	216
	2158	1.4	43
7 M ○	0407	7.5	229
	1022	0.9	27
	1632	7.4	226
	2236	1.1	34
8 Tu	0445	7.8	238
	1100	0.7	21
	1709	7.6	232
	2314	0.9	27
9 W	0523	8.0	244
	1137	0.6	18
	1745	7.8	238
	2351	0.7	21
10 Th	0602	8.1	247
	1214	0.5	15
	1823	7.9	241
11 F	0031	0.6	18
	0642	8.0	244
	1254	0.6	18
	1903	7.8	238
12 Sa	0113	0.7	21
	0725	7.9	241
	1336	0.8	24
	1947	7.7	235
13 Su	0159	0.8	24
	0812	7.6	232
	1423	1.1	34
	2035	7.5	229
14 M ◐	0251	1.1	34
	0906	7.2	219
	1517	1.5	46
	2131	7.2	219
15 Tu	0352	1.4	43
	1010	6.8	207
	1620	1.9	58
	2237	6.9	210
16 W	0503	1.6	49
	1123	6.6	201
	1734	2.0	61
	2352	6.9	210
17 Th	0620	1.6	49
	1240	6.6	201
	1850	2.0	61
18 F	0106	7.0	213
	0732	1.4	43
	1351	6.9	210
	1959	1.7	52
19 Sa	0212	7.3	223
	0835	1.1	34
	1450	7.2	219
	2057	1.3	40
20 Su	0309	7.7	235
	0928	0.8	24
	1541	7.6	232
	2147	1.0	30
21 M ●	0358	8.0	244
	1014	0.5	15
	1625	7.8	238
	2231	0.7	21
22 Tu	0442	8.2	250
	1055	0.4	12
	1705	8.0	244
	2312	0.5	15
23 W	0522	8.2	250
	1134	0.4	12
	1742	8.0	244
	2350	0.5	15
24 Th	0601	8.1	247
	1211	0.6	18
	1819	7.9	241
25 F	0028	0.6	18
	0638	7.9	241
	1247	0.8	24
	1854	7.7	235
26 Sa	0105	0.8	24
	0715	7.6	232
	1323	1.1	34
	1931	7.5	229
27 Su	0143	1.1	34
	0755	7.2	219
	1402	1.5	46
	2011	7.1	216
28 M	0225	1.5	46
	0838	6.8	207
	1445	1.9	58
	2056	6.7	204
29 Tu ◐	0314	1.9	58
	0929	6.4	195
	1537	2.3	70
	2150	6.3	192
30 W	0413	2.2	67
	1032	6.0	183
	1642	2.6	79
	2258	6.1	186
31 Th	0525	2.4	73
	1147	5.9	180
	1758	2.7	82

September

Day	Time (h m)	Height (ft)	Height (cm)
1 F	0014	6.1	186
	0640	2.3	70
	1301	6.0	183
	1910	2.5	76
2 Sa	0124	6.3	192
	0745	2.0	61
	1402	6.4	195
	2009	2.2	67
3 Su	0220	6.7	204
	0837	1.6	49
	1451	6.8	207
	2057	1.7	52
4 M	0307	7.2	219
	0921	1.2	37
	1532	7.3	223
	2138	1.2	37
5 Tu	0348	7.6	232
	1000	0.8	24
	1610	7.7	235
	2217	0.8	24
6 W ○	0426	8.0	244
	1037	0.5	15
	1646	8.0	244
	2254	0.4	12
7 Th	0503	8.3	253
	1113	0.3	9
	1722	8.2	250
	2331	0.2	6
8 F	0541	8.4	256
	1150	0.3	9
	1759	8.3	253
9 Sa	0010	0.1	3
	0621	8.3	253
	1229	0.4	12
	1838	8.3	253
10 Su	0051	0.2	6
	0703	8.0	244
	1310	0.7	21
	1920	8.0	244
11 M	0135	0.5	15
	0749	7.6	232
	1356	1.1	34
	2007	7.6	232
12 Tu	0226	1.0	30
	0842	7.1	216
	1449	1.6	49
	2102	7.2	219
13 W ◐	0327	1.4	43
	0946	6.6	201
	1555	2.1	64
	2211	6.7	204
14 Th	0441	1.8	55
	1105	6.3	192
	1716	2.4	73
	2334	6.6	201
15 F	0605	1.9	58
	1230	6.4	195
	1841	2.3	70
16 Sa	0056	6.7	204
	0722	1.6	49
	1342	6.7	204
	1951	1.9	58
17 Su	0204	7.1	216
	0823	1.3	40
	1439	7.2	219
	2047	1.4	43
18 M	0258	7.5	229
	0913	0.9	27
	1524	7.6	232
	2133	0.9	27
19 Tu	0343	7.8	238
	0954	0.7	21
	1604	7.9	241
	2213	0.6	18
20 W ●	0423	8.1	247
	1032	0.5	15
	1640	8.1	247
	2249	0.4	12
21 Th	0459	8.1	247
	1106	0.5	15
	1713	8.2	250
	2324	0.3	9
22 F	0533	8.1	247
	1139	0.6	18
	1746	8.1	247
	2357	0.4	12
23 Sa	0607	7.9	241
	1212	0.8	24
	1819	7.9	241
24 Su	0031	0.6	18
	0641	7.6	232
	1245	1.1	34
	1852	7.7	235
25 M	0106	0.9	27
	0717	7.3	223
	1321	1.5	46
	1929	7.3	223
26 Tu	0145	1.3	40
	0757	6.8	207
	1401	1.9	58
	2011	6.8	207
27 W ◐	0230	1.8	55
	0845	6.4	195
	1450	2.4	73
	2102	6.4	195
28 Th	0326	2.2	67
	0947	6.0	183
	1555	2.7	82
	2210	6.0	183
29 F	0440	2.5	76
	1106	5.8	177
	1718	2.9	88
	2334	6.0	183
30 Sa	0603	2.4	73
	1228	6.0	183
	1839	2.6	79

Time meridian 52° 30' W. 0000 is midnight. 1200 is noon. Times are not adjusted for Daylight Saving Time.
Heights are referred to the chart datum of soundings.
Seasonal variations in sea level have not been included in these predictions.

Suriname River Entrance, Surinam, 2017

Times and Heights of High and Low Waters

October

Day	Time (h m)	Height (ft)	Height (cm)
1 Su	0052	6.2	189
	0714	2.1	64
	1333	6.4	195
	1942	2.2	67
2 M	0152	6.7	204
	0808	1.6	49
	1422	6.9	210
	2031	1.6	49
3 Tu	0240	7.2	219
	0853	1.1	34
	1504	7.5	229
	2113	1.0	30
4 W	0323	7.7	235
	0933	0.7	21
	1542	8.0	244
	2152	0.5	15
5 Th ○	0402	8.2	250
	1011	0.4	12
	1619	8.4	256
	2230	0.1	3
6 F	0441	8.4	256
	1048	0.2	6
	1656	8.6	262
	2309	-0.2	-6
7 Sa	0520	8.5	259
	1126	0.2	6
	1734	8.7	265
	2348	-0.2	-6
8 Su	0600	8.4	256
	1205	0.4	12
	1814	8.5	259
9 M	0030	0.0	0
	0643	8.1	247
	1247	0.7	21
	1857	8.2	250
10 Tu	0115	0.4	12
	0729	7.6	232
	1334	1.2	37
	1945	7.7	235
11 W	0207	0.9	27
	0824	7.0	213
	1428	1.8	55
	2041	7.1	216
12 Th ◐	0309	1.5	46
	0930	6.5	198
	1537	2.3	70
	2153	6.6	201
13 F	0426	1.9	58
	1053	6.2	189
	1704	2.5	76
	2320	6.4	195
14 Sa	0551	2.0	61
	1218	6.3	192
	1830	2.3	70
15 Su	0044	6.5	198
	0706	1.8	55
	1326	6.7	204
	1937	1.9	58
16 M	0149	6.9	210
	0804	1.4	43
	1419	7.1	216
	2029	1.4	43
17 Tu	0239	7.3	223
	0850	1.1	34
	1501	7.5	229
	2112	0.9	27
18 W	0321	7.6	232
	0929	0.9	27
	1538	7.9	241
	2149	0.6	18
19 Th ●	0358	7.9	241
	1004	0.7	21
	1612	8.1	247
	2223	0.4	12
20 F	0432	7.9	241
	1036	0.7	21
	1644	8.2	250
	2256	0.3	9
21 Sa	0505	7.9	241
	1108	0.7	21
	1715	8.1	247
	2328	0.4	12
22 Su	0537	7.8	238
	1139	0.9	27
	1746	8.0	244
23 M	0000	0.6	18
	0610	7.6	232
	1212	1.1	34
	1819	7.7	235
24 Tu	0035	0.8	24
	0645	7.3	223
	1247	1.5	46
	1855	7.4	226
25 W	0113	1.2	37
	0725	6.9	210
	1327	1.9	58
	1936	7.0	213
26 Th	0157	1.6	49
	0811	6.5	198
	1415	2.3	70
	2026	6.5	198
27 F ◑	0251	2.0	61
	0911	6.1	186
	1517	2.7	82
	2131	6.2	189
28 Sa	0401	2.3	70
	1026	5.9	180
	1637	2.8	85
	2252	6.0	183
29 Su	0521	2.3	70
	1146	6.1	186
	1759	2.6	79
30 M	0012	6.3	192
	0633	2.0	61
	1253	6.5	198
	1905	2.1	64
31 Tu	0116	6.7	204
	0731	1.6	49
	1346	7.1	216
	1958	1.5	46

November

Day	Time (h m)	Height (ft)	Height (cm)
1 W	0208	7.2	219
	0819	1.1	34
	1431	7.6	232
	2044	0.8	24
2 Th	0254	7.8	238
	0902	0.7	21
	1513	8.1	247
	2126	0.3	9
3 F ●	0336	8.2	250
	0943	0.4	12
	1553	8.5	259
	2207	-0.1	-3
4 Sa ○	0418	8.4	256
	1023	0.2	6
	1632	8.8	268
	2248	-0.3	-9
5 Su	0459	8.5	259
	1104	0.2	6
	1713	8.8	268
	2330	-0.3	-9
6 M	0542	8.3	253
	1145	0.4	12
	1755	8.6	262
7 Tu	0014	0.0	0
	0627	8.0	244
	1230	0.8	24
	1840	8.2	250
8 W	0101	0.4	12
	0715	7.5	229
	1318	1.3	40
	1930	7.7	235
9 Th	0153	0.9	27
	0810	7.0	213
	1414	1.8	55
	2027	7.1	216
10 F ◐	0254	1.5	46
	0916	6.5	198
	1523	2.3	70
	2138	6.6	201
11 Sa	0408	1.9	58
	1033	6.3	192
	1645	2.5	76
	2300	6.4	195
12 Su	0527	2.0	61
	1151	6.4	195
	1805	2.3	70
13 M	0018	6.5	198
	0638	1.9	58
	1257	6.7	204
	1911	1.9	58
14 Tu	0122	6.7	204
	0735	1.7	52
	1349	7.0	213
	2002	1.5	46
15 W	0212	7.0	213
	0821	1.4	43
	1432	7.4	226
	2045	1.1	34
16 Th	0254	7.3	223
	0900	1.2	37
	1509	7.7	235
	2123	0.8	24
17 F	0331	7.5	229
	0935	1.0	30
	1543	7.9	241
	2157	0.6	18
18 Sa ●	0406	7.6	232
	1008	1.0	30
	1616	8.0	244
	2230	0.5	15
19 Su	0439	7.6	232
	1041	1.0	30
	1648	8.0	244
	2303	0.5	15
20 M	0512	7.6	232
	1113	1.0	30
	1721	7.9	241
	2336	0.7	21
21 Tu	0546	7.4	226
	1147	1.2	37
	1755	7.7	235
22 W	0012	0.9	27
	0622	7.2	219
	1223	1.4	43
	1832	7.5	229
23 Th	0050	1.1	34
	0701	6.9	210
	1303	1.7	52
	1913	7.1	216
24 F	0133	1.4	43
	0747	6.6	201
	1350	2.1	64
	2001	6.8	207
25 Sa	0224	1.8	55
	0841	6.4	195
	1447	2.3	70
	2100	6.5	198
26 Su ◑	0325	2.0	61
	0946	6.2	189
	1553	2.5	76
	2211	6.3	192
27 M	0435	2.1	64
	1058	6.3	192
	1711	2.3	70
	2325	6.4	195
28 Tu	0545	1.9	58
	1205	6.6	201
	1821	1.9	58
29 W	0033	6.7	204
	0648	1.6	49
	1304	7.1	216
	1920	1.4	43
30 Th	0132	7.2	219
	0742	1.2	37
	1356	7.6	232
	2012	0.9	27

December

Day	Time (h m)	Height (ft)	Height (cm)
1 F	0224	7.6	232
	0831	0.9	27
	1443	8.1	247
	2100	0.4	12
2 Sa	0312	8.0	244
	0917	0.6	18
	1528	8.5	259
	2146	0.0	0
3 Su ○	0358	8.2	250
	1002	0.4	12
	1613	8.7	265
	2231	-0.2	-6
4 M	0443	8.2	250
	1046	0.4	12
	1657	8.7	265
	2316	-0.2	-6
5 Tu	0528	8.1	247
	1131	0.5	15
	1742	8.5	259
6 W	0002	0.0	0
	0615	7.9	241
	1218	0.8	24
	1829	8.2	250
7 Th	0049	0.4	12
	0703	7.5	229
	1307	1.2	37
	1919	7.7	235
8 F	0141	0.9	27
	0756	7.1	216
	1401	1.6	49
	2014	7.2	219
9 Sa	0237	1.3	40
	0855	6.8	207
	1503	2.0	61
	2116	6.8	207
10 Su ◐	0340	1.8	55
	1000	6.5	198
	1612	2.2	67
	2226	6.5	198
11 M	0448	2.0	61
	1108	6.4	195
	1724	2.2	67
	2338	6.4	195
12 Tu	0555	2.1	64
	1213	6.5	198
	1830	2.1	64
13 W	0043	6.5	198
	0654	2.0	61
	1309	6.8	207
	1926	1.8	55
14 Th	0137	6.7	204
	0745	1.8	55
	1357	7.0	213
	2014	1.5	46
15 F	0224	6.9	210
	0828	1.6	49
	1439	7.3	223
	2055	1.2	37
16 Sa	0305	7.1	216
	0908	1.4	43
	1517	7.5	229
	2133	1.0	30
17 Su	0342	7.2	219
	0944	1.3	40
	1553	7.7	235
	2209	0.9	27
18 M ●	0418	7.3	223
	1020	1.2	37
	1628	7.7	235
	2244	0.8	24
19 Tu	0453	7.4	226
	1055	1.2	37
	1703	7.8	238
	2319	0.8	24
20 W	0529	7.4	226
	1130	1.2	37
	1739	7.7	235
	2355	0.9	27
21 Th	0605	7.3	223
	1207	1.3	40
	1816	7.6	232
22 F	0033	1.0	30
	0644	7.2	219
	1247	1.5	46
	1856	7.4	226
23 Sa	0114	1.2	37
	0726	7.0	213
	1330	1.6	49
	1941	7.2	219
24 Su	0200	1.4	43
	0813	6.8	207
	1420	1.8	55
	2033	7.0	213
25 M	0252	1.6	49
	0908	6.7	204
	1518	1.9	58
	2132	6.7	204
26 Tu ◑	0351	1.8	55
	1009	6.7	204
	1624	1.9	58
	2239	6.7	204
27 W	0456	1.8	55
	1115	6.8	207
	1734	1.8	55
	2349	6.7	204
28 Th	0603	1.7	52
	1221	7.0	213
	1841	1.5	46
29 F	0056	7.0	213
	0706	1.5	46
	1322	7.4	226
	1942	1.0	30
30 Sa	0156	7.3	223
	0804	1.2	37
	1417	7.8	238
	2038	0.6	18
31 Su	0251	7.6	232
	0857	0.9	27
	1509	8.2	250
	2129	0.3	9

Time meridian 52° 30' W. 0000 is midnight. 1200 is noon. Times are not adjusted for Daylight Saving Time.
Heights are referred to the chart datum of soundings.
Seasonal variations in sea level have not been included in these predictions.

Recife, Brazil, 2017

Times and Heights of High and Low Waters

January

Day	Time	ft	cm	Day	Time	ft	cm
1 Su	0000	1.0	30	16 M	0034	1.0	30
	0545	7.2	220		0636	7.2	220
	1147	1.3	40		1245	1.3	40
	1758	7.5	230		1854	7.5	230
2 M	0013	1.0	30	17 Tu	0117	1.3	40
	0626	6.9	210		0719	6.6	200
	1226	1.6	50		1330	2.0	60
	1843	7.2	220		1941	6.9	210
3 Tu	0058	1.3	40	18 W	0204	2.0	60
	0711	6.6	200		0808	6.2	190
	1311	2.0	60		1421	2.3	70
	1930	6.9	210		2032	6.2	190
4 W	0151	1.6	50	19 Th ◗	0258	2.3	70
	0806	6.2	190		0900	5.9	180
	1406	2.3	70		1521	2.6	80
	2026	6.6	200		2128	5.9	180
5 Th ◖	0251	2.0	60	20 F	0400	2.6	80
	0906	6.2	190		1002	5.6	170
	1513	2.3	70		1634	3.0	90
	2136	6.6	200		2236	5.6	170
6 F	0402	2.0	60	21 Sa	0509	3.0	90
	1015	6.2	190		1108	5.6	170
	1632	2.3	70		1747	3.0	90
	2249	6.6	200		2343	5.6	170
7 Sa	0519	2.0	60	22 Su	0613	2.6	80
	1126	6.2	190		1211	5.9	180
	1749	2.0	60		1847	2.6	80
8 Su	0000	6.6	200	23 M	0043	5.9	180
	0628	2.0	60		0706	2.6	80
	1232	6.6	200		1304	6.2	190
	1856	1.6	50		1936	2.3	70
9 M	0104	6.9	210	24 Tu	0130	6.2	190
	0726	1.6	50		0751	2.3	70
	1330	7.2	220		1351	6.6	200
	1954	1.0	30		2013	2.0	60
10 Tu	0202	7.5	230	25 W	0211	6.6	200
	0819	1.0	30		0828	2.0	60
	1421	7.5	230		1428	6.9	210
	2047	0.7	20		2053	1.3	40
11 W	0254	7.5	230	26 Th	0253	6.9	210
	0906	1.0	30		0904	1.3	40
	1509	7.9	240		1506	7.2	220
	2134	0.3	10		2126	1.0	30
12 Th ○	0341	7.9	240	27 F ●	0330	7.2	220
	0953	0.7	20		0941	1.3	40
	1556	8.2	250		1545	7.5	230
	2219	0.0	0		2202	0.7	20
13 F	0424	7.9	240	28 Sa	0408	7.5	230
	1036	0.7	20		1015	1.0	30
	1641	8.2	250		1623	7.9	240
	2304	0.3	10		2239	0.7	20
14 Sa	0508	7.9	240	29 Su	0449	7.5	230
	1117	0.7	20		1053	1.0	30
	1724	8.2	250		1700	7.9	240
	2349	0.3	10		2317	0.7	20
15 Su	0554	7.5	230	30 M	0526	7.5	230
	1200	1.0	30		1130	1.0	30
	1808	7.9	240		1741	7.9	240
					2358	0.7	20
				31 Tu	0606	7.5	230
					1209	1.0	30
					1823	7.9	240

February

Day	Time	ft	cm	Day	Time	ft	cm
1 W	0039	1.0	30	16 Th	0115	1.6	50
	0653	7.2	220		0719	6.6	200
	1254	1.3	40		1330	2.0	60
	1909	7.5	230		1943	6.6	200
2 Th	0126	1.3	40	17 F	0156	2.3	70
	0741	6.9	210		0804	6.2	190
	1343	1.6	50		1417	2.3	70
	2004	6.9	210		2030	5.9	180
3 F	0223	2.0	60	18 Sa ◗	0245	2.6	80
	0836	6.6	200		0858	5.9	180
	1445	2.0	60		1517	3.0	90
	2108	6.6	200		2130	5.6	170
4 Sa ◖	0332	2.3	70	19 Su	0353	3.0	90
	0945	6.2	190		1004	5.6	170
	1604	2.3	70		1641	3.0	90
	2224	6.2	190		2247	5.2	160
5 Su	0454	2.3	70	20 M	0517	3.0	90
	1100	6.2	190		1121	5.6	170
	1732	2.3	70		1804	3.0	90
	2347	6.2	190				
6 M	0613	2.3	70	21 Tu	0000	5.6	170
	1215	6.6	200		0632	3.0	90
	1849	1.6	50		1228	5.9	180
					1904	2.6	80
7 Tu	0058	6.6	200	22 W	0102	5.9	180
	0719	2.0	60		0723	2.6	80
	1319	6.9	210		1319	6.2	190
	1951	1.3	40		1951	2.0	60
8 W	0156	6.9	210	23 Th	0151	6.2	190
	0811	1.6	50		0806	2.0	60
	1411	7.5	230		1404	6.9	210
	2041	0.7	20		2028	1.6	50
9 Th	0247	7.2	220	24 F	0230	6.9	210
	0858	1.0	30		0843	1.6	50
	1500	7.9	240		1445	7.2	220
	2124	0.3	10		2104	1.0	30
10 F ○	0328	7.5	230	25 Sa	0308	7.2	220
	0941	0.7	20		0919	1.0	30
	1545	8.2	250		1523	7.9	240
	2206	0.3	10		2143	0.7	20
11 Sa	0409	7.9	240	26 Su ●	0349	7.9	240
	1019	0.7	20		0956	0.7	20
	1623	8.2	250		1602	8.2	250
	2247	0.3	10		2219	0.3	10
12 Su	0449	7.9	240	27 M	0424	7.9	240
	1058	0.7	20		1034	0.7	20
	1704	8.2	250		1641	8.5	260
	2323	0.3	10		2258	0.0	0
13 M	0524	7.5	230	28 Tu	0504	7.9	240
	1136	0.7	20		1109	0.3	10
	1743	7.9	240		1721	8.5	260
					2338	0.3	10
14 Tu	0000	0.7	20				
	0602	7.2	220				
	1211	1.0	30				
	1821	7.5	230				
15 W	0038	1.3	40				
	0641	6.9	210				
	1251	1.6	50				
	1900	6.9	210				

March

Day	Time	ft	cm	Day	Time	ft	cm
1 W	0547	7.9	240	16 Th	0000	1.3	40
	1153	0.7	20		0604	7.2	220
	1804	8.2	250		1215	1.3	40
					1824	7.2	220
2 Th	0019	0.7	20	17 F	0034	1.6	50
	0628	7.5	230		0643	6.9	210
	1236	1.0	30		1251	1.6	50
	1853	7.5	230		1902	6.6	200
3 F	0106	1.3	40	18 Sa ◗	0108	2.0	60
	0715	7.2	220		0721	6.2	190
	1324	1.3	40		1330	2.3	70
	1947	7.2	220		1947	5.9	180
4 Sa	0200	1.6	50	19 Su	0149	2.6	80
	0811	6.6	200		0808	5.9	180
	1426	2.0	60		1419	2.6	80
	2051	6.6	200		2041	5.6	170
5 Su ◖	0308	2.3	70	20 M ◗	0245	3.0	90
	0919	6.2	190		0908	5.6	170
	1549	2.3	70		1534	3.0	90
	2208	6.2	190		2154	5.2	160
6 M	0438	2.6	80	21 Tu	0411	3.3	100
	1043	5.9	180		1026	5.6	170
	1724	2.3	70		1709	3.0	90
	2338	5.9	180		2315	5.2	160
7 Tu	0606	2.6	80	22 W	0545	3.0	90
	1204	6.2	190		1145	5.6	170
	1845	2.0	60		1824	2.6	80
8 W	0054	6.2	190	23 Th	0026	5.9	180
	0711	2.3	70		0649	2.6	80
	1309	6.6	200		1245	6.2	190
	1945	1.3	40		1915	2.0	60
9 Th	0151	6.6	200	24 F	0117	6.2	190
	0802	1.6	50		0736	2.0	60
	1402	7.2	220		1334	6.9	210
	2032	1.0	30		1958	1.6	50
10 F	0234	7.2	220	25 Sa	0202	6.9	210
	0847	1.3	40		0813	1.6	50
	1447	7.5	230		1415	7.2	220
	2109	0.7	20		2038	1.0	30
11 Sa	0311	7.5	230	26 Su	0243	7.5	230
	0923	1.0	30		0853	1.0	30
	1526	7.9	240		1458	7.9	240
	2149	0.7	20		2115	0.3	10
12 Su ○	0349	7.5	230	27 M ●	0321	7.9	240
	0958	0.7	20		0932	0.7	20
	1602	8.2	250		1539	8.5	260
	2223	0.3	10		2156	0.0	0
13 M	0423	7.9	240	28 Tu	0402	8.2	250
	1034	0.7	20		1009	0.3	10
	1639	8.2	250		1619	8.5	260
	2256	0.7	20		2236	0.3	10
14 Tu	0456	7.9	240	29 W	0443	8.2	250
	1106	0.7	20		1053	0.0	0
	1713	7.9	240		1702	8.5	260
	2328	1.0	30		2317	0.3	10
15 W	0530	7.5	230	30 Th	0524	8.2	250
	1141	1.0	30		1136	0.3	10
	1751	7.5	230		1749	8.2	250
				31 F	0002	0.7	20
					0608	7.9	240
					1221	0.7	20
					1838	7.9	240

Time meridian 45° W. 0000 is midnight. 1200 is noon. Times are not adjusted for Daylight Saving Time.
Heights are referred to the chart datum of soundings.

Recife, Brazil, 2017

Times and Heights of High and Low Waters

April

Day	Time	Height (ft)	Height (cm)	Day	Time	Height (ft)	Height (cm)
1 Sa	0051	1.3	40	16 Su	0034	2.0	60
	0658	7.2	220		0651	6.6	200
	1313	1.0	30		1258	2.0	60
	1932	7.2	220		1913	6.2	190
2 Su	0145	2.0	60	17 M	0113	2.3	70
	0756	6.9	210		0734	6.2	190
	1419	1.6	50		1345	2.6	80
	2039	6.6	200		2006	5.9	180
3 M	0256	2.3	70	18 Tu	0204	3.0	90
	0904	6.2	190		0828	5.9	180
	1543	2.0	60		1447	2.6	80
	2200	5.9	180		2111	5.6	170
4 Tu	0424	2.6	80	19 W	0317	3.3	100
	1028	6.2	190		0939	5.6	170
	1715	2.3	70		1611	3.0	90
	2326	5.9	180		2230	5.6	170
5 W	0553	2.6	80	20 Th	0449	3.0	90
	1153	6.2	190		1056	5.9	180
	1834	2.0	60		1734	2.6	80
					2343	5.9	180
6 Th	0041	6.2	190	21 F	0600	2.6	80
	0658	2.3	70		1202	6.2	190
	1256	6.6	200		1834	2.0	60
	1930	1.6	50				
7 F	0134	6.6	200	22 Sa	0041	6.2	190
	0747	1.6	50		0654	2.3	70
	1347	6.9	210		1256	6.9	210
	2013	1.3	40		1921	1.6	50
8 Sa	0213	6.9	210	23 Su	0126	6.9	210
	0826	1.3	40		0741	1.6	50
	1426	7.5	230		1345	7.5	230
	2053	1.0	30		2006	1.0	30
9 Su	0251	7.2	220	24 M	0211	7.5	230
	0902	1.0	30		0823	1.0	30
	1504	7.5	230		1428	7.9	240
	2123	1.0	30		2049	0.3	10
10 M	0321	7.5	230	25 Tu	0254	7.9	240
	0936	1.0	30		0904	0.3	10
	1539	7.9	240		1513	8.5	260
	2156	0.7	20		2130	0.0	0
11 Tu	0354	7.5	230	26 W	0338	8.2	250
	1008	0.7	20		0949	0.0	0
	1611	7.9	240		1600	8.5	260
	2224	0.7	20		2213	0.0	0
12 W	0426	7.5	230	27 Th	0419	8.5	260
	1039	0.7	20		1034	0.0	0
	1647	7.5	230		1647	8.5	260
	2256	1.0	30		2258	0.3	10
13 Th	0500	7.5	230	28 F	0504	8.2	250
	1111	1.0	30		1119	0.0	0
	1719	7.5	230		1734	8.2	250
	2326	1.3	40		2345	0.7	20
14 F	0536	7.2	220	29 Sa	0554	7.9	240
	1147	1.3	40		1209	0.3	10
	1756	7.2	220		1824	7.5	230
15 Sa	0000	1.6	50	30 Su	0036	1.3	40
	0609	6.9	210		0645	7.5	230
	1221	1.6	50		1306	1.0	30
	1834	6.6	200		1921	7.2	220

May

Day	Time	Height (ft)	Height (cm)	Day	Time	Height (ft)	Height (cm)
1 M	0134	1.6	50	16 Tu	0053	2.3	70
	0743	6.9	210		0708	6.6	200
	1411	1.6	50		1323	2.3	70
	2026	6.6	200		1943	5.9	180
2 Tu	0243	2.3	70	17 W	0139	2.6	80
	0851	6.6	200		0800	6.2	190
	1532	2.0	60		1417	2.3	70
	2145	5.9	180		2041	5.9	180
3 W	0406	2.6	80	18 Th	0241	3.0	90
	1008	6.2	190		0900	5.9	180
	1656	2.0	60		1528	2.6	80
	2304	5.9	180		2149	5.6	170
4 Th	0526	2.6	80	19 F	0356	3.0	90
	1126	6.2	190		1008	5.9	180
	1808	2.0	60		1643	2.3	70
					2258	5.9	180
5 F	0013	6.2	190	20 Sa	0509	2.6	80
	0630	2.3	70		1117	6.2	190
	1232	6.6	200		1749	2.0	60
	1904	1.6	50		2358	6.2	190
6 Sa	0106	6.2	190	21 Su	0611	2.3	70
	0719	2.0	60		1217	6.9	210
	1321	6.9	210		1845	1.6	50
	1949	1.6	50				
7 Su	0147	6.6	200	22 M	0053	6.9	210
	0800	1.6	50		0704	1.6	50
	1402	6.9	210		1311	7.2	220
	2023	1.3	40		1936	1.0	30
8 M	0221	6.9	210	23 Tu	0141	7.2	220
	0838	1.3	40		0754	1.0	30
	1438	7.2	220		1402	7.9	240
	2056	1.3	40		2021	0.7	20
9 Tu	0254	7.2	220	24 W	0226	7.9	240
	0909	1.0	30		0843	0.3	10
	1509	7.5	230		1453	8.2	250
	2126	1.0	30		2108	0.3	10
10 W	0324	7.5	230	25 Th	0313	8.2	250
	0943	1.0	30		0930	0.0	0
	1545	7.5	230		1541	8.5	260
	2156	1.0	30		2154	0.3	10
11 Th	0400	7.5	230	26 F	0400	8.2	250
	1013	1.0	30		1017	0.0	0
	1617	7.5	230		1630	8.2	250
	2228	1.0	30		2243	0.3	10
12 F	0434	7.5	230	27 Sa	0449	8.2	250
	1049	1.0	30		1108	0.0	0
	1654	7.2	220		1719	8.2	250
	2300	1.3	40		2330	0.7	20
13 Sa	0508	7.2	220	28 Su	0539	8.2	250
	1123	1.3	40		1200	0.3	10
	1730	6.9	210		1811	7.5	230
	2336	1.6	50				
14 Su	0547	7.2	220	29 M	0021	1.0	30
	1158	1.6	50		0630	7.5	230
	1808	6.6	200		1256	0.7	20
					1908	7.2	220
15 M	0009	2.0	60	30 Tu	0117	1.6	50
	0624	6.9	210		0726	7.2	220
	1238	2.0	60		1358	1.3	40
	1853	6.2	190		2008	6.6	200
				31 W	0221	2.0	60
					0830	6.9	210
					1508	1.6	50
					2115	6.2	190

June

Day	Time	Height (ft)	Height (cm)	Day	Time	Height (ft)	Height (cm)
1 Th	0334	2.3	70	16 F	0208	2.3	70
	0939	6.6	200		0828	6.2	190
	1621	2.0	60		1451	2.0	60
	2226	5.9	180		2108	5.9	180
2 F	0449	2.6	80	17 Sa	0311	2.6	80
	1051	6.2	190		0932	6.2	190
	1730	2.0	60		1558	2.3	70
	2332	5.9	180		2211	6.2	190
3 Sa	0554	2.3	70	18 Su	0423	2.3	70
	1154	6.2	190		1039	6.6	200
	1826	2.0	60		1706	2.0	60
					2317	6.2	190
4 Su	0026	6.2	190	19 M	0532	2.0	60
	0649	2.3	70		1145	6.9	210
	1249	6.6	200		1809	1.6	50
	1913	2.0	60				
5 M	0111	6.2	190	20 Tu	0017	6.6	200
	0732	2.0	60		0636	1.6	50
	1332	6.6	200		1247	7.2	220
	1953	2.0	60		1908	1.3	40
6 Tu	0151	6.6	200	21 W	0113	7.2	220
	0809	1.6	50		0732	1.0	30
	1408	6.9	210		1343	7.5	230
	2026	1.6	50		2000	1.0	30
7 W	0224	6.9	210	22 Th	0206	7.5	230
	0845	1.3	40		0824	0.7	20
	1445	6.9	210		1436	7.9	240
	2058	1.6	50		2051	0.7	20
8 Th	0300	7.2	220	23 F	0256	7.9	240
	0919	1.3	40		0915	0.3	10
	1519	7.2	220		1526	8.2	250
	2132	1.3	40		2139	0.7	20
9 F	0336	7.2	220	24 Sa	0347	8.2	250
	0954	1.3	40		1006	0.0	0
	1556	7.2	220		1615	8.2	250
	2204	1.3	40		2228	0.7	20
10 Sa	0409	7.5	230	25 Su	0434	8.2	250
	1028	1.0	30		1058	0.0	0
	1634	7.2	220		1706	7.9	240
	2239	1.3	40		2315	0.7	20
11 Su	0449	7.2	220	26 M	0523	8.2	250
	1102	1.3	40		1149	0.3	10
	1709	6.9	210		1756	7.5	230
	2315	1.6	50				
12 M	0524	7.2	220	27 Tu	0006	1.0	30
	1141	1.3	40		0613	7.9	240
	1751	6.9	210		1241	0.7	20
	2353	1.6	50		1849	7.2	220
13 Tu	0604	6.9	210	28 W	0058	1.3	40
	1219	1.6	50		0706	7.5	230
	1834	6.6	200		1336	1.3	40
					1941	6.9	210
14 W	0032	2.0	60	29 Th	0153	1.6	50
	0647	6.9	210		0800	6.9	210
	1302	1.6	50		1434	1.6	50
	1917	6.2	190		2038	6.2	190
15 Th	0115	2.3	70	30 F	0254	2.3	70
	0734	6.6	200		0900	6.6	200
	1353	2.0	60		1538	2.0	60
	2009	6.2	190		2138	5.9	180

Time meridian 45° W. 0000 is midnight. 1200 is noon. Times are not adjusted for Daylight Saving Time.
Heights are referred to the chart datum of soundings.

Recife, Brazil, 2017

Times and Heights of High and Low Waters

July

Day	Time	ft	cm		Day	Time	ft	cm
1 Sa	0400	2.3	70		**16** Su	0238	2.3	70
	1004	6.2	190			0900	6.6	200
	1641	2.3	70			1521	2.0	60
	2241	5.9	180		◐	2138	6.2	190
2 Su	0506	2.6	80		**17** M	0347	2.3	70
	1108	5.9	180			1006	6.6	200
	1743	2.3	70			1632	2.3	70
	2341	5.9	180			2245	6.2	190
3 M	0608	2.3	70		**18** Tu	0502	2.0	60
	1206	5.9	180			1117	6.6	200
	1836	2.3	70			1745	2.0	60
						2353	6.6	200
4 Tu	0032	6.2	190		**19** W	0613	1.6	50
	0700	2.3	70			1226	6.9	210
	1258	6.2	190			1851	1.6	50
	1919	2.3	70					
5 W	0117	6.2	190		**20** Th	0054	6.9	210
	0745	2.0	60			0719	1.3	40
	1341	6.2	190			1328	7.2	220
	2000	2.0	60			1949	1.3	40
6 Th	0158	6.6	200		**21** F	0153	7.5	230
	0823	1.6	50			0815	0.7	20
	1419	6.6	200			1424	7.5	230
	2036	1.6	50			2039	1.0	30
7 F	0238	6.9	210		**22** Sa	0243	7.9	240
	0858	1.6	50			0906	0.3	10
	1458	6.9	210			1513	7.9	240
	2109	1.6	50			2126	0.7	20
8 Sa	0313	7.2	220		**23** Su	0332	8.2	250
	0934	1.3	40			0956	0.0	0
	1536	6.9	210			1602	7.9	240
	2147	1.3	40		●	2213	0.7	20
9 Su	0353	7.5	230		**24** M	0419	8.5	260
	1008	1.0	30			1043	0.0	0
	1613	7.2	220			1651	7.9	240
○	2221	1.3	40			2258	0.7	20
10 M	0426	7.5	230		**25** Tu	0506	8.2	250
	1045	1.0	30			1130	0.3	10
	1653	7.2	220			1736	7.5	230
	2258	1.3	40			2345	0.7	20
11 Tu	0504	7.5	230		**26** W	0553	8.2	250
	1121	1.0	30			1215	0.7	20
	1730	7.2	220			1819	7.2	220
	2334	1.3	40					
12 W	0545	7.5	230		**27** Th	0028	1.0	30
	1200	1.3	40			0638	7.5	230
	1809	6.9	210			1302	1.0	30
						1904	6.9	210
13 Th	0011	1.6	50		**28** F	0115	1.6	50
	0624	7.2	220			0724	7.2	220
	1241	1.3	40			1351	1.6	50
	1854	6.9	210			1953	6.6	200
14 F	0054	1.6	50		**29** Sa	0206	2.0	60
	0709	6.9	210			0815	6.6	200
	1324	1.6	50			1443	2.3	70
	1941	6.6	200			2045	6.2	190
15 Sa	0141	2.0	60		**30** Su	0304	2.3	70
	0800	6.9	210			0911	6.2	190
	1417	2.0	60			1541	2.6	80
	2036	6.2	190		◑	2143	5.9	180
					31 M	0409	2.6	80
						1013	5.9	180
						1649	2.6	80
						2249	5.6	170

August

Day	Time	ft	cm		Day	Time	ft	cm
1 Tu	0523	2.6	80		**16** W	0445	2.3	70
	1121	5.6	170			1102	6.2	190
	1754	2.6	80			1728	2.3	70
	2353	5.9	180			2336	6.2	190
2 W	0628	2.6	80		**17** Th	0606	2.0	60
	1223	5.9	180			1217	6.6	200
	1851	2.6	80			1841	2.0	60
3 Th	0047	5.9	180		**18** F	0043	6.9	210
	0719	2.3	70			0713	1.3	40
	1313	5.9	180			1323	6.9	210
	1936	2.3	70			1941	1.6	50
4 F	0134	6.2	190		**19** Sa	0143	7.2	220
	0800	2.0	60			0809	1.0	30
	1358	6.2	190			1415	7.2	220
	2013	2.0	60			2030	1.3	40
5 Sa	0213	6.9	210		**20** Su	0232	7.9	240
	0839	1.6	50			0858	0.7	20
	1438	6.6	200			1502	7.5	230
	2053	1.6	50			2113	1.0	30
6 Su	0253	7.2	220		**21** M	0317	8.2	250
	0913	1.3	40			0943	0.3	10
	1513	7.2	220			1547	7.9	240
	2126	1.3	40		●	2156	0.7	20
7 M	0328	7.5	230		**22** Tu	0402	8.2	250
	0949	1.0	30			1024	0.3	10
	1553	7.2	220			1626	7.9	240
○	2200	1.0	30			2238	0.7	20
8 Tu	0406	7.5	230		**23** W	0445	8.2	250
	1023	0.7	20			1104	0.3	10
	1630	7.5	230			1706	7.9	240
	2236	1.0	30			2317	0.7	20
9 W	0445	7.9	240		**24** Th	0524	8.2	250
	1100	0.7	20			1145	0.7	20
	1706	7.5	230			1747	7.5	230
	2311	1.0	30			2356	1.0	30
10 Th	0521	7.9	240		**25** F	0606	7.9	240
	1138	0.7	20			1223	1.0	30
	1747	7.5	230			1824	7.2	220
	2349	1.0	30					
11 F	0602	7.5	230		**26** Sa	0038	1.3	40
	1215	1.0	30			0649	7.2	220
	1828	7.2	220			1302	1.6	50
						1906	6.9	210
12 Sa	0030	1.3	40		**27** Su	0119	1.6	50
	0647	7.5	230			0732	6.6	200
	1300	1.3	40			1347	2.3	70
	1911	6.9	210			1954	6.2	190
13 Su	0115	1.6	50		**28** M	0208	2.3	70
	0736	7.2	220			0819	5.9	180
	1351	1.6	50			1436	2.6	80
	2004	6.6	200			2047	5.9	180
14 M	0209	2.0	60		**29** Tu	0309	2.6	80
	0834	6.6	200			0919	5.6	170
	1451	2.0	60			1543	3.0	90
◑	2104	6.2	190		◑	2153	5.6	170
15 Tu	0319	2.3	70		**30** W	0430	3.0	90
	0945	6.2	190			1034	5.2	160
	1606	2.3	70			1706	3.0	90
	2217	6.2	190			2306	5.6	170
					31 Th	0553	3.0	90
						1151	5.6	170
						1817	3.0	90

September

Day	Time	ft	cm		Day	Time	ft	cm
1 F	0013	5.9	180		**16** Sa	0038	6.6	200
	0653	2.6	80			0709	1.3	40
	1249	5.9	180			1317	6.6	200
	1909	2.6	80			1934	1.6	50
2 Sa	0106	6.2	190		**17** Su	0134	7.2	220
	0738	2.0	60			0802	1.0	30
	1336	6.2	190			1406	7.2	220
	1953	2.0	60			2019	1.3	40
3 Su	0151	6.6	200		**18** M	0219	7.5	230
	0813	1.6	50			0847	0.7	20
	1413	6.6	200			1449	7.5	230
	2026	1.6	50			2100	1.0	30
4 M	0226	7.2	220		**19** Tu	0302	7.9	240
	0849	1.3	40			0924	0.3	10
	1453	7.2	220			1524	7.5	230
	2102	1.3	40			2138	0.7	20
5 Tu	0304	7.5	230		**20** W	0343	8.2	250
	0923	0.7	20			1002	0.3	10
	1526	7.5	230			1602	7.9	240
	2138	1.0	30		●	2213	0.3	10
6 W	0343	7.9	240		**21** Th	0419	8.2	250
	0958	0.3	10			1038	0.3	10
	1604	7.9	240			1638	7.9	240
○	2211	0.7	20			2251	0.7	20
7 Th	0419	8.2	250		**22** F	0456	7.9	240
	1036	0.3	10			1109	0.7	20
	1643	7.9	240			1711	7.5	230
	2249	0.7	20			2324	0.7	20
8 F	0458	8.2	250		**23** Sa	0534	7.5	230
	1111	0.3	10			1145	1.0	30
	1721	7.9	240			1751	7.2	220
	2326	0.7	20					
9 Sa	0541	8.2	250		**24** Su	0000	1.3	40
	1154	0.7	20			0609	7.2	220
	1802	7.5	230			1219	1.6	50
						1826	6.9	210
10 Su	0008	1.0	30		**25** M	0039	1.6	50
	0624	7.5	230			0651	6.6	200
	1238	1.0	30			1256	2.0	60
	1849	7.2	220			1908	6.6	200
11 M	0056	1.3	40		**26** Tu	0121	2.3	70
	0713	7.2	220			0736	5.9	180
	1326	1.6	50			1339	2.6	80
	1939	6.6	200			1956	5.9	180
12 Tu	0153	1.6	50		**27** W	0213	2.6	80
	0813	6.6	200			0832	5.6	170
	1430	2.3	70			1439	3.0	90
	2043	6.2	190		◑	2058	5.6	170
13 W	0306	2.0	60		**28** Th	0330	3.0	90
	0930	6.2	190			0945	5.2	160
	1553	2.6	80			1608	3.3	100
◑	2200	6.2	190			2215	5.6	170
14 Th	0441	2.3	70		**29** F	0504	3.0	90
	1056	6.2	190			1106	5.2	160
	1723	2.6	80			1738	3.0	90
	2324	6.2	190			2334	5.6	170
15 F	0606	2.0	60		**30** Sa	0613	2.6	80
	1215	6.2	190			1213	5.6	170
	1838	2.3	70			1838	2.6	80

Time meridian 45° W. 0000 is midnight. 1200 is noon. Times are not adjusted for Daylight Saving Time.
Heights are referred to the chart datum of soundings.

Recife, Brazil, 2017

Times and Heights of High and Low Waters

October

Day	Time	ft	cm	Day	Time	ft	cm
1 Su	0032	5.9	180	16 M	0119	7.2	220
	0702	2.3	70		0749	1.3	40
	1304	6.2	190		1351	6.9	210
	1921	2.3	70		2002	1.3	40
2 M	0117	6.6	200	17 Tu	0204	7.5	230
	0743	1.6	50		0828	1.0	30
	1345	6.9	210		1428	7.2	220
	1958	1.6	50		2041	1.0	30
3 Tu	0158	7.2	220	18 W	0243	7.9	240
	0819	1.0	30		0902	0.7	20
	1423	7.2	220		1502	7.5	230
	2034	1.3	40		2115	0.7	20
4 W	0238	7.9	240	19 Th	0317	7.9	240
	0854	0.7	20		0938	0.7	20
	1500	7.9	240		1536	7.5	230
	2108	0.7	20	●	2151	0.7	20
5 Th O	0315	8.2	250	20 F	0354	7.9	240
	0932	0.3	10		1008	0.7	20
	1539	7.9	240		1608	7.9	240
	2147	0.3	10		2223	0.7	20
6 F	0356	8.5	260	21 Sa	0428	7.9	240
	1009	0.0	0		1039	1.0	30
	1615	8.2	250		1643	7.5	230
	2224	0.3	10		2256	0.7	20
7 Sa	0438	8.5	260	22 Su	0502	7.5	230
	1051	0.3	10		1111	1.3	40
	1658	8.2	250		1717	7.5	230
	2306	0.3	10		2332	1.0	30
8 Su	0519	8.2	250	23 M	0539	7.2	220
	1132	0.7	20		1145	1.6	50
	1741	7.9	240		1754	7.2	220
	2353	0.7	20				
9 M	0606	7.9	240	24 Tu	0006	1.6	50
	1217	1.0	30		0617	6.6	200
	1826	7.5	230		1219	2.0	60
					1834	6.6	200
10 Tu	0043	1.0	30	25 W	0047	2.0	60
	0700	7.2	220		0700	6.2	190
	1309	1.6	50		1300	2.3	70
	1921	6.9	210		1917	6.2	190
11 W	0143	1.6	50	26 Th	0134	2.6	80
	0802	6.6	200		0753	5.6	170
	1415	2.3	70		1353	3.0	90
	2026	6.6	200		2013	5.9	180
12 Th ◐	0302	2.0	60	27 F ◐	0238	3.0	90
	0921	6.2	190		0858	5.6	170
	1543	2.6	80		1506	3.3	100
	2151	6.2	190		2123	5.6	170
13 F	0436	2.0	60	28 Sa	0404	3.0	90
	1051	5.9	180		1015	5.2	160
	1713	2.6	80		1639	3.3	100
	2313	6.2	190		2241	5.6	170
14 Sa	0558	2.0	60	29 Su	0523	2.6	80
	1206	6.2	190		1128	5.6	170
	1824	2.3	70		1751	3.0	90
					2347	5.9	180
15 Su	0024	6.6	200	30 M	0619	2.3	70
	0700	1.6	50		1223	6.2	190
	1304	6.6	200		1841	2.3	70
	1919	1.6	50				
				31 Tu	0039	6.6	200
					0704	1.6	50
					1308	6.6	200
					1923	1.6	50

November

Day	Time	ft	cm	Day	Time	ft	cm
1 W	0123	7.2	220	16 Th	0221	7.2	220
	0747	1.3	40		0839	1.3	40
	1353	7.2	220		1439	7.2	220
	2002	1.3	40		2054	1.0	30
2 Th	0206	7.9	240	17 F	0256	7.5	230
	0826	0.7	20		0909	1.0	30
	1432	7.9	240		1509	7.5	230
	2043	0.7	20		2126	1.0	30
3 F	0251	8.2	250	18 Sa ●	0330	7.5	230
	0906	0.3	10		0943	1.0	30
	1511	8.2	250		1545	7.5	230
	2123	0.3	10		2200	1.0	30
4 Sa O	0334	8.5	260	19 Su	0404	7.5	230
	0949	0.3	10		1013	1.0	30
	1554	8.2	250		1617	7.5	230
	2206	0.0	0		2234	1.0	30
5 Su	0417	8.5	260	20 M	0439	7.2	220
	1030	0.3	10		1047	1.3	40
	1638	8.2	250		1654	7.5	230
	2253	0.0	0		2308	1.0	30
6 M	0504	8.2	250	21 Tu	0513	7.2	220
	1115	0.7	20		1119	1.6	50
	1723	8.2	250		1730	7.2	220
	2339	0.3	10		2345	1.3	40
7 Tu	0554	7.9	240	22 W	0554	6.9	210
	1204	1.0	30		1156	2.0	60
	1811	7.5	230		1808	6.9	210
8 W	0034	0.7	20	23 Th	0023	1.6	50
	0651	7.2	220		0636	6.2	190
	1258	1.6	50		1234	2.3	70
	1908	7.2	220		1851	6.6	200
9 Th	0136	1.3	40	24 F	0106	2.3	70
	0753	6.6	200		0721	5.9	180
	1404	2.3	70		1319	2.6	80
	2013	6.6	200		1939	6.2	190
10 F ◑	0253	1.6	50	25 Sa	0158	2.3	70
	0906	6.2	190		0817	5.6	170
	1524	2.6	80		1415	3.0	90
	2132	6.2	190		2038	5.9	180
11 Sa	0417	2.0	60	26 Su ◐	0304	2.6	80
	1028	5.9	180		0923	5.6	170
	1651	2.6	80		1530	3.0	90
	2253	6.2	190		2147	5.9	180
12 Su	0538	2.0	60	27 M	0419	2.6	80
	1145	6.2	190		1034	5.6	170
	1802	2.3	70		1647	3.0	90
					2254	5.9	180
13 M	0002	6.6	200	28 Tu	0526	2.3	70
	0639	1.6	50		1136	5.9	180
	1243	6.2	190		1753	2.3	70
	1858	2.0	60		2356	6.6	200
14 Tu	0058	6.9	210	29 W	0623	2.0	60
	0724	1.6	50		1230	6.6	200
	1326	6.6	200		1845	2.0	60
	1943	1.6	50				
15 W	0143	7.2	220	30 Th	0051	6.9	210
	0804	1.3	40		0711	1.3	40
	1404	6.9	210		1317	7.2	220
	2019	1.3	40		1934	1.3	40

December

Day	Time	ft	cm	Day	Time	ft	cm
1 F	0141	7.5	230	16 Sa	0236	6.9	210
	0800	1.0	30		0851	1.6	50
	1404	7.5	230		1449	7.2	220
	2019	0.7	20		2109	1.3	40
2 Sa	0228	7.9	240	17 Su	0309	7.2	220
	0845	0.7	20		0921	1.3	40
	1451	8.2	250		1523	7.5	230
	2106	0.3	10		2143	1.0	30
3 Su O	0315	8.2	250	18 M ●	0345	7.2	220
	0928	0.3	10		0954	1.3	40
	1536	8.2	250		1558	7.5	230
	2153	0.0	0		2215	1.0	30
4 M	0402	8.5	260	19 Tu	0419	7.2	220
	1015	0.3	10		1026	1.3	40
	1621	8.5	260		1634	7.5	230
	2241	0.0	0		2253	1.0	30
5 Tu	0453	8.2	250	20 W	0456	7.2	220
	1102	0.7	20		1102	1.3	40
	1709	8.2	250		1709	7.5	230
	2332	0.0	0		2326	1.3	40
6 W	0543	7.9	240	21 Th	0534	6.9	210
	1153	1.0	30		1138	1.6	50
	1800	7.9	240		1749	7.2	220
7 Th	0024	0.7	20	22 F	0002	1.3	40
	0638	7.2	220		0611	6.9	210
	1247	1.3	40		1213	2.0	60
	1856	7.5	230		1826	6.9	210
8 F	0124	1.0	30	23 Sa	0041	1.6	50
	0736	6.9	210		0656	6.6	200
	1347	2.0	60		1254	2.3	70
	1956	6.9	210		1909	6.6	200
9 Sa	0230	1.6	50	24 Su	0124	2.0	60
	0841	6.2	190		0743	6.2	190
	1456	2.3	70		1339	2.3	70
	2102	6.6	200		2000	6.2	190
10 Su ◑	0347	2.0	60	25 M	0217	2.3	70
	0953	5.9	180		0838	5.9	180
	1611	2.3	70		1436	2.6	80
	2217	6.2	190		2058	6.2	190
11 M	0500	2.0	60	26 Tu ◐	0319	2.3	70
	1102	5.9	180		0941	5.9	180
	1724	2.3	70		1545	2.6	80
	2328	6.2	190		2204	6.2	190
12 Tu	0604	2.0	60	27 W	0432	2.3	70
	1206	6.2	190		1047	5.9	180
	1826	2.3	70		1658	2.3	70
					2313	6.2	190
13 W	0028	6.6	200	28 Th	0541	2.0	60
	0658	2.0	60		1153	6.2	190
	1256	6.2	190		1808	2.0	60
	1917	2.0	60				
14 Th	0117	6.6	200	29 F	0017	6.9	210
	0741	2.0	60		0643	1.6	50
	1338	6.6	200		1251	6.9	210
	1958	1.6	50		1908	1.3	40
15 F	0158	6.9	210	30 Sa	0117	7.2	220
	0815	1.6	50		0738	1.3	40
	1413	6.9	210		1343	7.2	220
	2036	1.3	40		2002	1.0	30
				31 Su	0211	7.5	230
					0828	1.0	30
					1434	7.9	240
					2054	0.3	10

Time meridian 45° W. 0000 is midnight. 1200 is noon. Times are not adjusted for Daylight Saving Time.
Heights are referred to the chart datum of soundings.

Rio de Janeiro, Brazil, 2017

Times and Heights of High and Low Waters

January

Day	Time	Height (ft)	Height (cm)
1 Su	0436	3.9	120
	1134	1.3	40
	1628	3.9	120
	2345	0.3	10
2 M	0513	3.6	110
	1219	1.6	50
	1706	3.6	110
3 Tu	0038	0.7	20
	0558	3.6	110
	1311	1.6	50
	1751	3.6	110
4 W	0139	0.7	20
	0643	3.3	100
	1409	1.6	50
	1838	3.3	100
5 Th	0243	1.0	30
	0734	3.0	90
	1513	1.6	50
	1939	3.0	90
6 F	0349	1.0	30
	0836	3.0	90
	1619	1.6	50
	2111	3.0	90
7 Sa	0453	1.0	30
	1015	3.0	90
	1724	1.3	40
8 Su	0013	3.3	100
	0556	1.0	30
	1228	3.0	90
	1824	1.0	30
9 M	0100	3.6	110
	0658	1.0	30
	1241	3.0	90
	1919	0.7	20
10 Tu	0136	3.6	110
	0756	1.0	30
	1311	3.3	100
	2009	0.3	10
11 W	0209	3.9	120
	0849	1.0	30
	1347	3.6	110
	2100	0.0	0
12 Th	0241	3.9	120
	0938	1.0	30
	1421	3.6	110
	2149	0.0	0
13 F	0313	3.9	120
	1019	1.3	40
	1500	3.9	120
	2234	0.3	10
14 Sa	0353	3.9	120
	1102	1.3	40
	1539	3.9	120
	2315	0.3	10
15 Su	0426	3.6	110
	1143	1.6	50
	1615	3.9	120
16 M	0000	0.7	20
	0504	3.6	110
	1219	1.6	50
	1658	3.9	120
17 Tu	0049	1.0	30
	0545	3.3	100
	1258	1.6	50
	1739	3.6	110
18 W	0141	1.3	40
	0623	3.3	100
	1347	2.0	60
	1823	3.3	100
19 Th	0239	1.6	50
	0708	3.0	90
	1451	2.0	60
	1915	3.0	90
20 F	0341	1.6	50
	0804	3.0	90
	1558	1.6	50
	2032	3.0	90
21 Sa	0443	1.6	50
	0917	2.6	80
	1702	1.6	50
	2224	3.0	90
22 Su	0539	1.6	50
	1053	3.0	90
	1758	1.3	40
23 M	0004	3.0	90
	0628	1.6	50
	1202	3.0	90
	1845	1.0	30
24 Tu	0051	3.3	100
	0713	1.3	40
	1249	3.3	100
	1924	0.7	20
25 W	0126	3.6	110
	0756	1.3	40
	1324	3.6	110
	2002	0.3	10
26 Th	0202	3.9	120
	0834	1.0	30
	1400	3.9	120
	2041	0.3	10
27 F	0236	3.9	120
	0911	1.0	30
	1436	3.9	120
	2117	0.0	0
28 Sa	0309	4.3	130
	0951	1.0	30
	1508	4.3	130
	2156	0.0	0
29 Su	0345	4.3	130
	1026	1.0	30
	1543	4.3	130
	2239	0.0	0
30 M	0417	3.9	120
	1106	1.0	30
	1613	4.3	130
	2323	0.3	10
31 Tu	0454	3.9	120
	1151	1.3	40
	1653	3.9	120

February

Day	Time	Height (ft)	Height (cm)
1 W	0013	0.7	20
	0526	3.6	110
	1239	1.3	40
	1728	3.9	120
2 Th	0111	0.7	20
	0604	3.3	100
	1338	1.6	50
	1809	3.6	110
3 F	0215	1.0	30
	0647	3.0	90
	1443	1.6	50
	1902	3.3	100
4 Sa	0324	1.3	40
	0734	3.0	90
	1054	2.3	70
	1554*	1.6	50
5 Su	0006	2.6	80
	0438	1.3	40
	0839	2.6	80
	1100	2.3	70
	1254*	2.6	80
6 M	0100	3.3	100
	0549	1.3	40
	1319	2.6	80
	1811	1.0	30
7 Tu	0138	3.3	100
	0653	1.3	40
	1308	3.0	90
	1909	0.7	20
8 W	0156	3.6	110
	0749	1.3	40
	1308	3.3	100
	2002	0.3	10
9 Th	0209	3.6	110
	0836	1.0	30
	1338	3.6	110
	2051	0.0	0
10 F	0228	3.9	120
	0915	1.0	30
	1409	3.9	120
	2132	0.0	0
11 Sa	0258	3.9	120
	0956	1.0	30
	1449	4.3	130
	2211	0.0	0
12 Su	0328	3.9	120
	1032	1.0	30
	1523	4.3	130
	2251	0.3	10
13 M	0402	3.9	120
	1102	1.3	40
	1600	4.3	130
	2328	0.7	20
14 Tu	0438	3.6	110
	1134	1.3	40
	1639	3.9	120
15 W	0006	1.0	30
	0509	3.6	110
	1151	1.6	50
	1713	3.9	120
16 Th	0051	1.3	40
	0549	3.3	100
	1230	1.6	50
	1756	3.6	110
17 F	0151	1.6	50
	0623	3.0	90
	1343	1.6	50
	1839	3.3	100
	2309	2.0	60
18 Sa	0004	2.0	60
	0258	2.0	60
	0704	3.0	90
	1502	1.6	50
	1938*	3.0	90
19 Su	0024	2.3	70
	0402	2.0	60
	0802	2.6	80
	1617	1.6	50
	2119*	2.6	80
20 M	0030	2.6	80
	0506	2.0	60
	0945	2.6	80
	1723	1.3	40
21 Tu	0038	3.0	90
	0604	1.6	50
	1158	3.0	90
	1815	1.0	30
22 W	0058	3.3	100
	0653	1.3	40
	1241	3.3	100
	1900	0.7	20
23 Th	0123	3.6	110
	0734	1.3	40
	1315	3.6	110
	1941	0.3	10
24 F	0153	3.9	120
	0809	1.0	30
	1351	3.9	120
	2017	0.0	0
25 Sa	0221	3.9	120
	0847	1.0	30
	1421	4.3	130
	2056	0.0	0
26 Su	0253	4.3	130
	0923	0.7	20
	1454	4.3	130
	2138	0.0	0
27 M	0323	4.3	130
	1000	0.7	20
	1524	4.3	130
	2217	0.0	0
28 Tu	0354	4.3	130
	1039	0.7	20
	1558	4.3	130
	2302	0.3	10

March

Day	Time	Height (ft)	Height (cm)
1 W	0423	3.9	120
	1121	1.0	30
	1632	4.3	130
	2354	0.7	20
2 Th	0456	3.6	110
	1208	1.0	30
	1706	3.9	120
3 F	0053	1.0	30
	0526	3.3	100
	1304	1.3	40
	1751	3.6	110
4 Sa	0158	1.3	40
	0604	3.0	90
	1011	2.0	60
	1106	2.0	60
	1411*	1.6	50
5 Su	0308	1.6	50
	0653	2.6	80
	1011	2.0	60
	1213	2.0	60
	1534*	1.6	50
6 M	0028	3.0	90
	0424	1.6	50
	0751	2.6	80
	1039	2.0	60
	1258*	2.3	70
7 Tu	0108	3.3	100
	0539	1.6	50
	1051	2.3	70
	1321	2.6	80
	1800	1.0	30
8 W	0141	3.3	100
	0641	1.6	50
	1308	3.0	90
	1900	0.7	20
9 Th	0147	3.6	110
	0730	1.3	40
	1253	3.3	100
	1949	0.3	10
10 F	0147	3.6	110
	0811	1.0	30
	1319	3.6	110
	2032	0.3	10
11 Sa	0202	3.9	120
	0853	1.0	30
	1354	3.9	120
	2109	0.0	0
12 Su	0228	3.9	120
	0924	1.0	30
	1428	4.3	130
	2149	0.3	10
13 M	0300	3.9	120
	0956	1.0	30
	1504	4.6	140
	2221	0.7	20
14 Tu	0332	3.9	120
	1026	1.0	30
	1543	4.3	130
	2253	0.7	20
15 W	0404	3.9	120
	1047	1.0	30
	1613	4.3	130
	2328	1.0	30
16 Th	0439	3.6	110
	1115	1.3	40
	1653	3.9	120
17 F	0006	1.3	40
	0508	3.3	100
	1130	1.3	40
	1724	3.6	110
18 Sa	0102	1.6	50
	0545	3.3	100
	1123	1.6	50
	1804	3.3	100
	2223	2.0	60
19 Su	0000	2.0	60
	0215	2.0	60
	0617	3.0	90
	1113	1.6	50
	1413*	1.6	50
20 M	0017	2.3	70
	0332	2.0	60
	0704	2.6	80
	1536	1.6	50
	2008*	2.6	80
21 Tu	0036	2.6	80
	0439	2.0	60
	0819	2.6	80
	1645	1.3	40
22 W	0041	3.0	90
	0538	1.6	50
	1156	2.6	80
	1743	1.0	30
23 Th	0051	3.3	100
	0623	1.6	50
	1230	3.0	90
	1830	0.7	20
24 F	0108	3.6	110
	0704	1.3	40
	1300	3.6	110
	1911	0.3	10
25 Sa	0132	3.9	120
	0743	1.0	30
	1330	3.9	120
	1954	0.0	0
26 Su	0200	3.9	120
	0817	0.7	20
	1402	4.3	130
	2034	0.0	0
27 M	0226	4.3	130
	0856	0.7	20
	1434	4.6	140
	2115	0.0	0
28 Tu	0256	4.3	130
	0934	0.7	20
	1506	4.6	140
	2158	0.0	0
29 W	0323	3.9	120
	1013	0.7	20
	1539	4.6	140
	2247	0.3	10
30 Th	0354	3.9	120
	1058	0.7	20
	1611	4.3	130
	2339	0.7	20
31 F	0421	3.6	110
	1149	1.0	30
	1653	3.9	120

Time meridian 45° W. 0000 is midnight. 1200 is noon. Times are not adjusted for Daylight Saving Time.
Heights are referred to the chart datum of soundings.
* See Page 320 for the remaining tides on this day.

Rio de Janeiro, Brazil, 2017

Times and Heights of High and Low Waters

April

Day	Time	ft	cm
1 Sa	0039	1.3	40
	0458	3.3	100
	1247	1.3	40
	1730	3.6	110
2 Su	0149	1.6	50
	0534	3.0	90
	0945	1.6	50
	1104	1.6	50
	1356*	1.3	40
3 M ◑	0300	2.0	60
	0613	2.6	80
	0958	1.6	50
	1202	2.0	60
	1511*	1.3	40
4 Tu	0021	3.0	90
	0411	2.0	60
	0713	2.6	80
	1019	2.0	60
	1245*	2.3	70
5 W	0100	3.3	100
	0521	1.6	50
	0902	2.3	70
	1053	2.3	70
	1300*	2.6	80
6 Th	0121	3.3	100
	0617	1.6	50
	1211	3.0	90
	1841	0.7	20
7 F	0111	3.3	100
	0704	1.3	40
	1221	3.3	100
	1926	0.7	20
8 Sa	0108	3.6	110
	0747	1.0	30
	1256	3.6	110
	2008	0.3	10
9 Su	0128	3.9	120
	0819	1.0	30
	1332	3.9	120
	2047	0.3	10
10 M	0158	3.9	120
	0853	0.7	20
	1408	4.3	130
	2119	0.7	20
11 Tu ○	0230	3.9	120
	0923	0.7	20
	1447	4.3	130
	2153	0.7	20
12 W	0302	3.9	120
	0951	0.7	20
	1519	4.3	130
	2224	1.0	30
13 Th	0336	3.9	120
	1023	0.7	20
	1556	4.3	130
	2254	1.3	40
14 F	0404	3.6	110
	1047	1.0	30
	1628	3.9	120
	2336	1.6	50
15 Sa	0439	3.6	110
	1128	1.0	30
	1702	3.6	110
16 Su	0034	2.0	60
	0508	3.3	100
	1219	1.3	40
	1741	3.3	100
	2206*	2.0	60
17 M	0145	2.0	60
	0547	3.0	90
	1332	1.6	50
	1823	3.0	90
	2204*	2.3	70
18 Tu	0256	2.0	60
	0626	2.6	80
	1449	1.6	50
	1928	2.6	80
	2200	2.6	80
19 W ◐	0002	2.6	80
	0400	2.0	60
	0730	2.6	80
	1558	1.3	40
20 Th	0011	3.0	90
	0500	1.6	50
	1111	2.6	80
	1700	1.3	40
21 F	0023	3.3	100
	0549	1.6	50
	1158	3.0	90
	1756	0.7	20
22 Sa	0041	3.6	110
	0630	1.3	40
	1234	3.3	100
	1843	0.3	10
23 Su	0106	3.9	120
	0708	1.0	30
	1306	3.9	120
	1926	0.3	10
24 M	0132	3.9	120
	0751	0.7	20
	1341	4.3	130
	2009	0.0	0
25 Tu	0158	3.9	120
	0828	0.3	10
	1413	4.3	130
	2056	0.0	0
26 W ●	0224	3.9	120
	0909	0.3	10
	1449	4.6	140
	2143	0.3	10
27 Th	0256	3.9	120
	0956	0.3	10
	1521	4.3	130
	2234	0.7	20
28 F	0323	3.6	110
	1043	0.7	20
	1600	4.3	130
	2326	1.0	30
29 Sa	0358	3.6	110
	1136	0.7	20
	1639	3.9	120
30 Su	0026	1.6	50
	0432	3.3	100
	1236	1.0	30
	1719	3.6	110
	2154	2.6	80

May

Day	Time	ft	cm
1 M	0136	2.0	60
	0509	3.0	90
	1039	1.6	50
	1343	1.3	40
	1808*	3.0	90
2 Tu ○	0245	2.0	60
	0600	3.0	90
	1000	1.6	50
	1139	2.0	60
	1454*	1.3	40
3 W ◐	0002	3.0	90
	0354	2.0	60
	0702	2.6	80
	1036	2.0	60
	1211*	2.0	60
4 Th	0043	3.0	90
	0456	2.0	60
	0836	2.6	80
	1713	1.0	30
5 F	0049	3.0	90
	0551	1.6	50
	1034	3.0	90
	1811	1.0	30
6 Sa	0011	3.3	100
	0634	1.3	40
	1143	3.3	100
	1900	1.0	30
7 Su	0024	3.3	100
	0711	1.0	30
	1228	3.6	110
	1943	0.7	20
8 M	0056	3.6	110
	0749	1.0	30
	1309	3.9	120
	2019	0.7	20
9 Tu	0126	3.9	120
	0821	0.7	20
	1351	4.3	130
	2053	1.0	30
10 W ○	0200	3.9	120
	0854	0.7	20
	1426	4.3	130
	2126	1.0	30
11 Th	0236	3.9	120
	0928	0.7	20
	1502	4.3	130
	2158	1.0	30
12 F	0306	3.9	120
	1000	0.7	20
	1538	4.3	130
	2236	1.3	40
13 Sa	0341	3.6	110
	1023	0.7	20
	1609	3.9	120
	2315	1.6	50
14 Su	0409	3.6	110
	1113	1.0	30
	1649	3.6	110
15 M	0004	1.6	50
	0447	3.3	100
	1156	1.0	30
	1721	3.6	110
16 Tu	0104	2.0	60
	0519	3.0	90
	1254	1.3	40
	1804	3.3	100
17 W	0209	2.0	60
	0602	3.0	90
	1400	1.3	40
	1902	3.0	90
18 Th ◐	0313	2.0	60
	0700	2.6	80
	1508	1.3	40
	2041	3.0	90
	2200	3.0	90
19 F	0411	1.6	50
	0830	2.6	80
	1615	1.0	30
	2341	3.3	100
20 Sa	0504	1.6	50
	1054	3.0	90
	1715	1.0	30
21 Su	0006	3.3	100
	0553	1.3	40
	1200	3.3	100
	1809	0.7	20
22 M	0034	3.6	110
	0638	1.0	30
	1243	3.6	110
	1902	0.3	10
23 Tu	0100	3.6	110
	0721	0.7	20
	1323	3.9	120
	1953	0.3	10
24 W	0128	3.6	110
	0806	0.3	10
	1400	4.3	130
	2043	0.3	10
25 Th ●	0158	3.6	110
	0854	0.3	10
	1438	4.3	130
	2132	0.7	20
26 F	0226	3.6	110
	0943	0.3	10
	1511	4.3	130
	2221	1.0	30
27 Sa	0302	3.6	110
	1034	0.3	10
	1554	3.9	120
	2313	1.3	40
28 Su	0339	3.6	110
	1124	0.7	20
	1632	3.9	120
29 M	0009	1.6	50
	0415	3.3	100
	1219	0.7	20
	1713	3.6	110
30 Tu	0109	2.0	60
	0500	3.3	100
	1319	1.0	30
	1802	3.3	100
	2108*	2.6	80
31 W	0211	2.0	60
	0553	3.0	90
	1423	1.3	40
	1900	3.0	90
	2141*	2.6	80

June

Day	Time	ft	cm
1 Th ◑	0311	2.0	60
	0651	3.0	90
	1534	1.3	40
	2011	2.6	80
	2213	2.6	80
2 F	0019	2.6	80
	0409	2.0	60
	0802	3.0	90
	1641	1.3	40
	2151	2.6	80
3 Sa	0506	1.6	50
	0934	3.0	90
	1743	1.3	40
	2256	3.0	90
4 Su	0556	1.3	40
	1100	3.3	100
	1834	1.3	40
	2341	3.3	100
5 M	0639	1.0	30
	1202	3.3	100
	1913	1.3	40
6 Tu	0019	3.6	110
	0717	1.0	30
	1253	3.6	110
	1954	1.0	30
7 W	0100	3.6	110
	0754	0.7	20
	1334	3.9	120
	2028	1.0	30
8 Th	0138	3.9	120
	0832	0.3	10
	1409	3.9	120
	2102	1.0	30
9 F ○	0209	3.9	120
	0908	0.3	10
	1451	3.9	120
	2139	1.3	40
10 Sa	0249	3.9	120
	0943	0.3	10
	1521	3.9	120
	2213	1.3	40
11 Su	0319	3.9	120
	1021	0.7	20
	1558	3.9	120
	2254	1.3	40
12 M	0354	3.6	110
	1056	0.7	20
	1632	3.9	120
	2339	1.6	50
13 Tu	0428	3.6	110
	1138	0.7	20
	1708	3.6	110
14 W	0030	1.6	50
	0504	3.3	100
	1226	1.0	30
	1753	3.6	110
15 Th	0128	2.0	60
	0551	3.3	100
	1324	1.0	30
	1839	3.3	100
16 F ◑	0226	2.0	60
	0639	3.0	90
	1430	1.0	30
	1938	3.0	90
17 Sa ◐	0324	1.6	50
	0745	3.0	90
	1538	1.0	30
	2106	3.0	90
18 Su	0419	1.6	50
	0913	3.0	90
	1643	1.0	30
	2315	3.0	90
19 M	0513	1.3	40
	1121	3.3	100
	1747	1.0	30
	2356	3.3	100
20 Tu	0606	1.0	30
	1230	3.6	110
	1845	1.0	30
21 W	0030	3.3	100
	0700	0.7	20
	1317	3.9	120
	1939	0.7	20
22 Th	0102	3.3	100
	0753	0.3	10
	1358	3.9	120
	2030	0.7	20
23 F ●	0136	3.6	110
	0845	0.3	10
	1436	3.9	120
	2121	1.0	30
24 Sa	0209	3.6	110
	0934	0.0	0
	1511	3.9	120
	2209	1.0	30
25 Su	0251	3.6	110
	1023	0.3	10
	1551	3.9	120
	2300	1.3	40
26 M	0324	3.6	110
	1111	0.3	10
	1624	3.9	120
	2353	1.6	50
27 Tu	0406	3.6	110
	1202	0.7	20
	1702	3.6	110
28 W	0043	1.6	50
	0453	3.6	110
	1254	1.0	30
	1745	3.3	100
29 Th	0134	2.0	60
	0539	3.3	100
	1349	1.3	40
	1826	3.0	90
	2211*	2.3	70
30 F ◑	0226	2.0	60
	0626	3.3	100
	1451	1.3	40
	1915	3.0	90
	2302	2.3	70

Time meridian 45° W. 0000 is midnight. 1200 is noon. Times are not adjusted for Daylight Saving Time.
Heights are referred to the chart datum of soundings.
* See Page 320 for the remaining tides on this day.

Rio de Janeiro, Brazil, 2017

Times and Heights of High and Low Waters

July

Day	Time	ft	cm		Day	Time	ft	cm
1 Sa	0004	2.3	70		16 Su ◑	0243	1.6	50
	0323	2.0	60			0706	3.3	100
	0726	3.0	90			1502	1.3	40
	1556	1.6	50			1947	3.0	90
	2019	2.6	80					
2 Su	0419	1.6	50		17 M	0345	1.6	50
	0843	3.0	90			0811	3.0	90
	1700	1.6	50			1611	1.3	40
	2141	3.0	90			2056	3.0	90
3 M	0511	1.6	50		18 Tu	0447	1.3	40
	1011	3.0	90			1017	3.0	90
	1800	1.6	50			1723	1.3	40
	2256	3.0	90			2311	3.0	90
4 Tu	0602	1.3	40		19 W	0549	1.0	30
	1141	3.3	100			1300	3.3	100
	1851	1.6	50			1830	1.3	40
	2353	3.3	100					
5 W	0651	1.0	30		20 Th	0017	3.0	90
	1239	3.3	100			0647	0.7	20
	1930	1.3	40			1343	3.6	110
						1928	1.0	30
6 Th	0038	3.6	110		21 F	0049	3.3	100
	0732	0.7	20			0743	0.3	10
	1323	3.6	110			1415	3.9	120
	2006	1.3	40			2021	1.0	30
7 F	0115	3.6	110		22 Sa	0123	3.3	100
	0809	0.3	10			0836	0.0	0
	1402	3.9	120			1439	3.9	120
	2043	1.3	40			2108	1.0	30
8 Sa	0156	3.9	120		23 Su ●	0200	3.6	110
	0849	0.3	10			0923	0.0	0
	1438	3.9	120			1506	3.9	120
	2117	1.0	30			2156	1.0	30
9 Su ○	0230	3.9	120		24 M	0239	3.9	120
	0924	0.3	10			1009	0.0	0
	1509	3.9	120			1538	3.9	120
	2154	1.3	40			2239	1.3	40
10 M	0304	3.9	120		25 Tu	0315	3.9	120
	1000	0.3	10			1056	0.3	10
	1545	3.9	120			1606	3.9	120
	2230	1.3	40			2317	1.3	40
11 Tu	0339	3.9	120		26 W	0358	3.9	120
	1038	0.3	10			1139	0.3	10
	1617	3.9	120			1643	3.6	110
	2308	1.3	40			2358	1.6	50
12 W	0411	3.9	120		27 Th	0438	3.9	120
	1117	0.3	10			1221	1.0	30
	1654	3.9	120			1715	3.6	110
	2353	1.3	40					
13 Th	0453	3.6	110		28 F	0041	1.6	50
	1202	0.7	20			0517	3.6	110
	1728	3.6	110			1304	1.3	40
						1756	3.3	100
						2224*	2.0	60
14 F	0045	1.6	50		29 Sa	0128	1.6	50
	0530	3.6	110			0602	3.6	110
	1254	0.7	20			1356	1.6	50
	1806	3.6	110			1836	3.0	90
						2300	2.0	60
15 Sa	0141	1.6	50		30 Su ◐	0013	2.0	60
	0611	3.3	100			0224	2.0	60
	1356	1.0	30			0656	3.3	100
	1854	3.3	100			1123	2.0	60
						1251*	2.0	60
					31 M	0330	1.6	50
						0756	3.0	90
						1202	2.3	70
						1615	2.0	60
						2024	2.6	80

August

Day	Time	ft	cm		Day	Time	ft	cm
1 Tu	0434	1.6	50		16 W	0017	2.3	70
	0921	2.6	80			0421	1.3	40
	1726	2.0	60			0915	3.0	90
	2202	2.6	80			1249	3.0	90
						1709*	1.6	50
2 W	0530	1.3	40		17 Th	0053	2.6	80
	1141	3.0	90			0532	1.0	30
	1821	1.6	50			1332	3.3	100
	2328	3.0	90			1821	1.3	40
3 Th	0621	1.0	30		18 F	0049	2.6	80
	1245	3.3	100			0636	0.7	20
	1906	1.6	50			1400	3.6	110
						1919	1.3	40
4 F	0023	3.3	100		19 Sa	0047	3.0	90
	0706	0.7	20			0732	0.3	10
	1321	3.6	110			1417	3.9	120
	1947	1.3	40			2008	1.0	30
5 Sa	0104	3.6	110		20 Su	0115	3.6	110
	0747	0.3	10			0821	0.0	0
	1356	3.9	120			1426	3.9	120
	2019	1.3	40			2053	1.0	30
6 Su	0143	3.6	110		21 M ●	0151	3.9	120
	0824	0.3	10			0908	0.0	0
	1424	3.9	120			1447	3.9	120
	2054	1.0	30			2132	1.0	30
7 M ○	0215	3.9	120		22 Tu	0223	3.9	120
	0902	0.0	0			0953	0.0	0
	1458	4.3	130			1511	3.9	120
	2128	1.0	30			2208	1.0	30
8 Tu	0251	3.9	120		23 W	0302	4.3	130
	0939	0.0	0			1034	0.3	10
	1526	4.3	130			1545	3.9	120
	2202	1.0	30			2243	1.3	40
9 W	0323	4.3	130		24 Th	0341	4.3	130
	1015	0.0	0			1109	0.7	20
	1600	4.3	130			1611	3.9	120
	2239	1.0	30			2311	1.3	40
10 Th	0358	4.3	130		25 F	0415	4.3	130
	1056	0.3	10			1147	1.0	30
	1630	3.9	120			1649	3.6	110
	2319	1.0	30			2334	1.3	40
11 F	0434	3.9	120		26 Sa	0458	3.9	120
	1141	0.3	10			1221	1.3	40
	1702	3.9	120			1717	3.6	110
						2219	1.6	50
12 Sa	0004	1.3	40		27 Su	0539	3.6	110
	0508	3.9	120			1036	1.6	50
	1230	0.7	20			1756	3.3	100
	1736	3.6	110			2241	1.6	50
13 Su	0058	1.3	40		28 M	0621	3.3	100
	0553	3.6	110			1049	2.0	60
	1330	1.0	30			1251	2.0	60
	1809	3.3	100			1409	2.0	60
						1834*	3.0	90
14 M ◐	0202	1.3	40		29 Tu ◐	0243	1.6	50
	0639	3.3	100			0711	3.0	90
	1441	1.3	40			1104	2.3	70
	1856	3.0	90			1300	2.3	70
						1538*	2.0	60
15 Tu	0311	1.3	40		30 W	0354	1.6	50
	0738	3.0	90			0830	2.6	80
	1556	1.6	50			1106	2.6	80
	1951	2.6	80			1300	2.6	80
	2300	2.3	70			1654*	2.0	60
					31 Th	0456	1.3	40
						1253	3.0	90
						1756	2.0	60
						2319	2.6	80

September

Day	Time	ft	cm		Day	Time	ft	cm
1 F	0553	1.0	30		16 Sa	0051	2.6	80
	1256	3.3	100			0619	0.7	20
	1845	1.6	50			1349	3.6	110
						1904	1.3	40
2 Sa	0015	3.0	90		17 Su	0034	3.3	100
	0639	0.7	20			0715	0.3	10
	1315	3.6	110			1351	3.6	110
	1921	1.3	40			1951	1.0	30
3 Su	0053	3.3	100		18 M	0058	3.6	110
	0719	0.7	20			0804	0.3	10
	1341	3.9	120			1356	3.9	120
	1956	1.0	30			2028	1.0	30
4 M	0124	3.6	110		19 Tu	0130	3.9	120
	0758	0.3	10			0849	0.0	0
	1408	3.9	120			1415	3.9	120
	2028	1.0	30			2102	1.0	30
5 Tu	0200	3.9	120		20 W ●	0204	4.3	130
	0838	0.0	0			0928	0.3	10
	1438	4.3	130			1445	3.9	120
	2100	0.7	20			2138	1.0	30
6 W ○	0232	4.3	130		21 Th	0245	4.3	130
	0915	0.0	0			1004	0.3	10
	1504	4.3	130			1511	4.3	130
	2136	0.7	20			2204	1.0	30
7 Th	0304	4.3	130		22 F	0319	4.3	130
	0954	0.0	0			1041	0.7	20
	1536	4.3	130			1547	3.9	120
	2209	0.7	20			2230	1.0	30
8 F	0339	4.3	130		23 Sa	0358	4.3	130
	1036	0.3	10			1113	1.0	30
	1602	4.3	130			1615	3.9	120
	2249	0.7	20			2239	1.0	30
9 Sa	0411	4.3	130		24 Su	0438	3.9	120
	1121	0.3	10			1141	1.3	40
	1634	3.9	120			1651	3.6	110
	2336	1.0	30			2230	1.3	40
10 Su	0451	3.9	120		25 M	0511	3.6	110
	1211	1.0	30			1224	1.6	50
	1702	3.6	110			1721	3.3	100
						2236	1.3	40
11 M	0032	1.3	40		26 Tu	0556	3.3	100
	0528	3.6	110			1021	2.0	60
	1311	1.3	40			1202	2.0	60
	1739	3.3	100			1336	2.0	60
						1756	3.0	90
12 Tu	0139	1.3	40		27 W ◐	0156	1.6	50
	0611	3.3	100			0645	3.0	90
	1423	1.6	50			1024	2.3	70
	1813	3.0	90			1223	2.3	70
	2211*	2.0	60			1456*	2.3	70
13 W ◐	0254	1.3	40		28 Th	0309	1.6	50
	0709	3.0	90			0753	2.6	80
	0958	2.6	80			1026	2.6	80
	1158	2.6	80			1238	2.6	80
	1545*	2.0	60			1609*	2.0	60
14 Th	0021	1.3	40		29 F	0415	1.3	40
	0404	1.3	40			1241	3.0	90
	1253	3.3	100			1719	2.0	60
	1700	2.0	60			2308	2.6	80
	2024*	2.3	70					
15 F	0053	2.6	80		30 Sa	0511	1.0	30
	0515	1.0	30			1241	3.3	100
	1326	3.3	100			1811	1.6	50
	1809	1.6	50			2359	3.0	90

Time meridian 45° W. 0000 is midnight. 1200 is noon. Times are not adjusted for Daylight Saving Time.
Heights are referred to the chart datum of soundings.
* See Page 320 for the remaining tides on this day.

Rio de Janeiro, Brazil, 2017

Times and Heights of High and Low Waters

October

Day	Time	ft	cm
1 Su	0604	1.0	30
	1254	3.6	110
	1853	1.3	40
2 M	0034	3.3	100
	0649	0.7	20
	1317	3.9	120
	1926	1.0	30
3 Tu	0106	3.6	110
	0730	0.3	10
	1343	3.9	120
	2000	0.7	20
4 W	0139	3.9	120
	0809	0.0	0
	1409	4.3	130
	2034	0.7	20
5 Th ○	0211	4.3	130
	0853	0.0	0
	1439	4.3	130
	2108	0.3	10
6 F	0247	4.6	140
	0936	0.0	0
	1506	4.3	130
	2147	0.3	10
7 Sa	0319	4.6	140
	1017	0.3	10
	1536	4.3	130
	2228	0.7	20
8 Su	0356	4.3	130
	1106	0.7	20
	1604	3.9	120
	2315	0.7	20
9 M	0432	3.9	120
	1200	1.0	30
	1638	3.6	110
10 Tu	0011	1.0	30
	0511	3.6	110
	1300	1.6	50
	1708	3.3	100
11 W	0121	1.0	30
	0600	3.3	100
	1039	2.6	80
	1409	2.0	60
	1753*	3.0	90
12 Th ◐	0239	1.3	40
	0702	3.0	90
	0915	2.6	80
	1151	3.0	90
	1528*	2.0	60
13 F	0000	2.3	70
	0353	1.0	30
	1238	3.3	100
	1647	2.0	60
	2004*	2.6	80
14 Sa	0028	2.3	70
	0500	1.0	30
	1306	3.3	100
	1753	1.6	50
	2351	2.6	80
15 Su	0602	0.7	20
	1319	3.3	100
	1843	1.3	40
	2356	3.3	100
16 M	0656	0.7	20
	1306	3.6	110
	1923	1.3	40
17 Tu	0030	3.6	110
	0743	0.3	10
	1315	3.6	110
	2000	1.0	30
18 W	0106	3.9	120
	0824	0.3	10
	1343	3.9	120
	2036	0.7	20
19 Th ●	0147	4.3	130
	0902	0.7	20
	1411	3.9	120
	2106	0.7	20
20 F	0223	4.3	130
	0941	0.7	20
	1449	4.3	130
	2138	0.7	20
21 Sa	0302	4.3	130
	1013	1.0	30
	1517	3.9	120
	2204	0.7	20
22 Su	0341	4.3	130
	1047	1.3	40
	1554	3.9	120
	2234	1.0	30
23 M	0415	3.9	120
	1124	1.3	40
	1623	3.6	110
	2313	1.0	30
24 Tu	0456	3.6	110
	1204	1.6	50
	1656	3.6	110
25 W	0008	1.3	40
	0536	3.3	100
	1302	2.0	60
	1728	3.3	100
26 Th	0119	1.3	40
	0617	3.0	90
	1021	2.3	70
	1413	2.0	60
	1806	3.0	90
27 F ◑	0230	1.3	40
	0717	3.0	90
	1019	2.6	80
	1151	2.6	80
	1530*	2.0	60
28 Sa	0336	1.3	40
	1154	3.0	90
	1639	2.0	60
	2100	2.6	80
29 Su	0434	1.0	30
	1202	3.0	90
	1732	1.6	50
	2323	3.0	90
30 M	0524	1.0	30
	1221	3.3	100
	1813	1.3	40
31 Tu	0004	3.3	100
	0613	0.7	20
	1247	3.6	110
	1853	1.0	30

November

Day	Time	ft	cm
1 W	0041	3.6	110
	0700	0.3	10
	1313	3.9	120
	1928	0.7	20
2 Th	0115	3.9	120
	0747	0.3	10
	1343	3.9	120
	2006	0.3	10
3 F	0153	4.3	130
	0830	0.3	10
	1409	4.3	130
	2047	0.3	10
4 Sa ○	0226	4.6	140
	0917	0.3	10
	1441	3.9	120
	2128	0.3	10
5 Su	0304	4.3	130
	1004	0.7	20
	1508	3.9	120
	2213	0.3	10
6 M	0343	4.3	130
	1058	1.0	30
	1543	3.9	120
	2304	0.7	20
7 Tu	0421	3.9	120
	1154	1.3	40
	1613	3.6	110
8 W	0004	0.7	20
	0506	3.6	110
	1254	1.6	50
	1654	3.3	100
9 Th	0108	1.0	30
	0558	3.3	100
	0906	2.6	80
	1009	2.6	80
	1358*	2.0	60
10 F ◐	0219	1.0	30
	0700	3.0	90
	0904	2.6	80
	1126	3.0	90
	1504*	2.0	60
11 Sa	0330	1.0	30
	1213	3.0	90
	1613	2.0	60
	1951	2.6	80
12 Su	0438	1.0	30
	1245	3.0	90
	1715	1.6	50
	2145	3.0	90
13 M	0538	1.0	30
	1223	3.0	90
	1808	1.3	40
	2309	3.3	100
14 Tu	0630	1.0	30
	1209	3.3	100
	1854	1.3	40
15 W	0002	3.6	110
	0717	0.7	20
	1238	3.6	110
	1934	1.0	30
16 Th	0047	3.9	120
	0800	0.7	20
	1309	3.6	110
	2008	0.7	20
17 F	0124	3.9	120
	0839	1.0	30
	1347	3.9	120
	2043	0.7	20
18 Sa ●	0206	4.3	130
	0915	1.0	30
	1421	3.9	120
	2115	0.3	10
19 Su	0247	4.3	130
	0953	1.0	30
	1458	3.9	120
	2149	0.7	20
20 M	0323	3.9	120
	1028	1.3	40
	1530	3.9	120
	2224	0.7	20
21 Tu	0400	3.9	120
	1104	1.3	40
	1602	3.9	120
	2304	0.7	20
22 W	0441	3.6	110
	1149	1.6	50
	1638	3.6	110
	2349	1.0	30
23 Th	0517	3.6	110
	1239	2.0	60
	1708	3.3	100
24 F	0047	1.0	30
	0602	3.3	100
	1339	2.0	60
	1751	3.0	90
25 Sa	0151	1.3	40
	0656	3.0	90
	1443	2.0	60
	1841	3.0	90
26 Su ◑	0253	1.3	40
	0804	3.0	90
	1547	2.0	60
	1956	2.6	80
27 M	0353	1.0	30
	1019	3.0	90
	1645	1.6	50
	2158	3.0	90
28 Tu	0449	1.0	30
	1132	3.3	100
	1734	1.3	40
	2324	3.3	100
29 W	0543	0.7	20
	1209	3.3	100
	1817	1.0	30
30 Th	0015	3.6	110
	0634	0.7	20
	1243	3.6	110
	1900	0.7	20

December

Day	Time	ft	cm
1 F	0058	3.9	120
	0723	0.3	10
	1315	3.6	110
	1947	0.3	10
2 Sa	0138	4.3	130
	0813	0.3	10
	1349	3.9	120
	2030	0.3	10
3 Su ○	0217	4.3	130
	0904	0.7	20
	1417	3.9	120
	2115	0.0	0
4 M	0258	4.3	130
	0958	0.7	20
	1453	3.9	120
	2206	0.0	0
5 Tu	0339	3.9	120
	1051	1.0	30
	1524	3.6	110
	2258	0.3	10
6 W	0419	3.9	120
	1143	1.3	40
	1602	3.6	110
	2356	0.3	10
7 Th	0502	3.6	110
	1238	1.6	50
	1645	3.6	110
8 F	0056	0.7	20
	0551	3.3	100
	1336	2.0	60
	1726	3.3	100
9 Sa	0158	1.0	30
	0643	3.0	90
	0941	2.6	80
	1056	2.6	80
	1436*	2.0	60
10 Su ◐	0302	1.0	30
	0741	3.0	90
	1008	2.6	80
	1156	2.6	80
	1538*	2.0	60
11 M	0404	1.3	40
	0854	2.6	80
	1109	2.6	80
	1639	2.0	60
	2053	3.0	90
12 Tu	0506	1.3	40
	1011	3.0	90
	1736	1.6	50
	2223	3.0	90
13 W	0602	1.3	40
	1111	3.0	90
	1823	1.3	40
	2336	3.3	100
14 Th	0654	1.3	40
	1200	3.3	100
	1906	1.0	30
15 F	0026	3.6	110
	0738	1.3	40
	1245	3.6	110
	1947	0.7	20
16 Sa	0111	3.9	120
	0815	1.0	30
	1323	3.9	120
	2023	0.3	10
17 Su	0156	3.9	120
	0854	1.0	30
	1402	3.9	120
	2058	0.3	10
18 M ●	0234	3.9	120
	0932	1.0	30
	1441	3.9	120
	2134	0.3	10
19 Tu	0309	3.9	120
	1008	1.3	40
	1511	3.9	120
	2209	0.3	10
20 W	0351	3.9	120
	1047	1.3	40
	1549	3.9	120
	2247	0.7	20
21 Th	0423	3.9	120
	1126	1.3	40
	1619	3.6	110
	2328	0.7	20
22 F	0502	3.6	110
	1208	1.6	50
	1656	3.6	110
23 Sa	0015	1.0	30
	0543	3.6	110
	1256	1.6	50
	1734	3.3	100
24 Su	0109	1.0	30
	0624	3.3	100
	1353	2.0	60
	1813	3.3	100
25 M	0208	1.0	30
	0715	3.3	100
	1453	2.0	60
	1909	3.0	90
26 Tu ◑	0309	1.0	30
	0817	3.0	90
	1554	1.6	50
	2028	3.0	90
27 W	0411	1.0	30
	0941	3.0	90
	1653	1.3	40
	2228	3.0	90
28 Th	0511	1.0	30
	1126	3.0	90
	1749	1.0	30
29 F	0000	3.3	100
	0609	1.0	30
	1221	3.3	100
	1841	0.7	20
30 Sa	0054	3.6	110
	0706	0.7	20
	1258	3.3	100
	1930	0.3	10
31 Su	0141	3.9	120
	0802	0.7	20
	1332	3.6	110
	2019	0.3	10

Time meridian 45° W. 0000 is midnight. 1200 is noon. Times are not adjusted for Daylight Saving Time.
Heights are referred to the chart datum of soundings.
* See Page 320 for the remaining tides on this day.

Santos, Brazil, 2017

Times and Heights of High and Low Waters

January

Day	Time	ft	cm
1 Su	0428	4.6	140
	1024	1.6	50
	1600	3.9	120
	2338	0.3	10
2 M	0508	4.3	130
	1104	1.6	50
	1632	3.6	110
3 Tu	0023	0.7	20
	0556	3.9	120
	1151	2.0	60
	1717	3.3	100
4 W	0113	0.7	20
	0649	3.6	110
	1247	2.3	70
	2117	3.3	100
5 Th ☽	0208	1.0	30
	0751	3.3	100
	1400	2.3	70
	2226	3.6	110
6 F	0309	1.3	40
	0923	3.3	100
	1723	2.3	70
	2328	3.9	120
7 Sa	0415	1.3	40
	1202	3.3	100
	1753	1.6	50
8 Su	0024	3.9	120
	0523	1.3	40
	1256	3.6	110
	1832	1.3	40
9 M	0119	4.3	130
	0630	1.3	40
	1336	3.6	110
	1911	1.0	30
10 Tu	0209	4.6	140
	0728	1.3	40
	1356	3.6	110
	1953	0.7	20
11 W	0254	4.6	140
	0819	1.3	40
	1409	3.9	120
	2036	0.3	10
12 Th ○	0334	4.6	140
	0902	1.3	40
	1424	3.9	120
	2119	0.3	10
13 F	0400	4.6	140
	0943	1.3	40
	1451	4.3	130
	2200	0.3	10
14 Sa	0415	4.3	130
	1017	1.3	40
	1513	4.3	130
	2239	0.3	10
15 Su	0432	4.3	130
	1054	1.3	40
	1547	4.3	130
	2313	0.7	20
16 M	0456	3.9	120
	1124	1.6	50
	1615	4.3	130
	2353	1.0	30
17 Tu	0519	3.6	110
	1200	1.6	50
	1654	4.3	130
18 W	0028	1.3	40
	0551	3.6	110
	1241	2.0	60
	1738	3.6	110
19 Th ◐	0109	1.6	50
	0624	3.3	100
	1341	2.0	60
	1847	3.3	100
20 F	0204	2.0	60
	0713	3.0	90
	1502	2.0	60
	2051	3.3	100
21 Sa	0313	2.0	60
	1134	3.0	90
	1630	1.6	50
	2241	3.3	100
22 Su	0424	2.0	60
	1224	3.3	100
	1732	1.3	40
	2349	3.6	110
23 M	0528	2.0	60
	1302	3.6	110
	1817	1.0	30
24 Tu	0039	3.9	120
	0619	1.6	50
	1339	3.9	120
	1900	0.7	20
25 W	0119	4.3	130
	0704	1.6	50
	1408	3.9	120
	1941	0.3	10
26 Th	0158	4.6	140
	0747	1.3	40
	1438	4.3	130
	2023	0.0	0
27 F ●	0234	4.9	150
	0828	1.3	40
	1500	4.3	130
	2106	0.0	0
28 Sa	0308	4.9	150
	0909	1.0	30
	1523	4.3	130
	2151	0.0	0
29 Su	0341	4.9	150
	0949	1.0	30
	1545	4.3	130
	2234	0.0	0
30 M	0413	4.6	140
	1024	1.3	40
	1611	4.3	130
	2315	0.0	0
31 Tu	0451	4.6	140
	1102	1.3	40
	1645	3.9	120

February

Day	Time	ft	cm
1 W	0000	0.3	10
	0524	4.3	130
	1141	1.6	50
	1721	3.6	110
2 Th	0049	0.7	20
	0602	3.6	110
	1219	2.0	60
	1819	3.3	100
3 F	0139	1.3	40
	0649	3.3	100
	1315	2.0	60
	2213	3.3	100
4 Sa ◐	0243	1.6	50
	0741	3.0	90
	1456	2.3	70
	2334	3.6	110
5 Su	0358	2.0	60
	1223	3.0	90
	1817	2.0	60
6 M	0038	3.9	120
	0526	2.0	60
	1306	3.3	100
	1849	1.3	40
7 Tu	0128	4.3	130
	0643	1.6	50
	1343	3.6	110
	1923	1.0	30
8 W	0211	4.6	140
	0732	1.6	50
	1402	3.6	110
	1954	0.7	20
9 Th	0251	4.9	150
	0811	1.3	40
	1411	3.9	120
	2028	0.3	10
10 F ○	0319	4.9	150
	0847	1.3	40
	1421	4.3	130
	2104	0.3	10
11 Sa	0338	4.6	140
	0919	1.0	30
	1443	4.6	140
	2141	0.3	10
12 Su	0351	4.6	140
	0954	1.0	30
	1506	4.6	140
	2213	0.3	10
13 M	0406	4.3	130
	1026	1.0	30
	1538	4.9	150
	2251	0.7	20
14 Tu	0424	4.3	130
	1100	1.0	30
	1608	4.6	140
	2319	1.0	30
15 W	0451	3.9	120
	1136	1.3	40
	1645	4.6	140
	2351	1.3	40
16 Th	0511	3.6	110
	1208	1.6	50
	1721	3.9	120
17 F	0019	1.6	50
	0536	3.3	100
	1256	2.0	60
	1808	3.6	110
18 Sa ◐	0056	2.0	60
	0556	3.0	90
	1413	2.0	60
	1928	3.3	100
19 Su ◐	0219	2.3	70
	0611	2.6	80
	0921	2.6	80
	1139	2.6	80
	1556*	2.0	60
20 M	0409	2.3	70
	0747	2.6	80
	1221	3.0	90
	1709	1.6	50
	2345	3.6	110
21 Tu	0545	2.3	70
	1256	3.3	100
	1802	1.3	40
22 W	0036	3.9	120
	0630	2.0	60
	1330	3.9	120
	1847	0.7	20
23 Th	0115	4.3	130
	0709	1.6	50
	1400	4.3	130
	1926	0.3	10
24 F	0154	4.6	140
	0747	1.3	40
	1432	4.3	130
	2009	0.0	0
25 Sa	0226	4.9	150
	0826	1.0	30
	1500	4.6	140
	2053	-0.3	-10
26 Su ●	0258	4.9	150
	0906	1.0	30
	1524	4.6	140
	2134	-0.3	-10
27 M	0326	4.9	150
	0945	1.0	30
	1549	4.6	140
	2215	-0.3	-10
28 Tu	0356	4.9	150
	1019	1.0	30
	1611	4.6	140
	2258	0.0	0

March

Day	Time	ft	cm
1 W	0423	4.6	140
	1056	1.0	30
	1643	4.3	130
	2339	0.3	10
2 Th	0454	4.3	130
	1132	1.3	40
	1711	3.9	120
3 F	0021	1.0	30
	0523	3.6	110
	1208	1.6	50
	1754	3.6	110
4 Sa	0109	1.6	50
	0556	3.3	100
	1300	2.0	60
	2219	3.3	100
5 Su ◐	0215	2.0	60
	0626	3.0	90
	0956	2.3	70
	1106	2.3	70
	1415*	2.0	60
6 M	0404	2.3	70
	0849	2.3	70
	1211	2.6	80
	1826	2.0	60
7 Tu	0039	3.9	120
	0653	2.0	60
	1256	3.3	100
	1902	1.3	40
8 W	0121	4.6	140
	0713	2.0	60
	1323	3.6	110
	1928	1.0	30
9 Th	0158	4.6	140
	0726	1.6	50
	1341	3.9	120
	1947	0.7	20
10 F	0228	4.9	150
	0749	1.3	40
	1351	4.3	130
	2015	0.3	10
11 Sa	0251	4.9	150
	0817	1.0	30
	1406	4.6	140
	2045	0.3	10
12 Su ○	0306	4.6	140
	0853	0.7	20
	1428	4.9	150
	2117	0.3	10
13 M	0319	4.6	140
	0926	0.7	20
	1458	4.9	150
	2151	0.3	10
14 Tu	0339	4.6	140
	1002	0.7	20
	1526	4.9	150
	2221	0.7	20
15 W	0358	4.3	130
	1041	0.7	20
	1600	4.9	150
	2251	1.0	30
16 Th	0419	3.9	120
	1115	1.0	30
	1634	4.6	140
	2311	1.3	40
17 F	0441	3.6	110
	1154	1.3	40
	1708	4.3	130
	2317	2.0	60
18 Sa	0454	3.3	100
	1238	1.6	50
	1753	3.9	120
	2323	2.3	70
19 Su	0458	3.3	100
	1343	2.0	60
	1851	3.3	100
20 M ◐	0008	2.6	80
	0445	3.0	90
	0853	2.3	70
	1100	2.6	80
	1506*	2.0	60
21 Tu	0754	2.3	70
	1153	3.0	90
	1630	1.6	50
	2332	3.6	110
22 W	0724	2.3	70
	1228	3.3	100
	1734	1.3	40
23 Th	0023	3.9	120
	0708	2.0	60
	1302	3.9	120
	1823	0.7	20
24 F	0104	4.3	130
	0717	1.6	50
	1339	4.3	130
	1906	0.3	10
25 Sa	0141	4.6	140
	0741	1.3	40
	1411	4.6	140
	1951	0.0	0
26 Su	0213	4.9	150
	0815	1.0	30
	1445	4.9	150
	2034	-0.3	-10
27 M ●	0241	4.9	150
	0853	0.7	20
	1513	4.9	150
	2115	-0.3	-10
28 Tu	0308	4.9	150
	0930	0.7	20
	1539	4.9	150
	2158	0.0	0
29 W	0330	4.6	140
	1008	0.7	20
	1606	4.9	150
	2238	0.3	10
30 Th	0358	4.3	130
	1047	1.0	30
	1636	4.6	140
	2317	0.7	20
31 F	0419	3.9	120
	1124	1.0	30
	1706	4.3	130

Time meridian 45° W. 0000 is midnight. 1200 is noon. Times are not adjusted for Daylight Saving Time.
Heights are referred to the chart datum of soundings.
* See Page 320 for the remaining tides on this day.

Santos, Brazil, 2017

Times and Heights of High and Low Waters

April

Date	Time (h m)	Height (ft)	Height (cm)
1 Sa	0000	1.3	40
	0449	3.6	110
	1206	1.3	40
	1751	3.6	110
2 Su	0054	2.0	60
	0506	3.3	100
	1300	1.6	50
	2215	3.3	100
3 M ☾	0200	2.3	70
	0511	3.0	90
	0904	2.3	70
	1053	2.3	70
	1404*	2.0	60
4 Tu	0751	2.3	70
	1143	2.6	80
	1541	2.0	60
5 W	0024	3.9	120
	0654	2.3	70
	1213	3.0	90
	1841	1.6	50
6 Th	0102	4.3	130
	0649	2.0	60
	1239	3.3	100
	1908	1.3	40
7 F	0136	4.6	140
	0654	1.6	50
	1254	3.9	120
	1924	1.0	30
8 Sa	0158	4.6	140
	0715	1.3	40
	1313	4.3	130
	1943	0.7	20
9 Su	0217	4.6	140
	0745	1.0	30
	1341	4.6	140
	2015	0.7	20
10 M	0234	4.6	140
	0819	0.7	20
	1409	4.9	150
	2051	0.7	20
11 Tu ○	0254	4.6	140
	0858	0.3	10
	1445	4.9	150
	2123	0.7	20
12 W	0311	4.6	140
	0939	0.3	10
	1513	4.9	150
	2156	1.0	30
13 Th	0334	4.3	130
	1017	0.7	20
	1551	4.9	150
	2223	1.3	40
14 F	0353	3.9	120
	1058	0.7	20
	1623	4.6	140
	2239	1.6	50
15 Sa	0406	3.9	120
	1141	1.0	30
	1700	4.3	130
	2245	1.6	50
16 Su	0411	3.6	110
	1224	1.3	40
	1743	3.9	120
	2300	2.0	60
17 M	0409	3.3	100
	1317	1.6	50
	1834	3.6	110
	2339	2.3	70
18 Tu	0354	3.0	90
	0758	2.3	70
	1006	2.6	80
	1423	1.6	50
	1956	3.3	100
19 W ☽	0109	2.6	80
	0321	3.0	90
	0719	2.3	70
	1102	3.0	90
	1538*	1.6	50
20 Th	0704	2.0	60
	1149	3.3	100
	1645	1.3	40
	2358	3.9	120
21 F	0700	1.6	50
	1226	3.9	120
	1743	1.0	30
22 Sa	0045	4.3	130
	0706	1.3	40
	1306	4.3	130
	1836	0.7	20
23 Su	0123	4.6	140
	0724	1.0	30
	1347	4.6	140
	1923	0.3	10
24 M	0154	4.6	140
	0753	1.0	30
	1423	4.9	150
	2009	0.0	0
25 Tu	0223	4.6	140
	0828	0.7	20
	1458	4.9	150
	2054	0.0	0
26 W ●	0245	4.6	140
	0908	0.7	20
	1530	4.9	150
	2139	0.3	10
27 Th	0306	4.6	140
	0953	0.7	20
	1604	4.9	150
	2219	0.7	20
28 F	0328	4.3	130
	1036	0.7	20
	1636	4.6	140
	2302	1.0	30
29 Sa	0354	3.9	120
	1119	1.0	30
	1711	4.3	130
	2349	1.6	50
30 Su	0413	3.6	110
	1204	1.0	30
	1800	3.6	110

May

Date	Time (h m)	Height (ft)	Height (cm)
1 M	0034	2.0	60
	0436	3.3	100
	1258	1.3	40
	2153	3.6	110
2 Tu ☾	0134	2.6	80
	0438	3.0	90
	0853	2.3	70
	1004	2.3	70
	1353*	1.6	50
3 W	0321	2.6	80
	0753	2.6	80
	1053	2.6	80
	1454	1.6	50
4 Th	0000	3.9	120
	0619	2.3	70
	1115	3.0	90
	1602	1.6	50
5 F	0038	3.9	120
	0604	2.0	60
	1136	3.3	100
	1715	1.6	50
6 Sa	0102	4.3	130
	0611	1.6	50
	1202	3.9	120
	1813	1.3	40
7 Su	0124	4.3	130
	0638	1.0	30
	1238	4.3	130
	1858	1.0	30
8 M	0147	4.3	130
	0709	0.7	20
	1311	4.6	140
	1939	1.0	30
9 Tu	0206	4.6	140
	0751	0.3	10
	1353	4.6	140
	2019	1.0	30
10 W ○	0230	4.6	140
	0828	0.3	10
	1426	4.9	150
	2058	1.0	30
11 Th	0253	4.3	130
	0909	0.3	10
	1502	4.9	150
	2130	1.0	30
12 F	0309	4.3	130
	0956	0.3	10
	1539	4.9	150
	2156	1.3	40
13 Sa	0326	3.9	120
	1039	0.7	20
	1613	4.6	140
	2215	1.6	50
14 Su	0341	3.9	120
	1123	1.0	30
	1653	4.3	130
	2234	1.6	50
15 M	0351	3.6	110
	1208	1.0	30
	1732	4.3	130
	2258	2.0	60
16 Tu	0353	3.3	100
	1258	1.3	40
	1819	3.9	120
	2336	2.3	70
17 W	0343	3.0	90
	0724	2.6	80
	0921	2.6	80
	1354	1.3	40
	1923	3.6	110
18 Th ☽	0039	2.6	80
	0332	3.0	90
	0651	2.3	70
	1019	3.0	90
	1453*	1.3	40
19 F	0639	2.3	70
	1104	3.6	110
	1553	1.0	30
	2315	3.6	110
20 Sa	0641	2.0	60
	1151	3.9	120
	1654	1.0	30
21 Su	0019	3.9	120
	0645	1.6	50
	1236	4.3	130
	1754	0.7	20
22 M	0102	4.3	130
	0700	1.0	30
	1317	4.6	140
	1851	0.7	20
23 Tu	0139	4.3	130
	0728	1.0	30
	1402	4.6	140
	1945	0.7	20
24 W	0208	4.3	130
	0806	0.7	20
	1447	4.9	150
	2038	0.7	20
25 Th ●	0228	4.3	130
	0847	0.3	10
	1532	4.9	150
	2124	0.7	20
26 F	0249	4.3	130
	0934	0.3	10
	1615	4.6	140
	2208	1.0	30
27 Sa	0308	3.9	120
	1021	0.7	20
	1653	4.6	140
	2253	1.3	40
28 Su	0334	3.9	120
	1109	0.7	20
	1730	4.3	130
	2328	1.6	50
29 M	0356	3.6	110
	1158	1.0	30
	1815	3.9	120
30 Tu	0008	2.0	60
	0417	3.6	110
	1243	1.0	30
	1917	3.6	110
31 W	0056	2.3	70
	0441	3.3	100
	1324	1.3	40
	2209	3.3	100

June

Date	Time (h m)	Height (ft)	Height (cm)
1 Th ☽	0154	2.6	80
	0506	3.0	90
	1409	1.3	40
	2317	3.3	100
2 F	0315	2.6	80
	0941	3.0	90
	1504	1.6	50
3 Sa	0002	3.6	110
	0445	2.3	70
	1038	3.3	100
	1602	1.6	50
4 Su	0036	3.6	110
	0530	1.6	50
	1121	3.6	110
	1704	1.6	50
5 M	0058	3.9	120
	0608	1.3	40
	1206	3.9	120
	1804	1.6	50
6 Tu	0124	3.9	120
	0647	0.7	20
	1251	4.3	130
	1902	1.3	40
7 W	0153	4.3	130
	0723	0.3	10
	1334	4.6	140
	1951	1.3	40
8 Th	0215	4.3	130
	0804	0.3	10
	1411	4.6	140
	2032	1.3	40
9 F ○	0241	4.3	130
	0849	0.3	10
	1453	4.6	140
	2106	1.3	40
10 Sa	0300	4.3	130
	0932	0.3	10
	1528	4.6	140
	2138	1.3	40
11 Su	0313	3.9	120
	1015	0.3	10
	1604	4.6	140
	2202	1.3	40
12 M	0328	3.9	120
	1102	0.7	20
	1641	4.6	140
	2226	1.6	50
13 Tu	0345	3.6	110
	1149	0.7	20
	1719	4.3	130
	2256	1.6	50
14 W	0358	3.6	110
	1236	1.0	30
	1804	4.3	130
	2330	2.0	60
15 Th	0402	3.3	100
	1323	1.0	30
	1854	3.9	120
16 F ☾	0015	2.3	70
	0358	3.0	90
	0626	2.6	80
	0939	3.0	90
	1413*	1.0	30
17 Sa ☽	0143	2.6	80
	0349	2.6	80
	0608	2.3	70
	1032	3.6	110
	1509*	1.0	30
18 Su	0615	2.0	60
	1119	3.9	120
	1608	1.0	30
	2356	3.6	110
19 M	0628	1.6	50
	1209	3.9	120
	1713	1.3	40
20 Tu	0056	3.9	120
	0643	1.0	30
	1302	4.3	130
	1821	1.3	40
21 W	0138	3.9	120
	0713	1.0	30
	1356	4.6	140
	1928	1.0	30
22 Th	0208	3.9	120
	0751	0.7	20
	1451	4.6	140
	2028	1.0	30
23 F ●	0228	3.9	120
	0834	0.3	10
	1541	4.9	150
	2117	1.0	30
24 Sa ○	0243	3.9	120
	0921	0.3	10
	1630	4.6	140
	2200	1.0	30
25 Su	0300	3.9	120
	1008	0.3	10
	1711	4.6	140
	2238	1.3	40
26 M	0319	3.9	120
	1056	0.3	10
	1732	4.3	130
	2308	1.3	40
27 Tu	0349	3.9	120
	1138	0.7	20
	1747	3.9	120
	2345	1.6	50
28 W	0409	3.9	120
	1215	1.0	30
	1806	3.6	110
29 Th	0015	2.0	60
	0443	3.6	110
	1258	1.3	40
	1832	3.3	100
30 F ☾	0058	2.3	70
	0519	3.3	100
	1339	1.0	40
	1904	3.3	100

Time meridian 45° W. 0000 is midnight. 1200 is noon. Times are not adjusted for Daylight Saving Time.
Heights are referred to the chart datum of soundings.
* See Page 320 for the remaining tides on this day.

Santos, Brazil, 2017

Times and Heights of High and Low Waters

July

Day	Time	ft	cm	Day	Time	ft	cm
1 Sa	0158	2.3	70	**16** Su ○	0056	2.3	70
	0647	3.0	90		1000	3.3	100
	1423	1.6	50		1438	1.3	40
	2000	3.0	90		1958	3.3	100
	2208	3.0	90				
2 Su	0326	2.3	70	**17** M	0256	2.3	70
	0938	3.3	100		0400	2.3	70
	1515	2.0	60		0554	2.3	70
					1102	3.6	110
					1538*	1.3	40
3 M	0013	3.3	100	**18** Tu	0000	3.0	90
	0456	2.0	60		0619	2.0	60
	1053	3.6	110		1202	3.9	120
	1617	2.0	60		1649	1.6	50
4 Tu	0049	3.3	100	**19** W	0102	3.3	100
	0549	1.3	40		0643	1.3	40
	1149	3.9	120		1302	4.3	130
	1724	2.0	60		1811	1.6	50
5 W	0117	3.6	110	**20** Th	0145	3.6	110
	0628	1.0	30		0713	1.0	30
	1238	3.9	120		1400	4.6	140
	1830	1.6	50		1932	1.6	50
6 Th	0147	3.9	120	**21** F	0215	3.9	120
	0708	0.7	20		0747	0.7	20
	1321	4.3	130		1453	4.6	140
	1926	1.6	50		2028	1.3	40
7 F	0213	4.3	130	**22** Sa	0236	3.9	120
	0749	0.3	10		0826	0.3	10
	1404	4.6	140		1541	4.9	150
	2011	1.3	40		2109	1.3	40
8 Sa	0241	4.3	130	**23** Su ●	0245	4.3	130
	0828	0.3	10		0909	0.0	0
	1443	4.6	140		1621	4.9	150
	2051	1.3	40		2145	1.0	30
9 Su ○	0300	4.3	130	**24** M	0256	4.3	130
	0909	0.0	0		0951	0.0	0
	1517	4.6	140		1647	4.6	140
	2123	1.3	40		2215	1.0	30
10 M	0315	4.3	130	**25** Tu	0311	4.3	130
	0954	0.3	10		1030	0.3	10
	1554	4.6	140		1658	4.3	130
	2154	1.3	40		2249	1.3	40
11 Tu	0332	4.3	130	**26** W	0339	4.6	140
	1039	0.3	10		1108	0.7	20
	1626	4.6	140		1706	4.3	130
	2221	1.3	40		2315	1.3	40
12 W	0354	3.9	120	**27** Th	0404	4.3	130
	1123	0.3	10		1149	0.7	20
	1702	4.6	140		1721	3.9	120
	2253	1.6	50		2349	1.6	50
13 Th	0415	3.9	120	**28** F	0436	4.3	130
	1208	0.7	20		1221	1.3	40
	1741	4.3	130		1747	3.6	110
	2323	1.6	50				
14 F	0445	3.6	110	**29** Sa	0017	1.6	50
	1256	0.7	20		0508	3.9	120
	1819	3.9	120		1300	1.6	50
					1808	3.3	100
15 Sa	0000	2.0	60	**30** Su ☽	0100	2.0	60
	0517	3.3	100		0558	3.6	110
	0708	3.0	90		1351	2.0	60
	0836	3.3	100		1834	3.3	100
	1345*	1.0	30				
				31 M	0224	2.3	70
					0758	3.0	90
					1447	2.0	60
					1858	3.0	90
					2209	2.6	80

August

Day	Time	ft	cm	Day	Time	ft	cm
1 Tu	0008	2.6	80	**16** W	0008	2.6	80
	0417	2.0	60		0617	2.0	60
	1030	3.3	100		1208	3.9	120
	1554	2.3	70		1643	2.0	60
2 W	0047	3.3	100	**17** Th	0100	3.3	100
	0530	1.6	50		0651	1.3	40
	1141	3.6	110		1304	4.3	130
	1706	2.3	70		1841	2.0	60
3 Th	0111	3.6	110	**18** F	0139	3.6	110
	0615	1.0	30		0719	1.0	30
	1230	3.9	120		1356	4.6	140
	1819	2.0	60		1945	1.6	50
4 F	0143	3.9	120	**19** Sa	0204	3.9	120
	0656	0.7	20		0747	0.7	20
	1313	4.3	130		1441	4.9	150
	1917	1.6	50		2021	1.3	40
5 Sa	0208	4.3	130	**20** Su	0224	4.3	130
	0732	0.3	10		0819	0.3	10
	1354	4.6	140		1517	4.9	150
	2000	1.6	50		2051	1.3	40
6 Su	0236	4.3	130	**21** M ●	0230	4.3	130
	0809	0.0	0		0853	0.0	0
	1430	4.6	140		1547	4.9	150
	2038	1.3	40		2119	1.0	30
7 M ○	0258	4.6	140	**22** Tu	0243	4.6	140
	0853	0.0	0		0924	0.0	0
	1504	4.9	150		1606	4.6	140
	2113	1.3	40		2151	1.0	30
8 Tu	0319	4.6	140	**23** W	0300	4.9	150
	0934	0.0	0		1002	0.3	10
	1538	4.9	150		1611	4.3	130
	2147	1.0	30		2219	1.0	30
9 W	0338	4.6	140	**24** Th	0324	4.9	150
	1015	0.0	0		1038	0.7	20
	1608	4.9	150		1624	4.3	130
	2215	1.0	30		2253	1.0	30
10 Th	0400	4.3	130	**25** F	0354	4.9	150
	1058	0.0	0		1109	1.0	30
	1641	4.6	140		1647	3.9	120
	2247	1.3	40		2323	1.0	30
11 F	0423	4.3	130	**26** Sa	0423	4.6	140
	1143	0.3	10		1147	1.3	40
	1711	4.3	130		1706	3.9	120
	2315	1.3	40		2356	1.3	40
12 Sa	0456	3.9	120	**27** Su	0458	4.3	130
	1226	0.7	20		1219	1.6	50
	1749	3.9	120		1730	3.6	110
	2351	1.6	50				
13 Su	0532	3.6	110	**28** M	0034	1.6	50
	1313	1.0	30		0539	3.6	110
	1821	3.6	110		1300	2.0	60
					1749	3.3	100
14 M ☽	0032	2.0	60	**29** Tu ☽	0141	2.0	60
	0941	3.3	100		0647	3.3	100
	1408	1.6	50		1402	2.3	70
	1900	3.3	100		1800	3.0	90
					2208*	2.6	80
15 Tu	0153	2.3	70	**30** W	0336	2.0	60
	1102	3.6	110		1000	3.0	90
	1515	2.0	60		1528	2.6	80
	1958	3.0	90		1804	2.6	80
	2206	2.6	80		2049	2.6	80
				31 Th	0026	3.0	90
					0506	1.6	50
					1136	3.3	100
					1715	2.3	70
					2004	2.3	70

September

Day	Time	ft	cm	Day	Time	ft	cm
1 F	0056	3.3	100	**16** Sa	0108	3.6	110
	0558	1.3	40		0713	1.0	30
	1219	3.9	120		1339	4.6	140
	1838	2.0	60		1930	1.6	50
2 Sa	0121	3.9	120	**17** Su	0136	3.9	120
	0638	0.7	20		0734	0.7	20
	1300	4.3	130		1413	4.9	150
	1915	1.6	50		1947	1.3	40
3 Su	0153	4.3	130	**18** M	0151	4.3	130
	0711	0.3	10		0756	0.3	10
	1338	4.6	140		1443	4.9	150
	1947	1.3	40		2013	1.0	30
4 M	0219	4.6	140	**19** Tu	0202	4.6	140
	0751	0.0	0		0823	0.3	10
	1409	4.6	140		1502	4.6	140
	2023	1.3	40		2043	1.0	30
5 Tu	0247	4.6	140	**20** W ●	0217	4.9	150
	0828	-0.3	-10		0854	0.3	10
	1445	4.9	150		1515	4.6	140
	2056	1.0	30		2115	0.7	20
6 W	0308	4.9	150	**21** Th	0245	4.9	150
	0909	-0.3	-10		0928	0.3	10
	1513	4.9	150		1530	4.3	130
	2132	1.0	30		2153	0.7	20
7 Th	0330	4.9	150	**22** F	0309	5.2	160
	0953	-0.3	-10		1002	0.7	20
	1543	4.9	150		1551	4.3	130
	2204	1.0	30		2226	0.7	20
8 F	0354	4.9	150	**23** Sa	0341	4.9	150
	1034	0.0	0		1036	1.0	30
	1609	4.6	140		1609	3.9	120
	2238	1.0	30		2300	0.7	20
9 Sa	0417	4.6	140	**24** Su	0411	4.6	140
	1113	0.3	10		1100	1.3	40
	1641	4.3	130		1632	3.9	120
	2306	1.0	30		2339	1.0	30
10 Su	0451	4.3	130	**25** M	0449	4.3	130
	1200	1.0	30		1117	2.0	60
	1709	3.9	120		1651	3.6	110
	2345	1.3	40				
11 M	0521	3.6	110	**26** Tu	0017	1.3	40
	1253	1.3	40		0524	3.9	120
	1745	3.6	110		1043	2.3	70
					1700	3.3	100
12 Tu	0024	1.6	50	**27** W ☾	0111	1.6	50
	0621	3.3	100		0617	3.3	100
	0758	3.3	100		1126	2.6	80
	0943*	3.3	100		1700	3.0	90
	1353*	2.0	60				
13 W ○	0138	2.0	60	**28** Th	0245	2.0	60
	1106	3.6	110		0824	3.0	90
	1509	2.3	70		1449	2.6	80
	1900	2.6	80		1645	2.6	80
	2139*	2.6	80		2004*	2.6	80
14 Th	0604	2.0	60	**29** F	0417	1.6	50
	1206	3.9	120		1102	3.3	100
	1824	2.3	70		1932	2.3	70
15 F	0039	3.0	90	**30** Sa	0011	3.3	100
	0645	1.3	40		0521	1.3	40
	1258	4.3	130		1154	3.6	110
	1908	2.0	60		1858	2.0	60

Time meridian 45° W. 0000 is midnight. 1200 is noon. Times are not adjusted for Daylight Saving Time.
Heights are referred to the chart datum of soundings.
* See Page 320 for the remaining tides on this day.

Santos, Brazil, 2017

Times and Heights of High and Low Waters

October

Day	Time	ft	cm	Day	Time	ft	cm
1 Su	0049	3.9	120	16 M	0043	3.6	110
	0604	1.0	30		0653	1.0	30
	1234	4.3	130		1339	4.6	140
	1858	1.6	50		1856	1.3	40
2 M	0119	4.3	130	17 Tu	0102	4.3	130
	0645	0.3	10		0717	0.7	20
	1311	4.6	140		1400	4.6	140
	1923	1.3	40		1924	1.0	30
3 Tu	0153	4.6	140	18 W	0124	4.6	140
	0723	0.0	0		0745	0.7	20
	1347	4.6	140		1417	4.6	140
	1953	1.0	30		2000	0.7	20
4 W	0221	4.9	150	19 Th	0154	4.9	150
	0802	0.0	0		0817	0.7	20
	1417	4.9	150		1436	4.6	140
	2030	1.0	30	●	2039	0.7	20
5 Th ○	0251	4.9	150	20 F	0221	4.9	150
	0843	-0.3	-10		0853	0.7	20
	1445	4.9	150		1456	4.3	130
	2106	0.7	20		2117	0.3	10
6 F	0315	4.9	150	21 Sa	0254	4.9	150
	0924	0.0	0		0926	1.0	30
	1509	4.6	140		1513	4.3	130
	2145	0.7	20		2200	0.3	10
7 Sa	0341	4.9	150	22 Su	0326	4.9	150
	1006	0.3	10		0956	1.3	40
	1539	4.6	140		1539	3.9	120
	2221	0.7	20		2241	0.7	20
8 Su	0408	4.6	140	23 M	0400	4.6	140
	1053	0.7	20		1019	1.6	50
	1606	4.3	130		1558	3.9	120
	2300	1.0	30		2319	1.0	30
9 M	0443	4.3	130	24 Tu	0436	4.3	130
	1139	1.3	40		1024	2.0	60
	1636	3.6	110		1609	3.6	110
	2343	1.3	40				
10 Tu	0517	3.9	120	25 W	0002	1.3	40
	1228	1.6	50		0513	3.9	120
	1702	3.3	100		1034	2.0	60
					1617	3.3	100
11 W	0028	1.3	40	26 Th	0054	1.6	50
	0943	3.3	100		0604	3.6	110
	1334	2.3	70		1113	2.3	70
	1734	3.0	90		1611	3.0	90
12 Th ◑	0132	1.6	50	27 F ◐	0200	1.6	50
	1058	3.6	110		0726	3.3	100
	1506	2.6	80		1249	2.6	80
	1747	2.6	80		1558	3.0	90
	2053*	2.6	80		1919*	2.6	80
13 F	0308	1.6	50	28 Sa	0313	1.6	50
	1154	3.9	120		0949	3.3	100
	1821	2.3	70		1851	2.3	70
	2353	3.0	90		2321	3.3	100
14 Sa	0613	1.3	40	29 Su	0424	1.3	40
	1238	4.3	130		1109	3.6	110
	1834	2.0	60		1836	2.0	60
15 Su	0023	3.3	100	30 M	0002	3.9	120
	0639	1.0	30		0519	1.0	30
	1308	4.6	140		1200	3.9	120
	1838	1.6	50		1830	1.6	50
				31 Tu	0043	4.3	130
					0604	0.7	20
					1243	4.3	130
					1847	1.3	40

November

Day	Time	ft	cm	Day	Time	ft	cm
1 W	0117	4.6	140	16 Th	0053	4.6	140
	0649	0.3	10		0700	1.0	30
	1317	4.6	140		1343	4.3	130
	1919	1.0	30		1923	0.7	20
2 Th	0154	4.9	150	17 F	0126	4.6	140
	0730	0.0	0		0739	1.0	30
	1349	4.6	140		1404	4.3	130
	1956	0.7	20		2004	0.3	10
3 F	0228	4.9	150	18 Sa ●	0202	4.9	150
	0813	0.0	0		0817	1.0	30
	1415	4.6	140		1426	4.3	130
	2038	0.7	20		2051	0.3	10
4 Sa ○	0300	4.9	150	19 Su	0239	4.9	150
	0900	0.3	10		0854	1.0	30
	1443	4.6	140		1453	4.3	130
	2121	0.7	20		2134	0.3	10
5 Su	0330	4.9	150	20 M	0311	4.9	150
	0947	0.7	20		0920	1.3	40
	1506	4.3	130		1509	3.9	120
	2204	0.7	20		2215	0.7	20
6 M	0404	4.6	140	21 Tu	0349	4.6	140
	1032	1.0	30		0949	1.6	50
	1538	3.9	120		1528	3.9	120
	2253	0.7	20		2300	0.7	20
7 Tu	0441	4.3	130	22 W	0423	4.6	140
	1119	1.3	40		1008	1.6	50
	1602	3.6	110		1545	3.6	110
	2338	1.0	30		2345	1.0	30
8 W	0523	3.9	120	23 Th	0502	4.3	130
	1208	2.0	60		1030	2.0	60
	1632	3.3	100		1556	3.6	110
9 Th	0024	1.3	40	24 F	0030	1.3	40
	0913	3.6	110		0551	3.9	120
	1306	2.3	70		1108	2.3	70
	1658	3.0	90		1602	3.3	100
10 F ○	0117	1.3	40	25 Sa	0123	1.3	40
	1034	3.6	110		0653	3.6	110
	1419	2.6	80		1208	2.3	70
	1723	2.6	80		1602	3.0	90
	2056*	2.6	80		1858*	2.6	80
11 Sa	0221	1.6	50	26 Su ◑	0224	1.3	40
	1124	3.9	120		0819	3.3	100
	1624	2.6	80		1541	2.6	80
	2249	3.0	90	◐	1600	2.6	80
					1813*	2.6	80
12 Su	0336	1.6	50	27 M	0326	1.3	40
	1204	3.9	120		1004	3.6	110
	1717	2.3	70		1756	2.3	70
	2317	3.3	100		2321	3.6	110
13 M	0451	1.3	40	28 Tu	0426	1.0	30
	1239	3.9	120		1119	3.9	120
	1736	1.6	50		1751	1.6	50
	2343	3.6	110				
14 Tu	0539	1.3	40	29 W	0004	4.3	130
	1302	3.9	120		0521	0.7	20
	1808	1.3	40		1211	3.9	120
					1815	1.3	40
15 W	0015	3.9	120	30 Th	0049	4.6	140
	0621	1.0	30		0611	0.7	20
	1323	4.3	130		1253	4.3	130
	1845	1.0	30		1849	1.0	30

December

Day	Time	ft	cm	Day	Time	ft	cm
1 F	0132	4.6	140	16 Sa	0108	4.6	140
	0702	0.7	20		0708	1.3	40
	1326	4.3	130		1351	4.3	130
	1928	0.7	20		1943	0.3	10
2 Sa	0213	4.9	150	17 Su	0151	4.6	140
	0753	0.7	20		0753	1.3	40
	1354	4.3	130		1415	4.3	130
	2013	0.7	20		2024	0.3	10
3 Su ○	0253	4.9	150	18 M ●	0224	4.6	140
	0843	0.7	20		0828	1.3	40
	1421	4.3	130		1439	4.3	130
	2102	0.3	10		2108	0.3	10
4 M	0332	4.6	140	19 Tu	0300	4.9	150
	0932	1.0	30		0902	1.3	40
	1451	3.9	120		1458	4.3	130
	2153	0.3	10		2154	0.3	10
5 Tu	0411	4.6	140	20 W	0336	4.6	140
	1019	1.3	40		0932	1.3	40
	1513	3.9	120		1515	3.9	120
	2241	0.7	20		2238	0.7	20
6 W	0451	4.3	130	21 Th	0409	4.6	140
	1104	1.6	50		0958	1.6	50
	1547	3.9	120		1538	3.9	120
	2324	0.7	20		2319	0.7	20
7 Th	0528	3.9	120	22 F	0449	4.3	130
	1153	2.0	60		1026	1.6	50
	1611	3.6	110		1600	3.6	110
8 F	0009	1.0	30	23 Sa	0004	1.0	30
	0623	3.6	110		0528	4.3	130
	1236	2.3	70		1102	2.0	60
	1647	3.3	100		1621	3.3	100
9 Sa	0058	1.3	40	24 Su	0053	1.0	30
	0949	3.3	100		0615	3.9	120
	1323	2.3	70		1151	2.0	60
	1726	3.3	100		1647	3.3	100
10 Su ○	0147	1.3	40	25 M	0147	1.0	30
	1051	3.3	100		0715	3.6	110
	1426	2.3	70		1256	2.3	70
	1932	3.0	90		2151	3.3	100
11 M	0241	1.6	50	26 Tu ◑	0243	1.3	40
	1136	3.3	100		0830	3.3	100
	1541	2.3	70		1441	2.3	70
	2149	3.3	100		2249	3.6	110
12 Tu	0339	1.6	50	27 W	0345	1.3	40
	1206	3.6	110		1013	3.3	100
	1643	2.0	60		1713	2.0	60
	2253	3.6	110		2343	3.9	120
13 W	0441	1.6	50	28 Th	0445	1.0	30
	1232	3.6	110		1145	3.6	110
	1730	1.3	40		1751	1.6	50
	2341	3.9	120				
14 Th	0536	1.6	50	29 F	0034	4.3	130
	1256	3.9	120		0547	1.0	30
	1813	1.0	30		1243	3.6	110
					1832	1.0	30
15 F	0026	4.3	130	30 Sa	0124	4.6	140
	0623	1.3	40		0645	1.0	30
	1323	3.9	120		1326	3.9	120
	1858	0.7	20		1917	0.7	20
				31 Su	0215	4.6	140
					0741	1.0	30
					1356	3.9	120
					2006	0.3	10

Time meridian 45° W. 0000 is midnight. 1200 is noon. Times are not adjusted for Daylight Saving Time.
Heights are referred to the chart datum of soundings.
* See Page 320 for the remaining tides on this day.

Buenos Aires, Argentina, 2017
Times and Heights of High and Low Waters

January

Day	Time	Height ft	Height cm	Day	Time	Height ft	Height cm
1 Su	0428	2.3	70	16 M	0551	2.0	60
	0836	3.3	100		1005	3.3	100
	1551	1.3	40		1703	1.3	40
	2201	3.9	120		2315	4.9	150
2 M	0510	2.3	70	17 Tu	0648	2.0	60
	0912	3.3	100		1055	3.0	90
	1624	1.0	30		1748	1.3	40
	2239	4.3	130				
3 Tu	0552	2.3	70	18 W	0011	4.6	140
	0952	3.0	90		0740	2.0	60
	1702	1.0	30		1144	3.0	90
	2320	4.3	130		1829	1.3	40
4 W	0636	2.0	60	19 Th ◗	0103	4.6	140
	1035	3.0	90		0827	2.0	60
	1744	1.0	30		1233	2.6	80
					1906	1.3	40
5 Th ◖	0005	4.3	130	20 F	0152	4.3	130
	0724	2.0	60		0911	2.0	60
	1123	3.0	90		1324	2.6	80
	1830	1.0	30		1941	1.6	50
6 F	0053	4.6	140	21 Sa	0238	4.3	130
	0816	2.0	60		0953	2.0	60
	1216	3.0	90		1419	2.6	80
	1922	1.3	40		2018	1.6	50
7 Sa	0145	4.6	140	22 Su	0323	3.9	120
	0912	2.0	60		1036	2.0	60
	1316	3.0	90		1526	2.6	80
	2025	1.3	40		2103	2.0	60
8 Su	0239	4.6	140	23 M	0408	3.9	120
	1010	2.0	60		1120	2.0	60
	1421	3.0	90		1647	2.6	80
	2137	1.6	50		2201	2.0	60
9 M	0335	4.6	140	24 Tu	0451	3.6	110
	1107	2.0	60		1202	1.6	50
	1530	3.3	100		1802	3.0	90
	2253	1.6	50		2309	2.3	70
10 Tu	0433	4.6	140	25 W	0528	3.6	110
	1202	1.6	50		1240	1.6	50
	1642	3.6	110		1851	3.0	90
11 W	0009	2.0	60	26 Th	0022	2.3	70
	0532	4.6	140		0559	3.3	100
	1254	1.6	50		1314	1.6	50
	1753	3.9	120		1924	3.3	100
12 Th ○	0124	2.0	60	27 F ●	0129	2.3	70
	0629	4.3	130		0627	3.3	100
	1346	1.3	40		1344	1.3	40
	1903	4.3	130		1953	3.6	110
13 F	0236	2.0	60	28 Sa	0226	2.3	70
	0725	3.9	120		0657	3.3	100
	1437	1.3	40		1414	1.3	40
	2009	4.6	140		2025	3.9	120
14 Sa	0345	2.0	60	29 Su	0317	2.3	70
	0820	3.9	120		0732	3.3	100
	1527	1.3	40		1448	1.3	40
	2112	4.6	140		2101	3.9	120
15 Su	0450	2.0	60	30 M	0403	2.3	70
	0913	3.6	110		0810	3.3	100
	1616	1.3	40		1526	1.0	30
	2214	4.9	150		2140	4.3	130
				31 Tu	0448	2.3	70
					0850	3.3	100
					1608	1.0	30
					2222	4.3	130

February

Day	Time	Height ft	Height cm	Day	Time	Height ft	Height cm
1 W	0532	2.3	70	16 Th	0651	2.3	70
	0932	3.3	100		1104	3.3	100
	1653	1.0	30		1805	1.3	40
	2308	4.6	140				
2 Th	0617	2.3	70	17 F	0033	4.3	130
	1017	3.3	100		0721	2.3	70
	1741	1.0	30		1146	3.0	90
	2357	4.6	140		1835	1.3	40
3 F	0704	2.3	70	18 Sa ○	0114	4.3	130
	1105	3.3	100		0751	2.3	70
	1833	1.0	30		1228	3.0	90
					1904	1.6	50
4 Sa ◐	0048	4.6	140	19 Su	0154	3.9	120
	0754	2.0	60		0826	2.0	60
	1159	3.3	100		1314	3.0	90
	1929	1.3	40		1937	1.6	50
5 Su	0139	4.6	140	20 M	0233	3.9	120
	0847	2.0	60		0907	2.0	60
	1258	3.3	100		1406	2.0	60
	2032	1.3	40		2020	2.0	60
6 M	0231	4.6	140	21 Tu	0311	3.6	110
	0943	2.0	60		0953	2.0	60
	1403	3.6	110		1509	3.0	90
	2142	1.6	50		2113	2.0	60
7 Tu	0326	4.6	140	22 W	0347	3.3	100
	1041	2.0	60		1040	2.0	60
	1514	3.6	110		1621	3.0	90
	2255	1.6	50		2217	2.3	70
8 W	0423	4.3	130	23 Th	0423	3.3	100
	1138	1.6	50		1124	2.0	60
	1632	3.9	120		1728	3.3	100
					2329	2.3	70
9 Th	0009	2.0	60	24 F	0501	3.3	100
	0522	4.3	130		1205	1.6	50
	1234	1.6	50		1822	3.3	100
	1755	3.9	120				
10 F ○	0123	2.0	60	25 Sa	0042	2.3	70
	0621	3.9	120		0542	3.3	100
	1329	1.6	50		1246	1.6	50
	1912	4.3	130		1906	3.6	110
11 Sa	0235	2.0	60	26 Su ●	0147	2.3	70
	0717	3.9	120		0625	3.3	100
	1422	1.3	40		1330	1.3	40
	2018	4.6	140		1946	3.9	120
12 Su	0341	2.3	70	27 M	0243	2.3	70
	0808	3.6	110		0708	3.3	100
	1513	1.3	40		1417	1.3	40
	2117	4.6	140		2027	4.3	130
13 M	0440	2.3	70	28 Tu	0332	2.3	70
	0855	3.6	110		0750	3.6	110
	1602	1.3	40		1506	1.0	30
	2211	4.6	140		2111	4.3	130
14 Tu	0531	2.3	70				
	0939	3.3	100				
	1648	1.3	40				
	2302	4.6	140				
15 W	0615	2.3	70				
	1022	3.3	100				
	1729	1.3	40				
	2350	4.6	140				

March

Day	Time	Height ft	Height cm	Day	Time	Height ft	Height cm
1 W	0419	2.3	70	16 Th	0525	2.3	70
	0832	3.6	110		0954	3.3	100
	1557	1.0	30		1711	1.3	40
	2159	4.6	140		2318	4.3	130
2 Th	0504	2.3	70	17 F	0550	2.3	70
	0915	3.6	110		1030	3.3	100
	1649	1.0	30		1743	1.3	40
	2251	4.6	140		2355	3.9	120
3 F	0550	2.3	70	18 Sa	0617	2.0	60
	1001	3.6	110		1107	3.3	100
	1743	1.0	30		1812	1.3	40
	2346	4.6	140				
4 Sa	0636	2.3	70	19 Su	0032	3.9	120
	1051	3.6	110		0647	2.0	60
	1839	1.0	30		1144	3.3	100
					1840	1.6	50
5 Su ◖	0040	4.6	140	20 M ○	0107	3.6	110
	0725	2.3	70		0718	2.3	70
	1147	3.9	120		1223	3.3	100
	1938	1.3	40		1912	1.6	50
6 M	0132	4.6	140	21 Tu	0139	3.6	110
	0818	2.3	70		0749	2.0	60
	1248	3.9	120		1307	3.3	100
	2041	1.3	40		1953	1.6	50
7 Tu	0225	4.3	130	22 W	0207	3.3	100
	0914	2.0	60		0822	2.0	60
	1354	3.9	120		1359	3.3	100
	2149	1.6	50		2042	2.0	60
8 W	0320	4.3	130	23 Th	0236	3.3	100
	1014	2.0	60		0903	2.0	60
	1508	3.9	120		1503	3.3	100
	2259	2.0	60		2141	2.0	60
9 Th	0419	3.9	120	24 F	0316	3.0	90
	1116	2.0	60		0954	2.0	60
	1634	3.9	120		1612	3.3	100
					2249	2.3	70
10 F	0012	2.0	60	25 Sa	0408	3.0	90
	0522	3.6	110		1051	1.6	50
	1216	1.6	50		1716	3.6	110
	1806	4.3	130				
11 Sa	0124	2.0	60	26 Su	0002	2.3	70
	0624	3.6	110		0504	3.3	100
	1315	1.6	50		1151	1.6	50
	1921	4.3	130		1812	3.9	120
12 Su ○	0231	2.0	60	27 M ●	0109	3.3	100
	0718	3.6	110		0556	3.3	100
	1411	1.3	40		1251	1.3	40
	2021	4.3	130		1902	3.9	120
13 M	0329	2.0	60	28 Tu	0207	2.3	70
	0803	3.6	110		0644	3.6	110
	1503	1.3	40		1351	1.3	40
	2112	4.3	130		1949	4.3	130
14 Tu	0417	2.3	70	29 W	0259	2.0	60
	0842	3.6	110		0729	3.6	110
	1550	1.3	40		1449	1.3	40
	2158	4.3	130		2038	4.6	140
15 W	0455	2.3	70	30 Th	0347	2.0	60
	0918	3.3	100		0813	3.6	110
	1633	1.3	40		1547	1.0	30
	2239	4.3	130		2131	4.6	140
				31 F	0433	2.0	60
					0858	3.9	120
					1644	1.0	30
					2229	4.6	140

Time meridian 45° W. 0000 is midnight. 1200 is noon. Times are not adjusted for Daylight Saving Time.
Heights are referred to the chart datum of soundings.

Buenos Aires, Argentina, 2017

Times and Heights of High and Low Waters

April

Day	Time	ft	cm	Day	Time	ft	cm
1 Sa	0520	2.0	60	16 Su	0532	2.0	60
	0947	3.9	120		1035	3.6	110
	1742	1.0	30		1751	1.6	50
	2329	4.3	130		2344	3.6	110
2 Su	0607	2.0	60	17 M	0559	2.0	60
	1041	4.3	130		1110	3.6	110
	1841	1.0	30		1821	1.6	50
3 M ◐	0027	4.3	130	18 Tu	0013	3.3	100
	0656	2.0	60		0623	2.0	60
	1140	4.3	130		1147	3.6	110
	1942	1.3	40		1853	1.6	50
4 Tu	0123	4.3	130	19 W ○	0038	3.3	100
	0749	2.0	60		0648	2.0	60
	1246	4.3	130		1226	3.6	110
	2046	1.3	40		1930	1.6	50
5 W	0217	3.9	120	20 Th	0104	3.0	90
	0847	2.0	60		0721	1.6	50
	1355	4.3	130		1311	3.3	100
	2153	1.6	50		2016	1.6	50
6 Th	0314	3.6	110	21 F	0139	3.0	90
	0949	2.0	60		0806	1.6	50
	1513	3.9	120		1408	3.3	100
	2303	1.6	50		2111	2.0	60
7 F	0417	3.6	110	22 Sa	0227	3.0	90
	1054	1.6	50		0903	1.6	50
	1642	3.9	120		1515	3.6	110
					2216	2.0	60
8 Sa	0013	1.6	50	23 Su	0325	3.0	90
	0525	3.3	100		1006	1.6	50
	1159	1.6	50		1622	3.6	110
	1810	3.9	120		2327	2.0	60
9 Su	0120	2.0	60	24 M	0426	3.0	90
	0630	3.3	100		1113	1.3	40
	1301	1.6	50		1724	3.9	120
	1918	4.3	130				
10 M	0218	2.0	60	25 Tu	0034	2.0	60
	0721	3.3	100		0524	3.3	100
	1359	1.3	40		1221	1.3	40
	2012	4.3	130		1820	3.9	120
11 Tu ○	0306	2.0	60	26 W ●	0133	2.0	60
	0759	3.3	100		0616	3.6	110
	1450	1.3	40		1328	1.3	40
	2057	3.9	120		1914	4.3	130
12 W	0342	2.0	60	27 Th	0226	2.0	60
	0830	3.3	100		0704	3.6	110
	1536	1.3	40		1433	1.0	30
	2134	3.9	120		2008	4.3	130
13 Th	0410	2.0	60	28 F	0316	2.0	60
	0859	3.6	110		0751	3.9	120
	1616	1.3	40		1536	1.0	30
	2207	3.9	120		2105	4.3	130
14 F	0436	2.0	60	29 Sa	0404	2.0	60
	0930	3.6	110		0840	4.3	130
	1651	1.3	40		1637	1.0	30
	2239	3.6	110		2207	4.3	130
15 Sa	0503	2.0	60	30 Su	0452	2.0	60
	1002	3.6	110		0933	4.3	130
	1722	1.6	50		1738	1.0	30
	2312	3.6	110		2311	3.9	120

May

Day	Time	ft	cm	Day	Time	ft	cm
1 M	0541	2.0	60	16 Tu	0520	1.6	50
	1033	4.3	130		1042	3.6	110
	1839	1.0	30		1802	1.3	40
					2319	3.0	90
2 Tu ◐	0011	3.9	120	17 W	0542	1.6	50
	0632	1.6	50		1118	3.6	110
	1139	4.3	130		1834	1.3	40
	1942	1.0	30		2348	3.0	90
3 W	0108	3.6	110	18 Th ○	0610	1.3	40
	0726	1.6	50		1156	3.6	110
	1249	4.3	130		1909	1.6	50
	2047	1.3	40				
4 Th	0204	3.3	100	19 F	0022	2.6	80
	0825	1.6	50		0648	1.3	40
	1401	4.3	130		1240	3.6	110
	2152	1.3	40		1952	1.6	50
5 F	0302	3.3	100	20 Sa	0103	2.6	80
	0927	1.6	50		0737	1.3	40
	1519	3.9	120		1334	3.6	110
	2258	1.6	50		2044	1.6	50
6 Sa	0408	3.0	90	21 Su	0152	2.6	80
	1033	1.6	50		0835	1.3	40
	1643	3.9	120		1438	3.6	110
					2146	1.6	50
7 Su	0003	1.6	50	22 M	0249	3.0	90
	0519	3.0	90		0939	1.3	40
	1140	1.3	40		1544	3.6	110
	1800	3.9	120		2255	1.6	50
8 M	0103	1.6	50	23 Tu	0349	3.0	90
	0623	3.0	90		1048	1.3	40
	1243	1.3	40		1647	3.9	120
	1903	3.9	120				
9 Tu	0153	1.6	50	24 W	0001	1.6	50
	0711	3.3	100		0447	3.3	100
	1341	1.3	40		1159	1.0	30
	1953	3.6	110		1748	3.9	120
10 W ○	0231	1.6	50	25 Th ●	0101	1.6	50
	0746	3.3	100		0542	3.6	110
	1431	1.3	40		1310	1.0	30
	2033	3.6	110		1846	3.9	120
11 Th	0301	1.6	50	26 F	0155	1.6	50
	0812	3.3	100		0635	3.9	120
	1515	1.3	40		1418	1.0	30
	2105	3.6	110		1943	3.9	120
12 F	0328	1.6	50	27 Sa	0247	1.6	50
	0838	3.3	100		0726	4.3	130
	1553	1.3	40		1524	1.0	30
	2132	3.3	100		2044	3.9	120
13 Sa	0357	1.6	50	28 Su	0338	1.6	50
	0905	3.6	110		0821	4.3	130
	1627	1.3	40		1628	1.0	30
	2158	3.3	100		2147	3.6	110
14 Su	0427	1.6	50	29 M	0429	1.6	50
	0935	3.6	110		0920	4.3	130
	1700	1.3	40		1731	1.0	30
	2226	3.3	100		2251	3.6	110
15 M	0455	1.6	50	30 Tu	0521	1.6	50
	1008	3.6	110		1027	4.3	130
	1731	1.3	40		1834	1.0	30
	2253	3.0	90		2352	3.3	100
				31 W	0614	1.3	40
					1140	4.3	130
					1937	1.0	30

June

Day	Time	ft	cm	Day	Time	ft	cm
1 Th ◐	0049	3.3	100	16 F	0551	1.3	40
	0709	1.3	40		1134	3.3	100
	1252	4.3	130		1849	1.3	40
	2039	1.0	30		2355	2.6	80
2 F	0144	3.0	90	17 Sa ○	0634	1.0	30
	0807	1.3	40		1221	3.3	100
	1403	3.9	120		1930	1.3	40
	2140	1.3	40				
3 Sa	0240	3.0	90	18 Su	0038	2.6	80
	0907	1.3	40		0725	1.0	30
	1515	3.9	120		1315	3.6	110
	2240	1.3	40		2019	1.3	40
4 Su	0341	3.0	90	19 M	0125	2.6	80
	1010	1.3	40		0822	1.0	30
	1630	3.6	110		1416	3.6	110
	2338	1.6	50		2117	1.6	50
5 M	0448	3.0	90	20 Tu	0217	3.0	90
	1114	1.3	40		0927	1.0	30
	1739	3.6	110		1520	3.6	110
					2223	1.6	50
6 Tu	0029	1.6	50	21 W	0314	3.0	90
	0551	3.0	90		1035	1.0	30
	1216	1.3	40		1622	3.6	110
	1839	3.3	100		2328	1.6	50
7 W	0112	1.6	50	22 Th	0412	3.3	100
	0640	3.0	90		1146	1.0	30
	1313	1.3	40		1724	3.9	120
	1928	3.3	100				
8 Th	0147	1.6	50	23 F ●	0029	1.6	50
	0716	3.0	90		0510	3.6	110
	1403	1.3	40		1256	1.0	30
	2006	3.3	100		1826	3.9	120
9 F ○	0219	1.6	50	24 Sa	0127	1.6	50
	0743	3.3	100		0608	3.9	120
	1446	1.3	40		1406	1.0	30
	2034	3.0	90		1926	3.6	110
10 Sa	0252	1.6	50	25 Su	0222	1.6	50
	0810	3.3	100		0705	4.3	130
	1525	1.3	40		1513	1.0	30
	2058	3.0	90		2028	3.6	110
11 Su	0324	1.6	50	26 M	0316	1.6	50
	0838	3.3	100		0806	4.3	130
	1601	1.3	40		1619	1.0	30
	2121	3.0	90		2130	3.3	100
12 M	0355	1.3	40	27 Tu	0411	1.3	40
	0908	3.3	100		0912	4.3	130
	1636	1.3	40		1723	1.0	30
	2144	3.0	90		2232	3.3	100
13 Tu	0423	1.3	40	28 W	0505	1.3	40
	0942	3.3	100		1024	4.3	130
	1709	1.3	40		1824	1.0	30
	2211	2.6	80		2330	3.3	100
14 W	0448	1.3	40	29 Th	0600	1.3	40
	1017	3.3	100		1138	4.3	130
	1742	1.3	40		1922	1.0	30
	2241	2.6	80				
15 Th	0516	1.3	40	30 F ◐	0024	3.0	90
	1054	3.3	100		0655	1.0	30
	1814	1.3	40		1248	3.9	120
	2317	2.6	80		2018	1.3	40

Time meridian 45° W. 0000 is midnight. 1200 is noon. Times are not adjusted for Daylight Saving Time.
Heights are referred to the chart datum of soundings.

Buenos Aires, Argentina, 2017

Times and Heights of High and Low Waters

July

Day	Time	ft	cm	Day	Time	ft	cm
1 Sa	0116	3.0	90	**16** Su ☽	0630	1.0	30
	0749	1.0	30		1208	3.6	110
	1354	3.9	120		1910	1.3	40
	2110	1.3	40				
2 Su	0206	3.0	90	**17** M	0015	3.0	90
	0845	1.0	30		0722	1.0	30
	1458	3.6	110		1305	3.6	110
	2200	1.3	40		1957	1.3	40
3 M	0259	2.6	80	**18** Tu	0101	3.0	90
	0941	1.0	30		0820	1.0	30
	1602	3.3	100		1403	3.6	110
	2248	1.6	50		2051	1.6	50
4 Tu	0356	2.6	80	**19** W	0152	3.3	100
	1038	1.0	30		0924	1.0	30
	1706	3.3	100		1503	3.6	110
	2333	1.6	50		2153	1.6	50
5 W	0455	2.6	80	**20** Th	0247	3.3	100
	1137	1.3	40		1031	1.0	30
	1804	3.0	90		1605	3.6	110
					2258	1.6	50
6 Th	0016	1.6	50	**21** F	0345	3.6	110
	0547	3.0	90		1140	1.0	30
	1233	1.3	40		1708	3.6	110
	1854	3.0	90				
7 F	0057	1.6	50	**22** Sa	0001	1.6	50
	0630	3.0	90		0447	3.9	120
	1324	1.3	40		1249	1.0	30
	1933	3.0	90		1812	3.6	110
8 Sa	0137	1.6	50	**23** Su ●	0102	1.6	50
	0704	3.0	90		0550	4.3	130
	1410	1.3	40		1359	1.0	30
	2003	2.6	80		1915	3.3	100
9 Su ○	0214	1.6	50	**24** M	0201	1.6	50
	0735	3.3	100		0654	4.3	130
	1453	1.3	40		1507	1.0	30
	2025	2.6	80		2017	3.3	100
10 M	0249	1.3	40	**25** Tu	0259	1.3	40
	0807	3.3	100		0800	4.3	130
	1533	1.3	40		1612	1.0	30
	2045	2.6	80		2115	3.3	100
11 Tu	0320	1.3	40	**26** W	0356	1.3	40
	0840	3.3	100		0909	4.3	130
	1610	1.3	40		1712	1.0	30
	2109	2.6	80		2211	3.3	100
12 W	0350	1.3	40	**27** Th	0452	1.3	40
	0916	3.3	100		1020	4.3	130
	1646	1.3	40		1807	1.0	30
	2139	2.6	80		2304	3.0	90
13 Th	0422	1.3	40	**28** F	0546	1.0	30
	0953	3.3	100		1129	3.9	120
	1720	1.3	40		1857	1.3	40
	2215	2.6	80		2353	3.0	90
14 F	0500	1.0	30	**29** Sa	0638	1.0	30
	1033	3.3	100		1233	3.9	120
	1754	1.3	40		1940	1.3	40
	2253	2.6	80				
15 Sa	0542	1.0	30	**30** Su ☽	0040	3.0	90
	1118	3.3	100		0728	1.0	30
	1830	1.3	40		1332	3.6	110
	2333	2.6	80		2017	1.3	40
				31 M	0126	3.0	90
					0817	1.0	30
					1427	3.3	100
					2050	1.6	50

August

Day	Time	ft	cm	Day	Time	ft	cm
1 Tu	0212	3.0	90	**16** W	0041	3.3	100
	0905	1.0	30		0821	1.0	30
	1521	3.3	100		1353	3.6	110
	2127	1.6	50		2030	1.6	50
2 W	0300	3.0	90	**17** Th	0133	3.6	110
	0954	1.3	40		0925	1.0	30
	1616	3.0	90		1451	3.6	110
	2212	1.6	50		2129	1.6	50
3 Th	0351	3.0	90	**18** F	0229	3.9	120
	1047	1.3	40		1031	1.0	30
	1713	2.6	80		1552	3.3	100
	2303	1.6	50		2234	1.6	50
4 F	0445	3.0	90	**19** Sa	0331	3.9	120
	1143	1.3	40		1139	1.0	30
	1806	2.6	80		1657	3.3	100
	2355	1.6	50		2338	1.6	50
5 Sa	0535	3.0	90	**20** Su	0437	4.3	130
	1239	1.3	40		1248	1.0	30
	1850	2.6	80		1804	3.3	100
6 Su	0042	1.6	50	**21** M ●	0043	1.6	50
	0620	3.3	100		0547	4.3	130
	1332	1.3	40		1358	1.3	40
	1922	2.6	80		1909	3.3	100
7 M ○	0124	1.6	50	**22** Tu	0145	1.6	50
	0659	3.3	100		0658	4.3	130
	1420	1.3	40		1503	1.3	40
	1944	2.6	80		2007	3.3	100
8 Tu	0201	1.6	50	**23** W	0246	1.3	40
	0735	3.3	100		0806	4.3	130
	1504	1.3	40		1603	1.3	40
	2007	2.6	80		2100	3.3	100
9 W	0237	1.3	40	**24** Th	0344	1.3	40
	0812	3.6	110		0910	4.3	130
	1544	1.3	40		1656	1.3	40
	2036	2.6	80		2149	3.3	100
10 Th	0316	1.3	40	**25** F	0438	1.3	40
	0850	3.6	110		1012	3.9	120
	1622	1.3	40		1741	1.3	40
	2111	2.6	80		2234	3.3	100
11 F	0400	1.3	40	**26** Sa	0530	1.3	40
	0930	3.6	110		1111	3.9	120
	1658	1.3	40		1817	1.3	40
	2149	3.0	90		2318	3.3	100
12 Sa	0446	1.0	30	**27** Su	0617	1.3	40
	1014	3.6	110		1206	3.6	110
	1734	1.3	40		1846	1.6	50
	2229	3.0	90				
13 Su	0535	1.0	30	**28** M	0001	3.3	100
	1104	3.6	110		0701	1.3	40
	1812	1.3	40		1256	3.6	110
	2311	3.0	90		1912	1.6	50
14 M ○	0627	1.0	30	**29** Tu ☽	0043	3.3	100
	1159	3.6	110		0743	1.3	40
	1853	1.3	40		1343	3.3	100
	2354	3.3	100		1941	1.6	50
15 Tu	0722	1.0	30	**30** W	0125	3.3	100
	1256	3.6	110		0824	1.3	40
	1939	1.6	50		1428	3.0	90
					2015	1.6	50
				31 Th	0209	3.3	100
					0907	1.3	40
					1515	2.6	80
					2052	1.6	50

September

Day	Time	ft	cm	Day	Time	ft	cm
1 F	0256	3.3	100	**16** Sa	0225	4.3	130
	0957	1.3	40		1034	1.3	40
	1603	2.6	80		1542	3.3	100
	2133	1.6	50		2216	1.6	50
2 Sa	0348	3.3	100	**17** Su	0333	4.3	130
	1054	1.6	50		1143	1.3	40
	1654	2.3	70		1649	3.0	90
	2217	2.0	60		2322	1.6	50
3 Su	0443	3.3	100	**18** M	0447	4.3	130
	1155	1.6	50		1252	1.3	40
	1741	2.0	70		1800	3.0	90
	2306	1.6	50				
4 M	0535	3.3	100	**19** Tu	0028	1.6	50
	1255	1.6	50		0605	4.3	130
	1818	2.3	70		1358	1.3	40
	2359	1.6	50		1906	3.0	90
5 Tu	0622	3.6	110	**20** W ●	0133	1.6	50
	1348	1.6	50		0715	4.3	130
	1850	2.6	80		1457	1.3	40
					2000	3.3	100
6 W	0054	1.6	50	**21** Th	0234	1.6	50
	0704	3.6	110		0814	4.3	130
	1434	1.6	50		1548	1.3	40
	1925	2.6	80		2045	3.3	100
7 Th	0149	1.6	50	**22** F	0330	1.3	40
	0744	3.6	110		0907	4.3	130
	1515	1.6	50		1630	1.6	50
	2001	3.0	90		2125	3.3	100
8 F	0244	1.3	40	**23** Sa	0422	1.3	40
	0825	3.9	120		0956	3.9	120
	1554	1.6	50		1704	1.6	50
	2040	3.0	90		2204	3.3	100
9 Sa	0338	1.3	40	**24** Su	0509	1.3	40
	0908	3.9	120		1043	3.9	120
	1633	1.6	50		1731	1.6	50
	2121	3.3	100		2242	3.3	100
10 Su	0432	1.3	40	**25** M	0551	1.3	40
	0956	3.9	120		1127	3.6	110
	1712	1.6	50		1756	1.6	50
	2203	3.3	100		2322	3.6	110
11 M	0526	1.3	40	**26** Tu	0629	1.6	50
	1050	3.9	120		1210	3.3	100
	1753	1.6	50		1823	1.6	50
	2247	3.6	110				
12 Tu	0622	1.3	40	**27** W ☽	0002	3.6	110
	1148	3.9	120		0705	1.6	50
	1835	1.6	50		1250	3.3	100
	2335	3.6	110		1851	1.6	50
13 W ○	0720	1.0	30	**28** Th	0042	3.6	110
	1247	3.6	110		0742	1.6	50
	1922	1.6	50		1328	3.0	90
					1920	1.6	50
14 Th	0027	3.9	120	**29** F	0125	3.6	110
	0822	1.0	30		0824	1.6	50
	1343	3.6	110		1402	2.6	80
	2013	1.6	50		1947	1.6	50
15 F	0124	3.9	120	**30** Sa	0210	3.3	100
	0927	1.3	40		0913	1.6	50
	1441	3.3	100		1433	2.6	80
	2112	1.6	50		2019	1.6	50

Time meridian 45° W. 0000 is midnight. 1200 is noon. Times are not adjusted for Daylight Saving Time.
Heights are referred to the chart datum of soundings.

Buenos Aires, Argentina, 2017

Times and Heights of High and Low Waters

October

Day	Time	ft	cm		Day	Time	ft	cm
1 Su	0301	3.3	100		16 M	0349	4.3	130
	1011	1.6	50			1146	1.3	40
	1511	2.3	70			1644	3.0	90
	2102	1.6	50			2308	1.6	50
2 M	0356	3.6	110		17 Tu	0509	4.3	130
	1115	1.6	50			1252	1.6	50
	1604	2.3	70			1800	3.0	90
	2156	1.6	50					
3 Tu	0452	3.6	110		18 W	0016	1.6	50
	1219	1.6	50			0622	4.3	130
	1703	2.3	70			1352	1.6	50
	2258	1.6	50			1905	3.0	90
4 W	0543	3.6	110		19 Th	0121	1.6	50
	1313	1.6	50			0722	4.3	130
	1756	2.6	80			1442	1.6	50
					●	1954	3.3	100
5 Th	0003	1.6	50		20 F	0221	1.6	50
	0630	3.9	120			0811	4.3	130
	1400	1.6	50			1524	1.6	50
O	1843	3.0	90			2032	3.3	100
6 F	0110	1.6	50		21 Sa	0314	1.6	50
	0714	3.9	120			0853	3.9	120
	1443	1.6	50			1556	1.6	50
	1926	3.0	90			2105	3.3	100
7 Sa	0215	1.3	40		22 Su	0402	1.6	50
	0758	4.3	130			0930	3.9	120
	1524	1.6	50			1623	1.6	50
	2008	3.3	100			2137	3.6	110
8 Su	0318	1.3	40		23 M	0445	1.6	50
	0844	4.3	130			1006	3.6	110
	1605	1.6	50			1649	1.6	50
	2051	3.6	110			2212	3.6	110
9 M	0418	1.3	40		24 Tu	0523	1.6	50
	0934	4.3	130			1041	3.6	110
	1648	1.6	50			1716	1.6	50
	2136	3.9	120			2248	3.6	110
10 Tu	0517	1.3	40		25 W	0557	1.6	50
	1032	3.9	120			1115	3.3	100
	1731	1.6	50			1743	1.6	50
	2226	3.9	120			2326	3.6	110
11 W	0617	1.3	40		26 Th	0632	1.6	50
	1134	3.9	120			1146	3.0	90
	1816	1.6	50			1808	1.6	50
	2322	4.3	130					
12 Th	0718	1.3	40		27 F	0006	3.6	110
	1234	3.6	110			0708	1.6	50
	1904	1.6	50			1212	3.0	90
☾					☽	1829	1.6	50
13 F	0023	4.3	130		28 Sa	0047	3.6	110
	0823	1.3	40			0749	2.0	60
	1331	3.6	110			1233	2.6	80
	1957	1.6	50			1854	1.6	50
14 Sa	0127	4.3	130		29 Su	0131	3.6	110
	0930	1.3	40			0837	2.0	60
	1429	3.3	100			1304	2.6	80
	2057	1.6	50			1929	1.6	50
15 Su	0235	4.3	130		30 M	0220	3.6	110
	1038	1.3	40			0933	2.0	60
	1532	3.0	90			1349	2.6	80
	2201	1.6	50			2016	1.6	50
					31 Tu	0314	3.6	110
						1037	2.0	60
						1452	2.3	70
						2115	1.6	50

November

Day	Time	ft	cm		Day	Time	ft	cm
1 W	0409	3.9	120		16 Th	0000	1.6	50
	1141	2.0	60			0618	4.3	130
	1603	2.6	80			1334	1.6	50
	2220	1.6	50			1902	3.0	90
2 Th	0503	3.9	120		17 F	0105	1.6	50
	1235	1.6	50			0711	4.3	130
	1708	2.6	80			1417	1.6	50
	2329	1.6	50			1948	3.3	100
3 F	0553	4.3	130		18 Sa	0203	1.6	50
	1323	1.6	50			0754	3.9	120
	1804	3.0	90			1450	1.6	50
					●	2023	3.3	100
4 Sa	0041	1.6	50		19 Su	0255	2.0	60
	0641	4.3	130			0828	3.9	120
	1408	1.6	50			1518	1.6	50
O	1852	3.3	100			2051	3.6	110
5 Su	0152	1.6	50		20 M	0340	2.0	60
	0728	4.3	130			0856	3.6	110
	1452	1.6	50			1545	1.6	50
	1939	3.6	110			2118	3.6	110
6 M	0300	1.6	50		21 Tu	0420	2.0	60
	0817	4.3	130			0923	3.6	110
	1536	1.6	50			1614	1.6	50
	2026	3.9	120			2149	3.6	110
7 Tu	0404	1.6	50		22 W	0456	2.0	60
	0911	4.3	130			0949	3.3	100
	1621	1.6	50			1641	1.3	40
	2117	4.3	130			2223	3.9	120
8 W	0508	1.3	40		23 Th	0532	2.0	60
	1010	3.9	120			1014	3.3	100
	1708	1.6	50			1706	1.3	40
	2214	4.6	140			2259	3.9	120
9 Th	0612	1.3	40		24 F	0608	2.0	60
	1114	3.6	110			1038	3.0	90
	1756	1.6	50			1725	1.3	40
	2319	4.6	140			2338	3.9	120
10 F	0717	1.3	40		25 Sa	0645	2.0	60
	1216	3.6	110			1104	3.0	90
	1847	1.6	50			1745	1.3	40
☾								
11 Sa	0028	4.6	140		26 Su	0018	3.9	120
	0824	1.3	40			0724	2.0	60
	1315	3.3	100			1137	2.6	80
	1941	1.6	50		☽	1814	1.3	40
12 Su	0137	4.6	140		27 M	0100	3.9	120
	0931	1.6	50			0809	2.0	60
	1414	3.0	90			1216	2.6	80
	2041	1.6	50			1853	1.3	40
13 M	0247	4.6	140		28 Tu	0145	3.9	120
	1038	1.6	50			0901	2.0	60
	1520	3.0	90			1305	2.6	80
	2145	1.6	50			1942	1.3	40
14 Tu	0401	4.6	140		29 W	0235	3.9	120
	1143	1.6	50			1001	2.0	60
	1638	3.0	90			1407	2.6	80
	2252	1.6	50			2042	1.3	40
15 W	0514	4.3	130		30 Th	0328	4.3	130
	1243	1.6	50			1101	2.0	60
	1759	3.0	90			1517	2.6	80
						2150	1.6	50

December

Day	Time	ft	cm		Day	Time	ft	cm
1 F	0423	4.3	130		16 Sa	0040	2.0	60
	1156	1.6	50			0644	3.9	120
	1626	3.0	90			1342	1.6	50
	2302	1.6	50			1938	3.3	100
2 Sa	0516	4.3	130		17 Su	0139	2.0	60
	1246	1.6	50			0723	3.9	120
	1727	3.3	100			1412	1.3	40
						2015	3.3	100
3 Su	0018	1.6	50		18 M	0230	2.0	60
	0607	4.6	140			0753	3.6	110
	1334	1.6	50			1442	1.3	40
O	1822	3.6	110		●	2042	3.6	110
4 M	0134	1.6	50		19 Tu	0315	2.3	70
	0658	4.6	140			0817	3.6	110
	1421	1.6	50			1512	1.3	40
	1914	3.9	120			2106	3.6	110
5 Tu	0245	1.6	50		20 W	0356	2.3	70
	0751	4.3	130			0838	3.3	100
	1509	1.6	50			1541	1.3	40
	2008	4.3	130			2133	3.9	120
6 W	0354	1.6	50		21 Th	0435	2.3	70
	0847	3.9	120			0858	3.3	100
	1557	1.3	40			1608	1.3	40
	2107	4.6	140			2205	3.9	120
7 Th	0502	1.6	50		22 F	0513	2.3	70
	0947	3.9	120			0921	3.0	90
	1646	1.3	40			1630	1.3	40
	2213	4.9	150			2240	3.9	120
8 F	0608	1.6	50		23 Sa	0551	2.3	70
	1050	3.6	110			0949	3.0	90
	1737	1.3	40			1649	1.3	40
	2324	4.9	150			2318	3.9	120
9 Sa	0715	1.6	50		24 Su	0628	2.0	60
	1152	3.3	100			1023	3.0	90
	1830	1.3	40			1714	1.0	30
						2356	3.9	120
10 Su	0034	4.9	150		25 M	0705	2.0	60
	0821	1.6	50			1100	2.6	80
	1252	3.0	90			1748	1.0	30
☾	1925	1.3	40					
11 M	0141	4.9	150		26 Tu	0035	4.3	130
	0925	1.6	50			0745	2.0	60
	1352	3.0	90			1143	2.6	80
	2023	1.3	40		☽	1829	1.0	30
12 Tu	0247	4.6	140		27 W	0117	4.3	130
	1028	1.6	50			0831	2.0	60
	1459	2.6	80			1232	2.6	80
	2124	1.3	40			1916	1.3	40
13 W	0353	4.6	140		28 Th	0203	4.3	130
	1127	1.6	50			0925	2.0	60
	1620	2.6	80			1332	2.6	80
	2229	1.6	50			2015	1.3	40
14 Th	0457	4.3	130		29 F	0254	4.3	130
	1220	1.6	50			1023	2.0	60
	1745	3.0	90			1438	3.0	90
	2335	1.6	50			2125	1.6	50
15 F	0555	4.3	130		30 Sa	0347	4.6	140
	1305	1.6	50			1119	2.0	60
	1850	3.0	90			1547	3.0	90
						2243	1.6	50
					31 Su	0442	4.6	140
						1212	1.6	50
						1653	3.6	110

Time meridian 45° W. 0000 is midnight. 1200 is noon. Times are not adjusted for Daylight Saving Time.
Heights are referred to the chart datum of soundings.

Puerto Ingeniero White, Argentina, 2017

Times and Heights of High and Low Waters

January

Day	Time	Height (ft)	Height (cm)	Day	Time	Height (ft)	Height (cm)
1 Su	0255	3.6	110	16 M	0251	3.6	110
	0859	14.1	430		0858	13.1	400
	1515	1.6	50		1530	1.6	50
	2142	14.1	430		2211	13.8	420
2 M	0327	3.6	110	17 Tu	0344	3.0	90
	0925	14.1	430		1039	13.5	410
	1549	1.6	50		1621	1.3	40
	2159	14.4	440		2300	14.4	440
3 Tu	0359	3.3	100	18 W	0438	2.3	70
	0955	14.1	430		1142	13.8	420
	1623	1.3	40		1711	1.3	40
	2220	14.4	440		2351	14.8	450
4 W	0436	3.0	90	19 Th	0533	2.0	60
	1033	14.4	440		1237	14.4	440
	1659	1.3	40		1801	1.3	40
	2249	14.8	450	○			
5 Th	0517	2.3	70	20 F	0045	15.1	460
	1120	14.4	440		0629	2.0	60
	1739	1.0	30		1327	14.4	440
◐	2326	15.1	460		1851	2.0	60
6 F	0604	2.0	60	21 Sa	0140	15.1	460
	1212	14.8	450		0726	1.6	50
	1823	1.0	30		1416	14.4	440
					1942	2.3	70
7 Sa	0010	15.1	460	22 Su	0233	15.1	460
	0655	1.6	50		0821	1.6	50
	1308	14.8	450		1503	14.4	440
	1910	1.3	40		2035	3.0	90
8 Su	0100	15.1	460	23 M	0325	15.1	460
	0750	1.6	50		0916	1.6	50
	1404	14.8	450		1551	14.4	440
	2001	2.0	60		2131	3.6	110
9 M	0157	14.8	450	24 Tu	0413	15.1	460
	0848	1.6	50		1008	1.6	50
	1501	14.1	430		1640	14.1	430
	2056	3.0	90		2230	3.9	120
10 Tu	0258	14.4	440	25 W	0459	15.1	460
	0948	2.0	60		1059	1.6	50
	1559	13.8	420		1731	14.1	430
	2157	3.9	120		2326	4.3	130
11 W	0359	13.8	420	26 Th	0543	14.8	450
	1048	2.0	60		1149	1.6	50
	1702	13.1	400		1823	14.1	430
	2301	4.6	140				
12 Th	0455	13.5	410	27 F	0018	4.3	130
	1148	2.3	70		0626	14.8	450
	1810	12.8	390		1237	1.6	50
○				●	1914	14.1	430
13 F	0004	4.6	140	28 Sa	0105	3.9	120
	0544	13.1	400		0708	14.4	440
	1247	2.3	70		1322	2.0	60
	1922	12.8	390		2001	14.1	430
14 Sa	0103	4.6	140	29 Su	0146	3.9	120
	0631	13.1	400		0747	14.1	430
	1344	2.3	70		1404	2.0	60
	2027	12.8	390		2039	14.1	430
15 Su	0158	3.9	120	30 M	0222	3.9	120
	0725	13.1	400		0823	14.1	430
	1438	2.0	60		1442	2.0	60
	2122	13.5	410		2106	14.1	430
				31 Tu	0257	3.6	110
					0857	13.8	420
					1518	2.0	60
					2125	14.1	430

February

Day	Time	Height (ft)	Height (cm)	Day	Time	Height (ft)	Height (cm)
1 W	0334	3.3	100	16 Th	0422	2.0	60
	0933	13.8	420		1123	14.1	430
	1554	1.6	50		1649	1.3	40
	2147	14.4	440		2325	15.1	460
2 Th	0413	2.6	80	17 F	0513	1.6	50
	1014	14.1	430		1209	14.4	440
	1632	1.3	40		1734	1.6	50
	2217	14.8	450				
3 F	0457	2.0	60	18 Sa	0012	15.1	460
	1101	14.4	440		0604	1.3	40
	1714	1.3	40		1253	14.4	440
	2254	15.1	460	◐	1820	2.0	60
4 Sa	0545	1.6	50	19 Su	0100	15.1	460
	1153	14.4	440		0655	1.3	40
	1758	1.3	40		1335	14.4	440
◑	2338	15.1	460		1905	2.6	80
5 Su	0637	1.3	40	20 M	0148	15.1	460
	1248	14.4	440		0744	1.3	40
	1846	1.6	50		1417	14.4	440
					1953	3.3	100
6 M	0030	15.1	460	21 Tu	0235	15.1	460
	0732	1.3	40		0833	1.3	40
	1345	14.4	440		1500	14.1	430
	1937	2.3	70		2043	3.9	120
7 Tu	0133	14.8	450	22 W	0321	14.8	450
	0829	1.3	40		0922	1.6	50
	1445	13.8	420		1546	14.1	430
	2034	3.3	100		2137	4.3	130
8 W	0244	14.1	430	23 Th	0406	14.8	450
	0929	1.6	50		1010	1.6	50
	1549	13.5	410		1635	13.8	420
	2137	4.3	130		2234	4.6	140
9 Th	0357	13.8	420	24 F	0450	14.8	450
	1030	2.0	60		1100	2.0	60
	1700	12.8	390		1728	13.8	420
	2245	4.6	140		2330	4.6	140
10 F	0505	13.1	400	25 Sa	0535	14.4	440
	1132	2.3	70		1150	2.0	60
	1818	12.8	390		1822	13.8	420
○	2351	4.9	150				
11 Sa	0610	13.1	400	26 Su	0021	4.3	130
	1232	2.6	80		0621	14.4	440
	1930	12.8	390		1239	2.3	70
				●	1912	13.8	420
12 Su	0052	4.6	140	27 M	0106	3.9	120
	0718	12.8	390		0705	14.1	430
	1330	2.6	80		1325	2.3	70
	2028	13.1	400		1953	13.8	420
13 M	0148	3.9	120	28 Tu	0148	3.6	110
	0832	12.8	390		0749	13.8	420
	1424	2.3	70		1406	2.3	70
	2115	13.8	420		2023	13.8	420
14 Tu	0240	3.3	100				
	0938	13.1	400				
	1514	2.0	60				
	2158	14.1	430				
15 W	0331	2.6	80				
	1033	13.5	410				
	1602	1.6	50				
	2241	14.8	450				

March

Day	Time	Height (ft)	Height (cm)	Day	Time	Height (ft)	Height (cm)
1 W	0228	3.3	100	16 Th	0317	2.0	60
	0830	13.8	420		1017	13.8	420
	1446	2.3	70		1542	1.6	50
	2046	14.1	430		2217	15.1	460
2 Th	0308	3.0	90	17 F	0404	1.6	50
	0911	13.8	420		1058	14.1	430
	1525	2.3	70		1625	1.6	50
	2111	14.4	440		2255	15.1	460
3 F	0351	2.3	70	18 Sa	0451	1.0	30
	0955	13.8	420		1138	14.4	440
	1606	2.0	60		1706	2.0	60
	2142	14.8	450		2333	15.1	460
4 Sa	0437	1.6	50	19 Su	0537	1.0	30
	1043	14.1	430		1215	14.4	440
	1648	1.6	50		1747	2.3	70
	2220	15.1	460				
5 Su	0526	1.3	40	20 M	0013	15.1	460
	1135	14.1	430		0621	1.0	30
	1734	1.6	50		1251	14.4	440
◐	2306	15.1	460	○	1827	3.0	90
6 M	0618	1.0	30	21 Tu	0053	14.8	450
	1231	14.1	430		0705	1.0	30
	1823	2.3	70		1326	14.4	440
					1909	3.6	110
7 Tu	0002	14.8	450	22 W	0136	14.8	450
	0713	1.0	30		0748	1.3	40
	1331	14.1	430		1404	14.1	430
	1917	3.0	90		1953	3.9	120
8 W	0119	14.4	440	23 Th	0221	14.8	450
	0811	1.3	40		0832	1.3	40
	1436	13.5	410		1447	14.1	430
	2018	3.6	110		2043	4.3	130
9 Th	0255	13.8	420	24 F	0309	14.8	450
	0912	1.6	50		0918	1.6	50
	1549	13.1	400		1537	13.8	420
	2125	4.3	130		2139	4.6	140
10 F	0416	13.5	410	25 Sa	0357	14.4	440
	1014	2.3	70		1007	2.0	60
	1707	13.1	400		1631	13.8	420
	2236	4.6	140		2238	4.3	130
11 Sa	0528	13.1	400	26 Su	0447	14.4	440
	1118	2.6	80		1059	2.3	70
	1823	13.1	400		1727	13.8	420
	2344	4.6	140		2334	4.3	130
12 Su	0636	13.1	400	27 M	0537	14.1	430
	1220	2.6	80		1152	2.6	80
	1926	13.5	410		1819	13.8	420
○				●			
13 M	0044	3.9	120	28 Tu	0026	3.9	120
	0741	13.1	400		0626	14.1	430
	1317	2.6	80		1243	3.0	90
	2017	14.1	430		1903	13.8	420
14 Tu	0138	3.3	100	29 W	0113	3.3	100
	0839	13.1	400		0714	13.8	420
	1409	2.3	70		1330	3.0	90
	2100	14.4	440		1937	14.1	430
15 W	0229	2.6	80	30 Th	0158	3.0	90
	0931	13.5	410		0801	13.5	410
	1457	2.0	60		1414	3.0	90
	2139	14.8	450		2005	14.1	430
				31 F	0243	2.3	70
					0847	13.5	410
					1456	2.6	80
					2033	14.4	440

Time meridian 45° W. 0000 is midnight. 1200 is noon. Times are not adjusted for Daylight Saving Time.
Heights are referred to the chart datum of soundings.

Puerto Ingeniero White, Argentina, 2017

Times and Heights of High and Low Waters

April

Day	Time	ft	cm	Day	Time	ft	cm
1 Sa	0328	2.0	60	**16** Su	0427	0.7	20
	0934	13.5	410		1106	14.4	440
	1539	2.3	70		1638	2.3	70
	2105	14.8	450		2252	15.1	460
2 Su	0416	1.3	40	**17** M	0508	0.7	20
	1023	13.8	420		1137	14.4	440
	1624	2.3	70		1714	2.6	80
	2145	15.1	460		2322	15.1	460
3 M ☾	0507	1.0	30	**18** Tu	0547	0.7	20
	1117	13.8	420		1205	14.4	440
	1712	2.3	70		1750	3.3	100
	2234	14.8	450		2355	14.8	450
4 Tu	0600	1.0	30	**19** W ◐	0626	1.0	30
	1216	13.8	420		1235	14.4	440
	1804	2.6	80		1828	3.6	110
	2340	14.4	440				
5 W	0656	1.0	30	**20** Th	0036	14.8	450
	1321	13.8	420		0704	1.0	30
	1901	3.3	100		1311	14.4	440
					1909	3.9	120
6 Th	0135	13.8	420	**21** F	0125	14.8	450
	0754	1.3	40		0745	1.3	40
	1434	13.5	410		1354	14.1	430
	2005	3.9	120		1958	3.9	120
7 F	0310	13.8	420	**22** Sa	0217	14.8	450
	0855	2.0	60		0829	1.3	40
	1551	13.5	410		1443	14.1	430
	2117	4.3	130		2053	3.9	120
8 Sa	0423	13.5	410	**23** Su	0310	14.8	450
	0959	2.3	70		0918	2.0	60
	1706	13.5	410		1539	14.1	430
	2230	4.3	130		2152	3.9	120
9 Su	0530	13.5	410	**24** M	0403	14.4	440
	1103	2.6	80		1011	2.3	70
	1813	14.1	430		1635	14.1	430
	2337	3.9	120		2252	3.6	110
10 M	0633	13.5	410	**25** Tu	0457	14.1	430
	1206	2.6	80		1106	2.6	80
	1910	14.4	440		1729	14.1	430
					2348	3.3	100
11 Tu ○	0035	3.3	100	**26** W ●	0549	13.8	420
	0733	13.8	420		1201	3.0	90
	1302	2.6	80		1815	14.1	430
	1957	14.8	450				
12 W	0127	2.6	80	**27** Th	0040	3.0	90
	0826	13.8	420		0641	13.5	410
	1352	2.3	70		1253	3.3	100
	2038	15.1	460		1852	14.1	430
13 Th	0214	2.0	60	**28** F	0130	2.6	80
	0913	14.1	430		0732	13.5	410
	1438	2.3	70		1342	3.3	100
	2115	15.4	470		1924	14.4	440
14 F	0300	1.3	40	**29** Sa	0218	2.0	60
	0955	14.1	430		0822	13.1	400
	1520	2.0	60		1428	3.3	100
	2150	15.4	470		1955	14.8	450
15 Sa	0344	1.0	30	**30** Su	0307	1.6	50
	1032	14.4	440		0912	13.1	400
	1600	2.0	60		1514	3.0	90
	2222	15.4	470		2030	14.8	450

May

Day	Time	ft	cm	Day	Time	ft	cm
1 M	0357	1.3	40	**16** Tu	0439	0.7	20
	1004	13.5	410		1102	14.4	440
	1602	2.6	80		1643	3.3	100
	2114	14.8	450		2238	14.8	450
2 Tu ◐	0448	1.0	30	**17** W	0514	0.7	20
	1101	13.5	410		1124	14.4	440
	1652	3.0	90		1716	3.3	100
	2208	14.4	440		2309	14.8	450
3 W	0542	0.7	20	**18** Th ◐	0549	0.7	20
	1205	13.8	420		1150	14.4	440
	1747	3.0	90		1752	3.6	110
	2336	14.1	430		2351	14.8	450
4 Th	0638	1.0	30	**19** F	0625	0.7	20
	1315	13.8	420		1225	14.4	440
	1847	3.6	110		1834	3.6	110
5 F	0151	13.8	420	**20** Sa	0040	14.8	450
	0736	1.3	40		0705	1.0	30
	1430	13.8	420		1308	14.4	440
	1955	3.9	120		1922	3.6	110
6 Sa	0308	13.8	420	**21** Su	0134	14.8	450
	0836	2.0	60		0749	1.0	30
	1544	14.1	430		1357	14.4	440
	2107	3.9	120		2016	3.3	100
7 Su	0414	13.8	420	**22** M	0229	14.8	450
	0940	2.3	70		0837	1.6	50
	1652	14.4	440		1452	14.4	440
	2219	3.6	110		2115	3.3	100
8 M	0516	13.8	420	**23** Tu	0325	14.4	440
	1045	2.6	80		0929	2.3	70
	1752	14.8	450		1549	14.4	440
	2323	3.0	90		2215	3.0	90
9 Tu	0615	13.8	420	**24** W	0420	14.1	430
	1147	3.0	90		1025	3.0	90
	1844	15.1	460		1643	14.4	440
					2314	3.0	90
10 W ○	0019	2.3	70	**25** Th ●	0515	13.8	420
	0712	14.1	430		1123	3.3	100
	1242	2.6	80		1731	14.4	440
	1930	15.4	470				
11 Th	0110	1.6	50	**26** F	0010	2.6	80
	0803	14.1	430		0610	13.1	400
	1332	2.6	80		1219	3.6	110
	2011	15.7	480		1812	14.4	440
12 F	0156	1.3	40	**27** Sa	0103	2.3	70
	0849	14.4	440		0705	12.8	390
	1416	2.3	70		1312	3.6	110
	2048	15.7	480		1847	14.4	440
13 Sa	0240	1.0	30	**28** Su	0155	2.0	60
	0930	14.4	440		0800	12.8	390
	1457	2.3	70		1402	3.6	110
	2122	15.4	470		1921	14.4	440
14 Su	0322	0.7	20	**29** M	0247	1.6	50
	1006	14.4	440		0855	12.8	390
	1535	2.6	80		1452	3.3	100
	2151	15.4	470		2001	14.8	450
15 M	0402	0.7	20	**30** Tu	0338	1.3	40
	1037	14.4	440		0951	13.1	400
	1610	3.0	90		1542	3.3	100
	2215	15.1	460		2050	14.4	440
				31 W	0431	1.0	30
					1051	13.5	410
					1635	3.3	100
					2154	14.1	430

June

Day	Time	ft	cm	Day	Time	ft	cm
1 Th ◐	0524	1.0	30	**16** F	0516	0.7	20
	1156	13.8	420		1113	14.4	440
	1732	3.3	100		1723	3.3	100
					2318	14.8	450
2 F	0018	13.8	420	**17** Sa ◐	0552	0.7	20
	0619	1.0	30		1147	14.8	450
	1306	13.8	420		1805	3.0	90
	1834	3.3	100				
3 Sa	0145	13.8	420	**18** Su	0006	15.1	460
	0715	1.3	40		0631	0.7	20
	1416	14.1	430		1227	14.8	450
	1942	3.6	110		1853	3.0	90
4 Su	0251	14.1	430	**19** M	0059	15.1	460
	0814	2.0	60		0714	1.0	30
	1524	14.4	440		1315	15.1	460
	2052	3.3	100		1947	2.6	80
5 M	0352	14.1	430	**20** Tu	0154	14.8	450
	0916	2.3	70		0802	1.3	40
	1626	15.1	460		1409	14.8	450
	2159	3.0	90		2044	2.6	80
6 Tu	0450	14.1	430	**21** W	0250	14.4	440
	1020	2.6	80		0854	2.0	60
	1723	15.4	470		1506	14.8	450
	2301	2.3	70		2144	2.6	80
7 W	0547	14.1	430	**22** Th	0347	13.8	420
	1121	3.0	90		0950	3.0	90
	1813	15.7	480		1603	14.4	440
	2356	2.0	60		2244	2.3	70
8 Th	0642	14.1	430	**23** F ●	0444	13.5	410
	1217	3.0	90		1049	3.6	110
	1858	15.7	480		1654	14.4	440
					2343	2.3	70
9 F	0046	1.3	40	**24** Sa ○	0543	12.8	390
	0733	14.1	430		1150	4.3	130
	1307	3.0	90		1739	14.1	430
	1939	15.7	480				
10 Sa	0133	1.0	30	**25** Su	0040	2.3	70
	0820	14.4	440		0645	12.5	380
	1352	2.6	80		1247	4.3	130
	2018	15.7	480		1818	14.1	430
11 Su	0217	0.7	20	**26** M	0135	2.0	60
	0902	14.4	440		0748	12.5	380
	1433	3.0	90		1341	4.3	130
	2052	15.4	470		1857	14.1	430
12 M	0258	0.7	20	**27** Tu	0229	1.6	50
	0939	14.4	440		0850	12.5	380
	1509	3.0	90		1434	3.9	120
	2121	15.1	460		1943	14.1	430
13 Tu	0336	0.7	20	**28** W	0322	1.3	40
	1010	14.4	440		0948	12.8	390
	1543	3.3	100		1526	3.6	110
	2144	14.8	450		2040	14.1	430
14 W	0411	0.7	20	**29** Th	0414	1.0	30
	1031	14.4	440		1046	13.5	410
	1614	3.3	100		1621	3.3	100
	2206	14.8	450		2230	13.8	420
15 Th	0443	0.7	20	**30** F ☾	0506	1.0	30
	1049	14.4	440		1146	13.8	420
	1647	3.6	110		1718	3.0	90
	2237	14.8	450				

Time meridian 45° W. 0000 is midnight. 1200 is noon. Times are not adjusted for Daylight Saving Time.
Heights are referred to the chart datum of soundings.

Puerto Ingeniero White, Argentina, 2017
Times and Heights of High and Low Waters

July

Day	Time	ft	cm	Day	Time	ft	cm
1 Sa	0019	13.8	420	16 Su ☽	0522	0.7	20
	0558	1.0	30		1112	14.8	450
	1249	14.4	440		1741	2.6	80
	1820	3.0	90		2340	15.1	460
2 Su	0125	14.1	430	17 M	0601	0.7	20
	0652	1.3	40		1151	15.1	460
	1353	14.8	450		1829	2.3	70
	1923	2.6	80				
3 M	0224	14.1	430	18 Tu	0031	15.1	460
	0748	1.6	50		0645	0.7	20
	1455	15.1	460		1237	15.1	460
	2028	2.6	80		1922	2.0	60
4 Tu	0320	14.1	430	19 W	0124	14.8	450
	0846	2.3	70		0732	1.3	40
	1553	15.4	470		1330	15.1	460
	2131	2.3	70		2018	2.0	60
5 W	0415	14.1	430	20 Th	0220	14.4	440
	0947	3.0	90		0823	2.3	70
	1647	15.7	480		1429	14.8	450
	2230	2.0	60		2117	2.3	70
6 Th	0510	14.1	430	21 F	0317	13.8	420
	1049	3.3	100		0920	3.3	100
	1736	15.7	480		1530	14.4	440
	2325	1.6	50		2218	2.3	70
7 F	0604	13.8	420	22 Sa	0418	12.8	390
	1146	3.3	100		1022	3.9	120
	1821	15.7	480		1628	14.1	430
					2319	2.6	80
8 Sa	0017	1.3	40	23 Su ●	0525	12.5	380
	0658	14.1	430		1127	4.6	140
	1238	3.3	100		1719	13.8	420
	1904	15.7	480				
9 Su ○	0105	1.3	40	24 M	0020	2.6	80
	0747	14.1	430		0640	12.1	370
	1324	3.3	100		1228	4.6	140
	1944	15.7	480		1806	13.8	420
10 M	0150	1.0	30	25 Tu	0119	2.6	80
	0832	14.1	430		0755	12.1	370
	1406	3.3	100		1326	4.3	130
	2020	15.4	470		1853	13.5	410
11 Tu	0231	1.0	30	26 W	0214	2.3	70
	0911	14.1	430		0857	12.5	380
	1442	3.3	100		1421	3.9	120
	2052	15.1	460		1952	13.5	410
12 W	0308	1.0	30	27 Th	0307	1.6	50
	0942	14.1	430		0949	13.1	400
	1516	3.6	110		1514	3.3	100
	2118	14.8	450		2134	13.5	410
13 Th	0342	1.0	30	28 F	0358	1.3	40
	1002	14.1	430		1038	13.8	420
	1547	3.6	110		1608	3.0	90
	2143	14.8	450		2301	13.8	420
14 F	0413	1.0	30	29 Sa	0447	1.0	30
	1017	14.1	430		1130	14.1	430
	1620	3.3	100		1704	2.6	80
	2214	14.8	450				
15 Sa	0446	0.7	20	30 Su ☾	0003	14.1	430
	1040	14.4	440		0537	1.0	30
	1658	3.0	90		1226	14.8	450
	2254	14.8	450		1801	2.3	70
				31 M	0058	14.4	440
					0627	1.3	40
					1323	15.1	460
					1900	2.0	60

August

Day	Time	ft	cm	Day	Time	ft	cm
1 Tu	0150	14.4	440	16 W	0007	14.8	450
	0718	1.6	50		0618	1.0	30
	1419	15.1	460		1202	15.1	460
	1958	2.0	60		1900	1.6	50
2 W	0241	14.4	440	17 Th	0059	14.8	450
	0812	2.3	70		0706	1.6	50
	1514	15.4	470		1257	15.1	460
	2056	2.0	60		1956	1.6	50
3 Th	0332	14.1	430	18 F	0154	14.1	430
	0909	3.0	90		0759	2.6	80
	1605	15.4	470		1401	14.4	440
	2152	2.0	60		2055	2.0	60
4 F	0424	13.8	420	19 Sa	0255	13.5	410
	1009	3.6	110		0858	3.6	110
	1653	15.4	470		1512	14.1	430
	2247	2.0	60		2156	2.6	80
5 Sa	0518	13.8	420	20 Su	0403	12.5	380
	1108	3.6	110		1003	4.3	130
	1739	15.4	470		1623	13.8	420
	2339	1.6	50		2300	3.0	90
6 Su	0613	13.8	420	21 M ●	0525	12.1	370
	1202	3.9	120		1112	4.6	140
	1822	15.4	470		1731	13.5	410
7 M ○	0029	1.6	50	22 Tu	0004	3.0	90
	0706	13.8	420		0653	12.1	370
	1251	3.6	110		1217	4.6	140
	1904	15.1	460		1840	13.1	400
8 Tu	0117	1.6	50	23 W	0105	3.0	90
	0755	13.8	420		0804	12.5	380
	1334	3.6	110		1316	4.3	130
	1945	15.1	460		1954	13.1	400
9 W	0159	1.6	50	24 Th	0201	2.6	80
	0836	13.8	420		0857	12.8	390
	1412	3.6	110		1411	3.6	110
	2021	14.8	450		2104	13.5	410
10 Th	0237	1.6	50	25 F	0253	2.0	60
	0909	13.8	420		0942	13.5	410
	1447	3.6	110		1504	3.0	90
	2053	14.4	440		2203	13.8	420
11 F	0311	1.6	50	26 Sa	0341	1.6	50
	0929	13.8	420		1025	14.1	430
	1520	3.3	100		1556	2.3	70
	2123	14.4	440		2254	14.1	430
12 Sa	0344	1.3	40	27 Su	0428	1.3	40
	0945	14.1	430		1109	14.8	450
	1556	3.0	90		1648	2.0	60
	2155	14.4	440		2341	14.4	440
13 Su	0418	1.3	40	28 M	0513	1.0	30
	1007	14.4	440		1157	15.1	460
	1635	2.6	80		1740	1.6	50
	2234	14.8	450				
14 M ○	0454	1.0	30	29 Tu ☾	0027	14.8	450
	1038	15.1	460		0559	1.3	40
	1719	2.0	60		1247	15.1	460
	2318	15.1	460		1833	1.3	40
15 Tu	0535	0.7	20	30 W	0111	14.8	450
	1116	15.1	460		0646	2.0	60
	1808	1.6	50		1338	15.1	460
					1925	1.6	50
				31 Th	0156	14.4	440
					0734	2.6	80
					1428	15.1	460
					2016	1.6	50

September

Day	Time	ft	cm	Day	Time	ft	cm
1 F	0242	14.1	430	16 Sa	0137	13.8	420
	0826	3.3	100		0740	3.0	90
	1517	15.1	460		1351	14.1	430
	2108	2.0	60		2036	2.0	60
2 Sa	0330	13.8	420	17 Su	0244	13.1	400
	0921	3.9	120		0843	3.6	110
	1603	15.1	460		1524	13.8	420
	2159	2.0	60		2138	2.6	80
3 Su	0422	13.5	410	18 M	0406	12.5	380
	1019	4.3	130		0953	4.3	130
	1649	15.1	460		1646	13.5	410
	2252	2.3	70		2244	3.3	100
4 M	0518	13.5	410	19 Tu	0537	12.1	370
	1117	4.3	130		1104	4.6	140
	1734	15.1	460		1801	13.1	400
	2344	2.3	70		2351	3.3	100
5 Tu	0614	13.5	410	20 W ●	0656	12.5	380
	1209	3.9	120		1210	4.3	130
	1819	14.8	450		1912	13.5	410
6 W ○	0034	2.3	70	21 Th	0053	3.3	100
	0707	13.5	410		0757	13.1	400
	1255	3.9	120		1309	3.6	110
	1903	14.8	450		2015	13.5	410
7 Th	0120	2.3	70	22 F	0148	2.6	80
	0752	13.8	420		0844	13.5	410
	1337	3.6	110		1402	3.0	90
	1946	14.4	440		2109	13.8	420
8 F	0201	2.3	70	23 Sa	0237	2.3	70
	0826	13.8	420		0926	14.1	430
	1415	3.3	100		1452	2.3	70
	2025	14.4	440		2155	14.1	430
9 Sa	0238	2.3	70	24 Su	0323	1.6	50
	0848	13.8	420		1004	14.4	440
	1453	3.0	90		1540	1.6	50
	2101	14.4	440		2237	14.4	440
10 Su	0314	2.0	60	25 M	0407	1.3	40
	0908	14.1	430		1044	14.8	450
	1532	2.6	80		1629	1.3	40
	2136	14.4	440		2316	14.8	450
11 M	0350	1.6	50	26 Tu	0449	1.3	40
	0932	14.4	440		1125	15.1	460
	1614	2.0	60		1716	1.0	30
	2214	14.4	440		2354	15.1	460
12 Tu	0428	1.3	40	27 W ☽	0532	1.6	50
	1004	14.8	450		1208	15.1	460
	1659	1.6	50		1803	1.0	30
	2258	14.8	450				
13 W ☾	0510	1.3	40	28 Th	0032	14.8	450
	1043	15.1	460		0614	2.0	60
	1748	1.3	40		1253	15.1	460
	2346	14.8	450		1849	1.3	40
14 Th	0555	1.3	40	29 F	0109	14.4	440
	1131	15.1	460		0656	2.6	80
	1841	1.3	40		1338	15.1	460
					1934	1.3	40
15 F	0038	14.4	440	30 Sa	0147	14.1	430
	0645	2.0	60		0741	3.3	100
	1231	14.8	450		1422	14.8	450
	1937	1.6	50		2020	1.6	50

Time meridian 45° W. 0000 is midnight. 1200 is noon. Times are not adjusted for Daylight Saving Time.
Heights are referred to the chart datum of soundings.

Puerto Ingeniero White, Argentina, 2017

Times and Heights of High and Low Waters

October

Day	Time (h m)	Height (ft)	Height (cm)
1 Su	0229 / 0831 / 1507 / 2106	13.8 / 3.6 / 14.8 / 2.3	420 / 110 / 450 / 70
2 M	0318 / 0925 / 1553 / 2156	13.8 / 3.9 / 14.8 / 2.6	420 / 120 / 450 / 80
3 Tu	0412 / 1022 / 1641 / 2248	13.5 / 4.3 / 14.8 / 3.0	410 / 130 / 450 / 90
4 W	0510 / 1119 / 1729 / 2342	13.5 / 3.9 / 14.8 / 3.0	410 / 120 / 450 / 90
5 Th ○	0606 / 1210 / 1818	13.5 / 3.6 / 14.4	410 / 110 / 440
6 F	0033 / 0654 / 1257 / 1907	3.0 / 13.5 / 3.3 / 14.4	90 / 410 / 100 / 440
7 Sa	0120 / 0732 / 1341 / 1952	3.0 / 13.5 / 3.0 / 14.1	90 / 410 / 90 / 430
8 Su	0202 / 0800 / 1424 / 2034	3.0 / 13.8 / 2.6 / 14.1	90 / 420 / 80 / 430
9 M	0242 / 0825 / 1507 / 2114	2.6 / 14.1 / 2.3 / 14.1	80 / 430 / 70 / 430
10 Tu	0322 / 0854 / 1552 / 2155	2.3 / 14.4 / 2.0 / 14.1	70 / 440 / 60 / 430
11 W	0403 / 0928 / 1640 / 2239	2.0 / 14.8 / 1.3 / 14.4	60 / 450 / 40 / 440
12 Th ◐	0448 / 1011 / 1730 / 2329	2.0 / 14.8 / 1.3 / 14.4	60 / 450 / 40 / 440
13 F	0536 / 1105 / 1823	2.0 / 14.4 / 1.3	60 / 440 / 40
14 Sa	0025 / 0628 / 1224 / 1919	14.1 / 2.6 / 14.1 / 1.6	430 / 80 / 430 / 50
15 Su	0130 / 0727 / 1418 / 2019	13.5 / 3.3 / 13.8 / 2.3	410 / 100 / 420 / 70
16 M	0249 / 0834 / 1543 / 2122	13.1 / 3.9 / 13.5 / 3.0	400 / 120 / 410 / 90
17 Tu	0415 / 0947 / 1656 / 2229	12.8 / 4.3 / 13.5 / 3.3	390 / 130 / 410 / 100
18 W	0535 / 1058 / 1804 / 2336	13.1 / 3.9 / 13.8 / 3.6	400 / 120 / 420 / 110
19 Th ●	0642 / 1202 / 1908	13.5 / 3.6 / 13.8	410 / 110 / 420
20 F	0038 / 0736 / 1258 / 2005	3.3 / 13.8 / 3.0 / 14.1	100 / 420 / 90 / 430
21 Sa	0132 / 0822 / 1349 / 2054	3.0 / 14.4 / 2.3 / 14.1	90 / 440 / 70 / 430
22 Su	0219 / 0902 / 1436 / 2137	2.3 / 14.8 / 1.6 / 14.4	70 / 450 / 50 / 440
23 M	0303 / 0940 / 1523 / 2215	2.0 / 14.8 / 1.3 / 14.8	60 / 450 / 40 / 450
24 Tu	0345 / 1017 / 1607 / 2251	1.6 / 15.1 / 1.0 / 15.1	50 / 460 / 30 / 460
25 W	0425 / 1053 / 1651 / 2323	2.0 / 15.1 / 0.7 / 15.1	60 / 460 / 20 / 460
26 Th	0504 / 1129 / 1733 / 2353	2.0 / 15.1 / 0.7 / 14.8	60 / 460 / 20 / 450
27 F ○	0542 / 1206 / 1814	2.3 / 14.8 / 1.0	70 / 450 / 30
28 Sa	0023 / 0620 / 1244 / 1853	14.8 / 3.0 / 14.8 / 1.3	450 / 90 / 450 / 40
29 Su	0055 / 0701 / 1327 / 1933	14.4 / 3.3 / 14.8 / 1.6	440 / 100 / 450 / 50
30 M	0134 / 0746 / 1412 / 2016	14.4 / 3.6 / 14.8 / 2.0	440 / 110 / 450 / 60
31 Tu	0220 / 0836 / 1501 / 2102	14.1 / 3.6 / 14.8 / 2.3	430 / 110 / 450 / 70

November

Day	Time (h m)	Height (ft)	Height (cm)
1 W	0312 / 0932 / 1551 / 2153	13.8 / 3.6 / 14.8 / 3.0	420 / 110 / 450 / 90
2 Th	0408 / 1029 / 1642 / 2248	13.8 / 3.3 / 14.4 / 3.3	420 / 100 / 440 / 100
3 F	0504 / 1125 / 1734 / 2343	13.8 / 3.3 / 14.4 / 3.6	420 / 100 / 440 / 110
4 Sa ○	0554 / 1217 / 1826	13.8 / 3.0 / 14.1	420 / 90 / 430
5 Su	0036 / 0636 / 1307 / 1916	3.6 / 13.8 / 2.6 / 13.8	110 / 420 / 80 / 420
6 M	0125 / 0710 / 1355 / 2004	3.6 / 13.8 / 2.3 / 13.8	110 / 420 / 70 / 420
7 Tu	0210 / 0741 / 1443 / 2049	3.3 / 13.8 / 2.0 / 13.8	100 / 420 / 60 / 420
8 W	0255 / 0814 / 1531 / 2135	3.0 / 14.1 / 1.6 / 13.8	90 / 430 / 50 / 420
9 Th	0340 / 0854 / 1621 / 2223	2.6 / 14.4 / 1.3 / 13.8	80 / 440 / 40 / 420
10 F ○	0428 / 0944 / 1713 / 2317	2.6 / 14.4 / 1.3 / 13.8	80 / 440 / 40 / 420
11 Sa	0519 / 1052 / 1807	2.6 / 13.8 / 1.3	80 / 420 / 40
12 Su	0020 / 0616 / 1304 / 1903	13.8 / 3.0 / 13.8 / 1.6	420 / 90 / 420 / 50
13 M	0133 / 0718 / 1432 / 2002	13.8 / 3.3 / 13.8 / 2.3	420 / 100 / 420 / 70
14 Tu	0253 / 0827 / 1541 / 2105	13.5 / 3.3 / 13.8 / 3.0	410 / 100 / 420 / 90
15 W	0409 / 0939 / 1646 / 2211	13.8 / 3.3 / 14.1 / 3.3	420 / 100 / 430 / 100
16 Th	0518 / 1046 / 1748 / 2317	14.1 / 3.0 / 14.1 / 3.3	430 / 90 / 430 / 100
17 F	0617 / 1147 / 1848	14.4 / 2.6 / 14.1	440 / 80 / 430
18 Sa ●	0018 / 0708 / 1241 / 1943	3.3 / 14.8 / 2.0 / 14.4	100 / 450 / 60 / 440
19 Su	0111 / 0753 / 1331 / 2031	3.0 / 14.8 / 1.6 / 14.4	90 / 450 / 50 / 440
20 M	0159 / 0834 / 1417 / 2114	2.6 / 15.1 / 1.3 / 14.8	80 / 460 / 40 / 450
21 Tu	0242 / 0913 / 1502 / 2152	2.3 / 15.1 / 1.0 / 14.8	70 / 460 / 30 / 450
22 W	0323 / 0949 / 1545 / 2225	2.3 / 15.1 / 0.7 / 15.1	70 / 460 / 20 / 460
23 Th	0401 / 1022 / 1625 / 2254	2.3 / 14.8 / 0.7 / 15.1	70 / 450 / 20 / 460
24 F	0437 / 1053 / 1703 / 2318	2.6 / 14.8 / 1.0 / 14.8	80 / 450 / 30 / 450
25 Sa	0512 / 1123 / 1739 / 2342	2.6 / 14.4 / 1.0 / 14.8	80 / 440 / 30 / 450
26 Su ◐	0547 / 1158 / 1815	3.0 / 14.8 / 1.0	90 / 450 / 30
27 M	0011 / 0626 / 1240 / 1852	14.8 / 3.0 / 14.8 / 1.3	450 / 90 / 450 / 40
28 Tu	0048 / 0709 / 1327 / 1932	14.8 / 3.0 / 14.8 / 1.6	450 / 90 / 450 / 50
29 W	0132 / 0758 / 1417 / 2017	14.8 / 3.0 / 14.8 / 2.0	450 / 90 / 450 / 60
30 Th	0222 / 0851 / 1508 / 2107	14.4 / 2.6 / 14.8 / 2.6	440 / 80 / 450 / 80

December

Day	Time (h m)	Height (ft)	Height (cm)
1 F	0316 / 0948 / 1600 / 2201	14.4 / 2.6 / 14.8 / 3.3	440 / 80 / 450 / 100
2 Sa	0411 / 1045 / 1653 / 2258	14.1 / 2.6 / 14.1 / 3.6	430 / 80 / 430 / 110
3 Su ○	0501 / 1140 / 1747 / 2355	14.1 / 2.3 / 13.8 / 3.9	430 / 70 / 420 / 120
4 M	0546 / 1235 / 1841	13.8 / 2.3 / 13.5	420 / 70 / 410
5 Tu	0050 / 0624 / 1327 / 1934	4.3 / 13.8 / 2.3 / 13.1	130 / 420 / 70 / 400
6 W	0141 / 0700 / 1419 / 2026	3.9 / 13.8 / 2.0 / 13.1	120 / 420 / 60 / 400
7 Th	0230 / 0739 / 1511 / 2118	3.6 / 13.8 / 2.0 / 13.1	110 / 420 / 60 / 400
8 F	0319 / 0825 / 1603 / 2212	3.3 / 13.8 / 1.6 / 13.5	100 / 420 / 50 / 410
9 Sa	0411 / 0926 / 1656 / 2312	3.0 / 13.8 / 1.6 / 13.8	90 / 420 / 50 / 420
10 Su ◐	0506 / 1139 / 1750	3.0 / 13.5 / 1.6	90 / 410 / 50
11 M	0020 / 0605 / 1317 / 1845	13.8 / 2.6 / 13.8 / 1.6	420 / 80 / 420 / 50
12 Tu	0132 / 0709 / 1424 / 1943	14.1 / 2.6 / 14.1 / 2.3	430 / 80 / 430 / 70
13 W	0243 / 0816 / 1525 / 2044	14.1 / 2.6 / 14.4 / 2.6	430 / 80 / 440 / 80
14 Th	0350 / 0923 / 1624 / 2148	14.4 / 2.3 / 14.4 / 3.3	440 / 70 / 440 / 100
15 F	0451 / 1027 / 1722 / 2253	14.8 / 2.0 / 14.4 / 3.3	450 / 60 / 440 / 100
16 Sa	0546 / 1125 / 1819 / 2353	15.1 / 1.6 / 14.4 / 3.3	460 / 50 / 440 / 100
17 Su	0635 / 1218 / 1913	15.1 / 1.3 / 14.4	460 / 40 / 440
18 M ●	0047 / 0721 / 1308 / 2002	3.3 / 15.1 / 1.0 / 14.8	100 / 460 / 30 / 450
19 Tu	0135 / 0803 / 1354 / 2046	3.0 / 15.1 / 1.0 / 14.8	90 / 460 / 30 / 450
20 W	0219 / 0843 / 1439 / 2126	2.6 / 15.1 / 1.0 / 14.8	80 / 460 / 30 / 450
21 Th	0259 / 0920 / 1520 / 2159	2.6 / 14.8 / 1.0 / 14.8	80 / 450 / 30 / 450
22 F	0336 / 0953 / 1558 / 2226	3.0 / 14.4 / 1.0 / 14.8	90 / 440 / 30 / 450
23 Sa	0411 / 1021 / 1633 / 2246	3.0 / 14.4 / 1.0 / 14.8	90 / 440 / 30 / 450
24 Su	0444 / 1048 / 1706 / 2305	3.0 / 14.4 / 1.0 / 14.8	90 / 440 / 30 / 450
25 M	0518 / 1122 / 1740 / 2333	3.0 / 14.4 / 1.0 / 15.1	90 / 440 / 30 / 460
26 Tu ◐	0556 / 1204 / 1816	2.6 / 14.8 / 1.3	80 / 450 / 40
27 W	0008 / 0639 / 1251 / 1856	15.1 / 2.3 / 15.1 / 1.3	460 / 70 / 460 / 40
28 Th	0051 / 0727 / 1340 / 1940	15.1 / 2.0 / 15.1 / 1.6	460 / 60 / 460 / 50
29 F	0139 / 0819 / 1431 / 2029	15.1 / 2.0 / 14.8 / 2.3	460 / 60 / 450 / 70
30 Sa	0231 / 0914 / 1524 / 2122	14.8 / 2.0 / 14.4 / 3.0	450 / 60 / 440 / 90
31 Su	0325 / 1011 / 1618 / 2220	14.4 / 2.0 / 14.1 / 3.9	440 / 60 / 430 / 120

Time meridian 45° W. 0000 is midnight. 1200 is noon. Times are not adjusted for Daylight Saving Time.
Heights are referred to the chart datum of soundings.

Comodoro Rivadavia, Argentina, 2017
Times and Heights of High and Low Waters

January

Day	Time	ft	cm	Day	Time	ft	cm
1 Su	0118	2.6	80	**16** M	0145	1.3	40
	0712	17.7	540		0748	20.0	610
	1328	4.6	140		1353	3.3	100
	1909	17.4	530		1954	19.7	600
2 M	0156	2.3	70	**17** Tu	0227	1.0	30
	0748	17.7	540		0832	19.7	600
	1406	4.3	130		1436	3.0	90
	1945	17.7	540		2038	19.0	580
3 Tu	0230	2.3	70	**18** W	0305	1.3	40
	0824	17.7	540		0914	19.0	580
	1438	3.9	120		1519	3.0	90
	2022	17.7	540		2122	18.4	560
4 W	0259	2.3	70	**19** Th	0344	1.6	50
	0902	17.7	540		0955	18.4	560
	1506	3.9	120		1602	3.0	90
	2103	17.4	530	○	2206	17.4	530
5 Th	0324	2.0	60	**20** F	0426	2.3	70
	0943	17.7	540		1038	17.7	540
	1538	3.6	110		1650	3.3	100
☾	2148	17.1	520		2254	16.4	500
6 F	0358	2.3	70	**21** Sa	0511	3.0	90
	1028	17.4	530		1125	16.7	510
	1623	3.6	110		1742	3.6	110
	2241	16.7	510		2347	15.4	470
7 Sa	0446	2.6	80	**22** Su	0602	3.6	110
	1121	17.1	520		1217	16.1	490
	1721	3.9	120		1839	3.9	120
	2343	16.4	500				
8 Su	0546	3.3	100	**23** M	0048	15.1	460
	1221	16.7	510		0658	4.3	130
	1830	3.9	120		1314	15.4	470
					1939	4.3	130
9 M	0052	16.1	490	**24** Tu	0153	14.8	450
	0653	3.6	110		0756	4.6	140
	1324	17.1	520		1414	15.4	470
	1942	3.6	110		2039	3.9	120
10 Tu	0203	16.7	510	**25** W	0257	15.1	460
	0800	3.9	120		0853	4.9	150
	1429	17.7	540		1511	15.7	480
	2050	3.3	100		2137	3.9	120
11 W	0313	17.4	530	**26** Th	0353	15.7	480
	0904	3.9	120		0949	4.9	150
	1532	18.4	560		1603	16.1	490
	2157	2.6	80		2233	3.6	110
12 Th	0417	18.4	560	**27** F	0443	16.4	500
	1008	3.9	120		1044	4.9	150
	1631	19.0	580		1649	16.7	510
○	2303	2.3	70	●	2325	3.3	100
13 F	0516	19.0	580	**28** Sa	0529	17.1	520
	1111	3.9	120		1136	4.9	150
	1727	19.4	590		1731	17.1	520
14 Sa	0004	2.0	60	**29** Su	0014	3.0	90
	0610	19.7	600		0610	17.4	530
	1211	3.9	120		1225	4.6	140
	1819	19.7	600		1810	17.4	530
15 Su	0059	1.3	40	**30** M	0058	2.6	80
	0701	20.0	610		0649	17.7	540
	1305	3.6	110		1309	4.3	130
	1908	20.0	610		1848	17.7	540
				31 Tu	0138	2.3	70
					0725	18.4	560
					1348	3.9	120
					1927	18.0	550

February

Day	Time	ft	cm	Day	Time	ft	cm
1 W	0213	2.0	60	**16** Th	0242	1.6	50
	0802	18.4	560		0846	19.0	580
	1422	3.6	110		1456	2.6	80
	2006	18.4	560		2057	18.4	560
2 Th	0243	2.0	60	**17** F	0317	2.0	60
	0839	18.7	570		0922	18.4	560
	1452	3.3	100		1536	2.6	80
	2047	18.4	560		2138	17.7	540
3 F	0310	1.6	50	**18** Sa	0355	2.3	70
	0919	18.4	560		1001	17.7	540
	1524	3.0	90		1619	2.6	80
	2133	18.4	560	○	2221	16.7	510
4 Sa	0343	2.0	60	**19** Su	0437	3.0	90
	1003	18.0	550		1042	16.7	510
	1607	3.0	90		1706	3.3	100
☾	2224	17.7	540		2308	16.1	490
5 Su	0429	2.3	70	**20** M	0524	3.6	110
	1054	17.7	540		1129	16.1	490
	1702	3.0	90		1759	3.6	110
	2323	17.1	520				
6 M	0525	3.0	90	**21** Tu	0003	15.1	460
	1152	17.1	520		0617	4.3	130
	1809	3.3	100		1222	15.1	460
					1857	3.9	120
7 Tu	0031	16.4	500	**22** W	0106	14.8	450
	0631	3.9	120		0714	4.6	140
	1257	16.7	510		1322	14.8	450
	1921	3.6	110		1957	3.9	120
8 W	0144	16.4	500	**23** Th	0211	14.8	450
	0739	4.3	130		0813	4.9	150
	1407	16.7	510		1425	15.1	460
	2031	3.3	100		2057	3.9	120
9 Th	0258	16.7	510	**24** F	0313	15.4	470
	0845	4.6	140		0912	4.9	150
	1517	17.4	530		1524	15.4	470
	2141	3.0	90		2156	3.9	120
10 F	0406	17.7	540	**25** Sa	0408	16.1	490
	0951	4.6	140		1010	4.9	150
	1620	18.0	550		1615	16.1	490
○	2253	2.6	80		2252	3.6	110
11 Sa	0504	18.4	560	**26** Su	0455	16.7	510
	1057	4.3	130		1105	4.6	140
	1717	18.7	570		1701	16.7	510
	2357	2.3	70	●	2344	3.3	100
12 Su	0556	19.0	580	**27** M	0538	17.4	530
	1200	3.9	120		1157	4.3	130
	1808	19.0	580		1743	17.7	540
13 M	0048	2.0	60	**28** Tu	0031	2.6	80
	0644	19.4	590		0618	18.0	550
	1253	3.6	110		1243	3.9	120
	1855	19.4	590		1824	18.4	560
14 Tu	0130	1.6	50				
	0728	19.4	590				
	1337	3.3	100				
	1938	19.4	590				
15 W	0207	1.6	50				
	0701	19.4	590				
	1417	3.0	90				
	2018	19.0	580				

March

Day	Time	ft	cm	Day	Time	ft	cm
1 W	0112	2.3	70	**16** Th	0139	2.6	80
	0657	18.7	570		0738	18.7	570
	1325	3.3	100		1352	3.0	90
	1906	18.7	570		1954	18.7	570
2 Th	0150	2.0	60	**17** F	0213	2.6	80
	0735	19.0	580		0814	18.4	560
	1402	3.0	90		1431	2.6	80
	1948	19.4	590		2032	18.0	550
3 F	0224	2.0	60	**18** Sa	0249	2.6	80
	0815	19.4	590		0848	18.0	550
	1437	2.3	70		1510	2.3	70
	2032	19.4	590		2110	17.7	540
4 Sa	0256	1.6	50	**19** Su	0327	2.6	80
	0856	19.0	580		0925	17.4	530
	1514	2.0	60		1550	2.6	80
	2119	19.0	580		2151	17.1	520
5 Su	0333	2.0	60	**20** M	0407	3.3	100
	0941	18.7	570		1004	16.7	510
	1558	2.0	60		1634	3.0	90
☾	2210	18.4	560	○	2236	16.1	490
6 M	0419	2.3	70	**21** Tu	0451	3.6	110
	1032	17.7	540		1048	15.7	480
	1652	2.3	70		1723	3.3	100
	2309	17.4	530		2327	15.4	470
7 Tu	0514	3.3	100	**22** W	0541	4.3	130
	1130	17.1	520		1139	15.1	460
	1756	3.0	90		1817	3.6	110
8 W	0017	16.4	500	**23** Th	0026	15.1	460
	0618	3.9	120		0637	4.6	140
	1238	16.4	500		1238	14.4	440
	1906	3.3	100		1916	3.9	120
9 Th	0132	16.4	500	**24** F	0129	15.1	460
	0725	4.6	140		0736	4.9	150
	1353	16.4	500		1341	14.8	450
	2017	3.3	100		2016	3.9	120
10 F	0247	16.7	510	**25** Sa	0231	15.4	470
	0832	4.6	140		0835	4.9	150
	1506	16.7	510		1442	15.1	460
	2130	3.3	100		2115	3.9	120
11 Sa	0351	17.4	530	**26** Su	0326	16.1	490
	0940	4.6	140		0932	4.6	140
	1610	17.4	530		1537	16.1	490
	2243	3.0	90		2211	3.6	110
12 Su	0447	18.0	550	**27** M	0415	17.1	520
	1027	4.3	130		1027	4.3	130
	1704	18.0	550		1626	17.1	520
○	2342	2.6	80	●	2303	3.3	100
13 M	0536	18.4	560	**28** Tu	0500	17.7	540
	1146	3.9	120		1119	3.9	120
	1752	18.4	560		1712	18.0	550
					2352	3.0	90
14 Tu	0027	2.6	80	**29** W	0542	18.7	570
	0620	18.7	570		1209	3.3	100
	1233	3.6	110		1758	18.7	570
	1836	18.7	570				
15 W	0105	2.6	80	**30** Th	0038	2.6	80
	0701	18.7	570		0624	19.0	580
	1314	3.3	100		1255	3.0	90
	1916	18.7	570		1843	19.4	590
				31 F	0120	2.3	70
					0707	19.4	590
					1338	2.3	70
					1929	19.7	600

Time meridian 45° W. 0000 is midnight. 1200 is noon. Times are not adjusted for Daylight Saving Time.
Heights are referred to the chart datum of soundings.

Comodoro Rivadavia, Argentina, 2017

Times and Heights of High and Low Waters

April

Day	Time (h m)	Height (ft)	Height (cm)
1 Sa	0200	2.3	70
	0750	19.7	600
	1420	1.6	50
	2017	19.7	600
2 Su	0240	2.0	60
	0835	19.4	590
	1503	1.6	50
	2106	19.4	590
3 M ◑	0322	2.3	70
	0922	18.7	570
	1551	1.6	50
	2159	18.7	570
4 Tu	0410	2.6	80
	1015	17.7	540
	1644	2.0	60
	2259	17.7	540
5 W	0506	3.3	100
	1115	16.7	510
	1746	2.6	80
6 Th	0007	16.7	510
	0608	3.9	120
	1225	16.1	490
	1854	3.0	90
7 F	0121	16.4	500
	0715	4.3	130
	1343	16.1	490
	2004	3.3	100
8 Sa	0231	16.7	510
	0824	4.3	130
	1454	16.4	500
	2115	3.3	100
9 Su	0331	17.4	530
	0930	4.3	130
	1553	17.1	520
	2219	3.0	90
10 M	0423	17.7	540
	1031	3.9	120
	1644	17.7	540
	2309	3.3	100
11 Tu ○	0509	18.4	560
	1121	3.6	110
	1730	18.0	550
	2351	3.3	100
12 W	0551	18.4	560
	1204	3.3	100
	1811	18.4	560
13 Th	0028	3.6	110
	0629	18.4	560
	1245	3.3	100
	1851	18.4	560
14 F	0105	3.6	110
	0705	18.0	550
	1325	3.0	90
	1928	18.0	550
15 Sa	0143	3.6	110
	0740	17.7	540
	1404	3.0	90
	2006	17.7	540
16 Su	0221	3.6	110
	0815	17.4	530
	1444	2.6	80
	2044	17.4	530
17 M	0300	3.6	110
	0851	17.1	520
	1524	2.6	80
	2124	17.1	520
18 Tu	0340	3.9	120
	0929	16.4	500
	1605	3.0	90
	2208	16.4	500
19 W ◐	0422	3.9	120
	1012	15.7	480
	1650	3.3	100
	2256	15.7	480
20 Th	0509	4.6	140
	1101	15.1	460
	1740	3.6	110
	2351	15.4	470
21 F	0603	4.6	140
	1159	14.8	450
	1836	3.9	120
22 Sa	0051	15.4	470
	0700	4.9	150
	1302	14.8	450
	1934	3.9	120
23 Su	0150	15.7	480
	0757	4.6	140
	1403	15.4	470
	2029	3.6	110
24 M	0244	16.7	510
	0852	4.3	130
	1500	16.4	500
	2122	3.6	110
25 Tu	0334	17.4	530
	0945	3.6	110
	1552	17.4	530
	2213	3.3	100
26 W ●	0421	18.4	560
	1036	3.3	100
	1642	18.7	570
	2303	3.0	90
27 Th	0506	19.0	580
	1128	3.0	90
	1732	19.4	590
	2354	3.0	90
28 F	0552	19.7	600
	1221	2.3	70
	1821	20.0	610
29 Sa	0044	3.0	90
	0639	20.0	610
	1312	2.0	60
	1911	20.3	620
30 Su	0133	2.6	80
	0726	20.0	610
	1401	1.6	50
	2002	20.0	610

May

Day	Time (h m)	Height (ft)	Height (cm)
1 M	0221	2.6	80
	0815	19.4	590
	1450	1.3	40
	2054	19.7	600
2 Tu ◑	0309	3.0	90
	0906	18.7	570
	1540	1.3	40
	2149	19.0	580
3 W	0400	3.3	100
	1001	18.0	550
	1634	2.0	60
	2249	18.0	550
4 Th	0456	3.6	110
	1102	17.1	520
	1734	2.3	70
	2355	17.4	530
5 F	0558	3.9	120
	1212	16.1	490
	1839	3.0	90
6 Sa	0104	17.1	520
	0704	4.3	130
	1326	16.1	490
	1945	3.3	100
7 Su	0208	17.1	520
	0811	4.3	130
	1433	16.4	500
	2048	3.3	100
8 M	0304	17.4	530
	0911	3.9	120
	1530	16.7	510
	2142	3.3	100
9 Tu	0354	17.7	540
	1003	3.6	110
	1619	17.4	530
	2227	3.6	110
10 W ○	0438	18.0	550
	1049	3.3	100
	1703	17.7	540
	2308	3.9	120
11 Th	0518	18.0	550
	1132	3.3	100
	1744	17.7	540
	2349	4.3	130
12 F	0555	18.0	550
	1214	3.3	100
	1824	17.7	540
13 Sa	0031	4.3	130
	0631	17.7	540
	1257	3.3	100
	1902	17.7	540
14 Su	0112	4.6	140
	0707	17.4	530
	1339	3.0	90
	1941	17.7	540
15 M	0154	4.6	140
	0743	17.1	520
	1419	3.0	90
	2020	17.4	530
16 Tu	0235	4.6	140
	0820	16.7	510
	1459	3.0	90
	2059	17.1	520
17 W	0315	4.6	140
	0858	16.1	490
	1539	3.0	90
	2141	16.7	510
18 Th ◐	0355	4.6	140
	0940	15.7	480
	1620	3.3	100
	2227	16.1	490
19 F	0439	4.6	140
	1028	15.1	460
	1704	3.6	110
	2318	15.7	480
20 Sa	0529	4.9	150
	1124	15.1	460
	1755	3.6	110
21 Su	0013	15.7	480
	0624	4.6	140
	1226	15.1	460
	1850	3.6	110
22 M	0110	16.4	500
	0721	4.3	130
	1328	15.7	480
	1945	3.6	110
23 Tu	0204	17.1	520
	0815	3.9	120
	1427	16.7	510
	2037	3.3	100
24 W	0256	18.0	550
	0907	3.3	100
	1522	17.7	540
	2127	3.3	100
25 Th ●	0346	18.7	570
	0959	2.6	80
	1616	19.0	580
	2218	3.3	100
26 F	0435	19.4	590
	1053	2.3	70
	1709	19.7	600
	2312	3.3	100
27 Sa	0524	20.0	610
	1150	2.0	60
	1802	20.0	610
28 Su	0010	3.3	100
	0615	20.0	610
	1248	1.6	50
	1855	20.3	620
29 M	0107	3.3	100
	0706	20.0	610
	1343	1.3	40
	1949	20.3	620
30 Tu	0201	3.3	100
	0758	19.7	600
	1435	1.3	40
	2042	20.0	610
31 W	0253	3.3	100
	0850	19.0	580
	1526	1.3	40
	2137	19.4	590

June

Day	Time (h m)	Height (ft)	Height (cm)
1 Th ◑	0346	3.3	100
	0946	18.0	550
	1619	1.6	50
	2234	18.4	560
2 F	0441	3.6	110
	1045	17.1	520
	1715	2.3	70
	2334	17.7	540
3 Sa	0541	3.9	120
	1151	16.4	500
	1815	3.0	90
4 Su	0036	17.1	520
	0644	3.9	120
	1300	16.1	490
	1915	3.3	100
5 M	0136	17.1	520
	0745	3.9	120
	1404	16.1	490
	2011	3.6	110
6 Tu	0231	17.1	520
	0842	3.6	110
	1500	16.4	500
	2101	3.9	120
7 W	0320	17.4	530
	0931	3.3	100
	1550	17.1	520
	2147	3.9	120
8 Th	0405	17.7	540
	1017	3.0	90
	1635	17.4	530
	2231	4.3	130
9 F ○	0445	17.7	540
	1102	3.0	90
	1718	17.4	530
	2315	4.6	140
10 Sa	0523	17.7	540
	1146	3.3	100
	1758	17.4	530
11 Su	0000	4.9	150
	0601	17.4	530
	1231	3.3	100
	1838	17.4	530
12 M	0045	4.9	150
	0638	17.1	520
	1314	3.3	100
	1917	17.4	530
13 Tu	0129	4.9	150
	0715	16.7	510
	1356	3.3	100
	1956	17.4	530
14 W	0211	4.9	150
	0752	16.4	500
	1436	3.0	90
	2034	17.1	520
15 Th	0251	4.9	150
	0831	16.1	490
	1513	3.0	90
	2114	16.7	510
16 F ◑	0329	4.6	140
	0911	16.1	490
	1548	3.3	100
	2156	16.7	510
17 Sa ○	0407	4.6	140
	0958	15.7	480
	1624	3.3	100
	2243	16.4	500
18 Su	0451	4.6	140
	1051	15.4	470
	1710	3.3	100
	2335	16.4	500
19 M	0546	4.3	130
	1152	15.4	470
	1806	3.6	110
20 Tu	0031	16.7	510
	0645	3.9	120
	1255	16.1	490
	1905	3.6	110
21 W	0128	17.1	520
	0743	3.6	110
	1358	16.7	510
	2001	3.6	110
22 Th	0223	18.0	550
	0839	3.0	90
	1458	17.7	540
	2055	3.3	100
23 F ●	0317	18.7	570
	0934	2.3	70
	1556	18.7	570
	2149	3.3	100
24 Sa ○	0410	19.4	590
	1030	2.0	60
	1652	19.4	590
	2245	3.6	110
25 Su	0504	19.7	600
	1129	1.6	50
	1747	20.0	610
	2345	3.6	110
26 M	0557	20.0	610
	1229	1.3	40
	1841	20.3	620
27 Tu	0045	3.6	110
	0650	19.7	600
	1326	1.3	40
	1935	20.0	610
28 W	0142	3.3	100
	0742	19.4	590
	1419	1.3	40
	2026	19.7	600
29 Th	0235	3.3	100
	0834	19.0	580
	1509	1.3	40
	2118	19.4	590
30 F ◑	0327	3.3	100
	0927	18.0	550
	1557	1.6	50
	2209	18.4	560

Time meridian 45° W. 0000 is midnight. 1200 is noon. Times are not adjusted for Daylight Saving Time.
Heights are referred to the chart datum of soundings.

Comodoro Rivadavia, Argentina, 2017
Times and Heights of High and Low Waters

July

Day	Time (h m)	Height (ft)	Height (cm)
1 Sa	0419	3.3	100
	1022	17.4	530
	1647	2.3	70
	2302	17.7	540
2 Su	0514	3.6	110
	1120	16.4	500
	1740	3.0	90
	2358	17.1	520
3 M	0611	3.6	110
	1223	15.7	480
	1835	3.3	100
4 Tu	0055	16.7	510
	0710	3.6	110
	1326	15.4	470
	1929	3.9	120
5 W	0151	16.4	500
	0805	3.3	100
	1425	15.7	480
	2022	3.9	120
6 Th	0243	16.7	510
	0858	3.0	90
	1519	16.1	490
	2111	4.3	130
7 F	0331	16.7	510
	0947	3.0	90
	1607	16.7	510
	2159	4.3	130
8 Sa	0415	17.1	520
	1034	3.0	90
	1652	17.1	520
	2246	4.6	140
9 Su ○	0456	17.1	520
	1121	3.0	90
	1734	17.4	530
	2334	4.6	140
10 M	0535	17.1	520
	1207	3.0	90
	1815	17.4	530
11 Tu	0021	4.9	150
	0613	16.7	510
	1252	3.0	90
	1853	17.4	530
12 W	0106	4.9	150
	0650	16.7	510
	1334	3.0	90
	1931	17.4	530
13 Th	0148	4.6	140
	0728	16.7	510
	1413	3.0	90
	2008	17.4	530
14 F	0227	4.6	140
	0806	16.4	500
	1447	2.6	80
	2045	17.1	520
15 Sa	0301	4.3	130
	0846	16.4	500
	1515	2.6	80
	2124	17.1	520
16 Su ○	0333	3.9	120
	0930	16.4	500
	1545	3.0	90
	2208	16.7	510
17 M	0413	3.9	120
	1021	16.1	490
	1629	3.0	90
	2257	16.7	510
18 Tu	0506	3.6	110
	1121	15.7	480
	1726	3.3	100
	2354	16.4	500
19 W	0611	3.6	110
	1227	15.7	480
	1831	3.6	110
20 Th	0054	16.7	510
	0717	3.3	100
	1334	16.4	500
	1934	3.6	110
21 F	0156	17.1	520
	0818	2.6	80
	1440	17.1	520
	2034	3.6	110
22 Sa	0257	17.7	540
	0918	2.0	60
	1543	18.0	550
	2131	3.6	110
23 Su ●	0355	18.7	570
	1017	1.6	50
	1641	19.0	580
	2230	3.6	110
24 M	0451	19.0	580
	1117	1.3	40
	1736	19.7	600
	2330	3.3	100
25 Tu	0545	19.4	590
	1216	1.3	40
	1829	19.7	600
26 W	0029	3.3	100
	0637	19.4	590
	1311	1.0	30
	1918	20.0	610
27 Th	0125	3.0	90
	0727	19.4	590
	1400	1.0	30
	2006	19.7	600
28 F	0215	3.0	90
	0815	18.7	570
	1445	1.3	40
	2052	19.0	580
29 Sa	0302	2.6	80
	0903	18.0	550
	1528	1.6	50
	2137	18.4	560
30 Su ◐	0349	2.6	80
	0951	17.1	520
	1612	2.3	70
	2223	17.4	530
31 M	0438	3.0	90
	1043	16.4	500
	1659	3.0	90
	2311	16.4	500

August

Day	Time (h m)	Height (ft)	Height (cm)
1 Tu	0531	3.3	100
	1139	15.4	470
	1751	3.6	110
2 W	0005	15.7	480
	0628	3.3	100
	1242	14.8	450
	1846	3.9	120
3 Th	0103	15.4	470
	0726	3.3	100
	1346	14.8	450
	1942	4.3	130
4 F	0202	15.4	470
	0822	3.0	90
	1446	15.1	460
	2037	4.3	130
5 Sa	0257	15.4	470
	0917	3.0	90
	1539	15.7	480
	2130	4.3	130
6 Su	0347	16.1	490
	1008	2.6	80
	1627	16.4	500
	2222	4.3	130
7 M ○	0432	16.4	500
	1057	2.3	70
	1710	17.1	520
	2311	4.3	130
8 Tu	0512	16.4	500
	1144	2.3	70
	1750	17.4	530
	2359	4.3	130
9 W	0550	16.7	510
	1229	2.3	70
	1828	17.4	530
10 Th	0044	3.9	120
	0628	17.1	520
	1311	2.3	70
	1903	17.7	540
11 F	0125	3.9	120
	0705	17.1	520
	1348	2.3	70
	1939	17.7	540
12 Sa	0202	3.6	110
	0743	17.1	520
	1419	2.3	70
	2015	17.7	540
13 Su	0233	3.3	100
	0823	17.1	520
	1444	2.3	70
	2053	17.4	530
14 M ◐	0302	3.0	90
	0907	17.1	520
	1514	2.3	70
	2135	17.1	520
15 Tu	0341	3.0	90
	0957	16.4	500
	1558	2.6	80
	2223	16.7	510
16 W	0434	3.0	90
	1055	16.1	490
	1655	3.3	100
	2320	16.1	490
17 Th	0542	3.0	90
	1203	15.7	480
	1804	3.6	110
18 F	0025	16.1	490
	0654	3.0	90
	1316	15.7	480
	1914	3.9	120
19 Sa	0135	16.1	490
	0803	2.6	80
	1429	16.4	500
	2020	3.9	120
20 Su	0244	16.7	510
	0909	2.0	60
	1535	17.4	530
	2123	3.6	110
21 M ●	0347	17.4	530
	1012	1.6	50
	1633	18.4	560
	2224	3.3	100
22 Tu	0445	18.4	560
	1112	1.3	40
	1726	19.0	580
	2323	3.0	90
23 W	0536	18.7	570
	1207	1.0	30
	1814	19.4	590
24 Th	0018	2.6	80
	0625	19.0	580
	1255	1.0	30
	1859	19.4	590
25 F	0108	2.3	70
	0710	19.0	580
	1337	1.0	30
	1941	19.4	590
26 Sa	0152	2.3	70
	0754	18.7	570
	1416	1.3	40
	2021	18.7	570
27 Su	0235	2.3	70
	0837	18.0	550
	1455	1.6	50
	2101	18.0	550
28 M	0317	2.0	60
	0920	17.1	520
	1535	2.3	70
	2141	17.1	520
29 Tu ◐	0401	2.3	70
	1005	16.1	490
	1618	3.0	90
	2224	16.1	490
30 W	0450	2.6	80
	1056	15.1	460
	1707	3.6	110
	2312	15.1	460
31 Th	0545	3.0	90
	1154	14.4	440
	1803	4.3	130

September

Day	Time (h m)	Height (ft)	Height (cm)
1 F	0009	14.4	440
	0644	3.3	100
	1301	14.1	430
	1903	4.6	140
2 Sa	0114	14.1	430
	0745	3.3	100
	1408	14.4	440
	2003	4.6	140
3 Su	0219	14.4	440
	0844	3.0	90
	1508	15.1	460
	2102	4.3	130
4 M	0317	14.8	450
	0940	2.6	80
	1558	16.1	490
	2157	3.9	120
5 Tu	0405	15.4	470
	1032	2.3	70
	1642	16.7	510
	2249	3.6	110
6 W ○	0447	16.1	490
	1120	2.0	60
	1722	17.4	530
	2337	3.3	100
7 Th	0526	16.7	510
	1204	2.0	60
	1758	17.7	540
8 F	0021	3.0	90
	0604	17.4	530
	1244	2.0	60
	1834	18.0	550
9 Sa	0101	3.0	90
	0642	17.7	540
	1320	2.0	60
	1909	18.4	560
10 Su	0137	2.6	80
	0722	18.0	550
	1351	1.6	50
	1946	18.4	560
11 M	0208	2.0	60
	0803	18.0	550
	1419	1.6	50
	2025	18.0	550
12 Tu	0240	2.0	60
	0848	17.7	540
	1453	2.0	60
	2107	17.7	540
13 W ◐	0320	2.0	60
	0938	17.1	520
	1537	2.6	80
	2155	17.1	520
14 Th ◐	0413	2.0	60
	1036	16.4	500
	1634	3.3	100
	2253	16.1	490
15 F	0520	2.6	80
	1144	15.4	470
	1743	3.9	120
16 Sa	0002	15.4	470
	0636	2.6	80
	1303	15.4	470
	1859	4.3	130
17 Su	0120	15.1	460
	0751	2.6	80
	1421	15.7	480
	2012	4.3	130
18 M	0237	15.7	480
	0904	2.3	70
	1527	17.1	520
	2121	3.6	110
19 Tu	0343	16.7	510
	1012	1.6	50
	1622	18.0	550
	2226	3.3	100
20 W ●	0438	17.7	540
	1109	1.3	40
	1711	18.7	570
	2322	2.6	80
21 Th	0526	18.4	560
	1155	1.3	40
	1755	19.0	580
22 F	0008	2.3	70
	0611	18.7	570
	1234	1.3	40
	1836	19.0	580
23 Sa	0049	2.0	60
	0652	18.7	570
	1311	1.6	50
	1914	19.0	580
24 Su	0129	1.6	50
	0732	18.4	560
	1346	2.0	60
	1950	18.4	560
25 M	0207	1.6	50
	0811	17.7	540
	1423	2.0	60
	2025	17.7	540
26 Tu	0247	1.6	50
	0850	17.1	520
	1501	2.6	80
	2102	17.1	520
27 W ◐	0328	2.0	60
	0932	16.4	500
	1542	3.0	90
	2141	16.1	490
28 Th	0412	2.3	70
	1018	15.4	470
	1628	3.6	110
	2226	15.1	460
29 F	0503	2.6	80
	1112	14.4	440
	1721	4.3	130
	2319	14.1	430
30 Sa	0600	3.3	100
	1215	14.1	430
	1822	4.6	140

Time meridian 45° W. 0000 is midnight. 1200 is noon. Times are not adjusted for Daylight Saving Time.
Heights are referred to the chart datum of soundings.

Comodoro Rivadavia, Argentina, 2017

Times and Heights of High and Low Waters

October (Days 1–15)

Day	Time	ft	cm
1 Su	0022	13.5	410
	0703	3.3	100
	1324	14.1	430
	1926	4.9	150
2 M	0133	13.5	410
	0806	3.3	100
	1428	14.8	450
	2030	4.6	140
3 Tu	0238	14.1	430
	0906	3.0	90
	1523	15.7	480
	2129	3.9	120
4 W	0332	15.1	460
	1000	2.6	80
	1608	16.7	510
	2222	3.3	100
5 Th ○	0418	16.1	490
	1049	2.3	70
	1649	17.4	530
	2310	3.0	90
6 F	0459	17.1	520
	1133	2.0	60
	1726	18.0	550
	2354	2.6	80
7 Sa	0540	18.0	550
	1213	2.0	60
	1803	18.7	570
8 Su	0034	2.0	60
	0621	18.7	570
	1250	2.0	60
	1841	19.0	580
9 M	0112	1.6	50
	0703	19.0	580
	1325	1.6	50
	1920	19.0	580
10 Tu	0149	1.3	40
	0747	19.0	580
	1400	2.0	60
	2002	19.0	580
11 W	0227	1.0	30
	0834	18.7	570
	1439	2.0	60
	2046	18.4	560
12 Th ◑	0310	1.0	30
	0925	17.7	540
	1525	2.6	80
	2136	17.4	530
13 F	0401	1.6	50
	1022	16.7	510
	1620	3.3	100
	2233	16.1	490
14 Sa	0505	2.3	70
	1130	15.7	480
	1728	3.9	120
	2343	15.1	460
15 Su	0619	2.6	80
	1249	15.4	470
	1845	4.6	140

October (Days 16–31)

Day	Time	ft	cm
16 M	0106	14.8	450
	0738	2.6	80
	1406	16.1	490
	2005	4.3	130
17 Tu	0227	15.4	470
	0856	2.3	70
	1511	16.7	510
	2122	3.6	110
18 W	0331	16.4	500
	1002	2.0	60
	1605	17.7	540
	2226	3.0	90
19 Th ●	0425	17.4	530
	1053	2.0	60
	1651	18.4	560
	2313	2.6	80
20 F	0511	18.0	550
	1133	2.0	60
	1733	18.7	570
	2352	2.3	70
21 Sa	0554	18.4	560
	1208	2.3	70
	1811	18.7	570
22 Su	0029	2.0	60
	0633	18.4	560
	1243	2.6	80
	1846	18.7	570
23 M	0106	2.0	60
	0710	18.0	550
	1318	2.6	80
	1920	18.4	560
24 Tu	0143	1.6	50
	0747	17.7	540
	1355	3.0	90
	1954	17.7	540
25 W	0221	1.6	50
	0825	17.4	530
	1433	3.0	90
	2029	17.1	520
26 Th	0300	2.0	60
	0904	16.7	510
	1512	3.3	100
	2106	16.4	500
27 F ◐	0341	2.3	70
	0947	15.7	480
	1555	3.9	120
	2147	15.4	470
28 Sa	0425	2.6	80
	1035	15.1	460
	1643	4.3	130
	2235	14.4	440
29 Su	0517	3.3	100
	1131	14.4	440
	1740	4.9	150
	2334	13.8	420
30 M	0616	3.6	110
	1235	14.4	440
	1844	4.9	150
31 Tu	0041	13.5	410
	0720	3.6	110
	1339	14.8	450
	1950	4.9	150

November (Days 1–15)

Day	Time	ft	cm
1 W	0149	13.8	420
	0822	3.6	110
	1437	15.4	470
	2052	4.3	130
2 Th	0250	15.1	460
	0918	3.0	90
	1526	16.7	510
	2147	3.6	110
3 F	0342	16.1	490
	1008	3.0	90
	1610	17.7	540
	2236	3.0	90
4 Sa ○	0429	17.4	530
	1054	2.6	80
	1652	18.7	570
	2323	2.3	70
5 Su	0515	18.4	560
	1137	2.3	70
	1733	19.4	590
6 M	0007	1.6	50
	0600	19.0	580
	1220	2.3	70
	1816	19.7	600
7 Tu	0051	1.3	40
	0647	19.7	600
	1302	2.3	70
	1859	19.7	600
8 W	0134	1.0	30
	0734	19.7	600
	1345	2.3	70
	1944	19.7	600
9 Th	0217	0.7	20
	0823	19.4	590
	1430	2.3	70
	2032	19.0	580
10 F ○	0303	0.7	20
	0915	18.7	570
	1517	3.0	90
	2122	18.0	550
11 Sa	0354	1.3	40
	1011	17.7	540
	1611	3.3	100
	2219	16.7	510
12 Su	0452	2.0	60
	1116	16.7	510
	1715	3.9	120
	2326	15.7	480
13 M	0600	2.6	80
	1228	16.1	490
	1829	4.6	140
14 Tu	0046	15.1	460
	0714	3.0	90
	1341	16.4	500
	1948	4.3	130
15 W	0204	15.4	470
	0828	3.0	90
	1444	16.7	510
	2104	3.9	120

November (Days 16–30)

Day	Time	ft	cm
16 Th	0309	16.1	490
	0931	3.0	90
	1539	17.4	530
	2204	3.3	100
17 F	0404	16.7	510
	1021	3.0	90
	1626	18.0	550
	2249	2.6	80
18 Sa ●	0451	17.4	530
	1101	3.3	100
	1707	18.4	560
	2328	2.6	80
19 Su	0533	17.7	540
	1138	3.3	100
	1745	18.4	560
20 M	0006	2.3	70
	0613	18.0	550
	1215	3.6	110
	1821	18.4	560
21 Tu	0044	2.3	70
	0651	18.0	550
	1253	3.6	110
	1855	18.0	550
22 W	0122	2.0	60
	0728	17.7	540
	1332	3.9	120
	1929	17.7	540
23 Th	0201	2.0	60
	0805	17.4	530
	1411	3.9	120
	2003	17.1	520
24 F	0239	2.0	60
	0842	17.1	520
	1450	3.9	120
	2039	16.7	510
25 Sa	0317	2.3	70
	0922	16.7	510
	1529	3.9	120
	2118	16.1	490
26 Su ◐	0355	2.6	80
	1005	16.1	490
	1611	4.3	130
	2201	15.1	460
27 M	0436	3.0	90
	1053	15.4	470
	1658	4.6	140
	2252	14.4	440
28 Tu	0525	3.3	100
	1147	15.1	460
	1755	4.9	150
	2353	14.1	430
29 W	0623	3.6	110
	1246	15.1	460
	1900	4.9	150
30 Th	0059	14.4	440
	0725	3.9	120
	1344	15.7	480
	2003	4.6	140

December (Days 1–15)

Day	Time	ft	cm
1 F	0204	15.1	460
	0823	3.6	110
	1439	16.7	510
	2102	3.9	120
2 Sa	0303	16.4	500
	0917	3.6	110
	1530	17.7	540
	2156	3.3	100
3 Su ○	0359	17.4	530
	1008	3.3	100
	1618	18.7	570
	2249	2.6	80
4 M	0451	18.7	570
	1059	3.3	100
	1706	19.4	590
	2341	2.0	60
5 Tu	0543	19.4	590
	1151	3.0	90
	1754	20.0	610
6 W	0032	1.3	40
	0633	20.0	610
	1243	3.0	90
	1842	20.3	620
7 Th	0121	1.0	30
	0724	20.3	620
	1333	2.6	80
	1931	20.0	610
8 F	0209	0.7	20
	0814	20.0	610
	1421	2.6	80
	2021	19.7	600
9 Sa	0257	0.7	20
	0906	19.7	600
	1510	3.0	90
	2112	18.7	570
10 Su ◐	0345	1.0	30
	0959	18.7	570
	1602	3.3	100
	2206	17.7	540
11 M	0438	1.6	50
	1056	17.7	540
	1659	3.6	110
	2307	16.7	510
12 Tu	0536	2.3	70
	1159	17.1	520
	1805	4.3	130
13 W	0016	15.7	480
	0640	3.0	90
	1304	16.7	510
	1915	4.3	130
14 Th	0130	15.4	470
	0744	3.6	110
	1407	16.7	510
	2023	3.9	120
15 F	0237	15.7	480
	0843	3.9	120
	1504	16.7	510
	2123	3.6	110

December (Days 16–31)

Day	Time	ft	cm
16 Sa	0335	16.1	490
	0935	3.9	120
	1554	17.4	530
	2214	3.3	100
17 Su	0425	16.7	510
	1022	4.3	130
	1639	17.4	530
	2259	3.0	90
18 M ●	0511	17.1	520
	1105	4.6	140
	1719	17.7	540
	2341	3.0	90
19 Tu	0552	17.4	530
	1148	4.6	140
	1757	17.7	540
20 W	0023	2.6	80
	0632	17.7	540
	1231	4.6	140
	1833	17.7	540
21 Th	0104	2.6	80
	0710	17.7	540
	1313	4.6	140
	1908	17.4	530
22 F	0144	2.3	70
	0747	17.7	540
	1354	4.3	130
	1943	17.4	530
23 Sa	0222	2.3	70
	0823	17.4	530
	1432	4.3	130
	2018	17.1	520
24 Su	0258	2.3	70
	0859	17.1	520
	1509	4.3	130
	2055	16.7	510
25 M	0331	2.3	70
	0937	16.7	510
	1543	4.3	130
	2134	16.1	490
26 Tu ◐	0402	2.6	80
	1018	16.4	500
	1620	4.3	130
	2219	15.7	480
27 W	0438	3.0	90
	1104	16.1	490
	1706	4.6	140
	2313	15.4	470
28 Th	0525	3.6	110
	1157	16.1	490
	1804	4.6	140
29 F	0016	15.1	460
	0623	3.9	120
	1255	16.1	490
	1909	4.6	140
30 Sa	0122	15.4	470
	0726	3.9	120
	1354	16.7	510
	2013	3.9	120
31 Su	0228	16.4	500
	0826	3.9	120
	1452	17.4	530
	2115	3.3	100

Time meridian 45° W. 0000 is midnight. 1200 is noon. Times are not adjusted for Daylight Saving Time.
Heights are referred to the chart datum of soundings.

Punta Loyola, Argentina, 2017
Times and Heights of High and Low Waters

January

Day	Time (h m)	Height (ft)	Height (cm)	Day	Time (h m)	Height (ft)	Height (cm)
1 Su	0009	37.1	1130	16 M	0107	39.0	1190
	0636	8.2	250		0746	5.9	180
	1220	37.4	1140		1318	38.7	1180
	1903	5.9	180		2011	4.3	130
2 M	0053	37.4	1140	17 Tu	0146	38.1	1160
	0721	7.9	240		0824	7.2	220
	1304	37.4	1140		1358	37.1	1130
	1950	6.2	190		2049	6.2	190
3 Tu	0138	37.1	1130	18 W	0225	36.7	1120
	0808	8.2	250		0859	9.2	280
	1351	37.1	1130		1439	35.4	1080
	2038	6.9	210		2123	8.9	270
4 W	0226	36.7	1120	19 Th	0305	35.1	1070
	0857	9.2	280		0930	11.2	340
	1443	36.1	1100		1524	33.5	1020
	2130	8.2	250	◐	2156	11.2	340
5 Th	0319	35.8	1090	20 F	0350	33.5	1020
	0951	10.2	310		1006	13.1	400
	1542	35.1	1070		1615	31.8	970
◑	2227	9.5	290		2234	13.5	410
6 F	0418	35.1	1070	21 Sa	0439	32.2	980
	1052	11.5	350		1052	14.8	450
	1649	34.1	1040		1712	30.5	930
	2331	10.8	330		2322	15.1	460
7 Sa	0523	34.8	1060	22 Su	0533	31.2	950
	1201	11.8	360		1146	15.4	470
	1801	34.1	1040		1814	29.9	910
8 Su	0038	11.5	350	23 M	0016	16.1	490
	0630	35.1	1070		0628	30.8	940
	1312	11.2	340		1246	15.4	470
	1912	34.8	1060		1915	30.2	920
9 M	0145	10.8	330	24 Tu	0113	15.7	480
	0735	36.1	1100		0723	31.5	960
	1421	9.5	290		1346	14.4	440
	2017	36.1	1100		2007	31.5	960
10 Tu	0249	9.8	300	25 W	0209	14.8	450
	0836	37.4	1140		0814	32.5	990
	1523	7.5	230		1443	12.8	390
	2116	37.7	1150		2054	32.8	1000
11 W	0348	8.2	250	26 Th	0303	13.1	400
	0931	38.7	1180		0902	33.8	1030
	1620	5.2	160		1535	10.5	320
	2209	39.0	1190		2138	34.8	1060
12 Th	0442	6.9	210	27 F	0354	11.2	340
	1022	39.7	1210		0949	35.4	1080
	1712	3.6	110		1625	8.2	250
○	2257	39.7	1210	●	2222	36.4	1110
13 F	0532	5.9	180	28 Sa	0444	8.9	270
	1110	40.4	1230		1035	37.1	1130
	1801	2.6	80		1714	6.2	190
	2343	40.0	1220		2306	38.1	1160
14 Sa	0620	5.2	160	29 Su	0532	6.9	210
	1155	40.0	1220		1121	38.7	1180
	1847	2.3	70		1801	4.6	140
					2351	39.4	1200
15 Su	0026	39.7	1210	30 M	0620	5.6	170
	0704	5.2	160		1207	39.7	1210
	1237	39.7	1210		1848	3.6	110
	1930	2.6	80				
				31 Tu	0035	39.7	1210
					0706	4.9	150
					1253	40.0	1220
					1935	3.6	110

February

Day	Time (h m)	Height (ft)	Height (cm)	Day	Time (h m)	Height (ft)	Height (cm)
1 W	0120	39.7	1210	16 Th	0149	37.4	1140
	0753	5.2	160		0819	8.5	260
	1339	39.4	1200		1407	35.8	1090
	2021	4.6	140		2038	8.9	270
2 Th	0206	39.0	1190	17 F	0225	35.8	1090
	0840	6.6	200		0846	10.5	320
	1428	38.4	1170		1446	33.8	1030
	2110	6.6	200		2106	11.5	350
3 F	0255	37.7	1150	18 Sa	0303	33.8	1030
	0931	8.5	260		0919	12.5	380
	1522	36.4	1110		1529	31.8	970
	2203	9.2	280	○	2143	14.1	430
4 Sa	0349	36.1	1100	19 Su	0346	31.8	970
	1028	10.5	320		1001	14.4	440
	1624	34.8	1060		1618	30.2	920
◐	2305	11.5	350		2228	16.1	490
5 Su	0450	34.4	1050	20 M	0435	30.5	930
	1139	12.1	370		1050	15.7	480
	1737	33.5	1020		1715	29.2	890
					2321	17.1	520
6 M	0018	12.8	390	21 Tu	0531	29.5	900
	0603	33.8	1030		1149	16.1	490
	1259	12.1	370		1819	29.2	890
	1857	33.8	1030				
7 Tu	0133	12.8	390	22 W	0021	17.1	520
	0720	34.1	1040		0634	29.5	900
	1413	10.5	320		1256	15.4	470
	2010	35.1	1070		1924	30.2	920
8 W	0240	11.2	340	23 Th	0128	15.7	480
	0828	35.8	1090		0737	30.8	940
	1515	7.9	240		1406	13.1	400
	2109	37.1	1130		2021	32.5	990
9 Th	0338	8.9	270	24 F	0233	13.5	410
	0926	37.4	1140		0835	33.1	1010
	1609	5.2	160		1508	10.5	320
	2200	38.7	1180		2112	35.1	1070
10 F	0430	6.9	210	25 Sa	0330	10.5	320
	1015	39.0	1190		0927	35.8	1090
	1658	3.3	100		1603	7.5	230
○	2245	40.0	1220		2159	37.4	1140
11 Sa	0517	5.2	160	26 Su	0423	7.5	230
	1100	40.0	1220		1017	38.1	1160
	1743	2.0	60		1653	4.9	150
	2327	40.4	1230	●	2245	39.7	1210
12 Su	0601	4.3	130	27 M	0513	4.9	150
	1142	40.4	1230		1105	40.0	1220
	1826	2.0	60		1742	3.0	90
					2331	41.3	1260
13 M	0006	40.4	1230	28 Tu	0601	3.3	100
	0643	4.3	130		1151	41.7	1270
	1220	40.0	1220		1829	2.0	60
	1906	2.6	80				
14 Tu	0042	40.0	1220				
	0720	4.9	150				
	1257	39.0	1190				
	1942	4.3	130				
15 W	0116	39.0	1190				
	0753	6.6	200				
	1332	37.7	1150				
	2012	6.6	200				

March

Day	Time (h m)	Height (ft)	Height (cm)	Day	Time (h m)	Height (ft)	Height (cm)
1 W	0016	42.0	1280	16 Th	0044	39.0	1190
	0648	2.6	80		0722	6.2	190
	1237	42.0	1280		1304	37.4	1140
	1916	2.3	70		1937	7.5	230
2 Th	0100	42.0	1280	17 F	0116	37.7	1150
	0735	3.3	100		0745	8.2	250
	1324	41.3	1260		1338	35.8	1090
	2002	3.6	110		2001	9.8	300
3 F	0145	40.7	1240	18 Sa	0149	36.1	1100
	0822	4.9	150		0811	9.8	300
	1411	39.7	1210		1413	34.1	1040
	2050	6.2	190	○	2030	11.8	360
4 Sa	0231	39.0	1190	19 Su	0224	34.1	1040
	0911	7.2	220		0845	11.8	360
	1502	37.4	1140		1452	32.2	980
	2141	9.2	280		2106	14.1	430
5 Su	0320	36.7	1120	20 M	0303	32.2	980
	1008	9.8	300		0924	13.5	410
	1600	35.1	1070		1536	30.5	930
◑	2242	12.1	370	◐	2149	15.7	480
6 M	0418	34.4	1050	21 Tu	0346	30.5	930
	1121	11.8	360		1010	14.8	450
	1715	33.1	1010		1629	29.5	900
					2239	17.1	520
7 Tu	0000	13.8	420	22 W	0439	29.5	900
	0536	32.8	1000		1107	15.4	470
	1246	12.1	370		1733	29.2	890
	1847	33.1	1010		2341	17.1	520
8 W	0120	13.5	410	23 Th	0547	29.2	890
	0709	33.1	1010		1218	15.1	460
	1359	10.5	320		1844	30.2	920
	2000	34.8	1060				
9 Th	0226	11.8	360	24 F	0054	15.7	480
	0820	34.8	1060		0702	30.5	930
	1458	7.9	240		1335	13.1	400
	2056	36.7	1120		1948	32.8	1000
10 F	0322	9.2	280	25 Sa	0205	13.1	400
	0914	37.1	1130		0808	33.1	1010
	1550	5.6	170		1441	10.2	310
	2143	38.7	1180		2044	35.4	1080
11 Sa	0411	6.9	210	26 Su	0305	9.8	300
	1002	38.7	1180		0905	36.1	1100
	1637	3.6	110		1537	6.9	210
	2226	40.0	1220		2134	38.4	1170
12 Su	0457	5.2	160	27 M	0400	6.6	200
	1044	39.7	1210		0957	39.0	1190
	1721	2.6	80		1630	4.3	130
○	2305	40.7	1240	●	2222	41.0	1250
13 M	0540	4.3	130	28 Tu	0451	3.9	120
	1123	40.0	1220		1046	41.0	1250
	1802	2.6	80		1720	2.3	70
	2341	40.7	1240		2309	42.7	1300
14 Tu	0619	3.9	120	29 W	0541	2.3	70
	1159	39.7	1210		1133	42.7	1300
	1839	3.6	110		1809	1.6	50
					2354	43.3	1320
15 W	0014	40.0	1220	30 Th	0630	1.6	50
	0654	4.9	150		1220	42.7	1300
	1232	38.7	1180		1856	2.3	70
	1911	5.2	160				
				31 F	0039	43.0	1310
					0718	2.3	70
					1307	42.0	1280
					1944	3.9	120

Time meridian 45° W. 0000 is midnight. 1200 is noon. Times are not adjusted for Daylight Saving Time.
Heights are referred to the chart datum of soundings.

Punta Loyola, Argentina, 2017

Times and Heights of High and Low Waters

April

Day	Time (h m)	Height (ft)	Height (cm)
1 Sa	0123	41.7	1270
	0806	3.6	110
	1354	40.0	1220
	2032	6.2	190
2 Su	0208	39.7	1210
	0856	6.2	190
	1444	37.7	1150
	2123	9.2	280
3 M ☽	0256	37.1	1130
	0954	8.9	270
	1541	35.4	1080
	2224	12.1	370
4 Tu	0351	34.4	1050
	1107	10.8	330
	1658	33.5	1020
	2342	13.8	420
5 W	0513	32.5	990
	1226	11.2	340
	1829	33.5	1020
6 Th	0058	13.5	410
	0652	32.8	1000
	1334	9.8	300
	1937	34.8	1060
7 F	0202	11.8	360
	0800	34.4	1050
	1433	8.2	250
	2032	36.7	1120
8 Sa	0258	9.5	290
	0854	36.4	1110
	1524	6.2	190
	2119	38.4	1170
9 Su	0348	7.2	220
	0941	38.1	1160
	1611	4.9	150
	2201	39.7	1210
10 M	0434	5.9	180
	1023	39.0	1190
	1655	4.3	130
	2239	40.0	1220
11 Tu ○	0517	4.9	150
	1101	39.0	1190
	1736	4.6	140
	2312	40.0	1220
12 W	0555	4.9	150
	1135	38.7	1180
	1812	5.6	170
	2343	39.4	1200
13 Th	0628	5.9	180
	1206	37.7	1150
	1840	7.2	220
14 F	0012	38.4	1170
	0653	6.9	210
	1237	36.7	1120
	1904	8.9	270
15 Sa	0044	37.1	1130
	0716	8.2	250
	1310	35.4	1080
	1930	10.5	320
16 Su	0117	35.8	1090
	0744	9.5	290
	1345	34.1	1040
	2002	12.1	370
17 M	0151	34.1	1040
	0818	10.8	330
	1423	32.8	1000
	2038	13.8	420
18 Tu	0227	32.8	1000
	0856	12.1	370
	1504	31.5	960
	2119	14.8	450
19 W ◑	0307	31.5	960
	0941	13.1	400
	1553	30.8	940
	2208	15.7	480
20 Th	0355	30.5	930
	1037	14.1	430
	1655	30.5	930
	2310	15.7	480
21 F	0507	30.2	920
	1149	13.8	420
	1808	31.5	960
22 Sa	0025	14.8	450
	0630	31.2	950
	1307	12.1	370
	1916	33.5	1020
23 Su	0136	12.5	380
	0741	33.5	1020
	1412	9.5	290
	2015	36.1	1100
24 M	0239	9.5	290
	0841	36.4	1110
	1511	6.9	210
	2108	38.7	1180
25 Tu	0336	6.6	200
	0935	39.0	1190
	1605	4.9	150
	2158	41.0	1250
26 W ●	0430	4.3	130
	1025	41.0	1250
	1658	3.6	110
	2246	42.7	1300
27 Th	0523	2.6	80
	1115	42.0	1280
	1749	3.0	90
	2333	43.0	1310
28 F	0614	2.0	60
	1203	42.3	1290
	1839	3.3	100
29 Sa	0019	42.7	1300
	0705	2.0	60
	1251	41.3	1260
	1929	4.6	140
30 Su	0104	41.3	1260
	0755	3.3	100
	1339	40.0	1220
	2018	6.6	200

May

Day	Time (h m)	Height (ft)	Height (cm)
1 M	0149	39.4	1200
	0846	4.9	150
	1430	38.1	1160
	2110	8.9	270
2 Tu ◐	0237	37.4	1140
	0943	7.2	220
	1527	35.8	1090
	2209	11.2	340
3 W	0333	34.8	1060
	1048	8.9	270
	1638	34.1	1050
	2317	12.8	390
4 Th	0451	33.1	1010
	1157	9.8	300
	1757	34.1	1040
5 F	0027	12.8	390
	0621	33.1	1010
	1301	9.8	300
	1904	34.8	1060
6 Sa	0131	11.8	360
	0729	34.1	1040
	1400	8.9	270
	1959	36.1	1100
7 Su	0228	10.2	310
	0825	35.4	1080
	1453	7.9	240
	2047	37.4	1140
8 M	0320	8.5	260
	0914	36.7	1120
	1542	7.2	220
	2130	38.4	1170
9 Tu	0409	7.5	230
	0957	37.4	1140
	1627	7.2	220
	2207	38.7	1180
10 W ○	0453	6.9	210
	1035	37.4	1140
	1708	7.5	230
	2239	38.4	1170
11 Th	0531	6.9	210
	1107	37.1	1130
	1742	8.5	260
	2309	37.7	1150
12 F	0602	7.5	230
	1138	36.4	1110
	1809	9.5	290
	2341	37.1	1130
13 Sa	0625	8.2	250
	1210	35.4	1080
	1834	10.5	320
14 Su	0014	36.1	1100
	0651	8.5	260
	1244	34.8	1060
	1905	11.2	340
15 M	0049	35.1	1070
	0723	9.2	280
	1321	34.1	1040
	1939	11.8	360
16 Tu	0125	34.4	1050
	0759	9.8	300
	1359	33.5	1020
	2018	12.8	390
17 W	0202	33.8	1030
	0839	10.5	320
	1440	33.1	1010
	2100	13.1	400
18 Th ◑	0241	32.8	1000
	0925	11.2	340
	1528	32.5	990
	2148	13.8	420
19 F	0330	32.2	980
	1020	11.8	360
	1627	32.5	990
	2248	14.1	430
20 Sa	0441	31.8	970
	1128	12.1	370
	1737	32.8	1000
	2359	13.5	410
21 Su	0602	32.5	990
	1239	11.2	340
	1844	34.4	1050
22 M	0109	11.8	360
	0714	34.1	1040
	1344	9.8	300
	1945	36.4	1110
23 Tu	0213	9.5	290
	0816	36.4	1110
	1445	7.9	240
	2041	38.7	1180
24 W	0313	7.2	220
	0912	38.4	1170
	1543	6.6	200
	2134	40.4	1230
25 Th ●	0412	5.2	160
	1006	40.0	1220
	1639	5.6	170
	2224	41.3	1260
26 F	0508	3.6	110
	1058	40.7	1240
	1733	4.9	150
	2313	42.0	1280
27 Sa	0603	2.6	80
	1148	41.0	1250
	1826	4.9	150
28 Su	0001	41.7	1270
	0655	2.3	70
	1238	40.7	1240
	1917	5.2	160
29 M	0048	40.7	1240
	0746	2.6	80
	1327	39.4	1200
	2006	6.6	200
30 Tu	0135	39.4	1200
	0836	3.9	120
	1417	38.1	1160
	2056	7.9	240
31 W	0224	37.7	1150
	0927	5.6	170
	1510	36.7	1120
	2148	9.5	290

June

Day	Time (h m)	Height (ft)	Height (cm)
1 Th ◑	0317	35.8	1090
	1021	7.2	220
	1609	35.4	1080
	2245	11.2	340
2 F	0422	34.1	1040
	1120	8.9	270
	1714	34.8	1060
	2347	12.1	370
3 Sa	0537	33.5	1020
	1220	9.8	300
	1818	34.8	1060
4 Su	0050	12.1	370
	0648	33.5	1020
	1319	10.2	310
	1916	35.4	1080
5 M	0152	11.5	350
	0749	34.1	1040
	1415	10.5	320
	2008	35.8	1090
6 Tu	0249	10.8	330
	0842	34.8	1060
	1508	10.5	320
	2052	36.4	1110
7 W	0342	9.8	300
	0928	35.1	1070
	1555	10.5	320
	2129	36.4	1110
8 Th	0428	9.5	290
	1005	35.1	1070
	1636	10.8	330
	2202	36.1	1100
9 F ○	0505	9.2	280
	1036	35.1	1070
	1708	11.2	340
	2235	36.1	1100
10 Sa	0533	9.2	280
	1109	34.8	1060
	1736	11.2	340
	2311	35.8	1090
11 Su	0559	8.9	270
	1144	34.8	1060
	1808	11.2	340
	2348	35.4	1080
12 M	0631	8.5	260
	1221	34.8	1060
	1844	11.2	340
13 Tu	0026	35.1	1070
	0707	8.2	250
	1259	34.8	1060
	1923	10.8	330
14 W	0105	35.1	1070
	0747	8.2	250
	1340	34.8	1060
	2003	10.8	330
15 Th	0146	34.8	1060
	0829	8.5	260
	1423	34.8	1060
	2047	11.2	340
16 F ◑	0229	34.8	1060
	0916	9.2	280
	1511	34.8	1060
	2135	11.5	350
17 Sa ◑	0321	34.1	1040
	1008	9.8	300
	1606	34.4	1050
	2231	12.1	370
18 Su	0425	33.5	1020
	1108	10.5	320
	1708	34.4	1050
	2335	12.1	370
19 M	0537	33.5	1020
	1213	10.8	330
	1814	35.1	1070
20 Tu	0043	11.5	350
	0647	34.4	1050
	1319	10.5	320
	1916	36.4	1110
21 W	0151	10.2	310
	0753	35.8	1090
	1422	9.5	290
	2016	37.7	1150
22 Th	0256	8.5	260
	0853	37.1	1130
	1525	8.5	260
	2113	39.0	1190
23 F ●	0359	6.6	200
	0951	38.4	1170
	1625	7.5	230
	2207	40.0	1220
24 Sa ○	0458	4.6	140
	1045	39.4	1200
	1721	6.6	200
	2259	40.4	1230
25 Su	0553	3.0	90
	1137	39.7	1210
	1814	5.6	170
	2349	40.4	1230
26 M	0644	2.3	70
	1226	39.7	1210
	1904	5.6	170
27 Tu	0037	40.0	1220
	0733	2.0	60
	1313	39.4	1200
	1951	5.9	180
28 W	0123	39.4	1200
	0819	2.6	80
	1400	38.7	1180
	2037	6.9	210
29 Th	0210	38.1	1160
	0904	4.3	130
	1446	37.7	1150
	2122	8.2	250
30 F ◑	0257	36.7	1120
	0950	6.2	190
	1533	36.4	1110
	2207	9.8	300

Time meridian 45° W. 0000 is midnight. 1200 is noon. Times are not adjusted for Daylight Saving Time.
Heights are referred to the chart datum of soundings.

Punta Loyola, Argentina, 2017

Times and Heights of High and Low Waters

July

Day	Time	ft	cm	Day	Time	ft	cm
1 Sa	0348	35.1	1070	**16** Su	0311	36.1	1100
	1036	8.5	260		0952	8.5	260
	1623	35.4	1080		1544	36.1	1100
	2257	11.5	350	☽	2213	10.5	320
2 Su	0445	33.8	1030	**17** M	0409	35.1	1070
	1127	10.5	320		1048	9.8	300
	1718	34.8	1060		1641	35.4	1080
	2354	12.8	390		2314	11.5	350
3 M	0549	32.8	1000	**18** Tu	0515	34.4	1050
	1222	12.1	370		1150	11.2	340
	1814	34.1	1040		1745	35.1	1070
4 Tu	0100	13.1	400	**19** W	0023	11.8	360
	0657	32.5	990		0625	34.1	1040
	1321	13.1	400		1258	11.8	360
	1909	33.8	1030		1851	35.4	1080
5 W	0209	13.1	400	**20** Th	0136	10.8	330
	0800	32.5	990		0735	34.8	1060
	1419	13.5	410		1408	11.2	340
	1958	33.8	1030		1957	36.4	1110
6 Th	0309	12.8	390	**21** F	0247	9.2	280
	0849	32.8	1000		0841	36.1	1100
	1509	13.5	410		1514	10.2	310
	2041	34.1	1040		2059	37.4	1140
7 F	0355	11.8	360	**22** Sa	0351	7.2	220
	0926	33.1	1010		0941	37.4	1140
	1548	13.5	410		1614	8.5	260
	2122	34.1	1040		2156	38.4	1170
8 Sa	0426	11.2	340	**23** Su	0448	4.9	150
	1001	33.5	1020		1035	38.7	1180
	1622	12.8	390		1709	6.9	210
	2202	34.4	1050	●	2249	39.4	1200
9 Su	0455	10.2	310	**24** M	0540	3.0	90
	1038	34.1	1040		1124	39.4	1200
	1700	11.8	360		1759	5.6	170
○	2243	34.8	1060		2338	40.0	1220
10 M	0530	9.2	280	**25** Tu	0628	2.0	60
	1117	34.8	1060		1210	39.7	1210
	1741	10.8	330		1846	4.9	150
	2325	35.4	1080				
11 Tu	0609	7.9	240	**26** W	0023	40.0	1220
	1157	35.4	1080		0713	1.6	50
	1823	9.8	300		1254	39.7	1210
					1931	4.9	150
12 W	0007	36.1	1100	**27** Th	0107	39.4	1200
	0650	6.9	210		0756	2.3	70
	1239	36.1	1100		1335	39.0	1190
	1906	8.9	270		2012	5.9	180
13 Th	0050	36.4	1110	**28** F	0149	38.7	1180
	0733	6.2	190		0837	3.9	120
	1322	36.7	1120		1415	38.4	1170
	1949	8.5	260		2051	7.2	220
14 F	0134	36.7	1120	**29** Sa	0230	37.4	1140
	0817	6.6	200		0915	6.2	190
	1406	36.7	1120		1455	37.1	1130
	2034	8.5	260		2127	9.2	280
15 Sa	0220	36.7	1120	**30** Su	0313	35.8	1090
	0903	7.2	220		0949	8.9	270
	1452	36.7	1120		1536	35.8	1090
	2121	9.2	280	☾	2201	11.2	340
				31 M	0359	33.8	1030
					1024	11.2	340
					1621	34.4	1050
					2239	12.8	390

August

Day	Time	ft	cm	Day	Time	ft	cm
1 Tu	0452	32.2	980	**16** W	0455	34.4	1050
	1104	13.5	410		1132	12.1	370
	1711	33.1	1010		1719	34.8	1060
	2327	14.1	430				
2 W	0551	31.2	950	**17** Th	0011	11.8	360
	1152	15.1	460		0610	33.8	1030
	1805	32.2	980		1246	12.8	390
					1833	34.4	1050
3 Th	0023	14.8	450	**18** F	0130	11.2	340
	0654	30.8	940		0727	34.4	1050
	1247	15.7	480		1400	12.1	370
	1900	31.8	970		1947	35.1	1070
4 F	0128	14.8	450	**19** Sa	0239	9.2	280
	0753	31.2	950		0834	35.8	1090
	1345	15.4	470		1504	10.5	320
	1954	32.2	980		2052	36.4	1110
5 Sa	0235	13.8	420	**20** Su	0339	6.9	210
	0841	31.8	970		0931	37.4	1140
	1443	14.4	440		1601	8.5	260
	2044	32.8	1000		2147	38.1	1160
6 Su	0326	12.1	370	**21** M	0431	4.6	140
	0924	32.8	1000		1020	38.7	1180
	1536	13.1	400		1652	6.6	200
	2131	33.8	1030	●	2236	39.4	1200
7 M	0413	10.2	310	**22** Tu	0520	3.0	90
	1007	34.4	1050		1106	39.7	1210
	1626	11.2	340		1739	5.2	160
○	2217	35.1	1070		2322	40.0	1220
8 Tu	0458	8.2	250	**23** W	0606	2.3	70
	1050	35.8	1090		1148	40.0	1220
	1714	9.5	290		1824	4.6	140
	2303	36.4	1110				
9 W	0544	6.6	200	**24** Th	0004	40.0	1220
	1133	37.1	1130		0649	2.3	70
	1800	7.9	240		1227	40.0	1220
	2348	37.7	1150		1906	4.6	140
10 Th	0629	5.2	160	**25** F	0044	39.4	1200
	1216	38.1	1160		0729	3.3	100
	1846	6.6	200		1305	39.4	1200
					1944	5.6	170
11 F	0033	38.4	1170	**26** Sa	0122	38.4	1170
	0714	4.6	140		0805	4.9	150
	1300	38.7	1180		1340	38.4	1170
	1931	6.2	190		2018	7.2	220
12 Sa	0119	38.7	1180	**27** Su	0159	37.1	1130
	0759	4.9	150		0837	7.5	230
	1345	38.7	1180		1416	37.1	1130
	2017	6.6	200		2047	9.2	280
13 Su	0206	38.4	1170	**28** M	0238	35.4	1080
	0845	5.9	180		0905	9.8	300
	1431	38.4	1170		1454	35.4	1080
	2104	7.5	230		2116	11.2	340
14 M	0256	37.4	1140	**29** Tu	0320	33.5	1020
	0934	7.9	240		0936	12.5	380
	1520	37.1	1130		1535	33.5	1020
☾	2156	9.5	290	◐	2153	13.1	400
15 Tu	0351	35.8	1090	**30** W	0407	31.5	960
	1028	10.2	310		1016	14.4	440
	1615	35.8	1090		1621	31.8	970
	2256	11.2	340		2238	14.4	440
				31 Th	0501	30.2	920
					1103	16.1	490
					1714	30.5	930
					2331	15.4	470

September

Day	Time	ft	cm	Day	Time	ft	cm
1 F	0601	29.5	900	**16** Sa	0121	10.5	320
	1159	16.7	510		0721	34.4	1050
	1813	30.2	920		1349	11.8	360
					1942	34.8	1060
2 Sa	0032	15.1	460	**17** Su	0225	8.5	260
	0704	30.2	920		0823	36.1	1100
	1300	16.1	490		1448	9.8	300
	1913	30.8	940		2042	36.4	1110
3 Su	0140	14.1	430	**18** M	0319	6.2	190
	0800	31.5	960		0914	37.7	1150
	1403	14.4	440		1541	7.9	240
	2011	32.2	980		2132	38.1	1160
4 M	0242	11.8	360	**19** Tu	0409	4.3	130
	0850	33.5	1020		0959	39.4	1200
	1501	12.1	370		1630	6.2	190
	2103	34.1	1040		2218	39.4	1200
5 Tu	0336	9.5	290	**20** W	0456	3.3	100
	0936	35.4	1080		1041	40.0	1220
	1554	9.8	300		1715	4.9	150
	2152	36.1	1100	●	2300	40.0	1220
6 W	0427	7.2	220	**21** Th	0540	3.0	90
	1022	37.4	1140		1120	40.4	1230
	1645	7.5	230		1759	4.6	140
○	2240	38.1	1160		2340	39.7	1210
7 Th	0516	5.2	160	**22** F	0621	3.6	110
	1107	39.0	1190		1157	40.0	1220
	1735	5.6	170		1839	4.9	150
	2327	39.4	1200				
8 F	0604	3.9	120	**23** Sa	0017	39.0	1190
	1152	40.0	1220		0659	4.9	150
	1823	4.6	140		1231	39.0	1190
					1914	6.2	190
9 Sa	0013	40.4	1230	**24** Su	0052	38.1	1160
	0651	3.6	110		0732	6.9	210
	1237	40.7	1240		1304	38.1	1160
	1910	4.3	130		1944	7.9	240
10 Su	0100	40.4	1230	**25** M	0127	36.4	1110
	0738	4.3	130		0758	9.2	280
	1322	40.4	1230		1338	36.4	1110
	1958	5.2	160		2009	9.5	290
11 M	0148	39.7	1210	**26** Tu	0204	34.4	1050
	0825	5.9	180		0825	11.5	350
	1408	39.0	1190		1415	34.4	1050
	2047	6.6	200		2039	11.5	350
12 Tu	0238	38.1	1160	**27** W	0244	32.8	1000
	0915	8.2	250		0859	13.5	410
	1457	37.4	1140		1454	32.8	1000
	2141	8.9	270	◐	2117	13.1	400
13 W	0333	36.1	1100	**28** Th	0328	30.8	940
	1012	10.8	330		0939	15.4	470
	1551	35.4	1080		1538	30.8	940
◐	2246	10.5	320		2201	14.4	440
14 Th	0440	34.1	1040	**29** F	0419	29.9	910
	1121	12.8	390		1027	16.4	500
	1659	33.8	1030		1629	29.9	910
					2254	15.1	460
15 F	0006	11.5	350	**30** Sa	0518	29.2	890
	0603	33.5	1020		1123	16.7	510
	1239	13.1	400		1730	29.5	900
	1825	33.5	1020		2358	15.1	460

Time meridian 45° W. 0000 is midnight. 1200 is noon. Times are not adjusted for Daylight Saving Time.
Heights are referred to the chart datum of soundings.

Punta Loyola, Argentina, 2017

Times and Heights of High and Low Waters

October

Day	Time	ft	cm
1 Su	0624	30.2	920
	1227	15.7	480
	1838	30.2	920
2 M	0107	13.5	410
	0724	31.8	970
	1333	13.8	420
	1941	32.2	980
3 Tu	0210	11.2	340
	0817	34.1	1040
	1431	11.2	340
	2037	34.8	1060
4 W	0305	8.5	260
	0907	36.7	1120
	1526	8.5	260
	2128	37.4	1140
5 Th ○	0357	6.2	190
	0954	39.0	1190
	1618	5.9	180
	2217	39.4	1200
6 F	0448	4.3	130
	1040	40.7	1240
	1710	4.3	130
	2305	41.0	1250
7 Sa	0539	3.6	110
	1127	41.7	1270
	1800	3.3	100
	2353	41.3	1260
8 Su	0628	3.6	110
	1212	41.7	1270
	1850	3.3	100
9 M	0040	41.0	1250
	0717	4.6	140
	1258	41.0	1250
	1941	4.3	130
10 Tu	0129	40.0	1220
	0807	6.2	190
	1345	39.4	1200
	2033	5.9	180
11 W	0220	38.1	1160
	0900	8.5	260
	1435	37.4	1140
	2130	8.2	250
12 Th ◗	0318	35.8	1090
	0959	11.2	340
	1531	35.1	1070
	2239	9.8	300
13 F	0429	34.1	1040
	1111	12.8	390
	1645	33.5	1020
	2354	10.2	310
14 Sa	0554	33.8	1030
	1225	12.8	390
	1817	33.5	1020
15 Su	0103	9.5	290
	0705	34.8	1060
	1330	11.5	350
	1927	34.8	1060
16 M	0202	7.9	240
	0801	36.7	1120
	1426	9.5	290
	2023	36.7	1120
17 Tu	0254	6.2	190
	0850	38.4	1170
	1518	7.5	230
	2112	38.1	1160
18 W	0343	4.9	150
	0934	39.4	1200
	1605	6.2	190
	2156	39.4	1200
19 Th ●	0429	4.3	130
	1014	40.0	1220
	1651	5.2	160
	2236	39.7	1210
20 F	0512	4.6	140
	1051	40.4	1230
	1733	5.2	160
	2314	39.0	1190
21 Sa	0552	5.2	160
	1124	39.7	1210
	1812	5.9	180
	2349	38.4	1170
22 Su	0628	6.9	210
	1157	38.7	1180
	1845	6.9	210
23 M	0023	37.1	1130
	0657	8.9	270
	1229	37.1	1130
	1911	8.5	260
24 Tu	0057	35.4	1080
	0722	10.8	330
	1304	35.4	1080
	1937	9.8	300
25 W	0133	33.8	1030
	0752	12.5	380
	1340	33.8	1030
	2009	11.5	350
26 Th	0212	32.2	980
	0827	14.1	430
	1418	32.2	980
	2047	12.8	390
27 F ◑	0254	30.8	940
	0908	15.4	470
	1459	30.8	940
	2131	13.8	420
28 Sa	0342	29.9	910
	0956	16.1	490
	1549	29.9	910
	2225	14.4	440
29 Su	0441	29.9	910
	1052	16.1	490
	1652	29.5	900
	2329	14.1	430
30 M	0547	30.5	930
	1159	15.1	460
	1806	30.5	930
31 Tu	0038	12.8	390
	0650	32.5	990
	1305	13.1	400
	1913	32.8	1000

November

Day	Time	ft	cm
1 W	0141	10.5	320
	0746	35.1	1070
	1404	10.2	310
	2011	35.4	1080
2 Th	0237	8.2	250
	0838	37.7	1150
	1500	7.5	230
	2104	38.1	1160
3 F	0331	5.9	180
	0927	40.0	1220
	1554	5.6	170
	2154	40.4	1230
4 Sa ○	0424	4.6	140
	1016	41.7	1270
	1648	3.9	120
	2244	41.3	1260
5 Su	0516	3.9	120
	1103	42.3	1290
	1742	3.0	90
	2333	41.7	1270
6 M	0609	4.3	130
	1150	42.0	1280
	1835	3.0	90
7 Tu	0023	41.0	1250
	0701	5.2	160
	1238	41.0	1250
	1928	3.9	120
8 W	0113	39.7	1210
	0753	6.6	200
	1326	39.4	1200
	2022	5.2	160
9 Th	0205	37.7	1150
	0847	8.5	260
	1416	37.4	1140
	2120	6.9	210
10 F ◑	0303	36.1	1100
	0946	10.5	320
	1514	35.1	1070
	2224	8.2	250
11 Sa	0413	34.4	1050
	1052	11.8	360
	1630	33.8	1030
	2331	9.2	280
12 Su	0529	34.1	1040
	1159	12.1	370
	1754	33.5	1020
13 M	0035	8.9	270
	0636	35.1	1070
	1302	11.2	340
	1902	34.8	1060
14 Tu	0133	8.2	250
	0732	36.4	1110
	1359	9.8	300
	1958	36.1	1100
15 W	0226	7.2	220
	0821	37.7	1150
	1452	8.2	250
	2047	37.4	1140
16 Th	0315	6.6	200
	0906	39.0	1190
	1541	6.9	210
	2132	38.4	1170
17 F	0402	6.2	190
	0945	39.4	1200
	1627	6.2	190
	2213	38.4	1170
18 Sa ●	0445	6.9	210
	1021	39.4	1200
	1709	6.2	190
	2249	38.1	1160
19 Su	0525	7.5	230
	1053	38.7	1180
	1748	6.9	210
	2322	37.1	1130
20 M	0558	8.9	270
	1125	37.4	1140
	1819	7.9	240
	2355	36.1	1100
21 Tu	0625	10.2	310
	1158	36.1	1100
	1843	8.9	270
22 W	0029	34.8	1060
	0652	11.5	350
	1233	34.8	1060
	1911	9.8	300
23 Th	0105	33.5	1020
	0725	12.5	380
	1310	33.5	1020
	1945	10.8	330
24 F	0144	32.5	990
	0802	13.5	410
	1347	32.5	990
	2024	11.8	360
25 Sa	0225	31.8	970
	0843	14.1	430
	1427	31.5	960
	2109	12.5	380
26 Su ◗	0311	31.2	950
	0930	14.8	450
	1530	30.8	940
	2201	13.1	400
27 M	0406	31.2	950
	1025	14.8	450
	1619	30.8	940
	2303	13.1	400
28 Tu	0511	31.8	970
	1130	14.1	430
	1735	31.5	960
29 W	0010	12.1	370
	0616	33.1	1010
	1236	12.5	380
	1844	33.5	1020
30 Th	0112	10.5	320
	0716	35.4	1080
	1339	10.2	310
	1946	35.8	1090

December

Day	Time	ft	cm
1 F	0211	8.5	260
	0811	37.7	1150
	1438	7.9	240
	2042	38.1	1160
2 Sa	0308	6.9	210
	0903	40.0	1220
	1536	5.9	180
	2135	39.7	1210
3 Su ○	0404	5.9	180
	0954	41.3	1260
	1633	4.3	130
	2227	41.0	1250
4 M	0500	5.2	160
	1044	42.0	1280
	1730	3.3	100
	2318	41.3	1260
5 Tu	0555	4.9	150
	1133	41.7	1270
	1825	2.6	80
6 W	0009	40.7	1240
	0648	5.2	160
	1222	40.7	1240
	1918	3.0	90
7 Th	0100	39.7	1210
	0740	6.2	190
	1311	39.4	1200
	2011	3.9	120
8 F	0151	38.4	1170
	0832	7.5	230
	1402	37.7	1150
	2104	5.2	160
9 Sa	0245	36.7	1120
	0925	9.2	280
	1457	36.1	1100
	2159	6.9	210
10 Su ◗	0344	35.4	1080
	1022	10.5	320
	1601	34.4	1050
	2257	8.2	250
11 M	0449	34.8	1060
	1123	11.5	350
	1715	33.8	1030
	2358	9.2	280
12 Tu	0554	34.8	1060
	1226	11.5	350
	1825	34.1	1040
13 W	0057	9.5	290
	0655	35.4	1080
	1328	10.8	330
	1928	34.8	1060
14 Th	0154	9.5	290
	0749	36.4	1110
	1426	9.8	300
	2023	35.8	1090
15 F	0248	9.2	280
	0836	37.1	1130
	1519	8.9	270
	2111	36.7	1120
16 Sa	0337	9.2	280
	0917	37.7	1150
	1608	8.2	250
	2153	36.7	1120
17 Su	0422	9.2	280
	0952	37.4	1140
	1652	7.9	240
	2228	36.4	1110
18 M ●	0501	9.8	300
	1024	37.1	1130
	1728	8.2	250
	2259	36.1	1100
19 Tu	0532	10.5	320
	1058	36.4	1110
	1755	8.5	260
	2330	35.4	1080
20 W	0557	10.8	330
	1133	35.4	1080
	1820	8.9	270
21 Th	0005	34.8	1060
	0628	11.2	340
	1209	34.8	1060
	1851	9.2	280
22 F	0041	34.1	1040
	0703	11.5	350
	1247	34.1	1040
	1927	9.5	290
23 Sa	0120	33.8	1030
	0741	11.5	350
	1325	33.8	1030
	2007	9.8	300
24 Su	0200	33.5	1020
	0823	11.8	360
	1406	33.5	1020
	2051	10.5	320
25 M	0244	33.1	1010
	0908	12.5	380
	1453	32.8	1000
	2140	11.2	340
26 Tu ◗	0335	33.1	1010
	1000	12.8	390
	1553	32.5	990
	2237	11.8	360
27 W	0436	33.1	1010
	1101	13.1	400
	1704	32.5	990
	2341	12.1	370
28 Th	0541	33.8	1030
	1208	12.5	380
	1816	33.5	1020
29 F	0046	11.5	350
	0645	35.1	1070
	1316	11.2	340
	1922	35.1	1070
30 Sa	0150	10.2	310
	0746	36.7	1120
	1422	9.2	280
	2024	37.1	1130
31 Su	0252	8.9	270
	0844	38.4	1170
	1525	6.9	210
	2122	38.7	1180

Time meridian 45° W. 0000 is midnight. 1200 is noon. Times are not adjusted for Daylight Saving Time.
Heights are referred to the chart datum of soundings.

Bahia de Cienfuegos, Cuba 2017
Times and Heights of High and Low Waters

January

Day	Time	ft	cm
1 Su	0514	0.3	10
	1141	1.4	42
	1751	0.6	17
	2338	1.3	40
2 M	0605	0.4	12
	1230	1.4	42
	1848	0.5	16
3 Tu	0045	1.2	38
	0702	0.5	14
	1326	1.3	41
	1950	0.5	14
4 W	0203	1.2	38
	0806	0.5	15
	1428	1.3	41
	2056	0.4	12
5 Th	0323	1.2	38
	0914	0.5	16
	1531	1.3	41
	2202	0.3	9
6 F ☽	0437	1.3	39
	1023	0.5	16
	1633	1.3	41
	2305	0.2	6
7 Sa	0542	1.3	40
	1128	0.5	15
	1731	1.4	42
8 Su	0004	0.1	3
	0640	1.4	42
	1228	0.5	14
	1825	1.4	43
9 M	0058	0.0	1
	0732	1.4	44
	1323	0.4	13
	1917	1.4	44
10 Tu	0148	0.0	-1
	0821	1.4	44
	1414	0.4	12
	2006	1.4	44
11 W	0237	0.0	-1
	0907	1.5	45
	1503	0.4	12
	2054	1.4	44
12 Th ○	0323	0.0	0
	0952	1.4	44
	1550	0.4	12
	2142	1.4	42
13 F	0408	0.1	2
	1036	1.4	43
	1638	0.4	12
	2230	1.3	40
14 Sa	0453	0.2	5
	1120	1.3	41
	1726	0.4	12
	2321	1.2	38
15 Su	0538	0.3	8
	1206	1.3	39
	1817	0.4	13
16 M	0015	1.1	35
	0625	0.4	11
	1253	1.2	37
	1910	0.5	14
17 Tu	0118	1.0	32
	0714	0.5	14
	1343	1.1	35
	2008	0.5	14
18 W	0230	1.0	30
	0809	0.6	17
	1438	1.1	33
	2110	0.5	14
19 Th	0350	1.0	29
	0911	0.6	19
	1534	1.0	32
	2212	0.4	13
20 F ☽	0502	1.0	29
	1017	0.7	20
	1627	1.0	31
	2307	0.4	12
21 Sa	0559	1.0	30
	1119	0.7	20
	1714	1.0	31
	2352	0.3	10
22 Su	0642	1.0	31
	1209	0.7	20
	1755	1.0	32
23 M	0031	0.3	9
	0716	1.1	33
	1250	0.6	19
	1832	1.1	33
24 Tu	0106	0.2	7
	0747	1.1	34
	1326	0.6	18
	1908	1.1	35
25 W	0140	0.2	6
	0817	1.2	36
	1401	0.5	16
	1944	1.2	36
26 Th	0216	0.2	5
	0847	1.2	38
	1436	0.5	15
	2022	1.2	38
27 F	0252	0.1	4
	0919	1.3	39
	1514	0.4	13
	2103	1.3	39
28 Sa ●	0331	0.1	4
	0954	1.3	40
	1554	0.4	12
	2146	1.3	40
29 Su	0412	0.2	5
	1031	1.3	41
	1638	0.3	10
	2234	1.3	40
30 M	0456	0.2	6
	1112	1.3	41
	1726	0.3	9
	2327	1.3	39
31 Tu	0544	0.3	8
	1158	1.3	40
	1820	0.3	8

February

Day	Time	ft	cm
1 W	0028	1.2	37
	0638	0.3	10
	1250	1.3	39
	1920	0.3	8
2 Th	0140	1.2	36
	0739	0.4	12
	1351	1.2	38
	2026	0.2	7
3 F	0259	1.1	35
	0849	0.5	14
	1500	1.2	37
	2136	0.2	5
4 Sa ☽	0418	1.1	35
	1001	0.5	14
	1610	1.2	37
	2245	0.1	3
5 Su	0527	1.2	36
	1112	0.4	13
	1715	1.2	38
	2348	0.0	1
6 M	0627	1.2	38
	1216	0.4	12
	1814	1.3	39
7 Tu	0046	0.0	-1
	0719	1.3	39
	1312	0.3	10
	1908	1.3	40
8 W	0137	-0.1	-2
	0806	1.3	41
	1402	0.3	8
	1959	1.3	41
9 Th	0224	-0.1	-2
	0850	1.3	41
	1449	0.2	7
	2046	1.3	41
10 F	0309	0.0	-1
	0931	1.3	41
	1533	0.2	7
	2131	1.3	40
11 Sa ○	0351	0.0	1
	1010	1.3	40
	1616	0.2	7
	2216	1.2	38
12 Su	0431	0.1	4
	1049	1.2	38
	1658	0.3	8
	2301	1.1	35
13 M	0511	0.2	7
	1126	1.2	36
	1741	0.3	9
	2347	1.1	33
14 Tu	0551	0.4	11
	1204	1.1	34
	1826	0.3	10
15 W	0038	1.0	30
	0632	0.5	14
	1242	1.0	31
	1914	0.4	12
16 Th	0139	0.9	27
	0717	0.6	17
	1325	1.0	29
	2008	0.4	13
17 F	0256	0.9	26
	0813	0.6	19
	1420	0.9	28
	2109	0.4	13
18 Sa	0419	0.9	26
	0922	0.7	20
	1526	0.9	27
	2212	0.4	12
19 Su ☽	0524	0.9	27
	1036	0.7	20
	1629	0.9	27
	2308	0.3	10
20 M	0608	1.0	29
	1135	0.6	19
	1722	1.0	29
	2355	0.3	9
21 Tu	0643	1.0	31
	1220	0.6	17
	1808	1.0	31
22 W	0036	0.2	7
	0714	1.1	33
	1259	0.5	15
	1850	1.1	33
23 Th	0115	0.2	5
	0745	1.1	35
	1336	0.4	12
	1930	1.2	36
24 F	0154	0.1	3
	0817	1.2	37
	1413	0.3	10
	2011	1.3	39
25 Sa	0232	0.1	3
	0850	1.3	39
	1452	0.3	8
	2053	1.3	40
26 Su ●	0321	0.1	3
	0925	1.3	40
	1532	0.2	6
	2137	1.3	41
27 M	0354	0.1	4
	1003	1.3	41
	1616	0.2	5
	2224	1.3	41
28 Tu	0437	0.2	5
	1043	1.3	41
	1702	0.1	4
	2315	1.3	40

March

Day	Time	ft	cm
1 W	0524	0.3	8
	1127	1.3	40
	1754	0.1	4
2 Th	0013	1.2	38
	0617	0.3	10
	1218	1.2	38
	1835	0.1	4
3 F	0121	1.2	36
	0718	0.4	12
	1320	1.2	36
	1959	0.2	5
4 Sa	0239	1.1	34
	0828	0.5	14
	1434	1.1	35
	2112	0.2	5
5 Su ☽	0359	1.1	34
	0946	0.5	14
	1552	1.1	35
	2225	0.1	4
6 M	0510	1.1	35
	1100	0.4	12
	1704	1.2	36
	2333	0.1	2
7 Tu	0610	1.2	37
	1205	0.3	10
	1807	1.2	37
8 W	0032	0.0	1
	0701	1.2	38
	1300	0.3	8
	1901	1.2	38
9 Th	0123	0.0	0
	0745	1.3	39
	1348	0.2	6
	1950	1.3	39
10 F	0209	0.0	0
	0826	1.3	39
	1431	0.1	4
	2036	1.3	39
11 Sa	0251	0.0	1
	0904	1.3	39
	1511	0.1	4
	2118	1.3	39
12 Su ○	0330	0.1	3
	0939	1.2	38
	1550	0.1	4
	2159	1.2	37
13 M	0406	0.2	6
	1012	1.2	37
	1627	0.2	6
	2238	1.1	35
14 Tu	0442	0.3	9
	1043	1.1	35
	1703	0.2	7
	2318	1.1	33
15 W	0516	0.4	12
	1112	1.1	33
	1740	0.3	9
	2359	1.0	30
16 Th	0551	0.5	15
	1138	1.0	30
	1819	0.4	11
17 F	0048	0.9	28
	0629	0.6	18
	1204	1.0	29
	1904	0.4	12
18 Sa	0153	0.9	26
	0719	0.7	20
	1241	0.9	27
	2000	0.4	13
19 Su	0316	0.9	26
	0830	0.7	21
	1401	0.9	26
	2108	0.4	13
20 M ☽	0429	0.9	27
	0951	0.7	20
	1541	0.9	26
	2215	0.4	12
21 Tu	0520	1.0	29
	1058	0.6	18
	1651	0.9	28
	2314	0.3	10
22 W	0600	1.0	31
	1148	0.5	15
	1745	1.0	31
23 Th	0003	0.3	8
	0636	1.1	33
	1230	0.4	12
	1832	1.1	34
24 F	0048	0.2	6
	0710	1.2	36
	1310	0.3	9
	1916	1.2	37
25 Sa	0130	0.2	5
	0744	1.2	38
	1349	0.2	6
	1959	1.3	40
26 Su	0211	0.1	4
	0820	1.3	40
	1429	0.1	3
	2042	1.4	42
27 M	0252	0.1	4
	0856	1.3	41
	1511	0.0	1
	2126	1.4	43
28 Tu ●	0335	0.2	5
	0935	1.4	42
	1554	0.0	0
	2213	1.4	43
29 W	0419	0.2	7
	1016	1.3	41
	1641	0.0	0
	2303	1.3	41
30 Th	0507	0.3	9
	1101	1.3	40
	1732	0.0	1
	2359	1.3	39
31 F	0600	0.4	11
	1153	1.2	38
	1830	0.1	3

Time meridian 75° E. 0000 is midnight. 1200 is noon. Times are not adjusted for Daylight Saving Time.
Heights are referred to the chart datum of soundings.

Bahia de Cienfuegos, Cuba 2017

Times and Heights of High and Low Waters

April

Day	Time	Height (ft)	Height (cm)	Day	Time	Height (ft)	Height (cm)
1 Sa	0105	1.2	36	16 Su	0059	0.9	28
	0702	0.4	13		0641	0.6	19
	1257	1.1	35		1144	0.9	28
	1936	0.1	4		1903	0.4	11
2 Su	0221	1.1	35	17 M	0210	0.9	28
	0814	0.5	14		0750	0.7	20
	1416	1.1	33		1257	0.9	26
	2049	0.2	5		2010	0.4	12
3 M	0339	1.1	34	18 Tu	0324	0.9	28
	0933	0.4	13		0908	0.6	19
	1540	1.1	33		1454	0.9	26
	2205	0.2	5		2124	0.4	12
4 Tu	0449	1.1	35	19 W	0424	1.0	30
	1048	0.4	11		1017	0.5	16
	1655	1.1	34		1619	0.9	28
	2314	0.1	4		2230	0.3	10
5 W	0547	1.2	36	20 Th	0512	1.0	32
	1151	0.3	8		1112	0.4	13
	1758	1.1	35		1721	1.0	31
					2328	0.3	9
6 Th	0013	0.1	3	21 F	0554	1.1	34
	0636	1.2	37		1159	0.3	9
	1244	0.2	6		1813	1.1	35
	1852	1.2	37				
7 F	0104	0.1	3	22 Sa	0018	0.2	7
	0719	1.2	38		0633	1.2	37
	1329	0.1	4		1243	0.2	5
	1939	1.2	38		1900	1.2	38
8 Sa	0149	0.1	4	23 Su	0104	0.2	6
	0757	1.2	38		0711	1.3	39
	1410	0.1	2		1325	0.1	2
	2022	1.2	38		1945	1.3	41
9 Su	0229	0.2	5	24 M	0148	0.2	5
	0832	1.2	37		0750	1.3	41
	1447	0.1	2		1408	0.0	-1
	2102	1.2	37		2030	1.4	42
10 M	0305	0.2	7	25 Tu	0232	0.2	6
	0904	1.2	36		0829	1.4	42
	1522	0.1	3		1451	-0.1	-3
	2140	1.2	36		2115	1.4	43
11 Tu	0339	0.3	9	26 W	0317	0.2	7
	0934	1.1	35		0910	1.4	42
	1555	0.1	4		1536	-0.1	-3
	2215	1.1	35		2202	1.4	43
12 W	0412	0.4	12	27 Th	0403	0.3	8
	1000	1.1	34		0953	1.3	41
	1626	0.2	6		1624	-0.1	-2
	2250	1.1	33		2253	1.3	41
13 Th	0443	0.5	14	28 F	0452	0.3	10
	1022	1.0	32		1040	1.3	39
	1658	0.2	7		1715	0.0	-1
	2326	1.0	31		2348	1.3	39
14 F	0515	0.5	16	29 Sa	0547	0.4	11
	1043	1.0	30		1135	1.2	37
	1731	0.3	9		1812	0.1	2
15 Sa	0007	1.0	30	30 Su	0051	1.2	37
	0552	0.6	18		0650	0.4	13
	1107	1.0	29		1240	1.1	34
	1811	0.3	10		1915	0.1	4

May

Day	Time	Height (ft)	Height (cm)	Day	Time	Height (ft)	Height (cm)
1 M	0202	1.1	35	16 Tu	0118	1.0	30
	0801	0.4	13		0718	0.6	17
	1400	1.0	32		1237	0.9	27
	2026	0.2	6		1928	0.3	10
2 Tu	0314	1.1	34	17 W	0224	1.0	30
	0918	0.4	12		0829	0.5	16
	1525	1.0	31		1417	0.9	27
	2139	0.2	6		2039	0.4	11
3 W	0421	1.1	34	18 Th	0327	1.0	31
	1030	0.3	10		0936	0.4	13
	1642	1.0	32		1546	1.0	29
	2249	0.2	7		2148	0.3	10
4 Th	0518	1.1	35	19 F	0422	1.1	33
	1132	0.2	7		1036	0.3	9
	1745	1.1	33		1655	1.0	31
	2349	0.2	6		2251	0.3	9
5 F	0606	1.1	35	20 Sa	0512	1.1	35
	1223	0.1	4		1129	0.2	6
	1839	1.1	34		1752	1.1	34
					2347	0.3	8
6 Sa	0040	0.2	7	21 Su	0557	1.2	37
	0648	1.2	36		1217	0.1	2
	1307	0.1	2		1843	1.2	37
	1926	1.1	35				
7 Su	0125	0.2	7	22 M	0039	0.3	8
	0725	1.1	35		0641	1.3	39
	1346	0.0	1		1304	-0.1	-2
	2007	1.1	35		1931	1.3	40
8 M	0204	0.3	8	23 Tu	0127	0.2	7
	0759	1.1	35		0724	1.3	40
	1421	0.0	1		1350	-0.1	-4
	2045	1.1	35		2018	1.3	41
9 Tu	0239	0.3	10	24 W	0214	0.2	7
	0829	1.1	34		0807	1.3	41
	1453	0.1	2		1435	-0.2	-5
	2121	1.1	35		2105	1.4	42
10 W	0312	0.4	12	25 Th	0301	0.3	8
	0856	1.1	33		0851	1.3	41
	1524	0.1	3		1522	-0.2	-5
	2154	1.1	34		2153	1.4	42
11 Th	0343	0.4	13	26 F	0350	0.3	8
	0920	1.0	32		0937	1.3	40
	1553	0.1	4		1610	-0.1	-4
	2226	1.1	33		2243	1.3	41
12 F	0414	0.5	15	27 Sa	0440	0.3	10
	0949	1.0	31		1027	1.2	38
	1623	0.2	5		1701	-0.1	-2
	2259	1.0	32		2336	1.3	39
13 Sa	0447	0.5	16	28 Su	0535	0.4	11
	1007	1.0	31		1122	1.2	36
	1656	0.2	6		1755	0.0	1
	2336	1.0	31				
14 Su	0526	0.6	17	29 M	0034	1.2	37
	1039	1.0	30		0636	0.4	11
	1736	0.3	8		1227	1.1	33
					1854	0.1	4
15 M	0021	1.0	30	30 Tu	0137	1.1	35
	0615	0.6	18		0743	0.4	11
	1125	0.9	28		1343	1.0	31
	1826	0.3	9		1959	0.2	6
				31 W	0242	1.1	34
					0854	0.3	10
					1505	1.0	30
					2107	0.3	8

June

Day	Time	Height (ft)	Height (cm)	Day	Time	Height (ft)	Height (cm)
1 Th	0346	1.1	33	16 F	0235	1.1	33
	1003	0.3	8		0857	0.4	11
	1622	1.0	30		1513	1.0	30
	2215	0.3	9		2109	0.4	11
2 F	0442	1.1	33	17 Sa	0336	1.1	34
	1105	0.2	6		1000	0.2	7
	1726	1.0	30		1627	1.0	32
	2318	0.3	10		2216	0.4	11
3 Sa	0532	1.1	33	18 Su	0432	1.2	36
	1158	0.1	4		1059	0.1	4
	1823	1.0	31		1731	1.1	35
					2319	0.4	11
4 Su	0012	0.3	10	19 M	0525	1.2	37
	0615	1.1	33		1154	0.0	1
	1242	0.1	3		1827	1.2	37
	1910	1.0	32				
5 M	0058	0.4	11	20 Tu	0016	0.3	10
	0653	1.1	33		0615	1.3	39
	1321	0.1	2		1245	-0.1	-2
	1952	1.1	33		1919	1.3	40
6 Tu	0138	0.4	12	21 W	0109	0.3	9
	0726	1.1	33		0704	1.3	40
	1355	0.0	1		1335	-0.1	-4
	2028	1.1	33		2008	1.3	41
7 W	0213	0.4	13	22 Th	0200	0.3	9
	0756	1.0	32		0751	1.3	41
	1426	0.1	2		1423	-0.2	-5
	2101	1.1	33		2055	1.4	42
8 Th	0246	0.5	14	23 F	0249	0.3	9
	0823	1.0	32		0839	1.3	41
	1456	0.1	2		1511	-0.2	-5
	2132	1.1	33		2143	1.4	42
9 F	0317	0.5	15	24 Sa	0338	0.3	9
	0849	1.0	32		0927	1.3	41
	1526	0.1	3		1559	-0.1	-3
	2203	1.1	33		2230	1.3	41
10 Sa	0349	0.5	15	25 Su	0429	0.3	9
	0916	1.0	32		1017	1.3	39
	1557	0.1	4		1647	0.0	-1
	2235	1.1	33		2319	1.3	40
11 Su	0423	0.5	16	26 M	0521	0.3	10
	0948	1.0	32		1111	1.2	37
	1632	0.2	5		1738	0.1	2
	2310	1.1	33				
12 M	0504	0.5	16	27 Tu	0011	1.2	38
	1028	1.0	31		0617	0.4	11
	1712	0.2	6		1211	1.1	34
	2350	1.1	33		1831	0.2	6
13 Tu	0552	0.5	15	28 W	0105	1.2	36
	1118	1.0	31		0717	0.4	11
	1800	0.3	8		1320	1.0	32
					1928	0.3	9
14 W	0038	1.1	33	29 Th	0203	1.1	35
	0648	0.5	15		0821	0.4	11
	1225	1.0	30		1437	1.0	30
	1857	0.3	9		2029	0.4	12
15 Th	0134	1.1	33	30 F	0303	1.1	34
	0751	0.4	13		0927	0.3	10
	1348	1.0	29		1555	1.0	29
	2001	0.3	10		2135	0.5	14

Time meridian 75° E. 0000 is midnight. 1200 is noon. Times are not adjusted for Daylight Saving Time.
Heights are referred to the chart datum of soundings.

Bahia de Cienfuegos, Cuba 2017

Times and Heights of High and Low Waters

July

Day	Time	ft	cm	Day	Time	ft	cm
1 Sa ◐	0401	1.1	33	16 Su	0254	1.2	38
	1032	0.3	9		0927	0.3	9
	1706	1.0	30		1602	1.2	36
	2241	0.5	15		2146	0.5	15
2 Su	0454	1.0	32	17 M ☽	0358	1.3	39
	1128	0.2	7		1032	0.2	6
	1806	1.0	31		1712	1.2	38
	2341	0.5	16		2254	0.5	15
3 M	0540	1.0	32	18 Tu	0500	1.3	40
	1215	0.2	6		1133	0.1	3
	1854	1.0	32		1812	1.3	40
					2358	0.5	15
4 Tu	0031	0.5	16	19 W	0557	1.4	42
	0620	1.0	32		1230	0.0	1
	1255	0.2	5		1907	1.4	42
	1934	1.1	33				
5 W	0113	0.5	16	20 Th	0055	0.4	13
	0655	1.1	33		0650	1.4	43
	1329	0.2	5		1323	0.0	0
	2009	1.1	34		1956	1.4	44
6 Th	0149	0.6	17	21 F	0148	0.4	12
	0727	1.1	33		0741	1.4	44
	1400	0.2	5		1412	0.0	-1
	2039	1.1	35		2043	1.5	45
7 F	0221	0.6	17	22 Sa	0238	0.4	11
	0757	1.1	34		0831	1.5	45
	1431	0.2	5		1500	0.0	0
	2108	1.2	36		2128	1.5	45
8 Sa	0252	0.6	17	23 Su ●	0326	0.4	11
	0828	1.1	35		0920	1.4	44
	1502	0.2	5		1546	0.0	1
	2137	1.2	37		2212	1.5	45
9 Su ○	0325	0.5	16	24 M	0413	0.4	11
	0901	1.2	36		1008	1.4	43
	1536	0.2	5		1631	0.1	4
	2208	1.2	37		2256	1.4	44
10 M	0401	0.5	16	25 Tu	0501	0.4	12
	0938	1.2	36		1059	1.3	41
	1612	0.2	6		1717	0.2	7
	2242	1.2	38		2341	1.4	42
11 Tu	0441	0.5	15	26 W	0551	0.4	12
	1021	1.2	37		1152	1.2	38
	1653	0.2	7		1804	0.4	11
	2319	1.2	38				
12 W	0526	0.5	14	27 Th	0027	1.3	40
	1111	1.2	36		0643	0.4	13
	1739	0.3	9		1252	1.2	36
					1853	0.5	15
13 Th	0002	1.2	38	28 F	0117	1.2	38
	0618	0.5	14		0740	0.5	14
	1211	1.1	35		1401	1.1	33
	1831	0.4	11		1948	0.6	18
14 F	0052	1.2	38	29 Sa	0212	1.2	36
	0716	0.4	12		0842	0.5	15
	1323	1.1	35		1520	1.0	32
	1930	0.4	13		2049	0.7	21
15 Sa	0150	1.2	38	30 Su ◐	0311	1.1	35
	0820	0.4	11		0947	0.5	15
	1443	1.1	35		1639	1.0	32
	2036	0.5	15		2159	0.7	22
				31 M	0410	1.1	34
					1050	0.5	14
					1745	1.1	33
					2308	0.8	23

August

Day	Time	ft	cm	Day	Time	ft	cm
1 Tu	0504	1.1	34	16 W	0441	1.5	45
	1142	0.4	13		1116	0.3	10
	1835	1.1	34		1757	1.5	45
					2345	0.7	20
2 W	0005	0.8	23	17 Th	0545	1.5	46
	0549	1.1	35		1217	0.3	8
	1225	0.4	12		1852	1.5	47
	1913	1.2	36				
3 Th	0048	0.8	23	18 F	0044	0.6	18
	0628	1.2	36		0642	1.6	48
	1301	0.4	11		1311	0.2	7
	1943	1.2	38		1941	1.6	49
4 F	0123	0.7	22	19 Sa	0136	0.6	17
	0704	1.2	37		0735	1.6	49
	1334	0.4	11		1400	0.2	6
	2011	1.3	39		2026	1.6	50
5 Sa	0155	0.7	21	20 Su	0224	0.5	15
	0738	1.3	39		0824	1.6	50
	1407	0.3	10		1447	0.2	7
	2039	1.3	41		2108	1.6	50
6 Su	0227	0.7	20	21 M ●	0310	0.5	14
	0812	1.3	41		0911	1.6	50
	1440	0.3	10		1530	0.3	9
	2108	1.4	43		2148	1.6	50
7 M ○	0301	0.6	19	22 Tu	0354	0.5	14
	0849	1.4	43		0957	1.6	49
	1515	0.3	10		1612	0.4	12
	2138	1.4	44		2227	1.6	49
8 Tu	0337	0.6	17	23 W	0437	0.5	15
	0929	1.4	44		1043	1.5	47
	1553	0.4	11		1654	0.5	15
	2211	1.5	45		2306	1.5	47
9 W	0416	0.5	16	24 Th	0520	0.5	16
	1012	1.5	45		1130	1.5	45
	1633	0.4	12		1735	0.6	19
	2248	1.5	46		2345	1.5	45
10 Th	0500	0.5	15	25 F	0606	0.6	18
	1101	1.5	45		1221	1.4	42
	1718	0.5	14		1818	0.8	23
	2329	1.5	46				
11 F	0549	0.5	15	26 Sa	0025	1.4	43
	1156	1.4	44		0654	0.7	20
	1807	0.6	17		1321	1.3	39
					1905	0.9	26
12 Sa	0016	1.5	45	27 Su	0110	1.3	40
	0645	0.5	14		0748	0.7	22
	1301	1.4	42		1436	1.2	38
	1904	0.6	19		2001	1.0	29
13 Su	0112	1.4	44	28 M	0206	1.3	39
	0748	0.5	14		0850	0.8	23
	1418	1.3	41		1601	1.2	37
	2010	0.7	21		2112	1.0	31
14 M	0218	1.4	44	29 Tu ◐	0315	1.2	38
	0857	0.4	13		0957	0.8	23
	1539	1.4	42		1715	1.2	38
	2123	0.7	22		2231	1.0	31
15 Tu ○	0331	1.4	44	30 W	0423	1.2	38
	1008	0.4	12		1058	0.7	22
	1654	1.4	43		1805	1.3	40
	2237	0.7	22		2335	1.0	30
				31 Th	0518	1.3	39
					1148	0.7	21
					1839	1.3	41

September

Day	Time	ft	cm	Day	Time	ft	cm
1 F	0019	1.0	29	16 Sa	0032	0.7	22
	0603	1.3	41		0636	1.7	53
	1228	0.6	19		1257	0.5	15
	1908	1.4	43		1920	1.7	53
2 Sa	0054	0.9	27	17 Su	0122	0.7	20
	0643	1.4	43		0727	1.8	54
	1305	0.6	18		1345	0.5	15
	1936	1.5	46		2002	1.8	54
3 Su	0127	0.8	25	18 M	0208	0.6	18
	0720	1.5	46		0815	1.8	55
	1341	0.6	17		1429	0.5	15
	2005	1.6	48		2042	1.8	55
4 M	0200	0.8	23	19 Tu	0250	0.6	17
	0758	1.6	49		0900	1.8	55
	1417	0.6	17		1511	0.6	17
	2034	1.6	50		2119	1.8	54
5 Tu	0235	0.7	21	20 W ●	0330	0.6	17
	0837	1.7	51		0942	1.8	54
	1454	0.6	17		1550	0.7	20
	2106	1.7	52		2154	1.7	53
6 W ○	0312	0.6	19	21 Th	0410	0.6	18
	0918	1.7	53		1024	1.7	52
	1532	0.6	17		1628	0.8	23
	2140	1.7	53		2228	1.7	51
7 Th	0352	0.6	18	22 F	0448	0.7	20
	1001	1.7	53		1106	1.6	50
	1613	0.6	19		1705	0.9	26
	2217	1.7	53		2300	1.6	49
8 F	0436	0.6	17	23 Sa	0527	0.7	22
	1048	1.7	53		1150	1.5	47
	1657	0.7	21		1743	1.0	30
	2258	1.7	53		2331	1.5	46
9 Sa	0524	0.6	17	24 Su	0607	0.8	24
	1142	1.7	52		1240	1.5	45
	1747	0.8	23		1824	1.1	33
	2344	1.7	52				
10 Su	0618	0.6	17	25 M	0001	1.4	44
	1244	1.6	50		0652	0.9	26
	1843	0.9	26		1344	1.4	43
					1915	1.1	35
11 M	0041	1.6	50	26 Tu	0038	1.4	42
	0721	0.6	18		0746	0.9	28
	1358	1.6	48		1506	1.4	42
	1950	0.9	28		2024	1.2	36
12 Tu	0151	1.6	49	27 W	0150	1.3	41
	0832	0.6	19		0852	1.0	29
	1519	1.6	48		1622	1.4	43
	2107	0.9	28		2146	1.2	36
13 W ☽	0312	1.6	48	28 Th ☽	0331	1.3	41
	0947	0.6	18		1001	0.9	28
	1635	1.6	49		1715	1.4	44
	2224	0.9	27		2255	1.1	34
14 Th	0429	1.6	49	29 F	0443	1.4	42
	1058	0.6	17		1100	0.9	27
	1739	1.6	50		1752	1.5	46
	2333	0.8	25		2342	1.0	32
15 F	0537	1.7	51	30 Sa	0536	1.5	45
	1202	0.5	16		1149	0.8	25
	1833	1.7	52		1824	1.6	48

Time meridian 75° E. 0000 is midnight. 1200 is noon. Times are not adjusted for Daylight Saving Time.
Heights are referred to the chart datum of soundings.

Bahia de Cienfuegos, Cuba 2017
Times and Heights of High and Low Waters

October

Day	Time	Height (ft)	Height (cm)		Day	Time	Height (ft)	Height (cm)
1 Su	0020	1.0	29		16 M	0104	0.7	20
	0621	1.6	48			0717	1.8	55
	1232	0.8	24			1326	0.7	20
	1858	1.6	50			1934	1.8	55
2 M	0056	0.9	26		17 Tu	0148	0.6	18
	0702	1.7	51			0803	1.8	55
	1312	0.8	23			1409	0.7	21
	1927	1.7	53			2012	1.8	55
3 Tu	0132	0.8	23		18 W	0228	0.6	17
	0742	1.8	54			0846	1.8	55
	1352	0.7	22			1449	0.8	23
	2000	1.8	55			2047	1.8	54
4 W	0210	0.7	20		19 Th	0306	0.6	17
	0823	1.9	57			0927	1.8	54
	1431	0.7	22			1526	0.8	25
	2034	1.8	56			2120	1.7	53
5 Th ○	0249	0.6	18		20 F ●	0342	0.6	19
	0905	1.9	58			1006	1.7	53
	1512	0.7	22			1602	0.9	27
	2110	1.9	57			2150	1.7	51
6 F	0330	0.6	17		21 Sa	0416	0.7	20
	0950	1.9	59			1044	1.7	51
	1554	0.8	24			1636	1.0	30
	2149	1.9	57			2217	1.6	49
7 Sa	0414	0.5	16		22 Su	0450	0.7	22
	1037	1.9	58			1122	1.6	49
	1640	0.8	25			1711	1.1	33
	2231	1.9	57			2241	1.5	47
8 Su	0503	0.6	17		23 M	0524	0.8	24
	1130	1.8	56			1204	1.5	47
	1730	0.9	28			1759	1.1	35
	2320	1.8	55			2303	1.5	45
9 M	0557	0.6	18		24 Tu	0602	0.9	26
	1231	1.8	54			1255	1.5	45
	1829	1.0	29			1837	1.2	36
						2332	1.4	43
10 Tu	0018	1.7	53		25 W	0649	0.9	28
	0659	0.7	20			1359	1.4	44
	1342	1.7	52			1940	1.2	37
	1937	1.0	31					
11 W	0132	1.7	51		26 Th	0028	1.4	42
	0810	0.7	21			0749	1.0	29
	1500	1.7	51			1510	1.4	44
	2054	1.0	30			2056	1.2	36
12 Th ◐	0258	1.6	50		27 F	0229	1.3	41
	0925	0.7	22			0900	1.0	29
	1613	1.7	52			1609	1.5	45
	2211	1.0	29			2204	1.1	33
13 F	0419	1.6	50		28 Sa ◑	0401	0.6	17
	1038	0.7	21			1008	0.9	28
	1715	1.7	53			1656	1.5	47
	2319	0.9	26			2258	1.0	30
14 Sa	0528	1.7	52		29 Su	0505	1.5	45
	1143	0.7	21			1106	0.9	27
	1808	1.8	54			1736	1.6	49
						2343	0.9	27
15 Su	0016	0.7	22		30 M	0556	1.6	48
	0626	1.7	53			1156	0.8	25
	1238	0.7	20			1813	1.7	51
	1853	1.8	55					
					31 Tu	0024	0.8	23
						0642	1.7	52
						1242	0.8	24
						1850	1.7	53

November

Day	Time	Height (ft)	Height (cm)		Day	Time	Height (ft)	Height (cm)
1 W	0105	0.6	19		16 Th	0205	0.5	14
	0726	1.8	54			0832	1.6	50
	1326	0.8	23			1426	0.8	24
	1927	1.8	55			2015	1.6	49
2 Th	0146	0.5	16		17 F	0242	0.5	14
	0809	1.9	57			0910	1.6	50
	1409	0.8	23			1502	0.8	25
	2005	1.8	56			2046	1.6	48
3 F	0228	0.5	14		18 Sa ●	0315	0.5	15
	0853	1.9	58			0947	1.6	49
	1452	0.8	23			1537	0.9	27
	2045	1.9	57			2114	1.5	47
4 Sa ○	0312	0.4	13		19 Su	0347	0.6	17
	0939	1.9	58			1022	1.5	47
	1537	0.8	24			1610	1.0	29
	2126	1.9	57			2140	1.5	45
5 Su	0358	0.4	13		20 M	0418	0.6	18
	1027	1.9	57			1057	1.5	46
	1625	0.8	25			1644	1.0	30
	2212	1.8	55			2204	1.4	44
6 M	0447	0.5	14		21 Tu	0450	0.7	20
	1120	1.8	56			1133	1.5	45
	1718	0.9	27			1721	1.0	31
	2303	1.7	53			2230	1.4	42
7 Tu	0541	0.5	16		22 W	0525	0.7	21
	1218	1.7	53			1213	1.4	44
	1817	0.9	28			1806	1.0	32
						2307	1.3	41
8 W	0004	1.7	51		23 Th	0609	0.8	23
	0641	0.6	18			1303	1.4	43
	1324	1.7	51			1902	1.0	31
	1925	0.9	28					
9 Th	0119	1.6	48		24 F	0006	1.3	40
	0749	0.7	20			0703	0.8	24
	1436	1.6	50			1401	1.4	43
	2039	0.9	27			2007	1.0	30
10 F	0244	1.5	47		25 Sa	0141	1.3	39
	0901	0.7	21			0808	0.8	24
	1544	1.6	50			1502	1.4	43
	2153	0.8	25			2113	0.9	27
11 Sa ◑	0405	1.5	47		26 Su ◐	0316	1.3	40
	1012	0.7	22			0917	0.8	24
	1645	1.6	50			1557	1.4	44
	2259	0.7	22			2212	0.8	24
12 Su	0514	1.6	48		27 M	0430	1.4	42
	1117	0.7	21			1022	0.8	24
	1737	1.7	51			1646	1.5	46
	2355	0.6	19			2305	0.7	20
13 M	0613	1.6	49		28 Tu	0529	1.5	45
	1214	0.7	21			1120	0.8	23
	1823	1.7	51			1732	1.5	47
						2354	0.5	16
14 Tu	0044	0.5	16		29 W	0621	1.5	47
	0704	1.6	50			1213	0.7	22
	1303	0.7	22			1816	1.6	49
	1904	1.7	51					
15 W	0126	0.5	15		30 Th	0040	0.4	12
	0750	1.7	51			0709	1.6	50
	1346	0.7	22			1302	0.7	21
	1941	1.6	50			1858	1.7	51

December

Day	Time	Height (ft)	Height (cm)		Day	Time	Height (ft)	Height (cm)
1 F	0126	0.3	9		16 Sa	0218	0.3	10
	0756	1.7	52			0854	1.4	43
	1349	0.7	20			1440	0.7	22
	1942	1.7	52			2017	1.3	41
2 Sa	0211	0.2	7		17 Su	0250	0.3	10
	0842	1.7	53			0928	1.4	42
	1436	0.7	20			1513	0.8	23
	2025	1.7	52			2046	1.3	40
3 Su ○	0257	0.2	6		18 M ●	0321	0.4	11
	0929	1.7	53			0959	1.4	42
	1524	0.7	20			1545	0.8	24
	2111	1.7	52			2113	1.3	40
4 M	0345	0.2	7		19 Tu	0351	0.4	12
	1018	1.7	52			1030	1.3	41
	1614	0.7	21			1618	0.8	24
	2200	1.7	51			2142	1.3	39
5 Tu	0435	0.3	8		20 W	0423	0.4	13
	1108	1.7	51			1102	1.3	41
	1707	0.7	21			1654	0.8	24
	2253	1.6	48			2215	1.3	39
6 W	0527	0.3	10		21 Th	0459	0.5	14
	1203	1.6	49			1137	1.3	40
	1805	0.7	22			1736	0.8	24
	2354	1.6	48			2258	1.2	38
7 Th	0624	0.4	13		22 F	0540	0.5	15
	1302	1.5	47			1217	1.3	40
	1908	0.7	21			1826	0.8	23
						2355	1.2	37
8 F	0105	1.4	43		23 Sa	0630	0.6	17
	0725	0.5	15			1306	1.3	40
	1406	1.5	46			1924	0.7	21
	2016	0.7	20					
9 Sa	0225	1.3	41		24 Su	0110	1.2	36
	0832	0.6	18			0729	0.6	18
	1509	1.5	45			1402	1.3	39
	2126	0.6	18			2026	0.6	19
10 Su ◑	0345	1.3	41		25 M	0236	1.2	36
	0941	0.6	19			0834	0.6	19
	1609	1.4	44			1502	1.3	40
	2232	0.5	16			2129	0.5	16
11 M	0456	1.3	41		26 Tu ◐	0355	1.2	37
	1047	0.7	20			0942	0.6	19
	1703	1.4	44			1600	1.3	41
	2330	0.5	14			2230	0.4	12
12 Tu	0558	1.4	42		27 W	0503	1.3	39
	1146	0.7	20			1047	0.6	19
	1751	1.4	43			1655	1.4	42
						2326	0.3	9
13 W	0021	0.4	12		28 Th	0602	1.4	42
	0650	1.4	42			1147	0.6	18
	1238	0.7	20			1747	1.4	44
	1834	1.4	43					
14 Th	0104	0.3	10		29 F	0019	0.2	5
	0736	1.4	43			0655	1.4	44
	1324	0.7	21			1242	0.6	17
	1912	1.4	43			1837	1.5	45
15 F	0143	0.3	10		30 Sa	0110	0.1	3
	0817	1.4	43			0744	1.5	46
	1404	0.7	21			1334	0.5	16
	1946	1.4	42			1925	1.5	46
					31 Su	0158	0.0	1
						0832	1.5	47
						1423	0.5	15
						2013	1.5	47

Time meridian 75° E. 0000 is midnight. 1200 is noon. Times are not adjusted for Daylight Saving Time.
Heights are referred to the chart datum of soundings.

Havana, Cuba 2017

Times and Heights of High and Low Waters

January

Day	Time	ft	cm	Day	Time	ft	cm
1 Su	0537	0.2	5	16 M	0559	0.2	5
	1139	0.9	26		1203	1.0	30
	1604	0.5	15		1724	0.3	9
	2303	1.8	55				
2 M	0614	0.2	5	17 Tu	0008	1.4	43
	1223	0.9	28		0633	0.3	8
	1656	0.6	17		1252	1.1	33
	2344	1.7	51		1826	0.4	13
3 Tu	0652	0.2	7	18 W	0050	1.2	37
	1311	1.0	31		0707	0.3	9
	1801	0.6	19		1344	1.1	35
					1937	0.5	16
4 W	0030	1.5	46	19 Th	0135	1.0	31
	0732	0.3	8		0744	0.4	11
	1402	1.1	34		1442	1.2	37
	1922	0.7	20		2100	0.6	17
5 Th	0126	1.3	41	20 F	0229	0.9	26
	0814	0.3	10		0824	0.4	12
	1457	1.3	39		1541	1.3	39
	2055	0.6	19		2234	0.6	17
6 F	0234	1.1	34	21 Sa	0340	0.7	22
	0858	0.4	11		0909	0.4	13
	1553	1.4	44		1640	1.3	41
	2228	0.5	15				
7 Sa	0357	0.9	28	22 Su	0002	0.5	14
	0944	0.4	11		0510	0.7	20
	1649	1.6	49		0959	0.4	13
	2350	0.3	10		1733	1.4	43
8 Su	0524	0.8	24	23 M	0102	0.4	12
	1032	0.4	11		0631	0.7	20
	1744	1.8	54		1051	0.4	13
					1820	1.5	46
9 M	0059	0.2	5	24 Tu	0142	0.3	9
	0640	0.7	21		0727	0.7	20
	1121	0.3	9		1140	0.4	13
	1838	1.9	58		1903	1.6	49
10 Tu	0157	0.0	0	25 W	0215	0.2	7
	0741	0.6	19		0808	0.7	21
	1212	0.2	6		1227	0.4	12
	1930	2.0	61		1942	1.7	51
11 W	0248	-0.1	-3	26 Th	0247	0.2	5
	0830	0.6	18		0842	0.7	22
	1302	0.1	4		1312	0.4	11
	2020	2.0	62		2020	1.7	53
12 Th	0333	-0.1	-3	27 F	0318	0.1	4
	0913	0.6	19		0914	0.8	24
	1352	0.1	2		1356	0.3	9
	2109	2.0	61		2058	1.8	54
13 F	0413	-0.1	-2	28 Sa	0351	0.1	3
	0954	0.7	20		0947	0.8	25
	1443	0.0	1		1440	0.3	8
	2156	1.9	59		2136	1.8	54
14 Sa	0450	0.0	0	29 Su	0423	0.1	3
	1035	0.8	23		1021	0.9	28
	1535	0.1	2		1526	0.3	8
	2241	1.8	55		2216	1.7	52
15 Su	0525	0.1	3	30 M	0457	0.1	4
	1117	0.9	26		1057	1.0	31
	1628	0.2	5		1615	0.3	8
	2325	1.6	49		2257	1.6	49
				31 Tu	0530	0.2	6
					1136	1.1	34
					1709	0.3	9
					2341	1.5	45

February

Day	Time	ft	cm	Day	Time	ft	cm
1 W	0605	0.3	8	16 Th	0025	1.0	30
	1219	1.2	37		0606	0.3	9
	1811	0.4	11		1247	1.2	38
					1913	0.3	10
2 Th	0029	1.3	40	17 F	0107	0.8	25
	0640	0.3	10		0637	0.4	11
	1307	1.3	41		1336	1.2	38
	1924	0.4	12		2023	0.4	12
3 F	0125	1.1	34	18 Sa	0159	0.7	22
	0719	0.4	12		0712	0.4	13
	1402	1.4	44		1432	1.3	39
	2047	0.4	12		2145	0.5	14
4 Sa	0233	0.9	28	19 Su	0314	0.7	20
	0803	0.4	13		0757	0.5	15
	1504	1.5	47		1534	1.3	39
	2216	0.3	10		2312	0.4	13
5 Su	0355	0.8	23	20 M	1639	1.3	41
	0856	0.4	13				
	1611	1.6	49				
	2340	0.2	7				
6 M	0524	0.7	20	21 Tu	0019	0.4	12
	0958	0.4	12		0633	0.7	20
	1719	1.7	51		1014	0.6	17
					1738	1.4	43
7 Tu	0049	0.1	3	22 W	0103	0.3	10
	0637	0.6	18		0718	0.7	22
	1102	0.3	9		1118	0.6	17
	1822	1.7	53		1830	1.5	46
8 W	0144	0.0	0	23 Th	0137	0.3	8
	0730	0.6	18		0748	0.8	24
	1203	0.2	6		1213	0.5	15
	1920	1.8	54		1915	1.6	49
9 Th	0227	0.0	-1	24 F	0209	0.2	7
	0812	0.7	20		0816	0.9	27
	1300	0.1	2		1303	0.4	12
	2012	1.7	53		1958	1.6	50
10 F	0304	0.0	-1	25 Sa	0240	0.2	6
	0850	0.7	22		0845	1.0	29
	1354	0.0	0		1351	0.3	10
	2100	1.7	52		2039	1.7	51
11 Sa	0337	0.0	0	26 Su	0311	0.2	5
	0927	0.8	25		0915	1.1	33
	1446	0.0	-1		1439	0.2	7
	2145	1.6	49		2121	1.7	51
12 Su	0408	0.1	2	27 M	0342	0.2	6
	1004	1.0	29		0947	1.2	37
	1537	0.0	-1		1527	0.2	6
	2226	1.5	45		2203	1.6	50
13 M	0437	0.1	4	28 Tu	0413	0.3	8
	1042	1.0	32		1022	1.4	42
	1627	0.0	1		1618	0.2	6
	2306	1.3	40		2247	1.5	47
14 Tu	0506	0.2	5				
	1122	1.1	35				
	1718	0.1	4				
	2345	1.1	35				
15 W	0536	0.2	7				
	1203	1.2	37				
	1813	0.2	7				

March

Day	Time	ft	cm	Day	Time	ft	cm
1 W	0445	0.3	10	16 Th	0444	0.3	9
	1100	1.5	47		1123	1.4	44
	1713	0.2	7		1755	0.2	7
	2333	1.4	42		2358	0.9	28
2 Th	0516	0.4	13	17 F	0511	0.4	11
	1142	1.6	50		1202	1.4	44
	1814	0.3	8		1848	0.3	10
3 F	0023	1.2	37	18 Sa	0039	0.8	25
	0550	0.5	15		0538	0.5	14
	1230	1.7	53		1244	1.4	44
	1922	0.3	10		1949	0.4	13
4 Sa	0119	1.0	31	19 Su	0130	0.8	23
	0626	0.5	16		0604	0.5	16
	1326	1.8	54		1333	1.4	43
	2041	0.4	11		2102	0.5	15
5 Su	0227	0.9	26	20 M	0245	0.7	22
	0711	0.6	17		0634	0.6	19
	1432	1.8	54		1433	1.4	43
	2208	0.4	11		2222	0.5	15
6 M	0352	0.8	23	21 Tu	1543	1.4	43
	0814	0.6	17		2331	0.5	15
	1546	1.7	53				
	2331	0.3	10				
7 Tu	0521	0.7	22	22 W	1652	1.5	45
	0935	0.5	16				
	1701	1.7	52				
8 W	0035	0.3	8	23 Th	0017	0.4	13
	0627	0.8	23		0652	0.9	27
	1054	0.4	13		1055	0.7	21
	1810	1.7	52		1753	1.5	47
9 Th	0121	0.2	7	24 F	0054	0.4	11
	0713	0.8	25		0716	1.0	30
	1202	0.3	10		1158	0.6	18
	1910	1.7	51		1845	1.6	48
10 F	0157	0.2	6	25 Sa	0127	0.3	10
	0751	0.9	28		0742	1.1	33
	1302	0.2	7		1253	0.5	15
	2001	1.6	49		1934	1.6	50
11 Sa	0227	0.2	6	26 Su	0158	0.3	10
	0826	1.0	32		0810	1.2	38
	1356	0.1	4		1344	0.4	11
	2046	1.5	47		2020	1.6	50
12 Su	0255	0.2	6	27 M	0229	0.3	10
	0901	1.1	35		0841	1.4	44
	1446	0.1	2		1434	0.3	8
	2127	1.4	44		2105	1.6	50
13 M	0322	0.2	7	28 Tu	0300	0.4	12
	0935	1.3	39		0914	1.6	50
	1533	0.1	2		1524	0.2	6
	2206	1.3	40		2150	1.6	48
14 Tu	0349	0.2	7	29 W	0331	0.4	13
	1010	1.3	41		0951	1.8	55
	1620	0.1	2		1617	0.2	6
	2243	1.1	35		2236	1.4	44
15 W	0417	0.3	8	30 Th	0402	0.5	15
	1046	1.4	43		1031	2.0	60
	1707	0.1	4		1712	0.2	7
	2320	1.0	31		2323	1.3	40
				31 F	0434	0.6	17
					1116	2.1	63
					1811	0.3	9

Time meridian 75° E. 0000 is midnight. 1200 is noon. Times are not adjusted for Daylight Saving Time.
Heights are referred to the chart datum of soundings.

Havana, Cuba 2017

Times and Heights of High and Low Waters

April

Day	Time	ft	cm	Day	Time	ft	cm
1 Sa	0013 0508 1207 1917	1.2 0.6 2.1 0.4	36 18 63 12	**16** Su	0016 0453 1203 1917	0.9 0.6 1.6 0.5	26 17 49 14
2 Su	0108 0547 1305 2032	1.0 0.7 2.0 0.5	31 20 62 14	**17** M	0106 0519 1247 2020	0.8 0.7 1.6 0.5	25 20 48 16
3 M ☽	0214 0638 1412 2154	0.9 0.7 1.9 0.5	28 21 59 16	**18** Tu	0217 0550 1342 2129	0.8 0.7 1.5 0.6	25 22 47 17
4 Tu	0336 0754 1528 2309	0.9 0.7 1.8 0.5	27 22 56 16	**19** W ○	1449 2233	1.5 0.6	46 17
5 W	0500 0927 1647	0.9 0.7 1.7	28 21 53	**20** Th	1603 2323	1.5 0.5	45 15
6 Th	0004 0602 1053 1757	0.5 1.0 0.6 1.7	15 31 19 51	**21** F	0559 1035 1713	1.0 0.8 1.5	31 24 46
7 F	0044 0647 1204 1856	0.5 1.1 0.5 1.6	15 35 16 49	**22** Sa	0003 0630 1144 1815	0.5 1.1 0.7 1.5	14 35 20 46
8 Sa	0115 0725 1304 1946	0.5 1.3 0.4 1.5	14 39 12 46	**23** Su	0039 0700 1242 1911	0.5 1.3 0.5 1.5	14 40 15 47
9 Su	0142 0759 1355 2029	0.4 1.4 0.3 1.4	13 42 9 43	**24** M	0112 0731 1336 2003	0.5 1.5 0.3 1.5	14 47 10 46
10 M	0210 0833 1442 2108	0.4 1.5 0.2 1.3	12 46 7 40	**25** Tu	0145 0806 1428 2052	0.5 1.8 0.2 1.5	15 54 7 45
11 Tu ○	0237 0906 1526 2145	0.4 1.6 0.2 1.2	12 48 5 36	**26** W ●	0217 0843 1520 2139	0.5 2.0 0.1 1.4	16 60 4 43
12 W	0304 0939 1609 2221	0.4 1.6 0.2 1.1	11 50 5 33	**27** Th	0249 0924 1613 2226	0.6 2.2 0.1 1.3	17 66 4 40
13 Th	0332 1013 1651 2258	0.4 1.7 0.2 1.0	12 51 6 30	**28** F	0323 1009 1708 2313	0.6 2.3 0.2 1.2	17 69 6 36
14 F	0359 1048 1735 2335	0.4 1.7 0.3 0.9	13 51 8 28	**29** Sa	0359 1057 1805	0.6 2.3 0.3	18 70 9
15 Sa	0426 1124 1823	0.5 1.6 0.4	15 50 11	**30** Su	0001 0439 1150 1906	1.1 0.6 2.2 0.4	33 19 68 12

May

Day	Time	ft	cm	Day	Time	ft	cm
1 M	0054 0527 1249 2012	1.0 0.7 2.1 0.5	31 20 64 16	**16** Tu	0051 0456 1211 1940	0.9 0.7 1.6 0.5	27 21 50 14
2 Tu	0156 0628 1355 2120	1.0 0.7 1.9 0.6	31 22 59 19	**17** W	0152 0541 1259 2036	0.9 0.8 1.6 0.5	27 23 48 15
3 W ☽	0309 0752 1508 2222	1.0 0.8 1.8 0.7	32 24 54 20	**18** Th	0304 0701 1359 2131	1.0 0.8 1.5 0.5	29 25 45 15
4 Th	0424 0928 1625 2310	1.1 0.8 1.6 0.7	35 24 50 21	**19** F ○	0409 0849 1514 2221	1.0 0.8 1.4 0.5	31 25 43 15
5 F	0526 1056 1737 2349	1.3 0.7 1.5 0.7	39 22 47 20	**20** Sa	0458 1020 1633 2305	1.1 0.8 1.3 0.5	35 23 41 15
6 Sa	0614 1208 1837	1.4 0.6 1.4	43 19 43	**21** Su	0538 1133 1746 2344	1.3 0.6 1.3 0.5	40 18 40 15
7 Su	0022 0654 1306 1928	0.6 1.5 0.5 1.3	19 47 15 40	**22** M	0616 1235 1851	1.5 0.4 1.3	46 12 39
8 M	0052 0730 1354 2011	0.6 1.6 0.4 1.2	18 50 11 37	**23** Tu	0022 0654 1332 1949	0.5 1.7 0.2 1.2	16 53 7 38
9 Tu	0122 0803 1437 2051	0.5 1.7 0.3 1.1	16 52 8 34	**24** W	0058 0735 1425 2041	0.5 2.0 0.1 1.2	16 60 3 36
10 W	0152 0837 1517 2128	0.5 1.8 0.2 1.0	15 54 6 32	**25** Th	0134 0818 1518 2129	0.5 2.2 0.0 1.1	16 66 1 34
11 Th ○	0222 0910 1557 2205	0.5 1.8 0.2 1.0	14 55 6 30	**26** F ●	0212 0904 1611 2215	0.5 2.3 0.0 1.0	15 70 1 32
12 F	0252 0944 1636 2241	0.5 1.8 0.2 0.9	14 55 7 28	**27** Sa	0251 0952 1702 2301	0.5 2.3 0.1 1.0	15 71 3 31
13 Sa	0321 1018 1717 2319	0.5 1.8 0.3 0.9	15 55 8 28	**28** Su	0334 1043 1754 2347	0.5 2.3 0.2 1.0	15 70 6 30
14 Su	0352 1053 1801	0.6 1.8 0.4	17 54 11	**29** M	0422 1136 1846	0.5 2.2 0.4	16 66 11
15 M	0001 0422 1130 1848	0.9 0.6 1.7 0.4	27 19 52 13	**30** Tu	0038 0518 1232 1939	1.0 0.6 2.0 0.5	31 18 61 15
				31 W	0135 0626 1331 2030	1.1 0.7 1.8 0.6	33 21 55 18

June

Day	Time	ft	cm	Day	Time	ft	cm
1 Th ☽	0239 0750 1437 2118	1.2 0.8 1.6 0.7	36 24 49 20	**16** F	0217 0701 1322 2032	1.0 0.8 1.4 0.4	31 23 43 13
2 F	0346 0925 1548 2203	1.3 0.8 1.4 0.7	40 24 43 21	**17** Sa ◑	0311 0836 1431 2119	1.1 0.8 1.3 0.5	35 22 39 14
3 Sa	0447 1056 1702 2244	1.4 0.8 1.2 0.7	44 23 38 20	**18** Su	0402 1006 1554 2204	1.3 0.7 1.1 0.5	39 20 35 15
4 Su	0538 1212 1810 2323	1.6 0.6 1.1 0.6	48 19 35 19	**19** M	0451 1124 1718 2248	1.5 0.5 1.0 0.5	45 15 32 16
5 M	0621 1309 1907 2359	1.7 0.5 1.0 0.6	51 15 32 18	**20** Tu	0538 1231 1834 2331	1.7 0.3 1.0 0.5	51 10 30 16
6 Tu	0700 1354 1955	1.7 0.4 1.0	53 11 30	**21** W	0625 1330 1937	1.9 0.1 1.0	58 4 29
7 W	0034 0735 1433 2037	0.6 1.8 0.3 0.9	17 54 8 28	**22** Th	0014 0713 1424 2030	0.5 2.1 0.0 0.9	15 63 0 27
8 Th	0109 0810 1510 2115	0.5 1.8 0.2 0.9	16 56 7 27	**23** F	0058 0802 1515 2117	0.4 2.2 0.0 0.9	13 67 -1 26
9 F ○	0143 0845 1546 2152	0.5 1.9 0.2 0.9	15 57 6 27	**24** Sa ●	0143 0851 1604 2200	0.4 2.3 0.0 0.9	11 69 -1 26
10 Sa	0217 0920 1623 2228	0.5 1.9 0.2 0.9	15 57 6 27	**25** Su	0231 0942 1650 2242	0.3 2.3 0.0 0.9	10 69 1 27
11 Su	0252 0954 1701 2306	0.5 1.9 0.2 0.9	16 57 7 27	**26** M	0321 1032 1734 2326	0.3 2.2 0.2 1.0	10 66 5 29
12 M	0327 1030 1739 2346	0.6 1.8 0.3 0.9	17 56 8 27	**27** Tu	0415 1122 1816	0.4 2.0 0.3	12 62 9
13 Tu	0405 1105 1820	0.6 1.8 0.3	18 54 9	**28** W	0013 0514 1212 1856	1.1 0.5 1.8 0.4	33 15 56 13
14 W	0031 0448 1144 1902	0.9 0.7 1.7 0.3	28 20 51 10	**29** Th	0105 0621 1303 1936	1.2 0.6 1.6 0.5	36 19 49 16
15 Th	0122 0543 1227 1947	1.0 0.7 1.5 0.4	29 22 47 12	**30** F	0202 0740 1358 2015	1.3 0.7 1.4 0.6	40 22 42 18

Time meridian 75° E. 0000 is midnight. 1200 is noon. Times are not adjusted for Daylight Saving Time.
Heights are referred to the chart datum of soundings.

Havana, Cuba 2017
Times and Heights of High and Low Waters

July

Day	Time	ft	cm		Day	Time	ft	cm
1 Sa ◐	0302	1.4	43		16 Su	0216	1.4	42
	0910	0.8	23			0821	0.7	21
	1459	1.2	36			1406	1.2	37
	2057	0.6	19			2021	0.5	16
2 Su	0403	1.5	46		17 M ◐	0311	1.5	46
	1046	0.7	22			0951	0.6	19
	1612	1.0	31			1526	1.0	32
	2140	0.6	19			2107	0.6	17
3 M	0459	1.6	49		18 Tu	0408	1.7	51
	1210	0.6	19			1114	0.5	15
	1732	0.9	28			1657	0.9	28
	2224	0.6	19			2157	0.6	18
4 Tu	0548	1.7	51		19 W	0506	1.8	56
	1310	0.5	16			1227	0.3	10
	1844	0.9	26			1819	0.9	26
	2309	0.6	18			2250	0.6	17
5 W	0632	1.7	53		20 Th	0604	2.0	61
	1352	0.4	13			1327	0.2	5
	1940	0.9	26			1924	0.8	25
	2352	0.6	18			2344	0.5	14
6 Th	0711	1.8	55		21 F	0659	2.1	64
	1427	0.3	10			1420	0.1	2
	2023	0.8	25			2013	0.8	24
7 F	0033	0.6	17		22 Sa	0038	0.4	11
	0749	1.9	57			0753	2.2	66
	1500	0.3	9			1507	0.1	2
	2100	0.9	26			2055	0.8	25
8 Sa	0114	0.5	16		23 Su ●	0132	0.3	9
	0826	1.9	58			0845	2.2	67
	1533	0.3	8			1548	0.1	3
	2134	0.9	27			2135	0.9	27
9 Su ○	0154	0.5	16		24 M	0225	0.2	7
	0902	1.9	59			0934	2.1	65
	1605	0.2	7			1627	0.2	5
	2207	0.9	28			2214	1.0	30
10 M	0234	0.5	16		25 Tu	0318	0.3	8
	0937	1.9	58			1022	2.0	62
	1639	0.3	8			1702	0.3	8
	2242	1.0	29			2255	1.1	35
11 Tu	0316	0.5	16		26 W	0413	0.3	10
	1013	1.9	57			1108	1.9	57
	1713	0.3	8			1736	0.4	11
	2318	1.0	30			2338	1.3	39
12 W	0359	0.6	17		27 Th	0510	0.4	13
	1049	1.8	55			1153	1.7	51
	1747	0.3	9			1808	0.5	14
	2357	1.0	32					
13 Th	0448	0.6	19		28 F	0025	1.4	42
	1128	1.7	51			0611	0.6	17
	1823	0.3	10			1237	1.5	45
						1841	0.6	17
14 F	0040	1.1	35		29 Sa	0115	1.5	45
	0546	0.7	20			0719	0.7	20
	1210	1.5	47			1323	1.3	39
	1900	0.4	12			1916	0.6	19
15 Sa	0126	1.2	38		30 Su ◐	0209	1.5	47
	0657	0.7	21			0838	0.8	23
	1301	1.4	43			1416	1.1	33
	1939	0.5	14			1954	0.7	20
					31 M	0308	1.6	48
						1009	0.8	23
						1526	1.0	29
						2039	0.7	21

August

Day	Time	ft	cm		Day	Time	ft	cm
1 Tu	0409	1.6	49		16 W	0328	1.9	58
	1142	0.7	21			1059	0.6	17
	1657	0.9	27			1652	1.0	31
	2132	0.7	22			2120	0.8	24
2 W	0508	1.7	51		17 Th	0439	2.0	60
	1250	0.6	19			1213	0.5	14
	1827	0.9	27			1812	1.0	30
	2229	0.8	23			2230	0.7	22
3 Th	0601	1.7	53		18 F	0547	2.0	62
	1332	0.6	17			1313	0.4	12
	1924	0.9	28			1908	1.0	30
	2324	0.7	22			2337	0.6	19
4 F	0648	1.8	55		19 Sa	0651	2.1	64
	1405	0.5	16			1400	0.3	10
	2003	1.0	30			1951	1.0	31
5 Sa	0015	0.7	21		20 Su	0038	0.5	15
	0730	1.9	57			0747	2.1	64
	1435	0.5	14			1440	0.4	11
	2034	1.0	31			2028	1.1	34
6 Su	0101	0.7	20		21 M ●	0135	0.4	12
	0809	1.9	59			0839	2.1	63
	1504	0.4	13			1514	0.4	12
	2104	1.1	33			2105	1.2	38
7 M ○	0146	0.6	19		22 Tu	0229	0.3	10
	0847	2.0	60			0927	2.0	61
	1534	0.4	13			1546	0.5	14
	2134	1.1	35			2141	1.4	42
8 Tu	0230	0.6	18		23 W	0322	0.3	9
	0924	2.0	60			1012	1.9	57
	1604	0.4	13			1616	0.5	16
	2205	1.2	37			2219	1.5	46
9 W	0315	0.6	17		24 Th	0414	0.3	10
	1001	1.9	59			1055	1.7	52
	1635	0.5	14			1645	0.6	18
	2238	1.3	40			2258	1.6	50
10 Th	0401	0.6	17		25 F	0506	0.4	13
	1040	1.8	56			1137	1.5	47
	1706	0.5	15			1714	0.7	20
	2313	1.4	44			2338	1.7	52
11 F	0452	0.6	18		26 Sa	0559	0.5	16
	1121	1.7	53			1219	1.4	42
	1738	0.6	17			1744	0.7	22
	2351	1.5	47					
12 Sa	0548	0.6	19		27 Su	0021	1.7	53
	1206	1.6	49			0657	0.6	19
	1811	0.7	20			1303	1.2	38
						1815	0.8	24
13 Su	0034	1.6	50		28 M	0107	1.7	53
	0653	0.7	20			0801	0.7	22
	1258	1.4	44			1357	1.1	35
	1846	0.7	22			1849	0.9	26
14 M	0124	1.8	54		29 Tu ◐	0159	1.7	52
	0809	0.7	21			0915	0.8	24
	1401	1.3	39			1510	1.1	33
	1926	0.8	24			1933	1.0	29
15 Tu ○	0222	1.8	56		30 W	0301	1.7	52
	0934	0.7	20			1037	0.8	25
	1521	1.1	34					
	2016	0.8	25					
					31 Th	0410	1.7	52
						1148	0.8	24
						1828	1.1	35
						2202	1.0	32

September

Day	Time	ft	cm		Day	Time	ft	cm
1 F	0518	1.7	53		16 Sa	0530	2.0	62
	1238	0.8	24			1238	0.7	20
	1909	1.2	37			1851	1.3	41
	2312	1.0	31			2346	0.9	26
2 Sa	0816	1.8	55		17 Su	0639	2.0	61
	1315	0.7	22			1319	0.7	20
	1937	1.3	39			1928	1.5	45
3 Su	0010	1.0	29		18 M	0050	0.7	21
	0705	1.9	57			0739	2.0	60
	1347	0.7	21			1353	0.7	20
	2003	1.4	42			2002	1.6	49
4 M	0100	0.9	26		19 Tu	0147	0.6	17
	0748	1.9	59			0830	1.9	58
	1417	0.7	21			1424	0.7	21
	2029	1.4	44			2036	1.7	53
5 Tu	0147	0.8	23		20 W ●	0239	0.5	14
	0829	2.0	60			0917	1.8	54
	1447	0.7	21			1453	0.7	22
	2056	1.6	48			2110	1.9	57
6 W	0232	0.7	20		21 Th	0328	0.4	12
	0910	2.0	60			1000	1.7	51
	1517	0.7	21			1521	0.8	23
	2125	1.7	52			2144	2.0	60
7 Th	0318	0.6	18		22 F	0415	0.4	12
	0951	1.9	58			1042	1.5	47
	1547	0.8	23			1548	0.8	24
	2156	1.8	56			2218	2.0	62
8 F	0405	0.6	17		23 Sa	0501	0.4	13
	1034	1.8	56			1124	1.4	43
	1617	0.8	25			1615	0.9	26
	2230	2.0	61			2253	2.0	62
9 Sa	0456	0.6	17		24 Su	0548	0.5	15
	1120	1.7	53			1207	1.3	40
	1647	0.9	28			1642	0.9	28
	2307	2.1	64			2329	2.0	62
10 Su	0550	0.6	18		25 M	0637	0.6	17
	1209	1.6	49			1256	1.2	37
	1718	1.0	30			1707	1.0	30
	2350	2.2	67					
11 M	0651	0.6	19		26 Tu	0006	2.0	60
	1305	1.5	45			0731	0.7	20
	1751	1.0	32			1358	1.2	36
						1729	1.1	33
12 Tu	0039	2.2	68		27 W	0048	1.9	58
	0801	0.7	21			0831	0.8	23
	1412	1.3	41					
	1832	1.1	33					
13 W ◐	0139	2.2	67		28 Th ◐	0138	1.8	56
	0918	0.7	21			0937	0.8	25
	1535	1.2	38					
	1932	1.1	34					
14 Th	0251	2.1	65		29 F	0246	1.8	54
	1036	0.7	21			1040	0.9	26
	1703	1.2	38					
	2101	1.1	33					
15 F	0411	2.1	63		30 Sa	0407	1.7	53
	1145	0.7	20			1132	0.9	26
	1808	1.3	39			1853	1.5	45
	2230	1.0	31			2305	1.3	39

Time meridian 75° E. 0000 is midnight. 1200 is noon. Times are not adjusted for Daylight Saving Time.
Heights are referred to the chart datum of soundings.

Havana, Cuba 2017

Times and Heights of High and Low Waters

October

Day	Time	ft	cm
1 Su	0522	1.8	54
	1214	0.8	25
	1910	1.6	48
2 M	0008	1.1	35
	0625	1.8	54
	1249	0.8	24
	1930	1.7	52
3 Tu	0100	1.0	30
	0718	1.8	55
	1322	0.8	24
	1954	1.8	56
4 W	0147	0.9	26
	0807	1.8	55
	1354	0.8	25
	2020	2.0	61
5 Th ○	0233	0.7	21
	0854	1.8	55
	1424	0.9	27
	2050	2.2	67
6 F	0320	0.6	17
	0941	1.8	54
	1454	1.0	29
	2122	2.4	72
7 Sa	0408	0.5	15
	1029	1.7	52
	1524	1.0	31
	2157	2.5	77
8 Su	0458	0.5	15
	1119	1.6	49
	1554	1.1	33
	2237	2.6	80
9 M	0552	0.5	15
	1213	1.5	46
	1625	1.1	35
	2321	2.6	80
10 Tu	0651	0.6	17
	1313	1.4	43
	1659	1.2	37
11 W	0011	2.6	78
	0754	0.6	19
	1425	1.4	42
	1744	1.2	38
12 Th ◗	0109	2.4	73
	0902	0.7	21
13 F	0220	2.2	68
	1008	0.8	23
	1705	1.4	44
	2056	1.3	40
14 Sa	0342	2.1	63
	1105	0.8	24
	1754	1.6	48
	2239	1.2	37
15 Su	0505	1.9	59
	1150	0.8	24
	1832	1.7	52
16 M	0001	1.0	31
	0619	1.8	55
	1227	0.8	25
	1906	1.9	57
17 Tu	0106	0.9	26
	0721	1.7	52
	1259	0.8	25
	1939	2.0	61
18 W	0200	0.7	20
	0814	1.6	48
	1329	0.8	25
	2011	2.1	65
19 Th	0248	0.5	16
	0901	1.5	45
	1357	0.8	24
	2043	2.2	68
20 F ●	0332	0.4	13
	0944	1.3	41
	1425	0.8	24
	2115	2.3	69
21 Sa	0414	0.4	11
	1027	1.2	38
	1452	0.8	25
	2147	2.3	69
22 Su	0456	0.4	11
	1110	1.2	36
	1518	0.9	26
	2219	2.3	69
23 M	0538	0.4	12
	1156	1.1	35
	1542	0.9	28
	2251	2.2	67
24 Tu	0622	0.5	14
	1250	1.1	34
	1602	1.0	31
	2324	2.1	65
25 W	0709	0.6	17
	2357	2.0	62
26 Th	0800	0.6	19
27 F	0034	1.9	59
	0854	0.7	21
28 Sa ◖	0123	1.8	55
	0948	0.7	22
29 Su	0238	1.7	52
	1036	0.7	22
	1823	1.6	48
	2247	1.3	40
30 M	0410	1.6	49
	1117	0.7	21
	1835	1.7	51
	2358	1.1	35
31 Tu	0531	1.6	48
	1155	0.7	22
	1855	1.8	56

November

Day	Time	ft	cm
1 W	0053	1.0	29
	0640	1.5	47
	1229	0.7	22
	1920	2.0	62
2 Th	0143	0.8	23
	0740	1.5	46
	1302	0.8	24
	1948	2.3	69
3 F	0230	0.6	17
	0835	1.5	45
	1334	0.8	25
	2021	2.5	75
4 Sa ○	0318	0.4	13
	0928	1.4	44
	1406	0.9	27
	2057	2.7	81
5 Su	0408	0.3	10
	1019	1.4	42
	1438	0.9	28
	2137	2.8	84
6 M	0458	0.3	9
	1111	1.3	40
	1511	1.0	29
	2220	2.8	85
7 Tu	0552	0.3	10
	1205	1.2	38
	1547	1.0	30
	2307	2.7	83
8 W	0647	0.4	12
	1305	1.2	37
	1630	1.0	32
	2358	2.6	79
9 Th	0744	0.5	15
	1413	1.2	38
	1727	1.1	35
10 F ○	0055	2.4	72
	0841	0.6	18
	1528	1.3	41
	1858	1.2	38
11 Sa ○	0159	2.1	64
	0935	0.7	21
	1635	1.5	46
	2054	1.3	39
12 Su	0313	1.9	57
	1021	0.7	22
	1725	1.7	51
	2243	1.2	36
13 M	0433	1.6	50
	1101	0.8	23
	1806	1.8	56
14 Tu	0012	1.0	31
	0549	1.5	45
	1136	0.7	22
	1842	2.0	61
15 W	0119	0.8	25
	0654	1.3	40
	1209	0.7	22
	1916	2.1	64
16 Th	0210	0.6	19
	0750	1.2	37
	1240	0.7	21
	1949	2.2	67
17 F	0253	0.5	14
	0839	1.1	33
	1310	0.7	20
	2021	2.2	68
18 Sa ●	0332	0.4	11
	0923	1.0	31
	1340	0.6	19
	2053	2.3	69
19 Su	0409	0.3	9
	1006	1.0	29
	1410	0.6	19
	2125	2.2	68
20 M	0447	0.3	8
	1049	0.9	28
	1438	0.7	21
	2158	2.2	67
21 Tu	0525	0.3	9
	1135	0.9	28
	1505	0.7	22
	2230	2.1	65
22 W	0605	0.3	10
	1226	0.9	28
	1530	0.8	25
	2302	2.1	63
23 Th	0647	0.4	12
	2334	2.0	60
24 F	0731	0.4	13
25 Sa	0008	1.8	56
	0816	0.5	14
26 Su ◑	0049	1.7	51
	0902	0.5	14
27 M	0148	1.5	47
	0945	0.5	14
	1721	1.4	42
	2211	1.1	34
28 Tu	0312	1.4	42
	1027	0.5	15
	1745	1.5	47
	2333	1.0	29
29 W	0444	1.3	39
	1105	0.5	16
	1813	1.8	54
30 Th	0036	0.7	22
	0606	1.2	36
	1142	0.6	17
	1844	2.0	60

December

Day	Time	ft	cm
1 F	0131	0.5	15
	0716	1.1	35
	1218	0.6	17
	1919	2.2	68
2 Sa	0222	0.3	9
	0816	1.1	33
	1254	0.6	18
	1958	2.4	74
3 Su ○	0313	0.2	5
	0911	1.0	31
	1330	0.6	18
	2041	2.6	78
4 M	0403	0.1	3
	1001	1.0	30
	1409	0.6	18
	2126	2.6	80
5 Tu	0453	0.1	3
	1050	1.0	29
	1451	0.6	18
	2213	2.6	80
6 W	0543	0.1	4
	1139	1.0	29
	1538	0.6	19
	2303	2.5	76
7 Th	0633	0.2	7
	1232	1.0	30
	1631	0.7	21
	2354	2.3	70
8 F	0721	0.4	11
	1330	1.1	33
	1738	0.8	25
9 Sa	0048	2.1	63
	0807	0.5	14
	1434	1.2	37
	1903	1.0	29
10 Su ◑	0145	1.8	55
	0851	0.5	16
	1539	1.4	42
	2046	1.0	30
11 M	0248	1.5	47
	0932	0.6	18
	1638	1.6	48
	2233	1.0	29
12 Tu	0359	1.3	39
	1011	0.6	18
	1729	1.7	52
13 W	0010	0.8	24
	0515	1.1	33
	1049	0.6	17
	1812	1.8	56
14 Th	0120	0.6	19
	0626	1.0	29
	1125	0.5	16
	1851	1.9	58
15 F	0209	0.5	14
	0726	0.9	26
	1201	0.5	14
	1927	2.0	60
16 Sa	0248	0.3	10
	0816	0.8	24
	1237	0.4	13
	2001	2.0	61
17 Su	0322	0.2	7
	0900	0.7	22
	1312	0.4	13
	2036	2.0	61
18 M ●	0355	0.2	5
	0941	0.7	22
	1347	0.4	13
	2110	2.0	61
19 Tu	0429	0.2	5
	1020	0.7	22
	1422	0.4	13
	2144	2.0	60
20 W	0504	0.2	5
	1100	0.7	22
	1458	0.5	15
	2218	1.9	58
21 Th	0539	0.2	6
	1142	0.8	23
	1535	0.5	16
	2251	1.8	56
22 F	0616	0.2	6
	1229	0.8	24
	1615	0.6	19
	2324	1.7	52
23 Sa	0653	0.2	7
	1320	0.9	26
	1704	0.7	21
24 Su	0000	1.6	48
	0732	0.3	8
	1414	0.9	28
	1815	0.8	24
25 M	0041	1.4	44
	0812	0.3	9
	1507	1.0	32
	1953	0.8	25
26 Tu ◑	0135	1.3	39
	0853	0.3	10
	1555	1.2	37
	2134	0.8	23
27 W	0250	1.1	33
	0935	0.4	11
	1640	1.4	42
	2302	0.6	18
28 Th	0419	1.0	29
	1017	0.4	12
	1723	1.6	48
29 F	0014	0.4	13
	0546	0.9	26
	1059	0.4	12
	1807	1.8	55
30 Sa	0115	0.2	6
	0701	0.8	24
	1142	0.4	11
	1853	2.0	61
31 Su	0210	0.0	1
	0801	0.7	22
	1227	0.3	10
	1941	2.2	66

Time meridian 75° E. 0000 is midnight. 1200 is noon. Times are not adjusted for Daylight Saving Time.
Heights are referred to the chart datum of soundings.

Santiago de Cuba 2017

Times and Heights of High and Low Waters

January

Day	Time	ft	cm	Day	Time	ft	cm
1 Su	0345	0.2	7	16 M	0519	0.2	7
	1040	1.5	47		1146	1.2	36
	1711	0.3	10		1834	0.1	3
	2300	1.0	32				
2 M	0440	0.3	8	17 Tu	0038	0.9	27
	1125	1.5	45		0616	0.4	11
	1800	0.3	8		1229	1.1	33
					1922	0.1	4
3 Tu	0001	1.1	33	18 W	0145	0.9	26
	0543	0.3	10		0719	0.5	14
	1214	1.4	43		1312	1.0	29
	1853	0.2	6		2008	0.2	5
4 W	0107	1.1	34	19 Th	0300	0.9	27
	0654	0.4	12		0834	0.6	17
	1309	1.3	40		1358	0.9	27
	1949	0.1	4		2053	0.2	6
5 Th	0218	1.2	37	20 F ◑	0412	1.0	29
	0810	0.4	13		0958	0.6	19
	1408	1.2	38		1447	0.8	25
	2045	0.1	2		2134	0.2	6
6 F ◐	0329	1.3	40	21 Sa	0508	1.0	31
	0927	0.4	13		1117	0.6	19
	1512	1.2	36		1540	0.8	24
	2141	0.0	0		2211	0.2	7
7 Sa	0435	1.4	43	22 Su	0548	1.1	34
	1039	0.4	12		1213	0.6	19
	1616	1.1	35		1632	0.8	23
	2236	-0.1	-2		2247	0.2	7
8 Su	0535	1.5	46	23 M	0619	1.2	36
	1146	0.4	11		1245	0.6	18
	1718	1.1	34		1721	0.8	24
	2330	-0.1	-4		2322	0.2	6
9 M	0630	1.6	49	24 Tu	0647	1.3	39
	1247	0.3	9		1309	0.6	17
	1817	1.1	33		1805	0.8	25
					2359	0.2	5
10 Tu	0022	-0.2	-5	25 W	0716	1.3	41
	0720	1.6	50		1335	0.5	15
	1342	0.2	7		1848	0.9	26
	1912	1.1	33				
11 W	0112	-0.2	-5	26 Th	0038	0.1	3
	0808	1.6	50		0748	1.4	43
	1434	0.2	5		1404	0.4	12
	2005	1.0	32		1931	0.9	28
12 Th ○	0201	-0.2	-5	27 F	0120	0.1	2
	0854	1.6	49		0821	1.4	44
	1524	0.1	4		1438	0.3	10
	2057	1.0	31		2016	1.0	30
13 F	0250	-0.1	-3	28 Sa ●	0203	0.0	1
	0938	1.5	47		0857	1.5	45
	1612	0.1	3		1515	0.2	7
	2149	1.0	30		2102	1.0	31
14 Sa	0339	0.0	0	29 Su	0249	0.0	1
	1021	1.4	44		0936	1.4	44
	1659	0.1	3		1554	0.2	5
	2242	1.0	29		2151	1.0	32
15 Su	0428	0.1	3	30 M	0339	0.1	2
	1104	1.3	40		1017	1.4	43
	1747	0.1	3		1638	0.1	3
	2338	0.9	27		2243	1.1	33
				31 Tu	0432	0.1	3
					1101	1.3	41
					1725	0.0	1
					2340	1.1	34

February

Day	Time	ft	cm	Day	Time	ft	cm
1 W	0532	0.2	5	16 Th	0052	0.9	27
	1149	1.2	38		0637	0.5	14
	1817	0.0	0		1218	0.9	26
					1857	0.2	6
2 Th	0043	1.1	35	17 F	0152	0.9	27
	0639	0.3	8		0743	0.6	17
	1242	1.1	35		1255	0.8	23
	1914	0.0	-1		1939	0.3	8
3 F	0151	1.2	36	18 Sa	0300	0.9	27
	0754	0.3	9		0906	0.6	19
	1342	1.0	32		1340	0.7	22
	2014	-0.1	-2		2025	0.3	9
4 Sa ◐	0304	1.2	37	19 Su ○	0405	1.0	29
	0912	0.3	10		2113	0.3	9
	1449	1.0	30				
	2116	-0.1	-3				
5 Su	0414	1.3	40	20 M	0453	1.0	32
	1028	0.3	9		1126	0.6	18
	1559	1.0	29		1553	0.7	22
	2217	-0.1	-4		2203	0.3	9
6 M	0518	1.4	42	21 Tu	0532	1.1	35
	1136	0.2	7		1157	0.6	17
	1707	1.0	29		1655	0.8	24
	2316	-0.2	-5		2251	0.3	8
7 Tu	0615	1.4	44	22 W	0607	1.2	38
	1236	0.2	5		1225	0.5	15
	1809	1.0	30		1747	0.9	26
					2338	0.2	6
8 W	0012	-0.2	-6	23 Th	0641	1.3	40
	0706	1.5	45		1255	0.4	12
	1329	0.1	3		1834	1.0	29
	1906	1.0	31				
9 Th	0104	-0.2	-6	24 F	0023	0.1	4
	0753	1.5	45		0717	1.4	42
	1416	0.1	2		1328	0.3	9
	1958	1.0	31		1918	1.0	32
10 F	0154	-0.2	-5	25 Sa	0109	0.1	3
	0836	1.4	44		0753	1.4	43
	1501	0.0	1		1404	0.2	6
	2047	1.0	31		2003	1.1	35
11 Sa ○	0242	-0.1	-3	26 Su ●	0155	0.1	2
	0917	1.4	42		0832	1.4	44
	1543	0.0	0		1441	0.1	4
	2134	1.0	31		2048	1.2	37
12 Su	0327	0.0	0	27 M	0243	0.0	1
	0956	1.3	39		0911	1.4	43
	1623	0.0	1		1522	0.0	1
	2221	1.0	30		2135	1.3	39
13 M	0412	0.1	3	28 Tu	0332	0.1	2
	1034	1.1	35		0953	1.3	41
	1702	0.0	1		1605	0.0	0
	2309	1.0	29		2226	1.3	39
14 Tu	0457	0.2	7				
	1109	1.0	32				
	1740	0.1	3				
	2358	0.9	27				
15 W	0544	0.4	11				
	1144	0.9	28				
	1818	0.1	4				

March

Day	Time	ft	cm	Day	Time	ft	cm
1 W	0425	0.1	3	16 Th	0516	0.5	14
	1037	1.3	39		1059	0.9	28
	1651	0.0	-1		1708	0.3	8
	2320	1.3	39		2358	1.0	32
2 Th	0523	0.2	5	17 F	0601	0.6	17
	1126	1.2	36		1128	0.9	26
	1743	-0.1	-2		1738	0.3	10
3 F	0019	1.3	39	18 Sa	0044	1.0	31
	0629	0.2	7		0657	0.6	19
	1220	1.1	33		1200	0.8	24
	1841	0.0	-1		1815	0.4	12
4 Sa	0126	1.3	39	19 Su	0138	1.0	32
	0743	0.3	9		0809	0.7	20
	1323	1.0	30		1248	0.8	24
	1945	0.0	-1		1907	0.4	13
5 Su ◑	0238	1.3	39	20 M ◑	0239	1.1	33
	0901	0.3	9		0925	0.7	20
	1436	1.0	29		1404	0.8	24
	2054	0.0	0		2014	0.5	14
6 M	0352	1.3	40	21 Tu	0340	1.1	35
	1017	0.3	8		1021	0.6	19
	1553	1.0	29		1529	0.8	25
	2202	0.0	0		2122	0.5	14
7 Tu	0458	1.3	41	22 W	0433	1.2	37
	1123	0.2	7		1102	0.6	17
	1704	1.0	30		1637	0.9	28
	2307	0.0	-1		2224	0.4	13
8 W	0556	1.4	43	23 Th	0520	1.3	40
	1219	0.2	5		1138	0.5	15
	1806	1.0	32		1732	1.0	32
					2319	0.4	11
9 Th	0005	0.0	-1	24 F	0602	1.4	42
	0646	1.4	43		1215	0.4	12
	1307	0.1	3		1819	1.2	36
	1900	1.1	34				
10 F	0058	0.0	-1	25 Sa	0010	0.3	9
	0732	1.4	43		0643	1.4	44
	1350	0.1	2		1252	0.3	9
	1949	1.1	35		1904	1.3	40
11 Sa	0147	0.0	0	26 Su	0059	0.2	7
	0813	1.4	42		0724	1.5	45
	1430	0.1	2		1329	0.2	6
	2034	1.2	36		1948	1.4	44
12 Su ○	0233	0.1	2	27 M	0147	0.2	6
	0851	1.3	40		0804	1.5	45
	1506	0.1	2		1409	0.1	3
	2116	1.2	36		2034	1.5	46
13 M	0315	0.2	5	28 Tu ●	0235	0.2	5
	0926	1.2	37		0846	1.4	44
	1539	0.1	3		1450	0.1	2
	2157	1.1	35		2120	1.5	47
14 Tu	0356	0.3	8	29 W	0326	0.2	5
	0959	1.1	34		0929	1.4	42
	1610	0.1	4		1534	0.0	0
	2237	1.1	34		2209	1.6	48
15 W	0435	0.4	11	30 Th	0419	0.2	7
	1030	1.0	31		1015	1.3	39
	1640	0.2	6		1621	0.0	0
	2317	1.1	33		2302	1.5	47
				31 F	0517	0.3	8
					1106	1.2	36
					1713	0.0	1
					2359	1.5	45

Time meridian 75° E. 0000 is midnight. 1200 is noon. Times are not adjusted for Daylight Saving Time.
Heights are referred to the chart datum of soundings.

Santiago de Cuba 2017

Times and Heights of High and Low Waters

April

Day	Time	ft	cm	Day	Time	ft	cm
1 Sa	0623	0.3	10	16 Su	0624	0.7	22
	1204	1.1	33		1123	0.9	27
	1813	0.1	3		1708	0.5	15
2 Su	0103	1.4	44	17 M	0037	1.3	39
	0736	0.4	11		0725	0.7	22
	1311	1.0	31		1222	0.9	27
	1921	0.2	5		1805	0.6	17
3 M ☾	0213	1.4	43	18 Tu	0132	1.3	39
	0852	0.4	11		0829	0.7	21
	1430	1.0	30		1344	0.9	28
	2035	0.2	6		1924	0.6	19
4 Tu	0325	1.4	42	19 W ☽	0234	1.3	40
	1003	0.3	9		0925	0.7	20
	1551	1.0	31		1508	1.0	30
	2149	0.2	7		2046	0.6	19
5 W	0432	1.4	42	20 Th	0335	1.3	41
	1103	0.3	8		1013	0.6	17
	1702	1.1	34		1617	1.1	35
	2257	0.2	7		2158	0.6	18
6 Th	0530	1.4	43	21 F	0431	1.4	43
	1154	0.2	6		1055	0.5	14
	1801	1.2	37		1713	1.3	39
	2358	0.2	7		2300	0.5	16
7 F	0620	1.4	43	22 Sa	0521	1.5	45
	1239	0.2	5		1137	0.4	11
	1852	1.3	40		1802	1.4	44
					2355	0.5	14
8 Sa	0051	0.2	7	23 Su	0608	1.5	45
	0704	1.4	42		1217	0.3	8
	1318	0.2	5		1848	1.6	48
	1937	1.4	42				
9 Su	0139	0.3	8	24 M	0047	0.4	12
	0743	1.3	41		0653	1.5	46
	1353	0.2	5		1258	0.2	5
	2018	1.4	43		1934	1.7	52
10 M	0222	0.3	10	25 Tu	0138	0.4	11
	0819	1.3	39		0737	1.5	45
	1424	0.2	6		1340	0.1	3
	2056	1.4	43		2020	1.8	54
11 Tu ○	0302	0.4	12	26 W ●	0228	0.3	10
	0851	1.2	36		0822	1.4	44
	1452	0.2	7		1422	0.0	1
	2131	1.4	42		2106	1.8	55
12 W	0340	0.5	14	27 Th	0320	0.3	10
	0921	1.1	34		0908	1.3	41
	1517	0.3	8		1507	0.0	1
	2205	1.3	41		2155	1.8	55
13 Th	0416	0.6	17	28 F	0414	0.3	10
	0949	1.0	31		0957	1.3	39
	1541	0.3	10		1556	0.1	2
	2238	1.3	40		2246	1.7	53
14 F	0452	0.6	19	29 Sa	0513	0.4	11
	1016	1.0	30		1051	1.2	36
	1604	0.4	12		1649	0.1	4
	2313	1.3	40		2341	1.7	51
15 Sa	0533	0.7	20	30 Su	0618	0.4	12
	1045	0.9	28		1152	1.1	34
	1632	0.4	13		1749	0.2	7
	2351	1.3	39				

May

Day	Time	ft	cm	Day	Time	ft	cm
1 M	0041	1.6	48	16 Tu	0648	0.7	21
	0727	0.4	12		1208	1.0	31
	1304	1.0	32		1733	0.6	19
	1859	0.3	10				
2 Tu	0147	1.5	46	17 W	0047	1.5	45
	0837	0.4	11		0744	0.7	20
	1425	1.1	33		1324	1.0	32
	2016	0.4	12		1852	0.7	21
3 W ☽	0254	1.4	44	18 Th	0145	1.5	45
	0941	0.3	10		0838	0.6	18
	1546	1.1	35		1442	1.1	35
	2134	0.4	13		2016	0.7	22
4 Th	0359	1.4	43	19 F ☽	0246	1.5	45
	1036	0.3	9		0929	0.5	16
	1656	1.2	38		1552	1.3	39
	2245	0.5	14		2133	0.7	21
5 F	0457	1.4	42	20 Sa	0345	1.5	45
	1124	0.3	8		1016	0.4	13
	1752	1.4	42		1651	1.4	44
	2347	0.5	15		2240	0.7	20
6 Sa	0547	1.3	41	21 Su	0442	1.5	45
	1206	0.2	7		1102	0.3	9
	1840	1.4	44		1743	1.6	49
					2340	0.6	18
7 Su	0042	0.5	15	22 M	0534	1.5	45
	0631	1.3	40		1146	0.2	6
	1242	0.2	7		1832	1.8	54
	1922	1.5	46				
8 M	0130	0.5	16	23 Tu	0036	0.5	16
	0709	1.3	39		0624	1.5	45
	1314	0.3	8		1231	0.1	4
	2000	1.5	47		1920	1.9	57
9 Tu	0212	0.6	17	24 W	0129	0.5	14
	0743	1.2	37		0713	1.4	44
	1341	0.3	9		1315	0.1	2
	2034	1.6	48		2007	1.9	59
10 W	0250	0.6	19	25 Th	0222	0.4	13
	0814	1.1	35		0802	1.4	42
	1406	0.3	10		1401	0.0	1
	2105	1.6	48		2054	1.9	59
11 Th ○	0325	0.7	20	26 F ●	0315	0.4	12
	0843	1.1	34		0851	1.3	40
	1429	0.4	11		1448	0.1	2
	2135	1.5	47		2143	1.9	58
12 F	0358	0.7	21	27 Sa	0410	0.4	12
	0910	1.0	32		0944	1.2	38
	1452	0.4	12		1537	0.1	4
	2205	1.5	47		2232	1.8	56
13 Sa	0431	0.7	22	28 Su	0507	0.4	12
	0940	1.0	31		1040	1.2	36
	1518	0.5	14		1631	0.2	6
	2237	1.5	46		2324	1.7	53
14 Su	0510	0.7	22	29 M	0608	0.4	12
	1016	1.0	30		1143	1.1	34
	1551	0.5	15		1731	0.3	10
	2314	1.5	46				
15 M	0556	0.7	22	30 Tu	0019	1.6	50
	1104	1.0	30		0710	0.4	11
	1633	0.6	17		1253	1.1	34
	2357	1.5	45		1839	0.4	13
				31 W	0117	1.5	46
					0813	0.4	11
					1413	1.1	34
					1955	0.5	16

June

Day	Time	ft	cm	Day	Time	ft	cm
1 Th ☾	0218	1.4	44	16 F ☾	0107	1.5	47
	0911	0.3	10		0755	0.5	15
	1532	1.2	37		1412	1.3	39
	2113	0.6	18		1951	0.7	22
2 F	0319	1.3	41	17 Sa ☽	0205	1.5	46
	1003	0.3	9		0848	0.4	13
	1642	1.3	40		1522	1.4	43
	2227	0.7	20		2109	0.7	22
3 Sa	0417	1.3	40	18 Su	0306	1.5	45
	1049	0.3	9		0940	0.3	10
	1738	1.4	43		1626	1.5	47
	2334	0.7	20		2220	0.7	21
4 Su	0508	1.2	38	19 M	0407	1.4	44
	1130	0.3	9		1031	0.2	7
	1825	1.5	46		1724	1.7	52
					2325	0.7	20
5 M	0031	0.7	21	20 Tu	0505	1.4	43
	0553	1.2	37		1120	0.2	5
	1204	0.3	10		1817	1.8	55
	1905	1.6	48				
6 Tu	0121	0.7	22	21 W	0026	0.6	18
	0632	1.2	36		0601	1.4	43
	1234	0.3	10		1209	0.1	3
	1940	1.6	49		1907	1.9	58
7 W	0203	0.7	22	22 Th	0122	0.5	16
	0706	1.1	35		0655	1.4	42
	1300	0.4	11		1257	0.1	2
	2011	1.6	50		1955	2.0	60
8 Th	0238	0.8	23	23 F	0216	0.5	14
	0737	1.1	34		0747	1.3	41
	1325	0.4	12		1346	0.1	2
	2039	1.6	50		2043	2.0	60
9 F	0307	0.8	23	24 Sa ●	0308	0.4	13
	0808	1.1	33		0840	1.3	40
	1351	0.4	12		1435	0.1	3
	2107	1.6	50		2130	1.9	58
10 Sa	0336	0.8	23	25 Su	0401	0.4	12
	0840	1.1	33		0934	1.2	38
	1419	0.4	13		1525	0.2	5
	2137	1.6	50		2217	1.8	56
11 Su	0407	0.7	22	26 M	0454	0.4	11
	0916	1.1	33		1030	1.2	37
	1452	0.5	14		1618	0.3	8
	2209	1.6	50		2305	1.7	53
12 M	0443	0.7	21	27 Tu	0548	0.4	11
	0959	1.1	33		1130	1.2	36
	1531	0.5	15		1715	0.4	11
	2245	1.6	50		2354	1.6	49
13 Tu	0524	0.7	20	28 W	0643	0.3	10
	1051	1.1	33		1235	1.1	35
	1619	0.5	16		1818	0.5	15
	2327	1.6	49				
14 W	0611	0.6	19	29 Th	0045	1.5	45
	1151	1.1	34		0738	0.3	10
	1719	0.6	18		1349	1.2	36
					1928	0.6	19
15 Th	0014	1.6	48	30 F	0138	1.4	42
	0702	0.6	17		0832	0.4	11
	1300	1.2	36		1506	1.2	37
	1831	0.7	21		2045	0.7	22

Time meridian 75° E. 0000 is midnight. 1200 is noon. Times are not adjusted for Daylight Saving Time.
Heights are referred to the chart datum of soundings.

Santiago de Cuba 2017

Times and Heights of High and Low Waters

July

Day	Time (h m)	Height (ft)	Height (cm)	Day	Time (h m)	Height (ft)	Height (cm)
1 Sa ◑	0233	1.3	39	16 Su	0132	1.5	45
	0923	0.4	11		0811	0.4	11
	1619	1.3	40		1452	1.5	46
	2205	0.8	24		2048	0.7	22
2 Su	0330	1.2	37	17 M ◑	0234	1.4	44
	1009	0.4	11		0908	0.3	9
	1719	1.4	42		1601	1.6	49
	2319	0.8	24		2203	0.7	22
3 M	0424	1.1	35	18 Tu	0339	1.4	42
	1050	0.4	12		1004	0.2	7
	1806	1.5	45		1704	1.7	53
					2313	0.7	20
4 Tu	0023	0.8	25	19 W	0444	1.4	42
	0512	1.1	34		1100	0.2	5
	1125	0.4	13		1801	1.8	56
	1845	1.5	47				
5 W	0113	0.8	25	20 Th	0016	0.6	19
	0554	1.1	34		0546	1.3	41
	1155	0.4	13		1154	0.1	4
	1916	1.6	49		1854	1.9	58
6 Th	0150	0.8	25	21 F	0113	0.5	16
	0632	1.1	34		0644	1.4	42
	1224	0.4	13		1246	0.1	3
	1945	1.6	50		1943	1.9	59
7 F	0217	0.8	25	22 Sa	0205	0.5	14
	0706	1.1	34		0739	1.4	42
	1253	0.4	13		1337	0.1	4
	2011	1.7	51		2030	1.9	59
8 Sa	0240	0.8	24	23 Su ●	0255	0.4	13
	0741	1.1	34		0832	1.4	42
	1324	0.4	13		1427	0.2	5
	2039	1.7	52		2115	1.9	57
9 Su ○	0305	0.8	23	24 M	0343	0.4	12
	0818	1.1	35		0924	1.3	41
	1359	0.4	13		1517	0.2	7
	2110	1.7	53		2159	1.8	55
10 M	0334	0.7	21	25 Tu	0430	0.4	11
	0859	1.2	36		1017	1.3	40
	1438	0.4	13		1607	0.3	10
	2143	1.7	53		2242	1.7	51
11 Tu	0409	0.6	19	26 W	0517	0.4	11
	0945	1.2	37		1111	1.3	39
	1522	0.5	14		1700	0.5	14
	2220	1.7	52		2326	1.6	48
12 W	0448	0.6	18	27 Th	0605	0.4	11
	1035	1.2	38		1209	1.3	39
	1612	0.5	16		1756	0.6	18
	2301	1.7	51				
13 Th	0533	0.5	16	28 F	0009	1.4	44
	1131	1.3	39		0653	0.4	12
	1710	0.6	17		1313	1.2	38
	2346	1.6	50		1859	0.7	22
14 F	0622	0.5	14	29 Sa	0055	1.3	40
	1234	1.3	41		0743	0.5	14
	1816	0.7	20		1426	1.2	38
					2013	0.8	25
15 Sa	0036	1.6	48	30 Su ◑	0143	1.2	37
	0715	0.4	13		0832	0.5	15
	1342	1.4	43		1542	1.3	40
	1930	0.7	21		2138	0.9	27
				31 M	0237	1.1	35
					0920	0.5	16
					1648	1.4	42
					2305	0.9	28

August

Day	Time (h m)	Height (ft)	Height (cm)	Day	Time (h m)	Height (ft)	Height (cm)
1 Tu	0335	1.1	34	16 W	0322	1.4	42
	1003	0.6	17		0943	0.3	10
	1738	1.4	44		1644	1.8	54
					2302	0.7	22
2 W	0013	0.9	28	17 Th	0434	1.4	42
	0432	1.1	33		1045	0.3	9
	1042	0.6	18		1745	1.9	57
	1815	1.5	47				
3 Th	0056	0.9	28	18 F	0004	0.6	19
	0522	1.1	34		0540	1.4	43
	1118	0.6	18		1144	0.3	8
	1845	1.6	49		1838	1.9	58
4 F	0121	0.9	27	19 Sa	0059	0.6	17
	0605	1.1	35		0639	1.5	45
	1153	0.6	17		1239	0.3	8
	1912	1.7	51		1927	1.9	59
5 Sa	0139	0.9	26	20 Su	0148	0.5	15
	0644	1.2	37		0733	1.5	46
	1229	0.6	17		1331	0.3	8
	1940	1.7	53		2012	1.9	58
6 Su	0200	0.8	25	21 M ●	0233	0.5	14
	0723	1.2	38		0823	1.5	47
	1307	0.5	16		1421	0.3	10
	2010	1.8	54		2055	1.9	57
7 M ○	0226	0.8	23	22 Tu	0316	0.4	13
	0803	1.3	40		0912	1.5	47
	1347	0.5	15		1509	0.4	12
	2042	1.8	55		2136	1.8	54
8 Tu	0257	0.7	20	23 W	0357	0.4	13
	0844	1.4	42		1000	1.5	46
	1430	0.5	15		1556	0.5	15
	2117	1.8	55		2215	1.7	51
9 W	0333	0.6	18	24 Th	0438	0.5	14
	0929	1.4	44		1048	1.5	45
	1516	0.5	15		1644	0.6	18
	2154	1.8	54		2254	1.5	47
10 Th	0412	0.5	16	25 F	0518	0.5	15
	1018	1.5	46		1138	1.4	44
	1606	0.5	16		1734	0.7	22
	2235	1.7	53		2331	1.4	43
11 F	0455	0.5	14	26 Sa	0559	0.6	17
	1110	1.5	47		1231	1.4	43
	1701	0.6	18		1829	0.9	26
	2320	1.7	51				
12 Sa	0543	0.4	13	27 Su	0010	1.3	40
	1209	1.6	48		0641	0.6	19
	1804	0.7	20		1331	1.4	42
					1938	1.0	29
13 Su	0009	1.6	48	28 M	0051	1.2	37
	0637	0.4	12		0726	0.7	21
	1313	1.6	48		1440	1.4	42
	1915	0.7	22		2106	1.0	31
14 M	0106	1.5	45	29 Tu ◑	0140	1.1	35
	0736	0.4	12		0814	0.8	23
	1424	1.6	50		1552	1.4	44
	2033	0.8	23		2245	1.0	32
15 Tu ○	0211	1.4	43	30 W	0245	1.1	35
	0839	0.4	11		0905	0.8	24
	1536	1.7	52		1648	1.5	45
	2150	0.8	23		2345	1.0	31
				31 Th	0357	1.1	35
					0955	0.8	24
					1728	1.6	48

September

Day	Time (h m)	Height (ft)	Height (cm)	Day	Time (h m)	Height (ft)	Height (cm)
1 F	0012	1.0	31	16 Sa	0537	1.5	47
	0457	1.2	37		1137	0.5	14
	1042	0.8	24		1817	1.9	58
	1801	1.6	50				
2 Sa	0029	1.0	29	17 Su	0037	0.6	18
	0545	1.3	39		0634	1.6	49
	1127	0.8	23		1233	0.5	14
	1832	1.7	52		1905	1.9	58
3 Su	0049	0.9	28	18 M	0122	0.5	16
	0626	1.4	42		0725	1.7	51
	1210	0.7	21		1325	0.5	14
	1903	1.8	54		1949	1.9	57
4 M	0116	0.8	25	19 Tu	0204	0.5	15
	0706	1.5	46		0812	1.7	53
	1253	0.7	20		1414	0.5	16
	1937	1.8	56		2030	1.8	55
5 Tu	0146	0.7	22	20 W ●	0242	0.5	15
	0747	1.6	49		0857	1.7	53
	1337	0.6	19		1500	0.6	18
	2012	1.9	57		2108	1.7	52
6 W	0220	0.7	20	21 Th	0318	0.5	15
	0829	1.7	51		0940	1.7	52
	1422	0.6	18		1544	0.7	20
	2049	1.8	56		2144	1.6	49
7 Th	0256	0.6	17	22 F	0353	0.6	17
	0913	1.7	53		1022	1.7	51
	1509	0.6	18		1628	0.8	23
	2128	1.8	55		2218	1.5	46
8 F	0336	0.5	15	23 Sa	0426	0.6	18
	1000	1.8	55		1104	1.6	50
	1559	0.6	19		1714	0.9	27
	2210	1.7	53		2252	1.4	42
9 Sa	0420	0.5	14	24 Su	0457	0.7	21
	1051	1.8	55		1147	1.6	48
	1654	0.7	20		1804	1.0	29
	2256	1.7	51		2325	1.3	40
10 Su	0509	0.5	14	25 M	0529	0.8	23
	1146	1.8	55		1234	1.5	47
	1755	0.7	22		1905	1.0	32
	2347	1.6	48				
11 M	0603	0.5	14	26 Tu	0001	1.2	37
	1249	1.8	54		0605	0.8	25
	1905	0.8	24		1327	1.5	46
					2024	1.1	33
12 Tu	0047	1.5	45	27 W	0049	1.2	36
	0706	0.5	15		0651	0.9	27
	1358	1.8	54		1427	1.5	46
	2022	0.8	24		2149	1.1	33
13 W ◑	0157	1.4	44	28 Th ◑	0202	1.2	36
	0815	0.5	15		0755	1.0	29
	1511	1.8	55		1528	1.5	47
	2139	0.8	24		2236	1.1	33
14 Th	0315	1.4	43	29 F	0328	1.2	37
	0926	0.5	15		0904	1.0	29
	1621	1.8	56		1620	1.6	49
	2248	0.7	22		2303	1.0	31
15 F	0431	1.5	45	30 Sa	0435	1.3	40
	1034	0.5	15		1007	1.0	29
	1723	1.9	57		1704	1.7	51
	2347	0.7	20		2331	1.0	29

Time meridian 75° E. 0000 is midnight. 1200 is noon. Times are not adjusted for Daylight Saving Time.
Heights are referred to the chart datum of soundings.

Santiago de Cuba 2017

Times and Heights of High and Low Waters

October

Day	Time (h m)	Height (ft)	Height (cm)		Day	Time (h m)	Height (ft)	Height (cm)
1 Su	0524	1.4	44		16 M	0010	0.5	16
	1102	0.9	27			0627	1.7	52
	1744	1.7	53			1226	0.6	19
						1838	1.8	54
2 M	0000	0.9	27		17 Tu	0052	0.5	15
	0607	1.6	48			0715	1.8	55
	1152	0.8	25			1318	0.6	19
	1823	1.8	55			1921	1.7	52
3 Tu	0033	0.8	24		18 W	0130	0.5	14
	0649	1.7	52			0759	1.8	56
	1240	0.8	23			1406	0.7	20
	1902	1.8	56			2000	1.6	50
4 W	0108	0.7	20		19 Th	0205	0.5	15
	0730	1.8	56			0840	1.8	56
	1326	0.7	22			1451	0.7	22
	1941	1.8	56			2036	1.6	48
5 Th O	0144	0.6	18		20 F ●	0237	0.5	16
	0813	1.9	59			0919	1.8	56
	1413	0.7	20			1534	0.8	24
	2021	1.8	56			2110	1.5	45
6 F	0223	0.5	15		21 Sa	0307	0.6	17
	0857	2.0	61			0956	1.8	54
	1502	0.7	20			1615	0.9	26
	2103	1.8	54			2142	1.4	42
7 Sa	0305	0.5	14		22 Su	0333	0.6	19
	0943	2.0	62			1031	1.7	53
	1553	0.7	20			1657	0.9	28
	2147	1.7	52			2212	1.3	39
8 Su	0350	0.4	13		23 M	0358	0.7	21
	1033	2.0	61			1107	1.7	51
	1648	0.7	21			1742	1.0	30
	2236	1.6	49			2244	1.2	37
9 M	0439	0.5	14		24 Tu	0423	0.8	23
	1128	2.0	60			1144	1.6	50
	1750	0.7	22			1833	1.0	31
	2331	1.5	46			2321	1.2	36
10 Tu	0535	0.5	15		25 W	0453	0.8	25
	1228	1.9	58			1226	1.6	49
	1859	0.8	23			1933	1.0	31
11 W	0035	1.4	44		26 Th	0014	1.1	35
	0641	0.6	17			0537	0.9	28
	1334	1.8	56			1315	1.6	48
	2014	0.8	23			2031	1.0	31
12 Th ◑	0151	1.4	43		27 F	0131	1.2	36
	0754	0.6	19			0650	1.0	29
	1445	1.8	55			1412	1.6	48
	2126	0.7	22			2119	1.0	29
13 F	0313	1.4	44		28 Sa ◐	0256	1.2	38
	0911	0.6	19			0816	1.0	30
	1554	1.8	55			1510	1.6	49
	2229	0.7	20			2200	0.9	27
14 Sa	0429	1.5	46		29 Su	0405	1.4	42
	1024	0.6	19			0932	1.0	30
	1656	1.8	55			1605	1.6	50
	2323	0.6	18			2238	0.8	25
15 Su	0533	1.6	49		30 M	0459	1.5	46
	1129	0.6	19			1037	0.9	28
	1750	1.8	55			1655	1.7	51
						2316	0.7	22
					31 Tu	0545	1.7	51
						1133	0.9	26
						1742	1.7	52
						2354	0.6	18

November

Day	Time (h m)	Height (ft)	Height (cm)		Day	Time (h m)	Height (ft)	Height (cm)
1 W	0629	1.8	55		16 Th	0056	0.4	11
	1225	0.8	24			0744	1.8	54
	1826	1.7	53			1359	0.7	21
						1928	1.4	42
2 Th	0033	0.5	15		17 F	0128	0.4	12
	0713	1.9	59			0822	1.8	54
	1315	0.7	22			1443	0.7	22
	1910	1.7	52			2003	1.3	40
3 F	0114	0.4	12		18 Sa ●	0157	0.4	13
	0757	2.0	62			0857	1.8	54
	1404	0.7	20			1524	0.8	23
	1955	1.7	51			2036	1.2	38
4 Sa O	0155	0.3	10		19 Su	0223	0.5	14
	0842	2.1	63			0930	1.7	53
	1455	0.6	19			1603	0.8	24
	2040	1.6	49			2107	1.2	36
5 Su	0239	0.3	9		20 M	0248	0.5	16
	0930	2.1	63			1001	1.7	51
	1548	0.6	19			1639	0.8	25
	2128	1.5	47			2138	1.1	34
6 M	0326	0.3	9		21 Tu	0312	0.6	17
	1019	2.0	62			1032	1.6	50
	1644	0.6	19			1716	0.8	25
	2221	1.4	44			2212	1.1	33
7 Tu	0417	0.4	11		22 W	0339	0.6	19
	1112	2.0	60			1105	1.6	49
	1745	0.6	19			1757	0.8	25
	2319	1.4	42			2254	1.0	32
8 W	0514	0.4	13		23 Th	0413	0.7	20
	1209	1.9	57			1143	1.6	48
	1852	0.6	19			1842	0.8	25
						2351	1.0	32
9 Th	0027	1.3	40		24 F	0502	0.7	22
	0621	0.5	16			1226	1.5	47
	1310	1.8	54			1930	0.8	24
	2000	0.6	18					
10 F	0144	1.3	40		25 Sa	0102	1.1	33
	0736	0.6	18			0613	0.8	25
	1416	1.7	52			1317	1.5	46
	2105	0.5	16			2019	0.7	22
11 Sa ◐	0306	1.3	41		26 Su ◐	0218	1.2	36
	0855	0.6	19			0739	0.9	26
	1522	1.6	50			1414	1.5	46
	2203	0.5	14			2106	0.6	19
12 Su	0421	1.4	44		27 M	0329	1.3	39
	1010	0.7	20			0900	0.9	26
	1623	1.6	49			1513	1.5	46
	2254	0.4	13			2152	0.5	16
13 M	0523	1.5	47		28 Tu	0429	1.4	44
	1118	0.7	20			1011	0.8	24
	1718	1.6	48			1609	1.5	46
	2339	0.4	12			2236	0.4	13
14 Tu	0616	1.6	50		29 W	0521	1.6	49
	1217	0.7	20			1113	0.7	22
	1806	1.5	46			1703	1.5	45
						2320	0.3	10
15 W	0020	0.4	11		30 Th	0610	1.7	53
	0702	1.7	53			1210	0.7	20
	1311	0.7	20			1754	1.5	45
	1849	1.4	44					

December

Day	Time (h m)	Height (ft)	Height (cm)		Day	Time (h m)	Height (ft)	Height (cm)
1 F	0004	0.2	7		16 Sa	0053	0.2	7
	0657	1.9	57			0803	1.6	48
	1304	0.6	18			1437	0.6	19
	1844	1.4	44			1932	1.0	31
2 Sa	0048	0.1	4		17 Su	0121	0.3	8
	0743	1.9	59			0834	1.6	48
	1357	0.5	16			1513	0.6	19
	1933	1.4	43			2005	1.0	30
3 Su O	0134	0.1	3		18 M ●	0147	0.3	9
	0830	2.0	60			0904	1.5	47
	1449	0.5	15			1543	0.6	19
	2023	1.3	41			2037	1.0	29
4 M	0220	0.1	2		19 Tu	0214	0.3	10
	0917	2.0	60			0932	1.5	47
	1542	0.4	13			1611	0.6	19
	2115	1.3	39			2111	0.9	28
5 Tu	0309	0.1	3		20 W	0242	0.4	11
	1006	1.9	58			1001	1.5	46
	1638	0.4	12			1641	0.6	18
	2210	1.2	37			2149	0.9	28
6 W	0402	0.2	5		21 Th	0316	0.4	12
	1057	1.8	55			1033	1.5	45
	1736	0.4	12			1715	0.6	17
	2310	1.2	36			2235	0.9	28
7 Th	0500	0.3	8		22 F	0357	0.4	13
	1149	1.7	52			1109	1.4	44
	1836	0.4	11			1754	0.5	16
						2329	1.0	29
8 F	0017	1.1	34		23 Sa	0450	0.5	15
	0604	0.4	11			1150	1.4	43
	1245	1.6	48			1839	0.5	14
	1937	0.3	10					
9 Sa	0132	1.1	35		24 Su	0032	1.0	30
	0717	0.5	14			0555	0.6	17
	1344	1.5	45			1238	1.4	42
	2036	0.3	8			1928	0.4	12
10 Su ◑	0251	1.2	36		25 M	0141	1.1	33
	0835	0.5	16			0712	0.6	18
	1445	1.4	42			1331	1.3	40
	2131	0.2	7			2019	0.3	10
11 M	0405	1.3	39		26 Tu ◑	0251	1.2	36
	0952	0.6	17			0832	0.6	19
	1545	1.3	39			1430	1.3	39
	2221	0.2	6			2111	0.2	7
12 Tu	0509	1.4	42		27 W	0357	1.3	40
	1104	0.6	18			0947	0.6	18
	1641	1.2	37			1531	1.2	38
	2306	0.2	6			2201	0.1	4
13 W	0602	1.4	44		28 Th	0456	1.4	44
	1208	0.6	18			1055	0.6	17
	1731	1.2	36			1631	1.2	37
	2346	0.2	6			2252	0.0	1
14 Th	0647	1.5	46		29 F	0551	1.6	48
	1304	0.6	18			1157	0.5	15
	1816	1.1	34			1729	1.2	36
						2341	0.0	- 1
15 F	0022	0.2	7		30 Sa	0642	1.7	52
	0727	1.6	48			1254	0.4	12
	1354	0.6	19			1825	1.2	36
	1856	1.1	33					
					31 Su	0030	- 0.1	- 3
						0730	1.7	53
						1349	0.3	10
						1919	1.1	35

Time meridian 75° E. 0000 is midnight. 1200 is noon. Times are not adjusted for Daylight Saving Time.
Heights are referred to the chart datum of soundings.

Moa, Holguin, Cuba 2017
Times and Heights of High and Low Waters

January

Day	Time	ft	cm	Day	Time	ft	cm
1 Su	0318	0.2	7	**16** M	0433	-0.1	-3
	1002	2.4	72		1103	2.0	62
	1630	0.4	13		1725	-0.1	-2
	2213	1.6	49		2335	1.6	49
2 M	0407	0.2	7	**17** Tu	0527	0.1	2
	1046	2.3	69		1151	1.9	57
	1712	0.4	11		1813	0.0	-1
	2308	1.7	52				
3 Tu	0502	0.3	9	**18** W	0034	1.6	49
	1134	2.2	66		0626	0.3	8
	1758	0.3	8		1241	1.7	51
					1902	0.0	1
4 W	0007	1.8	55	**19** Th	0135	1.6	49
	0603	0.3	10		0730	0.4	13
	1226	2.1	63		1331	1.5	47
	1847	0.2	6		1652	0.1	3
5 Th	0110	1.9	58	**20** F	0236	1.7	51
	0710	0.4	12		0839	0.6	17
	1321	2.0	60		1423	1.4	44
	1940	0.1	4		2041	0.2	5
6 F	0214	2.1	63	**21** Sa	0334	1.8	54
	0821	0.4	13		0950	0.7	20
	1419	1.9	57		1515	1.3	41
	2036	0.0	1		2128	0.2	7
7 Sa	0317	2.2	68	**22** Su	0427	1.9	57
	0932	0.4	13		1054	0.7	20
	1518	1.8	55		1605	1.3	40
	2132	-0.1	-2		2213	0.3	8
8 Su	0417	2.4	73	**23** M	0512	2.0	60
	1039	0.4	11		1146	0.7	20
	1616	1.8	54		1652	1.3	40
	2228	-0.2	-6		2254	0.3	8
9 M	0515	2.6	78	**24** Tu	0553	2.1	63
	1140	0.3	9		1227	0.6	19
	1713	1.7	53		1735	1.3	40
	2322	-0.3	-9		2334	0.2	7
10 Tu	0609	2.6	80	**25** W	0629	2.1	65
	1236	0.2	6		1302	0.6	17
	1809	1.7	53		1815	1.3	41
11 W	0016	-0.4	-11	**26** Th	0013	0.2	5
	0702	2.7	81		0705	2.2	67
	1328	0.1	3		1335	0.5	15
	1903	1.7	53		1854	1.4	42
12 Th	0107	-0.4	-13	**27** F	0053	0.1	3
	0752	2.7	81		0740	2.2	68
	1417	0.0	1		1407	0.4	12
	1956	1.7	52		1935	1.4	44
13 F	0159	-0.4	-13	**28** Sa	0134	0.0	0
	0841	2.6	78		0817	2.2	68
	1505	0.0	-1		1441	0.3	9
	2049	1.7	52		2017	1.5	46
14 Sa	0249	-0.4	-11	**29** Su	0218	-0.1	-2
	0929	2.4	74		0856	2.2	67
	1552	-0.1	-2		1517	0.2	6
	2143	1.7	51		2103	1.6	49
15 Su	0341	-0.3	-8	**30** M	0305	-0.1	-3
	1016	2.2	68		0937	2.1	65
	1638	-0.1	-3		1556	0.1	2
	2238	1.6	50		2152	1.7	51
				31 Tu	0354	-0.1	-2
					1020	2.0	62
					1637	0.0	0
					2245	1.7	53

February

Day	Time	ft	cm	Day	Time	ft	cm
1 W	0448	0.0	-1	**16** Th	0000	1.6	49
	1107	1.9	58		0559	0.3	8
	1723	-0.1	-3		1204	1.5	45
	2342	1.9	58		1815	0.1	2
2 Th	0547	0.1	2	**17** F	0056	1.6	49
	1158	1.8	54		0658	0.4	13
	1812	-0.1	-4		1251	1.3	41
					1900	0.2	5
3 F	0044	1.9	58	**18** Sa	0152	1.6	49
	0652	0.1	4		0803	0.6	17
	1253	1.7	51		1342	1.2	38
	1907	-0.2	-5		1948	0.3	8
4 Sa	0148	2.0	61	**19** Su	0249	1.7	51
	0801	0.2	7		0913	0.7	20
	1353	1.6	49		1435	1.2	37
	2006	-0.2	-7		2037	0.3	10
5 Su	0254	2.1	65	**20** M	0343	1.8	54
	0913	0.2	7		1018	0.7	21
	1455	1.5	47		1528	1.2	37
	2107	-0.3	-8		2128	0.4	11
6 M	0357	2.2	68	**21** Tu	0431	1.9	57
	1021	0.2	6		1109	0.7	21
	1557	1.5	47		1618	1.2	38
	2208	-0.3	-10		2216	0.4	11
7 Tu	0457	2.3	71	**22** W	0514	2.0	60
	1123	0.1	4		1148	0.6	19
	1658	1.6	48		1705	1.3	41
	2307	-0.4	-12		2303	0.3	9
8 W	0554	2.4	73	**23** Th	0554	2.1	63
	1219	0.1	2		1223	0.6	17
	1758	1.6	50		1748	1.4	44
					2349	0.2	6
9 Th	0004	-0.4	-13	**24** F	0632	2.1	65
	0646	2.4	74		1256	0.5	14
	1309	0.0	-1		1830	1.6	48
	1851	1.7	51				
10 F	0057	-0.5	-14	**25** Sa	0034	0.1	3
	0736	2.4	73		0710	2.2	67
	1356	-0.1	-3		1330	0.3	10
	1944	1.7	53		1913	1.7	52
11 Sa	0149	-0.4	-13	**26** Su	0119	0.0	0
	0823	2.3	70		0749	2.2	67
	1441	-0.2	-5		1405	0.2	6
	2035	1.7	53		1957	1.8	56
12 Su	0238	-0.4	-11	**27** M	0206	-0.1	-2
	0908	2.2	66		0829	2.1	65
	1524	-0.2	-5		1442	0.1	3
	2126	1.7	53		2043	1.9	59
13 M	0327	-0.3	-8	**28** Tu	0253	-0.1	-3
	0952	2.0	61		0911	2.1	63
	1607	-0.2	-5		1521	0.0	-1
	2216	1.7	52		2131	2.0	61
14 Tu	0416	-0.1	-3				
	1036	1.8	55				
	1649	-0.1	-4				
	2308	1.6	50				
15 W	0506	0.1	2				
	1119	1.6	50				
	1732	0.0	-1				

March

Day	Time	ft	cm	Day	Time	ft	cm
1 W	0343	-0.1	-3	**16** Th	0445	0.3	9
	0955	2.0	60		1045	1.6	49
	1604	-0.1	-4		1646	0.2	6
	2224	2.1	63		2323	1.9	58
2 Th	0436	0.0	-1	**17** F	0534	0.5	14
	1042	1.8	56		1127	1.5	45
	1650	-0.2	-5		1724	0.3	9
	2320	2.1	64				
3 F	0534	0.0	1	**18** Sa	0012	1.8	56
	1134	1.7	53		0626	0.6	19
	1741	-0.2	-6		1211	1.4	42
					1805	0.4	13
4 Sa	0020	2.1	65	**19** Su	0103	1.8	56
	0636	0.2	5		0725	0.8	23
	1230	1.6	50		1300	1.3	40
	1838	-0.2	-5		1850	0.5	16
5 Su	0125	2.2	66	**20** M	0156	1.9	57
	0744	0.2	7		0828	0.8	25
	1332	1.6	48		1356	1.3	40
	1940	-0.2	-5		1943	0.6	18
6 M	0231	2.2	67	**21** Tu	0250	1.9	59
	0855	0.3	8		0929	0.9	26
	1438	1.6	48		1453	1.4	42
	2046	-0.1	-4		2041	0.6	19
7 Tu	0336	2.3	69	**22** W	0342	2.0	61
	1002	0.3	8		1019	0.8	25
	1544	1.6	49		1548	1.5	45
	2152	-0.2	-5		2140	0.6	19
8 W	0438	2.3	71	**23** Th	0430	2.1	64
	1103	0.2	6		1100	0.8	23
	1647	1.7	52		1637	1.6	50
	2255	-0.2	-6		2236	0.6	17
9 Th	0534	2.4	72	**24** F	0514	2.2	67
	1157	0.1	4		1138	0.7	21
	1745	1.8	56		1724	1.8	55
	2354	-0.2	-6		2328	0.4	13
10 F	0627	2.4	72	**25** Sa	0557	2.3	69
	1245	0.1	2		1214	0.6	17
	1839	1.9	59		1808	2.0	61
11 Sa	0048	-0.2	-6	**26** Su	0018	0.3	10
	0715	2.3	70		0638	2.3	70
	1330	0.0	0		1251	0.4	13
	1930	2.0	61		1853	2.2	66
12 Su	0139	-0.2	-5	**27** M	0106	0.2	5
	0800	2.2	68		0720	2.3	69
	1412	0.0	-1		1329	0.3	8
	2019	2.0	62		1938	2.3	71
13 M	0227	-0.1	-3	**28** Tu	0154	0.1	4
	0843	2.1	64		0802	2.2	68
	1452	0.0	-1		1408	0.1	4
	2105	2.0	62		2025	2.5	75
14 Tu	0313	0.0	0	**29** W	0242	0.1	3
	0925	1.9	59		0845	2.1	65
	1531	0.0	1		1450	0.0	1
	2151	2.0	61		2113	2.5	77
15 W	0359	0.2	5	**30** Th	0333	0.1	3
	1005	1.8	54		0931	2.0	62
	1609	0.1	3		1534	0.0	-1
	2237	1.9	59		2205	2.5	77
				31 F	0425	0.1	4
					1019	1.9	59
					1622	-0.1	-2
					2300	2.5	77

Time meridian 75° E. 0000 is midnight. 1200 is noon. Times are not adjusted for Daylight Saving Time.
Heights are referred to the chart datum of soundings.

Moa, Holguin, Cuba 2017

Times and Heights of High and Low Waters

April

Day	Time (h m)	ft	cm
1 Sa	0521	0.2	7
	1139	1.8	56
	1714	0.0	-1
	2359	2.5	75
2 Su	0622	0.3	9
	1212	1.7	53
	1813	0.0	1
3 M ◑	0102	2.4	74
	0728	0.4	11
	1317	1.7	53
	1918	0.1	3
4 Tu	0208	2.4	73
	0836	0.4	12
	1426	1.8	54
	2028	0.2	5
5 W	0313	2.4	73
	0940	0.4	12
	1533	1.9	57
	2138	0.2	6
6 Th	0414	2.4	73
	1039	0.3	10
	1636	2.0	62
	2244	0.2	6
7 F	0511	2.4	73
	1130	0.3	9
	1734	2.2	66
	2344	0.2	6
8 Sa	0602	2.4	72
	1217	0.2	7
	1826	2.3	70
9 Su	0038	0.2	7
	0650	2.3	71
	1300	0.2	7
	1915	2.4	73
10 M	0128	0.3	8
	0733	2.2	68
	1339	0.2	7
	2000	2.4	74
11 Tu ○	0214	0.3	10
	0815	2.1	64
	1417	0.2	7
	2043	2.4	74
12 W	0259	0.4	12
	0854	2.0	60
	1452	0.3	9
	2124	2.4	72
13 Th	0342	0.5	15
	0932	1.8	56
	1527	0.4	12
	2205	2.3	70
14 F	0425	0.6	19
	1010	1.7	52
	1601	0.5	15
	2246	2.3	69
15 Sa	0509	0.7	22
	1049	1.6	48
	1635	0.6	18
	2328	2.2	67
16 Su	0556	0.9	26
	1132	1.5	46
	1713	0.7	21
17 M	0014	2.2	66
	0647	0.9	28
	1221	1.5	45
	1758	0.8	24
18 Tu	0104	2.2	66
	0742	1.0	29
	1319	1.5	47
	1854	0.9	26
19 W ◐	0157	2.2	67
	0836	1.0	30
	1419	1.6	50
	1959	0.9	27
20 Th	0251	2.2	68
	0926	1.0	29
	1517	1.8	55
	2107	0.9	27
21 F	0344	2.3	70
	1011	0.9	26
	1610	2.0	61
	2210	0.8	25
22 Sa	0433	2.3	71
	1053	0.8	23
	1659	2.2	68
	2308	0.7	21
23 Su	0520	2.4	72
	1134	0.6	19
	1747	2.5	75
24 M	0001	0.6	18
	0606	2.4	72
	1214	0.5	14
	1834	2.7	81
25 Tu	0052	0.5	14
	0650	2.3	71
	1255	0.3	9
	1920	2.8	85
26 W ●	0142	0.4	11
	0735	2.3	70
	1338	0.2	5
	2008	2.9	88
27 Th	0232	0.3	10
	0821	2.2	67
	1422	0.1	2
	2057	2.9	89
28 F	0322	0.3	10
	0909	2.1	64
	1509	0.0	1
	2149	2.9	88
29 Sa	0414	0.3	10
	1000	2.0	61
	1559	0.1	2
	2243	2.8	86
30 Su	0510	0.4	12
	1056	1.9	59
	1653	0.1	4
	2340	2.7	83

May

Day	Time (h m)	ft	cm
1 M	0608	0.4	13
	1158	1.9	57
	1753	0.2	7
2 Tu	0041	2.6	80
	0710	0.5	14
	1304	1.9	58
	1859	0.4	11
3 W ◐	0143	2.5	77
	0813	0.5	15
	1414	2.0	60
	2011	0.5	14
4 Th	0246	2.5	75
	0914	0.5	14
	1521	2.1	64
	2123	0.5	16
5 F	0346	2.4	73
	1010	0.5	14
	1623	2.3	69
	2231	0.6	17
6 Sa	0442	2.4	72
	1100	0.4	13
	1720	2.4	74
	2331	0.6	17
7 Su	0533	2.3	71
	1146	0.4	12
	1811	2.6	78
8 M	0026	0.6	18
	0620	2.3	69
	1227	0.4	12
	1857	2.7	81
9 Tu	0115	0.6	19
	0703	2.2	66
	1305	0.4	13
	1940	2.7	82
10 W	0200	0.7	20
	0743	2.1	63
	1341	0.5	14
	2020	2.7	81
11 Th ○	0243	0.7	22
	0821	1.9	59
	1421	0.5	16
	2057	2.6	80
12 F	0324	0.8	24
	0858	1.9	58
	1447	0.6	17
	2134	2.6	79
13 Sa	0404	0.9	26
	0934	1.7	53
	1519	0.7	20
	2211	2.5	77
14 Su	0444	0.9	27
	1012	1.7	51
	1553	0.7	22
	2250	2.5	75
15 M	0525	1.0	29
	1055	1.6	50
	1632	0.8	24
	2332	2.4	74
16 Tu	0610	1.0	30
	1146	1.6	50
	1719	0.9	27
17 W	0019	2.4	73
	0657	1.0	30
	1244	1.7	52
	1818	1.0	29
18 Th	0111	2.4	72
	0746	1.0	29
	1345	1.8	56
	1926	1.0	30
19 F ◐	0205	2.4	72
	0836	0.9	28
	1445	2.0	62
	2037	1.0	30
20 Sa	0300	2.4	72
	0924	0.8	25
	1542	2.3	69
	2145	0.9	28
21 Su	0353	2.4	72
	1011	0.7	21
	1635	2.5	77
	2247	0.8	25
22 M	0444	2.4	72
	1056	0.6	17
	1726	2.8	84
	2345	0.7	22
23 Tu	0534	2.3	71
	1142	0.4	12
	1815	2.9	89
24 W	0038	0.6	19
	0622	2.3	70
	1227	0.3	8
	1904	3.1	93
25 Th	0130	0.5	16
	0710	2.3	69
	1313	0.1	4
	1954	3.1	95
26 F ●	0220	0.5	14
	0759	2.2	66
	1401	0.1	2
	2043	3.1	95
27 Sa	0311	0.4	13
	0850	2.1	64
	1449	0.0	1
	2134	3.1	93
28 Su	0402	0.4	12
	0944	2.0	62
	1541	0.1	3
	2227	3.0	90
29 M	0455	0.4	13
	1041	2.0	61
	1636	0.2	6
	2322	2.8	85
30 Tu	0551	0.4	13
	1144	2.0	60
	1736	0.3	10
31 W	0018	2.7	81
	0648	0.5	14
	1250	2.0	61
	1841	0.5	15

June

Day	Time (h m)	ft	cm
1 Th ◐	0117	2.5	76
	0746	0.5	14
	1357	2.1	63
	1952	0.6	19
2 F	0216	2.4	73
	0843	0.5	14
	1504	2.2	67
	2104	0.7	22
3 Sa	0313	2.3	70
	0937	0.5	14
	1605	2.4	72
	2213	0.8	24
4 Su	0409	2.2	68
	1027	0.5	14
	1701	2.5	76
	2316	0.8	25
5 M	0500	2.2	66
	1112	0.5	14
	1752	2.6	80
6 Tu	0012	0.9	26
	0547	2.1	64
	1153	0.5	15
	1837	2.7	82
7 W	0101	0.9	26
	0631	2.0	61
	1231	0.5	16
	1917	2.7	83
8 Th	0145	0.9	27
	0711	1.9	59
	1306	0.6	17
	1955	2.8	84
9 F ○	0225	0.9	27
	0748	1.9	57
	1339	0.6	18
	2030	2.7	83
10 Sa	0303	0.9	28
	0824	1.8	55
	1412	0.6	19
	2105	2.7	82
11 Su	0339	0.9	28
	0900	1.7	53
	1446	0.7	20
	2140	2.7	81
12 M	0415	0.9	28
	0939	1.7	52
	1523	0.7	21
	2217	2.6	79
13 Tu	0452	0.9	27
	1023	1.7	53
	1605	0.7	22
	2258	2.5	77
14 W	0532	0.9	27
	1114	1.8	54
	1655	0.8	24
	2342	2.5	75
15 Th	0615	0.9	26
	1211	1.9	57
	1753	0.9	26
16 F	0032	2.4	74
	0701	0.8	25
	1312	2.0	62
	1859	0.9	28
17 Sa ◐	0125	2.4	72
	0751	0.8	23
	1414	2.2	67
	2010	1.0	29
18 Su	0221	2.3	70
	0842	0.7	20
	1513	2.4	74
	2121	0.9	28
19 M	0317	2.3	69
	0933	0.5	16
	1611	2.7	81
	2227	0.9	26
20 Tu	0412	2.2	68
	1024	0.4	12
	1706	2.9	87
	2328	0.8	24
21 W	0505	2.2	68
	1114	0.3	8
	1758	3.0	92
22 Th	0024	0.7	21
	0558	2.2	67
	1204	0.1	4
	1850	3.1	95
23 F	0117	0.6	18
	0650	2.2	66
	1254	0.1	2
	1940	3.1	96
24 Sa ●	0208	0.5	15
	0742	2.1	65
	1345	0.0	0
	2030	3.1	95
25 Su	0257	0.4	13
	0835	2.1	64
	1436	0.0	0
	2120	3.1	93
26 M	0347	0.4	12
	0930	2.1	63
	1528	0.1	3
	2211	2.9	88
27 Tu	0437	0.4	11
	1027	2.1	63
	1622	0.2	6
	2302	2.7	83
28 W	0527	0.4	11
	1127	2.0	62
	1720	0.4	11
	2354	2.6	78
29 Th	0620	0.4	12
	1230	2.1	63
	1822	0.6	17
30 F	0048	2.4	73
	0713	0.4	13
	1335	2.1	65
	1929	0.7	22

Time meridian 75° E. 0000 is midnight. 1200 is noon. Times are not adjusted for Daylight Saving Time.
Heights are referred to the chart datum of soundings.

Moa, Holguin, Cuba 2017

Times and Heights of High and Low Waters

July

Day	Time	ft	cm	Day	Time	ft	cm
1 Sa ☽	0143	2.2	68	**16** Su	0051	2.3	71
	0807	0.5	14		0710	0.6	18
	1440	2.2	68		1343	2.4	73
	2041	0.9	26		1947	0.9	27
2 Su	0239	2.1	65	**17** M ☾	0147	2.2	68
	0900	0.5	15		0804	0.5	16
	1541	2.3	71		1446	2.6	78
	2152	1.0	29		2058	0.9	28
3 M	0333	2.0	62	**18** Tu	0246	2.2	67
	0951	0.5	16		0900	0.4	13
	1638	2.5	75		1547	2.8	84
	2258	1.0	30		2207	0.9	27
4 Tu	0426	2.0	60	**19** W	0345	2.2	66
	1037	0.6	17		0957	0.3	10
	1729	2.6	78		1646	2.9	89
	2355	1.0	31		2311	0.8	25
5 W	0514	1.9	59	**20** Th	0443	2.2	66
	1119	0.6	18		1053	0.2	7
	1813	2.7	81		1742	3.1	93
6 Th	0044	1.0	31	**21** F	0008	0.7	22
	0559	1.9	57		0540	2.2	67
	1158	0.6	19		1148	0.1	4
	1852	2.7	82		1835	3.1	95
7 F	0125	1.0	31	**22** Sa	0101	0.6	19
	0639	1.9	57		0635	2.2	67
	1234	0.7	20		1241	0.1	2
	1928	2.7	83		1926	3.1	96
8 Sa	0202	1.0	30	**23** Su ●	0151	0.5	16
	0717	1.8	56		0729	2.2	68
	1309	0.7	20		1334	0.1	2
	2002	2.7	83		2016	3.1	94
9 Su ○	0235	1.0	29	**24** M	0239	0.5	14
	0753	1.8	56		0822	2.3	69
	1344	0.6	19		1425	0.1	3
	2036	2.7	83		2104	3.0	91
10 M	0307	0.9	28	**25** Tu	0325	0.4	13
	0831	1.8	56		0916	2.3	69
	1421	0.6	19		1517	0.2	5
	2110	2.7	82		2152	2.8	86
11 Tu	0340	0.9	27	**26** W	0412	0.4	12
	0911	1.9	57		1011	2.2	68
	1502	0.6	19		1610	0.3	9
	2147	2.7	81		2239	2.7	81
12 W	0415	0.8	25	**27** Th	0458	0.4	12
	0955	1.9	59		1107	2.2	68
	1547	0.7	20		1704	0.5	14
	2227	2.6	79		2326	2.5	75
13 Th	0453	0.8	23	**28** F	0546	0.4	13
	1045	2.0	61		1205	2.2	68
	1638	0.7	21		1802	0.7	20
	2311	2.5	76				
14 F	0534	0.7	22	**29** Sa	0017	2.3	70
	1141	2.1	64		0635	0.5	15
	1735	0.8	23		1305	2.2	68
	2359	2.4	73		1905	0.9	26
15 Sa	0620	0.7	20	**30** Su ☽	0109	2.1	65
	1241	2.2	68		0726	0.6	18
	1838	0.9	26		1408	2.3	70
					2014	1.0	31
				31 M	0203	2.0	62
					0818	0.7	20
					1510	2.4	72
					2126	1.1	34

August

Day	Time	ft	cm	Day	Time	ft	cm
1 Tu	0258	1.9	59	**16** W	0222	2.2	68
	0910	0.7	22		0833	0.5	16
	1607	2.5	75		1524	2.9	88
	2235	1.2	36		2148	1.0	30
2 W	0352	1.9	58	**17** Th	0325	2.2	68
	0959	0.8	24		0935	0.5	14
	1659	2.6	78		1626	3.0	92
	2333	1.2	36		2252	0.9	28
3 Th	0443	1.9	58	**18** F	0427	2.3	70
	1044	0.8	25		1037	0.4	12
	1743	2.6	80		1725	3.1	94
					2350	0.8	25
4 F	0020	1.2	36	**19** Sa	0527	2.4	72
	0529	1.9	58		1136	0.3	10
	1126	0.9	26		1819	3.1	96
	1822	2.7	82				
5 Sa	0057	1.2	36	**20** Su	0042	0.8	23
	0610	1.9	59		0623	2.4	74
	1205	0.8	25		1232	0.3	9
	1857	2.8	84		1910	3.1	95
6 Su	0128	1.1	34	**21** M ●	0130	0.7	20
	0648	2.0	61		0717	2.5	77
	1244	0.8	24		1325	0.3	8
	1931	2.8	85		1958	3.1	94
7 M ○	0159	1.1	33	**22** Tu	0215	0.6	18
	0726	2.1	63		0809	2.6	78
	1323	0.7	22		1416	0.3	10
	2005	2.8	85		2044	3.0	90
8 Tu	0229	1.0	30	**23** W	0259	0.5	16
	0805	2.1	65		0900	2.6	79
	1404	0.7	21		1506	0.4	12
	2041	2.8	85		2129	2.8	85
9 W	0301	0.9	28	**24** Th	0342	0.5	16
	0846	2.2	68		0951	2.6	78
	1447	0.7	20		1556	0.5	16
	2119	2.7	83		2214	2.6	80
10 Th	0336	0.8	25	**25** F	0425	0.6	17
	0931	2.3	70		1043	2.5	77
	1534	0.7	20		1647	0.7	22
	2159	2.7	81		2259	2.5	75
11 F	0414	0.7	22	**26** Sa	0508	0.6	19
	1020	2.4	73		1136	2.5	76
	1624	0.7	21		1741	0.9	27
	2242	2.6	78		2345	2.3	69
12 Sa	0458	0.7	20	**27** Su	0553	0.7	22
	1114	2.5	76		1232	2.5	75
	1719	0.8	23		1839	1.1	33
	2330	2.5	75				
13 Su	0543	0.6	19	**28** M	0034	2.1	65
	1212	2.6	79		0640	0.9	26
	1821	0.9	26		1330	2.5	75
					1944	1.2	38
14 M	0022	2.4	72	**29** Tu ☾	0127	2.0	62
	0634	0.6	18		0730	1.0	30
	1315	2.7	81		1429	2.5	76
	1927	1.0	29		2056	1.3	41
15 Tu ☾	0120	2.3	69	**30** W	0223	2.0	60
	0731	0.6	17		0823	1.1	33
	1420	2.8	85		1527	2.5	77
	2038	1.0	30		2205	1.4	43
				31 Th	0320	2.0	60
					0916	1.1	35
					1619	2.6	80
					2301	1.4	43

September

Day	Time	ft	cm	Day	Time	ft	cm
1 F	0413	2.0	61	**16** Sa	0416	2.5	76
	1007	1.1	35		1025	0.7	20
	1704	2.7	83		1704	3.1	96
	2343	1.4	43		2327	1.0	29
2 Sa	0500	2.1	64	**17** Su	0517	2.6	80
	1055	1.1	35		1126	0.6	19
	1744	2.8	85		1759	3.1	96
3 Su	0016	1.3	41	**18** M	0017	0.9	26
	0542	2.2	67		0613	2.8	84
	1139	1.1	33		1223	0.6	18
	1821	2.9	87		1849	3.1	95
4 M	0046	1.3	39	**19** Tu	0103	0.8	24
	0622	2.3	71		0705	2.9	87
	1222	1.0	31		1316	0.6	18
	1857	2.9	88		1936	3.1	93
5 Tu	0117	1.2	37	**20** W ●	0147	0.7	22
	0701	2.5	75		0755	2.9	89
	1305	0.9	28		1406	0.6	19
	1924	2.9	88		2020	2.9	89
6 W ○	0148	1.1	33	**21** Th	0228	0.7	21
	0741	2.6	79		0843	3.0	90
	1349	0.9	26		1455	0.7	22
	2011	2.9	88		2104	2.8	84
7 Th	0222	1.0	30	**22** F	0309	0.7	22
	0823	2.7	83		0930	2.9	89
	1434	0.8	24		1542	0.9	26
	2050	2.8	86		2146	2.6	79
8 F	0259	0.9	26	**23** Sa	0348	0.8	24
	0909	2.8	86		1017	2.9	87
	1522	0.8	24		1631	1.0	30
	2131	2.7	83		2229	2.4	74
9 Sa	0338	0.8	23	**24** Su	0428	0.9	26
	0958	2.9	88		1105	2.8	85
	1612	0.8	25		1720	1.1	35
	2216	2.6	80		2312	2.3	69
10 Su	0422	0.7	21	**25** M	0508	1.0	30
	1051	2.9	89		1155	2.7	83
	1706	0.9	27		1814	1.3	39
	2304	2.5	77		2359	2.2	66
11 M	0510	0.7	20	**26** Tu	0551	1.1	34
	1148	3.0	90		1247	2.7	81
	1806	1.0	29		1913	1.4	43
	2359	2.4	74				
12 Tu	0604	0.7	20	**27** W	0051	2.1	63
	1250	3.0	91		0637	1.2	38
	1911	1.0	32		1341	2.7	81
					2018	1.5	46
13 W ☾	0059	2.4	72	**28** Th ☾	0148	2.0	62
	0704	0.7	21		0730	1.3	41
	1356	3.0	92		1436	2.7	81
	2020	1.1	33		2121	1.5	47
14 Th	0204	2.4	72	**29** F	0247	2.1	63
	0810	0.7	21		0828	1.4	43
	1502	3.1	93		1528	2.7	83
	2129	1.1	33		2213	1.5	47
15 F	0311	2.4	73	**30** Sa	0342	2.2	66
	0918	0.7	21		0928	1.4	44
	1605	3.1	94		1616	2.8	85
	2232	1.0	31		2252	1.5	46

Time meridian 75° E. 0000 is midnight. 1200 is noon. Times are not adjusted for Daylight Saving Time.
Heights are referred to the chart datum of soundings.

Moa, Holguin, Cuba 2017

Times and Heights of High and Low Waters

October

Day	Time	ft	cm	Day	Time	ft	cm
1 Su	0431	2.3	71	16 M	0506	2.8	86
	1023	1.4	42		1116	0.8	25
	1700	2.9	87		1734	3.0	91
	2327	1.4	44		2349	0.9	26
2 M	0514	2.5	76	17 Tu	0601	3.0	90
	1114	1.3	40		1214	0.8	25
	1741	2.9	88		1823	3.0	90
3 Tu	0000	1.3	41	18 W	0034	0.8	24
	0556	2.7	81		0651	3.1	94
	1202	1.2	36		1306	0.8	25
	1820	2.9	89		1910	2.9	87
4 W	0033	1.2	37	19 Th	0116	0.8	23
	0637	2.9	87		0739	3.1	95
	1249	1.1	33		1356	0.9	26
	1900	2.9	89		1953	2.7	83
5 Th O	0108	1.1	33	20 F ●	0156	0.8	23
	0719	3.0	92		0824	3.1	95
	1335	1.0	30		1443	0.9	28
	1940	2.9	88		2035	2.6	79
6 F	0145	1.0	29	21 Sa	0234	0.8	24
	0803	3.1	96		0908	3.1	94
	1422	0.9	28		1528	1.0	31
	2021	2.8	86		2116	2.4	74
7 Sa	0225	0.8	25	22 Su	0311	0.9	26
	0849	3.2	98		0951	3.0	91
	1510	0.9	27		1614	1.1	34
	2105	2.7	83		2157	2.3	69
8 Su	0307	0.7	22	23 M	0348	1.0	29
	0939	3.3	100		1033	2.9	89
	1601	0.9	27		1700	1.2	37
	2151	2.6	79		2239	2.1	65
9 M	0352	0.7	20	24 Tu	0424	1.1	33
	1031	3.2	99		1117	2.8	86
	1655	0.9	28		1748	1.3	40
	2242	2.5	76		2324	2.0	62
10 Tu	0443	0.7	20	25 W	0502	1.2	36
	1128	3.2	98		1202	2.7	83
	1753	1.0	30		1840	1.4	43
	2340	2.4	74				
11 W	0539	0.7	22	26 Th	0014	2.0	61
	1229	3.1	96		0546	1.3	40
	1855	1.0	32		1251	2.7	82
					1934	1.4	44
12 Th ☽	0043	2.4	73	27 F	0111	2.0	61
	0642	0.8	24		0638	1.4	43
	1333	3.1	95		1342	2.7	81
	2001	1.1	33		2027	1.5	45
13 F	0152	2.4	74	28 Sa ☽	0211	2.1	63
	0752	0.8	25		0741	1.5	45
	1438	3.1	94		1434	2.7	81
	2107	1.0	32		2115	1.4	44
14 Sa	0300	2.5	76	29 Su	0307	2.2	67
	0904	0.9	26		0848	1.5	45
	1541	3.1	93		1525	2.7	82
	2207	1.0	30		2157	1.4	42
15 Su	0406	2.7	81	30 M	0358	2.4	73
	1013	0.9	26		0951	1.4	43
	1640	3.0	92		1613	2.7	83
	2301	0.9	28		2236	1.3	39
				31 Tu	0445	2.6	80
					1049	1.3	40
					1659	2.8	84
					2314	1.1	35

November

Day	Time	ft	cm	Day	Time	ft	cm
1 W	0530	2.8	86	16 Th	0003	0.6	18
	1142	1.2	36		0635	3.0	91
	1743	2.8	84		1255	0.9	26
	2353	1.0	31		1841	2.4	74
2 Th	0614	3.0	92	17 F	0045	0.6	18
	1232	1.0	32		0721	3.0	92
	1826	2.7	83		1344	0.9	26
					1925	2.3	71
3 F	0032	0.9	26	18 Sa ●	0124	0.6	18
	0659	3.2	97		0804	3.0	92
	1321	1.0	29		1430	0.9	27
	1910	2.7	81		2006	2.2	67
4 Sa O	0113	0.7	21	19 Su	0201	0.7	20
	0745	3.3	101		0845	3.0	90
	1410	0.9	26		1513	1.0	29
	1954	2.6	79		2046	2.1	63
5 Su	0156	0.6	17	20 M	0236	0.7	22
	0833	3.3	102		0908	2.9	87
	1459	0.8	24		1556	1.0	30
	2041	2.5	76		2125	1.9	59
6 M	0241	0.5	15	21 Tu	0310	0.8	24
	0922	3.3	102		1002	2.8	84
	1550	0.8	24		1637	1.0	32
	2131	2.4	73		2205	1.8	56
7 Tu	0330	0.5	14	22 W	0345	0.9	27
	1015	3.3	100		1041	2.7	82
	1643	0.8	24		1719	1.1	33
	2225	2.3	71		2249	1.8	54
8 W	0422	0.5	15	23 Th	0422	1.0	29
	1110	3.2	97		1121	2.6	79
	1739	0.8	24		1802	1.1	34
	2325	2.3	69		2337	1.8	54
9 Th	0520	0.6	17	24 F	0505	1.0	32
	1209	3.1	93		1205	2.5	77
	1838	0.8	25		1846	1.1	34
10 F	0030	2.3	69	25 Sa	0032	1.8	55
	0625	0.7	20		0558	1.1	34
	1310	2.9	89		1252	2.5	75
	1940	0.8	25		1932	1.1	34
11 Sa ☽	0139	2.3	70	26 Su ☽	0130	1.9	58
	0735	0.8	23		0702	1.2	36
	1412	2.8	86		1442	2.4	74
	2041	0.8	24		2018	1.0	32
12 Su	0247	2.4	74	27 M	0228	2.1	63
	0848	0.8	25		0811	1.2	36
	1513	2.8	84		1436	2.4	73
	2138	0.7	22		2103	1.0	30
13 M	0352	2.6	78	28 Tu	0323	2.3	69
	0959	0.9	26		0920	1.1	35
	1611	2.7	82		1528	2.4	72
	2231	0.7	21		2148	0.9	26
14 Tu	0452	2.7	83	29 W	0415	2.5	76
	1104	0.9	26		1024	1.0	32
	1705	2.6	80		1618	2.4	72
	2319	0.6	19		2232	0.7	22
15 W	0546	2.9	88	30 Th	0505	2.7	83
	1202	0.9	26		1122	1.0	29
	1755	2.5	77		1707	2.3	71
					2317	0.6	17

December

Day	Time	ft	cm	Day	Time	ft	cm
1 F	0553	2.9	89	16 Sa	0014	0.3	9
	1216	0.8	25		0702	2.7	81
	1755	2.3	70		1331	0.7	21
					1856	1.8	55
2 Sa	0001	0.4	12	17 Su	0053	0.3	10
	0641	3.1	93		0743	2.7	81
	1307	0.7	21		1415	0.7	21
	1843	2.3	69		1937	1.7	52
3 Su O	0047	0.3	8	18 M ●	0129	0.4	11
	0729	3.1	96		0821	2.6	79
	1357	0.6	18		1455	0.7	21
	1932	2.2	67		2016	1.6	50
4 M	0134	0.1	4	19 Tu	0204	0.4	12
	0818	3.2	97		0857	2.5	77
	1447	0.5	16		1532	0.7	21
	2022	2.1	65		2054	1.5	47
5 Tu	0222	0.1	2	20 W	0238	0.5	14
	0908	3.1	95		0932	2.5	75
	1537	0.5	14		1608	0.7	21
	2114	2.1	63		2133	1.5	46
6 W	0313	0.1	2	21 Th	0314	0.5	15
	1000	3.0	92		1008	2.4	72
	1629	0.4	13		1644	0.7	21
	2211	2.0	61		2214	1.5	45
7 Th	0407	0.1	4	22 F	0353	0.6	17
	1053	2.9	87		1045	2.3	70
	1722	0.4	12		1720	0.7	21
	2311	2.0	60		2300	1.5	46
8 F	0506	0.2	7	23 Sa	0438	0.6	18
	1148	2.7	82		1126	2.2	67
	1817	0.4	12		1759	0.7	20
					2353	1.6	48
9 Sa	0016	2.0	60	24 Su	0531	0.7	20
	0609	0.4	11		1211	2.1	65
	1246	2.5	77		1841	0.6	18
	1913	0.4	11				
10 Su ☽	0123	2.0	62	25 M	0050	1.7	52
	0718	0.5	15		0632	0.7	22
	1344	2.4	72		1300	2.0	62
	2010	0.4	11		1927	0.6	17
11 M	0230	2.1	65	26 Tu ☽	0149	1.9	57
	0830	0.6	18		0741	0.8	23
	1442	2.3	69		1353	2.0	61
	2106	0.3	10		2015	0.5	14
12 Tu	0334	2.3	69	27 W	0248	2.1	63
	0942	0.7	20		0851	0.8	23
	1539	2.1	65		1447	1.9	59
	2159	0.3	9		2105	0.4	11
13 W	0434	2.4	74	28 Th	0345	2.3	69
	1049	0.7	20		0959	0.7	21
	1634	2.1	63		1542	1.9	58
	2247	0.3	9		2156	0.2	6
14 Th	0528	2.5	77	29 F	0440	2.5	75
	1149	0.7	21		1102	0.6	18
	1724	2.0	60		1636	1.9	57
	2333	0.3	9		2247	0.1	2
15 F	0617	2.6	80	30 Sa	0533	2.5	81
	1242	0.7	21		1159	0.5	15
	1812	1.9	58		1729	1.8	56
					2337	-0.1	-2
				31 Su	0625	2.8	84
					1252	0.4	11
					1822	1.8	56

Time meridian 75° E. 0000 is midnight. 1200 is noon. Times are not adjusted for Daylight Saving Time.
Heights are referred to the chart datum of soundings.

EXTRA TIDES, 2017

Woods Hole, Massachusetts

February
	h m	ft	cm
18	958	0.5	15
19	2048	0.5	15

March
	h m	ft	cm
19	1915	0.6	18
20	2016	0.6	18
21	2113	0.5	15

April
	h m	ft	cm
17	1844	0.6	18
18	1949	0.6	18
19	2050	0.6	18

May
	h m	ft	cm
17	1926	0.7	21
18	2029	0.6	18

June
	h m	ft	cm
14	2347	2.0	61

July
	h m	ft	cm
31	2310	0.6	18

August
	h m	ft	cm
29	2235	0.6	18

September
	h m	ft	cm
27	2150	0.6	18
28	2232	0.6	18
29	2253	0.6	18

October
	h m	ft	cm
26	2040	0.5	15
27	2113	0.5	15
28	2142	0.5	15

November
	h m	ft	cm
25	2013	0.4	12
26	2055	0.3	09

December
	h m	ft	cm
25	2014	0.2	06

Rio de Janeiro, Brazil

February
	h m	ft	cm
4	2013	3.0	90
	2245	2.6	80
5	1704	1.3	40
18	2313	2.3	70
19	2300	2.6	80

March
	h m	ft	cm
4	1838	3.3	100
	2202	2.6	80
	2326	2.6	80
5	1947	2.6	80
	2154	2.6	80
6	1653	1.3	40
19	1854	3.0	90
	2223	2.3	70
20	2208	2.6	80

April
	h m	ft	cm
2	1817	3.3	100
	2117	2.6	80
	2332	2.6	80
3	1926	2.6	80
	2115	2.6	80
4	1634	1.3	40
5	1745	1.0	30
16	2313	2.3	70
17	2353	2.3	70

May
	h m	ft	cm
1	2100	2.6	80
	2311	3.0	90
2	1917	2.6	80
	2106	2.6	80
3	1606	1.3	40
30	2253	2.6	80
31	2350	2.6	80

June
	h m	ft	cm
29	2334	2.3	70

July
	h m	ft	cm
28	2345	2.0	60
30	1502	2.0	60
	1919	3.0	90

August
	h m	ft	cm
16	2113	2.6	80
	2302	2.6	80
28	2319	1.6	50
29	1921	2.6	80
30	2051	2.6	80

September
	h m	ft	cm
12	2343	2.0	60
13	1904	2.6	80
	2223	2.0	60
14	2243	2.3	70
27	1839	3.0	90
28	1945	2.6	80

October
	h m	ft	cm
11	2156	1.6	50
	2315	2.0	60
12	1845	2.6	80
	2208	2.0	60
13	2238	2.3	70
27	1902	2.6	80

November
	h m	ft	cm
9	1738	3.0	90
10	1830	3.0	90
	2221	2.0	60
	2332	2.0	60

December
	h m	ft	cm
9	1817	3.3	100
10	1923	3.0	90

Santos, Brazil

February
	h m	ft	cm
19	2208	3.3	100

March
	h m	ft	cm
5	2345	3.6	110
20	2049	3.3	100

April
	h m	ft	cm
3	2336	3.6	110
19	2239	3.3	100

May
	h m	ft	cm
2	2304	3.6	110
18	2104	3.6	110

June
	h m	ft	cm
16	1954	3.6	110
17	2124	3.3	100

July
	h m	ft	cm
15	1904	3.6	110
17	2123	3.0	90

August
	h m	ft	cm
29	2354	2.6	80

September
	h m	ft	cm
12	1813	3.0	90
13	2353	2.6	80
28	2338	3.0	90

October
	h m	ft	cm
12	2302	2.6	80
27	2234	3.0	90

November
	h m	ft	cm
10	2208	2.6	80
25	2141	3.0	90
26	2236	3.3	100

TABLE 2. — TIDAL DIFFERENCES AND OTHER CONSTANTS

EXPLANATION OF TABLE

The publication of full daily predictions is necessarily limited to a comparatively small number of stations. Tide predictions for many other places, however, can be obtained by applying certain differences to the predictions for the reference stations in Table 1. The following pages list the places called "subordinate stations" for which such predictions can be made, and the differences or ratios to be used. These differences or ratios are to be applied to the predictions for the proper reference station which is listed in Table 2 in boldface type above the differences for the subordinate station. The stations in this table are arranged in geographical order. The index to stations at the end of this volume will assist in locating a particular station.

Caution.— The time and height differences listed in Table 2 are average difference derived from comparisons of simultaneous tide observations at the subordinate location and its reference station. Because these figures are constant, they may not always provide for the daily variations of the actual tide, especially if the subordinate station is some distance from the reference station. Therefore, although the application of the time and height differences will generally provide reasonable accurate approximations, they cannot result in predictions as accurate as those listed for the reference stations which are based upon much larger periods of analyses and which do provide for daily variations.

Time differences.—To determine the time of high water or low water at any station listed in this table there is given in the columns headed "Differences, Time" the hours and minutes to be added to or subtracted from the time of high or low water at some reference station. A plus (+) sign indicates that the tide at the subordinate station is later than at the reference station and the difference should be added; a minus (–) sign indicates that it is earlier and should be subtracted.

To obtain the tide at a subordinate station on any date, apply the difference to the tide at the reference station for that same date. In some cases, however, to obtain an a.m. tide it may be necessary to use the preceding day's p.m. tide at the reference station (or to obtain a p.m. tide it may be necessary to use the following day's a.m. tide). For example, if a high water at a reference station occurs at 0200 on July 17, and the tide at the subordinate station occurs 5 hour earlier, the high water at the subordinate station will occur at 2100 on July 16. For the second case, if a high water occurs at a reference station at 2200 on July 2, and the tide at the subordinate station occurs 3 hours later, then high water will occur at 0100 on July 3 at the subordinate station. The necessary allowance for change in date when the international date line is crossed is included in the time difference. In such cases use the same date at the reference station as desired for the subordinate station as explained above.

The results obtained by the application of the time differences will be in the kind of time indicated by the time meridian shown above the name of the subordinate station. Differences in time meridians between a subordinate station and its reference station have been accounted for and no further adjustment by the reader is necessary. Summer or daylight-saving time is not used in the tide tables.

Height differences.—The height of the tide, referred to the datum of charts, is obtained by means of the height differences or ratios. A plus (+) sign indicates that the difference should be added to the height at the reference station, and a minus (–) sign indicates that it should be subtracted. All height differences, ranges, and levels in Table 2 are in feet but may be converted to centimeters by the use of Table 7.

Ratio.— For some stations, use of predicted height difference would give unsatisfactory predictions. In such cases they have been omitted and one or two ratios are given (*). Where two ratios are given, one in the "height of high water" column and one in the "height of low water" column, the high waters and low waters at the reference station should be multiplied by these respective ratios. Where only one is given, the omitted ratio is either unreliable or unknown.

TABLE 2. — TIDAL DIFFERENCES AND OTHER CONSTANTS

For some subordinate stations there is given in parentheses a ratio as well as a correction in feet. In those instances, each predicted high and low water at the reference station should first be multiplied by the ratio and then the correction in feet is added to or subtracted from each product as indicated.

As an example, at Port of Spain, Trinidad, the values in the time and height difference columns in Table 2 are given as -0 44, -1 12, and (*0.31 + 1.4) as referred to the reference station at Punta Gorda, Venezuela. If we assume that the tide predictions in column (1) below are those of Ketchikan on a particular day, application of the time and height correction in columns (2) and (3) would result in the tide predictions for Treadwell Bay in column (4).

(1)		(2)	(3)	(4)		
Time h.m.	Height ft.	Time Corrections	Height Corrections	Time h.m.	Height ft.	centimeters
0326	0.6	$-1^h 12^m$	x0.31 + 1.4	0214	1.6	49
0900	5.1	$-0^h 44^m$	x0.31 + 1.4	0816	3.0	91
1608	-0.3	$-1^h 12^m$	x0.31 + 1.4	1456	1.3	40
2148	5.4	$-0^h 44^m$	x0.31 + 1.4	2104	3.1	94

Range. —The mean range is the difference in height between mean high water (MHW) and mean low water (MLW). The *spring range* is the average semidiurnal range occurring semimonthly as a result of the Moon being new or full. It is larger than the mean range where the type of tide is either semidiurnal or mixed, and is of not practical significance where the type of tide is diurnal. Where the tide is chiefly of the diurnal type the table gives the *diurnal range*, which is the difference in height between mean higher high water and mean lower low water.

Datum. — The datum of the predictions obtained through the height differences or ratios is also the datum of the largest scale chart for the locality. To obtain the depth at the time of high or low water, the predicted height should be added to the depth on the chart unless such height is negative (–), when it should be subtracted. To find the height at times between high and low water see Table 3. On some charts the depths are given in meters or centimeters and in such cases the heights of the tide can be converted to other units by the use of Table 7. Chart datums for the portion of the world covered by these tables are approximately as follows: *Mean lower low water* for the Pacific coast of the United States, Alaska, and the Hawaiian Islands, mean low water springs for Central American and Mexico. For the rest of the area covered by these tables the datums generally used are approximately *mean low water springs, Indian spring low water*, or the *lowest possible low water*.

Mean Tide Level (Half-Tide Level). — The mean tide level is a plane midway between mean low water and mean high water. Tabular values are reckoned from chart depth.

Observations Supporting Predictions.– All tidal predictions made by the National Ocean Service are based upon observations taken at the location in question. For most reference stations these observations often are of a continuing nature. As such, they are used to quality control the predictions and to update the harmonic constants used in generating annual predictions. For subordinate stations, the age and duration of their observations vary from a few days of observation taken decades ago to the most recent survey data.

The precision with which the position, ranges and mean tide level are reported in Table 2 is an indication of the age and analytical history of the supporting observation. Stations whose position is reported to the nearest tenth minute of latitude and longitude and whose ranges and mean tide level are reported to the nearest hundredth foot are supported by the most recent observations, analyzed with regard to current chart datums and the 1983-2001 National Tidal Datum Epoch. Stations whose position is reported to the nearest tenth minute but whose ranges and mean tide level are reported to the nearest tenth foot are typically supported by observations taken in the 1960's and 1970's with analysis based upon the previous National Tidal Datum Epochs. Finally, stations whose positions are reported to the

TABLE 2. — TIDAL DIFFERENCES AND OTHER CONSTANTS

nearest minute and whose ranges and mean tide level are reported to the nearest tenth foot indicated either older supporting observations or simply data not yet reviewed and entered into the Tables with full published precision. NOS is in the continuous process of updating the Tables with all available data.

Old observations are not in and of themselves an indication of poor present predictions. Certain coastal areas do not undergo much human or natural modification while other coastal areas are subject to nearly constant modification by both agents. Local knowledge of conditions is still very important to the wise use of these astronomical predictions.

NOTE. — Dashes are entered in the place of data which are unknown, unreliable, or not applicable.

TABLE 2 – TIDAL DIFFERENCES AND OTHER CONSTANTS

No.	PLACE	POSITION		DIFFERENCES				RANGES		Mean Tide Level
				Time		Height				
		Latitude	Longitude	High Water	Low Water	High Water	Low Water	Mean	Spring	
		North	West	h m	h m	ft	ft	ft	ft	ft
	ARCTIC ARCHIPELAGO Time meridian, local			on Hampton Roads, p.120						
1	Princess Royal Islands	72° 45'	117° 45'	+3 14	+3 32	0.0	+0.2	2.3	3.0	1.4
3	Mercy Bay, Banks Island	74° 07'	118° 15'	+4 05	+4 05	−0.8	+0.1	1.6	2.0	1.0
5	Winter Harbour, Melville Island	74° 47'	110° 48'	+4 44	+4 40	+0.2	+0.2	2.5	3.2	1.6
7	Bridport Inlet, Melville Island	74° 56'	108° 49'	+4 33	+4 33	+1.3	+1.0	2.8	4.1	2.5
9	Byam Martin Island	75° 10'	103° 34'	+3 42	+3 42	+1.8	+1.5	2.8	3.7	3.0
11	Cambridge Bay, Dease Strait	69° 07'	105° 07'	+2 35	+2 30	−0.4	+1.2	1.0	1.3	1.7
	Time meridian, 75° W			on Harrington Harbour, p.12						
13	Igloolik, Fury and Hecla Strait	69° 21'	81° 37'	+9 12	+9 12	+1.6	+0.8	4.6	6.0	4.7
15	Hall Beach, Foxe Basin	68° 45'	81° 13'	+9 45	+10 15	(*0.45+0.5)		1.7	2.0	2.1
	Time meridian, local									
17	Port Kennedy, Bellot Strait	72° 01'	94° 12'	+1 35	+1 44	+0.5	+0.8	3.5	4.5	4.2
19	Port Bowen, Prince Regent Inlet	73° 14'	88° 55'	+1 01	+1 06	+0.9	+1.3	3.4	4.5	4.6
21	Port Leopold, Prince Regent Inlet	73° 48'	90° 15'	+0 50	+0 45	+0.9	+0.1	4.6	5.9	4.0
23	Beechy Island, Barrow Strait	74° 43'	91° 54'	+1 30	+1 35	+1.0	−0.1	4.9	6.4	4.0
25	Assistance Bay, Barrow Strait	74° 37'	94° 15'	+1 56	+1 57	−0.1	+0.6	3.1	4.1	3.8
27	Griffith Island, Barrow Strait	74° 35'	95° 30'	+2 12	+2 13	−0.3	+0.5	3.0	3.9	3.6
29	Refuge Cove, Wellington Channel	75° 31'	92° 10'	+1 23	+1 38	+0.6	+0.2	4.2	5.5	3.9
31	Penny Strait	76° 52'	97° 00'	+1 53	+2 03	*0.39	*0.38	1.5	1.9	1.4
				on Hampton Roads, p.120						
33	Cape Columbia, Lincoln Sea	83° 14'	69° 55'	−0 55	−0 55	−1.8	0.0	0.8	1.1	0.5
35	Alert, Lincoln Sea	82° 30'	62° 20'	+1 26	+1 17	−0.4	+0.6	1.6	2.2	1.5
37	Cape Sheridan, Lincoln Sea	82° 29'	61° 30'	+1 37	+1 28	−0.5	+0.2	1.8	2.5	1.2
39	Cape Bryant, North Greenland	82° 21'	55° 30'	+3 33	+3 35	−1.4	+0.2	1.1	1.5	0.7
41	Cape Morris Jesup, North Greenland	83° 40'	34° 15'	+1 51	+1 43	−2.0	0.0	0.4	0.6	0.3
	GREENLAND, East Coast			on Harrington Harbour, p.12						
43	Danmarks Havn	76° 46'	18° 46'	−12 41	−12 32	−0.8	−0.6	3.6	4.7	2.8
45	Cape Borgen	75° 26'	18° 05'	−11 04	−11 03	*0.80	*0.81	3.0	3.9	2.8
47	Lille Pendulum	74° 37'	18° 29'	−11 40	−11 39	*0.80	*0.81	3.0	4.0	2.8
49	Finsch Islands	73° 59'	21° 08'	−12 18	−12 18	*0.81	*0.75	3.2	4.3	2.8
51	Myggbukta, Foster Bay	73° 28'	21° 33'	−11 57	−12 00	−0.9	−0.5	3.4	4.4	2.8
53	Blomsterbugten	73° 21'	25° 17'	−12 15	−12 27	−0.4	−0.3	3.7	4.8	3.2
	Time meridian, 30° W									
55	Danmarks Island, Scoresby Sound	70° 27'	26° 12'	−11 45	−11 45	*0.63	*0.62	2.4	3.3	2.2
	Time meridian, 45° W									
57	Angmagssalik (Kulusuk)	65° 36'	37° 09'	−7 00	−6 50	(*1.71−0.8)		6.5	8.8	5.2
				on Argentia, p.4						
59	Finnsbu	63° 24'	41° 17'	−4 09	−3 42	+0.8	−0.4	6.1	8.1	4.6
61	Kap Farvel	59° 45'	43° 53'	−2 21	−1 53	+0.2	−0.9	6.0	8.0	4.0
	GREENLAND, West Coast									
63	Frederiksdal	60° 00'	44° 40'	−2 10	−1 41	+1.5	−0.7	7.1	9.5	4.7
65	Nanortalik	60° 07'	45° 15'	−2 43	−2 16	+0.5	−0.9	6.3	8.4	4.2
67	Julianehaab	60° 43'	46° 01'	−2 09	−1 46	+0.3	−0.9	6.1	8.0	4.0
69	Narsarssuaq	61° 08'	45° 25'	−2 15	−1 46	+1.8	+0.1	6.6	8.6	5.3
71	Ivigtut, Arsuk Fjord	61° 12'	48° 11'	−1 49	−1 24	+0.7	−0.9	6.5	8.6	4.3
73	Frederikshaab	62° 00'	49° 43'	−1 22	−1 00	+3.0	−0.6	8.5	11.1	5.6
75	Godthaab	64° 10'	51° 44'	−1 21	−0 46	(*2.00−2.1)		9.8	13.0	6.5
77	Fishmaster's Harbour, Sondre Stromfjord	66° 01'	53° 29'	−1 41	−1 16	+3.6	−0.1	8.6	10.2	6.1
79	Camp Lloyd, Sondre Stromfjord	66° 58'	50° 57'	+2 21	+2 51	+1.7	−1.1	7.7	9.4	4.7
81	Holsteinsborg	66° 56'	53° 42'	−1 29	−1 00	+2.0	−0.8	7.7	10.0	5.0
83	Camp Michigan, Maligiak Fjord	66° 56'	52° 37'	−0 22	+0 10	+2.2	−0.8	7.9	10.2	5.1
				on Harrington Harbour, p.12						
85	Aningaq, Rifkol	67° 55'	53° 50'	−1 42	−1 42	+1.0	−0.8	5.6	7.4	3.6
87	Nunarssuaq, Kronprinsens Ejlanden	68° 59'	53° 21'	−0 48	−0 52	−0.5	−0.9	4.2	5.7	2.8
89	Godhavn, Disko Island	69° 15'	53° 33'	−1 37	−1 32	−0.4	−0.9	4.3	5.7	2.9
91	Ingnerit, Umanak Fjord	71° 00'	51° 00'	+0 00	+0 00	−1.6	−1.1	3.3	4.3	2.2
	Time meridian, local									
93	North Star Bay, Wolstenholme Fjord	76° 32'	68° 50'	+0 30	+0 32	*1.33	*1.12	5.4	7.0	4.5
95	Port Foulke	78° 18'	72° 45'	+0 28	+0 26	(*2.08−0.8)		7.9	10.7	6.5
97	Rensselaer Bugt	78° 37'	70° 53'	+1 05	+0 58	(*2.08−1.1)		7.9	10.8	6.2
99	Thank God Harbor, Polaris Bugt	81° 36'	61° 40'	+1 34	+1 31	−0.3	−0.4	3.9	5.4	3.2

Endnotes can be found at the end of table 2.

TABLE 2 – TIDAL DIFFERENCES AND OTHER CONSTANTS

No.	PLACE	POSITION		DIFFERENCES				RANGES		Mean Tide Level
		Latitude	Longitude	Time		Height		Mean	Spring	
				High Water	Low Water	High Water	Low Water			
		North	West	h m	h m	ft	ft	ft	ft	ft
	NORTHERN CANADA Baffin Bay, etc., West Side Time meridian, local			on Halifax, p.20						
101	Fort Conger, Discovery Harbor	81° 44'	64° 44'	+3 48	+3 25	−1.4	−1.3	4.3	5.9	3.0
103	Cape Lawrence	80° 21'	69° 15'	+3 46	+3 40	−0.2	−1.3	5.5	7.2	3.6
105	Payer Harbour, Cape Sabine	78° 43'	74° 25'	+3 36	+3 30	+1.7	−0.9	7.0	9.4	4.7
107	Cape Adair	71° 33'	71° 30'	+3 06	+3 06	+0.4	−1.2	6.0	7.8	3.9
109	Cape Hewett	70° 16'	67° 47'	+2 56	+2 56	+0.6	−0.5	5.5	7.2	4.4
	Davis Strait, West Side Time meridian, 60° W			on Pictou, p.8						
111	Cape Hooper, Baffin Island	68° 23'	66° 45'	−5 52	−5 41	*0.47	*0.43	1.6	1.9	1.8
113	Kivitoo, Baffin Island	67° 56'	64° 56'	−5 17	−5 10	*0.51	*0.43	1.8	2.4	1.9
				on Saint John, N. B., p.24						
115	Cape Dyer, Baffin Island	66° 34'	61° 40'	−6 19	−6 21	*0.31	*0.45	5.8	7.3	4.7
117	Clearwater Fiord, Cumberland Sound	66° 36'	67° 20'	−5 36	−5 38	−5.5	−0.6	15.9	20.6	11.4
119	Frobisher Bay	63° 29'	68° 02'	−4 13	−4 15	+5.5	+3.3	23.0	29.8	18.8
	Hudson Strait and Bay									
121	Pikyulik Island, Payne River	60° 00'	69° 55'	−2 15	−1 54	+3.7	+3.2	21.3	26.8	17.9
	Time meridian, 75° W									
123	Sorry Harbor, Resolution Island	61° 37'	64° 44'	−5 30	−5 30	−8.3	−0.9	13.4	17.6	9.8
125	Lower Savage Islands	61° 46'	65° 51'	−4 46	−4 55	−1.2	+2.0	17.6	25.4	14.8
127	Ashe Inlet, Big Island	62° 33'	70° 35'	−3 46	−3 43	+4.2	+2.2	22.8	30.9	17.6
129	Schooner Harbour, Baffin Island	64° 24'	77° 52'	−0 49	−0 44	−6.2	+0.4	14.2	18.9	11.5
131	Winter Island, Foxe Basin	66° 11'	83° 10'	+1 02	+1 10	−12.1	−0.8	9.5	12.4	8.0
	Time meridian, 90° W									
133	Coral Harbour, Southampton Island	64° 08'	83° 10'	−0 25	+0 04	−14.4	−1.5	7.9	10.3	6.5
135	Chesterfield Inlet	63° 20'	90° 42'	−8 17	−8 20	−12.4	−0.8	9.2	11.8	7.8
137	Churchill	58° 47'	94° 12'	−4 25	−4 36	−11.5	−1.4	10.7	13.4	7.9
				on Quebec, p.16						
139	Port Nelson, Nelson River entrance	57° 05'	92° 36'	+3 56	+4 35	−3.1	−0.9	11.5	12.9	6.4
	Time meridian, 75° W									
141	Moosonee, James Bay	51° 17'	80° 38'	+9 29	+9 32	*0.48	*1.81	4.5	5.4	5.2
143	Moose Factory, James Bay	51° 16'	80° 35'	+9 33	+10 37	*0.42	*1.56	4.0	5.4	4.5
145	Charlton Island, James Bay	51° 57'	79° 16'	+8 00	+6 38	*0.39	*1.06	4.3	5.3	3.9
				on Saint John, N. B., p.24						
147	Digges Harbour	62° 30'	77° 42'	−2 11	−2 05	*0.39	*0.62	7.1	9.3	6.1
149	Port de Boucherville, Nottingham Island	63° 12'	77° 28'	−2 07	−2 02	−11.6	−1.2	10.4	14.0	8.0
151	Wakeham Bay	61° 43'	71° 57'	−3 52	−3 55	−0.4	+2.2	18.2	27.0	15.3
153	Stupart Bay	61° 35'	71° 32'	−4 10	−4 17	0.0	+2.4	18.4	27.2	15.6
155	Diana Bay	60° 52'	70° 04'	−4 00	−4 03	+2.8	+3.1	20.5	26.8	17.4
157	Hopes Advance Bay, Ungava Bay	59° 21'	69° 38'	−3 59	−4 00	*1.44	*2.20	27.0	34.4	22.3
159	Leaf Bay, Ungava Bay	58° 55'	69° 00'	−4 00	−4 00	*1.49	*2.25	28.0	36.0	23.0
161	Leaf Lake, Ungava Bay	58° 45'	69° 40'	−3 00	−3 00	(*1.54+5.8)		32.0	40.0	28.0
163	Koksoak River entrance	58° 32'	68° 11'	−3 50	−3 53	*1.47	*2.00	28.5	36.4	22.3
165	Port Burwell, Ungava Bay	60° 25'	64° 52'	−4 13	−4 13	−6.5	−0.9	15.2	19.9	10.7
	LABRADOR Time meridian, 52° 30' W									
167	Button Islands	60° 37'	64° 44'	−2 38	−2 38	−9.5	−0.3	11.6	15.4	9.5
169	Williams Harbour	60° 00'	64° 19'	−3 07	−3 27	*0.32	*0.30	6.8	8.2	4.6
				on Halifax, p.20						
171	Eclipse Harbour	59° 48'	64° 09'	+0 25	+0 02	−2.4	−1.0	3.0	3.7	2.6
173	Kangalaksiorvik Fiord	59° 23'	63° 47'	+1 00	+0 42	−2.6	−1.5	3.3	4.1	2.2
175	Nachvak Bay	59° 03'	63° 35'	+0 04	−0 20	−1.5	−1.1	4.0	5.0	3.0
177	Port Manvers	56° 57'	61° 25'	−0 55	−0 55	−2.3	−1.2	3.3	4.2	2.6
179	Hebron, Hebron Fjord	58° 12'	62° 38'	−0 49	−1 05	−1.4	−0.9	3.9	4.7	3.2
181	Nain	56° 33'	61° 41'	−0 32	−0 54	+0.3	−0.5	5.2	6.5	4.2
183	Hopedale Harbour	55° 27'	60° 13'	−0 46	−1 09	−0.4	−0.3	4.3	5.6	4.0
185	Webeck Harbour	54° 54'	58° 02'	−1 07	−1 38	−1.3	−0.8	3.9	5.0	3.3
	Hamilton Inlet and Lake Melville									
187	Indian Harbour	54° 27'	57° 12'	−0 37	−1 33	−1.0	−0.9	4.3	5.7	3.4
189	Ticoralak Island	54° 17'	58° 12'	−0 35	−0 55	−0.9	−0.5	4.0	4.9	3.7
191	Rigolet	54° 11'	58° 25'	−0 02	−0 17	−1.9	−1.0	3.5	4.5	2.8
193	Goose Bay	53° 21'	60° 24'	+4 22	+4 24	(*0.27+0.4)		1.2	1.7	1.6
195	Cartwright Harbour	53° 42'	57° 02'	−0 03	−0 34	−1.3	−0.6	3.7	4.9	3.4
197	Curlew Harbour	53° 45'	56° 33'	−0 07	−0 38	−1.6	−0.9	3.7	4.9	3.1
199	Comfort Bight	53° 09'	55° 46'	−0 32	−1 03	−1.9	−1.0	3.5	4.6	2.9

Endnotes can be found at the end of table 2.

TABLE 2 – TIDAL DIFFERENCES AND OTHER CONSTANTS

No.	PLACE	POSITION		DIFFERENCES				RANGES		Mean Tide Level
				Time		Height				
		Latitude	Longitude	High Water	Low Water	High Water	Low Water	Mean	Spring	
		North	West	h m	h m	ft	ft	ft	ft	ft
	LABRADOR Time meridian, 52° 30' W			*on Halifax, p.20*						
201	Square Island Harbour	52° 44'	55° 49'	−0 34	−1 05	−2.0	−1.1	3.5	4.7	2.8
203	Port Marnham	52° 23'	55° 44'	−0 43	−1 14	−2.7	−1.0	2.7	3.6	2.5
205	Battle Harbour	52° 16'	55° 36'	−1 03	−1 30	−2.1	−0.3	2.6	3.8	3.1
	Strait of Bell Isle			*on Harrington Harbour, p.12*						
207	Chateau Bay	52° 00'	55° 50'	−3 08	−3 19	*0.69	*0.81	2.4	3.1	2.5
209	Red Bay	51° 43'	56° 25'	−2 00	−1 55	*0.56	*0.56	2.1	2.6	2.0
211	Forteau Bay	51° 27'	56° 53'	−0 26	−0 17	*0.78	*0.81	2.9	3.7	2.8
	NEWFOUNDLAND, East Coast			*on Halifax, p.20*						
213	Pistolet Bay	51° 30'	55° 44'	−0 14	−0 28	*0.46	*0.29	2.4	3.1	1.8
215	Ariege Bay	51° 10'	56° 00'	−0 34	−0 34	−2.6	−1.5	3.3	4.3	2.3
217	Wild Cove	50° 42'	56° 10'	−0 49	−1 01	−2.0	−1.1	3.5	4.7	2.8
219	Sops Island, White Bay	49° 50'	56° 46'	−0 49	−1 24	*0.46	*0.29	2.4	3.4	1.8
221	Exploits Lower Harbour	49° 32'	55° 04'	−0 34	−1 09	−3.1	−1.3	2.6	3.5	2.1
223	Fogo Harbour	49° 43'	54° 16'	−0 34	−0 42	−2.6	−1.3	3.1	4.2	2.4
225	Valleyfield	49° 10'	53° 37'	−0 46	−1 13	*0.45	*0.33	2.2	2.9	1.8
227	Port Union	48° 30'	53° 05'	−0 53	−1 15	*0.49	*0.48	2.2	3.0	2.1
229	Random Head Harbour, Trinity Bay	48° 06'	53° 34'	−0 53	−1 05	*0.48	*0.33	2.4	3.2	1.9
231	Harbour Grace, Conception Bay	47° 41'	53° 12'	−0 28	−0 46	*0.51	*0.33	2.6	3.5	2.0
233	St. John's	47° 34'	52° 42'	−0 34	−0 46	*0.52	*0.38	2.6	3.5	2.1
	NEWFOUNDLAND, South Coast			*on Argentia, p.4*						
235	Trepassey Harbour	46° 43'	53° 23'	−0 19	−0 11	−1.2	−0.5	4.2	5.6	3.5
237	St. Mary Harbour, St. Mary Bay	46° 55'	53° 35'	−0 14	−0 06	−1.2	−0.5	4.2	5.6	3.5
	Placentia Bay									
239	ARGENTIA	47° 18'	53° 59'	*Daily predictions*				4.9	6.3	4.4
241	Woody Island	47° 47'	54° 10'	+0 09	+0 09	−0.5	−0.3	4.7	6.0	4.0
243	Mortier Bay	47° 10'	55° 09'	+0 15	+0 26	−1.0	−0.8	4.7	6.0	3.5
245	Great St. Lawrence Harbour	46° 55'	55° 22'	+0 28	+0 55	−0.7	+0.3	3.9	5.0	4.2
	Time meridian, 60° W									
247	St. Pierre Harbor, St. Pierre Island	46° 47'	56° 10'	−0 09	+0 13	−0.8	+0.2	3.9	5.0	4.1
	Time meridian, 52° 30' W									
	Fortune Bay									
249	Grande le Pierre Harbour	47° 40'	54° 47'	+1 09	+1 09	−1.0	+0.2	3.7	4.8	4.0
251	Belleoram	47° 32'	55° 25'	+0 57	+0 57	(*0.67+0.8)		3.3	4.3	3.8
253	Ship Cove, Bay d'Espoir	47° 52'	55° 50'	+0 45	+0 53	−0.4	0.0	4.5	5.5	4.2
255	Great Jervis Harbour, Bay d'Espoir	47° 39'	56° 11'	+0 38	+1 05	−1.1	+0.1	3.7	4.8	3.9
257	Hare Bay	47° 37'	56° 32'	+0 41	+1 08	(*0.67+0.6)		3.3	4.3	3.6
259	Grey River	47° 34'	57° 07'	+0 45	+1 12	(*0.63+0.7)		3.1	4.0	3.5
261	Connoire Bay	47° 40'	57° 54'	+0 50	+0 50	(*0.59+0.7)		2.9	3.8	3.3
263	La Poile Bay	47° 40'	58° 24'	+1 15	+1 15	(*0.63+0.6)		3.1	4.0	3.4
				on Harrington Harbour, p.12						
265	Port Aux Basques	47° 35'	59° 09'	−1 24	−1 28	*0.80	*0.75	3.1	4.0	2.8
267	Codroy Road	47° 53'	59° 24'	−1 22	−1 27	*0.74	*0.75	2.8	3.7	2.6
	NEWFOUNDLAND, West Coast									
269	St. Georges Harbour	48° 27'	58° 30'	−0 28	−0 38	*0.78	*0.88	2.8	3.5	2.8
271	Port−au−Port	48° 33'	58° 45'	+0 05	+0 10	−1.3	−1.0	3.5	4.5	2.4
273	Frenchman's Cove, Bay of Islands	49° 04'	58° 10'	+0 10	+0 10	−0.5	0.0	3.3	4.2	3.3
275	Norris Cove, Bonne Bay	49° 31'	57° 52'	+0 10	+0 10	−0.7	−0.4	3.5	4.4	3.0
277	Portland Cove	50° 11'	57° 36'	+0 19	+0 19	−0.6	−0.4	3.6	4.6	3.0
279	Port Saunders	50° 39'	57° 18'	+0 07	+0 03	−0.3	−0.3	3.8	4.9	3.2
281	Castors Harbour, St. John Bay	50° 55'	56° 59'	+0 10	+0 10	*0.78	*0.75	3.0	4.1	2.7
283	St. Barbe Bay	51° 12'	56° 46'	+0 00	+0 00	*0.78	*0.56	3.3	4.4	2.6
	QUEBEC, Gulf of St. Lawrence Time meridian, 60° W									
285	Bradore Bay	51° 28'	57° 15'	−0 35	−0 30	−0.6	−0.1	3.3	4.4	3.1
287	Mistanoque Harbour	51° 16'	58° 12'	−0 15	−0 15	−0.4	−0.1	3.5	4.6	3.3
289	HARRINGTON HARBOUR	50° 30'	59° 28'	*Daily predictions*				3.8	4.9	3.5
291	Wapitagun Harbour	50° 12'	60° 01'	+0 15	+0 15	−0.3	+0.1	3.4	4.4	3.4
293	Kegaska	50° 12'	61° 14'	+0 40	+0 40	−0.9	−0.2	3.1	4.0	3.0
295	Natashquan	50° 12'	61° 50'	+1 00	+1 10	−0.8	−0.1	3.1	4.0	3.1
297	Betchewun Harbour	50° 14'	63° 11'	+2 09	+2 13	−0.7	−0.4	3.5	4.6	3.0
299	Havre St. Pierre	50° 14'	63° 36'	+2 23	+2 32	0.0	−0.1	3.9	4.8	3.5
301	Mingan	50° 18'	64° 03'	+2 35	+2 40	+0.9	0.0	4.7	5.8	3.9
	Anticosti Island									
303	Heath Point	49° 05'	61° 42'	+0 51	+0 52	(*0.61+0.3)		2.3	3.0	2.4
305	Southwest Point	49° 24'	63° 36'	+3 21	+3 26	−0.3	0.0	3.5	4.4	3.4
307	Ellis Bay	49° 48'	64° 22'	+3 37	+3 38	+0.3	−0.5	4.6	5.7	3.4
309	Moisie Bay	50° 12'	66° 05'	+3 43	+3 49	+2.3	+0.5	5.6	7.2	4.9
311	Sept Iles	50° 13'	66° 24'	+3 54	+3 58	+2.7	−0.1	6.6	8.6	4.8
313	Cawee Islands	49° 50'	67° 00'	+4 01	+4 07	+3.0	+0.6	6.2	8.0	5.3

Endnotes can be found at the end of table 2.

TABLE 2 – TIDAL DIFFERENCES AND OTHER CONSTANTS

No.	PLACE	POSITION Latitude	POSITION Longitude	DIFFERENCES Time High Water	DIFFERENCES Time Low Water	DIFFERENCES Height High Water	DIFFERENCES Height Low Water	RANGES Mean	RANGES Spring	Mean Tide Level
		North	West	h m	h m	ft	ft	ft	ft	ft
	QUEBEC, St. Lawrence River Time meridian, 75° W			on Harrington Harbour, p.12						
315	Ste. Anne des Monts	49° 08'	66° 29'	+3 17	+3 19	+3.4	+0.6	6.6	8.6	5.5
317	Cap Chat	49° 06'	66° 45'	+3 17	+3 21	+4.2	+1.0	7.0	9.0	6.1
319	Pointe des Monts	49° 20'	67° 22'	+3 10	+3 16	+4.3	+0.8	7.3	9.6	6.1
321	Matane	48° 51'	67° 32'	+3 18	+3 22	+4.7	+0.9	7.6	9.9	6.3
323	Metis–sur–Mer	48° 41'	68° 02'	+3 24	+3 28	+5.4	+1.1	8.1	10.6	6.8
				on Quebec, p.16						
325	Betsiamites River	48° 53'	68° 39'	−4 20	−5 08	−3.8	+1.4	8.5	11.2	7.3
327	Father Point	48° 31'	68° 28'	−4 22	−5 29	−3.4	+1.4	8.9	11.7	7.5
329	Old Bic Harbour	48° 22'	68° 44'	−4 12	−5 14	−3.3	+1.4	9.0	11.8	7.5
331	Tadoussac, Saguenay River	48° 08'	69° 43'	−3 47	−4 54	−1.8	+0.8	11.1	14.0	8.0
333	Chicoutimi, Saguenay River	48° 26'	71° 03'	−3 28	−3 40	−1.4	+1.3	11.0	14.4	8.4
335	Brandypot Islands	47° 52'	69° 41'	−3 36	−4 40	−0.5	+2.2	11.0	14.5	9.3
337	Murray Bay	47° 39'	70° 08'	−3 20	−4 22	+0.4	+2.3	11.8	15.3	9.8
339	Pointe aux Orignaux	47° 29'	70° 01'	−2 47	−3 41	−0.3	+2.2	11.2	14.7	9.4
341	Ile aux Coudres	47° 26'	70° 19'	−2 10	−3 21	+1.2	+2.0	12.9	15.8	10.1
343	L' Islet	47° 08'	70° 22'	−1 17	−2 05	0.0	+0.9	12.8	15.3	9.0
345	Beaujeu Channel	47° 05'	70° 29'	−1 10	−1 43	+0.6	+0.5	13.8	15.7	9.0
347	Grosse Ile	47° 02'	70° 40'	−0 57	−1 19	+1.3	0.0	15.0	17.1	9.1
349	Berthier	46° 56'	70° 44'	−0 47	−1 08	+1.3	0.0	15.0	16.9	9.1
351	St. Laurent d' Orleans	46° 52'	71° 00'	−0 20	−0 30	+0.3	+0.2	13.8	15.6	8.7
353	QUEBEC	46° 49'	71° 11'	Daily predictions				13.7	15.5	8.5
355	St. Nicolas	46° 43'	71° 24'	+0 35	+0 32	−0.7	− − −	12.6	14.3	− −
357	St. Augustin	46° 43'	71° 28'	+0 54	+0 53	−1.6	− − −	11.8	13.3	− −
359	Ste. Croix <1>	46° 37'	71° 45'	+1 31	+2 00	− − −	− − −	11.8	13.3	− −
361	Pointe Platon <1>	46° 40'	71° 51'	+1 43	+2 11	− − −	− − −	11.4	12.9	− −
363	Grondines <1>	46° 36'	72° 04'	+2 14	+3 18	− − −	− − −	6.7	8.1	− −
365	Cap a la Roche <1>	46° 33'	72° 10'	+2 37	+3 48	− − −	− − −	5.4	6.7	− −
367	Batiscan <1>	46° 31'	72° 15'	+3 32	+4 49	− − −	− − −	2.3	3.3	− −
369	Champlain <1>	46° 26'	72° 21'	+4 08	+5 30	− − −	− − −	1.8	2.8	− −
371	Trois Rivieres <1>	46° 20'	72° 33'	+4 45	+6 15	− − −	− − −	0.7	1.0	− −
	QUEBEC, Gulf of St. Lawrence–cont. Time meridian, 60° W			on Pictou, p.8						
373	GaspÖ Bay	48° 50'	64° 29'	+4 43	+4 58	−1.1	−0.5	2.6	3.3	3.1
375	Point St. Peter	48° 38'	64° 10'	+4 59	+5 11	*0.67	*0.52	2.5	3.2	2.5
	Chaleur Bay									
377	Port Daniel	48° 10'	64° 57'	+5 27	+5 42	−0.7	−0.6	3.1	3.8	3.3
379	Paspebiac	48° 01'	65° 14'	+5 22	+5 34	−0.4	−1.0	3.8	4.6	3.2
381	Carleton Point	48° 05'	66° 07'	+5 31	+5 36	+0.8	−0.7	4.7	6.2	4.0
	NEW BRUNSWICK, Gulf of St. Lawrence									
	Chaleur Bay–cont.									
383	Campbellton	48° 01'	66° 40'	+6 04	+6 40	+3.5	+0.9	5.8	7.2	6.1
385	Dalhousie	48° 04'	66° 22'	+5 42	+5 52	+2.2	−0.2	5.6	7.1	4.9
387	Bathurst	47° 37'	65° 39'	+6 04	+6 50	−0.3	−1.1	4.0	4.8	3.2
389	Caraquet Harbour	47° 48'	64° 56'	+5 49	+5 50	−1.0	−1.1	3.3	4.0	2.9
391	Miscou Harbour	47° 54'	64° 35'	+5 45	+5 57	−0.5	−1.1	3.8	5.0	3.1
393	Old Tracadie Gully entrance	47° 31'	64° 52'	+6 25	+6 36	−1.6	−1.2	2.8	3.5	2.5
395	Tracadie	47° 31'	64° 55'	+6 55	+7 06	*0.55	*0.35	2.2	2.8	1.9
								Mean Diurnal		
397	Portage Island, Miramichi Bay }	47° 09'	65° 03'	−5 11	−4 59	−1.7	−0.8	− −	3.3	2.2
399	Newcastle, Miramichi River }	47° 00'	65° 34'	−3 53	−3 13	−0.7	−0.5	− −	4.0	− −
401	Richibucto River entrance }	46° 43'	64° 48'	−4 45	− − −	−2.7	−0.8	− −	2.3	1.8
403	Shediac Bay }	46° 15'	64° 32'	− − −	+0 18	−1.9	−0.5	− −	2.8	2.8
								Mean Spring		
405	Cape Tormentine	46° 08'	63° 47'	+0 41	+1 03	+1.5	−0.1	4.8	5.7	4.6
407	Tidnish Head, Baie Verte	46° 01'	64° 01'	+0 33	+0 54	+1.7	−0.2	5.1	6.3	4.7
	PRINCE EDWARD ISLAND							Mean Diurnal		
409	Tignish }	46° 58'	64° 00'	−4 59	−5 27	−2.5	−0.8	− −	2.5	1.7
411	Alberton }	46° 49'	64° 03'	−4 27	−4 10	−2.8	−0.7	− −	2.1	1.7
413	Malpeque Bay }	46° 35'	63° 40'	−3 29	−3 13	−2.5	−0.8	− −	2.5	1.8
415	North Rustico }	46° 28'	63° 17'	−4 10	−4 04	−2.7	−1.0	− −	2.5	1.6
417	St. Peters Bay }	46° 26'	62° 44'	−3 52	−3 37	−3.3	−1.0	− −	1.9	1.5
419	Naufrage }	46° 28'	62° 25'	−3 09	−3 27	−2.6	−0.8	− −	2.4	2.0
								Mean Spring		
421	Souris Head	46° 20'	62° 17'	−1 23	−1 25	−0.6	−0.2	2.8	3.5	3.5
423	Georgetown Harbour	46° 11'	62° 32'	−1 03	−1 00	−0.5	−0.1	2.8	3.5	3.6
425	Cape Bear	46° 00'	62° 27'	−0 42	−0 40	−0.6	−0.5	3.1	4.0	3.4
427	Charlottetown	46° 13'	63° 08'	+0 33	+0 42	+2.5	+0.5	5.2	6.4	5.4
429	Summerside Harbour	46° 24'	63° 47'	+0 57	+1 19	+0.9	+0.3	3.8	4.5	4.5
	ISLANDS, Gulf of St. Lawrence									
431	St. Paul Island	47° 12'	60° 09'	−1 25	−1 22	*0.64	*0.57	2.2	2.8	2.4
433	Amherst Harbour, Magdalen Islands	47° 14'	61° 50'	−1 05	−1 07	*0.53	*0.57	1.6	2.0	2.1

Endnotes can be found at the end of table 2.

TABLE 2 – TIDAL DIFFERENCES AND OTHER CONSTANTS

No.	PLACE	POSITION		DIFFERENCES				RANGES		Mean Tide Level
		Latitude	Longitude	Time		Height		Mean	Spring	
				High Water	Low Water	High Water	Low Water			
		North	West	h m	h m	ft	ft	ft	ft	ft

NOVA SCOTIA, Gulf of St. Lawrence
Time meridian, 60° W

on Pictou, p.8

No.	PLACE	Latitude	Longitude	High Water	Low Water	High Water	Low Water	Mean	Spring	Mean Tide Level
435	Pugwash	45° 51'	63° 40'	+1 00	+1 03	+1.8	0.0	5.0	6.0	4.8
437	PICTOU	45° 41'	62° 42'	*Daily predictions*				3.2	3.9	3.9
439	Merigomish Harbour	45° 39'	62° 27'	−0 13	−0 01	−0.3	0.0	2.9	3.4	3.8
441	Cape George	45° 53'	61° 53'	−0 54	−0 51	−1.6	−0.8	2.4	3.2	2.7
443	Antigonish Harbour	45° 40'	61° 53'	+0 09	+0 17	−1.7	−0.5	2.0	2.5	2.8
445	Cape Jack	45° 42'	61° 33'	−1 11	−1 18	−1.8	−0.7	2.1	2.6	2.7
447	Auld Cove	45° 39'	61° 26'	−0 27	−0 33	(*0.62+1.3)		2.0	2.6	3.7
	Cape Breton Island									
449	Port Hood	46° 01'	61° 32'	−0 46	−0 45	−1.6	−0.9	2.5	3.2	2.7
451	Mabou River entrance	46° 06'	61° 28'	−0 53	−1 04	*0.66	*0.61	2.2	2.9	2.5
453	Cheticamp	46° 37'	61° 02'	−1 23	−1 20	*0.56	*0.74	1.4	1.8	2.4

NOVA SCOTIA, Outer Coast

Cape Breton Island-cont.

No.	PLACE	Latitude	Longitude	High Water	Low Water	High Water	Low Water	Mean	Spring	Mean Tide Level
455	Neil Harbour	46° 48'	60° 20'	−1 44	−1 45	*0.69	*0.65	2.4	3.1	2.7
457	Ingonish Island	46° 40'	60° 23'	−1 40	−1 33	−1.5	−0.9	2.6	3.2	2.7
459	St. Anns Harbour	46° 15'	60° 34'	−1 37	−1 40	−1.4	−1.0	2.8	3.5	2.7
461	North Sydney	46° 13'	60° 15'	−1 54	−1 49	*0.73	*0.61	2.6	3.2	2.7
463	Glace Bay	46° 12'	59° 55'	−1 59	−1 54	−1.6	−0.9	2.5	3.2	2.7

on Halifax, p.20

No.	PLACE	Latitude	Longitude	High Water	Low Water	High Water	Low Water	Mean	Spring	Mean Tide Level
465	Louisburg Harbour	45° 54'	59° 59'	−0 08	−0 14	−1.6	−0.7	3.5	4.2	3.2
467	Gabarus Cove	45° 51'	60° 10'	+0 08	+0 10	−1.4	−0.7	3.7	4.4	3.3
469	St. Peter Bay	45° 38'	60° 52'	−0 12	−0 07	−0.6	−0.4	4.2	5.1	3.8
471	Arichat	45° 31'	61° 02'	−0 25	−0 14	−0.9	−0.5	4.0	4.8	3.6
473	Port Hastings, Strait of Canso	45° 39'	61° 24'	−0 16	−0 12	0.0	+0.2	4.2	5.1	4.4
475	Guysborough	45° 23'	61° 29'	+0 06	+0 18	−1.1	−0.5	3.8	4.6	3.5
477	Canso Harbour	45° 21'	61° 00'	−0 05	−0 04	−1.1	−0.6	3.9	4.7	3.5
479	Whitehaven Harbour	45° 14'	61° 12'	−0 10	−0 02	−1.1	−0.4	3.7	4.7	3.6
481	Isaacs Harbour	45° 11'	61° 40'	−0 03	+0 04	−0.6	−0.1	3.9	4.6	4.0
483	Sonora, St. Mary River	45° 03'	61° 55'	−0 02	+0 09	−0.7	−0.6	4.3	5.2	3.7
485	Liscomb Harbour	45° 00'	62° 02'	−0 11	−0 05	−0.6	−0.4	4.2	5.0	3.8
487	Sheet Harbour	44° 54'	62° 30'	−0 08	−0 04	−1.1	−0.9	4.2	5.0	3.3
489	Ship Harbour	44° 47'	62° 49'	−0 07	−0 04	−0.6	−0.4	4.2	5.1	3.8
491	Jeddore Harbour	44° 45'	63° 01'	−0 06	−0 03	−0.5	−0.4	4.3	5.2	3.9
493	HALIFAX	44° 40'	63° 34'	*Daily predictions*				4.4	5.3	4.3
495	Sable Island, north side	43° 57'	60° 06'	−0 06	−0 12	−2.7	−0.9	2.6	3.2	2.5
497	Sable Island, south side	43° 56'	59° 54'	−0 02	−0 06	−2.1	−1.6	3.9	4.8	2.5
499	St. Margarets Bay	44° 31'	63° 56'	+0 08	+0 07	−0.5	−0.3	4.2	4.9	3.9
501	Chester, Mahone Bay	44° 34'	64° 18'	+0 01	−0 04	−0.2	−0.2	4.4	5.3	4.1
503	Mahone Harbour, Mahone Bay	44° 27'	64° 22'	+0 03	−0 01	−0.1	−0.2	4.5	5.5	4.2
505	Lunenburg	44° 22'	64° 19'	+0 07	+0 07	−0.1	+0.1	4.2	4.9	4.3
507	Riverport, La Have River	44° 17'	64° 20'	+0 12	+0 05	−0.3	−0.4	4.5	5.3	4.0
509	Bridgewater, La Have River	44° 23'	64° 31'	+0 09	+0 06	−0.2	−0.3	4.5	5.5	4.1
511	Liverpool Bay	44° 02'	64° 41'	+0 14	+0 04	−0.5	−0.4	4.3	5.1	3.9
513	Lockeport	43° 44'	65° 05'	+0 27	+0 02	−0.2	−0.4	4.6	5.4	4.0
515	Shelburne	43° 45'	65° 18'	+0 30	+0 35	+0.1	−0.3	4.8	5.8	4.2
517	Barrington Passage	43° 32'	65° 36'	+0 51	+0 30	+1.6	+0.6	5.4	6.2	5.4
519	Swim Point	43° 26'	65° 38'	+1 41	+1 03	+2.9	+0.1	7.2	8.4	5.8

NOVA SCOTIA, Bay of Fundy

on Saint John, N. B., p.24

No.	PLACE	Latitude	Longitude	High Water	Low Water	High Water	Low Water	Mean	Spring	Mean Tide Level
521	Lower East Pubnico	43° 38'	65° 46'	−1 52	−2 07	*0.43	*0.48	8.7	10.0	6.3
523	Yarmouth Harbour	43° 48'	66° 08'	−1 07	−1 15	*0.53	*0.42	11.5	13.4	7.5
525	Westport, St. Mary Bay	44° 16'	66° 21'	−0 35	−0 30	*0.72	*0.72	15.0	16.7	10.4
527	Tiverton, St. Mary Bay	44° 24'	66° 13'	−0 38	−0 30	−5.6	−0.7	15.9	18.3	11.3
529	Weymouth, St. Mary Bay	44° 27'	66° 01'	−0 26	−0 22	−6.5	−0.7	15.0	17.0	10.8
531	Digby, Annapolis Basin	44° 38'	65° 45'	−0 09	−0 07	+0.7	+0.3	21.2	24.6	14.9
533	Annapolis Royal, Annapolis River	44° 45'	65° 30'	+0 06	+0 10	+2.2	+0.4	22.6	25.7	15.7
535	Port George	45° 01'	65° 10'	−0 06	−0 06	+6.7	+0.8	26.7	30.5	18.2
537	Ile Haute	45° 15'	65° 00'	−0 02	−0 02	+7.4	+0.7	27.5	31.5	18.5
539	Spencer Island	45° 20'	64° 42'	+0 17	+0 21	*1.47	*1.50	30.5	35.0	21.2
	Minas Basin									
541	Parrsboro (Partridge Island) <2>	45° 22'	64° 20'	+0 51	+0 49	+14.7	– – –	34.4	39.0	22.3
543	Horton Bluff, Avon River	45° 06'	64° 13'	+0 58	+1 02	*1.76	*1.38	38.1	43.6	24.6
545	Windsor <2>	45° 00'	64° 08'	+1 03	– – –	+19.5	– – –	– –	– –	– –
547	Burntcoat Head	45° 18'	63° 49'	+1 06	+1 12	*1.90	*2.18	38.4	43.5	27.9
549	Truro <2>	45° 22'	63° 20'	+1 43	– – –	+26.1	– – –	– –	– –	– –
551	Spicer Cove, Chignecto Bay	45° 26'	64° 54'	+0 12	+0 16	+7.0	+0.8	27.0	30.0	18.3
553	Joggins <2>	45° 41'	64° 28'	+0 14	+0 26	+14.2	+1.8	33.2	37.0	22.4
555	Amherst Point, Cumberland Basin	45° 50'	64° 17'	+0 33	+0 45	*1.69	*1.55	35.6	40.5	24.0

NEW BRUNSWICK, Bay of Fundy

Petitcodiac River <3>

No.	PLACE	Latitude	Longitude	High Water	Low Water	High Water	Low Water	Mean	Spring	Mean Tide Level
557	Grindstone Island	45° 43'	64° 37'	+0 21	+0 28	*1.49	*1.45	31.1	35.6	21.4
559	Hopewell Cape	45° 52'	64° 35'	+0 14	+0 39	*1.64	*1.85	33.2	38.0	24.0
561	Moncton <2> <3>	46° 05'	64° 46'	+0 46	– – –	+17.2	– – –	– –	– –	– –
563	Salisbury	46° 01'	65° 03'	+1 31	– – –	+18.2	– – –	– –	– –	– –
565	Herring Cove	45° 35'	64° 58'	+0 22	+0 20	+8.4	+0.9	28.3	32.4	19.1
567	Quaco Bay	45° 20'	65° 32'	+0 11	+0 12	+2.0	−0.3	23.1	26.3	15.3
569	SAINT JOHN <4>	45° 15'	66° 04'	*Daily predictions*				20.8	23.7	14.4
571	Indiantown, St. John River	45° 16'	66° 05'	+1 30	+2 25	– – –	– – –	1.2	1.4	2.4

Endnotes can be found at the end of table 2.

TABLE 2 – TIDAL DIFFERENCES AND OTHER CONSTANTS

No.	PLACE	POSITION		DIFFERENCES				RANGES		Mean Tide Level
				Time		Height				
		Latitude	Longitude	High Water	Low Water	High Water	Low Water	Mean	Spring	
		North	**West**	h m	h m	ft	ft	ft	ft	ft
	NEW BRUNSWICK, Bay of Fundy Time meridian, 60° W			on Saint John, N. B., p.24						
573	Lepreau Harbour	45° 07'	66° 29'	−0 01	+0 03	−2.3	−0.5	19.0	21.7	13.0
575	L' Etang Harbour	45° 02'	66° 49'	+0 01	+0 05	−3.2	−0.8	18.4	21.0	12.4
577	North Head, Grand Manan Island	44° 46'	66° 45'	−0 05	−0 05	−4.5	−0.9	17.2	19.3	11.7
579	Seal Cove, Grand Manan Island	44° 37'	66° 51'	−0 15	−0 17	*0.68	*0.65	14.3	16.3	9.8
581	Outer Wood Island <5>	44° 36'	66° 48'	−0 25	−0 27	−7.8	−0.8	13.8	16.2	10.1
583	Machias Seal Island <5>	44° 30'	67° 06'	−0 01	− − −	−9.6	−1.7	12.9	14.5	8.8
585	Welshpool, Campobello Island <5>	44° 53'	66° 57'	−0 01	+0 06	−3.5	−1.0	18.3	21.2	12.1
587	Wilsons Beach, Campobello Island <5> ..	44° 56'	66° 56'	+0 00	+0 01	−3.7	+0.1	17.0	19.4	12.6
589	Back Bay, Letite Harbour <5>	45° 03'	66° 52'	+0 00	−0 03	−3.5	0.0	17.3	20.1	12.6
591	Midjik Bluff, Passamaquoddy Bay <5> ...	45° 07'	66° 54'	+0 12	+0 17	−2.0	−0.5	19.3	22.0	13.1
593	St. Andrews, Passamaquoddy Bay <5> ...	45° 04'	67° 03'	+0 14	+0 20	−2.3	0.0	18.5	21.2	13.2
	MAINE Time meridian, 75° W			on Eastport, p.28						
595	Pettegrove Point, Dochet Island	45° 07.7'	67° 08.6'	+0 08	+0 12	*1.07	*1.00	19.57	22.12	10.24
597	EASTPORT	44° 54.2'	66° 59.1'	Daily predictions				18.35	21.18	9.6
	Cobscook Bay									
599	Garnet Point, Pennamquan River	44° 55.4'	67° 07.8'	+0 11	+0 14	*1.04	*1.00	19.17	22.05	10.04
601	Coffins Point	44° 52.2'	67° 06.5'	+0 31	+0 33	*0.94	*0.77	17.3	19.7	9.0
603	Birch Islands, Whiting Bay	44° 52.5'	67° 09.5'	+0 59	+1 13	*0.94	*0.75	17.4	19.8	9.0
605	Gravelly Point, Whiting Bay	44° 49.4'	67° 09.1'	+1 07	+1 18	*0.97	*0.73	17.90	19.06	9.28
607	Cutler, Little River	44° 39.4'	67° 12.6'	−0 10	−0 19	*0.74	*0.74	13.5	15.4	7.1
609	Cutler, Naval Radio Station	44° 38.5'	67° 17.8'	−0 07	−0 14	*0.70	*0.84	12.78	14.67	6.76
611	Stone Island, Machias Bay	44° 36.2'	67° 22.1'	−0 11	−0 28	*0.68	*0.68	12.4	14.1	6.5
613	Machiasport, Machias River	44° 41.9'	67° 23.6'	+0 01	−0 09	*0.69	*0.69	12.6	14.4	6.6
615	Shoppee Point, Englishman Bay	44° 36.9'	67° 29.8'	−0 05	−0 13	*0.66	*0.66	12.1	13.8	6.2
				on Portland, p.36						
617	Steele Harbor Island	44° 29.6'	67° 32.6'	−0 28	−0 20	*1.27	*1.27	11.6	13.3	6.2
619	Millbridge, Narraguagus River, Maine ...	44° 32.4'	67° 52.5'	−0 15	+0 05	*1.23	*1.09	11.31	12.89	6.03
621	Green Island, Petit Manan Bar	44° 22.3'	67° 52.2'	−0 28	−0 24	*1.16	*1.16	10.6	12.2	5.7
623	Prospect Harbor	44° 24'	68° 01'	−0 24	−0 15	*1.15	*1.15	10.5	12.1	5.7
				on Bar Harbor, p.32						
625	Winter Harbor, Frenchman Bay	44° 23.3'	68° 05.2'	−0 01	+0 10	*0.95	*0.95	10.1	11.6	5.4
	Mount Desert Island									
627	BAR HARBOR	44° 23.5'	68° 12.3'	Daily Predictions				10.56	12.25	5.66
629	Southwest Harbor	44° 16.5'	68° 18.8'	+0 00	−0 27	*0.96	*0.95	10.2	11.7	5.5
631	Bass Harbor	44° 14.5'	68° 21.2'	+0 04	−0 27	*0.93	*0.93	9.9	11.3	5.4
	Blue Hill Bay									
633	Blue Hill Harbor	44° 24.5'	68° 33.8'	+0 09	+0 11	*0.95	*0.95	10.1	11.6	5.4
635	Mackerel Cove	44° 10.2'	68° 26.1'	+0 02	−0 27	*0.94	*0.93	10.0	11.5	5.4
637	Ellsworth, Union River	44° 32.1'	68° 25.3'	+0 15	+0 16	*1.00	*0.97	10.59	12.07	5.67
639	Burnt Coat Harbor, Swans Island	44° 08.7'	68° 27.0'	−0 01	+0 06	*0.89	*0.88	9.5	10.8	5.1
	Penobscot Bay									
	Eggemoggin Reach									
641	Center Harbor	44° 15.8'	68° 35.2'	+0 09	+0 12	*0.95	*0.95	10.1	11.5	5.4
643	Little Deer Isle	44° 17.5'	68° 41.6'	+0 16	+0 14	*0.94	*0.93	10.0	11.5	5.4
645	Isle Au Haut	44° 04.4'	68° 38.2'	−0 01	−0 27	*0.87	*0.88	9.3	10.7	5.0
647	Oceanville, Deer Isle	44° 11.5'	68° 37.2'	+0 08	+0 05	*0.93	*0.95	9.86	11.62	5.29
649	Stonington, Deer Isle	44° 09.2'	68° 39.7'	+0 08	+0 06	*0.91	*0.90	9.7	11.2	5.2
651	Matinicus Harbor, Wheaton Island	43° 51.7'	68° 52.9'	+0 05	−0 27	*0.85	*0.85	9.0	10.4	4.8
653	Vinalhaven, Vinalhaven Island	44° 02.6'	68° 50.4'	+0 09	+0 10	*0.87	*0.88	9.3	10.7	5.0
655	North Haven	44° 07.6'	68° 52.4'	+0 13	+0 09	*0.91	*0.90	9.7	11.2	5.3
657	Pulpit Harbor, North Haven Island	44° 09.4'	68° 53.2'	+0 12	+0 10	*0.93	*0.97	9.85	11.43	5.30
659	Castine	44° 23.2'	68° 47.8'	+0 15	+0 11	*0.95	*1.00	10.1	11.6	5.4
	Penobscot River									
661	Fort Point	44° 28.3'	68° 44.80'	+0 09	+0 06	*0.98	*0.95	10.39	11.67	5.55
663	Gross Point, Eastern Channel	44° 32.2'	68° 45.5'	−0 06	+0 10	*0.99	*0.98	10.4	12.0	5.6
665	Bucksport	44° 34.3'	68° 48.1'	−0 04	+0 11	*1.01	*1.00	10.8	12.4	5.8
667	Winterport	44° 38.2'	68° 50.5'	−0 09	+0 04	*1.11	*0.92	11.76	13.64	6.22
669	Sandy Point	44° 40.3'	68° 48.3'	+0 06	+0 08	*0.99	*0.98	10.5	12.1	5.6
671	Bangor	44° 47.7'	68° 46.3'	−0 06	+0 18	*1.25	*0.87	13.40	14.97	7.03
673	Belfast	44° 25.6'	69° 00.3'	+0 09	+0 04	*0.97	*1.03	10.23	11.66	5.51
675	Rockland	44° 06.3'	69° 06.1'	+0 09	+0 06	*0.93	*1.03	9.78	11.15	5.28
	MAINE, outer coast			on Portland, p.36						
677	Tenants Harbor	43° 57.9'	69° 13.0'	−0 11	−0 11	*1.02	*1.02	9.3	10.6	5.0
679	Monhegan Island	43° 45.9'	69° 19.3'	−0 13	−0 09	*0.97	*0.97	8.8	10.1	4.7
681	Burnt Island, Georges Islands	43° 52.3'	69° 17.7'	−0 13	−0 12	*0.98	*0.98	8.9	10.2	4.8
	St. George River									
683	Port Clyde	43° 55.5'	69° 15.6'	−0 11	−0 07	*0.98	*0.98	8.9	10.2	4.8
685	Otis Cove	43° 59.2'	69° 14.2'	−0 15	−0 14	*1.00	*1.00	9.1	10.5	4.9
687	Thomaston	44° 04.3'	69° 10.9'	−0 04	−0 03	*1.03	*1.03	9.4	10.8	5.0
689	New Harbor, Muscongus Bay	43° 52.5'	69° 29.4'	−0 10	−0 08	*0.97	*0.97	8.8	10.1	4.7
691	Muscongus Harbor, Muscongus Sound ..	43° 58.0'	69° 26.5'	−0 09	−0 03	*0.99	*0.99	9.0	10.4	4.8
693	Friendship Harbor	43° 58.2'	69° 20.5'	−0 18	−0 11	*0.99	*0.99	9.0	10.4	4.8

Endnotes can be found at the end of table 2.

330

TABLE 2 – TIDAL DIFFERENCES AND OTHER CONSTANTS

No.	PLACE	POSITION Latitude	POSITION Longitude	DIFFERENCES Time High Water	DIFFERENCES Time Low Water	DIFFERENCES Height High Water	DIFFERENCES Height Low Water	RANGES Mean	RANGES Spring	Mean Tide Level
		North	West	h m	h m	ft	ft	ft	ft	ft
	MAINE, outer coast Time meridian, 75° W				on Portland, p.36					
	Medomak River									
695	Jones Neck	44° 00.9'	69° 22.8'	−0 10	−0 05	*1.00	*1.00	9.1	10.5	4.9
697	Waldoboro	44° 05.6'	69° 22.6'	−0 16	−0 04	*1.04	*1.04	9.5	10.9	5.1
699	Pemaquid Harbor, Johns Bay	43° 52.6'	69° 31.5'	−0 05	−0 04	*0.97	*0.97	8.8	10.1	4.7
	Damariscotta River									
701	East Boothbay	43° 51.9'	69° 35.0'	−0 02	+0 01	*0.98	*0.98	8.9	10.2	4.8
703	Walpole	43° 56.0'	69° 34.8'	+0 06	+0 14	*1.03	*1.06	9.35	10.66	5.05
705	Newcastle	44° 02.0'	69° 32.2'	+0 16	+0 25	*1.02	*1.02	9.3	10.7	5.0
707	Damariscove Harbor, Damariscove Island	43° 45.5'	69° 36.9'	−0 09	−0 10	*0.97	*0.97	8.8	10.1	4.7
709	Boothbay Harbor	43° 51.1'	69° 37.7'	−0 06	−0 08	*0.97	*0.97	8.8	10.1	4.7
711	Southport, Townsend Gut	43° 50.8'	69° 39.7'	+0 01	+0 01	*0.98	*0.98	8.9	10.2	4.8
	Sheepscot River									
713	Isle of Springs	43° 51.6'	69° 41.2'	−0 02	−0 04	*0.98	*0.98	8.9	10.3	4.8
715	Cross River entrance	43° 55.5'	69° 40.2'	+0 07	+0 04	*1.00	*1.00	9.1	10.5	4.9
717	Wiscasset	44° 00.0'	69° 40.0'	+0 16	+0 04	*1.03	*1.03	9.4	10.8	5.0
719	Sheepscot (below rapids)	44° 03.0'	69° 37.1'	+0 20	+0 20	*1.05	*1.05	9.6	11.0	5.2
721	Back River	43° 57.5'	69° 41.1'	+0 34	+0 31	*1.00	*1.00	9.1	10.5	4.9
723	Robinhood, Sasanoa River	43° 51.2'	69° 44.0'	+0 14	+0 14	*0.97	*0.97	8.8	10.1	4.7
725	Mill Point, Sasanoa River	43° 53.2'	69° 45.8'	+0 35	+0 43	*0.97	*0.97	8.8	10.1	4.7
	Kennebec River									
727	Fort Popham, Hunniwell Point	43° 45.3'	69° 47.3'	+0 09	+0 04	*0.92	*0.92	8.4	9.7	4.5
729	Phippsburg	43° 49.1'	69° 48.6'	+0 26	+0 28	*0.88	*0.88	8.0	9.2	4.3
731	Bath	43° 55.1'	69° 48.8'	+1 01	+1 17	*0.70	*0.70	6.4	7.4	3.4
733	Sturgeon Island, Merrymeeting Bay	43° 58.9'	69° 50.1'	+2 00	+2 04	*0.58	*0.58	5.3	6.1	2.8
735	Androscoggin River entrance	43° 57.0'	69° 53.3'	+2 24	+3 26	*0.52	*0.52	4.7	5.4	2.5
737	Brunswick, Androscoggin River	43° 55.3'	69° 57.8'	+2 35	+4 36	*0.42	*0.42	3.8	4.4	2.0
739	Bowdoinham, Cathance River	44° 00.5'	69° 53.7'	+2 34	+2 42	*0.63	*0.63	5.7	6.6	3.1
	Casco Bay									
741	Cundy Harbor, New Meadows River	43° 47.3'	69° 53.6'	−0 01	−0 02	*0.98	*0.98	8.9	10.2	4.8
743	Howard Point, New Meadows River	43° 53.4'	69° 53.0'	−0 05	+0 01	*0.99	*0.99	9.0	10.3	4.8
745	South Harpswell, Potts Harbor	43° 44.3'	70° 01.4'	+0 02	+0 01	*0.98	*0.98	8.9	10.2	4.8
747	Wilson Cove, Middle Bay	43° 49.5'	69° 58.6'	+0 02	+0 02	*1.00	*1.00	9.1	10.5	4.9
749	South Freeport	43° 49.2'	70° 06.2'	+0 12	+0 10	*0.99	*0.99	9.0	10.3	4.8
751	Prince Point	43° 45.7'	70° 10.4'	+0 00	+0 01	*1.00	*0.99	9.19	10.57	4.90
753	Doyle Point	43° 45.1'	70° 08.4'	−0 02	−0 03	*1.00	*0.88	9.2	10.5	4.9
755	Falmouth Foreside	43° 43.9'	70° 12.3'	+0 01	+0 01	*1.00	*0.97	9.16	10.53	4.91
757	Great Chebeague Island	43° 43.3'	70° 08.5'	+0 02	+0 02	*1.00	*1.03	9.11	10.48	4.91
759	Cliff Island, Luckse Sound	43° 41.7'	70° 06.6'	−0 02	−0 02	*1.00	*1.00	9.1	10.4	4.9
761	Vaill Island	43° 40.6'	70° 09.3'	+0 05	+0 01	*0.98	*1.03	9.0	10.3	4.8
763	Long Island	43° 41.4'	70° 10.2'	−0 01	−0 01	*1.00	*1.00	9.09	10.45	4.89
765	Cow Island	43° 41.4'	70° 11.4'	−0 01	+0 00	*1.00	*1.00	9.11	10.48	4.89
767	Presumpscot River Bridge	43° 41.4'	70° 14.8'	+0 01	+0 04	*1.01	*1.06	9.2	10.6	5.0
769	Back Cove	43° 41'	70° 15'	+0 02	+0 06	*0.97	*0.97	9.1	10.5	4.9
771	Great Diamond Island	43° 40.2'	70° 12.0'	+0 00	+0 00	*1.00	*1.03	9.08	10.44	4.89
773	Peak Island	43° 39.3'	70° 12.0'	−0 04	−0 08	*0.99	*0.99	9.0	10.4	4.8
775	Cushing Island	43° 38.7'	70° 11.9'	+0 01	+0 01	*0.99	*1.03	9.02	10.37	4.87
777	PORTLAND	43° 39.6'	70° 14.8'		*Daily predictions*			9.12	10.53	4.91
779	Fore River	43° 38.5'	70° 17.1'	+0 02	+0 02	*1.00	*1.03	9.16	10.53	4.93
781	Portland Head Light	43° 37.4'	70° 12.4'	−0 02	−0 01	*0.97	*1.00	8.89	10.13	4.78
	MAINE, outer coast–cont.									
783	Pine Point, Scarborough River	43° 32.7'	70° 20.0'	+0 06	+0 16	*0.96	*0.97	8.77	9.72	4.71
785	Old Orchard Beach	43° 31'	70° 22'	+0 00	−0 06	*0.97	*0.97	8.8	10.1	4.7
787	Camp Ellis, Saco River Entrance	43° 27.7'	70° 22.9'	+0 03	+0 10	*0.97	*1.00	8.92	10.17	4.79
789	Biddeford, Saco River	43° 29.5'	70° 26.8'	+0 12	+0 26	*0.99	*0.97	9.06	10.33	4.86
791	Cape Porpoise	43° 22.0'	70° 25.9'	+0 12	+0 14	*0.95	*0.95	8.7	9.9	4.7
793	Kennebunkport	43° 21.5'	70° 28.6'	+0 07	+0 05	*0.97	*1.00	8.84	10.08	4.76
795	Wells, Webhannet River	43° 19.2'	70° 33.8'	+0 06	+0 02	*0.96	*1.00	8.77	10.09	4.72
797	Cape Neddick	43° 10.0'	70° 35.6'	+0 02	+0 08	*0.95	*1.00	8.69	9.99	4.68
799	York Harbor	43° 07.9'	70° 38.5'	+0 03	+0 13	*0.95	*0.95	8.6	9.9	4.6
801	Fort Point, York Harbor	43° 07.8'	70° 38.3'	−0 04	+0 10	*0.95	*0.94	8.69	9.99	4.66
803	Seapoint, Cutts Island	43° 05.1'	70° 39.7'	+0 01	−0 04	*0.96	*0.96	8.8	10.1	4.7
	MAINE and NEW HAMPSHIRE									
	Portsmouth Harbor									
805	Jaffrey Point	43° 03.4'	70° 43.9'	−0 03	−0 05	*0.95	*0.95	8.7	10.0	4.7
807	Gerrish Island	43° 04.0'	70° 41.7'	−0 02	−0 03	*0.95	*0.95	8.7	10.0	4.7
809	Fort Point	43° 04.3'	70° 42.7'	+0 09	+0 05	*0.95	*1.00	8.63	9.92	4.65
811	Kittery Point	43° 04.9'	70° 42.2'	−0 07	+0 01	*0.96	*0.96	8.7	10.0	4.7
813	Seavey Island	43° 05'	70° 45'	+0 20	+0 18	*0.89	*0.89	8.1	9.4	4.4
815	Portsmouth	43° 04.7'	70° 45.1'	+0 22	+0 17	*0.86	*0.86	7.8	9.0	4.2
	Piscataqua River									
817	Atlantic Heights	43° 05.4'	70° 46.0'	+0 37	+0 28	*0.82	*0.82	7.5	8.6	4.0
819	Dover Point	43° 07'	70° 50'	+1 33	+1 27	*0.70	*0.70	6.4	7.4	3.4
821	Dover, Cocheco River	43° 11.9'	70° 52.1'	+1 45	+1 39	*0.77	*0.76	7.04	8.03	3.78
823	Salmon Falls River	43° 11.4'	70° 49.5'	+1 35	+1 52	*0.75	*0.75	6.8	7.8	3.6
825	Squamscott River RR. Bridge	43° 03.2'	70° 54.8'	+2 19	+2 41	*0.75	*0.75	6.8	7.8	3.6
827	Gosport Harbor, Isles of Shoals	42° 58.7'	70° 36.9'	+0 02	−0 02	*0.93	*0.93	8.5	9.8	4.5
829	Hampton Harbor	42° 54'	70° 49'	+0 14	+0 32	*0.91	*0.91	8.3	9.5	4.5

Endnotes can be found at the end of table 2.

TABLE 2 – TIDAL DIFFERENCES AND OTHER CONSTANTS

No.	PLACE	POSITION		DIFFERENCES				RANGES		Mean Tide Level
				Time		Height				
		Latitude	Longitude	High Water	Low Water	High Water	Low Water	Mean	Spring	
		North	West	h m	h m	ft	ft	ft	ft	ft
	MASSACHUSETTS, outer coast Time meridian, 75° W			on Portland, p.36						
	Merrimack River									
831	Plum Island, Merrimack River Entrance	42° 49.0'	70° 49.2'	+0 06	+0 29	*0.88	*0.88	8.00	9.12	4.30
833	Newburyport	42° 48.7'	70° 51.9'	+0 31	+1 11	*0.86	*0.86	7.8	9.0	4.2
835	Salisbury Point	42° 50.3'	70° 54.5'	+0 55	+1 18	*0.83	*0.56	7.64	8.71	4.01
837	Merrimacport	42° 49.5'	70° 59.3'	+1 26	+2 08	*0.76	*0.50	7.05	8.04	3.70
839	Riverside	42° 45.8'	71° 04.6'	+1 56	+3 30	*0.62	*0.35	5.72	6.52	2.80
841	Plum Island Sound (south end)	42° 42.6'	70° 47.3'	+0 12	+0 37	*0.94	*0.94	8.6	9.9	4.6
843	Essex	42° 37.9'	70° 46.6'	+0 22	+0 31	*1.00	*0.94	9.18	10.47	4.90
845	Annisquam, Lobster Cove	42° 39.3'	70° 40.6'	+0 11	+0 03	*0.97	*0.97	8.81	10.04	4.74
847	Rockport	42° 39.5'	70° 36.9'	+0 06	+0 06	*0.95	*0.97	8.70	9.92	4.71
				on Boston, p.40						
849	Gloucester Harbor	42° 36.6'	70° 39.6'	+0 00	−0 04	*0.93	*0.97	8.80	10.03	4.73
851	Salem, Salem Harbor	42° 31.4'	70° 52.6'	−0 02	−0 05	*0.94	*0.97	8.93	10.18	4.79
853	Lynn, Lynn Harbor	42° 27.5'	70° 56.6'	+0 01	−0 03	*0.97	*1.00	9.16	10.44	4.92
	Boston Harbor									
855	Boston Light	42° 19.7'	70° 53.5'	−0 01	−0 02	*0.95	*0.97	9.05	10.03	4.85
857	Deer Island (south end)	42° 20.7'	70° 57.5'	+0 01	+0 00	*0.97	*0.97	9.3	10.8	4.9
859	BOSTON	42° 21.3'	71° 03.2'	*Daily predictions*				9.49	11.07	5.09
861	Charlestown, Charles River entrance	42° 22.5'	71° 03.0'	+0 00	+0 01	*1.00	*1.00	9.5	11.0	5.0
863	Amelia Earhart Dam, Mystic River	42° 23.7'	71° 04.6'	+0 01	+0 02	*1.01	*0.97	9.56	10.89	5.11
865	Chelsea St. Bridge, Chelsea River	42° 23.2'	71° 01.4'	+0 01	+0 06	*1.01	*1.01	9.6	11.1	5.1
867	Neponset, Neponset River	42° 17.1'	71° 02.4'	−0 02	+0 03	*1.00	*1.00	9.5	11.0	5.0
869	Moon Head	42° 18.5'	70° 59.3'	+0 01	+0 04	*0.99	*0.99	9.4	10.9	5.0
	Hingham Bay									
871	Nut Island, Quincy Bay	42° 16.8'	70° 57.3'	+0 01	+0 01	*0.99	*1.00	9.42	10.74	5.05
873	Weymouth Fore River Bridge	42° 14.7'	70° 58.1'	+0 09	+0 06	*1.00	*1.00	9.5	11.0	5.0
875	Crow Point, Hingham Harbor entrance	42° 15.7'	70° 53.6'	+0 02	+0 05	*0.99	*0.99	9.4	10.9	5.0
877	Hingham	42° 14.8'	70° 53.1'	+0 09	+0 08	*1.00	*1.00	9.5	11.0	5.0
879	Nantasket Beach, Weir River	42° 16.2'	70° 51.6'	+0 06	+0 07	*0.99	*0.99	9.4	10.9	5.0
881	Hull	42° 18.2'	70° 55.2'	+0 05	+0 07	*0.97	*0.97	9.3	10.8	5.0
	Cohasset Harbor to Davis Bank									
883	Cohasset Harbor (White Head)	42° 14.9'	70° 47.0'	+0 04	−0 02	*0.92	*0.92	8.8	10.2	4.7
885	Scituate, Scituate Harbor	42° 12.1'	70° 43.6'	+0 03	−0 01	*0.95	*1.03	8.94	10.19	4.83
887	Damons Point, North River	42° 09.6'	70° 44.0'	+0 20	+0 36	*0.89	*0.89	8.5	9.9	4.5
889	Brant Rock, Green Harbor River	42° 05.0'	70° 38.8'	+0 05	+0 03	*0.96	*1.03	9.08	10.35	4.89
	Cape Cod Bay									
891	Duxbury, Duxbury Harbor	42° 02.3'	70° 40.2'	+0 06	+0 33	*1.04	*1.03	9.89	11.27	5.30
893	Plymouth	41° 57.6'	70° 39.7'	+0 04	+0 18	*1.03	*1.00	9.76	11.13	5.22
895	Cape Cod Canal, east entrance	41° 46.3'	70° 30.4'	−0 01	−0 03	*0.91	*0.68	8.74	9.96	4.59
897	Cape Cod Canal, Sagamore (Sta. 115)	41° 46.5'	70° 32.1'	−0 15	−0 06	*0.83	*0.88	7.90	9.01	4.25
899	Cape Cod Canal, Bournedale (Sta. 200)	41° 46.2'	70° 33.7'	−0 29	−0 21	*0.66	*0.79	6.18	7.05	3.37
901	Cape Cod Canal, Bourne Bridge (Sta. 320)	41° 44.7'	70° 35.6'	−1 13	−0 24	*0.46	*0.79	4.29	4.89	2.42
903	Barnstable Harbor, Beach Point	41° 43.3'	70° 17.1'	+0 11	+0 30	*1.00	*1.00	9.5	11.0	5.0
905	Sesuit Harbor, East Dennis	41° 45.1'	70° 09.3'	+0 02	−0 01	*1.02	*0.82	9.73	11.09	5.14
907	Wellfleet	41° 55.8'	70° 02.5'	+0 14	+0 30	*1.05	*1.05	10.0	11.6	5.4
909	Provincetown	42° 03'	70° 11'	+0 16	+0 18	*0.95	*0.95	9.1	10.6	4.8
	Cape Cod									
911	Chatham, Stage Harbor	41° 40.0'	69° 58.0'	+0 46	+0 19	*0.43	*0.43	3.95	4.50	2.23
913	Chatham Harbor, Aunt Lydias Cove	41° 41.6'	69° 57.0'	+0 56	+1 10	*0.61	*0.71	5.77	6.58	3.12
915	Pleasant Bay	41° 44.2'	69° 58.9'	+2 28	+3 27	*0.34	*0.34	3.2	3.7	1.7
917	Georges Shoal, Texas Tower	41° 41.3'	67° 45.6'	−0 47	−0 43	*0.44	*0.44	4.2	4.8	2.2
	Nantucket Sound, north side									
919	Saquatucket Harbor	41° 40.1'	70° 03.4'	+0 46	+0 16	*0.41	*0.41	3.72	4.24	2.14
921	Wychmere Harbor	41° 39.9'	70° 03.9'	+0 52	+0 25	*0.39	*0.39	3.7	4.3	1.9
923	Dennisport	41° 39.5'	70° 06.9'	+1 03	+0 38	*0.36	*0.36	3.4	4.1	1.8
925	South Yarmouth, Bass River	41° 39.9'	70° 11.0'	+1 48	+1 46	*0.29	*0.29	2.8	3.4	1.5
927	Hyannis Port	41° 37.9'	70° 18.0'	+1 00	+0 26	*0.35	*0.76	3.20	3.80	1.85
929	Cotuit Highlands	41° 36.5'	70° 26.2'	+1 17	+0 47	*0.26	*0.26	2.5	3.0	1.3
931	Poponesset Island, Poponesset Bay	41° 35.2'	70° 27.8'	+2 03	+1 52	*0.24	*0.24	2.3	2.8	1.2
933	Falmouth Heights	41° 32.7'	70° 35.9'	−0 16	−0 09	*0.14	*0.14	1.3	1.6	0.6
	Nantucket Island									
935	Great Point	41° 23.2'	70° 02.8'	+0 43	+0 28	*0.32	*0.32	3.1	3.7	1.6
937	NANTUCKET	41° 17.1'	70° 05.8'	*Daily predictions, p.44*				3.0	3.36	1.7
939	Eel Point	41° 17.5'	70° 12.5'	+0 39	+0 07	*0.24	*0.24	2.3	2.7	1.2
941	Muskeget Island, north side	41° 20.2'	70° 18.3'	+0 25	+0 15	*0.21	*0.21	2.0	2.4	1.1
	Martha's Vineyard									
				on Newport, p.52						
943	Vineyard Haven	41° 27.5'	70° 36.0'	+3 39	+3 27	*0.48	*1.14	1.58	1.69	0.95
945	Oak Bluffs	41° 27.5'	70° 33.3'	+3 59	+3 47	*0.50	*0.71	1.7	2.0	0.9
947	Edgartown	41° 23.3'	70° 30.7'	+4 26	+4 16	*0.65	*1.64	2.13	2.68	1.29
949	Wasque Point, Chappaquiddick Island	41° 21.8'	70° 27.0'	+2 02	+3 20	*0.31	*0.31	1.1	1.4	0.6
951	Squibnocket Point	41° 18.7'	70° 46.1'	−0 45	−0 02	*0.82	*0.82	2.9	3.7	1.6

Endnotes can be found at the end of table 2.

TABLE 2 – TIDAL DIFFERENCES AND OTHER CONSTANTS

No.	PLACE	POSITION		DIFFERENCES				RANGES		Mean Tide Level
		Latitude	Longitude	Time High Water	Time Low Water	Height High Water	Height Low Water	Mean	Spring	
		North	West	h m	h m	ft	ft	ft	ft	ft
	MASSACHUSETTS, outer coast Martha's Vineyard–cont. Time meridian, 75° W			on Newport, p.52						
953	Nomans Land	41° 15.7'	70° 49.0'	−0 19	+0 18	*0.85	*0.85	3.0	3.6	1.6
955	Gay Head	41° 21.2'	70° 49.8'	−0 06	+0 45	*0.82	*0.82	2.9	3.5	1.5
957	Cedar Tree Neck	41° 26.1'	70° 41.8'	+0 10	+1 32	*0.62	*0.62	2.2	2.8	1.2
	Vineyard Sound									
	Woods Hole									
959	Little Harbor	41° 31.2'	70° 39.9'	+0 32	+2 21	*0.40	*0.40	1.4	1.8	0.8
961	OCEANOGRAPHIC INSTITUTION	41° 31.4'	70° 40.3'	Daily predictions, p.48				1.8	2.33	1.0
963	Uncatena Island (south side)	41° 30.9'	70° 42.2'	+0 12	+0 22	*1.02	*1.02	3.6	4.5	1.9
965	Quicks Hole, North side	41° 26.9'	70° 51.4'	−0 08	−0 08	*0.99	*0.99	3.5	4.4	1.8
967	Cuttyhunk	41° 25.5'	70° 55.0'	+1 20	+1 15	*0.97	*0.93	3.37	4.25	1.81
	Buzzards Bay									
969	Penikese Island	41° 27.0'	70° 55.3'	+0 02	+0 12	*0.98	*0.96	3.42	4.30	1.84
971	Chappaquoit Point, West Falmouth Harbor	41° 36.3'	70° 39.1'	+0 06	+0 08	*1.11	*1.14	3.82	4.70	2.07
973	Monument Beach	41° 42.9'	70° 37.0'	+0 16	+0 30	*1.15	*1.15	3.97	5.00	2.17
975	Gray Gables	41° 44.1'	70° 37.4'	+0 37	+1 16	*1.05	*1.21	3.62	4.45	1.98
977	Cape Cod Canal, RR. bridge <6>	41° 44.5'	70° 37.0'	+1 17	+2 50	*1.01	*1.01	3.43	4.22	1.93
979	Onset Beach, Onset Bay	41° 44.5'	70° 39.5'	+0 41	+1 25	*1.03	*1.03	3.50	4.41	1.97
981	Great Hill	41° 42.7'	70° 42.9'	+0 12	+0 12	*1.14	*1.21	3.96	4.99	2.15
983	Marion, Sippican Harbor	41° 43.2'	70° 45.6'	+0 10	+0 12	*1.13	*1.29	4.0	4.9	2.2
985	Piney Point	41° 41.7'	70° 43.2'	+0 10	+0 10	*1.13	*1.21	3.91	4.81	2.13
987	Mattapoisett, Mattapoisett Harbor	41° 39'	70° 49'	+0 11	+0 20	*1.09	*1.00	3.9	4.8	2.1
989	Clarks Point	41° 35.6'	70° 54.0'	+0 14	+0 23	*1.03	*1.07	3.56	4.49	1.93
991	New Bedford	41° 38.4'	70° 55.1'	+0 07	+0 07	*1.05	*1.05	3.7	4.6	1.9
993	Round Hill Point	41° 32.3'	70° 55.7'	+0 14	+0 22	*0.99	*1.00	3.43	4.32	1.85
	Westport River									
995	Westport Harbor	41° 31'	71° 05'	+0 09	+0 33	*0.85	*0.85	3.0	3.7	1.6
997	Hix Bridge, East Branch	41° 34.2'	71° 04.4'	+1 40	+2 30	*0.77	*0.77	2.7	3.4	1.4
	RHODE ISLAND, and MASSACHUSETTS Narragansett Bay									
	Sakonnet River									
999	Sakonnet	41° 27.9'	71° 11.6'	−0 09	+0 13	*0.91	*0.86	3.17	3.99	1.70
1001	Sachuest, Flint Point	41° 29.2'	71° 14.3'	−0 05	+0 15	*0.90	*0.93	3.13	3.94	1.69
1003	The Glen	41° 33.5'	71° 14.2'	−0 13	−0 03	*0.98	*1.00	3.40	4.28	1.84
1005	Nannaquaket Neck	41° 37.1'	71° 12.2'	−0 12	−0 13	*1.01	*1.01	3.50	4.41	1.91
1007	Anthony Point	41° 38.3'	71° 12.7'	+0 00	−0 01	*1.09	*1.09	3.75	4.73	2.05
1009	North End, Bay Oil pier	41° 39.1'	71° 12.6'	+0 20	+0 01	*1.20	*1.07	4.17	5.25	2.24
1011	Castle Hill	41° 27.8'	71° 21.7'	−0 05	+0 13	*0.94	*1.00	3.25	4.10	1.77
1013	NEWPORT	41° 30.3'	71° 19.6'	Daily predictions				3.47	4.38	1.87
	Conanicut Island									
1015	Beavertail Point	41° 27.1'	71° 24.1'	−0 05	+0 04	*0.98	*0.98	3.34	4.21	1.86
1017	West Jamestown, Dutch Island Harbor	41° 29.8'	71° 23.2'	+0 05	+0 04	*1.00	*1.00	3.46	4.36	1.87
1019	Conanicut Point	41° 34.4'	71° 22.3'	+0 07	−0 06	*1.07	*1.07	3.8	4.7	2.0
1021	Prudence Island, (south end)	41° 34.8'	71° 19.3'	+0 08	−0 03	*1.08	*1.14	3.74	4.71	2.03
1023	Bristol Ferry	41° 38.2'	71° 15.3'	+0 15	+0 00	*1.17	*1.14	4.08	5.14	2.20
1025	Bristol, Bristol Harbor	41° 40.1'	71° 16.7'	+0 13	+0 00	*1.16	*1.14	4.1	5.1	2.2
1027	Bristol Highlands	41° 41.8'	71° 17.6'	+0 11	−0 04	*1.19	*1.21	4.13	5.03	2.23
1029	Kickamuit River	41° 42.5'	71° 14.5'	+0 22	+0 14	*1.24	*1.29	4.30	5.01	2.33
1031	Fall River, Massachusetts	41° 42.3'	71° 09.8'	+0 18	+0 03	*1.25	*1.21	4.36	5.41	2.35
1033	Steep Brook, Taunton River	41° 44.4'	71° 07.9'	+0 26	+0 05	*1.30	*1.29	4.51	5.68	2.44
1035	Conimicut Light	41° 43.0'	71° 20.6'	+0 11	−0 02	*1.20	*1.19	4.17	5.25	2.25
1037	Bay Spring, Bullock Cove	41° 45.1'	71° 21.1'	+0 12	+0 01	*1.22	*1.21	4.25	5.23	2.30
1039	Pawtuxet, Pawtuxet Cove	41° 45.7'	71° 23.3'	+0 06	−0 11	*1.25	*1.29	4.35	5.35	2.35
1041	Providence, State Pier no.1	41° 48.4'	71° 24.1'	+0 13	+0 00	*1.27	*1.29	4.41	5.63	2.40
1043	Rumford, Seekonk River	41° 50.4'	71° 22.4'	+0 12	+0 06	*1.34	*1.29	4.66	5.73	2.51
1045	Pawtucket, Seekonk River	41° 52.1'	71° 22.8'	+0 18	+0 09	*1.31	*1.29	4.6	5.6	2.5
1047	Quonset Point	41° 35.2'	71° 24.7'	+0 06	−0 01	*1.07	*1.10	3.70	4.66	2.01
1049	East Greenwich	41° 39.9'	71° 26.7'	+0 12	+0 03	*1.18	*1.21	4.06	4.93	2.20
1051	Wickford	41° 34.3'	71° 26.7'	+0 03	−0 06	*1.07	*1.07	3.71	4.56	2.01
1053	Watson Pier, Boston Neck	41° 27.6'	71° 25.7'	−0 03	+0 16	*0.96	*0.93	3.32	4.18	1.79
1055	Narragansett Pier	41° 25.3'	71° 27.3'	−0 11	+0 11	*0.91	*0.93	3.2	4.0	1.7
	RHODE ISLAND, Outer Coast									
1057	Point Judith, Harbor of Refuge	41° 21.8'	71° 29.4'	+0 00	+0 33	*0.87	*0.93	3.00	3.13	1.63
1059	Block Island (Old Harbor)	41° 10.4'	71° 33.4'	−0 13	+0 15	*0.82	*0.86	2.85	3.51	1.54
1061	Southwest Point, Block Island	41° 09.8'	71° 36.6'	+0 05	+0 42	*0.75	*0.79	2.60	3.20	1.41
1063	Weekapaug Point, Block Island Sound	41° 19.7'	71° 45.7'	+0 41	+1 06	*0.74	*0.93	2.53	3.11	1.39
1065	Watch Hill Point	41° 18.3'	71° 51.6'	+0 41	+1 16	*0.74	*0.71	2.6	3.2	1.4
				on New London, p.60						
1067	Westerly, Pawcatuck River	41° 22.9'	71° 49.9'	−0 21	+0 03	*1.02	*1.00	2.6	3.1	1.5
	CONNECTICUT, Long Island Sound									
1069	West Mystic, Mystic River	41° 20.6'	71° 58.5'	−0 20	−0 16	*0.97	*1.00	2.50	2.97	1.44
1071	Silver Eel Pond, Fishers Island, N.Y.	41° 15.4'	72° 01.8'	−0 04	−0 04	*0.91	*1.00	2.33	2.83	1.37

Endnotes can be found at the end of table 2.

CAUTION

Cape Cod Canal, Railroad Bridge

Predictions of the times of low water must be used with caution because of the peculiarities in the behavior of the tide. Since the tide may be practically at a stand for as much as two hours before or after the predicted times of low water, the levels at other than high and low water times cannot be obtained in the usual way as in Table 3 (Height of Tide at Any Time). The peculiar behavior of the tide near low water, which is prevalent at this place, is illustrated by the first three curves; however there are brief periods each month when the behavior is as depicted by the fourth curve.

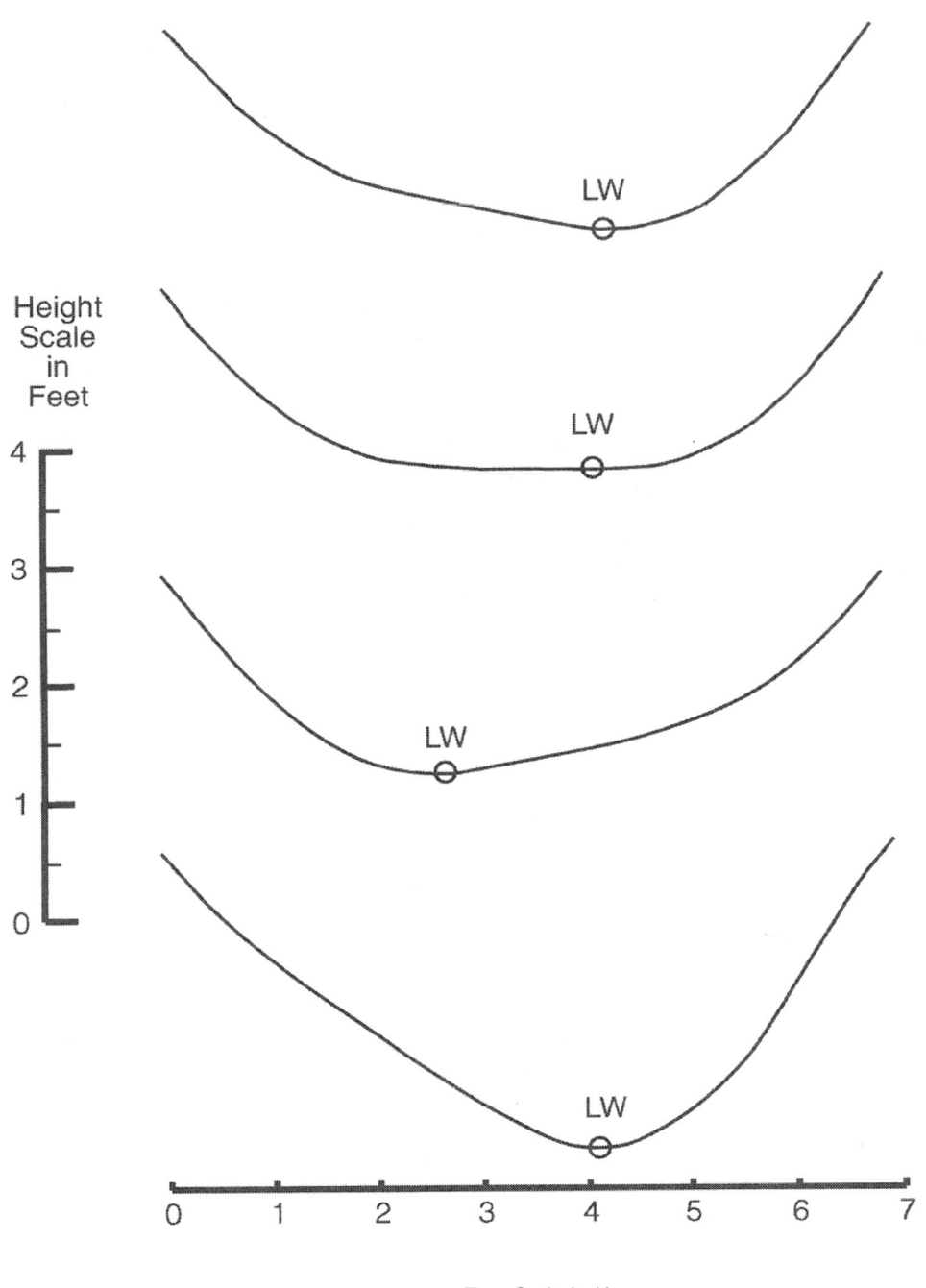

Time Scale in Hours

TABLE 2 – TIDAL DIFFERENCES AND OTHER CONSTANTS

No.	PLACE	POSITION		DIFFERENCES				RANGES		Mean Tide Level
		Latitude	Longitude	Time		Height		Mean	Spring	
				High Water	Low Water	High Water	Low Water			
		North	West	h m	h m	ft	ft	ft	ft	ft
	CONNECTICUT, Long Island Sound Time meridian, 75° W			on New London, p.60						
	Thames River									
1073	NEW LONDON, State Pier	41° 21.6'	72° 05.5'	*Daily predictions*				2.56	3.09	1.47
1075	Yale boathouse	41° 25.8'	72° 05.6'	+0 14	+0 10	*1.07	*1.11	2.73	3.22	1.57
1077	Norwich	41° 31.4'	72° 04.7'	+0 24	+0 19	*1.18	*1.21	3.03	3.57	1.75
1079	Niantic, Niantic River	41° 19.5'	72° 11.2'	+0 52	+0 57	*0.99	*0.84	2.58	3.04	1.44
	Connecticut River									
1081	Saybrook Jetty	41° 15.8'	72° 20.6'	+1 11	+0 45	*1.36	*1.35	3.5	4.2	2.0
1083	Saybrook Point	41° 17.0'	72° 21.0'	+1 11	+0 53	*1.24	*1.25	3.2	3.8	1.8
1085	Lyme, highway bridge	41° 19.3'	72° 21.0'	+1 36	+1 09	*1.26	*0.95	3.31	3.91	1.83
1087	Essex <7>	41° 20.9'	72° 23.1'	+1 39	+1 38	*1.16	*1.15	3.0	3.6	1.7
1089	Hadlyme <7>	41° 25.2'	72° 25.7'	+2 19	+2 23	*1.05	*1.05	2.7	3.2	1.5
1091	Tylerville <7>	41° 27.1'	72° 27.9'	+2 38	+2 51	*1.02	*1.02	2.71	3.20	1.46
1093	Haddam <7>	41° 28.9'	72° 30.4'	+2 48	+3 08	*0.97	*0.95	2.5	3.0	1.4
1095	Higganum Creek <7>	41° 30.2'	72° 33.2'	+3 08	+3 40	*0.91	*0.91	2.40	2.83	1.30
1097	Maromas <7>	41° 32.5'	72° 33.1'	+3 25	+4 01	*0.91	*0.91	2.41	2.84	1.31
1099	Middletown <7>	41° 33.6'	72° 38.7'	+3 54	+4 39	*0.83	*0.83	2.17	2.56	1.19
1101	Rocky Hill <7>	41° 39.8'	72° 37.8'	+4 30	+5 36	*0.72	*0.63	1.88	2.22	1.07
1103	South Hartford <7>	41° 45.3'	72° 39.5'	+5 24	+6 54	*0.74	*0.58	1.94	2.29	1.07
1105	Hartford <7>	41° 46.2'	72° 40.1'	+5 30	+6 52	*0.74	*0.75	1.9	2.3	1.1
				on Bridgeport, p.64						
1107	Westbrook, Duck Island Roads	41° 16.4'	72° 28.5'	−0 24	−0 32	*0.61	*0.60	4.1	4.7	2.2
1109	Clinton, Clinton Harbor	41° 16.1'	72° 31.9'	−0 11	−0 16	*0.67	*1.00	4.55	5.27	2.51
1111	Madison	41° 16.2'	72° 36.2'	−0 21	−0 30	*0.73	*0.72	4.9	5.6	2.6
1113	Guilford Harbor	41° 16.3'	72° 40.0'	−0 11	−0 21	*0.77	*0.96	5.19	5.92	2.83
1115	Sachem Head	41° 14.7'	72° 42.5'	−0 11	−0 15	*0.80	*0.80	5.4	6.2	2.9
1117	Branford, Branford River	41° 15.7'	72° 49.1'	−0 05	−0 13	*0.87	*0.96	5.85	6.67	3.15
1119	Lighthouse Point, New Haven Harbor	41° 15.1'	72° 54.3'	−0 04	−0 07	*0.91	*0.96	6.12	6.98	3.29
1121	New Haven Harbor, New Haven Reach	41° 17.0'	72° 54.5'	−0 01	−0 06	*0.92	*1.00	6.15	7.11	3.32
1123	Gulf Beach	41° 12.3'	73° 02.5'	−0 05	−0 08	*0.94	*1.04	6.29	7.17	3.40
1125	Milford Harbor	41° 13.1'	73° 03.3'	−0 02	−0 03	*0.94	*1.04	6.32	7.20	3.41
	Housatonic River									
1127	Sniffens Point	41° 11.2'	73° 06.8'	+0 10	+0 09	*0.96	*1.00	6.43	7.33	3.46
1129	Stratford, I-95 bridge	41° 12.2'	73° 06.7'	+0 23	+0 23	*0.98	*1.00	6.58	7.50	3.53
1131	Long Hill	41° 16.5'	73° 05.3'	+0 43	+1 13	*1.02	*1.04	6.85	7.81	3.67
1133	Shelton	41° 18.1'	73° 04.3'	+0 46	+1 19	*1.04	*0.96	7.01	7.99	3.74
1135	BRIDGEPORT	41° 10.4'	73° 10.9'	*Daily predictions*				6.74	7.80	3.61
1137	Black Rock Harbor	41° 09.4'	73° 12.8'	+0 00	+0 01	*1.00	*1.04	6.75	7.75	3.63
1139	Southport, Southport Harbor	41° 08.0'	73° 17.0'	−0 02	+0 02	*1.01	*1.00	6.84	8.18	3.66
1141	Saugatuck, Saugatuck River	41° 07.2'	73° 22.1'	+0 01	+0 09	*1.04	*1.00	6.99	8.14	3.74
1143	South Norwalk	41° 05.9'	73° 24.9'	+0 09	+0 15	*1.05	*1.04	7.1	8.2	3.8
1145	Rowayton, Fivemile River	41° 03.9'	73° 26.7'	+0 00	+0 05	*1.05	*1.08	7.09	8.08	3.80
1147	Long Neck Point	41° 02.3'	73° 28.8'	−0 09	+0 01	*1.06	*0.96	7.17	8.17	3.82
1149	Stamford	41° 02.3'	73° 32.8'	+0 03	+0 08	*1.07	*1.08	7.2	8.3	3.9
1151	Cos Cob Harbor	41° 01.0'	73° 35.8'	+0 05	+0 11	*1.07	*1.08	7.2	8.3	3.9
	NEW YORK Long Island Sound, north side			on Kings Point, p.68						
1153	Rye Beach	40° 57.7'	73° 40.3'	−0 20	−0 27	*1.00	*0.86	7.29	7.89	3.88
1155	New Rochelle	40° 53.6'	73° 46.9'	−0 16	−0 18	*1.01	*0.93	7.29	8.46	3.90
1157	Throgs Neck, Fort Schuyler	40° 48.3'	73° 47.7'	+0 01	+0 04	*1.00	*1.00	7.13	8.62	3.84
	East River									
1159	Whitestone	40° 47.9'	73° 48.8'	+0 07	+0 09	*1.00	*1.04	7.1	8.3	3.8
1161	College Point, Flushing Bay	40° 47.0'	73° 51.4'	+0 17	+0 16	*0.95	*1.04	6.8	7.9	3.7
1163	Worlds Fair Marina, Flushing Bay	40° 45.7'	73° 51.0'	+0 10	+0 16	*0.94	*1.00	6.75	8.10	3.65
1165	Hunts Point	40° 48.0'	73° 52.4'	+0 12	+0 10	*0.97	*1.07	6.92	7.57	3.75
1167	North Brother Island	40° 48.1'	73° 54.0'	+0 18	+0 18	*0.93	*1.11	6.6	7.8	3.6
1169	Port Morris (Stony Point)	40° 48.1'	73° 54.4'	+0 07	+0 10	*0.87	*0.96	6.24	6.85	3.39
				on New York, p.72						
1171	Hell Gate, Wards Island	40° 47.2'	73° 55.3'	+2 58	+3 45	*1.33	*1.59	6.0	7.3	3.4
1173	Horns Hook, East 90th Street	40° 46.6'	73° 56.5'	+1 54	+1 34	*1.03	*0.90	4.68	5.18	2.53
1175	Queensboro Bridge	40° 45.5'	73° 57.5'	+1 23	+0 57	*0.96	*1.00	4.33	5.24	2.38
1177	East 41st Street, New York City	40° 44.8'	73° 58.1'	+1 03	+0 46	*0.95	*1.09	4.31	4.89	2.40
1179	Hunters Point, Newtown Creek	40° 44.4'	73° 57.7'	+1 22	+0 56	*0.89	*0.90	4.1	4.9	2.2
1181	Williamsburg Bridge	40° 42.7'	73° 58.1'	+0 45	+0 28	*0.93	*0.95	4.22	5.11	2.31
1183	Wallabout Bay, Brooklyn Navy Yard	40° 42.4'	73° 58.5'	+0 32	+0 22	*0.94	*1.05	4.3	5.2	2.4
1185	Brooklyn Bridge	40° 42.2'	73° 59.3'	+0 24	−0 04	*0.99	*1.00	4.53	5.13	2.48
1187	Harlem River, Randalls Island	40° 48.0'	73° 55.6'	+1 55	+1 30	*1.00	*0.86	4.56	5.31	2.46
	Long Island, Long Island Sound			on Kings Point, p.68						
1189	Willets Point	40° 47.6'	73° 46.9'	−0 01	+0 00	*1.00	*1.04	7.15	8.21	3.88
1191	KINGS POINT	40° 48.6'	73° 45.9'	*Daily predictions*				7.16	8.46	3.86
1193	Port Washington, Manhasset Bay	40° 49.9'	73° 42.2'	−0 12	−0 12	*1.02	*0.96	7.29	8.46	3.92
1195	Glen Cove, Hempstead Harbor	40° 51.8'	73° 39.3'	−0 22	−0 26	*1.01	*0.82	7.27	7.87	3.87
1197	Harry Tappen Marina, Hempstead Harbor	40° 50.1'	73° 39.1'	−0 20	−0 23	*1.01	*0.82	7.29	8.87	3.88

Endnotes can be found at the end of table 2.

TABLE 2 – TIDAL DIFFERENCES AND OTHER CONSTANTS

No.	PLACE	POSITION		DIFFERENCES				RANGES		Mean Tide Level
				Time		Height				
		Latitude	Longitude	High Water	Low Water	High Water	Low Water	Mean	Spring	
		North	West	h m	h m	ft	ft	ft	ft	ft
	NEW YORK Long Island, Long Island Sound–cont. Time meridian, 75° W			on Bridgeport, p.64						
	Oyster Bay									
1199	Oyster Bay Harbor	40° 53'	73° 32'	+0 07	+0 13	*1.08	*1.08	7.3	8.4	3.9
1201	Bayville Bridge	40° 54.2'	73° 33.0'	−0 06	+0 04	*1.09	*1.04	7.37	7.99	3.94
1203	Cold Spring Harbor	40° 52.4'	73° 28.2'	−0 07	+0 02	*1.07	*0.92	7.27	7.86	3.86
1205	Eatons Neck Point	40° 57.2'	73° 24.0'	+0 02	+0 08	*1.05	*1.04	7.1	8.2	3.9
1207	Lloyd Harbor, Huntington Bay	40° 54.6'	73° 25.9'	−0 01	+0 07	*1.04	*0.88	7.02	7.60	3.73
1209	Northport, Northport Bay	40° 54.0'	73° 21.2'	−0 05	+0 04	*1.07	*0.92	7.25	7.84	3.86
1211	Port Jefferson Harbor entrance	40° 58'	73° 05'	+0 02	+0 01	*0.98	*0.98	6.6	7.6	3.5
1213	Port Jefferson	40° 57.0'	73° 04.6'	+0 04	+0 05	*0.98	*0.92	6.61	7.70	3.53
1215	Cedar Beach	40° 57.9'	73° 02.6'	+0 07	+0 05	*0.96	*1.00	6.43	7.01	3.46
1217	Mount Sinai Harbor	40° 57.8'	73° 02.4'	+0 04	+0 18	*0.89	*0.88	6.0	6.9	3.2
1219	Northville	40° 58.9'	72° 38.7'	+0 05	−0 03	*0.80	*0.92	5.35	6.10	2.89
1221	Mattituck Inlet	41° 00.9'	72° 33.7'	+0 11	+0 02	*0.76	*0.85	5.08	5.79	2.75
1223	Hashamomuck Beach	41° 05.7'	72° 23.9'	+0 03	−0 13	*0.64	*0.64	4.2	4.8	2.3
				on New London, p.60						
1225	Plum Gut Harbor, Plum Island	41° 10.3'	72° 12.3'	+0 33	+0 24	*1.01	*1.04	2.60	3.07	1.50
1227	Little Gull Island	41° 12.4'	72° 06.1'	+0 13	−0 22	*0.85	*0.85	2.2	2.6	1.3
	Shelter Island Sound									
1229	Orient	41° 08'	72° 18'	+0 37	+0 36	*0.97	*0.97	2.5	3.0	1.4
1231	Greenport	41° 06.1'	72° 21.7'	+1 12	+0 48	*0.95	*0.95	2.44	2.81	1.40
1233	Southold	41° 04'	72° 25'	+1 44	+1 33	*0.89	*0.89	2.3	2.7	1.3
1235	Noyack Bay	41° 00'	72° 20'	+2 06	+1 44	*0.89	*0.89	2.3	2.7	1.3
1237	Sag Harbor	41° 00.2'	72° 17.8'	+1 00	+0 48	*0.93	*0.89	2.41	2.78	1.37
	Peconic Bays									
1239	New Suffolk	41° 00'	72° 28'	+2 27	+2 11	*1.01	*1.00	2.6	3.1	1.5
1241	South Jamesport	40° 56.1'	72° 34.9'	+2 34	+2 43	*1.07	*0.95	2.79	3.29	1.57
1243	Threemile Harbor entrance, Gardiners Bay	41° 02.1'	72° 11.4'	+0 39	+0 19	*0.96	*1.00	2.48	2.98	1.44
1245	Lake Montauk	41° 04.4'	71° 56.1'	−0 26	−0 22	*0.77	*0.89	2.01	2.37	1.18
1247	Montauk Harbor entrance	41° 04.5'	71° 56.2'	−0 24	−0 16	*0.74	*0.75	1.9	2.3	1.0
1249	MONTAUK, FORT POND BAY	41° 02.9'	71° 57.6'	Daily Predictions, p.56				2.07	2.66	1.21
	Long Island, south shore			on Sandy Hook, p.84						
1251	Shinnecock Inlet (ocean)	40° 50.2'	72° 28.8'	−0 16	−1 11	*0.66	*0.68	3.08	3.68	1.67
	Shinnecock Bay									
1253	Shinnecock Bay entrance	40° 49.2'	72° 33.7'	+1 12	+1 51	*0.51	*0.37	2.41	2.89	1.27
1255	Ponquoque Point	40° 51.0'	72° 30.2'	−0 06	+0 03	*0.60	*0.65	2.81	3.20	1.53
1257	Shinnecock Yacht Club, Penniman Creek	40° 49.1'	72° 33.2'	+1 01	+1 45	*0.55	*0.55	2.56	2.93	1.39
1259	Moriches Inlet	40° 45.8'	72° 45.3'	−0 10	−1 08	*0.61	*0.79	2.83	3.40	1.56
1261	Moriches Inlet Coast Guard Station	40° 47.2'	72° 45.0'	+0 42	+0 48	*0.46	*0.63	2.15	2.51	1.19
1263	Smith Point Bridge, Narrow Bay	40° 44.3'	72° 52.1'	+1 58	+2 34	*0.27	*0.60	1.19	1.47	0.71
1265	Democrat Point, Fire Island Inlet	40° 38'	73° 18'	−0 39	−0 27	*0.56	*0.55	2.6	3.1	1.4
	Great South Bay									
1267	Fire Island Coast Guard Station	40° 37.6'	73° 15.6'	−0 04	−0 01	*0.42	*0.74	1.89	2.19	1.08
1269	Fire Island Light	40° 38.1'	73° 13.2'	+0 46	+1 22	*0.15	*0.15	0.7	0.8	0.3
1271	West Fire Island	40° 39.4'	73° 12.3'	+2 10	+2 18	*0.13	*0.13	0.6	0.7	0.3
1273	Seaview Ferry Dock	40° 38.9'	73° 09.0'	+2 20	+2 23	*0.27	*0.68	1.18	1.31	0.72
1275	Patchogue	40° 45.0'	73° 00.0'	+3 14	+3 33	*0.25	*0.53	1.11	1.33	0.66
1277	Great River, Connetquot River	40° 43.4'	73° 09.1'	+3 19	+3 32	*0.15	*0.15	0.7	0.8	0.3
1279	Bay Shore, Watchogue Creek Entrance	40° 43.0'	73° 14.4'	+2 15	+2 27	*0.22	*0.37	0.99	1.19	0.57
1281	Oak Beach	40° 38.5'	73° 17.2'	+2 23	+2 58	*0.15	*0.15	0.7	0.8	0.3
1283	Babylon	40° 41.1'	73° 18.9'	+2 11	+2 41	*0.13	*0.15	0.6	0.7	0.3
1285	Gilgo Heading	40° 37.2'	73° 23.7'	+2 22	+2 58	*0.24	*0.25	1.1	1.3	0.5
1287	Amityville	40° 39.3'	73° 25.1'	+2 20	+3 05	*0.26	*0.25	1.2	1.4	0.7
1289	Biltmore Shores, South Oyster Bay	40° 40'	73° 28'	+2 04	+2 32	*0.30	*0.30	1.4	1.7	0.8
1291	Point Lookout, Jones Inlet	40° 35.2'	73° 34.7'	−0 20	−0 25	*0.77	*0.75	3.6	4.3	2.0
1293	Point Lookout (marina), Jones Inlet	40° 35.6'	73° 35.0'	−0 02	−0 15	*0.89	*0.75	4.14	4.86	2.26
	Hempstead Bay									
1295	Deep Creek Meadow	40° 36.2'	73° 31.5'	+1 01	+1 11	*0.51	*0.50	2.4	2.9	1.3
1297	Green Island Drawbridge	40° 37.4'	73° 30.1'	+0 33	+0 31	*0.67	*0.89	3.11	3.56	1.72
1299	Cuba Island	40° 37.2'	73° 31.4'	+1 07	+1 22	*0.49	*0.50	2.3	2.8	1.2
1301	Bellmore, Bellmore Creek	40° 39.8'	73° 31.2'	+1 28	+1 58	*0.43	*0.45	2.0	2.4	1.1
1303	Neds Creek	40° 37.4'	73° 33.3'	+0 49	+0 54	*0.58	*0.60	2.7	3.3	1.4
1305	Freeport, Baldwin Bay	40° 38.0'	73° 35.2'	+0 37	+0 55	*0.64	*0.65	3.0	3.6	1.6
1307	Baldwin, Parsonage Cove	40° 38.0'	73° 37.0'	+0 10	+0 20	*0.93	*0.95	4.35	5.08	2.36
1309	Long Beach (Inside)	40° 36'	73° 39'	+0 18	+0 02	*0.84	*0.85	3.9	4.7	2.1
1311	Long Beach, Bridgewater Yacht Club	40° 35.7'	73° 39.3'	+0 06	+0 08	*0.94	*0.89	4.43	5.14	2.39
1313	Bay Park, Hewlett Bay	40° 37.7'	73° 40.1'	+0 20	+0 25	*0.99	*1.00	4.63	5.33	2.51
1315	Woodmere, Brosewere Bay	40° 37'	73° 42'	+0 34	+0 50	*0.84	*0.85	3.9	4.7	2.1
1317	East Rockaway Inlet, Atlantic Beach	40° 35.6'	73° 44.4'	−0 05	−0 21	*0.93	*1.00	4.37	5.16	2.38
	Jamaica Bay									
1319	Plumb Beach Channel	40° 35.1'	73° 55.5'	+0 02	−0 03	*1.05	*1.05	4.9	5.9	2.6
1321	Barren Island, Rockaway Inlet	40° 34.7'	73° 53.3'	−0 01	−0 04	*1.07	*1.05	5.0	6.0	2.7
1323	Beach Channel (bridge)	40° 35'	73° 49'	+0 37	+0 24	*1.09	*1.10	5.1	6.2	2.7
1325	Motts Basin	40° 37.0'	73° 45.5'	+0 39	+0 48	*1.16	*1.15	5.4	6.5	2.9
1327	Norton Point, Hook Creek	40° 38.1'	73° 44.8'	+0 38	+0 45	*1.16	*1.16	5.4	6.5	2.9
1329	J.F.K. International Airport	40° 37.4'	73° 47.0'	+0 25	+0 45	*1.14	*1.15	5.3	6.4	2.8
1331	North Channel Bridge, Grassy Bay	40° 39'	73° 50'	+0 43	+0 47	*1.12	*1.10	5.2	6.3	2.8
1333	Canarsie	40° 37.8'	73° 53.1'	+0 27	+0 08	*1.12	*1.10	5.2	6.3	2.8
1335	Mill Basin	40° 37'	73° 55'	+0 28	+0 04	*1.12	*1.10	5.2	6.3	2.8

Endnotes can be found at the end of table 2.

TABLE 2 – TIDAL DIFFERENCES AND OTHER CONSTANTS

No.	PLACE	POSITION		DIFFERENCES				RANGES		Mean Tide Level
		Latitude	Longitude	Time		Height		Mean	Spring	
				High Water	Low Water	High Water	Low Water			
		North	West	h m	h m	ft	ft	ft	ft	ft
	NEW YORK and NEW JERSEY New York Harbor Time meridian, 75° W			**on Sandy Hook, p.84**						
1337	Coney Island	40° 34'	73° 59'	−0 04	−0 17	*1.01	*1.00	4.7	5.7	2.5
1339	Norton Point, Gravesend Bay	40° 35.4'	73° 59.9'	−0 01	+0 03	*1.02	*1.15	4.7	5.7	2.6
1341	Fort Wadsworth, The Narrows	40° 36.4'	74° 03.3'	+0 06	+0 06	*0.98	*1.05	4.8	5.4	2.5
1343	Fort Hamilton, The Narrows	40° 36.5'	74° 02.1'	+0 02	+0 07	*1.01	*1.00	4.7	5.7	2.5
1345	U.S. Coast Guard Station, Staten Island	40° 36.7'	74° 03.6'	+0 12	+0 11	*0.96	*1.05	4.47	5.35	2.43
				on New York, p.72						
1347	St. George, Staten Island	40° 38.6'	74° 04.4'	−0 17	−0 15	*0.99	*0.99	4.5	5.4	2.4
1349	Gowanus Bay	40° 39.9'	74° 00.8'	−0 18	−0 12	*1.03	*0.95	4.7	5.7	2.6
1351	NEW YORK (The Battery)	40° 42.0'	74° 00.9'	*Daily Predictions*				4.53	5.50	2.47
	Hudson River <8>									
1353	Weehawken, Union City, N.J.	40° 45.9'	74° 01.1'	+0 13	+0 15	*0.96	*0.96	4.37	5.29	2.41
1355	Edgewater, N.J.	40° 48.8'	73° 58.7'	+0 31	+0 28	*0.93	*0.93	4.24	5.13	2.33
1357	Dyckman Street, Ferry Slip, N.Y.	40° 52.0'	73° 56.0'	+0 51	+0 44	*0.88	*0.81	3.98	4.66	2.16
1359	Spuyten Duyvil Creek ent., N.Y.	40° 52.7'	73° 55.5'	+0 52	+0 48	*0.84	*0.84	3.85	4.66	2.20
1361	Riverdale, N.Y.	40° 54.2'	73° 54.9'	+0 48	+0 49	*0.85	*0.85	3.86	4.67	2.13
1363	Alpine, N.J.	40° 56.7'	73° 55.1'	+1 05	+1 02	*0.83	*0.90	3.75	4.54	2.06
1365	Tarrytown	41° 04.7'	73° 52.2'	+1 49	+1 57	*0.70	*0.70	3.2	3.7	1.8
1367	Haverstraw	41° 13.1'	73° 57.8'	+2 15	+2 42	*0.72	*0.81	3.23	3.91	1.78
1369	Peekskill	41° 17'	73° 56'	+2 28	+3 03	*0.64	*0.64	2.9	3.4	1.8
1371	Newburgh	41° 30.0'	74° 00.4'	+3 46	+4 03	*0.62	*0.64	2.8	3.2	1.5
1373	Beacon	41° 30.3'	73° 58.2'	+3 37	+3 49	*0.70	*0.90	3.13	3.68	1.75
1375	New Hamburg	41° 35'	73° 57'	+4 04	+4 28	*0.64	*0.64	2.9	3.3	1.6
1377	Poughkeepsie	41° 42'	73° 57'	+4 34	+4 46	*0.68	*0.68	3.1	3.5	1.7
1379	Hyde Park	41° 47.2'	73° 57.8'	+5 00	+5 12	*0.70	*0.68	3.2	3.6	1.8
1381	Kingston	41° 55'	73° 59'	+5 20	+5 34	*0.81	*0.82	3.7	4.2	2.0
1383	Tivoli	42° 04'	73° 56'	+5 50	+6 04	*0.86	*0.86	3.9	4.4	1.9
1385	Hudson	42° 15'	73° 48'	+6 58	+7 12	*0.88	*0.86	4.0	4.4	2.2
				on Albany, p.80						
1387	Castleton	42° 32'	73° 46'	−0 17	−0 29	−0.2	+0.1	4.3	4.7	2.2
1389	ALBANY	42° 39.0'	73° 44.8'	*Daily predictions*				4.6	5.0	2.5
1391	Troy	42° 44'	73° 42'	+0 08	+0 10	*1.00	*1.00	4.7	5.1	2.3
	The Kills and Newark Bay			**on New York, p.72**						
	Kill Van Kull									
1393	Constable Hook	40° 39.3'	74° 05.2'	−0 18	−0 08	*1.02	*1.02	4.63	5.60	2.54
1395	BAYONNE BRIDGE, STATEN ISLAND	40° 38.4'	74° 08.8'	*Daily predictions, p.76*				4.98	5.52	2.70
1397	Port Elizabeth	40° 40.4'	74° 08.4'	−0 02	+0 13	*1.11	*0.95	5.05	6.11	2.73
1399	Port Newark Terminal	40° 41'	74° 08'	+0 03	+0 21	*1.12	*1.12	5.1	6.1	2.7
	Passaic River									
1401	Point No Point	40° 43.9'	74° 07.0'	+0 00	+0 22	*1.15	*1.04	5.21	6.30	2.83
1403	Belleville	40° 47.2'	74° 08.8'	+0 09	+0 49	*1.23	*1.19	5.60	6.78	3.08
1405	East Rutherford	40° 50.8'	74° 07.2'	+0 09	+1 06	*1.29	*1.29	5.87	7.10	3.20
1407	Garfield	40° 52.1'	74° 06.7'	+0 08	− − −	− − −	− − −	− −	− −	− −
	Hackensack River									
1409	Kearny Point	40° 43.7'	74° 06.2'	+0 11	+0 22	*1.15	*1.14	5.21	6.30	2.85
1411	Amtrak RR. swing bridge	40° 45.1'	74° 05.8'	+0 33	+0 39	*1.16	*1.10	5.27	6.38	2.87
1413	Fish Creek, Berrys Creek	40° 47.6'	74° 05.5'	+1 02	+1 00	*1.16	*1.00	5.31	6.43	2.86
1415	Carlstadt, Garretts Reach	40° 48.4'	74° 03.6'	+0 59	+0 45	*1.26	*1.29	5.71	6.89	3.12
1417	North Secaucus, Garretts Reach	40° 48.4'	74° 02.6'	+0 57	+0 57	*1.23	*1.23	5.61	6.79	3.06
1419	Mill Creek, 0.8 n.mi. above entrance	40° 47.9'	74° 03.0'	+1 34	− − −	− − −	− − −	− −	− −	− −
1421	Cromakill Creek, N.J. Turnpike	40° 48.2'	74° 02.0'	+1 00	− − −	− − −	− − −	− −	− −	− −
1423	Ridgefield Park	40° 51.0'	74° 01.8'	+1 00	+1 00	*1.26	*1.26	5.73	6.93	− −
1425	Hackensack	40° 52.8'	74° 02.4'	+1 06	+1 00	*1.33	*1.38	6.01	7.27	3.29
1427	New Millford	40° 56.1'	74° 01.8'	+1 17	+2 49	*1.02	*1.02	4.76	5.76	2.44
	Arthur Kill			**on Sandy Hook, p.84**						
1429	Port Ivory, Howland Hook, N.Y.	40° 38.7'	74° 10.8'	+0 27	+0 39	*1.09	*1.09	5.10	6.12	2.78
1431	Rahway River, RR. Bridge	40° 35.9'	74° 13.9'	+0 17	+0 30	*1.14	*1.16	5.36	6.49	2.91
1433	Chelsea	40° 36'	74° 12'	+0 23	+0 37	*1.07	*1.05	5.0	6.0	2.7
1435	Carteret	40° 35.2'	74° 12.6'	+0 22	+0 33	*1.09	*1.09	5.1	6.2	2.8
1437	Rossville, N.Y.	40° 33.3'	74° 13.4'	+0 20	+0 29	*1.12	*1.12	5.22	5.84	2.89
1439	Woodbridge Creek, 0.8 n.mi. above entrance	40° 32.7'	74° 15.9'	+0 09	+0 21	*1.10	*1.00	5.20	6.29	2.79
	Lower New York Bay, Raritan Bay, etc.									
1441	Great Kills Harbor	40° 32.6'	74° 08.4'	−0 01	+0 04	*1.05	*1.16	4.91	5.79	2.67
1443	Princes Bay	40° 30.7'	74° 12.0'	+0 00	+0 06	*1.05	*1.05	4.9	5.9	2.6
	Raritan River									
1445	South Amboy	40° 29.5'	74° 16.9'	−0 04	+0 08	*1.09	*1.09	5.09	6.11	2.77
1447	Keasbey	40° 30.5'	74° 18.7'	+0 06	+0 18	*1.10	*1.00	5.21	6.25	2.85
1449	Sayreville	40° 28.7'	74° 21.4'	+0 11	+0 25	*1.14	*1.21	5.43	6.57	2.95
1451	Old Bridge, South River	40° 25.0'	74° 21.8'	+0 48	+0 59	*1.18	*1.16	5.58	6.75	3.01
1453	New Brunswick	40° 29.3'	74° 26.1'	+0 32	+0 48	*1.21	*1.16	5.71	6.91	3.08
1455	Cheesequake Creek, Garden State Parkway	40° 27.2'	74° 16.4'	+0 12	+0 13	*1.09	*1.05	5.12	6.20	2.77

Endnotes can be found at the end of table 2.

TABLE 2 – TIDAL DIFFERENCES AND OTHER CONSTANTS

No.	PLACE	POSITION		DIFFERENCES				RANGES		Mean Tide Level
				Time		Height				
		Latitude	Longitude	High Water	Low Water	High Water	Low Water	Mean	Spring	
		North	West	h m	h m	ft	ft	ft	ft	ft
	NEW YORK and NEW JERSEY Lower New York Bay, Raritan Bay, etc.–cont. Time meridian, 75° W			on Sandy Hook, p.84						
1457	Keyport	40° 26.4'	74° 11.9'	−0 04	+0 06	*1.08	*1.10	5.05	6.06	2.74
1459	Matawan Creek, Route 35 bridge	40° 26.0'	74° 13.1'	−0 01	+0 07	*1.08	*1.08	5.06	6.12	2.77
1461	Waackaack Creek	40° 26.9'	74° 08.6'	−0 06	+0 21	*0.99	*0.99	4.62	5.54	2.47
	NEW JERSEY Sandy Hook Bay									
1463	Pews Creek	40° 26.5'	74° 06.3'	−0 08	− − −	− − −	− − −	− −	− −	− −
1465	Compton Creek	40° 25.9'	74° 05.1'	+0 13	− − −	− − −	− − −	− −	− −	− −
1467	Atlantic Highlands	40° 25.1'	74° 02.1'	−0 10	−0 10	*1.01	*1.01	4.71	5.65	2.55
1469	SANDY HOOK (Fort Hancock)	40° 28.0'	74° 00.6'	Daily predictions				4.70	5.71	2.54
	Shrewsbury River									
1471	Highlands, Route 36 bridge	40° 23.8'	73° 58.9'	+0 17	+0 14	*0.90	*0.90	4.19	5.03	2.27
1473	Oceanic Bridge, Navesink River	40° 22.6'	74° 00.9'	+1 13	+1 45	*0.72	*0.63	3.41	4.13	1.82
1475	Red Bank, Navesink River	40° 21.3'	74° 03.9'	+1 17	+1 57	*0.74	*0.63	3.51	4.25	1.87
1477	Sea Bright	40° 21.9'	73° 58.5'	+1 15	+1 07	*0.68	*0.68	3.15	3.78	1.74
1479	Gooseneck Point, bridge	40° 19.6'	74° 01.0'	+2 18	+2 41	*0.55	*0.55	2.57	3.08	1.44
1481	Long Branch Reach	40° 19.5'	73° 59.8'	+2 18	+2 41	*0.56	*0.63	2.60	3.15	1.42
	Outer Coast									
1483	Long Branch (fishing pier)	40° 18.2'	73° 58.6'	−0 26	−0 36	*0.94	*1.00	4.40	5.28	2.39
	Shark River									
1485	Shark River Island, fixed RR. bridge	40° 11.2'	74° 01.6'	−0 13	−0 08	*0.93	*0.93	4.32	5.18	2.32
1487	Shark River Hills	40° 11.6'	74° 02.3'	−0 13	−0 09	*0.94	*0.94	4.40	5.28	2.38
1489	New Bedford	40° 10.7'	74° 02.8'	−0 13	−0 07	*0.95	*0.95	4.41	5.29	2.40
1491	Belmar, Atlantic Ocean	40° 11.1'	74° 00.5'	−0 35	−0 45	*0.95	*0.95	4.43	5.32	2.38
1493	Manasquan Inlet, USCG Station	40° 06.1'	74° 02.1'	−0 12	−0 24	*0.86	*0.95	4.02	4.82	2.19
	Manasquan River									
1495	Brielle, Route 35 bridge	40° 06.3'	74° 03.3'	−0 06	−0 20	*0.83	*0.83	3.86	4.63	2.10
1497	Riviera Beach	40° 05.8'	74° 05.2'	+0 08	+0 38	*0.73	*0.73	3.39	4.07	1.83
	Metedeconk River									
1499	Beaverdam Creek entrance	40° 03.7'	74° 03.7'	+2 41	+2 40	*0.07	*0.37	0.30	0.36	0.22
1501	Beaverdam Creek, inside	40° 03.7'	74° 04.4'	+2 49	+2 47	*0.06	*0.06	0.29	0.35	0.25
1503	Forge Pond	40° 03.9'	74° 08.1'	+2 17	+2 07	*0.07	*0.07	0.31	0.37	0.23
1505	Tall Pines Camp	40° 03.5'	74° 07.0'	+2 23	+2 24	*0.06	*0.06	0.30	0.36	0.23
1507	Seaside Heights, ocean	39° 56.5'	74° 04.1'	−0 30	−0 32	*0.92	*0.92	4.29	5.15	2.33
	Barnegat Bay									
1509	Mantoloking	40° 02.2'	74° 03.2'	+4 28	+4 39	*0.07	*0.07	0.33	0.40	0.25
1511	Kettle Creek, Green Island	40° 00.8'	74° 06.8'	+4 23	+4 41	*0.08	*0.08	0.38	0.46	0.28
1513	Ocean Beach	39° 59.3'	74° 04.1'	+4 17	+4 36	*0.08	*0.08	0.37	0.44	0.27
1515	Silver Bay, Silver Bay Marina	39° 59.8'	74° 08.9'	+4 26	+4 39	*0.08	*0.08	0.37	0.44	0.27
1517	Goose Creek entrance	39° 57.8'	74° 06.9'	+4 06	+4 29	*0.08	*0.08	0.35	0.42	0.25
1519	Coates Point	39° 56.9'	74° 06.9'	+4 00	+4 21	*0.08	*0.08	0.37	0.44	0.25
1521	Toms River (town), Toms River	39° 57.0'	74° 11.9'	+3 33	+3 48	*0.18	*0.47	0.78	0.83	0.48
1523	Seaside Park	39° 55.3'	74° 05.0'	+3 40	+4 05	*0.08	*0.08	0.38	0.46	0.25
1525	Barnegat Pier	39° 55.1'	74° 06.6'	+3 35	+3 55	*0.08	*0.08	0.36	0.43	0.23
1527	Sloop Creek	39° 54.3'	74° 08.0'	+3 38	+4 01	*0.08	*0.08	0.35	0.42	0.22
1529	Cedar Creek	39° 52.2'	74° 09.3'	+3 23	+3 45	*0.08	*0.08	0.35	0.42	0.23
1531	Island Beach	39° 51.1'	74° 05.4'	+3 04	+3 28	*0.08	*0.08	0.35	0.42	0.24
1533	Stouts Creek	39° 50.7'	74° 09.1'	+3 16	+3 33	*0.06	*0.06	0.30	0.36	0.20
1535	Forked River	39° 49.5'	74° 10.4'	+3 08	+3 20	*0.07	*0.07	0.32	0.38	0.24
1537	Oyster Creek	39° 48.5'	74° 11.3'	+3 30	+3 36	*0.06	*0.06	0.29	0.35	0.20
1539	Island Beach, Sedge Islands	39° 47.3'	74° 05.9'	+3 00	+3 56	*0.07	*0.07	0.34	0.41	0.24
1541	Waretown	39° 47.5'	74° 10.9'	+2 43	+3 00	*0.07	*0.07	0.34	0.41	0.24
1543	Barnegat Inlet, USCG Station	39° 45.7'	74° 06.7'	−0 12	+0 02	*0.47	*0.63	2.16	2.59	1.20
1545	High Bar	39° 45.4'	74° 07.7'	+1 04	+1 55	*0.12	*0.12	0.54	0.65	0.39
1547	Double Creek	39° 44.7'	74° 12.1'	+3 03	+3 33	*0.07	*0.07	0.31	0.37	0.19
1549	Loveladies Harbor	39° 43.5'	74° 08.2'	+3 02	+3 39	*0.10	*0.10	0.46	0.55	0.30
	Manahawkin Bay									
1551	Flat Creek	39° 42.4'	74° 11.5'	+3 33	+4 35	*0.18	*0.18	0.84	1.01	0.49
1553	North Beach	39° 40.5'	74° 09.6'	+3 02	+4 07	*0.22	*0.22	1.02	1.22	0.58
1555	Manahawkin Creek	39° 40.0'	74° 12.9'	+2 50	+3 51	*0.27	*0.27	1.25	1.50	0.69
1557	Manahawkin Drawbridge	39° 39.2'	74° 11.1'	+2 47	+3 39	*0.27	*0.27	1.26	1.51	0.70
	Little Egg Harbor									
1559	Mill Creek, 1 n.mi. above entrance	39° 39.9'	74° 13.9'	+2 32	+3 33	*0.35	*0.35	1.61	1.93	0.87
1561	Cedar Run	39° 39.2'	74° 15.4'	+2 10	+2 56	*0.40	*0.40	1.86	2.23	1.01
1563	Dinner Point Creek, upper end	39° 39.4'	74° 16.2'	+2 41	+3 17	*0.40	*0.40	1.88	2.26	1.03
1565	Beach Haven Crest	39° 36.8'	74° 12.6'	+2 13	+2 59	*0.38	*0.32	1.81	2.19	0.96
1567	Westecunk Creek entrance, Long Point	39° 36.8'	74° 15.8'	+2 00	+2 40	*0.42	*0.47	1.97	2.38	1.07
1569	West Creek, Westecunk Creek	39° 37.9'	74° 17.8'	+2 10	+2 40	*0.44	*0.47	2.08	2.52	1.13
1571	Parker Run, upper end	39° 37.0'	74° 18.6'	+2 05	+2 39	*0.45	*0.47	2.09	2.53	1.13
1573	Tuckerton Creek entrance	39° 34.6'	74° 19.9'	+1 32	+1 59	*0.45	*0.45	2.11	2.53	1.15
1575	Tuckerton, Tuckerton Creek	39° 36.1'	74° 20.5'	+1 45	+2 15	*0.45	*0.47	2.11	2.55	1.14
1577	Beach Haven Coast Guard Station	39° 32.9'	74° 15.4'	+1 18	+1 23	*0.46	*0.58	2.15	2.60	1.19
	Great Bay									
1579	Shooting Thorofare, Little Egg Inlet	39° 30.5'	74° 19.5'	+0 38	+0 21	*0.62	*0.79	2.88	3.24	1.59
1581	Little Sheepshead Creek	39° 31.1'	74° 19.2'	+0 35	+0 44	*0.66	*0.68	3.10	3.75	1.68
1583	Seven Island, Newmans Thorofare	39° 31.0'	74° 20.2'	+0 32	+0 28	*0.73	*0.73	3.4	4.1	1.8
1585	Graveling Point	39° 32.4'	74° 23.2'	+0 44	+1 14	*0.68	*0.68	3.18	3.82	1.72

Endnotes can be found at the end of table 2.

TABLE 2 – TIDAL DIFFERENCES AND OTHER CONSTANTS

No.	PLACE	POSITION		DIFFERENCES				RANGES		Mean Tide Level
				Time		Height				
		Latitude	Longitude	High Water	Low Water	High Water	Low Water	Mean	Spring	
		North	West	h m	h m	ft	ft	ft	ft	ft
	NEW JERSEY Outer Coast–cont. Time meridian, 75° W					on Sandy Hook, p.84				
	Mullica River									
1587	Nacote Creek, U.S. Highway 9 bridge	39° 32.1'	74° 27.8'	+1 34	+1 55	*0.66	*0.68	3.09	3.74	1.68
1589	Chestnut Neck Boat Yard	39° 32.9'	74° 27.7'	+1 27	+2 01	*0.63	*0.79	2.94	3.53	1.74
1591	New Gretna, Bass River	39° 35.5'	74° 26.5'	+1 52	+2 06	*0.66	*0.74	3.10	3.75	1.69
1593	Wading River (town), Wading River	39° 37.1'	74° 29.8'	+2 48	+2 44	*0.64	*0.79	2.98	3.61	1.64
1595	Green Bank	39° 36.7'	74° 35.4'	+2 59	+3 16	*0.66	*0.66	3.07	3.68	1.70
1597	Sweetwater, Mullica River Marina	39° 37.5'	74° 38.5'	+3 23	+4 21	*0.56	*0.56	2.42	3.14	1.42
						on Atlantic City, p.88				
1599	Main Marsh Thorofare	39° 28.7'	74° 23.0'	+1 10	+1 52	*0.80	*0.76	3.21	3.92	1.74
1601	Brigantine Channel @ Hoffman Thorofare	39° 26.1'	74° 21.8'	+0 59	+0 58	*0.90	*0.88	3.63	4.43	1.97
1603	Reed Bay, Turtle Cove	39° 27.2'	74° 25.6'	+1 07	– – –	– – –	– – –	– –	– –	– –
1605	Absecon, Absecon Creek, U.S. Hwy. 30 bridge ...	39° 25.4'	74° 30.0'	+1 28	+1 37	*0.96	*0.94	3.87	4.72	2.09
1607	Absecon Channel, State Route 87 bridge	39° 23.1'	74° 25.5'	+0 38	+0 26	*0.96	*1.13	3.90	4.68	2.13
1609	ATLANTIC CITY, OCEAN	39° 21.3'	74° 25.1'		Daily predictions			4.02	4.90	2.18
1611	Ventnor City, ocean pier	39° 20.1'	74° 28.6'	−0 02	−0 02	*1.00	*1.00	4.04	4.92	2.19
1613	Longport (inside), Great Egg Harbor Inlet	39° 18.5'	74° 32.0'	+0 26	+0 32	*0.94	*0.88	3.78	4.61	2.04
1615	Dock Thorofare, Risley Channel	39° 21.1'	74° 32.4'	+0 55	+1 00	*0.98	*0.94	3.92	4.78	2.12
1617	Pleasantville, Lakes Bay, Great Egg Harbor Inlet .	39° 22.9'	74° 31.1'	+1 00	+1 37	*0.98	*0.82	3.96	4.83	2.12
	Great Egg Harbor Bay									
1619	Beesleys Point	39° 17.3'	74° 37.7'	+0 55	+1 32	*0.87	*1.00	3.55	4.26	1.93
1621	Steelmanville, Patcong Ck., 2.5 nm above ent. ..	39° 20.1'	74° 35.8'	+1 28	+1 50	*0.92	*0.94	3.70	4.51	2.01
1623	Tuckahoe, Tuckahoe River	39° 17.7'	74° 44.9'	+2 12	+2 40	*0.86	*1.25	3.47	4.16	1.93
1625	Cedar Swamp Creek, Tuckahoe River	39° 14.8'	74° 43.1'	+3 14	+3 03	*0.78	*1.53	2.99	3.65	1.75
1627	River Bend Marina, Great Egg Harbor River	39° 22.1'	74° 43.0'	+2 12	+2 25	*0.87	*1.00	3.47	4.23	1.90
1629	Mays Landing, Great Egg Harbor River	39° 26.9'	74° 43.7'	+2 50	+3 10	*1.01	*1.12	4.06	4.95	2.22
	Corson Inlet									
1631	Strathmere, Strathmere Bay	39° 12.0'	74° 39.4'	+0 31	+0 38	*0.95	*1.00	3.81	4.65	2.07
1633	Middle Thorofare, Ocean Drive bridge	39° 12.9'	74° 38.9'	+0 31	+0 30	*0.95	*0.94	3.80	4.64	2.06
1635	Ludlam Bay, west side	39° 10.6'	74° 42.6'	+0 56	+1 12	*0.98	*0.94	3.94	4.81	2.13
	Townsends Inlet									
1637	Ocean Drive bridge	39° 07.3'	74° 43.0'	+0 29	+0 21	*0.99	*1.06	3.96	4.62	2.16
1639	Townsend Sound	39° 08.8'	74° 45.0'	+1 08	+1 39	*0.90	*0.59	3.69	4.50	1.95
1641	Stites Sound	39° 07.2'	74° 45.3'	+0 49	+1 04	*0.97	*1.00	3.98	4.78	2.15
1643	Ingram Thorofare	39° 06.6'	74° 44.4'	+0 44	+0 50	*0.96	*1.00	3.93	4.72	2.12
1645	Long Reach, Ingram Thorofare	39° 06.1'	74° 45.3'	+1 06	+1 11	*0.98	*1.06	4.00	4.80	2.17
	Hereford Inlet									
1647	Great Sound, west side	39° 06.1'	74° 47.3'	+0 56	– – –	– – –	– – –	– –	– –	– –
1649	Stone Harbor, Great Channel	39° 03.4'	74° 45.9'	+1 01	+1 12	*1.08	*1.00	4.02	4.82	2.17
1651	Jenkins Sound	39° 03.9'	74° 48.5'	+0 52	– – –	– – –	– – –	– –	– –	– –
1653	Nummy Island, Grassy Sound Channel	39° 01.7'	74° 48.1'	+0 32	+0 45	*1.00	*1.00	4.09	4.91	2.21
1655	West Wildwood, Grassy Sound	39° 00.3'	74° 49.6'	+0 57	+1 11	*1.04	*1.00	4.27	5.12	2.30
1657	Old Turtle Thorofare, RR. bridge	39° 01.1'	74° 50.5'	+0 56	+1 10	*1.06	*1.00	4.33	5.20	2.33
1659	Wildwood Crest, ocean pier	38° 58.5'	74° 49.4'	+0 03	+0 03	*1.07	*1.06	4.31	5.15	2.34
	Cape May Inlet									
1661	Swain Channel, Taylor Sound	38° 58.8'	74° 51.8'	+0 55	+0 40	*1.09	*1.06	4.46	5.35	2.40
1663	Wildwood Crest, Sunset Lake	38° 58.7'	74° 50.2'	+0 52	+0 47	*1.10	*1.06	4.50	5.40	2.42
1665	Cape May Harbor	38° 56.9'	74° 53.5'	+0 33	+0 19	*1.10	*1.06	4.49	5.39	2.42
1667	Cape Island Creek, Cape May	38° 56.8'	74° 54.8'	+0 40	+0 20	*1.11	*1.19	4.51	5.41	2.44
1669	Cape May, Atlantic Ocean	38° 55.8'	74° 56.1'	+0 34	+0 21	*1.12	*1.06	4.59	5.51	2.46
	Delaware Bay, Eastern Shore					on Breakwater Harbor, p.92				
1671	Brandywine Shoal Light	38° 59.2'	75° 06.8'	+0 12	+0 17	*1.19	*1.06	4.89	5.77	2.61
1673	Cape May Point, Sunset Beach	38° 56.8'	74° 58.3'	−0 05	−0 08	*1.16	*1.16	4.80	5.66	2.56
1675	Cape May, ferry terminal	38° 58.1'	74° 57.5'	−0 06	−0 05	*1.18	*1.00	4.85	5.73	2.58
1677	North Highlands Beach	39° 01.1'	74° 57.2'	+0 04	+0 14	*1.26	*1.26	5.24	6.18	2.78
1679	Dias Creek, Route 47 bridge	39° 05.0'	74° 53.2'	+1 09	+3 18	*0.46	*0.46	1.89	2.23	1.04
1681	Bidwell Creek entrance	39° 07.7'	74° 53.5'	+0 15	+0 46	*1.39	*1.19	5.67	6.69	3.03
1683	Bidwell Creek, Route 47 bridge	39° 07.1'	74° 52.1'	+0 36	+0 48	*1.36	*1.36	5.66	6.68	3.01
1685	Dennis Creek, 2.5 n.mi. above entrance	39° 10.7'	74° 51.1'	+0 55	+1 17	*1.26	*1.26	5.23	6.17	2.88
1687	Sluice Creek, Route 47 bridge, Dennis Creek	39° 09.7'	74° 49.9'	+1 49	+1 36	*1.22	*1.22	5.05	5.96	2.82
1689	Dennis Creek, Route 47 bridge	39° 11.0'	74° 49.3'	+2 01	+1 30	*1.20	*1.20	4.96	5.85	2.79
1691	East Creek, Route 47 bridge	39° 12.5'	74° 54.1'	+1 46	+2 24	*0.94	*0.94	3.92	4.63	2.20
1693	West Creek, 0.7 n.mi. above entrance	39° 11.3'	74° 54.9'	+0 20	+1 31	*1.15	*1.15	4.76	5.33	2.55
1695	West Creek, Route 47 bridge	39° 13.0'	74° 55.5'	+2 20	+3 17	*0.58	*0.58	2.40	2.83	1.51
1697	Riggins Ditch, 0.5 n.mi. above entrance	39° 12.0'	74° 58.2'	+0 29	+1 29	*1.24	*1.24	5.14	6.07	2.79
1699	Riggins Ditch, Heislerville	39° 13.1'	74° 58.8'	+1 36	+1 40	*1.12	*1.12	4.65	5.49	2.55
1701	East Point, Maurice River Cove	39° 12.0'	75° 01.2'	+0 40	+1 08	*1.39	*1.39	5.75	6.78	3.08
	Maurice River									
1703	Bivalve	39° 13.8'	75° 02.2'	+0 39	+1 14	*1.35	*1.35	5.60	6.61	3.00
1705	Mauricetown	39° 17.1'	74° 59.5'	+2 17	+2 30	*1.05	*1.05	4.36	5.14	2.42
1707	Port Elizabeth, Manumuskin River	39° 18.8'	74° 59.1'	+2 52	+2 58	*1.05	*1.05	4.34	5.12	2.42
1709	Menantico Creek entrance	39° 20.6'	75° 00.5'	+3 06	+3 09	*1.10	*1.10	4.58	5.40	2.52
1711	Millville	39° 23.5'	75° 02.5'	+3 33	+3 36	*1.21	*1.21	5.01	5.91	2.75
1713	Dividing Creek entrance	39° 13.0'	75° 06.4'	+0 29	+1 05	*1.35	*1.35	5.62	6.63	2.99
1715	Weir Creek bridge, Dividing Creek	39° 15.0'	75° 07.7'	+1 38	+2 33	*0.71	*0.71	2.96	3.49	1.69
1717	Dividing Creek (town), Dividing Creek	39° 16.0'	75° 05.7'	+3 07	– – –	– – –	– – –	– –	– –	– –

Endnotes can be found at the end of table 2.

TABLE 2 – TIDAL DIFFERENCES AND OTHER CONSTANTS

No.	PLACE	POSITION		DIFFERENCES				RANGES		Mean Tide Level
		Latitude	Longitude	Time		Height		Mean	Spring	
				High Water	Low Water	High Water	Low Water			
		North	West	h m	h m	ft	ft	ft	ft	ft

NEW JERSEY
Delaware Bay, Eastern Shore–cont.
Time meridian, 75° W
on Reedy Point, p.96

No.	PLACE	Latitude	Longitude	High Water	Low Water	High Water	Low Water	Mean	Spring	Mean Tide Level
1719	Fishing Creek entrance	39° 12.9'	75° 09.6'	−1 51	−2 10	*1.02	*1.02	5.63	6.14	3.00
1721	Fortescue Creek	39° 14.3'	75° 10.5'	−1 57	−2 13	*1.09	*0.94	5.85	7.06	3.10
1723	Hollywood Beach, The Glades	39° 16.5'	75° 08.5'	+1 45	+1 13	*0.21	*0.21	1.16	1.26	0.71
1725	Money Island, Nantuxent Creek entrance	39° 17.1'	75° 14.3'	−1 43	−1 58	*1.10	*1.10	6.07	6.62	3.21
1727	Newport Landing, Nantuxent Creek	39° 17.5'	75° 11.9'	−0 03	−0 28	*0.74	*0.74	4.06	4.43	2.38
1729	Cedar Creek entrance, Nantuxent Cove	39° 17.9'	75° 14.8'	−1 37	−1 51	*1.08	*1.08	5.96	6.50	3.17
1731	Cedarville, Cedar Creek, Nantuxent Cove	39° 19.8'	75° 12.7'	−0 37	– – –	– – –	– – –	– –	– –	– –
1733	Back Creek entrance, Nantuxent Cove	39° 18.3'	75° 16.7'	−1 29	−1 34	*1.07	*1.07	5.91	6.44	3.11
1735	Husted Landing, Ogden Creek, Back Creek	39° 21.1'	75° 15.1'	−0 47	– – –	– – –	– – –	– –	– –	– –
1737	Greenwich Pier, Cohansey River	39° 23.0'	75° 21.0'	−0 42	−0 54	*0.99	*0.99	5.47	5.96	2.94
1739	Tindalls Wharf, Cohansey River	39° 22.7'	75° 14.1'	+1 01	−0 02	*1.09	*1.09	5.98	6.52	3.20

DELAWARE
Delaware Bay, Western Shore
on Breakwater Harbor, p.92

No.	PLACE	Latitude	Longitude	High Water	Low Water	High Water	Low Water	Mean	Spring	Mean Tide Level
1741	LEWES (BREAKWATER HARBOR)	38° 46.9'	75° 07.2'	*Daily predictions*			*1.00	4.08	4.94	2.19
1743	Mispillion River entrance	38° 56.9'	75° 18.9'	+0 22	+0 50	*1.13	*1.00	4.63	5.46	2.48
1745	Murderkill River entrance	39° 03.5'	75° 23.8'	+0 39	+1 11	*1.25	*0.94	5.12	6.04	2.71
1747	Mahon River entrance	39° 11.1'	75° 24.0'	+0 58	+1 29	*1.30	*1.13	5.33	6.29	2.84
1749	Leipsic, Leipsic River	39° 14.6'	75° 31.1'	+3 35	+3 49	*0.85	*0.63	3.50	4.13	1.80

DELAWARE and NEW JERSEY
Delaware River
on Reedy Point, p.96

No.	PLACE	Latitude	Longitude	High Water	Low Water	High Water	Low Water	Mean	Spring	Mean Tide Level
1751	Stathems Neck, Stow Creek, N.J.	39° 24.4'	75° 24.3'	−0 22	−0 37	*0.88	*0.88	4.85	5.29	2.65
1753	Woodland Beach, Del.	39° 20.2'	75° 28.3'	−1 07	−1 10	*1.11	*1.11	5.90	6.80	3.00
1755	Raccoon Ditch, Newport Meadows, Stow Creek, N.J.	39° 25.3'	75° 22.9'	+1 08	+0 33	*0.76	*0.76	4.17	4.55	2.30
1757	Canton, Stow Creek, N.J.	39° 27.7'	75° 24.2'	+1 36	+0 45	*0.80	*0.80	4.42	4.82	2.49
	Mad Horse Creek									
1759	1 n.mi. above entrance, N.J.	39° 25.9'	75° 26.8'	−0 20	−0 47	*1.07	*1.07	5.86	6.39	3.12
1761	Pine Island, Malapartis Creek, N.J.	39° 25.3'	75° 25.7'	+0 21	−0 18	*0.92	*0.92	5.08	5.54	2.76
1763	Silver Lake Fork, N.J.	39° 27.2'	75° 27.4'	+0 04	– – –	– – –	– – –	– –	– –	– –
1765	Hope Creek, 0.6 n.mi. above entrance, N.J.	39° 27.5'	75° 29.7'	−0 25	−0 36	*1.05	*1.05	5.78	6.30	3.07
1767	Hope Creek, upper end, N.J.	39° 29.1'	75° 29.6'	+0 49	– – –	– – –	– – –	– –	– –	– –
1769	Taylors Bridge, Blackbird Creek, Del.	39° 24.0'	75° 36.0'	+1 53	+0 57	*0.54	*0.56	2.90	3.30	1.50
1771	Artificial Island, Salem Nuclear Plant, N.J.	39° 27.7'	75° 31.9'	−0 35	−0 33	*1.08	*1.08	5.93	6.46	3.16
	Alloway Creek, New Jersey									
1773	0.8 n.mi. above entrance	39° 29.8'	75° 31.0'	+0 21	−0 10	*0.99	*0.99	5.44	5.93	3.18
1775	Abbots Meadow	39° 30.7'	75° 29.6'	+0 44	+0 12	*0.94	*0.94	5.15	5.61	2.76
1777	2.5 n.mi. above entrance	39° 30.3'	75° 29.0'	+0 51	+0 15	*0.90	*0.90	4.95	5.40	2.67
1779	Coopers Creek bridge	39° 30.8'	75° 26.8'	+1 51	+1 00	*0.78	*0.78	4.30	4.69	2.37
1781	Quinton	39° 32.9'	75° 24.9'	+2 24	+1 30	*0.69	*0.69	3.79	4.13	2.17
1783	Alloway	39° 33.9'	75° 21.8'	+3 37	– – –	– – –	– – –	– –	– –	– –
1785	Mill Creek, Elsinboro, N.J.	39° 32.1'	75° 30.7'	−0 04	– – –	– – –	– – –	– –	– –	– –
	Salem River, New Jersey									
1787	Sinnickson Landing	39° 34.2'	75° 29.9'	+0 04	+0 19	*0.97	*0.97	5.32	5.80	2.83
1789	Salem	39° 34.6'	75° 28.6'	+0 49	+0 41	*0.76	*0.76	4.19	4.57	2.29
1791	Kates Creek Meadow	39° 37.5'	75° 27.2'	+1 54	– – –	– – –	– – –	– –	– –	– –
1793	Winslow Farms	39° 37.7'	75° 28.9'	+2 09	– – –	– – –	– – –	– –	– –	– –
1795	Beaver Dam	39° 39.0'	75° 29.2'	+2 32	– – –	– – –	– – –	– –	– –	– –
1797	REEDY POINT	39° 33.5'	75° 34.4'	*Daily predictions*				5.34	5.81	2.85
	Chesapeake and Delaware Canal									
1799	St. Georges, Delaware	39° 33.3'	75° 38.9'	−0 16	−0 17	*0.83	*1.00	4.41	4.81	2.39
1801	Summit Bridge, Delaware	39° 32.0'	75° 44.0'	−0 28	−0 52	*0.65	*0.56	3.50	3.90	1.80
1803	Chesapeake City, Maryland	39° 31.6'	75° 48.6'	−0 45	−1 12	*0.56	*1.28	2.86	3.14	1.66
1805	Delaware City Branch Channel bridge	39° 34.2'	75° 35.4'	+0 00	+0 05	*1.02	*0.89	5.45	5.94	2.88
1807	Delaware City	39° 34.9'	75° 35.3'	+0 11	+0 14	*1.02	*1.00	5.44	5.93	2.90
1809	Pea Patch Island, Bulkhead Shoal Channel, Del.	39° 35.1'	75° 34.4'	+0 03	+0 00	*1.05	*1.00	5.62	6.13	2.99
1811	Mill Creek, Penns Neck, N.J.	39° 36.6'	75° 31.2'	+0 08	– – –	– – –	– – –	– –	– –	– –
1813	New Castle, Delaware	39° 39.4'	75° 33.7'	+0 29	+0 40	*0.98	*1.00	5.21	5.68	2.78
1815	Salem Canal entrance, N.J.	39° 41.0'	75° 30.6'	+0 36	+0 52	*1.00	*1.00	5.52	6.02	2.94
	Christina River, Delaware									
1817	Wilmington Marine Terminal	39° 43.1'	75° 31.2'	+0 50	+1 06	*0.99	*1.11	5.27	5.74	2.83
1819	Millside, RR. bridge	39° 43.5'	75° 33.6'	+1 08	+1 19	*0.99	*1.06	5.30	5.78	2.84
1821	Edgemoor, Del.	39° 45.0'	75° 29.6'	+0 52	+1 11	*1.02	*1.17	5.52	6.02	2.97
1823	Pedricktown, Oldmans Creek, N.J.	39° 45.7'	75° 24.2'	+2 11	+2 07	*0.75	*0.75	4.13	4.50	2.32
1825	Auburn, Oldmans Creek, N.J.	39° 42.9'	75° 21.6'	+4 12	+3 30	*0.55	*0.55	2.74	2.99	1.65

NEW JERSEY and PENNSYLVANIA
Delaware River–cont.
on Philadelphia, p.100

No.	PLACE	Latitude	Longitude	High Water	Low Water	High Water	Low Water	Mean	Spring	Mean Tide Level
1827	Marcus Hook, Pa.	39° 48.7'	75° 24.7'	−1 23	−1 07	*0.92	*0.95	5.53	5.86	2.96
1829	Bridgeport, Raccoon Creek, N.J.	39° 48.4'	75° 21.3'	−1 11	−0 50	*0.91	*1.00	5.42	5.66	2.91
1831	Swedesboro, Raccoon Creek, N.J.	39° 45.1'	75° 18.4'	+0 40	– – –	– – –	– – –	– –	– –	– –
	Darby Creek, Pennsylvania									
1833	Wanamaker Bridge	39° 52.6'	75° 18.3'	−0 46	−0 34	*0.95	*0.95	5.71	6.05	3.05
1835	Norwood City	39° 52.8'	75° 17.4'	−0 42	−0 35	*0.97	*1.00	5.79	6.13	3.09
1837	Tinicum National Wildlife Refuge	39° 52.7'	75° 16.6'	−0 22	−0 08	*0.91	*0.90	5.47	5.80	2.91
1839	Tinicum National Wildlife Refuge	39° 53.2'	75° 15.9'	−0 24	+0 27	*0.74	*0.74	4.51	4.78	2.33
1841	Tinicum Nat. Wildlife Refuge, Visitor Center	39° 53.5'	75° 15.5'	−0 10	– – –	– – –	– – –	– –	– –	– –
1843	Billingsport, N.J.	39° 51.0'	75° 15.0'	−0 35	−0 28	*0.93	*0.95	5.59	5.93	2.99
1845	Paulsboro, Mantua Creek, N.J.	39° 50.1'	75° 14.3'	−0 24	−0 19	*0.94	*0.90	5.64	5.88	3.01
1847	Mantua, Mantua Creek, N.J.	39° 47.8'	75° 10.6'	+1 28	+0 56	*0.71	*0.71	4.19	4.37	2.31
1849	Woodbury Creek, N.J.	39° 51.6'	75° 11.2'	−0 13	−0 14	*0.96	*0.95	5.75	6.10	3.07

Endnotes can be found at the end of table 2.

TABLE 2 – TIDAL DIFFERENCES AND OTHER CONSTANTS

No.	PLACE	POSITION		DIFFERENCES				RANGES		Mean Tide Level
				Time		Height				
		Latitude	Longitude	High Water	Low Water	High Water	Low Water	Mean	Spring	
		North	West	h m	h m	ft	ft	ft	ft	ft
	NEW JERSEY and PENNSYLVANIA Delaware River–cont. Time meridian, 75° W			on Philadelphia, p.100						
	Schuylkill River, Pennsylvania									
1851	Penrose Avenue Bridge	39° 53.9'	75° 12.7'	−0 22	−0 11	*0.96	*0.85	5.79	6.14	3.07
1853	Market Street Bridge	39° 57.3'	75° 10.8'	−0 20	+0 00	*0.99	*0.80	5.94	6.30	3.13
1855	Westville, Rt. 47 bridge, Big Timber Creek, N.J. ...	39° 52.5'	75° 07.4'	+0 02	+0 03	*0.97	*1.00	5.80	6.15	3.10
1857	Sunset Beach, Big Timber Creek, N.J.	39° 48.9'	75° 05.3'	+1 32	− − −	− − −	− − −	− −	− −	− −
1859	Philadelphia, Municipal Pier 11, Pa.	39° 57.2'	75° 08.3'	+0 02	+0 05	*1.04	*0.95	6.24	6.61	3.32
1861	PHILADELPHIA, US Coast Guard Station, Pa.	39° 56.0'	75° 08.5'	*Daily predictions*				5.99	6.32	3.30
1863	Pavonia, Cooper River, RR. bridge, N.J.	39° 56.8'	75° 06.3'	+0 14	+0 23	*1.04	*1.00	6.24	6.61	3.32
1865	Bridesburg, Philadelphia, Pa.	39° 59.0'	75° 04.5'	+0 12	+0 15	*1.06	*0.90	6.39	6.50	3.38
1867	Palmyra, Pennsauken Creek, Route 73 bridge, N.J.	39° 59.6'	75° 01.7'	+0 51	+1 03	*0.89	*0.89	5.25	5.48	2.86
1869	Cinnaminson, Pennsauken Ck., Rt. 130 bridge, N.J.	39° 59.1'	75° 00.9'	+1 37	− − −	− − −	− − −	− −	− −	− −
1871	Tacony–Palmyra Bridge	40° 00.7'	75° 02.6'	+0 24	+0 25	*1.10	*0.95	6.60	7.00	3.49
1873	Pompeston Creek, N.J.	40° 00.8'	75° 00.5'	+0 21	+0 43	*1.05	*1.05	6.39	6.68	3.30
	Rancocas Creek, New Jersey									
1875	Bridgeboro	40° 01.7'	74° 55.9'	+1 15	+1 18	*1.06	*1.00	6.35	6.73	3.38
1877	North Branch	39° 59.9'	74° 49.1'	+2 58	+3 29	*0.48	*0.60	2.86	3.03	1.55
1879	Hainesport, South Branch	39° 58.7'	74° 49.4'	+2 58	+3 05	*0.62	*0.62	3.63	3.85	2.05
1881	Cornwells Heights, Pa.	40° 04.1'	74° 56.3'	+0 46	+0 58	*1.17	*1.00	7.02	7.44	3.71
1883	Burlington, N.J.	40° 04.8'	74° 52.5'	+0 53	+1 07	*1.20	*1.00	7.24	7.63	3.83
1885	Assiscunk Creek, Route 130 bridge, N.J.	40° 04.4'	74° 50.9'	+1 04	+1 31	*1.12	*0.85	6.75	7.16	3.54
1887	Edgely, Pa.	40° 07.7'	74° 49.4'	+1 08	+1 28	*1.27	*1.15	7.64	8.10	4.05
1889	Fieldsboro, N.J.	40° 08.2'	74° 44.2'	+1 07	+1 39	*1.29	*1.10	7.78	8.25	4.11
1891	Newbold, N.J.	40° 08.2'	74° 45.1'	+1 08	+1 31	*1.30	*1.00	7.86	8.33	4.13
1893	Blacks Creek, Route 130 bridge, N.J.	40° 08.3'	74° 42.7'	+1 13	− − −	− − −	− − −	− −	− −	− −
1895	Sylvan Glen, Crosswicks Ck., Rt. 206 bridge, N.J.	40° 10.9'	74° 42.3'	+2 03	− − −	− − −	− − −	− −	− −	− −
1897	Crosswicks Creek, Route 130 bridge, N.J.	40° 10.4'	74° 40.8'	+3 07	− − −	− − −	− − −	− −	− −	− −
1899	Trenton, N.J.	40° 11.3'	74° 45.3'	+1 13	+1 54	*1.35	*1.00	8.18	8.47	4.29
	DELAWARE, outer coast			on Ocean City, p.104						
1901	Rehoboth Beach	38° 43.2'	75° 04.6'	+0 15	+0 08	*1.13	*1.33	3.9	4.7	2.1
1903	Indian River Inlet (Coast Guard Station)	38° 36.6'	75° 04.2'	+1 14	+0 45	*0.76	*1.00	2.51	2.94	1.41
	MARYLAND, outer coast									
1905	OCEAN CITY (FISHING PIER)	38° 19.6'	75° 05.0'	*Daily predictions*			*1.00	3.36	4.00	1.84
1907	Ocean City Inlet	38° 19.7'	75° 05.5'	+0 28	+0 14	*0.65	*1.00	2.13	2.62	1.23
1909	Ocean City (Isle of Wight Bay)	38° 19.9'	75° 05.4'	+0 25	+0 23	*0.67	*0.94	2.20	2.61	1.25
1911	Keydash, Isle of Wight Bay	38° 20.5'	75° 05.1'	−0 57	+0 54	*0.47	*0.81	1.53	1.82	0.89
	MARYLAND and VIRGINIA Chincoteague Bay									
1913	Assateague Beach, Toms Cove	37° 52.0'	75° 22.0'	+0 35	+0 48	*1.08	*1.25	3.60	4.28	2.00
1915	Harbor of Refuge	37° 54.2'	75° 24.4'	+0 31	+0 35	*0.73	*0.88	2.43	2.89	1.35
1917	Chincoteague Channel (south end)	37° 54.4'	75° 24.3'	+0 39	+0 47	*0.64	*0.69	2.16	2.57	1.19
1919	Wishart Point, Bogues Bay	37° 52.9'	75° 29.5'	+0 52	+1 13	*0.77	*0.63	2.60	3.09	1.40
1921	Chincoteague Island, USCG Station	37° 55.9'	75° 23.0'	+0 56	+1 11	*0.48	*0.56	1.59	1.89	0.89
1923	Chincoteague Island, Lewis Creek	37° 56.3'	75° 22.4'	+1 17	+1 38	*0.40	*0.63	1.32	1.57	0.76
1925	Chincoteague Island, Oyster Bay	37° 56.5'	75° 20.8'	+1 44	+2 05	*0.46	*0.56	1.54	1.83	0.86
1927	Chincoteague Island, Blake Cove	37° 57.1'	75° 21.3'	+1 51	+2 32	*0.28	*0.56	0.89	1.06	0.53
1929	Jesters Island	37° 58.9'	75° 18.1'	+2 32	+3 24	*0.24	*0.24	0.76	0.90	0.48
1931	Franklin City	38° 00.4'	75° 23.0'	+2 20	+3 00	*0.22	*0.63	0.66	0.79	0.43
1933	Public Landing	38° 08.9'	75° 17.1'	+4 41	+5 21	*0.18	*0.18	0.53	0.63	0.36
1935	South Point, Sinepuxent Neck	38° 12.9'	75° 11.5'	+5 16	+5 02	*0.16	*0.16	0.46	0.54	0.33
	VIRGINIA, outer coast									
1937	Wallops Island	37° 50.5'	75° 28.7'	+0 04	−0 04	*1.06	*0.31	3.67	4.37	1.89
1939	Gargathy Neck	37° 46.6'	75° 33.7'	+1 31	+1 27	*0.88	*0.63	3.01	3.58	1.60
1941	Metompkin Inlet	37° 40.3'	75° 35.7'	+1 01	+0 44	*1.08	*1.25	3.60	4.28	2.00
1943	Folly Creek, Metompkin Inlet	37° 41.8'	75° 38.1'	+1 24	+1 12	*0.97	*0.63	3.30	3.93	1.80
1945	Wachapreague, Wachapreague Channel	37° 36.4'	75° 41.2'	+1 10	+0 56	*1.19	*1.06	4.02	4.85	2.18
1947	Revel Creek, Revel Island	37° 29.8'	75° 41.0'	+0 35	+0 27	*1.19	*1.00	4.04	4.81	2.18
1949	Great Machipongo Inlet (inside)	37° 23.6'	75° 42.8'	+1 05	+0 56	*1.16	*1.25	3.86	4.59	2.10
1951	Upshur Neck, south end	37° 28.0'	75° 48.0'	+1 09	+1 14	*1.31	*1.25	4.40	5.24	2.40
1953	Sand Shoal Inlet (Coast Guard Station)	37° 18.1'	75° 46.7'	+0 32	+0 17	*1.18	*1.00	4.00	4.76	2.16
1955	Oyster Harbor	37° 17.3'	75° 55.5'	+1 00	+0 36	*1.34	*1.13	4.52	5.38	2.40
1957	Smith Island (Coast Guard Station)	37° 07.4'	75° 54.7'	+0 52	+1 29	*1.05	*1.25	3.50	4.17	1.90
	Chesapeake Bay, Eastern Shore			on Ches. Bay Bridge Tunnel, p.116						
1959	Fishermans Island	37° 05.8'	75° 58.9'	+0 02	+0 11	*1.19	*1.25	3.02	3.62	1.71
1961	Kiptopeke Beach	37° 10.0'	75° 59.3'	+0 23	+0 32	*1.01	*0.92	2.60	3.09	1.41
1963	Old Plantation Light	37° 14'	76° 03'	+0 33	+0 52	*0.92	*0.83	2.4	2.9	1.3
1965	Cape Charles Harbor	37° 15.8'	76° 00.9'	+0 45	+1 03	*0.90	*0.92	2.3	2.8	1.3
1967	Gaskins Point, Occohannock Creek	37° 33.3'	75° 55.2'	+2 35	+3 13	*0.66	*0.83	1.70	2.00	0.94
1969	Harborton, Pungoteague Creek	37° 40.0'	75° 50.0'	+3 11	+3 33	*0.70	*0.83	1.76	2.11	0.98
1971	Onancock, Onancock Creek	37° 42.7'	75° 45.4'	+3 55	+4 19	*0.71	*0.83	1.80	2.16	1.00
1973	Chesconessex Creek, Schooner Bay	37° 45.8'	75° 46.4'	+3 41	+3 59	*0.78	*1.25	1.94	2.33	1.12
1975	Watts Island	37° 47.9'	75° 53.8'	+4 02	+4 12	*0.64	*0.83	1.60	1.92	0.90

Endnotes can be found at the end of table 2.

TABLE 2 – TIDAL DIFFERENCES AND OTHER CONSTANTS

No.	PLACE	POSITION		DIFFERENCES				RANGES		Mean Tide Level
		Latitude	Longitude	Time High Water	Time Low Water	Height High Water	Height Low Water	Mean	Spring	
		North	West	h m	h m	ft	ft	ft	ft	ft

VIRGINIA, outer coast
Chesapeake Bay, Eastern Shore–cont.
Time meridian, 75° W

on Ches. Bay Bridge Tunnel, p.116

No.	PLACE	Latitude	Longitude	High Water	Low Water	High Water	Low Water	Mean	Spring	MTL
1977	Tangier Island	37° 49.7'	75° 59.6'	+3 58	+4 16	*0.60	*0.75	1.41	1.69	0.80
1979	Muddy Creek Entrance	37° 51.3'	75° 40.5'	+4 14	+4 51	*0.86	*0.83	2.20	2.64	1.20
1981	Guard Shore	37° 51.0'	75° 42.0'	+4 06	+4 47	*0.90	*0.83	2.30	2.76	1.27

MARYLAND
Chesapeake Bay, Eastern Shore

1983	Saxis, Starling Creek, Pocomoke Sound	37° 55.3'	75° 43.7'	+3 52	+4 36	*0.89	*1.17	2.24	2.69	1.26
1985	Ape Hole Creek, Pocomoke Sound	37° 57.7'	75° 49.3'	+4 27	+4 58	*0.90	*0.83	2.30	2.80	1.20
	Pocomoke River									
1987	Shelltown	37° 58.8'	75° 38.3'	+4 32	+5 16	*0.94	*1.00	2.40	2.90	1.30
1989	Snow Hill, city park	38° 10.7'	75° 23.8'	+7 26	+7 36	*0.70	*1.33	1.62	1.96	0.98
1991	Crisfield, Little Annemessex River	37° 58.6'	75° 51.8'	+4 34	+4 51	*0.75	*1.00	1.86	2.23	1.05
1993	Colburn Creek, Big Annemessex River	38° 02.9'	75° 48.2'	+4 59	+5 30	*0.78	*1.17	1.94	2.33	1.11
1995	Long Point, Big Annemessex River	38° 03.4'	75° 48.2'	+5 19	+5 47	*0.82	*0.83	2.10	2.50	1.10
1997	Teague Creek, Manokin River	38° 06.5'	75° 50.3'	+5 38	+6 05	*0.82	*0.83	2.10	2.50	1.10
1999	Ewell, Smith Island	37° 59.7'	76° 01.9'	+4 56	+5 19	*0.61	*1.00	1.53	1.84	0.88
2001	Holland Island Bar Light	38° 04.1'	76° 05.8'	+5 16	+5 30	*0.56	*0.58	1.40	1.70	0.80
2003	Chance	38° 10.2'	75° 56.8'	+5 29	+5 57	*0.78	*1.17	1.94	2.33	1.11
2005	Sharkfin Shoal Light	38° 12.1'	75° 59.2'	+5 46	+6 06	*0.86	*0.92	2.20	2.64	1.20
2007	Great Shoals Light, Monie Bay	38° 13.0'	75° 53.0'	+6 00	+6 22	*0.90	*0.92	2.30	2.80	1.30
	Wicomico River									
2009	Whitehaven	38° 16.0'	75° 47.0'	+6 26	+6 46	*0.94	*1.00	2.40	2.90	1.30
2011	Salisbury	38° 22.0'	75° 36.0'	+7 21	+7 24	*1.20	*1.25	3.00	3.60	1.70
	Nanticoke River									
2013	Roaring Point	38° 15.7'	75° 55.2'	+6 00	+6 35	*0.90	*0.92	2.30	2.76	1.30
2015	Vienna	38° 29.0'	75° 49.1'	+8 25	+8 32	*0.79	*1.33	1.94	2.33	1.13
2017	Sharptown	38° 32.5'	75° 43.4'	+9 19	+9 28	*0.97	*1.00	2.50	3.00	1.40
2019	McCreedy's Creek, Fishing Bay	38° 18.0'	76° 00.4'	+5 49	+6 22	*0.82	*1.17	2.05	2.46	1.16
2021	Hooper Strait Light	38° 13.6'	76° 04.6'	+5 26	+5 51	*0.61	*1.17	1.48	1.77	0.88
2023	Bishops Head, Hooper Strait	38° 13.2'	76° 02.3'	+5 32	+6 04	*0.70	*1.08	1.73	2.08	0.99

on Baltimore, p.108

2025	Middle Hooper Island	38° 17.8'	76° 12.3'	−4 40	−4 39	*1.32	*1.50	1.51	1.71	1.09
2027	Barren Island	38° 20.5'	76° 15.9'	−4 45	−4 56	*1.01	*0.68	1.22	1.38	0.77
	Little Choptank River									
2029	Smithville Road Bridge, Beaverdam Creek	38° 25.7'	76° 14.2'	−2 26	−2 49	*1.01	*0.82	1.19	1.34	0.78
2031	Taylors Island, Slaughter Creek	38° 28.0'	76° 17.7'	−3 15	−3 00	*1.10	*1.18	1.30	1.47	0.88
2033	Woolford, Church Creek	38° 30.4'	76° 10.4'	−3 11	−2 55	*1.25	*1.41	1.40	1.58	1.00
2035	Cherry Island, Beckwiths Creek	38° 33.7'	76° 12.5'	−3 07	−2 57	*1.18	*1.27	1.34	1.51	0.90
	Choptank River									
2037	Cambridge	38° 34.4'	76° 04.1'	−2 42	−2 28	*1.23	*0.95	1.62	1.83	1.02
2039	Dover Bridge	38° 45.4'	75° 59.9'	−0 18	−0 41	*1.54	*1.68	1.70	1.92	1.24
2041	Hillsboro, Tuckahoe Creek	38° 55.0'	75° 56.7'	+1 29	+1 19	*1.82	*0.86	2.29	2.59	1.33
	Tred Avon River									
2043	Oxford	38° 42.0'	76° 10.4'	−2 50	−2 45	*1.25	*1.41	1.40	1.58	1.00
2045	Easton Point	38° 46.1'	76° 05.9'	−2 45	−2 35	*1.47	*1.59	1.60	1.81	1.20
2047	Deep Neck Point, Broad Creek	38° 43.9'	76° 16.1'	−2 57	−2 47	*1.25	*1.41	1.40	1.58	1.00
2049	St. Michaels, San Domingo Creek	38° 46.5'	76° 14.0'	−2 55	−2 52	*1.25	*1.41	1.40	1.58	1.00
2051	Avalon, Dogwood Harbor	38° 42.5'	76° 19.8'	−2 54	−2 48	*1.18	*1.36	1.30	1.47	0.90
2053	Tilghman Island, Ferry Cove, Eastern Bay	38° 45.9'	76° 19.7'	−2 33	−2 42	*0.98	*1.00	1.10	1.24	0.78
2055	Poplar Island	38° 45.5'	76° 22.6'	−2 33	−2 41	*0.97	*0.95	1.10	1.54	0.77
2057	Claiborne, Eastern Bay	38° 50.2'	76° 16.8'	−2 26	−2 28	*0.96	*1.09	1.10	1.24	0.70
2059	St. Michaels, Miles River	38° 47.2'	76° 13.3'	−2 12	−2 02	*1.22	*1.18	1.40	1.58	0.96
2061	Kent Island Narrows	38° 58.0'	76° 14.6'	−1 30	−1 23	*1.10	*1.18	1.20	1.36	0.90
2063	Matapeake, Kent Island	38° 57.4'	76° 21.3'	−1 30	−1 49	*0.90	*0.95	1.02	1.15	0.72
2065	Kent Point Marina	38° 50.2'	76° 22.4'	−2 21	−2 29	*0.97	*0.95	1.11	1.25	0.76
	Chester River									
2067	Love Point	39° 01.9'	76° 18.1'	−0 25	−0 41	*1.03	*0.95	1.19	1.34	0.84
2069	Queenstown	38° 59.8'	76° 09.5'	+0 05	−0 08	*1.18	*1.27	1.30	1.47	0.90
2071	Centreville Landing, Corsica River	39° 03.2'	76° 04.5'	+0 20	+0 14	*1.47	*1.89	1.60	1.81	1.20
2073	Cliffs Point	39° 06.4'	76° 08.5'	+0 12	−0 02	*1.32	*1.50	1.50	1.70	1.00
2075	Cliffs Wharf	39° 06.7'	76° 08.3'	+0 09	−0 08	*1.33	*1.27	1.53	1.73	1.05
2077	Chestertown	39° 12.4'	76° 03.8'	+1 03	+0 36	*1.62	*1.77	1.80	2.03	1.31
2079	Crumpton	39° 14.7'	75° 55.5'	+1 10	+1 04	*1.82	*0.91	2.28	2.58	1.34
2081	Deep Landing, Swan Creek	39° 08.7'	76° 15.6'	+0 02	−0 04	*0.96	*1.09	1.13	1.28	0.70
2083	Tolchester Beach	39° 12.8'	76° 14.7'	+0 18	+0 11	*1.04	*0.95	1.21	1.35	0.81
2085	Worton Creek entrance	39° 17.8'	76° 10.3'	+1 22	+1 19	*1.18	*1.27	1.30	1.47	0.90
2087	Sassafras River, Betterton	39° 22.3'	76° 03.8'	+2 35	+2 15	*1.34	*1.00	1.60	1.81	1.02
	Elk River									
2089	Town Point Wharf	39° 30.2'	75° 55.0'	+3 18	+2 59	*1.74	*0.86	2.17	2.45	1.28
	C & D Canal (see Delaware River)	– –	– –	– – –	– – –	– – –	– – –	– –	– –	– –
	Chesapeake City, Maryland (see C & D Canal)	– –	– –	– – –	– – –	– – –	– – –	– –	– –	– –
2091	Old Frenchtown Wharf	39° 34.5'	75° 50.6'	+3 13	+3 00	*2.06	*2.27	2.30	2.60	1.60
2093	Charlestown, Northeast River	39° 34.4'	75° 58.2'	+3 52	+4 03	*1.69	*1.86	1.90	2.15	1.30

Chesapeake Bay, western shore

Susquehanna River

2095	Havre de Grace	39° 32.2'	76° 05.4'	+3 13	+3 27	*1.55	*0.95	1.90	2.15	1.16
2097	Port Deposit	39° 36.0'	76° 06.8'	+3 24	+3 49	*1.51	*1.14	1.81	2.04	1.16
2099	Pond Point, Bush River	39° 23.3'	76° 15.3'	+1 52	+1 31	*1.06	*0.86	1.25	1.41	0.81

Endnotes can be found at the end of table 2.

TABLE 2 – TIDAL DIFFERENCES AND OTHER CONSTANTS

No.	PLACE	POSITION Latitude	POSITION Longitude	DIFFERENCES Time High Water	DIFFERENCES Time Low Water	DIFFERENCES Height High Water	DIFFERENCES Height Low Water	RANGES Mean	RANGES Spring	Mean Tide Level
		North	West	h m	h m	ft	ft	ft	ft	ft
	C & D Canal (see Delaware River) Chesapeake Bay, western shore–cont. Time meridian, 75° W				on Baltimore, p.108					
	Patapsco River									
2101	North Point	39° 11.8'	76° 26.8'	+0 12	+0 04	*0.93	*1.09	1.03	1.16	0.75
2103	Stony Creek	39° 09.8'	76° 31.6'	+0 03	–0 05	*0.95	*0.91	1.09	1.23	0.75
2105	Hawkins Point	39° 12.5'	76° 32.0'	+0 00	+0 06	*1.03	*0.95	1.19	1.34	0.80
2107	Curtis Creek, US Coast Guard Station	39° 11.7'	76° 34.6'	+0 12	+0 08	*0.96	*1.14	1.06	1.20	0.78
2109	BALTIMORE, Fort McHenry	39° 16.0'	76° 34.7'		Daily predictions			1.14	1.25	0.79
2111	Fort McHenry Marsh	39° 15.7'	76° 35.1'	–0 01	–0 01	*1.00	*1.00	1.14	1.29	0.78
2113	Mountain Point, Gibson Is., Magothy River	39° 03.7'	76° 26.0'	–0 04	–0 04	*0.74	*0.77	0.80	0.90	0.60
2115	Cornfield Creek, Magothy River	39° 06.0'	76° 26.7'	–0 29	–0 38	*0.89	*0.95	0.99	1.12	0.71
	Severn River									
2117	Brewer Point	39° 01.6'	76° 32.0'	–0 45	–0 54	*0.74	*0.91	0.80	0.90	0.60
2119	Annapolis (US Naval Academy)	38° 59.0'	76° 28.8'	–1 30	–1 44	*0.88	*1.00	0.97	1.12	0.71
2121	Thomas Point Shoal Light	38° 54.0'	76° 26.0'	–1 56	–2 11	*0.81	*0.91	0.90	1.02	0.60
2123	Edgewater, South River	38° 57.0'	76° 33.0'	–1 51	–2 07	*0.81	*0.91	0.90	1.02	0.60
2125	Gingerville Creek, South River	38° 57.5'	76° 33.3'	–2 01	–2 06	*0.92	*1.00	1.03	1.16	0.74
2127	Rhode River (County Wharf)	38° 53.2'	76° 32.4'	–2 07	–2 17	*0.88	*1.00	0.98	1.10	0.70
2129	Galesville, West River	38° 50.0'	76° 32.0'	–1 39	–1 34	*0.81	*0.91	0.90	1.01	0.60
2131	Rose Haven, Herring Bay	38° 43.5'	76° 32.5'	–2 37	–2 44	*0.81	*0.91	0.90	1.01	0.60
2133	Chesapeake Beach	38° 41.0'	76° 32.0'	–2 47	–3 05	*0.88	*1.00	1.00	1.13	0.70
2135	Long Beach	38° 27.9'	76° 28.4'	–3 47	–4 04	*0.87	*0.77	1.01	1.14	0.67
2137	Cove Point	38° 23.5'	76° 23.9'	–4 10	–4 25	*0.83	*0.83	1.04	1.18	0.61
	Patuxent River									
2139	Solomons Island	38° 19.0'	76° 27.1'	–4 38	–4 46	*0.98	*0.73	1.17	1.34	0.74
2141	Broomes Island	38° 24.9'	76° 32.7'	–4 13	–4 19	*1.18	*1.36	1.30	1.47	0.94
2143	Benedict	38° 30.8'	76° 40.2'	–3 54	–3 54	*1.47	*1.82	1.60	1.81	0.81
2145	Lower Marlboro	38° 39.3'	76° 41.0'	–2 46	–2 54	*1.47	*0.77	1.82	2.06	1.09
2147	Point Lookout	38° 02.4'	76° 1.4'	–5 28	–5 37	*1.02	*0.77	1.22	1.38	0.78
	MD., VA. and DISTRICT OF COLUMBIA Potomac River				on Washington, p.112					
2149	Cornfield Harbor, Md.	38° 03.7'	76° 21.5'	–6 16	–7 35	*0.48	*0.53	1.30	1.43	0.76
2151	Lewisetta, Va.	37° 59.7'	76° 27.9'	–6 19	–7 31	*0.46	*0.80	1.25	1.42	0.74
2153	Travis Point, Coan River, Va.	37° 59.8'	76° 28.0'	–6 00	–7 05	*0.44	*0.67	1.20	1.32	0.70
2155	Kinsale, Yeocomico River, Va.	38° 01.9'	76° 34.6'	–5 46	–6 53	*0.44	*0.67	1.20	1.32	0.70
2157	Piney Point, Md.	38° 08.0'	76° 32.0'	–5 54	–7 16	*0.51	*0.60	1.40	1.54	0.80
2159	Ragged Point, Coles Neck, Va.	38° 08.5'	76° 36.8'	–5 35	–7 03	*0.54	*0.67	1.50	1.65	0.85
2161	Mount Holly, Nomini Creek, Va.	38° 05.9'	76° 44.1'	–4 51	–6 14	*0.54	*0.67	1.50	1.65	0.80
2163	Colton Point, Md.	38° 13.2'	76° 45.0'	–5 18	–6 43	*0.65	*0.73	1.80	1.98	1.03
2165	Mills Point (south of), Wicomico Riv., Md.	38° 19.6'	76° 50.0'	–5 05	–6 05	*0.65	*0.73	1.80	1.98	1.00
2167	Colonial Beach, Va.	38° 15.1'	76° 57.6'	–5 08	–6 13	*0.61	*0.93	1.63	1.79	0.96
2169	Dahlgren, Upper Machodoc Creek, Va.	38° 19.2'	77° 02.2'	–4 53	–5 59	*0.56	*0.93	1.58	1.87	0.93
2171	Lower Cedar Point, Md.	38° 20.5'	76° 58.6'	–4 48	–5 56	*0.54	*0.60	1.50	1.65	0.80
2173	Mathias Point, Va.	38° 23.9'	77° 03.2'	–4 00	–4 56	*0.44	*0.67	1.20	1.32	0.70
2175	Goose Creek, Port Tobacco River, Md.	38° 27.2'	77° 03.3'	–4 08	–5 07	*0.54	*0.60	1.46	1.61	0.82
2177	Riverside, Md.	38° 23.2'	77° 08.7'	–3 23	–4 24	*0.48	*0.53	1.28	1.41	0.78
2179	Aquia Creek, Va.	38° 25.1'	77° 21.2'	–1 28	–2 32	*0.48	*0.67	1.26	1.39	0.71
2181	Clifton Beach, Smith Point, Md.	38° 24.8'	77° 16.0'	–1 42	–2 46	*0.41	*0.67	1.10	1.21	0.60
2183	Liverpool Point, Md.	38° 27.6'	77° 16.2'	–0 39	–1 58	*0.44	*0.67	1.20	1.32	0.70
2185	Quantico, Va.	38° 31.2'	77° 17.2'	–0 52	–2 04	*0.51	*0.67	1.40	1.54	0.80
2187	Indian Head, Md.	38° 36.1'	77° 11.1'	–0 14	–1 33	*0.65	*0.73	1.80	1.98	1.03
2189	Marshall Hall, Md.	38° 41.2'	77° 06.1'	+0 10	–0 55	*0.82	*0.93	2.30	2.53	1.27
2191	Alexandria, Va.	38° 48.3'	77° 02.3'	+0 18	–0 11	*0.96	*1.33	2.62	2.88	1.51
2193	Bellevue, D.C.	38° 49.6'	77° 01.6'	+0 34	–0 11	*1.02	*1.33	2.80	3.08	1.60
2195	WASHINGTON, Washington Channel, D.C.	38° 52.3'	77° 01.2'		Daily predictions			2.77	3.07	1.55
	Anacostia River									
2197	Washington Naval Yard	38° 52.3'	76° 59.7'	+0 18	–0 06	*1.01	*1.20	2.80	3.08	1.57
2199	Kingman Lake	38° 53.7'	76° 58.1'	+0 22	+0 04	*1.03	*1.20	2.84	3.12	1.60
2201	Kenilworth Aquatic Garden	38° 54.6'	76° 57.3'	+0 29	+0 10	*1.05	*1.07	2.92	3.21	1.62
2203	Bladensburg, Md.	38° 56.0'	76° 56.3'	+0 31	+0 25	*1.06	*1.13	2.95	3.25	1.64
	VIRGINIA Chesapeake Bay, western shore–cont.				on Ches. Bay Bridge Tunnel, p.116					
2205	Sunnybank, Little Wicomico River	37° 53.2'	76° 16.0'	+6 41	+6 45	*0.30	*0.30	0.80	0.96	0.40
2207	Great Wicomico River Light	37° 48.3'	76° 16.1'	+3 58	+4 11	*0.41	*0.41	1.10	1.32	0.50
2209	Fleeton Point	37° 48.8'	76° 16.5'	+3 58	+4 11	*0.41	*0.41	1.10	1.32	0.59
2211	Glebe Point, Great Wicomico River	37° 50.8'	76° 22.1'	+4 15	+4 37	*0.49	*0.83	1.20	1.44	0.70
2213	Windmill Point Light	37° 35.8'	76° 14.2'	+2 48	+3 12	*0.41	*0.41	1.10	1.32	0.50
	Rappahannock River				on Hampton Roads, p.120					
2215	Windmill Point	37° 36.9'	76° 17.4'	+1 55	+2 14	*0.49	*0.83	1.16	1.40	0.68
2217	Mill Creek (Grey Point)	37° 35.0'	76° 25.1'	+2 28	+2 42	*0.55	*0.83	1.30	1.57	0.69
2219	Millenbeck, Corrotoman River	37° 40.1'	76° 29.2'	+2 37	+3 05	*0.55	*0.83	1.30	1.57	0.70
2221	Urbanna	37° 39.0'	76° 34.5'	+2 50	+3 09	*0.59	*0.83	1.40	1.69	0.79
2223	Bayport	37° 45.3'	76° 40.4'	+3 22	+3 51	*0.67	*0.83	1.60	1.94	0.90
2225	Wares Wharf	37° 52.4'	76° 47.0'	+4 04	+4 34	*0.75	*0.33	1.88	2.27	0.98
2227	Tappahannock	37° 55.8'	76° 51.4'	+4 40	+5 18	*0.71	*0.83	1.74	2.11	0.95

Endnotes can be found at the end of table 2.

TABLE 2 – TIDAL DIFFERENCES AND OTHER CONSTANTS

No.	PLACE	POSITION		DIFFERENCES				RANGES		Mean Tide Level
				Time		Height				
		Latitude	Longitude	High Water	Low Water	High Water	Low Water	Mean	Spring	
		North	West	h m	h m	ft	ft	ft	ft	ft
	VIRGINIA Chesapeake Bay, western shore–cont. Time meridian, 75° W			**on Washington, p.112**						
	Rappahannock River-cont.									
2229	Saunders Wharf	38° 05.4'	77° 02.0'	−3 53	−4 41	*0.54	*0.66	1.50	1.65	0.85
2231	Port Royal	38° 10.4'	77° 11.4'	−2 19	−3 02	*0.68	*0.67	1.90	2.09	1.10
2233	Park Turn	38° 12.8'	77° 14.6'	−1 35	−2 30	*0.73	*0.20	2.13	2.34	1.09
2235	Hopyard Landing	38° 14.6'	77° 13.6'	−1 07	−1 57	*0.75	*0.67	2.10	2.31	1.19
2237	Massaponax Sand & Gravel	38° 15.3'	77° 24.6'	−0 39	−0 41	*0.88	*1.33	2.50	2.75	1.39
	Piankatank River			**on Hampton Roads, p.120**						
2239	Jackson Creek, Deltaville	37° 32.9'	76° 19.9'	+1 36	+2 04	*0.51	*0.83	1.20	1.45	0.70
2241	Dixie	37° 30.5'	76° 25.0'	+1 34	+2 14	*0.55	*0.83	1.30	1.57	0.72
2243	Wolf Trap Light	37° 23.4'	76° 11.4'	−0 02	+0 32	*0.67	*0.83	1.60	1.94	0.90
	Mobjack Bay									
2245	Mobjack, East River	37° 22.4'	76° 20.8'	−0 17	+0 02	*0.98	*0.83	2.40	2.90	1.30
2247	Belleville	37° 24.7'	76° 26.3'	−0 06	+0 00	*1.02	*0.83	2.48	3.00	1.36
2249	Browns Bay	37° 18.1'	76° 24.2'	−0 11	−0 03	*0.98	*1.58	2.32	2.81	1.35
	York River									
2251	Tue Marshes Light	37° 14.1'	76° 23.1'	+0 03	+0 03	*0.90	*0.83	2.17	2.63	1.19
2253	Yorktown, Goodwin Neck	37° 13.4'	76° 26.4'	+0 18	+0 15	*0.90	*0.83	2.20	2.66	1.23
2255	Yorktown, USCG Training Center	37° 13.6'	76° 28.7'	+0 10	+0 15	*0.95	*1.08	2.29	2.77	1.28
2257	Gloucester Point	37° 14.8'	76° 30.0'	+0 10	+0 11	*0.98	*1.00	2.38	2.93	1.30
2259	Cheatham Annex	37° 17.5'	76° 35.2'	+0 48	+0 40	*1.02	*0.83	2.50	3.03	1.34
2261	Roane Point	37° 26.9'	76° 42.4'	+1 47	+1 50	*1.14	*0.83	2.81	3.40	1.54
2263	West Point	37° 32.1'	76° 47.6'	+2 12	+2 38	*1.14	*0.83	2.80	3.39	1.50
2265	Wakema (Fraziers Ferry), Mattaponi River	37° 39.0'	76° 54.0'	+3 34	+3 57	*1.41	*1.67	3.42	4.14	1.90
	Pamunkey River									
2267	Lester Manor	37° 35.0'	76° 59.4'	+4 45	+5 00	*1.05	*0.83	2.80	3.39	1.50
2269	Northbury	37° 37.5'	77° 07.3'	+6 03	+6 18	*1.37	*1.67	3.30	4.01	1.80
	Chesapeake Bay, western shore–cont.									
2271	Messick Point, Back River	37° 06.5'	76° 19.1'	−0 07	+0 02	*0.97	*0.97	2.30	2.78	1.33
	Hampton Roads									
2273	Old Point Comfort	37° 00.2'	76° 18.9'	+0 01	+0 09	*1.02	*0.83	2.52	3.05	1.38
2275	HAMPTON ROADS (Sewells Point)	36° 56.8'	76° 19.8'	*Daily predictions*				2.43	2.95	1.34
	Elizabeth River									
2277	Craney Island Light	36° 53.5'	76° 20.3'	+0 18	+0 04	*1.06	*0.83	2.60	3.15	1.40
2279	Lafayette River	36° 53.0'	76° 16.5'	+0 06	+0 10	*1.10	*1.17	2.67	3.14	1.47
2281	Western Branch, Rt 337 bridge	36° 49.3'	76° 23.9'	+0 11	+0 13	*1.14	*1.17	2.77	3.26	1.53
2283	Norfolk	36° 51.1'	76° 17.9'	+0 23	+0 20	*1.14	*0.83	2.82	3.41	1.50
2285	Portsmouth, Naval Shipyard	36° 49.3'	76° 17.6'	+0 08	+0 10	*1.13	*1.17	2.76	3.26	1.52
2287	Money Point	36° 46.7'	76° 18.1'	+0 15	+0 12	*1.18	*1.17	2.86	3.46	1.57
2289	Deep Creek Entrance	36° 45.3'	76° 17.6'	+0 22	+0 18	*1.21	*1.25	2.92	3.53	1.61
	Nansemond River									
2291	Pig Point	36° 55.0'	76° 26.1'	+0 42	+0 40	*1.05	*0.83	2.80	3.39	1.50
2293	Town Point	36° 53.0'	76° 30.5'	+0 37	+0 44	*1.22	*0.83	3.00	3.63	1.60
2295	Hollidays Point (Kings Highway bridge)	36° 50.3'	76° 33.0'	+0 56	+1 03	*1.25	*1.67	3.00	3.63	1.63
	James River									
2297	Newport News	36° 58.4'	76° 26.0'	+0 29	+0 28	*1.08	*0.83	2.60	3.15	1.40
2299	Huntington Park	37° 00.8'	76° 27.5'	+0 38	+0 39	*1.07	*0.92	2.62	3.17	1.42
2301	Menchville	37° 04.9'	76° 31.5'	+1 03	+1 19	*1.06	*0.83	2.60	3.15	1.40
2303	Smithfield, Pagan River	36° 59.1'	76° 37.8'	+1 34	+1 38	*1.14	*0.83	2.78	3.36	1.50
2305	Burwell Bay	37° 03.4'	76° 40.1'	+1 17	+1 39	*1.00	*1.17	2.42	2.93	1.35
2307	Fort Eustis	37° 08.2'	76° 37.3'	+1 44	+1 51	*0.92	*1.25	2.19	2.52	1.25
2309	Kingsmill	37° 13.2'	76° 39.8'	+2 05	+2 26	*0.94	*1.33	2.26	2.73	1.29
2311	Scotland	37° 11.1'	76° 47.0'	+2 44	+3 13	*0.78	*1.08	1.84	2.22	1.06
2313	Jamestown Wharf	37° 13.2'	76° 47.4'	+2 59	+3 15	*0.78	*1.42	1.81	2.09	1.08
	Chickahominy River									
2315	Ferry Point (bridge)	37° 15.8'	76° 52.7'	+4 01	+4 26	*0.78	*0.83	1.90	2.30	1.04
2317	Wright Island Landing	37° 20.7'	76° 52.5'	+4 44	+5 03	*0.90	*0.83	2.20	2.66	1.20
2319	Lanexa	37° 24.2'	76° 54.7'	+5 00	+4 51	*1.05	*1.08	2.56	2.77	1.41
2321	Claremont	37° 13.9'	76° 56.9'	+3 51	+4 25	*0.76	*1.17	1.79	2.11	1.06
2323	Tettington	37° 14.4'	76° 56.6'	+3 52	+4 17	*0.79	*1.13	1.87	2.26	1.07
2325	Sturgeon Point	37° 18.4'	77° 00.4'	+4 37	+5 09	*0.86	*0.83	2.10	2.54	1.10
2327	Willcox Wharf, Charles City	37° 19.0'	77° 05.9'	+5 30	+5 33	*0.89	*1.33	2.12	2.52	1.22
2329	Jordan Point	37° 18.8'	77° 13.4'	+6 16	+6 39	*1.02	*0.83	2.50	3.02	1.40
				on Washington, p.112						
2331	City Point, Hopewell	37° 18.8'	77° 16.2'	−4 31	−5 36	*0.87	*0.80	2.45	2.58	1.35
2333	Puddledock, Appomattox River	37° 16.0'	77° 22.3'	−3 49	−4 32	*1.00	*1.07	2.80	3.08	1.55
2335	Haxall	37° 22.4'	77° 14.6'	−4 10	−4 53	*0.99	*1.33	2.70	2.97	1.60
2337	Chester	37° 23.0'	77° 22.7'	−3 39	−3 59	*1.02	*0.67	2.90	3.19	1.60
2339	Meadowville	37° 22.7'	77° 19.4'	−3 46	−4 17	*1.05	*1.33	2.90	3.19	1.60
2341	Richmond Deepwater Terminal	37° 27.5'	77° 25.2'	−3 39	−3 51	*1.08	*0.93	3.05	3.25	1.66
2343	Richmond (river locks)	37° 31.5'	77° 25.2'	−3 16	−3 26	*1.16	*1.33	3.20	3.52	1.80

Endnotes can be found at the end of table 2.

TABLE 2 – TIDAL DIFFERENCES AND OTHER CONSTANTS

No.	PLACE	POSITION		DIFFERENCES				RANGES		Mean Tide Level
				Time		Height				
		Latitude	Longitude	High Water	Low Water	High Water	Low Water	Mean	Spring	
		North	West	h m	h m	ft	ft	ft	ft	ft
	VIRGINIA Chesapeake Bay, southern shore Time meridian, 75° W			**on Ches. Bay Bridge Tunnel, p.116**						
2345	Little Creek, NAB	36° 54.7'	76° 10.5'	+0 08	+0 09	*1.01	*1.17	2.57	3.08	1.42
2347	CHESAPEAKE BAY BRIDGE TUNNEL	36° 58.0'	76° 06.8'	*Daily predictions*				2.55	3.07	1.40
2349	Lynnhaven Inlet, Virginia Pilots Dock	36° 54.4'	76° 05.4'	+0 40	+0 38	*0.88	*1.08	2.22	2.66	1.24
	Lynnhaven Bay									
2351	Bayville	36° 53.6'	76° 06.3'	+1 52	+2 48	*0.67	*0.83	1.70	2.04	1.00
2353	Buchanan Creek entrance	36° 51.7'	76° 06.9'	+2 02	+2 56	*0.75	*0.83	1.90	2.28	1.00
2355	Brown Cove	36° 52.5'	76° 03.7'	+2 05	+2 43	*0.65	*0.83	1.64	1.96	0.92
2357	Broad Bay Canal	36° 54.1'	76° 03.7'	+2 05	+2 00	*0.56	*0.92	1.38	1.66	0.80
2359	Long Creek	36° 54.2'	76° 04.2'	+1 15	+1 15	*0.68	*1.08	1.68	2.02	0.97
	VIRGINIA, outer coast			**on Duck Pier, p.124**						
2361	Cape Henry	36° 55.8'	76° 00.4'	+0 31	+0 36	*0.96	*0.93	3.12	3.71	1.68
2363	Virginia Beach	36° 50.6'	75° 58.3'	+0 15	+0 16	*1.07	*1.07	3.34	3.97	1.85
2365	Rudee Inlet entrance	36° 49.9'	75° 58.1'	+0 02	+0 02	*1.01	*0.86	3.28	3.90	1.77
2367	Rudee Inlet, interior channel	36° 49.9'	75° 58.4'	+0 17	+0 17	*1.02	*0.94	3.29	3.92	1.78
2369	Rudee Heights, Lake Wesley	36° 49.5'	75° 58.5'	+0 18	+0 16	*1.03	*1.00	3.32	3.95	1.81
2371	Lake Rudee, south end	36° 49.5'	75° 58.9'	+0 20	+0 19	*1.05	*1.07	3.39	4.03	1.85
2373	Sandbridge	36° 41.5'	75° 55.2'	+0 07	+0 07	*1.04	*1.04	3.35	3.99	1.85
	NORTH CAROLINA, outer coast									
2375	DUCK PIER	36° 11.0'	75° 44.8'	*Daily predictions*				3.22	3.96	1.75
2377	Albemarle and Pamlico Sounds <9>	– – –	– – –	– – –	– – –	– – –	– – –	– –	– –	– –
2379	Kitty Hawk (ocean)	36° 06.1'	75° 42.6'	–0 01	+0 02	*1.01	*1.43	3.19	3.80	1.80
2381	Jennettes Pier, Nags Head (ocean)	35° 54.6'	75° 35.5'	–0 05	+0 01	*1.04	*1.43	3.26	3.88	1.80
				on Oregon Inlet, p.128						
2383	Roanoke Sound Channel	35° 48'	75° 35'	+1 37	+1 17	*0.47	*0.14	0.5	0.6	0.3
2385	OREGON INLET MARINA	35° 47.7'	75° 32.9'	*Daily predictions*				0.89	1.08	0.58
2387	Oregon Inlet	35° 46'	75° 31'	–0 03	–0 27	*1.98	*0.71	2.0	2.4	1.1
2389	Oregon Inlet (USCG Station)	35° 46.1'	75° 31.6'	–0 22	–0 51	*2.00	*0.69	1.97	2.30	1.07
2391	Oregon Inlet Bridge	35° 46.4'	75° 32.3'	–0 17	–0 55	*1.89	*0.64	1.9	2.3	1.1
2393	Oregon Inlet Channel	35° 46.5'	75° 33.5'	–0 09	–0 34	*1.23	*0.43	1.2	1.4	0.7
2395	Old House Channel	35° 46.5'	75° 34.9'	+0 34	+0 28	*0.66	*0.21	0.7	0.8	0.4
2397	Davis Slough	35° 44.9'	75° 33.2'	+0 09	–0 01	*0.85	*0.29	0.9	1.1	0.5
2399	Rodanthe, Pamlico Sound	35° 35.7'	75° 28.3'	+2 03	+1 36	*0.79	*0.69	0.72	0.84	0.45
2401	Roanoke Marshes Light, Croatan Sound	35° 48.7'	75° 42.0'	+2 10	+2 04	*0.50	*0.85	0.40	0.59	0.31
2403	Oyster Creek, Croatan Sound	35° 50.7'	75° 39.3'	+2 12	+2 06	*0.51	*0.77	0.41	0.60	0.31
2405	Manns Harbor, Croatan Sound	35° 54.2'	75° 46.2'	+2 31	+2 26	*0.37	*0.54	0.37	0.40	0.23
				on Cape Hatteras, p.132						
2407	Cape Hatteras	35° 14'	75° 31'	+0 01	+0 01	*1.00	*1.08	3.6	4.3	2.0
2409	CAPE HATTERAS FISHING PIER	35° 13.4'	75° 38.1'	*Daily predictions*				2.99	3.60	1.61
2411	Peters Ditch, Avon, Pamlco Sound	35° 21.0'	75° 30.7'	+3 20	+3 40	*0.17	*0.17	0.43	0.61	0.30
2413	Hatteras, Pamlico Sound	35° 12.3'	75° 42.2'	+1 16	+1 25	*0.17	*1.08	0.41	0.49	0.33
2415	Hatteras Inlet	35° 12'	75° 44'	+0 08	+0 13	*0.66	*0.83	2.0	2.4	1.1
2417	Ocracoke Inlet	35° 04'	76° 01'	+0 09	+0 11	*0.63	*0.83	1.9	2.3	1.0
2419	Ocracoke, Ocracoke Island	35° 06.9'	75° 59.3'	+0 15	+0 47	*0.34	*0.50	0.99	1.19	0.56
2421	Cape Lookout Bight	34° 36.8'	76° 32.3'	–0 17	–0 12	*1.35	*1.33	4.05	4.86	2.19
2423	Cape Lookout (ocean)	34° 36.5'	76° 31.7'	–0 22	–0 22	*1.15	*1.25	3.44	4.13	1.87
2425	Shell Point, Harkers Island	34° 41'	76° 32'	+1 52	+2 34	*0.54	*0.83	1.6	1.8	0.9
2427	Harkers Island Bridge	34° 43'	76° 35'	+2 08	+2 31	*0.52	*0.67	1.6	1.7	0.9
2429	Davis, Core Sound	34° 47.8'	76° 27.3'	+3 13	+3 39	*0.38	*0.75	1.08	1.23	0.64
2431	Channel Marker Lt. 59	34° 42'	76° 37'	+1 25	+1 27	*0.66	*0.83	2.0	2.3	1.1
2433	Lenoxville Point	34° 42.5'	76° 37.2'	+1 18	+1 11	*0.80	*1.00	2.37	2.84	1.31
2435	North River Bridge	34° 47'	76° 37'	+2 25	+3 08	*0.59	*0.67	1.8	2.0	1.0
2437	Beaufort Inlet Channel Range	34° 42'	76° 40'	+0 07	+0 11	*1.07	*1.67	3.2	3.8	1.6
2439	Beaufort, Taylor Creek	34° 42.7'	76° 38.7'	+0 52	+0 48	*0.95	*1.17	2.82	3.38	1.55
2441	Beaufort, Duke Marine Lab	34° 43.2'	76° 40.2'	+0 39	+0 36	*1.05	*1.17	3.11	3.58	1.70
2443	Gallant Channel	34° 44'	76° 40'	+0 49	+0 44	*1.01	*1.25	3.0	3.5	1.7
2445	Newport River (Yacht Club)	34° 46.1'	76° 40.3'	+1 03	+1 13	*1.03	*1.00	3.08	3.70	1.66
2447	Core Creek Bridge	34° 50'	76° 42'	+1 26	+1 46	*0.68	*0.83	2.1	2.3	1.1
2449	Fort Macon, USCG Station	34° 42'	76° 41'	+0 17	+0 18	*1.03	*1.25	3.1	3.7	1.7
2451	Morehead City	34° 43'	76° 42'	+0 26	+0 27	*1.04	*1.25	3.1	3.7	1.7
2453	Morehead City Harbor	34° 43.2'	76° 43.7'	+0 35	+0 37	*1.04	*1.17	3.08	3.70	1.68
2455	Atlantic Beach	34° 41.6'	76° 42.7'	–0 02	+0 01	*1.23	*1.25	3.65	4.38	1.98
2457	Triple S Marina, Bogue Sd.	34° 41.7'	76° 42.7'	+0 35	+0 28	*0.93	*1.17	2.8	3.3	1.5
2459	Atlantic Beach Bridge	34° 43'	76° 44'	+0 48	+1 02	*0.79	*0.83	2.4	2.8	1.2
2461	N.C. State Fisheries	34° 43'	76° 45'	+1 05	+1 32	*0.66	*0.83	2.0	2.3	1.1
2463	Coral Bay, Atlantic Beach	34° 42'	76° 46'	+1 47	+2 14	*0.53	*0.83	1.6	1.8	0.9
2465	Spooner Creek	34° 43.5'	76° 48.2'	+2 06	+2 20	*0.56	*1.08	1.27	1.85	0.94
2467	Bogue Inlet	34° 39'	77° 06'	+0 13	+0 15	*0.73	*0.83	2.2	2.6	1.2
2469	New River Inlet	34° 32'	77° 20'	+0 16	+0 17	*0.98	*0.83	3.0	3.6	1.6
2471	Ocean City Beach (fishing pier)	34° 27.1'	77° 29.7'	+0 03	–0 01	*1.40	*1.33	4.20	5.04	2.25
2473	New Topsail Inlet	34° 22'	77° 38'	+0 20	+1 00	*0.98	*0.83	3.0	3.5	1.6
2475	Wrightsville Beach	34° 12.8'	77° 47.2'	+0 18	+0 23	*1.27	*1.25	3.80	4.56	2.05
2477	Wilmington Beach	34° 01.9'	77° 53.6'	+0 18	+0 10	*1.40	*1.25	4.21	5.05	2.26
2479	Cape Fear	33° 51'	77° 58'	+0 04	+0 07	*1.47	*1.33	4.5	5.1	2.3

Endnotes can be found at the end of table 2.

TABLE 2 – TIDAL DIFFERENCES AND OTHER CONSTANTS

No.	PLACE	POSITION		DIFFERENCES				RANGES		Mean Tide Level
		Latitude	Longitude	Time		Height		Mean	Spring	
				High Water	Low Water	High Water	Low Water			
		North	**West**	h m	h m	ft	ft	ft	ft	ft
	NORTH CAROLINA, outer coast Time meridian, 75° W			on Wilmington, p.136						
	Cape Fear River									
2481	Bald Head	33° 52.8'	78° 00.1'	−2 06	−2 43	*1.05	*1.13	4.49	4.89	2.41
2483	Fort Caswell	33° 54'	78° 01'	−2 02	−2 45	*1.03	*1.25	4.2	4.8	2.3
2485	Southport	33° 54.9'	78° 01.1'	−1 49	−2 22	*0.99	*1.00	4.24	4.62	2.28
2487	Zekes Island	33° 57.0'	77° 57.1'	−1 12	−1 43	*0.96	*1.07	4.09	4.46	2.20
2489	Federal Point	33° 57.7'	77° 56.4'	−1 17	−1 52	*0.94	*0.93	4.04	4.40	2.16
2491	Sunny Point Army Base, Wharf no.1 . . .	33° 59.4'	77° 57.4'	−1 03	−1 45	*0.95	*0.93	4.06	4.43	2.17
2493	Reaves Point	34° 00.2'	77° 57.3'	−0 54	−1 18	*0.96	*1.07	4.09	4.46	2.21
2495	Sunny Point Army Base, Wharf no.3 . . .	34° 01.4'	77° 56.8'	−0 57	−1 15	*0.97	*1.07	4.15	4.52	2.24
2497	Orton Point	34° 03.4'	77° 56.4'	−0 36	−0 58	*0.98	*1.00	4.17	4.55	2.24
2499	WILMINGTON	34° 13.6'	77° 57.2'	Daily predictions				4.28	4.70	2.29
2501	Castle Hayne, Northeast River	34° 21'	77° 56'	+2 44	+2 54	*0.42	*0.42	1.7	1.9	0.9
2503	Bannermans Branch, Northeast River	34° 35'	77° 46'	+5 58	+6 08	*0.32	*0.31	1.3	1.4	0.6
				on Myrtle Beach, p.140						
2505	Oak Island	33° 54.1'	78° 04.9'	−0 05	−0 05	*0.94	*0.84	4.72	5.57	2.53
2507	Lockwoods Folly Inlet	33° 55'	78° 14'	+0 04	+0 15	*0.84	*1.00	4.2	4.8	2.3
2509	Shallotte Inlet (Bowen Point)	33° 55'	78° 22'	+0 43	+0 55	*0.91	*1.00	4.6	5.4	2.5
2511	Tubbs Inlet	33° 53'	78° 29'	+0 14	+0 15	*0.89	*1.00	4.5	5.1	2.4
2513	Sunset Beach Pier	33° 51.9'	78° 30.4'	+0 02	−0 03	*0.97	*1.11	4.82	5.78	2.62
2515	Sunset Beach Bridge	33° 52.9'	78° 30.6'	+0 34	+0 56	*0.94	*0.84	4.72	5.57	2.52
	SOUTH CAROLINA, outer coast									
2517	Dunn Sound, Little River Inlet	33° 51.5'	78° 34.2'	+0 15	+0 41	*0.91	*0.80	4.64	5.52	2.48
2519	Dunn Sound, north end	33° 51.6'	78° 34.8'	+0 25	+0 40	*0.93	*0.84	4.67	5.51	2.50
2521	Dunn Sound, west end	33° 51.1'	78° 35.3'	+0 29	+0 36	*0.96	*1.00	4.85	5.58	2.63
2523	Little River Neck, north end	33° 52.2'	78° 34.4'	+0 32	+0 46	*0.92	*0.84	4.63	5.56	2.47
2525	Cherry Grove (inside)	33° 50.1'	78° 38.0'	+0 40	+0 44	*0.92	*0.74	4.67	5.51	2.47
2527	Hog Inlet Pier	33° 50.2'	78° 36.4'	−0 06	−0 07	*0.99	*0.90	5.0	5.7	2.7
2529	MYRTLE BEACH, SPRINGMAID PIER	33° 39.3'	78° 55.1'	Daily predictions				5.02	6.00	2.70
2531	Garden City Pier (ocean)	33° 34.5'	78° 59.8'	+0 00	+0 00	*1.00	*1.00	5.07	5.88	2.74
	Murrells Inlet									
2533	Garden City Bridge, Main Creek	33° 34.7'	79° 00.2'	+1 19	+2 09	*0.84	*0.68	4.26	5.03	2.25
2535	Divine's Dock	33° 32.5'	79° 01.7'	+0 40	+1 18	*0.84	*0.84	4.22	5.06	2.27
2537	Smith's Dock	33° 32.7'	79° 02.7'	+1 01	+1 36	*0.86	*0.95	4.29	5.06	2.32
2539	Captain Alex's Marina, Parsonage Creek	33° 33.1'	79° 02.2'	+0 57	+1 28	*0.85	*0.68	4.30	5.16	2.28
2541	Oaks Creek, 0.5 mi. above entrance	33° 31.8'	79° 02.6'	+0 38	+1 03	*0.85	*0.95	4.27	5.12	2.32
2543	Allston Creek	33° 31.9'	79° 03.2'	+0 52	+1 32	*0.84	*0.95	4.24	4.92	2.31
2545	Oaks Creek, upper end	33° 30.7'	79° 04.1'	+1 10	+1 43	*0.87	*1.05	4.35	5.22	2.37
2547	Litchfield Beach bridge	33° 28.3'	79° 06.1'	+1 10	+3 02	*0.58	*0.75	2.89	3.35	1.59
2549	Midway Inlet North, Pawleys Island	33° 26.9'	79° 06.7'	+0 16	+0 42	*0.87	*1.00	4.40	5.10	2.40
2551	Bennet's Dock, Pawleys Island Creek	33° 26.1'	79° 07.6'	+0 55	+1 35	*0.78	*1.21	3.84	4.61	2.15
2553	Pawleys Island Pier (ocean)	33° 25.9'	79° 07.0'	+0 06	+0 06	*0.98	*0.95	4.92	5.81	2.65
2555	Ward's Dock, Pawleys Inlet	33° 24.7'	79° 08.1'	+0 35	+2 07	*0.67	*0.95	3.32	3.98	1.84
2557	Oyster Landing, Crab Haul Creek, North Inlet	33° 21.1'	79° 11.2'	+1 08	+0 52	*0.92	*1.00	4.58	5.50	2.48
2559	Clambank Creek, Goat Island, North Inlet	33° 20.0'	79° 11.6'	+1 01	+0 36	*0.94	*1.00	4.69	5.53	2.54
	Intercoastal Waterway Little River Inlet to Winyah Bay			on Charleston, p.144						
2561	Little River (town)	33° 52.2'	78° 36.5'	+0 13	+0 39	*0.84	*0.79	4.41	5.07	2.35
2563	Nixon Crossroads	33° 51.3'	78° 38.9'	+0 27	+0 51	*0.78	*0.68	4.10	4.55	2.18
2565	Myrtle Beach Airport	33° 49.2'	78° 43.1'	+1 09	+1 47	*0.56	*0.84	2.88	3.34	1.60
2567	North Myrtle Beach	33° 46.0'	78° 48.9'	+2 15	+3 12	*0.36	*0.84	1.78	2.10	1.25
2569	Myrtle Beach, Combination Bridge	33° 42.8'	78° 55.3'	+2 56	+4 18	*0.35	*0.89	1.71	2.02	1.03
2571	Socastee Bridge	33° 41.2'	79° 00.3'	+3 27	+4 41	*0.41	*0.74	2.08	2.45	1.18
	Winyah Bay									
2573	Winyah Bay Entrance (South Jetty)	33° 11'	79° 09'	−0 21	−0 24	*0.87	*0.89	4.6	5.4	2.5
2575	Georgetown Lighthouse	33° 13.4'	79° 11.1'	+0 26	+0 25	*0.75	*1.05	3.89	4.51	2.15
2577	South Island Plantation (C.G. Station)	33° 14.1'	79° 12.2'	+0 35	+0 36	*0.74	*0.84	3.81	4.38	2.07
2579	South Island Ferry, Intracoastal Waterway	33° 15.1'	79° 16.1'	+0 54	+1 25	*0.71	*0.74	3.69	4.24	1.99
2581	Frazier Point	33° 19'	79° 17'	+1 26	+2 07	*0.66	*0.68	3.5	4.1	1.8
	Sampit River									
2583	Georgetown	33° 21.7'	79° 16.8'	+1 25	+2 09	*0.71	*0.79	3.72	4.32	2.01
2585	Jacobs Wharf	33° 21.8'	79° 21.3'	+2 15	+2 22	*0.73	*0.74	3.84	4.45	2.06
2587	Cumberland	33° 22.2'	79° 26.0'	+2 42	+2 29	*0.77	*0.74	4.02	4.74	2.15
	Great Pee Dee River									
2589	Windsor Plantation, Black River	33° 24.9'	79° 15.0'	+2 00	+2 45	*0.66	*0.74	3.45	3.97	1.86
2591	Black River (south of Dunbar)	33° 30.7'	79° 20.5'	+3 29	+4 09	*0.47	*0.89	2.42	2.81	1.38
2593	Winea Plantation, Black River	33° 32.1'	79° 23.3'	+4 23	+4 39	*0.47	*0.84	2.37	2.73	1.34
2595	Mt. Pleasant Plantation, Black River	33° 29.7'	79° 27.7'	+5 38	+6 04	*0.37	*1.05	1.82	2.11	1.11
2597	Rhems, Black Mingo Creek, Black River	33° 36.2'	79° 25.6'	+6 00	+6 13	*0.36	*1.05	1.75	2.03	1.08
2599	Weymouth Plantation	33° 27.3'	79° 12.3'	+2 16	+3 02	*0.68	*0.89	3.56	4.13	1.95
2601	Carr Creek, 1 mile above entrance	33° 27.9'	79° 11.2'	+2 13	+3 00	*0.69	*0.84	3.62	4.20	1.97
2603	South of Sam Worth Game Management Area .	33° 28.1'	79° 11.3'	+2 21	+3 06	*0.69	*0.68	3.66	4.25	1.96
2605	Arundel Plantation	33° 29.0'	79° 10.7'	+2 38	+3 39	*0.53	*0.79	2.75	3.19	1.53
2607	Holly Grove Plantation	33° 33.1'	79° 10.6'	+3 20	+4 12	*0.50	*0.68	2.59	3.00	1.43
2609	Lower Topsaw Landing	33° 36.5'	79° 09.1'	+4 48	+5 20	*0.20	*0.53	0.96	1.13	0.58
2611	Yauhannah Bridge	33° 39.6'	79° 09.3'	+4 33	+5 24	*0.33	*0.68	1.66	1.91	0.96

Endnotes can be found at the end of table 2.

TABLE 2 – TIDAL DIFFERENCES AND OTHER CONSTANTS

No.	PLACE	POSITION Latitude	POSITION Longitude	DIFFERENCES Time High Water	DIFFERENCES Time Low Water	DIFFERENCES Height High Water	DIFFERENCES Height Low Water	RANGES Mean	RANGES Spring	Mean Tide Level
		North	**West**	h m	h m	ft	ft	ft	ft	ft
	SOUTH CAROLINA, outer coast Winyah Bay–cont. Time meridian, 75° W			**on Charleston, p.144**						
	Waccamaw River									
2613	Entrance	33° 22.0'	79° 15.3'	+1 19	+2 11	*0.69	*0.58	3.60	4.14	1.91
2615	Hagley Landing	33° 26.1'	79° 10.9'	+1 58	+2 53	*0.67	*0.79	3.47	3.99	1.88
2617	Thoroughfare Creek entrance	33° 30.4'	79° 08.8'	+2 32	+3 15	*0.64	*0.89	3.34	3.94	1.84
2619	Wachesaw Landing	33° 33.6'	79° 05.1'	+3 11	+4 00	*0.53	*0.84	2.74	3.18	1.53
2621	Bull Creek entrance	33° 35.8'	79° 05.9'	+3 36	+4 22	*0.48	*0.79	2.46	2.85	1.38
2623	Little Bull Creek entrance, Bull Creek	33° 36.1'	79° 07.1'	+3 59	+4 43	*0.46	*0.84	2.35	2.73	1.33
2625	Bucksport	33° 38.8'	79° 05.7'	+4 23	+4 53	*0.43	*0.89	2.16	2.48	1.25
2627	Enterprise Landing	33° 40'	79° 04'	+5 01	+5 35	*0.38	*0.37	2.0	2.4	1.1
2629	Keysfield	33° 44.7'	79° 03.9'	+6 09	+6 20	*0.28	*0.89	1.37	1.59	0.85
2631	Pitch Landing	33° 48.0'	79° 03.3'	+7 25	+7 30	*0.20	*0.74	0.94	1.09	0.61
2633	Conway, RR. bridge	33° 50.1'	79° 02.5'	+7 19	+7 28	*0.25	*0.74	1.24	1.44	0.76
2635	Grahamville	33° 49.8'	78° 57.2'	+8 17	+8 32	*0.20	*0.58	0.97	1.13	0.60
2637	North Santee River Inlet	33° 08'	79° 15'	−0 09	+0 04	*0.85	*0.84	4.5	5.3	2.3
2639	Cedar Island, North Santee Bay	33° 08.4'	79° 14.7'	−0 03	+0 17	*0.80	*0.95	4.19	4.86	2.28
2641	Minim Creek ent., ICWW, North Santee Bay	33° 11.7'	79° 16.5'	+0 16	+1 00	*0.77	*0.95	3.98	4.70	2.18
2643	North Santee Bridge	33° 12.6'	79° 23.1'	+1 09	+1 54	*0.72	*0.74	3.8	4.2	2.0
2645	Cedar Island Point, South Santee River	33° 07.2'	79° 16.2'	−0 16	+0 08	*0.78	*0.79	4.1	4.8	2.1
2647	Brown Island, South Santee River	33° 09'	79° 20'	+0 27	+1 31	*0.78	*0.79	4.1	4.8	2.1
2649	U.S. Highway 17 bridge, South Santee River	33° 11.1'	79° 24.4'	+0 43	+1 43	*0.78	*0.95	4.07	4.68	2.20
2651	Pleasant Hill Landing, Santee River	33° 14.7'	79° 31.3'	+2 28	+3 47	*0.45	*0.74	2.30	2.71	1.29
2653	Jamestown Bridge, Santee River	33° 18.3'	79° 40.7'	+4 15	+6 30	*0.22	*0.37	1.12	1.29	0.63
2655	Cape Romain	33° 01'	79° 21'	−0 22	−0 17	*0.89	*0.89	4.7	5.5	2.5
2657	Cape Romain, 46 miles east of	33° 06'	78° 26'	−1 05	−1 13	*0.78	*0.79	4.1	4.8	2.1
2659	Casino Creek, ICWW	33° 06.5'	79° 23.6'	+0 40	+0 53	*0.87	*0.79	4.55	5.37	2.42
	Bulls Bay									
2661	Five Fathom Creek entrance	33° 00'	79° 30'	−0 06	−0 07	*0.93	*0.95	4.9	5.8	2.6
2663	McClellanville, Jeremy Creek	33° 04.7'	79° 27.6'	+0 31	+0 24	*0.93	*0.89	4.86	5.59	2.60
2665	Harbor River entrance	33° 02.0'	79° 32.1'	+0 03	+0 36	*0.93	*0.95	4.9	5.8	2.6
2667	Buck Hall, Awendaw Creek	33° 02.4'	79° 33.6'	+0 22	+0 37	*0.95	*1.00	4.97	5.77	2.67
2669	Jack Creek entrance	32° 56'	79° 35'	−0 14	−0 15	*0.95	*0.95	5.0	5.9	2.7
2671	Wharf Creek entrance	32° 55'	79° 37'	+0 12	−0 08	*0.97	*0.95	5.1	6.0	2.7
2673	Moores Landing, ICWW, Sewee Bay	32° 56.2'	79° 39.3'	+0 11	+0 08	*0.96	*1.00	5.04	5.85	2.71
2675	Price Inlet, North Capers Island	32° 52.9'	79° 39.5'	−0 01	−0 21	*0.92	*0.89	4.80	5.52	2.57
2677	Old Capers Landing, Santee Pass, Capers Island	32° 52.2'	79° 41.2'	+0 21	−0 09	*0.94	*0.84	4.93	5.67	2.62
2679	North Dewees Island, Capers Inlet	32° 51.0'	79° 42.2'	−0 02	−0 11	*0.91	*0.95	4.76	5.62	2.56
2681	Capers Creek, South Capers Island	32° 51.4'	79° 42.4'	+0 04	−0 15	*0.94	*0.95	4.89	5.62	2.63
2683	South Dewees Island, Dewees Inlet	32° 50.0'	79° 43.6'	−0 01	−0 17	*0.94	*0.89	4.93	5.67	2.63
2685	Hamlin Sound	32° 49.6'	79° 47.2'	+0 13	−0 13	*0.99	*1.00	5.19	5.97	2.78
2687	Isle of Palms Pier	32° 47.0'	79° 47.1'	−0 25	−0 28	*0.95	*0.89	4.94	5.68	2.65
2689	Hamlin Creek, Isle of Palms	32° 47.2'	79° 47.5'	+0 06	−0 12	*0.97	*1.00	5.04	5.80	2.71
2691	Breach Inlet, Isle of Palms	32° 46.6'	79° 48.7'	−0 05	−0 14	*0.95	*1.05	4.94	5.68	2.66
2693	Sullivans Island (outer coast)	32° 46'	79° 50'	−0 08	−0 12	*0.99	*1.00	5.2	6.1	2.8
2695	Ben Sawyer Bridge, ICWW	32° 46.4'	79° 50.5'	+0 06	−0 12	*0.97	*1.00	5.05	5.81	2.71
	Charleston Harbor									
2697	Fort Sumter	32° 45.2'	79° 52.6'	+0 02	−0 01	*0.97	*0.95	5.09	5.90	2.72
2699	The Cove, Fort Moultrie	32° 45.8'	79° 51.4'	−0 01	−0 10	*0.97	*0.95	5.08	5.84	2.72
2701	Fort Johnson	32° 45.1'	79° 53.9'	−0 05	−0 02	*0.97	*1.00	5.09	5.90	2.74
2703	Shem Creek	32° 47.6'	79° 52.9'	−0 02	−0 03	*0.99	*1.00	5.20	6.03	2.79
2705	CHARLESTON (Customhouse Wharf)	32° 46.9'	79° 55.5'	Daily predictions				5.22	6.15	2.80
2707	Shipyard Creek, 0.8 mile above entrance	32° 50'	79° 57'	+0 34	+0 20	*1.01	*1.00	5.3	6.1	2.8
	Cooper River									
2709	Clouter Creek, south entrance	32° 51.6'	79° 56.3'	+0 25	+0 19	*1.02	*1.00	5.35	6.31	2.87
2711	Goose Creek entrance	32° 54.6'	79° 57.1'	+0 42	+0 33	*1.04	*1.00	5.41	6.22	2.90
2713	Yeamans Hall, Goose Creek	32° 55.5'	79° 59.2'	+2 06	+1 31	*1.00	*1.37	5.14	6.07	2.84
2715	Hanahan, Turkey Creek, Goose Creek	32° 55.1'	80° 00.7'	+2 51	+2 13	*0.90	*0.79	4.70	5.55	2.50
2717	Clouter Creek, north entrance	32° 54.4'	79° 56.1'	+0 45	+0 33	*1.04	*1.00	5.43	6.41	2.91
2719	Snow Point, 0.4 mi. North of	32° 56.9'	79° 55.9'	+0 59	+0 45	*1.02	*1.05	5.31	6.10	2.86
2721	General Dynamics Pier	33° 00.5'	79° 55.4'	+1 40	+1 24	*0.84	*1.11	4.35	5.03	2.39
2723	Dupont, Dean Hall	33° 03.5'	79° 56.2'	+2 21	+2 07	*0.68	*1.58	3.43	3.98	2.01
2725	Bonneau Ferry, East Branch	33° 04.3'	79° 53.0'	+3 14	+2 49	*0.63	*1.79	3.11	3.61	1.90
2727	Blessing Plantation, East Branch	33° 03.3'	79° 52.8'	+3 24	+3 20	*0.56	*1.32	2.79	3.29	1.64
2729	Richmond Plantation, East Branch	33° 04.6'	79° 51.3'	+3 43	+3 43	*0.54	*1.37	2.67	3.07	1.59
2731	Quinby Creek bridge, East Branch	33° 05.7'	79° 48.5'	+4 37	+4 12	*0.56	*1.42	2.75	3.25	1.65
2733	Huger Landing, East Branch	33° 07.8'	79° 48.7'	+4 46	− − −	− − −	− − −	− −	− −	− −
2735	Old Rice Mill, West Branch	33° 04.7'	79° 55.5'	+2 56	+2 51	*0.53	*1.63	2.60	3.02	1.61
2737	Back River Reservoir, West Branch	32° 59.7'	79° 56.2'	+5 44	+5 57	*0.17	*0.79	0.78	0.90	0.54
2739	Pimlico, West Branch	33° 05.7'	79° 57.2'	+3 19	+3 53	*0.34	*0.89	1.69	1.94	1.01
	Wando River									
2741	Hobcaw Point	32° 49.3'	79° 54.0'	+0 19	+0 13	*1.03	*0.95	5.39	6.20	2.88
2743	Parker Island, Horlbeck Creek	32° 53.1'	79° 50.7'	+0 43	+0 27	*1.09	*1.11	5.70	6.73	3.06
2745	Nowell Creek	32° 54.0'	79° 54.0'	+0 47	+0 23	*1.13	*1.05	5.91	6.80	3.16
2747	Cainhoy	32° 55.6'	79° 49.8'	+0 49	+0 31	*1.15	*1.00	6.02	6.92	3.20
2749	Big Paradise Island	32° 54.9'	79° 44.8'	+1 24	+0 52	*1.24	*1.11	6.48	7.45	3.45
2751	Woodville	32° 55.2'	79° 44.0'	+2 07	+1 22	*1.19	*1.19	6.3	7.3	3.4
	Ashley River									
2753	James Island Creek, 1 mi. above ent.	32° 44.7'	79° 56.9'	+0 17	+0 07	*1.02	*1.05	5.36	6.22	2.88
2755	Wappoo Creek, highway bridge	32° 46.0'	79° 58.4'	+0 22	+0 22	*0.99	*0.99	5.2	6.0	2.8
2757	South Ashley Bridge	32° 47.0'	79° 57.4'	+0 04	+0 07	*1.01	*1.05	5.34	6.19	2.87
2759	Duck Island	32° 49.8'	79° 58.0'	+0 23	+0 17	*1.06	*1.06	5.6	6 5	3.0
2761	Cosgrove Bridge	32° 50.1'	79° 59.2'	+0 25	+0 17	*1.07	*1.05	5.57	6.57	2.99
2763	I-526 bridge	32° 50.2'	80° 01.3'	+0 30	+0 29	*1.08	*1.11	5.68	6.53	3.05

Endnotes can be found at the end of table 2.

TABLE 2 – TIDAL DIFFERENCES AND OTHER CONSTANTS

No.	PLACE	POSITION		DIFFERENCES				RANGES		Mean Tide Level
				Time		Height				
		Latitude	Longitude	High Water	Low Water	High Water	Low Water	Mean	Spring	
		North	**West**	h m	h m	ft	ft	ft	ft	ft
	SOUTH CAROLINA, outer coast Charleston Harbor–cont. Time meridian, 75° W				**on Charleston, p.144**					
	Ashley River-cont.									
2765	Drayton, Bee's Ferry	32° 50.9'	80° 03.1'	+0 41	+0 39	*1.09	*1.05	5.69	6.54	3.05
2767	Magnolia Gardens	32° 52.6'	80° 04.9'	+1 02	+0 54	*1.10	*1.05	5.79	6.72	3.10
2769	Greggs Landing, Mateeba Gardens	32° 55.7'	80° 09.3'	+2 06	+1 42	*1.15	*1.16	6.06	7.03	3.25
2771	Bacon Bridge	32° 57.5'	80° 12.2'	+2 45	+3 41	*0.39	*0.16	2.10	2.48	1.08
	SOUTH CAROLINA, outer coast–cont.									
2773	Secessionville, Secessionville Creek	32° 42.4'	79° 56.2'	+0 22	– – –	– – –	– – –	– –	– –	– –
2775	Folly Island (outer coast)	32° 39'	79° 56'	−0 08	−0 14	*0.98	*1.00	5.2	6.1	2.8
2777	Folly River Bridge, Folly Island	32° 39.7'	79° 56.7'	+0 21	−0 03	*1.01	*0.95	5.27	6.06	2.22
2779	Folly Creek, Hwy. 171 bridge	32° 40.5'	79° 57.1'	+0 25	−0 06	*1.04	*1.00	5.41	6.22	2.89
2781	Folly River, north, Folly Island	32° 40.2'	79° 55.0'	+0 24	−0 05	*1.03	*0.95	5.38	6.19	2.87
	Stono River									
2783	Snake Island	32° 38.4'	80° 00.9'	+0 01	−0 12	*1.01	*1.00	5.27	6.06	2.83
2785	Abbapoola Creek entrance	32° 40.6'	80° 00.4'	+0 17	+0 02	*1.01	*0.95	5.36	6.22	2.86
2787	Elliott Cut entrance	32° 45.8'	80° 00.1'	+0 48	+0 52	*0.99	*1.16	5.14	5.91	2.79
2789	Pennys Creek, west entrance	32° 46.1'	80° 04.2'	+1 23	+1 20	*1.03	*1.32	5.32	6.12	2.91
2791	Sandblasters, Pennys Creek	32° 46.2'	80° 03.8'	+1 30	+1 18	*1.02	*1.02	5.26	6.21	2.91
2793	Limehouse Bridge	32° 47.2'	80° 06.3'	+1 43	+1 34	*1.08	*1.08	5.58	6.58	3.04
2795	Church Flats	32° 44.8'	80° 09.9'	+1 51	+1 14	*1.22	*1.16	6.37	7.33	3.41
2797	Kiawah River Bridge	32° 36.2'	80° 07.9'	+0 14	+0 06	*1.07	*0.89	5.60	6.44	2.97
	North Edisto River									
2799	Ocella Creek, 2 mi. above entrance	32° 33.7'	80° 14.3'	+0 32	+0 09	*1.08	*1.08	5.7	6.6	3.0
2801	Rockville, Bohicket Creek	32° 35.9'	80° 11.7'	+0 19	+0 07	*1.09	*1.11	5.76	6.68	3.09
2803	Ho–Non–Wah Boy Scout Camp, Bohicket Creek	32° 37.5'	80° 10.0'	+0 49	+0 30	*1.13	*1.11	5.93	6.82	3.17
2805	Oak Branch, Bohicket Creek	32° 41.0'	80° 05.8'	+1 39	+0 57	*1.26	*1.16	6.66	7.73	3.55
2807	Point of Pines	32° 35.1'	80° 13.7'	+0 15	+0 11	*1.08	*1.05	5.66	6.51	3.04
2809	Leadenwah Creek, 3 mi. above entrance	32° 38.2'	80° 12.1'	+0 54	+0 23	*1.15	*1.11	5.99	6.89	3.21
2811	Steamboat Landing, Steamboat Creek	32° 36.2'	80° 17.2'	+0 45	+0 25	*1.15	*1.11	6.02	6.92	3.22
2813	Windsor Plantation, Russel Creek	32° 35.9'	80° 20.7'	+1 16	+0 35	*1.21	*1.11	6.40	7.42	3.41
2815	Dawho Bridge, Dawho River	32° 38.2'	80° 20.5'	+0 56	+0 47	*1.18	*1.11	6.17	7.10	3.29
2817	Park Island, Tom Point Creek	32° 39.9'	80° 19.0'	+1 19	+0 34	*1.21	*1.21	6.40	7.42	3.43
2819	Toogoodoo Creek, 2 mi. above entrance	32° 40.1'	80° 17.6'	+1 06	+0 38	*1.21	*1.05	6.36	7.31	3.38
2821	Lower Toogoodoo Creek, 2 mi. above entrance	32° 42.2'	80° 16.7'	+1 26	+0 47	*1.29	*1.26	6.73	7.94	3.61
	Wadmalaw River									
2823	Bluff Point	32° 38.8'	80° 15.4'	+0 58	+0 31	*1.17	*1.11	6.13	7.05	3.28
2825	Yonges Island	32° 41.7'	80° 13.4'	+1 22	+0 45	*1.24	*1.16	6.50	7.48	3.47
2827	Johns Island, Church Creek	32° 42.4'	80° 09.4'	+1 43	+1 00	*1.30	*1.16	6.85	7.88	3.64
2829	Church Creek bridge	32° 42.9'	80° 05.5'	+1 58	+0 58	*1.30	*1.00	6.93	8.04	3.66
					on Savannah River Ent., p.148					
2831	Edisto Beach, Edisto Island	32° 30.1'	80° 17.8'	−0 21	−0 29	*0.84	*0.95	5.75	6.61	3.08
	South Edisto River									
2833	Edisto Marina, Big Bay Creek entrance	32° 29.6'	80° 20.4'	−0 06	−0 13	*0.86	*0.91	5.96	6.85	3.18
2835	Carters Dock, Big Bay Creek	32° 29.6'	80° 19.6'	+0 08	−0 07	*0.87	*0.91	5.97	6.87	3.18
2837	Scott Creek, 0.5 mi. above ent., Big Bay Creek	32° 30.1'	80° 19.1'	+0 29	– – –	– – –	– – –	– –	– –	– –
2839	Peters Point, St. Pierre Creek	32° 32.4'	80° 20.4'	+0 22	+0 09	*0.88	*0.95	6.09	7.00	3.25
2841	Fenwick Island	32° 33.6'	80° 25.1'	+0 15	+0 25	*0.90	*1.09	6.19	7.12	3.32
2843	Pine Landing	32° 36.2'	80° 23.3'	+0 29	+0 45	*0.92	*0.95	6.29	7.30	3.36
2845	Dawho River	32° 39.4'	80° 23.5'	+1 07	+1 31	*0.89	*0.95	6.15	7.07	3.29
2847	Willtown Bluff, Edisto River	32° 40.9'	80° 25.0'	+1 34	+2 03	*0.83	*1.00	5.69	6.54	3.06
2849	Hope Creek, Edisto River	32° 42.0'	80° 25.6'	+1 46	+2 13	*0.82	*1.05	5.62	6.46	3.04
2851	Penny Creek, south of, Edisto River	32° 42.9'	80° 26.2'	+2 10	+2 43	*0.73	*1.18	4.97	5.72	2.75
2853	Jacksonboro Camp	32° 45.2'	80° 27.0'	+2 46	+3 34	*0.59	*0.86	4.04	4.65	2.21
2855	Canaday Landing, south of, Edisto River	32° 48.8'	80° 24.4'	+4 20	+5 34	*0.13	*0.32	0.84	0.97	0.49
2857	Hart Bluff, Edisto River <24>	32° 55.6'	80° 23.9'	– – –	– – –	– – –	– – –	– –	– –	– –
	St. Helena Sound									
2859	Otter Island	32° 28.6'	80° 25.2'	+0 04	+0 07	*0.87	*0.95	6.01	6.91	3.21
2861	Johnson Creek Bridge, Hunting Island	32° 23.5'	80° 26.3'	+0 03	+0 03	*0.85	*0.86	5.88	6.76	3.13
2863	Harbor River Bridge	32° 24.2'	80° 27.2'	+0 03	−0 06	*0.88	*0.95	6.09	7.00	3.25
	Ashepoo River									
2865	Seabrook	32° 31.4'	80° 24.4'	+0 11	+0 18	*0.90	*0.91	6.2	7.3	3.3
2867	Ashepoo–Coosaw Cutoff, ICWW	32° 31.5'	80° 27.1'	+0 15	+0 23	*0.90	*0.91	6.20	7.19	3.30
2869	Musselboro Island, Mosquito Creek	32° 34.7'	80° 26.9'	+1 21	+0 57	*0.90	*0.91	6.22	7.15	3.31
2871	Hutchinson Island	32° 33.1'	80° 28.9'	+0 31	+0 44	*0.87	*0.91	6.01	6.97	3.20
2873	Bluff Islands	32° 34.7'	80° 29.6'	+0 46	+1 04	*0.84	*0.91	5.79	6.72	3.10
2875	Brickyard Ferry, swing bridge	32° 36.8'	80° 28.9'	+1 27	+1 34	*0.71	*0.86	4.82	5.59	2.60
2877	Airy Hall Plantation	32° 37.9'	80° 28.3'	+1 57	+1 59	*0.60	*1.00	4.16	4.71	2.25
2879	Ashepoo	32° 44.6'	80° 33.4'	+4 18	+4 00	*0.34	*1.05	2.18	2.53	1.32
	Morgan River									
2881	Village Creek Entrance	32° 26.7'	80° 30.2'	+0 17	+0 07	*0.93	*1.00	6.35	7.37	3.40
2883	Village Creek Cemetery	32° 25.0'	80° 31.2'	+0 36	+0 15	*0.94	*0.95	6.45	7.48	3.43
2885	Edding Point, Edding Creek	32° 26.8'	80° 32.0'	+0 31	+0 14	*0.93	*0.95	6.41	7.37	3.42
2887	Jenkins Creek, 1 mi. above entrance	32° 26.4'	80° 33.2'	+0 41	+0 17	*0.98	*0.95	6.80	7.82	3.61
2889	Jenkins Creek, Polawana Island	32° 25.2'	80° 34.6'	+0 55	+0 27	*1.01	*1.05	6.91	8.02	3.69
2891	Lucy Point Creek entrance	32° 27.1'	80° 36.6'	+0 53	+0 33	*0.90	*0.88	6.32	7.33	3.21
	Combahee River									
2893	Bowles Island, New Chehaw River	32° 33.9'	80° 31.0'	+1 02	+0 42	*0.96	*1.00	6.59	7.64	3.51
2895	Wiggins, Chehaw River	32° 36.1'	80° 32.5'	+1 45	+1 20	*0.88	*1.18	6.03	6.93	3.28
2897	Fields Point	32° 34.0'	80° 33.7'	+0 42	+0 52	*0.91	*0.91	6.2	7.3	3.3

Endnotes can be found at the end of table 2.

TABLE 2 – TIDAL DIFFERENCES AND OTHER CONSTANTS

No.	PLACE	POSITION Latitude	POSITION Longitude	DIFFERENCES Time High Water	DIFFERENCES Time Low Water	DIFFERENCES Height High Water	DIFFERENCES Height Low Water	RANGES Mean	RANGES Spring	Mean Tide Level
		North	West	h m	h m	ft	ft	ft	ft	ft
	SOUTH CAROLINA, outer coast–cont. St. Helena Sound–cont. Time meridian, 75° W			on Savannah River Ent., p.148						
	Combahee River-cont.									
2899	Railroad Bridge	32° 35.4'	80° 37.8'	+1 37	– – –	– – –	– – –	– –	– –	– –
2901	U.S. 17 Bridge	32° 39.1'	80° 41.0'	+3 00	+2 29	*0.71	*1.14	4.83	5.55	2.66
2903	Bluff Plantation	32° 41.0'	80° 44.3'	+4 17	+3 51	*0.50	*1.59	3.12	3.59	1.95
2905	Cuckolds Creek	32° 42.8'	80° 41.7'	+4 45	+4 12	*0.51	*1.73	3.26	3.81	2.01
	Coosaw River									
2907	Summerhouse Point, Bull River	32° 31.6'	80° 34.4'	+0 55	+0 37	*0.96	*0.95	6.58	7.63	3.50
2909	Briars Creek ent., Wimbee Creek, Bull River ...	32° 34.7'	80° 40.2'	+2 06	+1 24	*0.93	*0.95	6.39	7.35	3.41
2911	Sams Point, Lucy Point Creek	32° 29.0'	80° 35.9'	+0 55	+0 45	*0.97	*0.91	6.71	7.78	3.55
2913	Brickyard Point, Brickyard Creek	32° 29.6'	80° 41.1'	+1 27	+1 19	*1.08	*0.95	7.45	8.64	3.94
2915	Whale Branch entrance	32° 31.5'	80° 40.5'	+1 27	+1 20	*1.06	*0.95	7.32	8.49	3.87
2917	Lobeco, Whale Branch	32° 34.4'	80° 44.7'	+1 40	+1 28	*1.11	*0.95	7.75	8.91	4.08
2919	Sheldon, Huspa Creek, Whale Branch	32° 35.0'	80° 47.0'	+2 11	+1 52	*1.16	*0.77	8.07	9.28	4.21
2921	Fripps Inlet, Hunting Island Bridge	32° 20.4'	80° 27.9'	–0 10	–0 22	*0.88	*0.91	6.10	7.02	3.25
	Port Royal Sound									
2923	Capers Island, Trenchards Inlet	32° 16.4'	80° 35.1'	–0 01	–0 18	*0.93	*0.95	6.37	7.39	3.39
2925	Club Bridge Creek ent., Trenchards Inlet	32° 20.1'	80° 32.5'	+0 15	–0 24	*0.99	*1.00	6.78	7.86	3.61
2927	Port Royal Plantation, Hilton Head Island	32° 13.2'	80° 40.1'	+0 01	–0 11	*0.88	*1.00	6.10	7.02	3.27
2929	The Folly, Hilton Head Island	32° 11.4'	80° 42.1'	+0 03	– – –	– – –	– – –	– –	– –	– –
2931	Station Creek, west end	32° 16.8'	80° 38.3'	+0 16	+0 13	*0.96	*0.91	6.62	7.68	3.51
2933	Station Creek, County Landing	32° 19.5'	80° 36.1'	+0 27	–0 16	*0.99	*1.00	6.84	7.87	3.64
	Beaufort River									
2935	Fort Fremont	32° 18.4'	80° 38.7'	+0 19	+0 17	*0.95	*0.64	6.63	7.69	3.45
2937	Parris Island, Marine Corps Recruit Depot	32° 21.0'	80° 40.1'	+0 37	+0 26	*1.02	*0.91	7.02	8.14	3.71
2939	Distant Island, Cowen Creek	32° 22.7'	80° 38.0'	+0 43	+0 27	*1.06	*1.05	7.29	8.46	3.87
2941	Distant Island Creek, upper end, Cowen Creek .	32° 24.1'	80° 39.2'	+1 00	+1 08	*0.98	*0.36	6.92	7.96	3.54
2943	Capers Creek, Cowen Creek, St. Helena Island	32° 22.3'	80° 36.3'	+0 58	+0 34	*1.08	*0.95	7.44	8.63	3.93
2945	Cowen Creek, Rt. 21 bridge	32° 23.9'	80° 37.0'	+0 55	+0 58	*1.00	*0.55	6.97	8.09	3.61
2947	Battery Creek, 4 mi. above entrance	32° 24.8'	80° 42.0'	+1 14	+0 37	*1.10	*0.91	7.64	8.79	4.02
2949	Beaufort	32° 25.8'	80° 40.5'	+1 09	+0 51	*1.07	*0.95	7.39	8.17	3.90
2951	Marine Corps Air Station, Brickyard Creek	32° 27.9'	80° 41.5'	+1 27	+1 11	*1.10	*0.95	7.62	8.84	4.02
2953	Albergotie Creek, Rt. 21 bridge	32° 27.0'	80° 43.9'	+1 48	+2 02	*0.98	*0.45	6.83	7.92	3.52
2955	Skull Creek, north entrance, Hilton Head Island .	32° 16.0'	80° 44.2'	+0 15	+0 16	*0.99	*0.91	6.83	7.85	3.62
2957	Skull Creek, south entrance, Hilton Head Island ..	32° 13.4'	80° 46.3'	+0 34	+0 23	*1.05	*1.05	7.28	8.37	3.87
2959	Pinckney Island, Mackay Creek, Chechessee River	32° 15.6'	80° 46.0'	+0 36	+0 25	*1.04	*0.91	7.21	8.36	3.80
2961	Colleton River Entrance	32° 19.3'	80° 47.5'	+0 49	+0 37	*1.05	*1.05	7.2	8.4	3.8
2963	Callawassie Creek, Colleton River	32° 19.0'	80° 50.5'	+1 15	+0 53	*1.13	*1.14	7.8	9.1	4.1
2965	Callawassie Island, south, Colleton River	32° 18.8'	80° 51.6'	+1 09	+0 40	*1.19	*1.11	7.7	9.0	4.1
2967	Callawassie Island Bridge, Colleton River	32° 20.5'	80° 51.4'	+1 12	+0 49	*1.13	*1.14	7.8	9.1	4.2
2969	Baileys Landing, Okatee River, Colleton River ...	32° 20.8'	80° 53.4'	+1 25	+0 57	*1.17	*1.05	8.09	9.30	4.28
2971	Chechessee Bluff, Chechessee River	32° 22.4'	80° 50.2'	+1 06	+0 48	*1.10	*1.00	7.62	8.84	4.03
	Broad River									
2973	Hwy. 170 bridge	32° 23.2'	80° 46.6'	+0 51	+0 45	*1.06	*0.91	7.35	8.45	3.88
2975	Broughton Point, Hazzard Creek	32° 24.6'	80° 53.1'	+1 34	+1 30	*1.10	*0.82	7.61	8.83	3.99
2977	Euhaw Creek, 2.5 mi. above entrance	32° 26.1'	80° 51.1'	+1 33	+1 09	*1.14	*0.91	7.92	9.19	4.16
2979	Salvesbarg Landing, West Branch Boyds Creek	32° 28.5'	80° 51.0'	+1 29	– – –	– – –	– – –	– –	– –	– –
2981	Pilot Island, West Branch Boyds Creek	32° 30.3'	80° 51.8'	+1 50	+1 24	*1.15	*0.91	7.98	9.26	4.19
2983	Corning Landing, Whale Branch	32° 30.0'	80° 47.1'	+1 37	+1 25	*1.15	*0.77	8.00	9.28	4.17
2985	RR. Bridge, Hall Island	32° 31.3'	80° 50.3'	+1 39	+1 24	*1.17	*1.05	8.08	9.37	4.27
2987	Pocotaligo River, 4 mi. above entrance	32° 35.7'	80° 49.9'	+2 21	+1 48	– – –	– – –	– –	– –	– –
2989	North Dawson Landing, Coosawhatchie River ..	32° 33.7'	80° 54.6'	+2 34	+2 10	*1.12	*1.14	7.71	8.94	4.10
2991	Tulifiny River, I-95 bridge	32° 36.1'	80° 54.2'	+3 24	+3 31	*0.73	*0.73	5.01	5.81	2.66
	Calibogue Sound									
2993	Braddock Point, Hilton Head Island	32° 06.8'	80° 49.8'	+0 05	–0 02	*0.98	*1.00	6.74	7.82	3.59
2995	Calibogue Cay, Broad Creek, Hilton Head Island .	32° 09.2'	80° 47.7'	+0 20	+0 09	*1.04	*1.00	7.13	8.27	3.79
2997	Broad Creek, Hilton Head Island	32° 11.1'	80° 45.2'	+0 33	+0 17	*1.08	*1.05	7.48	8.60	3.97
2999	Haig Point, Daufuskie Island, Cooper River	32° 08.8'	80° 50.2'	+0 20	+0 10	*1.02	*1.00	7.05	8.18	3.74
3001	Bull Creek, Bull Island South, Cooper River	32° 09.9'	80° 51.4'	+0 28	+0 12	*1.05	*1.05	7.23	8.39	3.84
3003	Pine Island, Ramshorn Creek, Cooper River	32° 07.3'	80° 53.9'	+0 34	+0 28	*1.03	*0.91	7.17	8.25	3.78
3005	Savage I., Savage Creek, Bull Creek	32° 11.1'	80° 51.6'	+0 46	+0 19	*1.10	*1.00	7.56	8.77	4.00
	May River									
3007	Moreland Cemetery	32° 10.5'	80° 53.5'	+0 49	+0 23	*1.11	*0.77	7.73	8.97	4.04
3009	Bull Island North	32° 12.0'	80° 48.9'	+0 40	+0 25	*1.09	*1.05	7.52	8.72	3.99
3011	Bluffton	32° 13.8'	80° 51.7'	+1 00	+0 37	*1.16	*1.05	8.01	9.29	4.23
3013	Rose Dew Creek	32° 13.2'	80° 55.2'	+1 19	– – –	– – –	– – –	– –	– –	– –
	New River									
3015	Bloody Point, Daufuskie Island	32° 04.9'	80° 52.7'	+0 01	+0 19	*0.98	*0.91	6.77	7.79	3.59
3017	Hargray Pier, Daufuskie Island	32° 05.9'	80° 53.9'	+0 19	+0 27	*1.01	*1.05	6.96	8.07	3.71
3019	Daufuskie Landing, Daufuskie Island	32° 06.2'	80° 53.7'	+0 30	+0 33	*1.01	*0.95	7.02	8.07	3.72
3021	Doughboy Island	32° 08.3'	80° 55.9'	+1 04	+1 06	*1.01	*1.05	6.96	8.07	3.71
3023	Good Hope Landing, south of	32° 10.6'	80° 58.0'	+2 19	+2 06	*0.85	*1.55	5.71	6.62	3.20
3025	Cook Landing Cemetery	32° 11.7'	81° 00.0'	+3 09	+3 00	*0.69	*1.41	4.58	5.31	2.60
3027	Rt. 170 bridge	32° 14.2'	81° 00.7'	+4 12	+3 53	*0.51	*0.51	3.33	3.83	2.01
3029	Fields Cut, Wright River	32° 05.2'	80° 56.0'	+0 16	+0 29	*1.02	*1.05	6.98	8.10	3.72
3031	Turnbridge Landing, Salt Water Creek	32° 07.7'	81° 00.7'	+1 41	+0 59	*1.06	*1.09	7.27	8.43	3.87

Endnotes can be found at the end of table 2.

TABLE 2 – TIDAL DIFFERENCES AND OTHER CONSTANTS

No.	PLACE	Latitude	Longitude	Time High Water	Time Low Water	Height High Water	Height Low Water	Mean Range	Spring Range	Mean Tide Level
		North	West	h m	h m	ft	ft	ft	ft	ft
	GEORGIA Savannah River Time meridian, 75° W			on Savannah River Ent., p.148						
3033	Tybee Light	32° 02'	80° 51'	−0 10	−0 12	*0.99	*0.99	6.8	8.0	3.6
3035	SAVANNAH RIVER ENTRANCE, FORT PULASKI	32° 02.0'	80° 54.1'	*Daily predictions*				6.92	8.03	3.67
3037	Fort Jackson	32° 04.9'	81° 02.2'	+0 29	+0 42	*1.09	*1.09	7.50	8.70	4.04
3039	Savannah, Bull Street	32° 05'	81° 05'	+0 44	+0 33	*1.14	*1.14	7.9	8.8	4.2
3041	Port Wentworth	32° 08.6'	81° 08.5'	+0 44	+0 41	*1.17	*0.95	8.14	9.12	4.28
3043	Little Back River, Hwy. 17, Back River, S.C.	32° 09.9'	81° 07.8'	+1 28	+1 41	*1.10	*1.14	7.63	8.55	4.06
3045	S.C.L. RR. bridge	32° 14'	81° 09'	+1 51	+3 08	*0.90	*0.91	6.2	7.2	3.3
3047	Purrysburg Landing, S.C.	32° 18.2'	81° 07.3'	+2 14	+3 38	*0.44	*0.41	3.03	3.48	1.60
	Tybee Creek and Wassaw Sound									
3049	Tybee Creek entrance	31° 59'	80° 51'	−0 09	+0 05	*0.99	*1.00	6.8	8.0	3.6
3051	Beach Hammock	31° 57'	80° 56'	−0 01	−0 07	*1.00	*1.00	6.9	8.1	3.7
3053	Romerly Marsh Creek	31° 56'	81° 00'	+0 08	−0 03	*1.03	*1.03	7.1	8.3	3.7
	Wilmington River									
3055	Savannah Sheraton Resort Hotel	32° 00'	81° 00'	+0 14	+0 06	*1.13	*1.14	7.8	9.1	4.2
3057	Thunderbolt	32° 02'	81° 03'	+0 32	+0 12	*1.15	*1.14	7.9	9.2	4.2
3059	North entrance	32° 04'	81° 00'	+0 40	+0 44	*1.10	*1.09	7.6	8.9	4.0
3061	Isle of Hope, Skidaway River	31° 59'	81° 03'	+0 50	+0 28	*1.13	*1.13	7.8	9.1	4.1
	Ossabaw Sound									
3063	Egg Islands	31° 50'	81° 05'	+0 04	+0 10	*1.04	*1.04	7.2	8.4	3.8
3065	Vernon View, Burnside River	31° 56'	81° 06'	+0 40	+0 31	*1.09	*1.09	7.5	8.8	4.0
3067	Coffee Bluff, Forest River	31° 56'	81° 09'	+1 05	+0 42	*1.09	*1.09	7.5	8.8	3.9
3069	Fort McAllister, Ogeechee River	31° 53'	81° 13'	+0 48	+1 16	*1.00	*1.00	6.9	8.1	3.6
3071	Highway bridge, Ogeechee River	31° 59'	81° 17'	+3 19	+4 25	*0.15	*0.14	1.0	1.2	0.5
3073	Florida Passage, Ogeechee River	31° 51'	81° 09'	+0 34	+0 46	*1.05	*0.91	7.3	8.5	3.8
3075	Florida Passage, Bear River	31° 49'	81° 10'	+0 46	+0 49	*1.09	*0.95	7.6	8.8	4.0
3077	Cane Patch Creek entrance	31° 49'	81° 09'	+0 55	+0 43	*1.05	*1.05	7.2	8.4	3.8
3079	Bradley Point, Bradley River	31° 49'	81° 03'	+0 04	+0 13	*1.02	*0.95	7.0	8.2	3.7
	St. Catherines and Sapelo Sounds									
3081	Walburg Creek entrance	31° 42'	81° 09'	+0 16	+0 21	*1.03	*1.00	7.1	8.3	3.8
3083	Kilkenny Club, Kilkenny Creek	31° 47'	81° 12'	+0 48	+0 37	*1.09	*0.91	7.5	8.8	4.0
3085	Bear River, (Range 'A' Light)	31° 47.6'	81° 10.9'	+0 42	+0 29	*1.06	*0.95	7.36	8.46	3.89
3087	Bear River Entrance	31° 43.3'	81° 08.5'	+0 10	+0 13	*1.00	*0.86	6.97	8.12	3.67
3089	Sunbury, Medway River	31° 46.0'	81° 16.7'	+0 55	+0 49	*1.05	*1.00	7.28	8.27	3.87
3091	Belfast, Belfast River	31° 49'	81° 18'	+1 23	+1 10	*1.13	*1.14	7.8	9.1	4.2
3093	North Newport River (Daymark 119)	31° 41'	81° 12'	+0 35	+0 31	*1.05	*1.00	7.2	8.4	3.8
3095	North Newport River	31° 40'	81° 16'	+0 56	+0 36	*1.10	*1.09	7.6	8.9	4.0
3097	South Newport Cut, N. Newport River	31° 40'	81° 16'	+1 01	+0 54	*1.08	*1.04	7.5	8.7	4.0
3099	Halfmoon, Timmons River	31° 41.7'	81° 16.3'	+1 21	+1 09	*1.06	*1.05	7.35	8.45	3.90
3101	Eagle Neck, South Newport River	31° 39'	81° 18'	+1 16	+1 06	*1.09	*1.00	7.5	8.8	4.0
3103	Thomas Landing, S. Newport River	31° 39'	81° 15'	+0 57	+0 46	*1.06	*0.95	7.4	8.6	3.9
3105	South Newport River (Daymark 135)	31° 34.5'	81° 11.4'	+0 22	+0 13	*1.00	*0.95	7.11	7.99	3.66
3107	Dallas Bluff, Julienton River	31° 35'	81° 19'	+0 48	+1 04	*1.10	*1.09	7.6	8.9	4.0
3109	Harris Neck, Barbour Island River	31° 37'	81° 16'	+0 54	+0 32	*1.08	*1.00	7.5	8.8	4.0
3111	Barbour Island, Barbour Island River	31° 35'	81° 14'	+0 36	+0 24	*1.06	*1.00	7.3	8.5	3.9
3113	Blackbeard Island	31° 32'	81° 12'	+0 18	+0 22	*1.00	*1.00	6.9	8.1	3.6
3115	Dog Hammock, Sapelo River	31° 32'	81° 16'	+0 33	+0 22	*1.04	*0.91	7.2	8.4	3.8
3117	Bellville Point, Sapelo River	31° 32'	81° 22'	+1 12	+1 02	*1.08	*0.86	7.5	8.8	3.9
3119	Pine Harbor, Sapelo River	31° 33'	81° 22'	+1 03	+1 04	*1.05	*1.05	7.2	8.4	3.8
3121	Eagle Creek, Mud River	31° 31'	81° 17'	+0 21	+0 19	*1.05	*1.05	7.2	8.4	3.8
3123	Creighton Narrows Entrance, Crescent River	31° 29'	81° 20'	+0 49	+0 37	*1.08	*1.09	7.4	8.6	4.0
3125	Mud River, Old Teakettle Cr.(Daymark 156)	31° 29.2'	81° 19.2'	+0 46	+0 33	*1.08	*1.00	7.50	8.43	3.97
	Doboy and Altamaha Sounds									
3127	Old Tea Kettle Creek (Daymark 173)	31° 26'	81° 18'	+0 39	+0 39	*0.96	*0.82	6.7	7.8	3.5
3129	Blackbeard Creek, Blackbeard Island	31° 29'	81° 13'	+0 19	+0 47	*0.94	*0.95	6.5	7.6	3.5
3131	Old Tower, Sapelo Island	31° 23.4'	81° 17.3'	+0 15	+0 14	*0.99	*0.95	6.82	7.84	3.62
3133	Hudson Creek entrance	31° 27'	81° 21'	+0 37	+0 31	*1.05	*1.05	7.2	8.4	3.8
3135	Threemile Cut entrance, Darien River	31° 21'	81° 23'	+0 44	+0 55	*1.03	*1.05	7.1	8.3	3.7
3137	Darien, Darien River	31° 22'	81° 26'	+1 08	+1 15	*1.06	*1.05	7.3	8.5	3.9
3139	Rockdedundy River (Daymark 185)	31° 22.4'	81° 20.0'	+0 25	+0 26	*1.00	*1.00	6.86	8.03	3.68
3141	Wolf Island, south end	31° 20'	81° 19'	+0 25	+0 45	*0.97	*1.09	6.7	7.8	3.6
3143	Champney Island, South Altamaha River	31° 20'	81° 28'	+1 10	+2 33	*0.76	*0.77	5.2	6.1	2.8
3145	Hampton River entrance	31° 13'	81° 19'	+0 16	+0 04	*0.96	*0.95	6.6	7.8	3.5
3147	Jones Creek entrance, Hampton River	31° 18'	81° 20'	+1 03	+0 13	*1.05	*1.05	7.2	8.5	3.8
	St. Simons Sound									
3149	St. Simons Sound Bar	31° 06'	81° 19'	−0 01	−0 02	*0.95	*0.95	6.5	7.6	3.4
3151	St. Simons Light	31° 07.9'	81° 23.8'	+0 14	+0 16	*0.95	*0.91	6.60	7.72	3.50
3153	Frederick River Bridge	31° 10'	81° 25'	+0 43	+0 45	*1.00	*1.09	6.9	8.0	3.7
3155	Frederica River	31° 13'	81° 24'	+0 48	+0 56	*1.05	*1.05	7.2	8.4	3.8
3157	Mackay River (Daymark 239)	31° 13'	81° 26'	+0 58	+0 56	*1.03	*1.09	7.1	8.3	3.8
3159	Mackay River (ICWW), Buttermilk Sound	31° 17.1'	81° 23.1'	+0 58	+1 23	*1.00	*1.09	6.87	7.90	3.68
3161	Brunswick, East River, Howe Street Pier	31° 08.6'	81° 29.8'	+0 44	+0 35	*1.03	*1.00	7.13	8.27	3.78

Endnotes can be found at the end of table 2.

.

TABLE 2 – TIDAL DIFFERENCES AND OTHER CONSTANTS

No.	PLACE	POSITION Latitude	Longitude	DIFFERENCES Time High Water	Low Water	Height High Water	Low Water	RANGES Mean	Spring	Mean Tide Level
		North	West	h m	h m	ft	ft	ft	ft	ft
	GEORGIA St. Simons Sound–cont. Time meridian, 75° W			**on Savannah River Ent., p.148**						
	Turtle River									
3163	Crispen Island	31° 13'	81° 33'	+1 33	+0 55	*1.15	*1.05	7.9	9.3	4.2
3165	Allied Chemical Corp. docks	31° 11'	81° 31'	+1 03	+0 42	*1.10	*1.09	7.6	8.9	4.0
3167	Dillard Creek	31° 14'	81° 34'	+1 32	+1 02	*1.16	*1.18	8.0	9.4	4.3
3169	Buffalo River entrance	31° 13'	81° 35'	+1 37	+0 58	*1.16	*1.18	8.0	9.4	4.3
3171	Highway bridge, South Brunswick River	31° 09'	81° 34'	+1 07	+0 49	*1.10	*1.09	7.6	8.9	4.0
	St. Andrew Sound			**on Fernandina Beach, p.152**						
3173	Raccoon Key Spit	31° 00.8'	81° 27.3'	−0 19	+0 09	*1.09	*1.11	6.56	7.63	3.49
3175	Jekyll Island Marina, Jekyll Creek	31° 03.4'	81° 25.4'	+0 03	+0 36	*1.13	*1.16	6.83	7.85	3.63
3177	Jointer Island, Jointer Creek	31° 06'	81° 30'	+0 11	+0 31	*1.18	*1.18	7.2	8.4	3.8
	Little Satilla River									
3179	2.5 miles above mouth	31° 04'	81° 30'	−0 04	+0 31	*1.12	*1.12	6.8	7.9	3.6
3181	8 miles above mouth	31° 06'	81° 34'	+0 24	+1 02	*1.20	*1.20	7.3	8.5	3.8
3183	Below Spring Bluff	31° 10'	81° 37'	+1 09	+1 31	*1.23	*1.23	7.5	8.7	3.9
3185	Dover Bluff, Dover Creek	31° 01'	81° 32'	+0 06	+0 31	*1.15	*1.15	7.0	8.1	3.7
	Satilla River									
3187	Todd Creek entrance	30° 58'	81° 31'	−0 08	+0 41	*1.10	*1.10	6.7	7.8	3.5
3189	Bailey Cut, 0.8 mile west of	30° 59.1'	81° 35.5'	+0 28	+1 12	*1.13	*1.21	6.80	7.39	3.62
3191	Ceylon	30° 58'	81° 39'	+0 34	+1 35	*1.09	*1.09	6.6	7.7	3.5
3193	Burnt Fort	30° 57'	81° 54'	+3 55	+5 05	*0.53	*0.53	3.2	3.7	1.7
3195	Cumberland Wharf, Cumberland River	30° 55.8'	81° 26.8'	+0 00	+0 26	*1.12	*1.12	6.8	7.9	3.6
3197	Floyd Creek, 2.8 miles above entrance	30° 56'	81° 30'	+0 08	+0 21	*1.17	*1.17	7.1	8.2	3.7
	GEORGIA and FLORIDA Cumberland Sound									
3199	St. Marys Entrance, North Jetty	30° 43'	81° 26'	−0 36	−0 03	*0.96	*0.96	5.8	6.7	3.1
3201	Kings Bay, Navy Base	30° 48.1'	81° 30.9'	+0 12	+0 10	*1.09	*1.05	6.43	7.39	3.42
3203	Beach Creek ent., Cumberland Island	30° 43.6'	81° 28.6'	+0 00	−0 04	*0.98	*0.95	5.92	6.81	3.14
3205	Seacamp Dock, Cumberland Island	30° 45.8'	81° 28.3'	+0 12	+0 16	*1.04	*1.05	6.23	7.16	3.31
3207	Crooked River, Cumberland Dividings	30° 50.6'	81° 29.2'	+0 44	+0 56	*1.12	*1.12	6.8	7.9	3.6
3209	Harrietts Bluff, Crooked River	30° 52.2'	81° 35.1'	+1 29	+1 56	*1.05	*1.05	6.4	7.4	3.4
	St. Marys River									
3211	St. Marys	30° 43.2'	81° 32.9'	+0 38	+0 45	*0.98	*1.05	5.86	6.74	3.13
3213	Crandall	30° 43.3'	81° 37.3'	+1 06	+1 25	*0.81	*1.00	4.84	5.57	2.61
3215	U.S. Highway 17	30° 44.5'	81° 41.3'	+2 30	– – –	– – –	– – –	– –	– –	– –
3217	Little St. Marys River	30° 43.9'	81° 43.6'	+2 49	+2 36	*0.71	*0.79	4.27	4.91	2.29
3219	Kings Ferry	30° 47.2'	81° 50.4'	+4 05	+4 09	*0.49	*1.16	2.83	3.25	1.63
3221	Chester, Bells River	30° 41.0'	81° 32.0'	+0 27	+0 19	*1.04	*1.11	6.27	7.21	3.34
3223	Roses Bluff, Bells River	30° 42.2'	81° 34.6'	+0 35	+0 35	*1.03	*0.95	6.18	7.11	3.28
3225	Lofton, Lanceford Creek	30° 38.6'	81° 31.4'	+0 18	−0 01	*1.05	*1.05	6.33	7.28	3.36
3227	FERNANDINA BEACH, Amelia River	30° 40.5'	81° 27.9'	*Daily Predictions*				6.02	7.07	3.20
3229	Kingsley Creek, RR. bridge	30° 37.9'	81° 28.6'	+0 27	+0 25	*0.99	*1.00	5.97	6.87	3.18
	FLORIDA Nassau Sound and Fort George River									
3231	Amelia City, South Amelia River	30° 35.2'	81° 27.8'	+0 21	+0 42	*0.89	*0.89	5.39	6.20	2.86
	Nassau River									
3233	entrance	30° 31.1'	81° 27.2'	−0 18	+0 41	*0.86	*1.00	5.16	5.93	2.77
3235	Nassauville	30° 34.1'	81° 30.9'	+0 24	+1 09	*0.80	*1.00	4.75	5.46	2.56
3237	Tiger Point, Pumpkin Hill Creek	30° 30.1'	81° 29.7'	+1 22	+1 46	*0.82	*0.95	4.89	5.62	2.63
3239	Edwards Creek, 1 mi. above entrance	30° 30.1'	81° 32.5'	+1 24	+1 51	*0.77	*0.85	4.62	5.36	2.48
3241	Cuno, Lofton Creek	30° 34.6'	81° 34.3'	+2 14	+2 48	*0.60	*1.05	3.55	4.12	1.98
3243	Mink Creek entrance	30° 32.2'	81° 34.9'	+1 13	+2 05	*0.72	*1.05	4.26	4.90	2.33
3245	Halfmoon Island, highway bridge	30° 34.6'	81° 36.5'	+2 00	+2 39	*0.70	*1.05	4.16	4.78	2.28
3247	Boggy Creek, 2 mi. above entrance	30° 35.3'	81° 39.8'	+3 29	+3 50	*0.49	*0.89	2.90	3.34	1.62
3249	Sawpit Creek, bridge	30° 30.8'	81° 27.4'	−0 14	+0 21	*0.84	*1.00	5.05	5.81	2.71
3251	Sawpit Creek, 1 mi. above entrance	30° 30.2'	81° 28.3'	+0 05	+0 31	*0.84	*0.74	5.08	5.84	2.68
3253	Simpson Creek, A1A highway bridge	30° 27.9'	81° 25.9'	+0 04	+0 17	*0.84	*0.63	5.08	5.84	2.66
3255	Little Talbot Island, ocean	30° 25.8'	81° 24.3'	−0 36	−0 13	*0.91	*1.00	5.45	6.27	2.91
3257	Fort George Island, Fort George River	30° 26.4'	81° 26.3'	+0 10	+0 33	*0.79	*0.74	4.78	5.50	2.53
	FLORIDA, St. Johns River			**on Mayport, p.156**						
3259	Mayport Naval Station, Degaussing Structure	30° 23.8'	81° 23.7'	−0 21	−0 04	*1.07	*1.13	4.87	5.36	2.61
3261	Mayport Naval Station, Water Treatment Dock ...	30° 24.0'	81° 24.8'	−0 12	−0 06	*1.03	*1.00	4.72	5.17	2.51
3263	MAYPORT (BAR PILOT DOCK)	30° 23.8'	81° 25.8'	*Daily predictions*				4.57	5.32	2.44
3265	Pablo Creek entrance	30° 22.6'	81° 26.9'	+0 29	+0 33	*0.85	*0.73	3.89	4.24	2.05
3267	Pablo Creek, ICWW bridge	30° 19.4'	81° 26.3'	+1 14	+1 20	*0.84	*1.00	3.82	4.16	2.06
3269	Sisters Creek	30° 25.0'	81° 27.2'	+0 32	+0 50	*0.95	*0.93	4.34	4.70	2.31
3271	Clapboard Creek, Pelotes Island	30° 24.4'	81° 30.6'	+0 32	+0 56	*0.79	*0.80	3.64	3.94	1.94
3273	Fulton	30° 23.4'	81° 30.4'	+0 24	+0 40	*0.80	*0.73	3.66	3.97	1.94
3275	Blount Island Bridge	30° 24.8'	81° 32.7'	+0 42	+1 05	*0.77	*0.73	3.51	3.80	1.87
3277	Dame Point	30° 23.2'	81° 33.5'	+0 42	+1 12	*0.70	*0.67	3.19	3.44	1.70
3279	Mill Cove	30° 22.2'	81° 33.5'	+0 51	– – –	– – –	– – –	– –	– –	– –
3281	Cedar Heights, Broward River	30° 26.2'	81° 38.5'	+1 08	+1 53	*0.65	*0.53	2.99	3.47	1.58
3283	Jacksonville, Navy Fuel Depot	30° 24.0'	81° 37.6'	+1 14	+1 48	*0.56	*0.53	2.60	2.81	1.37
	Trout River									
3285	Moncrief Creek entrance	30° 23.5'	81° 39.7'	+1 11	+1 53	*0.55	*0.53	2.51	2.91	1.34
3287	Lake Forest, Ribault River	30° 23.9'	81° 41.9'	+1 13	+2 10	*0.58	*0.60	2.64	2.82	1.41
3289	Sherwood Forest	30° 25.2'	81° 43.7'	+1 42	+2 13	*0.58	*0.67	2.65	2.88	1.43

Endnotes can be found at the end of table 2.

TABLE 2 – TIDAL DIFFERENCES AND OTHER CONSTANTS

No.	PLACE	POSITION		DIFFERENCES				RANGES		Mean Tide Level
				Time		Height				
		Latitude	Longitude	High Water	Low Water	High Water	Low Water	Mean	Spring	
		North	West	h m	h m	ft	ft	ft	ft	ft
	FLORIDA, St. Johns River Time meridian, 75° W			**on Mayport, p.156**						
3291	Phoenix Park	30° 23.0'	81° 38.2'	+1 02	+1 47	*0.56	*0.60	2.54	2.75	1.36
3293	Jacksonville, Long Branch	30° 21.6'	81° 37.2'	+1 15	+1 54	*0.55	*0.73	2.49	2.89	1.35
3295	Little Pottsburg Creek	30° 18.6'	81° 36.6'	+1 31	+2 09	*0.44	*0.53	2.02	2.34	1.09
3297	Jacksonville, Main Street Bridge	30° 19.2'	81° 39.5'	+1 42	+2 13	*0.41	*0.73	1.83	2.03	1.03
3299	Ortega River entrance	30° 16.7'	81° 42.3'	+2 09	+2 47	*0.25	*0.47	1.11	1.26	0.63
3301	Piney Point	30° 13.7'	81° 39.8'	+2 39	+3 36	*0.20	*0.40	0.87	1.01	0.49
3303	I-295 bridge (west end)	30° 11.5'	81° 41.5'	+2 56	+3 43	*0.21	*0.60	0.91	1.06	0.55
3305	Orange Park Landing, Orange Park	30° 10.1'	81° 41.7'	+3 24	+4 44	*0.17	*0.53	0.74	0.87	0.45
3307	Peoria Point, Doctors Lake	30° 07.2'	81° 45.5'	+3 36	+4 56	*0.18	*0.33	0.80	0.93	0.45
3309	Julington Creek	30° 08.1'	81° 37.8'	+3 58	+5 13	*0.16	*0.47	0.71	0.83	0.43
3311	Black Creek, S.C.L. RR. bridge	30° 04.8'	81° 45.7'	+4 46	+5 52	*0.18	*0.33	0.82	0.92	0.46
3313	Green Cove Springs	29° 59.4'	81° 39.8'	+4 57	+5 55	*0.17	*0.27	0.78	0.90	0.43
3315	Tocoi	29° 51.5'	81° 33.2'	+6 02	+7 03	*0.21	*0.27	0.95	1.10	0.51
3317	Palmetto Bluff	29° 45.8'	81° 33.7'	+6 35	+7 36	*0.23	*0.47	1.04	1.18	0.59
3319	Palatka	29° 38.6'	81° 37.9'	+7 11	+8 38	*0.25	*0.53	1.09	1.22	0.63
3321	Sutherlands Still, Dunns Creek	29° 34.3'	81° 36.4'	+7 35	+9 05	*0.18	*0.20	0.84	0.97	0.45
3323	Buffalo Bluff	29° 35.7'	81° 40.9'	+7 27	+8 58	*0.21	*0.40	0.93	1.03	0.52
3325	Welaka	29° 28.6'	81° 40.5'	+7 16	+8 07	*0.10	*0.27	0.43	0.50	0.25
3327	Georgetown <24>	29° 23.1'	81° 38.2'	– – –	– – –	– – –	– – –	– –	– –	– –
	FLORIDA, East Coast			**on Fernandina Beach, p.152**						
3329	Atlantic Beach	30° 20.1'	81° 23.7'	–0 41	–0 23	*0.86	*0.86	5.2	6.0	2.8
3331	Jacksonville Beach	30° 17.0'	81° 23.2'	–0 50	–0 27	*0.84	*0.84	5.07	5.83	2.70
3333	Oak Landing, ICWW	30° 15.2'	81° 25.8'	+2 15	+2 03	*0.68	*0.80	4.07	4.72	2.20
3335	Palm Valley, ICWW	30° 08.0'	81° 23.2'	+2 00	+1 49	*0.79	*0.75	4.79	5.56	2.55
3337	Vilano Beach, Tolomato River	29° 55.0'	81° 18.0'	–0 20	–0 05	*0.74	*0.90	4.48	5.20	2.42
3339	St. Augustine, city dock	29° 53.5'	81° 18.6'	–0 20	+0 01	*0.75	*0.89	4.48	5.15	2.41
3341	St. Augustine Beach	29° 51.4'	81° 15.8'	–0 51	–0 32	*0.77	*0.84	4.61	5.48	2.47
	Matanzas River, ICWW									
3343	State Road 312	29° 52.0'	81° 18.4'	–0 03	+0 15	*0.72	*1.00	4.31	5.04	2.34
3345	Crescent Beach	29° 46.1'	81° 15.5'	+0 39	+1 14	*0.69	*0.95	4.09	4.79	2.23
3347	Fort Matanzas	29° 42.9'	81° 14.3'	+0 03	+0 49	*0.65	*0.95	3.86	4.44	2.11
3349	Matanzas Inlet, A1A bridge	29° 42.3'	81° 13.7'	–0 26	+0 00	*0.61	*0.84	3.64	4.21	2.05
3351	Bing Landing	29° 36.9'	81° 12.3'	+2 15	+2 52	*0.26	*0.68	1.46	1.71	0.86
3353	Smith Creek, Flagler Beach	29° 28.7'	81° 08.2'	+4 33	+5 00	*0.15	*0.30	0.86	1.00	0.49
3355	Ormond Beach, Halifax River	29° 17.1'	81° 03.2'	+3 17	+4 31	*0.11	*0.45	0.60	0.70	0.39
3357	Daytona Beach Shores, Sunglow Pier	29° 08.8'	80° 57.8'	–0 56	–0 42	*0.65	*0.84	3.90	4.49	2.11
				on Miami, Government Cut, p.164						
3359	Ponce de Leon Inlet	29° 03.8'	80° 54.9'	–0 11	+0 19	*1.17	*0.92	2.76	3.37	1.48
3361	Ponce Inlet, Halifax River	29° 04.9'	80° 56.2'	+0 05	+0 33	*1.18	*1.00	2.75	3.36	1.52
	Mosquito Lagoon									
3363	New Smyrna Beach	29° 01.4'	80° 55.1'	+0 19	+0 49	*1.04	*1.00	2.43	2.77	1.36
3365	Packwood Place	28° 56.4'	80° 52.2'	+1 43	+2 40	*0.44	*0.44	1.06	1.24	0.56
3367	Turtle Mound	28° 55.6'	80° 49.5'	+3 01	+4 30	*0.17	*0.17	0.45	0.51	0.23
3369	Oak Hill <21>	28° 52'	80° 50'	– – –	– – –	– – –	– – –	– –	– –	– –
3371	Cape Canaveral	28° 26'	80° 34'	–1 06	–0 44	*1.50	*1.42	3.5	4.1	2.0
3373	PORT CANAVERAL (TRIDENT PIER)	28° 24.9'	80° 35.6'	*Daily predictions, p.160*				3.47	4.13	1.89
3375	Cocoa Beach	28° 22.1'	80° 36.0'	–1 01	–0 38	*1.47	*1.14	3.46	4.22	1.89
3377	Patrick Air Force Base	28° 14.7'	80° 36.0'	–1 04	–0 38	*1.50	*1.43	3.50	4.20	1.95
	Banana River									
3379	Kennedy Pkwy., Banana Creek, Merritt I. <22>	28° 35.4'	80° 39.5'	– – –	– – –	– – –	– – –	– –	– –	– –
3381	VAB Turning Basin, Merritt Island <22>	28° 35.1'	80° 38.6'	– – –	– – –	– – –	– – –	– –	– –	– –
3383	Orsino Causeway <22>	28° 30.8'	80° 36.7'	– – –	– – –	– – –	– – –	– –	– –	– –
3385	Port Canaveral locks <22>	28° 24.5'	80° 38.3'	– – –	– – –	– – –	– – –	– –	– –	– –
3387	Sykes Creek <22>	28° 24.3'	80° 41.8'	– – –	– – –	– – –	– – –	– –	– –	– –
3389	Carter's Cut, Merritt Island <22>	28° 09.5'	80° 36.7'	– – –	– – –	– – –	– – –	– –	– –	– –
	Indian River									
3391	Titusville <22>	28° 37.2'	80° 48.0'	– – –	– – –	– – –	– – –	– –	– –	– –
3393	Williams Point <22>	28° 27.4'	80° 45.6'	– – –	– – –	– – –	– – –	– –	– –	– –
3395	Pineda <22>	28° 12.7'	80° 39.8'	– – –	– – –	– – –	– – –	– –	– –	– –
3397	Canova Beach	28° 08.3'	80° 34.7'	–0 53	–0 26	*1.49	*1.50	3.45	4.14	1.93
	Indian River - cont.									
3399	Eau Gallie <22>	28° 08.0'	80° 37.5'	– – –	– – –	– – –	– – –	– –	– –	– –
3401	Melbourne <22>	28° 06.0'	80° 36.7'	– – –	– – –	– – –	– – –	– –	– –	– –
3403	Palm Bay <22>	28° 02.5'	80° 34.9'	– – –	– – –	– – –	– – –	– –	– –	– –
3405	Micco	27° 52.4'	80° 29.8'	+1 14	+2 19	*0.14	*0.57	0.26	0.31	0.21
3407	Sebastian Inlet bridge	27° 51.6'	80° 26.9'	–0 48	–0 24	*0.93	*1.00	2.16	2.64	1.22
	Indian River - cont.									
3409	Sebastian	27° 48.7'	80° 27.8'	+1 32	+2 36	*0.15	*0.50	0.30	0.36	0.22
3411	Wabasso	27° 45.3'	80° 25.6'	+2 20	+3 24	*0.17	*0.42	0.37	0.44	0.25
3413	Vero Beach	27° 38.0'	80° 22.5'	+2 56	+3 41	*0.37	*0.79	0.80	0.96	0.51
3415	Oslo	27° 35.6'	80° 21.4'	+3 00	+3 59	*0.34	*0.50	0.77	0.92	0.46
3417	St. Lucie	27° 28.7'	80° 20.0'	+0 41	+1 46	*0.48	*1.00	1.05	1.26	0.66
3419	Vero Beach (ocean)	27° 40.2'	80° 21.6'	–0 55	–0 35	*1.45	*1.36	3.39	4.03	1.88
3421	Fort Pierce Inlet, south jetty	27° 28.2'	80° 17.3'	–0 31	–0 18	*1.14	*1.50	2.61	3.13	1.52
3423	Fort Pierce Inlet, Binney dock	27° 28.1'	80° 17.8'	–0 14	–0 01	*0.82	*1.28	1.85	2.22	1.11
	Indian River - cont.									
3425	Fort Pierce, North Beach Causeway	27° 28.3'	80° 19.5'	+0 21	+0 45	*0.67	*1.14	1.50	1.79	0.91
3427	Fort Pierce, South Beach Causeway	27° 27.4'	80° 19.4'	+0 35	+0 44	*0.64	*1.00	1.43	1.64	0.85
3429	Ankona	27° 21.3'	80° 16.5'	+2 16	+3 03	*0.52	*0.85	1.10	1.32	0.67
3431	Eden, Nettles Island	27° 17.2'	80° 13.6'	+2 35	+3 31	*0.45	*0.92	0.98	1.18	0.62
3433	Jensen Beach	27° 14.1'	80° 12.6'	+2 17	+3 04	*0.48	*0.92	1.05	1.26	0.65

Endnotes can be found at the end of table 2.

TABLE 2 – TIDAL DIFFERENCES AND OTHER CONSTANTS

No.	PLACE	POSITION Latitude	Longitude	DIFFERENCES Time High Water	Low Water	Height High Water	Low Water	RANGES Mean	Spring	Mean Tide Level
		North	West	h m	h m	ft	ft	ft	ft	ft
	FLORIDA, East Coast Time meridian, 75° W			on Miami, Government Cut, p.164						
	St. Lucie River									
3435	North Fork	27° 14.6'	80° 18.8'	+2 28	+3 28	*0.46	*0.92	0.99	1.19	0.63
3437	Stuart	27° 12.0'	80° 15.5'	+2 13	+3 30	*0.40	*0.86	0.88	1.06	0.56
3439	South Fork	27° 09.9'	80° 15.3'	+2 35	+3 32	*0.43	*0.92	0.93	1.12	0.59
3441	Sewall Point	27° 10.5'	80° 11.3'	+1 13	+2 10	*0.43	*0.93	0.93	1.11	0.59
3443	Port Salerno, Manatee Pocket	27° 09.1'	80° 11.7'	+0 51	+1 46	*0.42	*0.92	0.90	1.08	0.58
3445	Seminole Shores	27° 11.0'	80° 09.5'	−0 59	−0 35	*1.29	*1.28	3.00	3.60	1.68
3447	Great Pocket	27° 09.1'	80° 10.3'	+0 55	+1 42	*0.50	*1.00	1.08	1.30	0.68
3449	Peck Lake, ICWW	27° 06.8'	80° 08.7'	+1 13	+2 10	*0.58	*1.00	1.28	1.54	0.78
3451	Gomez, South Jupiter Narrows	27° 05.7'	80° 08.2'	+1 33	+2 37	*0.60	*1.07	1.32	1.58	0.81
3453	Hobe Sound bridge	27° 03.8'	80° 07.4'	+1 28	+2 25	*0.68	*1.00	1.53	1.84	0.90
3455	Hobe Sound, Jupiter Island	27° 02.2'	80° 06.4'	+1 16	+2 12	*0.75	*1.00	1.72	2.06	1.00
3457	Conch Bar, Jupiter Sound	26° 59.3'	80° 05.6'	+0 56	+1 34	*0.74	*1.07	1.68	2.02	0.99
3459	Jupiter Sound, south end	26° 57.1'	80° 04.7'	+0 22	+0 45	*0.88	*1.36	1.98	2.38	1.18
3461	Jupiter Inlet, south jetty	26° 56.6'	80° 04.4'	−0 10	−0 09	*1.08	*1.42	2.46	2.95	1.43
3463	Jupiter Inlet, U.S. Highway 1 Bridge	26° 56.9'	80° 05.1'	+0 28	+1 05	*0.86	*1.14	1.96	2.35	1.14
	Loxahatchee River									
3465	A1A highway bridge	26° 56.8'	80° 05.4'	+0 34	+0 54	*0.87	*1.14	2.00	2.40	1.16
3467	Tequesta	26° 57.0'	80° 06.1'	+0 59	+1 58	*0.80	*1.14	1.83	2.20	1.08
3469	Tequesta, North Fork entrance	26° 57.1'	80° 06.1'	+0 51	+1 42	*0.78	*0.92	1.80	2.16	1.03
3471	Tequesta, North Fork	26° 57.6'	80° 06.3'	+1 14	+2 13	*0.75	*1.00	1.72	2.06	1.00
3473	North Fork, 2 miles above entrance	26° 58.6'	80° 06.9'	+1 04	+1 55	*0.86	*1.14	1.95	2.34	1.14
3475	3 miles above A1A highway bridge	26° 58.2'	80° 07.5'	+0 56	+1 49	*0.86	*1.14	1.98	2.38	1.15
3477	Boy Scout Dock	26° 59.2'	80° 08.5'	+1 01	+1 57	*0.92	*1.36	2.09	2.51	1.23
3479	Southwest Fork, 0.5 mile above entrance	26° 56.6'	80° 07.2'	+0 41	+1 35	*0.89	*1.42	2.00	2.40	1.20
3481	Southwest Fork (spillway)	26° 56.1'	80° 08.6'	+0 52	+1 45	*0.86	*1.28	1.94	2.33	1.15
3483	Jupiter, Lake Worth Creek, ICWW	26° 56.1'	80° 05.1'	+0 34	+1 12	*0.91	*1.28	2.06	2.47	1.21
3485	Lake Worth Creek, Day Beacon 19, ICWW	26° 54.7'	80° 04.8'	+0 29	+1 08	*0.92	*1.21	2.10	2.52	1.22
3487	Donald Ross Bridge, ICWW	26° 52.9'	80° 04.2'	+0 20	+0 50	*1.00	*1.21	2.31	2.77	1.32
3489	PGA Boulevard Bridge, ICWW	26° 50.6'	80° 04.0'	−0 02	+0 31	*1.16	*1.36	2.68	3.22	1.53
	Lake Worth									
3491	North Palm Beach	26° 49.6'	80° 03.3'	−0 17	+0 15	*1.22	*1.29	2.81	3.34	1.59
3493	Port of Palm Beach	26° 46.2'	80° 03.1'	−0 21	+0 04	*1.18	*1.36	2.72	3.26	1.55
3495	Palm Beach	26° 44.0'	80° 02.5'	−0 11	+0 16	*1.17	*1.29	2.69	3.20	1.54
3497	Palm Beach, Highway 704 bridge	26° 42.3'	80° 02.7'	+0 18	+0 40	*1.10	*1.07	2.57	3.06	1.44
3499	West Palm Beach Canal	26° 38.7'	80° 02.7'	+0 48	+1 35	*1.07	*1.14	2.46	2.92	1.40
3501	Rt. 802 bridge	26° 36.8'	80° 02.8'	+0 42	+1 26	*1.18	*1.07	2.75	3.27	1.52
3503	Boynton Beach	26° 32.9'	80° 03.2'	+1 05	+2 07	*1.06	*1.07	2.47	2.94	1.38
3505	Lake Worth Pier (ocean)	26° 36.7'	80° 02.0'	−0 45	−0 19	*1.16	*1.00	2.73	3.25	1.50
3507	Ocean Ridge, ICWW	26° 31.6'	80° 03.2'	+1 16	+2 10	*1.10	*1.21	2.54	3.05	1.44
3509	Delray Beach, ICWW	26° 28.4'	80° 03.7'	+1 24	+2 07	*1.07	*1.14	2.47	2.94	1.40
3511	South Delray Beach, ICWW	26° 26.8'	80° 03.9'	+1 28	+2 03	*1.03	*1.10	2.37	2.82	1.34
3513	Yamato, ICWW	26° 24.2'	80° 04.2'	+1 22	+1 57	*1.02	*1.14	2.35	2.80	1.34
3515	Lake Wyman, ICWW	26° 22.2'	80° 04.2'	+1 24	+1 54	*0.93	*1.06	2.14	2.55	1.22
3517	Boca Raton, Lake Boca Raton	26° 20.6'	80° 04.6'	+0 23	+1 07	*0.97	*1.14	2.23	2.68	1.27
3519	Deerfield Beach, Hillsboro River	26° 18.8'	80° 04.9'	+0 28	+1 03	*1.02	*1.07	2.36	2.83	1.33
3521	Hillsboro Beach, ICWW	26° 16.5'	80° 04.8'	+0 02	+0 34	*1.06	*1.07	2.47	2.96	1.39
3523	Hillsboro Inlet, Coast Guard Light Station	26° 15.5'	80° 04.9'	−0 16	+0 03	*1.08	*1.14	2.49	2.96	1.41
3525	Hillsboro Inlet Marina	26° 15.6'	80° 05.1'	−0 06	+0 24	*1.06	*1.14	2.45	2.94	1.38
3527	Hillsboro Inlet (ocean)	26° 15.4'	80° 04.8'	−0 23	+0 00	*1.12	*1.21	2.60	3.12	1.47
3529	Lauderdale-by-the-Sea, Anglin Fishing Pier	26° 11.3'	80° 05.6'	−0 34	−0 13	*1.14	*1.28	2.64	3.17	1.50
	Fort Lauderdale									
3531	Bahia Mar Yacht Club	26° 06.8'	80° 06.5'	−0 05	+0 33	*1.05	*1.21	2.42	2.90	1.38
3533	Andrews Avenue bridge, New River	26° 07.1'	80° 08.7'	+0 15	+0 51	*0.92	*1.07	2.13	2.56	1.22
3535	Mayan Lake	26° 06.0'	80° 06.5'	+0 20	+1 02	*0.91	*1.00	2.11	2.53	1.19
3537	Port Everglades, Turning Basin	26° 05.5'	80° 07.4'	−0 29	−0 09	*1.09	*1.14	2.53	3.01	1.43
3539	South Port Everglades, ICWW	26° 04.9'	80° 07.0'	−0 23	−0 03	*1.10	*1.42	2.52	3.02	1.46
3541	Whiskey Creek, north end	26° 04.8'	80° 06.7'	−0 23	−0 06	*1.10	*1.28	2.52	3.02	1.44
3543	Port Laudania, Dania cut-off Canal	26° 03.6'	80° 07.8'	+0 01	+0 11	*1.00	*1.21	2.30	2.76	1.32
3545	Whiskey Creek, south entrance, ICWW	26° 03.3'	80° 06.8'	+0 04	+0 31	*0.96	*1.14	2.21	2.63	1.27
3547	Hollywood Beach, West Lake, north end	26° 02.6'	80° 07.6'	+1 08	+1 42	*0.85	*1.07	1.94	2.33	1.12
3549	Hollywood Beach, West Lake, south end	26° 02.0'	80° 07.4'	+1 02	+1 45	*0.88	*1.14	2.02	2.42	1.17
3551	Hollywood Beach	26° 02.4'	80° 06.9'	+0 37	+1 41	*0.91	*1.14	2.08	2.50	1.20
3553	Golden Beach, ICWW	25° 58.0'	80° 07.4'	+1 13	+1 57	*0.91	*1.07	2.10	2.52	1.20
3555	Dumfoundling Bay	25° 56.5'	80° 07.5'	+1 17	+2 07	*0.88	*1.00	2.02	2.40	1.15
3557	Sunny Isles, Biscayne Creek	25° 55.7'	80° 07.8'	+2 00	+2 24	*0.77	*0.71	1.8	2.2	1.0
3559	Biscayne Creek, ICWW	25° 52.8'	80° 09.8'	+0 47	+1 39	*0.93	*1.00	2.15	2.56	1.21
3561	North Miami Beach, Newport Fishing Pier	25° 55.8'	80° 07.2'	−0 22	+0 00	*1.08	*1.21	2.49	2.96	1.41
3563	Haulover Pier, N. Miami Beach	25° 54.2'	80° 07.2'	−0 29	−0 06	*1.06	*1.00	2.48	2.95	1.37
3565	Bakers Haulover Inlet (inside)	25° 54.2'	80° 07.5'	+0 57	+1 37	*0.87	*0.92	2.01	2.20	1.13
3567	Indian Creek Golf Club, ICWW	25° 52.5'	80° 08.6'	+1 13	+1 46	*0.92	*0.92	2.13	2.56	1.20
3569	Miami Harbor Entrance	25° 46.1'	80° 07.9'	−0 22	−0 02	*1.07	*1.14	2.46	2.93	1.39
3571	GOVERNMENT CUT, MIAMI HARBOR ENTRANCE	25° 45.8'	80° 07.8'	Daily predictions				2.32	2.83	1.32
	Biscayne Bay									
3573	San Marino Island	25° 47.6'	80° 09.8'	+0 37	+0 58	*0.92	*1.00	2.14	2.57	1.21
3575	Miami, Miamarina	25° 46.7'	80° 11.1'	+0 20	+0 49	*0.94	*0.92	2.18	2.59	1.22
3577	Dodge Island, Fishermans Channel	25° 46.2'	80° 10.1'	+0 34	+1 10	*0.91	*1.00	2.10	2.52	1.19
3579	Dinner Key Marina	25° 43.6'	80° 14.2'	+0 54	+1 48	*0.84	*0.92	1.94	2.33	1.10
	Florida Keys									
3581	Bear Cut, Virginia Key	25° 43.9'	80° 09.7'	+0 28	+0 51	*0.88	*0.86	2.05	2.44	1.15
3583	Key Biscayne Yacht Club, Biscayne Bay	25° 41.9'	80° 10.2'	+0 44	+1 31	*0.86	*0.92	2.00	2.40	1.13
3585	Coral Shoal, Biscayne Channel	25° 39.1'	80° 09.4'	+0 11	+0 37	*0.88	*0.92	2.05	2.46	1.15
3587	Cutler, Biscayne Bay	25° 36.9'	80° 18.3'	+1 01	+1 58	*0.84	*0.92	1.94	2.22	1.10

Endnotes can be found at the end of table 2.

TABLE 2 – TIDAL DIFFERENCES AND OTHER CONSTANTS

No.	PLACE	POSITION		DIFFERENCES				RANGES		Mean Tide Level
		Latitude	Longitude	Time		Height				
				High Water	Low Water	High Water	Low Water	Mean	Spring	
		North	**West**	h m	h m	ft	ft	ft	ft	ft

FLORIDA, East Coast
Florida Keys–cont.
Time meridian, 75° W

on Miami, Government Cut, p.164

No.	PLACE	Latitude	Longitude	High Water	Low Water	High Water	Low Water	Mean	Spring	Mean Tide Level
3589	Soldier Key	25° 35'	80° 10'	+0 30	+1 16	*0.81	*0.71	1.9	2.3	1.0
3591	Ragged Keys, Biscayne Bay	25° 32.0'	80° 10.3'	+0 43	+1 18	*0.73	*1.00	1.65	1.96	0.96
3593	Boca Chita Key, Biscayne Bay	25° 31.4'	80° 10.6'	+1 01	+1 39	*0.70	*1.14	1.57	1.88	0.94
3595	Sands Key, northwest point, Biscayne Bay	25° 30.3'	80° 11.3'	+1 25	+2 26	*0.63	*0.64	1.46	1.64	0.82
3597	Coon Point, Elliott Key, Biscayne Bay	25° 28.7'	80° 11.4'	+1 55	+2 56	*0.63	*0.71	1.44	1.63	0.82
3599	Elliott Key Harbor, Elliott Key, Biscayne Bay	25° 27.2'	80° 11.8'	+1 56	+3 00	*0.64	*0.64	1.48	1.67	0.83
3601	Turkey Point, Biscayne Bay	25° 26.2'	80° 19.7'	+2 11	+3 21	*0.70	*0.79	1.61	1.71	0.92
3603	Billys Point, south of, Elliott Key, Biscayne Bay	25° 24.9'	80° 12.6'	+2 08	+3 20	*0.63	*0.64	1.46	1.65	0.82
3605	Sea Grape Point, Elliott Key	25° 28.6'	80° 10.8'	−0 25	−0 05	*1.03	*1.03	2.30	2.74	1.39
3607	Christmas Point, Elliott Key	25° 23.5'	80° 13.8'	+0 13	+0 37	*0.80	*1.07	1.82	2.13	1.06
3609	Adams Key, south end	25° 23.8'	80° 14.0'	+1 01	+1 08	*0.67	*1.00	1.52	1.75	0.90
3611	Totten Key, west side, Biscayne Bay	25° 22.7'	80° 15.4'	+2 19	+3 21	*0.54	*0.57	1.26	1.41	0.71
3613	East Arsenicker, Card Sound	25° 22.4'	80° 17.5'	+2 26	+3 09	*0.40	*0.64	0.91	1.04	0.54
3615	Card Sound, western side	25° 20.7'	80° 19.9'	+2 51	+3 40	*0.30	*0.43	0.68	0.77	0.40
3617	Pumpkin Key, south end, Card Sound	25° 19.5'	80° 17.6'	+2 35	+2 52	*0.30	*0.78	0.63	0.71	0.43
3619	Wednesday Point, Key Largo, Card Sound	25° 18.6'	80° 17.9'	+2 38	+3 30	*0.34	*0.57	0.77	0.88	0.46
3621	Cormorant Point, Key Largo, Card Sound	25° 17.4'	80° 20.3'	+2 45	+3 01	*0.32	*0.50	0.73	0.82	0.43
3623	Little Card Sound bridge	25° 17.3'	80° 22.2'	+3 30	+4 03	*0.24	*0.43	0.53	0.63	0.33
3625	Ocean Reef Harbor, Key Largo	25° 18.6'	80° 16.8'	−0 08	+0 17	*1.02	*1.50	2.30	2.74	1.36
3627	Main Key, Barnes Sound	25° 14.4'	80° 24.0'	+5 04	+6 16	*0.19	*0.36	0.41	0.46	0.26
3629	Manatee Creek, Manatee Bay, Barnes Sound	25° 14.1'	80° 25.8'	+5 14	+6 20	*0.18	*0.36	0.39	0.44	0.25
3631	Manatee Creek, Hwy. 1 bridge, Long Sound <26>	25° 14.1'	80° 26.1'	– – –	– – –	– – –	– – –	– –	– –	– –
3633	Carysfort Reef	25° 13.3'	80° 12.7'	+0 19	+0 39	*1.03	*1.36	2.34	2.60	1.36
3635	Jewfish Creek entrance, Blackwater Sound <26>	25° 11.0'	80° 23.2'	– – –	– – –	– – –	– – –	– –	– –	– –
3637	Deep Six Marina, Blackwater Sound <26>	25° 08.4'	80° 24.2'	– – –	– – –	– – –	– – –	– –	– –	– –
3639	Garden Cove, Key Largo	25° 10.3'	80° 22.0'	−0 01	+0 25	*0.94	*1.14	2.16	2.53	1.24
3641	Largo Sound, Key Largo	25° 08.4'	80° 23.7'	+2 13	+3 03	*0.35	*0.50	0.80	0.96	0.47
3643	Key Largo, South Sound, Key Largo	25° 06.8'	80° 25.0'	+0 23	+1 49	*0.66	*0.64	1.55	1.86	0.85
3645	Point Charles, Key Largo	25° 04.9'	80° 27.0'	+0 25	+1 53	*0.77	*0.64	1.80	2.14	0.99
3647	Rock Harbor, Key Largo	25° 04.9'	80° 26.8'	+0 22	+0 36	*0.94	*1.21	2.14	2.57	1.24
3649	Sunset Cove, Key Largo, Buttonwood Sound <26>	25° 05.7'	80° 26.6'	– – –	– – –	– – –	– – –	– –	– –	– –
3651	Hammer Point, Key Largo, Florida Bay <26>	25° 02.1'	80° 30.3'	– – –	– – –	– – –	– – –	– –	– –	– –
3653	Tavernier, Key Largo, Florida Bay <26>	25° 00.9'	80° 30.9'	– – –	– – –	– – –	– – –	– –	– –	– –
3655	Tavernier Harbor, Hawk Channel	25° 00.3'	80° 31.0'	+0 07	+0 26	*0.90	*1.36	2.04	2.43	1.21
3657	Tavernier Creek, Hwy. 1 bridge, Hawk Channel	25° 00.2'	80° 31.8'	+0 25	+0 52	*0.60	*1.07	1.32	1.58	0.81
3659	Plantation Key, northern end, Florida Bay <26>	25° 00.1'	80° 32.6'	– – –	– – –	– – –	– – –	– –	– –	– –
3661	Crane Keys, north side, Florida Bay	25° 00.3'	80° 37.1'	+2 52	+4 35	*0.17	*0.21	0.39	0.46	0.22
3663	East Key, southern end, Florida Bay	24° 59.8'	80° 36.6'	+2 43	+4 06	*0.22	*0.14	0.52	0.62	0.28
3665	Plantation Key, Hawk Channel	24° 58.4'	80° 33.0'	+0 05	+0 12	*0.96	*1.21	2.20	2.64	1.27
3667	Yacht Harbor, Cowpens Anchorage, Plantation Key	24° 57.9'	80° 34.1'	+2 45	+4 00	*0.23	*0.29	0.53	0.64	0.31
3669	Snake Creek, Hwy. 1 bridge, Windley Key	24° 57.1'	80° 35.3'	+0 49	+0 56	*0.46	*0.50	1.07	1.28	0.61
3671	Snake Creek, USCG Station, Plantation Key	24° 57.2'	80° 35.2'	+1 08	+1 56	*0.36	*0.50	0.82	0.98	0.48
3673	Whale Harbor, Windley Key, Hawk Channel	24° 56.4'	80° 36.5'	+0 07	+0 51	*0.65	*0.36	1.56	1.87	0.83
3675	Whale Harbor Channel, Hwy. 1 bridge, Windley Key	24° 56.3'	80° 36.6'	+0 16	+1 00	*0.59	*0.71	1.36	1.63	0.78
3677	Upper Matecumbe Key, Hawk Channel	24° 54.9'	80° 37.9'	+0 34	+0 49	*0.87	*1.21	1.98	2.38	1.16
3679	Alligator Reef, Hawk Channel	24° 51.0'	80° 37.1'	+0 08	+0 24	*0.86	*1.36	1.93	2.37	1.15

on Key West, p.172

No.	PLACE	Latitude	Longitude	High Water	Low Water	High Water	Low Water	Mean	Spring	Mean Tide Level
3681	Flamingo, Florida Bay	25° 08.5'	80° 55.4'	+5 28	+7 20	*1.47	*1.08	2.02	2.52	1.27
3683	Upper Matecumbe Key, west end, Hawk Channel	24° 53.8'	80° 39.5'	−1 00	+0 14	*0.98	*0.33	1.44	1.80	0.80
3685	Indian Key, Hawk Channel	24° 52.6'	80° 40.6'	−0 58	−0 35	*1.30	*0.71	1.84	2.30	1.09
3687	Shell Key Channel, Florida Bay	24° 54.8'	80° 39.6'	−0 20	+0 45	*0.78	*0.78	1.02	1.28	0.58
3689	Lignumvitae Key, NE side, Florida Bay	24° 54.2'	80° 41.7'	+0 09	+1 31	*0.52	*0.52	0.68	0.85	0.37
3691	Lignumvitae Key, west side, Florida Bay	24° 54.0'	80° 42.3'	+0 32	+1 54	*0.47	*0.47	0.62	0.74	0.35
3693	Little Basin, Upper Matecumbe Key, Florida Bay	24° 54.9'	80° 38.4'	+0 08	+1 15	*0.61	*0.61	0.80	1.00	0.40
3695	Shell Key, northwest side, Lignumvitae Basin	24° 55.4'	80° 40.3'	+0 31	+1 57	*0.46	*0.46	0.60	0.75	0.33
3697	Islamorada, Upper Matecumbe Key, Florida Bay	24° 55.5'	80° 37.9'	+0 39	+2 07	*0.37	*0.37	0.49	0.57	0.30
3699	Indian Key Anchorage, Lower Matecumbe Key	24° 52.1'	80° 42.2'	−1 25	−0 54	*1.38	*0.88	1.89	2.34	1.16
3701	Matecumbe Bight, Lower Matecumbe Key, Fla. Bay	24° 51.9'	80° 43.0'	−0 18	+0 33	*0.55	*0.38	0.75	0.93	0.47
3703	Matecumbe Harbor, Lower Matecumbe Key, Fla. Bay	24° 51.1'	80° 44.4'	−0 25	+0 23	*0.59	*0.33	0.83	1.04	0.50
3705	Channel Two, east, Lower Matecumbe Key, Fla. Bay	24° 50.7'	80° 44.9'	−0 49	−0 42	*0.85	*0.54	1.18	1.48	0.72
3707	Channel Two, west side, Hawk Channel	24° 50.5'	80° 45.2'	−1 06	−0 54	*1.12	*0.75	1.55	1.94	0.96
3709	Channel Five, east side, Hawk Channel	24° 50.2'	80° 46.0'	−0 54	−0 42	*0.90	*0.58	1.25	1.56	0.77
3711	Channel Five, west side, Hawk Channel	24° 50.4'	80° 46.8'	−0 58	−0 41	*1.00	*0.67	1.39	1.74	0.85
3713	Jewfish Hole, Long Key, Florida Bay	24° 50.3'	80° 47.9'	−0 11	+1 32	*0.42	*0.38	0.56	0.70	0.37
3715	Long Key Bight, Long Key	24° 49.7'	80° 48.5'	−0 59	−0 43	*1.03	*0.62	1.44	1.80	0.87
3717	Long Key Lake, Long Key	24° 49.2'	80° 49.0'	+0 33	+0 57	*0.62	*0.46	0.85	1.06	0.53
3719	Long Key, western end	24° 48.1'	80° 51.0'	−1 01	−0 54	*0.82	*0.33	1.19	1.49	0.67
3721	Conch Key, eastern end	24° 47.5'	80° 53.0'	−1 09	−0 45	*0.85	*0.54	1.18	1.48	0.72
3723	Toms Harbor Cut	24° 47.0'	80° 54.4'	−1 19	−0 30	*0.37	*0.38	0.48	0.60	0.33
3725	Toms Harbor, Duck Key <26>	24° 46.4'	80° 54.9'	– – –	– – –	– – –	– – –	– –	– –	– –
3727	Duck Key, Hawk Channel	24° 45.9'	80° 54.8'	−1 11	−0 40	*0.97	*0.55	1.34	1.66	0.80
3729	Toms Harbor Channel, Hwy. 1 bridge	24° 46.6'	80° 54.5'	+5 07	+4 49	*0.38	*0.38	0.50	0.62	0.45
3731	Grassy Key, north side, Florida Bay	24° 46.3'	80° 56.4'	+5 40	+6 48	*0.73	*1.04	0.86	1.07	0.68
3733	Grassy Key, south side, Hawk Channel	24° 45.3'	80° 57.5'	−0 52	−0 26	*1.22	*0.71	1.72	2.15	1.03
3735	Fat Deer Key, Florida Bay	24° 44.0'	81° 01.1'	+5 09	+6 26	*0.87	*0.87	1.14	1.42	0.82
3737	Vaca Key–Fat Deer Key bridge	24° 43.8'	81° 01.8'	−1 11	−0 36	*0.95	*0.71	1.31	1.64	0.83
3739	Key Colony Beach	24° 43.1'	81° 01.0'	−1 17	−0 53	*1.22	*0.83	1.66	2.06	1.03
3741	VACA KEY, USCG STATION, FLORIDA BAY	24° 42.7'	81° 06.3'	Daily predictions, p.168				0.72	0.97	0.51
3743	Boot Key Harbor bridge, Boot Key	24° 42.2'	81° 06.3'	−1 03	−0 37	*1.13	*0.75	1.57	1.96	0.96
3745	Sombrero Key, Hawk Channel	24° 37.6'	81° 06.7'	−1 03	−0 39	*1.18	*0.79	1.64	2.02	1.01
3747	Knight Key Channel, Knight Key, Florida Bay	24° 42.4'	81° 07.5'	−0 02	−0 18	*0.54	*0.50	0.72	0.90	0.48
3749	Pigeon Key, south side, Hawk Channel	24° 42.2'	81° 09.3'	−0 55	−0 26	*0.81	*0.50	1.14	1.42	0.69

Endnotes can be found at the end of table 2.

TABLE 2 – TIDAL DIFFERENCES AND OTHER CONSTANTS

No.	PLACE	POSITION Latitude	POSITION Longitude	DIFFERENCES Time High Water	DIFFERENCES Time Low Water	DIFFERENCES Height High Water	DIFFERENCES Height Low Water	RANGES Mean	RANGES Spring	Mean Tide Level
		North	West	h m	h m	ft	ft	ft	ft	ft
	FLORIDA, East Coast Florida Keys–cont. Time meridian, 75° W					on Key West, p.172				
3751	Pigeon Key, north side, Florida Bay	24° 42.3'	81° 09.4'	−0 10	+0 45	*0.46	*0.46	0.60	0.75	0.44
3753	Molasses Key Channel, Molasses Keys	24° 41.0'	81° 11.5'	−0 56	−0 16	*0.79	*0.50	1.10	1.38	0.67
3755	Money Key	24° 41.0'	81° 12.9'	+0 03	+1 17	*0.58	*0.58	0.76	0.95	0.54
3757	Little Duck Key, east end, Hawk Channel	24° 40.9'	81° 13.7'	−0 49	+0 05	*0.67	*0.67	0.88	1.10	0.60
3759	East Bahia Honda Key, south end, Florida Bay ...	24° 46.5'	81° 13.6'	+4 04	+2 49	*0.69	*0.69	0.90	1.12	0.77
3761	Cocoanut Key, Florida Bay	24° 44.7'	81° 14.2'	+3 52	+2 50	*0.55	*0.55	0.72	0.90	0.66
3763	West Bahia Honda Key	24° 46.8'	81° 16.3'	+3 59	+4 01	*0.97	*1.00	1.27	1.59	0.88
3765	Horseshoe Keys, south end	24° 46.0'	81° 17.0'	+3 54	+3 09	*0.86	*1.00	1.09	1.36	0.79
3767	Johnson Keys, south end	24° 44.6'	81° 18.0'	+3 36	+2 33	*0.72	*0.96	0.88	1.10	0.67
3769	Johnson Keys, north end	24° 46.0'	81° 19.4'	+3 35	+4 22	*1.31	*1.38	1.70	2.12	1.18
3771	Missouri Key–Little Duck Key Channel	24° 40.8'	81° 14.1'	−0 52	+0 36	*0.70	*0.46	0.98	1.22	0.60
3773	Missouri Key–Ohio Key Channel, west side	24° 40.4'	81° 14.6'	−0 47	−0 22	*0.77	*0.50	1.08	1.35	0.66
3775	Ohio Key–Bahia Honda Key Channel, west side ..	24° 40.2'	81° 15.1'	−0 57	−0 14	*0.81	*0.62	1.10	1.38	0.70
3777	Bahia Honda Key, Bahia Honda Channel	24° 39.3'	81° 16.9'	−0 46	−0 28	*0.86	*0.63	1.16	1.44	0.73
3779	Big Pine Key, Spanish Harbor	24° 38.9'	81° 19.8'	−0 44	−0 03	*0.75	*0.42	1.07	1.34	0.64
3781	Big Pine Key, Doctors Arm, Bogie Channel	24° 41.4'	81° 21.4'	+0 41	+1 47	*0.63	*0.71	0.80	1.00	0.57
3783	Big Pine Key, Bogie Channel Bridge	24° 41.9'	81° 20.9'	+2 10	+2 11	*0.65	*0.83	0.80	1.00	0.60
3785	No Name Key, east side, Bahia Honda Channel ..	24° 41.9'	81° 19.1'	+1 35	+1 33	*0.58	*0.83	0.70	0.88	0.55
3787	Little Pine Key, south end	24° 42.8'	81° 18.2'	+1 07	+1 07	*0.56	*0.79	0.68	0.85	0.53
3789	Porpoise Key, Big Spanish Channel	24° 43.1'	81° 21.1'	+3 23	+2 29	*0.72	*1.00	0.88	1.10	0.68
3791	Water Key, west end, Big Spanish Channel	24° 44.4'	81° 20.5'	+3 23	+2 37	*0.81	*1.04	1.00	1.25	0.75
3793	Mayo Key, Big Spanish Channel	24° 44.0'	81° 21.7'	+3 35	+3 01	*0.92	*1.08	1.17	1.46	0.85
3795	Little Pine Key, north end	24° 45.0'	81° 19.7'	+3 38	+3 28	*1.05	*1.21	1.33	1.66	0.96
3797	Big Pine Key, northeast shore	24° 43.7'	81° 23.2'	+3 19	+2 30	*0.86	*1.08	1.08	1.35	0.80
3799	Crawl Key, Big Spanish Channel	24° 45.4'	81° 21.5'	+3 34	+4 13	*1.33	*1.33	1.74	2.18	1.19
3801	Big Pine Key, north end	24° 44.7'	81° 23.7'	+4 24	+5 56	*0.96	*0.83	1.29	1.61	0.85
3803	Annette Key, north end, Big Spanish Channel	24° 45.5'	81° 23.4'	+3 30	+4 33	*1.44	*1.29	1.92	2.40	1.27
3805	Little Spanish Key, Spanish Banks	24° 46.5'	81° 22.2'	+3 25	+4 30	*1.74	*1.62	2.30	2.88	1.54
3807	Big Spanish Key	24° 47.3'	81° 24.7'	+3 19	+4 29	*1.97	*1.50	2.69	3.36	1.71
3809	Munson Island, Newfound Harbor Channel	24° 37.4'	81° 24.2'	−0 40	−0 12	*0.98	*0.67	1.36	1.70	0.84
3811	Ramrod Key, Newfound Harbor	24° 39.0'	81° 24.2'	−0 41	+0 05	*0.90	*0.50	1.28	1.60	0.76
3813	Middle Torch Key, Torch Ramrod Channel	24° 39.7'	81° 24.1'	−0 16	+1 29	*0.69	*0.38	0.98	1.22	0.58
3815	Little Torch Key, Torch Channel	24° 39.9'	81° 23.7'	+0 11	+1 45	*0.57	*0.33	0.80	1.00	0.48
3817	Big Pine Key, Newfound Harbor Channel	24° 39.1'	81° 22.5'	−0 09	+0 44	*0.82	*0.46	1.16	1.45	0.69
3819	Big Pine Key, Coupon Bight	24° 39.1'	81° 21.0'	−0 20	+0 49	*0.87	*0.50	1.19	1.48	0.72
3821	Little Torch Key, Pine Channel Bridge, south side .	24° 39.9'	81° 23.3'	−0 15	+0 57	*0.68	*0.33	0.97	1.21	0.56
3823	Big Pine Key, Pine Channel Bridge, south side ...	24° 40.1'	81° 22.3'	−0 13	+1 03	*0.67	*0.33	0.96	1.20	0.56
3825	Big Pine Key, Pine Channel Bridge, north side ...	24° 40.2'	81° 22.1'	+0 03	+1 43	*0.57	*0.33	0.79	0.98	0.47
3827	Big Pine Key, west side, Pine Channel	24° 41.4'	81° 23.0'	+0 21	+1 52	*0.52	*0.42	0.71	0.89	0.45
3829	Howe Key, south end, Harbor Channel	24° 43.5'	81° 24.4'	+4 43	+4 49	*0.72	*0.62	0.96	1.20	0.63
3831	Big Torch Key, Harbor Channel	24° 44.3'	81° 26.6'	+3 47	+5 51	*1.58	*1.29	2.14	2.68	1.38
3833	Water Keys, south end, Harbor Channel	24° 44.8'	81° 27.0'	+3 42	+5 41	*1.52	*1.00	2.11	2.64	1.29
3835	Howe Key, northwest end	24° 45.5'	81° 25.7'	+3 29	+5 22	*1.68	*1.33	2.28	2.85	1.46
3837	Summerland Key, Niles Channel South	24° 39.1'	81° 26.1'	−0 36	+0 11	*0.85	*0.71	1.14	1.42	0.74
3839	Summerland Key, Niles Channel Bridge	24° 39.6'	81° 26.2'	−0 10	+0 56	*0.67	*0.58	0.90	1.12	0.59
3841	Ramrod Key, Niles Channel Bridge	24° 39.6'	81° 25.4'	−0 13	+1 12	*0.67	*0.46	0.93	1.16	0.58
3843	Big Torch Key, Niles Channel	24° 42.3'	81° 26.0'	+3 15	+2 05	*0.61	*0.71	0.77	0.96	0.56
3845	Knockemdown Key, north end	24° 42.9'	81° 28.7'	+3 30	+4 54	*1.35	*1.21	1.80	2.25	1.19
3847	Raccoon Key, east side	24° 44.5'	81° 29.0'	+3 20	+5 09	*1.50	*1.21	2.04	2.55	1.31
3849	Content Keys, Content Passage	24° 47.4'	81° 29.0'	+2 46	+3 49	*2.13	*1.83	2.79	3.46	1.84
3851	Key Lois, southeast end	24° 36.4'	81° 28.2'	−1 15	−0 45	*1.06	*0.75	1.46	1.82	0.91
3853	Sugarloaf Key, east side, Tarpon Creek	24° 37.7'	81° 30.6'	−0 41	+0 15	*0.89	*0.58	1.24	1.55	0.76
3855	Gopher Key, Cudjoe Bay	24° 38.5'	81° 29.1'	−0 46	+0 17	*0.90	*0.71	1.22	1.52	0.78
3857	Sugarloaf Key, Pirates Cove	24° 39.2'	81° 30.9'	−0 48	+1 41	*0.59	*0.75	0.74	0.92	0.55
3859	Cudjoe Key, Cudjoe Bay	24° 39.6'	81° 29.5'	−0 38	+0 41	*0.87	*0.71	1.18	1.48	0.76
3861	Summerland Key, southwest side, Kemp Channel	24° 39.0'	81° 26.8'	−0 26	+0 50	*0.81	*0.54	1.12	1.40	0.69
3863	Kemp Channel Viaduct, Hwy A1A bridge	24° 39.1'	81° 28.1'	+0 47	+2 04	*0.58	*0.46	0.77	0.95	0.50
3865	Cudjoe Key, Kemp Channel Bridge	24° 39.7'	81° 28.1'	− − −	− − −	*0.59	*0.50	0.79	0.99	0.52
3867	Cudjoe Key, northeast side, Kemp Channel	24° 41.2'	81° 29.0'	+3 45	− − −	− − −	− − −	− −	− −	− −
3869	Cudjoe Key, north end, Kemp Channel	24° 42.0'	81° 30.3'	+3 33	+4 40	*1.61	*1.46	2.10	2.60	1.41
3871	Sugarloaf Key, northeast side, Bow Channel	24° 40.3'	81° 32.0'	+3 47	+3 24	*1.01	*0.71	1.40	1.75	0.87
3873	Cudjoe Key, Pirates Cove	24° 39.7'	81° 30.9'	+3 50	+2 54	*0.77	*0.79	0.98	1.21	0.68
3875	Sugarloaf Key, north end, Bow Channel	24° 41.6'	81° 33.3'	+3 37	+5 20	*1.29	*0.75	1.82	2.28	1.09
3877	Pumpkin Key, Bow Channel	24° 43.0'	81° 33.7'	+3 17	+4 39	*1.56	*1.17	2.14	2.68	1.35
3879	Sawyer Key, outside, Cudjoe Channel	24° 45.5'	81° 33.7'	+2 45	+5 24	*1.57	*0.50	2.32	2.90	1.28
3881	Sawyer Key, inside, Cudjoe Channel	24° 45.5'	81° 33.7'	+2 37	+5 19	*1.43	*0.50	2.10	2.62	1.17
3883	Johnston Key, southwest end, Turkey Basin	24° 42.6'	81° 35.6'	+3 26	+5 38	*1.10	*0.50	1.59	1.99	0.92
	Upper Sugarloaf Sound									
3885	Perky	24° 38.9'	81° 34.2'	+5 37	+8 25	*0.28	*0.08	0.42	0.52	0.23
3887	Park Channel Bridge	24° 39.3'	81° 32.4'	+5 47	+8 33	*0.26	*0.29	0.34	0.42	0.24
3889	North Harris Channel	24° 39.0'	81° 33.2'	+5 32	+8 04	*0.25	*0.25	0.33	0.41	0.22
3891	Sugarloaf Shores East <26>	24° 38.6'	81° 33.6'	− − −	− − −	− − −	− − −	− −	− −	− −
3893	Tarpon Creek	24° 37.8'	81° 31.0'	−0 29	+0 17	*0.35	*0.38	0.46	0.58	0.32
	Lower Sugarloaf Sound <27>									
3895	Sugarloaf Shores <27>	24° 38.0'	81° 33.1'	− − −	− − −	− − −	− − −	− −	− −	− −
3897	Sugarloaf Beach <27>	24° 36.4'	81° 34.0'	− − −	− − −	− − −	− − −	− −	− −	− −
3899	Sugarloaf Shores North <27>	24° 38.4'	81° 34.2'	− − −	− − −	− − −	− − −	− −	− −	− −
3901	Saddlebunch Keys, south end <27>	24° 36.1'	81° 34.9'	− − −	− − −	− − −	− − −	− −	− −	− −
3903	Lower Sugarloaf Channel Bridge <27>	24° 38.0'	81° 35.2'	− − −	− − −	− − −	− − −	− −	− −	− −
3905	Saddlebunch Keys, Channel No. 2 <27>	24° 37.6'	81° 35.9'	− − −	− − −	− − −	− − −	− −	− −	− −
3907	Saddlebunch Keys <27>	24° 37.1'	81° 36.1'	− − −	− − −	− − −	− − −	− −	− −	− −
3909	Snipe Keys, southeast end, Inner Narrows	24° 39.5'	81° 36.5'	+3 25	+5 39	*1.28	*0.83	1.79	2.24	1.10
3911	Snipe Keys, Middle Narrows	24° 40.0'	81° 37.8'	+3 44	+5 54	*1.02	*0.67	1.42	1 78	0 87
3913	Snipe Keys, Snipe Point	24° 41.5'	81° 40.4'	+2 15	+3 33	*1.69	*1.29	2.31	2.89	1.47

Endnotes can be found at the end of table 2.

TABLE 2 – TIDAL DIFFERENCES AND OTHER CONSTANTS

No.	PLACE	POSITION		DIFFERENCES				RANGES		Mean Tide Level
		Latitude	Longitude	Time		Height		Mean	Spring	
				High Water	Low Water	High Water	Low Water			
		North	West	h m	h m	ft	ft	ft	ft	ft
	FLORIDA, East Coast Florida Keys–cont. Time meridian, 75° W			on Key West, p.172						
3915	Waltz Key, Waltz Key Basin	24° 38.8'	81° 39.2'	+3 53	+5 33	*1.03	*0.96	1.36	1.70	0.91
3917	Duck Key Point, Duck Key, Waltz Key Basin	24° 37.4'	81° 41.1'	+3 27	+4 57	*1.19	*0.96	1.61	2.01	1.03
3919	O'Hara Key, north end, Waltz Key Basin	24° 37.0'	81° 38.7'	+3 53	+5 39	*1.03	*0.83	1.40	1.75	0.90
3921	Saddlebunch Keys, Channel No. 5	24° 36.7'	81° 37.5'	+4 32	+6 58	*0.66	*1.12	0.76	0.95	0.65
3923	Saddlebunch Keys, Channel No. 4	24° 36.9'	81° 37.0'	+4 35	+5 36	*0.54	*0.29	0.76	0.95	0.45
3925	Saddlebunch Keys, Channel No. 3	24° 37.4'	81° 36.2'	+1 44	−0 10	*0.43	*0.21	0.62	0.78	0.36
3927	Bird Key, Similar Sound	24° 35.3'	81° 38.3'	−0 21	+1 03	*0.59	*0.42	0.82	1.02	0.51
3929	Shark Key, southeast end, Similar Sound	24° 36.2'	81° 38.7'	+0 18	+1 51	*0.52	*0.46	0.70	0.88	0.46
3931	Saddlebunch Keys, Similar Sound	24° 36.0'	81° 37.3'	+0 39	+2 41	*0.37	*0.21	0.52	0.65	0.31
3933	Geiger Key, inside <26>	24° 35.0'	81° 39.3'	– – –	– – –	– – –	– – –	– –	– –	– –
3935	Big Coppitt Key, northeast side, Waltz Key Basin .	24° 36.1'	81° 39.3'	+4 21	+6 54	*0.84	*0.33	1.22	1.52	0.69
3937	Rockland Key, Rockland Channel Bridge	24° 35.5'	81° 40.1'	+5 02	+6 06	*0.76	*0.88	0.97	1.21	0.69
3939	Boca Chica Key, Long Point	24° 36.2'	81° 41.9'	+3 54	+5 22	*0.94	*0.71	1.28	1.60	0.81
3941	Channel Key, west side	24° 36.2'	81° 43.5'	+3 09	+3 07	*0.70	*0.71	0.91	1.14	0.62
3943	Boca Chica Marina	24° 34.5'	81° 42.5'	+0 20	+1 11	*0.66	*0.71	0.83	1.03	0.58
3945	Boca Chica Key, Southwest end	24° 33.8'	81° 42.8'	−0 14	+0 16	*0.66	*0.63	0.87	1.08	0.58
3947	Boca Chica Channel Bridge	24° 34.6'	81° 43.2'	+1 23	+1 29	*0.57	*0.67	0.72	0.90	0.52
3949	Key Haven – Stock Island Channel	24° 34.8'	81° 44.3'	+2 25	+2 57	*0.73	*0.79	0.94	1.18	0.66
3951	Cow Key Channel	24° 34.2'	81° 45.0'	+1 55	+2 05	*0.65	*0.71	0.82	1.01	0.58
3953	Sigsbee Park, Garrison Bight Channel	24° 35.1'	81° 46.5'	+1 59	+2 06	*0.81	*0.88	1.04	1.30	0.73
3955	Fleming Key, north end	24° 35.5'	81° 47.7'	+1 38	+1 54	*0.79	*0.79	1.01	1.25	0.69
3957	Riveria Canal, Key West	24° 33.9'	81° 45.1'	−0 12	+1 00	*0.65	*0.63	0.84	1.04	0.57
3959	Key West, south side, White Street Pier	24° 32.7'	81° 47.0'	−0 53	−0 31	*1.07	*0.92	1.41	1.75	0.92
3961	KEY WEST	24° 33.2'	81° 48.5'	Daily predictions				1.28	1.65	0.88
3963	Sand Key Lighthouse, Sand Key Channel	24° 27.2'	81° 52.6'	−0 43	−0 32	*0.95	*0.88	1.23	1.53	0.83
3965	Garden Key, Dry Tortugas	24° 37.6'	82° 52.3'	+0 29	+0 33	*0.94	*1.33	1.14	1.42	0.89
3967	Smith Shoal Light	24° 43.1'	81° 55.2'	+1 43	+2 20	*2.10	*2.37	2.63	3.44	1.88
	Gulf Coast			on Naples, p. 176				Mean Diurnal		
3969	Cape Sable, East Cape	25° 07'	81° 05'	+1 33	+1 50	*1.30	*0.98	2.9	3.8	2.0
3971	Shark River entrance	25° 21'	81° 08'	+0 57	+1 45	*1.43	*0.98	3.6	4.5	2.4
3973	Whitewater Bay	25° 19'	81° 02'	+3 53	+4 38	*0.26	*0.33	0.5	0.8	0.4
3975	Lostmans River entrance	25° 33'	81° 13'	+1 09	+1 59	*1.33	*0.98	3.0	3.9	2.1
3977	Onion Key, Lostmans River	25° 37'	81° 08'	+3 09	+4 53	*0.26	*0.16	0.6	0.9	0.4
3979	Chatham River entrance	25° 41'	81° 17'	+0 59	+1 53	*1.43	*0.66	3.3	4.2	2.1
3981	Chokoloskee	25° 48.8'	81° 21.8'	+2 15	+3 14	*1.11	*0.62	2.53	3.18	1.63
3983	Everglades City, Barron River	25° 51.5'	81° 23.2'	+2 25	+3 26	*0.99	*0.57	2.26	2.84	1.47
3985	Indian Key	25° 48'	81° 28'	+0 55	+1 19	*1.48	*0.98	3.4	4.3	2.3
3987	Round Key	25° 50'	81° 32'	+0 54	+1 12	*1.48	*0.98	3.4	4.3	2.3
3989	Pumpkin Bay	25° 55'	81° 33'	+2 39	+3 07	*0.89	*0.49	2.1	2.7	1.3
3991	Marco Island, Caxambas Pass	25° 54.5'	81° 43.7'	+0 25	+0 18	*1.07	*0.98	2.22	3.05	1.70
3993	Coon Key	25° 53.8'	81° 38.2'	+1 06	+1 25	*1.34	*1.03	2.90	3.86	2.07
3995	Cape Romano	25° 51'	81° 41'	+0 43	+1 04	*1.19	*0.98	2.6	3.5	1.9
3997	Marco, Big Marco River	25° 58.3'	81° 43.7'	+1 00	+0 46	*0.98	*0.85	2.04	2.78	1.53
3999	McIlvanine Bay	25° 59.1'	81° 42.1'	+1 39	+1 55	*0.90	*0.75	1.92	2.61	1.41
4001	Keewaydin Island (inside)	26° 01.5'	81° 46.1'	+0 58	+0 55	*0.90	*0.78	1.90	2.61	1.42
4003	Naples, Naples Bay, north end	26° 08.2'	81° 47.3'	+0 43	+0 56	*0.97	*0.90	2.06	2.85	1.58
4005	NAPLES (outer coast)	26° 07.8'	81° 48.4'	Daily Predictions				2.01	2.87	1.61
4007	Wiggins Pass, Cocohatchee River	26° 17.4'	81° 49.1'	+0 44	+0 59	*0.77	*0.73	1.59	2.26	1.23
4009	Cocohatchee River, U.S. 41 bridge	26° 16.9'	81° 48.1'	+1 10	+1 28	*0.74	*0.65	1.54	2.18	1.17
	Estero Bay			on St. Petersburg, p.180						
4011	Little Hickory Island	26° 21'	81° 51'	−0 58	−1 05	*1.09	*1.09	– –	2.5	1.3
4013	Coconut Point	26° 24.0'	81° 50.6'	−1 21	−0 44	*1.12	*1.21	1.75	2.48	1.34
4015	Carlos Point	26° 24'	81° 53'	−1 08	−1 28	*1.17	*1.17	– –	2.7	1.4
4017	Estero River	26° 25.8'	81° 51.4'	−0 45	−0 10	*1.09	*1.11	1.74	2.45	1.29
4019	Hendry Creek	26° 28.2'	81° 52.6'	−0 25	+0 28	*0.89	*0.68	1.51	2.06	1.01
4021	Estero Island	26° 26.3'	81° 55.1'	−1 08	−0 43	*1.14	*1.30	1.77	2.52	1.37
4023	Matanzas Pass (fixed bridge) Estero Island	26° 27'	81° 57'	−1 10	−1 34	*1.22	*1.22	– –	2.8	1.4
4025	Point Ybel, San Carlos Bay entrance	26° 27'	82° 01'	−1 50	−1 12	*1.21	*1.21	– –	2.6	1.4
4027	Punta Rassa, San Carlos Bay	26° 29.3'	82° 00.8'	−1 06	−0 59	*1.02	*1.26	1.54	2.26	1.25
	Caloosahatchee River									
4029	Iona Shores	26° 31'	81° 58'	+1 08	+1 40	*0.43	*0.43	– –	1.0	0.5
4031	Cape Coral Bridge	26° 34'	81° 56'	+1 15	+2 02	*0.43	*0.43	– –	1.0	0.5
4033	Fort Myers	26° 38.8'	81° 52.3'	+1 56	+2 23	*0.56	*0.39	0.95	1.32	0.63
4035	Tarpon Bay, Sanibel Island	26° 26.6'	82° 04.9'	−0 46	−0 18	*1.02	*1.18	1.57	2.27	1.23
4037	St. James City, Pine Island	26° 30'	82° 05'	−0 30	−0 44	*1.04	*1.04	– –	2.4	1.2
4039	Galt Island, Pine Island Sound	26° 31'	82° 06'	−0 25	+0 16	*0.91	*0.91	– –	2.1	1.1
4041	Captiva Island (outside)	26° 29'	82° 11'	−2 20	−2 28	*1.13	*1.13	– –	2.6	1.3
4043	Captiva Island, Pine Island Sound	26° 31'	82° 11'	−0 46	−0 20	*0.91	*0.91	– –	2.1	1.1
4045	North Captiva Island	26° 36.3'	82° 12.1'	−1 42	−1 17	*0.92	*0.71	1.54	2.02	1.05
4047	Redfish Pass, Captiva Island (north end)	26° 33'	82° 12'	−0 55	−1 14	*0.91	*0.91	– –	2.1	1.0
4049	Tropical Homesites Landing, Pine Island	26° 33'	82° 05'	−0 08	+0 22	*0.87	*0.87	– –	2.0	1.0
4051	Matlacha Pass (bascule bridge) Pine Island	26° 38'	82° 04'	+0 43	+1 28	*0.83	*0.83	– –	1.9	1.0
4053	Pineland, Pine Island	26° 40'	82° 09'	−0 19	+0 26	*0.83	*0.83	– –	1.9	0.9
	Charlotte Harbor									
4055	Port Boca Grande	26° 43.1'	82° 15.5'	−0 50	−1 42	*0.67	*1.03	0.93	1.56	0.86
4057	Bokellia	26° 42.4'	82° 09.8'	−0 35	−0 09	*0.80	*0.63	1.34	1.73	0.91
4059	Turtle Bay	26° 47.8'	82° 11.0'	+0 51	+0 35	*0.69	*0.95	1.02	1.56	0.86
4061	Punta Gorda	26° 56'	82° 04'	+1 06	+1 27	*0.83	*0.83	– –	1.9	1.0
4063	Shell Point (Harbor Heights), Peace River	26° 59.3'	81° 59.6'	+1 42	+2 10	*0.89	*0.89	1.32	2.02	1.10
4065	Locust Point, Hog Islan	26° 55.8'	82° 08.2'	+1 15	+1 27	*0.82	*0.82	1.22	1.95	1.03

Endnotes can be found at the end of table 2.

TABLE 2 – TIDAL DIFFERENCES AND OTHER CONSTANTS

No.	PLACE	POSITION		DIFFERENCES				RANGES		Mean Tide Level
		Latitude	Longitude	Time High Water	Time Low Water	Height High Water	Height Low Water	Mean	Diurnal	
		North	West	h m	h m	ft	ft	ft	ft	ft
	FLORIDA, East Coast Gulf Coast–cont. Time meridian, 75° W			on St. Petersburg, p.180						
	Charlotte Harbor–cont.									
4067	El Jobean, Myakka River	26° 58'	82° 13'	+1 38	+1 56	*0.83	*0.83		1.9	1.0
4069	Myakka River, US 41 bridge	27° 02.7'	82° 17.6'	+2 48	+3 01	*0.83	*0.97	1.31	1.90	1.00
4071	Placida, Gasparilla Sound	26° 50.0'	82° 15.9'	−0 43	−0 56	*0.59	*0.94	0.82	1.41	0.77
4073	Don Pedro Island State Park, Cutoff (south)	26° 51.3'	82° 18.2'	−0 54	−0 53	*0.63	*0.84	0.91	1.49	0.78
4075	Englewood, Lemon Bay	26° 56.0'	82° 21.2'	−0 17	−0 17	*0.66	*0.82	1.00	1.57	0.81
4077	Manasota, Lemon Bay	27° 00.7'	82° 24.6'	−0 24	−0 11	*0.70	*0.89	1.05	1.68	0.86
4079	Venice Municipal Airport	27° 04.3'	82° 27.2'	−2 33	−2 43	*0.97	*0.97	1.56	2.20	1.15
4081	Venice Inlet (inside)	27° 07'	82° 28'	−2 02	−1 38	*0.91	*0.91	− −	2.1	1.1
4083	Sarasota, Sarasota Bay	27° 20'	82° 33'	−1 38	−0 58	*0.91	*0.91	− −	2.1	1.1
4085	Cortez, Sarasota Bay	27° 28'	82° 41'	−2 00	−1 25	*0.96	*0.96	− −	2.2	1.1
	Tampa Bay									
4087	Egmont Key, Egmont Channel	27° 36.1'	82° 45.6'	−2 15	−3 20	*0.96	*1.00	− −	2.16	1.14
4089	Anna Maria Key, Bradenton Beach	27° 29.8'	82° 42.8'	−2 27	−3 32	*0.99	*1.00	1.58	2.25	1.17
4091	Anna Maria Key, city pier	27° 32.0'	82° 43.8'	−2 10	−2 19	*0.99	*0.99	− −	2.22	1.11
4093	Bradenton, Manatee River	27° 30'	82° 34'	−1 24	−0 55	*0.97	*0.95	− −	2.3	1.2
4095	Redfish Point, Manatee River	27° 32'	82° 29'	−0 30	+0 14	*0.92	*1.00	− −	2.2	1.1
4097	Mullet Key Channel (Skyway)	27° 36.9'	82° 43.6'	−2 03	−2 01	*0.92	*0.92	1.48	2.08	1.09
4099	Port Manatee	27° 38.2'	82° 33.8'	−1 00	−0 48	*0.97	*0.95	1.56	2.19	1.14
4101	Shell Point	27° 43'	82° 29'	+0 08	+0 17	*0.91	*0.91	− −	2.3	1.2
4103	Little Manatee River, US 41 Bridge	27° 42.3'	82° 26.9'	+0 51	+1 15	*0.91	*0.68	1.55	1.99	1.03
4105	Point Pinellas	27° 42'	82° 38'	−0 22	−0 29	*0.86	*0.86	− −	2.0	1.0
4107	ST. PETERSBURG	27° 46.4'	82° 37.3'	Daily predictions				1.59	2.26	1.18
4109	Apollo Beach	27° 47.2'	82° 25.6'	−0 53	−0 32	*1.10	*1.18	1.72	2.46	1.31
4111	Newman Branch	27° 47.0'	82° 24.4'	−0 02	+0 12	*1.17	*1.11	1.89	2.61	1.37
4113	Ballast Point	27° 53.4'	82° 28.8'	+0 20	+0 23	*1.22	*1.16	1.98	2.73	1.43
4115	Pendola Point, Hillsborough Bay	27° 53.9'	82° 25.6'	+0 21	+0 05	*1.14	*1.18	1.81	2.61	1.36
4117	Davis Island, Hillsborough Bay	27° 54.5'	82° 27.1'	+0 03	+0 32	*1.16	*1.24	1.82	2.63	1.38
4119	McKay Bay entrance	27° 54.8'	82° 25.5'	+0 02	+0 28	*1.19	*1.26	1.89	2.69	1.42
4121	Old Port Tampa	27° 51.5'	82° 33.2'	+0 25	+0 39	*1.10	*1.18	1.73	2.48	1.31
4123	Gandy Bridge, Old Tampa Bay	27° 53.6'	82° 32.3'	+0 59	+0 57	*1.12	*1.24	1.75	2.55	1.35
4125	Bay Aristocrat Village, Old Tampa Bay	27° 56.5'	82° 43.2'	+1 01	+1 32	*1.24	*1.37	1.95	2.81	1.49
4127	Safety Harbor, Old Tampa Bay	27° 59.3'	82° 41.1'	+1 32	+1 34	*1.23	*1.39	1.91	2.79	1.48
4129	Mobbly Bayou	28° 01.3'	82° 39.3'	+2 38	+2 54	*0.71	*0.45	1.24	1.77	0.79
	Boca Ciega Bay									
4131	Pass-a-Grille Beach	27° 41'	82° 44'	−1 34	−1 30	*0.87	*0.87	− −	2.1	1.0
4133	Gulfport	27° 44'	82° 42'	−1 32	−1 05	*0.96	*0.96	− −	2.3	1.2
4135	Long Key, 0.5mi N. of Corey Causeway	27° 44.7'	82° 44.8'	−1 18	−0 44	*0.92	*1.00	− −	2.2	1.1
4137	Johns Pass	27° 47'	82° 47'	−2 14	−2 04	*0.97	*1.02	− −	2.3	1.2
4139	Madeira Beach Causeway	27° 48.5'	82° 47.7'	−1 32	−1 45	*1.08	*1.18	− −	2.42	1.29
	Gulf Coast–cont.			on Cedar Key, p.184						
4141	Indian Rocks Beach (inside)	27° 52'	82° 51'	−0 57	−0 53	*0.65	*0.63	1.8	2.6	1.3
4143	Clearwater	27° 57'	82° 48'	−1 48	−1 35	*0.65	*0.63	1.8	2.6	1.3
4145	Clearwater Beach	27° 58.7'	82° 49.9'	−2 07	−2 19	*0.69	*0.84	1.87	2.74	1.46
4147	Dunedin, St. Joseph Sound	28° 01'	82° 48'	−1 50	−1 45	*0.70	*0.79	1.9	2.8	1.4
4149	Anclote Key, southern end	28° 09.9'	82° 50.6'	−2 16	−2 11	*0.88	*0.60	2.65	3.32	1.71
4151	Anclote, Anclote River	28° 10.3'	82° 47.1'	−1 28	−1 24	*0.78	*0.87	2.16	3.07	1.63
4153	Tarpon Springs, Anclote River	28° 09.6'	82° 46.1'	−1 16	−1 03	*0.77	*0.83	2.10	3.00	1.57
4155	North Anclote Key	28° 12.6'	82° 50.4'	−1 55	−1 38	*0.80	*0.86	2.20	3.11	1.64
4157	Gulf Harbors	28° 14.6'	82° 45.8'	−1 15	−0 52	*0.84	*0.90	2.30	3.26	1.72
4159	Hwy. 19 bridge, Pithlachascotee River	28° 16.1'	82° 43.6'	−1 16	−0 40	*0.85	*0.84	2.36	3.27	1.71
4161	New Port Richey, Pithlachascotee River	28° 14.9'	82° 43.4'	−0 58	−0 11	*0.88	*0.87	2.44	3.40	1.77
4163	Hudson, Hudson Creek	28° 21.7'	82° 42.6'	−1 12	−1 02	*0.91	*0.89	2.53	3.48	1.82
4165	Aripeka, Hammock Creek	28° 26.0'	82° 40.1'	−0 37	+0 23	*0.81	*0.63	2.37	3.15	1.58
4167	Hernando Beach, Rocky Creek, Little Pine I. Bay .	28° 29.2'	82° 39.7'	−0 20	+0 58	*0.83	*0.83	2.16	− −	− −
4169	Bayport	28° 32.0'	82° 39.0'	−0 01	+0 43	*0.80	*0.71	2.33	3.16	1.61
4171	Johns Island, Chassahowitzka Bay	28° 41.5'	82° 38.3'	+1 09	+1 34	*0.62	*0.49	1.81	2.53	1.22
4173	Chassahowitzka, Chassahowitzka River	28° 42.9'	82° 34.6'	+3 59	+5 45	*0.14	*0.16	0.39	0.60	0.30
4175	Mason Creek, Homosassa Bay	28° 45.7'	82° 38.3'	+3 09	+4 44	*0.32	*0.25	0.96	1.35	0.64
4177	Tuckers Island, Homosassa River	28° 46.3'	82° 41.7'	+1 26	+2 23	*0.47	*0.33	1.38	1.92	0.90
4179	Halls River bridge, Homosassa River	28° 48.0'	82° 36.2'	+4 30	+5 41	*0.16	*0.13	0.45	0.72	0.30
4181	Ozello, St. Martins River	28° 49.5'	82° 39.5'	+4 25	+5 21	*0.17	*0.14	0.49	0.74	0.33
4183	Mangrove Pt., Crystal Bay	28° 52.2'	82° 43.4'	+0 22	+0 41	*0.95	*0.76	2.82	3.65	1.89
4185	Ozello north, Crystal Bay	28° 51.8'	82° 40.0'	+1 25	+3 17	*0.50	*0.25	1.53	2.03	0.93
4187	Dixie Bay, Salt River, Crystal Bay	28° 52.9'	82° 38.1'	+2 00	+3 06	*0.55	*0.33	1.66	2.15	1.04
	Crystal River									
4189	Florida Power	28° 57.6'	82° 43.5'	−0 03	+0 30	*1.04	*0.89	3.00	3.90	2.06
4191	Shell Island, north end	28° 55.4'	82° 41.5'	+0 36	+1 30	*0.79	*0.59	2.32	3.01	1.53
4193	Twin Rivers Marina	28° 54.3'	82° 38.3'	+1 46	+2 30	*0.64	*0.49	1.90	2.53	1.26
4195	Kings Bay	28° 53.9'	82° 35.9'	+2 20	+3 07	*0.59	*0.41	1.76	2.31	1.14
4197	Withlacoochee River entrance	29° 00'	82° 46'	+0 07	+0 55	*0.91	*0.95	2.5	3.5	1.8
4199	CEDAR KEY	29° 08.1'	83° 01.9'	Daily predictions				2.83	3.80	2.05
4201	Suwannee River entrance	29° 17'	83° 09'	+0 06	+0 18	*0.88	*0.95	2.4	3.4	1.8
4203	Suwannee, Salt Creek	29° 19.7'	83° 09.1'	−0 07	+0 24	*0.91	*0.83	2.65	3.47	1.84
4205	Horseshoe Point	29° 26.2'	83° 17.6'	−0 21	+0 08	*0.95	*0.94	2.69	3.58	1.94
4207	Pepperfish Keys	29° 30'	83° 22'	+0 12	+0 24	*0.88	*0.95	2.4	3.4	1.8
4209	Steinhatchee River ent., Deadman Bay	29° 40.3'	83° 23.4'	+0 02	+0 00	*1.03	*1.08	2.87	3.83	2.12

Endnotes can be found at the end of table 2.

TABLE 2 – TIDAL DIFFERENCES AND OTHER CONSTANTS

No.	PLACE	POSITION Latitude	POSITION Longitude	DIFFERENCES Time High Water	DIFFERENCES Time Low Water	DIFFERENCES Height High Water	DIFFERENCES Height Low Water	RANGES Mean	RANGES Diurnal	Mean Tide Level
		North	West	h m	h m	ft	ft	ft	ft	ft
	FLORIDA, East Coast Gulf Coast−cont. Time meridian, 75° W			on St. Marks River Ent., p.188						
4211	Fishermans Rest	29° 44'	83° 32'	−0 14	−0 02	*0.93	*0.86	2.4	3.4	1.8
4213	Spring Warrior Creek	29° 55.2'	83° 40.3'	−0 25	−0 06	*0.98	*0.84	2.68	3.46	1.86
4215	Rock Islands	29° 58'	83° 50'	−0 03	+0 04	*0.93	*0.91	2.4	3.3	1.8
	Apalachee Bay									
4217	Mandalay, Aucilla River	30° 07.6'	83° 58.5'	+0 25	+0 57	*0.69	*0.55	1.92	2.47	1.30
4219	ST. MARKS RIVER ENTRANCE	30° 04.7'	84° 10.7'	Daily predictions				2.63	3.49	1.94
4221	St. Marks, St. Marks River	30° 09'	84° 12'	+0 36	+1 04	*0.93	*0.91	2.4	3.3	1.8
4223	Shell Point, Walker Creek	30° 03.6'	84° 17.4'	−0 03	−0 03	*1.02	*1.08	2.65	3.56	2.00
4225	Bald Point, Ochlockonee Bay	29° 56.9'	84° 20.5'	+0 33	+0 19	*0.85	*0.70	2.28	3.07	1.60
4227	Panacea, Dickerson Bay	30° 01.7'	84° 23.2'	+0 16	+0 20	*1.01	*0.82	2.73	3.66	1.90
4229	Alligator Point, St. James Island	29° 54.2'	84° 24.8'	−0 08	+0 11	*0.75	*0.73	1.95	2.82	1.45
4231	Turkey Point, St. James Island	29° 54.9'	84° 30.7'	−0 16	−0 21	*0.78	*0.98	1.92	2.74	1.57
	St. George Sound			on Apalachicola, p.192						
4233	Dog Island, west end	29° 47'	84° 40'	−1 53	−2 38	*1.73	*1.40	− −	2.6	1.3
4235	Carrabelle, Carrabelle River	29° 51'	84° 40'	−1 25	−2 13	*1.60	*1.60	− −	2.6	1.3
4237	St. George Island, East End	29° 41.2'	84° 47.2'	−2 02	−2 48	*1.13	*1.00	− −	1.9	1.1
4239	St. George Island, Rattlesnake Cove	29° 41.5'	84° 47.5'	−1 00	−1 35	*1.33	*1.20	− −	2.2	1.3
4241	St. George Island, 12th St. W (Bayside)	29° 39'	84° 54'	−0 55	−1 08	*1.26	*1.26	− −	2.2	1.1
4243	St. George Island, Sikes Cut	29° 36.8'	84° 57.5'	+0 07	+0 07	*1.15	*1.30	1.22	1.97	1.13
	Apalachicola Bay									
4245	Cat Point	29° 43'	84° 53'	−0 40	−1 17	*1.07	*0.60	− −	2.2	1.1
4247	White Beach, East Bay	29° 47.1'	84° 53.9'	−0 11	+0 10	*1.21	*1.40	1.27	1.98	1.19
4249	APALACHICOLA	29° 43.6'	84° 58.9'	Daily predictions				1.11	1.61	0.96
4251	Apalachicola River (A&N RR bridge)	29° 45.8'	85° 02.0'	+0 28	+0 35	*0.85	*0.83	0.97	1.39	0.81
4253	Lower Anchorage	29° 36'	85° 03'	−0 17	−0 35	*0.93	*1.00	− −	1.5	0.8
4255	West Pass, St. Vincent Island	29° 38'	85° 06'	−0 27	−0 27	*0.87	*1.00	− −	1.4	0.7
				on Pensacola, p.196						
4257	Port Saint Joe, St. Joseph Bay }	29° 48.9'	85° 18.8'	−1 06	−1 45	*1.11	*1.11	1.15	1.65	0.78
4259	White City, ICWW }	29° 52.8'	85° 13.3'	−0 40	+1 31	*0.77	*0.77	0.86	1.01	0.52
	Time meridian, 90° W									
	St. Andrew Bay									
4261	Channel entrance }	30° 07.5'	85° 43.8'	−1 39	−1 50	*1.02	*1.02	1.20	1.29	0.67
4263	Panama City }	30° 09.1'	85° 40.0'	−0 57	−1 11	*1.05	*1.66	1.25	1.34	0.7
4265	Panama City Beach (outside) }	30° 12.8'	85° 52.7'	−2 17	−2 44	*1.05	*1.05	1.22	1.37	0.68
4267	Parker }	30° 08'	85° 37'	−0 05	+0 22	*1.20	*1.20	− −	1.5	0.7
4269	Laird Bayou, East Bay }	30° 07.3'	85° 32.7'	−0 28	−1 05	*1.13	*1.13	1.28	1.47	0.75
4271	Farmdale, East Bay }	30° 01.0'	85° 28.2'	−0 16	−0 59	*1.17	*1.17	1.31	1.56	0.78
4273	Allanton, East Bay }	30° 01.8'	85° 27.9'	−0 16	−1 01	*1.15	*1.15	1.30	1.53	0.76
4275	Wetappo Creek, East Bay }	30° 02'	85° 24'	+1 01	+1 40	*1.10	*1.10	− −	1.4	0.7
4277	Alligator Bayou }	30° 10.2'	85° 45.3'	−0 47	−1 10	*1.07	*1.07	1.25	1.37	0.68
4279	Lynn Haven, North Bay }	30° 15.3'	85° 38.9'	−0 31	−1 01	*1.10	*1.10	1.25	1.47	0.73
4281	West Bay Creek, West Bay }	30° 17.6'	85° 51.5'	−0 10	−0 47	*1.13	*1.13	1.30	1.46	0.74
	Choctawhatchee Bay <11>									
4283	East Pass (Destin) }	30° 23.7'	86° 30.8'	−0 33	−0 34	*0.49	*0.33	0.59	0.61	0.31
4285	Shalimar, Garnier Bayou }	30° 26.1'	86° 35.2'	+3 33	+3 03	*0.32	*0.32	0.36	0.41	0.21
4287	Harris, The Narrows}	30° 24'	86° 44'	+1 37	+2 51	*1.10	*1.10	− −	1.4	0.7
4289	Navarre Beach	30° 22.6'	86° 51.9'	−2 07	−2 26	*1.07	*1.67	1.26	1.38	0.69
4291	Fishing Bend, Santa Rosa Sound }	30° 20'	87° 08'	+0 41	+0 51	*1.10	*1.10	− −	1.4	0.7
	Pensacola Bay									
4293	Entrance }	30° 20'	87° 19'	−1 23	−0 34	*0.80	*0.80	− −	1.1	0.5
4295	Warrington, 2 miles south of }	30° 21'	87° 16'	−0 27	−0 30	*1.00	*1.00	− −	1.3	0.6
4297	PENSACOLA }	30° 24.2'	87° 13.8'	Daily predictions				1.20	1.26	0.63
4299	Lora Point, Escambia Bay }	30° 31'	87° 10'	+0 36	+1 03	*1.20	*1.20	− −	1.5	0.7
4301	East Bay }	30° 27'	86° 55'	+0 44	+1 17	*1.20	*1.20	− −	1.6	0.8
4303	Bay Point, Blackwater River }	30° 34'	87° 00'	+1 23	+1 27	*1.20	*1.20	− −	1.6	0.8
4305	Milton, Blackwater River }	30° 37'	87° 02'	+1 40	+1 47	*1.20	*1.20	− −	1.6	0.8
	Perdido Bay									
4307	Blue Angels Park }	30° 23.2'	87° 25.7'	+2 36	+4 00	*0.58	*0.58	0.71	0.73	0.35
4309	Nix Point }	30° 23.6'	87° 25.5'	+2 29	+3 37	*0.57	*0.33	0.69	0.71	0.35
4311	Millview }	30° 25.1'	87° 21.4'	+2 33	+4 33	*0.67	*0.67	0.82	0.85	0.41
4313	Alabama Point, Perdido Pass, Alabama	30° 16.7'	87° 33.3'	−1 26	−1 24	*0.67	*0.67	0.78	0.86	0.42
	ALABAMA			on Mobile, p.204						
4315	Mobile Point (Fort Morgan) }	30° 14'	88° 01'	−1 46	−1 32	*0.80	*0.80	− −	1.2	0.6
4317	DAUPHIN ISLAND }	30° 15.0'	88° 04.5'	Daily predictions, p.200				1.18	1.20	0.60
4319	Gulf Shores, ICWW }	30° 16.8'	87° 41.1'	−0 41	−0 16	*0.75	*0.90	1.03	1.15	0.60
4321	Bon Secour, Bon Secour River }	30° 18'	87° 44'	−1 13	−1 17	*1.07	*1.07	− −	1.6	0.8
4323	East Fowl River, Hwy 193 bridge, Mobile Bay }	30° 26.6'	88° 06.8'	−0 53	−0 58	*0.88	*0.30	1.28	1.36	0.68
4325	West Fowl River, Hwy 188 bridge }	30° 22.6'	88° 09.5'	−2 00	−2 01	*0.94	*1.48	1.33	1.61	0.79
4327	Point Clear, Mobile Bay }	30° 29.2'	87° 56.1'	−1 03	−0 34	*1.00	*1.00	1.50	1.52	0.77
4329	Dog River, Hwy 163 bridge, Mobile Bay }	30° 33.9'	88° 05.2'	−0 38	−0 47	*0.93	*0.60	1.39	1.44	0.72
4331	Meaher State Park, Mobile Bay }	30° 40.0'	87° 56.1'	−0 38	+0 25	*1.03	*0.50	1.48	1.54	0.79
4333	Coast Guard Station, Mobile Bay }	30° 38.9'	88° 03.5'	−0 38	−0 38	*1.03	*0.90	1.45	1.63	0.82
4335	MOBILE, Mobile River (State Dock) }	30° 42.3'	88° 02.4'	Daily predictions				1.38	1.61	0.80
4337	William Brooks Park, Chickasaw Creek }	30° 46.9'	88° 04.4'	−0 05	−0 07	*0.99	*1.00	1.39	1.56	0.79
4339	Lower Hall Landing, Tensaw River }	30° 49'	87° 55'	+2 16	+3 05	*0.87	*0.87	− −	1.3	0.6

Endnotes can be found at the end of table 2.

TABLE 2 – TIDAL DIFFERENCES AND OTHER CONSTANTS

No.	PLACE	POSITION Latitude	Longitude	DIFFERENCES Time High Water h m	Low Water h m	Height High Water ft	Low Water ft	RANGES Mean ft	Diurnal ft	Mean Tide Level ft
		North	West							
	ALABAMA Time meridian, 90° W			on South Pass, p.208						
4341	Bayou La Batre, Mississippi Sound }	30° 22'	88° 16'	+1 52	+1 14	*1.23	*1.23	– –	1.5	0.8
4343	Bayou La Batre, Hwy 188 Bridge }	30° 24.3'	88° 14.8'	+1 29	+0 56	*1.28	*1.28	1.46	1.60	0.82
	MISSISSIPPI									
4345	Grand Bay NERR }	30° 24.8'	88° 24.2'	+1 38	+0 54	*1.25	*1.25	1.37	1.59	0.81
4347	Point of Pines, Bayou Cumbest }	30° 23.2'	88° 26.4'	+1 49	+1 09	*1.25	*1.25	1.37	1.62	0.81
4349	Hollingsworth Point, Davis Bayou }	30° 23.2'	88° 46.4'	+2 24	+1 52	*1.42	*1.42	1.59	1.80	0.91
4351	Petit Bois Island, Mississippi Sound }	30° 12.2'	88° 26.5'	+1 14	+0 41	*1.18	*1.18	1.37	1.47	0.73
4353	Horn Island, Mississippi Sound }	30° 14.3'	88° 40.0'	+1 34	+0 59	*1.25	*1.25	1.38	1.60	0.81
4355	Ship Island, Mississippi Sound }	30° 12.8'	88° 58.3'	+1 48	+1 05	*1.32	*1.32	1.49	1.60	0.83
4357	Port of Pascagoula, Dock E }	30° 20.8'	88° 30.3'	+1 08	+0 44	*1.22	*1.22	1.37	1.55	0.78
4359	Pascagoula, Mississippi Sound }	30° 20.4'	88° 32.0'	+1 20	+0 48	*1.21	*1.21	1.37	1.53	0.86
4361	Graveline Bayou Entrance }	30° 21.7'	88° 39.8'	+1 43	+1 04	*1.29	*1.29	1.44	1.63	0.82
4363	Gulfport Harbor, Mississippi Sound }	30° 21.6'	89° 04.9'	+2 09	+1 09	*1.29	*1.29	1.38	1.64	0.86
4365	Biloxi (Cadet Point), Biloxi Bay }	30° 23.4'	88° 51.4'	+2 04	+1 30	*1.38	*1.38	1.55	1.76	0.88
4367	Turkey Creek, Bernard Bayou }	30° 25.6'	89° 03.2'	+3 23	+2 27	*1.54	*1.54	1.65	2.00	1.02
4369	Handsboro Bridge, Bernard Bayou }	30° 24.4'	89° 01.6'	+3 40	+2 06	*1.53	*1.53	1.64	1.98	1.01
4371	Cat Island }	30° 13.9'	89° 07.0'	+2 13	+2 00	*1.23	*1.23	1.39	1.57	0.78
4373	Pass Christian Yacht Club, Mississippi Sound } ...	30° 18.6'	89° 14.7'	+2 36	+2 04	*1.37	*1.37	1.53	1.73	0.87
4375	Wolf River, Henderson Avenue bridge	30° 21.5'	89° 16.4'	+3 18	+2 51	*1.36	*1.36	1.47	1.80	0.90
4377	St. Louis Bay entrance }	30° 19.5'	89° 19.5'	+3 17	+2 57	*1.36	*1.36	1.52	1.73	0.87
4379	Waveland }	30° 16.9'	89° 22.0'	+3 09	+2 49	*1.28	*1.28	1.44	1.60	0.81
4381	Pearlington, Pearl River }	30° 14.4'	89° 36.9'	+5 51	+5 31	*0.99	*0.99	1.15	1.23	0.62
	LOUISIANA									
4383	The Rigolets }	30° 09.9'	89° 44.4'	+6 22	+5 35	*0.64	*0.50	0.76	0.79	0.39
4385	Bayou BonFouca, Route 433 }	30° 16.3'	89° 47.6'	+11 12	+11 31	*0.43	*0.43	0.53	0.53	0.26
4387	Tchefuncta River, Lake Pontchartrain	30° 22.7'	90° 09.6'	+11 36	+12 21	*0.48	*0.48	0.57	0.57	0.28
4389	New Canal USCG station, Lake Pontchartrain	30° 01.6'	90° 06.8'	+11 47	+12 09	*0.43	*0.43	0.51	0.52	0.26
4391	Chef Menteur, Chef Menteur Pass }	30° 03.9'	89° 48.0'	+6 25	+6 27	*0.88	*0.88	0.97	1.06	0.56
4393	Michoud Substation, ICWW }	30° 00.4'	89° 56.2'	+6 37	+6 22	*1.09	*1.09	1.23	1.39	0.70
4395	Shell Beach, Lake Borgne }	29° 52.0'	89° 40.3'	+5 34	+5 13	*1.17	*1.17	1.35	1.45	0.73
4397	Grand Pass }	30° 07.6'	89° 13.3'	+3 01	+2 36	*1.18	*1.18	1.14	1.47	0.73
4399	Chandeleur Light }	30° 03'	88° 52'	+1 50	+1 54	*0.98	*0.98	– –	1.2	0.6
4401	Comfort Island }	29° 49.4'	89° 16.2'	+2 47	+2 14	*1.28	*1.28	1.45	1.57	0.80
4403	Bay Gardene }	29° 35.9'	89° 37.1'	+4 04	+4 04	*1.16	*1.16	1.34	1.44	0.75
4405	Breton Islands }	29° 29.6'	89° 10.4'	+2 07	+2 08	*1.14	*1.14	1.37	1.37	0.69
4407	Jack Bay }	29° 22.0'	89° 20.7'	+3 12	+2 48	*1.00	*1.00	– –	1.2	0.6
4409	Grand Bay }	29° 23.1'	89° 22.8'	+2 54	+2 56	*1.08	*1.08	1.25	1.34	0.67
4411	Lonesome Bayou (Thomasin) }	29° 14'	89° 03'	+0 34	-0 29	*0.90	*0.90	– –	1.1	0.5
	Mississippi River									
4413	North Pass, Pass a Loutre }	29° 12.3'	89° 02.2'	+0 42	+0 43	*0.91	*0.91	1.08	1.10	0.55
4415	Venice, Grand Pass }	29° 16.4'	89° 21.1'	+2 38	+2 54	*0.82	*0.82	0.98	0.98	0.50
4417	Pilottown }	29° 10.7'	89° 15.5'	+1 59	+2 15	*0.82	*1.00	0.96	1.06	0.50
4419	Southeast Pass }	29° 07.0'	89° 02.7'	+0 37	-0 28	*0.98	*0.98	– –	1.2	0.6
4421	SOUTH PASS }	28° 59.4'	89° 08.4'	Daily predictions				1.18	1.22	0.61
4423	Port Eads, South Pass }	29° 00.9'	89° 09.6'	+0 56	-0 17	*0.90	*0.90	– –	1.1	0.5
4425	Southwest Pass }	28° 55.9'	89° 25.7'	+0 35	-0 13	*1.07	*1.07	– –	1.3	0.6
4427	Joseph Bayou }	29° 03.5'	89° 16.3'	+0 37	-0 17	*1.15	*1.15	– –	1.4	0.7
4429	New Orleans <12> }	29° 55'	90° 04'	– – –	– – –	– – –	– – –	– –	– –	– –
				on Grand Isle, p.212						
4431	Paris Road Bridge (ICWW) }	30° 00'	89° 56'	+5 53	+5 58	*1.04	*1.04	– –	1.1	0.6
4433	Empire Jetty }	29° 15.0'	89° 36.5'	-1 03	-1 45	*1.23	*1.23	– –	1.3	0.7
4435	Bastian Island }	29° 17.2'	89° 39.8'	+0 41	+0 12	*1.13	*1.13	– –	1.2	0.6
4437	Quatre Bayous Pass }	29° 18.6'	89° 51.2'	+2 18	+0 17	*1.23	*1.23	– –	1.3	0.6
4439	Barataria Pass }	29° 16'	89° 57'	+1 00	-0 10	*1.13	*1.13	– –	1.2	0.6
	Barataria Bay									
4441	EAST POINT, GRAND ISLE	29° 15.8'	89° 57.4'	Daily predictions				1.04	1.06	0.53
4443	Bayou Rigaud, Grand Isle }	29° 16'	89° 58'	+1 32	+0 46	*0.94	*0.94	– –	1.0	0.5
4445	Independence Island }	29° 18.6'	89° 56.3'	+2 29	+1 59	*0.85	*0.85	– –	0.9	0.4
4447	Manilla }	29° 25.6'	89° 58.6'	+2 32	+3 13	*0.94	*0.94	– –	1.0	0.5
4449	Caminada Pass (bridge) }	29° 12.6'	90° 02.4'	+0 20	+0 12	*0.94	*0.94	0.99	0.99	0.50
4451	Port Fourchon, Belle Pass }	29° 06.8'	90° 11.9'	-0 27	-0 29	*1.16	*1.16	1.21	1.23	0.62
4453	Leeville, Bayou Lafourche }	29° 14.9'	90° 12.7'	+3 00	+3 00	*0.83	*0.83	0.85	0.88	0.44
4455	East Timbalier Island, Timbalier Bay}	29° 04.6'	90° 17.1'	+0 07	+0 53	*1.22	*1.22	1.25	1.32	0.66
4457	Timbalier Island, Timbalier Bay }	29° 05'	90° 32'	+0 19	+0 23	*1.13	*1.13	– –	1.2	0.6
4459	Pelican Islands, Timbalier Bay }	29° 07.7'	90° 25.4'	+2 26	+2 26	*1.13	*1.13	– –	1.2	0.6
4461	Wine Island, Terrebonne Bay }	29° 04.7'	90° 37.1'	+1 08	+1 02	*1.23	*1.23	– –	1.3	0.6
4463	Cocodrie, Terrebonne Bay }	29° 14.7'	90° 39.7'	+1 22	+1 33	*0.98	*0.98	1.01	1.05	0.53
4465	East Isle Dernieres, Lake Pelto }	29° 04.3'	90° 38.40'	-0 55	-0 43	*1.19	*1.19	1.22	1.28	0.64
4467	Caillou Boca }	29° 03.8'	90° 48.4'	+0 40	+0 48	*1.32	*1.32	– –	1.4	0.7
4469	Raccoon Point, Caillou Bay }	29° 03.5'	90° 57.7'	-0 03	-0 20	*1.60	*1.60	– –	1.6	0.8
4471	Texas Gas Platform, Caillou Bay }	29° 10.4'	90° 58.5'	-0 49	-0 20	*1.35	*1.35	1.22	1.51	0.81
4473	Ship Shoal Light }	28° 55'	91° 04'	-1 54	-1 50	*1.51	*1.51	– –	1.6	0.8
	Atchafalaya Bay			on Galveston, p.216						
4475	Eugene Island, north of	29° 22.4'	91° 23.0'	-1 48	-1 51	*1.34	*1.23	1.39	1.96	1.07
4477	Point Au Fer }	29° 20'	91° 21'	-0 21	-2 26	*1.40	*1.40	– –	2.0	1.0
4479	Shell Island }	29° 28'	91° 18'	+0 54	-0 39	*1.07	*1.07	– –	1.5	0.7
4481	Stouts Pass, Six Mile Lake }	29° 44.6'	91° 13.8'	+2 09	+2 32	*0.61	*0.23	0.74	0.89	0.44

Endnotes can be found at the end of table 2.

TABLE 2 – TIDAL DIFFERENCES AND OTHER CONSTANTS

No.	PLACE	POSITION		DIFFERENCES				RANGES		Mean Tide Level
				Time		Height				
		Latitude	Longitude	High Water	Low Water	High Water	Low Water	Mean	Diurnal	
		North	West	h m	h m	ft	ft	ft	ft	ft
	LOUISIANA Time meridian, 90° W			on Galveston, p.216						
	Atchafalaya Bay-cont.									
4483	Point Chevreuil }	29° 31'	91° 33'	+1 02	−0 54	*1.07	*1.07	– –	1.5	0.8
4485	Rabbit Island, 5 miles south of }	29° 25'	91° 36'	−0 13	−2 00	*1.40	*1.40	– –	2.0	1.0
4487	South Point, Marsh Island }	29° 29'	91° 46'	−0 19	−1 57	*1.30	*1.30	– –	1.8	0.9
4489	Lighthouse Point }	29° 31'	92° 03'	−1 16	−2 17	*1.40	*1.40	– –	2.0	1.0
4491	Cote Blanche Island, West Cote Blanche Bay }	29° 44'	91° 43'	+2 19	+2 16	*1.00	*1.00	– –	1.4	0.7
4493	Southwest Pass, Vermilion Bay }	29° 35'	92° 02'	−0 32	−0 33	*1.14	*1.14	– –	1.6	0.8
4495	Cypremort Point, Vermillion Bay }	29° 42.8'	91° 52.8'	+2 18	+1 52	*1.18	*0.80	1.32	1.70	0.90
4497	Weeks Bay, Vermilion Bay }	29° 50.2'	91° 50.3'	+3 47	+2 30	*1.15	*0.83	1.27	1.61	0.88
4499	Freshwater Canal Locks }	29° 33.3'	92° 18.3'	−2 32	−2 17	*1.52	*1.73	1.48	2.16	1.26
4501	Mermentau River entrance }	29° 45'	93° 06'	−1 54	−0 59	*1.79	*1.79	– –	2.5	1.2
4503	Calcasieu Pass, East Jetty }	29° 46.1'	93° 20.6'	−2 27	−1 23	*1.38	*1.80	1.28	1.93	1.18
4505	Calcasieu Ship Channel, Bulk Terminal }	30° 11.4'	93° 18.0'	+3 48	+3 59	*0.94	*0.91	1.03	1.33	0.73
4507	Lake Charles, Calcasieu River }	30° 13.4'	93° 13.3'	+3 03	+3 54	*0.99	*0.81	1.06	1.40	0.77
	TEXAS									
4509	Sabine Pass, Texas Point }	29° 40.6'	93° 50.2'	−1 51	−1 03	*1.41	*1.66	1.36	1.98	1.18
4511	Sabine Pass }	29° 43.8'	93° 52.2'	−1 18	−0 38	*1.14	*1.14	1.09	1.60	0.96
4513	Port Arthur, Sabine Naches Canal }	29° 52.0'	93° 55.8'	+1 08	+1 08	*0.75	*0.53	0.83	1.04	0.57
4515	Rainbow Bridge, Neches River }	29° 58.8'	93° 52.9'	+4 04	+3 23	*0.75	*0.33	0.90	1.06	0.55
4517	Galveston Bay Entrance, north jetty }	29° 21.2'	94° 43.4'	−1 06	−0 42	*1.20	*1.17	1.23	1.70	0.96
4519	GALVESTON, Galveston Channel }	29° 18.6'	94° 47.6'	*Daily predictions*				1.02	1.41	0.81
	Galveston Bay									
4521	Port Bolivar }	29° 21.9'	94° 46.8'	+0 57	+0 09	*1.00	*0.63	1.13	1.40	0.85
4523	Texas City, Turning Basin }	29° 23'	94° 53'	+0 33	+0 41	*1.00	*1.00	– –	1.4	0.7
4525	Eagle Point <20> }	29° 28.8'	94° 55.1'	+5 34	+2 38	*0.80	*0.80	1.01	1.09	0.60
4527	Clear Lake <20> }	29° 33.8'	95° 04.0'	+6 57	+5 19	*0.83	*0.83	1.05	1.16	0.63
4529	Morgans Point, Barbours Cut <20> }	29° 40.9'	94° 59.1'	+5 11	+4 17	*0.95	*0.40	1.14	1.31	0.72
4531	Lynchburg Landing, San Jacinto River <20> }	29° 45.9'	95° 04.7'	+4 55	+4 51	*1.06	*0.67	1.20	1.50	0.80
4533	Annie's Landing, San Jacinto River <20> }	29° 49.1'	95° 04.7'	+5 20	+5 16	*1.14	*0.83	1.26	1.59	0.88
4535	Manchester, Houston Ship Channel <20> }	29° 43.1'	95° 15.1'	+4 55	+5 05	*1.15	*0.83	1.27	1.64	0.90
4537	Round Point, Trinity Bay <20> }	29° 44'	94° 42'	+10 39	+5 15	*0.71	*0.71	– –	1.0	0.5
4539	Umbrella Point, Trinity Bay <20> }	29° 40.8'	94° 52.1'	+4 41	+3 39	*0.93	*0.33	1.14	1.27	0.67
4541	Point Barrow, Trinity Bay }	29° 44'	94° 50'	+5 48	+4 43	*0.79	*0.79	– –	1.1	0.5
4543	Rollover Pass, East Bay }	29° 30.9'	94° 30.8'	+4 25	+3 16	*0.95	*0.53	1.10	1.35	0.71
4545	High Island, ICWW }	29° 35.6'	94° 23.4'	+4 18	+4 05	*0.95	*0.60	1.07	1.35	0.72
4547	Gilchrist, East Bay }	29° 31'	94° 29'	+3 16	+4 18	*0.86	*0.86	– –	1.2	0.6
4549	Jamaica Beach, West Bay }	29° 12'	94° 59'	+2 38	+3 31	*0.71	*0.71	– –	1.0	0.5
4551	Alligator Point, West Bay }	29° 10'	95° 08'	+2 39	+2 33	*0.64	*0.64	– –	0.9	0.4
4553	Christmas Bay }	29° 02.5'	95° 10.5'	+4 47	+2 37	*0.58	*0.23	0.71	0.82	0.42
4555	Galveston Pleasure Pier }	29° 17.1'	94° 47.3'	−1 33	−1 03	*1.40	*1.30	1.46	2.04	1.12
4557	San Luis Pass }	29° 05.7'	95° 06.8'	+0 10	+0 11	*1.06	*0.80	1.16	1.50	0.81
4559	Freeport, US Coast Guard Station }	28° 56.6'	95° 18.1'	−1 18	−1 08	*1.23	*0.77	1.40	1.78	0.93
4561	Sargent, ICWW }	28° 46.3'	95° 37.0'	+3 04	+0 17	*0.51	*0.13	0.64	0.72	0.36
4563	Matagorda City, ICWW }	28° 46.2'	95° 54.8'	+3 13	+0 51	*0.41	*0.17	0.49	0.54	0.30
4565	PORT O'CONNOR, MATAGORDA BAY }	28° 27'	96° 24'	*Daily predictions, p.220*				– –	0.5	0.2
4567	Port Lavaca, Matagorda Bay }	28° 37'	96° 37'	– – –	– – –	– – –	– – –	– –	0.7	0.3
4569	Rockport, Aransas Bay }	28° 01.3'	97° 02.8'	– – –	– – –	– – –	– – –	0.36	0.36	0.18
4571	Port Aransas (H. Caldwell Pier) }	27° 49.6'	97° 03.0'	−0 46	−1 26	*1.15	*0.77	1.30	1.64	0.88
4573	Corpus Christi }	27° 34.8'	97° 13.0'	−1 09	−1 30	*1.17	*0.73	1.31	1.63	0.93
4575	Riviera Beach, Baffin Bay }	27° 17'	97° 40'	– – –	– – –	– – –	– – –	– –	0.3	0.1
				on Padre Island, p.224						
4577	PADRE ISLAND (south end) }	26° 04.1'	97° 09.4'	*Daily predictions*				1.25	1.47	0.87
4579	Queen Isabella Causeway (east end) }	26° 04.7'	97° 10.2'	+0 24	+0 21	*0.87	*0.75	1.11	1.28	0.68
4581	Queen Isabella Causeway (west end) }	26° 04.3'	97° 11.5'	+0 52	+0 30	*0.81	*0.63	1.05	1.19	0.62
4583	Port Isabel }	26° 03.6'	97° 12.9'	+0 10	+0 26	*0.92	*1.00	1.15	1.37	0.74
4585	South Bay entrance }	26° 03.1'	97° 10.9'	+0 14	+0 21	*0.91	*0.94	1.14	1.35	0.72
	MEXICO <13> Gulf of Mexico			on Tampico Harbor, p.228						
4587	Matamoros }	25° 53'	97° 31'	+0 55	+0 40	*1.00	*1.00	– –	1.4	0.7
4589	TAMPICO HARBOR (Madero) }	22° 13'	97° 51'	*Daily predictions*				– –	1.4	0.7
4591	Tuxpan }	21° 00'	97° 20'	+0 02	+0 04	*1.21	*1.21	– –	1.7	0.8
4593	Veracruz }	19° 12'	96° 08'	−0 19	−0 12	*1.21	*1.21	– –	1.7	0.8
4595	Alvarado }	18° 46'	95° 46'	+0 51	+0 27	*0.93	*0.93	– –	1.3	0.6
4597	Coatzacoalcos }	18° 09'	94° 25'	−0 40	+0 05	*1.07	*1.07	– –	1.5	0.7
4599	Frontera }	18° 32'	92° 39'	−0 18	−0 27	*1.14	*1.14	– –	1.6	0.8
4601	Progreso }	21° 18'	89° 40'	+1 19	+0 23	*1.29	*1.29	– –	1.8	0.9
	BELIZE			on Key West, p.172						
4603	Belize City	17° 30'	88° 11'	+0 14	+0 47	*0.46	*0.46	0.6	0.7	0.4
4605	Punta Gorda	16° 06'	88° 49'	−0 27	+0 30	*0.46	*0.46	0.6	0.8	0.4
	GUATEMALA <13>									
4607	Rio Dulce entrance	15° 50'	88° 49'	−1 25	−1 35	*0.92	*0.92	1.2	1.5	0.7

Endnotes can be found at the end of table 2.

TABLE 2 – TIDAL DIFFERENCES AND OTHER CONSTANTS

No.	PLACE	POSITION		DIFFERENCES				RANGES		Mean Tide Level
				Time		Height				
		Latitude	Longitude	High Water	Low Water	High Water	Low Water	Mean	Diurnal	
		North	**West**	h m	h m	ft	ft	ft	ft	ft
	HONDURAS <13> Time meridian, 90° W					on Key West, p.172				
4609	Puerto Cortes	15° 50'	87° 57'	−0 43	−0 02	*0.38	*0.38	0.5	0.6	0.2
4611	Port Royal, Isla de Roatan	16° 24'	86° 20'	−2 41	−2 35	*0.92	*0.92	1.2	1.4	0.6
4613	Puerto Castilla	16° 00'	86° 02'	−0 48	−0 13	*0.46	*0.46	0.6	0.8	0.4
4615	Isla de Guanaja	16° 29'	85° 54'	−1 26	−1 42	*0.72	*0.72	1.0	1.3	0.6
4617	Harbor Bay, Great Swan Island	17° 24'	83° 56'	−1 18	−0 33	*0.51	*0.51	0.7	0.9	0.4
	NICARAGUA <13>				on Hampton Roads, p.120					
4619	Cabo Gracias a Dios	15° 00'	83° 10'	+0 23	−0 32	*0.57	*0.57	1.2	1.6	0.8
4621	Puerto Cabezas	14° 01'	83° 23'	+3 05	+3 11	*0.56	*0.56	1.4	1.9	0.9
4623	Cayos de Perlas	12° 25'	83° 25'	+4 53	+4 33	*0.46	*0.46	0.9	1.3	0.6
4625	Isla del Maiz Grande	12° 10'	83° 03'	+4 38	+4 13	*0.46	*0.46	0.9	1.3	0.3
4627	Bluefields Lagoon entrance	12° 00'	83° 42'	+3 54	+3 27	*0.28	*0.28	0.7	1.0	0.4
4629	San Juan del Norte (Greytown)	10° 55'	83° 42'	+4 03	+4 03	*0.28	*0.28	0.7	1.1	0.5
	COSTA RICA <13>				on Cristobal, p.232					
4631	Limon	10° 00'	83° 02'	−0 32	−0 29	*1.00	*1.00	0.7	1.2	0.5
	PANAMA <13> Time meridian, 75° W									
4633	Bocas del Toro, Almirante Bay	9° 21'	82° 15'	+0 21	+0 24	*1.14	*1.14	0.8	1.2	0.6
4635	CRISTOBAL (COLON)	9° 21'	79° 55'		Daily Predictions			0.7	1.1	0.4
4637	Bahia de Caledonia	8° 54'	77° 41'	+0 12	+0 00	*1.00	*1.00	0.7	1.1	0.4
	BERMUDA ISLANDS Time meridian, 60° W				on St. Georges Island, p.236			Mean	Spring	
4639	Ireland Island	32° 19'	64° 50'	+0 11	+0 13	*1.07	*1.23	2.6	3.1	1.6
4641	Ferry Reach (Biological Station)	32° 22.2'	64° 41.7'	−0 04	+0 03	*0.93	*1.00	2.4	2.9	1.3
4643	ST. GEORGES ISLAND	32° 22.4'	64° 42.2'		Daily Predictions			2.5	3.0	1.3
	BAHAMAS Time meridian, 75° W				on Settlement Point, p.240					
4645	Guinchos Cay	22° 45'	78° 07'	+0 06	+0 16	*0.79	*1.11	2.1	2.6	1.2
4647	Elbow Cay, Cay Sal Bank	23° 57'	80° 28'	+1 18	+1 28	*0.79	*1.11	2.1	2.6	1.2
4649	Fresh Creek, Andros Island	24° 44'	77° 48'	+0 05	−0 08	*0.97	*1.11	2.4	2.9	1.3
4651	North Cat Cay	25° 33'	79° 17'	+0 22	+0 32	*0.86	*1.11	2.3	2.8	1.3
4653	North Bimini	25° 44'	79° 18'	+0 05	+0 22	*0.90	*1.11	2.4	2.9	1.3
4655	Memory Rock	26° 57'	79° 07'	+0 16	+0 26	*0.86	*1.11	2.3	2.7	1.3
4657	SETTLEMENT POINT, GRAND BAHAMAS ISLAND	26° 42.6'	78° 59.8'		Daily predictions			2.7	3.1	1.4
4659	Pelican Harbor	26° 23'	76° 58'	+0 18	+0 28	*0.97	*1.11	2.6	3.1	1.4
4661	Nassau, New Providence Island	25° 05'	77° 21'	−0 08	−0 03	*0.98	*1.44	2.6	3.1	1.9
4663	Eleuthera Island, west coast	25° 15'	76° 19'	+2 09	+2 33	*0.94	*1.11	2.4	2.9	1.3
4665	Eleuthera Island, east coast	24° 56'	76° 09'	+0 11	+0 23	*0.82	*1.11	2.2	2.6	1.2
4667	The Bight, Cat Island	24° 19'	75° 26'	−0 37	−0 27	*0.97	*1.11	2.6	3.1	1.4
4669	San Salvador	24° 03'	74° 33'	−0 08	−0 06	*0.86	*1.11	2.3	2.8	1.3
4671	Clarence Harbor, Long Island	23° 06'	74° 59'	+0 41	+0 51	*0.97	*1.11	2.6	3.1	1.4
4673	Nurse Channel	22° 31'	75° 51'	+0 00	+0 10	*0.79	*1.11	2.1	2.6	1.1
4675	Datum Bay, Acklin Island	22° 10'	74° 18'	−0 21	−0 11	*0.75	*1.11	2.0	2.6	1.1
4677	Mathew Town, Great Inagua Island	20° 57'	73° 41'	+0 08	+0 28	*0.79	*1.11	2.1	2.6	1.2
4679	Abraham Bay, Mayaguana Island	22° 22'	73° 00'	+0 02	−0 10	*0.79	*1.11	2.0	2.5	1.1
4681	Hawks Nest Anchorage, Turks Islands	21° 26'	71° 07'	−0 27	−0 17	*0.79	*1.11	2.1	2.6	1.1
	CUBA				on Hampton Roads, p.120					
4683	La Isabela	22° 56'	80° 00'	+0 20	+0 16	*0.64	*0.64	1.6	2.0	0.9
4685	Bahia de Nuevitas entrance	21° 38'	77° 07'	−0 05	−0 46	*0.52	*0.52	1.3	1.5	0.7
4687	Nuevitas, Bahia de Nuevitas	21° 35'	77° 15'	+1 32	+1 33	*0.56	*0.56	1.4	1.6	0.7
4689	Puerto Padre	21° 14'	76° 33'	−0 05	−0 10	*0.84	*0.84	2.1	2.4	1.1
4691	Puerto de Gibara	21° 07'	76° 07'	−1 06	−1 03	*0.76	*0.76	1.9	2.2	1.0
4693	Bahia de Nipe entrance	20° 47'	75° 34'	−0 55	−1 01	*0.81	*0.81	2.0	2.3	1.1
4695	Antilla, Bahia de Nipe	20° 50'	75° 44'	−0 37	−0 44	*0.89	*0.89	2.2	2.5	1.2
4697	Bahia de Levisa entrance	20° 45'	75° 28'	−1 03	−1 07	*0.77	*0.77	1.9	2.2	1.0
4699	Sagua de Tanamo, Bahia de	20° 43'	75° 19'	−1 00	−1 08	*0.76	*0.76	1.9	2.2	1.0
4701	MOA, HOLGUIN	20° 39.2'	74° 54.6'		Daily predictions, p.316			1.74	− −	
4703	Baracoa	20° 21'	74° 30'	−1 14	−1 18	*0.68	*0.68	1.7	2.0	0.9
4705	Punta Maisi	20° 15'	74° 08'	−1 16	−1 20	*0.88	*0.88	2.2	2.8	1.2
					on San Juan, p.248			Mean	Diurnal	
4707	Guantanamo Bay	19° 54'	75° 09'	−0 17	−0 23	*0.89	*0.89	− −	1.4	0.7
4709	SANTIAGO DE CUBA	19° 59.1'	75° 52.5'		Daily predictions, p.312			1.01	− −	− −
4711	Puerto de Pilon	19° 54'	77° 19'	+0 11	+0 13	*0.72	*0.72	− −	1.2	0.6
4713	Manzanillo, Golfo de Guacanayabo	20° 21'	77° 07'	+1 41	+1 38	+1.39	+1.39	− −	2.2	1.1
4715	Casilda	21° 45'	79° 59'	+1 04	+0 52	*0.65	*0.65	− −	1.0	0.5
	Bahia de Cienfuegos									
4717	Punta Pasacaballos	22° 04'	80° 27'	+0 49	+0 58	*0.80	*0.80	− −	1.3	0.6
4719	CIENFUEGOS	22° 09.1'	80° 27.3'		Daily predictions, p.304			0.89	− −	− −
4721	Carapachibey, Isla de Pinos	21° 27'	82° 55'	+0 43	+0 52	*0.54	*0.54	− −	0.9	0.4
4723	La Coloma	22° 14'	83° 34'	+2 04	+2 23	*0.54	*0.54	− −	0.9	0.4
4725	Cabo San Antonio	21° 52'	84° 58'	−0 50	−0 07	*0.92	*0.92	1.2	1.5	0.8

Endnotes can be found at the end of table 2.

TABLE 2 – TIDAL DIFFERENCES AND OTHER CONSTANTS

No.	PLACE	POSITION Latitude	POSITION Longitude	DIFFERENCES Time High Water	DIFFERENCES Time Low Water	DIFFERENCES Height High Water	DIFFERENCES Height Low Water	RANGES Mean	RANGES Spring	Mean Tide Level
		North	West	h m	h m	ft	ft	ft	ft	ft
	CUBA Time meridian, 75° W			**on Key West, p.172**						
4727	Bahia Honda	22° 58'	83° 13'	−1 04	−0 23	*0.76	*0.76	1.0	1.4	0.7
4729	HAVANA	23° 08.9'	82° 20.2'	*Daily predictions, p. 308*				0.95	− −	− −
4731	Matanzas	23° 04'	81° 32'	−0 59	−0 59	*0.92	*0.92	1.2	1.5	0.8
4733	Cardenas	23° 04'	81° 12'	−0 11	+0 34	*1.08	*1.08	1.4	1.8	1.0
	JAMAICA			**on Galveston, p.216**				Mean	Diurnal	
4735	Port Morant	17° 53'	76° 20'	−7 45	−7 45	*0.57	*0.57	− −	0.8	0.4
4737	Port Royal }	17° 56'	76° 51'	−7 07	−8 14	*0.50	*0.50	− −	0.7	0.3
4739	Galleon Harbour	17° 54'	77° 04'	− − −	− − −	− − −	− − −	− −	0.8	0.4
4741	South Negril Point }	18° 18'	78° 24'	−2 47	−2 47	*1.21	*1.21	− −	1.7	0.8
4743	Montego Bay	18° 28'	77° 55'	−6 44	−6 40	*0.71	*0.71	− −	1.0	0.5
4745	St. Anns Bay	18° 25'	77° 14'	−7 17	−7 17	*0.57	*0.57	− −	0.8	0.4
4747	Grand Cayman }	19° 20'	81° 20'	−8 01	−8 01	*0.93	*0.93	− −	1.3	0.6
	HAITI and DOMINICAN REPUBLIC			**on San Juan, p.248**						
4749	Port−au−Prince	18° 33'	72° 21'	−0 35	−0 38	*0.99	*0.99	− −	1.6	0.8
4751	Massacre, Riviere du entrance	19° 43'	71° 46'	−1 04	−1 07	*1.44	*1.44	− −	2.3	1.2
4753	Puerto Plata	19° 49'	70° 42'	−1 12	−1 20	*1.44	*1.44	− −	2.3	1.2
4755	Santa Barbara de Samana	19° 12'	69° 20'	−0 54	−0 53	*1.25	*1.25	− −	2.0	1.0
4757	Sanchez	19° 13'	69° 36'	−0 40	−0 43	*2.05	*2.05	− −	3.3	1.6
				on Galveston, p.216						
4759	Saona, Isla }	18° 10'	68° 40'	− − −	− − −	− − −	− − −	− −	0.6	0.3
4761	La Romana }	18° 25'	68° 57'	− − −	− − −	− − −	− − −	− −	0.6	− −
4763	Santo Domingo }	18° 27'	69° 53'	−6 28	−11 01	*0.57	*0.57	− −	0.8	0.4
4765	Barahona }	18° 12'	71° 05'	− − −	− − −	− − −	− − −	− −	0.7	0.3
4767	Jacmel }	18° 13'	72° 34'	−10 00	−10 00	*1.43	*1.43	− −	2.0	1.0
	PUERTO RICO Time meridian, 60° W			**on Magueyes, p.244**						
4769	MAGUEYES ISLAND }	17° 58.3'	67° 02.8'	*Daily predictions*				0.65	0.67	0.34
4771	Guanica }	17° 58'	66° 55'	−1 22	+0 18	*1.00	*1.00	− −	0.7	0.3
4773	Playa de Ponce }	17° 58'	66° 37'	−0 39	−0 13	*1.14	*1.14	− −	0.8	0.4
4775	Playa Cortada }	17° 59'	66° 27'	+0 16	−0 37	*1.14	*1.14	− −	0.8	0.4
4777	Arroyo }	17° 58'	66° 04'	+0 52	+0 13	*1.14	*1.14	− −	0.8	0.4
4779	Puerto Maunabo }	18° 00'	65° 53'	−0 56	+1 13	*1.00	*1.00	− −	0.7	0.4
4781	Culebrita, Isla }	18° 19'	65° 14'	−2 34	+2 40	*1.57	*1.57	− −	1.1	0.6
4783	Puerto Ferro, Isla de Vieques }	18° 06'	65° 26'	−2 26	+3 01	*1.14	*1.14	− −	0.8	0.4
				on San Juan, p.248						
4785	Punta Mulas, Isla de Vieques	18° 09'	65° 26'	−0 14	−0 17	*0.72	*0.72	− −	1.2	0.6
4787	Roosevelt Roads	18° 14'	65° 37'	+0 02	+0 20	*0.63	*0.63	− −	1.0	0.5
4789	Ensenada Honda, Culebra Island	18° 18'	65° 17'	−0 34	−0 15	*0.63	*0.63	− −	1.0	0.5
4791	Culebra	18° 18.05'	65° 18.15'	−0 19	+0 08	*0.72	*0.73	0.78	1.14	0.55
4793	Playa de Fajardo	18° 20'	65° 38'	−0 10	−0 13	*0.99	*0.99	− −	1.6	0.8
4795	SAN JUAN	18° 27.5'	66° 07.0'	*Daily predictions*				1.10	1.58	0.76
4797	Mayaguez	18° 13.2'	67° 09.6'	−0 09	−0 11	*0.93	*0.76	1.06	1.40	0.69
4799	Puerto Real	18° 05'	67° 11'	−0 33	−0 26	*0.72	*0.72	− −	1.2	0.6
	LESSER ANTILLES & VIRGIN ISLANDS			**on Charlotte Amalie, p.252**						
	St. Thomas Island									
4801	Botany Bay }	18° 21.8'	65° 02.1'	+0 01	−0 17	*1.39	*1.39	0.90	1.28	0.58
4803	Dorothea Bay, Ruy Point }	18° 22.2'	64° 57.8'	+0 03	−0 17	*1.41	*1.41	0.93	1.29	0.58
4805	Magens Bay }	18° 22'	64° 55'	−0 06	−0 17	*1.59	*1.59	1.0	1.4	0.7
4807	Water Bay }	18° 20.9'	64° 51.8'	−0 11	−0 14	*1.30	*1.30	0.81	1.19	0.56
4809	Redhook Bay }	18° 19.1'	64° 51.1'	−0 46	+0 44	*1.28	*1.28	0.82	1.09	0.54
4811	CHARLOTTE AMALIE }	18° 20.1'	64° 55.2'	*Daily predictions*				0.70	0.79	0.40
4813	Dog Island }	18° 17.8'	64° 49.0'	−0 09	+0 06	*0.97	*0.97	0.63	0.80	0.40
	St. Johns Island									
4815	Lovango Cay }	18° 21.6'	64° 48.2'	−0 27	−0 31	*1.13	*1.13	0.61	1.06	0.49
4817	Leinster Point }	18° 22.0'	64° 43.2'	−0 12	−0 20	*1.22	*1.22	0.90	1.12	0.51
4819	Coral Harbor }	18° 20.9'	64° 43.0'	−0 13	−0 13	*1.08	*1.08	0.72	0.90	0.44
4821	Lameshur Bay }	18° 19.0'	64° 43.4'	−0 04	−0 06	*1.04	*1.14	0.72	0.82	0.41
	St. Croix Island			**on Lime Tree Bay, p.256**						
4823	Christiansted Harbor }	17° 45.0'	64° 42.3'	−1 37	+0 23	*1.03	*1.03	0.69	0.73	0.37
4825	LIME TREE BAY, ST.CROIX ISLAND }	17° 41.8'	64° 45.2'	*Daily predictions*				0.69	0.71	0.36
4827	Fredericksted }	17° 42.8'	64° 53.0'	−0 14	+0 59	*1.01	*1.00	0.70	0.73	0.36
4829	St. Barthelemy }	17° 54'	62° 51'	−3 26	−1 11	*1.87	*1.00	− −	1.4	0.7
4831	Pointe−a−Pitre, Guadeloupe	16° 14'	61° 32'	−4 28	−0 33	*3.24	*1.80	− −	1.0	0.5
				on Key West, p.172						
4833	Roseau, Dominica	15° 18'	61° 24'	−6 29	−6 05	*0.65	*0.65	0.7	1.2	0.6
4835	Fort−de−France, Martinique	14° 35'	61° 03'	−6 55	−6 18	*0.38	*0.38	0.5	− −	0.5
4837	Castries, St. Lucia	14° 01'	61° 00'	−7 09	−7 05	*0.62	*0.62	0.8	1.2	0.6
4839	Vieux Fort Bay, St. Lucia	13° 44'	60° 58'	−6 02	−5 38	*0.69	*0.69	0.9	− −	0.7
4841	Kingstown, St. Vincent <15>	13° 10'	61° 13'	−7 09	−6 38	*1.53	*1.53	2.0	2.7	1.4

Endnotes can be found at the end of table 2.

TABLE 2 – TIDAL DIFFERENCES AND OTHER CONSTANTS

No.	PLACE	POSITION Latitude	Longitude	DIFFERENCES Time High Water	Low Water	Height High Water	Low Water	RANGES Mean	Diurnal	Mean Tide Level
		North	West	h m	h m	ft	ft	ft	ft	ft
	LESSER ANTILLES & VIRGIN ISLANDS Time meridian, 60° W			**on Key West, p.172**						
4843	Bridgetown, Barbados	13° 06'	59° 38'	−6 28	−5 47	*1.30	*1.30	1.7	2.1	1.0
4845	Grenada	12° 04'	61° 45'	−7 26	−6 51	*0.92	*0.92	1.2	1.5	0.8
4847	Scarborough, Tobago	11° 11'	60° 44'	−6 40	−6 22	*1.60	*1.60	2.1	2.7	1.4
				on Cristobal, p.232						
4849	Schottegat, Curacao }	12° 07'	68° 56'	+0 25	+1 09	*0.82	*0.82	− −	0.9	0.5
4851	St. Nicolaas Bay, Aruba }	12° 26'	69° 54'	− − −	− − −	− − −	− − −	− −	0.8	0.4
	COLOMBIA <13> Time meridian, 75° W			**on Hampton Roads, p.120**						
4853	Isla de Providencia	13° 20'	81° 23'	+7 53	+7 53	*0.28	*0.28	0.7	1.1	0.4
				on Cristobal, p.232						
4855	Turbo	8° 10'	76° 45'	−0 49	−0 30	*1.43	*1.43	1.0	1.4	0.6
4857	Covenas	9° 20'	75° 40'	−1 06	−0 46	*1.14	*1.14	0.8	1.2	0.5
4859	Cartagena, Bahia de Cartagena	10° 24'	75° 33'	−1 16	−0 48	*1.00	*1.00	0.7	1.1	0.4
4861	Puerto Colombia	11° 00'	74° 58'	−0 52	−1 08	*1.29	*1.29	0.9	1.3	0.5
4863	Santa Marta	11° 18'	74° 12'	−1 19	−1 08	*1.00	*1.00	0.7	1.1	0.4
4865	Riohacha	11° 33'	72° 55'	−1 54	−1 09	*1.00	*1.00	0.7	1.1	0.4
	VENEZUELA Time meridian, 60° 30' W			**on Isla Zapara, p.260**				**Mean Spring**		
4867	ISLA ZAPARA, Lake Maracaibo	11° 00'	71° 35'	*Daily predictions*				2.8	3.0	2.7
4869	Bahia de Tablazos, Lake Maracaibo	10° 53'	71° 35'	+0 30	+0 11	*0.61	*0.31	2.1	2.3	1.5
4871	Punta de Palmas	10° 48'	71° 37'	+0 35	+0 16	*0.49	*0.31	1.6	1.8	1.2
				on Amuay, p.264				**Mean Diurnal**		
4873	AMUAY	11° 45'	70° 13'	*Daily predictions*				− −	1.2	0.6
4875	La Guaira }	10° 36'	66° 56'	−2 29	−1 59	+0.8	+1.0	− −	1.0	1.5
4877	Carenero }	10° 32'	66° 07'	−1 51	−1 59	+0.8	+1.0	− −	1.0	1.5
4879	Cumana }	10° 28'	64° 11'	−2 37	−1 02	−0.1	0.0	− −	1.1	0.5
4881	Porlamar, Isla de Margarita }	10° 57'	63° 51'	−1 19	−0 59	+0.6	0.0	− −	1.8	0.9
4883	Carupano }	10° 40'	63° 15'	−1 17	−0 42	+0.2	0.0	− −	1.4	0.7
	Gulf of Paria			**on Punta Gorda, p.268**				**Mean Spring**		
4885	Macuro	10° 39'	61° 56'	−1 15	−2 05	*0.38	*0.38	2.2	2.7	1.4
4887	Puerto de Hierro	10° 37'	62° 05'	−0 46	−1 19	*0.59	*0.59	3.3	4.2	2.0
4889	Barra de Maturin, channel entrance ..	10° 18'	62° 31'	−0 22	−0 45	−1.0	+0.2	4.6	5.7	2.8
4891	PUNTA GORDA, Rio San Juan	10° 10'	62° 38'	*Daily predictions*				5.8	7.1	3.2
4893	Boca Pedernales entrance	10° 01'	62° 12'	−0 03	−0 34	−1.3	+0.2	4.3	5.4	2.6
4895	Rio Orinoco entrance, Isla Ramon Isidro	8° 39'	60° 35'	+0 07	−0 12	+0.2	+1.0	5.0	6.7	3.8
	TRINIDAD Time meridian, 60° W									
4897	Staubles Bay	10° 41'	61° 39'	−0 37	−1 32	(*0.33+1.7)		1.9	2.5	2.8
4899	Carenage Bay	10° 41'	61° 36'	−0 28	−1 10	(*0.34+1.6)		2.0	2.6	2.7
4901	Port of Spain	10° 39'	61° 31'	−0 14	−0 42	(*0.31+1.4)		1.8	2.3	2.4
4903	Bonasse pier	10° 05'	61° 52'	−0 13	−0 45	−1.0	+1.4	3.4	4.4	3.4
4905	Erin Bay	10° 04'	61° 39'	−0 20	−1 11	−0.3	+1.2	4.3	5.6	3.6
4907	Guayaguayare Bay	10° 09'	61° 01'	−1 02	−1 39	(*0.53+1.3)		3.1	3.8	3.0
4909	Nariva River	10° 24'	61° 02'	−0 36	−1 46	(*0.41+1.3)		2.4	3.1	2.5
	GUYANA Time meridian, 56° 15' W			**on Suriname Rivier, p.272**						
4911	Parika, Essequibo River	6° 52'	58° 25'	+0 07	+0 31	+1.6	+1.0	6.6	8.3	5.6
4913	Georgetown	6° 48'	58° 10'	−0 13	−0 29	+0.9	+1.1	5.8	8.0	5.3
	SURINAM Time meridian, 45° W									
4915	Nickerie River	5° 57'	56° 59'	+0 09	+0 21	+1.1	0.0	7.1	9.2	4.9
4917	SURINAME RIVIER ENTRANCE	6° 00'	55° 14'	*Daily predictions*				6.0	7.6	4.3
4919	Paramaribo, Suriname Rivier	5° 49'	55° 09'	+1 09	+1 42	0.0	0.0	6.0	7.3	4.3
	FRENCH GUIANA Time meridian, 60° W									
4921	Rio Maroni entrance	5° 45'	53° 58'	+0 18	+0 24	+0.7	+1.2	5.5	7.2	5.2
4923	Iles du Salut	5° 17'	52° 35'	−0 07	−0 07	+1.7	+2.2	5.5	7.2	6.2
4925	Cayenne	4° 56'	52° 20'	+0 15	+0 15	+2.4	+1.8	6.6	7.8	6.4
	BRAZIL <16> Time meridian, 45° W									
4927	Cape Cassipore	3° 49'	51° 01'	+1 24	+1 19	+1.5	+0.3	7.2	9.5	5.2
4929	Rio Cunanl entrance	2° 50'	50° 53'	+2 10	+2 24	(*2.42−0.2)		14.5	19.0	10.1

Endnotes can be found at the end of table 2.

TABLE 2 – TIDAL DIFFERENCES AND OTHER CONSTANTS

No.	PLACE	POSITION		DIFFERENCES				RANGES		Mean Tide Level
		Latitude	Longitude	Time		Height		Mean	Spring	
				High Water	Low Water	High Water	Low Water			
		South	**West**	h m	h m	ft	ft	ft	ft	ft
	BRAZIL <16> Time meridian, 45° W					on Suriname Rivier, p.272				
4931	Ilha de Maraca anchorage	2° 09'	50° 30'	+1 40	+1 52	(*2.42−0.2)		14.5	19.0	10.1
4933	Ilha do Brigue, Amazon River	0° 55'	50° 05'	+7 09	+7 40	+8.3	+1.1	13.2	15.7	9.0
4935	Ponta Pedreira, Amazon River	0° 11'	50° 43'	+6 31	+6 43	*2.08	*2.23	12.3	16.2	9.0
4937	Macapa, Amazon River	0° 03'	51° 11'	+10 57	+12 13	+2.8	+0.4	8.4	9.5	5.9
4939	Canal de Braganca, Rio Para entrance	0° 23'	47° 55'	+6 09	+6 09	+1.8	−0.1	7.9	10.4	5.1
4941	Salinopolis	0° 39'	47° 23'	+2 38	+2 52	*1.99	*1.54	12.5	15.9	8.3
4943	Belem (Para)	1° 27'	48° 30'	+6 34	+7 37	+2.9	+0.7	8.2	10.1	6.1
4945	Ilhas de Sao Joao	1° 17'	44° 55'	+1 31	+1 31	*1.70	*1.31	10.7	14.1	7.0
4947	Sao Luiz	2° 32'	44° 18'	+2 28	+2 25	(*2.35−0.7)		14.1	17.1	9.3
4949	Santana, Recifes de	2° 16'	43° 36'	+0 46	+0 45	*1.58	*1.15	10.0	13.1	6.5
4951	Tutoia, Baia da	2° 46'	42° 14'	+0 11	+0 10	+2.4	+0.4	8.0	10.0	5.7
4953	Luis Correia	2° 53'	41° 40'	+0 01	+0 13	+1.8	+0.4	7.4	9.4	5.4
4955	Camocim	2° 53'	40° 52'	+1 07	+1 06	+2.0	+0.4	7.6	9.7	5.5
4957	Rio Ceara (bar)	3° 41'	38° 37'	−0 13	−0 21	+0.2	−0.1	6.3	8.3	4.3
4959	Fortaleza	3° 43'	38° 29'	−0 08	−0 12	+0.2	−0.3	6.5	8.5	4.2
	Time meridian, 30° W					on Recife, p.276				
4961	Fernando de Noronha	3° 50'	32° 25'	+1 32	+1 33	−1.2	−0.5	4.5	6.0	2.9
4963	Rocas, Atol das	3° 51'	33° 49'	+1 43	+1 44	+2.3	0.0	7.5	10.0	4.9
	Time meridian, 45° W									
4965	Macau, Rio Acu	5° 06'	36° 41'	+1 29	+1 58	+0.6	−0.1	5.9	7.6	4.1
4967	Natal	5° 47'	35° 12'	+0 28	+0 30	+0.1	−0.2	5.5	7.3	3.7
4969	Cabedelo	6° 58'	34° 50'	+0 36	+0 37	+0.1	−0.2	5.5	7.2	3.7
4971	Tambau	7° 06'	34° 50'	−0 04	−0 03	+0.7	−0.1	6.0	7.6	4.1
4973	RECIFE	8° 03'	34° 52'		Daily predictions			5.3	7.1	3.8
4975	Maceio	9° 40'	35° 43'	+0 10	+0 14	−0.3	−0.2	5.1	6.8	3.6
4977	Rio Sao Francisco (bar)	10° 31'	36° 24'	+0 06	+0 14	−0.7	0.0	4.5	6.0	3.5
4979	Aracaju	10° 56'	37° 03'	+0 33	+0 48	−0.8	−0.3	4.7	6.1	3.3
4981	Salvador	12° 58'	38° 31'	−0 02	−0 08	+0.6	+0.4	5.5	7.4	4.3
4983	Ponta da Areia	12° 47'	38° 30'	+0 10	+0 06	+0.6	−0.1	5.9	7.6	4.0
4985	Morro de Sao Paulo	13° 21'	38° 54'	−0 11	−0 13	−0.6	0.0	4.6	6.0	3.5
4987	Camamu	13° 54'	38° 58'	−0 08	−0 04	−0.2	+0.1	4.9	6.5	3.8
4989	Ilheus	14° 48'	39° 02'	−0 33	−0 32	−0.9	−0.3	4.6	5.8	3.2
4991	Canavieiras	15° 40'	38° 56'	+0 16	+0 22	−1.0	−0.2	4.5	5.8	3.1
4993	Santa Cruz Cabralia	16° 17'	39° 02'	−0 35	−0 35	−1.2	−0.5	4.5	6.0	2.9
4995	Cumuruxatiba	17° 06'	39° 11'	−0 23	−0 09	+0.4	+0.3	5.3	7.2	4.2
4997	Caravelas	17° 43'	39° 09'	−0 50	−0 49	−0.8	−0.5	4.9	6.4	3.1
4999	Abrolhos Anchorage	17° 58'	38° 42'	−0 01	+0 04	+0.6	−0.1	5.7	7.6	4.2
5001	Vitoria	20° 19'	40° 19'	−0 34	−0 35	*0.66	*0.75	3.3	4.6	2.6
5003	Guarapari	20° 40'	40° 30'	+0 12	+0 17	*0.62	*0.75	3.1	4.2	2.5
						on Rio de Janeiro, p.280				
5005	Sao Joao da Barra	21° 38'	41° 03'	+0 34	−0 42	−0.1	−0.2	2.6	3.6	2.1
5007	Macae (Imbitiba Bay)	22° 23'	41° 46'	−0 23	−1 08	0.0	−0.2	2.7	3.6	2.1
5009	Armacao dos Buzios	22° 45'	41° 53'	−0 01	−0 55	−0.1	−0.1	2.5	3.4	2.1
5011	Cabo Frio	23° 00'	42° 03'	−0 03	−0 05	*0.91	*0.90	2.3	3.2	2.0
5013	RIO DE JANEIRO	22° 54'	43° 10'		Daily predictions			2.5	3.5	2.2
5015	Itacurussa	22° 56'	43° 55'	+0 50	−0 26	0.0	−0.1	2.6	3.3	2.2
5017	Angra dos Reis	23° 01'	44° 19'	−0 35	−0 40	*0.86	*0.86	2.1	3.0	1.9
5019	Parati	23° 14'	44° 43'	−0 09	−1 25	−0.1	0.0	2.4	3.4	2.2
5021	Sao Sebastiao	23° 49'	45° 24'	−0 28	−1 24	*0.94	*1.00	2.3	3.3	2.2
5023	SANTOS	23° 57'	46° 19'		Daily predictions, p.284			2.6	3.8	2.4
5025	Cananeia	25° 01'	47° 56'	+1 09	−1 09	+0.4	+0.2	2.7	4.1	2.6
5027	Paranagua	25° 31'	48° 27'	+1 51	−1 32	+1.8	+0.2	4.1	6.0	3.2
5029	Sao Francisco do Sul	26° 15'	48° 38'	+0 38	− − −	+0.8	−0.1	3.4	4.8	2.6
5031	Itajai	26° 54'	48° 39'	−0 08	−0 16	(*0.76+0.4)		1.9	2.8	2.1
5033	Porto Belo	27° 09'	48° 33'	−0 38	−0 28	*0.74	*0.74	1.8	2.5	1.7
5035	Florianopolis	27° 36'	48° 34'	−0 14	+0 15	*0.69	*0.70	1.7	2.4	1.6
5037	Imbituba	28° 14'	48° 39'	−0 17	−1 10	*0.54	*0.50	1.4	2.0	1.2
5039	Laguna	28° 30'	48° 47'	+1 10	−1 31	(*0.32+0.4)		0.8	1.2	1.1
5041	Barra do Rio Grande <18> }	32° 10'	52° 05'	− − −	− − −	− − −	− − −	− −	0.8	0.3
	URUGUAY					on Buenos Aires, p.288				
5043	Montevideo	34° 55'	56° 13'	−5 10	−7 11	(*0.52+1.6)		1.1	1.4	3.0
5045	Colonia, Rio de la Plata	34° 28'	57° 51'	+0 17	−0 33	(*0.52+1.2)		1.1	1.3	2.6
	ARGENTINA									
	Rio de la Plata									
5047	BUENOS AIRES	34° 34'	58° 23'		Daily predictions			2.1	2.5	2.6
5049	La Plata	34° 50'	57° 53'	−1 50	−2 04	+0.2	+0.6	1.7	2.0	3.0
5051	Banco Chico	34° 50'	57° 30'	−3 00	−3 24	+0.8	+0.8	2.1	2.5	3.4
5053	Banco Cuirassier	35° 06'	57° 08'	−5 25	−5 39	+0.8	+0.8	2.1	2.5	3.4
5055	Punta Piedras	35° 26'	57° 07'	−7 10	−7 23	+2.2	+1.1	3.2	3.8	4.2
5057	Punta Norte del Cabo San Antonio <17>	36° 18'	56° 47'	−8 50	−9 26	+1.2	+0.3	3.0	3.7	3.3
5059	Mar del Plata <17>	38° 03'	57° 33'	−0 02	+0 14	+0.7	+0.2	2.6	3.0	3.0
5061	Quequen <17>	38° 35'	58° 42'	−0 18	−0 22	+1.5	−0.3	3.9	4.2	3.2

Endnotes can be found at the end of table 2.

TABLE 2 – TIDAL DIFFERENCES AND OTHER CONSTANTS

No.	PLACE	POSITION		DIFFERENCES				RANGES		Mean Tide Level
				Time		Height				
		Latitude	Longitude	High Water	Low Water	High Water	Low Water	Mean	Spring	
		South	West	h m	h m	ft	ft	ft	ft	ft
	ARGENTINA Time meridian, 45° W			on Puerto Ingeniero White, p.292						
5063	Faro Recalada	39° 00'	61° 16'	−0 48	−0 28	−4.9	−1.3	6.5	7.1	5.3
5065	Monte Hermoso	38° 59'	61° 41'	−0 46	−0 40	−3.4	−1.2	7.9	9.1	6.2
	Bahia Blanca									
5067	Punta Ancla	38° 57'	62° 00'	−0 57	−0 21	−1.9	−0.9	9.1	9.9	7.1
5069	Puerto Rosales	38° 55'	62° 04'	−0 28	−0 06	−0.5	−0.5	10.1	11.0	8.0
5071	Puerto Belgrano	38° 53'	62° 06'	−0 22	−0 07	−0.5	−0.3	9.9	11.0	8.0
5073	PUERTO INGENIERO WHITE	38° 47'	62° 16'	Daily Predictions				10.1	11.6	8.5
5075	General Daniel Cerri	38° 45'	62° 24'	+0 16	+0 20	+1.8	+0.1	11.8	12.9	9.4
5077	Canal del Sur, Isla Bermejo	39° 01'	61° 58'	−0 55	−0 24	−2.2	−0.9	8.8	9.6	6.9
5079	Canal Bermejo, Isla Trinidad	39° 05'	61° 58'	−0 57	−0 26	−2.7	−1.0	8.4	9.2	6.6
5081	Punta Lobos, Isla Trinidad	39° 11'	61° 52'	−0 58	−0 41	−3.3	−1.2	8.0	8.8	6.2
5083	El Chara (Punta Laberinto)	39° 26'	62° 03'	−1 19	−0 51	−2.9	−1.0	8.3	9.2	6.5
5085	Bahia Anegada, Islote NW	40° 01'	62° 10'	−2 07	−2 00	(*0.63−0.6)		6.4	7.1	4.8
5087	Bahia San Blas	40° 33'	62° 14'	−3 47	−3 41	*0.50	*0.35	5.6	6.0	4.0
5089	Faro Segunda Barranca	40° 47'	62° 17'	−4 51	−4 40	(*0.53−0.5)		5.4	5.9	4.0
5091	Punta Redonda, Rio Negro entrance	41° 02'	62° 46'	−6 16	−6 10	−1.6	−1.4	9.9	11.2	7.0
	Golfo San Matias			on Comodoro Rivadavia, p.296						
5093	Caleta de los Loros	41° 02'	64° 06'	+7 14	+7 08	*1.45	*1.39	20.3	24.0	14.8
5095	Puerto San Antonio	40° 48'	64° 52'	+7 30	+7 23	(*1.57−1.6)		21.9	25.6	14.6
	Golfo San Jose									
5097	San Roman	42° 15'	64° 14'	+7 15	+7 18	(*1.42−1.1)		19.8	23.4	13.5
5099	Pueyrredon (Fondeadero)	42° 24'	64° 09'	+7 46	+7 40	(*1.52−2.2)		21.2	24.6	13.5
5101	La Argentina (Fondeadero)	42° 23'	64° 34'	+7 04	+6 58	*1.31	*1.36	18.0	23.3	13.5
5103	Punta Norte	42° 05'	63° 46'	+6 50	+6 44	−0.8	−1.4	14.5	17.0	9.5
5105	Caleta Valdes	42° 31'	63° 36'	+5 04	+4 58	−5.2	−1.9	10.6	12.4	6.7
5107	Punta Delgada	42° 46'	63° 38'	+4 08	+4 02	−5.8	−2.0	10.1	11.7	6.4
	Golfo Nuevo									
5109	Punta Ninfas (Fondeadero)	42° 57'	64° 25'	+2 48	+3 31	−2.3	−1.0	12.6	15.4	8.6
5111	Puerto Piramides	42° 35'	64° 17'	+2 56	+3 33	−2.7	−1.3	12.5	15.0	8.3
5113	Puerto Madryn	42° 46'	65° 02'	+3 08	+3 42	−0.8	−0.1	13.2	16.0	9.8
5115	Bahia Engano	43° 20'	65° 04'	+2 06	+2 00	−2.7	−1.3	12.5	15.2	8.2
5117	Isla Escondida	43° 43'	65° 17'	+2 10	+2 05	−3.3	−0.3	10.9	13.1	8.5
5119	Bahia Janssen	44° 02'	65° 14'	+1 48	+2 03	−4.1	−1.9	11.7	13.9	7.3
5121	Cabo Raso	44° 20'	65° 14'	+1 41	+1 26	−4.8	−1.6	10.7	12.4	7.0
5123	Bahia Cruz	44° 27'	65° 19'	+2 13	+2 07	−6.1	−2.1	9.9	11.5	6.2
5125	Santa Elena, Puerto	44° 31'	65° 22'	+1 45	+1 40	−3.1	−0.4	11.2	13.6	8.5
5127	Bahia Camarones	44° 54'	65° 36'	+1 10	+1 14	−2.3	+0.1	11.5	13.7	9.2
	Golfo San Jorge									
5129	Caleta Leones	45° 03'	65° 37'	+1 11	+1 05	−0.7	−0.2	13.4	14.7	9.8
5131	Bahia Gil (Caleta Horno)	45° 02'	65° 41'	+0 42	+0 36	−1.7	+0.3	11.9	14.1	9.6
5133	Puerto Melo	45° 01'	65° 50'	+0 27	+0 24	−1.5	+0.1	12.3	14.6	9.6
5135	Isla Tova	45° 06'	65° 59'	+0 27	+0 24	−1.5	+0.1	12.3	14.6	9.6
5137	Bahia Bustamante	45° 07'	66° 32'	+0 28	+0 23	−0.8	+0.7	12.4	14.7	10.2
5139	COMODORO RIVADAVIA	45° 52'	67° 29'	Daily predictions				14.0	16.3	10.3
5141	Cabo Blanco	47° 12'	65° 45'	−1 15	−1 20	−2.3	−0.3	11.9	13.2	9.0
5143	Puerto Deseado	47° 45'	65° 55'	−2 52	−2 44	−0.6	+1.0	12.4	14.5	10.5
5145	Bahia Oso Marino	47° 56'	65° 48'	−3 35	−3 40	−1.2	+1.2	11.5	14.1	10.3
5147	Bahia de los Nodales	48° 01'	65° 57'	−3 01	−3 06	−1.2	+0.1	12.6	15.3	9.7
5149	Bahia Laura	48° 23'	66° 29'	−5 28	−5 28	+6.7	−1.9	22.5	25.4	12.7
5151	Bahia San Julian (Punta Pena)	49° 15'	67° 40'	−4 58	−5 04	(*1.40−1.4)		19.5	23.6	13.0
				on Punta Loyola, p.300						
5153	Santa Cruz (Punta Quilla)	50° 07'	68° 25'	+0 43	+0 44	+0.2	+0.1	26.0	32.4	20.4
5155	Ria Coig	50° 57'	69° 10'	−0 05	−0 04	0.0	−0.7	26.6	32.2	19.9
5157	PUNTA LOYOLA	51° 36'	69° 01'	Daily predictions				25.9	32.4	20.3
5159	Rio Gallegos (Reduccion Beacon)	51° 37'	69° 13'	+0 21	+0 30	+4.2	+1.1	29.0	36.2	22.9
5161	Cabo Virgenes	52° 21'	68° 22'	−0 36	−0 55	−2.1	0.0	23.8	29.8	19.2
	Tierra del Fuego <19>			on Comodoro Rivadavia, p.296						
5163	Bahia San Sebastian	53° 10'	68° 30'	−7 50	−7 55	*1.69	*1.91	22.8	28.6	17.7
5165	Rio Grande (Muelle)	53° 48'	67° 41'	−7 50	−7 55	*1.15	*1.18	15.8	19.2	11.8
5167	Cabo San Pablo	54° 17'	66° 42'	−8 48	−8 53	*1.17	*1.27	16.0	19.3	12.2
				on Puerto Ingeniero White, p.292						
5169	Bahia Thetis	54° 38'	65° 15'	+1 00	+1 07	−2.0	−0.6	8.7	10.6	7.2
	SOUTH ATLANTIC OCEAN ISLANDS Time meridian, 60° W			on Pictou, p.8						
	Falkland Islands									
5171	Port Louis (Berkeley Sound)	51° 33'	58° 09'	+7 50	+7 47	−0.9	−1.0	3.3	4.2	3.0
5173	Stanley Harbor	51° 42'	57° 51'	+7 51	+7 48	−1.0	−1.0	3.2	4.2	2.9
	South Georgia									
5175	Royal Bay (Moltke Harbor)	54° 31'	36° 01'	+9 58	+10 19	*0.36	*0.13	1.7	2.3	1.2
5177	Leith Harbor	54° 08'	36° 41'	+9 15	+9 35	*0.64	*0.65	2.0	2.7	2.5
	Time meridian, local									
	South Orkneys									
5179	Scotia Bay, Laurie Island	60° 44'	44° 39'	+8 21	+8 32	−0.3	−0.6	3.5	5.0	3.5

Endnotes can be found at the end of table 2.

TABLE 2 – TIDAL DIFFERENCES AND OTHER CONSTANTS

No.	PLACE	POSITION		DIFFERENCES				RANGES		Mean Tide Level
				Time		Height				
		Latitude	Longitude	High Water	Low Water	High Water	Low Water	Mean	Spring	
	SOUTH ATLANTIC OCEAN ISLANDS Time meridian, local	**South**	**West**	h m	h m	ft	ft	ft	ft	ft
				on Pictou, p.8						
	South Shetlands									
5181	Port Foster, Deception Island	62° 58'	60° 34'	+8 26	+8 38	0.0	−0.1	3.3	4.3	3.9
	Time meridian, 45° W									
5183	Admiralty Bay	62° 03'	58° 24'	+9 49	+10 05	−0.5	−0.4	3.1	4.4	3.5

Endnotes can be found at the end of table 2.

ENDNOTES

* RATIO. If the ratio is accompanied by a correction factor multiply the heights of the high and low waters at the reference station by the ratio and then apply the correction factor. See note and example on pages 309 and 310.

† The tide at this location is chiefly diurnal. SEE CAUTION NOTE ON PAGE 305.

<1> Neap low water falls lower than spring low water.

<2> Wharves are dry at low water.

<3> There is a bore in the Petitcodiac River. It arrives at Moncton about 1h 38m before high water at St. John: its height is about 3 to 3 1/2 feet on average spring tides, but it sometimes exceeds 5 feet on highest tides. On small tides it is not much more than a large ripple.

<4> The Reversing Falls at St. John—The most turbulence in the gorge occurs on days when the tides are largest. On largest tides the outward fall is between 15 and 16 1/2 feet and is accompanied by a greater turbulence than the inward fall which is between 11 and 12 1/2 feet. The outward fall is at its greatest between 2 hours before and 1 hour after low water at St John: the inward fall is greater just before the time of high water.

<5> For Eastern Standard, time subtract one hour from the predictions obtained using these differences.

<6> Low water time difference is +2h 47m. SEE CAUTION NOTE ON PAGE FOLLOWING LISTING.

<7> Tidal information applies only during low river stages.

<8> Values for the Hudson River above the George Washington Bridge are based upon averages for the six months May to October, when the freshwater discharge is at a minimum.

<9> In Albermarle and Pamlico Sounds, except near the inlets, the periodic tide has a mean range of less than 0.5 foot.

<11> In Choctawhatchee and Perdido Bays the periodic tide has a mean range of less than 0.5 foot.

<12> At New Orleans the diurnal range of the tide during low river stages averages 0.8 foot. There is no periodic tide at high river stages.

<13> For places on the Pacific coast, see "Tide Tables, West Coast of North and South America."

<14> Inside, in the various bays, except near the inlets, the periodic tide has a mean range of less than 0.5 foot.

<15> Spring range is given instead of diurnal range.

<16> A "Pororoca", a bore, reported to vary from 5 to 15 feet at spring tides, occurs in the Araguary, Guama and Guajara Rivers.

<17> Predictions will be approximate.

<18> Diurnal range is given instead of spring range.

<19> For places in Magellan Strait, on the south coast of Tierra del Fuego and on the Pacific coast, see "Tide Tables, West Coast of North and South America."

<20> The time differences should be applied only to the higher high and the lower low water times of the reference station.

<21> From Oak Hill southward in Mosquito Lagoon the periodic tide is negligible.

<22> In Indian River north of Palm Bay, in Banana River and in Banana Creek, the periodic tides are negligible.

<24> The periodic tide is negligible, at this location and above.

<25> Data is for low river levels. At high levels the tidal range is reduced.

<26> The periodic range of the tide is negligible at this location.

<27> The periodic range of the tide is negligible inside Sugarloaf Sound.

<29> "The times listed for this reference station are the Greenwich Intervals for high water and low water respectively. Please see the discussion at the beginning of Table 2 under the heading "Time differences".

TABLE 3.—HEIGHT OF TIDE AT ANY TIME

EXPLANATION OF TABLE

Although the footnote of Table 3 may contain sufficient explanation for finding the height of tide at any time, two examples are given here to illustrate its use.

Example 1.—Find the height of the tide at 0755 at New York (The Battery), N.Y., on a day when the predicted tides from Table 1 are given as:

Low Water			High Water	
Time	*Height*		*Time*	*Height*
h.m.	*ft*		*h.m.*	*ft*
0522	0.1		1114	4.2
1741	0.6		2310	4.1

An inspection of the above example shows that the desired time falls between the two morning tides

The duration of rise is $11^h 14^m - 5^h 22^m = 5^h 52^m$.

The time after low water for which the height is required is $7^h 55^m - 5^h 22^m = 2^h 33^m$.

The range of tide is $4.2 - 0.1 = 4.1$ feet.

The duration of rise or fall in Table 3 is given in heavy-faced type for each 20 minutes from $4^h 10^m$ to $10^h 40^m$. The nearest tabular value to $5^h 52^m$, the above duration of rise, is $6^h 00^m$; and on the horizontal line of $6^h 00^m$, the nearest tabular time to $2^h 33^m$ after low water for which the height is required is $2^h 36^m$ Following down the column in which this $2^h 36^m$ is found to its intersection with the line of the range 4.0 feet (the nearest tabular value to the above range of 4.1 feet), the correction is found to be 1.6 feet, which being reckoned from low water, must be added, making $0.1 + 1.6 = 1.7$ feet or 52 centimeters which is the required height above mean lower low water, the datum for New York.

Example 2. —Find the height of the tide at 0300 at Somewhere, U.S.A. on a day when the predicted tides are given as:

High Water			Low Water	
Time	*Height*		*Time*	*Height*
h.m.	*ft*		*h.m.*	*ft*
0012	11.3		0638	-2.0
1251	11.0		1853	-0.8

The duration of fall is $6^h 38^m - 00^h 12^m = 6^h 26^m$.

The time after high water for which the height is required is $3^h 00^m - 00^h 12^m = 2^h 48^m$.

The range of tide is $11.3 - (-2.0) = 13.3$ feet.

Entering Table 3 at the duration of fall of $6^h 20^m$, which is the nearest value to $6^h 26^m$, the nearest value on the horizontal line to $2^h 48^m$ is $2^h 45^m$ after high water. Follow down this column to its intersection with a range of 13.5 feet which is the nearest tabular value to 13.3 feet, one obtains 5.3 which, being calculated from high water, must be subtracted from it. The approximate height at $03^h 00^m$ is, therefore, $11.3 - 5.3 = 6.0$ feet or 183 centimeters.

When the duration of rise or fall is greater than $10^h 40^m$, enter the table with one-half the given duration and with one-half the time from the nearest high or low water; but if the duration of rise or fall is less than 4 hours, enter the table with double the given duration and with double the time from the nearest high or low water.

TABLE 3.—HEIGHT OF TIDE AT ANY TIME

Similarly, when the range of tide is greater than 20 feet, enter the table with one-half the given range. The tabular correction should then be doubled before applying it to the given high or low water height. If the range of tide is greater than 40 feet, take one-third of the range and multiply the tabular correction by 3.

If the height at any time is desired for a place listed in Table 2 predictions of the high and low waters for the day in question should be obtained by the use of the difference given for the place in that table. Having obtained these predictions, the height for any intermediate time is obtained in the same manner as illustrated in the foregoing example.

GRAPHIC METHOD

If the height of the tide is required for a number of times on a certain day the full tide curve for the day may be obtained by the *one-quarter, one-tenth rule*. The procedure is as follows:

1. On cross-section paper plot the high and low water points in the order of their occurrence for the day, measuring time horizontally and height vertically. These are the basic points for the curve.

2. Draw light straight lines connecting the points representing successive high and low waters.

3. Divide each of these straight lines into four equal parts. The halfway point of each line gives another point for the curve.

4. At the quarter point adjacent to high water draw a vertical line above the point and at the quarter point adjacent to low water draw a vertical line below the point, making the length of these lines equal to one-tenth of the range between the high and low waters used. The points marking the ends of these vertical lines give two additional intermediate points for the curve.

5. Draw a smooth curve through the points of high and low waters and the intermediate points, making the curve well rounded near high and low waters. This curve will approximate the actual tide curve and heights for any time of the day may be readily scaled from it.

Caution.—Both methods presented are based on the assumption that the rise and fall conform to simple cosine curves. Therefore, the heights obtained will be approximate. The roughness of approximation will vary as the tide curve differs from a cosine curve.

An example of the use of the graphical method is illustrated below. Using the same predicted tides as in example 2, the approximate height at $3^h 00^m$ could be determined as shown below.

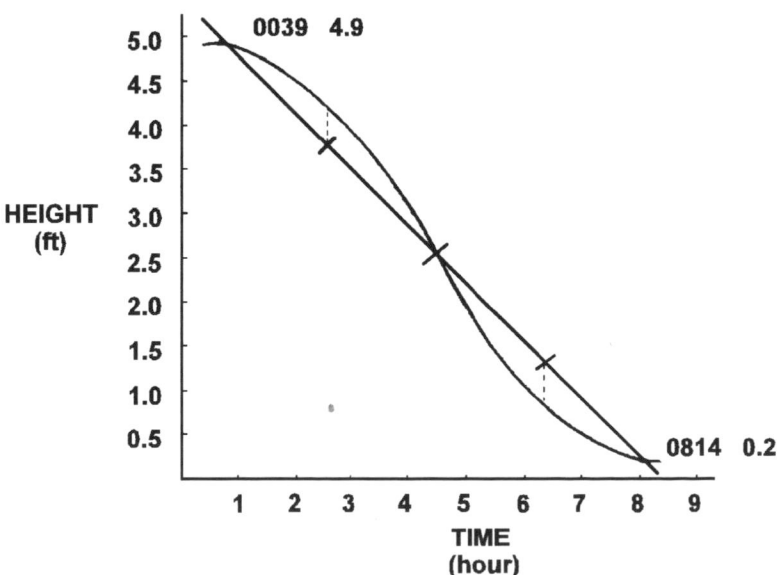

TABLE 3.—HEIGHT OF TIDE AT ANY TIME

Time from the nearest high water or low water

Duration of rise or fall, see footnote (h. m.)	h. m.	h. m.	h. m.	h. m.	h. m.	h. m.	h. m.	h. m.	h. m.	h. m.	h. m.	h. m.	h. m.	h. m.	h. m.
4 10	0 08	0 16	0 24	0 32	0 40	0 48	0 56	1 04	1 12	1 20	1 28	1 36	1 44	1 52	2 00
4 20	0 09	0 17	0 26	0 35	0 43	0 52	1 01	1 09	1 18	1 27	1 35	1 44	1 53	2 01	2 10
4 40	0 09	0 19	0 28	0 37	0 47	0 56	1 05	1 15	1 24	1 33	1 43	1 52	2 01	2 11	2 20
5 00	0 10	0 20	0 30	0 40	0 50	1 00	1 10	1 20	1 30	1 40	1 50	2 00	2 10	2 20	2 30
5 20	0 11	0 21	0 32	0 43	0 53	1 04	1 15	1 25	1 36	1 47	1 57	2 08	2 19	2 29	2 40
5 40	0 11	0 23	0 34	0 45	0 57	1 08	1 19	1 31	1 42	1 53	2 05	2 16	2 27	2 39	2 50
6 00	0 12	0 24	0 36	0 48	1 00	1 12	1 24	1 36	1 48	2 00	2 12	2 24	2 36	2 48	3 00
6 20	0 13	0 25	0 38	0 51	1 03	1 16	1 29	1 41	1 54	2 07	2 19	2 32	2 45	2 57	3 10
6 40	0 13	0 27	0 40	0 53	1 07	1 20	1 33	1 47	2 00	2 13	2 27	2 40	2 53	3 07	3 20
7 00	0 14	0 28	0 42	0 56	1 10	1 24	1 38	1 52	2 06	2 20	2 34	2 48	3 02	3 16	3 30
7 20	0 15	0 29	0 44	0 59	1 13	1 28	1 43	1 57	2 12	2 27	2 41	2 56	3 11	3 25	3 40
7 40	0 15	0 31	0 46	1 01	1 17	1 32	1 47	2 03	2 18	2 33	2 49	3 04	3 19	3 35	3 50
8 00	0 16	0 32	0 48	1 04	1 20	1 36	1 52	2 08	2 24	2 40	2 56	3 12	3 28	3 44	4 00
8 20	0 17	0 33	0 50	1 07	1 23	1 40	1 57	2 13	2 30	2 47	3 03	3 20	3 37	3 53	4 10
8 40	0 17	0 35	0 52	1 09	1 27	1 44	2 01	2 19	2 36	2 53	3 11	3 28	3 45	4 03	4 20
9 00	0 18	0 36	0 54	1 12	1 30	1 48	2 06	2 24	2 42	3 00	3 18	3 36	3 54	4 12	4 30
9 20	0 19	0 37	0 56	1 15	1 33	1 52	2 11	2 29	2 48	3 07	3 25	3 44	4 03	4 21	4 40
9 40	0 19	0 39	0 58	1 17	1 37	1 56	2 15	2 35	2 54	3 13	3 33	3 52	4 11	4 31	4 50
10 00	0 20	0 40	1 00	1 20	1 40	2 00	2 20	2 40	3 00	3 20	3 40	4 00	4 20	4 40	5 00
10 20	0 21	0 41	1 02	1 23	1 43	2 04	2 25	2 45	3 06	3 27	3 47	4 08	4 29	4 49	5 10
10 40	0 21	0 43	1 04	1 25	1 47	2 08	2 29	2 51	3 12	3 33	3 55	4 16	4 37	4 59	5 20

Correction to height

Range of tide, see footnote (Ft.)	Ft.	Ft.	Ft.	Ft.	Ft.	Ft.	Ft.	Ft.	Ft.	Ft.	Ft.	Ft.	Ft.	Ft.	Ft.
0.5	0.0	0.0	0.0	0.0	0.0	0.0	0.1	0.1	0.1	0.1	0.1	0.2	0.2	0.2	0.2
1.0	0.0	0.0	0.0	0.0	0.1	0.1	0.1	0.2	0.2	0.2	0.3	0.3	0.4	0.4	0.5
1.5	0.0	0.0	0.0	0.1	0.1	0.1	0.2	0.2	0.3	0.4	0.4	0.5	0.6	0.7	0.8
2.0	0.0	0.0	0.0	0.1	0.1	0.2	0.3	0.3	0.4	0.5	0.6	0.7	0.8	0.9	1.0
2.5	0.0	0.0	0.1	0.1	0.2	0.2	0.3	0.4	0.5	0.6	0.7	0.9	1.0	1.1	1.2
3.0	0.0	0.0	0.1	0.1	0.2	0.3	0.4	0.5	0.6	0.8	0.9	1.0	1.2	1.3	1.5
3.5	0.0	0.0	0.1	0.2	0.2	0.3	0.4	0.6	0.7	0.9	1.0	1.2	1.4	1.6	1.8
4.0	0.0	0.0	0.1	0.2	0.3	0.4	0.5	0.7	0.8	1.0	1.2	1.4	1.6	1.8	2.0
4.5	0.0	0.0	0.1	0.2	0.3	0.4	0.6	0.7	0.9	1.1	1.3	1.6	1.8	2.0	2.2
5.0	0.0	0.1	0.1	0.2	0.3	0.5	0.6	0.8	1.0	1.2	1.5	1.7	2.0	2.2	2.5
5.5	0.0	0.1	0.1	0.2	0.4	0.5	0.7	0.9	1.1	1.4	1.6	1.9	2.2	2.5	2.8
6.0	0.0	0.1	0.1	0.3	0.4	0.6	0.8	1.0	1.2	1.5	1.8	2.1	2.4	2.7	3.0
6.5	0.0	0.1	0.2	0.3	0.4	0.6	0.8	1.1	1.3	1.6	1.9	2.2	2.6	2.9	3.2
7.0	0.0	0.1	0.2	0.3	0.5	0.7	0.9	1.2	1.4	1.8	2.1	2.4	2.8	3.1	3.5
7.5	0.0	0.1	0.2	0.3	0.5	0.7	1.0	1.2	1.5	1.9	2.2	2.6	3.0	3.4	3.8
8.0	0.0	0.1	0.2	0.3	0.5	0.8	1.0	1.3	1.6	2.0	2.4	2.8	3.2	3.6	4.0
8.5	0.0	0.1	0.2	0.4	0.6	0.8	1.1	1.4	1.8	2.1	2.5	2.9-	3.4	3.8	4.2
9.0	0.0	0.1	0.2	0.4	0.6	0.9	1.2	1.5	1.9	2.2	2.7	3.1	3.6	4.0	4.5
9.5	0.0	0.1	0.2	0.4	0.6	0.9	1.2	1.6	2.0	2.4	2.8	3.3	3.8	4.3	4.8
10.0	0.0	0.1	0.2	0.4	0.7	1.0	1.3	1.7	2.1	2.5	3.0	3.5	4.0	4.5	5.0
10.5	0.0	0.1	0.3	0.5	0.7	1.0	1.3	1.7	2.2	2.6	3.1	3.6	4.2	4.7	5.2
11.0	0.0	0.1	0.3	0.5	0.7	1.1	1.4	1.7	2.3	2.8	3.3	3.8	4.4	4.9	5.5
11.5	0.0	0.1	0.3	0.5	0.8	1.1	1.5	1.8	2.3	2.9	3.4	4.0	4.6	5.1	5.8
12.0	0.0	0.1	0.3	0.5	0.8	1.1	1.5	1.9	2.5	3.0	3.6	4.1	4.8	5.4	6.0
12.5	0.0	0.1	0.3	0.5	0.8	1.2	2.6	1.9	2.6	3.1	3.7	4.3	5.0	5.6	6.2
13.0	0.0	0.1	0.3	0.6	0.9	1.2	1.7	2.2	2.7	3.2	3.9	4.5	5.1	5.8	6.5
13.5	0.0	0.1	0.3	0.6	0.9	1.3	1.7	2.2	2.8	3.4	4.0	4.7	5.3	6.0	6.8
14.0	0.0	0.2	0.3	0.6	0.9	1.3	1.8	2.3	2.9	3.5	4.2	4.8	5.5	6.3	7.0
14.5	0.0	0.2	0.4	0.6	1.0	1.4	1.9	2.4	3.0	3.6	4.3	5.0	5.7	6.5	7.2
15.0	0.0	0.2	0.4	0.6	1.0	1.4	1.9	2.5	3.1	3.8	4.4	5.2	5.9	6.7	7.5
15.5	0.0	0.2	0.4	0.7	1.0	1.5	2.0	2.6	3.2	3.9	4.6	5.4	6.1	6.9	7.8
16.0	0.0	0.2	0.4	0.7	1.1	1.5	2.1	2.6	3.3	4.0	4.7	5.5	6.3	7.2	8.0
16.5	0.0	0.2	0.4	0.7	1.1	1.6	2.1	2.7	3.4	4.1	4.9	5.7	6.5	7.4	8.2
17.0	0.0	0.2	0.4	0.7	1.1	1.6	2.2	2.8	3.5	4.2	5.0	5.9	6.7	7.6	8.5
17.5	0.0	0.2	0.4	0.8	1.2	1.7	2.2	2.9	3.6	4.4	5.2	6.0	6.9	7.8	8.8
18.0	0.0	0.2	0.4	0.8	1.2	1.7	2.3	3.0	3.7	4.5	5.3	6.2	7.1	8.1	9.0
18.5	0.1	0.2	0.5	0.8	1.2	1.8	2.4	3.1	3.8	4.6	5.5	6.4	7.3	8.3	9.2
19.0	0.1	0.2	0.5	0.8	1.3	1.8	2.4	3.1	3.9	4.8	5.6	6.6	7.5	8.5	9.5
19.5	0.1	0.2	0.5	0.8	1.3	1.9	2.5	3.2	4.0	4.9	5.8	6.7	7.7	8.7	9.8
20.0	0.1	0.2	0.5	0.9	1.3	1.9	2.6	3.3	4.1	5.0	5.9	6.9	7.9	9.0	10.0

Obtain from the predictions the high water and low water, one of which is before and the other after the time for which the height is required. The difference between the times of occurrence of these tides is the duration of rise or fall, and the difference between their heights is the range of tide for the above table. Find the difference between the nearest high or low water and the time for which the height is required.

Enter the table with the duration of rise or fall, printed in heavy-faced type, which most nearly agrees with the actual value, and on that horizontal line find the time from the nearest high or low water which agrees most nearly with the corresponding actual difference. The correction sought is in the column directly below, on the line with the range of tide.

When the nearest tide is high water, subtract the correction.

When the nearest tide is low, add the correction.

TABLE 4.—LOCAL MEAN TIME OF SUNRISE AND SUNSET

EXPLANATION OF TABLE

This table gives the local mean time of the rising and setting of the Sun's upper limb for every fifth day of the year. The times were computed for the instant when the true zenith distance of the Sun's center is 90° 50', 34' having been allowed for horizontal refraction and 16' for semidiameter. No allowance has been made for elevation of the observer.

Because of the sensible variations which may be made in the time of rising or setting of the Sun by a difference in elevation of the observer, and by changes in the refraction, any great refinement in the interpolation of intermediate dates or latitudes in this table is unnecessary.

The value obtained from Table 4 may be converted to standard time by means of Table 5, which follows it.

Date		0° Rise h. m.	0° Set h. m.	5° N. Rise h. m.	5° N. Set h. m.	10° N. Rise h. m.	10° N. Set h. m.	15° N. Rise h. m.	15° N. Set h. m.	20° N. Rise h. m.	20° N. Set h. m.	25° N. Rise h. m.	25° N. Set h. m.
Jan.	1	06 00	18 07	06 08	17 59	06 17	17 50	06 26	17 42	06 35	17 32	06 45	17 22
	6	06 02	18 10	06 11	18 01	06 19	17 53	06 28	17 44	06 37	17 35	06 46	17 26
	11	06 04	18 12	06 12	18 04	06 20	17 56	06 29	17 47	06 37	17 39	06 47	17 29
	16	06 06	18 13	06 14	18 06	06 22	17 58	06 30	17 50	06 38	17 42	06 47	17 33
	21	06 08	18 15	06 15	18 08	06 22	18 01	06 30	17 53	06 38	17 45	06 46	17 37
	26	06 09	18 16	06 16	18 09	06 23	18 03	06 30	17 56	06 37	17 48	06 45	17 41
	31	06 10	18 17	06 16	18 11	06 22	18 05	06 29	17 58	06 36	17 51	06 43	17 44
Feb.	5	06 11	18 17	06 16	18 12	06 22	18 06	06 28	18 00	06 34	17 54	06 41	17 48
	10	06 11	18 18	06 16	18 13	06 21	18 08	06 26	18 02	06 32	17 57	06 38	17 51
	15	06 11	18 17	06 15	18 13	06 20	18 09	06 24	18 04	06 29	17 59	06 34	17 54
	20	06 10	18 17	06 14	18 13	06 18	18 09	06 22	18 06	06 26	18 02	06 30	17 57
	25	06 10	18 16	06 13	18 13	06 16	18 10	06 19	18 07	06 23	18 04	06 26	18 00
Mar.	2	06 09	18 15	06 11	18 13	06 14	18 11	06 16	18 08	06 19	18 05	06 22	18 03
	7	06 08	18 14	06 09	18 13	06 11	18 11	06 13	18 09	06 15	18 07	06 17	18 05
	12	06 06	18 13	06 08	18 12	06 09	18 11	06 10	18 10	06 11	18 09	06 12	18 08
	17	06 05	18 12	06 05	18 11	06 06	18 11	06 06	18 11	06 07	18 10	06 07	18 10
	22	06 04	18 10	06 03	18 10	06 03	18 11	06 03	18 11	06 02	18 12	06 02	18 12
	27	06 02	18 09	06 01	18 10	06 00	18 11	05 59	18 12	05 58	18 13	05 57	18 14
Apr.	1	06 01	18 07	05 59	18 09	05 57	18 11	05 55	18 12	05 54	18 14	05 52	18 16
	6	05 59	18 06	05 57	18 08	05 54	18 10	05 52	18 13	05 49	18 16	05 47	18 19
	11	05 58	18 04	05 55	18 07	05 52	18 10	05 49	18 14	05 45	18 17	05 42	18 21
	16	05 56	18 03	05 53	18 07	05 49	18 11	05 45	18 14	05 41	18 19	05 37	18 23
	21	05 55	18 02	05 51	18 06	05 47	18 11	05 42	18 15	05 37	18 20	05 32	18 25
	26	05 54	18 01	05 50	18 06	05 45	18 11	05 39	18 16	05 34	18 22	05 28	18 28
May.	1	05 54	18 00	05 48	18 06	05 43	18 12	05 37	18 17	05 31	18 24	05 24	18 30
	6	05 53	18 00	05 47	18 06	05 41	18 12	05 35	18 19	05 28	18 25	05 21	18 33
	11	05 53	18 00	05 46	18 06	05 40	18 13	05 33	18 20	05 26	18 27	05 18	18 35
	16	05 53	18 00	05 46	18 07	05 39	18 14	05 31	18 22	05 24	18 29	05 15	18 38
	21	05 53	18 00	05 46	18 08	05 38	18 15	05 30	18 23	05 22	18 31	05 13	18 40
	26	05 53	18 01	05 46	18 08	05 38	18 16	05 30	18 25	05 21	18 33	05 11	18 43
	31	05 54	18 01	05 46	18 09	05 38	18 18	05 29	18 26	05 20	18 35	05 10	18 45
Jun.	5	05 55	18 02	05 47	18 11	05 38	18 19	05 29	18 28	05 20	18 37	05 10	18 47
	10	05 56	18 03	05 47	18 12	05 39	18 20	05 30	18 29	05 20	18 39	05 10	18 49
	15	05 57	18 04	05 48	18 13	05 39	18 22	05 30	18 31	05 20	18 41	05 10	18 51
	20	05 58	18 05	05 49	18 14	05 40	18 23	05 31	18 32	05 21	18 42	05 11	18 52
	25	05 59	18 06	05 50	18 15	05 41	18 24	05 32	18 33	05 23	18 43	05 12	18 53
	30	06 00	18 07	05 51	18 16	05 43	18 25	05 34	18 34	05 24	18 43	05 14	18 54
Jul.	5	06 01	18 08	05 53	18 17	05 44	18 25	05 35	18 34	05 26	18 44	05 15	18 54
	10	06 02	18 09	05 54	18 17	05 45	18 26	05 37	18 34	05 27	18 43	05 17	18 53
	15	06 02	18 10	05 55	18 17	05 46	18 25	05 38	18 34	05 29	18 43	05 20	18 52
	20	06 03	18 10	05 55	18 17	05 48	18 25	05 40	18 33	05 31	18 42	05 22	18 51
	25	06 03	18 10	05 56	18 17	05 49	18 24	05 41	18 32	05 33	18 40	05 24	18 48
	30	06 03	18 10	05 56	18 17	05 49	18 23	05 42	18 30	05 35	18 38	05 27	18 46
Aug.	4	06 03	18 10	05 56	18 16	05 50	18 22	05 44	18 28	05 37	18 35	05 29	18 43
	9	06 02	18 09	05 56	18 14	05 51	18 20	05 45	18 26	05 38	18 32	05 31	18 39
	14	06 01	18 08	05 56	18 13	05 51	18 18	05 45	18 24	05 40	18 29	05 34	18 35
	19	06 00	18 07	05 56	18 11	05 51	18 16	05 46	18 21	05 41	18 26	05 36	18 31
	24	05 59	18 06	05 55	18 09	05 51	18 13	05 47	18 18	05 43	18 22	05 38	18 26
	29	05 58	18 04	05 54	18 07	05 51	18 11	05 47	18 14	05 44	18 18	05 40	18 22
Sep.	3	05 56	18 03	05 53	18 05	05 51	18 08	05 48	18 11	05 45	18 13	05 42	18 17
	8	05 54	18 01	05 52	18 03	05 50	18 05	05 48	18 07	05 46	18 09	05 44	18 11
	13	05 53	17 59	05 51	18 00	05 50	18 02	05 49	18 03	05 47	18 04	05 45	18 06
	18	05 51	17 57	05 50	17 58	05 50	17 58	05 49	17 59	05 48	18 00	05 47	18 01
	23	05 49	17 56	05 49	17 55	05 49	17 55	05 49	17 55	05 49	17 55	05 49	17 55
	28	05 47	17 54	05 48	17 53	05 49	17 52	05 49	17 51	05 50	17 51	05 51	17 50
Oct.	3	05 46	17 52	05 47	17 51	05 49	17 49	05 50	17 48	05 51	17 46	05 53	17 45
	8	05 44	17 51	05 46	17 49	05 48	17 46	05 51	17 44	05 53	17 42	05 55	17 40
	13	05 43	17 49	05 46	17 47	05 48	17 44	05 51	17 41	05 54	17 38	05 57	17 35
	18	05 42	17 48	05 45	17 45	05 49	17 41	05 52	17 38	05 56	17 34	06 00	17 30
	23	05 41	17 48	05 45	17 44	05 49	17 39	05 53	17 35	05 58	17 31	06 02	17 26
	28	05 40	17 47	05 45	17 42	05 50	17 38	05 55	17 33	06 00	17 28	06 05	17 22
Nov.	2	05 40	17 47	05 45	17 42	05 51	17 36	05 56	17 31	06 02	17 25	06 08	17 19
	7	05 40	17 47	05 46	17 41	05 52	17 35	05 58	17 29	06 04	17 23	06 11	17 16
	12	05 41	17 48	05 47	17 41	05 54	17 35	06 00	17 28	06 07	17 21	06 15	17 14
	17	05 41	17 49	05 48	17 42	05 55	17 35	06 03	17 27	06 10	17 20	06 18	17 12
	22	05 43	17 50	05 50	17 42	05 57	17 35	06 05	17 27	06 13	17 19	06 22	17 11
	27	05 44	17 51	05 52	17 44	06 00	17 36	06 08	17 28	06 16	17 19	06 25	17 10
Dec.	2	05 46	17 53	05 54	17 45	06 02	17 37	06 10	17 28	06 19	17 20	06 29	17 10
	7	05 48	17 55	05 56	17 47	06 05	17 38	06 13	17 30	06 22	17 21	06 32	17 11
	12	05 50	17 58	05 59	17 49	06 07	17 40	06 16	17 31	06 25	17 22	06 35	17 12
	17	05 52	18 00	06 01	17 51	06 10	17 43	06 19	17 34	06 28	17 24	06 38	17 14
	22	05 55	18 02	06 04	17 54	06 12	17 45	06 21	17 36	06 31	17 26	06 41	17 16
	27	05 57	18 05	06 06	17 56	06 15	17 48	06 24	17 39	06 33	17 29	06 43	17 19

Local mean time. To obtain standard time of rise or set, see Table 5.

TABLE 4.-SUNRISE AND SUNSET, 2017   375

Date		30° N. Rise h. m.	30° N. Set h. m.	32° N. Rise h. m.	32° N. Set h. m.	34° N. Rise h. m.	34° N. Set h. m.	36° N. Rise h. m.	36° N. Set h. m.	38° N. Rise h. m.	38° N. Set h. m.	40° N. Rise h. m.	40° N. Set h. m.
Jan.	1	06 56	17 12	07 01	17 07	07 05	17 02	07 11	16 57	07 11	16 57	07 22	16 46
	6	06 57	17 15	07 01	17 11	07 06	17 06	07 11	17 01	07 11	17 01	07 22	16 50
	11	06 57	17 19	07 01	17 15	07 06	17 10	07 11	17 06	07 11	17 06	07 21	16 55
	16	06 56	17 23	07 01	17 19	07 05	17 15	07 10	17 10	07 10	17 10	07 20	17 00
	21	06 55	17 28	06 59	17 24	07 03	17 20	07 08	17 15	07 08	17 15	07 17	17 06
	26	06 53	17 32	06 57	17 29	07 01	17 25	07 05	17 21	07 05	17 21	07 14	17 12
	31	06 51	17 36	06 54	17 33	06 58	17 30	07 01	17 26	07 01	17 26	07 09	17 18
Feb.	5	06 48	17 41	06 51	17 38	06 54	17 35	06 57	17 31	06 57	17 31	07 04	17 24
	10	06 44	17 45	06 47	17 42	06 50	17 39	06 52	17 36	06 52	17 36	06 59	17 30
	15	06 40	17 49	06 42	17 46	06 45	17 44	06 47	17 42	06 47	17 42	06 53	17 36
	20	06 35	17 53	06 37	17 51	06 39	17 49	06 41	17 46	06 41	17 46	06 46	17 42
	25	06 30	17 56	06 32	17 55	06 33	17 53	06 35	17 51	06 35	17 51	06 39	17 47
Mar.	2	06 25	18 00	06 26	17 59	06 27	17 57	06 29	17 56	06 29	17 56	06 32	17 53
	7	06 19	18 03	06 20	18 02	06 21	18 01	06 22	18 00	06 22	18 00	06 24	17 58
	12	06 13	18 06	06 14	18 06	06 14	18 05	06 15	18 05	06 15	18 05	06 16	18 04
	17	06 07	18 10	06 08	18 09	06 08	18 09	06 08	18 09	06 08	18 09	06 08	18 09
	22	06 01	18 13	06 01	18 13	06 01	18 13	06 01	18 13	06 01	18 13	06 00	18 14
	27	05 55	18 16	05 55	18 16	05 54	18 17	05 53	18 18	05 53	18 18	05 52	18 19
Apr.	1	05 49	18 19	05 48	18 20	05 47	18 21	05 46	18 22	05 46	18 22	05 44	18 24
	6	05 43	18 22	05 42	18 23	05 41	18 25	05 39	18 26	05 39	18 26	05 36	18 29
	11	05 38	18 25	05 36	18 27	05 34	18 28	05 32	18 30	05 32	18 30	05 28	18 34
	16	05 32	18 28	05 30	18 30	05 28	18 32	05 26	18 35	05 26	18 35	05 21	18 40
	21	05 27	18 31	05 24	18 33	05 22	18 36	05 19	18 39	05 19	18 39	05 13	18 45
	26	05 22	18 34	05 19	18 37	05 16	18 40	05 13	18 43	05 13	18 43	05 06	18 50
May.	1	05 17	18 37	05 14	18 41	05 11	18 44	05 07	18 47	05 07	18 47	05 00	18 55
	6	05 13	18 41	05 10	18 44	05 06	18 48	05 02	18 52	05 02	18 52	04 54	19 00
	11	05 09	18 44	05 06	18 48	05 02	18 52	04 58	18 56	04 58	18 56	04 49	19 05
	16	05 06	18 47	05 02	18 51	04 58	18 55	04 53	19 00	04 53	19 00	04 44	19 09
	21	05 03	18 50	04 59	18 54	04 55	18 59	04 50	19 04	04 50	19 04	04 40	19 14
	26	05 01	18 53	04 57	18 58	04 52	19 02	04 47	19 07	04 47	19 07	04 36	19 18
	31	05 00	18 56	04 55	19 01	04 50	19 06	04 45	19 11	04 45	19 11	04 34	19 22
Jun.	5	04 59	18 59	04 54	19 03	04 49	19 08	04 44	19 14	04 44	19 14	04 32	19 25
	10	04 58	19 01	04 53	19 06	04 48	19 11	04 43	19 16	04 43	19 16	04 31	19 28
	15	04 59	19 03	04 54	19 08	04 48	19 13	04 43	19 18	04 43	19 18	04 31	19 31
	20	04 59	19 04	04 54	19 09	04 49	19 14	04 43	19 20	04 43	19 20	04 31	19 32
	25	05 01	19 05	04 56	19 10	04 50	19 15	04 45	19 21	04 45	19 21	04 32	19 33
	30	05 02	19 05	04 57	19 10	04 52	19 15	04 47	19 21	04 47	19 21	04 34	19 33
Jul.	5	05 04	19 05	04 59	19 10	04 54	19 15	04 49	19 20	04 49	19 20	04 37	19 32
	10	05 07	19 04	05 02	19 09	04 57	19 14	04 52	19 19	04 52	19 19	04 40	19 30
	15	05 09	19 03	05 05	19 07	05 00	19 12	04 55	19 17	04 55	19 17	04 44	19 28
	20	05 12	19 00	05 08	19 05	05 03	19 09	04 58	19 14	04 58	19 14	04 48	19 24
	25	05 15	18 58	05 11	19 02	05 07	19 06	05 02	19 11	05 02	19 11	04 52	19 20
	30	05 18	18 55	05 14	18 58	05 10	19 02	05 06	19 07	05 06	19 07	04 57	19 16
Aug.	4	05 21	18 51	05 17	18 54	05 14	18 58	05 10	19 02	05 10	19 02	05 01	19 10
	9	05 24	18 47	05 21	18 50	05 17	18 53	05 14	18 57	05 14	18 57	05 06	19 04
	14	05 27	18 42	05 24	18 45	05 21	18 48	05 18	18 51	05 18	18 51	05 11	18 58
	19	05 30	18 37	05 27	18 39	05 24	18 42	05 22	18 45	05 22	18 45	05 15	18 51
	24	05 33	18 32	05 30	18 34	05 28	18 36	05 26	18 38	05 26	18 38	05 20	18 44
	29	05 35	18 26	05 34	18 28	05 32	18 30	05 30	18 32	05 30	18 32	05 25	18 36
Sep.	3	05 38	18 20	05 37	18 21	05 35	18 23	05 33	18 25	05 33	18 25	05 30	18 28
	8	05 41	18 14	05 40	18 15	05 38	18 16	05 37	18 17	05 37	18 17	05 34	18 20
	13	05 44	18 08	05 43	18 08	05 42	18 09	05 41	18 10	05 41	18 10	05 39	18 12
	18	05 46	18 01	05 46	18 02	05 45	18 02	05 45	18 03	05 45	18 03	05 44	18 04
	23	05 49	17 55	05 49	17 55	05 49	17 55	05 49	17 55	05 49	17 55	05 49	17 55
	28	05 52	17 49	05 52	17 49	05 52	17 48	05 53	17 48	05 53	17 48	05 53	17 47
Oct.	3	05 55	17 43	05 55	17 42	05 56	17 41	05 57	17 41	05 57	17 41	05 58	17 39
	8	05 58	17 37	05 59	17 36	06 00	17 35	06 01	17 34	06 01	17 34	06 03	17 31
	13	06 01	17 31	06 02	17 30	06 04	17 28	06 05	17 27	06 05	17 27	06 08	17 23
	18	06 04	17 26	06 06	17 24	06 08	17 22	06 09	17 20	06 09	17 20	06 14	17 16
	23	06 07	17 21	06 09	17 19	06 12	17 16	06 14	17 14	06 14	17 14	06 19	17 09
	28	06 11	17 16	06 13	17 14	06 16	17 11	06 19	17 08	06 19	17 08	06 25	17 02
Nov.	2	06 15	17 12	06 18	17 09	06 20	17 06	06 24	17 03	06 24	17 03	06 30	16 56
	7	06 19	17 08	06 22	17 05	06 25	17 02	06 29	16 58	06 29	16 58	06 36	16 51
	12	06 23	17 05	06 26	17 02	06 30	16 58	06 34	16 54	06 34	16 54	06 42	16 46
	17	06 27	17 03	06 31	16 59	06 34	16 55	06 39	16 51	06 39	16 51	06 48	16 42
	22	06 31	17 01	06 35	16 57	06 39	16 53	06 44	16 49	06 44	16 49	06 53	16 39
	27	06 35	17 00	06 39	16 56	06 44	16 51	06 48	16 47	06 48	16 47	06 59	16 37
Dec.	2	06 39	17 00	06 44	16 55	06 48	16 51	06 53	16 46	06 53	16 46	07 04	16 35
	7	06 43	17 00	06 47	16 56	06 52	16 51	06 57	16 46	06 57	16 46	07 08	16 35
	12	06 46	17 01	06 51	16 56	06 56	16 52	07 01	16 46	07 01	16 46	07 12	16 35
	17	06 50	17 03	06 54	16 58	06 59	16 53	07 05	16 48	07 05	16 48	07 16	16 36
	22	06 52	17 05	06 57	17 00	07 02	16 55	07 07	16 50	07 07	16 50	07 19	16 39
	27	06 54	17 08	06 59	17 03	07 04	16 58	07 09	16 53	07 09	16 53	07 21	16 42

Local mean time. To obtain standard time of rise or set, see Table 5.

TABLE 4.-SUNRISE AND SUNSET, 2017

Date		42° N. Rise	42° N. Set	44° N. Rise	44° N. Set	46° N. Rise	46° N. Set	48° N. Rise	48° N. Set	50° N. Rise	50° N. Set	52° N. Rise	52° N. Set
		h. m.	h. m.	h. m.	h. m.	h. m.	h. m.	h. m.	h. m.	h. m.	h. m.	h. m.	h. m.
Jan.	1	07 28	16 39	07 35	16 33	07 42	16 26	07 50	16 18	07 58	16 09	08 08	15 59
	6	07 28	16 44	07 35	16 38	07 42	16 31	07 49	16 23	07 57	16 15	08 07	16 05
	11	07 27	16 49	07 33	16 43	07 40	16 36	07 47	16 29	07 55	16 21	08 04	16 12
	16	07 25	16 55	07 31	16 49	07 37	16 43	07 44	16 36	07 52	16 28	08 00	16 20
	21	07 22	17 01	07 28	16 56	07 34	16 50	07 40	16 43	07 47	16 36	07 55	16 28
	26	07 18	17 07	07 23	17 02	07 29	16 57	07 35	16 51	07 41	16 44	07 49	16 37
	31	07 14	17 14	07 18	17 09	07 23	17 04	07 29	16 59	07 35	16 53	07 41	16 46
Feb.	5	07 08	17 20	07 13	17 16	07 17	17 11	07 22	17 07	07 27	17 01	07 33	16 56
	10	07 02	17 27	07 06	17 23	07 10	17 19	07 14	17 15	07 19	17 10	07 24	17 05
	15	06 56	17 33	06 59	17 30	07 03	17 26	07 06	17 23	07 10	17 19	07 15	17 14
	20	06 49	17 39	06 51	17 37	06 54	17 34	06 58	17 31	07 01	17 27	07 05	17 24
	25	06 41	17 45	06 43	17 43	06 46	17 41	06 48	17 38	06 51	17 36	06 54	17 33
Mar.	2	06 33	17 51	06 35	17 50	06 37	17 48	06 39	17 46	06 41	17 44	06 43	17 42
	7	06 25	17 57	06 26	17 56	06 28	17 55	06 29	17 54	06 31	17 52	06 32	17 51
	12	06 17	18 03	06 18	18 03	06 18	18 02	06 19	18 01	06 20	18 00	06 21	17 59
	17	06 08	18 09	06 09	18 09	06 09	18 09	06 09	18 08	06 09	18 08	06 09	18 08
	22	06 00	18 14	05 59	18 15	05 59	18 15	05 59	18 16	05 58	18 16	05 58	18 17
	27	05 51	18 20	05 50	18 21	05 49	18 22	05 48	18 23	05 47	18 24	05 46	18 25
Apr.	1	05 43	18 26	05 41	18 27	05 40	18 29	05 38	18 30	05 37	18 32	05 35	18 34
	6	05 34	18 31	05 32	18 33	05 30	18 35	05 28	18 37	05 26	18 40	05 23	18 43
	11	05 26	18 37	05 24	18 39	05 21	18 42	05 18	18 45	05 15	18 48	05 12	18 51
	16	05 18	18 42	05 15	18 45	05 12	18 48	05 09	18 52	05 05	18 56	05 01	19 00
	21	05 10	18 48	05 07	18 51	05 03	18 55	04 59	18 59	04 55	19 03	04 50	19 08
	26	05 03	18 53	04 59	18 57	04 55	19 02	04 50	19 06	04 45	19 11	04 40	19 17
May.	1	04 56	18 59	04 52	19 03	04 47	19 08	04 42	19 13	04 36	19 19	04 30	19 25
	6	04 50	19 04	04 45	19 09	04 40	19 14	04 34	19 20	04 28	19 26	04 21	19 33
	11	04 44	19 10	04 38	19 15	04 33	19 21	04 27	19 27	04 20	19 34	04 12	19 41
	16	04 39	19 15	04 33	19 21	04 27	19 27	04 20	19 34	04 13	19 41	04 05	19 49
	21	04 34	19 20	04 28	19 26	04 21	19 32	04 14	19 40	04 06	19 48	03 58	19 57
	26	04 30	19 24	04 24	19 31	04 17	19 38	04 09	19 45	04 01	19 54	03 52	20 03
	31	04 27	19 28	04 21	19 35	04 13	19 43	04 05	19 51	03 57	19 59	03 47	20 09
Jun.	5	04 25	19 32	04 18	19 39	04 11	19 47	04 03	19 55	03 53	20 04	03 43	20 15
	10	04 24	19 35	04 17	19 42	04 09	19 50	04 01	19 59	03 51	20 08	03 41	20 19
	15	04 24	19 37	04 17	19 45	04 09	19 53	04 00	20 01	03 50	20 11	03 39	20 22
	20	04 24	19 39	04 17	19 46	04 09	19 54	04 00	20 03	03 51	20 13	03 40	20 24
	25	04 26	19 40	04 18	19 47	04 10	19 55	04 02	20 04	03 52	20 13	03 41	20 24
	30	04 28	19 39	04 21	19 47	04 13	19 55	04 04	20 03	03 55	20 13	03 44	20 23
Jul.	5	04 31	19 38	04 23	19 46	04 16	19 53	04 07	20 02	03 58	20 11	03 48	20 21
	10	04 34	19 37	04 27	19 43	04 20	19 51	04 11	19 59	04 02	20 08	03 52	20 18
	15	04 38	19 34	04 31	19 40	04 24	19 47	04 16	19 55	04 08	20 04	03 58	20 13
	20	04 42	19 30	04 36	19 36	04 29	19 43	04 22	19 50	04 14	19 58	04 05	20 07
	25	04 47	19 26	04 41	19 32	04 34	19 38	04 28	19 45	04 20	19 52	04 12	20 01
	30	04 52	19 21	04 46	19 26	04 40	19 32	04 34	19 38	04 27	19 45	04 19	19 53
Aug.	4	04 57	19 15	04 52	19 20	04 46	19 25	04 40	19 31	04 34	19 37	04 27	19 44
	9	05 02	19 09	04 57	19 13	04 52	19 18	04 47	19 23	04 41	19 29	04 35	19 35
	14	05 07	19 02	05 03	19 06	04 58	19 10	04 54	19 15	04 48	19 20	04 43	19 26
	19	05 12	18 54	05 08	18 58	05 05	19 02	05 00	19 06	04 56	19 10	04 51	19 15
	24	05 17	18 47	05 14	18 50	05 11	18 53	05 07	18 57	05 03	19 00	04 59	19 05
	29	05 23	18 38	05 20	18 41	05 17	18 44	05 14	18 47	05 11	18 50	05 07	18 54
Sep.	3	05 28	18 30	05 26	18 32	05 23	18 34	05 21	18 37	05 18	18 39	05 15	18 42
	8	05 33	18 22	05 31	18 23	05 30	18 25	05 28	18 27	05 26	18 29	05 23	18 31
	13	05 38	18 13	05 37	18 14	05 36	18 15	05 34	18 16	05 33	18 18	05 31	18 19
	18	05 43	18 04	05 43	18 05	05 42	18 05	05 41	18 06	05 40	18 07	05 40	18 07
	23	05 49	17 55	05 48	17 55	05 48	17 56	05 48	17 56	05 48	17 56	05 48	17 56
	28	05 54	17 47	05 54	17 46	05 55	17 46	05 55	17 45	05 56	17 45	05 56	17 44
Oct.	3	05 59	17 38	06 00	17 37	06 01	17 36	06 02	17 35	06 03	17 34	06 04	17 33
	8	06 05	17 30	06 06	17 28	06 08	17 27	06 09	17 25	06 11	17 23	06 13	17 21
	13	06 10	17 21	06 12	17 20	06 14	17 17	06 16	17 15	06 19	17 13	06 21	17 10
	18	06 16	17 14	06 18	17 11	06 21	17 09	06 24	17 06	06 27	17 03	06 30	16 59
	23	06 22	17 06	06 25	17 03	06 28	17 00	06 31	16 57	06 35	16 53	06 39	16 49
	28	06 28	16 59	06 31	16 56	06 35	16 52	06 39	16 48	06 43	16 44	06 48	16 39
Nov.	2	06 34	16 53	06 38	16 49	06 42	16 45	06 47	16 40	06 52	16 35	06 57	16 30
	7	06 40	16 47	06 45	16 42	06 49	16 38	06 54	16 33	07 00	16 27	07 06	16 21
	12	06 46	16 42	06 51	16 37	06 56	16 32	07 02	16 26	07 08	16 20	07 15	16 13
	17	06 52	16 37	06 58	16 32	07 03	16 26	07 09	16 20	07 16	16 13	07 24	16 06
	22	06 58	16 34	07 04	16 28	07 10	16 22	07 17	16 15	07 24	16 08	07 32	16 00
	27	07 04	16 31	07 10	16 25	07 17	16 18	07 24	16 11	07 31	16 04	07 40	15 55
Dec.	2	07 10	16 29	07 16	16 23	07 23	16 16	07 30	16 09	07 38	16 01	07 47	15 52
	7	07 14	16 28	07 21	16 22	07 28	16 15	07 36	16 07	07 44	15 59	07 54	15 49
	12	07 19	16 29	07 25	16 22	07 33	16 15	07 41	16 07	07 49	15 58	07 59	15 48
	17	07 22	16 30	07 29	16 23	07 37	16 16	07 45	16 08	07 54	15 59	08 03	15 49
	22	07 25	16 32	07 32	16 25	07 39	16 18	07 48	16 10	07 56	16 01	08 06	15 51
	27	07 27	16 35	07 34	16 29	07 41	16 21	07 49	16 13	07 58	16 04	08 08	15 55

Local mean time. To obtain standard time of rise or set, see Table 5.

TABLE 4.-SUNRISE AND SUNSET, 2017   377

Date	54° N. Rise h. m.	54° N. Set h. m.	56° N. Rise h. m.	56° N. Set h. m.	58° N. Rise h. m.	58° N. Set h. m.	60° N. Rise h. m.	60° N. Set h. m.	62° N. Rise h. m.	62° N. Set h. m.	64° N. Rise h. m.	64° N. Set h. m.
Jan. 1	08 19	15 49	08 31	15 36	08 45	15 22	09 02	15 06	09 23	14 45	09 49	14 18
6	08 17	15 55	08 29	15 43	08 43	15 30	08 59	15 14	09 18	14 54	09 43	14 30
11	08 14	16 02	08 25	15 51	08 38	15 39	08 53	15 23	09 11	15 05	09 34	14 43
16	08 09	16 11	08 20	16 00	08 32	15 48	08 46	15 35	09 02	15 18	09 23	14 58
21	08 03	16 20	08 13	16 10	08 24	15 59	08 37	15 46	08 52	15 31	09 10	15 13
26	07 56	16 29	08 05	16 21	08 15	16 11	08 27	15 59	08 40	15 46	08 56	15 30
31	07 48	16 39	07 56	16 31	08 05	16 22	08 16	16 12	08 28	16 00	08 42	15 46
Feb. 5	07 40	16 49	07 47	16 42	07 55	16 34	08 04	16 25	08 14	16 15	08 26	16 03
10	07 30	16 59	07 36	16 53	07 43	16 46	07 51	16 38	08 00	16 29	08 11	16 19
15	07 20	17 09	07 25	17 04	07 31	16 58	07 38	16 52	07 45	16 44	07 54	16 35
20	07 09	17 19	07 13	17 15	07 18	17 10	07 24	17 05	07 30	16 58	07 38	16 51
25	06 57	17 29	07 01	17 26	07 05	17 22	07 10	17 17	07 15	17 12	07 21	17 07
Mar. 2	06 46	17 39	06 49	17 37	06 52	17 34	06 55	17 30	06 59	17 26	07 03	17 22
7	06 34	17 49	06 36	17 47	06 38	17 45	06 40	17 43	06 43	17 40	06 46	17 37
12	06 22	17 59	06 23	17 58	06 24	17 56	06 25	17 55	06 27	17 54	06 29	17 52
17	06 10	18 08	06 10	18 08	06 10	18 08	06 10	18 08	06 11	18 07	06 11	18 07
22	05 57	18 17	05 57	18 18	05 56	18 19	05 55	18 20	05 54	18 21	05 53	18 22
27	05 45	18 27	05 44	18 28	05 42	18 30	05 40	18 32	05 38	18 34	05 36	18 37
Apr. 1	05 33	18 36	05 30	18 39	05 28	18 41	05 25	18 44	05 22	18 48	05 18	18 51
6	05 20	18 46	05 17	18 49	05 14	18 52	05 10	18 56	05 05	19 01	05 00	19 06
11	05 08	18 55	05 04	18 59	05 00	19 03	04 55	19 09	04 49	19 15	04 43	19 21
16	04 57	19 04	04 52	19 09	04 46	19 15	04 40	19 21	04 33	19 28	04 25	19 36
21	04 45	19 13	04 39	19 19	04 33	19 26	04 26	19 33	04 17	19 42	04 08	19 52
26	04 34	19 23	04 27	19 29	04 20	19 37	04 11	19 46	04 02	19 56	03 50	20 08
May. 1	04 23	19 32	04 16	19 40	04 07	19 48	03 58	19 58	03 46	20 10	03 33	20 23
6	04 13	19 41	04 05	19 50	03 55	19 59	03 44	20 11	03 32	20 24	03 16	20 39
11	04 04	19 50	03 55	19 59	03 44	20 10	03 32	20 23	03 17	20 38	03 00	20 56
16	03 55	19 58	03 45	20 09	03 33	20 21	03 20	20 35	03 04	20 51	02 44	21 12
21	03 48	20 06	03 37	20 18	03 24	20 31	03 09	20 46	02 51	21 04	02 28	21 28
26	03 41	20 14	03 29	20 26	03 15	20 40	02 59	20 56	02 39	21 17	02 13	21 43
31	03 36	20 21	03 23	20 33	03 08	20 48	02 51	21 06	02 29	21 28	02 00	21 57
Jun. 5	03 31	20 26	03 18	20 40	03 03	20 55	02 44	21 14	02 20	21 38	01 49	22 10
10	03 29	20 31	03 15	20 45	02 59	21 01	02 39	21 21	02 14	21 46	01 39	22 21
15	03 27	20 34	03 13	20 48	02 57	21 05	02 36	21 25	02 10	21 51	01 33	22 29
20	03 27	20 36	03 13	20 50	02 56	21 07	02 36	21 28	02 09	21 54	01 31	22 32
25	03 29	20 36	03 15	20 51	02 58	21 07	02 37	21 28	02 11	21 54	01 33	22 31
30	03 32	20 35	03 18	20 49	03 01	21 06	02 41	21 25	02 16	21 51	01 40	22 26
Jul. 5	03 36	20 33	03 22	20 46	03 06	21 02	02 47	21 21	02 23	21 45	01 50	22 18
10	03 41	20 29	03 28	20 42	03 13	20 57	02 55	21 15	02 32	21 37	02 02	22 07
15	03 47	20 24	03 35	20 36	03 21	20 50	03 04	21 07	02 43	21 27	02 16	21 54
20	03 54	20 17	03 43	20 29	03 30	20 42	03 14	20 57	02 55	21 16	02 31	21 39
25	04 02	20 10	03 51	20 20	03 39	20 32	03 25	20 47	03 08	21 03	02 46	21 24
30	04 10	20 01	04 00	20 11	03 49	20 22	03 36	20 35	03 21	20 50	03 02	21 08
Aug. 4	04 19	19 52	04 10	20 01	04 00	20 11	03 48	20 22	03 34	20 36	03 18	20 52
9	04 27	19 42	04 19	19 50	04 10	19 59	04 00	20 09	03 48	20 21	03 34	20 35
14	04 36	19 32	04 29	19 39	04 21	19 47	04 12	19 55	04 02	20 06	03 49	20 18
19	04 45	19 21	04 39	19 27	04 32	19 34	04 24	19 41	04 15	19 50	04 05	20 00
24	04 54	19 09	04 49	19 14	04 43	19 20	04 36	19 27	04 28	19 34	04 20	19 43
29	05 03	18 57	04 59	19 02	04 54	19 07	04 48	19 12	04 42	19 18	04 34	19 25
Sep. 3	05 12	18 45	05 08	18 49	05 04	18 53	05 00	18 57	04 55	19 02	04 49	19 08
8	05 21	18 33	05 18	18 36	05 15	18 39	05 12	18 42	05 08	18 46	05 03	18 50
13	05 30	18 21	05 28	18 23	05 26	18 25	05 23	18 27	05 21	18 29	05 18	18 32
18	05 39	18 08	05 38	18 09	05 36	18 10	05 35	18 12	05 34	18 13	05 32	18 15
23	05 48	17 56	05 47	17 56	05 47	17 56	05 47	17 56	05 47	17 57	05 46	17 57
28	05 57	17 44	05 57	17 43	05 58	17 42	05 59	17 41	05 59	17 40	06 00	17 39
Oct. 3	06 06	17 31	06 07	17 30	06 09	17 28	06 10	17 26	06 12	17 24	06 15	17 22
8	06 15	17 19	06 17	17 17	06 20	17 14	06 23	17 11	06 26	17 08	06 29	17 04
13	06 24	17 07	06 27	17 04	06 31	17 00	06 35	16 57	06 39	16 52	06 44	16 47
18	06 34	16 56	06 38	16 52	06 42	16 47	06 47	16 42	06 53	16 36	06 59	16 30
23	06 43	16 44	06 48	16 40	06 54	16 34	07 00	16 28	07 06	16 21	07 14	16 13
28	06 53	16 34	06 59	16 28	07 05	16 22	07 12	16 14	07 21	16 06	07 30	15 56
Nov. 2	07 03	16 24	07 09	16 17	07 17	16 10	07 25	16 01	07 35	15 52	07 46	15 40
7	07 13	16 14	07 20	16 07	07 28	15 58	07 38	15 49	07 49	15 38	08 02	15 24
12	07 22	16 05	07 31	15 57	07 40	15 48	07 51	15 37	08 03	15 24	08 18	15 09
17	07 32	15 58	07 41	15 49	07 51	15 38	08 03	15 26	08 17	15 12	08 34	14 55
22	07 41	15 51	07 51	15 41	08 02	15 30	08 15	15 16	08 31	15 01	08 50	14 42
27	07 49	15 46	08 00	15 35	08 12	15 22	08 27	15 08	08 44	14 51	09 05	14 30
Dec. 2	07 57	15 41	08 09	15 30	08 22	15 17	08 37	15 01	08 56	14 43	09 19	14 19
7	08 04	15 39	08 16	15 27	08 30	15 13	08 46	14 57	09 06	14 37	09 32	14 11
12	08 10	15 38	08 22	15 25	08 37	15 11	08 54	14 54	09 15	14 33	09 42	14 06
17	08 14	15 38	08 27	15 25	08 42	15 11	08 59	14 53	09 21	14 32	09 49	14 04
22	08 17	15 40	08 30	15 27	08 45	15 12	09 02	14 55	09 24	14 33	09 53	14 05
27	08 19	15 43	08 32	15 31	08 46	15 16	09 03	14 59	09 25	14 38	09 53	14 10

Local mean time. To obtain standard time of rise or set, see Table 5.

TABLE 4.-SUNRISE AND SUNSET, 2017

Date		66° N. Rise h. m.	66° N. Set h. m.	68° N. Rise h. m.	68° N. Set h. m.	70° N. Rise h. m.	70° N. Set h. m.	72° N. Rise h. m.	72° N. Set h. m.	74° N. Rise h. m.	74° N. Set h. m.	76° N. Rise h. m.	76° N. Set h. m.
Jan.	1	10 27	13 40	-- --	-- --	-- --	-- --	-- --	-- --	-- --	-- --	-- --	-- --
	6	10 17	13 56	11 20	12 53	-- --	-- --	-- --	-- --	-- --	-- --	-- --	-- --
	11	10 04	14 13	10 51	13 25	-- --	-- --	-- --	-- --	-- --	-- --	-- --	-- --
	16	09 49	14 31	10 27	13 53	-- --	-- --	-- --	-- --	-- --	-- --	-- --	-- --
	21	09 33	14 50	10 04	14 19	10 54	13 29	-- --	-- --	-- --	-- --	-- --	-- --
	26	09 16	15 10	09 42	14 44	10 19	14 07	11 34	12 53	-- --	-- --	-- --	-- --
	31	08 59	15 29	09 21	15 07	09 50	14 38	10 34	13 54	-- --	-- --	-- --	-- --
Feb.	5	08 41	15 48	08 59	15 30	09 23	15 07	09 55	14 34	10 49	13 41	-- --	-- --
	10	08 23	16 07	08 38	15 51	08 57	15 33	09 22	15 08	09 58	14 32	11 04	13 26
	15	08 05	16 25	08 17	16 12	08 33	15 57	08 52	15 37	09 19	15 11	09 59	14 31
	20	07 46	16 43	07 56	16 33	08 09	16 20	08 24	16 05	00 44	15 45	09 12	15 17
	25	07 27	17 00	07 35	16 52	07 45	16 43	07 57	16 31	08 12	16 16	08 33	15 56
Mar.	2	07 09	17 17	07 15	17 11	07 22	17 04	07 31	16 56	07 42	16 45	07 56	16 31
	7	06 50	17 34	06 54	17 30	06 59	17 25	07 04	17 20	07 12	17 12	07 21	17 03
	12	06 31	17 51	06 33	17 48	06 36	17 46	06 39	17 43	06 43	17 39	06 48	17 34
	17	06 11	18 07	06 12	18 07	06 12	18 06	06 13	18 06	06 14	18 06	06 15	18 05
	22	05 52	18 23	05 51	18 25	05 49	18 27	05 47	18 29	05 45	18 32	05 42	18 35
	27	05 33	18 40	05 30	18 43	05 26	18 47	05 21	18 52	05 16	18 58	05 08	19 06
Apr.	1	05 14	18 56	05 09	19 01	05 03	19 08	04 55	19 15	04 46	19 25	04 34	19 38
	6	04 54	19 12	04 47	19 20	04 39	19 29	04 29	19 39	04 15	19 53	03 58	20 12
	11	04 35	19 29	04 26	19 39	04 15	19 50	04 01	20 05	03 43	20 23	03 19	20 49
	16	04 16	19 46	04 04	19 58	03 50	20 13	03 33	20 31	03 09	20 56	02 35	21 32
	21	03 56	20 04	03 42	20 18	03 25	20 36	03 02	21 00	02 31	21 33	01 40	22 30
	26	03 37	20 22	03 20	20 39	02 58	21 01	02 29	21 32	01 45	22 20	** **	** **
May.	1	03 17	20 40	02 57	21 01	02 30	21 29	01 51	22 10	00 23		** **	** **
	6	02 57	20 59	02 33	21 24	01 59	22 00	00 59	23 08	** **	** **	** **	** **
	11	02 38	21 18	02 08	21 49	01 22	22 39	** **	** **	** **	** **	** **	** **
	16	02 18	21 38	01 41	22 17	00 17		** **	** **	** **	** **	** **	** **
	21	01 58	21 59	01 09	22 52	** **	** **	** **	** **	** **	** **	** **	** **
	26	01 37	22 21	00 14		** **	** **	** **	** **	** **	** **	** **	** **
	31	01 16	22 43	** **	** **	** **	** **	** **	** **	** **	** **	** **	** **
Jun.	5	00 54	23 08	** **	** **	** **	** **	** **	** **	** **	** **	** **	** **
	10	00 28	23 38	** **	** **	** **	** **	** **	** **	** **	** **	** **	** **
	15	** **	** **	** **	** **	** **	** **	** **	** **	** **	** **	** **	** **
	20	** **	** **	** **	** **	** **	** **	** **	** **	** **	** **	** **	** **
	25	** **	** **	** **	** **	** **	** **	** **	** **	** **	** **	** **	** **
	30	00 09	23 46	** **	** **	** **	** **	** **	** **	** **	** **	** **	** **
Jul.	5	00 48	23 16	** **	** **	** **	** **	** **	** **	** **	** **	** **	** **
	10	01 14	22 53	** **	** **	** **	** **	** **	** **	** **	** **	** **	** **
	15	01 36	22 32	** **	** **	** **	** **	** **	** **	** **	** **	** **	** **
	20	01 58	22 12	00 59	23 06	** **	** **	** **	** **	** **	** **	** **	** **
	25	02 18	21 51	01 36	22 31	** **	** **	** **	** **	** **	** **	** **	** **
	30	02 38	21 31	02 05	22 03	01 08	22 55	** **	** **	** **	** **	** **	** **
Aug.	4	02 58	21 12	02 31	21 37	01 52	22 14		23 31	** **	** **	** **	** **
	9	03 16	20 52	02 54	21 13	02 24	21 42	01 37	22 26	** **	** **	** **	** **
	14	03 34	20 32	03 16	20 50	02 52	21 13	02 18	21 45	01 20	22 37	** **	** **
	19	03 52	20 13	03 37	20 28	03 17	20 46	02 51	21 11	02 14	21 46	01 00	22 49
	24	04 09	19 53	03 56	20 05	03 41	20 21	03 20	20 40	02 53	21 06	02 11	21 45
	29	04 26	19 34	04 15	19 44	04 03	19 56	03 47	20 11	03 26	20 31	02 57	20 58
Sep.	3	04 42	19 14	04 34	19 22	04 24	19 32	04 12	19 43	03 56	19 58	03 35	20 18
	8	04 58	18 55	04 52	19 01	04 45	19 08	04 36	19 16	04 24	19 27	04 09	19 42
	13	05 14	18 36	05 10	18 40	05 05	18 44	04 59	18 50	04 51	18 57	04 41	19 07
	18	05 30	18 16	05 28	18 19	05 25	18 21	05 21	18 24	05 17	18 28	05 11	18 33
	23	05 46	17 57	05 45	17 58	05 44	17 58	05 44	17 59	05 43	17 59	05 41	18 00
	28	06 01	17 38	06 03	17 37	06 04	17 35	06 06	17 33	06 08	17 31	06 11	17 27
Oct.	3	06 17	17 19	06 20	17 16	06 24	17 12	06 28	17 07	06 34	17 02	06 41	16 54
	8	06 34	17 00	06 38	16 55	06 44	16 49	06 51	16 42	07 00	16 32	07 12	16 20
	13	06 50	16 41	06 57	16 34	07 05	16 26	07 15	16 15	07 28	16 02	07 45	15 45
	18	07 07	16 22	07 16	16 13	07 26	16 02	07 40	15 49	07 57	15 31	08 20	15 08
	23	07 24	16 04	07 35	15 52	07 49	15 39	08 06	15 21	08 28	14 58	09 01	14 26
	28	07 41	15 45	07 55	15 31	08 12	15 14	08 34	14 52	09 04	14 22	09 51	13 34
Nov.	2	07 59	15 27	08 16	15 10	08 36	14 50	09 04	14 22	09 46	13 40	-- --	-- --
	7	08 18	15 09	08 37	14 49	09 03	14 24	09 39	13 47	10 48	12 38	-- --	-- --
	12	08 36	14 51	09 00	14 28	09 31	13 56	10 23	13 04	-- --	-- --	-- --	-- --
	17	08 55	14 34	09 23	14 06	10 04	13 25	-- --	-- --	-- --	-- --	-- --	-- --
	22	09 14	14 17	09 48	13 44	10 46	12 45	-- --	-- --	-- --	-- --	-- --	-- --
	27	09 33	14 02	10 14	13 21	-- --	-- --	-- --	-- --	-- --	-- --	-- --	-- --
Dec.	2	09 51	13 48	10 43	12 55	-- --	-- --	-- --	-- --	-- --	-- --	-- --	-- --
	7	10 07	13 36	11 20	12 23	-- --	-- --	-- --	-- --	-- --	-- --	-- --	-- --
	12	10 21	13 26	-- --	-- --	-- --	-- --	-- --	-- --	-- --	-- --	-- --	-- --
	17	10 31	13 22	-- --	-- --	-- --	-- --	-- --	-- --	-- --	-- --	-- --	-- --
	22	10 35	13 22	-- --	-- --	-- --	-- --	-- --	-- --	-- --	-- --	-- --	-- --
	27	10 34	13 29	-- --	-- --	-- --	-- --	-- --	-- --	-- --	-- --	-- --	-- --

Local mean time. To obtain standard time of rise or set, see Table 5.

TABLE 4.-SUNRISE AND SUNSET, 2017

379

Date		0° S. Rise	0° S. Set	5° S. Rise	5° S. Set	10° S. Rise	10° S. Set	15° S. Rise	15° S. Set	20° S. Rise	20° S. Set	25° S. Rise	25° S. Set
		h. m.	h. m.	h. m.	h. m.	h. m.	h. m.	h. m.	h. m.	h. m.	h. m.	h. m.	h. m.
Jan.	1	06 00	18 07	05 51	18 16	05 43	18 25	05 34	18 34	05 24	18 43	05 14	18 53
	6	06 02	18 10	05 54	18 18	05 45	18 26	05 37	18 35	05 27	18 44	05 17	18 54
	11	06 04	18 12	05 56	18 20	05 48	18 28	05 40	18 36	05 31	18 45	05 21	18 55
	16	06 06	18 13	05 59	18 21	05 51	18 29	05 43	18 37	05 34	18 46	05 25	18 55
	21	06 08	18 15	06 00	18 22	05 53	18 30	05 45	18 37	05 37	18 45	05 29	18 54
	26	06 09	18 16	06 02	18 23	05 55	18 30	05 48	18 37	05 41	18 44	05 32	18 53
	31	06 10	18 17	06 04	18 23	05 57	18 30	05 51	18 36	05 44	18 43	05 36	18 51
Feb.	5	06 11	18 17	06 05	18 23	05 59	18 29	05 53	18 35	05 47	18 41	05 40	18 48
	10	06 11	18 18	06 06	18 23	06 00	18 28	05 55	18 33	05 49	18 39	05 43	18 45
	15	06 11	18 17	06 06	18 22	06 02	18 26	05 57	18 31	05 52	18 36	05 46	18 41
	20	06 10	18 17	06 06	18 21	06 03	18 25	05 58	18 29	05 54	18 33	05 49	18 38
	25	06 10	18 16	06 06	18 19	06 03	18 23	06 00	18 26	05 56	18 29	05 52	18 33
Mar.	2	06 09	18 15	06 06	18 18	06 04	18 20	06 01	18 23	05 58	18 26	05 55	18 29
	7	06 08	18 14	06 06	18 16	06 04	18 18	06 02	18 20	06 00	18 22	05 58	18 24
	12	06 06	18 13	06 05	18 14	06 04	18 15	06 03	18 16	06 01	18 18	06 00	18 19
	17	06 05	18 12	06 05	18 12	06 04	18 12	06 04	18 13	06 03	18 13	06 02	18 14
	22	06 04	18 10	06 04	18 10	06 04	18 09	06 04	18 09	06 04	18 09	06 05	18 09
	27	06 02	18 09	06 03	18 08	06 04	18 07	06 05	18 06	06 06	18 05	06 07	18 04
Apr.	1	06 01	18 07	06 02	18 05	06 04	18 04	06 05	18 02	06 07	18 00	06 09	17 58
	6	05 59	18 06	06 01	18 03	06 04	18 01	06 06	17 59	06 08	17 56	06 11	17 53
	11	05 58	18 04	06 01	18 01	06 04	17 58	06 07	17 55	06 10	17 52	06 13	17 49
	16	05 56	18 03	06 00	17 59	06 04	17 56	06 07	17 52	06 11	17 48	06 15	17 44
	21	05 55	18 02	06 00	17 58	06 04	17 53	06 08	17 49	06 13	17 44	06 18	17 39
	26	05 54	18 01	05 59	17 56	06 04	17 51	06 09	17 46	06 14	17 41	06 20	17 35
May.	1	05 54	18 00	05 59	17 55	06 05	17 49	06 10	17 44	06 16	17 38	06 22	17 32
	6	05 53	18 00	05 59	17 54	06 05	17 48	06 11	17 42	06 18	17 35	06 25	17 28
	11	05 53	18 00	05 59	17 53	06 06	17 47	06 13	17 40	06 20	17 33	06 27	17 25
	16	05 53	18 00	06 00	17 53	06 07	17 46	06 14	17 39	06 22	17 31	06 30	17 23
	21	05 53	18 00	06 00	17 53	06 08	17 45	06 16	17 38	06 24	17 29	06 32	17 21
	26	05 53	18 01	06 01	17 53	06 09	17 45	06 17	17 37	06 26	17 28	06 35	17 19
	31	05 54	18 01	06 02	17 53	06 10	17 45	06 19	17 37	06 28	17 28	06 37	17 18
Jun.	5	05 55	18 02	06 03	17 54	06 12	17 45	06 20	17 37	06 29	17 28	06 39	17 18
	10	05 56	18 03	06 04	17 55	06 13	17 46	06 22	17 37	06 31	17 28	06 41	17 18
	15	05 57	18 04	06 05	17 56	06 14	17 47	06 23	17 38	06 33	17 28	06 43	17 18
	20	05 58	18 05	06 07	17 57	06 15	17 48	06 24	17 39	06 34	17 29	06 44	17 19
	25	05 59	18 06	06 08	17 58	06 16	17 49	06 26	17 40	06 35	17 30	06 45	17 20
	30	06 00	18 07	06 09	17 59	06 17	17 50	06 26	17 41	06 36	17 32	06 46	17 22
Jul.	5	06 01	18 08	06 09	18 00	06 18	17 51	06 27	17 43	06 36	17 33	06 46	17 24
	10	06 02	18 09	06 10	18 01	06 18	17 53	06 27	17 44	06 36	17 35	06 45	17 26
	15	06 02	18 10	06 10	18 02	06 18	17 54	06 26	17 46	06 35	17 37	06 44	17 28
	20	06 03	18 10	06 10	18 02	06 18	17 55	06 26	17 47	06 34	17 39	06 43	17 30
	25	06 03	18 10	06 10	18 03	06 17	17 56	06 25	17 48	06 33	17 41	06 41	17 32
	30	06 03	18 10	06 10	18 03	06 16	17 57	06 23	17 50	06 31	17 42	06 38	17 35
Aug.	4	06 03	18 10	06 09	18 03	06 15	17 57	06 22	17 51	06 28	17 44	06 35	17 37
	9	06 02	18 09	06 08	18 03	06 13	17 58	06 19	17 52	06 25	17 46	06 32	17 39
	14	06 01	18 08	06 06	18 03	06 12	17 58	06 17	17 53	06 22	17 47	06 28	17 41
	19	06 00	18 07	06 05	18 02	06 09	17 58	06 14	17 53	06 19	17 49	06 24	17 43
	24	05 59	18 06	06 03	18 02	06 07	17 58	06 11	17 54	06 15	17 50	06 19	17 45
	29	05 58	18 04	06 01	18 01	06 04	17 58	06 08	17 54	06 11	17 51	06 15	17 47
Sep.	3	05 56	18 03	05 59	18 00	06 01	17 57	06 04	17 55	06 07	17 52	06 10	17 49
	8	05 54	18 01	05 56	17 59	05 58	17 57	06 00	17 55	06 02	17 53	06 04	17 51
	13	05 53	17 59	05 54	17 58	05 55	17 57	05 56	17 55	05 58	17 54	05 59	17 53
	18	05 51	17 57	05 51	17 57	05 52	17 56	05 53	17 56	05 53	17 55	05 54	17 55
	23	05 49	17 56	05 49	17 56	05 49	17 56	05 49	17 56	05 49	17 56	05 48	17 57
	28	05 47	17 54	05 47	17 55	05 46	17 56	05 45	17 56	05 44	17 57	05 43	17 58
Oct.	3	05 46	17 52	05 44	17 54	05 43	17 55	05 41	17 57	05 40	17 59	05 38	18 00
	8	05 44	17 51	05 42	17 53	05 40	17 55	05 38	17 58	05 35	18 00	05 33	18 03
	13	05 43	17 49	05 40	17 52	05 37	17 55	05 34	17 58	05 31	18 01	05 28	18 05
	18	05 42	17 48	05 38	17 52	05 35	17 56	05 31	17 59	05 27	18 03	05 23	18 07
	23	05 41	17 48	05 37	17 52	05 33	17 56	05 28	18 00	05 24	18 05	05 19	18 10
	28	05 40	17 47	05 36	17 52	05 31	17 57	05 26	18 02	05 21	18 07	05 15	18 13
Nov.	2	05 40	17 47	05 35	17 52	05 29	17 58	05 24	18 04	05 18	18 10	05 11	18 16
	7	05 40	17 47	05 34	17 53	05 28	17 59	05 22	18 06	05 15	18 12	05 08	18 19
	12	05 41	17 48	05 34	17 54	05 28	18 01	05 21	18 08	05 14	18 15	05 06	18 23
	17	05 41	17 49	05 35	17 56	05 27	18 03	05 20	18 10	05 12	18 18	05 04	18 26
	22	05 43	17 50	05 35	17 57	05 28	18 05	05 20	18 13	05 12	18 21	05 03	18 30
	27	05 44	17 51	05 36	17 59	05 28	18 07	05 20	18 15	05 11	18 24	05 02	18 34
Dec.	2	05 46	17 53	05 38	18 01	05 29	18 10	05 21	18 18	05 12	18 27	05 02	18 37
	7	05 48	17 55	05 39	18 04	05 31	18 12	05 22	18 21	05 13	18 31	05 03	18 41
	12	05 50	17 58	05 41	18 06	05 33	18 15	05 24	18 24	05 14	18 34	05 04	18 44
	17	05 52	18 00	05 44	18 09	05 35	18 18	05 26	18 27	05 16	18 36	05 05	18 47
	22	05 55	18 02	05 46	18 11	05 37	18 20	05 28	18 29	05 18	18 39	05 08	18 50
	27	05 57	18 05	05 49	18 14	05 40	18 22	05 31	18 32	05 21	18 41	05 11	18 52

Local mean time. To obtain standard time of rise or set, see Table 5.

TABLE 4.–SUNRISE AND SUNSET, 2017

Date		30° S. Rise h. m.	Set h. m.	32° S. Rise h. m.	Set h. m.	34° S. Rise h. m.	Set h. m.	36° S. Rise h. m.	Set h. m.	38° S. Rise h. m.	Set h. m.	40° S. Rise h. m.	Set h. m.
Jan.	1	05 03	19 05	04 58	19 10	04 52	19 15	04 47	19 20	04 41	19 26	04 35	19 32
	6	05 06	19 05	05 01	19 10	04 56	19 15	04 51	19 20	04 46	19 26	04 40	19 32
	11	05 10	19 05	05 06	19 10	05 01	19 15	04 56	19 20	04 50	19 25	04 45	19 31
	16	05 15	19 05	05 10	19 09	05 06	19 14	05 01	19 19	04 56	19 24	04 50	19 29
	21	05 19	19 03	05 15	19 08	05 10	19 12	05 06	19 16	05 01	19 21	04 56	19 26
	26	05 23	19 01	05 20	19 05	05 15	19 09	05 11	19 13	05 07	19 18	05 02	19 23
	31	05 28	18 59	05 24	19 02	05 21	19 06	05 17	19 10	05 12	19 14	05 08	19 18
Feb.	5	05 32	18 55	05 29	18 59	05 26	19 02	05 22	19 05	05 18	19 09	05 14	19 13
	10	05 36	18 52	05 33	18 54	05 30	18 57	05 27	19 01	05 24	19 04	05 20	19 07
	15	05 40	18 47	05 38	18 50	05 35	18 52	05 32	18 55	05 29	18 58	05 26	19 01
	20	05 44	18 43	05 42	18 45	05 40	18 47	05 37	18 49	05 35	18 52	05 32	18 54
	25	05 48	18 37	05 46	18 39	05 44	18 41	05 42	18 43	05 40	18 45	05 38	18 47
Mar.	2	05 52	18 32	05 50	18 33	05 49	18 35	05 47	18 36	05 45	18 38	05 44	18 40
	7	05 55	18 26	05 54	18 27	05 53	18 28	05 52	18 30	05 51	18 31	05 49	18 32
	12	05 58	18 20	05 58	18 21	05 57	18 22	05 56	18 23	05 55	18 23	05 55	18 24
	17	06 02	18 14	06 01	18 15	06 01	18 15	06 01	18 15	06 00	18 16	06 00	18 16
	22	06 05	18 08	06 05	18 08	06 05	18 08	06 05	18 08	06 05	18 08	06 05	18 08
	27	06 08	18 02	06 08	18 02	06 09	18 01	06 09	18 01	06 10	18 00	06 10	18 00
Apr.	1	06 11	17 56	06 12	17 56	06 12	17 55	06 13	17 54	06 14	17 53	06 15	17 52
	6	06 14	17 51	06 15	17 49	06 16	17 48	06 17	17 47	06 19	17 45	06 20	17 44
	11	06 17	17 45	06 18	17 43	06 20	17 42	06 22	17 40	06 23	17 38	06 25	17 36
	16	06 20	17 39	06 22	17 37	06 24	17 35	06 26	17 33	06 28	17 31	06 30	17 29
	21	06 23	17 34	06 25	17 32	06 27	17 30	06 30	17 27	06 32	17 24	06 35	17 22
	26	06 26	17 29	06 28	17 27	06 31	17 24	06 34	17 21	06 37	17 18	06 40	17 15
May.	1	06 29	17 25	06 32	17 22	06 35	17 19	06 38	17 16	06 42	17 12	06 45	17 09
	6	06 32	17 21	06 35	17 17	06 39	17 14	06 42	17 11	06 46	17 07	06 50	17 03
	11	06 35	17 17	06 39	17 14	06 43	17 10	06 46	17 06	06 50	17 02	06 55	16 58
	16	06 39	17 14	06 42	17 10	06 46	17 06	06 50	17 02	06 55	16 58	06 59	16 53
	21	06 42	17 11	06 46	17 07	06 50	17 03	06 54	16 59	06 59	16 54	07 04	16 49
	26	06 45	17 09	06 49	17 05	06 53	17 01	06 58	16 56	07 03	16 51	07 08	16 46
	31	06 47	17 08	06 52	17 04	06 56	16 59	07 01	16 54	07 06	16 49	07 12	16 43
Jun.	5	06 50	17 07	06 54	17 03	06 59	16 58	07 04	16 53	07 10	16 47	07 15	16 42
	10	06 52	17 07	06 57	17 02	07 02	16 57	07 07	16 52	07 12	16 47	07 18	16 41
	15	06 54	17 07	06 59	17 02	07 04	16 57	07 09	16 52	07 14	16 47	07 20	16 41
	20	06 55	17 08	07 00	17 03	07 05	16 58	07 10	16 53	07 16	16 47	07 22	16 41
	25	06 56	17 09	07 01	17 04	07 06	17 00	07 11	16 54	07 17	16 49	07 23	16 43
	30	06 57	17 11	07 01	17 06	07 06	17 01	07 11	16 56	07 17	16 51	07 23	16 45
Jul.	5	06 56	17 13	07 01	17 08	07 06	17 04	07 11	16 58	07 16	16 53	07 22	16 47
	10	06 56	17 15	07 00	17 11	07 05	17 06	07 10	17 01	07 15	16 56	07 20	16 51
	15	06 54	17 18	06 59	17 14	07 03	17 09	07 08	17 04	07 13	16 59	07 18	16 54
	20	06 52	17 21	06 56	17 17	07 01	17 12	07 05	17 08	07 10	17 03	07 15	16 58
	25	06 50	17 23	06 54	17 20	06 58	17 16	07 02	17 11	07 06	17 07	07 11	17 02
	30	06 47	17 26	06 50	17 23	06 54	17 19	06 58	17 15	07 02	17 11	07 07	17 07
Aug.	4	06 43	17 29	06 46	17 26	06 50	17 23	06 54	17 19	06 57	17 15	07 02	17 11
	9	06 39	17 32	06 42	17 29	06 45	17 26	06 49	17 23	06 52	17 19	06 56	17 16
	14	06 34	17 35	06 37	17 32	06 40	17 30	06 43	17 27	06 46	17 24	06 49	17 20
	19	06 30	17 38	06 32	17 36	06 34	17 33	06 37	17 31	06 40	17 28	06 43	17 25
	24	06 24	17 41	06 26	17 39	06 28	17 37	06 31	17 34	06 33	17 32	06 36	17 30
	29	06 19	17 43	06 20	17 42	06 22	17 40	06 24	17 38	06 26	17 36	06 28	17 34
Sep.	3	06 13	17 46	06 14	17 45	06 16	17 43	06 17	17 42	06 19	17 41	06 20	17 39
	8	06 07	17 49	06 08	17 48	06 09	17 47	06 10	17 46	06 11	17 45	06 12	17 44
	13	06 01	17 51	06 01	17 51	06 02	17 50	06 03	17 50	06 03	17 49	06 04	17 48
	18	05 54	17 54	05 55	17 54	05 55	17 54	05 55	17 53	05 56	17 53	05 56	17 53
	23	05 48	17 57	05 48	17 57	05 48	17 57	05 48	17 57	05 48	17 58	05 48	17 58
	28	05 42	18 00	05 42	18 00	05 41	18 01	05 40	18 01	05 40	18 02	05 39	18 03
Oct.	3	05 36	18 03	05 35	18 03	05 34	18 04	05 33	18 05	05 32	18 06	05 31	18 08
	8	05 30	18 06	05 29	18 07	05 27	18 08	05 26	18 10	05 25	18 11	05 23	18 13
	13	05 24	18 09	05 23	18 10	05 21	18 12	05 19	18 14	05 17	18 16	05 15	18 18
	18	05 19	18 12	05 17	18 14	05 15	18 16	05 12	18 18	05 10	18 21	05 08	18 23
	23	05 13	18 16	05 11	18 18	05 09	18 20	05 06	18 23	05 04	18 26	05 01	18 29
	28	05 09	18 19	05 06	18 22	05 03	18 25	05 00	18 28	04 57	18 31	04 54	18 34
Nov.	2	05 04	18 23	05 01	18 26	04 58	18 29	04 55	18 33	04 51	18 36	04 48	18 40
	7	05 01	18 27	04 57	18 31	04 54	18 34	04 50	18 38	04 46	18 42	04 42	18 46
	12	04 57	18 31	04 54	18 35	04 50	18 39	04 46	18 43	04 42	18 47	04 37	18 52
	17	04 55	18 36	04 51	18 40	04 47	18 44	04 42	18 48	04 38	18 53	04 33	18 58
	22	04 53	18 40	04 49	18 44	04 44	18 48	04 40	18 53	04 35	18 58	04 29	19 03
	27	04 52	18 44	04 47	18 48	04 43	18 53	04 38	18 58	04 32	19 03	04 27	19 09
Dec.	2	04 51	18 48	04 47	18 53	04 42	18 58	04 37	19 03	04 31	19 08	04 25	19 14
	7	04 51	18 52	04 47	18 57	04 42	19 02	04 36	19 07	04 31	19 13	04 24	19 19
	12	04 52	18 55	04 47	19 00	04 42	19 05	04 37	19 11	04 31	19 17	04 25	19 23
	17	04 54	18 59	04 49	19 03	04 44	19 09	04 38	19 14	04 32	19 20	04 26	19 27
	22	04 56	19 01	04 51	19 06	04 46	19 11	04 40	19 17	04 34	19 23	04 28	19 29
	27	04 59	19 03	04 54	19 08	04 49	19 13	04 43	19 19	04 37	19 25	04 31	19 31

Local mean time. To obtain standard time of rise or set, see Table 5.

TABLE 4.-SUNRISE AND SUNSET, 2017   381

Date		42° S. Rise h. m.	42° S. Set h. m.	44° S. Rise h. m.	44° S. Set h. m.	46° S. Rise h. m.	46° S. Set h. m.	48° S. Rise h. m.	48° S. Set h. m.	50° S. Rise h. m.	50° S. Set h. m.	52° S. Rise h. m.	52° S. Set h. m.
Jan.	1	04 28	19 39	04 21	19 46	04 13	19 54	04 05	20 02	03 55	20 12	03 45	20 22
	6	04 33	19 38	04 26	19 45	04 19	19 53	04 10	20 01	04 01	20 10	03 51	20 20
	11	04 38	19 37	04 32	19 44	04 24	19 51	04 17	19 59	04 08	20 08	03 58	20 17
	16	04 44	19 35	04 38	19 41	04 31	19 48	04 23	19 56	04 15	20 04	04 06	20 13
	21	04 50	19 32	04 44	19 38	04 38	19 44	04 31	19 51	04 23	19 59	04 15	20 07
	26	04 57	19 28	04 51	19 33	04 45	19 39	04 39	19 46	04 32	19 53	04 24	20 00
	31	05 03	19 23	04 58	19 28	04 53	19 33	04 47	19 39	04 40	19 46	04 33	19 53
Feb.	5	05 10	19 17	05 05	19 22	05 00	19 27	04 55	19 32	04 49	19 38	04 43	19 44
	10	05 16	19 11	05 12	19 15	05 08	19 20	05 03	19 24	04 58	19 29	04 52	19 35
	15	05 23	19 04	05 19	19 08	05 15	19 12	05 11	19 16	05 07	19 20	05 02	19 25
	20	05 29	18 57	05 26	19 00	05 23	19 04	05 19	19 07	05 15	19 11	05 11	19 15
	25	05 36	18 50	05 33	18 52	05 30	18 55	05 27	18 58	05 24	19 01	05 21	19 04
Mar.	2	05 42	18 42	05 40	18 44	05 38	18 46	05 35	18 48	05 33	18 51	05 30	18 53
	7	05 48	18 33	05 46	18 35	05 45	18 36	05 43	18 38	05 41	18 40	05 39	18 42
	12	05 54	18 25	05 53	18 26	05 52	18 27	05 50	18 28	05 49	18 29	05 48	18 31
	17	05 59	18 16	05 59	18 17	05 58	18 17	05 58	18 18	05 57	18 18	05 56	18 19
	22	06 05	18 08	06 05	18 08	06 05	18 08	06 05	18 08	06 05	18 08	06 05	18 07
	27	06 11	17 59	06 11	17 59	06 12	17 58	06 12	17 57	06 13	17 57	06 14	17 56
Apr.	1	06 16	17 51	06 17	17 50	06 18	17 49	06 20	17 47	06 21	17 46	06 22	17 44
	6	06 22	17 42	06 23	17 41	06 25	17 39	06 27	17 37	06 29	17 35	06 31	17 33
	11	06 27	17 34	06 29	17 32	06 31	17 30	06 34	17 27	06 36	17 25	06 39	17 22
	16	06 33	17 26	06 35	17 24	06 38	17 21	06 41	17 18	06 44	17 15	06 48	17 11
	21	06 38	17 19	06 41	17 16	06 44	17 12	06 48	17 09	06 52	17 05	06 56	17 01
	26	06 43	17 12	06 47	17 08	06 51	17 04	06 55	17 00	06 59	16 56	07 04	16 51
May.	1	06 49	17 05	06 53	17 01	06 57	16 56	07 02	16 52	07 07	16 47	07 12	16 41
	6	06 54	16 59	06 59	16 54	07 03	16 49	07 09	16 44	07 14	16 38	07 20	16 32
	11	06 59	16 53	07 04	16 48	07 09	16 43	07 15	16 37	07 21	16 31	07 28	16 24
	16	07 04	16 48	07 10	16 43	07 15	16 37	07 21	16 31	07 28	16 24	07 36	16 16
	21	07 09	16 44	07 15	16 38	07 21	16 32	07 28	16 25	07 35	16 18	07 43	16 10
	26	07 14	16 40	07 20	16 34	07 26	16 28	07 33	16 21	07 41	16 13	07 49	16 04
	31	07 18	16 38	07 24	16 31	07 31	16 24	07 38	16 17	07 46	16 09	07 55	16 00
Jun.	5	07 21	16 36	07 28	16 29	07 35	16 22	07 43	16 14	07 51	16 06	08 00	15 57
	10	07 24	16 35	07 31	16 28	07 38	16 21	07 46	16 13	07 55	16 04	08 04	15 54
	15	07 27	16 34	07 33	16 28	07 41	16 20	07 49	16 12	07 58	16 03	08 07	15 54
	20	07 28	16 35	07 35	16 28	07 42	16 21	07 51	16 13	07 59	16 04	08 09	15 54
	25	07 29	16 36	07 36	16 30	07 43	16 22	07 51	16 14	08 00	16 05	08 10	15 55
	30	07 29	16 39	07 36	16 32	07 43	16 25	07 51	16 17	08 00	16 08	08 09	15 58
Jul.	5	07 28	16 41	07 35	16 35	07 42	16 28	07 50	16 20	07 58	16 11	08 08	16 02
	10	07 26	16 45	07 33	16 38	07 40	16 31	07 47	16 24	07 55	16 16	08 05	16 07
	15	07 24	16 48	07 30	16 42	07 37	16 36	07 44	16 29	07 52	16 21	08 00	16 12
	20	07 20	16 53	07 26	16 47	07 33	16 41	07 39	16 34	07 47	16 26	07 55	16 18
	25	07 16	16 57	07 22	16 52	07 28	16 46	07 34	16 40	07 41	16 33	07 49	16 25
	30	07 11	17 02	07 16	16 57	07 22	16 51	07 28	16 46	07 34	16 39	07 41	16 32
Aug.	4	07 06	17 07	07 10	17 02	07 15	16 57	07 21	16 52	07 27	16 46	07 33	16 40
	9	07 00	17 12	07 04	17 08	07 08	17 03	07 13	16 58	07 18	16 53	07 24	16 47
	14	06 53	17 17	06 57	17 13	07 01	17 09	07 05	17 05	07 10	17 00	07 15	16 55
	19	06 46	17 22	06 49	17 19	06 53	17 15	06 56	17 11	07 00	17 07	07 05	17 03
	24	06 38	17 27	06 41	17 24	06 44	17 21	06 47	17 18	06 51	17 15	06 54	17 11
	29	06 30	17 32	06 32	17 30	06 35	17 27	06 38	17 25	06 40	17 22	06 44	17 19
Sep.	3	06 22	17 37	06 24	17 36	06 26	17 34	06 28	17 32	06 30	17 29	06 32	17 27
	8	06 13	17 42	06 15	17 41	06 16	17 40	06 18	17 38	06 19	17 37	06 21	17 35
	13	06 05	17 48	06 06	17 47	06 07	17 46	06 07	17 45	06 08	17 44	06 10	17 43
	18	05 56	17 53	05 56	17 52	05 57	17 52	05 57	17 52	05 57	17 52	05 58	17 51
	23	05 47	17 58	05 47	17 58	05 47	17 58	05 47	17 59	05 46	17 59	05 46	17 59
	28	05 39	18 03	05 38	18 04	05 37	18 05	05 36	18 06	05 35	18 07	05 35	18 08
Oct.	3	05 30	18 09	05 29	18 10	05 27	18 11	05 26	18 13	05 25	18 14	05 23	18 16
	8	05 21	18 14	05 20	18 16	05 18	18 18	05 16	18 20	05 14	18 22	05 11	18 25
	13	05 13	18 20	05 11	18 22	05 09	18 25	05 06	18 27	05 03	18 30	05 00	18 33
	18	05 05	18 26	05 02	18 29	05 00	18 32	04 56	18 35	04 53	18 38	04 49	18 42
	23	04 58	18 32	04 54	18 35	04 51	18 39	04 47	18 43	04 43	18 47	04 38	18 51
	28	04 50	18 38	04 47	18 42	04 43	18 46	04 38	18 50	04 34	18 55	04 28	19 00
Nov.	2	04 44	18 44	04 40	18 48	04 35	18 53	04 30	18 58	04 25	19 04	04 19	19 10
	7	04 38	18 50	04 33	18 55	04 28	19 00	04 22	19 06	04 16	19 12	04 10	19 19
	12	04 32	18 57	04 27	19 02	04 21	19 08	04 15	19 14	04 09	19 21	04 01	19 28
	17	04 28	19 03	04 22	19 09	04 16	19 15	04 09	19 22	04 02	19 29	03 54	19 37
	22	04 24	19 09	04 18	19 15	04 11	19 22	04 04	19 29	03 56	19 37	03 47	19 46
	27	04 21	19 15	04 14	19 21	04 07	19 29	04 00	19 36	03 51	19 45	03 42	19 54
Dec.	2	04 19	19 20	04 12	19 27	04 05	19 35	03 57	19 43	03 48	19 52	03 38	20 02
	7	04 18	19 25	04 11	19 32	04 03	19 40	03 55	19 49	03 46	19 58	03 35	20 08
	12	04 18	19 30	04 11	19 37	04 03	19 45	03 54	19 53	03 45	20 03	03 34	20 14
	17	04 19	19 33	04 12	19 41	04 04	19 49	03 55	19 57	03 46	20 07	03 35	20 18
	22	04 21	19 36	04 14	19 43	04 06	19 51	03 57	20 00	03 47	20 10	03 37	20 21
	27	04 24	19 38	04 17	19 45	04 09	19 53	04 00	20 02	03 51	20 11	03 40	20 22

Local mean time. To obtain standard time of rise or set, see Table 5.

TABLE 4.-SUNRISE AND SUNSET, 2017

Date		54° S.		56° S.		58° S.		60° S.	
		Rise	Set	Rise	Set	Rise	Set	Rise	Set
		h. m.	h. m.	h. m.	h. m.	h. m.	h. m.	h. m.	h. m.
Jan.	1	03 33	20 34	03 19	20 48	03 03	21 04	02 43	21 23
	6	03 39	20 32	03 26	20 45	03 11	21 00	02 52	21 19
	11	03 47	20 28	03 34	20 41	03 20	20 55	03 02	21 12
	16	03 56	20 23	03 44	20 35	03 30	20 48	03 14	21 04
	21	04 05	20 17	03 54	20 27	03 42	20 40	03 27	20 54
	26	04 15	20 09	04 05	20 19	03 54	20 30	03 40	20 43
	31	04 25	20 01	04 16	20 10	04 06	20 20	03 54	20 31
Feb.	5	04 35	19 51	04 27	19 59	04 18	20 08	04 08	20 18
	10	04 46	19 41	04 39	19 48	04 31	19 56	04 22	20 05
	15	04 56	19 31	04 50	19 37	04 43	19 43	04 35	19 51
	20	05 06	19 20	05 01	19 25	04 55	19 30	04 49	19 37
	25	05 17	19 08	05 12	19 12	05 08	19 17	05 02	19 22
Mar.	2	05 27	18 56	05 23	19 00	05 19	19 03	05 15	19 07
	7	05 37	18 44	05 34	18 47	05 31	18 49	05 28	18 52
	12	05 46	18 32	05 45	18 34	05 43	18 35	05 41	18 37
	17	05 56	18 20	05 55	18 20	05 54	18 21	05 53	18 22
	22	06 05	18 07	06 05	18 07	06 05	18 07	06 05	18 07
	27	06 14	17 55	06 15	17 54	06 16	17 53	06 17	17 52
Apr.	1	06 24	17 43	06 25	17 41	06 27	17 39	06 29	17 37
	6	06 33	17 31	06 36	17 28	06 38	17 25	06 41	17 22
	11	06 42	17 19	06 46	17 15	06 49	17 12	06 53	17 07
	16	06 51	17 07	06 56	17 03	07 00	16 58	07 05	16 53
	21	07 00	16 56	07 05	16 51	07 11	16 45	07 17	16 39
	26	07 09	16 45	07 15	16 39	07 22	16 33	07 29	16 25
May.	1	07 18	16 35	07 25	16 28	07 33	16 21	07 41	16 12
	6	07 27	16 25	07 35	16 18	07 43	16 09	07 53	15 59
	11	07 36	16 16	07 44	16 08	07 54	15 58	08 05	15 47
	16	07 44	16 08	07 53	15 59	08 04	15 48	08 16	15 36
	21	07 52	16 01	08 02	15 51	08 13	15 40	08 26	15 26
	26	07 59	15 55	08 10	15 44	08 22	15 32	08 36	15 17
	31	08 05	15 50	08 17	15 38	08 30	15 25	08 45	15 10
Jun.	5	08 11	15 46	08 23	15 34	08 36	15 20	08 53	15 04
	10	08 15	15 44	08 28	15 31	08 42	15 17	08 59	15 00
	15	08 18	15 42	08 31	15 30	08 46	15 15	09 03	14 58
	20	08 20	15 43	08 33	15 30	08 48	15 15	09 06	14 58
	25	08 21	15 44	08 34	15 32	08 49	15 17	09 06	15 00
	30	08 20	15 47	08 33	15 35	08 47	15 20	09 04	15 03
Jul.	5	08 18	15 51	08 30	15 39	08 44	15 25	09 01	15 09
	10	08 15	15 56	08 26	15 45	08 40	15 32	08 55	15 16
	15	08 10	16 02	08 21	15 52	08 33	15 39	08 48	15 24
	20	08 04	16 09	08 14	15 59	08 26	15 47	08 40	15 34
	25	07 57	16 17	08 06	16 07	08 17	15 56	08 30	15 44
	30	07 49	16 24	07 58	16 16	08 08	16 06	08 19	15 55
Aug.	4	07 40	16 33	07 48	16 25	07 57	16 16	08 07	16 06
	9	07 31	16 41	07 38	16 34	07 46	16 26	07 55	16 17
	14	07 20	16 50	07 27	16 43	07 34	16 36	07 42	16 29
	19	07 10	16 58	07 15	16 53	07 21	16 47	07 28	16 40
	24	06 59	17 07	07 03	17 02	07 08	16 57	07 14	16 52
	29	06 47	17 16	06 51	17 12	06 55	17 08	07 00	17 03
Sep.	3	06 35	17 24	06 38	17 22	06 41	17 18	06 45	17 15
	8	06 23	17 33	06 25	17 31	06 27	17 29	06 30	17 26
	13	06 11	17 42	06 12	17 41	06 13	17 39	06 15	17 38
	18	05 58	17 51	05 59	17 51	05 59	17 50	06 00	17 50
	23	05 46	18 00	05 46	18 00	05 45	18 01	05 45	18 01
	28	05 33	18 09	05 32	18 10	05 31	18 12	05 29	18 13
Oct.	3	05 21	18 18	05 19	18 20	05 17	18 23	05 14	18 25
	8	05 09	18 27	05 06	18 30	05 03	18 34	04 59	18 37
	13	04 57	18 37	04 53	18 41	04 49	18 45	04 44	18 50
	18	04 45	18 47	04 40	18 51	04 35	18 57	04 29	19 03
	23	04 34	18 56	04 28	19 02	04 22	19 08	04 15	19 15
	28	04 22	19 06	04 16	19 13	04 09	19 20	04 01	19 29
Nov.	2	04 12	19 16	04 05	19 24	03 56	19 32	03 47	19 42
	7	04 02	19 26	03 54	19 35	03 45	19 44	03 34	19 55
	12	03 53	19 37	03 44	19 46	03 33	19 57	03 21	20 09
	17	03 45	19 46	03 35	19 57	03 23	20 08	03 10	20 22
	22	03 38	19 56	03 27	20 07	03 14	20 20	02 59	20 35
	27	03 32	20 05	03 20	20 17	03 06	20 31	02 50	20 47
Dec.	2	03 27	20 13	03 14	20 26	03 00	20 41	02 42	20 58
	7	03 24	20 20	03 10	20 33	02 55	20 49	02 36	21 08
	12	03 22	20 26	03 08	20 40	02 52	20 56	02 32	21 16
	17	03 22	20 30	03 08	20 44	02 51	21 01	02 31	21 22
	22	03 24	20 33	03 10	20 47	02 53	21 04	02 33	21 25
	27	03 28	20 34	03 14	20 49	02 57	21 05	02 37	21 25

Local mean time. To obtain standard time of rise or set, see Table 5.

TABLE 5.—REDUCTION OF LOCAL MEAN TIME TO STANDARD TIME

Difference of longitude between local and standard meridian	Correction to local mean time to obtain standard time	Difference of longitude between local and standard meridian	Correction to local mean time to obtain standard time	Difference of longitude between local and standard meridian	Correction to local mean time to obtain standard time
° ′ ° ′	Minutes	° ′ ° ′	Minutes	°	Hours
0 00 to 0 07	0	7 23 to 7 37	30	15	1
0 08 to 0 22	1	7 38 to 7 52	31	30	2
0 23 to 0 37	2	7 53 to 8 07	32	45	3
0 38 to 0 52	3	8 08 to 8 22	33	60	4
0 53 to 1 07	4	8 23 to 8 37	34	75	5
1 08 to 1 22	5	8 38 to 8 52	35	90	6
1 23 to 1 37	6	8 53 to 9 07	36	105	7
1 38 to 1 52	7	9 08 to 9 22	37	120	8
1 53 to 2 07	8	9 23 to 9 37	38	135	9
2 08 to 2 22	9	9 38 to 9 52	39	150	10
2 23 to 2 37	10	9 53 to 10 07	40	165	11
2 38 to 2 52	11	10 08 to 10 22	41	180	12
2 53 to 3 07	12	10 23 to 10 37	42		
3 08 to 3 22	13	10 38 to 10 52	43		
3 23 to 3 37	14	10 53 to 11 07	44		
3 38 to 3 52	15	11 08 to 11 22	45		
3 53 to 4 07	16	11 23 to 11 37	46		
4 08 to 4 22	17	11 38 to 11 52	47		
4 23 to 4 37	18	11 53 to 12 07	48		
4 38 to 4 52	19	12 08 to 12 22	49		
4 53 to 5 07	20	12 23 to 12 37	50		
5 08 to 5 22	21	12 38 to 12 52	51		
5 23 to 5 37	22	12 53 to 13 07	52		
5 38 to 5 52	23	13 08 to 13 22	53		
5 53 to 6 07	24	13 23 to 13 37	54		
6 08 to 6 22	25	13 38 to 13 52	55		
6 23 to 6 37	26	13 53 to 14 07	56		
6 38 to 6 52	27	14 08 to 14 22	57		
6 53 to 7 07	28	14 23 to 14 37	58		
7 08 to 7 22	29	14 38 to 14 52	59		

If local meridian is east of standard meridian, subtract the correction from local time.

If local meridian is west of standard meridian, add the correction to local time.

For differences of longitude less than 15°, use the first part of the table. For greater differences use both parts thus: 47° 23' is equivalent to 45°+ 2° 23', the correction for 45° is 3 hours, the correction for 2° 23' is 10 minutes; therefore the total correction for the difference in longitude 47° 23' is 3 hours and 10 minutes.

TABLE 6.—MOONRISE AND MOONSET

EXPLANATION OF TABLE

This table gives the time of rising and setting of the Moon's upper limb for every day in the year, at each of the following places:

Boston, Massachusetts	New York, New York	Baltimore, Maryland
Washington, D.C.	Charleston, South Carolina	Savannah, Georgia
Galveston, Texas	Panama Canal	

All of Table 6 was supplied by the Nautical Almanac Office of the United States Naval Observatory. Since Baltimore, Md., and Washington, D.C., are comparatively near to each other, a single table was compiled for a point midway between the two cities. The difference in time of moonrise and moonset at the point selected and at either city may vary between 0 and 2 minutes. In a similar way, a single table was made for Charleston, S.C., and Savannah, Ga.; and the difference in time of the moonrise or moonset at the point selected and at either city may vary between 0 and 4 minutes, which differences are of no practical importance in this table. For the Panama Canal the times were computed for a point about midway between the two ends and are applicable to the entire canal and are accurate to within a minute or two.

TABLE 6.-MOONRISE AND MOONSET, 2017

Boston, Massachusetts

Day	JANUARY Rise h m	Set h m	FEBRUARY Rise h m	Set h m	MARCH Rise h m	Set h m	APRIL Rise h m	Set h m	MAY Rise h m	Set h m	JUNE Rise h m	Set h m	Day
1	0916	1959	0934	2213	0808	2112	0847	2336	0928	....	1135	0016	1
2	0952	2102	1007	2321	0844	2222	0939	....	1032	0018	1238	0048	2
3	1025	2207	1042	....	0922	2331	1036	0037	1137	0102	1338	0118	3
4	1058	2313	1121	0030	1004	....	1137	0132	1241	0140	1438	0146	4
5	1130	....	1205	0139	1051	0039	1240	0219	1343	0213	1536	0215	5
6	1204	0021	1254	0246	1144	0142	1344	0300	1445	0244	1634	0244	6
7	1241	0131	1350	0349	1242	0241	1448	0337	1545	0313	1731	0315	7
8	1322	0241	1451	0447	1344	0333	1550	0410	1644	0342	1826	0350	8
9	1410	0352	1556	0539	1448	0419	1652	0440	1742	0410	1920	0428	9
10	1504	0500	1702	0624	1553	0500	1752	0509	1840	0441	2010	0511	10
11	1604	0603	1808	0703	1657	0536	1851	0538	1936	0514	2057	0558	11
12	1709	0700	1913	0738	1800	0608	1950	0608	2031	0550	2139	0650	12
13	1816	0749	2016	0810	1902	0639	2047	0640	2123	0629	2218	0745	13
14	1923	0831	2116	0840	2002	0708	2143	0714	2212	0713	2253	0843	14
15	2028	0908	2216	0909	2102	0738	2236	0751	2257	0802	2326	0944	15
16	2131	0941	2314	0939	2159	0808	2327	0832	2338	0855	2358	1046	16
17	2232	1011	....	1010	2256	0841	....	0918	....	0952	....	1151	17
18	2331	1040	0011	1043	2351	0916	0015	1009	0016	1051	0029	1258	18
19	....	1109	0106	1120	....	0955	0059	1104	0051	1154	0102	1407	19
20	0029	1139	0201	1201	0043	1038	0139	1203	0124	1259	0136	1518	20
21	0126	1210	0253	1247	0133	1127	0217	1305	0157	1406	0215	1631	21
22	0222	1245	0342	1338	0220	1220	0252	1410	0230	1516	0300	1744	22
23	0317	1324	0428	1434	0304	1318	0326	1518	0304	1629	0352	1853	23
24	0411	1407	0511	1535	0344	1419	0400	1629	0342	1743	0451	1955	24
25	0502	1456	0550	1638	0421	1525	0434	1742	0425	1858	0556	2050	25
26	0550	1549	0626	1745	0457	1632	0511	1856	0514	2009	0704	2136	26
27	0635	1648	0701	1853	0531	1742	0552	2010	0610	2114	0813	2215	27
28	0716	1749	0734	2002	0605	1854	0638	2122	0712	2211	0921	2250	28
29	0753	1853	....	....	0641	2006	0729	2228	0817	2259	1026	2321	29
30	0828	1959	....	....	0719	2118	0826	2327	0925	2341	1129	2350	30
31	0901	2106	....	....	0800	2229	....	....	1031	....	....	....	31

Day	JULY Rise h m	Set h m	AUGUST Rise h m	Set h m	SEPTEMBER Rise h m	Set h m	OCTOBER Rise h m	Set h m	NOVEMBER Rise h m	Set h m	DECEMBER Rise h m	Set h m	Day
1	1230	....	1412	....	1530	0031	1527	0103	1536	0258	1513	0403	1
2	1329	0018	1507	0027	1614	0123	1602	0204	1608	0407	1555	0516	2
3	1427	0047	1600	0106	1654	0218	1635	0307	1644	0518	1643	0631	3
4	1524	0118	1650	0150	1731	0318	1707	0413	1723	0631	1738	0743	4
5	1620	0151	1736	0239	1805	0420	1739	0520	1807	0744	1841	0849	5
6	1715	0228	1818	0332	1837	0524	1813	0630	1858	0856	1949	0947	6
7	1806	0309	1857	0429	1909	0630	1849	0740	1956	1003	2059	1036	7
8	1855	0355	1932	0530	1941	0737	1930	0851	2058	1103	2207	1118	8
9	1939	0445	2005	0632	2015	0845	2016	1002	2205	1155	2314	1154	9
10	2019	0539	2036	0735	2051	0954	2107	1109	2312	1239	....	1226	10
11	2056	0637	2107	0840	2132	1103	2205	1211	....	1317	0019	1256	11
12	2130	0737	2139	0946	2219	1210	2308	1307	0018	1351	0122	1324	12
13	2202	0839	2213	1053	2312	1315	....	1355	0123	1422	0223	1353	13
14	2232	0943	2251	1202	....	1415	0013	1437	0226	1451	0323	1423	14
15	2303	1047	2333	1310	0011	1509	0119	1514	0328	1519	0422	1455	15
16	2336	1154	....	1418	0115	1556	0225	1547	0429	1549	0520	1530	16
17	....	1302	0023	1523	0222	1637	0331	1618	0530	1620	0616	1609	17
18	0012	1412	0119	1622	0330	1713	0434	1647	0629	1653	0709	1653	18
19	0052	1523	0222	1715	0437	1746	0537	1717	0726	1730	0758	1741	19
20	0139	1632	0329	1801	0543	1817	0639	1747	0821	1811	0843	1833	20
21	0233	1737	0439	1841	0647	1847	0739	1820	0913	1857	0924	1928	21
22	0334	1835	0548	1916	0750	1917	0838	1855	1001	1946	1001	2026	22
23	0441	1925	0655	1948	0851	1949	0934	1933	1044	2039	1034	2125	23
24	0551	2009	0800	2019	0950	2022	1028	2016	1123	2136	1105	2226	24
25	0700	2046	0903	2049	1048	2058	1118	2103	1159	2234	1135	2329	25
26	0808	2120	1005	2119	1143	2139	1204	2154	1232	2335	1204	....	26
27	0914	2151	1104	2151	1235	2223	1246	2249	1303	....	1234	0033	27
28	1017	2220	1202	2225	1324	2312	1324	2347	1333	0038	1307	0140	28
29	1118	2249	1258	2303	1408	....	1359	....	1404	0144	1344	0250	29
30	1217	2320	1352	2345	1449	0005	1432	0049	1437	0252	1427	0402	30
31	1316	2352	1443	....	....	....	1504	0152	....	....	1518	0515	31

Local Standard Time. Not adjusted for Daylight Savings Time.

TABLE 6.-MOONRISE AND MOONSET, 2017   387

New York, New York

Day	JANUARY Rise h m	JANUARY Set h m	FEBRUARY Rise h m	FEBRUARY Set h m	MARCH Rise h m	MARCH Set h m	APRIL Rise h m	APRIL Set h m	MAY Rise h m	MAY Set h m	JUNE Rise h m	JUNE Set h m	Day
1	0925	2014	0946	2225	0821	2123	0903	2344	0945	....	1149	0027	1
2	1002	2116	1020	2332	0858	2232	0956	....	1048	0026	1251	0059	2
3	1036	2220	1057	....	0937	2340	1053	0045	1152	0111	1351	0130	3
4	1109	2326	1136	0040	1020	....	1154	0140	1255	0150	1449	0159	4
5	1143	....	1221	0148	1107	0047	1256	0228	1357	0224	1547	0228	5
6	1218	0033	1311	0254	1200	0151	1359	0310	1457	0255	1644	0258	6
7	1256	0141	1407	0357	1258	0249	1502	0347	1557	0325	1740	0331	7
8	1338	0251	1508	0455	1400	0342	1604	0420	1655	0355	1835	0406	8
9	1426	0400	1612	0547	1504	0428	1704	0452	1752	0424	1927	0445	9
10	1521	0508	1718	0633	1608	0509	1803	0522	1849	0455	2018	0528	10
11	1621	0611	1823	0713	1711	0546	1902	0552	1945	0529	2104	0615	11
12	1726	0708	1927	0748	1814	0619	1959	0622	2039	0605	2147	0706	12
13	1832	0758	2028	0821	1914	0651	2056	0655	2131	0646	2227	0801	13
14	1938	0841	2128	0852	2014	0721	2151	0729	2220	0730	2303	0859	14
15	2042	0918	2227	0922	2112	0751	2245	0807	2305	0819	2336	0959	15
16	2144	0952	2324	0953	2209	0823	2335	0849	2347	0912	....	1100	16
17	2244	1023	....	1024	2305	0856	....	0935	....	1008	0009	1204	17
18	2342	1053	0020	1058	2359	0932	0023	1026	0025	1107	0041	1310	18
19	....	1123	0115	1136	....	1011	0107	1120	0101	1208	0115	1418	19
20	0039	1153	0209	1217	0051	1055	0148	1218	0135	1312	0150	1528	20
21	0135	1225	0301	1303	0141	1143	0226	1320	0208	1419	0230	1641	21
22	0231	1301	0350	1354	0228	1236	0302	1425	0242	1528	0316	1752	22
23	0326	1340	0436	1450	0312	1334	0337	1532	0318	1639	0408	1901	23
24	0419	1424	0519	1550	0353	1435	0412	1641	0357	1753	0508	2003	24
25	0510	1512	0559	1653	0431	1539	0447	1753	0441	1906	0613	2058	25
26	0558	1606	0636	1759	0507	1646	0525	1906	0530	2017	0721	2145	26
27	0643	1704	0712	1906	0542	1755	0607	2019	0627	2122	0829	2225	27
28	0725	1805	0746	2014	0618	1905	0654	2130	0729	2219	0936	2300	28
29	0803	1908	....	....	0654	2017	0746	2236	0834	2308	1040	2332	29
30	0838	2013	....	....	0733	2128	0843	2335	0940	2350	1142	....	30
31	0912	2118	....	....	0816	2238	....	....	1046	....	....	....	31

Day	JULY Rise h m	JULY Set h m	AUGUST Rise h m	AUGUST Set h m	SEPTEMBER Rise h m	SEPTEMBER Set h m	OCTOBER Rise h m	OCTOBER Set h m	NOVEMBER Rise h m	NOVEMBER Set h m	DECEMBER Rise h m	DECEMBER Set h m	Day
1	1241	0002	1421	0007	1538	0048	1536	0119	1548	0311	1528	0414	1
2	1340	0032	1515	0043	1622	0139	1612	0219	1621	0419	1610	0526	2
3	1437	0102	1608	0123	1703	0235	1646	0321	1658	0529	1659	0639	3
4	1533	0133	1658	0207	1740	0333	1719	0426	1738	0640	1755	0750	4
5	1629	0207	1744	0256	1815	0435	1752	0533	1823	0753	1858	0856	5
6	1723	0244	1826	0349	1848	0538	1827	0641	1915	0904	2006	0955	6
7	1814	0326	1905	0445	1921	0643	1904	0751	2013	1010	2114	1045	7
8	1902	0411	1941	0545	1954	0749	1945	0901	2115	1110	2222	1127	8
9	1947	0502	2015	0646	2029	0856	2032	1010	2221	1203	2328	1204	9
10	2028	0556	2047	0749	2106	1004	2124	1117	2327	1248	....	1237	10
11	2105	0653	2119	0853	2148	1112	2222	1219	....	1327	0032	1308	11
12	2140	0753	2152	0958	2235	1219	2324	1315	0032	1401	0134	1337	12
13	2212	0854	2227	1104	2329	1323	....	1403	0136	1433	0234	1407	13
14	2244	0956	2306	1211	....	1423	0029	1446	0239	1503	0333	1437	14
15	2316	1100	2349	1319	0028	1517	0135	1524	0340	1533	0431	1510	15
16	2350	1205	....	1426	0132	1604	0240	1558	0440	1603	0528	1546	16
17	....	1313	0039	1530	0238	1646	0344	1629	0540	1635	0624	1626	17
18	0026	1422	0136	1630	0345	1723	0447	1700	0638	1709	0716	1710	18
19	0108	1531	0239	1723	0451	1757	0548	1730	0735	1747	0806	1758	19
20	0155	1640	0346	1810	0556	1829	0649	1802	0829	1828	0851	1850	20
21	0250	1745	0454	1850	0659	1900	0748	1835	0921	1914	0932	1945	21
22	0351	1843	0602	1927	0801	1931	0846	1911	1008	2003	1009	2042	22
23	0457	1934	0708	2000	0901	2003	0942	1950	1052	2056	1044	2140	23
24	0606	2018	0813	2031	1000	2037	1035	2033	1132	2152	1115	2240	24
25	0715	2057	0915	2102	1056	2114	1125	2120	1208	2250	1146	2342	25
26	0822	2131	1015	2133	1151	2155	1212	2211	1242	2350	1216	....	26
27	0927	2203	1114	2206	1243	2240	1254	2305	1313	....	1247	0045	27
28	1029	2233	1211	2241	1331	2329	1333	....	1345	0052	1321	0151	28
29	1129	2303	1306	2319	1416	....	1409	0003	1417	0156	1359	0300	29
30	1228	2334	1400	....	1458	0022	1442	0103	1450	0304	1443	0411	30
31	1325	....	1451	0001	....	....	1515	0206	....	....	1535	0523	31

Local Standard Time. Not adjusted for Daylight Savings Time.

TABLE 6.-MOONRISE AND MOONSET, 2017

Baltimore, MD and Washington, DC

Day	JANUARY Rise h m	Set h m	FEBRUARY Rise h m	Set h m	MARCH Rise h m	Set h m	APRIL Rise h m	Set h m	MAY Rise h m	Set h m	JUNE Rise h m	Set h m	Day
1	0934	2028	0958	2236	0834	2133	0919	2352	1000	....	1203	0036	1
2	1011	2130	1033	2342	0911	2241	1011	....	1104	0034	1303	0110	2
3	1046	2233	1110	....	0951	2349	1109	0053	1207	0119	1402	0141	3
4	1120	2337	1151	0049	1034	....	1209	0147	1309	0159	1500	0211	4
5	1155	....	1236	0156	1123	0055	1311	0236	1410	0234	1556	0241	5
6	1231	0043	1326	0302	1216	0158	1414	0318	1509	0306	1653	0312	6
7	1309	0151	1422	0405	1314	0257	1515	0356	1608	0337	1748	0345	7
8	1353	0300	1523	0503	1415	0349	1616	0430	1705	0407	1842	0421	8
9	1441	0408	1627	0555	1519	0436	1716	0502	1802	0437	1935	0500	9
10	1536	0516	1732	0641	1622	0518	1814	0533	1858	0509	2025	0543	10
11	1637	0619	1837	0722	1725	0555	1912	0604	1953	0543	2112	0631	11
12	1741	0716	1939	0758	1826	0630	2009	0636	2047	0621	2155	0722	12
13	1847	0806	2040	0832	1926	0702	2105	0709	2139	0701	2235	0816	13
14	1952	0850	2139	0903	2024	0733	2159	0744	2227	0746	2311	0914	14
15	2055	0928	2237	0934	2122	0804	2252	0822	2313	0835	2346	1013	15
16	2157	1002	2333	1006	2218	0836	2343	0905	2355	0927	....	1114	16
17	2255	1034	....	1038	2313	0910	....	0951	....	1023	0019	1216	17
18	2353	1105	0029	1113	....	0947	0030	1041	0033	1121	0053	1321	18
19	....	1135	0123	1151	0007	1027	0115	1135	0110	1222	0127	1428	19
20	0049	1207	0216	1232	0059	1110	0156	1233	0145	1325	0204	1538	20
21	0144	1240	0308	1319	0149	1159	0235	1334	0219	1431	0244	1649	21
22	0239	1315	0357	1410	0236	1252	0312	1438	0254	1539	0331	1800	22
23	0334	1355	0444	1506	0320	1349	0347	1544	0330	1649	0424	1908	23
24	0426	1439	0527	1605	0401	1449	0423	1652	0410	1802	0523	2011	24
25	0518	1528	0608	1708	0440	1553	0500	1803	0455	1914	0628	2106	25
26	0606	1621	0646	1812	0517	1659	0539	1915	0546	2024	0736	2153	26
27	0651	1719	0722	1918	0553	1807	0621	2028	0643	2129	0843	2234	27
28	0733	1819	0758	2025	0629	1916	0709	2138	0744	2226	0949	2310	28
29	0812	1922	....	....	0707	2026	0801	2243	0850	2316	1052	2343	29
30	0848	2026	....	....	0747	2137	0859	2342	0955	2359	1153	....	30
31	0923	2130	....	....	0831	2246	....	....	1100	....	....	....	31

Day	JULY Rise h m	Set h m	AUGUST Rise h m	Set h m	SEPTEMBER Rise h m	Set h m	OCTOBER Rise h m	Set h m	NOVEMBER Rise h m	Set h m	DECEMBER Rise h m	Set h m	Day
1	1252	0014	1429	0022	1545	0104	1545	0134	1559	0324	1542	0423	1
2	1350	0044	1523	0058	1630	0155	1621	0233	1634	0430	1625	0535	2
3	1446	0115	1615	0138	1711	0250	1656	0335	1711	0539	1715	0647	3
4	1542	0147	1705	0223	1749	0348	1730	0439	1752	0650	1811	0758	4
5	1637	0222	1751	0311	1824	0449	1804	0544	1838	0801	1914	0904	5
6	1730	0259	1834	0404	1858	0551	1840	0652	1931	0911	2021	1002	6
7	1821	0341	1914	0501	1932	0655	1918	0800	2029	1018	2129	1053	7
8	1910	0427	1950	0559	2006	0800	2000	0910	2131	1118	2237	1136	8
9	1954	0517	2025	0700	2042	0906	2047	1018	2236	1210	2342	1214	9
10	2036	0611	2058	0802	2120	1013	2140	1125	2342	1256	....	1248	10
11	2114	0708	2131	0905	2203	1120	2238	1226	....	1336	0044	1319	11
12	2149	0807	2205	1009	2251	1227	2340	1322	0046	1411	0145	1349	12
13	2222	0907	2241	1114	2345	1331	....	1411	0149	1444	0244	1420	13
14	2255	1008	2320	1220	....	1430	0044	1455	0251	1515	0343	1451	14
15	2328	1111	....	1327	0044	1524	0149	1533	0351	1545	0440	1525	15
16	....	1216	0005	1434	0147	1612	0253	1608	0450	1616	0537	1601	16
17	0003	1322	0055	1538	0253	1655	0356	1640	0549	1649	0631	1642	17
18	0040	1431	0152	1637	0359	1733	0458	1712	0646	1724	0724	1726	18
19	0122	1540	0254	1731	0504	1808	0559	1743	0743	1802	0813	1814	19
20	0210	1648	0401	1818	0608	1841	0659	1815	0837	1844	0858	1906	20
21	0305	1752	0509	1900	0711	1912	0757	1849	0928	1930	0940	2000	21
22	0407	1850	0616	1937	0811	1944	0855	1926	1016	2019	1018	2056	22
23	0513	1942	0721	2011	0911	2017	0950	2005	1059	2111	1052	2154	23
24	0621	2027	0824	2043	1008	2052	1043	2049	1140	2207	1125	2253	24
25	0729	2106	0926	2115	1104	2130	1133	2136	1216	2304	1156	2354	25
26	0836	2141	1025	2147	1158	2211	1219	2227	1251	....	1227	....	26
27	0939	2214	1123	2220	1250	2256	1301	2321	1323	0003	1300	0056	27
28	1040	2245	1220	2256	1339	2345	1341	....	1356	0105	1335	0201	28
29	1140	2316	1314	2334	1424	....	1417	0018	1428	0208	1414	0309	29
30	1237	2348	1407	....	1506	0038	1452	0117	1503	0314	1458	0419	30
31	1334	....	1458	0017	....	....	1525	0219	....	....	1551	0530	31

Local Standard Time. Not adjusted for Daylight Savings Time.

TABLE 6.-MOONRISE AND MOONSET, 2017   389

Charleston, SC and Savannah, GA

Day	JANUARY Rise h m	JANUARY Set h m	FEBRUARY Rise h m	FEBRUARY Set h m	MARCH Rise h m	MARCH Set h m	APRIL Rise h m	APRIL Set h m	MAY Rise h m	MAY Set h m	JUNE Rise h m	JUNE Set h m	Day
1	0939	2053	1013	2249	0852	2144	0947	2353	1030	....	1224	0044	1
2	1019	2152	1052	2352	0932	2249	1041	....	1132	0036	1321	0121	2
3	1057	2252	1132	....	1015	2354	1139	0053	1233	0123	1417	0155	3
4	1134	2353	1216	0056	1101	....	1238	0148	1332	0205	1511	0228	4
5	1212	....	1303	0200	1152	0057	1339	0238	1430	0243	1605	0301	5
6	1251	0055	1356	0304	1246	0159	1438	0323	1526	0318	1659	0335	6
7	1333	0159	1452	0406	1344	0257	1537	0403	1621	0352	1752	0410	7
8	1419	0305	1553	0504	1444	0351	1635	0441	1716	0425	1844	0448	8
9	1510	0411	1655	0557	1545	0440	1731	0516	1810	0458	1935	0529	9
10	1606	0517	1758	0645	1646	0524	1827	0550	1903	0533	2025	0614	10
11	1707	0619	1859	0729	1745	0604	1922	0623	1956	0610	2112	0701	11
12	1810	0717	1959	0808	1843	0641	2016	0658	2048	0649	2156	0752	12
13	1914	0809	2056	0845	1940	0716	2109	0733	2139	0731	2238	0845	13
14	2016	0855	2152	0919	2036	0750	2202	0811	2227	0816	2317	0940	14
15	2116	0936	2247	0953	2130	0824	2253	0851	2313	0905	2355	1036	15
16	2214	1014	2341	1027	2224	0859	2343	0934	2357	0956	....	1134	16
17	2310	1049	....	1102	2317	0936	....	1021	....	1050	0031	1234	17
18	....	1122	0034	1139	....	1014	0031	1111	0038	1146	0107	1335	18
19	0005	1155	0126	1219	0009	1056	0116	1204	0117	1244	0145	1439	19
20	0058	1229	0218	1302	0100	1140	0159	1300	0155	1344	0225	1545	20
21	0151	1305	0309	1349	0149	1229	0240	1358	0232	1447	0309	1653	21
22	0243	1343	0358	1440	0237	1321	0320	1459	0310	1551	0359	1802	22
23	0336	1424	0445	1534	0322	1416	0359	1602	0350	1658	0454	1909	23
24	0427	1509	0530	1632	0405	1515	0438	1707	0434	1807	0554	2011	24
25	0518	1558	0613	1732	0447	1616	0518	1814	0522	1917	0659	2107	25
26	0607	1651	0654	1833	0527	1718	0601	1922	0615	2025	0804	2157	26
27	0653	1747	0734	1936	0606	1823	0646	2031	0713	2129	0909	2241	27
28	0737	1845	0812	2040	0646	1928	0737	2139	0815	2227	1012	2320	28
29	0818	1945	....	....	0727	2035	0831	2244	0919	2319	1112	2356	29
30	0858	2045	....	....	0810	2142	0929	2343	1022	....	1209	....	30
31	0936	2147	....	....	0857	2249	....	....	1124	0004	....	....	31

Day	JULY Rise h m	JULY Set h m	AUGUST Rise h m	AUGUST Set h m	SEPTEMBER Rise h m	SEPTEMBER Set h m	OCTOBER Rise h m	OCTOBER Set h m	NOVEMBER Rise h m	NOVEMBER Set h m	DECEMBER Rise h m	DECEMBER Set h m	Day
1	1305	0030	1432	0048	1546	0134	1549	0202	1614	0341	1605	0432	1
2	1400	0103	1525	0126	1631	0225	1628	0259	1652	0444	1652	0540	2
3	1453	0137	1616	0208	1714	0319	1706	0357	1733	0549	1744	0649	3
4	1547	0211	1705	0253	1754	0415	1743	0458	1818	0656	1842	0758	4
5	1639	0248	1752	0342	1833	0513	1821	0600	1907	0805	1945	0903	5
6	1731	0328	1836	0434	1910	0612	1900	0704	2001	0913	2051	1003	6
7	1821	0411	1918	0529	1947	0713	1941	0809	2100	1018	2157	1055	7
8	1910	0458	1957	0625	2024	0814	2027	0915	2202	1118	2301	1141	8
9	1955	0548	2034	0723	2103	0917	2116	1021	2305	1212	....	1222	9
10	2038	0640	2111	0822	2145	1020	2210	1125	....	1300	0003	1259	10
11	2119	0735	2147	0921	2230	1125	2309	1226	0008	1342	0102	1334	11
12	2156	0831	2224	1022	2320	1229	....	1323	0109	1421	0159	1407	12
13	2233	0929	2303	1124	....	1331	0010	1413	0209	1456	0255	1441	13
14	2309	1027	2346	1227	0015	1430	0112	1459	0307	1530	0351	1515	14
15	2345	1127	....	1331	0114	1525	0214	1540	0404	1604	0445	1551	15
16	....	1228	0033	1435	0216	1615	0315	1618	0500	1638	0539	1630	16
17	0023	1331	0125	1538	0320	1700	0415	1654	0556	1713	0632	1712	17
18	0104	1436	0223	1638	0423	1742	0514	1729	0651	1751	0723	1757	18
19	0149	1542	0325	1732	0525	1820	0611	1803	0745	1831	0812	1845	19
20	0239	1648	0429	1822	0626	1856	0708	1838	0837	1914	0858	1936	20
21	0336	1752	0534	1906	0725	1930	0803	1915	0928	2001	0941	2028	21
22	0437	1851	0638	1947	0822	2005	0858	1953	1015	2050	1021	2122	22
23	0542	1945	0740	2024	0918	2041	0951	2035	1100	2141	1058	2218	23
24	0649	2032	0840	2059	1013	2118	1043	2119	1142	2234	1133	2314	24
25	0754	2114	0938	2134	1107	2158	1132	2207	1221	2329	1208	....	25
26	0856	2153	1035	2209	1200	2241	1219	2257	1258	....	1242	0011	26
27	0957	2228	1130	2245	1250	2326	1303	2350	1333	0026	1318	0110	27
28	1055	2303	1224	2323	1339	....	1344	....	1409	0124	1356	0212	28
29	1151	2337	1316	....	1424	0015	1423	0044	1445	0224	1439	0316	29
30	1246	....	1408	0003	1508	0107	1500	0141	1523	0326	1527	0423	30
31	1339	0011	1458	0047	....	....	1537	0240	....	....	1621	0532	31

Local Standard Time. Not adjusted for Daylight Savings Time.

TABLE 6.-MOONRISE AND MOONSET, 2017

Galveston, Texas

Day	JANUARY Rise h m	JANUARY Set h m	FEBRUARY Rise h m	FEBRUARY Set h m	MARCH Rise h m	MARCH Set h m	APRIL Rise h m	APRIL Set h m	MAY Rise h m	MAY Set h m	JUNE Rise h m	JUNE Set h m	Day
1	0933	2056	1013	2248	0852	2142	0952	2347	1036	....	1225	0040	1
2	1014	2154	1052	2349	0934	2245	1047	....	1137	0030	1321	0118	2
3	1053	2252	1134	....	1018	2349	1144	0047	1237	0117	1416	0153	3
4	1132	2352	1219	0052	1106	....	1244	0142	1335	0200	1509	0227	4
5	1211	....	1308	0155	1157	0052	1343	0232	1431	0239	1602	0302	5
6	1252	0053	1401	0258	1252	0153	1442	0317	1526	0316	1654	0337	6
7	1335	0156	1458	0359	1350	0251	1539	0359	1620	0351	1746	0413	7
8	1423	0301	1558	0457	1449	0344	1636	0437	1713	0425	1838	0452	8
9	1515	0406	1700	0551	1549	0434	1731	0514	1806	0500	1928	0534	9
10	1612	0511	1801	0640	1649	0518	1825	0549	1858	0535	2018	0619	10
11	1713	0613	1902	0724	1747	0600	1918	0624	1950	0613	2105	0707	11
12	1815	0711	2000	0804	1844	0638	2011	0659	2042	0653	2150	0757	12
13	1918	0803	2056	0842	1939	0714	2104	0736	2132	0736	2232	0850	13
14	2019	0850	2151	0918	2033	0750	2156	0814	2220	0822	2312	0944	14
15	2118	0932	2244	0953	2127	0825	2246	0856	2306	0910	2350	1039	15
16	2215	1011	2337	1028	2219	0901	2336	0939	2350	1001	....	1136	16
17	2309	1047	....	1105	2311	0939	....	1026	....	1055	0028	1234	17
18	....	1121	0029	1143	....	1018	0024	1116	0032	1150	0106	1334	18
19	0002	1156	0120	1223	0003	1100	0109	1209	0112	1247	0145	1436	19
20	0055	1231	0211	1307	0053	1146	0153	1304	0151	1346	0227	1541	20
21	0146	1308	0302	1354	0142	1234	0235	1401	0230	1446	0313	1648	21
22	0238	1347	0351	1445	0230	1326	0316	1501	0310	1549	0403	1756	22
23	0330	1429	0439	1539	0316	1421	0356	1602	0351	1655	0459	1902	23
24	0421	1514	0524	1636	0400	1518	0436	1706	0436	1803	0600	2004	24
25	0511	1603	0608	1735	0442	1618	0518	1811	0526	1911	0704	2101	25
26	0600	1656	0650	1835	0523	1719	0602	1919	0620	2019	0809	2151	26
27	0647	1751	0731	1937	0604	1822	0650	2026	0719	2123	0913	2236	27
28	0731	1849	0811	2039	0645	1927	0741	2133	0821	2221	1014	2316	28
29	0814	1947	....	....	0728	2032	0837	2237	0924	2313	1113	2354	29
30	0854	2047	....	....	0813	2138	0935	2336	1027	2359	1209	....	30
31	0933	2147	....	....	0901	2243	....	....	1127	....	....	....	31

Day	JULY Rise h m	JULY Set h m	AUGUST Rise h m	AUGUST Set h m	SEPTEMBER Rise h m	SEPTEMBER Set h m	OCTOBER Rise h m	OCTOBER Set h m	NOVEMBER Rise h m	NOVEMBER Set h m	DECEMBER Rise h m	DECEMBER Set h m	Day
1	1303	0029	1427	0051	1538	0140	1543	0206	1613	0341	1608	0429	1
2	1357	0103	1518	0130	1624	0230	1623	0302	1653	0443	1656	0535	2
3	1449	0138	1609	0213	1708	0323	1702	0400	1735	0547	1749	0644	3
4	1541	0214	1658	0258	1749	0419	1741	0459	1821	0652	1849	0752	4
5	1633	0252	1745	0347	1829	0516	1820	0600	1911	0800	1952	0856	5
6	1724	0333	1830	0439	1907	0614	1901	0702	2007	0906	2057	0956	6
7	1814	0416	1912	0533	1945	0713	1944	0806	2106	1011	2201	1049	7
8	1902	0503	1952	0629	2024	0813	2031	0910	2208	1111	2304	1136	8
9	1949	0553	2031	0725	2105	0914	2121	1015	2310	1205	....	1218	9
10	2032	0645	2108	0823	2148	1017	2216	1119	....	1254	0004	1256	10
11	2113	0739	2146	0921	2235	1120	2315	1219	0012	1337	0102	1332	11
12	2152	0835	2224	1020	2326	1223	....	1316	0112	1417	0158	1407	12
13	2230	0931	2305	1121	....	1324	0015	1407	0210	1454	0253	1441	13
14	2307	1028	2349	1223	0021	1424	0117	1454	0307	1529	0347	1517	14
15	2344	1126	....	1326	0120	1519	0217	1536	0403	1604	0440	1555	15
16	....	1226	0037	1429	0222	1609	0317	1615	0457	1639	0533	1634	16
17	0024	1328	0130	1532	0324	1655	0416	1652	0552	1716	0625	1717	17
18	0106	1431	0228	1631	0426	1738	0513	1728	0645	1755	0716	1802	18
19	0153	1537	0330	1726	0527	1817	0609	1804	0738	1836	0805	1851	19
20	0244	1642	0434	1816	0626	1854	0704	1840	0830	1920	0851	1941	20
21	0342	1745	0538	1902	0723	1930	0759	1918	0920	2006	0934	2033	21
22	0443	1845	0641	1943	0819	2007	0852	1958	1008	2055	1015	2126	22
23	0548	1939	0741	2022	0914	2043	0945	2040	1053	2146	1053	2220	23
24	0653	2027	0840	2059	1008	2122	1036	2125	1135	2239	1129	2315	24
25	0757	2110	0936	2135	1101	2202	1125	2212	1215	2333	1205	....	25
26	0858	2150	1031	2211	1153	2246	1212	2302	1253	....	1241	0011	26
27	0957	2227	1125	2248	1243	2332	1256	2354	1330	0028	1318	0109	27
28	1054	2302	1218	2327	1331	....	1338	....	1407	0125	1358	0209	28
29	1148	2338	1310	....	1417	0020	1418	0048	1444	0224	1442	0312	29
30	1242	....	1401	0008	1501	0112	1456	0144	1524	0325	1531	0418	30
31	1335	0013	1451	0052	....	....	1534	0242	....	....	1627	0526	31

Local Standard Time. Not adjusted for Daylight Savings Time.

TABLE 6.-MOONRISE AND MOONSET, 2017   391

Panama Canal (East End)

Day	JANUARY Rise h m	Set h m	FEBRUARY Rise h m	Set h m	MARCH Rise h m	Set h m	APRIL Rise h m	Set h m	MAY Rise h m	Set h m	JUNE Rise h m	Set h m	Day
1	0908	2114	1012	2239	0856	2128	1020	2312	1105	2357	1236	0022	1
2	0955	2205	1100	2333	0946	2224	1117	....	1202	....	1325	0107	2
3	1041	2257	1149	....	1037	2321	1215	0011	1257	0050	1412	0149	3
4	1127	2349	1240	0029	1130	....	1311	0107	1349	0138	1458	0231	4
5	1213	....	1334	0126	1225	0019	1407	0201	1439	0224	1544	0311	5
6	1301	0042	1430	0224	1322	0118	1500	0252	1527	0307	1631	0353	6
7	1352	0138	1528	0324	1419	0215	1552	0339	1614	0349	1718	0435	7
8	1446	0235	1627	0422	1516	0311	1641	0424	1700	0430	1805	0518	8
9	1542	0335	1725	0519	1611	0404	1729	0508	1746	0511	1853	0603	9
10	1642	0436	1821	0612	1705	0455	1816	0550	1833	0553	1942	0650	10
11	1742	0537	1915	0703	1757	0542	1903	0631	1920	0636	2030	0738	11
12	1843	0637	2006	0750	1846	0628	1950	0713	2008	0720	2117	0827	12
13	1941	0733	2056	0835	1935	0711	2037	0755	2056	0806	2203	0916	13
14	2036	0826	2143	0918	2022	0753	2125	0839	2144	0853	2249	1006	14
15	2128	0914	2230	1000	2109	0835	2212	0924	2232	0941	2333	1055	15
16	2218	1000	2317	1041	2156	0917	2301	1010	2319	1030	....	1145	16
17	2306	1043	....	1123	2243	1000	2349	1057	....	1120	0018	1236	17
18	2352	1124	0003	1206	2331	1044	....	1146	0005	1210	0103	1328	18
19	....	1205	0050	1250	....	1129	0036	1236	0051	1300	0150	1422	19
20	0038	1246	0138	1336	0019	1216	0124	1327	0137	1352	0240	1519	20
21	0124	1328	0227	1425	0107	1305	0211	1418	0223	1445	0332	1619	21
22	0210	1412	0316	1514	0156	1355	0258	1511	0311	1539	0429	1722	22
23	0258	1457	0406	1606	0244	1446	0345	1604	0400	1637	0529	1825	23
24	0347	1544	0455	1658	0333	1538	0434	1700	0453	1737	0631	1928	24
25	0436	1634	0544	1752	0421	1631	0523	1757	0549	1840	0734	2028	25
26	0526	1725	0632	1845	0509	1725	0615	1856	0648	1943	0835	2124	26
27	0615	1817	0720	1939	0558	1820	0710	1957	0750	2046	0933	2215	27
28	0704	1909	0808	2033	0647	1916	0807	2100	0851	2146	1028	2302	28
29	0752	2001	....	....	0737	2014	0906	2201	0952	2242	1119	2347	29
30	0839	2054	....	....	0829	2113	1006	2301	1050	2334	1208	....	30
31	0926	2146	....	....	0923	2212	....	....	1144	....	....	....	31

Day	JULY Rise h m	Set h m	AUGUST Rise h m	Set h m	SEPTEMBER Rise h m	Set h m	OCTOBER Rise h m	Set h m	NOVEMBER Rise h m	Set h m	DECEMBER Rise h m	Set h m	Day
1	1255	0029	1357	0113	1503	0211	1517	0231	1611	0343	1625	0410	1
2	1342	0111	1445	0157	1551	0300	1603	0321	1658	0436	1720	0509	2
3	1428	0152	1533	0243	1638	0350	1649	0412	1749	0532	1819	0611	3
4	1515	0233	1622	0330	1725	0441	1735	0504	1842	0629	1920	0715	4
5	1602	0316	1710	0418	1811	0532	1822	0557	1938	0730	2023	0818	5
6	1650	0401	1758	0508	1857	0623	1910	0651	2037	0831	2126	0920	6
7	1738	0447	1845	0558	1943	0715	2001	0747	2138	0933	2225	1018	7
8	1827	0535	1931	0649	2029	0807	2054	0844	2238	1034	2321	1111	8
9	1915	0624	2016	0739	2117	0901	2150	0943	2337	1131	....	1200	9
10	2002	0713	2101	0830	2207	0955	2247	1043	....	1225	0014	1246	10
11	2048	0803	2146	0920	2300	1052	2346	1143	0033	1315	0105	1329	11
12	2133	0853	2232	1012	2355	1150	....	1240	0126	1402	0153	1411	12
13	2217	0943	2320	1105	....	1248	0044	1335	0217	1446	0241	1453	13
14	2301	1033	....	1159	0052	1347	0141	1427	0307	1529	0328	1535	14
15	2347	1123	0010	1256	0151	1444	0236	1516	0355	1611	0415	1618	15
16	....	1215	0104	1355	0249	1539	0329	1603	0443	1653	0503	1702	16
17	0033	1309	0200	1455	0347	1631	0420	1647	0530	1736	0551	1748	17
18	0123	1406	0300	1555	0442	1720	0510	1730	0618	1820	0640	1835	18
19	0216	1505	0400	1653	0536	1807	0559	1813	0706	1905	0728	1923	19
20	0312	1606	0500	1749	0627	1852	0647	1856	0755	1951	0815	2012	20
21	0412	1709	0558	1841	0717	1935	0735	1940	0843	2039	0901	2100	21
22	0514	1810	0654	1929	0806	2019	0824	2024	0931	2127	0946	2148	22
23	0616	1908	0747	2016	0855	2102	0912	2110	1018	2215	1030	2236	23
24	0716	2002	0838	2100	0943	2145	1000	2156	1104	2304	1113	2324	24
25	0814	2053	0927	2143	1031	2230	1048	2244	1148	2352	1156	....	25
26	0908	2140	1015	2225	1119	2316	1136	2333	1232	....	1239	0013	26
27	0959	2224	1103	2308	1207	....	1223	....	1316	0041	1324	0103	27
28	1048	2307	1151	2352	1255	0003	1309	0021	1400	0131	1411	0155	28
29	1136	2349	1238	....	1343	0052	1354	0111	1446	0221	1502	0250	29
30	1223	....	1326	0037	1430	0141	1439	0201	1534	0314	1558	0349	30
31	1310	0031	1415	0123	....	....	1524	0251	....	....	1657	0451	31

Local Standard Time. Not adjusted for Daylight Savings Time.

TABLE 7.—CONVERSION OF FEET TO CENTIMETERS

Feet	Tenths of a Foot										Feet
	0.0	0.1	0.2	0.3	0.4	0.5	0.6	0.7	0.8	0.9	
0	0	3	6	9	12	15	18	21	24	27	0
1	30	34	37	40	43	46	49	52	55	58	1
2	61	64	67	70	73	76	79	82	85	88	2
3	91	94	98	101	104	107	110	113	116	119	3
4	122	125	128	131	134	137	140	143	146	149	4
5	152	155	158	162	165	168	171	174	177	180	5
6	183	186	189	192	195	198	201	204	207	210	6
7	213	216	219	223	226	229	232	235	238	241	7
8	244	247	250	253	256	259	262	265	268	271	8
9	274	277	280	283	287	290	293	296	299	302	9
10	305	308	311	314	317	320	323	326	329	332	10
11	335	338	341	344	347	351	354	357	360	363	11
12	366	369	372	375	378	381	384	387	390	393	12
13	396	399	402	405	408	411	415	418	421	424	13
14	427	430	433	436	439	442	445	448	451	454	14
15	457	460	463	466	469	472	475	479	482	485	15
16	488	491	494	497	500	503	506	509	512	515	16
17	518	521	524	527	530	533	536	539	543	546	17
18	549	552	555	558	561	564	567	570	573	576	18
19	579	582	585	588	591	594	597	600	604	607	19
20	610	613	616	619	622	625	628	631	634	637	20
21	640	643	646	649	652	655	658	661	664	668	21
22	671	674	677	680	683	686	689	692	695	698	22
23	701	704	707	710	713	716	719	722	725	728	23
24	732	735	738	741	744	747	750	753	756	759	24
25	762	765	768	771	774	777	780	783	786	789	25
26	792	796	799	802	805	808	811	814	817	820	26
27	823	826	829	832	835	838	841	844	847	850	27
28	853	856	860	863	866	869	872	875	878	881	28
29	884	887	890	893	896	899	902	905	908	911	29
30	914	917	920	924	927	930	933	936	939	942	30
31	945	948	951	954	957	960	963	966	969	972	31
32	975	978	981	985	988	991	994	997	1000	1003	32
33	1006	1009	1012	1015	1018	1021	1024	1027	1030	1033	33
34	1036	1039	1042	1045	1049	1052	1055	1058	1061	1064	34
35	1067	1070	1073	1076	1079	1082	1085	1088	1091	1094	35
36	1097	1100	1103	1106	1109	1113	1116	1119	1122	1125	36
37	1128	1131	1134	1137	1140	1143	1146	1149	1152	1155	37
38	1158	1161	1164	1167	1170	1173	1177	1180	1183	1186	38
39	1189	1192	1195	1198	1201	1204	1207	1210	1213	1216	39
40	1219	1222	1225	1228	1231	1234	1237	1241	1244	1247	40
41	1250	1253	1256	1259	1262	1265	1268	1271	1274	1277	41
42	1280	1283	1286	1289	1292	1295	1298	1301	1305	1308	42
43	1311	1314	1317	1320	1323	1326	1329	1332	1335	1338	43
44	1341	1344	1347	1350	1353	1356	1359	1362	1366	1369	44
45	1372	1375	1378	1381	1384	1387	1390	1393	1396	1399	45
46	1402	1405	1408	1411	1414	1417	1420	1423	1426	1430	46
47	1433	1436	1439	1442	1445	1448	1451	1454	1457	1460	47
48	1463	1466	1469	1472	1475	1478	1481	1484	1487	1490	48
49	1494	1497	1500	1503	1506	1509	1512	1515	1518	1521	49
50	1524	1527	1530	1533	1536	1539	1542	1545	1548	1551	50

Feet to Meters = Centimeters divided by 100 (from above table)

Example: 09.40 feet = (287 centimeters) / (100) = 02.87 meters.

1 Meter = 100 centimeters	1 Foot = 0.30480061 meters
1 Meter = 3.2808399 feet	1 Foot = 30.480061 centimeters

TABLE 8.—TIDE PREDICTION ACCURACY

EXPLANATION OF TABLE

The accuracy of National Ocean Service tide predictions is determined by comparing predicted and observed high and low waters at all stations for which data exists, primarily the U.S. and its territories. Each water-level station is unique; there is no single standard of accuracy when comparing astronomic tide predictions with observed water levels. Water-level station locations are examined on an individual basis to determine if the predictions are adequate. Comparisons are based on 1989 data except for those locations where the stations were not in operation or the data acquired were unacceptable. If a station was not in operation in 1989, the last good year of data was used. Comparisons are made by subtracting the observed times and heights of the high and low waters from the predicted tides to compute a difference.

Table Legend

Station ID—Each water-level station in the United States and dependent territories has a unique seven digit identification number (ID). The ID is unrelated to the four digit station number used in the published prediction tables.

90% Distribution Level—90% of the absolute values of the differences are less than or equal to the values in these columns.

Standard Deviation of Differences—Standard deviation of all the differences.

Average Difference—Average of the signed sum of all the differences.

Notes

Albany—This station, located on the Hudson River, experiences a significant change in river level and corresponding times and heights of high and low waters throughout the year.

Baltimore—Winds greatly affect the times and heights of the high and low tides, owing to the large shallow bay and small tidal range.

Gulf of Mexico locations—Water level is difficult to predict because the Gulf, being large, relatively shallow, and with a small tidal range, is greatly influenced by weather conditions.

TABLE 8.—TIDE PREDICTION ACCURACY

Station ID	Station Name	Year	90% Distribution Level				Standard Deviation of Differences				Average Differences			
			Time Differences		Height Differences		Times		Heights		Times		Heights	
			High Water (Hours)	Low Water (Hours)	High Water (Feet)	Low Water (Feet)	High Water (Hours)	Low Water (Hours)	High Water (Feet)	Low Water (Feet)	High Water (Hours)	Low Water (Hours)	High Water (Feet)	Low Water (Feet)
841-0140	Eastport, ME	1998	0.2	0.2	0.7	0.6	0.09	0.11	0.41	0.40	-0.07	-0.10	-0.08	-0.10
841-8150	Portland, ME	1998	0.3	0.2	0.6	0.6	0.14	0.13	0.40	0.39	-0.10	-0.07	-0.11	0.06
844-3970	Boston, MA	1998	0.3	0.3	0.8	0.7	0.14	0.14	0.49	0.48	-0.10	-0.10	-0.10	-0.09
844-7930	Woods Hole, MA	2003	0.5	>1.0	0.7	0.7	0.48	0.77	0.43	0.40	-0.03	0.01	-0.02	-0.01
844-9130	Nantucket,Ma	2003	0.3	0.3	0.6	0.6	0.23	0.21	0.40	0.39	-0.03	0.03	-0.03	0.03
845-2660	Newport, RI	1997	0.3	0.6	0.7	0.7	0.19	0.14	0.41	0.40	-0.06	-0.04	-0.07	-0.05
846-1490	New London, CT	1998	0.4	0.3	0.7	0.7	0.25	0.22	0.47	0.47	-0.11	-0.08	-0.10	-0.09
846-7150	Bridgeport, CT	1998	0.3	0.3	0.8	0.8	0.13	0.13	0.55	0.56	-0.12	-0.15	-0.11	-0.16
841-6945	Kings Point, NY	1999	0.9	>1.0	0.8	0.8	0.59	0.54	0.55	0.56	-0.12	-0.15	-0.11	-0.16
851-8750	The Battery, NY	2003	0.6	0.5	0.9	0.9	0.37	0.31	0.59	0.60	-0.07	-0.06	0.03	-0.02
853-1680	Sandy Hook, NJ	2002	0.4	0.4	0.8	0.9	0.25	0.25	0.51	0.54	-0.13	-0.12	0.19	0.21
853-4720	Atlantic City, NJ	2000	0.3	0.4	0.9	0.9	0.24	0.24	0.57	0.57	-0.02	-0.01	0.02	-0.02
854-5530	Philadelphia, PA	1989	0.5	0.6	1.0	1.0	0.30	0.36	0.72	0.65	0.14	0.11	-0.12	0.28
855-1910	Reedy Point, DE	2002	0.5	0.7	0.9	0.9	0.23	0.31	0.55	0.56	-0.18	-0.35	0.09	-0.02
855-7380	Breakwater Harbor, DE	1998	0.3	0.3	0.9	0.9	0.18	0.18	0.62	0.68	-0.06	-0.03	-0.03	-0.01
857-4680	Baltimore, MD	1998	0.8	1.0	1.0	1.0	1.38	1.43	0.64	0.62	-0.21	-0.09	-0.21	-0.11
859-4900	Washington, DC	1998	0.5	0.8	1.0	1.0	0.33	0.48	0.73	0.83	-0.05	-0.19	-0.03	-0.23
863-8863	Chesapeake Bay Bri Tunnel	2002	0.3	0.4	0.8	0.8	0.25	0.27	0.50	0.52	-0.06	-0.08	-0.07	-0.08
863-8610	Hampton Roads, VA	1995	0.4	0.4	0.8	0.9	0.27	0.25	0.51	0.56	0.07	0.05	0.03	-0.01
865-8120	Wilmington, NC	2003	0.5	0.5	0.6	0.8	0.34	0.29	0.38	0.46	-0.01	-0.08	0.11	0.16
8661070	Myrtle Beach, SC	2003	0.4	0.4	0.8	0.8	0.28	0.29	0.48	0.50	0.00	0.01	0.00	0.00
866-5530	Charleston, SC	2000	0.4	0.4	0.6	0.7	0.19	0.20	0.42	0.47	0.14	-0.10	0.05	-0.02
867-0870	Savannah R. Ent., GA	1995	0.3	0.3	0.7	0.9	0.21	0.19	0.47	0.58	-0.01	-0.07	0.05	0.03
872-0030	Fernandina Beach, FL	1995	0.2	0.3	0.9	0.9	0.15	0.19	0.48	0.56	-0.02	0.06	0.33	0.30
872-0218	Mayport, FL	2003	0.2	0.3	0.6	0.8	0.14	0.21	0.41	0.51	-0.04	0.01	-0.02	0.01
872-3178	Miami, Government Cut, FL	1985	0.3	0.3	0.4	0.4	0.18	0.17	0.25	0.24	-0.07	0.01	-0.02	-0.01
872-4580	Key West, FL	2000	0.5	0.4	0.3	0.3	0.29	0.25	0.19	0.20	-0.18	-0.06	-0.15	-0.10
872-6520	St. Petersburg, FL	2003	0.7	0.7	0.6	0.5	0.56	0.44	0.38	0.34	0.07	0.00	0.01	0.2
872-9840	Pensacola, FL	1995	>1.0	>1.0	0.6	0.9	2.61	2.72	0.48	0.41	0.04	0.10	-0.04	0.07
873-7048	Mobile, AL	1984	>1.0	>1.0	0.8	0.7	2.56	2.49	0.48	0.45	0.05	-0.09	-0.05	0.04
876-1724	Grand Isle, LA	2003	>1.0	>1.0	0.5	0.5	1.21	1.22	0.30	0.30	-0.24	-0.33	0.00	0.00
877-1450	Galveston, TX	1995	>1.0	>1.0	0.7	0.8	1.29	1.25	0.50	0.54	-0.15	-0.12	-0.03	0.00

TABLE 9.— LOWEST/ HIGHEST ASTRONOMICAL TIDE AND OTHER TIDAL DATUMS

EXPLANATION OF TABLE

Lowest Astronomical Tide (LAT) and Highest Astronomical Tide (HAT) are the lowest and highest predicted values for the tides at a given location over a 19 year period. These values were calculated by generating tide predictions for the time period of the latest National Tidal Datum Epoch (1983-2001) using the latest set of tidal harmonic constituents. The highest and lowest values predicted were recorded to the nearest 0.1 foot. It is important to note that the LAT and HAT values are derived solely from predicted tides based on astronomical forces. Observed water levels can be above the HAT level or below the LAT level due to storms, winds, or other meteorological effects which are not accounted for in the tide predictions.

Table Legend

Station - Each water level station in the United States and its territories has a unique seven digit identification number (ID). The ID is unrelated to the four digit indexing number used in the published prediction tables.

LAT - Lowest Astronomical Tide - The lowest predicted tidal level

MLLW - Mean Lower Low Water

MLW - Mean Low Water

MHW - Mean High Water

MHHW - Mean Higher High Water

HAT - Highest Astronomical Tide - The highest predicted tidal level

Notes

All elevations are provided in feet relative to Mean Lower Low Water (MLLW), the reference datum for tide predictions and soundings on NOAA nautical charts. The other tidal datums (Mean Low Water, Mean High Water, and Mean Higher High Water) in this table are included to provide additional information.

TABLE 9.— LOWEST/ HIGHEST ASTRONOMICAL TIDE AND OTHER TIDAL DATUMS

RELATIVE TO MLLW (feet)

Station	Name	LAT	MLW	MHW	MHHW	HAT
8410140	Eastport, Maine	-3.4	0.4	18.8	19.3	22.9
8413320	Bar Harbor, Maine	-2.2	0.4	10.9	11.4	13.7
8418150	Portland, Maine	-2.0	0.3	9.5	9.9	11.9
8443970	Boston, Massachusetts	-2.2	0.3	9.8	10.3	12.4
8449130	Nantucket Island, Massachusetts	-0.8	0.2	3.2	3.6	4.5
8447930	Woods Hole, Massachusetts	-0.7	0.1	1.9	2.2	3.2
8452660	Newport, Rhode Island	-1.0	0.1	3.6	3.9	5.2
8510560	Montauk, Fort Pond, New York	-0.9	0.2	2.2	2.5	3.5
8461490	New London, Connecticut	-0.8	0.2	2.8	3.1	3.9
8467150	Bridgeport, Connecticut	-1.4	0.2	7.0	7.3	8.8
8516945	Kings Point, New York	-1.5	0.3	7.4	7.8	9.7
8518750	New York (The Battery), New York	-1.5	0.2	4.7	5.1	6.4
8519483	Bayonne Bridge, New York	-1.6	0.2	5.2	5.5	6.9
8518995	Albany, New York	-1.1	0.2	5.1	5.5	6.3
8531680	Sandy Hook, New Jersey	-1.4	0.2	4.9	5.2	6.6
8534720	Atlantic City, New Jersey	-1.3	0.2	4.2	4.6	5.8
8557380	Breakwater Harbor, Delaware	-1.1	0.2	4.2	4.7	5.8
8551910	Reedy Point, Delaware	-1.0	0.2	5.5	5.8	6.9
8545530	Philadelphia, Pennsylvania	-0.6	0.2	6.4	6.8	8.0
8570280	Ocean City, Maryland	-1.2	0.2	3.5	3.9	5.1
8574680	Baltimore, Maryland	-0.6	0.2	1.4	1.7	2.3
8594900	Washington, DC	-0.6	0.2	2.9	3.2	3.8
8638863	Chesapeake Bay Bridge Tunnel, Virginia	-0.9	0.1	2.7	2.9	4.0
8638610	Hampton Roads, Sewells Point, Virginia	-0.7	0.1	2.6	2.8	3.6
8651370	Duck Pier, North Carolina	-1.0	0.1	3.4	3.7	4.9
8652587	Oregon Inlet Marina, North Carolina	-0.2	0.1	1.0	1.2	1.7
8654400	Cape Hatteras, North Carolina	-1.0	0.1	3.1	3.5	4.7
8658120	Wilmington, North Carolina	-0.4	0.2	4.4	4.7	5.4
8661070	Myrtle Beach, South Carolina	-1.5	0.2	5.2	5.6	7.2
8665530	Charleston, South Carolina	-1.5	0.2	5.4	5.8	7.3
8670870	Savannah River Entrance, Georgia	-1.7	0.2	7.1	7.5	9.2
8670681	Savannah, Georgia	-1.9	0.3	8.1	8.6	10.1
8720030	Fernandina Beach, Florida	-1.7	0.2	6.2	6.6	8.2
8720218	Mayport, Florida	-1.6	0.2	4.7	5.0	6.4
8721604	Port Canaveral, Florida	-1.2	0.2	3.6	4.0	5.4
8723178	Miami, Government Cut, Florida	-0.9	0.1	2.5	2.5	3.6
8723970	Vaca Key, Florida	-0.5	0.2	0.9	1.0	1.7
8724580	Key West, Florida	-0.8	0.2	1.5	1.8	2.6
8725110	Naples, Florida	-1.4	0.6	2.6	2.9	3.8
8726520	St. Petersburg, Florida	-1.1	0.4	2.0	2.3	3.1
8727520	Cedar Key, Florida	-1.4	0.6	3.5	3.8	4.8
8728130	St. Marks River Entrance, Florida	-1.6	0.6	3.3	3.5	4.5
8728690	Apalachicola, Florida	-1.0	0.4	1.5	1.6	2.1
8729840	Pensacola, Florida	-1.2	0.0	1.2	1.3	2.2
8735180	Dauphin Island, Alabama	-1.0	0.0	1.2	1.2	2.0
8737048	Mobile, Alabama	-1.2	0.1	1.5	1.6	2.4
8760551	South Pass, Louisiana	-1.2	0.0	1.2	1.2	2.2
8761724	Grand Isle, Louisiana	-0.9	0.0	1.1	1.1	1.8
8771450	Galveston, Texas	-1.2	0.3	1.3	1.4	2.0
8773701	Port O'Connor, Texas	-0.9	0.0	0.8	0.8	1.7
8779750	Padre Island, Texas	-1.5	0.2	1.4	1.5	2.4
2695540	Bermuda Esso Pier, Bermuda	-0.8	0.1	2.6	2.9	3.9
9710441	Settlement Point, Grand Bahamas Island	-0.8	0.1	2.8	3.1	4.1
9759110	Magueyes Island, Puerto Rico	-0.5	0.0	0.7	0.7	1.1
9755371	San Juan, Puerto Rico	-0.6	0.2	1.3	1.6	2.2
9751639	Charlotte Amalie, St. Thomas Island	-0.5	0.0	0.7	0.8	1.2
9751401	Lime Tree Bay, St. Croix Island	-0.5	0.0	0.7	0.7	1.1

PUBLICATIONS RELATING TO TIDES AND TIDAL CURRENTS

TIDE TABLES

Advance information relative to the rise and fall of the tide is given in annual tide tables. These tables include the predicted times and heights of high and low waters for every day in the year for a number of reference stations and differences for obtaining similar predictions for numerous other places.

Tide Tables, Central and Western Pacific Ocean and Indian Ocean.

Tide Tables, East Coast of North and South America (Including Greenland).

Tide Tables, Europe and West Coast of Africa (Including the Mediterranean Sea).

Tide Tables, West Coast of North and South America (Including the Hawaiian Islands).

TIDAL CURRENT TABLES

Accompanying the rise and fall of the tide is a periodic horizontal flow of the water known as the tidal current. Advance information relative to these currents is made available in annual tidal current tables which include daily predictions of the times of slack water and the times and velocities of strength of flood and ebb currents for a number of waterways together with differences for obtaining predictions for numerous other places.

Tidal Current Tables, Atlantic Coast of North America.

Tidal Current Tables, Pacific Coast of North America and Asia.

OFFICIAL U.S. DATUMS

Privately Owned Uplands

AL, AK, CA, CT, FL, MD, MS,
NJ, NY, NC, OR, RI, SC, WA

Mean higher high water line

Mean high water line

Shoreline

Mean low water line

Coastline

Mean Lower low water line

Baseline

Privately
Owned
Uplands

TX

Privately
Owned

DE, MA, ME, NH, PA, VA, GA

Mean higher high water

Mean high water

Mean low water

Chart Datum
Mean Lower low water

Soundings

400

GLOSSARY OF TERMS

ANNUAL INEQUALITY—Seasonal variation in the water level or current, more or less periodic, due chiefly to meteorological causes.

APOGEAN TIDES OR TIDAL CURRENTS—Tides of decreased range or currents of decreased speed occurring monthly as the result of the Moon being in apogee (farthest from the Earth).

AUTOMATIC TIDE GAGE—An instrument that automatically registers the rise and fall of the tide. In some instruments, the registration is accomplished by recording the heights at regular intervals in digital format, in others by a continuous graph in which the height versus corresponding time of the tide is recorded.

BENCH MARK (BM)—A fixed physical object or marks used as reference for a vertical datum. A *tidal bench mark is* one near a tide station to which the tide staff and tidal datums are referred. A *Geodetic bench mark* identifies a surveyed point in the National Geodetic Vertical Network.

CHART DATUM—The tidal datum to which soundings on a chart are referred. It is usually taken to correspond to low water elevation of the tide, and its depression below mean sea level is represented by the symbol Zo.

CURRENT—Generally, a horizontal movement of water. Currents may be classified as *tidal* and *nontidal*. Tidal currents are caused by gravitational interactions between the Sun, Moon, and Earth and are a part of the same general movement of the sea that is manifested in the vertical rise and fall, called *tide*. Nontidal currents include the permanent currents in the general circulatory systems of the sea as well as temporary currents arising from more pronounced meteorological variability.

CURRENT DIFFERENCE—Difference between the time of slack water (or minimum current) or strength of current in any locality and the time of the corresponding phase of the tidal current at a reference station, for which predictions are given in the *Tidal Current Tables*.

CURRENT ELLIPSE—A graphic representation of a rotary current in which the velocity of the current at different hours of the tidal cycle is represented by radius vectors and vectorial angles. A line joining the extremities of the radius vectors will form a curve roughly approximating an ellipse. The cycle is completed in one-half tidal day or in a whole tidal day according to whether the tidal current is of the semidiurnal or the diurnal type. A current of the mixed type will give a curve of two unequal loops each tidal day.

CURRENT METER—An instrument for measuring the speed and direction or just the speed of a current. The measurements are usually Eulerian since the meter is most often fixed or moored at a specific location.

DATUM (vertical)—For marine applications, a base elevation used as a reference from which to reckon heights or depths. It is called a *tidal datum* when defined by a certain phase of the tide. Tidal datums are local datums and should not be extended into areas which have differing topographic features without substantiating measurements. In order that they may be recovered when needed, such datums are referenced to fixed points known as *bench marks*.

DAYLIGHT SAVING TIME—A time used during the summer in some localities in which clocks are advanced 1 hour from the usual standard time.

DIURNAL—Having a period or cycle of approximately 1 tidal day. Thus, the tide is said to be diurnal when only one high water and one low water occur during a tidal day, and the tidal current is said to be diurnal when there is a single flood and single ebb period in the tidal day. A rotary current is diurnal if it changes its direction through all points of the compass once each tidal day.

DIURNAL INEQUALITY—The difference in height of the two high waters or of the two low waters of each day; also the difference in speed between the two flood tidal currents or the two ebb tidal currents of each day. The difference changes with the declination of the Moon and to a lesser extent with the declination of the Sun. In general, the inequality tends to increase with an increasing declination, either north or south, and to diminish as the Moon approaches the Equator. *Mean diurnal high water inequality* (DHQ) is one-half the average difference between the two high waters of each day observed over a specific 19-year Metonic cycle (the National Tidal Datum Epoch). It is obtained by subtracting the mean of all high waters from the mean of the higher high waters. *Mean diurnal low water inequality* (DLQ) is one-half the average difference between the two low waters of each day observed over a specific 19-year Metonic cycle (the National Tidal Datum Epoch). It is obtained by subtracting the mean of the lower low waters from the mean of all low waters. *Tropic high water inequality* (HWQ) is the average difference between the two high waters of the day at the times of the tropic tides. *Tropic low water inequality* (LWQ) is the average difference between the two low waters of the day at the times of the tropic tides. Mean and tropic inequalities as defined above are applicable only when the type of tide is either semidiurnal or mixed. Diurnal inequality is sometimes called *declinational inequality*.

DOUBLE EBB—An ebb tidal current where, after ebb begins, the speed increases to a maximum called *first ebb*; it then decreases, reaching a *minimum ebb* near the middle of the ebb period (and at some places it may actually run in a flood direction for a short period); it then again ebbs to a maximum speed called second ebb after which it decreases to slack water.

DOUBLE FLOOD—A flood tidal current where, after flood begins, the speed increases to a maximum called first flood; it then decreases, reaching a minimum flood near the middle of the flood period (and at some places it may actually run in an ebb direction for a short period); it then again floods to a maximum speed called second flood after which it decreases to slack water.

DOUBLE TIDE—A double-headed tide, that is, a high water consisting of two maxima of nearly the same height separated by a relatively small depression, or a low water consisting of two minima separated by a relatively small elevation. Sometimes, it is called an agger.

DURATION OF FLOOD AND DURATION OF EBB—Duration of flood is the interval of time in which a tidal current is flooding, and the *duration of ebb* is the interval in which it is ebbing. Together they cover, on an average, a period of 12.42 hours for a semidiurnal tidal current or a period of 24.84 hours for a diurnal current. In a normal semidiurnal tidal current, the duration of flood and duration of ebb will each be approximately equal to 6.21 hours, but the times may be modified greatly by the presence of a nontidal flow. In a river the duration of ebb is usually longer than the duration of flood because of the freshwater discharge, especially during the spring when snow and ice melt are the predominant influences.

DURATION OF RISE AND DURATION OF FALL—*Duration of rise* is the interval from low water to high water, and *duration of fall* is the interval from high water to low water. Together they cover, on an average, a period of 12.42 hours for a semidiurnal tide or a period of 24.84 hours for a diurnal tide. In a normal semidiurnal tide, the duration of rise and duration of fall will each be approximately equal to 6.21 hours, but in shallow waters and in rivers there is a tendency for a decrease in the duration of rise and a corresponding increase in the duration of fall.

EBB CURRENT—The movement of a tidal current away from shore or down a tidal river or estuary. In the mixed type of reversing tidal current, the terms *greater ebb* and *lesser ebb* are applied respectively to the ebb tidal currents of greater and lesser speed of each day. The terms *maximum ebb* and *minimum ebb* are applied to the maximum and minimum speeds of a current running continuously ebb, the speed alternately increasing and decreasing without coming to a slack or reversing. The expression maximum ebb is also applicable to any ebb current at the time of greatest speed.

EQUATORIAL TIDAL CURRENTS—Tidal currents occurring semimonthly as a result of the Moon being over the Equator. At these times the tendency of the Moon to produce a diurnal inequality in the tidal current is at a minimum.

EQUATORIAL TIDES—Tides occurring semi monthly as the result of the Moon being over the Equator. At these times the tendency of the Moon to produce a diurnal inequality in the tide is at a minimum.

FLOOD CURRENT—The movement of a tidal current toward the shore or up a tidal river or estuary. In the mixed type of reversing current, the terms *greater flood* and *lesser flood* are applied respectively to the flood currents of greater and lesser speed of each day. The terms *maximum flood* and *minimum flood* are applied to the maximum and minimum speeds of a flood current, the speed of which alternately increases and decreases without coming to a slack or reversing. The expression maximum flood is also applicable to any flood current at the time of greatest speed.

GREAT DIURNAL RANGE (Gt)—The difference in height between mean higher high water and mean lower low water. The expression may also be used in its contracted form, *diurnal range*.

GREENWICH INTERVAL—An interval referred to the transit of the Moon over the meridian of Greenwich as distinguished from the local interval which is referred to the Moon's transit over the local meri-dian. The relation in hours between Greenwich and local intervals may be expressed by the formula:

Greenwich interval = local interval +0.069 L

where L is the west longitude of the local meridan in degrees. For east longitude, L is to be considered negative.

GULF COAST LOW WATER DATUM—A chart datum. Specifically, the tidal datum formerly designated for the coastal waters of the Gulf Coast of the United States. It was defined as *mean lower low water* when the type of tide was mixed and *mean low water* when the type of tide was diurnal.

HALF-TIDE LEVEL—See *mean tide level*.

GLOSSARY OF TERMS

HARMONIC ANALYSIS—The mathematical process by which the observed tide or tidal current at any place is separated into basic harmonic constituents.

HARMONIC CONSTANTS—The amplitudes and epochs of the harmonic constituents of the tide or tidal current at any place.

HARMONIC CONSTITUENT—One of the harmonic elements in a mathematical expression for the tide-producing force and in corresponding formulas for the tide or tidal current. Each constituent represents a periodic change or variation in the relative positions of the Earth, Moon, and Sun. A single constituent is usually written in the form y=A cos (at+α), in which y is a function of time as expressed by the symbol t and is reckoned from a specific origin. The coefficient A is called the amplitude of the constituent and is a measure of its relative importance. The angle (at+α) changes uniformly and its value at any time is called the phase of the constituent. The speed of the constituent is the rate of change in its phase and is represented by the symbol a in the formula. The quantity α is the phase of the constituent at the initial instant from which the time is reckoned. The period of the constituent is the time required for the phase to change through 360° and is the cycle of the astronomical condition represented by the constituent.

HIGH WATER (HW)—The maximum height reached by a rising tide. The height may be due solely to the periodic tidal forces or it may have superimposed upon it the effects of prevailing meteorological conditions. Use of the synonymous term, *high tide*, is discouraged.

HIGHER HIGH WATER (HHW)—The higher of the two high waters of any tidal day.

HIGHER LOW WATER (HLW)—The higher of the two low waters of any tidal day.

HYDRAULIC CURRENT—A current in a channel caused by a difference in the surface level at the two ends. Such a current may be expected in a strait connecting two bodies of water in which the tides differ in time or range. The current in the East River, N.Y., connecting Long Island Sound and New York Harbor, is an example.

KNOT—A unit of speed, one international nautical mile (1,852.0 meters or 6,076.11549 international feet) per hour.

LOW WATER (LW)—The minimum height reached by a falling tide. The height may be due solely to the periodic tidal forces or it may have superimposed

upon it the effects of meteorological conditions. Use of the synonymous term, *low tide*, is discouraged.

LOWER HIGH WATER (LHW)—The lower of the two high waters of any tidal day.

LOWER LOW WATER (LLW)—The lower of the two low waters of any tidal day.

LUNAR DAY—The time of the rotation of the Earth with respect to the Moon, or the interval between two successive upper transits of the Moon over the meridian of a place. The mean lunar day is approximately 24.84 solar hours long, or 1.035 times as long as the mean solar day.

LUNAR INTERVAL—The difference in time between the transit of the Moon over the meridian of Greenwich and over a local meridian. The average value of this interval expressed in hours is 0.069 L, in which L is the local longitude in degrees, positive for west longitude and negative for east longitude. The lunar interval equals the difference between the local and Greenwich interval of a tide or current phase.

LUNICURRENT INTERVAL—The interval between the Moon's transit (upper or lower) over the local or Greenwich meridian and a specified phase of the tidal current following the transit. Examples: *strength of flood interval and strength of ebb interval,* which may be abbreviated to *flood interval and ebb interval,* respectively. The interval is described as local or Greenwich according to whether the reference is to the Moon's transit over the local or Greenwich meridian. When not otherwise specified, the reference is assumed to be local.

LUNITIDAL INTERVAL—The interval between the Moon's transit (upper or lower) over the local or Greenwich meridian and the following high or low water. The average of all high water intervals for all phases of the Moon is known as *mean high water lunitidal interval* and is abbreviated to high water interval (HWI). Similarly the *mean low water lunitidal interval* is abbreviated to *low water interval* (LWI). The interval is described as local or Greenwich according to whether the reference is to the transit over the local or Greenwich meridian. When not otherwise specified, the reference is assumed to be local.

MEAN HIGH WATER (MHW)—A tidal datum. The arithmetic mean of the high water heights observed over a specific 19-year Metonic cycle (the National Tidal Datum Epoch). For stations with shorter series, simultaneous observational comparisons are made with a primary control tide station in order to derive the equivalent of a 19-year value.

GLOSSARY OF TERMS

MEAN HIGHER HIGH WATER (MHHW)—A tidal datum. The arithmetic mean of the higher high water heights of a mixed tide observed over a specific 19-year Metonic cycle (the National Tidal Datum Epoch). Only the higher high water of each pair of high waters, or the only high water of a tidal day is included in the mean.

MEAN HIGHER HIGH WATER LINE (MHHWL)—The intersection of the land with the water surface at the elevation of mean higher high water.

MEAN LOW WATER (MLW)—A tidal datum. The arithmetic mean of the low water heights observed over a specific 19-year Metonic cycle (the National Tidal Datum Epoch). For stations with shorter series, simultaneous observational comparisons are made with a primary control tide station in order to derive the equivalent of a 19-year value.

MEAN LOW WATER SPRINGS (MLWS)—A tidal datum. Frequently abbreviated *spring low water.* The arithmetic mean of the low water heights occurring at the time of the spring tides observed over a specific 19-year Metonic cycle (the National Tidal Datum Epoch).

MEAN LOWER LOW WATER (MLLW)—A tidal datum. The arithmetic mean of the lower low water heights of a mixed tide observed over a specific 19-year Metonic cycle (the National Tidal Datum Epoch). Only the lower low water of each pair of low waters, or the only low water of a tidal day is included in the mean.

MEAN RANGE OF TIDE (Mn)—The difference in height between mean high water and mean low water.

MEAN RIVER LEVEL—A tidal datum. The average height of the surface of a tidal river at any point for all stages of the tide observed over a 19-year Metonic cycle (the National Tidal Datum Epoch), usually determined from hourly height readings. In rivers subject to occasional freshets the river level may undergo wide variations, and for practical purposes certain months of the year may be excluded in the determination of tidal datums. For charting purposes, tidal datums for rivers are usually based on observations during selected periods when the river is at or near low water stage.

MEAN SEA LEVEL (MSL)—A tidal datum. The arithmetic mean of hourly water elevations observed over a specific 19-year Metonic cycle (the National Tidal Datum Epoch). Shorter series are specified in the name; e.g., monthly mean sea level and yearly mean sea level.

MEAN TIDE LEVEL (MTL)—Also called half-tide level. A tidal datum midway between mean high water and mean low water.

MIXED TIDE—Type of tide with a large inequality in the high and/or low water heights, with two high waters and two low waters usually occurring each tidal day. In strictness, all tides are mixed but the name is usually applied to the tides intermediate to those predominantly semidiurnal and those predominantly diurnal.

NATIONAL TIDAL DATUM EPOCH—The specific 19-year period adopted by the National Ocean Service as the official time segment over which tide observations are taken and reduced to obtain mean values (e.g., mean lower low water, etc.) for tidal datums. It is necessary for standardization because of periodic and apparent secular trends in sea level. The present National Tidal Datum Epoch is 1960 through 1978. It is reviewed annually for possible revision and must be actively considered for revision every 25 years.

NEAP TIDES OR TIDAL CURRENTS—Tides of decreased range or tidal currents of decreased speed occurring semimonthly as the result of the Moon being in quadrature. The *neap range* (Np) of the tide is the average semidiurnal range occurring at the time of neap tides and is most conveniently computed from the harmonic constants. It is smaller than the mean range where the type of tide is either semidiurnal or mixed and is of no practical significance where the type of tide is diurnal. The average height of the high waters of the neap tides is called *neap high water* or *high water neaps* (MHWN) and the average height of the corresponding low waters is called neap low water or low water neaps (MLWN).

PERIGEAN TIDES OR TIDAL CURRENTS—Tides of increased range or tidal currents of increased speed occurring monthly as the result of the Moon being in perigee or nearest the Earth. The *perigean range* (Pn) of tide is the average semidiurnal range occurring at the time of perigean tides and is most conveniently computed from the harmonic constants. It is larger than the mean range where the type of tide is either semidiurnal or mixed, and is of no practical significance where the type of tide is diurnal.

RANGE OF TIDE—The difference in height between consecutive high and low waters, the *mean range* is the difference in height between mean high water and mean low water. Where the type of tide is diurnal the mean range is the same as the diurnal range.

For other ranges, see great diurnal, spring, neap, perigean, apogean, and tropic tides.

REFERENCE STATION—A tide or current station for which independent daily predictions are given in the *Tide Tables and Tidal Current Tables,* and from which corresponding predictions are obtained for subordinate stations by means of differences and ratios.

REVERSING CURRENT—A tidal current which flows alternately in approximately opposite directions with a slack water at each reversal of direction. Currents of this type usually occur in rivers and straits where the direction of flow is more or less restricted to certain channels. When the movement is towards the shore or up a stream, the current is said to be flooding, and when in the opposite direction it is said to be ebbing. The combined flood and ebb movement including the slack water covers, on an average, 12.42 hours for the semidiurnal current. If unaffected by a nontidal flow, the flood and ebb movements will each last about 6 hours, but when combined with such a flow, the durations of flood and ebb may be quite unequal. During the flow in each direction the speed of the current will vary from zero at the time of slack water to a maximum about midway between the slacks.

ROTARY CURRENT—A tidal current that flows continually with the direction of flow changing through all points of the compass during the tidal period. Rotary currents are usually found offshore where the direction of flow is not restricted by any barriers. The tendency for the rotation in direction has its origin in the Coriolis force and, unless modified by local conditions, the change is clockwise in the Northern Hemisphere and counterclockwise in the Southern. The speed of the current usually varies throughout the tidal cycle, passing through the two maxima in approximately opposite directions and the two minima with the direction of the current at approximately 90° from the direction at time of maximum speed.

SEMIDIURNAL—Having a period or cycle of approximately one-half of a tidal day. The predominating type of tide throughout the world is semidiurnal, with two high waters and two low waters each tidal day. The tidal current is said to be semidiurnal when there are two flood and two ebb periods each day.

SET (OF CURRENT)—The direction *towards* which the current flows.

SLACK WATER—The state of a tidal current when its speed is near zero, especially the moment when a reversing current changes direction and its speed is zero. The term is also applied to the entire period of low speed near the time of turning of the current when it is too weak to be of any practical importance in navigation. The relation of the time of slack water to the tidal phases varies in different localities. For standing tidal waves, slack water occurs near the times of high and low water, while for progressive tidal waves, slack water occurs midway between high and low water.

SPRING TIDES OR TIDAL CURRENTS—Tides of increased range or tidal currents of increased speed occurring semimonthly as the result of the Moon being new or full. The *spring range* (Sg) of tide is the average semidiurnal range occurring at the time of spring tides and is most conveniently computed from the harmonic constants. It is larger than the mean range where the type of tide is either semidiurnal or mixed, and is of no practical significance where the type of tide is diurnal. The mean of the high waters of the spring tide is called *spring high water or mean high water springs* (MHWS), and the average height of the corresponding low waters is called *spring low water or mean low water springs* (MLWS).

STAND OF TIDE—Sometimes called a platform tide. An interval at high or low water when there is no sensible change in the height of the tide. The water level is stationary at high and low water for only an instant, but the change in level near these times is so slow that it is not usually perceptible. In general, the duration of the apparent stand will depend upon the range of tide, being longer for a small range than for a large range, but where there is a tendency for a double tide the stand may last for several hours even with a large range of tide.

STANDARD TIME—A kind of time based upon the transit of the Sun over a certain specified meridian, called the *time meridian*, and adopted for use over a considerable area. With a few exceptions, standard time is based upon some meridian which differs by a multiple of 15° from the meridian of Greenwich.

STRENGTH OF CURRENT—Phase of tidal current in which the speed is a maximum; also the speed at this time. Beginning with slack before flood in the period of a reversing tidal current (or minimum before flood in a rotary current), the speed gradually increases to flood strength and then diminishes to slack before ebb (or minimum before ebb in a rotary current), after which the current turns in direction, the speed increases to ebb strength and then diminishes to slack before flood completing the cycle. If it is assumed that the speed throughout the cycle varies as the ordinates of a cosine curve, it can be shown that the average speed for an entire flood or ebb period is equal to $2/\pi$ or 0.6366 of the speed of the corresponding strength of current.

SUBORDINATE CURRENT STATION—(1) A current station from which a relatively short series of observations is reduced by comparison with simultaneous observations from a control current station. (2) A station listed in the *Tidal Current Tables* for which predictions are to be obtained by means of differences and ratios applied to the full predictions at a reference station .

SUBORDINATE TIDE STATION—(1) A tide station from which a relatively short series of observations is reduced by comparison with simultaneous observations from a tide station with a relatively long series of observations. (2) A station listed in the *Tide Tables* for which predictions are to be obtained by means of differences and ratios applied to the full predictions at a reference station.

TIDAL CURRENT TABLES—Tables which give daily predictions of the times and speeds of the tidal currents. These predictions are usually supplemented by current differences and constants through which additional predictions can be obtained for numerous other places.

TIDAL DIFFERENCE—Difference in time or height of a high or low water at a subordinate station and at a reference station for which predictions are given in the *Tide Tables*. The difference, when applied according to sign to the prediction at the reference station, gives the corresponding time or height for the subordinate station .

TIDE—The periodic rise and fall of the water resulting from gravitational interactions between the Sun, Moon, and Earth. The vertical component of the particulate motion of a tidal wave. Although the accompanying horizontal movement of the water is part of the same phenomenon, it is preferable to designate the motion as tidal current.

TIDE TABLES—Tables which give daily predictions of the times and heights of high and low waters. These predictions are usually supplemented by tidal differences and constants through which additional predictions can be obtained for numerous other places.

TIME MERIDIAN—A meridian used as a reference for time.

TROPIC CURRENTS—Tidal currents occurring semimonthly when the effect of the Moon's maximum declination is greatest. At these times the tendency of the Moon to produce a diurnal inequality in the current is at a maximum.

TROPIC RANGES—The *great tropic range* (Gc), or *tropic range*, is the difference in height between tropic higher high water and tropic lower low water. The *small tropic range* (Sc) is the difference in height between tropic lower high water and tropic higher low water. The *mean tropic range* (Mc) is the mean between the great tropic range and the small tropic range. The small tropic range and the mean tropic range are applicable only when the type of tide is semidiurnal or mixed. Tropic ranges are most conveniently computed from the harmonic constants.

TROPIC TIDES—Tides occurring semimonthly when the effect of the Moon's maximum declination is greatest. At these times there is a tendency for an increase in the diurnal range. The tidal datums pertaining to the tropic tides are designated as *tropic higher high water* (TcHHW), *tropic lower high water* (TcLHW), *tropic higher low water* (TcHLW), and *tropic lower low water* (TcLLW).

TYPE OF TIDE—A classification based on characteristic forms of a tide curve. Qualitatively, when the two high waters and two low waters of each tidal day are approximately equal in height, the tide is said to be *semidiurnal*; when there is a relatively large diurnal inequality in the high or low waters or both, it is said to be *mixed*; and when there is only one high water and one low water in each tidal day, it is said to be *diurnal*.

VANISHING TIDE—In a mixed tide with very large diurnal inequality, the lower high water (or higher low water) frequently becomes indistinct (or vanishes) at time of extreme declinations. During these periods the diurnal tide has such overriding dominance that the semidiurnal tide, although still present, cannot be readily seen on the tide curve.

[Stations marked with an asterisk (*) are reference stations for which daily predictions are given in table 1. Page numbers of reference stations are given in parentheses.]

T

ASTRONOMICAL DATA, 2017

January

	d	h	m
E	5	04	..
◐	5	19	47
P	10	06	..
N	11	10	..
○	12	11	34
E	18	00	..
◑	19	22	13
A	22	00	..
S	25	13	..
●	28	00	07

February

	d	h	m
E	1	10	..
◐	4	04	19
P	6	14	..
N	7	19	..
○	11	00	33
E	14	10	..
◑	18	19	33
A	18	21	..
S	21	21	..
●	26	14	58
E	28	17	..

March

	d	h	m
P	3	08	..
◐	5	11	32
N	7	01	..
○	12	14	54
E	13	19	..
A	18	17	..
☉m	20	10	29
◑	20	15	58
S	21	06	..
E	28	02	..
●	28	02	57
P	30	13	..

April

	d	h	m
N	3	07	..
◐	3	18	39
E	10	02	..
○	11	06	08
A	15	10	..
S	17	14	..
◑	19	09	57
E	24	12	..
●	26	12	16
P	27	16	..
N	30	14	..

May

	d	h	m
◐	3	02	47
E	7	08	..
○	10	21	42
A	12	20	..
S	14	21	..
◑	19	00	33
E	21	23	..
●	25	19	44
P	26	01	..
N	28	00	..

June

	d	h	m
◐	1	12	42
E	3	15	..
A	8	22	..
○	9	13	10
S	11	04	..
◑	17	11	33
E	18	08	..
☉j	21	04	24
P	23	11	..
●	24	02	31
N	24	12	..
E	30	23	..

July

	d	h	m
◐	1	00	51
A	6	04	..
S	8	11	..
○	9	04	07
E	15	16	..
◑	16	19	26
P	21	17	..
N	21	23	..
●	23	09	46
E	28	08	..
◐	30	15	23

August

	d	h	m
A	2	18	..
S	4	19	..
○	7	18	11
E	11	21	..
◑	15	01	15
N	18	07	..
P	18	13	..
●	21	18	30
E	24	17	..
◐	29	08	13
A	30	11	..

September

	d	h	m
S	1	03	..
○	6	07	03
E	8	04	..
◑	13	06	25
P	13	16	..
N	14	14	..
●	20	05	30
E	21	02	..
☉s	22	20	02
A	27	07	..
◐	28	02	54
S	28	11	..

October

	d	h	m
E	5	12	..
○	5	18	40
P	9	06	..
N	11	19	..
◑	12	12	25
E	18	10	..
●	19	19	12
A	25	02	..
S	25	19	..
◐	27	22	22

November

	d	h	m
E	1	22	..
○	4	05	23
P	6	00	..
N	8	02	..
◑	10	20	36
E	14	16	..
●	18	11	42
A	21	19	..
S	22	03	..
◐	26	17	03
E	29	09	..

December

	d	h	m
○	3	15	47
P	4	09	..
N	5	12	..
◑	10	07	51
E	11	23	..
●	18	06	30
A	19	01	..
S	19	10	..
☉d	21	16	28
◐	26	09	20
E	26	19	..

LUNAR DATA

- ● — new Moon
- ◐ — first quarter
- ○ — full Moon
- ◑ — last quarter
- A — Moon in apogee
- P — Moon in perigee
- N — Moon farthest north of Equator
- E — Moon on Equator
- S — Moon farthest south of Equator

SOLAR DATA

- ☉m — March equinox
- ☉j — June solstice
- ☉s — September equinox
- ☉d — December solstice

Greenwich mean time (GMT) or universal time (UT) is the mean solar time on the Greenwich meridian reckoned in days 24 mean solar hours written as 00ʰ at midnight and 12ʰ at noon. To convert the above times to those of other standard time meridians, add 1 hour for each 15° of east longitude of the desired meridian and subtract 1 hour for each 15° of west longitude. This table was compiled from data supplied by the Nautical Almanac Office, United States Naval Observatory.

Made in the USA
Charleston, SC
08 December 2016